2011/12
Ninth Edition

Educators
Resource
Directory

- *Race to the Top* Summary
- Associations & Organizations
- Professional Development
- Consultants
- Financial Resources
- Conferences & Trade Shows
- Opportunities Abroad
- National & State Statistics

A SEDGWICK PRESS Book

Grey House
Publishing

PUBLISHER: Leslie Mackenzie
EDITOR: Richard Gottlieb
EDITORIAL DIRECTOR: Laura Mars

PRODUCTION MANAGER: Kristen Thatcher
STATISTICS: David Garoogian
MARKETING DIRECTOR: Jessica Moody

A Sedgwick Press Book
Grey House Publishing, Inc.
4919 Route 22
Amenia, NY 12501
518.789.8700
FAX 518.789.0545
www.greyhouse.com
e-mail: books @greyhouse.com

While every effort has been made to ensure the reliability of the information presented in this publication, Grey House Publishing neither guarantees the accuracy of the data contained herein nor assumes any responsibility for errors, omissions or discrepancies. Grey House accepts no payment for listing; inclusion in the publication of any organization, agency, institution, publication, service or individual does not imply endorsement of the editors or publisher.

Errors brought to the attention of the publisher and verified to the satisfaction of the publisher will be corrected in future editions.

First edition published 1994
Ninth edition published 2011
Printed in Canada

ISBN: 978-1-59237-743-5
ISSN: 1549-7224

Educators
Resource
Directory

Table of Contents

Introduction

This ninth edition of *Educators Resource Directory* is a comprehensive resource designed to provide educators, administrators, and other education professionals with immediate access to a unique combination of 6,191 educational information resources and 229 charts of educational statistics and rankings.

Race to the Top

Listings in *Educators Resource Directory* include associations, publications, trade shows, workshops and training programs designed not only to help educators advance professionally, but also to give them the resources they need to help their students, their schools, and their state win President Obama's *Race to the Top*. This competitive grant program, under the American Recovery and Reinvestment Act of 2009, is designed to encourage and reward states that 1. create conditions for education innovations and reform, 2. achieve significant improvement in student outcomes, and 3. implement ambitious plans in core education reform areas. Following this introduction is a comprehensive *Race to the Top* Executive Summary, followed by the winners of the second round of *Race to the Top* grants.

This premier directory provides tools for classroom and career management, and resources that truly make a difference in job, school, and student performance. Listings in this comprehensive volume are organized in 13 chapters and 76 subchapters, making the information in this directory significantly easier to access than the unfocused data available online or the information scattered in dozens of different sources. Statistics and rankings are designed to help states, school districts, and individual educators better understand their educational environment, crucial to making informed decisions on careers, curriculum and funding.

Educators Resource Directory includes 6,191 listings in **Section One,** with current contact information, including 6,594 key contact names, 4,205 fax numbers, 2,991 e-mail addresses, and 3,846 web sites. **Section Two** includes 229 charts in 9 main categories and 17 subcategories. From elementary to post-secondary levels, these statistics and rankings include data not only on the American educational system, but also on Canadian and international education.

SECTION ONE: RESOURCES

Associations & Organizations disseminates information, host seminars, provide educational literature and promote study councils. This chapter organizes 581 associations into 18 distinct categories from *Administration* to *Technology*.

The chapter on **Conferences & Trade Shows** lists everything from large conventions of classroom resources and equipment suppliers to small, specialized conferences that target rural education and specific teaching challenges. Events are listed regionally.

Consultants gives information on educational consulting services, including curriculum-building guidance, school district organizations, and facility format.

Teaching Opportunities Abroad includes not only U.S. government schools, but also American schools overseas. The chapter is organized geographically by region, and provides contact information, grade level and enrollment numbers on 1,223 schools.

Details on 627 grants, foundations and scholarships can be found in **Financial Resources**. Learn how to obtain funds for individual professional advancement, schools, programs, students, and education districts and communities.

The 462 **Professional Development** listings include *Associations, Awards, Conferences* and *Training Materials.*

Publications lists 972 directories, magazines and journals, divided into 17 subjects. Find where to publish your research findings, which testing materials best suit your needs, how to incorporate technology into your classroom, and where to find innovative classroom supplies.

Publishers includes 348 educational publishers of textbooks, testing resources and specific curriculums.

Research results on general learning and training issues, and data on specific subjects, like *Gifted & Talented, Educational Media* and *Scientific Learning*, are easy to find from the nearly 100 **Research Centers** profiled in this edition.

The chapter on **School Supplies** focuses on the latest in *Classroom Technology, Scientific Equipment, Furniture* and *Sports & Playground Equipment.*

Software, Hardware & Internet Resources includes 17 subchapters from *Administration* to *Technology in Education* that provide easy access to everything from educational computer programs to web sites with information on classroom resources for every level and subject.

Testing Resources includes resources for written materials and web sites in six categories: *Elementary Education, Language Arts, Mathematics, Music & Art, Reading* and *Secondary Education.*

SECTION TWO: STATISTICS, RANKINGS & GLOSSARY
This 282-page section provides 229 tables and charts (67 more than last edition) in nine categories, *Educational Attainment *Elementary & Secondary Education *Federal Programs *International Comparisons *Libraries & Educational Technology *Opinions on Education *Outcomes of Education *Post-secondary Education *Canadian Education. Specific topics include degrees, enrollment, completions, dropouts, faculty, revenues, expenditures, and student behavior. Many tables offer state-by-state rankings.

Using the most current data available, this section helps to complete the picture for educators making career development decisions, for school administrators interested in comparing fiscal health and educational scores, and for anyone doing educational research.

Following the statistics and rankings, and new to this edition, is a **Glossary** with over 100 education terms from Accountability to Vocational.

SECTION THREE: INDEXES
- ◼ *Entry & Publisher Name Index* – alphabetical list of both entry names and the companies that publish the listed material. Publishers and parent organizations are boldfaced.
- ◼ *Geographic Index* – state-by-state listing of all entries.
- ◼ *Subject Index* -- organized by core subjects plus Special Education, Technology, and No Child Left Behind (NCLB) related listings.

Educators Resource Directory 2011/12 is also available for subscription via Grey House OnLine Database. Subscribers can do customized searches that instantly locate needed information. Visit http://gold.greyhouse.com or call 800-562-2139 to set up a free trial.

Race to the Top Program
Executive Summary

> "It's time to stop just talking about education reform and start actually doing it.
> It's time to make education America's national mission."
> – President Barack Obama, November 4, 2009

BACKGROUND

On February 17, 2009, President Obama signed into law the American Recovery and Reinvestment Act of 2009 (ARRA), historic legislation designed to stimulate the economy, support job creation, and invest in critical sectors, including education. The ARRA lays the foundation for education reform by supporting investments in innovative strategies that are most likely to lead to improved results for students, long-term gains in school and school system capacity, and increased productivity and effectiveness.

The ARRA provides $4.35 billion for the Race to the Top Fund, a competitive grant program designed to encourage and reward States that are creating the conditions for education innovation and reform; achieving significant improvement in student outcomes, including making substantial gains in student achievement, closing achievement gaps, improving high school graduation rates, and ensuring student preparation for success in college and careers; and implementing ambitious plans in four core education reform areas:

- Adopting standards and assessments that prepare students to succeed in college and the workplace and to compete in the global economy;
- Building data systems that measure student growth and success, and inform teachers and principals about how they can improve instruction;
- Recruiting, developing, rewarding, and retaining effective teachers and principals, especially where they are needed most; and
- Turning around our lowest-achieving schools.

Race to the Top will reward States that have demonstrated success in raising student achievement and have the best plans to accelerate their reforms in the future. These States will offer models for others to follow and will spread the best reform ideas across their States, and across the country.

KEY TIMING

The Department plans to make Race to the Top grants in two phases. States that are ready to apply now may do so in Phase 1; States that need more time may apply in Phase 2. States that apply in Phase 1 but are not awarded grants may reapply for funding in Phase 2, together with States that are applying for the first time in Phase 2. Phase 1 grantees may not apply for additional funding in Phase 2.

Notices Published:	November 2009
Technical Assistance:	
Informational Conference Calls:	November and December 2009
Technical Assistance Workshops:	December 3 in Denver, CO; December 10 in Washington, D.C.
Other Events	TBD
Applications:	
Phase 1 Applications Due:	January 19, 2010
Phase 1 Awards Announced:	April 2010
Phase 2 Applications Due:	June 1, 2010
Phase 2 Awards Announced:	September 2010 *(see article on page xv)*

OVERVIEW OF PROGRAM AND POINTS

<u>Selection Criteria</u>
A. State Success Factors *(125 points)*
(A)(1) Articulating State's education reform agenda and LEAs' participation in it *(65 points)*
(A)(2) Building strong statewide capacity to implement, scale up, and sustain proposed plans *(30 points)*
(A)(3) Demonstrating significant progress in raising achievement and closing gaps *(30 points)*
B. Standards and Assessments *(70 points)*
(B)(1) Developing and adopting common standards *(40 points)*
(B)(2) Developing and implementing common, high-quality assessments *(10 points)*
(B)(3) Supporting the transition to enhanced standards and high-quality assessments *(20 points)*
C. Data Systems to Support Instruction *(47 points)*
(C)(1) Fully implementing a statewide longitudinal data system *(24 points)*
(C)(2) Accessing and using State data *(5 points)*
(C)(3) Using data to improve instruction *(18 points)*
D. Great Teachers and Leaders *(138 points)*
(D)(1) Providing high-quality pathways for aspiring teachers and principals *(21 points)*
(D)(2) Improving teacher and principal effectiveness based on performance *(58 points)*
(D)(3) Ensuring equitable distribution of effective teachers and principals *(25 points)*
(D)(4) Improving the effectiveness of teacher and principal preparation programs *(14 points)*
(D)(5) Providing effective support to teachers and principals *(20 points)*
E. Turning Around the Lowest-Achieving Schools *(50 points)*
(E)(1) Intervening in the lowest-achieving schools and LEAs *(10 points)*
(E)(2) Turning around the lowest- achieving schools *(40 points)*
F. General Selection Criteria *(55 points)*
(F)(1) Making education funding a priority *(10 points)*
(F)(2) Ensuring successful conditions for high-performing charters and other innovative schools *(40 points)*
(F)(3) Demonstrating other significant reform conditions *(5 points)*

<u>Priorities</u>
Priority 1: Absolute Priority – Comprehensive Approach to Education Reform
Priority 2: Competitive Preference Priority – Emphasis on Science, Technology, Engineering, and
Mathematics (STEM) *(15 points, all or nothing)*
Priority 3: Invitational Priority – Innovations for Improving Early Learning Outcomes
Priority 4: Invitational Priority – Expansion and Adaptation of Statewide Longitudinal Data Systems
Priority 5: Invitational Priority – P-20 Coordination, Vertical and Horizontal Alignment
Priority 6: Invitational Priority – School-Level Conditions for Reform, Innovation, and Learning

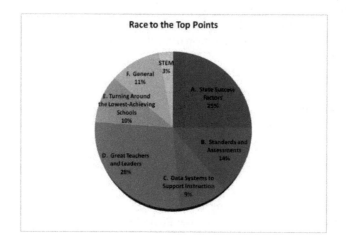

ELIGIBILITY REQUIREMENTS

A State must meet the following requirements in order to be eligible to receive funds under this program.

(a) The State's applications for funding under Phase 1 and Phase 2 of the State Fiscal Stabilization Fund program must be approved by the Department prior to the State being awarded a Race to the Top grant.

(b) At the time the State submits its application, there must not be any legal, statutory, or regulatory barriers at the State level to linking data on student achievement (as defined in this notice) or student growth (as defined in this notice) to teachers and principals for the purpose of teacher and principal evaluation.

PRIORITIES

Priority 1: Absolute Priority -- Comprehensive Approach to Education Reform

To meet this priority, the State's application must comprehensively and coherently address all of the four education reform areas specified in the ARRA as well as the State Success Factors Criteria in order to demonstrate that the State and its participating LEAs are taking a systemic approach to education reform. The State must demonstrate in its application sufficient LEA participation and commitment to successfully implement and achieve the goals in its plans; and it must describe how the State, in collaboration with its participating LEAs, will use Race to the Top and other funds to increase student achievement, decrease the achievement gaps across student subgroups, and increase the rates at which students graduate from high school prepared for college and careers.

Priority 2: Competitive Preference Priority -- Emphasis on Science, Technology, Engineering, and Mathematics (STEM). *(15 points, all or nothing)*

To meet this priority, the State's application must have a high-quality plan to address the need to (i) offer a rigorous course of study in mathematics, the sciences, technology, and engineering; (ii) cooperate with industry experts, museums, universities, research centers, or other STEM-capable community partners to prepare and assist teachers in integrating STEM content across grades and disciplines, in promoting effective and relevant instruction, and in offering applied learning opportunities for students; and (iii) prepare more students for advanced study and careers in the sciences, technology, engineering, and mathematics, including by addressing the needs of underrepresented groups and of women and girls in the areas of science, technology, engineering, and mathematics.

Priority 3: Invitational Priority – Innovations for Improving Early Learning Outcomes.

The Secretary is particularly interested in applications that include practices, strategies, or programs to improve educational outcomes for high-need students who are young children (pre-kindergarten through third grade) by enhancing the quality of preschool programs. Of particular interest are proposals that support practices that (i) improve school readiness (including social, emotional, and cognitive); and (ii) improve the transition between preschool and kindergarten.

Priority 4: Invitational Priority – Expansion and Adaptation of Statewide Longitudinal Data Systems.

The Secretary is particularly interested in applications in which the State plans to expand statewide longitudinal data systems to include or integrate data from special education programs, English language learner programs,[1] early childhood programs, at-risk and dropout prevention programs, and school climate and culture programs, as well as information on student mobility, human resources (*i.e.*, information on teachers, principals, and other staff), school finance, student health, postsecondary education, and other

---

[1] The term English language learner, as used in this notice, is synonymous with the term limited English proficient, as defined in section 9101 of the ESEA.

relevant areas, with the purpose of connecting and coordinating all parts of the system to allow important questions related to policy, practice, or overall effectiveness to be asked, answered, and incorporated into effective continuous improvement practices.

The Secretary is also particularly interested in applications in which States propose working together to adapt one State's statewide longitudinal data system so that it may be used, in whole or in part, by one or more other States, rather than having each State build or continue building such systems independently.

Priority 5: Invitational Priority -- P-20 Coordination, Vertical and Horizontal Alignment.

The Secretary is particularly interested in applications in which the State plans to address how early childhood programs, K-12 schools, postsecondary institutions, workforce development organizations, and other State agencies and community partners (*e.g.*, child welfare, juvenile justice, and criminal justice agencies) will coordinate to improve all parts of the education system and create a more seamless preschool-through-graduate school (P-20) route for students. Vertical alignment across P-20 is particularly critical at each point where a transition occurs (*e.g.*, between early childhood and K-12, or between K-12 and postsecondary/careers) to ensure that students exiting one level are prepared for success, without remediation, in the next. Horizontal alignment, that is, coordination of services across schools, State agencies, and community partners, is also important in ensuring that high-need students (as defined in this notice) have access to the broad array of opportunities and services they need and that are beyond the capacity of a school itself to provide.

Priority 6: Invitational Priority -- School-Level Conditions for Reform, Innovation, and Learning.

The Secretary is particularly interested in applications in which the State's participating LEAs (as defined in this notice) seek to create the conditions for reform and innovation as well as the conditions for learning by providing schools with flexibility and autonomy in such areas as--

(i) Selecting staff;

(ii) Implementing new structures and formats for the school day or year that result in increased learning time (as defined in this notice);

(iii) Controlling the school's budget;

(iv) Awarding credit to students based on student performance instead of instructional time;

(v) Providing comprehensive services to high-need students (as defined in this notice) (*e.g.*, by mentors and other caring adults; through local partnerships with community-based organizations, nonprofit organizations, and other providers);

(vi) Creating school climates and cultures that remove obstacles to, and actively support, student engagement and achievement; and

(vii) Implementing strategies to effectively engage families and communities in supporting the academic success of their students.

SELECTION CRITERIA

A. State Success Factors *(125 points)*

(A)(1) <u>Articulating State's education reform agenda and LEAs' participation in it</u> *(65 points)*
The extent to which—

(i) The State has set forth a comprehensive and coherent reform agenda that clearly articulates its goals for implementing reforms in the four education areas described in the ARRA and improving student outcomes statewide, establishes a clear and credible path to achieving these goals, and is consistent with the specific reform plans that the State has proposed throughout its application; *(5 points)*

(ii) The participating LEAs (as defined in this notice) are strongly committed to the State's plans and to effective implementation of reform in the four education areas, as evidenced by Memoranda of Understanding (MOUs) (as set forth in Appendix D)[2] or other binding agreements between the State and its participating LEAs (as defined in this notice) that include— *(45 points)*

(a) Terms and conditions that reflect strong commitment by the participating LEAs (as defined in this notice) to the State's plans;

(b) Scope-of-work descriptions that require participating LEAs (as defined in this notice) to implement all or significant portions of the State's Race to the Top plans; and

(c) Signatures from as many as possible of the LEA superintendent (or equivalent), the president of the local school board (or equivalent, if applicable), and the local teachers' union leader (if applicable) (one signature of which must be from an authorized LEA representative) demonstrating the extent of leadership support within participating LEAs (as defined in this notice); and

(iii) The LEAs that are participating in the State's Race to the Top plans (including considerations of the numbers and percentages of participating LEAs, schools, K-12 students, and students in poverty) will translate into broad statewide impact, allowing the State to reach its ambitious yet achievable goals, overall and by student subgroup, for— *(15 points)*

(a) Increasing student achievement in (at a minimum) reading/language arts and mathematics, as reported by the NAEP and the assessments required under the ESEA;

(b) Decreasing achievement gaps between subgroups in reading/language arts and mathematics, as reported by the NAEP and the assessments required under the ESEA;

(c) Increasing high school graduation rates (as defined in this notice); and

(d) Increasing college enrollment (as defined in this notice) and increasing the number of students who complete at least a year's worth of college credit that is applicable to a degree within two years of enrollment in an institution of higher education.

(A)(2) <u>Building strong statewide capacity to implement, scale up, and sustain proposed plans</u> *(30 points)*
The extent to which the State has a high-quality overall plan to—

(i) Ensure that it has the capacity required to implement its proposed plans by— *(20 points)*

(a) Providing strong leadership and dedicated teams to implement the statewide education reform plans the State has proposed;

(b) Supporting participating LEAs (as defined in this notice) in successfully implementing the education reform plans the State has proposed, through such activities as identifying promising practices, evaluating these practices' effectiveness, ceasing ineffective practices, widely disseminating and replicating the effective practices statewide, holding participating LEAs (as defined in this notice) accountable for progress and performance, and intervening where necessary;

(c) Providing effective and efficient operations and processes for implementing its Race to the Top grant in such areas as grant administration and oversight, budget reporting and monitoring, performance measure tracking and reporting, and fund disbursement;

---

[2] See Appendix D (omitted here) for more on participating LEA MOUs and for a model MOU.

(d) Using the funds for this grant, as described in the State's budget and accompanying budget narrative, to accomplish the State's plans and meet its targets, including, where feasible, by coordinating, reallocating, or repurposing education funds from other Federal, State, and local sources so that they align with the State's Race to the Top goals; and

(e) Using the fiscal, political, and human capital resources of the State to continue, after the period of funding has ended, those reforms funded under the grant for which there is evidence of success; and

(ii) Use support from a broad group of stakeholders to better implement its plans, as evidenced by the strength of statements or actions of support from— *(10 points)*

(a) The State's teachers and principals, which include the State's teachers' unions or statewide teacher associations; and

(b) Other critical stakeholders, such as the State's legislative leadership; charter school authorizers and State charter school membership associations (if applicable); other State and local leaders (*e.g.*, business, community, civil rights, and education association leaders); Tribal schools; parent, student, and community organizations (*e.g.*, parent-teacher associations, nonprofit organizations, local education foundations, and community-based organizations); and institutions of higher education.

(A)(3) <u>Demonstrating significant progress in raising achievement and closing gaps</u> *(30 points)*
The extent to which the State has demonstrated its ability to—

(i) Make progress over the past several years in each of the four education reform areas, and used its ARRA and other Federal and State funding to pursue such reforms; *(5 points)*

(ii) Improve student outcomes overall and by student subgroup since at least 2003, and explain the connections between the data and the actions that have contributed to— *(25 points)*

(a) Increasing student achievement in reading/language arts and mathematics, both on the NAEP and on the assessments required under the ESEA;

(b) Decreasing achievement gaps between subgroups in reading/language arts and mathematics, both on the NAEP and on the assessments required under the ESEA; and

(c) Increasing high school graduation rates.

B. Standards and Assessments *(70 points)*
State Reform Conditions Criteria

(B)(1) <u>Developing and adopting common standards</u> *(40 points)*
The extent to which the State has demonstrated its commitment to adopting a common set of high-quality standards, evidenced by (as set forth in Appendix B)—

(i) The State's participation in a consortium of States that— *(20 points)*

(a) Is working toward jointly developing and adopting a common set of K-12 standards (as defined in this notice) that are supported by evidence that they are internationally benchmarked and build toward college and career readiness by the time of high school graduation; and

(b) Includes a significant number of States; and

(ii) *(20 points)*

(a) For Phase 1 applications, the State's high-quality plan demonstrating its commitment to and progress toward adopting a common set of K-12 standards (as defined in this notice) by August 2, 2010, or, at a minimum, by a later date in 2010 specified by the State, and to implementing the standards thereafter in a well-planned way; or

(b) For Phase 2 applications, the State's adoption of a common set of K-12 standards (as defined in this notice) by August 2, 2010, or, at a minimum, by a later date in 2010 specified by the State in a high-quality plan toward which the State has made significant progress, and its commitment to implementing the standards thereafter in a well-planned way.[3]

---

[3] Phase 2 applicants addressing selection criterion (B)(1)(ii) may amend their June 1, 2010 application submission through August 2, 2010 by submitting evidence of adopting common standards after June 1, 2010.

(B)(2) Developing and implementing common, high-quality assessments *(10 points)*

The extent to which the State has demonstrated its commitment to improving the quality of its assessments, evidenced by (as set forth in Appendix B) the State's participation in a consortium of States that—

(i) Is working toward jointly developing and implementing common, high-quality assessments (as defined in this notice) aligned with the consortium's common set of K-12 standards (as defined in this notice); and

(ii) Includes a significant number of States.

Reform Plan Criteria

(B)(3) Supporting the transition to enhanced standards and high-quality assessments *(20 points)*

The extent to which the State, in collaboration with its participating LEAs (as defined in this notice), has a high-quality plan for supporting a statewide transition to and implementation of internationally benchmarked K-12 standards that build toward college and career readiness by the time of high school graduation, and high-quality assessments (as defined in this notice) tied to these standards. State or LEA activities might, for example, include: developing a rollout plan for the standards together with all of their supporting components; in cooperation with the State's institutions of higher education, aligning high school exit criteria and college entrance requirements with the new standards and assessments; developing or acquiring, disseminating, and implementing high-quality instructional materials and assessments (including, for example, formative and interim assessments (both as defined in this notice)); developing or acquiring and delivering high-quality professional development to support the transition to new standards and assessments; and engaging in other strategies that translate the standards and information from assessments into classroom practice for all students, including high-need students (as defined in this notice).

C. Data Systems to Support Instruction *(47 points)*

State Reform Conditions Criteria

(C)(1) Fully implementing a statewide longitudinal data system *(24 points)*

The extent to which the State has a statewide longitudinal data system that includes all of the America COMPETES Act elements (as defined in this notice).

Reform Plan Criteria

(C)(2) Accessing and using State data *(5 points)*

The extent to which the State has a high-quality plan to ensure that data from the State's statewide longitudinal data system are accessible to, and used to inform and engage, as appropriate, key stakeholders (*e.g.*, parents, students, teachers, principals, LEA leaders, community members, unions, researchers, and policymakers); and that the data support decision-makers in the continuous improvement of efforts in such areas as policy, instruction, operations, management, resource allocation, and overall effectiveness.[4]

(C)(3) Using data to improve instruction *(18 points)*

The extent to which the State, in collaboration with its participating LEAs (as defined in this notice), has a high-quality plan to—

(i) Increase the acquisition, adoption, and use of local instructional improvement systems (as defined in this notice) that provide teachers, principals, and administrators with the information and resources they need to inform and improve their instructional practices, decision-making, and overall effectiveness;

(ii) Support participating LEAs (as defined in this notice) and schools that are using instructional improvement systems (as defined in this notice) in providing effective professional development to teachers,

---

[4] Successful applicants that receive Race to the Top grant awards will need to comply with the Family Educational Rights and Privacy Act (FERPA), including 34 CFR Part 99, as well as State and local requirements regarding privacy.

principals, and administrators on how to use these systems and the resulting data to support continuous instructional improvement; and

(iii) Make the data from instructional improvement systems (as defined in this notice), together with statewide longitudinal data system data, available and accessible to researchers so that they have detailed information with which to evaluate the effectiveness of instructional materials, strategies, and approaches for educating different types of students (*e.g.*, students with disabilities, English language learners, students whose achievement is well below or above grade level).

D. Great Teachers and Leaders *(138 points)*
State Reform Conditions Criteria
(D)(1) <u>Providing high-quality pathways for aspiring teachers and principals</u> *(21 points)*
The extent to which the State has—

(i) Legal, statutory, or regulatory provisions that allow alternative routes to certification (as defined in this notice) for teachers and principals, particularly routes that allow for providers in addition to institutions of higher education;

(ii) Alternative routes to certification (as defined in this notice) that are in use; and

(iii) A process for monitoring, evaluating, and identifying areas of teacher and principal shortage and for preparing teachers and principals to fill these areas of shortage.

Reform Plan Criteria
(D)(2) <u>Improving teacher and principal effectiveness based on performance</u> *(58 points)*
The extent to which the State, in collaboration with its participating LEAs (as defined in this notice), has a high-quality plan and ambitious yet achievable annual targets to ensure that participating LEAs (as defined in this notice)—

(i) Establish clear approaches to measuring student growth (as defined in this notice) and measure it for each individual student; *(5 points)*

(ii) Design and implement rigorous, transparent, and fair evaluation systems for teachers and principals that (a) differentiate effectiveness using multiple rating categories that take into account data on student growth (as defined in this notice) as a significant factor, and (b) are designed and developed with teacher and principal involvement; *(15 points)*

(iii) Conduct annual evaluations of teachers and principals that include timely and constructive feedback; as part of such evaluations, provide teachers and principals with data on student growth for their students, classes, and schools; and *(10 points)*

(iv) Use these evaluations, at a minimum, to inform decisions regarding— *(28 points)*

(a) Developing teachers and principals, including by providing relevant coaching, induction support, and/or professional development;

(b) Compensating, promoting, and retaining teachers and principals, including by providing opportunities for highly effective teachers and principals (both as defined in this notice) to obtain additional compensation and be given additional responsibilities;

(c) Whether to grant tenure and/or full certification (where applicable) to teachers and principals using rigorous standards and streamlined, transparent, and fair procedures; and

(d) Removing ineffective tenured and untenured teachers and principals after they have had ample opportunities to improve, and ensuring that such decisions are made using rigorous standards and streamlined, transparent, and fair procedures.

(D)(3) <u>Ensuring equitable distribution of effective teachers and principals</u> *(25 points)*
The extent to which the State, in collaboration with its participating LEAs (as defined in this notice), has a high-quality plan and ambitious yet achievable annual targets to—

(i) Ensure the equitable distribution of teachers and principals by developing a plan, informed by reviews of prior actions and data, to ensure that students in high-poverty and/or high-minority schools (both as defined in this notice) have equitable access to highly effective teachers and principals (both as defined in this notice) and are not served by ineffective teachers and principals at higher rates than other students; and *(15 points)*

(ii) Increase the number and percentage of effective teachers (as defined in this notice) teaching hard-to-staff subjects and specialty areas including mathematics, science, and special education; teaching in language instruction educational programs (as defined under Title III of the ESEA); and teaching in other areas as identified by the State or LEA. *(10 points)*

Plans for (i) and (ii) may include, but are not limited to, the implementation of incentives and strategies in such areas as recruitment, compensation, teaching and learning environments, professional development, and human resources practices and processes.

(D)(4) <u>Improving the effectiveness of teacher and principal preparation programs</u> *(14 points)*
The extent to which the State has a high-quality plan and ambitious yet achievable annual targets to—

(i) Link student achievement and student growth (both as defined in this notice) data to the students' teachers and principals, to link this information to the in-State programs where those teachers and principals were prepared for credentialing, and to publicly report the data for each credentialing program in the State; and

(ii) Expand preparation and credentialing options and programs that are successful at producing effective teachers and principals (both as defined in this notice).

(D)(5) <u>Providing effective support to teachers and principals</u> *(20 points)*
The extent to which the State, in collaboration with its participating LEAs (as defined in this notice), has a high-quality plan for its participating LEAs (as defined in this notice) to—

(i) Provide effective, data-informed professional development, coaching, induction, and common planning and collaboration time to teachers and principals that are, where appropriate, ongoing and job-embedded. Such support might focus on, for example, gathering, analyzing, and using data; designing instructional strategies for improvement; differentiating instruction; creating school environments supportive of data-informed decisions; designing instruction to meet the specific needs of high-need students (as defined in this notice); and aligning systems and removing barriers to effective implementation of practices designed to improve student learning outcomes; and

(ii) Measure, evaluate, and continuously improve the effectiveness of those supports in order to improve student achievement (as defined in this notice).

E. Turning Around the Lowest-Achieving Schools *(50 points)*
State Reform Conditions Criteria
(E)(1) <u>Intervening in the lowest-achieving schools and LEAs</u> *(10 points)*
The extent to which the State has the legal, statutory, or regulatory authority to intervene directly in the State's persistently lowest-achieving schools (as defined in this notice) and in LEAs that are in improvement or corrective action status.

Reform Plan Criteria
(E)(2) <u>Turning around the lowest-achieving schools</u> *(40 points)*
The extent to which the State has a high-quality plan and ambitious yet achievable annual targets to—

(i) Identify the persistently lowest-achieving schools (as defined in this notice) and, at its discretion, any non-Title I eligible secondary schools that would be considered persistently lowest-achieving schools (as defined in this notice) if they were eligible to receive Title I funds; and *(5 points)*

(ii) Support its LEAs in turning around these schools by implementing one of the four school intervention models (as described in Appendix C): turnaround model, restart model, school closure, or transformation model (provided that an LEA with more than nine persistently lowest-achieving schools may not use the transformation model for more than 50 percent of its schools). *(35 points)*

F. General *(55 points)*

State Reform Conditions Criteria

(F)(1) Making education funding a priority *(10 points)*

The extent to which—

(i) The percentage of the total revenues available to the State (as defined in this notice) that were used to support elementary, secondary, and public higher education for FY 2009 was greater than or equal to the percentage of the total revenues available to the State (as defined in this notice) that were used to support elementary, secondary, and public higher education for FY 2008; and

(ii) The State's policies lead to equitable funding (a) between high-need LEAs (as defined in this notice) and other LEAs, and (b) within LEAs, between high-poverty schools (as defined in this notice) and other schools.

(F)(2) Ensuring successful conditions for high-performing charter schools and other innovative schools *(40 points)*

The extent to which—

(i) The State has a charter school law that does not prohibit or effectively inhibit increasing the number of high-performing charter schools (as defined in this notice) in the State, measured (as set forth in Appendix B) by the percentage of total schools in the State that are allowed to be charter schools or otherwise restrict student enrollment in charter schools;

(ii) The State has laws, statutes, regulations, or guidelines regarding how charter school authorizers approve, monitor, hold accountable, reauthorize, and close charter schools; in particular, whether authorizers require that student achievement (as defined in this notice) be one significant factor, among others, in authorization or renewal; encourage charter schools that serve student populations that are similar to local district student populations, especially relative to high-need students (as defined in this notice); and have closed or not renewed ineffective charter schools;

(iii) The State's charter schools receive (as set forth in Appendix B) equitable funding compared to traditional public schools, and a commensurate share of local, State, and Federal revenues;

(iv) The State provides charter schools with funding for facilities (for leasing facilities, purchasing facilities, or making tenant improvements), assistance with facilities acquisition, access to public facilities, the ability to share in bonds and mill levies, or other supports; and the extent to which the State does not impose any facility-related requirements on charter schools that are stricter than those applied to traditional public schools; and

(v) The State enables LEAs to operate innovative, autonomous public schools (as defined in this notice) other than charter schools.

(F)(3) Demonstrating other significant reform conditions *(5 points)*

The extent to which the State, in addition to information provided under other State Reform Conditions Criteria, has created, through law, regulation, or policy, other conditions favorable to education reform or innovation that have increased student achievement or graduation rates, narrowed achievement gaps, or resulted in other important outcomes.

DEFINITIONS

Alternative routes to certification means pathways to certification that are authorized under the State's laws or regulations, that allow the establishment and operation of teacher and administrator preparation programs in the State, and that have the following characteristics (in addition to standard features such as demonstration of subject-matter mastery, and high-quality instruction in pedagogy and in addressing the needs of all students in the classroom including English language learners and student with disabilities): (a) can be provided by various types of qualified providers, including both institutions of higher education and other providers operating independently from institutions of higher education; (b) are selective in accepting candidates; (c) provide supervised, school-based experiences and ongoing support such as effective mentoring and coaching; (d) significantly limit the amount of coursework required or have options to test out of courses; and (e) upon completion, award the same level of certification that traditional preparation programs award upon completion.

<u>College enrollment</u> refers to the enrollment of students who graduate from high school consistent with 34 CFR 200.19(b)(1) and who enroll in an institution of higher education (as defined in section 101 of the Higher Education Act, P.L. 105-244, 20 U.S.C. 1001) within 16 months of graduation.

<u>Common set of K-12 standards</u> means a set of content standards that define what students must know and be able to do and that are substantially identical across all States in a consortium. A State may supplement the common standards with additional standards, provided that the additional standards do not exceed 15 percent of the State's total standards for that content area.

<u>Effective principal</u> means a principal whose students, overall and for each subgroup, achieve acceptable rates (*e.g.*, at least one grade level in an academic year) of student growth (as defined in this notice). States, LEAs, or schools must include multiple measures, provided that principal effectiveness is evaluated, in significant part, by student growth (as defined in this notice). Supplemental measures may include, for example, high school graduation rates and college enrollment rates, as well as evidence of providing supportive teaching and learning conditions, strong instructional leadership, and positive family and community engagement.

<u>Effective teacher</u> means a teacher whose students achieve acceptable rates (*e.g.*, at least one grade level in an academic year) of student growth (as defined in this notice). States, LEAs, or schools must include multiple measures, provided that teacher effectiveness is evaluated, in significant part, by student growth (as defined in this notice). Supplemental measures may include, for example, multiple observation-based assessments of teacher performance.

<u>Formative assessment</u> means assessment questions, tools, and processes that are embedded in instruction and are used by teachers and students to provide timely feedback for purposes of adjusting instruction to improve learning.

<u>Graduation rate</u> means the four-year or extended-year adjusted cohort graduation rate as defined by 34 CFR 200.19(b)(1).

<u>Highly effective principal</u> means a principal whose students, overall and for each subgroup, achieve high rates (*e.g.*, one and one-half grade levels in an academic year) of student growth (as defined in this notice). States, LEAs, or schools must include multiple measures, provided that principal effectiveness is evaluated, in significant part, by student growth (as defined in this notice). Supplemental measures may include, for example, high school graduation rates; college enrollment rates; evidence of providing supportive teaching and learning conditions, strong instructional leadership, and positive family and community engagement; or evidence of attracting, developing, and retaining high numbers of effective teachers.

<u>Highly effective teacher</u> means a teacher whose students achieve high rates (*e.g.*, one and one-half grade levels in an academic year) of student growth (as defined in this notice). States, LEAs, or schools must include multiple measures, provided that teacher effectiveness is evaluated, in significant part, by student growth (as defined in this notice). Supplemental measures may include, for example, multiple observation-based assessments of teacher performance or evidence of leadership roles (which may include mentoring or leading professional learning communities) that increase the effectiveness of other teachers in the school or LEA.

<u>High-minority school</u> is defined by the State in a manner consistent with its Teacher Equity Plan. The State should provide, in its Race to the Top application, the definition used.

<u>High-need LEA</u> means an LEA (a) that serves not fewer than 10,000 children from families with incomes below the poverty line; or (b) for which not less than 20 percent of the children served by the LEA are from families with incomes below the poverty line.

<u>High-need students</u> means students at risk of educational failure or otherwise in need of special assistance and support, such as students who are living in poverty, who attend high-minority schools (as defined in this notice), who are far below grade level, who have left school before receiving a regular high school diploma, who are at risk of not graduating with a diploma on time, who are homeless, who are in foster care, who have been incarcerated, who have disabilities, or who are English language learners.

High-performing charter school means a charter school that has been in operation for at least three consecutive years and has demonstrated overall success, including (a) substantial progress in improving student achievement (as defined in this notice); and (b) the management and leadership necessary to overcome initial start-up problems and establish a thriving, financially viable charter school.

High-poverty school means, consistent with section 1111(h)(1)(C)(viii) of the ESEA, a school in the highest quartile of schools in the State with respect to poverty level, using a measure of poverty determined by the State.

High-quality assessment means an assessment designed to measure a student's knowledge, understanding of, and ability to apply, critical concepts through the use of a variety of item types and formats (e.g., open-ended responses, performance-based tasks). Such assessments should enable measurement of student achievement (as defined in this notice) and student growth (as defined in this notice); be of high technical quality (e.g., be valid, reliable, fair, and aligned to standards); incorporate technology where appropriate; include the assessment of students with disabilities and English language learners; and to the extent feasible, use universal design principles (as defined in section 3 of the Assistive Technology Act of 1998, as amended, 29 U.S.C. 3002) in development and administration.

Increased learning time means using a longer school day, week, or year schedule to significantly increase the total number of school hours to include additional time for (a) instruction in core academic subjects, including English; reading or language arts; mathematics; science; foreign languages; civics and government; economics; arts; history; and geography; (b) instruction in other subjects and enrichment activities that contribute to a well-rounded education, including, for example, physical education, service learning, and experiential and work-based learning opportunities that are provided by partnering, as appropriate, with other organizations; and (c) teachers to collaborate, plan, and engage in professional development within and across grades and subjects.[5]

Innovative, autonomous public schools means open enrollment public schools that, in return for increased accountability for student achievement (as defined in this notice), have the flexibility and authority to define their instructional models and associated curriculum; select and replace staff; implement new structures and formats for the school day or year; and control their budgets.

Instructional improvement systems means technology-based tools and other strategies that provide teachers, principals, and administrators with meaningful support and actionable data to systemically manage continuous instructional improvement, including such activities as: instructional planning; gathering information (e.g., through formative assessments (as defined in this notice), interim assessments (as defined in this notice), summative assessments, and looking at student work and other student data); analyzing information with the support of rapid-time (as defined in this notice) reporting; using this information to inform decisions on appropriate next instructional steps; and evaluating the effectiveness of the actions taken. Such systems promote collaborative problem-solving and action planning; they may also integrate instructional data with student-level data such as attendance, discipline, grades, credit accumulation, and student survey results to provide early warning indicators of a student's risk of educational failure.

Interim assessment means an assessment that is given at regular and specified intervals throughout the school year, is designed to evaluate students' knowledge and skills relative to a specific set of academic

---

[5] Research supports the effectiveness of well-designed programs that expand learning time by a minimum of 300 hours per school year. (See Frazier, Julie A.; Morrison, Frederick J. "The Influence of Extended-year Schooling on Growth of Achievement and Perceived Competence in Early Elementary School." Child Development. Vol. 69 (2), April 1998, pp.495-497 and research done by Mass2020.) Extending learning into before- and after-school hours can be difficult to implement effectively, but is permissible under this definition with encouragement to closely integrate and coordinate academic work between in-school and out-of school. (See James-Burdumy, Susanne; Dynarski, Mark; Deke, John. "When Elementary Schools Stay Open Late: Results from The National Evaluation of the 21st Century Community Learning Centers Program." <http://www.mathematica-mpr.com/publications/redirect_PubsDB.asp?strSite=http://epa.sagepub.com/cgi/content/abstract/29/4/296> Educational Evaluation and Policy Analysis, Vol. 29 (4), December 2007, Document No. PP07-121.)

standards, and produces results that can be aggregated (*e.g.*, by course, grade level, school, or LEA) in order to inform teachers and administrators at the student, classroom, school, and LEA levels.

Involved LEAs means LEAs that choose to work with the State to implement those specific portions of the State's plan that necessitate full or nearly-full statewide implementation, such as transitioning to a common set of K-12 standards (as defined in this notice). Involved LEAs do not receive a share of the 50 percent of a State's grant award that it must subgrant to LEAs in accordance with section 14006(c) of the ARRA, but States may provide other funding to involved LEAs under the State's Race to the Top grant in a manner that is consistent with the State's application.

Low-minority school is defined by the State in a manner consistent with its Teacher Equity Plan. The State should provide, in its Race to the Top application, the definition used.

Low-poverty school means, consistent with section 1111(h)(1)(C)(viii) of the ESEA, a school in the lowest quartile of schools in the State with respect to poverty level, using a measure of poverty determined by the State.

Participating LEAs means LEAs that choose to work with the State to implement all or significant portions of the State's Race to the Top plan, as specified in each LEA's agreement with the State. Each participating LEA that receives funding under Title I, Part A will receive a share of the 50 percent of a State's grant award that the State must subgrant to LEAs, based on the LEA's relative share of Title I, Part A allocations in the most recent year, in accordance with section 14006(c) of the ARRA. Any participating LEA that does not receive funding under Title I, Part A (as well as one that does) may receive funding from the State's other 50 percent of the grant award, in accordance with the State's plan.

Persistently lowest-achieving schools means, as determined by the State: (i) Any Title I school in improvement, corrective action, or restructuring that (a) Is among the lowest-achieving five percent of Title I schools in improvement, corrective action, or restructuring or the lowest-achieving five Title I schools in improvement, corrective action, or restructuring in the State, whichever number of schools is greater; or (b) Is a high school that has had a graduation rate as defined in 34 CFR 200.19(b) that is less than 60 percent over a number of years; and (ii) Any secondary school that is eligible for, but does not receive, Title I funds that (a) Is among the lowest-achieving five percent of secondary schools or the lowest-achieving five secondary schools in the State that are eligible for, but do not receive, Title I funds, whichever number of schools is greater; or (b) Is a high school that has had a graduation rate as defined in 34 CFR 200.19(b) that is less than 60 percent over a number of years.

To identify the lowest-achieving schools, a State must take into account both (i) The academic achievement of the "all students" group in a school in terms of proficiency on the State's assessments under section 1111(b)(3) of the ESEA in reading/language arts and mathematics combined; and (ii) The school's lack of progress on those assessments over a number of years in the "all students" group.

Rapid-time, in reference to reporting and availability of locally-collected school- and LEA-level data, means that data are available quickly enough to inform current lessons, instruction, and related supports.

Student achievement means—

(a) For tested grades and subjects: (1) a student's score on the State's assessments under the ESEA; and, as appropriate, (2) other measures of student learning, such as those described in paragraph (b) of this definition, provided they are rigorous and comparable across classrooms.

(b) For non-tested grades and subjects: alternative measures of student learning and performance such as student scores on pre-tests and end-of-course tests; student performance on English language proficiency assessments; and other measures of student achievement that are rigorous and comparable across classrooms.

Student growth means the change in student achievement (as defined in this notice) for an individual student between two or more points in time. A State may also include other measures that are rigorous and comparable across classrooms.

Total revenues available to the State means either (a) projected or actual total State revenues for education and other purposes for the relevant year; or (b) projected or actual total State appropriations for education and other purposes for the relevant year.

America COMPETES Act elements means (as specified in section 6401(e)(2)(D) of that Act): (1) a unique statewide student identifier that does not permit a student to be individually identified by users of the system; (2) student-level enrollment, demographic, and program participation information; (3) student-level information about the points at which students exit, transfer in, transfer out, drop out, or complete P–16 education programs; (4) the capacity to communicate with higher education data systems; (5) a State data audit system assessing data quality, validity, and reliability; (6) yearly test records of individual students with respect to assessments under section 1111(b) of the ESEA (20 U.S.C. 6311(b)); (7) information on students not tested by grade and subject; (8) a teacher identifier system with the ability to match teachers to students; (9) student-level transcript information, including information on courses completed and grades earned; (10) student-level college readiness test scores; (11) information regarding the extent to which students transition successfully from secondary school to postsecondary education, including whether students enroll in remedial coursework; and (12) other information determined necessary to address alignment and adequate preparation for success in postsecondary education.

Source: U.S. Department of Education, Race to the Top Executive Summary, November 2009

Nine States and the District of Columbia Win Second Round Race to the Top Grants

U.S. Secretary of Education Arne Duncan announced today that 10 applicants have won grants in the second phase of the Race to the Top competition. Along with Phase 1 winners Delaware and Tennessee, 11 states and the District of Columbia have now been awarded money in the Obama Administration's groundbreaking education reform program that will directly impact 13.6 million students, and 980,000 teachers in 25,000 schools.

The 10 winning Phase 2 applications in alphabetical order are: the District of Columbia, Florida, Georgia, Hawaii, Maryland, Massachusetts, New York, North Carolina, Ohio, and Rhode Island.

"These states show what is possible when adults come together to do the right thing for children," said Secretary Arne Duncan. "Every state that applied showed a tremendous amount of leadership and a bold commitment to education reform. The creativity and innovation in each of these applications is breathtaking," Duncan continued. "We set a high bar and these states met the challenge."

While peer reviewers rated these 10 as having the highest scoring plans, very few points separated them from the remaining applications. The deciding factor on the number of winners selected hinged on both the quality of the applications and the funds available.

"We had many more competitive applications than money to fund them in this round," Duncan said. "We're very hopeful there will be a Phase 3 of Race to the Top and have requested $1.35 billion dollars in next year's budget. In the meantime, we will partner with each and every state that applied to help them find ways to carry out the bold reforms they've proposed in their applications."

A total of 46 states and the District of Columbia put together comprehensive education reform plans to apply for Race to the Top in Phases 1 and 2. Over the course of the Race to the Top competition, 35 states and the District of Columbia have adopted rigorous common, college- and career-ready standards in reading and math, and 34 states have changed laws or policies to improve education.

Every state that applied has already done the hard work of collaboratively creating a comprehensive education reform agenda. In the coming months, the Department plans to bring all States together to help ensure the success of their work implementing reforms around college- and career-ready standards, data systems, great teachers and leaders, and school turnarounds.

In addition to the reforms supported by Race to the Top, the Department has made unprecedented resources available through reform programs like the Investing in Innovation Fund, the Teacher Incentive Fund, and the School Improvement Grants under Title I.

Through all of these programs, the Department of Education will be distributing almost $10 billion to support reform in states and local communities.

"As we look at the last 18 months, it is absolutely stunning to see how much change has happened at the state and local levels, unleashed in part by these incentive programs," Duncan said.

As with any federal grant program, budgets will be finalized after discussions between the grantees and the Department, and the money will be distributed over time as the grantees meet established benchmarks.

The $4.35 billion Race to the Top Fund is an unprecedented federal investment in reform. The program includes $4 billion for statewide reform grants and $350 million to support states working together to improve the quality of their assessments, which the Department plans to award in September. The Race to the Top state competition is designed to reward states that are leading the way in comprehensive, coherent, statewide education reform across four key areas:

- Adopting standards and assessments that prepare students to succeed in college and the workplace;
- Building data systems that measure student growth and success, and inform teachers and principals how to improve instruction;
- Recruiting, developing, rewarding, and retaining effective teachers and principals, especially where they are needed most; and
- Turning around their lowest-performing schools.

The 10 winning applicants have adopted rigorous common, college- and career-ready standards in reading and math, created pipelines and incentives to put the most effective teachers in high-need schools, and all have alternative pathways to teacher and principal certification.

	Phase 2 Grantee	Budget Not to Exceed...	Phase 2 Score	Phase 1 Score	Score Change
1	Massachusetts	$250,000,000	471.0	411.4	59.6
2	New York	$700,000,000	464.8	408.6	56.2
3	Hawaii	$75,000,000	462.4	364.6	97.8
4	Florida	$700,000,000	452.4	431.4	21
5	Rhode Island	$75,000,000	451.2	419.0	32.2
6	District of Columbia	$75,000,000	450.0	402.4	47.6
7	Maryland	$250,000,000	450.0	N/A	N/A
8	Georgia	$400,000,000	446.4	433.6	12.8
9	North Carolina	$400,000,000	441.6	414.0	27.6
10	Ohio	$400,000,000	440.8	418.6	22.2

In the first round of competition supporting state-based reforms, Delaware and Tennessee won grants based on their comprehensive plans to reform their schools and the statewide support for those plans.

The Department of Education has posted all Phase 2 applications online. Phase 2 peer reviewers' comments, and scores will be available on the website by August 25th; videos of states' presentations will be posted by September 10th. Phase 1 materials are available online.

Source: U.S. Department of Education, August 24, 2010

General

1 ASPIRA Association
1444 Eye Street NW
Suite 800
Washington, DC 20005-6543
202-835-3600
Fax: 202-835-3613
E-mail: info@aspira.org
http://www.aspira.org
Founded in 1961 ASPIRA promotes Latino youth leadership and education. Through its associate ASPIRA organizations and national demonstration projects, it provides a host of leadership development and education programs for Puerto Rican and other Latino youth.

Ronald Blackburn-Moreno, President/CEO
John Villamil-Casanova, Executive Vice President & C

2 Academy for Educational Development
1825 Connecticut Avenue, NW
Washington, DC 20009-5721
202-884-8000
Fax: 202-884-8400
E-mail: web@aed.org
http://www.aed.org
Assists schools, colleges and other educational institutions of developing countries in researching, planning, designing, implementing and evaluating development programs. In the US, manages the Center for Youth Development and Policy Research (disadvantaged youth), Disabilities Studies and Services Center (clearinghouse on special education and children with disabilities), National Institute for Work and Learning (school-to-work transition), and schools and Community Services Department.

Founded: 1961

George Ingram, President/CEO
Robert Murphy, Senior VP/COO

3 Advance Program for Young Scholars
Northwestern State University
PO Box 5671
Natchitoches, LA 71497
318-357-4500
Fax: 318-357-4547
E-mail: palmerh@nsula.edu
http://www.advanceprogram.org
From chemistry to history, from foreign languages to ecology, the program offers a broad spectrum of academic opportuities to the qualified 12-17 year old student.

David Wood PhD, Director
Harriette Palmer, Assistant Director

4 Alliance for Parental Involvement in Education
PO Box 59
East Chatham, NY 12060-59
518-392-6900
E-mail: allpie@taconic.net
http://www.allpie.org
Seeks to nurture parents' natural teaching abilities and offer tools and resources, public, private and home in becoming active participants in the education of their children.

Katharine Houk, Executive Director

5 American Academy of Pediatrics
141 NW Point Boulevard
Elk Grove Village, IL 60007-1098
847-434-4000
Fax: 847-434-8000
E-mail: kidsdoc@aap.org
http://www.aap.org
Committed to the attainment of optimal physical, mental and social health for all infants, children, adolescents and young adults.

O Marion Burton, MD/FAAP, President
Errol R Alden, MD, Executive Director

6 American Association for Vocational Instructional Materials (AAVIM)
220 Smithonia Road
Winterville, GA 30683-1418
706-742-5355
800-228-4689
Fax: 706-742-7005
E-mail: sales@aavim.com
http://www.aavim.com
Develops, produces and distributes qualtiy instructional materials for career education instructors, students, and administrators.

Gary Farmer, Director
Vicki J Eaton, Art Director/Production Coor

7 American Council for Drug Education
50 Jay Street
Brooklyn, NY 11201
718-222-6641
800-488-3784
Fax: 212-595-2553
E-mail: acde@phoenixhouse.org
http://www.acde.org
Distributes packaged information about drugs and the consequences of their use and identifies effective community programs to address the drug problem in the country.

Founded: 1977

William F Current, Executive Director

8 American Council on Education (ACE)
1 Dupont Circle NW
Suite 800
Washington, DC 20036-1193
202-939-9300
Fax: 202-833-4730
E-mail: comments@ace.nche.edu
http://www.acenet.edu
Represents accredited degree-granting colleges and universities directly and through national and regional higher education associations. Seeks to advance education and serves as an advocate for adult education.

Molly Corbett Broad, President
Tully R Cornick, Executive Director

9 American Council on Rural Special Education (ACRES)
Montana Center on Disabilities
MSU-B
1500 University Drive
Billings, MT 59101
406-657-2312
888-866-3822
Fax: 406-657-2313
E-mail: inquiries@acres-sped.org
http://www.acres-sped.org
The organization is comprised of special educators, general educators, related service providers, administrators, teacher trainers, researchers, and parents committed to the enhancement of services to students and individuals living in rural America.

Nancy Glomb, Chair
Cathy Galyon Keramidal, Chair Elect

10 American Driver and Traffic Safety Education Association (ADTSEA)
Highway Safety Services
1434 Trim Tree Road
Indiana, PA 15705
724-801-8246
877-485-7172
Fax: 724-349-5042
E-mail: support@hsc.iup.edu
http://www.adtsea.org
The purpose of the American Driver and Traffic Safety Education Association is to promote traffic safety and its concomitant benefits by improving and extending driver education/training activities in schools, colleges, universities, the private sector, industry and other institutions.

Fred Nagao, President
Dana Sosnick-Bowser, Executive Director

11 American Federation of Teachers
555 New Jersey Avenue NW
Washington, DC 20001
202-879-4400
Fax: 202-879-4556
E-mail: online@aft.org
http://www.aft.org
The AFT represents one million teachers, school support staff, higher education faculty and staff, health care professionals, and state and municipal employees. AFT is an affiliated international union of the AFL-CIO.

Randi Weingarten, President
Lorreta Johnson, Executive VP

12 American Montessori Society
281 Park Avenue S
New York, NY 10010-6102
212-358-1250
Fax: 212-358-1256
E-mail: ams@amshq.org
http://www.amshq.org
Provides the leadership and inspiration to make Montessori a significant voice in education.ÿ The Society advocates quality Montessori education, strengthens members through its services, and champions Montessori principles to the greater community.

Marilyn E Stewart, President
Kathy Roemer, Vice President

13 American School Health Association
4340 East West Highway
Suite 403
Bethesda, MD 20814
301-652-8072
Fax: 301-652-8077
E-mail: asha@ashaweb.org
http://www.ashaweb.org
A nonprofit organization founded to protect and improve the health and well-being of children and youth by supporting comprehensive, preschool-12 school health programs.

Jeffrey K Clark, President
Linda Morse RN, MA, President-Elect

14 American Society for Engineering Education
1818 N Street NW
Suite 600
Washington, DC 20036-2479
202-331-3500
Fax: 202-265-8504
E-mail: aseeexec@asee.org
http://www.asee.org
A nonprofit organization of individuals and institutions committed to furthering education in engineering and engineering technology.

Founded: 1893

Lyle Feisel, Executive Director

15 Association for Business Communication (ABC)
Baruch College
PO Box 6143
Nacogdoches, TX 75962-0001
936-468-6280
Fax: 936-468-6281
E-mail: abcjohnson@sfasu.edu
http://www.businesscommunication.org

Committed to fostering excellence in business communication scholarship, research, education, and practice.

Betty S Johnson, Executive Director
Jim Dubinsky, President

16 Association for Community-Based Education
1806 Vernon Street NW
Washington, DC 20009-1217
202-462-6333
Offers technical assistance on planning, management and program development for community-based education.

Christofer Zachariadis, Executive Director

17 Association for Disabled Students
University of Oklahoma
Disability Resource Center
620 Elm Avenue, Suite 166
Norman, OK 73019-0340
405-325-3852
Fax: 405-325-4491
E-mail: drc@ou.edu
http://drc.ou.edu/content/view/54
Also known as ADS, this student organization provides a forum for support, regular meetings, and social and recreational activities. ADS sponsors Disability Awareness Week each October and Disability Arts Week the first week of April. ADS also sponsors a wheelchair basketball team, affiliated with the Intercollegiate Wheelchair Division of the National Wheelchair Basketball Association. The team competes nationally.

Suzette Dyer, Director

18 Association for Environmental and OutdoorEducation (AEOE)
PO Box 187
Angelus Oaks, CA 92305
714-838-8990
714-474-1377
E-mail: TraciFesko@cusd.com
http://www.aeoe.org
The Association for Environmental and Outdoor Education supports and inspires educators in their quest for the knowledge, skills, and attitudes essential to help all learners understand, appreciate and care for their environment.

Ryan Brennan, President
Helen M De La Maza, Membership Chair

19 Association for Gender Equity Leadership in Education
317 S Division PMB 54
Ann Arbor, MI 48104
734-769-2456
Fax: 734-769-2456
E-mail: businessmgr@agele.org
http://www.agele.org
A national organization for gender equity specialists and educators. Individuals and organizations committed to reducing sex role stereotyping for females and males. Services include an annual national training conference, a quarterly newsletter and a membership directory. Members may join task forces dealing with equity related topics such as computer/technology issues, early childhood, male issues, sexual harassment prevention, sexual orientation and vocational issues.

Marta Larson, Business Manager
Keith Eccarius, Communications Manager

20 Association for Integrative Studies
School of Interdisciplinary Studies
Miami University
Oxford, OH 45056
513-529-2659
Fax: 513-529-5849
E-mail: newellwh@muohio.edu
http://www.units.muohio.edu/aisorg
The Association for Integrative Studies is an interdisciplinary professional organization founded in 1979 to promote the interchange of ideas among scholars and administrators in all of the arts and sciences on intellectual and organizational issues related to furthering integrative studies. Incorporated as a non-profit educational association in the State of Ohio, it has an international membership.

Bill Newell, Executive Director
Karen Moranski, President

21 Association for Play Therapy
3198 Willow Avenue
Suite 110
Clovis, CA 93612
559-294-2128
Fax: 559-294-2129
E-mail: info@a4pt.org
http://www.a4pt.org
Founded in 1982 APT promote the value of play, play therapy, and credentialed play therapists.

Annette Markowitz, President
Bill Burns, Executive Director/CEO

22 Association for Supervision & CurriculumDevelopment (ASCD)
1703 N Beauregard Street
Alexandria, VA 22311-1714
703-578-9600
800-933-2723
Fax: 703-575-5400
E-mail: member@ascd.org
http://www.ascd.org
A membership organization that develops programs, products, and services essential to the way educators learn, teach, and lead.

Founded: 1943

Sara Magana Shubel, President
Kathy Clayton, Executive Director

23 Association of Boarding Schools
9 SW Pack Square
Suite 201
Asheville, NC 28801
828-258-5354
Fax: 828-258-6428
E-mail: tabs@schools.com
http://www.schools.com
A marketing consortium founded in 1975 of 300 boarding schools that seeks to increase the applicant pool of member schools by increasing public awareness of benefits and advantages of boarding school education.

Founded: 1975

Steve Banks, Director of Operations
Peter Upham, Executive Director

24 Association of Educators in Private Practice
5909 Barbados Place
Suite 202
Rockville, MD 20852
800-252-3280
Fax: 301-468-3249
E-mail: spines@educationindustry.org
http://www.educationindustry.org
To promote increased public support for the education industry in order to improve educational opportunities and outcomes for all students.

Steven Pines, Executive Director
Jim Giovannini, Board President

25 Association of Teacher Educators
8505 Euclid Avenue
Suite 3
Manassas Park, VA 20111-2400
703-331-0911
Fax: 703-331-3666
E-mail: info@ate1.org
http://www.ate1.org
The mission of the Association of Teacher Educators is to improve the effectiveness of teacher education through leadership in the development of quality programs to prepare teachers, by analyzing issues and practices relating to professional development, and by providing opportunities for the personal and professional growth of Association members.

Founded: 1920

Jim Alouf, President-Elect
Terrell Peace, President

26 Attention Deficit Disorder Association
PO Box 7557
Wilmington, DE 19803-9997
800-939-1019
Fax: 800-939-1019
E-mail: adda@jmoadmin.com
http://www.add.org
ADDA, provides information, resources and networking opportunities to help adults with Attention Deficit/Hyperactivity Disorder (AD/HD) lead better lives.

Evelyn P Green, President
Ari Tuckman, VP

27 Awards and Recognition Association
4700 W Lake Avenue
Glenview, IL 60025
847-375-4800
800-344-2148
Fax: 888-374-7257
E-mail: info@ara.org
http://www.ara.org
The purpose of ARA is to advance the capabilities and growth of businesses whose primary focus is the manufacture, distribution or sales of awards and recognition goods and services. ARA is the essential component for success in the awards and recognition business.

B J Bailey Jr, President
Guy Barone, President-Elect

28 Better Chance
240 W 35th Street
Floor 9
New York, NY 10001-2506
646-346-1310
800-562-7865
Fax: 646-346-1311
http://www.abetterchance.org
Our mission is to substantially increase the number of well-educated young people of color who are capable of assuming positions of responsibility and leadership in American society.

Founded: 1963

Sandra E Timmons, President
Colin Lord, Director

29 CHADD: Children & Adults with Attention Deficit/Hyperactivity Disorder
8181 Professional Place
Suite 150
Landover, MD 20785
301-306-7070
800-233-4050
Fax: 301-306-7090
E-mail: conference@chadd.org
http://www.chadd.org
National nonprofit organization which offers advocacy, information and support for patients and parents of children with attention deficit disorders. Maintains support groups, provides

a forum for continuing education about ADHD, and maintains a national resource center for information about ADD.

Russell L Shipley, Chief Development Officer
E Clarke Ross, CEO

30 Cable in the Classroom

25 Massachusetts Avenue NW
Suite 100
Washington, DC 20001
202-222-2335
Fax: 202-222-2336
E-mail: help@ciconline.org
http://www.ciconline.org
Fosters the use of cable content and technology to expand and enhance learning for children and youth nationwide.

Frank Gallagher, Executive Director
Rhonda Yates, Senior Director

31 Center for Civic Education

5145 Douglas Fir Road
Calabasas, CA 91302-1440
818-591-9321
800-350-4223
Fax: 818-591-9330
E-mail: cce@civiced.org
http://www.civiced.org
Non-profit, nonpartisan educational corporation dedicated to fostering the development of informed, responsible participation in civic life by citizens committed to values and principles fundamental to American constitutional democracy.

Dick Kean, Director Publication Service
Margaret Branson, Associate Director

32 Center for Lifelong Learning

American Council on Education
One Dupont Circle NW
Washington, DC 20036-1193
202-939-9300
E-mail: comments@ace.nche.edu
http://www.acenet.edu
ACE's Center for Lifelong Learning (CLLL) has led the national movement to recognize and promote adult learner programs in higher education.

Susan Porter Robinson, Vice President
Mary Beth Lakin, Associate Director

33 Center on Education Policy

1001 Connecticut Avenue NW
Suite 522
Washington, DC 20036
202-822-8065
Fax: 202-822-6008
E-mail: cep-dc@cep-dc.org
http://www.cep-dc.org
Understand the role of public education in a democracy and the need to improve the academic quality of public schools.

Jack Jennings, President/CEO
Arturo Pacheco PhD, Director

34 Center on Human Policy

805 S Crouse Avenue
Syracuse, NY 13244-2280
315-443-3851
800-894-0826
Fax: 315-443-4338
E-mail: staylo01@syr.edu
http://disabilitystudies.syr.edu
Promotes its mission of inclusion by developing and sponsoring academic programs and courses, conferences and publications, research and training programs, and public education and advocacy efforts on behalf of, and with, people with disabilities.

Founded: 1971

Steven J Taylor, Co-Director
Arlene S Kanter, Co-Director

35 Citizens for Educational Freedom

498 Woods Mill Road
Manchester, OH 63011-4144
636-686-7101
Fax: 636-686-7173
E-mail: citedfree@educational-freedom.org
http://www.educational-freedom.org
Secures legal recognition for the right of parents to direct and control the education of their children; secures freedom of choice in education of their children, including an alternative to the government-established school system.

Founded: 1959

Mae Duggan, President/CEF
Herman Kriegshauser, Executive Director

36 Civic Practices Network

60 Turner Street
Waltham, MA 02154
617-736-4890
Fax: 617-736-4891
E-mail: cpn@cpn.org
http://www.cpn.org
Collaborative and nonpartisan project bringing together a diverse array of organizations and perspectives within the new citizenship movement.

Carmen Sirianni, Editor-in-Chief
Lewis Friedland, Research Director

37 Constitutional Rights Foundation

601 S Kingsley Drive
Los Angeles, CA 90005
213-487-5590
Fax: 213-386-0459
E-mail: crf@crf-usa.org
http://www.crf-usa.org
Seeks to instill in our nation's youth a deeper understanding of citizenship through values expressed in our Constitution and its Bill of Rights, and educate them to become active and responsible participants in our society. Dedicated to assuring our country's future by investing in our youth today.

Todd Clark, Executive Director Emeritus
JoAnn Burton, Development Director

38 Council for Advancement & Support of Education

1307 New York Avenue NW
Suite 1000
Washington, DC 20005
202-328-2273
Fax: 202-387-4973
E-mail: memberservicecenter@case.org
http://www.case.org
An international membership association, advances and supports educational institutions by providing knowledge, standards, advocacy and training designed to strengthen the combined efforts of alumni relations, communications, fundraising, marketing and allied professionals.

John Lippincott, President
Cassie McVeety, Chair

39 Council for Exceptional Children

2900 Crystal Drive
Suite 1000
Arlington, VA 22202-3557
703-620-3660
888-232-7733
Fax: 703-264-9494
E-mail: service@cec.sped.org
http://www.cec.sped.org
The Council for Exceptional Children works to improve the educational success of individuals with disabilities and/or gifts and talents.

Marilyn Friend, President
Bruce Ramirez, Executive Director

40 Council of Graduate Schools

1 Dupont Circle NW
Suite 230
Washington, DC 20036-1173
202-223-3791
Fax: 202-331-7157
E-mail: pmcallister@cgs.nche.edu
http://www.cgsnet.org
CGS has been the national voice for the graduate dean community. The only national organization in the United States that is dedicated solely to the advancement of graduate education and research.

Patricia McAllister, VP Government Relations
Belle Woods, Manager External Affairs

41 Council on Postsecondary Accreditation

1 Dupont Circle NW
Suite 230
Washington, DC 20036-1173
202-223-3791
Fax: 202-331-7157
E-mail: general_inquiries@cgs.nche.edu
http://www.cgsnet.org
Has been the national voice for the graduate dean community. The only national organization in the United States that is dedicated solely to the advancement of graduate education and research.

Patricia McAllister, VP Government Relations
Belle Woods, Manager External Affairs

42 Disability Rights Education & Defense Fund

3075 Adeline Street
Suite 210
Berkeley, CA 94703
510-644-2555
800-348-4232
Fax: 510-841-8645
E-mail: info@dredf.org
http://www.dredf.org
The mission of the Disability Rights Education and Defense Fund is to advance the civil and human rights of people with disabilities through legal advocacy, training, education, and public policy and legislative development.

Beverly Bertaina, President
Kim Connor, Treasurer

43 Drug Information & Strategy Clearinghouse

3109 Lubbock Ave
Fort Worth, TX 76109
800-955-2232
Provides housing officials, residents and community leaders with information and assistance on drug abuse prevention and trafficking control techniques.

Nancy Kay, Director

44 EF Educational Tours

1 Education Street
Cambridge, MA 02141-1883
800-637-8222
Fax: 617-619-1803
http://www.eftours.com
EF Educational Tours helps educators like you enrich what you teach in the classroom with international group travel. Your students actually learn it by living it by experiencing the world's very best historic, cultural and natural sights.

Founded: 1965

Martha H Doyle, President
Amy Connolly, Director of Customer Service

45 ERIC - Education Resources Information Center
655 15th Street NW
Suite 500
Washington, DC 20005
800-538-3742
http://www.eric.ed.gov/
The ERIC mission is to provide a comprehensive, easy-to-use, searchable, Internet-based bibliographic and full-text database of education research and information that also meets the requirements of the Education Sciences Reform Act of 2002.

Robert Boruch, Chairman
Alvin Walker, Jr, Product Development Manager

46 ERIC Clearinghouse on Assessment & Evaluation
University of Maryland
1129 Shriver Laboratory
College Park, MD 20742-5701
301-405-7449
800-464-3742
Fax: 301-405-8134
E-mail: feedback3@ericae.net
http://www.ericae.net
Disseminates education information on topics pertaining to tests and other measurement devices, research design and methodology.

Lawrence M Rudner, Director
Carol Boston, Associate Director

47 ERIC Clearinghouse on Rural Education & Small Schools
Edvantia
PO Box 1348
Charleston, WV 25325-1348
304-347-0400
800-624-9120
Fax: 304-347-0487
E-mail: info@edvantia.org
http://www.edvantia.org
Economic, cultural, social or other factors related to educational programs and practices for rural residents.

Doris Redfield, President

48 Easter Seals Communications
Easter Seals
233 South Wacker Drive
Suite 2400
Chicago, IL 60606-4703
312-726-6200
800-221-6827
Fax: 312-726-1494
E-mail: info@easter-seals.org
http://www.easterseals.com
Easter Seals provides exceptional services, education, outreach, and advocacy so that people living with autism and other disabilities can live, learn, work and play in our communities.

Gerard P Mattimore, Chairman
Dwane Brenneman, Treasurer

49 Education Commission of the States
700 Broadway
Suite 810
Denver, CO 80203-3442
303-299-3600
Fax: 303-296-8332
E-mail: ecs@ecs.org
http://www.ecs.org
To help states develop effective policy and practice for public education by providing data, research, analysis and leadership; and by facilitating collaboration, the exchange of ideas among the states and long-range strategic thinking

Roger Sampson, President
John Hickenlooper, Chairman

50 Education Development Center
55 Chapel Street
Newton, MA 02458-1060
617-969-7100
Fax: 617-969-5979
E-mail: comment@edc.org
http://www.edc.org
A nonprofit institution financed by the US government, private educational foundations, foreign governments, and sales of materials for the purpose of comprehensive educational improvement.

Founded: 1958

Luther Luedtke, President
Steve Anzalone, Vice President

51 Education Extension
Oklahoma State University-Stillwater
327 Willard
Stillwater, OK 74078-4034
405-744-6254
800-765-8933
Fax: 405-744-7713
E-mail: education.outreach@okstate.edu
http://education.okstate.edu
The school counseling specialization prepares students to work as school counselors in public schools, serving students, teachers, and parents.

Dr Pamela Fry, Dean
Dr C Robert Davis, Associate Dean

52 Education, Training and Research Associates
4 Carbonero Way
Scotts Valley, CA 95066
831-438-4060
Fax: 831-438-4284
http://www.etr.org
To maximize the physical, social and emotional health of all individuals, families and communities by advancing the work of health, education and social service providers through high-quality research, publications, information resources and programs.

Francisco Buchting PhD, Director of Development
Dave Kitchen, COO

53 Educational Equity Concepts
100 5th Avenue
8th Floor
New York, NY 10011
212-243-1110
Fax: 212-627-0407
E-mail: lcolon@aed.org
http://www.edequity.org
We provide professional development, consulting services, and community partnerships. Our goal is to eliminate inequities based on gender, race/ethnicity, disability, and level of family income.

Merle Froschl, Co-Founder/Co-Director
Linda Colén, Program Manager

54 Educational Register
Vincent-Curtis
29 Simpson Lane
Falmouth, MA 02540-2230
508-457-6473
Fax: 508-457-6499
E-mail: register@vincentcurtis.com
http://www.theeducationalregister.com
Hundreds of illustrated announcements describing a variety of private boarding schools and resident summer programs in the United States, Canada and Europe, together with articles by school heads and camp directors of interest to parents of students 10-18.

Stanford B Vincent, Editor

55 Equity Clearinghouse
Mid-Continent Regional Educational Laboratory
4601 DTC Boulevard
Suite 500
Denver, CO 80237
303-337-0990
Fax: 303-337-3005
http://www.mcrel.org
Provides information and literature on the topics of desegregation as it relates to education.

Timothy Waters, President/CEO
Louis Cicchinelli, Executive Vice President

56 Facing History & Ourselves
16 Hurd Road
Brookline, MA 2445-6919
617-232-1595
800-856-9039
Fax: 617-232-0281
http://www.facinghistory.org
Facing History is an international nonprofit that helps teachers and students link the past to moral choices they face today.

Founded: 1976

Margot Strom, President

57 Family Centered Learning Alternatives (FCLA)
Context Institute
PO Box 946
Langley, WA 98260
360-221-6044
Fax: 360-221-6045
http://www.context.org/ICLIB/IC06/Stewart
Supports parents' right to choose the educational environment best suited for their children's needs and to promote homeschooling as a legal nationwide learning alternative.

Eric Stewart, Founder/Director
Debra Stewart, Founder/Director

58 Foundation for Student Communication
Princeton University
48 University Place
Princeton, NJ 8544
609-258-1111
Fax: 609-258-1222
E-mail: Maggie@businesstoday.org
http://www.businesstoday.org
Student subscribers and conference participants who promote communication among students and business persons.

Founded: 1968

Michael Short, President
Maggie Orr, Publicity Director

59 Friends Council on Education
1507 Cherry Street
Philadelphia, PA 19102
215-241-7245
Fax: 215-241-7299
E-mail: Info@friendscouncil.org
http://www.friendscouncil.org
Founded in 1931 the Friends Council on Education acts as a clearinghouse for information on Quaker schools and colleges.

Founded: 1931

Irene McHenry, Executive Director
Sarah Sweeney-Denham, Associate Director

60 Gifted Child Society
190 Rock Road
Glen Rock, NJ 7452-1736
201-444-6530
Fax: 201-444-9099
E-mail: admin@gifted.org
http://www.giftedchildsociety.com
Educational enrichment and support services specifically designed for gifted children.As-

sistance to parents in raising gifted children to full and productive adulthood.

Founded: 1957

Gina G Riggs, Executive Director

61 Girls Incorporated
120 Wall Street
New York, NY 10005-3902
212-509-2000
Fax: 212-509-8708
E-mail: communications@girlsinc.org
http://www.girlsinc.org
A national nonprofit youth organization dedicated to inspiring all girls to be strong, smart, and bold.

Founded: 1864

Judy Vredenburgh, President
Bridgette P Heller, Chairman

62 HEATH Resource Center
George Washington University
2134 G Street NW
Washington, DC 20052-0001
202-973-0904
800-544-3284
Fax: 202-994-3365
E-mail: askheath@gwu.edu
http://www.HEATH.gwu.edu
The national clearinghouse on post-secondary education for individuals with disabilities. Support from the US Department of Education enables HEATH to serve as an information exchange for support services, policies, procedures and education opportunities.

Founded: 2000

Dr Lynda West, Principal Investigator
Dr Joel Gomez, Co-Principal Investigator

63 Independent Schools Association of theSouthwest (ISAS)
Energy Square
505 N Big Spring Street
Suite 406
Midland, TX 79701
432-684-9550
800-688-5007
Fax: 432-684-9401
E-mail: rdurham@isasw.org
http://www.isasw.org
Independent Schools Association of the Southwest (ISAS) is a voluntary membership association of private schools. The membership of ISAS consists of 84 schools located in Arizona, Kansas, Louisiana, Mexico, New Mexico, Oklahoma and Texas enrolling over 38,000 students. A central purpose of ISAS is to encourage, support and develop the highest standard for independent schools of the region and to recognize by formal accreditation those schools in which these standards are maintained.

Founded: 1955

Rhonda Durham, Executive Director
Jananne McLaughlin, Accreditation Director

64 Institute for Educational Leadership
4455 Connecticut Avenue NW
Suite 310
Washington, DC 20008
202-822-8405
Fax: 202-872-4050
E-mail: iel@IEL.ORG
http://www.iel.org
To build the capacity of individuals and organizations in education and related fields to work together - across policies, programs and sectors.

Martin J Blank, President/CEO

65 InterAction - American Council for VoluntaryInternational Action
1400 16th Street, NW
Suite 210
Washington, DC 20036
202-667-8227
Fax: 202-667-8236
E-mail: ia@interaction.org
http://www.interaction.org/
Collectively, InterAction's 172 members work in every developing country. Members meet people halfway in expanding opportunities and supporting gender equality in education, health care, agriculture, small business, and other areas.

Sam Worthington, President/CEO
Allen Abtahi, Director of Information Tech

66 International Association of Educators forWorld Peace
2013 Orba Drive NE
Huntsville, AL 35811-2414
256-534-5501
Fax: 256-536-1018
E-mail: info@iaewp.org
http://www.iaewp.org
To contribute to the improvement of man's ability to live at peace, to educate world citizens for peaceful co-existence and cooperation so that all people may have free access to the achievement of science and civilization.

Dr Charles Mercieca, President
Dr Surya Nath Prasad, Executive Vice President

67 International Society for Technology inEducation
1710 Rhode Island Avenue NW
Suite 900
Washington, DC 20036
202-861-7777
866-654-4777
Fax: 202-861-0888
http://www.iste.org
Providing leadership and service to improve teaching and learning by advancing the effective use of technology in education.

Don Knezek PhD, CEO
Leslie S Conery CAE, PhD, Deputy CEO

68 Jewish Education Council
Jewish Federation Greater Seattle
2031 Third Avenue
Seattle, WA 98121
206-443-5400
Fax: 206-443-0303
E-mail: info@jewishinseattle.org
http://www.jewishinseattle.org/JF/Education/AboutJEC.asp
Ensures Jewish survival and enhance the quality of Jewish life locally, in Israel and worldwide.

Liat Zaidenberg, Education Director

69 Jewish Education Service of North America
JESNA
318 W 39th Street
5th Floor
New York, NY 10018
212-284-6950
Fax: 212-284-6951
E-mail: info@jesna.org
http://www.jesna.org
Ensure that Jewish education is the best that it can be in all of its variety. JESNA's role is to strengthen communities and their educational offerings by providing tested solutions, leveraging partnerships, promoting synergies, and building the connections that strengthen us all.

David Steirman, President
Mandell L Berman, Honorary Chair

70 Jewish Educators Assembly
Broadway and Locust Avenue
PO Box 413
Cedarhurst, NY 11516
516-569-2537
Fax: 516-295-9039
E-mail: jewisheducators@jewisheducators.org
http://www.jewisheducators.org
Promotes excellence among educators committed to Conservative Jewish education by advancing professionalism, encouraging leadership, pursuing lifelong learning and building community.

Hedda S Morton, President
Edward Edelstein, Executive Director

71 John Dewey Society for the Study of Education & Culture
1801 NW 11th Road
Gainesville, FL 32605-5323
352-378-7365
http://www.johndeweysociety.org
Founded in 1935, John Dewey's commitment to the use of critical and reflective intelligence in the search for solutions to crucial problems in education and cuture.

Lynda Stone, President
Kyle Greenwalt, Secretary/Treasurer

72 Learning Disabilities Association of America
Learning Disabilities Association of America
4156 Library Road
Pittsburgh, PA 15234-1349
412-341-1515
888-300-6710
Fax: 412-344-0224
E-mail: info@ldaamerica.org
http://www.ldanatl.org
Largest non-profit volunteer organization advocating for individuals with learning disabilities and has over 200 state and local affiliates in 42 states and Puerto Rico. LDA's international membership of over 15,000 includes members from 27 countries around the world.

Founded: 1963

Patricia Lillie, President
B J Wierner, VP

73 Lutheran Education Association
7400 Augusta Street
River Forest, IL 60305
708-209-3343
Fax: 708-209-3458
E-mail: lea@lea.org
http://www.lea.org
Seeks to spark ideas, thoughts and practices among Lutherans.

Dr Jonathan Laabs, Executive Director
Kathy Slupik, Executive Assistant

74 MATRIX: A Parent Network and Resource Center
94 Galli Drive
Suite C
Novato, CA 94949
415-884-3535
800-578-2592
Fax: 415-884-3555
E-mail: info@matrixparnets.org
http://www.matrixparents.org
Matrix offers families of children with special needs support, information, training, and advice.

Nora Thompson, Executive Director
Jeanne Baunan, Technical Assistance Coord

75 Mississippi Library Association
PO Box 13687
Jackson, MS 39236-3687

601-981-4586
Fax: 601-981-4501
E-mail: info@misslib.org
http://www.misslib.org
Provides professional leadership for the development, promotion, and the improvement of library and information services and the profession of librarianship in order to enhance learning and ensure access to information for all.

Jennifer A Smith, President
Stephen Cunetto, VP

76 National Academy of Education
500 5th Street, NW
Suite 333
Washington, DC 20001-9580
202-334-2341
Fax: 202-334-2350
E-mail: info@naeducation.org
http://www.naeducation.org
Offers the Spencer Postdoctoral Fellowship which is designed to promote scholarship in the United States and abroad on matters relevant to the improvement of education in all its forms.

Susan Fuhrman, President
Edward Haertel, VP

77 National Alliance for Safe Schools
PO Box 335
Slanesville, WV 25444-0335
304-496-8100
888-510-6500
Fax: 304-496-8105
E-mail: nass@frontiernet.net
http://www.safeschools.org
Founded in 1977 NASS a non-profit corporation, ascribes to the belief that schools need to take back control and identify what the local issues are that may be causing fear and anxiety on the part of the students and staff. Once local issues have been identified, school administrators, working with students, teachers, parents and support staff, are able to effect change.

Peter D Blauvelt, CEO/President

78 National Association for Asian and Pacific American Education
PO Box 3471
Palos Verdes Peninsula, CA 90274
818-677-6853
Fax: 818-366-2714
E-mail: naapae@naapae.net
http://www.naapae.net
Objectives are to enhance awareness of multicultural studies in the United States as well as promoting inclusion of Asian and Pacific American culture and history into the school curriculum.
Founded: 1977

John N Tsuchida, President
Betty Jeung, Vice President

79 National Association for DevelopmentalEducation (NADE)
500 N Estrella Parkway
Suite B2 PMB 412
Goodyear, AZ 85338
877-233-9455
Fax: 623-792-5747
E-mail: office@nade.net
http://www.nade.net
Improves the theory and performance at all academic levels.

Marcella Davis, President
Joyce Adams, Vice President

80 National Association for Legal Support ofAlternative Schools (NALSAS)
PO Box 2823
Santa Fe, NM 87504-2823
505-474-0300
E-mail: nalsas@msn.com
http://www.nalsas.org/
It was originally designed to help interested persons/organizations locate/evaluate/create viable alternatives to traditional schooling approaches including home study.
Founded: 1973

Ed Nagel, CEO

81 National Association for Year-Round Education
PO Box 711386
San Diego, CA 92171-1386
619-276-5296
Fax: 858-571-5754
E-mail: info@nayre.org
http://www.NAYRE.org
Founded in 1972 NAYRE fosters and disseminates information about year-round education as a way to improve educational programs.

Richard Coleman, President
Sam Pepper, Executive Director

82 National Association of Catholic SchoolTeachers
1700 Sansom Street
Suite 903
Philadelphia, PA 19103
215-568-4175
800-996-2278
Fax: 215-568-8270
E-mail: Rita@NACST.com
http://www.nacst.com
Unifies, advises and assists Catholic school teachers in matters of collective bargaining.

Rita C Schwartz, President
Michael A Milz, Executive Vice President

83 National Association of Federally Impacted Schools
Hall of the States
444 N Capitol Street NW
Suite 419
Washington, DC 20001-1512
202-624-5455
Fax: 202-624-5468
E-mail: johnfork@nafisdc.org
http://www.nafisdc.org
Impact aid provides a payment to school districts in lieu of these lost taxes to assist with the basic educational needs of its students.

John Forkenbrock, Executive Director
John Deegan, President

84 National Association of Secondary School Principals
1904 Association Drive
Reston, VA 20191-1557
703-860-0200
800-253-7746
Fax: 703-476-5432
E-mail: nhs@nassp.org
http://www.nassp.org
Promotes leadership training for students involved in the creative process.

Charity Varnado, Principal

85 National Association of State Boards of Education
2121 Crystal Drive
Suite 350
Arlington, VA 22202
703-684-4000
Fax: 703-836-2313
E-mail: boards@nasbe.org
http://www.nasbe.org

Aims are to study problems of mutual interest and concern, improve communication among state boards, and exchange and collect information concerning all aspects of education.

Brenda L Welburn, Executive Director
Bradley Hall, Deputy Director

86 National Association of Student Councils (NASC)
1904 Association Drive
Reston, VA 20191-1537
703-860-0200
800-253-7746
Fax: 703-476-5432
E-mail: nasc@nasc.us
http://www.nasc.us/s_nasc/index.asp
Supports student councils, relations between teachers and students, as well as directing student-sponsored activities.

Scott D Thompson, Executive Officer

87 National Association of Trade & Industrial Instructors
Canadian Valley Vo Tech
6505 East Highway 66
El Reno, OK 73036-579
405-262-2629
Fax: 405-422-2354
Founded in 1965 the National Association of Trade and Industrial Instructors seeks to improve communication among members and to support the needs of classroom teachers.

Carol McNish, President
Greg Winters, Superintendent

88 National Catholic Educational Association
1005 N Glebe Rd
Suite 525
Arlington, VA 22201
800-711-6232
Fax: 703-243-0025
E-mail: nceaadmin@ncea.org
http://www.ncea.org
Rooted in the Gospel of Jesus Christ, the National Catholic Educational Association (NCEA) is a professional membership organization that provides leadership, direction and service to fulfill the evangelizing, catechizing and teaching mission of the Church.

Karen M Ristau, President
Wilton Gregory, Chairman

89 National Center for Learning Disabilities
381 Park Avenue S
Suite 1401
New York, NY 10016-8806
212-545-7510
888-575-7373
Fax: 212-545-9665
http://www.ncld.org
The National Center for Learning Disabilities (NCLD) works to ensure that the nation's 15 million children, adolescents and adults with learning disabilities have every opportunity to succeed in school, work and life.

Frederic M Poses, Chairman of the Board
James H Wendorf, Executive Director

90 National Coalition for Parent Involvement inEducation (NCPIE)
1400 L Street NW
Suite 300
Washington, DC 20005
202-289-6790
Fax: 202-289-6791
E-mail: ferguson@ncpie.org
http://www.ncpie.org/
National Coalition for Parent Involvement in Education (NCPIE) advocates the involvement of parents and families in their children's education, and to foster relationships

between home, school, and community to enhance the education of all our nation's young people.

Sue Ferguson, Chairperson
Hilda Crespo, Vice President

91 National Coalition of Advocates for Students
100 Boylston Street
Suite 737
Boston, MA 2116
617-357-8507
Fax: 617-357-9549
http://www.ncasboston.org
NCAS is a national education advocacy organization with 21 member groups in 14 states that works to achieve equal access to a quality public education for the most vulnerable students those who are poor, children of color, recently immigrated, or children with disabilities. Focusing on kindergarten through grade 12, NCAS informs and mobilizes parents, concerned educators, and communities to help resolve critical education issues. NCAS raises concerns that otherwise might not be addressed.

Judge Nancy Francis, Chairperson

92 National Coalition of Alternative Community Schools
1129 Gault Drive
Ypsilanti, MI 48198
734-483-7040
888-771-9171
Fax: 734-482-7436
E-mail: ncacs2@earthlink.net
http://www.ncacs.org
Our mission is to unite and organize a grassroots movement of learners and learning communities dedicated to participant control, liberation from all forms of oppression, and the pursuit of freedom.

Terri Wheeler, Treasurer

93 National Coalition of Independent Scholars
Box 838
St Helena, CA 94574
510-704-0990
E-mail: Info@NCIS.org
http://www.ncis.org
Provide information for the creation of local organizations of independent scholars
Founded: 1989

Lisa Purry, President
Guillermia Walas, Interim Vice President

94 National Commission for Cooperative Education
360 Huntington Avenue
384 CP
Boston, MA 02115-5096
617-373-3770
Fax: 617-373-3463
E-mail: ncce@co-op.edu
http://www.co-op.edu
Founded in 1962 the national commission for Copperative Education offers brochures and publications describing the structure and benefits of cooperative education. Co-op is an academic program which integrates classroom studies with paid work experience in a field related to a student's goals.
Founded: 1962

Dr Paul J Stonely, CEO
Frank Schettino, Director

95 National Consortium for Academics and Sports
University of Central Florida
PO Box 161400
Orlando, FL 32816-1400

407-823-4770
Fax: 407-823-3542
E-mail: rlapchick@bus.ucf.edu
http://www.ncasports.org
To create a better society by focusing on educational attainment and using the power and appeal of sport to positively affect social change.
Founded: 1985

Dr Richard Lapchick, President/CEO
Keith L Lee, VP

96 National Council for Black Studies
PO Box 4109
Atlanta, GA 30302-4109
404-413-5131
Fax: 404-413-5140
E-mail: info@ncbsonline.org
http://www.ncbsonline.org
Promote academic excellence and social responsibility in the discipline of Africana/Black Studies through the production and dissemination of knowledge, professional development and training, and advocacy for social change and social justice.

Sundiata Cha-Jua, Vice President
Shawnrece Champbell, Secretary

97 National Council for Science and theEnvironment
1101 17th Street NW
Suite 250
Washington, DC 20036
202-530-5810
Fax: 202-628-4311
E-mail: ncse@ncseonline.org
http://www.ncseonline.org
improve the scientific basis for environmental decisionmaking by bringing about the establishment of the National Institute for the Environment (NIE) and supporting the successful implementation of its principles and programs.
Founded: 1990

Dr Warren Washington, Senior Scientise
Peter Saundry, Executive Director

98 National Council for the Accreditation of Teacher Education
2010 Massachusetts Avenue NW
Suite 500
Washington, DC 20036-1023
202-466-7496
Fax: 202-296-6620
E-mail: ncate@ncate.org
http://www.ncate.org
Professional accrediting organization for schools, colleges, and departments of education in the United States.

James C Cibulka, President
Donna M Gollnick, Sr VP

99 National Council of Higher Education
National Education Association (NEA)
1201 16th Street NW
Room 410
Washington, DC 20036-3290
202-833-4000
Fax: 202-822-7974
E-mail: nche@nea.org
http://www.nea.org
Our mission is to advocate for education professionals and to unite our members and the nation to fulfill the promise of public education to prepare every student to succeed in a diverse and interdependent world

Dennis Van Roekel, President
Lily Eskelsen, VP

100 National Council of Urban EducationAssociations
National Education Association (NEA)
1201 16th Street NW
Washington, DC 20036-3290
202-833-4000
Fax: 202-822-7974
E-mail: ncuea@nea.org
http://www.nea.org
NCUEA is a caucus of local affiliates of the National Education Association (NEA), which is dedicated to strengthening member advocacy and making the NEA more responsive to member needs.

Dennis Van Roekel, President
Lily Eskelsen, VP

101 National Council on Measurement in Education
2424 American Lane
Suite 3800
Madison, WI 53704
608-443-2487
Fax: 608-443-2474
E-mail: plovelace@ncme.org
http://www.ncme.org
NCME is a professional organization for individuals involved in assessment, evaluation, testing, and other aspects of educational measurement

Plumer Lovelace III, Executive Director
Gerald Sroufe, Administrative Officer

102 National Council on Rehabilitation Education (NCRE)
5005 N Maple Avenue
MS ED 3
Fresno, CA 90740
559-906-0787
Fax: 559-412-2550
E-mail: charlesa@csufresno.edu
http://www.rehabeducators.org
A professional organization of educators dedicated to quality services for persons with disabilities through education and research.

Charles Arokiasamy, Administrative Officer
Charles Degeneffe, President

103 National Council on Student Development (NCSD)
PO Box 3948
Parker, CO 80134
866-972-0717
Fax: 303-755-7363
http://www.ncsdonline.org
NCSD is the nation's primary voice for sharing knowledge, expertise, professional development and student advocacy for community college student development professionals. Affiliate council of the American Association of Community Colleges (AACC)

Nicole Singleton, Executive Director
Tom Walter, President

104 National Dissemination Center for Children with Disabilities
1825 Connecticut Ave NW
Suite 700
Washington, DC 20009
202-884-8200
800-695-0285
Fax: 202-884-8441
E-mail: nichcy@aed.org
http://www.nichcy.org
The center that provides information to the nation on disabilities in children and youth; programs and services for infants, children, and youth with disabilities; IDEA, the nation's special education law; No Child Left Behind, the nation's general education law;

and research-based information on effective practices for children with disabilities.

Lisa Savard, Sales/Marketing Director
Suzanne Ripley, Project Director

105   National Education Association
1201 16th Street NW
Washington, DC 20036-3290
202-833-4000
Fax: 202-822-7974
E-mail: ncuea@nea.org
http://www.nea.org
The voice of education professionals. Advocate for education professionals

Dennis Van Roekel, President
Lily Eskelsen, VP

**106   National Education Association
Student Program**
National Education Association (NEA)
1201 16th Street NW
Washington, DC 20036-3290
202-833-4000
Fax: 202-822-7974
E-mail: ncuea@nea.org
http://www.nea.org
Strive to promote community partnerships; foster leadership through pre-professional opportunities and peer mentoring;

Dennis Van Roekel, President
Lily Eskelsen, VP

**107   National Education
Association-Retired**
National Education Association (NEA)
1201 16th Street NW
Washington, DC 20036-3290
202-833-4000
Fax: 202-822-7974
http://www.nea.org/retired
NEA-Retired exists to meet the needs of retired education employees.

Barbara Matteson, President
Tom Curran, Vice President

108   National Education Policy Institute
National Alliance of Black School Educators
310 Pennsylvania Avenue
Washington, DC 20003
202-608-6310
800-221-2654
Fax: 202-608-6319
E-mail: glawson@nabse.org
http://www.nabse.org
NABSE is the nation's premiere non-profit organization devoted to furthering the academic success for the nation's children - particularly children of African descent.

Carrol A Thomas, President
Bernard Hamilton, President-Elect

109   National Educational Service
1252 Loesch Rd
Box 8
Bloomington, IN 47402
812-336-7700
800-733-6786
Fax: 812-336-7790
E-mail: info@solution-tree.com
http://www.nes.org
Strive to be the premier provider of books, videos, multimedia resources, and professional development opportunities designed to help educators throughout the United States and Canada realize continuous school improvement and connect with youth at risk.

Founded: 1987

Karen Bailey, Representative
Deb McDonald, Representative

110   National Institute for Literacy (NIL)
1775 I Street NW
Suite 730
Washington, DC 20006-2401
202-233-2025
Fax: 202-233-2050
E-mail: lreddy@nifl.gov
http://nifl.gov
The National Institute for Literacy, a federal agency, provides leadership on literacy issues, including the improvement of reading instruction for children, youth, and adults. In consultation with the U.S. Departments of Education, Labor, and Health and Human Services, the Institute serves as a national resource on current, comprehensive literacy research, practice, and policy.

Donald D Deshler, Director
Susan Boorse, Executive Officer

111   National Lekotek Center
2001 N Clybourn
Chicago, IL 60614
773-528-5766
800-366-7529
Fax: 773-537-2992
E-mail: lekotek@lekotek.org
http://www.lekotek.org
Therapeutic toy lending library and play education for children ages 0-8 with disabilities.

Deidre Pate Omahen, Director of Programs
Macy Welch, Executive Director

112   National Middle School Association
4151 Executive Parkway
Suite 300
Westerville, OH 43081
614-895-4730
800-528-6672
Fax: 614-895-4750
E-mail: info@nmsa.org
http://www.nmsa.org
NMSA has been a voice for those committed to the educational and developmental needs of young adolescents. NMSA is the only national education association dedicated exclusively to those in the middle level grades.

Janet Vernon, President
Nancy Poliseno, President-Elect

113   National Organization on Disability
1625 K Street NW
Suite 850
Washington, DC 20006-2988
202-293-5960
800-248-ABLE
Fax: 202-293-7999
E-mail: ability@nod.org
http://www.nod.org
Expands the participation and contribution of America's 54 million men, women and children with disabilities in all aspects of life. By raising disability awareness through programs and information, together we can work toward closing the participation gaps.

Carol Glazer, President
Governor Tom Ridge, Chairman

114   National Rural Education Association
Purdue University
Beering Hall of Liberal Arts & Ed
100 N University St
W Lafayette, IN 47907
765-494-0086
Fax: 765-496-1228
E-mail: jehill@purdue.edu
http://www.nrea.net
Organization of rural school administrators, teachers, board members, regional service agency personnel, researchers, business and industry representatives and others interested

in maintaining the vitality of rural school systems across the country.

Founded: 1907

Scott Turney, Executive Director
Ray Patrick, President

115   National School Boards Association
1680 Duke Street
Alexandria, VA 22314-3455
703-838-6722
Fax: 703-683-7590
E-mail: info@nsba.org
http://www.nsba.org
Not-for-profit Federation of state associations of school boards across the United States. Its mission is to foster excellence and equity in public education through school board leadership.

Anne Bryant, Executive Director
Barbara L Bolas, President

**116   National School Public Relations
Association**
15948 Denwood Road
Rockville, MD 20855-1109
301-519-0496
Fax: 301-519-0494
E-mail: nspra@nspra.org
http://www.nspra.org
Professional membership organization of 2,000 members throughout the United States and Canada. Major mission is to build more support for education.

Ron Koehler, President
Frank Kwan, President-Elect

**117   National Society for Experiential
Education**
19 Mantua Road
Mt. Royal, NJ 08061
856-423-3427
Fax: 856-423-3420
E-mail: nsee.@talley.com
http://www.nsee.org
National Society for Experiential Education (NSEE) is a nonprofit membership association of educators, businesses, and community leaders.

Founded: 1971

James Walters, President
Mary King, VP

**118   National Society for the Study of
Education (NSSE)**
University of Illinois at Chicago
525 W 120th Street
New York, NY 10027
312-996-4529
773-702-7748
Fax: 773-702-9756
E-mail: nsse@uic.edu
http://www.nsse-chicago.org/
The National Society for the Study of Education (NSSE) is an organization of education scholars, professional educators, and policy makers dedicated to the improvement of education research, policy, and practice. NSSE's mission is to advance the study and practice of education by providing accessible scholarship and promoting informed discourse about the challenges and opportunities of education in a democratic society.

David Hansen, Board of Directors
Deborah Loewenberg Ball, Board of Directors

119   National Student Exchange
4656 W Jefferson Boulevard
Suite 140
Fort Wayne, IN 46804
260-436-2634
Fax: 260-436-5676

E-mail: bworley@nse2.org
http://www.nse.org
The National Student Exchange (NSE) is a program for undergraduate exchange within the United States and Canada. Instead of crossing oceans, NSE students cross state, regional, provincial, and cultural borders.

Founded: 1968

Bette Worley, President
Wendel Wickland, Vice President

120 National Student Program
National Education Association (NEA)
1201 16th Street NW
Washington, DC 20036-3290
202-833-4000
Fax: 202-822-7974
E-mail: ncuea@nea.org
http://www.nea.org
The National Education Association (NEA), the nation's largest professional employee organization

Dennis Van Roekel, President
Lily Eskelsen, Vice President

121 National Telemedia Council
517 N Segue Rd
Suite 210
Madison, WI 53703
608-257-7712
Fax: 608-257-7714
E-mail: ntc@danenet.wicip.org
http://www.danenet.org
A professional, non-profit organization promoting media literacy education through partnership with educators, informed citizens and media producers across the country.

Eric Howland, Director
John Jordan, Community Outreach

122 National Women's Student Coalition (NWSC)
United States Student Association
1211 Connecticut Avenue NW
Suite 406
Washington, DC 20006
202-640-6570
Fax: 202-223-4005
E-mail: ussa@usstudents.org
http://www.usstudents.org
National Women's Student Coalition (NWSC), an affiliate of the United States Student Association, provides a space for women of different economic backgrounds, races, sexual orientations, religions and abilities to come together and strategize ways to increase campus safety, diversity, fight against bias related violence and build women's leadership.

Lindsey McCluskey, President
Victor Sanchez, VP

123 National Women's Studies Association
University of Maryland
7100 Baltimore Avenue
Suite 203
College Park, MD 20740
301-403-0407
Fax: 301-403-4137
E-mail: nwsaoffice@nwsa.org
http://www.nwsa.org
The National Women's Studies Association leads the field of women's studies in educational and social transformation.

Founded: 1977

Allison Kimmich, Executive Director
Bonnie Thornton Dill, President

124 Native American Homeschool Association
474 Brush Creek Road
Fries, VA 24330
540-636-1020
Fax: 540-636-1464

http://www.expage.com/page/nahomeschool2
Association of Native American homeschoolers.
Misty Dawn Thomas Ruff, Tribal Chairwoman

125 North American Association for EnvironmentalEducation (NAAEE)
2000 P Street NW
Suite 540
Washington, DC 20036
202-419-0412
Fax: 202-419-0415
E-mail: info@naaee.org
http://www.naaee.org
Advances environmental education and supports environmental educators in Canada, the United States, and Mexico.

October

Brian A Day, Executive Director

126 North American Association of Educational Negotiators
PO Box 1068
Salem, OR 97308
503-588-2800
E-mail: execdir@naen.org
http://www.naen.org
Improves the knowledge and performance of K-12 school district, community college, and university, management negotiators by advancing their professional status, providing a forum for effective communication, and encourage information exchanges among educational negotiators.

Ann Chapman, President
Steven Talsky, President-Elect

127 North American Students of Cooperation
PO Box 180048
Chicago, IL 60618-7715
773-404-2667
Fax: 773-404-2668
E-mail: info@nasco.coop
http://www.nasco.coop
Organizes and educates affordable group equity co-ops and their members for the purpose of promoting a community oriented cooperative movement.

Tom Pierson, Executive Director
Jim Jones, Sr Director of Development

128 Northwest Association of Schools & Colleges
1910 University Drive
Boise, ID 83725
208-426-1000
Fax: 208-334-3228
E-mail: sclemens@boisestate.edu
http://www.boisestate.edu
The university offers more than 190 fields of interest. Undergraduate, graduate and technical programs are available in seven colleges: Arts and Sciences, Business and Economics, Education, Engineering, Graduate Studies, Health Sciences, and Social Sciences and Public Affairs. Students can also study abroad and participate in one of the largest internship programs in the Northwest.

Bob Kustra, President
Sona Andrews, Vice President for Academic

129 Odyssey of the Mind
Creative Competitions, Inc.
406 Ganttown Road
Sewell, NJ 8080
856-256-2797
Fax: 856-256-2798
E-mail: info@odysseyofthemind.com
http://www.odysseyofthemind.com

An international educational program that provides creative problem-solving opportunities for students from kindergarten through college.

Samuel Micklus, Founder

130 PACER Center
8161 Normandale Boulevard
Bloomington, MN 55437
952-838-9000
888-248-0822
Fax: 952-838-0199
E-mail: pacer@pacer.org
http://www.pacer.org
Founded in 1976 PACER a coalition of organizations founded on the concept of Parents Helping Parents. PACER strives to improve and expand opportunities that enhance the quality of life for children and young adults with disabilities and their families. Helps parents become informed and effective representatives for their children in early childhood, school-age and vocational settings through agencies and appropriate service.

Paula F Goldberg, Executive Director
Mary Schrock, Chief Operating and Developm

131 Parents, Let's Unite for Kids
516 N 32nd Street
Billings, MT 59101-6003
406-255-0540
800-222-7585
Fax: 406-255-0523
E-mail: info@pluk.orgÿ
http://www.pluk.org
Parent's Let's Unite for Kids unites parents, professionals, families and friends of children with special needs to support one another, and share information for the benefit of their children.

Founded: 1984

William J O'Connor II, President
Dave Rye, Vice President

132 Peace & Justice Studies Association
220 Grove Avenue
Prescott, AZ 86301
928-350-2008
E-mail: randall@peacejusticestudies.org
http://www.peacejusticestudies.org
Works to create a just and peaceful world through the promotion of peace studies within universities, colleges and K-12 grade levels.

Founded: 2001

Randall Amster, Executive Director
Michael Nagler, Board Co-Chair

133 Public Relations Student Society of America
33 Maiden Lane
11th Floor
New York, NY 10038-5150
212-460-1474
Fax: 212-995-0757
E-mail: prssa@prsa.org
http://www.prssa.org
The PRSSA 2003-04 National Committee proudly announces its theme for the year and the vision for the future of the Society. The Committee encourages you to Get Your G.E.A.R.S. in Motion! If each Chapter focuses on Growth, Education, Advancement, Relationships and Students, then our Society's G.E.A.R.S. will turn more efficiently and more productively than ever.

Nick Lucido, National President
Jeneen Garcia, VP

134 Religious Education Association (REA)
PO Box 200392
Evans, CO 80620-0392

765-225-5836
Fax: 970-351-1269
E-mail: reaapprre@msn.com
http://www.religiouseducation.net
Creates opportunities for exploring and advancing the interconnected practices of scholarship, research, teaching, and leadership in faith communities, academic institutions, and the wider world community.

Dr Lucinda Huffaker, REA Executive Secretary
Maureen O'Brien, President

135 Sexuality Information & Education Council of the US
90 John Street
Suite 704
New York, NY 10038-7802
212-819-9770
Fax: 212-819-9776
E-mail: pmalone@siecus.org
http://www.siecus.org
SIECUS affirms that sexuality is a fundamental part of being human, one that is worthy of dignity and respect. We advocate for the right of all people to accurate information, comprehensive education about sexuality, and sexual health services. SIECUS works to create a world that ensures social justice and sexual rights.

Monica Rodriguez, President/CEO
Jason Osher, COO

136 Society for the Advancement of Excellence inEducation (SAFE)
1889 Springfield Road
Suite 225
Kelowna, Canada
250-717-1163
Fax: 250-717-1134
E-mail: info@saee.ca
http://www.saee.ca/
Provides non-partisan education research and information to policy-makers, education partners and the public. Our purpose is to encourage higher performance throughout Canada's public education system.

Founded: 1996

Elizabeth Bredberg, Research Director
Mame McCrea Silva, General Manager

137 Southeastern Library Association
PO Box 950
Rex, GA 30273
770-961-3520
Fax: 770-961-3712
E-mail: gordonbaker@clayton.edu
http://selaonline.org
Holds a conference and publishes a journal.

Michael Seigler, President
Gordon Baker, Vice President

138 Summit Vision
5640 Lynx Drive
Westerville, OH 43081
614-403-3891
Fax: 614-895-8326
E-mail: tmcbane@wideopenwest.com
http://www.summit-vision.com
Summit Vision believes that through the use of adventure and experiential learning tools, people have the opportunity to reach their full potential—both individually and as part of a larger team.

Trey McBane, President
Laissa Kopestonsky, VP

139 Utah Library Association (ULA)
PO Box 708155
Sandy, UT 84070-8155
801-422-6763
Fax: 801-422-0466

E-mail: anna.neatrour@gmail.com
http://ula.org
The mission of the Utah Library Association is to serve the professional development and educational needs of its members and to provide leadership and direction in developing and improving library and information services in the state. The Association also initiates and supports legislation promoting library development and monitors legislation that might threaten Utah libraries and librarians. Holds a conference.

Andy Spackman, President
Anna Neatrour, Executive Director

140 Wilderness Education Association
Elgenman Hall 029
1900 E 10th St
Bloomington, IN 47406
812-855-4095
Fax: 812-855-8697
E-mail: cpelchat@ithaca.edu
http://www.weainfo.org
The Wilderness Education Association is a not-for-profit organization whose purpose is to educate the general public and outdoor leaders in the appropriate use of wildlands and protected areas by developing and implementing educational curricula, programs and by forming strategic alliances with federal land management agencies, conservation groups and all organizations that benefit from wildlands and feel that the existence of wildlands is important to the quality of life

Chris Pelchat, President
Mike McGowan, VP

141 Women's Educational & Industrial Union
Crittenton Women's Union
One Washington Mall
2nd Floor
Boston, MA 2108
617-259-2900
Fax: 617-247-8826
E-mail: info@liveworkthrive.org
http://www.weiu.org
Crittenton Women's Union transforms the course of low-income women's lives so that they can attain economic independence and create better futures for themselves and their families

Charles Carter Jr, COO
Nathalie Apchin, CFO

142 World Trade Centers Association
Greater Kansas City Chamber of Commerce
30 W Pershing Road
Suite 301
Kansas City, MO 64108-2423
816-221-2424
http://wtcaonline.com
Fosters a global Trade Center Network that enhances the brand and promotes prosperity through trade and investment.

Ghazi Abu Nahl, Chairman
Guy F Tozzoli, President

Administration

143 American Association of Collegiate Registrars & Admissions Officers
1 Dupont Circle NW
Suite 520
Washington, DC 20036
202-293-9161
Fax: 202-872-8857
E-mail: sullivanj@aacrao.org
http://www.aacrao.org
Promotes higher education and furthers the professional development of members working in admissions, enrollment management, financial aid, institutional research, records and registration.

Jerome Sullivan, Executive Director
Martha Henebry, Membership/Publications Dir

144 American Association of School Administrators
801 N Quincy Street
Suite 700
Arlington, VA 22203-1730
703-528-0700
Fax: 703-841-1543
E-mail: Info@aasa.org
http://www.aasa.org
The mission of the American Association of School Administrators is to support and develop effective school system leaders who are dedicated to the highest quality public education for all children

Daniel A Domenech, Executive Director
Sharon Adams-Taylor, Associate Executive Director

145 American Education Finance Association (AEFA)
258 Norman Hall
PO Box 117049
Gainesville, FL 32611-7049
352-392-2391
Fax: 303-670-8986
E-mail: AEFA@coe.ufl.edu
http://www.afajof.org
Promotes understanding of means by which resources are generated, distributed and used to enhance human learning.

Founded: 1976

Raghuram Rajan, President
Sheridan Titman, President-Elect

146 Association of School Business Officials International
ASBO International Annual Meetings and Exhibits
11401 N Shore Drive
Reston, VA 20190
866-682-2729
Fax: 703-708-7060
E-mail: jmusso@asbointl.org
http://www.asbointl.org
Provide programs and services to promote the highest standards of school business management practices, professional growth, and the effective use of educational resources.

Founded: 1910

John D Musso, Executive Director
Charles E Linderman, President

147 Council of Chief State School Officers
1 Massachusetts Avenue NW
Suite 700
Washington, DC 20001-1431
202-336-7000
Fax: 202-408-8072
E-mail: info@ccsso.org
http://www.ccsso.org
Envision a system of schooling in each state that ensures high standards of performance and prepares each child to succeed as a productive member of a democratic society.

Christopher Koch, President
Thomas Luna, President Elect

148 ERIC Clearinghouse on Educational Management
University of Oregon
5214 University of Oregon
Eugene, OR 97403-5214
541-346-5044
800-438-8841
Fax: 541-346-2565

E-mail: sales@cepm.uoregon.edu
http://www.eric.uoregon.edu
The Clearinghouse produces and disseminates books, monographs, and synthesis papers on topics of interest to our national clientele of educational policymakers, school administrators, researchers, and other personnel.

Philip K Piele, Director
Stuart C Smith, Associate Director

149 Independent Schools Association of the Central States
1165 N Clark Street
Suite 311
Chicago, IL 60610
312-255-1244
Fax: 312-255-1278
E-mail: info@isacs.org
http://www.isacs.org
The purpose of ISACS is to promote the development of strong learning communities characterized by high achievements, social responsibility, and independence of governance, programs and policies.

1165 pages

Keith Shahan, President
Amanda Brown, Program Manager

150 NASPA - Student Affairs Administrators inHigher Education
111 K Street, NE
10th Floor
Washington, DC 20002
202-265-7500
Fax: 202-898-5737
E-mail: office@naspa.org
http://www.naspa.org
NASPA is the leading voice for student affairs administration, policy, and practice, and affirms the commitment of the student affairs profession to educating the whole student and integrating student life and learning. With more than 12,000 members at 1,400 campuses, and representing 29 countries, NASPA is the foremost professional association for student affairs administrators, faculty, and graduate and undergraduate students.

Elizabeth Griego, President

151 National Association for Supervision andCurriculum Development (ASCD)
1703 N Beauregard Street
Alexandria, VA 22311-1714
703-578-9600
800-933-2723
Fax: 703-575-5400
E-mail: member@ascd.org
http://www.ascd.org
Represents administrators of pupil services, promotes the concept of pupil personnel services in school systems to serve the needs of children and youth. Provides communication and professional growth for members.

Kathy Clayton, Executive Director
Sara Magana Shubel, President

152 National Association of Elementary School Principals
1615 Duke Street
Alexandria, VA 22314-3483
703-684-3345
800-386-2377
Fax: 703-549-5568
E-mail: naesp@naesp.org
http://www.naesp.org
To lead in the advocacy and support for elementary and middle level principals and other education leaders in their commitment to all children.

Gail Connelly, Executive Director
Nancy Shaaribel, Office Manager

153 National Association of Principals of Schools for Girls (NAPSG)
23490 Caraway Lakes Drive
Bonita Springs, FL 34135-8441
239-947-6196
Fax: 239-390-3245
E-mail: napsg@mac.com
http://www.napsg.org
Founded in 1921, the association consists of principals and deans of private and secondary independent (private) co-ed and girls' schools in the U.S. and Canada. Presentations and an Annual Meeting focus on school issues, particularly as they affect girls and young women.

Bruce W Galbraith, Executive Director
Ellen Stein, President

154 National Association of Private Schools for Exceptional Children
601 Pennsylvania Ave NW
Suite 900, South Building
Washington, DC 20004
202-434-8225
Fax: 202-434-8224
E-mail: napsec@aol.com
http://www.napsec.org
Strives to ensure access to special education for individuals as a vital component of the continuum of appropriate placements and services in American education.

Founded: 1971

Dr Dorothy Verleur, President
Dr Donald Verleur, VP

155 National Association of Secondary School Principals
1904 Association Drive
Reston, VA 20191-1537
703-860-0200
800-253-7746
Fax: 703-476-5432
E-mail: membership@principals.org
http://www.nassp.org
To promote excellence in school leadership and to provide members with a wide variety of programs and services to assist them in administration, supervision, curriculum planning, and effective staff development.

Jana Frieler, President
Ken Griffith, President-Elect

156 National Association of State Directors of Special Education
1800 Diagonal Road
Suite 320
Alexandria, VA 22314
703-519-3800
Fax: 703-519-3808
E-mail: nasdse@nasdse.org
http://www.nasdse.org
A nonprofit corporation that promotes and supports education programs for students with disabilities in the United States and outlying areas.

Babbi Lockman, President
Stephanie Petska, Secretary/Treasurer

157 National Association of Student Financial Aid Administrators
1101 Connecticut Avenue NW
Suite 1100
Washington, DC 20036-4303
202-785-0453
Fax: 202-785-1487
E-mail: Web@NASFAA.org
http://www.nasfaa.org
A nonprofit corporation of postsecondary institutions, individuals, agencies and students interested in promoting the effective adminis-

tration of student financial aid in the United States.

Pamela Fowler, National Chair-Elect
Dr Laurie A Wolf, National Chair

158 National Council of State Directors of Adult Education
444 N Capitol Street, NW
Suite 422
Washington, DC 20001
202-624-5250
Fax: 202-624-1497
E-mail: dc2@ncsdae.org
http://www.ncsdae.org
to attend to legislative needs and concerns, to work with other adult education organizations, to exchange ideas and solve common problems, and to establish and maintain a nationwide communication network regarding national policy and legislative issues.

Founded: 1967

Denise Pottmeyer, Chairman
Dr Lennox McLendon, Executive Director

159 National Data Bank for Disabled StudentServices
University of Maryland
Room 0126, Shoemaker Building
College Park, MD 20742
301-314-7682
301-314-7682
Fax: 301-405-0813
http://www.inform.umd.edu
Provides assessment of statistics related to services, staff, budget and other components of disabled student services programs across the country.

Vivian S Boyd, Director
Jo Ann Hutchinson, Assistant Director, DSS

160 National Institute for School and Workplace Safety
257 Plaza Drive
Suite B
Oviedo, FL 32765-6457
407-366-4878
Fax: 407-977-1210
http://www.nisws.com
Believes that every school and workplace must implement school and workplace safety standards. Committed to enhance school and workplace safety and to increase awareness of school and workplace safety issues.

Steven Burhoe, CEO

161 National School Safety Center
141 Duesenberg Drive
Suite 7B
Westlake Village, CA 91362-3815
805-373-9977
Fax: 805-373-9277
E-mail: info@schoolsafety.us
http://www.schoolsafety.us
Serves as an advocate for safe, secure and peaceful schools worldwide and as a catalyst for the prevention of school crime and violence.

Founded: 1984

Ronald D Stephens, Executive Director
June Lane Arnette, Associate Director

162 Psychological Corporation
19500 Bulverde Road
San Antonio, TX 78259
210-339-8190
800-627-7271
Fax: 800-232-1223
http://www.pearsonassess.com
Our mission is to improve teaching and learning. We help student, families, educators, and professionals use assessment, research, and innovative technologies to promote learning and personal development, advance academic

achievement, and transform educational communities.

Doug Kubash, President/CEO
Satbir S Bedi, SVP/Chief Technology Officer

Early Childhood Education

163 Child Care Information Exchange
PO Box 3249
Redmond, WA 98073-3249
800-221-2864
800-221-2864
Fax: 425-861-9386
E-mail: infor@ChildCareExchange.com
http://www.ccie.com
Exchange has promoted the exchange of ideas among leaders in early childhood programs worldwide through its magazine, books, training products, trainig seminars, and international conferences for 27 years.

Debbie Goodeve, Manager
Debra Hartzell, Advertising

164 Dimensions of Early Childhood
Southern Early Childhood Association
PO 55930
Little Rock, AR 72215-5930
501-221-1648
800-305-SECA
Fax: 501-227-5297
E-mail: info@southernearlychildhood.org
http://www.southernearlychildhood.org
Southern Early Childhood Association has brought together preschool, kindergarten, and primary teachers and administrators, caregivers, program directors, and individuals working with and for families, to promote quality care and education for young children.

Janie Humphries, President
Crystal Campbell, Coordinator

165 Division for Early Childhood
The Council for Exceptional Children
27 Fort Missoula Road
Suite 2
Missoula, MT 59804
406-543-0872
Fax: 406-543-0887
E-mail: dec@dec-sped.org
http://www.dec-sped.org
The Division for Early Childhood promotes policies and advances evidence-based practices that support families and enhance the optimal development of young children who have or are at risk for developmental delays and disabilities.

Sarah Mulligan, Executive Director
Bethany Morris, Director of Member Services

166 Education Advisory Group
6239 Woodlawn Avenue North
Seattle, WA 98810
206-323-1838
Fax: 206-267-1325
E-mail: info@eduadvisory.com
http://www.eduadvisory.com
Specializes in matching children with learning environments. Helps families identify concerns and establish priorities about their child's education.

167 National Early Childhood Technical Assistance Center
517 S Greensboro Street
Carrboro, NC 27510
919-962-2001
919-843-3269
Fax: 919-966-7463
E-mail: nectac@unc.edu
http://www.nectac.org

NECTAC is the national early childhood technical assistance center supported by the U.S. Department of Education's Office of Special Education Programs.

Lynne Kahn, Director
Joan Danaher, Associate Director

168 National Educational Systems (NES)
6333 De Zavala
Suite 106
San Antonio, TX 78249
800-231-4380
Fax: 210-699-4674
E-mail: info@shopnes.com
http://www.shopnes.com
NES is committed to providing quality materials to its customers and prides itself on the friendly customer service that is readily available.

Lupe Garza, Owner
Diana Garza, Owner

169 National Head Start Association
1651 Prince Street
Alexandria, VA 22314-2818
703-739-0875
Fax: 703-739-0878
http://www.nhsa.org
The National Head Start Association is a private not-for-profit membership organization dedicated exclusively to meeting the needs of Head Start children and their families.

Ron Herndon, Chairman
Janis Santos, Vice- Chairperson

Elementary Education

170 Center for Play Therapy
University of North Texas
1400 Highland Street
Room 14
Denton, TX 76203-0829
940-565-3864
Fax: 940-565-4461
E-mail: cpt@unt.edu
http://www.centerforplaytherapy.com
Encourages the unique development and emotional growth of children through the process of play therapy, a dynamic interpersonal relationship between a child and a therapist trained in play therapy procedures. Provides training, research, publications, counseling services and acts as a clearinghouse for literature in the field.

Sue Bratton, Director
Garry Landreth, Founder

171 Clearinghouse on Early Education and Parenting (CEEP)
University of Illinois at Urbana-Champaign
51 Gerty Drive
Champaign, IL 61820-7469
217-333-1386
877-275-3227
Fax: 212-244-7732
E-mail: ceep@uiuc.edu
http://ceep.crc.uiuc.edu/
The Clearinghouse on Early Education and Parenting (CEEP) is part of the the Early Childhood and Parenting (ECAP) Collaborative at the University of Illinois at Urbana-Champaign. CEEP provides publications and information to the worldwide early childhood and parenting communities on topics relating to the physiological, psychological and cultural development of children from birth through early adolescence.

Lilian G Katz Ph.D, Co-Director
Jeanne C Bleuer, Associate Director

172 National Association for the Education of Young Children
1313 L Street, NW
Suite 500
Washington, DC 20005-4101
202-232-8777
800-424-2460
Fax: 202-328-1846
E-mail: naeyc@naeyc.org
http://www.naeyc.org
Supports those interested in serving and acting on behalf of the needs and rights of the education of young children.

Jarlean Daniel, Executive Director
Adele B Robinson, Deputy Executive Director

173 Tribeca Learning Center-PS 150
334 Greenwich Street
New York, NY 10013
212-732-4392
Fax: 212-766-5895
E-mail: Info@ps150.net
http://www.ps150.net
Tribeca Learning Center, PS 150 opened in 1987 as a public school that encourages student-centered learning and family involvement fostering the optimal development and learning of every child and reaffirming the pivotal role of the elementary school. The school offers specialized classes in art, music, dance, technology and library as well as daily classroom activities which encourage the integration of a child's academic development, emotional-social growth, and the arts.

Brian Fingeret, President
Laura Cohen, Coordinator

174 Voyager Expanded Learning
17855 Dallas Parkway
Suite 400
Dallas, TX 75287
214-932-3213
888-399-1995
Fax: 888-589-0085
E-mail: jnowakowski@voyagerlearning.com
http://www.voyagerlearning.com
Voyager Expanded Learningr is a leading provider of in-school core reading programs, reading and math intervention programs, and professional development programs for school districts throughout the United States
Founded: 1994

David Cappellucci, President
Ron Klausner, CEO

Employment

175 AAA Teacher's Agency
177 Main Street
Suite 364
Fort Lee, NJ 7024-2540
718-548-3267
Fax: 718-548-3315
A placement agency for teachers, administrators and others in the field of education.

Daniel Shea, Director/Owner

176 Aviation Information Resources
1001 Riverdale Court
Atlanta, GA 30337
800-247-2777
Fax: 404-592-6515
E-mail: airinfo@airapps.com
http://www.jet-jobs.com
Aviation Information Resources, is a Career Information Resource company for pilots who are on an airline pilot career track. We work with military pilots transitioning to the civilian sector, general aviation, corporate,

and commuter pilots seeking to get a job with an airline, from regional to major.

Kit Darby, President
Becky Dean, Vice President

177 English Language Fellow Program
Center for Intercultural Development Center
3300 Whitehaven Street
Suite 1000
Washington, DC 20007
202-687-2608
Fax: 202-687-2555
E-mail: elf@georgetown.edu
http://elf.georgetown.edu
The English Language Fellow Program provides American professional expertise in teaching English as a foreign language by sending American experts on ten-month fellowships to overseas academic institutions to improve foreign teachers' and students' access to diverse perspectives on a broad variety of issues, giving foreign teachers and students information enabling them to better understand and convey concepts about American values, democratic representative government, and free enterprise.

Magdalena Potocka, Director
Faith Jarmon, Program Officer

178 Graphic Arts Education & Research Foundation
1899 Preston White Drive
Reston, VA 20191
703-264-7200
866-381-9839
Fax: 703-620-3165
E-mail: gaerf@npes.org
http://www.gaerf.org
To advance knowledge and education in the field of graphic communications by supporting programs that prepare the workforce of the future. 1

Stephen L Johnson, Chairman

179 Graphic Arts Technical Foundation
200 Deer Run Road
Sewickley, PA 15143
412-741-6860
800-910-4283
Fax: 412-741-2311
E-mail: printing@printing.org
http://www.gain.net
Deliver products and services that enhance the growth, efficiency, and profitability of its members and the industry through: Advocacy,ÿ Education,ÿ Research, and Technical information

Denna Hower, Marketing Coordinator
Mary Garnett, Executive Vice President

180 Health Occupations Students of America
6021 Morriss Road
Suite 111
Flower Mound, TX 75028
972-874-0062
800-321-4672
Fax: 972-874-0063
http://www.hosa.org
Provides health occupations educators with a student organization used to recruit and develop a competent and motivated work force for the health care field.

Jim Koeninger, Executive Director
Kim Smith, Associate Director

181 Mountain Pacific Association of Colleges andEmployers
16 Santa Ana Place
Walnut Creek, CA 94598
925-934-3877
Fax: 925-906-0922

E-mail: d2@dobbsgroup.com
http://www.mpace.org
The Mountain-Pacific Association of Colleges and Employers, Inc. is committed to attaining a pluralistic, diverse membership, and providing access to all programs and resources to individu-als regardless of race, color, national origin, religion, gender, age, sexual orientation, veteran status, disability, or appearance

James Tarbox PhD, President
Margaret Paulin, Past President

182 NPES: Association for Suppliers of Printing, Publishing & Converting Technologies
1899 Preston White Drive
Reston, VA 20191
703-264-7200
Fax: 703-620-0994
E-mail: npes@npes.org
http://www.npes.org
A US trade association representing more than 400 companies that manufacture and distribute equipment, software and supplies used across the workflow of newarly every printing, publishing and converting process.

Ralph J Nappi, President
William K Smythe Jr, Vice President

183 National Association of Teachers' Agencies
799 Kings Highway
Fairfield, CT 6432
203-333-0611
Fax: 203-334-7224
E-mail: fairfieldteachers@snet.net
http://www.jobsforteachers.com
Provides placement services for those seeking professional positions at all levels of teaching/administration/support services worldwide.

Mark King, Secretary/Treasurer

184 National Business Education Association
1914 Association Drive
Reston, VA 20191-1596
703-860-8300
Fax: 703-620-4483
E-mail: nbea@nbea.org
http://www.nbea.org
NBEA is committed to the advancement of the professional interest and competence of its members and provides programs and services that enhance members' professional growth and development.

Madge Lewis Gregg, President
John J Olivo, President-Elect

185 Windsor Mountain International
One World Way
Windsor, NH 03244
603-369-6088
800-862-7760
Fax: 603-478-5260
E-mail: mail@WindsorMountain.org
http://www.windsormountain.org/
Windsor Mountain International was founded in 1961, as Interlocken International Camp, hosting young people from more than 60 countries through international youth travel programs where students learn by doing, thereby enriching their lives with lasting friendships, new skills, self discovery, and increased environmental and cross-cultural awareness.

Richard Herman, Executive Director
Jake Labovitz, Owner

186 Women's International League for Peace &Freedom
U.S. Section
565 Boylston Street 2nd Floor
Boston, MA 02116
617-266-0999
Fax: 617-266-1688
http://www.wilpf.org
Agency offering internships in the United States.

Marilyn Clement
Tanya Burovtseva, Project Coordinator

Guidance & Counseling

187 American Association of Sex Educators,Counselors & Therapists
14441 Street NW
Suite 700
Washington, DC 20005
202-449-1099
Fax: 202-216-9646
E-mail: info@aasect.org
http://www.aasect.org
The American Association of Sexuality Educators, Counselors and Therapists is a not-for-profit, interdisciplinary professional organization.
Founded: 1967

Deeann Walker, Executive Director/Conferenc
Dr Patricia Schiller, Founder

188 American Counseling Association
5999 Stevenson Avenue
Alexandria, VA 22304-3302
703-823-9800
800-347-6647
Fax: 703-823-0252
E-mail: membership@counseling.org
http://www.counseling.org
A not-for-profit, professional and educational organization that is dedicated to the growth and enhancement of the counseling profession.

Dr Marcheta Evans, President

189 American School Counselor Association
1101 King Street
Suite 625
Alexandria, VA 22314
703-683-2722
800-306-4722
Fax: 703-683-1619
E-mail: asca@schoolcounselor.org
http://www.schoolcounselor.org
Promotes human rights and child welfare, as well as educational rights for children.

Richard Wong, Executive Director
Stephanie J Wicks, Director of Administration

190 Association of Educational Therapists
11300 W Olympic Boulevard
Suite 600
Los Angeles, CA 90064
310-909-1490
800-286-4267
Fax: 310-437-0585
E-mail: aet@aetonline.org
http://www.aetonline.org
Founded in 1979 the Association of Educational Therapists establishes professional standards and defines roles, responsibilities and ethics of educational therapists; studies techniques, technologies, philosophies and research related to educational therapy; represents/defines educational therapy to the community, school and professional group;

provides opportunities for continued professional growth.

Marcy Dunn, President
Loren Deutsch, President-Elect

191 Counseling Association
5999 Stevenson Avenue
Alexandria, VA 22304-3302
703-823-9800
800-347-6647
Fax: 703-823-0252
E-mail: clogan@argosy.edu
http://www.counseling.org
Promotes public confidence and trust in the counseling profession so that professionals can further assist their clients and students in dealing with the challenges life presents.

Colleen R Logan, President
Richard Yep, Executive Director

192 ERIC/CASS Virtual Libraries: Online Resourcesfor Parents, Teachers, and Counselors
Computer Sciences Corporation
655 15th Street SW
Suite 500
Washington, DC 20005
800-538-3742
http://www.eric.ed.gov
Collects and disseminates information on counseling, guidance and student services. (ERIC/CASS) serves counseling and student professionals as well as parents who have an interest in personal and social factors that affect learning and development. ERIC/CASS has developed virtual libraries to provide online access to full-text documents on topics within its scope.

Robert Boruch, Chairman
John Collins, ERIC Steering Committee

193 International Association of Counseling Services
101 S Whiting Street
Suite 211
Alexandria, VA 22304-3415
703-823-9840
Fax: 703-823-9843
E-mail: iacsinc@earthlink.net
http://www.iacsinc.org
IACS is committed to furthering the visibility of the counseling profession and improving its quality. IACS has evolved standards that define professional quality and has established criteria for accreditation which reflect these standards.

Nancy E Roncketti, Executive Officer
Rattana Thanagosol, Administrative Assistant

194 National Association of School Psychologists
4340 E West Highway
Suite 402
Bethesda, MD 20814
301-657-0270
866-331-6277
Fax: 301-657-0275
E-mail: center@naspweb.org
http://www.nasponline.org
Founded in 1977 the National Association of School Psychologists is a professional association representing over 22,000 school psychologists and related professionals.

Janela Joseh, COO
Susan Gorin, Executive Director

195 National Association of Substance Abuse Trainers & Educators
1521 Hillary Street
New Orleans, LA 70118-4007
504-286-5000

Sustains an information network of substance abuse/chemical dependency training programs in higher education.

Thomas Lief, Director

International

196 Academic Travel Abroad
1920 N Street NW
Suite 200
Washington, DC 20036
202-785-9000
800-556-7896
Fax: 202-342-0317
http://www.academic-travel.com
Seeks to foster intercultural relations and educational cooperation between institutions of higher learning.

Founded: 1950

David Parry, Chairman
Kate Simpson, President

197 Alberta Association of Recreation FacilityPersonnel
Box 1000
Cochrane, AB T4C-1A4
403-851-7626
888-253-7544
Fax: 403-253-9181
E-mail: office@aarfp.com
http://www.aarfp.com
A provincial organization dedicated to providing excellence in training and professional development for individuals involved in the operation of recreation facilities.

Founded: 1978

Larry Golby, Executive Director
Kim Snell, President

198 Alberta Council on Admissions and Transfer
10155-102 Street
11th Floor
Edmonton, AB T5J-4L5
780-422-9021
800-232-7215
Fax: 780-422-3688
E-mail: acat@gov.ab.ca
http://www.acat.gov.ab.ca
To be a catalyst for necessary change and an advocate for learners in the areas of admission and transfer to educational programs.

Founded: 1974

Ron Woodward, Chairman
Marg Leathem, Director

199 American Friends Service Committee
Human Resources
1501 Cherry Street
Philadelphia, PA 19102-1429
215-241-7000
Fax: 215-241-7275
E-mail: afscinfo@afsc.org
http://www.afsc.org
The American Friends Service Committee carries out service, development, social justice, and peace programs throughout the world. Founded by Quakers in 1917 to provide conscientious objectors with an opportunity to aid civilian war victims, AFSC's work attracts the support and partnership of people of many races, religions, and cultures.

Arlene Kelly, Presiding Clerk
Phil Lord, Assistant Clerk

200 American Schools Association of Central America, Columbia-Caribbean and Mexico
Unit 5372-Box 004
APO AA, Quito
Ecuador 34039-3420
593-2-244-9141
Fax: 593-2-243-4985
E-mail: marsanc@uio.satnet.net
http://www.tri-association.org
Established to provide information to three regional educational associations: Association of American Schools of Central America, Association of Colombian-Caribbean American Schools, Association of Americann Schools of Mexico.

Mary Virginia Sanchez, Executive Director
Linda Niehaus, President

201 Aprovecho Research Center
PO Box 1175
Cottage Grove, OR 97424
541-767-0287
E-mail: dean@aprovecho.org
http://www.aprovecho.org
A non-profit organization whose purpose is To research, develop, and disseminate technological solutions for meeting the basic human needs of low income and impoverished people and communities in third world countries, in order to help relieve their suffering, improve their health, enhance their safety, and reduce their adverse impacts on their environment.

Dr Richard Zeller, President
Damon Ogle, VP

202 Associated Schools Project Network
UNESCO
7 Placede Fontenoy
Paris, France 75352
330-1-45-68-10-00
Fax: 331-43067925
E-mail: nathalie.hirschsprung@diplomatie.gouv.fr
http://www.unesco.org
Founded in 1953 the Associated Schools Project Network is of schools designed to conduct pilot projects in favor of a culture of peace.

Nathalie Hirschsprung, Coordinator

203 Association for Asian Studies
1021 E Huron Street
Ann Arbor, MI 48104
734-665-2490
Fax: 734-665-3801
E-mail: mpaschal@asian-studies.org
http://www.asian-studies.org
Founded in 1941 the Association for Asian Studies seeks through publications, meetings, and seminars to facilitate contact and an exchange of information among scholars to increase their understanding of East, South, and Southeast Asia.

K (Shivi) Slvaramakrishnan, President
Gail Hershatter, Vice President

204 Association for Canadian Education Resources
Unit 44, Flamewood Drive
Mississauga, ON L4Y-3P5
905-275-7685
Fax: 905-275-9420
E-mail: acerinfo@rogers.com
http://www.acer-acre.org
Initiate and facilitate development, production and promotion of Canadian materials to meet the needs of today's learners.

Alice Casselman, President
Irene Katkov, Chairman

205 Association for Canadian Studies in the US
2030 M Street NW
Suite 350
Washington, DC 20036
202-775-9007
Fax: 202-775-0061
E-mail: info@acsus.org
http://www.acsus.org
Devoted to the encouragement and support of the study of Canada and the United States-Canada bilateral relationship. Publishes a quarterly journal, American Review of Canadian Studies.

Tamara Woroby, President
Nadine Fabbi, Secretary/Treasurer

206 Association for International Practical Training
10400 Little Patuxent Parkway
Suite 250
Columbia, MD 21044-3519
410-997-2200
Fax: 410-992-3924
E-mail: aipt@aipt.org
http://www.aipt.org
Provides educational and professional exchange experiences that enhance cultural awareness, develop global competencies, mutual understanding, and international cooperation.

Dr Cheryl A Matherly, Board Chair
Prof Howard A Rollins Jr, Board Chair Elect

207 Association of American International Colleges & Universities
PO Box 21021
Pylea, Thessaloniki
Greece 555 1
33-4-42-23-39-35
Fax: 33-4-42-21-11-38
E-mail: rjackson@act.edu
http://www.aaicu.org
Founded in 1971 the Association of American International Colleges and Universities provides a unified source of information regarding accredited independent institutions in Europe and the Middle East offering a liberal arts or technical education.
Founded: 1971

Richard L Jackson, President

208 Association of American Schools of Brazil
Bloco E, Lotes 34/37
SGAS 605
Brasilia, DF, Brazil 70200-650
55-61-3442-9700
Fax: 55-61-3442-9729
E-mail: cjohnson@eabdf.br
http://www.eabdf.br
Provides a US accredited, pre-K through grade 12 program based on a comprehensive college preparatory curriculum taught in English to students of all nationalities.

Craig A Johnson, Headmaster
Paul Echaniz, Board President

209 Association of American Schools of Central America
c/o US Embassy Quito
Unit 5372, Box 004
Quito, Ecuador 34039
593-2-477-534
Fax: 593-2-434-985
E-mail: marsanc@uio.satnet.net
http://www.tri-association.org
Supports and encourage academic, artistic, athletic and cultural interaction between international schools that offer a US type education in Central America.

Mary Virginia Sanchez, Executive Director
William Scotti, Regional Education Officer

210 Association of American Schools of South America
1911 NW 150 Ave
Suite 101
Pembroke Pines, FL 33028
954-436-4034
Fax: 954-436-4092
E-mail: ppoore@aassa.com
http://www.aassa.com
Provide and promote programs and services to member schools to enhance the quality of American International Education. As an organization, AASSA values service leadership, quality and effectiveness.

Paul Joslin, President
Susan Barba, VP

211 Association of British Schools in Spain
c/o Urbanizacion Los Pinos
S-N 18690, Almunecar, Granada
Spain
34-958-639-003
Fax: 34-958-639-003
E-mail: info@nabss.org
http://www.nabss.org
Founded in 1978 to promote, uphold and defend British education in Spain.

Donat Morgan, President
Roger Deign, VP

212 Association of Christian Schools International
731 Chapel Hills Drive
PO Box 65130
Colorado Springs, CO 80920
719-528-6906
800-367-0798
Fax: 719-531-0631
E-mail: membership@acsi.org
http://www.acsi.org
Founded in 1978 the Association of Christian Schools International represents members in legislative efforts and legal confrontations with the government.

Brian S Simmons, President

213 Association of International Educators
1307 New York Avenue NW
8th Floor
Washington, DC 20005-4701
202-737-3699
800-836-4994
Fax: 202-737-3657
E-mail: inbox@nafsa.org
http://www.nafsa.org
A nonprofit membership association that provides training, information and other services to professionals in the field of international education and exchange.

Meredith M McQuaid, President
Susan M Thompson, VP Member Relations

214 Association of International Educators (NAFSA)
1307 New York Avenue NW
8th Floor
Washington, DC 20005-4701
202-737-3699
Fax: 202-737-3657
E-mail: inbox@nafsa.org
http://www.nafsa.org
Serves international educators and their institutions and organizations by setting standards of good practice, providing training and professional development opportunities, providing networking opportunities, and advocating for international education.

Marlene Johnson, Executive Director/CEO
Victor C Johnson, Senior Advisor Public Policy

215 Association of International Schools in Africa
Peponi Road
P O Box 14103, Nairobi
Kenya 00800
254-20-2697442
Fax: 254-20-4183272
E-mail: info@aisa.or.ke
http://www.aisa.or.ke
Facilitates communications, cooperation, and professional growth among member schools. Promotes intercultural understanding and friendships as well as facilitating collaboration between its members, host country schools, and other regional and professional groups.

Peter Bateman, Executive Director
Thomas P Shearer, Chairperson

216 Atlantic Provinces Special Education Authority
5940 S Street
Halifax, Nova Scotia
Canada B3H-1S6
902-424-8500
Fax: 902-424-0543
http://www.apsea.ca
APSEA is an interprovincial cooperative agency established in 1975 by joint agreement among the Ministers of Education of New Brunswick, New foundland, Nova Scotia, and Prince Edward Island.

Bertram Tulk, Superintendent
Lori Moore, Programs Director

217 British American Educational Foundation
520 Summit Avenue
Oradell, NJ 07649
201-261-4438
http://www.baef.org
Founded by a group of American alumni of British schools, the BAEF is a non-profit charitable foundation governed by a Board of Directors, comprised primarily of alumni, and a President.

Laurel Zimmermann, Executive Director
Denise Bryan, Founder

218 CARE
151 Ellis Street NE
Atlanta, GA 30303-2400
404-681-2552
800-422-7385
Fax: 404-589-2651
E-mail: managemyaccount@care.org
http://www.care.org
CARE is a leading humanitarian organization fighting global poverty
Founded: 1945

Helene D Gayle, President/CEO
W Bowman Cutter, Chair

219 CDS International
440 Park Avenue S
New York, NY 10016
212-497-3500
Fax: 212-497-3535
E-mail: info@cdsintl.org
http://www.cdsintl.org
CDS International, Inc. is committed to the advancement of international career training opportunities customized to provide individuals with in-depth practical knowledge of

other nations' business practices, cultures, and political traditions.

Robert Fenstermacher, Executive Director
Linda Boughton, Deputy Executive Director

220 Canadian Association of Communicators inEducation
2138 Blossom Drive
Ottawa, ON K1H-6G8
E-mail: strachan_d@sd36.bc.ca
http://www.cace-acace.org
The major goal of the organization was to provide networking opportunities for its members and acknowledge their contributions to the success of the education system in Canada.
Founded: 1984

Doug Strachan, President
Maxeen Jolin, VP

221 Canadian Association of Independent Schools
2 Ridley Road
PO Box 3013
St. Cathatines, ON L2R-7C3
905-657-5658
Fax: 905-684-5057
E-mail: execasst@cesi.edu
http://cais.ca
CAIS is a membership association for independent schools in Canada and abroad that offer a Canadian curriculum.

Anne-Marie Kee, Executive Director

222 Canadian Council for the Advancement ofEducation
4 Cataraqui Street
Suite 310
Kingston, ON K7K-1Z7
613-531-9213
613-421-7960
Fax: 613-531-0626
E-mail: admin@ccaecanada.org
http://www.ccaecanada.org
The Canadian Council for the Advancement of Education (CCAE) fosters excellence in Canadian education by providing bilingual programs and services to professionals in institutional advancement.

Mary Williams, President
Mark Hazlett, Executive Director

223 Canadian Memorial Chiropractic College
6100 Leslie Street
Toronto, ON M2H-3J1
416-482-2340
800-463-2923
Fax: 416-646-1114
E-mail: communications@cmcc.ca
http://www.cmcc.ca
CMCC is a registered organization in chiropractic education and research.
Founded: 1945

Jean A Moss, President

224 Canadian Society for the Study of Education
260 Dalhousie Street
Suite 204 Ottawa, Ontario
Canada K1N-7E4
613-241-0018
Fax: 613-241-0019
E-mail: csse-scee@csse.ca
http://www.csse.ca
To promote the advancement of Canadian research and scholarship in education. In order to fulfill its mandate
Founded: 1972

Fernand Gervais, President
Marc-Andre Ethier, VP

225 Catholic Medical Mission Board
10 W 17th Street
New York, NY 10011-5765
212-242-7757
800-678-5659
Fax: 212-807-9161
E-mail: info@cmmb.org
http://www.cmmb.org
To provide quality healthcare programs and services, without discrimination, to people in need around the world.
Founded: 1912

John F Galbraith, President/CEO
Michael Doring Connelly, Chairman

226 Central and Eastern European Schools Association
American School of Warsaw
Vocarska 106
Zagreb 10000
Croatia
385-1-460-9935
Fax: 385-1-460-9936
E-mail: office@ceesa.org
http://www.ceesa.org
Enhances school effectiveness and inspires student learning and development and provides extensive collaborative networks that improve school effectiveness

David M Cobb, Executive Director
Dr Robin Heslip, Chairman, Executive Committe

227 Commonwealth of Learning
1055 W Hastings Street
Suite 1200
Vancouver, BC V6E-2E9
604-775-8200
Fax: 604-775-8210
E-mail: info@col.org
http://www.col.org
An intergovernmental organization created by Commonwealth Heads of Government to encourage the development and sharing of open learning/distance education knowledge, resources and technologies.
Founded: 2001

Sir John Daniel, President/CEO
Professor Asha Kanwar, VP

228 Communicating for America
112 E Lincoln Avenue
PO Box 677
Fergus Falls, MN 56538-677
218-739-3241
800-432-3276
Fax: 218-739-3832
E-mail: memberbenefits@cain.org
http://www.communicatingforamerica.org
Agency offering international internships, financed and unfinanced, in agriculture, horticulture, equine and ecology of Western Europe, Eastern Europe, Australia, New Zealand, South America and South Africa.

Wayne Nelson, President

229 Concern-America Volunteers
2015 N Broadway Avenue
PO Box 1790
Santa Ana, CA 92706-1790
714-953-8575
800-266-2376
Fax: 714-953-1242
E-mail: concamerinc@earthlink.net
http://www.concernamerica.org
Concern America is a unique nonprofit, nonsectarian, nongovernmental development and refugee aid organization - unique in that its philosophy emphasizes the transference of skills and thus the creation of opportunity (seen as a more permanent solution), not just

the placement of resources into impoverished regions.
Founded: 1972

Marianne Loewe, Executive Director
Denis Garvey, Director of Development

230 Cordell Hull Foundation for International Education
501 Fifth Avenue
Third Floor
New York, NY 10017
212-300-2138
Fax: 646-349-3455
E-mail: cordellhull@aol.com
http://www.cordellhull.org
Not-for-profit organization dedicated to continuing the work of Cordell Hull. Offered programs to improve relations between the United States and other countries, primarily through educational and cultural exchange.

Marianne Mason, President

231 Council of British International Schools
Pambroke House
8 St Christophers Place
Fanborough, Hampshire, UK GU14-0NH
44-0-1252-513-930
Fax: 440-0-1252-516-00
E-mail: executive.director@cobis.org.uk
http://www.cobisec.org.uk
COBIS is a Membership Association of British Schools of quality and is a member of the Independent Schools Council (ISC) of the United Kingdom.

Roger Fry, Chairman
Sybil Melchers MBE, Honorary Vice President

232 Council of Education FacilityPlanners-International
9180 E Desert Cove
Suite 104
Scottsdale, AZ 85260
480-391-0840
Fax: 480-391-0940
E-mail: contact@cefpi.org
http://www.cefpi.org
CEFPI is the primary advocate and resource for effective educational facilities.Serve those who use, plan, design, construct, maintain, equip and operate educational facilities.

Don Gilmore, Chairman
David C Edwards, Vice-Chair

233 Council of Ministers of Education, Canada
95 St Clair Avenue W
Suite 1106
Toronto, Ontario, Canada M4V-1N6
416-962-8100
Fax: 416-962-2800
E-mail: information@cmec.ca
http://www.cmec.ca
CMEC provides leadership in education at the pan-Canadian and international levels and contributes to the fulfilment of the constitutional responsibility for education conferred on provinces and territories.

Jean-Gilles Pelletier, Administration Director
Colin Bailey, Communications Director

234 Council on Foreign Relations
58 E 68th Street
New York, NY 10065
212-434-9400
Fax: 212-434-9800
http://www.cfr.org
The Council on Foreign Relations is an independent, nonpartisan membership organization, think tank, and publisher dedicated to being a resource for its members, government

officials, business executives, journalists, educators and students, civic and religious leaders, and other interested citizens.

Richard Haass, President
Jeffrey Riche, Chief of Staff

235 Council on Hemisphere Affairs
1250 Connecticut Avenue NW
Suite 1C
Washington, DC 20036
202-223-4975
888-922-9261
Fax: 202-223-4979
E-mail: coha@coha.org
http://www.coha.org
It supports open and democratic political processes just as it consistently has condemned authoritarian regimes of any stripe that fail to provide their populations with even minimal standards of political freedoms, economic and social justice, personal security and civic guarantees.

Founded: 1975

Larry Birns, Director

236 Council on International Educational Exchange(CIEE)
300 Fore Street
Portland, ME 04101
207-553-4000
800-407-8839
Fax: 207-553-4299
E-mail: contact@ciee.org
http://www.ciee.org
CIEE is a United States non-governmental international education organization. CIEE creates and administers programs that allow high school and university students and educators to study and teach abroad.

James Pellow, President/CEO

237 Council on Islamic Education
10055 Slater Avenue
Suite 250
Fountain Valley, CA 92708
714-839-2929
Fax: 714-839-2714
E-mail: info@cie.org
http://www.cie.org
CIE is formally comprised of Muslim academic scholars of religion, history, political science, cultural studies, communications, education, and other fields, along with a full-time professional staff with expertise on matters related to U.S. education, civics, politics, the media, faith communities and other components of American society and the institutional system.

Founded: 1990

Shabbir Mansuri, Founding Director
Munir A Shaikh, Executive Director

238 East Asia Regional Council of Overseas Schools
Barangay Mamplasan
Binan, Laguna
Philippines 4024
63-49-511-5993
Fax: 63-49-511-4694
E-mail: lsills@earcos.org
http://www.earcos.org
To promote intercultural understanding and international friendship through the activities of member schools.

Tim Carr, President
Sean O'Maonaigh, Vice President

239 Global Learning
22 Mary Ann Drive
Brick, NJ 08723
732-281-8929
Fax: 723-528-1027

E-mail: globallearningnj@comcast.net
http://www.globallearningnj.org/
A non-profit educational organization that translates the world's growing interdependence into educational activities for teachers, students, librarians, and educational systems, from elementary school through college and in community settings

Jeffrey L Brown, Executive Director
Paula Gotsch, Associate Director

240 Institute of Cultural Affairs
4750 N Sheridan Road
Chicago, IL 60640
773-769-6363
800-742-4032
Fax: 773-944-1582
E-mail: Chicago@ica-usa.org
http://www.ica-usa.org/
Releasing the capacity for positive, sustainable futures.

Founded: 1962

Kathleen Kelley, Office Manager
Terry Bergda, CEO

241 Institute of International Education
809 United Nations Plaza
New York, NY 10017-3580
212-883-8200
Fax: 212-984-5452
http://www.iie.org
Seeks to develop better understanding between the people of the US and the peoples of other countries through educational exchange programs for students, scholars and specialists.

Allan Goodman, President
Peggy Blumenthal, VP

242 Inter-Regional Center
PO Box 020470
Tuscaloosa, AL 35402
205-391-0727
Fax: 205-391-0927

Founded: 1969

Dr Burton Fox, Director

243 International Association for Continuing Education & Training
1760 Old Meadow Road
Suite 500
McLean, VA 22102
703-506-3275
Fax: 703-506-3266
E-mail: info@iacet.org
http://www.iacet.org
The International Association for Continuing Education and Training is a non-profit association dedicated to quality continuing education and training programs. IACET certifies education providers that meet strict continuing education guidelines originally created in 1968 and recently updated by the IACET Council for Standards Development (ICSD).

Karen Niles, President
Fran Johnson, President-Elect

244 International Association for the Exchange of Students for Technical Experience
10400 Little Patuxent Parkway
Suite 250
Columbia, MD 21044-3519
410-997-3069
Fax: 410-997-5186
E-mail: iaeste@aipt.org
http://www.iaesteunitedstates.org
IAESTE (I-ess-tay)...is the International Association for the Exchange of Students for Technical Experience, a global organization established in 1948 at the Imperial College in London. For more than 50 years, IAESTE has

continued to grow and now includes more than 80 member countries.

Pamela Ruiz, Director

245 International Association of Students inEconomics & Business Management (AIESC)
127 West 26th Street
10th Floor
New York, NY 10001
212-757-3774
Fax: 212-757-4062
E-mail: missys@aiesecus.org
http://www.aiesecus.org/
Agency offering study abroad programs, exchange programs and international internships, financed and unfinanced.

Founded: 1956

Tiffany Curtiss, President
Janet Etsch, VP

246 International Baccalaureate American GlobalCentre
7510 Wisconsin Ave
Suite 200 W
Bethesda, MD 20814
212-696-4464
Fax: 212-889-9242
E-mail: iba@ibo.org
http://www.ibo.org
The IB is a nonprofit educational foundation, motivated by its mission, focused on the student. Our three programmes for students aged 3 to 19 help develop the intellectual, personal, emotional and social skills to live, learn and work in a rapidly globalizing world.

Steve Aronson, President
Louis Bouchard, Director General

247 International Baccalaureate Organization
Route des Morillons 15
Grand-Saconnex, Geneve
Switzerland CH-12
41-22-791-7740
Fax: 41-22-791-0277
E-mail: ibaem@ibo.org
http://www.ibo.org
The International Baccalaureate (IB) is more than its three educational programmes. At our heart we are motivated by a mission to create a better world through education.

Jeff Beard, Director General
Dr Ian Hill, Deputy Director General

248 International Graphic Arts EducationAssociation (IGAEA)
1899 Preston White Drive
Reston, VA 26191

http://www.igaea.org
The International Graphic Arts Education Association (IGAEA) is an association of educators in partnership with industry, dedicated to sharing theories, principles, techniques and processes relating to graphic communications and imaging technology.

Shaun Dudek, President elect
Pam Daniel, 1st Vice President Pub

249 International Physicians for the Prevention of Nuclear War
66-70 Union Square
#204
Somerville, MA 02143-1024
617-440-1733
Fax: 617-440-1734
E-mail: ippnwbos@ippnw.org
http://www.ippnw.org
Agency offering non profit organization working to ban nuclear weapons and ex-

17

change programs and international internships, and unfinanced.

Michael Christ, Executive Director
Douglas Kline, Director of Administration

250 International Research and Exchanges Board

IREX
2121 K Street NW
Suite 700
Washington, DC 20037
202-628-8188
Fax: 202-628-8189
E-mail: irex@irex.org
http://www.irex.org
IREX is an international nonprofit oraganization specializing in education, independent media, Internet development and civil society programs.

W Robert Pearson, President
Joyce Warner, VP

251 International Schools Services

15 Roszel Road
PO Box 5910
Princeton, NJ 08543
609-452-0990
Fax: 609-452-2690
E-mail: iss@iss.edu
http://www.iss.edu
The mission of International Schools Services is to advance the quality of education for children and to respond effectively to the educational needs of teachers and administrators abroad whether in cosmopolitan capital cities or remote rain forests.ÿ ISS accomplishes its mission by working closely with all constituencies and stakeholders in the education process.

Roger Hove, President
Jim New Frack, COO

252 International Society for Business Education

US Chapter
1914 Association Drive
Reston, VA 20191-1538
703-860-8300
Fax: 703-620-4483
E-mail: blivingston@cerritos.edu
http://www.isbeusa.org
Its purpose is to provide educational and business training, opportunities and programs for its member.

Janice Bosman, President
Marilyn Sherry, President-Elect

253 International Studies Association (ISA)

University of Arizona
324 Social Sciences
Tucson, AZ 85721
520-621-7715
Fax: 520-621-5780
E-mail: isa@isanet.org
http://www.isanet.org
Provides opportunities for communications among educators, researchers, and practitioners in order to continually share intellectual interests and meet the challenges of a changing global environment

Founded: 1959

Thomas J Volgy, Executive Director
Lyn Brabant, Director of Administration

254 Mediterranean Association of International Schools

Apartado 80
Madrid
Spain 28080
34-91-740-1900
Fax: 34-91-357-2678

E-mail: info@amerschmad.org
http://www.mais-web.org
Professional organization that strives to improve the quality of education in its Member Schools through several venues. It promotes the professional development of faculty, administrators and school board members; effects communication and interchange and creates international understanding.

Founded: 1981

Sister Anne M Hill, President
Saara Tatem, VP

255 National Registration Center for Study Abroad

PO Box 1393
Milwaukee, WI 53201-1393
414-278-0631
Fax: 414-271-8884
E-mail: study@nrcsa.com
http://www.nrcsa.com
Evaluating programs around the world - selecting those best able to meet your needs. Improves international understanding through educational exchanges. NRCSA welcomes participants of all ages, nationalities, and occupations.

Founded: 1968

Mike Wittig, General Manager

256 Near East-South Asia Council of Overseas Schools

Gravias 6 Aghia Paraskevi
Athens, Greece, GR 15342
30-210-600-9821
Fax: 30-210-600-9928
E-mail: nesa@nesacenter.org
http://www.nesacenter.org
NESA will create dynamic, collaborative professional relationships which transcend current barriers and boundaries in order to maximize student learning in member schools.

David J Chojnacki, Executive Director
Kevin Schafer, President

257 Ontario Business Education Partnership

170 Louisa Steert
Kitchener, ON N2H 5
519-208-5699
888-672-7996
Fax: 519-208-5919
E-mail: sherryl@obep.on.ca
http://www.obep.ca
OBEP strives to ignite ideas and provide positive changes for today's youth through supporting our 26 community based not for profit organizations across Ontario committed to advancing business-education co-operation in support of workforce and economic development.OBEP supports the local organizations who promote and facilitate alliances between education, business, community organizations and government.

Founded: 1999

Sherryl Petricevic, Executive Director
Jeremy Hill, Co-Chair

258 Ontario Operative Education Association

35 Reynar Drive
Quispamsis, NB E2G-1J9
Fax: 506-849-8375
E-mail: OCEA@Rogers.com
http://www.ocea.on.ca
A not-for-profit professional organization of Ontario Cooperative Education and Experiential Learning Professionals.

Mary Davis, President
Darrell Czop, VP

259 Operation Crossroads Africa

PO Box 5570
New York, NY 10027
212-289-1949
Fax: 212-289-2526
E-mail: oca@igc.org
http://www.operationcrossroadsafrica.org
Agency offering study abroad programs, exchange programs and international internships, financed and unfinanced.

Founded: 1958

James Robinson Ph.D, Founder
Willis Logan, President

260 Opportunities Industrialization CentersInternational (OIC)

1500 Walnut St
Suite 1304
Philadelphia, PA 19102-3295
215-842-0220
Fax: 215-842-2276
E-mail: info@oici.org
http://www.oicinternational.org
OIC International provides individuals with the education,skills and confidence they need to help themselves, their households and their communities.

Crispian Kirk, President/CEO
Edmund D Cooke Jr, Chair of the Board

261 People to People International

911 Main Street
Suite 2110
Kansas City, MO 64105
816-531-4701
Fax: 816-561-7502
E-mail: ptpi@ptpi.org
http://www.ptpi.org
Enhance international understanding and friendship through educational, cultural and humanitarian activities involving the exchange of ideas and experiences directly among peoples of different countries and diverse cultures.

Mary Eisenhower, President/CEO
Mark Stansberry, Chairman

262 Phi Delta Kappa International

408 N Union Street
Bloomington, IN 47405
812-339-1156
800-766-1156
Fax: 812-339-0018
E-mail: customerservice@pdkintl.org
http://www.pdkintl.org
The premier professional association for educators. For more than 100 years, educators have joined PDK to access professional development resources that help them excel in their work. PDK's vision is to be the experts in cultivating great educators for tomorrow while continuing to ensure high-quality education for today.

Sandee Crowther, President
William J Bushaw, Executive Director

263 School Milk Foundation of New Foundland andLabrador

27 Sagona Avenue
Mount Pearl
Canada, NL A1N-4P8
709-364-2776
Fax: 709-364-8364
E-mail: info@schoolmilkfdn.nf.net
http://www.schoolmilk.nf.ca
Was established in 1991 with a mandate to increase the consumption of milk amongst school aged children throughout Newfoundland and Labrador.

Founded: 1991

264 Teach Overseas
International Schools Services
15 Roszel Road
PO Box 5910
Princeton, NJ 8543
609-452-0990
Fax: 609-452-2690
E-mail: iss@iss.edu
http://www.iss.edu/
Placed over 17,000 K-12 teachers and administrators in overseas schools since 1955. Most candidates attend US-based International Recruitment Centers where ISS candidates interview with overseas school heads seeking new staff.

Sandra Logorda, CFO
Roger Hove, President

265 Teachers of English to Speakers of Other Languages
1925 Ballenger Ave
Suite 550
Alexandria, VA 22314-6820
703-836-0774
888-547-3369
Fax: 703-836-7864
E-mail: info@tesol.org
http://www.tesol.org
TESOL is an international professional organization whose mission is to ensure excellence in English language to speakers of other languages.

Brock Brady, President
Christine Loombe, President-Elect

266 United Nations Development Program
One United Nations Plaza
New York, NY 10017-3515
212-906-5000
Fax: 212-906-5001
E-mail: ohr.recruitment.hq@undp.org
http://www.undp.org
UNDP is the UN's global development network, an organization advocating for change and connecting countries to knowledge, experience and resources to help people build a better life. We are on the ground in 166 countries, working with them on their own solutions to global and national development challenges

Edita Hrda, President
Michel T Monthe, Vice-President

267 Visions in Action
2710 Ontario Road NW
Washington, DC 20009-2154
202-625-7402
Fax: 202-588-9344
E-mail: visions@visionsinaction.org
http://www.visionsinaction.org
Visions in Action is committed to achieving social and economic justice in the developing world through grassroots programs and communities of self-reliant volunteers

Shaun Skelton PhD, Director
Suzanne Bach, US Program Manager

268 World Association of Publishers, Manufacturers & Distributors
Worlddidac
Bollwerk 21, PO Box 8866 CH-3001
Bern
Switzerland
41-31-311-7682
Fax: 41-31-312-1744
E-mail: info@worlddidac.org
http://www.worlddidac.org
Founded in 1996 the World Association of Publishers, Manufacturers and Distributors is a worldwide listing of over 330 publishers, manufacturers and distributors of educational materials. Listings include all contact information, products and school levels/grades.

Beat Jost, Director General
Andrea Hofmann, Project Manager

Language Arts

269 American Association of Teachers of French
Southern Illinois University
Mailcode 4510
Carbondale, IL 62901-4510
618-453-5731
Fax: 618-453-5733
E-mail: abrate@siu.edu
http://www.frenchteachers.org
Founded in 1927, AATF is the largest national association of French teachers in the world with nearly 10,000 members.

Jayne Abrate, Executive Director
Ann Sunderland, President

270 American Council on Education in Journalismand Mass Communication (ACEJMC)
University of Kansas
Stauffer Flint Hall
1435 Jayhawk Blvd
Lawrence, KS 66045-7575
785-864-3986
Fax: 785-864-5225
E-mail: sshaw@ku.edu
http://www2.ku.edu/~acejmc
The Accrediting Council on Education in Journalism and Mass Communications, or ACEJMC, is the agency responsible for the evaluation of professional journalism and mass communications programs in colleges and universities. These programs offer education to prepare students for careers in advertising, newspaper or magazine journalism, photojournalism, public relations, radio and television broadcasting and related fields.

Susanne Shaw, Executive Director
William Allen White, Professor

271 American Council on the Teaching of Foreign Languages
1001 N Fairfax Street
Suite 200
Alexandria, VA 22314
703-894-2900
Fax: 703-894-2905
E-mail: headquarters@actfl.org
http://www.actfl.org
National organization dedicated to the improvement and expansion of the teaching and learning of all languages at all levels of instruction. Individual membership organization of more than 7,000 foreign language educators and administrators from elementary through graduate education, as well as government industry.

Barbara Mandloch, President
Bret Lovejoy, Executive Director

272 American Speech-Language-Hearing Association
2200 Research Boulevard
Rockville, MD 20852-3289
301-296-5700
800-498-2071
Fax: 301-296-8580
E-mail: actioncenter@asha.org
http://www.asha.org
A professional, scientific, and credentialing association for more than 130,000 members and affiliates who are speech-language pathologists, audiologists, and speech, language, and hearing scientists in the United States and internationally.

Paul R Rao, President
Shelly S Chabon, President Elect

273 Association of Schools of Journalism and MassCommunication (ASJMC)
234 Outlet Pointe Boulevard
Columbia, SC 29210-5667
803-798-0271
Fax: 803-772-3509
E-mail: aejmchq@aol.com
http://www.asjmc.org
The Association of Schools of Journalism and Mass Communication/ ASJMC seeks to extend collectively on an international level the individual leadership its members practice on their campuses, striving to ensure that its constituents innovate, manage and lead in a media marketplace undergoing fundamental change, ensuring that journalism and mass communication programs broaden, deepen and invigorate the professions they serve.

Jennifer McGill, Executive Director
Paul Persons, President

274 Center for Applied Linguistics
4646 40th Street NW
Washington, DC 20016-1859
202-362-0700
Fax: 202-362-3740
E-mail: info@cal.org
http://www.cal.org
The Center for Applied Linguistics (CAL) is a private, nonprofit organization working to improve communication through better understanding of language and culture. CAL's staff of researchers and educators conduct research, design and develop instructional materials and language tests, provide technical assistance and professional development, conduct needs assessments and program evaluations, and disseminate information and resources related to language and culture.

Joy Kreeft Peyton, Language & Culture VP
Deborah Kennedy, Direector of Development

275 ERIC Clearinghouse on Languages andLinguistics
4646 40th Street NW
Washington, DC 20016-1859
202-362-0700
800-276-9834
Fax: 202-362-3740
E-mail: info@cal.org
http://www.cal.org
Promotes and improves the teaching and learning of languages, Identifies and solves problems related to language and culture.

Donna Christian, President
Joy Kreeft Peyton, Vice President

276 International Dyslexia Association (IDA)
40 York Road
4th Floor
Baltimore, MD 21204-2044
410-296-0232
800-222-3123
Fax: 410-321-5069
E-mail: info@interdys.org
http://www.interdys.org/
The International Dyslexia Association (IDA) is an international organization that concerns itself with the complex issues of dyslexia.ÿ The IDA membership consists of a variety of professionals in partnership with dyslexics and their families and all others interested in The Association's mission.

Guinevere Eden, President
Eric Q Tridas, President-Elect

19

277 Journalism Education Association
Kansas State University
103 Kedzie Hall
Manhattan, KS 66506-1505
785-532-5532
866-532-5532
Fax: 785-532-5563
E-mail: jea@spub.ksu.edu
http://www.jea.org
Among JEA's 2,100 members are journalism teachers and publications advisers, media professionals, press associations, adviser organizations, libraries, yearbook companies, newspapers, radio stations and departments of journalism.

Jack Kennedy, President
Bob Bair, Vice President

278 National Association for Bilingual Education
National Education Association (NEA)
8701 Georgia Ave
Suite 611
Silver Spring, MD 20910
240-450-3700
Fax: 240-450-3799
E-mail: nabe@nabe.org
http://www.nabe.org
Recognizes, promotes and publicizes bilingual education.

Jose Agustin Ruiz-Escalante, President
Rossana Boyd, Vice President

279 National Council of Teachers of English
1111 W Kenyon Road
Urbana, IL 61801-1096
217-328-3870
877-369-6283
Fax: 217-328-9645
E-mail: public_info@ncte.org
http://www.ncte.org
The Council promotes the development of literacy, the use of language to construct personal and public worlds and to achieve full participation in society, through the learning and teaching of English and the related arts and sciences of language.

Yvonne Siu Runyan, President
Sandy Hayes, VP

280 National Federation of Modern Language Teachers Association (NFMLTA)
c/o University of Wisconsin-Madison
460 Pierce Street
Monterey, CA 93940
831-647-6510
Fax: 831-647-6514
E-mail: mlj@miis.edu
http://mlj.miis.edu/nfmlta.htm
The purposes of the National Federation of Modern Language Teachers Associations (NFMLTA) are the expansion, promotion, and improvement of the teaching of languages, literatures, and cultures throughout the United States, by a variety of activities including but not limited to the publication of The Modern Language Journal.

Carol Klee, President
Aleidine Moeller, VP

281 National Network for Early Language Learning (NELL)
PO Box 75003
Oklahoma City, OK 73147
405-604-0041
Fax: 405-604-0491
E-mail: nnell@wfu.edu
http://www.nnell.org

Provide leadership in support of successful early language learning and teaching.

Dr Jacqueline Bott VanHouten, President
Rita Oleksak, VP

282 National Research Center on English Learning and Achievement
School of Education
University of Albany
1400 Washington Avenue
Albany, NY 12222-100
518-442-4985
Fax: 518-442-4953
E-mail: educationdean@uamail.albany.edu
http://www.albany.edu
Conducting research dedicated to gaining knowledge to improve students' English and literacy achievement.

Janet I Angelis, Associate Director
Robert Bangert Drowns, Dean

283 Sigma Tau Delta
Northern Illinois University
Department of English
Northern Illinois University
DeKalb, IL 60115-2867
815-753-1612
E-mail: sigmatd@niu.edu
http://www.english.niu.edu
A unique entity that opens the doors of opportunity for its members and facilitates academic, professional, and personal growth.

Sidney Watson, President
Sarah Dangelantonio, VP

284 Teachers & Writers Collaborative
520 Eighth Avenue
Suite 2020
New York, NY 10018-3306
212-691-6590
888-BOO-KSTW
Fax: 212-675-0171
E-mail: info@twc.org
http://www.twc.org
Brings writers and educators together in collaborations that explore the connections between writing and reading literature and that generate new ideas and materials.

Amy Swauger, Director
B Jade Triton, Director of Operations

Library Services

285 American Library Association
50 E Huron
Chicago, IL 60611-2795
312-944-6780
800-545-2433
Fax: 312-440-9374
E-mail: ala@ala.org
http://www.ala.org
Founded on October 6, 1876 during the Centennial Exposition in Philadelphia, created to provide leadership for the development, promotion, and improvement of library and information services and the profession of librarianship in order to enhance learning and ensure access to information for all. The current strategic plan, ALA Ahead to 2010, calls for continued work in the areas of Advocacy and Value of the Profession, Education, Public Policy and Standards, Building the Profession, Membership

Molly Raphael, President-Elect
James G Neal, Treasurer

286 Asian American Curriculum Project
529 E Third Avenue
San Mateo, CA 94401
650-375-8286
800-874-2242

Fax: 650-375-8797
E-mail: aacpinc@asianamericanbooks.com
http://www.asianamericanbooks.com
Our mission is to educate the public about the greatdiversity of the Asian American experience, through the books that they distrbute; fostering cultural awareness and to educate Asian Americans about their own heritage,instilling a sense of pride. AACP believes that the knowledge which comes from the use of appropriate materials can accomplish these goals.

Florence M Hongo, President
Shizue Yoshina, Vice President

287 Association for Library & Information Science Education
65 E Wacker Place
Suite 1900
Chicago, IL 60601-7246
312-795-0996
Fax: 312-419-8950
E-mail: contact@alise.org
http://www.alise.org
Promotes excellence in education for library and information sciences as a means of increasing library services.

January

Lorna Peterson, President
Kathleen Combs, Executive Director

288 Council on Library Technical Assistants (COLT)
900 University Avenue
Riverside, CA 92521
951-872-1012
E-mail: jlakatos@lemontlibrary.org
http://colt.ucr.edu
An international organization which works to address the issues and concerns

Founded: 1967

Jackie Hite, President
Chris Egan, VP

289 International Association of SchoolLibrarianship
PMB 292
1903 W 8th Street
Erie, PA 16505
E-mail: pgenco@iu05trc.iu5.org
http://www.asi-onoline.org
Provides an international forum for those people interested in promoting effective school library media programmes as viable isntruments in the educational process. Also provides guidance and advice for the development of school library profession.

Dr Diljit Singh, President

290 Pacific Northwest Library Association
500 Hazel Avenue
Homer, AK 99603-7220
907-235-3180
Fax: 907-235-3136
E-mail: hhill@ci.homer.ak.us
http://www.pnla.org
Provide opportunities for emerging library leaders in the Pacific Northwest to cultivate their leadership skills and potential.

Michael Burris, President
Heidi Chittim, First VP

291 Pro Libra
436 Springfield Avenue
Suite 3
Summit, NJ 07901
908-918-0077
800-262-0070
Fax: 908-918-0977
E-mail: staffing@prolibra.com
http://www.prolibra.com

PRO LiBRA Associates Inc., is a library service company providing personnel staffing, project management and consulting services to corporations, public entities and individuals.

M Bennett Livingston

Mathematics

292 Eisenhower National Clearinghouse forMathematics and Science Education
1275 Kinnear Road
Columbus, OH 43212
614-378-4567
800-471-1045
Fax: 614-523-0883
E-mail: info@goENC.com
http://www.goenc.org
Provides excellent resources for professional development programs and for district curriculumcoordinators. We can help by providing carefully selected online resources to support effective teaching and learning in K-12 math and science.

Len Simutis, President

293 Mathematical Association of America
1529 18th Street NW
Washington, DC 20036-1358
202-387-5200
800-741-9415
Fax: 202-265-2384
E-mail: maahq@maa.org
http://www.maa.org
The MAA will be the leading professional association in collegiate mathematics, the preeminent provider of expository mathematics, the primary and best source for professional development programs for faculty, and the number one provider of resources for teaching and learning.

David Bressoud, President
Francis E Su, First VP

294 National Council of Teachers of Mathematics
1906 Association Drive
Reston, VA 20191-1502
703-620-9840
800-235-7566
Fax: 703-476-2970
E-mail: nctm@nctm.org
http://www.nctm.org
The National Council of Teachers of Mathematics is a public voice of mathematics education, providing vision, leadership and professional development to support teachers in ensuring equitable mathematics learning of the highest quality for all students.

J Michael Shaughnessy, President
Kichoon Yang, Executive Director

Music & Art

295 American Art Therapy Association
225 N Fairfax Street
Alexandria, VA 22314
888-290-0878
Fax: 571-333-5685
E-mail: info@arttherapy.org
http://www.arttherapy.org
Serves its members and the general public by providing standards of professional competence, and developing and promoting knowledge in, and of, the field of art therapy.

Joan Phillips, President
Mercedester Morat PhD, President-Elect

296 American Dance Therapy Association
10632 Little Patuxent Parkway
Suite 108
Columbia, MD 21044-3273
410-997-4040
Fax: 410-997-4048
E-mail: info@adta.org
http://www.adta.org
Founded in 1966, works to establish and maintain high standards of professional education and competence in the field of dance/movement therapy.

Sharon Goodill, President
Judy Wager, VP

297 American Musicological Society
6010 College Station
Brunswick, ME 04011
207-798-4243
877-679-7648
Fax: 207-798-4254
E-mail: ams@ams-net.org
http://www.ams-net.org
Founded in 1934 the American Musicological Society advances research and scholarship in music education and its related fields. Bestows awards and publishes journals.

Robert Judd, Executive Director
Al Hipkins, Office Manager

298 Future Music Oregon
School of Music
1225 University of Oregon
Eugene, OR 97403-1225
541-346-5652
Fax: 541-346-0723
E-mail: stolet@uoregon.edu
http://pages.uoregon.edu/fmo/home
Educational Institute dedicated to the exploration of sound and its creation, and to the innovative use of computers and other recent technologies to create expressive music and media composition.

Jeffrey Stolet, Director
Brad Foley, Dean, School of Music/Dance

299 International Technology and EngineeringEducators Association
1914 Association Drive
Reston, VA 22091-1539
703-860-2100
703-860-0353
Fax: 480-727-1089
E-mail: iteea@iteea.org
http://www.iteea.org
The Council on Technology Teacher Education (CTTE), formerly known as the American Council of Industrial Arts Teacher Education (ACIATE), strives to support and further the professional ideals of technology education in addition to stimulating research and the dissemination of information of professional interest.

Gary Wynn, President
Thomas Bell, President-Elect

300 International Thespian Society
Educational Theatre Association
2343 Auburn Avenue
Cincinnati, OH 45219-2819
513-421-3900
Fax: 513-421-7077
E-mail: info@schooltheatre.org
http://www.schooltheatre.org
Honoring excellence in the work of theatre students. Thespian troupes serve students in grades nine through twelve, and Junior Thespian troupes serve students in grades six through eight.

Founded: 1929

Michael J Peitz, Executive Director

301 Kennedy Center Alliance for Arts Education
John F Kennedy Center for the Performing Arts
2700 F Street NW
Washington, DC 20566-1
202-416-8817
800-444-1324
Fax: 202-416-8802
E-mail: kcaaen@kennedy-center.org
http://www.kennedy-center.org/education/kcaaen
Advances education in the arts, collects and disseminates information about arts education, offers technical assistance on arts education to general public and education field.

Nancy Welch w/Andrea Greene, Author
Michael Kaiser, President
Stephen A Schwarzman, Chairman

302 Music Teachers National Association
441 Vine Street
Suite 3100
Cincinnati, OH 45202-3004
513-421-1420
888-512-5278
Fax: 513-421-2503
E-mail: mtnanet@mtna.org
http://www.mtna.org
Founded in 1876, the Music Teachers National Association is a nonprofit association of independent and collegiate music teachers committed to furthering the art of music through teaching, performance, composition and scholarly research.

Gary Ingle, Executive Director
Ann Gipson, President

303 National Art Education Association
1806 Robert Fulton Drive
Suite 300
Reston, VA 20191-1590
703-860-8000
800-299-8321
Fax: 703-860-2960
E-mail: info@arteducators.org
http://www.naea-reston.org
The mission of NAEA is to promote art education through professional development, service, advancement of knowledge, and leadership.

Founded: 1947

R Barry Shauck, President
Dr Robert Sabol, President-Elect

304 National Association for Music Education
1806 Robert Fulton Drive
Reston, VA 20191
703-860-4000
800-336-3768
Fax: 703-860-1531
E-mail: mbrserv@menc.org
http://www.menc.org
The MENC serves millions of students through activities from pre-school and up and works to ensure every student has access to comprehensive, well-balanced, and high quality music instruction taught by qualified teachers.

72 pages
ISSN: 0027-4321

Michael Butera, Executive Director
Mike Blakeslee, Deputy Exec Dir/CEO

305 National Association of Schools of Music (NASM)
11250 Roger Bacon Drive
Suite 21
Reston, VA 20190-5248
703-437-0700
Fax: 703-437-6312

E-mail: info@arts-accredit.org
http://nasm.arts-accredit.org/
Founded in 1924 the National Association of Schools of Music interested in promoting and funding music schools and conservatories.

Samuel Hope, Executive Director
Don Gibson, Associate Director

306 National Guild of Community Schools of the Arts
520 8th Avenue
Suite 302
New York, NY 10018
212-268-3337
Fax: 212-268-3995
E-mail: jonathanherman@nationalguild.org
http://www.nationalguild.org
The national service organization for a diverse constituency of non-profit organizations providing arts education in urban, suburban and rural communities throughout the United States.

Jonathan Herman, Executive Director
Kenneth Cole, Associate Director

307 National Institute of Art and Disabilities
551 23rd Street
Richmond, CA 94804-1626
510-620-0290
Fax: 510-620-0326
E-mail: admin@niadart.org
http://www.niadart.org
NIAD is an innovative visual arts center assisting adults with developmental and other physical disabilities.

Deb Dyer, Executive Director
Brian Stechshschulte, Gallery Director

Physical Education

308 American Alliance for Health, PhysicalEducation, Recreation and Dance
1900 Association Drive
Reston, VA 20191-1598
703-476-3400
800-213-7193
Fax: 703-476-9527
E-mail: infor@aahperd.org
http://www.aahperd.org
Largest organization of professionals supporting and assisting those involved in physical education, leisure, fitness, dance, health promotion, and education and all specialties related to achieving a healthy lifestyle.

E Paul Roetert, CEO
Viki J Worrell, President

309 American Sports Education Institute
8505 Fenton Street
Suite 211
Silver Spring, MD 20910
301-495-6321
Fax: 301-495-6322
E-mail: mmay@sgma.com
Boosts amateur sports and physical education at all levels.

Mike May, Executive Director

310 International Council for Health, Physical Education and Recreation
1900 Association Drive
Reston, VA 20191-1598
703-476-3462
Fax: 703-476-9527
E-mail: ichper@aahperd.org
http://www.ichpersd.org
ICHPERúSD is committed to fostering the essence of education in HPERSD fields through international understanding and goodwill,

safeguarding peace, freedom, and respect for human dignity. ICHPERúSD is committed to promoting quality HPERSD programs, professional standards, scholarly pursuits, research, and exchanges of knowledge among its constituent members, as well as other concerned professionals and institutions.

Dr Dong Ja Yang, President
Dr Adel Elnashar, Secretary General

311 National Association for Girls and Women in Sports
1900 Association Drive
Reston, VA 20191-1598
703-476-3452
800-213-7193
Fax: 703-476-4566
E-mail: nagws@aahperd.org
http://www.aahperd.org/nagws
Its mission is to promote and support leadership, research, education, and best practices in the professions that support creative, healthy, and active lifestyles.

Shawn Ladda, President
Heidi Parker, VP

312 National Association of Academic Advisors for Athletics
240 Jeter Drive
300 Case Academic Center
Raleigh, NC 27695-9007
919-513-1007
Fax: 919-513-0541
E-mail: info@nfoura.org
http://www.nfoura.org
Aim is to promote academic achievement and personal development among student athletes.

Gerald Gurney, President
Joseph Luckey, President-Elect

313 National Athletic Trainers' Association
2952 Stemmons Freeway
Suite 200
Dallas, TX 75247-6196
214-637-6282
800-879-6282
Fax: 214-637-2206
E-mail: webmaster@nata.org
http://www.nata.org
The mission of the National Athletic Trainers' Association is to enhance the quality of health care provided by certified athletic trainers and to advance the athletic training profession.

Marjorie J Albohm, President
James Thornton, VP

314 President's Council on Fitness, Sports & Nutrition
President's Council on Fitness, Sports & Nutrition
Tower Bldg
1101 Wootton Pkwy, Suite 560
Rockville, MD 20852
202-276-9567
Fax: 202-276-9860
E-mail: fitness@hhs.gov
http://www.fitness.gov
Promotes and encourages the development of physical activity fitness and sports programs for all Americans.

Shellie Pfohl, Executive Director
Shannon Foster, Communications/Public Aff

Reading

315 Clearinghouse on Reading, English &Communication
Indiana University School of Education
201 N Rose Avenue
Bloomington, IN 47405-1006
812-856-8500
Fax: 812-856-8440
http://reading.indiana.edu/
Improve teaching, learning, and human development in a global, diverse, rapidly changing, and increasingly technological society.

Carl B Smith Ph.D, Director
Andy Wisemanane, Systems Administrator

316 International Reading Association
800 Barksdale Road
PO Box 8139
Newark, DE 19714-8139
302-731-1600
800-336-7323
Fax: 302-731-1057
E-mail: customerservice@reading.org
http://www.reading.org
The mission of the International Reading Association is to promote reading by continuously advancing the quality of literacy instruction and research worldwide.

Patricia A Edwards, President
Mark Mullen, Executive Director

317 National Center for ESL Literacy Education
Center for Applied Linguistics
4646 40th Street NW
Washington, DC 20016-1859
202-362-0700
Fax: 202-363-7204
E-mail: info@cal.org
http://www.cal.org/
CAL carries out a wide range of activities to accomplish its mission of improving communication through better understanding of language and culture.

Miriam Burt, Associate Director
Dora Johnson, Research Associate

318 National Contact Hotline
Contact Center, Inc.
PO Box 81826
Lincoln, NE 68501-1826
800-228-8813
A 25-year-old information and referral agency, to help individuals with literacy problems. Maintains a database of over 7,000 literacy programs across the country and the 7-day hotline.

319 ProLiteracy Worldwide
1320 Jamesville Avenue
Syracuse, NY 13210
315-422-9121
888-528-2224
Fax: 315-422-6369
E-mail: info@proliteracy.org
http://www.proliteracy.org
Now the oldest and largest non-governmental literacy organization in the world and pursues a mission of sponsoring educational programs that help adults and their families acquire the literacy practices and skills they need to function more effectively in their dialy lives.

David Harvey, President
Ann DuPrey, Secretary

320 Reading Recovery Council of North America
500 W Wilson Bridge Road
Suite 250
Worthington, OH 43085-5218

614-310-7323
Fax: 614-310-7345
E-mail: jjohnson@readingrecovery.org
http://www.readingrecovery.org
We prevent literacy failure by supporting specialized and continuous professional development that results in strong teaching to improve student achievement.

Jady Johnson, Executive Director
Linda Wilson, Executive Assistant

Secondary Education

321 American Driver & Traffic Safety Education Association
National Education Association (NEA)
Indiana University of Pennsylvania
1434 Trim Tree Road
Indiana, PA 15701
724-801-8246
877-485-7172
Fax: 724-349-5042
E-mail: office@adtsea.org
http://www.adtsea.org
Professional association which represents traffic safety educators throughout the United States and abroad. Serves as a national advocate for quality traffic safety education, conducts conferences, workshops and seminars and provides consultative services.

Fred Nagao, President
Kevin Kirby, President-Elect

322 Association for Institutional Research
Florida State University
1435 E Piedmont Drive
Suite 211
Tallahassee, FL 32308
850-385-4155
Fax: 850-385-5180
E-mail: rswing@airweb.org
http://www.airweb.org
Support members to continuously improve the practice of institutional research for postsecondary planning, management and operations, and to further develop and promote the institutional research profession.

Randy Swing, Executive Director
Donna Carlsen, Membership Coordinator

323 Close-Up Foundation
1330 Braddock Place
Suite 400
Alexandria, VA 22314
703-706-3300
800-336-5479
Fax: 703-706-0001
E-mail: info@closeup.org
http://www.closeup.org
Offers government studies programs for high school students, educators and older Americans.

Joel Jankowsky, Chairman, Board of Directors
Timothy S Davis, President

324 College Board
45 Columbus Avenue
New York, NY 10023-6917
212-713-8165
Fax: 212-713-8282
E-mail: store.help@collegeboard.org
http://www.collegeboard.com
The College Board is a not-for-profit membership association whose mission is to connect students to college success and opportunity. Founded in 1900, the association is composed of more than 5,400 schools, colleges, universities, and other educational organizations

Gaston Caperton, President
Herb Elish, COO

325 National Business Education Association
1914 Association Drive
Reston, VA 20191-1596
703-860-8300
Fax: 703-620-4483
E-mail: nbea@nbea.org
http://www.nbea.org
NBEA is committed to the advancement of the professional interest and competence of its members and provides programs and services that enhance members' professional growth and development.

Madge Lewis Gregg, President
John J Olivo, President-Elect

326 National Middle School Association
4151 Executive Parkway
Suite 300
Westerville, OH 43081
614-895-4730
800-528-6672
Fax: 614-895-4750
E-mail: info@nmsa.org
http://www.nmsa.org
NMSA has been a voice for those committed to the educational and developmental needs of young adolescents. NMSA is the only national education association dedicated exclusively to those in the middle level grades.

Joan Jarrett, President
Dr Betty Greene Bryant, Executive Director

Science

327 Academy of Applied Science
24 Warren Street
Concord, NH 03301
603-228-4530
Fax: 603-228-4730
E-mail: admin@aas-world.org
http://www.aas-world.org
The Academy of Applied Science, incorporated in 1963, is a private nonprofit, tax-exempt organization, chartered for the purpose of promoting creativity, invention and scientific achievement.

Sheldon Apsell, Chairman
Joanne Hayes-Rines, Vice-President

328 Association for Advancement of Computing inEducation (AACE)
PO Box 1545
Chesapeake, VA 23327-1545
757-366-5606
Fax: 703-997-8760
E-mail: info@aace.org
http://www.aace.org
Advance Information Technology in Education and E-Learning research, development, learning, and its practical application. Serves the profession with international conferences, high quality publications, leading-edge Digital Library, Career Center, and other opportunities for professional growth.

Gary H Marks Ph.D, Executive Director

329 Association for Science Teacher Education
Old Dominion University
113 Radcliff Drive
Pittsburgh, PA 15237
412-624-2861
E-mail: ExecutiveDirector@TheASTE.org
http://theaste.org

Promotes leadership in the professional development of teachers in science, including science teacher educators, staff developers, college-level science instructors, education policy makers, instructional material developers, science supervisors/specialists/coordinators, lead/mentor teachers, and all interested in promoting the development of teachers in science.

Randy Bell, President
Eugene Wagner, Executive Director

330 Association of Science-Technology Centers
1025 Vermont Avenue NW
Suite 500
Washington, DC 20005-6310
202-783-7200
Fax: 202-783-7207
E-mail: info@astc.org
http://www.astc.org
The Association of Science-Technology Centers (ASTC) is an organization of science centers and museums dedicated to furthering the public understanding of science among increasingly diverse audiences. ASTC encourages excellence and innovation in informal science learning by serving and linking its members worldwide and advancing their common goals.

Nancy Stueber, President
Chevy Humphrey, Vice President

331 California Biomedical Research Association
PO Box 19340
Sacramento, CA 95819-0340
916-558-1515
Fax: 916-558-1523
E-mail: info@ca-biomed.org
http://www.ca-biomed.org
To promote and protect the continued advancement of human and animal health through biomedical research, teaching, and testing

Linda Cork, Director
Boris Predovich, President and CEO

332 Educational REALMS-Resources for EngagingActive Learners in Mathematics and Science
Ohio State University
1929 Kenny Road
Columbus, OH 43210-1080
614-292-6717
800-276-0462
Fax: 614-292-0263
E-mail: haury.2@osu.edu
http://www.stemworks.org
Educational REALMS (Resources for Engaging Active Learners in Mathematics and Science) is a new organization created in 2004 after the discontinuation of the federally funded ERIC Clearinghouse for Science, Mathematics and Environmental Education (ERIC/CSMEE). Educational REALMS provides many of the same services, offering a variety of resources to anyone interested in science, mathematics, technology, and environmental education at all levels.

David L Haury, Project Director
Christopher Andersen, Associate Director

333 Eisenhower National Clearinghouse forMathematics and Science Education
1900 Polaris Parkway
Suite 450
Columbus, OH 43204
614-378-4567
800-471-1045
Fax: 877-656-0315

E-mail: info@goENC.com
http://www.goenc.org
Provides excellent resources for professional development programs and for district curriculumcoordinators. We can help by providing carefully selected online resources to support effective teaching and learning in K-12 math and science.

Len Simutis, President

334 Energy Education Group
664 Hilary Drive
Tiburon, CA 94920
415-435-4574
Fax: 415-435-7737
E-mail: energyforkeeps@aol.com
http://www.energyforkeeps.org
Provides information about where our electricity comes from and how energy choices affect our lives, our environment and future generations.

Marilyn Nemzer, Executive Director
Deborah Page, Lead Write

335 Geothermal Education Office
664 Hilary Drive
Tiburon, CA 94920
415-435-4574
Fax: 415-435-7737
E-mail: geo@marin.org
http://www.geothermal.marin.org
To promote public understanding about geothermal resources and its importance in providing clean sustainable energy while protecting our environment.

Marliyn L Nemzer, Executive Director

336 History of Science Society
University of Notre Dame
440 Gedds Hall
Notre Dame, IN 46556
574-631-1194
Fax: 574-631-1533
E-mail: Info@hssonline.org
http://www.hssonline.org
The Society's mission is to foster interest in the history of science and its social and cultural relations.

Founded: 1924

Robert J Malone, Executive Director
Greg Macklam, Society Coordinator

337 Institute for Earth Education
Cedar Cove
PO Box 115
Greenville, WV 24945
304-832-6404
Fax: 304-832-6077
E-mail: iee1@aol.com
http://www.eartheducation.org
An international network of individuals and organizations committed tot developing a serious educational response to the environmental problems of the earth.

Steve Van Matre, Chairman
David Dodson, Office Coordinator

338 National Association for Research in ScienceTeaching (NARST)
12100 Sunset Hills Road
Suite 130
Reston, VA 20190-3221
703-234-4138
Fax: 703-435-4390
E-mail: info@narst.org
http://www.narst.org
The National Association for Research in Science Teaching (NARST) is a worldwide organization of professionals committed to the improvement of science teaching and learning through research. Since its inception in 1928, NARST has promoted research in science education and the communication of

knowledge generated by the research. The ultimate goal of NARST is to help all learners achieve science literacy.

William C Kyle JR, Executive Director
Dana L Zeidler, President

339 National Association of Biology Teachers
1313 Dolley Madison Boulevard
Suite 402
McLean, VA 22101
703-264-9696
888-501-6227
Fax: 703-790-2672
E-mail: office@nabt.org
http://www.nabt.org
Interested in the advancement of biology education and awareness of new developments in the biology field by educators.

Daniel Ward, President
Donald French, President-Elect

340 National Center for Science Education
420 40th Street
Suite 2
Oakland, CA 94609-2509
510-601-7203
800-290-6006
Fax: 510-601-7204
E-mail: info@ncse.com
http://www.ncse.com
We educate the press and public about the scientific, educational, and legal aspects of the creation and evolution controversy, and supply needed information and advice to defend good science education at local, state, and national levels.

ISSN: 1064-2358

Eugenie C Scott, Executive Director

341 National Institute for Science Education
1025 W Johnson Street
Suite 753
Madison, WI 53706-1706
608-263-4200
E-mail: uw-wcer@education.wis.edu
http://www.wcer.wisc.edu/nise
A partnership of the University of Wisconsin-Madison and the National Center for Improving Science Education, Washington, DC, with funding from the National Science Foundation. Strives to strengthen the nation's science enterprise by helping to extend science, mathematics, engineering and technology literacy to all students.

Andrew C Porter, Director
Norman Webb, Associate Director

342 National Science Teachers Association
1840 Wilson Boulevard
Arlington, VA 22201-3000
703-243-7100
800-782-6782
Fax: 703-243-7177
E-mail: pubinfo@nsta.org
http://www.nsta.org
A member-driven organization that publish books and journals for science teachers from kindergarten through college.

Alan McCormick, President
Patricia Simms, President-Elect

343 Science Service
1719 N Street NW
Washington, DC 20036-2888
202-785-2255
Fax: 202-785-1243
E-mail: webmaster@societyforscience.org
http://www.societyforscience.org
Society for Science & the Public (SSP) is a nonprofit 501(c) (3) organization dedicated

to the public engagement in scientific research and education. Our vision is to promote the understanding and appreciation of science and the vital role it plays in human advancement: to inform, educate, inspire.

Elizabeth Marincola, President/Publisher
H Robert Horvitz, Chair

Social Studies

344 African-American Institute
420 Lexington Avenue
Suite 1706
New York, NY 10170-0002
212-949-5666
Fax: 212-682-6174
E-mail: aainy@aaionline.org
http://www.aaionline.org
Committed to developing African-American understanding and providing Americans with information regarding Africa. Offices in New York and Washington, D.C. lead a team in over 50 African countries.

Mora McLean, President
Kofi A Appenteng, Co-Founder

345 American Association for Chinese Studies
City College-CUNY
Convent Avenue/138th Street
New York, NY 10031
212-650-8268
Fax: 212-650-8287
E-mail: aacs@mail.com
http://www.ccny.cuny.edu/aacs
Promotes understanding and communication between Western and Eastern scholars involved in Chinese studies. AACS, founded in 1959, is the only academic society in America devoted exclusively to the general area of Chinese studies.

Shelly Rigger, President
Vincent Wang, VP

346 Center for Education Studies
American Textbook Council
1150 Park Ave
12th Floor
New York, NY 10128-599
212-870-2760
Fax: 212-870-3112
http://www.historytextbooks.org
Conducts independent reviews and studies of schoolbooks in the humanities and publishes a quarterly bulletin providing commentary and reviews of social studies textbooks for leading historians, educators and public officials.

Founded: 1989

Gilbert T Sewall, Director
Stapley W Emberling, Assistant Director

347 Council for Indian Education
1240 Burlington Avenue
Billings, MT 59102-4224
406-248-3465
Fax: 406-248-1297
E-mail: cie@cie-mt.org
http://www.cie-mt.org
Providing in-service training for teachers to help them better meet the needs of their Native American students by equipping the teachers with information on Native American culture and traditions and on ways in which their instruction can be adapted to the needs of their Native American students.

Hap Gilliland, President

348 ERIC Clearinghouse for Social StudiesEducation
Indiana University, Social Studies Dev. Center
2805 E Tenth Street
Suite 140
Bloomington, IN 47408-2698
812-855-3838
800-266-3815
Fax: 812-855-0455
E-mail: eric-cue@columbia.edu
http://www.indiana.edu/ssdc
The primary mission of the CSSIE is to improve education in the social studies (history, geography, economics, civics, anthropology, and the social sciences) in elementary and secondary schools. A secondary mission of the CSSIE is to meet professional development needs of the international community of educators through in-service training, content seminars, and curriculum workshops in all curriculum areas.

Dr Terrance Mason, Director
Jane E Henson, Associate Director

349 National Council for the Social Studies
8555 Sixteenth Street
Suite 500
Silver Spring, MD 20910
301-588-1800
800-683-0812
Fax: 301-588-2049
E-mail: sgriffin@ncss.org
http://www.ncss.org
Social studies educators teach students the content knowledge, intellectual skills, and civic values necessary for fulfills the duties of citizenship in a participatory democracy. The mission of National Council for the Social Studies is to provide leadership, service, and support for all social studies educators.

Susan Griffin, Executive Director
Steven S Lapham, Associate Editor

350 New England History Teachers Association
1154 Boyslton Street
Boston, MA 02215-3695
617-646-0557
E-mail: info@nehta.net
http://www.nehta.net
NEHTA provides teachers, students and academics opportunities to engage in meaningful conversations about the teaching and learning of history and its related disciplines.

Founded: 1897

Charles L Newhall, President
Amy George, Vice President

351 North American Association for Environmental Education
2000 P Street NW
Suite 540
Washington, DC 20036
202-419-0412
Fax: 202-419-0415
E-mail: communicator@naaee.org
http://www.naaee.org
Promotes professional excellence in nonformal organizations, K-12 classrooms, universities government agencies, and corporate settings throughout North America and in over 55 other countries.

October

Diane C Centrell, President
Pepe Marcos- Iga, President-Elect

352 Society for History Education
PO Box 1578
Borrego Springs, CA 92004
760-767-5938
562-985-8703

Fax: 760-767-5938
E-mail: conniegeorge@thehistoryteacher,org
http://www.csulb.edu/~histeach/ AND
www.thehistoryteacher.org/
Serves as a network for those interested in history and its importance in the classroom.

Connie George, General Manager
Troy Johnson, Board of Directors President

353 Western History Association
University of New Mexico
MSC04 2545
Albuquerque, NM 87131-0001
505-277-1989
Fax: 505-277-8978
E-mail: ucam@unm.edu
http://www.unm.edu/~wha
Founded in 1962 the Western History Association promotes the teaching of Western history.

Peter Iverson, President
Walter Nugent, President-Elect

Technology in Education

354 Agency for Instructional Technology
1800 N StoneLake Drive
Box A
Bloomington, IN 47402-0120
812-339-2203
800-457-4509
Fax: 812-333-4218
E-mail: info@ait.net
http://www.ait.net
Seeks to strengthen education through electronic technologies. Develops, produces and distributes instructional materials in a variety of media, including online instruction, CDs, DVDs, and instructional software.

Marie Wilson, Chair
Ruth Blankenbaker, Vice Chair

355 Alliance for Technology Access Conference
Alliance for Technology Access
1119 Old Hunboldt Road
Jackson, TN 38301
731-554-5282
Fax: 731-554-5283
E-mail: ATAinfo@ATAccess.org
http://www.ataccess.org
Providing technology information to children and adults with disabilities, and increasing their use of standard, assistive, and information technologies.

James Allison, President
Bob Van der Linde, VP

356 Association for Career and Technical Education
1410 King Street
Alexandria, VA 22314
703-683-3111
800-826-9972
Fax: 703-683-7424
E-mail: acte@acteonline.org
http://www.acteonline.org
Founded in 1926 the Association for Career and Technical Education, aims to provide leadership in developing an educated, prepared, adaptable and competitive workforce.

Gary Moore, President
Jim Comer, President-Elect

357 Association for Educational Communications & Technology
PO Box 2447
Bloomington, IN 47402-2447
812-335-7675
877-677-2328

Fax: 812-335-7678
E-mail: aect@aect.org
http://www.aect.org
Provide leadership in educational communications and technology by linking a wide range of professionals holding a common interest in the use of educational technology and its application learning process.

Barbara Lockee, President
Phillip Harris, Executive Director

358 Center for Educational Technologies
316 Washington Avenue
Wheeling, WV 26003-6243
304-243-2388
800-624-6992
Fax: 304-243-2497
E-mail: webmaster@cet.edu
http://www.cet.edu
the Center for Educational Technologiesr grew into the internationally recognized education facility that today serves thousands of teachers and students throughout the world.

Charles Wood, Executive Director
Laurie Ruberg, Associate Director

359 Computer Using Educators, Inc (CUE)
877 Ygnacio Valley Road
Suite 104
Walnut Creek, CA 94596
925-478-3460
Fax: 925-934-6799
E-mail: cueinc@cue.org
http://www.cue.org
Provides leadership and support to advance student achievement in the educational technology community.

Mike Lawrence, Executive Director
Marisol Valles, Director of Operations

360 Consortium for School Networking
1025 Vermont Avenue NW
Suite 1010
Washington, DC 20005-3007
202-861-2676
866-267-8747
Fax: 202-393-2011
E-mail: info@cosn.org
http://www.cosn.org
CoSN is the country's premier voice for K-12 education leaders who use technology strategically to improve teaching and learning.

Keith Krueger, CEO
Irene Spero, COO

361 EDUCAUSE
4772 Walnut Street
Suite 206
Boulder, CO 80301-2538
303-449-4430
Fax: 303-440-0461
E-mail: info@educause.edu
http://www.educause.edu
A nonprofit association whose mission is to advance higher education by promoting the intelligent use of information technology.

Gregory Jackson, VP
Diana G Oblinger, President and CEO

362 Educational Technology Center
Harvard Graduate School of Education
360 Huntington Avenue
215 Snell Library
Boston, MA 02115
617-373-3157
Fax: 617-373-7779
E-mail: edtech@neu.edu
http://www.edtech.neu.edu
To exploration, development and dissemination of technology to enhance teaching, learning and research goals. The Center is also an agent of change, helping to formulate policy

on technology-supported teaching and learning

Alicia K Russell, Director
Seth J Merriam, Web Services Manager/Multime

363 International Society for Technology in Education
180 West 8th Avenue
Suite 300
Eugene, OR 97401-2916
541-302-3777
800-336-5191
Fax: 541-302-3778
E-mail: iste@iste.org
http://www.iste.org
Providing leadership and service to improve teaching and learning by advancing the effective use of technology in education.

Helen Padgett, President
Holly Jobe, President-Elect

364 Learning Independence Through Computers
LINC
2301 Argonne Drive
Baltimore, MD 21218
410-554-9134
800-772-7372
Fax: 410-261-2907
E-mail: info@linc.org
http://www.linc.org
Learning Independence Through Computers (LINC) is a non-profit computer resource center that provides opportunities for people with disabilities, their families, professionals, and members of the business community to explore adaptive technology, computer systems, software, and the Internet.

Theo Pinette, Executive Director
John Walker, Project Coordinator

365 MarcoPolo
WorldCom Foundation
One Verizon Way
Basking Ridge, NJ 07920
509-374-1951
800-360-7955
Fax: 908-630-2660
E-mail: oposewa@edumedia.com
http://www.marcopolo-education.org
A non-profit consortium of premier national and international education organizations and the MCI Foundation dedicated to providing high quality internet and professional development to teachers and students throughout the United States.

Oksana Posewa, Project Manager
Della Cronin, Prog Officer Communications

366 National Association of Media and Technology Centers
PO Box 9844
Cedar Rapids, IA 52409
319-654-0608
Fax: 319-654-0609
http://www.namtc.org
Committed to promoting leadership among its membership through networking, advocacy, and support activities that will enhance the equitable access to media, technology, and information services to educational communities.

Jerry Schnabel, President
Beverly Knox-Pipes, President-Elect

367 National Institute on Disability andRehabilitation Research
U.S. Department of Education
400 Maryland Avenue SW
Washington, DC 20202-2572
202-245-7640
800-872-5327

Fax: 202-245-7323
http://www.ed.gov/about/offices/list/osers/nidrr
Promote student achievement and preparation for global competitiveness by fostering educational excellence and ensuring equal access.

Arne Duncan, Secretary of Education
Leonard L Haynes III, Executive Director

368 Technology & Media Division
The Council for Exceptional Children
1110 N Glede Road
Suite 300
Arlington, VA 22201-5704
703-620-3660
888-232-7733
Fax: 703-264-9494
E-mail: contactus@tamcec.org
http://www.tamcec.org
The purpose of TAM is to support educational participation and improved results for individuals with disabilities and diverse learning needs through the selection, acquisition, and use of technology.

Deborah Newton, President
Brenda Heiman, President-Elect

369 Technology Student Association
1914 Association Drive
Reston, VA 20191-1540
703-860-9000
888-860-9010
Fax: 703-758-4852
http://www.tsaweb.org
Leadership and opportunities in technology, innovation, design and engineering. Members apply STEM concepts through co-curricular programs.

Zachary Barnes, President
Austin Tatum, VP

370 Technology and Children
International Technology Education Association
1914 Association Drive
Suite 201
Reston, VA 20191-1539
703-860-2100
Fax: 703-860-0353
E-mail: itea@iteaconnect.org
http://iteaconnect.org
To advance technological capabilities for all people and to nurture and promote the professionalism of those engaged in these pursuits.ÿ ITEA seeks to meet the professional needs and interests of members as well as to improve public understanding of technology, innovation, design, and engineering education and its contributions.

Kendall N Starkweather, Executive Director
Brigitte Valesey, CATTS Director

371 Telemetrics
6 Leighton Place
Mahwah, NJ 07430-3198
201-848-9818
Fax: 201-848-9819
E-mail: info@telemetricsinc.com
http://www.telemetricsinc.com
offers a comprehensive line of camera robotics and control systems for broadcast, industrial, educational and military applications.

Founded: 1950

Anthony C Cuomo, President
Jim Wolfe, Sales Manager

372 Twenty First Century Teachers Network: TheMcGuffey Project
888 17th Street NW
12th Floor
Washington, DC 20006

202-429-0572
Fax: 202-296-2962
E-mail: info@mcguffey.org
http://www.21ct.org/
A nationwide, non-profit initiative of the McGuffey Project, dedicated to assisting K-2 teachers learn, use and effectively integrate technology in the curriculum for improved student learning.

Wade D Sayer, Project Director, Director Program Development

Alabama

373 Alabama Business Education Association
A&M University
School of Business
PO Box 429
Normal, AL 35762
256-372-4799
Fax: 256-851-5568
E-mail: karzetta@bellsouth.net
http://www.alabamabusinessed.org
A professional association for business and marketing educators at the secondary and post-secondary levels.

Karzetta Bester, President
Emma Fault, President-Elect

374 Alabama Education Association
422 Dexter Avenue
Montgomery, AL 36104-3743
334-834-9790
800-392-5839
Fax: 334-262-8377
E-mail: myaea@alaedu.org
http://www.myaea.org
Serves as an advocate for Alabama teachers and leads in the advancement of equitable and quality public education.

Paul R Hubbert, Executive SecretaryTreasurer
Joe L Reed, Associate Executive Secretar

375 Alabama Library Association
9154 Eastchase Parkway
Suite 418
Montgomery, AL 36117
334-414-0113
877-563-5146
Fax: 334-265-1281
E-mail: administrator@allanet.org
http://www.allanet.org
Non-profit corporation formed to encourage and promote the welfare of libraries and professional interests of librarians in Alabama.

Jodi W Poe, President
Steven Yates, President-Elect

Alaska

376 Alaska Association of School Librarians
344 W 3rd Avenue
Suite 125
Anchorge, AK 99501
907-269-6569
800-776-6566
Fax: 907-269-6580
E-mail: akasl@akla.org
http://www.akla.org/akasl
Advances a high standard for the school librarian profession and the library information program in the schools of Alaska.

Ann Morgeste, President
Kari Sagel, Secretary

377 Alaska Library Association
PO Box 81084
Fairbanks, AK 99708
907-459-1020
Fax: 907-459-1024
E-mail: webdeveloper@akla.org
http://www.akla.org
Holds a conference in March and publishes a journal.

David Ongley, President
Mary Jennings, Executive Officer

Arizona

378 Arizona Library Association
1030 E Baseline Road
Suite 105-1025
Tempe, AZ 85283
480-609-3999
Fax: 480-609-3939
E-mail: admin@azla.org
http://www.azla.org
Promotes library service and libarianship in libraries of all types in the state of Arizona.

Debbie Hanson, Executive Director
Kerrall Farmelant, Conference Administrator

379 Arizona School Boards Association
2100 N Central Avenue
Suite 200
Phoenix, AZ 85004-1441
602-254-1100
800-238-4701
Fax: 602-254-1177
http://www.azsba.org
Promotes community volunteer governance of public education and continuous improvement of student success by providing training, leadership and assistance to public school governing boards.ÿ

Dee Navarro, President
Michael Hughes, President Elect

380 Professional Office Instruction & Training
1325 W 16th Street
Suite 5
Yuma, AZ 85364
928-343-3076
Fax: 520-782-3211
E-mail: rthomp@c2i2.com
Computer software applications training.

Rochelle Thompson, Owner

Arkansas

381 Arkansas Business Education Association
Bryant Junior High School
201 Sullivan
Bryant, AR 72022
501-847-5620
Fax: 501-847-5627
E-mail: bengstonc@hssd.net
http://www.abea.us
A professional association comprised of business and marketing educators involved at the secondary and post-secondary levels.

Linda Burns, President
Kerry Ellason, President-Elect

382 Arkansas Education Association
1500 W 4th Street
Little Rock, AR 72201
501-375-4611
800-632-0624
Fax: 501-375-4620

E-mail: ldimond@nea.org
http://www.aeaonline.org
A member-driven organization.Improves the quality of education offered Arkansas school children and contribute to attracting and retaining the best and brightest teachers and support professionals for our public schools.

Donna Morey, President
Brenda Robinson, VP

383 Arkansas Library Association
PO Box 958
Benton, AR 72018-0958
501-860-7585
Fax: 501-776-9709
E-mail: arlib2@sbcglobal.net
http://www.arlib.org
Holds a conference in October and publishes a journal.
Founded: 1911

Lynda Hampel, Assistant
Barbara Martin, Executive Administrator

California

384 California Business Education Association
PO Box 2591
Walnut Creek, CA 94595
925-377-0939
Fax: 925-295-1104
E-mail: cbeaquestions@cbeaonline.org
http://www.cbeaonline.org
The prime mission of CBEA is to recognize, encourage, and promote excellence in business disciplines. Also, it is to collaborate with other disciplines and other groups dedicated to this mission.

Linda Snider, President
Edna Prigmore, Secretary

385 California Classical Association-Northern Section
San Francisco State University
Department of Classics
San Francisco, CA 94132
415-253-2267
Fax: 415-338-2514
E-mail: ccanorth@yahoo.com
http://www.ccanorth.org
Supports programs to enrich and promote Classics.
Founded: 1969

Michael Smith, President
Mary McCarthy, VP

386 California Foundation for Agriculture in theClassroom
2300 River Plaza Drive
Sacramento, CA 95833-3293
916-561-5625
800-700-2482
Fax: 916-561-5697
E-mail: info@learnaboutag.org
http://www.cfaitc.org
Our mission is to increase awarenes and understanding of agriculture among California's educators and students. Our vision is an appreciation of agriculture by all.

Judy Culbertson, Executive Director
Kelly Benarth, Communications Coordinator

387 California Library Association
950 Glenn Drive
Suite 150
Folsom, CA 95630
916-223-3298
Fax: 916-932-2209

E-mail: info@cla-net.org
http://www.cla-net.org
Provides leadership for the development, promotion, and improvement of library services, librarianship, and the library community. A resource for learning about new ideas and technology.

Paymaneh Maghsoudi, President
Wayne Disher, VP

388 California Reading Association
638 Camino De Los Mares
Suite H130/476
Costa Mesa, CA 92673
714-435-1983
Fax: 714-435-0269
E-mail: kathy@californiareads.org
http://www.californiareads.org
CRA is an independent, self-governing organization dedicated to increasing literacy in California.

Kathy Belanger, Administrative Director
Judy Miranda, President

389 California School Library Association
950 Glenn Drive Suite 150
Folsom, CA 95630
916-447-2684
Fax: 916-447-2695
E-mail: deidreb@csla.net
http://www.csla.net
Organized of library media teachers, classroom teachers, paraprofessionals, district and county coordinators of curriculum, media and technology and others committed to enriching student learning by building a better future for school libraries.

Deidre Bryant, Executive Director
Diane Alexander, President

390 California Teachers Association
1705 Murchison Drive
Burlingame, CA 94010
650-697-1400
Fax: 650-552-5002
E-mail: webmaster@cta.org
http://www.cta.org
Protects and promotes the well-being of California teachers by improving the conditions of teaching and learning and advancing the cause of universal education.

David A Sanchez, President
Dean E Vogel, Vice President

391 Northern California Comprehensive Assistance Center
730 Harrison Street
18th Floor
San Francisco, CA 94107
415-565-3000
877-493-7833
Fax: 415-565-3012
E-mail: plloyd@wested.com
http://www.wested.org
WestEd's Assessment and Standards Development Services program has helped shape effective statewide assessment and accountability systems nationwide

Sri Ananda, Chief Development Officer
Glen Harvey, Chief Executive Officer

392 WestEd
730 Harrison Street
San Francisco, CA 94107-1242
415-565-3000
877-493-7833
Fax: 415-565-3012
E-mail: dtorres@wested.org
http://www.WestEd.org
Nonprofit research, development and service agency working with education and other human services communities across the country. As one of the nation's Regional Educational Laboratories, WestEd also has a special rela-

tionship serving the states of Arizona, California, Nevada, and Utah. For complete listings of all WestEd developed resources visit us online at www.WestEd.org/catalog.

Danny Torres, Publications Manager
Liza Cardinal-Hand, Information/Outreach Manager

Colorado

393 Colorado Association of Libraries
3030 W 81st Ave
Westminster, CO 80031
303-463-6400
Fax: 303-458-0002
E-mail: jesse@imigroup.org
http://www.cal-webs.org
The Colorado Association of Libraries (CAL) is the common bond, voice, and power for the library community.

Teri Switzer, President
Linda Conway, VP

394 Colorado Business Educators
Prairie High School
300 Thomas
Box 82
New Rayemr, CO 80742
970-437-5386
Fax: 970-437-5732
E-mail: lucinda@creedek12.net
http://www.cbeweb.org
Association of Colorado Business Educators.

Jean Sykes, President
Addie Wallace, Secretary

395 Colorado Community College & Occupational Education System
9101 E Lowry Boulevard
Denver, CO 80230-6011
303-620-4000
Fax: 303-620-4030
E-mail: marybeth.noble@cccs.edu
http://www.cccs.edu
The Colorado Community College System comprises the state's largest system of higher education serving more than 117,000 students annually.

Nancy McCallin, President
Claire Kuhns, Executive Asst to President

396 Colorado Education Association
1500 Grant Street
Denver, CO 80203-1800
303-837-1500
800-332-5939
Fax: 303-837-9006
http://www.coloradoea.org
The Colorado Education Association is a voluntary membership organization of 38,000 K-12 teachers and education support professionals; higher education faculty and support professionals; retired educators; and students preparing to become teachers.

Beverly Ingle, President
Colleen Heinz, Vice President

397 Colorado Library Association
12081 W Alameda Parkway
Suite 427
Lakewood, CO 80228
303-463-6400
Fax: 303-431-9752
E-mail: executivedirector@cal-webs.org
http://www.cal-webs.org
The Colorado Association of Libraries (CAL) is the common bond, voice, and power for the library community.

Rachelle Logan, VP
Judy Barnett, President

Connecticut

398 Connecticut Business & Indusry Association (CBIA)
350 Church Street
Hartford, CT 06103-1126
860-244-1900
Fax: 860-278-8562
E-mail: bellj@cbia.com
http://www.cbia.com/home.htm
Serve as an advocate for the general business and industry community in Connecticut. Promote a state business climate that is globally competitive

Jim Bell, Business Consulting Director
Nancy Andrews, Media/Public Relations

399 Connecticut Education Association (CEA)
Capitol Place
21 Oak Street
Suite 500
Hartford, CT 06106-8001
860-525-5641
800-842-4316
Fax: 860-725-6323
E-mail: johny@cea.org
http://www.cea.org
CEA advocates for teachers and public education, lobbying legislators for the resources public schools need and campaigning for high standards for teachers and students.

John Yrchik, Executive Director
Janet Streckfus, Administration Asst Director

400 Connecticut Educational Media Association
25 Elmwood Avenue
Trumbull, CT 06611-3594
203-372-2260
E-mail: aweimann@snet.net
http://www.ctcema.org
Professional association of Connecticut school library media specialist.

Janet Roche, President
David Bilmes, Vice President

401 Connecticut School Library Association
New Haven Free Library
133 Elm Street
New Haven, CT 06510-2003
203-946-8130
http://www.newhavenlibrarypatrons.com
New Haven Free Public Library provides free and equal access to knowledge and information in an environment conducive to study and resource sharing. Through its collection of media, services and programs, the library promotes literacy, reading, personal development and cultural understanding for the individual and the community at large.

Maureen Grieco, President

Delaware

402 Delaware Business Education Association
Delcastle High School
140 Brennen Drive
Newwark, DE 19713
302-454-2164
E-mail: rhuddj@christina.k12.de.us
Fosters business education in the state of Delaware.

Jennifer Rhudd, President
Lisa Stoner, Membership Director

403 Delaware Library Association
PO Box 816
Dover, DE 19903-816
816-531-2468
Fax: 302-831-1631
E-mail: danbradbury@gossagesager.com
http://www2.lib.udel.edu/dla
The goal of the Delaware Library Association is to promote the profession of librarianship and provide library information and media services to the people of Delaware by developing a unified library association

Margery Cyr, President
Patty Langley, VP/Conference Planning Chair

404 Delaware State Education Association
136 East Water Street
Dover, DE 19901-3630
302-734-5834
866-734-5834
Fax: 392-674-8499
E-mail: pamela.nichols@dsea.org
http://www.dsea.org/
The Delaware State Education Association, a union of public school employees, advocates for the rights and interests of its members and outstanding public education for all students.

Diane Donohue, President
Mike Hoffman, VP

District of Columbia

405 American Council on Education Library & Information Service
American Council on Education
1 Dupont Circle NW
Suite 1B-20
Washington, DC 20036-1193
202-939-9300
Fax: 202-833-4730
E-mail: comments@ace.nche.edu
http://www.acenet.edu
The major coordinating body for all the nation's higher education institutions, seeks to provide leadership and a unifying voice on key higher education issues and to influence public policy through advocacy, research, and program initiatives.

John Sexto, Chair
Eduardo Padron, Vice Chair/Chair-elect

406 Associates for Renewal in Education (ARE)
Brenda Strong Nixon Community Complex
45 P Street NW
Brenda Strong Nixon Community Complex
Washington, DC 20001-1133
202-483-9424
Fax: 202-667-5299
E-mail: info@areinc.org
http://www.areinc.org
A multi project agency working to improve the quality of life and education of the young people of the District of Columbia, with an emaphasis on youth-at risk and under served populations.

Thomas W Gore, President/CEO
Evie Saunders Davis, Deputy Finance/HR

407 District of Columbia Library Association
Benjamin Franklin Station
PO Box 14177
Washington, DC 20044
202-872-1112
E-mail: April.King@dc.gov
http://www.dcla.org

Richard Huffine, President
Megan Sheils, VP

Florida

408 Florida Association for Media in Education
1876-B Eider Court
Tallahassee, FL 32308
850-531-8351
Fax: 850-531-8344
E-mail: info@floridamedia.org
http://www.floridamedia.org
FAME advocates for every student in Florida to be involved in and have open access to a quality school library media program administered by a highly competent, certified library media specialist. FAME is a collaborative, responsive, dynamic network for Florida library media professionals.
Pat Dedicos, President
Lou Greco, VP

409 Florida Business Technology EducationAssociation
c/o Palm Beach County School District
3310 Forest Hill Boulevard
C-225
West Palm Beach, FL 33406
561-434-7395
E-mail: sslarsen@bellsouth.net
http://www.fbtea.org
Fosters business education in the state of Florida.
Fran Tomarchio, President
Sue Larsen, Treasurer

410 Florida Education Association
213 South Adams Street
Tallahassee, FL 32301
850-201-2800
888-807-8007
Fax: 850-222-1840
http://www.feaweb.org
Advocates the right to a free, quality public education for all, Empower and support local affiliates. Advance professional growth, development and status of all who serve the students in Florida's public schools. Engage our members and communities to ensure that all students learn and succeed in a diverse world.
Andy Ford, President
Joanne McCall, Vice President

411 Florida Education Association (FEA)
213 South Adams Street
Tallahassee, FL 32301
850-201-2800
Fax: 850-222-1840
E-mail: ANDY.FORD@FLORIDAEA.ORG
http://www.feaweb.org
Advocates the right to a free, quality public education for all, Empower and support local affiliates. Advance professional growth, development and status of all who serve the students in Florida's public schools. Engage our members and communities to ensure that all students learn and succeed in a diverse world.
Aaron Wallace, Chief of Staff
Andy Ford, President

412 Florida Library Association (FLA)
164 NW Madison Street
Suite 104
Lake City, FL
386-438-5795
850-322-5005
Fax: 386-438-5796
E-mail: fla.admin@comcast.net
http://www.flalib.org
The Florida Library Association (FLA) develops programs and undertakes activities to earn it a leadership position for all areas of librarianship. To do this, the Association works with other professional organizations and professions that are relevant to librarianship;

provides increasing opportunities for librarians and support staff in Florida to advance their skills so that they can maintain their effectiveness in the new information age; works closely with the information industry, facilita
Faye C Roberts, Executive Director
Sharon Gray, Conference Manager

Georgia

413 Georgia Association of Educators
100 Crescent Center Parkway
Suite 500
Tucker, GA 30084
678-837-1118
800-282-7142
Fax: 678-837-1150
http://www.gae2.org
The Georgia Association of Educators is a professional organization for public education professionals
Richard J Hubbard, President
Sid Chapman, VP

414 Georgia Business Education Association (GBEA)
Perry High School
1307 N Avenue
Perry, VA 31069
478-988-6315
E-mail: lary.debra@newton.k12.ga.us
http://www.georgiagbea.org/
Fosters business education in the state of Georgia.
Beth Parks, President
Debra Lary, Public Relations Chair

415 Georgia Library Association
PO Box 793
Rex, GA 30273
678-466-4339
800-999-8558
Fax: 678-466-4349
E-mail: karamullen@clayton.edu
http://gla.georgialibraries.org
Developing an understanding of the place that libraries should take in advancing the educational, cultural, and economic life of the state
Cayoly Fuller, President
Elizabeth Bagley, VP

416 Georgia Parents & Teachers Association
114 Baker Street NE
Atlanta, GA 30308-3366
404-659-0214
800-782-8632
Fax: 404-525-0210
E-mail: gapta@bellsouth.net
http://www.georgiapta.org
A powerful voice for all children, a relevant resource for families and communities and a strong advocate for the education and well-being of every child
Sheila Cornelius, President
Donna Kosicki, President Elect

417 Southeastern Library Association
PO Box 950
Rex, GA 30273
678-466-4334
Fax: 678-466-4349
E-mail: fline@andersonlibrary.org
http://sela.jsu.edu
Holds a conference in October and publishes a journal.
Kathleen Imhoff, President
Michael Seigler, President-Elect

Hawaii

418 Hawaii Business Education Association
Leeward Community College
Normadeene Musick, Leeward Communit
96-045 Ala Ike
Pearl City, HI 96782-3393
808-455-0206
Fax: 808-453-6735
E-mail: president@hbea.org
http://www.hbea.org
HBEA is devoted exclusivlely to serving individuals and groups engaged in instruction, administration, research, and dissemination of information for and about business and technology. Hosts conferences and other professional improvement opportunities.
Kuuipo Lum, President
Frances Kwock, VP

419 Hawaii Education Association (HEA)
953 S Beretania Street
Suite 5C
Honolulu, HI 96826
808-949-6657
866-653-9372
Fax: 808-944-2032
E-mail: hea.office@heaed.com
http://www.heaed.com
The Hawaii Education Association (HEA) is an independent, nonprofit 501(c)(3) organization governed by its members. HEA focuses on the perpetuation and improvement of education in Hawaii, and the enhancement of the welfare of its members. HEA welcomes as members public and private school teachers, university and college personnel, educational administrators, retirees, and friends of education from all sectors of our local and national communities.
Sarah Moriyama, President
Laurie Togami, HEA Staff Specialist

420 Hawaii Library Association
PO Box 4441
Honolulu, HI 96814-4441
808-292-2068
Fax: 808-956-5968
E-mail: batesd@byuh.edu
http://www.hlaweb.org
Holds a conference in November and publishes a journal and a newsletter.
Stewart Chun, President
Kimball Boone, Secretary

421 Hawaii State Teachers Association (HSTA)
1200 Ala Kapuna Street
Honolulu, HI 96819
808-833-2711
Fax: 808-839-7106
E-mail: info@hsta.org
http://www.hsta.org
The Hawaii State Teachers Association's mission is to serve the needs of Hawaii's public school teachers, in all facets of their professional lives.
Wil OKabe, President
Alvin Nagasako, Executive Director

Idaho

422 Idaho Education Association
620 N 6th Street
PO Box 2638
Boise, ID 83701
208-344-1341
800-727-9922
Fax: 208-336-6967

E-mail: info@idahoea.org
http://www.idahoea.org
Advocates the professional and personal well-being of its members and the vision of excellence in public education.

Marty Meyer, VP
Sherri Wood, President

423 Idaho Library Association
PO Box 8533
Moscow, ID 83843-1033
208-334-2150
Fax: 208-334-4016
http://www.idaholibraries.org
Holds a conference in October.

Ben Hunter, President
Gena Marker, VP/President-Elect

424 Pacific Northwest Library Association
5849 W Hidden Springs Drive
Boise, ID 83714
907-235-3180
Fax: 907-235-3136
E-mail: iseborg@adalib.org
http://www.pnla.org
Provide opportunities for emerging library leaders in the Pacific Northwest to cultivate their leadership skills and potential.

Michael Burris, President
Hidi Chittim, First VP

Illinois

425 Illinois Affiliation of Private Schools for Exceptional Children
Lawrence Hall Youth Services
4833 N Francisco Avenue
Chicago, IL 60625-3640
773-769-3500
http://www.iapsec.org
A non-profit organization consisting of private schools serving Illionis children with exceptional needs and the quality of special education made available to them.

Ken Carwell, President
Sol Rappaport, Secretary

426 Illinois Association of School Business Officials
Northern Illinois University
108 Carroll Avenue
DeKalb, IL 60115
815-753-1276
Fax: 847-357-5001
E-mail: grizaffigi@vvsd.org
http://www.iasbo.org
Association of school business officials.

Garrick Grizaffi, President
Michael A Jacoby, Executive Director

427 Illinois Business Education Association (IBEA)
8536 E Jackson Street
Du Quoin, IL 62832-4078
Fax: 618-542-5528
E-mail: president@ibea.org
http://www.ibea.org
Promoting the profession and providing the environment and encouragement to improve professional endeavors

Ehtel Holladay, Executive Director
Deanna Hudgens, Business/Marketing Director

428 Illinois Citizens' Education Council
100 East Edwards Street
Springfield, IL 62704-1999
217-544-0706
Fax: 217-333-2736
Association of 120,000 members composed of Illinois elementary and secondary teachers, higher education faculty and staff, educational support professionals, retired educators, and college students preparing to become teachers.

Anne Davis, President
Ken Swanson, Vice President

429 Illinois Education Association
100 E Edwards Street
Springfield, IL 62704-1999
217-544-0706
800-252-8076
Fax: 217-544-7383
http://www.ieanea.org
Represents public, academic, and special libraries as well as librarians, library assistants, trustees, students and library vendors.

Ken Swanson, President
Robert Blade, Vice President

430 Illinois Library Association
33 W Grand Avenue
Suite 301
Chicago, IL 60654
312-644-1896
Fax: 312-644-1899
E-mail: ila@ila.org
http://www.ila.org
The Illinois Library Association is the voice for Illinois libraries and the millions who depend on them.

Donna Dziedzic, President
Bob Doyle, Executive Director

431 Illinois School Library Media Association
PO Box 598
Canton, IL 61520
309-649-0911
Fax: 309-649-0916
E-mail: islma@islma.org
http://www.islma.org
Promotes student interaction, continuing education of school library media specialists, and collaboration among parents, community members, teachers and administrators to prepare students for life-long learning.

Jeremy Dunn, President
Sarah Hill, President-Elect

Indiana

432 Indiana Association of School Business Officials
1 N Capital Avenue
Suite 1215
Indianapolis, IN 46204-2095
765-639-3586
Fax: 317-639-4360
E-mail: dcosterison@indiana-asbo.org
http://www.indiana-asbo.org
The Indiana Association of School Business Officials is a professional organization which strives for the promotion and union of those individuals involved in school business affairs such as finance, accounting, purchasing, maintenance and operations, human resources, facilities and grounds, food service, technology, and transportation.

Loren E Evans, President
Lynn Kwilasz, VP

433 Indiana Business Education Association
South Putnam High School
1780 E US Highway 40
Greencastle, IN 46135-9768
765-653-3149
Fax: 317-232-9121
E-mail: gvalenti@usi.edu
http://ind-ibea.org
Fosters business education in the state of Indiana.

Amber Reed, President
John Dawson, President-Elect

434 Indiana Library Federation
941 E 86th Street
Suite 260
Indianapolis, IN 46240
317-257-2040
Fax: 317-257-1389
http://www.ilfonline.org
ILF keeps its members at the cutting-edge of their profession, offering critical continuing education opportunities as well as opportunities for library community leadership and important networking.

Ken Swanson, President
Robert Blade, Vice President

435 Indiana State Teachers Association
150 W Market Street
Suite 900
Indianapolis, IN 46204
317-263-3400
800-382-4037
Fax: 317-655-3700
http://www.ista-in.org
With nearly 50,000 members, ISTA is committed to great public schools across Indiana.

Nathan Schnellenberger, President
Teresa Meredith, Vice President

Iowa

436 Iowa Business Education Association
Highway 150 S
PO Box 400
Calmar, IA 52132-400
515-471-8005
Fax: 563-562-4363
E-mail: rselwood@mchsi.com
http://www.ibeaonline.org
We are a group of people who are proud to be business educators and are preparing our students to be productive citizens.~

Deb Jons, President
Sharon Keehner, President-Elect

437 Iowa Library Association
3636 Westown Parkway
Suite 202
West Des Moines, IA 50266
515-273-5322
800-452-5507
Fax: 515-309-4576
http://www.iowalibraryassociation.org
The Iowa Library Association advocates for quality library services for all Iowans and provides leadership, education and support for members.

Dale Van De Harr, President
Lorraine Borowski, VP

438 Iowa State Education Association
777 Third Street
Des Moines, IA 50309
515-471-8000
800-445-9358
E-mail: ISEAnews@isea.org
http://www.isea.org
Designed to promote and support quality education.

Chris Bern, President
Tammy Wawro, Vice President

Kansas

439 Kansas Association of School Librarians
8517 W Nothridge
Wichita, KS 67205

http://kasl.typepad.com/kasl
Association of school librarians in the state of Kansas.

Judy Eller, Executive Secretary
Cindy Pfeiffer, President

440 Kansas Business Education Association
Fory Hays State University
600 Park Street
Hays, KS 67601
785-628-4019
Fax: 785-628-5398
http://www.ksbea.org
Fosters business education in the state of Kansas.

Jean Anna Sellers, Contact
Gina Stanley, President

441 Kansas Education Association
715 SW 10th Avenue
Topeka, KS 66612-1686
785-232-8271
Fax: 785-232-6012
E-mail: KNEAnews@knea.org
http://www.knea.org
Empowers its members to promote quality public schools, strengthen the teaching profession, and improve the well-being of members.

Blake West, President
Sherri Yourdon, Vice President

442 Kansas Library Association
1020 SW Washburn
Topeka, KS 66604
785-580-4581
Fax: 785-580-4595
E-mail: kansaslibraryassociation@yahoo.com
http://www.kansaslibraryassociation.org
KLA develops a legislative push card, tracks legislation and keeps association members and the library community at large informed on the status of bills related to library issues

Laura Loveless, President
Denise Smith, First Vice President

Kentucky

443 Kentucky Library Association
1501 Twilight Trail
Frankfort, KY 40601
502-223-5322
Fax: 502-223-4937
E-mail: info@kylibasn.org
http://www.kylibasn.org
Holds a conference in October and publishes a journal.

Kim Goff, Associate Director
John Underwood, Executive Secretary

444 Kentucky School Media Association
Scott County School
1080 Cardinal Drive
Georgetown, KY 40324
E-mail: mroberts@scott.k12.ky.us
http://www.kysma.org
Promotes the use of media in schools.

Evie Topcik, President
Crystal Smallwood, Secretary

445 Mountain-Plains Business Education Association(M-PBEA)
Newcastle High School
4771 West Scott Road
Beatrice, NE 68310
307-746-2713
E-mail: tlandenb@gmail.com
http://www.mpbea.org
The Mountain-Plains Business Education Association (M-PBEA) is an affiliate of the National Business Education Association (NBEA), a professional organization serving individuals and groups engaged in instruction, administration, research, and dissemination of information for and about business. M-PBEA is comprised of the following states and provinces: Colorado, Kansas, Manitoba, Nebraska, New Mexico, North Dakota, Oklahoma, Saskatchewan, South Dakota, Texas, and Wyoming.

Suzanne Sydow, President
Connie Lindell, Kansas State Representative

Louisiana

446 Louisiana Association of Business Educators
Alfred M Barbe High School
2200 W McNeese Street
Lake Charles, LA 70615
337-478-3628
Fax: 337-474-6782
http://www.laabe.org
Foster business education in the state of Louisiana.

Marilyn Gastineau, President
Joseph Lane Jr, Vice President

447 Louisiana Association of Educators
PO Box 479
Baton Rouge, LA 70821
225-343-9243
800-256-4523
Fax: 225-343-9272
E-mail: joyce.haynes@lae
http://www.lae.org
Dedicated to improving the education profession and the quality of education. Affiliated with National Education Association.

Joyce Haynes, President
Bruce Hunt, Executive Director

448 Louisiana Association of School BusinessOfficials (LASBO)
PO Box 1029
Gonzales, LA 70707-1029
225-644-0619
Fax: 225-644-0122
E-mail: cctripp@eatel.net
http://www.lasbo.org/
To promote excellence and professional ethical standards in the practice of public school business finance by educating and training our membership in the most efficient and economic methods of conducting our business affairs

Tami Austin, President-elect
Juanita Duke, President

449 Louisiana Library Association
8550 United Plaza Boulevard
Suite 1001
Baton Rouge, LA 70809
225-922-4642
877-550-7890
Fax: 225-408-4422
E-mail: office@llaonline.org
http://www.llaonline.org

Holds a conference in March and publishes a journal.

Beth Paskoff, Registration
Melissa Elrod, Chair

Maine

450 Eastern Business Education Association (EBEA)
1914 Association Drive
Reston, VA 20191-1596
703-860-8300
Fax: 703-620-4483
E-mail: nbea@nbea.org
http://www.nbea.org
NBEA is committed to the advancement of the professional interest and competence of its members and provides programs and services that enhance members' professional growth and development.

Sharon Fisher-Larson, President
Janet M Treichel, Executive Director

451 Maine Association of School Libraries
64 State House Station
Augusta, ME 4333
207-287-5620
Fax: 207-287-5624
E-mail: felicia.kennedy@state.me.us
http://www.maslibraries.org
Dedicated to total involvement between Library Media Specialists, support staff and students.

Molly Larson, President
Joyce Lucas, Secretary

452 Maine Education Association
35 Community Drive
Augusta, ME 04330
207-622-5866
800-452-8709
Fax: 207-623-2129
http://www.maine.nea.org
Advance the cause of public education, protect human and civil rights, advocate for professional excellence and autonomy of the profession. To guarantee the independence of the profession ane protect the rights of educators and advance their interests and welfare.

Chris Galgay, President
Lois Kilby-Chesley, Vice President

453 Maine Library Association
PO Box 634
Augusta, ME 4332-634
207-623-8428
Fax: 207-626-5947
E-mail: jscherma@thomas.lib.me.us
http://mainelibraries.org/home.php
is to promote and enhance the value of libraries and librarianship, to foster cooperation among those who work in and for libraries, and to provide leadership in ensuring that information is accessible to all citizens via their libraries

Molly Larson, President
Joan Kiszely, Executive Secretary

Maryland

454 Maryland Educational Media Organization
PO Box 21127
Baltimore, MD 21228

http://www.tcps.md.us

31

Brings students and information regarding educational media together.

Dorothy D'Ascanio, President
Patricia Goff, Secretary

455 Maryland Library Association
1401 Hollins Street
Baltimore, MD 21223
410-947-5090
Fax: 410-947-5089
E-mail: mla@mdlib.org
http://www.mdlib.org
Maryland Library Association provides leadership for those who are committed to libraries by providing opportunities for professional development and communication and by advocating principles and issues related to librarianship and library service.

Margaret Carty, Executive Director
Kate Monagan, Executive Assistant

456 Maryland State Teachers Association
140 Main Street
Annapolis, MD 21401-2003
410-263-6600
800-448-6782
Fax: 410-263-3605
E-mail: cfloyd@mstanea.org
http://www.mstanea.org/
Organization representing 60,000 Maryland teachers, support professionals, retired educators, school administers, higher education faculty, and future educators.

Clara B Floyd, President
Betty Weller, VP

Massachusetts

457 Massachusetts Business Educators Association
Amherst Regional High School
21 Mattoon Street
Amherst, MA 1002
413-549-9700
Fax: 413-549-9704
Fosters business education in the state of Massachusetts.

Mary Ann Shea, Contact

458 Massachusetts Library Association
PO Box 535
Bedford, MA 1730
781-275-7729
Fax: 781-998-0393
E-mail: mlaoffice@masslib.org
http://www.masslib.org
The mission of the Government Relations Advisory Board is to represent the interests of all libraries to the state legislature on behalf of the citizens of the Commonwealth

Elizabeth Hacala, Executive Manager
Margaret Cardello, Secretary

459 Massachusetts Teachers Association
20 Ashburton Place
Boston, MA 2108-2727
617-878-8000
800-392-6175
Fax: 617-742-7046
E-mail: awass@massteacher.org
http://www.massteacher.org
The MTA is a union, dedicated to improving the workplace and the quality of life for all education employees and to protecting their hard-won rights. MTA and local affiliates are highly democratic organizations in which members' views and concerns are vital to the development of policies and programs.

Anne Wass, President
Paul Toner, Vice President

460 New England Library Association
31 Connor Lane
Wilton, NH 03086
603-654-3533
Fax: 603-654-3526
E-mail: maryann@nelib.org
http://www.nelib.org
Initiate, plan and support regional activities to encourage the exchange of ideas to cooperate with regional and national agencies having related interests. Stimulate library-related research in the region.

Jen Leo, President
Mary Ann List, Vice President

Michigan

461 Michigan Association for Media in Education
1407 Rensen Street
Suite 3
Lansing, MI 48910
517-394-2808
Fax: 517-394-2096
E-mail: mame@mame.gen.mi.us
http://www.mame.gen.mi.us
Michigan Association for Media in Education is an independent, professional association of library media specialists dedicated to educational, literary and technological excellence in library / media services in Michigan's schools.

Roger Ashley, Executive Director
Diane Nye, Media Spectrum

462 Michigan Association of School Administrators
1001 Centennial Way
Suite 300
Lansing, MI 48917-9279
517-327-5910
Fax: 517-327-0771
E-mail: jscofield@gomasa.org
http://www.gomasa.org/
Professional organization serving superintendents and their first line of assistants.

Dan Pappas, Associate Executive Director
Jon Tomlanovich, Associate Executive Director

463 Michigan Education Association
1216 Kendale Boulevard
PO Box 2573
East Lansing, MI 48826-2573
517-332-6551
800-292-1934
Fax: 517-337-5598
E-mail: webmaster@mea.org
http://www.mea.org/
A self-governing education association, representing more than 157,000 teaches, faculty, and education support staff throughout the state.

Iris Salters, President
Steven Cook, Vice President

464 Michigan Elementary & Middle School Principals Association
1980 N College Road
Mason, MI 48854
517-694-8955
800-227-0824
Fax: 517-694-8945
E-mail: bob@memspa.org
http://www.memspa.org
Membership association of 1,600 Michigan elementary and middle school principals; sponsoring workshops, conferences, resource materials, job security, networking services

to members. Affiliated with National Association of Elementary School Principals.

Robert E Howe Jr, Executive Director
Darla Campbell, President

465 Michigan Library Association
1407 Rensen Street
Suite 2
Lansing, MI 48910
517-394-2774
Fax: 517-394-2675
E-mail: mla@mlcnet.org
http://www.mla.lib.mi.us
The Michigan Library Association is a professional organization dedicated to the support of its members, to the advancement of librarianship, and to the promotion of quality library service for all Michigan citizens.

Kathy Irwin, President
Larry Neal, President-Elect

Minnesota

466 Education Minnesota
41 Sherburne Avenue
St. Paul, MN 55103-2196
651-227-9541
800-652-9073
Fax: 651-292-4802
http://www.educationminnesota.org
Education Minnesota is the largest advocate for public education in the state. Our 70,000 members work at all levels from pre-kindergarten through post-secondary, at public schools, state residential schools and college campuses.

Thomas A Dooher, President
Paul Mueller, Vice President

467 Minnesota Business Educators
2620 Eleventh Avenue NW
Rochester, MN 55901-7722
507-282-7079
Fax: 507-282-4925
E-mail: rhmeyer@rconnect.com
http://www.mbei-online.org
To keep abreast with the state legislature and with issues related to business education

Mary Flesberg, Past President
Cindy Drahos, President

468 Minnesota Congress of Parents, Teachers &Students/Minnesota PTA
1667 Snelling Avenue
N Suite 111
Saint Paul, MN 55108
651-999-7320
800-672-0993
Fax: 651-999-7321
E-mail: mnptaofc@mnpta.org
http://www.mnpta.org
Minnesota PTA, an affiliate of the National PTA, extends the concept of a volunteer organization engaged in educating parents and teachers on issues affecting children and youth. It supports public education and the welfare of children.

Rosie Loeffler Kemp, President
Bonnie Beery, Secretary

469 Minnesota Library Association
1619 Dayton Avenue
Suite 314
Saint Paul, MN 55104
651-641-0982
877-867-0982
Fax: 651-649-3169
E-mail:
mlaoffice@mnlibraryassociation.org
http://www.mnlibraryassociation.org

MLA meets the interests of its members by facilitating educational opportunities, supportingstrong ethical standards, and fostering connections between the library community and various constituencies. An annual three-day conference, featuring approximately 70 programs held in the fall. Programs are planned and sponsored by Divisions, Sections, Round Tables, and Committees

Robin Chaney, Treasurer
Ken Behringer, President

470 Minnesota School Boards Association
1900 W Jefferson Avenue
Saint Peter, MN 56082-3015
507-934-2450
800-324-4459
Fax: 507-931-1515
E-mail: gabbott@mnmsba.org
http://www.mnmsba.org
The purpose of the Association is to support, promote and enhance the work of public school boards

Kent Thiesse, President
Greg Abbott, MSBA Dir. of Communications

Mississippi

471 Mississippi Advocate For Education
775 N State Street
Jackson, MS 39202-3086
601-354-4463
800-530-7998
Fax: 601-352-7054
E-mail: mmarks@nea.org
http://www.maetoday.nea.org
The Mississippi Association of Educators advocates great public schools for every child by empowering members, providing services and promoting parental/community environment.

Kevin F Gilbert, President
Seyed Darbandi, Vice President

472 Mississippi Business Education Association
Itawamba Community College
2176 S Eason Boulevard
Tupelo, MS 38801
662-620-5001
Fax: 601-982-5801
E-mail: acbrown@nmsd.k12.ms.us
http://www.ms-mbea.org
To establish and maintain active state leadership in promotion of all types of business and technology education

Aimee Brown, President
Judith Hurtt, President-Elect

Missouri

473 Missouri Association of Elementary School Principals
3550 Amazonas Drive
Jefferson City, MO 65109
57- 63- 269
Fax: 573-556-6270
E-mail: maesp@mcsa.org
http://www.mcsa.org
MAESP is a statewide professional association that has grown to include over 1,000 school administrators. The services provided by MAESP to its membership have also increased as members have identified and approved long-range plans incorporating key services.

Matthew Martz, President
Connie Browning, President-Elect

474 Missouri Association of Secondary School Principals
2409 W Ash Street
Columbia, MO 65203-45
573-445-5071
Fax: 573-445-6416
E-mail: massp@moassp.org
http://www.moassp.org
The mission of the Missouri Association of Secondary School Principals is to improve secondary education through positive leadership and the enhancement of student performance. In pursuing the mission of MASSP, the Association shall be involved in providing information and leadership; encouraging research and service; promoting high educational standards; focusing attention on state educational issues; providing for the general welfare of principals; and working with other educational organizati

Ron Helms, President
Ken Treaster, Past President

475 Missouri Congress of Parents &Teachers/Missouri PTA
2101 I-70 Drive, SW
Columbia, MO 65203
573-445-4161
800-328-7330
Fax: 573-445-4163
E-mail: kimw@mopta.org
http://www.mopta.org
A powerful voice for all children, A relevant resource for all families and communities,A strong advocate for the education and well-being of every child

Mary Oyler, President
Kim Weber, Vice President and Director

476 Missouri Library Association
3212-A Lemone Industrial Boulevard
Columbia, MO 65201-45
573-449-4627
Fax: 573-449-4655
E-mail: mla001@more.net
http://www.molib.org
A non-profit, educational organization operating to promote library service, the profession of librarianship, and cooperation among all types of libraries and organizations concerned with library service in Missouri.

Kimberlee Ried, President
Margaret Booker, Executive Director

477 Missouri National Education Association
1810 E Elm Street
Jefferson City, MO 65101-4174
573-634-3202
Fax: 573-634-5646
http://www.mnea.org
The Missouri National Education Association is an advocate for public schools, public school students and public school employees

November annual
1,500 attendees

Ben Simmons, Executive Director
Chris Guinther, President

478 Missouri State Teachers Association
PO Box 458
407 S Sixth Street
Columbia, MO 65205-4201
573-442-3127
800-392-0532
Fax: 573-443-5079
E-mail: membercare@msta.org
http://www.msta.org

A grassroots organization made up of local community teachers associations in each school district.

Tami Pasley, Board of Directors
Russell Smithson, Vice President

479 North Central Business Education Association (NCBEA)
Mineral Area College
803 Rambling Brook Circle
Elgin, IL 60124
573-243-9513
Fax: 573-243-9524
E-mail: satbfl@aol.com
http://www.ncbea.com
The objectives of this Association are to improve the relationship in business education at the state, regional, and national levels; to promote the professional growth of those in business education; to promote better business education through whatever means seem desirable; and to offer assistance and service to state associations within the region.

Kim Schultz, President
Susan Elwood, Secretary

Montana

480 Montana Association of County School Superintendents
1134 Butte Avenue
Helena, MT 59601
406-442-2510
http://www.sammt.org/macss
Organization of school superintendents.

Darrell Rud, Executive Director
Julia Sykes, Associate Director

481 Montana Association of School Librarians (MASL)
606 Dix Road
Jefferson City, MO 65109
E-mail: masl_org@earthlink.net
http://www.maslonline.org/
Montana Association of School Librarians/MASL is a professional organization for library media specialists who work in Missouri schools.

Linda Weatherspoon, President
Sandy Roth, Treasurer

482 Montana Library Association
169 W River Rock Road
Belgrade, MT 59714-3126
406-670-8446
Fax: 406-243-2060
http://www.mtlib.org
Holds a conference in April and publishes a journal.

Eva English, Vice President
Della Dubbe, President

483 Western Business and Information TechnologyEducators (WBITE)
Hardin High School
720 N Terry
Hardin, MT 59034
406-665-6300
Fax: 406-665-1909
E-mail: odellj@hardin.k12.mt.us
http://www.nbea.org/aboutrda.html
Western Business and Information Technology Educators, an affiliate of the National Business Education Association seeks to share educational experiences preparing individuals to excel as consumers, workers, and citizens in our economic systems. WBITE is comprised of Alaska, Alberta, American Samoa, Arizona, British Columbia, California, Guam, Hawaii, Idaho, Montana, Nevada, Northern Marianas Islands, Northwest

Territories, Oregon, Utah, Yukon and Washington.

Julie O'Dell, President
Roy Kamida, Treasurer

Nebraska

484 Nebraska Library Association
1402 N Jackson
Lexington, NE 68850
402-826-2636
Fax: 402-471-6244
E-mail: nebraskalibraries@gmail.com
http://www.nebraskalibraries.org
The Nebraska Library Association supports and promotes all libraries, library media centers and library services in the state.

Pam Bohmfalk, President
Scott Childers, Vice President

485 Nebraska State Business Education Association
Wayne State College
1111 Main Street-Gardner Hall 206F
Wayne, NE 68787
402-375-7255
E-mail: paarnes1@wsc.edu
http://www.nsbea.org
Foster business education in the state of Nebraska.

Patricia Arneson, Contact
Janelle Stansberry, President

486 Nebraska State Education Association
605 S 14th Street
Suite 200
Lincoln, NE 68508
402-475-7611
800-742-0047
Fax: 402-475-2630
http://www.nsea.org
NSEA is a member-directed union of professional educators and education support professionals dedicated to providing quality public education for the students of Nebraska.

Mark Shively, Director
Leann Widhalm, Director

Nevada

487 Nevada Library Association
West Charleston Library
Clark County Library District
Las Vegas, NV 89030
702-507-3941
Fax: 702-649-2576
E-mail: rjdebuff@hotmail.com
http://www.nevadalibraries.org
The purpose of NLA shall be to promote library service of the highest quality for all present and potential users of libraries in Nevada.

Jeanette Hammons, President
Robbie DeBuff, Executive Secretary

488 Nevada State Education Association
1890 Donald Street
Reno, NV 89502
775-828-6732
800-232-6732
Fax: 775-828-6745
http://www.nsea-nv.org
Advocate the professional rights and economic security of its members, while also serving as the prominent voice for excellence in public education in Nevada.

Terry Hickman, Executive Director
Lynn Warne, President

New Hampshire

489 New Hampshire Business Education Association
Newfound Regional High School
2500 N River Road
Manchester, NH 3106
603-926-3395
Fax: 603-926-5418
E-mail: mmatarazzo@rivier.edu
http://www.nhbea.org
Fosters business education in the state of New Hampshire.

Joyce White, President
Maria Matarazzo, Business Administration Dir

490 New Hampshire Education Association
9 S Spring Street
Concord, NH 3301-2425
603-224-7751
866-556-3264
Fax: 603-224-2648
http://www.neanh.org
To strengthen and support public education and to serve our members' professional, political, economic and advocacy needs.

Rhonda Wesolowski, President
Jim Sweeny, Executive Director

491 New Hampshire Library Association
LGC, PO Box 617
Concord, NH 3302-617
603-641-4123
Fax: 603-641-4124
E-mail: annie.donahue@unh.edu
http://www.nhlibrarians.org
advance the interests of its members through advocacy on library issues and increasing public awareness of library service; to support the professional development of its members; to foster communication and encourage the exchange of ideas among its members; and to promote participation in the association and its sections.

Annie Donahue, Conference Committee
Steven Butzel, President

New Jersey

492 Educational Media Association of New Jersey
PO Box 610
Trenton, NJ 8607
609-394-8032
Fax: 609-394-8164
http://www.emanj.org
Promotes the use of media in education.

Sue Henis, President

493 New Jersey Education Association (NJEA)
180 W State Street
Trenton, NJ 8607-1211
609-599-4561
800-359-6049
Fax: 609-392-6321
E-mail: lmaher@njea.org
http://www.njea.org
The mission of the New Jersey Education Association is to advance and protect the rights, benefits, and interests of members, and promote a quality system of public education for all students.

Joyce Powell, President
Stephen K Wollmer, Director of Communications

494 New Jersey Library Association
PO Box 1534
Trenton, NJ 8607
609-394-8032
Fax: 609-394-8164
E-mail: ptumulty@njla.org
http://www.njla.org
Established in 1890, the NJLA is the oldest and largest library organization in New Jersey.

Patricia A Tumulty, Executive Director
Susan Rice, Office Manager

495 New Jersey State Department of Education Resource Center
PO Box 500
Trenton, NJ 8625-500
609-292-4469
http://www.state.nj.us/education
provide leadership to prepare all students for their role as citizens and for the career opportunities of the 21st century.

Josephine Hernandez, President
Arcelio Aponte, Vice President

New Mexico

496 Mountain Plains Business Education Association (M-PBEA)
c/o Newcastle High School
4771 West Scott Road
Beatrice, NE 68310
307-746-2713
E-mail: tlandenb@gmail.com
http://www.mpbea.org
The Mountain-Plains Business Education Association (M-PBEA), an affiliate of the National Business Education Association (NBEA), is a professional organization serving individuals and groups engaged in instruction, administration, research, and dissemination of information for and about business. M-PBEA is comprised of the following states and provinces: Colorado, Kansas, Manitoba, Nebraska, New Mexico, North Dakota, Oklahoma, Saskatchewan, South Dakota, Texas, and Wyoming.

Suzanne Sydow, President
DeLayne Havlovic, M-PBEA Treasurer

497 National Education Association of New Mexico
2007 Botulph
Santa Fe, NM 87505
505-982-1916
Fax: 505-982-6719
http://www.nea-nm.org
The NEA-NM and its affiliates will be the recognized advocate for students, public education, and public education employees in New Mexico.

Eduardo Holg-un, Political Affairs Specialist
Sharon Morgan, President

498 New Mexico Library Association (NMLA)
PO Box 26074
Albuquerque, NM 87125
505-400-7309
Fax: 505-891-5171
E-mail: admin@nmla.org
http://www.nmla.org/
The New Mexico Library Association is a non-profit organization dedicated to the support and promotion of libraries and the development of library personnel through education and the exchange of ideas to enrich the lives of all New Mexicans.

Cassandra Osterloh, President
Lorie Christian, Administrator

New York

499 Business Teachers Association of New York State
5260 Rogers Road
Apt A-5
Hamburg, NY 14075
315-369-6133
Fax: 315-369-6216
E-mail: President@btanys.org
http://www.btanys.org
The Business Teachers Association of New York State provides networking, support, and professional growth opportunities for its members to effectively educate today's students for tomorrow's global economy.

Sharon L Keller, Secretary/Awards Director
Susan Hall, President

500 Eastern Business Education Association (EBEA)
c/o National Business Education Association
1914 Association Drive
Reston, VA 20191-1596
703-860-8300
Fax: 703-620-4483
E-mail: nbea@nbea.org
http://www.nbea.org
NBEA is committed to the advancement of the professional interest and competence of its members and provides programs and services that enhance members' professional growth and development.

Sharon Fisher-Larson, President
Janet M Treichel, Executive Director

501 New York Library Association (NYLA)
252 Hudson Avenue
Albany, NY 12210-1802
518-432-6952
800-252-6952
Fax: 518-427-1697
E-mail: info@nyla.org
http://www.nyla.org/
The Association was the first state-wide organization of librarians in the United States.

Michael J Borges, Executive Director
Johanna Geiger, Deputy Director

502 New York State United Teachers (NYSUT)
800 Troy-Schenectady Road
Latham, NY 12210-2455
518-213-6000
800-342-9810
Fax: 518-213-6409
E-mail: mediarel@nysutmail.org
http://www.nysut.org/cps/rde/xchg/nysut/hs.xsl/index.htm
Through a representative democratic structure, New York State United Teachers improves the professional, economic and personal lives of our members and their families, strengthens the institutions in which they work, and furthers the cause of social justice through the trade union movement.

Richard C Iannuzzi, President
Linda Stanczik, Regional Staff Director

North Carolina

503 North Carolina Association for Career and Technical Education
PO Box G
Catawba, NC 28609-5159
828-241-3910
Fax: 919-782-8096
E-mail: tony.bello@gmail.com
http://www.actenc.org

Act as a central agency in keeping the people of the state informed of the mission, scope, needs, quality, importance, and contributions of career and technical education .

Paul Heiderpiem, Author
Scot Whitfield, President
Tom H Jones, Executive Director

504 North Carolina Association of Educators (NCAE)
700 S Salisbury Street
Raleigh, NC 27601
919-832-3000
800-662-7924
Fax: 919-829-1626
E-mail: colleen.borst@ncae.org
http://www.ncae.org
NCAE's mission is is to advocate for members and students, to enhance the education profession, and to advance public education.

Colleen Borst, Executive Director
Kevin Spragley, Associate Executive Director

505 North Carolina Business Education Association(NCBEA)
King's College
700 E Stonewall Street
Suite 400
Charlotte, NC 28202
980-343-2738
Fax: 704-348-2029
E-mail: bpetersen@kingscollegecharlotte.edu
http://www.ncbea.org
NCBEA seeks to promote and improve the quality of business education at all levels through membership activities and meetings and through cooperation with public and private educational agencies and institutions with related professional organizations and with business and industry.

Becky Petersen, Executive Director
Cindi Sweeney, President Elect

506 North Carolina Department of PublicInstruction (DPI)
301 N Wilmington Street
Education Building, Suite 5540
Raleigh, NC 27601
919-807-3952
Fax: 919-807-3826
E-mail: information@dpi.state.nc.us
http://www.ncpublicschools.org
The North Carolina Department of Public Instruction (DPI) is the agency charged with implementing the State's public school laws and the State Board of Education's policies and procedures governing pre-kindergarten through 12th grade public education. DPI develops the Standard Course of Study which describes the subjects and course content that should be taught in North Carolina public schools and develops the assessments and accountability model used to evaluate school and district success.

Melissa E Bartlett, Executive Director
Peter Asmar, Chief Information Officer

507 North Carolina Library Association (NCLA)
1811 Capital Boulevard
Raleigh, NC 27604
919-839-6252
Fax: 919-839-6253
E-mail: nclaonline@ibiblio.org
http://www.nclaonline.org
An affiliate of the American Library Association and the Southeastern Library Association, the North Carolina Library Association (NCLA) is a statewide organization concerned with the total library community in North Carolina. NCLA's purpose is to promote libraries, library and information ser-

vices, librarianship, intellectual freedom and literacy. Holds conferences in September and October and publishes a journal.

Sherwin Rice, VP/President elect
Phil Barton, President

North Dakota

508 North Dakota Education Association (NDEA)
410 East Thayer Avenue
Bismarck, ND 58501-5005
701-223-0450
Fax: 701-224-8535
E-mail: Dakota.draper@ndea.org
http://nd.nea.org/
Since 1887, the North Dakota Education Association has been advocating on behalf of North Dakota students and their teachers. NDEA's mission is to improve the political climate and economic conditions for public education and the status of teaching professionals and educational employees, in addition to promoting educational excellence, innovation, and equal opportunity in working toward the elimination of all forms of discrimination.

Dakota Draper, President
Mark Berntson, Vice President

509 North Dakota Library Association
PO Box 1595
Bismarck, ND 58502-1595
701-231-8863
Fax: 701-231-7138
E-mail: NDLA@LISTSERV.NODAK.EDU
http://www.ndla.info
The North Dakota Library Association is concerned with the needs and rights of all citizens of North Dakota to have free access to library collections of sufficient scope and quality to provide the means for fruitful inquiry.

ISSN: 0882-4746
150 attendees and 25 exhibits
Cathy Langemo, Executive Secretary
Phyllis Ann K Bratton, President

Ohio

510 Ohio Association of School Business Officials
8050 North High Street
Suite 170
Columbus, OH 43235
614-431-9116
800-64 -2726
Fax: 614-431-9137
http://www.oasbo-ohio.org
The Ohio Association of School Business Officials is a not-for-profit educational management organization dedicated to learning, utilizing and sharing the best methods and technology of school business administration.

David A Varda, Executive Director
Mark Pepera, Treasurer

511 Ohio Association of Secondary School Administrators
8050 N High Street
Suite 180
Colcumbus, OH 43235-6484
614-430-8311
Fax: 614-430-8315
http://www.oassa.org
The Ohio Association of Secondary School Administrators is dedicated to the adnocacy and welfare of its members. Our mission is to

provide high standards of leadership through professional development, political astuteness, legislative influence, positive public relations and collaboration with related organization.

Craig S Kupferberg, President
James J Harbuck, Executive Director

512 Ohio Library Council
1105 Schrock Road
Suite 440
Columbus, OH 43229-1174
614-410-8092
Fax: 614-410-8098
E-mail: olc@olc.org
http://www.olc.org
The Ohio Library Council is the State wide professional associationwhich represents the interests of Ohio's public libraries as well as their trustess, friends and staff. The OLC is governed by a Board of Directors composed of three library employees with an MLIS degree, three library trustees currently serving on library boards, and seven a- l arge members.

Margaret Danziger, President
Douglas Evans, Executive Director

513 Ohio Technology Education Association (OTEA)
c/o State Supervisor
25 South Front Street
Room 509
Edison, OH 43320
419-946-2071
Fax: 614-995-5568
E-mail: william_s@treca.org
http://www.otea.info/
The mission of the Ohio Technology Education Association (OTEA) is to promote technological literacy for all Ohio students; provide leadership in curriculum and professional development; inform governmental and educational decision makers on technological literacy issues; advocate society wide the understanding of technological literacy and why it is vital; and form and maintain alliances with the business and industrial community.

Richard A Dieffenderfer Ph.D, State Supervisor
Timothy N Tryon, Executive Director

Oklahoma

514 Oklahoma Education Association (OEA)
323 East Madison Avenue
PO 18485
Oklahoma City, OK 73154
402-528-7785
800-522-8091
Fax: 405-524-0350
E-mail: lodom@okea.org
http://www.okea.org
The Oklahoma Education Association (OEA) supports public education as the cornerstone of a democratic society in that education employees, parents, community leaders and elected officials should work together to promote quality education. OEA has 40,000 members, comprised of public school teachers, coaches, counselors, and administrators; nurses, librarians, custodians, cafeteria workers, bus drivers, secretaries; retired teachers; and education majors at Oklahoma colleges and universities.

Roy Bishop, President
Lela Odom, Executive Director

515 Oklahoma Library Association (OLA)
300 Hardy Drive
Edmond, OK 73013
405-525-5100
Fax: 405-525-5103
E-mail: kboies@sbcglobal.net
http://www.oklibs.org
The Oklahoma Library Association works to strengthen the quality of libraries, library services and librarianship in Oklahoma. Members of OLA work in public, school, academic and special libraries of all sizes. Members include professional, paraprofessional and clerical library staff, library trustees, Friends, students, volunteers, vendors of library products and services and many others. Holds a conference in April and publishes a journal.

Kay Boies, Executive Director
Leslie Langley, Marketing/Communications

Oregon

516 AFT-Oregon (American Federation ofTeachers-Oregon)
7035 SW Hampton Street
Tigard, OR 97223-8313
503-595-3880
Fax: 503-595-3887
E-mail: AFTOregon@aft-oregon.org
http://or.aft.org/
Charted in 1952, AFT-Oregon, a state affiliate of the American Federation of Teachers, AFL-CIO, is a non-profit organization representing some 11,000 Oregon workers in K-12, community college and higher education in faculty and classified positions; and child care workers, in both public and private sectors. AFT-Oregon, in coalition with other unions and community groups, advocates for quality education and health care for all Oregonians, and gives working people a voice in our state's capitol.

Mark Schwebke, President
Phil Gilmore, Executive VP

517 Oregon Association of Student Councils (OASC)
707 13th Street SE
Suite 100
Salem, OR 97301-4035
503-480-7206
Fax: 503-581-9840
E-mail: nancy@oasc.org
http://www.oasc.org
The Oregon Association of Student Councils (OASC) is a non-profit member association, serving middle and high schools throughout the state, that provides leadership development to both students and advisors. OASC's program is sponsored by the Confederation of Oregon School Administrators.

Sara S Nilles, Program Director

518 Oregon Education Association (OEA)
6900 SW Atlanta Street
Portland, OR 97223
503-684-3300
800-858-5505
Fax: 503-684-8063
E-mail: larry.wolf@oregoned.org
http://www.oregoned.org
The mission of the Oregon Education Association (OEA) is to assure quality public education for every student in Oregon by providing a strong, positive voice for school employees. OEA's school funding priority, established in December 2002, seeks to restore stable and adequate funding for Oregon's schools and community colleges so that all Oregon students have access to a quality public education.

Larry Wolf, President
Jerry Caruthers, Executive Director

519 Oregon Educational Media Association
PO Box 277
Terrebonne, OR 97760
503-625-7820
E-mail: j23hayden@aol.com
http://www.oema.net
To provide progressive leadership to ensure that Oregon students and educators are effective users of ideas and information, and to pursue excellence in school library media programs by advocating information literacy for all student, supporting reading instruction and enjoyment of literature, supporting the highest levels of library media services in schools, strengthening member professionalism through communications and educational opportunities and promoting visibility in education, governme

Jim Hayden, Executive Director
Merrie Olson, President

520 Oregon Library Association (OLA)
PO Box 2042
Salem, OR 97308-2042
503-370-7019
Fax: 503-587-8063
E-mail: ola@olaweb.org
http://www.olaweb.org
The mission of the Oregon Library Association is to promote and advance library service through public and professional education and cooperation. Holds a conference in March and publishes two journals.

Mary Ginnane, President
Connie A Cohoon, Vice President

Pennsylvania

521 Pennsylvania Library Association (PaLA)
220 Cumberland Parkway
Suite 10
Mechanicsburg, PA 17055
717-766-7663
800-622-3308
Fax: 717-766-5440
E-mail: glenn@palibraries.org
http://www.palibraries.org
The Pennsylvania Library Association (PaLA) is a professional non-profit organization with strong volunteer leadership, dedicated to the support of its members, to the advancement of librarianship, and to the improvement and promotion of quality library service for citizens of the Commonwealth.

Glenn Miller, Executive Director
Mary O Garm, President

522 Pennsylvania School Librarians Association
9 Saint James Avenue
Somerville, MA 2144
617-628-4451
http://www.psla.org
Provides school librarians/media specialists with educational opportunities and current information through publications, workshops, seminars and conferences

Marg Foster, Secretary
Nancy S Latanision, President

523 Pennsylvania State Education Association (PSEA)
400 N 3rd Street
PO Box 1724
Harrisburg, PA 17105-1724
717-255-7000
800-944-7732
Fax: 717-255-7124
E-mail: cdumaresq@psea.org
http://www.psea.org
PSEA's mission is to advocate for quality public education and our members through collective action. PSEA is a member-driven organization, headed by elected officers, an executive director and a board of directors.

James P Testerman, President
John F Springer, Executive Director

Rhode Island

524 National Education Association Rhode Island (NEARI)
99 Bald Hill Road
Cranston, RI 2920
401-463-9630
Fax: 401-463-5337
E-mail: RWalsh@nea.org
http://www.neari.org/matriarch/default.asp
The NEA Rhode Island is both a union and a professional organization.

Robert A Walsh Jr, Executive Director
Vincent P Santaniello, Deputy Executive Director

525 Rhode Island Association of School Business Officials
600 Mount Pleasant Avenue
Building #16, RIC
Providence, RI 2908
401-272-9811
Fax: 401-272-9834
http://www.riasp.org
Is an umbrella association serving elementary, middle level, and high school leaders from all across Rhode Island. Affiliated with both the National Association of Elementary School Principals (NAESP) and the National Association of Secondary School Principals (NASSP)

Norma Cole, President
Arlene Miguel, Secretary

526 Rhode Island Educational Media Association
646 Camp Avenue
North Kingstown, RI 2852
401-295-9200
Fax: 401-295-8101
E-mail: www@ride.ri.net
http://www.ri.net
RINET provides complete Internet solutions for organizations that serve children, such as schools, libraries, municipalities, as well as high quality technology programs and services in support of K-12 teaching, learning and administration

Mike Mello, Membership Chairman
Sharon Hussey, Executive Director

527 Rhode Island Library Association
PO Box 6765
Providence, RI 2940
401-943-9080
Fax: 401-946-5079
E-mail: book_n@yahoo.com
http://www.rilibraryassoc.org
The Rhode Island Library Association is a profesional association of Librarians, Library Staff, Trustees, and library supporters whose purpose is to promote the profession of librarianship and to improve the visibility, accessibility, responsiveness and effectiveness of library and information services throughout Rhode Island.

Christopher Laroux, President
Laura Marlane, Vice President

South Carolina

528 South Carolina Education Association (SCEA)
421 Zimalcrest Drive
Columbia, SC 29210
803-772-6553
800-422-7232
Fax: 803-772-0922
E-mail: czullinger@thescea.org
http://www.thescea.org/
Professional association for educators in South Carolina.

Aaron Wallace, Executive Director
Carolyn Randolph, Assistant Executive Director

529 South Carolina Library Association
PO Box 1763
Columbia, SC 29202
803-252-1087
Fax: 803-252-0589
E-mail: scla@capconsc.com
http://www.scla.org
Informes members of issues and to provide training and networking opportunities.

Libby Young, President
Rayburne Turner, Vice President

South Dakota

530 Mountain Plains Library Association (MPLA)
14293 West Center Drive
Lakewood, CO 80228
303-985-7795
E-mail:
mpla_execsecretary@operamail.com
http://www.mpla.us
The Mountain Plains Library Association (MPLA) is a twelve state association of librarians, library paraprofessionals and friends of libraries in Arizona, Colorado, Kansas, Montana, Nebraska, Nevada, New Mexico, North Dakota, Oklahoma, South Dakota, Utah and Wyoming. Its purpose is to promote the development of librarians and libraries by providing significant educational and networking opportunities. Holds conferences in September, October and November. Also publishes a newsletter.

Judy Zelenski, Interim Executive Secretary
Dan Chaney, MPLA Webmaster

531 South Dakota Education Association (SDEA)
441 E Capitol Avenue
Pierre, SD 57501
605-224-9263
800-529-0090
Fax: 605-224-5810
E-mail: Bryce.Healy@sdea.org
http://www.sdea.org/
The South Dakota Education Association/SDEA advocates new directions for public education, providing professional services that benefit students, schools and the public.

Bryce Healy, Executive Director
Paul McCorkle, CFO/CIO

532 South Dakota Library Associations
PO Box 1212
Rapid City, SD 57709
605-343-3750
E-mail: bkstand@rap.midco.net
http://www.sdlibraryassociation.org
The SD Library Association strives to promote library service of the highest quality for present and potential SD library users; to provide opportunities for professional involvement of all persons engaged in any phase of librarianship within the state; and to further the professional development of SD librarians, trustees, and library employees.

Nancy Sabbe, President
Brenda Hemmelman, Secretary/Treasurer

Tennessee

533 Tennessee Association of Secondary School Principals (TASSP)
PO Box 18079
Knoxville, TN 37928
865-687-8965
866-737-2777
Fax: 865-687-2341
E-mail: tassp@bellsouth.net

The mission of the Tennessee Association of Secondary School Principals is: to promote professional standards of practice for secondary school administrators; provide high quality professional development experiences for rural, urban, and suburban administrators, statewide, based on their common and unique professional development needs; and advocate on behalf of secondary administrators in their efforts to provide high quality education for all students.

Dana Finch, President
Tommy Everette, Executive Director

534 Tennessee Library Association
PO Box 241074
Memphis, TN 38124-1074
901-485-6952
Fax: 615-269-1807
E-mail: arhuggins1@comcast.net
http://www.tnla.org
Promote the establishment, maintenance, and support of adequate library services for all people of the state.

Annelle R Huggins, Executive Director
Sue Szostak, President

535 Tennessee School Boards Association
525 Brick Church Park Drive
Nashville, TN 37207
615-815-3900
800-448-6465
Fax: 615-815-3911
E-mail: webadmin@tsba.net
http://www.tsba.net
The mission of the Tennessee School Boards Association is to assisst school boards in effectively governing school districts.

Tammy Grissom, Executive Director
David Pickler, President

Texas

536 Texas Association of Secondary School Principals (TASSP)
1833 S IH-35
Austin, TX 78741
512-443-2100
Fax: 512-442-3343
E-mail: aarguello@tassp.org
UELLO@TASSP.ORG
HTTP://WWW.TASSP.ORG/
TASSP provides proactive leadership to systemically change schools into learning com-

munities in which all students and other participants achieve their full potential as life long learners in a diverse and changing society. ˜

Archie E McAfee, Executive Director
Tom Leyden, Associate Executive Director

537 Texas Library Association (TLA)
3355 Bee Cave Road
Suite 401
Austin, TX 78746
512-328-1518
800-580-2852
Fax: 512-328-8852
E-mail: tla@txla.org
http://www.txla.org
The Texas Library Association/TLA is a professional organization that promotes librarianship and library service in Texas. Through legislative advocacy, continuing education events, and networking channels, TLA offers members opportunities for service to the profession as well as for personal growth. Holds conferences in March or April, also publishes a quarterly journal and a bimonthly newsletter.

Patricia H Smith, Executive Director
Gloria Meraz, Communications Director

Utah

538 Utah Education Association (UEA)
875 E 5180 S
Murray, UT 84107-5299
801-266-4461
800-594-8996
Fax: 801-265-2249
E-mail: mark.mickelsen@utea.org
http://www.utea.org
The mission of the Utah Education Association (UEA) is to advance the cause of public education in partnership with others: strengthen the teaching profession, promote quality schools for Utah's children, and advocate the well-being of members.

Kim Campbell, President
Mark Mickelsen, Executive Director

Vermont

539 Vermont Library Association
PO Box 803
Burlington, VT 5402
802-388-3845
Fax: 802-388-4367
E-mail: vlaorg@sover.net
http://www.vermontlibraries.org
The Vermont Library Association is an educational Organization working to develop, promote, and improve library and information services and librarianship in the state of Vermont.

Judah S Hamer, President
David Clark, Chapter Councilor

540 Vermont National Education Association (VTNEA)
10 Wheelock Street
Montpelier, VT 5602-3737
802-223-6375
800-649-6375
Fax: 802-223-1253
E-mail: vtnea@together.net
http://www.vtnea.org/
The Vermont National Education Association is a voluntary organization of 11,000 Vermont teachers and education support professionals, their purpose being to make sure that members have a satisfying work environment

where they are acknowledged for the work they perform and where the work they perform helps students do their best.

Joel D Cook, Executive Director
Darren M Allen, Communications Director

541 Volunteers for Peace
7 Kilburn Street
Suite 316
Burlington, VT 05401
802-259-2759
Fax: 802-259-2922
E-mail: vfp@vfp.org
http://www.vfp.org
Volunteers for Peace promotes International Voluntary Service as an effective means of intercultural education, service learning and community development. We provide projects where people from diverse backgrounds can work together to help overcome the need, violence and environmental challenges facing our planet

Meg Brook, President

Virginia

542 Action Alliance for Virginia's Children and Youth
701 E Franklin Street
Suite 807
Richmond, VA 23219
804-649-0184
Fax: 804-649-0161
E-mail: info@vakids.org
http://www.vakids.org
Nonprofit and non-partisan, Voices for Virginia's Children is a persistent voice of reason in advocating for better lives and futures for children. The Commonwealth's only statewide multi-issue organization advocating for children and youth, Voices promotes sound, far-reaching program and policy solutions, focusing on early care and education, health care, family economic success, and foster care and adoption.

James V Duty, Chairman
John R Morgan, Executive Director

543 Division of Student Leadership Services
PO Box K 170
Richmond, VA 23288-1
804-285-2829
Fax: 804-285-1379
http://www.vaprincipals.org
Organization that sponsors the Virginia Student Councils Association; the Virginia Association of Honor Societies; and the Virginia Association of Student Activity Advisers.

Dr. Randy Barrack, Executive Director

544 Organization of Virginia Homeschoolers
PO Box 5131
Charlottesville, VA 22905
866-513-6173
Fax: 804-946-2263
E-mail: info@vahomeschoolers.org
http://www.vahomeschoolers.org
The Organization of Virginia Homeschoolers' most effective action is screening legislation for potential impact on homeschoolers. We pay attention to a large list of topics: home instruction statute, tutor provision, religious exemption provision, driver training, truancy, curfews, tax credits, and more.

Parrish Mort, President
Kenneth L Payne, Executive Director

545 Southern Association of Colleges & Schools
Virginia Secondary & Middle School Committee
PO Box 7007
Radford, VA 24142-7007
540-831-5399
Fax: 540-831-6309
E-mail: mdalderm@runet.edu
Public and private school accreditation organization. 12,000 member schools in 11 southern state regions. 430 middle and secondary SACS member schools in Virginia.

Dr. Emmett Sufflebarger, President
Lanny Holsinger, President-Elect

546 Virginia Alliance for Arts Education
PO Box 70232
Richmond, VA 23255-232
804-740-7865
Fax: 804-828-2335
To promote aesthetic and creative art education for the development of the individual at all levels in the commonwealth of Virginia. To assist teachers in improving the quality of art education. To organize and conduct panels, forums, lectures, and tours for art educators and the general public on art and art instruction. To keep the public informed of the arts through whatever means are available.

Margaret Edwards, Division Director

547 Virginia Association for Health, Physical Education, Recreation & Dance
817 W Franklin Street
Box 842037
Richmond, VA 23284-2037
800-918-9899
Fax: 800-918-9899
VAHPERD is a professional association of educators that advocate quality programs in health, physical education, recreation, dance and sport. The association seeks to facilitate the professional growth and educational practices and legislation that will impact the profession.

Judith Clark, President

548 Virginia Association for Supervision and Curriculum Development
513 Half Mile Branch
Crozet, VA 22932
434-960-7732
Fax: 540-832-7666
E-mail: annetchison@earthlink.net
http://www.vaascd.org/
VASCD is an organization committed to excellence in education by providing programs and services to promote quality instruction for lifelong learning.

Ann Etchison, Executive Director
Judy Lam, Administrative Coordinator

549 Virginia Association for the Education of the Gifted
PO Box 26212
Richmond, VA 23260-6212
804-355-5945
Fax: 804-355-5137
E-mail: vagifted@comcast.net
http://www.vagifted.org
The Virginia Association for the Gifted supports research in gifted education and advocates specialized preparation for educators of the gifted. The association disseminates information, maintains a statewide network of communication, and cooperates with organizations and agencies to improve the quality of education in the Commonwealth of Virginia.

Liz Nelson, Executive Director

550 Virginia Association of Elementary School Principals
1805 Chantilly Street
Richmond, VA 23230
804-355-6791
Fax: 804-355-1196
E-mail: info@vaesp.org
http://www.vaesp.org
Nonprofit professional association advocating for public education and equal educational opportunities. Promotes leadership of school administrators, principals as educational leaders, and provides professional development opportunities.

Thomas L Shortt, Executive Director
Jeanne Grady, Operations Director

551 Virginia Association of Independent Specialized Education Facilities
6802 Paragon Place
Suite 525
Richmond, VA 23230
804-282-3592
Fax: 804-282-3596
E-mail: info@vais.org
http://www.vais.org
The Virginia Association of Independent Schools is a service organization that promotes educational, ethical and professional excellence. Through its school evaluation/accreditation program, attention to professional development and insistence on integrity, the Association safeguards the interests of its member schools.

Kimberly E Failon, Director Professional Develo
Sally K Boese, Executive Director

552 Virginia Association of Independent Schools
6802 Paragon Place
Suite 525
Richmond, VA 23230
804-282-3592
Fax: 804-282-3596
E-mail: info@vais.org
http://www.vais.org
The Virginia Association of Independent Schools is a service organization that promotes educational, ethical and professional excellence. Through its school evaluation/accreditation program, attention to professional development and insistence on integrity, the Association safeguards the interests of its member schools.

Kimberly E Failon, Director Professional Develo
Sally K Boese, Executive Director

553 Virginia Association of School Superintendents
405 Emmet Street
PO Box 400265
Charlottesville, VA 22904-4265
434-924-0538
Fax: 434-982-2942
http://vass.edschool.virginia.edu/
The Virginia Association of School Superintendents (VASS) is a professional organization dedicated to the mission of providing leadership and advocacy for public school education throughout the Commonwealth of Virginia.

J Andrew Stamp, Associate Executive Director
Alfred R Butler IV, Executive Director

554 Virginia Association of School Business Officials
Williamsburg-James City County Public Schools
PO Box 8783
Williamsburg, VA 23187-8783

757-253-6748
Fax: 757-253-0173
http://www.vasbo.org/
The mission of the Virginia Association of School Business Officials is to promote the highest standards of school business practices for its membership through professional development, continuing education, networking, and legislative impact.

David C Papenfuse, Division Director

555 Virginia Association of School Personnel Administrators
800 E City Hall Avenue
Norfolk, VA 23510-2723
757-340-1217
Fax: 757-340-1889
E-mail: president@vaspa.org
http://www.vaspa.org/
The Virginia Association of School Personnel Administrators helps personnel/human resources professionals improve their administrative skills and grow extensively in their profession.

Eddid P Antoine II, Division Director
Barbara Warren Jones, President

556 Virginia Congress of Parents & Teachers
1027 Wilmer Avenue
Richmond, VA 23227-2419
804-264-1234
866-482-497
Fax: 804-264-4014
E-mail: info@vapta.org
http://www.vapta.org
The Virginia Congress of Parents and Teachers, better known as the Virginia PTA is a volunteer child advocacy association working for ALL children and youth in the Commonwealth of Virginia.

Melissa S Nehrbass, President
Eugene A Goldberg, Executive Director

557 Virginia Consortium of Administrators for Education of the Gifted
RR 5 Box 680
Farmville, VA 23901-9011
804-225-2884
Fax: 814-692-3163

Catherine Cottrell, Division Director

558 Virginia Council for Private Education
1901 Huguenot Road
Suite 301
Richmond, VA 23235
804-423-6435
Fax: 804-423-6436
E-mail: jwebster@vcpe.org
http://www.vcpe.org
The Virginia Council for Private Education (VCPE) oversees accreditation of nonpublic preschool, elementary and secondary schools in the Commonwealth.

George McVey, President
Joanne L Webster, Vice President

559 Virginia Council of Administrators of Special Education
Franklin County Public Schools
25 Bernard Road
Rocky Mount, VA 24151
703-493-0280
Fax: 540-483-5806
E-mail: kkirst@k12albemarle.org
http://www.vcase.org
The Virginia Council of Administrators of Special Education is a professional organization that promotes professional leadership through the provision of collegial support and current information on recommended instruc-

tional practices as well as local, state and national trends in Special Education for professionals who serve students with disabilities in order to improve the quality and delivery of special education services in Virginia's public Schools

Susan Clark, President
Wyllys VanDerwerker, President-Elect

560 Virginia Council of Teachers of Mathematics
1033 Backwoods Road
Virginia Beach, VA 23455-6617
757-671-7316
E-mail: gnelson@vctm.org.
http://www.vctm.org/
The purpose of the Virginia Council of Teachers of Mathematics is to stimulate an active interest in mathematics, to provide an interchange of ideas in the teaching of mathematics, to promote the improvement of mathematics education in Virginia, to provide leadership in the professional development of teachers, to provide resources for teachers and to facilitate cooperation among mathematics organizations at the local, state and national levels

Ellen Smith Hook, Division Director

561 Virginia Council on Economic Education
301 W Main Street
Box 844000
Richmond, VA 23284-4000
804-828-1627
Fax: 804-828-7215
E-mail: shfinley@vcu.edu
http://www.vcee.org
Goal is for students to understand our economy and develop the life-long decision-making skills they need to be effective, informed citizens, consumers, savers, investors, producers and employees.

Yvonne Toms Allmond, Senior Vice President
Sallie Garrett, Contact

562 Virginia Education Association
116 S 3rd Street
Richmond, VA 23219
804-648-5801
Fax: 804-775-8379
E-mail: kboitnott@veanea.org
http://www.veanea.org
VEA is a statewide community of more than 60,000 teachers and school support professionals working for the betterment of public education in the Commonwealth. First organized in 1863, VEA has consistently advocated for quality instruction and curriculum, adequate funding, and excellent working conditions for Virginia public employees.

Robert Whitehead, Executive Director
Kitty Boitnott, President

563 Virginia Educational Media Association
PO Box 2743
Fairfax, VA 22031-2743
703-764-0719
Fax: 703-272-3643
E-mail: jremler@pen.k12.va.us
http://www.vema.gan.va.us
Aim is to promote literacy, information access and evaluation, love of literature, effective use of technology, collaboration in the teaching and learning process, intellectual freedom, professional growth, instructional leadership and lifelong learning.

Jean Remler, Executive Director
Terri Britt, President

564 Virginia Educational Research Association
3354 Taleen Court
Annandale, VA 22003-1161
703-698-1325
Fax: 703-698-0587
E-mail: mpowell@ctb.com
http://www.doe.virginia.gov/VDOE/dbpubs/
doedir/edorgs.html
The mission of the Educational Research Service is to improve the education of children and youth by providing educators and the public with timely and reliable research and information.

Dr. Edith Carter, Assistant Professor
Michaeline M Powell, President

565 Virginia High School League
1642 State Farm Boulevard
Charlottesville, VA 22911-8609
434-977-8475
Fax: 434-977-5943
E-mail: ktillry@vhsl.org
http://www.vhsl.org
The Virginia High School League is an alliance of Virginia's public high schools that promotes education, leadership, sportsmanship, character and citizenship for students by establishing and maintaining high standards for school activities and competitions.

Craig Barbrow, President
Ken Tilley, Executive Director

566 Virginia Library Association
PO Box 8277
Norfolk, VA 23503-277
757-583-0041
Fax: 757-583-5041
E-mail: lhahne@coastalnet.com
http://www.vla.org
The Virginia Library Association is a statewide organization whose purpose is to develop, promote, and improve library and information services and the profession of librarianship in order to advance literacy and learning and to ensure access to information in the Commonwealth of Virginia.

Linda Hahne, Executive Director

567 Virginia Middle School Association
11138 Marsh Road
Bealeton, VA 22712-9360
703-439-3207
Fax: 540-439-2051
http://www.vmsa.org/
Lisa Norris, President
Virginia Jones, President Elect

568 Virginia School Boards Association
200 Hansen Road
Charlottesville, VA 22911
434-295-8722
800-446-8722
Fax: 434-295-8785
http://www.vsba.org
The Virginia School Boards Association is a voluntary, nonpartisan association whose primary mission is the advancement of education through the unique American tradition of local citizen control of, and accountability for, the Commonwealth's public schools.

Gina Patterson, Assistant Executive Director
Frank E Barham, Executive Director

569 Virginia Student Councils Association
4909 Cutshaw Avenue
Richmond, VA 23230
804-355-2777
Fax: 804-285-1379
E-mail: rbarrack@vassp.org
http://www.vassp.org/vsca.html
Assist school principals and assistant principals in providing leadership to their schools and communities for the purpose of improving the education of Virginia's youth.

Randy D Barrack, Executive Director
Lawrence W Lenz, President

570 Virginia Vocational Association
10259 Lakeridge Square Court
Suite G
Ashland, VA 23005-8159
804-365-4556

Jean Holbrook, President
Kathy Williams, Executive Director

Washington

571 Washington Education Association
32032 Weyerhaeuser Way S
PO Box 9100
Federal Way, WA 98063-9100
253-941-6700
Fax: 253-946-4735
http://www.wa.nea.org
The mission of the Washington Education Association is to advance the professional interests of its members in order to make public education the best it can be for students, staff and communities

Mary Lindquist, President
Mike Ragan, VP

572 Washington Library Association
23607 Highway 99
Suite 2-C
Edmonds, WA 98026
425-967-0739
Fax: 425-771-9588
E-mail: info@wla.org
http://http://wla.org/
Washington's citizens rely upon libraries to further their education, enhance their skills in the work place, fully function in today's global society, and enrich and enjoy their daily lives. The Washington Library Association, with a membership of over 1300 individuals and 39 institutions, provides the leadership needed to develop, improve, and promote library services to all Washington residents

ISSN: 8756-4173

Gail Willis, Association Coordinator
Kristin Crowe, Executive Director

West Virginia

573 Edvantia
1031 Quarrier Street
PO Box 1348
Charleston, WV 25325-1348
304-347-0400
800-624-9120
Fax: 304-347-0487
E-mail: info@edvantia.org
http://www.edvantia.org
Edvantia is a nonprofit corporation committed to helping client-partners improve education and meet federal and state mandates. Schools, districts, and state education agencies-as well as publishers and service providers-rely on Edvantia's core capabilities in research, evaluation, professional development, and technical assistance to help them succeed.

Nancy Balow, Author
Patricia Hammer, Director of Communications
Carolyn Luzader, Communications Specialist

574 West Virginia Education Association
1558 Quarrier Street
Charleston, WV 25311-2497
304-346-5315
800-642-8261
Fax: 304-346-4325
http://www.wvea.org
We are education employees like you who care deeply about children and public education. We help employees throughout the state face the demands of their profession

Dale Lee, President
Wayne Spangler, Vice President

575 West Virginia Library Association
PO Box 5221
Charleston, WV 25361
304-558-2045
Fax: 304-558-2044
E-mail: webmaster@wvla.org
http://www.wvla.org
The West Virginia Library Association (WVLA) was established in 1914 to promote library service and librarianship in West Virginia. Since then, WVLA has offered leadership in the development and expansion of library services of all types

Ann Farr, Immediate Past President
Olivia L Bravo, Chairperson

Wisconsin

576 Wisconsin Education Association Council
33 Nob Hill Drive
PO Box 8003
Madison, WI 53708-8003
608-276-7711
800-362-8034
Fax: 608-276-8203
E-mail: AskOnWEAC@weac.org.
http://www.weac.org
To fulfill the promise of a democratic society, the mission of the Wisconsin Education Association Council is to promote respect and support for quality public education and to provide for the professional and personal growth and economic welfare of members.

Mary Bell, President
Dan Burkhalter, Executive Director

577 Wisconsin Educational Media Association
PO Box 206
Boscobel, WI 53809
608-375-6020
E-mail: wemtamanager@hughes.net
http://www.wemaonline.org
Providing programs and services that enhance the professional growth of all members

Courtney Rounds, Association Manager
Jo Ann Carr, President

578 Wisconsin Library Association
5250 E Terrace Drive
Suite A1
Madison, WI 53718-8345
608-245-3640
Fax: 608-245-3646
E-mail: wla@scls.lib.wi.us
http://www.wla.lib.wi.us/
WLA brings together and supports people from all types of libraries to advocate and work for the improvement and development of library and information services for all of Wisconsin

Pat Chevis, President
Lisa Strand, Executive Director

Wyoming

579 Wyoming Education Association
115 E 22nd Street
Suite 1
Cheyenne, WY 82001-3795
800-442-2395
Fax: 800-778-8161
E-mail: mkruse@nea.org
http://www.wyoea.org
Advance public education at all levels by creating equitable educational opportunity for all learners, promoting the highest quality standards for the profession,and expanding the rights and furthering the interests of educational personnel.

Kathryn Valido, President
Craig Williams, Vice President

580 Wyoming Library Association
PO Box 1387
Cheyenne, WY 82003-1387
307-632-7622
Fax: 307-638-3469
E-mail: grottski@aol.com
http://www.wyla.org
Promotes library service and profession of librarianship in Wyoming.

Cynthia Twing, President
Laura Grott, Executive Secretary

581 Wyoming School Boards Association
2323 Pioneer Avenue
Cheyenne, WY 82001-3274
307-634-1112
Fax: 307-634-1114
E-mail: wsba@wsba-wy.org
http://www.wsba-wy.org
The official voice of local school boards.

Gregg Blikre, President
Mike Eathorne, President-Elect

International

582 AISA School Leaders' Retreat and EducatorsConference

Association of International Schools in Africa
Peponi Road
PO Box 14103, Nairobi
Kenya 00800
254-20-2697442
Fax: 254-20-4183272
E-mail: info@aisa.or.ke
http://www.aisa.or.ke
Facilitates communications, cooperation, and professional growth among member schools. Promotes intercultural understanding and friendships as well as facilitating collaboration between its members, host country schools, and other regional and professional groups.

Annual/October

Peter Bateman, Executive Director
Thomas P Shearer, Chairperson

583 Association for Childhood Education International Annual Conference

Assn for Childhood Educational International
17904 Georgia Avenue
Suite 215
Olney, MD 20832
301-570-2111
800-423-3563
Fax: 301-570-2212
E-mail: headquarters@acei.org
http://www.acei.org
Symposium focusing on education for bi-lingual and culturally diverse children. International issues and over 200 workshops.

April
50 booths with 1000 attendees

James Hoot, President
Debra Wisneski, President Elec.

584 Association for Experiential Education Annual Conference

3775 Iris Avenue
Suite 4
Boulder, CO 80301-1043
303-440-8844
866-522-8337
Fax: 303-440-9581
E-mail: admin@aee.org
http://www.aee.org
Annual international and regional conference dedicated to promoting, defining, developing, and applying the theories and practices of experiential education.

November
1,200 attendees

Christian Itin, President
Paul Limoges, CEO

585 CIEE Annual Conference

Council on International Educational Exchange
300 Fore Street
Portland, ME 04101
207-553-7600
800-407-8839
Fax: 207-553-7699
http://www.ciee.org
Open to study-abroad advisors, administrators, faculty and other international education professionals. The conference is an opportunity to share ideas, keep up with developments in the field, and meet with colleagues from around the world.

November

586 Center for Critical Thinking and Moral Critique Annual International

Po Box196
Tomales, CA 94971
707-878-9100
800-833-3645
Fax: 707-878-9111
E-mail: cct@criticalthinking.org
http://www.criticalthinking.org
Over 1,200 educators participate to discuss critical thinking and educational change.

March, July

Dr Linda Elder, President

587 Childhood Education Association International

17904 Georgia Avenue
Suite 215
Olney, MD 20832-2277
301-570-2111
800-423-3563
Fax: 301-570-2212
E-mail: headquarters@acei.org
http://wwwacei.org
To promote and support in the global community the optimal education and development of children, from birth through early adolescence, and to influence the professional growth of educators and the efforts of others who are committed to the needs of children in a changing society.

April
35 booths

James Hoot, President
Debra Wisneski, President Elec.

588 Council for Learning Disabilities International Conference

1184 Antoich Road
Box 405
Overland Park, KS 66210-4303
913-491-1011
Fax: 913-491-1012
E-mail: cdlinfo@ie-events.com
http://www.cldinternational.org
Intensive interaction with and among professional educators and top LD researchers. Concise, informative and interesting forums on topics from effective instruction to self-reliance are presented by well-known professionals from across the country and around the world.

October
35 booths with 800 attendees

Brian Bryant, Conference Contact

589 Council of British Independent Schools in the European Communities Annual Conference

8 St. Christophers Place
Farnborough, Hampshire, UK GU14O-7JY
44-1252-513-930
Fax: 44-1252-516-000
E-mail: excecutive.director@cobis.org.uk
http://www.cobisec.org
Conference for Heads, Governors and members of Senior Management Teams of schools. Assurance of quality in member schools.

May
75 attendees and 20 exhibits

590 European Council of International Schools

21B Lavant Street
Petersfield, Hampshire GU32 3EL
United Kingdom
44-1730-268-244
Fax: 44-1730-267-914
E-mail: conferences@ecis.org
http://www.ecis.org
Support professional development, curriculum and instruction, leadership and good governance in international schools located in Europe and around the world.

April, November

Michelle Clue, Events Manager
Jean Vahey, Executive Officer

591 Hort School: Conference of the Association ofAmerican Schools

International School of Panama
P.O. Box 0819-02588
Panama City, Pa
507-293-3000
Fax: 507-266-7808
E-mail: isp@isp.edu.pa
http://www.isp.edu.pa
Founded in 1982 by a group of interested parents from the Panamanian and International community. ISP is a private, independent, non-profit educational institution providing instruction in English for the multinational and Panamanian population residing in Panama City, Panama.

October
600 attendees and 35 exhibits

Linda LaPine, Director
Terry McCoy, President

592 International Association of Teachers of English as a Foreign Language

Darwin College
University of Kent
Canterbury, Kent, UK CT2-7NY
44-1227-824430
Fax: 44-1227-824431
E-mail: generalenquires@iatefl.org
http://www.iatefl.org
Plenary sessions by eminent practitioners, a large number of workshops, talks and round tables given by other speakers, an ELT Resources Exhibition and Pre-Conference Events organized by Special Interest Groups.

April
80 booths with 1500 attendees

Alison Medland, Conference Organizer
Glenda Smart, Executive Officer

593 International Awards Market

Awards and Recognition Association
4700 W Lake Avenue
Glenview, IL 60025
847-375-4800
800-344-2148
Fax: 888-374-7257
E-mail: info@ara.org
http://www.ara.org
Providing outstanding business and educational opportunities for both retailers and suppliers. Retailers can view the latest industry products, take advantage of special show offers and benefit from a full educational program.

Feb, March, Nov
200 booths with 6,000 attendees

BJ Bailey Jr., President

594 International Conference
World Associaiton for Symphonic Bands &
Ensembles
1037 Mill Street
San Luis Obispo, CA 93401
805-541-8000
Fax: 805-543-9498
E-mail: admin@wasbe2005.com
http://www.wasbe.org
WASBE is a nonprofit, international association open to individuals, institutions, and industries interested in symphonic bands and
wind ensembles. Dedicated to enhancing the
quality of the wind band throughout the world
and exposing its members to new worlds of
repertoire, musical culture, people and
places.

Every 2 years
Leon Bly, President

**595 International Congress for School
Effectiveness & Improvement**
International Congress Secretariat
PO Box 527-Frankston, VC 3199
Australia
61-037844230
http://www.icsei.net
The purpose of building and using an expanded base for advancing research, practice
and policy in the area of school effectiveness
and improvement. The Congress offers the
opportunity to exchange information and networking for the educational community.

January
500 attendees
Tony Mackay, President

**596 International Dyslexia Association
Annual Conference**
40 York Road
4th Floor
Baltimore, MD 21204-2044
410-296-0232
800-ABC-D123
Fax: 410-321-5069
E-mail: info@interdys.org
http://www.interdys.org
Provide the most comprehensive range of information and services that address the full
scope of dyslexia and related difficulties in
learning to read and write.

November
3000 attendees
Darnella Parks, Conferences Coordinator
Kristen Penczek, Conference Director

597 International Exhibit
National Institute for Staff & Organizational
Dev.
University of Texas
1 University Station
Austin, TX 78712
512-471-7545
Fax: 512-471-9426
E-mail: mpg@mail.utexas.edu
http://www.nisod.org
The largest international conference to focus
specifically on the celebration of teaching,
learning, and leadership excellence. This conference has enjoyed steady growth since its
inception in 1978.

May
1500 attendees
Sheryl Powell, Conference Director

**598 International Listening Association
Annual Convention**
Center for Information & Communication
Ball State University
Ball Communication Bldg. room 221
Muncie, IN 47306-0001
765-285-1889
Fax: 765-285-1516
E-mail: cics@bcu.edu
http://www.bsu.edu/cic
Geared toward the teaching of listening in the
classroom and various techniques for increas-
ing effectiveness in the classroom setting.

March
Rita Stewart, Conference Director

**599 International Reading Association
Annual Convention**
800 Barksdale Road
PO Box 8139
Newark, DE 19714-8139
302-731-1600
800-336-7323
Fax: 302-731-1057
E-mail: conferences@reading.org
http://www.reading.org
Contains exhibitors involved in various lectures and workshops dealing with illiteracy,
literature and some library science courses.

May
800 booths with 13M attendees
Patricia A. Edwards, President

600 International Symposium
American Association of University Women
1111 16th Street NW
Washington, DC 20036
202-785-7700
800-326-2289
Fax: 202-872-1425
E-mail: convention@aauw.org
http://www.aauw.org
The nation's leading voice promoting education and equity for women and girls.

Katie Broendel, Media Relations
Christy Jones, Membership Director

**601 International Technology Education
Association Conference**
1914 Association Drive
Suite 201
Reston, VA 20191-1539
703-860-2100
Fax: 703-860-0353
E-mail: itea@iris.org
http://www.iteawww.org
Provides teachers with new and exciting ideas
for educating students of all grade levels. The
conference gives educators an opportunity for
better understanding of the constant changes
that take place in technology education.

April
150 booths with 2,200+ attendees
Katie de la Paz, Communications
Coordinator

602 International Trombone Festival
International Trombone Association
1 Broomfield Road
Conventry, UK CV5-6JW
903-886-8711
Fax: 903-886-7975
http://www.trombone.net
This annual festival takes place at The Crane
School of Music, State University of New
York College at Potsdam.

June
Tony Baker, Festival Director
Jon Bohls, ITF Exhibits Coordinator

603 Learner-Centered
Improving Learning and Teaching
8510 49th Avenue
College Park, MD 20740-2412
Fax: 301-474-3473
E-mail: iut2000@aol.com
http://www.iut2000.org
Provides a forum in which participants from
across the globe share discoveries, practices
and challenges relating to improving the effectiveness of postsecondary teaching and
learning. The conference will be held in Johannesburg, South Africa.

July

**604 Learning Disabilities Association of
America International Conference**
4156 Library Road
Pittsburgh, PA 15234-1349
412-341-1515
Fax: 412-344-0224
E-mail: info@ldaamerica.org
http://www.ldaamerica.org
The largest meeting on learning disabilities
(LD) in the world. Disabled, parents, various
educators and administrators. The conference
follows a general theme set by LDAA.

Febuary, March
95 booths with 2600 attendees and 300 exhibits
Mary Clare Reynolds, Conference
Coordinator

605 NELA Annual Conference
New England Library Association
31 Connor Lane
Wilton, NH 03086
603-654-3533
Fax: 603-654-3526
E-mail: maryann@nelib.org
http://www.nelib.org
600 attendees
Jen Leo, President
Mary Ann List, Vice President

606 NJLA Spring Conference
New Jersey Library Association
PO Box 1534
Trenton, NJ 08607
609-394-8032
Fax: 609-394-8164
E-mail: ptumulty@njla.org
http://www.njla.org
1139 attendees
Patricia A Tumulty, Executive Director
Susan Rice, Office Manager

National

607 ACSI Teachers' Convention
Assocation of Christian Schools
International
731 Chapel Hills Drive
Colorado City, CO 80920
719-528-6906
800-367-0798
Fax: 791-531-0716
E-mail: exhibitors@acsi.org
http://www.acsi.org
Educational convention for administrators,
school board members, and early educators to
assist and encourage staff and volunteer development throughout the year.
50000 attendees
Brian S. Simmons, President
Janet Stump, Public Relations

608 AIS Annual Conference
Association for Integrative Studies
Miami University
Oxford, OH 45056
513-529-2659
Fax: 513-529-5849
E-mail: www.units.muohio.edu/aisorg
http://aisorg@muohio.edu
Each year since 1979, AIS has attracted scholars and administrators from across the country with a keen interest in developing and promoting research, pedagogy, and programs in integrative and interdisciplinary studies. Attendees from over 30 states and 5 countries gather to present the products of their research and practice, to network with others about recent developments in integrative studies and to draw upon the resources of the AIS.

Annual/October
165 attendees

Bill Newell, Executive Director
Karen Moranski, President

609 ALA Annual Conference
American Library Association
50 E Huron
Chicago, IL 60611
312-944-6780
800-545-2433
Fax: 312-440-9374
E-mail: ala@ala.org
http://www.ala.org
Brings together librarians, educators, publishers, literacy experts, illustrators and the leading suppliers to the market. A once-a-year opportunity to advance your career and improve your library.

June
20000+ attendees

Alicia Babcock, Conference/Events Coordinat

610 ASCD Annual Conference & Exhibit Show
Association for Supervision & Curriculum
1703 N Beauregard Street
Alexandria, VA 22311
703-578-9600
800-933-2723
Fax: 703-575-5400
E-mail: member@ascd.org
http://www.ascd.org
Explore the big ideas in education today, or examine new developments in your content area or grade level. Stretch your professional development learning into new areas, or pick an issue you care about most and examine it in depth.

April
12000 attendees

Barbara Gleason, Public Information Director
Christy Guilfoyle, Public Relations Specialist

611 AZLA/MPLA Conference
Arizona Library Association
1030 E Baseline Road
Suite 105-1025
Tempe, AZ 85283
480-609-3999
Fax: 480-998-7838
E-mail: meetmore@aol.com
http://www.azla.org
Advance the education advantages of the state through libraries, and to promote general in-

terest in library extension (traveling libraries).

October
90+ booths with 2,000 attendees

Kerrell Farmelant, Conference Administrator
Debbie Hanson, Exhibitor & Registration Mgn

612 Advocates for Language Learning Annual Meeting
Kansas City School District
301 E Armour Boulevard #620
Kansas City, MO 64111-1259
301-808-8291
Designed for both language instruction and language learning, the Conference is attended by language teachers, school administrators, directors, principals and parents at the elementary level.

October

Pat Barr-Harrison, Conference Contact

613 American Association School Administrators National Conference on Education
801 N Quincy Street
Suite 700
Arlington, VA 22203
703-528-0700
Fax: 703-841-1543
E-mail: info@aasa.org
http://www.aasa.org
For school superintendents, assistant superintendents, central office staff and those aspiring to the superintendence.

Daniel Domenech, Executive Director
Marilyn Maury, Conference Assist. Director

614 American Association for Employment in Education Annual Conference
American Association for Employment in Education
1509 N High Street
Suite 300
Columbus, OH 43201
614-292-1050
800-678-6010
Fax: 614-292-6235
E-mail: aaee@osu.edu
http://www.aaee.org
Disseminate information on the educational marketplace, and job search process. Promote ethical standards and practices in the employment process. Promote dialogue and cooperation among institutions which prepare educators and institutions which provide employment opportunities.

November
20 booths with 150-200 attendees

Carol Newcomb, Executive Director
Matthew Gaul, Conference Manager

615 American Association for Higher Education -Learning to Change Conference
American Associations for Higher Education
1 Dupont Circle NW
Suite 360
Washington, DC 20036-1137
202-293-6440
Fax: 202-293-0073
E-mail: info@aahe.org
http://www.aahe.org
Widens the circle of faculty and administrators interested in higher education. You will

be engaged and excited by a rich mix of learning and networking events.

March
20 booths with 1000 attendees

Joyce DePass, Conference Director
Clara Lovett, President

616 American Association for Higher Education-Summer Academy, Organizing for Learning
American Associations for Higher Education
1 Dupont Circle NW
Suite 360
Washington, DC 20036-1137
202-293-6440
Fax: 202-293-0073
E-mail: info@aahe.org
http://www.aahe.org
Team-based, project-centered experience focused on undergraduate change initiatives that enhance student learning.

July
300 attendees

Joyce DePass, Convention Director

617 American Association for Higher Education:Annual Assessment Conference
American Associations for Higher Education
1 Dupont Circle NW
Suite 360
Washington, DC 20036-1137
202-293-6440
Fax: 202-293-0073
E-mail: info@aahe.org
http://www.aahe.org
Bringing together trendsetters - the individuals, institutions, and coalitions in North America and beyond - who demonstrates the courage and imagination to act on the pressing issues of our time.

20 booths with 1700 attendees

Joyce DePass, Conference Director
Robert Mundhenk, Assessment Director

618 American Association of Colleges for TeacherEd Annual Meeting and Exhibits
1307 New York Avenue NW
Suite 300
Washington, DC 20005-4701
202-293-2450
Fax: 202-457-8095
E-mail: aacte@aacte.org
http://www.aacte.org
Identifying and meeting the learning needs of teacher education deans and faculty.

Feb
75 booths with 2400 attendees

Sharon P Robinson, President/CEO
Gail M. Bozeman, VP Meetings and Events

619 American Association of French Teachers Conference
American Association of French Teachers
Mailcode 4510
Southern Illinois University
Carbondale, IL 62901-4510
618-453-5731
Fax: 618-453-5733
E-mail: aatf@frenchteachers.org
http://www.frenchteachers.org/convention
Takes place in French-speaking areas where our members can benefit from immersion in a French-speaking culture. Representing the French language in North America and to encourage the dissemination, both in the schools and in the general public, of knowledge concerning all aspects of the culture and civiliza-

tion of France and the French-speaking world.

July
1100 attendees
Dr Jayne Abrate, Executive Director

620 American Association of Physics Teachers National Meeting

One Physics Ellipse
College Park, MD 20740-4129
301-209-3311
Fax: 301-209-0845
E-mail: aapt-meet@aapt.org
http://www.aapt.org
Gives members the opportunity to network, discuss innovations in teaching methods and share the results of research about teaching and learning.

January & August
Tiffany Hayes, Director of Conferences
Cerena Cantrell, Associate Program Director

621 American Association of School Administrators Annual Convention

American Association of School Administrators
801 N Quincy Street
Suite 700
Arlington, VA 22203-1730
703-528-0700
Fax: 703-841-1543
E-mail: info@aasa.org
http://www.aasa.org
To support and develop effective school system leaders who are dedicated to the highest quality public education for all children.

February
Christopher Daw, Director of Conferences
Daniel Domenech, Executive Director

622 American Association of School Librarians National Conference

American Library Association
50 E Huron Street
Chicago, IL 60611
312-280-4382
800-545-2433
Fax: 312-280-5276
E-mail: aasl@ala.org
http://www.ala.org/aasl
An open conference holding seminars, workshops and tours of local libraries and facilities.

October
3,000 attendees
Julie Walker, Executive Director
Elise Fette, Manager, Professional Develo

623 American Association of Sex Educators, Counselors & Therapists Conference

1444 I Street NW
Suite 700
Washington, DC 20005-1960
202-449-1099
Fax: 202-216-9646
E-mail: aasect@aasect.org
http://www.aasect.org
For professionals and affiliated groups with a focus on continuing education for license renewal.

06/20-06/24
50 booths with 400-500 attendees
Dee Ann Walker, Executive Director
Christoper White, Conference Co Chair

624 American Camping Association National Conference

American Camping Association
5000 State Road 67 N
Martinsville, IN 46151-7902
765-342-8456
800-428-2267
Fax: 765-342-2065
E-mail: conference@ACAcamps.org
http://www.acacamps.org
Each year our community comes together to share the work we do and to explore opportunities for the future. With new directions, exciting and creative improvements, and added value for all attendees, the 2005 ACA National Conference offers you essential opportunities.

Ferbrurary
175 booths with 1500 attendees
Peg Smith, CEO
Kim Bruno, Marketing Manager

625 American Council on Education Annual Meeting

American Council on Education
1 Dupont Circle NW
Washington, DC 20036-1110
202-939-9410
Fax: 202-833-4760
E-mail: annualmeeting@ace.nche.edu
http://www.acenet.edu/meeting/index.cfm
The social compact that has governed and financed U.S. higher education for more than 50 years. A compact among government, citizens, and institutions has made postsecondary education broadly accessible. Join us as we explore the implications behind this highly politicized and provocative topic.

February
74 booths
Stephanie Marshall, Meeting Services Director
Wendy Bresler, Program Planning

626 American Council on the Teaching of Foreign Languages Annual Conference

101 N Fairfax Street
Suite 200
Alexandria, VA 22314
703-894-2900
Fax: 703-894-2905
E-mail: morehouse@actfl.org
http://www.actfl.org
Annual convention, the largest meeting of second language educators in the US and the only national convention in the continental US for teachers of Chinese, French, Russian, German, Italian, Japanese, Spanish and other languages. It is the professional forum for all languages, and all levels of instruction and the largest exhibition of teaching materials and technology in support of foreign language instruction in the US.

November
250 booths with 5,000+ attendees
Roberta Morehouse, Convention Coordinator
Bret Lovejoy, Executive Director

627 American Counseling Association Annual Conference & Expo

American Counseling Association
5999 Stevenson Avenue
Alexandria, VA 22304-3302
703-823-9800
800-347-6647
Fax: 703-823-0252

E-mail: rhayes@counseling.org
http://www.counseling.org

March
4000 attendees
Robin Hayes, Convention & Meeting Contact
Theresa Holmes, Convention & Meeting Contact

628 American Education Finance Association Annual Conference & Workshop

American Education Finance Association
5249 Cape Leyte Drive
Sarasota, FL 34242-1805
941-349-7580
Fax: 941-349-7580
http://www.aefa.cc
Information and discussion relating to critical issues in education finance for administrators, directors and principals.

March
3000 attendees
Marge Plecki, President
Ed Steinbrecher, Executive Director

629 American Educational Research Association Annual Meeting

1430 K Street
Suite 1200
Washington, DC 20005-3078
202-238-3200
Fax: 202-238-3250
E-mail: 2005annualmtg@aera.net
http://www.aera.net
Contains exhibiting college and secondary school text publishers, software and hardware manufacturers that emphasize such applications as test development, test scoring and applications.

April
120 booths with 12M attendees
Felice J Levine, Executive Director
Norman Tenorio, Director

630 American Educational Studies Association

Tennessee Technical University
PO Box 5193
Cookeville, TN 38505-0001
931-372-3101
Fax: 931-372-6319
Encourages research and the improvement of teaching in various curriculum areas.

November
Harvey Neufeldt, Conference Contact

631 American Indian Science & Engineering Society Annual Conference

AISES
PO Box 9828
Albuquerque, NM 87106
505-765-1052
Fax: 505-765-5608
E-mail: info@aises.org
http://www.aises.org
Issues of science and technological advances in regard to the various American Indian cultures and possible opportunities in North America. Workshops, seminars, cultural ceremonies, and a job fair with opportunities for employment or receiving scholarships for future academics.

November
3000 attendees
Anthony Kahn, Chair
Dr. Mary Jo Ondrechen, Vice Chair

632 American Library Association Annual Conference

American Library Association
50 E Huron Street
Chicago, IL 60611-2795
312-280-3219
800-545-2433
E-mail: ala@ala.org
http://www.ala.org
Bi-Annual conference for librarians.

June/January

Yvonne McLean, Conference Coordinator
Keith Michael Fiels, Executive Director

633 American Mathematical Society

American Mathematical Society
201 Charles Street
Providence, RI 02904
401-455-4000
800-321-4267
Fax: 401-331-3842
E-mail: meet@ams.org
http://www.ams.org
Information on joint mathematics meetings, publications, and professional services of the American Mathematical Society.

January

Dr. Donald McClure, Exceutive Director

634 American Montessori Society Conference

281 Park Avenue S
6th Floor
New York, NY 61020
212-358-1250
Fax: 212-358-1256
E-mail: east@amshq.org
http://www.amshq.org
Promotes quality Montessori education for all children from birth to 18 years of age.

May
75 booths with 1000 attendees

Marilyn E. Stewart, President
Kathy Roemer, Vice President

635 American Psychological Association Annual Conference

750 1st Street NE
Washington, DC 20002-4241
202-336-5500
800-374-2721
Fax: 202-336-5919
E-mail: convention@apa.org
http://www.apa.org
A national conference attended by psychologists from around the world. The conference has workshops, lectures, discussions, roundtables and symposiums.

August

13,000 attendees

Ronald F LeVant, President

636 American Public Health Association Annual Meeting

American Public Health Association
800 I Street NW
Washington, DC 20001
202-777-2742
Fax: 202-777-2534
E-mail: diane.lentini@apha.org
http://www.apha.org/meetings
The premier platform to share successes and failures, discover exceptional best practices and learn from expert colleagues and the latest research in the field.

November
650 booths with 13000 attendees

George C. Benjamin, Executive Director
Pamela M. Aaltonen, CoA Chair

637 American School Health Association's National School Conference

4340 East West Highway
Suite 403
Bethesda, MD 20814-5960
301-652-8072
Fax: 301-652-8077
E-mail: asha@ashaweb.org
http://www.ashaweb.org
Attendees include school nurses, health educators, health counselors, physicians and students. During the five-day conference, presentations are made by ASHA members, government officials and health education professionals.

October
40 booths with 700 attendees

Stephen Conley, Executive Director
Jeffery K. Clark, President

638 American Speech-Language-Hearing Association Annual Convention

ASHA
220 Reasearch Blvd.
Rockville, MD 20850-3226
301-897-5700
800-638-8255
Fax: 301-571-0457
E-mail: convention@asha.org
http://www.asha.org
A scientific and professional conference of speech-language pathology, audiology and other professionals.

Annual
November
400 booths with 12,000 attendees

Arlene A Pietranton, Executive Director
Paul Rao, President

639 American Technical Education Association Annual Conference

American Technical Education Association
800 6th Street N
Wahpeton,, ND 58076-0002
701-671-2301
Fax: 701-671-2260
E-mail: betty-krump@ndscs.nodak.edu
http://www.ateaonline.org
Over 350 administrators/directors and faculty of various technical institutes, junior colleges, universities and colleges, with 40 exhibitors. Topics cover all aspects of computer assisted instruction, distance education and technical education.

March
35 booths with 700 attendees and 75 exhibits

Betty Krump, Executive Director

640 Annual Academic-Vocational Integrated Curriculum Conference

National School Conference Institute
2525 East Arizona
Biltmore Circle, Suite 240
Phoenix, AZ 85069-7527
602-778-1030
800-242-3419
Fax: 602-778-1032
http://www.nscinet.com
Two pre-conference workshops: Comprehensive Career Guidance K-12, and Curriculum Integration: A New Level of Learning. Conference will also hold over 50 breakout sessions.

March

641 Annual Challenging Learners with Untapped Potential Conference

National School Conference Institute
2525 East Arizona
Biltmore Circle, Suite 240
Phoenix, AZ 85016
602-778-1030
800-242-3419
Fax: 602-778-1032
Two pre-conference workshops: The necessary ingredients for success, and Trends; identification strategies. Conference will also hold over 60 breakout sessions.

February

Carl Boyd, President

642 Annual Conference on Hispanic American Education

National School Conference Institute
2525 East Arizona
Biltmore Circle, Suite 240
Phoenix, AZ 85016
602-778-1030
800-242-3419
Fax: 602-778-1032
Two pre-conference workshops: Hispanic educational success: What schools can do to meet the challenge, and Closing the Hispanic achievement gap: A K-16 strategy using real data and standards-based professional development. Conference will also hold over 60 breakout sessions.

April

643 Annual Effective Schools Conference

National School Conference Institute
2525 East Arizona
Biltmore Circle, Suite 240
Phoenix, AZ 85069-7527
602-778-1030
800-242-3419
Fax: 602-778-1032
Two pre-conference workshops: Making the right changes at the district level to assure successful, sustainable school reform, and The challenges of high standards, accurate assessments, and meaningful accountability. Conference will also hold over 70 breakout sessions.

Bill Daggett

644 Annual Ethics & Technology Conference

Loyola University
820 N Michigan Avenue
School of Business
Chicago, IL 60611-2103
312-915-7394
E-mail: rkizior@luc.edu
http://www.ethicstechconference.org
The primary goal of the conference is to continue the interdisciplinary dialogue about ethical and social challenges triggered by the rapid diffusion of information technology.

June

Dr Ronald Kizior, Conference Chair
Dr Mary Malliaris, Program Chair

645 Annual Microcomputers in Education Conference

Arizona State University
1475 N. Scottsdale Rd
Suite 200
Scottsdale, AZ 85257-0908
480-884-1651
Fax: 480-965-4128

E-mail: info@mec.asu.edu
http://mec.asu.edu
The conference provides a forum to explore emerging educational technology and draws administrators, teachers, researchers, professionals and technology specialists from Arizona and throughout the country. Conference sessions cover K-12 through university-level applications, and target beginner through experienced users.

March
81 booths with 1,200+ attendees and 80+ exhibits
Dr Gary Bitter, Conference Director
Julie Solomon, Event Coordinator, Sr

646 Annual NCEA Convention & Exposition
National Catholic Educational Association
1005 North Glebe Road
Suite 525
Arlington, Va 22201-3852
202-337-6232
800-711-6232
Fax: 703-243-0025
E-mail: convasst@ncea.org
http://www.ncea.org
For all Catholic educators. 700 special exhibits, 400 engaging sessions and dozens of outstanding speakers.

Annually
April
Sue Arvo, Convention/Exposition Dir.
Stacey Svendgard, Exposition Coordinator

647 Annual Technology & Learning Conference
National School Boards Association
1680 Duke Street
Alexandria, VA 22314
703-838-6722
800-950-6722
Fax: 703-683-7590
E-mail: info@nsba.org
http://www.nsba.org
The latest education technology and the most innovative programming.

October
Anne L Bryant, Executive Director
Sandy Folks, General Conference Contact

648 Association for Advancement of Behavior Therapy Annual Convention
305 7th Avenue
New York, NY 10001-6008
212-647-1890
Fax: 212-647-1865
E-mail: mebrown@aabt.org
http://www.aabt.org
Psychologists, psychology faculty and students, and counselors with information on behavior modification, counseling and guidance and mental health issues.

November
2,000 attendees
Mary Ellen Brown, Convention Manager
Mary Jane Eimer, Executive Director

649 Association for Behavior Analysis Annual Convention
Association for Behavior Analysis
550 W. Centre Ave.
Portage, MI 49024
269-492-9310
Fax: 269-492-9316
E-mail: convention@abainternational.org
http://www.abainternational.org
Psychologists, psychology faculty and students, counselors and social workers are among the attendees of this conference offering over 25 exhibitors. The conference is research and education oriented.

43 booths
Maria E Malott, PhD, Conference Contact

650 Association for Education in Journalism and Mass Communication Convention
AEJMC
234 Outlet Pointe Boulevard
Columbia, SC 29210-5667
803-798-0271
Fax: 803-772-3509
http://www.aejmc.org
Featuring the latest in technology as well as special sessions on teaching, research and public service in the various components of journalism and mass communication — from advertising and public relations to radio and television journalism to media management and newspapers.

August
1,500 attendees
Fred Williams, Convention Manager
Jennifer McGill, Executive Director

651 Association for Persons with Severe Handicaps Annual Conference
1025 Vermont Avenue, NW
Suite 300
Washington, DC 20005
202-540-9020
Fax: 202-540-9019
E-mail: info@tash.org
http://www.tash.org
Provides a forum for individuals with disabilities, families, researchers, educators, scholars, and others to create dialogue around creating action for social and systems reform.

December
2,500 attendees
Kelly Nelson, Conference Coordinator
Nancy Weiss, Executive Director

652 Association for Play Therapy Conference
Association for Play Therapy
3198 Willow Avenue
Suite 110
Clovis, CA 93612-2831
559-294-2128
Fax: 559-294-2129
E-mail: info@a4pt.org
http://www.a4pt.org
Dedicated to the advancement of play therapy. APT is interdisciplinary and defines play therapy as a distinct group of interventions which use play as an integral component of the therapeutic process.

October
1000 attendees
Kathryn Lebby, Events Coordinator
Bill Burns, Executive Director

653 Association for Science Teacher Education Science Annual Meeting
The Association For Science Teacher Education
5040 Haley Center
Auburn, AL 36849
972-690-2496
http://www.aste.chem.pitt.edu
Offers programs in science, mathematics and environmental education with a wide variety of teachers and professors attending.

January
Paul Kuerbis, Conference Chair

654 Association for Supervision & Curriculum Development Annual Conference
ASCD
1703 N Beauregard Street
Alexandria, VA 22311-1717
703-578-9600
800-933-2723
Fax: 703-575-5400
E-mail: member@ascd.org
http://www.ascd.org
Explore the big ideas in education today, or examine new developments in your content area or grade level. Stretch your professional development learning into new areas, or pick an issue you care about most and examine it in depth.

300 booths with 1,100+ attendees
Barbara Gleason, Public Information Director
Christy Guilfoyle, Public Relations

655 Association for the Advancement ofInternational Education
San Diego State University
3970 RCA Blvd.
Suite 7000
Palm Beach Gardens, FL 33410
954-262-5691
Fax: 954- 26- 288
E-mail: aaie@nova.edu
http://www.aaie.org
Provides the organizational leadership to initiate and promote an understanding of the need for and the support of American/International education.

February
70 booths with 550 attendees
Elleana Austin, Executive Assistant
Elsa Lamb, Executive Director

656 Association for the Education of Gifted Underachieving Students Conference
6 Wildwood Street
Burlington, MA 01803
651-962-5385
http://www.aegus1.org
Attended by teachers, professors, administrators and social workers, this conference deals with cultural awareness and education of the disabled and gifted students.

April
Lois Baldwin, President
Terry Neu, Vice President

657 Association for the Study of Higher Education Annual Meeting
Michigan State University
4505 S. Maryland Parkway
Box 453002
Las Vegas, NV 89154
702-895-2737
Fax: 702-895-4269
E-mail: ashemsu@msu.edu
http://www.ashe.ws/index.htm
Promotes collaboration among its members and others engaged in the study of higher education.

November
Gary Rhoades, President

658 Association of American Colleges &Universities Annual Meeting
Association of American Colleges & Universities
1818 R Street NW
Washington, DC 20009-1604

202-387-3760
Fax: 202-265-9532
http://www.aacu-edu.org
Bringing together college educators from across institutional types, disciplines, and departments. Providing participants with innovative ideas and practices, and shaping the direction of their educational reform efforts.

January
1,200 attendees

Carol Geary, President
Ross Miller, Director of Programs

659 Association of Community College TrusteesConference
1233 20th Street NW
Suite 301
Washington, DC 20036-2907
202-775-4667
Fax: 202-223-1297
http://www.acct.org
Exists to develop effective lay governing board leadership to strengthen the capacity of community colleges to achieve their missions on behalf of their communities.

1000 attendees

Ray Taylor, President/CEO
Lila Farmer, Conference Logistics Coord.

660 Association of Science-Technology Centers Incorporated Conference
Association of Science-Technology Centers Incorp.
1025 Vermont Avenue NW
Suite 500
Washington, DC 20005-3516
202-783-7200
Fax: 202-783-7207
E-mail: conference@astc.org
http://www.astc.org
An organization of science centers and museums dedicated to furthering the public understanding of science. ASTC encourages excellence and innovation in informal science learning by serving and linking its members worldwide and advancing the common goals.

October
165 booths with 1600 attendees

Cindy Kong, Meetings/Conference Director
Gareth Rees, Meetings/Conference Coord.

661 CHADD: Children & Adults with Attention Deficit/Hyperactivity Disorder
CHADD
8181 Professional Place
Suite 150
Landover, MD 20785
301-306-7070
800-233-4050
Fax: 301-306-7090
http://www.chadd.org
National non-profit organization which offers advocacy, information and support for patients and parents of children with attention deficit disorders. Maintains support groups, provides a forum for continuing education about ADHD, and maintains a national resource center for information about ADD.

October
60 booths with 1,500 attendees

Alison Harris, Conference Coordinator
Peg Nichols, Communications Director

662 Center for Appalachian Studies & Services Annual Conference
East Tennessee University
PO Box 70556
Johnson City, TN 37614-0918

423-439-7865
Fax: 423-439-7870
E-mail: asa@marshal.edu
http://www.cass.etsu.edu/
Sponsor educational programs and public service activities that enhance the quality of life in Appalachia and that empower people to live more effectively within the region.

March

Elizabeth Fine, Conference Contact

663 Center for Applications of PsychologicalType Biennial Education Conference
2815 NW 13th Street
Suite 401
Gainesville, FL 32609
352-375-0160
800-777-2278
Fax: 352-378-0503
E-mail: fields@capt.org
Promotes the practical application and ethical use of psychological type. Conference sponsored by Center for Applications of Psychological Type (CAPT).

July

Jim Weir, Executive Director

664 Center for Gifted Education and Talent Development Conference
University of Connecticut
2131 Hillside Road
Unit 3007
Storrs Mansfield, CT 06269-3007
860-486-4826
Fax: 860-486-2900
http://www.gifted.uconn.edu
Conducts research on methods and techniques for teaching gifted and talented students.

Annual

Sally M Reis, Professor

665 Center for Rural Education and Small Schools Annual Conference
College of Education
124 Bluemont Hall
1100 Mid-Campus Drive
Manhattan, KS 66506
785-532-5886
Fax: 785-532-7304
E-mail: barbhav@ksu.edu
http://www.coe.ksu.edu/CRESS/conference.html
Annual conference is held which includes over 200 administrators, directors, principals, teachers and university faculty discussing all aspects of education in rural areas.

October
200 attendees and 20 exhibits

Barbara Havlicek, Assistant Director
Robert Newhouse, Director

666 Center on Disabilities Conference
Students with Disabilities Resources
1811 Nordhoff
Bayramian Hall 110
Northridge, CA 91330-8264
818-677-2578
Fax: 818-677-4929
E-mail: sdr@csun.edu
http://www.csun.edu/cod
This is a comprehensive, international conference, where all technologies across all ages; disabilities; levels of education and training; employment; and independent living are ad-

dressed. It is the largest conference of its kind!

March
130 booths with 4,000+ attendees

Marina Sanchez, Participant Coordinator
Sonya Hernandez, Speakers Coordinator

667 Choristers Guild's National Festival & Directors' Conference
Choristers Guild
12404 Park Central Drive
Suite 100
Dallas, TX 75251-2498
469-398-3606
800-246-7478
Fax: 469-398-3611
E-mail: conferences@mailcg.org
http://www.choristersguild.org
Enables leaders to nurture the spiritual and musical growth of children and youth.

September

Jim Rindelaub, Director

668 Closing the Gap
526 Main Street
PO Box 68
Henderson, MN 56044-0068
507-248-3294
Fax: 507-248-3810
E-mail: info@closingthegap.com
http://www.closingthegap.com
Provides information on the use of computer technology by and for persons with disabilities and the opportunities available for education and independent learning.

October
150+ booths with 2400 attendees

Sarah Anderson, Administrative Assistant
Connie Kneip, VP/General Manager

669 Computers on Campus National Conference
University of South Carolina
937 Assembly Street
Suite 108
Columbia, SC 29208
803-777-2260
Fax: 803-777-2663
E-mail: confs@rcce.scarolina.edu
http://www.rcce.sc.edu/coc
This conference provides a national forum for showcasing computer-based instructional models, discussing successful experiences in computer networking, making effective use of computer support in academic assessment, and using computer technology to enhance total student development.

November

Dr Andrew A Sorensen, President
Margaret M Lamb, Media Relations Director

670 Conference for Advancement of Mathematics Teaching
Texas Education Agency
William Travis Building
1701 N Congress Avenue
Austin, TX 78701-1402
512-463-9734
Fax: 512-463-9838
E-mail: teainfo@tea.state.tx.us
http://www.tea.state.tx.us
Exhibits educational materials useful to mathematics teachers.

July
175 booths with 7.5M-8M attendees

Anita Hopkins, Conference Contact

671 Conference on Information Technology
League for Innovation in the Community College
4505 East Chandler Boulevard
Suite 250
Phoenix, AZ 85048
480-705-8200
Fax: 480-705-8201
E-mail: harris@league.org
http://www.league.org
The premier showcase of the use of information technology to improve teaching and learning, student services, and institutional management. Celebrating 18 years of excellence, CIT features a technologically sophisticated and topically diverse program that enables educators to explore and expand their use of technology.

October
3,000 attendees
Mary K Harris, Conference Manager
Robin Piccilliri, Conference Specialist

672 Council for Advancement and Support ofEducation
1307 New York Avenue NW
Suite 1000
Washington, DC 20005-4701
202-328-2273
Fax: 202-387-4973
E-mail: conference@case.org
http://www.case.org
Offers numerous opportunities in the United States, Canada, Mexico, mainland Europe, the United Kingdom, and even online, to network with colleagues and learn about Institutional Advancement.

Fall/Winter
John Lippincott, President
Richard Salatiello, Sr Conference Program Coord.

673 Council for Exceptional Children Annual Convention
The Council for Exceptional Children
2900 Crystal Drive
Suite 1000
Arlington, VA 22202-3557
703-620-3660
888-232-7733
Fax: 703-264-1637
E-mail: service@cec.sped.org
http://www.cec.sped.org
Largest professional organization dedicated to improving educational results of individuals with disabilities and the gifted. 50,000 members

April
437 booths with 7000 attendees and 299 exhibits
Marilyn Friend, President
Bruce Ramirez, Executive Director

674 EDUCAUSE
4772 Walnut Street
Suite 206
Boulder, CO 80301-2408
303-449-4430
Fax: 303-440-0461
E-mail: info@educause.edu
http://www.educause.edu
EDUCAUSE is an international, nonprofit association whose mission is to help shape and enable transformational change in higher education through the introduction, use, and management of information resources and technologies in teaching, learning, scholarship, research, and institutional management. EDUCAUSE publishes books, magazines, monographs, executive briefings, white papers, and other materials that provide thoughtful leadership to effect transformational change in higher education.

October
4,000+ attendees and 180 exhibits
Diana Oblinger, President
Beverly Williams, Conference Director

675 Education Technology Conference
Society for Applied Learning Technology
50 Culpeper Street
Warrenton, VA 20186
540-347-0055
800-457-6812
Fax: 540-349-3169
E-mail: info@lti.org
http://www.salt.org
For over 30 years the Society has sponsored conferences which are educational in nature and cover a wide range of application areas such as distance learning, interactive multimedia in education and training, development of interactive instruction materials, performance support systems applications in education and training, interactive instruction delivery, and information literacy.

August
20 booths with 400 attendees
Raymond G Fox, President

676 Educational Publishing Summit
Association of Educational Publishers
510 Heron Drive
Suite 201
Logan Township, NJ 08085
856-241-7772
Fax: 856-241-0709
E-mail: mail@aepweb.org
http://www.aepweb.org
Professional association for publishers of supplemental educational materials. Its membership represents the breadth of educational content developers and service providers delivering progressive products in both print & electronic formats to today's schools and colleges. AEP now assists its members in navigating the global realities of publishing in the 21st century through its professional development programming, government relations efforts, & opportunities for collaboration & partnership

June
Charlene F Gaynor, CEO
JoAnn McDevitt, VP Sales/Mrktg/Business Dev.

677 Educational Theatre Association Conference
Educational Theatre Association
2343 Auburn Avenue
Cincinnati, OH 45219-2815
513-421-3900
Fax: 513-421-7077
E-mail: mpeitz@edta.org
http://www.edta.org
Promotes and strengthens theatre in education-primarily middle school and high school. Sponsors an honor society, various events, numerous publications, and arts education advocacy activities.

September
2,400 attendees
Michael J Peitz, Executive Director
Debbie Gibbs, President

678 Embracing an Inclusive Society: The Challenge for the New Millennium
National Multicultural Institute
1666 K Street NW
Suite 440
Washington, DC 20006-2556
202-483-0700
Fax: 202-483-5233
E-mail: nmci@nmci.org
http://www.nmci.org
Brings together practitioners from across the country and around the world to explore diversity and multiculturalism in both personal and professional contexts. Leaders from academia, business, and government present the latest thinking and action on diversity issues to conference participants.

June
Maria Morukian, Conference Coordinator
Elizabeth P Salett, President

679 Foundation for Critical Thinking Regional Workshop & Conference
Foundation for Critical Thinking
PO Box 196
Tomales, CA 94971
800-833-3645
Fax: 707-878-9111
E-mail: cct@criticalthinking.org
http://www.criticalthinking.org
Investigates and reports on the value and use of analytical thinking programs and curriculum in the classroom.

July
Dr Linda Elder, President

680 Gifted Child Society Conference
190 Rock Road
Glen Rock, NJ 07452-1736
201-444-6530
Fax: 201-444-9099
E-mail: admin@gifted.org
http://www.gifted.org
Provides educational enrichment and support for gifted children through national advocacy and various programs.

September
250 attendees
Janet L Chen, Executive Director

681 High School Reform Conference
National School Conference Institute
PO Box 37527
Phoenix, AZ 85069-7527
602-371-8655
Fax: 602-371-8790
http://www.nscinet.com
Annuan conference covers restructuring the high school schedule, designing curriculum and instruction, assessments and student motivation, and information and communication technology.

April
Robert Lynn Canady
Rick Stiggins

682 Hitting the High Notes of Literacy
Proliteracy Volunteers of America
1320 Jamesville Avenue
Syracuse, NY 13210
315-422-9121
888-528-2224
Fax: 315-422-6369
E-mail: lvanat@aol.com
http://www.literacyvolunteers.org

49

Conference dealing with literacy issues.

November
50 booths with 1,000 attendees
Peggy May, Conference Manager
David Harvey, President

683 INFOCOMM Tradeshow
8401 Eagle Creek Parkway
Suite 700
Savage, MN 55378
952-894-6280
800-582-6480
Fax: 877-894-6918
E-mail: chief@chiefmfg.com
http://www.chiefmfg.com
Chief Manufacturing is the leader in total mounting solutions for presentation systems. Based in Minnesota, Chief designs, manufactures and distributes worldwide, a full line of mounts, lifts and accessories for LCD/DLP/CRT projectors, large flat panel displays and small flat panel displays.

Cristy Sabatka, Sales Admin. Coordinator

684 Improving Student Performance
National Study of School Evaluation
9115 Westside Parkway
Alpharetta, GA 30009-4958
847-995-9080
888-413-3669
Fax: 847-995-9088
E-mail: schoolimprovement@nsse.org
http://www.nsse.org
A comprehensive guide for data-driven and research-based school improvement planning.

November

Dr. Mark A Elgart, President

685 Increasing Student Achievement in Reading, Writing, Mathematics, Science
National School Conference Institute
PO Box 37527
Phoenix, AZ 85069-7527
602-371-8655
Fax: 602-371-8790
http://www.nscinet.com

March

Orlando Taylor
George Nelson

686 Independent Education Consultants Association Conference
3251 Old Lee Highway
Suite 510
Fairfax, VA 22030-1504
703-591-4850
800-888-4322
Fax: 703-591-4860
E-mail: requests@IECAonline.com
http://www.IECAonline.com
National professional association of educational counselors working in private practice. Provides counseling in college, secondary schools, learning disabilities and wilderness therapy programs. Publishes a monthly newsletter called 'Insight'.

Spring & Fall
400 booths with 800 attendees
Mark H Sklarow, Executive Director
Susan Millburn, Conference Manager

687 Infusing Brain Research, Multi-Intelligence, Learning Styles and Mind Styles
National School Conference Institute
Crowne Plaza Hotel
Phoenix, AZ 85069-7527

602-371-8655
Fax: 602-371-8790
http://www.nscinet.com
Two pre-conference workshops: Intelligences in the curriculum and classroom, and What do educators need to know about the human brain? Conference will also hold over 50 breakout sessions.

February

Geoffrey Caine
Renate Caine

688 Instant Access: Critical Findings from the NRC/GT
University of Connecticut
2131 Hillside Road
Unit 3007
Storrs, CT 06269
860-486-4826
Fax: 860-486-2900
http://www.gifted.uconn.edu
Conference sponsored by the National Research Center on the Gifted and Talented.

March

689 Integrated/Thematic Curriculum and Performance Assessment
National School Conference Institute
Hyatt Regency Hotel
Phoenix, AZ 85069-7527
602-371-8655
Fax: 602-371-8790
http://www.nscinet.com
Two pre-conference workshops: The door to restructuring, aligning, and integrating the curriculum for the 21st century, and Moving assessment to the top of the charts. Conference will also hold over 50 breakout sessions.

February

Heidi Hayes Jacobs
Roger Taylor

690 International Performance Improvement Conference Expo
International Society for Performance
1400 Spring Street
Suite 260
Silver Spring, MD 20910
301-587-8570
Fax: 301-587-8573
E-mail: info@ispi.org
http://www.ispi.org

April
60 booths with 1500 attendees
Ellen Kaplan, Conference Manager

691 Iteachk
Society for Developmental Education
10 Sharon Road
PO Box 577
Peterborough, NH 03458
800-462-1478
Fax: 800-337-9929
http://www.iteachk.com
National conference for kindergarten teachers.

692 Journalism Education Association
Kansas State University
103 Kedzie Hall
Manhattan, KS 66506-1505
785-532-5532
866-532-5532
Fax: 785-532-5563
E-mail: lindarp@ksu.edu
http://www.jea.org
An organization of about 2,300 journalism teachers and advisers, offers two national teacher-student conventions a year, quarterly newsletter and magazines, bookstore and national certification program. This association

serves as a leader in scholastic press freedom and media curriculum.
Jack Kennedy, President

693 Literacy Volunteers of America National Conference
5795 Widewaters Parkway
Syracuse, NY 13214-1846
315-472-0001
Fax: 315-422-6369
Workshops to promote literacy and reading.
November
30 booths with 1000+ attendees
Peg Price, Conference Contact

694 Lutheran Education Association Convention
Lutheran Education Association
7400 Augusta Street
River Forest, IL 60305-1402
708-209-3343
Fax: 708-209-3458
E-mail: lea@crf.cuis.edu
http://www.lea.org
Equip, and affirms educators in Lutheran ministries, helping them become excellent educators.

Kathy Slupik, Executive Assistant
Jonathan C Laabs, Executive Director

695 MEMSPA Annual State Conference
Michigan Elementary & Middle School Principals
Association
1980 N. College Road
Mason, MI 48854
517-694-8955
Fax: 517-694-8945
E-mail: bob@memspa.org
http://www.memspa.org
Professional association for elementary & middle level principals.

Annual/December

Robert E Howe, Jr., Executive Director
Darla Campbell, President

696 Master Woodcraft Inc.
1312 College Street
Oxford, NC 27565
919-693-8811
800-333-2675
Fax: 919-693-1707
Announcement and classroom chalkboards, arts and craft supplies. Cork bulletin boards, dry erase melamine boards, easels, floor, table top, lap boards (white melamine dry erase, chalkboard and magnetic).

2 booths with 6 exhibits

Louis B Moss, Manager

697 Meeting the Tide of Rising Expectations
1225 Providence Road
PMB #116
Whitinsville, MA 01588-3267
508-380-1202
Fax: 508-278-5342
E-mail: nasdtec@attbi.com
http://www.nasdtec.org
NASDTEC is the National Association of State Directors of Teacher Education and Certification. It is the organization that represents professional standards boards and commissions and state departments of education in all 50 states.

October

Roy Einreinhofer, Executive Director

698 Modern Language Association Annual Conference
26 Broadway
3rd Floor
New York, NY 10004-6935
646-576-5000
Fax: 646-458-0030
http://www.mla.org
Promotes and explains the role of language, specifically second language training, in education.

December

Rosemary G Feal, Executive Director

699 Music Educators National Conference
1806 Robert Fulton Drive
Reston, VA 20191-4348
703-860-4000
800-336-3768
Fax: 703-860-1531
http://www.menc.org
Provides a forum for music educators and other musical development in the school setting.

April

700 Music Teachers Association National Conference
Music Teachers National Association
441 Vine Street
Suite 505
Cincinnati, OH 45202-2811
513-421-1420
888-512-5278
Fax: 513-421-2503
E-mail: mtnanet@mtna.org
http://www.mtna.org
Supports and supplies music teachers with information on development and training.

March
160 booths with 2000 attendees

Rachel Kramer, Assistant Executive Director

701 NAAEE Annual Conference
North American Assoc for Environmental Education
2000 P Street NW
Suite 540
Washington, DC 20036
202-419-0412
Fax: 212-419-0415
E-mail: info@naaee.org
http://www.naaee.org

October
1000+ attendees

Brian Bray, Executive Director
Bridget Chisholm, Conference Manager

702 NAAEE Member Services Office
2000 P Street NW
Suite 540
Washington, DC 20036
202-419-0412
Fax: 202-419-0415
E-mail: brian@naaee.org
http://www.naaee.org
Exhibitors seeking to integrate and expand environmental education in school systems and in nonformal settings as well.

September

Brian A Day, Executive Director

703 NAFSA: National Association of International Educators
1307 New York Ave. NW
8th Floor
Washington, DC 20005-5747
202-737-3699
800-836-4994
Fax: 202-737-3657
http://www. nafsa.org
Annual meeting of professionals in the field of international education, with exhibits of services and products relating to international education.

May
150 booths with 5,500 attendees

Marlene M Johnson, Director/CEO

704 NASDSE National Conference
National Association of State Directors of Special
Education
1800 Diagonal Road, Suite 320
Alexandria, VA 22314
703-519-3800
Fax: 703-519-3808
E-mail: nasdse@nasdse.org
http://www.nasdse.org
NASDSE has been providing leadership to improve educational services and outcomes for students with disabilities.

Bambi Lockman, President
Stephanie Petska, Secretary/Treasurer

705 NASPA Annual Conference
NASPA-Student Affairs Administrators in Higher
Education
111 K Street NE, 10th Floor
Washington, DC 20002
202-265-7500
Fax: 202-898-5737
E-mail: office@naspa.org
http://www.naspa.org
Educational sessions, speakers, workshops and networking

Annual/March
5000 attendees

Elizabeth Griego, President

706 NSTA Educational Workshops
National Science Teachers Association
1840 Wilson Boulevard
Arlington, VA 22201-3000
703-243-7100
888-400-6782
Fax: 703-243-7177
http://www.nsta.org
To promote excellence and innovation in science teaching and learning for all.

Alan McCormack, President

707 National Academy Foundation Annual Institute for Staff Development
National Academy Foundation
39 Broadway
Sutie 1640
New York, NY 10006
212-635-2400
Fax: 212-635-2409
http://cssrs.ou.edu
Features several days of intensive peer training, industry presentations, and networking opportunities, with the goal of ensuring that Academy programs are successful, focused on the improvement of public education, and dedicated toward helping young people of all backgrounds continue their education as a step toward building careers.

July

708 National Alliance of Black School Educators Conference
310 Pennsylvania Avenue SE
Washington, DC 20003-3819
202-608-6310
800-221-2654
Fax: 202-608-6319
E-mail: nabse@nabse.org
http://www.nabse.org
Teachers, principals, specialists, superintendents, school board members and higher education personnel. Workshops, plenary sessions, public forums, networking and fellowship.

November
300 booths with 3,500 attendees

Quentin R Lawson, Conference Manager/Executive

709 National Art Education Association Annual Convention
National Art Education Association
1806 Robert Fulton Drive
Suite 300
Reston, VA 20191-1590
703-860-8000
Fax: 703-860-2960
E-mail: naea@dgs.dgsys.com
http://www.naea-reston.org
Containing booths of art education products and services. New art techniques, skills, and knowledge; renowned speakers and teachers; new ideas for art instruction and curriculum.

March
171 booths with 5,000 attendees

Kathy Duse, Conference Manager

710 National Association for Bilingual Education
8701 Georgia Avenue
Suite 611
Silver Spring, MD 20910-4018
240-450-3700
Fax: 240-450-3799
E-mail: nabe@nabe.org
http://www.nabe.org
Contains publishers and Fortune 500 companies displaying educational materials and multi-media products.

March
350 booths with 8,000 attendees

Dr. Santiago Wood, Executive Director
Josephina Velasco, Conference Manager

711 National Association for College Admission Counseling Conference
Nat'l Association for College Admission Counseling
1050 N Highland Street
Suite 400
Arllington, VA 22201-2818
703-836-2222
Fax: 703-243-9375
http://www.nacac.com
Membership association offering information to counselors and guidance professionals working in the college admissions office.

September
142 booths with 4,000 attendees

Shanda T Ivory, Chief Officer Communications
Amy C Vogt, Assistant Director

712 National Association for Girls and Womenin Sports Yearly Conference
1900 Association Drive
Reston, VA 20191-1599
703-476-3400
800-213-7193
Fax: 703-476-4566
E-mail: nagws@aahperd.org
http://www.aahperd.org

An association providing information for girls and women in sports.

March/April
280 booths with 6,000 attendees
Vicki J. Worrell, President

713 **National Association for Multicultural Education**
NAME National Office
1511 K Street NW
Suite 430
Washington, DC 20005
202-628-6263
Fax: 202-628-6264
E-mail: nameorg@erols.com
http://www.inform.umd.edu/name
Keynote speakers and presenters are individuals and educators who value and appreciate diversity and multiculturalism, seek creative approaches to educative practices, and strive to promote social justice through education and training.

714 **National Association for Year-Round Education Annual Conference**
5404 Napa Street
Suite A
San Diego, CA 92110-7319
619-276-5296
Fax: 858-571-5754
E-mail: info@nayre.org
http://www.NAYRE.org
Fosters the study of year-round education as a way to improve educational programs in terms of providing quality education and adapting the school calendar to community and family living patterns Disseminates information about year-round education.

February
60 booths with 1200 attendees
Marilyn J Stenvall, Executive Director
Don Jeffries, Exhibit Coordinator

715 **National Association of Biology Teachers Conference**
1313 Dolley Madison Blvd.
Suite 402
McLean, VA 22101
703-264-9696
Fax: 703-790-2672
E-mail: office@nabt.org
http://www.nabt.org
Contains textbooks, laboratory and classroom supplies and equipment.

November
140 booths with 1,700 attendees
Donald French, President

716 **National Association of Elementary School Principals Conference**
1615 Duke Street
Alexandria, VA 22314-3406
703-684-3345
800-386-2377
Fax: 703-518-6281
E-mail: lburnett@naesp.org
http://www.naesp.org
Products and services in the educational market shopping area. Industry leaders offer practical ways from curriculum resources and instructional aids to fundraising ideas and playground equipment.

April
300 booths
Barbara Chester, President
Lani Burnett, Exhibit Manager

717 **National Association of Independent Schools Conference**
1620 L Street NW
11th Floor
Washington, DC 20036-5695
202-973-9700
Fax: 202-973-9790
E-mail: bassett@nais.org
http://www.nais.org
Publications, statistics, professional development for independent schools.

February/March
166 booths
Peter D Relic, President

718 **National Association of Private Schools for Exceptional Children Conference**
1522 K Street NW
Suite 1032
Washington, DC 20005-1211
202-408-3338
Fax: 202-408-3340
E-mail: napsec@aol.com
http://www.napsec.com
This in an annual conference that is held for administrators/directors/principals and private school educators.

January
300 attendees and 8 exhibits
Barb DeGroot, Manager

719 **National Association of School Psychologists Annual Convention**
4340 EW Highway
Suite 402
Bethesda, MD 20814
301-657-0270
Fax: 301-657-0275
E-mail: center@naspweb.org
http://www.nasponline.org
Gathering of school psychologists and related professionals, offering over 500 workshops, seminars, symposia, papers, presentations and exhibits.

April
100 booths with 4000 attendees
Kathleen Minke, President

720 **National Association of Student Financial Aid Administrators**
1101 Connecticut Avenue
Suite 1100
Washington, DC 20036-5020
202-785-0453
Fax: 202-785-1487
http://www.nasfaa.org
Exhibits computer hardware and software and banks participating in student loan programs.

July
105 booths
Babara Kay Gordon, Conference Contact
Justin Draeger, President

721 **National Association of Teachers' Agencies Conference**
National Association of Teachers' Agencies
799 Kings Highway
Fairfield, CT 06432
203-333-0611
Fax: 203-334-7224
E-mail: fairfieldteachers@snet.net
http://www.jobsforteachers.com
Mark King, Secretary/Treasurer

722 **National Black Child Development Institute Annual Conference**
1313 L Street NW
Suite 110
Washington, DC 20005-2618

202-833-2220
800-556-2234
Fax: 202-833-8222
E-mail: moreinfo@ndcdi.orh
http://www.nbcdi.org
Offers information to counselors and social service workers on African-American Children.

October
Vicki Pinkston, Vice President
Michael G Johnson, Board Chair

723 **National Catholic Education Association Annual Convention & Exposition**
National Catholic Educational Association
1005 North Glebe Road
Suite 525
Arlington, VA 22201-3852
202-337-6232
800-711-6232
Fax: 703-243-0025
http://www.ncea.org
The convention features general sessions with outstanding speakers, special convention liturgies, and a large exposition of many products and services to benefit the educator.

April
675 booths
Leonard DeFiore, President

724 **National Center for Montessori Education Conference**
PO Box 1543
Roswell, GA 30077-1543
770-434-1128
Focuses on developing and maintaining the Montessori Education system.
March
Kristen Cook, Conference Contact

725 **National Coalition for Sex Equity in Education**
PO Box 534
Annandale, NJ 08801-0534
908-735-5045
Fax: 908-735-9674
The only national organization for gender equity specialists and educators. Individuals and organizations committed to reducing sex role stereotyping for females and males. Services include an annual national training conference, a quarterly newsletter and a membership directory. Members may join task forces dealing with equity related topics such as computer/technology issues, early childhood, male issues, sexual harassment prevention, sexual orientation and vocational issues.

Theodora Martin, Business Manager

726 **National Coalition of Alternative Community Schools**
PO Box 15036
Santa Fe, NM 87506-5036
505-474-4312
888-771-9171
A clearinghouse for information regarding alternatives in education for all ages, including home education. Yearly conference, newsletters, mentored Teacher Education Program.

April
Ed Nagel, National Office Manager

727 National Coalition of Title 1-Chapter 1 Parents Conference
Edmonds School Building
9th & D Streets NE
#201
Washington, DC 20002
202-547-9286
Provides lectures and presentations aimed at Chapter 1 parents and professionals.
October

728 National Conference on Student Services
Magna Publications
2718 Dryden Drive
Madison, WI 53704
608-227-8109
800-206-4805
Fax: 608-246-3597
E-mail: carriej@magnapubs.com
http://www.magnapubs.com
Target hard to reach college audiences, and attract campus leaders. Each 4-day conference has potential for the right exhibitor. A second conference will be held in Boston.

October
15 booths with 500 attendees
Carrie Jenson, Conference Manager
David Burns, Associate Publisher

729 National Congress on Aviation and Space Education
Omni Rosen Hotel
Orlando, FL
334-953-5095
E-mail: bspick@cap.af.mil
http://www.cap.af.mil
Provides educators with the tools that make classroom learning fun.
April

730 National Council of Higher Education
National Education Association (NEA)
1201 16th Street NW
Washington, DC 20036-3207
202-822-7162
Fax: 202-822-7974
E-mail: nche@nea.org
http://www.nea.org
Assessing a 20 year journey of the academy.

February, March
400 attendees
Rachel Hendrickson, Coordinator

731 National Council on Alcoholism & Drug Abuse
8790 Manchester Road
Brentwood, MO 63144
314-962-3456
Fax: 314-968-7394
E-mail: ncada@ncada-stl.org
http://www.ncada-stl.org
A not-for-profit community health agency serving the metropolitan St. Louis area, provides educational materials on substance abuse and addiction, information and referral services, prevention and intervention.

Harriet Kopolow, Director Prevention

732 National Dropout Prevention Center/Network Conference
205 Martin Street
Clemson, SC 29631-1555
864-656-2599
800-443-6392
Fax: 864-656-0136
E-mail: ndpc@clemson.edu
http://www.dropoutprevention.com

Concentrating on programs and services for educators and counselors who deal with at-risk students.

October
100 booths with 1000 attendees
Jay Smink, Executive Director
John Peters, Network Coordinator

733 National Education Association-Retired
National Education Association (NEA)
1201 16th Street NW
Washington, DC 20036-3207
202-822-7125
Fax: 202-822-7974
http://www.nea.org/retired
Serves as a resource in the maintenance of quality public education, promotes improved services and legislation for members, provides training for members and serves as a vehicle for local input to the National Education Association.

150 attendees
Deborah C Jackson, Manager
Todd Crenshaw, Coordinator

734 National Guild of Community Schools of theArts Conference
520 8th Avenue
Suite 302, 3rd Floor
New York, NY 10018
212-268-3337
Fax: 212-268-3995
E-mail: info@natguild.org
http://www.nationalguild.org
The National Guild of Community Schools of the Arts fosters and promotes the creation and growth of high-quality arts education in communities across the country. The Guild provides community arts organizations with multiple levels of support, including training, advocacy, information resources, and high-profile leadership in arts education.

November
15 booths with 300 attendees and 15 exhibits
Noah Xifr, Director Membership/Oper.

735 National Head Start Association Annual Conference
1651 Prince Street
Alexandria, VA 22314-2818
703-739-0875
Fax: 703-739-0878
http://www.nhsa.org
Seeks to advance program development, policy and promote training of the Head Start program professionals.

May
A Renee Battle, CMP, Conference Contact
Ruby Lewis-Riar, Conference Assistant

736 National Institute for School and Workplace Safety Conference
160 Internation Parkway
Suite 250
Heathrow, FL 32746
407-804-8310
Fax: 407-804-8306
http://www.nisws.com/
Believes that every school and workplace must implement school and workplace safety standards.

April
80 attendees
Wolfgang Halbig, CEO/Manager

737 National Parent-Teacher Association Annual Convention & Exhibition
1787 Agate Street
Eugene, OR 97403-1923
503-346-4414
Addresses parent-teacher involvement in education. Includes lectures, workshops and seminars for parents and professionals.
June

738 National Reading Styles Institute Conference
PO Box 737
Syosset, NY 11791-3933
512-224-4555
800-331-3117
Fax: 516-921-5591
http://www.nrsi.com
This conference addresses reading instruction and the problems of illiteracy.
July
Juliet Carbo, Conference Contact

739 National Rural Education Annual Convention
National Rural Education Association
230 Education
Colorado State University
Fort Collins, CO 80523-0001
970-491-1101
Fax: 970-491-1317
Exchanges ideas, practices and better ways to enhance rural educational school systems.

October
30 booths with 400 attendees
Joseph T Newlin, PhD, Conference Contact

740 National Rural Education AssociationAnnual Convention
National Rural Education Association
820 Van Vleet Oval
Room 227
Norman, OK 73019
Fax: 405-325-7959
E-mail: bmooney@ou.edu
http://www.nrea.net
The NREA will be the leading national organization providing services which enhance educational opportunities for rural schools and their communities.

October
35 booths with 400 attendees
Bob Mooneyham, Executive Director

741 National School Boards Annual Conference
1680 Duke Street
Alexandria, VA 22314-3493
703-838-6722
Fax: 703-683-7590
http:// ww.nsba.org/itte
The nation's largest policy and training conference for local education officials on national and federal issues affecting public schools in the U.S.

March
7,000 attendees and 300 exhibits
Sandra Folks, Conference/Meetings Coord.
Karen Miller, Exhibit Services Manager

742 National School Conference Institute
11202 N 24th Street
Suite 103
Phoenix, AZ 85029
602-371-8655
888-399-8745
Fax: 602-371-8790
http://www.nscinet.com

Our purpose is to increase every student's opportunity for academic success.

743 National School Supply & Equipment Association
NSSEA Essentials
8380 Colesville Road
Silver Spring, MD 20910
301-495-0240
800-395-5550
Fax: 301-495-3330
E-mail: awatts@nssea.org
http://www.nessa.org
Lists 1,500 member dealers and manufacturers representatives for school supplies, equipment and instructional materials.

March
1200 booths with 5,000 attendees and 700 exhibits
Adrienne Dayton, VP of Marketing/Communicatio
DeShuna Spencer, Editor/Communications Manage

744 National Society for Experiential Education Conference
National Society for Experiential Education
3509 Haworth Drive
Suite 207
Raleigh, NC 27609-7235
919-787-3263
Fax: 919-787-3381
E-mail: info@nsee.org
http://www.nsee.org
To foster the effective use of experience as an integral part of education, in order to empower learners and promote the common good.

October
600-700 attendees

745 National Student Assistance Conference
1270 Rakin Drive
Suite F
Troy, MI 48033-2843
800-453-7733
Fax: 800-499-5718
Learn to maintain and improve safe, drug free schools, student assistance programs. Develop skills to implement the Principles of Effectiveness. Choose from workshops and skill building sessions.

746 National Women's History Project Annual Conference
3440 Airway Drive
Suite F
Santa Rosa, CA 95403-8518
707-636-2888
Fax: 707-636-2909
E-mail:
nwhp@aol.commailto:nwhp@nwhp.org
http://www.nwhp.org
Posters, reference books, curriculum materials and biographies of American women in all subjects for grades K-12.

July
72 attendees

Molly Murphy MacGregor, Conference Manager

747 New Learning Technologies
Society for Applied Learning Technology
50 Culpeper Street
Warrenton, VA 20186
540-347-0055
800-457-6812
Fax: 540-349-3169
E-mail: info@lti.org
http://www.salt.org

To provide a comprehensive overview of the latest in research, design, and development in order to furnish attendees information on systems that are applicable to their organizations.

748 North American Montessori Teachers' Association
13693 Butternnut Road
Burton, OH 44021
440-834-4011
Fax: 440-834-4016
E-mail: staff@montessori-namta.org
http://www.montessori-namta.org/
Professional organization for Montessori teachers and administrators. Services include The NAMTA Journal and other publications, videos and slide shows. Conferences in January and March.

David J Kahn, Executive Director

749 Parents as Teachers National Center Conference
2228 Ball Drive
Saint Louis, MO 63146
314-432-4330
Fax: 314-432-8963
E-mail: patnc@patnc.org
http://www.patnc.org
An international early childhood parent education and family support program designed to enhance child development and school achievement through parent education accessible to all families. Serves families throughout pregnancy and until their child enters kindergarten, usually age 5.

April-May
40 booths with 1400+ attendees
Susan S Stepleton, President/CEO
Cheryl Dyle-Palmer, Director Operations

750 Retention in Education Today for All Indigenous Nations
National Conference Logistics Center
University of Oklahoma
1639 Cross Center Drive, Suite 101
Norman, OK 73019-7820
405-325-3760
800-203-5494
Fax: 405-325-7075
E-mail: tmonnard@ou.edu
http://www.conferencepros.com
National conference designed to discuss and share retention strategies for indigenous students.

Theresa Monnard, Program Coordinator

751 SERVE Conference
SERVE
5900 Summit Avenue, #201
Browns Summit, NC 27214
336-315-7400
800-755-3277
Fax: 336-315-7457
E-mail: jsanders@serve.org
http://www.serve.org
The Regional Educational Laboratories are educational research and development organizations supported by contracts with the US Education Department, National Institute for Education Sciences. Specialty area: Expanded Learning Opportunities.

October-November
Jack Sanders, Executive Director

752 School Equipment Show
830 Colesville Road
Suite 250
Silver Spring, MD 20910-3297
301-495-0240
800-395-5550

Fax: 301-495-3330
E-mail: customerservice@nnsea.org
http://www.nnsea.org
Annual show featuring exhibits from manufacturers of school equipment such as bleachers, classroom furniture, lockers, playground and athletic equipment, computer hardware, software, etc.

February
Elizabeth Bradley, Conference Contact

753 Sexual Assault and Harassment on Campus Conference
c/o Sexual Conference
PO Box 1338
Holmes Beach, FL 34218-1338
800-537-4903
http://www.ed.mtu.edu
Topics include gender based hate crime, sexual assault investigators, generational legacy of rape, innovations in the military, sexual harassment in K-12, updates on date-rape drugs and many more. Hosted by the Hyatt Orlando Hotel in Kissimmee, Florida.

Karen McLaughlin, Conference Co-Chair
Alan McEvoy, Conference Co-Chair

754 Society for Research in Child Development Conference
5720 S Woodlawn Avenue
Chicago, IL 60637-1603
773-702-7700
Fax: 773-702-9756
Working to further research in the area of child development and education.

March/April
40 booths
Barbara Kahn, Conference Contact

755 Teacher Link: An Interactive National Teleconference
Center for the Study of Small/Rural Schools
555 E Constitution Street
Room 138
Norman, OK 73072-7820
405-325-1450
Fax: 405-325-7075
E-mail: jcsimmons@ou.edu
http://cssrs.ou.edu
Prevention Series

Spring
5 booths with 100 attendees
Jan C Simmons, Director

756 Teachers of English to Speakers of Other Languages Convention and Exhibit
1925 Ballenger Avenue
Suite 550
Alexandria, VA 22314
703-836-0774
888-547-3369
Fax: 703-836-6447
http://www.tesol.org
Leading worldwide professional development opportunity. Simulating program of presentations sponsored by nineteen interest sections, a half-dozen caucus groups and TESOL's advocacy division as well as sessions invited especially for their relevance to our work and our students.

March
245 booths with 8000 attendees
Bart Ecker, Manager
Rosa Aronson, Executive Director

757 Teaching for Intelligence Conference
SkyLight
2626 S Clearbrook Drive
Arlington Heights, IL 60005

847-290-6600
800-348-4474
Fax: 877-260-2530
E-mail: info@irisskylight.com
http://www.irisskylight.com
Focuses on student achievement, brain-based learning and multiple intelligences.

April

758   Technology & Learning Schooltech Exposition & Conference
212-615-6030
http://www.SchoolTechExpo.com
Over 150 targeted sessions specifically designed for all education professionals: technology directors, teachers, principals, superintendents and district administrators.

759   Technology Student Conference
Technology Student Association
1914 Association Drive
Reston, VA 20191-1538
703-860-9000
Fax: 703-758-4852
http://www.tsawww.org
Devoted to the needs of technology education students and supported by educators, parents, and business leaders who believe in the need for a technologically literate society.

June
2,500 attendees
Rosanne White, Conference Manager

760   Technology in 21st Century Schools
National School Conference Institute
PO Box 37527
Phoenix, AZ 85069-7527
602-371-8655
Fax: 602-371-8790
http://www.nscinet.com
Conference will cover managing the Internet, literacy skills, Web Site designs, short and long term planning, creating curriculum, and staff development. Being held at the Boston Park Plaza Hotel in Boston, Massachusetts.

July
Alan November

761   Technology, Reading & Learning Difficulties Conference
International Reading Association
19 Calvert Court
Piedmont, CA 94611
510-594-1249
888-594-1249
Fax: 510-594-1838
http://www.trld.com
Focuses on ways to use technology for reading, learning difficulties, staff development, adult literacy, and more.

January

762   Training of Trainers Seminar
Active Parenting Publishers
1955 Vaughn Road NW
Suite 108
Kennesaw, GA 30144-8943
770-429-0565
800-825-0060
Fax: 770-429-0334
E-mail: cservice@activeparenting.com
http://www.activeparenting.com
Delivers quality education programs for parents, children and teachers to schools, hospitals, social services organizations, churches and the corporate market.

Dana McKie, Training Coordinator

763   USC Summer Superintendents' Conference
University of Southern California, School of Ed.
Waite Room 901
Los Angeles, CA 90089-0001
213-740-2182
Fax: 213-749-2707
E-mail: lpicus@bcf.usc.edu
A select group of educational leaders nationwide engaged in reform practices offer discussions with nationally renowned speakers; tour innovative schools; and network with colleagues from the United States, Great Britain and Australia.

Lawrence O Picus, Conference Director
Carolyn Bryant, Conference Coordinator

Northeast

764   Clonlara School Annual Conference HomeEducators
Clonlara Home Based Education Programs
1289 Jewett Street
Ann Arbor, MI 48104-6201
734-769-4511
Fax: 734-769-9629
E-mail: info@clonlara.org
http://www.clonlara.org
Clonlara School is committed to illuminating educational rights and freedoms through our actions and deep dedication to human rights and dignity.

June
300 attendees
Terri Wheeler, Associate Director

765   Connecticut Library Association
PO Box 85
Williamantic, CT 06226-0085
860-465-5006
Fax: 860-465-5004
E-mail: kmcnulty@avon.lib.ct.us
Holds a conference in April and publishes a journal.
April
1000 attendees and 100 exhibits
Karen McNulty, President
Mary Rupert, Manager

766   Hoosier Science Teachers Association Annual Meeting
5007 W 14th Street
Indianapolis, IN 46224-6503
317-244-7238
Fax: 317-486-4838
Papers, workshops, demonstrations and presentations in each area of science.
February
78 booths
Edward Frazer, Conference Contact

767   Illinois Library Association Conference
Illinois Library Association
33 W Grand Avenue
Suite 301
Chicago, IL 60654-4306
312-644-1896
Fax: 312-644-1899
E-mail: ila@ila.org
http://www.ila.org
More than 70 program sessions, exploring nearly every facet of library services, from building projects and professional recruit-

ment to storytelling and the latest revisions of AACR2.

September
2,400+ attendees
Cyndi Robinson, Conference Manager
Bob Doyle, Executive Director

768   Illinois Vocational Association Conference
230 Broadway
Suite 150
Springfield, IL 62701-1138
217-585-9430
Fax: 217-544-0208
E-mail: iva@eosinc.com
Equipment and supplies, publications, teaching aids, computers and food services.

February
75 booths with 600 attendees
Karen Riddle, Conference Contact

769   National Association of Student Financial Aid Administrators
1101 Connecticut Avenue NW
Suite 1100
Washington, DC 20036-3453
202-785-0453
Fax: 202-785-1487
http://www.nasfaa.org
Exists to promote the professional preparation, effectiveness, and mutual support of persons involved in student financial aid administration.

May
40 booths
Suzy Allen, President

770   New Jersey School Boards Association Annual Meeting
413 W State Street
PO Box 909
Trenton, NJ 08605-0909
609-695-7600
888-886-5722
Fax: 609-695-0413
http://www.njsba.org
School/office supplies, furniture, equipment, counseling services and more.

October
630 booths with 9,000 attendees
Wendy L. Wilson, Conference Contact

771   New York State Council of Student Superintendents Forum
111 Washington Avenue
Suite 104
Albany, NY 12210-2210
518-449-1063
Fax: 518-426-2229
Offers educational products and related services.

February
12 booths
Dr. Claire Brown, Conference Contact

772   Northeast Regional Christian SchoolsInternational Association
845 Silver Spring Plaza
Suite B
Lancaster, PA 17601-1183
717-285-3022
Fax: 717-285-2128
http://www.acsi.org
40 booths.
November

Alan Graustein, Conference Contact

773 Ohio Library Council Trade Show
35 E Gay Street
Suite 305
Columbus, OH 43215-3138
614-221-9057
Fax: 614-221-6234
Exhibits will offer products and services for library administrators and professionals.
May
Lori Hensley, Exhibits Manager

774 Ohio School Boards Association Capital Conference & Trade Show
700 Brooksedge Boulevard
Westerville, OH 43081-2820
614-891-6466
Provides school officials from Ohio an opportunity to gain information about products, equipment, materials and services.

November
425 booths
Richard Lewis, Conference Contact

775 Satellites and Education Conference
189 Schmucker Science Center
W Chester University
West Chester, PA 19383
610-436-1000
Fax: 610-436-2790
http://www.sated.org/eceos
The Satellite Educators Association was established in 1988 as a professional society to promote the innovative use of satellite technology in education and disseminate information nationally to all members.

March
15 booths with 200 attendees
Nancy McIntyre, Director

776 UNI Overseas Recruiting Fair
University of Northern Iowa
102 Gilchrist Hall
Cedar Falls, IA 50614-0390
319-273-2083
Fax: 319-273-6998
E-mail: overseas.placement@uni.edu
http://www.uni.edu/placement/overseas
About 160 recruiters from 120 schools in 80 countries recruit at this fair for certified K-12 educators.
February
Tracy Roling, Coordinator

777 Wisconsin Vocational Association Conference
44 E Mifflin Street
Suite 104
Madison, WI 53703-2800
608-283-2595
Fax: 608-283-2589
Trade and industry vendor equipment and book publishers.
April
50 booths
Linda Stemper, Conference Contact

Northwest

778 Montana High School Association Conference
1 S Dakota Street
Helena, MT 59601-5111
406-442-6010
School athletic merchandise.
January
15 booths
Dan Freund, Conference Contact

779 Nebraska School Boards Association Annual Conference
140 S 16th Street
Lincoln, NE 68508-1805
402-475-4951
Fax: 402-475-4961
60 booths exhibiting products and services directed at the public school market.
November
60 booths
Burma Kroger, Conference Contact

780 North Dakota Vocational Educational Planning Conference
State Capitol
600 East Boulevard Avenue, Dept. 270
Bismarck, ND 58505
701-328-3180
Fax: 701-328-1255
E-mail: cte@nd.gov
http://www.nd.gov/cte/
August
30 booths
Ernest Breznay, Conference Contact

781 Pacific Northwest Library Association
Boise Public Library
715 Capitol Boulevard
Boise, ID 83702
208-384-4026
Fax: 208-384-4156
E-mail: sprice@pobox.ci.boise.id.us
Holds a conference in August and publishes a journal.
Susannah Price, President
Colleen Bell, Secretary

782 WA-ACTE Career and Technical Exhibition for Career and Technical Education
Washington Association for Career & Tech Education
PO Box 315
Olympia, WA 98507-0315
360-786-9286
Fax: 360-357-1491
E-mail: kal@wa-acte.org
http://www.wa-acte.org

August
40 booths with 1,000 attendees
Tim Knue, Executive Director

Southeast

783 Association for Continuing Higher Education Conference
Trident Technical College
PO Box 118067
Charleston, SC 29423-8067
843-722-5546
Fax: 843-574-6470
15 tabletops.
October
Dr. Wayne Whelan, Executive VP

784 Center for Play Therapy Summer Institute
University of North Texas
PO Box 311337
Denton, TX 76203
940-565-3864
Fax: 940-565-4461
E-mail: cpt@coefs.coe.unt.edu
http://www.centerforplaytherapy.com
Encourage the unique development and emotional growth of children through the process of play therapy, a dynamic interpersonal relationship between a child and a therapist trained in play therapy procedures. The therapist provides the child with selected play materials and facilitates a safe relationship to express feelings, thoughts, experiences and behaviors through play, the child's natural medium of communication.
July
500 attendees
Garry Landreth PhD, Director

785 Missouri Library Association Conference
1306 Business 63 S
Suite B
Columbia, MO 65201
573-449-4627
Fax: 573-449-4655
E-mail: jmccartn@mail.more.net
http://www.mlnc.com/~mla/
The mission of the Missouri Library Network Corporation (MLNC) is to organize and deliver to its member libraries and other contracting entities OCLC-based information services, related electronic services and content, and training in the management and use of information.

October
75 booths with 400 attendees
Margaret Conroy, President
Jean Ann McCartney, Executive Director

786 National Youth-At-Risk Conference
Georgia Southern University
PO Box 8124
Statesboro, GA 30460
912-681-5555
Fax: 912-681-0306
http://http://ceps.georgiasouthern.edu/conte d/nationalyouthatrisk.h
Stresses education and development for professionals working with at-risk students.

February
Sybil Fickle, Conference Contact

787 Technology and Learning Conference
National School Boards Association
1680 Duke Street
Alexandria, VA 22314
703-838-6722
Fax: 703-683-7590
E-mail: info@nsba.org
http://www.nsba.org
This conference offers programs, equipment, services, and ideas. It will be held at the Dallas Convention Center.

Southwest

788 Children's Literature Festival
Department of Library Science
Sam Houston State University
PO Box 2236
Huntsville, TX 77341-2236
936-294-1614
Fax: 936-294-3780
This annual event is sponsored by the Department of Library Science at Sam Houston State University.

789 Colorado Library Association Conference
3030 W 81st Avenue
Westminister, CO 80031
303-463-6400
Fax: 303-458-0002

E-mail: executivedirector@cal-web.org
http://www.cal-webs.org

October
60 booths with 450 attendees
Terri Switzer, President
Linda Conway, Vice President

**790 Phoenix Learning Resources
Conference**
12 W 31st Street
New York, NY 10001-4415
212-629-3887
800-221-1274
Fax: 212-629-5648
Supplemental and remedial reading and language arts programs for early childhood, K-12, and adult literacy programs.

Alexander Burke, President
John Rothermich, Executive VP

**791 Southwest Association College and
University Housing Officers**
Sam Houston State University
PO Box 2416
Huntsville, TX 77341-2416
936-294-1812
Fax: 936-294-1920
Products and services for college and university housing.

Febuary/March
45 booths

E Thayne King, Conference Contact

**792 Texas Classroom Teachers Association
Conference**
PO Box 1489
Austin, TX 78767-1489
512-477-9415
Fax: 512-469-9527
http://www.tcta.org
Educational materials, fundraising and jewelry.

February
150 booths

Jan Lanfear, Conference Contact

793 Texas Library Association Conference
3355 Bee Cave Road
Suite 401
Austin, TX 78746-6763
512-328-1518
800-580-2852
Fax: 512-328-8852
E-mail: pats@txla.org
http://www.txla.org
Established in 1902 to promote and improve library services in Texas.

March
750 booths with 6,000 attendees
Herman L Totten, President
Kathy Pustyovsky, Meetings Manager

**794 Texas Vocational Home Economics
Teachers Association Conference**
3737 Executive Center Drive
Suite 210
Austin, TX 78731-1633
512-794-8370

July/August

Terry Green, Conference Contact

**795 Western History Association Annual
Meeting**
University of New Mexico
Mesa Room 1080
Albuquerque, NM 87131-0001
505-277-5234
Fax: 505-277-6023

Exhibits by book sellers.
October
45 booths
Paul Hutton, Conference Contact

General

796 Accuracy Temporary Services Incorporated
1431 E 12 Mile Road
Madison Hieghts, MI 48071-2653
248-399-0220
Educational consultant for public and private schools.

Howard Weaver, President

797 Add Vantage Learning Incorporated
6805 Route 202
New Hope, PA 18938
800-230-2213
Fax: 215-579-8391
http://http://www.vantagelearning.com/
Management and educational consultant for the general public.

Jim Pepitone, Chairman

798 Advance Infant Development Program
2232 D Street
Suite 203
LaVerne, CA 91750-5409
909-593-3935
Fax: 909-593-7969
Business and educational consultant for general trade.

Diane Hinds, President
Jeanine Coleman, Executive Director

799 Aguirre International Incorporated
555 Airport Boulevard
Suite 400
Burlingame, CA 94010-3349
650-373-4900
Fax: 650-348-0260
E-mail: aguirre@aiweb.com
http://http://aguirre-1.interliant.com/aiweb/
home.nsf/Home?OpenPage
Educational, data, market analysis, statistical and research consultants for US Government Agencies.

Edward Aguirre, President
Ronald Rodgers, Senior VP Operations

800 American International Schools
2203 Franklin Road SW
Roanoak, VA 24014-1109
852-233-3812
Fax: 852-233-5276
E-mail: asisadmin@ais.edu.hk
American International School is pledged to preparing students to contribute to an increasingly international and interdependent world. AIS strives to provide an atmosphere conducive to building interpersonal relationships and global awareness. AIS is committed to working closely with students and families to attain academic excellence and to inspire the growth of well-rounded individuals.

Andrew Hurst, President
Lewis C Smith Jr, Executive VP

801 Area Cooperative Educational Services
350 State Street
North Haven, CT 06473
203-498-6881
Fax: 203-498-6817
http://http://www.aces.org
ACES is the regional educational service center for twenty-five school districts in south central Connecticut.

Robert D Parker, Marketing Specialist
Craig W Edmondson, Executive Director

802 Aspira of Penna
2726 N 6th Street
Philadelphia, PA 19133-2714
215-229-1226
Educational consultant for educational institutions.

Oscar Cardona, President

803 Association for Refining Cross-Cultured International
Japanese American Cultural Center
244 S San Pedro Street
Suite 505
Los Angeles, CA 90012
213-620-0696
Fax: 213-620-0930
E-mail: support@eryugaku.org
http://www.arcint.com
Educational consultants for international studies.

Chiey Nomura, Director

804 Association of Christian Schools International
PO Box 69103
Colorado Springs, CO 80962-3509
719-528-6906
Fax: 719-531-0631
E-mail: webmaster@acsi.org
http://www.acsi.org
Educational consultant for Christian Schools.

Brian S Simmons, President

805 Auerbach Central Agency for Jewish Education Incorporated
7607 Old York Road
Melrose Park, PA 19027-3010
215-635-8940
Fax: 215-635-8946
E-mail: lbalaban@acaje-jop.org
http://www.acaje.org
Educational consultants.

Lynne Balaban, Director

806 Basics Plus
921 Aris Avenue
Suite C
Metairie, LA 70005-2200
504-832-5111
Fax: 504-832-5110
Educational consultants.

Scott Green, President

807 Beacon Education Management
112 Turnpike Road
Suite 107
Westborough, MA 01581
508-836-4461
800-789-1258
Fax: 508-836-2604
http://www.beaconedu.com
A K-12, education services company that offers contracted management services to public schools and charter school boards. Currently operating 27 charter schools in Massachusetts, Michigan, Missouri and North Carolina.

808 Beverly Celotta
13517 Haddonfield Lane
Gaithersburg, MD 20878
301-330-8803
E-mail: drbev@comcast.net
http://www.celotta.net
Provides psychological and educational services to organizations that serve children and parents.

809 Bluegrass Regional Recycling Corporation
360 Thompson Road
Lexington, KY 40508-2045
859-233-7300
Fax: 859-233-7787
Consultants for educational, training, and services for governments and school systems.

Douglas Castle, Chairman

810 CPM Educational Program
1233 Noonan Drive
Sacramento, CA 95822-2569
916-446-9936
Fax: 916-444-5263
http://www.cpm.org
Educational and training consultants for school districts.

Gthomas Sallee, President Human Resource Dir
Carol Cho, Regional Coordinator

811 Caldwell Flores Winters
2187 Newcastle Avenue
Suite 201
Cardiff, CA 92007-1848
760-634-4239
800-273-4239
Fax: 760-436-7357
E-mail: cfw@cfwinc.com
http://http://www.cfwinc.com/index.html
Offers educational counsel to school districts.

Ernesto Flores, President
Scott Gaudineer, AIA, Program Executive

812 Career Evaluation Systems
1024 N Oakley Boulevard
Suite 4
Chicago, IL 60622-3586
773-772-9595
800-448-7552
Fax: 773-772-5010
Testing instruments for vocational evaluation.

813 Carnegie Foundation for the Advancement of Teaching
51 Vista Lane
Stanford, CA 94305
650-566-5100
Fax: 650-326-0278
E-mail:
publications@carnegiefoundation.org
http://http://www.carnegiefoundation.org/
Educational consultant for the educational field.

Anthony S Bryk, President

814 Carney Sandoe & Associates
44 Bromfield Street
Boston, MA 02108-4608
617-542-0260
Fax: 617-542-9400
http://www.carneysandoe.com/
Educational consultant for private schools.

James H Carney, Chairman/President

815 Carter/Tardola Associates
419 Pleasant Street
Suite 307
Beloit, WI 53511
608-365-3163
Fax: 608-365-5961
E-mail: tardola@tucm.net
http://http://www.carter-tardola.com/
Evaluates program, administration, staff, resource and time organization, and utilization of resources. Proposal development, language skills development, diversity training.

Betty Tardola, Educational Consultant

816 Center for Educational Innovation
28 W 44th Street
Suite 300
New York, NY 10036-6600
212-302-8800
Fax: 212-302-0088
E-mail: vchabrier@cei-pea.org
http://www.cei-pea.org/
Educational consultant for private and commercial accounts.

Vivian Chabrier, Director

817 Center for Professional Development & Services
408 N Union Street
Po Box 7888
Bloomington, IN 47407-0789
812-339-1156
800-766-1156
Fax: 812-339-0018
E-mail: information@pdkintl.org
http://www.pdkintl.org
Examines school district curriculum management system. Determines how effectively a school district designs and delivers its curriculum.

Sandra Crowther, Ed D, President
Kathleen Andreson, President-Elect

818 Center for Resource Management
200 International Drive
Suite 201
Portsmouth, NH 03801
603-427-0206
Fax: 603-427-6983
E-mail: info@crminc.com
Employment, human resources, educational, development, training, computer software, organizational and management consultants for Human Service Agencies and Educational Institutions/ Schools.

Mary Ann Lachat, Chairman/President
Martha Anderson, Vice President

819 Child Like Consulting Limited
700 E Rambling Drive
Wellington, FL 33414-5010
561-798-5847
800-487-6725
Fax: 866-468-4555
Training in literacy, music, classroom and learning center management.

820 Children's Educational Opportunity Foundation
901 McClain Road
Suite 802
Bentonville, AR 72712-9242
479-273-6957
Fax: 479-273-9362
Educational consultant for institutions.

Fritz Steiger, President

821 Childs Consulting Associates
514 Lakeside Drive
Mackinaw City, MI 49701
231-436-4099
Fax: 231-436-4101
E-mail: info@childs.com
http://www.childs.com
Educational, schools and technology consultants for schools, banking and automotive industries.

John W Childs, Chief Executive Officer
Jack Keck, Vice President

822 Classroom
245 5th Avenue
Room 1901
New York, NY 10016-8728
212-545-8400
800-258-0640
Fax: 212-481-7178
http://www.classroominc.org
Technology based curriculum and teacher professional development for middle school and high school use.

George Demarco, VP
Jane Canner, President

823 Coalition of Essential Schools
1814 Franklin Street
Suite 700
Oakland, CA 94612
510-433-1451
Fax: 510-433-1455

The Coalition of Essential Schools (CES) is a leading comprehensive school reform organization, fundamentally changing the way people think about teaching and learning and transforming American education.

Hudi Podolsky, Executive Director

824 College Bound
17316 Edwards Road
Suite 180
Cerritos, CA 90703
562-860-2127
Fax: 562-860-1957
E-mail: info@collegeboundca.org
http://www.collegeboundca.org
Educational consultants.

Johnnie Savoy, President
Cynthia Moore, Executive Assistant

825 College Entrance Examination Board
45 Columbus Avenue
New York, NY 10023-6917
212-713-8000
E-mail: emonts@umich.edu
http://www.collegeboard.com
Educational, research, testing and financial consultant for learning institutions and students.

Gaston Caperton, President
Lester P Monts, Chair

826 Community Connections
1695 Old West Broad Street
Athens, GA 30606
706-353-1313
800-924-5085
Fax: 706-353-1375
E-mail: jmeehan@communityconnection211.org
http://www.communityconnection211.org
Educational consultant for the general public.

Julie Meehan, Director

827 Community Foundation for Jewish Education
618 S Michigan Avenue
10th Floor
Chicago, IL 60605-1901
312-913-1818
Fax: 312-913-1763
Educational consultant for the general public and schools.

Howard Swibel, President

828 Connecting Link
387 Coopers Pond Drive
Siute 1
Lawrenceville, GA 30044-5231
770-979-5804
Fax: 770-931-6831
Business and educational consultants for teachers.

Dr. Bernard F Cleveland, President

829 Conover Company
4 Brookwood Court
Appleton, WI 54914-8618
920-231-4667
800-933-1933
Fax: 800-933-1943
E-mail: sales@conovercompany.com
http://www.conovercompany.com
Training and setting up workplace literacy programs; emotional intelligence assessment and skill enhancement; functional literacy software, career exploration and assessment software

Rebecca Schmitz, Member

830 Consortium on Reading Excellence
2560 Nineth Street
Suite 220
Berkley, CA 94710-1923

888-249-6165
Fax: 888-460-4520
E-mail: info@corelearn.com
http://www.corelearn.com
Educational consultant for public and private schools.

Bill Honing, President
Linda Diamond, CEO

831 Continuous Learning Group Limited Liability Company
500 Cherrington Corprate Center
Site 350
Pittsburgh, PA 15108
412-269-7240
Fax: 412-269-7247
E-mail: info@clg.com
http://www.clg.com
Educational consultants.

Hillary Potts, President, CEO

832 Corporate Design Foundation
20 Park Plaza
Suite 400
Boston, MA 02116-4303
617-566-7676
E-mail: admin@cdf.org
Educational consultant for universities and colleges.

Peter G Lawrence, Chairman

833 Corporate University Enterprise
7600 Leesburg Pike West Building
Suite 202
Falls Church, VA 22043
703-848-0070
866-848-1675
Fax: 703-848-0071
E-mail: info@cuenterprise.com
Corporate University Enterprise, Inc. is and educational consulting firm designed to bring a strategic approach to workforce education in both private and public organizations. The company was incorporated in 1998 and has since served clients throughout the United States, Europe, and Asia.

John H. Wells, Senior Advisor
Karen Barley, President

834 Council for Aid to Education
215 Lexington Avenue
21st floor
New York, NY 10016-1599
212-661-5800
Fax: 212-661-9766
http://www.cae.org
Non-profit educational consultant for government and commercial concerns.

Roger Benjamin, President
Michael Rich, Vice President

835 Council on Occupational Education
41 Perimeter Center E
#640
Atlanta, GA 30346-1903
770-396-3898
800-917-2081
Fax: 770-396-3790
E-mail: bowmanh@council.org
http://www.council.org
Managerial and educational consultant for post secondary technical education institutions.

Dr. Harry Bowman, President
Gary Puckett, CEO

836 Creative Learning Consultants
1990 Market Road
Marion, IL 62959-1906
800-729-5137
Fax: 800-844-0455
E-mail: info@piecesoflearning.com
http://www.piecesoflearning.com

Educational consulting for school districts, teachers, book stores and parents.

Stanley Balsamo, Secretary/Treasurer
Kathy Balsamo, President

837 Creative Learning Systems
2065 S Escondido Blvd
Suite 108
Escondido, CA 92025
800-458-2880
Fax: 858-592-7055
E-mail: info@creativelearningsystems.com
http://www.creativelearningsystems.com
Educational consulting firm.

Matt Dickstein, Chief Executive Officer

838 Dawson Education Cooperative
711 Clinton Street
Suite 201
Arkadelphia, AR 71923-5921
870-246-3077
Fax: 870-246-5892
E-mail: rds@dawson.dsc.k12.ar.us
http://www.dawson.dsc.k12.ar.us
Educational consulting group.

Nathan Gills, President

839 Dawson Education Service Cooperative
711 Clinton Street
Suite 201
Arkadelphia, AR 71923-5921
870-246-3077
Fax: 870-246-5892
http://www.dawson.dsc.k12.ar.us
Educational and organizational consultants for school districts

Becky Jester, Director

840 Designs for Learning
2233 University Ave W
Suite 450
St. Paul, MN 55114-1634
651-645-0200
Fax: 651-645-0240
E-mail: dalley@designlearn.net
http://www.designlearn.net
Educational consultants for primary schools and the private sector.

David Alley, President
Andrew Adelmann, Project Coordinator

841 Direct Instructional Support Systems
535 Lakeview Plaza Blvd.
Suite B
Worthington, OH 43085-4146
614-846-8946
Fax: 614-846-1794
Educational consultant for public and private agencies.

Gary Moore, President

842 Dr. Anthony A Cacossa
4300 N Charles Street
Apartment 9B
Baltimore, MD 21218-1052
410-889-1806
Fax: 410-889-1806
Assists schools in marketing academic programs that offer internship opportunities.

843 EPIE InstituteEducational Products Information Exchange Institut
103 West Montauk Highway
PO Box 590
Hampton Bays, NY 11946-4006
631-728-9100
E-mail: kkomoski@epie.org
http://www.epie.org
Curriculum development, training and evaluation of education products.

844 EPPA Consulting
1116 Comanche Trail
Georgetown, KY 40324-1071
502-863-6053
Fax: 502-867-0157
E-mail: eppa@juno.com
Strategic and operational planning.

Theo R Leverenz, PhD, Contact, Owner

845 East Bay Educational Collaborative
317 Market Street
Warren, RI 02885
401-245-4998
Fax: 401-253-6547
http://www.ebecri.org
Business and educational consultant for member school districts.

Gerald Kowalczyk, Executive Director

846 East Central Educational Service Center
1601 Indiana Avenue
Connersville, IN 47331
765-825-1247
Fax: 765-825-2532
E-mail: harrison@ecesc.k12.in.us
http://www.ecesc.k12.in.us
Educational services for school districts in East Central Indiana.

William J Harrison, Executive Director

847 Edge Learning Institute
2515 South Hood Street
Tacoma, WA 98402-3320
253-272-3103
800-858-1484
Fax: 253-572-2668
E-mail: cihrig@edgelearning.com
http://www.edgelearning.com
Educational consultants for the general public, commercial concerns, government agencies and school districts.

Chris Ihrig, CEO
Anita Paige, Vice President

848 Edison Schools
485 Lexington Avenue
2nd Floor
New York, NY 10017
212-419-1600
Fax: 212-419-1746
E-mail: information@edisonlearning.com
http://www.edisonschools.com
The country's largest private manager of public schools. Implemented its design in 79 public schools, including 36 charter schools, which it operates under management contracts with local school districts and charter school boards.

Jeff Wahl, President, CEO

849 Education Concepts
9861 Strausser Street
Canal Fulton, OH 44614
330-497-1055
Fax: 330-966-8000
E-mail: info@ed-concepts.com
http://www.ed-concepts.com
Professional development programs for early childhood educators.

850 Education Data
1305 E Waterman
Witchata, KS 67211
800-248-4135
Expertise in organizational needs assessments.

851 Education Development Center
55 Chapel Street
Newton, MA 02158
617-969-7100
Fax: 617-969-5979
http://www.edc.org

Developing programs in science, mathematics, reading, writing, health and special education.

852 Education Management Consulting LLC
49 Coryell Street
Lambertville, NJ 08530
609-397-8989
800-291-0199
Fax: 609-397-1999
E-mail: edragan@edmgt.com
http://www.edmgt.com
Consultation for schools on special education and administration consultation for lawyers working on education and school related issues.

Dr. Edward F Dragan, President

853 Educational Consultants of Oxford
10431 Highway 51 S
Courtland, MS 38620
601-563-8954
All areas of educational information services, tutoring, scholarship information, and non-traditional and overseas training.

854 Educational Credential Evaluators
260 East Highland Avenue
PO Box 514070
Milwaukee, WI 53202
414-289-3400
Fax: 414-289-3411
E-mail: eval@ece.org
http://www.ece.org
Evaluates foreign educational credentials.

James Frey, President
Margit Schatzman, VP

855 Educational Data Service
236 Midland Avenue
Saddle Brook, NJ 07663-4604
973-340-8800
Fax: 973-340-0078
http://www.ed-data.com
Educational and school consulting for Boards of Education.

Gil Wohl, President
Alan Wohl, Chairman

856 Educational Information & Resource Center
900 Hollydell Drive
Sewell, NJ 08080
856-582-7000
Fax: 856-582-4206
E-mail: info@eirc.org
http://www.eirc.org
Programs and consulting services for schools, on many topics from teaching techniques to technical assistance.

857 Educational Resources
8910 W 62nd Terrace
Shawnee Mission, KS 66202-2814
913-362-4600
Fax: 913-362-4627
Educational consulting for colleges.

Michael Frost, President
Karen Harrison, VP

858 Educational Services Company
3535 East 96th Street
Suite 126
Indianapolis, IN 46240-1754
317-818-3535
888-351-3535
Fax: 317-818-3533
http://www.educationalservicesco.com
Educational and management consulting for primary and secondary schools.

Douglas Cassman, President
William McMaster, Secretary

859 Educational Specialties
9923 S Wood Street
Chicago, IL 60643-1809
773-445-1000
Fax: 773-445-5574
http://www.educationalspecialties.com
Educational consultant for schools.

Elois W Steward, President

860 Educational Systems for the Future
14650 Viburnum Drive
Dayton, MD 21036
410-531-3737
Fax: 410-531-3939
E-mail: info@esf-protainer.com
http://www.esf-protainer,com
Development of teaching skills, training
needs analysis, and training management.

**861 Educational Technology Design
Consultants**
100 Allentown Parkway
Suite 110
Allen, TX 75002
972-727-1234
Fax: 972-727-1491
http://www.etdc.com/html/about_us.html
Developing system design for virtual campus
control and support.

862 Educational Testing Service
Rosedale Road
Princeton, NJ 08541-0001
609-921-9000
Fax: 609-734-5410
http://www.ets.org
Educational and professional consulting for
schools.

Kurt M. Landgraf, President
Sharon Robison, COO, Senior VP

863 Edusystems Export
820 Wisconsin Street
Walworth, WI 53184-9765
262-275-5761
Fax: 262-275-2009
E-mail:
sales@edusystems.com;admin@edusystems.
com
Expertise in educational systems.

864 Effective Schools Products
2199 Jolly Road
Suite 160
Okemos, MI 48864-5983
517-349-8841
800-827-8041
Fax: 517-349-8852
http://www.effectiveschools.com
Publishing consultants for schools, teachers,
directors of planning and others in this field.

Ruth Lezotte, PhD, President

865 Effective Training Solutions
103 Linden Street
Oakland, CA 94607-1447
510-834-1901
800-949-5035
Fax: 510-834-1905
E-mail: boris@trainingsuccess.com
http://www.trainingsuccess.com
Design and implementation of training strategies. Proficiency training-performance improvement training.

Ingrid Gudenas, CEO

866 Efficacy Institute
182 Felton Street
Waltham, MA 02453-4134
781-547-6060
Fax: 781-547-6077
E-mail: info@efficacy.org
http://www.efficacy.org

Non-profit, educational consultants for educational and community service institutions.

Jeff P Howard, President
Mike Hyter, Treasurer

867 Emerging Technology Consultants
216 Heritage Lane
New Brighton, MN 55112
651-639-3973
Fax: 651-639-3973
Serves as a connection between technology
producers and the education and training industries.

Richard Pollak, Chief Executive Officer
Rubyanna Pollak, President

868 Epistemological Engineering
5269 Miles Avenue
Oakland, CA 94618-1044
510-653-3377
866-341-3377
Fax: 866-879-7797
E-mail: publications@eeps.com
http://www.eeps.com
Educational consultants.

Tim Erickson, President

869 Examiner Corporation
600 Marshall Avenue
Suite 100
St. Paul, MN 55102-1723
651-451-7360
800-395-6840
Fax: 651-451-6563
E-mail: examine@xmn.com
Educational and certification evaluation in-
struments.

Gary C Brown, President
Michelle Smith, Sales and Marketing

870 Excell Education Centers
3807 Wilshire Boulevard
Los Angeles, CA 90010-3101
213-386-1953
Educational and planning consultants.

Raymond Hahl, Owner

871 FPMI Communications
707 Fiber Street NW
Huntsville, AL 35801-5833
256-539-1850
Fax: 256-539-0911
http://www.fmpi.com
Educational management consulting.

872 First District Resa
201 West Lee Street
P.O. Box 780
Brooklet, GA 30415
912-842-5000
Fax: 912-842-5161
http://www.fdresa.org
Educational consultants for the general public and commercial concerns.

Shelly Smith, Executive Director

**873 Foundation for Educational
Innovation**
401 M Street SW
2nd Floor, Suite 1
Washington, DC 20024-2610
202-554-7400
Fax: 202-554-7401
Educational consultant for educa-
tional/school systems.

Archie Prioleau, President

874 George Dehne & Associates
3331 Cotton Field Drive
Mt. Pleasant, SC 29466-3836
843-971-9088
800-942-7427

Fax: 843-971-7759
http://www.dehne.com
Educational and business consultants for
commercial concerns and colleges.

George Dehne, President

875 Health Outreach Project
825 Cascade Avenue
Atlanta, GA 30331-8362
404-755-6700
Educational consultants.

Sandra McDonald, President

876 Higher Education Consortium
2233 University Avenue W
Suite 210
St. Paul, MN 55104-1205
651-646-8831
Fax: 651-659-9421
Educational consultants.

Jenny Keyser, Executive Director

877 Highlands Program
PO Box 76168
Atlanta, GA 30358-3915
404-497-0835
Educational consultants for educational insti-
tutions, corporations and consumers.

Don Hutcheson, President

878 Howard Greene Associates
60 Post Road W
Westport, CT 06880-4208
203-226-4257
Fax: 203-226-5595
E-mail:
counseling@howardgreeneassociates.com
http://www.greenesguides.com
Educational consultants for school systems
and individuals.

Howard Greene, President

879 Huntley Pascoe
19125 N Creek Parkway
Bothel, WA 98011-8035
425-485-0900
Fax: 425-487-1825
Educational consultant for architects, utility
companies, computer facilities, school districts and hospitals.

Roger Huntley, President

880 Ingraham Dancu Associates
1265 Lakevue Drive
Butler, VA 16002
724-586-8761
Fax: 724-586-6638
E-mail: dedance@msn.com
Development planning for educational and
industrial clients.

Dr. Daniel Dancu, Contact

881 Innovative Learning Group
10261 Canteberry Street
Westchester, IL 60154-1780
708-865-7752
Educational consultants for schools and the
general public.

Joseph Elliott, President

882 Innovative Programming Systems
9001poplar Bridge Road
Bloomington, MN 55437
612-835-1290
Development of instructional and training
programs.

883 Insight
12 S 6th Street
Suite 510
Minneapolis, MN 55402-1510
612-338-5777

Educational consultants for commercial concerns.

Mark Kovatch, President

884 Institute for Academic Excellence
901 Deming Way
Suite 301
Madison, WI 53717-1964
608-664-0965
Fax: 608-664-382
Educational consultants for K-12 schools.

John Hickey, Chairman

885 Institute for Development of Educational Activities
259 Regency Ridge
Dayton, OH 45459
937-434-6969
Fax: 937-434-5203
E-mail: ideadayton@aol.com
http://www.idea.com
Assistance for administrators and teachers of elementary and secondary schools.

886 Institute for Global Ethics
91 Camden Street
Suite 403
Rockland, ME 04843-1703
207-594-6658
800-729-2615
Fax: 207-594-6648
E-mail: ethics@globalethics.org
http://www.globalethics.org
Educational consultants for the general public, corporations and educators.

Rushworth Kidder, President

887 Interface Network
321 SW 4th Avenue
Suite 502
Portland, OR 97204-2323
503-222-2702
Fax: 503-222-7503
E-mail: www.daggettt.com
http://info@leaderEd.com
Educational consultant for the United States Department of Education, businesses, school districts and other governmental agencies.

888 International Center for Leadership in Education
1587 Route 146
Rexford, NY 12148
518-399-2776
Fax: 518-399-7607
E-mail: info@leadered.com
http://www.leadered.com
Educational consultants for educational institutions, governments and commercial concerns.

Willard R Daggett, President

889 International Schools Association
3, Chemin des Tulipiers
CH-1208, Geneva
Switzerland
41 -9 3-8 94
39-011-645-967
Fax: 39-011-643-298
E-mail: info@isaschools.org
http://www.isaschools.org
Provides advisory and consultative services to its international and internationally minded member schools, as well as to other organizations in the field of education, such as UNESCO. The Association promotes innovations in international education, conducts conferences and workshops and publishes various educational materials.

Katherine Kastoryano, Executive Director

890 J&Kalb Associates
300 Pelham Road
Suite 5K
New Rochelle, NY 10805
914-636-6154
Consulting experience to school districts.

891 JCB/Early Childhood Education Consultant Service
813 Woodchuck Place
Bear, DE 19701
302-836-8505
Program design and cross-cultural staff development through seminars.

892 JJ Jones Consultants
1206 Harrison Avenue
Oxford, MS 38655-3904
662-234-6755
Educational consultant for high school and college students.

JJ Jones, Owner

893 JP Associates Incorporated
131 Foster Avenue
Valley Stream, NY 11580-4726
516-561-7803
Fax: 516-561-4066
Educational consultant for schools.

Jane Dinapoli, President

894 Janet Hart Heinicke
1302 W Boston Avenue
Indianola, IA 50125
515-961-8933
Fax: 515-961-8903
E-mail: heinicke@simpson.edu
Development of new programs and maintenance strategies.

895 Jobs for California Graduates
2525 O Street
Merced, CA 95340-3634
209-385-8466
Educational consultants for high school students.

Obie Obrien, Director

896 John McLaughlin Company
1524 S Summit Avenue
Sioux Falls, SD 57105
605-332-4900
Fax: 605-339-1662
http://www.mclaughlincompany.com
Advises companies regarding private-sector activities in K-12 and higher education.

John Laughlin, Owner

897 Johnson & Johnson Associates
3970 Chain Bridge Road
Fairfax, VA 22030-3316
703-359-5969
800-899-6363
Fax: 703-359-5971
E-mail: info@jjaconsultants.com
http://www.jjaconsultants.com
Educational consultants for governmental agencies and commercial concerns.

Dr. Johnson Edosomwan, President/CEO

898 Joseph & Edna Josephson Institute
9841 Airport Blvd.
Suite 300
Los Angeles, CA 90045-6621
310-846-4800
800-711-2670
Fax: 310-846-4858
http://charactercounts.org
Educational consultant for organizations, government, businesses and the general public.

Michael Josephson, President

899 Kaludis Consulting Group
1050 Conn Avenue NW
Suite 10
Washington, DC 20036
202-772-3120
Fax: 202-331-1428
E-mail: info@kaludisconsulting.com
http://www.kaludisconsulting.com
Educational consultants for colleges and universities.

George Kaludis, President/Chairman
Barry M Cohen, Senior Vice President

900 Kentucky Association of School Administrators
152 Consumer Lane
Suite 154
Frankfort, KY 40601-8489
502-875-3411
800-928-kasa
Fax: 502-875-4634
E-mail: webmaster@kasa.com
Educational consultant for school administrators.

V Wayne Young, Director

901 Kleiner & Associates
8636 SE 75th Place
Mercer Island, WA 98040-5235
206-236-0608
Educational consultants for public and private institutions.

Charles Kleiner, Owner

902 Lawrence A Heller Associates
324 Freeport Road
Pittsburgh, PA 15238-3422
412-820-0670
Fax: 412-820-0669
Development and implementation of educational programs.

903 Leona Group
4660 S Hagadorn Road
Suite 500
East Lansing, MI 48823-5353
517-333-9030
Fax: 517-333-4559
http://www.leonagroup.com
Currently manages more than 40 school sites in Michigan, Arizona, Ohio and Indiana

Dr. Bill Coats, CEO

904 Linkage
200 Wheeler Road
Burlington, MA 01803-7305
781-402-5400
Fax: 781-402-5556
E-mail: info@linkage-inc.com
http://www.linkageinc.com
Linkage, Inc. is a global organizational development company that specializes in leadership development.

Philip Harkins, President

905 Logical Systems
605 E 1st Street
Suite 101
Rome, GA 30161-3109
706-234-9896
Fax: 706-290-0998
http://www.logsysinc.com
Educational consultants for school districts.

Francis Ranwez, President

906 Los Angeles Educational Alliance forRestructuring Now
445 S Figueroa Street
Los Angeles, CA 90071
323-255-3276
Fax: 213-626-5830
E-mail: asant@ccf-la.org

Educational consulting for school systems.

Mary Chambers, Vice President
Michael Roos, President

907 Louisiana Children's Research Center for Development & Learning
1 Galleria Blvd.
Suite 903
Metairie, LA 70001-3036
504-840-9786
Fax: 504-840-9968
http://www.cdl.org
Educational consultants for the general public.

Alice P Thomas, President, CEO

908 MK & Company
132 Bronte Street
San Francisco, CA 94110
415-826-5923
Program development and project management for educational products, services and organizations.

909 MPR Associates
2150 Shattuck Avenue
Suite 800
Berkeley, CA 94704-1321
510-849-4942
Fax: 510-849-0794
E-mail: info@mprinc.com
http://www.mprinc.com
Educational consultants for governmental, educational and commercial concerns including law firms.

Gary Hoachlander, President

910 Magi Educational Services Incorporated
7-11 Broadway
Suite 402
White Plains, NY 10601-3546
914-682-1861
Fax: 914-682-1760
E-mail: info@westchesterinst.com
http://www.westchesterinst.org
Educational consultant for educational institutions.

Dr. Ronald Szczypkowski, President

911 Management Concepts
8230 Leesburg Pike
Suite 800
Vienna, VA 22182-2639
703-790-9595
800-506-4450
Fax: 703-790-1371
E-mail: csmith@managementconcepts.com
http://www.managementconcepts.com
Educational consultants for commercial and governmental concerns.

Thomas F. Dungan III, CEO

912 Management Simulations
540 W Frontage Road
Suite 3270
Winnetka, IL 60093-1250
877-477-8787
E-mail: welcome@capsim.com
http://www.capsim.com
Educational consultants for commercial concerns and universities.

Daniel Smith, President

913 Marketing Education Resource Center
1375 King Avenue
PO Box 12279
Columbus, OH 43212-2220
614-486-6708
800-448-0398
Fax: 614-486-1819
http://www.mbaresearch.org

Educational, development and curriculum consulting for high schools and post secondary schools.

James R Gleason Ph.D., President, CEO

914 Maryland Educational Opportunity Center
2700 Gwynns Falls
Baltimore, MD 21216
410-728-3400
888-245-2774
Fax: 410-523-6340
E-mail: edhoward@meoconline.com
http://www.meoconline.com
Consultant services for educational institutions.

Ellen Howard, Executive Director

915 Maryland Elco Incorporated Educational Funding Company
4740 Chevy Chase Drive
Chevy Chase, MD 20815-6461
301-654-8677
Fax: 301-654-7750
http://www.efconline.com
Educational, accounting and billing consultants for service and vocational schools and businesses.

Nicholas Cokinos, Chairman

916 Mason Associates
142 N Mountain Avenue
Montclair, NJ 07042
201-744-9143
Educational services for independent secondary schools, colleges and universities.

917 Matrix Media Distribution
28310 Roadside Drive
Suite 237
Agoura, CA 91301-4951
818-865-3470
Educational consultant for the educational market.

Paul Luttrell, President

918 McKenzie Group
1100 17th Street NW
Suite 1100
Washington, DC 20036-4638
202-466-1111
Fax: 202-466-3363
Educational consultant for commercial concerns and government.

Floretta D McKenzie, President

919 Measurement
423 Morris Street
Durham, NC 27701-2128
919-683-2413
Fax: 919-425-7726
http://www.measurementinc.com
Educational, research, testing and printing consultant for schools, state governments and private businesses.

Henry H Scherich, President/CEO

920 Measurement Learning Consultants
80920 Highway 10
Tolovana Park, OR 97145
503-436-1464
Business, educational, testing and development consultants for the general public and commercial concerns such as schools.

Albert G Bennyworth, Partner

921 Merrimack Education Center
101 Mill Road
Chelmsford, MA 01824-4844
978-256-3985
Fax: 978-937-5585
http://www.mec.edu

Educational consultant for educational facilities.

John Barranco, Executive Director

922 Michigan Education Council
40440 Palmer Road
Canton, MI 48188-2034
734-729-1000
Fax: 734-729-1004
Educational consultant for individuals.

Dawud Tauhidi, Director

923 Midas Consulting Group
4600 S Syracuse Street
Suite 900
Denver, CO 80237
303-256-6500
Fax: 866-790-9500
E-mail: info@midasconsultinggroup.com
http://www.midasconsultinggroup.com
Educational consultant for schools, universities, training centers and government agencies.

Michael Blimes, Executive Consultant

924 Miller, Cook & Associates
1606 Bellview Avenue
Suite 1
Roanoke, VA 24014-4923
540-345-4393
800-591-1141
Fax: 239-394-2656
E-mail: info@millercook.com
http://www.millercook.com
Educational consultants for colleges and universities.

William B Miller, President

925 Model Classroom
4095 173rd Place SW
Bellvue, WA 98008-5929
425-746-0331
Educational consultant for school districts, commercial concerns and the Department of Education.

Cheryl Avena, Owner

926 Modern Educational Systems
15 Limestone Terrace
Ridgefield, CT 06877-2621
203-431-4144
Educational consultant for schools.

Edward T McCormick, President

927 Modern Red Schoolhouse Institute
1901 21st Avenue
South Nashville, TN 37212-1502
615-320-8804
888-275-6774
Fax: 615-320-5366
E-mail: info@mrsh.com
http://www.mrsh.com
Educational consultant for school districts.

Sally B Kilgore, President

928 Montana School Boards Association
863 Great Northern Blvd.
Suite 301
Helena, MT 59601-5156
406-442-2180
Fax: 406-442-2194
E-mail: cwilson@mtsba.org
http://www.mtsba.org
Training, educational and school districts consultant for school boards.

Charles Wilson, President

929 Montgomery Intermediate Unit 23
1605 W Main Street
Suite B
Norristown, PA 19403-3268

610-539-8550
Fax: 610-539-5073
http://www.mciu.org
Educational consultants for professional associations, groups and student organizations.

Marc Lieberson, President

930 Moore Express
865 Pancheri Drive
Idaho Falls, ID 83402
208-523-6276
Educational consultant for public school districts, state and local governments and commercial concerns.

Lawry Wilde, President

931 Mosaica Education
42 Broadway
Suite 1039
New York, NY 10004
212-292-0305
Fax: 212-232-0309
http://www.mosaicaeducation.com
Manages public schools either under contract with local school districts or funded directly by states under charter school laws that permit private management.

Gene Eidelman, President

932 Multicorp
1912 Avenue K
Suite 210
Plano, TX 75074-5960
972-551-8899
Computer and educational consultant.

Fred Sammet, Chairman

933 National Center on Education & the Economy
2000 Pennsylvania Avenue NW
Suite 5300
Washington, DC 20006-4507
202-379-1800
Fax: 202-293-1560
E-mail: info@ncee.org
http://www.ncee.org
Educational consultant for schools.

Marc S Tucker, President

934 National Evaluation Systems
30 Gatehouse Road
PO Box 226
Amherst, MA 01004
Fax: 413-256-8221
Educational testing, test development, and assessment for education agencies.

935 National Heritage Academies
3850 Broadmoor Avenue SE
Suite 201
Grand Rapids, MI 49512
877-223-6402
Fax: 616-575-6801
E-mail: info@heritageacademies.com
http://www.heritageacademies.com
Manages 22 charter academies (K-8) in Michigan and North Carolina.

2007, Author
Jeff Clark, President, CEO

936 National Reading Styles Institute
179 Lafayette Drive
Syosset, NY 11791
516-921-5500
800-331-3117
Fax: 516-921-5591
E-mail: readingstyle@nrsi.com
http://www.nrsi.com
Educational consultants for schools and educators.

Marie Carbo, Executive Director

937 National School Safety and Security Services
PO Box 110123
Cleveland, OH 44111
216-251-3067
E-mail: kentrump@aol.com
http://www.schoolsecurity.org
National consulting firm specializing in school security and crisis preparedness training, security assessments, and related safety consulting for K-12 schools, law enforcement, and other youth safety providers.

Kenneth S Trump, President/CEO

938 Noel/Levitz Centers
2350 Oakdale Blvd.
Coralville, IA 52241-9581
319-626-8380
800-876-1117
Fax: 319-626-8388
http://www.noellevitz.com
Educational consultant for colleges and universities.

Tom Williams, President/CEO

939 Ome Resa
2023 Sunset Boulevard
Steubenville, OH 43952-1349
740-283-2050
Fax: 740-283-1500
E-mail: angie.underwood@omeresa.net
http://www.omeresa.net
Educational consultants for school districts.

Angela Underwood, Executive Director

940 Oosting & Associates
200 Seaboard Lane
Franklin, TN 37067-8237
615-771-7706
Fax: 615-771-7810
Educational consultants for colleges and universities.

Dr. Kenneth Oosting, President

941 Pamela Joy
1049 Whipple Avenue
Suite A
Redwood City, CA 94062-1414
650-368-9968
Fax: 650-368-2794
Educational consultants for schools.
Pamela Joy, Owner

942 Parsifal Systems
155 N Craig Street
Pittsburgh, PA 15213
412-682-8080
Fax: 412-682-6291
Educational consultants for commercial concerns and schools.

Marcia Morton, President

943 Paul H Rosendahl, PHD
240 Mohouli Street
Hilo, HI 96720-2445
808-935-5233
Fax: 808-961-6998
Science, archaeology, historical, resources and management consultant for developers, government agencies, educational institutions, groups and individuals.

Paul H Rosendahl, Owner

944 Perfect PC Technologies
15012 Red Hill Avenue
Tustin, CA 92780-6524
714-258-0800
Computer consultants for commercial concerns, schools and institutions.

Neil Lin, President

945 Performa
124 N Broadway
De Pere, WI 54115
920-336-9929
Fax: 920-336-2899
E-mail: jeffk@performaic.com
http://www.performainc.com
Planning and facility consultants for higher education, manufacturing and government agencies.

Jeff Kanzelberger, CEO
Doug Page, Chief Operating Officer

946 Poetry Alive!
70 Woodfin Place
Suite WW4C
Asheville, NC 28801
828-255-7636
800-476-8172
Fax: 828-232-1045
E-mail: poetry@poetryalive.com
http://www.poetryalive.com
Educational consultants for commercial concerns and school systems.

Bob Falls, President

947 Post Secondary Educational Assistance
1210 20th Street S
Suite 200
Birmingham, AL 35205-3814
205-930-4930
Fax: 205-930-4905
E-mail: clientservices@peaccorp.com
http://www.peaccorp.com
Educational consultant for commercial concerns.

Kenneth Horne, President

948 Prevention Service
7614 Morningstar Avenue
Harrisburg, PA 17112-4226
717-651-9510
Educational consultant for corporations, private health clubs, school districts and other organizations.

Mark Everest, President

949 Princeton Review
2315 Broadway
2nd Floor
New York, NY 10024-4332
212-874-8282
Fax: 212-874-0775
Educational consultants for commercial concerns.

John Katzman, President

950 Priority Computer Services
4001 Technology Drive
South Bend, IN 46628
574-236-5979
866-661-9049
E-mail: priority@pcserv-inc.com
http://www.prioritycomputer.biz
Computer consultant for commercial education.

Ben Hahaj, President

951 Prism Computer Corporation
2 Park Plaza
Suite 1060
Irvine, CA 92614-8520
800-774-7622
Fax: 949-553-6559
Educational consultant for manufacturers, government agencies and colleges.

Micheal A Ellis, President

952 Professional Computer Systems
849 E Greenville Avenue
Winchester, IN 47394-8441

765-584-2288
Fax: 765-584-1283
Computer consultants for businesses, schools and municipalities.
Steve Barnes, President

953 Professional Development Institute
280 S County Road
Suite 427
Longwood, FL 32750-5468
407-834-5224
Educational consultants for US Department of Transportation and commercial concerns.
Elsom Eldridge, Jr, President

954 Profiles
507 Highland Avenue
Iowa City, IA 52240-4516
319-354-7600
Fax: 319-354-6813
Educational consultants for school districts and commercial concerns.
Douglas Paul, President

955 Pyramid Educational Consultants
13 Garfield Way
Newark, DE 19713
302-368-2515
800-732-7462
Fax: 302-368-2516
E-mail: pyramid@pecs.com
http://www.pecsusa.com
Educational consultant for general trade, historical commissions and other public bodies.
Andrew Bondy, President
Lori Frost, Vice President

956 Quality Education Development
41 Central Park West
New York, NY 10023
212-724-3335
800-724-2215
Fax: 212-724-4913
E-mail: info@qedconsulting.com
Structures courses that promote knowledge and understanding through interactive learning, and communication programs.

957 Quantum Performance Group
5050 Rushmore Road
Palmyra, NY 14522-9414
315-986-9200
Educational consultant for commercial concerns, including schools.
Dr. Mark Blazey, President

958 Rebus
4111 Jackson Road
Ann Arbor, MI 48103-1827
734-668-4870
Fax: 734-913-4750
Educational consultant for schools and school districts.
Linda Borgsdorf, President

959 Records Consultants
10826 Gulfdale Street
San Antonio, TX 78216-3607
210-366-4127
Fax: 210-366-0776
Educational consultant for school districts and municipalities.
Lang Glotfelty, President

960 Regional Learning Service of Central New York
770 James Street Office
Syracuse, NY 13203-1644
315-446-0500
Fax: 315-446-5869
Educational consultants for commercial concerns.
Rebecca Livengood, Executive Director

961 Reinventing Your School Board
Aspen Group International,Inc
PO Box 260301
Highlands Ranch, CO 80163-0301
303-478-0125
Fax: 208-248-6084
Linda Dawson, Contact
Dr. Randy Quinn, Contact

962 Relearning by Design
447 Forcina Hall
PO Box 7718
Ewing, NJ 08628-0718
609-771-2921
Fax: 609-637-5130
E-mail: info@relearning.org
http://www.relearning.org
Grant Wiggins, Author/Editor
Jacquelyn Nance, Chair

963 Research Assessment Management
816 Camarillo Springs Road
Camarillo, CA 93012-9441
805-987-5538
Fax: 805-987-2868
Educational consultants for governmental agencies and commercial concerns.
Adrienne McCollum, PhD, President

964 Robert E Nelson Associates
120 Oak Brook Center
Suite 208
Oak Brook, IL 60523
630-954-5585
Fax: 630-954-5606
Consulting for private colleges, universities and secondary schools.

965 Rookey Associates
1740 Little York Xing
Little York, NY 13087
607-749-2325
Educational consultant for school districts, public utility companies and the government.
Ernest J Rookey, President

966 Root Learning
810 W S Boundary Street
Perrysburg, OH 43551-5200
419-874-0077
Fax: 419-874-4801
Business, educational, employment consultant for commercial concerns.
Randall Root, Chairman/CEO

967 School Management Study Group
1649 Lone Peoh Drive
Salt Lake City, UT 84117
801-277-3725
Fax: 801-277-4547
Organization seeking to promote improvement of schools and to involve educators in critical school problems.
Donald Thomas, President
Dale Holden, Associate

968 SchoolMatch by Public Priority Systems
110 Mohawk Trail
Wayne, NJ 07470
973-831-1757
An educational consultant for private and public schools.
John Pinto, President

969 Sensa of New Jersey
110 Mohawk Trail
Wayne, NJ 07470-5030
973-831-1757
An educational consultant for private and public schools.
John Pinto, President

970 Shirley Handy
19860 Bloss Avenue
Hilmar, CA 95324-8308
209-668-4142
Fax: 209-668-1855
http://www.n-e-n.com
Educational consultants for school districts and teachers.
Shirley Handy, Owner

971 Sidney Kreppel
704 E Benita Boulevard
Vestal, NY 13850-2629
607-754-6870
Educational consultants.
Sidney Kreppel, Owner

972 Solutions Skills
565 E Tennessee Street
Tallahassee, FL 32308-4981
850-681-6543
Fax: 850-681-6543
http://www.solutionskills.com
Business and educational consultants for state and governments, educational, medical and legal publishing companies.
Randall Vickers, President

973 Special Education Service Agency
3501 Denali Street
Suite 101
Anchorage, AK 99503-1068
907-562-7372
Fax: 907-561-7383
E-mail: sesa@sesa.org
http://www.sesa.org
Educational consultant for school districts.
Nancy Nagarkar, Executive Director

974 Sports Management Group
918 Parker Street
Suite A-13
Berkeley, CA 94710
510-849-3090
Fax: 510-849-3094
E-mail: tsmq@sportsmqmt.com
http://www.sportsmgnt.com
Educational consulting for universities.
Lauren Livingston, President

975 Stewart Howe Alumni Service of New York
3109 N Triphammer Road
Lansing, NY 14882
607-533-9200
E-mail: programs@stewarthowe.com
http://www.stewarthowe.com
Educational consultants for college organizations.
Peter McChesney, Director

976 Strategies for Educational Change
11 Whitby Court
Mount Holly, NJ 08060
609-261-1702
E-mail: barbd@prodigy.net
Development of programs for youths at risk.

977 Success for All Foundation
200 W Towsontown Boulevard
Baltimore, MD 21204-5200
410-616-2300
800-548-4998
Fax: 410-324-4444
E-mail: sfainfo@successforall.net
http://www.successforall.net
A not-for-profit organization dedicated to the development, evaluation and dissemination of proven reform models for preschool, elementary and middle schools.
Nancy Madden, Ph.D., CEO

978 Teachers Curriculum Institute
244 W El Cam
Mountain View, CA 94040-4234
650-856-0565
800-497-6138
Fax: 800-343-6828
E-mail: infor@teachtci.com
http://www.teachtci.com
Educational consultant for schools and teachers.

Bert Bower, President

979 Teachers Service Association
1107 E Lincoln Avenue
Orange, CA 92865-1939
714-282-6342
Educational consultants for schools and teachers.

Richard Ghysels, Secretary Treasurer

980 Tech Ed Services
One World Trade Center
8th Floor
Long Beach, CA 90831
562-869-1913
800-832-4411
Fax: 562-869-5673
E-mail: info@techedservices.com
http://techedservices.com
Computer, planning and training consultant for k-12 educators and adult educators.

Patricia K Sanford, President
Brenna Terrones, Corporate Specialists

981 Technical Education Research Centers
2067 Massachusetts Avenue
Cambridge, MA 02140-1340
617-873-9600
Fax: 617-873-9601
E-mail: communications@terc.edu
http://www.terc.edu
Educational consultant for the National Science Foundation and the Department of Education.

Arthur Nelson, Chairman

982 Tesseract Group
4111 E. Ray Road
Suite 2
Phoenix, AZ 85044
480-706-2500
Fax: 480-759-0160
http://www.tesseractgroup.org
An integrated education management company, serving private and public charter elementary, middle and high schools in six states.

Michael Lynch, CEO

983 Timothy Anderson Dovetail Consulting
936 Nantasket Avenue
Hull, MA 02045-1453
781-925-3078
Fax: 781-925-9830
Educational consultant for businesses.

Eric Anderson, Owner

984 University Research
7200 Wisconsin Avenue
Suite 600
Bethesda, MD 20814-4811
301-654-8338
Fax: 301-941-8427
Educational consultants for the federal government along with other government and private sectors.

Barbara M. Turner, President

985 University of Georgia-Instructional Technology
630 Aderhold Hall
Athens, GA 30602
706-542-4110
Fax: 706-542-4240
E-mail: coeinfo@uga.edu
http://www.coe.uga.edu
Instructional design and development.

Aurthur M. Horne, Dean
Pedro R Portes, Professor

986 Uplinc
48 Capital Drive
West Springfield, MA 01089
413-693-0700
E-mail: sales@uplinc.com
http://www.uplinc.com
Computer consultants for commercial, general public and educational concerns.

Ron Marino, President

987 William A Ewing & Company
505 S Main Street
Suite 700
Orange, CA 92868
714-245-1850
Fax: 714-456-1755
E-mail: ewingo@aol.com
http://www.members.aol.com/ewingo
Expertise in compensation and classification.

988 Wisconsin Technical College System Foundation
1 Foundation Circle
Waunakee, WI 53597-8914
608-849-2424
Fax: 608-849-2468
Educational consultant for educational institutions and businesses.

Loren Brumm, Executive Director

Africa

989 Alexandra House School
King George V Avenue
Floreal
Mauritius
230-696-4108
Fax: 230-696-4108
E-mail: admin@alexandrahouseschool.com
http://www.alexandrahouseschool.com
A private English Primary day school in Mauritius for boys and girls between 4 and 11 years of age. Cater for approximately 100 children and provide a British curriculum with a strong international flavour.

M Wrenn-Beejadhur, Principal

990 American International School-Dhaka
United Nations Road Baridhara
Dhaka
Bangladesh
880-2-882-2414
Fax: 880-2-883-3175
E-mail: info@ais-dhaka.net
http://www.ais-dhaka.net
Provides a program based on American educational principles to students from an international community, creates an academic and social environment that challenges students to achieve their potential, become life-long learners and contribute to changing global society.

Kyra Buchko, President
Diane Lindsey, Vice President

991 American International School-Johannesburg
Private Bag X 4
Bryanston 2021
Republic of South Africa
011 464 1505
Fax: 27-11-464-1327
E-mail: info@aisj-jhb.com
http://www.aisj-jhb.com
Serves a diverse community of students from around the world and provides a challenging education emphasizing academic excellence through a collaborative partnership with families and staff. Our program inspires and prepares the students to become responsible world citizens with a passion for life long learning.

Andy Page-Smith, Director
Ellinor Parkes, Admissions Coordinator

992 American International School-Lom
DOS/Administrative Officer
2300 Lome Place
Washington, DC 20521-2300
E-mail: aisl@cafe.tg
http://membres.lycos.fr/aisl
Established in 1967 as a private, coeducational day school offering an educational program to students of all nationalities in pre-kindergarten through grade 8.

Clover Afokpa, Director
Warace Tchamsi, Administrative Assistant

993 American International School-Zambia
PO Box 31617
Lusaka
Zambia
260-211-260509 (10
Fax: 260-211-260-538
E-mail: SpecialPerson@aislusaka.org
http://www.aislusaka.org
Committed to being a leading IB World School, offering a balanced, academically rigorous and internationally recognized college preparatory education and seeks to enable its students to become successful, lifelong learners, as well as humane, self-di-

rected, confident and well-rounded individuals.

Chris Muller, Director
Jim Anderson, Secondary Principal

994 American School of Kinshasa
Unit 31550
APO AE
9828
243-884-6619
Fax: 243-884-1161
E-mail: irene.epp@gmail.com
http://www.tasok.cd
rawing on the strengths of a committed and culturally diverse community, The American School of Kinshasa aims to provide a high quality American primary and secondary education for English speaking students living in the Democratic Republic of Congo

Irene Epp, Superintendent
Fiona M Merali, Business Manager

995 American School-Tangier
Rue Christophe Colomb
Tangier 9000
Morocco
212-39 93 98 27/28
Fax: 212-39 94 75 35
E-mail: ast@tangeroise.net.ma
http://http://www.theamericanschooloftangier.com/
An independent, coeducational day and boarding school which offers an educational program from prekindergarten through grade 12 for students of all nationalities.

Brian Horvath, Head of School

996 American School-Yaounde
BP 7475
Yaounde
Cameroon
237-2223-0421
Fax: 237-2223-6011
E-mail: school@asoy.org
http://asoy.org
Ensures that all students achieve high academic success, demonstrate critical thinking skills, and become responsible and compassionate, global citizens prepared for their next stage in life; as gained through an enriched, American curriculum and offered in a challenging, secure, and diverse environment.

Paul Sheppard, School Director

997 Arundel School
28 Arundel School Road
PO Box MP 91 Mount Pleasant
Harere, Zimbabwe
263-4-335654/7
Fax: 263 4 335671 / 304
E-mail: head@arundel.ac.zw
http://http://www.arundel.ac.zw/
Gives all students the opportunity to reach their full potential, both in and out of the classroom. This is achieved through an active educational program, which encompasses the search for excellence in the fields of academic endeavour, culture, sports and personal development.

G Alcock, Principal

998 Arusha International School
PO Box 733
Moshi, Kilimanjaro
Tanzania
255-27-275-5004
Fax: 255-27-275-2877
E-mail: director@ismoshi.net
http://www.ismoshi.org
Offers a fully accredited, academically rigorous international education for students of ages three to nineteen years old.

Barry Sutherland, CEO
Bob Woods, Director

999 Asmara International Community School
117-19 Street, #6
PO Box 4941, Asmara
Eritrea
291-1-161-705
Fax: 291-1-161-705
E-mail: johnston@gmail.com
http://www.aicsasmara.com
Grade levels pre K-12.

Paul Johnston, Director

1000 Banda School
PO Box 24722
Nairobi
Kenya 00502
254-20-8891220/260
Fax: 254-20-8890004
E-mail: bandaschool@swiftkenya.com
http://www.bandaschool.com
Meet the educational needs of children living in and around Nairobi whose parents required a Preparatory School education for their children but who did not wish them to go to boarding school overseas.

Michael D Dickson, Headmaster
W Rutter, Deputy Head

1001 Bishop Mackenzie International Schools
PO Box 102
Lilongwe
Malawi
265-1-756-364
Fax: 265-1-751-374
E-mail: info@bmismw.com
http://bmis.ecis.org
The mission of the school is to prepare students to become responsible, self-reliant, contributing and productive citizens of our ever-changing world.

Peter Todd, Director
Janette Johnson, Primary Head Teacher

1002 Braeburn High School
Kisongo Campus
Gitanga Road
PO Box 45112 GPO Nairobi
Kenya 100
254-20-5018000
Fax: 254-20-3872310
E-mail: andy.hill@braeburn.ac.ke
http://www.braeburn.com
This is a co-educational international boarding school following the British National Curriculum (University of Cambridge International General Certificate of Secondary Education Examinations IGCSE), with boarding options.

R E Diaper, Principal
Andy Hill, Headteacher

1003 Braeburn School
Gitanga Road
PO Box 45112 GPO Nairobi
Kenya 100
254-722 68557
Fax: 254-2-572310
E-mail: scott.webber@braeburn.ac.ke
http://www.braeburn.com
This school caters to close to 600 children from 61 different countries.

R E Diaper, Principal
Scott Webber, Headteacher

1004 British International School Cairo
km 38, Cairo-Alex Desert Road
Beverly Hills, 6th of October
Egypt, EG
202-3859-2000
Fax: 202-3859-1720
E-mail: info@bisc.edu.eg
http://www.bisc.edu.eg

The School was established in 1976 to provide a balanced and challenging education based on British principles and curricula to meet the needs of the children of the expatriate British and Anglo-Egyptian communities; children from the Commonwealth and other countries with educational systems based upon British standards; children of the English-speaking Egyptian community and other nationalities tied to British-type schooling.

Simon O'Grady, Principal
Ahmed Ezz, Chairman of the Board

1005 British School-Lom

BP 20050
Lome
Togo
002-8 2-6 46
Fax: 002-8 2-6 49
E-mail: admin@bsl.tg
http://www.bsl.tg
We value not only academic success but encourage talent of all kinds, whether in academic studies, art, drama, music or games; and that we take the position that the pupil who is kind and helpful, who has a positive attitude to school life and fellow pupils, is considered every bit as worthwhile as the brilliant scholar, artist or athlete.

1006 British School-Lom,

BP 20050
Lome
Togo
228-226-46-06
Fax: 228-226-49-89
E-mail: bsl@cafe.tg
http://www.bsl.tg
This school offers an English based curriculum for 120 day students and 95 boarding students (110 boys; 105 girls), ages 4-18. The school is an independent, co-educational day and boarding school. External exams from the University of London and Cambridge-UK plus International Baccalaureate (IB) is offered. Applications needed to teach include science, pre-school, French, math, social sciences, administration, Spanish, reading, German, English and physical education.

1007 British Yeoward School

Parque Taoro
Tenerife
Spain, ES 38400
00-34-922-384685
Fax: 00-34-922-37-35-65
E-mail: office@yeowardschool.org
http://www.yeowardschool.org
The International British Yeoward School provides a high quality British education for children of all ages in an open, multi-cultural environment; allowing each child to achieve their full potential in a positive learning community

Karen Hern~ndez, Head of Primary Grades
Alan Halstead, Head of School

1008 Broadhurst Primary School

Private Bag BR 114 Broadhurst
Garborone
Botswana, BW
267-3971-221
Fax: 267-307987
E-mail: broadhurst@info.bw
http://www.info.bw
To create, together with the family, a caring environment of learning and experience, in which children may develop their potential to the full, may acquire the knowledge and skills to equip them for living, may experience the best that the human spirit has achieved, may develop respect for themselves, for other peo-

ple and the world around them and have the courage to make a difference to future

Rehana Khan, Head Teacher
Michael Eisen, Deputy Headteacher

1009 Brookhouse Preparatory School

PO Box 24987- 00502
Nairobi
Kenya
254-20-2430260
Fax: 254-20-891641
E-mail: info@brookhouse.ac.ke
http://http://www.brookhouse.ac.ke/index.asp
Provides education in general computer literacy.

Eric Mulind, School Coordinator

1010 Cairo American College

PO Box 39
Maadi 11431
Cairo, EG 11431
20-2-755-5505
Fax: 20-2-2519-6584
E-mail: support@cacegypt.org
http://www.cacegypt.org
Cairo American College is a world class learning environment that affirms the voice, passions and talents of students and inspires them to use their hearts and minds as global citizens.

Nivine Captan-Amr, Board Chair
Elizabeth Bredin, Secretary

1011 Casablanca American School

Route de la Mecque,Lotissement Ougo
Casablanca, Morocco 20150
212-22-214-115
Fax: 212-22-212-488
E-mail: cas@cas.ac.ma
http://www.cas.ac.ma
To offer the best possible U.S. and international university preparatory education program, curriculum and instruction for its students.

Simohamed Erroussafi, President
Karima Abisourour, Vice President

1012 Cavina School

PO Box 43090
Nairobi
Kenya
254-2-3866011
Fax: 254-2-3866676
E-mail: cavina@iconnect.co.ke
http://www.cavina.ac.ke
Cavina aims to develop many qualities in the children who come through her gates - academic excellence, an inquiring mind, a sense of moral and social responsibility, and most of all a recognition of their relationship with their Creator who has revealed Himself through His son Jesus.

Massie Blomfield, Headmaster/Managing Director

1013 Dakar Academy

BP 3189 Route des Peres Maristes
Dakar, Senegal
West Africa
221-33-832-06-82
Fax: 221-33-832-17-21
E-mail: office@dakar-academy.org
http://www.dakar-academy.org
Dakar Academy exists to partner in the advancement of the Kingdom of God through serving missionary families by providing education services for their children

Charlie Campbell, Chairman
Joseph Rosa, Director

1014 Greensteds School

Private Bag
Nakuru
Kenya
254 50 50770
Fax: 254 50 50775
E-mail: office@greenstedsschool.com
http://http://www.greenstedsschool.com/
An international school for boys and girls.

MP Bentley, Headmaster

1015 Harare International School

66 Pendennis Road
Mount Pleasant
Harare, Zimbabwe
(263 4) 870514/5
Fax: 263-4-883-371
E-mail: his@his.ac.zw
http://www.his-zim.com
Grade levels prekindergarten through twelfth, with enrollment of 376.

Marcel Gerrmann, Board Chair
Shannon Brauchli, Vice Chair

1016 Hillcrest Secondary School

PO Box 24819
Nairobi
Kenya 00502
254-20-882-222
Fax: 254-20-882-350
E-mail: admin@hillcrest.ac.ke
http://http://www.hillcrest.ac.ke/secondary/
Mixed boarding school.

Christopher Drew, Head Teacher

1017 International Community School-Addis Ababa

PO Box 70282
Addis Adaba
Ethiopia
251-11-3-711-544
Fax: 251-11-371-0722
E-mail: info@icsaddis.edu.et
http://http://www.icsaddis.edu.et/
An independent, coeducational day school which offers an educational program from prekindergarten through grade 12 for students of all nationalities.

Jim Laney, Director

1018 International School-Kenya

PO Box 14103
Nairobi
Kenya 00800
254-20-418-3622
Fax: 254-20-418-3272
E-mail: info@isk.ac.ke
http://www.isk.ac.ke
Students from many backgrounds go to this school, which prepares them for successful transitions to other schools and universities around the world, offering both a North American Hogh School Diploma as well as the International Baccalaureate Diploma to its graduates.

John Roberts, Director
Jodi Lake, Curriculum Coordinator

1019 International School-Moshi

PO Box 733
Moshi, Kilimanjaro
Tanzania
255-27-275-5004
Fax: 255-27-275-2877
E-mail: school@ismoshi.org
http://www.ismoshi.org
The school inspires individuals to be lifelong learners in a global community.

Bob Woods, Director of ISM
Keiron White, Head, Moshi Campus

1020 International School-Tanganyika
United Nations Road
PO Box 2651, Dar es Salaam
Tanzania
255-22-2151817/8
Fax: 255-22-2152077
E-mail: ist@raha.com
http://www.istafrica.com
IST aspires to provide an outstanding international education. We value and respect cultural diversity and embrace the people and natural environment of Tanzania. Within this safe, secure and caring community students reach their full potential as citizens of the world.

David Shawver, Director
Nazir Thawer, General Manager

1021 John F Kennedy International School
CH-3792 Saanen
Switzerland
41-033-744-1372
Fax: 41- 033-744-8982
E-mail: lovell@jfk.ch
http://www.jfk.ch
Boarding day school for boys and girls aged 5-14 years.

William Lovell, Co-Director
Sandra Lovell, Co-Director

1022 Kabira International School
PO Box 34249
Kampala
Uganda
256-0414-530-472
Fax: 256-0414-543-444
E-mail: office@kisu.com
http://www.kabiraschool.com
Grade levels Pre-K through 8, school year - September - July

Emma Whitney, Admissions
Elaine Whelen, Principal

1023 Kestrel Manor School
Ring Road Westlands
PO Box 14489, Nairobi
Kenya 00200
254-20-3740-311
E-mail: info@kestrelmanorschool.com
http://www.kestrelmanorschool.com
Coeducational school for children Kindergarten through secondary schooling.

1024 Khartoum American School
PO Box 699
Khartoum
Sudan
249-15-577-0105
Fax: 249-183-512044
E-mail: kas@krtams.org
http://www.krtams.org
An independent, coeducational day school which offers an educational program from prekindergarten through grade 12 for students of all nationalities.

Gregory Hughes, Superintendent
Brad Waugh, Principal

1025 Kigali International School
Caisse Sociale Estates, Gaculiro
BP 6558
Kigali, Rwanda
250-033-7282
250-0783307282
Fax: 250-72128
E-mail: office.kics@gmail.com
http://www.kicsrw.org
Non-profit, co-educational day school

Bryan Hixson, Chairman
Mark Thiessen, Vice Chairman

1026 Kingsgate English Medium Primary School
Box 169
Mafeteng, 900 Lesotho
Africa
Kingsgate is the only non-denominational primary school in the district. The curriculum is English-based offered to a total of 460 day students (240 boys; 220 girls), PreK-7. Overseas teachers are welcome with the length of stay being one year, with housing provided. Applications needed to teach include pre-school and reading.

M Makhothe, Principal

1027 Kisumu International School
PO Box 1276
Kisumu
Kenya
254-35-21678
E-mail: admin@kis.co.ke
This school is located on the shores of Lake Victoria and offers a unique education to students of all nationalities and cultural backgrounds. The total enrollment of the school is 35 day students, in grades K-7. The school does participate in the teacher exchange programs, with the length of stay being two years with housing provided by the school. Applications needed to teach include science, pre-school, math, social sciences, English and physical education.

Neena Sharma, Principal

1028 Lincoln Community School
American Embassy Accra
N126/21 Dedeibaa Street
Abelemkpe, Accra
Ghana, West Africa
233 30 277 4018
Fax: 233 302 78 09 85
E-mail: headofschool@lincoln.edu.gh
http://www.lincoln.edu.gh
is committed to inspiring students to achieve the highest standards of intellectual and personal development through a stimulating and comprehensive program.

Dennis Larkin, Head of School
Sanjay Rughani Tanzanian, President

1029 Lincoln International School of Uganda
PO Box 4200
Kampala
Uganda
256-41-4200374/8/9
Fax: 256-41-200303
E-mail: dtodd@isumail.ac.ug
http://www.lincoln.ac.ug
Grade levels Pre-K through 12, school year August - June

Daniel Todd, Dean of Studied/Admission
Jim Campbell, Chairman

1030 Lincoln International School-Uganda
PO Box 4200
Kampala
Uganda
256-41-4200374/8/9
Fax: 256-41-200303
E-mail: dtodd@isumail.ac.ug
http://www.lincoln.ac.ug

Daniel Todd, Dean of Studied/Admission
Jim Campbell, Chairman

1031 Maru A Pula School
Plot 4725
Maruapula Way
Botswana 0045
267-391-2953
Fax: 267-397-3338
E-mail: principal.map@gmail.com
http://www.maruapula.org/

Maru-a-Pula is a dynamic, world-class school rooted in Botswana. We offer a rigorous curriculum that prepares students for entry to highly selective universities and to pursue challenging careers. Through programmes emphasizing self-discipline and community service, each student learns personal and social responsibility.

Andrew S Taylor, Principal

1032 Mombasa Academy
PO Box 86487
Mombasa
Kenya, KE
254-11-471629
Fax: 254-11-221484
E-mail: msaacademy@swiftmombasa.com
http://www.msaacademy.com
Our aim is to help our pupils to reach their true potential. Within the academic and extra-curricular frameworks, staff offer pupils considerable personal support; warm and productive working relations are a distinguishing feature of our community and are instrumental in helping each girl and boy on the road towards maturity and self-fulfillment

Kishor Joshi, Headmaster
FJ Bentley, Founder

1033 Northside Primary School
PO Box 897
Gaborone
Botswana
00-267-395-2440
Fax: 09-267-395-3573
E-mail: administration@northsideschool.net
http://www.northsideschool.net
In Gaborone, Botswana, Northside Primary School provides education in English and serves the needs of primary school children of all nationalities.

Mandy Watson, Headteacher

1034 Nsansa School
PO Box 70322
Ndola
Zambia
26-2-611753
Fax: 26-2-618465
This school offers an English curriculum to 185 day students (96 boys; 124 girls), in grades K-7. Length of stay for overseas teachers is one year with housing provided. Student/teacher ratio is 20:1.

Nel Mather, Principal

1035 Peterhouse
Private Bag 3741
Marondera
Zimbabwe
263 (0)279 - 22200
Fax: 263 (0)279 - 24200
E-mail: peterhouse@peterhouse.co.zw
http://www.peterhouse.org
This Anglican school offers an English based curriculum for 19 day students and 790 boarding students (535 boys; 255 girls), in Form I-Form VI. The school is willing to participate in a teacher exchange program with the length of stay being one year, with housing provided. Applications needed to teach include science, math, and physical education.

JB Calderwood, Rector

1036 Rabat American School
1 Bis Rue Emir Ibn Abdelkade
Agdal, Rabat
Morocco 10000
202-536-4442
212-537-671-476
Fax: 212-537-670-963
E-mail: info@ras.ma
http://www.ras.ma

We provide our students with a breadth of experiences which encourage them to realize their full potential and allow them to acquire the knowledge, skills, character, and confidence to contribute positively and responsibly to an ever-changing, interconnected world.

Paul W Johnson, Director

1037 Rift Valley Academy
PO Box 80
Kijabe, 00220
Kenya
254-20-3246-249
Fax: 254-20-3246-111
E-mail: rva@rva.org
http://www.rva.org
RVA is a Christian boarding school located in central Kenya. The academy, a branch of Africa Inland Mission International, exists to provide a quality education in a nurturing environment for the children of missionaries serving in Africa.

Roy E Entwistle, Principal
Tim Cook, Superintendent

1038 Rosslyn Academy
PO Box 14146
Nairobi
Kenya 800
254-20-263-5294
Fax: 254-20-263-5281
E-mail: info@rosslynacademy.com
http://www.rosslynacademy.com
The purpose of Rosslyn Academy is to provide a K-12 North American and Christian-oriented educational program for children of missionaries. Rosslyn also welcomes children from privately sponsored families who are in sympathy with the philosophy of the school.

Phil Dow, Superintendent
Don McGavran, Director of Operations

1039 Sandford English Community School
PO Box 30056 MA
Addis Ababa
Ethiopia
251-11-123-38-92
Fax: 251-11-123-3728
E-mail: admission@sandfordschool.org
http://www.sandfordschool.org
A co-educational, non-boarding, nursery to pre University institution. Its committed to providing a standard of education that is accepted within Ethiopia and by the international community.

Jon D P Lane, Head of Primary School
Tsegaye Kassa, Senior Manager

1040 Schutz American School
51 Schutz Street
PO Box 1000
Alexandria, Egypt 21111
(20) (3) 576-2205
Fax: (20) (3) 576-0229
E-mail: jlujan@schutzschool.org.eg
http://www.schutzschool.org.eg
A single campus houses PreK-3 through grade twelve in two main classroom buildings and an auditorium/ classroom complex, as well as the administrative center, dining room, resident staff housing, clinic, art room, computer labs, libraries and snack bar. Sports facilities on the campus include basketball, volleyball, tennis and football courts, a half-size grass soccer pitch, and a swimming pool and weight training room.

Dr Joyce Lujan, Head of School
Nathan Walker, Upper School Principal

1041 Sifundzani School
PO Box A286, Swazi Plaza
Mbabane
Swaziland
268-404-2465
Fax: 268-404-0320
E-mail: sifundzani@realnet.co.sz
A coeducational day school which offers an educational program from grades 1 through 10 for students of all nationalities.

Ella Magongo, Principal

1042 Sir Harry Johnston Primary School
Kalimbuka Road
Zomba PO Box 52
Malawi
265-1525280
Fax: 265 888202374
E-mail: admin@shjzomba.com
http://www.shjzomba.com

Una Barras-Hargan, Headteacher

1043 St. Barnabas College
34 Langeberg Avenue Bostmont Johann
PO Box 88188 Newclare
South Africa 2112
011-27-474-2055
Fax: 011-27-474-2249
E-mail: theronn@stbarnabas.co.za
http://www.stbarnabas.co.za
St Barnabas College is a co-educational secondary school in Johannesburg. It is well known as a centre of excellence. The school's mission is to provide quality secondary education to young people, the main criterion for admission being intellectual potential and the motivation to succeed.

Glynn Blignaut, Headmaster
Faizel Panker, Deputy Headmaster

1044 St. Mary's School
Rhapta Road, PO Box 40580- 00100
Nairobi
Kenya
254-020-4444569
Fax: 254-020-4446191
E-mail: info@stmarys.ac.ke
http://www.stmarys.ac.ke
We are a Catholic Private School committed to our international character in the provision of a spiritual, intellectual and physical education. We aim at developing the gifts of the young in an atmosphere which encourages the ethos of self-expression and mutual respect with a view to their facing the future responsibly, with confidence and courage.

John Awiti, Head of School
Rosemary Abuodha Omogo, Deputy Principal

1045 St. Paul's College
St. Paul's United Theological College
Po Private Bag
Limuru
Kenya 00217
254 - 20 - 2020505
Fax: 254-66-73033
E-mail:
assistantregistrar@stpaulslimuru.ac.ke
http://www.stpaulslimuru.ac.ke/
The school prepares men and women for ministry in the Christian Church and present day society.

Samuel Kobia, Chancellor .
Joseph Galgalo, Vice Chancellor

1046 Tigoni Girls Academy
Box 10
Limuru
Kenya
This Academy is a small, closely knit community of individuals from different cultures in which physical, emotional, creative and intellectual development is fortified in all aspects

of daily life. Total enrollment is 40 boarding students, ages 11-16. Applications from overseas include science, math, social sciences, French, Spanish and English. Length of stay for overseas teachers is 2 years with housing provided. The Academy is affiliated with the Church of England.

Duncan Kelly, Principal

1047 Waterford-Kamhlaba United World College
PO Box 52
Mbabane
Swaziland
011-268-422-0866
Fax: 011-268-422-0088
E-mail: admissions@waterford.sz
http://www.waterford.sz/index.php
This school offers a curriculum based in English for 181 day students and 295 boarding (251 boys; 226 girls), in grades 6-12. Overseas teachers length of stay is three years with housing provided. Applications needed to teach include math, English, and physical education.

Laurence Nodder, Principal
Bruce Wells, Deputy Principal

1048 Westwood International School
PO Box 2446
Gabarone
Botswana
011-267-390-6736
Fax: 011-267-390-6734
E-mail: westwood-admissions@info.bw
http://www.westwoodis.com
Westwood International School shall provide students with a quality international education that shall effectively prepare them for access to tertiary study and the world of work, and enable them to confidently meet future challenges as life long learners

Phyllis Hildebrandt, Principal
Michael Francis, Director

1049 Windhoek International School
Private Bag
Windhoek
Namibia 16007
264-61-241-783
Fax: 264-61-243-127
E-mail: k.jarman@wis.edu.na
http://www.wis.edu.na
The Windhoek International School prepares its students to be inquiring, knowledgeable and caring participants in the global arena through an international curriculum of the highest standard. WIS embraces the diversity of its students from the international community and Namibia, in an atmosphere of mutual respect, tolerance and educational enrichment for all

Maureen Rainey, Director
Neville Field, Chairperson

Asia, Pacific Rim & Australia

1050 Aiyura International Primary School
PO Box 407
Ukarumpa Papua
New Guinea

Perry Bradford, Principal

1051 Ake Panya International School
158/1 Moo 3 Hangdong-Samoeng Road
Banpong, Hangdong, Chiang Mai 50230
Thailand
66-53-36-5303
Fax: 66-53-365-304

E-mail: akepanya@cm.ksc.co.th
http://www.akepanya.co.th
Grade levels 1-12, school year August - June

Barry Sutherland, Headmaster
Holly Shaw, Director of Studies

1052 Alotau International Primary School

PO Box 154
Alotau, Milne Bay Province
Papua New Guinea
675-641-1078
Fax: 675-641-1627
E-mail: alotauis@iea.ac.pg
http://www.iea.ac.pg

Lucy Kula, Principal

1053 Amelia Earhart Intermediate School

Unit 5166
APO AP 96368
Okinawa
611-634-1329
011-81-611-734-132
Fax: 611-634-7207
Fax: 011-81-611-734-720
E-mail: aeis_okinawa@pac.dodea.edu
http://www.earhart-is.pac.dodea.edu
Success in Education is a Partnership in Responsibility characterized by the opportunities and the guidance necessary to motivate learners, the desire and ability to be successful in human interactions, to access and process information, and to accept personal responsibility for all decisions made throughout one's lifetime.

Deborah Carlson, Principal

1054 American International School-Dhaka

P.O. Box: 6106
Gulshan, Dhaka 1212
Bangladesh
880-2-882-2452
Fax: 880-2-882-3175
E-mail: info@ais-dhaka.net
http://www.ais-dhaka.net
Provides a program based on American educational principles to students from an international community, creates an academic and social environment that challenges students to achieve their potential, become life-long learners and contribute to changing global society.

Richard Boerner, Superintendent
Kyra Buchko, President

1055 American International School-Guangzhou

No 3 Yan Yu Street S
Ersha Island, Yuexiu District
Guangzhou PR China 51010
86-20-8735-3392
Fax: 86-20-8735-3339
E-mail: admissions@aisgz.org
http://http://www.aisgz.org/
Prepares students for entrance into the very best universities in the world is enhanced by being in the cultural center of Guangzhou and Southern China.

Joseph Stucker, Director
Katherine Farrell, Chair

1056 American School-Bombay

SF 2 G Block
Bandra Kurla Complex
Mumbai 400 0
91 22 6772 7272ÿ
Fax: 91 22 6252 6666
E-mail: admissions@asbindia.org
http://www.asbindia.org
ASB delivers a dynamic educational program that encourages each student to achieve her or his highest potential. While ASB is a U.S. style school, the Indian setting and multi-national community, representing over 51 countries, brings children who have varied experiences together to learn in a rich and unique environment

Paul M Fochtman, Superintendent

1057 American School-Guangzhou (China)

Number 3 Yan Yu Street S
Ersha Island, Yuexiu District
Guangzhou, China 51010
8620-8735-3393
Fax: 8620-8735-3339
E-mail: admissions@aisgz.org
http://http://www.aisgz.org/
An independent, coeducational day school which offers an educational program from kindergarten through grade 12

Joseph Stucker, Director
Paul Wood, Principal

1058 American School-Japan

1-1 Nomizu 1
Chofu-shi, Tokyo
Japan 182-0
011-81 -22 3
0422-34-5300
011-81 -22 3
Fax: 0422-34-5303
E-mail: info@asij.ac.jp
http://www.asij.ac.jp
The American School in Japan is a private, coeducational day school which offers an educational program from nursery through grade 12 for students of all nationalities, but it primarily serves the American community living in the Tokyo area. The school was founded in 1902. The school year comprises 2 semesters extending from September to January and January to June.

Ed Ladd, Headmaster

1059 Aoba International School

2-10-34 Aobadai
Meguro-Ku, Tokyo
Japan 153-0-42
03-3461-1442
Fax: 81-3-3463-9873
E-mail: meguro@aobajapan.jp
http://www.aobaonline.jp
A co-educational school located on campuses in Meguro and Suginami. Over 550 students are enrolled in classes from pre-kindergarten to grade nine.

Neal Dilk, Head of School
Chiharu Uemura, VP

1060 Ashgabat International School

Berzengi, Ata Turk Street
Ashgabat
Turkmenistan
386-12-007870
Fax: 386-12-007871
E-mail: ashgabat@qsi.org
http://tkm.qsi.org
Offers high quality education in the English language for elementary students from three years through thirteen years of age.

Brad Goth, Director

1061 Bali International School

PO Box 3259
Denpasar
Bali, Indonesia
62-361-288-770
Fax: 62-361-285-103
E-mail: admin@baliis.net
http://www.baliinternationalschool.com
Provides educational excellence in a supportive, secure environment, preparing students to thrive and succeed as responsible citizens in a changing world. Offers the three IB Programs (PYP, MYP and DP) and is accredited by WASC.

Chris Akin, Director
Russell McGrath, PS-12 Assistant Principal

1062 Bandung Alliance International School

Jalan Bujanggamanik Kav 2
Kota Baru Parahyangan
Bandung, Indonesia 40553
62-22-8681-3949
Fax: 62-22-8681-3953
E-mail: info@baisedu.org
http://www.baisedu.org
BAIS operates as a private non-profit school to serve the international community. BAIS provides quality education in the traditions of classic, conservative ethics and values.

Pete Simano, Director
Charity Lamertha, Elementary Principal

1063 Bandung International School

Jl Suria Sumantri No 61
Bandung
West Java, Indonesia 40164
62-22-201-4995
Fax: 62-22-201-2688
E-mail: bisadmin@poboxes.com
http://www.bisdragons.com
At Bandung International Scholl, it is our vision to be a preeminent school providing world class secular education in the English language to the children of expatriates and others while maintaining strong links with the Indonesian community

Henri Behelmans, Head of School
Mark Holland, Chair

1064 Bangalore International School

Geddalahalli, Hennur Bagalur Road
Kothanur Post
Bangalore, India 560 0
91-802-846-5060
Fax: 91-802-846-5059
E-mail: info@bisedu.co.in
http://www.bangaloreinternationalschool.com
Provides internationally recognized standards of education with an India ethos and enable students to fulfill their potential in a culturally rich atmosphere.

Anuradha Monga, Principal

1065 Bangkok Patana School

643 Lasalle road Sukhumvit 105 Bang
Bangkok, Thailand 10260
6602-398-0200
Fax: 6602-399-3179
E-mail: reception@patana.ac.th
http://www.patana.ac.th
We are an academically directed school, focussed on our commitment to offer all of our students the best intellectual and physical preparation for higher education.

Tej Bunnag, Chairman
Kulvadee Siribhadra, Director

1066 Beacon Hill School

23 Ede Road
Kowloon Tong, Hong Kong
China
852-233-65-221
Fax: 852-233-87-895
E-mail: bhs@bhs.esf.edu.hk
http://www.asioonline.net.hk/beacon
Aim to provide each child with a safe and secure school where everyone, irrespective of ability, is an valued individual.

John Brewster, Principal

1067 Beijing BISS International School

No 17, Area 4 An Zhen Xi Li
Chaoyang District, Beijing
China 10002
86-10-6443-3151
Fax: 86-10-6443-3156
E-mail: Admissions@biss.com.cn
http://www.biss.com.cn

To educate and empower our students to attain personal excellence and positively impact the world.

Chan Ching Oi, CEO
Ettie Zilber, Head of School

1068 Bob Hope Primary School
Unit 5166
APO AP 96368-5166
Okinawa, Japan 96368-5166
11-81-611-734-0093
Fax: 11-81-98-934-6806
E-mail: bhps.okinawa@pac.dodea.edu
http://www.bob-hope-ps.pac.dodea.edu
The Bob Hope Primary School community is committed to teaching basic skills using developmentally appropriate strategies.

Jim Journey, Principal
Luldes Giraud, Vice Principal

1069 Bogor Expatriate School
PO Box 258
Jalan Papandayan 7, Bogor 16151
Indonesia
62-251-324360
Fax: 62-251-328512
Mission is to provide opportunities to foster positive attitudes towards learning.

Chris Rawlins, Head of School
Lance Kelly, Principal

1070 Bontang International School
15 Roszel Road
Po Box 5910
Princeton, NJ 8543
62-548551176
E-mail: iss@iss.edu
An international school with an English/Japanese based curriculum for twenty day students (6 boys; 14 girls), grades PreK-8. Student/teacher ration 5:1.

Roger Hove, Executive Vice President

1071 Brent International School-Manila
Brentville Subdivision
Mamplasan, Bian, Laguna
Philippines 4024
63 (049) 511-4330
Fax: 632-633-8420
E-mail: webmaster@brent.edu.ph
http://www.brent.edu.ph
Brent Schools, in a Christian ecumenical environment in the Philippines, are committed to develop individual students as responsible global citizens and leaders in their respective communities, with a multicultural and international perspective, and equipped for entry to colleges and universities throughout the world.

Dick B Robbins, Headmaster
Jeffrey W Hammett, Deputy Headmaster

1072 Brent School
Brent Road
PO Box 35, Baguio City
Philippines 2600
63 (074) 442-3628
Fax: 63 (074) 442-2260
E-mail: webmaster@brent.edu.ph
http://www.brentschoolbaguio.com
Brent Schools, in a Christian ecumenical environment in the Philippines, are committed to develop individual students as responsible global citizens and leaders in their respective communities, with a multicultural and international perspective, and equipped for entry to colleges and universities throughout the world.

Dick B Robbins, Headmaster
Ursula Banga-an Daoey, Deputy Head

1073 British International School
Bintayo Jaya Sektor IX JI
Raya Jomabang Ciledug Pondok Aren
Jakarta, ID 15227
62-21-745-1670
Fax: 62-21-745-1671
E-mail: enquiries@bis.or.id
http://www.bis.or.id
The new premises and facilities enable the school to excel further in the range of opportunities and experiences that can be offered to its students.

Christian Barkei, Principal
Brian Dallamore, Chairman

1074 British School Manila
36th Street University Park Forth B
Fort Bonifacio Global City
Taguig, PH
63 2 860 4800
Fax: 63 2 860 4900
E-mail: admissions@britishschoolmanila.org
http://www.britishschoolmanila.org
The British School Manila will deliver the highest standard of education in the Philippines for British children and for English speaking children of other nationalities The British School Manila provides outstanding education for English speaking children of all nationalities aged 3-18, based on an adapted form of the National Curriculum of England, and the I.B. Diploma

Chris Mantz, Head of School
Glenn Hardy, Head of Primary School

1075 British School-Muscat
PO Box 1907
Ruwi
Oman 112
00968ÿ24600842ÿ
Fax: 00968 24601062
E-mail: admin@britishschoolmuscat.com
http://www.britishschoolmuscat.com
The Vision of the British School-Muscat is to offer the highest quality British education to children of wide ranging abilities and nationalities. It values cultural diversity and provides a caring, innovative and stimulating environment, realizing the full potential and celebrating the success of every student. The School's curriculum will also develop the child as a whole person, provide them with learning-to-learn skills and will prepare them to lead a successful life in an inter-cultural wor

Steve Howland, Principal
Deirdre Selway, Registrar

1076 Calcutta International School Society
18 Lee Road
Calcutta 700 020
India
This school offers an English-based curriculum to 480 day students (230 boys; 250 girls), grades Nursery-12. CIS follows GCE London Curriculum. The cultures represented by the student body include expatriates, NRIs, local children. The student body is mainly Indians. Highly qualified individuals offering excellent results. The school is willing to participate in a teacher exchange program with the length of stay being 1-2 years, with no housing provided.

N Chatterjee, Principal
L Chaturvedi, Faculty Head

1077 Caltex American School
CPI Rumbal
Pekanbaru, Sumatra Riau
Indonesia
62-765-995-501
Fax: 62-765-996-321

Grade level preK through 8.

Daniel Hovde, Superintendent

1078 Camberwell Grammar School
55 Mout Albert Road
Canterbury 3126, Victoria
Australia
61 3 9835 1777
Fax: 61 3 9836 0752
E-mail: registrar@cgs.vic.edu.au
http://http://www.cgs.vic.edu.au/index.asp
Independent boys school.

CF Black, Principal

1079 Canadian Academy
4-1 Koyo Cho Naka
Higashinada-Ku, Kobe
Japan 658-0-32
81-78-857-0100
Fax: 81-78-857-3250
E-mail: hdmstr@canacad.ac.jp
http://www.canacad.ac.jp/canacad/welcome.html
Canadian Academy inspires students to inquire, reflect, and choose to compassionately impact the world throughout their lives.

Fred Wesson, Headmaster
Charles Kite, Assistant Headmaster

1080 Canadian School-India
14/1 Kodigehalli Main Road
Sahakar Nagar, Bangalore 560 092
India
91-80-343-8414
Fax: 91-80-343-6488
E-mail: csib@vsnl.com
http://www.canschoolindia.org
Grade levels K-13, school year August - June

T Alf Mallin, Principal

1081 Canberra Grammar School
Monaro Crescent
Red Hill
Australia ACT 2
02-6260-9700
Fax: 02-6260-9701
E-mail: headmaster@cgs.act.edu.au
http://www.cgs.act.edu.au
To develop a cultured man, ready for today's world and the future, balanced in intellectual, spiritual, emotional and physical aspects, with a love of learning and a willingness to serve fellow students and the wider community

Justin Garrick, Headmaster
Alan Ball, Head of Senior School

1082 Carmel School-Hong Kong
10 Borrett Road
Mid-Levels
Hong Kong
852-2964-1600
Fax: 852-2813-4121
E-mail: admin@carmel.edu.hk
http://www.carmel.edu.hk
Carmel School is committed to providing children living in Hong Kong with the highest international standard of secular and Jewish education. Through small classes and individual attention, the school offers a supportive environment that develops students' confidence, imagination and skills, in both academic and social spheres.

Edwin Epstein, Head of School
Kaisha Chow, Operations Director

1083 Casa Montessori Internationale
17 Palm Avenue Forbes Park Makati
Etro Manila D-3117
Philippines
Pre-nursery, nursery and kindergarten classes.

Carina Lebron, Principal

1084 Cebu International School
Banilad Road
PO Box 735, Cebu City 6000
Philippines
(63 32)ÿ401-1900
Fax: (63 32) 401-1904
E-mail: deidref@cis.edu.ph
http://http://www.cis.edu.ph/main.aspx
The primary aim of Cebu International School is to develop well-balanced global citizens who are intelligent, dynamic, respectful of universal moral values within a multicultural environment, and able to cope responsibly in an ever-changing interdependent world.

Deidre Fischer, Superintendent
Jenny Basa, Dean of Student Services

1085 Central Java Inter-Mission School
Jl Nakula Sadewa Raya Number 55
Salatiga, Jateng
Indonesia 50722
62-298-311673
Fax: 62-298-321609
E-mail: office@mountainviewics.org
http://www.mountainviewics.org
Primary intent of the school is that all students be thoroughly exposed to Scripture and that they find and sustain a vital relationship to Jesus Christ through Holy Spirit.

Willliam J Webb III, Superintendent
Kirk Thornton, Assistant Superintendent

1086 Central Primary School
Winston Churchill Avenue
Port Vila
Republic of Vanuatu
678-23122
Fax: 678-22526
E-mail: central@vanuatu.com.vu
http://www.vanuatu.com.vu/~central
Meet the needs of children from most countries and to provide an equivalent level of education for local children in an 'English as a First Language' context.

John Path, Chairman
John Lee Solomon, PEO

1087 Chiang Mai International School
PO Box 38
13 Chetupon Road
Thailand, TH 50000
665-324-2027
Fax: 665-324-2455
E-mail: info@cmis.ac.th
http://www.cmis.ac.th
Encourage the development of students' abilities in critical, analytical, and independent thinking, demonstrated in fluent oral and written communication.

Lance Potter, Principal
Sinturong Pannavalee, Director

1088 Chinese International School
1 Hau Yuen Path
Braemar Hill, Hong Kong
China
852-2510-7288
Fax: 852-2510-7488
E-mail: cis_info@cis.edu.hk
http://www.cis.edu.hk
Committed to the achievement of academic excellence and is characterized and enriched by its dual-language program in Chinese and English.

Theodore S Faunce, Headmaster
Li Bin, Deputy Head of School

1089 Chittagong Grammar School
Sarson Valley, 448/B Joynagar,
Chiottagong
Bangladesh
88-031-632900
E-mail: cgslower@hotmail.com
http://www.chittagonggrammarschool.com

Dedicated to the total growth and development of each student. Provides the students a broad, challenging and sound education to enable children to achieve the highest standards of which they are capable.

Afran Sanchita, Teacher
Akther Sharmin, Teacher

1090 Colombo International School
28, Gregory's Road
Colombo 7
Sri Lanka
94-11-269-7587
Fax: 94-11-269-9592
E-mail: management@cis.lk
http://www.cis.lk
English medium co-educational day school with separate Infant, Junior and Secondary sections.

M.J. Chappell, Principal
Armyne Wirasinha, Chairman

1091 Concordia International School-Shanghai
999 Mingyue Road, Jinqiao, Pudong
Shanghai
201206, China
86-21-5899-0380
Fax: 86-21-5899-1685
E-mail: admissions@ciss.com.cn
http://www.ciss.com.cn
Concordia's vision to offer academic excellence in a faith-based, caring community finds its roots in the 150-year educational tradition of the Lutheran Church-Missouri Synod.

James Koerschen, Head of School
Carol Ann Tonn-Bourg, Director of Admissions

1092 Cummings Elementary School
Unit 5039
APO AP
Japan 96319-5039
81-3117-66-2226
Fax: 81-3117-62-5110
E-mail: pcumming@pac.dodea.edu
http://www.cummings-es.pac.dodea.edu
We, the community of Cummings Elementary School, are committed to guiding our students to become successful learners and responsible citizens in an ever-changing world

Scott Sterry, Principal

1093 Dalat School
11200 Penang
Tanjung Bunga
Malaysia
60-4-899-2105
Fax: 60-4-890-2141
E-mail: info@dalat.org
http://www.dalat.org
The mission of Dalat International School is to prepare young people to live fully for God in a rapidly changing world by enabling them to understand, evaluate, and reconcile that world with the foundation of God's unchanging values.

Karl Steinkamp, Director
Fred Colburn, High School Principal

1094 Dover Court Prep School
Dover Road
Singapore, 139644
Singapore
65-67757664
Fax: 65-67774165
E-mail: admin@dover.edu.sg
http://http://www.dovercourt.edu.sg/contact.htm
To teach goals of the learning process, which is facilitated through encouraging pupils to pose and solve problems, take risks, demonstrate responsible attitudes and behaviour,

adopt a critical and self-evaluative approach to their work.

Maureen Roach, Director
Catherine Alliott, Chief Executive Officer

1095 Ela Beach International School
PO Box 1137
Boroko
Papua New Guinea
675-325-2183
Fax: 675-325-7925
E-mail: bmackinlay@temis.iea.ac.pg
This school consists of 262 boys and 222 girl day students in PreK-Grade 6. The length of stay for overseas teachers is three years with housing provided. School enrollment is made up of 260 PNG children, 224 non PNG children, overseas and PNG staff team teaching in mixed age group classrooms.

Bruce E Mackinlay, Principal

1096 Elsternwick Campus-Wesley College
577 Street Kilda Road
Melbourne
Australia 3004
61-3-8102-6100
Fax: 61 3 8102 6054
E-mail: stkildaroad@wesleycollege.net
http://www.wesleycollege.net
Wesley College is a coeducational school of the Uniting Church which has enriched the lives of thousands of young people, since it opened on 18 January 1866 as a boy's boarding school. In its 140 year history, it has experienced the influence of 14 principals, each of whom has in turn, enriched the life of the College.

Jack Moshakis, Executive Director
Helen Drennen, Principal

1097 Faisalabad Grammar School
Kohinoor Nagar
Faisalabad 728593
Pakistan
This Islamic school offers a curriculum taught in both English and Urdu to 2,000 day students (1,000 boys; 1,000 girls), in Junior Nursery up to eighteen years of age. The school runs 50% of classes in Matriculation Streams Local, and 50% in 'O' and 'A' level University of Cambridge UK examinations. Applications needed to teach include science, math, English and computers, with the length of stay for overseas teachers being one year.

RY Saigol Sarfraz, Principal
N Akhtar, VP

1098 Faith Academy
MCPO Box 2016
Makati City
Philippines 0706
11-632-248-5000
Fax: 63-2-658-0026
E-mail: vanguard@faith.edu.ph
http://www.faith.edu.ph
Faith Academy envisions expanding children's educational delivery options to meet the needs of the missions enterprise throughout Asia.

Tom Hardeman, Superintendent
Mike Hause, Deputy Superindentent

1099 French International School
165 Blue Pool
Happy Valley, SAR, Hong Kong
China
852-257-76217
Fax: 852-257-79658
E-mail: lfi@lfis.edu.hk
http://www.fis.edu.hk
To provide, together with families, a nurturing, culturally diverse community that inspires our young people to realize their true potential as confident, independent learners

and responsible global citizens with moral values and integrity.

Francis Cauet, Headmaster
Samuel Hureau, Administrator

1100 Fukuoka International School

3-18-50 Momochi
Sawara-ku, Fukuoka
Japan 814-6
81-92-841-7601
Fax: 81-92-841-7602
E-mail: adminfis@fka.att.ne.jp
http://www.fis.ed.jp
To create a dynamic learning environment in which students can be educated in high international academic standards. We strive to be a model of unity in diversity in which the individual is respected in each student is challenged at his/her own level.

Linda Gush, Head of School
Daniel Habel, Dean of Students

1101 Garden International School

16 Jalan Kiara 3, Off Jalan Bukit K
Kuala Lumpur
Malaysia 50480
011-60-3-6209-6888
Fax: 011-60-3-6201-2468
E-mail: admissions@gardenschool.edu.my
http://www.gardenschool.edu.my
Grade levels Pre-K through eleventh.

Simon Mann, Principal
Dato' Loy Teik Ngan, Chairman

1102 Geelong Grammar School-Glamorgan

14 Douglas Street
Toorak, Victoria
Australia 3142
011-61-3-9829-1444
Fax: 011-61-3-9826-2829
E-mail: toorakcampus@ggs.vic.edu.au
http://www.ggs.vic.edu.au
Geelong Grammar School offers an exceptional Australian education. Our students are girls and boys who see the richness of the world through confident eyes.

Lisa Marchetti, Fundraising Coordinator
Stephen Meek, Principal

1103 German Swiss International School

11 Guildford Road, The Peak
Hong Kong
China
011-852-2849-6216
852-820- 621
Fax: 011-852-2849-6347
E-mail: gsis@gsis.edu.hk
http://www.gsis.edu.hk
Encourage and foster the talents of our students - as well-rounded individuals, responsible team members and open-minded citizens of the 21st century.

Hans PeterÿNaef, COO
Jens-Peter Green, Principal

1104 Glenunga International High School

99 L'Estrange Street
Glenuga
South Australia 5064
011-61-8-8379-5629
Fax: 011-61-8-8338-2518
E-mail: glenunga@gihs.sa.edu.au
http://www.gihs.sa.edu.au
Grade levels 8-12.

Wendy Johnson, Principal
Jeremy Cogan, Deputy Principal

1105 Good Hope School-Kowloon

303 Clear Water Bay Road
Kowloon
Hong Kong
011-852- 2321-0250
Fax: 011-852- 2324-8242

E-mail: goodhope@ghs.edu.hk
http://www.ghs.edu.hk
Provides equal opportunities to develop their moral, intellectual, physical, social, emotional and artistic aspects of life.

Pauline Yuen, Supervisor
Paul Chow, Principal

1106 Goroka International School

PO Box 845
Goroka EHP
Papua New Guinea
011-675-732-1452
Fax: 011-675-732-2146
E-mail: gorokais@online.net.pg
http://www.iea.ac.pg
Provide education of a high academic standard from early childhood to grade 12

James M Masa, Principal

1107 Hebron School-Lushington Hall

Lushington Hall, Ootacamund
Tamil Nadu
India 643 0
11-91-42-3244-2372
Fax: 11-91-42-3244-1295
E-mail: admin@hebronooty.org
http://www.hebronooty.org
Independent, international Christian school.

Mark Noonan, Principal

1108 Hillcrest International School

PO Box 248
Sentani 99352
Papua, Indonesia
011-62-967-591460
Fax: 011-62-967-592673
E-mail: director@hismk.org
http://www.hismk.org
HIS is a Christian international school. Teachers must raise their own support, normally with a mission. Enrollment consists of 97 day students and 24 boarding (53 boys; 68 girls), in grades K-12.

Margaret Hartzler, Director

1109 Hiroshima International School

3-49-1 Kurakake
Asakita-Ku
Hiroshima, Japan 739-1
011-81-82-843-4111
Fax: 011-81-82-843-6399
E-mail: info@hiroshima-is.ac.jp
http://www.hiroshima-is.ac.jp
The Hiroshima International School is an independent, coeducational day school which offers educational programs from preschool through grade 12. The school year comprises 2 semesters extending from early September to mid-June.

Peter MacKenzie, Principal

1110 Hokkaido International School

1-55, 5-Jo, 19-Chome
Hirahishi, Toyohira-Ku
Sapporo, Japan 062-0
011-81-11-816-5000
Fax: 011-81-11-816-2500
E-mail: his@his.ac.jp
http://www.his.ac.jp
A private, coeducational day and boarding school which offers an America-style education from preschool through grade 12.

Michael Branson, Headmaster
Eri Kashiwabara, Business Manager

1111 Hong Kong International School

1 Red Hill Road
Tai Tam, Hong Kong
Republic of China
011-852-3149-7000
Fax: 011-852-2813-8740
E-mail: Advancement@hkis.edu.hkÿ
http://www.hkis.edu.hk

The Hong Kong International School is a private, Christian, coeducational day school which offers an educational program from pre-primary through grade 12 for students of all nationalities and religious backgrounds. The school year comprises 2 semesters extending approximately from August 19 to January 16 and from January 19 to June 12.

Doug Werth, Chair
David Condon, Head of School

1112 Ikego Elementary School

PSC 474 Box 300
FPO, AP
Japan 96351-300
011-81-46-806-8320
Fax: 011-81-46-806-8324
E-mail: principal_ikegoes@pac.dodea.edu
http://www.ikego-es.pac.dodea.edu
Provides developmentally-appropriate learning experiences that teaches, problem solving, critical thinking, make responsible choices.

Scott Finlay, Principal

1113 Indianhead School

233-3, Howon-Dong
Uijeongbu City, Gyeonggi-Do
South Korea 480-7
011-82-31-870-3475
Fax: 011-82-31-826-3476
E-mail: info@iis.or.kr
http://www.iis.or.kr
Provides a comprehensive and enriched program of education for expatriate children and for those Korean nationals deemed eligible by the Korean Ministry of Education.

Jeong Jin Park, President
Stephen Ellis, Principal

1114 International Christian School

1 On Muk Lane
Shek Mun
N.T. Hong Kong
011-852-3920 0010
Fax: 011-852-2336-6114
E-mail: ics@ics.edu.hk
http://www.ics.edu.hk
International Christian School is an exceptional school for a number of reasons. Every ICS graduate has enrolled in a college or university somewhere in the world.

Jack Young, Board Chair
Noel Chu, Executive Assistant

1115 International Community School

1225 The Parkland Road
Khwaeng Bangna, Khet Bangna Bangkok
Thailand 10260
011-66-2-338-0777
Fax: 011-66-2-338-0778
E-mail: info@icsbangkok.com
http://www.icsbangkok.com
Based on the Bible, in partnership with parents, we teach the whole student to know and apply wisdom for the good of our world and the glory of God.

Darren Gentry, Headmaster
Gary Opfer, High School Principal

1116 International School Manila

University Parkway
Fort Bonifacio Global City, Taguig
Philippines 1634
011-63-2-840-8400
Fax: 011-63-2-840-8405
E-mail: superintendent@ismanila.com
http://www.ismanila.com
International School Manila is an independent international school whose structure, traditions and style emanate from the United States and whose curriculum and methodology reflect the best in worldwide educational research and practice. Our school is diverse

and dynamic, and our students have the highest aspirations for their education and future lives.

William Brown, High School Principal
David Toze, Superintendent

1117 International School of the Sacred Heart

4-3-1 Hiroo, Shibuya-ku
Tokyo
Japan 150-0
011-81-3-3400-3951
Fax: 011-81-3-3400-3496
E-mail: info@issh.ac.jp
http://www.issh.ac.jp
ISSH is a multicultural Catholic school that warmly welcomes students and families from many faiths. The Pre-Kindergarten and Kindergarten classes for 3, 4 and 5 year olds are for boys and girls, while grades 1-12 are for girls only.

Yvonne Hayes, Headmistress
Charmaine Young, High School Principal

1118 International School-Bangkok

39/7 Soi Nichada Thani,Samakee Road
Nonthaburi
Thailand 11120
011-66-2-963-5800
Fax: 011-66-2-583-5432
E-mail: daladk@isb.ac.th
http://www.isb.ac.th
Our Vision states that our students will make extraordinary academic progress. They become smart about their own learning processes, understanding what does and does not work for them as learners.

Dr Bill Gerritz, Head of School
Dr Ugo Costessi, Deputy Head of School/CFO

1119 International School-Beijing

10 An Hua Street
Shunyi District,,Beijing
China 10131
86-10-8046-2345
Fax: 86-10-8046-2001
E-mail: isb-info@isb.bj.edu.cn
http://www.isb.bj.edu.cn
Educate and inspire students to reach their unique potential and contribute positively to society by providing a world class education enriched by diversity and the Chinese culture.

Thomas Hawkins, Head of School
Rodney Fagg, High School Principal

1120 International School-Eastern Seaboard

PO Box 6
Banglamung, Chonburi
Thailand 20150
(6638) 372 591
Fax: (6638) 372 950
E-mail: ise@ise.ac.th
http://www.ise.ac.th
Prepare an international student population for higher education and lifelong learning by emphasizing higher level thinking skills, effective communication, global responsibilities, and personal wellness within a cooperative and supportive school community.

Robert Brewitt, Superintendent
Heather Naro, Elementary Principal

1121 International School-Fiji

PO Box 10828
Laucala Beach Estate, Suva
Fiji Islands
11-679-3393-560
Fax: 11-679-3340-017
E-mail: info@international.school.fj
http://www.international.school.fj

An independent co-educational day school offering pre-school, primary and secondary education and offers excellent education and a caring and nurturing environment for young people. The curriculum includes International Baccalaureate (Primary Years Programme, Middle Years Programme, Diploma Programme), University of Cambridge - International General Certificate of Secondary Education and the Australian Capital Territory Year 12 Certificate and University Admissions Index (UAI).

Dianne Korare, Principal
Sera Brown, Registrar

1122 International School-Ho Chi Minh City

16 Vo Truong Toan St
An Phu Ward, District 2, Ho Ci Minh City
Vietnam
84-8-898-9100
Fax: 84 (8) 3 519-4110
E-mail: admissions@ishcmc.edu.vn
http://www.ishcmc.com
The school provides and teaches the students about intellectual, emotional, social, creative, linguistic, cultural, moral, aesthetic and physical needs of each students. The school seeks to involve parents in the education of their children through regular communication.

Sean O'Maonaigh, Headmaster
Chris Byrne, Admissions/Marketing

1123 International School-Kuala Lumpur

PO Box 12645
Kuala Lumpur
Malaysia 50784
603-4259-5600
Fax: 603-4257-9044
E-mail: iskl@iskl.edu.my
http://www.iskl.edu.my
Offers its students a superior education to prepare them to be responsible world citizens who think creatively, reason critically, communicate effectively and learn enthusiastically throughout life.

Paul Chmelik, Headmaster
Amina O'Kane, Admissions Director

1124 International School-Lae

PO Box 2130
Lae, Morobe
Papua New Guinea 411
011-675-479-1425
Fax: 011-675-472-3485
E-mail: mail@tisol.iea.ac.pg
http://www.tisol.ac.pg
Offers high quality education, from ages 18 months to grade 8. The curriculum prepares students for national and international success.

Neal Mather, Principal

1125 International School-Manila

Univiersty Parkway
Fort Bonifacio, Taguig City
Philippines 1634
632-840-8488
Fax: 632-840-8489
E-mail: superintendent@ismanila.com
http://http://www.ismanila.org/portal/alias_/lang__en/tabID__1/Des
An independent international school whose structure, traditions and style emanate from the United States. It aims to build a community of reflective learners who are passionate, caring and responsible contributors to the world in which we live.

Ray Dempsey, President
David Toze, Superintendent

1126 International School-Penang-Uplands

Jalan Sungai Satu
Batu Feringgi, Penang
Malaysia 11100
011-604-8819-777
Fax: 011-604-8819-778
E-mail: info@uplands.org
http://www.uplands.org
Uplands aims to provide excellent international education for students of all nationalities in a challenging multi-cultural environment. It favours methods of teaching which foster the joys of learning, discovery and enquiry, aiming to nurture students into thinking, learning, caring and striving to meet the needs of a better world.

John Horsfall, Acting Principal
M R Chandran, Chair

1127 International School-Phnom Penh, Cambodia

146 Norodom Boulevard
PO Box 138, Phnom Penh
Cambodia
855-23-213-103
Fax: 855-23-213-104
E-mail: ispp@ispp.edu.kh
http://www.ispp.edu.kh
ISPP empowers students, in a caring international environment, to achieve their potential by pursuing personal and academic excellence, and to grow as responsible global citizens who celebrate diversity.

Barry Sutherland, Director
Laura Watson, Chairperson

1128 International School-Phnom Penh-Cambodia

146 Norodom Boulevard
PO Box 138, Phnom Penh
Cambodia
855-23-213-103
Fax: 855-23-361-002
E-mail: ispp@ispp.edu.kh
http://www.ispp.edu.kh
ISPP empowers students, in a caring international environment, to achieve their potential by pursuing personal and academic excellence, and to grow as responsible global citizens who celebrate diversity.

Barry Sutherland, Director
Laura Watson, Chairperson

1129 International School-Pusan

798 Nae-ri, Gijang-eup
Gijang-gun, Busan 619-902
South Korea
82 51 742-3332
Fax: 82 51 742 3375
E-mail: enquiries@bifskorea.org
http://www.isbusan.org
The school possess a caring, family-like ethos, giving the children a high level of self-confidence and esteem, and teaching them tolerance and respect for other cultures.

Stephen Palmer, Principal
Thomas Walker, Chairman

1130 International School-Singapore

25 Paterson Road
Singapore 23851
(65) 6235 5844
Fax: (65) 6732 5701
E-mail: admissions@iss.edu.sg
http://www.iss.edu.sg
ISS mission is to provide a multicultural educational environment for our students in which they achieve academic success, personal growth and become socially responsible and active global citizens with an appreciation of learning as a life-long process.

Mak Lai Ying, Principal
Anthony Race, Headmaster

1131 International School-Ulaanbaatar
Four Seasons Garden, Khan-Uul Distr
1st Khoroo, PO Box 36/10
Ulaanbaatar, Mongolia 17032
976-70160010
Fax: 976-70160012
E-mail:
administration@isumongolia.edu.mn
http://www.isumongolia.edu.mn
The International School of Ulaanbaatar
seeks to offer the best educational system possible, based on an international curriculum.

Gregory Rayl, Director
Tuul Arildii, Deputy Director

1132 Island School
20 Borrett Road
Mid Levels
Hong Kong
852-2524-7135
Fax: 852-2840-1673
E-mail: school@mail.island.edu.hk
http://www.island.edu.hk
An international, co-educational, comprehensive school, providing secondary education
for children of all nations who can benefit
from an education through the medium of
English.

Pinder Wong, Council Chairman
Chris Binge, Principal

1133 Ivanhoe Grammar School
PO Box 91
The Ridgeway, Ivanhoe, Victoria
Australia 3079
61 3 9490 1877
Fax: 61 3 9497 4060
E-mail: info@ivanhoe.com.au
http://www.igs.vic.edu.au
Our mission is to be a community of learning
that develops in students the skills and values
that will prepare them for the challenges and
responsibilities of adult citizenship.

Roderick D Fraser, Principal
Andrew Sloane, Head of School

1134 JN Darby Elementary School
PSC 485 Box 99
FPO, AP
Japan 96321
011-81-956-50-8800
Fax: 011-81-956-50-8804
E-mail: Darby_ES@pac.dodea.edu
http://http://www.darby-es.pac.dodea.edu/
The Darby Community promotes academic
and social excellence so all students can become positive contributors to society.

Joy Jaramillo, Principal

1135 Jakarta International School
PO Box 1078/JKS
Jakarta 12010
Indonesia
(62-21) 750-3644
Fax: 62-21-765-7852
E-mail: parentnet@jisedu.org
http://www.jisedu.org
JIS is a place where people from almost 60
countries come together to share ideas, experiences and values.

Tim Carr, Head of School

1136 Japan International School
2-10-7 Miyamae
Shibuya-Ku, Tokyo 168-0081
Japan
81-3-3335-6620
Fax: 81-3-3332-6930
E-mail: suginami@aobajapan.jp
http://http://www.aobaonline.jp/
Student of all nationalities, and religions are
welcome.

Charles S Barton, Headmaster

1137 John McGlashan College
2 Pilkington Street
Maori Hill, Dunedin
New Zealand
03-467-6620
Fax: 03-467-6622
http://www.mcglashan.school.nz
ohn McGlashan College is an integrated, Year
7-13, secondary school for boys. The roll
comprises approximately 380 dayboys from
Dunedin city and its surrounds and 110 boarders, most of whom come from rural Otago and
Southland. In addition, up to 20 international
students are enrolled each year

K Michael Corkery, Principal
Neil Garry, Deputy Principal

1138 Kansai Christian School
282-2 Oaza Misato, Heguri-cho, Ikom
Nara Ken 636-0904
Japan
0745-45-6422
Fax: 011-81-745-45-6422
E-mail: office@kansaichristianschool.com
http://http://www.kansaichristianschool.com
/index.php?page=contact-
Kansai Christian School was established in
1970 to provide a general education in a
Christian environment for children of the
evangelical missionary community

Albert Greeff, Principal

1139 Kaohsiung American School
35 Sheng Li Road
Tzuo-Ying District (813)
Taiwan
886-7-583-0112
Fax: 886-7-582-4536
E-mail: dchang@kas.kh.edu.tw
http://www.kas.kh.edu.tw
Kaohsiung American School (KAS) is a private, non-profit Pre-K - 12 institution with
330 students offering college preparatory
programs leading to a U.S. high school diploma. It is located in Kaohsiung, a city of 1.5
million in southwestern Taiwan.

Tom Farrell, Superintendent
Deborah Taylor, Assistant Director

1140 Kellett School
2 Wah Lok Path
Wah Fu, Pokfulam
Hong Kong
852-2551-8234
Fax: 852-2875-0262
E-mail: admissions@kellettschool.com
http://www.kellettschool.com/homealt.htm
Kellett School is an independent
non-for-profit school catering to the English-speaking children living in Hong Kong.
The school is operated by Kellett School Association Limited through a Board of Governors; seven of whom are parents, elected by
the Association, and the remaining three are
ex-officio members. All parents become
members of the Association.

Ann McDonald, Principal

1141 Kilmore International School
40 White Street
Kilmore, Victoria
Australia 3764
61-357-822-211
Fax: 61-357-822-525
E-mail: info@kilmore.vic.edu.au
http://www.kilmore.vic.edu.au
The Kilmore International School is an independent, non-denominational, co-educational boarding and day school for
academically motivated students undertaking
their secondary education (Years 7-12
inclusive).

John Settle, Principal

1142 Kinabalu International School
PO Box 12080
88822 Kota Kinabalu, Sabah
Malaysia
608-822-4526
Fax: 608-824-4203
E-mail: kismy@streamyx.com
http://www.kis.edu.my
This school offers an English-based curriculum for 100 day students (50 boys; 50 girls),
ages 3-13 years.

1973 pages

Stuart McLay, Principal
Elis Ho, Office Manager

1143 King George V School
2 Tin Kwong Road
Homantin, Kowloon
Hong Kong
852-2711-3029
Fax: 852-2760-7116
E-mail: office@kgv.edu.hk
http://www.kgv.edu.hk
Non selective secondary school which provides a broad.

Ed Wickins, Principal
Richard Bradford, Vice Principal

1144 Kitakyushu International School
Yahata Higashi-ku, Takami 2,
Shinnittetsu, Shijo, Kitakyushu
Japan
81-93-652-0682
This school offers an English based curriculum for 8 day students (2 boys; 6 girls), in kindergarten through elementary. The school is
always looking for dedicated and qualified
teachers to teach children and adults in school
and preschool (especially female teachers).
Applications needed include preschool and
English.

Ann Ratnayake, Principal

1145 Kodaikanal International School
Seven Roads Junction, PO Box 25
Kodaikanal, Tamil Nadu
India 624 1-101
91-4542-247-500
Fax: 91-4542-241-109
E-mail: contact@Kis.in
http://www.kis.in
Kodaikanal Internationa lSchool is an autonomous residential school with a broad college-oriented curriculum, serving young
people from a wide diversity of cultures. The
School's academic program is intentionally
set within a community life based on the life
and teaching of Jesus Christ and devoted to
service in India and the whole human
community.

Geoffrey Fisher, Principal
Gregg Faddegon, Vice Principal

1146 Kooralbyn International School
Shop 1, 29 Wellington Bundock Drive
Kooralbyn QLD 4285
Australia
61-7-5544-6111
Fax: 61-7-5544-6702
E-mail: info@kooralbyn.com
http://www.tkis.qld.edu.au
Aims to provide students with a broad liberal
education.

Geoff Mills, Principal

1147 Kowloon Junior School
20 Perth Street
Ho Man Tin, Kowloon
Hong Kong
852-2714-5279
Fax: 852 2760 4438
E-mail: office@kjs.edu.hk
http://www.kjs.edu.hk

Primary students learn English, math, science, technology, history, geography, art, music and physical education.

Mark Cripps, Principal
Deborah Graham, ESF Representative

1148 Kyoto International School
Kitatawara-cho,Nakadachiuri-sagaru
Yoshiyamachi-Dori, Kamigyo-ku, Kyoto
Japan 602-8247
81-75-451-1022
Fax: 81-75-451-1023
E-mail: kis@kyotointernationalschool.org
http://www.kyoto-is.org
Independent day school, offering education from Preschool level through to Middle School

Annette Levy, Head of School
Amanda Gillis-Furutaku, Board Chair

1149 Lahore American School
American Consulate General Lahore
15 Upper Mall, Canal Bank
Lahore
Pakistan 54000
92-42-576-2406
Fax: 92-42-571-1901
E-mail: las@las.edu.pk
http://www.las.edu.pk
An independent, coeducational day school which offers an educational program from nursery through grade 12 for students of all nationalities.

Kathryn Cochran, Superintendent
Imran Aslam, Board Chair

1150 Lanna International School Thailand
300 Grandview Moo 10
Chiang-Mai to Hang Dong, T Mae-hea, A. M
Thailand 50100
66-53-806-231
Fax: 66-53-271-159
E-mail: head@lannaist.ac.th
http://www.lannaist.ac.th
t is the goal of Lanna International School to prepare its students to be responsible world citizens who demonstrate a commitment to life-long learning and the application of that learning to the improvement of self, and local and global communities.

Roy Lewis, Head of School
Ajarn Kannika, School Director

1151 Lincoln School
PO Box 2673
Rabi Bhawan, Kathmandu
Nepal
977-1-4270482
Fax: 977-1-4272685
E-mail: info@lsnepal.com.np
http://www.lsnepal.com
is an independent, international school in Kathmandu, Nepal with an American Curriculum

Allan Bredy, Director
Craig Baker, Principal

1152 Makassar International School
PO Box 1327
Makassar, Sulawesi Selatan 90125
Indonesia
(0411) 315889
Fax: (0411) 313168
E-mail: info@mi-school.com
http://www.mischoolsulsel.tripod.com
Grade levels Pre-K through 7, school year August - June

Gordon Hall, Principal

1153 Malacca Expatriate School
2443-C Jalan Batang Tiga
Tanjung Kling, Melaka
Malaysia 76400
011-60-6-315-4970
Fax: 011-60-6-315-4970
E-mail: sossb@pd.jaring.my
http://www.meschool.virtualave.net
Mission is provide a high standard of learning. The students benefit from a high level of individual attention because of their low student to teacher ratio.

Susheila Samuel, Principal

1154 Marist Brothers International School
1-2-1 Chimori-cho
Suma-ku, Kobe
Japan 654-0
011-81-787-326266
Fax: 011-81-787-326268
E-mail: enquiries@marist.ac.jp
http://www.marist.ac.jp
The philosophy of MBIS is designed to awaken students to the realities of life and to prepare them for the future. school aims to give to each student a well-rounded education incorporating the academic, moral, social and physical aspects of life.

Ed Fitzgerald, Principal
Geraldo de Couto, Vice Principal

1155 Matthew C Perry Elementary School
PSC 561 Box 1874
FPO Iwakuni 96310 0019
Japan
011-81-827-79-3447
Fax: 011-81-827-79-6490
E-mail: principal.perryes@pac.dodea.edu
http://www.perry-es.pac.dodea.edu/
Committed to promoting student achievement in a positive safe environment. It provides a quality education for every student based on the needs of each child.

Shelia Cary, Principal
Christopher Racek, Asst. Principal

1156 Matthew C Perry Middle & High School
PSC 561 Box 1874
FPO Iwakuni 96310 1874
Japan
011-81-827-79-5449
Fax: 011-81-827-79-4600
E-mail: principal.perryhs@pac.dodea.edu
http://http://www.perry-hs.pac.dodea.edu/welcome/welcome.html

Morgan Nugent, Principal
Robert Funk, Assistant Principal

1157 Mentone Boys Grammar School
63 Venice Street
Mentone, Victoria
Australia 3194
011-61-3-9584-4211
Fax: 011-61-3-9581-3290
E-mail: enquiry@mentonegrammar.net
http://www.mentonegrammar.net
We are a school for boys and girls providing a flexible and sensitive approach which considers what boys and girls need at various stages of their development.

Mal Cater, Principal
Simon Appel, Chairman

1158 Mercedes College
540 Fullarton Road
Springfield 5062
South Australia
011-61-8-8372-3200
Fax: 011-61-8-8379-9540
E-mail: info@mercedes.adl.catholic.edu.au
http://www.mercedes.adl.catholic.edu.au/index.cfm

Mercedes College, in Adelaide, South Australia, is a Reception to Year 12 Catholic co-educational school in the Mercy tradition.

Peter Daw, Principal
Steve Bowley, Business Manager

1159 Methodist Ladies College
207 Barkers Road Kew
Victoria 3101
Australia
011-61-3-9274-6333
Fax: 011-61-3-9819-2345
E-mail: college@mlc.vic.edu.au
http://www.mlc.vic.edu.au
This college prepares its students for the world of tomorrow by liberating their talents through challenge, enrichment, and opportunity in a supportive Christian environment. Committed to technology and to student initiated learning so each girl from year five onward works with her personal computer to understand the present and shape the future. Total enrollment: 2,135 day students; 105 boarding. Grade range K-12. The school is willing to participate in a teacher exchange program.

Rosa Swtorelli, Principal
Louise Adler, Chairperson

1160 Minsk International School
DOS/Administrative Officer
7010 Minsk Place
Washington, DC 20521-7010
375-172-343-035
Fax: 375-172-343-035
E-mail: mis@open.by
An independent, coeducational day school which offers an educational program from kindergarten through grade 8 for students of all nationalities. Enrollment 11.

Stanley Harrison Orr, Director

1161 Moreguina International Primary School
PO Box 438
Konedobu Papua
New Guinea

Wayne Coleman, Principal

1162 Morrison Christian Academy
136-1 Shui Nan Road
Taichung 40679
Taiwan, TW 40679
11-886-4-2297-3927
Fax: 11-886-4-2292-1174
E-mail: mcgillt@mca.org.tw
http://www.mca.org.tw
Morrison Academy exists to meet the educational needs of the children of missionaries throughout Taiwan, helping fulfill Christ's commission to go into all the world. Morrison seeks to provide a Christ-centered school culture where all students, from missionary and non-missionary families, experience a Biblically-integrated quality education. Therefore, Morrison structures learning so that students may develop the knowledge, discernment, and ability to dynamically impact their world as Christian

Tim McGill, Superintendent
Matt Strange, Director of Curriculum

1163 Mount Hagen International School
PO Box 945
Mount Hagen
Papua New Guinea
675-542-1964
Fax: 675-542-1840
E-mail: mhis@online.net.pg
http://www.iea.ac.pg
It is envisaged that students enrolled at the Mount Hagen International School will always remain encouraged by their schooling. They will earn an education of International

standard, their learning will be contextualized within Papua New Guinea culture, and they will learn how to become productive members of their community

Bruce Imatana, Principal

1164 Mt Zaagham International School
PT Freeport
Tembagapura W Papua
Indonesia
62 901 407876
Fax: 62 901 403170
E-mail: joecuthbertson@efmi.com
http://mzis.org
Grade levels Pre-K through 98, school year September - June. Two campuses Tembagapura and Kuala Kencana

Barney Latham, Superintendent
Richard Ledger, Principal

1165 Murray International School
PO Box 1137
Boroko
Papua New Guinea
675-325-2183
Fax: 675-325-7925
E-mail: ssavage@temis.iea.ac.pg
http://www.elamurray.ac.pg
Non-profit, private, co-educational day school that provides quality international standard education for the expatriate and local community in Port Moresby.

Suzanne Savage, Principal
Marlene Filippi, Deputy Principal

1166 Murree Christian School
Jhika Gali, Murree Hills
Punjab
Pakistan 47180
0092-513-410321
Fax: 0092-513-411668
E-mail: mcs@mcs.org.pk
http://www.mcs.org.pk
This school offers an English-based curriculum for 20 day students and 140 boarding students (75 boys; 85 girls), in grades K-12. Murree Christian School educates the children of missionaries from 14 different countries working in Pakistan and the region. Living allowances rather than salaries are awarded. Overseas teacher stay is two years with housing provided by the school.

Phil Billing, Director
Linda Fisher, HS Faculty Head

1167 Mussoorie International School
Srinagar Estate, Mussoorie 248179
Uttarakhand
India
91-135-2632007
Fax: 91-135-2631160
E-mail: misadmission@gmail.com
http://www.misindia.net
One of the leading residential educational institutions for girls and is recognized for its progressive education with a definite account on India culture and traditions.

HK Rawal, Principal
A. Ghosh, Headmaster

1168 Nagoya International School
2686 Minamihara, Nakashidami
Moriyama-ku, Nagoya, 463-0002
Japan
81-52-736-2025
Fax: 81-52-736-3883
E-mail: info@nis.ac.jp
http://www.nagoyais.jp
Envisions a school community devoted to developing the skills, attitudes, and values that allow students to realize their full potential, lead lives of purpose, and become responsible, global citizens.

Rob Risch, Headmaster

1169 Narrabundah College
Jerrabomberra Avenue
Narrabundah, ACT 2604
Australia
61-2-6205-6999
Fax: 61-2-6205-6969
E-mail: laura.beacroft@cbit.net.au
http://www.narrabundahc.act.edu.au
This college is a government college for years 11 and 12 students - the final two years of secondary education. It offers a challenging curriculum in a caring environment and meets the needs of an international community.

Steve Kyburz, Head of School
Laura Beacroft, Board Chair

1170 New International School of Thailand
36 Sukhumvit Soi 15
Bangkok, TH 10110
66-2651-2065
Fax: 66-2253-3800
E-mail: nist@nist.ac.th
http://www.nist.ac.th
Co-educational, day school, IBO World School

Simon Leslie, Headmaster
Adrian Watts, Deputy Head

1171 Nile C Kinnick High School
PSC 473 Box 95
FPO, AP
96349-95
011-81-46816-7392
Fax: 011-81-46-816-7278
E-mail: Kinnick_Principal@pac.dodea.edu
http://www.kinnick-hs.pac.dodea.edu
The mission of Nile C. Kinnick High School is to challenge students to maximize potential in order to prepare them to be responsible and productive citizens in an ever-changing world.

Lorenzo Brown, Principal

1172 Nishimachi International School
2-14-7 Moto Azabu
Minato-ku Tokyo
Japan 106-0-46
81-3-3451-5520
Fax: 81-3-3456-0197
E-mail: info@nishimachi.org
http://www.nishimachi.ac.jp
Offers a dual-language, multicultural program ro 430 student k-9.

Terence Christian, Headmaster

1173 Okinawa Christian School International
1835 Zakimi, Yomitan-son
Okinawa 904-0301
Japan
81-098-958-3000
800-446-6423
Fax: 81-098-958-6279
E-mail: info@ocsi.org
http://www.ocsi.org
Provides a major educational support base for the international community living on Okinawa.

Rich Barnett, Contact
Randel J Hadley, Superintendent

1174 Osaka International School
4-4-16 Onohara Nishi
Mino-shi, Osaka, 562-0032
Japan
81-72-727-5050
Fax: 81-72-727-5055
E-mail: addmissions@senri.ed.jp
http://www.senri.ed.jp
OIS is an English-language-based, preK-12 grade coeducational college-preparatory school.

John Searle, Head of School

1175 Osaka YMCA International High School
1-2-2-800 Benten Minato-ku
Osaka 552-0007
Japan
06-4395-1002
Fax: 06-4395-1004
E-mail: general-inquiry@oyis.org
http://www.oyis.org
OYIS strives to be a leading provider of international education for the citizens and residents of Osaka and its environs.

John Murphy, Principal

1176 Osan American High School
Unit 2037
APO AP 96278-0005
Korea
011-82-31-661-9076
Fax: 011-82-31-661-9121
E-mail: PRINCIPAL.OSANHS@pac.dodea.edu
http://www.osan-hs.pac.dodea.edu
Provides student with successful, productive and rewarding educational experiences.

Timothy Erickson, Principal
Truly Schramm, Assistant Principal

1177 Osan Elementary School
Unit 2037
APO, AP 96278-2037
Korea
011-82-31-661-6912
Fax: 011-82-31-661-5733
E-mail: david.petree.pac.dodea.edu
http://www.osan-es.pac.dodea.edu
Provides quality and challenging educational opportunities for all students to become critical thinkers, life-long learners, and productive citizens in a global society.

Mia Plourde, Secretary
David Petree, Principal

1178 Overseas Children's School
PO Box 9, Pelawatte
Battaramulla
Sri Lanka
94 11 2784920-2
Fax: 94-11-2784999
E-mail: admin@osc.lk
http://www.osc.lk
OSC develops the whole person as a responsible learner striving for personal excellence within a culturally diverse school

Areta Williams, Head of School
Jerry Huxtable, Chair

1179 Overseas Family School
25 F Paterson Road
Singapore 23851
65-6738-0211
Fax: 65-6733-8825
E-mail: executive_director@ofs.edu.sg
http://www.ofs.edu.sg
To focus on the individual needs of every student and to provide a supportive atmosphere designed to help students achieve personal academic goals.

David Perry, Chairman
Irene Wong, Executive Director

1180 Overseas School of Colombo
Pelawatte
PO Box 9, Battaranmulla
Sri Lanka
94 11 2784920-2
Fax: 94 11 2784999
E-mail: admin@osc.lk
http://www.osc.lk

OSC develops the whole person as a responsible learner striving for personal excellence within a culturally diverse school.

Areta Williams, Head of School
Jerry Huxtable, Chair

1181 Pacific Harbour International School
PO Box 50
Pacific Harbour, Deuba
Fiji Islands

Janet Tuni, Principal

1182 Pasir Ridge International
Unocal-po Box 3-tampines S
Balikpapan 9152
Singapore
62-542-543-474
Fax: 62-542-767-126
E-mail: prschool@bpp.mega.net.id
Grade levels preK through 8.

Kathryn Carter-Golden PhD, Principal

1183 Peak School
20 Plunketts Road
The Peak
Hong Kong
852-2849 7211
Fax: 852-2849 7151
E-mail: office@peakschool.net
http://www.ps.edu.hk
Helping promote a better understanding of Americans on the part of the peoples served

Annette Ainsworth, Principal/Secretary
Bill Garnett, Vice Principal

1184 Phuket International Preparatory School
115/15 Moo 7 Thepkasattri Road
Thepkasattri, Thalang, Phuket 83110
Thailand
66 (0)76 336 000
Fax: 66 (0)76 336 081
E-mail: info@phuketinternationalacademy.com
http://http://www.phuketinternationalacademy.com

Agnes Hebler, Principal

1185 Popondetta International School
PO Box 10
Popondetta, Papua
New Guinea

Michael Whitting, Principal

1186 Prahram Campus-Wesley College
577 St Kilda Road-Prahran
Melbourne
Australia
61 3 8102 6100
Fax: 61 3 8102 6054
E-mail: stkildaroad@wesleycollege.net
http://http://www.wesleycollege.net

AB Conabere, Principal

1187 Pusan American School
Do DOS
Pusan 96259
South Korea
82-51-801-7528
Fax: 82-51-803-1729
E-mail: pas@pac.odedodea.edu

Alexia Venglek, Principal

1188 Pusan Elementary & High School
Unit 15625
APO AP 96259-0005, Pusan
Korea
82-52-801-7528
Fax: 82-51-803-1729

1189 QSI International School-Phuket
Box 432 A Muang
Phuket 83000
Thailand
66-076-354-077
Fax: 66-76-354077
E-mail: phuket@qsi.org
http://www.qsi.org
To keep this urge to learn alive in every child in QSI schools. Our schools are established to provide in the English language a quality education for students in the cities we serve.

Khun Janrita Hnobnorb, Administrative Coordinator
Alan Siporin, Director

1190 QSI International School-Zhuhai
Building 2B, HengXin Industry Distr
JiuZhou Dadao Xi #2001
Zuhai, China
86-756-815-6134
Fax: 86-756-8189021
E-mail: zhuhai@qsi.org
http://http://www.qsi.org/zhu_home/contact.htm
To keep this urge to learn alive in every child in QSI schools. Our schools are established to provide in the English language a quality education for students in the cities we serve.

Matthew Farwell, Director

1191 Quarry Bay School
6 Hau Yuen Path Braemar Hill
North Point, Hong Kong
China
852 2566 4242ÿ
Fax: 852 2887 9849
E-mail: debra.gardiner@qbs.edu.hk
http://www.qbs.edu.hk
Our aim is to encourage in our children the enjoyment of learning by providing activities both in and outside the classroom which help to develop confident, happy and successful individuals.

Debra Gardiner, Principal

1192 Rabaul International School
PO Box 571
Rabaul Enbp, Papua
New Guinea

Ian Smith, Principal

1193 Richard E Byrd Elementary School
PSC 472 Box 12
FPO
Japan, AP 96348-12
045-281-4815
011-81-45-281-4815
Fax: 045-281-4870
Fax: 011-81-45-281-4870
http://www.byrd-es.pac.dodea.edu
Richard E. . Byrd envisions a school unbound by traditional school concepts of time, location and age requirements. Byrd Elementary School will provide all students with vast opportunities for learning and civic involvement

Gwen Baxter-Oakley, Principal

1194 Robert D Edgren High School
Unit 5040
APO
Japan, AP 96319-5040
226-437-
011-81-176-77-4377
Fax: 226-495-
Fax: 011-81-176-77-4959
E-mail: principal_*edgren_hs@pac.dodea.edu
http://www.edgren-hs.pac.dodea.edu
Committed to helping students develop academically, socially, physically and emotionally in a global community.

Gerogia Watters, Principal

1195 Ruamrudee International School
6 Ramkamhaeng 184 Road
Minburi, Bangkok
Thailand 10510
66-2-518-0320
Fax: 66-2-518-0334
E-mail: info@rism.ac.th
http://www.rism.ac.th/risweb
Grade levels K-12, school year August - June

Fr. Leo Travis, Director
Dave Parsons HS Principal

1196 Saigon South International School
Nguyen Van Linh Parkway, Tan Phong
Ho Chi Minh City
Vietnam
(84-8) 5413-0901
Fax: (84-8) 5413-0902
E-mail: info@ssis.edu.vn
http://www.ssischool.org
Saigon South International School is a college preparatory school committed to the intellectual and personal development of each student in preparation for a purposeful life as a global citizen.

Robert Crowther, Headmaster
Charles Barton, Head of School

1197 Sancta Maria International School
41 Karasawa Minami-ku
Yokohama
Japan

Sr Mary Elizabeth Doll, Principal

1198 School at Tembagapura
PO Box 616 Cairns
Queensland 4870
Australia

Bruce Goforth, Principal

1199 Scots PGC College
60 Oxenham Street
Warwick, QLD
Australia 4370
61 7 4666 9811
Fax: 61 7 4666 9812
E-mail: postbox@scotspgc.qld.edu.au
http://www.scotspgc.qld.edu.au
Our philosophy of schooling rests squarely on the belief that a true education encourages young people to question and explore, to develop a strong sense of personal identity, to strive to achieve one's best, and to value the act of serving without losing one's desire to lead.

Michael Harding, Principal
Nigel Grant, Director of Learning

1200 Seisen International School
12-15 Yoga 1-chome
Setagaya-Ku, Tokyo
Japan 158-0-97
03-3704-2661
Fax: 033701-1033
E-mail: sisinfo@seisen.com
http://www.seisen.com
Seisen International School seeks to provide a happy, stable and secure environment in which students are prepared through teaching and example, to live in a world of tremendous challenge and rapid change.

Concesa Martin, Headmistress

1201 Semarang International School
Asad Ave-Mohammedpur
Semarang, Central Java
Indonesia 50254
62-24-8311-424
Fax: 62-24-8311-994
E-mail: info@semarangis.or.id
http://www.semarangis.or.id
Offer Semarang 's international community high quality and affordable education based

on the International Baccalaureate Organization's Primary Years Programme, (PYP) philosophy. Provide an educational and motivational base from which each pupil may take his or her place with confidence in any school in any country in the medium of English.

Barry Burns, Principal

1202 Seoul Academy
988-5, Daechi-dong
Kangamku Seoul
Korea 135-2
82-02-554-1690
Fax: 82-2-562-0451
E-mail: sais5541690@hanmail.net
http://http://www.seoulacademy.net/
Grade levels pre-K through eighth.

Thomas O'Connor, Director

1203 Seoul British School
55 Yonhi Dong Sudaemun Ku
Seoul
Korea

Philip Mayor-Smith, Principal

1204 Seoul Elementary School
Unit 15549
APO, AP
Korea 96205-5549
736-461-
011-82-2-7916-4613
Fax: 736-460-
Fax: 011-82-2-793-6925
E-mail: principal.seoules@pac.dodea.edu
http://www.seoul-es.pac.dodea.edu
Provides standards based instruction in a safe learning environment which fosters independent thinking and respects cultural diversity through collaboration among staff, students, parents and community

Catherine Yurica, Principal

1205 Seoul Foreign School
55 Yonhi-Dong Sodaemun-Gu
Seoul
Korea 120-8-113
82-2-330-3100
Fax: 82-2-335-1857
E-mail: sfsoffice@seoulforeign.org
http://www.sfs.or.kr
As has been true throughout our history, Seoul Foreign School is committed to academic excellence. Our rigorous college preparatory curriculum - which includes the International Baccalaureate diploma program - and our dynamic learning environment challenge students to achieve their full intellectual potential. Equally, we cherish Christian values which encourage our students to develop strong character, live and work with integrity, and accept responsibility for themselves and others.

John Engstrom, Head of School
Barry Benger, Director Human Resources

1206 Seoul High School
Unit 15549
APO, AP
South Korea 96205-5549
738-526-
011+82-2-7918-5261
Fax: 738-882-
Fax: 011+82-2-7918-8822
http://www.seoul-hs.pac.dodea.edu
Seoul American High School is located on Yongsan Army Base in the center of Seoul, Korea. The school complex is comprised of eight buildings containing over 60 classrooms and special purpose rooms.

Richard Schlueter, Principal

1207 Shanghai American School
258 Jin Feng Lu
Huacao Town, Minhang Dist. Shanghai
China 20110
86-21-6221-1445
Fax: 86-21-6221-1269
E-mail: admission@saschina.org
http://www.saschina.org
Shanghai American School, in partnership with parents, fosters the development of each student's personal potential through a balance of the academic, physical, social, emotional and ethical aspects of life. SAS provides a challenging American core curriculum with an international perspective that inspires a passion for learning and intellectual vitality.

Kerry Jacobson, Superintendent
Andrew Torris, Deputy Superintendent

1208 Shatin College
3 Lai Wo Lane
Sha Tin
Hong Kong
852-269- 181
852 26991811
Fax: 852 26950592
E-mail: info@shatincollege.edu.hk
http://www.shatincollege.edu.hk
Independent, coeducational, secondary school within the English Schools Foundation

David Cottam, Principal
Grahame Carder, Chairman

1209 Shatin Junior College
3A Lai Wo Lane
Fo Tan, New Terretories
Hong Kong
852 2692 2721
Fax: 852 2602 5572
E-mail: info@sjs.esf.edu.hk
http://http://www.sjs.edu.hk/
At Sha Tin Junior School we aim to provide a secure and happy environment in which a child can develop their academic, social and physical potential to the full.

Perry Tunesi, Principal

1210 Shirley Lanham Elementary School
PSC 477 Box 38
FPO AP
Japan 96306-5
264-366-
011-81-467-63-3664
Fax: 264-447-
Fax: 011-81-467-63-4476
E-mail: Principal.lanhames@pac.dodea.edu
http://www.lanham-es.pac.dodea.edu
We are preparing all students to be responsible, positive contributors within a diverse, global community.

Dave Russell, Principal

1211 Singapore American School
40 Woodlands Street 41
Singapore 73854
65-6363-3403
Fax: 65-6363-3408
E-mail: communications@sas.edu.sg
http://www.sas.edu.sg
The Singapore American School is committed to providing each student an exemplary American educational experience with an international perspective.

Brent Mutsch, Superintendent

1212 Sollars Elementary School
Unit 5041
APO, AP
Japan 96319-5041
226-393-
011-81-176-77-3933
Fax: 226-387-
Fax: 011-81-176-77-3873

E-mail:
PRINCIPAL.SOLLARSES@pac.dodea.edu
http://www.sollars-es.pac.dodea.edu
Dana Chandler, Principal

1213 South Island School
50 Nam Fung Road
Aberdeen
Hong Kong
852-255- 93
Fax: 852-553-811
E-mail: sis@mail.sis.edu.hk
http://www.sis.edu.hk
School Aims to develop students' confidence, self-esteem and a range of positive values and personal qualities and to produce enthusiastic, active, independent and lifelong learners.

Graham Silverthorne, Principal
Roberta Kam, Admission

1214 St. Andrews International School-Bangkok
Pridi Banomyong 20/1
Sukhumvit Soi 71, Prakanong, Bangkok
Thailand 10110
(+66) 23 81 23 87-
Fax: (+66) 23 91 52 27
E-mail: info@standrews.ac.th
http://http://www.standrews.ac.th/
Our mission is to provide an inclusive, international education in a happy, supportive and stimulating environment, where all the needs of the individual learner are met and students are inspired to achieve their full potential enabling them to become responsible global citizens

Paul Schofield, Head of School
Jamsai Anuvongchareon, Director

1215 St. Christopher's School
10 Nunn Road
Penang
Malaysia 10350
604-226-3589
Fax: 604-226-4340
E-mail: principal@scips.org.my
http://www.scips.org.my
St. Christopher's International Primary School of Penang, caters for expatriates' and also Malaysian children. It is located in one of the most sought after residential areas on the island of Penang Malaysia.

John G Jones, Principal

1216 St. John's International School
Ladprao
Bangkok
Thailand 10900
662-513-8575
Fax: +66 2 513 5273
E-mail: sjiadmin@stjohn.ac.th
http://www.international.stjohn.ac.th
A holistic British style school preparing students of all nationalities to become life long learners and effective communicators in the global community.

Chainarong Monthienvic, Principal

1217 St. Joseph International School
5-16-10 Shibamata, Katsushika-ku
Tokyo
Japan 125-0
03 -694-4550
E-mail: schray@stjoseph-k.org
http://www.stjoseph-k.org
Coeducational day/boarding school, preschool through grade 12.

James Mueller, Principal
Thomas Schray, Head Teacher

1218 St. Joseph's International Primary School
PO Box 5784
Boroko Papua
New Guinea
Barbara D'Arbon, Principal

1219 St. Mark's College
46 Pennington Terrace
North Adelaide
Australia, SA 5006
08-8334-5600
Fax: 08-8267-4694
E-mail: stmarks@stmarkscollege.com.au
http://www.stmarkscollege.com.au
Grade levels Pre-K through 12, school year
March - December

Rose Alwyn, Headmaster
James Raw, Dean

1220 St. Mary's International School
1-6-19 Seta Setagaya-ku
Tokyo
Japan 158-8
81 - 37-9 34
Fax: 81 - 37-7 19
E-mail: michelj@smis.ac.jp
http://www.smis.ac.jp
St. Mary's is committed to educating boys to
be lifelong learners of good character who
demonstrate academic, physical, artistic, and
moral excellence, respect for religious and
cultural beliefs, and responsibility as
international citizens.

Michel Jutras, Headmaster
Br Lawrence G Lambert, Elementary School
Principal

1221 St. Maur International School
83 Yamate-cho Naka-ku
Yokahama
Japan 231-8
81-45-641-5751
Fax: 81-45-641-6688
E-mail: office@stmaur.ac.jp
http://www.stmaur.ac.jp
he basic objective of Saint Maur International
School is to provide a Pre-school, Elementary
and Secondary education for international
students residing in Japan, by using the English language as the primary medium of instruction. An international student is defined
as a student whose life experiences span more
than one cultural dimension. From this basic
goal stem specific objectives which fall into
three conceptual categories: spiritual,
cultural, and academic.

Jeanette K Thomas, Head of School
Richard B Rucci, Coordinating Principal

1222 St. Michael's International School
17-2 Nakayamate-dori 3-chome
Chuo-ku, Kobe-shi 650-0004
Japan
078-231-8885
81-78-231-8885
Fax: 078-231-8899
Fax: 81-78-231-8899
E-mail: head@smis.org
http://www.smis.org
Provides a distinctive Primary education
within a positive culture of academic excellence and caring family community.

Aileen Pardon, Principal
Paul Grisewood, Head of School

1223 St. Stephen's International School
998 Viphavadi Rangsit Road
Lad Yao, Chatuchak, Bangkok
Thailand 10900
66-2-5130270
Fax: 66-2-9303307
E-mail: info@sis.edu
http://www.sis.edu

To encourage all students in their studies, personal life and in all their interactions to strive
for excellence on their journey to becoming
effective and compassionate citizens and
leaders. Our goal is to nurture a culture and a
community of learners creating a unique East
meets West environment .

Richard A Ralphs, School Director
Gary Rodbard, Principal

1224 St. Xavier's Greenherald School
Asad Ave-Mohammedpur
Dhaka 1207
Bangladesh
Mary Imelda, Principal

1225 Stearley Heights Elementary School
Unit 5166
APO Kadena 96368 5166
Okinawa 36368
634-452-
001-81-611-694-452
Fax: 98 -34 -168
Fax: 001-81- 98-934-681
E-mail:
Stearley-Heights.Principal@pac.dodea.edu
http://http://www.stearley-es.pac.dodea.edu

Thomas Godbold, Principal

1226 Sullivans Elementary School
PSC 473, Box 96
Yokosuka 96349 0096
Japan
243-733-
011-81-468-16-7336
Fax: 243-786-
Fax: 011-81-468-16-7865
E-mail:
principal_*sullivan_es@pac.dodea.edu
http://http://www.sullivans-es.pac.dodea.ed
u

Walter Wilhoit, Principal

1227 Surabaya International School
CitraRaya International Village
Citra Raya, Lakarsantri
Tromol Pos 2/SBDK, Surabaya
Indonesia 60225
62-31-741-4300
Fax: 62-31-741-4334
E-mail: sisadmin@sisedu.net
http://www.sisedu.net
The Surabaya International School Community is committed to developing the social,
emotional, physical, creative, and intellectual
abilities necessary for its students to become
reasoning, responsible, contributing, successful members of our global community.

Larry Jones, Superintendent
Christopher Burke, Chairperson

1228 TEDA International School-Tianjin
Number 72 Third Avenue Teda
Tianjin, CN 30045
86 -2 6-2261
Fax: 86 -2 6-0018
E-mail:
Principal@tedainternationalschool.net
http://www.tedainternationalschool.net
provide outstanding education to the students
of all nationalities.

Nick Bowley, Director
Joseph Azmeh, Headmaster

1229 Tabubil International School
PO Box 408 Tabubil
Tabubil
Papua New Guinea
675-548-9233
Fax: 675-542-9641
E-mail: tabis@online.net.pg
http://www.tis.ac.pg
To provides a high quality international
school education catering to the varied needs

of Tabubil's multicultural mining community.
The school employs a well motivated and productive staff, with good working conditions
and a high degree of community involvement

SE Walker, Principal

1230 Taegu Elementary & High School
Unit 15623
APO Taegu 96218 0005
Korea
Leon Rivers, Principal

1231 Taipei American School
800 Chung Shan N Road Section 6
Taipei
Taiwan 11152
886-2-287-39900
Fax: 886-2-287-31641
E-mail: admissions@tas.edu.tw
http://www.tas.edu.tw
Our mission is to inspire each student to be a
confident, creative, caring and moral individual prepared to adapt and succeed anywhere
in a rapidly changing world. We provide an
American-based education with a global perspective that results in a love of learning, academic excellence, a balanced life, and service
to others.

Sharon D Hennessy, Superintendent
Ira B Weislow, Business Manager

1232 Tanglin Trust Schools
95 Portsdown Road
Singapore 13929
65-67780711
Fax: 65-67775862
E-mail: admissions@tts.edu.sg
http://www.tts.edu.sg
Our vision is to be the premier school, providing the highest quality learning experiences
for 3 to 18 year olds, and cultivating strong relationships in an environment where the individual is important. Our students enjoy a rich
and stimulating all-round education which
prepares them thoroughly for life in a rap-
idly-changing and competitive world.

Ronald Stones, Head of School
Peter Derby-Crook, CEO

1233 Thai-Chinese International School
101/177 Moo 7 Soi Mooban Bangpleeni
Prasertsin Road Bangplee Yai
Samutprakarn, TH 10540
66-2-260-8202
E-mail: tcis@schoolmail.com
http://www.tcis.ac.th
provide an education which allows each student to develop his/her full being in all areas
of human development, academic, physical,
emotional, spiritual and social, to interact as
critical and compassionate thinkers, and to
become a responsible member of our global
society.

1234 Timbertop Campus
Timbertop PB-Mansfield
Victoria 3722
Australia
61 3 5733 6777
Fax: 61 3 5777 5772
E-mail: timbertop@ggs.vic.edu.au
http://http://www.ggs.vic.edu.au/Contact.as
px
Stephen Meek, Principal

1235 Traill Preparatory School
34-36 S01
18 Ramkhamheng Road, Huamark Bangkok
Thailand
AM Traill, Principal

1236 Ukarumpa High School
PO Box 406
Ukarumpa Via Lae, Papua
New Guinea

Steve Walker, Principal

1237 United Nations International School-Hanoi
Phu Thuong Ward Lac Long Quan Road
Tay Ho District
Veitnam, VN
(84 4) 3758 1551
Fax: (84 4) 3758 1542
E-mail: info@unishanoi.org
http://www.unishanoi.org
A private, nonprofit, English language, coeducational day school which offers an educational program from prekindergarten through grade 12 for the expatriate community of Hanoi.

Chip Barder, Head of School

1238 United World College-SE Asia
1207 Dover Road
PO Box 15, Singapore 9111
Singapore 13965
65 6775 5344
Fax: 65 6778 5846
E-mail: info@uwcsea.edu.sg
http://www.uwcsea.edu.sg
The United World College Movement makes education a force to unite people, nations and cultures for peace and a sustainable future. We educate individuals to take responsibility for shaping a better world

Julian Whiteley, Head of College
Geraint Jones, Assistant Head of College

1239 University Vacancies in Australia
Australian Vice-Chancellors' Committee
GPO Box 1142
Canberra City
Australia
61-02-6285-8200
Fax: 60-02-6285-8211
E-mail:
contact@universitiesaustralia.edu.au
Universities Australia was established on 22 May 2007 as the industry peak body representing the university sector.

G Withers, Chief Executive Officer
P Rodely, Committee Executive Officer

1240 Vientiane International School
PO Box 3180
Phonesavanh Road, Saphanthong Tai Villag
Lao PDR
856 21 486001
Fax: 856 21 486009
E-mail: contact@vislao.com
http://www.vislao.com/
Vientiane International School (VIS) is an independent, non-profit day school offering a quality international-standard curriculum from Preschool (3 year olds) through Grade 12 (18 year olds).

Greg Smith, Director

1241 Wellesley College
PO Box 41037
Eastbourne, Lower Hutt 5047, Wellington
New Zealand
64 - 56- 803
Fax: 64 - 56- 728
E-mail: office@wellesley.school.nz
http://www.wellesley.school.nz
Wellesley is a full independent primary day school for boys from Year 0 (aged five) to Year 8.

Warren Owen, Principal
Charlotte Gendall, Board member

1242 Wesley International School
Kotak Pos 275
Malang, East Java
Indonesia 65101
62-341-586410
Fax: 62-341-586413
E-mail: wesley@wesleyinterschool.org
http://www.wesleyinterschool.org
Our mission at Wesley International School is to provide students with a Christ-centered education: one that inspires them to live a Godly life, that instills a biblical worldview, and produces academic excellence-an education that will prepare our students to impact and bless their world with knowledge, insight, action and love

Paul Richardson, HS Principal
Jonathan Heath, Director

1243 Western Academy of Beijing
PO Box 8547
10 Lai Guang Ying dong Lu, Beijing 10010
China
86-10-8456-4155
Fax: 86 10 6433-3974
E-mail: wabinfo@wab.edu
http://www.wab.edu
The Western Academy of Beijing offers a challenging and caring, community based educational environment in which students are active participants in the learning process

Robert Landau, Director
Karen O'Connell, Deputy Chair

1244 Wewak International Primary School
PO Box 354
Wewak Esp, Papua
New Guinea

Darian Sullavan, Principal

1245 Woodstock School
Mussoorie
Uttarakhand
India 24817
91-135-632-610
Fax: 91-135-632-885
E-mail: mail@woodstock.ac.in
http://www.woodstock.ac.in
Woodstock aims to develop responsible global citizens and leaders by providing a world-class international education, rooted in its Christian heritage and values, for a diverse group of students, especially from families in Christian or public service, in an Indian Himalayan environment

David Laurenson, Principal
Thomas Chandy, President

1246 Xiamen International School
262 Xingbei San Lu, Xinglin
Jimei, Xiamen, Fujian
China
86-592-625-6581
Fax: 86-592-625-6584
E-mail: askxis@xischina.com
http://www.xischina.com
Develops confident, knowledgeable students who enjoy life-long learning, demonstrate global awareness and contribute compassionately to the world around them.

Paul Raschke, Headmaster
Yuan Yuan Deng, Vice Chairman

1247 Yew Chung Shanghai International School
18 W Rong Hua Road, Gubei New Area
Shanghai
China 20110
(8621) 6219 5910
Fax: (8621) 6219 0675
E-mail: enquiry@ycef.com
http://www.ycis-sh.com
Provide an all-round education that nurtures the whole person - spiritual, academic, physi-

cal, social and emotional that includes relationships with others.

Andrew Mellor, Co-Principal
Julie Zheng, Co-Principal

1248 Yogyakarta International School
P.O. Box 1175
Yogyakarta 55011, Jalan Cendrawasih No.1
Indonesia
62.274.625965
Fax: 62.274.625966
E-mail: board@ yis-edu.org
http://http://www.yis-edu.org/
Operates as a not for profit social foundation and is overseen by a School Board made up of both parents and non-parents.

Chris Scott, Principal

1249 Yokohama International School
258 Yamate-cho Naka-ku
Yokohama
Japan 231-0
81-45-622-0084
Fax: 81-45-621-0379
E-mail: yis@yis.ac.jp
http://www.yis.ac.jp
Provides the highest-quality, balanced education to internationally minded students in an inquiring and supportive environment.

Simon Taylor, Headmaster
John Inge, Chairman

1250 Yokota East Elementary School
DoDDS P J YE Unit 5072
APO, Yokota 96328 5072
Japan 96328
225-550-
81-3117-55-5503
Fax: 225-550-
Fax: 81-3117-55-5502
E-mail: principal.mendel@pac.dodea.edu
http://http://www.mendel-es.pac.dodea.edu
Yokota East Elementary School is located on Yokota Air Force Base near Tokyo, Japan. There are approximately 900 students grades K-6.

Hattie Phipps, Principal

1251 Yokota High School
DoDDS P J YH Unit 5072
APO AP
Japan 96328-5072
225-701-
011-81-3117-55-701
Fax: 225-722-
Fax: 011-81-3117-55-722
E-mail:
principal_*yokotahs@pac.dodea.edu
http://www.yokota-hs.pac.dodea.edu
Yokota High School, working in partnership with the family and local community, provides a safe, academically-inspiring environment in which all students will develop to their maximum potential as life-long learners and responsible participants in an ever-changing global society.

Darrell Mood, Principal

1252 Yokota West Elementary School
DoDDS P J YW Unit 5072
APO AP
Japan 96328-5072
225-761-
011-81-3117-55-761
Fax: 225-573-
Fax: 011-81-3117-55-573
E-mail:
principal_*yokota_west_es@pac.dodea.edu
http://www.ywes.pac.dodea.edu

Sharon Carter, Principal

1253 Yonggwang Foreign School
Ceii Site Office
PO Box 9, Yonggwang-Kun 513-880
Korea

Eleanor Jones, Principal

1254 Zama Junior High & High School
USA Garrison, Camp Zama
APO, Honshu 96343 0005
Japan

Samuel Menniti, Principal

1255 Zukeran Elementary School
Unit 35017
FPO AP
Japan 96379-5017
645-257-
011-81-611-7452576
Fax: 011-81-098-892-795
E-mail: Zukeran.Principal@pac.dodea.edu
http://www.zukeran-es.pac.dodea.edu
Zukeran Elementary School shares the vision of creating a community of learners actively engaged in the pursuit of the knowledge, skills and experiences necessary to empower all children to meet the challenges of the 21st century.

Cindy Templeton, Principal
Roger Reade, Assistant Principal

Central & South America

1256 Academia Cotopaxi American International School
De las Higuerillas y Alondras
Quito
Ecuador
593-2-246-7411
Fax: 593-2-244-5195
E-mail: info@cotopaxi.k12.ec
http://www.cotopaxi.k12.ec
Premier English-language school from early childhood through secondary school.

Kurt Kywi, President
Robert Moss, Vice President

1257 American Cooperative School
Lawton 20
Paramaribo
Suriname
597-49-9461
Fax: 597-498-853
E-mail: acs_suriname@sil.org
http://www.acs-suriname.com
A private, coeducational day school which offers an educational program from prekindergarten through grade 12 for students of all nationalities.

Frank Martens, Administrator

1258 American Elementary & High School
Caixa Postal 7432
01064-970, Sao Paulo
Brazil
55-11-3842-2499
Fax: 55-11-3842-9358
E-mail: graded@eagle.aegsp.br
A private, coeducational day school which offers a full college-preparatory educational program from preschool through grade 12 for students of all nationalities.

Dr Gunther Brandt, Principal

1259 American International School-Bolivia
Casilla 5309
Cochabamba
Bolivia
591-4-428-8577
Fax: 591-4-428-8576
E-mail: administracion@aisb.edu.bo
http://www.aisb.edu.bo
The American International School of Bolivia was founded in 1993 as an international, non-governmental, co-educational day school. The AIS/B educational system covers from Early Childhood education up to the IB program in grades 11 and 12 for students representing all nationalities and socio-economical levels.

Dr Silke Marina Scholer, Director General
Tatiana Jimenez BA, Chief Administrator

1260 American International School-Lincoln Buenos Aires
Andres Ferreyra 4073
B1637 AOS La Lucila, Buenos Aires
Argentina
(54)(11) 4851-1700
Fax: 54-11-479-02117
E-mail: pacha_c@lincoln.edu.ar
http://www.lincoln.edu.ar
Provides education based on United States accredited curriculum in an environment of academic excellence that develops ethical, responsible and globally conscious world citizens.

Phil T Joslin, Superintendent

1261 American School
PO Box (01) 35
El Salvador
503-26-38-330
Fax: 503-26-38-385
E-mail: recruiting@amschool.edu.sv
http://www.amschool.edu.sv
Founded in 1946 and is an independent, international, coeducational, college-preparatory institution

Yolanda de Lopez, Director of Admissions

1262 American School Foundation AC
Bondojito 215
Colonia Las Americas
Mexico City, Mexico 01120
52-55-5227-4900
Fax: 52-55-5273-4357
E-mail: asf@asf.edu.mx
http://www.asf.edu.mx
is an academically rigorous, international, university preparatory school, which offers students from diverse backgrounds the best of American independent education

Julie Hellmund, Director

1263 American School Foundation-Guadalajara
Colomos 2100, Coronel Providencia
Guadalajara, Jalisco
Mexico 44640
52 (33) 3648-0299
Fax: 52-33-3817-3356
E-mail: asfg@asfg.mx
http://www.asfg.mx
Educating students in a bilingual, bicultural and secular environment to be purposeful learners, critical and creative thinkers, effective communicators and community contributors, based on a foundation of honor, freedom and commitment

David McGrath, Principal
Jabet Heinze, Superintendent

1264 American School Foundation-Monterrey
Ave. Ignacio Morones Prieto No. 150
Col. San Isidro, Santa Catarina, N.L.
Nuevo Leon, Mexico 66190
(52)-81-5000-4400
Fax: (52)-81-5000-4428
E-mail: jeff.keller@asfm.edu.mx
http://www.asfm.edu.mx
A private, nonprofit, coeducational day school which offers an educational program from nursery through grade 12 for students of all nationalities.

Dr. Jeffrey Keller, Superintendent

1265 American School-Belo Horizonte
Avenida Deputado Cristovan Chiaradia 120
Caixa Postal 1701
Bairro Buritis, Belo Horizonte 30575-440
Brazil
55-31-378-6700
Fax: 55-31-378-6878
E-mail: eabh@eabh.com.br
http://http://www.eabh.com.br/eng/contact.html
A coeducational, private day school which offers an educational program from prekindergarten through grade 12 for students of all nationalities.

Sid Stewart, Principal

1266 American School-Brasilia
SGAS 605
Bloco E, Lotes 34/37
Brasilia,DF,Brazil 70200-650
55 (61) 3442-9700
Fax: 55 (61) 3442-9729
E-mail: kpuzic@eabdf.br
http://www.eabdf.br
A private, coeducational day school which offers an educational program from prekindergarten through grade 12 for students of all nationalities

Barry Dequanne, Headmaster
Beth Lopez, Lower School Principal

1267 American School-Campinas
Rua Cajamar, 35 - Jardim Alto da Ba
Campinas- SP
Brazil 13090
55 19 2102-1000
Fax: 55 19 2102-1016
http://www.escolaamericanadecampinas.com.br/?contact

Steve Herrara, Superintendent

1268 American School-Durango
Francisw Sarabia #416 Pte
Durango 34000
Mexico
(618) 813-36-36
Fax: (618) 811-28-39
E-mail: colegio_americano@cadurango.edu.mx
http://http://www.cadurango.edu.mx

Dr Jorge O Nelson, Principal

1269 American School-Guatemala
11 Calle 1579 Zona 15 Vista Hermosa
Guatemala
Guatemala
50- 2-6907
Fax: 50- 2-6983
E-mail: director@cag.edu.gt
http://www.cag.edu.gt
is to educate independent, critical-thinking, responsible, bilingual individuals prepared to meet the challenges of the future

Robert Gronniger, General Director
Edward Langlais, High School Principal

1270 American School-Guayaquil
PO Box 3304
Guayaquill
Ecuador
593-4-255-503
Fax: 593-4-250-453
E-mail: dir_asg@gye.satnet.net

Grade levels K-12, school year April - January

Francisco Andrade, Interim General Director
Patricia Ayala de Coronel, HS Principal

1271 American School-Laguna Verde
Veracruz, Mexico
Maurice H Blum, Principal

1272 American School-Lima
Apartado 18-0977
Lima 18
Peru
51-14-35-0890
Fax: 51 1 619-9301
E-mail: fdr@amersol.edu.pe
http://www.amersol.edu.pe/fdr/
is to empower our students to pursue their passion for learning, lead lives of integrity and create socially responsible solutions.

Carol Kluznik, Superintendent

1273 American School-Pachuca
Valle de Anahuac S/N Valle de San J
ZC: 42083 Pachuca de Soto Hidalgo
Mexico
01-771 713 9608
Fax: 52-771-85077
E-mail: admisiones@americana.edu.mx
http://http://www.americana.edu.mx/
Grade levels prekindergarten through ninth.

Nic,foro Ramirez, General Director

1274 American School-Puebla
Apartado 665
Puebla
Mexico

http://http://www.cap.edu.mx/english/
Dr Arthur W Chaffee, Principal

1275 American School-Puerto Vallarta
PO Box 2-280
Puerto Vallarta, Jalisco 48300
Mexico
52 322-221-1525
Fax: (52) 322-226-7677
E-mail: Info@aspv.edu.mx
http://http://www.aspv.edu.mx
Gerald Selitzer, Director

1276 American School-Recife
408 S⁻ e Souza Street
Boa Viagem
Brazil 51030-60
55 81 3341.4716
Fax: 55-81-341-0142
E-mail: info@ear.com.br
http://www.ear.com.br
A private, coeducational day school which offers an instructional program from prekindergarten through grade 12 for students of all nationalities.

George Takacks, Superintendent

1277 American School-Tampico
Hidalgo # 100
Tancol, Tampico
Mexico
833-2 2- 20
52-12-272-081
Fax: 52-12-280-080
E-mail: racevedo@ats.edu.mx
http://www.ats.edu.mx
Grade levels N through tenth.

Emma deSalazar, Headmaster

1278 American School-Torreon
Paseo del Algodn y Boulevard Carlo
Fracc Los Viedos Torren, Coahuila
Mexico 27019

222-51 -0
871ÿ222 51 00 TO 0
Fax: 871 733 26 68
E-mail: cat@cat.mx
http://www.cat.mx
A prestigious center of academic excellence dedicated to creating life-long learners and ethical leaders in a global and changing world.

Makhlouf Ouyed, Director General
Martha Martinez, Business Manager

1279 Anglo American School
PO Box 3188-1000
San Jose
Costa Rica
506-279-2626
Fax: 506-279-7894
E-mail: angloam@racsa.co.cr
Grade levels Pre-K through 6, school year February - November

Virginia Hine Barrantes, Principal

1280 Anglo Colombian School
Apaptado Aereo 253393
Bogota
Colombia
David Toze, Principal

1281 Anglo-American School
Calle 37
Avenida Central, 1000 San Jose
Costa Rica
E-mail: angloam@sd.racsa.co.cr

Virginia Hine, Principal

1282 Antofagasta International School
Avda. Jaime Guzman Errazurz #04300
Antofagasta
Chile
56 - 55 - 694900
Fax: 56 - 55 - 694912
E-mail: ais@ais.cl
http://www.ais.cl
A Pre-Kindergarten through 12th grade educational institution that is dedicated to offering a challenging, English-based curriculum to its students.

Carlos Ignacio Figueroa Ahumada, Principal
Carlos Arturo Calussen Calvo, Chairman

1283 Asociacion Colegio Granadino
AA 2138
Manizales, Caldas
Colombia
57-68-745-774
Fax: 57-68-746-066
E-mail: granadino@emtelsa.multi.net.co
Grade levels Pre-K through 12, school year August - June

Gonzalo Arango, General Director

1284 Asociacion Escuelas Lincoln
Andres Ferreyra 4073
B1636 AOS La Lucila, Buenos Aires
Argentina
(54)(11) 4851-1700
Fax: 54-11-4790-2117
E-mail: joslin_p@lincoln.edu.ar
http://www.lincoln.edu.ar
Provide an education based on United States accredited curriculum

Phil Joslin, Superintendent
Claudia Pacha, Admissions

1285 Balboa Elementary School
Unit 9025
APO Balboa 34002
Panama
Susan Beattie, Principal

1286 Balboa High School
Unit 9025
APO Balboa 34002
Panama
Ernest Holland, Principal

1287 Barker College
91 Pacific Highway
Hornsby
NSW, Australia 2077
02-98-7 83
Fax: 02-94-6 13
E-mail: reception@barker.nsw.edu.au
http://www.barker.nsw.edu.au
That Barker College be, and be recognized as, a leading Australian Christian independent school, which provides a broadly-based education and encourages young people to strive to fulfil their potential, and which is acknowledged as a centre of excellence in pastoral care and in teaching and learning

Jimmy Cappanera, Principal
Roderic Kefford, Headmaster

1288 Belgrano Day School
Juramento 3035
Ciudad de Buenos Aires
Argentina c1428
54-11 -781
Fax: 54-11 -4786
E-mail: rrpp@bdsnet.com.ar
http://www.bds.edu.ar
We cooperate with the family to offer bilingual education quality for the training of future leaders and citizens of the world committed to the common good, free, responsible, creative and respectful of diversity and dissent.

Maria Matilde V Green, President
Carol Halle, Faculty Head

1289 Bilingue School Isaac Newton
Chihuahua, Mexico
Lauya Gonzalez Valenzula, Principal

1290 British American School
AA 4368
Barranquilla
Colombia
Rafael Ortegon Rocha, Principal

1291 British School-Costa Rica
PO Box 8184-1000
San Jose
Costa Rica 2232-7833
50- 2-20 0
Fax: 50- 2-32 7
E-mail: britsch@racsa.co.cr
http://http://www.thebritishschoolofcostarica.com/

David John Lloyd, Principal

1292 British School-Rio de Janeiro
R Real Grandeza 99
Botafogo, Rio de Janeiro
Brazil, BR 22281-30
55-21-2539-2717
Fax: 55(21) 2244-5591
E-mail: edu@britishschool.g12.br
http://www.britishschool.g12.br
The British School aims to develop responsible, well-informed, open-minded, confident and caring individuals by providing an educational community within which all pupils are motivated to realize their full potential through a challenging British-based education in a non-discriminatory and bi-cultural environment

Paul Wiseman, Director
Adam Reid, Chairman

1293 British School-Venezuela
Sector 8 and Sector 12
Panchkula
India 13410
91-172-5028556
E-mail: tbs@thebritishschool.org
http://www.thebritishschool.org
aims to provide education with global standards. This will not only make students studying in the school eligible for higher education in the institutions across the world but also give NRI's settled abroad, an opportunity to send their children to such schools to have a better idea of the social system back home.

TBS Panchkula, Principal
U Sethi, Board Member

1294 Buenos Aires International Christian Academy
Red de Escuelas Mundiales Cristiana
Av Libertador General San Mart-n 2170
Buenos Aires, AR 1646
5411 4549 1300
Fax: 5411 4549 1300
E-mail: info@baica.com
http://www.baica.com
Our school is unique in that we are home to both Argentineans and the expat community.

Andy Simon, Principal
Robert Newman, Director

1295 Caribbean International School
Box 1594
Cristobal Colon
Panama

Anderson, Principal

1296 Centro Cultural Brazil-Elementary School
Rua Jorge Tibirica 5
11100 Santos, Sao Paulo
Brazil

Newton Antonio Martin, Principal

1297 Cochabamba Cooperative School
Casilla 1395
Cochabamba
Bolivia
591-42-987-61
Fax: 591-42-329-06
E-mail: Cwieburg@ccs.edu.bo
http://www.ccs.edu.bo
President

Provide attendees

Carl Wieburg, Director
Jos Leonis, Manager

1298 Colegio Abraham Lincoln
Calle 170, # 51A-81
SedePrimaria Avenue Calle 170 #65-31
Columbia
571-676-7360
http://www.abrahamlincoln.edu.co
Promoting human development within a humanistic philosophy and pruricultural.

Amparo Rueda, Director

1299 Colegio Alberto Einstein
PO Box 5018
Av. Diego V squez de Cepeda N77-157
Quito, Ecuador
(593-2)2477-901
Fax: 2470-144
E-mail: einstein@einstein.k12.ec
http://http://www.einstein.k12.ec/home-e.html
ml

Benjamin Tobar, Principal
Raquel Katzkowicz, General Director

1300 Colegio Americano De Guayaquil
Juan Tanca Marengo Avenue PO Box 33
Guayaquil
Ecuador

593-4-255-03
Fax: 593-4-250-453
E-mail: info@colegioamericano.edu.ec
http://www.colegioamericano.edu.ec
Provide an education with the highest standards of quality, thus contributing to the improvement of our society.

Stanley Whitman, Principal
Francisco Andrade, Association President

1301 Colegio Anglo Colombiano
Avenida 19 # 152A-48
Bogota
, DC
57- 2-9 57
E-mail:
admissions@anglocolombiano.edu.co
http://www.anglocolombiano.edu.co
Our purpose is to educate human beings with open minds, real social awareness and the power of critical thinking.

David Toze, Principal
Catherine Cushnan, Admission

1302 Colegio Bilingue Juan Enrigue
Pestalozzi AC
Veracruz
Mexico

Michael S Garber, Principal

1303 Colegio Bolivar
Calle 5 Number 122-21 V-a Pance
Cali
Colombia
(57-2) 684 8600
Fax: 57-2-555-2041
E-mail: cbinfo@colegiobolivar.edu.co
http://www.colegiobolivar.edu.co
Colegio Bolivar is an educational community whose mission is to educate its students in a bilingual, democratic environment to be autonomous, and to demonstrate a spirit of inquiry and collaboration, a commitment to excellence, and the highest aspirations for the welfare of both the individual and society.

Joseph Nagy, Director
Richard Martin, Dean of Students

1304 Colegio Columbo Britanico
Apartado Aereo 5774
Cali
Colombia

Ian Watson, Principal

1305 Colegio Gran Bretana
Carrera 51 #215-20
Bogota
Colombia
57-1-676-0391
Fax: 57-1-676-0426
E-mail: admissions@cgb.edu.co
http://http://www.cgb.edu.co/
Grade levels N-10, school year August-June

Daryl Barker, Director
David Simpson, Deputy Director

1306 Colegio Granadino
AA 2138 Manizales
Colombia
57-6-874-57-74
Fax: 57-6-874-60-66
E-mail: granadino@emtelsa.multi.net.com
http://gradino.edu.co
Early Childhood, Elementary, Middle School and High School

Gonzalo Arango, Principal
Robert Sims, Director

1307 Colegio Interamericano de la Montana
Boulevard La Montana
Finca El Socorro, Zona 16
Guatemala, GT 01016

502 2200.2990
Fax: 502-3-641-779
http://www.interamericano.edu.gt
The mission of Colegio Interamericano is to prepare its students for life and for studies anywhere in the world, by orienting them towards being responsible members of society.

Dr Michael Farr, General Director
Griselda de Amezquita, Head of Human Resources

1308 Colegio Jorge Washington
Zona Norte, Anillo Vial Km.12
Cartagena
Colombia, CO
57-5-673 5505
Fax: 57-5-665-6447
E-mail: director@cojowa.edu.co
http://cojowa.edu.co
The mission of the George Washington School is to form bilingual and bicultural citizens who possess high ethical values and commitment to the search for academic excellence and success in life.

Pete Nonnenkamp, Director
Maritza Garcia, Assistant Director

1309 Colegio Karl C Parrish
Kilometer 2 Antigua Via a Puerto Co
Barranquilla
Colombia, CO 52962
57-5-359-8929
Fax: 57-5-359-8828
E-mail: mail@kcparrish.edu.co
http://www.kcparrish.edu.co
strives to provide an environment that results in students displaying personal integrity and character in their relationships both within and outside the school.

Laura Horbal Rebolledo, Director
Hectalina Donado, Elementary School Principal

1310 Colegio Montelibano
AA 6823 Cerromatoso
Montelibano, Bogota
Colombia

Francisco Cajiao, Principal

1311 Colegio Nueva Granada
Carrera 2 Este Number 70-20
Bogota
Colombia, CO
57-1-2123511
Fax: 57-1-211-3720
E-mail: sngrana@COL1.telecom.com.co
http://www.cng.edu
Prepare tomorrow's leaders by educating the mind, nurturing the spirit, and strengthening the body.

Barry McCombs PhD, Director
Michael Adams, Deputy Director

1312 Colegio Peterson SC
Apartado Postal 10-900
DF 11000
Mexico
52-5-81-30-11-4
Fax: 52-5-81-31-38-5
E-mail: kapm@mail.internet.com.mx

Marvin Peterson, Principal

1313 Colegio San Marcus
61 Ourense
Buenas Aires
Argentina 32004
988-24 -7 94
Fax: 988-23 -9 85
E-mail: csmarcos@csmarcos.com
http://www.csmarcos.com
Collegio San Marcos was established in 1988, when it began its first year of dentures, being recognized by the Galician regional government, as accredited Vocational Training Sec-

ond Grade, under the Order of May 20 1.988 of the Department of Education and University (DOG num.110 June 1988).

Susana Raffo, Principal

1314 Colegio Ward
Hector Coucheiro 599
1706 DF Sarmiento, Ramos Mejia
Buenos Aires, Argentina
54-11 -4658
E-mail: info@ward.edu.ar
http://www.ward.edu.ar

Ruben Carlos Urcola, Principal
Daniel Campagna, Director

1315 Costa Rica Academy
Apartado Postal 4941
San Jose 1000
Costa Rica
506-239-03-76
Fax: 506-239-06-25
A private, coeducational school which offers an educational program from prekindergarten through grade 12 for students of all nationalities.

William D Rose, BS, Med, Principal

1316 Cotopaxi Academy
PO Box 17-11-6510
Quito
Ecuador
593-2-246-7411
Fax: 593-2-244-5195
E-mail: info@cotopaxi.k12.ec
http://www.cotopaxi.k12.ec
Premier English-language early childhood through secondary school in Ecuador. The internationally recognized program is aggressively sought out by all National and International parents who truly want to join a partnership to provide the very best education possible for their children.

Eddie Wexler, Principal
Kurt Kywi, President

1317 Country Day School
Apartado 1139 - 1250
Escazu
Costa Rica
(506) 2289 - 0919
Fax: (506) 2228 - 2076
E-mail: gloria_doll@cds.ed.cr
http://www.cds.ed.cr
CDS is an American School serving an international population. Accredited by the Middle States Association of Colleges and Schools in the United States, and by the Costa Rican Ministry of Education

Gloria Doll, Director
Maria Fernanda Cardona, Admissions Coordinator

1318 Crandon Institute
Casilla Correo 445
Montevideo
Uruguay
487-337-
http://www.crandon.edu.uy
This school offers a curriculum taught in Spanish for 2,000 day students (700 boys; 1,300 girls), in high school through junior college level (home economics, commercial). The school, affiliated with the Methodist church, employs 300 teachers.

Marcos Rocchietti, Principal

1319 Curundu Elementary School
Unit 0925
APO Curundu 34002 0005
Panama

Clifford Drexler, Principal

1320 Curundu Junior High School
Unit 0925
APO Curundu 34002 0005
Panama

Charles Renno, Principal

1321 Edron Academy-Calz Al Desierto
Desierto de los Leones 5578
Mexico City 01740
Mexico
5-585-30-49
Fax: 5-585-28-46

Richard Gilby Travers, Principal

1322 El Abra School
Phelps Dodge Corporation
Calama
Chile
56-55-313-600
Fax: 56-55-315-182
E-mail: elabraschool@hotmail.com
Grade levels K-11, school year August - June

Margaret Maclean, Head of School

1323 English School
AA 51284
Bogota
Colombia

Leonard Mabe, Principal

1324 Escola Americana do Rio de Janeiro
Estrada Da Gavea 132
Rio de Janeiro
Brazil 22451-263
55-21 -2125
(916) 458-5932
Fax: 55-21 -2259
Fax: 55-21-259-4722
E-mail: americanrio@ax.apc.org
http://www.earj.com.br
Escola Americana motivates engaged learners to become independent critical thinkers in a multicultural community.

Dr Dennis Klumpp, Principal
Caren Addis, Director of Admissions

1325 Escola Maria Imaculada
Rua Vig rio Joao de Pontes, 537, Ch
Sao Paulo
Brazil 04748
55 -1 -101
Fax: 55-1 -521
http://http://www.chapelschool.com/

Gerald Gates, Principal

1326 Escuela Anaco
Avenue Jose Antonio Anzoategui, KM
Anaco
Venezuela
58 -82 -22 2
E-mail: director@ESCUELAANACO.COM
Offers a United States High School Diploma with a full schooling program from Day Care through Grade 12. Also have on-line courses to enhance our program. Uses the best of the educational standards of the states of California, New York, and Virginia.

Francene Conte, Principal
Bill Kralovec, Director

1327 Escuela Bilingue Santa Barbara
Apartado 342-El Marchito
San Pedro Sila
Honduras
504-659-3053
Fax: 504-659-3059
E-mail: mochitoschool@breakwater.hn
Grade levels preK through 8.

John P Leddy, Principal

1328 Escuela Bilingue Valle De Sula
Apartado 735
San Pedro Sula
Honduras

Carole A Black, Principal

1329 Escuela International Sampedrana
Col Gracias A Dios 500 mts W Hospit
San Pedro Sula
Honduras
504-566-2722
Fax: 504-566-1458
E-mail: eperez@seishn.com
http://www.seishn.org
EIS seeks to be the premier school in the city of San Pedro Sula, the country of Honduras and region of Central America through the use of best teaching practices with the goal of reaching all of its students.

Gregorg E Werner, Principal
Ronald Vair, Superintendent

1330 Escuela Las Palmas
Apartdo 6-2637
Panama

Aleida Molina, Principal

1331 Foreign Students School
Avenue Station B
#6617-6615 Esquina 70
Miramar Havana City, Cuba

Gillian P Greenwood, Principal

1332 Fort Clayton Elementary School
Unit 0925
APO, Fort Clayton 34004 0005
Panama

Barbara Seni, Principal

1333 Fort Kobbe Elementary School
Unit 0714
APO, Fort Kobbe 34001 0005
Panama

Dr Vinita Swenty, Principal

1334 Fundacion Colegio Americano de Quito
Manuel Benigno Cueva N80 - 190 Urba
PO Box 17-01-157, Carcel,n, Quito
Ecuador
(593) 2 3976 300
Fax: 593-2-472-972
E-mail: dirgeneral@fcaq.k12.ec
http://www.fcaq.k12.ec
Grade levels Pre-K through 12, school year September - June.

Susan Barbara, Director General

1335 George Washington School
Apartado Aereo 2899
Cartagena
Colombia
57-5-665-3396
Fax: 57-5-665-6447
A private, coeducational day school which offers and educational program from prekindergarten through grade 12 for students of all nationalities.

Steven Fields, Principal

1336 Grange School
Casilla 218
Correo 12, Santiago
Chile
(56) 2- 5981500?
Fax: 56-2-227-1204
E-mail: admissions@grange.cl
http://www.grange.cl
Places great importance on the idea of 'fair play', a concept with connotations of sportsmanship, rule obedience, and honesty

Mike Freeman, Headmaster
Carolina Varela, Deputy Headmaster

1337 Greengates School
Avenue Circumbalacion Pte 102
Baliones De San Mateo, Naucalpah
Edo de Mexico, Mexico 53200
52-55-5373-0088
Fax: 52-55-5373-0765
E-mail: sarav@greengates.edu.mx
http://www.greengates.edu.mx
Grade levels prekindergarten through twelfth.

Susan E Mayer, Principal

1338 Howard Elementary School
Unit 0713
APO, Howard AFB 34001 0005
Panama

Jean Lamb, Principal

1339 Inst Tecnologico De Estudios
Apartado Postal 28B
Chihuahua
Mexico

Hector Chavrez Barron, Principal

1340 International Preparatory School
PO Box 20015-LC
Santiago
Chile
56-2-321-5800
Fax: 56-2-321-5821
E-mail: info@tipschool.com
Grade levels Pre-K through 12, school year March - December

Lesley Easton-Allen, Headmistress
Pamela Thomson, Curriculum Coordinator

1341 International School Nido de Aguilas
Casilla 162
Correo La Dehesa, Lo Barnechea, Santiago
Chile
(562) 339-8105
Fax: 56-2-216-7603
E-mail: abattistoni@nido.cl
http://www.nido.cl
The International School Nido de Aguilas is committed to offering each student excellence in the pursuit of academic achievement in preparation for attendance at a US, Chilean or other international university, all within the framework of a challenging US-based, English-language curriculum. We encourage open-mindedness, global diversity, environmental awareness, community service and the development of leadership skills, including integrity, responsibility and self-discipline.

Dr Don Bergman, Headmaster
Jared Harris, HS Principal

1342 International School-Curitiba
Av Dr Eug^nio Bertolli
3900 Santa Felicidade, Curitiba, Paran˜
Brazil 18241
55- 4- 35
Fax: 55- 4- 35
E-mail: isc@iscbrazil.com~
http://www.iscbrazil.com
It is a private, nonprofit, self-governed school that serves students and families from our local and international community; offers a U.S. based curriculum in English with American, Brazilian and International Baccalaureate diplomas; commits to academic and personal excellence and prepares students for universities around the world.

Elizabeth Mello, Principal 1-12
Bill Pearson, Superintendent

1343 International School-La Paz
CC1075870 Villa Dolores
La Paz, Cordoba
Argentina

LH Sullivan, Principal

1344 International School-Panama
PO Box 0819-02588
El Dorado
Panama
(507) 293-3000
Fax: 507-266-7808
E-mail: isp@isp.edu.pa
http://www.isp.edu.pa
A private, coeducational day school which offers an educational program from prekindergarten through grade 12 for students of all nationalities.

Linda LaPine, Director
Jania Jacob, Business Manager

1345 Karl C Parrish School
Km 2 Antigua via a Puerto
Barranquilla
Colombia
(57-5) 3598929
Fax: 57-5-3598828
E-mail: mail@kcparrish.edu.co
http://www.kcparrish.edu.co
Karl C. Parrish is a private, non-sectarian, non-profit elementary and secondary school that is open to children of all nationalities.

Laura H Rebolledo, Director

1346 Liceo Pino Verde
Vereda Los Planes kilometro 5
V¡a Cerritos Entrada 16, El Tigre
Colombia
57 -6 -1326
963-379368
E-mail: info@liceopinoverde.edu.co
http://http://72.167.105.89/site/
This school teaches English as a second language; builds strong human values; develops logical thinking skills and prepares students for the world of technology and communication. Enrollment consists of 110 day students (57 boys; 53 girls, in grades PK-12. Overseas teachers are welcome to apply with the length of stay being two years, with housing provided. Applications needed to teach include science, math and English.

Luz Stella Rios Patino, Principal

1347 Limon School
P.O. Box 249
847 F Avenue
Limon, CO 80828
719-775-2350
Fax: 719-775-9052
http://limonbadgers.com
strive to provide a safe environment and develop responsible and productive citizens who have the knowledge and skills to seize their chosen opportunities

Chris Selle, Principal

1348 Lincoln International Academy
PO Box 52-7444
Miami, FL 33152
50- 2-76 3
1 (305) 395-4825ÿ
Fax: 50- 2-76 1
E-mail: lincoln@lincoln.edu.ni
http://www.lincoln.edu.ni
instilling in them solid Christian and human virtues as taught by the Catholic faith, challenging them to reach their full intellectual capacity and achieve a high integral academic excellence in order to face the challenges of today's world. providing them with English instruction while preserving our Hispanic-Nicaraguan culture.

Hennington Hammond, Operation Manager
Adolfo Gonzalez, General Director

1349 Mackay School
Vicuna Mackenna 700
Renaca
Chile

56 -2 2-8660
http://www.mackay.cl
Nigel William Blackbur, Principal

1350 Marian Baker School
Apartado 4269
San Jose
Costa Rica 1000
560-273-3426
Fax: 506-273-4609
E-mail: mbschool@sol.racsa.co.cr
http://www.mbs.ed.cr/
Marian Baker School (MBS) is an International English speaking school educating pre-school through high school students.

Linda Niehaus, Director
Bonnie Heigold, Business Manager

1351 Marymount School
Apartado Aereo #1912
Barranquilla
Colombia

Dr. Kathleen Cunniffe, Principal

1352 Metropolitan School
7281 Sarah Avenue
Maplewood, MO 63143
314-644-0850
E-mail: nsmith@metroschool.org
The School is dedicated to providing a highly individualized educational experience for middle and senior high school students whose potential has not been recognized and/or meaningfully challenged in traditional school settings.

Judi Thomas, Head of School

1353 Modern American School
Cerro del Hombre 18
Col. Romero de Terreros
Mexico
565- 47-6
http://www.modernamerican.edu.mx
To provide our students with the educational elements which will promote the optimum development of the intellect, instill social awareness and emotional sensitivity, encourage artistic creativity, and emphasize physical well-being, aiming for excellence toward future success

1354 Northlands Day School
Roma 1210
1636 Olivos, Buenos Aires
Argentina
This bilingual day school for girls offers modern facilities, sports, etc. on a spacious campus. Languages spoken include English and Spanish and total enrollment is 1,100 students, ranging in grade from K1-12. Overseas teachers are accepted, with the length of stay being 2-6 years with housing provided.

Susan Brooke Jackson, MA, Principal

1355 Our Lady of Mercy School
Rua Visconde de Caravelas
48, Botafogo, Rio de Janeiro
Brazil
372- 82-8
Our Lady of Mercy School is an American Catholic English speaking school whose main purpose is to educate the whole student towards global understanding.

Charles Lyndaker, Superintendent

1356 Pan American Christian Academy
Rua C ssio de Campos Nogueira, 393
04829-310 Sao Paulo
Brazil
55 -1 5-29 9
480.471.5339
Fax: 55-11-59289591
E-mail: info@paca.com.br
http://www.paca.com.br

American international school located in the city of Sao Paulo, working with 350 students from different parts of the world with an American-style pre-school through high school education. Since 1960, we've served the local and international community of Sao Paulo.

Micheal Epp, Superintendent

1357 Pan American School-Bahia

Caixa Postal 231
Salvador
Brazil 40901-970
55-71-3368-8400
Fax: 55-71-3368-8441
E-mail: info@escolapanamericana.com
http://www.escolapanamericana.com
A private, coeducational day school which offers a program from preschool through grade 12 for students of all nationalities.

Mary Jo Heatherington, PhD,
Superintendent

1358 Pan American School-Costa Rica

Apartado 474
Monterrey
Costa Rica, NL 64000
(81) 83-42-07-78
Fax: (81) 83-40-27-49
E-mail: dadmission@pas.edu.mx
http://www.pas.edu.mx
Offer excellent educational programs in English that foster the integral development of students.

Robert Arpee, Director

1359 Pan American School-Monterrey

Hidalgo 656 Pte
Apartado Postal 474, Monterrey 64000
Mexico
(81) 83-42-07-78
http://www.pas.edu.mx
This school offers an English curriculum for 1,393 day students and 100 boarding students (709 boys; 684 girls), grades preschool through nine. The school is willing to participate in a teacher exchange program with the length of stay being one year. Applications needed to teach include science, preschool, math, reading, English, and physical education.

Tobert L Arpee, Principal
Lenor Arpee, Faculty Head

1360 Pan American School-Porto Alegre

Rua Joao Paetzel 440
91 330 Porto Alegre
Brazil

Jennifer Sughrue, Principal

1361 Panama Canal College

Unit 0925
APO Balboa 34002 0005
Panama

1362 Prescott Anglo American School

PO Box 1036
Arequipa
Peru
This school offers a Spanish/English curriculum for 1,050 day students (450 boys; 600 girls) in grades K-12. Students are taught English three hours a day, so they can reach an intermediate level in grade 9, and high intermediate in grades 11-12.

Jorge Pachecot, Principal

1363 Redland School

Camino El Alba 11357
Santiago
Chile
This school offers an English/Spanish curriculum to 820 day students (420 boys; 400 girls), in grades PreK-12. The student body is

mostly Chilean and 90% of the teachers are Chilean. However, overseas teachers are welcome, with the applications being pre-school and English.

Richard Collingwood-Selby, Principal

1364 Reydon School for Girls

5178 Cruz Chica
Sierras de Cordoba, Cordoba
Argentina

NJ Milman, Principal

1365 Saint George's School

Carrera 92 No 156-88, Suba
Bogota
Colombia
0-71 -6849
Fax: 0-71 -6849
E-mail: sanjorge@sgs.edu.co
http://www.sgs.edu.co

Mary De Acosta, Principal

1366 Santa Cruz Cooperative School

Barrio Las Palmas Calle Barcelona #
Casilla 753 Santa Cruz
Bolivia
(591) (3) 353-0808
Fax: (591) (3) 352-6993
E-mail: william.j.mckelligott@gmail.com
http://www.sccs.edu.bo
College preparatory school equipping students with the necessary skills and values to be citizens and leaders for the 21st century. Preparing students to become productive citizens, leaders and life-long learners.

William J McKelligott, Director General
Hugo Paz, Board Director

1367 Santa Margarita School

Avenue Manuel Olguin 961 El Derby
Surco, Lima
Peru

Guillermo Descalzi, Principal

1368 St. Albans College

110 Clearwater Road
Lynnwood Glen Pretoria
South Africa
27 -2 3-8 12
Fax: 27 -2 3-1 19
E-mail: robertr@stalbanscollege.com
http://www.stalbanscollege.com
St Alban's College is a learning community of boys, staff and parents. We are forward looking, committed to quality and service, and we pursue innovative strategies and encourage personal responsibility in the interest of all-round development of the boy as he journeys towards manhood.

Tom Hamilton, Headmaster
Carlos Palermo, Faculty Director

1369 St. Andrew's Scots School

Rosales 2809
Olivos
Argentina 1636
54-114-799-8318
Fax: 54-114-799-8318
E-mail: admissions@sanandres.esc.edu.ar
http://www.sanandres.esc.edu.ar
St. Andrew's Scots School aims to graduate responsible citizens committed to serving Argentina and contributing to its equitable development through a well-balanced, bilingual education which meets high international standards and fosters a joy for learning.

Gabriel Rshaid, Headmaster
Ana Repila, Admissions Director

1370 St. Catherine's School

Carbajal 3250
1426 Capital Federal, Buenos Aires
Argentina

54-114-552-4353
Fax: 54-114-554-4113
E-mail: stcath@ciudad.com.ar
http://www.redeseducacion.com.ar
Pre-K through 12, school year March-December

Mabel Manzitti, Principal

1371 St. George's College

Guido 800 CP
Quilmes, Buenos Aires
Argentina 1878
(5411) 4254-8237
Fax: 54-11-425-30030
E-mail: info@stgeorge.com.ar
http://www.stgeorge.com.ar
Our mission is to provide students of varying abilities and backgrounds between the ages of 3 - 18 with a bilingual, fully integrated education of the highest calibre in order that they may develop their potential to the full in an appropriately resourced co-educational environment which nurtures individual development, independent thinking and the highest moral standards.

Derek Pringle, Headmaster
Peter Ashton, Deputy Headmaster

1372 St. Hilda's College

Cowley Place Oxford
OX4 1DY
England
44-1865-276884
Fax: 44-1865-276816
E-mail: college.office@st-hildas.ox.ac.uk
http://www.st-hildas.ox.ac.uk
To promote the education of women within Oxford University and the tradition of excellence in women's education which it pioneered.

Sheila Forbes, Principal
Lucia Nixon, Senior Tutor

1373 St. John School

Casilla 284
Concepcion
Chile
St. John School is a bilingual school that caters to children from PK through grade twelve. The student body includes 1,170 day students (580 boys and 590 girls). The school does participate in teacher exchange programs with the length of stay for teachers being two years. The languages spoken include Spanish and English and the student/teacher ratio is 10:1.

Chris Pugh, Principal

1374 St. Margaret's British School-Girls

Calle Saint Margaret
150 Lomas de Montemar
Chile
451-00 -
E-mail: admissions@stmargarets.cl
http://www.stmargarets.cl
St. Margarets objective is to protect in its pupil its motto: Recte Fac Nec Time (Do Right , Fear not) This implies assigning value to great ideals, acting fairly and courteously, having sound judgement, enriched understanding, a discipline manner and making responsible use of their freedom.

Margery Byrne, Principal
Avril Cooper, Headmistress

1375 St. Paul's School

325 Pleasant Street
Concord, NH 03301-2591
603-229-4600
http://www.sps.edu
St. Paul's School is a fully residential academic community that pursues the highest ideals of scholarship. We strive to challenge our students intellectually and morally - to

nurture a love for learning and a commitment to engage as servant leaders in a complex world.

Richardo Pons, Principal
William R Matthews, Jr, Rector

1376 St. Pauls School
1600 St Paul's Drive
Clearwater, FL 33764
727-536-2756
Fax: 727-531-2276
http://www.st.pauls.edu
To educate and inspire young minds in a challenging and nurturing community of learning.

AH Thurn, Principal
Angel W Kytle, Head of the School

1377 St. Peter's School
Pacheco 715
1640 Martinez, Buenos Aires
Argentina

Joy Headland, Principal

1378 Teaching Opportunities in Latin America for US Citizens
Organization of American States
17th & Constitution Avenue NW
Washington, DC 20036
202-458-3000
Fax: 202-458-3967
Supports teaching abroad opportunities.

1379 The American School Foundation of Monterrey
Ave. Ignacio Morones Prieto No. 150
Santa Catarina, N.L., C.P.
Mexico, MX 66190
(52)-81-5000-4400
Fax: (52)-81-5000-4428
E-mail: jeff.keller@missouri.asfm.edu.mx
http://www.asfm.edu.mx
providing the type of learning environment which will prepare its students to successfully assume their role in the international community during the current millennium.

Jeff Keller, Superintendent
Jeff Farrington, Principal

1380 Uruguayan American School
Av Saldon de Rodriguez
Montevideo
Uruguay 11500-3360
598-2-600-7681
Fax: 598-2-606-1935
E-mail: MSchramm@uas.edu.uy
http://www.uas.edu.uy
Uruguayan American School is to provide, together with the family, a balanced college preparatory education. UAS integrates a US style curriculum with Uruguayan studies to equip our national and international students to be successful in a diverse, ever changing world

Mike Schramm, Director
Cecilia Burgueo, UP Coordinator

1381 William T Sampson
Elementary & High School
PSC 1005 Box 49
FPO, Guantanamo Bay 09593 0005
Cuba

Eastern Europe

1382 American Academy Larnaca
Gregory Afxentious Avenue
PO Box 40112, Larnaca
Cyprus 6301
357-248-5400
Fax: 357-246-1046
E-mail: info@academy.ac.cy
http://www.academy.ac.cy

Non-profit making school that is supported by an active multi-functional operation to achieve its core purpose: pre-school to University entrance education of the highest standard. It is a private, selective, co-educational, independent school, registered under the Private Schools' Law, 1971, of the Republic of Cyprus and uniquely, is run by its own graduates.

Doros Neocleous, Principal
Tom Widdows, Director

1383 American College-Sofia
PO Box 873
Sofia
Bulgaria 1000
(359-2) 434 10 08
Fax: (359-2) 434 10 09
E-mail: acs@acs.bg
http://www.acs.bg
The primary mission is to educate Bulgarian youth, it embraces qualified students of all nationalities, races and faiths in the belief that a wide variety of students will enrich educational opportunities for all.

Paul Johnson, President
Maria Angelova, Deputy Director

1384 American International School-Bucharest
Sos Pipera-Tunari 196
Voluntari Jud Ilfov 077190
Romania
40-21-2044300
Fax: 40-21-2044306
E-mail: office@aisb.ro
http://www.aisb.ro
The American International School of Bucharest is a multicultural and international learning community, located in Romania. English is the principal language of instruction.

David Ottaviano Ed D, Director
Tamara Shreve, Elementary Principal

1385 American International School-Budapest
PO Box 53
Budapest
Hungary 1525
06 -6 5-6 00
36 26 556 000
Fax: 06 -6 5-6 00
Fax: 36 26 556 003
E-mail: admissions@nk.aisb.hu
http://www.aisb.hu
The American International School of Budapest (AISB) is a private and independent co-educational day school governed by a Board of Directors elected and appointed from the parent community. Established in 1973 by the United States Embassy to serve United States Government employees' dependents, AISB currently serves the needs of a rapidly expanding international population, including children of the local and expatriate business and diplomatic communities.

Ray Holliday Bersegeay, School Director
Larry Kinde, Chairman

1386 American International School-Cyprus
PO Box 23847, 11 Kassos Street
1086 Nisocia
Cyprus
357-22-316345
Fax: 357-22-316549
E-mail: aisc@aisc.ac.cy
http://www.aisc.ac.cy
Founded in 1987, a private, coeducational, college preparatory day school providing a first class American and international university preparatory education within the Cyprus local community that incorporates a Greek as

a First Language program for our Cypriot students.

Michelle Kleiss, Director
Terry Wolfson, Principal

1387 American International School-Krakow
Lusina ul. sw. Floriana 57
30-698 Kraków
Poland
48 12 270-1409
Fax: 48 12 270-1409
E-mail: director@iskonline.org
http://www.aisk.kompit.com.pl
Affiliated with the American School of Warsaw, AISK is an independent, coeducational day school which offers an educational program from preschool through grade 8 for students of all nationalities.

Ellen Deitsch Stern, Director

1388 American International School-Vienna
Salmannsdorfer Strasse 47
A-1190 Vienna
Austria
43-1-40-132-0
Fax: 43-1-40-132-5
E-mail: info@ais.at
http://www.ais.at
Provide a culture of educational excellence, a nurturing environment, and an atmosphere of open communication and aims to prepare a diverse student body for higher education; to inspire the youth to realize their potential; to foster life-long learning, tolerance, personal integrity, and democratic values; and to prepare students to become responsible adults, with respect for different cultures and beliefs.

Carol Kluznik, Director
Gail McMillan, HS Principal

1389 American School of Bucharest
Sos Pipera-Tunari 196
Voluntari Jud Ilfov
Romania 07719
40-21-2044300
Fax: 40-21-2044306
E-mail: office@aisb.ro
http://www.aisb.ro
An independent, international, coeducational day school which offers an educational program from prekindergarten through grade 12 for students of all nationalities.

David Ottaviano, Director
Jeri Guthrie Corn, Chair

1390 Asuncion Christian Academy
Avenida Santisimo Sacramento
1181 Casilla 1562
Asuncion, Paraguay-1209
011-595-21-607-378
Fax: 011-595-21-604-855
E-mail: aca@aca.edu.py
http://http://www.acaknights.org/
Asuncion Christian Academy believes that the best education to prepare a student for adult life is an education based upon the truth of God's Word and having a growing and personal relationship with Jesus Christ.

Bethany Abreu, Director

1391 Falcon School
PO Box 23640
Nicosia
Cyprus 1685
357 22 424781
Fax: 357 22 313764
E-mail: falconschool@cytanet.com.cy
http://http://www.falconschool.ac.cy/default.asp?id=261

Nikolas Michael Ieride, Principal

1392 Gimnazija Bezigrad
Periceva ulica 4
PO Box 2504
Ljubljana 1001-1001
Fax: 01 -00 -4 40
E-mail: info@gimb.org
http://www.gimb.org
Assistance to parents in raising gifted children to full and productive adulthood

Cyril Dominko, Principal
Janez Sustersic, Director

1393 International Elementary School-Estonia
Juhkentali 18
Tallinn
Estonia 10132
372-666-4380
Fax: 372-666-4383
E-mail: office@ise.edu.ee
http://www.ise.edu.ee
Provide high-quality, international education; maximize personal potential; develop life-long learners who appreciate diversity; foster active, compassionate world citizens

Don Fitzmahan, Director
Terje Akke, PYP Coordinator

1394 International School-Belgrade
Temisvarska 19
Belgrade
Serbia 11040
381 11 206-9999
Fax: 381 11 206-9940
E-mail: isb@isb.rs
http://http://www.isb.rs/main/?pgid=263
An independent, coeducational day school which offers an educational program from kindergarten through grade 8 for students of all nationalities.

Dr. Eric Sands, Director
Sanja Ilic, Admissions Director

1395 International School-Budapest
P.O. Box 53
Budapest
Hungary 1525
36 26 556 000
Fax: 36 26 556 003
E-mail: admissions@aisb.hu
http://http://www.aisb.hu/DOCS/1/contact.html
Grade levels N-8, school year August - June

Ray Holliday-Bersegeay, Director

1396 International School-Estonia
Juhkentali 18
Tallinn
Estonia 10132
372-666-4380
Fax: 372-666-4383
E-mail: office@ise.edu.ee
http://www.ise.edu.ee
Provides high-quality, international education, maximize personal potential, develop life-long learners who appreciate diversity and foster active, compassionate world citizens.

Don Fitzmahan, Terje
Akke PYP Coordinator

1397 International School-Latvia
Viestura iela 6a
Jurmala
Latvia LV 20
(+371) 6775 5146
Fax: (+371) 6775 5009
E-mail: merliha@isl.edu.lv
http://www.isl.edu.lv
Offers English-language, academically challenging programmes designed to develop life-long learners who are critical, creative and open-minded thinkers prepared and motivated to meet the diverse challenges of an

ever-changing environment; act with integrity and responsibility locally and globally to transform their world in positive ways and appreciate and respect human diversity.

Larry Molacek, Director
Kevin Reimer, Deputy Director

1398 International School-Paphos
100 Aristotelous Savva Avenue
PO Box 62018, Paphos
Cyprus 8025
26 821700ÿ
Fax: 26 942541
E-mail: info@isop-ed.org
http://www.isop-ed.org
The school caters for the needs of children from Kindergarten to Year 13. Its mission is to serve each and every one of the pupils as part of our school family and as an individual.

Litsa Olympiou, Headmistress

1399 International School-Prague
Nebusicka 700
164 00 Prague 6
Czech Republic
420 2 2038 4111
Fax: 420-2-2038-4555
E-mail: ispmail@isp.cz
http://www.isp.cz
Educates students to be responsible, productive, ethical and healthy citizens with the ability to think creatively, reason critically, and communicate effectively through a variety of educational philosophies and methods, combining the best methodology and practices from a variety of national systems with an international perspective.

Arnie Bieber, Director
Barry Freckmann, Business Manager

1400 International Teachers Service
47 Papakyriazi Street
Larissa, Greece
41-253856
Fax: 41-251022
A recruitment service for teachers of English in Greece. Must have a BA/BS in education preferably English and/or EFL training or past experience in EFL and be a native speaker of English.

Fani Karatzou

1401 Kiev International School
3A Svyatoshinsky Provuluk
Kyiv
Ukraine 3115
380-44-452-2792
Fax: 380-44-452-2998
E-mail: kiev@qsi.org
http://www.qsi.org
Kyiv International School, a private non-profit institution

Scott D'Alterio, Director
David Pera, Director Instruction

1402 Limassol Grammar-Junior School
10 Manoli Kalomiri & Theklas Lisiot
PO Box 51340
Limassol, Cyprus 3504
357-257-7933
Fax: 357-257-7818
E-mail: junior@grammarschool.com.cy
http://www.grammarschool.com.cy/services.htm
The primary goal of the Grammar School is to provide its students with a solidly grounded liberal education. Thus, it seeks to encourage the intellectual, spiritual, and physical development of its students.

EWP Foley, Principal
Demetris Gregoriou, Director

1403 Logos School of English Education
33-35 Yialousa Street
PO Box 51075 Limassol
Cyprus 3501
357-25336061
Fax: 357-25335578
E-mail: Principal@Logos.ac.cy
http://www.logos.ac.cy

Gary Love, Principal

1404 Magyar British International School
H-1519 Budapest
PO Box 219, Budapest
Hungary

Mary E Pazsit, Principal

1405 Melkonian Educational Institute
PO Box 1907
Nicosia
Cyprus
An Armenian boarding school with high academic standards.

S Bedikan, Principal

1406 Private English Junior School
P.O Box 23575
Nicosia
Cyprus 1684
357-22 -9930
Fax: 357-22 -9930
E-mail: info@englishschool.ac.cy
http://http://www.englishschool.ac.cy/?link=contact.php

Vassos Hajierou, BA, Principal

1407 QSI International School-Bratislava
Karloveska 64
Bratislava
Slovak Republic 842-2
421-2-6542-2844
Fax: 421-2-6541-1646
E-mail: bratislava@qsi.org
http://www.qsi.org
To keep this urge to learn alive in every child in QSI schools. Our schools are established to provide in the English language a quality education for students in the cities we serve.

Britt Brantley, Director

1408 QSI International School-Ljubljana
Dolgi most 6A
1000 Ljubljana
Solvenia
386-1-2441750
Fax: 386-1-2441754
E-mail: ljubljana@qsi.org
http://www.qsi.org
To keep this urge to learn alive in every child in QSI schools. Our schools are established to provide in the English language a quality education for students in the cities we serve.

Jay Loftin, Director

1409 QSI International School-Tbilisi
Village Zurgovani
Tbilisi
Republic of Georgia
995-32-53767
Fax: 995-32-322607
E-mail: tbilisi@qsi.org
http://www.qsi.org
To keep this urge to learn alive in every child in QSI schools. Our schools are established to provide in the English language a quality education for students in the cities we serve.

James Rehberg, Director

1410 QSI International School-Yerevan
PO Box 82, Ashtarok Highway
Yerevan
Republic of Armenia 37501
374-10-349130
Fax: 374-10-397599

E-mail: yerevan@qsi.org
http://www.qsi.org/arm_home
To keep this urge to learn alive in every child in QSI schools. Our schools are established to provide in the English language a quality education for students in the cities we serve.

Douglas Shippert, Director

Middle East

1411 ACI & SEV Elementary School
Inonu Caddesi No 476
Goztepe, Izmir
Turkey 35290
90-232-285-3401
Fax: 90-232-246-1674
E-mail: channa@aci.k12.tr
http://www.aci.k12.tr
Contribute to the growth of individuals who combine self-confidence with a firm sense of personal, social, and environmental responsibility. Enable students to be strong bilinguals in English and Turkish, well-educated adults, lifelong learners, and efficient communicators, who have developed skills, accountability, and attitudes for leading a fulfilling life and for serving their country and humanity.

Charles C Hanna, Director
Anet Gomel, Turkish First Vice Principal

1412 Abdul Hamid Sharaf School
PO Box 6008
Amman
Jordan 11118
962-6 5-2418
Fax: 962-6 5-2462
E-mail: ahss@go.com.jo
http://www.ahss.edu.jo
A private, coeducational, K-12 day school serving the needs of a diverse group of students, international and local. Languages of instruction for the basic subjects are Arabic and English.

Sue Dahdah, Director

1413 Abquaiq Academy
PO Box 31677
Al-Khobar
Saudi Arabia 31952
966-3 5-6 04
Fax: 966-3 5-6 23
E-mail: abqaiq@isgdh.org
The sole purpose of the school is for serving the educational needs of children from expatriate families.

Vineeta Dambal, Administrator/Principal

1414 Al Ain English Speaking School
PO Box 17939
Al Ain
United Arab Emirates
00971-3-7678636
Fax: 00971-3-767-1973
E-mail: school@aaess.sch.ae
http://www.aaess.com
Al Ain English Speaking School is a member of the Association of British Schools in the Middle East and the Incorporated Association of Preparatory Schools (UK). The basic curriculum is that of the National Curriculum of England.

Peter Hodge, Principal

1415 Al Bayan Bilingual School
PO Box 24472
Safat 13105
Kuwait
965 2227 - 5000
Fax: 965 2227 - 5002
E-mail: bbsjadm@bbs.edu.kw
http://www.bbs.edu.kw

A non-profit Arabic-English university preparatory educational institution, which fosters an environment for students to develop the intellectual qualities, ethical values, and positive attitudes required for effective participation and leadership in the overall development of Kuwait and the rapidly changing world.

Brian L McCauley, Director

1416 Al Khubairat Community School
PO Box 4001
Abu Dhabi
United Arab Emirates
971-2 4-6 22
Fax: 971-2 4-6 19
E-mail: principal@britishschool.sch.ae
http://www.britishschool.sch.ae
British curriculum school for children aged 3 to 18.It is a non-profit school administered by a Board consisting of parent representatives and nominees of the British Ambassador.

Paul Coackley, Principal

1417 Al Rabeeh School
PO Box 41807
Abu Dhabi
United Arab Emirates
971 2 4482856
Fax: 971 2 4482854
http://http://www.alrabeeh.sch.ae/

HJ Kadri, Principal

1418 Al-Nouri English School
PO Box 46901
Fahaheel
Kuwait

PD Oldfield, Principal

1419 Al-Worood School
PO Box 46673
Abu Dhabi
United Arab Emirates
971-2-444-7655
Fax: 971-2-444-9732
E-mail: alworood@emirates.net.ae
http://http://www.alworood.sch.ae/alworood/StaticContentDetails.asp
Grade levels N-12, school year September - June

Ahmed Osman, Academic Principal
Abdulla Al Nuwais, President

1420 American Collegiate Institute
Inonu Caddesi #476 Goztepe
Izmir
Turkey 35290
90-232-285-3401
Fax: 90-232-246-4128
E-mail: channa@aci.k12.tr
http://www.aci.k12.tr
Offers a 1 + 4 year academic program. Students enter the school based upon a competitive national high-school entrance exam needing to improve their English language skills go into the intensive English one-year preparatory program before entering the school's rigorous four-year educational program.

Charles C Hanna, Director
Anet Gomel, First Vice Principal

1421 American Community School
Rue de Paris, Jel El Bahr
PO Box 11-8129, Riad El Solh
Beirut, Lebanon 1107-2260
961-1-374-370
Fax: 961-1-366-050
E-mail: gdamon@acs.edu.lb
http://www.acs.edu.lb

Founded in 1905, an independent, non-profit, non-sectarian, pre-K-12 coeducational day school.

George Damon, Headmaster
David Warren, Deputy Headmaster

1422 American Community School-Abu Dhabi
PO Box 42114
Abu Dhabi
United Arab Emirates
971-2-681-5115
Fax: 971-2-681-6006
E-mail: acs@acs.sch.ae
http://www.acs.sch.ae
The mission is to empower and inspire all students to define and shape their futures, pursue their dreams and contribute to society.

Dr George Robinson, Superintendent
Waheeda Al Tamimi, Administrative Assistant

1423 American Community School-Beirut
Rue de Paris, Jel El Bahr
PO Box 11-8129, Riad El Solh
Beirut, Lebanon 1107-2260
961-1-374-370
Fax: 961-1-366-050
E-mail: gdamon@acs.edu.lb
http://www.acs.edu.lb
Founded in 1905, an independent, non-profit, non-sectarian, pre-K-12 coeducational day school. It draws students from both the Lebanese and international communities in Lebanon and embraces diversity in race, gender, religion, national origin and economic background.

George Damon, Headmaster
David Warren, Deputy Headmaster

1424 American International School
PO Box 22090
Doha
Qatar
974-445- 150
Fax: 974-445- 157
E-mail: info@asd.edu.qa
http://http://www.asd.edu.qa/
The American School of Doha is an independent, U.S. accredited, college preparatory school, committed to provide the highest standard of educational excellence, through an enriched American curriculum.

Deborah Welch, Director
Michael Shahen, High School Principal

1425 American International School-Abu Dhabi
PO Box 5992
Abu Dhabi
United Arab Emirates
971-2-444-4333
Fax: 971-2-444-4005
E-mail: admissions@aisa.sch.ae
http://www.aisa.sch.ae
Founded in 1995 to serve the needs of the local and expatriate residents of Abu Dhabi who want their children to pursue both American and International Baccalaureate curricula in an international setting.

Gareth Jones, Director
Abdulla Al-Hashly, Chairman

1426 American International School-Israel
PO Box 484, 65 Hashomron St
Even Yehuda
Israel 40500
972-9-890-1000
Fax: 972-9-890-1001
E-mail: aisrael@wbais.org
http://http://www.wbais.org/~joomla/index.php?option=com_frontpage&
An independent, coeducational day school which offers an educational program from

kindergarten through grade 12 for students of all nationalities.

Richard Detwiler, Principal

1427 American International School-Kuwait
PO Box 3267
Salmiya
Kuwait 22033
(965) 22255155
Fax: (965) 22255156
E-mail: director@aiskuwait.org
http://www.aiskuwait.org
Grade levels kindergarten through twelfth.

Samera Al Rayes, Owner/Director
Noreen Hawley, Superintendent

1428 American International School-Muscat
PO Box 584
Azaiba Postal Code 130
Sultanate of Oman
968 24 595 180
Fax: 968 24 503 815
E-mail: taism@omantel.net.com
http://www.taism.com
Pursues academic excellence for students in the international community through an American-based education that develops ethical, responsible, and globally conscious life-long learners.

Kevin Schafer, Director
Nelson File, High School Principal

1429 American International School-Riyadh
PO Box 990
Riyadh
Saudi Arabia 11421
966-1-491-4270
Fax: 966-1-491-7101
E-mail: registration@ais-r.edu.sa
http://www.aisr.org
As a school committed to excellence, we will educate and inspire our students to be responsible, productive and ethical world citizens with the skills and passion to think creatively, reason critically, communicate effectively and learn continuously. We will accomplish this in an American educational environment characterized by high measurable standards and a clearly defined, appropriately interrelated college preparatory curriculum, implemented by a superior staff in partnership with parents a

Dr. Dennis Larkin, Superintendent

1430 American School-Doha
PO Box 22090
Doha
Qatar
974-4459-1500
Fax: 974-4459-1570
E-mail: dwelch@asd.edu.ga
http://www.asd.edu.qa/pages/sitepage.cfm?page=32659
is an independent, U.S. accredited, college preparatory school, committed to provide the highest standard of educational excellence, through an enriched American curriculum

Deborah Welch, Director
Colin Boudreau, High School Principal

1431 American School-Kuwait
PO Box 6735
Hawalli
Kuwait 32040
965-266-4341
Fax: 965-265-0438
E-mail: ask@ask.edu.kw
http://www.ask.edu.kw
It is a privately owned, independent coeducational day school which offers a general academic curriculum for students of all nationalities.

Bernard Mitchell, Superintendent
Fawsi Hasan, Arabic Studies Principal

1432 American-British Academy
PO Box 372
Medinat Al Sultan Qaboos
Sultanate of Oman PC 11
968-24603646
Fax: 968-24603544
E-mail: admin@abaoman.edu.om
http://www.abaoman.edu.om
Provides an international education of the highest quality to enable students to be confident, responsible, caring life-long learners.

Mona Nashman-Smith, Superintendent
Rod Harding, Director of Operations

1433 Amman Baccalaureate School
PO Box 441
Sweileh Amman
Jordan 11910
962-6-541-1191/7
Fax: 962-6-541-2603
E-mail: info@abs.edu.jo
http://www.abs.edu.jo
A coeducational and non-profit school which caters to students aged 3-18 years that offers an academically rigorous programme, enriched by extensive co-curricular activities, that culminates in the International Baccalaureate Diploma or Certificates.

Stuart Bryan, Principal
Robert Jones, Vice-Principal

1434 Anglican International School-Jerusalem
82 Rechov Haneviim
PO Box 191 Jerusalem
Israel 91001
972-2-567-7200
Fax: 972-2-538-474
E-mail: hoskino@aisj.co.il
http://www.aisj.co.il
An internationally accredited, pre-Kindergarten to Grade 12 [ages 3-18] school. It creates student-focused academic and educational environment which aspires to achieve excellence.

Owen Hoskin, Director
Matthew Dufty, Deputy Principal

1435 Ankara Elementary & High School
PSC 89 Unit 7010
APO, Ankara 09822 7010
Turkey
011-90-312-287-253
Fax: 011-90-312-285-179
E-mail:
AnkaraEHS.Principal@eu.dodea.edu
http://http://www.anka-ehs.eu.dodea.edu/

Kathleen Reiss, Principal
Rosie Uluer, Assistant Principal

1436 Arab Unity School
PO Box 10563
Rashidiya, Dubai
United Arab Emirates
971-4-886-226
Fax: 971 4 2886321
E-mail: auschool@amirates.net.ae
http://www.arabunityschool.com/aus/home.htm
Provide an equal opportunity, to all students, to develop their intellectual faculties and to awaken their latent, creative talents, irrespective of their ethnic background.

Zainab A Taher, Founder Director

1437 Baghdad International School
PO Box 571
Baghdad
Iraq

Amen A Rihani, Principal

1438 Bahrain Bayan School
PO Box 32411
Isa Town
Bahrain
973-682-227
Fax: 973-780-019
E-mail: bayanschool@bayan.edu.bh
http://www.bayanschool.edu.bh
A bilingual, coeducational, college preparatory school with an international curriculum and faculty. It aims to preserve the tenets of Arabic /Islamic values, to assist students to a depth of cross-cultural knowledge and to promote the global perspective necessary for future world citizens.

Dr Nakhle Wehbe, Director General
Gilbert Daoura, Operations Manager

1439 Bahrain Elementary & High School
Psc 451 Box 690
FPO Bahrain
Bahrain 09834-5200
973 1772-7828
Fax: 973 1772-8583
http://http://www.bahr-ehs.eu.dodea.edu/
Grade levels K-12.

Gail Anderson, Principal

1440 Bahrain School
PO Box 934
Juffair
Bahrain
973 1772-7828
Fax: 973 1772-8583
E-mail:
BahrainEHS.Principal@eu.dodea.edu
http://http://www.bahr-ehs.eu.dodea.edu/
To provide a safe environment in which our students are challenged to their maximum potential as responsible members of a multi-cultural society.

Gail Anderson, Principal
Laura Bleck, Assistant Principal

1441 Bilkent University Preparatory School-Bilkent International School
East Campus
Bilkent Ankara
Turkey 06800
90 312 290 53 61
Fax: 90 312 266 49 63
E-mail: school@bups.bilkent.edu.tr
http://www.bupsbis.bilkent.edu.tr
BUPS serves the educational needs of selected Turkish students while BIS serves the needs of selected international students in the Ankara area.

James Swetz, Director
Dan Keller, Associate Director

1442 Bishop's School
PO Box 2001
Amman
Jordan
962-6-653668
This Episcopal boy's school, founded in 1936, teaches both the Jordanian Curricula and the London University General Certification of Education Curriculum. Total enrollment is 855 day students in grades 1-12. Length of stay for teachers is one year with no housing provided. Languages spoken are English and Arabic.

Najib F Elfarr, Principal
Jamil Ismair, Faculty Head

1443 British Aircraft Corp School
PO Box 3843
Riyadh
Saudi Arabia
MR Pound, Principal

1444 British Embassy Study Group
Sehit Ersan Caddesi 46A, 06680
Cankaya Ankara
Turkey 6680
90 (312) 468 6563
Fax: 90 (312) 468 6239
E-mail: admin@besg.org
http://www.besg.org
BESG is a co-educational primary school with 135 children aged between 3 and 11, representing nearly 26 countries. We are known as a friendly and caring British school, which values a holistic approach to education

Dawn Akyurek, Head Teacher
Katie Vincent, Deputy Head Teacher

1445 British International School-Istanbul
Dilhayat Sokak No:18 Etiler
Istanbul
Turkey, TR
90 (0) 212 257 51
Fax: 90-0-212-257 53 33
E-mail: registrar2@bis.k12.tr
http://www.bis.k12.tr
The British International School Istanbul (BISI) provides a wide range of educational choices for international families. We are a private, coeducational school providing British-style international education for 520 students of 40 nationalities between the ages of 2r and 18.

Graham Pheby, Principal
Roger Short, Governor of the School

1446 Cairo American College
PO Box 39
Maadi 11431
Cairo, EG 11431
(20-2) 2755-5507
Fax: 20-2-519-6584
E-mail: support@cacegypt.org
http://www.cacegypt.org
Cairo American College is a world class learning environment that affirms the voice, passions and talents of students and inspires them to use their hearts and minds as global citizens.

Nivine Captan-Amr, Board Chair
Elizabeth Bredin, Secretary

1447 Cambridge High School
PO Box 60835
Dubai
United Arab Emirates
971 - 4 282 4646
Fax: 971 - 4 282 4109
E-mail: cambridge@cis-dxb.ae
http://www.gemscis-garhoud.com

David Mcaughlin, Principal
Nigel Cropley, Vice Principal

1448 Continental School (Sais British)
PO Box 6453
Jeddah 21442
Saudi Arabia
966- 69- 001
Fax: 966- 69- 194
E-mail: conti@conti.sch.sa
http://www.continentalschool.com
Inspire in students a love of learning using a child centered, British style of education. Strive for excellence, recognizing, celebrating and encouraging a spirit of internationalism.

Bruce Gamwell, Director
Marina Alibhai, Registrar

1449 Dhahran Academy International School Group
PO Box 31677
Al Khobar 31952
Saudi Arabia
966-3-330-0555
Fax: 966-3-330-2450
E-mail: info@isgdh.org
http://www.isgdh.org
Grades preSchool-11, enrollment 994.

Norma Hudson, Superintendent

1450 Dhahran Central School
PO Box 31677
Dhahran 31311
Saudi Arabia
966-3-330-0555
Fax: 966-3-330-2450
E-mail: info@isgdh.org
http://www.isgdh.org

Norma Hudson, Principal

1451 Dhahran Hills School
PO Box 31677
Dhahran 31311
Saudi Arabia
966-3-330-0555
Fax: 966-3-330-2450
E-mail: info@isgdh.org
http://www.isgdh.org

Norma Hudson, Principal

1452 Doha College-English Speaking
PO Box 22090
Doha Qatar
Arabian Gulf
974-806-770
Fax: 974-806-311
E-mail: asdoha@qatar.net.qa
An independent, coeducational day school which offers an educational program from children of all nationalities from kindergarten through grade12.

E Goodwin, Principal

1453 Doha English Speaking School
PO Box 7660
Doha
Qatar
(974) 44592750
Fax: ÿ(974) 44592761
E-mail: ÿdess@dess.org
http://www.dess.org
Create a happy, secure, stimulating and supportive learning environment

Emad Turkman, Chairman
Eddie Liptrot, Head Teacher

1454 Doha Independent School
PO Box 5404
Doha Qatar
Arabian Gulf

SJ Williams, Principal

1455 Emirates International School
PO Box 6446
Dubai
United Arab Emirates
971-4-348-9804
Fax: 971-4-348-2813
E-mail: mail@eischools.ae
http://www.eischools.ae
We offer a broad international education, in English, designed for local and expatriate students, that promotes excellence in all academic activities. It is our mission to enhance the educational, social and physical development of our students encouraging them to think analytically and creatively in preparation for the next stage of their education.

Daryle Russell, EdD, Headmaster
Jason Kirwin, HS Principal

1456 English School-Fahaheel
PO Box 7209
Fahaheel
Kuwait 64003
96- 23-1 10
Fax: 96- 23-1 54
E-mail: esf@skee.com
http://www.skee.com
The English School Fahaheel recognizes the need for all students to be made aware of the demands placed upon them for Further Education and the world of work.

Ibrahim J Shuhaiber, Chairman
John J MacGregor, Principal

1457 English School-Kuwait
PO Box 379
Safat
Kuwait 13004
965-256-7205
Fax: 965-256-7147
http://www.tes.edu.kw
The English School was founded in 1953 under the auspices of the British Embassy and is the longest established school in Kuwait catering for the expatriate community. The School operates as a not-for-profit independent co-educational establishment providing the highest standards in education for children of Pre-Preparatory and Preparatory School age.

William James Strath, Principal
Richard Davis, Chair

1458 English Speaking School
PO Box 2002
Dubai
United Arab Emirates
04 - 33-1457
Fax: 04 - 33-8932
E-mail: dess@dessdubai.com
http://www.dessdxb.com
The school opened in 1963 in the upstairs room of a villa where expatriate workers were housed. There was one class which was taught by parents and a British Officer called Flight Lieutenant F. Loughman.

Bernadette McCarty, Principal
David Hammond, Headteacher

1459 Enka Okullari-Enka Schools
Sadi Gulcelik Spor Sitesi
Istinye, Istanbul
Turkey 34460
90-212-276-05-4547
Fax: 90-212-286-59-3035
E-mail: mailbox@enkaschools.com
http://www.enkaschools.com
Enka Schools provide an international education for our students. We have a well qualified and passionate group of teachers from Turkey and overseas. Most of our students are Turkish while some of them have international backgrounds.

Darlene Fisher, Director
Ayten Yilmaz, Preschool Principal

1460 Gulf English School
PO Box 2440
Doha
Qatar
974-445-8 77
Fax: 974-448-1 25
E-mail: info@gulfenglishschool.com
http://www.gulfenglishschool.com
Provide a positive and stimulating environment which facilitates individual learning, encourages experimentation, and develops critical thinking and problem solving skills. We must enable each student to achieve his or her best in the pursuit of academic excellence, and give them the confidence to be independent thinkers, able to assume responsibility

and leadership and to take their place in the wider world

Paul Andrews, Principal
Tim Brosnan, Faculty Head

1461 Habara School
PO Box 26516
Bahrain

PM Wrench, Principal

1462 IBN Khuldoon National School
Po Box 20511
Manama
Bahrain
973-16-687-073
Fax: 973-17-689-028
E-mail: info@ikns.edu.bh
http://www.ikns.edu.bh
This IBN school is a private, fee paying, non-profit, coeducational, accredited middle states school. The curriculum offered to the 1,210 day students (630 boys and 580 girls) in grades K-12, is English/Arabic. The school is willing to participate in a teacher exchange program with the applications needed being science, math, social sciences, pre-school and English.

Kamal Abdel-Nour, President
Ghada R Bou Zeineddine, Principal

1463 Incirlik Elementary School
Unit 7180 Box 270
APO AE 09824
Turkey
011-90-322-316-310
Fax: 011-90-322-332-757
E-mail:
IncirlikEHS.Principal@eu.dodea.edu
http://http://www.inci-ehs.eu.dodea.edu/

Mary Davis, Principal

1464 Incirlik High School
Unit 7180 Box 270
APO AE 09824
Turkey
011-90-322-316-310
Fax: 011-90-322-332-757
E-mail:
IncirlikEHS.Principal@eu.dodea.edu
http://http://www.inci-ehs.eu.dodea.edu/

Dr. Donald Torrey, Principal

1465 Infant School-House #45
Khalil Kando Gardens Road, 5651
Manama
Bahrain

Maria Stiles, Principal

1466 International Community School
PO Box 2002
Amman
Jordan 11181
962-6 5-2 10
Fax: 962-6 5-2 71
E-mail: office@ics-amman.edu.jo
http://www.ics-amman.edu.jo
Ours is a school where people matter. ~We want good results for each student, according to his or her own abilities in the classroom, in sport , music, drama or art.

John Light, Principal
Sue Hill, Primary Head

1467 International School of Choueifat
PO Box 7212
Abu Dhabi
United Arab Emirates
971-2-446-1444
Fax: 971-2-446-1048
E-mail: iscad@sabis.net
http://www.iscad-sabis.net
Over the last 27 years hundreds of students have graduated from The International

Schools of Choueifat in the region and then graduated from top universities in the world. In the UK, these universities include Oxford, Cambridge, LSE, Bristol, Edinburgh, Bath, Birmingham, Liverpool, The Imperial College of Science and Technology and all other Colleges of London University.

Marilyn Abu-Esber, Director

1468 Istanbul International Community School
Karaagac Mahallesi, G 72 Sokak No:1
Buyukcekmece , Istanbul
Turkey 34866
90-212-857-8264
Fax: 90-212-857-8270
E-mail: jlewis@iics.k12.tr
http://www.iics.k12.tr
Through its challenging curriculum and strong staff-student relationships, IICS provides a caring environment that inspires each student to excel and to be inquisitive, creative, compassionate, balanced and internationally-minded.

Peter Welch, Headmaster
Sean Murphy, Primary Principal

1469 Izmir Elementary & High School
PSC 88
APO, Izmir 09821 0005
Turkey

Terry Emerson, Principal

1470 Jeddah Preparatory School
British Consulate, Box 6316
Jeddah 21442 Saudi Arabia
265-235-
Fax: ÿÿ0- 65-1836
E-mail: registrar@jpgs.org
http://http://www.jpgs.org/

John GF Parsons, Principal

1471 Jubail British Academy
PO Box 10059 Madinat Al Jubail
Jubail 31961
Saudi Arabia
966.3.341.7550
Fax: 966.3.341.6990
E-mail: mmcdougall@isgdh.org
http://http://www.isg-jubail.org/

Norman Edwards, Principal

1472 Jumeirah English Speaking School
PO Box 24942, Dubai
United Arab Emirates
971-4-394-5515
Fax: 971-4-394-3531
E-mail: jess@jess.sch.ae
http://http://www.jess.sch.ae/Home.aspx

CA Branson, Headmaster
RD Stokoe, Director

1473 King Faisal School
PO Box 94558, Riyadh 11614
Saudia Arabia
966-1-482-0802
Fax: 966-1-482-1521
E-mail: kfs@kfs.sch.sa
http://www.kfs.sch.sa/English/adefault.aspx
Grade levels preK-12, enrollment 600.

Mohammed Al-Humood, Director General

1474 Koc School
PK 60-Tuzla
Istanbul
Turkey 34941
(90)216 585 6200
Fax: 90-216-304-1048
E-mail: info@kocschool.k12.tr
http://www.kocschool.k12.tr
The goal of KoO School is to be respected nationally and internationally as a model K-12

school, offering an educational program of the highest academic and ethical standards.

Suna Kirac, Chairman

1475 Kuwait English School
PO Box 8640
Salmiya 22057
Kuwait
256-552-6
Fax: 256-293-6
E-mail: keschool@kes.edu.kw
http://http://www.kes.edu.kw/?page_id=69

Craig Halsall, Principal

1476 Mohammed Ali Othman School
PO Box 5713
Taiz Yeman
Arab Republic
Mohammed Ali Othman School is a well established school which has been running for over thirty years. At present it has around a thousand students from the Foundation Stage through to Year 12

Abdulla Ahmad, Principal
Fowzia Abdo Saeed, Deputy Head

1477 Nadeen Nursery & Infant School
PO Box 26367
Adliya
Bahrain
973-17 -2888
Fax: 973-17 -2888
E-mail: info@nadeenschool.com
http://www.nadeenschool.info/
Nadeen School is dedicated to providing a caring, nurturing, and stimulating environment in which all children can learn and thrive. All of our students are treated with respect, care, and with the utmost sensitivity to their individual needs and requirements.

Pauline Puri, Principal

1478 New English School
PO Box 6156
Hawalli
Kuwait, KW 32036
[00965] 25318060
Fax: [00965] 25319924
E-mail: admin@neskt.com
http://www.neskt.com
Private, co-educational day-school to offer a British style curriculum from Kindergarten to 'A' level.

Tareq S Rajab, Founder

1479 Pakistan International School-Peshawar
PO Box 3797
Riyadh
Saudi Arabia
92-441-4428
Fax: 92-441-7272
An independent, coeducaional day school which offers an educational program from prekindergarten through grade 8 and supervised correspondence study for the high school grades for all expatriate nationalities.

Angela Coleridge, Principal

1480 Rahmaniah-Taif-Acad International School
American Consulate General, Dhahran
District Saudi Arabia

Dean May, Principal

1481 Ras Al Khaimah English Speaking School
PO Box 975
Ras Al Khaimah
United Arab Emirates

971-7-362-441
Fax: 971-7-362-445
http://www.rakess.net
Roy Burrows, Principal

1482 Ras Tanura School
PO Box 6140
Ras Tanura
Saudi Arabia 31311
673-676-
E-mail: david.weston@aramco.com
http://www.saudiaramco.com
David Weston, Principal

1483 Sanaa International School
PO Box 2002
Sanaa
Yemen
967-1-370192
Fax: 967-1-370-193
E-mail: qsi-sanaa@qsi.org
http://www.qsi.org/yem_home/yem_home.htm
Sanaa International School, a non-profit institution that opened in September 1971 offers a high quality education in the English language for pre-school, elementary, and secondary students. The Campus is located on 34 acres on the outskirts of Sanaa constructed and entered in September 1978.
Martin Avelsgaard, Director

1484 Saudi Arabian International British School
PO Box 85769
Riyadh
Saudi Arabia 11612
966-1 2-8 23
Fax: 966-1 2-8 03
E-mail: principal@britishschoolriyadh.com
http://www.britishschoolriyadh.com
Improve standards of teaching, learning and citizenship within a safe and secure environment. Our Mission Statement and School Improvement Plan provide the direction for the future development of our pupils and the continuous improvement of our school.
Peter Wiles, Acting Principal
Terry Sayce, Chairman

1485 Saudi Arabian International School-Dhahran
SAIS-DD, Box 677
Dhahran International Airport
Dhahran 31932, Saudi Arabia
996-3-330-0555
Fax: 966-3-330-0555
E-mail:
brent_mutsch%sais@macexpress.org
http://http://www.isgdh.org/
Dr. Leo Ruberto, Principal

1486 Saudi Arabian International School-Riyadh
PO Box 990
Riyadh
Kingdom of Saudi Arabia 11421
966-1-491-4270
Fax: 966-1-491-7101
E-mail: registration@ais-r.edu.sa
http://www.aisr.org
Educate and inspire our students to be responsible, productive and ethical world citizens with the skills and passion to think creatively, reason critically, communicate effectively and learn continuously. We will accomplish this in an American educational environment characterized by high measurable standards and a clearly defined, appropriately interrelated college preparatory curriculum, imple-

mented by a superior staff in partnership with parents and community.
Daryle Russell, EdD, Principal
Brian Matthews, Superintendent

1487 Saudia-Saudi Arabian International School
PO Box 167, CC 100
Jeddah 21231
Saudi Arabia
John Hazelton, Principal

1488 Sharjah English School
PO Box 1600
Sharjah
United Arab Emirates
971- 55- 930
Fax: 971- 55- 930
E-mail: seschool@emirates.net.ae
http://www.seschool.ae
Not for profit school. It is self-supporting and financed by fees paid by parents for the education of their children.
David Throp, Principal
Jenefer Race, Primary Headteacher

1489 Sharjah Public School
PO Box 6125, Sharjah
United Arab Emirates
Nazim Khan, Principal

1490 St. Mary's Catholic High School
PO Box 52232
Dubai
United Arab Emirates
009-1 4-3370
Fax: 009-1 4-3368
E-mail: maryscol@emirates.net.ae
http://www.stmarysdubai.com
St. Mary's Catholic High School is reputed for its high standards in academic work and also in the standards of discipline which we try to inspire in the children.
Sr Anne Marie Quigg, Principal
U D'Souza, Vice Principal

1491 Sultan's School
PO Box 665
Seeb
Sultanate of Oman 121
968-24 -36 7
Fax: 968-24 -36 2
E-mail: admissions@sultansschool.org
http://www.sultansschool.org
The Sultan's School is a co-educational school offering a bilingual Arabic-English education from early childhood to pre-university.
Anthony J Cashin, Principal

1492 Sunshine School
2 Dutcher Avenue
Pawling, NY 12564
845-855-9238
Fax: 845-855-0222
http://sunshineschool-pawling.org
Our goal is to provide a quality pre-school education for young children. We do this by addressing both the social and the intellectual development of the child.
David Brinded, Principal

1493 Tarsus American College and SEV Primary
Cengiz Topel Cd Caminur Mah 201 Sk
Tarsus/Mersin
Turkey 33440
90-324-613-5402
Fax: 90-324-624-6347
E-mail: info@tac.k12.tr
http://www.tac.k12.tr
The mission of Tarsus American Schools is to contribute to the growth of individuals who

combine self-confidence with a firm sense of personal and social responsibility.
Bernard Mitchell, PhD, Superintendent
Jale Sever, Primary School Principal

1494 Universal American School
PO Box 17035
Khalidiya
Kuwait 72451
965-562-0297/561
Fax: 965-562-5343
E-mail: uas@qualitynet.net
http://www.uas.edu.kw
The Universal American School is a private, college-preparatory, N-12 school serving a multinational student body from the diverse populations residing in Kuwait
Nora Al-Ghanim, Administrative Director
Mike Church, Assistant Principal

1495 Uskudar American Academy
Vakif Sokak Number 1
Baglarbasi Istanbul
Turkey, TR
90-216-310-6823
Fax: 90-216-333-1818
E-mail: wshepard@uaa.k12.tr
http://www.uaa.k12.tr
The mission of SEV/ABH Schools is to contribute to the growth of individuals who combine self-confidence with a firm sense of personal, social, and environmental responsibility. We aim to enable our students to be strong bilinguals in English and Turkish, well-educated adults, lifelong learners, and efficient communicators, who have developed skills, accountability, and attitudes for leading a fulfilling life and for serving their country and humanity
Whitman Shepard, Director
Dilek Yakar, Primary Principal

1496 Walworth Barbour American International School in Israel
65 Hashomron Street
PO Box 484
Israel 40500
972-9-961-8100
Fax: 972-9-961-8111
E-mail: aisrael@wbais.org
http://www.american.hasharon.k12.il
Through a rigorous and dynamic American international curriculum, AIS, a private secular school in Israel, inspires each student to cultivate a respect for diversity, develop a passion for life-long learning, achieve academic potential, assume leadership, contribute actively to society, and resolve conflict through dialogue and understanding
Robert A Sills, Superintendent
John Chere, Chairman

Western Europe

1497 AC Montessori Kids
Route De Renipont 4
Lasne B-1380
Belgium
32-2-633-6652
Fax: 32-2-633-6652
E-mail: info@acmontessorikids.com
http://www.acmontessorikids.com
A bilingual English/French Montessori School for children aged 18 months - 12 years.
Laurence Randoux, Director
Mark Ciepers, Director

1498 AFCENT Elementary & High School
Unit 21606
APO AE 09703
Brunssum, Netherlands

http://www.afcent.org

1499 Abbotsholme School
Rocester (Uttoxeter, Staffordshire)
ST14 5BS
England
01889-590217
Fax: 01889-590001
E-mail: enquiries@abbotsholme.co.uk
http://www.abbotsholme.com
This interdenominational school offers an English-based curriculum for 78 day students and 166 boarding (152 boys; 92 girls), in grades 7-13.

Darrell J Farrant, MA, FRSA, Principal
Steve Fairclough, Head

1500 Academy-English Prep School
Apartado 1300 Palma D Mallorca
07080 Palma de Mallorca
Spain

CA Walker, Principal

1501 Ackworth School, Ackworth
Pontefract, West Yorkshire
England WF7 7
0977-611401
E-mail: admissions@ackworthschool.com
http://www.ackworthschool.com
This school offers an English-based curriculum to 264 day students and 111 boarding students (180 boys; 195 girls), ages 11-18 years of age.

Peter J Simpson, Head
Jeffrey Swales, Deputy Head, Curriculum

1502 Alconbury Elementary School
Unit 5570 Box 60
APO AE 09470
Great Britain
011-44-1480-843620
Fax: 011-44-1480-843172
E-mail:
AlconburyES.Principal@eu.dodea.edu
http://www.alco-es.eu.dodea.edu
To provide a safe and productive learning environment in which all students reach their fullest potential by developing knowledge and skills.

Ora C Flippen-Casper, Principal

1503 Alconbury High School
Unit 5570 Box 60
APO AE 09470
Great Britain
44 -480-8437
Fax: 44 -480-8431
http://www.alco-hs.eu.dodea.edu
To develop healthy, adaptable, independently thinking, and socially responsible members of the global community.

Gael Coyle, Principal
Lance Posey, Assistant Principal

1504 Alexander M Patch Elementary School
Unit 30401
APO AE 09107
Germany
49 -711-680
Fax: 49 -711-6877
http://www.patch-es.eu.dodea.edu
Provide a standards-based curriculum that develops lifelong learners and promotes highest student achievement in partnership with our community.

Robert Allen, Principal
Ronald Lathrop, Assistant. Principal

1505 Alexander M Patch High School
Unit 30401
APO AE 09107-0401
Germany
49 -711-680
Fax: 49 -711-682
http://www.stut-hs.eu.dodea.edu
Prepares all students to exceed challenging academic standards, know how to learn, communicate effectively, and make responsible decisions so that they can be continuous learners and productive citizens in a diverse society.

Susan Page, Principal

1506 Alfred T Mahan Elementary School
PSC 1003 Box 48
FPO Keflavik 09728
Iceland

Jan Long, Principal

1507 Alfred T Mahan High School
PSC 1003 Box 52
FPO Keflavik 09728 0352
Iceland

M Deatherage, Principal

1508 Amberg Elementary School
CMR 414
APO, Amberg 09173 0005
Germany

Letcher Connell, Principal

1509 Ambrit Rome International School
Via Filippo Tajani, 50
Rome, Italy 149
39-06-559-5305
Fax: 39-06-559-5309
E-mail: ambrit@ambrit-rome.com
http://www.ambrit-rome.com
Grade levels Pre-K through 8, school year September - June

Bernard C Mullane, Director
Loretta Nanini, Admissions Director

1510 American College-Greece
6 Gravias Street
Aghia Paraskevi
Athens, Greece GR-15
30-1-600-9800
Fax: 30-1-600-9811
E-mail: info@acg.edu
http://www.acg.edu
Founded in 1875, combining the best of American education with the intellectual and cultural heritage of Greece, provide a unique foundation for international educational excellence.

David G Horner, President
Nicholas Jiavaras, Executive Vice President

1511 American Community School-Cobham
Heywood, Portsmouth Road
Cobham, Surrey
United Kingdom KT11
44-1932-869-744
Fax: 44-1932-869-789
E-mail: hayoub@acs-england.co.uk
http://www.acs-england.co.uk
Promotes a high standard of scholarship, responsibility, and citizenship in a supportive, international community.

Tom Lehman, Head of School
Heidi Ayoub, Dean of Admissions

1512 American Community School-Egham
Woodlee London Road (A30)
Egham, Surrey
United Kingdom TW20
44-1784-430-611
Fax: 44-1784-430-626
E-mail: jlove@acs-england.co.uk
http://www.acs-england.co.uk
Promotes high standards of scholarship, responsibility and citizenship in a supportive, international community

Julia Love, Dean of Admissions
Moyra Hadley, Head of School

1513 American Community School-Hillingdon
108 Vine Lane
Hillingdon, Middlesex
United Kingdom UB10
44-189-581-3734
Fax: 44-189-581-0634
E-mail:
HillingdonAdmissions@acs-england.co.uk
http://www.acs-england.co.uk
Foundes in 1978, has endeavoured to provide a quality education for a multi-national community in the London area.

Ginger Apple, Head of School
Rudianne Soltis, Dean of Admissions

1514 American Community Schools
108 Vine Court
Hillingdon, Uxbridge, Middlesex UB100BE
England
44-189-581-3734
Fax: 44-189-581-0634
E-mail: hmulkey@acs-england.co.uk
http://www.acs-england.co.uk
This school serves the needs of the international business families in Greater London. Programs are nonsectarian, coeducational day schools with lower, middle and high school divisions offering coordinate college preparatory curricula from pre-kindergarten through grade twelve.

Paul Berg, Headmaster

1515 American Community Schools-Athens
129 Aghias Paraskevis Avenue and Ka
Halandri, Athens
Greece 15343
301-639-3200
Fax: 301-639-0051
E-mail: gialamas@acs.gr
http://www.acs.gr
Provides a student-centered environment where individuals excel academically and develop intellectually, socially and ethically to thrive as healthy, responsible members of global society.

Stefanos Gialamas, President
Steve Kakaris, Business Manager

1516 American Embassy School-Reykjavik
L"ngul-nu 8
210 Gardab'r
Iceland
354-590-3106
Fax: 354-590-3110
E-mail: isi@internationalschool.is
http://www.internationalschool.is
The International School of Iceland (ISI)~is a private elementary school housed in an Icelandic public school, Sjÿlandssk⟩li. The school offers an international educational program to children in grades 1-7.

Berta Faber, Headmistress
Hanna Hilmarsdottir, Assistant Headmistress

1517 American International School-Carinthia
Friesacher Strasse 3 Audio ICC
A-9330 Althofen
Austria

Ron Presswood, Principal

1518 American International School-Florence
Villa le Tavernule - via del Carota
Bagno a Ripoli, Florence
Italy 50012
39-055-646-1007
Fax: 39-055-644-226
E-mail: admin.tav@isfitaly.org
http://www.isfitaly.org
Business Manager
Provide attendees
Christopher Maggio, Head of School
Marie Jos, Manzini

1519 American International School-Genoa
Via Quarto 13-C
Genoa
Italy 16148
39-010-386-528
Fax: 39-010-398-700
E-mail: info@aisge.it
http://www.aisge.it
Provides students of internationally- minded families with a high quality education in the English language, from Pre-School through to the 12th Grade.

Sheldon Friedman, Director
Raffaele Boccardo, President

1520 American International School-Lisbon
Rua Antonio Dos Reis, 95
Linho, 2710-301 Sintra
Portugal
351-21-923-98-00
Fax: 351-21-923-98-26
E-mail: tesc0893@mail.telepac.pt
http://www.ecis.org/aislisbon/index.html
An independent, coeducational day school which offers an educational program from early childhood through grade 12 for student of all nationalities.

Blannie M Curtis, Director

1521 American International School-Rotterdam
Verhulstlaan 21
3055 WJ Rotterdam
Netherlands
31-10-422-5351
Fax: 31-10-422-4075
E-mail: queries@aisr.nl
http://www.aisr.nl
Provides a comprehensive program of learning, with well-qualified and experienced faculty who prepare students Pre-School through Grade 12 for the ever-changing world in which we live.

Brian Atkins, Director
Anne-Marie Blitz, Elementary Principal

1522 American International School-Salzburg
Moosstrasse 106
Salzburg A-5020
Austria
43-662-824-617
Fax: 43-662-824-555
E-mail: office@ais.salzburg.at
http://www.ais-salzburg.at
A boarding and day school committed to the college-preparatory education of conscientious young men and women. The academic and boarding programs nurture the students' intellectual growth and artistic potential, as well as their social, physical, and personal development.

Paul McLean, Headmaster
Felicia Gundringer, Admissions Coordinator

1523 American International School-Vienna
Salmannsdorfer Strasse 47
A-1190 Vienna
Austria
43-1-401-320
Fax: 43-1-401-325
E-mail: info@ais.at
http://www.ais.at
Provide a culture of educational excellence, a nurturing environment, and an atmosphere of open communication and aims to prepare a diverse student body for higher education; to inspire the youth to realize their potential; to foster life-long learning, tolerance, personal integrity, and democratic values; and to prepare students to become responsible adults, with respect for different cultures and beliefs.

Ellen Stern, Director
Dr Greg Moncada, HS Principal

1524 American Overseas School-Rome
Via Cassia 811
Rome, IT 189
39-06-3326-4841
Fax: 39-06-3326-2608
E-mail: aosr@aosr.org
http://www.aosr.org
An independent, coeducational day school for students of all nationalities in prekindergarten through grade 13 and offers a boarding program for select students in grades 9-12.

Beth Kempler, Head of School

1525 American School of the Hague
Rijksstraatweg 200
2241 BX Wassenaar
The Netherlands
31-70-512-1060
Fax: 31-70-511-2400
E-mail: info@ash.nl
http://www.ash.nl
educates students to excel in critical inquiry, creative thinking, clear communication, and commitment to others.

Paul De Minico, Superintendent
Douglas Buckley, Chair

1526 American School-Barcelona
Jaume Balmes 7
Esplugues de Llobregat
Spain 8950
34-93-371-4016
Fax: 34-93-473-4787
E-mail: info@a-s-b.com
http://www.a-s-b.com
fully develop each student's unique potential by providing a high quality American/Spanish curriculum in an English-language based, respectful and diverse environment

Nancy Boyd, Elementary School Principal
Bill Volckok, Secondary School Principal

1527 American School-Bilbao
Soparda Bidea 10
Berang (Bizkaia)
Spain 48640
34-94-668-0860
Fax: 34-94-668-0452
E-mail: asob@asob.es
http://www.asob.es/en
s a private, non-profit, International School, Offers students an American-style educational programme taught in English. The curriculum has an international focus and leads to the American High School Diploma

Roger West, Director

1528 American School-Las Palmas
Carretera de los Hoyos, Km 1.7
Las Palmas de Gran Canaria
Las Palmas, Spain 35017
34-928-430-023
Fax: 34-928-430-017
E-mail: info@dns.aslp.org
http://www.aslp.org
upports students in becoming life long learners in the tradition of American education

Nathan Walker, Director
Conchita Neyra, Assistant Director

1529 American School-London
One Waverly Place
London
United Kingdom NW8 0
44-207-449-1200
Fax: 44-207-449-1350
E-mail: admissions@asl.org
http://www.asl.org
is to develop the intellect and character of each student by providing an outstanding American education with a global perspective.

Jodi Coats, Dean of Admissions

1530 American School-Madrid
Apartado 80
Madrid
Spain 28080
34-91-740-1900
Fax: 34-91-357-2678
E-mail: info@asmadrid.org
http://www.amerschmad.org
Grade levels Pre-K through 12, school year September - June

Robert Thompson, Director
William O'Hale, Headmaster

1531 American School-Milan
Via K Marx 14
Noverasco di Opera, Milan
Italy 20090
39-02-530-001
Fax: 39-02-576-06274
E-mail: director@asmilan.org
http://www.asmilan.org
s to provide a fulfilling educational environment where learners can discover and develop their capacities and achieve personal excellence.

Alen P Austen, Director
Samer Khoury, High School Principal

1532 American School-Paris
41, rue Pasteur
Saint Cloud
France 92210
33-1-411-28282
Fax: 33-1-460-22390
E-mail: webteam@asparis.fr
http://www.asparis.org
We develop lifelong learners with an international focus who use their social, thinking and problem-solving skills to contribute constructively to a changing global society

Pilar Cabeza de Vaca, Headmistress
Jack Davis, Head of the School

1533 American School-Valencia
Avenida Sierra Calderona 29
Urb Los Monasterios, Puzol
Spain 46530
34-96-140-5412
Fax: 34-96-140-5039
E-mail: asvalencia@asvalencia.org
http://www.asvalencia.org
An international, private, bilingual, university- preparatory school that provides a broad and balanced curriculum in a safe and positive learning environment that encourages students to seek challenges.

Saara Tatem, Director
Ildefonso Segura, Financial Director

1534 American School-the Hague
Rijkstraatweg 200
BX Wassenaar
Netherlands 2241
31-70-514-0113
Fax: 31-70-511-2400
E-mail: info@ash.nl
http://www.ash.nl
Educates students to excel in critical inquiry,
creative thinking, clear communication, and
commitment to others.

Rick Spradling, Director

1535 Anatolia College
PO Box 21021
Pylea Thessaloniki
Greece 55510
30-31-398-201
Fax: 30-31-327-500
E-mail: admissions@act.edu
http://www.anatolia.edu.gr
Offers undergraduate and graduate programs
of study characterized by reasoned and open
inquiry, acquisition of the breadth and depth
of knowledge associated with traditional university curricula, and achievement of the
highest possible standards in student-centered teaching and faculty scholarship, with
emphasis on individual growth.

Richard L Jackson, President
Panayiotis Kanellis, Executive Vice
President

1536 Anglo-American School-Moscow
American Embassy
Itainen Puistotie 14
Finland 140
7-095-231-4488
Fax: 7-095-231-4477
E-mail: director@aas.ru
http://www.aas.ru
An international learning community where
students, teachers and parents demand excel-
lence and engagement from one another.

Drew Alexander, Director
Nicolette Kirk, Admissions Officer

**1537 Anglo-American School-St.
Petersburg**
c/o American Embassy
Itainen Puistotie 14, Box L, Helsinki
Finland
7-812-320-8925
Fax: 7-812-320-8926
E-mail: nastia.smirnova@aas.ru
http://www.aas.ru/stpetersburg
An international learning community where
students, teachers and parents demand excel-
lence and engagement from one another.

Ronald Gleason, Principal
Ellen D Stren, Director

1538 Ansbach Elementary School
Unit 28614 APO AE 09177
Germany
011-49 -802
Fax: 011-46 -802
E-mail:
AnsbachES.Principal@eu.odedodea.edu
http://www.ansb-es.eu.dodea.edu
Provides many excellent opportunities to
encouage and support all students intellectual, physical, social, emotional and creative
developments and prepare them to meet the
challengges of a dynamic and diverse world
community.

Essie Grant, Principal

1539 Ansbach High School
Unit 28614
APO AE 09177
Germany
49-9802-223
Fax: 49-9802-1496

E-mail:
AnsbachHS.Principal@eu.dodea.edu
http://www.ansb-hs.eu.dodea.edu
A public school serving the children of American Army units.

Jennifer Rowland, Principal

1540 Antwerp International School
Veltwijcklaan 180
2180 Ekeren-Antwerpen
Belgium
32-3-543-9300
Fax: 32-3-541-8201
E-mail: ais@ais-antwerp.be
http://www.ais-antwerp.be
Educates young people to be responsible, caring, and productive members of a democratic
society in a global community, and to prepare
them for continued education. It promotes integrity, self-realization, mutual respect and
understanding in a multi-cultural environment of students and teachers.

Alun Cooper, Headmaster

1541 Argonner Elementary School
Unit 20193 Box 0015
APO, Hanau 09165 0015
Germany

Christine Holsten, Principal

1542 Athens College
420 Madison Avenue
New York, NY 10017
212-697-7071
Fax: 212-697-7093
E-mail: trustees@athenscollege.org
http://www.athenscollege.org
The mission of Athens College is to provide,
by international standards, the highest quality
education to the most deserving candidates
and to cultivate in its students those habits of
mind, body, and spirit necessary for responsible citizenship in GReece and the world;
moral courage, intellectual discipline, com-
passion, and an unswerving devotion to justice and truth. Our goal is to instill in our
students, by teaching and by example, a
strong sense of measure.

Walter McCanny Eggleston, Principal
Dr Nicholas G Bacopoulos, President

1543 Aviano Elementary School
Unit 6210 Box 180
APO, AE 09604-0180
Italy
011-39-0434-660921
E-mail: avianoes.principal@eu.dodea.edu
http://www.avia-es.eu.dodea.edu

Lillian Hiyama, Principal
Phyllis Fuglaar, Assistant Principal

1544 Aviano High School
Unit 6210 Box 180
APO, AE 09604-0180
Italy
011-39 -434
Fax: 011-39 -434
E-mail: avianohs.principal@eu.dodea.edu
http://www.avia-hs.eu.dodea.edu

Debra K Johnson, Principal

1545 BEPS 2 Limal International School
23 Avenue Franklin Roosevelt
Brussels
Belgium 1050
32-10-417-227
Fax: 32-2-687-2968
E-mail: info@beps.com
http://www.beps.com
The schools share a common philosophy and
approach to education. An average class size
of 16 allows for a high level of individual at-

tention in a caring and supportive
environment.

Charles A Gellar, Head
Henny de Waal, Headmistress

1546 Babenhausen Elementary School
CMR 426 Unit 20219
APO, Babenhausen 09089 0005
Germany

Ida Rhodes, Principal

1547 Bad Kissingen Elementary School
CMR 464
APO, Bad Kissingen 09226 0005
Germany

Beatrice McWaters, Principal

1548 Bad Kreuznach Elementary School
CMR 441
APO, Bad Kreuznach 09525 0005
Germany

Peter Grenier, Principal

1549 Bad Kreuznach High School
Unit 24324
APO, Bad Krueznach 09252 0005
Germany

Jennifer Beckwith, Principal

1550 Bad Nauheim Elementary School
Unit 21103
APO, Bad Nauheim 09074 0005
Germany

Raymond Burkard, Principal

1551 Badminton School
Westbury-on-Trym, Bristol
BS9 3BA
England
0272-623141
E-mail:
admissions@badminton.bristol.sch.uk
http://www.badminton.bristol.sch.uk
The school combines excellent facilities and
teaching standards with a friendly atmosphere and a strong emphasis on pastoral care.
Badminton is also focused on ensuring that
girls realise their potential so that they can be
capable of achieving whatever they want to be
when they leave school.

Jan Scarrow, Headmistress

1552 Bamberg Elementary School
USAG Bamberg, Unit 27539
APO AE 09139
Germany
011-49 -51 3
Fax: 095- 31-15
E-mail:
BambergES.Principal@eu.dodea.edu
http://www.bamb-es.eu.dodea.edu
John G Rhyne, Principal

1553 Bamberg High School
Unit 27539
APO AE 09139
Germany
469-887-
Fax: 095- 3-669
E-mail:
BambergHS.Principal@eu.dodea.edu
http://www.bamb-hs.eu.dodea.edu/
Preparing all students to achieve success and
personal fulfillment in a dynamic global envi-
ronment.

Dominick Calabria, Principal
Richard Jimenez, Assistant Principal

1554 Barrow Hills School
Roke Lane
Witley, Godalming
Surrey, England GU8 5

01428-683639
Fax: 01428-683639
E-mail: sec@barrowhills.org.uk
http://www.barrowhills.org.uk

Michael Connolly, Headmaster

1555 Baumholder High School

Unit 23816 Box 30
APO, AE 09034-0034
Germany
011-49 -783
Fax: 011-49 -783
E-mail:
BaumholderHS.Principal@eu.dodea.edu
http://www.baum-hs.eu.dodea.edu

Danny Robinson, Principal
Patrick McDonald, Assistant Principal

1556 Bavarian International School

Haputstrasse 1
Schloss Haimbausen
Haimhausen, Germany 85778
49-8133-9170
Fax: 49-8133-917-135
E-mail: k.lippacher@bis-school.com
http://www.bis-school.com
Inspiring young minds and challenging young
individuals to achieve their intellectual and
personal potential within a caring international environment

Bryan Nixon, Director

1557 Bedales School

Church Road Steep
Petersfield Hampshire
England, UK GU32
01730-300100
Fax: 01730-300500
E-mail: admin@bedales.org.uk
http://www.bedales.org.uk

Keith Budge, Headmaster
Leo Winkley, Deputy Head

1558 Bedford School

De Parys Avenue Bedford
England, UK MK40
44-0-1234-362200
Fax: 44-0-1234-362283
E-mail: info@bedfordschool.org.uk
http://www.bedfordschool.org.uk
We pride ourselves on the pursuit of excellence, on encouraging boys to develop their
talent, discover new interests and prepare for
the world beyond school.

John Moule, Head Master

1559 Bedgebury School

Goudhurst
Cranbrook
Kent TN17
0580-211954
E-mail: bedgebury@bell-centres.com
http://www.bedgeburyschool.co.uk
Our goal at Bell Bedgebury is a simple one - to
offer all our students the best possible preparation for their future educational careers.

Eric Squires, Headmaster
David Morse, Principal

1560 Belgium Antwerp International School

Veltwijcklaan 180
Ekeren-Antwerp
Belgium 2180
32-3-543-9300
Fax: 32-3-541-8201
E-mail: ais@ais-antwerp.be
http://www.ais-antwerp.be
The school is concerned with the student's so-
cial, physical, emotional and intellectual de-
velopment. It is committed to excellence and

to providing the best possible opportunities
for growth for each student.

Alun Cooper, Headmaster
Matthew Cox, Elementary School Principal

1561 Benjamin Franklin International School

Martorell i Pena 9
Barcelona
Spain 8017
34-93-434-2380
Fax: 34-93-417-3633
E-mail: bfranklin@bfis.org
http://www.bfis.org
We view education as an opportunity for chil-
dren to live fully and become global citizens
able to build a more humane world.

David Penberg, Director
James Duval, Elementary Principal

1562 Berlin International School

Lentzeallee 8/14
Berlin
Germany 14195
49-30-790-00370
Fax: 49-30-3790-00370
E-mail:
office@berlin-international-school.de
http://www.berlin-international-school.de
Berlin International School is a private,
non-profit, non-denominational day school
offering student-centered learning to international and local students from pre-school
through university entrance preparation.

Hubert Keulers, Acting Director
Michael Cunningham, Principal

1563 Berlin Potsdam International School

Am Hochwald 30, Haus 2
14 532 Kleinmachnow
Germany
49-332-086-760
Fax: 49-332-086-7612
E-mail: office@bpis.de
http://www.bpis.de
Grade levels N-12, school year August - June

Stephen Middlebrook, Director

1564 Bitburg Elementary School

52 MSG/CCSE-B Unit 3820 Box 45
APO, AE
Germany 9126-45
11 -9 6-61 5
Fax: 11 -9 6-61 1
E-mail: BitburgES.Principal@eu.dodea.edu
http://www.bitb-es.eu.dodea.edu

Joseph Lovett, Principal

1565 Bitburg High School

52 MSG/CCSH-B Unit 3820 Box 50
APO, AE
Germany 9126-50
065-5 6- 920
Fax: 065-1 9-0 90
E-mail: webmaster@eu.dodea.edu
http://www.bitb-hs.eu.dodea.edu

David W Carlisle, Principal
Jennifer Remoy, Assistant Principal

1566 Bitburg Middle School

52 MSG/CCSM-B Unit 3820 Box 55
APO, AE
Germany 9126
065-1 5-66
Fax: 065-1 1-091
E-mail: webmaster@eu.dodea.edu
http://www.bitb-ms.eu.dodea.edu

Douglas Carlson, Principal

1567 Bjorn's International School

Gartnerivej 5
Copenhagen
Denmark 2100

45 -9 2- 29
Fax: 45 -9 1- 38
E-mail: kontoret.101152@skolekom.dk
http://www.b-i-s.dk

Lea Kroghly, Principal

1568 Black Forest Academy

Postfach 1109
Kandern
Germany 79396
49-7626-91610
Fax: 49-7626-8821
http://www.bfacademy.com
Black Forest Academy's vision is glob-
ally-minded Christians changing their world
for Christ.

George Durance, Principal
Tim Shuman, Director

1569 Bloxham School

Bloxham
Banbury
Oxfordshire, UK OX15
01295-720206
Fax: 01295-721897
E-mail: registar@bloxhamschool.com
http://www.bloxhamschool.com
As the largest group of Church of England
Schools in the UK, Woodard was established
in 1847 and today is known for providing academic excellence and an unrivalled supportive environment where individuals can
flourish.

Mark Allbrook, Headmaster
B Hurst, Chairman

1570 Blue Coat School

Birmingham Street
Walsall
West Midlands, UK WS1 2
0121-456-3966
E-mail: postbox@blue-coat-s.walsall.sch.uk
http://www.bluecoatschool.org

Brian Bissell, Principal
Ken Yeates, Headteacher

1571 Boeblingen Elementary School

Unit 30401
APO
AE 9107
070-1 1-2715
Fax: 070-1 2-1368
http://www.stut-esb.eu.dodea.edu
To inspire curiosity and ambition for life-long
learning in every student.

Dale Moore, Principal
Toufy Haddad, Assistant Principal

1572 Bonn International School

Martin-Luther-King Strasse 14
Bonn
Germany 53175
49-228-308-540
Fax: 49-228-308-5420
E-mail: admin@bis.bonn.org
http://www.bis.bonn.org
The mission of Bonn International School is
to inspire and empower students, aged 3-19,
to become balanced, responsible global citizens who are successful, independent thinkers with a passion for learning.

Peter Murphy, Director
Diane Lewthwaite, Secondary School
Principal

1573 Bordeaux International School

252 rue Jadaique
Bordeaux
France 33000
33-557-870-211
Fax: 33-556-790-047
E-mail: bis@bordeaux-school.com
http://www.bordeaux-school.com

Conveniently located in the centre of historic Bordeaux, the school is purpose-built around a secure, enclosed and partially covered courtyard, which provides a space for pupils across the school to socialise with each other.

Christine Cussac, Head Teacher

1574 Brillantmont International School
16, avenue Charles-Secretan
Lausanne
Switzerland, CH 1005
41-21-310-0400
Fax: 41-21-320-8417
E-mail: info@brillantmont.ch
http://www.brillantmont.ch
Brillantmont International School houses some 100 boarding boys and girls and about 50 day students.

Philippe Pasche, Director
Geraldine Boland, Deputy Director

1575 British Council School-Madrid
Prado de Somosaguas
Pozuelo de Alarcon
Madrid, UK 28223
34-91-337-3500
Fax: 34-91-337-3573
E-mail:
general.enquiries@britishcouncil.org
http://www.britishcouncil.org
The British Council School is one of the leading bilingual, bi-cultural schools in the world, offering the very best of British and Spanish education. The school is divided into three departments (Early Years, Primary and Secondary) and offers education from children aged three to eighteen years old.

Jack Cushman, Principal
Norman Roddom, Head of School

1576 British Kindergarten
Ctra Del La Coruna Km 17
Las Rozas, 28230 Madrid
Spain

Mary Jane Maybury, Principal

1577 British Primary School
Stationsstraat 3 Vossem
Tervuren, BE 3080
32-2-767-3098
Fax: 32-2-767-0351
E-mail: info@stpaulsbps.com
http://www.britishprimary.com
Our aim at St Paul's is to provide 'The Best Possible Start in Life '. We offer a secure, nurturing and truly caring environment for children, whether settling into a new country or going to school for the first time.

Katie Tyrie, Headteacher
Bruce Guy, Financial Manager

1578 British Primary School-Stockholm
Vossem
S182 62 Djursholm
Sweden

Gaye Elliot, Principal

1579 British School-Amsterdam
Anthonie van Dijckstraat 1
Amsterdam, ME 1077
31-20-347-1111
Fax: 31-20-347-1222
http://www.britishschoolofamsterdam.nl
Our school is commited to providing the best possible eduction for our students. This is achieved in a calm, friendly, purposeful learning environment. Our strong and experieced team of teaching professionals are supported with excellent resources and facilities.

MWG Roberts, Principal
K McCarthy, Chairman

1580 British School-Bern
Hintere Dorfgasse 20
Gumligen
Switzerland 3073
41-31-951-2358
Fax: 41-31-951-1710
E-mail: britishschool@bluewin.ch
http://www.britishschool.ch
We aim to provide a high quality programme for children of all abilities that promotes the social, emotional, cognitive, moral, physical and aesthetic development of each child

Enid Potts, Head Teacher/Administrator
Joe Quinn, Support Staff

1581 British School-Brussels
Leuvensesteenweg 19
Tervuren
Belgium, BE 3080
322-767-4700
Fax: 322-767-8070
E-mail: reception@britishschool.be
http://www.britishschool.be
The British School of Brussels, situated 30 minutes from the city centre on a beautiful campus, offers a British education to International families in the heart of Europe, with pupils from some 70 nationalities on roll.

Roland Chant, Principal
Brenda Despontin, Principal

1582 British School-Netherlands
Wheatfields
Tarwekamp 3
Netherlands 2592
071-616958
Fax: 071-617144
E-mail: foundation@britishschool.nl
http://www.britishschool.nl
BSN provides the opportunity of becoming part of a student community defined by an ethos of mutual understanding and cultural harmony. We have high expectations of our students, so whilst appreciating the difference in the ability and achievement of individual children within the classroom, we expect the same high level of behaviour from all. Good behaviour, manners and a respect for teachers and other adults are everyday expectations of our students.

Martin Coles, Principal
Nigel Collins, Assistant Principal

1583 British School-Oslo
PO Box 7531, Skillebekk 0205
Oslo 2
Norway

Margaret Stark, Principal

1584 British School-Paris
21B Lavant Street
Petersfield
Hampshire GU32-3EL
01-34-80-45-94
Fax: 01-39-76-12-69
E-mail: ecis@ecis.org
http://www.ecis.org
The European Council of International Schools (ECIS) is a collaborative network promoting the ideals and best practice of international education.

Pilar Cabeza de Vaca, Executive Director
Mary Langford de Donoso, Deputy Executive Director

1585 Bromsgrove School
Worcester Road
Bromsgrove
Worcestershire B61-7DU
44-0-1527-579679
Fax: 44-0-1527-576177
E-mail:
headmaster@bromsgrove-school.co.uk
http://www.bromsgrove-school.co.uk

This school offers an English curriculum to 840 day students and 350 boarding (700 boys; 490 girls), ages 3 to 18. The curriculum is English based but french, german and Spanish are also taught. Teachers from overseas are welcome with the length of stay being 1-2 years. Applications needed to teach include science, French, math, Spanish, reading, German, English and physical education.

Chris Edwards, Headmaster
John Rogers, Foundation Director

1586 Brooke House College
Market Harborough Leicestershire
Leicestershire
England LE16-7AU
44-0-1852-462452
Fax: 44-0-1858-462487
E-mail: enquiries@brookehouse.com
http://www.brookehouse.com
Brooke House College is a co-educational, international boarding college, specialising in preparing students from all over the globe, and from Britain, for entrance to the most prestigious universities to which they can aspire in both the U.K. and U.S.A

K Anderton, Academic Tutor
A Burditt, Diploma Personal Assistant

1587 Brussels American School
Unit 8100 Box 13
APO AE 09714-9998
Belgium, BE
320- 71- 955
Fax: 320- 7-7 95
E-mail:
BrusselsEHS.Principal@eu.dodea.edu
http://www.brus-ehs.eu.dodea.edu
Brussels American School (BAS) serves students in Kindergarten through Grade 12. The elementary section of the school consists of Kindergarten through Grade 5. It is housed in one of the four major buildings and has a playground and special learning facilities. Grades 6-8 serve as transitional grades between the elementary and secondary programs; students attend classes in both the elementary and high school buildings

Walter G Seely, Principal
Cheryl A Aeillo, Assistant Principal

1588 Brussels English Primary School
23 Avenue Franklin Roosevelt
Brussels
Belgium 1050
62-010-41-72-27
Fax: 62-010-40-10-43
E-mail: info@beps.com
http://www.beps.com
Offering the Primary Years Programme, a prestigious programme supported by many international schools around the world (ages 3 to 11).

Henny de Waal, Head of School
Dominique Floridor, Secretary

1589 Bryanston School
Blandford
Dorset
UK DT11-0PX
0258-452411
E-mail: development@bryanston.co.uk
http://www.bryanston.co.uk
Bryanston they are those which encourage independence, individuality, and thinking, as well as being able to learn from living in a loving community which fast becomes, and remains, a family

Paul Speakman, Treasurer
Robert Ware, Chair

1590 Buckswood Grange International School
Broomham Hall Rye Road Guestling
Nr Hastings E Suxxex
England TN35- 4LT
44-182-574-7000
Fax: 44-182-576-5010
E-mail: achieve@buckswood.co.uk
http://www.buckswood.co.uk
A multinational boarding school for British and foreign students which combines the British curriculum with specialist EFL tution and close attention to social skills in an international environment.

Michael Reiser, Principal
David Walker, Marketing Manager

1591 Butzbach Elementary School
CMR 452 Box 5500
APO, Butzbach 09045 0005
Germany

Carl Ford, Principal

1592 Byron Elementary School
202 New Dunbar Road
Byron, GA 31008
478-956-5020
E-mail: dmartin@peachschools.org
http://bes.peachschools.org
Our teachers are dedicated, hard working educators who are life learners themselves. An enriched, standards-based instruction is provided through collegial partnerships and staff development. Teachers continue to refine their instructional skills through book study discussions, grade level meetings, and attending various workshops.

Martin Dannelly, Principal
Dennis Teresia, Assistant Principal

1593 CIV International School-Sophia Antipolis
BP 97, 190 rue Frederic Mistral
Sophia Antipolis 06902
France
33-4-929-65224
Fax: 33-4-936-52215
E-mail: secretary@civissa.org
http://www.civissa.org
Grade levels 1-12, school year September-June

Andrew Derry, Head of Section

1594 Calpe College International School
Cta de Cadiz Km 171
29670 Malaga
Spain
95-278-1479
Fax: 95-278-9416
E-mail: calpe@activanet.es

Luis Proetta, Principal

1595 Campion School
PO Box 67484
Pallini GR-15302
Greece
301-813-5901
Fax: 301-813-6492
E-mail: dbaker@hol.gr

Dennis MacKinnon, Principal

1596 Canadian College Italy-The Renaissance School
59 Macamo Courte
Maple, Ontario
Canada L6A-1G1
905-508-7108
800-422-0548
Fax: 905-508-5480
E-mail: cciren@rogers.com
http://www.ccilanciano.com
A unique source of highest-quality English-language education, preparing students for university entrance in the U.S.A., U.K., Canada and Europe, become one of the pre-eminent high school boarding schools in Europe. Graduates from CCI's founding years earned acceptances, and a variety of scholarships

1597 Cascais International School
Rua Das Faias, Lt 7 Torre
2750 Cascais
Portugal
An international nursery school, founded in 1996, that caters to children ages 1-6 years on a fulltime or part-time basis. The first language of the school is English and Portuguese is the second. Many other languages are spoken throughout the school. Offers an individual approach, flexible hours and transport. Total enrollment is 75 day students (45 boys; 30 girls).

Evan Lerven Sixma, Principal

1598 Castelli Elementary School
Via Dei Laghi, 8.60
Ligetta Di Marinus, Ag, 00047 Marina
Italy
39-06-9366-1311
Fax: 39-06-9366-1311

Diana Jaworska, Principal

1599 Castelli International School
Via Degli Scozzesi
13-Grottaferrata
Rome, Italy
39-06-943-15779
Fax: 39-06-943-15779
E-mail: maryac@castelli-international.it
http://www.castelli-international.it/
To provide a stimulating educational environment for international families living south of Rome and in the Castelli Romani area. CIS believes that the children, being naturally curious, are eager to learn, and that they learn best through inquiry, experience, and trial and error

Marianne Palladino, BA, MA, PhD, Director of Studies

1600 Casterton School
Kirkby Lonsdale, Via Carnforth
Lancashire, United Kingdom LA6-2SG
052-42-71202
E-mail: admissions@castertonschool.co.uk
http://www.castertonschool.co.uk
One of the most established academic girls boarding and day schools in the UK, with a national and international reputation.

P McLaughlin, Headmaster
G A Sykes, Deputy Head

1601 Caxton College
Ctra De Barcelona S/N 46530
Puzol Valencia
Spain
34-96-146-4500
Fax: 34-96142-0930
E-mail: caxton@caxtoncollege.com
http://www.caxtoncollege.com
Aim to provide pupils with the skills necessary to form independent opinions enabling them to make personal decisions in response to situations which will arise in their lives.

Amparo Gil, Principal
Marta Gil, Vice Principal

1602 Center Academy
92 St John's Hill Battersea
London SW11 1SH
England
071-821-5760
http://www.centeracademy.com
To provide students with a learning environment that facilitates the development of self-confidence, motivation, and academic skills, and gives students the opportunity to achieve success in life.

Robert Detweiler, Principal
Mack R Hicks, Founder and Chairman

1603 Centre International De Valbonne
Civ-bp 097 06902 Sophia
Antipolis Cedex
France
33-4-929-652-24
Fax: 33-4-936-522-15
E-mail: greta.antipolis languages @ ac-nice.fr
http://www.civfrance.com

Ian Hill, Principal

1604 Charters-Ancaster School
Penland Road, Bexhill on Sea
TN40 2JQ
England
0424-730499
Boarding girls ages eleven to eighteen; day school for boys three to eight and girls three-eighteen.

K Lewis, MA, Headmaster

1605 Children's House
Kornbergvegen 23-4050 Sola
Stavanger
Norway

Christine Grov, Principal

1606 Cite Scolaire International De Lyon
2 Place De Montreal
69007 Lyon
France
33-04-78-69-60-06
Fax: 33-04-78-69-60-36
E-mail: csi-lyon-gerland@ac-lyon.fr
Grade levels 1-12.

Donna Galiana, Director

1607 Cobham Hall
Cobham (Nr Gravesend, Kent)
DA12 3BL
England, UK
0474-82-3371
E-mail: enquiries@cobhamhall.com
http://www.cobhamhall.com
Encouraged and supported to make the most of your talents, whether these are academic, musical, sporting ... or as yet undiscovered!

Paul Mitchel, Headmaster
C Sykes, Chairman

1608 Colegio Ecole
Santa Rosa 12
Lugo Llanera
Asturias 33690
985-77 -758
E-mail: ecole1@colegioecole.com
http://www.colegioecole.com

Patrick Wilson, Principal

1609 Colegio International-Meres
Apartado 107
33080 Oviedo, Asturias
Spain

Belen Orejas Fernandez, Principal

1610 Colegio International-Vilamoura
Apt 856, 8125 Vilamoura
Loule Algarve
Portugal

Lawrence James, Principal

1611 College Du Leman International School
74 Route De Sauverny
CH-1290 Versoix, Geneva
Switzerland, GE

41-22-775-5555
Fax: 41-22-775-5559
E-mail: admissions@cdl.ch
http://www.cdl.ch
Grade levels include N-13 with an enrollment of 1700.

Francis Clivaz, General Director
Cedric Chaffois, Director of Admission

1612 College International-Fontainebleau
48 Rue Guerin 77300
Fontainebleau
France
01-64-22-11-77
Fax: 01-64-23-43-17
E-mail: glenyskennedy@compuserve.com

Mrs. G Kennedy, Principal

1613 College Lycee Cevenol International
43400 Le Chambon sur Lignon
France
04-71-59-72-52
Fax: 04-71-65-87-38
E-mail: contact@lecevenol.org
http://www.lecevenol.org
he CollSge Lyc,e International C,venol (a private establishment under a contract of state sponsorship since 1971) today welcomes boarders and day students of local, regional, national and international origins.

Christiane Minssen, Principal
Robert Lassey, Headmaster

1614 Copenhagen International School
Hellerupvej 22-26
2900 Hellerup
Denmark
45-39-463-300
Fax: 45-39-612-230
E-mail: cis@cisdk.dk
http://www.cis-edu.dk
Develop the potential of each student in a stimulating environment of cultural diversity, academic excellence and mutual respect.

Peter Wellby, Director
Simon Watson, Senior School Principal

1615 Croughton High School
Unit 5485 Box 15
APO Croughton, 09494 0005
Great Britain

Dr. Charles Recesso, Principal

1616 Danube International School
Josef Gall-Gassee 2
1020 Vienna
Austria
00-43-1-720-3110
Fax: 43-1-720-3110-40
E-mail: info@ danubeschool.at
http://www.danubeschool.at
DIS started off life in 1992 in Schrutkagasse in the 13th District. The school had another name, then - 'Pawen International Community School' that now houses a Rudolf Steiner school

Peter Harding, Director
Sabine Biber-Brussmann, Registrar

1617 Darmstadt Elementary School
CMR 431
APO, Darmstadt 09175 0005
Germany

Sherry Templeton, Principal

1618 Darmstadt Junior High School
CMR 431
APO, Darmstadt 09175 0005
Germany

Daniel Basarich, Principal

1619 De Blijberg
Graaf Florisstraat 56
Rotterdam
Netherlands 3032C
010-448-2266
Fax: 010-448-2270
E-mail: deblijberg_international@hotmail.com
http://www.blijberg.nl

Barbera Everaars, Director
Bart Loman, Director

1620 Dean Close School
Lansdown Road
Cheltenham
England GL51
0242-522640
E-mail: squirrels@deanclose.org.uk
http://www.deanclose.co.uk
Aim to provide a rich variety of opportunities that will enable your son or daughter to develop in confidence and independance within our happy and caring community.

Sue Bennett, Headmistress
Anthony R Barchand, Faculty Head

1621 Dexheim Elementary School
Unit 24027
APO, Dexheim 09110 0005
Germany

Gary Waltner, Principal

1622 Downside School
Stratton-on-the-Fosse, Bath (Avon)
Radstock Bath
England, UK BA3
0761-232-206
E-mail: admin@downside.co.uk
http://www.downside.co.uk
Downside is an independent Catholic co-educational boarding school for pupils aged 9 to 18.

Dom Leo Maidlow Davis, Head Master
AR Hobbs, Deputy Head Master

1623 Dresden International School
Annenstr 9
D-01067 Dresden
Germany
49-351-3400428
Fax: 49-351-3400430
E-mail: dis@dredsen-is.de
http://www.dresden-is.de
Committed to the aim of continuous improvement, which has been such a feature of the school since it opened in 1996.

Chrissie Sorenson, Director
Steve Ellis, Secondary School Principal

1624 ECC International School
Jacob Jordaensstraat 85-87
2018 Antwerp
Belgium

Dr. X Nieberding, Principal

1625 Ecole Active Bilingue
70 rue du Theatre
Paris
France 75015
01-44-37-00-80
Fax: 01-45-79-06-66
E-mail: info@eabjm.net
http://www.eabjm.org
An associated UNESCO school, EABJM is also contractually part of the French national education system. The high school prepares students for the French Baccalaureate, the French Baccalaureate with Option Internationale, or the International Baccalaureate. An official testing site for the SAT, EABJM is also accredited by the College En-

trance Examination Board and the Cambridge University Local Examination Syndicate.

Danielle Monod, Principal

1626 Ecole Active Bilingue Jeannine Manuel
70 rue du Theatre
75015 Paris
France 75015
45-44-37-00-80
Fax: 01-45-79-06-66
E-mail: info@eabjm.net
http://www.eabjm.com
Grade levels k-12.

Elizabeth Zeboulon, Directrice

1627 Ecole D'Humanite
CH-6085 Hasliberg-Goldern
Switzerland
41-33-972-9292
Fax: 41-33-972-9211
E-mail: us.office@ecole.ch
150 boys and girls, aged 6 to 20 and faculty live in small family-style groups. International, inter-racial student body. Main language is German, with special classes for beginners.

Kathleen Hennessy, Interim Director

1628 Ecole Des Roches & Fleuris
3961 Bluche
Valais
Switzerland

Marcel Clivez, Principal

1629 Ecole Lemania
Chemin de Preville 3
CP500 1001 Lausanne
Switzerland
41-0-21-320-15-01
Fax: 41-0-21-312-67-00
E-mail: info@lemania.com
http://www.lemania.com
This international college represents over 65 nationalities offering French and English intensive courses, summer programs, American academic studies at graduate and undergraduate levels, sports and cultural activities, and accommodation in boarding school. Total enrollment: 800 day students; 100 boarding (450 boys; 450 girls), in grades 1-10.

M JP du Pasquier, Principal

1630 Ecole Nouvelle Preparatoire
Route Du Lac 22, Ch-1094
Paudex
Switzerland

Marc Desmet, Principal

1631 Ecole Nouvelle de la Suisse Romande
Ch de Rovereaz 20, CP-161
CH-1000 Lausanne 12
Switzerland
41-21-654-65-00
Fax: 41-21-654-65-05
E-mail: info@ensr.ch
http://www.ensr.ch
The mission of the school is to prepare its students

Isabel Matos, Director Administrative/Fina
Beth Krasna, President

1632 Edinburgh American School
29 Chester Street
Edinburgh EH37EN
Scotland

AW Morris, Principal

1633 Edradour School
Edradour House - Pitlochry
Perthshire PH165JW,
Scotland
JPA Romanes, Principal

**1634 El Plantio International School
Valencia**
Urbanizacion El Plantio
Calle 233, N36, La Canada, Paterna
Spain
96-132-14-10
Fax: 96-132-18-41
E-mail: plantiointernational@retemail.es
http://www.plantiointernational.com
To educate young people who can adapt to
their environment and therefore our objective
is based on providing our students with the
necessary skills to enable a better knowledge
of the modem world and maximising the ability to communicate in an ever-changing and
broadening society.

Anthony C Nelson, Principal

1635 Ellerslie School
Abbey Road, Malvern
WR14 3HF
England
0684-575701

Elizabeth M Baker, BA, Headmaster

1636 English Junior School
Lilla Danska Vagen 1
412 74 Gothenburg
Sweden
31-401819

Patricia Gabrielsson, Principal

1637 English Kindergarten
Valenjanpolku 2
05880 Hyvinkaa
Finland

Riva Rentto, Principal

1638 English Montessori School
C/ de la Salle S/N
Aravaca, Madrid
Spain 28023
91-357-26-67
Fax: 91-307-15-43
E-mail: t.e.m.s@teleline.es
http://englishmontessorischool.com
Each year of school up to and including Year
10 at The English Montessori School is vali-
dated with the Spanish Educational System.
The importance of this is that a students enter-
ing or leaving the school can transfer to the
equivalent level in any other school.

Elaine Fitzpatrick, Headmistress
Milagros Alonso, Director

1639 English School-Helsinki
Mantytie 14
Helinski
Finland 270
358-9-477-1123
Fax: 358-9-477-1980
E-mail: english.school@edu.hel.fi
http://www.eschool.edu.hel.fi
The English School is a private, national language school based on Christian values. The
Ministry of Education has placed a special responsibility on the school to familiarize the
students with Finnish and English languages
as well as the culture of Finnish and An-
glo-Saxon language areas.

Erkki Lehto, Principal
Riitta Volanen, Secretary

1640 English School-Los Olivos
Avda Pino Panera 25, 46110 Godella
Valencia
Spain

96-363-99-38
Fax: 96-364-48-63
http://www.school-losolivos.es
Jane Rodriguez, Principal

**1641 European Business & Management
School**
Frederik de Merodestraat, 12-16
Antwerp
Belgium 2600
323-218-8182
Fax: 323-218-5868
E-mail: info@ebms.edu
http://www.ebms.edu
Once a year, European Business and Manage-
ment School organizes a cross-cultural busi-
ness tour, providing our students with another
opportunity to strengthen their competencies
in global thinking in international business.

Luc Van Meli, Director

1642 European School Culham
Thame Lane, Abingdon
Oxfordshire
Great Britain OX14
44 -235-5226
Fax: 44 -235-5546
E-mail: esculham@eursc.org
http://www.esculham.net
Educated side by side, untroubled from infancy by divisive prejudices, acquainted with
all that is great and good in different cultures,
it will be borne in upon them as they mature
that they belong together.

T Hyem, Principal
Simon Sharron, Head

1643 European School-Brussels I
Avenue Du Vert Chasseur 46
Brussels
Belgium 1180
02-374-58-44
E-mail: kari.kivinen@eursc.org
http://www.eeb1.org
The European Schools fulfil a task that national schools are unable to fulfil: to teach pupils from different countries in their
respective mother tongues and to instil in
them the cultural values of their home country
room a European perspective.

J Marshall, Principal
Kari Kivinen, Director

1644 European School-Italy
Via Montello 118
21100 Varese
Italy

Jorg Hoffman, Principal

1645 Evangelical Christian Academy
Calle La Manda 47
Camarma de Esteruelas, Madrid
Spain 28816
34-91-741-2900
Fax: 34-91-320-8606
E-mail: secretary@ecaspain.com
http://www.ecaspain.com
The vision drives every facet of ECA's existence. ECA offers a challenging, college
preparatory curriculum in an American-based
system. Students at ECA study Bible each
year, and a Christian worldview is integrated
into every aspect of the curriculum.

Beth Hornish, Principal
Scot Musser, Business Manager

1646 Feltwell Elementary School
CCSE/F Unit 5185 Box 315
APO AE
Great Britain 9461-5315
011-44 -842
Fax: 018-2 8-7931

E-mail: feltwell.attendance@eu.dodea.edu
http://www.felt-es.eu.dodea.edu
School where teachers, parents, and community share the responsibility for each child's
learning.

Tom LaRue, Principal

1647 Frankfurt International School
An der Waldlust 15
Oberursel
Germany 61440
49-6171-2020
Fax: 49-6171-202384
E-mail: admissions@fis.edu
http://www.fis.edu
To be the leading culturally diverse and fam-
ily-oriented international school with English
as the principal language of instruction. We
inspire young individuals to develop their intellect, creativity and character to grow into
adaptable, socially responsible global citizens by ensuring a dynamic, 21st-century, in-
quiry-driven education of the highest
standard.

Jutta Kuehne, Director
Mark Ulfers, Head of School

1648 Frederiksborg Gymnasium
Carlsbergvej 15
3400 Hillerod
Denmark
482- 10-0
Fax: 482- 07-1
E-mail: post@frborg-gymhf.dk
http://www.frborg-gymhf.dk

Peter Kuhlman, Principal

1649 Friends School
Saffron Walden, Essex
England CB11
0642-722141
E-mail: admissions@friends.org.uk
http://www.friends.org.uk
Friends' School strives to be a unique community where the potential and talent of each individual is realised within a friendly and
challenging environment based on Quaker
principles.

Graham Wigley, Head

1650 Gaeta Elementary & Middle School
PSC Box 811
FPO Gaeta 09609 0005
Italy

Dr. Robert Kirkpatrick, Principal

1651 Garmisch Elementary School
Unit 24511
APO AE, Garmisch
Germany 9053
440-261-
Fax: 088-1 7-949
E-mail:
GarmischEMS.Webmaster@eu.dodea.edu
http://www.garm-es.eu.dodea.edu
To provide a challenging curriculum in an at-
mosphere respectful of individual needs and
cultural diversity.˜ All students will learn the
academic and social skills necessary for their
future success.

Debbie Strong, Principal

1652 Geilenkirchen Elementary School
Unit 8045
APO AE, Geilenkirchen 09104 0005
Germany 9104
024-1 9- 308
Fax: 024-1 9- 308
E-mail:
GeilenkirchenES.Webmaster@eu.dodea.edu
http://www.geil-es.eu.dodea.edu/
Educating our students to be responsible, pro-
ductive and ethical citizens with the skills to

think creatively, reason critically, communicate effectively and learn continuously.

James V Dierendonck, Principal

1653 Gelnhausen Elementary School
CMR 465
APO, Gelnhausen 09076 0005
Germany

Jim Harrison, Principal

1654 Geneva English School
36 Route de Malagny
1294 Genthod
Switzerland
41-22-755-18-55
Fax: 41-22-779-14-29
E-mail: admin@genevaenglishschool.ch
http://www.geneva-english-school.ch
A private, nonprofit primary school that is owned and managed by an association which is composed of parents whose children attend the school. The main objective of the school is to offer education on British lines for children of primary school age living in or near Geneva, and to prepare them for secondary education in any English-speaking school.

Denis Unsworth, Principal
Gareth Davies, Headmaster

1655 Giessen Elementary School
414th BSB GSN, Unit 20911
APO, Giessen 09169 0005
Germany

Mary Ann Burkard, Principal

1656 Giessen High School
414th BSB GSB, Unit 20911
APO, Giessen 09169 0005
Germany

Gordon Gartner, Principal

1657 Grafenwoehr Elementary School
Unit 28127
APO AE
Germany 9114-8127
096-1 3-54
Fax: 096-1 3-54
E-mail:
GrafenwoehrES.Principal@eu.dodea.edu
http://www.graf-es.eu.dodea.edu
To maintain a meaningful partnership with the community through which physical well being, cognitive growth, and emotional support are provided to all learners.

Crystal Bailey, Principal
David Eldredge, Assistant Principal

1658 Greenwood Garden School
Via Vito Sinisi 5
Rome
Italy
39-06-332-66703
Fax: 39-06-332-66703
E-mail: greenwoodgarden@libero.it
http://www.greenwoodgardenschool.com
An international pre-school and kindergarten for children aging from 2-6 with teaching being done in English by mother-tongue educators experienced with young children

Donna Seibert, Directress

1659 Gstaad International School
Ahorn
Gstaad
Switzerland CH-37
41-33-744-2373
Fax: 41-33-744-3578
E-mail: gis@gstaad.ch
http://www.gstaadschool.ch
The school's mission includes the building of endurance and stamina in both academics and sports, as well as stimulating personal achievement by teaching the values of re-

spect, gratitude, humour and real caring for others. Students are continually presented with challenges and the opportunities to achieve where perhaps before they thought impossible.

Alain Souperbiet, Director

1660 Haagsche School Vereeniging
Nassaulaan 26
Den Haag-2514
003-170-363
E-mail: info@hsvdenhaag.nl
http://www.hsvdenhaag.nl
HM Jongeling, Principal
Lorraine Dean, Director

1661 Hainerberg Elementary School
Unit 29647 Box 0086
APO AE, Wiesbaden
Germany 9096-86
337-516-
Fax: 011-49 -11 7
E-mail:
Wiesbadenes.principal@eu.dodea.edu
http://www.wies-esh.eu.dodea.edu
Provide exemplary educational programs that inspire and prepare all students for success in a global environment.

Maren James, Principal

1662 Halvorsen Tunner Elementary and Middle School
Unit 7565
APO, Rhein Main 09050 0005
Germany

Julie Gaski, Principal

1663 Hanau High School
Unit 20235
APO, Hanau 09165 0005
Germany

Allen Davenport, Principal

1664 Hanau Middle School
Unit 20193
APO, Hanau 09165 0016
Germany

Robert Sennett, Principal

1665 Harrow School
5 High Street
Harrow on the Hill
England HA1 3
01-423-2366
E-mail: harrow@harrowschool.org.uk
http://www.harrowschool.org.uk
Barnaby Lenon, Headmaster

1666 Hatherop Castle School
Hatherop, Cirencester
England GL7 3
028-575-206
http://www.hatheropcastle.com
Paul Easterbrook, Headmaster

1667 Heidelberg High School
Unit 29237
APO AE
Germany 9102
062-1 5- 800
Fax: 062-1 3- 587
http://www.heid-hs.eu.dodea.edu
Kevin J Brewer, Principal

1668 Heidelberg Middle School
Unit 29237
APO AE
Germany 9102
062-1 3-8 93
http://www.heid-ms.eu.dodea.edu
Donald Johnson, Principal

1669 Hellenic College-London
67 Pont Street
London SWIX OBD
England
0171-581-5044
Fax: 0171-589-9055
E-mail: hellenic@rmplc.co.uk
http://www.rmplc.co.uk/eduweb/sites/hellen ic
James Wardrobe, Principal

1670 Hellenic-American Education Foundation Athens College-Psychico College
15 Stefanou Delta
Psychico
Greece 154 5
30-1-671-2771
Fax: 30-1-674-8156
E-mail: info@haef.gr
http://www.haef.gr
Grade levels 1-12, school year September - June

David William Rupp, President

1671 Helsingin Suomalainen
Isonnevantie 8
Helinski, Finland 320
358-9 4-74 1
Fax: 358-9 4-74 1
http://www.syk.fi
Helsingin Suomalainen Yhteiskoulu (SYK) is an independent coeducational, which prepares its students either for the national matriculation exam or the International Baccalaureate, both of which give a student general university entry qualifications.

Anja-Liisa Alanko, Principal

1672 Het Nederlands Lyceum
Wijndaelerduin 1
Hague, Netherlands 2554
31 -0 3-8 45
Fax: 31 -0 3-8 20
E-mail: primary@ishthehague.nl
http://www.ishthehague.nl
Offers young people of all nationalities between the ages of 4 and 18 top quality international education in a caring environment, which aim for academic success and encourage sporting and creative abilities in a community based on honesty, fairness, open-mindedness and tolerance.

Graeme Scott, Principal Primary School

1673 Het Rijnlands Lyceum
Appollolaan 1 2341 BA
Oegstgeest
Netherlands
31-3771-5155640
E-mail:
administratie@rijnlandslyceum-rlo.nl
http://www.rlo.nl
Lyceum is a state subsidized school with an international department offering IBMYP and IB. Offers an English/Dutch spoken curriculum to 1,190 day students and 60 boarding (650 boys; 600 girls), in grades 6 through 12. Student/teacher ratio is 15:1, and the school is willing to participate in a teacher exchange program, however, housing will not be provided by the school.

Drs LE Timmerman, Principal

1674 Hillhouse Montessori School
Avenida Alfonso Xiii 30 Y 34
Madrid 2
Spain

Judy Amick, Principal

1675 Hohenfels Elementary School
Unit 28214
APO AE
Germany 9173
466-282-
Fax: 094-2 8-32
http://www.hohe-es.eu.dodea.edu
Olaf Zwicker, Principal

1676 Hohenfels High School
CMR 414
APO, AE
Germany 9173
094-2 -9096
Fax: 094-2 8- 316
http://www.hohe-hs.eu.dodea.edu
Daniel J Mendoza, Principal

1677 Holmwood House
Chitts Hill, Lexden
Colchester, Essex
England CO3 9
44-0-1904-626183
Fax: 44-0-1904-670899
E-mail: hst@holmwood.essex.sch.uk
http://www.holmwood.essex.sch.uk
Holmwood House is an independent coeducational day and boarding preparatory school. The total enrollment of the school is 310 day students and 50 boarding students (240 boys and 120 girls), ages 4 1/2 to 13 1/2.
Alexander Mitchell, Headmaster

1678 Hvitfeldtska Gymnasiet
Rektorsgatan 2, SE-411 33
Goteborg
Sweden
46-31-367-0623
Fax: 46-31-367-0602
E-mail: agneta.santesson@educ.goteborg.se
http://www.hvitfeldt.educ.goteborg.se
State school, founded 1647, offers the International Baccalaureate curriculum to a total enrollment of 90 girls and 90 boys, in grades 10-12.
Christen Holmstrom, Principal
Agneta Santesson, Deputy Headmaster

1679 Illesheim Elementary and Middle School
CMR 416 Box J
APO, Hohenfels 09140 0005
Germany
49-9841-8408
Fax: 49-9841-8987
Donald J Ness, Principal

1680 Independent Bonn International School
Tulpenbaumweg 42
Bonn 53177
Germany
49-228-32-31-66
Fax: 49-228-32-39-58
E-mail: ibis@ibis-school.com
http://www.ibis-school.com
IBIS is an international primary school.
Irene Bolik, Headteacher

1681 Independent Schools Information Service
Grosveror Gardens House 35-37
Frosvernor Gardens, London SW1W 0BS
England
020-77981575
Fax: 020-77981561
E-mail: national@isis.org.uk
http://www.isis.org.uk
Provides information on 1400 elementary and secondary schools in the United Kingdom and Ireland.
David J Woodhead

1682 Innsbruck International High School
Schonger, Austria A-6141
0-5225-4201
Fax: 0-5225-4202
An accredited coeducational boarding and day school. The school offers an American college preparatory high school curriculum for grades 9-12.
Gunther Wenko, Director
John E Wenrick, Headmaster

1683 Institut Alpin Le Vieux Chalet
1837 Chateau D'oex
Switzerland
Jean Bach, Principal

1684 Institut Auf Dem Rosenberg
Hohenweg 60-9000 St Gallen
Switzerland
417- 27- 777
Fax: 417- 27- 982
E-mail: info@instrosenberg.ch
http://www.instrosenberg.ch
Felicitas Scharli, Principal

1685 Institut Chateau Beau-Cedre
57 Av De Chillion
CH-1820 Territet Montreux
Switzerland
41-21-963-5341
Fax: 41-21-963-4783
E-mail: info@monterosaschool.com
This Institut is an exclusive boarding and finishing international school for girls. American high school with a general culture section for 30 boarding students in grades 9 through twelve. Languages spoken include French and English and the student/teacher ratio is 1:6.
Pierre Gay, Principal

1686 Institut Le Champ Des Pesses
1618 Chatel-st-denis
Montreux
Switzerland
PL Racloz, Principal

1687 Institut Le Rosey
Chateau du Rosey
1180 Rolle
Switzerland
41-21-822-5500
Fax: 41-21-822-5555
E-mail: rosey@rosey.ch
http://www.rosey.ch
Le Rosey's philosophy is inspired by what Harvard educationalist Howard Gardner has called multiple intelligences: its aim is to develop all Roseans' talents through academic, sporting and artistic programs.
Philippe Gudin, General Director
Michael Gray, Headmaster

1688 Institut Montana Bugerbug-American Schools
Zugerberg
CH 6300 Zug
Switzerland
41-41-711-1722
Fax: 41-41-711-5465
E-mail: kob@montana.zug.ch
http://www.montana.zug.ch
Grade levels include 7-13 with a total enrollment of 111.
Daniel Fredez, Director

1689 Institut Monte Rosa
57, Ave de Chillon,
CH-1820 Territet/Montreux
Switzerland
021-963-5341
Fax: 021-963-4783

E-mail: info@monterosa.ch
http://www.monterosa.ch
Bernhard Gademann, BS, MS, Principal

1690 Inter-Community School
Strubenacher 3 Postfach
Zumikon
Switzerland 8126
41-1-919-8300
Fax: 41-1-919-8320
http://www.icsz.ch
The Inter-Community School is committed to providing a supportive and enabling learning environment in which all members of the community are challenged to achieve their individual potential, encouraged to pursue their passions, and expected to fulfil their responsibilities
Michael Matthews, Head of School
Martin Hall, Secondary Principal

1691 International Academy
Via di Grottarossa 295
00189 Rome
Italy
39-340-731-4195
Joan Bafaloukas Bulgarini, Principal

1692 International College Spain
C/Vereda Norte 3
La Moraleja, Madrid
Spain 28109
34-91-650-2398
Fax: 34-91-650-1035
E-mail: admissions@icsmadrid.org
http://www.icsmadrid.org
The philosophy of the school is to provide students with a high quality international education which places a strong emphasis on fostering respect for the world's nations and cultures.
Terry Hedger, Director
Hubert Keulers, Head of Primary School

1693 International Management Institute
Garden Square Building, Block-C Laa
Antwerp
Belgium 2610
32-3-21-85-431
Fax: 32-3-21-85-868
E-mail: info@timi.edu
http://www.timi.edu
Our vision is to empower our students in terms of all the faculties required to pursue a career in the competitive globalized world. The focus of our curriculum is to enhance the learning perspective through customized modules and simulation exercises from globally renowned academicians and professionals.
Luc Van Mele, Director

1694 International Preparatory School
Rua Do Boror 12 Carcavelos
2775 Parede
Portugal
56-2-321-5800
Fax: 56-2-321-5821
E-mail: info@tipschool.com
http://www.tipschool.com

1695 International School Beverweerd
Beverweerdseweg 60, 3985 RE
Werkhoven
Netherlands
03437-1341
Fax: 03437-2079
Ray Kern, BA, MA, Principal

1696 International School-Aberdeen
296 N Deeside Road
Milltimber, Aberdeen
Scotland, UK AB13

44-1224-732267
Fax: 44-1224-735648
E-mail: admin@isa.aberdeen.sch.uk
http://www.isa.aberdeen.sch.uk
The International School of Aberdeen (ISA) is an independent, non-profit school (K-12) that delivers excellence in education. We do this through a safe and caring learning environment where students are challenged to reach their maximum potential through academic success and personal growth, becoming socially responsible and active global citizens.

Daniel A Hovde PhD, Director
Don Newbury, Elementary Principal

1697 International School-Algarve

Apartado 80 Porches 8400
Lagoa Algarve
Portugal

Peter Maddison, Principal

1698 International School-Amsterdam

PO Box 920
AX Amstelveen
The Netherlands 1180
31-20-347-1111
Fax: 31-20-347-1222
E-mail: info@isa.nl
http://www.isa.nl
The International School of Amsterdam (ISA) was founded in 1964 to serve the educational needs of the children of the international community living in and around Amsterdam. ISA is a nonsectarian, non-profit coeducational day school, enrolling students in Pre-School through Grade 12 (from 3 to 18 years of age).

Dr Edward Greene, Director
Sarah Grace, Head of Lower School

1699 International School-Basel

Fleischbachstrasse 2
4153 Reinach BL
Switzerland
41-61-426-96-26
Fax: 41-61-426-96-25
http://www.isbasel.ch
mission of the International School Basel is to provide an international education to the highest recognized academic standards

Geoff Tomlinson, Principal

1700 International School-Bergen

Vilhelm Bjerknesvei 15
Bergen
Norway 5081
47-55-30-63-30
Fax: 47-55-30-63-31
E-mail: post@isob.no
http://www.isb.gs.hl.no
Provide an education for the children of expatriate oil company personnel in Bergen and to attract further corporate investment in the Bergen area.

June Murison, Director

1701 International School-Berne

Mattenstrasse 3
Gumligen
Switzerland 3073
41-31-951-2358
Fax: 41-31-951-1710
E-mail: office@isberne.ch
http://www.isberne.ch
Creative learning community for students from all over the world, within the framework of the three International Baccalaureate Programmes, guided by ISBerne teachers and staff, students aged 3 - 18 have the opportunity to become open-minded, principled, knowledgeable, confident lifelong learners

and multilingual citizens of the world, who respect themselves and others.

Kevin Page, Director
Cory Etchberger, Chair

1702 International School-Brussels

Kattenberg 19
Brussels 1170
Belguim
32-2-661-4211
Fax: 32-2-661-4200
E-mail: admissions@isb.be
http://www.isb.be
Offers a challenging, inclusive international education designed to give every student opportunities for success within and beyond our school.

Kevin Bartlett, Director
Andrei Teixeira, Chairman

1703 International School-Cartagena

Manga Club Cp 30385 Cartagena
Los Belones Murcia
Spain
34-68-175000
E-mail: isc@sendanet.es

Robert Risch, Principal

1704 International School-Curacao

PO Box 3090
Koninginnelaan Emmastad, Curacao
Netherlands Antilles
599-9-737-3633
Fax: 599-90737-3142
E-mail: iscmec@attglobal.net
http://www.isc.an
Offers a rigorous academic program in order to prepare students planning to pursue higher learning at colleges and universities around the world. The School's curriculum includes International Baccalaureate (IB) coursework that allows students the opportunity to receive the IB Diploma.

Margie Elhage, Director
Rene Romer, President

1705 International School-Dusseldorf

Niederrheinstrasse 336
Dusseldorf
Germany 40489
49-211-94066-799
Fax: 49-211-4080-744
E-mail: nmcw@isdedu.de
http://www.isdedu.eu
Provide the students of the International School of D sseldorf with the best possible program of academic and personal development in a challenging and supportive environment.

Neil A McWilliam, Director
Michael Coffey, Senior School Principal

1706 International School-Eerde

Kasteellaan 1
PJ Ommen
The Netherlands 7731
031-0529-451452
Fax: 031-0529-456377
E-mail: info@eerde.nl
http://www.eerde.nl
Offers numerous programmes tailored to the individual needs of each student, including children with learning difficulties and dyslexia, as well as highly gifted children. Eerde carefully monitors the personal, academic, athletic and creative development of each individual student ages 4 to 19.

Herman Voogd, Principal

1707 International School-Friuli

Via Delle Grazie 1/A
Pordenone 33170
Italy

Susan Clarke, Principal

1708 International School-Geneva

62 route de Chene
Geneva
Switzerland CH-12
41-22-787-2400
Fax: 41-22-787-2410
E-mail: administration@ecolint.ch
http://www.ecolint.ch
Aims to provide a distinctive high quality international education that prepares pupils for membership of a world community based on mutual understanding, tolerance and shared humanitarian values.

Nicholas Tate, Director General
John Douglas, Director

1709 International School-Hamburg

Holmbrook 20
Hamburg
Germany 22605
49-40-883-1101
Fax: 49-40-1881-1405
E-mail: info@ishamburg.org
http://www.international-school-hamburg.de

A co-educational day school enrolling students from Primary 1 (age 3) to Grade 12. The school was founded in 1957 as the first international school in Germany.

Peter Gittins, Headmaster
Nick Ronai, Junior School Director

1710 International School-Hannover Region

Bruchmeisterstrasse 6
Hannover
Germany D-301
49-511-27041650
Fax: 49-511-557934
E-mail: adminoffice@is-hr.de
http://www.is-hr.de
Provides a high quality, balanced educational program in the English language for children of internationally-minded families.Offer a dynamic environment where each student is challenged and supported to become a dedicated learner for life and a contributing member of the local and global community.

Patricia Baier, Director
Steffen Stegemann, Business Manager

1711 International School-Helsinki

Selkamerenkatu 11
Helsinki
Finland 180
358-9-686-6160
Fax: 358-9-685-6699
E-mail: mainoffice@ish.edu.hel.fi
http://www.ish.edu.hel.fi
Office Manager

Provide attendees

Bob Woods, Headmaster
Therese Thibault, Director

1712 International School-Iita

Carolyn House, 26 Dingwall Road
Croydon
England CR9 3
E-mail: iita@cgiar.org
http://www.iita.org
Provide a comprehensive, international curriculum in an environment which promotes confidence, caring and understanding, and prepares our students for successful learning here and in schools around the world.

Neil Jackson, Principal

1713 International School-Lausanne
Chemin de la Grangette 2
Le Mont-sur-Lausanne
Switzerland CH -
41-21-728-1733
Fax: 41-21-728-7868
E-mail: info@isl.ch
http://www.isl.ch
The school is committed to excellence in education, it strives to fulfill the unique potential of each student in a supportive and challenging holistic learning environment that prepares the student for continuing education and an active and responsible role in a multicultural world.

Lyn Cheetham, Director
John Ivett, Assistant Director

1714 International School-Le Chaperon Rouge
3963 Crans Sur Sierre
Crans/Montana
Switzerland
41-27-4812-500
Fax: 41-27-4812-502

Prosper Bagnoud, Principal

1715 International School-London
139 Gunnersbury Avenue
London
England W3 8L
44-20-8992-5823
Fax: 44-20-8993-7012
E-mail: mail@ISLondon.com
http://www.islondon.com
Aims to maximize the achievement of its students throughout the curriculum and in personal and social fields. Drawing on the rich variety of cultures represented at the school, ISL aims to develop in each student a global outlook which seeks to understand and appreciate the attitudes and values of others.

Amin Makarem, Director
Sergio Pawel, Deputy Head, Curriculum

1716 International School-Lyon
80 chemin du Grand Roule
Ste-Foy-LSs-Lyon
France F-691
33 - 4 -8 86
Fax: 33 - 4 -8 86
E-mail: info@islyon.org
http://www.islyon.org
The school's curriculum is based on the programmes and pedagogy of the International Baccalaureate Organization which aims to develop in the students the skills, values and knowledge that will help them to become responsible citizens in an increasingly interconnected world.

Donna Philip, Director
Michael Ford, Curriculum Coordinator

1717 International School-Naples
Viale della Liberazione, 1
Bagnoli, Napoli 80125
Italy
39-081-721-2037
Fax: 39-081-570-0248
E-mail: info@isnaples.it
http://www.isnaples.it
Provide a nurturing environment where students can grow intellectually, socially, psychologically and physically. Through a dedicated partnership of parents and educators, we strive to prepare our students to become productive, global citizens of the twenty-first century.

Josephine Sessa, Principal
Patricia Montesano, Vice Principal

1718 International School-Nice
15 Avenue Claude Debussy
Nice
France 6200
33-493-210-400
Fax: 33-493-216-911
E-mail: robert.silvetz@cote-azur.cci.fr
http://www.isn-nice.org
The school offers Pre-Kindergarten through grade 12 instruction and college preparatory education and provides an intellectually challenging programme of studies which aims to promote analytic understanding with an integrated view of the various academic disciplines and to encourage creativity and self-expression. Serves both the international community and local families who wish to offer their children an education in English, which is both international and versatile.

Wylie Michael, Director

1719 International School-Paris
6 Rue Beethoven
Paris
France 75016
33-1-422-40954
Fax: 33-1-452-71593
E-mail: info@isparis.edu
http://www.isparis.edu
ISP create a challenging and motivating English-speaking environment where students and staff from around the world use the programs of the International Baccalaureate Organisation and work in harmony to develop every student's full intellectual and human potential.

Audrey Peverelli, Headmaster
Catherine Hard, Head of Admissions

1720 International School-Sotogrande
Apartado 15
Sotogrande San Roque Cadiz
Spain 11310
34-956-79-59-02
Fax: 34-956-79-48-16
E-mail: director@sis.ac
http://www.sis.ac
Our school is a learning organisation with a passion for learning. Learning is a complex process and it is vitally important that our teachers know how pupils learn best and that they create exciting opportunities for learning to take place.

Geroge O'Brien, Headmaster
Christopher TJ Charleson, Head of School

1721 International School-Stavanger
Treskeveien 3
Hafrsfjord
Norway 4043
47-51-559-100
Fax: 47-51-552-962
E-mail: LDuevel@isstavanger.no
http://www.isstavanger.no
The International School of Stavanger is dedicated to providing its students with an English language education in a supportive, academically stimulating, and multi-cultural environment.

Linda Duevel, PhD, Director
Gareth Jones, High School Principal

1722 International School-Stockholm
Johannesgatan 18
Stockholm SE-111 38
Sweden
46-8-412-4000
Fax: 46-8-412-4001
E-mail: admin@intsch.se
http://www.intsch.se
SIS vision is to enable students to learn, develop, grow, and fulfill their potential in an international environment, which is student-centered, safe, nurturing and rich with opportunities to learn.

Chris Mockrish, Principal
Richard Mast, Director

1723 International School-Stuttgart
Sigmaringer Street 257
Stuttgart
Germany 70597
49-7-11-76-9600-0
Fax: 49-7-11-76-9600-0
E-mail: iss@issev.de
http://www.international-school-stuttgart.de
The International School of Stuttgart provides students of internationally-minded families with a high quality, English language education.

Timothy Kelley, Director
Sarah Kupke, Head of School

1724 International School-Trieste
Via Conconello 16 Opicina
Trieste Friuli - Venezia Giulia
Italy 34151
39-040-211-452
Fax: 39-040-213-122
E-mail: istrieste@interbusiness.it
http://www.istrieste.org
It is our mission to provide students from the international and local community with a broad, balanced education using English both in curricular and extra-curricular life of the school.

Peter Metzger, Principal
Jim Pastore, Director

1725 International School-Turin
Vicolo Tiziano 10
Moncalieri
Italy 10024
39 -11 -45 9
Fax: 39 -11 -43 2
E-mail: info@acat-ist.it
http://www.acat-ist.it
The school's goal is to create self-motivated, independent learners who strive for excellence. The school community feels that this is best achieved in an environment which fosters trust and respect between the educational staff and the student body, demands accountability and team-work, while inspiring a general sense of well-being and self-confidence.

George Selby, BA, MA, Principal

1726 International School-Venice
Via Terraglio 30
Mestre, Venice
Italy 30174
39 -41 -83 7
Fax: 39 -41 -86 0
E-mail: info@isvenice.com
http://www.isvenice.com
The fundamental aim of The International School of Venice is to give its pupils a bilingual education and an intellectual education based on tolerance, open-mindedness and an acceptance of diversity.

John Millerchip, Principal

1727 International School-Zug
Walterswil
Baar 6340
Switzerland
41-41-768-1188
Fax: 41-41-768-1189
E-mail: office@isoz.ch
Grade levels include preK-8 with a total enrollment of 354.

Martin Latter, Head of School

1728 International Schule-Berlin, Potsdam
Seestrasse 45
14467 Potsdam
Germany

49-332-086-760
Fax: 49-332-086-7612
E-mail: office@isbp.p.bb.schule.de
http://www.shuttle.de/p/isbp
This school offers an English curriculum to
157 day students (87 boys and 64 girls) in
grades PreK-12. Applications needed to teach
include science, pre-school, math, social sciences, reading, English and physical
education.

Matthias Truper, Principal

**1729 International Secondary
School-Eindhoven**
Venetiestraat 43
RM Eindhoven
Netherlands 5632
040-413600
E-mail: isse@issehv.nl~
http://www.issehv.nl
By striving for excellence in education and by
engaging with the international community,
the ISSE seeks to be an asset to Eindhoven and
the Noord-Brabant region.

JM Westerhout, Principal
M Watts, Acting Head of School

**1730 Internationale Schule
Frankfurt-Rhein-Main**
Strasse zur Internationalen Schule
Frankfurt
Germany 65931
49-69-954-3190
Fax: 49-69-954-31920
E-mail: isf@sabis.net
http://www.isf-net.de
ISF Internationale Schule-Rhein-Main, as a
member of the SABISr School Network, is ac-
ademically oriented without being highly se-
lective.

Angus Slesser, School Director
Carl Bistany, Managing Director

1731 Interskolen
Engtoften 22
8260 Viby J
Denmark
45-8611-4560
Fax: 45-8614-9670
E-mail: adm@interskolen.dk
http://www.interskolen.dk
Coeducational day program for ages five to
seventeen.

Tommy Schou Christesen, Principal

1732 John F Kennedy International School
CH-3792 Saanen
Switzerland
41-33-744-1372
Fax: 41-33-744-8982
E-mail: lovell@jfk.ch
http://www.jfk.ch
Boarding day school for boys and girls aged
5-14 years.

William Lovell, Co-Director
Sandra Lovell, Co-Director

1733 John F Kennedy School-Berlin
Teltower Damm 87-93
Berlin
Germany 14167
49-30-6321-5711
Fax: 49-30-6321-6377
E-mail: jfks-el-adm@t-online.de
http://www.jfks.de
The John F. Kennedy School is a bilingual,
bicultural German-American tuition-free
public school.

Herr Ulrich Schurmann, Managing Principal
HR Roth, German Principal

1734 Joppenhof/Jeanne D'arc Clg
PO Box 4050, 6202 Rb Maastricht
Netherlands

L Spronck, Principal

1735 Kaiserslautern Elementary School
Unit 3240 Box 425
APO
Germany, AE 9021
063- 54-89
Fax: 063- 58-06
http://www.kais-es.eu.dodea.edu

Matt J Syarto, Principal

1736 Kaiserslautern High School
Unit 3240 Box 425
APO
Germany, AE 9021
063- 54-54
Fax: 063- 99-46
http://www.kais-hs.eu.dodea.edu

Jennifer J Beckwith, Principal
Richard Nicholson, Assistant Principal

1737 Kaiserslautern Middle School
Unit 3240 Box 425
APO
Germany, AE 9021
063- 59-71
Fax: 063- 99-25
http://www.kais-ms.eu.dodea.edu

Susan P Hargis, Principal
Marion Sutton, Assistant Principal

1738 Kendale Primary International School
Via Gradoli 86, Via Cassia Km 10300
00189 Rome
Italy
39-06-332-676-08
Fax: 39-06-332-676-08
E-mail: kendale@diesis.com
http://www.diesis.com/kendale

Veronica Said Tani, Principal

1739 Kensington School
Carrer Dels Cavallers 31-33 Pedralb
Barcelona
Spain 8034
93 -03 -457
Fax: 93 -80 -067
E-mail: info@kensingtonschoolbcn.com
http://www.kensingtonschoolbcn.com
EP Giles, Principal

1740 King Fahad Academy
Bromyard Avenue, Acton
London
United Kingdom W3-7HD
020-7259-3350
E-mail: academy@thekfa.org.uk
http://www.thekfa.org.uk
The idea for the establishment of an academy
that caters for the educational needs of the
Saudi Arabian, Arab and Muslim communities in the UK took its genesis in the creation
of the King Fahad Academy in London in
1985 AD/1405 H

Dr. Ibtissam Al-Bassam, Dean
Mohammed Bin Na Al Saud, Chairman

1741 King's College
Paseo de los Andes, 35
Soto De Viuelas, Madrid
Spain
91-803-48-00
Fax: 91-803-65-57
E-mail: info@kingscollege.es
http://www.kingscollege.es
to sustain and develop an educational envi-
ronment in which all students are able to fulfil

their maximum potential, both as individuals
and as members of a community.
CA Clark, Principal
David Johnson, Headmaster

1742 Kitzingen Elementary School
Unit 26124
APO, Kitzingen 09031 0005
Germany

Fred Paesel, Principal

1743 Kleine Brogel Elementary School
701 MUNSS
Unit 8150, APO AE
Belgium 9719
003- 11-2 25
Fax: 011-79 -0 91
E-mail: terry.emerson@eu.dodea.edu
http://www.kbro-es.eu.dodea.edu

Terry Emerson, Principal

1744 La Chataigneraie International School
Geneva La Chataigneraie, 1297
Founex Vaud
Switzerland

Michael Lee, Principal

1745 La Maddalena Elementary School
PSC 816 Box 1755
FPO, La Maddalena, Sardinia 09612 0005
Italy

Janice Barber, Principal

1746 Lajes Elementary School
Unit 7725
APO AE
Portugal 9720
050-547-73
Fax: 011-351-295
http://www.laje-ehs.eu.dodea.edu/index.htm
Mary Waller, Principal

1747 Lajes High School
Unit 7725
APO AE
Portugal 9720
351-295-5741
Fax: 351-295-5425
http://www.laje-hs.eu.dodea.edu/main1.htm
Virginia Briggs, Principal

1748 Lakenheath Elementary School
Unit 5185 Box 40
APO AE
Great Britain 9464-8540
016-8 5-3 72
Fax: 016-8 5-3943
http://www.lake-es.eu.dodea.edu/index.htm
Lakenheath Elementary School serves the US
Military overseas as part of the Department of
Defense Dependent Schools

Charles Yahres, Principal
Rhonda Bennett, Assistant Principal

1749 Lakenheath High School
Unit 5185 Box 45
APO AE
Great Britain 9461-8545
44 - 16-8523
Fax: 44 - 16-8533
E-mail:
lakenheathhs.attendance@eu.dodea.edu
http://www.lake-hs.eu.dodea.edu
Lakenheath High School (LHS) serves three
U.S. Air Force bases located in the East
Anglia region of England; about 1.5 hours
drive northeast of London. LHS is
coeducational.

Kent Worford, Principal
Barbara Lee, Assistant Principal

1750 Lakenheath Middle School
Unit 5185 Box 55
APO AE
Great Britain 9461-8555
011-44 -638
Fax: 226-737-
E-mail:
LakenheathMS.Principal@eu.dodea.edu
http://www.lake-ms.eu.dodea.edu
Mary Zimmerman-Bayer, Principal
D J LaFon, Assistant Principal

1751 Lancing College
Lancing, West Sussex
BN15 ORW
England
0273-452213
Fax: 01273-464720
E-mail: admissions@lancing.org.uk
http://www.lancingcollege.co.uk
One of Britain's leading independent schools
for boys and girls aged 13 to 18
Jonathan W J Gillespie, Headmaster
Harry Brunjes, Chairman

1752 Landstuhl Elementary and Middle School
CMR 402
APO AE
Germany 9180-402
637-192-6508
Fax: 637-192-6514
E-mail:
LandstuhlEMS.Principal@eu.dodea.edu
http://www.lans-ems.eu.dodea.edu
Susan Ransom, Principal
Stephen Austin, Assistant Principal

1753 Leighton Park School
Shinfield Road
Reading RG2 7DH
England
4-118-987-9600
Fax: 44-118-987-9625
E-mail: info@leightonpark.com
http://www.leightonpark.com
Life at Leighton Park reflects the school's
Quaker foundation and is influenced by
Quaker thinking and practice. We seek to create a community of tolerance and understanding within which a balance between discipline, especially self-discipline, freedom and exploration is maintained.
John Dunston, Headmaster
Elizabeth Thomas, Deputy Head

1754 Leipzig International School
Konneritzstrasse 47
Leipzig
Germany 4229
49-341-421-0574
Fax: 49-341-421-2154
E-mail: admin@intschool-leipzig.com
http://www.intschool-leipzig.com
The Leipzig International School provides a
quality education conducted primarily in
English for children of all nationalities and
cultures living in the Leipzig region.˜ We seek
to give all students the opportunity to discover and develop their intellectual, creative,
social and physical potential to the full.
Michael Webster, Headmaster
Clemens Gerteiser, Commercial Editor

1755 Lennen Bilingual School
65 Quai d'Orsay
Paris
France 75007
01-47-05-66-55
Fax: 01-47-05-17-18
http://www.lennenbilingual.com
This school teaches a curriculum in English
and French to 120 day students. The school is
willing to participate in a teacher exchange

program with the length of stay being one
year, with no housing provided by the school.
Bilingual education is offered in the pre-
school and grade school (until Grade 3).
Michelle Lennen, Principal

1756 Leys School
The Leys School
Cambridge CB2 7AD
England
44-1223-508-900
Fax: 44-1223-505-333
E-mail: office@theleys.net
http://www.theleys.cambs.sch.uk
The Leys is one of England's premier independent schools.
Mark Slater, Headmaster

1757 Leysin American School
1854 Leysin
Switzerland
41-24-493-3777
Fax: 41-24-493-3790
E-mail: admissions@las.ch
http://www.las.ch
At the core of Leysin American School is a
guiding set of principles and beliefs that set
the highest standards for our efforts every
day.
Steven Oh, Executive Director
Vladimir Kuskovski, Headmaster

1758 Livorno Elementary School
Unit 31301 Box 65
APO, Livorno 09613 0005
Italy
Dr. Robert Kethcart, Principal

1759 Livorno High School
Unit 31301 Box 65
APO, Livorno 09613 0005
Italy, AE 9613-5
Dr. Frank Calvano, Principal

1760 London Central High School
PSC 821 Box 119
APO, High Wycombe 09421 0005
Great Britain, AE 9421-5

http://www.londoncentral.org
Dr. Charles Recesso, Principal

1761 Lorentz International School
Groningensingel 1245, 6835HZ
Arnhem
Netherlands
31-26-320-0110
Fax: 31-26-320-0113
Jan M Meens, Principal

1762 Lusitania International College Foundation
Apartado 328
8600 Lagos
Portugal
Krisine Byrne, Principal

1763 Lyce International-American Section
BP 230, rue du Fer A Cheval
St Germain-En-Laye, 78104 Cedex
France
33 - 1 -4 51
Fax: 33 - 1 -0 87
E-mail: american.lycee@wanadoo.fr
http://lycee-intl-american.org
pursues this mission through a rigorous and
rewarding American curriculum which culminates in the French Baccalaureate with International Option, as well as through a broad
and enriching co-curricular program includ-

ing such activities as drama, community service, sports and student publications.
Sean Lynch, Director
Beth Heudebourg, President

1764 Lycee Francais De Belgique
9 Avenue Du Lycee Francais
1180 Brussels
Belgium
02-374-58-78
Jean-Claude Giudicelli, Principal

1765 Lycee International-American Section
Rue du Fer a Cheval
BP 230 Germain En Laye
France
33-34-51-74-85
Fax: 33-30-87-00-49
E-mail: american.lycee.intl@wanadoo.fr
http://www.lycee-intl-american.org
pursues this mission through a rigorous and
rewarding American curriculum which culminates in the French Baccalaureate with International Option, as well as through a broad
and enriching co-curricular program including such activities as drama, community service, sports and student publications.
Yves Lemarie, Head of School
Ted Fauance, Head of Section

1766 Lyc,e International-American Section
BP 230, rue du Fer A Cheval
St. Germain-En-Laye, 78104 Cedex
France
33-1-345-17485
Fax: 33-1-308-70049
E-mail: american.lycee@wanadoo.fr
http://http://lycee-intl-american.org
Grade levels Pre-K through 12, school year
September - June
Theodore Faunce, PhD, Director

1767 Malvern College
College Road, Malvern
Worcestershire WR14 3DF
England
01684-581-500
E-mail: inquiry@malcol.org
http://www.malcol.org
Roy de C Chapman, MA, Headmaster

1768 Mannheim Elementary School
Unit 29938
APO AE
9086
380-4705
Fax: 0621-723-905
E-mail: esmannattend@eu.dodea.edu
http://www.mann-es.eu.dodea.edu
Dr. Ardelle Hamilton PhD, Principal
Dr. Ellen Minette, Assistant Principal

1769 Mannheim High School
Unit 29939
APO AE
9267
380-409-
Fax: 062- 73-901
E-mail:
MannheimHS.Principal@eu.dodea.edu
http://www.mann-hs.eu.dodea.edu
is to equip all students to be conscientiously
contributing citizens through a challenging
curriculum and effective instruction
Sharon O'Donnell, Principal

1770 Margaret Danyers College
N Downs Road, Cheadle Hulme
Cheadle SK8 5HA
England
061-485-4372
Harry Tomlinson, BA, MA, MS,
Headmaster

1771 Mark Twain Elementary School
Unit 29237
APO, Heidelberg 09102 0005
Germany

Joseph Newbury, Principal

1772 Marymount International School-Rome
Via di Villa Lauchli 180
00191 Rome
Italy
33-1-462-41051
Fax: 33-1-463-70750
E-mail: marymount@marymountrome.org
http://www.marymountrome.org/
Marymount International School provides an education based on Christian values. Marymount is dedicated to fostering individual dignity in an atmosphere of love and respect in which students, faculty, staff and parents work and pray together.

Anne Marie Clancy, Headmistress

1773 Marymount International School-United Kingdom
George Road
Kingston upon Thames, Surrey, KT2 7PE
Surrey , United Kingdom KT2 7
44-20-8949-0571
Fax: 44-20-8336-2485
E-mail:
admissions@marymount.kingston.sch.uk
http://www.marymountlondon.com/home.php
Marymount London is a vibrant and dynamic learning community where all are respected and encouraged to contribute,committed to developing individuals.

Kathleen Fagan, Headmistress

1774 Mattlidens Gymnasium
Mattliden 1
02230 Esbo
Finland
09 -16 -30 5
Fax: 09 -16 -30 5
E-mail: gun-maj.roiha@esbo.fi
http://www.mattliden.fi/gym/
Mattlidens Gymnasium is a coeducational Swedish-speaking upper secondary school

Tom Ginman, Headmaster

1775 Mayenne English School
Chateau les Courges 53420
Chailland
France

J Braillard, Principal

1776 Menwith Hill Estates & Middle School
PSC 45 Unit 8435
APO, High Wycombe 09468 0005
Great Britain

Dr. Arnold Watland, Principal

1777 Millfield School
Butleigh Road Street
Somerset
England BA16-0YD
145-844-2291
E-mail: office@millfieldschool.com
http://www.millfieldschool.com
With its outstanding facilities, a staff:pupil ratio of 1:7.5, an extraordinary range of academic courses and the unrivalled strength of its extra-curricular programme, Millfield strives to achieve all these aims. It also seeks to move with the times whilst maintaining the important traditions of good manners, discipline and respect for others

Craig Considine, Headmaster
Adrian E White, Chairman of the Governors

1778 Monkton Combe School
Church Lane
Monkton Combe, Bath
England BA2-7HG
01225-721102
Fax: 01225-721208
E-mail: reception@monkton.org.uk
http://www.monktoncombeschool.com
Boarding and day school for girls and boys ages two to nineteen.

Chris Stafford, Headmaster
Richard Backhouse, Principal

1779 Monti Parioli English School
Via Monti Parioli 50
00197 Rome
Italy

Lynette Surtees, Principal

1780 Mougins School
615 Avenue Drive, Maurice Donat
BP 401, 06251 Mougins Cedex
France
33-4-93-90-15-47
Fax: 33-4-93-75-31-40
E-mail: information@mougins-school.com
http://www.mougins-school.com
The School has a capacity of 460 students, large enough to provide a stimulating environment and small enough to retain a caring family atmosphere. With thirty-five nationalities the School is culturally rich and its philosophy is designed to encourage pupils to develop morally, emotionally, culturally, intellectually and physically

Brian G Hickmore, Headmaster
Jane Hart, Deputy Head

1781 Mountainview School
Bosch 35-6331 Hunenberg
Switzerland

Brenda Moors, Principal

1782 Munich International School
Schloss Buchhof
Starnberg
Germany 82319
49-8151-366-100
Fax: 49-8151-366-109
E-mail: admissions@mis-munich.de
http://www.mis-munich.de
MIS caters for the physical, social, emotional and educational development of its children by providing a student-centred, inquiry-based learning environment which fosters an appreciation in its students of their cultural heritage and the cultural richness of the global community.

Mary Sepalla, Head of School
Maha Kattoura, Chairman

1783 Naples Elementary School
PSC 808 Box 39
FPO, AE
Italy 9618
011-39 -81 8
Fax: 011-39 -81 8
E-mail: NaplesES.Principal@eu.dodea.edu
http://www.napl-es.eu.dodea.edu

Dr. Jacqueline Hulbert, Principal

1784 Naples High School
PSC 808 Box 15
FPO, AE
Italy 9618
011-39 -81 8
Fax: 011-39 -81 8
E-mail: NaplesHS.Principal@eu.dodea.edu
http://www.napl-hs.eu.dodea.edu
Students will be prepared to be critical thinkers, effective communicators, and accountable members in a global society.

Carl Albrecht, Principal

1785 Neubruecke Elementary School
Unit 23825
APO, Neubruecke 09034 0005
Germany

Margaret Hoffman-Otto, Principal

1786 Neuchatel Junior College
44 Victoria Street
Suite 1310
Toronto, ON M5C-1Y2
038-25-27-00
800-263-2923
Fax: 038-24-42-59
E-mail: info@neuchatel.org
http://www.njc.ch
To provide students a rigorous university preparatory programme in a culturally rich and multi-lingual European setting where learning through educational travel, engagement with world affairs and service to others fosters personal growth and leadership.

Norman Southward, Principal
Dayle Leishman, Director

1787 New School Rome
Via Della Camilluccia 669
Roma
Italy 135
39-329-4269
E-mail: info@newschoolrome.com
http://www.newschoolrome.com
The School is a non-profit making organisation run by the Academic Council (all staff and seven student representatives) which also elects the headteacher, and by the Executive Council (three elected teachers and four elected parents).

Josette Fusco, Head Teacher
Richard Lydiker, Executive Chairman

1788 Newton College
Av Ricardo El-as Aparicio 240
La Molina
Lima-Peru, PE
511-479-0460
Fax: 511-479-0430
E-mail: college@newton.edu.pe
http://www.newton.edu.pe
Newton College is an Anglo-Peruvian, co-educational, bilingual, day school for students aged 2 to 18.

David Few, Principal

1789 Norra Reals Gymnasium
Roslagsgatan 1
Stockholm
Sweden 113 5
08 -74 -2 00
Fax: 08 -73 -2 84
E-mail:
infonorrareal@utbildning.stockholm.se
http://www.norrareal.stockholm.se
Offers two preparatory study programs: the science and social science.

Per Engback, Principal
Maria Sellberg, Assistant Principal

1790 Numont School
C/ Parma 16
Madrid
Spain 28043
349-130- 243
Fax: 349- 75- 94
E-mail: numont@telefonica.net
http://eoficina.e.telefonica.net
Provide a warm, happy and challenging atmosphere where children can derive pleasure from learning and achieving their personal goals. The emphasis is on the individual, so that all of the children, regardless of strengths and weaknesses, colour, creed or sex, feel valued and able to reach their full potential.

Margaret Ann Swanson, Principal

1791 Oak House School
Sant Pere Claver 12-18
Barcelona
Spain 8017
349-325- 402
Fax: 349-325- 402
E-mail: sec@oakhouseschool.com
http://www.oakhouseschool.com
The training of students both personal and social is one of the main objectives of the educational work.

Teresa Armadans, Director of Finance
VicenØ Orobitg, Information Technology

1792 Oakham School
Chapel Close
Market Place
Oakham,Rutland, UK LE15
44-0-1572-758758
Fax: 44-0-1572-758595
E-mail: registrar@oakham.rutland.sch.uk
http://www.oakham.rutland.sch.uk
A pioneer of full co-education, a boarding and day school for boys and girls aged 10 to 18 years that has become widely known for developing new ideas and making them work to the benefit of all Oakham's pupils.

Joseph AF Spence, Headmaster
Jon Wills, Registrar

1793 Oporto British School
Rua Da Cerca 326/338
PORTO
Portugal 4150-
226-666-0
E-mail: school@obs.edu.pt
http://www.obs.edu.pt
As the oldest British School in Continental Europe, the Oporto British School is committed to providing a high quality international education for its students.

Mark Rogers, Principal
David Butcher, Headmaster

1794 Oslo American School
Gml Ringeriksv 53, 1340 Bekkestua
Oslo
Norway

James Mcneil, Principal

1795 Panterra American School
Via Ventre D'oca 41, Fontanella
Pescara 65131
Italy

Virginia Simpson, Principal

1796 Paris American Academy
277 Rue Street Jacques
Paris
France 75005
01 -4 4- 99
Fax: 01 -4 4- 99
http://www.parisamericanacademy.edu
To create and maintain a system of higher education that contributes to the transformation of students into

Peter Carman, President/Executive Director
Jean-Michel Ageron-Blanc, General Director

1797 Patrick Henry Elementary School
Unit 29237
APO, Heidelberg
Germany, AE 9102
388-905-
Fax: 062-1 7-5 49
E-mail:
PatrickHenryES.Principal@eu.dodea.edu
http://www.heid-esp.eu.dodea.edu
To educate all children by providing a nurturing environment and standards-based curric-

ulum dedicated to meeting he diverse needs of every child.

Russ Claus, Principal
Marie Granger, Assistant Principal

1798 Perse School
Hills Road
Cambridge CB2 8QF
England
0223-248127
E-mail: office@perse.co.uk
http://www.perse.co.uk

Edward Elliott, Head of Politics
Dan Cross, Deputy Head

1799 Pinewood Schools of Thessaloniki
PO Box 21001
555 10 Pilea
Greece
30-31-301-221
Fax: 30-31-323-196
E-mail: pinewood@spark.net.gr
Independent, coeducational schools which offer an educational program from prekindergarten through grade 12 and boarding facilities from grade 7 though grade 12 for students of all nationalities. The school year comprises 2 semesters extending from September to January and from January to June.

Peter B Baiter, Director

1800 Pordenone Elementary School
PSC 1
Aviano
Italy
39-0434-28462
Fax: 39-0434-28761

D Jean Waddell, Principal

1801 Priory School
West Bank, Dorking
Surrey RH4 3DG
England
130-688-7337
Fax: 130-688-8715
E-mail:
enquiries@staff.priorycofe.surrey.sch.uk
http://www.priorycofe.surrey.sch.uk
To provide an educational environment which encourages pupils to become confident, competent, self-reliant and happy members of society, fully prepared for adult life and the world of work

A C Sohatski, Headteacher
M Pinchin, Senior Deputy Headteacher

1802 Queen Elizabeth School
Queen's Road, Barnet
Hertfordshire
England, UK EN5 4
020-844- 464
Fax: 020-844- 750
E-mail: enquiries@qebarnet.co.uk
http://www.qebarnet.co.uk
To produce boys who are confident, able and responsible.

John Marincowitz, Headmaster

1803 Queens College the English School
Juan De Saridakis 64
Palma de Malorca
Spain
809-393-2153
This Methodist affiliated school offers an English-based curriculum to a total of 1,200 female students, grades K1-12. The school does recruit from overseas, offering three year contracts with housing provided for one week at the beginning of the contract, while they find accommodations. Applications needed to teach include science, pre-school,

French, math, Spanish, English and physical education.

Philip Cash, Principal

1804 Rainbow Elementary School
Unit 28614 Box 0040
APO, Ansbach 09177 0005
Germany

Thomas Murdock, Principal

1805 Ramstein Elementary School
Unit 3240 Box 430
APO AE
Germany 9094
067- 14- 399
Fax: 067- 15- 835
http://www.rams-es.eu.dodea.edu
To provide a quality education for eligible minor dipendents of DoD military and civilian personnel stationed overseas.

Kathy Downs, Principal

1806 Ramstein High School
Unit 3240 Box 445
APO AE
Germany 9094-445
067-1 4-6 95
Fax: 067-1 4-9 86
http://www.rams-hs.eu.dodea.edu
To provide a varied and challenging curriculum that will allow students to be life-long learners and responsible participants in a global community.

Greg Hatch, Principal

1807 Ramstein Intermediate School
Unit 3240 Box 600
APO AE
Germany 9094-600
067-1 4-6023
Fax: 067-1 5-238
http://www.rams-is.eu.dodea.edu
To provide an educational environment designed to maximize the potential of all Students.

Stanley B Caldwell, Principal

1808 Ramstein Junior High School
86 SPTG CCSI R, Unit 3240 Box 455
APO, Ramstein 09094 0005
Germany

Richard Snell, Principal

1809 Rathdown School
Upper Glenageary Road Glenageary
Co Dublin
Ireland
01-853133
E-mail: admin@rathdownschool.ie
http://www.rathdownschool.ie/contact_us.p
hp
Our aim is to offer a high-quality, modern, challenging and liberal education. In an inclusive and friendly environment, Rathdown School hopes to foster a love of learning which will enable each student to develop her own unique potential. Our purpose is to support and promote the student's academic, cultural, sporting, creative, musical and spiritual capabilities.

Barbara Ennis, Principal

1810 Regionale Internationale School
Humperdincklaan 4, 5654 PA
Eindhoven
Netherlands
040-2519437
E-mail: info@riseindhoven.nl
http://ise2008.stedelijkcollege.nl
This school teaches a curriculum in Dutch, English, and French for 360 day students (180 boys; 180 girls), 4-12 years of age. The enroll-

ment and teaching staff represent 43 nationalities, and the student/teacher ratio is 14:1.

HA Schol, Principal
R van Elderen, Chairman

1811 Rikkyo School in England
Guildford Road, Rudgwick, W Sussex
RH12 3BE
Great Britain
014-3 8-2107
Fax: 014-3 8-2535
E-mail: eikoku@rikkyo.w-sussex.sch.uk
http://www.rikkyo.co.uk

M Usuki, Principal

1812 Riverside School
Walterswil
6340 Baar
Switzerland
41-41-724-5690
Fax: 41-41-724-5692
E-mail: office.zug@iszl.ch
http://www.iszl.ch
The International School of Zug and Luzern (ISZL) provides a high quality Pre-School to Grade 12 international education to day students resident in the Cantons of central Switzerland.

Dominic Currer, Director
Elaine Tomlinson, Headmaster

1813 Robinson Barracks Elementary School
Unit 30401
APO
Germany, AE 9107
49 -11 -19 7
Fax: 071- 85- 473
E-mail:
RobinsonBarracksES.Principal@eu.dodea.e du
http://www.rbar-es.eu.dodea.edu
The Robinson Barrack's school community provides a respectful environment where all members learn to recognize their strengths and gain confidence to become lifelong learners and leaders in an ever-changing world.

Shirley Sheck, Principal

1814 Rome International School
Via Panama 25
00198 Rome
Italy
039-06 -4482
Fax: 039-06 -4482
E-mail: office@romeinternationalschool.it
http://www.romeinternationalschool.it
Provides a nurturing environment, in which children of all nationalities and faiths can explore and respect their own and each other's cultural and religious heritage.

Patricia Martin-Smith, Principal Primary School
Ivano Boragine, Managing Director

1815 Rosall School
Fleetwood
Lancashire
United Kingdom FY7 8
012- 37- 420
Fax: 012- 37- 205
E-mail: enquiries@rossallcorporation.co.uk
http://www.rossall.co.uk
Providing a unique educational experience we offer a wide ranging choice of curriculums underpinned by a commitment to academic excellence.

RDW Rhodes, Principal
GSH Penelley, Faculty Head

1816 Rosemead
East Street, Littlehampton
BN17 6AL
England
0903-716065

J Bevis, BA, Headmaster

1817 Rota Elementary School
PSC 819 Box 19
FPO AE 09645 0019
Spain
34 -56 -2 41
Fax: 011-34 -56 8
E-mail: rotaes.principal@eu.dodea.edu
http://www.rota-es.eu.dodea.edu
Provides a standards-based educational program, which creates lifelong learners and responsible citizens.

Charles Callahan, Principal

1818 Rota High School
PSC 819 Box 63
FPO AE 09645 0005
Spain
956-82 -181
Fax: 011-34 -56 8
E-mail: RotaHS.Principal@eu.dodea.edu
http://www.rota-hs.eu.dodea.edu

Lynne Michael, Principal

1819 Roudybush Foreign Service School
Place des Arcades, Sauveterre de Rouergue (Averyon)
France
This European school prepares men for the foreign service.

Franklin Roudybush, AB, MA, Headmaster

1820 Rugby School
Rugby, Warwickshire
United Kingdom CV22
44-178-854-3465
Fax: 44-178-856-9124
E-mail: enquiries@rugbyschool.net
http://www.rugbyschool.net
Rugby School is an educational community whose philosophy embraces the challenges of academic excellence, spiritual awareness, responsibility and leadership, friendships and relationships and participation in a wide variety of activities

Patrick Derham, Headmaster
SK Fletcher, Deputy Head

1821 Runnymede College School
Calle Salvia 30
28109 La Moraleja, Madrid
Spain
34-91-650-8302
Fax: 34-91-650-8236
E-mail: office@runnymede-college.com
http://www.runnymede-college.com
Provides an all-round, academic, liberal humanist education to all students regardless of their sex, race, religion or nationality. There is no religious instruction.

Frank M Powell, Headmaster
FJ Murphy, Deputy Head

1822 Rygaards International School
Bernstorffsvej 54, DK-2900
Hellerup
Denmark
45-39-62-10-53
Fax: 45-39-62-10-81
E-mail: admin@rygaards.com
http://www.rygaards.com
Rygaards School is a private, Christian/Catholic, co-educational establishment. It is recognised by and subject to, Danish law and receives a subsidy from the Danish State.

Mathias Jepsen, Principal
Charles Dalton, Headmaster

1823 Salzburg International Preparatory School
Moosstrasse 106
A-5020 Salzburg
Austria
662-844485
Fax: 662-847711
A coeducational boarding school offering an American college preparatory high school curriculum for grades 7 to 12 as well as a post graduate course.

1824 Schiller Academy
51-55 Waterloo Road
London, SE1 8TX
United Kingdom
44-207-928-1372
Fax: 44-207-928-8089
E-mail: office@schiller-academy.org.uk
http://www.schiller-academy.org.uk
Grade levels 9-12, school year August - June

George Selby, Headmaster
Renee Miller, Director Studies

1825 Schools of England, Wales, Scotland & Ireland
J. Burrow & Company
Imperial House, Lypiatt Road
Cheltenham 50201
England

1826 Schweinfurt American Elementary School
CMR 457
AP, AE
Germany 9033
09721-81893
Fax: 09721-803905
E-mail:
schweinfurtes.principal@eu.dodea.edu
http://www.schw-es.eu.dodea.edu
The mission of Schweinfurt Elementary School is to help all students become respectful, responsible citizens and life-long learners.

Wilma Holt, Principal
Beverly Erdmann, Assistant Principal

1827 Schweinfurt Middle School
CMR 457
AP, AE
Germany 9033-5
354-681-
Fax: 097-1 8-363
E-mail:
SchweinfurtMS.Principal@eu.dodea.edu
http://www.schw-ms.eu.dodea.edu
Schweinfurt Middle School will engage all students in meaningful experiences that develop 21st Century Skills, preparing them to be successful and responsible citizens in a technological, global society.

Dr George P Carpenter, Principal

1828 Sembach Elementary School
Unit 4240 Box 325
APO, AE
Germany 9136
063-2 6- 700
Fax: 063-2 7-12
E-mail:
SembachES.Principal@eu.dodea.edu
http://www.semb-es.eu.dodea.edu

Monica Harvey, Principal

1829 Sembach Middle School
Unit 4240 Box 320
APO, AE
Germany 9136
063-2 5-98
Fax: 063-2 7-86
E-mail:

SembachMS.Principal@eu.dodea.edu
http://www.semb-ms.eu.dodea.edu
Bonnie B Hannan, Principal

1830 Sevenoaks School
Sevenoaks
Kent TN13 IHU
England
44 - 17-2 45
Fax: 44 - 17-2 45
E-mail: enq@sevenoaksschool.org
http://www.sevenoaksschool.org
Sevenoaks School is an independent, co-educational boarding and day school, set in 100 acres in the heart of Southeast England. Half an hour from Central London, and half an hour from Gatwick International Airport, we are situated on the edge of Sevenoaks, overlooking the 15th century deer park of the Knole Estate.

Katy Ricks, Head of School
Tony Evans, Chairman

1831 Sevilla Elementary & Junior High School
496 ABS DODDS Unit 6585
APO Moron AB 09643 0005
Spain

Robert Ludwig, Principal

1832 Shape Elementary School
Unit 21420
APO, AE
Belgium 9705
011-32 -5 44
Fax: 011-32 -5 31
E-mail: ShapeES.Principal@eu.dodea.edu
http://www.shap-es.eu.dodea.edu
It is the mission of SHAPE Elementary School to educate all students in an integrated, multi-cultural environment to become productive thinkers, to achieve their maximum physical and mental potential, and to be literate, responsible members of a global society through excellence in teaching and learning.

Charlene Leister, Principal
Miles Shea, Assistant Principal

1833 Shape High School
Unit 21420
APO, AE
Belgium 9705
32 -5 4- 571
Fax: 32 -5 3- 166
E-mail: david.tran@eu.dodea.edu
http://www.shap-hs.eu.dodea.edu
David Tran, Principal
Arlena Ray, Assistant Principal

1834 Shape International School
Avenue de Reijkjavik 717
SHAPE
Belgium 7010
65-44-52-83
http://www.nato.int/shape/community/school.htm
Performs the operational duties previously undertaken by Allied Command Europe and Allied Command Atlantic

Jacques Laurent, Principal

1835 Sherborne School
Abbey Road
Sherborne, Dorset DT9 3AP
England
44-193-581-2249
Fax: 44-193-581-6628
E-mail: enquiries@sherborne.org
http://www.sherborne.org/home
Ralph Mowat, Principal
Simon Eliot, Headmaster

1836 Sidcot School
Winscombe
N Somerset BS25 1PD
England
44-193-484-3102
Fax: 44-193-484-4181
E-mail: addmissions@sidcot.org.uk
http://www.sidcot.org.uk
This friendly school with an international enrollment of 277 day students and 149 boarding students (255 boys; 171 girls), in grades K-12, is set in over one hundred acres of Somerset countryside. The school offers an English-based curriculum and the student/teacher ratio is 10:1.

John Walmsley, Headteacher
Ross Wallis, Head of Art

1837 Sierra Bernia School
La Caneta s/n
Alfaz del Pi Alicante
Spain 3580
96-687-51-49
Fax: 96-687-36-33
E-mail: duncan@ctv.es
http://sierraberniaschool.com/news.php
Forefront of modern education. Combining both traditional and innovative methods of teaching made possible by the wealth and immense knowledge base of its fully qualified teaching body

Duncan Allan, Owner/Director
Iain Macinnes, Headteacher

1838 Sigonella Elementary & High School
PSC 824 Box 2630
FPO Signoella, Sicily 09627 2630
Italy

Dr. Peter Price, Principal

1839 Sigtunaskolan Humanistiska Laroverket
Manfred Bjorkquists Alle 6
Box 508, Sigtuna
Sweden 19328
46-8-592-57100
Fax: 46-8-592-57250
E-mail: info@sshl.se
http://www.sshl.se
Grade levels include 7-12 with an enrollment of 543.

Kent Edberg, Principal
Rune Svaninger, Director

1840 Sir James Henderson School
Via Pisani Dossi 16
Milano
Italy 20134
39-02-264-13310
Fax: 39-02-264-13515
E-mail: sirjames@bbs.infosquare.it
http://www.sjhschool.com
To ensure that its diverse student body grows to its full potential as independent learners in a caring British and international community, uniting the best of British educational tradition with the values, practices and beliefs of the International Baccalaureate

Stephen Anson, Principal
Jim Noble, Chairman

1841 Skagerak Gymnas
PO Box 1545-Veloy
3206 Sandefjord
Norway

Elisabeth Norr, Principal

1842 Smith Elementary School
Unit 23814 Box 30
APO, AE
Germany 9034-3814
067-783-5693
Fax: 067-783-8874

E-mail: SmithES.Principal@eu.dodea.edu
http://www.baum-ess.eu.dodea.edu
Kent Bassett, Principal

1843 Southlands English School
Via Teleclide 40
Casalapalocco, Rome
Italy 124
39 -6 5-5 39
Fax: 06 -091-7192
http://www.southlands.it
Our aim is to give you a flavour of the quality educational experience available at Southlands and encourage you to visit the school so you can see for yourself the happy, successful community that Southlands nurtures.

Deryck M Wilson, Principal

1844 Spangdahlem Elementary School
52 MSG/CCSE S, Unit 3640 Box 50
APO, AE
Germany 9126-4050
065- 56- 688
Fax: 065- 56- 710
E-mail:
SpnagdahlemES.Principal@eu.dodea.edu
http://www.spang-es.eu.dodea.edu
Richard R Alix, Principal

1845 Spangdahlem Middle School
52 CSG CCSM, Unit 3640 Box 45
APO, AE
Germany 9126-4045
065-5 6- 725
Fax: 065-5 6- 279
E-mail:
SpangdahlemMS.Principal@eu.dodea.edu
http://www.spang-ms.eu.dodea.edu
Spangdhalem Middle School promotes high achievement and lifelong learning for all students through positive interactions and standards-based educational program.

Joseph Malloy, Principal

1846 Sportfield Elementary School
Unit 20193 Box 0014
APO, Hanau
Germany, AE 9165-14
John O'Reilly, Jr, Principal

1847 St. Andrew's College
19 Carillon Avenue
Newtown NSW
Australia 2042
02-9626-1999
E-mail:
principalassist@standrewscollege.edu.au
http://www.standrewscollege.edu.au
St Andrew's is proud of its reputation as a leading academic institution, fostering leaders within the community and moulding the leaders of tomorrow. The College places emphasis on academic and intellectual development and excellence as core to the development of the individual.

Wayne Erickson, Principal
Donna Wiemann, Development Manager

1848 St. Anne's School
Jarama 9
Madrid 2
Spain

Margaret Raines, Principal

1849 St. Anthony's International College
Camino de Coin km 53.5
Mijas-Costa, Malaga
Spain 29649
00 -4 9-2 47
Fax: 00 -4 9-2 46
E-mail: info@stanthonyscollege.com
http://www.stanthonyscollege.com

The school with its friendly, family atmosphere provides opportunities for our students to achieve their best. Trying not to cater just for high achievers we endeavour, through a broad and balanced education, to find courses for all abilities.

1850 St. Catherine's British School

PO Box 51019
Kifissia 145 10 Athens
Greece
30 -10 -8297
Fax: 30 -10 -8264
E-mail: administrator@stcatherines.gr
http://www.stcatherines.gr
The school endeavors to foster a love of learning through a well taught, appropriately challenging, clearly defined and balanced curriculum. Our aim is to fully develop intellectual, social, physical and creative potential, giving students the foundatin to develop into sensitive, informed, and capable global citizens of the future.

Michael Toman, Principal
R Morton, Headmaster & CEO

1851 St. Christopher School

Barrington Road, Letchworth
Hertfordshire SG6 3JZ
England
0462-679301
Fax: 0462-481578
E-mail: school.admin@stchris.co.uk
http://www.stchris.co.uk
St Christopher has a distinctive ethos, based on the development of each child's individuality whilst teaching a sense of responsibility towards others, towards the School and towards the local and global community.

Richard Palmer, Head of School
Emma-Kate Henry, Deputy Head of St Christophe

1852 St. Clare's Oxford

139 Banbury Road
Oxford OX2 7AL
England
44-186-555-2031
Fax: 44-186-551-3359
E-mail: admissions@stclares.ac.uk
http://www.stclares.ac.uk
St. Clare's welcomes students and staff of all nationalities and cultures who will benefit from, and contribute to, our learning community. Living and studying together, we learn from one another. We are enriched and challenged by a diversity of views and ideas.

Paula Holloway, Principal
Tom Walsh, Vice Principal

1853 St. David's School

Justin Hall, Beckenham Road
West Wickham BR4 0QS
England
01784-252494
Fax: 01784-252494
E-mail: office@stdavidsschool.com
Boarding school for girls ages nine to eighteen; day school for girls ages four to eighteen.

Judith G Osborne, BA, Headmaster

1854 St. Dominic's International School

Outeiro de Polima-Arneiro
2785-816 Sao Domingos da Rana
Portugal
351-21-448-0550
Fax: 351-21-444-3027
E-mail: school@dominics-int.org
http://www.dominics-int.org
Our school mission is to offer an international education of the highest calibre enriched and enlivened by the Dominican tradition of study and education;~ promoting the development of each student's potential:~ physical, emotional, social, intellectual, moral and spiritual.

Maria do Rosÿri Empis, Principal
Manuel Lucas, President of Supervision

1855 St. Dominic's Sixth Form College

Mount Park Avenue Harrow on the Hil
Middlesex HA1 3HX
England
020-84228084
Fax: 020-8422-3759
E-mail: stdoms@stdoms.ac.uk
http://www.stdoms.ac.uk
St. Dominic's is a Roman Catholic Sixth Form College committed to the pesonal and spiritual growth of all its members based on Christian values, academic excellence and high quality pastoral care.

Patrick Harty, Principal

1856 St. Georges English School

Via Cassia Km 16
La Storta Rome
Italy 123
06-3790141
Fax: 06-3792490
E-mail: Secretary@stgeorge.school.it
http://www.stgeorge.school.it
To develop the individual talents of young people and teach them to relate the experience of the classroom to the realities of the world outside.

Martyn Hales, Principal

1857 St. Georges School

Vila Goncalve, Quinta Loureiras
2750 Cascais
Portugal
MPB Hoare, Principal

1858 St. Georges School-Switzerland

Chemin de St Georges 19
Clarens Montreux
Switzerland 1815
21-964-34-11
Fax: 21-964-49-32
E-mail: office@st-georges.ch
http://www.st-georges.ch
St. George's School encourages students to lift their eyes and recognise positive qualities within themselves and others and to nurture a caring and dynamic attitude in today's demanding world.

Dr Ilya V Eigenbrot, Principal
Francis Kahn, President of Directors

1859 St. Gerard's School

Thornhill Road, Bray Co Wicklow
Republic of Ireland
353-0 1-2821
Fax: 353-0 1-2821
E-mail: info@stgerards.ie
http://www.stgerards.ie
To provide an opportunity for each student to realise his or her potential in all areas: academic, moral, personal, physical, social, spiritual and sporting.

Tom Geraghty, Headmaster
Victor Drummy, Deputy Principal

1860 St. Helen's School

Eastbury Road Northwood, Middlesex
England HA6-3AS
09274-28511
Fax: 0923-835824
E-mail: enquiries@sthn.co.uk
http://www.sthn.co.uk
We aim to give every pupil an academic, innovative and stimulating education, developing her intellectual, creative and physical talents to the full. We provide a friendly, supportive and well-ordered environment in which every girl is treated as an individual and where in-

tegrity, personal responsibility and respect for others are highly valued.

YA Burne, Principal

1861 St. John's International School

Dreve Richelle 146
Waterloo
Belguim 1410
32-2-352-0610
Fax: 32-2-352-0630
E-mail: contact@stjohns.be
http://www.stjohns.be
we exist to provide an English-speaking education that emphasizes Christian values, encourages academic excellence and stimulates social development within a culturally diverse environment. St. John's is also a caring environment where students are encouraged to reach their full potential, prepared to think globally, with a commitment to justice and challenged to act responsibly in a consistently changing society.

Joseph Doenges, Director
Judith Hoskins, Director Admissions

1862 St. Mary's School

Rhapta Road, PO Box 40580- 00100
Nairobi
Kenya
0990-23721
E-mail: info@stmarys.ac.ke
http://www.stmarys.ac.ke
We are a Catholic Private School committed to our international character in the provision of a spiritual, intellectual and physical education. We aim at developing the gifts of the young in an atmosphere which encourages the ethos of self-expression and mutual respect with a view to their facing the future responsibly, with confidence and courage.

M Mark Orchard, IBVM, BA, Principal

1863 St. Michael's School

Otford Court
Otford TN14 5SA
England
095-92-2137
http://www.stmichaels-otford.co.uk
Keith Crombie, Headmaster

1864 St. Stephen's School

Via Aventina 3
Rome
Italy 153
39-06-575-0605
Fax: 39-06-574-1941
E-mail: ststephens@ststephens-rome.com
http://www.ststephens-rome.com
Philip Allen, Headmaster
Lesley Murphey, Head of the School

1865 Stavenger British School

Gauselbakken 107
4032 Gausel
Norway
Zelma Roisli, Principal

1866 Stover School

Newton Abbot
Devon
England TQ12
0626-54505
E-mail: mail@stover.co.uk
http://www.stover.co.uk
Susan Bradley, Principal

1867 Stowe School

Stowe
Buckingham
England MK18
44-1280-818000
Fax: 44-1280-818181

E-mail: enquiries@stowe.co.uk
http://www.stowe.co.uk
Our vision for Stowe, a co-educational independent boarding and day school in the heart of the English countryside, is of a school that delivers the highest academic and cultural achievement; and a school that continues to foster the development of Stoics who are as original and individual as their school.

Anthony Wallersteiner, Headmaster
GM Hornby, Faculty Head

1868 Summerfield School SRL
Via Tito Poggi 21 Divino Amore
00134 Rome
Italy

Vivien Franceschini, Principal

1869 Summerhill School
Westward Ho
Leiston, Suffolk
England IP16
0728-830540
E-mail: zoe@summerhillschool.co.uk
http://www.summerhillschool.co.uk
A S Neill's Summerhill School, a co-educational boarding school in Suffolk, England, is the original alternative 'free' school. Founded in 1921, it continues to be an influential model for progressive, democratic education around the world.

Zoe Readhead, Principal

1870 Sunny View School
C/ Teruel No 32, Cerro del Toril
Torremolinos Malaga
Spain 29620
34 -52 -8 31
Fax: 34 -52 -7 26
E-mail: sunny@acade.es
http://www.sunnyviewschool.com
Sunny View is a privately owned day school, which accepts students of all nationalities from the age of 3 years to 18 years. It is a long-established International School.

Jane Barbadillo, Principal
David McConnell, HS Principal

1871 Sutton Park School
St Fintan's Road
Sutton, Dublin 13
Ireland
353-1-832-2940
Fax: 353-1-832-5929
E-mail: info@sps.ie
http://www.suttonparkschool.com
Sutton Park School aims to provide its pupils with an educational environment that is intellectually, physically and culturally challenging, so that they can grow into balanced, mature and confident adults.

Laurence J Finnegan, Chief Executive
Michael Moretta, Head of School

1872 Sutton Valence School
Maidstone
Kent
England ME17
0622-842281
E-mail: enquiries@svs.org.uk
http://www.svs.org.uk
Our aim today is to give our girls and boys an excellent all round education in an atmosphere of togetherness and trust, where day and boarding pupils benefit from the same supportive ethos.

Joe Davies, Headmaster
Kathy Webster, Admissions Officer

1873 Swans School
Capricho s/n
Marbella, Malaga
Spain 29600

95 -77 -248
Fax: 95 -77 -431
E-mail: info@swansschool.net
http://www.swansschool.net
Swans' motto is Constancy and Truth.

TJ Swan, Principal
Nick Lee, Head Teacher

1874 TASIS Hellenic International School
PO Box 51051
Kifissia Gr-145 10
Greece
30-1-623-3888
Fax: 30-1-623-3160
E-mail: info@tasis.edu.gr
http://www.tasis.com
Grade levels Pre-K through 12, school year September - June

Basile Daskalakis, President

1875 TASIS The American School in England
Coldharbour Lane
Thorpe, Surrey, TW20 8TE
England
44-1932-565-252
Fax: 44-1932-564-644
E-mail: ukadmissions@tasis.com
http://www.tasis.com
Grade levels Pre-K through 12, school year August - June

Barry Breen, Headmaster

1876 Taunus International Montessori School
Altkonigstrasse 1 6370
Oberursel
Germany

Kathleen Hauer, Principal

1877 Teach in Great Britain
5 Netherhall Gardens
London, NW3, England

1878 Thessaloniki International High School & Pinewood Elementary School
PO Box 21001
555 10 Pilea, Thessaloniki
Greece
30-31-301-221
Fax: 30-31-323-196
E-mail: pinewood@spark.net.gr
http://www.users.otenet.gr/~pinewood
Grades preK-12, enrollment 256.

Peter B Baiter, Director

1879 Thomas Jefferson School
4100 South Lindbergh Boulevard
Saint Louis
Missouri, MO 63127
314-843-4151
http://www.tjs.org
The mission of Thomas Jefferson School is to give its students the strongest possible academic background, responsibility for their own learning, a concern for other people, and the resources to live happily as adults and become active contributors to society

William C Rowe, Head of School
Susan S Stepleton, Chair, Board of Trustees

1880 United Nations Nursery School
40 Rue Pierre Guerin
75016 Paris
France
33-1-452-72024
Fax: 33-1-428-87146
Pre-K and kindergarten levels.

Brigitte Weill, Directrice

1881 United World College-Adriatic
Via Treste 29
Duino (TS)
Italy 34011
39 -40 -7391
Fax: 39 -40 -7392
http://www.uwcad.it
The United World Colleges offer students of all races and creeds the opportunity of developing international understanding through programmes which combine high quality academic study and activities which encourage

DB Sutcliffe, Principal
David Sutcliffe, Headmaster

1882 United World College-Atlantic
St Donats Castle Llantwit
Major S Glamorgan
United Kingdom
a sense of adventure and social responsibility

Colin Jenkins, Principal

1883 Vajont Elementary School
PSC 1
Aviano
Italy
427-701553

Nick Suida, Principal

1884 Verdala International School
Fort Pembroke
Pembroke, STJ 14
Malta
356-332-361
Fax: 356-372-387
E-mail: vis@maltanet.net
http://www.verdala.org
An independent, coeducational day and boarding school which offers an educational program from play school through grade 12 for students of all nationalities.

Adam Pleasance, Headmaster
Charles Zerafa, Business Manager

1885 Verona Elementary School
1011 Lee Highway
Verona, VA 24482
540-248-0141
Fax: 540-248-0562
http://www.augusta.k12.va.us/veronaes/site/default.asp

Marguerite McDonald, Principal

1886 Vicenza Elementary School
Unit 31401 Box 11
APO, Vicenza
Italy 9630-5
011-39 -444
Fax: 011-39 -444
E-mail: VicenzaES.Principal@eu.dodea.edu
http://www.vice-es.eu.dodea.edu/index.htm
Increase student achievement, we are committed to improving our children's ability to communicate in writing across all curricular areas, and to reason mathematically.

Martha Parsons, Principal

1887 Vicenza High School
Unit 31401 Box 11
APO, Vicenza
Italy 9630
011-39 -444
Fax: 011-39 -444
E-mail: VicenzaHS.Principal@eu.dodea.edu
http://www.vice-hs.eu.dodea.edu/
Lauri Kenney, Principal
Chris Beane, Assistant Principal

1888 Vicenza International School
Viale Trento 141
Vicenza 36100
Italy

39-0444-288-475
Fax: 39-0444-963-633
E-mail: vix-ib@vip.it
Grade levels 11-13, school year September - June

Dionigio Tanello, PhD, Director

1889 Vienna Christian School
Wagramerstrasse 175
Panthgasse 6A
Wien, Austria A-122
43-1-25122-501
E-mail: office@vcs-austria.org
http://www.viennachristianschool.org/
VCS is an international school with a United States-based curriculum.

Ken Norman, Director
Nancy L Deibert, Athletic Director/PE

1890 Vienna International School
Strasse der Menschenrechte 1
Vienna, Austria 1220
43-1-203-5595
Fax: 43-1-203-0366
E-mail: visinfo@vis.ac.at.
http://www.vis.ac.at
To serve the children of the United Nations and diplomatic community in Vienna. It is also open to children of the international business community and of Austrian families.

James S Walbran, Director
Neil Tomalin, Head Primary School

1891 Vilseck Elementary School
Unit 28040
APO, Vilseck
Germany 9112-14
011-49 -662
Fax: 011-49 -662
E-mail: VilseckES.Principal@eu.dodea.edu
http://www.vils-es.eu.dodea.edu/
Vilseck Elementary School prepares students for lifelong learning within a safe, nurturing environment. Honoring the uniqueness of our military community, we foster respect for all people and for cultural diversity

Hammack, Principal, Assistant Principal

1892 Vilseck High School
Unit 20841
APO, Vilseck
Germany 9112-5
011-49 -662
Fax: 096-2 8- 248
E-mail: Duane.Werner@eu.dodea.edu
http://www.vils-hs.eu.dodea.edu/
VHS is home to approximately 520 students, grades 9-12, who have the opportunity to participate in Engaged Learning projects in academic areas. They have a wide range of choices in elective areas to include art, band, chorus, German, Spanish, home economics and technical education.

Duane Werner, Principal

1893 Violen School, International Department
Violenstraat 3, 1214
CJ Hilversum
Netherlands
This school offers an enrollment of 240 day students (125 boys and 115 girls), in grades K through 6. The primary education is in the English language for international mobile families, set up and supported by the Dutch government.

Atse R Spoor, Principal

1894 Vogelweh Elementary School
Unit 3240 Box 435
APO
Germany, AE 9021

011-49 -31 9
Fax: 011-49 -31 5
http://www.voge-es.eu.dodea.edu
Vogelweh Elementary School is committed to creating an environment that supports life-long learning in order for students to be successful in a global society.

Donna E Donaldson, Principal
Janie Page, Assistant Principal

1895 Volkel Elementary School
752 MUNSS Unit 6790
APO, Volkel 09717 5018
Netherlands

Claudia Holtzclaw, Principal

1896 Westwing School
Kyneton House
Thornbury BS122JZ
England
0454-412311

Marjorie Crane, MA, Headmaster

1897 Wetzel Elementary School
Unit 23815
APO, Baumholder 09034 0005
Germany

Robert Richards, Principal

1898 Wiesbaden Middle School
Unit 29647
APO, AE
Germany 9096
011-49 -11 7
Fax: 011-49 -11 7
E-mail: wiesbadenMS.Webmaster@eu.dodea.edu
http://www.wies-ms.eu.dodea.edu
The entire WMS community strives to provide a positive school climate through which all students can mature socially, academically and physically, while developing a lifelong love of learning.

Alexia Venglik, Principal

1899 Wolfert Van Borselen
Bredewater 24, Postbus 501
2700 AM Zoetermeer
Netherlands
E-mail: info@owinsp.nl
http://http://www.wolfert.nl/

Gilles Schuilenburg, Principal

1900 Worksop College
Worksop, Nottinghamshire
S80 3AP
England
0909-472391
E-mail: enquiries@worksopcollege.notts.sch.uk
http://http://www.worksopcollege.notts.sch.uk/
Worksop College was founded as St Cuthbert's School in 1890 by Nathaniel Woodard. As a parish priest working in London in the 1840s Woodard was dismayed by the ignorance of the middle classes and believed that there was a need for something comparable to the National School's Christian schools for the poor in order to serve the needs of the trade classes.

Roy Collard, Headmaster

1901 Worms Elementary School
CMR 455
APO, Worms 09058 0005
Germany

Charles Raglan, Principal

1902 Wuerzburg Elementary School
CMR 475 Box 6
APO, Wuerzburg 09244 6627
Germany

Dee Ann Edwards, Principal

1903 Wuerzburg High School
CMR 475 Box 8
APO, Wuerzburg 09036 0005
Germany

Robert Kubarek, Principal

1904 Wuerzburg Middle School
CMR 475 Box 7
APO, Wuerzburg 09036 0005
Germany

Karen Kroon, Principal

1905 Zurich International School
Steinacherstrasse 140
8820 Wadenswill
Switzerland
41-43-833-2222
Fax: 41-43-833-2223
E-mail: zis@zis.ch
http://www.zis.ch
Zurich International School is a co-educational international day school in the Zurich area for students aged 3 to 18 and is fully accredited by both the Council of International Schools and the New England Association of Schools and Colleges and is an IB World School.

Peter C Mott, Director
Jennifer Saxe, Director Development

West Indies & Carribean

1906 American School-Santo Domingo
Apartado 20212
Santo Domingo
Dominican Republic
809-565-7946
809-549-5841
E-mail: info@assd.edu.do
http://www.assd.edu.do
The American School of Santo Domingo provides all students with quality educational opportunities to make life long learners while fostering moral values and physical development.

Lourdes Tomas, School Director

1907 Aquinas College
1607 Robinson Road SE
Grand Rapids, MI 49506-1799

http://www.aquinas.edu
Emphasizes career preparation with a focus on leadership and service to others.

Vincent Ferguson, Principal

1908 Belair School
43 Decarteret Road
Mandeville
Jamaica
1-876-962-2168
Fax: 1-876-962-3396
E-mail: admissions@belairschool.com
http://www.belairschool.com
The Belair School seeks to promote the academic, social and emotional development of students and a value system of integrity through an integrated curriculum, so that students will become self-assured and responsible citizens.

Sylvan Shields, Director

1909 Bermuda High School
19 Richmond Road
Pembroke
Bermuda HM 08
1-441-295-6153
Fax: 1-441-295-2754
E-mail: info@bhs.bm
http://www.bhs.bm
This girls school offers an English-based curriculum for 620 total day students in grades 1-12.

Martina Harris, Primary Head
Jennifer Howarth, Primary Assistant

1910 Bermuda Institute-SDA
234 Middle Road
Southampton
Bermuda SN BX
441-238-1566
http://www.bermudainstitute.bm
The Bermuda Institute family exists to show children Jesus, nurture their love for Him and others, teach them to think, and empower them to serve.

Lois Tucker, Principal
Kathleen Allers, Elementary Vice Principal

1911 Bishop Anstey Junior School
Ariapita Road
Port of Spain
Trinidad and Tobago
868-624-1177
E-mail: admin@bishopansteyjunior.edu.tt
http://www.bishopansteyjunior.edu.tt
To stimulate learning within the spiritual, academic, social , cultural and sporting disciplines aimed at developing rounded individuals, within an environment that allows the flexibility to cope with the challenges of the changing education landscape.

Grace Campbell, Principal

1912 Capitol Christian School
C-11 #3 Urb Real Santo Domingo
Dominican Republic

Stacy Lee Blossom, Principal

1913 Ecole Flamboyant
PO Box 1744-A Schweitzer Hosp
Port-au-Prince
Haiti
509-381-141/2
Fax: 509-381-141
E-mail: has-pap@acn.com

William Dunn, Principal

1914 International School-Aruba
Wayaca 238 A
Aruba
Dutch Caribbean
297-845-365
Fax: 297-847-341
E-mail: info@isaruba.com
http://www.isaruba.com
A nonprofit, coeducational English-speaking day school serving students from prekindergarten to grade 12.

Paul D Sibley, Headmaster
Mary B Sibley, Academic Dean/Counselor

1915 International School-Curacao
PO Box 3090
Koninginnelaan Emmastad, Curacao
Netherlands Antilles
5-999-737-3633
Fax: 5-999-737-3142
E-mail: iscmec@attglobal.net
http://www.isc.an
Offers a rigorous academic program in order to prepare students planning to pursue higher learning at colleges and universities around the world. The School's curriculum includes International Baccalaureate (IB) coursework

that allows students the opportunity to receive the IB Diploma.
Margie Elhage PhD, Director
Rene Romer, President

1916 International School-West Indies
PO Box 278 Leeward
Providenciales
British West Indies

Alison Hodges, Principal

1917 Kingsway Academy
PO Box N-4378
Nassau
Bahamas
242-324-6887
Fax: 242-393-6917
http://www.kingswayacademy.com
Kingsway Academy endeavours to provide children with a sound education that is thoroughly Christian in its outlook and practices - Training Children in the King's Way .

Carol Harrison, Principal

1918 Mount Saint Agnes Academy
PO Box HM 1004
Hamilton HMDX
Bermuda
441-292-4134
Fax: 441-295-7265
E-mail: msaoffice@msa.bm
http://www.msa.bm
The Mission of Mount Saint Agnes Academy is to provide quality education in a caring, Christian environment. Belief in Christ and fidelity to the Roman Catholic Church form the foundation upon which all academic learning and social interaction take place. To this end we make a strong commitment to recognize each child as an individual and to help him/her to develop according to his/her own potential in order to become a responsible member of the community

Sue Moench, Principal
Margaret DiGiacomo, Assistant Principal

1919 Queens College
PO Box N7127
Nassau
Bahamas
242-393-1666
Fax: 242-393-3248
E-mail: info@qchenceforth.com
http://www.qchenceforth.com
Our interests lie not only in academic excellence but also in raising well-rounded, courteous, spiritually grounded global citizens.

Andrea Gibson, Principal

1920 Saltus Cavendish School
PO Box DV 209
Devonshire DV BX
Bermuda
441-236-3215
Fax: 441-292-0438
E-mail: head.cavendish@saltus.bm
http://www.saltus.bm
Saltus Grammar School is a co-educational, independent day school of excellent reputation. It is the premier independent school in Bermuda and is well known in the international community.

Susan Furr, Headteacher
Stephanie Queary, Secretary

1921 St. Andrew's School
16 Valleton Avenue
Marraval Trinidad West Indies
Trinidad and Tobago
868-622-2630
Fax: 868-628-1857
E-mail: principal@standrews.edu.tt
http://www.standrews.edu.tt

St. Andrew's is a progressive school that produces a caring, confident and responsible child. St. Andrew's also supports the development of social and moral values that allow the child to appreciate and respect diversity.

Sandra Farinha, Principal
Paula Moses, Vice Principal

1922 St. Anne's Parish School
PO Box SS6256
Nassau
Bahamas

Rev. Patrick Adderley, Principal

1923 St. John's College
PO Box N4858
Nassau
Bahamas

Arlene Ferguson, Principal

1924 St. Paul's Methodist College
PO Box F897
Freeport
Grand Bahamas

Annette Poitier, Principal

1925 Sunland Lutheran School
PO Box F2469
Freeport
Bahamas

J Pinder, Principal

1926 Tapion School
PO Box 511 La Toc
Castries, St Lucia
West Indies
758-452-2902
Fax: 758-453-0582
E-mail: tapionsch@candw.lc
http://tapionschool.com
The Tapion School will endeavour to produce individuals who would be empowered to meet the demands of a changing society.

Laurena Primus, Principal
Margaret Francois, Administration Officer

U.S. Branches

1927 Aisha Mohammed International School
Washington, DC 20521-1

Daryl Barker, Principal

1928 Albania Tirana International School
DOS/Administrative Officer
9510 Tirana Place
Washington, DC 20521-9510
E-mail: qsialb@albaniaonline.net
http://www1.qsi.org/alb
Provides a quality education in the English language for expatriates living in Tirana and Albanian citizens who want their children to be educated in English.

Scott D'Alterio, Director
Sotiraq Trebicka, Administrative Coordinator

1929 Alexander Muss High School Israel
78 Randall Avenue
Rockville Centre, NY 11570
212-472-9300
800-327-5980
Fax: 212-472-9301
E-mail: info@amiie.org
http://amiie.org
Provide a superior Israel education experience to learners of all ages in Israel and within communities throughout North America and abroad. The Institute promotes, builds and strengthens lifelong bonds between Jews and

Israel through education, experiences and understanding.

Gideon Shavit, CEO
Chaim Fischgrund, Headmaster

1930 Almaty International School
DOS/Administrative Officer
7030 Almaty Place
Washington, DC 20521-7030
E-mail: director@ais.almaty.kz
http://www.state.gov/www/about_state/schools/oalmaty.html
Grades preK-12, enrollment 169.

Robert B Draper, Director

1931 American School
Col Lomas del Guijarro Avenue Repœb
Tegucigalpa
Honduras 2134
504-239-3333
Fax: 504-239-6162
E-mail: eagurcia@amschool.org
http://www.amschool.org
Provides a student-centered, enriching, college-preparatory education that emphasizes social responsibility in a safe, bicultural, and disciplined learning environment.

Liliana F Jenkins, Superintendent
David Mendoza, Business Administrator

1932 American Cooperative School
Calle 10 y Pasaje Kantutas, Calacot
c/o American Embassy, La Paz, Bolivia
La Paz, Bolivia
519-2-792-302
Fax: 591-2-797-218
E-mail: acs@acslp.org
http://www.acslp.org
Offers college prepatory North American education that enables our graduates to enter the best universities in the United States, Canada, Europe and Latin America.

Matthew Kirby, Superintendent
Robert Boni, Chair

1933 American Cooperative School of Tunis
6360 Tunis Place
Washington, DC 20521-6360
216-71-760-905
Fax: 216-71-761-412
E-mail: acst@acst.intl.tn
http://www.acst.net

Dennis Sheehan, Superintendent

1934 American Embassy School
Department of State/AES
9000 New Delhi Place
Washington, DC 20521-9000
91-11-611-7140
Fax: 91-11-687-3320
E-mail: aesindia@aes.ac.in
http://www.serve.com/aesndi
Grade levels Pre-K through 12, school year August - May

Rob Mochrish, PhD, Director

1935 American Embassy School of New Delhi
Chandragupta Marg
Chanakyapuri, New Delhi
India 11002
91-11-611-7140
Fax: 91-11-687-3320
E-mail: aesindia@del2.vsnl.net.in
http://aes.ac.in/splash.php
Serves students from the United States and other nations. It provides a quality American education that enables students to be inspired learners and responsible global citizens

through the collaboration of a dedicated faculty and a supportive community.

Dr Robert Hetzel, Director
Linda McGinnis, Secretary, AES School Board

1936 American International School of Nouakchott
DOS/Administrative Officer
2430 Nouakchott Place
Washington, DC 20521-2430
222-2-52967
Fax: 222-2-52967
E-mail: aisnsahara@yahoo.com
http://www.aisn.mr
At the American International School of Nouakchott, a partnership of educators and parents is committed to providing our culturally diverse students a safe, nurturing and respectful learning environment. We promote academic achievement through a curriculum founded on an American educational philosophy.

Sharon Orlins PhD, Director

1937 American International School-Abuja
DOS/Administrative Officer
8300 Abuja Place
Washington, DC 20521-8300
234-9-413-4464
Fax: 234-9-413-4464
E-mail: info@aisabuja.com
http://www.aisabuja.com
Provide a quality education, utilizing an American curriculum for students of all nationalities from preschool through 12th grade.

Amy Uzoewulu, Director
Peter Williams, Primary Principal

1938 American International School-Bamako
DOS/Administrative Officer
2050 Bamako Place
Washington, DC 20189-2050
223-222-4738
Fax: 223-222-0853
E-mail: aisb@aisbmali.org
http://www.aisbmali.org
An independent, coeducational day school which offers an educational program from prekindergarten through grade 10. Supervised study using the University of Nebraska High School correspondence courses for grades 12 may also be arranged.

David Henry, Director
Rob Van Doeselaar, Chairman

1939 American International School-Chennai
100 Feet Road
Taramani
Chennai 600-113
91-44-499-0881
Fax: 91-44-466-0636
E-mail: HeadofSchool@aisch.org
http://www.aisch.org
Embraces international diversity and strives to provide an academically challenging environment in order to foster intellectual curiosity and a sense of responsibility in our students. To fully educate the whole person, we are committed to cultivating lifelong learners and balanced, service-oriented citizens, who are thereby prepared to positively contribute in a globally competitive world.

Barry Clough, Head of School
Dr James R Fellabaum, High School Principal

1940 American International School-Costa Rica
Interlink 249
PO Box 02-5635
Miami, FL 33102
506-229-3256
Fax: 506-223-9062
E-mail: ais@aiscr.com
http://www.aiscr.com
A private, non-profit school that was founded in 1970 under the name of Costa Rica Academy. AIS serves approximately 200 students from pre-school through 12th grade.

Austin Briggs Jr, Headmaster
Neli Santiago, Principal

1941 American International School-Freetown
Department of State/MGT
2160 Freetown Place
Washington, DC 20521-2160
232-22-232-480
Fax: 232-22-225-471
E-mail: aisfinfo@yahoo.com
http://www.aisfreetown.websiteanimal.com
A private, non-profit, PreK-8th grade school providing an American curriculum to a multinational community in Freetown, Sierra Leone.

Ndye Njie, Director
Nielette Gordon, Administrative Assistant

1942 American International School-Kingston
1a Olivier Road
Kingston 8
Jamaica
876-977-3625
Fax: 876-977-3625
E-mail: aiskoff@cwjamaica.com
http://www.aisk.com
A non-profit, non-sectarian, private day school funded by tuition income receiving small annual grants from the U.S. Government through it Office of Overseas Schools.

Sean Goudie, Director
Anna Wallace, Lower School Coordinator

1943 American International School-Lesotho
DOS/Administrative Officer
2340 Maseru Place
Washington, DC 20521-2340
266-322-987
Fax: 266-311-963
E-mail: aisl@lesoff.co.za
http://www.aisl.lesoff.co.za
An independent, coeducational day school which offers an American education from preschool through grade 8. The school was founded in 1991 to serve the needs of the American community and other students seeking an English-language education.

Harvey Cohen, Principal

1944 American International School-Libreville
2270 Libreville Place
Washington, DC 20521-2270
241-76-20-03
Fax: 241-74-55-07
E-mail: aisl@internetgabon.com

Paul Sicard, Director

1945 American International School-Lome
DOS/Administrative Officer
2300 Lome Place
Washington, DC 20521-2300
E-mail: aisl@cafe.tg
http://membres.lycos.fr/aisl
Established in 1967 as a private, coeducational day school offering an educa-

tional program to students of all nationalities in pre-kindergarten through grade 8.

Clover Afokpa, Director
Warace Tchamsi, Administrative Assistant

1946 American International School-Lusaka

PO Box 31617
Lusaka
Zambia
260-1-260-509
Fax: 260-1-260-538
E-mail: SpecialPerson@aislusaka.org
http://www.aislusaka.org
Committed to being a leading IB World School, offering a balanced, academically rigorous and internationally recognized college preparatory education.

Chris Muller, Director
Shirley Mee, Business Manager

1947 American International School-Mozambique

DOS/Administrative Officer
2330 Maputo Place
Washington, DC 20521-2330
258-1-49-1994
Fax: 258-1-49-0596
E-mail: aism@aism-moz.com

Don Reeser, Director

1948 American International School-N'Djamena

DOS/Administrative Officer
2410 N'Djamena Place
Washington, DC 20521-2410
235-52-2103
Fax: 235-51-5654
E-mail: aisn@intent.td

Gay Mickle, Director

1949 American International School-Nouakchott

2430 Nouakchott Place
Washington, DC 20521-2430
222-2-52967
Fax: 222-2-52967
E-mail: aisnsahara@yahoo.com
http://www.aisn.mr
Committed to provide culturally diverse students a safe, nurturing and respectful learning environment and promotes academic achievement through a curriculum founded on an American educational philosophy.

Sharon Orlins PhD, Director

1950 American Nicaraguan School

c/o American Embassy
Unit No 2710 Box 7, APO AA 34021
Washington, DC 20521-3240
505-278-0029
Fax: 505-267-3088
E-mail: director@ans.edu.ni
http://www.ans.edu.ni
A private, nonsectarian coeducaitonal day school which offers an educaional program from prekindergarten through grade 12 for students of all nationalities.

Fredy Ramirez, Elementary School Principal
Joseph Azmeh, Secondary Principal

1951 American Samoa Department of Education

Pago Pago
American Samoa 96799
011-684-633-5237
Fax: 011-684-633-5733
http://www.doe.as
Is to ensure student success by providing high quality teaching and learning opportunities to all our children

Sili K Sataua

1952 American School Honduras

American Embassy Tegucigalpa
Department of State
Washington, DC 20521-3480
504-239-333
Fax: 504-239-6162
A private, coeducational day school which offers an educational program from nursery through grade 12 for students of all nationalities.

James Szoka, Principal

1953 American School-Algiers

American Embassy Algiers
Washington, DC 20520-1
202-265-2800
Fax: 202-667-2174

Richard Gillogly, Principal

1954 American School-Antananarivo

2040 Antananarivo Place
Dulles, VA 20189-2040
261-20-22-420-39
Fax: 261-20-22-345-39
E-mail: miasaadm@gmail.com
http://www.asamadagascar.org
As the only English language institution in Madagascar offering a K-12 diploma program, we challenge our students to actively engage with the exceptional educational opportunities that are available to them in our school.

Jay Long, Director

1955 American School-Asuncion

Avenida Esapaa 1175
PO Box 10093
Asuncion, Paraguay
595-21-600-476
Fax: 595-21-603-518
E-mail: asagator@asa.edu.py
http://www.asa.edu.py
A bilingual learning community of International and Paraguayan families, is to prepare responsible proactive world citizens in a student-centered, caring environment through a college preparatory program that adheres to the highest U.S. and Paraguayan standards of excellence

Dennis Klumpp, Director
David Warken, Elementary Principal

1956 American School-Dschang

Washington, DC 20521-1

Jane French, Principal

1957 American School-Guatemala

11 Calle 1579 Zona 1511 calle 15-79
Guatemala
Guatemala
502-236- 079
Fax: 502-236- 833
E-mail: director@cag.edu.gt
http://www.cag.edu.gt
The school's goal is to educate independent, critical-thinking, responsible, bilingual individuals prepared to meet the challenges of the future.

Tracy Berry-Lazo, General Director
Fabio Corvaglia, High School Principal

1958 American School-Niamey

DOS/Administrative Officer
2420 Niamey Place
Dulles, VA 20189-2420
227-723-942
Fax: 227-723-457
E-mail: asniger@intnet.ne
http://www.geocities.com/asniamey

A coeducational day school offering an educational program from prekindergarten through grade 9, and 10-12 correspondence.

Deborah M Robinson, Director

1959 American School-Port Gentil

1100 Louisiana Street
Suite 2500
Houston, TX 77002-5215

Keith Marriott, Principal

1960 American School-Tegucigalpa

Coronel Lomas del Guijarro
Avenue Repœblica Dominicana Calle Costa
Tegucigalpa, Honduras
504-239-3333
Fax: 504-239-6162
http://www.amschool.org
Provides a Student Centered, enriching, college-preparatory education that emphasizes social responsibility in a safe, bicultural, and disciplined learning enviroment

James Shepherd, Principal
Liliana Jerkins, Superintendent

1961 American School-Warsaw

Ul Warszawska 202
Konstancin-Jeziorna
Poland 5520
48-22-651-9611
Fax: 48-22-642-1506
E-mail: admissions@asw.waw.pl
http://www.asw.waw.pl
Offers a rigorous, supportive and balanced PK-12 program in English for the international community of Warsaw that is driven by a strong commitment to prepare students for lives as responsible world citizens

Tony Gerlicz, Director
Rebecca Brown, Finance/Operations Director

1962 American School-Yaounde

BP 7475
Yaounde
Cameroon
234-223-0421
Fax: 237-223-6011
E-mail: school@asoy.org
http://asoy.org
Ensures that all students achieve high academic success, demonstrate critical thinking skills, and become responsible and compassionate, global citizens prepared for their next stage in life; as gained through an enriched, American curriculum and offered in a challenging, secure, and diverse environment.

Nanci Shaw, School Director

1963 American-Nicaraguan School

Frente al Club Lomas de Monserrat
PO Box 2670, Managua
Nicaragua
505-2-782-565
Fax: 505-2-673-088
E-mail: elementary@ans.edu.ni
http://www.ans.edu.ni
Provides its multicultural student community with a US-accredited college preparatory program, based on democratic and universal values, that develops critical thinkers and ethical individuals capable of realizing their leadership potential by making meaningful contributions to society.

Stan Key, Director General
Roberto Cardenal, Director of Finance

1964 Amoco Galeota School

PO Box 4381
Houston, TX 77210-4381

Barbara Punch, Principal

1965 Andersen Elementary & Middle School
Unit 14057
APO, Mariana Islands 96543 4057
Guam

1966 Anzoategui International School
PO Box 020010, M-42
Jet Cargo International
Miami, FL 33102-10
58-82-22683
Fax: 58-82-22683
E-mail: aishead@telcel.net.ve
http://www.anaco.net
Grade levels Pre-K through 12, school year
August - June

Jorge Nelson EdD, Superintendent

1967 Armenia QSI International School-Yerevan
DOS/Administrative Officer
7020 Yerevan Place
Washington, DC 20521-7020
374-1-391-030
Fax: 374-1-151-438
E-mail: qsiy@arminco.com
An independent, coeducational day school which offers an educational program from preschool (3-4 years) through grade 12 for students of all nationalities. Enrollment 45.

Arthur W Hudson, Director

1968 Atlanta International School
2890 N Fulton Drive NE
Atlanta, GA 30305-3155
404-841-3840
Fax: 404-841-3873
E-mail: info@aischool.org
http://www.aischool.org
Continuing to develop and deserve a worldwide reputation as an exemplary center of teaching and learning, a school that achieves and sets, within the framework of the International Baccalaureate.Maintaining an optimal size composition of faculty and students so that opportunities for individual learning, mutual understanding, and community feeling are maximized.

Robert Brindley, Headmaster
Charlotte Smith, Executive Assistant

1969 Awty International School
7455 Awty School Lane
Houston, TX 77055-7222
713-686-4850
Fax: 713-686-4956
E-mail: admissions@awty.org
http://www.awty.org
Grade level prekindergarten through twelfth, with total enrollment of 900 students.

David Watson, Headmaster
John Ransom, Chairman

1970 Azerbaijan Baku International School
Darnagul Qasabasi Street Ajami Nakc
Block 3097
Baku, Azerbaijan 1108
994-12-90-63-52
Fax: 994-12-90-63-51
E-mail: baku@qsi.org
http://www.qsi.org
the primary purpose of the school is to meet the needs of the children in Baku who require this type of education with a view to continuing their education in their home countries with a minimum of adjustment problems.

Scott Root, Director

1971 Baku International School
Darnagul Qasabasi Street Ajami Nakc
Block 3097
Baku, Azerbaijan, AZ 1108
994-12-656352
Fax: 991-12-4105951

E-mail: baku@qsi.org
http://www.qsi.org
the primary purpose of the school is to meet the needs of the children in Baku who require this type of education with a view to continuing their education in their home countries with a minimum of adjustment problems.

Scott Root, Director

1972 Ball Brothers Foundation
222 S Mulberry Street
Muncie, IN 47305
765-741-5500
Fax: 765-741-5518
E-mail: info@ballfdn.org
http://www.ballfdn.org
The Foundation's primary focus is Muncie and East Central Indiana.The Foundation has been a philanthropic leader, serving as initiator, convener, and catalyst among donors and nonprofit organizations. Within Muncie, the Foundation seeks to forge active partnerships with effective nonprofit agencies by providing consultation and financial support to promote their success.

Jud Fisher, Executive Director/ COO
John W Fisher, Chairman & President

1973 Banjul American Embassy School
2070 Banjul Place
Dulles, VA 20189-2070
220-495-920
Fax: 220-497-181
E-mail: baes@qanet.gm
http://www.baes.gm
The school demonstrates U.S. education abroad to a multi-ethnic, multi-cultural, diverse student body and otherwise increases mutual understanding through its emphasis on an American-based curriculum, use of American textbooks and supplemental materials, and its teaching staff, of whom four are American nationals trained in American universities.

Dianne Zemichael, Director
Leah Moore, Administrative Secretary

1974 Bingham Academy Ethiopia
SIM International
PO Box 4937
Addis Ababa, Ethiopia
East Africa
251-11 -791
Fax: 251-11 -791
E-mail: director@binghamacademy.net
http://www.binghamacademy.net
The purpose of Bingham Academy is to provide high quality, culturally sensitive education, within a Christian environment, which challenges each student to impact the world for God's glory.

Murray Overton, Director

1975 Bishkek International School
14A Tynystanova Street
Bishkek
Kyrgyzstan 72005
996-312-66-35-03
Fax: 996-312-66-35-03
E-mail: bishkek@qsi.org
http://www.qsi.org
The primary purpose of the school is to meet the needs of the children in Bishkek who require this type of education with a view to continuing their education in their home countries with a minimum of adjustment problems.

MaryKay Gudkova, Director

1976 Bosnia-Herzegovina QSI InternationalSchool Sarajevo
Omladinska #12
Vogosca-Saravejo
Bosnia & Herzegovina 71320

387-33-434-756
Fax: 387-33-434-756
E-mail: saravejo@qsi.org
http://www.qsi.org
The primary purpose of the school is to meet the needs of the expatriate children living in Sarajevo who require this type of education.

Jay Hamric, Director

1977 Bratislava American International School
American Embassy Bratislava
Karloveska 64
Bratislava
Slovak Republic 842-2
421-7-722-844
Fax: 721-7-722-844
E-mail: bratislava@qsi.org
http://www.qsi.sk
The primary purpose of the school is to meet the needs of the children in Bratislava who require this type of education with a view to continuing their education in their home countries with a minimum of adjustment problems.

Ronald Adams, Principal
Matthew Lake, Director

1978 Bulgaria Anglo-American School-Sofia
DOS/Administrative Officer
5740 Sophia Place
Washington, DC 20521-5740
359-2-974-4575
Fax: 359-2-974-4483
E-mail: aasregist@infotel.bg
http://www.geocities.com/angloamericanschool
An independent, coeducational day school which offers an educational program from prekindergarten through grade 8 for students of all nationalities. The school year comprises 2 semesters extending from August to December and from January to June. Enrollment 140.

Brian M Garton, Director

1979 Burma International School Yangon
DOS/Administrative Officer
4250 Rangoon Place
Washington, DC 20521-4250
95-1-512-793/795
Fax: 95-1-525-020
E-mail: ISYDIRECTOR@mptmail.net.mm
Grades PK-12, enrollment 331.

Merry Wade, Director

1980 Burns Family Foundation
410 N Michigan Avenue
Room 1600
Chicago, IL 60611-4213
Offers support in secondary school education, higher education and youth services.

1981 Caribbean American School
5 Gates Court
Cranbury, NJ 8512-2926

Ernestine Rochelle, Principal

1982 Caribbean-American School
PO Box 407139
Lynx Air
Ft Lauderdale, FL 33340-7139
509-257-7961
Grade levels Pre-K through 12, school year
September - June

Ernestine Roche Robinson, Director

1983 Chinese American International School
150 Oak Street
San Francisco, CA 94102
415-865-6000
Fax: 415-865-6089

E-mail: caishead@aol.com
http://www.cais.org
Educates students for academic excellence, moral character and international perspective through immersion in American and Chinese culture and language.

Andrew W Corcoran, Executive Director

1984 Colegio Albania
PO Box 25573
Miami, FL 33102-5573

Eric Spindler, Principal

1985 Colegio Corazon de Maria
Ferrer y Ferrer-Santiago Igles
San Juan
Puerto Rico

M Cyril Stauss, Principal

1986 Colegio De Parvulos
263 Calle San Sebastian
San Juan 00901-1205
Puerto Rico

Maria Dolores Vice, Principal

1987 Colegio Del Buen Pastor
Camino Alejandrino Km 3.4
Rio Piedras 00927
Puerto Rico

Adria M Borges, Principal

1988 Colegio Del Sagrado Corazon
Obispado Final Urb La Alhambra
Ponce 00731
Puerto Rico

Joan G Dedapena, Principal

1989 Colegio Espiritu Santo
Box 191715 San Juan
Puerto Rico 19-1715
787-754-0555
Fax: 754-715-
E-mail: admision@colespiritusanto.com
http://www.colespiritusanto.com

Carmen Jovet, Principal

1990 Colegio Inmaculada
Carr Militar 2 Km 49.6
Manati 00674
Puerto Rico

Sor Nichlasa Maderea, Principal

1991 Colegio Inmaculada Concepcion
2 Calle Isabela
Guayanilla 00656-1703
Puerto Rico

Sor Alejandrina Torres, Principal

1992 Colegio Internacional-Carabobo
VLN 1010
PO Box 025685
Miami, FL 33102-5685
58-41-421-807
Fax: 58-41-426-510
E-mail: admin@cic-valencia.org.ve
http://www.cic-valencia.org.ve
To develop young men and women of character through an international college-preparatory program, in English, based on high intellectual and moral standards

Frank Anderson, Superintendent
Joe Walker, Director

1993 Colegio Internacional-Caracas
PAKMAIL 6030
PO Box 025323
Miami, FL 33102-5304
58-2-945-0444
Fax: 58-2-945-0533
E-mail: cic@cic-caracas.org
http://www.cic-caracas.org

Colegio Internacional de Caracas is an English-medium, Pre-Nursery to Grade 12 school dedicated to the intellectual and personal development of each student in a caring and supportive environment. CIC offers a challenging program to prepare an international student body to excel in a variety of the world's finest schools and universities.

Alan Benson, Superintendent
Carmen Sweeting, Director of Academics

1994 Colegio Internacional-Puerto La Cruz
11010 NW 30th Street
Suite 104
Miami, FL 33172-5032
58-281-277-6051
Fax: 58-281-274-1134
E-mail: ciplc@telcel.net.ve
http://www.ciplc.net
Inspiring students to learn and serve by cultivating each student's full potential as an effective communicator, problem solver, and contributing global citizen.

Mike Martell, Superintendent
Frank Capuccio, Administrative Assistant

1995 Colegio La Inmaculada
1711 Ave Ponce De Leon
San Juan 00909-1905
Puerto Rico

Sor Teresa Del Rio, Principal

1996 Colegio La Milagrosa
107 Calle De Diego
San Juan 00925-3303
Puerto Rico

Maria Flores, Principal

1997 Colegio Lourdes
Box 190847
San Juan, PR 919-847
787-767-6106
Fax: 787-767-5282
E-mail: clourdes@coqui.net
http://www.colegiolourdes.net
Forming strong Christian faith and critical, able to make a commitment within the society and the church that is open to the realities and needs of his time, able to integrate into an attitude of service in a democratic society, as understand and explain the Preamble to the Constitution of Puerto Rico.

Paz Asiain, Director
Thalia Lopez, Principal

1998 Colegio Madre Cabrini
1564 Calle Encarnacion
San Juan 00920-4739
Puerto Rico

Anne Marie Gavin, Principal

1999 Colegio Maria Auxiliadora
PO Box 797
Carolina 00986-0797
Puerto Rico

Leles Rodriguez, Principal

2000 Colegio Marista
Final Santa Ana Alt Torrimar
Guaynabo 00969
Puerto Rico

Hilario Martinez, Principal

2001 Colegio Marista El Salvador
PO Box 462
Manati 00674-0462
Puerto Rico

Hnio Efrain Romo, Principal

2002 Colegio Mater Salvatoris
RR 3 Box 3080
San Juan 00926-9601
Puerto Rico

Maria Luisa Benito, Principal

2003 Colegio Notre Dame Nivel
PO Box 967
Caguas 00726-0967
Puerto Rico

Francisca Suarez, Principal

2004 Colegio Nuestra Senora de La Caridad
PO Box 1164
Caparra Heigh 00920
Puerto Rico

Madre Esperanza Sanchez, Principal

2005 Colegio Nuestra Senora de La Merced
PO Box 4048
San Juan 00936-4048
Puerto Rico

Ivette Lopez, Principal

2006 Colegio Nuestra Senora de Lourdes
1050 Demetrio Odaly-Country Club
Rio Piedras 00924
Puerto Rico

Rita Manzano, Principal

2007 Colegio Nuestra Senora de Valvanera
53 Calle Jose I Quinton # 53
Coamo 00769-3108
Puerto Rico

Cruz Victor Colon, Principal

2008 Colegio Nuestra Senora del Carmen
RR 2, Box 9KK, Carr Trujillo Alt
Rio Piedras 00721
Puerto Rico

Candida Arrieta, Principal

2009 Colegio Nuestra Senora del Pilar
PO Box 387
Canovanas 00729-0387
Puerto Rico

Sor Leonilda Mallo, Principal

2010 Colegio Nuestra Senora del Rosario
Aa7 Calle 5
Bayamon 00959-3719
Puerto Rico

Theresita Miranda, Principal

2011 Colegio Nuestra Sra del Rosario
PO Box 1334
Ciales 00638-0414
Puerto Rico
787-871-1318
Fax: 787-871-5797
Parrochial School - Prekindergarten to 9th grade.

Angel Mendoza, Principal
Padre Gabriel M Jorres, Director

2012 Colegio Padre Berrios
PO Box 7717
San Juan 00916-7717
Puerto Rico

Sor Enedina Santos, Principal

2013 Colegio Parroquial San Jose
PO Box 1386
Aibonito 00705-1386
Puerto Rico

Maria Maria Malave, Principal

2014 Colegio Ponceno
Coto Laurel, Puerto Rico 644

809-848-2525
Rev. Jose A Basols, MA, Principal

2015 Colegio Puertorriqueno de Ninas
Calle Turquessa 208
Golden Gate
Guaynabo, PR 968
787-782-2618
Fax: 787-782-8370
E-mail: Info@cpnpr.org
http://www.cpnpr.org
Ivette Nÿter, School Director
Millie Suau, Principal

2016 Colegio Reina de Los Angeles
M-19 Calle Frontera
San Juan, PR 926
787-761-7455
Fax: 787-761-7440
E-mail: info@reinaangeles.org
http://www.reinaangeles.org
Train Students education with a focus on physical, moral, intellectual, religious and social development within a framework of faith.
Victorina Ortega, Principal
Juana F Gomez, Director

2017 Colegio Rosa Bell
Calle Oviedo Number 42
Torrimar-Guaynabo, PR 966
787-781-4240
Fax: 787-792-5415
E-mail: exalumno@rosabell.com
http://rosabell.wordpress.com
The purpose of a good education is to maximize the capabilities of the individual: intellectually, socially, emotionally and physically.
Rose Rodriquez, Director
Miguel Arzola-Barris, Executive Director

2018 Colegio Sacred Heart
Palma Real Urb, Univ Gardens
San Juan 00927
Puerto Rico
Paul Marie, CSB, Principal

2019 Colegio Sagrada Familia
7 Hostos
Ponce
Puerto Rico 731
Sor Pilar Becerra, Principal

2020 Colegio Sagrados Corazones
A Esmeralda Urb, Ponce De Leon
Guaynabo 00969
Puerto Rico

http://home.coqui.net/sagrado
Ana Arce de Marrer, Principal

2021 Colegio San Agustin
PO Box 4263
Bayamon 00958-1263
Puerto Rico
Georgina Ortiz, Principal

2022 Colegio San Antonio
PO Box 21350
San Juan 00928-1350
Puerto Rico
809-764-0090
Rev. Paul S Brodie, Principal

2023 Colegio San Antonio Abad
PO Box 729
Humacao 00792-0729
Puerto Rico
Padre Eduardo Torrella, Principal

2024 Colegio San Benito
PO Box 728
Humacao 00792-0728
Puerto Rico
Hermana Carmen Davila, Principal

2025 Colegio San Conrado (K-12)
PO Box 7111
Ponce 00732-7111
Puerto Rico
Fax: 787-841-7303
E-mail: sanconrado@pucpr.edu
Sister Nildred Rodriguez, Principal
Sister Wilma de Echevarria, Assistant Principal

2026 Colegio San Felipe
566 Ave San Luis # 673
Arecibo 00612-3600
Puerto Rico
809-878-3532
Veronica Oravec, Principal

2027 Colegio San Francisco De Asis
PO Box 789
Barranquitas
Puerto Rico 794
787-857-2123
Fax: 787-857-2123
E-mail: info@csfabarranquitas.com
http://www.csfabarranquitas.com
Founded in August 7, 1985
Hermana Maria Carbonell, Principal
Carlos Colon-Bernadi, Director

2028 Colegio San Gabriel
Gpo Box 347
San Juan 00936
Puerto Rico
Sor Antonia Garatachea, Principal

2029 Colegio San Ignacio de Loyola
Urb Santa Mar-a, 1940 Calle Sæceo
San Juan
Puerto Rico 927
787-765-3814
Fax: 787-758-4145
http://www.sanignacio.org
Dr Luis O Pino, Principal
Mario Alberto Torres, President

2030 Colegio San Jose
PO Box 21300
San Juan
Puerto Rico 928-1300
787-751-8177
Fax: 787-767-7146
E-mail: sanjose@csj-rpi.org
http://www.csj-rpi.org
Bro Francisco T Gonzalez, Principal
Sra Elaine Torrens, Vice Principal

2031 Colegio San Juan Bautista
PO Box E
Orocovis 00720
Puerto Rico
Sor Maria Antonia Miya, Principal

2032 Colegio San Juan Bosco
PO Box 14367
San Juan 00916-4367
Puerto Rico
Rev. P Jose Luis Gomez, Principal

2033 Colegio San Luis Rey
43 Final SE, Urb Reparto Metro
San Juan 00921
Puerto Rico
Rosario Maria, Principal

2034 Colegio San Miguel
GPO Box 1714
San Juan 00936
Puerto Rico
Elvira Gonzalez, Principal

2035 Colegio San Rafael
PO Box 301
Quebradillas 00678-0301
Puerto Rico

2036 Colegio San Vicente Ferrer
PO Box 455
Catano 00963-0455
Puerto Rico
Maria Soledad Colon, Principal

2037 Colegio San Vicente de Paul
Calle Bolivar 709, Parada 24
San Juan
Puerto Rico 909
787-727-4273
Fax: 787-728-2263
http://www.csvp-sj.org
Dra Isabel C Machado, Principal
P Evaristo Oliveras, Director

2038 Colegio Santa Clara
Via 14-2JL-456 Villa Fontana
Carolina 00983
Puerto Rico
Elsie Mujica, Principal

2039 Colegio Santa Cruz
PO Box 235
Trujillo Alto 00977-0235
Puerto Rico
Maria Ramon Santiago, Principal

2040 Colegio Santa Gema
PO Box 1705
Carolina 00984-1705
Puerto Rico
Lilia Luna De Anaya, Principal

2041 Colegio Santa Rita
Calle 9, Apartado 1557
Bayamon 00958
Puerto Rico
Elba N Villalba, Principal

2042 Colegio Santa Rosa
Calle Marti, 15 Esquina Maceo
Bayamon 00961
Puerto Rico
Ana Josefa Colon, Principal

2043 Colegio Santa Teresita
342 Victoria
Ponce 00731
Puerto Rico
Mary Terence, Principal

2044 Colegio Santiago Apostol
Calle 23 Bloque 23 #17, Urb Sierra
Bayamon
Puerto Rico 961
787-786- 917
Fax: 787-269-3965
E-mail:
colegiosantiagoapostol@onlinkpr.net
http://www.colegiosantiagoapostol.net
Hilda Velazquez, Principal

2045 Colegio Santisimo Rosario
PO Box 26
Yauco 00698-0026
Puerto Rico
Judith Negron, Principal

2046 Colegio Santo Domingo
192 Calle Comerio
Bayamon 00959-5358
Puerto Rico

Pura Huyke, Principal

2047 Colegio Santo Nino de Praga
PO Box 25
Penuelas 00624-0025
Puerto Rico

Aminta Santos, Principal

2048 Colegio Santos Angeles Custod
3 Sicilia Urb, San Jose
San Juan 00923
Puerto Rico

Roberto Rivera, Principal

2049 Colegio de La Salle
PO Box 518
Bayamon 00960-0518
Puerto Rico

Wilfredo Perez De, Principal

2050 Commandant Gade Special Education School
St. Thomas, Virgin Islands 801

Miss Jeanne Richards, Principal

2051 Community United Methodist School
PO Box 681
Frederiksted 00841-0681
Virgin Islands

Marva Oneal, Principal

2052 Country Day
RR 1 Box 6199
Kingshill, VI 850
340-778-1974
Fax: 340-779-3331
E-mail: bsinfield@stxcountryday.com
http://www.stxcountryday.com
An independent, multicultural, college preparatory educational community set on a 34-acre tropical campus.

William Sinfield, Headmaster
Mariska Nurse, Dean of Guidance

2053 Croatia American International School-Zagreb
Vocarska 106
10 000 Zagreb
Croatia-5080
385-1-4680-133
Fax: 385-1-4680-171
E-mail: asz@asz.hr
http://www.aisz.hr
Grades K-8, enrollment 112.

Robin Heslip, Director

2054 Dallas International School
6039 Churchill Way
Dallas, TX 75230
972-991-6379
Fax: 972-991-6608
E-mail: rwkdis@metronet.com
http://www.dallasinternationalschool.org
DIS students will have the skills to continue their studies at universities in the United States or abroad and launch a professional career which will take advantage of all the opportunities created by globalization

Mea Ahlberg, Director of Admissions
MylSne Dumont, Middle School Coordinator

2055 Dominican Child Development Center
PO Box 5668
Agana
Guam 96910
617-477-7228
Fax: 671-472-4782

Kindergarten and nursery school.

Lednor Flores, Principal

2056 Dorado Academy
Urb Dorado del Mar Calle Madre Perl
Dorado
Puerto Rico 646
787-796-2180
Fax: 787-796-7398
E-mail: mescabi@doradoacademy.org
http://www.doradoacademy.org
Its objective is to provide to all students an education that reflects the school's philosophy. The teachers strive to implement by instruction the school's philosophy and meet instructional goals and objectives.

Liutma Caballero, Principal
Nancy Escabi, Headmaster

2057 Dwight School
291 Central Park W
New York, NY 10024
212-724-7524
Fax: 212-724-2539
E-mail: admissions@dwight.edu
http://www.dwight.edu
Dwight's rigorous IB program and world-class faculty prepare a future generation of well-educated and ethical global leaders who will seek to create an environment of equality and respect for all human beings.

Marina Bernstein, Director Admissions
Alyson Waldman, Associate Director

2058 Educare
4235 Reserve Road
Unit 202
Lexington, KY 40514
859-396-7087
Fax: 859-201-1064
E-mail: mnaidu@educare.org
http://www.educare.org
To inspire children to achieve their very best; to educate children in character and leadership by drawing out their hidden character traits and leadership qualities.

Sara Connell, Principal

2059 Episcopal Cathedral School
PO Box 13305
Santurce
Puerto Rico 908-3305
787-721-5478
Fax: 787-724-6668
E-mail: esc@gocougars.com
http://www.gocougars.com
Founded in 1946.

Gary J DeHope, Director

2060 Escole Tout Petit
PO Box 1248
San Juan 00902
Puerto Rico

Vivian Aviles, Principal

2061 Escuela Beata Imelda
PO Box 804
Guanica 00653-0804
Puerto Rico

P Salvador Barber, Principal

2062 Escuela Bella Vista
Avenido Cecilio Acosta Calle 67 Ent
Maracaibo
Venezuela
58-61-966-696
Fax: 58-61-969-417
E-mail: ebvnet@ebv.org.ve
http://www.ebv.org.ve
At EBV we offer an internationally enriched accredited U.S. program that prepares our students to participate actively, independently, cooperatively, and effectively in a multicul-

tural, multilingual world. It is our commitment to educate each student to his/her maximum potential.

Steve Sibley, Superintendent
Todd Zukewich, High School Principal

2063 Escuela Campo Alegre
8424 NW 56th Street
Suite CCS 00007
Miami, FL 33166
58-2-993-3230
Fax: 58-2-993-0219
E-mail: info@eca.com.ve
http://www.eca.com.ve
ECA seeks to inspire its students toward the highest standards and expectations through a stimulating and comprehensive program of intellectual and personal development.

Bambi Betts, Director

2064 Escuela Campo Alegre-Venezuela
8424 NW 56th Street
Suite CCS00007
Miami, FL 33166
58-2-993-7135
Fax: 58-2-993-0219
E-mail: info@eca.com.ve
A private, coeducational day school offering a program for students from prekindergarten through grade 12.

Dr. Forest Broman, Principal

2065 Escuela Caribe Vista School
New Horizon-100 S & 350 E
Marion, IN 46953
765-668-4009

Phil Redwine, Principal

2066 Escuela Las Morochas
Apartado Postal # 235
Ciudad Ojeda, Estado Zulia
Venezuela
58-265-6315-539
Fax: 58-265-6315-539
E-mail: jtrudeau@escuelalasmorochas.com
http://www.escuela-lasmorochas.com
Escuela Las Morochas is an English medium international school that offers a challenging U.S. education that encourages students to be life-long learners and responsible global citizens.

Jeff Trudeau, Director
Zulay Marcano, Assistant Secretary

2067 Escuela Nuestra Senora Del Carmen
PO Box 116, Playa De Ponce
Ponce 00731
Puerto Rico 731

Paquita Alvarado, Principal

2068 Escuela Superior Catolica
PO Box 4245
Bayamon 00958-1245
Puerto Rico

Eledis Diaz, Principal

2069 Evangelical School for the Deaf
HC-01 Buzon 7111
Luquillo
Puerto Rico 773-9602
787-889-3488
866-928-2836
E-mail: esdluquillo@gmail.com
http://www.esdluquillo.com
We believe that it is the obligation of the saved to witness by life and by words to the truths of Scripture, and to seek to proclaim the Gospel to all mankind.

Pamela Eadie, Principal
Hector Saroza, President

2070 Fajardo Academy
55 Calle Federico Garcia
PO Box 1146, Fajardo 00648
Puerto Rico
809-863-1001
http://fajardoacademy.org
Miguel A Rivera, BA, MA, MEd, Principal

2071 Freewill Baptist School
PO Box 6265
Christiansted 00823-6265
Virgin Islands
Joe Postlewaite, Principal

2072 French-American International School
150 Oak Street
San Francisco, CA 94102
415-558-2000
Fax: 415-558-2024
E-mail: fais@fais-ihs.org
http://www.fais-ihs.org
Grade levels preK-12, with total student enrollment of 813.
Jane Camblin, Head of School

2073 George D Robinson School
5 Nairn Condado
Santurce 00907
Puerto Rico
Daniel W Sheehan, Principal

2074 Georgetown American School
3170 Georgetown Place
Washington, DC 20521-3170
592-225-1595
Fax: 592-226-1459
E-mail: admin@amschoolguyana.net
http://www.geocities.com/Athens/Atlantis/6811
Thurston Riehl, Director

2075 Georgia QSI International School-Tbilisi
Village Zurgovani
Tbilisi
Republic of Georgia
995-32-982909
Fax: 995-32-322-607
E-mail: tbilisi@qsi.org
http://www.qsi.org/grg_home
A private non-profit organization, organizes and operates schools of excellence, identifies quality educators for these schools, and provides educational consulting services
Merry Wade, Director
Manana Parulava, Coordinator

2076 Glynn Christian School
Club 6, Christian Hill
St Croix, Kingshill 00851
Virgin Islands
Muriel Francis, Principal

2077 Good Hope School-St. Croix
Estate Good Hope Frederiksted
St Croix 00840
Virgin Islands
Tanya L Nichols, Principal

2078 Good Shepherd School
PO Box 1069
St Croix, Kingshill 00851
Virgin Islands 851
340-772-2280
Fax: 340-772-1021
Mary Ellen Mcencil, Director
Susan P Eversley, Assistant Director

2079 Grace Baptist Academy
7815 Shallowford Road
Chattanooga, TN 37421

423-892-8223
Fax: 423-892-1194
E-mail: jmccurdy@gracechatt.org
http://www.gracechatt.org
Helen Yasper, Principal

2080 Guam Adventist Academy
1200 Aguilar Road
Yoa
Guam 96915
617-789-1515
Fax: 617-789-3547
E-mail: Office@GAAsda.org
http://www.gaasda.org
Learn about God and His character through Bible study, aided by the study of nature and E.G. White's writings. Develop a personal friendship with Jesus Christ
John N Youngberg, Principal
Dori Talon, Accountant

2081 Guam Department of Education
PO Box DE
Hagatna, Guam 96932
011-671-475-0457
Fax: 011-671-472-5003
Develop a personal friendship with Jesus Christ
Rosie R Tainatongo, Director

2082 Guam High School
PSC 455 Box 192
FPO, Mariana Islands 96540 1192
Guam

2083 Guam S Elementary & Middle School
PSC 455 Box 168
FPO
Mariana Islands, Guam 96540-1054

2084 Guamani School
PO Box 3000
Guayama
Puerto Rico 785
787-864-6880
Fax: 787-866-4947
E-mail: edelgado@guamani.com
http://www.guamani.com
A private non-profit, co-educational, non-sectarian school committed in offering an English-based academic college preparatory program geared in preparing students to become knowledgeable and responsible individuals for today's changing society.
Eduardo Delgado, Director
Pedro A Dominguez, Administrator

2085 Harvest Christian Academy
PO Box 23189
Barrigada
Guam 96921
671-477-6341
Fax: 671-477-7136
http://www.harvestministries.net
Harvest Christian Academy is a K-12th grade school. It is a ministry of Harvest Baptist Church.
John McGraw, Principal

2086 Hogar Colegio La Milagrosa
Ave Cotto 987 Barrio Cotto
Arecibo 00612
Puerto Rico 612
Sor Trinidad Ibizarry, Principal

2087 India American Embassy School-New Delhi
Chandragupta Marg Chanakyapuri
New Delhi
India 11002
91-11-611-7140
Fax: 91-11-687-3320
E-mail: aesindia@aes.ac.in
http://aes.ac.in

The American Embassy School serves students from the United States and other nations. It provides a quality American education that enables students to be inspired learners and responsible global citizens through the collaboration of a dedicated faculty and a supportive community.
Bob Hetzel, Director

2088 India American International School-Bombay
6240 Mumbai Place
Dulles, VA 20189
91-22-652-1837
Fax: 91-22-652-1838
E-mail: personnel@asbindia.org
http://www.asbindia.org
We inspire all of our students to continuous inquiry, empowering them with the skills, courage, optimism, and integrity to pursue their dreams and enhance the lives of others.
Paul M Fochtman, Superintendent
Julie A Cox, Elementary School Principal

2089 Inter-American Academy
Suite 8227
6964 NW 50th Street
Miami, FL 33166-5632
593-4-871-790
Fax: 593-4-873-358
E-mail: bgoforth@acig.k12.ec
http://www.acig.k12.ec
Dr. Bruce Goforth, Executive Director

2090 International Community School-Abidjan
DOS/Administrative Officer
2010 Abidjan Place
Washington, DC 20521-2010
225-22-47-11-52
Fax: 225-22-47-19-96
E-mail: rmockrish@icsa.ac.ci
http://www.icsa.ac.ci
American style curriculum from kindergarten through grade 12 for children of all nationalities.
Rob Mockrish, Director

2091 International High School-Yangon
4250 Rangoon Place
Department of State
Washington, DC 20521-4250
95-1-512-793
Fax: 95-1-525-020
E-mail: isydirector@mptmail.net.mm
Merry Wade, Director

2092 International School of Port-of-Spain
#POS 1369 1601 NW 97th Avenue
PO Box 025307
Miami, FL 33102-5307
868-632-4591
Fax: 868-632-4595
E-mail: elarson@isps.edu.tt
http://www.isps.edu.tt
ISPS will provide an outstanding educational programme for both international and resident families who want their children to pursue higher education.
Eric Larson, Director
John Horsfall, High School Principal

2093 International School-Conakry
2110 Conakry Place
Washington, DC 20521-2110
224-12-661-535
Fax: 224-41-15-22
E-mail: isc@biasy.net
http://www.iscguinea.org
A private, coeducational school offering an educational program from pre-kindergarten through grade 12 for children from expatriate and host country families. Develop pupils' ac-

ademic knowledge; learning, thinking, social, and communication skills; international attitudes; and appreciation for cultural diversity.

Greg Hughes, Director
Robert Merritt, Management Officer

2094 International School-Dakar
BP 5136
Dakar
Senegal
221-33 -25 0
Fax: 221-33 -25 5
E-mail: admin_isd@orange.sn
http://www.isd.sn
An independent English-medium international school, which offers, in a nurturing environment, a rigorous, US-based, PK-12 curriculum enriched to reflect the needs and diversity of its international student body and faculty.

Wayne Rutherford, Director

2095 International School-Grenada
Washington, DC 20521-1

Mary Delaney Dunn, Principal

2096 International School-Havana
Department of State
18 Street, 315 and 5th Avenue
Miramar, Havana City
Cuba 10600
53 - 20-2818
Fax: 53 - 20-2740
E-mail: office@ish.co.cu
http://www.ishav.org
The school offer high quality education to the children of the expatriate community in Cuba. Serves and can admit students who have a foreign (non-Cuban) citizenship, and are temporarily living in Cuba with their parent(s) or guardian(s), and as such form part of the diplomatic or expatriate non-diplomatic community in the country.

Ian Morris, Principal
Richard Fluit, Head, Secondary School

2097 International School-Islamabad
H-9/1, PO Box 1124
Islamabad
Pakistan 44000
92-51-434-950
Fax: 92-51-440-193
E-mail: school@isoi.edu.pk
http://www.isoi.edu.pk
Offers an American- based curriculum to students of over 29 nationalities.

Rose C Puffer, Superintendent

2098 International School-Ouagadougou
s/c Ambassade des, Etats Unis
01 BP35, Ouagadougou
Burkina Faso
226-36-21-43
Fax: 226-36-22-28
E-mail: iso@iso.bf
http://www.iso.bf
ISO strives to cultivate a student's intellect and character in an English-speaking environment, offering strong academic programs and promoting cultural understanding.

Larry Ethier, Director
Kim Overton, Curriculum Coordinator

2099 International School-Port of Spain
1601 NW 97th Avenue
PO Box 025307
Miami, FL 33102-5307
868-633-4777
Fax: 868-632-4595
E-mail: elarson@isps.edu.tt
http://www.isps.edu.tt
Provides a college preparatory, holistic education for children in grades pre-kindergarten through grade 12, providing them with the

skills, knowledge, and values necessary to be productive individuals in an interdependent world.

Eric Larson, Director
Jackie Fung-Kee-Fung, Admission Director/PR

2100 International School-Sfax
Brit Gas 1100 Louisiana
Houston, TX 77002

Sidney Norris, Principal

2101 International School-Yangon
20 Shwe Taungyar
Bahan Township, Yangon
Myanmar-1
512-93 -
Fax: 95 - 52-020
E-mail: director@isy.net.mm
http://www.isy.net.mm
We inspire students with a challenging, international education, based on an American curriculum, in a nurturing learning environment that promotes respondibility and respect. We aim to develop socially engaged, self-motivated, creative, compassionate individuals who will be a force for positive change in their communities and the world.

DJ Condon, Middle/High School Principal
Dennis MacKinnon, Director

2102 Izmir American Institute
Friends-850 Third Avenue
18th Floor
New York, NY 10022

Richard Curtis, Principal

2103 John F Kennedy School-Queretaro
Sabinos #272, Jurica
Queretaro
Mexico 76100
442-218-0075
Fax: 442-218-1784
E-mail: admissions@jfk.edu.mx
http://www.jfk.edu.mx
The American School of Queretaro, is to provide the whole individual an opportunity for high quality U.S. type, bilingual education that recognizes individual talents and encourages lifelong learning

Dr. Francisco Galicia, Principal
Mirtha Stappung, General Director

2104 Jordan American Community School
PO Box 310, Dahiat Al-Amir Rashid
Amman 11831
Jordan
962-6-581-3944
Fax: 962-6-582-3357
E-mail: school@acsamman.edu.jo
http://www.acsamman.edu.jo
ACS is fully accredited K-12 by the Middle States Association of Colleges and Schools and is a member in good standing of NESA, the Near East South Asia Association of Overseas Schools

Dr. Gray Duckett, Superintendent

2105 Karachi American Society School
American Consulate General Karachi
6150 Karachi Place
Washington, DC 20521-6150
92-21-453-909619
Fax: 92-21-453-7305

David Holmer, Principal

2106 Kongeus Grade School
44-46 Gade
St Thomas 00802
Virgin Islands 802

Veronica Miller, Principal

2107 Lincoln International School-Kampala
Co of State
Washington, DC 20521-1

Margaret Bell, Principal

2108 Lincoln School
Lincoln School 565-20
PO Box 025331
Miami, FL 33102-5331
506-224- 660
Fax: 506-224- 670
E-mail: director@ns.lincoln.ed.cr
http://www.lincoln.ed.cr
offer an integrated education, using English as the primary language of instruction, to motivate a continuing search for excellence and stimulate students to fully develop their potential to become responsible, enterprising, creative, open-minded citizens with solid ethical values, committed to democracy, and capable of being successful in a multicultural, global society.

Charles Prince, Principal

2109 Lincoln-Marti Schools
2700 SW 8 Street
Miami, FL 33135
305-643-4888
877-874-1999
Fax: 305-649-2767
E-mail: info@lincoln-marti.com
http://www.lincolnmarti.com
Lincoln-Mart- is an institution dedicated to educating the future of our community, both academically and socially.

Demitrio Perez, President

2110 Little People's Learning Center
9605 SE 7th Street
Vancouver, WA 98664
360-892-7570
E-mail: info@lplc.net
http://www.lplc.net/home.html

Daphne Maynard, Principal
Becky Dolan, Director

2111 Little School House
47 Kongens Gade
St Thomas 00802
Virgin Islands

Carol Struiell, Principal

2112 Luanda International School
Rua da Talatona Caixa 1566
Barrio da Talatona Luanda Sul Samba
Republica de Angola
244-2-44-3416
Fax: 244-2-44-3416
E-mail: officesec@lisluanda.com
http://www.lisluanda.com
offers a balanced, academically challenging, English language education to the international community of Luanda, designed to develop individuals who are both independent learners and international citizens.

Anthony Baron, Director
Di Atkinson, Senior Administrator

2113 Lutheran Parish School
#1 Lille Taarne Gade
Charlotte Aml 00802
Puerto Rico 802

Nancy Gotwalt, Principal

2114 Manor School
236 La Grande Princesse
Christiansted, VI 820-4449
340-718-1448
Fax: 340-718-3651
E-mail: jgadd@manorschoolstx.com
http://www.manorschoolstx.com

is dedicated to personal and academic growth in an extended-family environment. We promote academic confidence, creativity, community involvement and citizenship, a sense of respon-sibility, and positive decision-making. We strive to ensure that our graduates are person-ally and academically prepared to succeed in their future endeavors.

Judith C Gadd, Headmistress
Hanley Hamed, Office Manager

2115 Maranatha Christian Academy
9201 75th Avenue N
Brooklyn Park, MN 55428
612- 58- 285
Fax: 763-315-7294
E-mail: info@mca.lwcc.org
http://www.maranathachristianacademy.org
is to offer a pre-kindergarten through 12th grade traditional classroom education providing a quality educational experience, which encourages and enables students to mature spiritually, intellectually, physically, emotionally, and socially in accordanc

Rev. Gary Sprunger, Principal
Brian Sullivan, Chief Administrator

2116 Martin De Porress Academy
621 Elmont Road
Elmont, NY 11003
516-502-2840
Fax: 516-502-2841
E-mail: sfagin@mdp.org
http://www.mdp.org/
The Martin De Porress Academy program provides academic instruction based upon the NY State Learning Standards as well as hands on experiences in business enterprises, performing arts, home improvement skills, life skills, culinary arts, maintenance services and community services.

Raymond R Blixt, Executive Director
Philip E Chance, Assistant Executive Director

2117 Montessori House of Children
572 Dunholme Way
Suite 103
Sunnyvale, CA 94086
408-749-1602
http://www.sunnyvalemontessori.com
Our program is based on the premise that every child is an individual with his own needs and abilities. All children need affection and friendliness. They require affirmation, encouragement and understanding

William Myers, Principal
Priya Medelberg, Founder-Director

2118 Moravian School
PO Box 1777
Chrisyiansted 00821-1777
Virgin Islands
809-773-8921
This Moravian affiliated school offers a curriculum based in English for 200 day students (96 boys; 104 girls), in grades K-6. The school is willing to participate in a teacher exchange program, with the length of stay being one year, with housing provided. Applications include science, Spanish and computer skills.

Condon L Joseph, Principal

2119 Morrocoy International
MUN 4051
PO Box 025352
Miami, FL 33102-5352
58-286-9520016
Fax: 58-286-9521861
E-mail: kempenich@telcel.net.ve
http://www.geocities.com/minaspov

Grade levels Pre-K through 10, school year August - June
Michael Kempenich, Headmaster

2120 Mount Carmel Elementary School
PO Box 7830
Agat 96928 0830
Guam-b830
This Catholic school offers an English (primary) curriculum for 206 day students (100 boys; 106 girls), in Kinder 4 - 8th grade. Overseas teachers are accepted, with the length of stay being one year. Applications needed to teach include reading, English and counseling/counselor.

Bernadette Quintanilla, Sr, SSND, Principal
Augustin Gumataotao, Administrator

2121 Nazarene Christian School
385 Hazel Mill Road
Asheville, NC 28806
828-252-9713
E-mail:
ncsoffice@ashevillefirstnazarene.org
http://www.ashevillefirstnazarene.org
The Nazarene International Center provides support services to more than 1.2 million members worshiping in more than 11,800 churches in the United States, Canada, and 135 other world areas

Peggy Neighbors, Administrator

2122 Nepal Lincoln School
Kathmandu (LS)
Department of State
Washington, DC 20521-6190
977-1-270-482
Fax: 977-1-272-685
E-mail: info@lsnepal.com.np
http://www.lsnepal.com
Lincoln School is an independent, international school in Kathmandu, Nepal with an American Curriculum. We are committed to nurture of the individual student, excellence in all spheres of achievement, pursuit of personal responsibility, appreciation of diversity, and love of learning

Allan Bredy, Director
Craig Baker, Principal

2123 Northern Mariana Islands Department of Education
PO Box 501370 CK
Siapan, MP 96950
011-670-664-3720
Fax: 011-670-664-3798

Rita Hocog Inos, Commissioner

2124 Notre Dame High School
480 S San Miguel Street
Talofofo
Guam 96930-4699
671-789-1676
Notre Dame is a co-educational, year-round high school run by the School Sisters of Notre Dame. This Roman Catholic affiliated school offers a curriculum in English for 191 day students and 9 boarding (32 boys; 168 girls), in grades 9-12. Student/teacher ratio is 10:1, and the applications needed to teach include science, math, social sciences, and English.

Regina Paulino, SSND, Principal

2125 Nuestra Senora de La Altagracia
672 Calle Felipe Gutierrez #672
San Juan 00924-2225
Puerto Rico

2126 Nuestra Senora de La Providencia
PO Box 11610
San Juan 00922-1610
Puerto Rico

2127 Okinawa Christian School
1835 Zakimi
Yomitan, Okinawa
Japan 904-0
098-958-3000
Fax: 098-958-6279
E-mail: info@ocsi.org
http://www.ocsi.org
A non-denominational mission whose purpose is to partner with families of the international community of Okinawa by offering an excellent Christian education in the English language.

Paul Gieschen, Principal

2128 Open Classroom
PO Box 4046
St Thomas 00803
Virgin Islands 803

Janie Lang, Principal

2129 Osaka International School
4-16 Onohar Nishi 4-Chome
Mino, Osaki, 562-0032
Japan
072-727-5050
Fax: 072-727-5055
E-mail: addmissions@senri.ed.jp
http://www.senri.ed.jp
OIS is an english-language-based, preK-12 grade coeducational college-preparatory school.

John Searle, Head of School

2130 Palache Bilingual School
PO Box 1832
Arecibo 00613-1832
Puerto Rico

Rev. David Valez, Principal

2131 Peace Corp
1111 20th Street NW
Washington, DC 20526
202-692-1470
800-424-8580
Fax: 202-692-1897
E-mail: psa@peacecorps.gov
http://www.peacecorps.gov
Helping the people of interested countries in meeting their need for trained men and women. Helping promote a better understanding of Americans on the part of the peoples served

2132 Pine Peace School
PO Box 1657
St John, VI 831
340-776-6595
E-mail: pinepeace@viaccess.net
http://www.pinepeaceschool.k12.vi
An independent, non-profit, English language school that serves students without regard to sex, race, religion, or nationality.˜

Beth Knight, Headmistress

2133 Ponce Baptist Academy
72 Calle 1 Belgica
Ponce 00731
Puerto Rico

Vivian Medina, Principal

2134 Prophecy Elementary School
PO Box 10497
APO St Thomas 00801-3497
Virgin Islands 801
340-775-7223
Fax: 340-714-5354
E-mail: pai@prophecyacademy.org
http://http://www.prophecyacademy.net
Church of God of Prophecy Academy, Inc. offers a Christian atmosphere which develops the physical, spiritual, intellectual and the social skills of every student. Our primary pur-

pose is to help train students while teaching them the Christian way of life.

Anne E Bramble-Johnson, Principal
VeronaCeleste Hutchinson, Secretary/Office Manager

2135 Puerto Rico Department of Education
PO Box 190759
San Juan
Puerto Rico 919-759
787-759-2000
http://www.de.gobierno.pr

Cesar A Rey-Hernandez, Secretary

2136 QSI International School-Chisinau
18 Anton Crihan Street
Chisinau
Moldova 20521-7080
373-24-2366
E-mail: chisinau@qsi.org
http://www.qsi.org
To keep this urge to learn alive in every child in QSI schools. Our schools are established to provide in the English language a quality education for students in the cities we serve.

Sandra Smith, Director

2137 QSI International School-Skopje
Inlindenska BB, Reon 55
1000 Skopie
Macedonia 20521-7120
389-91-367-678
Fax: 389-91-362-250
E-mail: skopje@qsi.org
http://www.qsi.org
To keep this urge to learn alive in every child in QSI schools. Our schools are established to provide in the English language a quality education for students in the cities we serve.

Robert Tower, Director
Aleksandar Kostadinovski, Finance Manager

2138 QSI International School-Vladivostok
DOS/Administrative Officer
5880 Vladivostok Place
Washington, DC 20521-5880
7-4232-321-292
Fax: 7-4232-313-684
E-mail: qsiisv@fastmail.vladivostok.ru
Grades preK-9, enrollment 18.

Harold M Strom Jr, Director

2139 Rainbow Development Center
PO Box 7618
Christiansted 00823-7618
Virgin Islands

Gloria Henry, Principal

2140 Rainbow Learning Institute
PO Box 75
Christiansted 00821-0075
Virgin Islands

Alda Lockhart, Principal

2141 Rainbow School
PO Box 422
Charlotte Aml 00801
Virgin Islands

Louise Thomas, Principal

2142 Robinson School
5 Nairn Street Condado
San Juan 00907
Puerto Rico 907
1-787-728-6767
Fax: 1-787-727-7736
E-mail: robinson_school@hotmail.com
http://www.robinsonschool.org

The Heart of Educational Excellence. Robinson offers its students a solid foundation for their future academic and career pursuits.

Giberto Quintana, Executive Director
Hugh Andrews, President

2143 Roosevelt Roads Elementary School
PO Box 420132
Roosevelt Roads 00742-0132
Puerto Rico
787-865-3073
Fax: 787-865-4891
http://www.netdial.caribe.net

2144 Roosevelt Roads Middle & High School
PO Box 420131
Roosevelt Roads 00742-0131
Puerto Rico
787-865-4000
Fax: 787-865-4893
E-mail: wjames@caribe.net
http://www.antilles.odedodea.edu

Waynna James, Principal

2145 Saint Anthony School
529 Chalan San Antonio
Tamuning
Guam 96913
671-647-1140
Fax: 471-649-7130
http://stanthonyschoolguam.org/index.php
A Catholic co-educational elementary school in the Archdiocese of Agana, exists to educate the whole person by providing a rich integrated curriculum served by enabling adults.

Doris San Agustin, Principal
Elizabeth E San Nicolas, Vice-Principal

2146 Saint Eheresas Elementary School
Leone
Pago Apgo 96799
American Samoa

Sister Katherine, Principal

2147 Saint Francis Elementary School
520130 Lepua
Pago Pago 96799
American Samoa

Sister Gaynor Ana, Principal

2148 Saint John's School
911 N Marine Corps Drive
Tumon Bay 96913
Guam
671-646-8080
Fax: 617-649-6791
E-mail: info@stjohns.edu.gu
http://www.stjohns.edu.gu
St. John's students on average score in the top 20% on national scholastic achievement tests in all academic subjects in all grades K-12, a tangible result of an integrated academic program supported by a dedicated faculty, many with advanced degrees in their respective areas of instruction

Glenn Chapin, Headmaster
Imelda D Santos, Dean of Students

2149 Saint John's School, Puerto Rico
1454-66 Ashford Avenue
San Juan 00907
Puerto Rico
787-728-5343
Fax: 787-268-1454
http://www.sjspr.org/home.aspx
Saint John's School is a college preparatory, nonsectarian, coeducational day school founded in 1915. The school, located in a residential area of the Condado, has an enrollment of approximately 750 students from preschool to grade twelve. 84% come from Hispanic backgrounds, 8% percent from diverse backgrounds and 8% from the continen-

tal United States. With the exception of Spanish and French classes, instruction is in English.

Louis R Christiansen, Principal
Barry Farnham, Headmaster

2150 Saints Peter & Paul High School
900 High Street
Easton, MD
410-822-2275
Fax: 410-822-1767
E-mail: jnemeth@ssppeaston.org
http://www.ssppeaston.org/schools/high_school
Saints Peter and Paul High School is a parochial, Catholic, college preparatory,

James Nemeth, Principal
Carolyn Hayman, Administrative Assistant

2151 Samoa Baptist Academy
Tafuna
Pago Pago 96799
American Samoa

Janice Yerton, Principal

2152 San Carlos & Bishop McManus High School
PO Box Loo 9, Yumet
Aguadilla 00605
Puerto Rico

Nydia U Nieves, Principal

2153 San Vincente Elementary School
San Vincente School Drive
Barrigada 96913
Puerto Rico 96913
671-734-4242
This campus is on five acres of outside Barrigada Village. The average enrollment of 460 students consists of 234 boys and 226 girls in grades PreK-8. SVS holds a Certificate of Accreditation from the Western Association of Schools and Colleges until 1998. Length of stay for overseas teachers is two years, with housing provided. Applications needed to teach include English and physical education.

Adrian Cristobal, Principal
Tarcisia Sablan SSND, Faculty Head

2154 Santa Barbara School
274A W Santa Barbara Avenue
Dededo
Guam 96929
671-632-5578
Fax: 671-632-1414
http://www.santabarbaraschool.org
To ensure that each student is given the opportunity to realize his or her full potential according to God's design by recognizing and affirming the gifts of each child.

Sr Jeanette Mar Pangelinan, Principal
Sr Maria Rosari Gaite, Vice Principal

2155 Santiago Christian School
PO Box 5600
Fort Lauderdale, FL 33310-5600

Lloyd Haglund, Principal

2156 School of the Good Shepherd
1069 Kinghill
St Croix 00851
Virgin Islands 851

Linda Navarro, Principal

2157 Seventh Day Adventist
PO Box 7909
St Thomas 00801-0909
Virgin Islands

Josiah Maynard, Principal

2158 Shekou International School
Jing Shan Villas, Nan Hai Road Shek
Guangdong Province
China 51806
86-755-2669-3669
Fax: 86-755-2667-4099
E-mail: sis@sis.org.cn
http://www.sis.org.cn
Shekou International School follows a rigorous college preparatory US style curriculum and is dedicated to meeting the outcomes of the Expected Student Learning Results.

Robert Dunseth, Director
Jennifer Lees, Curriculum Coordinator

2159 Slovak Republic QSI International School of Bratislava
Karloveska 64
Bratislava
Slovak Republic 84220
421-2-6541-1636
Fax: 421-2-6541-1646
E-mail: bratislava@qsi.org
http://www.qsi.sk
THE PRIMARY PURPOSE of the school is to meet the needs of the children in Bratislava who require this type of education with a view to continuing their education in their home countries with a minimum of adjustment problems.

Matthew Lake, Director

2160 Slovenia QSI International School-Ljubljana
Dolgi Most 6A
Ljubljana
Slovenia 1000
386-1-439-6300
Fax: 386-1-439-6305
E-mail: ljubljana@qsi.org
http://www.qsi.org/sln_home
THE PRIMARY PURPOSE of the school is to meet the needs of the children in Ljubljana who require this type of education with a view to continuing their education in their home countries with a minimum of adjustment problems.

Steve Miner, Director

2161 South Pacific Academy
PO Box 520
Pago Pago 96799 0520
American Samoa

Tina Senrud, Principal

2162 Southern Peru Staff Schools-Peru
180 Maiden Lane
New York, NY 10038-4925

John Dansdill, Principal

2163 St. Croix Christian Academy
26-28 Golden Rock, Christiansted, S
PO Box 716
Virgin Islands, US 821
340-718-4974
Fax: 340-718-6768
E-mail: stccacademy@vipowernet.net
http://www.stcroixchristianacademy.com
The mission of the school is to foster knowledge of God and to give the children a solid academic foundation, along with effective Christian training.

Linus Gittens, Principal

2164 St. Croix Country Day School
Rt-01, Box 6199
Kingshill
Virgin Islands, US 850
1-340-778-1974
Fax: 1-340-779-3331
E-mail: bsinfield@stxcountryday.com
http://www.stxcountryday.com

It is dedicated to providing students with an enriched and challenging education, encouraging them to love learning, grow as individuals and be prepared for a productive and responsible future.

Bill Sinfield, Headmaster
Susan Gibbons, Business Manager

2165 St. Croix Moravian School
PO Box 117
St Thomas 00801
Virgin Islands

Condon L Joseph, Principal

2166 St. Croix SDA School
PO Box 930
Kingshill 00851-0930
Virgin Islands

Peter Archer, Principal

2167 St. Joseph High School
PO Box 517
Frederiksted 00841-0517
Virgin Islands

Kevin Marin, Principal

2168 St. Patrick School
PO Box 988
Frderiksted 00841-0988
Virgin Islands

Juliette Clarke, Principal

2169 St. Peter & Paul Elementary School
PO Box 1706
St Thomas 00803
Virgin Islands

Annamay Komment, Principal

2170 Sunbeam
36 Hospital Ground
St Thomas 00803
Virgin Islands

Ione Leonard, Principal

2171 Syria Damascus Community School
6110 Damascus Place
Dulles, VA 20189-6110
963-11-333-0331
Fax: 963-11-332-1457
E-mail: dcs-dam@net.sy
http://www.dcssyria.org
An independent, coeducational day school which offers an American educational program from preschool through grade 12 for students of all nationalities.

John Gates, Director
Maura Connelly, Chairman

2172 Tashkent International School
7117 Tashkent Place
Dulles, VA 20189-7110
998-71-191-9671
Fax: 998-71-120-6621
E-mail: office@tashschool.org
http://www.tashschool.org
To provide a high academic standard of education, educating students to become ethical, responsible, productive citizens of the world with the skills to think creatively, reason critically, and to communicate effectively

John Thomas, Director

2173 Teaching in Austria
Austrian Institute
11 E 52nd Street
New York, NY 10022-5301
212-579-5165

2174 Temple Christian School
PO Box 3009
Agana 96910
Guam 96910

Rev. Ray Fagan, Principal

2175 Tirana International School-Albania
Kutia Postare
Tirana
Albania, DC 1527-9510
355-4-365-239
Fax: 335-4-227-734
E-mail: tirana@qsi.org
http://www.qsi.org
The school's educational philosophy, which includes a personalized approach to instruction, leads to teaching for mastery.

Mark Hemphill, Director

2176 Trinity Christian School
1231 East Pleasant Run Road
Yiga 96929 0343
Cedar Hill, TX 75104
972-291-2505
Fax: 972-291-4739
http://www.trinitychristianschool.com
Being a Christian school means we assist parents in fulfilling their divine responsibility to thoroughly train each child to obey God in every area of life and make him or her a true disciple of Jesus Christ. Our program is designed to challenge and educate students of good moral character who are in the middle to upper range of academic ability

Kathleen L Watts, Superintendent
Rhonda Parker, Executive Assistant

2177 Turkmenistan Ashgabat International School
Box 2002
7070 Ashgabat Place
Washington, DC 20521-7070
967-1-234-437
Fax: 967-1-234-438
E-mail: director@ais.cat.glasnet.ru
Grades K-11, enrollment 75.

Scott Root, Director

2178 Ukraine Kiev International School-An American Institution
EOS/Administrative Officer
5850 Kiev Place
Washington, DC 20521-5850
380-44-452-2792
Fax: 380-44-452-2998
E-mail: kisukr@sovamua.com
An independent, coeducational day school which offers an educational program from prekindergarten through high school for students of all nationalities.

E Michael Tewalthomas, Director

2179 United Nations International School
24-50 FDR Drive
New York, NY 10010-4046
212-684-7400
Fax: 212-685-5023
E-mail: admissions@unis.org
http://www.unis.org
The United Nations International School provides an international education that emphasizes academic excellence within a caring community for kindergarten through twelfth grade students from families of the United Nations, as well as from other families seeking a similar education for their children

Kenneth Wrye, EdD, Executive Director
Satya Nandan, Chairperson

2180 University del Sagrado Corazon
PO Box 12383
San Juan
Puerto Rico 914-383
787-728-1515
http://www.sagrado.edu

2181 Uruguayan American School
Av Saldœn de Rodriguez
Montevideo
Uruguay, DC 11500-3360
598-2-600-7681
Fax: 598-2-600-1935
E-mail: info@uas.edu.uyuy
http://www.uas.edu.uy
Uruguayan American School is to provide, together with the family, a balanced college preparatory education. UAS integrates a US style curriculum with Uruguayan studies to equip our national and international students to be successful in a diverse, ever changing world

Thomas Oden, Director
Cecilia Burgueo, UP Coordinator

2182 Uruguayan American School-Montevideo
Av Saldœn de Rodriguez
Montevideo
Uruguay, DC 11500-3360
598-2-600-7681
Fax: 598-2-606-1935
E-mail: info@uas.edu.uyuy
http://www.uas.edu.uy
Uruguayan American School is to provide, together with the family, a balanced college preparatory education. UAS integrates a US style curriculum with Uruguayan studies to equip our national and international students to be successful in a diverse, ever changing world

Thomas Oden, Director
Cecilia Burgueo, UP Coordinator

2183 Uzbekistan Tashkent International School
38 Sarikul Street
Tashkent, Uzbekistan 10000
998-71-191-9671
Fax: 998-71-120-6621
E-mail: office@tashschool.org
http://www.tashschool.org
Tashkent International School (TIS), an IB World School, is a private, not for profit, independent, co-educational day school governed by a Board of Directors elected and appointed from the parent community. TIS offers an American based international curriculum from Kindergarten - grade 12. TIS is an IB World School offering: the full International Baccalaureate Diploma in grades 11 - 12, the Primary Years Program for Kindergarten - grade 5, and is a candidate school for the Middle Years Program

Kevin Glass, Director
John Zohrab, Treasurer

2184 Venezuela Colegio Internacional-Carabobo
PO Box 025685
Miami, FL 33102-5685
58-41-426-551
Fax: 58-41-426-510
E-mail: admin@cic-valencia.org.ve
Colegio Internacional de Carabobo (CIC) is a school dedicated to the development of the whole child. Our teachers are innovative, skilled, and dedicated. Creativity and self-esteem are essential qualities for students to develop as they ascend the academic ladder.

Frank Anderson, Superintendent
Joe Walker, Director

2185 Venezuela Escuela Campo Alegre
8424 NW 56th Street
Suite CCS 00007
Miami, FL 33166
58-2-993-7135
Fax: 58-2-993-0219
E-mail: info@eca.com.ve
http://www.eca.com.ve
Escuela Campo Alegre is a private non-profit English language school, designed primarily to serve the needs of the children from ages 3-18 of its shareholding members.

Jean K Vahey, Superintendent

2186 Venezuela International School-Caracas
Pakmail 6030
PO Box 025304
Miami, FL 33102-5304
58-2-945-0422
Fax: 58-2-945-0533
E-mail: cic@cic-caracas.org
http://www.cic-caracus.org
Colegio Internacional de Caracas is an English-medium, Pre-Nursery to Grade 12 school dedicated to the intellectual and personal development of each student in a caring and supportive environment.

Alan Benson, Superintendent

2187 Virgin Island Montessori School
6936 Vessup Lane
Saint Thomas, VI 802
340-775-6360
Fax: 340-775-3080
E-mail: info@vimontessori.com
http://www.vimontessori.com/
Virgin Islands Montessori School and International Academy offers a unique environment and learning experience to over 200 students from two years of age through High School

Shournagh Mcweeney, Administrator
Michael Bornn, President

2188 Virgin Islands Department of Education
44-46 Kongens Gade
Saint Thomas, Virgin Islands 802
340-774-2810
Fax: 340-774-7153
http://www.doe.vi/
The mission of the Department of Education is to provide the Territory's students with an education that makes them competitive with their peers in the rest of the Caribbean, the United States, and the World; take advantage of our uniqueness of being geographically Caribbean and politically American; integrate all discipline; and educate the whole child.

LaVerne Terry, Commissioner
Donna Frett-Gregory, Assistant Commissioner

2189 Washington International School
3100 Macomb Street NW
Washington, DC 20008-3324
202-243-1800
Fax: 202-243-1802
E-mail: admissions@wis.edu
http://www.wis.edu
Washington International School (WIS) is a coeducational day school offering 890 students a challenging curriculum and rich language program from Pre-Kindergarten through Grade 12

Clayton W. Lewis, Head of School
Sandra Bourne, Middle School Principal

2190 We Care Child Development Center
PO Box 818
Christiansted 00821-0818
Virgin Islands

Pauline Canton, Principal

2191 Wesleyan Academy
PO Box 1489
Guaynabo
Puerto Rico 970-1489
78- 7-0 89
Fax: 787-790-0730
http://www.wesleyanacademy.org

We are a nonprofit, private, coeducational, English Christian school providing a Pre-Pre Kinder through Twelfth grade college preparatory education.

Jack Mann, Principal

2192 Yakistan International School-Karachi
DOS/Administrative Officer
6150 Karachi Place
Washington, DC 20521-6150
92-21-453-9096
Fax: 92-21-454-7305
E-mail: ameschl@cyber.net.pk
http://www.isk.edu.pk
Grades N-12, enrollment 338.

Glen Shapin, Superintendent

2193 Zion Academy
7629 199th Street SW
Lynnwood, WA 98036
425-640-3311
E-mail: info@zionacademy.com
http://www.zionacademy.com
Zion Academy is a fully accredited private school. Consists of students that wish to work at home and desire complete oversight and administrative services.

Evelyn Williams, Principal
Marigene Lindsey, Founder and Headmaster

International

2194 Center for Strategic & International Studies
1800 K Street NW
Suite 400
Washington, DC 20006-2202
202-887-0200
Fax: 202-775-3199
E-mail: books@csis.org
http://www.csis.org
Provides strategic insights and policy solutions to decisionmakers in government, international institutions, the private sector, and civil society. A bipartisan, nonprofit organization headquartered in Washington, DC, CSIS conducts research and analysis and develops policy initiatives that look into the future and anticipate change.

John J Hamre, President/CEO
Sam Nunn, Cochairman & CEO

2195 Council for International Exchange of Scholars
3007 Tilden Street NW
Suite 5-L
Washington, DC 20008-3009
202-686-4000
Fax: 202-362-3442
E-mail: apprequest@cies.iie.org
http://www.cies.org
Helped administer the Fulbright Scholar Program on behalf of the United States Department of State, Bureau of Educational and Cultural Affairs.

Michael A Brintnall, Executive Director
Judy Pehrson, Director External Relations

2196 Defense Language Institute-English Language Branch
US Civil Service Commission, San Antonio Area
2235 Andrews Avenue
Lackland, TX 78236-5514
210-671-3783
Fax: 210-671-5362
http://www.dlielc.org
The DLIELC is a Department of Defense (DOD) agency responsible for the management and operation of the Defense English

Language Program (DELP) to train international military and civilian personnel to speak and teach English, manage the English as a second language program for the US military

2197 Education Information Services which Employ Americans
Education Information Services
PO Box 620662
Newton, MA 2462-662
781-433-0125
Fax: 781-237-2842
Devoted to helping Americans who wish to teach in American overseas schools and International Schools in which English is the primary teaching language. Supports those wishing to teach English as a second language. Publish papers covering every country in the world, list of recruiting fairs, internships, volunteers, jobs, summer overseas jobs.

Frederic B Viaux, President

2198 Educational Information Services
PO Box 662
Newtown Lower Falls, MA 2162
617-964-4555
Offers information on employment opportunities including books, periodicals and more for the teaching professional who wishes to teach in American overseas schools, international schools, language (ESL) schools, and Department of Defense Dependencies Schools (DODDS).

Frederick B Viaux, President
Michelle V Curtin, Editor

2199 Educational Placement Sources-US
Education Information Services/Instant Alert
PO Box 620662
Newton, MA 2462-662
617-433-0125
Lists 100 organizations in the United States that find positions for teachers, educational administrators, counselors and other professionals. Listings are classified by type, listed alphabetically and offer all contact information.

4 pages Annual

FB Viaux, President

2200 Educational Staffing Program
International Schools Services
15 Roszel Road
PO Box 5910
Princeton, NJ 8543
609-452-0990
Fax: 609-452-2690
E-mail: edustaffing@iss.edu
http://www.iss.edu/edustaff/edstaffingprog.html
The Educational Staffing Program has placed almost 15,000 K-12 teachers and administrators in overseas schools since 1955. Most candidates obtain their overseas teaching positions by attending our US-based International Recruitment Center where ISS candidates have the potential to interview with overseas school heads seeking new staff. You must be an active ISS candidate to attend an IRC. Applicants must have a bachelor's degree and two years of current relevant experience.

2201 European Council of International Schools
21B Lavant Street
Petersfield, Hampshire GU3 23EL
United Kingdom GU32
44-0-1730-268244
Fax: 44-0-1730-267914
E-mail: ecis@ecis.org
http://www.ecis.org

The European Council of International Schools (ECIS) is a collaborative network promoting the ideals and best practice of international education.

T Michael Maybury, Executive Secretary
Pilar Cabeza de Vaca, CEO

2202 FRS National Teacher Agency
PO Box 298
Seymour, TN 37865-298
865-577-8143
Offers employment options to educators in the United States and abroad.

2203 Foreign Faculty and Administrative Openings
Education Information Services
PO Box 620662
Newton, MA 2462-662
617-433-0125
150 specific openings in administration, counseling, library and other professional positions for American teachers in American schools overseas and in international schools in which teaching language is English.

15 pages Every 6 Weeks

FB Viaux, Coordinating Education

2204 Fulbright Teacher Exchange
600 Maryland Avenue SouthWest
Suite 320
Washington, DC 20024-2520
202-314-3520
800-726-0479
Fax: 202-479-6806
E-mail: fulbright@grad.usda.gov
http://www.fulbrightexchanges.org
An organization that offers opportunities for two-year college faculty and secondary school teachers who would like to exchange with teachers in Eastern or Western Europe, Latin America, Australia, Africa, and Canada. To qualify, teachers must be US citizens, have three years full-time teaching experience and be employed in a full-time academic position.

2205 International Educators Cooperative
212 Alcott Road
East Falmouth, MA 2536-6803
508-540-8173
Fax: 508-540-8173
In addition to year round recruitment, International Educators Cooperative hosts Recruitment Centers in the United States each year.

Dr. Lou Fuccillo, Director

2206 National Association of Teachers' Agencies
National Association of Teachers' Agencies
799 Kings Highway
Fairfield, CT 6432
203-333-0611
Fax: 203-334-7224
E-mail: fairfieldteachers@snet.net
http://www.jobsforteachers.com
Provides placement services for those seeking professional positions at all levels of teaching/administration/support services worldwide.

Mark King, Secretary/Treasurer

2207 National Council of Independent Schools' Associations
Curtin ACT 2605
PO Box 324
Australia
06-282-3488
Fax: 06-282-2926
Services include career placement.

Fergus Thomson

2208 Overseas Employment Opportunities for Educators
Department of Defense, Office of Dependent Schools
2461 Eisenhower Avenue
Alexandria, VA 22331-3000
703-325-0867
This publication tells about teaching jobs in 250 schools operated for children of US military and civilian personnel stationed overseas. Applicants usually must qualify in two subject areas.

2209 Recruiting Fairs for Overseas Teaching
Education Information Services/Instant Alert
PO Box 620662
Newton, MA 2462-662
781-433-0125
Fax: 781-237-2842
Recruiting fairs and sponsors in the US and elsewhere for American educators who wish to teach outside of the United States.

FB Viaux, Coordinating Education

2210 UNI Overseas Recruiting Fair
University of Northern Iowa
102 Gilchrist Hall
Cedar Falls, IA 50614-390
319-273-2083
Fax: 319-273-6998
E-mail: overseas.placement@uni.edu
http://www.uni.edu/placement/overseas
UNI is home to the oldest international recruitment event in the world. The event began in 1976 after the UNI Career Services staff and several school headmasters recognized the need for more efficient and cost-effective recruitment techniques. It became readily apparent that UNI was meeting a need for school recruiters and interested educators all over the globe. In addition to inventing the international recruitment fair, UNI developed fact sheets, credential files, vacancy listings, referral

February

Brian Atkins, Advisory Board
Susan Barba, Advisory Board

2211 WorldTeach
Center for International Development
79 John F Kennedy Street
Box 122
Cambridge, MA 2138
617-495-5527
800-483-2240
Fax: 617-495-1599
E-mail: info@worldteach.org
http://www.worldteach.org
WorldTeach is a non-profit, non-governmental organization that provides opportunities for individuals to make a meaningful contribution to international education by living and working as volunteer teachers in developing countries

Laurie Roberts Belton, Executive Director
Eric Weiss, Program Manager

Alabama

2212 Auburn University at Montgomery Library
PO Box 244023
Montgomery, AL 36124-4023
334-244-3649
Fax: 334-244-3720
http://www.aumnicat.aum.edu
Member of The Foundation Center network, maintaining a collection of private foundation tax returns which provide information on the scope of grants dispensed by that particular foundation.

R Best, Dean Administration
T Bailey, ILL/ Reference

2213 Benjamin & Roberta Russell Educational and Charitable Foundation
PO Box 272
Alexander City, AL 35010-0272
256-329-4224
Offers giving in the areas of higher and public education, youth programs and a hospital.

James D Nabors, Executive Director

2214 Birmingham Public Library
Government Documents
2100 Park Place
Birmingham, AL 35203-2794
205-226-3600
Fax: 205-226-3729
http://www.bplonline.org/resources/subjects/gov/deault
Member of The Foundation Center network, maintaining a collection of private foundation tax returns which provide information on the scope of grants dispensed by that particular foundation.

2215 Carolina Lawson Ivey Memorial Foundation
PO Box 340
Smiths, AL 36877-0340
334-826-5760
Scholarships are offered to college juniors and seniors who are pursuing careers of teaching social studies in middle or secondary grades. The grants are also offered to teachers in Alabama and west Georgia for curriculum planning and development, in-service training, the development of instructional materials for use in elementary and secondary schools, and other projects that focus on the cultural approach method of teaching.

2216 Huntsville Public Library
915 Monroe Street SW
Huntsville, AL 35801-5007
256-532-5940
http://www.hpl.lib.al.us/
Member of The Foundation Center network, maintaining a collection of private foundation tax returns which provide information on the scope of grants dispensed by that particular foundation.

Donna B Schremser, Library Director

2217 JL Bedsole Foundation
PO Box 1137
Mobile, AL 36633-1137
251-432-3369
Fax: 251-432-1134
http://www.jlbedsolefoundation.org
The foundation's primary interest is the support of educational institutions within the state of Alabama and civic and economic development which is limited to the geographical area of Southwest Alabama. The arts, social service and health programs receive limited grants. Organizations or projects out-

side of the State of Alabama are not considered for funding by the Foundation.
Mabel B Ward, Executive Director
Scott A Morton, Assistant Director

2218 Mildred Weedon Blount Educational andCharitable Foundation
PO Box 607
Tallassee, AL 36078-0007
334-283-4931
Support for Catholic schools, public schools and a scholarship fund for secondary school students.

Arnold B Dopson, Executive Director

2219 Mitchell Foundation
PO Box 1126
Mobile, AL 36633
251-432-1711
Fax: 334-432-1712
Places an emphasis on secondary and higher education, social services programs, youth agencies, and aid for the handicapped.

Augustine Meaher, Executive Director

2220 University of South Alabama
307 University Boulevard
Mobile, AL 36688-0002
251-460-7025
Fax: 251-460-7636
http://http://library.southalabama.edu
Richard Wood, Dean Of Libraries

Alaska

2221 University of Alaska-Anchorage Library
3211 Providence Drive
Anchorage, AK 99508-8000
907-786-1848
Fax: 907-786-6050
http://www.lib.uaa.alaska.edu/
Member of The Foundation Center network, maintaining a collection of private foundation tax returns which provide information on the scope of grants dispensed by that particular foundation.

Stephen J Rollins, Dean Of Library

Arizona

2222 Arizona Department of Education
1535 W Jefferson Street
Phoenix, AZ 85007
602-542-5393
800-352-4558
Fax: 602-542-5440
http://www.ade.state.az.us
Implements procedures that ensure the proper allocation, distribution, and expenditure of all federal and state funds administerd by the department. The following links to our web pages contain information pertaining to educational grants funded from the state or federal programs.

Tom Horne, Superintendent

2223 Arizona Governor's Committee on Employment of People with Disabilities
Samaritan Rehabilitation Institute
1012 E Willetta Street
Phoenix, AZ 85006-3047
602-239-4762
Fax: 602-239-5256

Jim Bruzewski, Executive Director

2224 Education Services
Arizona Department of Education
1535 W Jefferson Street
Phoenix, AZ 85007-3280
602-364-1961
Fax: 602-542-5440
http://www.ade.state.az.us/edservices
Provides quality services and resources to schools, parent groups, government agencies, and community groups to enable them to achieve their goals.

Lillie Sly, Associate Superintendent

2225 Evo-Ora Foundation
2525 E Broadway Boulevard
Suite 111
Tucson, AZ 85716-5398
Giving is primarily aimed at education, especially Catholic high schools and universities.

2226 Flinn Foundation
1802 N Central Avenue
Suite 2300
Phoenix, AZ 85012-2513
602-744-6800
Fax: 602-744-6815
http://www.flinn.org
Supports nonprofit organizations in the state of Arizona for programs in health care, as well as an annual awards competition for Arizona's principal arts institutions and a college scholarship program for Arizona high school graduates. Scholarship provides expenses for four years, two summers of study-related travel abroad and other benefits.

John W Murphy, Executive Director

2227 Phoenix Public Library
Business & Sciences Department
12 E McDowell Road
Phoenix, AZ 85004-1627
602-262-4636
Fax: 602-261-8836
http://www.phxlib.org
Member of The Foundation Center network, maintaining a collection of private foundation tax returns which provide information on the scope of grants dispensed by that particular foundation.

2228 Special Programs
Arizona Department of Education
1535 W Jefferson Street
Phoenix, AZ 85007-3280
602-542-5393
Fax: 602-542-5440

Tom Horne, Superintendent

2229 Support Services
Arizona Department of Education
1535 W Jefferson Street
Phoenix, AZ 85007-3280
602-542-5393
Fax: 602-542-5440

Rachel Arroyo, School Finance

2230 Vocational Technological Education
Arizona Department of Education
1535 W Jefferson Street
Phoenix, AZ 85007-3280
602-542-5393
Fax: 602-542-5440

Tom Horne, Superintendent

Arkansas

2231 Charles A Frueauff Foundation
900 S Shackleford Road
Suite 300
Little Rock, AR 72211-3848
501-219-1410
http://www.frueauffoundation.com

Will review proposals from private four-year colleges and universities.

Zoe Cole Galloway

2232 Roy and Christine Sturgis Charitable andEducational Trust
PO Box 92
Malvern, AR 72104-0092
501-337-5109
Giving is offered to Baptist and Methodist organizations, including schools, churches and higher and secondary education.

Katie Speer, Executive Director

2233 The Jones Center For Families
922 East Emma Avenue
Springdale, AR 72765
479-756-8090
Focuses funds on education, medical resources and religious organizations in Arkansas.

HG Frost Jr, Executive Director
Grace Donoho, Director Of Education

2234 Walton Family Foundation
125 W Central Avenue
Room 217 Po Box 2030
Bentonville, AR 72712-5248
479-464-1570
Fax: 479-464-1580
http://www.wffhome.com
Offers giving for systemic reform of primary education (K-12) and early childhood development.

Stewart T Springfield, Executive Director

2235 Westark Community College
Borham Library
5210 Grand Avenue
Fort Smith, AR 72904-7397
479-788-7200
Fax: 479-788-7209
Member of The Foundation Center network, maintaining a collection of private foundation tax returns which provide information on the scope of grants dispensed by that particular foundation.

2236 William C & Theodosia Murphy Nolan Foundation
200 N Jefferson Avenue
Suite 308
El Dorado, AR 71730-5853
870-863-7118
Fax: 870-863-6528
Supports education and the arts (historic preservation, arts centers) as well as religious welfare and youth organizations in Northern Louisiana and Southern Arkansas.

William C Nolan, Executive Director

2237 Winthrop Rockefeller Foundation
308 E 8th Street
Little Rock, AR 72202-3999
501-376-6854
Fax: 501-374-4797
Dedicated to improving the quality of life and education in Arkansas. Grants go to schools that work to involve teachers and parents in making decisions; to universities and local schools to strengthen both levels of education; and for projects that promote stakeholder participation in the development of educational policy.

Mahlon Martin, President
Jackie Cox-New, Sr Program Officer

California

2238 Ahmanson Foundation
9215 Wilshire Boulevard
Beverly Hills, CA 90210-5538
310-278-0770
Concentrates mainly on education, health and social services in Southern California.

Lee E Walcott, Executive Director

2239 Alice Tweed Tuohy Foundation
205 E Carrillo Street
Suite 219
Santa Barbara, CA 93101-7186
805-962-6430
Priority consideration is given to applications from organizations serving: young people; education; selected areas of interest in health care and medicine; and community affairs.

Harris W Seed, President
Eleanor Van Cott, Executive VP

2240 Arrillaga Foundation
2560 Mission College Boulevard
Suite 101
Santa Clara, CA 95054-1217
408-980-0130
Fax: 408-988-4893
Giving is aimed at secondary schools and higher education in the state of California.

John Arrillaga, Executive Director

2241 Atkinson Foundation
1100 Grundy Lane
Suite 140
San Bruno, CA 94066-3030
650-876-0222
Fax: 650-876-0222
Provides opportunities for people in San Mateo County, California to reach their highest potential and to improve the quality of their lives and to assist educational institutions and supporting organizations with the implementation of effective programs that reach and serve their target populations.

Elizabeth Curtis, Executive Director

2242 BankAmerica Foundation
Bank of America Center
PO Box 37000
San Francisco, CA 94137-0001
415-953-3175
Fax: 415-622-3469
E-mail: bacef@consumer-action.org
Fields of interest include arts/cultural programs, higher education, community development and general federated giving programs.

Elizabeth Nachbaur, Program Director

2243 Bechtel Group Corporate Giving Program
Po Box 193965
San Francisco, CA 94119-3965
415-768-5974
Offers support for higher education and programs related to engineering and construction, math and science in grades K-12 and general charitable programs.

Kathryn M Bandarrae, Executive Director

2244 Bernard Osher Foundation
909 Montgomery
#300
San Francisco, CA 94133
415-861-5587
Fax: 415-677-5868
E-mail: nagle@osherfoundation.org
Funds in the arts, post-secondary education and environmental education on San Francisco and Alameda Counties.

Patricia Nagle, Sr VP

2245 Boys-Viva Supermarkets Foundation
955 Carrillo Drive
Suite 103
Los Angeles, CA 90048-5400
Wide range of support for education of school-aged children, especially the at-risk population, tutoring, and social opportunities.

Fred Snowden, Executive Director

2246 California Community Foundation
445 S Figueroa Street
Suite 3400
Los Angeles, CA 90071-1638
210-413-4130
Fax: 213-622-2979
http://www.calfund.org
Improving human condition through nonprofit agencies in Los Angeles County. Integral parts of eligible proposals are, hosting conferences, incurring debt, individuals, sectarian purposes or regranting.

Judy Spiegel, Sr VP of Programs
Antonia Hernandez, President/CEO

2247 Carrie Estelle Doheny Foundation
707 Wilshire Boulevard
Suite 4960
Los Angeles, CA 90017-2659
213-488-1122
Fax: 213-488-1544
http://www.dohenyfoundation.org
This foundation funds a myriad of organizations ranging from the education and medicine field to public health and science areas.

Robert A Smith III, Executive Director

2248 Dan Murphy Foundation
PO Box 711267
Los Angeles, CA 90071-9767
213-623-3120
Fax: 213-623-1421
Funds Roman Catholic institutions, with a primary interest in religious orders and schools.

Daniel J Donohue, Executive Director

2249 David & Lucile Packard Foundation
300 2nd Street
Suite 200
Los Altos Hills, CA 94022-3643
650-948-7658
Fax: 650-941-3151
http://www.packard.org
Concentrates on four categories: education, the arts, conservation and child health. Also allocates funds to companies interested in public improvement and public policy.

Colburn S Wilbur, Executive Director

2250 Evelyn & Walter Haas Jr Fund
One Market Landmark
Suite 400
San Francisco, CA 94105
415-856-1400
Fax: 415-856-1500
Interested in strengthening neighborhoods, communities, and human services. Funds mainly in San Francisco Bay Area.

Ira Hirschfield, President
Clayton Juan, Grants Administrator

2251 Foundation Center-San Francisco
312 Sutter Street
Suite 606
San Francisco, CA 94108-4323
415-397-0902
Fax: 415-397-7670
http://www.fdncenter.org
One of five Foundation Centers nationwide, the Foundation Center - San Francisco is a library which collects information on private foundations, corporate philanthropy, non-

profit management, fundraising and other topics of interest to nonprofit organization representatives.

2252 Foundations Focus
Marin Community Foundation
5 Hamilton Landing
Suite 200
Novato, CA 94949
415-464-2500
Fax: 415-464-2555
http://www.marincf.org
Grants support projects that benefit residents of Marin County, CA.

Don Jen, Program Officer/Education
Thomas Peters, President/CEO

2253 Francis H Clougherty Charitable Trust
500 Newport Center Drive
Suite 720
Newport Beach, CA 92660-7007
Offers grants in the areas of elementary, secondary school and higher education in Southern California.

2254 Freitas Foundation
C/O Fiduciary Resources
1120 Nye Street
Suite 320
San Rafael, CA 94901-2945
Offers giving in the areas of elementary and secondary education, as well as theological education.

Margaret Boyden, Executive Director

2255 Fritz B Burns Foundation
4001 W Alameda Avenue
Suite 201
Burbank, CA 91505-4338
818-840-8802
Fax: 818-840-0468
Grants are primarily focused on education, hospitals and medical research organizations.

Joseph E Rawlinson, Executive Director

2256 George Frederick Jewett Foundation
235 Montgomery Street
Suite 612
San Francisco, CA 94104-2909
415-421-1351
Fax: 415-421-1351
Concerns itself mainly with voluntary, nonprofit organizations that promote human welfare.

2257 Grant & Resource Center of Northern California
2280 Benton Drive, Building C
Suite A
Redding, CA 96003
530-244-1219
Fax: 530-244-0905
E-mail: library@grcnc.org
Member of The Foundation Center network, maintaining a collection of private foundation tax returns which provide information on the scope of grants dispensed by that particular foundation.

2258 Greenville Foundation
283 2nd Street E
Suite A
Sonoma, CA 95476-5708
707-938-9377
Fax: 707-939-9311
This foundation focuses its support on education, the environment and human rights. The main focus of the educational grants lie within the areas of elementary, secondary and higher education.

Virginia Hubbell, Executive Director

2259 HN & Frances C Berger Foundation
PO Box 3064
Arcadia, CA 91006
626-447-3351
Provides scholarships and endowments to colleges and universities.

2260 Harry & Grace Steele Foundation
441 Old Newport Boulevard
Suite 301
Newport Beach, CA 92663-4231
949-631-0418
Grants are given in the areas of secondary education, including scholarship funds in the fine arts and youth agencies.

Marie F Kowert, Executive Director

2261 Henry J Kaiser Family Foundation
Quadrus
2400 Sand Hill Road
Menlo Park, CA 94025-6941
650-854-9400
Fax: 650-854-4800
http://www.kff.org
Concentrates on health care, minority groups and South Africa.

Drew Altman, President/CEO

2262 Hon Foundation
25200 La Paz Road
Suite 210
Laguna Hills, CA 92653-5110
949-586-4400
Offers giving in the areas of elementary, secondary and higher education in the states of Hawaii and California.

2263 Hugh & Hazel Darling Foundation
520 S Grand Avenue
7th Floor
Los Angeles, CA 90071-2645
213-683-5200
Fax: 213-627-7795
Supports education in California with special emphasis on legal education; no grants to individuals; grants only to 501(c)(3) organizations.

Richard L Stack, Trustee

2264 Ingraham Memorial Fund
C/O Emrys J. Ross
301 E Colorado Boulevard
Suite 900
Pasadena, CA 91101-1916
Offers giving in the areas of elementary, secondary and higher education, as well as theological education in Claremont and Pasadena, California.

2265 James G Boswell Foundation
101 W Walnut Street
Pasadena, CA 91103-3636
626-583-3000
Fax: 626-583-3090
Funds hospitals, pre-college private schools, public broadcasting and youth organizations.

James G Boswell II, Chairman
Sherman Railsback, EVP/COO

2266 James Irvine Foundation
1 Market, Steuart Tower
Suite 2500
San Francisco, CA 94105-1017
415-777-2244
Fax: 415-777-0869
Giving is primarily aimed at the areas of education, youth and health.

James E Canales, President/CEO
Kristin Nelson, Executive Assistant

2267 James S Copley Foundation
7776 Ivanhoe Avenue #1530
La Jolla, CA 92037-4520
858-454-0411
Fax: 858-729-7629

Support is offered for higher and secondary education, child development, cultural programs and community services.

Anita A Baumgardner, Executive Director

2268 John Jewett & H Chandler Garland Foundation
PO Box 550
Pasadena, CA 91102-0550
Support given primarily for secondary and higher education, social services and cultural and historical programs.

GE Morrow, Executive Director

2269 Joseph Drown Foundation
1999 Avenue of the Stars
Suite 2330
Los Angeles, CA 90067-4611
310-277-4488
Fax: 310-277-4573
http://www.jdrown.org
The Foundation's goal is to assist individuals in becoming successful, self-sustaining, contributing citizens. The foundation is interested in programs that break down any barrier that prevents a person from continuing to grow and learn.

Norman Obrow, Executive Director

2270 Jules & Doris Stein Foundation
PO Box 30
Beverly Hills, CA 90213-0030
213-276-2101
Supports charitable organizations.

2271 Julio R Gallo Foundation
PO Box 1130
Modesto, CA 95353-1130
209-579-3373
Offers grants and support to secondary schools and higher education universities.

Sam Gallo, Chairman

2272 Kenneth T & Eileen L Norris Foundation
11 Golden Shore Street
Suite 450
Long Beach, CA 90802-4214
562-435-8444
Fax: 562-436-0584
E-mail: gerringer@ktn.org
http://www.norrisfoundation.org
Funding categories include medical, education/science, youth, cultural and community.

Ronald Barnes, Executive Director

2273 Koret Foundation
33 New Montgomery Street
Suite 1090
San Francisco, CA 94105-4526
415-882-7740
Fax: 415-882-7775
E-mail: sandyedwards@koretfoundation.org
http://www.koretfoundation.org
Funding includes; public policy and selected programs in K-12 public education, higher education, youth programs, Jewish studies at colleges and universities, and Jewish education. The geographical area for grant-making is the San Francisco Bay area.

Tad Taube, President

2274 Lane Family Charitable Trust
500 Almer Road
Apartment 301
Burlingame, CA 94010-3966
Offers giving in the areas of secondary schools and higher education facilities in California.

Ralph Lane, Trustee
Joan Lane, Trustee

2275 Levi Strauss Foundation
1155 Battery Street
Floor 7
San Francisco, CA 94111-1230
415-501-6000
Fax: 415-501-7112
http://www.levistrauss.com
Grants are made in four areas: AIDS prevention and care; economic empowerment; youth empowerment; and social justice. Grants are limited to communities where Levi Strauss and Company has plants or customer service centers.

Theresa Fay-Buslillos, Executive Director

2276 Louise M Davies Foundation
580 California Street
Suite 1800
San Francisco, CA 94104-1039
Offers giving in the areas of elementary, secondary and higher education, as well as scholarship funding for California students.

Donald Crawford Jr, Executive Director

2277 Lowell Berry Foundation
3685 Mount Diablo Boulevard
Lafayette, CA 94549
925-284-4427
Fax: 925-284-4332
Assists Christian ministry at local church levels.

Debbie Coombe, Office Manager

2278 Luke B Hancock Foundation
360 Bryant Street
Palo Alto, CA 94301-1409
650-321-5536
Fax: 650-321-0697
E-mail: lhancock@lukebhancock.org
http://www.fdcenter.org/grantmaker/hancock
Provides funding for programs which promote the well being of children and youth. Priority is given to programs which address the needs of youth who are at risk of school failure. Additional funding is provided for early childhood development, music education and homeless families.

Ruth M Ramel, Executive Director

2279 Margaret E Oser Foundation
1911 Lyon Court
Santa Rosa, CA 95403-0974
949-553-4202
Offers grants in the areas of elementary and secondary and higher education, which will benefit women.

Carl Mitchell, Executive Director

2280 Marin Community Foundation
17 E Sir Francis Drake Boulevard
Suite 200
Larkspur, CA 94939-1736
415-461-3333
Fax: 415-464-2555
http://www.marincf.org
Established as a nonprofit public benefit corporation to engage in educational and philanthropic activities in Marin County, California.

2281 Mary A Crocker Trust
233 Post Street
Floor 2
San Francisco, CA 94108-5003
415-982-0138
Fax: 415-982-0141
http://www.mactrust.org
Giving is aimed at precollegiate education, as well as conservation and environmental programs.

Barbaree Jernigan, Executive Director

2282 Maurice Amado Foundation
3940 Laurel Canyon Boulevard
Suite 809
Studio City, CA 91604
818-980-9190
Fax: 818-980-9190
E-mail: pkaizer@mauriceamadofdn.org
Concentrates on the Jewish heritage.

Pam Kaizer, Executive Director

2283 McConnell Foundation
PO Box 492050
Redding, CA 96049-2050
530-226-6200
Fax: 530-226-6210
http://www.mcconnellfoundation.org
Interested in cultural, community and health care related projects.

Ana Diaz, Program Assistant

2284 McKesson Foundation
1 Post Street
San Francisco, CA 94104-5203
415-983-8300
http://www.mckesson.com/foundation.html
Giving is primarily to programs for junior high school students and for emergency services such as food and shelter.

Marcia M Argyris, Executive Director

2285 Milken Family Foundation
C/O Foundations of the Milken Families
1250 4th Street
Floor 6
Santa Monica, CA 90401-1350
310-570-4800
http://www.mff.org
Offers support to the educational community to reward educational innovators, stimulate creativity among students, involve parents and other citizens in the school system, and help disadvantaged youth.

Dr. Julius Lesner, Executive Director

2286 Miranda Lux Foundation
57 Post Street
Suite 510
San Francisco, CA 94104-5020
415-981-2966
http://ww.mirandalux.org
Offers support to promising proposals for pre-school through junior college programs in the fields of pre-vocational and vocational education and training.

Kenneth Blum, Executive Director

2287 Northern California Grantmakers
625 Market Street
15th Floor
San Francisco, CA 94105
415-777-4111
Fax: 415-777-1741
E-mail: ncg@ncg.org
Northern California Grantmakers is an association of foundations, corporate contributions programs and other private grantmakers. Its mission is to jpromote the well being of people and their communities in balance with a healthy environment by the thoughtful and creative use of private wealth and resources for the public benefit. To this end, NCG works to enhance the effectiveness of philanthropy, including nonprofit organizations, government, business, media, academia and the public at large.

Colin Lacon, President

2288 Pacific Telesis Group Corporate Giving Program
130 Kearny Street
San Francisco, CA 94108-4818
415-394-3000
Primary areas of interest include K-12 education reform, education of minorities, women

and disabled individuals in the math, science, engineering, education and MBA fields; and specific K-12 issues such as dropouts, information technology and parent involvement.

Jere A Jacobs, Executive Director

2289 Peninsula Community Foundation
1700 S El Camino Real
Suite 300
San Mateo, CA 94402-3049
650-358-9369
Fax: 650-358-9817
http://www.pcf.org
Serving a population from Daly City to Mountain View, the foundations focus is on children and youth, adult services, programs serving homeless families and children, prevention of homelessness and civic and public benefit grants.

Sterling K Speirn, Executive Director

2290 Peter Norton Family Foundation
225 Arizona Avenue
Floor 2
Santa Monica, CA 90401-1243
310-576-7700
Fax: 310-576-7701
Offers giving in the areas of early childhood education, elementary school education, higher education, childrens services and AIDS research.

Anne Etheridge, ED, Executive Director

2291 RCM Capital Management Charitable Fund
4 Embarcadero Center
Suite 2900
San Francisco, CA 94111-4189
415-954-5474
Fax: 415-954-8200
Giving is offered in many areas including youth development, early childhood education and elementary education.

Jami Weinman, Executive Director

2292 Ralph M Parsons Foundation
1055 Wilshire Boulevard
Suite 1701
Los Angeles, CA 90017-5600
213-482-3185
Fax: 213-482-8878
http://www.rmpf.org
Giving is focused on higher and pre-collegiate education, with an emphasis on engineering, technology, and science; social impact programs serving families, children and the elderly; health programs targeting underserved populations; civic and cultural programs.

Wendy G Hoppe, Executive Director

2293 Riordan Foundation
300 S Grand Avenue
Suite 29
Los Angeles, CA 90071-3110
213-229-8402
Fax: 213-229-5061
http://www.riordanfoundation.org
Priorities of the foundation include early childhood literacy, youth programs, leadership programs, job training, direct medical services to young children, and cyclical, targeted mini-grants. When determining levels of support, priority is always given to programs which impact young children.

Nike Irvin, President

2294 Royal Barney Hogan Foundation
PO Box 193809
San Francisco, CA 94119-3809
Offers grants specifically for secondary education in the state of California.

2295 SH Cowell Foundation
120 Montgomery Street
Suite 2570
San Francisco, CA 94104-4303
415-397-0285
Fax: 415-986-6786
http://www.shcowell.org
Offers support for educational programs, including pre-school and primary public educational programs.

JD Erickson, Executive Director
Mary S Metz, President

2296 Sacramento Regional Foundation
555 Capitol Mall
Suite 550
Sacramento, CA 95814-4502
916-492-6510
Fax: 916-492-6515
http://www.sacregfoundation.org
Primary interests of this foundation include the arts, humanities and education.

Stephen F Boutin, President
Janice Gow Pettey, CEO

2297 San Diego Foundation
1420 Kettner Boulevard
Suite 500
San Diego, CA 92101-2434
619-235-2300
Fax: 619-239-1710
E-mail: info@sdfoundation.org
http://www.sdfoundation.org
Offers grants in the areas of social services with emphasis on children and families, education and health for San Diego County.

Robert A Kelly, President/CEO
Rebecca Reichmann, VP Programs

2298 San Francisco Foundation
225 Bush Street
Suite 500
San Francisco, CA 94104-4224
415-733-8500
Fax: 415-477-2783
E-mail: rec@sff.org
http://www.sff.org
Addresses community needs in the areas of community health, education, arts and culture, neighborhood revitalization, and environmental justice. Works to support families and communities to help children and youth succeed in school and provide opportunities for them to become confident, caring and contributing adults.

Sandra R Hernandez MD, CEO
Sara Ying Kelley, Director Public Affairs

2299 Santa Barbara Foundation
15 E Carrillo Street
Santa Barbara, CA 93101-2780
805-963-1873
Fax: 805-966-2345
http://www.sbfoundation.org
Offers a student aid program with no interest-1/2 loan and 1/2 scholarship. Funding limited to long-term Santa Barbara County residents.

Claudia Armann, Program Officer
Charles O Slosserm, President/CEO

2300 Sega Youth Education & Health Foundation
255 Shoreline Drive
Suite 200
Redwood City, CA 94065-1428
Offers support only to organizations that address and promote youth education and health issues.

Trizia Carpenter, Executive Director

2301 Sidney Stern Memorial Trust
PO Box 893
Pacific Palisades, CA 90272-0893
310-459-2117
Funding offered includes education, community action groups, the arts and the disabled.

2302 Sol & Clara Kest Family Foundation
5150 Overland Avenue
Culver City, CA 90230-4914
213-204-2050
Offers support for Jewish organizations in the areas of education.

Sol Kest, Executive Director

2303 Szekely Family Foundation
3232 Dove Street
San Diego, CA 92103
619-295-2372
Offers giving in the areas of early childhood education, child development, elementary education, higher education, and adult and continuing education.

Deborah Szekely, Executive Director

2304 Thomas & Dorothy Leavey Foundation
10100 Santa Monica Boulevard
Suite 610
Los Angeles, CA 90067
310-551-9936
Focus is placed on college scholarships, medical research, youth groups and programs, and secondary and higher education purposes.

J Thomas McCarthy, Executive Director

2305 Times Mirror Foundation
202 West First Street
Los Angeles, CA 90012
213-237-3945
Fax: 213-237-2116
http://www.timesmirrorfoundation.org
Giving is largely for higher education purposes including liberal arts and business education.

Cassandra Malry, Executive Director

2306 Timken-Sturgis Foundation
7421 Eads Avenue
La Jolla, CA 92037-5037
619-454-2252
Offers support for education in Southern California and Nevada.

Joannie Barrancotto, Executive Director

2307 Toyota USA Foundation
19001 S Western Avenue
Torrance, CA 90501-1106
310-715-7486
Fax: 310-468-7809
E-mail: b_pauli@toyota
http://www.toyota.com/foundation
Supports K-12 education programs, with strong emphasis on math and science.

William Pauli, National Manager

2308 Turst Funds Incorporated
100 Broadway Street
Floor 3
San Francisco, CA 94111-1404
415-434-3323
Offers grants for Catholic Schools, including elementary and secondary education, in the San Francisco Bay Area.

James T Healy, President

2309 Ventura County Community Foundation
Funding & Information Resource Center
1317 Del Norte Road
Suite 150
Camarillo, CA 93010-8504
805-988-0196
Fax: 805-485-5537
http://www.vccf.org
Member of The Foundation Center network, maintaining a collection of private foundation tax returns which provide information on the scope of grants dispensed by that particular foundation.

Hugh J Ralston, President/CEO
Virginia Weber, Program Officer

2310 WM Keck Foundation
550 S Hope Street
Suite 2500
Los Angeles, CA 90071
213-680-3833
Fax: 213-614-0934
E-mail: info@wmkeck.org
http://www.wmkeck.org
The Foundation also gives some consideration, limited to Southern California, for the support of arts and culture, civic and community services, health care and precollegiate education. The foundation's grant-making is focused primarily on pioneering research efforts in the areas of science, engineering and medical research, and on higher education, including liberal arts.

Maria Pellegrini, Program Director

2311 Walter & Elise Haas Fund
1 Lombard Street
Suite 305
San Francisco, CA 94111-1130
415-398-4474
Fax: 415-986-4779
http://www.haassr.org
Supports education, arts, environment, human services, humanities and public affairs; is especially in projects which have a wide impact within their respective fields through enhancing public education and access to information, serving a central organizing role, addressing public policy, demonstrating creative approaches toward meeting human needs, or supporting the work of a major institution in the field.

Pamela H David, Executive Director
Peter E Hass Jr, President

2312 Walter S Johnson Foundation
525 Middlefield Road
Suite 160
Menlo Park, CA 94025-3447
650-326-0485
Fax: 650-326-4320
http://www.wsjf.org
Giving is centered on education in public schools and social service agencies concerned with the quality of public education in Northern California and Washoe County, Nevada.

Pancho Chang, Executive Director

2313 Wayne & Gladys Valley Foundation
1939 Harrison Street
Suite 510
Oakland, CA 94612-3535
510-466-6060
Fax: 510-466-6067
Supports four areas: education, medical research, community services and special projects.

Michael D Desler, Executive Director

2314 Weingart Foundation
1055 W 7th Street
Suite 3050
Los Angeles, CA 90017-2509
213-688-7799
Fax: 213-688-1515
http://www.weingartfnd.org
Offers support for community services including a student loan program.

William D Schulte, Chairman & CEO
Fred J Ali, President/Chief Adm. Officer

2315 Wells Fargo Foundation
550 California Street
7th Floor MAC A0112-073
San Francisco, CA 94104
415-396-5830
Fax: 415-975-6260
http://www.wellsfargo.com
Offers support for elementary school education, secondary school education and community development.

Tim Hanlon, Executive Director

2316 Wilbur D May Foundation
C/O Brookhill Corporation
2716 Ocean Park Boulevard
Suite 2011
Santa Monica, CA 90405
Gives to youth organizations and hospitals.

2317 William & Flora Hewlett Foundation
2121 Sand Hill Road
Menlo Park, CA 94025-3448
650-234-4500
Fax: 650-234-4501
http://www.hewlett.org
The Hewlett Foundation concentrates its resources on the performing arts, education, population issues, environmental issues, conflict resolution and family and community development. Grants in the education program, specifically the elementary and secondary education part of it, are limited to K-12 areas in California programs, with primary emphasis on public schools in the San Francisco Bay area. The program favors schools, school districts and universities.

Paul Brest, President

2318 William C Bannerman Foundation
9255 Sunset Boulevard
Suite 400
West Hollywood, CA 90069
310-273-9933
Fax: 310-273-9931
Offers grants in the fields of elementary school, secondary schools, education, human services and youth programs K-12 in Los Angeles County, Adult Education and Vocational Training.

Elliot Ponchick, President

2319 Y&H Soda Foundation
2 Theatre Square
Suite 211
Orinda, CA 94563-3346
925-253-2630
Fax: 925-253-1814
E-mail: jNM@silcom.com
Offers support in the areas of early childhood education, child development, elementary education and vocational and higher education.

Judith Murphy, Executive Director

2320 Zellerbach Family Fund
120 Montgomery Street
Suite 1550
San Francisco, CA 94104-4318
415-421-2629
Fax: 415-421-6713
Provides funds to nonprofit organizations in the San Francisco Bay Area.

Cindy Rambo, Executive Director
Linda Avidan, Program Director

Colorado

2321 Adolph Coors Foundation
4100 East Mississippi Avenue
Suite 1850
Denver, CO 80246

303-388-1636
Fax: 303-388-1684
http://www.adolphcoors.org
Giving is primarily offered for programs with an emphasis on education, human services, youth and health.

Sally W Rippey, Executive Director
Jeanne L Bistranin, Program Officers

2322 Boettcher Foundation
600 17th Street
Suite 2210
Denver, CO 80202-5402
303-534-1937
800-323-9640
http://www.boettcherfoundation.org
Offers grants to educational institutions, with an emphasis on scholarships and fellowships.

Timothy W Schultz, President/Executive Director

2323 Denver Foundation
950 S Cherry Street
Suite 200
Denver, CO 80246
303-300-1790
Fax: 303-300-6547
http://www.denverfounation.org
The Foundation serves as the steward and the administrator of the endowment, charged with investing its earned income in programs that meet the community's growing and changing needs. The Foundation has a solid history of supporting a broad array of community efforts. Grants are awarded to nonprofit organizations that touch nearly every meaningful artistic, cultural, civic, educational, human service and health interest of metro Denver's citizens.

David Miller, President/CEO
Betsy Mangone, VP Philanthropic Services

2324 El Pomar Foundation
10 Lake Circle
Colorado Springs, CO 80906-4201
719-633-7733
800-554-7711
Fax: 719-577-5702
http://www.elpomar.org
Founded in 1937, the philosophy of this foundation is simply to help foster a climate for excellence in Colorado's third sector, the nonprofit community, as well as the foundation's own responsibility to improve the quality of life for all residents of Colorado. The foundation gives grants to the arts and humanities, civic and community, education, health, human services, and youth in community service.

William J Hybl, Executive Director

2325 Gates Foundation
3575 Cherry Creek N Drive
Suite 100
Denver, CO 80209-3247
303-722-1881
Fax: 303-698-9031
The purpose of this foundation is to aid, assist, encourage, initiate, or carry on activities that will promote the health, well-being, security and broad education of all people. Because of a deep concern for and confidence in the future of Colorado, the foundation will invest primarily in institutions and programs that will enhance the quality of life for those who live and work in the state.

Thomas C Stokes, Executive Director

2326 Ruth & Vernon Taylor Foundation
518 17th Street
Suite 1670
Denver, CO 80202
303-893-5284
Fax: 303-893-8263

Offers support for education, the arts, human services and conservation.

Friday A Green, Executive Director

2327 US West Foundation
7800 E Orchard Road
Suite 300
Englewood, CO 80111-2526
303-799-3852
Grants are given in the areas of health and human services, including programs for youth, early childhood, elementary, secondary, higher and other.

Janet Rash, Executive Director

Connecticut

2328 Aetna Foundation
151 Farmington Avenue
Hartford, CT 06156-0001
860-273-0123
Fax: 860-273-4764
http://www.aetna.com/foundation/
Aetna gives grants in various areas that improve the community and its citizens. Certain areas include; children's health, education for at-risk students, and community initiatives. Geographic emphasis is placed on organizations and initiatives in Aetna's Greater Hartford headquarters communities; organizations in select communities across the country where Aetna has a significant local presence; and national organizations that can influence state, local or federal policies and programs.

Marilda L Gandara, President
Dave Wilmont, Executive Assistant

2329 Community Foundation of Greater New Haven
70 Audubon Street
New Haven, CT 06510-1248
203-777-2386
Fax: 203-787-6584
http://www.cfgnh.org
Offers a wide variety of giving with an emphasis on social services, youth services, AIDS research and education.

William W Ginsberg, President/CEO
Ronda Maddox, Administrative Assistant

2330 Connecticut Mutual Financial Services
140 Garden Street
Hartford, CT 06154-0200
860-987-6500
Giving is aimed at education, primarily higher education, equal opportunity programs and social services.

Astrida R Olds, Executive Director

2331 Hartford Foundation for Public Giving
85 Gillett Street
Hartford, CT 06105-2693
860-548-1888
Fax: 860-524-8346
E-mail: www.hfpg.org
Offers grants for demonstration programs and capital purposes with emphasis on educational institutions, social services and cultural programs.

Michael R Bangser, Executive Director

2332 Loctite Corporate Contributions Program
Hartford Square North
10 Columbus Boulevard
5th Floor
Hartford, CT 06106-1976

860-571-5100
Fax: 860-571-5430
Offers support in various fields of interest including funding for educational programs for inner city youths in grades K-12.

Kiren Cooley, Corporate Contributions

2333 Louis Calder Foundation
175 Elm Street
New Canaan, CT 06840
203-966-8925
Fax: 203-966-5785
http://www.louiscalderfdn.org
Offers support to organizations who promote education, health and welfare of children and youth in New York City.

Holly Nuechterlein, Program Manager

2334 Sherman Fairchild Foundation
71 Arch Street
Greenwich, CT 06830-6544
203-661-9360
Fax: 203-661-9360
Offers grants in higher education, fine arts and cultural institutions.

Patricia A Lydon, Executive Director

2335 Smart Family Foundation
74 Pin Oak Lane
Wilton, CT 06897-1329
203-834-0400
Fax: 203-834-0412
The foundation is interested in educational projects that focus on primary and secondary school children.

Raymond Smart, Executive Director

2336 Worthington Family Foundation
411 Pequot Avenue
Southport, CT 06490-1386
203-255-9400
Offers grants in the areas of elementary school education and secondary school education in Connecticut.

Worthington Johnson, Executive Director

Delaware

2337 Crystal Trust
Po Box 39
Montchanin, DE 19710-0039
302-651-0533
Grants are awarded for higher and secondary education and social and family services.

Stephen C Doberstein, Executive Director

2338 HW Buckner Charitable Residuary Trust
JP Morgan Services
PO Box 8714
Wilmington, DE 19899-8714
302-633-1900
Focuses giving on educational and cultural organizations in New York, Rhode Island and Massachusetts.

2339 Longwood Foundation
100 W 10th Street
Suite 1109
Wilmington, DE 19801-1694
302-654-2477
Fax: 302-654-2323
Limited grants are offered to educational institutions and cultural programs.

David D Wakefield, Executive Director

District of Columbia

2340 Abe Wouk Foundation
3255 N Street NW
Washington, DC 20007-2845
Offers grants in elementary, secondary education and federated giving programs.

Herman Wouk, Executive Director

2341 Eugene & Agnes E Meyer Foundation
1400 16th Street NW
Suite 360
Washington, DC 20036-2215
202-483-8294
Fax: 202-328-6850
http://www.meyerfoundation.org
Offers grants in the areas of development and housing, education and community services, arts and humanities, law and justice, health and mental health.

Julie L Rogers, President

2342 Foundation Center-District of Columbia
1627 K Street NW
3rd Floor
Washington, DC 20006-1708
202-331-1400
Fax: 202-331-1739
http://www.fdncenter.org/washington/index.jhtml
Member of The Foundation Center network, maintaining a collection of private foundation tax returns which provide information on the scope of grants dispensed to nonprofit organizations by those particular foundations.

2343 Foundation for the National Capitol Region
1201 15th Street NW
Suite 420
Washington, DC 20005
202-955-5890
Fax: 202-955-8084
http://www.cfncr.org
Grants are focused on organization strengthening and regional collaboration. The Foundation wishes to foster collaborations that identify, address, and increase awareness of regional issues, as well as help strengthen the region's existing nonprofit organizations to improve their financial stability. The Foundation welcomes requests from organizations serving the Greater Washington area that are tax-exempt under Section 501(c)(3) of the Internal Revenue Code.

Terry Lee Freeman, President

2344 Gilbert & Jaylee Mead Family Foundation
2700 Virginia Avenue NW #701
Washington, DC 20037-1908
202-338-0208
Offers support for education (K-12), the performing arts and community service programs for Washington, DC, Montgomery County, Maryland, and Geneva, Switzerland.

Linda Smith, Executive Director

2345 Hitachi Foundation
1509 22nd Street NW
Washington, DC 20037-1073
202-457-0588
Fax: 202-296-1098
http://www.hitachi.org
The majority of projects supported by the foundation: promote collaboration across sectors and among institutions, organizations and individuals; reflect multi-or-interdisciplinary perspectives; respect and value diversity of thought, action, and ethnicity. Grants are given in the areas of community develop-

ment, education, global citizenship and program related investments.

Barbara Dyer, President/CEO

2346 Morris & Gwendolyn Cafritz Foundation
1825 K Street NW
Suite 1400
Washington, DC 20006-1202
202-223-3100
Fax: 202-296-7567
http://www.cafritzfoundation.org
Gives grants to organizations in the metropolitan area, focusing on arts, humanities and scholarships.

Sara Cofrin, Program Assistant

2347 Public Welfare Foundation
1200 U Street NW
Washington, DC 20009-4443
202-965-1800
Fax: 202-265-8851
http://www.publicwelfare.org
Offers grants to grass roots organizations in the US and abroad with emphasis on the environment and education.

Larry Kressley, Executive Director
Teresa Langston, Director Of Programs

2348 Washington Post Company Educational Foundation
1150 15th Street NW
Washington, DC 20071-0002
202-334-6000
Offers support for pre-college and higher education including student scholarships and awards for academic excellence.

Eric Grant, Director Contributions

Florida

2349 Applebaum Foundation
1111 Biscaynees Boulevard
Tower 3, Room 853
North Miami, FL 33181
Offers an emphasis on higher education.

2350 Benedict Foundation for Independent Schools
607 Lantana Lane
Vero Beach, FL 32963-2315
Support is offered primarily for independent secondary schools that have been members of the National Association of Independent Schools for ten consecutive years.

Nancy H Benedict, Executive Director

2351 Chatlos Foundation
PO Box 915048
Longwood, FL 32791-5048
407-862-5077
Fax: 407-862-0708
http://www.chatlos.org
Bible colleges and seminaries, liberal arts colleges, vocation and domestic education, medical education; children, elderly, disabled and learning disabled. The Foundation is non-receptive to primary or secondary education, the arts, medical research, individual churches. No direct scholarship support to individuals.

William J Chatlos, Executive Director

2352 Citibank of Florida Corporate Giving Program
8750 Doral Boulevard
7th Floor
Miami, FL 33718
305-599-5775
Fax: 305-599-5520

Offers support for K-12 education for at-risk children. Funding is also available through the program for housing and community development in the state of Florida.

Susan Yarosz, Executive Director

2353 Dade Community Foundation
200 S Biscayne Boulevard
Suite 505
Miami, FL 33131-2343
305-371-2711
Fax: 305-371-5342
http://www.dadecommunityfoundation.org
Offers support for projects in the fields of education, arts and culture.

Ruth Shack, Executive Director

2354 Innovating Worthy Projects Foundation
Lakeview Corporate Center
6415 Lake Worth Road
Suite 208
Lake Worth, FL 33463-2904
561-439-4445
Offers grants and support for education in the areas of childhood education and elementary education.

Dr. Irving Packer, Executive Director

2355 Jacksonville Public Library
Business, Science & Documents
122 N Ocean Street
Jacksonville, FL 32202-3374
904-630-1994
Fax: 904-630-2431
http://www.neflin.org/members/libraries/jackspub.htm
Member of The Foundation Center network, maintaining a collection of private foundation tax returns which provide information on the scope of grants dispensed by that particular foundation.

Gretchen Mitchell, Business/Science Department

2356 Jessie Ball duPont Fund
One Independent Drive
Suite 1400
Jacksonville, FL 32202-5011
904-353-0890
800-252-3452
Fax: 904-353-3870
E-mail: smagill@dupontfund.org
http://www.dupontfund.org
Grants limited to those institutions to which the donor contributed personally during the five year period ending December 31, 1964. Among the 325 institutions eligible to recieve funds are higher and secondary education intitutions, cultural and historic preservation programs, social services organizations, hospitals, health agencies, churches and church-related organizations and youth agencies.

Dr. Sherry P Magill, President
JoAnn Bennett, Director Administration

2357 Joseph & Rae Gann Charitable Foundation
10185 Collins Avenue
Apartment 317
Bal Harbour, FL 33154-1606
Offers support in the areas of elementary, secondary and theological education.

2358 Orlando Public Library-Orange County Library System
Social Sciences Department
101 E Central Boulivard
Orlando, FL 32801-2471
407-835-7323
Fax: 407-835-7646
E-mail: ajacobe@ocls.lib.fl.us
http://www.ocls.lib.fl.us

Member of The Foundation Center network, maintaining a collection on microfiche of Florida private foundation tax returns which provide information on the scope of grants dispensed by that particular foundation. Other available resources include directories of foundations, guide to funding, and materials on successful grant acquisition. FC Search Foundation Center CD Rom.

Angela C Jacobe, Head Social Science Dpt

2359 Peter D & Eleanore Kleist Foundation
12734 Kenwood Lane
Suite 89
Fort Myers, FL 33907-5638
Support is given to secondary school education and higher education.

Peter D Kleist, Executive Director

2360 Robert G Friedman Foundation
76 Isla Bahia Drive
Fort Lauderdale, FL 33316-2331
Giving is offered to elementary and high schools, with minor support to indigent individuals and charitable activities.

Robert G Friedman, Executive Director

2361 Southwest Florida Community Foundation
8260 College Parkway
Suite 101
Fort Myers, FL 33919
239-274-5900
Fax: 239-274-5930
E-mail: swflcfo@earthlink.net
http://www.floridacommunity.com
Offers grants and support in the areas of education, higher education, children and youth services and general charitable giving to Lee, Charlotte, Hendry, Glades, and Collier Counties, Florida.

Paul B Flynn, Executive Director
Carol McLaughlin, Program Director

2362 Student Help and Assistance Program toEducation
C/O Michael Bienes
141 Bay Colony Drive
Fort Lauderdale, FL 33308-2024
Offers grants and support in the areas of elementary and secondary education, music and dance.

2363 Thomas & Irene Kirbo Charitable Trust
1112 W Adams Street
Suite 1111
Jacksonville, FL 32202
904-354-7212
Favors smaller colleges in Florida and Georgia.

Murray Jenks, Executive Director

2364 Thompson Publishing Group
PO Box 26185
Tampa, FL 33623
800-876-0226
http://www.thompson.com or
www.grantsandfunding.com
Assists education administrators and grant seekers in successful fundraising in the public and private sectors.

Joel M Drucker, Executive Director

Georgia

2365 Atlanta-Fulton Public Library
Foundation Collection/Ivan Allen Department
1 Margaret Mitchell Square NW
Atlanta, GA 30303-1089

404-730-1700
Fax: 404-730-1990
http://www.af.public.lib.ga.us
Member of The Foundation Center network, maintaining a collection of private foundation tax returns which provide information on the scope of grants dispensed by that particular foundation.

2366 BellSouth Foundation
C/O BellSouth Corporation
1155 Peachtree Street NE
Sutie 7H08
Atlanta, GA 30309-3600
404-249-2396
Fax: 404-249-5696
http://www.bellsouthfoundation.org
The foundation's purpose is to improve education in the South and to address the problem of the inadequate schooling in the region.

Mary D Boehm, President
Beverly Fleming, Administrative Assistant

2367 Bradley Foundation
PO Box 1408
Savannah, GA 31402-1408
404-571-6040
Focuses on higher educational facilities, elementary and secondary education, human services and federated giving programs.

2368 Callaway Foundation
209 W Broome Street
#790
Lagrange, GA 30240-3101
706-884-7348
Fax: 706-884-0201
Offers giving in the areas of elementary, higher and secondary education, including libraries and community giving.

JT Gresham, Executive Director

2369 Coca-Cola Foundation
Po Box 1734
Atlanta, GA 30301
404-676-2568
Fax: 404-676-8804
http://www.thecoca-colacompany.com
Committed to serving communities through education. The foundation supports programs for early childhood education, elementary and secondary schools, public and private colleges and universities, teacher training, adult learning and global education programs, among others.

Donald R Greene, Executive Director

2370 J Bulow Campbell Foundation
50 Hurt Plaza
Suite 312
Atlanta, GA 30303
404-658-9066
Fax: 404-659-4802
The purpose of this foundation is to offer grants and support to privately supported education, human welfare, youth services and the arts in the state of Georgia.

John W Stephenson, Executive Director

2371 JK Gholston Trust
C/O NationsBank of Georgia
PO Box 992
Athens, GA 30603-0992
706-357-6271
Support is offered to elementary school and higher education facilities in the Comer, Georgia area.

Janey M Cooley, Executive Director

2372 John & Mary Franklin Foundation
C/O Bank South N.A.
PO Box 4956
Atlanta, GA 30302
404-521-7397

Offers grants in secondary school/education, higher education and youth services.

Virlyn Moore Sr, Executive Director

2373 John H & Wilhelmina D Harland CharitableFoundation
2 Piedmont Center NE
Suite 106
Atlanta, GA 30305-1502
404-264-9912
Fax: 404-266-8834
Children and higher education.

2374 Joseph B Whitehead Foundation
50 Hurt Plaza SE
Suite 1200
Atlanta, GA 30303-2916
404-522-6755
Fax: 404-522-7026
http://www.jbwhitehead.org
Offers grants in education, cultural programs, the arts and civic affairs.

Charles H McTier, Executive Director

2375 Lettie Pate Evans Foundation
50 Hurt Plaza SE
Suite 1200
Atlanta, GA 30303-2916
404-522-6755
Fax: 404-522-7026
http://www.lpevans.org
Offers grants in the areas of higher education, and support for educational and cultural institutions.

Charles H McTier, Executive Director
Russell Hardin, Vice President/Secretary

2376 McCamish Foundation
1 Buckhead Loop NE #3060
Atlanta, GA 30326-1528
Offers grants for conservation and educational institutions.

2377 Metropolitan Atlanta Community Foundation
50 Hurt Plaza
Suite 449
Atlanta, GA 30303
404-688-5525
Fax: 404-688-3060
http://www.atlcf.org
This foundation was organized for the administration of funds placed in trust for the purposes of improving education, community development and civic health of the 19-county metropolitan area of Atlanta.

Winsome Hawkins Sr, Executive Director
Alicia Phillip, President

2378 Mill Creek Foundation
PO Box 190
115 North Racetrack Street
Swainsboro, GA 30401-0190
478-237-0101
Fax: 478-237-6187
The foundation's primary interests are educational programs in all levels of study in Emanuel County, Georgia.

James H Morgan, Executive Director

2379 Mills Bee Lane Memorial Foundation
Nations Bank of Georgia
PO Box 9626
Savannah, GA 31412-9626
Offers support in various areas of education, including higher, secondary, and elementary.

2380 Peyton Anderson Foundation
577 Mulberry Street
Suite 105
Macon, GA 31201
478-743-5359
Fax: 912-742-5201

Supports organizations and programs that center on elementary education, higher education, adult education, literacy and basic skills and youth services, in Bibb County, Georgia only.

Juanita T Jordan, Executive Director

2381 Rich Foundation
11 Piedmont Avenue NE
Atlanta, GA 30303
404-262-2266
Funds are allocated to social services, health, the arts and education.

Anne Berg, Executive Director

2382 Robert & Polly Dunn Foundation
PO Box 723194
Atlanta, GA 31139-0194
404-816-2883
Fax: 404-237-2150
Offers support in the areas of child development, education, higher education, and children and youth services.

Karen C Wilbanks, Executive Director

2383 Sapelo Foundation
1712 Ellis Street
2nd Floor
Brunswick, GA 31520
912-265-0520
Fax: 912-265-1888
The Sapelo Foundation's scholarship program, The Richard Reynolds Scholarship Program offers college scholarships only to students who are legal residents of McIntosh County, Georgia.

Phyllis Bowen, Administrative Assistant
Alan McGregor, Executive Director

2384 Tull Charitable Foundation
50 Hurt Plaza SE
Suite 1245
Atlanta, GA 30303-2916
404-659-7079
http://www.tullfoundation.org
Offers support to secondary schools, elementary schools and higher education facilities in the state of Georgia.

Barbara Cleveland, Executive Director

2385 Warren P & Ava F Sewell Foundation
PO Box 645
Bremen, GA 30110-0645
Offers support in elementary school, secondary school education and religion.

Jack Worley, Executive Director

Hawaii

2386 Barbara Cox Anthony Foundation
1132 Bishop Street #120
Honolulu, HI 96813-2807
Offers support to secondary schools, higher education, and human service organizations in Hawaii.

Barner Anthony, Executive Director

2387 Cooke Foundation
1164 Bishop Street
Suite 800
Honolulu, HI 96813
808-566-5524
888-731-3863
Fax: 808-521-6286
E-mail: foundations@hcf-hawaii.org
http://www.hawaiicommunityfoundation.org

The environment, the arts, education and social services are the priority areas for this foundation.

Lisa Schiff, Private Foundation Service
Samuel Cooke, President & Trustee

2388 Harold KL Castle Foundation
146 Hekili Street
Suite 203A
Kailua, HI 96734-2835
808-262-9413
http://www.castlefoundation.org
Grants are given in the area of education, community and cultural/community affairs.

Terrence R George, Executive Director
H Mitchell D'Olier, President

2389 Hawaiian Electric Industries CharitableFoundation
PO Box 730
Honolulu, HI 96808-0730
808-532-5862
http://www.hei.com/heicf/heicf.html
Offers support for education, including higher education, business education, educational associations and secondary schools.

Scott Shirai, Executive Director
Robert F Clark, President

2390 James & Abigail Campbell Foundation
1001 Kamokila Boulevard
Kapolei, HI 96707-2014
808-674-6674
888-322-2232
Fax: 808-674-3111
Offers support in education for schools and educational programs related to literacy or job training in Hawaii.

Theresia McMurdo, Public Relations

2391 Oceanic Cablevision Foundation
200 Akamainui Street
Mililani, HI 96789-3999
808-625-8359
Offers support in a variety of areas with an emphasis on education, especially early childhood and cultural programs.

Kit Beuret, Executive Director

2392 Samuel N & Mary Castle Foundation
733 Bishop Street
Suite 1275
Honolulu, HI 96813-2912
808-522-1101
Fax: 808-522-1103
E-mail: acastle@aloha.net
http://www.fdncenter.org
Funding is offered in the areas of education, human services and the arts for the state of Hawaii.

Annually

Al Castle, Executive Director

2393 University of Hawaii
Hamilton Library
2550 The Mall
Honolulu, HI 96822-2233
808-956-7214
Fax: 808-956-5968
http://www.libweb.hawaii.edu/uhmlib
Member of The Foundation Center network, maintaining a collection of private foundation tax returns which provide information on the scope of grants dispensed by that particular foundation.

Idaho

2394 Boise Public Library
715 S Capitol Boulevard
Boise, ID 83702-7115
208-384-4076
http://www.boisepubliclibrary.org
Member of The Foundation Center network, maintaining a collection of private foundation tax returns which provide information on the scope of grants dispensed by that particular foundation.

2395 Claude R & Ethel B Whittenberger Foundation
PO Box 1073
Caldwell, ID 83606-1073
208-459-0091
E-mail: whittfnd@cableone.net
http://www.whittenberger.org
Offers support for youth and children in higher and secondary education.

William J Rankin, Executive Director

2396 Walter & Leona Dufresne Foundation
1150 W State Street
Boise, ID 83702-5327
Offers support in the areas of secondary school education and higher education.

Royce Chigbrow, Executive Director

Illinois

2397 Ameritech Foundation
30 S Wacker Drive
Floor 34
Chicago, IL 60606-7487
312-750-5223
Fax: 312-207-1098
http://www.ntlf.com
A foundation that offers grants to elementary school/education, secondary school/education and higher education.

Michael E Kuhlin, Executive Director

2398 Carus Corporate Contributions Program
315 5th Street
Peru, IL 61354-2859
815-223-1500
Offers support for higher, secondary, elementary and early childhood education.

Robert J Wilmot, Executive Director

2399 Chauncey & Marion Deering McCormick Foundation
410 N Michigan Avenue
Suite 590
Chicago, IL 60611-4220
312-644-6720
Preschool education, journalism and the improvement of socio-economic condition of Metropolitan Chicago are the main areas of giving for this foundation.

Charles E Schroeder, Executive Director

2400 Chicago Community Trust
11 East Wacker Drive
Suite 1400
Chicago, IL 60601-1088
312-616-8000
Fax: 312-616-7955
E-mail: sandy@cct.org
http://www.cct.org
A community foundation that offers support for general operating projects and specific programs and projects in areas including child development, education and higher education.

Sandy Chears, Grants Manager
Terry Mazany, President

2401 Coleman Foundation
575 W Madison Street
Suite 4605-Ii
Chicago, IL 60661-2515
312-902-7120
Fax: 312-902-7124
http://www.colemanfoundation.org
A nonprofit, private foundation established in the state of Illinois in 1951. Major areas of support include health, educational, cultural, scientific and social programs. Grants generally focus on organizations within the Midwest and particularly within the state of Illinois and the Chicago Metropolitan area. No grants are made for programs outside of the United States. Ongoing support is not available, continuing programs must indicate how they will be sustained in the future.

Rosa Janus, Program Manager
Michael W Hennessy, President/CEO

2402 Dellora A & Lester J Norris Foundation
PO Box 4325
Saint Charles, IL 60174-9075
630-377-4111
Education, health and social services are the main concerns of this foundation, with Illinois, Colorado and Florida being their priority.

Eugene W Butler, Executive Director

2403 Dillon Foundation
2804 West Le Fevre Road
Sterling, IL 61081-0537
815-626-9000
Offers support for educational purposes, including higher education and community services.

Peter W Dillon, Executive Director

2404 Dr. Scholl Foundation
1033 Skokie Boulevard
Suite 230
Northbrook, IL 60062
847-559-7430
http://www.drschollfoundation.com
Applications for grants are considered in the following areas: private education at all levels including elementary, secondary schools, colleges and universities and medical and nursing institutions; general charitable organizations and programs, including grants to hospitals and programs for children, developmentally disabled and senior citizens; civic, cultural, social services, health care, economic and religious activities.

Pamela Scholl, Executive Director

2405 Evanston Public Library
1703 Orrington Avenue
Evanston, IL 60201-3886
847-866-0300
Fax: 847-866-0313
http://www.evanston.lib.il.us
Member of The Foundation Center network, maintaining a collection of private foundation tax returns which provide information on the scope of grants dispensed by that particular foundation.

Neal J Ney, Director

2406 Farny R Wurlitzer Foundation
PO Box 418
Sycamore, IL 60178-0418
Offers support in the areas of education, including programs for minorities, early child-hood, elementary and secondary institutions, music education and organizations.

William A Rolfing, Executive Director

2407 Grover Hermann Foundation
1000 Hill Grove
Suite 200
Western Springs, IL 60558-6306
708-246-8331
Focus of giving is on higher education and private schooling activities.

Paul K Rhoads, Executive Director

2408 Joyce Foundation
70 W Madison Street
Suite 2750
Chicago, IL 60602
312-782-2464
Fax: 312-782-4160
E-mail: info@joycefdn.org
http://www.joycefdn.org
Based in Chicago with assets of $1 billion, the Joyce foundation supports efforts to strengthen public policies in ways that improve the quality of life in the Great Lakes region. Last year the foundation made nearly $17 million in grants to groups working to inprove public education in Chicago, Cleveland, Detroit and Milwaukee.

Ellen Alberding, President

2409 Lloyd A Fry Foundation
120 S Lasalle Street
Suite 1950
Chicago, IL 60603-4204
312-580-0310
Fax: 312-580-0980
http://www.fryfoundation.org
The foundation primarily supports education, higher education, the performing arts, and social service organizations.

Unmi Song, Executive Director

2410 Northern Trust Company Charitable Trust
Community Affairs Division
50 S Lasalle Street
Chicago, IL 60603-1006
312-630-6000
http://www.ntrs.com
Offers grants in the areas of community development, education and early childhood education.

Marjorie W Lundy, Executive Director

2411 Palmer Foundation
C/O Jay L. Owen
824 N Western Avenue
Lake Forest, IL 60045-1703
Offers grants in elementary and secondary education, as well as youth services and Protestant churches.

2412 Philip H Corboy Foundation
33 N Dearborn Street
Chicago, IL 60602-2502
312-346-3191
http://www.corboydemetrio.com
Offers grants in the areas of elementary, secondary, law school education and health care.

2413 Polk Brothers Foundation
20 W Kinzie Street
Suite 1100
Chicago, IL 60610-4600
312-527-4684
Fax: 312-527-4681
http://www.polkbrosfdn.org
Offers grants for new or ongoing programs to organizations whose work is based in the areas of education, social services and health care.

Nikki W Stein, Executive Director
Shiela A Robinson, Grants Administrator

2414 Prince Charitable Trust
303 West Madison Street
Suite 1900
Chicago, IL 60606-7407
312-419-8700
Fax: 312-419-8558
http://www.fdncenter.org/grantmaker/prince
/chicago.html
Offers support for cultural programs, public
school programming and social service organizations.

Benna B Wilde, Managing Director
Sharon L Robison, Grants Manager

2415 Regenstein Foundation
8600 W Bryn Mawr Avenue
Suite 705N
Chicago, IL 60631-3579
773-693-6464
Fax: 773-693-2480
Offers grants for educational and general
charitable institutions within the metropolitan Chicago area and the state of Illinois.

Joseph Regenstein Jr, Executive Director

2416 Richard H Driehaus Foundation
77 W Wacker Drive
Chicago, IL 60601-1604
312-641-5772
Fax: 312-641-5736
Offers support in elementary, secondary and
higher education in the state of Illinois.

Susan M Levy, Executive Director

**2417 Robert R McCormick Tribune
Foundation**
435 N Michigan Avenue
Suite 770
Chicago, IL 60611-4066
312-222-3512
Fax: 312-222-3523
http://www.rrmtf.org
Offers contributions for private higher education and rehabilitation services.

Nicholas Goodban, Senior VP/Philanthropy
Richard A Behrenhausen, President/CEO

2418 Sears-Roebuck Foundation
Sears Tower
Department 903-BSC 51-02
Chicago, IL 60684
312-875-8337
The foundation focuses its giving primarily
on projects that address education and
volunteerism.

Paula A Banke, Executive Director

2419 Spencer Foundation
875 N Michigan Avenue
Suite 3930
Chicago, IL 60611-1803
312-337-7000
Fax: 312-337-0282
http://www.spencer.org
Supports research aimed at the practice of understanding and expanding knowledge in the
area of education.

Michael McPherson, President

2420 Sulzer Family Foundation
1940 W Irving Park Road
Chicago, IL 60613-2437
312-321-4700
Offers giving for education, including higher,
secondary, elementary and adult education in
the areas of Chicago, Illinois.

John J Hoellen, Executive Director

2421 United Airlines Foundation
PO Box 66919
Chicago, IL 60666-0919
847-952-5714

Offers a wide variety of support programs
with an emphasis on education and educational reform.

Eileen Younglove, Executive Director

2422 Valenti Charitable Foundation
Valenti Builders
225 Northfield Road
Northfield, IL 60093-3311
847-446-2200
Fax: 847-446-2610
Offers support in elementary education, secondary school education, higher education
and children and youth services.

Valenti Sr Trustee, Executive Director

Indiana

2423 Allen County Public Library
Po Box 2270
Fort Wayne, IN 46802-3699
260-421-1200
Fax: 260-421-1386
http://www.acpl.lib.in.us
Member of The Foundation Center network,
maintaining a collection of private foundation tax returns which provide information on
the scope of grants dispensed by that particular foundation.

2424 Arvin Foundation
1 Noblitt Plaza #3000
Columbus, IN 47201-6079
812-379-3207
Fax: 812-379-3688
Giving is offered primarily to primary, secondary and higher education and technical
training.

E Fred Meyer, Executive Director

2425 Clowes Fund
320 N Meridian Street Suite 316
The Chamber of Commerce Building
Indianapolis, IN 46204-1722
800-943-7209
Fax: 800-943-7286
http://www.clowesfund.org
Offers giving for higher and secondary education; the performing arts; marine biology and
social service organizations.

Elizabeth Casselman, Executive Director

2426 Dekko Foundation
PO Box 548
Kendallville, IN 46755-0548
260-347-1278
Fax: 260-347-7103
Offers support for all levels of education and
human service organizations.

Linda Speakman, Executive Director

**2427 Eli Lilly & Company Corporate
Contribution Program**
Lilly Corporate Center D.C. 1627
Indianapolis, IN 46285
317-276-2000
Offers support in the areas of secondary
school/education, higher education and
health care programs.

Thomas King, President

2428 Foellinger Foundation
520 E Berry Street
Fort Wayne, IN 46802-2002
260-422-2900
Fax: 260-422-9436
http://www.foellinger.org
Giving is aimed at higher education and other
secondary and elementary projects, commu-

nity programs and social service organizations.

Harry V Owen, Executive Director

2429 Indianapolis Foundation
615 N Alabama Street
Suite 119
Indianapolis, IN 46204-1498
317-634-2423
Fax: 317-684-0943
http://www.indyfund.org
Offers support in the areas of education and
neighborhood services.

Kenneth Gladish, Executive Director

2430 John W Anderson Foundation
402 Wall Street
Valparaiso, IN 46383-2562
219-462-4611
Fax: 219-531-8954
Offers grants in the areas of higher education,
youth programs, human services, and arts and
humanities. Grants are limited primarily to
Northwest Indian organizations.

William Vinovich, Vice Chairman/Trustee

2431 Lilly Endowment
2801 N Meridian Street
Indianapolis, IN 46208-4712
317-924-5471
Fax: 317-926-4431
http://www.lillyendowment.org
Supports the causes of religion, education and
community development. Although the Endowment supports efforts of national significance, especially in the field of religion, it is
primarily committed to its hometown, Indianapolis, and home state, Indiana.

Sue Ellen Walker, Communications
Associate

2432 Moore Foundation
9100 Keystone Xing
Suite 390
Indianapolis, IN 46240-2158
317-848-2013
Fax: 317-571-0744
Offers support in elementary school and secondary school education, higher education,
business school education and youth services
in Indiana.

Eileen C Ryan, Executive Director

2433 W Brooks Fortune Foundation
7933 Beaumont Green W Drive
Indianapolis, IN 46250-1652
317-842-1303
Support is limited to education-related programs in Indiana.

William Brooks Fortune, Executive Director

Iowa

2434 Cedar Rapids Public Library
Funding Information Center
500 1st Street SE
Cedar Rapids, IA 52401-2095
319-398-5123
Fax: 319-398-0476
http://www.crlibrary.org
Member of The Foundation Center network,
maintaining a collection of private foundation tax returns which provide information on
the scope of grants dispensed by that particular foundation.

Tamara Glise, Public Services Manager
Eileen C Ryan, Executive Director

2435 RJ McElroy Trust
425 Cedar Street
Suite 312
Waterloo, IA 50701
319-287-9102
312
Fax: 319-287-9105
http://www.mcelroytrust.org
The trust funds grants to educational youth programs in the northeast quarter of Iowa. The trust guidelines do not include grants to individuals.

Linda L Klinger, Executive Director

Kansas

2436 Mary Jo Williams Charitable Trust
PO Box 439
Garden City, KS 67846-0439
Offers support in the areas of early childhood education, higher education, and children and youth services.

Michael E Collins, Executive Director

2437 Sprint Foundation
2330 Shawnee Mission Parkway
Westwood, KS 66205-2090
913-624-3343
Offers grants in a variety of areas with an emphasis on education, including business education, secondary education and higher education.

Don G Forsythe, Executive Director

2438 Wichita Public Library
223 S Main Street
Wichita, KS 67202-3795
316-261-8500
Fax: 316-262-4540
http://www.wichita.lib.ks.us
Member of The Foundation Center network, maintaining a collection of private foundation tax returns which provide information on the scope of grants dispensed by that particular foundation.

Kentucky

2439 Ashland Incorporated Foundation
50 E River Center Boulevard
Covington, KY 41012
859-815-3630
Fax: 859-815-4496
http://www.ashland.com
Offers support to educational organizations, colleges and universities, as well as giving an employee matching gift program to higher education and community funding.

James O'Brien, CEO

2440 Gheens Foundation
One Riverfront Plaza
Suite 705
Louisville, KY 40202
502-584-4650
Fax: 502-584-4652
The foundation's support is aimed at higher and secondary education, ongoing teacher education, and social service agencies.

James N Davis, Executive Director

2441 James Graham Brown Foundation
4350 Brownsboro Road
Suite 200
Louisville, KY 40207
502-896-2440
Fax: 502-896-1774
http://www.jgbf.org

Offers grants in the areas of higher education and social services.

Mason Rummel, Executive Director
Dodie L McKenzie, Program Officer

2442 Louisville Free Public Library
301 York Street
Louisville, KY 40203-2257
502-574-1611
Fax: 502-574-1657
http://www.lfpl.org
Member of The Foundation Center network, maintaining a collection of private foundation tax returns which provide information on the scope of grants dispensed by that particular foundation.

2443 Margaret Hall Foundation
291 S Ashland Avenue
Lexington, KY 40502-1727
859-269-2236
http://www.margarethallfoundation.org
Awards grants and scholarships to private, nonprofit secondary schools for innovative programming.

Helen R Burg, Executive Director

2444 VV Cooke Foundation Corporation
220 Mount Mercy Drive
Pewee Valley, KY 40056
502-241-0303
Offers support in education and youth services with an emphasis on Baptist church and school support.

John B Gray, Executive Director

Louisiana

2445 Baton Rouge Area Foundation
406 N 4th Street
Baton Rouge, LA 70802
225-387-6126
877-387-6126
Fax: 225-387-6153
Offers grants in the area of elementary and secondary education and health.

John G Davies, President

2446 Booth-Bricker Fund
826 Union Street
Suite 300
New Orleans, LA 70112-1421
504-581-2430
Fax: 504-566-4785
Does not have a formal grant procedure or grant application form; nor does it publish an annual report. The Booth-Bricker Fund makes contributions for the purposes of promoting, developing and fostering religious, charitable, scientific, literary or educational programs, primarily in the state of Louisiana. It does not make contributions to individuals.

Gray S Parker, Chairman

2447 East Baton Rouge Parish Library
Centroplex Branch Grants Collection
7711 Goodwood Boulevard
Baton Rouge, LA 70806
225-231-3750
Member of The Foundation Center network, maintaining a collection of private foundation tax returns which provide information on the scope of grants dispensed by that particular foundation.

2448 Fred B & Ruth B Zigler Foundation
PO Box 986
Zigler Building
Jennings, LA 70546-0986
337-824-2413
Fax: 337-824-2414
http://www.ziglerfoundation.org

Offers support to higher, secondary and primary education.

Julie G Berry, President

2449 New Orleans Public Library
Business & Science Division
219 Loyola Avenue
New Orleans, LA 70112-2044
504-529-7323
Fax: 504-596-2609
Member of The Foundation Center network, maintaining a collection of private foundation tax returns which provide information on the scope of grants dispensed by that particular foundation.

2450 Shreve Memorial Library
424 Texas Street
Shreveport, LA 71101-5452
318-226-5897
Fax: 318-226-4780
http://www.shreve-lib.org
Member of The Foundation Center network, maintaining a collection of private Louisiana foundation tax returns which provide information on the scope of grants dispensed by that particular foundation.

Carlos Colon, Reference Supervisor

Maine

2451 Clarence E Mulford Trust
PO Box 290
Fryeburg, ME 04037-0290
207-935-2061
Fax: 207-935-3939
Offers grants to charitable, educational and scientific organizations for the purpose of improving education.

David R Hastings II, Executive Director

2452 Harold Alfond Trust
C/O Dexter Shoe Company
PO Box 353
Dexter, ME 04930-0353
Grants are offered to secondary and higher education in Maine and Maryland.

Keith Burden, Executive Director

Maryland

2453 Abell Foundation
111 S Calvert Street
Suite 2300
Baltimore, MD 21202-6182
410-547-1300
Fax: 410-539-6579
http://www.abell.org
The foundation supports education with an emphasis on public education, including early childhood and elementary, research, and minority education.

Robert C Embry Jr, Executive Director

2454 Aegon USA
1111 N Charles Street
Baltimore, MD 21201-5505
410-576-4571
Fax: 410-347-8685
http://www.aegonins.com
Offers grants in elementary school, secondary school, higher education and medical school education.

Larry G Brown, Executive Director

2455 Clarence Manger & Audrey Cordero Plitt Trust
C/O First National Bank of Maryland
PO Box 1596
Baltimore, MD 21203-1596
410-566-0914
Offers grants to educational institutions for student loans and scholarships.
Mary M Kirgan, Executive Director

2456 Clark-Winchcole Foundation
Air Rights Building
3 Bethesda Metro Center
Suite 550
Bethesda, MD 20814
301-654-3607
Fax: 301-654-3140
Offers grants in the areas of higher education and social service agencies.
Laura E Philips, Executive Director

2457 Commonwealth Foundation
9737 Colesville Road
Suite 800
Silver Spring, MD 20910
301-495-4400
Offers grants in the areas of early childhood education, child development, elementary schools, secondary schools and youth services.
Barbara Bainum, Executive Director

2458 Dresher Foundation
4940 Campbell Boulevard
Suite 110
Baltimore, MD 21236
410-933-0384
http://www.jdgraphicdesign.com/dresher/dr esherfoundation/
Offers giving in the areas of elementary school, early childhood education, meals on wheels, and food distribution.

2459 Edward E Ford Foundation
1122 Kenilworth Drive
Suite 105
Towson, MD 21204
410-823-2201
Fax: 410-823-2203
http://www.eeford.org
Offers giving to secondary schools and private education in the US and its protectorates.
Robert Hallett, Executive Director

2460 Enoch Pratt Free Library
Social Science & History Department
400 Cathedral Street
Baltimore, MD 21201-4484
301-396-5430
http://www.pratt.lib.md.us
Member of The Foundation Center network, maintaining a collection of private foundation tax returns which provide information on the scope of grants dispensed by that particular foundation.

2461 France-Merrick Foundation
The Exchange
1122 Kenilworth Drive
Suite 118
Baltimore, MD 21204-2139
410-832-5700
Fax: 410-832-5704
Offers grants in the areas of public education, private and higher education, health, social services and cultural activities.
Frederick W Lafferty, Executive Director

2462 Grayce B Kerr Fund
117 Bay Street
Easton, MD 21601-2769
410-822-6652
Fax: 410-822-4546
E-mail: gbkf@bluecrab.org

The major area of interest to the fund is education, including higher, elementary and early childhood education for the state of Maryland with focus on the Eastern Shore Counties.
Margaret van den Berg, Administrative Assistant

2463 Henry & Ruth Blaustein Rosenberg Foundation
Blaustein Building
10 East Baltimore Street
Suite 1111
Baltimore, MD 21202
410-347-7201
Fax: 410-347-7210
http://www.blaufund.org
Offers grants in the areas of secondary and higher education.
Betsy F Ringel, Executive Director
Henry A Rosenberg Jr, President

2464 James M Johnston Trust for Charitable and Educational Purposes
2 Wisconsin Circle
Suite 600
Chevy Chase, MD 20815-7003
301-907-0135
Grants are given to higher and secondary educational institutions located in Washington, DC and North Carolina.
Julie Sanders, Executive Director

2465 John W Kluge Foundation
6325 Woodside Court
Columbia, MD 21046-1017
Offers grants in higher education and secondary education.

2466 Marion I & Henry J Knott Foundation
3904 Hickory Avenue
Baltimore, MD 21211-1834
410-235-7068
Fax: 410-889-2577
http://www.knottfoundation.org
Grantmaking limited to private nonsectarian schools and Catholic schools geographically located within the Archdiocese of Baltimore, Maryland.
Greg Cantori, Executive Director

2467 Robert G & Anne M Merrick Foundation
The Exchange
1122 Kenilworth Drive
Suite 118
Baltimore, MD 21204-2142
410-832-5700
Fax: 410-832-5704
Offers grants for public education, higher education and social services.
Frederick W Lafferty, Executive Director

Massachusetts

2468 Associated Grantmakers of Massachusetts
55 Court Street
Suite 520
Boston, MA 02108-4304
617-426-2606
Fax: 617-426-2849
http://www.agmconnect.org
Member of The Foundation Center network, maintaining a collection of private foundation tax returns which provide information on the scope of grants dispensed by that particular foundation.
Ron Ancrum, President
Martha Moore, Director Center Philanthropy

2469 Boston Foundation
75 Arlington Street
10th Floor
Boston, MA 02108-4407
617-338-1700
Fax: 617-338-1604
http://www.tbf.org
Supports local educational, social and housing programs and institutions.
Paul Grogan, President

2470 Boston Globe Foundation II
135 Morrissey Boulevard
Boston, MA 02107
617-929-2895
Fax: 617-929-7889
http://www.bostonglobe.com/community/fo undation/partner.stm
The foundation's highest priority is community based agencies which understand, represent and are part of the following populations; children and youth with disabilities, children and youth with AIDS, refugees, low-birth weight babies, pregnant and nursing mothers and incarcerated youth.
Suzanne W Maas, Executive Director
Leah P Bailey

2471 Boston Public Library
Social Sciences Reference
700 Boylston Street
Boston, MA 02116-2813
617-536-5400
http://www.bpl.org
Member of The Foundation Center network, maintaining a collection of private foundation tax returns which provide information on the scope of grants dispensed by that particular foundation.
Bernard Margolis, President

2472 Dean Foundation for Little Children
C/O Boston Safe Deposit & Trust Company
1 Boston Pl
Boston, MA 02108-4407
Giving is centered on little children age twelve and under for the care and relief of destitute children. Provides support for preschools, day care, summer camps and other programs.
Nancy Criscitiello, Executive Director

2473 Hyams Foundation
175 Federal Street
Floor 14
Boston, MA 02110-2210
617-426-5600
Fax: 617-426-5696
http://www.hyamsfoundation.org
The foundation seeks to promote understanding and appreciation of diversity, including race, ethnicity, gender, sexual orientation, age, physical ability, class and religion. The foundation's primary objective is to meet the needs of low-income and other underserved populations, striving to address the causes of those needs, whenever possible. Foundation supports low-income communities in their efforts to identify their own problems, solve these problems and improve people's lives.
Elizabeth B Smith, Executive Director

2474 Irene E & George A Davis Foundation
C/O Ann T Keiser
1 Monarch Place
Suite 1450
Springfield, MA 01144-1450
413-734-8336
Fax: 413-734-7845
http://www.davisfdn.org

Education and social service organizations and programs in Western Massachusetts are the primary concern of this foundation.

Mary E Walachy, Executive Director

2475 James G Martin Memorial Trust
122 Pond Street
Jamaica Plain, MA 02130-2714
Giving is centered on elementary education and higher education in Massachusetts.

Ms Martin, Executive Director

2476 Jessie B Cox Charitable Trust
Grants Management Association
60 State Street
Boston, MA 02109-1899
617-227-7940
Fax: 617-227-0781
http://www.hemenwaybarnes.com/selectsrv/jbcox/cox.html
This trust makes grants for projects which will address important social issues in the trust's fields of interest and for which adequate funding from other sources cannot be obtained. The trust funds projects in New England in the areas of health, education and the environment. The trustees look to support special projects which will assist the applicants to achieve their long-range organizational goals.

Michaelle Larkins, Executive Director
Susan M Fish, Grants Administrator

2477 LG Balfour Foundation
Fleet Bank of Massachusetts
75 State Street
Boston, MA 02109-1775
617-346-4000
Offers support for scholarships and innovative projects designed to eliminate barriers and improve access to education for all potentially qualified students.

Kerry Herliney, Executive Director

2478 Little Family Foundation
33 Broad Street
Suite 10
Boston, MA 02109-4216
617-723-6771
Fax: 617-723-7107
Offers scholarships at various business schools and Junior Achievement programs in secondary schools.

Arthur D Little, Executive Director

2479 Rogers Family Foundation
29 Water Street
Newburyport, MA 01950-4501
978-465-6100
Fax: 978-685-1588
Offers support in the areas of secondary and higher education in the Lawrence, Massachusetts area.

Stephen Rogers, President

2480 State Street Foundation
225 Franklin Street
12th Floor
Boston, MA 02110
617-664-1937
http://www.statestreet.com
Offers grants to organizations that help improve the quality of life in the greater Boston area. Interest includes human services, public and secondary education, vocational education, and arts and culture programs.

Madison Thompson, Executive Director

2481 Sudbury Foundation
278 Old Sudbury Road
Sudbury, MA 01776-1843

978-443-0849
Fax: 978-579-9536
http://www.sudburyfoundation.org
Offers college scholarships to local high school seniors who meet eligibility criteria.

Fredericka Tanner, Executive Director
Marilyn Martino, Program Officer

2482 Trustees of the Ayer Home
PO Box 1865
Lowell, MA 01853-1865
978-452-5914
Fax: 978-452-5914
Funding (greater Lowell, MA only) educational programs (RLF, SMARTS). Primary interests are women and children.

D Donahue, Assistant Treasurer

2483 Weld Foundation
Peter Loring/Janice Palumbo
Loring, Wolcott & Coolidge
30 Congress Street
Boston, MA 02110-2409
617-523-6531
Fax: 617-523-6535
Grants are offered in the areas of elementary, secondary and higher education in Massachusetts.

2484 Western Massachusetts Funding Resource Center
65 Elliot Street
Springfield, MA 01105-1713
413-732-3175
Fax: 413-452-0618
http://www.diospringfield.org/wmfrc.html
Member of The Foundation Center network, maintaining a collection of private foundation tax returns which provide information on the scope of grants dispensed by that particular foundation.

Kathleen Dowd, Director
Jean Los, Administrative Assistant

2485 William E Schrafft & Bertha E SchrafftCharitable Trust
1 Financial Center
Floor 26
Boston, MA 02111-2621
617-457-7327
Giving is primarily allocated to educational programs in the Boston metropolitan area.

2486 Woodstock Corporation
Woodstock Corporation
27 School Street
Suite 200
Boston, MA 02108-2301
617-227-0600
Fax: 617-523-0229
Offers support in the area of secondary school education in the state of Massachusetts.

2487 Worcester Public Library
Grants Resource Center
Salem Square
Worcester, MA 01608
508-799-1655
Fax: 508-799-1652
http://www.worcpublib.org
Member of The Foundation Center network, maintaining a collection of private foundation tax returns which provide information on the scope of grants dispensed by that particular foundation.

J Peck, Director Grants Resource

Michigan

2488 Alex & Marie Manoogian Foundation
21001 Van Born Road
Taylor, MI 48180-1340

313-274-7400
Fax: 313-792-6657
Supports higher and secondary education, cultural programs and human service organizations.

Alex Manoogian, Executive Director

2489 Charles Stewart Mott Foundation
Office of Proposal Entry
503 S Saginaw Street
Suite 1200
Flint, MI 48502-1851
810-238-5651
800-645-1766
Fax: 810-237-4857
E-mail: infocenter@mott.org
http://www.mott.org
Grants are given to nonprofit organizations with an emphasis on programs of volunteerism, at-risk youth, environmental protection, economic development and education.

2490 Chrysler Corporate Giving Program
12000 Chrysler Drive
Detroit, MI 48288-0001
810-576-5741
Offers support for education, especially secondary education and leadership development.

Lynn A Feldhouse, Executive Director

2491 Community Foundation for Southeastern Michigan
333 W Fort Street
Suite 2010
Detroit, MI 48226-3134
313-961-6675
Fax: 313-961-2886
http://www.cfsem.org
Supports projects in the areas of education, culture and social services.

Mariam C Noland, President

2492 Community Foundation of Greater Flint
502 Church Street
Flint, MI 48502-2013
810-767-8270
Fax: 810-767-0496
E-mail: cfgf@cfgf.org
http://www.cfgf.org
A community foundation that makes grants to benefit residents of Genessee County, Michigan. Areas of interest include: arts, education, environment, community services and health and social services.

Kathi Horton, President
Evan M Albert, VP Program

2493 Cronin Foundation
203 E Michigan Avenue
Marshall, MI 49068-1545
616-781-9851
Fax: 616-781-2070
Offers support to expand educational, social and cultural needs of the community within the Marshall, Michigan school district.

Joseph E Schroeder, Executive Director

2494 Detroit Edison Foundation
2000 2nd Avenue
Room 1046
Detroit, MI 48226-1279
313-235-9271
Fax: 313-237-9271
http://www.my.dteenergy.com
Offers support for all levels of education, and local community social services and cultural organizations in Southeast Michigan.

Katharine W Hunt, Executive Director

2495 Ford Motor Company Fund
One American Road
PO Box 1899
Dearborn, MI 48126-2798
888-313-0102
Fax: 313-337-6680
http://www.ford.com
Ford Motor Company Fund continues the legacy of Henry Ford's commitment to innovative education at all levels. We remain dedicated to creating and enriching educational opportunities, especially in the areas of science, engineering, math and business, while promoting diversity in education.

Sandra E Ulsh, President
Jim Graham, Manager Education Programs

2496 Frey Foundation
40 Pearl Street NW
Suite 1100
Grand Rapids, MI 49503-3023
616-451-0303
Fax: 616-451-8481
http://www.freyfdn.org
Awards grants and supports the needs of children in their early years, support for environmental education, and protection of our natural resources.

Milton W Rohwer, President
Teresa J Crawford, Grants Manager

2497 General Motors Foundation
13-145 General Motors Building
Detroit, MI 48202
313-556-4260
http://www.gm.com/company/gmability/philanthropy
Offers support for higher education, cultural programs and civic affairs.

Ronald L Theis, Executive Director

2498 Grand Rapids Foundation
209-C Water Building
161 Ottawa Avenue NW
Grand Rapids, MI 49503
616-454-1751
Fax: 616-454-6455
E-mail: mrapp@grfoundation.org
http://www.grfoundation.org
A community foundation established in 1922. The foundation actively serves the people of Kent County by administering funds it receives and by making philanthropic grants to non-profit organizations in response to community needs. Various educational scholarships are offered on the basis of a competitive process which considers academic achievement, extracurricular activities, a statement of one's own personal aspirations and educational goals, and financial need. Kent County Residency required.

Ruth Bishop, Program Associate-Education
Diana Sieger, President

2499 Harry A & Margaret D Towsley Foundation
3055 Plymouth Road
Suite 200
Ann Arbor, MI 48105-3208
312-662-6777
Areas of support include pre-school education, social services, and continuing education.

Margaret Ann Riecker, Executive Director

2500 Henry Ford Centennial Library
Adult Services
16301 Michigan Avenue
Dearborn, MI 48126-2792
313-943-2330
Fax: 313-943-3063
http://www.dearborn.lib.mi.us/aboutus/adult.htm

Member of The Foundation Center network, maintaining a collection of private foundation tax returns which provide information on the scope of grants dispensed by that particular foundation.

2501 Herbert H & Grace A Dow Foundation
1018 W Main Street
Midland, MI 48640
989-631-3699
Fax: 989-631-0675
http://www.hhdowfdn.org
Limited to organizations within Michigan. Has charter goals to improve the educational, religious, economic and cultural lives of Michigan's people.

Margaret Ann Riescker, President
Elysa M Rogers, Assistant VP

2502 Herrick Foundation
150 W Jefferson Avenue
Suite 2500
Detroit, MI 48226-4415
313-496-7585
Offers grants to colleges and universities, health agencies and social service organizations.

Dolores de Galleford, Executive Director

2503 Kresge Foundation
2701 Troy Center Drive
Suite 150
Troy, MI 48084
248-643-9630
Fax: 313-643-0588
http://www.kresge.org
Giving is aimed at areas of interest including arts and humanities, social services and public policy.

John E Marshall III, Executive Director
Sandra McAlister Ambrozy, Senior Program Officer

2504 Malpass Foundation
PO Box 1206
East Jordan, MI 49727-1206
Offers giving in the areas of education and community development.

William J Lorne, Executive Director

2505 McGregor Fund
333 W Fort Street
Suite 2090
Detroit, MI 48226-3134
313-963-3495
Fax: 313-963-3512
http://www.mcgregorfund.org
Social services, health and education grants awarded to organizations located in Ohio, primarily the Detroit area.

C David Campbell, President
Kate Levin Markel, Program Officer

2506 Michigan State University Libraries
Social Sciences/Humanities
Main Library
East Lansing, MI 48824
517-353-8700
Fax: 517-432-3532
http://www.lib.msu.edu
Member of The Foundation Center network, maintaining a collection of private foundation tax returns which provide information on the scope of grants dispensed by that particular foundation.

2507 Richard & Helen DeVos Foundation
190 Muncie NW
Suite 500
Grand Rapids, MI 49503
616-454-4114
Fax: 616-454-4654

Strong geographical preference to Western Michigan. Funding includes Christian education, cultural, community, education (not an individual basis) and government services. Donations are also made on a national level to organizations based in Washington, DC.

Stephanie Roy, Executive Director

2508 Rollin M Gerstacker Foundation
PO Box 1945
Midland, MI 48641-1945
989-631-6097
Fax: 517-832-8842
http://www.tamu.edu/baum/gerstack.html
Primary purpose of this foundation is to carry on, indefinitely, financial aid to charities concentrated in the states of Michigan and Ohio. Grants are given in the areas of community support, schools, education, social services, music and the arts, youth activities, health care and research, churches and other areas.

Carl A Gerstacker, Executive Director

2509 Steelcase Foundation
PO Box 1967, CH-4E
Grand Rapids, MI 49501-1967
616-246-4695
Fax: 616-475-2200
E-mail: sbroman@steelcse.com
http://www.steelcase.com
Offers support for human services and education, to improve the quality of life for children, the elderly and the disabled in the areas where there are manufacturing plants.

Susan Broman, Executive Director

2510 Wayne State University
Purdy-Kresge Library
5265 Cass Avenue
Detroit, MI 48202-3930
313-577-6424
http://www.lib.wayne.edu
Member of The Foundation Center network, maintaining a collection of private foundation tax returns which provide information on the scope of grants dispensed by that particular foundation.

2511 Whirlpool Foundation
2000 N M 63
Benton Harbor, MI 49022-2632
269-923-5580
Fax: 269-925-0154
Giving centers on learning, cultural diversity, adult education, and scholarships for children of corporation employees.

Ddaniel Hopp, President & Chairman
Barbara Hall, Program Officer

Minnesota

2512 Andersen Foundation
Andersen Corporation
100 4th Avenue N
Bayport, MN 55003-1096
651-264-5150
Fax: 651-264-5537
Grants are given in the areas of higher education, health, youth and the arts in Minnesota.

2513 Bush Foundation
E-900 First National Bank Building
332 Minnesota Street
Saint Paul, MN 55101-1314
651-227-0891
Fax: 651-297-6485
http://www.bushfoundation.org
The foundation is predominantly a regional grantmaking foundation, with broad interests in education, human services, health, arts and

humanities and in the development of leadership.

Anita M Pampusch, President
John Archabal, Senior Program Officer

2514 Cargill Foundation
PO Box 9300
Minneapolis, MN 55440-9300
952-742-4311
Fax: 612-742-7224
http://www.cargill.com
Offers grants in the areas of education, health, human service organizations, arts and cultural programs and social service agencies.

Audrey Tulberg, Executive Director

2515 Charles & Ellora Alliss Educational Foundation
332 Minnesota Street #64704
Saint Paul, MN 55101-1314
651-244-4581
Fax: 651-244-0860
The foundation is organized exclusively for support of the education of young people, up to and including the period of postgraduate study. As a matter of policy, the foundation generally has limited its program to universities and colleges located in Minnesota. Grants are made to such institutions in support of undergraduate scholarship programs administered by their student aid offices. The foundation makes no direct grants to individuals.

John Bultena, Executive Director

2516 Duluth Public Library
520 W Superior Street
Duluth, MN 55802-1578
218-723-3802
Fax: 218-723-3815
http://www.duluth.lib.mn.us
Member of The Foundation Center network, maintaining a collection of private foundation tax returns which provide information on the scope of grants dispensed by that particular foundation.

Elizabeth Kelly, Library Director

2517 FR Bigelow Foundation
600 Fifth Street
Center 55th Street East
St. Paul, MN 55101-1797
651-224-5463
Fax: 651-224-8123
http://www.frbigelow.org
Offers support in early childhood education, elementary and secondary education, higher and adult education and human services.

Jon A Theobald, Chair
Carleen K Rhodes, Secretary

2518 First Bank System Foundation
PO Box 522
Minneapolis, MN 55480-0522
612-973-2440
Offers support for public elementary and secondary education, arts and cultural programs.

Cheryl L Rantala, Executive Director

2519 Hiawatha Education Foundation
360 Vila Street
Winona, MN 55987-1500
507-453-5550
Giving is centered on Catholic high schools and colleges, as well as awarding scholarships to college-bound high school graduates.

Robert Kierlin, Executive Director

2520 IA O'Shaughnessy Foundation
First Trust
PO Box 64704
Saint Paul, MN 55164-0704
612-291-5164

Giving is centered on cultural programs, secondary and higher education, human services and medical programs.

John Bultena, Executive Director

2521 Marbrook Foundation
730 2nd Avenue
1450 US Trust Building
Minneapolis, MN 55402
612-752-1783
Fax: 612-752-1780
E-mail: marbrook@brooksinc.net
Offers grants in the areas of the environment, the arts, social empowerment, spiritual endeavors, basic human needs and health.

Annual Report

Conley Brooks Jr, Executive Director
Julie S Hara, Program Officer

2522 Medtronic Foundation
7000 Central Avenue NE
Minneapolis, MN 55432-3576
763-514-4000
800-328-2518
Fax: 763-514-8410
http://www.medtronic.com
Offers grants in the areas of education (especially at the pre-college level), community funding and social services.

Penny Hunt, Executive Director

2523 Minneapolis Foundation
800 Ids Center 80 S 8th Street
Minneapolis, MN 55402
612-672-3878
Fax: 612-672-3846
http://www.minneapolisfoundation.org
The foundation strives to strengthen the community for the benefit of all citizens. Grants are awarded for the purposes of achieving this goal in the areas of early childhood education, child development, and education.

Karen Kelley-Ariwoola, VP Community Philanthropy

2524 Minneapolis Public Library
Music, Art, Sociology & Humanities
250 S Marquette
Minneapolis, MN 55401-2188
612-630-6000
Fax: 612-630-6220
http://www.mplib.org
Member of The Foundation Center network, maintaining a collection of private foundation tax returns which provide information on the scope of grants dispensed by that particular foundation.

Katherine G Hadle, Director

2525 Otto Bremer Foundation
445 Minnesota Street
Suite 2250
Saint Paul, MN 55101-2135
651-227-8036
Fax: 651-312-3665
http://www.fdncenter.org/grantmaker/bremer/
Offers support for post-secondary education, human services and community affairs.

John Kostishack, Executive Director
Karen Starr, Senior Program Officer

2526 Saint Paul Foundation
55 Fifth Street East
Suite 600
St. Paul, MN 55101-1797
651-224-5463
Fax: 651-224-8123
http://www.saintpaulfoundation.org
Offers support for educational, charitable and cultural purposes of a public nature.

Carleen K Rhodes, President
Mindy K Molumby, Grants Administrator

2527 TCF Foundation
Code EXO-02-C
200 Lake Street
East Wayzata, MN 55391-1693
952-745-2757
Fax: 612-661-8554
http://www.tcfexpress.com
Giving is primarily for education through grants and employee matching gifts, including secondary schools, higher education and organizations that increase public knowledge.

Neil I Whitehouse, Executive Director

Mississippi

2528 Foundation for the Mid South
1230 Raymond Road
Box 700
Jackson, MS 39204
601-355-8167
Fax: 601-355-6499
http://www.fndmidsouth.org
Makes grants in the area of education, as well as economic development and families and children.

George Penick, Executive Director

2529 Jackson-Hinds Library System
300 N State Street
Jackson, MS 39201-1705
601-968-5803
http://www.jhlibrary.com
Member of The Foundation Center network, maintaining a collection of private foundation tax returns which provide information on the scope of grants dispensed by that particular foundation.

Carolyn McCallum, Executive Director

2530 Mississippi Power Foundation
PO Box 4079
Gulfport, MS 39502-4079
228-864-1211
http://www.southerncompany.com/mspower/edufound
The foundation is dedicated to the improvement and enhancement of education in Mississippi from kindergarten to twelfth grade.

Huntley Biggs, Executive Director

2531 Phil Hardin Foundation
Citizens National Bank
1921 24th Avenue
Meridian, MS 39301-5800
601-483-4282
Fax: 601-483-5665
http://www.philhardin.org
Offers giving in Mississippi for schools and educational institutions and programs.

C Thompson Wacaster, Executive Director

Missouri

2532 Ameren Corporation Charitable Trust
Ameren Corporation
PO Box 66149
MC 100
Saint Louis, MO 63166-6149
314-554-2789
877-426-3736
Fax: 314-554-2888
E-mail: sbell@ameren.com
http://www.ameren.com
Offers giving in the areas of education, environment, youth and seniors; giving restricted

to nonprofits located in Ameren service area in Missouri and Illinois.

Annually

Susan M Bell, Sr Community Relations
Otis Cowan, Community Relations Manger

2533 Clearinghouse for Midcontinent Foundations
University of Missouri
5110 Cherry Street
Suite 310
Kansas City, MO 64110-2426
816-253-1176
Fax: 816-235-5727
Member of The Foundation Center network, maintaining a collection of private foundation tax returns which provide information on the scope of grants dispensed by that particular foundation.

2534 Danforth Foundation
211 N Broadway
Suite 2390
Saint Louis, MO 63102-2733
314-588-1900
Fax: 314-588-0035
E-mail: banderson@info.csd.org
http://www.orgs.muohio.edu/forumscp/index.html
This foundation is aimed at enhancing human life through activities which emphasize the theme of improvement in teaching and learning. Serves the pre-collegiate education through grantmaking and program activities.

Dr. Bruce J Anderson, President

2535 Enid & Crosby Kemper Foundation
C/O UMB Bank, N.A.
PO Box 419692
Kansas City, MO 64141-6692
816-860-7711
Fax: 816-860-5690
Giving is primarily allocated to organizations and programs focusing on educational and cultural needs.

Stephen J Campbell, Executive Director

2536 Hall Family Foundation
Charitable & Crown Investment - 323
PO Box 419580
Kansas City, MO 64141-8400
816-274-8516
Fax: 816-274-8547
Offers grants in the areas of all levels of education, performing and visual arts, community development, and children, youth and families.

Wendy Burcham, Program Officer
Peggy Collins, Program Officer

2537 James S McDonnell Foundation
1034 S Brentwood Boulevard
Suite 1850
Saint Louis, MO 63117-1284
314-721-1532
Fax: 314-721-7421
http://www.jsmf.org
Foundation Program, Cognitive Studies for Educational Practice, funding available through competition in broadly announced requests for proposals. Program grant guidelines are announced in 3 year cycles.

John T Bruer, President
Cheryl A Washington, Grants Manager

2538 Kansas City Public Library
14 West 10th Street
Kansas City, MO 64105
816-701-3400
Fax: 816-701-3401
http://www.kclibrary.org
Member of The Foundation Center network, maintaining a collection of private foundation tax returns which provide information on the scope of grants dispensed by that particular foundation.

2539 Mary Ranken Jordan & Ettie A Jordan Charitable Foundation
Mercantile Bank
PO Box 387
Saint Louis, MO 63166-0387
314-231-7626
Giving is limited to charitable institutions with an emphasis on secondary education and cultural programs, as well as higher education and social services.

Fred Arnold, Executive Director

2540 McDonnell Douglas Foundation
PO Box 516
MC S100-1510
Saint Louis, MO 63166-0516
314-234-0360
Fax: 314-232-7654
Offers various grants with an emphasis on higher and other education and community funding.

AM Bailey, Executive Director

2541 Monsanto Fund
800 N Lindbergh Boulevard
Saint Louis, MO 63167-0001
314-694-1000
Fax: 314-694-7658
E-mail: monsanto.fund@monsanto.com
http://www.monsanto.com/monsanto/about_us/monsanto_fund
Giving is offered primarily in the area of education, specifically science and math.

Deborah J Patterson, President

Montana

2542 Eastern Montana College Library
Special Collections-Grants
1500 N 30th Street
Billings, MT 59101-0245
406-657-1662
Fax: 406-657-2037
http://www.msubillings.edu/library
Member of The Foundation Center network, maintaining a collection of private foundation tax returns which provide information on the scope of grants dispensed by that particular foundation.

Joan Bares, Grants Manager

2543 Montana State Library
Library Services
1515 E 6th Avenue
Helena, MT 59601-4542
406-444-3115
Fax: 406-444-5612
http://www.msl.state.mt.us/
Member of The Foundation Center network, maintaining a collection of private foundation tax returns which provide information on the scope of grants dispensed by that particular foundation.

Barbara Duke, Administrative Assistant

Nebraska

2544 Dr. CC & Mabel L Criss Memorial Foundation
US Bank
1700 Farnam Streets
Omaha, NE 68102
800-441-2117
Fax: 402-348-6666
Offers support for educational and scientific purposes, including higher education.

2545 Thomas D Buckley Trust
PO Box 647
Chappell, NE 69129-0647
308-874-2212
Fax: 308-874-3491
Offers giving in the areas of education, health care and youth and religion. Grants awarded in Chappell, NE, community and surrounding area.

Connie Loos, Secretary

2546 W Dale Clark Library
Social Sciences Department
215 S 15th Street
Omaha, NE 68102-1601
402-444-4826
Fax: 402-444-4504
http://www.omahapubliclibrary.org
Member of The Foundation Center network, maintaining a collection of private foundation tax returns which provide information on the scope of grants dispensed by that particular foundation.

Angela Green-Garland, President

Nevada

2547 Conrad N Hilton Foundation
100 W Liberty Street
Suite 840
Reno, NV 89501-1988
775-323-4221
Fax: 775-323-4150
http://www.hiltonfoundation.org
Founded in 1944 as a Trust, this foundation is dedicated to fulfilling and expanding Conrad Hilton's philanthropic vision by carrying out grantmaking activities. The foundation's giving is focused primarily in two areas: the alleviation of human suffering, particularly among disadvantaged children; and the human services works of the Catholic Sisters through a separate entity as described under Major Projects (supportive housing, disabled, education and prevention of domestic violence).

Donald H Hubbs, Executive Director
Steven M Hilton, President

2548 Cord Foundation
E.L. Cord Foundation Center For Learning Literacy
College Of Education/Mail Stop 288
University Of Nevada, Reno
Reno, NV 89557-0215
775-784-4951
Fax: 775-784-4758
http://www.unr.edu/cll
Offers support for secondary and higher education, including youth organizations and cultural programs.

Donald Bear, Director/Professor

2549 Donald W Reynolds Foundation
1701 Village Center Circle
Las Vegas, NV 89134
702-804-6000
Fax: 702-804-6099
E-mail: generalquestions@dwrf.org
http://www.dwreynolds.org
Devotes funds to further the cause of free press and journalism education.

Fred Smith, Chairman

2550 EL Wiegand Foundation
Wiegand Center
165 W Liberty Street
Reno, NV 89501-1915
775-333-0310
Fax: 775-333-0314
Offers grants in of culture and the arts, organizations, health and medical institutions, with

an emphasis on Roman Catholic organizations.

Kristen A Avansino, Executive Director

2551 Las Vegas-Clark County
Library District
833 Las Vegas Boulevard N
Las Vegas, NV 89101-2030
702-382-5280
Fax: 702-382-5491
http://www.lvccld.org
Member of The Foundation Center network, maintaining a collection of private foundation tax returns which provide information on the scope of grants dispensed by that particular foundation.

Daniel L Walters, Executive Director

2552 Washoe County Library
301 S Center Street
Reno, NV 89501-2102
775-327-8349
Fax: 775-327-8341
http://www.washoe.lib.nv.us/
Member of The Foundation Center network, maintaining a collection of private foundation tax returns which provide information on the scope of grants dispensed by that particular foundation.

New Hampshire

2553 Lincolnshire
Liberty Lane
Hampton, NH 03842
Giving is primarily for secondary school education, business school education and recreation.

William Coffey, Executive Director

2554 New Hampshire Charitable Foundation
37 Pleasant Street
Concord, NH 03301-4005
603-225-6641
Fax: 603-225-1700
E-mail: scg@nhcf.org
http://www.nhcf.org
Offers grants for charitable and educational purposes including college scholarships, existing charitable organizations, child welfare, community services, health and social services and new programs that emphasize programs rather than capital needs.

Racheal Stuart, VP Program

2555 Plymouth State College
Herbert H. Lamson Library
Highland Street MSC #47
Plymouth, NH 03264
603-535-2258
Fax: 603-535-2445
http://www.plymouth.edu/psc/library
Member of The Foundation Center network, maintaining a collection of private foundation tax returns which provide information on the scope of grants dispensed by that particular foundation.

New Jersey

2556 Community Foundation of New Jersey
Knox Hill Road
PO Box 338
Morristown, NJ 07963-0338
973-267-5533
Fax: 973-267-2903
E-mail: cfnj@bellatlantic.net
http://www.cfnj.org

Offers support for programs that offer a path of solution of community problems in the areas of education, leadership development and human services.

Hans Dekker, President

2557 Fund for New Jersey
Kilmer Square
94 Church Street
Suite 303
New Brunswick, NJ 08901-1242
732-220-8656
Fax: 732-220-8654
http://www.fundfornj.org
Offers grants on projects which provide the basis of action in education, AIDS research, minorities/immigrants, public policy and community development.

Mark M Murphy, Executive Director

2558 Hoechst Celanese Foundation
Route 202-206 N
PO Box 2500
Somerville, NJ 08876
908-522-7500
Fax: 908-598-4424
Provides support for education, particularly in the sciences.

Lewis F Alpaugh, Executive Director

2559 Honeywell Foundation
101 Columbia Road
Morristown, NJ 07960-4658
973-455-2000
Fax: 973-455-4807
http://www.honeywell.com/about/foundation.html
Offers support for education, including fellowship and scholarship aid to colleges.

2560 Hyde & Watson Foundation
437 Southern Boulevard
Chatham, NJ 07928-1454
973-966-6024
Fax: 973-966-6404
http://www.fdncenter.org/grantmaker/hydeandwatson
Support of capital projects of lasting value which tend to increase quality, capacity, or efficiency of a grantee's programs or services, such as purchase or relocation of facilities, capital equipment, instructive materials development, and certain medical research areas. Broad fields include health, education, religion, social services, arts, and humanities. Geographic areas served include the New York City Metropolitan region and primarily Essex, Union, and Morris Counties in New Jersey.

Hunter W Corbin, President

2561 Mary Owen Borden Memorial Foundation
160 Hodge Road
Princeton, NJ 08540-3014
609-924-3637
Fax: 609-252-9472
E-mail: tborden@ibm.net
http://www.fdncenter.org/grantmaker/borden/index.htm
Offers grants in the areas of childhood education, child development, education, conservation and health and human services.

Thomas Borden, Executive Director

2562 Merck Company Foundation
1 Merck Drive #100
Whitehouse Station, NJ 08889-3400
908-423-2042
http://www.merck.com
Offers support of education, primarily medical through community programs, grants and

matching gift programs for colleges and secondary education.

John R Taylor, Executive Director

2563 Prudential Foundation
Prudential Plaza
751 Broad Street
Floor 15
Newark, NJ 07102-3714
973-802-4791
http://www.prudential.com
Focus is on children and youth for services that can better their lives. Grants are made in the areas of education, health and human services, community and urban development, business and civic affairs, culture and the arts. Emphasis is placed on programs that serve the city of Newark and the surrounding New Jersey urban centers, programs in cities where The Prudential has a substantial presence and national programs that further the company's objectives.

Barbara L Halaburda, Executive Director

2564 Turrell Fund
21 Van Vleck Street
Montclair, NJ 07042-2358
201-783-9358
Fax: 973-783-9283
E-mail: turrell@bellatlantic.net
http://www.fdncenter.org/grantmaker/turrell
Offers grants to organizations and agencies that are dedicated to the care of children and youth under twelve years of age, with an emphasis on education, early childhood education, delinquency prevention and child and youth services.

E Belvin Williams, Executive Director

2565 Victoria Foundation
946 Bloomfield Avenue
Glen Ridge, NJ 07028
973-748-5300
Fax: 973-748-0016
E-mail: cmcfarvic@aol.com
http://www.victoriafoundation.org
Grants are limited to Newark, New Jersey in the following areas: elementary and secondary education, after school enrichment programs, teacher training and academic enrichment.

Catherine M McFarland, Executive Officer
Nancy K Zimmerman, Senior Program Officer

2566 Warner-Lambert Charitable Foundation
201 Tabor Road
Morris Plains, NJ 07950-2614
212-573-2323
Fax: 212-573-7851
Grants are given in the areas of education, health care, culture and the arts. Supports higher institutions of learning which concentrate on pharmacy, medicine, dentistry, the sciences and mathematics. Current support is aimed at the higher levels of education, but the foundation has begun to place more of its attention on the growing needs that impact elementary and secondary training.

Evelyn Self, Community Affairs
Richard Keelty, VP Investor Affair

2567 Wilf Family Foundation
820 Morris Tpke
Short Hills, NJ 07078-2619
973-467-5000
Awards grants in the areas of Jewish higher education and religion.

Joseph Wilf, Executive Director

New Mexico

2568 Dale J Bellamah Foundation
PO Box 36600
Albuquerque, NM 87176-6600
858-756-1154
Fax: 858-756-3856
Offers grants for higher education including military academies, hospitals and social service organizations.

AF Potenziani, Executive Director

2569 New Mexico State Library
Information Services
1209 Camino Carlos Rey
Santa Fe, NM 87507
505-476-9700
Fax: 505-476-9701
http://www.stlib.state.nm.us
Member of The Foundation Center network, maintaining a collection of private foundation tax returns which provide information on the scope of grants dispensed by that particular foundation.

2570 RD & Joan Dale Hubbard Foundation
PO Box 1679
Ruidoso Downs, NM 88346-1679
505-378-4142
Giving is offered in the areas of childhood education, elementary, secondary and higher education as well as other cultural programs.

Jim Stoddard, Executive Director

New York

2571 Achelis Foundation
767 3rd Avenue
4th Floor
New York, NY 10017
212-644-0322
Fax: 212-759-6510
E-mail: achelis@aol.com
http://fdncenter.org/grantmaker/achelis-bodman
Grants include biomedical research at Rockefeller University, rebuilding the Hayden Planetarium at the American Museum of Natural History, support for the arts and culture, the charter school movement, youth organizations, and special efforts to curb father absence and strengthen family life with awards.

Russell P Pennoyer, President
Joseph S Dolan, Executive Director

2572 Adrian & Jessie Archbold Charitable Trust
401 East 60th Street
New York, NY 10022
212-371-1152
Eastern United States educational institutions and health care service organizations are the main recipients of the Trust.

Myra Mahon, Executive Director

2573 Alfred P Sloan Foundation
630 5th Avenue
Suite 2550
New York, NY 10111-0100
212-649-1649
Fax: 212-757-5117
E-mail: www.sloan.org
A nonprofit foundation offering Sloan Research Fellowships which are awarded in chemistry, computer science, economics, mathematics, neuroscience and physics. These are competitive grants given to young faculty members with high research potential

on the recommendation of department heads and other senior scientists.

Ralph E Gomory, President

2574 Altman Foundation
521 5th Avenue
35th Floor
New York, NY 10175
212-682-0970
http://www.altmanfoundation.org
In education, the Altman Foundation supports programs that identify, sponsor and tutor talented disadvantaged youngsters and help them to obtain educations in non-public and independent schools. The Foundation awards grants only in New York State with an almost-exclusive focus on the five boroughs of New York City. The Foundation does not award grants or scholarships to individuals.

Karen L Rosa, VP/Executive Director

2575 Ambrose Monell Foundation
C/O Fulton, Duncombe & Rowe
1 Rockefeller Plaza
Room 301
New York, NY 10020-2002
212-586-0700
Fax: 212-245-1863
http://www.monellvetlesen.org
Broad range of allocation including education, social service, cultural organizations and the environment.

Ambrose K Monell, Executive Director

2576 American Express Foundation
American Express Company
World Financial Center
New York, NY 10285
212-640-5661
http://www.home3.americanexpress.com/corp/philanthropy/contacts.asp
The foundation's giving focuses on three areas including community service, education and employment.

Mary Beth Salerno, Executive Director
Angela Woods, Philanthropic Program

2577 Andrew W Mellon Foundation
140 E 62nd Street
New York, NY 10021-8187
212-838-8400
Fax: 212-223-2778
http://www.mellon.org
Offers grants in the areas of higher education, cultural affairs and public affairs.

William G Bowen, President

2578 Arnold Bernhard Foundation
220 E 42nd Street
Floor 6
New York, NY 10017-5806
212-907-1500
Offers funding in the areas of education with the emphasis placed on college and universities as well as college preparatory schools.

Jean B Buttner, Executive Director

2579 Atran Foundation
23-25 East 21st Street
3rd Floor
New York, NY 10010
212-505-9677
Offers grants and funding to nonprofit educational and religious organizations.

2580 Beatrice P Delany Charitable Trust
The Chase Manhattan Bank
1211 Avenue of the Americas
34th Floor
New York, NY 10036
212-935-9935

Giving is offered for education, especially higher education and religion.

John HF Enteman, Executive Director

2581 Bodman Foundation
767 3rd Avenue
4th Floor
New York, NY 10017
212-644-0322
Fax: 212-759-6510
E-mail: bodmanfnd@aol.com
Grants include biomedical research at Rockefeller University, building the Congo Gorilla Forest Education Center at the Bronx Zoo through the Wildlife Conservation Society, rebuilding of the Hayden Planetarium for Science and Technology at the American Museum of Natural History, support for Symphony Space, the charter school movement, youth organizations, and the Rutgers University Foundation.

John N Irwin III, President
Joseph S Dolan, Executive Director

2582 Bristol-Myers Squibb Foundation
345 Park Avenue
Floor 43
New York, NY 10154-0004
212-546-4331
http://www.bms.com
Offers support for elementary and secondary school, math and science education reform, civic affairs and health care.

Cindy Johnson, Executive Director

2583 Buffalo & Erie County Public Library
History Department
Lafayette Square
Buffalo, NY 14203
716-858-8900
Fax: 716-858-6211
http://www.buffalolib.org/libraries/central
Member of The Foundation Center network, maintaining a collection of private foundation tax returns which provide information on the scope of grants dispensed by that particular foundation.

Michael C Mahaney, Director

2584 Caleb C & Julia W Dula Educational & Charitable Foundation
C/O Chemical Bank
270 Park Avenue
Floor 21
New York, NY 10017-2014
212-270-9066
Offers grants to charities with an emphasis on secondary and higher education.

G Price-Fitch, Executive Director

2585 Capital Cities-ABC Corporate Giving Program
77 W 66th St
New York, NY 10023-6201
212-456-7498
Fax: 212-456-7909
Offers support in adult education, literary and basic skills, reading, and AIDS research.

Bernadette Longford Williams, Executive Director

2586 Carl & Lily Pforzheimer Foundation
476 5th Avenue
New York, NY 10018
212-764-0655
Offers support primarily for higher and secondary education, cultural programs, public administration, and health care.

Carl H Pforzheimer III, Executive Director

2587 Carnegie Corporation of New York
437 Madison Avenue
New York, NY 10022-7001

212-374-3200
Fax: 212-754-4073
http://www.carnegie.org
The foundation has several program goals including education and healthy development of children and youth, including early childhood health and education, early adolescence educational achievement, science education and education reform.

Vartan Gregorian, President

2588 Chase Manhattan Corporation Philanthropy Department
1 Chase Manhattan Plaza
Floor 9
New York, NY 10005-1401
212-552-7087
Offers support to various organizations to enhance the well-being of the communities Chase Manahattan serves. Grants are awarded in the areas of education, youth services, community and economic development, homeless, library science, health care and housing development.

Steven Gelston, Executive Director

2589 Christian A Johnson Endeavor Foundation
1060 Park Avenue
New York, NY 10128-1008
212-534-6620
http://www.csuohio.edu/uored/funding/johnson.htm
Offers support to private institutions of higher education at the baccalaureate level and on educational outreach programs.

Wilmot H Kidd, Executive Director

2590 Cleveland H Dodge Foundation
670 W 247th Street
Bronx, NY 10471-3292
212-543-1220
Fax: 718-543-0737
http://www.chdodgefoundation.org
Bestows funding for nonprofit organizations aimed at improving higher education and youth organizations.

William D Rueckert, President

2591 Cowles Charitable Trust
630 5th Avenue
Suite 1612
New York, NY 10111-0100
212-765-6262
Funding for higher education and cultural organizations.

2592 Daisy Marquis Jones Foundation
1600 S Avenue
Suite 250
Rochester, NY 14620
585-461-4950
Fax: 585-461-9752
http://www.dmjf.org
Offers grants for nonprofit organizations focusing on improving the lives of children, youth and the elderly, in Monroe and Yates counties in New York State.

Roger L Gardner, President
Marless A Honan, Administrative Assistant

2593 DeWitt Wallace-Reader's Digest Fund
2 Park Avenue
Floor 23
New York, NY 10016-9301
212-251-9700
Fax: 212-679-6990
E-mail: www.wallacefoundation.org
The mission of this foundation is to invest in programs and projects that enhance the quality of educational and career development opportunities for all school-age youth.

M Christine De Vita, President

2594 Edna McConnell Clark Foundation
415 Madison Avenue
10th Floor
New York, NY 10017
212-551-9100
Fax: 212-421-9325
http://www.emcf.org
Supports select youth, serving organizations working with children 9-24 during the non-school hours.

Michael Bailin, President

2595 Edward John Noble Foundation
32 E 57th Street
Floor 19
New York, NY 10022-2513
212-759-4212
Fax: 212-888-4531
Offers grants to major cultural organizations in New York City, especially for arts educational programs and management training internships.

June Noble Larkin, Chairman

2596 Edward W Hazen Foundation
90 Broad Street
Suite 604
New York, NY 10004
212-889-3034
E-mail: hazen@hazenfoundation.org
http://www.hazenfoundation.org
The foundation focuses giving on public education and youth development in the area of public education.

Lori Bezahler, President

2597 Edwin Gould Foundation for Children
126 East 31st Street
New York, NY 10016
212-251-0907
Fax: 212-982-6886
Supports projects that promote the welfare and education of children. Interests lies in early childhood education, higher education, children and youth services and family services.

Michael W Osheowitz, Executive Director

2598 Elaine E & Frank T Powers Jr Foundation
81 Skunks Misery Road
Locust Valley, NY 11560-1306
Offers support in the areas of secondary and higher education as well as youth services.

2599 Elmer & Mamdouha Bobst Foundation
Elmer Holmes Bobst Library, NYU
70 Washington Square S
New York, NY 10012-1019
212-998-2440
Fax: 212-995-4070
Offers grants and funding in the areas of youth, community development and the arts.

2600 Equitable Foundation
787 7th Avenue
Floor 39
New York, NY 10019-6018
212-554-3511
Offers grants in the areas of secondary school education, arts, community services, art and cultural programs, and higher education.

Kathleen A Carlson, Executive Director

2601 Ford Foundation
320 E 43rd Street
New York, NY 10017-4890
212-573-5000
Fax: 212-351-3677
E-mail: offsec@fordfound.rog
http://www.fordfound.org
Offers grants to advance public well-being and educational opportunities. Grants are given in the areas of education, secondary school/education, early childhood education, development services, human services, citizenship, academics and more.

Barron M Tenny, Secretary

2602 Frances & Benjamin Benenson Foundation
708 3rd Avenue
Floor 28
New York, NY 10017-4201
212-867-0990
Offers grants in elementary/secondary education, higher education and human services.

Charles B Benenson, Executive Director

2603 George F Baker Trust
477 Madison Avenue
New York, NY 10022
212-755-1890
Fax: 212-319-6316
Offers giving in the areas of higher and secondary education, social services, civic affairs and international affairs.

Rocio Suarez, Executive Director

2604 George Link Jr Foundation
C/O Emmet, Marvin & Martin
120 Broadway
32nd Floor
New York, NY 10271
212-238-3000
Fax: 212-238-3100
Giving is primarily centered on higher education, secondary school/education and medical research.

Michael J Catanzaro, Executive Director

2605 Gladys & Roland Harriman Foundation
63 Wall Street
Floor 23
New York, NY 10005-3001
212-493-8182
Fax: 212-493-5570
Giving is centered on education and support for youth and social service agencies.

William F Hibberd, Executive Director

2606 Gladys Brooks Foundation
1055 Franklin Avenue
Garden City, NY 11530
212-943-3217
http://www.gladysbrooksfoundation.org
The purpose of this foundation is to provide for the intellectual, moral and physical welfare of the people of this country by establishing and supporting nonprofit libraries, educational institutions, hospitals and clinics. In the area of education, grant applications will be considered generally for (a) educational endowments to fund scholarships based solely on leadership and academic ability of the student; (b) endowments to support salaries of educators.

Harman Hawkins, Chairman
Robert E Hill, Executive Director

2607 Green Fund
14 E 60th Street
Suite 702
New York, NY 10022-1006
212-755-2445
Fax: 212-755-0021
Offers grants in the area of higher and secondary education.

Cynthia Green Colin, Executive Director

2608 Hagedorn Fund
C/O JPMorgan Private Bank
Global Foundations Group
345 Park Avenue 4th Floor
New York, NY 10154

212-473-1587
http://www.fdncenter.org/grantmaker/haged
orn/
Offers support for higher and secondary education, youth agencies and social service agencies.

Monica J Neal, Vice President

2609 Hasbro Children's Foundation
10 Rockefeller Plaza
16th Floor
New York, NY 10020
212-713-7654
Fax: 212-645-4055
http://www.hasbro.org
Offers support to improve the quality of life for children. Areas of interest include education, AIDS research, literacy, special education, and youth services.

Eve Weiss, Executive Director

2610 Henry Luce Foundation
111 W 50th Street
Room 3710
New York, NY 10020-1202
212-489-7700
Fax: 212-581-9541
http://www.hluce.org
Offers grants for specific programs and projects in the areas of higher education and scholarship, social sciences at private colleges and universities, American arts and public affairs.

Michael Gilligan, President

2611 Herman Goldman Foundation
61 Broadway
Floor 18
New York, NY 10006-2701
212-797-9090
Fax: 212-797-9161
This foundation offers grants in the areas of social, legal and organizational approaches to aid for deprived or handicapped people; education for new or improved counseling for effective pre-school, vocational, and paraprofessional training; and the arts.

Richard K Baron, Executive Director

2612 Hess Foundation
1185 Avenue of the Americas
New York, NY 10036-2601
212-997-8500
Fax: 212-536-8390
E-mail: webmaster@hess.com
http://www.hess.com
Offers grants that focus on higher education, performing arts, and welfare organizations.

Leon Hess, Executive Director

2613 Horace W Goldsmith Foundation
375 Park Avenue
Suite 1602
New York, NY 10152-1699
212-319-8700
800-319-2881
Fax: 212-319-2881
Offers giving and support for education, higher education, cultural programs and museums.

James C Slaughter, Executive Director

2614 IBM Corporate Support Program
Old Orchard Road
Armonk, NY 10504
914-765-1900
The mission of this fund is to improve the areas and the communities that IBM operates in. Grants are awarded in various areas including early childhood education, elementary education, secondary education, business

school/education, and engineering school/education.

Stanley Litow, Executive Director

2615 JI Foundation
C/O Patterson, Belknap, Webb & Tyler
1133 Avenue of the Americas
New York, NY 10036
212-336-2000
Offers grants in the areas of elementary education, higher education, and general charitable giving.

2616 JP Morgan Charitable Trust
60 Wall Street
Floor 46
New York, NY 10005-2836
212-648-9673
Offers support in the area of education, housing, economic development, advocacy and international affairs.

Roberta Ruocco, Executive Director

2617 Joukowsky Family Foundation
410 Park Avenue
Suite 1610
New York, NY 10022-4407
212-355-3151
Fax: 212-355-3147
http://www.joukowsky.org
Giving is focused on higher and secondary education.

Nina J Koprulu, Director/President
Emily R Kessler, Executive Director

2618 Julia R & Estelle L Foundation
1 HSBC Center
Suite 3650
Buffalo, NY 14203-1217
716-856-9490
Fax: 716-856-9493
http://www.oisheifdt.org
This fund offers grants in the areas of higher and secondary education, medical research, social services and support agencies.

Thomas E Baker, President

2619 Leon Lowenstein Foundation
575 Madison Avenue
New York, NY 10022-3613
212-605-0444
Fax: 212-688-0134
Support is given for New York City public education and medical research.

John F Van Gorder, Executive Director

2620 Levittown Public Library
1 Bluegrass Lane
Levittown, NY 11756-1292
516-731-5728
Fax: 516-735-3168
http://www.nassaulibrary.org/levtown/
Member of The Foundation Center network, maintaining a collection of private foundation tax returns which provide information on the scope of grants dispensed by that particular foundation.

Margaret Santer, President

2621 Louis & Anne Abrons Foundation
C/O First Manhattan Company
437 Madison Avenue
New York, NY 10022-7001
212-756-3376
Fax: 212-832-6698
Offers support in the areas of education, improvement programs, environmental and cultural projects.

Richard Abrons, Executive Director

2622 Margaret L Wendt Foundation
40 Fountain Plaza
Suite 277
Buffalo, NY 14202-2200
716-855-2146
Fax: 716-855-2149
Offers various grants with an emphasis on education, the arts and social services in Buffalo and Western New York.

Robert J Kresse, Executive Director

2623 McGraw-Hill Foundation
1221 Avenue of the Americas
Room 2917
New York, NY 10020
212-512-6113
800-442-9685
Offers support to educational organizations in the areas of company operations or to national organizations.

Susan A Wallman, Executive Director

2624 New York Foundation
350 5th Avenue
Suite 2901
New York, NY 10118-2996
212-594-8009
Fax: 212-594-5918
http://www.nyf.org
Provides support for the implementation of programs that offer support for the quality of life including educational services, health organizations, centers and services, civil rights, public policy, research and more.

Madeline Lee, Executive Director

2625 Palisades Educational Foundation
C/O Gibney, Anthony & Flaherty
665 5th Avenue
Floor 2
New York, NY 10022-5305
Offers support for secondary and higher education in New York, New Jersey and Connecticut.

Ralph F Anthony, Executive Director

2626 Robert Sterling Clark Foundation
135 E 64th Street
New York, NY 10021-7307
212-288-8900
Fax: 212-288-1033
http://www.rsclark.org
For more than 15 years, this foundation has provided support to New York City's cultural community. During this time, the Foundation has tried to structure a grants program so that it is flexible and meets the needs of the institutions and organizations. Grants are given in the areas of cultural institutions, arts advocacy, family planning services and supporting new initiatives in the area of arts and education.

Winthrop R Munyan, President
Margaret C Ayers, Executive Director

2627 Rochester Public Library
Business, Economics & Law
115 S Avenue
Rochester, NY 14604-1896
585-428-8045
Fax: 585-428-8353
http://www.rochester.lib.ny.us/central
Member of The Foundation Center network, maintaining a collection of private foundation tax returns which provide information on the scope of grants dispensed by that particular foundation.

Emeterio M Otero, President

2628 Ronald S Lauder Foundation
767 5th Avenue
42nd Floor
New York, NY 10153-0023
212-572-6966

151

Offers giving in the areas of elementary/secondary education, human services and religion.

Marjorie S Federbush, Executive Director

2629 SH & Helen R Scheuer Family Foundation
350 5th Avenue
Suite 3410
New York, NY 10118-0110
212-947-9009
Fax: 212-947-9770
Offers support in the areas of higher education, welfare funding and cultural programs.

2630 Samuel & May Rudin Foundation
345 Park Avenue
New York, NY 10154-0004
212-407-2544
Fax: 212-407-2540
Offers support for higher education, social services, religious welfare agencies, hospitals and cultural programs.

Susan H Rapaport, Executive Director

2631 Seth Sprague Educational and Charitable Foundation
C/O U.S. Trust Company of New York
114 W 47th Street
New York, NY 10036-1510
212-852-3683
Fax: 212-852-3377
Offers support in the areas of education, culture, the arts, human services, community development and government/public administration.

Maureen Augusciak, Executive Director

2632 Starr Foundation
70 Pine Street
New York, NY 10270-0002
212-770-6881
Fax: 212-425-6261
http://www.fdncenter.org/grantmaker/starr
Support is given for educational projects with an emphasis on higher education, including scholarships under specific programs.

Ta Chun Hsu, Executive Director

2633 Tiger Foundation
101 Park Avenue
47th Floor
New York, NY 10178-0002
212-984-2565
Fax: 212-949-9778
http://www.tigerfoundation.org
Support is given primarily for early childhood education, youth programs and job training.

Phoebe Boyer, Executive Director

2634 Tisch Foundation
667 Madison Avenue
New York, NY 10021-8029
212-545-2000
Support is given in the area of education, especially higher education, and includes institutions in Israel and research-related programs.

Laurence A Tisch, Executive Director

2635 Travelers Group
388 Greenwich Street
New York, NY 10013-2375
212-816-8000
Fax: 212-816-5944
The main purpose of this foundation is to support public education, offering grants in the communities that the company serves.

Dee Topol, Executive Director

2636 White Plains Public Library
100 Martine Avenue
White Plains, NY 10601-2599

914-422-1400
Fax: 914-422-1462
http://www.whiteplainslibrary.org
Member of The Foundation Center network, maintaining a collection of private foundation tax returns which provide information on the scope of grants dispensed by that particular foundation.

2637 William Randolph Hearst Foundation
888 7th Avenue
Floor 45
New York, NY 10106-0001
212-586-5404
Fax: 212-586-1917
http://www.hearstfdn.org
Offers support to programs that aid priority-level and minority groups, educational programs especially private secondary and higher education, health systems and cultural programs.

Robert M Frehse Jr, Executive Director
Ilene Mack, Senior Program Officer

2638 William T Grant Foundation
570 Lexington Avenue
Floor 18
New York, NY 10022-6837
212-752-0071
Fax: 212-752-1398
E-mail: info@wtgrantfdn.org
http://www.wtgrantfoundation.org
The goal of the foundation is to help create a society that values people and helps them to reach their potenial. The Foundation is interested in environmentally friendly approaches

Edward Seidman, Senior VP Programs
Robert Granger, President

North Carolina

2639 AE Finley Foundation
1151 Newton Road
Raleigh, NC 27615
919-782-0565
Fax: 919-782-6978
Private foundation contributing and supporting to charitable, scientific, literary, religious and educational organizations. It endeavors to contribute to soundly managed and operated qualifying organizations which fundamentally give service with a broad scope and impact, aid all kinds of people and contribute materially to the general welfare.

Robert C Brown, Executive Director

2640 Cannon Foundation
PO Box 548
Concord, NC 28026-0548
704-786-8216
Fax: 704-785-2052
http://www.thecannonfoundationinc.org
Offers support for higher and secondary education, cultural programs, and grants to social service and youth agencies.

Frank Davis, Executive Director
William C Cannon Jr, President

2641 Dickson Foundation
301 S Tryon Street
Suite 1800
Charlotte, NC 28202
704-372-5404
Fax: 704-372-6409
Main focus is on areas of education & healthcare. Considers funding programs in the Southeast.

Susan Patterson, Secretary/Treasurer

2642 Duke Endowment
100 N Tryon Street
Suite 3500
Charlotte, NC 28202-4012
704-376-0291
Fax: 704-376-9336
http://www.dukeendowment.org
Support is given to higher education, children and youth services, churches and hospitals.

Eugene W Cochrane Jr, Executive Director

2643 First Union University
Two 1st Union Center
Charlotte, NC 28288
704-374-6868
Fax: 704-374-4147
Offers support for higher education and special programs for public elementary and secondary schools.

Ann D Thomas, Executive Director

2644 Foundation for the Carolinas
PO Box 3479
Charlotte, NC 28234
704-973-4500
800-973-7244
Fax: 704-376-1243
http://www.fftc.org
Offers support for education, the arts and health in North Carolina and South Carolina.

Michael Marsicano, President/CEO

2645 Kathleen Price and Joseph M Bryan Family Foundation
3101 N Elm Street
Greensboro, NC 27408-3184
336-288-5455
Grants are primarily offered in the fields of higher, secondary, and early childhood education.

William Massey, Executive Director

2646 Mary Reynolds Babcock Foundation
2920 Reynolda Road
Winston Salem, NC 27106-4618
336-748-9222
Fax: 336-777-0095
http://www.mrbf.org
This foundation traditionally provides funds to programs in education, social services, the environment, the arts and citizen participation in the development of public policy. The foundation prefers to fund programs of two kinds: those particularly sensitive to the changing and emerging needs of society and those addressing society's oldest needs in new and imaginative ways.

Gayle W Dorman, Executive Director
Sandra H Mikush, Assitant Director

2647 Non-Profit Resource Center/Pack Memorial Library
Learning Resources Center
67 Haywood Street
Asheville, NC 28801-4897
828-254-4960
Fax: 828-251-2258
http://www.buncombecounty.org
Cooperating collection of the Foundation Center. Other resources for non-profit organizations are also available.

Ed Sheary, Library Director

2648 State Library of North Carolina
Government & Business Services
109 E Jones Street
Raleigh, NC 27601-2806
919-807-7450
Fax: 919-733-5679
http://www.statelibrary.dcr.state.nc.us
Member of The Foundation Center network, maintaining a collection of private foundation tax returns which provide information on

the scope of grants dispensed by that particular foundation.

2649 William R Kenan Jr Charitable Trust
Kenan Center
PO Box 3858
Chapel Hill, NC 27515-3858
919-962-0343
Fax: 919-962-3331
The focus of this foundation is on education, primarily at private institutions in the US. The emphasis now is on national literacy and the importance of early childhood education. Grants have just established an institute for the arts and an institute for engineering, technology and science. No grants are given to individuals for scholarships, for research or other special projects or for medical, public health or social welfare projects. This Trust does not accept unsolicited requests.

William C Friday, Executive Director

2650 Winston-Salem Foundation
860 W 5th Street
Winston Salem, NC 27101-2506
336-725-2382
Fax: 336-727-0581
http://www.wsfoundation.org
Educational grants and loans to residents of Forsyth County, North Carolina in most areas.

Scott Wierman, President
Donna Rader, VP Grants & Programs

2651 Z Smith Reynolds Foundation
147 S Cherry Street
Suite 200
Winston Salem, NC 27101
336-725-7541
800-443-8319
Fax: 336-725-6069
http://www.zsr.org
Grants are limited to the state of North Carolina. General purpose foundation provides for their current priorities including community economic development, women's issues, minority issues, environment and pre-collegiate education. No grants are given to individuals.

Thomas W Ross, Executive Director

North Dakota

2652 Myra Foundation
PO Box 13536
Grand Forks, ND 58208-3536
701-775-9420
Offers grants in the areas of secondary school, and higher education to residents of Grand Forks County, North Dakota.

Edward C Gillig, Executive Director

2653 Tom & Frances Leach Foundation
PO Box 1136
Bismarck, ND 58502-1136
701-255-0479
Offers grants in the areas of higher and other education in North Dakota.

Clement C Weber, Executive Director

Ohio

2654 Akron Community Foundation
345 W Cedar Street
Akron, OH 44307-2407
330-376-8522
Fax: 330-376-0202
E-mail: acf_fund@ix.netcom.com
http://www.akroncommunityfdn.org

The foundation receives donations to permanent endowment and makes grants to qualified nonprofit organizations within Summit County, Ohio.

Jody Bacon, President

2655 American Foundation Corporation
720 National City Bank Building
Cleveland, OH 44114
216-241-6664
Fax: 216-241-6693
Offers support in the areas of higher and secondary education, the arts and community funds.

Maria G Muth, Executive Director

2656 Burton D Morgan Foundation
PO Box 1500
Akron, OH 44309-1500
330-258-6512
Fax: 330-258-6559
http://www.bdmorganfdn.org
The foundation's present areas of interest include economics, education, mental health and organizations principally located in Northeast Ohio. No grants are made to individuals and few grants are made to social service organizations.

John V Frank, President

2657 Dayton Foundation
2300 Kettering Tower
Dayton, OH 45423-1395
937-222-0410
Fax: 937-222-0636
http://www.daytonfoundation.org
Educational and community service grants.

Michael M Parks, President

2658 Eva L & Joseph M Bruening Foundation
1422 Euclid Avenue
Suite 627
Cleveland, OH 44115-1952
216-621-2632
Fax: 216-621-8198
http://www.fmscleveland.com/bruening
Support is offered in the fields of education, early childhood education, education fund-raising, higher education, youth services and health agencies.

Janet E Narten, Executive Director

2659 GAR Foundation
50 S Main Street #1500
Akron, OH 44308-1828
330-643-0201
800-686-2825
Fax: 330-252-5584
http://www.garfdn.org
Established in 1967 as a charitable trust, the foundation offers grants to organizations located primarily in Akron, Ohio area or, secondarily, in Northeastern Ohio or elsewhere in the United States at the discretion of the Distribution Committee. Grants for research projects of educational or scientific institutions, capital improvement projects, or matching campaigns are the priorities of this foundation.

Richard A Chenoweth, Executive Director
Robert W Briggs, Co-Trustee

2660 George Gund Foundation
1845 Guildhall Building
45 Prospect Avenue
West Cleveland, OH 44115
216-241-3114
Fax: 216-241-6560
E-mail: info@gundfdn.org
http://www.gundfdn.org
The primary interest of this foundation is in educational projects, with an emphasis on in-

ventive movements in teaching and learning, and on increasing educational opportunities for the disadvantaged.

David Abbott, Executive Director
Marcia Egbert, Senior Program Officer

2661 Hoover Foundation
101 E Maple Street
North Canton, OH 44720-2517
330-499-9200
Fax: 330-966-5433
Offers grants for elementary education, secondary and higher education and youth agencies.

LR Hoover, Executive Director

2662 Kettering Fund
40 N Main Street
Suite 1440
Dayton, OH 45423-1001
937-228-1021
Support is offered for social and educational studies and research as well as community development and cultural programs.

Richard F Beach, Executive Director

2663 Kulas Foundation
Tower City Center
50 Public Square
Suite 924
Cleveland, OH 44113-2203
216-623-4770
Fax: 216-623-4773
http://www.fdncenter.org/grantmaker/kulas/
A major general interest foundation, but with an emphasis on music. Giving is limited to Cuyahoga County and its surrounding area. Provides support to musical educational programs at Baldwin Wallace College, Case Western Reserve University and Cleveland Institute of Music. Also provides tickets to cultural programs to students in 16 colleges and universities in the area. The Foundation does not provide grants or loans to individuals. Support is geared to local primary and secondary schools.

Nancy W McCann, President/Treasurer

2664 Louise H & David S Ingalls Foundation
20600 Chagrin Boulevard
Suite 301
Shaker Heights, OH 44122-5334
216-921-6000
Offers support to organizations whose primary interest in the improvement of the educational, physical and mental condition of humanity throughout the world. Grants are given in secondary, elementary, and educational research.

Jane W Watson, Executive Director

2665 Louise Taft Semple Foundation
425 Walnut Street
Suite 1800
Cincinnati, OH 45202-3948
513-381-2838
Fax: 513-381-0205
Support is offered in the areas of secondary school/education, higher education, human services and health care organizations.

Dudley S Taft, Executive Director

2666 Martha Holden Jennings Foundation
Advisory & Distribution Committee Office
1228 Euclid Avenue
Suite 710
Cleveland, OH 44115-1831
216-589-5700
Fax: 216-589-5730
http://mhjf.org
The purpose of this foundation is to foster the development of young people to the maxi-

mum possible extent through improving the quality of teaching in secular elementary and secondary schools.

William T Hiller, Executive Director
Kathy L Kooyman, Grants Manager

2667 Mead Corporation Foundation
Courthouse Plz NE
Dayton, OH 45463-0001
937-495-3883
Fax: 937-495-4103
Grants are given to elementary, secondary, higher and minority education.

Ronald F Budzik, Executive Director

2668 Nord Family Foundation
747 Milan Avenue
Amherst, OH 44001
440-984-3939
Fax: 440-984-3934
http://www.nordff.org
Offers support for a variety of programs, including giving for early childhood, secondary, and higher education, social services, cultural affairs and civic activities.

David R Ashenhurst, Executive Director

2669 Ohio Bell Telephone Contribution Program
45 Erieview Plaza
Room 870
Cleveland, OH 44114-1814
216-822-4445
800-257-0902
Offers support of elementary school/education, secondary school/education, higher education, literacy and basic skills.

William W Boag Jr, Executive Director

2670 Ohio State Library Foundation Center
Kent H. Smith Library
1422 Euclid Avenue
Suite 1356
Cleveland, OH 44115-2001
216-861-1933
Fax: 216-861-1936
Member of The Foundation Center network, maintaining a collection of private foundation tax returns which provide information on the scope of grants dispensed by that particular foundation.

2671 Owens-Corning Foundation
PO Box 1688
Toledo, OH 43603-1688
419-248-8000
Fax: 419-325-4273
Offers support for education, including religious schools and science and technology programs.

Emerson J Ross, Executive Director

2672 Procter & Gamble Fund
PO Box 599
Cincinnati, OH 45201-0599
513-983-1100
Fax: 513-983-8250
Always considers the interests of the company's employees helping in the community, the arts, improving of schools and universities and to meet the needs of the less-fortunate neighbors. Some donations into the education program include grants to the United Negro College Fund, The National Hispanic Scholarship Fund, The Leadership Conference on Civil Rights Education Fund and more than 600 colleges and universities.

RL Wehling, President
G Talbot, VP

2673 Public Library of Cincinnati
Grants Resource Center
800 Vine Street #Library
Cincinnati, OH 45202-2009
513-369-6940
Fax: 513-369-6993
http://www.cincinnatilibrary.org
Member of The Foundation Center network, maintaining a collection of private foundation tax returns which provide information on the scope of grants dispensed by that particular foundation.

Kimber L Fender, Director

2674 Thomas J Emery Memorial
Frost & Jacobs
201 E 5th Street
Suite 2500
Cincinnati, OH 45202-4113
513-621-3124
Offers support in secondary school/education, higher education, health care, human services and arts/cultural programs.

Henry W Hobson Jr, Executive Director

2675 Timken Foundation of Canton
200 Market Avenue N
Suite 210
Canton, OH 44702-1622
330-452-1144
Fax: 330-455-1752
Offers support to promote the broad civic betterment including the areas of education, conservation and recreation. Grants restricted to caption projects only.

Don D Dickes, Secretary
Nancy Kuvdsen

2676 Wolfe Associates
34 S 3rd Street
Columbus, OH 43215-4201
614-461-5220
Fax: 614-469-6126
The foundation supports those organizations whose programs educate the individual and cultivate the individual's ability to participate in and contribute to the community or which enhance the quality of life which the community can offer to its citizens. The foundation has six general program areas in which it focuses its support: health and medicine, religion, education, culture, community service and environment.

AK Pierce Jr, Executive Director

Oklahoma

2677 Grace & Franklin Bernsen Foundation
15 W 6th Street
Suite 1308
Tulsa, OK 74119-5407
918-584-4711
Fax: 918-584-4713
E-mail: gfbersen@aol.com
http://www.bernsen.org
The foundation is limited by its policies to support of nonprofit organizations within the metropolitan area of Tulsa. The foundation discourages applications for general support or reduction of debt or for continuing or additional support for the same programs, although a single grant may cover several years. No grant is made to individuals or for the benefit of specific individuals and the applications must be received before the twelfth of each month.

John Strong Jr, Trustee

2678 Mervin Bovaird Foundation
100 W 5th Street
Suite 800
Tulsa, OK 74103-4291
918-583-1777
Fax: 918-592-5809
Awards scholarships to the University of Tulsa. Recipients are selected by Tulsa Area high schools and by Tulsa Junior College. No individual grants are made.

R Casey Cooper, President

2679 Oklahoma City University
Dulaney Brown Library
2501 N Blackwelder Avenue
Oklahoma City, OK 73106-1493
405-521-5000
Fax: 405-521-5291
Member of The Foundation Center network, maintaining a collection of private foundation tax returns which provide information on the scope of grants dispensed by that particular foundation.

Victoria Swinney, Director

2680 Public Service Company of Oklahoma Corporate Giving Program
212 E 6th Street #201
Tulsa, OK 74119-1295
918-586-0420
Offers support in the areas of elementary, secondary and higher education.

Mary Polfer, Executive Director

2681 Samuel Roberts Noble Foundation
PO Box 2180
Ardmore, OK 73402-2180
580-223-5810
Fax: 580-224-6380
http://www.noble.org
Offers support in the areas of higher education, agricultural research, human services and educational grants for health research pertaining to degenerative diseases, cancer and for health delivery systems.

Michael A Cawley, Executive Director

Oregon

2682 Collins Foundation
1618 SW 1st Avenue
Suite 305
Portland, OR 97201-5708
503-227-7171
Fax: 503-295-3794
http://www.collinsfoundation.org
Offers general support with an emphasis on higher education, hospices and health agencies, youth programs and arts and culture.

Jerry E Hudson, Executive Vice President
Cynthia G Adams, Director Of Programs

2683 Ford Family Foundation
1600 NW Stewart Parkway
Roseburg, OR 97470-0252
541-957-5574
Fax: 541-957-5720
E-mail: info@tfff.org
http://www.tfff.org
Giving is centered on education, youth organizations and human service programs in Oregon and Siskiyou County in California.

Bart Howard, Director Scholarship Program
Sarah Reeve, Scholarship Program Officer

2684 Meyer Memorial Trust
425 NW 10th Avenue
Suite 400
Portland, OR 97209
503-228-5512
Fax: 503-228-5840

E-mail: mmt@mmt.org
http://www.mmt.org
The Trust operates three different funding programs, all of which are restricted primarily to Oregon: 1) a broad-based General Purpose program that provides funds for education, arts, and humanities, health, social welfare, community development, and other activities; 2) a Small Grants program that provides up to $12,000 for small projects in the general purpose categories; and 3) the Support for Teacher Initiatives program, which provides grants of up to $7,000- to teachers.

Doug Stamm, Executive Director

2685 Multnomah County Library
Government Documents
801 SW 10th Avenue
Portland, OR 97205-2597
503-988-5123
Fax: 503-988-8014
http://www.multcolib.org
Member of The Foundation Center network, maintaining a collection of private foundation tax returns which provide information on the scope of grants dispensed by that particular foundation.

2686 Oregon Community Foundation
1221 SW Yamhill
Suite 100
Portland, OR 97205
503-227-6846
Fax: 503-274-7771
http://www.ocfl.org
The purpose of this foundation is to improve the cultural, educational and social needs in all levels of society throughout the state of Oregon.

Gregory A Chaille, Executive Director

2687 Tektronix Foundation
PO Box 1000
Wilsonville, OR 97070-1000
503-627-7111
http://www.tek.com
Offers support for education, especially science, math and engineering, and some limited art grants.

Jill Kirk, Executive Director

Pennsylvania

2688 Alcoa Foundation
201 Isabella Street
Pittsburgh, PA 15212-5858
412-553-2348
Fax: 412-553-4498
http://www.alcoa.com
Grants are given for education, arts and cultural programs.

F Worth Hobbs, Executive Director

2689 Annenberg Foundation
St. David's Center
150 N Radnor Chester Road
Suite A200
Saint Davids, PA 19087-5293
610-341-9066
Fax: 610-964-8688
E-mail: info@annenbergfoundation.org
http://www.annenbergfoundation.org
Primary support is given to childhood and K-12 education.

Dr. Gail C Levin Sr, Executive Director

2690 Arcadia Foundation
105 E Logan Street
Norristown, PA 19401-3058
215-275-8460
Gives only in Eastern Pennsylvania, no personal scholarships, accepts proposals only

between June 1-August 15. These will be considered for the following calendar year. Proposal has to be no more than 2 pages long and longer submissions will be discarded. Must have a copy of the IRS tax-identified letter with no other enclosures.

Marilyn Lee Steinbright, Executive Director

2691 Audrey Hillman Fisher Foundation
2000 Grant Building
Pittsburgh, PA 15219
412-338-3466
Fax: 412-338-3463
Offers support for secondary school/education, higher education, rehabilitation, science and engineering.

Ronald W Wertz, Executive Director

2692 Bayer Corporation
100 Bayer Court
Pittsburgh, PA 15205
412-777-2000
Fax: 412-777-3468
http://www.bayerus.com/about/community/
Support is given primarily in education, especially science programs, chemistry and the arts.

Rebecca Lucore, Executive Director

2693 Buhl Foundation
650 Smithfield Street
Pittsburgh, PA 15222-1207
412-566-2711
Fax: 412-566-2714
Grants are given to colleges and universities, secondary schools and educational associations, community educational and training programs, and other community programs offering health and education to the community. Grants are not made for building funds, overhead costs, accumulated deficits, ordinary operating budgets, general fund-raising campaigns, loans, scholarships and fellowships, other foundations, nationally funded organized groups or individuals.

Dr. Doreen Boyce, President

2694 Connelly Foundation
One Tower Bridge
Suite 1450
West Conshohocken, PA 19428
610-834-3222
Fax: 610-834-0866
http://www.connellyfdn.org
Offers support for education, health, human service, culture and civic programs to nonprofit organizations located in the city of Philadelphia and the greater Delaware Valley region.

Victoria K Flaville, VP Administration
Josephine C Mandeville, President/CEO

2695 Eden Hall Foundation
Pittsburgh Office And Research Park
600 Grant Street
Suite 3232
Pittsburgh, PA 15219
412-642-6697
Fax: 412-642-6698
http://www.edenhallfdn.org
This foundation offers support for higher education, social welfare and the improvement of conditions of the poor and needy.

Sylvia V Fields, Program Director
George C Greer, Chairman/President

2696 Erie County Library System
160 E Front Street
Erie, PA 16507-1554
814-451-6927
Fax: 814-451-6969
http://www.ecls.lib.pa.us
Member of The Foundation Center network, maintaining a collection of private founda-

tion tax returns which provide information on the scope of grants dispensed by that particular foundation.

2697 Foundation Center-Carnegie Library ofPittsburgh
Foundation Collection
4400 Forbes Avenue
Pittsburgh, PA 15213-4080
412-281-7143
Fax: 412-454-7001
E-mail: foundati@carnegielibrary.org
http://www.clpgh.org/clp/Foundation
Member of the Foundation Center network, of cooperating collections; providing current, factual information about grants and grantmaking organizations, and other aspects of philanthropy to the local nonprofit community.

Jim Lutton, Manager
Herb Elish, Director

2698 HJ Heinz Company Foundation
PO Box 57
Pittsburgh, PA 15230-0057
412-456-5772
Fax: 412-456-7859
E-mail: heinz.foundation@hjheinz.com
http://www.heinz.com/jsp/foundation.jsp
Offers support for higher education, employee matching gifts, social service agencies and cultural programs.

Loretta M Oken, Executive Director

2699 John McShain Charities
540 N 17th Street
Philadelphia, PA 19130-3988
215-564-2322
Offers support for higher and secondary education, Roman Catholic church support and social welfare.

Mary McShain, Executive Director

2700 Mary Hillman Jennings Foundation
625 Stanwix Street
Apt 2203
Pittsburgh, PA 15222-1408
412-434-5606
Fax: 412-434-5907
Offers grants to schools, youth agencies, and hospitals and health associations.

Paul Euwer Jr, Executive Director

2701 McCune Foundation
750 Six PPG Place
Pittsburgh, PA 15222
412-644-8779
Fax: 412-644-8059
http://www.mccune-db.mccune.org
The foundation provides support to independent higher education and human services.

Henry S Beukema, Executive Director

2702 Pew Charitable Trusts
One Commerce Square
2005 Market Street
Suite 1700
Philadelphia, PA 19103-7077
215-575-9050
Fax: 215-575-4939
http://www.pewtrusts.com
Offers support for education (including theology), arts culture, as well as public policy and religion.

Rebecca W Rimel, Executive Director

2703 Richard King Mellon Foundation
One Mellon Bank Center
500 Grant Street
Suite 4106
Pittsburgh, PA 15219-2502
412-392-2800
Fax: 412-392-2837
http://fdncenter.org/grantmaker/rkmellon/

Offers local grant programs with an emphasis on education, social services and the environment.

Seward Prosser Mellon, Trustee/President

2704 Rockwell International Corporation Trust
625 Liberty Avenue
Pittsburgh, PA 15222-3110
414-212-5200
Fax: 414-212-5201
Offers support in the areas of K-12 math and science education, and higher education in the field of engineering and science.

William R Fitz, Executive Director

2705 Samuel S Fels Fund
1616 Walnut Street
Suite 800
Philadelphia, PA 19103-5308
215-731-9455
Fax: 215-731-9457
http://www.samfels.org
Offers grants in continuing support that help prevent, lessen or resolve contemporary social problems including education, arts/cultural programs, and community development.

Helen Cunningham, Executive Director
Nell Williams, Office Administrator

2706 Sarah Scaife Foundation
Three Mellon Bank Center
301 Grant Street
Suite 3900
Pittsburgh, PA 15219-6402
412-392-2900
http://www.scaife.com
Offers grants in the areas of education and community development.

Joanne B Beyer, Executive Director
Michael W Gleba, Executive Vice President

2707 Shore Fund
C/O Melton Bank N.A.
PO Box 185
Pittsburgh, PA 15230-0185
412-234-4695
Fax: 412-234-3551
Although the foundation appreciates funding opportunities within the field of education, most grants given out have been to schools with which the foundation's trustees have been personally involved.

Helen M Collins, Executive Director

2708 Stackpole-Hall Foundation
44 S Saint Marys Street
Saint Marys, PA 15857-1667
814-834-1845
Fax: 814-834-1869
Offers support for higher education and secondary education, literacy and vocational projects, social services, arts and cultural programs, and community development.

William C Conrad, Executive Director

2709 United States Steel Foundation
600 Grant Street
Suite 639
Pittsburgh, PA 15219-2800
412-433-5237
Fax: 412-433-2792
http://www.psc.uss.com/usxfound
Grants are awarded for capital development, special projects or operating needs. Support is limited to organizations within the United States, with preference to those in the US Steel Corporation's operating areas. US Steel does not award grants for religious purposes. Additionally, grants are not awarded for conferences, seminars or symposia, travel, publication of papers, books or magazines, or

production of films, videotapes or other audiovisual materials.

Craig D Mallick, General Manager
Pamela E DiNardo, Program Administrator

2710 William Penn Foundation
2 Logan Square 11th Floor
100 North 18th Street
Philadelphia, PA 19103-2757
215-988-1830
Fax: 215-988-1823
http://www.williampennfoundation.org
The foundation supports culture, environment, human development, including programs for youth and elderly, education, including early childhood, secondary, elementary and higher.

Kathryn J Engebretson, President

Rhode Island

2711 Champlin Foundations
300 Centerville Road
Suite 300 S
Warick, RI 02868
401-736-0370
Fax: 401-736-7248
E-mail: champlinfons@worldnet.att.net
http://www.fdncenter.org/grantmaker/champlin
Offers giving in the areas of higher, secondary and other education. Exclusively in Rhode Island.

David A King, Executive Director

2712 Providence Public Library
Reference Department
150 Empire Street
Providence, RI 02903-3219
401-455-8005
http://www.provlib.org
Member of The Foundation Center network, maintaining a collection of private foundation tax returns which provide information on the scope of grants dispensed by that particular foundation.

Dale Thompson, Director

2713 Rhode Island Foundation
One Union Station
Providence, RI 02903-4630
401-274-4564
Fax: 401-331-8085
http://www.rifoundation.org
Promotes charitable activities which tend to improve the living conditions and well-being of the residents of Rhode Island.

Ronald V Gallo, President

South Carolina

2714 Charleston County Library
68 Calhoun Street
Charleston, SC 29401
843-805-6801
Fax: 843-727-3741
http://www.ccpl.org
Member of The Foundation Center network, maintaining a collection of private foundation tax returns which provide information on the scope of grants dispensed by that particular foundation.

Jan Buvinger, Director

2715 South Carolina State Library
1500 Senate Street
Columbia, SC 29201-3815

803-734-8666
Fax: 803-734-8676
http://www.state.sc.us/scsl/
Member of The Foundation Center network, maintaining a collection of private foundation tax returns which provide information on the scope of grants dispensed by that particular foundation.

James B Johnson Jr, Director

South Dakota

2716 South Dakota Community Foundation
207 E Capitol Avenue
Suite 296
Pierre, SD 57501-3159
605-224-1025
800-888-1842
Fax: 605-224-5364
http://www.sdcommunityfoundation.org
The mission of the foundation is to promote philanthropy, receive and administer charitable gifts and invest in a wide range of programs promoting the social and economic well being of the people of the South Dakota. Grants given in South Dakota only.

Bob Sutton, Executive Director

2717 South Dakota State Library
Reference Department
800 Governors Drive
Pierre, SD 57501-2294
605-773-5070
Fax: 605-773-4950
http://www.sdstatelibrary.com
Member of The Foundation Center network, maintaining a collection of private foundation tax returns which provide information on the scope of grants dispensed by that particular foundation.

Tennesse

2718 Benwood Foundation
736 Market Street
Chattanooga, TN 37402-4803
423-267-4311
Fax: 423-267-9049
The general purpose of this foundation is to support such religious, charitable, scientific, literary and educational activities as will promote the advancement of mankind in any part of the United States of America. It should be recognized by all prospective grantees that while the foundation is not limited to the Chattanooga, Tennessee area, the bulk of the grants are made to organizations in the immediate area.

Jean R McDaniel, Executive Director

2719 Christy-Houston Foundation
1296 Dow Street
Murfreesboro, TN 37130-2413
615-898-1140
Fax: 615-895-9524
Offers grants for education, arts, culture and health care to residents and organizations of Rutherford County, Tennessee.

James R Arnhart, Executive Director

2720 Frist Foundation
3100 West End Avenue
Suite 1200
Nashville, TN 37203
615-292-3868
Fax: 615-292-5843
http://www.fristfoundation.org

Broad general-purposed charitable foundation whose grants are restricted primarily to Nashville.

Peter F Bird Jr, President/CEO

2721 JR Hyde Foundation
First Tennessee Bank
PO Box 84
Memphis, TN 38101-0084
901-523-4883
Fax: 901-523-4266
Offers grants for higher education, including scholarships for the children of Malone and Hyde employees, community funds, secondary education and youth services.

JR Hyde III, Executive Director

2722 Lyndhurst Foundation
517 E 5th Street
Chattanooga, TN 37403
423-756-0767
Fax: 423-756-0770
http://www.lyndhurstfoundation.org
Support local arts and culture and downtown revitalzation efforts in Chattanooga. Support the protection and enhancement of the natural environment of the Southern Appalachian Region. Support the elementary and secondary public schools in Chattanooga.

Jack E Murrah, President

2723 Nashville Public Library
Business Information Division
615 Church Street
Nashville, TN 37219
615-862-5800
http://www.library.nashville.org
Member of The Foundation Center network, maintaining a collection of private foundation tax returns which provide information on the scope of grants dispensed by that particular foundation.

2724 Plough Foundation
6410 Poplar Avenue
Suite 710
Memphis, TN 38119-5736
901-761-9180
Fax: 901-761-6186
Offers grants for community projects, including a community fund, early childhood and elementary education, social service agencies and the arts.

Noris R Haynes Jr, Executive Director

2725 RJ Maclellan Charitable Trust
Provident Building
Suite 501
Chattanooga, TN 37402
423-755-1366
Supports higher and theological education, social services and youth programs.

Hugh O Maclellan Jr, Executive Director

Texas

2726 Albert & Ethel Herzstein Charitable Foundation
6131 Westview Drive
Houston, TX 77055-5421
713-681-7868
Fax: 713-681-3652
http://www.herzsteinfoundation.org
Concentrates support on temples and medical research with grants offered to medical schools.

L Michael Hajtman, President

2727 Burlington Northern Foundation
3800 Continental Plaza
777 Main Street
Fort Worth, TX 76102
817-352-6425
Fax: 817-352-7924
The major channel of philanthropy for Burlington Northern and its subsidiaries. The foundation administers a consistent contribution program in recognition of the company's opportunity to support and improve the general welfare and quality of life in communities it serves.

Beverly Edwards, President
Becky Blankenship, Grant Administrator

2728 Burnett Foundation
801 Cherry Street
Suite 1400
Fort Worth, TX 76102-6814
817-877-3344
Fax: 817-338-0448
Focus is on Fort Worth and Santa Fe, NM, seeking to be a positive force in the community, supporting the energy and creativity that exist in the nonprofit sector, and building capacity in organizations and people in the fields of education, health, community affairs, human services and arts and humanities.

Thomas F Beech, Executive Director

2729 Cooper Industries Foundation
PO Box 4446
Houston, TX 77210-4446
713-209-8607
Fax: 713-209-8982
E-mail: evans@cooperindustries.com
http://www.cooperindustries.com
The policy of this foundation is to carry out the responsibilities of corporate citizenship, by supporting nonprofit organizations in areas where employees are located, which best serve the educational, health, welfare, civic, cultural and social needs of the foundation's communities. All gifts are consistent with the company's objectives to enhance the quality of life and to honor the principles and freedoms that have enabled the company to prosper and grow. Average Grant: $5,000.

Victoria Guennewig, President
Jennifer L Evans, Secretary

2730 Corpus Christi State University
Library-Reference Department
805 Comanche
Corpus Christi, TX 78401
361-880-7000
Fax: 361-880-7005
http://www.library.ci.corpus-christi.tx.us
Member of The Foundation Center network, maintaining a collection of private foundation tax returns which provide information on the scope of grants dispensed by that particular foundation.

Denise Landry

2731 Cullen Foundation
601 Jefferson Street
Floor 40
Houston, TX 77002-7900
713-651-8837
Fax: 713-651-2374
http://www.cullenfdn.org
Supports educational, medical purposes, community funds and conservation.

Alan M Stewart, Executive Director
Sue A Alexander, Grants Administrator

2732 Dallas Public Library
Urban Information
1515 Young Street
Dallas, TX 75201-5499

214-670-1487
Fax: 214-670-1451
http://www.dallaslibrary.org
Member of The Foundation Center network, maintaining a collection of private foundation tax returns which provide information on the scope of grants dispensed by that particular foundation.

2733 El Paso Community Foundation
Historic Cortez Building
310 North Mesa 10th Floor
El Paso, TX 79901
915-533-4020
Fax: 915-532-0716
http://www.epcf.org
Grants to 501(c)(3) organizations in the El Paso geographic area. Fields of interest are arts and humanities, education, environment, health and disabilities, human services and civic benefits. No grants to individuals are offered.

Janice Windle, President
Virginia Martinez, Executive VP

2734 Ellwood Foundation
PO Box 52482
Houston, TX 77052-2482
713-739-0763
Scholarships for social services and education.

H Wayne Hightower, Executive Director

2735 Eugene McDermott Foundation
3808 Euclid Avenue
Dallas, TX 75205-3102
214-521-2924
Offers support primarily for higher and secondary education, health, cultural programs, and general community interests.

Eugene McDermott, Executive Director

2736 Ewing Halsell Foundation
711 Navarro Street
Suite 535
San Antonio, TX 78205-1786
210-223-2649
Fax: 210-271-9089
Offers grants in the areas of art and cultural programs, education, medical research, human services and youth services.

2737 Exxon Education Foundation
5959 Las Colinas Boulevard
Irving, TX 75039-2298
972-444-1106
Fax: 972-444-1405
http://www.exxon.mobile.com
Grants are given in the areas of environment, education, public information and policy research, united appeals and federated drives, health, civic and community service organizations, minority and women-oriented service organizations, arts, museums and historical associations. In the education area grants are awarded to mathematics education programs, elementary and secondary school improvement programs, undergraduate general education programs, research, training and support programs.

EF Ahnert, Executive Director

2738 Fondren Foundation
7 TCT 37
PO Box 2558
Houston, TX 77252
713-236-4403
Provides support in various areas of interest with an emphasis on higher and secondary education, social services and cultural organizations.

Melanie Scioneaus, Executive Director

2739 George Foundation
310 Morton Street
PMB Suite C
Richmond, TX 77469-3135
281-342-6109
Fax: 281-341-7635
http://www.thegeorgefoundation.org
Offers giving for religious, educational, charitable or scientific purposes.

Roland Adamson, Executive Director

2740 Gordon & Mary Cain Foundation
8 E Greenway Plaza
Suite 702
Houston, TX 77046-0892
713-960-9283
Fax: 713-877-1824
The foundation is not limited to education but does contribute a large amount to that area. For a company to apply for a grant they must offer a statement of purpose or a summary of the project needing funding; budget with balance sheet, fund balance, distribution of funds, audited statement and number of employees; latest copy of IRS tax-exempt status letter 501(c)(3); current projects needing funding with amounts needed for entire project and the amount of the grant being requested.

James D Weaver, Executive Director

2741 Haggar Foundation
6113 Lemmon Avenue
Dallas, TX 75209-5715
214-352-8481
Fax: 214-956-4446
Offers support in various areas with an emphasis on higher and secondary education, including a program for children of company employees.

Mary Vaughan Rumble, Executive Director

2742 Hobby Foundation
2131 San Felipe Street
Houston, TX 77019-5620
713-521-4694
Fax: 713-521-3950
Offers grants to educational facilities in the state of Texas.

Oveta Culp Hobby, Executive Director

2743 Houston Endowment
600 Travis Street
Suite 6400
Houston, TX 77002-3000
713-238-8100
Fax: 713-238-8101
E-mail: info@houstonendowment.org
http://www.houstonendowment.org
Offers support for charitable, religious or educational organizations.

H Joe Nelson III, Executive Director

2744 Houston Public Library
Bibliographic Information Center
500 McKinney Street
Houston, TX 77002-2534
832-238-9640
Fax: 832-393-1383
http://www.hpl.lib.tx.us/hpl/hplhome
Member of The Foundation Center network, maintaining a collection of private foundation tax returns which provide information on the scope of grants dispensed by that particular foundation.

2745 James R Dougherty Jr Foundation
PO Box 640
Beeville, TX 78104-0640
361-358-3560
Fax: 361-358-9693

Offers support for Roman Catholic church-related industries including education, higher, secondary and other education.

Hugh Grove Jr, Executive Director

2746 Leland Fikes Foundation
3050 Lincoln Plaza
500 N Akard
Dallas, TX 75201
214-754-0144
Fax: 214-855-1245
Giving is focused on education, youth services, family planning, public interest and cultural programs.

Nancy Solana, Executive Director

2747 MD Anderson Foundation
PO Box 2558
Houston, TX 77252-2558
713-658-2316
The purpose of this foundation is to improve lives in the areas of health care, education, human service, youth and research.

John W Lowrie, Executive Director

2748 Meadows Foundation
3003 Swiss Avenue
Wilson Historic Block
Dallas, TX 75204-6049
214-826-9431
800-826-9431
Fax: 214-824-0642
E-mail: besterline@mfi.org
http://www.mfi.org
Support is given in the area of arts and culture, civic and public affairs, education, health, including mental health, and human services.

Bruce Esterline, VP Grants
Carol Stabler, Director Communications

2749 Moody Foundation
2302 Post Office Street
Suite 704
Galveston, TX 77550-1994
409-763-5333
Fax: 409-763-5564
http://www.moodyf.org
Provides major support for two foundation-initiated projects: the Transitional Learning Center, a residential rehabilitation and research facility for the treatment of traumatic brain injury, and Moody Gardens, a world-class education and recreation complex that includes a 1-acre enclosed rainforest, the area's largest aquarium, a space museum, IMAX theater, and the Moody Hospitality Institute.

Peter M Moore, Grants Director

2750 Paul & Mary Haas Foundation
PO Box 2928
Corpus Christi, TX 78403-2928
361-887-6955
Offers scholastic grants to graduating high school seniors from Corpus Christi, Texas. The student must have above average grades and ability to prove financial need. The Foundation asks that the senior contact them in the Fall of his/her senior year in order to begin the in-house application process. The grant is a maximum of $1,500 per semester and is renewable for a total of eight semesters if the student maintains a 3.0 GPA. The student may attend college or university of his choice.

Karen Wesson, Executive Director

2751 Perot Foundation
12377 Merit Drive
Suite 1700
Dallas, TX 75251-2239
972-788-3000
Fax: 972-788-3091

Educational grants, medical research funding and grantmaking for the arts and cultural organizations.

Bette Perot, Executive Director

2752 RW Fair Foundation
PO Box 689
Tyler, TX 75710-0689
903-592-3811
Grants are given for secondary and higher education, church-related programs and legal education.

Wilton H Fair, Executive Director

2753 Sid W Richardson Foundation
309 Main Street
Fort Worth, TX 76102-4006
817-336-0494
Fax: 817-332-2176
E-mail: www.sidrichardson.org
This foundation was established for the purpose of supporting organizations that serve the people of Texas. Grants are given in the areas of education, health, the arts and human services.

Valleau Wilkie Jr, Executive Director

2754 Strake Foundation
712 Main Street
Suite 3300
Houston, TX 77002-3210
713-546-2400
Fax: 713-216-2401
Foundation gives primarily in Texas in the areas of operating budgets, continuing support, annual campaigns, special projects, research, matching funds and general purposes.

George W Strake Jr, Executive Director

2755 Trull Foundation
404 4th Street
Palacios, TX 77465-4812
361-972-5241
Fax: 361-972-1109
E-mail: trullfdn@ncnet.net
http://www.trullfoundation.org
1. A concern for the needs of the Palacios, Matagorda county are, where the foundation has its roots. Local health care, the senior center, and other local projects were considered and supported. 2. A concern for children and families. Grants are given to direct and channel lives away from child abuse, neglect from hunger, and poverty. 3. A concern for those persons and families devastated by the effects of substance abuse.

Gail Purvis, Executive Director
Lucja White, Administrative Assistant

Utah

2756 Marriner S Eccles Foundation
79 S Main Street
Salt Lake City, UT 84111-1901
801-246-5155
General support for Utah's human services, education and the arts programs.

Erma E Hogan, Executive Director

2757 Ruth Eleanor Bamberger and John Ernest Bamberger Memorial Foundation
136 S Main Street
Salt Lake City, UT 84101
801-364-2045
Fax: 801-322-5284
Offers support for secondary education, especially undergraduate scholarships for student nurses and for schools.

William H Olwell, Executive Director

2758 Salt Lake City Public Library
210 East 400 south
Salt Lake City, UT 84111-3280
801-524-8200
Fax: 801-524-8272
http://www.slcpl.lib.ut.us
Member of The Foundation Center network, maintaining a collection of private foundation tax returns which provide information on the scope of grants dispensed by that particular foundation.

Dana Tumtowsky, Comm Relations Coordinator
Nancy Tessman, Director

Vermont

2759 Vermont Community Foundation
PO Box 30
Three Court Street
Middlebury, VT 05753-0030
802-388-3355
Fax: 802-388-3398
http://www.vermontcf.org
Offers support for the arts and education, the environment, preservation of the community, public affairs and more for the betterment of Vermont.

Brian T Byrnes, President/CEO
Mary Conlon, Program Director

2760 Vermont Department of Libraries
Reference Services
109 State Street
Montpelier, VT 05609-0001
802-828-3268
Fax: 802-828-2199
http://www.dol.state.vt.us
Member of The Foundation Center network, maintaining a collection of private foundation tax returns which provide information on the scope of grants dispensed by that particular foundation.

2761 William T & Marie J Henderson Foundation
PO Box 600
Stowe, VT 05672-0600
Offers grants in the areas of elementary and secondary education.

William T Henderson, Executive Director

Virginia

2762 Beazley Foundation
3720 Brighton Street
Portsmouth, VA 23707-3902
757-393-1605
Fax: 757-393-4708
http://www.beazleyfoundation.org
The purpose of this foundation to further the causes of charity, education and religion. Offers support for higher, secondary and medical education, youth agencies, community agencies and development.

Richard Bray, President
Donna Russell, Associate Director

2763 Flagler Foundation
PO Box 644
Richmond, VA 23205
804-648-5033
Offers support for secondary and higher education, cultural programs and restoration.

Lawrence Lewis Jr, Executive Director

2764 Hampton Public Library
4207 Victoria Boulevard
Hampton, VA 23669-4200

757-727-1154
Fax: 757-727-1152
http://www.hampton.va.us
Member of The Foundation Center network, maintaining a collection of private foundation tax returns which provide information on the scope of grants dispensed by that particular foundation.

2765 Jeffress Memorial Trust
Bank Of America Private Bank
Po Box 26688
Richmond, VA 23261-6688
804-788-3698
Fax: 804-788-2700
http://www.wm.edu/grants/opps/jeffress.htm

Funds research in higher education.
Richard B Brandt, Advisor

2766 Kentland Foundation
PO Box 837
Berryville, VA 22611-0837
540-955-1082
Focuses on civic affairs organizations and education.

Helene Walker, Executive Director

2767 Longview Foundation for Education in World Affairs/International Understanding
8639 B Sixteenth Street
Box 211
Silver Spring, MD 20910
301-681-0899
Fax: 301-681-0925
http://www.fdncenter.org/grantmaker/longview/index.html
Offers grants and scholarships with an emphasis on pre-collegiate education, primarily elementary education, and also supports teacher education.

Betsy Devlin-Foltz, Director

2768 Richmond Public Library
Business, Science & Technology Department
101 E Franklin Street
Richmond, VA 23219-2193
804-646-7223
Fax: 804-646-4757
http://www.richmondpubliclibrary.org
Member of The Foundation Center network, maintaining a collection of private foundation tax returns which provide information on the scope of grants dispensed by that particular foundation.

2769 Virginia Foundation for Educational Leadership
2204 Recreation Drive
Virginia Beach, VA 23456-6178
757-430-2412
Fax: 757-430-3247

George E McGovern, Division Director

Washington

2770 Comstock Foundation
S 2607 SE Boulevard #B115
Spokane, WA 99223
509-534-6499
The Foundation contributes only to 501(c)(3) organizations, limited to Spokane County and its environs. In the field of general education, Comstock Foundation favors grants only to private institutions of higher learning, and no grants are made to individuals.

Horton Herman, Trustee
Charles M Leslie, Trustee

2771 Foster Foundation
1201 3rd Avenue
Suite 2101
Seattle, WA 98101-3086
206-624-5200
Offers support in art, culture, higher education, adult education, literacy and basic reading, health care and children and youth services.

Jill Goodsell, Executive Director

2772 MJ Murdock Charitable Trust
703 Broadway Street
Suite 701
Vancouver, WA 98660-3308
360-694-8415
Fax: 360-694-1819
http://www.murdock-trust.org
Offers support primarily for special projects of private organizations in the areas of education, higher education, human services and program development.

John Van Zytveld, Senior Program Director

2773 Seattle Foundation
200 5th Avenue
Suite 1300
Seattle, WA 98101-3151
206-622-2294
Fax: 206-622-7673
http://www.seattlefoundation.org
A community foundation that facilitates charitable giving; administers charitable funds, trusts and bequests; and distributes grants to non-profit organizations that are making a positive difference in our community. Grants are awarded to organizations working in areas that include social service, children and youth, civic, culture, elderly, conservation, education and health/rehabilitation.

Phyllis J Campbell, President/CEO
Molly Stearns, Senior Vice President

2774 Seattle Public Library
Science, Social Science
1000 4th Avenue
Seattle, WA 98104-1193
206-386-4636
Fax: 206-386-4634
http://www.spl.org
Member of The Foundation Center network, maintaining a collection of private foundation tax returns which provide information on the scope of grants dispensed by that particular foundation.

2775 Spokane Public Library
Funding Information Center
906 West Main Street
Spokane, WA 99201-0903
509-444-5300
Fax: 509-444-5365
http://www.spokanelibrary.org
Member of The Foundation Center network, maintaining a collection of private foundation tax returns which provide information on the scope of grants dispensed by that particular foundation.

Pat Partovi, Director

West Virginia

2776 Clay Foundation
1426 Kanawha Boulevard E
Charleston, WV 25301-3084
304-344-8656
Fax: 304-344-3805
Private charitable foundation making grants for health, education and programs for the aging or disadvantaged children.

Charles M Avampao, Executive Director

159

2777 Kanawha County Public Library
123 Capitol Street
Charleston, WV 25301-2686
304-343-4646
Fax: 304-348-6530
http://www.kanawha.lib.wv.us
Member of The Foundation Center network, maintaining a collection of private foundation tax returns which provide information on the scope of grants dispensed by that particular foundation.

2778 Phyllis A Beneke Scholarship Fund
Security National Bank & Trust Company
PO Box 511
Wheeling, WV 26003-0064
Offers support and scholarships for secondary education.

GP Schramm Sr, Executive Director

Wisconsin

2779 Faye McBeath Foundation
1020 N Broadway
Suite 112
Milwaukee, WI 53202-3157
414-272-2626
Fax: 414-272-6235
http://www.fayemcbeath.org
The purpose of the foundation is to provide Wisconsin people the best in education, child welfare, homes and care for the elderly and research in civics and government.

Scott E Gelzer, Executive Director
Aileen Mayer, Executive Assistant

2780 Lynde & Harry Bradley Foundation
1241 N Franklin Place
Milwaukee, WI 53202-2901
414-291-9915
Fax: 414-291-9991
http://www.bradleyfdn.org
The Foundation encourages projects that focus on cultivating a renewed, healthier and more vigorous sense of citizenship among the American people, and among peoples of all nations, as well. Grants are awarded to organizations and institutions exempt from federal taxation under Section 501(c)(3) and publicly supported under section 509(a), favor projects which are not normally financed by public tax funds, consider requests from religious organizations and institutions as well.

Michael W Grebe, President/CEO
Terri L Famer, Director Of Administration

2781 Marquette University Memorial Library
1415 W Wisconsin Avenue
Milwaukee, WI 53233-2287
414-288-1515
Fax: 414-288-5324
http://www.marquette.edu/library/
Member of The Foundation Center network, maintaining a collection of private foundation tax returns which provide information on the scope of grants dispensed by that particular foundation.

2782 Siebert Lutheran Foundation
2600 N Mayfair Road
Suite 390
Wauwatosa, WI 53226-1392
414-257-2656
Fax: 414-257-1387
E-mail: rdjslf@execpc.com
http://www.siebertfoundation.org
Offers support in elementary and secondary, higher education and early childhood education.

Ronald D Jones, President
Deborah Engel, Administrative Assistant

2783 University of Wisconsin-Madison
Memorial Library
728 State Street
Madison, WI 53706-1418
608-262-3242
Fax: 608-262-8569
E-mail: grantsinfo@library.wisc.edu
http://www.grants.library.wisc.edu
Member of The Foundation Center network, maintaining a collection of private foundation tax returns which provide information on the scope of grants dispensed by that particular foundation.

Wyoming

2784 Natrona County Public Library
307 E 2nd Street
Casper, WY 82601-2598
307-237-4935
Fax: 307-266-3734
http://www.library.natrona.net
Member of The Foundation Center network, maintaining a collection of private foundation tax returns which provide information on the scope of grants dispensed by that particular foundation.

Grants, Federal & Private

2785 American Honda Foundation
PO Box 2205
Torrance, CA 90509-2205
310-781-4090
Fax: 310-781-4270
http://www.hondacorporate.com/community
Offers support for national organizations whose areas of interest include youth and scientific education. Grants reach private elementary, secondary, higher, vocational and scientific education.

Kathryn A Carey, Manager

2786 Awards for University Administrators and Librarians
Association of Commonwealth Universities
John Foster House
36 Gordon Square
London WC1H OPF, England
171 3878572
Fax: 171 3872655
E-mail: pubinfo@acu.ac.uk;
acusales@acu.ac.uk
Lists approximately 40 sources of financial assistance for administrative and library staff for universities worldwide. Includes name, address, phone, fax, tenure place and length, amount of aid, requirements for eligibility and application procedure, and frequency and number of grants available.

40 pages Biennial
ISSN: 0964-2714

Moira Hunter, Editor

2787 Awards for University Teachers and Research Workers
Association of Commonwealth Universities
36 Gordon Square
London
WC1H OPF, England
44-20-7380-6700
Fax: 44-20-7387-2655
E-mail: info@devry.edu
http://www.devry.edu
Lists approximately 740 awards open to university teachers and research workers in one country for research, study visits or teaching at a university in another country. Offers fel-

lowships, visiting professorships and lectureships and travel grants.

364 pages Biennial
ISSN: 0964-2706

2788 Educational Foundation of America
35 Church Lane
Westport, CT 06880-3515
203-226-6498
Fax: 203-227-0424
http://www.efaw.org
Funds projects in arts, education and programs benefiting Native Americans.

Diane M Allison, Executive Director

2789 Foundation Center
79 5th Avenue
Floor 8
New York, NY 10003-3076
212-620-4230
Fax: 212-807-3677
http://www.fdncenter.org
A national service organization which disseminates information on private giving through public service programs, publications, and through a national network of library reference collections for free public use. Over 100 network members have sets of private foundation information returns, and the New York, Washington, DC, Cleveland and San Francisco reference collections operated by the Foundation offer a wide variety of services and collections of information on foundations and grants.

Cheryl Loe, Director Of Communications
Laura Cascio, Fulfillment Management

2790 GTE Foundation
PO Box 152257
Irving, TX 75015-2257
972-507-5434
Fax: 972-615-4310
http://www.gte.com
The emphasis of giving for the foundation is on higher education in math, science and technology. It also sponsors scholarships and supports community funds and social service agencies that emphasize literacy training.

Maureen Gorman, VP

2791 George I Alden Trust
370 Main Street
Worcester, MA 01608-1714
508-798-8621
Fax: 508-791-6454
http://www.aldentrust.org
Gives to higher education organizations and facilities with an emphasis on scholarship endowments.

Francis H Dewey III, Executive Director

2792 Gershowitz Grant and Evaluation Services
505 Merle Hay Tower
Des Moines, IA 50310
515-270-1718
Fax: 515-270-8325
E-mail: gershowitz@netins.net
To give schools an edge in funding their technology programs

Michael V Gershowitz, PhD
Steve Panyan, PhD

2793 Grants and Contracts Service
Department of Education/Regional Office Building
7th & D Streets
Suite 3124
Washington, DC 20202-0001
202-401-2000
Fax: 202-260-7225
To support improvements in teaching and learning and to help meet special needs of

schools and students in elementary and secondary education

Gary J Rasmussen, Director

2794 Grantsmanship Center
PO Box 17220
Los Angeles, CA 90017-0220
213-482-9860
Fax: 213-482-9863
E-mail: norton@tgci.com
http://www.tgci.com
The world's oldest and largest training organization for the nonprofit sector. Since it was founded in 1972, the has trained trains more than 75,000 staff members of public and private agencies; training provided includes grantsmanship, program management and fundraising. Center also produces publications on grantsmanship, fundraising, planning, management and personnel issues for nonprofit agencies.

Norton Kiritz, President

2795 John S & James L Knight Foundation
Wachovia Financial Center
Suite 3300
200south Biscayne Boulevard
Miami, FL 33131-2349
305-908-2635
http://www.knightfdn.org
The foundation makes national grants in journalism, education and the field of arts and culture. It also supports organizations in communities where the Knight brothers were involved in publishing newspapers but is wholly separate from and independent of those newspapers.

James D Spaniolo, Executive Director

2796 National Academy of Education
School of Education
Ceras 108
Stanford, CA 94305
212-998-9035
Fax: 212-995-4435
Offers the Spencer Postdoctoral Fellowship which is designed to promote scholarship in the United States and abroad on matters relevant to the improvement of education in all its forms.

Debbie Leong-Childs, Executive Director

2797 National Science Foundation
4201 Wilson Boulevard
Arlington, VA 22230
703-292-5111
Fax: 703-292-9184
http://www.nsf.gov
Offers grants, workshops and curricula for all grade levels.

Arden L Bement Jr, Director

2798 Trust to Reach Education Excellence
1904 Association Drive
Reston, VA 20191-1537
703-860-0200
800-253-7746
Fax: 703-476-5432
E-mail: tree@principals.org
http://http://tree.principals.org
Founded to make grants to educators and students who would ordinarily not have access to outstanding NASSP programs, such as camps, programs and workshops on leadership, technology and school reform.

Dr. Anne Miller, Executive Director

2799 Union Carbide Foundation
39 Old Ridgebury Road
Danbury, CT 06817-0001
203-794-6945
Fax: 203-794-7031
Offers grants in the areas of elementary and secondary education, with an emphasis on

systemic reform; higher education with a focus on science and engineering; and environmental protection awareness.

Nancy W Deibler, Executive Director

2800 United States Institute of Peace
1200 17th Street NW
Washington, DC 20036
202-457-1700
Fax: 202-429-6063
http://www.usip.org
Includes grants, fellowships, a National Peace Essay Contest for high school students and teacher training institutes.

Richard H Solomon, President

2801 United States-Japan Foundation
145 E 32nd Street
Floor 12
New York, NY 10016-6055
212-481-8753
Fax: 212-481-8762
E-mail: info@us-jf.org
http://www.us-jf.org
A nonprofit, philanthropic organization with the principal mission of promoting a greater mutual knowledge between United States and Japan and to contribute to a strengthened understanding of important public policy issues of interest to both countries. Currently the focus is on precollegiate education, policy studies, and communications and public opinion.

2802 Westinghouse Foundation
Westinghouse Electric Corporation
Po Box 355
ECE 575C
Pittsburgh, PA 15230-0355
412-374-6824
Fax: 412-642-4874
http://www.westinghousenuclear.com
Makes charitable contributions to community priorities primarily where Westinghouse has a presence. Areas of emphasis include: education, health and welfare, culture and the arts and civic and social grants. Support for education is central to Westinghouse's contributions program, particularly higher education in the areas of engineering, applied science and business. Also encourages educational programs that strengthen public schools through enhanced student learning opportunities.

G Reynolds Clark, Executive Director

2803 Xerox Foundation
800 Long Ridge Road #1600
Stamford, CT 06902-1227
203-968-3445
http://www.xerox.com
Offers giving in the areas of higher education to prepare qualified men and women for careers in business, government and education.

Joseph M Cahalan, Executive Director

Fundraising

2804 A&L Fund Raising
95 Leggett Street
East Hartford, CT 06108-1140
860-242-2476
800-286-7247
Offers many successful fundraising programs including Christmas gifts, designer gift wraps from Ashley Taylor and Geoffrey Boehm chocolates. A&L sells only the highest quality items at affordable prices with great service to schools and organizations.

Anita Brown

2805 A+ Enterprises
1426 Route 33
Hamilton Square, NJ 08690-1704
609-587-1765
800-321-1765
A promotional corporation offering a variety of fundraising programs for schools and educational institutions, ranging from Christmas campaigns to chocolates, as well as magnets and gift campaigns.

2806 Aid for Education
CD Publications
8204 Fenton Street
Sliver Spring, MD 20910
301-588-6380
800-666-6380
Fax: 301-588-0519
E-mail: afe@cdpublications.com
http://cdpublications.com
18 pages Newsletter
ISSN: 1058-1324

Frank Kimko, Editor

2807 All Sports
21 Round Hill Road
Wethersfield, CT 06109
860-721-0273
800-829-0273
Fax: 860-257-9609
http://www.graduationshirts.com
Fundraising and school promotion company offering crew sweatshirts, hoods, tees, jackets, caps, gymwear and specialty signature shirts for graduating classes.

Wally Schultz, Owner

2808 Art to Remember
5535 Macy Drive
Indianapolis, IN 46236
317-826-0870
800-895-8777
Fax: 317-823-2822
E-mail: brackney@arttoremember.com
http://www.arttoremember.com
Raises funds for art departments and special school programs.

2809 Childrens Youth Funding Report
CD Publications
8204 Fenton Street
Sliver Spring, MD 20910
301-588-6380
800-666-6380
Fax: 301-588-0519
E-mail: cye@cdpublications.com
http://cdpublications.com
Detailed coverage of federal and private grant opportunities and legislative initiatives effecting childrens programs in such areas as child welfare, education healthcare.

18 pages Monthly

Steve Albright, Editor

2810 Dutch Mill Bulbs
PO Box 407
Hershey, PA 17033-1386
717-868-3120
800-533-8824
Fax: 800-556-0539
E-mail: info@dutchmillbulbs.com
http://www.dutchmillbulbs.com
Spring and Fall fundraising with flower bulbs program.

Jeffrey E Ellenberger, President

2811 E-S Sports Screenprint Specialists
47 Jackson Street
Holyoke, MA 01040-5512
413-534-5634
800-833-3171
Fax: 413-538-8648
Scholastic Spirit Division offers screenprinted T-shirts, sweatshirts, shorts

and apparel. This program offers schools and organizations an easy way to increase school spirit with no risk, no minimum orders and prompt delivery.

Aaron Porchelli, Division Director

2812 Fundraising USA
1395 State Route 23
Butler, NJ 07405-1736
973-283-1946
800-428-6178
Fundraiser offering a variety of programs for schools and organizations including Walk-A-Thons. This program is fast becoming the most popular way for schools to raise money. The walks are designed to take place at your own school, and children are not responsible for collecting any money. Fundraising USA collects all donations through the mail.

2813 Gold Medal Products
10700 Medallion Drive
Cincinnati, OH 45241-4807
513-769-7676
800-543-0862
Fax: 513-769-8500
E-mail: info@gmpopcorn.com
http://www.gmpopcorn.copm
Offers a full line of fundraising products popcorn poppers and supplies and programs including candy, clothing and sports programs for schools and colleges.

Chris Petroff
Dan Kroeger, President

2814 Human-i-Tees
400 Columbus Avenue
Valhalla, NY 10595-1335
800-275-2638
Fax: 914-745-1799
http://www.humanitees.com
Environmental T-shirt fundraisers that provide large profits while raising environmental awareness for thousands of school, youth and service organizations across the country.

2815 Hummel Sweets
PO Box 232
Forestville, MD 20747
800-998-8115
Offer fundraising programs with 45% to 50% profit.

2816 M&M Mars Fundraising
800 High Street
Hackettstown, NJ 07840-1552
908-852-1000
Fax: 908-850-2734
Offers America's favorite candies for fundraising programs throughout the year.

2817 QSP
Subsidiary of the Reader's Digest Association
PO Box 2003
Ridgefield, CT 06877-0903
203-756-3022
For twenty-seven years, this fundraiser has helped students raise more than $900,000,000 for extracurricular programs and projects that are essential to a meaningful, well-rounded education. With QSP programs, students earn money to fund worthwhile projects and learn about the business world at the same time. QSP offers various fundraising programs including: Family Reading Programs; The Music Package; Delightful Edibles; and The Parade of Gifts.

Robert L Metivier, Sales Manager

2818 Sally Foster Gift Wrap
PO Box 539
Duncan, SC 29334-0539
800-552-5875
Fax: 800-343-0809

Fundraiser offers gift wrap packages to schools. Offers high quality merchandise, including the heaviest papers and foils available. This proven two-week program is quick, easy and profitable offering your school or organization the opportunity to raise thousands of dollars to buy computers, books, athletic equipment and more. Organizations and schools keep 50% of all the profits, and there are no up-front costs or risks.

Mark Metcalfe, Sr VP

2819 School Identifications
Chas. E. Petrie Comapny
PO Box 12
Long Beach, CA 90801-0012
562-591-0666
800-772-0798
Fax: 562-591-0071
E-mail: info@schoolidents.com
http://www.schoolidents.com
An easy fundraising project for schools, offering school identification cards and tags for students.

2820 School Memories Collection
Fundcraft Publishing
PO Box 340
Collierville, TN 38027
901-853-7070
800-390-2129
Fax: 901-853-6196
E-mail: info@schoolplanners.com
http://www.schoolmemories.com
Memory books with games and activities.

Chris Bradley, Marketing Director

2821 Sports Shoes & Apparel
3 Moulton Drive
Londonderry, NH 03053-4061
603-437-7844
800-537-7844
Fax: 603-437-2300
Offers customized sweatshirts, T-shirts and beach towels at group discount, with several complete fund raising programs being available as well. Beach towels for fundraising.

Bill McMahon, Regional Manager

2822 Steve Wronker's Funny Business
39 Boswell Road
W Hartford, CT 06107-3708
860-233-6716
800-929-swfb
Fax: 860-561-8910
http://www.swfb.net/swfb.htm
Comedy and educational magic shows available for preschool and elementary school aged children. Award winning programs such as The Magic of Books and Magic from Around the World are available for any size audience. For middle schools and high schools, comedy hypnosis is a perfect venue for entertainment as a fundraising program, for high school after-prom parties, graduation parties, or just for an evening's entertainment.

Steve Wronker

2823 T-Shirt People/Wearhouse
10722 Hanna Street
Beltsville, MD 20705-2123
301-937-4843
800-638-7070
Fax: 301-937-2916
Fundraiser offering customized T-shirts to boost school spirit, raise funds, instill school pride and save money.

2824 Troll Book Fairs
100 Corporate Drive
Mahwah, NJ 07430-2041
201-529-4000
Fax: 201-529-8282

A profit-making program designed to introduce children to the wonderful world of books.

2825 Union Pen Company
70 Riverdale Avenue
Greenwich, CT 06831
800-846-6600
Fax: 800-688-4877
E-mail: unionpen@aol.com
http://www.unionpen.com
This company offers advertising gifts including customized pens and key chains that will increase confidence, school spirit and community goodwill in education. Group discounts are available.

Matt Roberts, General Manager
Morton Tenny, President

2826 www.positivepins.com
802 E 6th Streetve
PO Box 52528
Tulsa, OK 74152
918-587-2405
800-282-0085
Fax: 918-382-0906
E-mail: pinrus@aol.com
http://www.thepinman-pins.com
Fundraising organization used by educational organizations. Designer and manufacturer of lapel pins used for employee service, appreciation, volunteer recognition, donor incentives and recognition, public relations and spirit.

Bern L Gentry, President
Michelle Anderson, VP

Scholarships & Financial Aid

2827 AFL-CIO Guide to Union Sponsored Scholarships, Awards & Student Aid
AFL-CIO
815 16th Street NW
Suite 407
Washington, DC 20006-4104
202-637-5000
http://www.unionplus.org
Lists international and national unions, local unions, state federations and labor councils offering scholarships, awards or financial aid to students.

100 pages Annual

2828 American-Scandinavian Foundation
58 Park Avenue
New York, NY 10016
212-779-3587
E-mail: info@amscan.org
http://www.amscan.org
The Foundation provides information, scholarships and grants on the study programs in Scandinavia.

Edward Gallagher, President
Christian Sonne, Deputy Chairman

2829 Arts Scholarships
Jewish Foundation for Education of Women
135 E 64th Street
New York, NY 10019-1827
212-288-3931
Fax: 212-288-5798
E-mail: fdnscholar@aol.com
http://www.jfew.org
These scholarships are being offered at the Julliard School, Tisch School, of the Arts at New York University, and the Manhattan School of Music to qualified students enrolled in their programs. Faculty members will select recipients.

Marge Goldwater, Executive Director

2830 CUNY Teacher Incentive Program
Jewish Foundation for Education of Women
135 E 64th Street
New York, NY 10019-1827
212-288-3931
Fax: 212-288-5798
E-mail: fdnscholar@aol.com
http://www.jfew.org
Provide stipends to CUNY graduates who are studying for a master's degree in education and interested in a teaching career in the New York City public school system. Contact the office of the Vice Chancellor for Academic Affairs at CUNY for further information.

Marge Goldwater, Executive Director

2831 College Board
45 Columbus Avenue
New York, NY 10023-6992
212-713-8000
Fax: 212-713-8282
http://www.collegeboard.org
The College Board is a national, nonprofit membership association that supports educational transitions through programs and services in assessment, guidance, admission, placement, financial aid, and educational reform.

2832 Dissertation Fellowships in the Humanities
Jewish Foundation for Education of Women
330 W 58th Street
New York, NY 10019-1827
212-883-9315
Fax: 212-288-5798
E-mail: fdnscholar@aol.com
http://www.jfew.org
A small number of fellowships will be awarded through the CUNY Graduate Center to qualified applicants.

Marge Goldwater, Executive Director

2833 George & Mary Kremer Foundation
1100 5th Avenue S
Suite 411
Naples, FL 34102-7415
941-261-2367
Fax: 941-261-1494
Provides scholarship funding for needy children in elementary Catholic schools throughout the Continental United States.

Mary Anderson Goddard, Director
Sister MT Ballrach, Assistant Director

2834 Intel Science Talent Search Scolarship
1719 N Street NW
Washington, DC 20036-2888
202-785-2255
Fax: 202-785-1243
E-mail: sciedu@sciserv.org
http://www.sciserv.org
Offers a variety of services to teachers and students, including Intel Science Talent Search Scholarship competition, science fairs and publications.

2835 Jewish Foundation for Education of Women
330 W 58th Street
New York, NY 10019-1827
212-288-3931
Fax: 212-288-5798
E-mail: fdnscholar@aol.com
http://www.jfew.org
The Jewish Foundation for Education of Women is a private, nonsectarian foundation providing scholarships to women for higher education in the New York City area. A variety of specific programs are available. Most programs are administered collaboratively with area schools and organizations; the Foundation's mission is to help women of all ages attain the education and training needed to make them productive, economically independent members of the community.

Marge Goldwater, Executive Director

2836 Octameron Associates
1900 Mount Vernon Avenue
Alexandria, VA 22301-0748
703-836-5480
Fax: 703-836-5650
E-mail: info@octameron.com
http://www.octameron.com
Octameron is a publishing and consulting firm with over 25 years experience in financial aid and admissions.

2837 Scholarship America
One Scholarship Way
Saint Peter, MN 56082-1556
507-931-1682
800-537-4180
Fax: 507-931-9250
E-mail: dsnatoff@aol.com
http://dollarsforscholars.org
Provides community volunteers with the tools and support to create, develop and sustain legally constituted community-based scholarship foundations. Over 15,000 volunteers are active on 760 Dollars for Scholars chapter boards and committees throughout the United States. In addition, 20,000 high school youth and community residents are active in fund-raising events and academic support programs. Since the late 1950's, over 155,000 students have received Dollars for Scholars scholarships.

David Bach, VP

2838 Scholarships in the Health Professions
Jewish Foundation for Education of Women
135 E 64th Street
New York, NY 10021
212-288-3931
Fax: 212-288-5798
E-mail: fdnscholar@aol.com
http://www.jfew.org
Provides scholarships to emigres from the former Soviet Union who are studying medicine, dentistry, nursing, pharmacy, OT, PT, dental hygiene, and physician assistanceship.

Marge Goldwater, Executive Director

Federal Listings

2839 Accounting & Financial Management Services
Department of Education/1175 Main Building
400 Maryland Avenue SW
Washington, DC 20202-0001
Fax: 202-401-0207

Mitchell L Laine, Chief Officer

2840 Assistance to States Division
Department of Education/3042 Mary E. Switzer Bldg.
330 C Street
Washington, DC 20202
202-401-2000
Fax: 202-260-7225

Tom Irvin, Acting Director

2841 Brody Professional Development
Brody Communications Ltd.
115 West Avenue
Suite 114
Jenkintown, PA 19046
215-886-1688
Fax: 215-886-1699
E-mail: info@brodypro.com
http://www.brodypro.com
Brody offers tailored training programs, executive coaching and presentations in the areas of communication skills and professional development.

Miryam Roddy, Manager of Maximum Exposure

2842 Compensatory Education Program
US Department of Education
400 Maryland Avenue SW
Washington, DC 20202
202-260-0826
Fax: 202-260-7764

Mary Jean LeTendre, Director

2843 Elementary Secondary Bilingual & Research Branch
Department of Education/Regional Office Bldg.
7th & D Streets
Suite 3653
Washington, DC 20202
202-401-0113
Fax: 202-260-7225

Queenola Tyler, Bureau Chief

2844 Elementary, Secondary & Vocational Analysis
Department of Education
400 Maryland Avenue SW
3043 Main Building
Washington, DC 20202-0001
202-401-0318
Fax: 202-260-7225

Thomas Corwin, Division Director

2845 Human Resources and Administration
Department of Education/3181 Main Building
400 Maryland Avenue SW
Washington, DC 20202-0001
202-401-0470
Fax: 202-260-7225

Rodney A McCowan, Assistant Secretary

2846 International Educational Exchange
U.S. Department of State
Bureau Educational/Cultural Affairs
Washington, DC 20202
202-632-3238
E-mail: fulbright@state.gov

Offers educational information on student and teacher exchanges abroad.

2847 Management Services
Department of Education/3005 Main Building
400 Maryland Avenue SW
Washington, DC 20202-0001
202-401-0500
Fax: 202-260-7225

2848 National Center for Education Statistics
1990 K Street NW
Washington, DC 20006
202-502-7300
Fax: 202-260-7225
http://www.nces.ed.gov

Sean P. "Jack" Buckley, Commissioner

2849 National Council on Disability
1331 F Street NW
Suite 850
Washington, DC 20004-1107
202-272-2004
Fax: 202-272-2022
E-mail: ncd@ncd.gov
http://www.ncd.gov/
An independent federal agency comprised of 15 members appointed by the President and confirmed by the Senate.

Jonathan M. Young, Ph.D., Chairman
Aaron Bishop, Executive Director

2850 National Institute of Child Health and Human Development
Bldg.31, Room 2A32, MSC 2425
31 Center Drive
Bethesda, MD 20892-2425
800-370-2943
Fax: 866-760-5947
E-mail: NICHDInformationResourceCenter@mail.nih.gov
http://www.nichd.nih.gov
Develops research to solve problems in the physical and mental evolution of development. Including some of the most emotionally draining disorders, learning disabilities, behavioral disabilities, birth defects and infant mortality. Acts as a clearinghouse of materials, information and referrals and more.

Ellie Brown Hochman, Administrative Officer
Brenda Hanning, Program Management Officer

2851 National Library of Education
U.S. Department of Education
400 Maryland Avenue, SW
Washington, DC 20202
800-424-1616
Fax: 202-401-0547
E-mail: library@ed.gov
http://www.ed.gov

Dr. Rebecca Maynard, Commissioner

2852 National Trust for Historic Preservation: Office of Education Initiatives
1785 Massachusetts Avenue NW
Washington, DC 20036-2117
202-588-6000
800-944-6847
Fax: 202-588-6038
http://www.nationaltrust.org
Teaching with Historic Places, a program offered by the National Park Service's National Register of Historic Places, and the National Trust for Historic Preservation Press.

Stephanie Meeks, President & CEO

2853 No Child Left Behind
U.S. Department of Education
400 Maryland Avenue, SW
Washington, DC 20202
202-401-2000
800-872-5327
Fax: 202-401-0689
http://www.ed.gov/nclb
Provides education standards and incentives for states in adopting academic standards that prepare students to succeed in college and the workplace.

Arne Duncan, Secretary of Education
Tony Miller, Deputy Secretary

2854 Office for Civil Rights
U.S. Department of Education
400 Maryland Avenue SW
Lyndon Baines Johnson Dept of Ed Bldg.
Washington, DC 20202-1100
800-421-3481
Fax: 202-453-6012
E-mail: ocr@ed.gov
http://www.ed.gov

Russlynn Ali, Assistant Secretary
Ricardo Soto, Deputy Assistant Secretary

2855 Office of Bilingual Education and MinorityLanguages Affairs
U.S. Department of Education
600 Independence Avenue, SW
Washington, DC 20202-6510
202-205-5463
Fax: 202-260-7225
E-mail: askncbe@ncbe.gwu.edu

Delia Pompa, Director
Dang T. Pham, Deputy Director

2856 Office of Elementary & Secondary Education
U.S. Department of Education
400 Maryland Avenue SW
Washington, DC 20202
202-401-0113
Fax: 202-205-0310
E-mail: oese@ed.gov
http://www2.ed.gov

Thelma Melendez De Santa Ana, Assistant Secretary

2857 Office of Indian Education
U.S. Department of Education
400 Maryland Avenue SW
LBJ Building, 3E205
Washington, DC 20202-6335
202-260-3774
Fax: 202-260-7779
E-mail: indian.education@ed.gov
http://www.2.ed.gov

Jenelle Leonard, Acting Director
Terrie Nelson, Administrative Assistant

2858 Office of Legislation & Congressional Affairs
U.S. Department of Education
400 Maryland Avenue SW
Washington, DC 20202-3100
202-401-0020
Fax: 202-401-1438
E-mail: olca@ed.gov
http://www.2.ed.gov

Gabriella Gomez, Assistant Secretary
Lloyd Horwich, Deputy Assistant Secretary

2859 Office of Migrant Education
U.S. Department of Education
400 Maryland Avenue SW
Room 3E317 FOB-6
Washington, DC 20202-6135
202-260-1164
800-872-5327

Fax: 202-205-0089
http://www.2.ed.gov
Arne Duncan, Secretary Of Education
Lisa Ramirez, Director

2860 Office of Overseas Schools
US Department of State
Room H328, SA-1
Washington, DC 20522-0132
202-261-8200
Fax: 202-261-8224
E-mail: OverseasSchools@state.gov
http://www.state.gov
Maintains detailed information on 190 overseas elementary and secondary schools which receive some assistance from the US Department of State. These schools provide an American-type education which prepares students for schools, colleges and universities in the United States.

Dr. Keith D Miller, Director

2861 Office of Planning, Evaluation and PolicyDevelopment
U.S. Department of Education
330 C Street SW
Suite 4022
Washington, DC 20201-0001
202-205-9960
Fax: 202-260-7225
E-mail: judy.wurtzel.ed.gov
http://www.2.ed.gov

Carmel Martin, Assistant Secretary
Judy Wurtzel, Deputy Assistant Secretary

2862 Office of Public Affairs
Department of Education/4181 Main Building
400 Maryland Avenue SW
Washington, DC 20202-0001
202-401-3026
Fax: 202-260-7225

Kay Kahler, Division Director

2863 Office of Special Education Programs
Department of Education/3086 Mary E. Switzer Bldg.
600 Independence Avenue SW
Washington, DC 20202-2570
202-205-5507
Fax: 202-260-7225
E-mail: thomas_hehir@ed.gov
http://www.ed.gov./offices/osers/idea/index.htm

Thomas Hehir, Director

2864 Office of Student Financial Assistance Programs
U.S. Department of Education
400 Maryland Avenue SW
Washington, DC 20202-0001
319-337-5665
800-433-3243

2865 Planning & Evaluation Service
Department of Education
Elementary Secondary Division
3127 Main Building, 400 Maryland
Washington, DC 20202
202-401-1968
Fax: 202-260-7225

Val Ptisko, Division Director

2866 Programs for the Improvement of Practice
Department of Education
500 N Capitol Street NW
Suite 555
Washington, DC 20001-1531
202-219-2164
Fax: 202-260-7225

Ronald W Cartwright, Sr Program Manager

2867 Rehabilitation Services Administration
U.S. Department of Education
400 Maryland Avenue SW
Washington, DC 20202-2800
202-245-7488
Fax: 202-260-7225
E-mail: rsa.ed.gov
http://www.2.ed.gov

Lynnae M. Ruttledge, Commissioner
Edward Anthony, Deputy Commissioner

2868 Research to Practice Division
U.S. Department of Education
Ofc of Special Ed/Rehabilitative Sv
400 Maryland Avenue SW
Washington, DC 20202-7100
202-245-7459
http://www2.ed.gov

Alexa Posny, Assistant Secretary

2869 School Assistance Division
Department of Education/4200 Portals Building
1250 Maryland Avenue SW
Washington, DC 20024-2141
202-260-2270
Fax: 202-260-7225

Catherine Schagh, Division Director

2870 School Improvement Grants
U.S. Department Of Education
400 Maryland Avenue SW
Washington, DC 20202
800-872-5327
http://www.ed.gov

Arne Duncan, Secretary of Education
Tony Miller, Deputy Secretary

2871 School Improvement Programs-Equity and Educational Excellence Division
Department of Education/4500 Portals Building
1250 Maryland Avenue SW
Washington, DC 20024-2141
202-260-3693
Fax: 202-260-7225

Janice Williams-Madison, Division Director

2872 School Improvement Programs-Safe and Drug FreeSchools
Office of Safe and Drug Free Schools
550 12th Street, SW
10th Floor
Washington, DC 20202-6450
202-245-7896
Fax: 202-485-0013
E-mail: osdfs.safeschl@ed.gov
http://www.ed.gov
Works to promote safe schools that are free from drug abuse and violence.

Kevin Jennings, Assistant Deputy Director
Tina Hunter, Executive Officer

2873 US Department of Defense Dependents Schools
2461 Eisenhower Avenue
Alexandria, VA 22331-3000
571-325-0867

Marilyn Witcher

2874 US Department of Education
400 Maryland Avenue SW
Washington, DC 20202
800-872-5327
Fax: 202-401-0689
E-mail: customerservice@inet.ed.gov
http://www.ed.gov

Ensures equal access to education and promotes educational excellence for all Americans.

Margaret Spellings, Secretary of Education

2875 Vocational & Adult Education
Department of Education/4090 Mary E. Switzer Bldg.
330 C Street
Washington, DC 20202
202-205-5451
Fax: 202-260-7225

Augusta Souza Kappner, Assistant Secretary

2876 Washington DC Department of Education
825 N Capitol Street NE
Suite 900
Washington, DC 20202-4210
202-442-5885
Fax: 202-442-5026

Paul L Varce, Superintendent

Alabama

2877 Alabama State Department of Education
50 N Ripley Street
PO Box 302101
Montgomery, AL 36104
334-242-9700
E-mail: astarks@alsde.edu
http://www.alsde.edu
Mission is to provide a state system of education which is committed to academic excellence and which provides education of the highest quality to all Alabama students, preparing them for the 21st century. For certification information contact the Alabama certification office at 334-242-9977.

Dr. Joseph B Morton, State Superintendent of Ed.
Dr. Craig Pouncey, Deputy State Superintendent

2878 Assistant Superintendent & Financial Services
Alabama Department of Education
50 N Ripley Street
PO Box 302101
Montgomery, AL 36104
334-242-9741
E-mail: astarks@alsde.edu
http://www.alsde.edu

Dr. Craig Pouncy, Deputy State Superintendent
Feagin Johnson, Jr., Asst. State Superintendent

2879 Deputy Superintendent
Alabama Department of Education
50 N Ripley Street
Montgomery, AL 36130-0624
334-242-9700
Fax: 334-242-9708

Thomas Ingram, Assistant Superintendent

2880 Disability Determination Division
Alabama Department of Education
50 N Ripley Street
PO Box 302101
Montgomery, AL 36104
334-242-9700
E-mail: www.alsde.edu

Tommy Warren, General Counsel

2881 General Administrative Services
Alabama Department of Education
50 N Ripley Street
Montgomery, AL 36130-0624
334-242-9700
Fax: 334-242-9708

William J Rutherford, Assistant
Superintendent

2882 General Counsel
Alabama Department of Education
50 N Ripley Street
Montgomery, AL 36130-0624
334-242-1899
E-mail: studor@alsde.edu
http://www.alsde.edu
Provides legal counsel to the State Superintendent of Education, State Board of Education and State Department of Education.

Larry Craven, General Counsel
Susan Tudor Crowther, Assoc General
Counsel/Admin.

2883 Instructional Services
Alabama Department of Education
50 N Ripley Street
Montgomery, AL 36130-0624
334-242-9700
Fax: 334-242-9708

Charlie G Williams, Assistant
Superintendent

2884 Professional Services
Alabama Department of Education
50 N Ripley Street
Montgomery, AL 36130-0624
334-242-9700
Fax: 334-242-9708

Eddie R Johnson, Assistant Superintendent

2885 Rehabilitation Services
Alabama Department of Rehabilitation
Services
2129 E S Boulevard
PO Box 11586
Montgomery, AL 36111-0586
334-281-8780
800-441-7607
Fax: 334-281-1973
http://www.rehab.state.al.us
State agency that provides and services and assistance to Alabama's children and adults with disabilities and their families.

Steve Shrivers, Commissioner

2886 Special Education Services
Alabama Department of Education
50 N Ripley Street
Montgomery, AL 36130-0624
334-242-8114
Fax: 334-242-9192

Bill East, Division Director

2887 Student Instructional Services
Alabama Department of Education
50 N Ripley Street
Montgomery, AL 36130-0624
334-242-8256
Fax: 334-242-9708

Martha V Beckett, Assistant Superintendent

2888 Superintendent
Alabama Department of Education
50 N Ripley Street
Montgomery, AL 36130-0624
334-242-9700
Fax: 334-242-9708

Ed Richardson, Superintendent

2889 Vocational Education
Alabama Department of Education
50 N Ripley Street
Montgomery, AL 36130-0624

334-242-9111
Fax: 334-353-8861

Stephen B Franks, Division Director

Alaska

2890 Alaska Commission on Postsecondary Education
PO Box 110510
Juneau, AK 99811-0510
907-465-2962
800-441-2962
Fax: 907-465-5316
E-mail: customer.service@alaska.gov
http://www.akadvantage.alaska.gov
This state agency coordinates administration of state-funded educational financial assistance for students and their families. This agency is also responsible for licensing and regulating postsecondary institutions to operate in Alaska.

Diane Barrans, Executive Director
Kenneth Dodson, Dir. Information Support
Svc

2891 Alaska Department of Education Administrative Services
801 W 10th Street
Suite 200
Juneau, AK 99801-1894
907-465-2802
Fax: 907-465-4156
For certification information visit www.eed.state.ak.us/TeacherCertification/ or contact 907-465-2831.

Shirley J Halloway, Commissioner

2892 Alaska Department of Education & Early Development
801 W 10th Street
Suite 200
Juneau, AK 99801
907-465-2800
Fax: 907-465-3452
http://www.educ.state.ak.us

Gerald Covey, Commissioner

2893 Libraries, Archives & Museums
Alaska Department of Education & Early
Development
PO Box 110500
Juneau, AK 99811-0500
907-465-2800
Fax: 907-465-4156
E-mail: asl@alaska.gov
http://www.lam.alaska.gov
Summer reading programs

Linda Thibodeau, Director
Bob Banghart, Chief Curator

2894 School Finance & Data Management
Alaska Department of Education & Early
Development
801 W 10th Street, Suite 200
PO Box 110500
Juneau, AK 99811-0500
907-465-2800
Fax: 907-465-4156
E-mail: eed.webmaster@alaska.gov
http://www.eed.state.ak.us
Public school funding programs

Cynthia Curran, Director
Paul Prussing, Deputy Director

2895 Teaching And Learning Support Program
Alaska Department of Education & Early
Development
801 W 10th Street, Suite 200
PO Box 110500
Juneau, AK 99811-0500

907-465-2800
Fax: 907-465-4156
E-mail: eed.webmaster@alaska.gov
http://www.eed.state.ak.us
To improve students performance as well as the administering of a variety of federal, state and private programs that provide support to school district staff across the state.

Cynthia Curran, Director
Paul Prussing, Deputy Director

2896 Vocational Rehabilitation
Alaska Department of Labor & Workforce
Development
801 W 10th Street
Suite A
Juneau, AK 99801-1894
907-465-2814
800-478-2815
Fax: 907-465-2856
E-mail: dawn.duval@alaska.gov
http://www.labor.state.ak.us
Helping individuals with disabilities to find employment

Cheryl Walsh, Director
John Cannon, Chairperson

Arizona

2897 National Council of State Supervisors of Music
Arizona Department of Education
1535 W Jefferson Avenue
1st Floor
Phoenix, AZ 85007-3209
602-542-5393
800-352-4558
Fax: 602-542-3590
E-mail: mgiffor@mail1.ade.state.az.com
http://http://ade.state.az.us/
Strives to improve the supervision and education of music on the state level and to encourage coordination between states.

John Huppenthal, Superintendent Public
Instr.

Arkansas

2898 Arkansas Department of Education
4 Capitol Mall
Room 403-A
Little Rock, AR 72201-1071
501-683-4786
E-mail: virginia.hill@arkansas.gov
http://www.arkansased.org
Mission is to provide the highest quality leadership, service, and support to school districts and schools in order that they may provide equitable, quality education for all to ensure that all public schools comply with the standards.

Dr. Naccaman Williams, Chair
Virginia Hill, Administrative Assistant

2899 Arkansas Department of Education: Special Education
4 Capitol Mall
Room 403-A
Little Rock, AR 72201-1071
501-683-4786
E-mail: virginia.hill@arkansas.gov
http://www.arkansased.org

Dr. Naccaman Williams, Chair
Virginia Hill, Administrative Assistant

2900 Federal Programs
Arkansas Department of Education
4 Capitol Mall
Room 403-A
Little Rock, AR 72201-1011

501-682-4475
E-mail: virginia.hill@arkansas.gov
http://www.arkansased.org
Dr. Naccaman Williams, Chair
Virginia Hill, Administrative Assistant

2901 Human Resources Office
Arkansas Department of Education
4 Capitol Mall
Room 403-A
Little Rock, AR 72201-1011
501-682-4475
E-mail: virginia.hill@arkansas.gov
http://www.arkansased.org
Dr. Naccaman Williams, Chair
Virginia Hill, Administrative Assistant

California

2902 California Department of Education
1430 N Street
Sacramento, CA 95814-5901
916-319-0800
Fax: 916-657-4975
http://www.cde.ca.gov
Works to encourage the highest achievement for students by defining the knowledge, concepts and skills that students should aquire in each grade level.

Tom Torlakson, St Superintendent Public Ins
Richard Zeiger, Chief Deputy Superintendent

2903 California Department of Education'sEducational Resources Catalog
CDE Press Sales
1430 N Street
Suite 3207
Sacramento, CA 95814
916-323-4583
800-995-4099
Fax: 916-323-0823
E-mail: sales@cde.ca.gov
http://www.cde.ca.gov
Offers new techniques and fresh perspectives in handbooks, guides, videos and more.

Tom Torlakson, St Superintendent Public Ins

2904 California Department of Special Education
1430 N Street
Sacramento, CA 95814-5901
913-319-0800
Fax: 916-327-3516
Resources and information that serve the unique needs of persons with disabilities by helping them to meet or exceed high standards of achievement in both academic and nonacademic skills.

Tom Torlakson, St Superintendent Public Ins

2905 Curriculum & Instructional Leadership Branch
California Department of Education
1430 N Street
Sacramento, CA 95814
916-657-3043
http://www.cde.ca.gov
Works to improve students academic achievements

Harvey Hunt, Deputy

2906 Department Management Services Branch
California Department of Education
721 Capitol Mall
Sacramento, CA 95814-4785
916-657-5474
Fax: 916-319-0106

Diane Kirkham, Deputy

2907 Executive Office & External Affairs
California Department of Education
721 Capitol Mall
Sacramento, CA 95814-4702
916-657-3027
Fax: 916-657-4975

Susie Lange, Division Director

2908 Field Services Branch
California Department of Education
721 Capitol Mall
Sacramento, CA 95814-4702
916-657-4748
Fax: 916-319-0155

Robert W Agee, Division Director

2909 Governmental Policy Branch
California Department of Education
721 Capitol Mall
Sacramento, CA 95814-4702
916-657-5461

Joe Holsinger, Deputy

2910 Legal & Audits Branch
California Department of Education
1430 N Street
Suite 5319
Sacramento, CA 95814-4702
916-319-0860
Fax: 916-319-0155

Marsha Bedwell, General Counsel

2911 Region 9: Education Department
San Diego COE
6401 Linda Vista Road
Suite 321
North San Diego, CA 92111
858-569-5304
E-mail: dbrashear@sdcoe.net
Part of a statewide system of school support established to meet state and federal requirements, the support system works within county offices offering intensive and sustained assistance to local schools and educational agencies receiving Title I funds, helping to increase the opportunity for all student's to meet the state academic content standards.

David Brashear, Director

2912 Specialized Programs Branch
California Department of Education
1430 N Street
Sacramento, CA 95814
916-319-0854
E-mail: mpayne@cde.ca.gov
http://www.cde.ca.gov
Works to ensure that all children have the opportunity to obtain high-quality education.

Tom Torlakson, St Superintendent Public Ins
Mary Payne, District/School Improvement

Colorado

2913 Colorado Department of Education
201 E Colfax Avenue
Denver, CO 80203-1799
303-866-6600
Fax: 303-866-6938
http://www.cde.state.co.us

For certification information visit www.cde.state.co.us/index_license.htm or contact 303-866-6628.

William T Moloney, Commissioner

2914 Educator Licensing Unit
Colorado Department of Education
201 E Colfax Avenue
Denver, CO 80203-1704
303-866-6628
Fax: 303-866-6866
Licensing applications for educators, career and technical education. Issues educators licenses, reviews content, induction/professional development and disciplinary actions

Ed Almon, Educator Licensing

2915 Management, Budget & Planning
Colorado Department of Education
201 E Colfax Avenue
Denver, CO 80203-1704
303-866-6822
Fax: 303-866-6938

Karen Stroup, Division Director

2916 Office of Federal Program Administration
Colorado Department of Education
1560 Broadway
Suite 1450
Denver, CO 80202-5149
303-866-6600
Fax: 303-866-6637
Administers funds under the elementary and secondary education act as well as a variety of other state and federal competitive awards and grants with the main goal to help all students to reach proficiency in English language arts, mathematics and reading.

Patrick Chapman, Executive Director
Lynn Bamberry, Director

2917 Public School Finance
Colorado Department of Education
201 E Colfax Avenue
Denver, CO 80203-1704
303-866-6845

Dan Stewart, Division Director

2918 Special Services
Colorado Department of Education
201 E Colfax Avenue
Denver, CO 80203-1704
303-866-6782
Fax: 303-866-6785

Brian McNulty, Assistant Commissioner

2919 State Library
Colorado Department of Education
201 E Colfax Avenue
Room 309
Denver, CO 80203-1704
303-866-6900
Fax: 303-866-6940
http://www.cde.state.co.us
Provides leadership and expertise in library related activities and policies and provides assistance to public and academic schools.

Eugene Hainer, Assistant Commissioner
Sharon Morris, Director

2920 Supplemental Educational Services
Colorado Department of Education
1560 Broadway
Suite 1450
Denver, CO 80202
303-866-6600
Fax: 303-866-6637
E-mail: medler_l@cde.state.co.us
http://www.cde.state.co.us
SES offers tutoring outside the regular school day that is designed to increase the academic achievement in reading/mathematics and lan-

167

guage arts to low-income students in low-income schools

Patrick Chapman, Executive Director
Lisa Medler, Title IIA Coordinator

2921 US Department of Education: Region VIII
1244 Speer Boulevard
Suite 310
Denver, CO 80204-3582
303-844-3544
Fax: 303-844-2524
http://www.ed.gov

Helen Littlejohn, Public Affairs Officer

Connecticut

2922 Connecticut Early Childhood Unit
Connecticut State Department of Education
165 Capital Avenue
Hartford, CT 06106
860-713-6740
Fax: 860-713-7018
E-mail: www.sde.ct.gov
Offers programs for children, infants and toddlers with disabilities.

Steven Adamowski, Superintendent

2923 Connecticut Governor's Committee on Employment of the Handicapped
Labor Department Building
200 Folly Brook Boulevard
Wethersfield, CT 06109-1153
860-263-6774
Fax: 860-263-6039
http://www.dol.gov

2924 Connecticut State Department of Education
165 Capitol Avenue
Hartford, CT 06106
860-713-6543
Fax: 860-722-8502
http://www.sde.ct.gov

Steven Adamowski, Superintendent

2925 Education Programs & Services
Connecticut Department of Education
25 Industrial Park Road
Middletown, CT 06457-1520
860-807-2005
Fax: 860-635-7125

Theodore S Sergi, Division Director

2926 Finance & Grants Department
Connecticut State Department of Education
Grants Management
165 Capitol Avenue
Hartford, CT 06106
860-713-0466
Fax: 860-713-7046
http://www.sde.ct.gov

Eugene Croce, Manager
Candace Madison, Secretary

2927 Human Services
Connecticut Department of Education
165 Capitol Avenue Office Building
Hartford, CT 06106-1659
860-713-6690
Fax: 860-713-7011

Dick Wilber, Division Director

2928 Information Systems
Connecticut Department of Education
165 Capitol Avenue Office Building
Hartford, CT 06106-1659
860-647-5064
Fax: 860-647-5027

Greg Vassar, Division Director

2929 Office of State Coordinator of Vocational Education for Disabled Students
Vocational Prgs. for the Disabled & Disadvantaged
PO Box 2219
Hartford, CT 06145
860-807-2001
Fax: 860-807-2196

2930 Teaching & Learning Division
Connecticut State Department of Education
165 Capital Avenue
Hartford, CT 06106-1659
860-713-6740
Fax: 860-713-7018
E-mail: ciquest@ct.gov
http://www.sde.ct.gov

George Coleman, Acting Commissioner

2931 Vocational-Technical School Systems
Connecticut Technical High School System
25 Industrial Park Road
Middletown, CT 06457-1520
800-822-6832
Fax: 860-807-2196
E-mail: cthsinternet@ct.gov
http://www.cttech.org

Patricia Ciccone, Superintendent
Robert Lombardi, Assistant

Delaware

2932 Assessments & Accountability Branch Delaware Department of Education
John G. Townsend Bldg.
401 Federal St (Federal & Lockerman Sts)
Dover, DE 19901
302-735-4000
Fax: 302-739-4654
http://www.doe.k12.de.us

Teri Quinn Gray, Ph.D., President/St. Board Of Educ.
Jorge L. Melendez, VP, State Board of Education

2933 Delaware Department of Education
John G. Townsend Bldg.
401 Federal St (Federal & Lockerman Sts)
Dover, DE 19901
302-735-4000
Fax: 302-739-4654
E-mail: dedoe@doe.k12.de.us
http://www.doe.k12.de.us
Our mission is to promote the highest quality education for every Delaware student by providing visionary leadership and superior service.

Teri Quinn Gray, Ph.D., President State Board of Ed.
Jorge L. Melendez, VP State Board of Ed

2934 Delaware Department of Education:Administrative Services
John G. Townsend Bldg.
401 Federal St (Federal & Lockerman Sts)
Dover, DE 19901
302-735-4000
Fax: 302-739-4654
E-mail: dedoe@doe.k12.de.us
http://www.doe.k12.de.us

Teri Quinn Gray, Ph.D., President State Board of Ed
Jorge L. Melendez, VP State Board of Ed

2935 Improvement & Assistance Branch Delaware Department of Education
John G. Townsend Bldg.
401 Federal St (Federal & Lockerman Sts)
Dover, DE 19901

302-735-4000
Fax: 302-739-4654
E-mail: dedoe@doe.k12.de.us
http://www.doe.k12.de.us

Teri Quinn Gray, Ph.D., President School Board of Ed
Jorge J. Melendez, VP State Board of Ed

District of Columbia

2936 DC Office of Special Education
District of Columbia Public Schools
1200 First Street, NE
9th Floor
Washington, DC 20002
202-442-4800
http://www.ocp.dc.gov

Richard Nyankori, Deputy Chancellor

2937 District of Columbia Department of Education
1200 First Street, NE
Washington, DC 20002
202-442-5885
Fax: 202-442-5026
E-mail: ocao.dc.gov
http://www.ocp.dc.gov

Dr. Carey Wright, Chief Academic Officer

2938 Grants Administration Branch
District of Columbia Public Schools
1200 First Street, NE
Washington, DC 20002
202-442-5885
Fax: 202-442-5026
E-mail: ocao.dc.gov
http://www.dcps.dc.gov

Barbara Jackson, Division Director

2939 Management Systems & Technology Services Division
District of Columbia
415 12th St NW, Presidential Building
Washington, DC 20004
202-724-4062

Ulysses Keyes, Division Director

2940 State Services Division District of Columbia
415 12th Street NW
Presidential Building
Washington, DC 20004
202-624-5490
Fax: 202-624-8588

Andrew E Jenkins, Division Director

Florida

2941 Florida Department of Education
Turlington Building Suite 1514
325 West Gaines Street
Tallahassee, FL 32399
850-245-0505
Fax: 850-245-9667
E-mail: commissioner@fldoe.org
http://www.fldoe.org
Offers information on community colleges, vocational education, public schools, human resources, financial assistance, adult education and more.

Dr. Eric J. Smith, Commissioner/Fl. Dept of Ed

Georgia

2942 Georgia Department of Education
2054 Twin Towers East
205 Jesse Hill Jr. Drive SE
Atlanta, GA 30334
404-656-2800
800-311-3627
Fax: 404-651-6867
E-mail: askdoe@doe.k12.ga.us
http://www.gadoe.org
Among many other features, this organization offers agriculture education, federal programs, Leadership Development Academy, school and community nutrition progams, Spanish language and cultural program, technology/career (vocational) education and more.

Dr. John D. Barge, Superintendent
Sue Goodman, Manager

Hawaii

2943 Business Services Office
Hawaii Department of Education
1390 Miller Street
PO Box 2360
Honolulu, HI 96804
808-586-3230
Fax: 808-586-3314
E-mail: doe_info@notes.k12.hi.us
http://www.doe.k12.hi.us

Kathryn Matayoshi, Superintendent

2944 Career & Technical Education Center
University of Hawaii
Lunalilo Portable 1
Lower Campus Road
Honolulu, HI 96822-2489
808-956-7461
Fax: 808-956-9096
E-mail: hicte@hawaii.edu
http://www.hawaii.edu/cte

Angela Meixell, Interim Director

2945 Hawaii Department of Education
1390 Miller Street
PO Box 2360
Honolulu, HI 96804
808-586-3230
Fax: 808-586-3314
E-mail: doe_info@notes.k12.hi.us
http://www.doe.k12.hi.us

Kathryn Matayoshi, Superintendent

2946 Information & Telecommunications ServicesBranch
Hawaii Department of Education
1390 Miller St., Room 417
PO Box 2360
Honolulu, HI 96804
808-586-3222
Fax: 808-586-3227
E-mail: doe_info@notes.k12.hi.us
http://www.doe.k12.hi.us

Kathryn Matayoshi, Superintendent

2947 Office of Curriculum, Instruction and StudentSupport
Hawaii Department of Education
Queen Liliuokalani Bldg, Rm 316
1390 Miller St,
Honolulu, HI 96813
808-586-3446
Fax: 808-586-3429
E-mail: doe_info@notes.k12.hi.us
http://www.ociss.k12.hi.us

Kathryn Matayoshi, Superintendent

2948 Special Education Department
Hawaii Department of Education
475 22nd Ave, Room 115
Ofc Curriculum/Instruction/Student Supp.
Honolulu, HI 96804
808-203-5560
Fax: 808-733-4475
E-mail: doe_info@notes.k12.hi.us
http://www.doe.k12.hi.us

Kathryn Matayoshi, Superintendent
Debra Farmer, Administrator

2949 State Public Library System
Hawaii State Public Library System
478 South King Street
Honolulu, HI 96813-2901
808-586-3617
Fax: 808-586-3314
http://www.librarieshawaii.org

Richard P. Burns, State Librarian

Idaho

2950 Idaho State Department of Education
650 West State Street
PO Box 83720
Boise, ID 83720-0027
208-332-6800
800-432-4601
Fax: 208-334-2228
E-mail: trluna@sde.idaho.gov
http://www.sde.idaho.gov

Tom Luna, Superintendent

2951 Special Education Division
Idaho State Department of Education
650 W. State Street
PO Box 83720
Boise, ID 83720-0027
208-332-6806
E-mail: rhenderson@sde.idaho.gov
http://sde.idaho.gov
Committed to empower people with disabilities with appropriate resources to make informed choices about their futures.

Richard Henderson, Director
Casandra Myers, Administrative Assistant

Illinois

2952 Educator & School Development
Illinois Department of Education
100 N. 1st Street
Springfield, IL 62777
217-782-4321
866-262-6663
http://www.isbe.state.il.us

Dr. Christopher Koch, State Superintendent
Jesse Ruiz, Board Chair

2953 Educator Certification
Illinois Department of Education
100 N. 1st Street
Springfield, IL 62777
217-782-4321
866-262-6663
http://www.isbe.state.il.us

Dr. Christopher Koch, State Superintendent
Jesse Ruiz, Board Chair

2954 Executive Deputy Superintendent
Illinois Department of Education
100 N 1st Street
Springfield, IL 62777
217-782-0342
Fax: 217-782-5333

2955 Finance & Support Services
Illinois Department of Education
100 N. 1st Street
Springfield, IL 62777
217-782-4321
866-262-6663
E-mail: finance@isbe.net
http://www.isbe.state.il.us

Dr. Christopher Koch, State Superintendent
Jesse Ruiz, Board Chair

2956 Illinois Department of Education
100 N 1st Street
Springfield, IL 62777
217-782-4321
866-262-6663
http://www.isbe.state.il.us

Dr. Christopher Koch, State Superintendent
Jesse Ruiz, Board Chair

2957 Planning, Research & Evaluation
Illinois Department of Education
100 N 1st Street
Springfield, IL 62702-5199
217-782-3950
Fax: 217-524-7784

Connie Wise, Division Director

2958 Recognition & Supervision of Schools
Illinois Department of Education
100 N 1st Street
Springfield, IL 62702-5199
217-782-4123
Fax: 217-524-6125

Dick Haney, Division Director

2959 Region 5: Education Department
6130 W Walcott Avenue
Chicago, IL 60636
773-535-9570
Fax: 773-535-9582

2960 School Finance
Illinois State Department of Education
100 N. 1st Street
Springfield, IL 62777
217-782-4321
866-262-6663
E-mail: finance@isbe.net
http://www.isbe.state.il.us

Dr. Christopher Koch, State Superintendent
Jesse Ruiz, Board Chair

2961 School Improvement & Assessment Services
Illinois State Board of Education
100 N 1st Street
Springfield, IL 62777
217-782-4321
866-262-6663
http://www.isbe.state.il.us

Chris Koch, Superintendent

2962 Special Education
Illinois State Board of Education
100 N 1st Street
Springfield, IL 62777
217-782-4321
866-262-6663
http://www.isbe.state.il.us

Dr. Christopher Koch, State Superintendent

2963 Student Development Services
Illinois Department of Education
100 N 1st Street
Springfield, IL 62702-5199
217-782-0995
Fax: 217-785-7849

Frank Llano, Division Director

2964 Teacher Education & Certification
Illinois Department of Education
100 N 1st Street
Springfield, IL 62702-5199
217-782-3774
Fax: 217-524-1289

Sue Bentz, Division Director

Indiana

2965 Center for School Assessment & Research
Indiana Department of Education
100 N Capitol Avenue, Room 229
Indianapolis, IN 46204-2203
317-232-9050
Fax: 317-233-2196

Wes Bruce, Director

2966 Community Relations & Special Populations
Indiana Department of Education
100 N Capitol Avenue, Room 229
Indianapolis, IN 46204-2203
317-232-0520
Fax: 317-233-6502

Linda Miller, Senior Officer

2967 External Affairs
Indiana Department of Education
100 N Capitol Avenue, Room 229
Indianapolis, IN 46204-2203
317-232-6614
Fax: 317-232-8004

Joe DiLaura, Division Director

2968 Indiana Department of Education
200 W Washington Street
State House, Room 229
Indianapolis, IN 46204-2798
317-232-6665
Fax: 317-232-8004
http://www.doe.state.in.us
For certification information visit www.in.gov/psb or contact 866-542-3672.

Suellen K Reed, Superintedent

2969 Office of Legal Affairs
Indiana Department of Education
Office of Legal Affairs
151 West Ohio Street
Indianapolis, IN 46204-2203
317-232-6676
Fax: 317-232-0744
E-mail: legal@doe.in.gov
http://www.doe.in.gov

Dr. Tony Bennett, Superintendent
Susie Langston, Office Manager

2970 Office of School Financial Management
Indiana Department of Education
151 West Ohio Street
Indianapolis, IN 46204-2203
317-232-0840
Fax: 317-232-0504
E-mail: webmaster@doe.in.gov
http://www.doe.in.gov

Dr. Tony Bennett, Superintendent

2971 Office of the Deputy Superintendent
Indiana Department of Education
100 N Capitol Avenue, Room 229
Indianapolis, IN 46204-2203
317-232-0510
Fax: 317-232-0589

Robert Dalton, Division Director

2972 Policy & Planning
Indiana Department of Education
151 West Ohio Street
Indianapolis, IN 46204-2203
317-232-6648
Fax: 317-232-8004
E-mail: webmaster@doe.in.gov
http://www.doe.in.gov

Dr. Tony Bennett, Superintendent/Public Inst.
Heather Neal, Chief of Staff

2973 School Improvement & Performance Center
Indiana Department of Education
100 N Capitol Avenue, Room 229
Indianapolis, IN 46204-2203
317-232-9100
Fax: 317-232-9121

Phyllis Land Usher, Division Director

Iowa

2974 Community Colleges Division
Iowa Department of Education
14th E & Grand Streets
Des Moines, IA 50319-0001
515-281-8260

Harriet Custer, Division Director

2975 Division of Library Services
Iowa Department of Education
14th E & Grand Streets
Des Moines, IA 50319-0001
515-281-4105

Sharman B Smith, Administrator

2976 Educational Services for Children & Families
Iowa Department of Education
14th E & Grand Streets
Des Moines, IA 50319-0001
515-281-3575

Susan J Donielson, Administrator

2977 Elementary & Secondary Education
Iowa Department of Education
400 E. 14th Street
Des Moines, IA 50319-0146
515-281-5294
http://www.iowa.gov
Strives for higher levels of learning and achievement for students in public elementary and secondary schools

Jason Glass, Director
Kathy Petosa, Administrative Assistant

2978 Financial & Information Services
Iowa Department of Education
Grimes State Office Buildings
Des Moines, IA 50319-0001
515-281-5293
Fax: 515-242-5988
E-mail: lee.tack@ed.state.ia.us
http://www.state.ia.us/educate

Leland Tack, Administrator

2979 Iowa Department of Education
Grimes State Office Building
400 E 14th & Grand Streets
Des Moines, IA 50319-0146
515-281-5294
Fax: 515-281-5988
E-mail: webmaster@ed.state.ia.us
http://www.state.ia.us/educate
Serves the students of Iowa by providing leadership and resources for schools, area education agencies and community colleges.
For certification information visit

www.state.ia.us/boee or contact 515-281-3245.

Ted Stilwill, Director

2980 Iowa Public Television
Iowa Department of Education
14th E & Grand Streets
Des Moines, IA 50319-0001
515-242-3150

David Bolender, Executive Director

2981 Vocational Rehabilitation Services
Iowa Department of Education
14th E & Grand Streets
Des Moines, IA 50319-0001
515-281-6731

Margaret Knudsen, Administrator

Kansas

2982 Kansas Department of Education
120 SE Tenth Avenue
Topeka, KS 66612-1182
785-296-3201
Fax: 785-796-7933
E-mail: ddebacker@ksde.org
http://www.ksde.org

Dr. Diane DeBacker, Commissioner of Education

2983 Office of the Commissioner
Kansas State Department of Education
120 SE 10th Avenue
Topeka, KS 66612-1182
785-296-3201
Fax: 785-296-7933
E-mail: price@ksde.org
http://www.ksde.org

Dr. Diane DeBacker, Commissioner of Education
Penny Rice, Administrative Officer

2984 Special Education Services Department
Kansas State Department of Education
120 SE 10th Avenue
Topeka, KS 66612-1182
785-296-3201
Fax: 785-296-7933
E-mail: khaag@ksde.org
http://www.ksde.org

Dr. Diane DeBacker, Commissioner of Education
Kerry Haag, SES Assistant Director

2985 Teacher Education & Licensure
Kansas State Department of Education
120 SE 10th Avenue
Topeka, KS 66612-1182
785-296-3201
Fax: 785-296-7933
E-mail: pcoleman@ksde.org
http://www.ksde.org

Dr. Diane DeBacher, Commissioner of Education
Pamela Coleman, Director

Kentucky

2986 Chief of Staff Bureau
Kentucky Department of Education
500 Mero Street, 19th Floor
Frankfort, KY 40601-1957
502-564-3141
Fax: 502-564-6470

Hunt Helm, Office Communications

2987 Communications Services
Kentucky Department of Education
15 Fountain Place
Frankfort, KY 40601-1957
502-564-2020
E-mail: andrew.liaupsin@education.ky.gov
http://www.education.ky.gov
Terry Holliday, Ph.D, Commissioner of
Education
Andrew Liaupsin

**2988 Curriculum, Assessment &
AccountabilityCouncil**
Kentucky Department of Education
500 Mero Street
18th Floor
Frankfort, KY 40601-1957
502-564-4394
Fax: 502-564-7749
E-mail: rhonda.sims@education.ky.gov
Terry Holliday, Ph.D, Commissioner of
Education
Rhonda Sims

2989 Education Technology Office
Kentucky Department of Education
500 Mero Street
16th Floor CPT
Frankfort, KY 40601-1957
502-564-1976
E-mail: lauren.moore@education.ky.gov
http://www.education.ky.gov
Terry Holliday, Ph.D, Commissioner of
Education
Lauren Moore

2990 Kentucky Department of Education
500 Mero Street
Capital Plaza Tower
Frankfort, KY 40601-1957
502-564-3141
Fax: 502-564-5680
http://www.education.ky.gov
For certification information visit
www.kyepsb.net or contact 502-573-4606.
Terry Holliday PhD, Commissioner

2991 Learning Results Services Bureau
Kentucky Department of Education
500 Mero Street, 19th Floor
Frankfort, KY 40601-1957
502-564-2256
Fax: 502-564-7749
Vickie Basham, Division Director

**2992 Office of Learning Programs
Development**
Kentucky Department of Education
500 Mero Street, 19th Floor
Frankfort, KY 40601-1957
502-564-3010
Fax: 502-564-6952
Linda Hargan, Division Director

2993 Regional Services Centers
Kentucky Department of Education
500 Mero Street
18th Floor CPT
Frankfort, KY 40601-1957
502-564-2106
E-mail: michael.miller@education.ky.gov
http://www.kde.state.ky.us
Terry Holliday, Ph.D, Commissioner of
Education
Michael Miller

2994 Special Education Services
Kentucky Department of Education
500 Mero Street
8th Floor
Frankfort, KY 40601-1957
502-564-4970
Fax: 502-564-6721

E-mail: larry.taylor@education.ky.gov
http://www.education.ky.gov
Terry Holliday, Ph.D, Commissioner of
Education
Larry Taylor, Special Education Services

2995 Support Services Bureau on Learning
Kentucky Department of Education
500 Mero Street, 19th Floor
Frankfort, KY 40601-1957
502-564-3301
Fax: 502-564-6952
Lois Adams-Rodgers, Division Director

2996 Teacher Education & Certification
Kentucky Department of Education
500 Mero Street, 17th Floor
Frankfort, KY 40601-1957
502-564-7056
E-mail:
annie.rooney-french@education.ky.gov
http://www.education.ky.gov
Terry Holliday, Ph.D, Commissioner of
Education

Louisiana

2997 Academic Programs Office
Louisiana Department of Education
PO Box 94064
Baton Rouge, LA 70804-9064
877-453-2721
Fax: 225-342-0193
E-mail: customerservice@la.gov
http://www.louisianaschools.net
Paul Pastorek, State Superintendent of Educ
Rene Greer, Director, Public Affairs

2998 Louisiana Department of Education
2758-D Brightside Drive
PO Box 94064
Baton Rouge, LA 70804-9064
504-342-3607
Fax: 504-342-7316
http://www.doe.state.la.us
Provides leadership and enacts policies that
result in improved academic achievement and
responsible citizenship for all students. For
certification information visit
www.louisianaschools.net or contact
225-342-3490.
Cecil J Picard, Superintendent

2999 Management & Finance Office
Louisana State Department of Education
PO Box 64064
Baton Rouge, LA 70804-9064
225-342-3617
877-453-2721
Fax: 225-219-7538
E-mail: mlangley@doe.state.la.us
http://www.doe.state.la.us
Marlyn J Langley, Deputy Superintendent

3000 Office of Educator Support
Louisiana Department of Education
PO Box 94064
Baton Rouge, LA 70804-9064
877-453-2721
Fax: 225-342-0193
E-mail: customerservice@la.gov
http://www.louisianaschools.net
Paul Pastorek, State Superintendent of Educ
Karen Burke, Acting Asst. Superintendent

3001 Research & Development Office
Louisiana Department of Education
PO Box 94064
Baton Rouge, LA 70804-9064
877-453-2721
Fax: 225-342-0193

E-mail: customerservice@la.gov
http://www.louisianaschools.net
Paul Pastorek, State Superintendent of Educ
Rene Greer, Director, Public Affairs

3002 Special Education Services
Louisiana Department of Education
PO Box 94064
Baton Rouge, LA 70804-9064
877-453-2721
Fax: 225-342-0193
E-mail: customerservice@la.gov
http://www.louisianaschools.net
Paul Pastorek, State Superintendent of Educ
Rene Greer, Director, Public Affairs

**3003 Standards, Assessments &
Accountability**
Louisiana Department of Education
PO Box 94064
Baton Rouge, LA 70804-9064
877-453-2721
Fax: 225-342-3600
E-mail: customerservice@la.gov
http://www.louisianaschools.net
Paul Pastorek, State Superintendent of Educ
Scott Norton, Assistant Superintendent

Maine

**3004 Administrator and Teacher
Certification**
Maine Department of Education
Certification Office
23 State House Station
Augusta, ME 04333-0023
207-624-6603
Fax: 207-624-6604
E-mail: cert.doe@maine.gov
http://www.maine.gov
Angela Faherty, Commissioner
Mark Cyr, Team Coordinator

3005 Adult Education
Maine Department of Education
23 State House Station
Augusta, ME 04333-0023
207-624-6600
Fax: 207-624-6700
E-mail: jeff.fantine@maine.gov
http://www.maine.gov
Angela Faherty, Commissioner
Jeff Fantine, State Director Adult Educ.

3006 Maine Department of Education
23 State House Station
Augusta, ME 04333-0023
207-624-6620
Fax: 207-624-6601
http://www.state.me.us/education
Susan Gendron, Commissioner

Maryland

3007 Career & Technology Education
Maryland State Department of Education
200 W Baltimore Street
Baltimore, MD 21201
410-767-0186
Fax: 410-333-2099
E-mail: pmikos@msde.state.md.us
http://www.marylandpublicschools.org
Pat Mikos, Program Manager

3008 Certification & Accreditation
Maryland State Department of Education
200 W. Baltimore Street
Baltimore, MD 21201-2502

410-767-0412
866-772-8922
http://www.marylandpublicschools.org
Nancy S. Grasmick, St Superintendent of
Schools

**3009 Compensatory Education & Support
Services**
Maryland Department of Education
200 W Baltimore Street
Baltimore, MD 21201-2502
410-333-2400

Ellen Gonzales, Division Director

3010 Division of Business Services
Maryland Department of Education
200 W Baltimore Street
Baltimore, MD 21201-2502
410-333-2648

Raymond H Brown, Division Director

3011 Instruction Division
Maryland State Department of Education
200 W Baltimore Street
Baltimore, MD 21201-2502
410-767-0316
http://www.marylandpublicschools.org

Mary Cary, Assistant Superintendent

3012 Library Development & Services
Maryland State Department of Education
200 West Baltimore Street
Baltimore, MD 21201-2502
410-333-2113
E-mail: www.marylandpublicschools.org

Irene Padilla, Asst St Superintendent Lib.

3013 Maryland Department of Education
200 W Baltimore Street
Baltimore, MD 21201-2502
410-767-0600
888-246-0016
Fax: 410-333-6033
http://www.msde.state.md.us
Mission of MSDE is to provide leadership,
support, and accountability for effective systems of public education, library services and
rehabilitation services. For certification information visit www.certifica-
tion.msde.state.md.us or contact
410-767-0412.

Nancy S Grasmick, Superintendent

**3014 Office of Special Education and
RehabilitativeServices**
U.S. Department of Education
400 Maryland Avenue SW
Washington, DC 20202-7100
202-245-7459
http://www.2.ed.gov

Melody Musgrove, Director
Bill Wolf, Acting Deputy Director

**3015 Planning, Results & Information
Management**
Maryland Department of Education
200 W Baltimore Street
Baltimore, MD 21201-2502
410-333-2045

Mark Moody, Division Director

**3016 Special Education/Early Intervention
ServicesDivision**
Maryland State Department of Education
200 W Baltimore Street
9th Floor
Baltimore, MD 21201-2502
410-767-0261
800-535-0182

Fax: 410-333-8165
http://www.marylandpublicschools.org
Nancy S. Grasmick, St Superintendent of
Schools

Massachusetts

**3017 Massachusetts Department of
Education**
350 Main Street
Malden, MA 02148-5023
781-338-3000
Fax: 781-338-3770
http://www.doe.mass.edu

David P Driscoll, Commissioner

**3018 Massachusetts Department of
Educational Improvement**
350 Main Street
Malden, MA 02148-5089
781-388-3300

Andrea Perrault, Division Director

3019 Region 1: Education Department
J.W. McCormick Post Office & Courthouse
540 McCormick Courthouse
Boston, MA 02109-4557
617-223-9317
Fax: 617-223-9324

Michael Sentance

Michigan

3020 Administrative Services Office
Michigan Department of Education
608 W Allegan Street
Lansing, MI 48933-1524
517-373-3324
Fax: 517-335-4565
http://www.michigan.gov

Calvin C Cupidore, Director

3021 Adult Extended Learning Office
Michigan Department of Education
608 W Allegan Street
Lansing, MI 48933-1524
517-373-3324
Fax: 517-335-4565
http://www.michigan.gov

Ronald Gillum, Director

3022 Career & Technical Education
Michigan Department of Education
608 W Allegan Street
Lansing, MI 48933-1524
517-373-3324
Fax: 517-373-8776
http://www.michigan.gov

William Welsgerber, Director

3023 Higher Education Management Office
Michigan Department of Education
608 W Allegan Street
Lansing, MI 48933-1524
517-373-3324
Fax: 517-373-2759
http://www.michigan.gov

Ronald L Root, Director

3024 Instructional Programs
Michigan Department of Education
608 W Allegan Street
Lansing, MI 48933-1524
517-373-3324
Fax: 517-335-4565
http://www.michigan.gov

3025 Michigan Department of Education
608 W Allegan Street
PO Box 30008
Lansing, MI 48909
517-373-3324
Fax: 517-335-4565
E-mail: MDEweb@michigan.gov
http://www.michigan.gov/mde

Thomas D Watkins, Superintendent

3026 Office of School Management
Michigan Department of Education
608 W Allegan Street
Lansing, MI 48933-1524
517-373-3324
Fax: 517-335-4565
http://www.michigan.gov

Roger Lynas, Director

3027 Office of the Superintendent
Michigan Department of Education
608 W Allegan Street
Lansing, MI 48933-1524
517-373-3324
Fax: 517-335-4565
http://www.michigan.gov

3028 Postsecondary Services
Michigan Department of Education
608 W Allegan Street
Lansing, MI 48909
517-373-3324
Fax: 517-335-4565
http://www.michigan.gov

3029 School Program Quality
Michigan Department of Education
608 W Allegan Street
Lansing, MI 48933-1524
517-373-3324
Fax: 517-373-4565
http://www.michigan.gov

Anne Hansen, Division Director

3030 Special Education
Michigan Department of Education
608 W Allegan Street
Lansing, MI 48933-1524
517-373-3324
Fax: 581-733-5456

Richard Baldwin, Director

3031 Student Financial Assistance
Michigan Department of Education
608 W Allegan Street
Lansing, MI 48933-1524
517-373-3324
Fax: 517-335-4565

Jack Nelson, Director

**3032 Teacher & Administrative
Preparation**
Michigan Department of Education
608 W Allegan Street
Lansing, MI 48933-1524
514-373-3324
Fax: 517-335-4565
http://www.michigan.gov

Carolyn Logan, Director

Minnesota

3033 Data & Technology
Minnesota Department of Education
550 Cedar Street
Saint Paul, MN 55101-2233
612-297-3151

Mark Manning, Division Director

3034 Data Management
Minnesota Department of Education
1500 Highway 39 W
Roseville, MN 55113
651-582-8296
Fax: 651-582-8873
Carol Hokenson, Manager Data
Management

3035 Education Funding
Minnesota Department of Education
550 Cedar Street
Saint Paul, MN 55101-2233
651-297-2194
Tom Melcher, Division Director

3036 Financial Conditions & Aids Payment
Minnesota Department of Education
550 Cedar Street
Saint Paul, MN 55101-2233
612-296-4431
Gary Farland, Division Director

3037 Government Relations
Minnesota Department of Education
550 Cedar Street
Saint Paul, MN 55101-2233
612-296-5279
Sliv Carlson, Division Director

3038 Human Resources Office
Minnesota Department of Education
550 Cedar Street
Saint Paul, MN 55101-2233
651-582-8200
William O'Neill, Division Director

3039 Minnesota Department of Children, Families & Learning
1500 Highway 36 W
Roseville, MN 55113-4266
651-582-8204
Fax: 651-582-8724
http://cfl.state.mn.us
Works to help communities to measurably improve the well-being of children through programs that focus on education, community services, prevention, and the preparation of young people for the world of work. All department efforts emphasize the achievement of positive results for children and their families.
Dr.Cheri Pierson, Commissioner

3040 Minnesota Department of Education
1500 Highway 36 W
Roseville, MN 55113-4266
651-582-8204
Fax: 651-582-8724
http://www.education.state.mn.us
Christine Jax, Commissioner

3041 Residential Schools
Minnesota Department of Education
550 Cedar Street
Saint Paul, MN 55101-2233
507-332-3363
Wade Karli, Division Director

Mississippi

3042 Community Outreach Services
Mississippi Department of Education
PO Box 771
Jackson, MS 39205-1113
601-359-3513
Fax: 601-359-3033
Sarah Beard, Division Director

3043 Educational Innovations
Mississippi Department of Education
PO Box 771
Jackson, MS 39205-0771
601-359-3499
Fax: 601-359-2587
David Robinson, Division Director

3044 External Relations
Mississippi Department of Education
PO Box 771
372 Central High Building
Jackson, MS 39201
601-359-3515
Fax: 601-359-3033
Andrew P Mullins, Division Director

3045 Management Information Systems
Mississippi Department of Education
PO Box 771
Jackson, MS 39205
601-359-3487
Fax: 601-359-3033
Rusty Purvis, Division Director

3046 Mississippi Department of Education
359 NW Street
PO Box 771
Jackson, MS 39205-0771
601-359-3512
Fax: 601-359-3242
http://www.mde.k12.ms.us
Dr.Henry Johnson, Superintendent

3047 Mississippi Employment Security Commission
PO Box 1699
Jackson, MS 39215-1699
601-961-7400
Fax: 601-961-7405
http://www.mesc.state.ms

3048 Office of Accountability
Mississippi Department of Education
PO Box 771
Jackson, MS 39205
601-359-2038
Fax: 601-359-1748
Judy Rhodes, Division Director

3049 Vocational Technical Education
Mississippi Department of Education
359 NW Street
PO Box 771
Jackson, MS 39292
601-359-3090
Fax: 601-359-3989
Samuel McGee, Division Director

Missouri

3050 Deputy Commissioner
Missouri Department of Education
205 Jefferson Street
PO Box 480 Floor 6
Jefferson City, MO 65101-2901
573-751-3503
Fax: 573-751-1179
Dr.Bert Schulte, Deputy Commissioner

3051 Division of Instruction
Missouri Department of Education
205 Jefferson Street
Floor 6
Jefferson City, MO 65101-2901
573-751-4234
Fax: 573-751-8613
Otis Baker, Division Director

3052 Missouri Department of Education
205 Jefferson Street, 6th Floor
PO Box 480
Jefferson City, MO 65102-0480
573-751-4212
Fax: 573-751-8613
E-mail: pubinfo@mail.dese.state.mo.us
http://www.dese.state.mo.us
A team of dedicated individuals working for the continuous improvement of education and services for all citizens. We believe that we can make a positive difference in the quality of life for all Missourians by providing exceptional service to students, educators, schools and citizens.
D Kent King, Commissioner

3053 Region 7: Education Department
10220 NW Executive Hills Boulevard
Kansas City, MO 64153-2312
816-891-7972
Fax: 816-891-7972

3054 Special Education Division
Missouri Department of Education
205 Jefferson Street
PO Box 480 Floor 6
Jefferson City, MO 65102-2901
573-751-5739
Fax: 573-526-4404
John F Allan, Division Director

3055 Urban & Teacher Education
Missouri Department of Education
205 Jefferson Street
Floor 6
Jefferson City, MO 65101-2901
573-751-2931
Fax: 573-751-8613
L Celestine Ferguson, Division Director

3056 Vocational & Adult Education
Missouri Department of Education
205 Jefferson Street, 5th Floor
PO Box 480
Jefferson City, MO 65102-0480
573-751-2660
Fax: 573-526-4261
E-mail: nheadrick@mail.dese.state.mo.us
http://www.dese.state.mo.us
Nancy J Headrick, Assistant Commissioner

3057 Vocational Rehabilitation
Missouri Department of Education
3024 Dupont Circle
Jefferson City, MO 65109-0525
573-751-3251
Fax: 573-751-1441
Don L Gann, Division Director

Montana

3058 Accreditation & Curriculum Services Department
Montana Department of Education
106 State Capitol
Helena, MT 59620
406-444-5726
Fax: 406-444-2893
Dr.Linda Vrooman, Administrator

3059 Division of Information-Technology Support
Montana Department of Education
106 State Capitol
Helena, MT 59620
406-444-4326
Fax: 406-444-2893
Scott Buswell, Division Director

3060 Montana Department of Education
1227 11th Avenue
PO Box 202501
Helena, MT 59620-2501
406-444-3095
Fax: 406-444-2893
http://www.opi.state.mt.us
For certification information visit
www.opi.state.mt.us or contact
406-444-3150.

Linda McCulloch, Superindtendent

3061 Operations Department
Montana Department of Education
106 State Capitol
Helena, MT 59620
406-444-3095
Fax: 406-444-2893

Nebraska

3062 Administrative Services Office
Nebraska Department of Education
301 Centennial Mall S
Lincoln, NE 68508-2529
402-471-2295
Fax: 402-471-6351
http://www.nde.state.ne.us/ADSS/index.html
To provide quality services and support in the areas of finance human resource management continuous quality improvement, office/building services,and technical assistant.

Mike Stefkovich, Division Director

3063 Division of Education Services
Nebraska Department of Education
301 Centennial Mall S
Lincoln, NE 68508-2529
402-471-2783
Fax: 402-471-0117

Marge Harouff, Division Director

3064 Nebraska Department of Education
301 Centennial Mall S
PO Box 94987
Lincoln, NE 68509-4987
402-471-5020
Fax: 402-471-4433
http://www.nde.state.ne.us

Douglas D Christensen, Commissioner

3065 Rehabilitation Services Division
Nebraska Department of Education
301 Centennial Mall S 6th Floor
PO Box 94987
Lincoln, NE 68509-2529
402-471-3649
877-637-3422
Fax: 402-471-0788
http://www.bocrehab.state.ne.us

Frank C Lloyd, Director

Nevada

3066 Administrative & Financial Services
Nevada Department of Education
400 W King St
Carson City, NV 89703-4204
775-687-9102
888-590-6726
Fax: 702-486-5803

Douglas Thunder

3067 Instructional Services Division
Nevada Department of Education
400 W King St
Carson City, NV 89703-4204

775-687-3104
Mary L Peterson, Division Director

3068 Nevada Department of Education
700 E 5th Street
Carson City, NV 89701-5096
775-687-9200
Fax: 775-687-9101
http://www.nsn.k12.nv.us
Mission is to lead Nevada's citizens in accomplishing lifelong learning and educational excellence.

Jack McLaughlin, Superintendent

New Hampshire

3069 Information Services
New Hampshire Department of Education
101 Pleasent Street
Concord, NH 03301-3852
603-271-2778
Fax: 603-271-1953
http://www.ed.state.nh.us
New Hampshire schools enrollment, financial, assessment information.

Dr.Judith Fillion, Division Director

3070 New Hampshire Department of Education
101 Pleasant Street
State Office Park S
Concord, NH 03301-3860
603-271-3494
800-339-9900
Fax: 603-271-1953
E-mail: llovering@ed.state.nh.us
http://www.state.nh.us/doe
Mission is to provide educational leadership and services which promote equal educational opportunities and quality practices and programs than enable New Hampshire residents to become fully productive members of society.

Nicholas C Donohue, Commissioner

3071 New Hampshire Division of Instructional Services
101 Pleasant Street
Concord, NH 03301-3852
603-271-3880

William B Evert, Division Director

3072 Standards & Certification Division
New Hampshire Dept of Education
101 Pleasant St
Concord, NH 03301-3852
603-271-3453
Fax: 603-271-8709

Judith D Fillion, Divisions Director

New Jersey

3073 New Jersey Department of Education
100 Riverview Plaza
PO Box 500
Trenton, NJ 08625-0500
609-292-4450
Fax: 609-777-4099
http://www.state.nj.us/education
Develops and implements policies that address the major education issues in New Jersey. The State Board will engage in an effort to ensure that all children receive a quality public education that prepares them to succeed as responsible, productive citizens in a global society.

William L Librera, Commissioner

3074 New Jersey Department of Education: Finance
100 Riverview Plaza
PO Box 500
Trenton, NJ 08625-0500
609-292-4421
Fax: 609-292-6794
http://www.state.nj.us/education

Richard Rosenberg, Assistant Commissioner

3075 New Jersey Division of Special Education
100 Riverview Plaza
PO Box 500
Trenton, NJ 08625
609-292-0147
Fax: 609-984-8422

Jeffrey Osowski, Divsion Director

3076 New Jersey State Library
PO Box 520
Trenton, NJ 08625-0520
609-292-6200
Fax: 609-292-2746
E-mail: nblake@njstatelib.org
http://www.njstatelib.org

Norma E Blake, State Librarian

3077 Professional Development & Licensing
New Jersey Department of Education
100 Riverview Plaza, PO Box 500
Trenton, NJ 08625
609-292-2070
Fax: 609-292-3768

Hilda Hidalgo, Division Director

3078 Urban & Field Services
New Jersey Department of Education
100 Riverview Plaza, PO Box 500
Trenton, NJ 08625
609-292-4442
Fax: 609-292-3830

Elena Scambio, Division Director

New Mexico

3079 Agency Support
New Mexico Department of Education
300 Don Gaspar, Education Building
Santa Fe, NM 87501-2786
505-827-6330

Tres Giron, Division Director

3080 Learning Services
New Mexico Department of Education
300 Don Gaspar, Education Building
Santa Fe, NM 87501
505-827-6508
Fax: 505-827-6689

Albert Zamora, Division Director

3081 New Mexico Department of Education
300 Don Gaspar
Education Building
Santa Fe, NM 87501-2786
505-827-6688
Fax: 505-827-6520
http://www.sde.state.nm.us

Michael J Davis, Superintendent

3082 New Mexico Department of School-Transportation & Support Services
300 Don Gaspar, Education Building
Santa Fe, NM 87501
505-827-6683

Susan Brown, Division Director

3083 School Management Accountability
New Mexico Department of Education
300 Don Gaspar, Education Building
Santa Fe, NM 87501
505-827-3876
Fax: 505-827-6689

Michael J Davis, Division Director

3084 Vocational Education
New Mexico Department of Education
300 Don Gaspar, Education Building
Santa Fe, NM 87501
505-827-6511

Tom Trujillo, Division Director

New York

3085 Cultural Education
New York Department of Education
Madison Avenue
Albany, NY 12230
518-474-5976
Fax: 518-474-2718
E-mail: CISINFO@mail.nysed.gov

Carole F Huxley, Division Director

3086 Elementary, Middle & Secondary Education
New York Department of Education
89 Washington Avenue
Room 875 EBA
Albany, NY 12234-0001
518-474-5915
Fax: 518-474-2718
E-mail: emscgen@mail.nysed.gov

James Kadamus, Deputy

3087 Higher & Professional Education
New York Department of Education
111 Education Avenue W Mezzanine
2nd Floor
Albany, NY 12234-0001
518-474-5851
Fax: 518-474-2718

Johanna Duncan-Poitier, Deputy
Commissioner

3088 New York Department of Education
89 Washington Avenue
Education Building, Room 111
Albany, NY 12234
518-474-5844
Fax: 518-473-4909
E-mail: rmills@mail.nysed.gov
http://www.nysed.gov

Richard P Mills, President

3089 Professional Responsibility Office
New York Department of Education
89 Wolf Road Suite 204
Albany, NY 12205-2643
518-485-9350
Fax: 518-485-9361

3090 Region 2: Education Department
75 Park Place
New York, NY 10007
212-264-7005
Fax: 212-264-4427

3091 Vocational & Educational Services for Disabled
New York Department of Education
80 Wolf Road Suite 200
Albany, NY 12205
518-473-8097
800-272-5448
Fax: 518-457-4562

David Segalla, Regional Coordinator

North Carolina

3092 Auxiliary Services
North Carolina Department of Education
301 N Wilmington Street
Raleigh, NC 27601-2825
919-733-1110
Fax: 919-733-5279

Charles Weaver, Division Director

3093 Financial & Personnel Services
North Carolina Department of Education
301 N Wilmington Street
Raleigh, NC 27601-2825
919-807-3600

James O Barber, Division Director

3094 North Carolina Department of Education
301 N Wilmington Street
Raleigh, NC 27601-2825
919-715-1299
Fax: 919-807-3279
http://www.ncpublicschools.org

Bob R Etheridge, Division Director

3095 North Carolina Department of Instructional Services
301 N Wilmington Street
Raleigh, NC 27601-2825
919-715-1506
Fax: 919-807-3279

Henry Johnson, Division Director

3096 Staff Development & Technical Assistance
North Carolina Department of Education
301 N Wilmington Street
Raleigh, NC 27601-2825
919-715-1315

Nancy Davis, Division Director

North Dakota

3097 North Dakota Department of Education
600 E Boulevard Avenue
State Capitol Building, Floor 11
Bismarck, ND 58505-0440
701-328-4572
Fax: 701-328-2461
http://www.state.nd.us/espb

Wayne G Sanstead, Superintendent

3098 North Dakota Department of Public Instruction Division
600 E Boulevard Avenue, Dept. 201
Floor 9,10, & 11
Bismarck, ND 58505-0440
701-328-2260
Fax: 701-328-2461
E-mail: wsanstea@mail.dpi.state.nd.us
http://www.dpi.state.nd.us/dpi/index.htm

Dr. Wayne G Sanstead, State Superintendent

3099 North Dakota State Board for Vocational & Technical Education
600 E Boulevard Avenue
Floor 15
Bismarck, ND 58505-0660
701-224-2259
Fax: 701-328-2461

Reuben Guenthner, Division Director

3100 Study & State Film Library
North Dakota Department of Education
600 E Boulevard Avenue
Floor 11
Bismarck, ND 58505-0660
701-237-7282

Robert Stone, Division Director

Ohio

3101 Blind School
Ohio Department of Education
65 S Front Street
Columbus, OH 43215-4131
614-466-3641
Fax: 614-752-1713

Dennis Holmes, Division Director

3102 Curriculum, Instruction & Professional Development
Ohio Department of Education
65 S Front Street
Columbus, OH 43215-4131
614-466-2761
Fax: 704-992-5168

Nancy Eberhart, Division Director

3103 Early Childhood Education
Ohio Department of Education
65 S Front Street
Columbus, OH 43215-4131
614-466-0224
Fax: 614-728-2338

Jane Wiechel, Division Director

3104 Federal Assistance
Ohio Department of Education
65 S Front Street
Columbus, OH 43215-4131
614-466-4161
Fax: 704-992-5168

William Henry, Division Director

3105 Ohio Department of Education
25 S Front Street
7th Floor
Columbus, OH 43215-4183
614-466-7578
877-644-6338
Fax: 614-728-4781
http://www.ode.state.oh.us
Works in partnership with school districts to
assure high achievements for all learners, promote a safe and orderly learning environment,
provide leadership, support, and build capacity, and provide support to school districts
particularly those who need it most.

Susan T Zelman, Superintendent

3106 Personnel Services
Ohio Department of Education
65 S Front Street
Columbus, OH 43215-4131
614-466-3763
Fax: 704-992-5168

Larry Cathell, Division Director

3107 School Finance
Ohio Department of Education
65 S Front Street
Columbus, OH 43215-4131
614-466-6266
Fax: 704-992-5168
E-mail: sf_tavakolia@ode.ohio.gov
http://www.ode.state.ohio.us/foundation/ww
w_.html

Susan Tavakolian, Division Director

3108 School Food Service
Ohio Department of Education
65 S Front Street
Columbus, OH 43215-4131
614-466-2945
Fax: 704-992-5168

Lorita Myles, Division Director

3109 School for the Deaf
Ohio Department of Education
65 S Front Street
Columbus, OH 43215-4131
614-466-3641
Fax: 704-992-5168

Edward C Corbett Jr, Division Director

3110 Special Education
Ohio Department of Education
933 High Street
Worthington, OH 43085
614-466-2650
Fax: 704-992-5168
E-mail: se_herner@ode.ohio.gov

John Herner, Director Special Education

3111 Student Development
Ohio Department of Education
65 S Front Street
Columbus, OH 43215-4131
614-466-3641
Fax: 704-992-5168

Hazel Flowers, Division Director

3112 Teacher Education & Certification
Ohio Department of Education
65 S Front Street
Columbus, OH 43215-4131
614-466-3430
Fax: 704-992-5168

Darrell Parks, Division Director

3113 Vocational & Career Education
Ohio Department of Education
65 S Front Street
Columbus, OH 43215-4131
614-466-3430
Fax: 704-992-5168

Darrell Parks, Division Director

Oklahoma

3114 Accreditation & Standards Division
Oklahoma Department of Education
2500 N Lincoln Boulevard
Oklahoma City, OK 73105-4503
405-521-3333
Fax: 405-521-6205

Sharon Lease, Division Director

3115 Federal/Special/Collaboration Services
Oklahoma Department of Education
2500 N Lincoln Boulevard
Oklahoma City, OK 73105-4503
405-521-4873
Fax: 405-522-3503

Sid Hudson, Division Director

3116 Oklahoma Department of Career and Technology Education
1500 W 7th Avenue
Stillwater, OK 74074-4398
405-743-5444
Fax: 405-743-5541

Roy Peters Jr, Division Director

3117 Oklahoma Department of Education
2500 N Lincoln Boulevard
Hodge Education Building
Oklahoma City, OK 73105-4599

405-521-4485
Fax: 405-521-6205
http://http://sde.state.ok.us

Sandy Garrett, Superindentdent

3118 Oklahoma Department of Education; Financial Services
Oklahoma Department of Education
2500 N Lincoln Boulevard
Oklahoma City, OK 73105-4503
405-521-3371
Fax: 405-521-6205

Don Shive, Division Director

3119 Professional Services
Oklahoma Department of Education
2500 N Lincoln Boulevard
Oklahoma City, OK 73105-4503
405-521-4311
Fax: 405-521-6205

Paul Simon, Division Director

3120 School Improvement
Oklahoma Department of Education
2500 N Lincoln Boulevard
Oklahoma City, OK 73105-4503
405-521-4869
Fax: 405-521-6205

Hugh McCrabb, Division Director

Oregon

3121 Assessment & Evaluation
Oregon Department of Education
255 Capitol Street NE
Salem, OR 97310-0203
503-378-3600
Fax: 503-378-5156
E-mail: firstname.lastname@state.or.us
http://www.ode.state.or.us

Doug Kosty, Assistant Superintendent

3122 Community College Services
Oregon Department of Education
225 Capitol Street NE
Salem, OR 97310-1341
503-378-3600
Fax: 503-378-5156

Stan Bunn, Superintendent

3123 Compensatory Education Office
Oregon Department of Education
225 Capitol Street NE
Salem, OR 97310-1341
503-378-3569
Fax: 503-378-5156

Jerry Fuller, Division Director

3124 Deputy Superintendent Office
Oregon Department of Education
225 Capitol Street NE
Salem, OR 97310-1341
503-378-3573
Fax: 503-378-5156

Bob Burns, Division Director

3125 Early Childhood Council
Oregon Department of Education
225 Capitol Street NE
Salem, OR 97310-1341
503-378-5585
Fax: 503-378-5156

Judy Miller, Division Director

3126 Government Relations
Oregon Department of Education
225 Capitol Street NE
Salem, OR 97310-1341

503-378-8549
Fax: 503-378-5156

Greg McMurdo, Division Director

3127 Management Services
Oregon Department of Education
225 Capitol Street NE
Salem, OR 97310-1341
503-378-8549
Fax: 503-378-5156

Chris Durham, Division Director

3128 Office of Field, Curriculum & Instruction Services
Oregon Department of Education
225 Capitol Street NE
Salem, OR 97310-1341
503-378-8004
Fax: 503-378-5156

Roberta Hutton, Division Director

3129 Oregon Department of Education
225 Capitol Street NE
Salem, OR 97310-0203
503-378-3569
Fax: 503-378-5156
E-mail: ode.frontdesk@ode.state.or.us
http://www.ode.state.or.us

Susan Castillo, Superintendent

3130 Professional Technical Education
Oregon Department of Education
225 Capitol Street NE
Salem, OR 97310-1341
503-378-3584
Fax: 503-378-5156

JD Hoye, Division Director

3131 Special Education
Oregon Department of Education
225 Capitol Street NE
Salem, OR 97310-1341
503-378-3600
Fax: 503-378-5156
http://www.ode.state.or.us

Steve Johnson, Division Director

3132 Student Services Office
Oregon Department of Education
225 Capitol Street NE
Salem, OR 97310-1341
503-378-5585
Fax: 503-378-5156

Judy Miller, Division Director

3133 Twenty First Century Schools Council
Oregon Department of Education
225 Capitol Street NE
Salem, OR 97310-1341
503-378-3600
Fax: 503-378-5156

Joyce Reinke, Division Director

Pennsylvania

3134 Chief Counsel
Pennsylvania Department of Education
333 Market Street
Harrisburg, PA 17101-2210
717-787-5500
Fax: 717-783-0347

Jeffrey Champagne, Division Director

3135 Chief of Staff Office
Pennsylvania Department of Education
333 Market Street
Harrisburg, PA 17101-2210
717-787-9744
Fax: 717-787-7222

Terry Dellmuth, Chief of Staff

3136 Higher Education/Postsecondary Office
Pennsylvania Department of Education
333 Market Street
Harrisburg, PA 17101-2210
717-787-5041
Fax: 717-783-0583

Charles Fuget, Division Director

3137 Office of Elementary and Secondary Education
Pennsylvania Department of Education
333 Market Street
5th Floor
Harrisburg, PA 17101
717-787-2127
Fax: 717-783-6802
E-mail: dhaines@state.pa.us
http://www.pde.state.pa.us

Debra Haines, Executive Secretary

3138 Office of the Comptroller
Pennsylvania Department of Education
333 Market Street
Harrisburg, PA 17101-2210
717-787-5506
Fax: 717-787-3593

William Hardenstine, Division Director

3139 Pennsylvania Department of Education
333 Market Street
Harrisburg, PA 17126
717-783-6788
Fax: 717-787-7222
http://www.education.state.pa.us

Ronald J Tomalis, Acting Secretary

3140 Region 3: Education Department
3535 Market Street
Philadelphia, PA 19104-3309
215-596-1001

Rhode Island

3141 Career & Technical Education
Rhode Island Department of Education
255 Westminster Street
Providence, RI 02903-3414
401-222-4600
Fax: 401-222-2537
http://www.ridoe.net

Frank M Santoro, Division Director

3142 Equity & Access Office
Rhode Island Department of Education
255 Westminster Street
Providence, RI 02903-3414
401-222-4600
Fax: 401-222-2537
http://www.ridoe.net

Frank R Walker III, Division Director

3143 Human Resource Development
Rhode Island Department of Education
255 Westminster Street
Providence, RI 02903-3414
401-222-4600
Fax: 401-222-2537
http://www.ridoe.net

Paula A Rossi, Division Director

3144 Instruction Office
Rhode Island Department of Education
255 Westminster Street
Providence, RI 02903-3414
401-222-4600
Fax: 401-222-2537
http://www.ridoe.net

Marie C DiBiasio, Division Director

3145 Office of Finance
Rhode Island Department of Education
255 Westminster Street
Providence, RI 02903-3414
401-222-4600
Fax: 401-222-2537
http://www.ridoe.net

Frank A Pontarelli, Division Director

3146 Outcomes & Assessment Office
Rhode Island Department of Education
255 Westminster Street
Providence, RI 02903-3414
401-222-4600
Fax: 401-222-2537
http://www.ridoe.net

Pasquale J DeVito, Division Director

3147 Resource Development
Rhode Island Department of Education
255 Westminster Street
Providence, RI 02903-3414
401-222-4600
Fax: 401-222-6033
http://www.ridoe.net

Edward T Costa, Division Director

3148 Rhode Island Department of Education
255 Westminster Street
Providence, RI 02903
401-222-4600
Fax: 401-222-6178
E-mail: ride0001@ride.ri.net
http://www.ridoe.net
Goal of all our work is to improve student performance and help all students meet or exceed a high level of performance. Standards, instruction, and assessment intertwine to provide a system that ensures a strong education for our students.

Peter McWalters, Commissioner

3149 School Food Services Administration
Rhode Island Department of Education
255 Westminster Street
Providence, RI 02903-3414
401-222-4600
Fax: 401-222-3080
http://www.ridoe.net

Virginia da Mora, Dir Integrated Soc Service

3150 Special Needs Office
Rhode Island Department of Education
255 Westminster Street
Providence, RI 02903-3414
401-456-9331
Fax: 401-456-8699
http://www.ridoe.net

Dr.Frances Gallo, Acting Dirctor

3151 Teacher Education & Certification Office
Rhode Island Department of Education
255 Westminster Street
Providence, RI 02903-3414
401-222-4600
Fax: 401-222-2048
http://www.ridoe.net

Louis E DelPapa, Division Director

South Carolina

3152 Budgets & Planning
South Carolina Department of Education
1201 Main Street
Suite 950
Columbia, SC 29201-3730

803-734-2280
Fax: 803-734-0645

Les Boles, Division Director

3153 Communications Services
South Carolina Department of Education
1429 Senate Street
Columbia, SC 29201-3730
803-734-8500
Fax: 803-734-3389

Jerry Adams, Division Director

3154 General Counsel
South Carolina Department of Education
1429 Senate Street
Columbia, SC 29201-3730
803-734-8500
Fax: 803-734-4384

Shelly Carrigg, Esq, Division Director

3155 Internal Administration
South Carolina Department of Education
1429 Senate Street
Columbia, SC 29201-3730
803-734-8500
Fax: 803-734-6225

Jackie Rosswurm, Division Director

3156 Policy & Planning
South Carolina Department of Education
1429 Senate Street
Columbia, SC 29201-3730
803-734-8500
Fax: 803-734-8624

Valerie Truesdale, Division Director

3157 South Carolina Department of Education
1429 Senate Street
Columbia, SC 29201
803-734-8492
Fax: 803-734-3389
http://www.state.sc.us
Provides leadership and services to ensure a system of public education in which all students become educated, responsible, and contributing citizens. For certification information visit www.myscschools.com or contact 803-734-5280.

Inez M Tenenbaum, Superintendent

3158 Support Services
South Carolina Department of Education
1429 Senate Street
Columbia, SC 29201-3730
803-734-8500
Fax: 803-734-8254

Donald Tudor, Division Director

South Dakota

3159 Finance & Management
South Dakota Department of Education
700 Governors Drive
Pierre, SD 57501-2291
605-773-3248
Fax: 605-773-6139

Stacy Krusemark, Division Director

3160 Services for Education
South Dakota Department of Education
700 Governors Drive
Pierre, SD 57501-2291
605-773-4699
Fax: 605-773-3782

Donlynn Rice, Division Director

3161 South Dakota Department of Education & Cultural Affairs
700 Governors Drive
Pierre, SD 57501-2291
605-773-2291
Fax: 605-773-6139
E-mail: ray.christensen@state.sd.us
http://www.state.sd.us/deca/
Advocates for education, facilitate the delivery of statewide educational and cultural services, and promote efficient, appropriate, and quality educational opportunities for all persons residing in South Dakota.

Ray Christensen, Secretary
Patrick Keating, Division Director

3162 South Dakota State Historical Society
South Dakota Dept of Education & Cultural Affairs
900 Governors Drive
Pierre, SD 57501-2291
605-773-3458
Fax: 605-773-6041
E-mail: jay.vogt@state.sd.us
http://www.state.sd.us/deca/
Program areas: Archaeology, archives, historic preservation, museum, research, and publishing

Jay D Vogt, History Manager

3163 Special Education Office
South Dakota Department of Education
700 Governors Drive
Pierre, SD 57501-2291
605-773-3678
Fax: 605-773-3782

Michelle Powers, Division Director

Tennessee

3164 Special Education
Tennessee Department of Education
710 John Robertson Parkway
6th Floor
Nashville, TN 37243
615-741-2851
Fax: 615-532-9412

Joe Fisher, Division Director

3165 Teaching and Learning
Tennessee Department of Education
710 James Robertson Parkway
5th Floor
Nashville, TN 37243
615-532-6195
Fax: 615-741-1837
E-mail: wprotoe@mail.state.tn.us
http://www.state.tn.us/education

Wilma Protoe, Assitant Commissioner

3166 Tennessee Department of Education
710 James Robertson Parkway
6th Floor
Nashville, TN 37243-0375
615-741-2731
Fax: 615-741-6236
E-mail: jwalters@mail.state.tn.us
http://www.state.tn.us/education

Lana Seivers, Commissioner

3167 Vocational Education
Tennessee Department of Education
710 John Robertson Parkway
4th Floor
Nashville, TN 37243-0383
615-532-2800
Fax: 615-532-8226

Ralph Barnett, Assistant Commissioner

Texas

3168 Accountability Reporting and Research
Texas Education Agency
1701 Congress Avenue
WBT Building Room 3-111
Austin, TX 78701-1494
512-475-3523
Fax: 512-475-0028
E-mail: ccloudt@tmail.tea.state.tx.us
http://www.tea.state.tx.us

Criss Cloudt, Associate Commissioner

3169 Chief Counsel
Texas Department of Education
1701 Congress Avenue
Austin, TX 78701-1402
512-463-9720
Fax: 512-463-9838

Kewin O'Hanlon, Division Director

3170 Continuing Education
Texas Education Agency
1701 Congress Avenue
Austin, TX 78701-1402
512-463-9322
Fax: 512-463-6782
E-mail: wtillian@tea.state.tx.us

Walter Tillian, Manager

3171 Curriculum Development & Textbooks
Texas Department of Education
1701 Congress Avenue
Austin, TX 78701-1402
512-463-9581
Fax: 512-463-8057

Ann Smisko, Division Director

3172 Curriculum, Assessment & Professional Development
Texas Department of Education
1701 Congress Avenue
Austin, TX 78701-1402
512-463-9328
Fax: 512-475-3640

Linda Cimusz, Division Director

3173 Curriculum, Assessment and Technology
Texas Department of Education
1701 Congress Avenue
Austin, TX 78701-1402
512-463-9087
Fax: 512-475-3667
E-mail: asmisko@tea.tetn.net

Ann Smisko, Associate Commissioner

3174 Education of Special Populations & Adults
Texas Department of Education
1701 Congress Avenue
Austin, TX 78701-1402
512-463-8992
Fax: 512-463-9176

Jay Cummings, Division Director

3175 Field Services
Texas Department of Education
1701 Congress Avenue
Austin, TX 78701-1402
512-463-9354
Fax: 512-463-9227

3176 Internal Operations
Texas Department of Education
1701 Congress Avenue
Austin, TX 78701-1402
512-463-9437
Fax: 512-475-4293

3177 Operations & School Support
Texas Department of Education
1701 Congress Avenue
Austin, TX 78701-1494
512-463-8994
Fax: 512-463-9227

Roberto Zamora, Division Director

3178 Permanent School Fund
Texas Department of Education
1701 Congress Avenue
Room 5-120
Austin, TX 78701-1402
512-463-9169
Fax: 512-463-9432

Carlos Resendez, Division Director

3179 Region 6: Education Department
1200 Main Tower
Dallas, TX 75202-4325
214-767-3626

3180 Texas Department of Education
1701 N Congress Avenue
William B Travis Building
Austin, TX 78701-1494
512-463-8985
Fax: 512-463-9008
http://www.sbec.state.tx.us

Dr.Shirley Neeley, Commissioner

Utah

3181 Applied Technology Education Services
Utah Department of Education
250 E 500 S
Salt Lake City, UT 84111-4200
801-538-7840
Fax: 801-538-7868
E-mail: rbrems@usoe.kiz.ut.us
http://www.usoe.k12.ut.us
State agency for career and technical education.

Rod Brems, Associate Superintendent
Leslee Andelean, Administrative Assistant

3182 Instructional Services Division
Utah Department of Education
250 E 500 S
Salt Lake City, UT 84111-3204
801-538-7515
Fax: 801-538-7768

Jerry P Peterson, Division Director

3183 Schools for the Deaf & Blind
Utah Department of Education
250 E 500 S
Salt Lake City, UT 84111-3204
801-629-4700
Fax: 801-629-4896

Wayne Glaus, Division Director

3184 Utah Office of Education
250 E 500 South
PO Box 144200
Salt Lake City, UT 84111
801-538-7510
Fax: 801-538-7768
http://www.usoe.k12.ut.us

Steven O Laing, Superintendent

3185 Utah Office of Education; Agency Services Division
250 E 500 S
PO Box 144200
Salt Lake City, UT 84114-4200
801-538-7500
Fax: 801-538-7768
http://www.usoe.k12.ut.us

Patrick Ogden, Associate Superintendent

Vermont

3186 Career & Lifelong Learning
Vermont Department of Education
120 State Street
Montpelier, VT 05620-0001
802-828-3101
Fax: 802-828-3146

Charles Stander, Division Director

3187 Core Services
Vermont Department of Education
120 State Street
Montpelier, VT 05620-0001
802-828-3135
Fax: 802-828-3140

Eleanor Perry, Division Director

3188 Family & School Support
Vermont Department of Education
120 State Street
Montpelier, VT 05620-0001
802-828-2447
Fax: 802-828-3140

Jo Busha, Division Director

3189 Financial Management Team
Vermont Department of Education
120 State Street
Montpelier, VT 05620-0001
802-828-3155
Fax: 802-828-3140

Mark O'Day, Division Director

3190 School Development & Information
Vermont Department of Education
120 State Street
Montpelier, VT 05620-0001
802-828-2756
Fax: 802-828-3140

Douglas Chiappetta, Division Director

3191 Teaching & Learning
Vermont Department of Education
120 State Street
Montpelier, VT 05620-0001
802-828-3111
Fax: 802-828-3140

Marguerite Meyer, Division Director

3192 Vermont Department of Education
120 State Street
Montpelier, VT 05620-2501
802-828-3135
Fax: 802-828-3140
http://Vermont.gov
For certification information visit
www.pen.k12.va.us or contact
804-225-2022.

Richard Cate, Commissioner

3193 Vermont Special Education
120 State Street
Montpelier, VT 05602-2703
802-828-3141

Theodore Riggen, Division Director

Virginia

3194 Administrative Services
Virginia Department of Education
14th & Franklin Streets
PO Box 2120
Richmond, VA 23216
804-225-3252
Fax: 804-786-5828

Edward W Carr, Division Director

3195 Policy, Assessment, Research & Information Systems
Virginia Department of Education
101 N 4th Street
PO Box 2120
Richmond, VA 23218-2120
804-225-2102
800-292-3820
Fax: 804-371-8978
E-mail: charris@pen.k12.va.us
http://www.pen.k12.va.us

Anne Wescott, Assistant Superintendent

3196 Student Services
Virginia Department of Education
14th & Franklin Streets
PO Box 2120
Richmond, VA 23216
804-225-2757
Fax: 804-786-5828

Dr.Cynthia Cave, Division Director

3197 Virginia Centers for Community Education
Virginia Department of Education
PO Box 2120
Richmond, VA 23218-2120
804-225-2293
Fax: 804-786-5828

Dr. Lenox L McLendon, Division Director

3198 Virginia Department of Education
James Monroe Building
101 N 14th Street
Richmond, VA 23219
804-225-2023
800-292-3820
Fax: 804-371-2099
E-mail: rlayman@pen.k12.va.us
http://www.pen.k12.va.us

Jo Lynne DeMary, Superintendent

Washington

3199 Region 10: Education Department
915 2nd Avenue
Room 3362
Seattle, WA 98174-1001
206-220-7800
Fax: 202-220-7806
http://www.ed.gov

3200 Washington Department of Education
PO Box 47200
Olympia, WA 98504-7200
360-725-6000
Fax: 360-753-6712
http://www.k12.wa.us

Theresa Bergeson, Superintendent

3201 Washington Department of Education; Instruction Program
PO Box 47200
Olympia, WA 98504-7200
206-753-1545
Fax: 360-586-0247

John Pearson, Division Director

3202 Washington Department of Education; Commission on Student Learning Administration
PO Box 47200
Olympia, WA 98504-7200
360-664-3155
Fax: 360-664-3028

Terry Bergeson, Division Director

3203 Washington Department of Education; Executive Services
PO Box 47200
Olympia, WA 98504-7200
360-586-9056
Fax: 360-753-6754

Ken Kanikeberg, Division Director

3204 Washington Department of Education; School Business & Administrative Services
PO Box 47200
Olympia, WA 98504-7200
206-753-6742

David Moberly, Division Director

West Virginia

3205 Division of Administrative Services
West Virginia Department of Education
1900 Kanawha Boulevard E
Building 6
Charleston, WV 25305-0009
304-558-2441
Fax: 304-558-8867

Carolyn Arrington, Division Director

3206 Research, Accountability & Professional
West Virginia Department of Education
1900 Kanawha Boulevard E
Building 6
Charleston, WV 25305-0009
304-558-3762
Fax: 304-558-8867

William J Luff Jr, Division Director

3207 Student Services & Instructional Services
West Virginia Department of Education
1900 Kanawha Boulevard E
Building 6
Charleston, WV 25305-0009
304-558-2691
Fax: 304-558-8867

Keith Smith, Division Director

3208 Technical & Adult Education Services
West Virginia Department of Education
1900 Kanawha Boulevard E
Building 6
Charleston, WV 25305-0009
304-558-2346
Fax: 304-558-8867

Adam Sponaugle, Division Director

3209 West Virginia Department of Education
1900 Kanawha Boulevard E
Building 6, Room B-358
Charleston, WV 25305-0330
304-558-2681
Fax: 304-558-0048
http://www.wvde.state.wv.us
The constitutional mission is to provide supervision of the K-12 education system.

David Stewart, Superintendent
Audrey Horne, President

Wisconsin

3210 Division for Learning Support: Equity & Advocacy
Wisconsin Department of Education
125 S Webster Street
PO Box 7841
Madison, WI 53707-7841

608-266-1649
Fax: 608-267-3746
http://www.dpi.state.wi.us
Carolyn Stanford-Taylor, Division Director

3211 Instructional Services Division
Wisconsin Department of Education
125 S Webster Street
PO Box 7841
Madison, WI 53707-7841
608-266-3361
Fax: 608-267-3746
http://www.dpi.state.wi.us
Pauline Nikolay, Division Director

3212 Library Services Division
Wisconsin Department of Education
125 S Webster Street
PO Box 7841
Madison, WI 53707-7841
608-266-2205
Fax: 608-267-3746
http://www.dpi.state.wi.us
William Wilson, Division Director

3213 School Financial Resources & Management
Wisconsin Department of Education
125 S Webster Street
PO Box 7841
Madison, WI 53707-7841
608-266-3851
Fax: 608-267-3746
http://www.dpi.state.wi.us
Bambi Statz, Division Director

3214 Wisconsin College System Technical
310 Price Place
PO Box 7874
Madison, WI 53707-7874
608-266-1770
Fax: 608-266-1285
E-mail: wtcsb@board.tec.wi.us
http://www.board.tec.wi.us
Richard Carpenter, President

3215 Wisconsin Department of Public Instruction
125 S Webster Street
PO Box 7841
Madison, WI 53707-7841
608-266-1771
800-441-4563
Fax: 608-266-5188
E-mail: statesuperintendent@dpi.wi.gov
http://www.dpi.wi.gov
Tony Evers, Superintendent
Mike Thompson, Deputy State Superintendent

Wyoming

3216 Accounting, Personnel & School Finance Unit
Wyoming Department of Education
2300 Capitol Avenue
Floor 2
Cheyenne, WY 82001-3644
307-777-6392
Fax: 307-777-6234
Barry Nimmo, Division Director

3217 Applied Data & Technology Unit
Wyoming Department of Education
2300 Capitol Avenue
Floor 2
Cheyenne, WY 82001-3644
307-777-6213
Fax: 307-777-6234
Steven King, Division Director

3218 Services for Individuals with Hearing Loss
Wyoming Department of Education
2300 Capitol Avenue
Floor 2
Cheyenne, WY 82001-3644
307-777-4686
Fax: 307-777-6234
Tim Sanger, Division Director

3219 Support Programs & Quality Results Division
Wyoming Department of Education
2300 Capitol Avenue
Floor 2
Cheyenne, WY 82001-3644
307-777-6213
Fax: 307-777-6234
Dr. Alan Sheinker, Division Director

3220 Wyoming Department of Education
2300 Capitol Avenue
Hathaway Building, 2nd Floor
Cheyenne, WY 82002-0050
307-777-7675
Fax: 307-777-6234
http://www.k12.wy.us
Dr.Trent Blankenship, Superintendent

Associations

3221 Agency for Instructional Technology
1800 N StoneLake Drive
Box A
Bloomington, IN 47402-0120
812-339-2203
800-457-4509
Fax: 812-333-4218
E-mail: info@ait.net
http://www.ait.net
AIT's mission is to be the premier provider of services and products to enhance student learning. A nonprofit organization and is one of the largest providers of instructional TV programs in North America.

Ruth Blankenbaker, Vice Chair
Chuck Wilson, Executive Director

3222 American Association for Higher Education & Accreditation
2020 Pennsylvania Avenue NW
#975
Washington, DC 20006
202-293-6440
Fax: 877-510-4240
E-mail: admin@aahea.org
http://www.aahea.org
The individual membership organization that promotes the changes higher education must make to ensure its effectiveness in a complex, interconnected world. The association equips individuals and institutions committed to such changes with the knowledge they need to bring those changes about.

Jose Luis Gomez, President

3223 American Association of Colleges for Teacher Education
1307 New York Avenue NW
Suite 300
Washington, DC 20005
202-293-2450
Fax: 202-457-8095
E-mail: aacte@aacte.org
http://www.aacte.org
A national alliance of educator preparation programs dedicated to the highest quality professional development of teachers and school leaders in order to enhance PK-12 student learning.

Sharon P Robinson, President/CEO
Sandy L Monroe, Executive Assistant

3224 American Educational Research Association
1430 K Street NW
Suite 1200
Washington, DC 20005
202-238-3200
Fax: 202-238-3250
E-mail: flevine@aera.net
http://www.aera.net
Supports improvement of the educational process through the encouragement of scholarly inquiry related to education, the dissemination of research results, and their practical application. Holds a conference and publishes books, videos, and magazines.

Kris D Gutierrez, President
Felice J Levine PhD, Executive Director

3225 American Educational Studies Association
Department of Education
235 Morton Hall
Huntsville, AL 35899
330-972-7111
http://www.educationalstudies.org
An international learned society for students, teachers, research scholars, and administrators who are interested in the foundations of education. A society primarily comprised of college and university professors who teach and research in the field of education utilizing one or more of the liberal arts disciplines of philosophy, history, politics, sociology, anthropology, or economics as well as comparative/international and cultural studies.

Audrey Thompson, President
Sofia Villenas, President-Elect/Prog Chair

3226 American Foundation for Negro Affairs
117 S 17th Street
Suite 1200
Philadelphia, PA 19103-5011
215-854-1470
Fax: 215-854-1487
Offers a model for educational programs preparing minority students for professional careers.

Samuel L Evans, President

3227 American Society for Training and Development Information Center
1640 King Street
Box 1443
Alexandria, VA 22313-1443
703-683-8100
800-628-2783
Fax: 703-683-8103
E-mail: customercare@astd.org
http://www.astd.org
Dedicated to workplace learning and performance professionals. Members come from more than 100 countries and connect locally in more than 130 U.S. chapters and with more than 30 international partners.

Tony Bingham, President/CEO

3228 Association of Teacher Educators
8503 Euclid Avenue
Suite 3
Manassas Park, VA 20111-2407
703-331-0911
Fax: 703-331-3666
E-mail: info@ate1.org
http://www.ate1.org
The mission of the Association of Teacher Educators is to improve the effectiveness of teacher education through leadership in the development of quality programs to prepare teachers, by analyzing issues and practices relating to professional development, and by providing opportunities for the personal and professional growth of Association members.

David A Ritchey PhD, Executive Director
Terrell Peace, President

3229 Center for Rural Studies
University of Vermont
206 Morrill Hall
146 University Place
Burlington, VT 05405
802-656-3021
Fax: 802-656-1423
E-mail: crs@uvm.edu
http://www.uvm.edu/crs
A nonprofit, fee-for-service research and resource center that works with people and communities to address social, economic, and resource-based challenges. CRS supports the research and teaching missions of the university through its work in applied research, community outreach, program evaluation, and consulting services.

Jane Kolodinsky, Director
Fred Schmidt, Founder/Director Emeritus

3230 Committee on Continuing Education for School Personnel
Kean College of New Jersey
Academic Services
Union, NJ 7083
908-737-5326
Fax: 908-737-5845
Develops activities for professional and personal growth among teachers and educators.

George Sisko, Director

3231 Council for Learning Disabilities
11184 Antioch Road
PO Box 405
Overland Park, KS 66210
913-491-1011
Fax: 913-491-1012
E-mail: CLDInfo@ie-events.com
http://www.cldinternational.org
An international organization that promotes evidence-based teaching, collaboration, research, leadership, and advocacy. Comprised of professionals who represent diverse disciplines and are committed to enhancing the education and quality of life for individuals with learning disabilities and others who experience challenges in learning.

Cari Dunn, President
Linda Nease, President-Elect

3232 Council of Administrators of Special Education
Osigian Office Centre
101 Katelyn Circle, Suite E
Warner Robins, GA 31088
478-333-6892
Fax: 478-333-2453
E-mail: lpurcell@casecec.org
http://www.casecec.org
An international professional educational organization which is affiliated with the Council for Exceptional Children (CEC) whose members are dedicated to the enhancement of the worth, dignity, potential, and uniqueness of each individual in society.

Dr Mary V Kealy, President
Luann Purcell, Executive Director

3233 Distance Education & Training Council
1601 18th Street NW
Suite 2
Washington, DC 20009
202-234-5100
Fax: 202-332-1386
E-mail: mike@detc.org
http://www.detc.org
A voluntary, non-governmental, educational organization that was founded to promote sound educational standards and ethical business practices within the correspondence field.

Michael P Lambert, Executive Director

3234 ERIC Clearinghouse on Teaching and Teacher Education
American Association of Colleges for Teacher Ed.
1307 New York Avenue NW
Suite 300
Washington, DC 20055-4701
202-293-2450
Fax: 202-457-8095
E-mail: aacte@aacte.org
http://www.aacte.org
To promote the learning of all PK-12 students through high-quality, evidence-based preparation and continuing education for all school personnel.

Mary Dilworth, Director
Deborah Newby, Associate Director

3235 Educational Leadership Institute
4455 Connecticut Avenue NW
Suite 310
Washington, DC 20008
202-822-8405
Fax: 202-872-4050
E-mail: iel@iel.org
http://www.iel.org
A non-profit, nonpartisan organization that envisions a society that uses its resources effectively to achieve better futures for all children and youth. IEL's mission continues to be to build the capacity of individuals and organizations in education and related fields to work together, across policies, programs and sectors.

Martin J Blank, President
Louise A Clark, Chief Administrative Officer

3236 International Council on Education for Teaching
National-Louis University
1000 Capitol Drive
Wheeling, IL 60090
847-947-5881
Fax: 847-947-5881
E-mail: contact@icet4u.org
http://icet4u.org
An international association of policy and decision-makers in education, government and business dedicated to global development through education. ICET provides programs and services that give its members access to a worldwide resource base of organizations, programs, specialized consultative services and research and training opportunities at the university level.

Darrell Bloom, President

3237 National Association of State Directors of Teacher Education & Certification
1225 Providence Road
PMB #116
Whitinsville, MA 01588
508-380-1202
Fax: 508-278-5342
E-mail: rje@nasdtec.com
http://www.nasdtec.org
The organization that represents professional standards boards and commissions and state departments of education in all 50 states, the District of Columbia, the Department of Defense Education Activity, the U.S. Territories, Alberta, British Columbia, and Ontario that are responsible for the preparation, licensure, and discipline of educational personnel.

Roy Einreinhofer, Executive Director

3238 National Center for Community Education
1017 Avon Street
Flint, MI 48503-2797
810-238-0463
800-811-1105
Fax: 810-238-9211
E-mail: info@nccenet.org
http://www.nccenet.org
It is the mission of the National Center for Community Education to promote community and educational change emphasizing community schools by providing state-of-the-art leadership development, training and technical assistance.

Maxine Murray, Operations Director
Marion Baldwin, Chief Administrator

3239 National Middle School Association
4151 Executive Parkway
Suite 300
Westerville, OH 43081
614-895-4730
800-528-6672
Fax: 614-895-4750

E-mail: info@nmsa.org
http://www.nmsa.org
NMSA has been a voice for those committed to the educational and developmental needs of young adolescents. NMSA is the only national education association dedicated exclusively to those in the middle level grades.

Joan Jarrett, President
Dr Drew Allbritten, Executive Director

3240 National Staff Development Council
504 S Locust Street
Oxford, OH 45056
513-523-6029
800-727-7288
Fax: 513-523-0638
E-mail: NSDCoffice@nsdc.org
http://www.nsdc.org
The largest non-profit professional association committed to ensuring success for all students through staff development and school improvement. The purpose of the NSDC is that every educator engages in effective professional learning every day so every student achieves.

Stephanie Hirsh, Executive Director
Carol Francois, Director of Learning

3241 National Women's Studies Association
7100 Baltimore Avenue
Suite 203
College Park, MD 20740
301-403-0407
Fax: 301-403-4137
E-mail: nwsaoffice@nwsa.org
http://www.nwsa.org
A professional organization dedicated to leading the field of women's studies and gender studies, as well as its teaching, learning, research and service wherever they be found.

Allison Kimmich, Executive Director
Bonnie Thornton Dill, President

3242 Recruiting New Teachers
385 Concord Avenue
Suite 103
Belmont, MA 2478-3037
617-489-6000
800-45 -EACH
Fax: 617-489-6005
E-mail: rnt@rnt.org
http://www.rnt.org/channels/clearinghouse
Conducts public service advertising campaign encouraging people to consider teaching careers.

Mildred Hudson, CEO

3243 Search Associates
PO Box 636
Dallas, PA 18612-636
570-696-4600
Fax: 570-696-9500
E-mail: SearchCentralHQ@cs.com
http://www.search-associates.com
Each year Search Associates places over 1,500 teachers, administrators and interns in international schools throughout the world, making us the largest of the International School placement organizations. However, it is our personalized approach to the schools and candidates we serve which we would most like to emphasize.

John Magagna, Founding Director

Awards & Honors

3244 Apple Education Grants
Apple Computer
2420 Ridge Point Drive
Austin, TX 78754

800-800-2775
Fax: 512-919-2992
http://www.apple.com
Awarded each year to teams of K-12 educators working on educational technology plans. Potential awardees find innovative uses of technology in the classroom and come from schools that would otherwise have limited access to technology.

3245 Bayer/NSF Award for Community Innovation
105 Terry Drive
Suite 120
Newtown, PA 18940
215-579-8590
800-291-6020
Fax: 215-579-8589
E-mail: success@edumedia.com
A community-based science and technology competition to give all sixth, seventh and eighth-graders a hands-on experience with real-world problems using the scientific method.

Stephanie Hallman, Program Manager
Stacey Gall, Competition Coordinator

3246 Excellence in Teaching Cabinet Grant
Curriculm Associates
PO Box 2001
North Billerica, MA 1862
800-225-0248
Fax: 800-366-1158
Awarded to educators who wish to implement unique educational projects. Potential awardees propose projects using a variety of teaching tools, including technology and print.

3247 Magna Awards
American School Board Journal
1680 Duke Street
Alexandria, VA 22314
703-838-6722
http://www.asbj.com
A national recognition program co-sponsored by American School Board Journal, the National School Boards Association, and Sodexo School Services that honors school board best practices and innovative programs that advance student learning.

3248 NSTA Fellow Award
National Science Teachers Association
1840 Wilson Boulevard
Arlington, VA 22201
703-243-7100
Fax: 703-243-7177
http://www.nsta.org
This award recognizes NSTA members who have made extraordinary contributions to science education through personal commitment to education, specifically science teaching or science; educational endeavors and original work that position recipients as exemplary leaders in their field; significant contributions to the profession that reflect dedication to NSTA as well the entire educational community.

Dr Alan J McCormack, President
Dr Francis Q Eberle, Executive Director

3249 NSTA Legacy Award
National Science Teachers Association
1840 Wilson Boulevard
Arlington, VA 22201
703-243-7100
Fax: 703-243-7177
http://www.nsta.org
This NSTA award posthumously recognizes long-standing members of NSTA for significant lifelong service to NSTA and contributions to science education.

Dr Alan J McCormack, President
Dr Francis Q Eberle, Executive Director

3250 National Teachers Hall of Fame
National Teachers Hall of Fame
1200 Commercial
Box 4017
Emporia, KS 66801
620-341-5660
800-968-3224
Fax: 620-341-5912
E-mail: hallfame@emporia.edu
http://www.nthf.org
The mission of The National Teachers Hall of Fame is to recognize and honor exceptional career teachers, encourage excellence in teaching, and preserve the rich heritage of the teaching profession in the United States.

Roberts T Jones, President
Dr Anne L Bryant, Executive Director

3251 Presidential Awards for Excellence in Mathematics and Science Teaching
National Science Foundation
4201 Wilson Boulevard
Arlington, VA 22230
703-292-8620
Fax: 703-292-9044
E-mail: msaul@nsf.gov
http://www.ehr.nsf.gov
This award is the nation's highest commendation for K-12 math and science teachers. Approximately 108 teachers are recognized annually with this prestigious award.

Mark Saul, Director

3252 Senior Researcher Award
Music Education Research Council
Deptartment of Music
138 Fine Arts Center
Columbia, MO 65211
573-884-1604
Fax: 573-884-7444
For recognition of a significant scholarly achievement maintained over a period of years.

3253 Toyota Tapestry Grants for Teachers
National Science Teachers Association
1840 Wilson Boulevard
Arlington, VA 22201
703-243-7100
Fax: 703-243-7177
http://www.nsta.org
Awards 50 grants of up to $10,000 each to K-12 teachers of science in the fields of environmental science education.

Dr Alan J McCormack, President
Dr Francis Q Eberle, Executive Director

Conferences

3254 AASA National Conference on Education
American Association of School Administrators
801 N Quincy Street
Suite 700
Arlington, VA 22203-1730
703-528-0700
Fax: 703-841-1543
E-mail: info@aasa.org
http://www.aasa.org
Where America's school leaders go for a vision of the future in public education; to explore new thinking, new products, new services and new technologies.

February

Daniel A Domenech, Executive Director
Christopher Daw, Meetings Director

3255 ACE Fellows Program
American Council on Education
One Dupont Circle NW
Washington, DC 20036-1193
202-939-9420
E-mail: fellows@ace.nche.edu
http://www.acenet.edu
The nation's premier higher education leadership development program in preparing senior leaders to serve American colleges and universities. Enables participants to immerse themselves in the culture, policies, and decision-making processes of another institution.

Sharon A McDade, Director
Brian Madden, Program Coordinator

3256 AFT Convention
American Federation of Teachers AFL-CIO
555 New Jersey Avenue NW
Washington, DC 20001
202-879-4400
E-mail: online@aft.org
http://www.aft.org
The AFT represents one million teachers, school support staff, higher education faculty and staff, health care professionals, and state and municipal employees. AFT is an affiliated international union of the AFL-CIO.

Randi Weingarten, President

3257 ASQ Annual Koalaty Kid Conference
ASQ
600 N Plankinton Avenue
Milwaukee, WI 53203
414-272-8575
800-248-1946
Fax: 414-272-1734
http://www.asq.org
A professional association headquartered in Milwaukee, Wisconsin, creates better workplaces and communities worldwide by advancing learning, quality improvement, and knowledge exchange.

April

Paul E Borawski, Executive Director/Chief Str
Peter L Andres, President-Elect

3258 Alaska Department of Education Bilingual & Bicultural Education Conference
University of Alaska, Conference & Special Events
117 Eielson Building
Fairbanks, AK 99775
907-474-7396
Stresses the importance of literacy and multicultural education for Alaskan educators.

February

3259 American Association of Collegiate Registrars & Admissions Officers
American Assoc of Collegiate Registrars/Admissions
1 Dupont Circle NW
Suite 520
Washington, DC 20036
202-293-9161
Fax: 202-872-8857
E-mail: meetings@aacrao.org
http://www.aacrao.org
Provides the opportunity to reflect on where the association has been, where it currently stands, and what we can do to lead our colleagues, our students, and our institutions into the future.

March

Jerome Sullivan, Executive Director
Melissa Ficek, Meeetings/Conferences

3260 American Society for Training & Development International Conference & Exposition
American Society for Training & Development
1640 King Street
Box 1443
Alexandria, VA 22313-1443
703-683-8100
Fax: 703-683-8103
E-mail: customercare@astd.org
http://www.astd.org
This premier event for workplace learning and performance professionals welcomes attendees from more than 70 countries. The conference features 200+ educational sessions from industry leading experts, and a world-class EXPO filled with the latest products and services available from top suppliers.

Annual/May

Tony Bingham, President/CEO

3261 Annual Building Championship Schools Conference
Center for Peak Performing Schools
2021 Clubhouse Drive
Greeley, CO 80634
970-339-9277
Interested in curriculum development and instructional assessment. Members include administrators at all levels of education.

February

3262 Annual New England Kindergarten Conference
Lesley University
29 Everett Street
Cambridge, MA 2138
617-349-8544
800-999-1959
Fax: 617-349-8125
E-mail: hr@lesley.edu
http://www.lesley.edu
Committed to active learning, scholarly research, critical inquiry, and diverse forms of artistic practice through close mentoring relationships among students, faculty, and practitioners in the field

November
1000 attendees

Mary Mindess, Conference Coordinator
Kari Nygaard, Conference Manager

3263 Annual State Convention of Association of Texas Professional Educators
Association of Texas Professional Educators
305 E Huntland Drive
Suite 300
Austin, TX 78752
800-777-2873
Fax: 512-467-2203
E-mail: meetings@atpe.org
http://www.atpe.org
A member-owned, member-governed professional association with more than 112,000 members leading educators' association in the state and the largest independent association for public school educators in the nation.

March
100 booths with 1,300 attendees

Doug Rogers, Executive Director
Andrea Davis, Meetings/Conferences

3264 Association for Educational Communications & Technology Annual Convention
Assoc for Educational Communications & Technology
1800 N Stonelake Drive, Suite 2
PO Box 2447
Bloomington, IN 47402-2447
812-335-7675
Fax: 812-335-7678
E-mail: aect@aect.org
http://www.aect.org
Provide leadership in educational communications and technology by linking a wide range of professionals holding a common interest in the use of educational technology and its application learning process.

November

Dr Phillip Harris, Executive Director

3265 Association for Library & Information Science Education Annual Conference
ALISE
65 E Wacker Place
Suite 1900
Chicago, IL 60601-7246
312-795-0996
Fax: 312-419-8950
E-mail: contact@alise.org
http://www.alise.org
Promotes excellence in education for library and information sciences as a means of increasing library services.

January

Kathleen Combs, Executive Director
Ewanya Clark, Executive Assistant

3266 Association of Teacher Educators Annual Meeting
Association of Teacher Educators
PO Box 793
Manassas, VA 20113
703-331-0911
Fax: 703-331-3666
E-mail: info@ate1.org
http://www.ate1.org

February

David A Ritchey, Executive Director
Terrell Peace, President

3267 CASE Annual Convention
Colorado Association of School Executives
4101 S Bannock Street
Englewood, CO 80110-4606
303-762-8762
Fax: 303-762-8697
E-mail: case@co-case.org
http://www.co-case.org

July

Bruce Caughey, Executive Director

3268 CCAE/COABE National Conference
California Council for Adult Education
19332 Peachtree Lane
Huntington Beach, CA 92648
626-825-9363
Fax: 714-960-8764
E-mail: sprantalos@socal.rr.com
http://www.ccaestate.org

April
1200 attendees

Steve Prantalos, Executive Director

3269 CSBA Education Conference & Trade Show
California School Boards Association
3100 Beacon Boulevard
West Sacramento, CA 95691
800-266-3382
Fax: 916-371-3407
E-mail: dfernandes@csba.org
http://www.csba.org
Premier continuing education program - delivering practical solutions to help governance teams from districts and county offices of education improve student learning and achievement.

Annual/December
200 booths

Deanna Fernandes, Conference Coordinator
Laura Bohannon, Exhibit Manager

3270 California Kindergarten Conference andPreConference Institute
California Kindergarten Association
1014 Chippendale Way
Roseville, CA 95661
916-780-5331
Fax: 916-780-5330
E-mail: cka@ckanet.org
http://www.ckanet.org
The original conference for teachers by teachers.

January
120 booths with 2,000 attendees and 100 exhibits

Laura Darcy, Conference Co-Chair
Meredith Yeh, Principal

3271 Careers Conference
University of Wisconsin-Madison
Center on Education & Work
1025 W Johnson Street, Room 964
Madison, WI 53706-1796
608-265-6700
800-862-1071
Fax: 608-262-3063
E-mail: cewconf@education.wisc.edu
http://www.cew.wisc.edu
Designed to serve everyone and anyone who is involved with career development, careers education, and related fields. This national conference presents learning opportunities at all levels, from a basic introduction for those starting out. to the very latest practices, strategies, and resources for those who are advanced in the field.

Annual/Januaray
40 booths with 1500 attendees

Carol Edds, Conference Manager

3272 Center for Play Therapy Fall Conference
University of North Texas
1400 Highland Street
Room 114
Denton, TX 76203-0829
940-565-3864
Fax: 940-565-4461
E-mail: cpt@unt.edu
http://cpt.unt.edu
Features a one day workshop led by a recognized authority in the field of play therapy. This workshop enables professionals in the field of mental health to broaden their knowledge and clinical skills in play therapy.

Annual/October
350 attendees

Sue Bratton, Director

3273 Central States Conference on the Teaching of Foreign Languages
Central States Conference on the Teaching
PO Box 251
Milwaukee, WI 53201-0251
414-405-4645
Fax: 414-276-4650
E-mail: csctfl@aol.com
http://www.csctfl.org
Includes approximately 140 workshops and sessions presented by world language teachers at all levels of instruction. Serves Arkansas, Colorado, Illinois, Indiana, Iowa, Kansas, Kentucky, Michigan, Minnesota, Missouri, Nebraska, North Dakota, Ohio, Oklahoma, South Dakota, Tennessee and Wisconsin.

Annual/March

Patrick T Raven, Executive Director

3274 Chicago Principals Association Education Conference
221 N Lasalle Street
Suite 3316
Chicago, IL 60601-1505
312-263-7767
Fax: 312-263-2012
Educational or fund raising products including copy machines, computers, book companies, etc.
February

Beverly Tunney, Conference Coordinator

3275 Classroom Connect
6277 Sea Harbor Drive
Orlando, FL 32887
800-638-1639
888-801-8299
Fax: 650-351-5300
E-mail: help@classroom.com
http://www.classroom.com
A leading provider of professional development programs and online instructional content for K-12 education.

October

Jim Bowler, President
Melinda Cook, Vice President Sales

3276 Florida Elementary School Principals Association Conference
206 S Monroe Street
Suite B
Tallahassee, FL 32301-1801
800-593-3626
Fax: 850-224-3892
Exhibitors from fundraisers to computer companies.
November
50 booths

Lisa Begue, Conference Coordinator

3277 Florida School Administrators Association Summer Conference
Florida Association of School Administrators
326 Williams Street
Tallahassee, FL 32303
850-224-3626
800-593-3626
Fax: 850-224-3892
http://www.fasa.net
Exhibits include computer software, textbooks and school supplies, fundraising companies, schoolyear book and ring companies, video and audio companies, furniture suppliers and other school related products.

Annual/July

Juhan Mixon, Executive Director

3278 Florida Vocational Association Conference
1420 N Paul Russell Road
Tallahassee, FL 32301-4835
850-878-6860
Fax: 850-878-5476
Curriculum materials, industrial equipment and supplies, computer hardware and software, medical equipment and other materials utilized by vocational educators.

July
150 booths

Donna Harper, Conference Coordinator

3279 Foundation for Critical Thinking AnnualConference
PO Box 196
Tomales, CA 94971
707-878-9100
800-833-3645
Fax: 707-878-9111
E-mail: cct@criticalthinking.org
http://www.criticalthinking.org
Provides a unique opportunity to improve understanding of critical thinking, as well as one's ability to foster it in the classroom and other aspects in work/life.

July-August
1200 attendees

Dr. Richard Paul, Fellow
Dr. Linda Elder, Fellow

3280 IASB Convention
Iowa Association of School Boards
6000 Grand Avenue
Des Moines, IA 50312-1417
515-288-1991
800-795-4272
Fax: 515-243-4992
http://www.ia-sb.org
IASB is an organization of elected school board members dedicated to assisting school boards in achieving their goal of excellence and equity in public education.

Annual/November

LouAnn Gvist, Convention Director
Veronica Stalker, Interim Executive Director

3281 IASB Joint Annual Conference
Illinois Association of School Boards
2921 Baker Drive
Springfield, IL 62703-5929
217-528-9688
http://www.iasb.com
Recognized as one of the nation's largest state education conferences, the event was open to local school board members, superintendents and secretaries, school administrators, state and regional educators and officials, school attorneys, university professors, exhibitors, and guests.

November
235 booths with 9500+ attendees

Dr Michael D Johnson, Executive Director Emeritus
Sandra Boston, Asst Director/Exhibit Mgr

3282 IASSIST Annual Conference
Int'l Assoc for Social Science Info Service & Tech
405 Hilgard Avenue
Attn: Wendy Treadwell
Los Angeles, CA 90095-9000
612-624-4389
Fax: 612-626-9353
E-mail: melanie@essex.ac.uk
http://www.iassistdata.org
IASSIST is an international organization of professionals working with information technology and data services to support research and teaching in the social sciences. Its 300 members work in a variety of settings, including data archives, statistical agencies, research centers, libraries, academic departments, government departments, and non-profit organizations.

May-June

Melanie Wright, President
William Block, Vice President

3283 ISBA/IAPSS Annual Conference
Indiana School Board Association
1 N Capitol Avenue
Suite 1215
Indianapolis, IN 46204-2225
317-639-0330
Fax: 317-639-3591
E-mail: mwagers@isba-ind.org
http://www.isba-ind.org
Jointy sponsored by the Indiana School Boards Association and Indiana Association of Public School Superintendents. A comprehensive program, designed by the ISBA and IAPPS, that brings the latest information and some of the most informed experts on current topics in education.

Fall

Dr Frank A Bush, Executive Director
Leanne R Waters, Conference Coordinator

3284 Illinois Assistant Principals Conference
Illinois Principals Association
2940 Baker Drive
Springfield, IL 62703
217-525-1383
Fax: 217-525-7264
E-mail: support@ilprincipals.org
http://www.ilprincipals.org
Where assistant principals and deans attend annually to hear outstanding educational leaders; participate in educational sessions and to network with colleagues across the state

Annual/February
120 booths with 200 attendees

Jason Leahy, Executive Director
Jean Smith, Professional Development Dir

3285 Illinois Principals Professional Conference
2990 Baker Drive
Springfield, IL 62703-2800
217-525-1383
Fax: 217-525-7264
http://http:ipa.vsat.net
Professional member association dedicated to the improvement of elementary and secondary education.

October
120 booths with 800 attendees

Julie Weichert, Associate Director
David Turner, Executive Director

3286 Illinois Resource Center Conference of Teachers of Linguistically Diverse Students
Illinois Resource Center
1855 S Mount Prospect Road
Des Plaines, IL 60018-1805
847-803-3112
Fax: 847-803-2828
A conference that caters to those educators involved with teaching multi-licensed pupils.

March

3287 Iowa Council Teachers of Math Conference
Iowa Council of Teachers of Mathematics
1712 55th Street
Des Moines, IA 50310-1548
515-242-7846
http://www.iowamath.org
Math teachers conference.

Annual/February
48 booths

Ruth Avazian, President

3288 Iowa Reading Association Conference
Iowa Reading Association
512 Lynn Avenue
Ames, IA 50014-7320
712-754-3636
E-mail: jneal@jefferson0scranton.k12.ia.us
http://www.iowareading.org
Nationally prominent speakers, published authors, and experienced instructors will anchor the conference, sharing current research and creative reading strategies.

Annual/April

Julie Neal, Conference Chair
Clark Goltz, Executive Director

3289 KSBA Annual Conference
Kentucky School Boards Association
260 Democrat Drive
Frankfort, KY 40601
800-372-2962
Fax: 502-695-5451
http://www.ksba.org

February

William G Scott, Executive Director

3290 Kansas School Boards Association Conference
1420 SW Arrowhead Road
Topeka, KS 66604-4001
785-273-3600
800-432-2471
Fax: 785-273-7580
E-mail: ahartzell@kasb.org
http://www.kasb.org
Wide variety of school district vendors and contacts for products and services.

December
70 booths

Pam Robinson, President
Rodney Roush, President-Elect

3291 Kentucky School Superintendents Association Meeting
152 Consumer Lane
Frankfort, KY 40601
502-875-3411
800-928-5272
Fax: 502-875-4634
E-mail: webmaster@kasa.org
http://www.kasa.org
KASA is dedicated to serving school administrators throughout Kentucky through advocacy, professional development, research and leadership.

June
36 booths

Dr. Roland Haun, Conference Contact
Wayne Young, Executive Director

3292 LSBA Convention
Louisiana School Boards Association
7912 Summa Avenue
Baton Rouge, LA 70809
225-769-3191
877-664-5722

Fax: 225-769-6108
http://www.lsba.com

Annual/March
Nolton Senegal, Executive Director

3293 Lilly Conference on College Teaching
Miami University
303 S Patterson Ave
Oxford, OH 45056
513-529-9266
Fax: 513-529-9984
E-mail: lillycon@muohio.edu
http://www.units.muohio.edu/lillycon
One of the nation's most renowned conferences presenting the scholarship of teaching and learning. Teacher-scholars from across the U.S. and internationally gather to share innovative pedagogies and discuss questions, challenges, and insights about teaching and learning.

Annual/November
660 attendees

Melody Barton, Administrative Associate
Milton Cox, Conference Director

3294 Lilly Conferences on College and University Teaching
International Alliance of Teacher Scholars
Box 1000
Claremnont, CA 91711
800-718-4287
Fax: 909-621-8270
E-mail: alliance@iats.com
http://lillyconferences.com/
Lilly Conferences are retreats that combine workshops, discussion sessions and major addresses, with opportunities for informal discussion about excellence in college and university teaching and learning. Internationally known scholars join new and experienced faculty members and administrators from all over the world.

November

Laurie Richlin, Director

3295 MASB Annual Fall Conference
Michigan Association of School Boards
1001 Centennial Way
Suite 400
Lansing, MI 48917-8249
517-327-5900
Fax: 517-327-0775
E-mail: info@masb.org
http://www.masb.org
The premier leadership event that features nationally acclaimed speakers addressing current education topics.

October
110 booths with 500 attendees and 110 exhibits
Kathy Hayes, Executive Director
Deborah Keys, Conference Director

3296 MESPA Spring Conference
Massachusetts Elementary School Principals Assoc
28 Lord Road
Suite 125
Marlborough, MA 01752
508-624-0500
Fax: 508-485-9965
E-mail: mespa@mespa.org
http://www.mespa.org
Features nationally-known speakers, numerous workshops on relevant topics, awards pre-

sentation, and an outstanding exhibition of school-related vendors.

Annual/May
100 booths

Nadya Aswad Higgins, Executive Director
Eileen Gallant, Exhibit Coordinator

3297 MNEA Fall Conference
Missouri National Education Association
1810 E Elm Street
Jefferson City, MO 65101
573-634-3202
Fax: 573-634-5646
E-mail: chris.guinther@mnea.org
http://www.mnea.org
Free and open to the public. Includes workshops, exhibits and features a keynote address presented by Diane Ravitch

Annual/November
95 booths with 1,500 attendees
Chris Guinther, President

3298 MSBA Annual Conference
Missouri School Boards Association
2100 I-70 Drive SW
Columbia, MO 65203
800-221-6722
Fax: 573-445-9981
E-mail: info@msbanet.org
http://www.msbanet.org

September/October
125 booths

Dr Carter Ward, Executive Director
Jaime Fessler, Conference/Events Manager

3299 Maine Principals Association Conference
50 Industrial Drive
PO Box 2468
Augusta, ME 4338-2468
207-622-0217
Fax: 207-622-1513
E-mail: mpa@mpa.cc
http://www.mpa.cc
To assure a quality education for all students, promote the principalship

April

Barbara Proko, Conference Contact
Mary Martin, President

3300 Massachusetts School Boards Association Meeting
90 Topsfield Road
Ipswich, MA 1938-1650
978-356-5453

May
100 booths

Capt. Edward Bryant, NCCC, Conference Contact

3301 Michigan Association of Elementary and Middle School Principals Conference
1405 S Harrison Road
Suite 210
East Lansing, MI 48823-5245
517-353-8770
Fax: 517-432-1063
Exhibits offer books, fundraisers, camps, insurance groups and non-profit organizations.

October
100 booths

William Hays, Jr, Conference Contact

3302 Michigan Science Teachers Association Annual Conference
Michigan Science Teachers Association
1390 Eisenhower Place
Ann Arbor, MI 48108
734-973-0433
Fax: 734-677-3287
http://www.msta-mich.org
A conference that aims to supply science teachers with information and research.

February

Robby Cramer, Executive Director
Paul Drummond, Conference Chair

3303 Mid-South Educational Research Association Annual Meeting
Louisiana State University, School of Dentistry
1100 Florida Avenue
#223
New Orleans, LA 70119-2714
504-619-8700
Fax: 504-619-8740
Focuses on assessment and involvement in education by releasing research and statistics.
November

Diana Gardiner PhD, Conference Contact

3304 Middle States Council for the Social Studies Annual Regional Conference
Rider College
2083 Lawrenceville Road
Lawrenceville, NJ 8648-3001
717-865-2117
Seeks to develop and implement new curriculum into the social studies area.
April

Dan Sidelnick, Conference Contact

3305 Minnesota Leadership Annual Conference
Minnesota School Boards Association
1900 W Jefferson Avenue
Saint Peter, MN 56082-3015
507-934-2450
800-324-4459
Fax: 507-931-1515
E-mail: gabbott@mnmsba.org
http://www.mnmsba.org
The purpose of the Association is to support, promote and enhance the work of public school boards

January
200+ booths with 2,000+ attendees
Kent Thiesse, President
Greg Abbott, MSBA Dir. of Communications

3306 Minnesota School Administrators Association
1884 Como Avenue
Saint Paul, MN 55108-2715
651-645-6272
Fax: 651-645-7518
E-mail: members@mnasa.org
http://www.mnasa.org
MASA's Educational Leaderswill establish the statewide agenda for children, serve as the preeminent voice for public education and empower members through quality services and support.

October
70 booths

Charles Kyte, Executive Director
Mia Urick, Director of Communications

3307 Minnesota School Boards Association Annual Meeting
1900 W Jefferson Street
Saint Peter, MN 56082-3014
507-931-2450
Fax: 507-931-1515
School supplies and services as diverse as buses and architectural services.

January
190 booths

Mike Torkelson, Conference Contact

3308 Missouri State Teachers Association Conference
PO Box 458
Columbia, MO 65205-458
573-442-3127
Fax: 573-443-5079
Educational materials.

November
280 booths

Kent King, Conference Contact

3309 Montana Association of Elementary School Principals Conference
1134 Butte Avenue
Helena, MT 59601-5178
406-442-2510
Fax: 406-442-2518
January/Febuary
20 booths

Loran Frazier, Conference Contact

3310 NAAEE Annual Conference
North American Assoc for Environmental Education
2000 P Street NW
Suite 540
Washington, DC 20036
202-419-0412
Fax: 202-419-0415
E-mail: communicator@naaee.org
http://www.naaee.org

October

Brian A Day, Executive Director
Bridget Chicholm, Conference Manager

3311 NCASA Annual Conference
North Carolina Association of School Administrator
PO Box 27711
Raleigh, NC 27611
919-828-1426
Fax: 919-828-6099
E-mail: info@ncasa.net
http://www.ncasa.net
Delivers a powerful agenda packed with essential training and sessions led by key education leaders and political insiders in the state and nation.

March-April
40 booths

Bill McNeal, Executive Director
Katherine Joyce, Assistant Executive Director

3312 NCTM Annual Meeting & Exposition
National Council of Teachers of Mathematics
1906 Association Drive
Reston, VA 20191-1502
703-620-9840
800-235-7566
Fax: 703-476-2970
E-mail: nctm@nctm.org
http://www.nctm.org

Covers topics like differentiated instruction, common core standards, intervention, technology and more

April
650 booths with 18M attendees

Michael J Shaughnessy, President
Kichoon Yang, Executive Director

3313 NELMS Annual Conference
New England League of Middle Schools
120 Water Street
Suite 403
North Andover, MA 01845
978-557-9311
Fax: 978-557-9312
E-mail: nelms@nelms.org
http://www.nelms.org

April
160+ booths with 3800+ attendees

Brenda Needham, Executive Director

3314 NMSA Annual Education Conference & Exhibit
National Middle School Association
4151 Executive Parkway
Suite 300
Westerville, OH 43016
614-895-4730
800-528-6678
Fax: 614-895-4750
E-mail: info@nmsa.org
http://www.nmsa.org
Provides information, tools, and encouragement necessary to provide a high-quality education for every young adolescent.

November

Dr Betty Greene Bryant, Interim Executive Director
Sally Ann DeBolt, Meetings/Events Manager

3315 NSBA Annual Confernce & Exposition
National School Boards Association
1680 Duke Street
Alexandria, VA 22314
703-838-6722
Fax: 703-683-7590
E-mail: conference@nsba.org
http://www.nsba.org
The largest national gathering of elected officials and offers an impressive collection of professional development opportunities for school board members and other education leaders. Offers a great opportunity to improve leadership skills and learn what is happening in public education.

April
550 booths

Dr Anne L Bryant, Executive Director
Robin Preston, Conference Management

3316 NSTA National Conference
National Science Teachers Association
1840 Wilson Boulevard
Arlington, VA 22201
703-312-9232
Fax: 703-243-7177
E-mail: conferences@nsta.org
http://www.nsta.org

March

Dr Alan J McCormack, President
Dr Francis Q Eberle, Executive Director

3317 NYSSBA Annual Convention & Expo
New York School Board Association
24 Century Hill Drive
Suite 200
Latham, NY 12210-2125
518-783-0200
Fax: 518-783-0211
E-mail: info@nyssba.org
http://www.nyssba.org
Join your fellow school board colleagues from all corners of the state for an unsurpassed opportunity to learn, network with peers, and hear about the latest products and services impacting education at this all-important event.

October

Kate Chauvin, Trade Show Manager

3318 National Association of Secondary School Principals Annual Convention and Exposition
1904 Association Drive
Reston, VA 20191-1537
703-860-0200
800-253-7746
Fax: 703-476-5432
E-mail: membership@principals.org
http://www.nassp.org
Offers workshops for principals on leadership training, student personnel services, and how to deal with at-risk students. Convention highlights include more than 200 educational sessions, special interest forums and luncheons and spotlights on the latest education products and services.

Phoenix
March
290 booths

Gayle Mercer, Conference Contact

3319 National Association of State Boards of Education Conference
National Association of State Boards of Education
2121 Crystal Drive
Suite 350
Arlington, VA 22202
703-684-4000
Fax: 703-836-2313
E-mail: boards@nasbe.org
http://www.nasbe.org
Aims are to study problems of mutual interest and concern, improve communication among state boards, and exchange and collect information concerning all aspects of education.

October
24 booths with 150 attendees

Doris Cruel, Conventions/Meetings Dir

3320 National Career Development Association Conference
National Career Development Association
305 N Beech Circle
Broken Arrow, OK 74012
918-663-7060
Fax: 918-663-7058
E-mail: webeditor@ncda.org
http://www.ncda.org

Deneen Pennington, Executive Director
Bobbi Carter, Convention/Education Dir

3321 National Conference on Education
American Association of School Administrators
801 N Quincy Street
Suite 700
Arlington, VA 22203-1730
703-528-0700
E-mail: info@aasa.org
http://www.aasa.org

Rich with content about the issues and challenges in public education. Take this opportunity to hear recognized speakers discuss solutions, beest practices, challenges and more.

Annual/February

Molly O'Neill, Meetings Manager

3322 National Conference on Standards and Assessment

National School Conference Institute
Riviera Hotel
Las Vegas, NV 89101
602-371-8655
Fax: 602-371-8790
http://www.nscinet.com
Two pre-conference workshops: The five most important things that educators need to know when using information for continuous program improvement, and The key to sustained leadership effectiveness. Conference will also hold over 60 breakout sessions.

April

Bill Daggett
Bob Marzano

3323 National Council for Geographic Education Annual Meeting

National Council for Geographic Education
1710 Sixteenth Street NW
Washington, DC 20009-3198
202-360-4237
Fax: 202-234-2744
http://www.ncge.org
Where geography educators from across the country and around the world meet to exchange ideas, research, resources, and best practices in geogrpahy education.

October
45 booths with 800 attendees

Jacqueline Waite, Program Manager

3324 National Council for History Education Conference

National Council for History Education
7100 Baltimore Avenue
Suite 510
College Park, MD 20740
440-835-1776
E-mail: nche@nche.net
http://www.nche.net
bring school and university people together to tackle all the issues that concern them—from curricular design, K to Ph.D., through state, local, and university standards and requirements, teacher education, certification, and professional development, to the implications of the assessment movement, of new technologies, and of school re-structuring.

March-April
750 attendees and 75 exhibits

Peter Seibert, Executive Director
John Csepegi, Conferences/Events Director

3325 National Council for Social Studies Annual Conference

National Council for the Social Studies
8555 Sixteenth Street
Suite 500
Silver Spring, MD 20910
301-588-1800
Fax: 301-588-2049
E-mail: sgriffin@ncss.org
http://www.socialstudies.org
Provides new ideas, resources, techniques, and skills that will pay off in the classroom, school, district, and invigorate your career. Features more than 400 sessions, workshops, poster presentations, clinics, tours, speakers and panels, and social events.

December

David Bailor, Meetings/Exhibits Director
Susan Griffin, Executive Director

3326 National Council of English Teachers Conference

National Council of Teachers of English
1111 W Kenyon Road
Urbana, IL 61801-1096
217-328-3870
800-369-6283
Fax: 217-328-9645
E-mail: public_info@ncte.org
http://www.ncte.org

Annual/November

Keith Gilyard, Program Chair

3327 National Council of Teachers of English Annual Convention

1111 W Kenyon Road
Urbana, IL 61801-1096
217-328-3870
800-369-6283
Fax: 217-328-9645
E-mail: public_info@ncte.org
http://www.ncte.org
The Council promotes the development of literacy, the use of language to construct personal and public worlds and to achieve full participation in society, through the learning and teaching of English and the related arts and sciences of language.

290+ booths

Lori Bianchini, Communications
Jacqui Joseph-Biddle, Convention Director

3328 National Council of Teachers of Mathematics Conference

1906 Association Drive
Reston, VA 20191-1502
703-620-9840
800-235-7566
Fax: 703-476-2970
E-mail: nctm@nctm.org
http://www.nctm.org
The National Council of Teachers of Mathematics is a public voice of mathematics education, providing vision, leadership and professional development to support teachers in ensuring equitable mathematics learning of the highest quality for all students.

January

Henry S Kepner, President
James M Rubillo, Executive Director

3329 National Education Association Annual Meeting

National Education Association (NEA)
1201 16th Street NW
Washington, DC 20036-3290
202-833-4000
Fax: 202-822-7974
E-mail: ncuea@nea.org
http://www.nea.org
A general conference that addresses all facets and concerns of the educator.

July

Gloria Durgin, Conference Contact
Dennis Van Roekel, President

3330 National Educational Computing Conference

Washington State Convention & Trade Center
Walter E Washington Convention Cent
Washington, DC 20001

800-336-5191
Fax: 206-694-5399
E-mail: neccinfo@iste.org
http://center.uoregon.edu/ISTE
NECC has been the premier forum in which to learn, exchange, and survey the field of educational technology.

June
417 booths with 12,500 attendees

Dr Heidi Rogers, First Executive Director
Trina Davis, President

3331 National Occupational Information Coordinating Committee Conference

2100 M Street NW
Suite 156
Washington, DC 20037-1207
202-653-7680
Focuses on policy, social issues and social services addressing career development and occupational information.

August

Mary Susan Vickers, Conference Contact

3332 New England Kindergarten Conference

Lesley University
29 Everett Street
Cambridge, MA 2138
617-349-8525
Fax: 617-349-8526
E-mail: info@lesley.edu
http://www.lesley.edu/kc
Lesley University is committed to active learning, scholarly research, critical inquiry, and diverse forms of artistic practice through close mentoring relationships among students, faculty, and practitioners in the field.

November
100 booths with 2000 attendees

Joseph B Moore, President
Nathaniel G Mays, Dean

3333 New Mexico School Boards AssociationConference

New Mexico School Boards Association
300 Galisteo Street
Suite 204
Santa Fe, NM 87501
505-983-5041
Fax: 505-983-2450
E-mail: nmsba1@nm.net
http://www.nmsba.org
The New Mexico School Boards Association aspires to be recognized as the premier source of development and support for local boards of education in New Mexico.

February
20 booths

Elizabeth Egelhoff, Programs Director

3334 New York School Superintendents Association Annual Meeting

111 Washington Avenue
Suite 404
Albany, NY 12210-2210
518-449-1063
Fax: 518-426-2229
Provides leadership and membership services through a professional organization of school superintendents.

October
50 booths

Dr. Claire Brown, Conference Contact

3335 New York Science Teachers Association Annual Meeting
2449 Union Boulevard
Apartment 20B
Islip, NY 11751-3117
516-783-5432
Fax: 516-783-5432
Education related publications, equipment, supplies and services.

November
110 booths

Harold Miller, Conference Contact

3336 New York State United Teachers Conference
159 Wolf Road
Albany, NY 12205-1106
518-213-6000
Fax: 518-213-6415
http://www.nysut.org

February
40 booths

Anthony Bifaro, Conference Contact

3337 New York Teachers Math Association Conference
92 Governor Drive
Scotia, NY 12302-4802
518-399-0149

October-November
50 booths

Phil Reynolds, Conference Contact

3338 North Carolina Association for Career andTechnical Education Conference
Association for Career and Technical Education
1410 King Street
Alexandria, VA 22314
703-683-3311
800-826-9972
Fax: 703-683-7424
http://www.acteonline.org

July
110 booths with 3000 + attendees

Gary Moore, President
Tom H Jones, Executive Director

3339 North Central Association Annual Meeting
North Central Association Commission on Accred.
Arizona State University
PO Box 874705
Tempe, AZ 85287-1008
866-837-2229
800-525-9517
Fax: 480-773-6901
E-mail: denz@ncacasi.org
http://www.ncacasi.org
Founded in 1895, NCA CASI accredits over 8,500 public and private schools in 19 states, the Navajo Nation, and the Department of Defense Schools. NCA CASI is an accreditation division of AdvancED.

April
30 booths with 1,800 attendees

Judy Catchpole, CEO
Jay Cummings, Dean, College of Education,

3340 North Central Conference on Summer SessionsConference
North Central Conference on Summer Sessions
University of Wisconsin
410 S 3rd Street
River Falls, WI 54022

715-425-3851
Fax: 715-425-3785
http://www.nccss.org
This conference attracts a wide variety range of attendees, from faculty, admissions personnel, registrars, business office and marketing representatives, and a wide variety of academic and student affairs administrators with responsibility for overseeing or direecting some aspect of their institution's summer session activities.

Annual/March

William V Weber, President
Robert Griggs, President-Elect

3341 Northeast Conference on the Teaching of Foreign Languages
Northeast Conference at Dickinson College
PO Box 1773
Carlisle, PA 17013-2896
717-245-1977
Fax: 717-245-1976
E-mail: nectfl@dickinson.edu
http://www.dickinson.edu
NECTFL aspires to serve the diverse community of language professionals through responsive leadership in its outreach activities and its annual conference.

April
160 booths with 2500 attendees

Rebecca Kline, Executive Director
Susan M Shaffer, Associate Executive Director

3342 Northeast Teachers Foreign Language Conference
St. Michael's College
29 Ethan Allen Avenue
Dupont Building
Colchester, VT 5446
802-654-2000
Fax: 802-654-2595
Foreign language textbooks, supplementary materials, audio equipment, computer software, travel abroad program materials and other related teaching aids and publications.

April
130 booths

Elizabeth L Holekamp, Conference Contact

3343 Northwest Association of Schools & Colleges Annual Meeting
1910 University Drive
Boise, ID 83725-1060
208-426-5727
Fax: 208-334-3228
http://www.boisestate.edu
The university offers more than 190 fields of interest. Undergraduate, graduate and technical programs are available in seven colleges: Arts and Sciences, Business and Economics, Education, Engineering, Graduate Studies, Health Sciences, and Social Sciences and Public Affairs. Students can also study abroad and participate in one of the largest internship programs in the Northwest.

December
120 attendees

Bob Kustra, President
Sona Andrews, Vice President for Academic

3344 Northwest Regional Educational Laboratory Conference
101 SW Main Street
Suite 500
Portland, OR 97204-3213
503-275-9500
800-547-6339

Fax: 503-275-0660
E-mail: info@nwrel.org
http://www.nwrel.org
The mission of the Northwest Regional Educational Laboratory (NWREL) is to improve learning by building capacity in schools, families, and communities through applied research and development

October/November

Jerry Colonna, Chairperson
Rob Larson, Vice Chairperson

3345 Ohio Business Teachers Association
Wright State University, Lake Campus
2350 Westbelt Drive
Colcumbus, OH 43228-2921
419-586-0337
Fax: 419-586-0368
E-mail: MCWhite@itt-tech.edu
http://www.obta-ohio.org
Promote among educators the desire to find better techniques and methods in an effort to improve instruction in the field of business so that the students are well prepared to take their place in the business world.

October
40 booths

Joy Dougherty, President
Mary Deloe, Treasurer

3346 Ohio Public School Employees Association Convention
6805 Oak Creek Drive
Columbus, OH 43229
614-890-4770
800-786-2773
Fax: 614-890-3540
http://www.oapse.org
Committed in developing the most effective programs in the labor movement today.

May
15 booths

Joseph P Rugola, Executive Director
JoAnn Johntony, State President

3347 Ohio Secondary School Administrators Association Conference
Ohio Association of Secondary School Administrator
8050 N High Street
Suite 180
Columbus, OH 43235-6484
614-430-8311
Fax: 614-430-8315
http://www.oassa.org
Offers school secretaries the opportunity to network with colleagues while gaining valuable information that will add to their performance. Current administrators, representatives from the business community, OASSA legal counsel, and fellow secretaries combine to update these valuable employees.

April
42 booths

James J Harbuck, Executive Director
JoAnne Rubsam, Conference Secretary

3348 Oklahoma School Boards Association & School Administrators Conference
2801 N Lincoln Boulevard
Suite 125
Oklahoma City, OK 73105-4223
405-528-3571
888-528-3571
Fax: 405-528-5695
http://www.ossba.org
The mission of the Oklahoma State School Boards Association shall be to offer services to safeguard,represent and improve public education.The Association shall represent the

interests of public school boards before the legislature; provide training programs for school board members; provide school system services; and provide to the individual school board members a variety of other services and information that will improve the quality of educational leadership for each school district in Okla

August
195 booths

Joann Yandell, Conference Contact
Beth Schieber, President

3349 Oregon School Boards Association Annual Convention
Oregon School Boards Association
1201 Court Street NE
Suite 400
Salem, OR 97301
503-588-2800
800-578-6722
Fax: 503-588-2813
E-mail: info@osba.org
http://www.osba.org
To improve student achievement through advocacy, leadership and services to Oregon public school boards.

November

Kevin McCann, Executive Director

3350 PDK International Conference
Int'l Honor and Professional Assoc in Education
PO Box 7888
Bloomington, IN 47407-7888
812-339-1156
800-766-1156
Fax: 812-339-0018
E-mail: plt@pdkintl.org
http://www.pilambda.org
Conference on Innovations in Teaching and Learning was selected because of its relevance to educators everywhere as new and effective educational practices continue to emerge. Includes interactive sessions, research presentations, and networking events.

Annual/February
400 attendees

Bill Bushaw, Executive Director

3351 PSBA School Board Secretaries and AffiliatesConference
Pennsylvania School Boards Association
PO Box 2042
Mechanicsburg, PA 17055
717-506-2450
Fax: 717-506-2451
http://www.psba.org
To promote excellence in school board governance through leadership, service and advocacy for public education.

October
140 booths

Thomas J Gentzel, Executive Director

3352 Pacific Northwest Council on Languages Annual Conference
5290 University of Oregon
Eugene, OR 97403
541-346-5699
Fax: 541-346-6303
E-mail: pncfl@uoregon.edu
http://www.pncfl.org
The Pacific Northwest Council for Languages unites, serves, and supports all world language educators in Alaska, Idaho, Montana, Oregon, Washington, and Wyoming.

April

Brenda Gaver, President
Greg Hopper-Moore, Executive Director

3353 Pennsylvania Council for the Social Studies Conference
Pennsylvania Council for the Social Studies
1212 Smallman Street
Senator John Heinz Regional Histiry Cnt
Pittsburgh, PA 15222-4200
717-238-8768
E-mail: JKEARNEY@CBSD.ORG
http://www.pcssonline.org
The PCSS promotes quality Social Studies education from kindergarten to higher learning by advocating the Social Studies at all levels of education in Pennsylvania.

October
50 booths with 500 attendees

David Trevaskis, President elect
Ken Kubistek, Executive Secretary

3354 Pennsylvania Science Teachers Association
Center for Science & Technology Education
PO Box 330
Shippenville, PA 16254-330
814-782-6301
http://www.pascience.org
Work towards the advancement, improvement, and coordination of science education in all areas of science at all educational levels.

December
70 booths

Keith Butler, President
Kathleen Conn, President-Elect

3355 Principals' Center Spring Institute Conference
Harvard Graduate School of Education
6 Appian Way
#336
Cambridge, MA 2138-3704
617-495-1825
Fax: 617-495-5900
Administrative professionals get together to discuss issues, policy and procedures.

April

Nindy Leroy, Conference Contact

3356 Restructuring Curriculum Conference
National School Conference Institute
PO Box 35099
Phoenix, AZ 85069-5099
602-674-8990
Presents research, studies, and new information relevant to curriculum development.

January

3357 SAI Annual Conference
School Administrators of Iowa
12199 Stratford Drive
Clive, IA 50325
515-267-1115
Fax: 515-267-1066
E-mail: dsmith@sai-iowa.org
http://www.sai-iowa.org

August

Dr Dan Smith, Executive Director

3358 SchoolTech Forum
Miller Freeman
600 Harrison Street
San Francisco, CA 94109

415-947-6657
Fax: 415-947-6015
National forum for educational technology professional development and exhibits, devoted to intensive instruction by today's leading practitioners, eye-opening special events, unparalleled networking opportunities, and exposure to products and services.

3359 South Carolina Library Association Conference
South Carolina Library Association
PO Box 1763
Columbia, SC 29202
803-252-1087
Fax: 803-252-0589
E-mail: scla@capconsc.com
http://www.scla.org

Annual/October
125 booths with 350 attendees

Adam Haigh, President
Donald Wood, Executive Secretary

3360 Southern Association Colleges & Schools
1866 Southern Lane
Decatur, GA 30033-4097
404-679-4500
Fax: 404-679-4556
http://www.sacs.org
Exhibits publications, data and word processing equipment, school photography, charter bus services and more.

December
50 booths with 3700 attendees

Dr. James Rogers, Chief Academic Officer

3361 Southern Early Childhood Annual Convention
Southern Early Childhood Association
PO Box 55930
Little Rock, AR 72215-5930
501-221-1648
800-305-7322
Fax: 501-227-5297
E-mail: info@southernearlychildhood.org
http://www.southernearlychildhood.org
Southern Early Childhood Association has brought together preschool, kindergarten, and primary teachers and administrators, caregivers, program directors, and individuals working with and for families, to promote quality care and education for young children.

January
2,500 attendees

Janie Humphries, President
Glenda Bean, Executive Director

3362 Superintendents Work Conference
Teachers College, Columbia University
525 W 120th Street
PO Box 7
New York, NY 10027-6696
212-678-3783
Fax: 212-678-3682
E-mail: TCSuper@columbia.edu
http://www.conference.tc.columbia.edu
Offers practicing school superintendents a unique opportunity for professional growth in stimulating surroundings.

July
60 attendees

Thomas Sobol, Conference Chair
Gibran Matdalany, Associate Chair

3363 TASA/TASB Convention
Texas Association of School Boards
PO Box 400
Austin, TX 78767-0400

512-467-0222
800-580-8272
Fax: 512-467-3554
E-mail: tasb@tasb.org
http://www.tasb.org
Offers school board members and school administrators the opportunity to earn almost 17 hours of continuing education credit, hear outstnading keynote speakers, explore a tradeshow with hundreds of exhibitors, and network with more than 6,000 public school officials.

September-October

James B Crow, Executive Director

3364 Teachers Association in Instruction Conference
150 W Market Street
Indianapolis, IN 46204-2806
317-634-1515
Exhibits a wide variety of teaching materials and information from Grades K-12.
October
150 booths

Barbara Stainbrook, Conference Contact

3365 Tennessee School Boards Association Conference
525 Brick Church Park Drive
Nashville, TN 37207-2884
615-815-3900
800-448-6465
Fax: 615-815-3911
E-mail: webadmin@tsba.net
http://www.tsba.net
The mission of the Tennessee School Boards Associationis to assisst school boards in effectively governing school districts.

November
60 booths with 1,000 attendees

Tammy Grissom, Executive Director
David Pickler, President

3366 Texas Middle School Association Conference
Texas Middle School Association
PO Box 152499
Austin, TX 78715-2499
512-462-1105
888-529-8672
Fax: 512-462-0991
E-mail: tmsa@austin.rr.com
http://www.tmsanet.org
To promote the implementation of student-centered programs and highly effective practices by providing vision, knowledge, and resources which meet the unique individual needs of adolescents in an ever-changing society.

February

Cecil Floyd, Executive Director

3367 Texas State Teachers Association
316 W 12th Street
Austin, TX 78701-1815
877-275-8782
Fax: 512-476-9555
http://www.tsta.org
The Texas State Teachers Association will unite, organize and empower public education advocates to shape public education in Texas thus providing a quality public school for every child
April
120 booths

Carla Bond, Conference Contact
Rita Haecker, President

3368 Training & Presentations
Chief Manufacturing, Inc.
8401 Eagle Creek Parkway
Savage, MN 55378-4839
612-894-6280
800-582-6480
Fax: 877-894-6918
E-mail: chief@chiefmfg.com
http://www.chiefmfg.com
Providing top quality mounting solutions for projectors, monitors, and flat panel TVs. Committed to responding to industry needs in Commercial, Residential and Workstation/IT markets, Chief is dedicated to producing solutions that packed with form, function, and flexibility
Chicago, Illinois
February

Kris Murray, Director Customer Service/Pr
Yvette Danz, Manager Customer Service

3369 UPCEA Annual Conference
University Professional/Continuing Education Assoc
One Dupont Circle
Suite 615
Washington, DC 20036
202-659-3130
Fax: 202-785-0374
E-mail: nkats@upcea.edu
http://www.ucea.edu
The largest single gathering of higher education professionals who develop, implement, and promote professional and continuing education and online learning in North America.

April
70 booths with 1,000 attendees

Robert Hansen, CEO/Executive Director
Natalia Kats, Conference Director

3370 USA Kansas Annual Convention
United School Administrators of Kansas
515 S Kansas Avenue
Suite 201
Topeka, KS 66603
785-232-6566
Fax: 785-232-9776
E-mail: usaoffice@usa-ks.org
http://www.usakansas.org
Offers quality professional development opportunities for education administrators and leaders. During the convention, administrators are able to participate in professional workshops or learning clusters.
180 booths

Cheryl Semmel, Executive Director

3371 VAIS Conference
Virginia Association of Independent Schools
6802 Paragon Place
Suite 525
Richmond, VA 23230
804-282-3592
Fax: 804-282-3596
E-mail: info@vais.org
http://www.vais.org
The Virginia Association of Independent Schools is a service organization that promotes educational, ethical and professional excellence. Through its school evaluation/accreditation program, attention to professional development and insistence on integrity, the Association safeguards the interests of its member schools.

November
1,500 attendees

Dr Sally K Boese, Executive Director

3372 Virginia ASCD Conference
Virginia ASCD
513 Half Mile Branch
Crozet, VA 22932
434-960-7732
E-mail: annetchison@earthlink.net
http://vaascd.org
Dedicated to advancing excellence in Teaching, Learning and Leadership.

December
30 booths with 600 attendees

Ann Etchison, Executive Director
Judy Lam, Administrative Coordinator

3373 Virginia Association of Elementary School Principals Conference
Virginia Assoc of Elementary School Principals
1805 Chantilly Street
Richmond, VA 23230
804-355-6791
Fax: 804-355-1196
E-mail: info@vaesp.org
http://www.vaesp.org
Nonprofit professional association advocating for public education and equal educational opportunities. Promotes leadership of school administrators, principal as educational leaders, and provides professional development opportunities.
50 booths with 300 attendees

James Baldwin, Interim Executive Director

3374 Virginia School Boards Association Conference
Virginia School Boards Association
200 Hansen Road
Charlottesville, VA 22911
434-295-8722
800-446-8722
Fax: 434-295-8785
http://www.vsba.org
A voluntary, self-supporting and nonpartisan organization that promotes quality education through its services for local school boards. Provides member boards with services, training, and advocacy so that they may exercise effective leadership in public school governance on behalf of public education for all the children of the Commonwealth.

Annual/November

Barbara J Coyle, Executive Director
Gina G Patterson, Assistant Executive Director

3375 Wisconsin Association of School Boards Annual Conference
Wisconsin Association of School Boards
122 W Washington Avenue
Suite 400
Madison, WI 53703
608-257-2622
Fax: 608-257-8386
E-mail: convention@wasb.org
http://www.wasb.org
The WASB provides background and support for elected school leaders as they do the difficult work of democracy: weighing and balancing the unique values of their communities.

January
370 booths with 3,000 attendees

John Ashley, Executive Director

3376 Wisconsin Association of School District Administrators Conference
Wisconsin Assoc of School District
Administrators
4797 Hayes Road
Suite 201
Madison, WI 53704
608-242-1090
Fax: 608-242-1290
E-mail: mturner@wasda.org
http://www.wasda.org
The premiere collaborative leadership association, serves superintendents by providing professional support and expanding their capacity to be effective, innovative leaders.

Annual/May
70 booths

Miles Turner, Executive Director
Nancy Lund, Executive Assistant

3377 Wisconsin School Administrators Association Conference
Association of Wisconsin School
Administrators
4797 Hayes Road
Suite 103
Madison, WI 53704
608-241-0300
Fax: 608-249-4973
E-mail: patricia@awsa.org
http://www.awsa.org
The Association of Wisconsin School Administrators exists to coordinate the collective interests and needs of school administrators and to enhance their professional growth and competency for the purpose of improving the quality of educational opportunities for the youth of Wisconsin

October
60 booths

Jim Lynch, Executive Director
Kelly Meyers, Associate Executive Director

Directories & Handbooks

3378 BBX Teacher Clearinghouse
175 Norwood Road
Silver Spring, MD 20905
301-628-9776
Fax: 301-879-8060
E-mail: CEO@BBXOnline.com
http://www.teachersclearinghouse.com
BBX's Teacher Clearinghouse is a comprehensive resume databank where elementary and secondary school teachers, administrators, and education majors can post their resumes at no charge for review by subscribing school districts. Subscribers are public and private schools with an interest in receiving applications from, and importantly, a commitment to hiring, members of the African American/Black communities.

J R Moore, Administrator

3379 Education Index
H.W. Wilson Company
950 University Avenue
Bronx, NY 10452-4224
718-588-8400
800-367-6770
Fax: 718-590-1617
E-mail: rsky@hwwilson.com
http://www.hwwilson.com
Contains more than 456,000 citations to articles, interviews, editorials and letters, reviews of books, educational films, and software for approximately 427 English-language periodicals, monographs and yearbooks in the field of education. Available electronically on the Web with index, abstracts and full text versions.

Monthly

Roseward Sky, Assistant
Manager/Marketing
Harold Regan, President

3380 Educational Administration Resource Centre Database
University of Alberta
Department of Chemistry
Edmonton, AB, Canada, T6 G 2G2
780-492-3254
Fax: 780-492-8231
Over 3,650 bibliographic descriptions of the Centre's collection of educational administration print and audiovisual materials.

Directories & Handbooks

3381 American Association of Colleges for Teacher Education-Directory
American Association of Colleges for
Teacher Ed.
1307 New York Avenue NW
Suite 300
Washington, DC 20005
202-293-2450
Fax: 202-457-8095
E-mail: aacte@aacte.org
http://www.aacte.org
Promote the learning of all PK-12 students through high-quality, evidence-based preparation and continuing education for all school personnel.

144 pages Annual
ISSN: 0516-9313

Sharon P Robinson, President/CEO
Jeannette Knight-Mills, Associate Director
Executive

3382 American Society for Training/Development-Training Video
American Society for Training &
Development
1640 King Street
Box 1443
Alexandria, VA 22313-1443
703-683-8100
800-628-2783
Fax: 703-683-8103
E-mail: customercare@astd.org
http://www.astd.org
Serves as the educational society for persons engaged in training and development of business, industry, education and government personnel.

Tony Bingham, President/CEO
Cindy Huggett, Chair

3383 Appropriate Inclusion and Paraprofessionals
National Education Association (NEA)
1201 16th Street NW
Washington, DC 20036-3207
202-822-7364
Fax: 202-822-7624
E-mail: ncuea@nea.org
http://www.nea.org
A book offering information on mainstreaming disabled students and the work of paraprofessionals in the education process.

10 pages

3384 Assessing Student Performance: Exploring thePurpose and Limits of Testing
Jossey-Bass/Pfeiffer
989 Market Street
San Francisco, CA 94103-1741
415-433-1740
Fax: 415-433-0499
E-mail: info@wiley.com
http://www.josseybass.com
Clarifies the limits of testing in an assessment system. Analyzes problematic practices in test design and formats that prevent students from explaining their answers by showing that assessment is more than testing and intellectual performance is more than right answers.

336 pages Softcover
ISBN: 0-7879-5047-5

3385 Association for Continuing Higher Education Directory
1700 Asp Avenue
Norman, OK 73072-6400
405-329-0249
800-807-2243
Fax: 405-325-7196
E-mail: admin@acheinc.org
http://www.acheinc.org
Dedicated to promoting lifelong learning and excellence in continuing higher education. Encourage professional development, research and exchange of information for its members and continuing higher education as a means of enhancing and improving society.

102 pages Annual/March
10 booths with 250 attendees

James P Pappas, Executive VP
Rick E Osborn, President

3386 Before the School Bell Rings
Phi Delta Kappa Educational Foundation
408 N Union Street
PO Box 789
Bloomington, IN 47402-789
812-339-1156
800-766-1156
Fax: 812-339-0018
http://www.pdkintl.org
Early childhood teachers and administrators, childcare providers and parents will enjoy and learn from this practical, insightful book.

84 pages Paperback
ISBN: 0-87367-476-6

Carol B Hillman, Author
George Kersey, Executive Director
Donovan R Walling, Editor, Special
Publications

3387 Beyond Tracking: Finding Success in Inclusive Schools
Phi Delta Kappa Educational Foundation
PO Box 789
Bloomington, IN 47402-789
812-339-1156
800-766-1156
Fax: 812-339-0018
http://www.pdkintl.org
Research data, practical ideas and reports from educators involved in untracking schools make this an authoritative and useful collection of important articles.

293 pages Hardcover
ISBN: 0-87367-470-7

Harbison Pool and Jane A Page, Author
George Kersey, Executive Director
Donovan R Walling, Dir
Publications/Research

3388 Book of Metaphors, Volume II
AEE and Kendall/Hunt Publishing Company
4050 Westmark Drive
Dubuque, IA 52004-1840

563-589-1000
800-228-0810
Fax: 800-772-9165
http://www.kendallhunt.com
A compilation of presentations designed to enhance learning for those participating in adventure-based programs. Practitioners share how they prepare experiences for presentations.

256 pages Paperback
ISBN: 0-7872-0306-8

AEE, Author
Karen Berger, Customer Service Assistant

3389 Brief Legal Guide for the Independent Teacher
441 Vine Street
Suite 505
Cincinnati, OH 45202-2811
Offering insights into the most common legal issues faced by independent music teachers.

28 pages

3390 Building Life Options: School-Community Collaborations
Academy for Educational Development
1255 23rd Street NW
Washington, DC 20037-1125
202-884-8800
Fax: 202-884-8400
A handbook for family life educators on how to prevent pregnancy in the middle grades.

3391 Closing the Achievement Gap
Master Teacher
Leadership Lane
PO Box 1207
Manhattan, KS 66505-1207
785-539-0555
800-669-9633
Fax: 800-669-1132
http://www.masterteacher.com
A complete step-by-step approach to building a system that narrows the gap between student potential and student performance— between success and failure.

162 pages
ISBN: 0-914607-73-1

Kristy Meeks, Author

3392 Coming Up Short? Practices of Teacher Educators Committed to Character
Character Education Partnership
1025 Connecticut Avenue NW
Suite 1011
Washington, DC 20036
202-296-7743
800-988-8081
Fax: 202-296-7779
E-mail: rsipos@character.org
http://www.character.org
Nonprofit, nonpartisan, nonsectarian coalition of organizations and individuals committed to fostering effective character education in our nation's K-12 schools.

Henry Huffman, Author
Rebecca Sipos, Director Communications
Joe Mazzola, Executive Director

3393 Competency-Based Framework for Professional Development of Certified Health Specialists
Nat'l Health Education Credentialing
Columbia University
Department of Health Education
New York, NY 10027
212-854-1754
Fax: 212-678-4048
Aims to help the health education profession provide the leadership necessary for improving health in a rapidly changing, culturally

pluralistic and technologically complex society. Provides universities, professional organizations, and accreditation a common basis of skills for the development, assessment, and improvement of professional preparation for health educators.

3394 Contracting Out: Strategies for Fighting Back
National Education Association (NEA)
1201 16th Street NW
Washington, DC 20036-3290
202-833-4000
Fax: 202-822-7974
E-mail: ncuea@nea.org
http://www.nea.org
The voice of education professionals. Advocate for education professionals

John I Wilson, Executive Director
Dennis Van Roekel, President

3395 Directory of Curriculum Materials Centers
Association of College & Research Libraries
PO Box 8013
Statesboro, GA 30460-5295
912-681-5528
Fax: 513-529-1719
E-mail: jbedell@gaous.edu
http://acrl.telusys.com
Listing of over 275 centers that have collections of curriculum materials to aid in elementary and secondary teaching preparation.

200 pages

Jackie Bedell, Supervisor
Ruth Miller, Supervisor

3396 Distance Learning Directory
Virginia A Ostendorf
PO Box 2896
Littleton, CO 80161-2896
303-797-3131
Fax: 303-797-3524
E-mail: ostendorf@vaostendorf.com
Comprehensive list of distance learning practitioners and vendors. Each listing includes names, addresses, e-mail, fax and phones, credits awarded, program content, peripherals and technologies used, class configurations and more. Includes a lists of vendors offering descriptions of distance learning products, services and programming.

308 pages Annual

Virginia A Ostendorf, President
Ronald Ostendorf, VP

3397 Ethical Issues in Experiential Education
AEE and Kendall/Hunt Publishing Company
4050 Westmark Drive
Dubuque, IA 52002-2624
319-589-1000
800-228-0810
Fax: 800-772-9165
http://www.kendallhunt.com
An examination of ethical issues in the field of adventure programming and experiential education. Topics include ethical theory, informed consent, sexual issues, student rights, environmental concerns and programming practices.

144 pages
ISBN: 0-7872-93083

Karen Berger, Customer Service Assistant

3398 Finishing Strong: Your Personal Mentoring & Planning Guide for the Last 60 Days of Teaching
Master Teacher
Leadership Lane
PO Box 1207
Manhattan, KS 66505-1207

785-539-0555
800-669-9633
Fax: 800-669-1132
In this book we've selected from the 32 years of The Master Teacher, the writings we know you would most like your teachers to have to support that last 60 days of the school year.

132 pages
ISBN: 1-58992-095-3

Robert L De Bruyn, Author

3399 How to Plan and Develop a Career Center
Center on Education and Work
1025 W Johnson Street
Room 964
Madison, WI 53706-1796
608-265-6700
800-446-0399
Fax: 608-262-9197
E-mail: cewmail@soemadison.wisc.edu
http://www.cew.wisc.edu
High school, postsecondary, adult, and virtual career centers-a comprehensive blueprint that covers all the bases.

3400 How to Raise Test Scores
Skylight Professional Development
1900 E Lake Avenue
Glenview, IL 60025
847-657-7450
800-348-4474
Fax: 847-486-3183
E-mail: info@skylightedu.com
http://www.skylightedu.com
Addresses the teaching and learning process at its most basic and important level-the classroom.

30 pages Softcover
ISBN: 1575171635

Robin Fogarty, Author

3401 Inclusion: The Next StepDVD
Master Teacher
Leadership Lane
PO Box 1207
Manhattan, KS 66505-1207
785-539-0555
800-669-9633
Fax: 800-669-1132
http://www.masterteacher.com
Offers practical help for regular classroom teachers and special education teachers in meeting the challenges of inclusion.

225 pages
ISBN: 0-914607-69-3

Wendy Dover, Author

3402 Law of Teacher Evaluation: A Self-Assestment Handbook
Phi Delta Kappa Educational Foundation
PO Box 789
Bloomington, IN 47402-789
812-339-1156
800-766-156
Fax: 812-339-0018
http://www.pdkintl.org
This handy guidebook provides a concise, authoritative overview of US state statutes, regulations and guidelines regarding the performance evaluation of educators.

51 pages Paperback
ISBN: 0-87367-488-X

Perry A. Zirkel, Author
DR Walling, Director Publications/Resear

3403 Learning for Life
1329 W Walnut Hill Lane
PO Box 152225
Irving, TX 75015-2225

972-580-2433
Fax: 972-580-2137
E-mail: janthony@lflmail.org
http://www.learning-for-life.org
Learning for Life is designed to support schools and other youth-serving organizations in their efforts toward preparing youth to successfully handle the complexities of today's society and to enhance their self-confidence, motivation, and self-worth.

John Anthony, National Director
William Taylor, Director of Criminal Justice

3404 Lesson Plans for the Substitue Teacher: Elementary Edition
Master Teacher
Po Box 1207
Manhattan, KS 66505-1207
785-539-0555
800-669-9633
Fax: 800-669-1132
http://www.masterteacher.com
Gives you more than 100 lessons developed and tested by teachers across the curriculum and at all grade levels.

145 pages
ISBN: 1-58992-107-0

Robert L DeBruyn, Author

3405 Libraries Unlimited
PO Box 1911
Santa Barbara, CA 93116-1911
800-368-6868
800-225-5800
Fax: 805-685-9685
E-mail: lu-books@lu.com
http://www.lu.com
Publisher of resource books written by educators for educators. The books offer innovative ideas, practical lessons, and classroom-tested activities in the areas of math, science, social studies, whole language literature and library connections.

Debby LaBoon, Manager of Authors/Workshops

3406 Life Skills Training
711 Westchester Avenue
White Plains, NY 10604
914-421-2525
800-293-4969
Fax: 914-421-2007
E-mail: lstinfo@nhpamail.com
http://www.LifeSkillsTraining.com
Botvin LifeSkills Training (LST) is a research-validated substance abuse prevention program proven to reduce the risks of alcohol, tobacco, drug abuse, and violence by targeting the major social and psychological factors that promote the initiation of substance use and other risky behaviors.

Gilbert J Botvin, Developer

3407 List of Regional, Professional & Specialized Accrediting Association
Educational Information Services
PO Box 662
Newton Lower Falls, MA 2162
617-964-4555
A list of those associations involved in accreditation for the education fields.

3408 MacMillan Guide to Correspondence Study
MacMillan Publishing Company
1633 Broadway
New York, NY 10019
212-512-2000
Fax: 800-835-3202

Listing of 175 colleges, accredited trade, technical and vocational schools that offer home study courses.

500 pages

3409 Middle Grades Education in an Era of Reform
Academy for Educational Development
1255 23rd Street NW
Washington, DC 20037-1125
202-884-8800
Fax: 202-884-8400
Reviews middle-grades educational reform policies and practices.

3410 Middle School Teachers Guide to FREE Curriculum Materials
Educators Progress Service
214 Center Street
Randolph, WI 53956-1408
920-326-3126
888-951-4469
Fax: 920-326-3127
E-mail: epsinc@centurytel.net
http://www.freeteachingaids.com
Lists and describes free supplementary teaching aids for the middle school and junior high level.

290 pages Annual
ISBN: 87708-401-7

Kathy Nehmer, President

3411 NASDTEC Knowledge Base
1225 Providence Road
PMB # 1116
Whitinsville, MA 1588-3267
508-380-1202
Fax: 508-278-5342
E-mail: rje@nasdtec.com
http://www.nasdtec.org
It is the organization that represents professional standards boards and commissions and state departments of education in all 50 states, the District of Columbia, the Department of Defense Education Activity, the U.S. Territories, Alberta, British Columbia, and Ontario that are responsible for the preparation, licensure, and discipline of educational personnel.

Annually
ISBN: 0-9708628-3-0

Roy Einreinhofer, Executive Director

3412 Orators & Philosophers: A History of the Idea of Liberal Education
College Board Publications
45 Columbus Avenue
New York, NY 10023-6917
212-713-8165
800-323-7155
Fax: 212-713-8143
http://www.collegeboard.org
A cogent study of the historical evolution of the idea of liberal education. Clearly and forcefully argued, the book portrays this evolution as a struggle between two contending points of view, one oratorical and the other philosophical.

308 pages

Bruce A Kimball, Author

3413 Parent Training Resources
PACER Center
8161 Normandale Boulevard
Bloomington, MN 55437
952-838-0190
800-537-2237
Fax: 952-838-0199
E-mail: pacer@pacer.org
http://www.pacer.org
A Minnesota nonprofit, tax-exempt organization that provides information, training, and

assistance to parents of children and young adults with all disabilities; physical, learning, cognitive, emotional, and health

130 pages

Paula F Goldberg, Executive Director
Mary Schrock, Chief Operating and Developm

3414 Personal Planner and Training Guide for the Paraprofessional
Master Teacher
Po Box 1207
Manhattan, KS 66505-1207
785-539-0555
800-669-9633
Fax: 800-669-1132
http://www.masterteacher.com
Includes numerous forms which allow each para to keep track of vital information he or she will need in working with specific teachers and their special students.

128 pages
ISBN: 0-914607-39-1

Wendy Dover, Author

3415 Practical Handbook for Assessing Learning Outcomes in Continuing Education
International Association for Continuing Education
Departmant #3087
Washington, DC 20042-1
202-463-2905
Fax: 202-463-8498
Innovative guide offers readers a series of steps to help select an assessment plan which will work for any organization.

3416 Principles of Good Practice in Continuing Education
International Association for Continuing Education
Department #3087
Washington, DC 20042-1
202-463-2905
Fax: 202-463-8498
Principles from many sources for the field of continuing education, placing a pervasive emphasis on learning outcomes for the individual learner.

3417 Professional Learning Communities at Work
National Educational Service
304 W Kirkwood Avenue
Suite 2
Bloomington, IN 47404-5132
812-336-7700
800-733-6786
Fax: 812-336-7790
E-mail: nes@nesonline.com
http://www.nesonline.com
This publication provides specific, practical, how-to information on the best practices in use in schools through the US and Canada for curriculum development, teacher preparation, school leadership, professional development programs, school-parent partnerships, assessment practices and much more.

3418 Programs for Preparing Individuals for Careers in Special Education
The Council for Exceptional Children
1920 Association Drive
Reston, VA 20191-1545
703-620-3660
800-232-7323
Fax: 703-264-1637
This directory offers over 600 colleges and universities with programs in special education. Information includes institution name, address, contact person, telephone, fax,

Internet, accreditation status, size of faculty, level of program, and areas of specialty.

256 pages

3419 Quality School Teacher
National Professional Resources
25 South Regent Street
Port Chester, NY 10573-8295
914-937-8897
800-453-7461
Fax: 914-937-9327
E-mail: info@nprinc.com
http://www.nprinc.com
Provides the specifics that classroom teachers are asking for as they begin the move to quality schools. It is written for educators who are trying to give up the old system of boss-managing, and to create classrooms that produce quality work.

144 pages
ISBN: 0060-952857

William Glasser, Author
Robert Hanson, President
Helene Hanson, VP

3420 Requirements for Certification of Teachers & Counselors
University of Chicago Press
5801 S Ellis Avenue
Floor 4
Chicago, IL 60637-5418
312-702-7700
800-621-2736
Fax: 800-621-8476
A list of state and local departments of education for requirements including teachers, counselors, librarians, and administrators for elementary and secondary schools.

256 pages Annual
ISBN: 0-226-42850-8

Elizabeth Kaye, Author
John Tryneski, Coordinating Education

3421 Research for Better Schools Publications
112 N Broad Street
Philadelphia, PA 19102-2471
215-568-6150
Fax: 215-568-7260
E-mail: info@rbs.org
http://www.rbs.org
RBS is a private, nonprofit educational organization funded primarily through grants and contracts from the U.S. Department of Education, the National Science Foundation, Mid-Atlantic state departments of education, institutions of higher education, foundations, and school districts.

Dr. Keith M Kershner, Executive Director
Rev. John F Bloh, President

3422 Resources for Teaching Middle School Science
National Academy Press
901 D Street SW
Suite 704B
Washington, DC 20024-403
202-633-2966
Fax: 202-287-7309
E-mail: shulers@si.edu
http://www.nsrconline.org
The NSRC is an intermediary organization that bridges research on how children learn with best practices for the classroom.

496 pages

National Science Resources Center, Author
Sally Goetz Shuler, Executive Director
Tanya Miller, Executive Assistant

3423 Restructuring in the Classroom: Teaching, Learning, and School Organization
Jossey-Bass/Pfeiffer
989 Market Street
San Francisco, CA 94103-1741
415-433-1740
Fax: 415-433-0499
http://www.josseybass.com
Teaching, learning and school organization.

288 pages Hardcover
ISBN: 0-7879-0239-X

Riched Elmore, Penelope Peterson & Sara McCarthey, Author

3424 Revolution Revisited: Effective Schools and Systemic Reform
Phi Delta Kappa Educational Foundation
408 N Union Street
Bloomington, IN 47405-3800
812-339-1156
800-766-1156
Fax: 812-339-0018
E-mail: customerservice@pdkintl.org
http://www.pdkintl.org
The authors examine the Effective Schools movement of the past quarter century as a school reform philosophy and renewal process for today and for the coming years.

132 pages Paperback
ISBN: 0-873674-83-9

BO Taylor and P Bullard, Author
Donovan R Walling, Director Publications/Resear
John Amato, President

3425 Seminar Information Service
250 El Camino Real
Suite 112
Tustin, CA 92780-4469
714-508-0340
877-736-4636
Fax: 714-734-8027
E-mail: info@seminarinformation.com
http://www.seminarinformation.com
In 1981, Catherine Bellizzi and Mona Piontkowski founded Seminar Information Service, Inc. (SIS). Their idea was to fill a void - thousands of seminars were taking place, but there wasn't any one central source to tell someone where and when they were being held.

1,000 pages Annual

Mona Pointkowski, Co-Founder
Catherine Bellizzi, Co-Founder

3426 Service-Learning and Character Education: One Plus One is More Than Two
Character Education Partnership
1025 Connecticut Avenue NW
Suite 1011
Washington, DC 20036
202-296-7743
800-988-8081
Fax: 202-296-7779
E-mail: jmazzola@character.org
http://www.character.org
Leading the nation in helping schools develop people of good character for a just and compassionate society.

Rebecca Sipos, Director Communications
Joe Mazzola, Executive Director

3427 Teacher Created Resources
Teacher Created Resources
6421 Industry Way
Westminster, CA 92683-3652
714-891-7895
800-662-4321
Fax: 714-892-0283

E-mail: custserv@teachercreated.com
http://www.teachercreated.com
We publish quality resource books at the early childhood, elementary, and middle school levels. Our books cover all aspects of the curriculum—language arts, social studies, math, science, technology, and the arts.

Ina Levin, Managing Editor
Karen Goldfluss, Managing Editor

3428 Teachers as Educators of Character: Are the Nations Schools of Education Coming Up Short?
Character Education Partnership
1025 Connecticut Avenue NW
Suite 1011
Washington, DC 20036
202-296-7743
800-988-8081
Fax: 202-296-7779
E-mail: rsipos@character.org
http://www.character.org
Leading the nation in helping schools develop people of good character for a just and compassionate society.

Henry Huffman, Author
Rebecca Sipos, Director Communications
Joseph W Mazzola, Executive Director

3429 Teachers as Leaders
Phi Delta Kappa Educational Foundation
PO Box 789
Bloomington, IN 47402-789
812-339-1156
800-766-1156
Fax: 812-339-0018
http://www.pdkintl.org
Examines teacher recruitment, retention, professional development and leadership. The central theme of these twenty essays is excellence in education and how to achieve it.

320 pages Hardcover
ISBN: 0-873674-68-5

Donovan R Walling, Author
Donovan R Walling, Director Publications/Resear

3430 Teachers in Publishing
Pike Publishing Company
221 Town Center W
Suite 112
Santa Maria, CA 93458-5083
Editorial, research, sales, consulting, in office positions or travel to learn teachers' needs and instruct new texts.

3431 Teaching About Islam & Muslims in the Public School Classroom
9300 Gardenia Avenue
#B3
Fountain Valley, CA 92708-2253
714-839-2929
Fax: 714-839-2714

117 pages
ISBN: 1-930109-008

Susan Douglas, Author
Shabbir Mansuri, Founding Director

3432 Teaching as the Learning Profession: Handbook of Policy and Practice
Jossey-Bass/Pfeiffer
989 Market Street
San Francisco, CA 94103-1741
415-433-1740
Fax: 415-433-0499
Provides the best essays about the status of teaching, and the contributing writers are among the best thinkers in education today.

426 pages Hardcover

Linda Darling-Hammond, Editor
Gary Sykes, Editor

195

3433 Teaching for Results
Master Teacher
Leadership Lane
PO Box 1207
Manhattan, KS 66505-1207
800-669-9633
Fax: 800-669-1132
http://www.masterteacher.com
An easy-to-implement powerful method for helping to ensure sucess in the classroom.

45 pages
ISBN: 1-58992-120-8

3434 Their Best Selves: Building Character Education and Service Learning Together
Character Education Partnership
1025 Connecticut Avenue NW
Suite 1011
Washington, DC 20036
202-296-7743
800-988-8081
Fax: 202-296-7779
http://www.character.org
Character Education Partnership (CEP) is one of the world's premier character education organizations. It is recognized as a leader in the field and a foremost advocate for developing young people of good character and civic virtue

Joseph Mazzola, Executive Director
David W Fisher, Chairman

3435 Theory of Experiential Education
AEE and Kendall/Hunt Publishing Company
4050 Westmark Drive
PO Box 1840
Dubuque, IA 52004-2624
319-589-1000
800-228-0810
Fax: 563-589-1253
http://www.kendallhunt.com
This groundbreaking resource looks at the theoretical foundations of experiential education from philosophical, historical, psychological, social and ethical perspectives.

496 pages
ISBN: 0-7872-0262-2
AEE, Author
Karen Berger, Customer Service Assistant

3436 Time to Teach, Time to Learn: Changing the Pace of School
Northeast Foundation for Children
39 Montague City Road
Greenfield, MA 1301
413-772-2066
800-360-6332
Fax: 413-774-1129
E-mail: info@responsiveclassroom.org
Giving students the chance to learn and their teachers the chance to teach.

322 pages Softcover
Chip Wood, Author

3437 Top Quality School Process (TQSP)
National School Services
390 Holbrook Drive
Wheeling, IL 60090-5812
847-541-2768
800-262-4511
Fax: 847-541-2553
A customized School Improvement Program that incorporates input from all stakeholders in the educational process to establish baseline data, implement a continuous process of school improvement, and select quality programs for professional development.

3438 US Department of Education: Office of Educational Research & Improvement
National Library of Education
555 New Jersey Avenue NW
Washington, DC 20001-2029
877-433-7827
800-424-1616
Fax: 202-401-0457
Offers a variety of publications for professional development. The list of sources includes statistical reports, topical reports and effective programs, schools and practices.

John Blake, Reference/Information
Nancy Cavanaugh, Collection Development

3439 Understanding and Relating To Parents Professionally
Master Teacher
Leadership Lane
PO Box 1207
Manhattan, KS 66505-1207
800-669-9633
Fax: 800-669-1132
http://www.masterteacher.com
From one man with a mission to over sixty employees and growing, The MASTER Teacher has developed and matured. We will continue to provide educators with cutting-edge professional development solutions as we advance into the future.

70 pages
ISBN: 0-914607-65-0

Robert L DeBruyn, Author

3440 Welcome to Teaching and our Schools
Master Teacher
Leadership Lane
PO Box 1207
Manhattan, KS 66505-1207
800-669-9633
800-669-9633
Fax: 800-669-1132
http://www.masterteacher.com
Sets the stage for teachers so that they can have an enthusiastic and successful year in the classroom.

50 pages
ISBN: 0-914607-49-9

Robert L DeBryon, Author

3441 World Exchange Program Directory
Center for U.N. Studies, GPO Box 2786
Ramna
Dacca 1000, Bangladesh
Offers listings, by geographical location, of exchange programs available to United States and abroad students. Listings include all contact information, schedules, fields and levels of study and bilingual information.

Biennial

3442 You Can Handle Them All
Master Teacher
Leadership Lane
PO Box 1207
Manhattan, KS 66505-1207
800-669-9633
Fax: 800-669-1132
http://www.masterteacher.com
Encyclopedia of student misbehaviors offering answers that work. one hundred seventeen student misbehaviors are covered.

320 pages
ISBN: 0-914607-04-9

Robert L DeBruyn, Author

3443 Your Personal Mentoring & Planning Guide for the First 60 Days of Teaching
Master Teacher
Leadership Lane
PO Box 1207
Manhattan, KS 66505-1207
800-669-9633
Fax: 800-669-1132
http://www.masterteacher.com
In this book we've selected from 32 years of The Master Teacher, the writings we know you would most like your teachers to have to support the first 60 days of the school year.

116 pages
ISBN: 1-58992-056-2

Periodicals

3444 AACTE Briefs
American Association of Colleges for Teacher Ed.
1307 New York Avenue NW
Suite 300
Washington, DC 20005-4701
202-293-2450
Fax: 202-457-8095
E-mail: aacte@aacte.org
http://www.aacte.org
To promote the learning of all PK-12 students through high-quality, evidence-based preparation.

4-12 pages Monthly
ISSN: 0731-602x

Kristin McCabe, Publications Specialist/Edit
Aimee J Hall, Meetings Coordinator

3445 ATEA Journal
American Technical Education Association
800 N 6th Street N
Wahpeton, ND 58076-2
701-671-2301
Fax: 701-671-2260
E-mail: betty.krump@ndscs.edu
http://www.ateaonline.org
To be recognized as the preeminent international organization dedicated to the professional growth and development of postsecondary educators and industrial trainers. Provide leadership in assessing the needs of targeted technology initiatives and providing an array of professional growth and development opportunities to meet or exceed the expectation of institutional and individual members.

32 pages Quarterly
ISSN: 0889-6488

Betty M Krump, Executive Director
Edward Mann, Editor

3446 Action in Teacher Education
University of Georgia, College of Education
427 Aderhold Hall
Athens, GA 30602
706-542-4238
Fax: 706-542-4277
http://www.ou.edu/action
The official publication of the Association of Teacher Educators, serving as a forum for the exchange of information and ideas related to the improvement of teacher education at all levels.

Quarterly
John J Chiodo, Editor
Laura Bolf-Beliveau, Editor

3447 American Educational Research Journal
Columbia University Teachers College
PO Box 51
New York, NY 10027-51
212-678-3498
Fax: 212-678-4048
http://aer.sagepub.com
Publishes research articles that explore the processes and outcomes of teaching, learning, and human development at all educational levels and in both formal and informal settings.
Quarterly
Lois Weis, Editor
Philip Altbach, Associate Editor

3448 American Educator
American Federation of Teachers
555 New Jersey Avenue NW
Washington, DC 20001-2029
202-879-4420
E-mail: amered@aft.org
http://www.aft.org/pubs-reports/american_educator/index.htm
Professional journal of the American Federation of Teachers, is a quarterly magazine published for classroom teachers and other education professionals from preschool through university
Quarterly
Elizabeth McPike, Editor
Mary Kearney, Advertising/Sales

3449 Arts Management in CommunityInstitutions: Summer Training
National Guild of Community Schools of the Arts
520 8th Avenue
Suite 302
New York, NY 10018
212-268-3337
Fax: 212-268-3995
E-mail: info@natguild.org
http://www.nationalguild.org
Advances high-quality, community arts education so all people may participate in the arts according to their interests and abilities. Support the creation and development of community arts education organizations by providing research and information resources, professional development and networking opportunities, advocacy, and high-profile leadership.
June
Jonathan Herman, Executive Director
Kenneth T Cole, Associate Director

3450 Balance Sheet
ITP South-Western Publishing
5101 Madison Road
Cincinnati, OH 45227-1427
513-271-8811
800-824-5179
Fax: 800-487-8488
Informational publication for high school accounting educators. Articles contain information about innovations in teaching accounting, producing an extensive line of educational texts and software for K-postsecondary markets.
2x Year
Larry Qualls, Editor
Carol Bross-McMahon, Coordinating Editor

3451 Better Teaching
The Parent Institute
PO Box 7474
Fairfax Station, VA 22039-7474
703-323-9170
Fax: 703-323-9173
http://www.parent-institute.com

Newsletter for teachers (grades 1-12) that offers tips and techniques to improve student learning.
Monthly
ISSN: 1061-1495
John Wherry, Publisher

3452 C/S Newsletter
Center for Instructional Services
Purdue University
W. Lafayette, IN 47907
317-494-9454
Contains descriptions of CIS services and articles about instructional techniques.
4 pages 7x Year
Vickie Lojek

3453 Curriculum Brief
International Technology Education Association
1914 Association Drive
Reston, VA 20191-1538
703-860-2100
Fax: 703-860-0353
Seeks to advance technological literacy through professional development activities and publications.
4x Year
Kendall Starkweather, Executive Director

3454 Education & Treatment of Children
Pressley Ridge School
PO Box 6295
Morgantown, WV 26506-3016
304-293-8400
Fax: 304-293-6585
E-mail: fdowney@wvu.edu
http://www.educationandtreatmentofchildren.net
A journal devoted to the dissemination of information concerning the development and improvement of services for children and youth. Its primary criterion for publication is that the material be of direct value to educators and other child care professionals in improving their teaching/training effectiveness. Various types of material are appropriate for publication including originial experimental research, experimental replications, adaptations of previously reported research and reviews.
Quarterly
Bernie Fabry, Managing Editor
Daniel E Hursh, Senior Editor

3455 Educational Placement Sources-US
Education Information Services/Instant Alert
PO Box 620662
Newton, MA 2462-662
617-433-0125
Lists 100 organizations in the United States that find positions for teachers, educational administrators, counselors and other professionals. Listings are classified by type, listed alphabetically and offers all contact information.
4 pages Annual
FB Viaux, President

3456 Exceptional Child Education Resources
The Council for Exceptional Children
1920 Association Drive
Reston, VA 20191-1545
703-620-3660
800-328-0272
Fax: 703-264-1637
E-mail: askeric@ericir.syr.edu
A quarterly abstract journal that helps teachers stay abreast of the book, nonprint media,

and journal literature in special and gifted education.
Quarterly
ISSN: 0160-4309

3457 Extensions - Newsletter of the High/Scope Curriculum
High/Scope Educational Research Foundation
600 N River Street
Ypsilanti, MI 48198-2898
734-485-2000
800-40P-RESS
Fax: 734-485-0704
E-mail: info@highscope.org
http://www.highscope.org
Teacher guide for users of the High/Scope curriculum. Articles on classroom strategies, training techniques, problem-solving ideas, and news from the field. Also includes updated training data.
8 pages BiMonthly
ISSN: 0892-5135
Sharon Adams-Taylor, Associate Executive Director
A Clay Shouse, Vice President

3458 Guild Notes Bi-Monthly Newswletter
National Guild of Community Schools of the Arts
520 8th Avenue
Suite 302, 3rd Floor
New York, NY 10018
212-268-3337
Fax: 212-268-3995
E-mail: info@natguild.org
http://www.nationalguild.org
Bi-Monthly
Noah Xifr, Director Membership/Operatio

3459 Infocus: A Newsletter of the University Continuing Education Association
University Continuing Education Association
1 Dupont Circle NW
Suite 615
Washington, DC 20036-1134
202-659-3130
Fax: 202-785-0374
E-mail: kjkohl@ucea.edu
http://www.ucea.edu
Reports on higher education activities, federal legislation and government agencies, innovative programming at institutions across the country; member institutions; trends in continuing and part-time education; resources; professional development opportunities within the field; and changes in member personnel.
12-20 pages Monthly
Roger Whitaker, President
Kay J Kohl, Executive Director/CEO

3460 Innovator
University of Michigan Association
4001 School of Education Building
Ann Arbor, MI 48104
734-764-0394
Fax: 734-763-6934
For professional educators and alumni of University of Michigan's School of Education.
20 pages Quarterly
Eric Warden, Contact

3461 International Journal of Instructional Media
Westwood Press
149 Goose Lane
Tolland, CT 6084-3822

860-875-5484
E-mail: PLSleeman@aol.com
http://www.adprima.com/ijim.htm
A professional journal directly responsive to the need for precise information on the application of media to your instructional and training needs.

Quarterly

Dr Phillip J Sleeman, Executive Editor
Dr Bruce R Ledford, Associate Editor

3462 Intervention in School and Clinic
Pro-Ed., Inc.
8700 Shoal Creek Boulevard
Austin, TX 78757-6897
512-451-3246
800-897-3202
Fax: 800-397-7633
E-mail: general@proedinc.com
http://www.proedinc.com
The hands-on how-to resource for teachers and clinicians working with students (especially LD and BD) for whom minor curiculum and environmental medications are ineffective.

64 pages 5x Year Magazine
ISSN: 1053-4512

Judith K Voress, Periodicals Director
Brenda Smith Myles, Editor

3463 Journal of Classroom Interaction
University of Houston-University Park
442 Farish Hall
University of Houston
Houston, TX 77204-5026
713-743-5919
Fax: 713-743-8664
E-mail: jci@bayou.uh.edu
http://cmcd.coe.uh.edu/coejci/index.htm
The Journal is a semi-annual publication devoted to empirical investigations and theoretical papers dealing with observation techniques, research on student and teacher behavior, and other issues relevant to the domain of classroom interaction.

Bi-Annually

Dr. Jerome Freiberg, Editor
Stacey Lamb, Assistant to the Editor

3464 Journal of Economic Education
Heldref Publications
1319 18th Street NW
Washington, DC 20036-1802
202-296-6267
800-365-9753
Fax: 202-296-5149
http://www.indiana.edu/~econed/index.html
The Journal of Economic Education offers original articles on innovations in and evaluations of teaching techniques, materials, and programs in economics

Quarterly

William E Becker, Executive Editor

3465 Journal of Experiential Education
Association for Experiental Education
3775 Iris Avenue
Suite 4
Boulder, CO 80301-2043
303-440-8844
866-522-8337
Fax: 303-440-9581
E-mail: webmaster@aee.org
http://www.aee.org
Association for Experiential Education develops and promotes experiential education. The association is committed to supporting professional development, theoretical ad-

vancement and the evaluation of experiential education worldwide.

64 pages 3x Year
ISSN: 1053-8259

Paul Limoges, CEO
Laurie Frank, President

3466 Journal on Excellence in College Teaching
Miami University
Miami University
Oxford, OH 45056
513-529-9265
Fax: 531-529-9264
E-mail: wentzegw@muohio.edu
http://celt.muohio.edu/ject
A peer-reviewed journal published by and for faculty at colleges and universities to increase student learning through effective teaching, interest in and enthusiasm for the profession of teaching, and communication among faculty about their classroom experiences. The Journal provides a scholarly forum for faculty to share proven, innovative pedagogies and thoughtful, inspirational insights about teaching.

Journal 3x/Yr
ISSN: 1052-4800

Gregg Wentzell, Author
Gregg Wentzell, Managing Editor
Milton Cox, Editor-in-Chief

3467 Journalism Education Association
Kansas State University
103 Kedzie Hall
Manhattan, KS 66506-1505
785-532-5532
866-532-5532
Fax: 785-532-5563
E-mail: jea@spub.ksu.edu
http://www.jea.org
Among JEA's 2,100 members are journalism teachers and publications advisers, media professionals, press associations, adviser organizations, libraries, yearbook companies, newspapers, radio stations and departments of journalism.

April & November
25-30 booths with 4700 attendees

Jack Kennedy, President
Bob Bair, Vice President

3468 NCRTL Special Report
National Center for Research on Teacher Education
Michigan State University
East Lansing, MI 48824
517-355-9302
E-mail: floden@msu.edu
http://www.ncrtb.msu.edu
Membership news and updates.

3469 NCSIE Inservice
National Council of States on Inservice Education
Syracuse University
402 Huntington Hall
Syracuse, NY 13244
315-443-1870
Fax: 315-443-9082
Professional development, staff development and inservice education.

20 pages Quarterly

James Collins

3470 On The Go! for the Educational OfficeProfessional
Master Teacher
Leadership Lane
PO Box 1207
Manhattan, KS 66505-1207

800-669-9633
Fax: 800-669-1132
http://www.masterteacher.com
Positive, practical, and successful insights and techniques to help you manage and work with your support staff.

1 pages Monthly Newsletter

Tracey H DeBruyn, Executive Editor

3471 On-The-Go For Educational Office Professionals
Master Teacher
Leadership Lane
PO Box 1207
Manhattan, KS 66505-1207
785-539-0555
800-669-9633
Fax: 800-669-1132
http://www.masterteacher.com
The publication that provides you with great articles to complete your in-house newsletters and newsletters to parents, without fear of copyright violations.

1 pages Monthly Newsletter

Erica Parkinson, Executive Editor

3472 Paraeducator's Guide to Instructional & Curricular Modifications
Master Teacher
Leadership Lane
PO Box 1207
Manhattan, KS 66505-1207
800-669-9633
Fax: 800-669-1132
http://www.masterteacher.com
An indispensible tool your paras can use to understand, plan for and carry out appropriate modification for students with all types of special needs.

100 pages
ISBN: 0-914607-88-X

Wendy Dover, Author

3473 Pennsylvania Education
Pennsylvania Department of Education
333 Market Street
Harrisburg, PA 17126-2210
717-783-6788
Fax: 717-783-8230
http://www.pde.state.pa.us
The mission of the Pennsylvania Department of Education is to assist the General Assembly, the Governor, the Secretary of Education and Pennsylvania educators in providing for the maintenance and support of a thorough and efficient system of education.

8-10 pages 8x Year

Gary Tuma, Press Secretary
Beth Boyer, Information Specialist

3474 Performance Improvement Journal
International Society for Performance
1400 Spring Street
Suite 260
Silver Spring, MD 20910-2753
301-587-8570
Fax: 301-587-8573
E-mail: info@ispi.org
http://www.ispi.org
To develop and recognize the proficiency of its members and advocate the use of Human Performance Technology.

48 pages Monthly
ISSN: 1090-8811

April Davis, Executive Director
Matthew T Peters, President

3475 Preventing School Failure
Heldref Publications
1319 Eighteenth Street, NW
Washington, DC 20036-1802

202-296-6267
800-365-9753
Fax: 202-296-5149
E-mail: psf@heldref.org
http://www.heldref.org
The journal for educators and parents seeking strategies to promote the success of students who have learning and behavior problems. It includes practical examples of programs and practices that help children and youth in schools, clinics, correctional institutions, and other settings. Articles are written by educators and concern teaching children with various kinds of special needs.

48 pages Quarterly
ISSN: 1045-988X

Mary O'Donnell, Managing Editor

3476 Prevention Researcher

Integrated Research
66 Club Road
Suite 370
Eugene, OR 97401
541-683-9278
800-929-2955
Fax: 541-683-2621
E-mail: orders@TPRonline.org
http://www.TPRonline.org
A quarterly journal that uses a straightforward and easy-to-read approach to present the most current research and developments in adolescent behavioral research. In addition to cutting-edge, evidence-based research it also examines exemplary prevention programs and strategies that can help youth workers see which of today's best practices are most successful.

24 pages Magazine/Quarterly
ISSN: 1086-4385

Steven Ungerleider PhD, Editor
Jasmine Hunter, Office Manager & Contributin

3477 Progressive Teacher

Progressive Publishing Company
2678 Henry Street
Augusta, GA 30904-4656
770-868-1691
Offers new information and updates for the improvement and development of higher education.

Quarterly
ISSN: 0033-0825

MS Adcock

3478 Retaining Great Teachers

Master Teacher
Leadership Lane
PO Box 1207
Manhattan, KS 66505-1207
800-669-9633
Fax: 800-669-1132
http://www.masterteacher.com
The Retaining Great Teachers Book is a systemic approach for attracting, mentoring, supporting, and retaining new and veteran teacher.

85 pages
ISBN: 1-58992-097-X

Michael J Lovett PhD, Author

3479 Rural Educator-Journal for Rural and Small Schools

National Rural Education Association
Colorado State University
Fort Collins, CO 80523-1588
970-491-6444
Fax: 970-491-1317
E-mail: presofc@lamar.colostate.edu
http://www.colostate.edu
Official journal of the NREA. A nationally recognized publication that features timely

and informative articles written by leading rural educators from all levels of education. All NREA members are encouraged to submit research articles and items of general information for publication.

40 pages Quarterly Magazine
ISSN: 0273-446X

Joseph T Newlin, Editor
Anthony A Frank, President

3480 TED Newsletter

The Council for Exceptional Children
1920 Association Drive
Reston, VA 20191-1545
703-620-3660
888-232-7733
Fax: 703-264-9494
Newsletter of the Teacher Education Division offering information about TED activities, upcoming events, current trends and practices, state and national legislation, recently published materials and practical information of interest to persons involved in the preparation and continuing professional development of effective professionals in special education and related service fields.

3x Year

Diana Hammitte, Co-Editor
Laurence O'Shea, Editor

3481 TESOL Journal: A Journal of Teaching and Classroom Research

Teachers of English to Speakers of Other Languages
1600 Cameron Street
Suite 300
Alexandria, VA 22314-2705
703-836-0774
Fax: 703-836-7864
E-mail: tescol@tesol.edu
http://www.tesol.edu
TESOL's mission is to develop the expertise of its members and others involved in teaching English to speakers of other languages to help them foster communication in diverse settings. The association advances standards for professional preparation and employment, continuing education, and student programs, produces programs, services, and products, and promotes advocacy to further the profession. TESOL has 91 affiliates worldwide.

50 pages Quarterly

Christian J Faltis, Editor
Marilyn Kupetz, Managing Editor

3482 Teacher Education Reports

Feistritzer Publishing
4401-A Connecticut Avenue NW
#212
Washington, DC 20008-2302
202-362-3444
Fax: 202-362-3493
Covers the field of teacher education for elementary and secondary schools, including pre-service preparation, in-service training and professional development, related federal programs, legislation and funding.

8 pages BiWeekly

David T Chester, Editor

3483 Teacher Education and Special Education

The Council for Exceptional Children
1920 Association Drive
Reston, VA 20191-1545
703-620-3660
Fax: 352-392-7159
Contains information on current research, exemplary practices, timely issues, legislation, book reviews, and new programs and materials relative to the preparation and continuing professional development of effective profes-

sionals in special education and related service fields.

Quarterly

Vivian Correa, Editor

3484 Teacher Magazine

6935 Arlington Road
Suite 100
Bethesda, MD 20814-5233
301-280-3100
800-346-1834
Fax: 301-280-3250
E-mail: webeditors@epe.org
http://www.edweek.org
Our primary mission is to help raise the level of awareness and understanding among professionals and the public of important issues in American education.

Anthony Rebora, Managing Editor
Elizabeth Rich, Online Editor

3485 Teacher's Guide to Classroom Management

Economics Press
12 Daniel Road
Fairfield, NJ 7004-2507
973-227-1224
Bulletins showing teachers how to solve problems and avoid problematic situations.

BiWeekly

Robert Guder

3486 Teachers in Touch

ISM Independent School Management
1316 N Union Street
Wilmington, DE 19806-2534
302-656-4944
800-955-4944
Fax: 302-656-0647
Faculty professional development publication with strategies for career satisfaction, good teaching practices and stress-reducing techniques. The forum for professional sharing for private-independent school educators.

4 pages 5x Year

Rozanne S Elliott, Publisher
Kelly Rawlings, Editor

3487 Teaching Education

University of South Carolina, College of Education
Wardlaw College
Room 231
Columbia, SC 29208-1
803-777-6301
Fax: 803-777-3068
Focuses on the actual profession of teaching and new methodology by which to learn.

2x Year

James T. Sears, PhD, Editor

3488 Teaching Exceptional Children

The Council for Exceptional Children
1920 Association Drive
Reston, VA 20191-1545
703-620-3660
800-232-7323
Fax: 703-264-1637
A practical classroom-oriented magazine that explores instructional methods, materials and techniques for working with children who have disabilities or who are gifted.

BiMonthly
ISSN: 0040-0599

H William Heller, Editor
Fred Spooner, Editor

3489 Techniques-Connecting Education and Careers
Association for Career and Technical Education
1410 King Street
Alexandria, VA 22314-2749
703-683-3111
800-826-9972
Fax: 703-683-7424
E-mail: sackley@acteonline.org
http://www.acteonline.org
To provide leadership in developing an educated, prepared, adaptable and competitive workforce.
Newsletter/Magazine
Peter Magnuson, Director of Programs/Communi
Jan Bray, Executive Director

3490 Technology Integration for Teachers
Master Teacher
Po Box 1207
Manhattan, KS 66505-1207
785-539-0555
800-669-9633
Fax: 800-669-1132
http://www.masterteacher.com
The publication that provides teachers with innovative strategies for integratinjg technology into the classroom.
Monthly Newsletter
Brad Roberts, Executive Editor

3491 The Board
Master Teacher
Po Box 1207
Manhattan, KS 66505-1207
785-539-0555
800-669-9633
Fax: 800-669-1132
http://www.masterteacher.com
A complete program of in-service training for school board members.
Robert DeBruyn, Executive Editor

3492 The Professor In The Classroom
Master Teacher
Leadership Lane
PO Box 1207
Manhattan, KS 66505-1207
785-539-0555
800-669-9633
Fax: 800-669-1132
http://www.masterteacher.com
From one man with a mission to over sixty employees and growing, The MASTER Teacher has developed and matured. We will continue to provide educators with cutting-edge professional development solutions as we advance into the future.
1 pages Semi-Monthly
Robert DeBruyn, Author

3493 Today's Catholic Teacher
2621 Dryden Road
Suite 300
Dayton, OH 45439
937-293-1415
800-523-4625
Fax: 937-293-1310
E-mail: service@peterli.com
http://www.catholicteacher.com
Today's Catholic Teacher magazine is written for you, a teacher in a Catholic school. Each issue is filled with information that will help you succeed in the classroom
72 pages Bimonthly
ISSN: 0040-8441
Mary C Noschang, Editor-in-chief
Peter Li, President/Publisher

3494 Training Research Journal: The Science and Practice of Training
Educational Technology Publications
700 Paliside Avenue
Englewood Cliffs, NJ 7632
Fax: 201-871-4009
Peer-reviewed publication, published once yearly by Educational Technology Publications, is now in its fourth volume. Provides a high-quality, peer-reviewed forum for theoretical and empirical work relevant to training.
Annually

Software, Hardware & Internet Resources

3495 Analog & Digital Peripherals
PO Box 499
Troy, OH 45373-3585
937-339-2241
800-758-1041
Fax: 937-339-0070
E-mail: info@adpi.com
Established in 1978 to provide OEM manufacturers and end users with practical solutions in data logging, storage, and retrieval as well as program loading and back-up.
Lyle Ellicott

3496 E-Z Grader Software
E-Z Grader Company
PO Box 23608
Chagrin Falls, OH 44023
800-432-4018
http://www.ezgrader.com
Electronic guidebook designed by teachers for teachers.

3497 K12jobs.Com
PO Box 210811
West Palm Beach, FL 33421
E-mail: beth@k12jobs.com
To provide schools with an efficient and cost-effective recruiting tool, providing service and opportunities to institutions and job seekers alike.
Also: K-12jobs.Com
Beth Jones, CSR & General Information

3498 KidsCare Childcare Management Software
770 Cochituate Road
Framingham, MA 1701-4672
508-875-3451
Sells software programs to education professionals involved in childcare to aid their development and understanding.

3499 Mental Edge
Learning ShortCuts
PO Box 382367
Germantown, TN 38183-2367
901-218-8163
Fax: 309-406-5358
E-mail: feedback@learningshortcuts.com
http://www.learningshortcuts.com
The Mental Edge is specifically designed to facilitate review and reinforcement. It is the quickest, easiest, and most thorough way to bring the things that have been learned back to mind in preparation for any testing scenario.

3500 The Center For The Future Of Teaching AndLearning
Center for the Future of Teaching & Learning
133 Mission Street
Suite 220
Santa Cruz, CA 95060
831-427-3628
Fax: 831-427-1612

E-mail: info@cftl.org
http://www.cftl.org
A not-for-profit organization dedicated to strengthening teacher development policy and practice.
Margaret Gaston, President/Executive Director
Harvey Hunt, Vice President

3501 www.aasa.org
American Association of School Administrators
801 N Quincy Street
Suite 700
Arlington, VA 22203-1730
703-528-0700
Fax: 703-841-1543
E-mail: info@aasa.org
http://www.aasa.org
Supports and develops effective school system leaders who are dedicated to the highest quality public education for all children.
Randall H Collins, President
Mark T Bielang, President-Elect

3502 www.classbuilder.Com
Class Builder

http://www.classbuilder.com
Free teachers toolbox! Grade book, Create tests, Reports, Lessons, Distance Learning Courseware, and more.
Internet Only Access
Edhelper.Com, Author

3503 www.ed.gov/free
Federal Resources for Educational Excellence
Teaching and learning resources from Federal Agencies

3504 www.eduverse.com
eduverse.com
Leading Internet e-Knowledge software developer building core technologies for powering international distance education.

3505 www.freeteachingaids.com
Free Teaching Aids.com
214 Center Street
Randolph, WI 53956
888-951-4469
http://www.freeteachingaids.com
Guides for finding free resources for teachers.

3506 www.gsn.org
Global Schoolhouse
132 N El Camino Real
Suitte 395
Encinitas, CA 92024
760-635-0001
Fax: 760-635-0003
E-mail: helper2009@globalschoolnet.org
http://www.gsn.org
Collaborative projects, communication tools and professional development.
Yvonne Marie Andres, President
John St. Clair, Vice President

3507 www.imagescape.com/helpweb/www/oneweb.html
An Overview of the World Wide Web
E-mail: help@imagescape.com
http://www.imagescape.com/helpweb/www/oneweb.html

3508 www.learningpage.com
1840 E River Road
Suite 320
Tucson, AZ 85718
E-mail: learningpage@learningpage.com
http://www.learningpage.com

LearningPage provides a huge collection of professionally produced instructional materials you can download and print.

3509 www.mmhschool.com
McGraw Hill School Division
220 E Danieldale Road
Desoto, TX 75115
800-442-9685
Fax: 972-228-1982
http://www.mhschool.com
Dedicated to educating children and to helping educational professionals by providing the highest quality materials and services.

John Predmore, Privacy Official

3510 www.nprinc.com
National Professional Resources
25 S Regent Street
Port Chester, NY 10573
800-453-7461
Fax: 914-937-9327
E-mail: service@nprinc.com
http://www.nprinc.com
Produces videos/DVDs and publishes books on the most significant and current topical areas in the educational arena. New to this product line are laminated reference guides that provide a succinct summary of the topic being addressed.

Angela Hanson, Director of Marketing

3511 www.onlinelearning.net
OnlineLearning.net
12975 Coral Tree Place
Los Angeles, CA 90066
800-784-8436
E-mail: customerservice@laureate-inc.com
http://www.onlinelearning.net
Source for teacher education online.

Susan Ko, Vice President

3512 www.pagestarworld.com
Pagestar
E-mail: orders@pagestarworld.com
http://www.scrase.com/pagestar
Software products that are specifically designed for teachers. Over 600 electronic forms that are commonly used by teachers for planning, administering, delivering and assessing student learning.

3513 www.pbs.org
PBS TeacherSource

http://www.pbs.org
Offers all Americans the opportunity to explore new ideas and new worlds through television and online content.

3514 www.pbs.org/uti/quicktips.html
QuickTips
On understanding and using the Internet, you'll find tips on navigating the Web.

3515 www.rhlschool.com
RHL School
E-mail: contact2@rhlschool.com
http://www.rhlschool.com
Free ready to use quality worksheets for teaching, reinforcement,and review.

3516 www.sanjuan.edu/select/structures.html
San Juan Select - Structures
A Web site that examines various ways to structure and facilitate student projects using Internet capabilities. Each suggestion is accompanied by a specific example of how that structure can be or is being used on the Internet.

3517 www.schoolrenaissance.com
School Renaissance Model
PO Box 8036
Wisconsin Rapids, WI 54495-8036
715-424-3636
800-338-4204
Fax: 715-424-4242
E-mail: answers@renlearn.com
http://www.renlearn.com
Advance technology for essential practice. Makes the practice component of reading, math, and writing curriculum more personalized and effective.

3518 www.teachingjobs.com
The Teachers Employment Network

http://
Leading resource for education employment.

3519 www.usajobs.opm.gov/b1c.htm
Overseas Employment Info- Teachers
US Office of Personnel Management

Covers eligibility, position categories and special requirements, application procedures, program information and entitlement, housing, living/working conditions, shipment of household goods, and complete application forms and guidance.

3520 www.webworkshops.com
Web Work Shops

http://www.webworkshops.com
A series of on-line courses, designed to prepare teachers to integrate both the Internet and classroom computer applications into daily lessons.

Training Materials

3521 At-Risk Students: Identification and Assistance Strategies
Center for the Study of Small/Rural Schools
555 E Constitution Street
Room 138
Norman, OK 73072-7820
405-325-1450
Fax: 405-325-7075
E-mail: jcsimmons@ou.edu
http://cssrs.ou.edu
The Center for the Study of Small/Rural Schools is a cooperative effort between the University of Oklahoma's Colleges of Education and Continuing Education. Endorsed by the National Rural Education Association as one of its five recognized rural education research

Video

Jan C Simmons, Program Director

3522 Character Education: Making a Difference
Character Education Partnership
1025 Connecticut Avenue NW
Suite 1011
Washington, DC 20036
202-296-7743
800-988-8081
Fax: 202-296-7779
http://www.character.org
Leading the nation in helping schools develop people of good character for a just and compassionate society.

Rebecca Sipos, Director Communications
Joseph W Mazzola, Executive Director

3523 Character Education: Restoring Respect & Responsibility in our Schools
Master Teacher
Po Box 1207
Manhattan, KS 66505-1207
785-539-0555
800-669-9633
Fax: 800-669-1132
http://www.masterteacher.com
Provides a comprehensive model for character education in our nations schools. Specific classroom stategies as well as school wide approaches are outlines in a clear and compelling fashion.

Thomas Lickona PhD, Author

3524 Cisco Educational Archives
University of North Carolina at Chapel Hill
170 W Tasman Drive
San Jose, CA 95134-3455
408-526-4000
800-553-6387
http://www.cisco.com/web/siteassets
Focus on business operations, product innovation and design, and customer solutions. We develop products with minimal environmental impact and extend our technology to reduce environmental footprints globally.

John T Chambers, Chairman / CEO
Frank Calderoni, Executive VP/CFO

3525 Classroom Teacher's Guide for Working withParaeducators Video Set
Master Teacher
Po Box 1207
Manhattan, KS 66505-1207
785-539-0555
800-669-9633
Fax: 800-669-1132
http://www.masterteacher.com
Covers a range of nuts-and-bolts topics including why the job duties of paras have changed so much over the years, what a classroom teacher needs to know to get started working effectively with a para. Useful tips for managing another adult, and how para factor into the planning process.

Wendy Dover, Author

3526 Clinical Play Therapy Videos: Child-Centered Developmental & Relationship Play Therapy
University of North Texas
PO BOX 310829
Denton, TX 76203-829
940-565-3864
Fax: 940-565-4461
E-mail: cpt@unt.edu
http://www.centerforplaytherapy.com
Encourage the unique development and emotional growth of children through the process of play therapy, a dynamic interpersonal relationship between a child and a therapist trained in play therapy procedures.

Garry Landreth PhD, Founder
Sue Bratton PhD, Director

3527 Conferencing with Students & Parents Video Series
Master Teacher
PO Box 1207
Manhattan, KS 66505-1207
800-669-9633
800-669-9633
Fax: 800-669-1132
http://www.masterteacher.com
Will help teachers turn both formal and informal conferences with students and parents into opportunities for student success.

Robert L DeBruyn, Author/Publisher

3528 Conflict Resolution Strategies in Schools
Center for the Study of Small/Rural Schools
555 E Constitution Street
Room 138
Norman, OK 73072-7820

405-325-1450
Fax: 405-325-7075
E-mail: jcsimmons@ou.edu
http://cssrs.ou.edu
Series IV

Video

Jan C Simmons, Director

3529 Conover Company
4 Brookwood Court
Appleton, WI 54914-8618
800-933-1933
Fax: 800-933-1943
E-mail: sales@conovercompany.com
http://www.conovercompany.com
Developing training programs for industry. Provide off-the-shelf as well as custom sales and marketing, training, presentation, and application programs that connect learning to the workplace

Rebecca Schmitz, Member

3530 Cooperative Learning Strategies
Center for the Study of Small/Rural Schools
555 E Constitution Street
Room 138
Norman, OK 73072-7820
405-325-1450
Fax: 405-325-7075
E-mail: jcsimmons@ou.edu
http://cssrs.ou.edu
Series I

Video

Jan C Simmons, Program Director

3531 Creating Schools of Character Video Series
Master Teacher
PO Box 1207
Manhattan, KS 66505-1207
785-539-0555
800-669-9633
Fax: 800-669-1132
http://www.masterteacher.com
Visit a Blue Ribbon School of excellence and hear staff and others discuss how to create or improve a whole school character education program.

ISBN: 0-914607-90-1

3532 Crisis Management in Schools
Center for the Study of Small/Rural Schools
555 E Constitution Street
Room 138
Norman, OK 73072-7820
405-325-1450
Fax: 405-325-7075
E-mail: jcsimmons@ou.edu
http://cssrs.ou.edu
Series IV

Video

Jan C Simmons, Director

3533 Critical Thinking Video Set
Master Teacher
PO Box 1207
Manhattan, KS 66505-1207
785-539-0555
800-669-9633
Fax: 800-669-1132
http://www.masterteacher.com
Will help teachers challange students to think in a new way. Research shows that when we engage students in critical and creative though, retention increases tremendously.

ISBN: 1-58992-079-1

3534 Curriculum Alignment: Improving Student Learning
Center for the Study of Small/Rural Schools
555 E Constitution Street
Room 138
Norman, OK 73072-7820
405-325-1450
Fax: 405-325-7075
E-mail: jcsimmons@ou.edu
http://cssrs.ou.edu
Series I

Video

Jan C Simmons, Director

3535 Datacad
20 Tower Lane
Avon, CT 6001
860-677-4004
800-394-2231
Fax: 860-677-2610
E-mail: info@datacad.com
http://www.datacad.com
DATACAD's product development, sales, and marketing activities are managed at the corporate headquarters in Avon, Connecticut

Mark F Madura, President/CEO
David A Giessleman, Senior Vice President and CT

3536 Discipline Techniques you can Master in a Minute Video Series
Master Teacher
Leadership Lane
PO Box 1207
Manhattan, KS 66505-1207
800-669-9633
Fax: 800-669-1132
http://www.masterteacher.com
he MASTER Teacher provides essential solutions to meet the professional development needs of educators at all levels-from the paraeducator to the superintendent. For over 30 years, we have provided practical strategies to inspire, enrich, and motivate educators.

ISBN: 1-58992-040-6

Robert L DeBruyn, Founder

3537 Educational Productions Inc
7101 Wisconsin Avenue
Suite 700
Bethesda, MD 20814
800-950-4949
800-950-4949
Fax: 301-634-0826
E-mail: custserv@edpro.com
http://www.edpro.com
To increase the skills and understanding of the adults who work with, teach and care for young children.

Linda Freedman, President
Rae Latham, Vice-President

3538 Eleven Principals of Effective CharacterEducation
Master Teacher
Leadership Lane
PO Box 1207
Manhattan, KS 66505-1207
800-669-9633
Fax: 800-669-1132
http://www.masterteacher.com
Takes you to schools in Maryland, New York, and Missouri, where quality character education programs are being implemented by skilled and resourceful staff.

ISBN: 1-887943-13-7

Thomas Lickona PhD, Author

3539 Eleven Principles of Effective CharacterEducation
Character Education Partnership
1025 Connecticut Avenue NW
Suite 1011
Washington, DC 20036
202-296-7743
800-988-8081
Fax: 202-296-7779
E-mail: jmazzola@character.org
http://www.character.org
Leading the nation in helping schools develop people of good character for a just and compassionate society.

Rebecca Sipos, Director Communications
Joseph W Mazzola, Executive Director

3540 Eye on Education
6 Depot Way West
Larchmont, NY 10538
888-299-5350
Fax: 914-833-0761
E-mail:
customer-service@eyeoneducation.com
http://www.eyeoneducation.com
Books on performance-based learning and assessment.

3541 Great Classroom Management SeriesDVD
Master Teacher
Leadership Lane
PO Box 1207
Manhattan, KS 66505-1207
800-669-9633
Fax: 800-669-1132
http://www.masterteacher.com
Effetive classroom management is getting more difficult everday. teachers face increasing demands and expectations in ebery aspect of their jobs.

ISBN: 0-914607-90-1

3542 Great Classroom Management Video SeriesVHS
Master Teacher
Leadership Lane
PO Box 1207
Manhattan, KS 66505-1207
800-669-9633
Fax: 800-669-1132
http://www.masterteacher.com
Effective classroom management is getting more difficult everyday. teachers face increasing demands and expectations in everyday. Teachers face increasing demands and expectations in every aspect of their jobs.

ISBN: 1-58992-121-6

3543 Handling Chronically Disruptive Students at Risk Video Series
Master Teacher
Leadership Lane
PO Box 1207
Manhattan, KS 66505-1207
800-669-9633
Fax: 800-669-1132
http://www.masterteacher.com
Implement and utlize a CARE couscil, develop and individual Action plan, strategies for enhancing individual action plan.

ISBN: 1-58992-031-7

3544 Hearlihy & Company
Po Box 1747
Pittaburg, KS 66762-1747
866-622-1003
Fax: 800-443-2260
E-mail: kbolte@hearlihy.com
http://www.hearlihy.com

Training and installation for schools purchasing modular labratories.

Kevin Bolte, Contact

3545 Improving Parent/Educator Relationships

Center for the Study of Small/Rural Schools
555 E Constitution Street
Room 138
Norman, OK 73072-7820
405-325-1450
Fax: 405-325-7075
E-mail: jcsimmons@ou.edu
http://cssrs.ou.edu
Series I

Video

Jan C Simmons, Director

3546 Improving Student Thinking in the Content Area

Center for the Study of Small/Rural Schools
555 E Constitution Street
Room 138
Norman, OK 73072-7820
405-325-1450
Fax: 405-325-7075
E-mail: jcsimmons@ou.edu
http://cssrs.ou.edu
Series II

Video

Jan C Simmons, Director

3547 Inclusion: The Next Step the Video Series

Master Teacher
Leadership Lane
PO Box 1207
Manhattan, KS 66505-1207
800-669-9633
Fax: 800-669-1132
http://www.masterteacher.com
Will help you propel your inclusion efforts to a new level of success giving you the necessary insights and stategies for building consensus; weighing your program, curriculum, and instructional options.

ISBN: 1-58992-012-0

Wendy Dover, Author

3548 Integrating Technology into the Curriculum Video Series

Master Teacher
Leadership Lane
PO Box 1207
Manhattan, KS 66505-1207
800-669-9633
Fax: 800-669-1132
http://www.masterteacher.com
Gives teachers the tools and strategies they need to make information technology work for then and for students while empowering then to teach the skills necessary for students to be productive in a technology driven world.

ISBN: 1-58992-007-Y

3549 International Clearinghouse for the Advancement of Science Teaching

University of Maryland
Benjamin Building
Room 226
College Park, MD 20742-1100
301-405-3161
Fax: 301-314-9055
Provides curriculum information about science and mathematics teaching.

Dr. David Lockard, Director

3550 Lesson Plans and Modifications for Inclusionand Collaborative Classrooms

Master Teacher
Leadership Lane
PO Box 1207
Manhattan, KS 66505-1207
800-669-9633
Fax: 800-669-1132
http://www.masterteacher.com
Discover specific strategies lesson plans and activity modifications to enhance learning for all students in the inclusive classroom.

ISBN: 1-58992-022-8

3551 Managing Students Without Coercion

Center for the Study of Small/Rural Schools
555 E Constitution Street
Room 138
Norman, OK 73072-7820
405-325-1450
Fax: 405-325-7075
E-mail: jcsimmons@ou.edu
http://cssrs.ou.edu
Series II

Video

Jan C Simmons, Director

3552 Mentoring Teachers to MasteryVideo Series

Master Teacher
Leadership Lane
PO Box 1207
Manhattan, KS 66505-1207
800-669-9633
Fax: 800-669-1132
http://www.masterteacher.com
The MASTER Teacher's e-learning solutions provide cost-effective, subscription-based systems that help meet educators' time demands and continuous learning needs.

ISBN: 1-58992-001-5

3553 Motivating Students in the Classroom VideoSeries

Master Teacher
Leadership Lane
PO Box 1207
Manhattan, KS 66505-1207
800-669-9633
Fax: 800-669-1132
http://www.masterteacher.com
The MASTER Teacher has developed and matured.We will continue to provide educators with cutting-edge professional development solutions as we advance into the future

ISBN: 1-58992-074-0

3554 Multicultural Education: Teaching to Diversity

Center for the Study of Small/Rural Schools
555 E Constitution Street
Room 138
Norman, OK 73072-7820
405-325-1450
Fax: 405-325-7075
E-mail: jcsimmons@ou.edu
http://cssrs.ou.edu
Series II

Video

Jan C Simmons, Director

3555 Outcome-Based Education: Making it Work

Center for the Study of Small/Rural Schools
555 E Constitution Street
Room 138
Norman, OK 73072-7820
405-325-1450
Fax: 405-325-7075

E-mail: jcsimmons@ou.edu
http://cssrs.ou.edu
Series III

Video

Jan C Simmons, Director

3556 Overview of Prevention: A Social Change Model

Center for the Study of Small/Rural Schools
555 E Constitution Street
Room 138
Norman, OK 73072-7820
405-325-1450
Fax: 405-325-7075
E-mail: jcsimmons@ou.edu
http://cssrs.ou.edu
Prevention Series

Video

Jan C Simmons, Director

3557 Quality School

Center for the Study of Small/Rural Schools
555 E Constitution Street
Room 138
Norman, OK 73072-7820
405-325-1450
Fax: 405-325-7075
E-mail: jcsimmons@ou.edu
http://cssrs.ou.edu
Series II

Video

Jan C Simmons, Director

3558 SAP Today

Performance Resource Press
1270 Rankin Drive
Suite F
Troy, MI 48083-2843
800-453-7733
Fax: 800-499-5718
Overview offers the basics of student assistance.

3559 School-Wide Strategies for Retaining GreatTeachers Video Series

Master Teacher
Leadership Lane
PO Box 1207
Manhattan, KS 66505-1207
800-669-9633
Fax: 800-669-1132
http://www.masterteacher.com
You will hear proven strategies for supporting new teachers through all those typical expirences that cansabatage their efforts and cause them to leave your district or even abandon teaching all together.

ISBN: 1-58992-098-8

3560 Site-Based Management

Center for the Study of Small/Rural Schools
555 E Constitution Street
Room 138
Norman, OK 73072-7820
405-325-1450
Fax: 405-325-7075
E-mail: jcsimmons@ou.edu
http://cssrs.ou.edu
Series III

Video

Jan C Simmons, Director

3561 Strategic Planning for Outcome-Based Education

Center for the Study of Small/Rural Schools
555 E Constitution Street
Room 138
Norman, OK 73072-7820
405-325-1450
Fax: 405-325-7075

E-mail: jcsimmons@ou.edu
http://cssrs.ou.edu
Series II

Video

Jan C Simmons, Director

3562 Strengthening the Family: An Overview of aHolistic Family Wellness Model
Center for the Study of Small/Rural Schools
555 E Constitution Street
Room 138
Norman, OK 73072-7820
405-325-1450
Fax: 405-325-7075
E-mail: jcsimmons@ou.edu
http://cssrs.ou.edu
Prevention Series

Video

Jan C Simmons, Director

3563 Students-at-Risk Video Series
Master Teacher
Leadership Lane
PO Box 1207
Manhattan, KS 66505-1207
800-669-9633
Fax: 800-669-1132
http://www.masterteacher.com
Gives you specific stategies for reaching those students who are giving up.

ISBN: 1-58992-060-0

Mildred Odom Bradley, Author

3564 Superintendent/School Board Relationships
Center for the Study of Small/Rural Schools
555 E Constitution Street
Room 138
Norman, OK 73072-7820
405-325-1450
Fax: 405-325-7075
E-mail: jcsimmons@ou.edu
http://cssrs.ou.edu
Series I

Video

Jan C Simmons, Director

3565 TQM: Implementing Quality Management in Your School
Center for the Study of Small/Rural Schools
555 E Constitution Street
Room 138
Norman, OK 73072-7820
405-325-1450
Fax: 405-325-7075
E-mail: jcsimmons@ou.edu
http://cssrs.ou.edu
Series III

Video

Jan C Simmons, Program Director

3566 Teachers as Heros
Center for the Study of Small/Rural Schools
555 E Constitution Street
Room 138
Norman, OK 73072-7820
405-325-1450
Fax: 405-325-7075
E-mail: jcsimmons@ou.edu
http://cssrs.ou.edu
Series IV

Video

Jan C Simmons, Director

3567 Teaching for Intelligent Behavior
Center for the Study of Small/Rural Schools
555 E Constitution Street
Room 138
Norman, OK 73072-7820
405-325-1450
Fax: 405-325-7075
E-mail: jcsimmons@ou.edu
http://cssrs.ou.edu
Series IV

Video

Jan C Simmons, Director

3568 The Master Teacher
Master Teacher
Leadership Lane
PO Box 1207
Manhattan, KS 66505-1207
800-669-9633
Fax: 800-669-1132
http://www.masterteacher.com
From one man with a mission to over sixty employees and growing, The MASTER Teacher has developed and matured. We will continue to provide educators with cutting-edge professional development solutions as we advance into the future.

2 pages Weekly

3569 Training Video Series for the Substitute Teacher
Master Teacher
Leadership Lane
PO Box 1207
Manhattan, KS 66505-1207
800-669-9633
Fax: 800-669-1132
http://www.masterteacher.com
From one man with a mission to over sixty employees and growing, The MASTER Teacher has developed and matured. We will continue to provide educators with cutting-edge professional development solutions as we advance into the future.

ISBN: 0-914607-95-2

3570 Voices in the Hall: High School Principals at Work
Phi Delta Kappa Educational Foundation
PO Box 789
408 N Union Street
Bloomington, IN 47405-3800
812-339-1156
800-766-1156
Fax: 812-339-0018
E-mail: customerservice@pdkintl.org
http://www.pdkintl.org
The mission of Phi Delta Kappa International is to promote high-quality education, in particular publicly supported education, as essential to the development and maintenance of a democratic way of life. This mission is accomplished through leadership, research, and service in education

William E Webster, Author
Donovan R Walling, Director
Publications/Resear
John Amato, President

3571 Wavelength
4753 N Broadway
Suite 808
Chicago, IL 60640
773-784-1012
877-528-47 2
Fax: 773-784-1079
E-mail: info@wavelengthinc.com
http://www.wavelengthinc.com
Wavelength offers a fresh perspective on the key challenges in education today. Our programs are founded on the tenet that humor heals and enlightens. Of course, we also real-

ized that by focusing our humor on education, we'd never run out of material

3572 You Can Handle Them All Discipline Video Series
Master Teacher
Leadership Lane
PO Box 1207
Manhattan, KS 66505-1207
800-669-9633
Fax: 800-669-1132
http://www.masterteacher.com
Based upon the best selling books You Can Handle Them All and BEfore you can Discipline by Robert L Debruyn. It contains the vital professional foundations that must underpin and solid philosophy of discipline.

ISBN: 1-58992-035-X

Robert L DeBruyn, Author

Workshops & Programs

3573 ACE Fellows Program
American Council on Education
1 Dupont Circle NW
Washington, DC 20036-1193
202-939-9300
Fax: 202-785-8056
E-mail: comments@ace.nche.edu
http://www.acenet.edu
Provides comprehensive leadership development for senior faculty and administrators of universities and colleges. Offers mentor-intern relationships programs. Special institutional grants available for candidates from community colleges, tribal colleges and private historical black universities and colleges.

Andrew K Benton, Chairman
Judy Genshaft, Vice Chair

3574 ART New England Summer Workshops
Massachusetts College of Art and De
621 Huntington Avenue
Boston, MA 2115-5801
617-879-7175
E-mail: Nancy.Mccarthy@massart.edu
http://massart.edu/ane
Offers painting, drawing, photography, jewelry making, sculpting, computer imaging and ceramics.

Nancy McCarthy, Administrator

3575 Annual Conductor's Institute of South Carolina
University of South Carolina
School of Music
Columbia, SC 29208
803-777-7500
Fax: 803-777-9774
E-mail: CI@mozart.sc.edu
http://www.conductorsinstitute.com
Since its inception, more than 600 conductors have traveled to Columbia to study with guest conductors and composers. Academic credit is available.

Donald Portnoy, Director

3576 Annual Summer Institute for Secondary Teachers
Rock and Roll Hall of Fame
E-mail: soehler@rockhall.org
http://www.rockhall.com/programs/institute.asp
The institute provides teachers with the knowledge and tools needed to bring popular music into the curriculum. The program in-

cludes a rock and roll history survey; guest speakers; discussions and workshops.

June
Susan Oehler, Education Programs Manager

3577 Ball State University
2000 W University Avenue
Muncie, IN 47306
765-289-1241
800-382-8540
E-mail: askus@bsu.edu
http://cms.bsu.edu
At Ball State, we're more than just educators-we're educational entrepreneurs. Combining top-flight talent with the top-notch resources Ball State has to offer, our students and faculty inject endless energy and creativity into what they teach and how they learn. The result-a university The Princeton Review calls one of the best in the Midwest.~

Jo Ann M Gora, President
Terry King, Provost and Vice President f

3578 Bryant and Stratton College
1259 Central Avenue
Albany, NY 12205-142
518-437-1802
Fax: 716-821-9343
E-mail: rpferrell@bryantstratton.edu
http://www.bryantstratton.edu
For 150 years, Bryant & Stratton College has been helping students develop meaningful career skills in a concise, contemporary and effective manner - providing graduates with the marketable job skills they need to succeed in an increasingly competitive marketplace

Bryant H Prentice, Chairman of the Board
David J Ament, Managing Partner

3579 Center for Educational Leadership Trinity University
Trinity University
One Trinity Place
San Antonio, TX 78212-7200
210-999-7207
Fax: 210-999-8164
E-mail: admissions@trinity.edu
http://www.carme.cs.trinity.edu/education/index.asp
Offers three Masters degree programs for Arts, Teaching, Psychology and School Administration. The school also offers summer institutes and training programs for educators and administrators. Also see information regarding the Master of Education: School Administration at http://carme.cs.trinity.edu/education/graduate/medschoolleadership.htm

Paul Kelleher, Chairman
Sonia L Mireles, Senior Secretary

3580 Center for Global Education
Augsbury College
2211 Riverside Avenue
Minneapolis, MN 55454-1350
612-330-1159
800-299-8889
Fax: 612-330-1695
E-mail: globaled@augsburg.edu
http://www.augsburg.edu/global
To provide cross-cultural educational opportunities in order to foster critical analysis of local and global conditions so that personal and systemic change takes place leading to a more just and sustainable world.

Orval Gingerich, Associate Dean
Regina McGoff, Associate Director

3581 Center for Image Processing in Education
PO Box 13750
Tucson, AZ 85732-3750
520-322-0118
800-322-9884
Fax: 520-327-0175
E-mail: kRISR@evisual.org
http://www.cipe.com
CIPE promotes computer-aided visualization as a tool for inquiry-based learning. In support of that mission, it develops instructional materials and conducts workshops that use digital image analysis and geographic information systems technologies as platforms for teaching about science, mathematics, and technology.

Steve Moore, Chief Executive Director
Kristine Rees, Secretary/Treasurer

3582 Center for Learning Connections
Highline Community College
PO Box 98000
Des Moines, WA 98198-9800
206-870-3759
Fax: 206-870-5915
E-mail: jjacob@highline.edu
http://www.learningconnections.org
The mission of the Center for Learning Connections is to prepare learners to manage change and create successful futures.

3583 Center for Occupational Research & Development
601 Lake Air Drive
PO Box 21689
Waco, TX 76710
254-772-8756
800-231-3015
Fax: 254-772-8972
E-mail: twarner@cord.org
http://www.cord.org
The Center for Occupational Research and Development (CORD) is a national nonprofit organization dedicated to leading change in education

Teemus Warner, Coordinator Professional Dev
Richard Hinckley, President and CEO

3584 Center for Play Therapy
University of North Texas
PO Box 310829
Denton, TX 76203-829
940-565-3864
Fax: 940-565-4461
E-mail: cpt@unt.edu
http://www.centerforplaytherapy.com
Encourages the unique development and emotional growth of children through the process of play therapy, a dynamic interpersonal relationship between a child and a therapist trained in play therapy procedures. Provides training, research, publications, counseling services and acts as a clearinghouse for literature in the field.

Sue Bratton, Director
Garry Landreth, Founder

3585 Classroom Connect
6277 Sea Harbor Drive
Orlando, FL 32887
800-638-1639
888-801-8299
Fax: 650-351-5300
E-mail: help@classroom.com
http://www.classroom.com
A leading provider of professional development programs and online instructional content for K-12 education.

October
Jim Bowler, President
Melinda Cook, Vice President Sales

3586 College of the Ozarks
PO Box 17
Point Lookout, MO 65726
417-334-6411
800-222-0525
Fax: 417-335-2618
E-mail: webmaster@cofo.edu
http://www.cofo.edu
The College of the Ozarks began as a dream. In 1905, young Presbyterian missionary James Forsythe was assigned to serve the region that encompassed Sparta, Mansfield, and Forsyth, Missouri

Jerry C Davis, President

3587 Connect
Synergy Learning
116 Birge Street
PO Box 60
Brattleboro, VT 5302-60
800-769-6199
800-769-6199
Fax: 802-254-5233
E-mail: info@synergylearning.org
http://www.synergylearning.org
To engage in publishing and professional development for educators, pre-K through middle school

28 pages
ISSN: 1041-682X

Casey Murrow, Director
Susan Hathaway, Circulation Manager

3588 Critical Issues in Urban Special Education: The Implications of Whole-School Change
Harvard Graduate School of Education
44 Brattle Street
Fifth Floor
Cambridge, MA 2138
617-495-3572
800-545-1849
Fax: 617-496-8051
E-mail: ppe@gse.harvard.edu
http://www.gse.harvard.edu/~ppe
A one-week summer seminar that examines the implications of whole-school change on students with disabilities, policy, procedure, and practice. The program will clarify competing agendas, illuminate various models, and identify unified approaches to ensuring measurable benefits to all children.

Genet Jeanjean, Program Coordinator
Al Written, Interim Director

3589 Critical and Creative Thinking in the Classroom
National Center for Teaching Thinking
815 Washington Street
Suite 8
Newtonville, MA 2460
617-965-4604
Fax: 617-965-4674
A unique summer program of courses for K-12 teachers, curriculum developers, staff-development specialists, school/district administrators, teacher educators and college faculty.

3590 Curriculum Center - Office of Educational Services
3430 Constitution Drive
Suite 114
Springfield, IL 62707-9402
217-786-3010
Fax: 217-786-3020
E-mail: oesiscc@siu.edu
http://www.oes.siu.edu
Programs in vocational areas, career awareness, career development, integration, technology, tech preparation.

3591 Darryl L Sink & Associates
1 Cielo Vista Place
Suite 101
Monterey, CA 93940

831-649-8384
800-650-7465
Fax: 831-649-3914
E-mail: jane@dsink.com
http://www.dsink.com
DSA encourages customers to evaluate such adult learning strategies as cognitive apprenticeship, problem-based learning, goal-based scenarios, and real world authentic learning activities as the cornerstones of efficient, effective, and appealing learning experiences.

3592 DeVry University
One Tower Lane
Oakbrook Terrace, IL 60181
602-216-7700
800-295-8694
Fax: 602-943-4108
http://www.devry.edu
Subjects include communications, computer technology, electronics, graphic communications, and training and development.

Peter Anderson, Chief Strategist
Richard L Ehrlickman, Executive Vice President

3593 Delmar Thomson Learning
3 Columbia Circle
Albany, NY 12212
518-464-3500
Fax: 518-464-7000
E-mail: info@delmar.com
http://www.delmar.com
Subjects include welding, HVAC-R, electrical, electronics, automotive, CADD and drafting, construction, blueprint reading, and fire science.

3594 Depco
3305 Airport Drive
PO Box 178
Pittsburg, KS 66762
620-231-0019
800-767-1062
Fax: 620-231-0024
E-mail: tcoon@depcollc.com
http://www.depcoinc.com
DEPCO (Dependable Education Products Company) was introduced as a manufacturers' representative organization, which represented manufacturers of vocational education products

3595 Eastern Illinois University School of Technology
600 Lincoln Avenue
Charleston, IL 61920
217-581-3226
Fax: 217-581-6607
http://www.eiu-edu/~tech1
Subjects include manufacturing, construction, electronics, graphic communications, training and development.

3596 Edison Welding Institute
EWI
1250 Arthur E Adams Drive
Columbus, OH 43221-3585
614-688-5000
Fax: 614-688-5001
E-mail: info@ewi.org
http://www.ewi.org
The NJC's mission is to enhance the life-cycle affordability and mission capability of critical Navy weapon systems through the implementation of materials joining technology

Henry Cialone, President/CEO
Jim Tighe, CFO/Vice-President

3597 Educational Summit
The Principals' Center
20 Nassau Street
Suite 211
Princeton, NJ 8542-4509
609-497-1907
Fax: 609-497-1927

An educational summit held in August for school principals to explore, debate and design new models for schooling in America with implications for choice, charters and the community.

3598 Effective Strategies for School Reform
Harvard Graduate School of Education
44 Brattle Street
5th Floor
Cambridge, MA 2138
617-495-3572
800-545-1849
Fax: 617-496-8051
E-mail: ppe@gse.harvard.edu
http://www.gse.harvard.edu/~ppe
To enrich the professional practice of individuals and institutions worldwide that share our commitment to improving education.

Rosanne Boyle, Program Coordinator
Jennifer Stine, Managing Director/Profession

3599 Electronics Industries Alliance/CEA
2500 Wilson Boulevard
Arlington, VA 22201-3834
703-907-7670
Fax: 703-907-7968
http://www.CEMAweb.org
Electronics workshops.

3600 Elementary Education Professional DevelopmentSchool
Pennsylvania State University
148 Chambers Building
Pennsylvania State University
University Park, PA 16802
814-865-2243
E-mail: n78@psu.edu
http://www.ed.psu.edu/pds
The first goal is to enhance the educational experiences of all children. The second goal focuses on ensuring high quality field experiences for new teachers.

James Nolan, Professor of Education

3601 Emco Maier Corporation
2841 Charter Street
Columbus, OH 43228
614-771-5991
Fax: 614-771-5990
E-mail: info@emcomaier-usa.com
http://www.emcomaier-usa.com
The EMCO success story began in 1947 with the production of conventional lathes. In the years to follow, EMCO repeatedly impressed the market with extraordinary, innovative solutions.

Josh Dack, Sales Manager
Karen Fahy, Sales/Marketing Coordinator

3602 Energy Concepts
404 Washington Boulevard
Mundelein, IL 60060
847-837-8191
800-621-1247
Fax: 847-837-8171
http://www.energy-concepts-inc.com
Subjects include material science technology, principles of technology year I&II.

3603 Fastech
1750 Westfield Drive
Findlay, OH 45840
419-425-2233
Fax: 419-425-9431
E-mail: info@fastechinc.net
http://www.fastechinc.net
Subjects include mastercam training, and FMMT CD's.

3604 Festo Corporation
395 Moreland Road
PO Box 18023
Hauppauge, NY 11788

631-435-0800
Fax: 631-435-8026
E-mail: customer.service@us.festo.com
http://www.festo-usa.com
Subjects include fluid power, PLC, industrial automation.

Fred Zieram, Sales Manager
Petra Milks, Product Coordinator

3605 Foundation for Critical Thinking
PO Box 196
Tomales, CA 94971
707-878-9100
800-833-3645
Fax: 707-878-9111
E-mail: cct@criticalthinking.org
http://www.criticalthinking.org
The work of the Foundation is to integrate the Center's research and theoretical developments, and to create events and resources designed to help educators improve their instruction. Materials developed through the Foundation for Critical Thinking include books, thinker's guides, videos, and other teaching and learning resources.

Dr Richard Paul, Fellow
Dr Linda Elder, Fellow

3606 Four State Regional Technology Conference
Pittsburg State University
College of Technology
1701 S Broadway
Pittsburg, KS 66762
620-235-4365
800-854-7488
Fax: 620-235-4343
E-mail: tbaldwin@pittstate.edu
http://www.pittstate.edu
Subjects include educational technology and technology management.

November
30 booths with 250 attendees

Tom Baldwin, Dean, College of Technology

3607 Graduate Programs for Professional Educators
North Central Association of Colleges & Schools
Walden University
155 5th Avenue S
Minneaoplis, MN 55401
800-444-6795
Fax: 941-498-4266
E-mail: request@waldenu.edu
Both the MS and PhD in Education allow study from home or work. The Master of Science in Education serves classroom teachers and the PhD in education serves the advanced learning needs of educators from a wide range that serves practice fields and levels.

3608 Grand Canyon University College of Education
3300 W Camelback Road
Phoenix, AZ 85017-1097
602-639-7500
877-860-3951
Fax: 312-263-7462
E-mail: cmosby@gcu.edu
http://www.gcu.edu
Prepares learners to become global citizens, critical thinkers, effective communicators, and responsible leaders by providing an academically challenging, values-based curriculum from the context of our Christian heritage.

Kathy Player, Provots and Chief Academic O
Cheri St Arnauld, Senior VP of Academic Affair

3609 Harvard Institute for School Leadership
Harvard Graduate School of Education
44 Brattle Street
Fifth Floor
Cambridge, MA 2138
617-495-3572
800-545-1849
Fax: 617-496-8051
E-mail: ppe@harvard.edu
http://www.gse.harvard.edu/ppe
An intensive residential program for leadership teams from school districts. Participants will gain new perspectives on the processes and goals of school reform and practical skills for leading change in their districts.

July

3610 Harvard Seminar for Superintendents
Harvard Graduate School of Education
44 Brattle Street
Fifth Floor
Cambridge, MA 2138
617-495-3572
800-545-1849
Fax: 617-496-8051
E-mail: ppe@harvard.edu
http://www.gse.harvard.edu/ppe
Veteran superintendents from around the country participate in a week of intellectually stimulating conversations with Harvard faculty and networking with colleagues. Topics discussed include the arts, science, social science, and current events.

July

Julia Bean, Program Assistant

3611 Hobart Institute of Welding Technology
400 Trade Square East
Troy, OH 45373
800-332-9448
Fax: 937-332-5200
http://www.welding.org
Preparation course for CWI/CWE exams. Instructor course devoted to welding theory and hand-son practice.

Elmer Swank, Contact

3612 Indiana University-Purdue University of Indianapolis, IUPUI
Department of Construction Technology
799 W Michigan Street
ET 209
Indianapolis, IN 46202-5160
317-274-2533
Fax: 317-274-4567
E-mail: pmay2@iupui.edu
http://www.engr.iupui.edu/cnt
Subjects include architectural technology, civil engineering technology, construction technology, interior design.

H Tner Yurtseven, Dean
Lisa Jones, Administrative Assistant to

3613 Industrial Training Institute
3385 Wheeling Road
Lancaster, OH 43130
740-687-5262
800-638-4180
Fax: 740-687-5262
E-mail: drbillstevens1@msn.com
http://www.trainingrus.com
Subjects include basic electricity, motors, controls, PLC's, NEC and process control; custom designed training and consulting.

3614 Institute of Higher Education
General Board of Higher Education & Ministry/UMC
1001 19th Avenue S
Nashville, TN 37212

615-340-7406
Fax: 615-340-7379
E-mail: scu@gbhem.org
http://www.gbhem.org/highed.html
An annual seminar for administrators and faculty of United Methodist-related educational institutions addressing current themes related to the college's mission.

June
125 attendees

Cynthia Bond Hopson, Assistant General Secretary
Wanda Bigham, Interim Associate General

3615 International Curriculum Management Audit Center
Phi Delta Kappa International
408 N Union Street
Bloomington, IN 47405-3800
812-339-1156
800-766-1156
Fax: 812-339-0018
E-mail: customerservice@pdkintl.org
http://www.pdkintl.org
The mission of Phi Delta Kappa International is to promote high-quality education, in particular publicly supported education, as essential to the development and maintenance of a democratic way of life. This mission is accomplished through leadership, research, and service in education.

William Bushaw, Executive Director
Diana Daugherty, Administrative Assistant

3616 International Graduate School
Berne University
35 Center Street
Suite 18
Wolfeboro Falls, NH 3896-1080
603-569-8648
866-755-5557
Fax: 603-569-4052
E-mail: berne@berne.edu
http://www.berne.edu
Doctoral Degrees in one to two years, Specialist Diplomas in six to twelve months in: business, education (all specialties), government, health services, international relations, psychology, religion, social work and human services.

3617 International Workshops
187 Aqua View Road
Cedarburg, WI 53012
262-377-7062
Fax: 262-377-7096
E-mail: thintz@internationalworkshops.org
http://www.internationalworkshops.org
International Workshops creates an international community of artists and teachers in a site that combines touristic and cultural interest.

400 attendees

Tori Hintz, Manager
Gerald F Fischbach, Director

3618 Island Drafting & Technical Institute
128 Broadway
Amityville, NY 11701-2704
631-691-8733
Fax: 631-691-8738
E-mail: info@idti.edu
http://www.idti.edu
Our aim is to graduate students well-trained and technically qualified so that they may enter their chosen field or continue their education at the baccalaureate or higher level.

John G Diliberto, VP

3619 Janice Borla Vocal Jazz Camp
N Central College, Music Department
30 N Brainard Street
Naperville, IL 60540

630-416-3911
Fax: 630-416-6249
E-mail: jborla@aol.com
http://www.janiceborlavocaljazzcamp.org
The camp's mission is to enable jazz vocalists to develop and enhance their individual performing skills and musical creativity, regardless of prior experience level, by studying with and attending performances of professional artists actively engaged in the field of jazz performance.

Janice Borla, Director
Jay Clayton, Faculty

3620 Jefferson State Community College
2601 Carson Road
Birmingham, AL 35215
205-853-1200
800-239-5900
Fax: 205-856-8572
E-mail: workforcedev@jeffstateonline.com
http://www.jeffstateonline.com
Certificate and degree programs in automated manufacturing, electromechanical systems, industrial maintenance, and CAD.

3621 July in Rensselaer
St Joseph's College, Graduate Dept
PO Box 984
Rensselaer, IN 47978
219-866-6352
Fax: 219-866-6102
E-mail: jamesc@saintjoe.edu
Solo, ensemble, liturgy, accompanying, history, improvisation, private lessons, technique, repertoire, sight reading, workshops, theory and sacred choral music.

Rev. James Challancin, Director

3622 K'nex Education Division
2990 Bergey Road
PO Box 700
Hatfield, PA 19440
888-ABC-KNEX
Fax: 215-996-4222
E-mail: abcknex@knex.com
http://www.knexeducation.com
Introductory, set specific, regional and design your own professional development programs offered for any/all K-12 technology, math and science sets.

3623 Kaleidoscope
Consulting Psychologists Press
3803 E Bayshore Road
Palo Alto, CA 94303-4300
800-624-1765
Fax: 650-969-8608
An institute for educators that develops insights into teaching styles and learning styles; administers and interprets the Myers-Briggs Type Indicator (personality inventory); learn new techniques to help children understand and value their unique qualities; create and deliver lessons that enlighten all students and more.

July

3624 Kent State University
375 Terrace Drive
Van Deusen Hall
Kent, OH 44242
330-672-2892
Fax: 330-672-2894
E-mail: lepps@kent.edu
http://www.tech.kent.edu
Subjects include aeronautics, electronics, manufacturing engineering, computer technology, and automotive engineering technology.

Verna Fitzsimmons, Interim Dean
Isaac Richmond Nettey, Associate Dean

3625 Kentucky State University
400 East Main Street
Frankfort, KY 40601
502-597-6000
Fax: 502-227-6236
E-mail: webadmin@kysu.edu
http://www.kysu.edu
Associates in applied science in drafting and design technology and applied science in electronics technology.

Mary Evans Sias, President
Stephen Mason, Executive Assistant to the P

3626 Kodaly Teaching Certification Program
DePaul University, School of Music
804 West Belden Avenue
Chicago, IL 60614
773-325-4355
Fax: 773-325-7263
Music education, pedagogy and workshops.

Robert Krueger, Director Operations

3627 Lab Volt Systems
1710 State Highway 34
Farmingdale, NJ 7727
732-938-2000
800-522-2658
Fax: 732-774-8573
E-mail: us@labvolt.com
http://www.labvolt.com
Global leader in the design and manufacture of hands-on training laboratories for public education, industry, and the military.

Eric Maynard, Contact

3628 Leadership and the New Technologies
Harvard Graduate School of Education
Programs in Professional Education
339 Gutman Library
Cambridge, MA 2138
617-495-3572
800-545-1849
Fax: 617-496-8051
E-mail: ppe@harvard.edu
http://www.gse.harvard.edu/~ppe
Programs designed to help teams of school leaders anticipate the far-reaching impacts that new technologies can have on students, teachers, curriculum, and communication. Participants make long-term plans for the use of technology in their schools and districts and learn how to take advantage of federal and state technology initiatives.

July

Ann Doyle, Program Coordinator

3629 Learning & The Enneagram
National Enneagram Institute at Milton Academy
230 Atherton Street
Milton, MA 2186-2424
617-898-1798
Fax: 617-898-1712
An educational enterprise dedicated to guiding individuals and organizations in the most responsible and effective format for their needs. Programs include exploration of what every educator needs to know; why we learn in the way we do; and how we teach.

July

Regina Pyle, Coordinator

3630 Learning Materials Workshop
274 N Winooski Avenue
Burlington, VT 5401
800-693-7164
Fax: 802-862-8399
E-mail: info@learningmaterialswork.com
http://www.learningmaterialswork.com

Learning Materials Workshop Blocks are learning tools in the hands of young children. They are open-ended, yet carefully designed in a variety of colors, sizes, shapes, and textures that stimulate and develop perpetual, motor, and language skills. Learning Materials Workshops are designed for early childhood/primary grade teachers, paraprofessionals, curriculum coordinators, special education teachers, ESL teachers, and teachers of the gifted and talented to help develop the learning process.

Karen Hewitt, President

3631 Light Machines
444 E Industrial Park Avenue
Manchester, NH 3109-5317
800-221-2763
Fax: 603-625-2137
E-mail: industrialsales@intelitek_usa.com
http://www.lightmachines.com
Subjects include demonstrations and comprehensive training on CNC routers, turning machines and milling machines, and CAD/CAM software.

3632 MPulse Maintenance Software
PO Box 22906
Eugene, OR 97402
541-302-6677
800-944-1796
Fax: 541-302-6680
E-mail: info@mpulsesoftware.com
http://www.mpulsesoftware.com
Deliver simply better EAM / CMMS software that is easier to use and faster to implement. Keep it affordable by controlling the cost of sales and marketing. Design it to keep up with their needs today, their challenges of tomorrow, while maintaining the history of what they did yesterday. And do it better than anyone else

3633 Marcraft International Corporation
100 N Morain Street
Suite 302
Kennwick, WA 99336
509-374-1951
800-441-6006
Fax: 509-374-9250
E-mail: sales@mic-inc.com
http://www.mic-inc.com
s to develop exceptional products for effectively teaching and training people the technical IT, computer, and electronics training skills in demand today and in the future.

Robert Krug, National Sales Manager

3634 Maryland Center for Career and Technology Education
1415 Key Highway
Baltimore, MD 21230
410-685-1648
Fax: 410-685-0032
Subjects include technology education and occupational education certification.

3635 Media and American Democracy
Harvard Graduate School of Education
Programs in Professional Education
339 Gutman Library
Cambridge, MA 2138
617-495-3572
800-545-1849
Fax: 617-496-8051
E-mail: ppe@harvard.edu
http://www.gse.harvard.edu/~ppe
Participants learn about the interaction between the media and American democratic process, develop curriculum units, and examine ways to help students become thoughtful consumers of media messages about politics. Designed for secondary school teachers of

history, social studies, English, journalism, and humanities.

August

Tracy Ryder, Program Assistant

3636 Millersville University
PO Box 1002
1 South George Street
Millersville, PA 17551
717-872-3011
800-426-4553
Fax: 877-327-8132
http://www.millersville.edu
With a student population of 7,259 undergraduate and 1,047 graduate students, Millersville University offers all the advantages you would expect from a university: competitive programs, great facilities, a diverse student community and a variety of campus programming all offered in an accessible, intimate and close-knit atmosphere more frequently found at a smaller college

Michael G Warfel, Chairman
Paul G Wedel, Vice Chairman

3637 Morehead State University
150 University Boulevard
Morehead, KY 40351
606-783-2221
Fax: 606-783-5030
E-mail: admissions@moreheadstate.edu
http://www.morehead-st.edu
Morehead State University was founded upon and continues to embrace the ideal that all persons should have opportunity to participate in higher education. With immense pride in its past and great promise for its future, the University intends to emerge in the first decade of the 21st century as an even stronger institution recognized for superb teaching and learning with exemplary programs in teacher education, space-related science and technology, entrepreneurship, visual and performing arts, r

Beth Patrick, Vice President
Dayna Seelig, Special Assistant to the Pre

3638 Musikgarten
507 Arlington Street
Greensboro, NC 27406
336-272-5303
800-216-6864
Fax: 336-272-0581
E-mail: musgarten@aol.com
http://www.musikgarten.org
Early childhood music education workshops teaching music and understanding children.

Lorna Heyge, President

3639 NASA Educational Workshop
NSTA
1840 Wilson Boulevard
Arlington, VA 22201-3000
703-243-7100
888-400-6782
Fax: 703-243-7177
E-mail: businessoffice@nsta.org
http://www.nsta.org
Two week workshop at a NASA Center, professional development opportunity for K-12 teachers in mathematics, science, and technology, teachers and curriculum specialists at the K-12 levels; media specialists, resource teachers, elementary curriculum developers, counselors, and others with special interest in mathematics, science, technology, and geography.

Page Keeley, President
Pat Shane, President-Elect

3640 NCSS Summer Workshops
National Council for the Social Studies
8555 Sixteenth Street
Suite 500
Siver Spring, MD 20910
301-588-1800
800-683-0812
Fax: 301-588-2049
E-mail: sgriffin@ncss.org
http://www.socialstudies.org
Social studies educators teach students the content knowledge, intellectual skills, and civic values necessary for fulfilling the duties of citizenship in a participatory democracy.

July

Susan Griffin, Executive Director
Sojan Alex, Finance Assistant

3641 National Center for Construction Education & Research
3600 NW 43rd Street
Building G
Gainsville, FL 32606
352-334-0911
888-622-3720
Fax: 352-334-0932
E-mail: info@nccer.org
http://www.nccer.org
Our mission is to build a safe, productive, and sustainable workforce of craft professionals.

Don Whyte, President
Cathy Tyler, Executive Assistant

3642 National Computer Systems
4401 L Street NW
Suite 550
Edina, MN 55435
612-995-8997
800-328-6172
Fax: 952-830-8564
http://www.ncs.com
Programs offer skills to teach technology in the classroom.

3643 National Head Start Association
1651 Prince Street
Alexandria, VA 22314-2818
703-739-0875
Fax: 703-739-0878
http://www.nhsa.org
The National Head Start Association is a private not-for-profit membership organization dedicated exclusively to meeting the needs of Head Start children and their families.

Ron Herndon, Chairman
Janis Santos, Vice- Chairperson

3644 Northern Arizona University
South San Francisco Street
Flagstaff, AZ 86011
928-523-9011
Fax: 520-523-6395
E-mail: tlc2@dana.ucc.nau.edu
http://www.nau.edu
Provide an outstanding undergraduate residential education strengthened by research, graduate and professional programs, and sophisticated methods of distance delivery.

John D Haeger, President
Tracy Cooper, Lab Assistant

3645 Orff-Schulwerk Teacher Certification Program
DePaul University, School of Music
804 West Belden Avenue
Chicago, IL 60614
773-325-7260
Fax: 773-325-7264
E-mail: ahutchen@wppost.depaul.edu.
Music education, pedagogy and workshops.

Judy Bundra, Associate Dean

3646 Owens Community College
PO Box 10000
Toledo, OH 43699-1947
567-661-7000
800-466-9367
Fax: 419-661-7664
http://www.owens.edu
We believe in serving our students and our communities. Your success is our misssion.

John C Moore, Chairman
Diana H Talmage, Vice Chair

3647 Paideia Group
608 Garden Leaf Court
St. Louis, M 63011
636-220-9300
Fax: 919-932-3905
E-mail: bethsymes@psideiagroup.com
http://www.paideiagroup.com
To help people understand what it means to be customer-focused. Participants focus on the skills, attitudes, and automatic behaviors that must be developed to reach a common goal of becoming a customer-focused organization.

Beth Symes, Principal and Founder

3648 Pamela Sims & Associates
54 Mozart Crescent
Brampton, Ontario
Canada L6Y-2W7
905-455-7331
888-610-7467
Fax: 905-455-0207
E-mail: loveofkids@aol.com
http://www.pamelasims.com
Seminars and workshops for educators and parents.

Pamela Sims, President
Kelly Smith, Marketing Director

3649 Pennsylvania State University-WorkforceEducation & Development Program
301 Keller Building
University Park, PA 16802
814-863-3858
Fax: 814-863-7532
E-mail: eif1@psu.edu
http://www.ed.psu.edu/wfed
To promote excellence, opportunity, and leadership among professionals in the workforce education and development field including, but not limited to, those employed in secondary or postsecondary education institutions, social services industries, and employee groups and private businesses.

Edgar I Farmer, Department Head
Judith A Kolb, Professor-in-Charge

3650 Performance Learning Systems
72 Lone Oak Drive
Cadiz, KY 42211
270-522-2000
866-757-2527
Fax: 270-522-2010
E-mail: info@plsweb.com
http://www.plsweb.com
The mission of Performance Learning Systems, Inc. is to enhance education through the development of educational services.

Jackie Futrell, Resource Manager
Stephen G Barkley, Master teacher-of-teachers

3651 Piano Workshop
Goshen College
1700 S Main Street
Goshen, IN 46526
574-535-7361
Fax: 574-535-7949
E-mail: beverlykl@goshen.edu
http://www.goshen.edu/music/Piano%20Workshop/Main

The Goshen College Piano Workshop and Academy comprises lectures, master classes and recital performances presented by distinguished clinicians, composers and performers.˜ Teachers participating in the Workshop hear inspiring lectures relevant to piano pedagogy, performance and literature.

Beverly K Lapp, Associate Professor of Music

3652 Pittsburg State University
College of Technology
1701 S Broadway
Pittsburg, KS 66762
620-231-7000
800-854-7488
Fax: 620-235-4343
E-mail: psuinfo@pittstate.edu
http://www.pittstate.edu
A comprehensive regional university, provides undergraduate and graduate programs and services to the people of southeast Kansas, but also to others who seek the benefits offered.

Bruce Dallman, Dean, College of Technology
Tom Bryant, President

3653 Polaroid Education Program
565 Technology Square
#3B
Cambridge, MA 2139-3539
781-386-2000
Fax: 781-386-3925
This program offers workshops for professional educators, preK-12; the Visual Learning Workshop and an Instant Image Portfolio Workshop.

3654 Professional Development Institutes
Center for Professional Development & Services
2730 University Boulevard
Suite 200
Wheaton, MD 20902
301-949-1771
800-766-1156
Fax: 301-949-5441
E-mail: info@pditraining.net
http://www.pditraining.net
Offers a wide variety of courses for Real Estate professionals around the US to meet their pre-licensing, post-licensing, and continuing education needs. Also offers non-credit courses on Technology, Business, Accounting, and Project Management, among others to further any career.

3655 Professional Development Workshops
Rebus
4111 Jackson Road
Ann Arbor, MI 48103
734-668-4870
800-435-3085
Fax: 734-668-4728
http://www.rebusinc.com
Workshops that promote success by assessing children in the context of active learning.

June/July

Sam Meisels, CEO
Linda Borgsdorf, President

3656 Project Zero Classroom
Harvard Graduate School of Education
Programs in Professional Education
44 Brattle Street, 5th floor
Cambridge, MA 2138
617-495-3572
800-545-1849
Fax: 617-496-8051
E-mail: ppe@gse.harvard.edu
http://www.gse.harvard.edu/~ppe
Renowned educators Howard Gardner and David Perkins and their Project Zero colleagues work with K-12 educators to help

209

them reshape their classroom practices to promote student understanding. The week focuses on five concepts: teaching for understanding, multiple intelligences, the thinking classroom, authentic assessment, and learning with and through the arts.

July

Julia Bean, Program Assistant

3657 Robert McNeel & Associates
3670 Woodland Park Avenue N
Seattle, WA 98103
206-545-7000
Fax: 206-545-7321
E-mail: bob@mcneelcom
http://www.en.na.mcneel.com
3D modeling workshop for design, drafting, graphics, and technology educators.

3658 Rockford Systems
4620 Hydraulic Road
Rockford, IL 61109-2695
815-874-7891
800-922-7533
Fax: 815-874-6144
E-mail: sales@rockfordsystems.com
http://www.rockfordsystems.com
Machine safegaurding seminar for technology educators.

3659 SUNY College at Oswego
7060 Route 104
Oswego, NY 13126-3599
315-312-2500
Fax: 315-312-2863
E-mail: stanley@oswego.edu
http://www.oswego.edu
The chief goal of the Oswego College Foundation, Inc. is to raise and manage private support to advance SUNY~Oswego's mission.

October
26 booths with 350-400 attendees
Deborah F Stanley, President
Howard Gordon, Executive Assistant to Presi

3660 School of Music
Georgia State University
PO Box 4097
Atlanta, GA 30302-4097
404-413-5900
Fax: 404-413-5910
E-mail: music@gsu.edu
http://www.music.gsu.edu
The mission of the School of Music is to provide a comprehensive, rigorous, and innovative academic program that is consistent with the urban context and mission of Georgia State University, and that serves the pursuit of artistic, professional, and scholarly excellence through experiences of lasting value to all stakeholders.

W Dwight Coleman, Director
Robert J Ambrose, Associate Director

3661 Southern Polytechnic State University
1100 S Marietta Parkway
Marietta, GA 30060
678-915-7240
Fax: 678-915-7490
E-mail: coned@spsu.edu
http://www.oce.spsu.edu
Specialize in the delivery of comprehensive real-world training on a grand scale. Whether it be High-Tech, Business Professional or Engineering

3662 Southwestern Oklahoma State University
Industrial and Engineering Technology Department
100 Campus Drive
Weatherford, OK 73096

580-772-6611
Fax: 580-774-3795
E-mail: admissions@swosu.edu
http://www.swosu.edu
The mission of Southwestern Oklahoma State University is to provide educational opportunities in higher education that meet the needs of the state and region; contribute to the educational, economic, and cultural environment; and support scholarly activity.

Gary Bell, Chair
Jeff Short, Program Coordinator

3663 Specialized Solutions
24703 US Highway 19-N
Suite 200
Clearwater, FL 33763
240-252-5070
800-942-1660
Fax: 877-200-5959
E-mail: sales@quickcert.com
http://www.specializedsolutions.com
Technology based training and certification self study programs.

Sheri Nash, Contact

3664 Staff Development Workshops & Training Sessions
National School Conference Institute
PO Box 37527
Phoenix, AZ 85069-7527
602-371-8655
Fax: 602-371-8790
Offers twenty relevant and leading edge programs including curriculum instruction assessment, restructuring your school, improving student performance and gifted at-risk students. Ten monthly sessions of each program are available, with monthly feedback to follow-up. Accelerates restructuring efforts and also offers graduate credit.

3665 Standards and Accountability: Their Impact on Teaching and Assessment
Harvard Graduate School of Education
Programs in Professional Education
339 Gutman Library
Cambridge, MA 2138
617-495-3572
800-545-1849
Fax: 617-496-8051
E-mail: ppe@harvard.edu
http://www.gse.harvard.edu/~ppe
Examines educational and policy issues by new approaches to standards, assessment, and accountability. Focuses on issues of excellence and equity, aligning assessments with standards, strengthening professional development, impacts of challenges on school communities, and political and legal issues surrounding standards and forms of accountability. Designed for public school leaders whose responsibilities include evaluation and testing.

July

Tracy Ryder, Program Assistant

3666 Storytelling for Educational Enrichment The Magic of Storytelling
2709 Oak Haven Drive
San Marcos, TX 78666-5065
512-392-0669
800-322-3199
Fax: 512-392-9660
E-mail: krieger@corridor.net
Teacher in-service and training in storytelling and puppetry for teachers of Pre-K through third grades. The Magic of Storytelling is for all ages and levels, specializing in original stories of enlightenment and environmental education. Over ten years experiences with

many national and regional conferences and training.

Cherie Krieger, President

3667 Summer Institute in Siena
University of Siena-S/American Universities
595 Prospect Road
Waterbury, CT 6706
203-754-5741
Fax: 203-753-8105
E-mail: siena@sienamusic.org
http://www.sienamusic.org
Programs offered in cooperation with the University of Siena-S and American Universities and Colleges. The program in Siena Italy is open to qualified graduates, undergraduates, professionals, teachers, 19 years of age or above. Special diploma; credit or non-credit; in-service credit; auditions; trips to Rome, Florence, Assisi, Venice, Pisa, three days in Switzerland; a Puccini Opera.

Joseph Del Principe, Music Director

3668 Summer Programs for School Teams
National Association of Elementary School Principa
1615 Duke Street
Alexandria, VA 22314-3406
703-684-3345
800-386-2377
Fax: 703-518-6281
http://www.naesp.org
Events focused on the key to exceptional instruction. Effective teaching and learning for school teams, must include the principal.

Ann R Walker, Assistant Executive Director
Herrie Hahn, Director Programs

3669 Supplemental Instruction, Supervisor Workshops
University of Missouri-Kansas City
5100 Rockhill Road
SASS 210
Kansas City, MO 64110-2499
816-235-1174
Fax: 816-235-5156
E-mail: cad@umkc.edu
http://www.umkc.edu/cad/si
Supplemental Instruction (SI) is an academic assistance program that utilizes peer-assisted study sessions.

Kim Wilcox, Coordinator of Training
Glen Jacobs, Executive Director

3670 THE Institute & Knowvation
16261 Laguna Canyon Road
Suite 130
Irvine, CA 92618
949-265-1520
800-840-0003
Fax: 949-265-1528
E-mail: kodell@1105media.com
http://www.thejournal.com/institute
T.H.E. Institute believes that in order for students to be successful in the 21st century, technology must be an integral part of every aspect of education.

Geoffrey H Fletcher, Executive Director

3671 TUV Product Service
Westendstra e 199
Munich, MA D-806
49 -9 5-91 0
800-TUV-0123
Fax: 978-762-7637
E-mail: info@tuev-sued.de
http://www.tuvglobal.com
As process partners with comprehensive industry knowledge our teams of specialists provide early consultation and continuous

guidance, thus achieving the optimisation of technology, systems and expertise

Axel Stepken, Chief Executive Officer
Manfred Bayerlein, Chief Operations Officer

3672 Teacher Education Institute
1079 W Morse Boulevard
Winter Park, FL 32789-3751
800-331-2208
Fax: 800-370-2600
E-mail: tei@teachereducation.com
http://www.teachereducation.com
TEI was founded in 1981 to meet the needs of classroom teachers for quality education and training in practical, proven skills and methods that make a tangible and positive difference in their relationships and interactions with students and colleagues.

Vince Welsh, President

3673 Teachers College: Columbia University
Center for Technology & School Change
525 W 120th Street
New York, NY 10027
212-678-3000
Fax: 212-678-4048
E-mail: webcomments@tc.columbia.edu
http://www.tc.columbia.edu
bring educational opportunities to all members of society, and whose faculty and students, time and again during more than a century of leadership, have demonstrated the power of ideas to change the world.

Howard Budin, Director Center for Technolo
Susan Fuhrman, President

3674 Technology Training for Educators
Astronauts Memorial Foundation
321-452-2887
800-792-3494
Fax: 321-452-6244
http://www.amfcse.org
Microsoft NT Administration; Technology Specialist; Management of Technology; Advanced Technology Specialist.

3675 Tooling University
15700 S Waterloo Road
Cleveland, OH 44110-3898
216-706-6600
866-706-8665
Fax: 216-706-6601
E-mail: info@toolingu.com
http://www.toolingu.com
Toolingu.com is the leading online training provider focused on the unique needs of manufacturers. Our roots are in manufacturing, and our business started by recognizing the industry's specific needs

Gene Jones, Director Marketing

3676 Total Quality Schools Workshop
Pennsylvania State University
302F Rackley Building
University Park, PA 16802
814-843-3765
E-mail: hli@psu.edu
http://www.ed.psu.edu/ctqs/index.html
Designed for public school educators at the state, national, and international level, this training program provides information in the philosophy, tools, and techniques of total quality management in education. The three day-six week program focuses on leadership, reform models, and education decision making.

William Hartman, Director

3677 University of Arkansas at Little Rock
2801 S University Avenue
Little Rock, AR 72204-1099

501-683-7302
Fax: 501-683-7304
E-mail: admissions@ualr.edu
http://www.ualr.edu
With more than 100 programs of study, UALR has an academic program to suit your interests. We offer everything from computer science to fine arts, and we're sure you will find your niche on our campus

Sandra Bates, President
Tammy Starks, Vice President

3678 University of Central Florida
3100 Technology Parkway
Suite 264
Orlando, FL 32816-3271
407-823-2000
Fax: 407-270-4911
http://www.distrib.ucf.edu
The University of Central Florida is one of the most dynamic universities in the country. Offering 223 degree programs, it has become an academic and research leader in numerous fields, such as optics, modeling and simulation, engineering and computer science, business administration, education, science, hospitality management and digital media.

John C Hitt, President/Corporate Secretar
John Schell, Vice President

3679 University of Michigan-Dearborn Center for Corporate & Professional Development
4901 Evergreen Road
CCPD-2000
Dearborn, MI 48128-2406
313-593-5000
Fax: 313-593-5111
E-mail: info@umich.edu
http://www.umd.umich.edu
We offer undergraduate, graduate, and professional education to a diverse, highly motivated, and talented student body. Our programs are responsive to the changing needs of society; relevant to the goals of our students and community partners; rich in opportunities for independent and collaborative study, research, and practical application; and reflective of the traditions of excellence, innovation, and leadership that distinguish the University of Michigan

Daniel Little, Chancellor
Ray Metz, Chief of Staff

3680 Wavelength
4753 N Broadway
Suite 808
Chicago, IL 60640
773-784-1012
877-528-47 2
Fax: 773-784-1079
E-mail: info@wavelengthinc.com
http://www.wavelengthinc.com
Wavelength offers a fresh perspective on the key challenges in education today. Our programs are founded on the tenet that humor heals and enlightens.

3681 Wids Learning Design System
1 Foundation Circle
Waunakee, WI 53597
800-677-9437
800-821-6313
Fax: 608-849-2468
E-mail: info@wids.org
http://www.wids.org
WIDS strives to enhance the quality of learning through the development, implementation, support, and continuous improvement of the WIDS Learning Design System, a comprehensive methodology, supported by application and professional development tools, for

designing and planning performance-based assessment learning and teaching.

Lisa Laabs, Office Manager
Judy Neill, Director

3682 Workforce Education and Development
Southern Illinois University Carbondale
475 Clocktower Drive
Mailcode 4605
Carbondale, IL 62901-4605
618-453-3321
Fax: 618-453-1909
E-mail: wed@siu.edu
http://http://wed.siu.edu/Public/
The Department of Workforce Education and Development is one of the largest education, training, and development departments in the United States. A recent external evaluation team recognized the Department as among the top ten in the nation.

Keith Waugh, Associate Professor/Chairman

Directories & Handbooks

3683 Integrated Pathways
Association of Integrative Studies
Miami University
Oxford, OH 45056
513-529-2659
Fax: 513-529-5849
E-mail: aisorg@muohio.edu
http://www.units.muohio.edu/aisorg
AIS news, including updates on AIS conferences, decisions of the AIS Board of Directors, and membership announcements. Published quarterly.

ISSN: 1081-647X
William H Newell, Editor

3684 Journal of Reading Recovery
Reading Recovery Council of North America
500 W. Wilson Bridge Road
Suite 250
Worthington, OH 43085-5218
614-310-7323
Fax: 614-310-7345
E-mail: jjohnson@readingrecovery.org
http://www.readingrecovery.org
The Journal of Reading Recovery is published twice per year, and is primarily a practitioners journal offering current information on Reading Recovery teaching theory, implementation and research for K-6 classroom literacy.

Jady Johnson, Executive Director
Linda Wilson, Executive Assistant

3685 Teaching Exceptional Children
Council for Exceptional Children
2900 Crystal Drive
Suite 1000
Arlington, VA 22202-3557
703-620-3660
888-232-7733
Fax: 703-264-9494
E-mail: service@cec.sped.org
http://www.cec.sped.org
Features practical articles that present methods and materials for classroom use as well as current issues in special education teaching and learning. Published four times per year, free with membership or $86.00 for individual subscription.

Marilyn Friend, President
Bruce Ramirez, Executive Director

Directories & Handbooks / *General*

3686 106 Ways Parents Can Help Students Achieve
American Association of School Administrators
801 N Quincy Street
Suite 700
Arlington, VA 22203-1730
703-528-0700
Fax: 703-841-1543
http://www.aasa.org
Provides parents with useful information about the importance of parental involvement, concrete ways to work with children and schools to promote success, and a list of resources for further reading.

Set of 10
ISBN: 0-8108-4220-3

3687 A Personal Planner & Training Guide for the Substitute Teacher
Master Teacher
Leadership Lane
PO Box 1207
Manhattan, KS 66505-1207
800-669-9633
Fax: 800-669-1132
http://www.masterteacher.com
Helps substitute teachers set the tone for a positive experience.

90 pages
ISBN: 0-914607-89-8
John Eller, Author

3688 Academic Year & Summer Programs Abroad
American Institute for Foreign Study
102 Greenwich Avenue
Greenwich, CT 06830-5504
203-869-9090
800-727-2437
Fax: 203-399-5590
E-mail: college.info@aifs.com
http://www.aifs.com
Offers school names, addresses, courses offered, tuition and fee information.

224 pages Annual

3689 Accredited Institutions of Postsecondary Education
MacMillan Publishing Company
1633 Broadway
New York, NY 10019
212-654-8500
Fax: 800-835-3202
Lists over 5,000 accredited institutions and programs for postsecondary education in the United States.

600 pages Annual

3690 Activities and Strategies for Connecting Kids with Kids: Elementary Edition
Master Teacher
Leadership Lane
PO Box 1207
Manhattan, KS 66505-1207
800-669-9633
Fax: 800-669-1132
http://www.masterteacher.com
Activities, lesson plans, and strategies that celebrate each student's individual differences while developing cooperation, tolerance, understanding, sharing and caring.

159 pages
ISBN: 0-914607-74-X

3691 Activities and Strategies for Connecting Kids with Kids: Secondary Edition
Master Teacher
Leadership Lane
PO Box 1207
Manhattan, KS 66505-1207
800-669-9633
Fax: 800-669-1132
http://www.masterteacher.com
Activities, lesson plans, and strategies that celebrate each student's individual differences while developing cooperation, tolerance, understanding, sharing and caring.

136 pages
ISBN: 0-914607-75-8

3692 American School Directory
PO Box 20002
Murfreesboro, TN 37129
866-273-2797
Fax: 800-929-3408
E-mail: asdwebmaster@asd.com
http://www.asd.com
More than 104,000 school sites are loaded with pictures, art, calendars, menus, local links and notes from students, parents and alumni. Choose the school by name, state list, or by ASD number.

3693 Amusing and Unorthodox Definitions
Careers/Consultants Consultants in Education
3050 Palm Aire Drive N
#310
Pompano Beach, FL 33069
954-974-5477
Fax: 954-974-5477
E-mail: carconed@aol.com
Collection of amusing and unorthodox definitions. The meanings, purposes and implications assigned to the words appearing here will delight audiences, enliven conversations and keep you chuckling.

ISBN: 0-7392-0089-5
ISSN: 99-94623
Dr. Robert M Bookbinder, President/Author

3694 Associated Schools Project in Education for International Co-operation
UNESCO Associated Schools Project Network
7 Place de Fontenoy
F-75700 Paris
France
1-45681000
Lists 1,970 secondary and primary schools, teacher training institutions and nursery schools in 95 countries that participate in the UNESCO Associated School Project.

200 pages Annual

3695 Association for Community-Based Education Directory of Members
Association for Community Based Education
1805 Florida Avenue NW
Washington, DC 20009-1708
202-462-6333
Offers information on 100 private community organizations concerned with alternative education including colleges that award degrees without residency requirements and more.

115 pages Annual

3696 Awakening Brilliance: How to Inspire Children to Become Successful Learners
Pamela Sims & Associates
54 Mozart Crescent
Canada L6Y 2W7
905-455-7331
888-610-7467
Fax: 905-455-0207
E-mail: loveofkids@aol.com
http://www.pamelasims.com
Seminars and workshops for educators and parents. Upcoming workshops include themes of awakening students' potential and team leadership skills.

248 pages Paperback
ISBN: 0-9651126-0-8
Pamela Sims, Author/Editor
Kelly Smith, Marketing Director

3697 Beyond the Bake Sale
Master Teacher
Leadership Lane
PO Box 1207
Manhattan, KS 66505-1207
800-669-9633
Fax: 800-669-1132
http://www.masterteacher.com
A notebook containing 101 detailed plans that not only provide you with fundraising ideas,

but get you started, keep you on track, and lead your team through the finishing touches.

101 pages
ISBN: 1-58992-119-4

3698 Biographical Membership Directory

American Educational Research Association
1230 17th Street NW
Washington, DC 20036-3078
202-223-9485
Fax: 202-775-1824
Membership directory of more than 23,000 persons involved in education research and development, including the names, addresses, phone numbers, highest degree held and year received, occupational specialization areas, e-mail addresses and more.

420 pages Bi-Annual

Thomas J Campbell, Director Publications

3699 CASE Directory of Advancement Professionals in Education

Council for Advancement & Support of Education
1307 New York Avenue NW
Suite 1000
Washington, DC 20005-4701
202-328-2273
Fax: 202-387-4973
E-mail: info@case.org
http://www.case.org
Membership directory of 16,000 professionals in alumni relations, communications and fund raising at educational institutions worldwide.

Publication Date: 1995 200 pages Annual
ISBN: 0-899643-10-8

Cedric Calhoun, Membership Director

3700 Cabells Directory of Publishing Opportunities in Educational Curriculum & Methods

Cabell Publishing Company
Box 5428
Tobe Hahn Station
Beaumont, TX 77726
409-898-0575
Fax: 409-866-9554
E-mail: publish@cabells.com
http://www.cabells.com
Provides information on editor's contact information, manuscript guidelines, acceptance rate, review information and circulation data for over 350 academic journals.

799 pages Annual
ISBN: 0-911753-27-3

David WE Cabell, Editor
Deborah L English, Editor

3701 Cadet Gray: Your Guide to MilitarySchools-Military Colleges & Cadet Programs

Reference Desk Books
PO Box 22925
Santa Barbara, CA 93121
805-772-8806
This is a comprehensive reference book which describes 55 American military schools, grade schools, high schools, junior colleges, senior colleges, and the federal service academies. Descriptions include school histories, academic requirements, military environment, extracurricular activities and costs.

Publication Date: 1990 212 pages
ISBN: 0-962574-90-2

3702 Character Education Evaluation Tool Kit

Character Education Partnership
1025 Connecticut Avenue NW
Suite 1011
Washington, DC 20036
202-296-7743
800-988-8081
Fax: 202-296-7779
http://www.character.org
Julea Posey, Matthew Davison, Meg Korpi, Author
Andrea Grenadier, Director Communications
Esther Schaeffer, CEO/Executive Director

3703 Character Education Kit: 36 Weeks of Success: Elementary Edition

Master Teacher
Leadership Lane
PO Box 1207
Manhattan, KS 66505-1207
800-669-9633
Fax: 800-669-1132
http://www.masterteacher.com
Takes the guesswork out of delivering your character education message by providing you with all the pieces of a well-rounded program including important components for 36 character traits.

428 pages
ISBN: 1-58992-096-1

3704 Choosing Your Independent School in the United Kingdom & Ireland

Independent Schools Information Service
56 Buckingham Gate
London SW1E 6AG
England
71-63087934
1,400 independent schools in the United Kingdom and Ireland with contact information, entry requirements, fees, scholarships available, subjects and exam boards.

293 pages Annual/September

3705 Classroom Teacher's Guide for Working with Paraeducators

Master Teacher
Leadership Lane
PO Box 1207
Manhattan, KS 66505-1207
800-669-9633
Fax: 800-669-1132
http://www.masterteacher.com
This workbook includes numerous forms that allow teachers to communicate more effectively to paras the vital information they will need in working with special students.

60 pages
ISBN: 1-58992-127-5

Wendy Dover, Author

3706 Commonwealth Universities Yearbook

Association of Commonwealth Universities
36 Gordon Square
London WC1H 0PF
England
44-20-7380-6700
Fax: 44-20-738-2655
E-mail: info@acu.ac.uk
http://www.acu.ac.uk
Offers information on over 700 university institutions of recognized academic standing in 36 Commonwealth countries or regions, including Africa, Asia, Australia, Britain, Canada and the Pacific.

2,600 pages Annual
ISBN: 0-85143-188-7
ISSN: 0069-7745

3707 Complete Learning Disabilities Directory

Grey House Publishing
185 Millerton Road
Millerton, NY 12546
518-789-8700
800-562-2139
Fax: 518-789-0545
E-mail: books@greyhouse.com
http://www.greyhouse.com
A one-stop sourcebook for people of all ages with learning disabilities and those who work with them. This comprehensive database in print includes information about associations and organizations, schools, government agencies, testing materials, camps, books, newsletters and more.

800 pages Annual/Softcover
ISBN: 1-59237-049-7

Leslie Mackenzie, Publisher
Richard Gottlieb, Editor

3708 Computer and Web Resources for People with Disabilities

Alliance for Technology Access/Hunter House
1304 Southpoint Boulevard
Suite 240
Petaluma, CA 94954
707-778-3011
800-914-3017
Fax: 707-765-2080
E-mail: atainfo@ataccess.org
http://www.ataccess.org
This directory shows how America's forty-five million people with disabilities can potentially benefit from using computer technology to achieve goals and change their lives. Written by experts in the field, this important work provides a comprehensive, step-by-step guide to approaching computer innovations. It explains how to identify the appropriate technology, how to seek funding, how to set it up and what to consider.

Publication Date: 1996 400 pages Paperback/CD ROM
ISBN: 0-89793-433-4

Libbie Butler, Information/Referral Assista

3709 Conservation Education and Outreach Techniques

North American Assoc for Environmental Education
2000 P Street NW
Suite 540
Washington, DC 20036
202-419-0412
Fax: 212-419-0415
E-mail: info@naaee.org
http://www.naaee.org
Presents the theory and practice for creating effective education and outreach programmes for conservation. An exciting array of techniques for enhancing school resources, marketing environmental messages, using mass media, developing partnerships for conservation, and designing on-site programmes for natural areas and community centres.

ISBN: 0-19-856772-3

Susan Jacobson, Author
Martha C Monroe, Author

3710 Contemporary World Issues: Public Schooling in America

ABC-CLIO
130 Cremona Drive
#1911
Santa Barbara, CA 93117-5599
805-963-4221
800-368-6868
Fax: 805-685-9685

Offers information on organizations and agencies involved with public education systems.

3711 Cornocopia of Concise Quotations
Careers/Consultants Consultants in Education
3050 Palm Aire Drive N
#310
Pompano Beach, FL 33069
954-974-5477
Fax: 954-974-5477
E-mail: carconed@aol.com
Wealth of practical reminders of the enduring ideas. The book furthers humane understandings by gathering and preserving the wisdom of the wise and experienced.

ISBN: 0-7392-0275-8
ISSN: 99-95201

Dr. Robert M Bookbinder, President

3712 Council for Educational Development and Research Directory
National Education Association (NEA)
1201 16th Street NW
Washington, DC 20036-3290
202-833-4000
Fax: 202-822-7974
E-mail: ncuea@nea.org
http://www.nea.org
Offers 15 member educational research and development institutions.

50 pages Annual

3713 Digest of Supreme Court Decisions
Phi Delta Kappa Educational Foundation
PO Box 789
408 N Union Street
Bloomington, IN 47402-0789
812-339-1156
800-786-1156
Fax: 812-339-0018
http://www.pdkintl.org
Designed as a ready reference, this edition of a popular digest provides a concise set of individual summaries of cases decided by the Supreme Court. Fully indexed.

256 pages Paperback
ISBN: 0-87367-835-4

Perry A Zirkel, Author
George Kersey, Executive Director
Donovan R Walling, Dir Publications/Research

3714 Directory for Exceptional Children
Porter Sargent Publishers, Inc.
11 Beacon Street
Suite 1400
Boston, MA 02108-3028
617-523-1670
800-342-7470
Fax: 617-523-1021
E-mail: info@portersargent.com
http://www.portersargent.com
A comprehensive survey of 2,500 schools, facilities and organizations across the country serving children and young adults with developmental, physical and medical disabilities. With 15 distinct chapters covering a range of disabilities, this work is an invaluable aid to parents and professionals seeking the optimal environment for special-needs children. Hardcover.

Publication Date: 1994 1152 pages BiAnnual
ISSN: 0070-5012

Dan McKeever, Senior Editor

3715 Directory of Catholic Special Educational Programs & Facilities
National Catholic Educational Association
1077 30th Street NW
Suite 100
Washington, DC 20007-3829
202-337-6232
Fax: 202-333-6706
Lists approximately 950 Catholic schools and day and residential school programs for children and adolescents with special education needs.

Publication Date: 1989 100 pages

3716 Directory of Central Agencies for Jewish Education
Jewish Education Service of North America
111 8th Avenue
New York, NY 10011
212-284-6882
Fax: 212-284-6951
E-mail: info@jesna.org
http://www.jesna.org
Offers educational resources for professionals in Jewish education, including general education information, materials and services.

Rika Levin, Director Marketing/Communica

3717 Directory of College Cooperative Education Programs
National Commission for Cooperative Education
360 Huntington Avenue
#384CP
Boston, MA 02115-5096
617-373-3770
Fax: 617-373-3463
E-mail: ncce@neu.edu
http://www.co-op.edu
A publication providing detailed information on cooperative education programs at 460 colleges throughout the United States.

Publication Date: 1962 219 pages
ISBN: 0-89774-998-4

Polly Hutcheson, VP
Paul Stonely, President

3718 Directory of ERIC Information Service Providers
Educational Resources Information Ctr./Access ERIC
1600 Research Boulevard
Rockville, MD 20850-3172
301-656-9723
Offers information on more than 1,000 government agencies, nonprofit and profit organizations, individuals and foreign organizations that provide access to ERIC microfiche collections, search services and abstract journal collections.

100 pages Biennial

3719 Directory of Graduate Programs
Graduate Record Examinations Program/ETS
PO Box 6014
Princeton, NJ 08541-6014
609-951-1542
Accredited institutions that offer graduate degrees.

1,400 pages 4 Volumes

3720 Directory of Indigenous Education
Floyd Beller - Wested
730 Harrison Street
San Francisco, CA 94107
415-565-3000
877-4we-sted
Fax: 415-565-3012
E-mail: fbeller@WestEd.org
http://www.wested.org
This revised and expanded edition incorporates a wider scope of information, including

a list of Head Start, Child Care and Title IX programs and JOM contractors, which enhances our principal goal of improving educational services to native students and communities.

Publication Date: 1998 94 pages

Floyd Beller, Research Associate

3721 Directory of International Internships: A World of Opportunities
International Studies & Programs
209 International Center
Michigan State University
East Lansing, MI 48824-1035
517-353-5589
Fax: 517-353-7254
E-mail: gliozzo@msu.edu
http://www.isp.msu.edu
A directory containing information about a wide range of overseas internship oppotunities. Over 500 entries of international internships sponsored by educational institutions, government agencies, and private organizations. There are indexes of topics in geographical areas listed by countries and geographical areas listed by topic.

Charles Gliozzo

3722 Directory of Member Institutions and Institutional Representatives
Council of Graduate Schools
1 Dupont Circle NW
Suite 430
Washington, DC 20036-1136
202-223-3791
Fax: 202-331-7157
Offers listings of over 400 member graduate schools in the US and Canada.

85 pages Annually

Nancy A Goffney, Administrator/Editor
Kathy Baker, Assistant

3723 Directory of Overseas Educational Advising Centers
College Board Publications
45 Columbus Avenue
New York, NY 10023-6917
212-713-8165
800-323-7155
Fax: 800-525-5562
http://www.collegeboard.org
This directory has been developed as a means through which institutions of higher education can communicate directly with overseas education advisers and through which advisers can communicate more directly with each other.

Publication Date: 1995 165 pages

3724 Directory of Postsecondary Institutions
National Center for Education Statistics
K Street NW
Washington, DC 20006
202-502-7300
877-4ED-PUBS
Fax: 301-470-1244
E-mail: edpubs@inet.ed.gov
http://www.ed.pubs/
Postsecondary institutions in the US, Puerto Rico, Virgin Islands and territories in the Pacific United States. Two volumes: Volume I Degree-Granting Institutions, Volume II Non-Degree-Granting Institutions.

Publication Date: 1990 500 pages Biennial

3725 Directory of Youth Exchange Programs
UN Educational, Scientific & Cultural Association
Youth Division, 1 Rue Miollis
Paris F-75015
France

1-4563842
Offers about 370 nonprofit organizations and governmental agencies in 95 countries that organize youth and student exchanges, study tours and correspondence exchanges.

Publication Date: 1992 225 pages

3726 Diversity, Accessibility and Quality

College Board Publications
45 Columbus Avenue
New York, NY 10023-6917
212-713-8165
800-323-7155
Fax: 800-525-5562
http://www.collegeboard.org
Primarily for non-Americans, this overview is designed to examine aspects of US education that have particular importance in programs of student exchange.

Publication Date: 1995 47 pages
ISBN: 0-874474-24-8

Clifford F Sjogren, Author

3727 Education Sourcebook: Basic Information about National Education Expectations and Goals

Omnigraphics
615 Griswold Street
Detroit, MI 48226
313-961-1340
800-234-1340
Fax: 313-961-1383
E-mail: info@omnigraphics.com
http://www.omnigraphics.com
A collection of education-related documents and articles for parents and students.

1123 pages
ISBN: 0-7808-0179-2

Jeanne Gough, Author
Paul Rogers, Publicity Associate

3728 Educational Placement Sources-Abroad

Education Information Services/Instant Alert
PO Box 620662
Newton, MA 02462-0662
617-433-0125
Lists 150 organizations, arranged by type, in the United States and abroad that place English-speaking teachers and education administrators in positions abroad.

19 pages Annual

FB Viaux, President

3729 Educational Rankings Annual

Gale Group
27500 Drake Road
Farmington Hills, MI 48331-3535
248-699-GALE
800-414-5043
Fax: 248-699-8069
E-mail: galeord@galegroup.com
http://www.galegroup.com
Top 10 lists from popular and scholarly periodicals, government publications, and others. The lists cover all facets of education.

890 pages Annual Hardcover
ISBN: 0-7876-7419-2

Lynn C Hattendorf Westney, Author
Kathleen Maki Petts, Coordinating Editor

3730 Educational Resources Catalog

CDE Press
PO Box 271
Sacramento, CA 95812-0271
916-445-1260
800-995-4099
Fax: 916-323-0823
http://www.cde.ca.gov/cdepress
Resource catalog from the California Department of Education.

3731 Educator's Desk Reference: A Sourcebook of Educational Information & Research

MacMillan Publishing Company
1633 Broadway
New York, NY 10019
212-654-8500
Fax: 800-835-3202
Directory includes national and regional education organizations.

Publication Date: 1989

3732 Educator's Scrapbook

Careers/Consultants Consultants in Education
3050 Palm Aire Drive N
#310
Pompano Beach, FL 33069
954-974-5477
Fax: 954-974-5477
E-mail: carconed@aol.com
Collection of education morsels offered to those who who would seek to redefine and clarify the aims and purposes of today's education. The book attepts to help its readers refocus upon the real purposes of education and their relationships to current education practices.

ISBN: 0-9703623-0-7
ISSN: 00-93185

Dr. Robert M Bookbinder, President

3733 Educators Guide to FREE Computer Materials and Internet Resources

Educators Progress Service
214 Center Street
Randolph, WI 53956-1408
920-326-3126
888-951-4469
Fax: 920-326-3127
E-mail: epsinc@centurytel.net
http://www.freeteachingaids.com
Lists and describes almost 2000 web sites of educational value. Available in two grade specific editions.

317 pages Annual
ISBN: 87708-362-2

Kathy Nehmer, President

3734 Educators Guide to FREE Films, Filmstrips and Slides

Educators Progress Service
214 Center Street
Randolph, WI 53956-1408
920-326-3126
888-951-4469
Fax: 920-326-3127
E-mail: epsinc@centurytel.net
http://www.freeteachingaids.com
Lists and describes free and free-loan films, filmstrips, slides, and audiotapes for all age levels.

135 pages Annual
ISBN: 87708-400-9

Kathy Nehmer, President

3735 Educators Guide to FREE Multicultural Material

Educators Progress Service
214 Center Street
Randolph, WI 53956-1408
920-326-3126
888-951-4469
Fax: 920-326-3127
E-mail: epsinc@centurytel.net
http://www.freeteachingaids.com
Lists and describes FREE films, videotapes, filmstrips, slides, web sites, and hundreds of free printed materials in the field of multicul-

tural and diversity education for all age levels.

198 pages Annual
ISBN: 87708-412-2

Kathy Nehmer, President

3736 El-Hi Textbooks and Serials in Print

RR Bowker Reed Reference
121 Chanlon Road
New Providence, NJ 07974-1541
908-464-6800
Fax: 908-665-6688
Listing of about 995 publishers of elementary and secondary level textbooks and related teaching materials.

Annual

3737 Environmental Education Materials: Guidelines for Excellence

North American Assoc for Environmental Education
2000 P Street NW
Suite 540
Washington, DC 20036
202-419-0412
Fax: 212-419-0415
E-mail: info@naaee.org
http://www.naaee.org
A set of recommendations for developing and selecting environmental education materials. These guidelines aim to help developers of activity guides, lesson plans, and other instructional materials produce high wuality products, and to provide educators with a tool to evaluate the wide array of available environmental education materials.

23 pages
ISBN: 1-884008-41-0

Bora Simmons, Author

3738 Evaluating Your Environmental EducationPrograms: A Workbook for Practitioners

North American Assoc for Environmental Education
2000 P Street NW
Suite 540
Washington, DC 20036
202-419-0412
Fax: 212-419-0415
E-mail: info@naaee.org
http://www.naaee.org
Walks you through how to design and conduct an evaluation. Throughout the workbook, 23 exercises as you to check your understanding (the answers are included). In addition, 47 application exercises point you to tasks that will help you develop your own evaluation.

Julie A Ernst, Author
Martha C Monroe, Author

3739 Excellence in Environmental Education:Guidelines for Learning (PreK-12)

North American Assoc for Environmental Education
2000 P Street NW
Suite 540
Washington, DC 20036
202-419-0412
Fax: 212-419-0415
E-mail: info@naaee.org
http://www.naaee.org
The guidelines support state and local environmental education efforts by: setting expectations for performance and achievement in fourth, eighth, and twelfth grades; suggesting a framework for effective and comprehensive environmental education programs and curricula; demonstrating how environmental edcuation can be used to meet standards set by the traditional disciplines and to give students

opportunities to synthesize knowledge and experience across disciplines.

121 pages
ISBN: 1-884008-75-5

Bora Simmons, Author

3740 Exceptional Children Education Resources
The Council for Exceptional Children
110 N Glebe Road
Suite 300
Arlington, VA 22201-5704
703-620-3660
800-232-7323
Fax: 703-264-9494
E-mail: cec@cec.sped.org
http://www.cec.sped.org/bk/catalog/journals.htm
A proprietary database that includes bibliographic data and abstract information on journal articles, and audiovisual materials in special education, and gifted education.

ISSN: 0160-4309

3741 Family Services Report
CD Publications
8204 Fenton Street
Sliver Spring, MD 20910
301-588-6380
301-666-6380
Fax: 301-588-0519
E-mail: fsr@cdpublications.com
http://cdpublications.com
Private grants for family service programs

18 pages
ISSN: 1524-9484

Ray Sweeney, Editor

3742 Fifty State Educational Directories
Career Guidance Foundation
8090 Engineer Road
San Diego, CA 92111-1906
619-560-8051
A collection on microfiche consisting of reproductions of the state educational directories published by each individual state department of education.

3743 Funny School Excuses
Careers/Consultants Consultants in Education
3050 Palm Aire Drive N
#310
Pompano Beach, FL 33069
954-974-5477
Fax: 954-974-5477
E-mail: carconed@aol.com
Collection of illustrations, cartoons and excuses gathered from authentic notes written by parents and sometimes their children. The book is wonderfully entertaining and recommended for its unusual humor, variety, and revelations of human nature.

ISBN: 0-7392-0309-6
ISSN: 99-95349

Dr. Robert M Bookbinder, President

3744 Ganley's Catholic Schools in America
Fisher Publishing Company
PO Box 15070
Scottsdale, AZ 85267-5070
800-759-7615
Fax: 480-657-9422
E-mail: publisher@ganleyscatholicschools.com
http://www.ganleyscatholicschool.com
Comprehensive listings on all Catholic Schools in America. Listings include phone numbers, addresses, names of administrators, number of students, complete diocesan, state, regional and national statistics. Includes an extensive analysis of demographic trends within Catholic elementary and secondary education, prepared by the National Catholic Education Association.

450+ pages Annual/June
ISBN: 1-558331-59-0

Millard T Fischer, Publisher

3745 Graduate & Undergraduate Programs & Courses in Middle East Studies in the US, Canada
Middle East Studies Association of North America
University of Arizona
1643 E Helen Street
Tucson, AZ 85721
520-621-5850
Fax: 520-626-9095
E-mail: mesana@u.arizona.edu
http://www.acls.org

3746 Guide to International Exchange, Community Service & Travel for Persons with Disabilities
Mobility International USA
45 W Broadway Suite 202
PO Box 10767
Eugene, OR 97401
541-343-1284
Fax: 541-343-6812
E-mail: info@miusa.org
http://www.miusa.org
This directory lists an impressive array of information regarding international study, living, travel, funding and contact organizations for people with disabilities.

Publication Date: 1997
ISBN: 1-880034-24-7

Christa Bucks, Editor

3747 Guide to Schools and Departments of Religion and Seminaries
MacMillan Publishing Company
1633 Broadway
New York, NY 10019
800-858-7674
Fax: 201-767-5029
Over 700 accredited programs and institutions granting degrees in theology, divinity and religion.

3748 Guide to Summer Camps & Schools
Porter Sargent Publishers
11 Beacon Street
Suite 1400
Boston, MA 02108-3028
617-523-1670
800-342-7470
Fax: 617-523-1021
E-mail: info@portersargent.com
http://www.portersargent.com
Covers the broad spectrum of recreational and educational summer opportunities. Current facts from 1,500 camps and schools, as well as programs for those with special needs or learning disabilities, makes the guide a comprehensive and convenient resource.

816 pages Biannual
ISBN: 0-875581-33-1

HJ Lane Coordinating Editor, Author
J Yonce, General Manager
Daniel McKeever, Sr Editor

3749 Guidelines for Effective Character Education Through Sports
Character Education Partnership
1025 Connecticut Avenue NW
Suite 1011
Washington, DC 20036
202-296-7743
800-988-8081
Fax: 202-296-7779
http://www.character.org
Guidelines for turning sports and physical education programs into the powerful, positive forces they should be.

Andrea Grenadier, Director Communications
Esther Schaeffer, CEO/Executive Director

3750 Guidelines for the Preparation andProfessional Development of Environmental Educator
North American Assoc for Environmental Education
2000 P Street NW
Suite 540
Washington, DC 20036
202-419-0412
Fax: 212-419-0415
E-mail: info@naaee.org
http://www.naaee.org
Recommendations about the basic knowledge and abilities educators need to provide high quality environmental education. The guidelines are designed to apply: within the context of pre-service teacher education programs and environmental education courses offered to students with varied backgrounds such as environmental studies, geography, liberal studies, or natural resources.

43 pages
ISBN: 1-884008-78-X

Bora Simmons, Author

3751 Handbook of Private Schools
Porter Sargent Publishers
11 Beacon Street
Suite 1400
Boston, MA 02108-3028
617-523-1670
800-342-7470
Fax: 617-523-1021
E-mail: info@portersargent.com
http://www.portersargent.com
Continuing a tradition that began in 1915, this handbook provides optimal guidance in the choice of educational environments and opportunities for students. Totally revised and updated, this 83rd edition presents current facts on 1,700 elementary and secondary boarding and day schools across the United States. Complete statistical data on enrollments, tuition, graduates, administrators and faculty have been compiled and objectively reported. Hardcover.

1472 pages Annual
ISBN: 0-875581-44-7

J Yonce, General Manager
Daniel McKeever, Sr Editor

3752 Handbook of United Methodist-Related Schools, Colleges, Universities & Theological Schools
General Board of Higher Education & Ministry/UMC
1001 19th Avenue
PO Box 340007
Nashville, TN 37203-0007
615-340-7406
Fax: 615-340-7379
E-mail: scu@gbhem.org
http://www.gbhem.org/highed.html
Includes two pages of information about each of United Methodist's 123 institutions, a chart indicating major areas of study, information about United Methodist loan and scholarship programs, as well as information about how to select a college. Published every four years.

344 pages Paperback

Dr. James A Noseworthy, Assistant General Secretary

3753 Hidden America
Place in the Woods
3900 Glenwood Avenue
Golden Valley, MN 55422-5302
763-374-2120
Fax: 952-593-5593
E-mail: placewoods@aol.com
Set of five reference-essay books on American minorities (African America; Hispanic America, the People (Native Americans); American women; My Own Book! classroom reference for elementary through secondary).

36+ pages Paperback Book

Roger Hammer, Publisher

3754 Higher Education Directory
Higher Education Publications
6400 Arlington Boulevard
Suite 648
Falls Church, VA 22042-2342
703-532-2300
888-349-7915
Fax: 703-532-2305
E-mail: info@hepinc.com
http://www.hepinc.com
Lists over 4,364 degree granting colleges and universities accredited by approved agencies, recognized by the US Secretary of Education successor to the Department of Education's: Education Directory, Colleges and Universities and Council for Higher Education Accreditation (CHEA).

Publication Date: 1994 1,040 pages Annual/Paperback
ISBN: 0-914927-44-2
ISSN: 0736-0197

Jeanne Burke, Editor
Fred Hafner JR, Vice President Operations

3755 Higher Education Opportunities for Women & Minorities: Annotated Selections
U.S. Office of Postsecondary Education
400 Maryland Avenue SW
Room 3915
Washington, DC 20202-0001
202-708-9180
Programs of public and private organizations and state and federal government agencies that offer loans, scholarships and fellowship opportunities for women and minorities.

143 pages Biennial

3756 Home from Home (Educational Exchange Programs)
Central Bureau for Educational Visits & Exchanges
10 Spring Gardens
London, SW1A 2BN, England
171-389-4004
Fax: 171-389-4426
150 organizations and agencies worldwide that arrange stays with families for paying guests or on an exchange basis. Organizations are geographically listed including a description of program, costs, insurance information, overseas representation and language instruction.

216 pages

3757 Homeschooler's Guide to FREE Teaching Aids
Educators Progress Service
214 Center Street
Randolph, WI 53956-1408
920-326-3126
888-951-4469
Fax: 920-326-3127
E-mail: epsinc@centurytel.net
http://www.freeteachingaids.com

Lists and describes free print materials specifically available to homeschoolers with students of all age levels.

277 pages
ISBN: 87708-375-4

Kathy Nehmer, President

3758 Homeschooler's Guide to FREE Videotapes
Educators Progress Service
214 Center Street
Randolph, WI 53956-1408
920-326-3126
888-951-4469
Fax: 920-326-3127
E-mail: epsinc@centurytel.net
http://www.freeteachingaids.com
Lists and describes free and free-loan videotapes specifically available to homeschoolers with students of all age levels.

248 pages Annual
ISBN: 87708-411-4

Kathy Nehmer, President

3759 IIEPassport: Academic Year Abroad 2007
Institute of International Education
809 United Nations Plaza
New York, NY 10017-3580
412-741-0930
Fax: 212-984-5496
E-mail: iiebooks@abdintl.com
http://www.iiebooks.org
Over 3,100 undergraduate and graduate study-abroad programs conducted worldwide during the academic year by United States and foreign colleges, universities, and private organizations.

Publication Date: 2007 Annual
ISBN: 87206-279-1

Marie O'Sullivan, Author
Daniel Obst, Sr Editor

3760 ISS Directory of Overseas Schools
International Schools Services
15 Roszel Road
PO Box 5910
Princeton, NJ 08540-6729
609-452-0990
Fax: 609-452-2690
E-mail: jlarsson@iss.edu
http://www.iss.edu
The only comprehensive guide to American and international schools around the world. The Directory is carefully researched and compiled to include current and complete information on over 600 international schools.

590 pages Paperback
ISBN: 0-913663-13-1

Jane Larsson, Director Of Education

3761 Inclusion Guide for Handling Chronically Disruptive Behavior
Master Teacher
Leadership Lane
PO Box 1207
Manhattan, KS 66505-1207
800-669-9633
Fax: 800-669-1132
http://www.masterteacher.com
A comprehensive process for ensuring that no disruptive behavior is tolerated, no student is turned away, and all students are served.

150 pages
ISBN: 0-914607-40-5

Teresa VanDover, Author

3762 Incorporating Multiple Intelligences into the Curriculum and into the Classroom: Elementary
Master Teacher
Leadership Lane
PO Box 1207
Manhattan, KS 66505-1207
800-669-9633
Fax: 800-669-1132
http://www.masterteacher.com
Contains lesson plans and teaching methods that address the needs of students and help them identify their strengths according to the domains of multiple intelligences.

181 pages
ISBN: 0-914607-63-4

3763 Incorporating Multiple Intelligences into the Curriculum and into the Classroom: Secondary
Master Teacher
Leadership Lane
PO Box 1207
Manhattan, KS 66505-1207
800-669-9633
Fax: 800-669-1132
http://www.masterteacher.com
Contains lesson plans and teaching methods that address the needs of students and help them identify their strengths according to the domains of multiple intelligences.

147 pages
ISBN: 0-914607-64-2

3764 Independent Schools Association of the Southwest-Membership List
Independent Schools Association of the Southwest
PO Box 52297
Tulsa, OK 74152-0297
817-569-9200
Fax: 817-569-9103
A geographical index of 65 independent elementary and secondary schools accredited by the association.

5 pages Annual/August

Richard W Ekdahl, Coordinating Education

3765 Independent Study Catalog
Peterson's Guides
PO Box 2123
Princeton, NJ 08543-2123
800-338-3282
Fax: 609-896-4531
A comprehensive listing of over 10,000 correspondence course offerings at 100 accredited colleges and universities nationwide, for those seeking the flexibility and convenience of at-home study.

293 pages
ISBN: 1-560794-60-7

3766 Industry Reference Handbooks
Gale Group
27500 Drake Road
Farmington Hills, MI 48331
248-699-4253
Fax: 248-699-8064
http://www.galegroup.com
Brings together and supplements Gale and D&B data on specific industries for reference use in public and academic libraries.

Hardcover
ISBN: 0787639567

Alen W Paschal, President

3767 International Federation of Organizations for School Correspondence/Exchange
FIOCES
29, rue d'ulm, F-75230 Paris
F-75230 Paris
France
Governmental agencies and other organizations concerned with scholastic correspondence and student exchange programs.

Publication Date: 1991 3 pages

3768 International Schools Directory
European Council of International Schools
21B Lavant Street, Petersfield,
Hampshire GU3 23EL
United Kingdom
1730-268244
Fax: 1730-267914
E-mail: 100412.242@compuserve.com
Over 420 ECIS schools in more than 90 countries; 300 affiliated colleges and universities worldwide; educational publishers and equipment suppliers.

550 pages Annual

JS Henleu, Coordinating Education

3769 International Study Telecom Directory
WorldWide Classroom
PO Box 1166
Milwaukee, WI 53201-1166
414-224-3476
Fax: 414-224-3466
E-mail: info@worldwide.edu
http://www.worldwide.edu
Comprehensive directory for locating educational resources both internationally and throughout the US Provides contact information on educational institutions including address, phone, fax, e-mail and URL. New icon system offers additional information on the type of programs offered. Resource guide at beginning includes useful web sites, airline and car rental contact numbers, currency converters, international organizations and international publications.

Mike Witley, President
Stacy Hargarten, Classroom Publications

3770 International Voluntary Service Directory
Volunteers for Peace
1034 Tiffany Road
Belmont, VT 05730
802-259-2759
Fax: 802-259-2922
E-mail: vfp@vfp.org
http://www.vfp.org
Comprehensive listing of over 3,400 workcamps in 100 countries around the world. Organized by country.

289 pages Annual
ISBN: 0-945617-20-B

Peter Coldwell, Director

3771 International Who's Who in Education
International Biographical Centre/Melrose Press
3 Regal Lane, Soham, Ely
Cambridgeshire CB7 5BA
United Kingdom
353-721091
Lists about 5,000 persons at all levels of teaching and educational administration.

1,000 pages

3772 International Yearbook of Education: Education in the World
UN Educational, Scientific & Cultural Assn.
7, place de Fontenoy
F-75700 Paris
France
1-45681000
Describes and offers information on educational systems worldwide.

Publication Date: 1989 200 pages

3773 Job Search Handbook for Educators
American Association for Employment in Education
3040 Riverside Drive
Suite 117
Columbus, OH 43221
614-485-1111
Fax: 360-244-7802
E-mail: execdir@aaee.org
http://www.aaee.org
Resume writing, interviewing tips, as well as articles on how to select the kind of school system you want, job fair networking and other related articles.

212 pages Bi-Annually

Neil Shnider, Executive Director
Diane Sledden Reed, Board President

3774 Legal Basics: A Handbook for Educators
Phi Delta Kappa International
408 N Union Street
PO Box 789
Bloomington, IL 47402-0789
812-339-1156
800-766-1156
Fax: 812-339-0018
http://www.pdkintl.org
Superintendents, principals, counselors, teachers, and paraprofessionals need to pay close attention to their actions in schools and classrooms because, from a legal standpoint, those settings may contain hazardous conditions. Legal Basics points out the pitfalls and how to avoid them.

Publication Date: 1998 120 pages Paperback
ISBN: 0-8736-806-0

Evelyn B Kelly, Author
DR Walling, Dir Publications/Research

3775 Lesson Plans and Modifications for Inclusion and Collaborative Classrooms
Master Teacher
Leadership Lane
PO Box 1207
Manhattan, KS 66505-1207
800-669-9633
Fax: 800-669-1132
http://www.masterteacher.com
Each modification is a complete lesson plan that gives the teacher a description of the activity and objetive the materials need and a step-by-step guide of how to carry out the learning process.

Publication Date: 0 242 pages
ISBN: 0-914607-37-5

3776 Lesson Plans for Character Education: Elementary Edition
Master Teacher
Leadership Lane
PO Box 1207
Manhattan, KS 66505-1207
800-669-9633
Fax: 800-669-1132
http://www.masterteacher.com
Gives you more than 140 practical lessons developed and tested by teachers across the curriculum and in all grade levels.

207 pages
ISBN: 0-914607-53-7

3777 List of Over 70 Higher Education Association
Educational Information Services
PO Box 662
Newton Lower Falls, MA 02162
617-964-4555
Provides descriptions and contact information on associations for individuals in higher education.

3778 List of State Boards of Higher Education
Educational Information Services
PO Box 662
Newton Lower Falls, MA 02162
617-964-4555
A compilation of the boards of education for all the states in the union.

3779 List of State Community & Junior College Board Offices
Educational Information Services
PO Box 662
Newton Lower Falls, MA 02162
617-964-4555
A list of the board officers and state officers within community, junior and university institutions.

3780 MDR School Directory
Market Data Retrieval
1 Forest Parkway
Shelton, CT 06484-6216
203-926-4800
800-333-8802
Fax: 203-929-5253
E-mail: msubrizi@dnb.com
MDR's school directories provide comprehensive data on every public school district and school, Catholic and other independent schools, regional and county centers in all fifty states and the District of Columbia. Updated each year, each state directory contains current names and job titles of key decision makers, school and district addresses, phone numbers, current enrollments and much more. Also available on CD-ROM and diskette.

51 Volume Set

Mike Subrizi, Director Marketing

3781 Minority Student Guide to American Colleges
Paoli Publishing
1708 E Lancaster Avenue
Suite 287
Paoli, PA 19301-1553
215-640-9889
Covers colleges, military schools, and financial aid information for minority students.

89 pages

3782 Monograph 1-Using a Logic Model to Review andAnalyze an Environmental Education Program
North American Assoc for Environmental Education
2000 P Street NW
Suite 540
Washington, DC 20036
202-419-0412
Fax: 212-419-0415
E-mail: info@naaee.org
http://www.naaee.org
Reviews and analyzes a long-standing and well-documented program in environmental education, Hungerford et al.'s issue-and-action instruction program (1973-). Logic models provide conceptual guidance and visual support for this review and analysis. These models were adapted from work in Aquatic

Resource Education by Peyton, and the literature on logic modeling in program evaluation.

72 pages
ISBN: 1-884008-86-0

Thomas C Marcinkowski, Author

3783 Monograph 2-Preparing Effective Environmental Educators

North American Assoc for Environmental Education
2000 P Street NW
Suite 540
Washington, DC 20036
202-419-0412
Fax: 212-419-0415
E-mail: info@naaee.org
http://www.naaee.org
Focuses on the methods used to prepare those who teach environmental education. Research and evaluation related to three main audiences for environmental education preparedness training - pre-service teachers, in-service teachers, and nonformal education - are examined. The five papers presented represent an interesting and instructive array of research and evaluation that can be used to spur our thinking about the preparation of environmental educators.

89 pages
ISBN: 1-884008-88-7

Bora Simmons, Author

3784 NAFSA's Guide to Education Abroad for Advisers & Administrators

NAFSA: Association of International Educators
1307 New York Avenue NW
8th Floor
Washington, DC 20005-4701
202-737-3699
800-836-4994
Fax: 202-737-3657
E-mail: inbox@nafsa.org
http://www.nafsa.org

Marlene M Johnson, Director/CEO

3785 NEA Almanac of Higher Education

National Education Association (NEA)
1201 16th Street NW
Washington, DC 20036-3207
202-833-4000
Fax: 202-822-7624
E-mail: nche@nea.org
http://www.nea.org
Annually
ISSN: 0743-670X

Con Lehane, Author

3786 National Directory of Children, Youth & Families Services

Contexo Media
2755 E Cottonwood Parkway
Suite 400
Salt Lake City, UT 84120
800-343-6681
Fax: 801-365-0710
E-mail:
customersupport@contexomedia.com
http://www.contexomedia.com
Organized by state and county, this directory lists over 30,000 organizations and 46,000 contacts that focus on helping anyone who is committed to providing the best possible service to our nation's at-risk children, youth and families.

Publication Date: 0 1456 pages Annually

Treavor Peterson, President
Kim Luna, Product Manager

3787 National Guide to Educational Credit for Training Programs

American Council on Education
1 Dupont Circle NW
Suite 535
Washington, DC 20036-1110
202-939-9430
Fax: 202-833-4762
More than 4,500 courses offered by over 280 government agencies, business firms and nonprofit groups.

1,018 pages Annual

3788 National Reference Directory of Year-Round Education Programs

National Association for Year-Round Education
PO Box 711386
San Diego, CA 92171-1386
619-276-5296
Fax: 858-571-5754
E-mail: info@nayre.org
http://www.nayre.org
Six hundred fifty school districts in the US with year-round programs are covered in this directory, listed by geographical location, including all contact information and descriptions.

178 pages Annual Paperback

Shirley Jennings, Directory Editor
Samuel Pepper, Executive Director

3789 National Schools of Character: Best Practices and New Perspectives

Character Education Partnership
1025 Connecticut Avenue NW
Suite 1011
Washington, DC 20036
202-296-7743
800-988-8081
Fax: 202-296-7779
http://www.character.org

Andrea Grenadier, Director Communications
Esther Schaeffer, CEO/Executive Director

3790 National Schools of Character: Practices to Adopt & Adapt

Character Education Partnership
1025 Connecticut Avenue NW
Suite 1011
Washington, DC 20036
202-296-7743
800-988-8081
Fax: 202-296-7779
http://www.character.org

Andrea Grenadier, Director Communications
Esther Schaeffer, CEO/Executive Director

3791 National Society for Experiential Education

515 King Street
Suite 420
Alexandria, VA 22314
703-706-9552
Fax: 703-684-6048
E-mail: info@nsee.org
http://www.nsee.org
28 pages Quarterly

Linda Goff, Author

3792 New England Association of Schools and Colleges

New England Association of Schools and Colleges
209 Burlington Road
Bedford, MA 01730-1433
781-271-0022
Fax: 781-271-0950
Listing of over 1,575 institutions of higher education, public and independent schools and vocational-technical schools in New England.

65 pages Annual

3793 Nonformal Environmental Education Programs: Guidelines for Excellence

North American Assoc for Environmental Education
2000 P Street NW
Suite 540
Washington, DC 20036
202-419-0412
Fax: 212-419-0415
E-mail: info@naaee.org
http://www.naaee.org
A set of recommendations for developing and administering high quality nonformal environmental education programs. These recommendations provide a tool that can be used to ensure a firm foundation for new programs or to trigger improvements in existing ones. The overall goal of these guidelines is to facilitate a superior educational process leading to the environmental quality that people desire.

ISBN: 1-884008-89-5

Bora Simmons, Author

3794 Overseas American-Sponsored Elementary and Secondary Schools

US Department of State, Office Overseas Schools
Room 245, SA-29
Washington, DC 20522
202-647-4000
Fax: 202-261-8224
Lists nearly 180 independent schools overseas and 10 regional associations of schools.

30 pages Annual

3795 Paradigm Lost: Leading America Beyond It'sFear of Educational Change

American Association of School Administrators
801 N Quincy Street
Suite 700
Arlington, VA 22203-1730
703-528-0700
Fax: 703-841-1543
E-mail: info@aasa.org
http://www.aasa.org
Explores the beliefs and assumptions upon which schools operate, provides powerful and practical insights and improvement strategies.

Publication Date: 1998 158 pages Softcover
ISBN: 0-87652-232-0

William G Spady, Editor

3796 Patterson's American Education

Educational Directories Inc
Po Box 68097
Schaumburg, IL 60168
847-459-0605
800-357-6183
Fax: 847-891-0945
E-mail: info@ediusa.com
http://www.ediusa.com
Lists more than 11,000 public school districts; 300 parochial superintendents; 400 territorial schools; 400 state department of education personnel; and 400 educational associations in one easy to use consistent format. Arranged alphabetically by state then by city. City listings include the city name, telephone area code, city population, county name, public school district name, enrollment, grade range, superintendent's name, ad-

dress and phone number. Index of secondary schools included.

Publication Date: 1994 974 pages Annual
ISBN: 0-9771602-3-8
ISSN: 0079-0230

Linda Moody, Office Manager

3797 Patterson's Schools Classified
Educational Directories Inc.
1025 W Wise Road
PO Box 68097
Schaumburg, IL 60168
847-891-1250
800-357-6183
Fax: 847-891-0945
E-mail: info@ediusa.org
http://www.ediusa.org
Contains 7,000 accredited postsecondary schools, the broadest assortment available in a single directory. Universities, colleges, community colleges, junior colleges, career schools and teaching hospitals are co-mingled under 50 academic disciplines but retain their school type identification. School professional accreditation is shown in 32 classifications. The basic entry includes school name, mailing address and contact person, with additional descriptive material supplied by the school.

Publication Date: 2006 302 pages Annual
ISBN: 0-9771602-2-X

Wayne Moody, Coordinating Education

3798 Persons as Resources
World Council for Curriculum & Instruction
School of Education
Indiana University
Bloomington, IN 47405
812-336-4702
Fax: 812-856-8088
Listing of about 600 member individuals and institutions concerned with curriculum and instruction in schools, colleges, universities and non-school agencies.

75 pages Triennial

3799 Peterson's Competitive Colleges
Peterson's, A Nelnet Company
Princeton Pike Corporate Center
2000 Lenox Drive PO Box 67005
Lawrenceville, NJ 08648
609-896-1800
800-338-3282
Fax: 609-896-4531
E-mail: custsvc@petersons.com
http://www.petersons.com
The most trusted source of advice for excellent students searching for high-quality schools. Provides objective criteria to compare more than 440 leading colleges and universities.

524 pages
ISBN: 1-560795-98-0

3800 Peterson's Guide to Four-Year Colleges
Peterson's, A Nelnet Company
Princeton Pike Corporate Center
2000 Lenox Drive PO Box 67005
Lawrenceville, NJ 08648
609-896-1800
800-338-3282
Fax: 609-896-1811
E-mail: custsvc@petersons.com
http://www.petersons.com
Includes descriptions of over 2,000 colleges, providing guidance on selecting the right school, getting in and financial aid.

2,922 pages

3801 Peterson's Guide to Two-Year Colleges
Peterson's, A Nelnet Company
Princeton Pike Corporate Center
2000 Lenox Drive PO Box 67005
Lawrenceville, NJ 08648
609-896-1800
800-338-3282
Fax: 609-896-4531
E-mail: custsvc@petersons.com
http://www.petersons.com
The only two-year college guide available, this new and expanded directory is the most complete source of information on institutions that grant an associate as their highest degree.

Publication Date: 2006 712 pages
ISBN: 1-560796-05-7

3802 Peterson's Regional College Guide Set
Peterson's, A Nelnet Company
Princeton Pike Corporate Center
2000 Lenox Drive PO Box 67005
Lawrenceville, NJ 08648
609-896-1800
800-338-3282
Fax: 609-896-4531
E-mail: custsvc@petersons.com
http://www.petersons.com
Six individual regional guides that help students compare colleges in a specific geographic area.

3803 Power of Public Engagement Book Set
Master Teacher
Leadership Lane
PO Box 1207
Manhattan, KS 66505-1207
800-669-9633
Fax: 800-669-1132
http://www.masterteacher.com
Learn how to engage your community to make the changes needed to ensure the best education for its children.

ISBN: 1-58992-128-3

William G O'Callaghan Jr, Author

3804 PreK-12 Excellence In Environmental EducatioEducation
North American Assoc for Environmental Education
2000 P Street NW
Suite 540
Washington, DC 20036
202-419-0412
Fax: 212-419-0415
E-mail: info@naaee.org
http://www.naaee.org
Offers a vision of environmental education and promotes progress toward sustaining a healthy environment and quality of life. The Guidelines support state and local environmental efforts by: setting expectations for performance and achievement in fourth, eighth, and twelfth grades; suggesting a framework for effective and comprehensive environmental education programs.

ISBN: 1-884008-77-1

Bora Simmons, Author

3805 Private Independent Schools
Bunting & Lyon
238 N Main Street
Wallingford, CT 06492-3728
203-269-3333
Fax: 203-269-5697
E-mail: BuntingandLyon@aol.com
http://www.buntingandlyon.com
Provides information on more than 1,100 elementary and secondary private schools and summer programs in the United States and

abroad. This annual guide, now in its 56th edition, is the most concise, current resource available on private school programs.

Publication Date: 1996 644 pages Annual
Hardcover
ISBN: 0-913094-56-0
ISSN: 0079-5399

Peter G Bunting, Publisher

3806 Private School Law in America
Progressive Business Publications
370 Technology Drive
Malvern, PA 19355
800-220-5000
Fax: 610-647-8089
E-mail: customer_service@pbp.com
http://www.pbp.com
An up-to-date compilation of summarized federal and state appellate court decisions which affect private education. The full legal citation is supplied for each case. A brief introductory note on the American judicial system is provided along with updated appendices of recent US Supreme Court cases and recently published law review articles. Also included are portions of the US Constitution which are most frequently cited in private education cases.

500 pages Annually
ISBN: 0-939675-80-3

3807 Public Schools USA: A Comparative Guide to School Districts
Peterson's, A Nelnet Company
Princeton Pike Corporate Center
2000 Lenox Drive PO Box 67005
Lawrenceville, NJ 08648
609-896-1800
800-338-3282
Fax: 609-896-4531
E-mail: custsvc@petersons.com
http://www.petersons.com
Lists over 400 school districts in 52 metropolitan areas throughout the United States.

490 pages Annual

Charles Hampton Harrison, Author

3808 School Foodservice Who's Who
Information Central
PO Box 3900
Prescott, AZ 86302-3900
520-778-1513
Listing of over 2,500 food service programs in public and Catholic school systems.

110 pages Triennial

3809 School Guide
School Guide Publications
210 N Avenue
New Rochelle, NY 10801-6402
914-632-7771
800-433-7771
Fax: 914-632-3412
E-mail: info@schoolguides.com
http://schoolguides.com
Listing of over 3,000 colleges, vocational schools and nursing schools in the US.

280 pages Annual/Paperback
ISBN: 1-893275-30-2

Janette Aiello, Editor

3810 Schools Abroad of Interest to Americans
Porter Sargent Publishers
11 Beacon Street
Suite 1400
Boston, MA 02108-3028
617-523-1670
800-342-7470
Fax: 617-523-1021
E-mail: info@portersargent.com
http://www.portersargent.com

Lists and authoritatively describes 800 elementary and secondary schools in 130 countries. Written for the educator, personnel advisor, student and parent as well as diplomatic and corporate officials, this unique guide is an indispensable reference for American students seeking preparatory schooling overseas. Hardcover.

Publication Date: 1991 544 pages BiAnnual

J Yonce, General Manager
Daniel McKeever, Sr Editor

3811 Schools-Business & Vocational Directory
American Business Directories
5711 S 86th Circle
Omaha, NE 68127-4146
402-593-4600
888-999-1307
Fax: 402-331-5481
A complete listing of business and vocational schools nationwide. Includes phone numbers, contact names, employee sizes and more.

Annual

Jerry Venner, Coordinating Education

3812 Treasury of Noteworthy Proverbs
Careers/Consultants Consultants in Education
3050 Palm Aire Drive N
#310
Pompano Beach, FL 33069
954-974-5477
Fax: 954-974-5477
E-mail: carconed@aol.com
Tapestry of maxims, aphorisims, and pithy sayings. A revealing picture of the wisdom, philosophy, and humor of the people of this and many other nations throughout the world.

ISBN: 0-7392-0208-1
ISSN: 99-943-75

Dr. Robert M Bookbinder, President

3813 US Supreme Court Education Cases
Progressive Business Publications
370 Technology Drive
Malvern, PA 19355
800-220-5000
Fax: 610-647-8089
E-mail: customer_service@pbp.com
http://www.pbp.com
A compilation of summarized US Supreme Court decisions since 1954 which affect education. The full legal citation is supplied for each case. Also included are portions of the US Constitution which are most frequently cited in education cases.

Annually

3814 VincentCurtis Educational Register
Vincent-Curtis
PO Box 724
Falmouth, MA 02541-0724
508-457-6473
Fax: 508-457-6499
E-mail: stan@vincentcurtis.com
http://www.vincentcurtis.com
An online guide to a variety of private boarding and day schools and resident summer programs in the United States, Canada and Europe, together with articles by school heads and camp directors of interest to educators and parents of students 10-18.

Publication Date: 1994 236 pages Annual/June

Stan Vincent, Editor

3815 Western Association of Schools and Colleges
Western Association of Schools and Colleges
3060 Valencia Avenue
#70
Aptos, CA 95003-4126
831-688-7575
Listing of schools and colleges in California, Hawaii, Guam, American Samoa and East Asia.

130 pages Annual

3816 What's Fair Got to Do With It
North American Assoc for Environmental Education
2000 P Street NW
Suite 540
Washington, DC 20036
202-419-0412
Fax: 212-419-0415
E-mail: info@naaee.org
http://www.naaee.org
Educators will find these cases a powerful tool for professional development. Each case is a candid, dramatic, and highly readable first-person account that makes concrete the challenges of fairness, expectations, respect, and communication when people who share goals, perhaps, but not cultures, interact.

119 pages
ISBN: 0-914409-20-4

Tania D Madfes, Editor

3817 Whole Nonprofit Catalog
Grantmanship Center
PO Box 17720
Los Angeles, CA 90017
Offers information on training programs offered by the Center, publications and other services available to the nonprofit sector.

3818 Working Together: A Guide to Community-Based Educational Resources
Research, Advocacy & Legislation/Council of LaRaza
810 1st Street NE
Suite 300
Washington, DC 20002-4227
202-289-1380
Listing of about 30 community-based organizations nationwide providing educational services to Hispanic Americans.

35 pages

3819 World of Learning
Gale Group
27500 Drake Road
Farmington Hills, MI 48331
248-699-4253
800-877-4253
Fax: 248-699-8064
E-mail: galeord@galegroup.com
http://www.galegroup.com
Contains information for over 26,000 universities, colleges, schools of art and music, libraries, archives, learned societies, research institutes, museums and art galleries in more than 180 countries.

ISBN: 0-7876-5004-8

Allen W Paschal, President

Directories & Handbooks / *Administration*

3820 American Association of Collegiate Registrars & Admissions Officers
American Association of Collegiate Registrars
1 Dupont Circle NW
Suite 330
Washington, DC 20036-1137
202-293-9161
Fax: 202-872-8857
Offers more than 2,300 member institutions and 8,400 college and university registrars, financial aid information and admissions officers.

Publication Date: 1995 224 pages Annual

3821 American School & University - Who's Who Directory & Buyer's Guide
Prism Business Media
9800 Metcalf Avenue
Overland Park, KS 66212-2286
913-967-1960
Fax: 913-967-1905
E-mail: jagron@asumag.com
http://www.asumag.com
Comprehensive directory of suppliers and products for facility needs; listings of architects by region; listing of associations affiliated with the education industry; article index for quick and easy reference; in-depth calendar of events.

Annual

Joe Agron, Editor-In-Chief
Susan Lustig, Executive Editor

3822 Bricker's International Directory
Peterson's, A Nelnet Company
Princeton Pike Corporate Center
2000 Lenox Drive PO Box 67005
Lawrenceville, NJ 08648
609-896-1800
800-338-3282
Fax: 609-896-4531
E-mail: custsvc@petersons.com
http://www.petersons.com
Offers over 400 residential management development programs at academic institutions in the United States and abroad.

Annual

3823 Cabells Directory of Publishing Opportunities in Educational Psychology and Administration
Cabell Publishing Company
Box 5428
Tobe Hahn Station
Beaumont, TX 77726
409-898-0575
Fax: 409-866-9554
E-mail: publish@cabells.com
http://www.cabells.com
Provides information on editor contact information, manuscript guidelines, acceptance rate, review information and circulation data for over 225 academic journals.

799 pages Annual
ISBN: 0-911753-28-1

David WE Cabell, Editor
Deborah L English, Associate Editor

3824 Character Education Questions & Answers
Character Education Partnership
1025 Connecticut Avenue NW
Suite 1011
Washington, DC 20036
202-296-7743
800-988-8081

Fax: 202-296-7779
http://www.character.org
Andrea Grenadier, Director
Communications
Esther Schaeffer, CEO/Executive Director

3825 Character Education Resource Guide
Character Education Partnership
1025 Connecticut Avenue NW
Suite 1011
Washington, DC 20036
202-296-7743
800-988-8081
Fax: 202-296-7779
http://www.character.org
Andrea Grenadier, Director
Communications
Esther Schaeffer, CEO/Executive Director

3826 Character Education: The Foundation for Teacher Education
Character Education Partnership
1025 Connecticut Avenue NW
Suite 1011
Washington, DC 20036
202-296-7743
800-988-8081
Fax: 202-296-7779
http://www.character.org
Andrea Grenadier, Director
Communications
Esther Schaeffer, CEO/Executive Director

3827 Continuing Education Guide
International Association for Continuing Education
Department #3087
Washington, DC 20042-0001
202-463-2905
Fax: 202-463-8498
Explores how to interpret and use the Continuing Education Unit or other criteria used for continuing education programs. This guide, written by continuing education and training consultant, Louis Phillips, is a reference source complete with sample forms, charts, checklists and everything you need to plan, develop and evaluate your school's continuing education program.

3828 Creating Quality Reform: Programs, Communities and Governance
Pearson Education Communications
1 Lake Street
Upper Saddle River, NJ 07458
201-236-7000
Fax: 877-260-2530
E-mail: communications@pearsoned.com
http://www.pearsoned.com
Publication Date: 2002
J Thomas Owens, Editor
Jan C Simmons, Editor

3829 Designing & Implementing a Leadership Academy in Character Education
Character Education Partnership
1025 Connecticut Avenue NW
Suite 1011
Washington, DC 20036
202-296-7743
800-988-8081
Fax: 202-296-7779
http://www.character.org
Andrea Grenadier, Director
Communications
Esther Schaeffer, CEO/Executive Director

3830 Deskbook Encyclopedia of American School Law
Progressive Business Publications
370 Technology Drive
Malvern, PA 19355

800-220-5000
Fax: 610-647-8089
E-mail: customer_service@pbp.com
http://www.pbp.com
An up-to-date compilation of summarized federal and state appellate court decisions which affect education. The full legal citation is supplied for each case with a brief introductory note on the American judicial system is provided along with updated appendices of recent US Supreme Court cases and recently published law review articles.
Annually

3831 Developing a Character Education Program
Character Education Partnership
1025 Connecticut Avenue NW
Suite 1011
Washington, DC 20036
202-296-7743
800-988-8081
Fax: 202-296-7779
http://www.character.org
Henry Huffman, Author
Andrea Grenadier, Director
Communications
Esther Schaeffer, CEO/Executive Director

3832 Development Education: A Directory of Non-Governmental Practitioners
U.N. Non-Governmental Liaison Service
Palais des Nations, CH 1211
Geneva 10
Switzerland
Lists about 800 national non-governmental organizations in industrialized countries and international non-governmental networks concerned with developmental education.
Publication Date: 1992 400 pages

3833 Directory of Chief Executive Officers of United Methodist Schools, Colleges & Universities
General Board of Higher Education & Ministry/UMC
1001 19th Avenue
PO Box 340007
Nashville, TN 37203-0007
615-340-7406
Fax: 615-340-7379
E-mail: scu@gbhem.org
http://www.gbhem.org/highed.html
123 United Methodist educational institutions including theology schools, professional schools, two year colleges and colleges and universities with all contact information arranged by institution type. Paperback.
32 pages Annual
Dr. James A Noseworthy, Assistant General Secretary

3834 Directory of Organizations in Educational Management
ERIC Clearinghouse on Educational Management
1787 Agate Street
Eugene, OR 97403-1923
541-346-5043
800-438-8841
Fax: 541-346-2334
E-mail: sales@oregon.uoregon.edu
http://www.eric.uoregon.edu
Offers listings of 163 organizations in the field of educational management at the elementary and secondary school levels.
Dr. Philip Piele, Director
Stuart C Smith, Associate Director

3835 Directory of State Education Agencies
Council of Chief State School Officers
1 Massachusette Avenue NW
Suite 700
Washington, DC 20001-1431
202-336-7000
Fax: 202-408-8072
http://www.ccsso.org
A reference to state and national education agency contracts. Arranged state-by-state, it includes state education agency personnel titles, addresses, phone numbers, and fax numbers when applicable. National information includes key contacts and information for 33 national education associations and 5 pages of names, titles, addresses, and numbers for the US Department of Education.
103 pages
ISBN: 1-884037-66-6
Kathleen Neary, Editor

3836 Educating for Character
Master Teacher
Leadership Lane
PO Box 1207
Manhattan, KS 66505-1207
800-669-9633
Fax: 800-669-1132
http://www.masterteacher.com
Dr. Licona has developed a 12 point program that offers practical strategies designed to create a working coalition of parents, teachers and communities.
428 pages
ISBN: 0-553-37052-9
Thomas Lickona PhD, Author

3837 Educating for Character: How Our Schools Can Teach Respect and Responsibility
Character Education Partnership
1025 Connecticut Avenue NW
Suite 1011
Washington, DC 20036
202-296-7743
800-988-8081
Fax: 202-296-7779
http://www.character.org
Tom Likona, Author
Andrea Grenadier, Director
Communications
Esther Schaeffer, CEO/Executive Director

3838 Education Budget Alert
Committee for Education Funding
122 C Street NW
Suite 280
Washington, DC 20001-2109
202-383-0083
Fax: 202-383-0097
E-mail: jchang@cef.org
http://www.cef.org
Federal programs currently help over 63 million Americans to engage in formal learning. This guidebook explains what these programs do, what types of activities are supported, the reasons the federal government initiated these programs, and their level at funding.
150 pages Annually
Jennifer Chang, Administrative Assistant
Michael Pons, Editor

3839 Educational Consultants Directory
American Business Directories, Inc.
5711 S 86th Circle
PO Box 27347
Omaha, NE 68127
402-593-4600
800-555-6124
Fax: 402-331-5481
E-mail: directory@abi.com

A list of more than 5,000 entries, including name, address, phone, size of advertisement, name of owner or manager and number of employees.

3840 Educational Dealer-Buyers' Guide Issue
Fahy-Williams Publishing
171 Reed Street
Geneva, NY 14456-2137
315-789-0458
Fax: 315-789-4263
List of approximately 2,000 suppliers of educational materials and equipment.

Annual

3841 Executive Summary Set
Master Teacher
Leadership Lane
PO Box 1207
Manhattan, KS 66502
800-669-9633
Fax: 800-669-1132
http://www.masterteacher.com
An easy, effective and practical way to orient new board members before they attend their first meeting. Executive Summary Sets cover the vital information board members must have in eight areas: tenets of education; powers and responsibilities; decision making; communication for maximum results; resource management; assessment of programs; assessment of personnel and conflict resolution.

Robert DeBruyn, Editor

3842 Grants and Contracts Handbook
Association of School Business Officials Int'l
11401 N Shore Drive
Reston, VA 20190-4232
703-478-0405
Fax: 703-478-0205
This is a basic reference for grant applicants, executors, project managers, administrators and staff. The ideas are school-tested and based on information gathered from institutions and agencies over the past two decades.

32 pages
ISBN: 0-910170-52-5

Peg D Kirkpatrick, Editor/Publisher
Robert Gluck, Managing Editor

3843 Hispanic Yearbook-Anuario Hispano
TIYM Publishing
6718 Whittier Avenue
Suite 130
McLean, VA 22101
703-734-1632
Fax: 703-356-0787
E-mail: TIYM@aol.com
http://www.tiym.com
This guide lists Hispanic organizations, publications, radio and TV stations, through not specifically for grant-giving purposes.

Annually

John O Zavala, COO
Ramon Palencia, Director PR

3844 Leading to Change: The Challenge of the New Superintendency
Jossey-Bass/Pfeiffer
989 Market Street
San Francisco, CA 94103-1741
415-433-1740
Fax: 415-433-0499
http://www.josseybass.com
The challenge of the new superintendency.

352 pages
ISBN: 0-7879-0214-4

Susan Moore Johnson, Author

3845 Legal Basics: A Handbook for Educators
Phi Delta Kappa International
PO Box 789
Bloomington, IL 47402-0789
812-339-1156
Fax: 812-339-0018
http://www.pdkintl.org
Superintendents, principals, counselors, teachers, and paraprofessionals need to pay close attention to their actions in schools and classrooms because, from a legal standpoint, those settings may contain hazardous conditions. Legal Basics points out the pitfalls and how to avoid them.

120 pages Paperback
ISBN: 8-87367-806-0

Evelyn B Kelly, Author
DR Walling, Dir Publications/Research

3846 Legal Issues and Education Technology
National School Board Association
PO Box 161
Annapolis Junction, MD 20701
800-706-6722
Fax: 703-683-7590
Helps administrators craft an acceptable-use policy.

Publication Date: 1999
ISSN: 0314510

3847 Lifeworld of Leadership: Creating Culture,Community, and Personal Meaning in Our Schools
Jossey-Bass Publishers
989 Market Street
San Francisco, CA 94103-1741
415-433-1740
Fax: 415-433-0499
http://www.josseybass.com
Explores the crucial link between school improvement and school character.

Publication Date: 2004 240 pages Paperback
ISBN: 0-7879-7277-6

Thomas J Sergiovanni

3848 Looking at Schools: Instruments & Processes for School Analysis
Research for Better Schools
112 N Broad Street
Philadelphia, PA 19102
215-568-6150
Fax: 215-568-7260
http://www.rbs.org
Thirty-five institutions that offer instruments and processes to assess the performance of students, teachers and administrators, school climate effectiveness and school-community relations.

Publication Date: 1991 140 pages

Carol Crociante, Executive Secretary
Keith M Kershner, Executive Co-Director

3849 Market Data Retrieval-National School Market Index
Market Data Retrieval
1 Forest Parkway
Shelton, CT 06484-0947
203-926-4800
800-333-8802
Fax: 203-929-5253
E-mail: msubrizi@dnb.com
An annual report on school spending patterns for instructional materials in the United States. The Index now in its twenty-fifth year of publication, lists the expenditures for instructional materials for all 15,000 US senior districts.

Publication Date: 1996
ISBN: 0-897708-25-3

Mike Subrizi, Marketing Director

3850 National Association of Principals of Schools for Girls Directory
National Association of Principals/Girls Schools
4050 Little River Road
Hendersonville, NC 28739-8317
828-693-8248
Fax: 828-693-1490
List of 575 principals and deans of private and secondary schools for girls and coeducational schools, colleges and admissions officers.

Annual

3851 National School Public Relations Association Directory
National School Public Relations Association
1501 Lee Highway
Arlington, VA 22209-1109
703-528-6713
Lists over 2,800 school system public relations directors and school administration officers.

100 pages Annual

3852 National School Supply & Equipment Association Membership/Buyers' Guide Directory
National School Supply & Equipment Association
830 Colesville Road
Suite 250
Silver Spring, MD 20910
301-495-0240
800-395-5550
Fax: 301-495-3330
E-mail: awatts@nssea.org
http://www.nssea.org
Lists 1,500 member dealers, manufacturers and manufacturers' representatives for school supplies, equipment and instructional materials.

200 pages Annual

Adrienne Watts, Author
Adrienne Watts, VP Marketing
Kathy Jentz, Director Communications

3853 National Schools of Character
Character Education Partnership
1025 Connecticut Avenue NW
Suite 1011
Washington, DC 20036
202-296-7743
800-988-8081
Fax: 202-296-7779
http://www.character.org

Andrea Grenadier, Director Communications
Esther Schaeffer, CEO/Executive Director

3854 Proactive Leadership in the 21st Century
Master Teacher
Leadership Lane
PO Box 1207
Manhattan, KS 66505-1207
800-669-9633
Fax: 800-669-1132
http://www.masterteacher.com
Contain the laws and principals of leadership and people management as they had never been defined and described before giving school administrators a set of guidelines that if followed would guarantee success.

ISBN: 0-914607-44-8

Robert L DeBruyn, Author

3855 QED's State School Guides
Quality Education Data
1625 Broadway Street
Suite 250
Denver, CO 80203
303-860-1832
800-525-5811
Fax: 303-209-9444
E-mail: info@qeddata.com
http://www.qeddata.com
Complete directories of every US school district and public, Catholic and private school. Directories are available for individual states, geographic regions and the entire United States. Each directory includes names of district administrators, school principals and school librarians, as well as addresses, phone numbers and enrollment information. QED's State school guide also includes key demographic and instructional technology data for each district and school.

Publication Date: 1993 Yearly
ISBN: 0-887476-49-0

Liz Stephens, Marketing

3856 School Promotion, Publicity & Public Relations: Nothing but Benefits
Master Teacher
Leadership Lane
PO Box 1207
Manhattan, KS 66505-1207
785-539-0555
800-669-9633
Fax: 785-539-7739
http://www.masterteacher.com
Contains the vital foundations an administrator must have to understand and implement a program of publicity, promotion and public relations, in a school or school district.

327 pages
ISBN: 0-914607-25-1

Tracey H DeBruyn, Author

3857 Schoolwide Discipline Strategies that Make a Difference in Teaching & Learning
Master Teacher
Leadership Lane
PO Box 1207
Manhattan, KS 66505-1207
800-669-9633
Fax: 800-669-1132
http://www.masterteacher.com
This approach to discipline will help your school or district eliminate the dependecy on one individual, provide guidance for present and new teachers, allow disipline to become a K-12 program, an bring about consistancy in the handling of all student misbehaviors.

150 pages
ISBN: 1-58992-000-7

Larry Dixon, Author

3858 The Teaching Professor
Magna Publications
2718 Dryden Drive
Madison, WI 53704
608-246-3590
Fax: 608-246-3597
E-mail: billh@magnapubs.com
http://www.magnapubs.com
This newsletter has been a leading source of information and inspiration for educators committed to creating a better learning environment.

Publication Date: 1995 530 pages Paperback November
1000 attendees and 10+ exhibits

William Haight, President
Jody Glynn Patrick, Vice President

Directories & Handbooks / *Early Childhood Education*

3859 Early Childhood Environmental EducationPrograms: Guidelines for Excellence
North American Assoc for Environmental Education
2000 P Street NW
Suite 540
Washington, DC 20036
202-419-0412
Fax: 212-419-0415
E-mail: info@naaee.org
http://www.naaee.org
A set of recommendations for developing and administering high-quality environmental education programs for young children from birth to age eight, with a focus on ages three to six. These guidelines provide a tool that can be used to ensure a firm foundation for new programs or to trigger improvements in existing ones.

Bora Simmons, Author

Directories & Handbooks / *Elementary Education*

3860 Educational Impressions
PO Box 77
Hawthorne, NJ 07507-0077
973-423-4666
800-451-7450
Fax: 973-423-5569
E-mail: awpeller@worldnet.att.net
Educational workbooks, activity books, literature guides, and audiovisuals. Grades K-8, with emphasis on intermediate and middle grades.

Paperback/Video/Audi

Neil Peller, Marketing Director
Lori Brown, Sales/Marketing

3861 Educators Guide to FREE Videotapes-Elementary/ Middle School Edition
Educators Progress Service
214 Center Street
Randolph, WI 53956-1408
920-326-3126
888-951-4469
Fax: 920-326-3127
E-mail: epsinc@centurytel.net
http://www.freeteachingaids.com
Lists and describes free and free-loan videotapes for the elementary and middle school level.

Annual
ISBN: 0-877082-67-7

Kathy Nehmer, President

3862 Educators Guide to FREE Videotapes-Secondary Edition
Educators Progress Service
214 Center Street
Randolph, WI 53956-1408
920-326-3126
888-951-4469
Fax: 920-326-3127
E-mail: epsinc@centurytel.net
http://www.freeteachingaids.com
Lists and describes free and free-loan videotapes for the elementary and middle school level.

Annual
ISBN: 0-877082-67-7

Kathy Nehmer, President

3863 Elementary Teachers Guide to FREE Curriculum Materials
Educators Progress Service
214 Center Street
Randolph, WI 53956-1408
920-326-3126
888-951-4469
Fax: 920-326-3127
E-mail: epsinc@centurytel.net
http://www.freeteachingaids.com
Lists and describes free supplementary teaching aids for the elementary level.

Annual
ISBN: 0-877082-64-2

Kathy Nehmer, President

3864 KIDSNET Media Guide and News
KIDSNET
6856 Eastern Avenue NW
Suite 208
Washington, DC 20012
202-291-1400
Fax: 202-882-7315
E-mail: kidsnet@kidsnet.org
http://www.kidsnet.org
Contains children's television, radio and video listings. Also lists related teaching materials and copyright guidelines.

150 pages Monthly

3865 Lesson Plans, Integrating Technology into the Classroom: Elementary Edition
Master Teacher
Leadership Lane
PO Box 1207
Manhattan, KS 66505-1207
800-669-9633
Fax: 800-669-1132
http://www.masterteacher.com
Gives teachers practical lessons developed and tested by teachers across the curriculum, with students of all levels of ability in using technology.

130 pages
ISBN: 0-914607-59-6

3866 Nursery Schools & Kindergartens Directory
American Business Directories
5711 S 86th Circle
Omaha, NE 68127-4146
402-593-4600
888-999-1307
Fax: 402-331-5481
A geographical listing of 34,900 nursery schools and kindergartens including all contact information, first year in Yellow Pages and descriptions. Also available are regional editions and electronic formats.

Annual

Jerry Venner, Coordinating Education

3867 Parent Involvement Facilitator: Elementary Edition
Master Teacher
Leadership Lane
PO Box 1207
Manhattan, KS 66505-1207
800-669-9633
Fax: 800-669-1132
http://www.masterteacher.com
Packed with ideas for you and your teachers to implement along with the exact steps for you to follow.

169 pages
ISBN: 0-914607-45-6

3868 Patterson's Elementary Education
Educational Directories Inc.
1025 W Wise Road
PO Box 68097
Schaumburg, IL 60168

847-891-1250
800-357-6183
Fax: 847-891-0945
E-mail: info@ediusa.org
http://www,ediusa.org
A directory to more than 13,000 public school districts; 71,000 public, private and Catholic elementary and middle schools; 1,600 territorial schools; and 400 state department of education personnel in one easy to use consistent format. Arranged alphabetically by state then city. City listings include city name, telephone area code, city population, county name, public school district name, enrollment, grade range, superintendent's name, address and phone number.

Publication Date: 1994 870 pages Annual
ISBN: 0-910536-59-7

Douglas Moody, Coordinating Education

3869 Teaching Our Youngest-A Guide for PreschoolTeachers and Child Care and Family Providers
PO Box 1398
Jessup, MD 20794-1398
877-4ED-PUBS
Fax: 301-470-1244
E-mail: edpubs@inet.ed.gov
http://www.edpubs.org
This booklet draws from scientifically based research about what can be done to help children develop their language abilities, increase their knowledge, become familiar with books and other printed materials,learn letters and sounds, recognize numbers and learn to count.

Directories & Handbooks / *Employment*

3870 AAEE Job Search Handbook for Educators
American Association for Employment in Education
3040 Riverside Drive
Suite 117
Columbus, OH 43221
614-485-1111
Fax: 614-485-9609
E-mail: aaee@osu.edu
http://www.aaee.org
Information for those pursuing work as educators.

72 pages Annually

Neil Shnider, Executive Director
Diane Sledden Reed, Board President

3871 Cabell's Directory of Publishing Opportunities in Education
Cabell Publishing
Box 5428
Tobe Hahn Station
Beaumont, TX 77726-5428
409-898-0575
Fax: 409-866-9554
E-mail: publish@cabells.com
http://www.cabells.com
Includes list of more than 430 education journals that consider manuscripts for publication. Includes contact names and addresses for submitting manuscripts, topics considered, publication guidelines, fees, and circulation information.

1,200 pages

David WE Cabell, Editor
Deborah L English, Associate Editor

3872 Cabell's Directory of Publishing Opportunities in Accounting
Cabell Publishing Company
Box 5428
Tobe Hahn Station
Beaumont, TX 77726
409-898-0575
Fax: 409-866-9554
E-mail: publish@cabells.com
http://www.cabells.com
Contains information on 130 journal. Entries include manuscript guidelines for authors: editor's address, phone, fax and e-mail. Review process and the time required, acceptance rates, readership circulation and subscription prices. The Index classifies journals by 15 topics areas and provides information on type of review, acceptance rate and review time.

425 pages Annual
ISBN: 0-911753-13-3

David WE Cabell, Editor
Deborah L English, Editor

3873 Cabell's Directory of Publishing Opportunities in Economics & Finance
Cabell Publishing Company
Box 5428
Tobe Hahn Station
Beaumont, TX 77726-5428
409-898-0575
Fax: 409-866-9554
E-mail: publish@cabells.com
http://www.cabells.com
Contains information on 350 journals. Each journal entry includes manuscript guidelines for authors: editor's address, phone, fax and e-mail, review process and time required, acceptance rates, readership, circulation and subscription prices. The Index classifies journals by 15 topic areas and provides information on type of review, acceptance rate and review time.

Publication Date: 1995 1100 pages Annual
ISBN: 0-911753-14-1

David WE Cabell, Editor
Deborah L English, Associate Editor

3874 Cabells Directory of Publishing Opportunities in Management
Cabell Publishing Company
Box 5428
Tobe Hahn Station
Beaumont, TX 77726
409-898-0575
Fax: 409-866-9554
E-mail: publish@cabells.com
http://www.cabells.com
Provides editor contact information, acceptance rates, review information, manuscript guidelines and circulation data for over 540 academic journals.

Publication Date: 1973 648 pages
ISBN: 0-911753-15-X

David WE Cabell, Editor
Deborah L English, Associate Editor

3875 Career Book
VGM Career Books
4255 W Touhy Avenue
Lincolnwood, IL 60712
732-329-6991
Fax: 732-329-6994
Offers information on educational employment opportunities in America and abroad.

BiAnnual Hard/Paper

Joyce Lain Kennedy & Darryl Laramore, Author

3876 Career Development Activities for Every Classroom
University of Wisconsin-Madison
1025 W Johnson Street
Madison, WI 53706-1796
608-263-3696
800-446-0399
Fax: 608-262-9197
E-mail: cewmail@soemadison.wisc.edu
http://www.cew.wisc.edu
Four volumes containing hundreds of career development activities, and separate activity masters to duplicate. All lessons are keyed to National Career Development Guidelines Competencies and subject matter areas. Each volume is available individually.

3877 Career Information Center; 13 Volumes
MacMillan Publishing Company
1633 Broadway
New York, NY 10019
212-512-2000
Fax: 800-835-3202
13 volumes covering 3,000 careers, 633 job summaries with 800 photos. Up-to-date information on salaries and occupational outlooks for nearly 3,000 careers.

2.6M pages Triennial
ISBN: 0-028974-52-2

3878 Careers Information Officers in Local Authorities
Careers Research & Advisory
Centre/Hobsons Pub.
Bateman Street
Cambridge CB2 1LZ England
223-354551
1,100 United Kingdom institutions offering collections of career information and audio-visual materials covering career opportunities and current job markets. Arranged alphabetically listing address, phone, contact name and titles, type of materials held and a description of the facilities.

165 pages 12.95 pounds

3879 Certification and Accreditation Programs Directory
Gale Research
27500 Drake Road
Farmington Hills, MI 48331-3535
248-699-4253
800-877-4253
Fax: 248-699-8064
E-mail: galeord@gale.com
http://www.galegroup.com
Directory of private organizations that offer more than 1,700 voluntary certification programs and approximately 300 accreditation programs. Also on CD-ROM.

Publication Date: 1995 620 pages
ISSN: 1084-2128

Allen W Paschal, President

3880 Council of British Independent Schools in the European Communities-Members Directory
Lucy's Hill
Hythe, Kent CT21 5ES
England
44-1303-260857
Fax: 44-1303-260857
E-mail: secretariat@cobisec.org
http://www.cobisec.org
Annual

Roger Fry CBE, Chairman
Sybil Melchers MBE, Honorary Secretary

3881 Directory of English Language Schools in Japan Hiring English Teachers

Information Career Opportunities Research Center
Box 1100, Station F
Toronto M4Y 2T7
Canada
416-925-8878
English-language schools in Japan.

15 pages Annual

3882 Directory of International Internships Michigan State University

MSU: Dean's Office of Int'l Studies and Programs
209 International Center
East Lansing, MI 48824
517-355-2350
Fax: 517-353-7254
E-mail: gliozzo@pilot.msu.edu
http://www.isp.msu.edu
International internships sponsored by academic institutions, private corporations and the federal government.

Publication Date: 1994 168 pages Paperback

Charles A Gliozzo, Coordinating Editor

3883 Directory of Schools, Colleges, and Universities Overseas

Overseas Employment Services
EBSCO Industries
PO Box 1943
Birmingham, AL 35201
205-991-1330
Fax: 205-995-1582
Directory of 300 educational institutions worldwide that hire teachers to teach different subjects in English.

21 pages Annual

Leonard Simcoe, Editor

3884 Directory of Work and Study in Developing Countries

Vacation-Work Publishers
9 Park End Street
Oxford OX1 1HJ
England
865-241978
Offers information on about 420 organizations worldwide offering employment and study opportunities in over 100 developing countries.

215 pages

3885 Earn & Learn: Cooperative Education Opportunities

Octameron Associates
1900 Mount Vernon Avenue
PO Box 2748
Alexandria, VA 22301-0748
703-836-5480
Fax: 703-836-5650
E-mail: info@octameron.com
http://www.octameron.com
Explains how students may participate in cooperative work-study education programs with federal government agencies.

Publication Date: 1997 48 pages BiAnnual
ISBN: 1-57509-023-6

3886 English in Asia: Teaching Tactics for New English Teachers

Global Press
697 College Parkway
Rockville, MD 20850-1135
303-393-7645
Directory covering 1,000 private English-language schools in Asia, to which applications can be sent to teach.

Publication Date: 1992 180 pages

3887 European Council of International Schools Directory

European Council of International Schools
21 Lavant Street, Petersfield
Hampshire GU3 23EL
United Kingdom
44-1730-26-8244
Fax: 44-1730-267914
E-mail: 100412.242@compuserve.com
More than 420 member elementary and secondary international schools in Europe and worldwide.

480 pages Annual

JS Henley, President

3888 Faculty Exchange Center Directory and House Exchange Supplement

Faculty Exchange Center
962 Virginia Avenue
Lancaster, PA 17603-3116
717-393-1130
Offers information for college and faculty members wishing to exchange positions and/or homes temporarily with faculty members at other institutions.

35 pages Annual

3889 Foreign Faculty and Administrative Openings

Education Information Services
PO Box 620662
Newton, MA 02462-0662
617-433-0125
150 specific openings in administration, counseling, library and other professional positions for American teachers in American schools overseas and in international schools in which teaching language is English.

15 pages Every 6 Weeks

FB Viaux, Coordinating Education

3890 Guide to Educational Opportunities in Japan

Embassy of Japan
2520 Massachusetts Avenue NW
Washington, DC 20008
202-238-6700
Fax: 202-328-2187
http://www.embjapan.org
This guide describes opportunities for study in Japan and outlines different forms of financial assistance.

3891 How to Create a Picture of Your Ideal Job or Next Career

Ten Speed Press
PO Box 7123
Berkeley, CA 94707-0123
415-845-8414
800-841-BOOK
Fax: 510-524-4588
Offers handy tips on how to choose the right career, and then go out and get it.

Publication Date: 1989

Richard Nelson Bolles, Author

3892 How to Plan and Develop a Career Center

Center on Education and Work
964 Educational Sciences Building
1025 W Johnson Street
Madison, WI 53706-1796
800-446-0399
Fax: 608-262-9197
E-mail: cewmail@soemadison.wisc.edu
http://www.cew.wisc.edu
High school, postsecondary, adult, and virtual career centers-a comprehensive blueprint that covers all the bases.

3893 Jobs in Russia & the Newly Independent States

Impact Publications
9104 Manassas Drive
Sutie N
Manassas Park, VA 20111-5211
703-361-7300
Fax: 703-335-9486
E-mail: info@impactpublications.com
http://www.impactpublications.com
This guide provides background information on the Russian Federation, the Baltics, the Eastern Slavic Republics, the Transcaucasian Republics and the Asiatic Republics.

3894 Leading Educational Placement Sources in the US

Educational Information Services
PO Box 662
Newton Lower Falls, MA 02162
617-964-4555
An index of the host placement agencies in America for education professionals.

3895 List of Over 200 Executive Search Consulting Firms in the US

Educational Information Services
PO Box 662
Newton Lower Falls, MA 02162
617-964-4555
Covers companies with active search committees in America.

3896 List of Over 600 Personnel & Employment Agencies

Educational Information Services
PO Box 662
Newton Lower Falls, MA 02162
617-964-4555
Contains information on personnel and employment agencies.

3897 Living in China: A Guide to Studying, Teaching & Working in the PRC & Taiwan

China Books & Periodicals
360 Swift Avenue
Suite 48
South San Francisco, CA 94080
650-872-7076
800-818-2017
Fax: 650-872-7808
E-mail: info@chinabooks.com
http://www.chinabooks.com
America's #1 source of publications about China since 1960.

284 pages Paperback
ISBN: 0835125823
November

Chellis Ying, Marketing Director
Jane Lau, Customer Support Specialist

3898 National Directory of Internships

National Society for Experiential Education
3509 Haworth Drive
Suite 207
Raleigh, NC 27609-7235
631-728-9100
Fax: 631-728-9228
E-mail: info@nsee.org
http://www.nsee.org
Directory contains internship descriptions for hundreds of organizations in 85 fields in non-profit organizations, government and corporations. Lists work and service experiences for high school, college and graduate students, people entering the job market, mid-career professionals and retired persons. Includes indexes by field of interest, location and host organization.

Publication Date: 1995 703 pages
ISBN: 0-536-01123-0

3899 Opening List in US Colleges, Public & Private Schools
Education Information Services/Instant Alert
PO Box 620662
Newton, MA 02462-0662
617-433-0125
Offers about 150 current professional openings in US colleges and public and private schools.

10 pages Every 6 weeks
FB Viaux, Coordinating Education

3900 Opening List of Professional Openings in American Overseas Schools
Education Information Services/Instant Alert
PO Box 620662
Newton, MA 02462-0662
617-433-0125
About 150 current professional openings for teachers, administrators, counselors, librarians and educational specialists in American overseas schools and international schools at which the teaching language is primarily English.

FB Viaux, Coordinating Education

3901 Overseas Employment Opportunities for Educators
Department of Defense, Office of Dependent Schools
2461 Eisenhower Avenue
Alexandria, VA 22331-3000
703-325-0867
This publication tells about teaching jobs in 250 schools operated for children of US military and civilian personnel stationed overseas. Applicants usually must qualify in two subject areas.

3902 Private School, Community & Junior College Four Year Colleges & Universities
Educational Information Services
PO Box 662
Newton Lower Falls, MA 02162
617-964-4555
Names, addresses and phones for any state or region in the United States offering employment opportunities.

3903 Research, Study, Travel, & Work Abroad
US Government Printing Office
732 N Capitol Street NW
Washington, DC 20401
202-512-1999
Fax: 202-512-1293
E-mail: admin@access.gpo.gov
http://www.access.gpo.gov

3904 Teaching Overseas
KSJ Publishing Company
PO Box 2311
Sebastopol, CA 95473-2311
A directory of information on how to find jobs teaching overseas.

Publication Date: 1992 89 pages 2nd Edition
ISBN: 0-962044-55-5

3905 Thirty-Four Activities to Promote Careers in Special Education
The Council for Exceptional Children
1920 Association Drive
Reston, VA 20191-1545
703-620-3660
800-232-7323
Fax: 703-264-1637
This guide introduces individuals to the opportunities, rewards and delights of working with children with exceptionalities. It provides directions on how to plan, develop, and implement activities in the school and community that will increase people's awareness

of careers in special education and related services.

Publication Date: 1996 120 pages
ISBN: 0-865862-77-0

3906 VGM's Careers Encyclopedia
VGM Career Books/National Textbook Company
4255 W Touhy Avenue
Lincolnwood, IL 60646-1933
708-679-5500
A list of over 200 professional associations that provide career guidance information.

3907 Work Abroad: The Complete Guide to Finding a Job Overseas
Transitions Abroad
PO Box 745
Bennington, VT 05201
802-442-4827
Fax: 802-442-4827
E-mail: editor@transitionsabroad.com
http://www.transitionsabroad.com
Resource for finding both short- and long-term jobs abroad. Organized by region and country, includes websites and phone numbers.

3908 Workforce Preparation: An International Perspective
PO Box 8623
Ann Arbor, MI 48107-8623
800-530-9673
Fax: 734-975-2787
Excellent collection of material by 20 prominent educators describes efforts in developed and developing countries worldwide to prepare youth and adults for work.

3909 World of Learning
Europa Publications
18 Bedford Square
London WC1B 3JN
England
171-580-8236
Fax: 171-636-1664
Details over 26,000 educational, cultural and scientific institutions throughout the world, together with an exhaustive directory of over 150,000 people active within them.

2,072 pages Annual
ISBN: 0-946653-92-5

Directories & Handbooks / *Financial Aid*

3910 Catalog of Federal Domestic Assistance
Office of Management & Budget
Washington, DC 20402
Offers information from all federal agencies that have assistance programs (loans, scholarships and technical assistance as well as grants) and compiles these into the CFDA. The individual entries are grouped by Department of Agency and includes an excellent set of instructions and several indices. Indices allow the user to search for grants by subject matter, agency, deadline date or eligibility criteria.

3911 Chronicle Financial Aid Guide
Chronicle Guidance Publications
66 Aurora Street
Moravia, NY 13118-3576
315-497-0330
800-622-7284
Fax: 315-497-3359
E-mail: customerservice@chronicleguidance.com
http://www.chronicleguidance.com

Financial aid programs offered primarily by noncollegiate organizations, independent and AFL-CIO affiliated labor unions and federal and state governments for high school seniors and undergraduate and graduate students.

460 pages Annual
ISBN: 1-5563-310-1

Janet Seemann, Author
Janet Seemann, Author/Editor

3912 College Costs and Financial Aid Handbook
College Board Publications
PO Box 869010
Plano, TX 75074-6917
800-323-7155
Fax: 888-321-7183
http://www.collegeboard.org
A step-by-step guide providing the most up-to-date facts on costs plus financial aid and scholarship availability at 3,200 two- and four-year institutions.

Publication Date: 2003
ISBN: 0-874476-83-6

3913 College Financial Aid Annual
Arco/Macmillan
1633 Broadway
Floor 7
New York, NY 10019-6708
212-654-8933
Lists of private businesses, academic institutions and other organizations that provide awards and scholarships for financial aid; guide to federal and state financial aid.

3914 Directory of Educational Contests for Students K-12
ABC-CLIO
130 Cremona Drive
#1911
Santa Barbara, CA 93117-5599
805-968-1911
800-368-6868
Fax: 805-685-9685
Offers about 200 competitive scholarship programs and other educational contests for elementary and secondary school students.

Publication Date: 1991 253 pages

3915 Directory of Financial Aid for Women
Reference Service Press
5000 Windplay Drive
Suite 4
El Dorado Hills, CA 95762
916-939-9620
Fax: 916-939-9626
E-mail: rspinfo@aol.com
http://www.rspfunding.com
Offers information on more than 1,500 scholarships, fellowships, loan sources, grants, awards and internships.

490 pages

3916 Directory of Institutional Projects Funded by Office of Educational Research
U.S. Office of Educational Research & Improvement
555 New Jersey Avenue NW
Washington, DC 20001-2029
202-219-2050

Publication Date: 1990 60 pages

3917 Directory of International Grants & Fellowships in the Health Sciences
National Institutes of Health
31 Center Drive MSC 2220
Building 31, Room B2C29
Bethesda, MD 20892-2220
301-496-2075
Fax: 301-594-1211

E-mail: ficinfo@nih.gov
http://www.nih.gov/fic
Fellowships and grants listed separately in
this guide. Each listing includes a complete
program description with contact information.

**3918 Don't Miss Out: The Ambitous
Students Guide to Financial Aid**
Octameron Associates
1900 Mt Vernon Avenue
Alexandria, VA 22301-0748
703-836-5480
Fax: 703-836-5650
E-mail: info2octameron.com
http://www.octameron.com
Publication Date: 0 192 pages Anually

**3919 Fellowships in International Affairs-A
Guide to Opportunities in the US &
Abroad**
Lynne Rienner Publishing
1800 30th Street
Suite 314
Boulder, CO 80301
303-444-6684
Fax: 303-444-0824
E-mail: questions@rienner.com
http://www.rienner.com
This guide lists fellowships meant to encour-
age women to pursue careers in international
security.

**3920 Fellowships, Scholarships and Related
Opportunities**
Center for International Ed./University of
TN
201 Aconda Court
Knoxville, TN 37996
865-974-1000
Fax: 865-974-2985
140 grants, scholarships and fellowships
available to citizens of the United States for
study or research abroad.
50 pages Biennial

**3921 Financial Aid for Research & Creative
Activities Abroad**
Reference Service Press
5000 Windplay Drive
Suite 4
El Dorado Hills, CA 95762
916-939-9620
Fax: 916-939-9626
E-mail: webagent@rspfunding.com
http://www.rspfunding.com
This book lists opportunities fir high school
students and undergraduates, graduates, post-
doctoral students, professionals and others.
432 pages
ISBN: 1588410625
Gail Schlachter, Author
R.David Weber, Author

**3922 Financial Aid for Study Abroad: a
Manual for Advisers &
Administrators**
NAFSA: Association of International
Educators
1307 New York Avenue NW
8th Floor
Washington, DC 20005-4701
202-737-3699
800-836-4994
Fax: 202-737-3657
E-mail: inbox@nafsa.org
http://www.nafsa.org
Publication Date: 1989 105 pages
Marlene M Johnson, Director/CEO

**3923 Financial Resources for International
Study**
Institute of International Education
809 United Nations Plaza
New York, NY 10017-3580
412-741-0930
Fax: 212-984-5452
E-mail: iiebooks@abdintl.com
http://www.iiebooks.org
Directory of more than 600 awards that can be
used for international study.
Publication Date: 1996 320 pages
ISBN: 087206-220-1

3924 Foundation Grants to Individuals
Foundation Center
79 Fifth Avenue
New York, NY 10003-3076
212-260-4230
Fax: 212-807-3677
Features current information for grant seek-
ers.

3925 Free Money for College: Fifth Edition
Facts On File
132 West 31st Street
17th Floor
New York, NY 10001
800-678-3633
E-mail: llikoff@factsonfile.com
http://www.factsonfile.com
1,000 grants and scholarships.
*Publication Date: 1999 240 pages Annual
Hardcover*
ISBN: 081603947X
Laurie Blum, Author
Laurie Likoff, Editorial Director

**3926 Free Money for Foreign Study: A
Guide to 1,000 Grants for Study
Abroad**
Facts On File
132 West 31st Street
17th Floor
New York, NY 10001
800-678-3633
E-mail: llikoff@factsonfile.com
http://www.factsonfile.com
Lists organizations and institutions worldwide offering scholarships and grants for
study outside the United States.
262 pages
Laurie Likoff, Editorial Director

**3927 Fulbright and Other Grants for USIA
Graduate Study Abroad**
U.S. Student Programs Division
809 United Nations Plaza
New York, NY 10017-3503
212-984-5330
Fax: 212-984-5325
http://www.iie.org
Mutual educational exchange grants for
pre-doctoral students offered by foreign governments.
90 pages Annual

**3928 Fund Your Way Through College:
Uncovering 1,100 Opportunities in
Aid**
Visible Ink Press/Gale Research
830 Penobscot Building
Detroit, MI 48226
313-961-2242
1,100 scholarships, grants, loans, awards and
prizes for undergraduate students.
470 pages

**3929 German-American Scholarship
Guide-Exchange Opportunities for
Historians and Social Scientist**
German Historical Institute
1607 New Hampshire Avenue NW
Washington, DC 20009-2562
202-387-3355
Fax: 202-483-3430
http://www.ghi-dc.org
This guide is divided into two sections: scholarships for study and research in the US and
scholarships for study and research in Germany.

**3930 Getting Funded: The Complete Guide
to WritingGrant Proposals**
Continuing Education Press
PO Box 1394
Portland, OR 97207-1394
503-725-4891
866-647-7377
Fax: 503-725-4715
E-mail: press@pdx.edu
http://www.cep.pdx.edu
A step-by-step guide to writing successful
grants and proposals. An indispensible refer-
ence for experienced and first-time grant writ-
ers alike.
180 pages Paperback
ISBN: 0-87678-071-0
Mary Hall, Author
Mary Hall, Author

3931 Graduate Scholarship Book
Pearson Education
1 Lake Street
Upper Saddle River, NJ 07458
201-909-6200
Fax: 201-767-5029
A complete guide to scholarships, grants and
loans for graduate and professional study.
441 pages Biennial

**3932 Grant Opportunities for US Scholars
& Host Opportunities for US
Universities**
International Research & Exchange Board
2121 K Street NW
Suite 700
Washington, DC 20037
202-628-8188
Fax: 202-628-8189
E-mail: irex@irex.org
http://www.irex.org
This pamphlet lists programs in advanced re-
search, language and development,
short-term travel, special projects and institu-
tional opportunities.

**3933 Grant Writing Beyond The Basics:
ProvenStrategies Professionals Use To
Make Proposals**
Continuing Education Press
PO Box 1394
Portland, OR 97207-1394
503-725-4891
866-647-7377
Fax: 503-725-4840
E-mail: press@pdx.edu
http://www.cep.pdx.edu
Designed to inspire those with grant writing
experience who want to take their develop-
ment strategies to the next level.
128 pages Paperback
ISBN: 0-87678-117-2
Michael K Wells, Author
Alba Scholz, Manager
Martha Ketchum, Customer Service

3934 Grants & Awards Available to American Writers
PEN American Center
588 Broadway
Suite 303
New York, NY 10012
212-334-1660
Fax: 212-334-2181
E-mail: ftw@pen.org
http://www.pen.org
Includes a full program description and is then broken down by type of writing. Awards for work in a particular country are listed alphabetically by country.
340 pages Paperback
ISBN: 0-934638-20-9

3935 Grants Register
St. Martin's Press
175 5th Avenue
New York, NY 10010
212-674-5151
888-330-8477
Fax: 800-672-2054
E-mail: firstname.lastname@stmartins.com
http://www.vhpsva.com
This directory offers a comprehensive list of programs organized alphabetically with special attention to eligibility requirements. Index by subject.

3936 Grants, Fellowships, & Prizes of Interest to Historians
American Historical Association
400 A Street SE
Washington, DC 20003-3889
202-544-2422
Fax: 202-544-8307
E-mail: aha@theaha.org
http://www.theaha.org
This guide offers information on awards for historians from undergraduate to postgraduate grants, fellowships, prizes, internships and awards.

3937 Guide to Department of Education Programs
US Department of Education
400 Maryland Avenue SW
Washington, DC 20202-0001
202-401-0765
Programs of financial aid offered by the Department of Education.
35 pages Annual

3938 Harvard College Guide to Grants
Office of Career Services
Harvard University
54 Dunster Street
Cambridge, MA 02138
617-495-2595
Fax: 617-496-6880
http://www.ocs.fas.harvard.edu
This guide describes national and regional grants and fellowships for study in the US, study abroad and work and practical experience.
234 pages Paperback

3939 How to Find Out About Financial Aid & Funding
Reference Service Press
5000 Windplay Drive
Suite 4
El Dorado Hills, CA 95762
916-939-9620
Fax: 916-939-9626
E-mail: rspinfo@aol.com
http://www.rspfunding.com

Over 700 financial aid directories and Internet sites described and evaluated.
432 pages Hardcover
ISBN: 1588410935
Gail A Schlachter, Author

3940 International Foundation Directory
Europa Publications
11 New Fetter Lane
London
England EC4P 4EE
44-0-20-7842-2110
Fax: 44-0-20-7842-2249
http://www.europapublications.co.uk
A world directory of international foundations, trusts and similar non-profit institutions. Provides detailed information on over 1,200 institutions in some 70 countries throughout the world.
Publication Date: 1994 736 pages
ISBN: 1-857430-01-8
Paul Kelly, Editorial Director

3941 International Scholarship Book: The Complete Guide to Financial Aid
Pearson Education
1 Lake Street
Upper Saddle River, NJ 07458
201-909-6200
Fax: 201-767-5029
Offers information on private organizations providing financial aid for university students interested in studying in foreign countries.
335 pages Cloth

3942 Journal of Student Financial Aid
University of Notre Dame
Office of Financial Aid
Notre Dame, IN 46556
574-631-6436
Offers a listing of private and federal sources of financial aid for college bound students.
3x Year
Joseph A Russo, Editor

3943 Loans and Grants from Uncle Sam
Octameron Associates
1900 Mount Vernon Avenue
PO Box 2748
Alexandria, VA 22301-0748
703-836-5480
Fax: 703-836-5650
E-mail: info@octameron.com
http://www.octameron.com
Offers information on federal student loan and grant programs and state loan guarantee agencies.
72 pages Annual
ISBN: 1-57509-097-X
Anna Leider, Author

3944 Money for Film & Video Artists
American for the Art
1000 Vermont Avenue NW
6th Floor
Washington, DC 20005
202-371-2830
Fax: 202-371-0424
http://www.artsusa.org
The listings are organized by sponsoring organization and entries include basic application and program information.

3945 Money for International Exchange in the Arts
American for the Art
1000 Vermont Avenue NW
12th Floor
Washington, DC 20005

202-371-2830
Fax: 202-371-0424
http://www.artsusa.org
A guide to the various resources available to support artists and arts organizations in international work.

3946 Money for Visual Artists
America for the Art
1000 Vermont Avenue NW
6th Floor
Washington, DC 20005
202-371-2830
Fax: 202-371-0424
http://www.artsusa.org
Programs are listed alphabetically by sponsor with detailed program description.

3947 National Association of State Scholarship and Grant Program Survey Report
National Association of State Scholarship Programs
660 Boas Street
Harrisburg, PA 17102-1324
717-257-2794
Listing of over 50 member state agencies administering scholarship and grant programs for student financial aid.
150 pages

3948 National Association of Student Financial Aid Administrators Directory
1129 20th Street NW
Suite 400
Washington, DC 20036-5001
202-785-0453
Fax: 202-785-1487
Offers information on over 3,000 institutions of postsecondary education and their financial aid administrators.
230 pages Annual

3949 Need A Lift?
The American Legion
700 N Pennsylvania Street
PO Box 1055
Indianapolis, IN 46206-1050
317-630-1200
888-453-4466
Fax: 317-630-1223
http://www.EMBLEM.legion.org
Sources of career, scholarship and loan information or assistance.
144 pages Annual/Paperback
Robert Caudell, Author

3950 Peterson's Grants for Graduate and Postdoctoral Study
Peterson's, A Nelnet Company
Princeton Pike Corporate Center
2000 Lenox Drive PO Box 67005
Lawrenceville, NJ 08648
609-698-1800
800-338-3282
Fax: 609-896-4531
E-mail: custsvc@petersons.com
http://www.petersons.com
Only comprehensive source of current information on grants and fellowships exclusively for graduate and postdoctoral students.
Publication Date: 1998 5th Edition
ISBN: 1-560794-01-1

3951 Peterson's Sports Scholarships and College Athletic Programs
Peterson's, A Nelnet Company
Princeton Pike Corporate Center
2000 Lenox Drive
Lawrenceville, NJ 08648
609-896-1800
800-338-3282

Fax: 609-896-4531
E-mail: custsvc@petersons.com
http://www.petersons.com
A college-by-college look at scholarships designated exclusively for student athletes in 32 men's and women's sports.

Publication Date: 2004 624 pages 5th Edition
ISBN: 0768915244

3952 Scholarship Handbook
The College Board
45 Columbus Avenue
New York, NY 10023
800-323-7155
http://www.collegeboard.org
Useful text for college-bound students, their families and guidance counselors. Offers more than 2,000 descriptions of national and state level award programs, public and private education loan programs, intership opportunities and more.

3953 Scholarships for Emigres Training for Careers in Jewish Education
Jewish Foundation for Education of Women
135 E 64th Street
New York, NY 10021
212-288-3931
Fax: 212-288-5798
E-mail: fdnscholar@aol.com
http://www.jfew.org
Open to emigres from the former Soviet Union who are pursuing careers in Jewish education. Candidates in Jewish education, rabbinical and cantorial studies, and Jewish studies are invited to write the Foundation.

Marge Goldwater, Executive Director

3954 Scholarships, Fellowships and Loans
Gale Research
PO Box 33477
Detroit, MI 48232-5477
800-877-GALE
Fax: 800-414-5043
http://www.galegroup.com
Written especially for professionals, students, counselors, parents and others interested in education. This resource provides more than 3,700 sources of education-related financial aid and awards at all levels of study.

Publication Date: 1995 1,290 pages Annual
ISBN: 0-810391-14-7

3955 Student Guide
Federal Student Aid Information Center
PO Box 84
Washington, DC 20044-0084
800-433-3243
800-433-3243
Describes the federal student aid programs, and general information about the eligibility criteria, application procedures and award levels, and lists important deadlines and phone numbers.

54 pages

John J McCarthy, Director

3956 Study Abroad
U.N. Educational, Scientific & Cultural Assn.
7, place de Fontenoy
F-75700 Paris
France
1-45681123
Listing of over 200,000 scholarships, fellowships and educational exchange opportunities offered for study in 124 countries.

1,300 pages Biennial

3957 Write Now: A Complete Self-Teaching Programfor Better Handwriting
Continuing Education Press
PO Box 1394
Portland, OR 97207-1394

503-725-4891
866-647-7377
Fax: 503-725-4840
E-mail: press@pdx.edu
http://www.cep.pdx.edu
A step-by-step guide to improving one's handwriting. Develop clean and legible italic handwriting with regular practice.

128 pages Paperback
ISBN: 0-87678-089-3

Barbara Getty & Inga Dubay, Author
Alba Scholz, Manager
Martha Ketchum, Customer Service

Directories & Handbooks / *Guidance & Counseling*

3958 Accredited Institutions of Postsecondary Education
MacMillan Publishing Company
1633 Broadway
New York, NY 10019
212-512-2000
Fax: 800-835-3202
Lists over 5,000 accredited institutions and programs for postsecondary education in the United States.

600 pages Annual

3959 Adolescent Pregnancy Prevention Clearinghouse
Children's Defense Fund Education & Youth Develop.
122 C Street NW
#400
Washington, DC 20001-2109
202-628-8787
Fax: 202-662-3560
Provides information and clarification on the connection between pregnancy and broader life questions for youth.

Marian Wright Edelman, Coordinating Education

3960 COLLEGESOURCE
Career Guidance Foundation
8090 Engineer Road
San Diego, CA 92111-1906
800-854-2670
Fax: 858-278-8960
http://www.collegesource.org
CD-ROM and Web College Catalog Collection. Contains colleges and universitie's catalogs from throughout the US, over 2,600. Also a college search program that can be searched by major, tuition costs, and more. Foreign catalogs available.

Annette Crone, Account Coordinator
David Hunt, Account Coordinator

3961 Cabells Directory of Publishing Opportunities in Educational Psychology and Administration
Cabell Publishing Company
Box 5428
Tobe Hahn Station
Beaumont, TX 77726
409-898-0575
Fax: 409-866-9554
E-mail: publish@cabells.com
http://www.cabells.com
Provides information on editor contact information, manuscript guidelines, acceptance rate, review information and circulation data for over 225 academic journals.

799 pages Annual
ISBN: 0-911753-19-2

David WE Cabell, Editor
Deborah L English, Associate Editor

3962 Career & Vocational Counseling Directory
American Business Directories
5711 S 86th Circle
Omaha, NE 68127-4146
402-593-4600
888-999-1307
Fax: 402-331-5481
Nationwide listing of 3,300 companies/consultants available in print, computer magnetic tape and diskette, mailing labels, and index cards listing the name, address, phone, size of advertisement, contact person and number of employees.

Annual

Jerry Venner, Coordinating Education

3963 College Handbook
College Board Publications
45 Columbus Avenue
New York, NY 10023-6992
212-713-8000
Fax: 800-525-5562
E-mail: puborderinfo@collegeboard.org
http://www.collegeboard.org
Descriptions of 3,200 colleges and universities.

Publication Date: 1994 1728 pages Annually

Kea Waithe, Director Customer Service

3964 College Handbook Foreign Student Supplement
College Board Publications
45 Columbus Avenue
New York, NY 10023-6917
212-713-8000
Fax: 800-525-5562
Lists about 2,800 colleges and universities that are open to foreign students.

Publication Date: 1994 288 pages Annual
ISBN: 0-877474-83-3

3965 College Transfer Guide
School Guide Publications
210 N Avenue
New Rochelle, NY 10801-6402
914-632-7771
800-433-7771
Fax: 914-632-3412
Five hundred four-year colleges in the Northeast and Midwest that accept transfer students listing transfer requirements, deadlines, fees, enrollment, costs and contact information. Circulation, 60,000.

125 pages Annual/January

3966 Community College Exemplary Instructional Programs
Massachusetts Bay Community College Press
50 Oakland Street
Wellsley Hills, MA 02181
781-237-1100
Fax: 781-237-1061
Community college programs identified as outstanding by the National Council of Instructional Administrators.

3967 Comparative Guide to American Colleges for Students, Parents & Counselors
HarperCollins
10 E 53rd Street
New York, NY 10022-5244
212-207-7000
Fax: 212-207-7145
Accredited four-year colleges in the United States.

800 pages Cloth

3968 Directory of Play Therapy Training
University of North Texas
PO Box 310829
Denton, TX 76203
940-565-3864
Fax: 940-565-4461
E-mail: cpt@coefs.coe.unt.edu
http://www.centerforplaytherapy.com
Provides training, research publications and serves as a clearinghouse for literature in the field.

Paperback

Rinda Thomas, Office Manager
Sue C Bratton, Center Director

3969 Educators Guide to FREE Guidance Materials
Educators Progress Service
214 Center Street
Randolph, WI 53956-1408
920-326-3126
888-951-4469
Fax: 920-326-3127
E-mail: epsinc@centurytel.net
http://www.freeteachingaids.com
Lists and describes free films, videotapes, filmstrips, slides, web sites, and hundreds of free printed materials in the field of career education and guidance for all age levels.

190 pages Annual
ISBN: 87708-406-8

Kathy Nehmer, President

3970 Index of Majors and Graduate Degrees
College Board Publications
45 Columbus Avenue
New York, NY 10023-6992
212-713-8000
Fax: 800-525-5562
http://www.collegeboard.org
Includes descriptions of over 600 majors and identifies the 3,200 colleges, universities, and graduate schools that offer them.

Annual
ISBN: 0-87447-592-9

3971 Tests: a Comprehensive Reference forPsychology, Education & Business
PRO-ED
8700 Shoal Creek Boulevard
Austin, TX 78757-6897
512-451-3246
800-897-3202
Fax: 800-397-7633
E-mail: info@proedinc.com
http://www.proedinc.com
This fifth edition groups updated information on approximately 2,000 assessment instruments into three primary classifications-psychology, education, and business-and 89 subcategories, enabling users to readily identify the tests that meet their assessment needs. Each entry contains a statement of the instrument's purpose, a concise description of the instrument, scoring procedures, cost, and publisher information.

Publication Date: 1991 809 pages Paperback/Hardcover
ISBN: 0-89079-709-9

Taddy Maddox, General Editor

3972 Vocational Biographies
PO Box 31
Sauk Centre, MN 56378-0031
320-352-6516
800-255-0752
Fax: 320-352-5546
E-mail: careers@vocbio.com
http://www.vocbio.com
Real life career success stories of persons in every walk of life that allow students to see a career through the eyes of a real person. New

for 2005: Internet Access to 1001 Career Success Stories.

Toby Behnen, President
Roxann Behnen, Customer Service/Sales

3973 What Works and Doesn't With at Risk Students
BKS Publishing
3109 150th Place SE
Mill Creek, WA 98012-4864
425-745-3029
Fax: 425-337-4837
E-mail: DocBlokk@aol.com
http://www.literacyfirst.com

Publication Date: 1919 162 pages Paperback
ISBN: 0-9656713-0-5

Jan Glaes, Author
Bill Blokker, Owner

3974 World of Play Therapy Literature
Center for Play Therapy
PO Box 311337
Denton, TX 76203
940-565-3864
Fax: 940-565-4461
E-mail: cpt@coefs.coe.unt.edu
http://www.centerforplaytherapy.com
Author and topical listings of over 6,000 books, dissertations, documents, and journal articles on play therapy, updated every two years.

Publication Date: 1995 306 pages

Landreth, Homeyer, Bratton, Kale, Hipl, Schumann, Author

Directories & Handbooks / *Language Arts*

3975 Classroom Strategies for the English Language Learner
Master Teacher
Leadership Lane
PO Box 1207
Manhattan, KS 66505-1207
800-669-9633
Fax: 800-669-1132
http://www.masterteacher.com
A practical model for accelerating both oral language and literacy development, based on the latest research for effective instruction of both Native English speakers and English language learners.

266 pages
ISBN: 1-58992-068-6

Socrro Herrera EdD, Author

3976 Italic Handwriting Series-Book A
Continuing Education Press
PO Box 1394
Portland, OR 97207-1394
503-725-4891
866-647-7377
Fax: 503-725-4840
E-mail: press@pdx.edu
http://www.cep.pdx.edu
Book A is the first workbook of a seven-part series. Designed for the beginning reader and writer, it introduces the alphabet one letter at a time. Illustrated.

64 pages Paperback
ISBN: 0-87678-092-3

Barbara Getty & Inga Dubay, Author
Alba Scholz, Manager

3977 Italic Handwriting Series-Book B
Continuing Education Press
PO Box 1394
Portland, OR 97207-1394
503-725-4891
866-647-7377
Fax: 503-725-4840
E-mail: press@pdx.edu
http://www.cep.pdx.edu
Book B is the second workbook of a seven-part series. Designed for the beginning reader and writer. Introduces words and sentences, lowercase and capitol print script, one letter per page. Illustrated.

59 pages Paperback
ISBN: 0-87678-093-1

Barbara Getty & Inga Dubay, Author
Alba Scholz, Manager

3978 Italic Handwriting Series-Book C
Continuing Education Press
PO Box 1394
Portland, OR 97207-1394
503-725-4891
866-647-7377
Fax: 503-725-4840
E-mail: press@pdx.edu
http://www.cep.pdx.edu
Book C is the third workbook of a seven-part series. Covers basic italic and introduces the cursive. Words and sentences include days of week, months of year, modes of transportation, and tongue twisters. Illustrated.

60 pages Paperback
ISBN: 0-87678-094-X

Barbara Getty & Inga Dubay, Author
Alba Scholz, Manager

3979 Italic Handwriting Series-Book D
Continuing Education Press
PO Box 1394
Portland, OR 97207-1394
503-725-4891
866-647-7377
Fax: 503-725-4840
E-mail: press@pdx.edu
http://www.cep.pdx.edu
Book D is the fourth workbook of a seven-part series. Reviews basic italic and covers the total cursive program. Includes prefixes, suffixes, capitalization, and playful poems. Explores history of the alphabet. Illustrated.

80 pages Paperback
ISBN: 0-87678-095-8

Barbara Getty & Inga Dubay, Author
Alba Scholz, Manager

3980 Italic Handwriting Series-Book E
Continuing Education Press
PO Box 1394
Portland, OR 97207-1394
503-725-4891
866-647-7377
Fax: 503-725-4840
E-mail: press@pdx.edu
http://www.cep.pdx.edu
Book E is the fifth workbook of a seven-part series. Reviews basic italic and covers the total cursive program. Writing practice covers natural history— plants, volcanoes, cities. Explores history of the alphabet. Illustrated.

56 pages Paperback
ISBN: 0-87678-096-6

Barbara Getty & Inga Dubay, Author
Alba Scholz, Manager

3981 Italic Handwriting Series-Book F
Continuing Education Press
PO Box 1394
Portland, OR 97207-1394
503-725-4891
866-647-7377
Fax: 503-725-4840

E-mail: press@pdx.edu
http://www;.cep.pdx.edu
Book F is the sixth workbook of a seven-part series. Reviews basic italic and covers the total cursive program. Writing practice emphasizes figures of speech (e.g. homophones, puns, metaphors, acronyms). Explores history of the alphabet. Illustrated.

56 pages Paperback
ISBN: 0-87678-097-4

Barbara Getty & Inga Dubay, Author
Alba Scholz, Manager

3982 Italic Handwriting Series-Book G
Continuing Education Press
PO Box 1394
Portland, OR 97207-1394
503-725-4891
866-647-7377
Fax: 503-725-4840
E-mail: press@pdx.edu
http://www.cep.pdx.edu
Book G is the seventh workbook of a seven-part series. A comprehensive self-instruction program in basic and cursive italic. Writing content follows a central theme-the history of our alphabet. Suitable for older students. Illustrated.

56 pages Paperback
ISBN: 0-87678-098-2

Barbara Getty & Inga Dubay, Author
Alba Scholz, Manager

3983 Language Schools Directory
American Business Directories
5711 S 86th Circle
Omaha, NE 68127-4146
402-593-4600
888-999-1307
Fax: 402-331-5481
A listing of language schools, arranged by geographic location, offering contact information which is updated on a continual basis, and printed on request. Directory is also available in electronic formats.

Jerry Venner, Coordinating Education

3984 Picture Book LearningVolume-1
Picture Book Learning Inc.
PO Box 270075
Louisville, CO 80027
303-548-2809
E-mail: todd@picturebooklearning.com
http://www.picturebooklearning.com
Teachers can use this fun method of teaching elementary children basic language arts skills through the use of picture books.

60 pages
ISBN: 0-9760725-0-5

Todd Osborne, Co-President
Corinne Osborne, Editor

3985 Process of Elimination - a Method of Teaching Basic Grammar - Teacher Ed
Scott & McCleary Publishing Company
2482 11th Street SW
Akron, OH 44314-1712
702-566-8756
800-765-3564
Fax: 702-568-1378
E-mail: jscott7576@aol.com
http://www.scottmccleary.com
Series of 7 steps designed to teach basic grammar skills to students in middle grades

through college. Available in a teacher edition and a student workbook.

50 pages
ISBN: 0-9636225-2-8
ISSN: 0-9636225-

Milton Metheny, Author
Janet Scott, Publisher
Sheila McCleary, Publisher

3986 Process of Elimination: A Method of Teaching Basic Grammar - Student Ed
Scott & McCleary Publishing Company
2482 11th Street SW
Akron, OH 44314-1712
702-566-8756
800-765-3564
Fax: 702-568-1378
E-mail: jscott7576@aol.com
http://www.scottmccleary.com
Series of 7 steps designed to teach basic grammar skills to students in middle grades through college. Available in a teacher edition and a student workbook.

Milton Metheny, Author
Janet Scott, Publisher
Sheila McCleary, Publisher

3987 Put Reading First: The Research BuildingBlocks For Teaching Children To Read
PO Box 1398
Jessup, MD 20794-1398
877-4ED-PUBS
Fax: 301-470-1244
E-mail: edpubs@inet.ed.gov
http://www.edpubs.org
Provides analysis and discussion in five areas of reading instruction: phonemic awareness, phonics, fluency, vocabulary and text comprehension.

3988 Write Now: A Complete Self Teaching Program for Better Handwriting
Continuing Education Press
PO Box 1394
Portland, OR 97207-1394
503-725-4891
866-647-7377
Fax: 503-725-4840
E-mail: press@pdx.edu
http://www.cep.pdx.edu
Finally, a handwriting improvement book for adults. Teach yourself to write legibly and retain it over time using this step-by-step guide to modern italic handwriting with complete instructions as well as practice exercises and tips. The secret to legible handwriting is the absence of loops in letterform, making it easier to write and easier to read.

96 pages Paperback
ISBN: 0-87678-089-3

Barbara Getty & Inga Dubay, Author
Alba Scholz, Manager
Wendi Johnson, Customer Service

Directories & Handbooks / *Library Services*

3989 Directory of Manufacturers & Suppliers
Special Libraries Association
331 S Patrick Street
Alexandria, VA 22314-3501
703-647-4900
Fax: 703-647-4901
E-mail: sla@sla.org
http://www.sla.org
The SLA network consists of nearly 15,000 librarians and information professionals who

specialize in the arts, communication, business, social science, biomedical sciences, geosciences and environmental studies, and industry, business, research, educational and technical institutions, government, special departments of public and university libraries, newspapers, museums, and public or private organizations that provide or require specialized information.

3990 Directory of Members of the Association for Library and Information Science Education
1009 Commerce Park Drive Suite 150
PO Box 4219
Oak Ridge, TN 37830
865-425-0155
Fax: 865-481-0390
E-mail: contact@alise.org
http://www.alise.org
The Directory is designed to serve as a handbook for the association, including a list of officers, committees, and interest groups and strategic planning information for the association. Also listed are graduate schools of library and information science and their faculty.

Annual Paperback

Rand Price, Executive Director
Maureen Thompson, Administrator

3991 Libraries Unlimited Academic Catalog
88 Post Road W
Westport, CT 06881
203-226-3571
Fax: 203-222-1502
E-mail: lu-books@lu.com
http://www.lu.com
Catalog includes reference, collection development, library management, cataloging, and technology.

3992 Managing Info Tech in School Library Media Center
Libraries Unlimited
88 Post Road West
Westport, CT 06881
203-226-3571
800-225-5800
Fax: 203-222-1502
E-mail: lu-books@lu.com
http://www.lu.com

Publication Date: 2000 290 pages Hardcover
ISBN: 1-56308-724-3

L Anne Clyde

3993 Managing Media Services Theory and Practice
Libraries Unlimited
88 Post Road West
Westport, CT 06881
203-226-3571
800-225-5800
Fax: 203-222-1502
E-mail: lu-books@lu.com
http://www.lu.com

Publication Date: 2002 418 pages Cloth
ISBN: 1-56308-530-5

L Anne Clyde

Directories & Handbooks / *Music & Art*

3994 College Guide for Visual Arts Majors
Peterson's, A Nelnet Company
Princeton Pike Corporate Center
2000 Lenox Drive PO Box 67005
Lawrenceville, NJ 08648

609-896-1800
800-338-3282
Fax: 609-896-4531
E-mail: custsvc@petersons.com
http://www.petersons.com
Offers descriptions of over 700 accredited US colleges and universities, music conservatories, and art/design schools that grant undergraduate degrees in the areas of studio art.

Publication Date: 2006 404 pages
ISBN: 1-560795-36-0

3995 Community Outreach and Education for the Arts Handbook
Music Teachers National Association
441 Vine Street
Cincinnati, OH 45202
513-421-1420
888-512-5278
Fax: 513-421-2503
E-mail: mtnanet@mtaa.org
http://www.mtaa.org
Resource booklet for independent music teachers.

Paperback
March
150 booths with 2500 attendees

Chad Schwatbach, Pr/Marketing Associate

3996 Italic Letters
Continuing Education Press
PO Box 1394
Portland, OR 97207-1394
503-725-4891
866-647-7377
Fax: 503-725-4840
E-mail: press@pdx.edu
http://www.cep.pdx.edu
Italic Letters is for professional and amateur calligraphers, art teachers, and enthusiasts of the book arts. Numerous tips on letter shapes, spacing, slant, pen edge angle, and other secrets to handsome writing.

128 pages Paperback
ISBN: 0-87678-091-5

Barbara Getty & Inga Dubay, Author
Alba Scholz, Manager

3997 Money for Film & Video Artists
American for the Art
1000 Vermont Avenue NW
6th Floor
Washington, DC 20005
202-371-2830
Fax: 202-371-0424
http://www.artsusa.org
The listings are organized by sponsoring organization and entries include basic application and program information.

3998 Money for Visual Artists
America for the Art
1000 Vermont Avenue NW
12th Floor
Washington, DC 20005
202-371-2830
Fax: 202-371-0424
http://www.artsusa.org
Programs are listed alphabetically by sponsor with detailed program description.

3999 Music Teachers Guide to Music Instructional Software
Music Teachers National Association
441 Vine Street
Suite 505
Cincinnati, OH 45202-2811
888-512-5278
Fax: 513-421-2503
E-mail: mtnanet@mtna.org
http://www.mtna.org
Evaluations of music software for the macintosh and PC, including CD-ROMs, music skills and keyboard technique drill soft-

ware, sequencers and soundequipment controllers.

4000 Resource Booklet for Independent Music Teachers
Music Teachers National Association
441 Vine Street
Suite 505
Cincinnati, OH 45202-2811
888-512-5278
Fax: 513-421-2503
E-mail: mtnanet@mtna.org
http://www.mtna.org
A booklet for organizing information about community resources.

4001 School Arts
50 Portland Street
Worcester, MA 01608
800-533-2847
Fax: 508-753-3834
Companies offering products, materials, and art education resources or programs that focus on the history of art, multicultural resources such as Fine Art, reproductions, CD-Roms, museum education, programs, slides, books, videos, exhibits, architecture, timelines, and resource kits.

Directories & Handbooks / *Physical Education*

4002 Educators Guide to FREE HPER Materials
Educators Progress Service
214 Center Street
Randolph, WI 53956-1408
920-326-3126
888-951-4469
Fax: 920-326-3127
E-mail: epsinc@centurytel.net
http://www.freeteachingaids.com
Lists and describes free films, videotapes, filmstrips, slides, web sites, and hundreds of free printed materials in the field of health, physical education, and recreation for all age levels.

184 pages Annual
ISBN: 87708-407-6

Kathy Nehmer, President

4003 Schools & Colleges Directory
Association for Experiential Education
3775 Iris Avenue
Suite 4
Boulder, CO 80301-2043
303-440-8844
Fax: 303-440-9581
E-mail: publications@aee.org
http://www.aee.org
Provides information about many schools, colleges and universities that have programs or offer degrees related to the field of outdoor/experiential education. Listings include programs in high schools and independent organizations as well as institutions of higher learning. Paperback.

Publication Date: 1995 Paperback

Natalie Kurylke, Publications Manager

Directories & Handbooks / *Reading*

4004 Diagnostic Reading Inventory for Bilingual Students in Grades 1-8
Scott & McCleary Publishing Company
2482 11th Street SW
Akron, OH 44314-1712

702-566-8756
800-765-3564
Fax: 702-568-1378
E-mail: jscott7576@aol.com
http://www.scottmccleary.com
Series of 13 tests designed to access reading performance. IRI, spelling, phonics, visual and auditory discrimination and listening comprehension are just some of the tests included.

155 pages
ISBN: 0-9636225-1-X

Janet M Scott, Co-Author
Sheila C McCleary, Co-Author

4005 Diagnostic Reading Inventory for Primary and Intermediate Grades K-8
Scott & McCleary Publishing Company
2482 11th Street SW
Akron, OH 44314-1712
702-566-8756
800-765-3564
Fax: 702-568-1378
E-mail: jscott7576@aol.com
http://www.scottmccleary.com
Designed to assess reading performance in grades K-8. Tests include: word recognition, oral reading inventory, comprehension, listening comprehension, auditory and visual discrimination, auditory and visual memory, learning modalities inventory, phonics mastery tests, structural analysis, word association and a diagnostic spelling test.

260 pages
ISBN: 0-9636225-4-4

Janet M Scott, Co-Author
Sheila C McCleary, Co-Author

4006 Educational Leadership
Assn. for Supervision & Curriculum Dev. (ASCD)
1703 N Beauregard Street
Alexandria, VA 22311-1714
703-578-9600
800-933-2723
Fax: 703-575-5400
E-mail: el@ascd.org
http://www.ascd.org
For educators by educators. With a circulation of 175,000, Educational Leadership is acknowledged throughout the world as an authoritative source of information about teaching and learning, new ideas and practices relevant to practicing educators, and the latest trends and issues affecting prekindergarten through higher education.

Marge Scherer, Executive Editor

4007 Laubach Literacy Action Directory
Laubach Literacy Action
1320 Jamesville Avenue
Syracuse, NY 13210
315-422-9121
888-528-2224
Fax: 315-422-6369
E-mail: info@laubach.org
http://www.laubach.org
Listing of over 1,100 local literacy councils and associates who teach the Laubach Method.

90 pages Annual

4008 Ready to Read, Ready to Learn
PO Box 1398
Jessup, MD 20794-1398
877-4ED-PUBS
Fax: 301-470-1244
E-mail: edpubs@inet.ed.gov
http://www.edpubs.org

4009 Tips for Reading Tutors
PO Box 1398
Jessup, MD 20794-1398

877-4ED-PUBS
Fax: 301-470-1244
E-mail: edpubs@inet.ed.gov
http://www.edpubs.org
Basic tips for reading tutors

Directories & Handbooks / *Secondary Education*

4010 College Board Guide to High Schools
College Board Publications
45 Columbus Avenue
New York, NY 10023-6917
212-713-8165
800-323-7155
Fax: 800-525-5562
http://www.collegeboard.org
Offers listings and information on over
25,000 public and private high schools nationwide.
Publication Date: 1994 2,024 pages
ISBN: 0-874474-66-3

**4011 Compendium of Tertiary & Sixth
Forum Colleges**
SCOTVIC: S McDonald, Principal
Ridge College
Manchester
England
61-4277733
Offers listings of over 200 Sixth Form and
Tertiary Colleges in the United Kingdom of-
fering courses preparing secondary students
for university study.
Publication Date: 1990 200 pages Biennial

**4012 Directory of Public Elementary and
Secondary Education Agencies**
US National Center for Education Statistics
555 New Jersey Avenue NW
Washington, DC 20208-5651
202-219-1916
800-424-1616
Fax: 202-502-7466
Directory of approximately 17,000 local education agencies that operate their own schools
or pay tuition to other local education
agencies.
400 pages Annual
John Sietsema, Statistician
Lena McDowell, Contact

**4013 Educators Guide to FREE Family and
Consumer Education Materials**
Educators Progress Service
214 Center Street
Randolph, WI 53956-1408
920-326-3126
888-951-4469
Fax: 920-326-3127
E-mail: epsinc@centurytel.net
http://www.freeteachingaids.com
Lists and describes free films, videotapes,
filmstrips, slides, web sites, and hundreds of
free printed materials in the field of home
economics and consumer education for all
age levels.
161 pages Annual
ISBN: 87708-408-4
Kathy Nehmer, President

4014 Focus on School
ABC-CLIO
130 Cremona Drive
#1911
Santa Barbara, CA 93117-5599
805-968-1911
800-368-6868
Fax: 805-685-9685

Hotlines, print and nonprint resources on education for young adults.
Publication Date: 1990

4015 Great Source Catalog
Great Source Education Group
PO Box 7050
Wilmington, MA 01887
800-289-4490
Fax: 800-289-3994
http://www.greatsource.com
Alternative, affordable, student-friendly
K-12 materials to make teaching and learning
fun for educators and students.

**4016 Helping Your Child Succeed In
School:Elementary and Secondary
Editions**
Master Teacher
Po Box 1207
Manhattan, KS 66505-1207
785-539-0555
800-669-9633
Fax: 800-669-1132
http://www.masterteacher.com
Provides a way for school administrators to
help parents help their children succeed in
school. Published in English and Spanish.
Erica Paronson, Executive Editor

**4017 Lesson Plans for Integrating
Technology into the Classroom:
Secondary Edition**
Master Teacher
Leadership Lane
PO Box 1207
Manhattan, KS 66505-1207
800-669-9633
Fax: 800-669-1132
http://www.masterteacher.com
Gives teachers practical lessons developed
and tested by teachers across the curriculum,
with students of all levels of ability in using
technology.
104 pages
ISBN: 1-58992-152-6

**4018 Lesson Plans for Problem-Based
Learning: Secondary Edition**
Master Teacher
Leadership Lane
PO Box 1207
Manhattan, KS 66505-1207
800-669-9633
Fax: 800-669-1132
http://www.masterteacher.com
An instructional technique which organizes
the curriculum around a major problem that
students work to solve over the weeks or
months.
117 pages
ISBN: 0-914607-87-1

**4019 Lesson Plans for the Substitute
Teacher: Secondary Edition**
Master Teacher
Leadership Lane
PO Box 1207
Manhattan, KS 66505-1207
800-669-9633
Fax: 800-669-1132
http://www.masterteacher.com
Gives you more than 100 lessons developed
and tested by teachers across the curriculum
and at all grade levels.
177 pages
ISBN: 1-58992-108-9

4020 Peterson's Private Secondary Schools
Peterson's, A Nelnet Company
Princeton Pike Corporate Center
2000 Lenox Drive PO Box 67005
Lawrenceville, NJ 08648-2123

609-896-1800
800-338-3282
Fax: 609-896-4531
E-mail: custsvc@petersons.com
http://www.petersons.com
Listing of over 1,400 accredited and state-ap-
proved private secondary schools in the US
and abroad.
1,300 pages Annual

**4021 Secondary Teachers Guide to FREE
Curriculum Materials**
Educators Progress Service
214 Center Street
Randolph, WI 53956-1408
920-326-3126
888-951-4469
Fax: 920-326-3127
E-mail: epsinc@centurytel.net
http://www.freeteachingaids.com
Lists and describes free supplementary teach-
ing aids for the high school and college level.
296 pages Annual
ISBN: 87708-399-1
Kathy Nehmer, President

Directories & Handbooks / *Science*

4022 Earth Education: A New Beginning
Institute for Earth Education
Cedar Cove
PO Box 115
Greenville, WV 24945
304-832-6404
Fax: 304-832-6077
E-mail: iee1@aol.com
http://www.eartheducation.org
This book proposes another direction-an alternative that many environmental leaders
and teachers around the world have already
taken. It is called The Earth Education Path,
and anyone can follow it in developing a gen-
uine program made up of magical learning
adventures.
334 pages Paperback
ISBN: 0917011023
Steve Van Matre, Chairman

4023 Earthkeepers
Institute for Earth Education
Cedar Cove
PO Box 115
Greenville, WV 24945
304-832-6404
Fax: 304-832-6077
E-mail: iee1@aol.com
http://www.eartheducation.org
This book will give you the best picture of
what a complete earth education program in-
volves. Even if you can't set up the complete
Earthkeepers program, there are many activi-
ties you can use to build an earth education
program in your own setting and situation.
108 pages Paperback
ISBN: 0917011015
Bruce Johnson, Chairman

**4024 Educators Guide to FREE Science
Materials**
Educators Progress Service
214 Center Street
Randolph, WI 53956-1408
920-326-3126
888-951-4469
Fax: 920-326-3127
E-mail: epsinc@centurytel.net
http://www.freeteachingaids.com
Lists and describes free films, videotapes,
filmstrips, slides, web sites, and hundreds of

free printed materials in the field of science for all age levels.

Annual

Kathy Nehmer, President

4025 K-6 Science and Math Catalog
Carolina Biological Supply Co.
2700 York Road
Burlington, NC 27215-3398
336-584-0381
800-334-5551
Fax: 800-222-7112
http://www.carolina.com
Service teaching materials for grades Pre K through 8, including charts, computers, software, books, living animals and plants, microscopes, microscope slides, models, teaching kits and more.

4026 Science for All Children; A Guide to Improving Science Education
National Academy Press
Arts & Industries Bldg Room 1201
900 Jefferson Drive SW
Washington, DC 20560-0403
202-287-2063
Fax: 202-287-2070
E-mail: outreach@nas.edu
http://www.si.edu/nsrc
Provides concise and practical guidelines for implementing science education reform at local level, including the elements of an effective, inquiry-based, hands-on science program. Produced by the National Science Resources Center. Published by National Academy Press.

240 pages
ISBN: 0-309-05297-1

National Science Resources Center, Author
Douglas Lapp, Executive Director

4027 Sunship Earth
Institute for Earth Education
Cedar Cove
PO Box 115
Greenville, WV 24945
304-832-6404
Fax: 304-832-6077
E-mail: iee1@aol.com
http://www.eartheducation.org
Contains clear descriptions of key ecological concepts and concise reviews of important learning principals, plus over 200 additional pages of ideas, activities and guidelines for setting up a complete Sunship Earth Study Station.

265 pages Paperback
ISBN: 0876030460

Bruce Johnson, Chairman

4028 Sunship III
Institute for Earth Education
Cedar Cove
PO Box 115
Greenville, WV 24945
304-832-6404
Fax: 304-832-6077
E-mail: iee1@aol.com
http://www.eartheducation.org
Examines perception and choice in our daily habits and routines. It is about exploration and discovery in the larger context of where and how we live, and examining alteratives and making sacrifices on behalf of a healthier home planet.

133 pages Paperback
ISBN: 0917011031

Bruce Johnson, Chairman

4029 UNESCO Sourcebook for Out-of-School Science & Technology Education
U.N. Educational, Scientific & Cultural Assn.
7, place de Fontenoy
F-75700 Paris
France
Offers information on science clubs, societies and congresses, science fairs and museums.

145 pages

Directories & Handbooks / *Social Studies*

4030 Directory of Central America Classroom Resources
Central American Resource Center
317 17th Avenue SE
Minneapolis, MN 55414-2012
612-627-9445
Offers information on suppliers of education resource materials about Central America, including curricula, materials, directories and organizations providing related services.

Publication Date: 1990 200 pages

4031 Educators Guide to FREE Social Studies Materials
Educators Progress Service
214 Center Street
Randolph, WI 53956-1408
920-326-3126
888-951-4469
Fax: 920-326-3127
E-mail: epsinc@centurytel.net
http://www.freeteachingaids.com
Lists and describes free films, videotapes, filmstrips, slides, web sites, and hundreds of free printed materials in the field of social studies for all age levels.

287 pages Annual
ISBN: 87708-405-X

Kathy Nehmer, President

4032 Geography: A Resource Guide for Secondary Schools
ABC-CLIO
130 Cremona Drive
#1911
Santa Barbara, CA 93117-5599
805-968-1911
800-368-6868
Fax: 805-685-9685
List of organizations and associations to use as resources for secondary education geography studies.

Directories & Handbooks / *Technology in Education*

4033 American Trade Schools Directory
Croner Publications
10951 Sorrento Valley Road
Suite 1D
San Diego, CA 92121
858-546-1954
800-441-4033
Fax: 858-546-1955
E-mail: paul@croner.com
http://ww.croner.com
Loose leaf binder directory listing trade and technical schools throughout the United

States, in alphabetical order, by state, then city, then school name.

411 pages
ISBN: 0-875140-02-5

Rosa Padilla, Office Manager

4034 Association for Educational Communications & Technology: Membership Directory
Association for Educational Communications & Tech.
1025 Vermont Avenue NW
Suite 820
Washington, DC 20005-3516
202-965-2059
Five thousand audiovisual and instructional materials specialists and school media specialists, with audio-visual and TV production personnel. Also listed are committees, task force divisions, auxiliary affiliates, state organizations and directory of corporate members.

200 pages Annual/Spring

4035 Chronicle Vocational School Manual
Chronicle Guidance Publications
66 Aurora Street
Moravia, NY 13118-3569
315-497-0330
800-899-0454
Fax: 315-497-3359
E-mail: customerservice@chronicleguidance.com
http://www.chronicleguidance.com
A geographical index of more than 3,500 vocational schools including all contact information, programs, admissions requirements, costs, financial aid programs and student services.

Publication Date: 1996 300 pages Annual
ISBN: 1-556312-50-4

Patricia F Hammon, Research Associate
Stephen Thompson, Managing Editor

4036 Directory of Public Vocational-Technical Schools & Institutes in the US
Media Marketing Group
PO Box 611
DeKalb, IL 60115-0611
360-576-5864
Offers information on over 1,400 post secondary vocational and technical education programs in public education; private trade and technical schools are not included.

Publication Date: 1994 400 pages Biennial
ISBN: 0-933474-51-2

4037 Directory of Vocational-Technical Schools
Media Marketing Group
PO Box 611
DeKalb, IL 60115-0611
360-576-5864
Offers information on public, postsecondary schools offering degree and non-degree occupational education.

Publication Date: 1996 450 pages Biennial
ISBN: 0-933474-52-0

4038 Educational Film & Video Locator
RR Bowker Reed Reference
121 Chanlon Road
New Providence, NJ 07974-1541
908-464-6800
Fax: 908-665-6688
Producers and distributors of educational films.

Publication Date: 1990

4039 Guide to Vocational and Technical Schools East & West
Peterson's, A Nelnet Company
Princeton Pike Corporare Center
2000 Lenox Drive PO Box 67005
Lawrenceville, NJ 08648
609-896-1800
800-338-3282
Fax: 690-896-4531
E-mail: custsvc@petersons.com
http://www.petersons.com
These two directories cover the full range of training programs in over 240 career fields divided into the categories of Business, Technology, Trade, Personal Services, and Health Care. East edition covers East of Mississippi; West edition covers West of the Mississippi.
Publication Date: 2006 579 pages Per Volume

4040 Industrial Teacher Education Directory
National Assn. of Industrial Teacher Educators
University of Northern Iowa
Cedar Falls, IA 50614-0001
319-273-2561
Fax: 319-273-5818
http://www.uni.edu/indtech
Listing of about 2,800 industrial education faculty members at 250 universities and four-year colleges in the United States, Canada, Australia, Japan and Taiwan.
108 pages Annual
M Fahmy, Professor/Head of Department
Charles Johnson, Coordinator of Tech Ed. Prog

4041 Information Literacy: Essential Skills for the Information Age
Syracuse University
4-194 Center for Science & Tech.
Syracuse, NY 13244-0001
315-443-3640
800-464-9107
Fax: 315-443-5448
E-mail: eric@ericir.sye.edu
Traces history, development, and economic necessity of information literacy. Reports on related subject matter standards. Includes reports on the National Educational Goals (1991), the Secretary's Commission on Achieving Necessary Skills Report (1991), and the latest updates from ALA's Information Power (1998).
377 pages
ISBN: 0-937597-44-9
Kathleen L Spitzer, Editor

4042 Internet Resource Directory for Classroom Teachers
Regulus Communications
140 N 8th Street
Suite 201
Lincoln, NE 68508-1358
402-432-2680
Directory offering information on all resources available on-line for classroom teachers, including e-mail addresses, Home Page URL's, phone and fax numbers, surface-mail addresses, classroom contacts and teaching resources. Available in paper and electronic formats.
Publication Date: 1996 272 pages Paper Format
Jane A Austin, Coordinating Education

4043 K-12 District Technology Coordinators
Quality Education Data
1625 Broadway
Suite 250
Denver, CO 80202-4715
303-860-1832
800-525-5811
Fax: 303-209-9444
E-mail: info@qeddata.com
http://www.qeddata.com
The first in QED's National Educator Directories, this comprehensive directory of technology coordinators combines QED's exclusive database of technology and demographic data with names of technology coordinators in the 7,000 largest US school districts. The directory includes district phone number, number of students in the district, number of computers, student/computer ratio and predominant computer brand.
Publication Date: 1994 400 pages
Laurie Christensen, Coordinating Education

4044 NetLingo Internet Dictionary
805-794-8687
E-mail: info@netlingo.com
http://www.netlingo.com
A smart looking easy-to-understand dictionary of 3000 internet terms, 1200 chat acronyms, and much more. Modem reference book for international students, educators, industry professionals and online businesses and organizations.
Publication Date: 0
Erin Jansen, Author

4045 Quick-Source
AM Educational Publishing
3745 Suffolk Drive
Suite D
Tallahassee, FL 32308-3048
850-668-4148
Educational technology directory with over 1,100 names, addresses, phones/faxes, and brief descriptions of the products/services of companies/organizations; supports major works/word processors (MS-DOS/MAC); conferences and other educational technology listings.
Annual/September

4046 Schools Industrial, Technical & Trade Directory
American Business Directories
5711 S 86th Circle
Omaha, NE 68127-4146
402-593-4600
888-999-1307
Fax: 402-331-5481
A geographical listing of over 3,750 schools with all contact information, size of advertisement and first year in Yellow Pages. Also available in electronic formats.
Annual
Jerry Venner, Coordinating Education

4047 TESS: The Educational Software Selector
EPIE Institute
103 W Montauk Highway
PO Box 590
Hampton Bays, NY 11946-4003
631-728-9100
Fax: 631-728-9228
E-mail: kkomoski@epie.org
http://www.epie.org
A list of over 1,200 suppliers of educational software and over 18,000 educational software products (on CD-ROM) for pre-school through college information. Includes description of program, grade level data, price, platform and review citations.
Nancy Boland, Coordinating Education

4048 Tech Directions-Directory of Federal & Federal and State Officials Issue
Prakken Publications
416 Longshore Drive
Ann Arbor, MI 48105-1624
313-577-4042
Fax: 313-577-1672
Listing of federal and state officials concerned with vocational, technical, industrial trade and technology education in the United States and Canada.
Annual

4049 Technology in Public Schools
Quality Education Data
1624 Broadway
Suite 250
Denver, CO 80202-4715
303-860-1832
800-525-5811
Fax: 303-209-9444
E-mail: info@qeddata.com
http://www.qeddata.com
Annual survey of instructional technology represents more than 67% of all US K-12 students. Includes computer brand and processor type market share, CD-ROM, networks, LAN, modem, cable and in-depth internet access installed base information.
Publication Date: 1994 160 pages Yearly
ISBN: 0-88947-925-1
Liz Stephens, Marketing Coordinator

Periodicals

4050 ConneXions
Association of International Schools in Africa
Peponi Road
PO Box 14103, Nairobi
Kenya 00800
254-20-2697442
Fax: 254-20-4183272
E-mail: info@aisa.or.ke
http://www.aisa.or.ke
Published twice per year, ConneXions is AISA's print and online newsletter
Peter Bateman, Executive Director
Thomas Shearer, Chairperson

4051 Connections/EdTech News
Commonwealth of Learning
1055 W. Hastings Street
Suite 1200
Vancouver BC-V6E
604-775-8200
Fax: 604-775-8210
E-mail: info@col.org
http://www.col.org/connections
Published three times per year to, these newsletters provide a continually updated mailing list of over 9,000 government officials, education leaders and international agencies with information on COL's work with its partners as well as other developments worldwide.
Dave Wilson, Editor-In-Chief

4052 Issues in Integrative Studies
Association for Integrative Studies
Miami University
Oxford, OH 45056
513-529-2659
Fax: 513-529-5849
E-mail: aisorg@muohio.edu
http://www.units.muohio.edu/aisorg
An annual, refereed professional journal for members.
ISBN: 1081-4760
Rick Szostak, Editor

Periodicals / *General*

4053 AACS Newsletter
American Association of Christian Schools
4500 S Selsa Road
Blue Springs, MO 64015-2221
816-252-9900
Fax: 703-252-6700
Association news offering the most
up-to-date information relating to Christian
education.
4 pages Monthly
Dr. Carl Herbster, Contact

4054 AAHE Bulletin
American Association for Higher Education
1 Dupont Circle
Suite 360
Washington, DC 20036
202-293-6440
Fax: 202-293-0073
http://www.aahebulletin.com
Electronic newsletter
16 pages Monthly
Vicky Hendly Dobin, Manager

4055 ACJS Today
Academy of Criminal Justice Services
7339 Hanover Parkway
Suite A
Greenbelta, MD 20770
301-446-6300
800-757-2257
Fax: 301-446-2819
http://www.acjs.org
Provides upcoming events, news releases,
ACJS activities, ads, book reviews and mis-
cellaneous information.
24-32 pages Quarterly
Laura Myers, Editor
Laura Monaco, Association Manager

4056 ASCD Update
Assn. for Supervision & Curriculum
Development
1703 N Beauregard Street
Alexandria, VA 22311
703-578-9600
Fax: 703-575-5400
News on contemporary education issues and
information on ASCD programs.
Ronald Brandt, Publisher
John O'Neil, Editor

4057 ASSC Newsletter
Arkansas School Study Council
255 Graduate Education Building
Fayetteville, AR 72701
479-442-8464
Fax: 479-442-2038
Monthly up-date on education, finance, new
legislation, mandates for Arkansas public
schools.
3-10 pages
Martin Schoppmeyer, Editor

4058 AV Guide Newsletter
Educational Screen
380 E NW Highway
Des Plaines, IL 60016-2201
847-298-6622
Fax: 847-390-0408
Provides concise and practical information on
audiovisually oriented products with an emphasis on new ideas and methods of using

learning media, including educational
computer software.
Monthly
ISSN: 0091-360X
HS Gillette, Publisher
Natalie Ferguson, Editor

4059 Academe
American Association of University
Professors
1012 14th Street NW
Suite 500
Washington, DC 20005-3406
202-737-5900
Fax: 202-737-5526
E-mail: academe@aaup.org
http://www.aaup.org
A thoughtful and provocative review of de-
velopments affecting higher education fac-
ulty. With timely features and informative
departments, Academe delivers the latest on
the state of the profession, legal and legisla-
tive trends, and issues in academia.
BiMonthly
Lawrence Hanley, Editor, Author
Gwendolyn Bradley, Managing Co-Director
Wendi Maloney, Managing Editor

4060 Aero Gramme
Alternative Education Resource
Organizations
417 Roslyn Road
Roslyn Heights, NY 11577-2620
516-621-2195
800-769-4171
Fax: 516-625-3257
Networks all forms of educational alterna-
tives, from public and private alternative
schools to homeschooling.
Quarterly
Jerry Mintz, Editor

4061 Agenda: Jewish Education
Jewish Education Service of North America
111 Eighth Avenue
Suite 11E
New York, NY 10011
212-284-6950
Fax: 212-284-6951
E-mail: info@jesna.org
http://www.jesna.org
Seeks to create a community of discourse on
issues of Jewish public policy dealing with
Jewish education and the indications of pol-
icy options for the practice of Jewish
education.
Quarterly
ISSN: 1072-1150
Amy Skin, Dir Marketing/Communication

**4062 American Council on Education:
GED Testing Service**
American Council on Education
1 Dupont Circle NW
Suite 800
Washington, DC 20036-1193
202-939-9300
Fax: 202-833-4760
Information relating to GED items and test-
ing.
8 pages 5x Year
Colleen Allen, Contact

4063 American Journal of Education
University of Chicago
5835 S Kimbark Avenue
Chicago, IL 60637

773-702-1555
Fax: 773-702-6207
E-mail: aje@uchicago.edu
Quarterly
Robert Dreeben and Zalman Usiskin,
Author
John E Craig, Editor
Susan S Stodolsky, Editor

4064 American Scholar
1785 Massachusetts Avenue NW
4th Floor
Washington, DC 20036-2117
202-265-3808
A general interest magazine that includes articles on science, literature, and book reviews.
Quarterly
Anne Fadiman, Editor

**4065 American Students & Teachers
Abroad**
US Government Printing Office
732 N Capitol Street NW
Washington, DC 20401
202-512-0000
Fax: 202-512-1293
E-mail: admin@access.gpo.gov
http://www.access.gpo.gov

4066 Annual Report
Jessie Ball duPont Fund
One Dependent Drive
Suite 1400
Jacksonville, FL 32202-5011
904-353-0890
800-252-3452
Fax: 904-353-3870
E-mail: contactus@dupontfund.org
http://www.dupontfund.org
Focused on a variety of good work aimed at
growing the capacity of the nonprofit sector.
Publication Date: 0 Annually

**4067 Association of Orthodox Jewish
Teachers of the New York Public
Schools**
Association of Orthodox Jewish Teachers of
the NY
1577 Coney Island Avenue
Brooklyn, NY 11230
718-258-3585
Fax: 718-258-3586
E-mail: aojt@juno.com
Newsletter representing observant Jewish
teachers in the New York City Public Schools.
8-12 pages Quarterly Newsletter
Max Zakon, Executive Director

4068 Between Classes-Elderhostel Catalog
Elderhostel
75 Federal Street
Boston, MA 02110-1913
617-426-7788
Fax: 617-426-8351
http://www.elderhostel.org
Seasonal listings of elderhostel educational
programs offered by educational cultural institutions in the US and 60 countries overseas.
120 pages Quarterly
Heather Baynes, Contact

4069 Blumenfeld Education Newsletter
PO Box 45161
Boise, ID 83711-5161
Providing knowledge to parents and educa-
tors who want to save children of America
from destructive forces that endanger them.
Children in public schools are at grave risk in
4 ways: academically, spiritually, morally,

physically, and only a well-informed public will be able to reduce these risks.

8 pages

Peter F Watt, Publisher
Samuel L Blumenfeld, Editor

4070 Brighton Times
Brighton Academy/Foundation of Human Understanding
1121 NE 7th Street
Grants Pass, OR 97526-1421
541-474-6865
Fax: 541-474-6866
Home schooling information.

Monthly

Cynthia Coumoyer, Contact

4071 Brochure of American-Sponsored Overseas Schools
Office of Overseas Schools, Department of State
Room 245
SA-29
Washington, DC 20522
202-261-8200
Fax: 202-261-8224

4072 Business-Education Insider
Heritage Foundation
214 Massachusetts Avenue NE
Washington, DC 20002-4958
202-546-4400
Fax: 202-546-8328
Deals with issues relating to the corporate/business world, and the effects it has on education.

Monthly

Jeanne Allen, Contact

4073 CBE Report
Association for Community Based Education
1806 Vernon Street NW
Washington, DC 20009-1217
202-462-6333
Educational institutions covering news, workshops and resources.

Monthly

4074 CEDS Communique
The Council for Exceptional Children
1920 Association Drive
Reston, VA 20191-1545
703-620-3660
888-232-7733
Fax: 703-264-9494
Reports on the activities of the Council for Educational Diagnostic Services and information about special programs, upcoming events, current trends and practices, and other topical matters.

Quarterly

Lamoine Miller, Contact

4075 Center Focus
Center of Concern
1225 Otis Street NE
Washington, DC 20017-2516
202-635-2757
Fax: 202-832-9494
E-mail: coc@coc.org
http://www.coc.org
Newsletters addressing the everchanging needs and concerns in the education field.

6 pages BiMonthly

Jane Deren, Publisher/Editor

4076 Center for Continuing Education of Women Newsletter
University of Michigan
Ann Arbor, MI 48109

734-763-1400
Fax: 734-936-1641
Association news focusing on the concerns of women in education.

4 pages

4077 Center for Parent Education Newsletter
81 Wyman Street
Wapham, MA 02160
617-964-2442
Offers information and tips to address parent involvement in the education of their children.

BiMonthly

4078 Change
Heldref Publications
1319 18th Street NW
Washington, DC 20036-1802
202-296-6267
800-365-9753
Fax: 202-296-5149
http://www.heldref.org
Perspectives on the critical issues shaping the world of higher education. It is not only issue-oriented and reflective, but challenges the status quo in higher education.

BiMonthly

Margaret A Miller, President
Theodore J Marchese, VP/Editor

4079 Clearing House: A Journal of Educational Research
Heldref Publications
1319 18th Street NW
Washington, DC 20036-1826
202-296-6267
800-365-9753
Fax: 202-296-5149
E-mail: tch@heldfred.org
Each issue offers a variety of articles for teachers and administrators of middle schools and junior and senior high schools. It includes experiments, trends and accomplishments in courses, teaching methods, administrative procedures and school programs.

4 pages BiMonthly
ISSN: 0009-8655

Deborah N Cohen, Promotions Manager
Judy Cusick, Managing Editor

4080 Commuter Perspectives
National Clearinghouse for Commuter Programs
1195 Stamp Union
College Park, MD 30314-9634
301-405-0986
Fax: 301-314-9874
E-mail: nccp@accmail.umd.edu
http://www.umd.edu/NCCP
A quarterly newsletter published by the National Clearinghouse for Commuter Programs for professionals who work for, with, and on behalf of commuter students.

8 pages Quarterly

Barbara Jacoby, Contact

4081 Congressional Digest
Congressional Digest Corp.
4416 East West Highway
Suite 400
Bethesda, MD 20814-4568
301-634-3113
800-637-9915
Fax: 301-634-3189
E-mail: griff.thomas@pro-and-con.org
http://www.pro-and-con.org

An independent publication featuring controversies in Congress, pro-and-con.

ISSN: 0010-5899

Delores Baisden, Assistant

4082 Contemporary Education
Indiana State University, School of Education
SE 1005th
Terre Haute, IN 47809-0001
877-856-8005
Fax: 812-856-8088
A readable and currently informative journal of topics in the mainstream of educational thought.

Quarterly
ISSN: 0010-7476

Todd Whitaker, Editor
Beth Whitaker, Editor

4083 Creative Child & Adult Quarterly
Nat'l Assn. for Creative Children & Adults
8080 Springvalley Drive
Cincinnati, OH 45236-1352
513-631-1777

Quarterly

Anne Fabe Isaacs, Editor

4084 Creativity Research Journal
Lawrence Erlbaum Associates
10 Industrial Avenue
Mahwah, NJ 07430-2262
201-258-2200
800-926-6579
Fax: 201-236-0072
E-mail: journals@erlbaum.com
http://www.erlbaum.com
A peer-reviewed journal covering a full range of approaches including behavioral, cognitive, clinical developmental, educational, social and organizational. Online access is available by visiting LEAonline.com

Quarterly
ISSN: 1040-0419

Mark A Runco, PhD., Editor

4085 Currents
Council for Advancement & Support of Education
1307 New York Avenue NW
Suite 1000
Washington, DC 20005-4726
703-379-4611
Fax: 202-387-4973
E-mail: memberservicecenter@case.org
http://www.case.org
Published nine times a year and distributed to 19,000 professional members, Currents delivers essential information, insight and ideas that empower those who support education to master challenges and act decisively to create a better future for their institutions and the world.

Liz Reilly, Editor-in-Chief

4086 DCDT Network
The Council for Exceptional Children
1920 Association Drive
Reston, VA 20191-1545
703-620-3660
888-232-7733
Fax: 703-264-9494
Newsletter of the Division on Career Development and Transition. Provides the latest information on legislation, projects, resource materials and implementration strategies in the field of career development and transition for persons with disabilities and/or who are gifted. Carries information about Division activities, upcoming events, announcements

and reports of particular interest to DCDT members.

3x Year

Sherrilyn Fisher, Contact

4087 DECA Dimensions
1908 Association Drive
Reston, VA 20191-1503
703-860-5000
Fax: 703-860-4013
http://www.deca.org
An educational nonprofit association news management for marketing education students across the country, Canada, Guam and Puerto Rico. Offers information on DECA activities, leadership, business and career skills, which help develop future leaders in business, marketing and management.

36 pages Quarterly
ISSN: 1060-6106

Carol Lund, Author

Carol Lund, Editor

4088 DLD Times
The Council for Exceptional Children
1920 Association Drive
Reston, VA 20191-1589
703-620-3660
800-CEC-SPED
Fax: 703-264-1637
Information concerning education and welfare of children and youth with learning disabilities.

8 pages TriQuarterly

Katherine Garnett, Editor

4089 Decision Line
Decision Sciences Institute
University Plaza
Atlanta, GA 30303
404-651-4000
Fax: 404-651-2896
Contains articles on education, business and decision sciences as well as available positions and textbook advertising.

32 pages 5x Year

K Roscoe Davis

4090 Desktop Presentations & Publishing
Doron & Associates
1213 Ridgecrest Circle
Denton, TX 76205-5421
940-320-0068
Fax: 940-591-9586
Computer generated presentations and visual aids for education and business.

16 pages BiMonthly

Tom Doron, Contact

4091 Development and Alumni Relations Report
LRP Publications
1901 N Moore Street
Suite 700
Arlington, VA 22209
703-516-7002
800-341-7874
Fax: 703-516-9313
E-mail: custserve@lrp.com
http://www.lrp.com
Provides colleges and universities with innovative ideas for improving: alumni relations; the involvement of alumni in clubs and chapters; annual giving; endowment and capital campaigns; and planned giving. Plus, you can recieve free e-mail updates on crucial news affecting your job with your paid subscription.

Monthly Newsletter

4092 Different Books
Place in the Woods
3900 Glenwood Avenue
Golden Valley, MN 55422-5302
763-374-2120
Fax: 952-593-5593
E-mail: differentbooks@aol.com
Special imprint of books by, for and about persons on a different path. Features main characters with disabilities as heroes and heroines in storyline. For hi-lo reading in early elementary grades (3-7).

Paperback

Roger Hammer, Publisher

4093 Directions
AFS Intercultural Programs USA
198 Madison Avenue
Floor 8
New York, NY 10016
212-299-9000
Fax: 212-299-9090
News of AFS US volunteers.

6 pages Monthly

Pedro Valez, Contact

4094 Disability Compliance for Higher Education
LRP Publications
1901 N Moore Street
Suite 700
Arlington, VA 22209
703-516-9313
800-341-7874
Fax: 703-516-9313
E-mail: custserve@lrp.com
http://www.lrp.com
Newsletter helps colleges determine if they're complying with the Americans with Disabilities Act (ADA) and Section 504 of the Rehabilitation Act- so they can avoid costly litigation. Gives tips on how to provide reasonable accommodations in test-taking, grading, admissions, and accessibility to programs and facilities.

Monthly
ISSN: 1086-1335

Edward Filo, Author

4095 Diversity 2000
Holocaust Resource Center
Kean College
1000 Morris Avenue
Union, NJ 07083
Offers ideas and issues on multicultural school education programs.

BiMonthly

J Preill, Contact

4096 ERIC/CRESS Bulletin
AEL, Inc.
PO Box 1348
Charleston, WV 25325-1348
304-347-0437
800-624-9120
Fax: 304-347-0467
E-mail: ericrc@ael.org
Announces new developments in the ERIC system nationally, and publications and events relevant to American Indians, Alaska Natives, Mexican Americans, migrants, outdoor education and rural, small schools.

3x Year Newsletter

Patricia Hammer Cahape, Associate Director

4097 Eagle Forum
Eagle Education Fund
8383 E 123rd Avenue
Brighton, CO 80601-8110

News on the Eagle Education Fund.

Quarterly

Jayne Schindler, Editor

4098 EdPress News
Association of Educational Publishers
510 Heron Drive
Suite 201
Logan Township, NJ 08085
856-241-7772
Fax: 856-241-0709
E-mail: mail@edpress.org
http://www.edpress.org
The Association supports the growth of educational publishing and it's positive effects on learning and teaching. EdPress provides information and analysis of markets and trends, education and legislative policy, learning and teaching research, and intellectual property. The Association also provides training and staff development programs, promotes supplemental learning resources as essential curriculum materials, and advocates on issues relevant to its constituents.

Charlene F Gaynor, Executive Director
Stacey Pusey, Communications Director

4099 Education
Project Innovation
1362 Santa Cruz Court
Chula Vista, CA 91910-7114
760-630-9938
E-mail: rcassel5@aol.com
http://www.rcassel.com
Original investigations and theoretical articles dealing with education. Preference given to innovations, real or magical, which promise to improve learning.

160 pages Quarterly
ISSN: 0013-1172

Dr. Russell Cassel, Editor
Lan Mieu Cassel, Managing Editor

4100 Education Digest
Prakken Publications
PO Box 8623
3970 Varsity Drive
Ann Arbor, MI 48107-8623
734-975-2800
800-530-9673
Fax: 734-975-2787
E-mail: publisher@techdirectories.com
http://www.eddigest.com
Offers outstanding articles condensed for quick review from over 200 magazines, monthlies, books, newsletters and journals, timely and important for professional educators and others interested in the field.

80 pages Monthly
ISSN: 0013-127X

George F Kennedy, Publisher
Kenneth Schroeder, Managing Editor

4101 Education Hotline
6935 Arlington Road
Suite 100
Bethesda, MD 20814
301-280-3100
800-346-1834
Fax: 301-280-3250
E-mail: ads@epe.org
http://www.edweek.org
Education newsletter.

4102 Education Newsletter LibraryCounterpoint
LRP Publications
1901 N Moore Street
Suite 700
Alington, VA 22209
703-516-7002
800-341-7874
Fax: 703-516-9313

E-mail: custserve@lrp.com
http://www.lrp.com
Offers its readers concise, informative and timely articles covering innovative practices in special education. Covers: special education news from the states; updates on curriculum; developments in special education technology; classified ads; descriptions of new products and publications; and more.

On-Line

4103 Education Newsline
National Association of Christian Educators
PO Box 3200
Costa Mesa, CA 92628-3200
949-251-9333
Articles pertinent to public education for teachers and parents, current trends and solutions and the work of Citizens for Excellence in Education.

8 pages BiMonthly

Robert Simonds, Publisher
Kathi Hudson, Editor

4104 Education Now and in the Future
Northwest Regional Educational Laboratory
101 SW Main Street
Suite 500
Portland, OR 97204-3213
503-275-9500
800-597-6339
Fax: 503-275-0458
E-mail: info@nwrel.org
http://www.nwrel.org
Contains articles about products, events, research and publications produced or sponsored by the NW Regional Educational Laboratory, a private nonprofit educational institution whose mission is to help schools improve outcomes for all students.

Carol F Thomas, CEO

4105 Education Quarterly
New Jersey State Department of Education
100 Riverview Plaza
PO Box 500
Trenton, NJ 08625
609-292-4040
New Jersey education information and updates.

6 pages Quarterly

Richard Vespucci, Contact

4106 Education USA
LRP Publications
1901 N Moore Street
Suite 1106
Arlington, VA 22209
703-516-7002
800-341-7874
Fax: 703-516-9313
E-mail: custserve@lrp.com
http://www.lrp.com
Offers information on court decisions, federal funding, the national debate over standards, education research, school finance, and more. Subscribers receive biweekly reports on Education Department policies on Title I, special education, bilingual education, drug-free schools and other issues affecting schools nationwide.

8-10 pages BiWeekly

4107 Education Update
Heritage Foundation
214 Massachusetts Avenue NE
Washington, DC 20002-4958
202-546-4400
Fax: 202-544-7330
http://www.heritage.org
Contains analyses of policy issues and trends in US education.

4108 Education Week
6935 Arlington Road
Suite 100
Bethesda, MD 20814
301-280-3100
800-346-1834
Fax: 301-280-3250
E-mail: ads@epe.org
http://www.edweek.org
For principals, superintendents, director, managers and other administrators.

4109 Education in Focus
Books for All Times
PO Box 2
Alexandria, VA 22313-0002
703-548-0457
E-mail: jdavid@bfat.com
Examines failures and successes of public and private education by looking beneath the surface for answers and explanations.

6 pages BiAnnually
ISSN: 1049-7250

Joe David, Editor

4110 Educational Forum
University of Colorado-Denver, School of Education
PO Box 173364
Campus Box 106
Denver, CO 80217-3364
303-556-3402
Fax: 303-556-4479
E-mail: education@cudenver.edu
http://www.cudenver.edu/sehd
The university is recognized as one of the leading public universities in the nation and offers a broad range of academic opportunities to students.

Quarterly

Hank Brown, President
Michel Dahlin, Interim Vice President

4111 Educational Freedom Spotlight On Homeschooling
Clonlara Home Based Education Programs
1289 Jewett Street
Ann Arbor, MI 48104-6201
734-769-4511
Fax: 734-769-9629
E-mail: clonlara@wash.k12.mi.us
http://www.clonlara.org
Clonlara School is committed to illuminating educational rights and freedoms through our actions and deep dedication to human rights and dignity.

12 pages Monthly

Susan Andrews, Editor
Carmen Amabile, Coordinator

4112 Educational Horizons
P. Lambda Theta, Int'l Honor & Professional Assn.
PO Box 6626
Bloomington, IN 47407-6626
812-339-3411
Fax: 812-339-3462
E-mail: root@pilambda.org
http://www.pilambda.org
Founded in the spirit of academic excellence in order to provide leadership in addressing educational, social and cultural issues of national and international significance and to enhance the status of educators by providing a recognized forum for sharing new perspectives, research findings and scholarly essays.

48 pages Quarterly
ISSN: 0013-175X

Juli Knutson, Editor

4113 Educational Research Forum
American Educational Research Association
1230 17th Street NW
Washington, DC 20036-3078
202-223-9485
Fax: 202-775-1824
E-mail: aera@gmu.edu
Contains news and information on educational research, teaching, counseling and school administration.

4114 Educational Researcher
American Educational Research Association
1230 17th Street NW
Washington, DC 20036-3078
202-223-9485
Fax: 202-775-1824
E-mail: aera@gmu.edu
Publishes research news and commentary on events in the field of educational research and articles of a wide interest to anyone involved in education.

9x Year

Robert Donmoyer, Editor
Leannah Harding, Managing Editor

4115 Educational Theory
University of Illinois at Urbana
1310 S 6th Street
Champaign, IL 61820-6925
217-333-3003
Fax: 217-244-3711
E-mail: edtheory@uiuc.edu
http://www.ed.uiuc.edu/educational-theory
The purpose of this journal is to foster the continuing development of educational theory and encourage wide and effective discussion of theoretical problems with the educational profession. Publishes articles and studies in the foundations of education and in related disciplines outside the field of education which contribute to the advancement of education theory.

570 pages Quarterly
ISSN: 0013-2004

Nicholas C Burbules, Editor
Diane E Beckett, Business Manager

4116 Exceptional Children
The Council for Exceptional Children
2900 Crystal Drive
Suite 100
Arlington, VA 22202-3557
703-620-3660
888-232-7733
Fax: 703-264-3494
E-mail: service@cec.sped.org
http://www.cec.sped.org
Original research on the education and development of infants, toddlers, children and youth with exceptionalities and articles on professional issues of concern to special educators. Published quarterly, free to members or $86.00 per year to individuals.

Quarterly
ISSN: 0014-4029

Margo Mastropieri, Editor
Thomas Scruggs, Editor

4117 Focus on Autism
Pro-Ed., Inc.
8700 Shoal Creek Boulevard
Austin, TX 78757-6816
512-451-3246
800-897-3202
Fax: 512-302-9129
http://www.proedinc.com
Hands-on tips, techniques, methods and ideas from top authorities for improving the quality of assessment, instruction and management.

Brenda Smith Myles, PhD, Editor

4118 Focus on Research
The Council for Exceptional Children
1920 Association Drive
Reston, VA 20191-1545
703-620-3660
888-232-7733
Fax: 703-264-9494
Contains member opinion articles, debates on research issues, descriptions and dates of specific projects, notices of funded program priorities in special education, the availability of research dollars, and the discussion of emerging issues that may affect research in special education.

3x Year

Mavis Donahue, Co-Editor
Eileen Ball, Co-Editor

4119 Foreign Student Service Council
2263 12th Place NW
Washington, DC 20009-4405
202-232-4979
Non-profit organization dedicated to promoting understanding between international students and Americans.

Quarterly

4120 Fortune Education Program
105 Terry Drive
Suite 120
Newtown, PA 18940-1872
800-448-3399
Fax: 215-579-8589
Professional program that offers 75% off the cover price of Fortune magazine, a free educator's desk reference, a free 2-page teaching guide, fast delivery, choice of billing options. Plus quality customer service.

Pat Sproehnle, Editor

4121 Forum
Educators for Social Responsibility
23 Garden Street
Cambridge, MA 02138-3623
617-492-1764
Fax: 617-864-5164
E-mail: educators@esrnational.org
http://www.esrnational.org
Edited for educators concerned with teaching in the nuclear age.

12 pages Quarterly

Susan Pittman, Contact

4122 Foundation for Exceptional Children: Focus
The Council for Exceptional Children
1920 Association Drive
Reston, VA 20191-1545
703-620-3660
888-232-7733
Fax: 703-264-9494
Membership and association news.

6 pages TriQuarterly

Ken Collins, Contact

4123 Fulbright News
Metro International Program Services of New York
285 W Broadway
Room 450
New York, NY 10013-2269
212-431-1195
Fax: 212-941-6291
A four page newsletter distributed 5 times a year to visiting Fulbright scholars in the New York area. Contains a scholar profile, information about activities, tips for living in the United States, events in the New York area, and relevant announcements.

4 pages

Kristen Pendleton, Publisher

4124 GED Items
Center for Adult Learning & Education Credentials
1 Dupont Circle NW
Washington, DC 20036-1110
202-939-9490
Newsletter of the GED Testing Service with articles focusing on adult education programs, teaching tips, GED graduate success stories and administration of GED testing.

12 pages BiMonthly

4125 Gifted Child Society Newsletter
190 Rock Road
Glen Rock, NJ 07452-1736
201-444-6530
Fax: 201-444-9099
E-mail: admin@gifted.org
http://www.gifted.org
Provides educational enrichment and support for gifted children through national advocacy and various programs.

Bi-Annual

Janet L Chen, Executive Director

4126 Harvard Education Letter
8 Story Street
5th Floor
Cambridge, MA 02138
617-495-3432
800-513-0763
Fax: 617-496-3584
E-mail: editor@edletter.org
http://www.edletter.org
Published by the Harvard Graduate School of Education and reports on current research and innovative practice in PreK-12.

8 pages Bi-Monthly
ISSN: 8755-3716

Douglas Clayton, Publisher
David T Gordon, Editor

4127 Health in Action
American School Health Association
PO Box 708
Kent, OH 44240-0013
330-678-1601
800-445-2742
Fax: 330-678-4526
E-mail: asha@ashaweb.org
http://www.ashaweb.org

24 pages Quarterly
ISSN: 1540-2479

Tom Reed, Assistant Executive Director

4128 Help! I'm in Middle School... How Will I Survive?
NRS Publications
1482 51st Road
Douglass, KS 67039
620-986-5472
E-mail: info@englishthrough.com
http://www.nsrpublications.com
The goal of NRS Publications is the success of every child. We provide a varity of books, educational games, posters, educational dice, overhead tiles, science kits, the SHAPES parts of speech learning system and creative play toys to help meet that goal.

Merry L Gumm, President
Tanya L Hein, Vice President

4129 Higher Education & National Affairs
American Council on Education
1 Dupont Circle NW
Suite 800
Washington, DC 20036-1132
202-939-9365
National newsletter with Capitol Hill and Administration updates on issues that affect colleges and universities. Includes stories on the federal budget, student financial aid, tax laws, Education Department regulations and re-

search, legal issues and minorities in higher education.

Janetta Hammock, Contact

4130 History of Education Quarterly
Indian University
School of Education
Bloomington, IN 47405
812-855-9334
Fax: 812-855-3631
Discusses current and historical movements in education.

Quarterly

Amy Schutt, Editor

4131 Homeschooling Marketplace Newsletter
13106 Patrici Circle
Omaha, NE 68164
Offers information, strategies and tips for homeschooling.

Clarice Routh, Contact

4132 IDRA Newsletter
Intercultural Development Research Association
5835 Callaghan Road
Suite 350
San Antonio, TX 78228-1125
210-444-1710
Fax: 210-444-1714
E-mail: idra@txdirect.net
http://www.idra.org
Mini-journal covering topics in the education of minority, poor and language-minority students in public institutions. It provides research-based solutions and editorial materials for education.

Monthly

Maria Robledo Montecel, Executive Director

4133 IEA Reporter
Idaho Education Association
620 N 6th Street
Boise, ID 83702-5542
208-344-1341
Fax: 208-336-6967
http://www.idahoea.org

Quarterly

Diana Mikesell, VP
Kathy Phelan, President

4134 Inclusive Education Programs
LRP Publications
1901 N Moore Street
Suite 700
Arlington, VA 22209
703-516-7002
800-341-7874
Fax: 703-516-9313
E-mail: custserve@lrp.com
http://www.lrp.com
Newsletter covers the legal and practical issues of educating children with disabilities in regular education environments. It provides practical, how-to-advice, real life examples, and concise case summaries of the most recent judicial case laws.

Monthly
ISSN: 1076-8548

4135 Independent Scholar
National Coalition of Independent Scholars
PO Box 5743
Berkeley, CA 94705-0743
510-704-0990
A newsletter for independent scholars and their organizations.

Quarterly

Murray Wax, Contact

4136 Innovative Higher Education
Kluwer Academic/Human Sciences Press
233 Spring Street
New York, NY 10013
212-620-8000
800-221-9369
Fax: 212-463-0742
http://www.wkpa.nl
Provides educators and scholars with the latest creative strategies, programs and innovations designed to meet contemporary challenges in higher education. Professionals throughout the world contribute high-quality papers on the changing rules of vocational and liberal arts education, the needs of adults reentering the education process, and the reconciliation of faculty desires to economic realities, among other topics.

Quarterly
ISSN: 0742-5627

Carol Bischoff, Publisher
Ronald Simpson, Editor

4137 Insight
Independent Education Consultants
Association
3251 Old Lee Highway
Suite 510
Fairfax, VA 22030-1504
703-591-4850
800-888-4322
Fax: 703-591-4860
E-mail: requests@IECAonline.com
http://www.IECAonline.com
Publication of national professional association of educational counselors working in private practice. Association provides counseling in college, secondary schools, learning disabilities and wilderness therapy programs.

Rebecca Peek, Author
Mark H Sklarow, Executive Director

4138 International Debates
Congressional Digest Corp.
4416 East West Highway
Suite 400
Bethesda, MD 20814-4568
301-634-3113
800-637-9915
Fax: 301-634-3189
E-mail: griff.thomas@pro-and-con.org
http://www.pro-and-con.org
An independent publication featuring global controversies in the United Nations and other international forums, pro and cons.

ISSN: 1542-0345

Delores Baisden, Assistant

4139 International Education
University of Tennessee
College of Education
Health & Human Services
Knoxville, TN 37996-3400
865-974-5252
Fax: 865-974-8718
E-mail: scarey@utk.edu
Publishes articles related to various international topics.

Publication Date: 1997 BiAnnual/Paperback
ISSN: 0160-5429

Sue Carey, Managing Editor

4140 International Journal of Qualitive Studies in Education
Sanchez 310
University of Texas at Austin
Austin, TX 78712
512-232-1552
Fax: 512-471-5975
E-mail: 8se@uts.cc.utexas.edu
http://www.tandF.co.uk/journals

Aims to enhance the theory of qualitative research in education.

6 Issues Per Year

Jim Scheurich, Editor
Angela Valenzuela, Editor

4141 International Volunteer
Volunteers for Peace
1034 Tiffany Road
Belmont, VT 05730-9988
802-259-2759
Fax: 802-259-2922
E-mail: vfp@vfp.org
http://www.vfp.org
Newsletter of Volunteers for Peace, which provides intercultural education and community services.

8 pages Annual

Peter Coldwell, Author

4142 It Starts in the Classroom
National School Public Relations
Association
1501 Lee Highway
Suite 201
Arlington, VA 22209-1109
703-528-5840
Devoted to classroom and teacher public relations techniques and ideas.

8 pages Monthly

Joseph Scherer, Publisher
Judi Cowan, Editor

4143 Journal of Behavioral Education
Kluwer Academic/Human Sciences Press
233 Spring Street
New York, NY 10013
212-620-8000
800-221-9369
Fax: 212-463-0742
http://www.wkpa.nl
Provides the first single-source forum for the publication of research on the application of behavioral principles and technology to education. Publishes original empirical research and brief reports covering behavioral education in regular, special and adult education settings. Subject populations include handicapped, at-risk, and non-handicapped students of all ages.

Quarterly
ISSN: 1053-0819

Carol Bischoff, Publisher
Christopher Skinner, Co-Editor

4144 Journal of Creative Behavior
Creative Education Foundation
289 Bay Road
Hadley, MA 01035
413-559-6614
800-447-2774
Fax: 413-559-6615
E-mail:
contact@creativeeducationfoundation.org
http://www.cef-cpsi.org
Devoted to the serious general reader with vocational/avocational interests in the fields of creativity and problem solving. Its articles are authored not only by established writers in the field, but by up-and coming contributors as well. The criteria for selecting articles include reference, clarity, interest and overall quality.

Quarterly

Grace A Guzzetta, Managing Editor
Mary Pokojowczyk, Circulation Manager

4145 Journal of Curriculum Theorizing
Colgate University
Department of Education
Hamilton, NY 13346

315-228-1000
Fax: 315-228-7998
Analyzes and provides insights to curriculum movements and evolution.

Quarterly

JoAnne Pagano, Editor

4146 Journal of Disability Policy Studies
Pro-Ed., Inc.
8700 Shoal Creek Boulevard
Austin, TX 78757-6816
512-451-3246
800-897-3202
Fax: 512-302-9129
E-mail: proed1@aol.com
http://www.proedinc.com
Devoted exclusively to disability policy topics and issues.

Quarterly Magazine
ISSN: 1044-2073

Craig R Fiedler, JD, PhD, Editor
Billie Jo Rylance, PhD, Editor

4147 Journal of Educational Research
Heldref Publications
1319 18th Street NW
Washington, DC 20036-1826
202-296-6267
800-365-9753
Fax: 202-296-5149
http://www.heldref.org
Since 1920, this journal has contributed to the advancement of educational practice in elementary and secondary schools. Authors experiment with new procedures, evaluate traditional practices, replicate previous research for validation and perform other work central to understanding and improving the education of today's students and teachers. This Journal is a valuable resource for teachers, counselors, supervisors, administrators, planners and educational researchers.

64 pages BiMonthly
ISSN: 0022-0671

Deborah Cohen, Promotions Editor

4148 Journal of Experimental Education
Heldref Publications
1319 18th Street NW
Washington, DC 20036-1826
202-296-6267
800-365-9753
Fax: 202-296-5149
E-mail: jxe@heldref.org
http://www.heldref.org
Aims to improve educational practice by publishing basic and applied research studies using the range of quantitative and qualitative methodologies found in the behavioral, cognitive and social sciences. Published studies address all levels of schooling, from preschool through graduate and professional education, and various educational context, including public and private education in the United States and abroad.

96 pages Quarterly

Paige Jackson, Managing Editor

4149 Journal of Law and Education
University of South Carolina Law School
Columbia, SC 29208
803-777-4155
Fax: 803-777-9405
A periodical offering information on the newest laws and legislation affecting education.

Quarterly

Eldon D Wedlock Jr, Editor

4150 Journal of Learning Disabilities
Pro-Ed., Inc.
8700 Shoal Creek Boulevard
Austin, TX 78757-6816

512-451-3246
800-897-3202
Fax: 512-302-9129
E-mail: proed1@aol.com
http://www.proedinc.com
Special series, feature articles and research articles.

Bi-Monthly Magazine
ISSN: 0022-2194

Wayne P Hresko, PhD, Editor-in-Chief

4151 Journal of Negro Education
Howard University
PO Box 311
Washington, DC 20059-0001
202-806-8120
Fax: 202-806-8434
E-mail: jne@howard.edu
A Howard University quarterly review of issues incident to the education of Black people; tracing educational developments and presenting research on issues confronting Black students in the US and around the world.

120+ pages Quarterly
ISSN: 0022-2984

D. Kamili Anderson, Associate Editor
Dr. Sylvia T. Johnson, Editor-in-Chief

4152 Journal of Positive Behavior Interventions
Pro-Ed., Inc.
8700 Shoal Creek Boulevard
Austin, TX 78757-6816
512-451-3246
800-897-3202
Fax: 512-302-9129
http://www.proedinc.com
Sound, research-based principles of positive behavior support for use in home, school and community settings for people with challenges in behavioral adaptation.

Glen Dunlap, PhD, Editor
Robert L Koegel, PhD, Editor

4153 Journal of Research and Development in Education
University of Georgia, College of Education
427 Tucker Hall
Athens, GA 30602
404-542-1154
A magazine offering insight and experimental and theoretical studies in education.

Quarterly

4154 Journal of Research in Character Education
Character Education Partnership
1025 Connecticut Avenue NW
Suite 1011
Washington, DC 20036
202-296-7743
800-988-8081
Fax: 202-296-7779
http://www.character.org

Andrea Grenadier, Director Communications
Esther Schaeffer, CEO/Executive Director

4155 Journal of Research in Rural Education
University of Maine, College of Education
5766 Shibles Hall
Orono, ME 04469-5766
207-581-2493
Fax: 207-581-2423
http://www.umaine.edu
Publishes the results of educational research relevant to rural settings.

3x Year Journal

Theodore Coladarci, Editor
Sara Sheppard, Managing Editor

4156 Journal of School Health
American School Health Association
PO Box 708
Kent, OH 44240-0013
330-678-1601
800-445-2742
Fax: 330-678-4526
E-mail: asha@ashaweb.org
http://www.ashaweb.org
Contains material related to health promotion in school settings. A non-profit organization founded in 1927, ASHA's mission is to protect and improve the health and well-being of children and youth by supporting comprehensive, preschool-12 school health programs. ASHA and its 4,000 members (school nurses, health educators, and physicians) work to improve school health services and school health environments.

40 pages Monthly
ISSN: 0022-4391

Tom Reed, Assistant Executive Director

4157 Journal of Special Education
Pro-Ed., Inc.
8700 Shoal Creek Boulevard
Austin, TX 78757-6816
512-451-3246
800-897-3202
Fax: 512-302-9129
http://www.proedinc.com
Timely, sound special education research.

Lynn S Fuchs, PhD, Editor
Douglas Fuchs, PhD, Editor

4158 Journal of Urban & Cultural Studies
University of Massachusetts at Boston
Department of English
Harbor Campus
Boston, MA 02125
617-287-5760
Fax: 617-287-6511
Explores various issues in education that deal with urban and cultural affairs.

Donaldo Macedo, Editor

4159 Kaleidoscope
Evansville-Vanderburgh School Corporation
1 SE 9th Street
Evansville, IN 47708-1821
812-435-8453
A staff publication for and about employees of the Evansville-Vanderburgh School Corporation.

8 pages Monthly

Patti S Coleman, Contact

4160 LD Forum
Council for Learning Disabilities
PO Box 40303
Overland Park, KS 68204
913-492-8755
Fax: 913-492-2546
Provides updated information and research on the activities of the Council for Learning Disabilities.

60 pages Quarterly
ISSN: 0731-9487

4161 Learning Disability Quarterly
Council for Learning Disabilities
PO Box 40303
Overland Park, KS 66204-4303
913-492-8755
Fax: 913-492-2546
Aimed at learning disabled students, their parents and educators. Accepts advertising.

Quarterly

4162 Learning Point MagazineLaboratory
North Central Regional Educational Laboratory
1900 Spring Road
Suite 300
Oak Brook, IL 60523-1447
630-649-6500
Fax: 630-649-6700
E-mail: info@ncrel.org
http://www.ncrel.org
Applies research and technology to learning.

16 pages Quarterly

Jeri Nowakowski, Director

4163 Learning Unlimited Network of Oregon
31960 SE Chin Street
Boring, OR 97009-9708
503-663-5153
Cuts through all barriers to communication and learning; institutional, personal, physical, psychological, spiritual. It focuses on basic communication/language skills but sets no limits on means or tools, subjects or participants in seeking maximum balance and productivity for all.

10 pages 9x Year

Gene Lehman, Contact

4164 Let It Grow. Let It Grow. Let It Grow.Hands-on Activities to Explore the Planet Kingdom
NSR Publications
1482 51st Road
Douglass, KS 67039
620-986-5472
E-mail: info@englishthrough.com
http://www.nsrpublications.com
The goal of NSR Publication is the success of every child. We provide a variety of books, educational games, posters, educational dice, overhead tiles, science kits, the SHAPES parts of speech learning system and creative play toys to help meet that goal.

58 pages

Merry L Gumm, President
Tanya L Hein, Vice President

4165 Liaison Bulletin
National Assn. of State Directors of Special Ed.
1800 Diagonal Road
Suite 320
Alexandria, VA 22314-2840
703-519-3800
Fax: 703-519-3808
Membership news for persons affiliated with the National Association of State Directors of Special Education.

BiWeekly

Dr. William Schipper, Editor

4166 Liberal Education
Association of American Colleges & Universities
1818 R Street NW
Washington, DC 20009-1604
202-387-3760
Fax: 202-265-9532
http://www.aacu-edu.org
Concentrates on issues currently affecting American higher education. Promotes and strengthens undergraduate curriculum, classroom teaching and learning, collaborative leadership, faculty leadership, diversity. Other publications on higher education in-

clude books, monographs, peer review, and on campus with women.

64 pages Quarterly
ISSN: 0024-1822

Bridget Puzon, Editor
Debra Humphreys, Comm/Public Affairs VP

4167 Link
AEL, Inc.
PO Box 1348
Charleston, WV 25325-1348
304-347-0400
800-624-9120
Fax: 304-347-0487
E-mail: aelinfo@ael.org
http://www.ael.org
A newsletter for educators providing research summaries, education news, and news of AEL products, services and events.

12 pages Quarterly Newsletter

Carolyn Luzader, Communications Associate

4168 Lisle-Interaction
433 W Sterns Street
Temperance, MI 48182-9568
734-847-7126
800-477-1538
Fax: 512-259-0392
Reports on domestic and international programs, annual meetings and board meetings of the Lisle Fellowship which seeks to broaden global awareness and appreciation of different cultures. Occasional special articles on topics such as racism, book reviews. News of members are also included.

16 pages Quarterly

Mark Kinney, Executive Director
Dianne Brause, VP

4169 MEA Today
Montana Education Association
1232 E 6th Avenue
Helena, MT 59601-3927
406-442-4250
Fax: 406-443-5081
National and state association news, legislative policies, and classroom features.

8 pages Monthly

Nancy Robbins

4170 Massachusetts Home Learning Association Newsletter
23 Mountain Street
Sharon, MA 02067-2234
781-784-8006
A source for information gleaned from all the major national magazines and many state newsletters. Calendar of events for Massachusetts homeschooling and several feature articles on legal, educational or familial issues.

24 pages Quarterly

Sharon Terry, Editor
Patrick Terry, Editor

4171 Mel Gabler's Newsletter
Educational Research Analysts
PO Box 7518
Longview, TX 75607-7518
972-753-5993
Educational information pertaining to curricula used in schools.

8 pages SemiAnnually

Mel Gabler, Publisher
Chad Rosenberger, Editor

4172 Minnesota Education Update
Office of Library Development & Services
440 Capital Square
550 Cedar Street
St. Paul, MN 55101
651-296-2821
Policies and activities in elementary and secondary education in the state of Minnesota.

8 pages Monthly

James Lee

4173 Missouri Schools
Missouri Department of Education
PO Box 480
Jefferson City, MO 65102-0480
573-751-3469
Fax: 573-751-8613
State education policy.

28 pages BiMonthly

James L Morris

4174 Momentum
National Catholic Educational Association
1077 30th Street NW
Suite 100
Washington, DC 20007-3852
202-337-6232
Fax: 202-333-6706
http://www.ncea.org
The association offers a quarterly publication, conducts research, works with voluntary groups and government agencies on educational problems, conducts seminars and workshops for all levels of educators.

Quarterly

Catherine T McNamee, CSJ, Publisher

4175 Montana Schools
Montana Office of Public Instruction
State Capitol
Helena, MT 59620
406-444-3095
Fax: 406-444-2893
Information about people and programs in the Montana education system.

12 pages 5x Year

Ellen Meloy

4176 Montessori Observer
International Montessori Society
9525 Georgia Avenue
Suite 200
Silver Spring, MD 20910-4570
301-589-1127
800-301-3131
Fax: 301-589-0733
E-mail: havis@erols.com
http://http://imsmontessori.org
Provides news and information about Montessori education and the work of the International Montessori Society.

ISSN: 0889-5643

Lee Havis, Editor

4177 NAEIR Advantage
Nat'l Assn. for Exchange of Industrial Resources
560 McClure Street
Galesburg, IL 61401-4286
309-343-0704
800-562-0955
Fax: 309-343-3519
E-mail: member.naeir@misslink.net
http://www.freegoods.com
News of the National Association for the Exchange of Industrial Resources, which collects donations of new excess inventory from

corporations and redistributes them to American schools and nonprofits.

8 pages BiMonthly

Gary C Smith, President/CEO
Jack Zavada, Communications Director

4178 NAEN Bulletin
Nort American Association of Education Negotiators
NAEN
PO Box 1068
Salem, OR 97308
503-588-2800
Fax: 503-588-2813
E-mail: naen@osba.org
http://www.naen.org
Association news and notes.

Members Only

4179 NAFSA Newsletter
NAFSA: Association of International Educators
1875 Connecticut Avenue NW
8th Floor
Washington, DC 20009-5728
202-737-3699
800-836-4994
Fax: 202-737-3657
E-mail: inbox@nafsa.org
http://www.nafsa.org
Publishes news and information related to international education and exchange.

40 pages Weekly & Quarterly

Marlene M Johnson, Director/CEO

4180 NAPSEC News
Assn. of Private Schools for Exceptional Children
1522 K Street NW
Suite 1032
Washington, DC 20005-1202
202-408-3338
Fax: 202-408-3340
Association news and events.

8-12 pages Quarterly

Sherry L Kolbe, Executive Director/CEO
Barb DeGroot, Manager

4181 NEA Higher Education Advocate
National Education Association (NEA)
1201 16th Street NW
Washington, DC 20036-3207
202-822-7364
Fax: 202-822-7624
E-mail: ncuea@nea.org
http://www.nea.org
Reports on NEA and general higher education news.

4 pages Monthly

Alicia Sandoual, Publisher
Rebecca Robbins, Editor

4182 NEA Today
National Education Association (NEA)
1201 16th Street NW
Washington, DC 20036-3290
202-822-7364
Fax: 202-822-7624
E-mail: ncuea@nea.org
http://www.nea.org
Contains news and features of interest to classroom teachers and other employees of schools.

8x Year

Bill Fischer, Editor
Suzanne Wade, Advertising Coordinator

4183 NEWSLINKS
International Schools Services
15 Roszel Road
Princeton, NJ 08540-6248

609-452-0990
Fax: 609-452-2690
E-mail: newslinks@iss.edu
http://www.iss.edu
Regularly published newspaper of International Schools Services that is distributed free of charge to overseas teachers, school administrators and libraries, US universities, educational organizations, multinational corporations, school supply companies and educational publishers.

32-40 pages Quarterly

Judy Seltz, Director Communications

4184 NJEA Review
New Jersey Education Association
180 W State Street
PO Box 1211
Trenton, NJ 08607
609-599-4561
Fax: 609-392-6321
Monthly educational journal of the New Jersey Education Association which focuses on educational news and issues related to New Jersey public schools. Its readers are active and retired teaching staff members and support staff, administrators, board members, teacher education students, and others in New Jersey public schools and colleges.

80 pages Monthly
ISSN: 0027-6758

Martha O DeBlieu, Editor
Rosemary Kaub, Conference Manager

4185 NREA News
National Rural Education Association
Education Room 246
Fort Collins, CO 80523-0001
Fax: 970-491-1317
E-mail: jnewlin@lamar.colostate.edu
http://www.colostate.edu
Keeps all members up-to-date on Association activities, events, rural education conferences and meetings, and research projects in progress.

8 pages Quarterly Newsletter
ISSN: 0273-4460

Joseph T Newlin, Editor

4186 National Accrediting Commission of Cosmetology, Arts and Sciences
National Accrediting Commission of Cosmetology
901 N Stuart Street
Suite 900
Arlington, VA 22203-1816
703-527-7600
Fax: 703-379-2200
E-mail: naccas@naccas.org
http://www.naccas.org
Information on accreditation, cosmetology schools and any federal regulations affecting accreditation and postsecondary education.

20 pages 6x Year

Clifford A Culbreath, Editor

4187 National Alliance of Black School Educators (NABSE)
2816 Georgia Avenue NW
Washington, DC 20001-3819
202-483-1549
800-221-2654
Fax: 202-608-6319
E-mail: nabse@nabse.org
http://www.nabse.org
For teachers, principals, specialists, superintendents, school board members and higher education personnel.

15-25 pages 3x Year

4188 National Homeschool Association Newsletter
National Homeschool Association
PO Box 290
Hartland, MI 48353-0290
425-432-1544
Information on what's happening in the homeschooling community.

28 pages Quarterly

4189 National Monitor of Education
CA Monitor of Education
1331 Fairmount Avenue
Suite 61
El Cerrito, CA 94530
510-527-4430
Fax: 510-528-9833
E-mail: jsod@aol.com
http://www.e-files.org
Supports traditional moral and academic values in education. Reports on litigation and reviews various education publications. Issues reported on include parents' rights and movement to restore basic academics.

8 pages Bi-Monthly/Paperback

Susan O'Donnell, Publisher
Susan Sweet, Newsletter Design

4190 New Hampshire Educator
National Education Association, New Hampshire
103 N State Street
Concord, NH 03301-4334
603-224-7751
Fax: 603-224-2648
Reports on the advancements in education in the state and nation and promotes the welfare of educators.

10 pages Monthly

Carol Carstarphen

4191 New Images
METCO
55 Dimock Street
Boston, MA 02119-1029
617-427-1545
Mailed to METCO parents and educational institutions local and national.

4 pages Quarterly

JM Mitchell

4192 New York Teacher
New York State United Teachers
PO Box 15008
Albany, NY 12212-5008
518-213-6000
800-342-9810
Fax: 518-213-6415
Edited primarily for teaching personnel in elementary, intermediate and high schools and colleges. News and features cover organizations' development, progress of legislation affecting education at local state and national levels and news of the labor movement.

BiWeekly

Nicki Rhue, Advertising Director
Bob Fitzpatrick, Production Manager

4193 News N' Notes
NTID at Rochester Institute of Technology
LBJ 2264
Box 9687
Rochester, NY 14623
716-475-6201
Convention news, membership information, education legislation advocacy and personal contributions to the scholarly society.

12 pages Quarterly

Judy Egleston

4194 Non-Credit Learning News
Learning for All Seasons
6 Saddle Club Road
#579X
Lexington, MA 02420-2115
781-861-0379
Marketing information for directors and marketers of non-credit programs.

8 pages 10x Year

Susan Capon

4195 Notes from the Field
Jessie Ball duPont Fund
One Dependent Drive
Suite 1400
Jacksonville, FL 32202-5011
904-353-0890
800-252-3452
Fax: 904-353-3870
E-mail: contactus@dupontfund.org
http://www.dupontfund.org
Provides information on the various organizations and institutes the Jessie Ball duPont Fund reaches out to every year.

Publication Date: 0 3x

4196 Occupational Programs in California Community Colleges
Leo A Myer Associates/LAMA Books
2381 Sleepy Hollow Avenue
Hayward, CA 94545
510-785-1091
888-452-6244
Fax: 510-785-1099
E-mail: lama@lmabooks.com
http://www.lamabooks.com
Writers and publishers of HVAC books.

186 pages Bi-Annually
ISBN: 0-88069

Steve Meyer, President

4197 Our Children: The National PTA Magazine
330 N Wabash Avenue
Suite 2100
Chicago, IL 60611-3603
312-670-6782
Fax: 312-670-6783
http://www.pta.org
Written by, for and about the National PTA. A nonprofit organization of parents, educators, students, and other citizens active in their schools and communities.

5x Year

Douglas Seibold, Editor
Laura Martinelli, Graphic Designer

4198 PTA National Bulletin
National Association of Hebrew Day School PTA'S
160 Broadway
New York, NY 10038-4201
212-227-1000
Fax: 212-406-6934
Educational events in day school relating to PTA movement. News of national and regional groups.

Quarterly

4199 PTA in Pennsylvania
Pennsylvania PTA
4804 Derry Street
Harrisburg, PA 17111-3440
717-564-8985
Fax: 717-564-9046
E-mail: info@papta.org
http://www.papta.org
Topical articles about issues affecting education and children, such as safety and health,

AIDS, parents involvement and guidance, environmental concerns and special education.

24 pages Quarterly
ISSN: 1072-3242
250 attendees and 40-50 exhibits

Peg Fallon, Executive Director
Mary Hess, Membership Coordinator

4200 Parents as Teachers National Center
2228 Ball Drive
Saint Louis, MO 63146
314-432-4330
Fax: 314-432-8963
E-mail: patnc@patnc.org
http://www.patnc.org
Provides information, training and technical assistance for those interested in adopting the home-school-community partnership program. Offers parents the information and support needed to give their children the best possible start in life.

Quarterly

Julie Robbens, Editor, Author
Susan S Stepleton, President/CEO
Cheryl Dyle-Palmer, Director Operations

4201 Passing Marks
San Bernadino City Unified School District
777 N F Street
San Bernardino, CA 92410-3017
909-381-1250
Fax: 909-388-1451
Educational resume of school activities, covering instruction, personnel, administration, board of education, etc.

12 pages Monthly

Jan Bell

4202 Pennsylvania Home Schoolers Newsletter
RR 2 Box 117
Kittanning, PA 16201-9311
724-783-6512
Fax: 724-783-6512
A support newsletter directed to homeschooling families in Pennsylvania. Articles, reviews of curriculum, advice, calendar, support group listing, children's writing section.

32 pages Quarterly

Howard Richman, Publisher
Susan Richman, Editor

4203 Pennsylvania State Education Association
400 N 3rd Street
Harrisburg, PA 17101-1346
717-255-7000
Fax: 717-255-7124
http://www.psea.org

16 pages 9x Year
ISSN: 0896-6605

William H Johnson, Editor

4204 Phi Delta Kappa Educational Foundation
PO Box 789
Bloomington, IN 47402-0789
812-339-1156
800-766-1156
Fax: 812-339-0018
E-mail: information@pdkintl.org
http://www.pdkintl.org

Articles concerned with educational research, service, and leadership; issues, trends and policy are emphazied.

350 pages 10x Year
ISBN: 0-87367-835-4
November
600 attendees and 30 exhibits

Perry A. Zirkel, Author
William Bushaw, Executive Director
Donovan Walling, Director Publications

4205 Phi Delta Kappan
Phi Delta Kappa International
408 N Union Street
Bloomington, IN 47405
812-339-1156
800-766-1156
Fax: 812-339-0018
E-mail: customerservice@pdkintl.org
http://www.pdkintl.org
Published 8 times a year and is Phi Delta Kappa International's professional education magazine distributed to more than 35,000 individuals. Addresses policy/practice for teachers, administrators, education faculty. Advocates research-based school reform and covers professinal development, research, federal policy, and standards. Includes annual PDK/Gallup poll on public education and features full text of current issues available to online subscribers.

ISBN: 0031-7217

Joan Richardson, Editor

4206 Planning for Higher Education
Society for College and University Planning (SCUP)
399 East Liberty Street
Suite 300
Ann Arbor, MI 48104
734-998-7832
Fax: 734-998-6532
E-mail: info@scup.org
http://www.scup.org/phe
A quarterly, peer-reviewed journal devoted to the advancement and application of the best planning practices for colleges and universities.

70+ pages Quarterly Journal
ISSN: 0736-0983
July
150 booths with 1,200 attendees and 150 exhibits

Tom Longin, Executive Editor
Chantelle Neumann, Managing Editor

4207 Policy & Practice
American Public Human Services Association
810 1st Street NE
Suite 500
Washington, DC 20002-4207
202-682-0100
Fax: 202-289-6555
http://www.aphsa.org
This quarterly magazine presents a comprehensive look at issues important to public human services administrators. It also features a wide spectrum of views by the best thinkers in social policy.

52 pages Quarterly
ISSN: 1520-801X

Sybil Walker Barnes, Editor

4208 Population Educator
Population Connection
1400 16th Street NW
Suite 320
Washington, DC 20036-2215
202-332-2200
800-767-1956
Fax: 202-332-2302

E-mail: poped@populationconnection.org
http://www.populationeducation.org
Offers population education news, classroom activities and workshop schedules for grades K-12.

4 pages Quarterly

Pamela Wasseman

4209 Public Education Alert
Public Education Association
39 W 32nd Street
New York, NY 10001-3803
212-868-1640
Fax: 212-302-0088
E-mail: info@peaonline
http://www.pea-online.org
Provides information and consumer-oriented analysis of law policy issues and current developments in New York City public education. PEA Alert back issues; e-guide to New York City's public high school offering comparative data.

Ray Domanico, Publisher
Jessica Wolfe, Editor

4210 QEG
Friends Council on Education
1507 Cherry Street
Philadelphia, PA 19102-1403
215-241-7245
Informal news sheet for Quaker schools.

4 pages BiMonthly

Irene McHenry

4211 QUIN: Quarterly University International News
University of Minnesota, Office in Education
149 Nicholson Hall
Minneapolis, MN 55455
612-625-1915
Fax: 612-624-6839
International campus update for students, faculty, staff and the community.

TriQuarterly

Gayla Marty

4212 Reclaiming Children and Youth
Pro-Ed., Inc.
8700 Shoal Creek Boulevard
Austin, TX 78757-6816
512-451-3246
800-897-3202
Fax: 512-302-9129
E-mail: proed1@aol.com
http://www.proedinc.com
Provides positive, creative solutions to professionals serving youth in conflict.

Quarterly Magazine

Nicholas J Long, PhD, Editor
Larry K Brendtro, PhD, Editor

4213 Recognition Review
Awards and Recognition Association
4700 W Lake Avenue
Glenview, IL 60025
847-375-4800
Fax: 877-734-9380
E-mail: rbloch@accessgroup.com
http://www.ara.org
Published monthly by the Awards and Recognition Association. Recognition Review is the leading voice of the awards, engraving and recognition industry.

Monthly

Stacy McTaggert, Editor

4214 Regional Spotlight
Southern Regional Education Board
592 10th Street NW
Atlanta, GA 30318-5776
404-875-9211

News of educational interest directed to 15 SREB-member states.

9 pages

Margaret Sullivan

4215 Remedial and Special Education

Pro-Ed., Inc.
8700 Shoal Creek Boulevard
Austin, TX 78757-6816
512-451-3246
800-897-3202
Fax: 512-302-9129
E-mail: proed1@aol.com
http://www.proedinc.com
Highest-quality interdisciplinary scholarship that bridges the gap between theory and practice involving the education of individuals for whom typical instruction is not effective.

Bi-Monthly Magazine
ISSN: 0741-9325

Edward A Polloway, EdD, Editor-in-Chief

4216 Renaissance Educator

Renaissance Educational Associates
4817 N County Road 29
Loveland, CO 80538-9515
970-679-4300
Quarterly publication highlighting educators around the world who are revealing the effectiveness of integrity in education.

8 pages Quarterly

Kristy Clark

4217 Research in Higher Education

Kluwer Academic/Human Sciences Press
233 Spring Street
New York, NY 10013
212-620-8000
800-221-9369
Fax: 212-463-0742
http://www.wkpa.nl
Essential source of new information for all concerned with the functioning of postsecondary educational institutions. Publishes original, quantitative research articles which contribute to an increased understanding of an institution, aid faculty in making more informed decisions about current or future operations, and improve the efficiency of an institution.

Bimonthly
ISSN: 0361-0365

Carol Bischoff, Publisher
John C Smart, Editor

4218 Research in the Schools

Mid-South Educational Research Association
University of Alabama
Tuscaloosa, AL 35487-0001
Fax: 205-348-6873
A nationally refereed journal sponsored by the Mid-South Educational Research Association and the University of Alabama. RITS publishes original contributions in the following areas: 1) Research in practice; 2) Topical Articles; 3) Methods and Techniques; 4) Assessment and 5) Other topics of interest dealing with school-based research. Contributions should follow the guidelines in the latest edition of the Publications Manual of the American Psychological Association.

James E McLean, Co-Editor
Alan S Kaufman, Co-Editor

4219 Roeper Review: A Journal on Gifted Education

Roeper Institute
PO Box 329
Bloomfield Hills, MI 48303-0329
248-203-7321
Fax: 248-203-7310

E-mail: tcross@bsu.edu
http://www.roeperreview.org
A journal that focuses on gifted and talented education, the Roeper Review applies the highest standards of peer review journalism to cover a broad range of issues. For professionals who work with teachers and for professionals who work directly with gifted and talented children and their families, the journal provides readable coverage of policy issues. Each issue covers one or more subjects. Regular departments include research reports and book reviews.

60-80 pages Quarterly
ISSN: 0278-3193

Tracy L Cross PhD, Editor
Vicki Rossbach, Subsciption

4220 Rural Educator: Journal for Rural and Small Schools

National Rural Education Association
246 E Ed Building
Colorado State University
Fort Collins, CO 80523-1588
970-491-7022
Fax: 970-491-1317
E-mail: jnewlin@lamar.colostate.edu
http://www.colostate.edu
Official journal of the NREA. A nationally recognized publication that features timely and informative articles written by leading rural educators from all levels of education. All NREA members are encouraged to submit research articles and items of general information for publication.

40 pages TriAnnual

Joseph T Newlin, Editor

4221 SEDL Letter

Southwestern Educational Development Laboratory
4700 Mueller Boulevard
Austin, TX 78701
512-476-6861
800-476-6861
Fax: 512-476-2286
E-mail: info@sedl.org
http://www.sedl.org
A biannual letter that complements and draws on work and performed by SEDL under a variety of funding sources, including the US Department of Education and the US government.

ISBN: 520-7315

Laura Shankland, Editor

4222 SKOLE: A Journal of Alternative Education

Down-To-Earth Books
72 Philip Street
Albany, NY 12202-1729
518-432-1578
Publishes articles, poems, and research by people engaged in alternative education.

200 pages SemiAnnually

Mary Leue

4223 SNEA Impact: The Student Voice of the Teaching Profession

National Education Association (NEA)
1201 16th Street NW
Washington, DC 20036-3207
202-822-7131
Fax: 202-822-7624
Offers articles and views on current events and the educational system through students' eyes for education professionals.

7x Year

4224 Safety Forum

Safety Society
1900 Association Drive
Reston, VA 20191-1502
703-476-3440
Offers articles and up-to-date information on school safety.

4 pages TriQuarterly

Linda Moore

4225 School Bus Fleet

Bobit Business Media
3520 Challenger Street
Torrance, CA 90503
310-533-2400
Fax: 310-533-2512
E-mail: sbf@bobit.com
http://www.schoolbusfleet.com
Coverage of federal vehicle and education regulations that affect pupil transportation, policy and management issues and, of course, how to improve the safety of children riding yellow buses. Special sections include how to transport students with disabilities, a state report on regulations and legislation, and various other departments. School officials that manage finance operations at school districts, private contractors, school bus manufacturers are the audience.

Frank Di Giacomo, Publisher
Steve Hirano, Editor/Associate Publisher

4226 School Foodservice & Nutrition

1600 Duke Street
Floor 7
Alexandria, VA 22314-3421
703-739-3900
800-877-8822
Fax: 703-739-3915
For foodservice professionals presenting current articles on industry issues, management events, legislative issues, public relations programs and professional development news.

11x Year

Adrienne Gall Tufts, Editor

4227 School Law Bulletin

Quinlan Publishing
23 Drydock Avenue
Boston, MA 02210-2336
617-542-0048
Covers cases and laws pertaining to schools.

8 pages Monthly

4228 School Safety

National School Safety Center
141 Duesenberg Drive
Suite 11
Westlake Village, CA 91362-3815
805-373-9977
800-453-7461
Fax: 805-373-9277
E-mail: rstephens@nssc1.org
http://www.nssc1.org
For educators, law enforcers, judges and legislators on the prevention of drugs, gangs, weapons, bullying, discipline problems and vandalism; also on-site security and character development as they relate to students and schools.

Monthly

Dr. Ronald D Stephens, Executive Director
June Lane Arnette, Editor

4229 School Transportation News

STN Media Company Inc.
700 Torrance Boulevard
Suite C
Redondo Beach, CA 90277
310-792-2226
Fax: 310-792-2231

E-mail: bpaul@stnonline.com
http://www.stnonline.com
Covers school district and contractor fleets, special needs and prekindergarten transportation, Head Start, and more on a monthly basis. Reports developments affecting public school transportation supervisors and directors, state directors of school transportation, school bus contractors, special needs transportation, Head Start transportation, private school transportation, school business officials responsible for transportation and industry suppliers.

Magazine/Monthly
100 booths
Bill Paul, Author
Colette Paul, VP
Bill Paul, Publisher/Editor

4230 School Zone
West Aurora Public Schools, District 129
80 S River Street
#14
Aurora, IL 60506-5178
630-844-4400
Informs the community of what is happening in their schools, with their students, and with their tax dollars.

4 pages 5x Year
Laurel Chivari

4231 Shaping the Future
Lutheran Education Association
7400 Augusta Street
River Forest, IL 60305-1402
708-209-3343
Fax: 708-209-3458
E-mail: lea@lea.org
http://www.lea.org
Newsletter for LEA members to focus on the unique spiritual and professional needs of church workers and to celebrate life in the ministry. Resource information for the organization, upcoming events, encouragement for pre-planning.

Dr. Johnathan Laabs, Contact

4232 Sharing Space
Creative Urethanes, Children's Creative Response
PO Box 271
Nyack, NY 10960-0271
845-358-4601
Trains all those working with children to communicate positivity and cooperation.

12 pages TriAnnually

4233 Special Education Leadership
LifeWay Church Resources
One LifeWay Plaza
Nashville, TN 37234
615-251-2000
Fax: 615-251-5933
Covers special education issues relating to religious education.

52 pages Quarterly
Ben Garner, Editor-in-Chief
Ellen Beene, Editor

4234 Special Educator
LRP Publications
1901 N Moore Street
Suite 700
Arlington, VA 22209
703-516-7002
800-341-7874
Fax: 703-516-9313
E-mail: custserve@lrp.com
http://www.lrp.com

Covers important issues in the field of special education, including such topics as law and administrative policy.

22 pages 22 Issues Per Year
ISSN: 1047-1618

4235 Star News
Jefferson Center for Character Education
PO Box 1283
Monrovia, CA 91017-1283
949-770-7602
Fax: 949-450-1100
Mission is to produce and promote programs to teach children the concepts, skills and behavior of good character, common core values, personal and civic responsibility, workforce readiness and citizenship.

Quarterly
Robert Jamieson, CEO
Sharon McClenahan, Administrative Assistant

4236 Statewise: Statistical & Research Newsletter
State Board of Education, Planning & Research
PO Box 1402
Dover, DE 19903-1402
302-736-4601
Fax: 302-739-4654
Statistical data relating to Delaware public schools.

2 pages

4237 Street Scenes
(APO Street College of Education
610 W 112th Street
New York, NY 10025-1898
212-222-6700
Fax: 212-222-6700
New ideas in education.

8 pages SemiAnnually
Renee Creange

4238 Supreme Court Debates
Congressional Digest Corp.
4416 East West Highway
Suite 400
Bethesda, MD 20814-4568
301-634-3113
800-637-9915
Fax: 301-634-3189
E-mail: griff.thomas@pro-and-con.org
http://www.pro-and-con.org
An independent publication featuring controversies before the U.S. Supreme Court, pro-and-con.

ISSN: 1099-5390
Delores Baisden, Assistant

4239 Teacher$ Talk
Teachers Insurance and Annuity Association
730 3rd Avenue
New York, NY 10017-3206
212-490-9000
Fax: 800-914-8922
Offers timely information and helpful hints about savings, investments, finance and insurance for teachers and educators.

Quarterly
Robert D Williams, Editor

4240 Telluride Newsletter
217 W Avenue
Ithaca, NY 14850-3980
607-273-5011
Fax: 607-272-2667
News of interest to alumni of Telluride Association sponsored programs.

8 pages TriQuarterly
Eric Lemer

4241 Tennessee Education
University of Tennessee
College of Education
Knoxville, TN 37996-0001
865-974-5252
Fax: 865-974-8718
E-mail: scarey@utk.edu
Publishes articles on topics related to K through higher education.

BiAnnually
ISSN: 0739-0408
Sue Carey, Editor

4242 Tennessee School Board Bulletin
Tennessee School Boards Association
500 13th Avenue N
Nashville, TN 37203-2884
Articles of interest to boards of education.

6 pages
Daniel Tollett, Publisher
Holly Hewitt, Editor

4243 The Sounds and Spelling Patterns of English: PHonics for Teachers and Parents
Oxton House Publishers, LLC
Po Box 209
Farmington, ME 04938
207-779-1923
800-539-7323
Fax: 207-779-0623
E-mail: info@oxtonhouse.com
http://www.oxtonhouse.com
A clear, concise, practical, jargon-free overview of the sounds that make up the English language and the symbols that we use to represent them in writing. It includes a broad range of strategies for helping beginning readers develop fluent decoding skills.

62 pages
William Berlinghoff, Managing Editor
Bobby Brown, Marketing Director

4244 Theory Into Practice
Ohio State University, College of Education
122 Ramseyer Hall
29 W Woodruff Avenue
Columbus, OH 43210
614-292-3407
Fax: 614-292-7900
E-mail: tip@osu.edu
http://www.coe.ohio-state.edu
Nationally recognized for excellence in educational journalism; thematic format, providing comprehensive discussion of single topic with many diverse points of view.

Quarterly
ISSN: 0040-5841
Anita Woolfolk Hey, Author
Anita Woolfolk Hey, Editor

4245 This Active Life
National Education Association (NEA)
1201 16th Street NW
Washington, DC 20036-3207
202-822-7125
Fax: 202-822-7624
http://www.nea.org/retired
Serves as a resource in the maintenance of quality public education.

20 pages Bi-Monthly
ISSN: 1526-9342
John O'Neil, Editor

4246 Three R'S for Teachers: Research, Reports & Reviews
Master Teacher
Po Box 1207
Manhattan, KS 66502
785-539-0555
800-669-9633

Fax: 800-669-1132
http://www.masterteacher.com
The publication that synthesizes the most recent educational research, data and trends on specific topics for teachers.

Quarterly

Alice King, Executive Editor

4247 Tidbits
Assn. for Legal Support of Alternative Schools
PO Box 2823
Santa Fe, NM 87504-2823
505-471-6928
Information and legal advice to those involved in non-public educational facilities.

12 pages Quarterly

Ed Nagel

4248 Transitions Abroad: The Guide to Learning, Living, & Working Abroad
Transitions Abroad
PO Box 745
Bennington, VT 05201
802-442-4827
Fax: 802-442-4827
E-mail: editor@transitionsabroad.com
http://www.transitionsabroad.com
This magazine contains articles and bibliographies on travel, study, teaching, internships and work abroad.

Bi-Monthly

4249 Unschoolers Network
2 Smith Street
Farmingdale, NJ 07727-1006
732-938-2473
Information and support for families teaching their children at home.

14 pages Monthly

Nancy Plent

4250 VSBA Newsletter
Vermont School Boards Association
2 Prospect Street
Montpelier, VT 05602-3555
802-223-3580
General information.

16 pages Monthly

Donald Jamieson

4251 WCER Highlights
Wisconsin Center for Education Research
1025 W Johnson Street
Suite 785
Madison, WI 53706-1706
608-263-8814
Fax: 608-263-6448
News about research conducted at the Wisconsin Center for Education Research.

8 pages Quarterly
ISSN: 1073-1882

Paul Baker, Editor

4252 WestEd: Focus
WestEd
730 Harrison Street
San Francisco, CA 94107-1242
415-615-3144
877-493-7833
Fax: 415-512-2024
E-mail: info@WestEd .org
http://www.WestEd.org
Improving education through research, development and service.

Mark Kerr, Manager of Organizational
Danny Torres, Publications Manager

4253 Western Journal of Black Studies
Washington State University
Heritage House
Pullman, WA 99164-0001
509-335-8681
Fax: 509-335-8338
A journal which canvasses topical issues affecting Black studies and education.

Quarterly

Talmadge Anderson, Editor

4254 World Gifted
World Council for Gifted & Talented Children
Purdue University
1446 S Campus
West Lafayette, IN 47907
Offers information and articles on gifted education for the professional.

4255 Young Audiences Newsletter
115 E 92nd Street
New York, NY 10128-1688
212-831-8110
Fax: 212-289-1202
Organization news of performing arts education programs in schools and communities.

Annual

Jane Bak

Periodicals / *Administration*

4256 AACRAO Data Dispenser
American Association of Collegiate Registrars
1 Dupont Circle NW
Suite 330
Washington, DC 20036-1137
202-293-9161
Fax: 202-872-8857
Association newsletter for US and foreign postsecondary education institution professionals involved in admissions, records and registration.

12 pages 10x Year

Eileen Kennedy, Editor

4257 AASA Bulletin
American Association of School Administrators
801 N Quincy Street
Suite 700
Arlington, VA 22203-1730
703-528-0700
Fax: 703-841-1543
E-mail: info@aasa.org
http://www.aasa.org
The AASA Bulletin is a supplement to The School Administrator. It contains the Job Bulletin and information for school leaders about the many products, services and events available to them from AASA.

Ginger O'Neil, Editor
Kari Arfstrom, Project Director

4258 ACCT Advisor
Association of Community College Trustees
1233 20th Street NW
Suite 605
Washington, DC 20036-2907
202-775-4667
Fax: 202-223-1297
http://www.acct.org
Provides news of association events, federal regulations, activities, state activities, legal issues and other news of interest to community college governing board members.

Ray Taylor, ACCT President
Alvin Major II, Director
Mktg/Communications

4259 AVA Update
Association for Volunteer Administration
PO Box 4584
Boulder, CO 80306-4584
303-447-0558
Information of value to administrators of volunteer services.

4 pages BiMonthly

Martha Martin

4260 Accreditation Fact Sheet
NAPNSC Accrediting Commission for Higher Education
182 Thompson Road
Grand Junction, CO 81503-2246
970-243-5441
Fax: 970-242-4392
E-mail: director@napnsc.org
http://www.napnsc.org
Newsletter reporting on the origin, history, developments, procedures and changes of educational institution accreditation.

Annually

H. Earl Heusser, Author
H Earl Heusser, Executive Director

4261 Administrative Information Report
Nat'l Association of Secondary School Principles
1904 Association Drive
Reston, VA 20191-1502
703-860-0200
800-253-7746
Fax: 703-620-6534
Offers school statistics and administrative updates for secondary school principals and management officers.

4 pages Monthly

Thomas Koerner, Editor

4262 American School & University Magazine
Intertec Publishing
PO Box 12960
Overland Park, KS 66282-2960
913-967-1960
Fax: 913-967-1905
Directed at business and facilities administrators in the nation's public and private schools.

Monthly

Joe Agron, Editor

4263 American School Board Journal
National School Boards Association
1680 Duke Street
Alexandria, VA 22314-3455
703-838-6722
Fax: 703-549-6719
E-mail: editor@asbj.com
Published primarily for school board members and school system superintendents serving public elementary and secondary schools in the United States and Canada.

Monthly

Anne L Bryant, Executive Publisher
Harold P Seamon, Deputy Executive Publisher

4264 Board
Master Teacher
Leadership Lane
PO Box 1207
Manhattan, KS 66502
800-669-9633
Fax: 800-669-1132
http://www.masterteacher.com
Designed to be a continuous form of communication to help board members know and understand the duties, responsibilities, and commitments of the office; view the superintendent of schools as the educational leader; improve administrator-board working rela-

tionships; better understand the purpose of education; and work at their responsibilities in a prudent, calm, and rational manner.

Monthly

Robert DeBruyn, Editor

4265 Building Leadership Bulletin

2990 Baker Drive
Springfield, IL 62703-2800
217-525-1383
Fax: 217-525-7264
http://www.ipa.vsta.net
Topical, timely issues.

8 pages 11x Year

Julie Weichert, Associate Director

4266 Business Education Forum

National Business Education Association
1914 Association Drive
Reston, VA 20191-1538
703-860-8300
Fax: 703-620-4483
A journal of distinctive articles dealing with current issues and trends, future directions and exemplary programs in business education at all instructional levels. Articles focus on international business, life-long learning, cultural diversity, critical thinking, economics, state-of-the-art technology and the latest research in the field.

200 pages Quarterly

Janet M Treichel, Executive Director
Regina McDowell, Editor

4267 CASE Currents

1307 New York Avenue NW
Suite 1000
Washington, DC 20036-1226
202-328-2273
Fax: 202-387-4973
Covers the world of fund raising, alumni administration, public relations, periodicals, publications and student recruitment in higher education.

10x Year

Karla Taylor, Editor

4268 CASE Newsletter

The Council for Exceptional Children
1920 Association Drive
Reston, VA 20191-1545
703-620-3660
888-232-7733
Fax: 703-264-9494
News about CASE activities, upcoming events, current trends and practices, state and national legislation, and other practical information relevant to the administration of special education programs.

5x Year

Jo Thomason, Editor

4269 CASE in Point

The Council for Exceptional Children
1920 Association Drive
Reston, VA 20191-1545
703-620-3660
888-232-7733
Fax: 703-264-9494
A journal reporting on emerging promising practices, current research, contact points for expanded information, and field-based commentary relevant to the administration of special education programs.

BiAnnual

Donnie Evans, Editor

4270 California Schools Magazine

California School Boards Association
3100 Beacon Boulevard
West Sacramento, CA 95691

916-371-4691
Fax: 916-372-3369
For school board members, superintendents and school business managers, responsible for the operation of California's public schools. Articles of interest to parents, teachers, community members and anyone else concerned with public education.

20 pages Quarterly
ISSN: 1081-8936

Mina G Fasulo, Executive Editor

4271 Clearing House: A Journal of Educational Research

Heldref Publications
1319 18th Street NW
Washington, DC 20036-1826
202-296-6267
800-365-9753
Fax: 202-296-5149
E-mail: tch@heldfred.org
Each issue offers a variety of articles for teachers and administrators of middle schools and junior and senior high schools. It includes experiments, trends and accomplishments in courses, teaching methods, administrative procedures and school programs.

4 pages BiMonthly
ISSN: 0009-8655

Deborah N Cohen, Promotions Manager
Judy Cusick, Managing Editor

4272 Connection

National Association of State Boards of Education
277 S Washington Street
Suite 100
Alexandria, VA 22314
703-684-4000
Fax: 703-836-2313
Quarterly magazine for state board of education members.

10 pages

David Kysilko, Editor

4273 Developer

National Staff Development Council
PO Box 240
Oxford, OH 45056-0240
513-523-6029
Fax: 513-523-0638
Devoted to staff development for educational personnel.

8 pages 10x Year

Dennis Sparks

4274 ERS Spectrum

Educational Research Service
1001 N. Fairfax Street
Suite 500
Arlington, VA 22314-1587
703-243-2100
800-791-9308
Fax: 703-243-1985
E-mail: ers@ers.org
http://www.ers.org
A quarterly journal of school research and information. Publishes practical research and information for school decisions. Authors include practicing administrators and other educators in local school districts.

48 pages Quarterly
ISSN: 0740-7874

John C Draper, Ed.D., CEO
Katherine A Behrens, COO

4275 Education Daily

LRP Publications
1901 N Moore Street
Suite 1106
Arlington, VA 22209

703-516-7002
800-341-7874
Fax: 703-516-9313
E-mail: custserve@lrp.com
http://www.lrp.com
News on national education policy. Offers daily reports of Education Department policies, initiatives and priorities— how they are developed and how they affect school programs.

6-8 pages Daily

4276 Educational Administration Quarterly

University of Wisconsin, Milwaukee
PO Box 413
Milwaukee, WI 53201-0413
414-229-4740
Fax: 414-229-5300
Deals with administrative issues and policy.

Quarterly

Dr. James Cibulka, Editor

4277 Electronic Learning

Scholastic
555 Broadway
New York, NY 10012-3919
212-343-6100
800-724-6527
Fax: 212-343-4801
Published for the administrative level, education professionals who are directly responsible for the implementing of electronic technology at the district, state and university levels.

8x Year

Lynn Diamond, Advertising Director
Therese Mageau, Editor

4278 Enrollment Management Report

LRP Publications
1901 N Moore Street
Suite 700
Arlington, VA 22209
703-516-7002
800-341-7874
Fax: 703-516-9313
E-mail: custserve@lrp.com
http://www.lrp.com
Provides colleges and universities with solutions and strategies for recruitment, admissions, retention and financial aid. Reviews the latest trends, research studies and their findings and gives a profile on how other institutions are handling their enrollment management issues.

Monthly
ISSN: 1094-3757

4279 Galileo For Superintendents And District LevelAdministrators

Master Teacher
Po Box 1207
Manhattan, KS 66505-1207
785-539-0555
800-669-9633
Fax: 800-669-1132
http://www.masterteacher.com
The monthly web and print service provides direction & strategies for superintendents and district level administrators.

Monthly Newsletter

Rick Stultz, Executive Editor

4280 HR on Campus

LRP Publications
1901 N Moore Street
Suite 700
Arlington, VA 22209
703-516-7002
800-341-7874
Fax: 703-516-9313

E-mail: custserve@lrp.com
http://www.lrp.com
This monthly newsletter provides coverage of the latest and most inovative programs higher education institutions use to handle their human resource challenges. Plus, you can recieve free e-mail updates on crucial news affecting your job with your paid subscription.

Monthly
ISSN: 1098-9293

4281 IPA Newsletter
2990 Baker Drive
Springfield, IL 62703-2800
217-525-1383
Fax: 217-525-7264
http://www.ipa.vsta.net
Provides current information on Illinois principals and the profession.

8 pages 11x Year

David Turner, Author
Julie Weichert, Associate Director

4282 Journal of Curriculum & Supervision
Association for Supervision & Curriculum Develop.
1703 N Beauregard Street
Alexandria, VA 22311-1714
512-471-4611
Fax: 512-471-8460
E-mail: oldavisjr@mail.uteyas.edu
http://www.ascd.org/framejcs.html
Offers professional updates and news as well as membership/association information.

Quarterly Paperback

OL Davis Jr, Editor

4283 Journal of Education for Business
Heldref Publications
1319 18th Street NW
Washington, DC 20036-1802
202-296-6267
800-365-9753
Fax: 202-296-5149
http://www.heldref.org
Offers information to instructors, supervisors, and administrators at the secondary, postsecondary and collegiate levels. The journal features basic and applied research-based articles in accounting, communications, economics, finance, information systems, management, marketing and other business disciplines.

BiMonthly

4284 Keystone Schoolmaster Newsletter
Pennsylvania Assn. of Secondary School Principals
PO Box 953
Easton, PA 18044-0953
215-253-8516
Reports achievements, honors, problems and innovations by officers and established authorities.

4 pages Monthly

Joseph Mamana, Contact

4285 LSBA Quarter Notes
Louisiana School Boards Association
7912 Summa Avenue
Baton Rouge, LA 70809-3416
News articles relative to the association, feature stories on research.

6 pages BiMonthly

Victor Hodgkins

4286 Legal Notes for Education
Progressive Business Publications
370 Technology Drive
Malvern, PA 19355

800-220-5000
Fax: 610-647-8089
E-mail: customer_service@pbp.com
http://www.pbp.com
Reports the latest school law cases and late-breaking legislation along with the most recent law review articles affecting education. Federal and state appellate court decisions are summarized and the full legal citation is supplied for each case.

Monthly

4287 Maintaining Safe Schools
LRP Publications
1901 N Moore Street
Suite 700
Arlington, VA 22209
703-516-7002
800-341-7874
Fax: 703-516-9313
E-mail: custserve@lrp.com
http://www.lrp.com
Focuses on the legal and practical issues involved in preventing and responding to violent acts by students in schools, and highlights successful violence prevention programs in school districts across the country. Offers strategies for mediation, discipline and crisis managment.

Monthly
ISSN: 1082-4774

4288 Managing School Business
LRP Publications
1901 N Moore Street
Suite 700
Arlington, VA 22209
703-516-7002
800-341-7874
Fax: 703-516-9313
E-mail: custserve@lrp.com
http://www.lrp.com
Newsletter provides school business managers with tips on how to solve the problems they face in managing finance, operations, personnel, and their own career.

Biweekly
ISSN: 1092-2229

Angela Childers, Author

4289 Memo to the President
American Assn. of State Colleges & Universities
1307 New York Avenue
Washington, DC 20005
202-293-7070
Fax: 202-296-5819
http://www.aascu.org
Monitors public policies at national, state and campus level on higher education issues. Reports on activities of the Association and member institutions.

20 pages Monthly
November

Susan Chilcott, Director Communications

4290 NASPA Forum
National Assn. of Student Personnel Administrators
1875 Connecticut Avenue NW
Suite 418
Washington, DC 20009-5737
202-265-7500
Fax: 202-797-1157
Offers information for personnel administrators and strategies, updates and tips on the education system.

Monthly

Sybil Walker, Editor

4291 National Faculty Forum
National Faculty of Humanities, Arts & Sciences
1676 Clifton Road NE
Atlanta, GA 30329-4050
404-727-5788
Offers administrative news and updates for persons in higher education.

TriQuarterly

4292 Network
National School Public Relations Association
1501 Lee Highway
Suite 201
Arlington, VA 22209-1109
301-519-0496
Fax: 301-519-0494
E-mail: nspra@nspra.org
http://www.nspra.org
Monthly newsletter for and about our members. Some articles about school public relations, issues that affect school public relations people.

Andy Grunig, Editorial Coordinator
Tommy Jones, Advertising/Sales

4293 OASCD Journal
Oklahoma Curriculum Development
3705 S. 98th East Avenue
Tulsa, OK 74146
918-627-4403
Fax: 918-627-4433
A refereed journal which prints contributions on curriculum theory and practices, leadership in education, staff development and supervision. The Editorial Board welcomes photographs, letters to the editor, program descriptions, interviews, research reports, theoretical pieces, reviews of books and non-print media, poetry, humor, cartoons, satire and children's art and writing, as well as expository articles.

Annual

Blaine Smith, Executive Secretary

4294 On Board
New York State School Boards Association
24 Century Hill Drive
Suite 200
Latham, NY 12110-2125
518-783-0200
800-342-3360
Fax: 518-783-0211
E-mail: info@nyssba.org
http://www.nyssba.org
Contains general educational news, state and federal legislative activity, legal and employee relations issues, commentary, issues in education, and successful education programs around the state.

21x Year

4295 Perspectives for Policymakers
New Jersey School Boards Association
413 W State Street
#909
Trenton, NJ 08618-5617
609-695-7600
Each issue focuses on a specific topic in education providing background, activities and resources.

8 pages SemiAnnually

Missy Martin

4296 Planning & Changing
Illinois State University
Dept. of Ed. Admin. & Foundations
Normal, IL 61790-5900
309-438-2399
Fax: 309-438-8683
http://http://coe.ilstu.edu/eafdept/pandc.htm

An educational leadership and policy journal. This journal attempts to disseminate timely and useful reports of practice and theory with particular emphasis on change, and planning in K-12 educational settings and higher education settings. Paperback.

64 pages Quarterly
ISSN: 0032-0684

Judith Mogilka, Editor
Lilly J Meiner, Publications Manager

4297 Principal

Nat'l Association of Elementary School Principals
1615 Duke Street
Alexandria, VA 22314-3406
703-684-3345
Fax: 800-396-2377
A professional magazine edited for elementary and middle school principals and others interested in education.

5x Year

Leon E Greene, Editor
Louanne M Wheeler, Production Manager

4298 Principal Communicator

National School Public Relations Association
15948 Derwood Road
Rockville, MD 20855
301-519-0496
Fax: 301-519-0494
E-mail: nspra@nspra.org
http://www.napra.org
Tips for building public relations people.

6 pages Monthly

Andy Grunig, Manager of Communications

4299 Private Education Law Report

Progressive Business Publications
370 Technology Drive
Malvern, PA 19355
800-220-5000
Fax: 610-647-8089
E-mail: customer_service@pbp.com
http://www.pbp.com
Reports the latest school law cases and late-breaking legislation along with the most recent law review articles affecting private education. Federal and state appellate court decisions are summarized and the full legal citation is supplied for each case.

Monthly

4300 Public Personnel Management

International Personnel Management Association
1617 Duke Street
Alexandria, VA 22314-3406
703-549-7100
Fax: 703-684-0948
Caters to those professionals in human resource management.

Quarterly

Sarah AI Shiffert, Editor

4301 Rural Educator-Journal for Rural and Small Schools

National Rural Education Association
246 E Ed Building
Colorado State University
Ft. Collins, CO 80523-1588
970-491-7022
Fax: 970-491-1317
E-mail: jnewlin@lamar.colostate.edu
http://www.colostate.edu
Official journal of the NREA. A nationally recognized publication that features timely and informative articles written by leading rural educators from all levels of education. All NREA members are encouraged to submit re-

search articles and items of general information for publication.

40 pages Quarterly Magazine
ISSN: 0273-446X

Joseph T Newlin, Editor

4302 School Administrator

American Association of School Administrators
801 N Quincy Street
Suite 700
Arlington, VA 22203-1730
703-528-0700
Fax: 703-841-1543
E-mail: info@aasa.org
http://www.aasa.org
Ensures the highest quality education systems for all learners through the support and development of leadership on the building, district and state levels.

52 pages Monthly

Paul D Houston, Executive Director

4303 School Business Affairs

Association of School Business Officials Int'l
11401 N Shore Drive
Reston, VA 20190-4232
703-478-0405
Fax: 703-478-0205
For school business administrators responsible for the administration and purchase of products and services for the schools.

Monthly

Peg D Kirkpatrick, Editor/Publisher
Robert Gluck, Managing Editor

4304 School Law Briefings

LRP Publications
1901 N Moore Street
Suite 700
Arlington, VA 22209
703-516-7002
800-341-7874
Fax: 703-516-9313
E-mail: custserve@lrp.com
http://www.lrp.com
Gives you summaries of general education, special education, and early childhood court cases, as well as administrative hearings.

Monthly
ISSN: 1094-3749

4305 School Law News

LPR Publications
1901 N Moore Street
Suite1106
Arlington, VA 22209
703-516-7002
800-341-7874
Fax: 703-516-9313
E-mail: custserve@lrp.com
http://www.lrp.com
Advises administrators to avoid legal pitfalls by monitoring education-related court action across the nation. With School Law News, administrators receive the latest information on issues like sexual harassment liability, special education, religion in the schools, affirmative action, youth violence, student-faculty rights, school finance, desegregation and much more.

8-10 pages Monthly

4306 School Planning & Management

Peter Li Education Group
330 Progress Road
Dayton, OH 45449-2322
937-293-1415
800-523-4625
Fax: 415-626-0554
For the business needs of school administrators featuring issues, ideas and technology at

work in public, private and independent schools.

Monthly
ISSN: 1086-4628

Peter J Li, Publisher
Deborah Moore, Editor

4307 Section 504 Compliance Advisor

LRP Publications
1901 N Moore Street
Suite 700
Arlington, VA 22209
703-516-7002
800-341-7874
Fax: 703-516-9313
E-mail: custserve@lrp.com
http://www.lrp.com
Newsletter examines the requirements of Section 504 of the Rehabilitation Act and analyzes their impact on disciplining students. Provides educators and administrators with detailed tips and advice to help them solve the discipline problems they face everyday and keep their policies and programs in compliance.

Monthly
ISSN: 1094-3730

4308 Special Education Law Monthly

LRP Publications
1901 N Moore Street
Suite 700
Arlington, VA 22209
703-516-7002
800-341-7874
Fax: 703-516-9313
E-mail: custserve@lrp.com
http://www.lrp.com
Covers court decisions and administrative rulings affecting the education of students with disabilities.

Monthly
ISSN: 1094-3773

4309 Special Education Law Report

Progressive Business Publications
370 Technology Drive
Malvern, PA 19355
800-220-5000
Fax: 610-647-8089
E-mail: customer_service@pbp.com
http://www.pbp.com
Reports the latest school law cases and late-breaking legislation along with the most recent law review articles affecting special education. Federal and state appellate court decisions are summarized and the full legal citation is supplied for each case.

Monthly

4310 Special Education Report

LPR Publications
1901 N Moore Street
Suite 1106
Arlington, VA 22209
703-516-7002
800-341-7874
Fax: 703-516-9313
E-mail: custserve@lrp.com
The special education administrator's direct pipeline to federal legislation, regulation and funding of programs for children and youths with disabilities.

6-8 pages Monthly

4311 Student Affairs Today

LRP Publications
1901 N Moore Street
Suite 700
Arlington, VA 22209
703-516-7002
800-341-7874
Fax: 703-516-9313

E-mail: custserve@lrp.com
http://www.lrp.com
Newsletter provides strategies and tips for handling higher education institutions' student affairs challenges and problems involving: sexual harassment, binge drinking, fraternity and sorority activities, student housing and more. Gives profiles of other colleges programs.

Monthly
ISSN: 1098-5166

4312 Superintendents Only Notebook

Master Teacher
Leadership Lane
PO Box 1207
Manhattan, KS 66502
800-669-9633
Fax: 800-669-1132
http://www.masterteacher.com
Offers superintendents hundreds of solid ideas to help their jobs run more smoothly. Written by practicing superintendents and business executives, this publication saves hundreds of hours of anguish over the course of the year.

Monthly

4313 THE JournalTechnology Horizons in Education

T.H.E Journal
16261 Laguna Canyon Road
Suite 130
Irvine, CA 92618
949-265-1520
Fax: 949-265-1528
E-mail: wladuke@1105media.com
http://www.thejournal.com
A forum for administrators and managers in school districts to share their experiences in the use of technology-based educational aids.

Wendy LaDuke, Publisher/CEO
Matthew Miller, Editor

4314 Thrust for Educational Leadership

Association of California School Administrators
1517 L Street
Sacramento, CA 95814-4004
916-444-3216
Fax: 916-444-3245
Designed for school administrators who must stay abreast of educational developments, management and personnel practices, social attitudes and issues that impact schools.

7x Year

Tom DeLapp, Communications Director
Susan Davis, Editor

4315 Title I Handbook

Thompson Publishing Group, Inc.
Customer Service Center
PO Box 26185
Tampa, FL 33623-6185
800-677-3789
Fax: 800-759-7179
http://www.titleionline.com
Two-volume looseleaf provides complete, up-to-date coverage of Title I, the largest federal program of aid for elementary and secondary education. The book contains all the laws, regulations and guidance needed to successfully operate the grant program, and insightful articles on key Title I topics, ongoing budget coverage, and special reports on issues like Title I testing, schoolwide programs, and audits. Also included is a compilation of official Title I policy letters, found nowhere else.

1,500 pages Quarterly
Cheryl L. Sattler, Author

4316 Title I Monitor

Thompson Publishing Group, Inc.
Customer Service Center
PO Box 26185
Tampa, FL 33623-6185
202-872-4000
800-876-0226
Fax: 202-739-9578
http://www.titleionline.com
This newsletter provides continuing coverage of Title I, the largest federal program of aid for elementary and secondary education. Title I is at the heart of the debate over education reform, and the Monitor ensures that educators have the most up-to-date information about developments in this ever-changing program. Breaking news about the Title I budget, new legislation and regulations, court cases and other issues.

Monthly
ISSN: 1086-2455
Cheryl L Sattler, Author

4317 Training Magazine

Lakewood Publications
50 S 9th Street
Minneapolis, MN 55402-3118
612-333-0471
800-328-4329
Fax: 612-333-6526
Focuses on corporate training and employee development, as well as management and human performance issues.

Monthly
Jack Gordon, Editor

4318 Updating School Board Policies

National School Boards Association
1680 Duke Street
Alexandria, VA 22314-3455
703-838-6722
Fax: 703-683-7590
Offers information and statistics for school boards and administrative offices across the country.

16 pages BiMonthly
ISSN: 1081-8286
Michael Wessely, Editor

Periodicals / *Early Childhood Education*

4319 Child Development

Arizona State University
Department of Psychology
Tempe, AZ 85287
480-965-3326
Fax: 480-965-8544
http://www.asu.edu
Offers professionals working with children news on childhood education, books, reviews, questions and answers and professional articles of interest.

BiMonthly
Susan C Somerville

4320 Child Study Journal

Buffalo State College
1300 Elmwood Avenue
#306
Buffalo, NY 14222-1004
716-878-5302
Articles of interest related to childhood education.

Quarterly
Donald E Carter

4321 Children Today

ACF Office of Public Affairs
370 Lenfant Plaza SW
Floor 7
Washington, DC 20560-0002
202-401-9218
Fax: 202-205-9688
An interdisciplinary magazine published by the Administration for Children and Families (ACF). The content is a mix of theory and practice, research and features, news and opinions for its audience.

Quarterly

4322 Children and Families

National Head Start Association
1651 Prince Street
Alexandria, VA 22314-2818
703-739-0875
Fax: 703-739-0878
http://www.nhsa.org
Designed to support the Head Start programs, directors, staff, parents and volunteers.

Quarterly
ISSN: 1091-7578
Julie Konieczny, Editor

4323 Division for Children with Communication Disorders Newsletter

The Council for Exceptional Children
1920 Association Drive
Reston, VA 20191-1545
703-620-3660
800-232-7323
Fax: 703-264-1637
Information concerning education and welfare of children with communication disorders.

12 pages SemiAnnually
Christine DeSouza, Editor

4324 Early Childhood Education Journal

Kluwer Academic/Human Sciences Press
233 Spring Street
New York, NY 10013
212-620-8000
Fax: 212-463-0742
http://www.wkpa.nl
Provides professional guidance on instructional methods and materials, child development trends, funding and administrative issues and the politics of day care.

Quarterly
ISSN: 1082-3301
Carol Bischoff, Publisher
Mary Renck Jalongo, Editor

4325 Early Childhood Report

LRP Publications
1901 N Moore Street
Suite 700
Arlington, VA 22209
703-516-7002
800-341-7874
Fax: 703-516-9313
E-mail: custserve@lrp.com
http://www.lrp.com
Educational newsletter for parents and professionals involved at the local state and federal levels responsible for the design and implementation of early childhood programs.

Monthly
ISSN: 1058-6482

4326 Early Childhood Research Quarterly

Department of Individuals & Family Syudies
111 Alison Annex
University of Delaware
Newark, DE 19716
302-831-8552
Fax: 302-831-8776

Addresses various topics in the development and education of young children.

Quarterly

Dr. Marion Hyson, Editor

4327 Early Childhood Today

Scholastic
555 Broadway
New York, NY 10012
212-343-6100
800-724-6527
Fax: 212-343-4801
E-mail: ect@scholastic.com
http://www.scholastic.com
The magazine for all early childhood professionals working with infants to six-year-olds. Each issue provides child development information resources, staff development information and parent communication information.

8x Year
ISSN: 1070-1214

Ellen Christian, Publisher
Jill Strauss, Managing Editor

4328 Highlights for Children

PO Box 269
Columbus, OH 43216
800-255-9517
Magazine featuring Fun with a Purpose, to all children preschool to preteen. Features stories, hidden pictures, reading and thinking exercises, crafts, puzzles, and more.

4329 Journal of Early Intervention

The Council for Exceptional Children
1920 Association Drive
Reston, VA 20191-1545
703-620-3660
800-232-7323
Fax: 703-264-1637

Quarterly
ISSN: 0885-3460

4330 Journal of Research in Childhood Education

Association for Childhood Education International
17904 Georgia Avenue
Suite 215
Olney, MD 20832
301-570-2111
800-423-3563
Fax: 301-570-2212
Current research in education and related fields. It is intended to advance knowledge and theory of the education of children, from infancy through early adolescence. The journal seeks to stimulate the exchange of research ideas through publication of: reports of empirical research; theroretical articles; ethnographic and case studies; cross-cultural studies and studies addressing international concerns; participant observation studies and, studies, deriving data collected.

142 pages BiAnnual
ISSN: 0256-8543

4331 NHSA Journal

National Head Start Association
1651 Prince Street
Alexandria, VA 22314-2818
703-739-0875
Fax: 703-739-0878
Edited for Head Start communities serving children 3 to 5 years of age throughout the country. The journal is an invaluable resource containing current research, innovative programming ideas, details on the Head Start conferences and training events.

Quarterly

Ethan Salwen, Editor

4332 National Guild of Community Schools of the Arts

National Guild of Community Schools of the Arts
520 8th Avenue
Suite 302, 3rd Floor
New York, NY 10018
212-268-3337
Fax: 212-268-3995
E-mail: info@natguild.org
http://www.nationalguild.org
National association of community based arts education institutions employment opportunities, guildnotes newsletter, publications catalog. See www.nationalguild.org.

Monthly

Noah Xifr, Director Membership/Oper.

4333 Parents Make the Difference!: School Readiness Edition

The Parent Institute
PO Box 7474
Fairfax Station, VA 22039-7474
703-323-9170
Fax: 703-323-9173
http://www.parent-institute.com
Newsletter focusing on parent involvement in education. Focuses on parents of children ages infant to five.

Monthly
ISSN: 1089-3075

John Wherry, Publisher

4334 Pre-K Today

Scholastic
555 Broadway
New York, NY 10012-3919
212-343-6100
800-724-6527
Fax: 212-343-4801
Edited to serve the needs of early childhood professionals, owners, directors, teachers and administrators in preschools and kindergarten.

8x Year

Ellen Christian, Editor

4335 Report on Preschool Programs

Business Publishers
8737 Colesville Road
Suite 1100
Silver Spring, MD 20910-3928
301-587-6300
800-274-6737
Fax: 301-585-9075
E-mail: bpinews@bpinews.com
http://www.bpinews.com
Reports on information about Head Start regulations, federal funding policies, state trends in Pre-K and research news. Also covers information on grant and contract opportunities.

8 pages BiWeekly

Eric Easton, Publisher
Chuck Devarics, Editor

4336 Topics in Early Childhood Special Education

Pro-Ed
8700 Shoal Creek Boulevard
Austin, TX 78757-6816
512-451-3246
800-897-3202
Fax: 512-302-9129
http://www.proedinc.com
Provides program developers, advocates, researchers, higher education faculty and other leaders with the most current, relevant research on all aspects of early childhood education for children with special needs.

Judith J Carta, PhD, Editor

4337 Totline Newsletter

Frank Schaffer Publications
23740 Hawthorne Boulevard
Torrance, CA 90505
310-378-1137
800-421-5533
Fax: 800-837-7260
E-mail: fspcustsrv@aol.com
http://www.frankschaffer.com
Creative activities for working with toddlers and preschool children.

32 pages BiMonthly

4338 Vision

SERVE
PO Box 5367
Greensboro, NC 27435
336-315-7400
800-755-3277
Fax: 336-315-7457
E-mail: cahearn@serve.org
http://www.serve.org
Publication of the Regional Educational Laboratories, an educational research and development organization supported by contracts with the US Education Department, National Institute for Education Sciences. Specialty area: Extended Learning Opportunity including Before and After School programs and Early Childhood.

Quarterly

Charles Ahearn, Author
Jack Sanders, Executive Director

Periodicals / *Elementary Education*

4339 Children's Literature in Education

Kluwer Academic/Human Sciences Press
233 Spring Street
New York, NY 10013
212-620-8000
Fax: 212-463-0742
http://www.wkpa.nl
Source for stimulating articles and interviews on noted children's authors, incisive critiques of classic and contemporary writing for young readers, and original articles describing successful classroom reading projects. Offers timely reviews on a variety of reading-related topics for teachers and teachers-in-training, librarians, writers and interested parents.

Quarterly
ISSN: 0045-6713

Margaret Mackey & Geoff Fox, Editors, Author
Carol Bischoff, Publisher

4340 Creative Classroom

Creative Classroom Publishing
149 5th Avenue
12th Floor
New York, NY 10010
212-353-3639
Fax: 212-353-8030
http://www.creativeclassroom.com
A magazine for teachers of K-8, containing innovative ideas, activities, classroom management tips and information on contemporary social problems facing teachers and students.

BiMonthly

Susan Eveno, Editorial Director
Laura Axler, Associate Editor

4341 Dragonfly

National Science Teachers Association
1840 Wilson Boulevard
Arlington, VA 22201-3000

703-243-7100
800-782-6782
Fax: 703-243-7177
http://www.nsta.org
A fun-filled interdisciplinary magazine for children grades 3-6. A teacher's companion is also available. The teacher's companion is designed to help you integrate Dragonfly into your curriculum.

Dr. Gerald Wheeler, Executive Director
Shelley Johnson Carey, Managing Editor

4342 Educate@Eight
US Department of Education, Region VIII
1244 Speer Boulevard
Suite 310
Denver, CO 80204-3582
303-844-3544
Fax: 303-844-2524
http://www.ed.gov

8 pages

Helen Littlejohn, Author

4343 Elementary School Journal
University of Missouri
1507 E Broadway
Hillcrest Hall
Columbia, MO 65211
573-882-7889
Academic journal publishing primarily original studies but also reviews of research and conceptual analyses for researchers and practitioners interested in elementary schooling. Emphasizes papers dealing with educational theory and research and their implications.

5x Year

Thomas L Good, Editor
Gail M Hinkel, Managing Editor

4344 Elementary Teacher's Ideas and Materials Workshop
Princeton Educational Publishers
117 Cuttermill Road
Great Neck, NY 11021-3101
516-466-9300
Articles on teaching for elementary schools.

16 pages 10x Year

Barry Pavelec

4345 Helping Your Child Succeed in Elementary School
Rowman & Littlfield Education
4501 Forbes Boulevard
Suite 200
Lanham, MD 20706
301-459-3366
Fax: 301-429-5748
http://www.rowmaneducation.com
Provides parents with useful information about the importance of parental involvement, concrete ways to work with children and schools to promote success, and a list of resources for further reading.

4346 Highlights for Children
PO Box 269
Columbus, OH 43216-0269
800-255-9517
Fax: 614-876-8564
Magazine featuring Fun with a Purpose, to all children preschool to preteen. Features stories, hidden pictures, reading and thinking exercises, crafts, puzzles, and more.

4347 Independent School
National Association of Independent Schools
75 Federal Street
Boston, MA 02110-1913
617-451-2444

Contains information and opinion about secondary and elementary education in general and independent education in particular.

TriAnnually

Thomas W Leonhardt, Editor
Kurt R Murphy, Advertising/Editor

4348 Instructor
Scholastic
555 Broadway
New York, NY 10012-3919
212-343-6100
800-724-6527
Fax: 212-343-4801
http://www.scholastic.com/instructor
Edited for teachers, curriculum coordinators, principals and supervisors of primary grades through junior high school.

Monthly

Claudia Cohl, Publisher
Lynn Diamond, Advertising Director

4349 Journal of Research in Childhood Education
Association for Childhood Education International
17904 Georgia Avenue
Suite 215
Olney, MD 20832
301-570-2111
800-423-3563
Fax: 301-570-2212
Current research in education and related fields. It is intended to advance knowledge and theory of the education of children, from infancy through early adolescence. The journal seeks to stimulate the exchange of research ideas through publication of: reports of empirical research; theroretical articles; ethnographic and case studies; cross-cultural studies and studies addressing international concerns; participant observation studies and, studies, deriving data collected.

142 pages BiAnnual
ISSN: 0256-8543

4350 Montessori LIFE
American Montessori Society
281 Park Avenue S
6th Floor
New York, NY 10010
212-358-1250
Fax: 212-358-1256
E-mail: kate@amshq.org
http://www.amshq.org
Magazine for parents and educators.

Quarterly
ISSN: 1054-0040

Joy Turner, Author
Eileen Roper, Executive Assistant

4351 Parents Make the Difference!
The Parent Institute
PO Box 7474
Fairfax Station, VA 22039-7474
703-323-9170
Fax: 703-323-9173
http://www.parent-institute.com
Newsletter focusing on parent involvement in children's education. Focuses on parents of preschool-aged children.

9x Year

John Wherry, Publisher

4352 Teaching K-8 Magazine
Early Years
40 Richards Avenue
Norwalk, CT 06854-2319
203-855-2650
800-249-9363
Fax: 203-855-2656

E-mail: patricia@teachingk-8.com
http://www.teachingk-8.com
Written for teachers in the elementary grades, kindergarten through eighth, offering classroom tested ideas and methods.

Monthly Magazine
ISSN: 0891-4508
November-December

Allen A Raymond, Publisher
Patricia Broderick, Editorial Director

Periodicals / *Employment*

4353 AACE Careers Update
American Association for Career Education
2900 Amby Place
Hermosa Beach, CA 90254
310-376-7378
Fax: 310-376-2926
Connects careers, education and work through career education for all ages. Career awareness, exploration, decision making, and preparation. Employability, transitions, continuing education, paid and nonpaid work, occupations, career tips, resources, partnerships, conferences and workshops. Awards and recognition, trends and futures. A newsletter is published.

8+ pages Quarterly/Newsletter
ISBN: 1074-9551

Dr.Pat Nellor Wickwire, Author
Dr. Pat Nellor Wickwire, Editor

4354 Career Development for Exceptional Individuals
The Council for Exceptional Children
1920 Association Drive
Reston, VA 20191-1545
703-620-3660
888-232-7733
Fax: 703-264-9494
Contains articles dealing with the latest research activities, model programs, and issues in career development and transition planning for individuals with disabilities and/or who are gifted.

2x Year

Gary Greene, Executive Editor

4355 Career Education News
Diversified Learning
72300 Vallat Road
Rancho Mirage, CA 92270-3906
619-346-3336
Reports on programs, materials and training for career educators.

4 pages BiWeekly

Webster Wilson Jr, Publisher
Webster Wilson, Editor

4356 Careers Bridge Newsletter
St. Louis Public Schools
901 Locust Street
Saint Louis, MO 63101-1401
314-231-3720
Available to educators and business/community persons on collaborative activities and promotion of career and self-awareness education in preschool to grade 12.

BiMonthly

Susan Katzman, Contact

4357 Chronicle of Higher Education
Subscription Department
PO Box 1955
Marion, OH 43305-1955
800-347-6969

Newspaper published weekly advertising many teaching opportunities overseas.

Weekly

4358 Current Openings in Education in the USA
Education Information Services
PO Box 620662
Newton, MA 02462-0662
617-433-0125
This publication is a booklet listing about 140 institutions or school systems, each with one to a dozen or more openings for teachers, librarians, counselors and other personnel.

15 pages Every 6 Weeks

F Viaux, Coordinating Education

4359 Education Jobs
National Education Service Center
PO Box 1279
Riverton, WY 82501-1279
307-856-0170
Offers information on employment in the education field.

Weekly

Lucretia Ficht, Contact

4360 Employment Opportunities
National Guild of Community Schools of the Arts
520 8th Avenue
Suite 302, 3rd Floor
New York, NY 10018
212-268-3337
Fax: 212-268-3995
E-mail: info@natguild.org
http://www.nationalguild.org

Monthly

Noah Xifr, Director Membership/Oper.

4361 Faculty, Staff & Administrative Openings in US Schools & Colleges
Educational Information Services
PO Box 662
Newton Lower Falls, MA 02162
617-964-4555
A listing of available positions in the educational system in the United States.

Monthly

4362 International Educator
PO Box 513
Cummaquid, MA 02637-0513
508-580-1880
A newspaper listing over 100 teaching positions overseas.

Quarterly

4363 Jobs Clearinghouse
Association for Experiential Education
2305 Canyon Boulevard
Suite 100
Boulder, CO 80302-5651
303-440-8844
Fax: 303-440-9581
E-mail: jch@aee.org
http://www.aee.org
A newsletter that is one of the most comprehensive and widely-used monthly listings of full-time, part-time, and seasonal employment and internship opportunities in the experiential/adventure education field for both employers and job seekers.

Monthly

Kristen Cherry

4364 Journal of Cooperative Education
University of Waterloo
200 University Avenue
Waterloo, ON N2L 3G1 Canada

519-888-4567
519-885-1211
Fax: 519-746-8631
Dedicated to the publication of thoughtful and timely articles concerning work-integrated education. It invites manuscripts which are essays that analyze issues, reports of research, descriptions of innovative practices.

3x Year

Patricia M Rowe, Editor

4365 Journal of Vocational Education Research
Colorado State University
202 Education
Fort Collins, CO 80523-0001
970-491-6835
Fax: 970-491-1317
Publishes refereed articles dealing with research and research-related topics in vocational education. Manuscripts based on original investigations, comprehensive reviews of literature, research methodology and theoretical constructs in vocational education are encouraged.

Quarterly

Brian Cobb, Editor

4366 New Jersey Education Law Report
Whitaker Newsletters
313 S Avenue
#340
Fanwood, NJ 07023-1364
908-889-6336
800-359-6049
Fax: 908-889-6339
Court decisions and rulings on employment in New Jersey schools.

8 pages
ISSN: 0279-8557

Joel Whitaker, Publisher
Fred Rossu, Editor

4367 SkillsUSA Champions
Vocational Industrial Clubs of America
PO Box 3000
Leesburg, VA 20177-0300
703-777-8810
Fax: 703-777-8999
E-mail: anyinfo@skillsusa.org
http://www.skillsusa.org
To individuals interested in cultivating leaderships skills, SkillsUSA is a dynamic resource that inspires and connencts all members creating a virtual community through its revalent and useful content.

28 pages Quarterly
ISSN: 1040-4538

E Thomas Hah, Director Office Publications
Timothy W Lawrence, Executive Director

4368 VEWAA Newsletter
Vocational Evaluation & Work Adjustment Assn.
1234 Haley Circle
Auburn University
Auburn, AL 36849
334-844-3800
News and information about the practice of vocational evaluation and work adjustment.

8 pages Quarterly

Ronald Fru, Publisher
Clarence D Brown, Editor

4369 Views & Visions
Wisconsin Vocational Association
44 E Mifflin Street
Suite 104
Madison, WI 53703-2800
608-283-2595
Fax: 608-283-2589

For teachers of vocational and adult education.

8 pages BiMonthly

Linda Stemper

4370 Vocational Training News
Aston Publications
701 King Street
Suite 444
Alexandria, VA 22314-2944
703-683-4100
800-453-9397
Fax: 703-739-6517
Contains timely, useful reports on the federal Job Training Partnership Act and the Carl D Perkins Vocational Education Act. Other areas include literacy, private industry councils and training initiatives.

10 pages Weekly

Cynthia Carter, Publisher
Matthew Dembicki, Editor

Periodicals / *Financial Aid*

4371 American-Scandinavian Foundation Magazine
American-Scandinavian Foundation
58 Park Avenue
New York, NY 10016-5025
212-779-3587
E-mail: info@amscan.org
http://www.amscan.org
Covers politics, culture and lifestyles of Denmark, Finland, Iceland, Norway and Sweden.

100 pages Quarterly Magazine

Edward P Gallagher, President
Christian Sonne, Deputy Chairman

4372 Education Grants Alert
LPR Publications
1901n Moore Street
Suite 700
Arlington, VA 22209-2944
703-516-7002
800-341-7874
Fax: 703-516-9313
E-mail: custserve@lrp.com
http://www.lrp.com
Dedicated to helping schools increase funding for K-12 programs. This newsletter will uncover new and recurring grant competitions from federal agencies that fund school projects, plus scores of corporate and foundation sources.

Weekly

4373 Federal Research Report
Business Publishers
8737 Colesville Road
Suite 1100
Silver Spring, MD 20910-3928
301-587-6300
800-274-6737
Fax: 301-585-9075
E-mail: bpinews@bpinews.com
http://www.bpinews.com
Identifies critical funding sources supplying administrator's with contact names, addresses, telephone numbers, RFP numbers and other vital details.

8 pages Weekly

Eric Easton, Publisher
Leonard Eiserer, Editor

4374 Foundation & Corporate Grants Alert
LRP Publishing
1901 N Moore Street
Suite 1106
Arlington, VA 22209

703-516-7002
800-341-7874
Fax: 703-516-9313
E-mail: custserve@lrp.com
http://www.lrp.com
Offers information on funding trends, new foundations and hard-to-find regional funders. You'll also get to foundation and corporate funders from the inside, with foundation profiles and interviews with program officers.

Monthly

4375 Grants for School Districts Monthly
Quinlan Publishing
23 Drydock Avenue
Boston, MA 02210-2336
617-542-0048
Listing of grants available for schools across the country.

Monthly

4376 Informativo
LASPAU (Latin America Scholarship Program)
25 Mount Auburn Street
Cambridge, MA 02138-6028
617-495-5255
Administers scholarships for staff members nominated by Latin American and Caribbean education and development organizations and other public and private sector entities.

8 pages SemiAnnually

Carole Biederman, Contact

4377 NASFAA Newsletter
National Assn. of Student Financial Aid Admin.
1920 L Street NW
Suite 200
Washington, DC 20036-5010
202-785-0453
Fax: 202-785-1487
News covering student financial aid legislation and regulations.

24 pages SemiMonthly

Madeleine McLean, Editor

4378 United Student Aid Funds Newsletter
PO Box 6180
Indianapolis, IN 46206-6180
317-578-6094
USA Funds Education Loan products and services information.

8 pages BiMonthly

Nelson Scharadin, Publisher
Dena Weisbard, Editor

Periodicals / *Guidance & Counseling*

4379 ASCA Counselor
American Counseling Association
5999 Stevenson Avenue
Alexandria, VA 22304-3302
703-823-9800
Fax: 703-823-0252
Aimed at the guidance counselor.

16 pages BiMonthly

Dolores Ehrlich, Editor

4380 Adolescence
Libra Publishers
3089C Clairemont Drive
San Diego, CA 92117-6802
858-571-1414
Fax: 858-571-1414
E-mail: librapublishers@juno.com

Articles contributed by professionals spanning issues relating to teenage education, counseling and guidance. Paperback.

256 pages Quarterly
ISSN: 0001-8449

Jon Kroll, Editor
William Kroll, Author

4381 Association for Play Therapy Newsletter
2050 N Winery Avenue
Suite 101
Fresno, CA 93703-2831
559-252-2278
Fax: 559-252-2297
E-mail: info@a4pt.org
http://www.a4pt.org
Dedicated to the advancement of play therapy. APT is interdisciplinary and defines play therapy as a distinct group of interventions which use play as an integral component of the therapeutic process.

Quarterly

William S Burns CAE, Executive Director
Kathryn Lebby MS, General Manager

4382 Attention
CHADD
8181 Professional Place
Suite 150
Landover, MD 20785
301-306-7070
800-233-4050
Fax: 301-306-7090
E-mail: attention@chadd.org
http://www.chadd.org
Magazine for children and adults with Attention Deficit/Hyperactivity Disorder, and their families.

48 pages Bi-Monthly
ISSN: 1551-0980
70+ booths with 1,400 attendees and 70+ exhibits

Marsha Bokman, Manager

4383 Before You Can Discipline
Master Teacher
Leadership Lane
PO Box 1207
Manhattan, KS 66505-1207
800-669-9633
Fax: 800-669-1132
http://www.masterteacher.com
Understand exactly how student's primary and secondary needs can and do influence acceptable and unacceptable behavior. Develop professional attitudes toward discipline problems and learn the laws and principals of managing people.

170 pages
ISBN: 0-914607-03-0

Robert L DeBruyn, Author

4384 Child Psychiatry & Human Development
Kluwer Academic/Human Sciences Press
233 Spring Street
New York, NY 10013
212-620-8000
800-221-9369
Fax: 212-463-0742
http://www.wkpa.nl
Interdisciplinary international journal serving the groups represented by child and adolescent psychiatry, clinical child/pediatric/family psychology, pediatrics, social science, and human development. Publishes research on diagnosis, assessment, treatment, epidemiology, development, advocacy, training, cultural factors, ethics, policy, and professional issues as related to clinical

disorders in children, adolescents and families.

Quarterly
ISSN: 0009-398X

Carol Bischoff, Publisher
Kenneth J Tarnowski, Editor

4385 Child Welfare
Child Welfare League of America
440 1st Street NW
Suite 310
Washington, DC 20001-2085
202-638-2952
Fax: 202-638-4004

BiMonthly

Eve Klein, Editor

4386 Child and Adolescent Social Work Journal
Kluwer Academic/Human Sciences Press
233 Spring Street
New York, NY 10013
212-620-8000
800-221-9369
Fax: 212-463-0742
http://www.wkpa.nl
Features original articles that focus on clinical social work practice with children, adolescents and their families. The journal addresses current issues in the field of social work drawn from theory, direct practice, research, and social policy, as well as focuses on problems affecting specific populations in special settings.

Bimonthly
ISSN: 0738-0151

Carol Bischoff, Publisher
Thomas Kenemore, Editor

4387 College Board News
College Board Publications
45 Columbus Avenue
New York, NY 10023-6992
212-713-8165
800-323-7155
Fax: 800-525-5562
http://www.collegeboard.org
Sent free to schools and colleges several times a year, the News reports on the activities of the College Board. Its articles inform readers about the Board's services in such areas as high school, guidance, college admission, curriculum and placement, testing, financial aid, adult education and research.

4388 College Board Review
College Board Publications
45 Columbus Avenue
New York, NY 10023-6992
212-713-8165
800-323-7155
Fax: 800-525-5562
http://www.collegeboard.org
Each issue of the Review probes key problems and trends facing education professionals concerned with student transition from high school to college.

4389 College Times
College Board Publications
45 Columbus Avenue
New York, NY 10023-6917
212-713-8165
800-323-7155
Fax: 800-525-5562
http://www.collegeboard.org
This annual magazine is a one-stop source to college admission. It provides valuable advice to help students through the complex college selection, application and admission process.

Publication Date: 1995 32 pages Package of 50

4390 Communique
National Association of School
Psychologists
4340 EW Highway
Suite 402
Bethesda, MD 20814
301-657-0270
Fax: 301-657-0275
E-mail: center@naspweb.org
http://www.nasponline.org
50 pages 8x Year
ISSN: 0164-775X

4391 Counseling & Values
American Counseling Association
5999 Stevenson Avenue
Alexandria, VA 22304-3302
703-823-9800
Fax: 703-823-0252
Editorial content focuses on the roles of values and religion in counseling and psychology.
3x Year
Stephen Brooks, Advertising Director
Susan Lausch, Advertising/Sales

4392 Counseling Today
American Counseling Association
5999 Stevenson Avenue
Alexandria, VA 22304-3302
703-823-9800
Fax: 703-823-0252
Covers national and international counseling issues and reports legislative and governmental activities affecting counselors.
Monthly
Kathy Maguire, Advertising Director
Mary Morrissey, Editor-in-Chief

4393 Counselor Education & Supervision
American Counseling Association
5999 Stevenson Avenue
Alexandria, VA 22304-3302
703-823-9800
Fax: 703-823-0252
Covers counseling theories, techniques and skills, teaching and training.
Quarterly
Stephen Brooks, Advertising Director
Susan Lausch, Advertising/Sales

4394 ERIC Clearinghouse on Counseling & Student Services
201 Ferguson Building UNCG
Greensboro, NC 27402-6171
336-334-4114
800-414-9769
Fax: 336-334-4116
E-mail: ericcass@uncg.edu.edu
http://ericcass.uncg.edu
Covers news about ERIC and the counseling clearinghouse and developments in the fields of education and counseling.
4 pages Quarterly
Garry R Walz, Co-Director
Jeanne C Bleuer, Co-Director

4395 Educational & Psychological Measurement
Sage Publications
2455 Telle Road
Thousand Oaks, CA 91320
805-499-9774
Fax: 805-375-1700
E-mail: order@sagepub.com
http://www.sagepub.com
Quarterly

4396 Elementary School Guidance & Counseling
American Counseling Association
5999 Stevenson Avenue
Alexandria, VA 22304-3300
703-823-9800
Fax: 703-823-0252
http://www.counseling.org
Journal concerned with enhancing the role of the elementary, middle school and junior high school counselor.
Quarterly
ISSN: 0013-5976
Michael Comlish, Editor

4397 Family Relations
Miami University
Family & Child Studies Center
Oxford, OH 45056
513-529-4909
Fax: 513-529-7270
Quarterly
Timothy H Brubaker, Editor

4398 Family Therapy: The Journal of the California Graduate School of Family Psychology
Libra Publishers
3089C Clairemont Drive
PNB 383
San Diego, CA 92117-6802
858-571-1414
Fax: 858-571-1414
Articles contributed by professionals spanning issues relating to teenage education, counseling and guidance. Paperback.
96 pages Quarterly
ISSN: 0091-6544
William Kroll, Editor

4399 Health & Social Work
National Association of Social Workers
750 First Street NE
Suite 700
Washington, DC 20002-4241
202-408-8600
800-638-8799
Fax: 202-336-8311
http://www.socialworkers.org
Covers practice, innovation, research, legislation, policy , planning, and all the professional issues relevant to social work services in all levels of education.
Mal Milburn, Marketing/Sales Associate
Lyn Carter, Advertising Specialist

4400 ICA Quarterly
Western Illinois University
Counseling Center
Memorial Hall
Macomb, IL 61455
309-298-2453
Fax: 309-298-3253
Official publication of the Illinois Counseling Association. Focus is on material of interest and value to professional counselors.
Quarterly
Michael Illovsky, Editor

4401 International Journal of Play Therapy
2050 N Winery Avenue
Suite 101
Fresno, CA 93703-2831
559-252-2278
Fax: 559-252-2297
E-mail: info@a4pt.org
http://www.a4pt.org
Dedicated to the advancement of play therapy. APT is interdisciplinary and defines play therapy as a distinct group of interventions which use play as an integral component of the therapeutic process.
Publication Date: 1982 BiAnnual
William S Burns CAE, Executive Director
Kathryn Lebby MS, General Manager

4402 Journal for Specialists in Group Work
American Counseling Association
5999 Stevenson Avenue
Alexandria, VA 22304-3302
703-823-9800
Fax: 703-823-0252
Contains theory, legal issues and current literature reviews.
Quarterly
Stephen Brooks, Editor

4403 Journal of At-Risk Issues
Clemson University
209 Martin Street
Clemson, SC 29631-1555
864-656-2599
800-443-6392
Fax: 864-656-0136
E-mail: NDPC@clemson.edu
http://www.dropoutprevention.org
36 pages
ISBN: 1098-1608
Dr. Judy Johnson, Author
Dr. Judy Johnson, Author
Dr. Alice Fisher, Editor

4404 Journal of Child and Adolescent Group Therapy
Kluwer Academic/Human Sciences Press
233 Spring Street
New York, NY 10013
212-620-8000
800-221-9369
Fax: 212-463-0742
http://www.wkpa.nl
Addresses the whole spectrum of professional issues relating to juvenile and parent group treatment. Promotes the exchange of new ideas from a wide variety of disciplines concerned with enhancing treatments for this special population. The multidisciplinary contributions include clinical reports, illustrations of new technical methods, and studies that contribute to the advancement of therapeutic results, as well as articles on theoretical issues, applications, and the group process.
Quarterly
ISSN: 1053-0800
Carol Bischoff, Publisher
Edward S Soo, Editor

4405 Journal of College Admission
Nat'l Association for College Admission Counseling
1631 Prince Street
Alexandria, VA 22314-2818
703-836-2222
Fax: 703-836-8015
http://www.nacac.com
Membership association offering information to counselors and guidance professionals working in the college admissions office.
32 pages Quarterly
ISSN: 0734-6670
Elaina Loveland, Author
Shanda T Ivory, Chief Officer Communications
Amy C Vogt, Assistant Director

4406 Journal of Counseling & Development
American Counseling Association
5999 Stevenson Avenue
Alexandria, VA 22304
703-823-9800
Fax: 703-823-0252

E-mail: jc-d@psu.edu
http://www.counseling.org
A quarterly journal that publishe articles that have broad interest for a readership composed mostly of couselors and other mental health professionals who work in private practice, schools, colleges, community agencies, hospitals and government.

ISBN: 0748-9633

Spencer Niles, Editor

4407 Journal of Counseling and Development
American Counseling Association
5999 Stevenson Avenue
Alexandria, VA 22304-3302
703-823-9800
Fax: 703-823-0252
Edited for counseling and human development specialists in schools, colleges and universities.

Monthly

Stephen Brooks, Editor

4408 Journal of Drug Education
California State University
Department of Health Science
Northridge, CA 91330-8285
818-677-3101
Fax: 818-677-2045
Offers information to counselors and guidance professionals dealing with areas of drug and substance abuse education in the school system.

Quarterly

Robert Huff, Contact

4409 Journal of Emotional and Behavioral Disorders
Pro-Ed
8700 Shoal Creek Boulevard
Austin, TX 78757-6816
512-451-3246
800-897-3202
Fax: 512-302-9129
http://www.proedinc.com
Presents high-quality interdisciplinary scholarship in the area of emotional and behavioral disabilities. Explores issues including youth violence, emotional problems among minority children, long-term foster care placement, mental health services, social development and educational strategies.

Michael H Epstein, EdD, Editor
Douglas Cullinan, EdD, Editor

4410 Journal of Employment Counseling
American Counseling Association
5999 Stevenson Avenue
Alexandria, VA 22304-3302
703-823-9800
Fax: 703-823-0252
Editorial content includes developing trends in case studies and newest personnel practices.

Quarterly

Stephen Brooks, Editor

4411 Journal of Humanistic Education and Development
Ohio University
201 McCracken Hall
Athens, OH 45701
740-593-4000
Fax: 740-593-0569
Focuses on the humanities and promotes their place in the educational system.

Quarterly

4412 Journal of Multicultural Counseling & Development
American Counseling Association
5999 Stevenson Avenue
Alexandria, VA 22304-3302
703-823-9800
Fax: 703-823-0252
Contains articles with focus on research, theory and program application related to multicultural counseling.

Quarterly

Stephen Brooks, Editor

4413 Journal of Sex Education & Therapy
American Association of Sex Educators
PO Box 5488
Richmond, VA 23220-0488
804-644-3288
Fax: 804-644-3290
E-mail: aasect@worldnet.att.net
http://www.aasect.org
Provides education and training in all areas of sexual health.

110 pages Quarterly
ISSN: 0161-4576

Michael Plant, Author

4414 Measurement & Evaluation in Counseling and Development
American Counseling Association
5999 Stevenson Avenue
Alexandria, VA 22304-3302
703-823-9800
Fax: 703-823-0252
Editorial focuses on research and applications in counseling and guidance.

Quarterly

Stephen Brooks, Editor
Susan Lausch, Advertising/Sales

4415 NACAC Bulletin
Nat'l Association for College Admission Counseling
1631 Prince Street
Alexandria, VA 22314-2818
703-836-2222
Fax: 703-836-8015
http://www.nacac.com
Membership association offering information to counselors and guidance professionals working in the college admissions office.

Monthly

Shanda T Ivory, Chief Officer Communications
Amy C Vogt, Assistant Director

4416 NASW News
National Association of Social Workers
PO Box 431
Annapolis Junction, MD 20701-0431
301-317-8688
800-638-8799
Fax: 301-206-7989
Features in-depth coverage of developments in social work practice, news of national social policy developments, political and legislative news in social services, noteworthy achievements of social workers and association news.

Monthly

Scott Moss, Editor

4417 National Coalition for Sex Equity in Education
PO Box 534
Annandale, NJ 08801
908-735-5045
Fax: 908-735-9674
E-mail: info@ncsee.org
http://www.ncsee.org

The only national organization for gender equity specialists and educators. Individuals and organizations committed to reducing sex role stereotyping for females and males. Services include an annual national training conference, a quarterly newsletter and a membership directory. Members may join task forces dealing with equity related topics such as computer/technology issues, early childhood, male issues, sexual harassment prevention, sexual orientation and vocational issues.

Quarterly Newsletter

Theodora Martin, Business Manager

4418 New Horizons
National Registration Center for Study Abroad
PO Box 1393
Milwaukee, WI 53201-1393
414-278-0631
Fax: 414-271-8884
E-mail: info@nrcsa.com
http://www.nrcsa.com
Provides information about member institution's programs and establishes standards for treatment of visitors from abroad including the appointment of bilingual housing officers and counselors to deal with culture shock.

16 pages Quarterly
ISBN: 1-977864-43-3

Anne Wittig, Author
Mike Wittig, General Manager

4419 Rehabilitation Counseling Bulletin
Pro-Ed
8700 Shoal Creek Boulevard
Austin, TX 78757-6816
512-451-3246
800-897-3202
Fax: 512-302-9129
E-mail: proed1@aol.com
http://www.proedinc.com
International journal providing original empirical research, essays of a theoretical nature, methodological treatises and comprehensive reviews of the literature, intensive case studies and research critiques.

Quarterly Magazine
ISSN: 0034-3552

Douglas Strohmer, PhD, Editor

4420 School Counselor
American Counseling Association
5999 Stevenson Avenue
Alexandria, VA 22304-3302
703-823-9800
Fax: 703-823-0252
Includes current issues and information affecting teens and how counselors can deal with them.

5x Year

Stephen Brooks, Editor
Susan Lausch, Advertising/Sales

4421 School Psychology Review
National Association of School Psychologists
4340 EW Highway
Suite 402
Bethesda, MD 20814
301-657-0270
Fax: 301-657-0275
E-mail: center@naspweb.org
http://www.nasponline.org

170 pages Quarterly
ISSN: 0279-6015

4422 Social Work Research Journal
National Association of Social Workers
750 1st Street NE
Suite 700
Washington, DC 20002-4241

202-408-8600
800-638-8799
Fax: 202-336-8311
http://www.socialworkers.org
Contains orginal research papers that contribute to knowledge about social work issues and problems. Topics include new technology, strategies and methods, and resarch results.

Quarterly
ISSN: 1070-5309

Stuart A Kirk, Editor

4423 Social Work in Education

National Association of Social Workers
750 1st Street NE
Suite 700
Washington, DC 20002-4241
202-408-8600
Fax: 202-336-8310
http://www.socialworkers.org
Covers practice, innovation, research, legislation, policy, planning, and all the professional issues relevant to social work services in all levels of education.

Mal Milburn, Marketing/Sales Associate
Lyn Carter, Advertising Specialist

4424 SocialWork

National Association of Social Workers
750 1st Street NE
Suite 700
Washington, DC 20002-4241
202-408-8600
800-638-8799
Fax: 202-336-8311
http://www.socialworkers.org
Covers important research findings, critical analyses, practice issues, and information on current social issues such as AIDS, homelessness, and federal regulation of social programs. Case management, third-party reimbursement, credentialing, and other professional issues are addressed.

Mal Milburn, Marketing/Sales Associate
Lyn Carter, Advertising Specialist

4425 Today's School Psychologist

LRP Publications
1901 N Moore Street
Suite 700
Arlington, VA 22209
703-516-7002
800-341-7874
Fax: 703-516-9313
E-mail: custserve@lrp.com
http://www.lrp.com/ed
An in-depth guide to a school psychologist's job, offering practical strategies and tips for handling day-to-day responsibilites, encouraging change, and improving professional standing and performance.

Monthly
ISSN: 1098-9277

4426 Washington Counseletter

Chronicle Guidance Publications
66 Aurora Street
Moravia, NY 13118-1190
315-497-0330
800-622-7284
Fax: 315-497-3359
E-mail:
customerservice@chronicleguidance.com
http://www.chronicleguidance.com
Monthly report highlighting federal, state, and local developments affecting the counseling and education professions. Items list events, programs, activities and publications of interest to counselors and educators.

8 pages 8x Year

Gary Fickeisen, President
Priscilla Lorah, Coordinator

Periodicals / *Language Arts*

4427 AATF National Bulletin

American Association of Teachers of French
Mailcode 4510
Southern Illinois University
Carbondale, IL 62901
618-453-5731
Fax: 618-453-5733
E-mail: abrate@siu.edu
http://www.frenchteachers.org
Announcements and short articles relating to the association on French language and cultural activities.

30-50 pages 5x Year

Jayne Abrate, Executive Director
Marie-Christine Koop, President

4428 ACTFL Newsletters

American Council on the Teaching of Foreign Lang.
6 Executive Plaza
Yonkers, NY 10701-6832
914-963-8830
Fax: 914-963-1275
A quarterly newsletter containing topical and timely information on matters of interest to foreign language educators. Regular columns include Languages in the News and Washington Watch.

20 pages Quarterly

C Edward Scebold, C-Editor
Jamie Draper, Co-Editor

4429 ADE Bulletin

Association of Departments of English
26 Broadway
Third Floor
New York, NY 10004-1789
646-576-5133
Fax: 646-458-0033
http://www.ade.org
This bulletin concentrates on developments in scholarship, curriculum and teachers in English.

64 pages
ISSN: 0001-0888

4430 Beyond Words

1534 Wells Drive NE
Albuquerque, NM 87112-6383
505-275-2558
Offers information on literature, language arts and English for the teaching professional.

10x Year

4431 Bilingual Research Journal

National Association for Bilingual Education
1030 15th Street NW
Suite 470
Washington, DC 20005-4018
202-898-1829
Fax: 202-789-2866
E-mail: nabe@nabe.org
http://www.nabe.org
Journal published by National Association for Bilingual Education.

Quarterly
8,000 attendees

Delia Pompa, Executive Director
Alicia Sosa, Membership Director

4432 Bilingual Review Press

Arizona State University
Hispanic Research Center
Tempe, AZ 85287
480-965-3990
Fax: 480-965-0315

Offers information and reviews on books, materials and the latest technology available to bilingual educators.

3x Year

Gary D Keller, Editor

4433 CEA Forum

College English Association
English Department
Youngstown State University
Youngstown, OH 44555-0001
330-941-3415
Fax: 330-941-2304
E-mail: Daniel.Robinson@widener.edu
http://www.as.ysu.edu/~english/cea/forum1.htm
Publishes articles on professional issues and pedagogy related to the teaching of English. Subscription includes CEA Critic, a scholarly journal that appears 3x annually.

Newsletter
ISSN: 0007-8034

Daniel Robinson, Editor

4434 Classroom Notes Plus

National Council of Teachers of English
1111 W Kenyon Road
Urbana, IL 61801-1010
217-328-3870
800-369-6283
Fax: 217-278-3761
E-mail: notesplus@ncte.org
http://www.ncte.org
Secondary periodical for English/Language Arts featuring usable teaching ideas for teachers by teachers.

16 pages Quarterly

Felice Kaufmann, Communications Director

4435 Communication Disorders Quarterly

Pro-Ed., Inc.
8700 Shoal Creek Boulevard
Austin, TX 78757-6816
512-451-3246
800-897-3202
Fax: 512-302-9129
E-mail: proed1@aol.com
http://www.proedinc.com
Research, intervention and practice in speech, language and hearing.

Quarterly Magazine
ISSN: 1525-7401

Alejandro Brice, Editor

4436 Communication: Journalism Education Today

Truman High School
3301 S Noland Road
Independence, MO 64055-1318
816-521-2710
Fax: 816-521-2913
A quarterly journal for the Journalism Education Association, based at Kansas State University, Manhattan, KS. Most articles are designed to relate to a theme. The magazine focuses on secondary and collegiate journalism educators.

Quarterly

Molly J Clemons, Editor

4437 Composition Studies Freshman English News

De Paul University
802 W Belden Avenue
Chicago, IL 60614
312-362-8000
Fax: 773-325-7328
Theoretical and practical articles on rhetorical theory.

44 pages SemiAnnually

Peter Vandenberg, English Department

4438 Council-Grams
National Council of Teachers of English
1111 W Kenyon Road
Urbana, IL 61801-1010
217-328-3870
800-369-6283
Fax: 217-328-9645
http://www.ncte.org
Offers information and updates in the areas of English, language arts and reading.

16 pages 5x Year

Michael Spooner

4439 Counterforce
Society for the Advancement of Good English
4501 Riverside Avenue
#30
Anderson, CA 96007-2759
530-365-8026
Offers updates and information for English teachers and professors.

Quarterly

4440 English Education
New York University
635 E Building
New York, NY 10003
212-998-8857
Fax: 212-995-4376
Offers updates and information for reading and English teachers, and professors.

Quarterly

Gordon M Pradl, Editor

4441 English Journal
National Council of Teachers of English
1111 W Kenyon Road
Urbana, IL 61801-1010
217-328-3870
800-369-6283
Fax: 217-328-9645
http://www.ncte.org
An ideal magazine for middle school, junior and senior high school English teachers.

Biannual
ISSN: 0013-8274

Carrie Stewart, Editor

4442 English Leadership Quarterly
National Council of Teachers of English
1111 W Kenyon Road
Urbana, IL 61801-1010
217-328-3870
800-369-6283
Fax: 217-328-9645
http://www.ncte.org
Teaching of English for secondary school English Department chairpersons.

12 pages Quarterly

James Strickland

4443 English for Specific Purposes
University of Michigan
Ann Arbor, MI 48109
619-594-6331
Fax: 619-594-6530
Concerned with English education and its importance to the developing student.

3x Year

John Swales, Editor

4444 Foreign Language Annals
American Council on the Teaching of Foreign Lang.
6 Executive Plaza
Yonkers, NY 10701-6832
914-963-8830
Fax: 914-963-1275
Dedicated to advancing all areas of the profession of foreign language teaching. It seeks primarily to serve the interests of teachers, ad-ministrators and researchers, regardless of educational level of the language with which they are concerned. Preference is given in this scholarly journal to articles that describe innovative and successful teaching methods, that report educational research or experimentation, or that are relevant to the concerns and problems of the profession.

128 pages Quarterly

C Edward Scebold, Executive Director

4445 Journal of Basic Writing
City University of NY, Instructional Resource Ctr.
535 E 80th Street
New York, NY 10021-0767
212-794-5445
Fax: 212-794-5706
Publishes articles of theory, research and teaching practices related to basic writing. Articles are referred by members of the Editorial Board and the editors.

Spring & Fall

Karen Greenberg, Editor
Trudy Smoke, Editor

4446 Journal of Children's Communication Development
The Council for Exceptional Children
1920 Association Drive
Reston, VA 20191-1545
703-620-3660
800-232-7323
Fax: 703-264-1637
Provides in-depth research and practical application articles in communication assessment and intervention. The journal frequently contains a practitioner's section that addresses professional questions, reviews tests and therapy materials, and describes innovative programs and service delivery models.

2x Year
ISSN: 0735-3170

Richard Nowell, Editor

4447 Journal of Teaching Writing
Indiana Teachers of Writing
IUPUI Department of English CA502L
425 University Boulevard
Indianapolis, IN 46202-5148
317-278-2054
Fax: 317-278-1287
E-mail: sfox@iupui.edu
http://www.iupui.edu/~jtw
A refereed journal for classroom teachers and researchers at all academic levels whose interest or emphasis is the teaching of writing. Appearing semiannually, JTW publishes articles on the theory, practice, and teaching of writing throughout the curriculum. Each issue covers a range of topics, from composition theory and discourse analysis to curriculum development and innovative teaching techniques. Contributors are reminded to tailor their writing for a diverse readership.

12-20 pages Semiannually

4448 Journalism Quarterly
George Washington University
School of Journalism
Washington, DC 20052-0001
202-994-6227
Fax: 202-994-5806
Information on all facets of writing and journalism for the student and educator.

Quarterly

Jean Folkerts, Editor

4449 Language & Speech
Kingston Press Services, Ltd.
43 Derwent Road, Whitton
Twickenham, Middlesex TW2 7HQ
United Kingdom
0-20-8893-3015
Fax: 208-893-3015
E-mail: sales@kingstonepress.com
http://www.kingstonepress.com
Psychological research articles, speech perception, speech production, psycholinguistics and reading.

Quarterly

4450 Language Arts
National Council of Teachers of English
1111 W Kenyon Road
Urbana, IL 61801-1010
217-328-3870
800-369-6283
Fax: 217-328-9645
http://www.ncte.org
Edited for instructors in language arts at the elementary level.

Monthly

Kent Williamson, Editor

4451 Language, Speech & Hearing Services in School
Ohio State University
110 Pressey Hall
1070 Carmack Road
Columbus, OH 43210
614-292-8207
Fax: 614-292-7504
Interested in innovative technology and growth in language development in schools.

Wayne A Secord, PhD, Editor

4452 Merlyn's Pen: Fiction, Essays and Poems by America's Teens
PO Box 910
East Greenwich, RI 02818-0964
401-885-5175
800-247-2027
Fax: 401-885-5199
E-mail: merlynspen@aol.com
http://www.merlynspen.com
Merlyns' Pen magazine is a selective publisher of model writing by America's students in grades 6-12. Products include Merlyn's Pen magazine (a reproducible annual magazine) and the American Teen Writer Series, collections of anthologized short fiction and nonfiction by brilliant teen writers. Used for models, inspiration, and instruction in literature and writing.

100 pages Annually
ISSN: 0882-2050

Jim Stahl, Editor

4453 Modern Language Journal
Case Western Reserve University
Department of Modern Languages
Cleveland, OH 44106
216-368-2000
Fax: 216-368-2216

Quarterly

David P Benseler, Editor

4454 NABE News
National Association for Bilingual Education
1030 15th Street NW
Suite 470
Washington, DC 20005-4018
202-898-1829
Fax: 202-789-2866
E-mail: nabe@nabe.org
http://www.nabe.org

Magazine published by the National Association for Bilingual Education.

Bi-Monthly

Delia Pompa, Executive Director
Alicia Sosa, Membership Director

4455 NASILP Journal

National Assn. of Self-Instructional
Language
Temple University
Philadelphia, PA 19122
215-204-7000
Articles, news and book reviews on language instructional methodology.

12 pages SemiAnnually

Dr. John Means

4456 National Clearinghouse for Bilingual Education Newsletter

George Washington University
2121 K Street NW
Suite 260
Washington, DC 20037-1214
202-467-0867
800-321-6223
E-mail: askncbe@ncbe.gwu.edu
http://www.ncbe.gwu.edu
Provides information to practitioners on the education of language minority students.

Weekly

Dr. Minerva Gorena, Director

4457 PCTE Bulletin

Pennsylvania Council of Teachers of English
Williamsport Area Community College
Williamsport, PA 17701
Focuses on Pennsylvania literacy issues.

SemiAnnually

Robert Ulrich

4458 Quarterly Journal of Speech

National Communication Association
1765 N Street NW
Washington, DC 20036
202-464-4622
Fax: 202-464-4600
http://www.natcom.org
Main academic journal in the speech/communication field of education.

Quarterly

James Gaudino, Executive Director

4459 Quarterly Review of Doublespeak

National Council of Teachers of English
1111 W Kenyon Road
Urbana, IL 61801-1010
217-328-3870
800-369-6283
Fax: 217-328-9645
http://www.ncte.org
Provides information on the misuses and abuse of language.

8 pages Quarterly

Harry Brent

4460 Quarterly of the NWP

National Writing Project
2105 Bancroft Way
Suite 1042
Berkeley, CA 94720-1042
510-642-0963
Fax: 510-642-4545
E-mail: writingproject.org
http://www.writingproject.org
Journal on the research in and practice of teaching writing at all grade levels.

40 pages Quarterly Magazine
ISSN: 0896-3592

Art Peterson, Amy Bauman; Editors, Author
Art Peterson, Senior Editor
Amy Bauman, Managing Editor

4461 Quill and Scroll

University of Iowa School of Journalism
100 Adler Journalism Builing
Room E346
Iowa City, IA 52242
319-335-3457
Fax: 319-335-3989
E-mail: quill-scroll@uiowa.edu
http://www.uiowa.edu/~quill-sc
Founded and distributed for the purpose of encouraging and rewarding individual achievements in journalism and allied fields. This magazine is published bimonthly during the school year and has a variety of pamphlets and lists of publications available as resources.

BiMonthly

Richard P Johns, Executive Director

4462 Research in the Teaching of English

Harvard Graduate School of Education
Larsen Hall
Appian Way
Cambridge, MA 02138
617-495-3521
Fax: 617-495-0540
A research journal devoted to original research on the relationships between teaching and learning for language development in reading, writing and speaking at all age levels.

Quarterly

Sandra Stotsky, Editor

4463 Rhetoric Review

University of Arizona
Department of English
Tucson, AZ 85721-0001
520-621-3371
Fax: 520-621-7397
http://http://members.aol.com/sborrowman/rr/html
A journal of rhetoric and composition publishing scholarly and historical studies, theoretical and practical articles, views of the profession, review essays of professional books, personal essays about writing and poems.

200+ pages Quarterly
ISSN: 0735-0198

Theresa Enos, Editor

4464 Slate Newsletter

National Council of Teachers of English
1111 W Kenyon Road
Urbana, IL 61801-1010
217-328-3870
800-369-6283
Fax: 217-328-9645
http://www.ncte.org
Short articles on topics such as censorship, trends and issues and testing.

4465 Studies in Second Language Acquisition

Cambridge University Press
1105 Atwater
Bloomington, IN 47401-5020
812-855-6874
Fax: 812-855-2386
E-mail: ssla@indiana.edu
http://www.indiana.edu/~ssla
Referred journal devoted to problems and issues in second and foreign language acquisition of any language.

140 pages Quarterly Paperback
ISSN: 0272-2631

Albert Valdman, Editor

4466 TESOL Journal: A Journal of Teaching and Classroom Research

Teachers of English to Speakers of Other Languages
1600 Cameron Street
Suite 300
Alexandria, VA 22314-2705
703-836-0774
Fax: 703-836-7864
E-mail: tesol@tesol.edu
http://www.tesol.edu
TESOL's mission is to develop the expertise of its members and others involved in teaching English to speakers of other languages to help them foster communication in diverse settings. The association advances standards for professional preparation and employment, continuing education, and student programs, produces programs, services, and products, and promotes advocacy to further the profession. TESOL has 91 affiliates worldwide.

50 pages Quarterly

Christian J Faltis, Editor
Marilyn Kupetz, Managing Editor

4467 TESOL Quarterly

Teachers of English to Speakers of Other Languages
1600 Cameron Street
Suite 300
Alexandria, VA 22314-2705
703-836-0774
Fax: 703-836-7864
E-mail: tesol@tesol.edu
http://www.tesol.com
TESOL Quarterly is our scholarly journal containing articles on academic research, theory, reports, reviews. Articles about linguistics, ethnographies, and more describe the theoretic basis for ESL/EFL teaching practices. Readership is approximately 23,400.

830 pages Quarterly

Carol Chapelle, Editor

4468 Writing Lab Newsletter

Purdue University, Department of English
500 Oval Drive
W. Lafayette, IN 47907-2038
765-494-7268
Fax: 765-494-3780
E-mail: wln@purdue.edudue.edu
http://www.owl.english.purdue.edu/lab/newsletter/index.html
Monthly newsletter for readers involved in writing centers and/or one-to-one instruction in writing skills.

16 pages Monthly/Newsletter
ISSN: 1040-3779

Muriel Harris, Editor
Shawna McCaw, Managing Editor

Periodicals / *Library Services*

4469 ALA Editions Catalog

Membership Services American Library Association
50 E Huron Street
Chicago, IL 60611
800-545-2433
Fax: 312-836-9958
http://www.ala.org
Contains over 1,000 job listings, news and reports on the latest technologies in 11 issues annually. Also scholarships, grants and awards are possibilities.

Annually

4470 American Libraries
American Library Association
50 E Huron Street
Chicago, IL 60611-2795
312-944-6780
800-545-2433
Fax: 312-440-9374
E-mail: ala@ala.org
http://www.ala.org
The magazine of the American Library Association that is published six times a year and distributed to more than 65,000 individuals.

ISBN: 0002-9769

Leonard Kniffel, Editor

4471 Booklist
American Library Association
50 E Huron Street
Chicago, IL 60611-5295
312-944-6780
Fax: 312-440-9374
http://www.ala.org/booklist
A guide to current print and audiovisual materials worthy of consideration for purchase by small and medium-sized public libraries and school library media centers.

Semimonthly

Bill Ott, Editor

4472 Catholic Library World
Catholic Library Association
461 W Lancaster Avenue
Haverford, PA 19041-1412
734-722-7185
A periodical geared toward the professional librarian in order to keep them abreast of new publications, library development, association news and technology.

Quarterly

Allen Gruenke, Executive Director

4473 Choice
Current Reviews for Academic Libraries
100 Riverview Center
Middletown, CT 06457-3445
860-347-6933
Fax: 860-346-8586
E-mail: adsales@ala-choice.org
http://www.ala.org/acrl/choice
A magazine distributed to librarians and other organizations that analyzes various materials, offers book reviews and information on the latest technology available for the library acquisitions departments.

11x Year

Steven Conforti, Subscriptions Manager
Stuart Foster, Advertising Manager

4474 Emergency Librarian
Ken Haycock and Associates
101-1001 W Braodway
Vancouver
British Columbia
604-925-0266
604-925-056
Professional journal targeted to the specific needs and concerns of teachers and teacher-librarians.

5x Year

Dr. Ken Haycock

4475 ILA Reporter
33 W Grand Avenue
Suite 301
Chicago, IL 60610-4306
312-644-1896
Fax: 312-644-1899

E-mail: ila@ila.org
http://www.ila.org
30 pages
ISSN: 0018-9979

Robert P Doyle, Arthor

4476 Information Technology & Libraries
University of the Pacific
William Knox Holt Library
Stockton, CA 95211-0001
209-946-2434
Fax: 209-946-2805
Offers information on the latest technology, systems and electronics offered to the library market.

Quarterly

Thomas W Leonhardt, Editor
Karen Hope

4477 Journal of Education for Library and Information Sciences
Kent State University
School of Library Science
Kent, OH 44242-0001
330-672-2782
Fax: 330-672-7965
The latest information on books, publications, electronics and technology for the librarian.

Quarterly

4478 Libraries & Culture
University of Texas at Austin/Univ. of Texas Press
PO Box 7819
Austin, TX 78713-7819
512-232-7618
Fax: 512-232-7178
E-mail: dgdavis@gslis.utexas.edu
An interdisciplinary journal that explores the significance of collections of recorded knowledge. Scholarly articles and book reviews cover international topics dealing with libraries, books, reviews, archives, personnel, and their history; for scholars, librarians, historians, readers interested in the history of books and libraries.

100 pages Quarterly
ISSN: 0894-8631

Dr. Donald G Davis Jr, Editor
Colleen Daly, Assistant Editor

4479 Library Collections, Acquisitions & Technical Services
Pergamon Press, Elsevier Science
The Boulevard, Lanngford Lane
Kidlington, Oxford
United Kingdom
614-292-4738
Fax: 614-292-7859
E-mail: deidrichs.1@osu.edu
http://www.elsvier.com
Offers information on policy, practice, and research on the collection management and technical service areas of libraries.

500 pages Quarterly
ISSN: 1464-9055

Carol Pitts Diedrichs, Editor

4480 Library Issues: Briefings for Faculty and Administrators
Mountainside Publishing Company
PO Box 8330
Ann Arbor, MI 48107-8330
734-662-3925
Fax: 734-662-4450
E-mail: apdougherty@compuserve.com
http://www.libraryissues.com
Offers overviews of the trends and problems affecting campus libraries. Explained in lay-

man's terms as they relate to faculty, administrators and the parent institution.

4-6 pages Bi-Monthly
ISSN: 0734-3035

Dr. Richard M Dougherty, Editor
Ann Dougherty, Managing Editor

4481 Library Quarterly
Indiana University, School of Library Science
Lib 013
Bloomington, IN 47405
812-855-5113
Fax: 812-855-6166
Updates, information, statistics, book reviews and publications for librarians.

Quarterly

Stephen P Harter, Editor

4482 Library Resources & Technical Services
Columbia University, School of Library Sciences
516 Butler Library
New York, NY 10027
212-854-3329
Fax: 212-854-8951

Quarterly

Richard P Smirgalia, Editor

4483 Library Trends
Grad. School Library & Info. Science
501 E Daniel Street
Champaign, IL 61820
217-333-1359
Fax: 217-244-7329
E-mail: puboff@alexia.lis.uiuc.edu
http://www.edfu.lis.uiuc.edu/puboff
A scholarly quarterly devoted to invited papers in library and information science. Each issue is devoted to a single theme.

208 pages Quarterly

FW Lancaster, Editor
James Dowling, Managing Editor

4484 Media & Methods Magazine
American Society of Educators
1429 Walnut Street
Philadelphia, PA 19102-3218
215-563-6005
Fax: 215-587-9706
E-mail: claudette@media-methods.com
http://www.media-methods.com
Leading pragmatic magazine for K-12 educators and administrators. The focus is on how to integrate today's technologies and presentation tools into the curriculum. Very up-to-date and well respected national source publication. Loyal readers are media specialists, school librarians, technology coordinators, administrators and classroom teachers.

5x Year

Michele Sokoloff, Publisher
Christine Weiser, Editor

4485 NEWSletter
New Jersey Library Association
PO Box 1534
Trenton, NJ 08607
609-394-8032
Fax: 609-394-8164
E-mail: ptumulty@njla.org
http://www.njla.org
A quarterly newsletter and distributed to more than 1,800 members, serves as a vehicle for communication of library issues and activities among members of NJLA.

Anita O'Malley, Production Manager

263

4486 Read, America!
Place in the Woods
3900 Glenwood Avenue
Golden Valley, MN 55422-5302
763-374-2120
Fax: 952-593-5593
E-mail: readamerica10732@aol.com
News, book reviews, ideas for librarians and reading program leaders; short stories and poetry pages for adults and children; and an annual Read America! collection with selections of new books solicited from 350 publishers.
12 pages Quarterly Newsletter
ISSN: 0891-4214

Roger Hammer, Editor/Publisher

4487 School Library Journal
360 Park Avenue
New York, NY 10010
646-746-6759
Fax: 646-746-6689
E-mail: slj@reedbusiness.com
http://www.schoollibraryjournal.com
For children, young adults and school librarians.

Francine Fialkoff, Editorial Director
Brian Kenney, Editor-in-Chief

4488 School Library Media Activities Monthly
LMS Associates
17 E Henrietta Street
Baltimore, MD 21230-3910
301-685-8621
Monthly

Paula Montgomery, Editor

4489 School Library Media Quarterly
American Library Association
50 E Huron Street
Chicago, IL 60611-5295
312-944-6780
Fax: 312-280-3255
For elementary and secondary building level library media specialists, district supervisors and others concerned with the selection and purchase of print and nonprint media.
Quarterly

Judy Pitts, Editor
Barbara Stripling, Editor

4490 Southeastern Librarian (SELn)
Southeastern Library Association
PO Box 950
Rex, GA 30273
770-961-3520
Fax: 770-961-3712
E-mail: gordonbaker@clayton.edu
http://seaonline.org
This quarterly publication seeks to publish articles, announcements and news of professional interest to the library community in the southeast. The publication also represents a significant means for addressing the Association's research objective. Two newsletter-style issues serve as a vehicle for conducting Association business, and two issues include juried articles.

Perry Bratcher, Editor

4491 Special Libraries
Special Libraries Association
1700 18th Street NW
Washington, DC 20009-2514
202-234-4700
Fax: 202-265-9317
Includes information and manuscripts on the administration, organization and operation of special libraries.
Quarterly

Maria Barry, Editor

4492 Specialist
Special Libraries Association
1700 18th Street NW
Washington, DC 20009-2514
202-234-4700
Fax: 202-265-9317
Contains news and information about the special library/information field.
Monthly

Alisa Nesmith Cooper, Editor

4493 TLACast
Texas Library Association
3355 Bee Cave Road
Suite 401
Austin, TX 78746
512-328-1518
800-580-2852
Fax: 512-328-8852
E-mail: tla@txla.org
http://www.txla.org
The association's online newsletter that is published several times a year to keep members informed on TLA issues and events.

Patricia A Smith, Executive Director
Gloria Meraz, Communications Director

4494 Texas Library Journal
Texas Library Association
3355 Bee Cave Road
Suite 401
Austin, TX 78746
512-328-1518
800-580-2852
Fax: 512-328-8852
E-mail: tla@txla.org
http://www.txla.org

ISBN: 0040-4446

Patricia A Smith, Executive Director
Gloria Meraz, Editor

Periodicals / *Mathematics*

4495 Focus on Learning Problems in Math
Center for Teaching/Learning Math
PO Box 3149
Framingham, MA 01701-3149
508-877-7895
Fax: 508-788-3600
E-mail: msharma@rea.com
An interdisciplinary journal. Edited jointly by the Research Council for Diagnostic and Prescription Mathematics and the Center for Teaching/Learning of Mathematics. The objective of focus is to make available the current research, methods of identification, diagnosis, and remediation of learning problems in mathematics. Contribution from the fields of education psychology and mathematics having the potential to import on classroom or clinical practice are valued.
64-96 pages Quarterly

Mahesh Sharma, Editor

4496 Journal for Research in Mathematics Education
National Council of Teachers of Mathematics
1906 Association Drive
Reston, VA 20191-1502
703-620-9840
Fax: 703-476-2970
E-mail: nctm@nctm.org
http://www.nctm.org
A forum for disciplined inquiry into the teaching and learning of math at all levels— from

preschool through adult. Available in print or online version.
5x Year
ISSN: 0021-8251

Harry B Tunis, Publications Director
Rowena G Martelino, Promotions Manager

4497 Journal of Computers in Math & Science
PO Box 2966
Charlottesville, VA 22902-2966
804-973-3087
Fax: 703-997-8760
Quarterly

4498 Journal of Recreational Mathematics
4761 Bigger Road
Kettering, OH 45440-1829
631-691-1470
Fax: 631-691-1770
Promotes the creative practice of mathematics for educational learning.
Quarterly

Joseph S Madachy, Editor

4499 Math Notebook
Center for Teacher/Learning Math
PO Box 3149
Framingham, MA 01705-3149
508-877-7895
Fax: 508-788-3600
A publication for teachers and parents to improve mathematics instruction.
4x/5x Year

Mahesh Sharma, Editor

4500 Mathematics & Computer Education
MAYTC Journal
PO Box 158
Old Bethpage, NY 11804-0158
516-822-5475
Contains a variety of articles pertaining to the field of mathematics.
TriAnnually

George Miller, Editor

4501 Mathematics Teacher
National Council of Teachers of Mathematics
1906 Association Drive
Reston, VA 20191-1502
703-620-9840
Fax: 703-295-0973
E-mail: nctm@nctm.org
http://www.nctm.org
Devoted to the improvement of mathematics instruction in grades 9 and higher.
Monthly
ISSN: 0025-5769

Harry B Tunis, Publications Director
Rowena G Martelino, Promotions Manager

4502 Mathematics Teaching in the Middle School
National Council of Teachers of Mathematics
1906 Association Drive
Reston, VA 20191-1593
703-620-9840
Fax: 703-476-2970
E-mail: nctm@nctm.org
http://www.nctm.org
Addresses the learning needs of students in grades 5-9.
Monthly
ISSN: 1072-0839

Harry B Tunis, Publications Director
Rowena G Martelino, Promotions Manager

4503 NCTM News Bulletin
National Council of Teachers of
Mathematics
1906 Association Drive
Reston, VA 20191-9988
703-620-9840
Fax: 703-476-2970
E-mail: nctm@nctm.org
http://www.nctm.org
Publication that reaches all of NCTM's individual and institutional members of more than
107,000 math teachers and school personnel.

Harry B Tunis, Director Publications
Krista Hopkins, Director Marketing
Services

4504 Notices of the American Mathematical Society
American Mathematical Society
PO Box 6248
Providence, RI 02940-6248
401-455-4000
Fax: 401-331-3842
Announces programs, meetings, conferences
and symposia of the AMS and other mathematical groups.

10x Year

Dr. John S Bradley, Managing Editor
Anne Newcomb, Avertising Coordinator

4505 SSMart Newsletter
School Science & Mathematics Association
Curriculum & Foundations
Bloomsburg, PA 17815
570-389-3894
Fax: 570-389-3894
Membership news offering information, updates, reviews, articles and association news
for professionals in the science and mathematics fields of education.

8 pages Quarterly

Darrel Fyffe, Publisher
Norbert Kuenzi, Editor

4506 Teaching Children Mathematics
National Council of Teachers of
Mathematics
1906 Association Drive
Reston, VA 20191-1502
703-620-9840
Fax: 703-476-2970
E-mail: nctm@nctm.org
http://www.nctm.org
Concerned primarily with the teaching of
mathematics from Pre-K through grade 6.

Monthly
ISSN: 1073-5836

Harry B Tunis, Publications Director
Rowena G Martelino, Promotions Manager

Periodicals / *Music & Art*

4507 American Academy of Arts & Sciences Bulletin
Norton Woods, 136 Irving Street
Cambridge, MA 02138
617-576-5000
Fax: 617-576-5050
Covers current news of the Academy as well
as developments in the arts and sciences.

Alexandra Oleson

4508 Art Education
National Art Education Association
1916 Association Drive
Reston, VA 20191-1590
703-860-8000
Fax: 703-860-2960

A professional journal in the field of art education devoted to articles on all education
levels.

6x Year

Thomas A Hatfield, Editor
Beverly Jeanne Davis, Managing Editor

4509 Arts & Activities
Arts & Activities Magazine
12345 World Trade Drive
San Diego, CA 92128
858-605-0242
E-mail: subs@artsandactivities.com
http://www.artsandactivities.com
For classroom teachers, art teachers and other
school personnel teaching visual art from kindergarten through college levels.

Monthly
ISSN: 0004-3931

4510 Arts Education Policy Review
Heldref Publications
1319 18th Street NW
Washington, DC 20036-1826
202-296-6267
800-365-9753
Fax: 202-296-5149
http://www.heldref.org
Discusses major policy issues concerning
K-12 education in the various arts. The journal presents a variety of views rather than taking sides and emphasizes analytical
exploration. Its goal is to produce the most insightful, comprehensive and rigorous exchange of ideas ever available on arts
education. The candid discussions are a valuable resource for all those involved in the arts
and concerned about their role in education.

40 pages BiWeekly
ISSN: 1063-2913

Leila Saad, Managing Editor

4511 CCAS Newsletter
Council of Colleges of Arts & Sciences
186 University Hall
Columbus, OH 43210
614-292-1882
Fax: 614-292-8666
Membership newsletter to inform deans about
arts and sciences issues in education.

4-10 pages BiMonthly

Richard J Hopkins, Contact

4512 Choral Journal
American Choral Directors Association
PO Box 6310
Lawton, OK 73506-0310
903-935-7963
Fax: 903-934-8114
E-mail: jmoore@etbu.edu
Publishes scholarly, practical articles and regular columns of importance to professionals
in the fields of choral music and music education. Articles explore conducting teachnique,
rehearsal strategies, historical performance
practice, choral music history and teaching
materials.

Monthly

James A Moore, President

4513 Clavier
200 Northfield Road
Northfield, IL 60093
847-446-5000
Fax: 847-446-6263
Published 10 times each year for piano and organ teachers, with issues in all months except
June and August.

Monthly

4514 Dramatics
Educational Theatre Association
2343 Auburn Avenue
Cincinnati, OH 45219-2815
513-421-3900
Fax: 513-421-7055
E-mail: info@etassoc.org
http://www.etassoc.org
Magazine published by Educational Theatre
Association, a professional association for
theatre educators/artists.

Monthly

David LaFleche, Dir
Membership/Leadership

4515 Flute Talk
200 Northfield Road
Northfield, IL 60093
847-446-5000
Fax: 847-446-6263
Published 10 times each year for flute teachers and intermediate or advanced students,
with issues every month except June and
August.

Monthly

4516 Instrumentalist
200 Northfield Road
Northfield, IL 60093
847-446-5000
Fax: 847-446-6263
Published 12 times each year for band and orchestra directors and teachers of instruments
in these groups.

Monthly

4517 Journal of Experiential Education
Association of Experiential Education
2305 Canyon Boulevard
Suite 100
Boulder, CO 80302
303-440-8844
Fax: 303-440-9581
E-mail: aewert@indiana.edu
http://www.aee.org
A professional journal that publishes articles
in outdoor adventure programming, service
learning, environmental education, therapeutic applications, research and theory, the creative arts, and much more. An invaluable
reference tool for anyone in the field of
experiential education.

3x Year
ISSN: 1053-8259

Alan Ewert, Editor

4518 Music Educators Journal
National Association for Music Education
1806 Robert Fulton Drive
Reston, VA 20191-4348
703-860-4000
Fax: 703-860-1531
http://www.menc.org
Offers informative, timely and accurate articles, editorials, and features to a national audience of music educators.

BiMonthly
ISSN: 0027-4321

Frances Ponick, Editor, Author

4519 Music Educators Journal and Teaching Music
National Association for Music Education
1806 Robert Fulton Drive
Reston, VA 20191-4348
703-860-4000
Fax: 703-860-4826
http://www.menc.org

Informative, timely and accurate articles, editorials, and features to a national audience of music educators.

BiMonthly
ISSN: 1069-7446

Jeanne Spaeth, Editor

4520 NAEA News
National Art Education Association
1916 Association Drive
Reston, VA 20191-1502
703-860-8000
Fax: 703-860-2960
E-mail: naea@dgs.dgsys.com
http://www.naea-reston.org
National, state and local news affecting visual arts education.

24 pages BiMonthly

Dr. Thomas Hatfield, Executive Director

4521 National Guild of Community Schools of the Arts
National Guild of Community Schools of the Arts
520 8th Avenue
Suite 302, 3rd Floor
New York, NY 10018
212-268-3337
Fax: 212-268-3995
E-mail: info@natguild.org
http://www.nationalguild.org
National association of community based arts education institutions employment opportunities, guildnotes newsletter, publications catalog. See www.nationalguild.org.

Monthly

Noah Xifr, Director Membership/Oper.

4522 Oranatics Journal
Educational Theatre Association
2343 Auburn Avenue
Cincinnati, OH 45219-2815
513-451-3900
Fax: 513-421-7077
http://www.etassoc.org
Promotes and strengthens theatre in education - primarily middle school and high school. Sponsors an honor society, various events, numerous publications, and arts education advocacy activities.

9x Year

David LaFleche, Director Membership

4523 SchoolArtsDavis Publications
50 Portland Street
Worcester, MA 01682
800-533-2847
Fax: 508-791-0779
http://www.davis-art.com/
Davis has promoted and advocated for art education at both the local and national levels, providing good ideas for teachers and celebrating cultural diversity and the contributions of world cultures through a wide range of art forms.

Wyatt Wade, Publisher
Claire Mowbray Golding, Managing Editor

4524 SchoolArts Magazine
Davis Publications
50 Portland Street
Worcester, MA 01608-2013
508-754-7201
800-533-2847
Fax: 508-791-0779
Aimed at art educators in public and private schools, elementary through high school. Articles offer ideas and information involving

art media for the teaching profession and for use in classroom activities.

Monthly
ISSN: 0036-3463

Wyatt Wade, Publisher
Eldon Katter, Editor

4525 Studies in Art Education
Louisiana State University, Dept. of Curriculum
Baton Rouge, LA 70803-0001
225-578-3202
Fax: 225-578-9135
Reports on developments in art education.

Quarterly

Karen A Hamblen, Editor

4526 Teaching Journal
Educational Theatre Association
2343 Auburn Avenue
Cincinnati, OH 45219-2815
513-421-3900
Fax: 513-421-7055
E-mail: info@etassoc.org
http://www.etassoc.org
Journal published by Educational Theatre Association, a professional association for theatre educators/artists.

Quarterly

David LaFleche, Dir
Membership/Leadership

4527 Teaching Music
National Association for Music Education
1806 Robert Fulton Drive
Reston, VA 20191-4348
703-860-4000
Fax: 703-860-4826
http://www.menc.org
Offers informative, timely and accurate articles, editorials, and features to a national audience of music educators.

BiMonthly
ISSN: 1069-7446

Christine Stinson, Editor

4528 Ultimate Early Childhood Music Resource
Miss Jackie Music Company
10001 El Monte Street
Shawnee Mission, KS 66207-3631
913-381-3672
Designed to assist parents and teachers engaged in early childhood.

16 pages Quarterly

Jackie Weissman, Publisher
Emily Smith, Editor

Periodicals / *Physical Education*

4529 Athletic Director
National Association for Sport & Physical Ed.
1900 Association Drive
Reston, VA 20191-1502
703-476-3410
Fax: 703-476-8316
Of interest to athletic directors and coaches.

4 pages SemiAnnually

4530 Athletic Management
College Athletic Administrator
2488 N Triphammer Road
Ithaca, NY 14850-1014
607-272-0265
Fax: 607-273-0701

Offers information on how athletic managers can improve their operations, focusing on high school and college athletic departments.

BiMonthly

Mark Goldberg, Publisher
Eleanor Frankel, Editor

4531 Athletic Training
National Athletic Trainers' Association
2952 N Stemmons Freeway
Dallas, TX 75247-6103
214-637-6282
800-879-6282
Fax: 214-637-2206
http://www.nata.org
Edited for athletic trainers.

100 pages Quarterly Magazine

4532 Athletics Administration
NACDA
PO Box 16428
Cleveland, OH 44116
440-892-4000
Fax: 440-892-4007
E-mail: jwork@nacda.com
http://www.nacda.com
The official publication of the National Association of Collegiate Directors of Athletics (NACDA), Athletics Administration focuses on athletics facilities, new ideas in marketing, promotions, development, legal ramifications and other current issues in collegiate athletics administrations.

44-48 pages BiMonthly
ISSN: 0044-9873

Julie Work, Editor

4533 Journal of Environmental Education
Heldref Publications
1319 18th Street NW
Washington, DC 20036-1826
202-296-6267
800-365-9753
Fax: 202-296-5149
E-mail: jee@heldref.org
http://www.heldref.org
An excellent resource for department chairpersons and directors of programs in environmental, resources, and outdoor education.

48 pages Quarterly
ISSN: 0095-8964

B Alison Panko, Managing Editor

4534 Journal of Experiential Education
Association for Experiential Education
2305 Canyon Boulevard
Suite 100
Boulder, CO 80302
303-440-8844
800-787-7979
Fax: 303-440-9581
E-mail: simps_sv@mail.uwlax.edu
http://www.aee.org
A professional journal that publishes articles in outdoor adventure programming, service learning, environmental education, therapeutic applications, research and theory, the creative arts, and much more. An invaluable reference tool for anyone in the field of experiential education.

3x Year

Steve Simpson, Editor

4535 Journal of Physical Education, Recreation and Dance
American Alliance for Health, Phys. Ed. & Dance
1900 Association Drive
Reston, VA 20191-1502
703-476-3495
Fax: 703-476-9527

Presents new books, teaching aids, facilities, equipment, supplies, news of the profession and related groups.

9x Year

Fran Rowan, Editor

4536 Journal of Teaching in Physical Education
Human Kinetics Incorporation
1607 N Market Street
Champaign, IL 61820
217-351-5076
800-747-4457
Fax: 217-351-2674
http://www.humankinetics.com/jtpe
Journal for in-service and pre-service teachers, teacher educators, and administrators, that presents research articles based on classroom and laboratory studies, descriptive and survey studies, summary and review articles, as well as discussions of current topics.

132 pages Quarterly
ISSN: 0273-5024

M Solmon, Author/Editor
R McBride, Author/Editor

4537 Marketing Recreation Classes
Learning Resources Network
1550 Hayes Drive
Manhattan, KS 66502-5068
785-539-5376
800-678-5376
Successful new class ideas and promotion techniques for recreation instructors.

8 pages Monthly

William Draves, Publisher
Julie Coates, Production Manager

4538 National Association for Sport & Physical Education News
National Association for Sport & Physical Ed.
1900 Association Drive
Reston, VA 20191-1502
703-476-3410
800-321-0789
Fax: 703-476-8316
News of conventions, new publications, workshops, and more, all tailored for people in the field of sports, physical education, coaching, etc. Legislative issues are covered as well as news about the over 20 structures in NASPE.

12 pages Monthly

Paula Kun, Editor

4539 National Standards for Dance Education News
National Dance Association
1900 Association Drive
Reston, VA 20191-1502
703-476-3400
Fax: 703-476-9527
E-mail: nda@aahperd.org
http://www.aahperd.org/nda
News of the National Dance Association activities, national events in dance education and topics of interest to recreation and athletic directors.

12 pages Quarterly

Barbara Hernandez, Executive Director

4540 Physical Education Digest
11 Cerilli Crescent
Sudbury
Ontario, Canada P3E5R5
705-523-3331
800-455-8782
Fax: 705-523-3331
E-mail: coach@pedigest.com
http://www.pedigest.com

Edited for physical educators and scholastic coaches. Condenses practical ideas from periodicals and books.

36 pages Quarterly
ISSN: 0843-2635

Dick Moss, Editor

4541 Physical Educator
Arizona State University
Editorial Office
Department of ESPE
Tempe, AZ 85287
480-965-3875
Fax: 480-965-2569
Offers articles for the physical educator.

Quarterly

Robert Pangrazi, Editor

4542 Quest
Louisiana State University/Dept. of Kinesiology
Huey Room 112
Baton Rouge, LA 70803-0001
225-388-2036
Fax: 225-388-3680
Publishes articles concerning issues critical to physical education in higher education. Its purpose is to stimulate professional development within the field.

Quarterly

4543 Teaching Elementary Physical Education
Human Kinetics Publishers
1607 N Market Street
Champaign, IL 61820-2220
217-351-5076
800-747-4457
Fax: 217-351-2674
A resource for elementary physical educators, by physical educators. Each 32-page issue includes informative articles on current trends, teaching hints, activity ideas, current resources and events, and more.

32 pages BiMonthly Magazine
ISSN: 1045-4853

G Jake Jaquet, Director Journal Division
Margery Robinson, Managing Editor

Periodicals / _Reading_

4544 Beyond Words
1534 Wells Drive NE
Albuquerque, NM 87112-6383
505-275-2558
Offers information on literature, language arts and English for the teaching professional.

10x Year

4545 Christian Literacy Outreach
Christian Literacy Association
541 Perry Highway
Pittsburgh, PA 15229-1851
412-364-3777
Association news offering membership information, convention news, books and articles for the Christian education professional.

4 pages Quarterly

Joseph Mosca

4546 Exercise Exchange
Appalachian State University
222 Duncan Hall
Boone, NC 28608-0001
828-262-2234
Fax: 828-262-2128
Bi-annual journal which features classroom-tested approaches to the teaching of English language arts from middle school

through college; articles are written by classroom practitioners.

BiAnnual
ISSN: 0531-531X

Charles R Duke, Editor

4547 Forum for Reading
Fitchburg State College, Education Department
160 Pearl Street
Fitchburg, MA 01420-2631
978-343-2151
Offers articles, reviews, question and answer columns and more for educators and students.

2x Year

Rona F Flippo, Editor

4548 Journal of Adolescent & Adult Literacy
International Reading Association
800 Barksdale Road
#8139
Newark, DE 19714
302-731-1600
800-336-7323
Fax: 302-731-1057
E-mail: journals@reading.org
http://www.reading.org
Carries articles and departments for those who teach reading in adolescent and adult programs. Applied research, instructional techniques, program descriptions, training of teachers and professional issues.

80-96 pages 8x Year
ISSN: 1081-3004

John Elleins, Editor

4549 Laubach LitScape
Laubach Literacy Action
1320 Jamesville Avenue
Syracuse, NY 13210
315-422-9121
888-528-2224
Fax: 315-422-6369
E-mail: info@laubach.org
http://www.laubach.org
Includes articles about national literacy activities as well as support and information on tutoring, resources, training, new readers, program management, and recruitment and retention of students and volunteers.

12 pages Quarterly

Linda Church, Managing Editor

4550 Literacy Advocate
Laubach Literacy Action
1320 Jamesville Avenue
Syracuse, NY 13210
315-422-9121
888-528-2224
Fax: 315-422-6369
E-mail: info@laubach.org
http://www.laubach.org
Covers United States and international programs and membership activities.

8 pages Quarterly

Beth Kogut, Editor

4551 News for You
Laubach Literacy Action
1320 Jamesville Avenue
Syracuse, NY 13210
315-422-9121
888-528-2224
Fax: 315-422-6369
E-mail: info@laubach.org
http://www.laubach.org
A newspaper for older teens and adults with special reading needs. Includes US and world

news written at a 4th to 6th grade reading level.

4 pages Weekly
ISSN: 0884-3910

Heidi Stephens, Editor

4552 Phonics Institute
PO Box 98785
Tacoma, WA 98498-0785
253-588-3436
E-mail: mah@readingstore.com
http://www.readingstore.com
Restoration of intensive phonics to beginning reading instruction.

8 pages 5x Year

4553 RIF Newsletter
Smithsonian Institution
900 Jefferson Drive SW
Washington, DC 20560-0004
202-357-2888
Fax: 202-786-2564
Describes RIF's nationwide reading motivation program.

TriQuarterly

4554 Read, America!
Place in the Woods
3900 Glenwood Avenue
Golden Valley, MN 55422-5302
763-374-2120
Fax: 952-593-5593
E-mail: readamerica10732@aol.com
News, book reviews, ideas for librarians and reading program leaders; short stories and poetry pages for adults and children; and an annual Read America! collection with selections of new books solicited from 350 publishers.

12 pages Quarterly Newsletter
ISSN: 0891-4214

Roger Hammer, Editor/Publisher

4555 Reading Improvement
Project Innovation of Mobile
PO Box 8508
Mobile, AL 36689-0508
334-633-7802
A journal dedicated to improving reading and literacy in America.

Quarterly

Dr. Phil Feldman, Editor

4556 Reading Psychology
Texas A&M University, College of Education
Department of Education
College Station, TX 77843-0001
979-845-7093
Fax: 979-845-9663

Quarterly

Dr. William H. Rupley, Editor

4557 Reading Research Quarterly
Ohio State University
1945 N High Street
Columbus, OH 43210-1120
614-292-8054
Fax: 614-292-1816
Delves into reading ratings and special concerns in the field of literacy.

Quarterly

Dr. Robert Tierney, Editor

4558 Reading Research and Instruction
Appalachian State University, College of Education
Dept. of Curriculum & Instruction
Boone, NC 28608-0001

828-262-6055

Quarterly

William E Blanton, Editor

4559 Reading Teacher
International Reading Association
800 Barksdale Road
#8139
Newark, DE 19711-3204
302-731-1600
800-336-READ
Fax: 301-731-1057
Carries articles and departments for those who teach reading in preschool and elementary schools. Applied research, instructional techniques, program descriptions, the training of teachers, professional issues and special feature reviews of children's books and ideas for classroom practice.

8x Year

Dr. James Baumann, Journal Editor
Linda Hunter, Advertising Manager

4560 Reading Today
International Reading Association
800 Barksdale Road
#8139
Newark, DE 19711-3204
302-731-1600
800-336-READ
Fax: 302-731-1057
Edited for IRA individual and institutional members offering information for teachers, news of the education profession and information for and relating to parents, councils and international issues.

36-44 pages BiMonthly

Linda Hunter, Advertising Manager
John Mickles, Editor

4561 Recording for the Blind & Dyslexic
69 Mapleton Road
Princeton, NJ 08540
609-750-1830
Fax: 609-750-9653
E-mail: scampbell@rfbd.org
http://www.rfbd.org
Textbooks on tape for students who cannot read standard print.

Stephanie Campbell, Executive Director

4562 Report on Literacy Programs
Business Publishers
8737 Colesville Road
Suite 1100
Silver Spring, MD 20910-3928
301-587-6300
800-274-6737
Fax: 301-585-9075
E-mail: bpinews@bpinews.com
http://www.bpinews.com
Reports on the efforts of business and government to provide literacy training to adults—focusing on the effects of literacy on the workforce.

8-10 pages BiWeekly

Eric Easton, Publisher
Dave Speights, Editor

4563 Visual Literacy Review & Newsletter
International Visual Literacy Association
Virginia Tech
Old Security Building
Blacksburg, VA 24061
540-231-8992
Forum for sharing research and practice within an educational context in the area of visual communication.

8 pages BiMonthly

Richard Couch

4564 WSRA Journal
University of Wisconsin - Oshkosh
1863 Doty Street
Oshkosh, WI 54901-6978
920-424-7231
Fax: 920-326-6280
E-mail: wsra@centurytel.net
A quarterly publication of the Wisconsin State Reading Association that publishes articles about literacy for academicians, teachers, libraries and literary workers.

Quarterly

Dr. Margaret Humadi Genisio, Editor

4565 What's Working in Parent Involvement
The Parent Institute
PO Box 7474
Fairfax Station, VA 22039-7474
703-323-9170
Fax: 703-323-9173
http://www.parent-institute.com
Focuses on parent involvement in children's reading education.

10x Year

John Wherry, Publisher

Periodicals / *Secondary Education*

4566 ACTIVITY
American College Testing
2201 Dodge
Iowa City, IA 52243-0001
319-337-1410
Fax: 319-337-1014
Distributed free of charge to more than 100,000 persons concerned with secondary and postsecondary education. ACT, an independent nonprofit organization provides a broad range of educational programs and services throughout this country and abroad.

Quarterly

Dan Lechay, Editor

4567 Adolescence
Libra Publishers
3089C Clairemont Drive
PNB 383
San Diego, CA 92117-6802
858-571-1414
Fax: 858-571-1414
Articles contributed by professionals spanning issues relating to teenage education, counseling and guidance. Paperback.

256 pages Quarterly
ISSN: 0001-8449

William Kroll, Editor

4568 American Secondary Education
Bowling Green State University
Education Room 531
Bowling Green, OH 43403-0001
419-372-7379
Fax: 419-372-8265
Serves those involved in secondary education— administrators, teachers, university personnel and others. Examines and reports on current issues in secondary education and provides readers with information on a wide range of topics that impact secondary education professionals. Professionals are provided with the most up-to-date theories and practices in their field.

Quarterly

Gregg Brownell, Editor
Madu Ireh, Graduate Editor

4569 Child and Youth Care Forum
Kluwer Academic/Human Sciences Press
233 Spring Street
New York, NY 10013
212-620-8000
800-221-9369
Fax: 212-463-0742
http://www.wkpa.nl
Independent, professional publication committed to the improvement of child and youth care practice in a variety of day and residential settings and to the advancement of this field. Designed to serve child and youth care practitioners, their supervisors, and other personnel in child and youth care settings, the journal provides a channel of communication and debate including material on practice, selection and training, theory and research, and professional issues.
Bimonthly
ISSN: 1053-1890

Carol Bischoff, Publisher
Doug Magnuson, Co-Editor

4570 Family Therapy: The Journal of the California Graduate School of Family Psychology
Libra Publishers
3089C Clairemont Drive
PNB 383
San Diego, CA 92117-6802
858-571-1414
Fax: 858-571-1414
Articles contributed by professionals spanning issues relating to teenage education, counseling and guidance. Paperback.
96 pages Quarterly
ISSN: 0091-6544

William Kroll, Editor

4571 High School Journal
University of North Carolina
212-D #3500
Chapel Hill, NC 27599-0001
919-962-1395
Fax: 919-962-1533
The Journal publishes articles dealing with adolescent growth, development, interests, beliefs, values, learning, etc., as they effect school practice. In addition, it reports on research dealing with teacher, administrator and student interaction within the school setting. The audience is primarily secondary school teachers and administrators, as well as college level educators.
60 pages Quarterly
ISSN: 0018-1498

Dr. George Noblit, Editor

4572 Independent School
National Association of Independent Schools
75 Federal Street
Boston, MA 02110-1913
617-451-2444
Contains information and opinion about secondary and elementary education in general and independent education in particular.
TriAnnually

Thomas W Leonhardt, Editor
Kurt R Murphy, Advertising/Editor

4573 Journal of At-Risk Issues
Clemson University
209 Martin Street
Clemson, SC 29631-1555
864-656-2599
800-443-6392
Fax: 864-656-0136

E-mail: NDPC@clemson.edu
http://www.dropoutprevention.org
Publication Date: 0 36 pages
ISBN: 1098-1608

Dr. Judy Johnson, Author
Dr. Judy Johnson, Author
Dr. Alice Fisher, Editor

4574 NASSP Bulletin
National Assn. of Secondary School Principals
1904 Association Drive
Reston, VA 20191-1537
703-860-0200
800-253-7746
Fax: 703-620-6534
E-mail: nassp@nassp.org
For administrators at the secondary school level dealing with subjects that range from the philosophical to the practical.
TriAnnual

Eugenia Cooper Potter, Editor

4575 Parents Still Make the Difference!
The Parent Institute
PO Box 7474
Fairfax Station, VA 22039-7474
703-323-9170
Fax: 703-323-9173
http://www.parent-institute.com
Newsletter focusing on parent involvement in children's education. Focuses on parents of children in grades 7-12.
Monthly
ISSN: 1523-2395

Betsie Millar, Author
John Wherry, Publisher

4576 Parents Still Make the Difference!: MiddleSchool Edition
The Parent Institute
PO Box 7474
Fairfax Station, VA 22039-7474
703-323-9170
Fax: 703-323-9173
http://www.parent-institute.com
Newsletter focusing on parent involvement in children's education. Focuses on parents of children in grades 7-12.
Monthly
ISSN: 1071-5118

John Wherry, Publisher

Periodicals / *Science*

4577 American Biology Teacher
National Association of Biology Teachers
12030 Sunrise Valley Drive
Reston, VA 20191
703-264-9696
800-406-0775
Fax: 703-264-7778
E-mail: office@nabt.org
http://www.nabt.org
Edited for elementary, secondary school, junior college, four-year college and university teachers of biology.
80 pages 9 times a year

Cheryl Merrill, Managing Editor
Kay Acevedo, Publications Specialist

4578 AnthroNotes
Smithsonian Institution Anthropology Outreach Offi
PO Box 37012
Washington, DC 20013-7012
202-633-1917
Fax: 202-357-2208
E-mail: anthroutreach@si.edu
http://www.nmnsi.edu/anthro

Offers archeological, anthropological research in an engaging style.
20 pages

Ann Krupp, Editor

4579 Appraisal: Science Books for Young People
Children's Science Book Review Committee
Boston University
School of Education
Boston, MA 02215
617-353-4150
This is a journal dedicated to the review of science books for children and young adults. Now in its 27th year of publication, Appraisal reviews nearly all of the science books published yearly for pre-school through high-school age young people. Each book is examined by a children's librarian and by a specialist in its particular discipline.
Quarterly

Diane Holzheimer, Editor

4580 Association of Science-Technology Centers Dimensions
1025 Vermont Avenue NW
Suite 500
Washington, DC 20005-3516
202-783-7200
Fax: 202-783-7207
E-mail: info@astc.org
http://www.astc.org
20 pages
ISSN: 1528-820X

Carolyn Sutterfield, Author
Bonnie VanDorn, Executive Director
Wendy Pollock, Dir Communication/Research

4581 CCAS Newsletter
Council of Colleges of Arts & Sciences
186 University Hall
Columbus, OH 43210
614-292-1882
Fax: 614-292-8666
Membership newsletter to inform deans about arts and sciences issues in education.
4-10 pages BiMonthly

Richard J Hopkins, Contact

4582 Journal of College Science Teaching
National Science Teachers Association
1840 Wilson Boulevard
Arlington, VA 22201-3000
703-243-7100
800-782-6782
Fax: 703-243-7177
http://www.nsta.org
Professional journal for college and university teachers of introductory and advanced science with special emphasis on interdisciplinary teaching of nonscience majors. Contains feature articles and departments including a science column, editorials, lab demonstrations, problem solving techniques and book reviews.
6x Year

Dr. Gerald Wheeler, Executive Director
Michael Byrnes, Managing Editor

4583 Journal of Environmental Education
Heldref Publications
1319 18th Street NW
Washington, DC 20036-1826
202-296-6267
800-365-9753
Fax: 202-296-5149
A vital research journal for everyone teaching about the environment. Each issue features case studies of relevant projects, evaluation of new research, and discussion of public policy and philosophy in the area of environmen-

tal education. The Journal is an excellent resource for department chairpersons and directors of programs in outdoor education.

Quarterly

Kerri P Kilbane, Editor

4584 Journal of Research in Science Teaching

Wiley InterScience
Wiley Corporate Headquarters
111 River Street
Hoboken, NJ 07030-5774
201-748-6000
Fax: 201-748-6088
http://www.interscience.wiley.com

10x Year

4585 NSTA Reports!

National Science Teachers Association
1840 Wilson Boulevard
Arlington, VA 22201-3000
703-243-7100
800-782-6782
Fax: 703-243-7177
http://www.nsta.org
The association's timely source of news on issues of interest to science teachers of all levels. Includes national news, information on teaching materials, announcements of programs for teachers and students, and advance notice about all NSTA programs, conventions and publications.

52 pages BiMonthly

Dr. Gerald Wheeler, Executive Director
Jodi Peterson, Editor

4586 Odyssey

Cobblestone Publishing
30 Grove Street
Suite C
Peterborough, NH 03458-1453
603-924-7209
800-821-0115
Fax: 603-924-7380
E-mail: custsvc@cobblestonepub.org
http://www.odysseymagazine.com
Secrets of science are probed with each theme issues's articles, interviews, activities and math puzzles. Astronomical concepts are experienced with Jack Horkheimer's Star Gazer cartoon and Night-Sky Navigation.

48 pages Monthly
ISSN: 0163-0946

Elizabeth E Lindstrom, Editor

4587 Physics Teacher

American Association of Physics Teachers
One Physics Ellipse
College Park, MD 20740-3845
301-209-3300
Fax: 301-209-0845
E-mail: aapt-web@aapt.org
http://www.aapt.org
Published by the American Association of Physics Teachers and dedicated to the improvement of the teaching of introductory physics at all levels.

9x Year

Karl C Mamola, Editor
Pamela R Brown, Senior Editorial Associate

4588 Quantum

National Science Teachers Association
1840 Wilson Boulevard
Arlington, VA 22201-3000
703-243-7100
800-782-6782
Fax: 703-243-7177
http://www.nsta.org
Illustrated magazine containing material translated from Russian magazine Kvant as well as original material specifically targeted

to American students. In addition to feature articles and department pieces, Quantum offers olympiad-style problems and brainteasers. Each issue also contains an answer section.

BiMonthly

Dr. Gerald Wheeler, Executive Director
Mike Donaldson, Managing Editor

4589 Reports of the National Center for Science Education

National Center for Science Education
925 Kearney Street
El Cerrito, CA 94530-2810
510-601-7203
800-290-6006
Fax: 510-601-7204
E-mail: ncse@ncseweb.org
http://www.ncseweb.org
An examination of issues and current events in science education with a focus on evolutionary science, and the evolution/creation controversy.

36-44 pages BiMonthly Newsletter
ISSN: 1064-2358

Eugenie C Scott, PhD, Publisher
Andrew J Petto PhD, Editor

4590 Science Activities

Heldref Publications
1319 18th Street NW
Washington, DC 20036-1826
202-296-6267
800-365-9753
Fax: 202-296-5149
E-mail: sa@heldref.org
http://www.heldref.org
A storehouse of up-to-date creative science projects and curriculum ideas for the K-12 classroom teacher. A one-step source of experiments, projects and curriculum innovations in the biological, physical and behavioral sciences, the journal's ideas have been teacher tested, providing the best of actual classroom experiences. Regular departments feature news notes, computer news, book reviews and new products and resources for the classroom.

48 pages Quarterly
ISSN: 0036-8121

Betty Bernard, Managing Editor

4591 Science News Magazine

1719 N Street NW
Washington, DC 20036-2888
202-785-2255
Fax: 202-659-0365
Information and programs in all areas of science.

Weekly

4592 Science Scope

National Science Teachers Association
1840 Wilson Boulevard
Arlington, VA 22201-3000
703-243-7100
800-782-6782
Fax: 703-243-7177
http://www.nsta.org
Specifically for middle-school and junior-high science teachers. Science Scope addresses the needs of both new and veteran teachers. The publication includes classroom activities, posters and teaching tips, along with educational theory on the way adolescents learn.

8x Year

Dr. Gerald Wheeler, Executive Director
Ken Roberts, Managing Editor

4593 Science Teacher

National Science Teachers Association
1840 Wilson Boulevard
Arlington, VA 22201-3000
703-243-7100
800-782-6782
Fax: 703-243-7177
http://www.nsta.org
Professional journal for junior and senior high school science teachers. Offers articles on a wide range of scientific topics, innovative teaching ideas and experiments, and current research news. Also offers reviews, posters, information on free or inexpensive materials, and more.

9x Year

Dr. Gerald Wheeler, Executive Director
Shelley Johnson Carey, Managing Editor

4594 Science and Children

National Association of Science Teachers
1840 Wilson Boulevard
Arlington, VA 22201-3000
703-243-7100
800-782-6782
Fax: 703-243-7177
http://www.nsta.org
Dedicated to preschool through middle school science teaching provides lively how-to articles, helpful hints, software and book reviews, colorful posters and inserts, think pieces and on-the-scene reports from classroom teachers.

8x Year

Dr. Gerald Wheeler, Executive Director
Linda L Roswog, Managing Editor

4595 Sea Frontiers

International Oceanographic Foundation
4600 Rickenbacker Causeway
Key Biscayne, FL 33149-1031
305-361-4888
A general interest magazine about science education including underwater studies.

BiMonthly

Bonnie Gordon, Editor

4596 Universe in the Classroom

Astronomical Society of the Pacific
390 Ashton Avenue
San Francisco, CA 94112-1722
415-337-1100
Fax: 415-337-5205
E-mail: astroed@astrosociety.org
http://www.astrosociety.org/uitc
On teaching astronomy in grades 3-12, including astronomical news, plain-English explanations, teaching resources and classroom activities.

8 pages Quarterly

Noel Encaracian, Customer Service

Periodicals / *Social Studies*

4597 Alumni Newsletter

Jewish Labor Committee
25 E 21st Street
Floor 2
New York, NY 10010-6207
212-477-0707
Fax: 212-477-1918
Newsletter of American public secondary school teachers who teach about the Holocaust and Jewish Resistance to the Nazis during World War II.

8 pages SemiAnnually

Arieh Lebowitz

4598 American Sociological Review
Pennsylvania State University
206 Oswald Tower, Sociology Dept
University Park, PA 16802
814-865-5021
Fax: 814-865-0705
Addresses most aspects of sociology in a general range of categories for academic and professional sociologists.

Bimonthly

Glenn Firebaugh, Editor

4599 AnthroNotes
Anthropology Outreach Office
PO Box 37012
Washington, DC 20013-7012
202-357-1592
Fax: 202-357-2208
Offers archeological, anthropological research in an engaging style.

4600 AppleSeeds
Cobblestone Publishing
30 Grove Street
Suite C
Peterborough, NH 03458-1453
603-924-7209
800-821-0115
Fax: 603-924-7380
E-mail: custsvc@cobblestonepub.com
http://www.cobblestonepub.com
A delightful way to develop love of non-fiction reading in grades 2-4. Full color articles, photographs, maps, activities that grab student and teacher interest. Children's doings and thinking around the world in Mail Bag.

32 pages Monthly
ISSN: 1099-7725

Susan Buckey, Barb Burt, Editors, Author
Lou Waryncia, Managing Editor

4601 Boletin
Center for the Teaching of the Americas
Immaculata College
Immaculata, PA 19345
610-647-4400
School teaching of the Americas.

Quarterly

Sr. Mary Consuela

4602 California Weekly Explorer
California Weekly Reporter
285 E Main Street
Suite 3
Tustin, CA 92780-4429
714-730-5991
Fax: 714-730-3548
Resources, events, awards and reviews relating to California history.

16 pages Weekly

Don Oliver

4603 Calliope
Cobblestone Publishing
30 Grove Street
Suite C
Peterborough, NH 03458-1453
603-924-7209
800-821-0115
Fax: 603-924-7380
E-mail: custsvc@cobblestonepub.com
http://www.cobblestonepub.com
Invests in world history with reality not only through articles, stories and maps but also current events and resource lists. Calliope's themes are geared to topics studied in world history classrooms.

48 pages Monthly
ISSN: 1058-7086

Lou Waryncia, Managing Editor
Charles F Baker, Editors

4604 Capitalism for Kids
National Schools Commitee for Economic Education
330 East 70th Street
Suite 5J
New York, NY 10021-8641
212-535-9534
Fax: 212-535-4167
E-mail: info@nscee.org
http://www.nscee.org
Teaches young people about capitalism and the free enterprise system in a clear and entertaining styl. Disscusses the practical aspects of starting a small business.

247 pages

John E Donnelly, Executive Director

4605 Cobblestone
Cobblestone Publishing
30 Grove Street
Suite C
Peterborough, NH 03458-1445
603-924-7209
800-821-0115
Fax: 603-924-7380
E-mail: custsvc@cobblestonepub.com
http://www.cobblestonepub.com
Blends sound information with excellent writing, a combination that parents and teachers appreciate. Cobblestone offers imaginative approaches to introduce young readers to the world of American history.

48 pages Monthly
ISSN: 0199-5197

Lou Waryncia, Managing Editor
Meg Chorlian, Editor

4606 Colloquoy on Teaching World Affairs
World Affairs Council of North California
312 Sutter Street
Suite 200
San Francisco, CA 94108-4311
415-982-3263
Fax: 415-982-5028
Offers information, articles and updates for the history teacher.

3x Year

Cassie Todd

4607 Faces
Cobblestone Publishing
30 Grove Street
Suite C
Peterborough, NH 03458-1453
603-924-7209
800-821-0115
Fax: 603-924-7380
E-mail: custsvc@cobblestonepub.com
http://www.cobblestonepub.com
The world is brought to the classroom through the faces of its people. World culture encourages young readers' perspectives through history, folk tales, news and activities.

48 pages Monthly
ISSN: 0749-1387

Lou Waryncia, Managing Editor
Elizabeth Crooker Carpentiere, Editor

4608 Focus
Freedoms Foundation at Valley Forge
PO Box 706
Valley Forge, PA 19482-0706
215-933-8825
800-896-5488
Fax: 610-935-0522
E-mail: tsueta@ffvf.org
http://www.ffvf.org
Strives to teach America and promote responsible citizenship through educational programs and awards designed to recognize outstanding Americans.

6 pages Quarterly

Thomas M Sueat, Editor

4609 Footsteps
Cobblestone Publishing
30 Grove Street
Suite C
Peterborough, NH 03458-1453
603-924-7209
800-821-0115
Fax: 603-924-7380
E-mail: custsvc@cobblestonepub.com
http://www.cobblestonepub.com
Celebrates heritage of African Americans and explores their contributions to culture from colonial times to present. Courage, perseverance mark struggle for freedom and equality in articles, maps, photos, etc.

48 pages 9x Year
ISSN: 1521-5865

Lou Waryncia, Managing Editor
Charles Baker, Editor

4610 History Matters Newsletter
National Council for History Education
26915 Westwood Road
Suite B-2
Westlake, OH 44145-4657
440-835-1776
Fax: 440-835-1295
E-mail: nche@nche.nett
http://www.history.org/nche
Serves as a resource to help members improve the quality and quantity of history learning.

8 pages Monthly
ISSN: 1090-1450

Elaine W Reed, Executive Director

4611 Inquiry in Social Studies: Curriculum, Research & Instruction
University of North Carolina-Charlotte
Dept of Curriculum & Instruction
Charlotte, NC 28223
704-547-4500
Fax: 704-547-4705
An annual journal of North Carolina Council for the Social Studies with a readership of 1,400.

Annual

John A Gretes, Editor
Jeff Passe, Editor

4612 Journal of American History
Organization of American Historians
121 N Bryan Street
Bloomington, IN 47408-4136
812-855-7311
800-446-8923
Fax: 812-855-0696
Contains articles and essays concerning the study and investigation of American history.

Quarterly

Tamzen Meyer, Editor

4613 Journal of Economic Education
Heldref Publications
1319 18th Street NW
Washington, DC 20036-1826
202-296-6267
800-365-9753
Fax: 202-296-5149
Offers original articles on innovations in and evaluations of teaching techniques, materials and programs in economics.

Quarterly
ISSN: 0022-4085

4614 Journal of Geography
National Council for Geographic Education
700 Pelham Road N
Jacksonville, AL 36265
256-782-5293
Fax: 256-782-5336
E-mail: ncge@jsu.edu
http://www.ncge.org
Stresses the essential value of geographic education and knowledge in schools.

Quarterly
ISSN: 0022-1341

Michal LeVasseur, Executive Director
Allison Newton, Associate Director

4615 Magazine of History
Organizations of American History
112 N Bryan Avenue
Bloomington, IN 47408-4199
812-855-7311
800-446-8923
Fax: 812-855-0696
E-mail: oah@oah.org
http://www.oah.org
Includes informative articles, lesson plans, current historiography and reproducible classroom materials on a particular theme. In addition to topical articles, such columns as Dialogue, Studentspeak and History Headlines allow for the exchange of ideas from all levels of the profession.

70-90 pages Quarterly Magazine
ISSN: 0882-228X

Michael Regoli, Managing Editor

4616 New England Journal of History
Bentley College
Dept of History
Waltham, MA 02254
781-891-2509
Fax: 781-891-2896
Covers all aspects of American history for the professional and student.

3x Year

Joseph Harrington, Editor

4617 News & Views
Pennsylvania Council for the Social Studies
11533 Clematis Boulevard
Pittsburgh, PA 15235-3105
717-238-8768
E-mail: lguru1@aol.com
http://www.pcss.org
Offers news, notes, and reviews of interest to social studies educators.

20 pages 5x Year
ISSN: 0894-8712

Jack Suskind, Executive Secretary
Leo R West, Editor

4618 Perspective
Association of Teachers of Latin American Studies
PO Box 620754
Flushing, NY 11362-0754
718-428-1237
Fax: 718-428-1237
Promotes the teaching of Latin America in US schools and colleges.

10 pages BiMonthly

Daniel Mugan

4619 Social Education
National Council for the Social Studies
8555 Sixteenth Street
Suite 500
Silver Spring, MD 20910
301-588-1800
800-683-0812
Fax: 301-588-2049
E-mail: sgriffin@ncss.org
http://www.socialstudies.org

Journal for the social studies profession serves middle school, high school and college and university teachers. Social Education features research on significant topics relating to social studies, lesson plans that can be applied to various disciplines, techniques for using teaching materials in the classroom and information on the latest instructional technology.

7x Year
ISSN: 0337-7724

Michael Simpson, Editor
Robin Hayes, Manager

4620 Social Studies
Heldref Publications
1319 18th Street NW
Washington, DC 20036-1826
202-296-6267
800-365-9753
Fax: 202-296-5149
Offers K-12 classroom teachers, teacher educators and curriculum administrators an independent forum for publishing their ideas about the teaching of social studies at all levels. The journal presents teachers' methods and classroom-tested suggestions for teaching social studies, history, geography and the social sciences.

48 pages BiMonthly

Helen Kress, Managing Editor

4621 Social Studies Journal
Pennsylvania Council for the Social Studies
11533 Clematis Boulevard
Pittsburgh, PA 15235-3105
717-238-8768
E-mail: lguru1@aol.com
http://www.pcss.org
Delves into matters of social studies, history, research and statistics for the education professional and science community.

80 pages Annual

Leo R West, Editor
Dr. Saundra McKee, Editor

4622 Social Studies Professional
National Council for the Social Studies
8555 Sixteenth Street
Suite 500
Silver Spring, MD 20910
301-588-1800
800-683-0812
Fax: 301-588-2049
E-mail: sgriffin@ncss.org
http://www.socialstudies.org
Newsletter focusing on strategies, tips and techniques for the social studies educator. New product announcements, professional development opportunities, association news, state and regional meetings.

6 Times

Terri Ackermann, Editor

4623 Social Studies and the Young Learner
National Council for the Social Studies
8555 Sixteenth Street
Suite 500
Silver Spring, MD 20910
301-588-1800
800-683-0812
Fax: 301-588-2049
E-mail: sgriffin@ncss.org
http://www.socialstudies.org
This publication furthers creative teaching in grades K-6, meeting teachers' needs for new information and effective teaching activities.

Quarterly

Martharose Laffey, Editor

4624 Society For History Education/History Teacher
California State University - Long Beach
CSULB, 1250 Bellflower Blvd.
Long Beach, CA 90840-1601
562-985-2573
Fax: 562-985-5431
E-mail: historyteacherjournal@gmail.com
http://www.thehistoryteacher.org
The most widely recognized journal in the United States suppoting all areas of history education, pre-collegiate through university level, with practical and insightful professional analyses of both traditional and innovative teaching techniques.

150 pages Quarterly
ISSN: 0018-2745

Jane Dabel, Editor
Elisa Herrera, Executive Director

4625 Teaching Georgia Government Newsletter
Carl Vinson Institute of Government
201 N Milledge Avenue
Athens, GA 30602-5027
706-542-2736
Fax: 706-542-6239
Substantive and supplementary material for social studies teachers in Georgia. Topics of government, history, archaeology, geography, citizenship, etc. are covered. Publications available and upcoming social studies meetings in the state are also announced.

8 pages TriAnnually

Inge Whittle, Editor
Ed Jackson, Editor

4626 Theory and Research in Social Education
National Council for the Social Studies
8555 Sixteenth Street
Suite 500
Silver Spring, MD 20910
301-588-1800
800-683-0812
Fax: 301-588-2049
E-mail: sgriffin@ncss.org
http://www.socialstudies.org
Features articles covering a variety of topics: teacher training, learning theory, and child development research; instructional strategies; the relationship of the social sciences, philosophy, history and the arts to social education; models and theories used in developing social studies curriculum; and schemes for student participation and social action.

Quarterly

4627 Wall Street Journal - Classroom Edition
PO Box 7019
Chicopee, MA 01021
800-544-0522
Fax: 413-598-2332
E-mail: classroom.edition@wsj.com
http://www.wsjclassroom.com
Monthly student newspaper, with stories drawn from the daily journal that show international, business, economic, and social issues affect students' lives and futures. The newspaper is supported by posters, monthly teacher guides, and videos. Regular features on careers, enterprise, marketing, personal finance and technology. Helps teachers prepare students for the world of work by combining timely articles with colorful graphics, etc.

Monthly

Krishnan Anantharamanz, Editor

4628 Women's History Project News
National Women's History Project
3343 Industrial Drive
Suite #4
Santa Rosa, CA 95403
707-636-2888
Fax: 707-636-2909
E-mail: nwhp@aol.com
http://www.nwhp.org
Monthly E-mail newsletter about US women's history, for educators, researchers, program planners, and general women's history enthusiasts.

Monthly

Molly Murphy MacGregor, Exec. Dir./Co-Founder

Periodicals / *Technology in Education*

4629 Cable in the Classroom
CCI/Crosby Publishing
214 Lincoln Street
Suite 112
Boston, MA 02134
617-254-9481
Fax: 617-254-9776
http://www.ciconline.org
Most comprehensive guide to integrating educational video with the Internet and other curriculum resources for K-12 educators.

54 pages Monthly
ISSN: 1054-5409

Stephen P Crosby, Publisher
Al Race, Executive Editor

4630 EDUCAUSE Quarterly
EDUCAUSE
4772 Walnut Street
Suite 206
Boulder, CO 80301-2538
303-544-5665
Fax: 303-440-0461
E-mail: pdeblois@educause.edu
http://www.educause.edu
Strategic policy advocacy; teaching and learning initiatives; applied research; special interest collaboration communities; awards for leadership and exemplary practices; and extensive online information services.

Quarterly Magazine
ISSN: 1528-5324

Nancy Hays, Author
Peter DeBlois, Director Communications

4631 EDUCAUSE Review
EDUCAUSE
4772 Walnut Street
Suite 206
Boulder, CO 80301-2408
303-544-5665
Fax: 303-440-0461
E-mail: pdeblois@educause.edu
http://www.educause.edu
Strategic policy advocacy; teaching and learning initiatives applied research; special interest collaboration communities; awards for leadership and exemplary practices; and extensive online information services.

Monthly
ISSN: 1527-6619

Nancy Hays, Author
Peter DeBlois, Director Communications

4632 Education Technology News
Business Publishers
8737 Colesville Road
Suite 1100
Silver Spring, MD 20910-3928

301-587-6300
800-274-6737
Fax: 301-585-9075
E-mail: bpinews@bpinews.com
http://www.bpinews.com
Offers information on computer hardware, multimedia products, software applications, public and private funding and integration of technology into K-12 classrooms.

8 pages BiWeekly

Eric Easton, Publisher
Brian Love, Editorial Coordinato

4633 Educational Technology
700 E Palisade Avenue
Englewood Cliffs, NJ 07632-3040
201-871-4007
800-952-BOOK
Fax: 201-871-4009
Published since 1961, periodical covering the entire field of educational technology. Issues feature essays by leading authorities plus a Research Section. With many special issues covering aspects of the field in depth. Readers are found in some 120 countries.

9x Year

Lawrence Lipsitz, Editor

4634 Electronic Learning
Scholastic
555 Broadway
New York, NY 10012-3919
212-343-6100
800-724-6527
Fax: 212-343-4801
Published for the administrative level, education professionals who are directly responsible for the implementing of electronic technology at the district, state and university levels.

8x Year

Lynn Diamond, Advertising Director
Therese Mageau, Editor

4635 Electronic School
1680 Duke Street
Alexandria, VA 22314
703-838-6722
Fax: 703-683-7590
E-mail: cwilliams@nsba.org
http://www.electronic-school.com
The school technology authority.

Cheryl S Williams, Director
Ann Lee Flynn, Director Education

4636 Information Searcher
Datasearch Group
14 Hadden Road
Scarsdale, NY 10583-3328
914-723-1995
Fax: 914-723-1995
http://www.infosearcher.com
Quarterly newsletter for the Internet and curriculum-technology integration in school.

32 pages

Pam Berger, President
Bill Berger, Treasurer

4637 Journal of Computing in Childhood Education
AACE
PO Box 2966
Charlottesville, VA 22902-2966
757-623-7588
Fax: 703-997-8760
Discusses the realm of software and technology now merging with primary education.

Quarterly

4638 Journal of Educational Technology Systems
58 New Mill Road
Smithtown, NY 11787-3342
516-632-8767
A compendium of articles submitted by professionals regarding the newest technology in the educational field.

Quarterly

Dr. Thomas Liao, Editor

4639 Journal of Information Systems Education
Bryant University
1150 Douglas Pike
Smithfield, RI 02917-1291
401-232-6393
Fax: 401-232-6319
Publishes original articles on current topics of special interest to Information Systems Educators and Trainers. Focus is applications-oriented articles describing curriculum, professional development or facilities issues. Topics include course projects/cases, lecture materials, curriculum design and/or implementation, workshops, faculty/student intern/extern programs, hardware/software selection and industry relations.

Quarterly

Richard Glass, Contact

4640 Journal of Research on Computing in Education
International Society for Technology in Education
480 Charnelton Street
Eugene, OR 97401-2626
541-302-3777
800-336-5191
Fax: 541-302-3778
E-mail: cust_serv@ccmail.uoregon.edu
http://www.iste.org
A quarterly journal of original research and detailed system and project evaluations. It also defines the state of the art and future horizons of educational computing.

Quarterly

Diane McGrath, Editor

4641 Journal of Special Education Technology
The Council for Exceptional Children
1920 Association Drive
Reston, VA 20191-1545
703-620-3660
888-232-7733
Fax: 703-264-9494
Provides professionals in the field with information on new technologies, current research, exemplary practices, relevant issues, legislative events and more concerning the availability and effective use of technology and media for individuals with disabilities and/or who are gifted.

Quarterly

Herbert Rieth, Editor

4642 Matrix Newsletter
Department of CCTE, Teachers College/Communication
PO Box 8
New York, NY 10027-0008
212-678-3344
Fax: 212-678-8227
Newsletter describing activities and interests of Department of Communication, Computing and Technology.

14 pages SemiAnnually

Marie Sayer

4643 MultiMedia Schools
Information Today
143 Old Marlton Pike
Medford, NJ 08055-8750
609-654-6266
800-300-9868
Fax: 609-654-4309
E-mail: custserv@infotoday.com
http://www.infotoday.com
A practical journal of multimedia, CD-Rom, online and Internet in K-12.

Thomas H Hogan, Publisher
Ferdi Serim, Editor

4644 National Forum of Instructional Technology Journal
McNeese State University
324 Prewitt Street
Lake Charles, LA 70601-5915
337-475-5000
Fax: 318-475-5467

Dr. J Mark Hunter, Editor

4645 Society for Applied Learning Technology
50 Culpeper Street
Warrenton, VA 20186
540-347-0055
800-457-6812
Fax: 540-349-3169
E-mail: info@lti.org
http://www.salt.org
Quarterly

4646 TAM Connector
The Council for Exceptional Children
1920 Association Drive
Reston, VA 20191-1545
703-620-3660
888-232-7733
Fax: 703-264-9494
Contains information about upcoming events, current trends and practices, state and national legislation, recently published materials and practical information relative to the availability and effective use of technology and media for individuals who are gifted or are disabled.

Quarterly

Cynthia Warger, Editor

4647 TECHNOS Quarterly for Education & Technolgy
Agency for Instructional Technology
PO Box A
Bloomington, IN 47402-0120
812-339-2203
Fax: 812-333-4218
E-mail: info@technos.net
http://www.technos.net
TECHNOS Quarterly is a forum for the discussion of ideas about the use of technology in education, with a focus on reform.

36 pages Quarterly
ISSN: 1060-5649

Michael F Sullivan, Executive Director
Carole Novak, Manager TECHNOS Press

4648 Tech Directions
Prakken Publications
275 Meity Drive
Suite 1
Ann Arbor, MI 48107
734-975-2800
Fax: 734-975-2787
E-mail: publisher@techdirections.com
http://www.eddigest.com
Issues programs, projects for educators in career-technical and technology education and

monthly features on technology, computers, tech careers.

Monthly
ISSN: 1062-9351

Tom Bowden, Managing Editor

4649 Technology & Learning
CMP Media
600 Harrison Street
San Francisco, CA 94107
516-562-5000
800-607-4410
Fax: 516-562-7013
http://www.techlearning.com
Product reviews; hard-hitting, straightforward editorial features; ideas on challenging classroom activities; and more. Tailor made to the special needs of a professional and an educator.

60-80 pages Monthly Magazine
ISSN: 1053-6728
March & October

Susan McLester, Author
Judy Salpeter, Editor-in-Chief
Jo-Ann McDevitt, Publisher

4650 Technology Integration for Teachers
Master Teacher
Leadership Lane
PO Box 1207
Manhattan, KS 66505-1207
800-669-9633
Fax: 800-669-1132
http://www.masterteacher.com

4 pages Monthly

4651 Technology Teacher
International Technology Education Association
1914 Association Drive
Suite 201
Reston, VA 20191-1538
703-860-2100
Fax: 703-860-0353
E-mail: itea@iris.org
http://www.iteawww.org
Seeks to advance technological literacy through professional development activities and publications.

40 pages 8x Year

Kendall Starkweather, Executive Director
Kathleen de la Paz, Editor

4652 Technology in Education Newsletter
111 E 14th Street
#140
New York, NY 10003-4103
800-443-7432
This newsletter for K-12 educators and administrators, covers national trends of technology in education.

4653 Web Feet Guides
Thomson Gale
Thomson Gale World Headquarters
27500 Drake Road
Farmington Hills, MI 48331-3535
248-699-4253
http://www.webfeetguides.com
The premier subject guides to the Internet, rigorously reviewed by librarians and educators, fully annotated, expanded and updated monthly. Appropriate for middle school through adult. Available in print, online, or MARC records. For more information, free trials and free samples.

Monthly

4654 eSchool News
7920 Norfolk Avenue
Suite 900
Bethesda, MD 20814

301-913-0115
800-394-0115
Fax: 301-913-0119
http://www.eschoolnews.com
Monthly newspaper dedicated to providing news and information to help educators use technology to improve education.

Monthly

Gregs Downey, Publisher

General

4655 ABC Feelings Adage Publications
Po Box 7280
Ketchum, ID 83340
208-788-5399
Fax: 208-788-4195
E-mail: info@theattitudedoc.com
http://www.abcfeelings.com
Interactive line of children's products that relate feelings to each letter of the alphabet. Encourages dialogue, understanding, communication, enhances self-esteem. Books, audiotape, poster, placemats, charts, activity cards, t-shirts and multicultural activity guides, floor puzzles,feelings dictionary, carpets.

Ages 3-10

Dr. Alexandra Delis-Abrams, President

4656 ABDO Publishing Company
4940 Viking Drive
Suite 622
Edina, MN 55435-5300
452-831-2120
800-800-1312
Fax: 952-831-1632
E-mail: info@abdopub.com
http://www.abdopub.com
K-8 nonfiction books, including Abdo and Daughters imprint, high/low books for reluctant readers and Checkerboard Library with K-3 science, geography, and biographics for beginning readers. Sand Castle for pre-K to second grade, graduated reading program.

Jill Abdo Hansen, President
James Abdo, Publisher

4657 AGS
4201 Woodland Road
Circle Pines, MN 55014-1796
763-786-4343
800-328-2560
Fax: 800-471-8457
Major test publisher and distributor of tests for literature, reading, English, mathematics, sciences, aptitude, and various other areas of education. Includes information on timing, scoring, teacher's guides and student's worksheets.

4658 AIMS Education Foundation
1595 S Chestnut Avenue
Fresno, CA 93702-4706
559-255-4094
888-733-2467
Fax: 559-255-6396
E-mail: aimsed@fresno.edu
http://www.aimsedu.org
A nonprofit educational foundation that focuses on preparing materials for science and mathematics areas of education.

4659 Ablex Publishing Corporation
PO Box 811
Stamford, CT 06904-0811
201-767-8450
Fax: 201-767-8450
Publishes academic books and journals dealing with many different subject areas. Some of these include: education, linguistics, psychology, library science, computer and cognitive science, writing research and sociology.

Kristin K Butter, President

4660 Acorn Naturalists
155 El Camino Real
Tustin, CA 92780
714-838-4888
800-422-8886
Fax: 714-838-5309
http://www.acornnaturalists.com
Publishes and distributes science and environmental education materials for teachers, naturalists and outdoor educators. A complete catalog is available.

World Wildlife Fund, Author
Jennifer Rigby, Director
Mika Stonehawk, Operations Manager

4661 Active Child
PO Box 2346
Salem, OR 97308-2346
503-371-0865
Publishes creative curriculum for young children.

4662 Active Learning
10744 Hole Avenue
Riverside, CA 92505-2867
909-689-7022
Fax: 909-689-7142
Interactive learning center publishing materials for childhood education.

4663 Active Parenting Publishers
1955 Vaughn Road NW
Suite 108
Kennesaw, GA 30144-7808
770-429-0565
800-825-0060
Fax: 770-429-0334
E-mail: cservice@activeparenting.com
http://www.activeparenting.com
Produces and sells books and innovative video-based programs for use in parent education, self-esteem education and loss education groups/classes.

4664 Addison-Wesley Publishing Company
2725 Sand Hill Road
Menlo Park, CA 94025-7019
650-854-0300
Publisher and distributor of a wide range of fiction, nonfiction and textbooks for grades K-12 in the areas of mathematics, reading, language arts, science, social studies and counseling.

4665 Advance Family Support & Education Program
301 S Frio Street
Suite 103
San Antonio, TX 78207-4422
210-270-4630
Fax: 210-270-4612
Offers books and publications on counseling and support for the family, student and educator.

4666 Alarion Press
PO Box 1882
Boulder, CO 80306-1882
303-443-9039
800-523-9177
Fax: 303-443-9098
E-mail: info@alarion.com
http://www.alarion.com
Video programs, posters, activities, manuals and workbooks dealing with History Through Art and Architecture for grades K-12.

4667 Albert Whitman & Company
6340 Oakton Street
Morton Grove, IL 60053-2723
847-581-0033
Children's books.

4668 Allyn & Bacon
160 Gould Street
Needham Heights, MA 02194
781-455-1250
Fax: 781-455-1220
Publisher of college textbooks and professional reference books.

4669 Alpha Publishing Company
1910 Hidden Point Road
Annapolis, MD 21401-6002
410-757-5404
Educational materials for K-12 curricula.

4670 American Association for State & Local History
1717 Church Street
Nashville, TN 37203-2921
615-320-3203
Fax: 615-327-9013
How-to books for anyone teaching history or social studies.

4671 American Association of School Administrators
1801 N Moore Street
Arlington, VA 22209-1813
703-528-0700
Fax: 703-528-2146
http://www.aasa.org

Paul Houston, Executive Director

4672 American Guidance Service
4201 Woodland Road
Circle Pines, MN 55014-1796
612-786-4343
800-328-2560
Fax: 763-783-4658
Largest distributor of educational materials focusing on guidance counselors and educators in the field of counseling. Materials include books, pamphlets, workshops and information on substance abuse, childhood education, alcoholism, inner-city subjects and more.

Matt Keller, Marketing Director

4673 American Institute of Physics
2 Huntington Quadrangle
Suite 1NO1
Melville, NY 11747
516-576-2200
Fax: 516-349-9704
Physics books.

Marc Brodsky, Executive Director

4674 American Nuclear Society
Outreach Department
555 N Kensington Avenue
La Grange Park, IL 60526-5592
708-352-6611
800-323-3044
Fax: 708-352-0499
E-mail: outreach@ans.org
http://www.aboutnuclear.com
Nuclear science and technology, supplemental educational materials for grades K-12. Re-Actions newsletters.

4675 American Physiological Society
9050 Rockville Pike
Bethesda, MD 20814
301-530-7132
Fax: 301-634-7098
Videotapes, tracking materials and free teacher resource packets.

4676 American Technical Publishers
1155 W 175th Street
Homewood, IL 60430-4600
708-957-1100
800-323-3471
Fax: 708-957-1101
E-mail: service@americantech.net
http://www.go2atp.com
Offers instructional materials for a variety of vocational and technical training areas.

4677 American Water Works Association
6666 W Quincy Avenue
Denver, CO 80235-3098
303-794-7711
Fax: 303-795-1989
Activity books, teacher guides and more on science education.

4678 Ampersand Press
750 Lake Street
Port Townsend, WA 98368
360-379-5187
800-624-4263
Fax: 360-379-0324
E-mail: info@ampersandpress.com
http://www.ampersandpress.com
Nature and science educational games.

Lou Haller, Owner

4679 Amsco School Publications
315 Hudson Street
New York, NY 10013-1009
212-675-7000
Fax: 212-675-7010
Basal textbooks, workbooks and supplementary materials for grades 7-12.

4680 Anderson's Bookshops
PO Box 3832
Naperville, IL 60567-3832
630-355-2665
The very latest and best trade books to use in the classroom.

4681 Annenberg/CPB Project
901 E Street NW
Washington, DC 20004-2037
202-393-7100
Fax: 202-879-6707
Offers teaching resources in chemistry, geology, physics and environmental science.

4682 Art Image Publications
PO Box 568
Champlain, NY 12919-0568
800-361-2598
Fax: 800-559-2598
Offers various products including art appreciation kits, art image mini-kits and visual arts programs for grades K-12.

Rachel Ross, President

4683 Art Visuals
PO Box 925
Orem, UT 84059-0925
801-226-6115
Fax: 801-226-6115
E-mail: artvisuals@sisna.com
http://www.members.tripod.com
Social studies and art history products including an Art History Timeline, 20 feet long that represents over 50 different styles, ranging from prehistoric to contemporary art; Modern Art Styles, set of 30 posters depicting 20th century styles; Multicultural Posters, Africa, India, China, Japan and the World of Islam, with 18 posters in each culture. Sets on women artists and African American Artists. Each set is printed on hard cardstock, laminated and ultraviolet protected.

Diane Asay, Owner

4684 Asian American Curriculum Project
83-37th Avenue
San Mateo, CA 94403
650-357-1088
800-874-2242
Fax: 650-357-6908
E-mail: aacpinc@best.com
http://www.asianamericanbooks.com
Develops, promotes and disseminates Asian-American books to schools, libraries and Asian-Americans. Over 1,500 titles.

Florence M Hongo, General Manager

4685 Association for Science Teacher Education
University of Florida
11000 University Parkway
Pensacola, FL 32514-5732
850-474-2000
Fax: 850-474-3205

Yearbooks, journals, newsletters and information on AETS.

4686 Association for Supervision & Curriculum Development
ASCD
1703 N Beauregard Street
Alexandria, VA 22311-1717
703-578-9600
800-933-2723
Fax: 703-575-5400
E-mail: member@ascd.org
http://www.ascd.org
Publishers of educational leadership books, audios and videos focusing on teaching and learning in all subjects and grade levels.

4687 Association of American Publishers
71 5th Avenue
Floor 12
New York, NY 10003
212-255-0200
Fax: 212-255-7007
Association for the book publishing industry.

4688 Atheneum Books for Children
MacMillan Publishing Company
1633 Broadway
New York, NY 10019
212-512-2000
Fax: 800-835-3202
Hardcover trade books for children and young adults.

4689 Australian Press-Down Under Books
15235 Brand Boulevard
Suite A107
Mission Hills, CA 91345-1423
818-837-3755
Big Books, models for writing, small books and teacher's ideas books from Australia.

4690 Avon Books
1350 Avenue of the Americas
New York, NY 10019-4702
212-481-5600
Fax: 212-532-2172
Focuses on middle grade paperbacks for the classroom and features authors such as Cleary, Avi, Borks, Hous, Reeder, Hobbs, Hahn, Taylor and Prish.

4691 Ballantine/Del Rey/Fawcett/Ivy
201 E 50th Street
New York, NY 10022-7703
212-782-9000
800-638-6460
Fax: 212-782-8438
Offer paperback books for middle school and junior and senior high.

4692 Barron's Educational Series
250 Wireless Boulevard
Hauppauge, NY 11788-3924
631-434-3311
800-645-3476
Fax: 631-434-3217
E-mail: barrons@barronseduc.com
http://www.barronseduc.com
Educational books, including a full line of juvenile fiction and non-fiction, and titles for test prep and guidance, ESL, foreign language, art history and techniques, business, and reference.

Frederick Glasser, Director School/Library Sale

4693 Baylor College of Medicine
One Baylor Plaza
Houston, TX 77030
713-798-4951
Fax: 713-798-6521
http://www.bcm.edu

Offers materials and programs in the scientific area from Texas Scope, Sequence and Coordination projects.

Peter G Traber, President
Robert H Allen, Chairman

4694 Beech Tree Books
1350 Avenue of the Americas
New York, NY 10019-4702
212-261-6500
Fax: 212-261-6518
Curriculum offering reading materials, fiction and nonfiction titles.

4695 Black Butterfly Children's Books
625 Broadway
Floor 10
New York, NY 10012-2611
212-982-3158
A wide variety of books focusing on children, hardcover and paperback.

4696 Blake Books
2222 Beebee Street
San Luis Obispo, CA 93401-5505
805-543-7314
800-727-8550
Fax: 805-543-1150
Photo books on nature, endangered species, habitats, etc. for ages 10 and up.

Paige Torres, President

4697 Bluestocking Press Catalog
Bluestocking Press
PO Box 1014
Placerville, CA 95997-1014
530-622-8586
800-959-8586
Fax: 530-642-9222
E-mail: Jane@bluestockingpress.com
http://www.bluestockingpress.com
Approximately 800 items with a concentration in American History, economics and law. That includes fiction, nonfiction, primary source material, historical documents, facsimile newspapers, historical music, hands-on-kits, audio history, coloring books and more.

Jane A Williams, Coordinating Editor

4698 Boyds Mill Press
815 Church Street
Honesdale, PA 18431-1889
570-253-1164
Fax: 570-253-0179
Publishes books for children from preschool to young adult.

4699 BridgeWater Books
100 Corporate Drive
Mahwah, NJ 07430-2041
Distinctive children's hardcover books featuring award-winning authors and illustrators, including Laurence Yep, Babette Cole, Joseph Bruchac and others. An imprint of Troll Associates.

4700 Bright Ideas Charter School
2507 Central Freeway East
Wichita Falls, TX 76302-5802
940-767-1561
Fax: 940-767-1904
E-mail: lydiaplmr@aol.com
K-12 curriculum framework for educators struggling to move toward a global tomorrow.

Lynda Plummer, President

4701 Brown & Benchmark Publishers
25 Kessel Court
Madison, WI 63711
608-273-0040
College textbooks in language arts and reading.

4702 Bureau for At-Risk Youth Guidance Channel
Guidance Channel
135 Dupont Street
PO Box 760
Plainview, NY 11803-0760
516-349-5520
800-999-6884
Fax: 800-262-1886
E-mail: info@at-risk.com
http://www.at-risk.com
Publisher and distributor of educational curriculums, videos, publications and products for at-risk youth and the counselors and others who work with them. Bureau products focus on areas such as violence and drug prevention, character education, parenting skills and more.

Sally Germain, Editor-in-Chief

4703 Business Publishers
PO Box 17592
Baltimore, MD 21297
301-587-6300
800-274-6737
Fax: 301-585-9075
E-mail: bpinews@bpinews.com
http://www.bpinews.com
Publishes education related materials.

4704 CLEARVUE/eav
6465 N Avondale Avenue
Chicago, IL 60631
773-775-9433
800-253-2788
Fax: 773-775-9855
E-mail: slucas@clearvue.com
http://www.clearvue.com
CLEARVUE/eav offers educators the largest line of curriculum-oriented media in the industry. CLEARVUE/eav programs have, and will continue to enhance students' interest, learning, motivation and skills.

Sarah M Lucas, Communications Coordinator
Kelli Campbell, VP

4705 Calculators
7409 Fremont Avenue S
Minneapolis, MN 55423-3971
800-533-9921
Fax: 612-866-9030
Calculators and calculator books for K thru college level instruction. Calculator products by Texas Instruments, Casio, Sharp and Hewlett-Packard.

Richard Nelson, President

4706 Cambridge University Press
Edinburgh Building
Shaftesbury Road
Cambridge, England CB22RU

http://www.cup.cam.ac.uk
Curriculum materials and textbooks for science education for grades K-12.

4707 Candlewick Press
2067 Massachusetts Avenue
Cambridge, MA 02140-1340
617-661-3330
Fax: 617-661-0565
High quality trade hardcover and paperback books for children and young adults.

4708 Capstone Press
151 Good Counsel Drive
Mankato, MN 56001-3143
952-224-0529
888-262-6135
Fax: 888-262-0705
E-mail: timadsen@capstone-press.com
http://www.capstonepress.com
PreK-12 Nonfiction publisher

Tim Mandsen, Director Marketing

4709 Careers/Consultants in Education Press
3050 Palm Aire Drive N
#310
Pompano Beach, FL 33069
954-974-3511
Fax: 954-974-5477
E-mail: carconed@aol.com
Current education job lists for teacher and administrator positions in schools and colleges. Plus nine differently titled desk/reference paperback books.

Dr. Robert M Bookbinder, President

4710 Carolrhoda Books
A Division of Lerner Publishing Group
241 1st Avenue N
Minneapolis, MN 55401-1607
612-332-3344
800-328-4929
Fax: 612-332-7615
http://www.lernerbooks.com
Fiction and nonfiction for readers K through grade 6. List includes picture books, biographies, nature and science titles, multicultural and introductory geography books, and fiction for beginning readers.

Rebecca Poole, Submissions Editor

4711 Carson-Dellosa Publishing Company
PO Box 35665
Greensboro, NC 27425-5665
336-632-0084
800-321-0943
Fax: 336-632-087
Textbooks, manuals, workbooks and materials aimed at increasing students reading skills.

4712 Center for Play Therapy
University of North Texas
PO Box 311337
Denton, TX 76203
940-565-3864
Fax: 940-565-4461
E-mail: cpt@coefs.coe.unt.edu
http://www.centerforplaytherapy.com
Encourages the unique development and emotional growth of children through the process of play therapy, a dynamic interpersonal relationship between a child and a therapist trained in play therapy procedures. Provides training, research, publications, counseling services and acts as a clearinghouse for literature in the field.

Garry Landreth PhD, Director

4713 Central Regional Educational Laboratory
2550 S Parker Road
Suite 500
Aurora, CO 80014
303-337-0990
Fax: 303-337-3005
E-mail: twaters@mcrel.org
The Regional Educational Laboratories are educational research and development organizations supported by contracts with the US Education Department, Office of Educational Research and Improvement. Specialty area: curriculum, learning and instruction.

Dr. J Timothy Waters, Executive Director

4714 Charles Scribner & Sons
MacMillan Publishing Company
1633 Broadway
New York, NY 10019
212-632-4944
Fax: 800-835-3202
Hardcover trade books for children and young adults.

4715 Chicago Board of Trade
141 W Jackson Boulevard
Chicago, IL 60604-2992
312-435-3500
Educational materials including a new economics program entitled Commodity Challenge.

4716 Children's Book Council
12 West 37th Street
2nd Floor
New York, NY 10018-7480
212-966-1990
800-999-2160
Fax: 212-966-2073
E-mail: staff@cbcbooks.org
http://www.cbcbooks.org
The Children's Book Council, Inc is the nonprofit trade association of publishers and packagers of trade books and related materials for children and young adults.

JoAnn Sabatino-Falkenstein, VP Marketing

4717 Children's Press
Grolier Publishing
90 Sherman Turnpike
Danbury, CT 06816
800-621-1115
Fax: 800-374-4329
http://publishing.grolier.com
Leading supplier of reference and children's nonfiction and fiction books.

4718 Children's Press/Franklin Watts
PO Box 1330
Danbury, CT 06813-1330
203-797-3500
Fax: 203-797-3197
K-12 curriculum materials.

4719 Children's Television Workshop
1 Lincoln Plaza
New York, NY 10023-7129
212-875-6809
Fax: 212-875-7388
Hands-on books for elementary school use in the area of science education.

Brenda Pilson, Review Coordinator
Elaine Israel, Editor-in-Chief

4720 Chime Time
2440-C Pleasantdale Road
Atlanta, GA 30340-1562
770-662-5664
Early childhood products and publications.

4721 Choices Education Project
Watson Institute for International Studies
Brown University
PO Box 1948
Providence, RI 02912-1948
401-863-3155
Fax: 401-863-1247
E-mail: choices@brown.edu
http://www.choices.edu
Develops interactive, supplementary curriculum resources on current and historical international issues. Makes complex current and historic international issues accessible for secondary school students. Materials are low-cost, reproducible, updated annually.

Annually

4722 Close Up Publishing
44 Canal Center Plaza
Alexandria, VA 22314-1592
800-765-3131
Fax: 703-706-3564
Offers textbooks, workbooks and other publications focusing on self-esteem, learning and counseling.

4723 Cognitive Concepts
PO Box 1363
Evanston, IL 60204-1363
888-328-8199
Fax: 847-328-5881
http://www.cogcon.com

Leading provider of language and literacy software, books, internet services and staff development. Specialize in integrating technology with scientific principles and proven instructional methods to offer effective and affordable learning solutions for educators, specialists and families.

4724 College Board
45 Columbus Avenue
New York, NY 10023-6992
212-713-8000
Fax: 212-713-8282
http://www.collegeboard.org
Publishers of books of interest to educational researchers, policymakers, students, counselors, teachers; products to prepare students for college and test prep materials.

4725 Coloring Concepts
1732 Jefferson Street
Suite 7
Napa, CA 94559-1737
707-257-1516
800-257-1516
Fax: 707-253-2019
E-mail: chris@coloringconcepts.com
http://www.coloringconcepts.com
Colorable active learning books for middle school through college that combine scientifically correct text with colorable illustrations to provide an enjoyable and educational experience that helps the user retain more information than during normal reading. Subjects include Anatomy, Marine Biology, Zoology, Botany, Human Evolution, Human Brain, Microbiology and biology.

Christopher Elson, Operations

4726 Comprehensive Health Education Foundation
22419 Pacific Hwy S
Seattle, WA 98198-5106
206-824-2907
800-833-6388
E-mail: info@chef.org
http://www.chef.org
Primarily Health gives K-3 kids a dynamic, hands-on health program while teaching academic skills.

Larry Clark, President
Marvin Hamanishi, Vice President

4727 Computer Learning Foundation
PO Box 60007
Palo Alto, CA 94306-0007
408-720-8898
Fax: 408-730-1191
E-mail: clf@computerlearning.org
http://www.computerlearning.org
Publishes books and videos on using technology.

4728 Computer Literacy Press
Computer Literacy Press
PO Box 562
Earlysville, VA 22936
513-600-3455
513-530-0110
Fax: 800-833-5413
E-mail: info@complitpress.com
http://www.complitpress.com
Instructional materials using hands-on, step-by-step format, appropriate for courses in adult and continuing education, business education, computer literacy and applications, curriculum integration, Internet instruction, and training and staff development. Products are available for ranging from middle school through high school as well as post secondary, teacher training and adult/senior courses.

Robert First

4729 Concepts to Go
PO Box 10043
Berkeley, CA 94709-5043
510-848-3233
Fax: 510-486-1248
Develops and distributes manipulative activities for language arts and visual communications for ages 3-8.

4730 Congressional Quarterly
1414 22nd Street NW
Washington, DC 20037-1003
202-887-8500
Fax: 202-293-1487
Comprehensive publications and reference and paperback books pertaining to Congress, US Government and politics, the presidency, the Supreme Court, national affairs and current issues.

4731 Continental Press
520 E Bainbridge Street
Elizabethtown, PA 17022-2299
717-367-1836
800-233-0759
Fax: 717-367-5660
E-mail: cpeducation@continentalpress.com
http://www.continentalpress.com
Publisher of print for PreK-12 (plus adult education). Programs relate to skill areas in reading, math, comprehension, phonics, etc. Producers of Testlynx Software.

4732 Cottonwood Press
107 Cameron Drive
Suite 398
Fort Collins, CO 80525
970-204-0715
800-864-4297
Fax: 970-204-0761
E-mail: cottonwood@cottonwwodpress.com
http://www.cottonwoodpress.com
Publishes books focusing on teaching language arts and writing, grades 5-12.

Cheryl Thurston

4733 Council for Exceptional Children
The Council for Exceptional Children
2900 Crystal Drive
Suite 1000
Arlington, VA 22202-3557
703-620-3660
888-232-7733
Fax: 703-264-9494
E-mail: service@cec.sped.org
http://www.cec.sped.org
The Council for Exceptional Children is a major publisher of special education literature and produces a catalog semiannually.

Marilyn Friend, President
Bruce Ramirez, Executive Director

4734 Creative Teaching Press
Po Box 2723
Huntington Beach, CA 92647-0723
800-287-8879
Fax: 800-229-9929
E-mail:
customerservice@creativeteaching.com
http://www.creativeteaching.com
Offers language and literature-based books including Teaching Basic Skills through Literature, Literature-Based Homework Activities, I Can Read! I Can Write!, Multicultural Art Activities, Responding to Literature, and Linking Math and Literature.

Jim Connelly, President
Luella Connelly, Co-Founder

4735 Cricket Magazine Group
315 5th Street
Peru, IL 61354-2859
815-223-1500
Magazines of high quality children's literature.

4736 Curriculum Associates
PO Box 2001
North Billerica, MA 01862-0901
978-667-8000
800-225-0248
Fax: 800-366-1158
E-mail: cainfo@curriculumassociates.com
http://www.curriculumassociates.com
Supplementary educational materials; cross-curriculum, language arts, reading, study skills, test preparation, diagnostic assessments, emergent readers, videos, and software.

4737 DC Heath & Company
125 Spring Street
Lexington, MA 02421-7801
781-862-6650
Publishes resources for all academic levels ranging from textbooks, fiction and nonfiction titles to business and college guides.

4738 DLM Teaching Resources
PO Box 4000
Allen, TX 75013-1302
972-248-6300
800-527-4747
Offers a variety of teacher's resources and guides for testing in all areas of education.

4739 Dawn Publications
14618 Tyler Foote Road
Nevada City, CA 95959-9316
530-478-7540
800-545-7475
Fax: 530-478-0112
Specializes in nature, children and health and healing books, tapes and videos and dedicated to helping people experience unity and harmony.

Bob Rinzler, Publisher
Glenn Hoveman, Editor

4740 Delta Education
80 Northwest Blvd.
Nashua, NH 03061-3000
800-258-1302
Fax: 800-282-9560
Science programs, materials and curriculum kits.

4741 Dial Books for Young Readers
345 Hudson Street
New York, NY 10014-3658
212-366-2800
Fax: 212-366-2938
http://www.penguinputnam.com
General hardcover, children's books, from toddler through young adult, fiction and nonfiction.

4742 Didax Educational Resources
PO Box 507
Rowley, MA 01969-0907
978-948-2340
800-458-0024
Fax: 978-948-2813
E-mail: info@didaxinc.com
http://www.didaxinc.com
High quality educational materials featuring Unifix and hundreds of math and reading supplements.

Brian Scarlett, President
Martin Kennedy, VP

4743 Dinah-Might Activities
PO Box 39657
San Antonio, TX 78218-6657
210-698-0123
Fax: 210-698-0095
Learn how to integrate language arts, math, map and globe skills and more into a science curriculum. Books include The Big Book of Books and Activities, Organizing the Integrated Classroom, Write Your Own Thematic Units and Reading and Writing All Day Long.

4744 Dinocardz Company
146 5th Avenue
San Francisco, CA 94118-1310
415-751-5809
Dinosaur curriculums for grades 1-3 and 4-6.

4745 Disney Press
Disney Juvenile Publishing
114 5th Avenue
New York, NY 10011-5604
212-633-4400
Fax: 212-633-5929
Hardcover trade and library editions and paperback books for children, grades K-12.

Liisa-Ann Fink, President

4746 Dominic Press
1949 Kellogg Avenue
Carlsbad, CA 92008-6582
619-481-3838
Offers a range of materials for the Reading Recovery Program and Chapter 1 programs.

4747 Dorling Kindorley Company
95 Madison Avenue
New York, NY 10016
212-213-4800
Fax: 212-689-5254
Science books for all grade levels.

4748 Dover Publications
31 E 2nd Street
Mineola, NY 11501
516-294-7000
Fax: 516-742-6953
Fun and educational storybooks, coloring, activity, cut-and-assemble toy books, science for children.

Clarence Strowbridge, President

4749 Dutton Children's Books
375 Hudson Street
New York, NY 10014-3658
212-366-2000
Fax: 212-366-2948
General hardcover children's books from toddler through young adult, fiction and nonfiction.

4750 DynEd International
1350 Bayshore Highway
Suite 850
Burlingame, CA 94010
800-765-4375
Fax: 650-375-7017
http://www.dyned.com
Pre-K-adult listening and speaking skill development English language acquisition software.

Steven Kearney, Sales
Sue Young, Operations

4751 ETA - Math Catalog
620 Lakeview Parkway
Vernon Hills, IL 60061-1828
847-816-5050
800-445-5985
Fax: 847-816-5066
E-mail: info@etauniverse.com
http://www.etauniverse.com
Offers a full line of mathematics products, materials, books, textbooks and workbooks for grades K-12.

Mary Cooney, Product Development Manager
Monica Butler, Director Marketing

4752 ETR Associates
4 Carbonero Way
Scotts Valley, CA 95066
831-438-4060
800-321-4407
Fax: 800-435-8433
http://www.etr.org

ETR Associate's mission is to enhance the well-being of individuals, families and communities by providing leadership, educational resources, training and research in health promotion with an emphasis on sexuality and health education.

Robert Keet, President
Arnold W. Kriegel, Vice President

4753 EVAN-Motor Corporation
18 Lower Ragsdale Drive
Monterey, CA 93940-5728
831-649-5901
Fax: 800-777-4332
Resource materials for K-6 science educational programs.

4754 Early Start-Fun Learning
PO Box 350187
Jacksonville, FL 32235-0187
904-641-6138
Preschool materials for the educator.

4755 Earth Foundation
5151 Mitchelldale
B11
Houston, TX 77092-7200
713-686-9453
Fax: 713-686-6561
Join the largest active network of educators working to save endangered ecosystems and their species! Multi-disciplinary, hands-on curriculum and videos for the classroom.

Cynthia Everage, President

4756 Editorial Projects in Education
6935 Arlington Road
Suite 100
Bethesda, MD 20814-5233
301-280-3100
800-346-1834
Fax: 301-280-3250
E-mail: customercare@epe.org
http://www2.edweek.org
Publishes various newsletters and publications in the fields of history and education.

Christopher B Swanson, Director
Carole Vinograd Bausell, Assistant Director

4757 Edmark
Riverdeep Inc.
100 Pine Street
Suite 1900
San Francisco, CA 94111
415-659-2000
888-242-6747
Fax: 415-659-2020
E-mail: info@riverdeep.net
http://www.edmark.com
Develops innovative and effective educational materials for children.

Barry O'Callaghan, Chairman
Tony Mulderry, Executive Vice President

4758 Education Center
3515 W Market Street
Greensboro, NC 27403-1309
336-273-9409
Publishers of the Mailbox, teacher's helper magazines, learning centers clubs, classroom beautiful bulletin board clubs, the storybook club and more.

4759 Educational Marketer
SIMBA Information
11 Riverbend Drive
PO Box 4234
Stamford, CT 06907-0234
800-307-2529
Fax: 203-358-5824
Contains a range of print and electronic tools, including software and multimedia materials for educational institutions.

4760 Educational Press Association of America
Glassboro State College
Glassboro, NJ 08028
609-445-7349
Offers various publications and bibliographic data focusing on all aspects of education.

4761 Educational Productions
9000 SW Gemini Drive
Beaverton, OR 97008
503-644-7000
800-950-4949
Fax: 503-350-7000
E-mail: custserv@edpro.com
http://www.edpro.com
Video training programs that help increase parenting skills and help every teacher meet performance standards. Offers training on preventing discipline problems, increasing parenting skills, supporting literacy efforts and more.

4762 Educational Teaching Aids
620 Lakeview Pkwy
Vernon Hills, IL 60061-1838
847-816-5050
800-445-5985
Fax: 847-816-5066
E-mail: info@etauniverse.com
http://www.etauniverse.com
Manipulatives to enhance understanding of basic concepts and to help bridge the gap between the concrete and the abstract.

4763 Educators Progress Service
214 Center Street
Randolph, WI 53956
920-326-3127
888-951-4469
Fax: 920-326-3126
http://www.freeteachingaids.com
A complete spectrum of curriculum and mixed media resources for allgrade levels.

4764 Educators Publishing Service
31 Smith Place
Cambridge, MA 02138-1089
617-547-6706
800-225-5750
Fax: 617-547-0412
http://www.epsbooks.com
Supplementary workbooks and teaching materials in reading, spelling, vocabulary, comprehension, and elementary math, as well as materials for assessment and learning differences.

4765 Edumate-Educational Materials
2231 Morena Boulevard
San Diego, CA 92110-4134
619-275-7117
Multicultural and multilingual materials in the form of toys, puzzles, books, videos, music, visuals, games, dolls and teacher resources. Special emphasis on Spanish and other languages. Literature offered from North and South America.

Gustavo Blankenburg, President

4766 Ellis
406 W 10600 S
Suite 610
Salt Lake City, UT 84003
801-374-3424
888-756-1570
Fax: 801-374-3495
http://www.ellis.com
Publish software that teaches English.

4767 Encyclopaedia Britannica
333 N La Salle Street
Chicago, IL 60610
312-347-7159
800-323-1229
Fax: 312-294-2104
http://www.britannica.com

279

Books and related educational materials.

4768 Energy Learning Center
USCEA
1776 I Street NW
Suite 400
Washington, DC 20006-3700
703-741-5000
Fax: 703-741-6000
Energy learning materials.

4769 Essential Learning Products
PO Box 2590
Columbus, OH 43216-2590
800-357-3570
Fax: 614-487-2272
Publishers of phonics workbooks.

4770 Ethnic Arts & Facts
PO Box 20550
Oakland, CA 94620-0550
510-465-0451
888-278-5652
Fax: 510-465-7488
E-mail: eaf@ethnicartsnfacts.com
http://www.ethnicartsnfacts.com
Kit titles include: Traditional Africa, Urban Africa, China, Guatemala, Peru, Huichol Indians of Mexico, Chinese Shadow Puppet Kit. African-American Music History Mini-Kit. Artifact kits/resource booklets designed to enhance appreciation of cultural diversity, improve geographic literacy and sharpen critical thinking and writing skills.

Susan Drexler, Curriculum Specialist

4771 Evan-Moor Corporation
18 Lower Ragsdale Drive
Monterey, CA 93940-5728
How to Make Books with Children and other fine teacher resources and reproducible materials for all curriculum areas grades PreK-6.

4772 Everyday Learning Corporation
PO Box 812960
Chicago, IL 60681-2960
800-382-7670
Fax: 312-233-7860
University of Chicago school mathematics project. Everyday Mathematics enriched curriculum for grades K-6.

4773 Exploratorium
3601 Lyon Street
San Francisco, CA 94123-1099
415-563-7337
Fax: 415-561-0307
http://www.exploratorium.edu
Exploratorium is dedicated to the formal and informal teaching of science using innovative interactive methods of inquiry. It publishes materials for educators and provides professional development opportunities both in print and online.

Quarterly/Monthly

4774 Extra Editions K-6 Math Supplements
PO Box 38
Urbana, IL 61803-0038
Fax: 614-794-0107
Special needs math supplements offering 70 single-topic units from K-6 that reach students your basic math program misses. Extra Editions newspaper-like format uses animation with a hands-on approach to show real life necessity for computational skills, time, money, problem solving, critical thinking, etc. Ideal for Chapter One, Peer-Tutoring, Parental Involvement, Home Use, and more.

Craig Rucker, General Manager
Earl Ockenga, Author/Owner

4775 F(G) Scholar
Future Graph
538 Street Road
Suite 200
Southhampton, PA 18966-3780
215-396-0721
Fax: 215-396-0724
A revolutionary program for teaching, learning and using math. This single program allows students and teachers easy answers to Algebra, Trigonometry, Pre-Calculus, Calculus, Statistics, Probability and more. It combines all of the power of a graphing calculator, spreadsheet, drawing tools, mathematics and programming/scripting language and much more, and makes it simple and fun to use.

4776 Facts on File
11 Penn Plaza
New York, NY 10001
212-967-8800
800-322-8755
Fax: 212-967-9196
E-mail: llikoff@factsonfile.com
http://www.factsonfile.com
Reference books for teacher education, software, hardware and educational computer systems.

9 Hardcover Books

Laurie Likoff, Editorial Director

4777 Farrar, Straus & Giroux
19 Union Square W
New York, NY 10003-3304
212-741-6900
Fax: 212-633-9385
Children's, young adult and adult trade books in hardcover and paperback, including Sunburst Books, Aerial Miraso/libros juveniles and Hill and Wang.

4778 First Years
1 Kiddie Drive
Avon, MA 02322-1171
508-588-1220
Early childhood books, hardcover and paperback.

4779 Forbes Custom Publishing
60 5th Avenue
New York, NY 10011-8802
513-229-1000
800-355-9983
Fax: 800-451-3661
E-mail: fcpinfo@forbes.com
http://www.forbescp.com
Offers educators and teachers the opportunity to select unique teaching material to create a book designed specifically for their courses.

4780 Formac Distributing
5502 Atlantic Street
Halifax, NS E3HIG-4
902-421-7022
800-565-1905
Fax: 902-425-0166
Contemporary and historical fiction for ages 6-15. Multicultural themes featuring Degrassi Y/A series; first novel chapter books.

4781 Frank Schaffer Publications
3195 Wilson Drive NW
Grand Rapids, MI 49534
800-417-3261
Fax: 888-203-9361
E-mail: cpg_custserve@schoolspecialty.com
http://www.frankschaffer.com
Best-selling supplemental materials including charts, literature notes, resource materials and more.

4782 Franklin Watts
Grolier Publishing
Sherman Turnpike
Danbury, CT 06816
800-621-1115
800-843-3749
Fax: 800-374-4329
Publisher of library bound books, paperback and Big Books for literature based, multicultural classrooms and school libraries.

4783 Free Spirit Publishing
217 Fifth Avenue North
Suite 200
Minneapolis, MN 55401-1299
612-338-2068
800-736-7323
Fax: 612-337-5050
Free Spirit is the leading publisher of learning tools that support young people's social and emotional health.

4784 Frog Publications
PO Box 280996
Tampa, FL 33682
813-935-5845
Fax: 813-935-3764
http://www.frog.com
An organized system of cooperative games for K-5 reading, language arts, thinking skills, math, social studies, Spanish and multicultural studies. Parental Involvement Program, Learning Centers, Test Preperation, Afterschool Program Materials. Drops in the Bucket daily practice books.

4785 Gareth Stevens
330 W Olive Street
Suite 100
Milwaukee, WI 53212
414-332-3520
800-542-2595
Fax: 414-336-0156
E-mail: info@gsinc.com
http://garethstevens.com
Complete display of supplemental children's reading material for grades K-6, including our New World Almanac Library imprint grades 6-12.

Bi-Annually
ISSN: 0-8368

Mark Sachner, Author
Juanita Jones, Marketing Manager
Jonathan Strickland, National Sales Manager

4786 Glencoe/Div. of Macmillan/McGraw Hill
936 Eastwind Drive
Westerville, OH 43081-3329
708-615-3360
800-442-9685
Fax: 972-228-1982
Secondary science programs.

4787 Goethe House New York
1014 5th Avenue
New York, NY 10028-0104
Teaching materials on Germany for the social studies classroom in elementary, middle and high schools.

4788 Goodheart-Willcox Publisher
18604 W Creek Drive
Tinley Park, IL 60477-6243
800-323-0440
Fax: 888-409-3900
E-mail: custerv@goodheartwillcox.com
http://www.goodheartwillcox.com
Comprehensive text designed to help young students learn about themselves, others, and the environment. Readers will develop skills in clothing, food, decision making, and life management. Case studies throughout allow students to apply learning to real-life situations.

4789 Greenhaven Press
PO Box 9187
Farmington Hills, MI 48333-9187

800-231-5163
800-231-5163
Fax: 248-699-8035
E-mail: info@greenhaven.com
Publishers of the Opposing Viewpoints Series, presenting viewpoints in an objective, pro/con format on some of today's controversial subjects.

4790 Greenwillow Books
1350 Avenue of the Americas
New York, NY 10019-4702
212-261-6500
Fax: 212-261-6518
Offers publications for all reading levels.

4791 Grey House Publishing
4419 Route 22
Amenia, NY 12501
518-789-8700
800-562-2139
Fax: 518-789-0545
E-mail: books@greyhouse.com
http://www.greyhouse.com
Publisher of educational reference directories, and encyclopedias.

Richard Gottlieb, President
Leslie Mackenzie, Publisher

4792 Grolier Publishing
90 Sherman Turnpike
Danbury, CT 06816
203-797-3500
800-621-1115
Fax: 203-797-3197
http://www.publishing.grolier.com
Publisher of library bound and paperback books in the areas of social studies, science, reference, history, and biographies for schools and libraries for grades K-12.

4793 Gryphon House
Gryphon House
PO Box 275
Mount Rainier, MD 20712-0275
301-779-6200
Fax: 301-595-0051
E-mail: info@ghbooks.com
http://www.ghbooks.com
Resource and activity books for early childhood teachers and directors.

Cathy Callootte, Marketing Director

4794 Hands-On Prints
PO Box 5899-268
Berkeley, CA 94705
510-601-6279
Fax: 510-601-6278
Specializes in cultural and language materials for children with an emphasis on internationalism and multiculturalism.

Christina Cheung, President

4795 Hardcourt Religion Publishers
6277 Sea Harbor Drive
Orlando, FL 32887
563-557-3700
800-922-7696
Fax: 563-557-3719
E-mail: hardcourtreligion.com
Publishers of religion education materials for schools and parishes.

4796 Hazelden Educational Materials
PO Box 176
Center City, MN 55012-0176
651-257-4010
Fax: 651-213-4590
Educational publisher of materials supporting both students and faculty in areas of substance abuse and related topics.

4797 Heinemann
361 Hanover Street
Portsmouth, NH 03801-3959

603-431-7894
Fax: 203-750-9790
Holistic/student-centered publications, videotapes and workshops for parents, teachers and administrators.

4798 Henry Holt & Company
175 Fifth Avenue
New York, NY 10010
646-307-5095
800-628-9658
Fax: 212-633-0748
Books and materials for classroom teachers, grades 6-adult, including programs on science literacy.

4799 Henry Holt Books for Young Readers
115 W 18th Street
New York, NY 10011-4113
800-628-9658
Fax: 212-647-0490
Hardcover and paperback trade books for preschool through young adult, fiction and nonfiction. Also, big books and promotional materials are available.

4800 High Touch Learning
PO Box 754
Houston, MN 55943-0754
507-896-3500
800-255-0645
Fax: 507-896-3243
Classroom interactive learning maps promoting the hands-on approach to the teaching of social studies.

4801 High/Scope Educational Research Foundation
600 N River Street
Ypsilanti, MI 48198-2821
734-485-2000
800-40 -RESS
Fax: 734-485-4467
Early childhood, elementary, movement and music, and adolescent materials. Over 300 titles of books, videos, cassettes and CDs from which to choose. Research and training materials as well as curriculum and development materials are based on the acclaimed High/Scope active learning approach.

Emily Koepp, President

4802 Holiday House
425 Madison Avenue
New York, NY 10017-1110
212-688-0085
Fax: 212-688-0395
Hardcover and paperback children's books. General fiction and nonfiction, preschool through high school.

4803 Hoover's
5800 Airport
Dallas, TX 78752-3812
512-374-4500
Fax: 512-374-4501
Everything educational, for the early childhood and K-12 market. As a partner for over 100 years, the company is eager to extend their commitment to produce quality, timely shipping and customer service to the public. Offer over 10,000 products for infants, toddlers, pre-school and school age educational needs.

4804 Horn Book Guide
Horn Book
56 Roland Street
Suite 200
Boston, MA 02129
617-628-0225
800-325-1170
Fax: 617-628-0882
E-mail: info@hbook.com
http://http://www.hbook.com
The most comprehensive review source of children's and young adult books available.

Published each spring and fall, the Guide contains concise, critical reviews of almost every hardcover trade children's and young adult book published in the United States - nearly 2,000 books each issue.
BiAnnually
ISSN: 1044-405X

Anne Quirk, Marketing Manager
Roger Sutton, Editor

4805 Houghton Mifflin Books for Children
222 Berkeley Street
Boston, MA 02116-3748
617-351-5000
800-225-3362
Fax: 617-351-1111
http://www.hmco.com
Wide variety of children's and young adult books, fiction and nonfiction.

4806 Houghton Mifflin Company: School Division
222 Berkeley Street
Boston, MA 02116-3748
617-351-5000
Fax: 617-651-1106
Children's literature; K-12 reading and language arts print and software programs; and testing and evaluation for K-12.

4807 Hyperion Books for Children
114 5th Avenue
New York, NY 10011-5604
212-633-4400
Fax: 212-633-5929
Children's books in paperback and hardcover editions.

4808 ITP South-Western Publishing Company
5101 Madison Road
Cincinnati, OH 45227-1427
800-824-5179
Fax: 800-487-8488
Innovative instructional materials for teaching integrated science.

4809 Idea Factory
10710 Dixon Drive
Riverview, FL 33569-7406
813-677-6727
Teacher resource books, science project ideas, materials and more for elementary and middle school teachers.

4810 Institute for Chemical Education
University of Wisconsin
1101 University Avenue
Madison, WI 53706-1322
608-262-3033
800-991-5534
Fax: 608-265-8094
E-mail: ice@chem.wisc.edu
http://ice.chem.wisc.edu
Hands-on activities, publications, kits and videos.

4811 Institute for Educational Leadership
1001 Connecticut Avenue NW
Suite 310
Washington, DC 20036-5541
202-822-8405
Fax: 202-872-4050
The Institute's list of publications on educational trends and policies is available to the public.

Michael C Usdan, President

4812 IntelliTools
1720 Corporate Circle
Petaluma, CA 94954
707-773-2000
800-899-6687
Fax: 707-773-2001
http://www.intellitools.com

Provider of hardware and software giving students with special needs comprehensive access to learning.

4813 Intellimation
130 Cremona Drive
Santa Barbara, CA 93117-5599
805-968-2291
800-346-8355
Fax: 805-968-8899
Educational materials in all areas of curriculum for early learning through college level. Over 400 titles are available in video, and software and multimedia exclusively for the Macintosh. Free catalogs avaiable.

Karin Fisher, Marketing Associate
Marlene Carlyle, Marketing Supervisor

4814 Intercultural Press
100 City Hall Plaza
Suite 501
Boston, MA 02108
617-523-3801
888-273-2539
Fax: 617-523-3708
E-mail: books@interculturalpress.com
http://www.interculturalpress.com
Publishes over 100 titles.

Judy Carl-Hendrick, Managing Editor

4815 J Weston Walch, Publisher
PO Box 658
Portland, ME 04104-0658
207-772-2846
800-558-2846
Fax: 207-772-3105
http://www.walch.com
Walch Publishing is an independent, family-owned publisher of educational supplemental materials for grades 3 through 12 and adult makets.

4816 Jacaranda Designs
3000 Jefferson Street
Boulder, CO 80304-2638
707-374-2543
Fax: 707-374-2543
Authentic African children's books from Kenya, including modern concept stories for K-3 in bilingual editions, folktales, and traditional cultural stories for older readers. All books are written and illustrated by African Kenyans.

Carrie Jenkins Williams, President

4817 Jarrett Publishing Company
PO Box 1460
Ronkonkoma, NY 11779
631-981-4248
Fax: 631-588-4722
Offers a wide range of books for today's educational needs.

4818 JayJo Books
Guidance Channel
135 Dupont Street
PO Box 760
Plainview, NY 11803
516-349-5520
800-999-6884
Fax: 516-349-5521
E-mail: jayjobooks@guidancechannel.com
http://www.jayjo.com
Publisher of books to help teachers, parents and children cope with chronic illnesses, special needs and health education in classroom, family and social settings.

Sally Germain, Editor-in-Chief

4819 John Wiley & Sons
111 River Street
Hoboken, NJ 07030-5774
201-748-6000
Fax: 201-748-6088

Publish science and nature books for children and adults.

4820 Jossey-Bass: An Imprint of Wiley
Jossey-Bass/Pfeiffer
989 Market Street
San Francisco, CA 94103-1741
415-433-1740
Fax: 415-433-0499
http://www.josseybass.com
Creating educational incentives that work.

Adrianne Biggs, Publicity/Manager
Jennifer A O'Day, Editor

4821 Junior Achievement
1 Education Way
Colorado Springs, CO 80906-4477
719-540-8000
Fax: 719-540-6127
Provides business and economics-related materials and programs to students in grades K-12. All programs feature volunteers from the local business community. Materials are free, but available only from local Junior Achievement offices.

4822 Kaeden Corporation
PO Box 16190
19915 Lake Road
Rocky River, OH 44116
440-356-0030
800-890-7323
Fax: 440-356-5081
E-mail: lcowan@kaedeen.com
http://www.kaeden.com
Books for emergent readers at the K, 1 and 2 levels, ideal for Title 1 and Reading Recovery and other at-risk reading programs.

Laura Cowan, Sales Manager
Joan Hoyer, Office Manager

4823 Kane/Miller Book Publishers
PO Boxn 8515
La Jolla, CA 92038-0529
858-456-0540
Fax: 858-456-9641
E-mail: info@kanemiller.com
http://www.kanemiller.com
English translation of foreign children's picture books. Distributors of Spanish language children's books.

Byron Parnell, Sales Manager
Kira Lynn, President

4824 Keep America Beautiful
1010 Washington Boulevard
Stamford, CT 06901
203-323-8987
Fax: 203-325-9199
E-mail: info@kab.org
http://www.kab.org
K-12 curriculum specializing in litter prevention and environmental education. Education posters with lesson plans printed right on the back of each poster and school recycling guides.

4825 Kendall-Hunt Publishing Company
4050 Westmark Drive
Dubuque, IA 52002-2624
319-589-1000
800-228-0810
Fax: 800-772-9165
E-mail: webmaster@kendallhunt.com
http://www.kendallhunt.com
A leading custom publisher in the United States with over 6,000 titles in print. Kendall/Hunt publishes educational materials for kindergarten through college to continuing education creditation and distance learning courses.

Karen Berger, Customer Service Assistant

4826 Knowledge Adventure
2377 Crenshaw Blvd
Suite 302
Torrance, CA 90501
310-533-3400
Fax: 310-533-3700
E-mail: editorial@education.com
http://www.knowledgeadventure.com
Develops, publishes, and distributes best-selling multimedia educational software for use in both homes and schools.

4827 Knowledge Unlimited
PO Box 52
Madison, WI 53701-0052
800-356-2303
Fax: 608-831-1570
http://www.newscurrents.com
NewsCurrents, the most effective current events programs for grades 3-12. Now available on DVD or Online.

4828 Kraus International Publications
358 Saw Mill River Road
Millwood, NY 10546-1035
914-762-2200
800-223-8323
Fax: 914-762-1195
Offers teacher resource notebooks with complete resource information for teachers and administrators at all levels. Great for program planning, quick reference, inservice training. Also offers books on early childhood education, English/language arts, mathematics, science, health education and visual arts.

Barry Katzen, President

4829 Lake Education
AGS/Lake Publishing Company
500 Harbor Boulevard
Belmont, CA 94002-4075
650-592-1606
800-328-2560
Fax: 800-471-8457
Alternative learning materials for underachieving students grades 6-12, RSL and adult basic education. High interest, low readability fiction, adapted classic literature, lifeskills and curriculum materials to supplement and support many basal programs.

Phil Schlenter
Carol Hegarty, VP Editorial

4830 Landmark Editions
PO Box 270169
Kansas City, MO 64127-0169
816-241-4919
Books written and illustrated by children.

4831 Langenseheidt Publishing
515 Valley Street
Maplewood, NJ 07040-1337
800-526-4953
Fax: 908-206-1104
E-mail: edusales@hammond.com
http://www.hammondmap.com
World maps, atlases, general reference guides and CD-Roms.

4832 Lawrence Hall of Science
University of California
Berkeley, CA 94720
510-642-5132
Fax: 510-642-1055
E-mail: lhsinfo@uclink.berkeley.edu
http://www.lawrencehallofscience.org
Offers programs and materials in the field of science and math education for teachers, families and interested citizens. Exhibits include Equals, Family Math, CePUP and FOSS.

Linda Schneider, Marketing Manager
Mike Salter, Marketing/PR Associate

4833 Leap Frog Learning Materials
6401
Suite 100
Emeryville, CA 94608-1071
510-596-3333
800-701-5327
Learning materials, books, posters, games and toys for children.

4834 Learning Connection
19 Devane Street
Frostproof, FL 33843-2017
863-635-5610
800-338-2282
Fax: 863-635-4676
Thematic, literature-based units with award-winning books, media and hands-on for PK-12 including parent involvement, early childhood, bilingual, literacy, math, writing, science and multicultural.

4835 Learning Disabilities Association of America
Learning Disabilities Association of America
4156 Library Road
Pittsburgh, PA 15234-1349
412-341-1515
888-300-6710
Fax: 412-344-0224
E-mail: info@ldaamerica.org
http://www.ldaamerica.org
Has 50 state affiliates with more than 300 local chapters. The national office has a resource center of over 500 publications for sale.

4836 Learning Links
2300 Marcus Avenue
New Hyde Park, NY 11042-1083
516-437-9075
800-724-2616
Fax: 516-437-5392
E-mail: learningLx@aol.com
http://www.learinglinks.com
All you need for literature based instruction; Noveltie, study guides, thematic units books and more.

4837 Lee & Low Books
95 Madison Avenue
Suite 606
New York, NY 10016-3303
212-779-4400
Fax: 212-683-1894
E-mail: info@leeandlow.com
http://www.leeandlow.com
A multicultural children's book publisher. Our primary focus is on picture books, especially stories set in contemporary America. Spanish language titles are available.

Craig Low, VP Publisher
Louise May, Executive Editor

4838 Leo A Myer Associates/LAMA Books
20956 Corsair Boulevard
Hayward, CA 94545-1002
510-785-1091
Fax: 510-785-1099
E-mail: lama@lmabooks.com
Writers and publishers of HVAC books.

Barbara Ragura, Marketing Assistant

4839 Lerner Publishing Group
A Division Lerner Publications Group
241 1st Avenue N
Minneapolis, MN 55401-1607
612-332-3344
800-328-4929
Fax: 612-332-7615
http://www.lernerbooks.com
Primarily nonfiction for readers of all grade levels. List includes titles encompassing nature, geography, natural and physical science, current events, ancient and modern history, world art, special interests, sports, world cultures, and numerous biography series. Some young adult and middle grade fiction.

Jennifer Martin, Submissions Editor

4840 Linden Tree Children's Records & Books
170 State Street
Los Altos Hills, CA 94022-2863
650-949-3390
Fax: 650-949-0346
Offers a wide variety of books, audio cassettes and records for children.

4841 Listening Library
One Park Avenue
Old Greenwich, CT 06870-1727
203-637-3616
800-243-4504
Fax: 800-454-0606
E-mail: moreinfo@listeninglib.com
http://www.listeninglib.com
A producer of quality unabridged audiobooks for listeners of all ages. Specializing in children's literature and adult classics.

BiAnnually

Annette Imperati, Director Sales/Marketing

4842 Little, Brown & Company
3 Center Plaza
Boston, MA 02108-2084
617-227-0730
Fax: 617-263-2854
Trade books for children and young adults, hardcover and paper, including Sierra Club Books for Children.

4843 Lodestar Books
375 Hudson Street
New York, NY 10014-3658
212-366-2000
General hardcover children's books from toddler through young adult, fiction and nonfiction.

4844 Lothrop, Lee & Shepard Books
1350 Avenue of the Americas
New York, NY 10019-4702
212-261-6500
Fax: 212-261-6518
Children's books.

4845 Lynne Rienner Publishing
1800 30th Street
Suite 314
Boulder, CO 80301
303-333-3003
800-803-8488
Fax: 303-333-4037
E-mail: karen-hemmes@mindspring.com
http://www.fireflybooks.com
Publishes academic-level books with a focus on international and domestic social sciences.

Karen Hemmes, Publicist
Mary Kay Opicka, Publicist

4846 MHS
PO Box 950
North Tonawanda, NY 14120-0950
416-492-2627
800-456-3003
Fax: 416-492-3343
E-mail: customer_service@mhs.com
http://www.mhs.com
Publishers and distributors of professional assessment materials.

Steven J Stein, PhD, President

4847 MacMillan Children's Books
1633 Broadway
New York, NY 10019
212-512-2000
Fax: 800-835-3202
Hardcover trade books for children and young adults.

4848 MacMillan Reference
1633 Broadway
New York, NY 10019
212-512-2000
Fax: 800-835-3202
A wide variety of titles for students and teachers of all grade levels.

4849 Macmillan/McGraw-Hill School Division
1633 Broadwaty
New York, NY 10019
212-654-8500
800-442-9685
Fax: 800-835-3202
Quality literature for the student and excellent support for the teacher. Programs and educational materials for all grade levels.

4850 Macro Press
18242 Peters Court
Fountain Valley, CA 92708-5873
310-823-9556
Fax: 310-306-2296
Includes resources to conduct thematic hands-on science lessons and integrated curriculum; and, student materials offering a Scientist's Notebook and reading materials to integrate hands-on (grade specific) scientific thinking, problem solving and documenting skills to benefit all students. Nine award-winning K-6 teachers (200+ years combined experience) joined together to address the real needs of today's high student load.

Leigh Hoven Swenson, President

4851 Magna Publications
2718 Dryden Drive
Madison, WI 53704
608-227-8109
800-206-4805
Fax: 608-246-3597
E-mail: carriej@magnapubs.com
http://www.magnapubs.com
Produces eight subscriptions newsletters in the field of higher education.

Carrie Jenson, Conference Manager
David Burns, Associate Publisher

4852 Major Educational Resources Corporation
10153 York Road
Suite 107
Hunt Valley, MD 21030-3340
800-989-5353
Multimedia curriculum tools for educators.

4853 Margaret K McElderry Books
1633 Broadway
New York, NY 10019
212-512-2000
Fax: 800-835-3202
Hardcover trade books for children and young adults.

4854 Mari
3215 Pico Boulevard
Santa Monica, CA 90405-4603
310-829-2212
800-955-9494
Fax: 310-829-2317
http://www.mariinc.com
The best literature learning materials for K-12. Offers Mini-Units for writing and critical thinking skills, Literature Extenders that extend literature across the curriculum and Basic Skills Through Literature that combine literature and skill work.

4855 MasterTeacher
Leadership Lane
PO Box 1207
Manhattan, KS 66505-1207
800-669-9633
Fax: 800-669-1132
http://www.masterteacher.com

283

A publisher of videotapes for the professional. Offers programs on inclusion, tests and testing, student motivation, discipline and more.

4856 MathSoft
101 Main Street
Cambridge, MA 02142
617-577-1017
800-628-4223
Fax: 617-577-8829
http://www.mathsoft.com
Provider of math, science and engineering software for business, academia, research and government.

4857 McCracken Educational Services
PO Box 3588
Blaine, WA 98231
360-332-1881
800-447-1462
Fax: 360-332-7332
E-mail: mes@mccrackened.com
http://www.mccrackened.com
Materials for beginning reading, writing and spelling. Big Books, manipulative materials, teacher resource books, spelling through phonics, posters and both audio and video tapes.

Robert & Marlene McCracken, Author

4858 McGraw Hill Children's Publishing
PO Box 1650
Grand Rapids, MI 49501-1650
616-363-1290
Fax: 800-543-2690
New self-esteem literature based reading and multicultural literature based reading.

4859 Mel Bay Publications
4 Industrial Drive
PO Box 66
Pacific, MO 63069-0066
637-257-3970
800-863-5229
Fax: 636-257-5062
E-mail: email@melbay.com
http://www.melbay.com
Music supply distributors.

Sheri Stephens, Customer Service Supervisor

4860 Merriam-Webster
47 Federal Street
#281
Springfield, MA 01105-3805
413-734-3134
Fax: 413-734-0257
A wide variety of titles for students and teachers of all grade levels.

4861 Millbrook Press
1251 Washington Avenue N
Minneapolis, MN 55401
203-740-2220
800-328-4929
Fax: 800-332-1132
http://www.millbrookpress.com
Exceptional nonfiction juvenile and young adult books for schools and public libraries.

4862 Milton Roy Company
820 Linden Avenue
Rochester, NY 14625-2710
716-248-4000
Teacher support materials, scientific kits and manuals.

4863 Mimosa Publications
90 New Montgomery Street
San Francisco, CA 94105-4501
415-982-5350
A language based K-3 math program featuring big books, language and activity based math topics and multicultural math activities.

4864 Model Technologies
2420 Van Layden Way
Modesto, CA 95356-2454
209-575-3445
Curriculum guides and scientific instruction kits.

4865 Mondo Publishing
980 Avenue Of The Americas
New York, NY 10018
Fax: 888-532-4492
E-mail: mondopub@aol.com
http://www.mondopub.com
Offers multicultural big books and music cassettes: Folk Tales from Around the World series; Exploring Habitats series; and, Let's Write and Sing a Song, whole language activities through music.

4866 Morning Glory Press
6595 San Haroldo Way
Buena Park, CA 90620-3748
714-828-1998
888-612-8254
Fax: 714-828-2049
E-mail: info@morningglorypress.com
http://www.morningglorypress.com
Publishes books and materials for teenage parents.

Quarterly

Jeanne Lindsay, President
Carole Blum, Promotion Director

4867 Music for Little People
PO Box 1460
Redway, CA 95560-1460
707-923-3991
Fax: 707-923-3241
Science and environmental education materials set to music for younger students.

4868 N&N Publishing Company
18 Montgomery Street
Middletown, NY 10940-5116
Low-cost texts and workbooks.

4869 NASP Publications
National Association of School Psychologists
4340 EW Highway
Suite 402
Bethesda, MD 20814
301-657-0270
Fax: 301-657-0275
E-mail: center@naspweb.org
http://www.naspionline.org
Over 100 hard-to-find books and videos centering on counseling, psychology and guidance for students.

Betty Somerville, President

4870 NCTM Educational Materials
National Council of Teachers of Mathematics
1906 Association Drive
Reston, VA 20191-1502
703-620-9840
Fax: 703-476-2970
E-mail: nctm@nctm.org
http://www.nctm.org
Publications, videotapes, software, posters and information to improve the teaching and learning of mathematics.

Harry B Tunis, Publications Director
Cynthia C Rosso, Director Marketing Services

4871 NYSTROM
3333 N Elston Avenue
Chicago, IL 60618-5898
773-463-1144
800-621-8086
Fax: 773-463-0515
Maps, globes, hands-on geography and history materials.

4872 Narrative Press
PO Box 145
Crabtree, OR 97335
800-315-9005
Fax: 541-259-2154
E-mail: service@narrativepress.com
http://www.narrativepress.com
Publisher of first person narratives of adventure and exploration.

Vickie Zimmer, Editor

4873 National Aeronautics & Space Administration
NASA Headquarters
300 E Street SW
Washington, DC 20546
202-358-0000
Fax: 202-358-3251
Over 10 different divisions offering a wide variety of classroom and educational materials in the areas of science, physics, aeronautics and more.

4874 National Center for Science Teaching & Learning/Eisenhower Clearinghouse
1929 Kenny Road
Columbus, OH 43210-1015
Collects and creates the most up-to-date listing of science and mathematics curriculum materials in the nation.

4875 National Council for the Social Studies
8555 Sixteenth Street
Suite 500
Silver Spring, MD 20910
301-588-1800
800-683-0812
Fax: 301-588-2049
E-mail: sgriffin@ncss.org
http://www.ncss.org
Publishes books, videotapes and journals in the area of social education and social studies.

4876 National Council of Teachers of English
1111 W Kenyon Road
Urbana, IL 61801-1096
217-328-3870
800-369-6283
Fax: 217-328-9645
E-mail: public_info@ncte.org
http://www.ncte.org
Devoted to the advancement of English language and literature studies at all levels of education. Publishes 12 periodicals, a member newspaper, and 20-25 books a year, and holds conventions and workshops.

Lori Bianchini, Public Affairs

4877 National Council on Economic Education
1140 Avenue of the Americas
New York, NY 10036-5803
212-730-7007
Offers various programs including their latest, US History: Eyes on the Economy, a council program for secondary education teachers.

4878 National Geographic School Publishing
1145 17th Street NW
Washington, DC 20036
800-368-2728
Fax: 515-362-3366
Books, magazines, videos, and software in the areas of science, geography and social studies.

4879 National Geographic Society
PO Box 10041
Des Moines, IA 50340-0597
800-548-9797
Fax: 301-921-1575
http://www.nationalgeographic.com

Science materials, videos, CD-ROM's and telecommunications program.

4880 National Head Start Association
1651 Prince Street
Alexandria, VA 22314-2818
703-739-0875
Fax: 703-739-0878
http://www.nhsa.org
Dedicated to promoting and protecting the Head Start program. Advocates on the behalf of America's low-income children and families. Publishes many books, periodicals and resource guides. Offers a legislative hotline as well as training programs through the NHSA Academy.

Ron Herndon, President
Blanche Russ-Glover, VP

4881 National Textbook Company
4255 W Touhy Avenue
Lincolnwood, IL 60646-1975
847-679-5500
800-323-4900
Fax: 847-679-2494
Offers various textbooks for students grades K-college level.

4882 National Women's History Project
3343 Industrial Drive
Suite #4
Santa Rosa, CA 95403
707-636-2888
Fax: 707-636-2909
E-mail: nwhp@aol.com
http://www.nwhp.org
Non-profit organization, the clearinghouse for information about multicultural US women's history. Initiated March as National Women's History Month; issues a catalog of women's history materials. Provides teacher-training nationwide; coordinates the Women's History Network; produces videos, posters, curriculum units and other curriculum materials.

Molly Murphy MacGregor, Exec. Dir./Co-Founder

4883 National Writing Project
University of California, Berkeley
2105 Bancroft Way
#1042
Berkeley, CA 94720-1042
510-642-6096
Fax: 510-642-4545
http://www.writingproject.org
Technical reports and occasional paper series: a series of research reports and essays on the research in and practice of teaching writing at all grade levels.

4884 New Canaan Publishing Company
PO Box 752
New Canaan, CT 06840
203-966-3408
800-705-5698
Fax: 203-966-3408
http://www.newcanaanpublishing.com
Children's publications.

4885 New Press
38 Greene Street
4th Floor
New York, NY 10013
212-629-8802
Fax: 212-629-8617
Multicultural teaching materials, focusing on the social studies.

4886 NewsBank
5020 Tamiami Trail N
Suite 110
Naples, FL 34103-2837
941-263-6004
Electronic information services that support the science curriculum.

4887 North South Books
11 E 26th Street
17 Floor
New York, NY 10010-2007
212-706-4545
Fax: 212-706-4544
Publisher of quality children's books by authors and illustrators from around the world.

4888 Nystrom, Herff Jones
3333 N Elston Avenue
Chicago, IL 60618-5811
913-432-8100
Fax: 913-432-3958
Charts for earth, life and physical science for upper elementary and high school grades.

4889 Options Publishing
PO Box 1749
Merrimack, NH 03054
603-429-2698
800-782-7300
Fax: 603-424-4056
E-mail: serviceoptionspublishing.com m
http://www.optionspublishing.com
Publishers of supplemental materials in reading, math and language arts.

Marty Furlong, VP

4890 Organization of American Historians
112 N Bryan Avenue
Bloomington, IN 47408-4136
812-855-7311
800-446-8923
Fax: 812-855-0696
E-mail: oah@oah.org
http://www.oah.org
Offers various products and literature dealing with American history, as well as job registries, Magazine of History, Journal of American History, OAH Newsletter, and more.

Damon Freeman, Marketing Manager
Michael Regoli, Publications Director

4891 Oxton House Publishers, LLC
Po Box 209
Farmington, ME 04938
207-779-1923
800-539-7323
Fax: 207-779-0623
E-mail: info@oxtonhouse.com
http://www.oxtonhouse.com
Publishes high quality, innovative, affordable materials for teaching, reading and mathematics and for dealing with learning disabilities.

William Berlinghoff, Managing Editor
Bobby Brown, Marketing Director

4892 PF Collier
1315 W 22nd Street
Suite 250
Oak Brook, IL 60523-2061
A leading educational publisher for more than 110 years, creating the home learning center. Products include: Collier's Encyclopedia, Quickstart and Early Learning Fun.

4893 PRO-ED
8700 Shoal Creek Boulevard
Austin, TX 78757-6897
512-451-3246
800-897-3202
Fax: 800-397-7633
E-mail: info@proedinc.com
http://www.proedinc.com
A leading publisher of assessments, therapy materials and resource/reference books in the areas of speech, language, and hearing; psychology; special education; and occupational therapy.

4894 Parenting Press
PO Box 75267
11065 5th Avenue NE
Seattle, WA 98125-0267

206-364-2900
800-992-6657
Fax: 206-364-0702
E-mail: office@ParentingPress.com
http://www.ParentingPress.com
Publishes books for parents, children, and professionals who work with them. Nonfiction books include topics on parenting, problem solving, dealing with feelings, safety, and special issues.

Carolyn J Threadgill, Publisher

4895 Penguin USA
375 Hudson Street
New York, NY 10014-3658
212-366-2000
Fax: 212-366-2934
http://www.penguinputnam.com
Children's and adult hardcover and paperback general trade books, including classics and multiethnic literature.

4896 Perfection Learning Corporation
Perfection Learning
10520 New York Avenue
Des Moines, IA 50322
303-333-3003
800-803-8488
Fax: 303-333-4037
E-mail: karen-hemmes@mindspring.com
http://www.fireflybooks.com
Perfection Learning publishes high interest-low reading level fiction and non-fiction books for young adults.

Karen Hemmes, Publicist
Mary Kay Opicka, Publicist

4897 Perma Bound Books
E Vandalia Road
Jacksonville, IL 62650
217-243-5451
800-637-6581
Fax: 800-551-1169
Thematically arranged for K-12 classroom use with 480,000 titles available in durable Perma-Bound bindings; related library services also available.

Ben Mangum, President

4898 Personalizing the Past
1534 Addison Street
Berkeley, CA 94703-1454
415-388-9351
Museum quality artifact history kits complete with integrated lesson plan teachers guide. Copy-ready student worksheets, literature section, videos and audio tapes. United States and ancient world history.

4899 Perspectives on History Series
Discovery Enterprises, Ltd.
31 Laurelwood Drive
Carlisle, MA 01741
978-287-5401
800-729-1720
Fax: 978-287-5402
E-mail: ushistorydocs@aol.com
http://www.ushistorydocs.com
Primary and secondary source materials for middle school to college levels; bibliographies; plays for grades 5-9 on American history topics. Educators curriculum guides for using primary source documents. 75-volumes of primary source documents on American history may be purchased individually or in sets. New Researching American History Series presents documents with summaries and vocabulary on each page (20 volumes) sold individually or in sets.

JoAnne Deitch, President

4900 Peytral Publications Inc
PO Box 1162
Minnetonka, MN 55345

285

952-949-8707
877-739-8725
Fax: 952-906-9777
E-mail: inquiry@peytral.com
http://www.peytral.com
Books and videos for educators.

Peggy Hammeken, Owner

4901 Phelps Publishing
PO Box 22401
Cleveland, OH 44122
216-752-4938
Fax: 216-752-4941
E-mail: earl@phelpspublishing.com
http://www.phelpspublishing.com
Publisher of art instruction books for ages 8 to 108.

Earl Phelps, President

4902 Phoenix Learning Resources
12 W 31st Street
New York, NY 10001-4415
212-629-3887
800-221-1274
Fax: 212-629-5648
Phoenix Learning Resources provides all students with the skills to be successful, lifelong learners.

Alexander Burke, President
John Rothermich, Executive VP

4903 Pleasant Company Publications
8400 Fairway Pl
Middleton Branch, WI 53562-2554
608-836-4848
800-233-0264
Fax: 800-257-3865
The American Girls Collection historical fiction series.

4904 Pocket Books/Paramount Publishing
1230 Avenue of the Americas
New York, NY 10020-1513
212-698-7000
Books for children and young adults in hardcover and paperback originals and reprints of bestselling titles.

4905 Population Connection
1400 16th Street NW
Suite 320
Washington, DC 20036-2290
800-767-1956
Fax: 202-332-2302
E-mail: poped@populationconnection.org
http://www.populationconnection.org
Curriculum materials for grades K-12 to teach students about population dynamics and their social, political and environmental effects in the United States and the world.

Pamela Wasserman, Director Education

4906 Prentice Hall School Division
340 Rancheros Drive
Suite 160
San Marcos, CA 92069
760-510-0222
Fax: 760-510-0230
Superb language arts textbooks and ancillaries for students grades 6-12.

4907 Prentice Hall School Division - Science
1 Lake Street
Upper Saddle River, NJ 07458
201-236-7000
Fax: 201-236-3381
Science textbooks and ancillaries for grades 6-12 and advanced placement students.

4908 Prentice Hall/Center for Applied Research in Education
1 Lake Street
Upper Saddle River, NJ 07458
201-236-7000
Fax: 201-236-3381

Publisher of practical, time and work saving teaching/learning resources for PreK-12 teachers and specialists in all content areas.

4909 Project Learning Tree
American Forest Foundation
1111 19th Street NW
Suite 780
Washington, DC 20036-3603
202-463-2462
Fax: 202-463-2461
Pre-K through grade 12 curriculum materials containing hundreds of hands-on science activities. PLT uses the forest as a window into the natural world to increase students' understanding of our complex environment. Stimulates critical and creative thinking; develops the ability to make informed decisions on environmental issues; and instills the confidence and commitment to take action on them.

Kathy McGlauflin, President

4910 Prufrock Press
PO Box 8813
Waco, TX 76714
800-998-2208
Fax: 800-240-0333
http://www.prufrock.com
Exciting classroom products for gifted and talented education.

4911 Puffin Books
375 Hudson Street
New York, NY 10014-3658
212-366-2819
Fax: 212-366-2040
Offers the Puffin Teacher Club set.

Lisa Crosby, President

4912 RR Bowker
Reed Reference Publishing Company
121 Chanlon Road
New Providence, NJ 07974-1541
908-464-6800
Fax: 908-665-6688
A leading information provider to schools and libraries for over one hundred years, RR Bowker provides quality resources to help teachers and librarians make informed reading selections for children and young adults.

4913 Raintree/Steck-Vaughn
Harcourt Achieve
6277 Sea Harbor Drive
Orlando, FL 32887
800-531-5015
Fax: 800-699-9459
http://www.steck-vaughn.com
Reference materials for K-8 students and texts for underachieving students K-12.

Tim McEwen, President
Martijn Tel, Chief Financial Officer

4914 Rand McNally
8255 Central Park Avenue
Skokie, IL 60076-2970
847-674-2151
Cross-curricular products featuring reading/language arts in the social studies.

4915 Random House
201 E 50th Street
New York, NY 10022-7703
212-751-2600
Fax: 212-572-8700
Offers a line of science trade books for grades K-8.

4916 Random House/Bullseye/Alfred A Knopf/CrownBooks for Young Readers
201 E 50th Street
New York, NY 10022-7703
212-751-2600
Fax: 212-572-8700

Publisher of hardcover books, paperbacks, books and cassettes and videos for children.

4917 Recorded Books
270 Skipjack Road
Prince Frederick, MD 20678-3410
800-638-1304
Professionally narrated, unabridged books on standard-play audio cassettes, classroom ideas and combinations of print book, cassettes and teacher's guides.

Linda Hirshman, President

4918 Redleaf Press
10 Yorkton Court
Saint Paul, MN 55117-1065
800-428-8309
Fax: 800-641-0115
E-mail: jward@redleafpress.org
http://www.redleafpress.org
Publisher of curriculum, activity, and childrens books for early childhood professionals.

Sid Farrer, Editor In Chief
JoAnne Voltz, Marketing Manager

4919 Reference Desk Books
430 Quintana Road
Suite 146
Morro Bay, CA 93442-1948
805-772-8806
Offers a variety of books for the education professional.

4920 Rhythms Productions
PO Box 34485
Los Angeles, CA 90034-0485
310-836-4678
800-544-7244
Fax: 310-837-1534
Producer and publisher of songs and games for learning through music. Cassettes, CDs, books for birth through elementary featuring rhythms, puppet play, art activities, and more. Titles include Lullabies, Singing Games, Watch Me Grow series, Mr. Windbag concept stories, phonics, First Reader's Kit, Hear-See-Say-Do Musical Math series, Themes, and more. Also publishes a line of folk dances from elementary through adult.

Audio

Ruth White, President

4921 Richard C Owen Publishers
PO Box 585
Katonah, NY 10536
914-232-3903
800-336-5588
Fax: 914-232-3977
E-mail: mfrund@rcowen.com
http://www.rcowen.com
Focus child-centered learning, Books for Young Learners, professional books, the Learning Network and Meet the Author series.

Mary Frundt, Marketing

4922 Riverside Publishing Company
425 Spring Lake Drive
Ithaca, IL 60143
630-467-7000
800-323-9540
Fax: 630-467-7192
http://www.riverpub.com
Offers a full line of reading materials, including fiction and nonfiction titles for all grade levels.

4923 Roots & Wings Educational Catalog-Australia for Kids
PO Box 19678
Boulder, CO 80308-2678
303-776-4796
800-833-1787
Fax: 303-776-6090

E-mail: roos@boulder.net
http://www.rootsandwingscatalog.com/
www.australiaforkids.com
Catalog company providing materials for the education of the young child, specializing in the following topics: Australia, multiculturalism, parenting and families, teaching, special needs, environment and peace.

Susan Ely, President/Sales
Anne Wilson, VP/Marketing

4924 Rosen Publishing Group
29 E 21st Street
New York, NY 10010-6209
212-777-3017
800-237-9932
Fax: 888-436-4643
Nonfiction books on self-help and guidance for young adults. Books also available for reluctant readers on self-esteem, values and drug abuse prevention.

4925 Routledge/Europa Library Reference
Taylor & Francis Books
29 W 35 Street
New York, NY 10001-2299
212-216-7800
800-634-7064
Fax: 212-564-7854
E-mail: reference@routledge-ny.com
http://www.reference.routlege-ny.com
Publisher of a wide range of print and online library reference titles, including the renowned Europa World Yearbook and the award-winning Routledge Encyclopedia of Philosophy (both available in online and print formats), Garland Encyclopedia of World Music, Routledge Religion and Society Encyclopedias, Chronological History of US Foreign Relations, and many other acclaimed resources.

Koren Thomas, Sr Marketing/Library Ref
Elizabeth Sheehan, Marketing/Library Reference

4926 Runestone Press
A Divisions of Lerner Publishing Group
241 1st Avenue N
Minneapolis, MN 55401-1607
612-332-3344
800-328-4929
Fax: 612-332-7615
http://www.lernerbooks.com
Nonfiction for readers in Grades 5 and up. Newly revised editions of previously out-of-print books. List includes Buried Worlds archaeology series and titles of Jewish and Native American interest. Complete catalog is available.

Harry J Lerner, President
Mary M Rodgers, Editorial Director

4927 Saddleback Educational
Three Watson
Irvine, CA 92618-2767
949-860-2500
800-637-8715
Fax: 888-734-4010
Supplementary curriculum materials for K-12 and adult students.

4928 SafeSpace Concepts
1424 N Post Oak Road
Houston, TX 77055-5401
713-956-0820
800-622-4289
Fax: 713-956-6416
E-mail: safespacec@aol.com
http://www.safespaceconcepts.com
Manufactures young children's play equipment and furnishings.

Barbara Carlson, PhD, President
Jerry Johnson, Marketing Director

4929 Sage Publications
Sage Publications
2455 Teller Road
Thousand Oaks, CA 91320
303-333-3003
800-803-8488
Fax: 303-333-4037
E-mail: karen-hemmes@mindspring.com
http://www.fireflybooks.com
Sage Publications publishes handbooks and guides with a focus on research and science.

Karen Hemmes, Publicist
Mary Kay Opicka, Publicist

4930 Santillana Publishing
901 W Walnut Street
Compton, CA 90220-5109
310-763-0455
800-245-8584
Fax: 305-591-9145
Publishers of K-12 and adult titles in Spanish.Imprints include: Altea, Alfagunea, Taurus and Aguilar.

Marla Norman, Publisher/Trade Book
Antonio de Marco, President

4931 Scholastic
555 Broadway
New York, NY 10012
212-343-6100
800-724-6527
Fax: 212-343-4801
http://www.scholastic.com
Publisher and distributor of children's books. Provides professional and classroom resources for K-12.

4932 School Book Fairs
PO Box 835105
Richardson, TX 75083
972-231-9838
A children's book publisher that provides distribution of leisure reading materials to elementary and middle schools through book fair fund-raising events via a North American network with 97 locations.

4933 Science Inquiry Enterprises
14358 Village View Lane
Chino Hills, CA 91709-1706
530-295-3338
Fax: 530-295-3334
Selected science teaching materials.

4934 Scott & McCleary Publishing Company
2482 11th Street SW
Akron, OH 44314-1712
702-566-8756
800-765-3564
Fax: 702-568-1378
E-mail: jscott7576@aol.com
http://www.scottmccleary.com
Diagnostic reading and testing material.

Janet M Scott, Publisher
Sheila C McCleary, Publisher

4935 Scott Foresman Company
1900 E Lake Avenue
Glenview, IL 60025-2086
800-554-4411
Fax: 800-841-8939
Science tests and reading/language arts materials for teachers and students. Celebrate Reading! is the K-8 literature-based reading/integrated language arts program designed to meet the needs of all children. Book Festival is a literature learning center that offers teachers a collection of trade books for independent reading.

Bert Crossland, Reading Product Manager
Jim Fitzmaurice, VP Editor Group

4936 Sharpe Reference
M.E. Sharpe, Inc.
80 Business Park Drive
Armonk, NY 10504
914-273-1800
800-541-6563
Fax: 914-273-2106
E-mail: custserv@mesharpe.com
http://www.mesharpe.com
Historical, political, geographical and art reference books.

Diana McDermott, Director Marketing

4937 Signet Classics
375 Hudson Street
New York, NY 10014-3658
212-366-2000
Fax: 212-366-2888
Publishes books on literature, poetry and reading.

4938 Silver Moon Press
160 5th Avenue
Suite 622
New York, NY 10010-7003
212-242-6499
800-874-3320
Fax: 212-242-6799
Informational and entertaining books for young readers. Subjects include history, multiculturalism and science.

4939 Simon & Schuster Children's Publishing
1230 Avenue of the Americas
New York, NY 10020
212-698-7000
Fax: 212-698-7007
http://www.simonsayskids.com
Fiction and nonfiction, in hardcover and paperback editions, for preschool through young adult.

4940 Social Issues Resources Series
1100 Holland Drive
Boca Raton, FL 33487-2701
561-994-0079
Fax: 561-994-2014
Provides information systems in print format and CD-ROM format.

4941 Social Science Education Consortium
Box 21270
Boulder, CO 80308-4270
303-492-8154
Fax: 303-449-3925
E-mail: singletl@stripe.colorado.edu
http://www.ssecinc.org
Produces curriculum guides, instructional units and collections of lesson plans on US history, law-related education, global studies, public issues and geography. Develops projects for social studies teachers and evaluates social studies programs.

James Cooks, Executive Director
Laurel Singleton, Associate Director

4942 Social Studies School Service
10200 Jefferson Boulevard
Culver City, CA 90232-3598
310-839-2436
800-421-4246
Fax: 310-839-2249
E-mail: access@socialstudies.com
http://www.socialstudies.com
Supplemental materials in all areas of social studies, language arts.

4943 Special Education & Rehabilitation Services
330 C Street
Washington, DC 20202
202-205-5465
Fax: 202-260-7225

Judith E Heuman, Assistant Secretary

4944 Speech Bin
1965 25th Avenue
Vero Beach, FL 32960-3000
561-770-0007
800-477-3324
Fax: 561-770-0006
Publisher and distributor of books and materials for professionals in rehabilitation, speech-language pathology, occupational and physical therapy, special education, and related fields. Major product lines include professional and children's books, computer software, diagnostic tests.

Jan J Binney, VP

4945 Stack the Deck Writing Program
PO Box 5352
Chicago, IL 60680-0429
312-675-1000
Fax: 312-765-0453
E-mail: stockthedeck@sbcglobal.net
http://www.stackthedeck.com
Composition textbooks, grades 1-12, plus computer software.

4946 Stenhouse Publishers
477 Congress Street
Suite 4B
Portland, ME 04101-3417
888-363-0566
Fax: 800-833-9164
http://www.stenhouse.com
Professional materials for teachers by teachers.

4947 Story Teller
PO Box 921
Salem, UT 84653-0921
801-423-2560
Fax: 801-423-2568
E-mail: patti@thestoryteler.com
http://www.thestoryteller.com
Felt board stories books and educational sets.

Patti Gardner, VP Sales

4948 Summit Learning
7755 Rockwell Avenue
PO Box 755
Fort Atkinson, WI 53538-0755
800-777-8817
800-777-8817
Fax: 800-317-2194
E-mail: info@summitlearning.com
http://www.summitlearning.com
Summit learning is a distributor of manipulative-based math and science materials, provides you with a carefully selected group of the most popular high-quality products at low prices.

Gary Otto, Marketing Manager

4949 Sunburst Technology
1550 Executive Drive
Elgin, IL 60123
914-747-3310
800-338-3457
Fax: 914-747-4109
http://www.sunburst.com
K-12 educational software, guidance and health materials, and online teacher resources.

4950 Sundance Publishing
234 Taylor Street
PO Box 1326
Littleton, MA 01460
978-486-9201
800-343-8204
Fax: 978-486-8759
E-mail: kjasmine@sundancepub.com
http://www.sindancepub.com
A supplementary educational publisher of instructional materials for shared, guided, and independent reading, phonics, and comprehension skills for grades K-9. Some of its pro-

grams include AlphKids, SunLit Fluency, Popcorns and Little Readers. Its Second Chance Reading Program for below-level readers features high-interest titles, written for upper elementary/middle school students. It also distributes paperback editions of some of the most widely taught literature titles for grades K-1

Katherine Jasmine, VP Marketing

4951 Synergistic Systems
2297 Hunters Run Drive
Reston, VA 20191-2834
703-758-9213
Science education curriculum materials.

4952 TASA
PO Box 382
Brewster, NY 10509-0382
845-277-8100
800-800-2598
Fax: 845-277-3548
Degrees of Literacy Power Program; English Language Profiles, primary, standard and advanced DRP tests, Degrees of World Meaning Tests.

4953 TL Clark Incorporated
5111 SW Avenue
St. Louis, MO 63110
314-865-2525
800-859-3815
Fax: 314-865-2240
E-mail: general@tlclarkinc.com
http://www.tlclarkinc.com
Educational products for grades Pre-K-3. Rest time products including cots and mats, sand and water play tubs, active play items including tunnels, tricycles and foam play items.

Jim Fleminla, President

4954 TMC/Soundprints
353 Main Avenue
Norwalk, CT 06851-1508
203-846-2274
800-228-7839
Fax: 203-846-1776
E-mail: sndprnts@ixinctcom.com
http://www.soundprints.com
Children's story books for children ages 4 through 8 under the license of the Smithsonian Institute and the National Wildlife Federation. Each 32 page four color book highlights a unique aspect of the animal featured in the book so as to provide education while still being entertaining. Each book can be bought with an audiocassette read-a-long and plush toy. Over 80 books in print.

Ashley Anderson, Associate Publisher
Chelsea Shriver

4955 Tambourine Books
1350 Avenue of the Americas
New York, NY 10019-4702
212-261-6500
Fax: 212-261-6518
A wide variety of books to increase creativity and reading skills in students.

4956 Taylor & Francis Publishers
7625 Empire Drive
Florence, KY 41042
800-624-7064
Fax: 800-248-4724
Publisher of professional texts and references in several fields including the behavioral sciences; arts, humanities, social sciences, science technology and medicine.

Chris Smith, Customer Service Manager

4957 Teacher's Friend Publications
3240 Trade Center Drive
Riverside, CA 92507

909-682-4748
800-343-9680
Fax: 909-682-4680
Complete line of the original monthly and seasonal Creative Idea Books. Plus, two new cooperative-learning language series and much more.

Karen Sevaly, Author
Richard Sevaly, President/CEO
Kim Marsh, National Sales Manager

4958 Teaching Comprehension: Strategies for Stories
Oxton House Publishers, LLC
Po Box 209
Farmington, ME 04938
207-779-1923
800-539-7323
Fax: 207-779-0623
E-mail: info@oxtonhouse.com
http://www.oxtonhouse.com
A detailed roadmap for providing students with effective strategies for comprehending and remembering stories. It includes story-line masters for helping students to organize their thinking and to accurately depict character and sequence events.

62 pages

William Berlinghoff, Managing Editor
Bobby Brown, Marketing Director

4959 Theme Connections
Perfection Learning
PO Box 500
Logan, IA 51546-0500
800-831-4190
Fax: 712-644-2392
Features 135 best-selling literature titles and related theme libraries for students to develop lifelong learning strategies.

4960 Ther-A-Play Products
PO Box 2030
Lodi, CA 95241-2030
209-368-6787
800-308-6749
Fax: 209-365-2157
E-mail: madgic@attbi.com
Children's books, play therapy books, sandplay and sandtray manipulatives, puppets, games, doll houses and furniture. Playmobile and educational toys, specializing in counselors' tools. Books on abuses, illness, death, behavior and parenting.

Madge Geiszler, Owner

4961 Thomson Learning
115 5th Avenue
New York, NY 10003-1004
212-979-2210
800-880-4253
Fax: 248-699-8061
Book publisher of library and classroom-oriented educational resources for children and young adults. Over 200 books are available in 30 different subjects.

4962 Time-Life Books
2000 Duke Street
Alexandria, VA 22314-3414
703-838-7000
Fax: 703-838-7166
A wide-ranging selection of quality reference and supplemental books for students from elementary to high school.

4963 Tiny Thought Press
1427 S Jackson Street
Louisville, KY 40208-2720
502-637-6916
Fax: 502-634-1693
Children's books that build character and self-esteem.

4964 Tom Snyder Productions
80 Coolidge Hill Road
Watertown, MA 02472
800-342-0236
Fax: 800-304-1254
E-mail: ask@tomsnyder.com
http://www.tomsnyder.com
Developer and publisher of educational software.

John McAndrews, Contact

4965 Tor Books/Forge/SMP
175 5th Avenue
New York, NY 10010-7703
212-388-0100
Fax: 212-388-0191
Science-fiction and fantasy children's books, mysteries, Westerns, general fiction and classics publications.

4966 Tricycle Press
PO Box 7123
Berkeley, CA 94707-0123
510-559-1600
800-841-2665
Fax: 510-559-1637
Publisher of books and posters for children ages 2-12 and their grown-ups. Catalog available.

Christine Longmuir, Publicity/Marketing

4967 Troll Associates
100 Corporate Drive
Mahwah, NJ 07430-2322
201-529-4000
Fax: 201-529-8282
Publisher of children's books and products, including paperbacks and hardcovers, special theme units, read-alongs, videos, software and big books.

4968 Trumpet Club
1540 Broadway
New York, NY 10036-4039
212-492-9595
School book club featuring hardcover and paperback books, in class text sets and author video visits.

4969 Turn-the-Page Press
203 Baldwin Avenue
Roseville, CA 95678-5104
916-786-8756
800-959-5549
Fax: 916-786-9261
E-mail: mleeman@ibm.net
http://www.turnthepage.com
Books, cassettes and videos focusing on early childhood education.

Michael Leeman, President

4970 USA Today
1000 Wilson Boulevard
Arlington, VA 22209-3901
703-276-3400
Fax: 703-854-2103
Educational programs focusing on social studies.

4971 Upstart Books
PO Box 800
Fort Atkinson, WI 53538-0800
920-563-9571
800-558-2110
Fax: 920-563-7395
http://www.hpress.highsmith.com
Publishes teacher activity resources, reading activities, library and information seeking skills, Internet.

Matt Mulder, Director
Virginia Harrison, Editor

4972 Useful Learning
711 Meadow Lane Court
Apartment 12
Mount Vernon, IA 52314-1549
319-895-6155
800-962-3855
The Useful Spelling Textbook series for Grades 2-8, represents a curriculum based upon the scientific knowledge of research studies conducted during the past 80 years at The University of Iowa, Iowa City, IA. Incorporates the New Iowa Spelling Scale and is composed of qualitative curriculum, qualitative learning practices and qualitative instructional procedures.

Larry D. Zenor, PhD, President
Bradley M Loomer, PhD, Board Chairman

4973 VIDYA Books
PO Box 7788
Berkeley, CA 94707-0788
510-527-9932
Fax: 510-527-2936
Supplemental materials about India and the surrounding region for K-12 lesson plans.

4974 Viking Children's Books
375 Hudson Street
New York, NY 10014-3658
212-941-8780
General hardcover children's books, from toddler through young adult, fiction and non-fiction.

4975 Vision 23
Twenty-Third Publications
185 Willow Street
Mystic, CT 06355-2636
860-536-2611
Fax: 800-572-0788
A wide variety of children's products including books, games, clothing and toys.

4976 WH Freeman & Company
41 Madison Avenue
New York, NY 10010-2202
212-576-9400
Fax: 212-481-1891
Books relating to the world of mathematics.

4977 Wadsworth Publishing School Group
10 Davis Drive
Belmont, CA 94002-3002
650-595-2350
Fax: 800-522-4923
College and advanced placement/honors high school materials in biology, chemistry and environmental science.

4978 Walker & Company
104 Fifth Avenue
New York, NY 10011
212-727-8300
800-289-2553
Fax: 212-727-0984
http://www.walkerbooks.com
Hardcover and paperback trade titles for Pre-K-12th grade, including picture books, photo essays, fiction and nonfiction titles appropriate for every curriculum need.

4979 Warren Publishing House
11625-G Airport Road
Everett, WA 98204-3790
425-353-3100
New Totline Teaching Tales with related activities plus quality whole language teacher activity books including Alphabet Theme-A-Saurus and Piggyback Songs.

4980 Waterfront Books
85 Crescent Road
Burlington, VT 05401-4126
802-658-7477
800-639-6063
Fax: 802-860-1368

E-mail: helpkids@waterfrontbooks.com
http://www.waterfrontbooks.com
Publishes and distributes books on special issues for children: barriers to learning, coping skills, mental health, prevention strategies, family/parenting, etc. for grades K-12. Titles include: The Divorce Workbook; Josh, a Boy with Dyslexia; What's a Virus, Anyway? The Kids' Book About AIDS and more.

Sherrill N Musty, Publisher
Michelle Russell, Order Fulfillment

4981 Web Feet Guides
Rock Hill Communications
14 Rock Hill Road
Bala Cynwyd, PA 19004
610-667-2040
888-762-5445
Fax: 610-667-2291
E-mail: info@rockhillcommunications.com
http://www.webfeetguides.com
The premier subject guides to the Internet, rigorously reviewed by librarians and educators, fully annotated, expanded and updated monthly. Appropriate for middle school through adult. Available in print, online, or marc records. For more information, free trials and Web casts, and free interactive Web Quests for your K-8 students, visit our Web site.

Linda Smith, Marketing Coordinator

4982 West Educational Publishing
620 Opperman Drive
#645779
Saint Paul, MN 55123-1340
A leader in quality social studies textbooks and ancillaries for grades K-12.

4983 Western Psychological Services
12031 Wilshire Boulevard
Los Angeles, CA 90025-1251
310-478-2061
800-648-8857
Fax: 310-478-7838
http://www.wpspublish.com
Assessment tools for professionals in education, psychology and allied fields. Offer a variety of tests, books, software and therapeutic games.

4984 Wildlife Conservation Society
Bronx Zoo
Education Department
2300 Southern Boulevard
Bronx, NY 10460
718-220-5131
800-937-5131
Fax: 718-733-4460
E-mail: sscheio@wes.org
http://www.wcs.com
Environmental science and conservation biology curriculum materials and information regarding teacher training programming for Grades K-12, on site or off site, nationally and locally. Science programming for grades pre-K-12 available on site.

Sydell Schein, Manager/Program Services
Ann Robinson, Director National Programs

4985 William Morrow & Company
1350 Avenue of the Americas
New York, NY 10019-4702
212-261-6500
Fax: 212-261-6518
High quality hardcover and paperback books for children.

4986 Winston Derek Publishers
101 French Landing Drive
Nashville, TN 37228-1511
615-321-0535
A cross section of African American books and educational materials, including preschool and primary grade books.

289

4987 Wolfram Research, Inc.
100 Trade Center Drive
Champaign, IL 61820-7237
217-398-0700
800-965-3726
Fax: 217-398-0747
E-mail: info@wolfram.com
http://www.wolfram.com
Offers mathematics publications, statistics and information to educators of grades K-12.

Stephen Wolfram, Founder/CEO
Jean Buck, Dir., Corp Communications

4988 Workman Publishing
708 Broadway
New York, NY 10003-9508
212-254-5900
Fax: 212-254-8098
Children's curriculum, books, textbooks, workbooks, fiction and nonfiction titles.

4989 World & I
News World Communications
2800 New York Avenue NE
Washington, DC 20002-1945
202-636-3365
800-822-2822
Fax: 202-832-5780
E-mail: ckim@worldandimag.com
http://www.worldandi.com
With over 40 articles each month, The World & I presents an enlightening look at our changing world through the eyes of noted scholars and experts covering current issues, the arts, science, book reviews, lifestyles, cultural perspectives, philosophical trends, and the millennium. For educators, students and libraries. Free teacher's guides year round. Also, online archives available at www.worldandi.com.

Charles Kim, Business Director

4990 World Association of Publishers, Manufacturers & Distributors
Worlddidac
Bollwerk 21, PO Box 8866 CH-3001
Berne
Switzerland
41-31-3121744
Fax: 41-31-3121744
E-mail: info@worlddidac.org
A worldwide listing of over 330 publishers, manufacturers and distributors of educational materials. Listings include all contact information, products and school levels/grades.

160 pages Annual

Beat Jost, Coordinating Education

4991 World Bank
1818 H Street NW
Room T-8061
Washington, DC 20433-0002
202-477-1234
Fax: 202-477-6391
Maps, poster kits, case studies and videocassettes that teach about life in developing countries.

4992 World Book Educational Products
525 W Monroe Street
20th Floor
Chicago, IL 60661
312-729-5800
Fax: 312-729-5600
Reference books and the World Book Encyclopedia on CD-Rom.

4993 World Eagle
111 King Street
Littleton, MA 01460-1527
978-486-9180
800-854-8273
Fax: 978-486-9652
E-mail: info@ibaradio.org
http://www.worldeagle.com

Publishes an online, social studies educational resource magazine: comparative data, graphs, maps and charts on world issues. Publishes world regional atlases, and supplies maps and curriculum materials.

Valentina Bardawil Powers, Author
Martine Crandall-Hollick, President

4994 World Resources Institute
10 G Street, NE
Suite 800
Washington, DC 20002
202-729-7600
Fax: 202-729-7610
The world Resources Institute is an envoronmental think tank that goes beyond research to create practical ways to protect the Earth and improve people's lives. our mission is to move human society to live in ways that protect Earth's environment for surrent and future generations.

Jonathan Lash, President

4995 World Scientific Publishing Company
27 Warren Street
Suite 401-402
Hackensack, NJ 07601
201-487-9655
Fax: 201-487-9695
E-mail: wspc@wspc.com
http://www.wspc.com
This is one of the world's leading academic publishers. It now publishes more than 400 books and 100 journals a year in diverse fields of science technology, medicine, business and management.

Ruth Zhou, Marketing Executive

4996 World of Difference Institute
Anti-Defamation League
823 United Nations Plaza
New York, NY 10017-3518
212-490-2525
Fax: 212-867-0779
E-mail: webmaster@adl.org
http://www.adl.org
Materials and training, as well as Pre K-12 curriculum resources, Anti-bias and diversity.

Lindsay J Friedman, Director

4997 Worth Publishers
33 Irving Plaza
New York, NY 10003-2332
212-475-6000
Fax: 212-689-2383
A balanced and comprehensive account of the U.S. past is accompanied by an extensive set of supplements.

4998 Wright Group
19201 120th Avenue NE
Bothell, WA 98011-9507
800-523-2371
Fax: 425-486-7704
http://www.wrightgroup.com
Supplementary program materials for reading education.

4999 Write Source Educational Publishing House
PO Box 460
Burlington, WI 53105-0460
262-763-8258
Fax: 262-763-2651
Publishes Writers Express, a writing, thinking and learning handbook series for grades 4 and 5. Also offer the latest editions of Write Source 2000 and Writers INC for grades 6-8 and 9-12.

5000 Zaner-Bloser K-8 Catalog
2200 W 5th Avenue
Columbus, OH 43215

614-486-0221
800-421-3018
Fax: 614-487-2699
http://www.zaner-bloser.com
Publisher of handwriting materials and reading, writing, spelling and study skills programs.

Robert Page, President

5001 Zephyr Press
814 North Franklin Street
Chicago, IL 60610-3109
312-337-5985
800-232-2187
Fax: 312-337-5985
E-mail: neways2learn@zephyrpress.com
http://www.zephyrpress.com
Zephyr Press publishes effective, state-of-the-art-teaching materials for classroom use.

Joey Tanner MEd, President

5002 ZooBooks
ZooBooks/Wildlife Education. Ltd.
12233 Thatcher Court
Poway, CA 92064-6880
619-513-7600
800-477-5034
Fax: 858-513-7660
E-mail: animals@zoobooks.com
http://www.zoobooks.com
Reference books offering fascinating insights into the world of wildlife. Created in collaboration with leading scientists and educators, these multi-volume Zoobooks make important facts and concepts about nature, habitat and wildlife understandable to children. From alligators to zebras, aquatic to exotic, each Zoobook is colorful, scientifically accurate and easy to read.

General

5003 AVKO Educational Research Foundation
3084 Willard Road
Birch Run, MI 48415-9404
810-686-9283
866-285-6612
Fax: 810-686-1101
E-mail: avkoemail@aol.com
http://www.avko.org
Comprised of teachers and individuals interested in helping others learn to read and spell. Develops reading training materials for individuals with dyslexia or other learning disabilities using a method involving audio, visual, kinesthetic and oral diagnosis and remediation. Conducts research into the causes of reading, spelling, and writing disabilities.

Don McCabe, Research Director
Devorah Wolf, President

5004 Assistive Technology Clinics
Children's Hospital
1056 E 19th Avenue
#030
Denver, CO 80218-1007
303-861-6250
Fax: 303-764-8214
A diagnostic clinic providing evaluation, information and support to families with children with disabilities in the areas of seating and mobility. Offers augmentative communication and assistive technology access.

Tracey Kovach, Coordinator

5005 Center for Equity and Excellence in Education
George Washington University
1555 Wilson Boulevard
Suite 515
Arlington, VA 22209-2004
703-528-3588
800-925-3223
Fax: 703-528-5973
E-mail: ceeeinfo@ceee.gwu.edu
http://www.ceee.gwu.edu
Mission is to advance education reform so that all students achieve high standards. Operates under the umbrella of the Institute for Education Policy Studies within the Graduate School of Education and Human Development. Designs and conducts program evaluation for states, districts and schools and conducts program evalutaion, policy and applied research effecting equitable educational opportunities for all students.

Charlene Rivera, Executive Director
Kristina Anstrom, Assistant Director

5006 Center for Learning
The Center for Learning
PO Box 910
2105 Evergreen Road
Villa Maria, PA 16155
724-964-8083
800-767-9090
Fax: 724-964-8992
E-mail: customerservice@centerforlearning.org
http://www.centerforlearning.org
To improve education by writing and publishing values-based curriculum materials that enable teachers to foster student responsibility for learning

5007 Center for Organization of Schools
Johns Hopkins University
2701 N Charles Street
Suite 300
Baltimore, MD 21218-2404

410-516-8810
Fax: 410-516-8890
E-mail: mmaushard@csos.jhu.edu
http://www.csos.jhu.edu
Conduct research, development, evaluation, and dissemination of replicable strategies designed to transform low-performing schools so that al lstudents graduate ready for college, career and life. Products include curricula that help all students achieve at a high level. Programs in early learning; school, family and community partnerships; a financial literacy program called Stocks ain the Future, and the Baltimore Education Research Consortium, plus Talent development Secondary reform

James McPartland, Co-Director
Mary Maushard, Communication Director

5008 Center for Research on the Context of Teaching
Stanford University
CERAS Building
4th Floor 520 Galvez Mall
Stanford, CA 94305-3084
650-725-1845
Fax: 650-736-2296
http://www.stanford.edu/group/CRC/
Conducts research on ways in which secondary school teaching and learning are affected by their contexts.

Milbrey W McLaughlin, Co-Director
Joan E Talbert, Co-Director

5009 Center for Social Organization of Schools
Johns Hopkins University
3003 N Charles Street
Suite 200
Baltimore, MD 21218-3888
410-516-8800
Fax: 410-516-8890
E-mail: jmcpartland@csos.jhu.edu
http://www.csos.jhu.edu
Conduct programmatic research to improve the education system, as well as full-time support staff engaged in developing curricula and providing technical assistance to help schools use the Center's research.

Jim McPartland, Director
Mary Maushard, Communication Director

5010 Center for Technology in Education
Bank Street College of Education
6740 Alexander Bell Drive
Suite 302
Columbia, MD 21046-1898
410-516-9800
Fax: 410-516-9818
E-mail: cte@jhu.edu
http://cte.jhu.edu
Improve the quality of life of children and youth, particularly those with special needs, through teaching, research, and leadership in the use of technology.

Jacqueline A Nunn, Director
K Lynne Harper Mainzer, Deputy Director

5011 Center for the Study of Reading
University of Illinois
158 Children's Research Center
51 Gerty Drive
Champaign, IL 61820
217-333-2552
Fax: 217-244-4501
E-mail: csrrca@uiuc.edu
http://csr.ed.uiuc.edu
Conduct reading research and development must be to discover and put into practice the means for reaching children who are failing to read.

Richard C Anderson, Director
Kim Nguyen-Jahiel, Associate Director

5012 Center for the Study of Small/Rural Schools
University of Oklahoma
555 E Constitution Street
Suite 138
Norman, OK 73072-7820
405-325-1450
Fax: 405-325-7075
E-mail: jcsimmons@ou.edu
http://cssrs.ou.edu
Assists small and rural schools in building and maintaining necessary knowledge bases, founded on state-of-the-art research in the areas of school improvement and reform, restructuring, staff development, administration, and teaching.

Jan C Simmons, Director

5013 Center on Families, Schools, Communities & Children's Learning
Northeastern University
50 Nightingale Hall
Boston, MA 2215
617-373-2595
Fax: 617-373-8924
Examines how families, communities and schools can work in partnership to promote children's motivation, learning and development, including disseminating information.

Nancy Ames, Vice President

5014 Center on Organization & Restructuring of Schools
1025 W Johnson Street
Madison, WI 53706-1706
608-263-7575
Fax: 608-263-6448
Focuses on restructuring K-12 schools in various areas of student development and progress.

Fred M Newman, Director

5015 Council for Educational Development and Research
National Education Association (NEA)
1201 16th Street NW
Washington, DC 20036-3290
202-833-4000
Fax: 202-822-7974
http://www.nea.org
The voice of education professionals. Advocate for education professionals

John I Wilson, Executive Director
Dennis Van Roekel, President

5016 Curriculum Research and Development Group
1776 University Avenue
Honolulu, HI 96822-2463
808-956-4949
800-799-8111
Fax: 808-956-6730
E-mail: crdg@hawaii.edu
http://www.hawaii.edu/crdg
Conducts research and creates, evaluates, disseminates, and supports educational programs that serve students, teachers, parents, and other educators in grades preK-12.

Helen Au, Assistant Director

5017 Division for Research
The Council for Exceptional Children
2000 Broadway
Oakland, CA 94612
510-891-3400
http://www.dor.kaiser.org
The Division of Research aims to conduct, publish, and disseminate high-quality epidemiologic and health services research to improve the health and medical care of Kaiser Permanente members and the society at large.

Joe Selby, Director
Morris Collen, Founder

5018 Educational Information & Resource Center
Research Department
606 Delsea Drive
Sewell, NJ 8080-9399
856-582-7000
Fax: 856-582-4206
E-mail: info@eirc.org
http://www.eirc.org
EIRC is committed to continuously improving the education, safety, physical and emotional health of children. EIRC meets this commitment by developing and delivering a comprehensive array of support services to those who teach, raise, care for and mentor children.

Charles Ivory, Executive Director
John Henry, Program Director

5019 Educational Research Service
1001 N Fairfax Street
Suite 500
Alexandria, VA 22314-1587
703-243-2100
800-791-9308
Fax: 703-243-1985
E-mail: ers@ers.org
http://www.ers.org
For over 30 years Educational Research Service has been the nonprofit organization serving the research and information needs of the nation's K-12 education leaders and the public.

John C Draper EdD, CEO
Katherine A Behrens, Chief Operating Officer

5020 Educational Testing Service
Rosedale Road
Princeton, NJ 8541
609-921-9000
Fax: 609-734-5410
http://www.ets.org
To advance quality and equity in education by providing fair and valid assessments, research and related services. Our products and services measure knowledge and skills, promote learning and educational performance, and support education and professional development for all people worldwide.

Susan Keipper, Program Director
Kurt Landgraf, President and CEO

5021 Florida Atlantic University-Multifunctional Resource Center
1515 W Commercial Boulevard
Suite 303
Boco Raton, FL 33309-3095
561-297-3000
800-328-6721
Fax: 561-297-2141
Provides training and technical assistance to Title VII-funded classroom instructional projects and other programs serving limited-English proficient students.

Dr Ann C Willig, Director
Elaine Sherr, Research Assistant

5022 Higher Education Center
National Education Association (NEA)
1201 16th Street NW
Washington, DC 20036-3290
202-833-4000
Fax: 202-822-7974
E-mail: ncuea@nea.org
http://www.nea.org
The center provides data and other research products to NEA higher education affiliates. The Research Advisory Group, composed of higher education leaders and staff, meets twice a year to review products from the NEA Research Center for Higher Education and make recommendations about additional research needs. The center currently provides salary reports, Higher Education Contract Analysis System, and budget analysis.

Dennis Van Roekel, President
John I Wilson, Executive Director

5023 Information Center on Education
Eba Room 385
Albany, NY 12234-1
518-474-8716
Fax: 518-473-7737
Coordinates data collection procedures within the New York State Education Department.

Leonard Powell, Director

5024 Information Exchange
Maine State Library
64 State House Station
Augusta, ME 4333-64
207-287-5620
800-322-8899
Fax: 207-287-5624
Provides access to the latest education research and information for teachers.

Edna M Comstock, Director

5025 Institute for Research in LearningDisabilities
The University of Kansas
3060 Robert
Lawrence, KS 66045-1
785-864-4780
Fax: 785-864-5728
Although the focus of the Institute's research is children, they have a sizeable publication list with some of their research having relevance for adults.

5026 Instructional Materials Laboratory
University of Missouri-Columbia
8 London Hall
Columbia, MO 65211-2230
800-669-2465
800-669-2465
Fax: 573-882-1992
E-mail: iml@missouri.edu
http://www.iml.missouri.edu/
Prepares and disseminates instructional materials for the vocational education community.

Dana Tannehill, Director
Richard Branton, Assistant Director

5027 Learning Research and Development Center
University of Pittsburgh
3939 O'Hara Street
Pittsburgh, PA 15260
412-624-7487
Fax: 412-624-3051
E-mail: lrangel@pitt.edu
http://www.lrdc.pitt.edu
LRDC fosters an environment in which research initiatives relating to the science, practice, organization and technology of learning, teaching and training are born and thrive.

Charles Perfetti, Director
Alan Lesgold, Senior Scientist/Research Sc

5028 Life Lab Science Program
1156 High Street
Santa Cruz, CA 95064
831-459-2001
Fax: 831-459-3483
E-mail: lifelab@lifelab.org
http://www.lifelab.org
Life Lab Science Program is nationally acknowledged as an expert leader in the development and dissemination of garden-centered educational programs.

Gail Harlamoff, Executive Director
Whitney Cohen, Education Director

5029 Merrimack Education Center
101 Mill Road
Chelmsford, MA 1824-4899
978-256-3985
Fax: 978-256-6890
E-mail: cjeffers@meccorp.mec.edu
http://www.mec.edu/
Merrimack Education Center (MEC) is a diversified educational and technological resource for schools, cities and towns and other non-profit organizations. MEC offers a broad range of special education, professional development, facilities management and technology programs and solutions.

John Barranco, Director

5030 Mid-Atlantic Regional Educational Laboratory
1301 Cecil B Moore Avenue
Philadelphia, PA 19122-6091
215-204-3000
Fax: 215-204-5130
E-mail: robert.sullivan@temple.edu
http://www.temple.edu/lss
The Regional Educational Laboratories are educational research and development organizations supported by contracts with the US Education Department. Specialty area: Education Leadership.

William Evans, Director

5031 Mid-Continent Regional Educational Laboratory
2550 S Parker Road
Suite 500
Aurora, CO 80014-1678
303-337-0990
Fax: 303-337-3005
Focuses on improvement of education practices in Colorado, Kansas, Missouri, Nebraska, Wyoming, North Dakota and South Dakota.

C. Lawrence Hutchins, Director

5032 Midwestern Regional Educational Laboratory
1900 Spring Road
Suite 300
Oak Brook, IL 60521
630-649-6500
Fax: 630-649-6700
E-mail: nowakows@ncrel.org
The Regional Educational Laboratories are educational research and development organizations supported by contracts with the US Education Department, Office of Educational Research and Improvement. Specialty area: Technology.

Dr. Jeri Nowakowski, Executive Director

5033 Missouri LINC
401 E Stewart Road
Columbia, MO 65211
573-882-2733
800-392-0533
Fax: 573-882-5071
Serves students with special needs through a resource and technical assistance center.

Linda Bradley, Director

5034 Music Teachers National Association
441 Vine Street
Suite 3100
Cincinnatti, OH 45202-3004
513-421-1420
888-512-5278
Fax: 513-421-2503
E-mail: mtnanet@mtna.org
http://www.mtna.org
Research reports dealing with any aspects of music, music teaching, music learning and related subjects.

Rachel Kramer, Member Liaison

5035 NEA Foundatrion for the Improvement ofEducation
1201 16th Street NW
Washington, DC 20036
202-822-7840
Fax: 202-822-7779
E-mail: info@neafoundation@list.nea.org
http://www.neafoundation.org
The NEA Foundation, through the unique strength of its partnership with educators, advances student achievement by investing in public education that will prepare each of America's children to learn and thrive in a rapidly changing world.

Aaron J Pope, Communications Associate
John I Wilson, Executive Director

5036 National Black Child Development Institute
1313 L Street, NW
Suite 110
Washington, DC 20005-4110
202-833-2220
800-556-2234
Fax: 202-833-8222
E-mail: moreinfo@nbcdi.org
http://www.nbcdi.org
NBCDI's mission is to improve and protect the quality of life of Black children and families.

Carol Brunson Day, President
Gillian Shurland, Contact

5037 National Center for Improving Science Education
2000 L Street NW
Suite 616
Washington, DC 20036-4917
202-467-0652
Fax: 202-467-0659
Promotes change in state and local policies and practices in science curricula, teaching, and assessment.

Senta A Raizen, Director

5038 National Center for Research in Mathematical Sciences Education
University of Wisconsin-Madison
1025 W Johnson Street
#557
Madison, WI 53706-1706
608-263-4285
Fax: 608-263-3406
Provides a research base for the reform of school mathematics.

Thomas A Romberg, Director

5039 National Center for Research in Vocational Education
University of California, Berkeley
2030 Addison Street
Suite 500
Berkeley, CA 94720-1674
510-642-4004
800-762-4093
Fax: 510-642-2124
E-mail: NCRVE@berkeley.edu
http://vocserve.berkeley.edu
The mission of the National Center for Research in Vocational Education (NCRVE) is to strengthen education to prepare all individuals for lasting and rewarding employment and lifelong learning.

David Stern, Director
Phyllis Hudecki, Associate Director

5040 National Center for Research on Teacher Learning
Michigan State University, College of Education
116 Erickson Hall
East Lansing, MI 48824-1034

517-355-9302
Fax: 517-432-2795
E-mail: floden_@_msu.edu
http://ncrtl.msu.edu
The NCRTL extended its findings about learning from students-as-learners to teachers-as-learners in order to understand how teachers learn to teach.

Robert E Floden, Director
G Williamson McDiarmid, Director

5041 National Center for Science Teaching & Learning
Ohio State University
1314 Kinnear Road
Columbus, OH 43212-1156
614-292-3339
Fax: 614-292-0263
Seeks to understand how non-curricular factors affect how science is taught in grades K-12.

Arthur L White, Director

5042 National Center for the Study of Privatization in Education
525 W 120th Street
Box 181, 230 Thompson Hall
New York, NY 10027-6696
212-678-3259
Fax: 212-678-3474
E-mail: ncspe@columbia.edu
http://www.ncspe.org
The goal of the National Center for the Study of Privatization in Education is to provide an independent, non-partisan source of analysis and information on privatization in education.

Henry M Levin, Director
Clive Belfield, Associate Director

5043 National Center on Education & the Economy
555 13th Street, NW
Suite 500 W
Washington, DC 20004
202-783-3668
888-361-6233
Fax: 202-783-3672
E-mail: info@ncee.org
http://www.ncee.org
NCEE is committed not just to research, analysis and advocacy, but also to following through on its recommendations by creating the training, professional development, technical assistance and materials that professionals in the system need to implement the proposals we make.

Marc Tucker, President/Founder
Rich Moglia Cannon, Chief Financial Officer

5044 National Center on Education in the Inner Cities
Temple University
13th Street & Cecil B Moore Avenue
Philadelphia, PA 19122
215-893-8400
Fax: 215-735-9718
Conducts systematic studies of innovative initiatives for improving the quality and outcomes of schooling and broad-based efforts to strengthen and improve education.

Margaret C Wang, Director

5045 National Child Labor Committee
1501 Broadway
Suite 1908
New York, NY 10036-5592
212-840-1801
Fax: 212-768-0963
E-mail: info@nationalchildlabor.org
http://www.nationalchildlabor.org

The National Child Labor Committee (NCLC) is a private, non-profit organization founded in 1904 and incorporated by an Act of Congress in 1907 with the mission of promoting the rights, awareness, dignity, well-being and education of children and youth as they relate to work and working.

Jeffrey F Newman, President/Executive Director
Erik Butler, President

5046 National Clearinghouse for Alcohol & Drug Information
PO Box 2345
Rockville, MD 20847-2345
240-221-4019
800-729-6686
Fax: 240-221-4292
http://ncadi.samhsa.gov
SAMHSA's National Clearinghouse for Alcohol and Drug Information (NCADI) is the Nation's one-stop resource for information about substance abuse prevention and addiction treatment.

John Noble, Director

5047 National Clearinghouse for Bilingual Education
George Washington University
2011 Eye Street NW
Suite 300
Washington, DC 20006
202-467-0867
800-321-6223
Fax: 202-467-4283
E-mail: askncela@ncela.gwu.edu
http://www.ncela.gwu.edu
OELA's National Clearinghouse collects, coordinates and conveys a broad range of research and resources in support of an inclusive approach to high quality education for ELLs.

Nancy Zelasko, Director
Minerva Gorena, Director

5048 National Clearinghouse for Information on Business Involvement in Education
National Association for Industry-Education Co-op
235 Hendricks Boulevard
Buffalo, NY 14226-3304
716-834-7047
Fax: 718-834-7047
E-mail: www2.pecom/naiec
http://www2.pecom.net/naiec
Seeks to foster industry-education cooperation in the US and Canada in the areas of school improvement, career education and human resource/economic development.

Dr. Donald Clark, Director

5049 National Dropout Prevention Center
Clemson University
209 Martin Street
Clemson, SC 29631-1555
864-656-2599
Fax: 864-656-0136
E-mail: ndpc@clemson.edu
http://www.dropoutprevention.org
Provide knowledge and promote networking for researchers, practitioners, policymakers, and families to increase opportunities for youth in at-risk situations to receive the quality education and services to successfully graduate from high school.

Jay Smink, Executive Director
Marty Duckenfield, Public Information Director

5050 National Early Childhood Technical Assistance System
517 S Greensboro Street
Carrboro, NC 27510
919-962-2001
919-843-3269
Fax: 919-966-7463
E-mail: nectac@unc.edu
http://www.nectac.org
NECTAC is the national early childhood technical assistance center supported by the U.S. Department of Education's Office of Special Education Programs.

Lynne Kahn, Director
Joan Danaher, Associate Director

5051 National Information Center for Educational Media
PO Box 8640
Albuquerque, NM 87198-8640
505-998-0800
800-926-8328
Fax: 505-256-1080
E-mail: mhlava@accessinn.com
http://www.nicem.com/index.html
The world's most comprehensive audiovisual database for over 35 years and a crucial reference tool for librarians, media specialists, training directors, faculty, teachers and researchers.

Marjorie Hlava, President
Jay Van Eman, Chief Executive Officer

5052 National Research Center on the Gifted & Talented
University of Connecticut
2131 Hillside Road
Unit 3007
Storrs, CT 6269-3007
860-486-4826
Fax: 860-486-2900
http://www.gifted.uconn.edu
Studies focusing on meeting the needs of gifted and talented youth have received national and international attention for over 40 years.

Joseph S Renzulli, Director
Phillip E Austin, President

5053 National Resource Center on Self-Care & School-Age Child Care
American Home Economics Association
1555 King Street
Alexandria, VA 22314-2738
703-706-4620
800-252-SAFE
Fax: 703-706-4663
Provides materials to parents, educators, child care professionals and others concerned about the number of latchkey children and about quality school-age child care.

Dr. Margaret Plantz, Director

5054 National School Boards Association Library
1680 Duke Street
Alexandria, VA 22314-3455
703-838-6731
Fax: 703-683-7590
Maintains up-to-date collection of resources concerning education issues, with an emphasis on school board policy issues.

Adria Thomas, Director

5055 National School Safety Center
141 Duesenberg Drive
Suite 11
Westlake Village, CA 91362-3815
805-373-9977
Fax: 805-373-9277
E-mail: info@schoolsafety.us
http://www.schoolsafety.us

Serves as an advocate for safe, secure and peaceful schools worldwide and as a catalyst for the prevention of school crime and violence.

Ronald D Stephens, Executive Director
June Lane Arnette, Associate Director

5056 National Science Resources Center
901 D Street SW
Suite 704B
Washington, DC 20024
202-633-2966
Fax: 202-287-2070
E-mail: nsrcinfo@si.edu
http://www.nsrconline.org
Intermediary organization that bridges research on how children learn with best practices for the classroom.

Sally Shuler, Executive Director
Jennifer Childress, Director

5057 North Central Regional Educational Laboratory
1120 East Diehl Road
Suite 200
Naperville, IL 60563-1486
630-649-6500
Fax: 630-649-6700
E-mail: info@ncrel.org
http://www.ncrel.org
Being an educator is a great responsibility. At Learning Point Associates, we accept responsibility in order to deserve the trust that has been placed in us and our work

Gina Burkhard, Chief Executive Officer
Robert Davis, Chief Financial Officer

5058 Northeast Regional Center for Drug-Free Schools & Communities
12 Overton Avenue
Sayville, NY 11782-2437
718-340-7000
Fax: 516-589-7894
Works to support the prevention of alcohol and other drug use in the northeast region of the United States.

Dr. Gerald Edwards, Director

5059 Northeast and Islands Regional Educational Laboratory
222 Richmond Street
Suite 300
Providence, RI 2903
401-274-9548
800-521-9550
Fax: 401-421-7650
E-mail: info@lab.brown.edu
http://www.lab.brown.edu
Promotes educational change to provide all students equitable opportunities to succeed. We advocate for populations whose access to excellent education has been limited or denied.

Oaxaca Schroder, Administrative Assistant
Sunitha Appikatla, Senior Programmer/Analyst

5060 Northwest Regional Educational Laboratory
101 SW Main Street
Suite 500
Portland, OR 97204-3213
503-275-9500
800-547-6339
Fax: 503-275-0660
E-mail: info@nwrel.org
http://www.nwrel.org
The mission of the Northwest Regional Educational Laboratory (NWREL) is to improve learning by building capacity in schools, fam-

ilies, and communities through applied research and development

Jerry Colonna, Chairperson
Rob Larson, Vice Chairperson

5061 Pacific Regional Educational Laboratory
1099 Alakea Street
Suite 2500
Honolulu, HI 96813
808-969-3482
Fax: 808-969-3483
E-mail: kofelj@prel.hawaii.edu
The Regional Educational Laboratories are educational research and development organizations supported by contracts with the U.S. Education Department, Office of Educational Research and Improvement. Specialty area: Language and Cultural Diversity.

Dr. John Kofel, Executive Director

5062 Parent Educational Advocacy Training Center
100 N Washington Street
Suite 234
Falls Church, VA 22046
804-819-1999
E-mail: partners@peatc.org
http://www.peatc.org
Mission is to build positive futures for children in Virginia by working collaboratively with families, schools and communities in order to improve opportunities for excellence in education and success in school and community life.

Cathy Healy, CEO
Michael Heaney, President

5063 Parents as Teachers National Center
2228 Ball Drive
Saint Louis, MO 63146
314-432-4330
866-728-4968
Fax: 314-432-8963
E-mail: info@parentsasteachers.org
http://www.patnc.org
To provide the information, support and encouragement parents need to help their children develop optimally during the crucial early years of life.

Sue Stepleton, President/CEO
Cheryl Dyle-Palmer, COO

5064 Public Education Fund Network
601 13th Street NW
Suite 710 S
Washington, DC 20005-3808
202-628-7460
Fax: 202-628-1893
E-mail: PEN@PublicEducation.org
http://www.publiceducation.org
To build public demand and mobilize resources for quality public education for all children through a national constituency of local education funds and individuals.

Wendy D Puriefoy, Director
Richard J. Vierk, Chairman

5065 Quality Education Data
1050 Seventeenth Street
Suite 1100
Denver, CO 80265
303-209-9400
800-525-5811
Fax: 303-209-9444
E-mail: info@qeddata.com
http://www.qeddata.com
Gathers information about K-12 schools, colleges and other educational institutions, offers an on-line database on education,

directories of public and nonpublic schools and research reports.

Jeanne Hayes, President
Katie Bukovsky, Sales Executive

5066 Regional Laboratory for Educational Improvement of the Northeast
555 New Jersey Ave NW
Washington, DC 20208
800-347-4200
Fax: 781-481-1120
Seeks to improve education in Connecticut, Maine, Massachusetts, New Hampshire, New York, Rhode Island, Vermont, Puerto Rico and the Virgin Islands.

David P Crandall, Director

5067 Research for Better Schools
112 N Broad Street
Philadelphia, PA 19102-2471
215-568-6150
Fax: 215-568-7260
E-mail: info@rbs.org
http://www.rbs.org
RBS is a private, nonprofit educational organization funded primarily through grants and contracts from the U.S. Department of Education, the National Science Foundation, Mid-Atlantic state departments of education, institutions of higher education, foundations, and school districts.

Dr. Keith M Kershner, Executive Director
Rev. John F Bloh, President

5068 SERVE
PO Box 5367
Greensboro, NC 27435
336-315-7400
800-755-3277
Fax: 336-315-7457
E-mail: info@serve.org
http://www.serve.org
Its mission is to support and promote teaching and learning excellence in the Pre-kindergarten to Grade 12 education community.

Ludwig Van Broekhuizen, Executive Director
Francena Cummings, Director, Technical Assistan

5069 SIGI PLUS
Educational Testing Service
105 Terry Drive
Suite 120
Newtown, PA 18940-1872
800-257-7444
Fax: 215-579-8589
A computerized career guidance program developed by Educational Testing Service. Covers all the major aspects of career decision making and planning through a carefully constructed system of nine separate but interrelated sections, including a Tech Prep module and Internet Hydrolink Connectivity.

Annie Schofer, Sales Manager

5070 Satellite Educational Resources Consortium
939 S Stadium Road
Columbia, SC 29201-4724
803-252-2782
Fax: 803-252-5320
http://www.serc.org
Seeks to expand educational opportunities by employing the latest telecommunication technologies to make quality education in math, science, and foreign languages available equally and cost-effectively to students regardless of their geographic location.

Wilbur H Hinton, Executive Director

5071 Scientific Learning
300 Frank H Ogawa Plaza
Suite 600
Oakland, CA 94612-2040
888-665-9707
888-665-9707
Fax: 510-444-3580
E-mail: customerservice@scilearn.com
http://www.scientificlearning.com
Scientific Learning bases their products and services on neuroscience research and scientifically validated efficacy and deliver them using the most efficient technologies. We also provide beneficial products and services to our customers that are easy to use and access.

Robert C Bowen, Chairman/CEO
Andy Myers, President/COO

5072 Smithsonian Institution/Office of Elementary & Secondary Education
PO Box 37012
SI Building, Room 153, MRC 010
Washington, DC 20013-7012
202-633- 100
Fax: 202-357-2116
E-mail: info@si.edu
http://si.edu
Helps K-12 teachers incorporate museums and other community resources into their curricula.

Ann Bay, Director
G Wayne Clough, Secretary

5073 Society for Research in Child Development
University of Chicago Press
2950 S State Street
Suite 401
Ann Arbor, MI 48104
734-926-0600
Fax: 734-926-0601
E-mail: info@srcd.org
http://www.srcd.org
The Society is a multidisciplinary, not-for-profit, professional association with a membership

Barbara Kahn, Business Manager
Lonnie Sherrod, Executive Director

5074 Southeast Regional Center for Drug-Free Schools & Communities
Spencerian Office Plaza
Louisville, KY 40292-1
502-588-0052
800-621-7372
Fax: 502-588-1782
Works to support the prevention of alcohol and drug use among youth in the Southeast region.

Nancy J Cunningham, Director

5075 Southern Regional Education Board
592 10th Street NW
Atlanta, GA 30318-5776
404-875-9211
Fax: 404-872-1477
E-mail: evalutech@sreb.org
http://www.sreb.org
Nonprofit, nonpartisan organization that helps government and education leaders in its 16 member states work together to advance education and improve the social and economic life of the region.

Mark D Musick, Director
David S Spence, President

5076 Southwest Comprehensive Regional Assistance Center-Region IX
New Mexico Highlands University
121 Tijeras Avenue NE
Suite 2100
Albuquerque, NM 87102-3461

800-247-4269
Fax: 505-243-4456
National network of 15 technical assistance centers, funded through the US Department of Education, designed to support federally funded educational programs. Specifically, these centers will provide comprehensive training and technical assistance under the Improving America's Schools Act (IASA) to States, Tribes, community based organizations, local education agencies, schools and other recipients of funds under the Act.

Paul E Martinez EdD, Director

5077 Southwestern Educational Development Laboratory
4700 Mueller Boulevard
Austin, TX 78723
512-476-6861
800-476-6861
Fax: 512-476-2286
E-mail: info@sedl.org
http://www.sedl.org
SEDL is a private, nonprofit corporation dedicated to fulfilling its mission with clients and other education stakeholders on a national, regional, state, and local basis through diverse and interrelated funding, partnerships, and projects.

Dr. Wesley A Hoover, Executive Director
Christine A Moses, Director of Communications

5078 Special Interest Group for Computer Science Education
Computer Science Department
University of Texas at Austin
Austin, TX 78712
512-471-9539
Fax: 512-471-8885
Provides a forum for solving problems common in developing, implementing and evaluating computer science education programs and courses.

Nell B Dale, Director

5079 TACS/WRRC
1268 University of Oregon
Eugene, OR 97403
541-346-5641
Fax: 541-346-0322
E-mail: wrrc@oregon.uoregon.edu
http://wrrc.uoregon.edu/tacs
Supports state education agencies in their task of ensuring quality programs and services for children with disabilities and their families.

Richard Zeller, Co-Director
Caroline Moore, Project Director

5080 TERC
2067 Massachusetts Avenue
Cambridge, MA 2140-1340
617-873-9600
Fax: 617-873-9601
E-mail: communications@terc.edu
http://www.terc.edu
We imagine a future in which learners from diverse communities engage in creative, rigorous, and reflective inquiry as an integral part of their lives.

24 pages
ISSN: 0743-0221

Ken Mayer, Communications Director
Arthur Nelson, Chairman/Founder

5081 UCLA Statistical Consulting
University of California, Los Angeles
8130 MSB, UCLA
PO Box 951554
Los Angeles, CA 90095-1554
310-825-8299
Fax: 310-206-5658

Provides statistical consulting services to UCLA and off-campus students. The staff is faculty members, graduate students and the Department of Statistics. Specializes in the quantitative analysis of research problems in a wide variety of fields.

Debbie Barrera, Administrator
Richard Berk, Director

Audio Visual Materials

5082 AGC/United Learning
Discovery Education
1560 Sherman Avenue
Suite 100
Evanston, IL 60201
847-328-6700
800-323-9084
Fax: 847-328-6706
http://www.discoveryed.com
A publisher/producer of educational videos and digital content K-College curriculum based.

Coni Rechner, Director Marketing
Ronald Reed, Sr. Vice President

5083 Active Parenting Publishing
810 Franklin Court
Suite B
Marietta, GA 30067
800-825-0060
Fax: 770-429-0334
E-mail: cservice@activeparenting.com
http://www.activeparenting.com
Videos and books on parenting, character education, substance abuse prevention, divorce and step-parenting, ADHD and more.

5084 Agency for Instructional Technology/AIT
PO Box A
Bloomington, IN 47402-0120
800-457-4509
Videodiscs, videocassettes, films and electronics.

5085 Allied Video Corporation
PO Box 702618
Tulsa, OK 74170-2618
918-587-6477
800-926-5892
Fax: 918-587-1550
E-mail: allied@farpointer.net
http://www.alliedvd.com
Produces the educational video series, The Assistant Professor. Animations and three-dimensional graphics clearly illustrate concepts in mathematics, science and music. Companion supplementary materials are also available.

Video

Charles Brown, President

5086 Altschul Group Corporation
1560 Sherman Avenue
Suite 100
Evanston, IL 60201-4817
800-323-9084
Video and film educational programs.

5087 Ambrose Video Publishing Inc
145 West 45th Street
New York, NY 10036
212-768-7373
800-526-4663
Fax: 212-768-9282
http://www.ambrosevideo.com
A leading distributor of broadcast quality documentation/educational videos to individuals (in the home) and schools, libraries and other institutions. The company also sells through catalog, sales staff and television advertising.

5088 Anchor Audio
3415 Lomita Boulevard
Torrance, CA 90505-5010
310-784-2300
800-262-4671
Fax: 310-784-0533
http://www.anchoraudio.com
Various audio visual products for the school and library.

5089 Association for Educational Communications & Technology
1025 Vermont Avenue NW
Suite 820
Washington, DC 20005-3516
202-347-7834
Offers a full line of videotapes and films for the various educational fields including language arts, science and social studies.

5090 BUILD Sucess Through the Values of Excellence
Center for the Study of Small/Rural Schools
555 E Constitution Street
Room 138
Norman, OK 73072-7820
405-325-1450
Fax: 405-325-7075
E-mail: jcsimmons@ou.edu
http://cssrs.ou.edu
Series IV

Video

Jan C Simmons, Director

5091 Bergwall Productions
540 Baltimore Pike
Chadds Ford, PA 19317-9304
800-645-3565
Educational videotapes and films.

5092 Cedrus
1420 Buena Vista Avenue
McLean, VA 22101-3510
703-883-0986
Videodiscs, videocassettes and filmstrips for educational purposes.

5093 Character Education
Center for the Study of Small/Rural Schools
555 E Constitution Street
Room 138
Norman, OK 73072-7820
405-325-1450
Fax: 405-325-7075
E-mail: jcsimmons@ou.edu
http://cssrs.ou.edu
Series IV

Video

Jan C Simmons, Director

5094 Chip Taylor Communications
2 E View Drive
Derry, NH 03038-5728
603-434-9262
800-876-2447
Fax: 603-432-2723
E-mail: sales@chiptaylor.com
http://www.chiptaylor.com
Quality educational videotapes and DVDs and multimedia in all areas of interest.

Video

Chip Taylor, President

5095 Churchill Media
6677 N NW Highway
Chicago, IL 60631-1304
310-207-6600
800-334-7830
Fax: 800-624-1678
Videos, videodiscs and curriculum packages for schools and libraries.

5096 College Board Publications
College Board Publications
45 Columbus Avenue
New York, NY 10023-6992
212-713-8165
800-323-7155
Fax: 800-525-5562
http://www.collegeboard.org
Offers a variety of educational videotapes and publications focusing on college issues.

5097 Computer Prompting & Captioning Company
1010 Rockville Pike
Suite 306
Rockville, MD 20852-3035
301-738-8487
800-977-6678
Fax: 301-738-8488
E-mail: info@cpcweb.com
http://www.cpcweb.com
Closed captioning systems and service.

Sid Hoffman, Project Manager

5098 Concept Media
2493 Du Bridge Avenue
Irvine, CA 92606-5022
949-660-0727
800-233-7078
Fax: 949-660-0206
E-mail: info@conceptmedia.com
http://www.conceptmedia.com
Videos for students and professionals focused on child development, early childhood education, and the challenges facing many young children. Effective educational media for development specialists, regular and special education staff in elementary school, preschool teachers, childcare providers, health care workers and parents.

Dennis Timmerman, Sr Account Executive

5099 Crystal Productions
PO Box 2159
Glenview, IL 60025-6159
847-657-8144
800-255-8629
Fax: 800-657-8149
E-mail: custserv@crystalproductions.com
http://www.crystalproductions.com
Producer and distributor of educational resource material in art and sciences. Resources include videotapes, posters, books, videodiscs, CD-Rom, reproductions, games.

132 pages

Amy Woodworth, President

5100 Dukane Corporation
Audio Visual Products Division
2900 Dukane Drive
St Charles, IL 60174-3395
630-584-2300
Fax: 630-584-5156
Full line of audio visual products, LCD display panels, computer data projectors, overhead projectors, microfilm readers and silent and sound filmstrip projectors.

Stew deLacey

5101 Early Advantage
270 Monroe Turnpike
PO Box 4063
Monroe, CT 06468-4063
888-999-4670
Fax: 800-301-9268
E-mail:
customerservice@early-advantage.com
http://www.earlyadvantage.com
Features the Muzzy video collection for teaching children beginning second language skills.

5102 Educational Video Group
291 S Wind Way
Greenwood, IN 46142-9190
317-888-6581
Fax: 317-888-5857
E-mail: evg@insightbb.com
http://www.evgonline.com
Award-winning video programs and textbooks in education, presenting new offerings in speech, government and historic documentaries.

Roger Cook, President

5103 English as a Second Language Video Series
Master Teacher
Leadership Lane
PO Box 1207
Manhattan, KS 66505-1207
800-669-9633
Fax: 800-669-1132
http://www.masterteacher.com
Assessing the needs of culturally diverse learners, you will learn what must be done to evaluate the learning needs and progress of ESL students.

ISBN: 1-58992-045-7

5104 Fase Productions
4801 Wilshire Boulevard
Suite 215
Los Angeles, CA 90010-3813
213-965-8794
Educational videotapes and films.

5105 Films for Humanities & Sciences
PO Box 2053
Princeton, NJ 08543-2053
609-419-8000
800-257-5126
Fax: 609-419-8071
A leading publisher/distributor of over four thousand educational programs, including NOVA and TV Ontario, for school and college markets. Also a leader in the production and distribution of videotapes and videodiscs to the educational, institutional and government markets.

5106 First Steps/Concepts in Motivation
18105 Town Center Drive
Olney, MD 20832-1479
301-774-9429
800-947-8377
Educational videotapes and accessories promoting physical fitness for preschoolers and young children. Using choreographed dance movement, familiar and fun children's music, colorful mats, bean bags and rhythm sticks, First Steps teaches balance, gross and fine motor skills, rhythm, coordination, and primary learning skills.

Dale Rimmey, Marketing Director
Larry Rose, President/Owner

5107 Future of Rural Education
Center for the Study of Small/Rural Schools
555 E Constitution Street
Room 138
Norman, OK 73072-7820
405-325-1450
Fax: 405-325-7075
E-mail: jcsimmons@ou.edu
http://cssrs.ou.edu
Series I

Video

Jan C Simmons, Director

5108 GPN Year 2005 Literacy Catalog
GPN Educational Media
PO Box 80669
Lincoln, NE 68501-0669
402-472-2007
800-228-4630
Fax: 402-472-4076
E-mail: gpn@unl.edu
http://www.gpn.unl.edu
DVD, VHS, CD-ROM and slides for K-12 libraries and higher education. Free previews and satisfaction guaranteed. The sole source of Reading Rainbow and many other quality programs seen on PBS.

Annually/Video

Stephen C Lenzen, Executive Director
John Vondracek, Director Marketing

5109 Gangs in Our Schools: Identification, Response, and Prevention Strategies
Center for the Study of Small/Rural Schools
555 E Constitution Street
Room 138
Norman, OK 73072-7820
405-325-1450
Fax: 405-325-7075
E-mail: jcsimmons@ou.edu
http://cssrs.ou.edu
Series III

Video

Jan C Simmons, Director

5110 Guidance Associates
PO Box 1000
Mount Kisco, NY 10549-7000
800-431-1242
Fax: 914-666-5319
E-mail: sales@guidanceassociates.com
http://www.guidanceassociates.com
Curriculum based videos in health/guidance, social studies, math, science, English, the humanities and career education.

Will Goodman, President

5111 Health Connection
55 W Oak Ridge Drive
Hagerstown, MD 21740
800-548-8700
Fax: 888-294-8405
E-mail: sales@healthconnection.org
http://www.healthconnection.org
Tools for freedom from tobacco and other drugs.

5112 Human Relations Media
175 Tompkins Avenue
Pleasantville, NY 10570-3144
800-431-2050
Fax: 914-244-0485
Offers a wide variety of videotapes and videodiscs in the areas of guidance, social services, human relations, self-esteem and student services.

5113 IIEPassport: Short Term Study Abroad
Institute of International Education
809 United Nations Plaza
New York, NY 10017-3580
412-741-0930
Fax: 212-984-5496
E-mail: iiebooks@abdintl.com
http://www.iiebooks.org
Over 2,900 short-term study abroad programs offered by universities, schools, associations and other organizations.

Annual
ISBN: 087206-296-1

Daniel Obst, Sr Editor

5114 INSIGHTS Visual Productions
374-A N Highway 101
Encinitas, CA 92024-2527
760-942-0528
Fax: 760-944-7793
Science video for K-12 and teacher training.

5115 INTELECOM Intelligent Telecommunications
150 E Colorado Boulevard
Suite 300
Pasadena, CA 91105-3710
626-796-7300
Fax: 626-577-4282
Videos and educational films.

Bob Miller, VP Marketing/Sale

5116 In Search of Character
Performance Resource Press
1270 Rankin Drive
Suite F
Troy, MI 48083-2843
800-453-7733
Fax: 800-499-5718
http://www.pronline.net
Character education videos.

5117 Instructional Resources Corporation
1819 Bay Ridge Avenue
Annapolis, MD 21403-2835
American History Videodisc.

5118 Intermedia
1165 Eastlake Ave East
Suite 400
Seattle, WA 98109-3571
206-284-2995
800-553-8336
Fax: 206-283-0778
http://www.intermedia-inc.com
Distributes a wide range of high-quality, social interest videos on topics such as teen pregnancy prevention, substance abuse prevention, domestic violence, sexual harassment, dating violence, date rape, gang education, cultural diversity, AIDS prevention and teen patenting. Offer free 30 day previews of the programs which are developed to address the needs of educators who must deal with the pressing social problems of today.

Paperback/Video

Susan Hoffman, President
Ted Fitch, General Manager

5119 International Historic Films
3533 S Archer Avenue
Chicago, IL 60609-1135
773-927-2900
Fax: 773-927-9211
E-mail: info@ihffilm.com
http://www.ihffilm.com
Military, political and social history of the 20th century.

Video/Audio

5120 January Productions
PO Box 66
Hawthorne, NJ 07507-0066
973-423-4666
800-451-7450
Fax: 973-423-5569
E-mail: anpeller@worldnet.att.net
Educational videotapes, read-a-long books, and CD-Rom.

Paperback/Video/Audi

Lori Brown, Sales/Marketing

5121 Karol Media
350 N Pennsylvania Avenue
Wilkes Barre, PA 18702-4415
570-822-8899
Fax: 570-822-8226
Science videos.

5122 Kimbo Educational
PO Box 477
Long Branch, NJ 07740-0477
800-631-2187
Manufacturer of children's audio-musical learning fun. Also offers videos and music by other famous children's artists such as Raffi, Sharon, Lois and Bram.

5123 Leadership: Rethinking the Future
Center for the Study of Small/Rural Schools
555 E Constitution Street
Room 138
Norman, OK 73072-7820
405-325-1450
Fax: 405-325-7075
E-mail: jcsimmons@ou.edu
http://cssrs.ou.edu
Series IV

Video

Jan C Simmons, Director

5124 MPC Multimedia Products Corp
1010 Sherman Avenue
Hamden, CT 06514
203-407-4623
800-243-2108
Fax: 203-407-4636
E-mail: sales@800-pickmpc.com
http://www.800-pickmpc.com
Over 5,000 most frequently requested high quality audio, visual and video products and materials offered at deep discount prices. Manufacturer of high quality tape records, CD's record players, PA systems, headphones
148 pages BiAnnual
T. Guercia, Author
T Guercia, VP
A Melillo, Sales Manager

5125 Main Street Foundations: Building Community Teams
Center for the Study of Small/Rural Schools
555 E Constitution Street
Room 138
Norman, OK 73072-7820
405-325-1450
Fax: 405-325-7075
E-mail: jcsimmons@ou.edu
http://cssrs.ou.edu
Prevention Series
Video
Jan C Simmons, Director

5126 Marshmedia
Marsh Media
8025 Ward Parkway Plaza
Kansas City, MO 64114
816-523-1059
800-821-3303
Fax: 816-333-7421
E-mail: order@marshmedia.com
http://www.marshmedia.com
Children's educational videotapes, books and teaching guides.
32 pages Bi-Annual
ISBN: 1-55942-xxx
Joan K Marsh, President

5127 Media Projects
5215 Homer Street
Dallas, TX 75206-6623
214-826-3863
Fax: 214-826-3919
E-mail: mediaprojects@noval.net
http://www.mediaprojects.org
Educational videotapes in all areas of interest, including drug education, violence prevention, women's studies, history, youth issues and special education.

5128 Middle School: Why and How
Center for the Study of Small/Rural Schools
555 E Constitution Street
Room 138
Norman, OK 73072-7820
405-325-1450
Fax: 405-325-7075
E-mail: jcsimmons@ou.edu
http://cssrs.ou.edu
Series III
Video
Jan C Simmons, Director

5129 Multicultural Educations: Valuing Diversity
Center for the Study of Small/Rural Schools
555 E Constitution Street
Room 138
Norman, OK 73072-7820
405-325-1450
Fax: 405-325-7075
E-mail: jcsimmons@ou.edu
http://cssrs.ou.edu

Series I
Video
Jan C Simmons, Director

5130 NUVO, Ltd.
PO Box 1729
Chula Vista, CA 91912
619-426-8440
Fax: 619-691-1525
E-mail: nuvoltd@aol.com
Produces and distributes how-to videotapes for teens and adults on beginning reading and decorative napkin folding useful in classroom instruction and individual practice. Also distributes two bilingual (Spanish/English) books by psychologist Dr. Jorge Espinoza.

5131 National Film Board
1251 Avenue of the Americas
New York, NY 10020-1104
800-542-2164
Fax: 845-774-2945
Educational films and videos ranging from documentaries on nature and science to social issues such as teen pregnancy.

5132 National Geographic School Publishing
PO Box 10579
Washington, DC 20090-8019
800-368-2728
Fax: 515-362-3366
Offers a wide variety of videodiscs, videotapes and educational materials in the area of social studies, geography, science and social sciences.

5133 PBS Video
1320 Braddock Pl
Alexandria, VA 22314-1649
703-739-5380
800-424-7963
Fax: 703-739-5269
Award-winning programs from PBS, public television's largest video distributors. Video and multimedia programming including interactive videodiscs for schools, colleges and libraries. The PBS Video Resource Catalog is organized into detailed subject categories.

5134 PICS Authentic Foreign Video
University of Iowa
270 International Center
Iowa City, IA 52242-1802
319-335-2335
800-373-PICS
Fax: 319-335-0280
Provides educators with authentic foreign language videos in French, German and Spanish on videotapes and videodisc. Also offers software to accompany the videodiscs as well as written materials in the form of transcripts and videoguides with pedagogical hints and tips.
Becky Bohde, German Coll Editor
Anny Ewing, French Coll Editor

5135 Penton Overseas
2470 Impala Drive
Carlsbad, CA 92008-7226
800-748-5804
Fax: 760-431-8110
Educational videotapes and videodiscs in a wide variety of interests for classroom use.

5136 Phoenix Films/BFA Educ Media/Coronet/MII
Phoenix Learning Group
2349 Chaffee Drive
St. Louis, MO 63146
314-569-0211
800-777-8100
Fax: 314-569-2834
E-mail: phoenixdealer@aol.com
http://www.phoenixlearninggroup.com

Educational multi-media - VHS, CD-Rom, DVD, streaming & broadcast.
Video
Kathy Longsworth, Vice President, Market Dev

5137 Presidential Classroom
119 Oronoco Street
Alexandria, VA 22314-2015
703-683-5400
800-441-6533
Fax: 703-548-5728
E-mail: eriedel@presidentialclassroom.org
http://www.presidentialclassroom.org
Video of civic education programs in Washington, DC for high school juniors and seniors. Each one week program provides students with an inside view of the federal government in action and their role as responsible citizens and future leaders.
Annual
400 attendees
Jack Buechner, President/CEO
Emily Davisriedel, Director Marketing

5138 Rainbow Educational Media Charles Clark Company
4540 Preslyn Drive
Raleigh, NC 27616
919-954-7550
800-331-4047
Fax: 919-954-7554
E-mail: karencf@rainbowedumedia.com
http://www.rainbowedumedia.com
Educational videocassettes and CD-Roms.
Karen C Francis, Business Analyst

5139 Rainbow Educational Video
170 Keyland Court
Bohemia, NY 11716-2638
800-331-4047
Producer and distributor of educational videos.
Wesley Clark, Marketing Director

5140 Reading & O'Reilly: The Wilton Programs
PO Box 302
Wilton, CT 06897-0302
800-458-4274
Producers and distributors of award-winning audiovisual educational programs in art appreciation, history, multicultural education, social studies and music. Titles include: African-American Art and the Take-a-Bow, musical production series. Free catalog is available of full product line.
Lee Reading, President
Gretchen O'Reilly, VP

5141 SAP Today
Performance Resource Press
1270 Rankin Drive
Suite F
Troy, MI 48083-2843
800-453-7733
Fax: 800-499-5718
Overview offers the basics of student assistance.

5142 SVE: Society for Visual Education
55 E Monroe Street
Suite 3400
Chicago, IL 60603-5710
312-849-9100
800-829-1900
Fax: 800-624-1678
Producer and distributor of curriculum based instructional materials including videodisc, microcomputer software, video cassettes and filmstrips for grade levels PreK-12.

299

5143 Slow Learning Child Video Series
Master Teacher
Leadership Lane
PO Box 1207
Manhattan, KS 66505-1207
800-669-9633
Fax: 800-669-1132
http://www.masterteacher.com
Provides a full understandging of the slow learning child and allows all educators to share in the excitment of teaching this invidual in ways that develop his or her emerging potenial to the fullest.

ISBN: 1-58992-157-0

Mildred Odom Bradley, Author

5144 Spoken Arts
PO Box 100
New Rochelle, NY 10802-0100
727-578-7600
Literature-based audio and visual products for library and K-12 classrooms.

5145 Teacher's Video Company
8150 S Krene Road
Tempe, AZ 85284
800-262-8837
Fax: 800-434-5638
http://www.teachersvideo.com
Video for teachers.

5146 Teen Court: An Alternative Approach toJuvenile Justice
Center for the Study of Small/Rural Schools
555 E Constitution Street
Room 138
Norman, OK 73072-7820
405-325-1450
Fax: 405-325-7075
E-mail: jcsimmons@ou.edu
http://cssrs.ou.edu
Prevention Series

Video

Jan C Simmons, Director

5147 Tools to Help Youth
529 S 7 Street
Suite 570
Minneapolis, MN 55415
800-328-0417
Fax: 612-342-2388
http://www.communityintervention.com
Books and videos on counseling, character education, anger management, life skills, and achohol, tobacco and other drug uses.

5148 Training Video Series for the Professional School Bus Driver
Master Teacher
Leadership Lane
PO Box 1207
Manhattan, KS 66505-1207
800-669-9633
Fax: 800-669-1132
http://www.masterteacher.com
Will help you provide bus drivers with consistent direction and training for the many situations thay will encounter beyond driving safety.

ISBN: 1-58992-082-1

5149 True Colors
Center for the Study of Small/Rural Schools
555 E Constitution Street
Room 138
Norman, OK 73072-7820
405-325-1450
Fax: 405-325-7075
E-mail: jcsimmons@ou.edu
http://cssrs.ou.edu

Series III

Video

Jan C Simmons, Director

5150 United Transparencies
435 Main Street
Johnson City, NY 13790-1935
607-729-6368
800-477-6512
Fax: 607-729-4820
A full line of overhead transparencies for Junior-Senior high school and colleges and technical programs.
D Hetherington

5151 Video Project
200 Estates Drive
Ben Lomond, CA 95005
800-475-2638
Fax: 905-278-2801
E-mail: videoproject@igc.org
http://www.videoproject.org
Distributor of environmental videos with a collection of over 500 programs for all grade levels, including Oscar and Emmy award winners. Many videotapes come with teacher's guides. Free catalogs available.
Terry Thiermann, Administrative Director
Ian Thiermann, Executive Director

5152 Weston Woods Studios
265 Post Road West
Westport, CT 06880
203-845-0197
800-243-5020
Fax: 203-845-0498
E-mail: wstnwoods@aol.com
Audiovisual adaptations of classic children's literature.

Video

Cindy Cardozo, Marketing Coordinator

Classroom Materials

5153 ABC School Supply
3312 N Berkeley Lake Road NW
Duluth, GA 30096-3024
Instructional materials and supplies.

5154 ADP Lemco
5970 W Dannon Way
West Jordan, UT 84088
801-280-4000
800-575-3626
Fax: 801-280-4040
E-mail: sales@adplemco.com
http://www.adplemco.com
Announcement boards, schedule boards, chalkboards, tackboard, marker boards, trophy cases, athletic equipment, gym divider curtains and basketball backstops.
David L Hall, Sr VP

5155 APCO
388 Grant Street SE
Atlanta, GA 30312-2227
404-688-9000
Fax: 404-577-3847
Classroom supplies including announcement and chalkboards.
Anne M Gallup

5156 AbleNet
2808 Fairview Avenue N
Roseville, MN 55113-1308
651-294-2200
800-322-0956
Fax: 651-294-2259
http://www.ablenetinc.com

Adaptive devices for students with disabilities from Pre-K through adult, as well as activities and games for students of all abilities.

5157 Accounter Systems USA
1107 S Mannheim Road
Suite 305
Westchester, IL 60154-2560
800-229-8765
Sports timers and clocks and classroom supplies.

5158 Accu-Cut Systems
1035 E Dodge Street
Fremont, NE 68025
402-721-4134
800-288-1670
Fax: 402-721-5778
E-mail: info@accucut.com
http://www.accucut.com
Manufacturer of die cutting machines dies.

5159 Airomat Corporation
2916 Engle Road
Fort Wayne, IN 46809-1198
260-747-7408
800-348-4905
Fax: 260-747-7409
E-mail: airomat@airomat.com
http://www.airomat.com
Mats and matting.
Jody Feasel, VP
Janie Feasel, President/CEO

5160 Airspace USA
89 Patton Avenue
Asheville, NC 28801
828-258-1319
800-872-1319
Fax: 828-258-1390
E-mail: sales@airspace-usa.com
http://www.airspacesolutions.com
Airspace Soft Center Play and Learn Systems provide a comprehensive range of play, learning and physical development opportunities using commercial grade and foam filled play equipment. Play manual provided.
Daniel Brenman, VP Sales/Marketing
Tracy Syxes, Administrator

5161 All Art Supplies
Art Supplies Wholesale
4 Enon Street
North Beverly, MA 01915
800-462-2420
Fax: 800-462-2420
E-mail: info@allartsupplies.com
http://www.allartsupplies.com
Art supplies at wholesale prices.

5162 American Foam
HC 37 Box 317 H
Lewisburg, WV 24901
304-497-3000
800-344-8997
Fax: 304-497-3001
http://www.bfoam.com
Carving blocks of foam.

5163 American Plastics Council
1300 Wilson Boulevard
Arlington, VA 22209
800-243-5790
http://www.plastics.org
Offers classroom materials on recycling and environmental education.

5164 Anatomical Chart Company
8221 Kimball Avenue
Skokie, IL 60076-2956
847-679-4700
http://www.anatomical.com
Maps and charts for educational purposes.

5165 Angels School Supply
600 E Colorado Boulevard
Pasadena, CA 91101-2006

626-584-0855
Fax: 626-584-0888
http://www.angelschoolsupply.com
School and classroom supplies.

Jennifer , Sales Representitive

5166 Aol@School
22070 Broderick Drive
Dulles, VA 20166
888-468-3768
E-mail: aol at school@aol.com
http://www.school.aol.com
Age-appropriate, high-quality educational
content tailored for K-12 students and educators. Aol@School focuses and filters the Web
for us, providing appropriate, developmental
access to the vast educational resources on the
internet.

5167 Armada Art Materials
Armada Art Inc.
142 Berkeley Street
Boston, MA 02116
617-859-3800
800-435-0601
Fax: 617-859-3808
E-mail: info@armadaart.com
http://www.armadaart.com

5168 Art Materials Catalog
United Art and Education
PO Box 9219
Fort Wayne, IN 46899
800-322-3247
Fax: 800-858-3247
http://www.unitednow.com
Art materials.

5169 Art Supplies Wholesale
4 R Enon Street
N Beverly, MA 01915
800-462-2420
Fax: 978-922-1495
E-mail: info@allartsupplies.com
http://www.allartsupplies.com
Wholesale art supplies.

5170 Art to Remember
10625 Deme Drive
Unit E
Indianapolis, IN 46236
317-826-0870
800-895-8777
Fax: 317-823-2822
http://www.arttoremember.com
A unique program that encourages your students' artisic creativity while providing an
opportunity to raise funds for schools.

5171 Artix
PO Box 25008
Kelowna, BC V1W3Y
250-861-5345
800-665-5345
http://www.artix.bc.ca
Papermaking kits.

5172 Assessories by Velma
PO Box 2580
Shasta, CA 96087-2580
Multicultural education-related products.

5173 At-Risk Resources
135 Dupont Street
PO Box 760
Plainview, NY 11803-0706
800-999-6884
Fax: 800-262-1886
Dealing with drug violence prevention, character education, self-esteem, teen sexuality,
dropout prevention, safe schoolks, career development, parenting crisis and trauma, and
professional development.

5174 Atlas Track & Tennis
19495 SW Teton Avenue
Tualatin, OR 97062-8846

800-423-5875
Fax: 503-692-0491
Specialty sport surfaces; synthetic running
tracks, tennis courts, and athletic flooring for
schools.

5175 Audio Forum
69 Broad Street
Guildford, CT 06437
203-453-9794
Fax: 203-453-9774
E-mail: info@audioforum.com
http://www.audioforum.com
Cassettes, CD's and books for language study.

5176 Badge-A-Minit
PO Box 800
La Salle, IL 61301-0800
815-883-8822
800-223-4103
Fax: 815-883-9696
E-mail: questions@badgeaminit.com
http://www.badgeaminit.com
Awards, trophies, emblems and badges for ed-
ucational purposes.

5177 Bag Lady School Supplies
9212 Marina Pacifica Drive N
Long Beach, CA 90803-3886
Classroom supplies.

5178 Bale Company
PO Box 6400
Providence, RI 02940-6400
800-822-5350
Fax: 401-831-5500
http://www.bale.com
Awards, medals, pins, plaques and trophies.

5179 Bangor Cork Company
William & D Streets
Pen Argyl, PA 18072
610-863-9041
Fax: 610-863-6275
Announcement boards.

Janice Cory, Customer Services Rep

5180 Baumgarten's
144 Ottley Drive
Atlanta, GA 30324-4016
404-874-7675
800-247-5547
Fax: 800-255-5547
E-mail: mlynch@baumgartens.com
http://www.baumgartens.com
Products available include pencil sharpeners,
pencil grips, pocket binders, disposable
aprons, American flags, practical colorful
clips, fastening devices in a variety of shapes
and sizes, identification security items, lami-
nation, magnifiers and key chains.

Michael Lynch, National Sales Manager

5181 Best Manufacturing Sign Systems
PO Box 577
Montrose, CO 81402-0577
970-249-2378
800-235-2378
Fax: 970-249-0223
E-mail: sales@bestsigns.com
http://www.bestsigns.com
Architectural and ADA signs, announcement
boards.

Mary Phillips, Sales Manager

5182 Best-Rite
201 N Crockett Avenue
#713
Cameron, TX 76520-3376
254-778-4727
800-749-2258
Fax: 866-888-7483
E-mail: boards@bestrite.com
http://www.bestrite.com
Quality visual display products which include
a complete line of chalk, marker, tack, bulle-

tin, fabric and projection boards. Display and
trophy cases, beginner boards, reversible
boards, mobile easels, desk-top and floor carrels and early childhood products are also
manufactured.
Bob Wilson, VP
Greg Moore, Executive VP

5183 Binney & Smith
1100 Church Lane
Easton, PA 18044
610-253-6271
800-CRA-YOLA
Fax: 610-250-5768
http://www.crayola.com
Crayons.

5184 Black History Month
Guidance Channel
135 Dupont Street
PO Box 760
Plainview, NY 44803-0706
800-999-6884
Fax: 800-262-1886
Products to celebrate Black history,
multicultutral resources.

5185 Blackboard Resurfacing Company
50 N 7th Street
Bangor, PA 18013-1731
610-588-0965
Fax: 610-863-1997
Chalk and announcement boards.

Karin Karpinski, Administrative Assistant

5186 Bob's Big Pencils
1848 E 27th Street
Hays, KS 67601-2108
Large novelty pencils, plaques, bookends and
many pencil related items.

5187 Book It!/Pizza Hut
9111 E Douglas Avenue
Wichita, KS 67207-1205
316-687-8401
National reading incentive program with materials, books and incentive display items to
get students interested in reading.

5188 Borden
Home & Professional Products Group
180 E Broad Street
Columbus, OH 43215-3799
614-225-7479
Fax: 614-225-7167
Arts and crafts supplies, maintenance and re-
pair supplies.

5189 Bulman Products
1650 McReynolds NW
Grand Rapids, MI 49504
616-363-4416
Fax: 616-363-0380
E-mail: bulman@macatawa.com
Art craft paper.

5190 Bydee Art
8603 Yellow Oak Street
Austin, TX 78729-3739
512-474-4343
Fax: 512-474-5749
Prints, books, T-shirts with the Bydee People
focusing on education.

5191 C-Thru Ruler Company
6 Britton Drive
Bloomfield, CT 06002-3632
860-243-0303
Fax: 860-243-1856
http://www.CThruRuler.com
Arts, crafts and classroom supplies.

Ross Zachs, Manager

5192 CHEM/Lawrence Hall of Science
University of California
Berkeley, CA 94720

301

510-642-6000
Fax: 510-642-1055
E-mail: lhsinfo@uclink.berkley.edu
http://www.lawrencehallofscience.org
Activities for grades 5-6 and helps students understand the use of chemicals in our daily lives.

Linda Schnieder, Marketing Manager
Mike Slater, Marketing/PR Associate

5193 CORD Communications
324 Kelly Street
Waco, TX 76710-5709
254-776-1822
Fax: 254-776-3906
Instructional materials for secondary and postsecondary applications in science education.

5194 Califone International
21300 Superior Street
Chatsworth, CA 91311-4328
818-407-2400
800-722-0500
Fax: 818-407-2491
http://www.califone.com
Multisensory, supplemental curricula on magnetic cards for use with all Card Reader/Language master equipment.

Nelly Spievak, Sales Coordinator

5195 Cardinal Industries
PO Box 1430
Grundy, VA 24614-1430
276-935-4545
800-336-0551
Fax: 276-935-4970
Awards, emblems, trophies and badges.

5196 Carousel Productions
1100 Wilcrest Drive
Suite 100
Houston, TX 77042-1642
281-568-9300
Fax: 281-568-9498
Moments in History T-shirts, as well as other various educational gifts and products.

5197 Cascade School Supplies
1 Brown Street
PO Box 780
North Adams, MA 01247
800-628-5078
Fax: 413-663-3719
Offers a variety of school supplies and more.

5198 Celebrate Diversity
Guidance Channel
135 Dupont Street
PO Box 760
Plainview, NY 44803-0706
800-999-6884
Fax: 800-262-1886
Educational resources that celebrate diversity.

5199 Celebrate Earth Day
Guidance Channel
135 Dupont Street
PO Box 760
Plainview, NY 44803-0706
800-999-6884
Fax: 800-262-1886
Educational resources for celebrating earth day.

5200 Center Enterprises
PO Box 33161
West Hartford, CT 06110
860-953-4423
Fax: 800-373-2923
Clifford individual curriculum and storybook stamp sets, individual, grading, curriculum based and Sweet Arts rubber stamp line, stamp pads, embossing inks and powders.

5201 Center for Learning
21590 Center Ridge Road
Rocky River, OH 44116-3963
440-331-1404
800-767-9090
Fax: 888-767-8080
E-mail: cfl@stratos.net
http://www.centerforlearning.org
Supplementary curriculum units for all grade levels in biography, language arts, novel/drama and social studies.

5202 Center for Teaching International Relations
University of Denver
Denver, CO 80208
303-871-3106
Reproducible teaching activities and software promoting multicultural understanding and international relations in the classroom for grades K-adult.

5203 Childcraft Education Corporation
20 Kilmer Avenue
Edison, NJ 08817
732-572-6100
Distributes children's toys, products, materials and publications to schools.

5204 Childswork/Childsplay
The Guidence Channel
135 Dupont Street
PO Box 760
Plainview, NY 11803-0760
800-962-1141
Fax: 800-262-1886
http://www.childswork.com
Contains over 450 resources to address the social and emotional needs of children and adolescents.

Lawrence C Shapiro, PhD, President
Constance H Logan, Development Coordinator

5205 Chroma
205 Bucky Drive
Lititz, PA 17543
717-626-8866
800-257-8278
Fax: 717-626-9292
http://www.chromaonline.com
Tempera and acrylic paints.

5206 Chroma-Vision Sign & Art System
PO Box 434
Greensboro, NC 27402-0434
336-275-0602
Refillable and renewable felt tip markers used with non-toxic, water soluable, fast drying colors for making signs, posters, and general art work with no messy cleanup.

S Gray, President

5207 Citizenship Through Sports and Fine Arts Curriculum
National Federation of State High School Assoc.
PO Box 20626
Kansas City, MO 64195-0626
816-464-5400
800-776-3462
Fax: 816-891-2414
http://www.nfhs.org
High school activities curriculum package that includes an introductory video, Rekindling the Spirit, along with the Overview booklet, plus two insightful books covering eight targets of the curriculum.

5208 Claridge Products & Equipment
Claridge Products & Equipment
601 Highway 62-65 S
PO Box 910
Harrison, AR 72601-0910
870-743-2200
Fax: 870-743-1908

E-mail: claridge@claridgeproducts.com
http://www.claridgeproducts.com
Claridge manufactures chalkboards, markerboards, bulletin boards, display and trophy cases, bulletin and directory board cabinets, easels, lecterns, speakers' stands, wood lecture units with matching credenzas and much more.

Terry McCutchen, Sales Manager

5209 Collins & Aikman Floorcoverings
311 Smith Industrial Boulevard
Dalton, GA 30722
800-248-2878
Fax: 706-259-2666
E-mail: tellis@powerbond.com
http://www.powerbond.com
An alternative to conventional carpet to improve indoor air quality and reduce maintenance cost. Powerboard floor covering.

T Ellis, General Manager/Edu Markets

5210 Columbia Cascade Company
1975 SW 5th Avenue
Portland, OR 97201-5293
503-223-1157
Fax: 503-223-4530
E-mail: hq@timberform.com
http://www.timberform.com
Playground equipment and site furniture.

Dale Gordon, Sales Manager

5211 Creative Artworks Factory
19031 McGuire Road
Perris, CA 92570-8305
909-780-5950
Screenprinted T-shirts, posters and gifts for educational purposes.

5212 Creative Educational Surplus
9801 James Avenue S
#C
Bloomington, MN 55431-2919
Art and classroom materials.

5213 Crizmac Art & Cultural Education Materials Inc
PO Box 65928
Tucson, AZ 85728
520-323-8555
800-913-8555
Fax: 520-323-6194
E-mail: customerservice@crizmac.com
http://www.crizmac.com
Publisher of art and cultural education materials includes curriculum, books, music, and folk art.

Stevie Mack, President

5214 Crown Mats & Matting
2100 Commerce Drive
Fremont, OH 43420-1048
419-332-5531
800-628-5463
Fax: 800-544-2806
E-mail: sales@crown-mats.com
http://www.crown-mats.com
Mats, matting and flooring for schools.

5215 Dahle USA
375 Jaffrey Road
Peterborough, NH 03458
603-924-0003
800-243-8145
Fax: 603-924-1616
E-mail: info@dahleusa.com
http://www.dahleusa.com
Arts and crafts supplies, school and office products, office shreddars and more.

5216 Designer Artwear I
8475 C-1 Highway 6 N
Houston, TX 77095
281-446-6641

Specialty clothing, accessories, etc. all educationally designed.

5217 Dexter Educational Toys
Dexter Educational Toys, Inc.
PO Box 630861
Aventura, FL 33163-0861
305-931-7426
Fax: 305-931-0552
Manufacturer and distributor of education material. Dress-ups for children 2-7 years. Multicultural hand puppets, finger puppets, head masks puppet theaters, rag dolls, dress-ups for teddy bears and dolls, cloth books, export manufacturing under special designs and orders.

Genny Silverstein, VP Secretary

5218 Dick Blick Art Materials
PO Box 1267
Galesburg, IL 61402
800-828-4584
Fax: 800-621-8293
E-mail: info@dickblick.com
http://www.dickblick.com
Classroom art supplies.

5219 Dinorock Productions
407 Granville Drive
Silver Spring, MD 20901-3238
301-588-9300
Musical, Broadway puppet shows for early childhood fun and education.

5220 Discovery Toys
12443 Pine Creek Road
Cerritos, CA 90703-2044
562-809-0331
Fax: 562-809-0331
http://www.discoverytoyslink.com/elizabeth
Emphasizes child physical, social and educational development through creative play. Educational toys, games and books are available for all ages. Services include home demonstrations, fund raisers, phone and catalog orders. New Book of Knowledge Encyclopedia and patenting video tapes are also available.

5221 Disney Educational Productions
500 S Buena Vista Street
Burbank, CA 91521-0001
800-777-8100
Creates and manufactures classroom aids for the educational field.

5222 Dixie Art Supplies
2612 Jefferson Highway
New Orleans, LA 70121
800-783-2612
Fax: 504-831-5738
http://www.dixieart.com
Fine art supplier.

5223 Dr. Playwell's Game Catalog
Guidance Channel
135 Dupont Street
PO Box 760
Plainview, NY 44803-0706
800-999-6884
Fax: 800-262-1886
Games that develop character and life skills.

5224 Draper
125 S Pearl Street
Spiceland, IN 47385
765-987-7999
800-238-7999
Fax: 765-987-7142
E-mail: draper@draper.com
http://www.draperinc.com
Projection screens, video projector mounts and lifts, plasma display mounts, presentation easels, window shades and gymnasium equipment.

Chris Broome, Contract Market Manager
Bob Mathes, AV/Video Market Manager

5225 Draw Books
Peel Productions
PO Box 546
Columbus, NC 28722-0546
828-859-3879
800-345-6665
Fax: 801-365-9898
http://www.drawbooks.com
How-to-draw books for elementary and middle school.

Paperback
ISBN: 0-939217

5226 Dupont Company
Corlan Products
CRP-702
Wilmington, DE 19880
302-774-1000
800-436-7426
Fax: 800-417-1266
Arts and crafts supplies.

5227 Durable Corporation
75 N Pleasant Street
Norwalk, OH 44857-1218
419-668-8138
800-537-1603
Fax: 419-668-8068
Furniture, classroom supplies, arts and crafts and educational products.

5228 EZ Grader
PO Box 23608
Chagrin Falls, OH 44023
800-732-4018
Fax: 800-689-2772
Electronic gradebook designed by teachers for teachers. It is an incredible time saver and computes percentage scores accurately, quickly and easily.

5229 Early Ed
3110 Sunrise Drive
Crown Point, IN 46307-8905
Teacher sweatshirts, cardigans, T-shirts, tote bags and jewelry.

5230 Education Department
Wildlife Conservation Society
2300 Southern Boulevard
Bronx, NY 10460
718-220-5131
800-937-5131
Fax: 718-733-4460
http://www.wcs.com
Year round programs for school and general audience. Teacher training, grades K-12.

Sydell Schein, Manager/Program Services
Ann Robinson, Director/National Programs

5231 Educational Equipment Corporation of Ohio
845 Overholt Road
Kent, OH 44240-7529
330-673-4881
Fax: 330-673-4915
E-mail: mkaufman@mkco.com
Chalkboards, tackboards, trophy cases, announcement boards.

Michael Kaufman, General Manager
Eric Baughman, Sales Manager

5232 Electronic Book Catalog
Franklin Learning Resources
1 Franklin Plaza
Burlington, NJ 08016-4908
800-BOO-MAN
Fax: 609-387-1787
Electronic translation machines, calculators and supplies.

5233 Ellison Educational Equipment
25862 Commercentre Drive
Lake Forest, CA 92630-8804
800-253-2238
Fax: 888-270-1200

E-mail: info@ellison.com
http://www.ellison.com
Serves the educational and craft community with time-saving equipment, supplies and ideas.

5234 Endura Rubber Flooring
2 University Office Park
Waltham, MA 02453-3421
781-647-5375
Fax: 781-647-4543
Floorcoverings, mats and matting for schools.

5235 Fairgate Rule Company
22 Adams Avenue
Cold Spring, NY 10516-1501
845-265-3677
Fax: 845-265-4128
Arts and crafts supplies.

5236 Family Reading Night Kit
Renaissance Learning
PO Box 8036
Wisconsin Rapids, WI 54495-8036
715-424-3636
800-338-4204
Fax: 715-424-4242
E-mail: answers@renlearn.com
http://www.renlearn.com
Kit to start a family reading night where parents and children spent quality time together sharing enthusiasm over books.

5237 Fascinating Folds
PO Box 10070
Glendale, AZ 85318
602-375-9979
Fax: 602-375-9978
http://www.fascinating-folds.com
World's large supplier of origami and paper arts products.

5238 Fiskars Corporation
636 Science Drive
Madison, WI 53711
608-233-1649
Fax: 608-294-4790
http://www.fiskars.com
School scissors.

5239 Fox Laminating Company
84 Custer Street
W Hartford, CT 06110-1955
860-953-4884
800-433-2468
Fax: 860-953-1277
E-mail: sales@foxlam.com
http://www.foxlam.com
Easy, simple, and inexpensive do-it-yourself laminators. A piece of paper can be laminated for just pennies. Badges, ID's and luggage tags can also be made. Also laminated plaques for awards, diplomas, and mission statements.

Joe Fox, President
John Mills, Marketing Manager

5240 George F Cram Company
PO Box 426
Indianapolis, IN 46206-0426
317-635-5564
Fax: 317-687-2845
Classroom geography maps, state maps, social studies skills and globes.

5241 Gift-in-Kind Clearinghouse
PO Box 850
Davidson, NC 28036-0850
704-892-7228
Fax: 704-892-3825
Educational and classroom supplies, computers and gifts for teachers.

5242 Gold's Artworks
2100 N Pine
Lumberton, NC 28358

910-739-9605
800-356-2306
Fax: 910-739-9605
http://www.goldsartworks.20m.com
Papermaking supplies.

5243 Golden Artist Colors
188 Bell Road
New Berlin, NY 13411-9527
800-959-6543
E-mail: goldenart@goldenpaints.com
http://www.goldenpaints.com
Acrylic paints.

5244 Graphix
19499 Miles Road
Cleveland, OH 44128-4109
216-581-9050
Fax: 216-581-9041
E-mail: sales@grafixarts.com
http://www.grafixarts.com
Art and crafts supplies and a source for creative plastic films.

Tanya Lutz, National Sales Manager

5245 Grolier Multimedial Encyclopedia
Grolier Publishing
PO Box 1716
Danbury, CT 06816
203-797-3703
800-371-3908
Fax: 203-797-3899
Encyclopedia software.

5246 Hands-On Equations
Borenson & Associates
PO Box 3328
Allentown, PA 18106
800-993-6284
Fax: 610-398-7863
http://www.borenson.com
System to teach algebraic concepts to elementary and middle school students.

5247 Harrisville Designs
Center Village
PO Box 806
Harrisville, NH 03450
603-827-3333
800-938-9415
Fax: 603-827-3335
http://www.harrisville.com
Award-winning weaving products for children.

5248 Hayes School Publishing
321 Penwood Avenue
Pittsburgh, PA 15221
800-245-6234
Fax: 800-543-8771
E-mail: info@hayespub.com
http://www.hayespub.com
Suppliers of certificates and awards.

5249 Henry S Wolkins Company
605 Myles Standish Boulevard
Taunton, MA 02780
800-233-1844
Fax: 877-965-5467
http://www.wolkins.com
Art and craft materials, teaching aids, early learning products, furniture, general school equipment.

5250 Hooked on Phonics Classroom Edition
665 3rd Street
Suite 225
San Francisco, CA 94107
714-437-3450
800-222-3334
E-mail: customerservice@hop.com
http://www.hop.com
Program that teaches students to learn letters and sounds to decoding words, and then reading books.

5251 Hydrus Galleries
PO Box 4944
San Diego, CA 92164-4944
800-493-7299
Fax: 619-283-7466
E-mail: info@hydra9.com
http://www.hydra9.com
Curriculum-based classroom activities including papyrus outlines for students to paint.

5252 Insect Lore
PO Box 1535
Shafter, CA 93263
800-548-3284
Fax: 661-746-0334
E-mail: livebug@insectlore.com
http://www.insectlore.com
Science materials for elementary and preschool students.

5253 J&A Handy-Crafts
165 S Pennsylvania Avenue
Lindenhurst, NY 11757-5058
631-226-2400
888-252-1130
Fax: 631-226-2564
E-mail: info@jacrafts.com
http://www.jacrafts.com
Arts, crafts and educational supplies.

Paul Siegelman, Marketing

5254 Jiffy Printers Products
35070 Maria Road
Cathedral City, CA 92234
760-321-7335
Fax: 760-770-1955
E-mail: jiffyprod@aol.com
Adhesive wax sticks.

Ivan Zwelling, Owner

5255 Key-Bak
Division of West Coast Chain
Manufacturing Co.
4245 Pacific Privado
Ontario, CA 91761
909-923-7800
800-685-2403
Fax: 800-565-6202
E-mail: sales@keybak.com
http://www.keybak.com
Badges, awards and emblems for educational purposes.

5256 Keyboard Instructor
Advanced Keyboard Technology, Inc.
PO Box 2418
Paso Robles, CA 93447-2418
805-237-2055
Fax: 805-239-8973
http://www.keyboardinstructor.com
Mobile keyboarding lab with individualized instruction.

5257 Kids Percussion Buyer's Guide
Percussion Marketing Council
818-753-1310
E-mail: DLevine360@aol.com
http://www.playdrums.com
This guide is divided into two sections- recreational instruments and those for beginning traditional drummers.

5258 Kids at Heart & School Art Materials
PO Box 94082
Seattle, WA 98124-9482
Classroom and art materials.

5259 Kidstamps
PO Box 18699
Cleveland Heights, OH 44118-0699
216-291-6884
Fax: 216-291-6887
E-mail: kidstamps@apk.net
http://www.kidstamps.com
Rubber stamps, T-shirts, bookplates and mugs designed by leading children's illustrators.

5260 Knex Education Catalog
Knex Education
2990 Bergey Road
PO Box 700
Hatfield, PA 19440-0700
888-ABC-KNEX
E-mail: abcknex@knex.com
http://www.knexeducation.com
Hands-on, award-winning curriculum supported K-12 math, science and technology sets.

5261 Lauri
PO Box 0263
Smethport, PA 16749
800-451-0520
Fax: 207-639-3555
Lacing puppets craft kits, crepe rubber picture puzzles, phonics kits and math manipulatives for pre- K and up. Catalog offers 200 manipulatives for early childhood.

5262 Learning Materials Workshop
274 N Winooski Avenue
Burlington, VT 05401-3621
802-802-8399
800-693-7164
Fax: 802-862-0794
E-mail: mail@learningmaterialswork.com
http://www.learningmaterialswork.com
Designs and produces open-ended blocks and construction sets for early childhood classrooms. An education guide and video, as well as training workshops are offered.

Karen Hewitt, President

5263 Learning Needs Catalog
Riverdeep Interactive Learning
PO Box 97021
Redmond, WA 98073-9721
800-362-2890
http://www.learningneeds.com
Hardware, software and print products designed for specialized student needs for Pre-K to grade 12.

5264 Learning Power and the Learning Power Workbook
Great Source Education Group
181 Ballardvale
Willmington, MA 01887
800-289-4490
Student materials for 8th and 9th grade critical thinking, study skills, life management, and other student success course.

218 pages
ISBN: 0-963813-33-1

5265 Learning Well
111 Kane Street
Baltimore, MD 21224-1728
800-645-6564
Fax: 800-413-7442
E-mail: learningwell@wclm.com
Drawing compass/ruler.

5266 Linray Enterprises
167 Corporation Road
Hyannis, MA 02601-2204
800-537-9752
Mats and matting for gym classes.

5267 Loew-Coenell
563 Chestnut Avenue
Teaneck, NJ 07666-2491
201-836-8110
Fax: 201-836-7070
E-mail: sales@loew-cornell.com
http://www.loew-cornell.com
Leader in art and craft brushes, painting accessories and artists' tools.

5268 Longstreth
PO Box 475
Parker Ford, PA 19457-0475
610-495-7022
Fax: 610-495-7023

Awards, emblems, badges and trophies, sports timers and clocks.

5269 Love to Teach
693 Glacier Pass
Westerville, OH 43081-1295
614-899-2118
800-326-8361
Fax: 614-899-2070
http://www.lovetoteach.com
Gifts for teachers.

Linda Vollmer, Contact

5270 Lyra
78 Browne Street
Suite 3
Brookline, MA 02146
888-PEN-LYRA
E-mail: mshoham@aol.com
Drawing supplies.

5271 MPI School & Instructional Supplies
PO Box 24155
Lansing, MI 48909-4155
517-393-0440
Fax: 517-393-8884
School and classroom supplies, arts and crafts.

5272 Magnetic Aids
133 N 10th Street
Paterson, NJ 07522-1220
973-790-1400
800-426-9624
Fax: 973-790-1425
E-mail: magneticaids@worldnet.att.com
http://www.magneticaids.com
Announcement and chalkboards, office supplies and equipment. Magnetic book supports.

Paul Pecka, VP Sales

5273 Mailer's Software
970 Calle Negocio
San Clemente, CA 92673-6201
949-492-7000
Fax: 949-589-5211
Charts, maps, globes and software for the classroom.

5274 Marsh Industries
Div. of Marsh Lumber Company
PO Box 509
Dover, OH 44622-1935
330-343-8825
800-426-4244
Fax: 330-343-9515
E-mail: wdsinghaus@marsh-ind.com
http://www.marsh-ind.com
Marker boards chalkboards, and tacknoards for new rennovative construction projects. Glass enclosed bulletin and directory boards. Map rail and accessories.

William Singhaus, Sales Manager

5275 Master Woodcraft
1312 College Street
Oxford, NC 27565
919-693-8811
800-333-2675
Fax: 919-693-1707
Announcement and classroom chalkboards, arts and craft supplies. Cork bulletin boards, dry erase melamine boards, easels, floor and table top.

J Moss, VP

5276 Material Science Technology
Energy Concepts
595 Bond Street
Lincolnshire, IL 60069
800-621-1247
http://www.energy-concepts-inc.com
Provides practical knowledge of the use and development of materials in todays world.

Each unit combines theory with hands-on experience.

5277 Midwest Publishers Supply
4640 N Olcott Avenue
Harwood Heights, IL 60706
800-621-1507
Fax: 800-832-3189
E-mail: info@mps-co.com
http://www.mps-co.com
Arts and crafts supplies.

Bonnie Cready, Sales Manager

5278 Miller Multiplex
1555 Larkin Williams Road
Fenton, MO 63026-3008
636-343-5700
800-325-3350
Fax: 636-326-1716
E-mail: info@millermultiplex.com
Announcement boards, classroom displays, charts and photography, books towers, posters, frames, kiosk displays, presentation displays.

12 pages Annually

Kathy Webster, Director Marketing

5279 Monsanto Company
800 N Lindbergh Boulevard
Saint Louis, MO 63167-0001
314-694-3902
Fax: 314-694-7625
Arts and crafts supplies.

5280 Morrison School Supplies
304 Industrial Road
San Carlos, CA 94070-6285
650-592-3000
Fax: 650-592-1679
School supplies, classroom equipment, furniture and toys.

5281 Names Unlimited
2300 Spikes Lane
Lansing, MI 48906-3996
Chalkboard and markerboard slates and tablets.

5282 Nasco Arts & Crafts Catalog
Nasco
901 Janesville Avenue
PO Box 901
Fort Atkinson, WI 53538-0901
920-563-2446
800-558-9595
Fax: 920-563-8296
http://www.eNASCO.com
Complete line of arts and craft materials for the art educator and individual artist.

Kris Bakke, Arts & Crafts Director

5283 Nasco Early Learning & Afterschool EssentialCatalogs
Nasco
901 Janesville Avenue
PO Box 901
Fort Atkinson, WI 53538-0901
920-563-2446
800-558-9595
Fax: 920-563-8296
E-mail: info@enasco.com
http://www.eNasco.com
Features low prices on classroom supplies, materials, furniture and equipment for early childhood and afterschool programs.

Scott J Beyer, Director, Sales & Marketing

5284 Nasco Math Catalog
Nasco
901 Janesville
PO Box 901
Fort Atkinson, WI 53538-0901
920-563-2446
800-558-9595

Fax: 920-563-8296
http://www.nascofa.com
Features hands-on manipulatives and real-life problem-solving projects.

5285 National Teaching Aids
PO Box 2121
Fort Collins, CO 80522
970-484-7445
800-289-9299
Fax: 970-484-1198
E-mail: bevans@amep.com
http://www.hubbardscientific.com
Learning math, alphabet, and geography skills is easy with our Clever Catch Balls. These colorful 24-inch inflatable vinyl balls provide an excellent way for children to practice math, alphabet and geography skills. Excellent learning tool in organized classroom activities, on the playground, or at home.

Barbara Evans, Customer Service Manager
Candy Coffman, National Sales Manger

5286 New Hermes
2200 Northmont Parkway
Duluth, GA 30096
770-623-0331
800-843-7637
Fax: 800-533-7637
E-mail: sales@newhermes.com
http://www.newhermes.com
Announcement boards, trophies, badges, emblems.

5287 Newbridge Discovery Station
PO Box 5267
Clifton, NH 07015
Monthly quick tips and activities for teachers.

5288 Newbridge Jumbo Seasonal Patterns
PO Box 5267
Clifton, NJ 07015
Art projects, games, bulletin boards, flannel boards, story starters, learning center displays, costumes, masks and more for grades Pre K-3.

5289 NewsCurrents
Knowledge Unlimited
PO Box 52
Madison, WI 53701
800-356-2303
Fax: 608-831-1570
E-mail: sales@newscurrents.com
http://www.newscurrents.com
Current issues discussion programs for grades 3 and up.

5290 Partners in Learning Programs
1065 Bay Boulevard
Suite H
Chula Vista, CA 91911-1626
619-407-4744
Fax: 619-407-4755
Manufacturers and produces books, manuals, materials, supplies and gifts, such as banners for classroom purposes.

5291 Pearson Education Technologies
827 W Grove Avenue
Mesa, AZ 85210
520-615-7600
800-222-4543
Fax: 520-615-7601
http://www.pearsonedtech.com
SuccessMaker is a multimedia K-Adult learning system which includes math, reading, language arts and science courseware.

5292 Pentel of America
2805 Columbia Street
Torrance, CA 90509-3800
310-320-3831
800-421-1419
Fax: 310-533-0697
http://www.pentel.com
Office supplies and equipment.

5293 Pin Man
Together Inc.
802 E 6th Street
PO Box 52528
Tulsa, OK 74105-3264
918-587-2405
800-282-0085
Fax: 918-382-0906
http://www.thepinmanok.com
Manufacturer of custom designed lapel pins, totes for Chapter 1, reading, scholastic achievement, honor roll, parent involvement, staff awards and incentives with over 25,000 items available for imprint.

Bern Gentry, CEO

5294 PlayConcepts
2275 Huntington Drive
#305
San Marino, CA 91108-2640
800-261-2584
Fax: 626-795-1177
Creative, 3-D scenery that stimulates dramatic play. The scenes complement integrated curriculum. They are age and developmentally appropriate, non-biased, and effective for groups or individuals.

5295 Polyform Products Company
1901 Estes Avenue
Elk Grove Village, IL 60007
847-427-0020
Fax: 847-427-0020
E-mail: polyform@sculpey.com
http://www.sculpey.com
Manufacturer of sculpey modeling clay.

5296 Presidential Classroom
119 Oronoco Street
Alexandria, VA 22314-2015
703-683-5400
800-441-6533
Fax: 703-548-5728
E-mail: eriedel@presidentialclassroom.org
http://www.presidentialclassroom.org
Civic education programs in Washington, DC for high school juniors and seniors. Each one week program provides students with an inside view of the federal government in action and their role as responsible citizens and future leaders.

Jan-March, June+July
400 attendees

Jack Buechner, President/CEO
Ginger King, Dean

5297 Professor Weissman's Software
Professor Weissman's Software
246 Crafton Avenue
Staten Island, NY 10314-4227
718-698-5219
Fax: 718-698-5219
E-mail: mathprof@hotmail.com
http://www.math911.com
Algebra comic books, learn by example algebra flash cards, step-by-step software tutorials for algebra, trigonometry, precalculus, statistics, network versions for all software.

Martin Weissman, Owner
Keith Morse, VP

5298 Pumpkin Masters
PO Box 61456
Denver, CO 80206-8456
303-860-8006
Fax: 303-860-9826
Classroom pumpkin carving kits featuring whole language curriculum with safer and easier carving tools and patterns.

5299 Puppets on the Pier
Pier 39
Box H4
San Francisco, CA 94133
415-781-4435
800-443-4463
Fax: 415-379-9544
E-mail: onepuppet@earthlink.net
http://www.puppetdream.com
Puppets, arts, crafts and other creative educational products for children.

Arthur Partner

5300 Qwik-File Storage Systems
1000 Allview Drive
Crozet, VA 22932-3144
804-823-4351
Schedule boards and classroom supplies.

5301 RC Musson Rubber Company
1320 E Archwood Avenue
Akron, OH 44306-2825
330-773-7651
800-321-3281
Fax: 330-773-3254
E-mail: info@mussonrubber.com
http://www.mussonrubber.com
Rubber floorcoverings, mats and athletic matting.

Mark Reese, Customer Service Manager
Robert Segers, VP

5302 RCA Rubber Company
1833 E Market Street
Akron, OH 44305-4214
330-784-1291
Fax: 330-784-2899
Floorcoverings, athletic mats and more for the physical education class.

5303 Reading is Fundamental
600 Maryland Avenue SW
Suite 600
Washington, DC 20024-2520
202-673-1641
Fax: 202-673-1633
Distributor of posters, bookmarks, and parent guide brochures.

5304 Reconnecting Youth
National Educational Service
304 W Kirkwood Avenue
Suite 2
Bloomington, IN 47404-5132
812-336-7700
800-733-6786
Fax: 812-336-7790
E-mail: nes@nesonline.com
http://www.nesonline.com
Curriculum to help discouraged learners achieve in school, manage their anger, and decrease drug use, depression, and suicide risk. The program was piloted for five years with over 600 urban Northwestern public high school students with funding from the National Institute on Drug Abuse and the National Institute of Mental Health, and has since been successful in many educational settings.

3 Ring Binder Circul
ISBN: 1-879639-42-4

Jane St. John, Sales Marketing Director

5305 Red Ribbon Resources
135 Dupont Street
PO Box 760
Plainview, NY 11803
800-646-7999
Fax: 800-262-1886
http://ww.redribbonresources.com
Over 250 low cost giveaways to promote your safe and drug-free school and community.

5306 Renaissance Graphic Arts
69 Steamwhistle Drive
Ivyland, PA 18974
888-833-3398
Fax: 215-357-5258
E-mail: pat@printmaking-materials.com
http://www.printmaking-materials.com
Tools, papers, plates, inks and assorted products necessary for printmaking.

5307 Rock Paint Distributing Corporation
PO Box 482
Milton, WI 53563
608-868-6873
Fax: 800-715-7625
E-mail: handyart@handyart.com
http://www.handyart.com
Tempera paint, India ink, acrylic paint, block inc, washable paint, fabric paint.

5308 S&S Worldwide
S&S Arts & Crafts
75 Mill Street
Department 2030
Colchester, CT 06415-1263
800-243-9232
Fax: 800-566-6678
Arts and crafts, classroom games and group paks.

5309 Safe & Drug Free Catalog
Performance Resource Press
1270 Rankin Drive
Suite F
Troy, MI 48083-2843
800-453-7733
Fax: 800-499-5718
http://www.pronline.net
Books, videos, CD-Roms, phamlets and posters toassist students with social skills, counseling, drug and violence prevention.

5310 Sakura of America
30780 San Clemente Street
Hayward, CA 94544-7131
510-475-8880
800-776-6257
Fax: 510-475-0973
E-mail: express@sakuraofamerica.com
http://www.gellyroll.com
Gelly Roll pens, Cray pas oil pastels, Fantasia watercolors, Pigma micron pens, Pentouch and Aqua Wipe markers and other art supplies for the classroom.

John Crook
Donna Wilson, Marketing Director

5311 Sanford Corporation
A Lifetime of Color
2711 Washington Boulevard
Bellwood, IL 60104-1970
708-547-6650
800-323-0749
Fax: 708-547-6719
E-mail: consumer.service@sanfordcorp.com
http://www.sanfordcorp.com
Writing instruments, art supplies.

Angela Nigl, Author
Sharon Meyers, PR Manager

5312 Sax Visual Art Resources
Sax Arts and Crafts
2725 S Moorland Road
bept. SA
New Berlin, WI 53151
800-558-6696
Fax: 800-328-4729
E-mail: catalog@saxfcs.com
http://www.saxfcs.com
Variety of resources for slides, books, videos, fine art posters and CD-Roms.

5313 School Mate
PO Box 2225
Jackson, TN 38302
731-935-2000
Fax: 800-668-7610
E-mail: school@schoolmateinc.com
Pre-school and elementary art products.

5314 SchoolMatters
Current
The Current Building
Colorado Springs, CO 80941-0001
800-525-7170
Fax: 800-993-3232
Offers a variety of creative classroom ideas including stickers, mugs, posters, signs and more for everyday and holidays and everyday of the year.

5315 Scott Sign Systems
PO Box 1047
Tallevast, FL 34270-1047
941-355-5171
800-237-9447
Fax: 941-351-1787
E-mail: mail@scottsigns.com
http://www.scottsigns.com
Educational supplies including announcement, letters, signs, graphics and chalkboards.

5316 Scratch-Art Company
PO Box 303
Avon, MA 02322
508-583-8085
800-377-9003
Fax: 508-583-8091
E-mail: info@scratchart.com
http://www.scratchart.com
Offers materials for drawing, sketching and rubbings.

5317 Sea Bay Game Company
PO Box 162
Middletown, NJ 07748-0162
732-583-7902
Fax: 732-583-7284
Manufacturer and distributor of products, games and creative play to nursery schools and preschools.

5318 Seton Identification Products
20 Thompson Road
PO Box 819
Branford, CT 06405
203-488-8059
800-243-6624
Fax: 203-488-4114
http://www.seton.com
Manufacturer of all types of identification products including signs, tags, labels, traffic control, OSHA, ADA and much more.

5319 Shapes, Etc.
PO Box 400
Dansville, NY 14437-0400
585-335-6619
Fax: 585-335-6070
Notepads and craft materials for creative writing projects. Coordinates with literature themes. Perfect for storystarters, bulletin boards, awards and motivators.

5320 Sign Product Catalog
Scott Sign Systems, Inc.
PO Box 1047
Tallevast, FL 34270-1047
845-355-5171
800-237-9447
Fax: 941-351-1787
E-mail: scottsigns@mindspring.com
http://www.scottsigns.com
Educational supplies including announcement, letters, signs, graphics and chalkboards.

Robert Lew, Account Executive

5321 Small Fry Originals
2700 S Westmoreland Road
Dallas, TX 75233-1312
214-330-8671
800-248-9443
Children's original artwork preserved in plastic plates and mugs.

5322 Southwest Plastic Binding Corporation
109 Millwell Drive
Maryland Heights, MO 63043-2509
800-986-2001
Fax: 800-942-2010
Overhead transparencies, maps, charts and classroom supplies.

5323 Spectrum Corporation
10048 Easthaven Boulevard
Houston, TX 77075-3298
800-392-5050
Fax: 713-944-1290
Announcement boards, scoreboards and sports equipment, sports timers and clocks.

5324 Speedball Art Products Company
2226 Speedball Road
PO Box 5157
Statesville, NC 28687
704-838-1475
800-898-7224
Fax: 704-838-1472
E-mail: tonyahill@speedballart.com
http://www.speedballart.com
Art products for stamping, calligraphy, printmaking, drawing and painting.

Rita Madsen, Manager
Tonya Hill, Director of Sales

5325 Sponge Stamp Magic
525 S Anaheim Hills Road
Apartment C314
Anaheim, CA 92807-4726
Rubber stamps and games for classroom use.

5326 Staedtler
PO Box 2196
Chatsworth, CA 91313-2196
818-882-6000
800-776-5544
Fax: 818-882-3767
E-mail: rhoye@staedtler-usa.com
http://www.staedtler-usa.com
Arts and crafts supplies, office supplies and equipment.

Dick Hoye, National Sales Manager

5327 Sylvan Learning Systems
1000 Lancaster Street
Baltimore, MD 21202
410-843-6828
888-779-5826
Fax: 410-783-3832
http://www1.sylvan.net
Provides public school academic programs that are traditional sylvan programs modified to fit the needs of individual school districts and performance guarantees.

Jody Madron, Contact

5328 Tandy Leather Company
PO Box 791
Fort Worth, TX 76101-0791
817-451-1480
Fax: 817-451-5254
Arts and crafts supplies, computer peripherals and systems.

5329 Teacher Appreciation
Guidance Channel
135 Dupont Street
PO Box 760
Plainview, NY 44803-0706
800-999-6884
Fax: 800-262-1886
Products for celebrating teacher appreciation week.

5330 Teachers Store
PO Box 24155
Lansing, MI 48909-4155
517-393-0440
Fax: 517-393-8884

School and classroom supplies, arts and crafts.

5331 Texas Instruments
12500 TI Boulevard
Dallas, TX 75243-4136
800-336-5236
Fax: 972-995-4360
http://www.ti.com
Manufacturer of calculators.

5332 Triarco Arts & Crafts
14650 28th Avenue N
Plymouth, MN 55447
763-559-5590
800-328-3360
Fax: 736-559-2215
E-mail: info@triarcoarts.com
Art supplies.

5333 Vanguard Crafts
1081 E 48th Street
Brooklyn, NY 11234
718-377-5188
800-662-7238
Fax: 888-692-0056
Arts and crafts supplier.

5334 Wagner Zip-Change
3100 W Hirsch Avenue
Melrose Park, IL 60160-1741
800-323-0744
Fax: 708-681-4165
Non-lighted changeable letter message activity signs, changeable letters in all sizes and colors.

CJ Krasula, Marketing VP
Jim Leone, Sales Manager

5335 Walker Display
6520 Grand Avenue
Duluth, MN 55807-2242
218-624-8990
Fax: 888-695-4647
Arts, crafts, classroom supplies and displays.

5336 Wellness Reproductions
Guidance Channel
135 Dupont Street
PO Box 760
Plainview, NY 44803-0706
800-999-6884
Fax: 800-262-1886
Mental and life skills educational materials.

5337 Wikki Stix One-of-a-Kind Creatables
Omnicor
2432 W Peoria Avenue #1188
Suite 1188
Phoenix, AZ 85029-4735
602-870-9937
800-869-4554
Fax: 602-870-9877
E-mail: info@wikkistix.com
http://www.wikkistix.com
Unique, one-of-a-kind twistable, stickable, creatable, hands-on teaching tools. Ideal for Pre-K through 8 for science, language arts, math, arts and crafts, positive behavior rewards, rainy day recess, classroom display, diagrams and 3-D work. Self-stick; no glue needed.

Kem Clark, President

5338 Wilson Language Training
175 W Main Strete
Millbury, MA 01527-1441
508-865-5699
Fax: 508-865-9644
Multisensory language program.

5339 Wilton Art Appreciation Programs
Reading & O'Reilley
PO Box 646
Botsford, CT 06404
203-270-6336
800-458-4274

Fax: 203-270-5569
E-mail: ror@wiltonart.com
http://www.wiltonart.com
Materials for art appreciation including
CD-ROMS, videos, fine art prints, slides,
workbooks, teacher' guides, lessons, puzzles
and games.

Diana O'Neill, President

5340 Young Explorers
1810 E Eisenhower Boulevrd
Loveland, CO 80539
800-239-7577
Fax: 888-876-8847
http://www.youngexplorers.com
Educational material for children.

Classroom Materials

5341 Math Through the Ages: A Gentle History forTeachers and Others
Oxton Publishers, LLC
Po Box 209
Farmington, ME 04938
207-779-1923
800-539-7323
Fax: 207-779-0623
E-mail: info@oxtonhouse.com
http://www.oxtonhouse.com
An easy-to-use tool for teachers who want
some history for their math classes, this book
contains 25 independent 4-to-6 page historical summaries of particular topics from elementary and secondary math, a 56-page
overview and an extensive bibliography.

224 pages

William Berlinghoff, Managing Editor
Bobby Brown, Marketing Director

Electronic Equipment

5342 AIMS Multimedia
9710 De Soto Avenue
Chatsworth, CA 91311-4409
818-773-4300
800-367-2467
Fax: 818-341-6700
E-mail: info@aimsmultimedia.com
http://www.aimsmultimedia.com
Film, video, laserdisc producer and distributor, offering a free catalog available materials. Also provides internet video streaming
via www.digitalcurriculum.com.

David Sherman, President
Biff Sherman, President

5343 Advance Products Company
1101 E Central Avenue
Wichita, KS 67214-3922
316-263-4231
Fax: 316-263-4245
Manufacturer of steel mobile projection and
television tables, video cabinets, easels, computer furniture, wall and ceiling TV mounts,
and study tables and carrels.

Paul Keck

5344 All American Scoreboards
Everbrite
401 S Main Street
Pardeeville, WI 53954
608-429-2121
800-356-8146
Fax: 608-429-9216
E-mail: score@everbrite.com
http://www.allamericanscoreboards.com
Scoreboards.

Doug Winkelmann, Product Manager

5345 American Time & Signal Company
140 3rd Avenue S
Dassel, MN 55325
800-328-8996
Fax: 800-789-1882
Sports timers and clocks.

5346 Arts & Entertainment Network
235 E 45th Street
Floor 9
New York, NY 10017-3354
212-210-1400
Fax: 212-210-9755
Cable network offering free educational pro-
gramming to schools.

5347 Barr Media/Films
12801 Schabarum Avenue
Irwindale, CA 91706-6808
626-338-7878
K-12 film, video and interactive Level I and
III laserdisc programs.

5348 Buhl Optical Company
1009 Beech Avenue
Pittsburgh, PA 15233-2013
412-321-0076
Fax: 412-322-2640
Overhead projectors and transparencies.

5349 C-SPAN Classroom
4000 N Capitol Street NW
Washington, DC 20001
800-523-7586
Fax: 202-737-6226
C-SPAN School Bus travels through more
than 80 communities during each school year.
This bus is a mobile television production studio and learning center designed to give
hands-on experience with C-SPAN's
programming.

5350 CASIO
570 Mount Pleasant Avenue
Dover, NJ 07801-1631
973-361-5400
Fax: 570-868-6898
Cameras, overhead projectors and electronics.

5351 CASPR
100 Park Center Plaza
Suite 550
San Jose, CA 95113-2204
800-852-2777
http://www.caspr.com
Leader in the field of library automation for
schools. Integrated library automation-cross
platforms: Macintosh, Windows, Apple
IIe/IIGS. Multimedia source.

Norman Kline, President

5352 Cable in the Classroom
1800 N Beauregard Street
Suite 100
Alexandria, VA 22311-1710
703-845-1400
Fax: 703-845-1409
http://www.ciconline.org
Represents the cable tele-communications industry's commitment to improving teaching
and learning for children in schools, at home
and in their communities.

5353 Canon USA
1 Canon Plaza
New Hyde Park, NY 11042-1198
516-488-1400
Fax: 516-328-5069
School equipment and supplies including a
full line of electronics, cameras, calculators
and other technology.

5354 Caulastics
5955 Mission Street
Daly City, CA 94014-1397
415-585-9600

Overhead projectors, transparencies and electronics.

5355 Cheshire Corporation
Cheshire Corporation
PO Box 61109
Denver, CO 80206-8109
303-333-3003
Fax: 303-333-4037
E-mail: karen-hemmes@mindspring.com
Cheshire corporation is a publicist for book,
video, CD-ROM and internet publishers in
the school and library market.

Karen Hemmes, Publicist
Mary Kay Opicka, Publicist

5356 Chief Manufacturing
14310 Ewing Avenue S
Burnsville, MN 55306-4839
612-894-6280
800-582-6480
Fax: 877-894-6918
E-mail: chief@chiefmfg.com
http://www.chiefmfg.com
Manufacturer of Communications Support
Systems for audio visual and video equipment. Chief's product includes a full-line of
mounts, electric lifts, carts, and accessories
for LCD/DLP projectors, plasma displays and
TV/monitors.

Liz Sorensen, Marketing Assistant
Sharon McCubbin, Marketing Manager

5357 Chisholm
7019 Realm Drive
San Jose, CA 95119-1321
800-888-4210
Computer peripherals, overhead projectors
and overhead transparencies.

5358 Daktronics
331 32nd Avenue
Brookings, SD 57006-4704
605-697-4300
888-325-8766
Fax: 605-697-4300
E-mail: sales@daktronics.com
http://www.daktronics.com
Scoreboards, electronic message displays statistics software.

Gary Gramm, HSPR Market Manager

5359 Depco- Millennium 3000
3305 Airport Drive
PO Box 178
Pittsburg, KS 66762
316-231-0019
800-767-1062
Fax: 316-231-0024
E-mail: sales@depcoinc.com
http://www.depcoinc.com
Program tracks and schedules for you, the test
taker delivers tests electronically, as well as,
automatic final exams. There are workstation
security features to help keep students focused on their activities.

5360 Discovery Networks
7700 Wisconsin Avenue
Bethesda, MD 20814-3578
301-986-0444
Manages and operates The Discovery Channel, offering the finest in nonfiction documentary programming, as well as The
Learning Channel, representing a world of
ideas to learners of all ages.

5361 Echolab
175 Bedford Street
Burlington, MA 01803-2794
781-273-1512
Fax: 978-250-3335
Cameras, equipment, projectors and electronics.

5362 Eiki International
Audio Visual/Video Products
26794 Vista Terrace Drive
Lake Forest, CA 92630
949-457-0200
Fax: 949-457-7878
Video projectors, overhead projectors and transparencies.

5363 Elmo Manufacturing Corporation
1478 Old Country Road
Plainview, NY 11803-5034
516-501-1400
800-654-7628
Fax: 516-501-0429
Overhead projectors and transparencies.

5364 Fair-Play Scoreboards
1700 Delaware Avenue
Des Moines, IA 50317-2999
800-247-0265
Fax: 515-265-3364
E-mail: sales@fair-play.com
http://www.fair-play.com
Scoreboards and sports equipment.

5365 Festo Corporation
395 Moreland Road
PO Box 18023
Hauppauge, NY 11788
631-435-0800
Fax: 631-435-3847
http://www.festo-usa.com

5366 General Audio-Visual
333 W Merrick Road
Valley Stream, NY 11580-5219
516-825-8500
Fax: 516-568-2057
Offers a full line of audio-visual equipment and supplies, cameras, projectors and various other electronics for the classroom.

5367 Hamilton Electronics
2003 W Fulton Street
Chicago, IL 60612-2365
312-421-5442
Fax: 312-421-0818
Electronics, equipment and supplies.

5368 JR Holcomb Company
3205 Harvard Avenue
Cleveland, OH 44101
216-341-3000
800-362-9907
Fax: 216-341-5151
A full line of electronics including calculators, overhead projectors and overhead transparencies.

5369 JVC Professional Products Company
41 Slater Drive
Elmwood Park, NJ 07407-1311
201-794-3900
Electronics line including cameras, projectors, transparencies and other technology for the classroom.

5370 Labelon Corporation
10 Chapin Street
Canandaigua, NY 14424-1589
585-394-6220
800-428-5566
Fax: 585-394-3154
Electronics, supplies and equipment for schools.

5371 Learning Channel
7700 Wisconsin Avenue
Bethesda, MD 20814
800-346-0032
Offers educational programming for schools.

5372 Learning Station/Hug-a-Chug Records
3950 Bristol Court
Melbourne, FL 32904-8712

321-728-8773
800-789-9990
Fax: 321-722-9121
http://www.learningstationmusic.com
Early childhood products including OMH, cassettes, CD's and videos. Also, the Learning Station performs children and family concerts and are internationally acclaimed for their concert/keynote presentations for early childhood conferences and other educational organizations.
Don Monopoli, President
Laurie Monopoli, VP

5373 Learning Well
2200 Marcus Avenue
#3759
New Hyde Park, NY 11042-1042
800-645-6564
Fax: 800-638-6499
Instructional material including computer and board games, videos, cassettes, audio tapes, theme units, manipulatives for grades PreK-8.
Mona Russo, President

5374 Leightronix
2330 Jarco Drive
Holt, MI 48842-1210
517-694-5589
Fax: 517-694-1600
Educational cable programming for schools and institutions.

5375 MCM Electronics
650 Congress Park Drive
Centerville, OH 45459
800-543-4330
Fax: 800-765-6960
http://www.mcmelectronics.com
Offers a full line of electronics products and components for use in the classroom or at home. Over 40,000 parts.

5376 Magna Plan Corporation
1320 Route 9
Champlain, NY 12919-5007
518-298-8404
800-361-1192
Fax: 518-298-2368
E-mail: info@visualplanning.com
http://www.visualplanning.com
Overhead projectors.
Joseph P Josephson, Managing Director
Joel Boloten, Manager Consultation Service

5377 Mitsubishi Professional Electronics
200 Cottontail Lane
Somerset, NJ 08873-1231
732-563-9889
Video projectors and electronics.

5378 Multi-Video
PO Box 35444
Charlotte, NC 28235-5444
704-563-4279
800-289-0111
Fax: 704-568-0219
Cameras, projectors and equipment.

5379 Naden Scoreboards
505 Fair Avenue
PO Box 636
Webster City, IA 50595-0636
515-832-4290
800-467-4290
Fax: 515-832-4293
E-mail: naden@ncn.net
http://www.naden.com
Electronic scoreboards for sports.
Russ Naden, President

5380 Neumade Products Corporation
30 Pecks Lane
Newtown, CT 06470-2361

203-270-1100
Fax: 203-270-7778
E-mail: neumadeGJ@aol.com
http://www.neumade.com
Overhead projectors, overhead transparencies, video projectors and electronics.
Gregory Jones, VP Sales

5381 Nevco Scoreboard Company
301 E Harris Avenue
Greenville, IL 62246-2151
618-664-0360
800-851-4040
Fax: 618-664-0398
E-mail: info@nevco.com
http://www.nevco.com
Nevco is a premier manufacturer and distributor of scoreboards, message centers and video displays.
Phil Robertson, Sales Manager

5382 Panasonic Communications & System Company
1 Panasonic Way
Secaucus, NJ 07094-2917
201-392-4818
800-524-1064
Fax: 201-392-4044
Cameras, projectors, equipment, players, CD-ROM equipment and school supplies.

5383 Quickset International
3650 Woodhead Drive
Northbrook, IL 60062-1895
800-247-6563
Fax: 847-498-1258
Telecommunication equipment, cameras, projectors and electronics.

5384 RMF Products
PO Box 520
Batavia, IL 60510-0520
630-879-0020
Fax: 630-879-6749
E-mail: mail@rmfproducts.com
http://www.rmfproducts.com
Complete line of slide-related products including two and three-projector dissolve controls, programmers, multi-track tape recorders, audio-visual cables, remote controls and slide mounts.
Richard Frieders, President

5385 RTI-Research Technology International
4700 W Chase Avenue
Lincolnwood, IL 60646-1608
800-323-7520
Fax: 800-784-6733
TapeChek Videotape Cleaner/Inspector/Rewinders make videotapes last longer and perform better. Find damage before tape is circulated. Also available is videotape/laser disc storage, shipping and care products.
Bill Wolavka, Marketing Director

5386 Recreation Equipment Unlimited
PO Box 4700
Pittsburgh, PA 15206-0700
412-731-3000
Fax: 412-731-3052
Scoreboards and sports/recreation equipment.

5387 Reliance Plastics & Packaging
25 Prospect Street
Newark, NJ 07105-3300
973-473-7200
Fax: 973-589-6440
Vinyl albums for audio or video cassettes, video discs, slides, floppy disks, CDs Protect, store and circulate valuable media properly.

309

5388 Resolution Technology
26000 Avenida Aeropuerto Spc 22
San Juan Capistrano, CA 92675-4736
949-661-6162
Fax: 949-661-0114
Video systems and videomicroscopy equipment.

5389 RobotiKits Direct
17141 Kingsview Avenue
Suite B
Carson, CA 90746
310-515-6800
877-515-6652
Fax: 310-515-0927
E-mail: info@owirobot.com
http://www.robotikitsdirect.com
New science and robotic kits for the millenium.

Craig Morioka, President
Armer Amante, General Manger

5390 S'Portable Scoreboards
3058 Alta Vista Drive
Fallbrook, CA 92028-8738
800-323-7745
Fax: 270-759-0066
Portable scoreboards, manual and electronic, sports timers and clocks.

5391 SONY Broadcast Systems Product Division
1 Sony Drive
Park Ridge, NJ 07656
800-472-SONY
Interactive videodisc players for multimedia applications, VTRs, monitors, projection systems, video cameras, editing systems, printers and scanners, video presentation stands, audio cassette duplicators and video library systems.

5392 Scott Resources/ Hubbard Scientific
National Training Aids
PO Box 2121
Fort Collins, CO 80522-2121
970-484-7445
800-289-9299
Fax: 970-484-1198
E-mail: sgranger@amep.com
http://www.hubbardscientific.com
Microslide system is a comprehensive, classroom-ready to help students learn. The microslide system combines superb photo-materials with detailed curriculum material and reproducible student activity sheets at an affrdable price.

Shelley Granger, OEM/Retail Sales Manager
Candy Coffman, National Sales Manager

5393 Shure Brothers
222 Hartrey Avenue
Evanston, IL 60202-3696
847-866-2200
Fax: 847-866-2551
Electronics, hardware and classroom supplies.

5394 Swift Instruments
1190 N 4th Street
San Jose, CA 95112
408-293-2380
800-523-4544
Fax: 408-292-7967
http://www.swiftmicroscope.com
Capture live or still microscopic images through your compound or stereo microscope and background sound images through your VCR or computer.

5395 Tech World
Lab-Volt
PO Box 686
Farmingdale, NJ 07727
732-938-2000
800-522-8658
Fax: 732-774-8573
E-mail: us@labvolt.com
http://www.labvolt.com
Tech World provides superior hands-on instruction using state-of-the-art technology and equipment. Lab-Volt also offers a full line of attractive, durable, and flexible modular classroom furniture.

5396 Technical Education Systems
814 Chestnut Street
PO Box 1203
Rockford, IL 61102
815-966-2525
800-451-2169
Fax: 815-965-4836
http://www.tii-tech.com
Hands-on application-oriented training systems integrating today's real world technologies in a flexible and easy-to-understand curriculum format.

5397 Telex Communications
12000 Portland Avenue S
Burnsville, MN 55337
952-884-4051
800-828-6107
Fax: 952-884-0043
http://www.telex.com
Telex manufactures a variety of products for the educational market, including multimedia headphones, headsets and microphones; LCD computer and multimedia projection panels, group listening centers, video projectors, slide projectors, portable sound systems, wired and wireless intercoms, and wired and wireless microphones.

Dawn Wiome, Marketing Coordinator

5398 The Transcription Studio
The Transcription Studio, LLC
210 N. Pass Avenue
Suite 206
Burbank, CA 91505
818-846-8973
Fax: 818-846-8933
E-mail: www.transcriptionstudio.com
http://jeff@transcriptionstudio.com
We transcribe and provide closed-captioning services to the education and academic fields.

Jeff Zedlar, CEO
Deborah Hargreaves, Director of Operations

5399 Three M Visual Systems
3M Austin Center
6801 River Place Boulevard
Austin, TX 78726-4530
800-328-1371
Fax: 512-984-6529
Overhead projectors, audiovisual carts and tables, and overhead transparencies.

5400 Tom Snyder Productions
80 Coolidge Hill Road
Watertown, MA 02472-7013
617-926-6000
800-342-0236
Fax: 800-304-1254
E-mail: ask@tpmsnyder.com
http://www.tomsnyder.com
Educational videotapes, videodiscs and computer programs.

5401 Varitronics Systems
PO Box 234
Minneapolis, MN 55440
800-637-5461
Fax: 800-543-8966
Computer electronics, hardware, software and systems.

5402 Wholesale Educational Supplies
PO Box 120123
East Haven, CT 06512-0123
800-243-2518
Fax: 800-452-5956
E-mail: wes4@snet.net
http://www.discountav.com
Over 5,000 audio visual and video equipment and supplies offered at deep discount prices. Free 148 page catalog.

J Fields, President

Furniture & Equipment

5403 ASRS of America
225 W 34th Street
Suite 1708
New York, NY 10122-0049
212-760-1607
Fax: 212-714-2084
E-mail: elecompack@erols.com
http://www.elecompack.com
Offers Elecompack, high density compact shelving which offers double storage capacity, automatic passive safety systems and custom front panels.

Walter M Kaufman

5404 Adden Furniture
26 Jackson Street
Lowell, MA 01852-2199
978-454-7848
800-625-3876
Fax: 978-453-1449
E-mail: fsafran@addenfurniture.com
http://www.addenfurniture.com
Manufacturer of dormitory furniture, bookcases and shelving products.

Frank Safran, Education/Sales Director

5405 Air Technologies Corporation
27130 Paseo Espada
Suite 1405-A
San Juan Capistrano, CA 92675
949-661-5060
800-759-5060
Fax: 949-661-2454
E-mail: sales@airtech.net
http://www.airtech.net
Develop and manufacture professional ergonomic computer products.

5406 Alma Industries
1300 Prospect Street
High Point, NC 27260-8329
336-578-5700
Fax: 336-578-0105
Bookcases and shelving for educational purposes.

5407 Angeles Group
Dailey Industrial Park
9 Capper Drive
Pacific, MO 63069
636-257-0533
Fax: 636-257-5473
http://www.angeles-group.com
Housekeeping furniture and children play kitchen's made of durable and sturdy molded polyethylene. Baseline Furniture: tables, chairs, lockers, cubbies, bookcases, bookracks, silver rider trikes, spaceline cots, basic trikes, and bye bye buggies.

Dianna Pritcjett, Customer Service Manager
Tami Warren, Customer Service Manager

5408 Anthro Corporation Technology Furniture
10450 SW Manhasset
Tualatin, OR 97062
503-691-2556
800-325-3841
Fax: 800-325-0045
http://www.anthro.com

Durable computer workstations and accessories; educational discounts; and dozens of shapes and sizes.

Mila Graham, Educational Sales

5409 Architectural Precast
10210 Winstead Lane
Cincinnati, OH 45231
513-772-4670
Fax: 513-772-4672
Furniture, tables, playground equipment, desks.

5410 Blanton & Moore Company
PO Box 70
Barium Springs, NC 28010-0070
704-528-4506
Fax: 704-528-6519
http://www.blantonandmoore.com
Standard and custom library furniture crafted from fine hardwoods.

Billy Galliher, Manager Sales Administration

5411 Borroughs Corporation
3002 N Burdick Street
Kalamazoo, MI 49004-3483
616-342-0161
800-627-6767
Bookcases and shelving products for educational purposes.

5412 Brady Office Machine Security
11056 S Bell Avenue
Chicago, IL 60643-3935
773-779-8349
800-326-8349
Fax: 773-779-9712
E-mail: b.brady1060@aol.com
The Brady Office Machine Security physically protects all office machines, computer components, faxes, printers, VCRs, have wall and ceiling mounts for TVs.

Bernadette Brady, President
Don Brady, VP

5413 Bretford Manufacturing
9715 Soreng Avenue
Schiller Park, IL 60176-2186
540-678-2545
Manufacturer of a full line of AV and computer projection screens, television mounts, wood office furniture and a full line of combination wood shelving and steel library shelving.

5414 Brixey
30414 Ganado Drive
Suite A
Palos Verdes Estates, CA 90275-6221
310-544-6098
Furniture for the classroom.

5415 Brodart Company, Automation Division
500 Arch Street
Williamsport, PA 17701
570-326-2461
800-233-8467
Fax: 570-327-9237
E-mail: salesmkt@brodart.com
http://www.brodart.com
Brodart's Automation Division has been providing library systems, software, and services for over 25 years. Products include: library management systems, media management systems, Internet solutions, cataloged web sites, cataloging resource tools, union catalog solutions, public access catalogs, and bibliographic services.

Kasey Dibble, Marketing Coordinator
Sally Wilmoth, Director Marketing/Sales

5416 Buckstaff Company
Buckstaff Company
1127 S Main Street
PO Box 2506
Oshkosh, WI 54902
920-235-5890
800-755-5890
Fax: 920-235-2018
E-mail: tmugerauer@buckstaff.com
http://www.buckstaff.com
The premier manufacturer of library furniture in the United States. Quality and durability has been the Buckstaff trademark for 150 years.

Tom Mugerauer, Sales Manager, National

5417 Carpets for Kids Etc...
115 SE 9th Avenue
Portland, OR 97214-1301
503-232-1203
Fax: 503-232-1394
http://www.carpetforkids.com
Carpets, flooring and floorcoverings for educational purposes.

5418 Children's Factory
505 N Kirkwood Road
Saint Louis, MO 63122-3913
314-821-1441
Fax: 877-726-1714
Manufactures children's indoor play furniture.

5419 Children's Furniture Company
Gressco Ltd.
328 Moravian Valley Road
Waunakee, WI 53597
800-697-3408
Fax: 608-849-6300
E-mail: caroline@gresscoltd.com
http://www.gressco.com
Commercial quality furniture for children of all ages.

Robert Childers, President
Caroline Ashmore, Marketing/Sales

5420 Community Playthings
PO Box 901
Rifton, NY 12471-0901
800-777-4244
Fax: 800-336-5948
E-mail: sales@bruderhof.com
Unstructured maple toys and furniture including innovative products, especially for infants and toddlers.

5421 Continental Film
PO Box 5126
Chattanooga, TN 37406-0126
423-622-1193
888-909-3456
Fax: 423-629-0853
E-mail: cfpc@chattanooga.net
http://www.continentalfilm.com
LCD projectors, distance learning systems, interactive white boards, document cameras.

Jim Webster, President
Courtney Sisk, VP

5422 Counterpoint
17237 Van Wagoner Road
Spring Lake, MI 49456-9702
800-628-1945
Fax: 616-847-3109
Audiovisual carts and tables.

5423 CyberStretch By Jazzercise
2460 Impala Drive
Carlsbad, CA 92008
760-476-1750
Fax: 760-602-7180
E-mail: cyberstretch@cyberstretch.com
http://www.jazzercize.com
To foster and promote wellness through the production of free interactive software pro-

grams for business, government, educational and personal use.

Kathy Missett, Contact

5424 Da-Lite Screen Company
3100 N Detroit Street
Warsaw, IN 46582
574-267-8101
800-622-3737
Fax: 574-267-7804
E-mail: info@dalite.com
http://www.da-lite.com
Projection screens, monitor mounts, audiovisual carts and tables, overhead projectors and transparencies.

5425 DeFoe Furniture 4 Kids
910 S Grove Avenue
Ontario, CA 91761-8011
909-947-4459
Fax: 909-947-3377
Furniture, floorcoverings, toys, constructive playthings and more for children grades PreK-5.

5426 Decar Corporation
7615 University Avenue
Middleton Branch, WI 53562-3142
606-836-1911
Library shelving, storage facilities and furniture.

5427 DecoGard Products
Construction Specialties
Route 405
PO Box 400
Muncy, PA 17756
570-546-5941
Fax: 570-546-5169
Physical fitness and athletic floorcoverings and mats.

5428 Engineering Steel Equipment Company
1307 Boissevain Avenue
Norfolk, VA 23507-1307
757-627-0762
Fax: 757-625-5754
Audiovisual carts and tables, bookcases and library shelving.

5429 Environments
PO Box 1348
Beaufort, SC 29901-1348
843-846-8155
800-348-4453
Fax: 843-846-2999
Publishes a catalog featuring equipment and materials for child care and early education. Offers durable and easy-to-maintain products with values that promote successful preschool, kindergarden, special needs and multi-age programs.

5430 Flagship Carpets
PO Box 1189
Chatsworth, GA 30705-1189
Carpets, flooring and floorcoverings.

5431 Fleetwood Group
PO Box 1259
Holland, MI 49422-1259
616-396-1142
800-257-6390
Fax: 616-820-8300
E-mail: www.fleetwoodfurniture.com
Offers library and school furniture including shelving, check out desks and multimedia units.

5432 Fordham Equipment Company
3308 Edson Avenue
New York, NY 10469
718-379-7300
800-249-5922
Fax: 718-379-7312

E-mail: alrobbi@attglobal.net
http://www.fordhamequip.com
Distributor and manufacturer of complete line of library supplies. Specialize in professional library shelving and furniture (wood and metal), mobile shelving and displayers. Catalog on request.

Al Robbins, President

5433 Good Sports
6031 Broad Street Mall
Pittsburgh, PA 15206-3009
412-661-9500
Mats, matting, floorcoverings and athletic training mats.

5434 Grafco
ERD
PO Box 71
Catasauqua, PA 18032-0071
800-367-6169
Fax: 610-782-0813
E-mail: info@grafco.com
http://www.grafco.com
GRAFCO manufacturers sturdy and durable computer furniture and tables designed for the educational environment.

Art Grafenberg, President

5435 Grammer
6989 N 55th Street
Suite A
Oakdale, MN 55128
651-770-6515
800-367-7328
http://www.grammerusa.com
Leading manufacturer and designer of ergonomically sound seating. Offers a chair designed especially for children.

5436 Greeting Tree
2709 Oak Haven Drive
San Marcos, TX 78666
512-392-0669
800-322-3199
Fax: 512-392-9660
E-mail: krieger@corridor.net
http://www.greetingtree.com
Solid wood furniture for Reading Recovery, Reading Library, Primary and Early Childhood. Specializes in quality and customized furniture for today's classroom. Kitchen learning centers, storage units of all sizes and sorts, easels with over fourteen different display front possibilities.

BiAnnually

Cherie Krieger, Owner

5437 Gressco Ltd.
Gressco
328 Moravian Valley Road
PO Box 339
Waunakee, WI 53597
608-849-6300
800-345-3480
Fax: 608-849-6304
E-mail: custserv@gresscoltd.com
http://www.gressco.com
Gressco is a supplier of a complete line of commercial children's HABA furniture and library displays for all types of medias. Kwik-case for the security protection of CDs, videos, and audiocassettes. Catalog available.

Caroline Ashmore, Marketing/Sales

5438 H Wilson Company
555 W Taft Drive
South Holland, IL 60473-2071
708-339-5111
800-245-7224
Fax: 800-245-8224
E-mail: sales@wilson.com
http://www.hwilson.com

Manufacturer of furniture for audio, video, and computers. Complete line of TV wall and ceiling mounts. Makers of the famous Tuffy color carts.

Matthew Glowiak, Director
Sales/Marketing

5439 HON Company
200 Oak Street
#769
Muscatine, IA 52761-4341
563-264-7100
Fax: 563-264-7505
Bookcases and shelving units.

5440 Haworth
One Haworth Center
Holland, MI 49423-9570
616-393-3000
800-344-2600
Fax: 616-393-1570
http://www.haworth.com
Steel and wood desks, systems furniture, seating, files, bookcases, shelving units, and tables.

5441 Joy Carpets
104 W Forrest Road
Fort Oglethorpe, GA 30742-3675
706-866-3335
800-645-2787
Fax: 706-866-7928
E-mail: joycarpets@joycarpets.com
http://www.joycarpets.com
Manufacturer of recreational and educational carpet for the classroom, home, or business. With a 10 year wear warranty, Class #1 Flammability rating, anti-stain and anti-bacterial treatment.

Joy Dobosh, Director Marketing

5442 KI
PO Box 8100
Green Bay, WI 54308-8100
920-468-8100
Fax: 920-468-2232
Library shelving, furniture, bookcases and more.

5443 Kensington Technology Group
2855 Campus Drive
San Mateo, CA 94403
650-572-2700
Fax: 650-572-9675
http://www.kensington.com
Offers several ergonomic mice.

5444 Kimball Office Furniture Company
1600 Royal Street
Jasper, IN 47549-1022
812-482-1600
Fax: 812-482-8300
Bookcases, office equipment and shelving units for educational institutions.

5445 Lee Metal Products
PO Box 6
Littlestown, PA 17340-0006
717-359-4111
Fax: 717-359-4414
http://www.leemetal.com
Carts, tables, bookcases and storage cabinets.

Richard Kemper, President

5446 Library Bureau
172 Industrial Road
Fitchburg, MA 01420
978-345-7942
800-221-6638
Fax: 978-345-0188
E-mail: melvil@librarybureau.com
http://www.librarybureau.com
Library shelving, bookcases, cabinets, circulation desks, carrels, computer workstations, upholstered seating.

Dennis Ruddy, Sr Project Manager

5447 Library Store
Library Store
112 E S Street
PO Box 964
Tremont, IL 61568
309-925-5571
800-548-7204
Fax: 800-320-7706
E-mail: libstore@thelibrarystore.com
http://www.thelibrarystore.com
The Library Store offers through its full-line catalog, supplies and furniture items for librarians, schools, and churches. Free catalog available containing special product discounts.

Janice Smith, Marketing Director

5448 Little Tikes Company
2180 Barlow Road
Hudson, OH 44236-4199
330-656-3906
800-321-4424
Fax: 330-650-3221
Offers a wide variety of furniture, educational games and toys and safety products for young children.

5449 Lucasey Manufacturing Company
2744 E 11th Street
Oakland, CA 94601-1429
510-534-1435
800-582-2739
Fax: 510-534-6828
E-mail: janrence@lucasey.com
Audiovisual carts, tables, and TV mounts.

Jan RenceTurnbull, National Accountant

5450 Lundia
600 Capitol Way
Jacksonville, IL 62650-1096
800-726-9663
Fax: 800-869-9663
Bookcases and shelving products, as well as furniture for educational institutions.

5451 Lyon Metal Products
PO Box 671
Aurora, IL 60507-0671
630-892-8941
Fax: 630-892-8966
Bookcases and library shelving.

5452 Mateflex-Mele Corporation
1712 Erie Street
Utica, NY 13502-3337
315-733-4600
800-926-3539
Fax: 315-733-3183
http://www.mateflex.com
Manufacturers of Mateflex gymnasium flooring for basketball/gym courts. Mateflex II tennis court surfaces and Mateflex/Versaflex gridded safety floor tiles.

Gabe Martini, Sales Manager

5453 Microsoft Corporation
One Microsoft Way
Redmond, WA 98502-6399
425-882-8080
Fax: 206-703-2641
http://www.microsoft.com
Strives to produce innovative products and services that meet our costomers' evolving needs.

5454 Miller Multiplex
1555 Larkin Williams Road
Fenton, MO 63026-3008
636-343-5700
800-325-3350
Fax: 636-326-1716
E-mail: info@millermultiplex.com
Announcement boards, classroom displays, charts and pghtography, books towers, post-

ers, frames, kiosk displays, presentation displays.

12 pages

Kathy Webster, Director Marketing

5455 ModuForm
ModuForm, Inc.
172 Industry Road
Fitchburg,, MA 01420
978-345-7942
800-221-6638
Fax: 978-345-0188
E-mail: guestlog@moduform.com
http://www.moduform.com
Residence hall furniture, loung seating, tables, stacking chairs, fully upholstered seating.

Robert Kushnir, Nationals Sales Manager
Darlene Bailey, VP Sales/Marketing

5456 Morgan Buildings, Pools, Spas, RV's
PO Box 660280
Dallas, TX 75266-0280
972-864-7300
800-935-0321
Fax: 972-864-7382
E-mail: rmoran@morganusa.com
http://www.morganusa.com
Classrooms, campus and other buildings custom designed to meet your projects needs. Permanent and relocatable modular classrooms or complete custom facilities. Rent, lease or purchase options available.

5457 Norco Products
Division of USA McDonald Corporation
PO Box 4227
Missoula, MT 59806
406-251-3800
800-662-2300
Fax: 406-251-3824
E-mail: john@norcoproducts.com
http://www.norcoproducts.com
Mobile cabinets, YRE funiture, tables, science labs, home economics displays, bookcases and shelving units, laboratory equipment, casework, cabinets, computer labs, podiums, award display cabinets, flags and flag poles.

Jim McDonald, President
John Schrom, Office Manger

5458 Nova
421 W Industrial Avenue
PO Box 725
Effingham, IL 62401
800-730-6682
Fax: 800-940-6682
E-mail: novadesk@effingham.net
http://www.novadesk.com
Patented furniture solution for computer mounting incorporates the downward gaze, our visual system's natural way of viewing close objects. Scientific evidence indicates that viewing a computer monitor at a downward gaze angle is a better solution than with traditional monitor placement.

5459 Oscoda Plastics
5585 N Huron Avenue
PO Box 189
Oscoda, MI 48750
989-739-6900
800-544-9538
Fax: 800-548-7678
E-mail: sales@oscodaplastics.com
http://www.oscodaplastics.com
Oscoda Plastics manufactures Protect-All Specialty Flooring from 100% recycled post-industrial vinyls. Protect-All is perfect for use in locker rooms, kitchen/walk-in

cooler floors, fitness areas, weight rooms, gym floors, or as a temporary gym floor cover.

Joe Brinn, National Sales Manager
Rick Maybury, Sales Coordinator

5460 Palmer Snyder
201 High Street
Conneautville, PA 16406
814-587-6313
800-762-0415
Fax: 814-587-2375
Tables are built with the highest quality materials for long life and low maintenance. A complete range of rugged options.

5461 Paragon Furniture
2224 E Randol Mill Road
Arlington, TX 76011
817-633-3242
800-451-8546
Fax: 817-633-2733
E-mail: customerservice@paragoninc.com
http://www.paragoninc.com
Offers a line of furniture for classroom, labs, science, and libraries.

Carl Brockway, VP Sales
Mark Hubbard, President

5462 Pawling Corporation
Borden Lane
Wassaic, NY 12592
845-373-9300
800-431-3456
Fax: 800-451-2200
E-mail: sales@pawling.com
Pawling is an approved manufacturer by E&I cooperative buying for athletic flooring, traffic safety products, wall and corner protection and entrance mat systems.

Richard Meyer, Sales Manager

5463 Peerless Sales Company
1980 N Hawthorne Avenue
Melrose Park, IL 60160-1167
708-865-8870
Fax: 708-865-2941
Auidovisual carts and tables.

5464 RISO
300 Rosewood Drive
Suite 210
Danvers, MA 01923-4527
978-777-7377
800-876-7476
Fax: 978-777-2517
The Risograph digital printer offers high speed copy/duplicating at up to 130 pages per minute. A 50-sheet document feeder lets people print multi-page documents quickly and inexpensively. Specifically designed to handle medium run length jobs that are too strenuous for copiers. Offers various other products and office equipment available to the education community.

5465 Research Technology International
4700 Chase Avenue
Lincolnwood, IL 60646-1689
847-677-3000
800-323-7520
Fax: 847-677-1311
E-mail: sales@rtico.com
http://www.ritco.com
Tape check, Video tape cleaner, disk chack optical, disc rejestor.

5466 Russ Bassett Company
8189 Byron Road
Whittier, CA 90606-2615
800-350-2445
Fax: 562-689-8972
Shelving units, furniture and bookcases for educational institutions.

5467 SNAP-DRAPE
2045 Westgate
Suite 100
Carrollton, TX 75006-5116
972-466-1030
800-527-5147
Fax: 800-230-1330
E-mail: mecton@snapdrape.com
http://www.snapdrape.com
Table and stage skirting

Melissa Acton, Marketing/Sales Assistant

5468 Screen Works
2201 W Fulton Street
Chicago, IL 60612
312-243-8265
800-294-8111
Fax: 312-243-8290
E-mail: daveh@thescreenworks.com
http://www.thescreenworks.com
Manufacturers the E-Z Fold brand of portable projection screens and offers a full line of portable presentation accessories and services, including: an extensive screen rental inventory; audio-visula roll carts; lecterns and PaperStand flip charts. Custom screen sizes, screen surface cleaning and frame repair service also available.

David Hull, National Sales Manager

5469 Spacemaster Systems
155 W Central Avenue
Zeeland, MI 49464-1601
616-772-2406
Fax: 616-772-2100
Standard and Custom Shelving Systems and USEFUL AISLE Storage Systems.

5470 Spacesaver Corporation
1450 Janesville Avenue
Fort Atkinson, WI 53538-2798
920-563-6362
800-492-3434
Fax: 920-563-2702
E-mail: ssc@spacesaver.com
http://www.spacesaver.com
Flexible Spacesaver custom designs high-density mobile storage systems. Will double your storage and filing capacity while increasing usable floor space. Store files, supplies, manuals, books, drawings, multi-media, etc.

5471 Synsor Corporation
1920 Merrill Creek Pkwy
Everett, WA 98203-5859
800-426-0193
Fax: 425-551-1313
Offers a full line of educational furniture.

5472 Tab Products Company
1400 Page Mill Road
Palo Alto, CA 94304-1124
800-672-3109
Fax: 920-387-1802
Bookcases and shelving products for library/media centers.

5473 Tepromark International
206 Mosher Avenue
Woodmere, NY 11598-1662
516-569-4533
800-645-2622
Fax: 516-295-5991
Trolley Rail wall guards, corner guards, wall guards with hand rails, door plates, chair rolls, kick plates, vinyl floor mats and carpet mats. All mats promote safety from slipping in wet areas.

Robert Rymers

5474 Tesco Industries
1038 E Hacienda Street
Bellville, TX 77418-2828
979-865-3176
Fax: 979-865-9026

313

Bookcases and shelving units.

5475 Texwood Furniture
1353 N 2nd Street
Taylor, TX 76574
512-352-3000
888-878-0000
Fax: 512-352-3084
E-mail: ajohnson@texwood.com
http://www.texwood.com
Wood library furniture, shelving, computer tables and circulation desks and early childhood furniture.

Andrea Johnson, Director Marketing
Dave Gaskers, VP Sales/Marketing

5476 Tot-Mate by Stevens Industries
704 W Main Street
Teutopolis, IL 62467-1212
217-857-6411
800-397-8687
Fax: 217-857-3638
E-mail: timw@stevens.com
Early learning furniture manufactured by Stevens Industries. Features include 16 color choices, plastic laminate surfacing, rounded corners, beveled edges, safe and strong designs. Items offered include change tables, storage shelving, book displays, teacher cabinets, housekeeping sets and locker cubbies.

Randy Ruholl, Sales Representative
Paul Jones, Customer Service

5477 University Products
University Products
517 Main Street
PO Box 101
Holyoke, MA 01041-0101
413-532-3372
800-628-1912
Fax: 413-532-9281
E-mail: info@universityproducts.com
http://www.universityproducts.com
University Products specializes in top-quality archival materials for conservation and preservation as well as library and media centers supplies, equipment, and furnishings.

John A Dunphy

5478 W. C. Heller & Company
Heller
201 W Wabash Avenue
Montpelier, OH 43543
419-485-3176
Fax: 419-485-8694
E-mail: wcheller@hotmail.com
Complete line of wood library furniture in oak and birch, custom cabinetry and special modifications. Over 110 years in business.

Robert L Heller II, VP Sales

5479 Wheelit
PO Box 352800
Toledo, OH 43635-2800
419-531-4900
800-523-7508
Fax: 419-531-6415
Carts and storage containers.

5480 White Office Systems
50 Boright Avenue
Kenilworth, NJ 07033-1015
908-272-8888
Fax: 908-931-0840
Shelving, bookcases, furniture and products for libraries, media centers, schools and offices.

5481 Whitney Brothers Company
PO Box 644
Keene, NH 03431-0644
603-352-2610
Fax: 603-357-1559
Manufactures children's furniture products for preschools and day care centers.

5482 Winsted Corporation
10901 Hampshire Avenue S
Minneapolis, MN 55438-2385
952-944-9050
800-447-2257
Fax: 800-421-3839
E-mail: racks@winsted.com
http://www.winsted.com
Video furniture, accessories, tape storage systems and lan rack systems.

Randy Smith, President

5483 Wood Designs
PO Box 1308
Monroe, NC 28111-1308
704-283-7508
800-247-8465
Fax: 704-289-1899
E-mail: p.schneider@tip-me-not.com
Manufactures wooden educational equipment and teaching toys for early learning environments. Sold through school supply dealers and stores.

Dennis Gosney, President
Paul Schneider, VP Sales/Marketing

5484 Worden Company
199 E 17th Street
Holland, MI 49423-4298
800-748-0561
Fax: 616-392-2542
Furniture for office, business, school or library.

Maintenance

5485 American Locker Security Systems
608 Allen Street
Jamestown, NY 14701-3966
716-664-9600
800-828-9118
Fax: 716-664-2949
E-mail: 103303.1432@compuserve.com
http://www.americanlocker.com
Lockers featuring coin operated lockers.

David L Henderson, VP/General Manager

5486 Atlantic Fitness Products
PO Box 300
Linthicum Hts, MD 21090-0300
800-445-1855
School lockers and fitness/physical education products and equipment.

5487 Barco Products
11 N Batavia Avenue
Batavia, IL 60510-1961
800-338-2697
Maintenance and safety products made from recycled materials.

Kitt Pittman, Office Manager
Judy Leonard, Marketing Manager

5488 Blaine Window Hardware
17319 Blaine Drive
Hagerstown, MD 21740-2394
800-678-1919
Fax: 301-797-2510
E-mail: user533955@aol.com
http://www.blainewindow.com
Window and door parts including window repair hardware, custom screens locker hardware, chair glides, panic exit hardware, balance systems, door closers and motorized operators.

William Pasquerette, VP
Robert Slick, Purchasing Agent

5489 Bleacherman, M.A.R.S.
105 Mill Street
Corinth, NY 12822-1021
518-654-9084

School lockers.

5490 Burkel Equipment Company
14670 Hanks Drive
Red Bluff, CA 96080-9475
800-332-3993
School lockers, hardware and security equipment, maintenance and repair supplies.

5491 Chemtrol
Santa Barbara Control Systems
5375 Overpass Road
Santa Barbara, CA 93111-5879
800-621-2279
Fax: 805-683-1893
E-mail: chemtrol@slocontrol.com
http://www.chemtrolcontrol.com
Maintenance supplies for educational institutions.

Kevin R Smith, Sales Manager

5492 Contact East
335 Willow Street S
N Andover, MA 01845-5995
978-682-2000
800-225-5370
Fax: 978-688-7829
E-mail: sales@contacteast.com
http://www.contacteast.com
Maintenance supplies and equipment.

5493 DeBourgh Manufacturing Company
27505 Otero Avenue
La Junta, CO 81050-9403
719-384-8161
Fax: 719-384-7713
Security equipment, hardware, storage and school lockers.

5494 Dow Corning Corporation
PO Box 0994
Midland, MI 48686-0001
989-496-4000
Fax: 989-496-4572
Maintenance supplies and equipment.

5495 Dri-Dek Corporation
2706 Horseshoe Drive S
Naples, FL 34104-6142
941-643-0578
800-348-2378
Fax: 800-828-4248
E-mail: dri-dek@kictr.com
http://www.dri-dek.com
Oxy-BI vinyl compound in the Dri-Dek flooring systems helps halt the spread of infectious fungus and bacteria in areas with barefooted traffic. This compound makes Dri-Dek's anti-skid, self-draining surface ideal for use in the wettest conditions.

5496 Esmet
Tufloc Group
1406 5th Street SW
Canton, OH 44702-2062
330-452-9132
Fax: 330-452-2557
Lockers for the educational institution.

5497 Ex-Cell Metal Products
11240 Melrose Avenue
Franklin, IL 60131
847-451-0451
Fax: 847-451-0458
Maintenance supplies and repair equipment.

5498 Facilities Network
PO Box 868
Mahopac, NY 10541-0868
845-621-1664
School lockers and security system units.

5499 Fibersin Industries
37031 E Wisconsin Avenue
Oconomowoc, WI 53066
262-567-4427
Fax: 262-567-4814

School lockers and maintenance supplies. Desks, cradenzas, bookcases for school adm. Tables for cafeteria and adm.

5500 Flagpole Components
4150A Kellway Circle
Addison, TX 75001-4205
972-250-0893
800-634-4926
Fax: 972-380-5143
Maintenance and repair supplies and equipment.

5501 Flexi-Wall Systems
PO Box 89
Liberty, SC 29657-0089
Maintenance and repair supplies for educational institutions.

5502 Flo-Pac Corporation
700 Washington Avenue N
Suite 400
Minneapolis, MN 55401-1130
612-332-6240
Fax: 612-344-1663
Maintenance and repair supplies.

5503 Four Rivers Software Systems
2400 Ardmore Boulevard
7th Floor
Pittsburgh, PA 15221-1451
412-273-6400
Fax: 412-273-6420
Maintenance and repair supplies, business and administrative software and supplies.

5504 Friendly Systems
3878 Oak Lawn Avenue
#1008-300
Dallas, TX 75219-4460
972-857-0399
Maintenance and repair supplies.

5505 GE Capitol Modular Space
40 Liberty Boulevard
Malvern, PA 19355
610-225-2836
800-523-7918
Fax: 610-225-2762
School lockers, shelving and storage facilities.

5506 Glen Products
13765 Alton Parkway
Suite A
Irvine, CA 92618-1627
800-486-4455
Storage facilities, lockers and security systems.

5507 Global Occupational Safety
22 Harbor Park Drive
Port Washington, NY 11050-4650
516-625-4466
Safety storage facilities, shelving, lockers and hardware.

5508 Graffiti Gobbler Products
6428 Blarney Stone Court
Springfield, VA 22152-2106
800-486-2512
Educational maintenance and repair supplies and equipment.

5509 H&H Enterprises
PO Box 585
Grand Haven, MI 49417-9430
616-846-8972
800-878-7777
Fax: 616-846-1004
E-mail: hhenterprises@novagate.com
Maintenance and repair supplies.

5510 HAZ-STOR
2454 Dempster Street
Des Plaines, IL 60016
217-345-4422
800-727-2067
Fax: 217-345-4475
E-mail: info@hazstor.com
http://www.hazstor.com
Manufacturer of pre-fabricated steel structures including hazardous material storage buildings and outdoor flammables lockers as well as waste compactors and drum crushers, secondary containment products and process shelters.

Roger Quinlan, National Sales Manager
Antoinette Balthazor, Marketing Coordinator

5511 HOST/Racine Industries
1405 16th Street
Racine, WI 53403-2249
800-558-9439
Fax: 262-637-1624
Maintenance and repair supplies.

5512 Hako Minuteman
111 S Rohlwing Road
Addison, IL 60101-4244
630-627-6900
Fax: 630-627-1130
Maintenance and repair supplies for educational institutions.

5513 Haws Corporation
PO Box 2070
Sparks, NV 89432-2070
775-359-4712
Fax: 775-359-7424
E-mail: haws@hawsco.com
http://www.hawsco.com
Manufacturer of drinking fountains, electric water coolers, emergency drench showers and eyewashes.

Jim Bowers, Marketing Manager

5514 Honeywell
Home & Building Control
PO Box 524
Minneapolis, MN 55440-0524
973-455-2001
Fax: 973-455-4807
Maintenance and cleaning products for educational purposes.

5515 Insta-Foam Products
2050 N Broadway Street
Joliet, IL 60435-2571
800-800-FOAM
Fax: 800-326-1054
Maintenance supplies, cleaning products and repair hardware.

5516 Interstate Coatings
1005 Highway 301 S
Wilson, NC 27895
800-533-7663
Hardware, repair, maintenance and cleaning supplies.

5517 J.A. Sexauer
PO Box 1000
White Plains, NY 10602-1000
800-431-1872
Fax: 856-439-1333
Cleaning and maintenance supplies for educational institutions.

5518 Karnak Corporation
330 Central Avenue
Clark, NJ 07066-1199
732-388-0300
800-526-4236
Fax: 732-388-9422
Maintenance and cleaning supplies.

5519 Kool Seal
Unifex Professional Maintenance Products
1499 Enterprise Pkwy
Twinsburg, OH 44087-2241
800-321-0572
Fax: 330-425-9778
Maintenance, repair and cleaning supplies.

5520 LDSystems
9535 Monroe Road
Suite 140
Charlotte, NC 28270
704-847-1338
Fax: 704-847-1354
E-mail: ds@starkpr.com
http://www.bottompump.com
Environmentally-safe bottom pump air powered spray containers to dispense cleaning supplies such as window sprays, for cooling during workouts and general storage containers.

Dick Stark

5521 List Industries
401 NW 12th Avenue
Deerfield Beach, FL 33442-1707
954-429-9155
Fax: 954-428-3843
School lockers and storage facilities.

5522 Maintenance
1051 W Liberty Street
Wooster, OH 44691-3307
330-264-6262
800-892-6701
Fax: 800-264-2578
Provides pavement maintenance products for parking lots, driveways, tennis courts, etc.

Robert E Huebner

5523 Master Bond
PO Box 522
Teaneck, NJ 07666
201-343-8983
Fax: 201-343-2132
E-mail: main@masterbond.com
http://www.masterbond.com
Repair hardware, maintenance and cleaning products for schools.

5524 Master Builders
Admixture Division
23700 Chagrin Boulevard
Cleveland, OH 44122-5554
216-831-5500
Fax: 216-839-8815
School hardware, maintenance and repair supplies and equipment.

5525 Medart
Division of Carriage Industries
PO Box 435
Garrettsville, OH 44231-0435
662-453-2506
School lockers.

5526 Modular Hardware
8190 N Brookshire Court
Tucson, AZ 85741-4037
520-744-4424
800-533-0042
Fax: 800-533-7942
School hardware, for repair and maintenance purposes.

5527 Penco Products
99 Brower Avenue
PO Box 378
Oaks, PA 19456-0378
610-666-0500
800-562-1000
Fax: 610-666-7561
E-mail: general@pencoproducts.com
http://www.pencoproducts.com
School lockers.

5528 Permagile Industries
910 Manor Lane
Bay Shore, NY 11706-7512
516-349-1100
Maintenance and cleaning products and supplies.

5529 Powr-Flite Commercial Floor Care Equipment
3301 Wichita Court
Fort Worth, TX 76140
817-551-0700
800-880-2913
Fax: 817-551-0719
http://www.powrflite.com
School maintenance supplies focusing on floor care equipment products, accessories and parts.

Curtis Walton, Contact

5530 ProCoat Products
260 Centre Street
Suite D
Holbrook, MA 02343-1074
781-767-2270
Fax: 781-767-2271
E-mail: info@procoat.com
http://www.procoat.com
Designed to restore aged and discolored acoustical ceiling tiles. Acoustical and fire retarding qualities are maintained. Ceiling restoration is cost effective, time efficient and avoids solid waste disposal. Products available also for preventative maintenance programs.

Kenneth Woolf, President

5531 Rack III High Security Bicycle Rack Company
675 Hartz Avenue
Suite 306
Danville, CA 94526-3859
800-733-1971
Lockers, bicycle racks, storage facilities and hardware.

5532 Republic Storage Systems Company
1038 Belden Avenue NE
Canton, OH 44705-1454
330-438-5800
Fax: 330-452-5071
Storage facilities, containers, maintenance products, shelving and lockers.

5533 Safety Storage
2301 Bert Drive
Hollister, CA 95023-2547
800-344-6539
Fax: 831-637-7405
Equipment, supplies and storage containers for maintenance and educational purposes.

5534 Salsbury Industries
1010 E 62nd Street
Los Angeles, CA 90001-1598
800-624-5269
Fax: 800-624-5299
E-mail: salsbury@mailboxes.com
http://www.mailboxes.com
School lockers, maintenance products and storage facilities.

5535 Servicemaster
Education Management Services
One Servicemaster Way
Downers Grove, IL 60515
800-926-9700
http://www.servicemaster.com
A provider of facility management support services to education.

5536 Sheffield Plastics
DSM Engineered Plastics Company
119 Salisbury Road
Sheffield, MA 01257-9706
413-229-8711
Maintenance and cleaning products for schools.

5537 Southern Sport Surfaces
PO Box 1817
Cumming, GA 30028-1817
770-887-3508
800-346-1632
Maintenance and cleaning products for schools.

5538 System Works
3301 Windy Ridge Parkway
Marietta, GA 30067
770-952-8444
800-868-0497
Fax: 770-955-2977
Addresses the capacity, quality and safety requirements of maintenance operations. Comprehensive and interactive it maximizes maintenance resources, people, tools and replacement parts, for increased productivity and equipment reliability, reduced inventories and accurate cost accounting.

Karen Kharlead

5539 TENTEL Corporation
4475 Golden Foothill Parkway
El Dorado Hills, CA 95762-9638
800-538-6894
Fax: 916-939-4114
Cleaning, repair and maintenance products for educational institutions.

5540 Tiffin Systems
450 Wall Street
Tiffin, OH 44883-1366
419-447-8414
800-537-0983
Fax: 419-447-8512
E-mail: tiffin@bpsom.com
http://www.tiffinmetal.com
Lockers, storage containers and shelving.

5541 Topog-E Gasket Company
1224 N Utica Avenue
Tulsa, OK 74110-4682
918-587-6649
Fax: 918-587-6961
Maintenance supplies and products.

5542 Tru-Flex Recreational Coatings
Touraine Paints
1760 Revere Beach Pkwy
Everett, MA 02149-5906
800-325-0017
Maintenance, floor care, coatings and repair supplies for upkeep of schools and institutions.

5543 Wagner Spray Tech Corporation
1770 Fernbrook Lane N
Plymouth, MN 55447-4663
763-553-7000
Fax: 763-553-7288
Maintenance supplies, floor care, cleaning and repair products and equipment.

5544 Wilmar
303 Harper Drive
Moorestown, NJ 08057
609-439-1222
800-523-7120
Fax: 800-220-3291
Maintenance and repair products, hardware and supplies.

5545 Witt Company
4454 Steel Place
Cincinnati, OH 45209-1184
513-979-3127
800-543-7417
Fax: 513-979-3134
Lockers, maintenance supplies and storage containers for educational purposes.

5546 Zep Manufacturing
1310 Seaboard Industrial Blvd NW
Atlanta, GA 30318-2807
404-352-1680
Maintenance and cleaning supplies.

Scientific Equipment

5547 Adventures Company
435 Main Street
Johnson City, NY 13790-1935
607-729-6512
800-477-6512
Fax: 607-729-4820
A full line of supplies and equipment for science and technology education.

D Hetherington

5548 Alfa Aesar
30 Bond Street
Ward Hill, MA 01835-8042
800-343-0660
Laboratory equipment and supplies.

5549 American Chemical Society
1155 16th Street NW
Washington, DC 20036-4800
202-872-4600
800-ACS-5558
Fax: 202-833-7732
Exhibits hands-on activities and programs for K-12 and college science curriculum.

5550 Arbor Scientific
PO Box 2750
Ann Arbor, MI 48106-2750
800-367-6695
Fax: 734-477-9570
E-mail: mail@arborsci.com
http://www.arborsci.com
Innovative products for Science Education.

56 pages Bi-Annual Catalog

Dave Barnes, Marketing Director

5551 Astronomy to Go
1115 Melrose Avenue
Melrose Park, PA 19027-3017
215-782-8970
Fax: 215-831-0486
E-mail: astro2go@aol.com
http://www.astronomytogo.com
Programs include Starlab Planetarium presentations, hands-on demonstrations, slides and lecture shows and energy observing sessions with our many telescopses. We are funded through our traveling museum shop which carries a large assortment of t-shirts, jewelry, gifts, books, and teaching supplies as well as an extensive selection of meterorites.

Bob Summerfield, Director

5552 CEM Corporation
3100 Smith Farm Road
Matthews, NC 28104-5044
704-821-7015
Fax: 704-821-7894
Laboratory and scientific supplies, furniture, casework and equipment.

5553 Carolina Biological Supply Company
2700 York Road
Burlington, NC 27215-3398
336-584-0381
800-334-5551
Fax: 800-222-7112
E-mail: carolina@carolina.com
http://www.carolina.com
Educational products for teachers and students of biology, molecular biology, biotechnology, chemistry, earth science, space science, physics, and mathematics. Carolina serves elementary schools through universities with living and preserved animals and plants, prepared microscope slides, microscopes, audiovisuals, books, charts, models, computer software, games, apparatus, and much more.

5554 Challenger Center for Space Science Education
1250 N Pitt Street
Alexandria, VA 22314
703-683-9740
Fax: 703-683-7546
E-mail: mail@challenger.org
http://www.challenger.org
Is a global not-for-profit education organization created in 1986 by familes of the astronauts tragically lost during the last flight of the Challenger Space Shuttle. Dedicated to the educaltional spirit of that mission, Challenger center develops Learning Centers and othe educational programs worldwide to continue the mission to engage students in science and math education
Glenn Ono, Marketing/Communications
Tracy Martin, Marketing Assistant

5555 ChronTrol Corporation
9975 Businesspark Avenue
San Diego, CA 92131-1644
619-282-8686
Fax: 619-563-6563
Scientific equipment, laboratory supplies and furniture.

5556 Classic Modular Systems
1911 Columbus Street
Two Rivers, WI 54241-2898
920-793-2269
800-558-7625
Fax: 920-793-2896
E-mail: cms@dataplusnet.com
http://www.dct.com/cms
Laboratory equipment, shelving, cabinets and markerboards.
Cathy Albers, Advertising Manager

5557 Columbia University's Biosphere 2 Center
Highway 77 & Biosphere Road
Oracle, AZ 85623
520-896-6200
Fax: 520-896-6471
Educational programs and products.

5558 Connecticut Valley Biological Supply Company
82 Valley Road
PO Box 326
Southampton, MA 01073-9536
413-527-4030
800-628-7748
Fax: 800-355-6813
E-mail: connval@ctvalleybio.com
Cultures and specimens, instruments, equipment, hands-on kits, books, software, audiovisuals, models and charts for teaching botany, zoology, life science, anatomy, physiology, genetics, astronomy, entomology, microscopy, AP Biology, microbiology, horticulture, biotechnology, earth science, natural history and environmental science.

5559 Crow Canyon Archaeological Center
23390 County Road K
Cortez, CO 81321-9408
970-565-8975
800-422-8975
Fax: 970-565-4859
E-mail: jsimpson@crowcanyon.org
http://www.crowcanyon.org
Experiential education programs in archaeology and Native American history. Programs offered for school groups, teachers and other adults.

ISBN: 0-7872-6748-1
M Elaine Davis and Marjorie R Connelly, Author
Joyce Simpson, Director Marketing
Elaine Davis, Director Education

5560 Cuisenaire Company of America
10 Bank Street
#5026
White Plains, NY 10606-1933
914-997-2600
Fax: 914-684-6137
Science materials and equipment.

5561 DISCOVER Science Program
105 Terry Drive
Suite 120
Newtown, PA 18940-1872
800-448-3399
Fax: 215-579-8589
Features the newest developments in a wide range of science topics and provides an easy way for teachers to stay current and up-to-date in the world of science. The DISCOVER Program offers the DISCOVER magazine at the lowest possible price.

5562 Delta Biologicals
PO Box 26666
Tucson, AZ 85726-6666
520-790-7737
800-821-2502
Fax: 520-745-7888
E-mail: sales@deltabio.com
http://www.deltabio.com
Products and supplies for science and biology educators for over 30 years. Preserves specimens, laboratory furniture, microscopes, anatomy models, balances and scales, dissection supplies, lab safety supplies, multimedia, plant presses.
Lynn Hugins, Marketing
Darlene Harris, Customer Service Manager

5563 Delta Biologicals Catalog
PO Box 26666
Tucson, AZ 85726-6666
520-790-7737
800-821-2502
Fax: 520-745-7888
E-mail: sales@deltabio.com
http://www.deltabio.com
96 pages
Lynn Hugins, Marketing
Darlene Harris, Customer Service Manager

5564 Detecto Scale Corporation
203 E Daugherty Street
Webb City, MO 64870-1929
417-673-4631
800-641-2008
Fax: 417-673-5001
E-mail: detecto@cardet.com
http://www.detectoscale.com
Scientific equipment and supplies for educational laboratories.

5565 Dickson Company
930 S Westwood Avenue
Addison, IL 60101-4997
630-543-3747
Laboratory instruments, electronics, furniture and equipment.

5566 Donald K. Olson & Associates
PO Box 858
Bonsall, CA 92003-0858
Mineral and fossil samples for educational purposes.

5567 Dranetz Technologies
1000 Durham Road
Edison, NJ 08818
732-287-3680
Fax: 732-287-9014
Laboratory instruments, equipment and supplies.

5568 Edmund Scientific - Scientifics Catalog
E726 Edscorp Building
Department 16A1
Barrington, NJ 08007
856-547-3488
Fax: 856-573-6295
Over 5,000 products including a wide selection of microscopes, telescopes, astronomy aids, fiber optic kits, demonstration optics, magnets and science discover products used in science fair projects.
Nancy McGonigle, President

5569 Educational Products
1342 N I35 E
Carrollton, TX 75006
972-245-9512
Fax: 972-245-5468
Science display boards, workshop materials and science fair accessories.

5570 Edwin H. Benz Company
73 Maplehurst Avenue
Providence, RI 02908-5324
401-331-5650
Fax: 401-331-5685
E-mail: sales@benztesters.com
http://www.benztesters.com
Laboratory equipment.

5571 Electro-Steam Generator Corporation
1000 Bernard Street
Alexandria, VA 22314-1299
703-549-0664
800-634-8177
Fax: 703-836-2581
E-mail: jharlineclectrostream.com
http://www.electrosteam.com
Laboratory equipment and supplies. Manufacture steam generators for sterilizers, autoclaves, clean rooms, pure steam humidification, laboratories, steam rooms, and cleaning of all kinds.
Jack Harlin, Sales/Marketing Associate

5572 Estes-Cox Corporation
1295 H Street
Penrose, CO 81240-9676
719-372-6565
800-820-0202
Fax: 719-372-3217
E-mail: info@esteseducator.com
http://www.esteseducator.com
Supplier of model rockets, engines and supporting videos, curriculums and educational publications for K-12.
Ann Grimm, Director Education

5573 FOTODYNE
950 Walnut Ridge Drive
Hartland, WI 53029-9388
262-369-7000
800-362-3642
Fax: 262-369-7017
Biotechnology curriculum equipment.

5574 First Step Systems
PO Box 2304
Jackson, TN 38302-2304
800-831-0877
Fax: 216-361-0829
Developed an effective, safe and less expensive approach to blood exposure safety for schools and classrooms that both help comply with OSHA requirements and is easy to purchase and resupply.
Susan Staples, Account Manager
Renee Carr, Bid Support

5575 Fisher Scientific Company
1410 Wayne Avenue
Indiana, PA 15701-3940
724-357-1000
Fax: 724-357-1019

A full line of laboratory and scientific supplies and equipment for educational institutions.

5576 Fisher Scientific/EMD
3970 John Creek Court
Suite 500
Suwanee, GA 30024
770-871-4500
800-766-7000
Fax: 800-926-1166
Supplier of chemistry, biology and physics laboratory supplies and equipment.

5577 Fisons Instruments
8 Forge Parkway
Franklin, MA 02038-3157
978-524-1000
Laboratory equipment and instruments for the scientific classroom.

5578 Flinn Scientific
PO Box 219
Batavia, IL 60510-0219
630-879-6900
800-452-1261
Fax: 630-879-6962
Laboratory safety supplies.

5579 Forestry Supplies
PO Box 8397
Jackson, MS 39284-8397
601-354-3565
800-647-5368
Fax: 800-543-4203
E-mail: fsi@forestry-suppliers.com
http://www.forestry-suppliers.com
Field and lab equipment for earth, life and environmental sciences.

Ken Peacock, VP Marketing
Debbie Raddin, Education Specialist

5580 Frank Schaffer Publications
23740 Hawthorne Boulevard
Torrance, CA 90505-5927
310-378-1133
800-421-5565
Fax: 800-837-7260
Charts, animal posters, floor puzzles, resource books and more.

5581 Frey Scientific
905 Hickory Lane
Mansfield, OH 44905-2862
800-225-FREY
Fax: 419-589-1522
Name brand scientific products including Energy Physics, Earth Science, Chemistry and Applied Science. Over 12,000 products and kits for grades 5-14 are available.

5582 Great Adventure Tours
1717 Old Topanga Canyon Road
Topanga, CA 90290-3934
800-642-3933
Educational science field trips and adventures.

5583 Guided Discoveries
PO Box 1360
Claremont, CA 91711-1360
Outdoor educational science programs.

5584 HACH Company
PO Box 389
Loveland, CO 80539-0389
970-669-3050
Fax: 970-669-2932
Water and soil test kits for field and laboratory work.

5585 Heathkit Educational Systems
455 Riverview Drive
Benton Harbor, MI 49022-5015
616-925-6000
800-253-0570
Fax: 616-925-3895

Electronics educational products from basic electricity to high-tech lasers and microscopes and beyond. Comprehensive line of different media to fit varied applications. Including Computer-Aided Instruction and Computer-Aided Troubleshooting services and Heathkit's PC Servicing, Troubleshooting and Networking courses.

Carolyn Feltner, Sales Coordinator
Patrick Beckett, Marketing Manager

5586 Holometrix
25 Wiggins Avenue
Bedford, MA 01730-2314
781-275-3300
Fax: 781-275-3705
Laboratory instruments.

5587 Howell Playground Equipment
1714 E Fairchild Street
Danville, IL 61832-3616
217-442-0482
800-637-5075
Fax: 217-442-8944
E-mail: howellequipment@aol.com
http://www.primestripe.com
Playground equipment and bicycle racks.

Nina Payne, President

5588 Hubbard Scientific
PO Box 2121
Fort Collins, CO 80522-2121
Earth science and life science models, kits, globes and curriculum materials.

5589 Innova Corporation
115 George Lamb Road
Bernardston, MA 01337-9742
Science kits and globes.

5590 Insect Lore
PO Box 1535
Shafter, CA 93263-1535
661-746-6047
800-548-3284
Fax: 661-746-0334
E-mail: orders@insectlore.com
http://www.insectlore.com
Science and nature materials for preschool through grade 6. Raises butterflies, frogs, ladybugs and more. Features books, curriculum units, videos, puppet, posters, and other nature oriented products.

5591 Insights Visual Productions
PO Box 230644
Encinitas, CA 92023-0644
800-942-0528
Laboratory instruments, manuals, and supplies.

5592 Instron Corporation
100 Royall Street
Canton, MA 02021-1089
781-828-2500
Fax: 781-575-5776
Laboratory and scientific equipment, supplies and furniture.

5593 Johnsonite
16910 Munn Road
Chagrin Falls, OH 44023-5493
800-899-8916
Fax: 440-632-5643
Physical education mats, matting and floors.

5594 Justrite Manufacturing Company
2454 E Dempster Street
Des Plaines, IL 60016-5315
847-298-9250
Fax: 847-298-3429
E-mail: justrite@justritemfg.com
http://www.justritemfg.com
Supplies and equipment aimed at the scientific classroom or laboratory.

5595 KLM Bioscientific
8888 Clairemont Mesa Boulevard
Suite D
San Diego, CA 92123
858-571-5562
Fax: 858-571-5587
A mail order company that provides high quality, reasonably priced, on time living and preserved biological specimens. The Biology Store also carries a wide range of instructional materials including books, charts, models and videos. Also available is a wide range of general labware.

Loli Victorio, President

5596 Ken-a-Vision Manufacturing Company
5615 Raytown Road
Kansas City, MO 64133-3388
816-353-4787
Fax: 816-358-5072
E-mail: info@ken-a-vision.com
http://www.ken-a-vision.com
Video Flex, Vison Viewer, Pupil CAM, Microscopes and Microrojectors

Steve Dunn, Domestic/International Op.
Ben Hoke, Sales Manger

5597 Kepro Circuit Systems
3640 Scarlet Oak Boulevard
Kirkwood, MO 63122-6606
800-325-3878
Fax: 636-861-9109
Laboratory equipment.

5598 Kewaunee Scientific Corporation
2700 W Front Street
Statesville, NC 28677-2894
704-873-7202
Fax: 704-873-1275
E-mail: humanresources@kewaunee.com
http://www.kewaunee.com
Science and laboratory supplies.

Bob Neals, Human Resources

5599 Knex Education Catalog
Knex Education
2990 Bergey Road
PO Box 700
Hatfield, PA 19440-0700
888-ABC-KNEX
E-mail: abcknex@knex.com
http://www.knexeducation.com
Hands-on, award-winning curriculum supported K-12 math, science and technology sets.

5600 Koffler Sales Company
100A Oakwood Road e
Lake Zurich, IL 60047-1524
847-438-1152
800-323-0951
Fax: 847-438-1514
http://www.kofflersales.com
Floor mats, Matting and stair treads.

5601 Komodo Dragon
PO Box 822
The Dalles, OR 97058-0822
541-773-5808
Museum-quality fossils and minerals.

5602 Kreonite
715 E 10th Street N
Wichita, KS 67214-2918
316-263-1111
Fax: 316-263-6829
Laboratory equipment, furniture and hardware.

5603 Kruger & Eckels
1406 E Wilshire Avenue
Santa Ana, CA 92705-4423
714-547-5165
Fax: 714-547-2009

Laboratory and scientific instruments for institutional or educational use.

5604 LEGO Data
PO Box 1600
Enfield, CT 06083-1600
860-749-2291
Fax: 860-763-7477
Curriculum programs and materials for science education.

5605 LINX System
Science Source
PO Box 727
Waldoboro, ME 04572-0727
207-832-6344
800-299-5469
Fax: 207-832-7281
E-mail: info@thesciencesource.com
http://www.thesciencesource.com
A building system that integrates science, mathematics and technology at the K-9 level.

5606 Lab Safety Supply
PO Box 1368
Janesville, WI 53547-1368
608-754-2345
Fax: 800-543-9910
Extensive variety of school products, including lab and safety apparel and floorcoverings.

5607 Lab Volt Systems
PO Box 686
Farmingdale, NJ 07727-0686
Educational materials and equipment for the science educator.

5608 Lab-Aids
17 Colt Center
Ronkonkoma, NY 11779-6949
631-737-1133
800-381-8003
Fax: 631-737-1286
E-mail: mkt@lab-aids.com
http://www.lab-aids.com
Science kits, published curriculum materials.

John Weatherby, Sales/Marketing Director
David M Frank, President

5609 Labconco Corporation
8811 Prospect Avenue
Kansas City, MO 64132-2696
816-333-8811
Fax: 816-363-0130
Laboratory equipment and supplies.

5610 Lakeside Manufacturing
1977 S Allis Street
Milwaukee, WI 53207-1295
414-481-3900
Fax: 414-481-9313
Laboratory and scientific instruments, equipment, furniture and supplies.

5611 Lane Science Equipment Company
225 W 34th Street
Suite 1412
New York, NY 10122-1496
212-563-0663
Fax: 212-465-9440
Scientific equipment, technology and supplies.

5612 Lasy USA
1309 Webster Avenue
Fort Collins, CO 80524-2756
800-444-2126
Fax: 970-221-4352
Building sets that encourage children to encounter technology through problem solving activities, planning, co-operation and perseverance. Allows students to build and learn programming skills in areas of communication, construction, manufacturing and transportation.

Dave Nayak

5613 Learning Technologies
40 Cameron Avenue
Somerville, MA 02144-2404
617-628-1459
800-537-8703
Fax: 617-628-8606
E-mail: starlab@starlab.com
http://www.starlab.com
STARLAB portable planetarium systems and the Project STAR hands-on science materials.

Jane Sadler, President

5614 Leica Microsystems EAD
PO Box 123
Buffalo, NY 14240-0123
716-686-3000
Fax: 716-686-3085
Educational microscopes for elementary through university applications.

5615 Life Technologies
7335 Executive Way
Suite A
Frederick, MD 21704-8354
716-774-6700
800-952-9166
Fax: 716-774-6727
Supplier of biology and cell culture products.

5616 Lyon Electric Company
1690 Brandywine Avenue
Chula Vista, CA 91911-6021
619-216-3400
Fax: 619-216-3434
Electrical tabletop incubators for science classrooms and tabletop animal intensive care units, hatchers and brooders.

Caroline Vazquez, Sales Manager
Jose Madrigal, Marketing Manager

5617 Magnet Source
607 S Gilbert Street
Castle Rock, CO 80104-2221
303-688-3966
888-293-9190
Fax: 303-688-5303
E-mail: magnet@magnetsource.com
http://www.magnetsource.com
Educational magnetic products and magnetic toys designed to stimulate creativity and encourage exploration of science with fun magnets. Kits include experiments, fun games, activities and powerful magnets. Moo Magnets, rare earth magnets, horseshoes, and bulk magnets.

Jim Madsen, Sales Manager

5618 Meiji Techno America
Meiji Techno America
2186 Bering Drive
San Jose, CA 95131-2041
408-428-9654
800-832-0060
Fax: 408-428-0472
http://www.meijitechno.com
A full line of elementary, secondary, grade school and college-level microscopes and accessories.

James J Dutkiewicz, General Manager

5619 Metrologic Instruments
Coles Road at Route 42
Blackwood, NJ 08012
800-436-3876
Fax: 856-228-0653
Manufactures low-power lasers and laser accessories for the classroom, a range of helium-neon lasers, a modulated VLD laser, optics lab, sandbox holography kit, speed of light lab, optics bench system and digital laser power meter, as well as a selection of pin carriers, mounting pins, lenses and mirrors. Sponsors the Physics Bowl, a yearly national physics competition for high school students

by the American Association of Physics Teachers.

Betty Williams

5620 Modern School Supplies
PO Box 958
Hartford, CT 06143-0958
860-243-9565
Fax: 800-934-7206
Products for hands-on science education.

5621 Mohon International
1600 Porter Court
Paris, TN 38242
731-642-4251
Fax: 731-642-4262
Classroom equipment and supplies, directed at the scientific classroom and laboratory.

5622 Museum Products Company
84 Route 27
Mystic, CT 06355-1226
860-536-6433
800-395-5400
Fax: 860-572-9589
E-mail: museumprod@aol.com
http://www.museumproducts.net
Field guides, rock collections, environmental puzzles, posters, charts, books, magnets, magnifiers, microscopes and other lab equipment. Also weather simulators, physics demonstration, games, toys in space, animal track replicas and fossils. Free catalog.

John Bannister, President

5623 Nalge Company
PO Box 20365
Rochester, NY 14602-0365
585-586-8800
800-625-4327
Fax: 585-586-8987
Plastic labware and safety products for the scientific classroom.

5624 National Instruments
6504 Bridge Point Parkway
Austin, TX 78730-5039
512-794-0100
Fax: 512-683-5794
Laboratory/scientific instruments.

5625 National Optical & Scientific Instruments
11113 Landmark 35 Drive
San Antonio, TX 78233-5786
210-590-7010
800-275-3716
Fax: 210-590-1104
E-mail: natlopt@sbcglobal.net
http://www.nationaloptical.com
Wholesale distributor of national compound, stero and digital miocroscopes for K-12 and college.

Michael Hart, Director Sales/Marketing

5626 Ohaus Corporation
19 A Chapin Road
Pine Brook, NJ 07058-1408
973-377-9000
800-672-7722
Fax: 973-593-0359
Scientific supplies and equipment for the classroom or laboratory.

5627 PASCO Scientific
10101 Foothills Boulevard
Roseville, CA 95747-7100
916-786-3800
800-772-8700
Fax: 916-786-7565
E-mail: jbrown@pasco.com
http://www.pasco.com

US manufacturers of physics apparatus and probe warer that enable teachers to improve science literacy and meet the standards

Justine Brown, Copy Writer

5628 Quest Aerospace Education
350 E 18th Street
Yuma, AZ 85364
602-595-9506
Fax: 520-783-9534
A complete line of model rockets and related teaching materials.

5629 Resources for Teaching Elementary School Science
National Academy Press
Arts & Industries Bldg Room 1201
900 Jefferson Drive SW
Washington, DC 20560-0403
202-287-2063
Fax: 202-287-2070
E-mail: outreach@nas.edu
http://www.si.edu
Resource guides for elementary, middle school, and high school science teachers. Annotated guides to hands-on, inquiry-centered curriculum materials and sources of help in teaching science from kindergarten through sixth grades. Produced by the National Science Resources Center.

National Science Resources Center, Author
Douglas Lapp, Executive Director

5630 Rheometrics
1 Possumtown Road
Piscataway, NJ 08854-2100
732-560-8550
Laboratory/science supplies and equipment.

5631 SARUT
107 Horatio Street
New York, NY 10014-1569
212-691-9453
Science and nature-related educational tools.

5632 Safe-T-Rack Systems
4325 Dominguez Road
Suite A
Rocklin, CA 95677-2146
916-632-1121
Fax: 916-632-1173
Laboratory furniture, safety storage containers and equipment.

5633 Sargent-Welch Scientific Company
911 Commerce Court
Buffalo Grove, IL 60089-2375
847-459-6625
Models, books and instruments for the scientific classroom.

5634 Science Instruments Company
6122 Reisterstown Road
Baltimore, MD 21215-3423
410-358-7810
Develops, manufactures and markets unique hands-on programs in biotechnology, biomedical instrumentation, telecommunications, electronics and industrial controls.

5635 Science Source
PO Box 727
Waldoboro, ME 04572-0727
207-832-6344
800-299-5469
Fax: 207-832-7281
E-mail: info@thesciencesource.com
http://www.thesciencesource.com
Design technology books, teacher resource and student books on design and technology, design technology materials, equipment and supplies used in the construction of design challenges.

Michelle Winter, Sales/Marketing Support
Rudolf Graf, President

5636 Science for Today & Tomorrow
1840 E 12th Street
Mishawaka, IN 46544
574-258-5397
Fax: 574-258-5594
Hands-on science activities packaged for K-3 students.

5637 Scientific Laser Connection, Incorporated
5021 N 55th Avenue
Suite 10
Glendale, AZ 85301-7535
623-939-6711
877-668-7844
Fax: 623-939-3369
E-mail: sales@slclaser.com
http://www.slclasers.com
Laser education modules.

Don Morris, President
Travis Gatrin, Service

5638 Shain/Shop-Bilt
509 Hemlock Street
Philipsburg, PA 16866-2937
814-342-2820
Fax: 814-342-6180
Laboratory casework and cabinets.

5639 Sheldon Lab Systems
PO Box 836
Crystal Springs, MS 39059-0836
601-892-2731
Fax: 601-892-4364
Laboratory casework and technical equipment for K-12, college and university level.

5640 Skilcraft
CRAFT House Corporation
328 N Westwood Avenue
Toledo, OH 43607-3317
419-537-9090
Fax: 419-537-9160
Microchemistry sets.

5641 Skullduggery Kits
624 S B Street
Tustin, CA 92780-4318
800-336-7745
Fax: 714-832-1215
Social studies kits offers hands-on learning, art projects, complete lesson plans, authentic replicas, and challenging products designed for small groups of students with increasing levels of difficulty.

5642 Skulls Unlimited International
10313 S Sunnylane Road
Oklahoma City, OK 73160
405-794-9300
800-659-SKUL
Fax: 405-794-6985
E-mail: sales@skullsunlimited.com
http://www.skullsunlimited.com
Leading supplier of specimen supplies to the educational community.

5643 Society of Automotive Engineers
400 Commonwealth Drive
Warrendale, PA 15086-7511
724-776-4841
877-606-7323
Fax: 724-776-5760
E-mail: info@sae.org
http://www.sae.org
Award-winning science unit for grades 4-6.

Steve Yaeger, Corporate PR Manager
Kathleen O'Conner, K-12 Education Program Mgr

5644 Southern Precision Instruments Company
3419 E Commerce Street
San Antonio, TX 78220-1322
210-212-5055
800-417-5055
Fax: 210-212-5062
E-mail: spico@flash.net
http://www.flash.net/spico
Microscopes and microprojectors for grades K-1-K-12 and college levels. Stereo and compound microscopes, along with CCTV color systems.

Victor Spiroff, VP/General Manager

5645 Southland Instruments
17741 Metzler Lane
Unit A
Huntington Beach, CA 92647-6246
714-847-5007
Fax: 714-893-3613
Microscopes.

5646 Spectronics Corporation
956 Brush Hollow Road
Westbury, NY 11590-1714
516-333-4840
800-274-8888
Fax: 800-491-6868
E-mail: vvvv@aol.com
http://www.spectroline.com
Laboratory and scientific classroom equipment, hardware and shelving.

Gloria Blusk, Manager Customer Service
Vincent McKenna, Publicist

5647 Spitz
Transnational Industries
PO Box 198
Chadds Ford, PA 19317-0198
215-459-5200
Offers scientific and laboratory instruments and accessories.

5648 Swift Instruments
1190 N 4th Street
San Jose, CA 95112-4946
408-293-2380
Educational microscopes and other laboratory instruments.

5649 TEDCO
498 S Washington Street
Hagerstown, IN 47346-1596
765-489-4527
800-654-6357
Fax: 765-489-5752
E-mail: sales@tedcotoys.com
http://www.tedcotoys.com
Bill Nye Extreme Gyro, Prisms, Educational Toys Solar Science Kit.

Jane Shadle

5650 Telaire Systems
6489 Calle Real
Goleta, CA 93117-1538
805-964-1699
Fax: 805-964-2129
Laboratory instruments and hardware.

5651 Tooltron Industries
103 Parkway
Boerne, TX 78006-9224
830-249-8277
800-293-8134
Fax: 830-755-8134
E-mail: easyleut@gvtc.comt
http://www.tooltron.com
Scientific hardware and laboratory equipment, including instruments and accessories. School scissors and craft supplies.

Thomas Love, Owner/VP Marketing

5652 Triops
PO Box 10852
Pensacola, FL 32524-0852
850-479-4415
800-200-DINO
Fax: 850-479-3315
E-mail: triopsinc@aol.com
http://www.triops.com

Classroom activities and kits in environmental, ecological and biological sciences.

Dr. Eugene Hull, President
Peter Bender, Office Manager

5653 Trippense Planetarium Company
Science First
95 Botsford Place
Buffalo, NY 14216
716-874-0133
800-875-3214
Fax: 716-874-9853
E-mail: info@sciencefirst.com
http://www.sciencefirst.com
Astronomy and earth science models and materials, including the Trippense planetarium, Elementary planetarium, Copernican and Ptolemic solar systems, Milky Way model, Explore Celestial Globes and the patented top quality educational astronomy models since 1905.

Kris Spors, Customer Service Manager
Nancy Bell, President

5654 Unilab
967 Mabury Road
San Jose, CA 95133
800-288-9850
Fax: 408-975-1035
E-mail: unilab@richnet.net
http://www.unilabinc.com
Designs and manufactures products for teaching science and technology.

Gerald A Beer, VP

5655 Vibrac Corporation
16 Columbia Drive
Amherst, NH 03031-2304
603-882-6777
Fax: 603-271-3454
Scientific instruments and hardware.

5656 Wild Goose Company
5181 S 300 W
Murray, UT 84107-4709
801-466-1172
Hands-on science kits for elementary-aged students 3 and up and resource books for all levels of general science.

5657 Wildlife Supply Company
95 Botsford Place
Buffalo, NY 14216-d
716-877-9518
800-799-8301
Fax: 716-874-9853
E-mail: goto@wildco.com
http://www.wildco.com
Aquatic sampling equipment including Fieldmaster Field Kits, Water Bottle Kits, Secchi Disks, line and messengers and a NEW Mini Ponar bottom grab. Also, a variety of professional Wildco bottom grabs, water bottles, plankton nets, hand corers and other materials.

Aaron Bell, Product Manager
Bruce Izard, Customer Service Manager

5658 WoodKrafter Kits
PO Box 808
Yarmouth, ME 04096-0808
207-846-3722
Fax: 207-846-1019
Science kits, hands-on curriculum-based science kits for ages 4 and up, classroom packs, supplies and science materials also available.

Sports & Playground Equipment

5659 American Playground Corporation
6406 Production Drive
Anderson, IN 46013-9408
765-642-0288
800-541-1602
Fax: 765-649-7162
E-mail: sales@american-playgroud.com
http://www.american-playground.com
Playground equipment and supplies.

Julie Morson, Inside Sales Manager
Marty Bloyd, General Manager

5660 American Swing Products
2533 N Carson Street
Suite 1062
Carson City, NV 89706-0147
800-433-2573
800-433-2573
Fax: 775-883-4874
E-mail: play@americanswing.com
http://www.americanswing.com
Replacement playground parts, including commercial and residential swing sets, swing hangers for pipes and wood beams, spring animals, S-hooks, spring connectors, and more.

Susan Watson, President

5661 BCI Burke Company
660 Van Dyne Road
Fond Du Lac, WI 54937-1447
920-921-9220
Fax: 920-921-9566
Playground equipment.

5662 Belson Manufacturing
111 N River Road
North Aurora, IL 60542-1396
800-323-5664
Playground equipment.

5663 Colorado Time Systems
1551 E 11th Street
Loveland, CO 80537-5056
970-667-1000
800-279-0111
Fax: 970-667-5876
E-mail: sales@coloradotimes.com
http://www.coloradotime.com
Been the system of choice for sports timing and scoring. Has a timing system for almost every sport including swimming, basketball, football, baseball, track, soccer and most others. Has a wide variety of displays ranging from fixed digit scoreboards to animation LED boards to fullcolor video displays and ribbon boards.

Randy Flint, Sr Sales Representative
Rick Connell, CDS Sales Manager

5664 Constructive Playthings
1227 E 119th Street
Grandview, MO 64030-1178
Playground, recreational and indoor fun equipment for children grades PreK-3.

5665 Creative Outdoor Designs
142 Pond Drive
Lexington, SC 29073-8009
803-957-9259
Fax: 803-957-7152
Playground equipment.

5666 Curtis Marketing Corporation
2550 Rigel Road
Venice, FL 34293-3200
941-493-8085
Playground equipment.

5667 GameTime
PO Box 680121
Fort Payne, AL 35968-0099

256-845-5610
800-235-2440
Fax: 256-845-9361
E-mail: info@gametime.com
http://www.gametime.com
Playground equipment.

Doris Dellinger, Marketing Service Manager

5668 Gared Sports
707 N 2nd Street
Suite 220
Saint Louis, MO 63102
800-325-2682
Fax: 314-421-6014
E-mail: laura@garedsports.com
http://www.garedsports.com
Basketball, Volleyball, Soccer, Equipment and training aids for indoor and outdoor facilities.

Laura St George, Sales/Marketing Manager

5669 Gerstung/Gym-Thing
6308 Blair Hill Lane
Baltimore, MD 21209-2102
800-922-3575
Physical education mats, matting and floorcoverings.

5670 Grounds for Play
1401 E Dallas Road
Mansfield, TX 76063
817-477-5482
800-552-7529
Fax: 817-477-1140
E-mail: jimdempsey@groundsforplay.com
http://www.groundsforplay.com
Playground equipment, flooring, floorcoverings, play eviroment design, lanscape architecure, insatllation, and safety inepection.

Jim Dempsey, Senior VP
Emily Smith, Office Manager

5671 Iron Mountain Forge
One Iron Mountain Drive
Farmington, MO 63640
800-325-8828
Fax: 573-760-7441
Playground equipment.

5672 JCH International
978 E Hermitage Road NE
Rome, GA 30161-9641
800-328-9203
Coverings, mats and physical education matting.

5673 Jaypro
Jaypro Sports
976 Hartford Tpke
Waterford, CT 06385-4002
860-447-3001
800-243-0533
Fax: 860-444-1779
E-mail: info@jaypro.com
http://www.jaypro.com
Sports equipment.

Linda Andels, Marketing Manager
Bill Wild, VP Sales/Marketing

5674 Kidstuff Playsystems
5400 Miller Avenue
Gary, IN 46403-2844
800-255-0153
Fax: 219-938-3340
E-mail:
rhagelberg@kidstuffplaysystems.com
http://www.fun-zone.com
Preschool and grade school playground equipment, Health Trek Fitness Course, park site furnishings.

Dick Hagelberg, CEO

5675 Kompan
7717 New Market Street
Olympia, WA 98501
360-943-6374
800-426-9788
Fax: 360-943-5575
http://www.kompan.com
Unique playgrond equipment.

Tom Grover, Marketing Director

5676 LA Steelcraft Products
1975 Lincoln Avenue
Pasadena, CA 91103-1395
626-798-7401
800-371-2438
Fax: 626-798-1482
E-mail: info@lasteelcraft.com
http://www.lasteelcraft.com
Manufacturer of quality athletic, park and playground equipment for schools, parks and industry. Features indoor/outdoor fiberglass furniture, court and field equipment, site furnishings, bike racks, flagpoles, baseball and basketball backstops.

James D Holt, President
John C Gaudesi, COO

5677 Landscape Structures
PO Box 198
Delano, MN 55328-0198
612-972-3391
Playground equipment.

5678 MMI-Federal Marketing Service
PO Box 241367
Montgomery, AL 36124-1367
334-286-0700
Fax: 334-286-0711
Playground equipment, sports timers, clocks and school supplies.

5679 Matworks
Division of Janitex Rug Service Corporation
11900 Old Baltimore Pike
Beltsville, MD 20705-1265
800-523-5179
Fax: 301-595-0740
Mats, matting and floorcoverings for entrances, gymnasiums, and all other facilities where the potential for slip and fall exists.

5680 Miracle Recreation Equipment Company
PO Box 420
Monett, MO 65708-0420
417-235-6917
Fax: 417-235-6816
Playground and recreation equipment.

5681 National Teaching Aids
PO Box 2121
Fort Collins, CO 80522
970-484-7445
800-289-9299
Fax: 970-484-1198
E-mail: bevans@amep.com
http://www.hubbardscientific.com
Learning math, alphabet, and geography skills is easy with our Clever Catch Balls. These colorful 24-inch inflatable vinyl balls provide an excellent way for children to practice math, alphabet and geography skills. Excellent learning tool in organized classroom activities, on the playground, or at home.

Barbara Evans, Customer Service Manager
Candy Coffman, National Sales Manger

5682 New Braunfels General Store International
3150 Interstate H 35 S
New Braunfels, TX 78130-7927
830-620-4000
Fax: 830-620-0598
Playground equipment, supplies and classroom supplies.

5683 Outback Play Centers
1280 W Main Street
Sun Prairie, WI 53590-0010
608-825-2140
800-338-0522
Fax: 608-825-2114
http://www.outbackplaycenters.com
Playground equipment.

Jack Garczynskl, President

5684 PlayDesigns
1000 Buffalo Road
Lewisburg, PA 17837-9795
800-327-7571
Fax: 570-522-3030
E-mail: webmaster@playdesigns.com
http://www.playdesigns.com
Playground and recreational equipment, flooring and matting.

5685 Playground Environments
22 Old Country Road
PO Box 578
Quogue, NY 11959
631-231-1300
800-662-0922
Fax: 631-231-1329
E-mail: peplay@mindspring.com
Designs and manufactures integrated play and recreational areas for children, providing them with new experiences in a safe, accessible, educationally supportive and fun environment.

5686 Playnix
3530 S Logan Street
Englewood, CO 80110-3731
303-761-5630
Fax: 303-781-6749
Wood products and playground equipment.

5687 Playworld Systems
1000 Buffalo Road
Lewisburg, PA 17837-9795
570-522-9800
800-233-8404
Fax: 570-522-3030
E-mail: webmaster@playworldsystems.com
http://www.playworldsystems.com
Playground and recreational equipment.

5688 Porter Athletic Equipment Company
Porter Athletic Equipment Company
2500 S 25th Avenue
Broadview, IL 60155-3870
708-338-2000
800-947-6783
Fax: 708-338-2060
E-mail: porter@porter-ath.com
http://www.porter-ath.com
Athletic equipment, floorcoverings, mats and supplies.

Dan Morgan, VP Sales/Marketing

5689 Quality Industries
PO Box 765
Hillsdale, MI 49242-0765
800-766-9458
Fax: 517-439-1878
Recycled plastic park and playground equipment.

5690 Real ACT Prep Guide
Peterson's, A Nelnet Company
Princeton Pike Corporate Center
2000 Lenox Drive PO Box 67005
Lawrenceville, NJ 08648
609-896-1800
800-338-3282
Fax: 609-896-4531

Familiarizes students with the test's format, reviews skills, and provides the all-important practice that helps build confidence.

621 pages
ISBN: 0-768919-75-4
Elaine Bender, Mark Weinfeld, et al., Author

5691 Recreation Creations
PO Box 955
Hillsdale, MI 49242-0955
517-439-0300
800-888-0977
Fax: 517-439-0303
Heavy duty park and playground equipment for school and public use. Equipment is both colorful and safe.

DC Shaneour

5692 Roppe Corporation
1602 N Union Street
Fostoria, OH 44830-1958
419-435-8546
Fax: 419-435-1056
Floorcoverings, mats and matting.

5693 Safety Play
10460 Roosevelt Boulevard
#295
St Petersburgh, FL 33716-3818
727-522-0061
888-878-0244
Fax: 727-522-0061
http://www.mindspring.com
Playground and recreational accident consultants. Experienced in insepctions, design, expert witness. Creators of Playground Safety Signs as required to be on the playground.

Scott Burmon, Contact

5694 Sport Court
939 S 700 W
Salt Lake City, UT 84104-1504
801-972-0260
800-421-8112
Fax: 801-975-7752
E-mail: info@sportcourt.com
http://www.sportcourt.com
Sport flooring, portable flooring, outdoor-indoor educational institutions.

Finnika Lundmark, Director Marketing

5695 Sport Floors
PO Box 1478
Cartersville, GA 30120-1478
800-322-3567
Fax: 574-293-2381
Sport floors, flooring, floorcoverings, mats and matting.

5696 Sportmaster
6031 Broad Street Mall
Pittsburgh, PA 15206-3009
412-243-5100
Fax: 412-731-3052
Playground equipment, sports timers and clocks.

5697 Stackhouse Athletic Equipment Company
1505 Front Street NE
Salem, OR 97303-6949
503-363-1840
Fax: 503-363-0511
E-mail: bob@stackhouseathletic.com
http://www.stackhouseathletic.com
Volleyball, soccer, football and baseball hardgoods.

Greg Henshaw, VP Marketing

5698 Swedes Systems - HAGS Play USA
2180 Stratingham Drive
Dublin, OH 43016-8907

Fax: 614-889-9026
Playground safety consultants.

5699 Ultra Play Systems
Parek Stuff
425 Sycamore Street
Anderson, IN 46016-1000
800-45 -LTRA
Playground and recreational equipment.

5700 Wausau Tile
PO Box 1520
Wausau, WI 54402-1520
715-359-3121
800-388-8728
Fax: 715-355-4627
E-mail: wtile@wausautile.com
http://www.wausautile.com
Playground and recreation equipment.

Rob Geurink, Furnishings Division
Manager

5701 Wear Proof Mat Company
2156 W Fulton Street
Chicago, IL 60612-2392
312-733-4570
Fax: 800-322-7105
http://www.notracks.com
Mats, matting and floorcoverings for the
physical education class.

5702 Wolverine Sports
745 State Circle
Ann Arbor, MI 48108-1647
734-761-5690
Fax: 800-654-4321
Playground, sports and physical fitness furniture and equipment.

General

5703 A-V Online
National Information Center for Educational Media
PO Box 8640
Albuquerque, NM 87198
505-265-3591
800-926-8328
Fax: 505-256-1080
E-mail: nicem@nicem.com
http://www.nicem.com
A CD-ROM that contains over 400,000 citations with abstracts, to non-print educational materials for all educational levels. It is available on an annual subscription basis and comes with semiannual updates.

Lisa Savard, Marketing and Sales

5704 AASA Daily News
American Association of School Administrators
801 N Quincy Street
Suite 700
Arlington, VA 22203-1730
703-528-0700
Fax: 703-841-1543
E-mail: info@aasa.org
http://www.aasa.org

Jay Goldman, Editor

5705 ACT
2201 N Dodge Street
PO Box 168
Iowa City, IA 52243-0168
319-337-1000
Fax: 319-339-3021
http://www.act.org
Help individuals and organizations make informed decisions about education and work.

5706 AMX Corporation
11995 Forestgate Drive
Dallas, TX 75243-5481
972-644-3048
Fax: 972-624-7153
Multiple products, equipment and supplies.

5707 ASC Electronics
2 Kees Pl
Merrick, NY 11566-3625
516-623-3206
Fax: 516-378-2672
High tech multimedia system. Completely software driven, featuring interactive video, audio and data student drills. Novell network. System includes CD-ROM, laserdisc and digital voice card technology.

5708 Accelerated Math
Renaissance Learning
PO Box 8036
Wisconsin Rapids, WI 54495-8036
715-424-3636
800-338-4204
Fax: 715-424-4242
E-mail: answers@renlearn.com
http://www.renlearn.com
Math management software that helps teachers increase student math achievement in grades 1 through calculus.

5709 Accelerated Reader
Renaissance Learning
PO Box 8036
Wisconsin Rapids, WI 54495-8036
715-424-3636
800-338-4204
Fax: 715-424-4242
E-mail: answers@renlearn.com
http://www.renlearn.com
Software program that helps teachers manage literature-based reading.

5710 Actrix Systems
6315 San Ignacio Avenue
San Jose, CA 95119-1202
800-422-8749
Fax: 509-744-2851
Computer networks.

5711 Allen Communications
5 Triac Center
5th Floor
Salt Lake Cty, UT 84180
801-537-7800
Fax: 801-537-7805
Software.

5712 Alltech Electronics Company
602 Garrison Street
Oceanside, CA 92054-4865
760-721-0093
Fax: 760-732-1460
Computer hardware.

5713 Anchor Pad Products
Anchor Pad Products
11105 Dana Circle
Cypress, CA 90630-5133
714-799-4071
800-626-2467
Fax: 714-799-4094
E-mail: kris@anchor.com
http://www.anchorpad.com
Cost effective physical security systems for computers, computer peripherals and office equipment.

Kris Jones, Marketing Associate
Melanie Rustle, Marketing Associate

5714 Apple Computer
1 Infinite Loop
Cupertino, CA 95014-2084
408-996-1010
Fax: 408-974-2786
Offers a wide selection of software systems and programs for the student, educator, professional and classroom use. Program areas include reading, science, social studies, history, language arts, mathematics and more.

5715 Ascom Timeplex
400 Chestnut Ridge Road
Woodcliff Lake, NJ 07675-7604
201-646-1571
Fax: 201-646-0485
Computer networks.

5716 BGS Systems
128 Technology Drive
Waltham, MA 02453-8909
617-891-0000
Facility planning and evaluation software.

5717 BLS Tutorsystems
5153 W Woodmill Drive
Wilmington, DE 19808-4067
800-545-7766
Computer software.

5718 Broderbund Software
500 Redwood Boulevard
Novato, CA 94947-6921
319-395-9626
800-223-8941
Fax: 319-395-7449
Educational software.

5719 Bulletin Boards for Busy Teachers

http://www.geocities.com/VisionTeacherwv/
Bulletin board tips and education links.

5720 CASL Software
6818 86th Street E
Puyallup, WA 98371-6450
206-845-7738
Educational software for schools and institutions in all areas of interest.

5721 CCU Software
PO Box 6724
Charleston, WV 25362-0724
800-843-5576
Fax: 800-321-4297
Educational software.

5722 CCV Software
5602 36th Street S
Fargo, ND 58104-6768
800-541-6078
Fax: 800-457-6953
All varieties of software and hardware for the educational fields of interest including language arts, math, social studies, science, history and more.

5723 Cambridge Development Laboratory
86 West Street
Waltham, MA 02451-1110
800-637-0047
Fax: 781-890-2894
E-mail: customerservice@edumatch.com
http://www.edumatch.com
Meets all educational software needs in language arts, mathematics, science, social studies early learning and special education.

5724 Chariot Software Group
123 Camino De La Reina W Building
San Diego, CA 92108-3002
619-298-0202
800-242-7468
Fax: 619-491-0021
E-mail: info@chariot.com
http://www.chariot.com
Academic software.

5725 Child's Play Software
5785 Emporium Square
Columbus, OH 43231-2802
614-833-1836
Fax: 614-833-1837
Markets learning games and creative software to schools.

5726 Claris Corporation
5201 Patrick Henry Drive
Santa Clara, CA 95054-1171
800-747-7483
Educational software.

5727 Classroom Direct
20200 E 9 Mile Road
Saint Clair Shores, MI 48080-1791
800-777-3642
Fax: 800-628-6250
Full line of hardware and software for Mac, IBM and Apple II at discount prices.

5728 College Board/SAT
45 Columbus Avenue
New York, NY 10023-6992
217-713-8000
http://http://sat.org/

5729 Computer City Direct
2000 Two Tandy Center
Fort Worth, TX 76102
800-538-0586
Hardware.

5730 Computer Friends
10200 SW Eastridge Street
Portland, OR 97225
800-547-3303
Fax: 503-643-5379
E-mail: cfi@cfriends.com
http://www.cfriends.com
Computer hardware, software and networks, printer support products.

Jimmy Moglia, Marketing Director

5731 Data Command
PO Box 548
Kankakee, IL 60901-0548
800-528-7390
Educational software.

5732 Davidson & Associates
19840 Pioneer Avenue
Torrance, CA 90503-1690
800-545-7677
Educational software and systems.

5733 Dell Computer Corporation
9595 Arboretum Boulevard
Austin, TX 78759-6337
512-338-4400
800-388-1450
Hardware.

5734 Digital Divide Network

http://www.digitaldividenetwork.org
Knowledge to help everyone succeed in the
digital age.

5735 Digital Equipment Corporation
Educational Computer Systems Group
2 Iron Way
Marlboro, MA 01752
Computer hardware and networks.

**5736 Don Johnston Developmental
Equipment**
1000 N Rand Road
Suite 115
Wauconda, IL 60084-1190
847-526-2682
800-999-4660
Develops educational software for special
needs. Products include the Ukandu Series for
emergent literacy, LD, ESL, students
Co-Writer and Write: OutLoud.

5737 Edmark Corporation
6727 185th Avenue NE
PO Box 97021
Redmond, WA 98052-5037
425-556-8400
800-691-2986
Fax: 425-556-8430
Markets educational software.

5738 EduQuest, An IBM Company
PO Box 2150
Atlanta, GA 30301-2150
Offers exciting educational software in various fields of interest including history, social
studies, reading, math and language arts, as
well as computers.

5739 Educational Activities
1937 Grand Avenue
Baldwin, NY 11510-2889
516-223-4666
800-645-3739
Fax: 516-623-9282
http://www.edact.com
Supplemental materials.

Roni Hofbauer, Office Manager
Carol Stern, VP

5740 Educational Resources
1550 Executive Drive
Elgin, IL 60123-9330
630-213-8681
Fax: 630-213-8681
The largest distributor of educational software and technology in the education market.
Features Mac, APL, ligs and IBM school versions, lab packs, site licenses, networking and
academic versions. Hardware, accessories
and multimedia is also available.

5741 Electronic Specialists Inc.
PO Box 389
Natick, MA 01760-0004
508-655-1532
810-225-4876
Fax: 508-653-0268
E-mail: esp@elect-spec.com
http://www.elect-spec.com

Computer and electronics, including networks and computer systems plus transform-
ers and power converters.

F Stifter, President

**5742 Environmental Systems Research
Institute**
380 New York Street
Redlands, CA 92373-8118
Demonstrates a full range of geographic in-
formation system software products.

5743 Eversan Inc.
34 Main Street
Whitesboro, NY 13492
800-383-6060
Fax: 315-736-4058
E-mail: sales&eversan.com
http://www.eversan.com
Announcement boards, scoreboards and
classroom supplies, sports timers and clocks.

Michelle Moran, Sales Representative
Elsa Kucherna, Sales Representative

5744 GAMCO Educational Materials
PO Box 1911
Big Spring, TX 79721-1911
800-351-1404
Publishes software in math, language arts,
reading, social studies, early childhood education and teacher tools for Macintosh, Apple, IBM and MS-DOS compatible.

5745 Games2Learn
1936 East Deere Avenue
Suite 120
Santa Ana, CA 92705
714-751-4263
888-713-4263
Fax: 714-442-0869
E-mail:
CustomerService@Games2Learn.com
http://www.games2learn.com
Develops, markets and provides children and
adults with quality, fun, interactive educational products designed to increase their
skills in language, math and general knowledge. Creator of The Phonics Game.

5746 Gateway Learning Corporation
665 3rd Street
Suite 225
San Francisco, CA 94107
800-544-7323
http://www.hop.com
Develop and sell innovative educational
products for home learning.

5747 Greene & Associates
1834 E Manhatton Drive
Tempe, AZ 85282-5857
480-491-1151
Educational software.

5748 Grolier
PO Box 1716
Danbury, CT 06816
800-371-3908
Fax: 800-456-4402
Multimedia software for education.

5749 Hubbell
Kellems Division
14 Lords Hill Road
Stonington, CT 06378-2604
860-535-5350
Fax: 860-535-1719
Computer hardware, software, systems, and
networks.

5750 Indiana Cash Drawer
1315 S Miller Street
Shelbyville, IN 46176-2424
317-398-6643
Fax: 317-392-0958
Computer peripherals.

5751 Ingenuity Works
1123 Fir Avenue
Blaine, WA 98230-9702
604-412-1555
800-665-0667
Fax: 604-431-7996
E-mail: info@ingenuityworks.com
http://www.ingenuityworks.com
Publishes K-12 educational software for
classroom use. Key curriculum areas include
geography, keyboarding, and math (K-9).
Network and district licenses are available.

Brigetta , Director Marketing

5752 Instructional Design
WIDS-Worldwide Instructional Design
System
1 Foundation Circle
Waunakee, WI 53597-8914
608-849-2411
800-677-9437
Fax: 608-849-2468
E-mail: info@wids.org
http://www.wids.org
Performance-based curriculum design software and professional devlopment tools. Use
software to write curriculum, implement standards, create assessments, and build in learning styles. Excellent upfront online design
tool.

Robin Nickel, Associate Director

5753 Instructor
Scholastic
555 Broadway
New York, NY 10012-3919
212-343-6100
800-724-6527
Fax: 212-343-4801
http://www.scholastic.com/instructor
Edited for teachers, curriculum coordinators,
principals and supervisors of primary grades
through junior high school.

Monthly

Claudia Cohl, Publisher
Lynn Diamond, Advertising Director

5754 Jostens Learning Corporation
4920 Pacific Heights Boulevard
Suite 500
San Diego, CA 92121
858-587-0087
800-521-8538
Fax: 858-587-1629
Educational software and CD-ROM's.

5755 Journey Education
1325 Capital Parkway
Suite 130
Carrollton, TX 75006
800-874-9001
Fax: 972-245-3585
E-mail: sales@journeyed.com
http://www.journeyed.com
Software for students.

5756 Ken Cook Education Systems
9929 W Silver Spring Drive
PO Box 25267
Milwaukee, WI 53225-1024
800-362-2665
Fax: 414-466-0840
Classroom curricular software.

5757 Kensington Microwave
2855 Campus Drive
San Mateo, CA 94403-2510
650-572-2700
800-535-4242
Fax: 650-572-9675
http://www.kensington.com
Computer systems and peripherals.

5758 Lapis Technologies
1100 Marina Village Parkway
Alameda, CA 94501-1043
510-748-1600
Computer peripherals.

5759 Laser Learning Technologies
120 Lakeside Avenue
#3240
Seattle, WA 98122-6533
800-722-3505
Educational CD-ROM's and interactive videos.

5760 Lawrence Productions
1800 S 35th Street
Galesburg, MI 49053-9687
800-421-4157
Fax: 616-665-7060
More than 60 proven software titles for PreK to adult, covering problem solving, early learning and leadership skills.

5761 Learning Company
500 Redwood Boulevard
Novato, CA 94947
800-825-4420
Fax: 877-864-2275
http://www.learningcompanyschool.com
School educational software.

5762 Library Corporation, Sales & Marketing
1501 Regency Way
Woodstock, GA 30189-5487
Computer networks.

5763 LinkNet
Introlink
1400 E Touhy Avenue
Suite 260
Des Plaines, IL 60018-3339
847-390-8700
Fax: 847-390-9435
Computer networks.

5764 MECC
6160 Summit Drive N
Minneapolis, MN 55430-2100
800-685-MECC
Educational software, hardware and overhead projectors.

5765 Mamopalire of Vermont
PO Box 24
Warren, VT 05674
802-496-4095
888-496-4094
Fax: 802-496-4096
E-mail: bethumpd@wcvt.com
http://www.bethumpd.com
Provides quality educational books and board games for the whole family.

Rebecca Cahilly, President
Glenn Cahilly, CEO

5766 McGraw-Hill Educational Resources
11 W 19th Street
New York, NY 10011-4209
800-442-9685
Fax: 972-228-1982
Educational software for all areas of interest including social studies, science, mathematics and reading.

5767 Microsoft Corporation
1 Microsoft Way
Redmond, WA 98052-8300
425-882-8080
Fax: 425-936-7329
One of the largest publishers and distributors of educational software, hardware, equipment and supplies.

5768 Misty City Software
11866 Slater Avenue NE
Kirkland, WA 98034-4103

206-820-2219
800-795-0049
Fax: 425-820-4298
Publisher of Grade Machine, gradebook software for Macintosh, MS-DOS, and Apple II. Grade Machine used by thousands of teachers in hundreds of schools worldwide. Grade Machine has full-screen editing, flexible reports, large class capacity, excellent documentation and reasonable cost.

Roberta Spiro, Business Manager
Russell Cruickshanks, Sales Manager

5769 NCR Corporation
1700 S Patterson Boulevard
Dayton, OH 45479-0002
937-445-5000
Computer networks, systems (large, mini, micro, medium and personal).

5770 NetLingo The Internet Dictionary
PO Box 627
Ojai, CA 93024
805-640-3754
Fax: 805-640-3654
E-mail: info@netlingo.com
http://www.NetLingo.com
A smart-looking and easy to understand dictionary of 3000 internet terms, 1200 chat acronyms, and much more. NetLingo is a modern reference book fo international students, educators, industry professionals, and online businesses and organizations.

528 pages Paperback
ISBN: 0-9706396-7-8

Erin Jansen, Author
Erin Jansen, Author/Publisher

5771 NetZero
2555 Townsgate Road
Westlake Village, CA 91361-2650
805-418-2020
Fax: 805-418-2075
http://www.netzero.com
Free Internet access.

5772 New Century Education Corporation
220 Old New Brunswick Road
Piscataway, NJ 08854
732-981-0820
800-833-6232
Fax: 732-981-0552
E-mail: jharrison@ncecorp.com
http://www.ncecorp.com
ILS systems.

Janice Harrison, Marketing Representative

5773 OnLine Educator

http://faldo.atmos.uiuc.edu/CLA
A comprehensive archive of educational sites with useful search capabilities and descriptions of the sites.

5774 Online Computer Systems
1 Progress Drive
Horsham, PA 19044-3502
CD-ROM networking, CD-ROM titles and CD-ROM tower units.

5775 PBS TeacherSource

http://www.pbs.org/teachersource
Includes an on-line inventory of more than 1,000 free lesson plans, teacher guides and other activities designed to complement PBS television programs.

5776 Parent Link
Parlant Technology
290 N University Avenue
Provo, UT 84601
801-373-9669
800-735-2930
Fax: 801-373-9697

E-mail: info@parlant.com
http://www.parlant.com
School to home communication systems allow scholls to create messages — emails, telephone calls, web content, printed letters, about student information, grades, attendance, homework, and activities. Also provides inbound access via internet and telephone.

George Joeckel, Marketing

5777 Peopleware
1621 114th Avenue SE
Suite 120
Bellevue, WA 98004-6905
425-454-6444
Fax: 425-454-7634
Classroom curricular software.

5778 Phillips Broadband Networks
100 Fairgrounds Drive
Manlius, NY 13104-2437
315-682-9105
Fax: 315-682-1022
Computer networks.

5779 Pioneer New Media Technologies
2265 E 220th Street
Long Beach, CA 90810-1639
800-LAS-R ON
DRM-604X CD-ROM mini-changer, world's fastest CD-ROM drive for multimedia. Also offers special packages including The Mystery Reading Bundle, CLD-V2400RB which includes the CLD-V2400 LaserDisc player, educator's remote control, UC-V109BC barcode reader and membership in the Pioneers in Learning Club and The Case of the Missing Mystery Writer videodisc from Houghton Mifflin.

5780 Polaroid Corporation
575 Tech Square
Cambridge, MA 02139
781-386-2000
Fax: 781-386-3925
Computer repair, hardware and peripherals, equipment and various size systems.

5781 Power Industries
37 Walnut Street
Wellsley Hills, MA 02181
800-395-5009
Educational software.

5782 Quetzal Computers
1708 E 4th Street
Brooklyn, NY 11223-1925
718-375-1186
Computer systems and networks, peripherals and hardware.

5783 RLS Groupware
Realtime Learning Systems
2700 Connecticut Avenue NW
Washington, DC 20008-5330
202-483-1510
Classroom curricular software.

5784 Radio Shack
100 Throckmorton Street
Suite 1800
Ft. Worth, TX 76102
817-415-3700
Fax: 817-415-2335
Computer networks and peripherals.

Laura Moore, Sr VP Public Relations

5785 Rose Electronics
10850 Wilcrest Drive
Suite 900
Houston, TX 77099-3599
281-933-7673
Fax: 281-933-0044
Computer peripherals and hardware.

5786 STAR Reading & STAR Math
Renaissance Learning
PO Box 8036
Wisconsin Rapids, WI 54495-8036
715-424-3636
800-338-4204
Fax: 715-424-4242
E-mail: answers@renlearn.com
http://www.renlearn.com
Computer-adaptive tests provide instructional levels, grade equivalents and percentile ranks.

5787 SVE & Churchill Media
6677 N NW Highway
Chicago, IL 60631
773-775-9550
800-829-1900
Fax: 773-775-5091
E-mail: slucas@svemedia.com
http://www.svemedia.com
Has brought innovative media technology into america's pre-K through high school classrooms. By producing programs to satisfy state curriculum standards, SVE consistently provides educators with high-quality and award-winning videos, CD-ROMs, eLMods, and DVDs in science, social studies, english and health/guidance.

Sarah M Lucas, Communications Coordinator
Kelli Campbell, VP Marketing/Development

5788 School Cruiser
Time Cruiser Computing Corporation
9 Law Drive
3rd Floor, Ottawa, Ontario
Canada K1N 7G1
613-562-9847
877-450-9482
Fax: 613-562-4768
http://www.epals.com
School Cruiser provides online tools and resources to promote academic and community interaction. It lets you access and share school calenders, lesson plans, homework assignments, announcements and other school related information.

5789 SchoolHouse

http://www.encarta.msn.com/schoolhouse/maincontent.asp
The Encarta Lesson Collection and other educational resources.

5790 Seaman Nuclear Corporation
7315 S 1st Street
Oak Creek, WI 53154-2095
414-762-5100
Fax: 414-762-5106
Facility planning and evaluation software.

5791 Skills Bank Corporation
7104 Ambassador Road
Suite 1
Baltimore, MD 21244-2732
800-451-5726
Educational manufacturing company offering computer and electronic resources, software, programs and systems focusing on home education and tutoring.

5792 Sleek Software Corporation
2404 Rutland Drive
Suite 600
Austin, TX 78758
800-337-5335
Fax: 888-353-2900
http://www.sleek.com
Specializes in Algorithm-Based tutorial and test-generating software.

5793 Smartstuff Software
PO Box 82284
Portland, OR 97282-0284
415-763-4799
800-671-3999
Fax: 877-278-7456
E-mail: info@smartstuff.com
http://www.smartstuff.com
Foolproof Security is a dual platform desktop security product that prevents unwanted changes to the desktop and a product line for the internet that protects browser settings, filters content, and allows guided activities.

5794 Society for Visual Education
1345 W Diversey Parkway
Chicago, IL 60614-1249
773-775-9550
Fax: 800-624-1678
Educational software dealing specifically with special education.

5795 SofterWare
540 Pennsylvania Avenue
Suite 200
Fort Washington, PA 19034-3388
215-628-0400
800-220-4111
Fax: 215-628-0585
E-mail: info@softerware.com
http://www.softerware.com
Offers software, support and administrative solutions to four markets: childcare centers, public and private schools, nonprofit organizations and institutions, and camps.

5796 SpecialNet
GTE Educational Network Services
5525 N Macarthur Boulevard
Suite 320
Irving, TX 75038-2600
214-518-8500
800-927-3000
Fax: 757-852-8277
Contains news and information on trends and developments in educational services and programs. Databases, bulletin boards, school packages, student/teacher packages, online magazines, distance learning, vocational education, school health, educational laws, and more.

5797 Student Software Guide
800-874-9001
E-mail: journey.com
Discounts on a variety of software materials.

5798 Sun Microsystems
2550 Garcia Avenue
#6-13
Mountain View, CA 94043-1100
714-643-2688
800-555-9786
Fax: 650-934-9776
Computer networks and peripherals.

5799 Sunburst/Wings for Learning
101 Castleton Street
Pleasantville, NY 10570-3405
914-747-3310
800-338-3457
Fax: 914-747-4109
Educational materials, including software, print materials, videotapes, videodisc and interdisciplinary packages.

5800 Support Systems International Corporation
136 S 2nd Street
Richmond, CA 94804-2110
510-234-9090
800-777-6269
Fax: 510-233-8888
E-mail: info@support-systems-intl.com
http://www.fiberopticcableshop.com

Fiber optic patch cables, converters, and switches.

Ben Parsons, General Manager

5801 Surfside Software
PO Box 1112
East Orleans, MA 02643-1112
800-942-9008
Educational software.

5802 Target Vision
1160 Pittsford Victor Road
Suite K
Pittsford, NY 14534-3825
800-724-4044
Fax: 585-248-2354
TVI DeskTop expands your show directly to desktop PC utilizing existing LANS. View information by topics or as a screen saver. Features: graphic importing, VCR interface, advanced scheduling and more.

5803 Teacher Universe
5900 Hollis Street
Suite A
Emeryville, CA 94608
877-248-3224
Fax: 415-763-4917
E-mail: info@teacheruniverse.com
http://www.teacheruniverse.com
Creates technology-rich solutions for improving the quality of life and work for teachers worldwide.

5804 Technolink Corporation
24 Depot Square
Tuckahoe, NY 10707-4004
914-961-1900
Computer systems and electronics.

5805 Tom Snyder Productions
80 Coolidge Hill Road
Watertown, MA 02472
800-342-0236
Fax: 800-304-1254
E-mail: ask@tomsnyder.com
http://www.tomsnyder.com
Educational CD-ROM products and Internet services for schools.

5806 Tripp Lite
500 N Orleans Street
Chicago, IL 60610-4117
312-329-1601
Peripherals, hardware and computer systems.

5807 True Basic
12 Commerce Avenue
West Lebanon, NH 03784-1669
800-436-2111
Fax: 603-298-7015
E-mail: john@truebasic.com
http://www.truebasic.com
Educational software.

5808 U.S. Public School Universe Database
U.S. National Center for Education Statistics
555 New Jersey Avenue NW
Washington, DC 20001-2029
202-219-1335
85,000 public schools of elementary and secondary levels, public special education, vocational/technical education and alternative education schools.

5809 USA CityLink Project
USA CityLink Project
Floppies for Kiddies
4060 Highway 59
Mandevelle, LA 70471
985-898-2158
Fax: 985-892-8535
Collects used and promotional disketts from the masses for redistribution to school groups and nonprofits throughout the county.

Carol Blake, Contact

327

Software, Hardware & Internet Resources / General

5810 Unisys
PO Box 500
Blue Bell, PA 19424-0001
215-986-3501
Fax: 215-986-3279
A full line of computers (sizes ranging from mini/micro to medium/large and personal).

5811 Ventura Educational Systems
910 Ramona Avenue
Suite E
Grover Beach, CA 93433-2154
805-473-7383
800-336-1022
Fax: 805-473-7382
E-mail: sales@venturaes.com
http://www.venturaes.com
Publishers of curriculum based educational software for all grade levels, specializing in interactive math and science software. Programs include teacher's guide with student worksheets.

5812 Viziflex Seels
16 E Lafayette Street
Hackensack, NJ 07601-6895
201-487-8080
Peripherals, hardware and electronics, floorcoverings, mats and matting.

5813 Waterford Institute
1590 E 9400 S
Sandy, UT 84093-3009
800-767-9976
Fax: 801-572-1667
Produces children's educational software for math and reading.

5814 Web Connection
Education Week
301-280-3100
E-mail: ads@epe.org
http://www.edweek.org
Information about education suppliers.

5815 Wiremold Company
60 Woodlawn Street
W Hartford, CT 06110-2383
800-243-8421
Computer networks and peripherals.

5816 Wisconsin Technical College System Foundation
1 Foundation Cir
Waunakee, WI 53597-8914
800-821-6313
Fax: 608-849-2468
E-mail: foundation@wtcsf.tec.wi.us
Interactive videodiscs, self-paced instruction or with barcodes. Students learn faster, become more motivated and retain more information. Math, algebra and electronics courseware are also available.

5817 Word Associates
3226 Robincrest Drive
Northbrook, IL 60062-5125
847-291-1101
Fax: 847-291-0931
E-mail: microlrn@aol.com
http://www.wordassociates.com
Software tutorials featuring lessons in question format, with tutorial and test mode. 15 titles include Math SAT, 2 English SAT; US Constitution Tutor; Phraze Maze; Geometry: Planely Simple, Concepts and Proofs, Right Triangles; Life Skills Math; Algebra; Reading: Myths and More Myths, Magic and Monsters; Economics; American History. Windows, Macintosh, CD's or disks.

Software

Myrna Helfand, President
Sherry Azaria, Marketing

5818 Ztek Company
PO Box 11768
Lexington, KY 40577-1768

859-281-1611
800-247-1603
Fax: 859-281-1521
E-mail: cs@ztek.com
http://www.ztek.com
Offers physics multimedia lessons on CD-ROM, DVD, videodisc and videotape. Also, carries Pioneer New Media DVD and videodisc players as well as Bretford Manufacturing's line of audio-visual furniture.

5819 ePALS.com
Classroom Exchange

http://www.epals.com
World's largest online classroom community, connecting over 3 million students and teachers through 41,044 profiles.

5820 http://ericir.syr.edu
AskERIC
Ask a question about education and receive a personalized e-mail response in two business days.

5821 http://gsn.bilkent.edu.tr
Ballad of an EMail Terrorist
Global SchoolNet Foundation

One pitfall of the internet is danger of vulgarity and/or obscenity to a child via e-mail.

5822 http://suzyred.home.texas.net
The Little Red School House
Offers sections on music, writing, quotes, web quests, jokes, poetry, games, activities and more.

5823 www.FundRaising.Com
FundRaising.Com
800-443-5353
Internet fundraising company.

5824 www.abcteach.com
E-mail: sandkems@abcteach.com
Offers ideas and activities for kids, parents, students and teachers. Features section on many topics in education, including writing, poetry, word searches, crosswords, games, maps, mazes and more.

5825 www.abctooncenter.com
ABC Toon Center
This family orientated site offers games, cartoons, storybook, theater, information stations and more. This site is open to children of differnt languages. Can be translated into Italian, French, Spanish, German and Russian.

5826 www.americatakingaction.com
America Taking Action
Provides every school with a free, 20 page website with resources for teachers, parents, students and the community. Created entirely by involved parents, teachers and community leaders as a public service.

5827 www.awesomelibrary.org
Awesome Library
Organizes the Web with 15,000 carefully reviewed resources, including the top 5 percent in education. Offers sections of mathematics, science, social studies, english, health, physical education, technology, languages, special education, the arts and more. Features a section involved with today's current issues facing our world, like pollution, gun control, tobacco, and other changing 'hot' topics. Site can be browsed in English, German, Spanish, French or Portuguese.

5828 www.bigchalk.com
Big Chalk-The Education Network
Educational web site tailored to fit teachers' and students' needs.

5829 www.brunchbunch.org
Brunch Bunch
The foundation names all of the grants it makes after teachers who have demonstrated excellence. The foundation regularly makes significant grants to aid teachers' efforts.

5830 www.busycooks.com
BusyCooks.com
A hit with home economics teachers, enjoying free recipes and online cooking shows. Tapping into the experience of thousands to nuture your culinary creativity.

5831 www.chandra.harvard.edu
Chandra X-ray Observatory Center
Find teacher-developed, classroom-ready materials based on results from the Chandra mission. Classroom-ready activities, interactive games, activities, quizzes, and printable activities which will keep students absorbed with interest.

5832 www.cherrydale.com
Cherrydale Farms
Website offers company information, fund raising products and information, online mega mall, card shop, career opportunities and much more. Produces fine chocolates and confections. Many opportunities for schools to raise funds with various Cherrydale programs.

5833 www.cleverapple.com
Education Station
Offers links to many sites involved with education.

5834 www.edhelper.com
edhelper.com
Keeps you up to date with the latest educational news.

5835 www.education-world.com
Education World
Features and education-specific search engine with links to over 115,000 sites. Offers monthly reviews of other educational web sites, and other original content on a weekly basis.

5836 www.eduverse.com
Software developer building core technologies for powering international distance education. Features an online distance education engine, product information, news releases and more.

5837 www.efundraising.com
efundraising.com
Provides non-profit groups with quality products, low prices and superior service. Helping thousands of schools, youth sports teams and community groups reach their fundraising goals each year.

5838 www.embracingthechild.com
Embracing the Child
Educational resource for teachers and parents that provides a structural resource for home and classroom use, lesson planning, as well as a child-safe site, for children's research, classroom use and homework fulfillment.

5839 www.enc.org
Eisenhower National Clearinghouse
For math and science teachers-anywhere in the K-12 spectrum. This organization contains a wealth of information, activities, resources, and demonstrations for the sciences and math.

5840 www.englishhlp.com
English Help
E-mail: englishhlpr@hotmail.com
This page is a walk through of Microsoft Power Point. The goal is to show in a few simple steps how to make your own website. Created by Rebecca Holland.

5841 www.expage.com/Just4teachers
Just 4 Teachers
The ultimate website for educators! Teaching tips, resources, themeunits, search engines, classroom management and sites for kids.

5842 www.fraboom.com
Fraboom
This site's tools let you specify areas within your state's standards and search for a list of 'Flying Rhinoceros' lessons that meet your criteria. Offers other information sources for teachers and students.

5843 www.globalschoolnet.org
Global Schoolhouse
Connects teachers, administrators, and parents with options and possibilities the Internet has to offer the schools of the world.

5844 www.gradebook.org/
The Classroom
Dedicated to the students and teachers of the world.

5845 www.homeworkspot.com
HomeworkSpot
A free online homework resource center developed by educators, students, parents and journalists for K-12 students. It simplifies the search for homework help, features a top-notch reference cetner, current events, virtual field trips and expeditions, extracurricular activities and study breaks, parent and teacher resources and much more.

5846 www.iearn.org
iEARN USA
Utilizes projects for students ages 6 through 19. Projects are concerned with the environment as well as arts, politics, and the health and welfare of all the Earth's citizens.

5847 www.jasonproject.org
Jason Project
Founded in 1989 as a tool for live, interactive programs for students in the fourth through eighth grades. Annual projects are funded through a variety of public corporations and governmental organizations.

5848 www.junebox.com
JuneBox.com
A classroom superstore that features the leading suppliers of educational products and services. A gateway to project ideas and educational links.

5849 www.k12planet.com
Chancery Software
Chancery Software is announcing a new school to home extension that will provide student information systems to give parents, students, and educators access to accurate information about students in one, easy-to-use website.

5850 www.kiddsmart.com
Institute for Child Development
E-mail: dcornell@kiddsmart.com
The ICD develops educational materials and resources designed to facilitate children's social and emotional development. Offers the previous materials as well as research summaries, lesson plans, training, workshops, games, multi-cultural materials and other resources to teachers, educational centers, parents, counselors, corporations, non-profits and others involved in the child-care professions.

5851 www.lessonplansearch.com
Lesson Plan Search
220 lesson plans from cooking to writing.

5852 www.lessonplanspage.com
lessonplanspage.com
A collection of over 1,000 free lesson plans for teachers to use in their classrooms. Lesson plans are organized by subject and grade level.

5853 www.library.thinkquest.org
Think Quest Library of Entries
The Arti FAQS 2100 Project is designed to predict how art will influence our lives in the next hundred years. Students can use available data to make reasonable predictions for the future.

5854 www.ncspearson.com
NCS Pearson
E-mail: info@ncs.com
NCS Pearson is at the forefront of the education space with curriculum, contant, tools, assessment, and interface to enterprise systems

5855 www.negaresa.org
LearningGate
For teachers, electronic web-based grade book aplication eGRader 2000. Many educational resource links as well has discussion groups, a news and events section, and even links to online shopping.

5856 www.netrover.com/~kingskid/108.html
Room 108

An educational activity center for kids. Offers lots of fun for children with educational focus; like songs, art, math, kids games, children's stories and much more. Sections with pen pal information, puzzles, crosswords, teachers store, spelling, kids sites, email, music, games and more.

5857 www.pcg.cyberbee.com
Postcard Geography
Offered to classes all over the world via the internet. Your class commits to exchanging picture postcards with all other participants. Appropriate for all ages, for public and private schools, for youth groups and for home-schools.

5858 www.pitt.edu
EdIndex
E-mail: poole@pitt.edu
A web resource for teachers and students, offers course information, MS Office tutorials, personal and professional pages, and more.

5859 www.riverdeep.net
Riverdeep Interactive Learning
Riverdeep's interactive science, language and math arts programs deliver high quality educational experiences.

5860 www.safedayeducation.com
Safe Day Education
The leader in bully prevention and street proofing education for kids; safe dating preparation programs for teens; and re-empowerment and assault prevention training for women.

5861 www.safekids.com/child_safety.htm
SafeKids.Com
Cyberspace is a fabulous tool for learning, but some of it can be exploitative and even criminal.

5862 www.sdcoe.k12.ca.us
Researches a coral reef and creates a diorama for The Cay by Theodore Taylor.

5863 www.shop2gether.com
Collective Publishing Service
We are committed to helping all schools buy better by shopping together. Building upon a scalable, dynamic procurement platform and group buying technology, we also provide a unique ecommerce system, delivering next generation procurement services over the Internet.

5864 www.spaceday.com
Space Day
Program engineered to build problem-solving and teamwork skills.

5865 www.specialednews.com
Special Education News
E-mail: info@specialednews.com
Consists of breaking news stories from Washington and around the country. These stories are complied together in the Special Education News letter is sent via e-mail once a week.

5866 www.straightscoop.org
Straight Scoop News Bureau
SSNB increases the frequency of anti-drug themes and messages in junior high and high school student media.

5867 www.tcta.org
Texas Classroom Teachers Association
Compromised of Texas educators, provides interest for teachers everywhere. Education laws and codes are presented here.

5868 www.teacherszone.com
TeachersZone.Com
Lesson plans, free stuff for teachers, contests, sites for kids, conferences and workshops, schools and organizations, job listings, products for school.

5869 www.teacherweb.com
TeacherWeb
TeacherWeb, your free personal website that's as easy to use as the bulletin board in your classroom. This site offers a secure, password-protected service.

5870 www.teachingheart.com
Teaching is A Work of Heart
Chock-full of ideas, projects, motivational thoughts, behavior ideas.

5871 www.thelearningworkshop.com
Learning Workshop.com
Services for teachers, students, and parents. For teachers online gradebooks and grade tracking, students can check their grades online, parents enjoy articles written expressly for them and a tutor search by zip code.

5872 www.tutorlist.com
TutorList.com
Offers information on tips on how to find and choose a tutor, what a tutor does, educational news and more.

5873 www.worksafeusa.org
WorkSafeUSA
Addresses the alarming injury and death rates experienced by America's adolescent workers. This non-profit site publishes and distributes A Teen Guide to Workplace Safety, available in English and Spanish.

5874 www1.hp.com
Compaq Computer Corporation
Compaq is one of the leading corporations in educational technology, working on developing solutions that will connect students, teachers and the community.

Administration

5875 ASQC
611 E Wisconsin Avenue
Milwaukee, WI 53202-4695
800-248-1946
Fax: 414-272-1734
Business and administrative software.

5876 Anchor Pad
Anchor Pad Products
11105 Dana Cir
Cypress, CA 90630-5133

714-799-4071
800-626-2467
Fax: 714-799-4094
E-mail: anchor@anchor.com
http://www.anchorpad.com
Computer and office security

Caroline Jones, COO
Melanie Ruste, Sales/Marketing Associate

5877 Applied Business Technologies
4631 W Chester Pike
Newtown Square, PA 19073-2225
610-359-0700
800-220-2281
Fax: 610-359-9420
Computer networks and administrative software.

5878 AskSam Systems
121 S Jefferson Street
Perry, FL 32347-3232
850-584-6590
800-800-1997
Fax: 850-584-7481
E-mail: info@asksam.com
http://www.asksam.com
Business and administrative free form database software.

Dottie Sheffield, Sales Manager

5879 Autodesk Retail Products
1725 220th Street
Suite C101
Bothell, WA 98021-8809
425-487-2233
Fax: 425-486-1636
Administrative and business software.

5880 Avcom Systems
250 Cox Lane
PO Box 977
Cutchogue, NY 11935-1303
631-734-5080
800-645-1134
Fax: 631-734-7204
Supplies for making and mounting transparencies. Products includes economy and self-adhesive mounts; transparent rolls and sheets; markers, pens and cleaners; thermo, computer graphics and plain-paper copier transparency films and laminating supplies.

Joseph K Lukas

5881 Bobbing Software
67 Country Oaks Drive
Buda, TX 78610-9338
800-688-6812
Administrative software and systems.

5882 Bull HN Information Systems
Technology Park
Billerica, MA 01821
978-294-6000
Fax: 978-294-7999
Computer networks, computers (large, medium, micro and mini), and supplies.

5883 Bureau of Electronic Publishing
745 Alexander Road
#728
Princeton, NJ 08540-6343
973-808-2700
Administrative software, hardware and systems.

5884 CRS
17440 Dallas Parkway
Suite 120
Dallas, TX 75287-7307
800-433-9239
Administrative software and systems.

5885 Campus America
900 E Hill Avenue
Suite 205
Knoxville, TN 37915-2580

865-523-4477
877-536-0222
Fax: 617-492-9081
http://www.campus.com
Computer supplies, equipment, systems and networks.

5886 Century Consultants
150 Airport Road
Suite 1500
Lakewood, NJ 08701-3309
732-363-9300
Fax: 732-363-9374
E-mail: marketing@centuryltd.com
http://www.centuryltd.com
Develops, markets, and services Oracle based web-enabled Management software, STAR_BASE, for school districts K-12.

5887 Computer Resources
PO Box 60
Barrington, NH 03825-0060
603-664-5811
Fax: 603-664-5864
The Modular Management System for Schools is a school administrative software system designed to handle all student record keeping and course scheduling needs. A totally integrated modular system built around a central Student Master File. Additional modules handle student scheduling, grades, attendance and discipline reporting.

Raymond J Perreault, VP Marketing
Robert W Cook, National Sales Manager

5888 Cyborg Systems
2 N Riverside Plaza
Chicago, IL 60606-2600
312-454-1865
Administrative and business software programs.

5889 Diskovery Educational Systems
1860 Old Okeechobee Road
Suite 105
West Palm Beach, FL 33409-5281
561-683-8410
800-331-5489
Fax: 561-683-8416
http://www.diskovery.com
Computer supplies, equipment, and various size systems.

5890 Doron Precision Systems
Doron Precision Systems
174 Court Street
PO Box 400
Binghamton, NY 13902-0400
607-772-1610
Fax: 607-772-6760
http://www.doronprecision.com
Business and classroom curriculum software. Driving Simulation Systems and Entertainment Simulation Systems.

5891 Educational Data Center
180 De La Salle Drive
Romeoville, IL 60446-1895
800-451-7673
Fax: 815-838-9412
Administration software.

5892 EnrollForecast: K-12 Enrollment Forecasting Program
Association of School Business Officials Int'l
11401 N Shore Drive
Reston, VA 20190-4232
703-478-0405
Fax: 703-478-0205
A powerful planning tool that helps project student enrollment.

Peg D Kirkpatrick, Editor/Publisher
Robert Gluck, Managing Editor

5893 Epson America
20770 Madrona Avenue
Torrance, CA 90503-3778
800-289-3776
Computer repair and peripherals.

5894 FMJ/PAD.LOCK Computer Security Systems
741 E 223rd Street
Carson, CA 90745-4111
310-549-3221
800-322-3365
Fax: 310-549-2921
E-mail: info@fmjpadlock.com
Computer peripherals, supplies and equipment.

Tom Separa

5895 Geist
Geist Manufacturing
1821 Yolande Avenue
Lincoln, NE 68521-1835
402-474-3400
Fax: 402-474-4369
E-mail: products@geistmfg.com
http://www.geistmfg.com
Power distribution for racks, cabinets and data centers.

Terri Rockeman, Customer Service Supervisor

5896 Global Computer Supplies
11 Harbor Park Drive
Port Washington, NY 11050-4622
516-625-6200
Fax: 516-484-8533
Computer supplies, equipment, hardware, software and systems.

5897 Harrington Software
658 Ridgewood Road
Maplewood, NJ 07040-2536
201-761-5914
Administrative and business software.

5898 Information Design
7009 S Potomac Street
Suite 110
Englewood, CO 80112
303-792-2990
800-776-2469
Fax: 303-792-2378
E-mail: sales@idesgninc.com
http://www.idesignic.com
Administrative and business software including systems focusing on payroll, personnel, financial accounting, purchasing, budgeting, fixed asset accounting and salary administration.

5899 International Rotex
7171 Telegraph Road
Los Angeles, CA 90040-3227
800-648-1871
Computer supplies.

5900 Jay Klein Productions Grade Busters
1695 Summit Point Court
Colorado Springs, CO 80919-3444
719-599-8786
Fax: 719-599-8312
A line of teacher productivity tools, the most highly recognized integrated gradebooks, attendance records, seating charts and scantron packages in K-12 education today (Mac, DOS, Windows, Apple II).

Jay A Klein, President
Angela C Wormley, Office Manager

5901 Jostens Learning Corporation
5521 Norman Center Drive
Minneapolis, MN 55437-1040
800-635-1429
The leading provider of comprehensive multimedia instruction, including hardware, software and service.

5902 MISCO Computer Supplies
1 Misco Plaza
Holmdel, NJ 07733-1033
800-876-4726
Computer supplies, networks, equipment and accessories.

5903 Mathematica
Wolfram Research, Inc.
100 Trade Centre Drive
Champaign, IL 61820-7237
217-398-0700
800-965-3726
Fax: 217-398-0747
E-mail: info@wolfram.com
http://www.wolfram.com
Classroom curricular software and business/administrative software.

Stephen Wolfram, Founder/CEO
Jean Buck, Dir., Corp Communications

5904 Media Management & Magnetics
N94W14376 Garwin Mace Drive
Menomonee Falls, WI 53051-1629
262-251-5511
800-242-2090
Fax: 262-251-4737
E-mail: medmgt@execpc.com
http://www.computersupplypeople.com
Computer supplies, equipment and systems, Koss headphones.

John Schimberg, Education Sales

5905 MicroAnalytics
Student Transportation Systems
2300 Clarendon Boulevard
Suite 404
Arlington, VA 22201-3331
703-841-0414
Fax: 703-527-1693
Automates bus routing and scheduling for school districts with fleets of 5 to 500 buses. BUSTOPS is flexible, affordable and easy to use. Offers color maps and graphics, efficient routing, report writing, planning and more to improve your pupil transportation system.

Mary Buchanan, Sales Manager

5906 MicroLearn Tutorial Series
Word Associates
3226 Robincrest Drive
Northbrook, IL 60062-5125
847-291-1101
Fax: 847-291-0931
E-mail: microlrn@aol.com
http://www.wordassociates.com
Software tutorials featuring lessons in question format, with tutorial and test mode. 15 titles include Math SAT, 2 English SAT; US Constitution Tutor; Phraze Maze; Geometry: Planely Simple, Concepts and Proofs, Right Triangles; Life Skills Math; Algebra; Reading: Myths and More Myths, Magic and Monsters; Economics; American History. Windows, Macintosh, CD's or disks.

Software

Myrna Helfand, President

5907 NCS Marketing
11000 Prairie Lakes Drive
Eden Prairie, MN 55344-3885
800-447-3269
Fax: 612-830-7788
http://www.ncspearson.com
OpScan optical mark reading scanners from NCS process data at speeds of up to 10,000 sheets per hour for improved accuracy and faster turnaround. Also provides software and scanning applications and services that manage student, financial, human resources, instructional and assessment information.

Sheryl Kyweriga

5908 National Computer Systems
11000 Prairie Lakes Drive
Minneapolis, MN 55440
800-447-3269
Fax: 952-830-8564
Administrative software and systems.

5909 Parlant Technologies
290 N University Avenue
Provo, UT 84601-2821
800-735-2930
Fax: 801-373-9697
Administrative software and systems.

5910 Quill Corporation
100 Schelter Road
Lincolnshire, IL 60069-3621
847-634-4800
Fax: 847-634-5708
Computer and office supplies and equipment.

5911 Rauland Borg
3450 Oakton Street
Skokie, IL 60076-2958
847-679-0900
Fax: 800-217-0977
Administrative software and systems.

5912 Rediker Administration Software
2 Wileraham Road
Hampden, MA 01036-9685
800-882-2994
Fax: 413-566-2274
E-mail: sales@rediker.com
School administrative software for the teaching professional.

5913 Scantron Corporation
PO Box 2411
Tustin, CA 92781-2411
714-259-8887
Computer peripherals, administrative software and services.

5914 SourceView Software International
PO Box 578
Concord, CA 94522-0578
925-825-1248
Classroom curricular, business and administrative software.

5915 Systems & Computer Technology Services
4 Country View Road
Malvern, PA 19355-1408
610-647-5930
Fax: 610-578-7778
Administrative and business software programs and services.

5916 Trapeze Software
23215 Commerce Park Drive
Suite 200
Beachwood, OH 44122
216-595-3100
Fax: 216-595-3113
E-mail: clint@mail.trapezesoftware.com
http://www.trapezesoftware.com
Computerized bus routing, boundary planning and redistricting software and services, and AVL (automatic vehicle locator software).

Clint Rooley, Director of Sales

5917 University Research Company
4724 W 2100 N
Cedar City, UT 84720-7846
800-526-4972
Supplies Quiz-A-Matic electronics for quiz competitions.

5918 Velan
4153 24th Street
Suite 1
San Francisco, CA 94114-3667
415-949-9150
Administrative software and systems.

5919 WESTLAW
West Group
610 Opperman Drive
Eagan, MN 55123-1340
612-687-7000
800-757-9378
Fax: 651-687-5827
http://www.westlaw.com
Online service concerning the complete text of U.S. federal court decisions, state court decisions from all 50 states, regulations, specialized files, and texts dealing with education.

5920 http://teacherfiles.homestead.com/index~ns4
Offers sections on clip art, quotes, slogans, lesson plans, organizations, web quests, political involvement, grants, publications, special education, professional development, humor and more.

5921 www.abcteach.com
Abcteach
E-mail: sandkems@abcteach.com
Free printable materials for kids, parents, student teachers and teachers. Theme units, spelling word searches, research help, writing skills and much more.

5922 www.apple.com
PowerSchool
PowerSchool's web-based architecture makes it easy to learn and easy to use.

5923 www.atozteacherstuff.com
A to Z Teacher Stuff
E-mail: webmaster@atozteacherstuff.com
Features quick indexes to online lesson plans and teacher resources, educational sites for teachers, articles, teacher store and more.

5924 www.awesomelibrary.org
Awesome Library
Organizes the Web with 15,000 carefully reviewed resources, including the top 5 percent in education. Offers sections of mathematics, science, social studies, english, health, physical education, technology, languages, special education, the arts and more. Features a section involved with today's current issues facing our world, like pollution, gun control, tobacco, and other changing 'hot' topics. Site can be browsed in English, German, Spanish, French or Portuguese.

5925 www.easylobby.com
EasyLobby
The complete electronic visitor management system.

5926 www.fraboom.com
Stan D. Bird's WhizBang Thang
This site's tools let's you specify areas within your state's standards and search for a list of 'Flying Rhinoceros' lessons that meet your criteria. Offers other information sources for teachers and students.

5927 www.fundraising.com
800-443-5353
http://www.fundraising.com
Internet fundraising company.

5928 www.hoagiesgifted.org
Hoagies Gifted Education Page
Features the latest research on parenting and educating gifted children. Offers ideas, solutions and other things to try for parents of gifted children. Sections with world issues facing children and other important social topics.

5929 www.kiddsmart.com
Institute for Child Development
E-mail: dcornell@kiddsmart.com
The ICD develops educational materials and resources designed to facilitate children's so-

331

cial and emotional development. Offers the previous materials as well as research summaries, lesson plans, training, workshops, games, multi-cultural materials and other resources to teachers, educational centers, parents, counselors, corporations, non-profits and others involved in the child-care professions.

5930 www.nycteachers.com
NYCTeachers.com
Designed for NYC teachers that work within public school systems. Speaks out on controversial issues facing the broadening, funding, development, staffing and other concerns about public schools. Welcomes your suggestions and comments about the site and the issues involved.

5931 www.songs4teachers.com
O'Flynn Consulting
E-mail: oflynn4@home.com
Offers many resources for teachers including songs made especially for your classroom. Sections with songs and activities for holidays, seasons and more. Features books and audios with 101 theme songs for use in the classroom or anywhere children gather to sing.

5932 www.thecanadianteacher.com
Free Stuff for Canadian Teachers
Site where educators can find the latest links to free resources, materials, lesson plans, software, samples and computers. Some links are for Canadians only.

5933 www.welligent.Com
Welligent
A web-based software program that improves student health management and your school's finances at the same time.

Early Childhood Education

5934 Jump Start Math for Kindergartners
Knowledge Adventure
Torrance, CA
800-545-7677
http://www.knowledgeadventure.com
The program covers important and essential kindergarten math skills such as, writing numbers, sorting, and problem solving/following directions.

5935 Mindplay
160 W Fort Lowell Road
Tucson, AZ 85705
520-888-1800
800-221-7911
Fax: 520-888-7904
E-mail: mail@mindplay.com
http://www.mindplay.com
Educational software focusing on early childhood education and adult literacy.

Stacie Johnson, Communication Coordinator

5936 Nordic Software
PO Box 5403
Lincoln, NE 68505
402-489-1557
800-306-6502
Fax: 402-489-1560
E-mail: info@nordicsoftware.com
http://www.nordicsoftware.com
Specializes in developing and publishing educational software titles. Well-known for its software titles that make it easy for children to learn while playing on the computer. Develops and publishes elementary software products for the Macintosh and Windows platforms. Products include Turbo Math

Facts, Clock Shop, Coin Critters, Language Explorer and Preschool Parade, and more.

Tammy Hurlbut, Finance/Operations

5937 Personalized Software
PO Box 359
Phoenix, OR 97535
541-535-8085
Fax: 541-535-8889
Offers a full line of childcare management and development software programs.

5938 Science for Kids
9950 Concord Church Road
Lewisville, NC 27023-9720
336-945-9000
800-572-4362
Fax: 336-945-2500
E-mail: sci4kids@aol.com
http://www.scienceforkids.com
Developers and publishers of CD-ROM science and early learning programs for children ages 5-14; for Macintosh and Windows computers; school and home programs available.

Charles Moyer, Executive VP

5939 http://daycare.about.com/parenting/daycare
About Parenting/Family Daycare

5940 www.booksofwonder.com
New and vintage childrens books.

5941 www.lil-fingers.com
Lil' Fingers
A computer storybook site for toddlers. Parents and children are encouraged to enjoy the colorful drawings and animations. Offers games, storybooks, coloring pages, the Lil' Store and more.

Elementary Education

5942 Educational Institutions Partnership Program
Defense Information Systems Agency
Automation Resources Information
701 S Courthouse Road
Arlington, VA 22204-2199
703-607-6900
Fax: 703-607-4371
Makes available used computer equipment for donation of transfer to eligible schools, including K-12 schools recognized by the US Department of Education, Universities, colleges, Minority Institutions and nonporfit groups.

5943 Houghton Mifflin Company
222 Berkeley Street
Boston, MA 02116-3748
617-351-5000
Fax: 617-351-1106
Offers literature-based technology products for grades K-8 including CD's Story Time, a Macintosh based CD-ROM programs for grades 1 and 2 and Channel R.E.A.D., a videodisc series for grades 3-8.

5944 Kid Keys 2.0
Knowledge Adventure
800-545-7677
Keyboarding for grades K-2.

5945 Kinder Magic
1680 Meadowglen Lane
Encinitas, CA 92024-5652
760-632-6693
Fax: 760-632-9995
Educational software for ages 4-11.

Dr. Ilse Ortabasi, President

5946 Micrograms Publishing
9934 N Alpine Road
Suite 108
Machesney Park, IL 61115-8240
800-338-4726
Fax: 815-877-1482
http://www.micrograms.com
Micrograms develops educational software for schools and homes.

5947 Tudor Publishing Company
17218 Preston Road
Suite 400
Dallas, TX 75252-4018
Grade level evaluation (GLE) is a computer-adaptive assessment program for elementary and secondary students.

5948 Wordware Publishing
2320 Los Rios Boulevard
#200
Plano, TX 75074-8157
214-423-0090
Fax: 972-881-9147
Publisher of computer reference tutorials, regional Texas and Christian books. Educational division produces a diagnostic and remediation software for grade levels 3-8. Content covers over 3,000 objectives in reading, writing and math. Contact publisher for dealer information.

Eileen Schnett, Product Manager

5949 World Classroom
Global Learning Corporation
PO Box 201361
Arlington, TX 76006-1361
214-641-3356
800-866-4452
An educational telecommunications network that prepares students, K-12 to use real-life data to make real-life decisions about themselves and their environment. Participating countries have included Argentina, Australia, Belgium, Canada, Denmark, France, Germany, Hungary, Iceland, Indonesia, Kenya, Russia, Lithuania, Mexico, Singapore, Taiwan, the Netherlands, the United States and Zimbabwe.

5950 http://k-6educators....education/k-6educators
About Education Elementary Educators

5951 http://www.etacuisenaire.com/index.htm
ETA Cuisenaire
Over 5,000 manipulative-based education and supplemental materials for grades K-12.

5952 http://www.wnet.org/wnetschool
wNet School
212-560-2713
Helps K-12 teachers by providing free standards based lesson plans, classroom activities, multimedia primers, online mentors, links to model technology schools, and more. Online workshops are also included in the WNET TV site.

5953 www.cherrydale.com/
Cherrydale Farms
Website offers company information, fund raising products and information, online mega mall, card shop, career opportunities and much more. Produces fine chocolates and confections. Many opportunities for schools to raise funds with various Cherrydale programs.

5954 www.efundraising.com
eFundraising
Provides non-profit groups with quality products, low prices and superior service. Helping thousands of schools, youth sports teams and community groups reach their fundraising goals each year.

5955 www.hoagiesgifted.org
Hoagies' Gifted Education Page
Features the latest research on parenting and educating gifted children. Offers ideas, solutions and other things to try for parents of gifted children. Sections with world issues facing children and other important social topics.

5956 www.netrover.com/~kingskid/108.html
Room 108
An educational activity center for kids. Offers lots of fun for children with educational focus; like songs, art, math, kids games, children's stories and much more. Sections with pen pal information, puzzles, crosswords, teachers store, spelling, kids sites, email, music, games and more.

5957 www.netrox.net
Dr. Labush's Links to Learning
General links for teachers with internet help, coloring pages, and enrichment programs.

5958 www.primarygames.com
PrimaryGames.com
Contains educational games for elementary students.

5959 www.usajobs.opm.gov/b1c.htm
Overseas Employment Info-Teachers

Employment

5960 Educational Placement Service
90 S Cascade
Suite 1110
Colorado Springs, CO 80903

http://www.teacherjobs.com
Largest teacher placement service in the U.S.

5961 Job Bulletin
American Association of School Administrators
801 N Quincy Street
Arlington, VA 22203-1730
703-528-0700
Fax: 703-841-1543
E-mail: info@aasa.org
http://www.aasa.org
The Job Bulletin was made to help employers and job candidates save time finding one another.

Jay Goldman, Editor

5962 Teachers@Work
PO Box 430
Vail, CO 81658
970-476-5008
Fax: 970-476-1496
http://www.teachersatwork.com
Electronic employment service designed to match the professional staffing needs of schools with teacher applicants.

5963 www.SchoolJobs.com
SchoolJobs.com
Provides principals, superintendents and other administrators the ability to market their job openings to a national pool of candidates, also gives educational professionals the chance to search for opportunities matching their skills.

5964 www.aasa.org
American Association of School Administrators
801 N Quincy Street
Suite 700
Arlington, VA 22203-1730
703-528-0700
Fax: 703-841-1543

E-mail: info@aasa.org
http://www.aasa.org
Leadership news online.

Guidance & Counseling

5965 Alcohol & Drug Prevention for Teachers, Law Enforcement & Parent Groups
PO Box 4656
Reading, PA 19606
610-582-2090
Fax: 610-404-0406
E-mail: nodrugs@earthlink.net
http://www.nodrugs.com
Local organizations and international groups against drugs.

5966 Live Wire Media
3450 Sacramento Street
619
San Francisco, CA 94118
800-359-5437
Fax: 415-665-8006
E-mail: info@livewiremedia.com
http://www.livewiremedia.com/
Videos for youth guidance and character development, and teacher training.

Christine Hollander, Director Marketing

5967 Phillip Roy Multimedia Materials
PO Box 130
Indian Rocks Beach, FL 34635
727-593-2700
800-255-9085
Fax: 727-595-2685
E-mail: info@philliproy.com
http://www.philliproy.com
Multimedia materials for use with alternative education, Chapter 1, dropout prevention, Even Start, Head Start, JTPA/PIC, special education students, at-risk students, transition to work programs. Focuses on basic skills, conflict resolution, remediation, vocational education, critical thinking skills, communication skills, reasoning and decision making skills. Materials can be duplicated networked at no cost.

Phil Padol, Consultant
Regina Jacques, Customer Support

5968 www.goodcharacter.com
Character Education
Teaching guides for k-12 character education, packed with discussion questions, assignments, and activities that you can use as your own lesson plans.

International

5969 www.aed.org
Academy for Educational Development
The site provides information on international exchange, fellowshipand training.

5970 www.asce.org
American Society of Civil Engineers
This site lists scholarships and fellowships available only to ASCE members.

5971 www.cie.uci.edu
International Opportunities Program
Valuable links for exploring opportunities for study and research abroad.

5972 www.ciee.org
Council on International Educational Exchange
Study abroad programs by region, work abroad opportunities, international volunteer

projects and Council-administered financial aid and grant information .

5973 www.cies.org
Council for International Exchange of Scholars
Information on the Fulbright Senior Scholar Program which is made available to Fulbright alumni,grantees, prospective applicants and public at large.

5974 www.daad.org
German Academic Exchange Service (DADD)
Promotes international academic relations and contains links to research grants, summer language grants,annual grants, grants in German studies andspecial programs.

5975 www.ed.gov
US Department of Education
Office of Higher Education Programs

This site describes programs and fellowships offered by the International Education and Graduate Programs office of the US Department of Education.

5976 www.finaid.org
FinAid
A free, comprehensive, independent and ojective guide to student financial aid.

5977 www.iie.org
Institute of International Education
809 United Nations Plaza
New York, NY 10017-3580
412-741-0930
Fax: 212-984-5452
E-mail: iiebooks@abdintl.com
http://www.iiebooks.org
The largest not-for-profit international educational organization in the United States. This site provides information regarding IIE's programs, services and resources, including the Filbright Fellowship.

5978 www.iiepasspport.org
Institute of International Education
IIE Passport: Study Abroad
1350 Edgmont Avenue Suite 1100
Chester, PA 19013
877-404-0338
Fax: 610-499-9205
E-mail: info@iiepassport.org
http://www.iiepassport.org
A student guide on the web to 5,000 learning oppurtunities worldwide.

5979 www.irex.org
International Research and Exchange Board
Academic exchanges between the United States and Russia. Lists a variety of programs as well as grant and fellowship oppurtunities.

5980 www.isp.msu.edu/ncsa
Michigan State University
National Consortium for Study
in Africa

Provides a comprehensive lists of sponsors for African exchange.

5981 www.istc.umn.edu/
University of Minnesota
International Study and Travel Center

Comprehensive and searchable links to study, work and travel abroad opportunities.

5982 www.languagetravel.com
Language Travel Magazine
Resource for finding study abroad language immersion courses.

5983 www.nsf.gov/
National Science Foundation

Encourages exchange in science and engineering. The site has inter-national component, providing links with valuable information on fellowships grants and awards, summer institutes, workshops,research and education projects and international programs.

5984 www.si.edu/
Smithsonian Institution
Fellowships link to Smithsonian Oppurtunities for research and study.

5985 www.studiesinaustralia.com/study
Studies in Australia
Listing of study abroad oppurtunities in Australia, providing details of academic and training institutions and the programs they offer to prospective international students and education professionals.

5986 www.studyabroad.com/
Educational Directories Unlimited, Inc.
Study abroad information resource listing study abroad programs worldwide.

5987 www.studyabroad.com/.
StudyAbroad.com
A commercial site with thousands of study abroad programs in over 100 countries with links to study abroad program home pages.

5988 www.ucis.pitt.edu/crees
University of Pittsburgh
Center for Russian/European Studies

Index of electronic resources for the student interested in Russian and European language and culture study.

5989 www.upenn.edu/oip/scholarships.html
University of Pennsylvania
Scholarships/Graduate Study Abroad

Provides links for graduate study abroad and scholarship opportunities.

5990 www.usc.edu
University of Southern California
Resources for Colleges and Universities in International Exchange

Links for browsing all aspects of international exchange, including study, research, work and teaching abroad, financial aid, grants and scholarships.

5991 www.usinfo.state/gov
US Department of State International Information Programs

Comprehensive desriptions of all IIP programs, sections on policy issues, global and regional issues and IIP publications.

5992 www.wes.org
World Education Services
Features information on WES' foreign credentials evaluation services, world education workshops, and the journals World Education and News Reviews.

5993 www.world-arts-resources.com/
World Wide Arts Resources
Focuses solely on the arts, this site provides links for funding sources, university programs and arts organizations all over the world.

5994 www.yfu.org/
Youth for Understanding (YFU)
Oppurtunities for young people around the world to spend a summer, semester or year with a host family in another country.

5995 wwww.sas.upenn.edu
African Studies Center, University of Pennsylvania
African Studies WWW

Links to Africa-related internet sources, African Studies Association and UPenn African Studies Center.

Language Arts

5996 Advantage Learning Systems
Renaissance Learning
PO Box 8036
Wisconsin Rapids, WI 54495-8036
715-424-3636
800-338-4204
Fax: 715-424-4242
E-mail: answers@renlearn.com
http://www.renlearn.com
Accelerated Reader software and manuals that motivate K-12 students to read more and better books. The program boosts reading scores and library circulation. Lets educators quickly and accurately assess student reading while motivating students to read more and better books.

5997 Bytes of Learning Incorporated
150 Consumers Road
Suite 2021
Willowdale, ON, Canada, M2 J 1P9
800-465-6428
Single and site licensed software for Macintosh, Apple II, DOS and Windows-network compatible too. Keyboarding, language arts, career exploration and more on diskette and CD-ROM.

5998 Humanities Software
408 Columbia Street
#950
Hood River, OR 97031-2044
503-386-6737
800-245-6737
Fax: 541-386-1410
Over 150 whole language, literature-based language arts software titles for grades K-12.
Karen Withrow, Marketing Assistant
Charlotte Arnold, Marketing Director

5999 Teacher Support Software
3542 NW 97th Boulevard
Gainesville, FL 32606-7322
352-332-6404
800-228-2871
Fax: 352-332-6779
E-mail: tss@tssoftware.com
http://www.tssoftware.com
Language arts, Title 1, special ed, at-risk and ESL, curriculum-based networkable software for grades K-12. Vocabulary software that develops sight word recognition, provides basal correlated databases, tests reading comprehension, tracks student's progress and provides powerful teacher tools.

6000 Weaver Instructional Systems
6161 28th Street SE
Grand Rapids, MI 49546-6931
616-942-2891
Fax: 616-942-1796
Reading and language arts computer software programs for K-college.

6001 www.caslt.org
Canadian Association of Second Language Teachers
Promotes the advancement of second language education throughout Canada.

6002 www.riverdeep.net
Riverdeep Interactive Learning
Riverdeep's interactive science, language and math arts programs deliver high quality educational experiences.

6003 www.signit2.com
Aylmer Press
Website hosted by Aylmer Press which produces video's to teach kids sign language as well as music.

6004 www.usajobs.opm.gov/b1c.htm1
Overseas Employment Info- Teachers
US Office of Personnel Management

Library Services

6005 American Econo-Clad Services
2101 N Topeka
Topeka, KS 66601
800-255-3502
Fax: 785-233-3129
A full service supplier of educational materials for the library, curriculum and software resource needs including MatchMaker, CD-ROM and ABLE (Analytically Budgeted Library Expenditures) computer systems.

6006 Anchor Audio
3415 Lomita Boulevard
Torrance, CA 90505-5010
310-784-2300
800-262-4671
Fax: 310-784-0533
http://www.anchoraudio.com
Various audio visual products for the school and library.

6007 Baker & Taylor
8140 Lehigh Avenue
Morton Grove, IL 60053-2627
847-965-8060
Nation's leading wholesale supplier of audio, computer software, books, videocassettes and other accessories to schools and libraries.

6008 Brodart Company, Automation Division
500 Arch Street
Williamsport, PA 17701
570-326-2461
800-233-8467
Fax: 570-327-9237
E-mail: salesmkt@brodart.com
http://www.brodart.com
Brodart's Automation Division has been providing library systems, software, and services for over 25 years. Products include: library management systems, media management systems, Internet solutions, cataloged web sites, cataloging resource tools, union catalog solutions, public access catalogs, and bibliographic services.
Kasey Dibble, Marketing Coordinator
Sally Wilmoth, Director Marketing/Sales

6009 Catalog Card Company
12219 Nicollet Avenue
Burnsville, MN 55337-1650
612-882-8558
800-442-7332
Fax: 785-290-1223
MARC records compatible with all software for retrospective conversions and new book orders. Catalog Card's conversion services include barcode labels to complement circulation software. MARC records generated from Dewey/Sears and Library of Congress databases are in standard USMARC or MicroLIF format.

6010 Chancery Student Management Solutions
3001 Wayburne Drive
Burnbay
Canada V5G 4W3
604-294-1233
800-999-9931
Fax: 604-294-2225
http://www.chancery.com
Online catalog searches and checking materials in and out.

6011 Data Trek
5838 Edison Place
Carlsbad, CA 92008-6519
800-876-5484
Turn-key library automation systems and computer networks.

6012 Demco
PO Box 7488
Madison, WI 53707-7488
800-356-1200
Fax: 608-241-1799
A leader in educational and library supplies for more than 80 years, Demco offers library audio and visual supplies and equipment plus display furniture.

6013 Dewey Decimal Classification
OCLC Forest Press
6565 Frantz Road
Dublin, OH 43017-3395
800-848-5878
Fax: 888-339-3921
E-mail: orders@oclc.org
http://www.oclc.org/fp
OCLC Forest Press publishes the Dewey Decimal Classification (DDC) system and many related print and CD-ROM products that teach librarians and library users about the DDC.

Libble Clawford, Marketing Manager

6014 Ebsco Subscription Services
International Headquarters
PO Box 1943
Birmingham, AL 35201-1943
205-991-1480
Fax: 205-980-6700
Periodical subscription and ordering and customer service equipment, computer and CD-ROM supplies, products and hardware for libraries.

Shannon Hayslip

6015 Electronic Bookshelf
5276 S Country Road, 700 W
Frankfort, IN 46041
765-324-2182
Fax: 765-324-2183
Reading motivation, testing management system and various computer systems and networks for educational purposes.

Rosalie Carter

6016 Filette Keez Corporation/Colorworks Diskette Organizing System
3204 Channing Lane
Bedford, TX 76021-6506
817-283-5428
Produces ten filing inventions for classroom library, lab and district technology resources management. SelecTsideS folders store multimedia in Press-an-Inch Technology Slings and keep instruction, printouts, pamphlets and blackliners altogether. The diskette/CD portfolio color coordinates with the student/magazine Spbinder, plastic LaceLox fastener and all systems paper supplies: CD envelopes, storage box dividers, sheeted cards, perforated tractor labels and keys, available in 7 tech colors.

Roxanne Kay Harbert, Founder/President
Ray L Harbert, VP

6017 Follett Software Company
1391 Corporate Drive
McHenry, IL 60050
815-344-8700
800-323-3397
Fax: 815-344-8774
E-mail: marketing@fsc.follett.com
http://www.fsc.follett.com
Helping K-12 schools and districts create a vital library-to-classroom link to improve student achievement. FSC combines award-winning library automation with practical applications of the Internet. From OPAC data enhancement and easy-to-implement Internet technology to innovative information literacy solutions, FSC helps simplify resource management, increase access to resources inside and outside your collection and provide tools to integrate technology into the curriculum.

Patricia Yonushonis, Marketing Manager
Ann Reist, Conference Manager

6018 Foundation for Library Research
1200 Bigley Avenue
Charleston, WV 25302-3752
304-343-6480
Fax: 304-343-6489
The Automated Library Systems integrated library automation software.

Robert Evans

6019 Gaylord Brothers
PO Box 4901
Syracuse, NY 13221-4901
800-448-6160
Fax: 315-457-8387
Library, AV supplies and equipment; security systems; and library furniture.

Tim Krein

6020 Highsmith Company
W5527 Highway 106
Fort Atkinson, WI 53538
414-563-9571
Catalog of microcomputer and multimedia curriculum products and software.

Barbara R Endl

6021 Information Access Company
362 Lakeside Drive
Foster City, CA 94404-1171
800-227-8431
Offers automation products and electronics for library/media centers.

6022 LePAC NET
Brodart Automation
500 Arch Street
Williamsport, PA 17705
570-326-2461
800-233-8467
Fax: 570-327-9237
E-mail: salesmkt@brodart.com
http://www.brodart.com
Software for searching thousands of library databases with a single search. Schools can use to take multiple individual library databases and consolidate them, while deleting duplicate listings, into a union database.

Shawn Knight, Assistant Marketing Manager
Denise Macafee, Marketing Manager

6023 Library Corporation
Library Corporation
Research Park
Inwood, WV 25428-9733
800-325-7759
http://www.tlcdelivers.com
Web-based library management systems allows patrons to have easy and immediate access to books and other library resources.

6024 Lingo Fun
International Software
PO Box 486
Westerville, OH 43086-0486
800-745-8258
Providers of microcomputer software including CD-ROM's for Macintosh and MPC, on-line dictionaries, translation assistants; teaching programs for elementary presentation, review and reinforcement, test preparation, and literary exploration.

6025 MARCIVE
PO Box 47508
San Antonio, TX 78265-7508
210-646-6161
800-531-7678
Fax: 210-646-0167
E-mail: info@marcive.com
http://www.marcive.com
Economical, fast 100% conversion. Full MARC records with SEARS or LC headings. Free authorities processing smart barcode labels, reclassification, MARC Record enrichment

6026 Medianet/Dymaxion Research Limited
5515 Cogswell Street
Halifax, Nova Scotia, B3 J 1R2
902-422-1973
Fax: 902-421-1267
E-mail: info@medianet.ns.ca
http://www.medianet.ns.ca
Medianet is the scheduling system for equipment and media that has consistently been rated as best in its class. Features include book library system integration, time-of-day booking, catalog production, WWW and touch tone phone booking by patrons.

Peter Mason, President

6027 Mitinet/Marc Software
6409 Odana Road
Madison, WI 53719-1125
800-824-6272
Fax: 608-270-1107
Import/export USMARC, MICROLIF to USMARC conversions.

6028 Orange Cherry Software
69 Westchester Avenue
PO Box 390
Pound Ridge, NY 10576-1702
914-764-4104
800-672-6002
Fax: 914-764-0104
http://www.orangecherry.com
Educational software products for libraries and media centers.

Biannual

Nicholas Vazzana, President

6029 Right on Programs
778 New York Avenue
Huntington, NY 11743-4240
631-424-7777
Fax: 631-424-7207
E-mail: friends@rightonprograms.com
http://www.rightonprograms.com
Computer software for Windows and networks for library management including circulation, cataloging, periodicals, catalog cardmaking, inventory and thirty more. Used in more than 24,000 schools and libraries of all sizes.

D Farren, VP

6030 SOLINET, Southeastern Library Network
1438 W Peachtree Street NW
Suite 200
Atlanta, GA 30309-2955
404-892-0943
800-999-8558

Fax: 404-892-7879
E-mail: information@solinet.net
http://www.solinet.net
SOLINET provides access, training and support for OCLC products and services; offers discounted library products and services, including licensed databases; provides electronic information solutions; workflow consulting, training and customized workshops; and supports a regional preservation of materials program.

Cathie Gharing, Marketing Coordinator
Liz Hornsby, Editor

6031 Sirsi Corporation
101 Washington Street SE
Huntsville, AL 35801-4827
256-704-7000
800-917-4774
Fax: 256-704-7007
E-mail: sales@sirsi.com
http://www.sirsi.com
Unicorn Collection Management Systems are fully integrated UNIX-based library systems, automating all of a library's operation. Modules include: cataloging, authority control, public access, materials booking, circulation, academic reserves, acquisitions, serials control, reference database manager and electronic mail. Modules can be configured for all types and sizes of libraries.

Vicki Smith, Communication Specialist

6032 Social Issues Resources Series
PO Box 2348
Boca Raton, FL 33427
561-994-0079
800-232-SIRS
Fax: 561-994-4704
Publisher of CD-ROM reference systems for PC and Macintosh computers. Databases of full-text articles carefully selected from 1,000 domestic and international sources. Also provides PC-compatible and stand-alone and network packages.

Paula Jackson, Marketing Director
Suzanne Panek, Customer Service

6033 TekData Systems Company
1111 W Park Avenue
Libertyville, IL 60048-2952
847-367-8800
Fax: 847-367-0235
E-mail: tekdata@tekdata.com
http://www.tekdata.com
Scheduling and booking systems for intranets and internets.

Randy Kick, Sales Manager

6034 Three M Library Systems
Three M Center
Building 225-4N-14
St. Paul, MN 55144
800-328-0067
Fax: 800-223-5563
Materials Flow Management system is the first comprehensive system for optimizing the handling, processing and security of your library materials - from processing to checkout to check-in. The SelfCheck System and Staff Workstation automate the processing of virtually all of your library materials, while the Tattle-Tape Security Strips and Detection Systems help ensure the security of those materials.

6035 UMI
300 N Zeeb Road
Ann Arbor, MI 48103-1553
800-521-0600
Fax: 800-864-0019
Information products in microform, CD-ROM, online and magnetic tape.

6036 University Products
517 Main Street
#101
Holyoke, MA 01040-5514
413-532-3372
800-628-1912
Fax: 413-452-0618
Complete selection of library and media center supplies and equipment.

Juhn Dunpay

6037 WLN
PO Box 3888
Lacey, WA 98509-3888
360-923-4000
800-342-5956
Fax: 360-923-4009
School and media librarians experience 95% hit rates with WLN's LaserCat, CD-ROM database, a cataloging product and MARC record service.

6038 Winnebago Software Company
457 E S Street
Caledonia, MN 55921-1356
800-533-5430
Fax: 507-725-2301
E-mail: sales@winnebago.com
http://www.winnebago.com
Comprehensive, user-friendly circulation and catalog software for Windows, Mac OS, and MS-DOS systems-plus Internet technology, online periodical databases, outstanding customer support, and retrospective conversion services-all developed within the quality guidelines of Winnebago's ISO 9001 certification with TickIT accreditation.

6039 www.awesomelibrary.org
Awesome Library
Organizes the Web with 15,000 carefully reviewed resources, including the top 5 percent in education. Offers sections of mathematics, science, social studies, english, health, physical education, technology, languages, special education, the arts and more. Features a section involved with today's current issues facing our world, like pollution, gun control, tobacco, and other changing 'hot' topics. Site can be browsed in English, German, Spanish, French or Portuguese.

6040 www.techlearning.com
Technology & Learning
Open 24 hours, every day of the week, with an extensive and up-to-date catalog of over 53,000 software and hardware products. Powerful search engine will help you find the right education-specific products.

Mathematics

6041 Accelerated Math
Renaissance Learning
PO Box 8036
Wisconsin Rapids, WI 54495-8036
715-424-3636
800-338-4204
Fax: 715-424-4242
E-mail: answers@renlearn.com
http://www.renlearn.com
Accelerated Math provides 17 different reports, providing individualized, constructive feedback to students, parents, and teachers.

6042 Applied Mathematics Program
Prime Technology Corporation
PO Box 2407
Minneola, FL 34755-2407
352-394-7558
Fax: 352-394-3778
http://www.primetechnology.net
Provides students with comprehensive instruction in 11 math areas. In working with

this program, students develop employment and life skills. The program will also lead the student to greater success on the mathematics sections of any standardized test.

Paul Scime, President

6043 CAE Software
3608 Shepherd Street
Chevy Chase, MD 20815-4132
301-907-9845
800-354-3462
Provides educational software for mathematics, grades 3-12. Simulations, tutorials, games, and problem solving. Titles include Mathematics Life Skills Services, Reading and Making Graphs Series, MathLab Series, Meaning of Fractions, Using Fractions and Using Decimals, ALG Football, GEO Pool and GEO Billiards, Paper Route, Mathematics Achievement Project, and others.

Alan R Chap, President

6044 EME Corporation
PO Box 1949
Stuart, FL 34995-1949
800-848-2050
Fax: 561-219-2209
E-mail: emecorp@aol.com
http://www.emescience.com
Publishers of award-winning science and math software, elementary through high school levels.

6045 Logal Software
125 Cambridgepark Drive
Cambridge, MA 02140-2329
617-491-4440
Fax: 617-491-5855
Math and science products for high school through college.

Martha Cheng, President

6046 MathType
Design Science
4028 E Broadway
Long Beach, CA 90803-1502
562-433-0685
800-827-0685
Fax: 562-433-6969
http://www.mathtype.com
Designed to make the creation of complex equations on a computer simple and fast. It works in conjunction with the software applications you already own, such as word processing programs, graphics programs, presentation programs, and web-authoring applications. Create research papers, tests, slides, books or web pages quickly and easily. MathType is the powerful, professional version of the Equation Editor in Microscoft Word, and Wordperfect.

Bruce Virga, VP Sales/Marketing
Nicole Jessey, Sale/Marketing Coordinator

6047 Mathematica
Wolfram Research, Inc.
100 Trade Center Drive
Champaign, IL 61820-7237
217-398-0700
800-965-3726
Fax: 217-398-0747
E-mail: info@wolfram.com
http://www.wolfram.com
Mathematica is an indispensable tool for finding and communicating solutions quickly and easily.

Stephen Wolfram, Founder/CEO
Jean Buck, Dir., Corp Communications

6048 MindTwister Math
Edmark Corporation
PO Box 97021
Redmond, WA 98073-9721

425-556-8400
800-691-2986
Fax: 425-556-8430
E-mail: edmarkteam@edmark.com
http://www.edmark.com
Software to help students in grade 3 and 4 build math fact fluency, practice mental math and improve estimating skills as they compete in a series of math challenges.

6049 Multimedia - The Human Body
Sunburst Technology
101 Castleton Street
Pleasantville, NY 10570
914-747-3310
800-321-7511
Fax: 914-747-4109
http://www.sunburst.com
Multimedia production of the intricate workings of the human body.

6050 Texas Instruments
Consumer Relations
PO Box 53
Lubbock, TX 79408-0053
800-842-2737
Fax: 972-917-0874
Instructional calculators offer features matched to math concepts taught at each of conceptional development. Classroom accessories and teacher support programs that support the Texas Instruments products enhance instruction and learning. TI also offers a complete range of powerful notebook computers and laser printers for every need.

6051 William K. Bradford Publishing Company
35 Forest Ridge Road
Concord, MA 01742-5414
800-421-2009
Fax: 978-318-9500
http://www.wkbradford.com
Educational software for grades K-12. Especially math and grade book.

Hal Wexler, VP

6052 www.mathgoodies.com
Mrs. Glosser's Math Goodies
Free educational site featuring interactive math lessons. Use a problem-solving approach and actively engage students in the learning process.

6053 www.mathstories.com
MathStories.com
The goal of this site is to help grade school children improve their math problem-solving and critical thinking skills. Offers over 4000 math word problems for children.

6054 www.riverdeep.net
Riverdeep Interactive Learning
Riverdeep's interactive science, language and math arts programs deliver high quality educational experiences.

6055 www.themathemagician.8m.com
The Mathemagician
Offers the help of a real live person to help students correct and understand math and other home work problems.

Music & Art

6056 Harmonic Vision
68 E Wacker Place
Chicago, IL 60610
312-332-9200
800-474-0903
http://www.harmonicvision.com
Leading musical education software to teach effectiveness of music in the home, school and studio.

6057 Midnight Play
Simon & Schuster Interactive
800-793-9972
http://www.simonandschuster.com
Electronic picture book with an unusual look at creativity.

6058 Music Teacher Find
33 W 17th Street
10th Floor
New York, NY 10011
212-242-2464
http://www.MusicTeacherFind.com
Comprehensive Music Teacher Database designed to help music students find quality teachers in their neighborhood.

6059 Music and Guitar

http://www.nl-guitar.com
Original music programs for schools, courses and encounterswith music.

6060 Pure Gold Teaching Tools
PO Box 16622
Tuscon, AZ 85732
520-747-5600
866-692-6500
Fax: 520-571-9077
E-mail: info@puregoldteachingtools.com
http://www.puregoldteachingtools.com
Exciting teaching methods and fabulous gifts for teachers, parents, students, pre-schoolers, homeschoolers and music therapists.

Heidi Goldman, President

6061 http://library.thinkquest.org
Think Quest
The Arti FAQS 2100 Project is designed to predict how art will influence our lives in the next hundred years. Students can use available data to make reasonable predictions for the future.

6062 http://members.truepath.com/headoft heclass
Head of The Class
Offers three galleries with clip art for teachers and children, several lesson plans, teaching tips, songs for teachers, lounge laughs, teacher tales and more.

6063 www.billharley.com
BillHarley.com
Humerous, yet meaningful songs which chronicle the lives of children at school and at home. His recordings of songs and stories can be used most effectively in the classroom as inspirational tools for the motivation of learning.

6064 www.sanford-artedventures.com
Sanford- A Lifetime of Color
800-323-0749
Teaches students about art and color theory while they play a game. Lessons plans, newsletter and product information.

6065 www.songs4teachers.com
O'Flynn Consulting
E-mail: oflynn4@home.com
Offers many resources for teachers including songs made especially for your classroom. Sections with songs and activities for holidays, seasons and more. Features books and audios with 101 theme songs for use in the classroom or anywhere children gather to sing.

6066 www.ushistory.com
History Happens
Teaches integrating art, music, literature, science, math, library skills, and American history. The Primary source is stories from American history presented in musci video style.

Physical Education

6067 InfoUse
2560 9th Street
Suite 216
Berkeley, CA 94710-2557
510-549-6520
Fax: 510-549-6512
An award-winning, multimedia development and products firm, features CD-ROM, websites on health, education and disability. For training, education or presentations, our services include: research, instructional design, interface design, graphics, animation, content acquisition, videoing, analog and digital editing and evaluation. Products include SafeNet, (HIV prevention for fifth and sixth grade children), Place Math and Math Pad (math tools and lessons for students with disabilities).

Lewis E Kraus, VP
Susan Stoddard, President

6068 www.sports-media.org
Sports Media
A tool for p.e. teachers, coaches, students and everyone who is interested in p.e./fitness and sports. Interactive p.e. lesson plans, sports pen-apls for the kids, European p.e. mailing list, and developing teaching skills in physical education.

Reading

6069 Accelerated Reader
Renaissance Learning
PO Box 8036
Wisconsin Rapids, WI 54495-8036
715-424-3636
800-338-4204
Fax: 715-424-4242
E-mail: answers@renlearn.com
http://www.renlearn.com
Helps teachers increase literature-based reading practice for all k-12 students

Secondary Education

6070 New York Times
New York, NY
646-698-8000
Fax: 646-698-8344
http://www.nytimes.com/learning
A resource for educators, parents and students in grades six through 12. Provides a daily lesson plan and comprehensive interactive resources based on newspaper content.

Rob Larson, Education Editor
Diane Morgan, Director Marketing

6071 Wm. C. Brown Communications
2460 Kerper Boulevard
Dubuque, IA 52001-2224
College textbooks, software, CD-ROM and more for grades 10-12.

6072 http://adulted.about.com/education/ad ulted
Adult/Continuing Education

6073 http://englishhlp.www5.50megs.com
English Help
E-mail: englishhlpr@hotmail.com
This page is a walk through of Microsoft Power Point. The goal is to show in a few simple steps how to make your own website. Created by Rebecca Holland.

6074 www.number2.com
Number2.com
Currently offer SAT and GRE prep along with a vocabulary builder. Practice questions and word drill are adapted to the ability level of the user.

Science

6075 Academic Software Development Group
University of Maryland
University of Maryland
Computer Science Center
College Park, MD 20742-0001
301-405-5100
Fax: 301-405-0726
Offers BioQuest Library which is a set of peer-reviewed resources for science education.

6076 Accu-Weather
385 Science Park Road
State College, PA 16803-2215
814-237-0309
Fax: 814-238-1339
Offers a telecommunications weather and oceanography database.

6077 AccuLab Products Group
614 Senic Drive
Suite 104
Modesto, CA 95350
209-522-8874
Fax: 209-522-8875
Science laboratory software.

6078 Learning Team
10 Long Pond Road
Armonk, NY 10504-2625
914-273-2226
800-793-TEAM
Fax: 914-273-2227
Offers CD-ROM, including MathFinder, Science Helper and Small Blue Planet and Redshift, the Learning Team edition.

Thomas Laster

6079 Problem Solving Concepts
611 N Capitol Avenue
Indianapolis, IN 46204-1205
317-267-9827
800-755-2150
Fax: 317-262-5044
Pro Solv provides students with a new approach to learning introductory physics problem solving techniques. Multi-experiential exercises with supporting text introduce students to relevant variables and their interrelations, principles, graphing and the development of problem solving skills through the quiz/tutorial mode.

Thomas D Feigenbaum, President
Gean R Shelor, Administrative Assistant

6080 Quantum Technology
PO Box 8252
Searcy, AR 72145-8252
A microcomputer database collection system that allows users to perform experiments in chemistry, biology and applied physics.

6081 SCI Technologies
SCI Technologies
105 Terry Drive
Suite 120
Newtown, PA 18940
215-579-8590
800-421-9881
Fax: 215-579-8589
E-mail: cgreenblatt@scitechnologies.com
http://www.scitechnologies.com
A computer-based interface with an integrated hardware and software package that al-

lows the focus of a science lab to shift from data collection to data analysis and experiment design.

Colleen Greenblatt, Sales Manager
Michelle Trexler, Event Coordinator

6082 Videodiscovery
1700 Westlake Avenue N
Suite 600
Seattle, WA 98109-3040
206-285-5400
800-548-3472
Fax: 206-285-9245
Publishers of award winning science videodiscs and multimedia software for kindergarten through post-secondary classes.

6083 www.kidsastronomy.com
KidsAstronomy.com
Offers information on astronomy, deep space, the solar system, space exploration, a teachers corner and more.

6084 www.riverdeep.net
Riverdeep Interactive Learning
Riverdeep's interactive science, language and math arts programs deliver high quality educational experiences.

Social Studies

6085 AccuNet/AP Multimedia Archive
AccuWeather, Inc.
385 Science Park Road
State College, PA 16803
814-235-8600
800-566-6606
Fax: 814-231-0453
E-mail: salesmail@accuwx.com
http://www.ap.accuweather.com
The Photo Archive is an on-line database containing almost a half-million of Associated Press's current and historic images for the last 150 years.

Michael Warfield, Southeastern Sales Manager
Richard Towne, Northeastern Sales Manager

6086 Gale Research
PO Box 33477
Detroit, MI 48232-5477
800-877-GALE
Fax: 800-414-5043
Offers CD-Rom information that offer students contextual understanding of the most commonly-studies persons, events and social movements in U.S. history; concepts, theories, discoveries and people involved in the study of science; current geopolitical data with cultural information on 200 nations of the world as well as all U.S. states and dependencies; poetry and literary information; and more in various databases for education.

6087 World Geography Web Site
ABC-CLIO Schools
130 Cremona Drive
#1911
Santa Barbara, CA 93117-5599
805-968-1911
800-368-6868
Fax: 805-685-9685
Provides convenient internet access to curriculum-based reference and research materials for media specialist, educators and students.

CD-ROM

Judy Fay, Managing Editor
Valerie Mercado, Customer Service

6088 WorldView Software
76 N Broadway
Suite 4009
Hicksville, NY 11801-4241
516-681-1773
800-347-8839
Fax: 516-681-1775
E-mail: history@worldviewsoftware.com
WorldView Software's interactive social studies programs for middle school and high school are comprehensive, curriculum-based tools that may be used along with or in place of textbooks. Each dynamic program contains Socratic learning sessions, writing activities and exams with instant feedback. Resource materials in every program include sketches and artwork. Used nationally in classrooms, computer labs and learning centers.

Grades 7-12

Jerrold Kleinstein, President

6089 http://faculty.acu.edu
M.I. Smart Program
Site designed for teacher and students. Offers electronic resources for historical and cultural geography. Features games, quizzes, trivia and virtual tours for students and thier teachers.

Technology in Education

6090 BLINKS.Net
PO Box 79321
Atlanta, GA 30357
404-243-5202
Fax: 404-241-4992
E-mail: info@blinks.net
http://www.blinks.net
Fastest growing free Internet service provider and community portal for information and resources for the African American, Caribbean, Latino, and African markets.

6091 Boyce Enterprises
360 Sharry Lane
Santa Maria, CA 93455
805-937-4353
Fax: 805-934-1765
Development of computer-based vocational curriculums.

6092 Center for Educational Outreach and Innovation
Teachers College-Columbia University
525 W 120th Street
Box 132
New York, NY 10027
212-678-3987
800-209-1245
Fax: 212-678-8417
E-mail: ceoi-mail@tc.columbia.edu
http://www.tc.columbia.edu
Lifelong learning programs, including distance learning courses, certificates and workshoops in education related topics.

6093 Depco
3305 Airport Drive
PO Box 178
Pittsburg, KS 66762
316-231-0019
800-767-1062
Fax: 316-231-0024
E-mail: sales@depcoinc.com
http://www.depcoinc.com
Program tracks and schedules for you, the test taker delivers tests electronically, as well as, automatic final exams. There are workstation security features to help keep students focused on their activities.

6094 Dialog Information Services
Worldwide Headquaters
3460 Hillview Avenue
#10010
Palo Alto, CA 94304-1338
415-858-3785
800-334-2564
Fax: 650-858-7069
The world's most comprehensive online information source offering over 450 databases containing over 330 million articles, abstracts and citations - covering an unequaled variety of topics, with particular emphasis on news, business, science and technology. Dialog has offices throughout the United States and around the world.

6095 Distance Education Database
International Centre for Distance Learning
Open University, Walton Hall
Milton Keynes
England
441-085-3537
Fax: 441-086-4173
Contains information on distance education, including more than 22,000 distance-taught programs and courses in the Commonwealth of Learning, an organization created by the Commonwealth Heads of Government. On-line and CD-Rom versions of the database contain detailed information on over 30,000 distance-taught courses, 900 distance teaching instructions, and nearly 9,000 books, journals, reports and papers.

Keith Harry, Director

6096 EDUCAUSE
1112 16th Street NW
Suite 600
Washington, DC 20036-4822
202-872-4200
Fax: 202-872-4318
http://www.educause.edu
Aims to link practitioners in primary and secondary education through computer-mediated communications networks.

John Clement, Director

6097 Educational Structures
NCS Pearson
827 W Grove Avenue
Mesa, AZ 85210
800-736-4357
http://www.ncspearson.com
Features complete lesson plans and resources in social studies, mathematics, science, and language arts.

6098 Gibson Tech Ed
1216 S 1580 West
Building C
Orem, UT 84058
800-422-1100
Fax: 800-470-1606
E-mail: gary@gibsonteched.com
http://www.gibsonteched.com
Educational materials to teach electronics, from middle, junior, high school and college.

Gary Gibson, Manager
Tim Gibson, President

6099 Grolier Interactive
Grolier Publishing
90 Sherman Turnpike
Danbury, CT 06816
800-371-3908
Fax: 800-456-4402
http://http://publishing.grolier.com
Instructional software including reference, science, mathematics, music, social studies, early learning, art and art history, language arts/literature.

6100 Heifner Communications
4451 Interstate 70 Drive NW
Columbia, MO 65202-3271
573-445-6163
800-445-6164
Fax: 512-527-2395
Offers educational-merit, cable-programming available via satellite. HCI Distance Learning systems are designed for dependable services and ease of operation and competitive prices.

Vicky Roberts

6101 In Focus
27700 B SW Parkway Avenue
Wilsonville, OR 97070-9215
503-685-8887
800-294-6400
Fax: 503-685-8887
LCD panels, video projectors and systems.

6102 JonesKnowledge.com
9697 E Mineral Avenue
Englewood, CO 80112
800-701-6463
For administrators, that means and integrated solution-with no minimum commitment, or upfront investment. For instructors, it means getting your course online your way, without being a web expert, and for students it means, an accessible and convenient online experience.

6103 Mastercam
CNC Software
5717 Wollochet Drive NW
Suite 2A
Gig Harbor, WA
800-275-6226
Fax: 253-858-6737
E-mail: mcinfo@mastercam.com
http://www.mastercamedu.com

6104 Merit Audio Visual
Merit Software
132 W 21st Street
New York, NY 10011-3203
212-675-8567
800-753-6488
Fax: 212-675-8607
E-mail: sales@meritsoftware.com
http://www.merutsoftware.com
Easy to use, interactive basic skills software for Windows 9x/ME/NT/2000/XP computers. Lessons for reading, writing, grammar and math with appropriate graphics for teens and adults.

Ben Weintraub, Marketing Manager

6105 National Information Center for Educational Media
PO Box 8640
Albuquerque, NM 87198
505-265-3591
800-926-8328
Fax: 505-256-1080
E-mail: nicem@nicem.com
http://www.nicem.com
NICEM maintains a comprehensive database describing educational media materials for all ages and subjects. It is available on CD-ROM and online.

Lisa Savard, Sales/Marketing Director

6106 NoRad Corporation
4455 Torrance Boulevard
#2806513
Torrance, CA 90503-4398
310-605-0808
Fax: 323-934-2101
Mini, personal, medium and large computer systems for educational institutions.

6107 Proxima Corporation
9440 Carroll Park Drive
San Diego, CA 92121
858-457-5500
800-294-6400
Fax: 503-685-7239
http://www.proxima.com
Proxima Corporation is a global leader in the multimedia projection market, providing world class presentation solutions to corporate enterprises, workgroups, mobile professionals, trainers, and professional public speakers.

Kim Gallagher, Public Relations Manager
Kathy Bankerd, Director Marketing Programs

6108 RB5X: Education's Personal Computer Robot
General Robotics Corporation
760 S Youngfield Court
Suite 8
Lakewood, CO 80228-2813
303-988-5636
800-422-4265
Fax: 303-988-5303
E-mail: cbrown@generalrobotics.com
http://www.edurobot.com
RB5X: Education's Personal Computer Robot. All grade levels. Self learn, self teach, hands on modular system. Problem solving, basic learning skills, increases self-esteem. Expanable open-ended, motivation at its best.

Constant Brown, President

6109 SEAL
550 Spring Street
Naugatuck, CT 06770-1906
203-729-5201
Complete line of systems and electronics for schools.

6110 Sharp Electronics Corporation
LCD Products Group
Sharp Plaza
Mall Stop One
Mahwah, NJ 07430
201-529-8731
Fax: 201-529-9636
E-mail: prolcd@sharpsec.com
http://www.sharplcd.com
Offers a full line of LCD-based video and computer multimedia projectors and projection panels for use in a wide range of educational applications. Sharp's product line also includes industrial VHS format VCRs, color TV monitors.

J Ganguzza, Director/Marketing

6111 Valiant
PO Box 3171
S Hackensack, NJ 07606-1171
800-631-0867
Fax: 201-814-0418
Distributors of LCD projection panels, P/A systems, overhead/slide and filmstrip projectors, cassette recorders, classroom record players, laser pointers, laminating equipment, lecturns, listening centers and headphones.

Sheldon Goldstein

6112 Vernier Software
8565 SW Beaverton Hillsdale Hwy
Portland, OR 97225-2429
Laboratory interacting software for the Macintosh, IBM and Apple II.

6113 Websense
10240 Sorrento Valley Road
San Diego, CA 92121
858-320-8000
800-723-1166
Fax: 858-458-2950
http://www.websense.com
Internet filtering.

6114 http://di...elearn/cs/eductechnology/index.htm
About Education Distance Learning

6115 http://futurekids.com
FUTUREKIDS School Technology
Solutions
http://www.futurekids.com
Helping schools use technology to transform
education.

6116 http://online.uophx.edu
University of Phoenix Online
Offers you the convenience and flexibility of
attending classes from your personal computer. Students are discussing issues, sharing
ideas, testing theories, essentially enjoying
all of the advantages of an on-campus degree
programs. Interaction is included like e-mail,
so you practice at your convenience.

6117 http://www.crossteccorp.com
NetOp
800-675-0729
Fax: 561-391-5820
http://www.crossteccorp.com
A powerful combination of seven essential
tools for networked classrooms. Based on the
award winning technology of NetOp Remote
Control and is easy-to-use software only
solution.

6118 http://www.growsmartbrains.com
GrowSmartBrains.com
Website for parents and educators who want
research based information and practical
stradegies for raising children in a media age.

6119 http://www.zdnet.com
ZDNet
Full-service destination for people looking to
buy, use and learn more about technology.

6120 www.21ct.org
Twenty First Century Teachers Network
A nationwide, non-profit initiative of the
McGuffey Project, dedicated to assisting k-12
teachers learn, use and effectively integrate
technology in the curriculum for improved
student learning.

6121 www.aboutonehandtyping.com/
One Hand Typing and Keyboarding
Resources
This site dishes up a blend of messages and
stories, resources for one-hand typists, links
to alternative keyboards, teaching links, and
more.

6122 www.digitaldividenetwork.org
Digital Divide Network
E-mail: ddivide@benton.org
The goal of bridging the divide is to use communications technology to help improve the
quality of life of all communities and their citizens; provide them with the tools, skills and
information they need to help them realize
their socioeconomic, educational and cultural
potential.

6123 www.getquizzed.com
GetQuizzed
Designed as a free service that provides a database that allows users to create, store and
edit Multiple Choice or Question and Answer
quizzes, under password protected
conditions.

6124 www.guidetogeekdom.com
Guide to Geekdom
E-mail: info@guidetogeekdom.com
Designed especially for Homeschoolers,
step-by-step lessons teach students how to
use the computer and troubleshoot computer
problems. Offers workbooks, sample lesson
and more.

6125 www.happyteachers.com
HappyTeachers.com
Information about technical and vocational
education programs, products and curriculum.

6126 www.integratingit.com
Integrating Information Technology for the
Classroom, School, & District

Dedicated to providing the education community a place to find real world strategies, solutions, and resources for integrating
technology. Organized by the perspective of
the classroom teacher, the school administrator, and the district.

6127 www.livetext.com
LiveText Curriculum Manager
Provides tools for engaged learning classroom projects and provides online professional development for teachers.

6128 www.ncrel.org
North Central Regional Educational
Laboratory
Offers research results regarding the effective
use of technology.

6129 www.ncrtec.org
N Central Regional Technology
in Education Consortiums

Provides a variety of tools and information to
improve technology-related professional development programs.

Elementary Education

6130 Curriculum Associates
153 Rangeway Road
No. Billerica, MA 01862
800-225-0248
Fax: 800-366-1158
http://www.curriculumassociates.com
Test preparation material with a guarantee of success; skill instruction and assessment.

6131 Diagnostic Reading Inventory for Primaryand Intermediate Grades K-8
Scott and McCleary Publishing Co.
2482 11th Street SW
Akron, OH 44314-1712
702-566-8756
800-765-3564
Fax: 702-568-1378
E-mail: jscott7576@aol.com
http://www.scottmccleary.com
A series of 13 tests at each grade level, 10 can be given in a group setting. 3 Forms of the IRI teacher friendly. Easy to administer.

Spiral Paperback
ISBN: 0-9636225-4-4

Janet M. Scott and Sheila C. McCeary, Author
Janet Scott, Co-Author
Sheila McCleary, Co-Author

6132 Lexia Learning Systems
PO Box 466
Lincoln, MA 01773-0466
781-259-8752
Fax: 781-259-1349
E-mail: info@lexialearning.com
http://www.lexialearning.com
Reading software and assessment programs for children and adults, professional development programs for teachers, principals and administrators.

6133 LinguiSystems
3100 4th Avenue
East Moline, IL 61244-9700
800-776-4332
Fax: 800-577-4555
E-mail: service@linguisystems.com
http://www.linguisystems.com
Offers tests and print materials for speech language pathologists, teachers of the learning disabled, middle school language arts and reading teachers.

6134 National Study of School Evaluation
1699 E Woodfield Road
Suite 406
Schaumburg, IL 60173-4958
847-995-9080
800-843-6773
Fax: 847-995-9088
E-mail: schoolimprovement@nsse.org
http://www.nsse.org
Provides educational leaders with state-of-the-art assessment and evaluation materials to enhance and promote student growth and school improvement.

Dr. Kathleen A. Fitzpatrick, Executive Director

6135 Testing Miss Malarky
Walker And Company
435 Hudson Street
New York, NY 10014
212-727-8300
800-289-2553
Fax: 212-727-0984
http://www.walkerbooks.com

Author and artist exploit the mania that accompanies the classes first standardized test.
32 pages
ISBN: 0-8027-8737-1
Judy Finchler, Contact

Language Arts

6136 CTB/McGraw-Hill
20 Ryan Ranch Road
Monterey, CA 93940-5703
831-393-0700
800-538-9547
Fax: 800-282-0266
http://www.ctb.com
K-12 achievement tests, early literacy assessment, language proficiency evaluation, adult basic skills tests, and test management and instructional planning software.

6137 SLEP Program Office
PO Box 6155
Princeton, NJ 08541-6155
Offers information on the Secondary Level English Proficiency Test.

Mathematics

6138 Psychological Assessment Resources
PO Box 998
Odessa, FL 33556
800-331-TEST
Fax: 800-727-9329
http://www.parinc.com
Catalog of professional testing resources.

6139 Summing It Up: College Board Mathematics Assessment Programs
College Board Publications
45 Columbus Avenue
New York, NY 10023-6917
212-713-8165
800-323-7155
Fax: 800-525-5562
http://www.collegeboard.org
An overview of SAT I: Reasoning Tests and PSAT/NMSQT, SAT II: Subject Tests, Descriptive Tests of Mathematical Skills (DTMS), CPTs in Mathematics, CLEP Mathematics Examinations, AP Exams in Mathematics, AP Exams in Computer Sciences, and Pacesetter Mathematics.
30 pages

Music & Art

6140 A&F Video's Art Catalog
PO Box 264
Geneseo, NY 14454

http://www.aandfvideo.com
New listing of titles for Art Teachers and Art Lovers.

6141 All Art Supplies
Art Supplies Wholesale
4 Enon Street
North Beverly, MA 01915
800-462-2420
http://www.allartsupplies.com
Art supplies at wholesale prices.

6142 American Art Clay Company
6060 Guion Road
Indianapolis, IN 46254
317-244-6871
800-374-1600
Fax: 317-248-9300

E-mail: catalog@amaco.com
http://www.amaco.com
Provides ceramic materials and equipment.

6143 Arnold Grummer
PO Box 13245
Milwaukee, WI 53213
800-453-1485
Fax: 414-453-1495
E-mail: webmaster@arnoldgrummer.com
http://www.arnoldgrummer.com
Products and information to meet most any papermaking need.

6144 Arrowmont School of Arts & Crafts
556 Parkway
Gainsburg, TN 37738
865-438-5860
Fax: 865-438-4101
http://www.arrowmont.org
The art school of tomorrow.

6145 Art & Creative Materials Institute
PO Box 479
Hanson, MA 02341
781-293-4100
Fax: 781-294-0808
E-mail: debbieg@acminec.org
http://www.acminec.org
A non-profit trade association whose memebers are manufacturers of art and creative materials. Sponsors a certification program to ensure that art materials are non-toxic or affixed with health warning labels where appropriate. Publishes a booklet on the safe use of art materials and a listing of products that are approved under its certification program. Both of these publications are free of charge.

Deborah Fanning, Executive Vice President
Deborah Gustafson, Associate Director

6146 Art Instruction Schools
3309 Broadway Street NW
Minneapolis, MN 55413

http://www.artists-ais.com

6147 Art to Remember
10625 Deme Drive
Unit E
Indianapolis, IN 46236
317-826-0870
800-895-8777
Fax: 317-823-2822
http://www.arttoremember.com
A unique program that encourages your students' artisic creativity while providing an oppurtunity to raise funds for schools.

6148 ArtSketchbook.com
487 Hulsetown Road
Campbell Hall, NY 10916
845-496-4709
http://www.artsketchbook.com
Provides instructions and work examples by an elementary student, secondary student and a professional artist.

6149 Arts Institutes International
Education Management Corporation
300 6th Avenue
Suite 800
Pittsburgh, PA 15222
800-275-2440
Post-secondary career education. Offers associate's, bachelor's and non-degree programs in design, media arts, technology, culinary arts and fashion.

6150 Museum Stamps
PO Box 356
New Canaan, CT 06840
800-659-2787
Fax: 203-966-2729
http://www.museumstamps.com

Rubber stamps of famous works of art, stamp accessories, classroom projects.

6151 Music Ace 2
Harmonic Vision
68 E Wacker Place
8th Floor
Chicago, IL 60610
312-332-9200
800-474-0903
Fax: 312-726-1946
http://www.harmonicvision.com
Introduces concepts such as standard notation, rhythm, melody, time signatures, harmony, intervals and more.

6152 http://www.ilford.com
Ilford
Partners in imaging.

6153 www.schoolrenaissance.com
School Renaissance Model
The School Renaissance Model combines the #1 software in education with professional development and consulting services to help you dramatically improve student performance.

6154 www.speedballart.com
Speedball lesson plans and teaching aids for calligraphy, stamping, printmaking, drawing, painting and more.

Reading

6155 Advantage Learning Systems
2911 Peach Street
PO Box 8036
Wisconsin Rapids, WI 54495-8036
800-338-4204
Fax: 715-424-4242
http://www.advlearn.com
New computer-adaptive tests that assess student reading and math levels in just 15 minutes or less.

6156 Educational Testing Service/Library
Test Collection
Rosedale Road
Princeton, NJ 08541
609-734-5686
Fax: 609-734-5410
Provides information on tests and related materials to those in research and advisory services and educational activities.
Janet Williams, President

6157 National Foundation for Dyslexia
4801 Hermitage Road
Richmond, VA 23227-3332
804-262-0586
800-SOS-READ
Provides screenings for schools or individuals and assists individuals with IEP's. Provides information about support groups and organizations and teacher training workshops.
Jo Powell, Executive Director

6158 Psychological Assessment Resources
PO Box 998
Odessa, FL 33556
800-331-TEST
Fax: 800-727-9329
http://www.parinc.com
Catalog of professional testing resources.

6159 www.schoolrenaissance.com
Renaissance Learning and School
Renaissance Inst.
The School Renaissance Model combines the #1 software in education with professional development and consulting services to help

you dramatically improve student performance.

6160 www.voyagerlearning.com
Voyager Expanded Learning
Improves students performance in reading for those at different grade levels.

Secondary Education

6161 ACT
PO Box 4060
Iowa City, IA 52243-0001
319-337-1000
800-498-6065
Offers a full-service catalog of tests for intermediate and secondary schools organized by assessment, career and educational planning, study skills, surveys and research services.
Catalog

6162 Admission Officer's Handbook for the New SAT Program
College Board Publications
45 Columbus Avenue
New York, NY 10023-6917
212-713-8165
800-323-7155
Fax: 800-525-5562
http://www.collegeboard.org
Designed to help college admission staff quickly find information on the new SAT program, the Handbook has detailed descriptions of score reports and special services for colleges.
56 pages

6163 American College Testing
ACT
2201 Dodge
#168
Iowa City, IA 52243-0001
319-337-1028
Fax: 319-337-1014
E-mail: gullettk@act.org
http://www.act.org
Provides educational assessment services to students and their parents, high schools, colleges and professional associations. Also workforce development services, including a network of ACT Centers and the Workkeys program.
Ken Gullette, Director,Media Relations

6164 College-Bound Seniors
College Board Publications
45 Columbus Avenue
New York, NY 10023-6917
212-713-8165
800-323-7155
Fax: 800-525-5562
http://www.collegeboard.org
Profile of SAT and achievement test takers, national report.
13 pages

6165 CollegeChoice, StudentChoice
College Board Publications
45 Columbus Avenue
New York, NY 10023-6917
212-713-8165
800-323-7155
Fax: 800-525-5562
http://www.collegeboard.org
This video provides a reassuring perspective on the SAT's importance and how the college admission process really works. It shows how SAT scores are only one of many elements in the admission picture and emphasizes academic preparation for college and discusses

the SAT within the context of the entire admission process.
15 Minutes

6166 Counselor's Handbook for the SAT Program
College Board Publications
45 Columbus Avenue
New York, NY 10023-6917
212-713-8165
800-323-7155
Fax: 800-525-5562
http://www.collegeboard.org
Easy-to-use reference provides details on the new SAT program tests and services.
64 pages

6167 Destination College: Planning with the PSAT/NMSQT
College Board Publications
45 Columbus Avenue
New York, NY 10023-6917
212-713-8165
800-323-7155
Fax: 800-525-5562
http://www.collegeboard.org
This new video offers schools an ideal format for explaining the features and benefits of the PSAT/NMSQT Score Report to groups of students.
18 Minutes

6168 Educational Testing Service
Rosedale Road
MS 26-C
Princeton, NJ 08541
609-921-9000
Fax: 609-734-5410
Private educational measurement institution and a leader in educational research.
Susan Keipper, Program Director

6169 Focus on the SAT: What's on it, How to Prepare & What Colleges Look For
College Board Publications
45 Columbus Avenue
New York, NY 10023-6917
212-713-8165
800-323-7155
Fax: 800-525-5562
http://www.collegeboard.org
The authoritative video for students on how to prepare for the SAT and PSAT/NMSQT. It provides test-taking tips, sample test questions, and an explanation of how SAT is developed.
20 Minutes

6170 GED Testing Service
American Council on Education
1 Dupont Cir NW
Washington, DC 20036-1110
202-939-9490
Fax: 202-775-8578
The largest testing service in the United States. Maintains a full line of tests and testing resources for all areas of education and all grade levels K-college level testing.

6171 Guide to the College Board Validity Study Service
College Board Publications
45 Columbus Avenue
New York, NY 10023-6917
212-713-8165
800-323-7155
Fax: 800-525-5562
http://www.collegeboard.org
The purpose of this manual is to assist Validity Study Service users in designing and interpreting validity studies. It provides design suggestions, sample admission and place-

ment studies, advice on interpreting studies, and a discussion of basic statistical concepts.

60 pages

6172 Look Inside the SAT I: Test Prep from the Test Makers Video
College Board Publications
45 Columbus Avenue
New York, NY 10023-6917
212-713-8165
800-323-7155
Fax: 800-525-5562
http://www.collegeboard.org
Brings the College Board's test-taking tips to life through interviews with people from different backgrounds who recount their SAT experiences.

30 Minutes
ISBN: 0-874475-29-5

6173 Master The GMAT
Peterson's, A Nelnet Company
Princeton Pike Corporate Center
2000 Lenox Drive PO Box 67005
Lawrenceville, NJ 08648
609-896-1800
800-338-3282
Fax: 690-896-4531
E-mail: custsvc@petersons.com
http://www.petersons.com
Helps test takers get ready, develop test-preparation strategies and manage test anxiety constructively, whether they have seven weeks to prepare or just one day.

672 pages Book & Disk

Martinson, Author

6174 Master The SAT
Peterson's, A Nelnet Company
Princeton Pike Corporate Center
2000 Lenox Drive PO Box 67005
Lawrenceville, NJ 08648
609-896-1800
800-338-3282
Fax: 609-896-4531
E-mail: custsvc@petersons.com
http://www.petersons.com
Features easily accessible Red Alert sections offering essential tips for test-taking success. Provides students with the critical skills they need to tackle the SAT.

821 pages Book & Disk
ISBN: 1-560796-06-5

John Davenport Carris with Michael R. Crystal, Author

6175 National Center for Fair & Open Testing
342 Broadway
Cambridge, MA 02139-1843
617-864-4810
Fax: 617-497-2224
Dedicated to ensuring that America's students and workers are assessed using fair, accurate, relevant and open tests.

Cinthia Schuman, President

6176 National Study of School Evaluation
1699 E Woodfield Road
Suite 406
Schaumburg, IL 60173-4958
847-995-9080
800-843-6773
Fax: 847-995-9088
E-mail: schoolimprovement@nsse.org
http://www.nsse.org
Provides educational leaders with state-of-the-art assessment and evaluation

materials to enhance and promote student growth and school improvement.

Dr. Kathleen A. Fitzpatrick, Executive Director

6177 Official Guide to the SAT II: Subject Tests
College Board Publications
45 Columbus Avenue
New York, NY 10023-6917
212-713-8165
800-323-7155
Fax: 800-525-5562
http://www.collegeboard.org
The authoritative preparation guide for students taking the SAT II: Subject Tests. The guide includes full-length practice Subject Tests, along with answer sheets, answer keys, and scoring instructions for Writing, Literature, American History, World History, Math I, Math IIC, Biology, Chemistry and Physics. It also includes minitests in French (reading only), German (reading only), Italian, Latin, Modern Hebrew, and Spanish.

380 pages
ISBN: 0-874474-88-4

6178 One-On-One with the SAT
College Board Publications
45 Columbus Avenue
New York, NY 10023-6917
212-713-8165
800-323-7155
Fax: 800-525-5562
http://www.collegeboard.org
Gives students easy access to proven advice and test-taking strategies direct from the test makers, as well as a unique chance to take a real SAT on computer. This program also includes password protection for each student record and toll-free technical support.

Home License

6179 Panic Plan for the SAT
Peterson's, A Nelnet Company
Princeton Pike Corporate Center
2000 Lenox Drive PO Box 67005
Lawrenceville, NJ 08648
609-896-1800
800-338-3282
Fax: 609-896-4531
E-mail: custsvc@petersons.com
http://www.petersons.com
An excellent, two-week review, featuring actual questions from the SAT. Helps students make the most out of the limited time they have left to study.

368 pages
ISBN: 1-560794-32-1

Michael R Crystal, Author

6180 Preventing School Failure
Heldref Publications
1319 Eighteenth Street NW
Washington, DC 20036-1802
202-296-6267
800-365-9753
Fax: 202-296-5149
http://www.heldref.org
The articles cover a broad array of specific topics, from important technical aspects and adaptions of functional behavioral assessment to descriptions of projects in which functional behavioral assessment is being used to provide technical assistance to preschools, schools, and families who must deal eith children and adolescents who present serious challenging behaviors.

Quarterly
ISSN: 1045-988X

Sheldon Braaten, Executive Editor

6181 Psychological Corporation
555 Academic Court
San Antonio, TX 78204-2498
210-921-8701
Assessment materials for teachers in all areas of curricula.

6182 Psychometric Affiliates
PO Box 807
Murfreeboro, TN 37133
615-890-6296
Testing instruments for use by educational institutions.

Jeannette Heritage

6183 Real SAT's
College Board Publications
45 Columbus Avenue
New York, NY 10023-6917
212-713-8165
800-323-7155
Fax: 800-525-5562
http://www.collegeboard.org
The only preparation guide that contains actual scorable tests. It has been developed to help the millions of students taking the tests each year to do their best on the PSAT/NMSQT and SAT and to improve their scores.

396 pages
ISBN: 0-874475-11-2

6184 Registration Bulletin
College Board Publications
45 Columbus Avenue
New York, NY 10023-6917
212-713-8165
800-323-7155
Fax: 800-525-5562
http://www.collegeboard.org
Available in five regional and a New York State edition, the Bulletin provides information on how to register for the SAT I and SAT II, and on how to use the related services.

24 pages

6185 SAT Services for Students with Disabilities
College Board Publications
45 Columbus Avenue
New York, NY 10023-6917
212-713-8165
800-323-7155
Fax: 800-525-5562
http://www.collegeboard.org
Describes arrangements for students with physical, hearing, visual and learning disabilities who wish to take the SAT I and/or SAT II.

6 pages

6186 Scholastic Testing Service
480 Meyer Road
Bensenville, IL 60106-1617
630-766-7150
800-642-6STS
Fax: 630-766-8054
E-mail: stslh25@aol.com
http://www.ststesting.com
Publisher of assessment materials from birth into adulthood, ability and achievement tests for kindergarten through grade twelve. Tests are also constructed on contract for educational agencies and school districts. Publish the Torrance Tests of Creative Thinking, Thinking Creatively in Action and Movement, the STS High School Placement Test and Educational Development Series.

OF Anderhalter, President
John D Kauffman, VP Marketing

6187 TOEFL Test and Score Manual
College Board Publications
45 Columbus Avenue
New York, NY 10023-6917

212-713-8165
800-323-7155
Fax: 800-525-5562
http://www.collegeboard.org
Focuses on information that college admissions officers, foreign student advisers and other users of TOEFL score reports need to know about the operation of the TOEFL program, the test itself, and the interpretation of scores.

48 pages

6188 Taking the SAT I: Reasoning Test
College Board Publications
45 Columbus Avenue
New York, NY 10023-6917
212-713-8165
800-323-7155
Fax: 800-525-5562
http://www.collegeboard.org
A complete guide for students who plan to take the SAT I: Reasoning Test.

80 pages

6189 Taking the SAT II: The Official Guide to the SAT II: Subject Tests
College Board Publications
45 Columbus Avenue
New York, NY 10023-6917
212-713-8165
800-323-7155
Fax: 800-525-5562
http://www.collegeboard.org
Provides information about the content and format of each of the SAT II: Subject Tests, as well as test-taking advice and sample questions.

95 pages

6190 TestSkills
College Board Publications
45 Columbus Avenue
New York, NY 10023-6917
212-713-8165
800-323-7155
Fax: 800-525-5562
http://www.collegeboard.org
A preparation program for the PSAT/NMSQT that helps students, particularly those from minority and disadvantaged groups, sharpen skills and increase confidence needed to succeed on the tests.

Spiral-Bound

6191 Think Before You Punch: Using Calculators on the New SAT I and PSAT/NMSQT
College Board Publications
45 Columbus Avenue
New York, NY 10023-6917
212-713-8165
800-323-7155
Fax: 800-525-5562
http://www.collegeboard.org
This video looks at the pros and cons of calculators usage on a test. In it, students talk about using them, and College Board and ETS staff explain the new calculator policy. It works through math questions that may or may not best be answered with the help of a calculator.

12 Minutes

NATIONAL & STATE STATISTICS

Percentage of persons age 25 and over and 25 to 29, by race/ethnicity, years of school completed, and sex: Selected years, 1910 through 2009

Age, year, and sex	Total			White[1]			Black[1]			Hispanic		
	Less than 5 years of elementary school	High school completion or higher[2]	Bachelor's or higher degree[3]	Less than 5 years of elementary school	High school completion or higher[2]	Bachelor's or higher degree[3]	Less than 5 years of elementary school	High school completion or higher[2]	Bachelor's or higher degree[3]	Less than 5 years of elementary school	High school completion or higher[2]	Bachelor's or higher degree[3]
1	2	3	4	5	6	7	8	9	10	11	12	13
Total, 25 and over												
1910[4]	23.8 (—)	13.5 (—)	2.7 (—)	— (†)	— (†)	— (†)	— (†)	— (†)	— (†)	— (†)	— (†)	— (†)
1920[4]	22.0 (—)	16.4 (—)	3.3 (—)	— (†)	— (†)	— (†)	— (†)	— (†)	— (†)	— (†)	— (†)	— (†)
1930[4]	17.5 (—)	19.1 (—)	3.9 (—)	— (†)	— (†)	— (†)	— (†)	— (†)	— (†)	— (†)	— (†)	— (†)
April 1940	13.7 (—)	24.5 (—)	4.6 (—)	10.9 (—)	26.1 (—)	4.9 (—)	41.8 (—)	7.7 (—)	1.3 (—)	— (†)	— (†)	— (†)
April 1950	11.1 (—)	34.3 (—)	6.2 (—)	8.9 (—)	36.4 (—)	6.6 (—)	32.6 (—)	13.7 (—)	2.2 (—)	— (†)	— (†)	— (†)
April 1960	8.3 (—)	41.1 (—)	7.7 (—)	6.7 (—)	43.2 (—)	8.1 (—)	23.5 (—)	21.7 (—)	3.5 (—)	— (†)	— (†)	— (†)
March 1970	5.3 (—)	55.2 (—)	11.0 (—)	4.2 (—)	57.4 (—)	11.6 (—)	14.7 (—)	36.1 (—)	6.1 (—)	— (†)	— (†)	— (†)
March 1975	4.2 (—)	62.5 (—)	13.9 (—)	2.6 (—)	65.8 (—)	14.9 (—)	12.3 (—)	42.6 (—)	6.4 (—)	18.2 (—)	38.5 (—)	6.6 (—)
March 1980	3.4 (0.08)	68.6 (0.20)	17.0 (0.16)	1.9 (0.07)	71.9 (0.21)	18.4 (0.18)	9.1 (0.47)	51.4 (0.81)	7.9 (0.44)	15.8 (0.87)	44.5 (1.18)	7.6 (0.63)
March 1985	2.7 (0.07)	73.9 (0.18)	19.4 (0.16)	1.4 (0.05)	77.5 (0.19)	20.8 (0.19)	6.1 (0.36)	59.9 (0.74)	11.1 (0.47)	13.5 (0.68)	47.9 (0.99)	8.5 (0.55)
March 1986	2.7 (0.07)	74.7 (0.18)	19.4 (0.16)	1.4 (0.05)	78.2 (0.19)	20.9 (0.19)	5.3 (0.33)	62.5 (0.72)	10.9 (0.47)	12.9 (0.64)	48.5 (0.96)	8.4 (0.53)
March 1987	2.4 (0.06)	75.6 (0.17)	19.9 (0.16)	1.3 (0.05)	79.0 (0.18)	21.4 (0.19)	4.9 (0.32)	63.6 (0.71)	10.8 (0.46)	11.9 (0.61)	50.9 (0.94)	8.6 (0.53)
March 1988	2.4 (0.06)	76.2 (0.17)	20.3 (0.16)	1.2 (0.05)	79.8 (0.18)	21.8 (0.19)	4.8 (0.31)	63.5 (0.70)	11.2 (0.46)	12.2 (0.60)	51.0 (0.92)	10.0 (0.55)
March 1989	2.5 (0.06)	76.9 (0.17)	21.1 (0.16)	1.2 (0.05)	80.7 (0.18)	22.8 (0.19)	5.2 (0.32)	64.7 (0.69)	11.7 (0.46)	12.2 (0.58)	50.9 (0.89)	9.9 (0.53)
March 1990	2.4 (0.06)	77.6 (0.17)	21.3 (0.16)	1.1 (0.05)	81.4 (0.17)	23.1 (0.19)	5.1 (0.31)	66.2 (0.67)	11.3 (0.45)	12.3 (0.58)	50.8 (0.88)	9.2 (0.51)
March 1991	2.4 (0.06)	78.4 (0.16)	21.4 (0.16)	1.1 (0.05)	82.4 (0.17)	23.3 (0.19)	4.7 (0.30)	66.8 (0.66)	11.5 (0.45)	12.5 (0.57)	51.3 (0.86)	9.7 (0.51)
March 1992	2.1 (0.06)	79.4 (0.16)	21.4 (0.16)	0.9 (0.04)	83.4 (0.16)	23.2 (0.19)	3.9 (0.27)	67.7 (0.65)	11.9 (0.45)	11.8 (0.55)	52.6 (0.85)	9.3 (0.49)
March 1993	2.1 (0.06)	80.2 (0.16)	21.9 (0.16)	0.8 (0.04)	84.1 (0.16)	23.8 (0.19)	3.7 (0.26)	70.5 (0.63)	12.2 (0.45)	11.8 (0.54)	53.1 (0.83)	9.0 (0.48)
March 1994	1.9 (0.05)	80.9 (0.15)	22.2 (0.16)	0.8 (0.04)	84.9 (0.16)	24.3 (0.19)	2.7 (0.22)	73.0 (0.61)	12.9 (0.46)	10.8 (0.48)	53.3 (0.79)	9.1 (0.45)
March 1995	1.8 (0.05)	81.7 (0.15)	23.0 (0.16)	0.7 (0.04)	85.9 (0.16)	25.4 (0.19)	2.5 (0.21)	73.8 (0.61)	13.3 (0.47)	10.6 (0.48)	53.4 (0.78)	9.3 (0.45)
March 1996	1.8 (0.05)	81.7 (0.16)	23.6 (0.17)	0.6 (0.04)	86.0 (0.16)	25.9 (0.20)	2.2 (0.18)	74.6 (0.53)	13.8 (0.42)	10.3 (0.42)	53.1 (0.68)	9.3 (0.40)
March 1997	1.7 (0.05)	82.1 (0.14)	23.9 (0.16)	0.6 (0.03)	86.3 (0.15)	26.2 (0.19)	2.0 (0.17)	75.3 (0.52)	13.3 (0.41)	9.4 (0.32)	54.7 (0.54)	10.3 (0.33)
March 1998	1.6 (0.05)	82.8 (0.14)	24.4 (0.16)	0.6 (0.03)	87.1 (0.14)	26.6 (0.19)	1.7 (0.15)	76.4 (0.50)	14.8 (0.42)	9.3 (0.31)	55.5 (0.53)	11.0 (0.33)
March 1999	1.6 (0.05)	83.4 (0.14)	25.2 (0.16)	0.6 (0.03)	87.7 (0.14)	27.7 (0.19)	1.7 (0.15)	77.4 (0.49)	15.5 (0.43)	9.0 (0.30)	56.1 (0.52)	10.9 (0.33)
March 2000	1.6 (0.05)	84.1 (0.13)	25.6 (0.16)	0.5 (0.03)	88.4 (0.14)	28.1 (0.19)	1.6 (0.15)	78.9 (0.48)	16.6 (0.44)	8.7 (0.29)	57.0 (0.51)	10.6 (0.32)
March 2001	1.6 (0.05)	84.3 (0.13)	26.1 (0.16)	0.5 (0.03)	88.7 (0.13)	28.6 (0.19)	1.3 (0.13)	79.5 (0.47)	16.1 (0.43)	9.3 (0.29)	56.5 (0.50)	11.2 (0.32)
March 2002	1.6 (0.03)	84.1 (0.09)	26.7 (0.11)	0.5 (0.02)	88.7 (0.10)	29.4 (0.14)	1.6 (0.11)	79.2 (0.34)	17.2 (0.31)	8.7 (0.19)	57.0 (0.34)	11.1 (0.21)
March 2003	1.6 (0.03)	84.6 (0.09)	27.2 (0.11)	0.5 (0.02)	89.4 (0.09)	30.0 (0.14)	1.5 (0.10)	80.3 (0.33)	17.4 (0.31)	8.2 (0.18)	57.0 (0.33)	11.4 (0.21)
March 2004	1.5 (0.03)	85.2 (0.09)	27.7 (0.11)	0.4 (0.02)	90.0 (0.09)	30.6 (0.14)	1.3 (0.09)	81.1 (0.32)	17.7 (0.31)	8.1 (0.18)	58.4 (0.32)	12.1 (0.21)
March 2005	1.6 (0.03)	85.2 (0.09)	27.6 (0.11)	0.5 (0.02)	90.1 (0.09)	30.5 (0.14)	1.5 (0.10)	81.5 (0.32)	17.7 (0.31)	7.9 (0.17)	58.5 (0.32)	12.0 (0.21)
March 2006	1.5 (0.03)	85.5 (0.09)	28.0 (0.11)	0.4 (0.02)	90.5 (0.09)	31.0 (0.14)	1.5 (0.10)	81.2 (0.32)	18.6 (0.31)	7.6 (0.17)	59.3 (0.31)	12.4 (0.21)
March 2007	1.5 (0.03)	85.7 (0.09)	28.7 (0.11)	0.4 (0.02)	90.6 (0.09)	31.8 (0.14)	1.2 (0.09)	82.8 (0.30)	18.7 (0.31)	6.9 (0.16)	60.3 (0.30)	12.7 (0.20)
March 2008	1.3 (0.03)	86.6 (0.08)	29.4 (0.11)	0.4 (0.02)	91.5 (0.08)	32.6 (0.14)	1.0 (0.08)	83.3 (0.30)	19.7 (0.32)	6.3 (0.15)	62.3 (0.29)	13.3 (0.21)
March 2009	1.4 (0.03)	86.7 (0.08)	29.5 (0.11)	0.4 (0.02)	91.6 (0.08)	32.9 (0.14)	1.1 (0.08)	84.2 (0.29)	19.4 (0.31)	6.6 (0.15)	61.9 (0.29)	13.2 (0.20)
Total, 25 to 29												
1920[4]	— (†)	— (†)	— (†)	12.9 (—)	22.0 (—)	4.5 (—)	44.6 (—)	6.3 (—)	1.2 (—)	— (†)	— (†)	— (†)
April 1940	5.9 (—)	38.1 (—)	5.9 (—)	3.4 (—)	41.2 (—)	6.4 (—)	27.0 (—)	12.3 (—)	1.6 (—)	— (†)	— (†)	— (†)
April 1950	4.6 (—)	52.8 (—)	7.7 (—)	3.3 (—)	56.3 (—)	8.2 (—)	16.1 (—)	23.6 (—)	2.8 (—)	— (†)	— (†)	— (†)
April 1960	2.8 (—)	60.7 (—)	11.0 (—)	2.2 (—)	63.7 (—)	11.8 (—)	7.2 (—)	38.6 (—)	5.4 (—)	— (†)	— (†)	— (†)
March 1970	1.1 (—)	75.4 (—)	16.4 (—)	0.9 (—)	77.8 (—)	17.3 (—)	2.2 (—)	58.4 (—)	10.0 (—)	— (†)	— (†)	— (†)
March 1975	1.0 (—)	83.1 (—)	21.9 (—)	0.6 (—)	86.6 (—)	23.8 (—)	0.5 (—)	71.1 (—)	10.5 (—)	8.0 (—)	53.1 (—)	8.8 (—)
March 1980	0.8 (0.10)	85.4 (0.40)	22.5 (0.47)	0.3 (0.07)	89.2 (0.40)	25.0 (0.55)	0.6 (0.31)	76.7 (1.64)	11.6 (1.24)	6.7 (1.31)	58.0 (2.59)	7.7 (1.39)
March 1985	0.7 (0.09)	86.1 (0.37)	22.2 (0.45)	0.2 (0.06)	89.5 (0.38)	24.4 (0.53)	0.4 (0.23)	80.5 (1.42)	11.6 (1.15)	6.0 (1.05)	60.9 (2.17)	11.1 (1.39)
March 1986	0.9 (0.10)	86.1 (0.37)	22.4 (0.45)	0.4 (0.07)	89.6 (0.37)	25.2 (0.53)	0.5 (0.26)	83.5 (1.32)	11.8 (1.15)	5.6 (0.97)	59.1 (2.07)	9.0 (1.21)
March 1987	0.9 (0.10)	86.0 (0.37)	22.0 (0.44)	0.4 (0.08)	89.4 (0.38)	24.6 (0.53)	0.4 (0.23)	83.4 (1.32)	11.5 (1.13)	4.8 (0.88)	59.8 (2.04)	8.7 (1.17)
March 1988	1.0 (0.11)	85.9 (0.37)	22.7 (0.45)	0.3 (0.07)	89.7 (0.38)	25.1 (0.54)	0.3 (0.21)	80.9 (1.39)	12.0 (1.15)	6.0 (0.96)	62.3 (1.96)	11.3 (1.28)
March 1989	1.0 (0.11)	85.5 (0.38)	23.4 (0.45)	0.3 (0.07)	89.3 (0.38)	26.3 (0.55)	0.5 (0.26)	82.3 (1.35)	12.6 (1.17)	5.4 (0.89)	61.0 (1.92)	10.1 (1.19)
March 1990	1.2 (0.12)	85.7 (0.38)	23.2 (0.46)	0.3 (0.07)	90.1 (0.37)	26.4 (0.55)	1.0 (0.36)	81.7 (1.37)	13.4 (1.20)	7.3 (1.02)	58.2 (1.94)	8.1 (1.07)
March 1991	1.0 (0.11)	85.4 (0.39)	23.2 (0.46)	0.4 (0.08)	89.8 (0.39)	26.7 (0.56)	0.5 (0.26)	81.8 (1.36)	11.0 (1.10)	5.8 (0.93)	56.7 (1.96)	9.2 (1.15)
March 1992	0.9 (0.10)	86.3 (0.38)	23.6 (0.47)	0.3 (0.07)	90.7 (0.38)	27.2 (0.58)	0.8 (0.32)	80.9 (1.41)	11.0 (1.12)	5.2 (0.88)	60.9 (1.93)	9.5 (1.16)
March 1993	0.7 (0.09)	86.7 (0.38)	23.7 (0.48)	0.3 (0.07)	91.2 (0.37)	27.2 (0.59)	0.2 (0.18)	82.6 (1.36)	13.3 (1.22)	4.0 (0.76)	60.9 (1.90)	8.3 (1.08)
March 1994	0.8 (0.10)	86.1 (0.39)	23.3 (0.47)	0.2 (0.07)	91.1 (0.38)	27.1 (0.60)	0.6 (0.28)	84.1 (1.31)	13.6 (1.23)	3.6 (0.66)	60.3 (1.75)	8.0 (0.97)
March 1995	0.9 (0.11)	86.8 (0.39)	24.7 (0.49)	0.3 (0.08)	92.5 (0.36)	28.8 (0.62)	0.2 (0.17)	86.7 (1.23)	15.4 (1.31)	4.9 (0.79)	57.1 (1.76)	8.9 (1.04)
March 1996	0.8 (0.11)	87.3 (0.40)	27.1 (0.53)	0.2 (0.07)	92.6 (0.38)	31.6 (0.67)	0.4 (0.20)	86.0 (1.14)	14.6 (1.16)	4.3 (0.65)	61.1 (1.58)	10.0 (0.97)
March 1997	0.8 (0.10)	87.4 (0.37)	27.8 (0.50)	0.1 (0.05)	92.9 (0.35)	32.6 (0.63)	0.6 (0.25)	86.9 (1.10)	14.2 (1.14)	4.2 (0.51)	61.8 (1.24)	11.0 (0.80)
March 1998	0.7 (0.09)	88.1 (0.36)	27.3 (0.50)	0.1 (0.05)	93.6 (0.34)	32.3 (0.64)	0.4 (0.21)	88.2 (1.04)	15.8 (1.18)	3.7 (0.48)	62.8 (1.23)	10.4 (0.78)
March 1999	0.6 (0.09)	87.8 (0.37)	28.2 (0.51)	0.1 (0.05)	93.0 (0.35)	33.6 (0.66)	0.2 (0.15)	88.7 (1.03)	15.0 (1.16)	3.2 (0.45)	61.6 (1.26)	8.9 (0.74)
March 2000	0.7 (0.09)	88.1 (0.37)	29.1 (0.52)	0.1 (0.04)	94.0 (0.33)	34.0 (0.67)	# (†)	86.8 (1.13)	17.8 (1.28)	3.8 (0.48)	62.8 (1.22)	9.7 (0.75)
March 2001	0.8 (0.11)	87.7 (0.38)	28.6 (0.52)	0.2 (0.06)	93.3 (0.36)	33.0 (0.68)	0.1 (0.10)	87.0 (1.11)	17.8 (1.27)	4.7 (0.54)	63.2 (1.23)	11.1 (0.80)
March 2002	1.1 (0.08)	86.4 (0.28)	29.3 (0.37)	0.1 (0.04)	93.0 (0.26)	35.9 (0.50)	0.6 (0.19)	87.6 (0.80)	18.0 (0.94)	4.7 (0.34)	62.4 (0.78)	8.9 (0.46)
March 2003	1.0 (0.08)	86.5 (0.27)	28.4 (0.36)	0.2 (0.04)	93.7 (0.25)	34.2 (0.49)	0.6 (0.19)	88.5 (0.78)	17.5 (0.93)	4.0 (0.30)	61.7 (0.75)	10.0 (0.47)
March 2004	1.1 (0.08)	86.6 (0.27)	28.7 (0.36)	0.3 (0.05)	93.3 (0.26)	34.5 (0.49)	0.3 (0.13)	88.7 (0.76)	17.1 (0.90)	4.1 (0.31)	62.4 (0.75)	10.9 (0.48)
March 2005	1.0 (0.08)	86.1 (0.27)	28.6 (0.36)	0.3 (0.05)	92.8 (0.26)	34.1 (0.48)	0.4 (0.15)	86.9 (0.79)	17.5 (0.89)	3.6 (0.28)	63.3 (0.74)	11.2 (0.48)

See notes at end of table.

Percentage of persons age 25 and over and 25 to 29, by race/ethnicity, years of school completed, and sex: Selected years, 1910 through 2009—Continued

Age, year, and sex	Total			White[1]			Black[1]			Hispanic		
	Less than 5 years of elementary school	High school completion or higher[2]	Bachelor's or higher degree[3]	Less than 5 years of elementary school	High school completion or higher[2]	Bachelor's or higher degree[3]	Less than 5 years of elementary school	High school completion or higher[2]	Bachelor's or higher degree[3]	Less than 5 years of elementary school	High school completion or higher[2]	Bachelor's or higher degree[3]
1	2	3	4	5	6	7	8	9	10	11	12	13
March 2006.....	0.9 (0.07)	86.4 (0.27)	28.4 (0.35)	0.2 (0.04)	93.4 (0.25)	34.3 (0.48)	0.4 (0.14)	86.3 (0.79)	18.7 (0.90)	3.5 (0.28)	63.2 (0.72)	9.5 (0.44)
March 2007.....	1.0 (0.08)	87.0 (0.26)	29.6 (0.35)	0.2 (0.04)	93.5 (0.25)	35.5 (0.47)	0.2 (0.11)	87.7 (0.75)	19.5 (0.90)	3.9 (0.29)	65.0 (0.71)	11.6 (0.47)
March 2008.....	0.6 (0.06)	87.8 (0.25)	30.8 (0.35)	0.1 (0.03)	93.7 (0.24)	37.1 (0.47)	0.3 (0.12)	87.5 (0.74)	20.4 (0.91)	2.5 (0.23)	68.3 (0.68)	12.4 (0.48)
March 2009.....	0.6 (0.06)	88.6 (0.24)	30.6 (0.35)	0.1 (0.03)	94.6 (0.22)	37.2 (0.47)	0.3 (0.13)	88.9 (0.70)	18.9 (0.87)	2.6 (0.23)	68.9 (0.68)	12.2 (0.48)
Males, 25 and over												
April 1940	15.1 (—)	22.7 (—)	5.5 (—)	12.0 (—)	24.2 (—)	5.9 (—)	46.2 (—)	6.9 (—)	1.4 (—)	— (†)	— (†)	— (†)
April 1950	12.2 (—)	32.6 (—)	7.3 (—)	9.8 (—)	34.6 (—)	7.9 (—)	36.9 (—)	12.6 (—)	2.1 (—)	— (†)	— (†)	— (†)
April 1960	9.4 (—)	39.5 (—)	9.7 (—)	7.4 (—)	41.6 (—)	10.3 (—)	27.7 (—)	20.0 (—)	3.5 (—)	— (†)	— (†)	— (†)
March 1970.....	5.9 (—)	55.0 (—)	14.1 (—)	4.5 (—)	57.2 (—)	15.0 (—)	17.9 (—)	35.4 (—)	6.8 (—)	— (†)	— (†)	— (†)
March 1980.....	3.6 (0.12)	69.2 (0.30)	20.9 (0.26)	2.0 (0.10)	72.4 (0.31)	22.8 (0.29)	11.3 (0.78)	51.2 (1.23)	7.7 (0.66)	16.5 (1.30)	44.9 (1.74)	9.2 (1.01)
March 1990.....	2.7 (0.09)	77.7 (0.24)	24.4 (0.25)	1.3 (0.07)	81.6 (0.25)	26.7 (0.29)	6.4 (0.53)	65.8 (1.03)	11.9 (0.70)	12.9 (0.85)	50.3 (1.27)	9.8 (0.76)
March 1995.....	2.0 (0.08)	81.7 (0.22)	26.0 (0.25)	0.8 (0.06)	86.0 (0.22)	28.9 (0.29)	3.4 (0.37)	73.5 (0.91)	13.7 (0.71)	10.8 (0.69)	52.9 (1.11)	10.1 (0.67)
March 1996.....	1.9 (0.08)	81.9 (0.23)	26.0 (0.26)	0.7 (0.06)	86.1 (0.21)	28.8 (0.30)	2.9 (0.31)	74.6 (0.80)	12.5 (0.61)	10.1 (0.59)	53.0 (0.97)	10.3 (0.59)
March 1997.....	1.8 (0.07)	82.0 (0.21)	26.2 (0.24)	0.6 (0.05)	86.3 (0.21)	29.0 (0.28)	2.9 (0.30)	73.8 (0.79)	12.5 (0.60)	9.2 (0.44)	54.9 (0.76)	10.6 (0.47)
March 1998.....	1.7 (0.07)	82.8 (0.20)	26.5 (0.24)	0.7 (0.05)	87.1 (0.21)	29.3 (0.28)	2.3 (0.27)	75.4 (0.77)	14.0 (0.62)	9.3 (0.44)	55.7 (0.74)	11.1 (0.47)
March 1999.....	1.6 (0.07)	83.4 (0.20)	27.5 (0.24)	0.6 (0.05)	87.7 (0.20)	30.6 (0.28)	2.0 (0.25)	77.2 (0.74)	14.3 (0.62)	9.0 (0.43)	56.0 (0.75)	10.7 (0.46)
March 2000.....	1.6 (0.07)	84.2 (0.19)	27.8 (0.24)	0.6 (0.05)	88.5 (0.20)	30.8 (0.28)	2.1 (0.25)	79.1 (0.72)	16.4 (0.65)	8.2 (0.40)	56.6 (0.73)	10.7 (0.45)
March 2001.....	1.6 (0.07)	84.4 (0.19)	28.0 (0.24)	0.6 (0.05)	88.6 (0.19)	30.9 (0.28)	1.7 (0.22)	80.6 (0.69)	15.9 (0.64)	9.4 (0.42)	55.6 (0.72)	11.1 (0.45)
March 2002.....	1.7 (0.05)	83.8 (0.14)	28.5 (0.17)	0.5 (0.03)	88.5 (0.14)	31.7 (0.20)	1.9 (0.17)	79.0 (0.51)	16.5 (0.47)	9.0 (0.28)	56.1 (0.48)	11.0 (0.30)
March 2003.....	1.7 (0.05)	84.1 (0.13)	28.9 (0.17)	0.5 (0.03)	89.0 (0.14)	32.3 (0.20)	1.9 (0.17)	79.9 (0.50)	16.8 (0.47)	8.3 (0.26)	56.3 (0.46)	11.2 (0.29)
March 2004.....	1.7 (0.05)	84.8 (0.13)	29.4 (0.17)	0.5 (0.03)	89.9 (0.13)	32.9 (0.20)	1.5 (0.15)	80.8 (0.49)	16.6 (0.46)	8.4 (0.25)	57.3 (0.45)	11.8 (0.30)
March 2005.....	1.7 (0.05)	84.9 (0.13)	28.9 (0.17)	0.5 (0.03)	89.9 (0.13)	32.3 (0.20)	1.7 (0.16)	81.4 (0.48)	16.1 (0.45)	8.0 (0.24)	58.0 (0.44)	11.8 (0.29)
March 2006.....	1.6 (0.05)	85.0 (0.13)	29.2 (0.16)	0.4 (0.03)	90.2 (0.13)	32.8 (0.20)	1.7 (0.16)	80.7 (0.48)	17.5 (0.46)	7.8 (0.23)	58.5 (0.43)	11.9 (0.28)
March 2007.....	1.6 (0.04)	85.0 (0.13)	29.5 (0.16)	0.4 (0.03)	90.2 (0.13)	33.2 (0.20)	1.3 (0.14)	82.5 (0.46)	18.1 (0.47)	7.3 (0.22)	58.2 (0.42)	11.8 (0.28)
March 2008.....	1.4 (0.04)	85.9 (0.12)	30.1 (0.16)	0.4 (0.03)	91.1 (0.12)	33.8 (0.20)	1.1 (0.12)	82.1 (0.46)	18.7 (0.47)	6.5 (0.21)	60.9 (0.41)	12.6 (0.28)
March 2009.....	1.4 (0.04)	86.2 (0.12)	30.1 (0.16)	0.4 (0.03)	91.4 (0.12)	33.9 (0.20)	1.2 (0.13)	84.2 (0.43)	17.9 (0.45)	6.6 (0.21)	60.6 (0.41)	12.5 (0.27)
Females, 25 and over												
April 1940	12.4 (—)	26.3 (—)	3.8 (—)	9.8 (—)	28.1 (—)	4.0 (—)	37.5 (—)	8.4 (—)	1.2 (—)	— (†)	— (†)	— (†)
April 1950	10.0 (—)	36.0 (—)	5.2 (—)	8.1 (—)	38.2 (—)	5.4 (—)	28.6 (—)	14.7 (—)	2.4 (—)	— (†)	— (†)	— (†)
April 1960	7.4 (—)	42.5 (—)	5.8 (—)	6.0 (—)	44.7 (—)	6.0 (—)	19.7 (—)	23.1 (—)	3.6 (—)	— (†)	— (†)	— (†)
March 1970.....	4.7 (—)	55.4 (—)	8.2 (—)	3.9 (—)	57.7 (—)	8.6 (—)	11.9 (—)	36.6 (—)	5.6 (—)	— (†)	— (†)	— (†)
March 1980.....	3.2 (0.11)	68.1 (0.28)	13.6 (0.21)	1.8 (0.09)	71.5 (0.30)	14.4 (0.23)	7.4 (0.58)	51.5 (1.10)	8.1 (0.60)	15.3 (1.20)	44.2 (1.66)	6.2 (0.80)
March 1990.....	2.2 (0.08)	77.5 (0.23)	18.4 (0.22)	1.0 (0.06)	81.3 (0.24)	19.8 (0.25)	4.0 (0.38)	66.5 (0.92)	10.8 (0.60)	11.7 (0.81)	51.3 (1.25)	8.7 (0.70)
March 1995.....	1.7 (0.07)	81.6 (0.21)	20.2 (0.22)	0.6 (0.05)	85.8 (0.22)	22.1 (0.26)	1.7 (0.24)	74.1 (0.81)	13.0 (0.62)	10.4 (0.67)	53.8 (1.09)	8.4 (0.61)
March 1996.....	1.7 (0.07)	81.6 (0.22)	21.4 (0.23)	0.5 (0.05)	85.9 (0.22)	23.2 (0.27)	1.6 (0.21)	74.6 (0.71)	14.8 (0.58)	10.5 (0.59)	53.3 (0.97)	8.3 (0.53)
March 1997.....	1.6 (0.06)	82.2 (0.20)	21.7 (0.21)	0.5 (0.04)	86.3 (0.20)	23.7 (0.25)	1.3 (0.18)	76.5 (0.68)	14.0 (0.56)	9.5 (0.45)	54.6 (0.76)	10.1 (0.46)
March 1998.....	1.6 (0.06)	82.9 (0.19)	22.4 (0.21)	0.6 (0.04)	87.1 (0.20)	24.1 (0.25)	1.2 (0.17)	77.1 (0.67)	15.4 (0.58)	9.2 (0.44)	55.3 (0.75)	10.9 (0.47)
March 1999.....	1.5 (0.06)	83.3 (0.19)	23.1 (0.22)	0.5 (0.04)	87.6 (0.19)	25.0 (0.26)	1.5 (0.19)	77.5 (0.66)	16.5 (0.59)	9.0 (0.42)	56.3 (0.73)	11.0 (0.46)
March 2000.....	1.5 (0.06)	84.0 (0.19)	23.6 (0.22)	0.4 (0.04)	88.4 (0.19)	25.5 (0.26)	1.1 (0.17)	78.7 (0.64)	16.8 (0.59)	9.3 (0.42)	57.5 (0.71)	10.6 (0.44)
March 2001.....	1.5 (0.06)	84.2 (0.18)	24.3 (0.22)	0.4 (0.04)	88.8 (0.19)	26.5 (0.26)	1.0 (0.16)	78.6 (0.64)	16.3 (0.58)	9.1 (0.41)	57.4 (0.70)	11.3 (0.45)
March 2002.....	1.5 (0.04)	84.4 (0.13)	25.1 (0.15)	0.5 (0.03)	88.9 (0.13)	27.3 (0.19)	1.4 (0.13)	79.4 (0.45)	17.7 (0.42)	8.3 (0.27)	57.9 (0.48)	11.2 (0.31)
March 2003.....	1.5 (0.04)	85.0 (0.13)	25.7 (0.15)	0.4 (0.03)	89.7 (0.13)	27.9 (0.19)	1.2 (0.12)	80.7 (0.44)	18.0 (0.43)	8.1 (0.26)	57.8 (0.46)	11.6 (0.30)
March 2004.....	1.4 (0.04)	85.4 (0.12)	26.1 (0.15)	0.4 (0.02)	90.1 (0.12)	28.4 (0.19)	1.1 (0.12)	81.2 (0.43)	18.5 (0.43)	7.8 (0.25)	59.5 (0.46)	12.3 (0.31)
March 2005.....	1.5 (0.04)	85.4 (0.12)	26.5 (0.15)	0.4 (0.03)	90.3 (0.12)	28.9 (0.19)	1.3 (0.12)	81.5 (0.42)	18.9 (0.43)	7.8 (0.25)	58.9 (0.45)	12.1 (0.30)
March 2006.....	1.5 (0.04)	85.9 (0.12)	26.9 (0.16)	0.4 (0.03)	90.8 (0.12)	29.3 (0.19)	1.3 (0.12)	81.5 (0.42)	19.5 (0.43)	7.4 (0.23)	60.1 (0.44)	12.9 (0.30)
March 2007.....	1.4 (0.04)	86.4 (0.12)	28.0 (0.16)	0.4 (0.03)	91.0 (0.12)	30.6 (0.19)	1.1 (0.11)	83.0 (0.40)	19.2 (0.42)	6.6 (0.22)	62.5 (0.43)	13.7 (0.30)
March 2008.....	1.3 (0.04)	87.2 (0.11)	28.8 (0.16)	0.4 (0.02)	91.8 (0.11)	31.5 (0.19)	1.0 (0.10)	84.2 (0.39)	20.5 (0.43)	6.1 (0.21)	63.7 (0.42)	14.1 (0.30)
March 2009.....	1.4 (0.04)	87.1 (0.11)	29.1 (0.16)	0.4 (0.02)	91.9 (0.11)	31.9 (0.19)	1.0 (0.10)	84.2 (0.39)	20.6 (0.43)	6.7 (0.21)	63.3 (0.41)	14.0 (0.30)

—Not available.
†Not applicable.
#Rounds to zero.
[1]Includes persons of Hispanic ethnicity for years prior to 1980.
[2]Data for years prior to 1993 are for persons with 4 or more years of high school. Data for later years are for high school completers—i.e., those persons who graduated from high school with a diploma, as well as those who completed high school through equivalency programs, such as a GED program.
[3]Data for years prior to 1993 are for persons with 4 or more years of college.

[4]Estimates based on Census Bureau reverse projection of 1940 census data on education by age.
NOTE: Totals include other racial/ethnic groups not separately shown. Race categories exclude persons of Hispanic ethnicity except where otherwise noted. Standard errors appear in parentheses.
SOURCE: U.S. Department of Commerce, Census Bureau, *U.S. Census of Population: 1960,* Vol. I, Part 1; 1960 Census Monograph, *Education of the American Population,* by John K. Folger and Charles B. Nam; Current Population Reports, Series P-20; various years; and Current Population Survey (CPS), March 1970 through March 2009. (This table was prepared September 2009.)

Number of persons age 18 and over, by highest level of education attained, age, sex, and race/ethnicity: 2009
[In thousands]

Age, sex, and race/ethnicity	Total	Elementary — Less than 7 years	Elementary — 7 or 8 years	High school — 1 to 3 years	High school — 4 years	High school — Completion	College — Some college	College — Associate's degree	College — Bachelor's degree	College — Master's degree	College — Professional degree	College — Doctor's degree
1	2	3	4	5	6	7	8	9	10	11	12	13
Total, 18 and over	226,973	6,634	4,766	17,265	3,323	70,044 (244.8)	44,241	19,303	40,276 (201.2)	15,260 (131.3)	3,236	2,624
18 and 19 years old	8,056	56	79	2,533	561	2,257 (51.9)	2,504	46	16 (4.4)	‡ (†)	5	‡
20 to 24 years old	20,632	246	190	1,517	391	6,161 (85.1)	7,905	1,420	2,625 (56.0)	142 (13.1)	25	10
25 years old and over	198,285	6,332	4,496	13,216	2,371	61,626 (235.2)	33,832	17,838	37,635 (195.7)	15,118 (130.7)	3,206	2,614
25 to 29 years old	21,256	444	282	1,411	282	6,113 (84.8)	4,361	1,856	4,927 (76.3)	1,258 (38.9)	204	117
30 to 34 years old	19,264	555	265	1,246	263	5,239 (78.6)	3,422	1,770	4,314 (71.5)	1,622 (44.1)	341	228
35 to 39 years old	20,445	664	283	1,247	251	5,506 (80.6)	3,472	2,086	4,487 (72.9)	1,754 (45.8)	403	290
40 to 49 years old	43,589	1,102	688	2,494	563	13,684 (124.8)	7,211	4,556	8,716 (100.7)	3,261 (62.3)	684	630
50 to 59 years old	40,409	1,092	588	2,281	463	12,621 (120.1)	7,118	4,176	7,448 (93.3)	3,377 (63.4)	691	554
60 to 64 years old	15,534	466	351	801	142	4,681 (74.4)	2,695	1,323	2,908 (58.9)	1,579 (43.5)	311	278
65 years old and over	37,788	2,007	2,039	3,737	407	13,782 (125.2)	5,553	2,071	4,836 (75.6)	2,268 (52.1)	573	516
Males, 18 and over	110,026	3,375	2,383	8,774	1,764	34,710 (189.3)	20,954	8,180	19,205 (146.0)	7,061 (90.9)	1,970	1,648
18 and 19 years old	4,088	36	45	1,425	288	1,179 (37.6)	1,081	23	7 (3.0)	‡ (†)	2	‡
20 to 24 years old	10,420	175	103	849	223	3,506 (64.5)	3,780	616	1,097 (36.3)	53 (8.0)	15	5
25 years old and over	95,518	3,164	2,235	6,500	1,253	30,025 (178.1)	16,093	7,541	18,101 (142.1)	7,009 (90.6)	1,953	1,643
25 to 29 years old	10,867	246	148	804	164	3,565 (65.1)	2,196	856	2,228 (51.6)	516 (24.9)	93	52
30 to 34 years old	9,574	330	155	688	151	2,931 (59.1)	1,683	773	1,931 (48.1)	637 (27.7)	160	136
35 to 39 years old	10,169	378	167	669	143	2,957 (59.4)	1,753	884	2,100 (50.1)	754 (30.1)	206	157
40 to 49 years old	21,484	554	405	1,370	343	7,148 (91.5)	3,346	1,904	4,102 (69.7)	1,546 (43.0)	377	389
50 to 59 years old	19,694	589	300	1,124	240	6,195 (85.3)	3,478	1,761	3,674 (66.1)	1,550 (43.1)	448	335
60 to 64 years old	7,423	247	176	356	67	2,013 (49.1)	1,261	581	1,526 (42.8)	791 (30.8)	231	174
65 years old and over	16,308	820	884	1,490	146	5,217 (78.5)	2,377	782	2,539 (55.0)	1,215 (38.2)	437	401
Females, 18 and over	116,947	3,259	2,383	8,491	1,559	35,334 (190.7)	23,287	11,123	21,071 (152.3)	8,199 (97.7)	1,266	976
18 and 19 years old	3,968	20	34	1,108	273	1,077 (36.0)	1,422	23	8 (3.2)	‡ (†)	3	‡
20 to 24 years old	10,212	71	88	668	168	2,656 (56.3)	4,125	804	1,528 (42.8)	89 (10.4)	10	5
25 years old and over	102,767	3,167	2,262	6,715	1,117	31,601 (182.0)	17,739	10,297	19,534 (147.1)	8,110 (97.2)	1,253	971
25 to 29 years old	10,389	198	134	607	118	2,548 (55.1)	2,165	1,000	2,699 (56.7)	743 (29.9)	111	65
30 to 34 years old	9,691	225	110	558	112	2,308 (52.5)	1,739	997	2,383 (53.3)	985 (34.4)	180	92
35 to 39 years old	10,275	287	116	578	108	2,549 (55.2)	1,719	1,202	2,387 (53.4)	1,000 (34.6)	197	133
40 to 49 years old	22,106	547	284	1,124	220	6,536 (87.6)	3,865	2,652	4,614 (73.9)	1,715 (45.3)	307	241
50 to 59 years old	20,715	503	287	1,157	224	6,426 (86.9)	3,640	2,415	3,774 (66.9)	1,827 (46.8)	242	220
60 to 64 years old	8,112	220	174	445	75	2,668 (56.4)	1,435	742	1,382 (40.7)	787 (30.8)	80	104
65 years old and over	21,480	1,187	1,155	2,247	261	8,565 (99.8)	3,176	1,289	2,296 (52.4)	1,053 (35.6)	135	115
White, 18 and over	155,631	1,139	2,487	9,083	1,551	48,511 (216.2)	31,120	14,314	30,908 (180.3)	11,936 (117.0)	2,555	2,026
18 and 19 years old	4,932	26	38	1,510	287	1,372 (40.6)	1,658	26	12 (3.8)	‡ (†)	4	‡
20 to 24 years old	12,785	21	72	612	171	3,639 (65.7)	5,245	954	1,961 (48.4)	85 (10.1)	16	9
25 years old and over	137,914	1,092	2,378	6,962	1,092	43,500 (207.4)	24,217	13,335	28,935 (175.2)	11,851 (116.6)	2,535	2,018
25 to 29 years old	12,727	16	75	487	106	3,370 (63.3)	2,680	1,253	3,610 (65.5)	898 (32.9)	158	74
30 to 34 years old	11,464	31	60	402	74	2,966 (59.4)	2,147	1,216	3,049 (60.3)	1,143 (37.0)	232	143
35 to 39 years old	12,569	45	90	467	81	3,311 (62.8)	2,191	1,438	3,213 (61.8)	1,225 (38.3)	300	206
40 to 49 years old	29,386	78	284	1,181	233	9,275 (103.7)	4,946	3,347	6,612 (88.1)	2,463 (54.2)	525	442
50 to 59 years old	29,591	162	255	1,254	231	9,368 (104.2)	5,301	3,349	5,874 (83.1)	2,765 (57.4)	564	468
60 to 64 years old	12,029	89	204	446	86	3,680 (66.1)	2,145	1,044	2,439 (54.0)	1,384 (40.7)	268	247
65 years old and over	30,149	672	1,410	2,725	282	11,530 (115.1)	4,807	1,687	4,137 (70.0)	1,972 (48.6)	487	439
Black, 18 and over	25,910	461	482	2,892	582	9,134 (99.4)	5,779	2,098	3,013 (61.9)	1,186 (39.7)	161	121
18 and 19 years old	1,163	‡	12	420	92	352 (21.8)	280	7	‡ (†)	‡ (†)	‡	‡
20 to 24 years old	2,835	26	15	316	80	1,005 (36.6)	1,031	132	216 (17.1)	11 (3.9)	4	‡
25 years old and over	21,911	435	455	2,157	411	7,778 (93.5)	4,467	1,959	2,797 (59.8)	1,175 (39.5)	158	121
25 to 29 years old	2,762	12	19	245	30	982 (36.2)	707	244	407 (23.4)	92 (11.2)	11	13
30 to 34 years old	2,395	10	11	192	36	853 (33.8)	538	206	380 (22.7)	142 (13.9)	13	14
35 to 39 years old	2,478	24	14	153	48	865 (34.0)	558	259	372 (22.4)	157 (14.6)	22	6
40 to 49 years old	5,204	31	52	385	137	1,943 (50.3)	1,090	521	689 (30.4)	276 (19.3)	43	36
50 to 59 years old	4,414	50	53	442	86	1,583 (45.6)	905	417	567 (27.6)	264 (18.9)	30	16
60 to 64 years old	1,492	43	42	180	21	513 (26.3)	291	135	155 (14.5)	85 (10.7)	17	12
65 years old and over	3,166	265	264	559	53	1,040 (37.2)	378	176	228 (17.6)	158 (14.7)	22	24
Hispanic, 18 and over	31,028	4,496	1,577	4,465	933	9,229 (74.4)	4,852	1,806	2,719 (47.4)	671 (24.6)	186	94
18 and 19 years old	1,459	27	26	468	137	418 (19.5)	372	10	‡ (†)	‡ (†)	‡	‡
20 to 24 years old	3,614	192	95	510	125	1,200 (32.5)	1,035	214	226 (14.4)	14 (3.5)	1	2
25 years old and over	25,956	4,276	1,455	3,487	671	7,611 (70.6)	3,445	1,582	2,493 (45.6)	658 (24.3)	185	92
25 to 29 years old	4,260	406	184	610	123	1,468 (35.8)	686	263	441 (20.0)	56 (7.2)	15	8
30 to 34 years old	3,867	497	187	600	132	1,155 (31.9)	519	250	393 (18.9)	92 (9.2)	37	5
35 to 39 years old	3,768	550	167	581	102	1,056 (30.6)	503	261	392 (18.9)	110 (10.1)	26	21
40 to 49 years old	6,095	929	317	794	148	1,856 (39.3)	774	410	627 (23.7)	177 (12.7)	38	26
50 to 59 years old	4,044	776	248	457	106	1,082 (30.9)	596	235	370 (18.4)	131 (11.0)	31	13
60 to 64 years old	1,204	277	74	130	25	319 (17.0)	154	62	104 (9.8)	49 (6.7)	7	4
65 years old and over	2,717	843	278	316	35	676 (24.6)	213	102	166 (12.3)	43 (6.3)	31	16

†Not applicable.
‡Reporting standards not met.
NOTE: Total includes other racial/ethnic groups not shown separately. Although cells with fewer than 75,000 weighted persons are subject to relatively wide sampling variation, they are included in the table to permit various types of aggregations; see Appendix A: Guide to Sources or http://www.census.gov/apsd/techdoc/cps/cps-main.html for information on calculating standard errors. Race categories exclude persons of Hispanic ethnicity. Detail may not sum to totals because of rounding. Standard errors appear in parentheses.
SOURCE: U.S. Department of Commerce, Census Bureau, Current Population Survey (CPS), March 2009. (This table was prepared August 2009.)

Persons age 18 and over who hold at least a bachelor's degree in specific fields of study, by sex, race/ethnicity, and age: 2001

Field of study	Total	Sex		Race/ethnicity					Age		
		Males	Females	White	Black	Hispanic	Asian/Pacific Islander	American Indian/ Alaska Native	18 to 29 years old	30 to 49 years old	50 years old and over
1	2	3	4	5	6	7	8	9	10	11	12
Total population, 18 and over (in thousands)	208,762 (680.6)	99,811 (484.3)	108,951 (477.6)	151,898 (779.3)	23,314 (234.3)	23,580 (273.6)	8,097 (252.9)	1,873 (135.5)	44,447 (572.0)	85,830 (721.6)	78,485 (703.0)
Degree holders											
Number (in thousands)											
Total	49,144 (595.5)	24,977 (422.6)	24,166 (419.3)	40,138 (548.5)	3,192 (142.5)	2,189 (145.7)	3,389 (177.9)	235 (49.2)	7,016 (245)	24,666 (444)	17,461 (378.5)
Agriculture/forestry	540 (68.7)	421 (60.6)	‡ (†)	473 (64.3)	‡ (†)	‡ (†)	‡ (†)	‡ (†)	‡ (†)	254 (47.1)	239 (45.7)
Art/architecture	1,450 (112.4)	649 (75.2)	801 (83.5)	1,156 (100.4)	‡ (†)	‡ (†)	‡ (†)	‡ (†)	259 (47.6)	748 (80.8)	443 (62.2)
Business/management	8,976 (275.8)	5,679 (218.3)	3,297 (167.9)	7,254 (248.7)	623 (65.4)	426 (66.1)	633 (80.2)	‡ (†)	1,202 (102.4)	5,102 (209.4)	2,672 (152.2)
Communications	1,164 (100.7)	577 (70.9)	586 (71.5)	945 (90.8)	‡ (†)	‡ (†)	‡ (†)	‡ (†)	301 (51.3)	706 (78.5)	157 (37.1)
Computer and information sciences	1,249 (104.3)	871 (87.0)	378 (57.4)	895 (88.4)	‡ (†)	‡ (†)	166 (41.4)	‡ (†)	268 (48.4)	828 (85.0)	152 (36.5)
Education	7,102 (246.1)	1,750 (123.0)	5,351 (212.3)	6,160 (229.6)	490 (58.1)	234 (49.1)	181 (43.2)	‡ (†)	663 (76.1)	2,891 (158.2)	3,548 (175.1)
Engineering	3,959 (184.8)	3,558 (174.2)	401 (59.2)	3,085 (163.4)	‡ (†)	173 (42.3)	559 (75.5)	‡ (†)	459 (63.3)	2,057 (133.7)	1,443 (112.1)
English/literature	1,527 (115.3)	597 (72.1)	930 (89.9)	1,316 (107.1)	‡ (†)	‡ (†)	‡ (†)	‡ (†)	241 (45.9)	633 (74.3)	654 (75.6)
Foreign languages	448 (62.6)	135 (34.4)	313 (52.3)	344 (54.9)	‡ (†)	‡ (†)	‡ (†)	‡ (†)	‡ (†)	219 (43.7)	189 (40.6)
Health sciences	2,298 (141.3)	482 (64.8)	1,817 (125.5)	1,811 (125.5)	173 (34.8)	‡ (†)	213 (46.9)	‡ (†)	382 (57.8)	1,247 (104.2)	670 (76.5)
Liberal arts/humanities	2,846 (157.0)	1,150 (99.9)	1,695 (121.1)	2,444 (145.6)	146 (31.9)	‡ (†)	142 (38.3)	‡ (†)	400 (59.1)	1,308 (106.7)	1,137 (99.6)
Mathematics/statistics	869 (87.1)	507 (66.5)	362 (56.2)	567 (70.4)	‡ (†)	‡ (†)	149 (39.2)	‡ (†)	‡ (†)	386 (58.1)	363 (56.3)
Natural sciences (biological and physical)	2,910 (158.8)	1,756 (123.2)	1,153 (100.1)	2,260 (140.1)	190 (36.4)	‡ (†)	345 (59.5)	‡ (†)	413 (60.1)	1,426 (111.4)	1,071 (96.6)
Philosophy/religion/theology	628 (74.1)	437 (61.8)	191 (40.9)	533 (68.3)	‡ (†)	‡ (†)	‡ (†)	‡ (†)	‡ (†)	268 (48.4)	255 (47.2)
Pre-professional	596 (72.1)	397 (58.9)	199 (41.7)	448 (62.6)	‡ (†)	‡ (†)	‡ (†)	‡ (†)	‡ (†)	306 (51.7)	216 (43.4)
Psychology	1,903 (128.6)	606 (72.7)	1,297 (106.1)	1,561 (116.6)	157 (33.0)	‡ (†)	‡ (†)	‡ (†)	428 (61.2)	940 (90.6)	535 (68.3)
Social sciences/history	2,436 (145.4)	1,026 (94.4)	1,410 (110.5)	1,981 (131.2)	260 (42.5)	‡ (†)	‡ (†)	‡ (†)	359 (56.0)	1,092 (97.6)	985 (92.7)
Other fields	8,243 (264.6)	4,377 (192.6)	3,866 (181.5)	6,907 (242.8)	417 (53.7)	337 (58.8)	559 (75.5)	‡ (†)	1,253 (104.5)	4,256 (191.5)	2,734 (153.9)
Percentage distribution of degree holders, by field											
Total	100.0 (†)	100.0 (†)	100.0 (†)	100.0 (†)	100.0 (†)	100.0 (†)	100.0 (†)	100.0 (†)	100.0 (†)	100.0 (†)	100.0 (†)
Agriculture/forestry	1.1 (0.14)	1.7 (0.24)	‡ (0.13)	1.2 (0.16)	0.7 (0.38)	1.1 (0.73)	0.5 (0.40)	4.4 (4.32)	0.7 (0.29)	1.0 (0.19)	1.4 (0.26)
Art/architecture	3.0 (0.23)	2.6 (0.30)	3.3 (0.34)	2.9 (0.25)	3.3 (0.83)	4.8 (1.47)	2.2 (0.81)	17.5 (7.98)	3.7 (0.67)	3.0 (0.32)	2.5 (0.35)
Business/management	18.3 (0.52)	22.7 (0.78)	13.6 (0.65)	18.1 (0.57)	19.5 (1.86)	19.5 (2.72)	18.7 (2.16)	‡ (†)	17.1 (1.33)	20.7 (0.76)	15.3 (0.81)
Communications	2.4 (0.20)	2.3 (0.28)	2.4 (0.29)	2.4 (0.22)	3.2 (0.82)	3.3 (1.23)	1.2 (0.60)	‡ (†)	4.3 (0.72)	2.9 (0.31)	0.9 (0.21)
Computer and information sciences	2.5 (0.21)	3.5 (0.34)	1.6 (0.24)	2.2 (0.22)	3.9 (0.91)	2.6 (1.10)	4.9 (1.19)	16.0 (7.69)	3.8 (0.68)	3.4 (0.34)	0.9 (0.21)
Education	14.5 (0.47)	7.0 (0.48)	22.1 (0.79)	15.3 (0.53)	15.3 (1.69)	10.7 (2.13)	5.3 (1.24)	11.4 (6.67)	9.5 (1.03)	11.7 (0.61)	20.3 (0.90)
Engineering	8.1 (0.36)	14.2 (0.65)	1.7 (0.24)	7.7 (0.39)	3.6 (0.87)	7.9 (1.86)	16.5 (2.05)	‡ (†)	6.5 (0.87)	8.3 (0.52)	8.3 (0.62)
English/literature	3.1 (0.23)	2.4 (0.23)	3.8 (0.37)	3.3 (0.26)	2.6 (0.75)	3.1 (1.19)	1.7 (0.71)	2.1 (2.99)	3.4 (0.64)	2.6 (0.30)	3.7 (0.43)
Foreign languages	0.9 (0.13)	0.5 (0.14)	1.3 (0.22)	0.9 (0.14)	0.8 (0.42)	1.7 (0.90)	1.0 (0.56)	4.5 (4.37)	0.6 (0.27)	0.9 (0.18)	1.1 (0.23)
Health sciences	4.7 (0.28)	1.9 (0.26)	7.5 (0.50)	4.5 (0.31)	5.4 (1.06)	4.4 (1.41)	6.3 (1.34)	10.4 (6.41)	5.4 (0.80)	5.1 (0.41)	3.8 (0.43)
Liberal arts/humanities	5.8 (0.31)	4.6 (0.39)	7.0 (0.49)	6.1 (0.35)	4.6 (0.98)	4.7 (1.45)	4.2 (1.11)	2.7 (3.41)	5.7 (0.82)	5.3 (0.42)	6.5 (0.55)
Mathematics/statistics	1.8 (0.18)	2.0 (0.26)	1.5 (0.23)	1.4 (0.17)	2.4 (0.72)	2.4 (1.05)	4.4 (1.13)	‡ (†)	1.7 (0.46)	1.6 (0.23)	2.1 (0.32)
Natural sciences (biological and physical)	5.9 (0.31)	7.0 (0.48)	4.8 (0.41)	5.6 (0.34)	6.0 (1.11)	4.9 (1.49)	10.2 (1.67)	‡ (†)	5.9 (0.83)	5.8 (0.44)	6.1 (0.54)
Philosophy/religion/theology	1.3 (0.15)	1.8 (0.25)	0.8 (0.17)	1.3 (0.17)	0.9 (0.45)	1.8 (0.90)	0.8 (0.49)	‡ (†)	1.5 (0.43)	1.1 (0.20)	1.5 (0.27)
Pre-professional	1.2 (0.15)	1.6 (0.23)	0.8 (0.17)	1.1 (0.16)	1.6 (0.59)	2.0 (0.97)	1.5 (0.67)	‡ (†)	1.1 (0.36)	1.2 (0.21)	1.2 (0.25)
Psychology	3.9 (0.26)	2.4 (0.29)	5.4 (0.43)	3.9 (0.29)	4.9 (1.01)	5.0 (1.50)	1.7 (0.72)	7.9 (5.65)	6.1 (0.85)	3.8 (0.36)	3.1 (0.39)
Social sciences/history	5.0 (0.29)	4.1 (0.37)	5.8 (0.45)	4.9 (0.32)	8.1 (1.28)	4.7 (1.45)	2.4 (0.85)	4.7 (4.45)	5.1 (0.78)	4.4 (0.39)	5.6 (0.52)
Other fields	16.8 (0.50)	17.5 (0.71)	16.0 (0.70)	17.2 (0.56)	13.1 (1.58)	15.4 (2.48)	16.5 (2.05)	9.9 (6.26)	17.9 (1.35)	17.3 (0.71)	15.7 (0.81)

†Not applicable.
‡Reporting standards not met.
NOTE: Race categories exclude persons of Hispanic ethnicity. Detail may not sum to totals because of rounding. Standard errors appear in parentheses.

SOURCE: U.S. Department of Commerce, Census Bureau, Survey of Income and Program Participation, 2001, unpublished tabulations. (This table was prepared September 2005.)

Educational attainment of persons 18 years old and over, by state: 2000 and 2005–07

State	Percent of 18- to 24-year-olds who were high school completers[1] 2000	Percent of 18- to 24-year-olds who were high school completers[1] 2005–07 (3-year average)[2]	2000 Less than high school completion	2000 High school completion or higher	2000 Bachelor's or higher degree Total	2000 Bachelor's degree	2000 Graduate or professional degree	2005–07 Less than high school completion	2005–07 High school completion or higher	2005–07 Bachelor's or higher degree Total	2005–07 Bachelor's degree	2005–07 Graduate or professional degree
1	2	3	4	5	6	7	8	9	10	11	12	13
United States	**74.7 (0.02)**	**82.3 (0.06)**	**19.6 (0.01)**	**80.4 (0.01)**	**24.4 (0.01)**	**15.5 (0.01)**	**8.9 (#)**	**15.9 (0.03)**	**84.1 (0.03)**	**27.0 (0.04)**	**17.1 (0.03)**	**9.9 (0.02)**
Alabama	72.2 (0.15)	79.3 (0.46)	24.7 (0.06)	75.3 (0.06)	19.0 (0.05)	12.1 (0.04)	6.9 (0.03)	20.0 (0.20)	80.0 (0.20)	21.0 (0.17)	13.4 (0.13)	7.7 (0.09)
Alaska	76.9 (0.40)	81.1 (1.22)	11.7 (0.12)	88.3 (0.12)	24.7 (0.16)	16.1 (0.13)	8.6 (0.10)	9.5 (0.36)	90.5 (0.36)	26.2 (0.45)	16.2 (0.42)	10.0 (0.40)
Arizona	69.2 (0.19)	77.8 (0.44)	19.0 (0.06)	81.0 (0.06)	23.5 (0.07)	15.1 (0.06)	8.4 (0.04)	16.6 (0.16)	83.4 (0.16)	25.3 (0.14)	16.0 (0.13)	9.2 (0.10)
Arkansas	75.4 (0.19)	81.8 (0.63)	24.7 (0.07)	75.3 (0.07)	16.7 (0.06)	11.0 (0.05)	5.7 (0.04)	19.3 (0.20)	80.7 (0.20)	18.7 (0.26)	12.5 (0.20)	6.2 (0.13)
California	70.7 (0.07)	81.3 (0.17)	23.2 (0.03)	76.8 (0.03)	26.6 (0.03)	17.1 (0.02)	9.5 (0.02)	20.0 (0.06)	80.0 (0.06)	29.1 (0.07)	18.7 (0.06)	10.4 (0.04)
Colorado	75.1 (0.15)	82.3 (0.46)	13.1 (0.05)	86.9 (0.05)	32.7 (0.06)	21.6 (0.06)	11.1 (0.04)	11.7 (0.15)	88.3 (0.15)	34.7 (0.17)	22.5 (0.16)	12.2 (0.13)
Connecticut	78.2 (0.21)	86.7 (0.47)	16.0 (0.06)	84.0 (0.06)	31.4 (0.08)	18.1 (0.07)	13.3 (0.06)	12.2 (0.16)	87.8 (0.16)	34.2 (0.24)	19.4 (0.17)	14.8 (0.16)
Delaware	77.6 (0.41)	80.8 (1.28)	17.4 (0.14)	82.6 (0.14)	25.0 (0.16)	15.6 (0.14)	9.4 (0.11)	14.5 (0.35)	85.5 (0.35)	26.8 (0.48)	16.2 (0.36)	10.6 (0.30)
District of Columbia	79.4 (0.40)	85.8 (0.87)	22.2 (0.18)	77.8 (0.18)	39.1 (0.21)	18.1 (0.17)	21.0 (0.18)	16.0 (0.43)	84.0 (0.43)	45.3 (0.42)	20.0 (0.43)	25.3 (0.35)
Florida	71.7 (0.11)	80.2 (0.25)	20.1 (0.04)	79.9 (0.04)	22.3 (0.04)	14.2 (0.03)	8.1 (0.02)	15.5 (0.08)	84.5 (0.08)	25.2 (0.09)	16.5 (0.07)	8.8 (0.05)
Georgia	70.0 (0.15)	77.8 (0.37)	21.4 (0.05)	78.6 (0.05)	24.3 (0.05)	16.0 (0.05)	8.3 (0.04)	17.8 (0.13)	82.2 (0.13)	26.4 (0.14)	17.2 (0.11)	9.2 (0.08)
Hawaii	85.8 (0.25)	91.0 (0.63)	15.4 (0.10)	84.6 (0.10)	26.2 (0.12)	17.8 (0.10)	8.4 (0.08)	11.2 (0.29)	88.8 (0.29)	28.5 (0.36)	18.8 (0.31)	9.7 (0.21)
Idaho	77.3 (0.25)	82.1 (0.85)	15.3 (0.09)	84.7 (0.09)	21.7 (0.10)	14.9 (0.09)	6.8 (0.06)	12.7 (0.30)	87.3 (0.30)	23.8 (0.34)	16.3 (0.26)	7.5 (0.21)
Illinois	76.0 (0.09)	83.7 (0.25)	18.6 (0.03)	81.4 (0.03)	26.1 (0.03)	16.6 (0.03)	9.5 (0.02)	14.7 (0.10)	85.3 (0.10)	29.0 (0.12)	18.2 (0.09)	10.8 (0.07)
Indiana	76.5 (0.15)	81.2 (0.35)	17.9 (0.05)	82.1 (0.05)	19.4 (0.05)	12.2 (0.04)	7.2 (0.04)	14.7 (0.12)	85.3 (0.12)	21.7 (0.15)	13.8 (0.11)	7.9 (0.10)
Iowa	81.4 (0.16)	87.0 (0.53)	13.9 (0.06)	86.1 (0.06)	21.2 (0.07)	14.7 (0.06)	6.5 (0.04)	10.9 (0.17)	89.1 (0.17)	23.9 (0.25)	16.7 (0.20)	7.3 (0.15)
Kansas	78.3 (0.18)	85.6 (0.56)	14.0 (0.06)	86.0 (0.06)	25.8 (0.08)	17.1 (0.06)	8.7 (0.05)	11.4 (0.19)	88.6 (0.19)	28.5 (0.25)	18.7 (0.22)	9.7 (0.16)
Kentucky	74.9 (0.15)	82.0 (0.52)	25.9 (0.06)	74.1 (0.06)	17.1 (0.05)	10.2 (0.04)	6.9 (0.03)	20.4 (0.18)	79.6 (0.18)	19.7 (0.17)	11.9 (0.14)	7.9 (0.11)
Louisiana	72.3 (0.15)	77.2 (0.52)	25.2 (0.06)	74.8 (0.06)	18.7 (0.05)	12.2 (0.04)	6.5 (0.03)	20.8 (0.20)	79.2 (0.20)	20.0 (0.19)	13.2 (0.15)	6.8 (0.11)
Maine	78.9 (0.28)	84.6 (0.97)	14.6 (0.08)	85.4 (0.08)	22.9 (0.10)	15.0 (0.09)	7.9 (0.06)	11.1 (0.23)	88.9 (0.23)	25.9 (0.40)	16.8 (0.31)	9.1 (0.24)
Maryland	79.6 (0.16)	84.8 (0.46)	16.2 (0.05)	83.8 (0.05)	31.4 (0.07)	18.0 (0.06)	13.4 (0.05)	13.1 (0.14)	86.9 (0.14)	34.8 (0.18)	19.2 (0.13)	15.6 (0.12)
Massachusetts	82.2 (0.13)	86.7 (0.36)	15.2 (0.05)	84.8 (0.05)	33.2 (0.06)	19.5 (0.05)	13.7 (0.04)	12.0 (0.12)	88.0 (0.12)	37.0 (0.16)	21.3 (0.13)	15.7 (0.12)
Michigan	76.5 (0.10)	83.8 (0.33)	16.6 (0.03)	83.4 (0.03)	21.8 (0.04)	13.7 (0.03)	8.1 (0.02)	12.9 (0.12)	87.1 (0.12)	24.7 (0.13)	15.3 (0.09)	9.4 (0.10)
Minnesota	79.3 (0.13)	86.0 (0.41)	12.1 (0.04)	87.9 (0.04)	27.4 (0.06)	19.1 (0.06)	8.3 (0.03)	9.3 (0.13)	90.7 (0.13)	30.4 (0.21)	20.8 (0.17)	9.6 (0.12)
Mississippi	71.3 (0.18)	77.3 (0.57)	27.1 (0.08)	72.9 (0.08)	16.9 (0.06)	11.1 (0.05)	5.8 (0.04)	22.0 (0.21)	78.0 (0.21)	18.6 (0.20)	12.2 (0.16)	6.5 (0.12)
Missouri	76.5 (0.13)	82.0 (0.42)	18.7 (0.05)	81.3 (0.05)	21.6 (0.05)	14.0 (0.04)	7.6 (0.03)	15.0 (0.13)	85.0 (0.13)	24.1 (0.17)	15.4 (0.14)	8.7 (0.10)
Montana	78.6 (0.31)	83.1 (1.13)	12.8 (0.10)	87.2 (0.10)	24.4 (0.13)	17.2 (0.11)	7.2 (0.08)	10.1 (0.35)	89.9 (0.35)	26.4 (0.46)	18.4 (0.37)	8.0 (0.25)
Nebraska	80.0 (0.21)	87.0 (0.64)	13.4 (0.07)	86.6 (0.07)	23.7 (0.09)	16.4 (0.08)	7.3 (0.06)	10.4 (0.22)	89.6 (0.22)	26.6 (0.32)	18.3 (0.24)	8.3 (0.20)
Nevada	66.7 (0.32)	76.7 (0.70)	19.3 (0.10)	80.7 (0.10)	18.2 (0.10)	12.1 (0.08)	6.1 (0.06)	16.6 (0.21)	83.4 (0.21)	20.9 (0.24)	13.9 (0.20)	7.0 (0.13)
New Hampshire	77.8 (0.29)	85.8 (0.78)	12.6 (0.08)	87.4 (0.08)	28.7 (0.11)	18.7 (0.10)	10.0 (0.07)	10.3 (0.24)	89.7 (0.24)	31.4 (0.39)	20.2 (0.33)	11.2 (0.23)
New Jersey	76.3 (0.14)	85.0 (0.33)	17.9 (0.04)	82.1 (0.04)	29.8 (0.05)	18.8 (0.04)	11.0 (0.04)	13.7 (0.11)	86.3 (0.11)	33.6 (0.15)	21.1 (0.11)	12.5 (0.09)
New Mexico	70.5 (0.24)	77.3 (0.88)	21.1 (0.09)	78.9 (0.09)	23.5 (0.09)	13.7 (0.07)	9.8 (0.06)	18.1 (0.27)	81.9 (0.27)	24.8 (0.30)	14.3 (0.22)	10.5 (0.20)
New York	76.1 (0.09)	83.4 (0.22)	20.9 (0.03)	79.1 (0.03)	27.4 (0.04)	15.6 (0.03)	11.8 (0.03)	16.2 (0.08)	83.8 (0.08)	31.2 (0.11)	17.8 (0.09)	13.4 (0.07)
North Carolina	74.2 (0.11)	81.8 (0.31)	21.9 (0.04)	78.1 (0.04)	22.5 (0.04)	15.3 (0.04)	7.2 (0.04)	17.8 (0.12)	82.2 (0.12)	25.1 (0.14)	16.8 (0.11)	8.3 (0.08)
North Dakota	84.4 (0.24)	91.2 (0.79)	16.1 (0.10)	83.9 (0.10)	22.0 (0.12)	16.5 (0.10)	5.5 (0.06)	12.0 (0.41)	88.0 (0.41)	26.3 (0.60)	19.3 (0.50)	7.0 (0.35)
Ohio	76.8 (0.09)	83.7 (0.29)	17.0 (0.03)	83.0 (0.03)	21.1 (0.03)	13.7 (0.03)	7.4 (0.02)	13.7 (0.11)	86.3 (0.11)	23.4 (0.11)	14.9 (0.09)	8.5 (0.06)
Oklahoma	74.8 (0.16)	81.2 (0.60)	19.4 (0.06)	80.6 (0.06)	20.3 (0.06)	13.5 (0.05)	6.8 (0.04)	15.9 (0.18)	84.1 (0.18)	22.2 (0.22)	15.0 (0.17)	7.3 (0.12)
Oregon	74.2 (0.17)	82.4 (0.49)	14.9 (0.05)	85.1 (0.05)	25.1 (0.06)	16.4 (0.06)	8.7 (0.04)	12.4 (0.16)	87.6 (0.16)	27.5 (0.22)	17.6 (0.17)	10.0 (0.14)
Pennsylvania	79.8 (0.09)	85.4 (0.28)	18.1 (0.03)	81.9 (0.03)	22.4 (0.03)	14.0 (0.03)	8.4 (0.02)	13.7 (0.09)	86.3 (0.09)	25.6 (0.12)	15.8 (0.09)	9.8 (0.08)
Rhode Island	81.3 (0.32)	86.7 (0.79)	22.0 (0.13)	78.0 (0.13)	25.6 (0.14)	15.9 (0.12)	9.7 (0.10)	17.5 (0.40)	82.5 (0.40)	29.1 (0.34)	17.8 (0.27)	11.3 (0.26)
South Carolina	74.3 (0.18)	81.5 (0.43)	23.7 (0.07)	76.3 (0.07)	20.4 (0.07)	13.5 (0.06)	6.9 (0.04)	18.5 (0.19)	81.5 (0.19)	23.0 (0.18)	15.0 (0.14)	8.0 (0.10)
South Dakota	78.2 (0.33)	82.8 (0.89)	15.4 (0.12)	84.6 (0.12)	21.5 (0.13)	15.5 (0.12)	6.0 (0.08)	12.4 (0.33)	87.6 (0.33)	24.4 (0.52)	17.4 (0.42)	7.0 (0.29)
Tennessee	75.1 (0.16)	82.1 (0.42)	24.1 (0.06)	75.9 (0.06)	19.6 (0.06)	12.8 (0.05)	6.8 (0.03)	19.1 (0.12)	80.9 (0.12)	21.8 (0.16)	14.2 (0.12)	7.6 (0.09)
Texas	68.6 (0.08)	78.6 (0.20)	24.3 (0.03)	75.7 (0.03)	23.2 (0.03)	15.6 (0.03)	7.6 (0.02)	21.4 (0.09)	78.6 (0.09)	24.8 (0.09)	16.7 (0.08)	8.1 (0.05)
Utah	80.3 (0.16)	86.4 (0.48)	12.3 (0.07)	87.7 (0.07)	26.1 (0.09)	17.8 (0.08)	8.3 (0.06)	9.7 (0.19)	90.3 (0.19)	28.3 (0.25)	19.2 (0.21)	9.1 (0.16)
Vermont	83.0 (0.28)	90.5 (0.95)	13.6 (0.10)	86.4 (0.10)	29.4 (0.13)	18.3 (0.11)	11.1 (0.09)	9.5 (0.29)	90.5 (0.29)	32.9 (0.58)	20.1 (0.47)	12.8 (0.36)
Virginia	79.4 (0.13)	85.9 (0.29)	18.5 (0.05)	81.5 (0.05)	29.5 (0.06)	17.9 (0.05)	11.6 (0.04)	14.7 (0.11)	85.3 (0.11)	32.9 (0.16)	19.5 (0.13)	13.4 (0.10)
Washington	75.3 (0.16)	81.9 (0.39)	12.9 (0.05)	87.1 (0.05)	27.7 (0.06)	18.4 (0.05)	9.3 (0.04)	11.0 (0.11)	89.0 (0.11)	30.0 (0.15)	19.5 (0.13)	10.5 (0.10)
West Virginia	78.2 (0.22)	83.8 (0.68)	24.8 (0.09)	75.2 (0.09)	14.8 (0.07)	8.9 (0.06)	5.9 (0.05)	19.0 (0.26)	81.0 (0.26)	17.0 (0.25)	10.2 (0.19)	6.8 (0.17)
Wisconsin	78.9 (0.13)	85.7 (0.43)	14.9 (0.04)	85.1 (0.04)	22.4 (0.05)	15.2 (0.04)	7.2 (0.03)	11.5 (0.14)	88.5 (0.14)	25.5 (0.19)	16.9 (0.14)	8.6 (0.12)
Wyoming	79.0 (0.41)	85.3 (1.28)	12.1 (0.13)	87.9 (0.13)	21.9 (0.16)	14.9 (0.14)	7.0 (0.10)	9.5 (0.39)	90.5 (0.39)	22.7 (0.51)	15.1 (0.48)	7.6 (0.28)

#Rounds to zero.

[1]High school completers include diploma recipients and those completing through alternative credentials, such as a GED.

[2]Use of a 3-year average increases the sample size, thereby reducing the size of sampling errors and producing more stable estimates.

NOTE: Detail may not sum to totals because of rounding. Standard errors appear in parentheses.

SOURCE: U.S. Department of Commerce, Census Bureau, Census 2000 Summary File 3, retrieved October 11, 2006, from http://factfinder.census.gov/servlet/DatasetMainPage Servlet?_ds_name=DEC_2000_SF3_U&_program=DEC&_lang=en; Census Briefs, *Educational Attainment: 2000;* and 2005–2007 American Community Survey (ACS) 3-Year Public Use Microdata Sample (PUMS) data. (This table was prepared July 2009.)

Educational attainment of persons 25 years old and over, by race/ethnicity and state: 2005–07

State	Percent with high school completion or higher								Percent with bachelor's degree or higher							
	Total	White	Black	Hispanic	Asian	Native Hawaiian/Pacific Islander	American Indian/Alaska Native	Two or more races	Total	White	Black	Hispanic	Asian	Native Hawaiian/Pacific Islander	American Indian/Alaska Native	Two or more races
1	2	3	4	5	6	7	8	9	10	11	12	13	14	15	16	17
United States	84.1 (0.03)	88.9 (0.02)	79.4 (0.07)	60.0 (0.10)	85.6 (0.10)	85.0 (0.60)	78.1 (0.27)	86.6 (0.18)	27.0 (0.04)	30.0 (0.04)	16.8 (0.07)	12.3 (0.06)	49.2 (0.14)	15.4 (0.59)	13.4 (0.21)	24.6 (0.24)
Alabama	80.0 (0.20)	82.5 (0.22)	74.2 (0.38)	56.3 (1.75)	86.3 (1.43)	‡ (†)	75.9 (2.23)	75.8 (1.80)	21.0 (0.17)	23.3 (0.22)	13.7 (0.33)	13.3 (1.10)	52.3 (2.33)	‡ (†)	14.0 (1.58)	15.9 (1.28)
Alaska	90.5 (0.36)	94.3 (0.31)	90.2 (2.68)	75.9 (3.27)	78.9 (2.57)	80.8 (6.77)	78.5 (1.06)	88.5 (2.07)	26.2 (0.45)	31.7 (0.58)	16.9 (2.63)	14.7 (2.27)	21.8 (2.29)	‡ (†)	5.8 (0.83)	16.5 (2.43)
Arizona	83.4 (0.16)	92.0 (0.12)	86.7 (0.78)	59.5 (0.49)	88.0 (0.89)	85.3 (4.20)	71.0 (1.06)	89.2 (1.20)	25.3 (0.14)	31.0 (0.19)	22.4 (0.98)	9.1 (0.25)	51.6 (1.36)	16.0 (2.79)	8.5 (0.53)	23.7 (1.46)
Arkansas	80.7 (0.20)	83.0 (0.19)	76.1 (0.60)	48.2 (1.77)	85.4 (1.77)	‡ (†)	74.9 (2.82)	77.5 (2.26)	18.7 (0.26)	20.2 (0.28)	12.2 (0.63)	8.6 (0.82)	40.2 (3.10)	‡ (†)	15.4 (1.97)	11.8 (1.71)
California	80.0 (0.06)	92.4 (0.06)	86.0 (0.23)	55.5 (0.17)	85.4 (0.17)	84.5 (1.13)	82.0 (0.86)	88.9 (0.45)	29.1 (0.07)	37.4 (0.10)	20.8 (0.29)	9.6 (0.10)	47.0 (0.22)	14.8 (0.98)	15.1 (0.74)	29.5 (0.55)
Colorado	88.3 (0.15)	94.0 (0.11)	87.3 (0.86)	62.3 (0.68)	86.6 (1.04)	84.3 (5.61)	83.6 (1.98)	92.1 (1.15)	34.7 (0.17)	40.1 (0.20)	22.2 (1.22)	11.3 (0.33)	48.2 (1.42)	22.3 (5.45)	19.5 (2.38)	27.9 (2.00)
Connecticut	87.8 (0.16)	90.8 (0.14)	81.0 (0.84)	67.8 (0.95)	89.6 (0.89)	‡ (†)	74.3 (5.56)	91.1 (1.39)	34.2 (0.24)	37.4 (0.26)	17.2 (0.73)	13.8 (0.62)	61.8 (1.44)	‡ (†)	23.0 (3.83)	30.7 (2.63)
Delaware	85.5 (0.35)	88.2 (0.37)	82.3 (1.08)	52.8 (2.66)	90.8 (1.80)	‡ (†)	70.9 (8.16)	92.6 (1.90)	26.8 (0.48)	28.7 (0.53)	17.9 (1.14)	12.1 (1.53)	61.0 (3.38)	‡ (†)	8.8 ! (3.71)	24.2 (3.81)
District of Columbia	84.0 (0.43)	98.3 (0.32)	78.2 (0.70)	56.4 (2.28)	91.9 (1.69)	‡ (†)	‡ (†)	92.8 (2.30)	45.3 (0.42)	85.1 (0.73)	20.2 (0.53)	30.3 (2.04)	72.2 (3.00)	‡ (†)	‡ (†)	54.5 (5.57)
Florida	84.5 (0.08)	89.3 (0.07)	76.7 (0.24)	72.6 (0.26)	85.9 (0.50)	84.6 (3.88)	80.5 (1.31)	84.2 (0.89)	25.2 (0.09)	27.7 (0.11)	15.4 (0.25)	20.8 (0.22)	45.7 (0.73)	15.2 (3.24)	16.1 (1.06)	23.6 (1.01)
Georgia	82.2 (0.13)	86.0 (0.14)	79.3 (0.28)	54.3 (0.84)	84.5 (0.71)	84.8 (5.95)	76.8 (2.33)	82.7 (1.49)	26.4 (0.14)	30.3 (0.16)	18.1 (0.26)	12.9 (0.47)	48.5 (0.99)	17.0 ! (5.61)	20.5 (2.37)	26.1 (1.84)
Hawaii	88.8 (0.29)	94.8 (0.29)	97.3 (1.32)	87.7 (1.32)	85.0 (0.48)	83.8 (1.09)	90.2 (5.08)	91.4 (0.52)	28.5 (0.36)	40.8 (0.68)	24.5 (2.91)	13.9 (1.01)	28.8 (0.54)	12.5 (0.93)	22.1 ! (7.49)	18.4 (0.95)
Idaho	87.3 (0.30)	90.4 (0.27)	85.8 (4.42)	51.3 (1.69)	88.5 (2.10)	72.6 (12.94)	78.4 (3.15)	82.9 (2.37)	23.8 (0.34)	25.1 (0.37)	23.5 (5.84)	8.9 (0.88)	40.8 (3.69)	‡ (†)	8.0 (1.58)	18.1 (2.71)
Illinois	85.3 (0.10)	90.4 (0.10)	80.6 (0.34)	58.8 (0.45)	90.9 (0.41)	99.4 (0.69)	78.2 (3.14)	86.6 (1.14)	29.0 (0.12)	32.2 (0.15)	17.9 (0.33)	11.2 (0.32)	61.2 (0.68)	63.8 (9.51)	21.8 (2.76)	29.7 (1.49)
Indiana	85.3 (0.12)	86.8 (0.12)	81.1 (0.51)	59.7 (1.08)	91.1 (1.12)	‡ (†)	77.8 (2.88)	82.0 (1.83)	21.7 (0.15)	22.3 (0.15)	13.6 (0.52)	12.1 (0.56)	62.0 (1.87)	‡ (†)	15.6 (2.50)	17.7 (1.87)
Iowa	89.1 (0.17)	90.4 (0.15)	79.5 (1.95)	54.0 (2.29)	82.7 (2.14)	‡ (†)	87.3 (2.64)	89.4 (2.64)	23.9 (0.25)	24.0 (0.26)	18.8 (1.76)	11.7 (1.43)	53.0 (2.68)	‡ (†)	18.1 (3.98)	22.8 (3.99)
Kansas	88.6 (0.19)	91.5 (0.16)	86.0 (0.98)	56.7 (1.36)	84.1 (2.28)	‡ (†)	86.7 (3.55)	84.3 (1.70)	28.5 (0.25)	30.2 (0.25)	17.6 (1.24)	10.8 (0.69)	48.8 (2.29)	‡ (†)	18.6 (2.43)	19.4 (2.09)
Kentucky	79.6 (0.18)	79.8 (0.19)	79.4 (0.72)	61.7 (1.95)	86.8 (1.70)	74.9 (8.00)	80.3 (4.46)	76.6 (2.25)	19.7 (0.17)	19.9 (0.18)	13.5 (0.59)	16.5 (1.27)	54.1 (2.15)	20.6 ! (7.93)	12.8 (3.30)	16.4 (2.19)
Louisiana	79.2 (0.20)	83.5 (0.21)	70.6 (0.46)	71.0 (1.55)	79.0 (1.76)	‡ (†)	63.1 (3.07)	81.3 (1.72)	20.0 (0.19)	23.3 (0.23)	11.6 (0.30)	20.0 (1.09)	40.9 (2.10)	‡ (†)	10.7 (1.43)	17.9 (1.90)
Maine	88.9 (0.23)	89.2 (0.25)	88.4 (3.87)	81.3 (4.69)	82.2 (3.05)	‡ (†)	76.7 (3.98)	79.6 (4.00)	25.9 (0.40)	26.0 (0.40)	22.0 (5.16)	20.5 (3.96)	42.5 (4.66)	‡ (†)	10.5 (2.55)	14.3 (2.55)
Maryland	86.9 (0.14)	89.9 (0.14)	83.8 (0.30)	64.2 (0.96)	89.9 (0.57)	86.8 (6.80)	83.9 (2.67)	90.3 (0.97)	34.8 (0.18)	38.7 (0.22)	23.9 (0.35)	20.6 (0.73)	60.4 (0.95)	29.5 (8.37)	21.4 (3.17)	32.3 (1.67)
Massachusetts	88.0 (0.12)	90.3 (0.12)	82.7 (0.67)	65.8 (0.91)	83.0 (0.73)	‡ (†)	87.3 (2.23)	87.3 (1.22)	37.0 (0.16)	38.8 (0.17)	20.8 (0.75)	15.4 (0.59)	56.2 (1.01)	‡ (†)	21.4 (2.62)	34.5 (1.81)
Michigan	87.1 (0.12)	89.1 (0.11)	80.0 (0.45)	60.6 (0.99)	88.7 (0.62)	96.9 (2.84)	80.8 (1.68)	85.2 (0.99)	24.7 (0.13)	25.6 (0.15)	14.5 (0.38)	14.7 (0.57)	63.0 (1.08)	33.1 ! (11.65)	13.0 (1.35)	21.9 (1.37)
Minnesota	90.7 (0.13)	92.6 (0.10)	70.6 (0.72)	55.6 (0.78)	87.2 (0.92)	‡ (†)	81.5 (1.88)	87.7 (2.03)	30.4 (0.24)	31.2 (0.22)	20.1 (1.25)	15.1 (1.07)	35.2 (1.13)	10.2 (2.79)	11.2 (1.70)	23.4 (2.43)
Mississippi	78.0 (0.21)	89.2 (0.25)	69.9 (0.39)	57.9 (2.49)	77.0 (2.48)	‡ (†)	70.3 (4.11)	83.3 (3.02)	18.6 (0.20)	22.2 (0.28)	11.5 (0.27)	11.7 (1.34)	39.3 (3.06)	‡ (†)	12.3 (2.55)	19.8 (2.81)
Missouri	85.0 (0.13)	86.2 (0.14)	82.0 (0.39)	68.0 (1.45)	84.6 (1.65)	80.1 (6.80)	80.2 (2.10)	80.9 (1.48)	24.1 (0.17)	25.0 (0.17)	14.7 (0.48)	17.1 (1.09)	55.3 (1.89)	7.6 ! (5.63)	17.2 (2.21)	17.5 (1.54)
Montana	89.9 (0.35)	90.7 (0.34)	73.4 (8.79)	84.0 (2.74)	89.0 (3.50)	‡ (†)	76.6 (1.75)	90.2 (2.17)	26.4 (0.46)	27.2 (0.49)	19.0 ! (9.36)	17.3 (3.34)	43.1 (6.20)	‡ (†)	11.1 (1.43)	19.7 (3.19)
Nebraska	89.6 (0.22)	92.5 (0.20)	82.2 (1.66)	50.6 (2.03)	83.2 (2.91)	‡ (†)	77.2 (3.36)	88.9 (3.06)	26.6 (0.32)	27.8 (0.36)	15.9 (1.43)	9.4 (1.06)	49.1 (3.47)	‡ (†)	16.5 (3.97)	21.4 (1.37)
Nevada	83.4 (0.21)	90.8 (0.18)	86.9 (0.72)	55.6 (0.78)	87.2 (0.92)	87.4 (2.39)	81.5 (1.88)	89.0 (1.26)	20.9 (0.24)	24.3 (0.32)	14.5 (0.79)	7.8 (0.32)	35.2 (1.13)	10.2 (2.79)	11.8 (1.70)	20.9 (1.86)
New Hampshire	89.7 (0.24)	89.9 (0.24)	83.3 (4.91)	79.4 (2.88)	94.6 (1.45)	‡ (†)	85.0 (4.92)	79.5 (4.19)	31.4 (0.39)	30.9 (0.37)	34.3 (5.13)	24.8 (3.24)	63.3 (4.64)	‡ (†)	34.4 (9.59)	21.2 (4.02)
New Jersey	86.3 (0.11)	90.3 (0.10)	82.0 (0.39)	68.3 (0.46)	91.7 (0.35)	91.7 (5.47)	82.5 (2.99)	85.7 (1.37)	33.6 (0.15)	36.3 (0.17)	20.1 (0.45)	15.1 (0.32)	65.9 (0.64)	15.9 ! (7.47)	20.7 (3.94)	33.8 (1.71)
New Mexico	81.9 (0.27)	92.8 (0.25)	85.8 (2.22)	70.0 (0.47)	87.3 (2.06)	‡ (†)	72.2 (1.28)	89.2 (2.03)	24.8 (0.30)	36.8 (0.48)	23.2 (2.31)	12.2 (0.37)	46.0 (2.95)	‡ (†)	8.9 (0.69)	28.7 (3.45)
New York	83.8 (0.08)	89.8 (0.06)	79.5 (0.26)	63.9 (0.39)	79.8 (0.41)	77.2 (9.41)	79.4 (2.08)	85.3 (0.75)	31.2 (0.11)	36.0 (0.13)	19.6 (0.26)	14.8 (0.23)	45.1 (0.46)	21.3 ! (6.82)	16.3 (1.53)	32.5 (1.07)
North Carolina	82.2 (0.12)	85.8 (0.13)	78.2 (0.29)	50.4 (0.82)	84.6 (0.92)	80.4 (8.69)	67.0 (1.47)	83.1 (1.33)	25.1 (0.14)	28.2 (0.15)	15.6 (0.29)	11.4 (0.50)	52.7 (1.08)	6.3 ! (3.81)	10.6 (0.87)	23.0 (1.67)
North Dakota	88.0 (0.41)	88.5 (0.42)	‡ (†)	75.1 (4.94)	89.8 (3.99)	‡ (†)	80.6 (2.06)	88.7 (4.33)	26.3 (0.60)	26.3 (0.63)	‡ (†)	20.5 (4.96)	64.0 (7.31)	‡ (†)	17.7 (2.19)	24.8 (7.18)

See notes at end of table.

Educational attainment of persons 25 years old and over, by race/ethnicity and state: 2005–07—Continued

State	Percent with high school completion or higher								Percent with bachelor's degree or higher							
	Total	White	Black	Hispanic	Asian	Native Hawaiian/ Pacific Islander	American Indian/Alaska Native	Two or more races	Total	White	Black	Hispanic	Asian	Native Hawaiian/ Pacific Islander	American Indian/ Alaska Native	Two or more races
1	2	3	4	5	6	7	8	9	10	11	12	13	14	15	16	17
Ohio..............	86.3 (0.11)	87.5 (0.11)	79.1 (0.39)	69.1 (0.89)	88.9 (0.77)	‡ (†)	80.1 (2.63)	84.6 (1.01)	23.4 (0.11)	24.1 (0.12)	14.0 (0.32)	16.3 (0.70)	60.2 (1.11)	‡ (†)	14.8 (2.26)	18.7 (1.20)
Oklahoma........	84.1 (0.18)	86.6 (0.19)	81.9 (1.00)	54.1 (1.35)	84.6 (1.46)	89.4 (5.35)	81.5 (0.79)	83.0 (0.81)	22.2 (0.22)	24.0 (0.25)	15.9 (0.86)	9.9 (0.61)	40.4 (2.20)	7.7 ! (6.53)	14.5 (0.64)	17.5 (0.95)
Oregon...........	87.6 (0.16)	90.9 (0.13)	86.0 (1.22)	53.1 (1.17)	85.0 (0.95)	88.1 (3.95)	82.8 (1.57)	87.1 (1.23)	27.5 (0.22)	28.8 (0.21)	17.5 (1.67)	10.1 (0.56)	44.6 (1.50)	16.8 (4.41)	14.1 (1.64)	22.7 (1.43)
Pennsylvania....	86.3 (0.09)	88.0 (0.09)	79.5 (0.43)	63.6 (0.82)	84.9 (0.67)	‡ (†)	83.8 (2.43)	85.6 (1.30)	25.6 (0.12)	26.5 (0.13)	14.3 (0.35)	12.9 (0.53)	53.7 (1.33)	‡ (†)	21.9 (3.27)	23.8 (1.75)
Rhode Island....	82.5 (0.40)	85.3 (0.39)	80.5 (1.60)	58.4 (1.86)	77.6 (2.73)	‡ (†)	78.9 (5.92)	87.3 (2.26)	29.1 (0.34)	30.8 (0.39)	19.7 (1.99)	14.6 (1.11)	45.5 (3.29)	‡ (†)	16.0 ! (5.75)	24.6 (3.22)
South Carolina..	81.5 (0.19)	85.4 (0.20)	73.7 (0.41)	57.3 (1.29)	85.4 (1.57)	80.3 (9.13)	73.0 (3.49)	82.9 (2.36)	23.0 (0.18)	27.3 (0.21)	11.9 (0.29)	12.3 (0.70)	45.9 (1.98)	‡ (†)	13.7 (2.64)	22.0 (2.26)
South Dakota....	87.6 (0.33)	89.0 (0.31)	78.9 (7.50)	57.2 (4.83)	94.6 (2.57)	‡ (†)	77.2 (1.65)	81.1 (4.40)	24.4 (0.52)	25.7 (0.55)	13.7 ! (4.43)	9.4 (2.36)	51.4 (7.64)	‡ (†)	10.0 (1.65)	14.6 (3.87)
Tennessee.......	80.9 (0.12)	82.1 (0.14)	78.0 (0.42)	55.0 (1.13)	86.3 (1.17)	‡ (†)	72.2 (3.22)	80.1 (1.71)	21.8 (0.16)	23.0 (0.16)	14.7 (0.39)	11.8 (0.83)	51.6 (1.79)	‡ (†)	12.7 (1.98)	18.0 (1.33)
Texas............	78.6 (0.09)	90.2 (0.08)	82.4 (0.23)	55.6 (0.22)	86.5 (0.41)	90.2 (2.99)	85.4 (1.06)	88.9 (0.78)	24.8 (0.09)	32.6 (0.11)	17.6 (0.24)	10.4 (0.12)	52.2 (0.53)	23.8 (3.62)	23.5 (1.21)	27.8 (0.93)
Utah..............	90.3 (0.19)	93.5 (0.17)	87.2 (2.90)	64.7 (1.14)	84.7 (1.51)	93.2 (2.28)	75.7 (3.04)	91.6 (1.76)	28.3 (0.25)	30.3 (0.30)	23.7 (3.01)	11.7 (0.63)	40.2 (2.54)	13.1 (2.58)	11.4 (2.00)	28.9 (3.80)
Vermont..........	90.5 (0.29)	90.6 (0.30)	‡ (†)	95.2 (1.89)	81.3 (4.49)	‡ (†)	78.8 (7.04)	94.5 (2.19)	32.9 (0.58)	32.6 (0.59)	‡ (†)	39.7 (6.66)	57.4 (5.63)	‡ (†)	11.7 ! (5.19)	30.1 (5.99)
Virginia..........	85.3 (0.11)	88.0 (0.12)	78.7 (0.31)	67.5 (0.84)	88.7 (0.53)	91.1 (5.14)	80.7 (2.26)	88.5 (1.18)	32.9 (0.16)	36.1 (0.18)	17.7 (0.35)	21.6 (0.69)	55.5 (0.79)	36.5 (9.33)	21.6 (2.18)	33.0 (1.58)
Washington.......	89.0 (0.11)	92.2 (0.11)	85.7 (1.08)	57.7 (0.80)	84.6 (0.62)	81.5 (2.37)	80.7 (1.29)	90.2 (0.82)	30.0 (0.15)	31.5 (0.16)	18.7 (0.97)	11.2 (0.46)	43.2 (0.88)	11.2 (2.08)	11.7 (0.90)	22.6 (1.19)
West Virginia....	81.0 (0.26)	80.8 (0.26)	85.4 (1.20)	73.3 (3.38)	93.6 (1.96)	‡ (†)	77.7 (5.23)	79.3 (3.32)	17.0 (0.25)	16.7 (0.25)	15.0 (1.46)	20.6 (3.03)	62.1 (5.03)	‡ (†)	17.1 (4.63)	20.3 (3.24)
Wisconsin........	88.5 (0.14)	90.4 (0.11)	76.2 (1.07)	62.2 (1.52)	80.1 (1.62)	‡ (†)	83.5 (1.68)	87.9 (1.73)	25.5 (0.19)	26.3 (0.19)	12.4 (0.85)	13.6 (0.80)	49.1 (1.99)	‡ (†)	12.2 (1.63)	22.6 (2.61)
Wyoming..........	90.5 (0.39)	92.0 (0.37)	79.2 (10.28)	71.1 (2.66)	84.5 (6.42)	‡ (†)	88.5 (2.35)	91.5 (2.92)	22.7 (0.51)	23.9 (0.51)	13.5 ! (6.83)	9.9 (1.89)	49.9 (10.14)	‡ (†)	9.5 ! (3.26)	13.8 ! (4.66)

†Not applicable.
!Interpret data with caution.
‡Reporting standards not met.

NOTE: Estimates are 3-year averages of 2005–07 data. Use of a 3-year average increases the sample size, thereby reducing the size of sampling errors and producing more stable estimates. Race categories exclude persons of Hispanic ethnicity. Standard errors appear in parentheses.
SOURCE: U.S. Department of Commerce, Census Bureau, 2005–2007 American Community Survey (ACS) 3-Year Public Use Microdata Sample (PUMS) data. (This table was prepared July 2009.)

Educational attainment of persons 25 years old and over, by sex and state: 2005–07

State	Number of persons 25 years old and over (in thousands)						Percent with high school completion or higher						Percent with bachelor's or higher degree					
	Total		Males		Females		Total		Male		Female		Total		Male		Female	
1	2		3		4		5		6		7		8		9		10	
United States	195,632	(48.7)	94,204	(31.5)	101,428	(28.0)	84.1	(0.03)	83.5	(0.03)	84.6	(0.03)	27.0	(0.04)	27.9	(0.04)	26.2	(0.04)
Alabama	3,018	(4.6)	1,421	(2.9)	1,597	(3.4)	80.0	(0.20)	79.1	(0.25)	80.7	(0.22)	21.0	(0.17)	21.7	(0.22)	20.4	(0.21)
Alaska.................	416	(2.7)	212	(1.8)	204	(1.6)	90.5	(0.36)	90.0	(0.53)	91.1	(0.45)	26.2	(0.45)	24.6	(0.52)	28.0	(0.75)
Arizona	3,961	(4.8)	1,945	(3.4)	2,017	(2.8)	83.4	(0.16)	82.5	(0.20)	84.3	(0.18)	25.3	(0.14)	26.4	(0.17)	24.2	(0.18)
Arkansas.............	1,845	(4.2)	880	(3.0)	965	(2.5)	80.7	(0.20)	79.8	(0.31)	81.5	(0.23)	18.7	(0.26)	18.9	(0.33)	18.6	(0.33)
California	23,052	(11.7)	11,323	(7.9)	11,729	(8.0)	80.0	(0.06)	79.7	(0.09)	80.3	(0.08)	29.1	(0.07)	30.1	(0.10)	28.1	(0.08)
Colorado	3,134	(4.8)	1,559	(3.5)	1,575	(3.6)	88.3	(0.15)	87.5	(0.19)	89.0	(0.19)	34.7	(0.17)	35.7	(0.23)	33.8	(0.23)
Connecticut...........	2,355	(3.7)	1,116	(2.8)	1,239	(2.3)	87.8	(0.16)	87.7	(0.22)	87.9	(0.19)	34.2	(0.24)	35.3	(0.32)	33.3	(0.27)
Delaware............	565	(2.1)	267	(1.5)	299	(1.4)	85.5	(0.35)	84.4	(0.48)	86.5	(0.43)	26.8	(0.48)	27.5	(0.64)	26.2	(0.53)
District of Columbia ...	397	(1.7)	184	(1.3)	213	(1.1)	84.0	(0.43)	84.0	(0.48)	84.0	(0.57)	45.3	(0.42)	47.0	(0.61)	43.8	(0.60)
Florida................	12,417	(5.5)	5,961	(4.9)	6,456	(4.2)	84.5	(0.08)	83.7	(0.12)	85.3	(0.09)	25.2	(0.09)	26.8	(0.12)	23.7	(0.12)
Georgia.................	5,947	(5.6)	2,848	(4.4)	3,099	(3.6)	82.2	(0.13)	81.0	(0.17)	83.2	(0.16)	26.4	(0.14)	26.8	(0.16)	26.1	(0.18)
Hawaii................	867	(2.5)	426	(1.7)	441	(1.7)	88.8	(0.29)	89.9	(0.35)	87.7	(0.35)	28.5	(0.36)	28.2	(0.44)	28.8	(0.49)
Idaho.................	917	(2.9)	454	(2.0)	463	(1.8)	87.3	(0.30)	86.6	(0.38)	88.0	(0.35)	23.8	(0.34)	25.3	(0.42)	22.3	(0.42)
Illinois................	8,296	(8.0)	3,994	(4.4)	4,302	(5.8)	85.3	(0.10)	85.0	(0.13)	85.6	(0.12)	29.0	(0.12)	30.0	(0.15)	28.1	(0.16)
Indiana................	4,106	(6.0)	1,977	(3.8)	2,130	(3.9)	85.3	(0.12)	84.9	(0.17)	85.7	(0.17)	21.7	(0.15)	22.6	(0.20)	20.9	(0.18)
Iowa	1,955	(5.1)	943	(3.3)	1,012	(3.3)	89.1	(0.17)	88.3	(0.24)	89.8	(0.19)	23.9	(0.25)	24.5	(0.30)	23.4	(0.33)
Kansas...............	1,772	(4.3)	861	(2.9)	911	(2.9)	88.6	(0.19)	88.2	(0.26)	89.1	(0.21)	28.5	(0.25)	29.3	(0.33)	27.6	(0.33)
Kentucky	2,807	(4.5)	1,341	(3.2)	1,466	(2.9)	79.6	(0.18)	78.2	(0.26)	80.8	(0.21)	19.7	(0.17)	19.8	(0.24)	19.7	(0.22)
Louisiana	2,766	(4.9)	1,308	(3.2)	1,458	(3.2)	79.2	(0.20)	77.6	(0.27)	80.7	(0.27)	20.0	(0.19)	19.7	(0.26)	20.3	(0.21)
Maine................	923	(3.0)	439	(1.9)	483	(2.2)	88.9	(0.23)	87.8	(0.34)	89.9	(0.28)	25.9	(0.40)	25.4	(0.47)	26.3	(0.49)
Maryland.............	3,700	(5.1)	1,738	(3.6)	1,962	(3.4)	86.9	(0.14)	86.0	(0.20)	87.7	(0.15)	34.8	(0.18)	35.8	(0.25)	33.9	(0.23)
Massachusetts........	4,354	(4.9)	2,058	(3.1)	2,296	(3.3)	88.0	(0.12)	87.4	(0.18)	88.5	(0.13)	37.0	(0.16)	37.8	(0.23)	36.3	(0.19)
Michigan	6,644	(8.0)	3,204	(5.0)	3,440	(5.0)	87.1	(0.12)	86.4	(0.18)	87.8	(0.13)	24.7	(0.13)	25.6	(0.16)	23.9	(0.14)
Minnesota	3,397	(7.1)	1,666	(5.0)	1,731	(4.3)	90.7	(0.13)	90.0	(0.20)	91.4	(0.15)	30.4	(0.21)	30.8	(0.25)	30.1	(0.26)
Mississippi	1,828	(3.6)	857	(2.1)	971	(2.5)	78.0	(0.21)	76.6	(0.30)	79.3	(0.26)	18.6	(0.20)	18.5	(0.26)	18.8	(0.26)
Missouri	3,839	(5.6)	1,827	(4.6)	2,012	(3.2)	85.0	(0.13)	84.7	(0.19)	85.2	(0.18)	24.1	(0.17)	24.8	(0.23)	23.4	(0.19)
Montana	632	(2.9)	309	(1.7)	323	(2.0)	89.9	(0.35)	89.1	(0.43)	90.6	(0.43)	26.4	(0.46)	27.1	(0.70)	25.6	(0.50)
Nebraska.............	1,122	(3.8)	543	(2.6)	579	(2.4)	89.6	(0.22)	89.1	(0.28)	90.0	(0.29)	26.6	(0.32)	27.0	(0.43)	26.2	(0.39)
Nevada	1,642	(2.7)	829	(2.0)	812	(1.6)	83.4	(0.21)	83.3	(0.27)	83.5	(0.29)	20.9	(0.24)	22.0	(0.32)	19.9	(0.28)
New Hampshire	890	(2.4)	429	(1.9)	461	(1.5)	89.7	(0.24)	88.7	(0.34)	90.6	(0.31)	31.4	(0.39)	32.4	(0.50)	30.5	(0.43)
New Jersey	5,835	(5.7)	2,777	(3.4)	3,058	(3.7)	86.3	(0.11)	86.1	(0.15)	86.4	(0.14)	33.6	(0.15)	35.5	(0.19)	31.9	(0.17)
New Mexico	1,240	(3.3)	599	(2.1)	641	(2.1)	81.9	(0.27)	81.5	(0.37)	82.4	(0.39)	24.8	(0.30)	25.5	(0.41)	24.2	(0.35)
New York.............	12,859	(10.2)	6,068	(7.3)	6,791	(6.5)	83.8	(0.08)	83.7	(0.11)	84.0	(0.10)	31.2	(0.11)	31.7	(0.16)	30.6	(0.12)
North Carolina	5,846	(5.2)	2,774	(4.3)	3,072	(3.5)	82.2	(0.12)	80.6	(0.18)	83.7	(0.14)	25.1	(0.14)	25.3	(0.16)	24.8	(0.17)
North Dakota	411	(2.3)	204	(1.7)	207	(1.6)	88.0	(0.41)	87.3	(0.51)	88.7	(0.48)	26.3	(0.60)	26.6	(0.77)	25.9	(0.73)
Ohio..................	7,603	(6.9)	3,617	(5.3)	3,985	(4.2)	86.3	(0.11)	86.1	(0.15)	86.5	(0.11)	23.4	(0.11)	24.4	(0.15)	22.5	(0.12)
Oklahoma	2,313	(5.2)	1,115	(3.2)	1,198	(3.6)	84.1	(0.18)	83.6	(0.24)	84.6	(0.23)	22.2	(0.22)	23.0	(0.26)	21.5	(0.26)
Oregon................	2,498	(3.7)	1,220	(2.3)	1,278	(2.5)	87.6	(0.16)	86.8	(0.20)	88.3	(0.21)	27.5	(0.22)	28.4	(0.28)	26.7	(0.25)
Pennsylvania..........	8,394	(7.6)	3,979	(5.6)	4,415	(5.0)	86.3	(0.09)	86.3	(0.13)	86.4	(0.12)	25.6	(0.12)	27.0	(0.15)	24.4	(0.14)
Rhode Island	711	(1.7)	334	(1.3)	377	(1.2)	82.5	(0.40)	81.8	(0.54)	83.1	(0.43)	29.1	(0.34)	29.8	(0.46)	28.5	(0.50)
South Carolina........	2,851	(4.0)	1,348	(2.7)	1,503	(2.7)	81.5	(0.19)	80.4	(0.21)	82.4	(0.23)	23.0	(0.18)	23.9	(0.23)	22.3	(0.22)
South Dakota.........	510	(2.7)	249	(1.7)	261	(1.9)	87.6	(0.33)	86.9	(0.47)	88.3	(0.43)	24.4	(0.52)	24.9	(0.64)	24.0	(0.64)
Tennessee	4,062	(4.8)	1,934	(3.6)	2,128	(3.1)	80.9	(0.12)	80.1	(0.19)	81.6	(0.15)	21.8	(0.16)	22.7	(0.21)	21.0	(0.18)
Texas	14,486	(10.0)	7,080	(7.2)	7,405	(5.5)	78.6	(0.09)	78.1	(0.11)	79.1	(0.11)	24.8	(0.09)	25.7	(0.10)	23.8	(0.12)
Utah..................	1,448	(3.8)	714	(2.5)	734	(2.4)	90.3	(0.19)	90.0	(0.28)	90.5	(0.24)	28.3	(0.25)	31.6	(0.32)	25.1	(0.31)
Vermont	424	(2.2)	205	(1.3)	219	(1.6)	90.5	(0.29)	88.9	(0.50)	92.0	(0.37)	32.9	(0.58)	31.6	(0.74)	34.1	(0.70)
Virginia................	5,056	(5.5)	2,417	(4.0)	2,639	(3.7)	85.3	(0.11)	84.6	(0.17)	85.9	(0.14)	32.9	(0.16)	33.8	(0.19)	32.1	(0.19)
Washington............	4,240	(4.3)	2,080	(3.2)	2,160	(3.2)	89.0	(0.11)	88.6	(0.15)	89.3	(0.15)	30.0	(0.15)	31.5	(0.21)	28.7	(0.21)
West Virginia..........	1,257	(2.6)	601	(1.9)	656	(1.8)	81.0	(0.26)	80.2	(0.33)	81.6	(0.32)	17.0	(0.25)	17.4	(0.30)	16.6	(0.31)
Wisconsin	3,688	(7.6)	1,803	(4.6)	1,885	(5.7)	88.5	(0.14)	87.8	(0.19)	89.2	(0.17)	25.5	(0.19)	25.5	(0.23)	25.4	(0.23)
Wyoming..............	336	(1.7)	167	(1.2)	169	(1.2)	90.5	(0.39)	90.2	(0.60)	90.9	(0.49)	22.7	(0.51)	23.5	(0.73)	22.0	(0.59)

NOTE: Estimates are 3-year averages of 2005–07 data. Use of a 3-year average increases the sample size, thereby reducing the size of sampling errors and producing more stable estimates. Standard errors appear in parentheses. Detail may not sum to totals because of rounding.

SOURCE: U.S. Department of Commerce, Census Bureau, 2005–2007 American Community Survey (ACS) 3-Year Public Use Microdata Sample (PUMS) data. (This table was prepared July 2009.)

Educational attainment of persons 25 years old and over for metropolitan areas with more than 1 million persons, by sex: 2009

| Metropolitan area | Number of persons 25 years old and over (in thousands) | | | Percent with high school completion or higher | | | Percent with bachelor's or higher degree | | |
| | Total | Males | Females | Total | Male | Female | Total | Male | Female |
1	2	3	4	5	6	7	8	9	10
Atlanta-Sandy Springs-Marietta, GA CBSA	3,571 (65.1)	1,731 (45.5)	1,840 (46.9)	90.6 (0.54)	90.6 (0.77)	90.6 (0.75)	38.8 (0.90)	39.4 (1.29)	38.3 (1.24)
Austin-Round Rock, TX CBSA	1,207 (38.1)	624 (27.4)	583 (26.5)	87.6 (1.04)	88.3 (1.42)	86.8 (1.54)	46.6 (1.58)	48.9 (2.20)	44.1 (2.26)
Birmingham-Hoover, AL CBSA	910 (33.1)	418 (22.4)	493 (24.3)	83.0 (1.37)	82.4 (2.04)	83.5 (1.84)	26.8 (1.61)	27.0 (2.38)	26.7 (2.19)
Boston-Worcester-Manchester, MA-NH-CT-ME CSA[1]	3,797 (67.1)	1,825 (46.7)	1,972 (48.6)	91.7 (0.49)	91.7 (0.71)	91.8 (0.68)	43.9 (0.88)	45.9 (1.28)	42.1 (1.22)
Buffalo-Niagara Falls, NY CBSA	760 (30.2)	347 (20.5)	412 (22.3)	88.1 (1.29)	86.9 (1.99)	89.1 (1.68)	18.8 (1.56)	18.4 (2.28)	19.1 (2.12)
Charlotte-Gastonia-Concord, NC-SC CBSA	1,149 (37.1)	576 (26.3)	573 (26.3)	83.8 (1.19)	84.5 (1.66)	83.2 (1.72)	32.9 (1.52)	34.6 (2.18)	31.3 (2.13)
Chicago-Naperville-Michigan City, IL-IN-WI CSA	6,090 (84.6)	2,910 (58.9)	3,180 (61.5)	88.1 (0.46)	88.2 (0.66)	88.0 (0.63)	35.4 (0.67)	35.9 (0.98)	35.0 (0.93)
Cincinnati-Middletown, OH-KY-IN CBSA[1]	1,350 (40.2)	644 (27.8)	706 (29.1)	87.6 (0.98)	89.1 (1.35)	86.3 (1.42)	28.8 (1.35)	30.5 (1.99)	27.4 (1.84)
Cleveland-Akron-Elyria, OH CSA	1,915 (47.9)	943 (33.7)	972 (34.2)	90.2 (0.75)	88.6 (1.14)	91.7 (0.97)	27.4 (1.12)	26.8 (1.58)	27.9 (1.58)
Columbus, OH CSA	1,071 (35.9)	512 (24.8)	560 (25.9)	85.8 (1.17)	83.5 (1.80)	87.9 (1.51)	28.5 (1.51)	30.2 (2.23)	26.9 (2.06)
Dallas-Fort Worth-Arlington, TX CBSA	4,041 (69.2)	1,990 (48.8)	2,052 (49.5)	84.2 (0.63)	83.5 (0.91)	84.8 (0.87)	31.3 (0.80)	32.8 (1.16)	29.9 (1.11)
Denver-Aurora-Boulder, CO CSA	1,932 (48.1)	968 (34.1)	964 (34.0)	91.5 (0.70)	91.8 (0.97)	91.1 (1.00)	45.3 (1.24)	48.0 (1.76)	42.6 (1.75)
Detroit-Warren-Flint, MI CSA	3,525 (64.7)	1,657 (44.5)	1,868 (47.3)	90.1 (0.55)	89.9 (0.81)	90.3 (0.75)	32.8 (0.87)	34.9 (1.29)	30.9 (1.17)
Fresno-Madera, CA CSA	658 (33.2)	342 (23.1)	317 (19.5)	75.9 (1.83)	75.3 (2.56)	76.6 (2.61)	22.6 (1.79)	21.1 (2.42)	24.2 (2.64)
Grand-Rapids-Muskegon-Holland, MI CSA	916 (33.2)	444 (23.1)	472 (23.8)	93.5 (0.89)	93.7 (1.27)	93.4 (1.25)	23.6 (1.54)	25.3 (2.27)	22.0 (2.10)
Greensboro-Winston-Salem-High Point, NC CSA	882 (32.5)	435 (22.9)	447 (23.2)	87.3 (1.23)	86.1 (1.82)	88.4 (1.66)	21.7 (1.52)	19.9 (2.10)	23.5 (2.20)
Hartford-West Hartford, CT CSA	781 (30.6)	370 (21.1)	411 (22.2)	90.4 (1.16)	90.8 (1.65)	90.0 (1.63)	38.2 (1.91)	40.4 (2.80)	36.2 (2.60)
Houston-Baytown-Sugarland, TX CBSA	3,544 (64.9)	1,740 (45.6)	1,804 (46.5)	78.2 (0.76)	78.3 (1.09)	78.1 (1.07)	24.6 (0.79)	23.9 (1.12)	25.1 (1.12)
Indianapolis-Anderson-Columbus, IN CSA	1,259 (38.9)	574 (26.3)	685 (28.7)	88.5 (0.99)	90.7 (1.33)	86.6 (1.43)	28.8 (1.40)	31.6 (2.13)	26.4 (1.85)
Jacksonville, FL CBSA	956 (33.9)	457 (23.5)	500 (24.5)	92.9 (0.91)	93.9 (1.23)	92.0 (1.33)	36.4 (1.71)	38.5 (2.50)	34.5 (2.34)
Kansas City, MO-KS CSBA	1,188 (37.8)	565 (26.1)	624 (27.4)	92.2 (0.85)	91.8 (1.27)	92.6 (1.15)	37.7 (1.54)	36.4 (2.22)	38.8 (2.14)
Las Vegas-Paradise, NV CBSA	1,248 (38.7)	620 (27.3)	628 (27.5)	87.1 (1.04)	86.2 (1.52)	88.0 (1.42)	23.6 (1.32)	25.8 (1.93)	21.5 (1.80)
Los Angeles-Long Beach-Riverside, CA CSA	11,169 (113.3)	5,432 (80.0)	5,737 (82.2)	78.3 (0.43)	78.4 (0.61)	78.1 (0.60)	28.6 (0.47)	29.7 (0.68)	27.7 (0.65)
Louisville, KY-IN CBSA	730 (29.6)	369 (21.1)	361 (20.8)	87.9 (1.33)	89.4 (1.76)	86.3 (1.99)	24.9 (1.76)	22.5 (2.39)	27.3 (2.58)
Memphis, TN-MS-AR CBSA[1]	792 (30.9)	374 (21.2)	418 (22.4)	83.9 (1.43)	82.2 (2.17)	85.5 (1.89)	28.5 (1.76)	26.2 (2.50)	30.6 (2.48)
Miami-Fort Lauderdale-Miami Beach, FL CBSA	3,714 (66.4)	1,769 (46.0)	1,945 (48.2)	85.6 (0.63)	84.9 (0.94)	86.3 (0.86)	31.1 (0.83)	31.7 (1.21)	30.5 (1.15)
Milwaukee-Racine-Waukesha, WI CSA	1,181 (37.7)	564 (26.0)	618 (27.3)	86.9 (1.08)	85.9 (1.61)	87.8 (1.45)	31.0 (1.48)	32.5 (2.17)	29.6 (2.02)
Minneapolis-St. Paul-St. Cloud, MN-WI CSA[1]	2,151 (50.7)	1,026 (35.1)	1,124 (36.7)	92.8 (0.61)	92.9 (0.88)	92.7 (0.85)	38.4 (1.15)	39.4 (1.68)	37.6 (1.59)
Nashville-Davidson-Murfreesboro, TN CBSA	1,129 (36.8)	548 (25.7)	582 (26.5)	88.5 (1.04)	87.1 (1.57)	89.8 (1.38)	35.2 (1.56)	35.9 (2.25)	34.5 (2.16)
New Orleans-Metairie-Kenner, LA CBSA	704 (29.1)	317 (19.5)	387 (21.6)	85.9 (1.44)	82.3 (2.36)	88.9 (1.76)	29.1 (1.78)	24.7 (2.66)	32.6 (2.62)
New York-Newark, NY-NJ-PA CSA	14,464 (128.1)	6,862 (89.7)	7,602 (94.2)	86.6 (0.31)	86.7 (0.45)	86.5 (0.43)	36.7 (0.44)	37.4 (0.64)	36.1 (0.61)
Oklahoma City, OK CBSA	880 (32.5)	408 (22.2)	472 (23.8)	89.5 (1.14)	86.9 (1.83)	91.6 (1.40)	29.3 (1.69)	29.9 (2.49)	28.8 (2.29)
Orlando, FL CBSA	1,372 (40.6)	665 (28.3)	707 (29.2)	88.6 (0.94)	89.1 (1.33)	88.2 (1.33)	32.1 (1.38)	33.0 (2.00)	31.3 (1.92)
Philadelphia-Camden-Vineland, PA-NJ-DE-MD CSA	3,784 (67.0)	1,749 (45.8)	2,036 (49.3)	88.2 (0.58)	87.1 (0.88)	89.1 (0.76)	32.7 (0.84)	33.6 (1.24)	31.9 (1.13)
Phoenix-Mesa-Scottsdale, AZ CBSA	2,784 (57.6)	1,394 (40.9)	1,390 (40.8)	84.2 (0.76)	81.6 (1.14)	86.8 (1.00)	29.9 (0.95)	30.4 (1.35)	29.5 (1.34)
Pittsburgh-New Castle, PA CBSA	1,564 (43.3)	722 (29.5)	842 (31.8)	90.5 (0.81)	92.3 (1.09)	89.0 (1.18)	29.1 (1.26)	34.3 (1.94)	24.7 (1.63)
Portland-Vancouver-Beaverton, OR-WA CBSA	1,350 (40.2)	650 (28.0)	700 (29.0)	92.8 (0.77)	91.1 (1.23)	94.4 (0.96)	37.1 (1.44)	35.9 (2.07)	38.2 (2.02)
Providence-Fall River-Warwick, RI-MA CBSA	854 (33.8)	405 (22.1)	449 (23.2)	85.4 (1.33)	87.3 (1.82)	83.7 (1.91)	32.2 (1.76)	34.2 (2.59)	30.4 (2.38)
Raleigh-Durham-Cary, NC CSA	1,058 (35.6)	523 (25.1)	535 (25.4)	86.3 (1.16)	83.6 (1.78)	88.9 (1.49)	41.4 (1.66)	39.3 (2.34)	43.4 (2.35)
Richmond, VA CBSA	841 (31.8)	403 (22.0)	438 (23.0)	87.7 (1.24)	87.2 (1.83)	88.2 (1.69)	33.0 (1.78)	33.9 (2.59)	32.1 (2.45)
Rochester, NY CBSA	743 (29.9)	370 (21.1)	373 (21.2)	89.0 (1.26)	91.0 (1.63)	87.0 (1.91)	28.7 (1.82)	26.4 (2.52)	31.0 (2.63)
Sacramento-Arden-Arcade-Roseville, CA CBSA	1,306 (39.6)	640 (27.7)	666 (28.3)	86.2 (1.05)	85.6 (1.52)	86.8 (1.44)	34.2 (1.44)	34.8 (2.07)	33.5 (2.01)
Salt Lake City-Ogden-Clearfield, UT CSA	981 (34.3)	498 (24.5)	483 (24.1)	89.7 (1.07)	88.3 (1.58)	91.1 (1.42)	28.4 (1.58)	35.0 (2.35)	21.7 (2.06)
San Antonio, TX CBSA	1,296 (39.4)	597 (26.8)	699 (29.0)	79.7 (1.23)	78.4 (1.85)	80.8 (1.64)	26.3 (1.34)	26.7 (1.99)	25.8 (1.82)
San Diego-Carlsbad-San Marcos, CA CBSA	1,885 (47.5)	939 (33.6)	946 (33.7)	86.3 (0.87)	87.7 (1.18)	84.9 (1.28)	33.5 (1.19)	35.9 (1.72)	31.2 (1.65)
San Jose-San Francisco-Oakland, CA CSA	5,299 (79.1)	2,641 (56.1)	2,657 (56.3)	88.9 (0.47)	89.1 (0.67)	88.7 (0.68)	45.5 (0.75)	46.7 (1.07)	44.2 (1.06)
Seattle-Tacoma-Olympia, WA CSA	2,778 (57.6)	1,383 (40.7)	1,395 (40.9)	94.6 (0.47)	94.0 (0.70)	95.2 (0.63)	36.7 (1.00)	36.8 (1.42)	36.6 (1.42)
St. Louis, MO-IL CBSA	1,894 (47.6)	893 (32.8)	1,001 (34.3)	90.7 (0.73)	91.0 (1.05)	90.4 (1.02)	28.9 (1.14)	30.7 (1.69)	27.3 (1.55)
Tampa-St. Petersburg-Clearwater, FL CBSA	1,947 (48.3)	871 (32.4)	1,076 (35.9)	91.2 (0.70)	91.4 (1.04)	91.0 (0.96)	29.1 (1.13)	30.0 (1.71)	28.3 (1.51)
Virginia Beach-Norfolk-Newport News, VA-NC CSA[1]	1,045 (35.4)	482 (24.1)	564 (26.0)	93.1 (0.86)	95.8 (1.01)	90.8 (1.34)	32.7 (1.59)	27.9 (2.24)	36.8 (2.23)
Washington-Baltimore-Northern Virginia, DC-MD-VA-WV CSA[1]	5,316 (79.2)	2,525 (54.9)	2,791 (57.7)	90.9 (0.43)	90.0 (0.66)	91.7 (0.57)	44.7 (0.75)	46.5 (1.09)	43.1 (1.03)

[1] Information on metropolitan status was suppressed for a small portion of sample observations. As a result, population estimates for these areas may be slightly underestimated.

NOTE: CSA = Combined Statistical Area; CBSA = Core Based Statistical Area. Detail may not sum to totals because of rounding. Standard errors appear in parentheses.

SOURCE: U.S. Department of Commerce, Census Bureau, Current Population Survey (CPS), March 2009. (This table was prepared November 2009.)

Average scores and achievement-level results in NAEP reading for public school students at grade 4, by state/jurisdiction: 2009

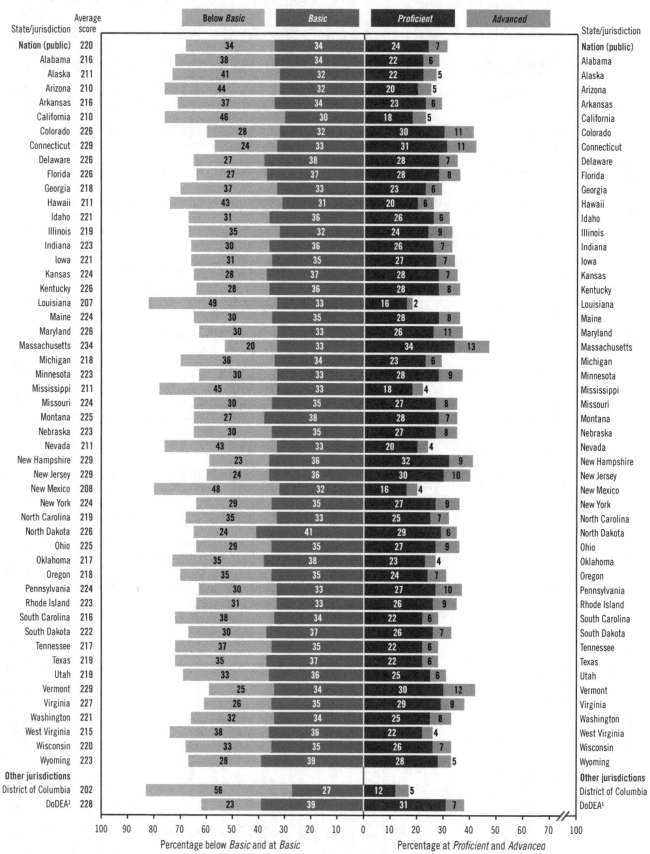

State/jurisdiction	Average score
Nation (public)	220
Alabama	216
Alaska	211
Arizona	210
Arkansas	216
California	210
Colorado	226
Connecticut	229
Delaware	226
Florida	226
Georgia	218
Hawaii	211
Idaho	221
Illinois	219
Indiana	223
Iowa	221
Kansas	224
Kentucky	226
Louisiana	207
Maine	224
Maryland	226
Massachusetts	234
Michigan	218
Minnesota	223
Mississippi	211
Missouri	224
Montana	225
Nebraska	223
Nevada	211
New Hampshire	229
New Jersey	229
New Mexico	208
New York	224
North Carolina	219
North Dakota	226
Ohio	225
Oklahoma	217
Oregon	218
Pennsylvania	224
Rhode Island	223
South Carolina	216
South Dakota	222
Tennessee	217
Texas	219
Utah	219
Vermont	229
Virginia	227
Washington	221
West Virginia	215
Wisconsin	220
Wyoming	223
Other jurisdictions	
District of Columbia	202
DoDEA[1]	228

Percentage below *Basic* and at *Basic*   Percentage at *Proficient* and *Advanced*

[1] Department of Defense Education Activity (overseas and domestic schools).
NOTE: The shaded bars are graphed using unrounded numbers. Detail may not sum to totals because of rounding.
SOURCE: U.S. Department of Education, Institute of Education Sciences, National Center for Education Statistics, National Assessment of Educational Progress (NAEP), 2009 Reading Assessment.

Average scores and achievement-level results in NAEP reading for fourth-grade public school students, by race/ethnicity and state/jurisdiction: 2009

State/jurisdiction	White — Average scale score	White — Below Basic	White — At or above Basic	White — At or above Proficient	White — At Advanced	Black — Average scale score	Black — Below Basic	Black — At or above Basic	Black — At or above Proficient	Black — At Advanced	Hispanic — Average scale score	Hispanic — Below Basic	Hispanic — At or above Basic	Hispanic — At or above Proficient	Hispanic — At Advanced
Nation (public)	**229**	**23**	**77**	**41**	**10**	**204**	**53**	**47**	**15**	**2**	**204**	**52**	**48**	**16**	**2**
Alabama	225	27	73	36	8	201	56	44	13	1	215	36	64	27	4
Alaska	226	25	75	38	8	204	50	50	13	1	198	58	42	14	2
Arizona	225	27	73	37	8	206	48	52	20	5	202	53	47	16	2
Arkansas	224	28	72	35	8	199	57	43	14	1	196	62	38	11	1
California	227	26	74	39	8	200	58	42	14	1	204	50	50	18	3
Colorado	236	16	84	51	14	213	43	57	27	5	204	50	50	18	2
Connecticut	238	15	85	52	15	209	46	54	22	4	205	49	51	15	2
Delaware	235	16	84	47	11	213	43	57	19	2	216	37	63	24	4
Florida	233	19	81	45	11	211	44	56	18	2	223	29	71	31	6
Georgia	229	24	76	40	10	204	53	47	15	2	208	48	52	20	3
Hawaii	226	28	72	42	13	‡	‡	‡	‡	‡	215	38	62	27	6
Idaho	225	27	73	36	7	198	60	40	11	1	201	55	45	14	2
Illinois	231	22	78	44	12	206	49	51	15	2	203	52	48	16	2
Indiana	227	25	75	38	9	203	51	49	22	3	203	50	50	15	2
Iowa	224	28	72	36	8	210	44	56	20	2	207	47	53	20	3
Kansas	229	22	78	40	8	204	55	45	13	1	210	45	55	20	2
Kentucky	228	25	75	39	9	196	63	37	9	1	215	42	58	22	5
Louisiana	219	34	66	28	4	198	58	42	18	3	206	52	48	16	1
Maine	225	29	71	36	8	210	47	53	19	3	‡	‡	‡	‡	‡
Maryland	237	19	81	50	16	210	47	53	19	3	221	33	67	30	7
Massachusetts	241	13	87	56	17	216	38	62	23	3	211	44	56	20	3
Michigan	225	28	72	36	8	194	65	35	9	1	206	49	51	17	2
Minnesota	230	22	78	43	11	195	61	39	12	2	194	62	38	13	3
Mississippi	225	28	72	35	7	198	61	39	10	1	212	40	60	19	4
Missouri	228	25	75	40	10	204	54	46	16	3	216	36	64	26	3
Montana	228	24	76	37	7	‡	‡	‡	‡	‡	207	47	53	20	3
Nebraska	228	24	76	40	9	203	52	48	19	3	199	56	44	13	2
Nevada	222	30	70	34	7	201	54	46	14	2	217	37	63	30	8
New Hampshire	230	22	78	42	9	216	38	62	28	5	213	42	58	19	2
New Jersey	237	14	86	51	13	213	43	57	18	3	201	55	45	14	1
New Mexico	224	30	70	35	9	205	50	50	13	1	210	44	56	22	4
New York	233	19	81	45	11	209	47	53	18	3	204	50	50	17	3
North Carolina	230	23	77	44	11	204	52	48	14	1	‡	‡	‡	‡	‡
North Dakota	228	21	79	37	6	‡	‡	‡	‡	‡	215	44	56	30	9
Ohio	230	22	78	42	10	203	54	46	13	1	207	47	53	17	3
Oklahoma	223	28	72	33	5	197	59	41	11	1	196	59	41	13	2
Oregon	223	28	72	35	7	202	53	47	17	3	199	56	44	14	2
Pennsylvania	230	23	77	42	11	201	56	44	15	2	200	55	45	14	2
Rhode Island	231	22	78	44	12	207	48	52	17	2	205	47	53	17	1
South Carolina	226	26	74	38	9	200	56	44	11	1	216	36	64	29	4
South Dakota	227	25	75	37	7	‡	‡	‡	‡	‡	202	52	48	16	2
Tennessee	224	28	72	34	7	197	62	38	12	1	210	46	54	18	2
Texas	232	20	80	43	11	213	42	58	20	2	194	63	37	10	#
Utah	225	27	73	36	7	202	54	46	14	2	‡	‡	‡	‡	‡
Vermont	229	25	75	42	12	214	39	61	29	9	214	40	60	26	5
Virginia	234	18	82	47	11	210	44	56	18	2	201	55	45	14	2
Washington	229	24	76	40	10	209	46	54	21	2	‡	‡	‡	‡	‡
West Virginia	215	37	63	26	4	204	53	47	16	2	202	54	46	16	2
Wisconsin	227	25	75	38	8	192	66	34	9	1	212	42	58	22	2
Wyoming	224	26	74	34	5	‡	‡	‡	‡	‡	207	49	51	17	4
Other jurisdictions															
District of Columbia	256	6	94	75	36	196	63	37	11	2	207	49	51	17	4
DoDEA[1]	234	17	83	48	10	218	34	66	22	3	223	27	73	30	4

See notes at end of table.

Average scores and achievement-level results in NAEP reading for fourth-grade public school students, by race/ethnicity and state/jurisdiction: 2009—Continued

State/jurisdiction	Asian/Pacific Islander					American Indian/Alaska Native				
	Average scale score	Percentage of students				Average scale score	Percentage of students			
		Below Basic	At or above Basic	At or above Proficient	At Advanced		Below Basic	At or above Basic	At or above Proficient	At Advanced
Nation (public)	**234**	**21**	**79**	**48**	**17**	**206**	**48**	**52**	**22**	**5**
Alabama	‡	‡	‡	‡	‡	‡	‡	‡	‡	‡
Alaska	208	49	51	19	3	179	73	27	9	1
Arizona	228	24	76	41	13	190	64	36	12	3
Arkansas	‡	‡	‡	‡	‡	‡	‡	‡	‡	‡
California	234	22	78	48	16	‡	‡	‡	‡	‡
Colorado	238	19	81	53	17	‡	‡	‡	‡	‡
Connecticut	239	18	82	55	21	‡	‡	‡	‡	‡
Delaware	242	12	88	57	19	‡	‡	‡	‡	‡
Florida	237	16	84	56	15	‡	‡	‡	‡	‡
Georgia	238	17	83	53	15	‡	‡	‡	‡	‡
Hawaii	208	46	54	22	4	‡	‡	‡	‡	‡
Idaho	225	26	74	33	9	‡	‡	‡	‡	‡
Illinois	249	9	91	63	27	‡	‡	‡	‡	‡
Indiana	‡	‡	‡	‡	‡	‡	‡	‡	‡	‡
Iowa	229	28	72	46	16	‡	‡	‡	‡	‡
Kansas	234	21	79	50	13	‡	‡	‡	‡	‡
Kentucky	243	15	85	56	22	‡	‡	‡	‡	‡
Louisiana	‡	‡	‡	‡	‡	‡	‡	‡	‡	‡
Maine	‡	‡	‡	‡	‡	‡	‡	‡	‡	‡
Maryland	245	11	89	59	25	‡	‡	‡	‡	‡
Massachusetts	241	15	85	56	22	‡	‡	‡	‡	‡
Michigan	234	21	79	42	17	‡	‡	‡	‡	‡
Minnesota	219	37	63	34	9	200	57	43	20	7
Mississippi	‡	‡	‡	‡	‡	‡	‡	‡	‡	‡
Missouri	‡	‡	‡	‡	‡	‡	‡	‡	‡	‡
Montana	‡	‡	‡	‡	‡	206	50	50	16	3
Nebraska	230	25	75	40	12	‡	‡	‡	‡	‡
Nevada	225	28	72	38	7	‡	‡	‡	‡	‡
New Hampshire	232	23	77	45	12	‡	‡	‡	‡	‡
New Jersey	246	11	89	62	24	‡	‡	‡	‡	‡
New Mexico	226	29	71	39	12	191	66	34	10	1
New York	238	17	83	52	17	‡	‡	‡	‡	‡
North Carolina	241	10	90	52	15	202	53	47	18	6
North Dakota	‡	‡	‡	‡	‡	204	53	47	16	3
Ohio	‡	‡	‡	‡	‡	‡	‡	‡	‡	‡
Oklahoma	‡	‡	‡	‡	‡	215	37	63	27	5
Oregon	227	28	72	43	14	210	44	56	17	3
Pennsylvania	243	16	84	61	23	‡	‡	‡	‡	‡
Rhode Island	219	34	66	30	9	‡	‡	‡	‡	‡
South Carolina	‡	‡	‡	‡	‡	‡	‡	‡	‡	‡
South Dakota	‡	‡	‡	‡	‡	196	62	38	11	2
Tennessee	‡	‡	‡	‡	‡	‡	‡	‡	‡	‡
Texas	242	12	88	52	22	‡	‡	‡	‡	‡
Utah	217	37	63	30	7	195	58	42	17	2
Vermont	‡	‡	‡	‡	‡	‡	‡	‡	‡	‡
Virginia	242	13	87	57	22	‡	‡	‡	‡	‡
Washington	221	33	67	35	10	212	40	60	27	7
West Virginia	‡	‡	‡	‡	‡	‡	‡	‡	‡	‡
Wisconsin	220	36	64	36	7	197	58	42	18	3
Wyoming	‡	‡	‡	‡	‡	205	48	52	19	2
Other jurisdictions										
District of Columbia	‡	‡	‡	‡	‡	‡	‡	‡	‡	‡
DoDEA[1]	224	25	75	34	4	‡	‡	‡	‡	‡

Rounds to zero.

‡ Reporting standards not met. Sample size insufficient to permit a reliable estimate.

[1] Department of Defense Education Activity (overseas and domestic schools).

NOTE: Black includes African American, Hispanic includes Latino, and Pacific Islander includes Native Hawaiian. Race categories exclude Hispanic origin. Results are not shown for students whose race/ethnicity was unclassified. Detail may not sum to totals because of rounding.

SOURCE: U.S. Department of Education, Institute of Education Sciences, National Center for Education Statistics, National Assessment of Educational Progress (NAEP), 2009 Reading Assessment.

Average scores and achievement-level results in NAEP reading for fourth-grade public school students, by gender and state/jurisdiction: 2009

State/jurisdiction	Male					Female				
	Average scale score	Percentage of students				Average scale score	Percentage of students			
		Below Basic	At or above Basic	At or above Proficient	At Advanced		Below Basic	At or above Basic	At or above Proficient	At Advanced
Nation (public)	**216**	**38**	**62**	**28**	**6**	**223**	**31**	**69**	**35**	**9**
Alabama	212	43	57	25	4	221	32	68	32	7
Alaska	207	45	55	24	4	216	37	63	31	7
Arizona	207	47	53	22	4	213	40	60	27	6
Arkansas	211	42	58	25	4	222	31	69	33	7
California	207	49	51	22	4	213	43	57	26	6
Colorado	222	31	69	36	8	229	25	75	44	13
Connecticut	225	29	71	38	9	234	20	80	47	14
Delaware	223	30	70	33	6	228	24	76	38	8
Florida	223	30	70	33	6	229	23	77	39	9
Georgia	214	41	59	26	5	221	34	66	33	7
Hawaii	205	49	51	22	4	217	37	63	30	7
Idaho	217	36	64	28	5	226	26	74	37	8
Illinois	215	40	60	29	7	224	30	70	36	10
Indiana	218	35	65	29	6	227	25	75	38	8
Iowa	217	36	64	29	6	226	26	74	39	9
Kansas	222	29	71	34	6	226	26	74	37	8
Kentucky	222	31	69	32	7	229	25	75	40	10
Louisiana	203	54	46	15	2	212	44	56	22	3
Maine	220	34	66	31	6	228	25	75	40	10
Maryland	223	33	67	34	9	229	26	74	40	13
Massachusetts	231	23	77	45	12	236	17	83	50	15
Michigan	214	39	61	26	5	222	32	68	34	8
Minnesota	220	33	67	34	8	227	26	74	41	11
Mississippi	208	49	51	20	3	213	42	58	24	4
Missouri	219	34	66	31	6	229	25	75	41	11
Montana	222	31	69	32	5	228	24	76	37	8
Nebraska	220	33	67	33	7	225	27	73	37	9
Nevada	208	46	54	22	4	214	39	61	26	5
New Hampshire	226	26	74	37	8	233	20	80	46	11
New Jersey	227	27	73	37	9	232	21	79	44	12
New Mexico	203	53	47	17	3	213	43	57	23	4
New York	221	33	67	32	7	228	25	75	40	10
North Carolina	215	39	61	29	6	224	30	70	36	8
North Dakota	223	28	72	30	4	229	21	79	39	7
Ohio	222	32	68	32	7	227	26	74	40	10
Oklahoma	214	38	62	26	4	220	31	69	29	5
Oregon	214	38	62	28	5	223	30	70	34	8
Pennsylvania	221	33	67	35	9	226	28	72	38	11
Rhode Island	218	36	64	31	8	228	26	74	40	11
South Carolina	213	40	60	26	6	219	36	64	29	6
South Dakota	220	34	66	31	6	225	27	73	35	8
Tennessee	214	40	60	26	4	220	34	66	30	7
Texas	216	39	61	25	5	222	31	69	30	7
Utah	217	36	64	28	5	222	31	69	34	6
Vermont	226	27	73	38	10	231	23	77	45	13
Virginia	223	30	70	35	8	230	22	78	42	11
Washington	217	36	64	29	6	226	29	71	38	10
West Virginia	211	42	58	23	3	218	35	65	29	5
Wisconsin	217	36	64	29	6	224	29	71	37	8
Wyoming	219	33	67	30	4	226	23	77	36	6
Other jurisdictions										
District of Columbia	198	60	40	16	4	206	52	48	18	5
DoDEA[1]	224	27	73	33	5	233	18	82	44	9

[1] Department of Defense Education Activity (overseas and domestic schools).
NOTE: Detail may not sum to totals because of rounding.
SOURCE: U.S. Department of Education, Institute of Education Sciences, National Center for Education Statistics, National Assessment of Educational Progress (NAEP), 2009 Reading Assessment.

Average scores and achievement-level results in NAEP reading for public school students at grade 8, by state/jurisdiction: 2009

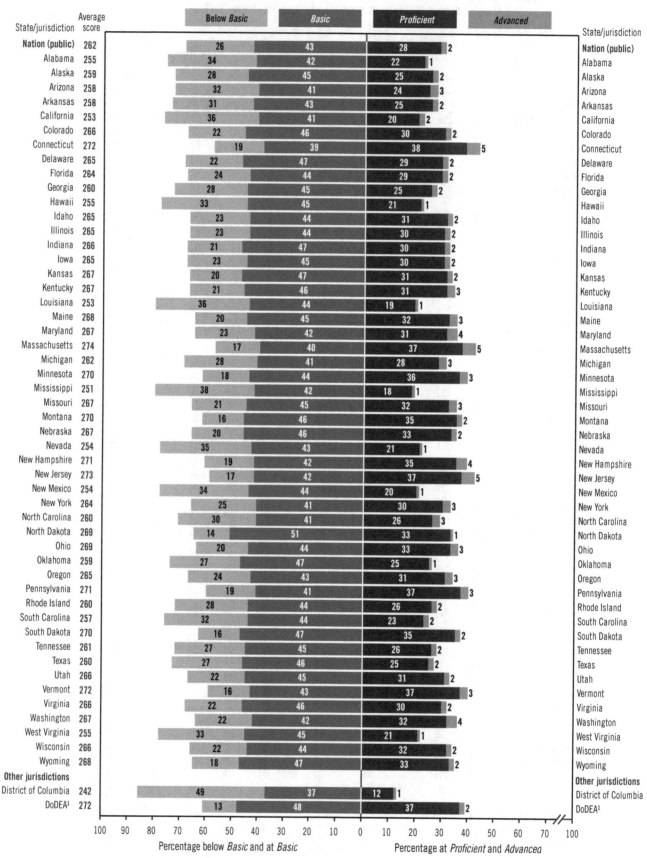

State/jurisdiction	Average score	Below Basic	Basic	Proficient	Advanced
Nation (public)	262	26	43	28	2
Alabama	255	34	42	22	1
Alaska	259	28	45	25	2
Arizona	258	32	41	24	3
Arkansas	258	31	43	25	2
California	253	36	41	20	2
Colorado	266	22	46	30	2
Connecticut	272	19	39	38	5
Delaware	265	22	47	29	2
Florida	264	24	44	29	2
Georgia	260	28	45	25	2
Hawaii	255	33	45	21	1
Idaho	265	23	44	31	2
Illinois	265	23	44	30	2
Indiana	266	21	47	30	2
Iowa	265	23	45	30	2
Kansas	267	20	47	31	2
Kentucky	267	21	46	31	3
Louisiana	253	36	44	19	1
Maine	268	20	45	32	3
Maryland	267	23	42	31	4
Massachusetts	274	17	40	37	5
Michigan	262	28	41	28	3
Minnesota	270	18	44	36	3
Mississippi	251	38	42	18	1
Missouri	267	21	45	32	3
Montana	270	16	46	35	2
Nebraska	267	20	46	33	2
Nevada	254	35	43	21	1
New Hampshire	271	19	42	35	4
New Jersey	273	17	42	37	5
New Mexico	254	34	44	20	1
New York	264	25	41	30	3
North Carolina	260	30	41	26	3
North Dakota	269	14	51	33	1
Ohio	269	20	44	33	3
Oklahoma	259	27	47	25	1
Oregon	265	24	43	31	3
Pennsylvania	271	19	41	37	3
Rhode Island	260	28	44	26	2
South Carolina	257	32	44	23	2
South Dakota	270	16	47	35	2
Tennessee	261	27	45	26	2
Texas	260	27	46	25	2
Utah	266	22	45	31	2
Vermont	272	16	43	37	3
Virginia	266	22	46	30	2
Washington	267	22	42	32	4
West Virginia	255	33	45	21	1
Wisconsin	266	22	44	32	2
Wyoming	268	18	47	33	2
Other jurisdictions					
District of Columbia	242	49	37	12	1
DoDEA[1]	272	13	48	37	2

Percentage below *Basic* and at *Basic*   Percentage at *Proficient* and *Advanced*

[1] Department of Defense Education Activity (overseas and domestic schools).
NOTE: The shaded bars are graphed using unrounded numbers. Detail may not sum to totals because of rounding.
SOURCE: U.S. Department of Education, Institute of Education Sciences, National Center for Education Statistics, National Assessment of Educational Progress (NAEP), 2009 Reading Assessment.

Average scores and achievement-level results in NAEP reading for eighth-grade public school students, by race/ethnicity and state/jurisdiction: 2009

State/jurisdiction	White					Black					Hispanic				
	Average scale score	Percentage of students				Average scale score	Percentage of students				Average scale score	Percentage of students			
		Below Basic	At or above Basic	At or above Proficient	At Advanced		Below Basic	At or above Basic	At or above Proficient	At Advanced		Below Basic	At or above Basic	At or above Proficient	At Advanced
Nation (public)	**271**	**17**	**83**	**39**	**3**	**245**	**44**	**56**	**13**	**#**	**248**	**41**	**59**	**16**	**1**
Alabama	264	23	77	31	2	238	54	46	9	#	245	47	53	23	4
Alaska	269	17	83	36	2	249	39	61	12	#	260	30	70	25	2
Arizona	270	19	81	39	4	249	42	58	21	2	246	43	57	15	1
Arkansas	266	22	78	33	3	234	57	43	8	#	249	42	58	19	1
California	269	20	80	37	4	243	47	53	11	#	241	48	52	13	1
Colorado	274	13	87	41	3	250	38	62	15	#	250	39	61	16	1
Connecticut	279	12	88	51	6	245	45	55	11	#	252	36	64	19	1
Delaware	273	14	86	41	3	254	34	66	16	#	256	31	69	21	1
Florida	272	18	82	40	4	250	38	62	15	#	260	27	73	27	1
Georgia	268	19	81	35	3	249	40	60	15	#	254	33	67	20	1
Hawaii	267	20	80	35	2	256	31	69	20	1	252	38	62	24	1
Idaho	269	18	82	37	2	‡	‡	‡	‡	‡	241	50	50	11	#
Illinois	274	14	86	42	3	243	46	54	10	#	252	35	65	18	#
Indiana	269	17	83	36	3	250	40	60	15	#	251	34	66	15	#
Iowa	267	20	80	34	2	241	49	51	12	#	249	39	61	18	1
Kansas	272	14	86	39	2	248	43	57	14	1	250	39	61	16	1
Kentucky	269	19	81	35	3	249	40	60	15	1	265	21	79	30	2
Louisiana	263	25	75	28	2	241	50	50	10	#	‡	‡	‡	‡	‡
Maine	268	19	81	35	3	254	32	68	22	#	‡	‡	‡	‡	‡
Maryland	279	12	88	48	7	250	39	61	16	1	258	29	71	25	1
Massachusetts	279	13	87	49	6	251	36	64	17	1	250	38	62	17	1
Michigan	268	21	79	36	3	238	54	46	9	#	253	40	60	26	2
Minnesota	275	13	87	44	3	244	46	54	10	#	247	39	61	16	#
Mississippi	264	23	77	31	2	239	53	47	8	#	‡	‡	‡	‡	‡
Missouri	270	17	83	38	3	246	45	55	14	#	260	29	71	25	4
Montana	273	14	86	40	2	‡	‡	‡	‡	‡	‡	‡	‡	‡	‡
Nebraska	272	14	86	39	2	242	49	51	12	#	253	35	65	19	1
Nevada	264	23	77	31	2	241	50	50	10	#	242	47	53	13	#
New Hampshire	271	18	82	40	4	‡	‡	‡	‡	‡	257	36	64	27	3
New Jersey	281	8	92	51	6	250	40	60	17	1	256	32	68	20	1
New Mexico	271	16	84	38	4	246	44	56	16	1	248	42	58	14	#
New York	275	15	85	44	4	246	44	56	13	#	247	42	58	16	#
North Carolina	270	19	81	39	4	243	47	53	12	#	249	42	58	19	2
North Dakota	271	12	88	35	1	‡	‡	‡	‡	‡	‡	‡	‡	‡	‡
Ohio	273	14	86	42	4	247	44	56	13	#	251	39	61	16	#
Oklahoma	264	22	78	29	1	247	43	57	16	1	246	43	57	14	#
Oregon	269	19	81	37	3	‡	‡	‡	‡	‡	247	42	58	14	1
Pennsylvania	276	13	87	46	4	249	40	60	16	1	247	42	58	12	#
Rhode Island	267	21	79	34	2	238	50	50	9	#	241	50	50	11	#
South Carolina	267	21	79	34	3	243	48	52	10	#	259	30	70	30	4
South Dakota	273	12	88	40	2	‡	‡	‡	‡	‡	‡	‡	‡	‡	‡
Tennessee	267	20	80	34	2	243	48	52	11	#	252	38	62	21	2
Texas	273	14	86	42	3	249	39	61	13	#	251	36	64	17	1
Utah	270	17	83	37	2	‡	‡	‡	‡	‡	246	45	55	13	#
Vermont	272	16	84	41	3	‡	‡	‡	‡	‡	‡	‡	‡	‡	‡
Virginia	272	15	85	40	3	250	39	61	14	#	256	30	70	22	1
Washington	273	17	83	41	5	245	39	61	13	#	248	40	60	17	1
West Virginia	255	32	68	22	1	250	41	59	18	2	‡	‡	‡	‡	‡
Wisconsin	271	16	84	39	3	238	52	48	9	#	250	40	60	15	#
Wyoming	269	17	83	36	2	‡	‡	‡	‡	‡	259	28	72	23	#
Other jurisdictions															
District of Columbia	‡	‡	‡	‡	‡	239	52	48	10	#	249	40	60	21	1
DoDEA[1]	278	9	91	48	2	262	20	80	22	1	269	16	84	35	1

See notes at end of table.

Average scores and achievement-level results in NAEP reading for eighth-grade public school students, by race/ethnicity and state/jurisdiction: 2009—Continued

	Asian/Pacific Islander					American Indian/Alaska Native				
	Average scale score	Percentage of students				Average scale score	Percentage of students			
State/jurisdiction		Below *Basic*	At or above *Basic*	At or above *Proficient*	At *Advanced*		Below *Basic*	At or above *Basic*	At or above *Proficient*	At *Advanced*
Nation (public)	**273**	**18**	**82**	**44**	**6**	**252**	**37**	**63**	**21**	**2**
Alabama	‡	‡	‡	‡	‡	‡	‡	‡	‡	‡
Alaska	254	34	66	21	1	239	52	48	11	1
Arizona	280	13	87	56	13	244	48	52	13	2
Arkansas	‡	‡	‡	‡	‡	‡	‡	‡	‡	‡
California	266	23	77	35	3	‡	‡	‡	‡	‡
Colorado	274	14	86	43	3	‡	‡	‡	‡	‡
Connecticut	290	9	91	64	15	‡	‡	‡	‡	‡
Delaware	272	15	85	38	3	‡	‡	‡	‡	‡
Florida	288	6	94	64	8	‡	‡	‡	‡	‡
Georgia	286	10	90	61	10	‡	‡	‡	‡	‡
Hawaii	252	36	64	19	1	‡	‡	‡	‡	‡
Idaho	‡	‡	‡	‡	‡	‡	‡	‡	‡	‡
Illinois	284	8	92	60	8	‡	‡	‡	‡	‡
Indiana	‡	‡	‡	‡	‡	‡	‡	‡	‡	‡
Iowa	‡	‡	‡	‡	‡	‡	‡	‡	‡	‡
Kansas	272	17	83	36	4	258	31	69	25	2
Kentucky	‡	‡	‡	‡	‡	‡	‡	‡	‡	‡
Louisiana	‡	‡	‡	‡	‡	‡	‡	‡	‡	‡
Maine	‡	‡	‡	‡	‡	‡	‡	‡	‡	‡
Maryland	286	7	93	60	10	‡	‡	‡	‡	‡
Massachusetts	281	11	89	50	10	‡	‡	‡	‡	‡
Michigan	‡	‡	‡	‡	‡	‡	‡	‡	‡	‡
Minnesota	260	31	69	30	1	259	28	72	26	4
Mississippi	‡	‡	‡	‡	‡	‡	‡	‡	‡	‡
Missouri	‡	‡	‡	‡	‡	‡	‡	‡	‡	‡
Montana	‡	‡	‡	‡	‡	253	36	64	20	1
Nebraska	‡	‡	‡	‡	‡	‡	‡	‡	‡	‡
Nevada	262	23	77	28	2	‡	‡	‡	‡	‡
New Hampshire	‡	‡	‡	‡	‡	‡	‡	‡	‡	‡
New Jersey	291	5	95	64	13	‡	‡	‡	‡	‡
New Mexico	‡	‡	‡	‡	‡	239	50	50	12	1
New York	277	17	83	49	8	‡	‡	‡	‡	‡
North Carolina	272	20	80	46	8	235	54	46	16	2
North Dakota	‡	‡	‡	‡	‡	246	40	60	22	1
Ohio	‡	‡	‡	‡	‡	‡	‡	‡	‡	‡
Oklahoma	‡	‡	‡	‡	‡	258	29	71	25	1
Oregon	276	15	85	48	4	259	32	68	28	4
Pennsylvania	287	12	88	60	15	‡	‡	‡	‡	‡
Rhode Island	270	19	81	35	6	‡	‡	‡	‡	‡
South Carolina	‡	‡	‡	‡	‡	‡	‡	‡	‡	‡
South Dakota	‡	‡	‡	‡	‡	248	40	60	16	1
Tennessee	‡	‡	‡	‡	‡	‡	‡	‡	‡	‡
Texas	280	13	87	53	7	‡	‡	‡	‡	‡
Utah	266	26	74	33	6	235	62	38	10	1
Vermont	‡	‡	‡	‡	‡	‡	‡	‡	‡	‡
Virginia	279	8	92	48	3	‡	‡	‡	‡	‡
Washington	272	17	83	42	6	254	40	60	25	3
West Virginia	‡	‡	‡	‡	‡	‡	‡	‡	‡	‡
Wisconsin	265	25	75	34	3	‡	‡	‡	‡	‡
Wyoming	‡	‡	‡	‡	‡	‡	‡	‡	‡	‡
Other jurisdictions										
District of Columbia	‡	‡	‡	‡	‡	‡	‡	‡	‡	‡
DoDEA[1]	272	13	87	39	2	‡	‡	‡	‡	‡

\# Rounds to zero.

‡ Reporting standards not met. Sample size insufficient to permit a reliable estimate.

[1] Department of Defense Education Activity (overseas and domestic schools).

NOTE: Black includes African American, Hispanic includes Latino, and Pacific Islander includes Native Hawaiian. Race categories exclude Hispanic origin. Results are not shown for students whose race/ethnicity was unclassified. Detail may not sum to totals because of rounding.

SOURCE: U.S. Department of Education, Institute of Education Sciences, National Center for Education Statistics, National Assessment of Educational Progress (NAEP), 2009 Reading Assessment.

Average scores and achievement-level results in NAEP reading for eighth-grade public school students, by gender and state/jurisdiction: 2009

State/jurisdiction	Male Average scale score	Below Basic	At or above Basic	At or above Proficient	At Advanced	Female Average scale score	Below Basic	At or above Basic	At or above Proficient	At Advanced
Nation (public)	**258**	**30**	**70**	**26**	**2**	**267**	**22**	**78**	**35**	**3**
Alabama	249	41	59	19	1	261	28	72	28	2
Alaska	254	34	66	21	1	265	23	77	33	2
Arizona	254	34	66	24	2	261	29	71	30	3
Arkansas	254	35	65	23	1	262	27	73	30	3
California	248	40	60	19	1	257	33	67	26	3
Colorado	262	25	75	28	1	270	18	82	37	3
Connecticut	267	23	77	37	4	277	15	85	48	6
Delaware	260	27	73	25	1	270	17	83	37	3
Florida	259	29	71	27	2	269	19	81	37	3
Georgia	255	34	66	22	1	266	22	78	32	2
Hawaii	248	42	58	16	1	262	25	75	28	2
Idaho	259	29	71	26	1	271	17	83	40	3
Illinois	260	28	72	28	2	269	19	81	37	3
Indiana	263	24	76	29	2	269	18	82	35	3
Iowa	261	26	74	26	1	269	19	81	38	3
Kansas	265	23	77	31	2	269	18	82	36	2
Kentucky	263	26	74	29	2	271	16	84	38	4
Louisiana	248	41	59	16	1	258	31	69	24	2
Maine	262	24	76	28	2	273	16	84	41	4
Maryland	262	28	72	31	3	272	18	82	41	6
Massachusetts	269	20	80	37	4	279	13	87	49	7
Michigan	257	33	67	25	2	267	23	77	36	4
Minnesota	265	22	78	32	2	275	13	87	45	4
Mississippi	248	43	57	17	1	255	34	66	21	1
Missouri	262	25	75	28	1	272	17	83	41	4
Montana	265	21	79	30	1	276	12	88	45	3
Nebraska	263	23	77	28	1	272	16	84	41	3
Nevada	248	41	59	16	1	260	28	72	28	2
New Hampshire	264	24	76	32	2	277	13	87	47	6
New Jersey	269	20	80	36	3	277	13	87	47	6
New Mexico	251	37	63	20	1	257	32	68	23	2
New York	259	30	70	28	2	270	21	79	39	4
North Carolina	253	36	64	22	1	267	24	76	36	4
North Dakota	265	18	82	27	1	274	11	89	41	2
Ohio	265	22	78	32	2	272	17	83	41	5
Oklahoma	255	32	68	21	#	264	22	78	31	2
Oregon	260	28	72	28	2	270	19	81	39	4
Pennsylvania	267	22	78	35	3	274	15	85	45	4
Rhode Island	255	33	67	23	1	265	23	77	32	2
South Carolina	251	38	62	19	1	264	26	74	30	3
South Dakota	266	19	81	30	1	275	12	88	44	3
Tennessee	257	31	69	24	1	265	24	76	32	3
Texas	256	31	69	23	1	264	23	77	31	2
Utah	260	26	74	27	1	271	17	83	39	3
Vermont	267	21	79	34	2	278	12	88	48	5
Virginia	260	27	73	25	1	271	17	83	39	3
Washington	261	26	74	30	3	273	18	82	42	5
West Virginia	248	40	60	17	1	262	25	75	28	2
Wisconsin	260	26	74	27	1	271	18	82	41	3
Wyoming	265	21	79	30	1	271	16	84	39	2
Other jurisdictions										
District of Columbia	236	56	44	11	1	248	43	57	16	1
DoDEA[1]	269	15	85	34	1	276	11	89	44	2

Rounds to zero.

[1] Department of Defense Education Activity (overseas and domestic schools).

NOTE: Detail may not sum to totals because of rounding.

SOURCE: U.S. Department of Education, Institute of Education Sciences, National Center for Education Statistics, National Assessment of Educational Progress (NAEP), 2009 Reading Assessment.

Average reading scale score, by age and selected student and school characteristics: Selected years, 1971 through 2008

Selected student and school characteristic	1971		1975		1980		1984		1988		1990		1994		1996		1999		2004		2008	
1	2		3		4		5		6		7		8		9		10		11		12	
9-year-olds																						
All students	208	(1.0)	210	(0.7)	215	(1.0)	211	(0.8)	212	(1.1)	209	(1.2)	211	(1.2)	212	(1.0)	212	(1.3)	216	(1.0)	220	(0.9)
Sex																						
Male	201	(1.1)	204	(0.8)	210	(1.1)	207	(1.0)	207	(1.4)	204	(1.7)	207	(1.3)	207	(1.4)	209	(1.6)	212	(1.1)	216	(1.1)
Female	214	(1.0)	216	(0.8)	220	(1.1)	214	(0.9)	216	(1.3)	215	(1.2)	215	(1.4)	218	(1.1)	215	(1.5)	219	(1.1)	224	(0.9)
Race/ethnicity																						
White	214[1]	(0.9)	217	(0.7)	221	(0.8)	218	(0.9)	218	(1.4)	217	(1.3)	218	(1.3)	220	(1.2)	221	(1.6)	224	(0.9)	228	(1.0)
Black	170[1]	(1.7)	181	(1.2)	189	(1.8)	186	(1.3)	189	(2.4)	182	(2.9)	185	(2.3)	191	(2.6)	186	(2.3)	197	(1.8)	204	(1.7)
Hispanic	[2]	(†)	183	(2.2)	190	(2.3)	187	(3.0)	194	(3.5)	189	(2.3)	186	(3.9)	195	(3.4)	193	(2.7)	199	(1.5)	207	(1.5)
Region																						
Northeast	213	(1.7)	215	(1.3)	221	(2.1)	216	(2.2)	215	(2.6)	217	(2.2)	217	(2.9)	220	(1.8)	222	(3.5)	221	(2.5)	225	(1.6)
Southeast	194	(2.9)	201	(1.2)	210	(2.3)	204	(2.0)	207	(2.1)	197	(3.2)	208	(3.0)	206	(2.8)	205	(2.3)	214	(1.6)	220	(2.1)
Central	215	(1.2)	215	(1.2)	217	(1.4)	215	(1.9)	218	(2.2)	213	(2.0)	214	(2.3)	215	(2.6)	215	(3.9)	217	(2.5)	218	(1.6)
West	205	(2.0)	207	(2.0)	213	(1.8)	209	(2.0)	208	(2.6)	210	(2.8)	205	(2.8)	210	(1.9)	206	(1.8)	213	(1.6)	218	(1.3)
13-year-olds																						
All students	255	(0.9)	256	(0.8)	258	(0.9)	257	(0.6)	257	(1.0)	257	(0.8)	258	(0.9)	258	(1.0)	259	(1.0)	257	(1.0)	260	(0.8)
Sex																						
Male	250	(1.0)	250	(0.8)	254	(1.1)	253	(0.7)	252	(1.3)	251	(1.1)	251	(1.2)	251	(1.2)	254	(1.3)	252	(1.1)	256	(1.0)
Female	261	(0.9)	262	(0.9)	263	(0.9)	262	(0.7)	263	(1.0)	263	(1.1)	266	(1.2)	264	(1.2)	265	(1.2)	262	(1.2)	264	(0.9)
Race/ethnicity																						
White	261[1]	(0.7)	262	(0.7)	264	(0.7)	263	(0.6)	261	(1.1)	262	(0.9)	265	(1.1)	266	(1.0)	267	(1.2)	265	(1.0)	268	(1.0)
Black	222[1]	(1.2)	226	(1.2)	233	(1.5)	236	(1.2)	243	(2.4)	241	(2.2)	234	(2.4)	234	(2.6)	238	(2.4)	239	(1.9)	247	(1.6)
Hispanic	[2]	(†)	232	(3.0)	237	(2.0)	240	(2.0)	240	(3.5)	238	(2.3)	235	(1.9)	238	(2.9)	244	(2.9)	241	(2.1)	242	(1.5)
Parents' highest level of education																						
Did not finish high school	—	(†)	—	(†)	239	(1.1)	240	(1.2)	246	(2.1)	241	(1.8)	237	(2.4)	239	(2.8)	238	(3.4)	238	(2.3)	239	(1.9)
Graduated high school	—	(†)	—	(†)	253	(0.9)	253	(0.8)	253	(1.2)	251	(0.9)	251	(1.4)	251	(1.5)	251	(1.8)	249	(1.1)	251	(1.1)
Some education after high school	—	(†)	—	(†)	268	(1.0)	266	(1.1)	265	(1.7)	267	(1.7)	266	(1.9)	268	(2.3)	269	(2.4)	261	(1.4)	265	(1.1)
Graduated college	—	(†)	—	(†)	273	(0.9)	268	(0.9)	265	(1.6)	267	(1.1)	269	(1.2)	269	(1.4)	270	(1.2)	266	(1.2)	270	(1.2)
Region																						
Northeast	261	(2.0)	259	(1.8)	260	(1.8)	261	(0.8)	259	(2.4)	259	(1.8)	269	(2.0)	259	(2.6)	263	(2.9)	264	(2.5)	266	(1.7)
Southeast	245	(1.7)	249	(1.5)	253	(1.6)	256	(1.9)	258	(2.2)	256	(2.2)	253	(2.5)	251	(3.3)	254	(2.4)	253	(1.8)	258	(1.9)
Central	260	(1.8)	261	(1.4)	265	(1.4)	258	(1.3)	256	(2.0)	257	(1.5)	259	(3.3)	267	(1.8)	261	(1.9)	259	(1.8)	262	(1.9)
West	254	(1.3)	253	(1.7)	256	(2.0)	254	(1.1)	258	(2.1)	256	(1.6)	253	(2.1)	257	(1.7)	259	(2.2)	253	(1.7)	256	(1.5)
17-year-olds																						
All students	285	(1.2)	286	(0.8)	285	(1.2)	289	(0.8)	290	(1.0)	290	(1.1)	288	(1.3)	288	(1.1)	288	(1.3)	283	(1.1)	286	(0.9)
Sex																						
Male	279	(1.2)	280	(1.0)	282	(1.3)	284	(0.8)	286	(1.5)	284	(1.6)	282	(2.2)	281	(1.3)	281	(1.6)	276	(1.4)	280	(1.1)
Female	291	(1.3)	291	(1.0)	289	(1.2)	294	(0.9)	294	(1.5)	296	(1.2)	295	(1.5)	295	(1.2)	295	(1.4)	289	(1.2)	291	(1.0)
Race/ethnicity																						
White	291[1]	(1.0)	293	(0.6)	293	(0.9)	295	(0.9)	295	(1.2)	297	(1.2)	296	(1.5)	295	(1.2)	295	(1.4)	289	(1.2)	295	(1.0)
Black	239[1]	(1.7)	241	(2.0)	243	(1.8)	264	(1.2)	274	(2.4)	267	(2.3)	266	(3.9)	266	(2.7)	264	(1.7)	262	(1.9)	266	(2.4)
Hispanic	[2]	(†)	252	(3.6)	261	(2.7)	268	(2.9)	271	(4.3)	275	(3.6)	263	(4.9)	265	(4.1)	271	(3.9)	267	(2.5)	269	(1.3)
Parents' highest level of education																						
Did not finish high school	—	(†)	—	(†)	262	(1.5)	269	(1.4)	267	(2.0)	270	(2.8)	268	(2.7)	267	(3.2)	265	(3.6)	259	(2.7)	266	(2.1)
Graduated high school	—	(†)	—	(†)	277	(1.0)	281	(0.8)	282	(1.3)	283	(1.4)	276	(1.9)	273	(1.7)	274	(2.1)	271	(1.4)	274	(1.4)
Some education after high school	—	(†)	—	(†)	295	(1.2)	298	(0.9)	299	(2.2)	295	(1.9)	294	(1.6)	295	(2.2)	295	(1.8)	285	(1.5)	288	(1.1)
Graduated college	—	(†)	—	(†)	301	(1.0)	302	(0.9)	300	(1.4)	302	(1.5)	300	(1.7)	299	(1.5)	298	(1.3)	295	(1.2)	298	(1.1)
Region																						
Northeast	291	(2.8)	289	(1.7)	286	(2.4)	291	(2.5)	295	(2.9)	296	(1.8)	297	(4.2)	292	(2.8)	295	(4.0)	286	(2.1)	290	(1.6)
Southeast	271	(2.4)	277	(1.4)	280	(2.2)	284	(2.1)	286	(2.1)	285	(2.5)	283	(2.8)	279	(2.6)	279	(2.4)	278	(1.6)	281	(1.8)
Central	291	(2.1)	292	(1.4)	287	(2.2)	290	(1.8)	291	(1.9)	294	(2.4)	286	(3.7)	293	(2.1)	292	(1.5)	289	(1.8)	290	(2.1)
West	284	(1.8)	282	(1.9)	287	(2.1)	289	(1.6)	289	(1.8)	287	(2.6)	288	(2.8)	287	(2.4)	286	(3.0)	280	(2.7)	284	(1.5)

—Not available.

†Not applicable.

[1]Data for 1971 include persons of Hispanic ethnicity.

[2]Test scores of Hispanics were not tabulated separately.

NOTE: The NAEP reading scores have been evaluated at certain performance levels. Scale ranges from 0 to 500. Students scoring 150 (or higher) are able to follow brief written directions and carry out simple, discrete reading tasks. Students scoring 200 are able to understand, combine ideas, and make inferences based on short uncomplicated passages about specific or sequentially related information. Students scoring 250 are able to search for specific information, interrelate ideas, and make generalizations about literature, science, and social studies materials. Students scoring 300 are able to find, understand, summarize, and explain relatively complicated literary and informational material. Includes public and private schools. Excludes persons not enrolled in school and students who were unable to be tested due to limited proficiency in English or due to a disability. Beginning in 2004, data are for a revised assessment format that provides accommodations for students with disabilities and English language learners. Race categories exclude persons of Hispanic ethnicity, except where noted. Totals include other racial/ethnic groups not shown separately. Some data have been revised from previously published figures. Standard errors appear in parentheses.

SOURCE: U.S. Department of Education, National Center for Education Statistics, National Assessment of Educational Progress (NAEP), *NAEP 2004 Trends in Academic Progress*; and 2008 NAEP Long-Term Trend Reading Assessment, retrieved May 4, 2009, from Long-Term Trend NAEP Data Explorer (http://nces.ed.gov/nationsreportcard/naepdata/). (This table was prepared May 2009.)

Average reading scale scores and percentage distribution of 9-, 13-, and 17-year-olds, by amount of reading for school, frequency of reading for fun, and time spent doing homework and watching TV/video: Selected years, 1984 through 2008

Standard errors appear in parentheses.

Average scale score

Time spent on reading and homework	9-year-olds 1984	1994	1999	2004	2008	13-year-olds 1984	1994	1999	2004	2008	17-year-olds 1984	1994	1999	2004	2008
	2	3	4	5	6	7	8	9	10	11	12	13	14	15	16
Pages read daily in school and for homework															
5 or fewer	208 (0.9)	203 (2.3)	202 (1.8)	206 (1.5)	210 (1.1)	250 (0.8)	249 (1.7)	249 (2.0)	245 (1.4)	250 (1.1)	273 (0.8)	271 (1.9)	273 (2.7)	269 (1.4)	271 (1.3)
6–10	215 (1.4)	214 (1.7)	220 (1.7)	217 (1.5)	219 (1.3)	261 (1.0)	261 (1.8)	262 (2.1)	257 (1.5)	258 (1.3)	287 (0.9)	284 (2.1)	285 (1.7)	283 (1.5)	284 (1.4)
11–15	220 (1.4)	217 (2.3)	224 (2.4)	222 (1.6)	224 (1.4)	264 (1.0)	266 (1.8)	263 (2.1)	263 (1.5)	263 (1.4)	294 (0.9)	288 (1.9)	292 (2.2)	290 (1.6)	296 (1.6)
16–20	215 (1.4)	209 (2.3)	220 (2.0)	220 (1.4)	224 (1.4)	263 (1.1)	263 (2.0)	264 (2.1)	266 (1.4)	267 (1.5)	296 (1.1)	298 (2.8)	292 (2.9)	293 (1.6)	295 (1.5)
More than 20	215 (1.6)	217 (2.4)	217 (2.1)	218 (1.1)	226 (1.2)	261 (1.5)	261 (2.0)	265 (2.0)	261 (1.6)	267 (1.4)	300 (1.2)	304 (2.2)	302 (1.9)	298 (1.9)	303 (1.3)
Frequency of reading for fun															
Almost every day	214 (1.1)	215 (2.3)	215 (2.4)	‡	225 (1.2)	264 (1.4)	272 (3.2)	272 (3.2)	‡	274 (1.4)	302 (1.5)	302 (4.2)	301 (4.9)	‡	302 (1.7)
Once or twice a week	212 (1.7)	214 (3.1)	215 (2.6)	‡	225 (1.3)	255 (2.1)	255 (3.1)	263 (2.7)	‡	264 (1.1)	290 (1.7)	286 (4.5)	286 (2.9)	‡	288 (1.5)
Once or twice a month	204 (3.3)	213 (5.8)	211 (4.2)	‡	217 (1.7)	252 (3.6)	255 (5.4)	253 (3.7)	‡	261 (1.3)	290 (1.8)	286 (5.2)	288 (4.8)	‡	287 (1.5)
A few times a year	197 (4.2)	‡	‡	‡	212 (2.0)	252 (2.5)	255 (4.1)	253 (4.4)	‡	254 (1.3)	269 (2.4)	262 (5.2)	262 (5.0)	‡	269 (1.1)
Never or hardly ever	198 (2.7)	193 (3.9)	195 (3.3)	‡	211 (1.2)	239 (2.5)	237 (5.3)	242 (5.3)	‡	247 (0.9)	—	—	—	—	—
Time spent on homework yesterday															
No homework assigned	212 (1.0)	213 (1.9)	210 (1.9)	215 (1.7)	201 (1.7)	254 (1.7)	250 (1.7)	251 (2.0)	248 (1.7)	251 (1.2)	276 (0.8)	273 (2.3)	275 (2.3)	268 (1.6)	272 (1.2)
Didn't do assignment	199 (2.3)	200 (4.3)	204 (4.4)	194 (3.0)	201 (2.6)	247 (1.7)	243 (5.6)	259 (4.2)	258 (1.1)	242 (2.4)	287 (1.4)	285 (1.6)	282 (3.1)	277 (0.4)	284 (1.1)
Less than 1 hour	217 (0.8)	214 (1.7)	214 (1.5)	219 (1.2)	223 (1.6)	261 (0.6)	261 (1.3)	263 (1.6)	266 (1.2)	260 (1.3)	290 (0.9)	288 (1.7)	288 (2.0)	294 (0.7)	288 (1.1)
1 to 2 hours	216 (1.9)	214 (3.0)	215 (3.2)	218 (1.9)	269 (1.2)	264 (0.8)	268 (1.7)	269 (1.6)	266 (1.4)	269 (1.2)	296 (0.8)	297 (3.1)	296 (2.0)	300 (0.6)	295 (1.2)
More than 2 hours	201 (1.9)	193 (6.1)	197 (3.5)	198 (3.6)	207 (3.1)	270 (1.0)	270 (2.4)	269 (3.0)	259 (2.3)	277 (1.9)	303 (1.4)	306 (3.1)	300 (2.8)	—	306 (2.2)
TV/video watched on school day															
1 hour or less	212 (3.4)	216 (4.8)	221 (4.6)	—	223 (3.0)	264 (2.7)	270 (5.1)	265 (6.0)	—	267 (3.0)	300 (1.6)	308 (3.4)	300 (2.8)	—	292 (2.4)
2 hours	217 (1.5)	216 (1.8)	218 (2.1)	—	225 (1.2)	269 (1.1)	268 (1.5)	268 (1.6)	—	266 (1.1)	295 (0.9)	299 (1.8)	298 (2.1)	—	293 (1.2)
3 hours	222 (1.1)	219 (1.8)	217 (1.7)	—	209 (1.1)	268 (1.0)	263 (1.4)	265 (1.5)	—	262 (1.3)	288 (1.0)	284 (1.0)	282 (2.1)	—	284 (1.3)
4 hours	220 (1.2)	218 (2.2)	218 (2.3)	—	207 (1.4)	262 (0.9)	254 (2.0)	254 (2.4)	—	255 (2.6)	284 (1.0)	276 (1.0)	273 (2.2)	276 (0.6)	276 (2.3)
5 hours	214 (1.4)	212 (1.8)	208 (3.0)	—	223 (2.6)	257 (1.0)	234 (3.1)	238 (1.8)	—	238 (1.4)	273 (1.5)	269 (4.1)	273 (3.8)	—	273 (2.4)
6 hours or more	199 (0.8)	192 (2.7)	191 (1.7)	—	205 (1.2)	245 (1.0)	234 (3.1)	238 (1.8)	—	238 (1.2)	269 (1.5)	256 (3.7)	256 (5.2)	—	256 (2.3)

Percentage distribution

Time spent on reading and homework	9-year-olds 1984	1994	1999	2004	2008	13-year-olds 1984	1994	1999	2004	2008	17-year-olds 1984	1994	1999	2004	2008
Pages read daily in school and for homework															
5 or fewer	27 (0.7)	28 (1.4)	28 (1.4)	25 (0.9)	25 (0.9)	27 (0.7)	26 (0.9)	23 (1.0)	25 (0.8)	26 (0.8)	21 (0.8)	21 (1.2)	23 (1.4)	31 (0.9)	30 (0.9)
6–10	34 (0.5)	26 (0.6)	24 (0.9)	20 (0.7)	20 (0.5)	34 (0.5)	31 (0.6)	31 (1.1)	20 (0.7)	24 (0.5)	18 (0.6)	25 (0.9)	17 (0.6)	24 (0.6)	23 (0.5)
11–15	16 (0.2)	14 (0.9)	15 (0.7)	14 (0.6)	14 (0.6)	17 (0.3)	17 (0.5)	18 (0.7)	16 (0.5)	17 (0.5)	14 (0.5)	13 (0.6)	14 (0.8)	11 (0.5)	16 (0.5)
16–20	11 (0.5)	14 (1.0)	16 (1.0)	12 (0.5)	14 (0.6)	11 (0.2)	13 (0.5)	13 (0.7)	12 (0.5)	13 (0.4)	21 (0.9)	23 (1.5)	22 (1.2)	19 (0.6)	19 (0.4)
More than 20	13 (0.5)	17 (1.0)	19 (1.0)	29 (1.0)	28 (0.8)	11 (0.5)	14 (0.8)	16 (1.0)	21 (0.7)	22 (0.9)	26 (0.9)	18 (0.9)	24 (1.0)	15 (0.6)	19 (0.7)
Frequency of reading for fun															
Almost every day	53 (1.0)	58 (1.6)	54 (1.6)	‡	48 (0.7)	35 (1.2)	32 (1.8)	36 (1.7)	‡	26 (0.6)	31 (1.1)	30 (2.6)	25 (1.7)	‡	20 (0.6)
Once or twice a week	28 (0.8)	25 (1.8)	26 (1.5)	‡	28 (0.6)	28 (0.8)	34 (1.7)	31 (1.6)	‡	25 (0.6)	17 (0.5)	15 (1.5)	19 (1.4)	‡	22 (0.5)
Once or twice a month	7 (0.6)	5 (0.6)	6 (0.6)	‡	8 (0.3)	14 (0.8)	14 (0.8)	17 (1.6)	‡	13 (0.4)	12 (0.5)	12 (1.5)	12 (1.4)	‡	16 (0.5)
A few times a year	9 (0.5)	3 (0.8)	4 (0.7)	‡	14 (0.6)	8 (0.6)	10 (0.7)	9 (1.2)	‡	24 (0.7)	9 (0.6)	9 (1.5)	16 (2.4)	‡	24 (0.6)
Never or hardly ever	3 (0.5)	9 (0.8)	10 (0.8)	‡	14 (0.6)	6 (0.6)	12 (1.2)	12 (1.4)	‡	24 (0.7)	9 (0.6)	9 (1.5)	16 (2.4)	‡	24 (0.6)
Time spent on homework yesterday															
No homework assigned	35 (1.3)	32 (2.1)	26 (1.6)	23 (1.5)	18 (1.3)	22 (0.7)	23 (1.4)	24 (1.2)	20 (1.2)	23 (1.2)	22 (0.9)	23 (1.4)	26 (1.7)	26 (1.0)	28 (0.8)
Didn't do assignment	4 (0.3)	4 (1.0)	4 (0.3)	4 (0.3)	6 (1.0)	36 (0.6)	34 (1.0)	5 (0.4)	42 (0.8)	7 (2.4)	36 (0.6)	11 (0.6)	13 (0.8)	8 (0.7)	12 (0.5)
Less than 1 hour	41 (1.0)	48 (1.7)	53 (1.4)	55 (1.2)	60 (1.2)	36 (0.6)	34 (1.0)	37 (0.4)	42 (0.8)	43 (1.2)	29 (0.3)	27 (1.2)	26 (1.0)	29 (0.7)	27 (0.5)
1 to 2 hours	13 (0.4)	11 (0.7)	12 (0.7)	13 (0.6)	12 (0.3)	29 (0.3)	28 (0.7)	28 (0.8)	24 (0.7)	21 (0.4)	13 (0.5)	13 (0.9)	12 (0.6)	10 (0.6)	10 (0.5)
More than 2 hours	6 (0.2)	4 (0.4)	5 (0.5)	6 (0.3)	14 (0.6)	9 (0.4)	9 (0.3)	4 (0.6)	8 (0.3)	6 (0.4)	13 (0.5)	13 (0.9)	12 (0.6)	10 (0.6)	10 (0.5)
TV/video watched on school day															
None	14 (0.3)	2 (0.5)	4 (0.6)	4 (0.9)	4 (0.6)	9 (0.4)	3 (0.3)	4 (0.6)	4 (0.6)	5 (0.3)	5 (0.3)	6 (0.8)	6 (0.3)	6 (0.3)	6 (0.3)
1 hour or less	23 (1.0)	23 (1.0)	24 (0.9)	24 (1.0)	24 (0.6)	12 (0.4)	20 (0.7)	29 (0.9)	29 (0.9)	25 (0.7)	26 (0.5)	31 (0.8)	34 (0.9)	26 (0.7)	33 (0.6)
2 hours	16 (0.3)	23 (0.5)	14 (0.6)	14 (0.6)	18 (0.4)	23 (0.4)	22 (0.8)	20 (0.6)	20 (0.6)	18 (0.4)	23 (0.3)	18 (0.8)	17 (0.5)	21 (0.5)	16 (0.5)
3 hours	15 (0.3)	16 (0.3)	14 (0.4)	14 (0.4)	13 (0.4)	17 (0.4)	16 (0.8)	20 (0.9)	24 (0.7)	18 (0.5)	12 (0.3)	12 (0.8)	8 (0.5)	11 (0.5)	10 (0.4)
4 hours	12 (0.3)	6 (0.4)	9 (0.4)	11 (0.5)	9 (0.3)	10 (0.3)	7 (0.4)	11 (0.3)	11 (0.5)	10 (0.3)	6 (0.2)	5 (0.5)	4 (0.6)	4 (0.4)	4 (0.2)
5 hours	12 (0.3)	6 (0.4)	6 (0.4)	6 (0.4)	9 (0.3)	8 (0.3)	5 (0.5)	5 (0.3)	5 (0.3)	5 (0.3)	4 (0.2)	5 (0.4)	5 (0.6)	—	4 (0.2)
6 hours or more	30 (0.7)	20 (0.8)	22 (1.2)	26 (0.8)	13 (0.4)	13 (0.4)	14 (0.9)	16 (1.0)	21 (0.5)	13 (0.4)	20 (0.7)	13 (1.0)	8 (0.6)	—	4 (0.4)

—Not available.
†Not applicable.
‡Reporting standards not met.

NOTE: The NAEP reading scores have been evaluated at certain performance levels. Scale ranges from 0 to 500. Students scoring 150 (or higher) are able to follow brief written directions and carry out simple, discrete reading tasks. Students scoring 200 able to understand, combine ideas, and make inferences based on short uncomplicated passages about specific or sequentially related information. Students scoring 250 are able to search for specific information, interrelate ideas, and make generalizations about literature, science, and social studies materials. Students scoring 300 are able to find, understand, summarize, and explain relatively complicated literary and informational material. Includes public and private schools.

Excludes persons not enrolled in school and students who were unable to be tested due to limited proficiency in English or due to a disability. Beginning in 2004, data are for a revised assessment format that provides accommodations for students with disabilities and English language learners. Detail may not sum to totals because of rounding. Some data have been revised from previously published figures. Standard errors appear in parentheses.

SOURCE: U.S. Department of Education, National Center for Education Statistics, National Assessment of Educational Progress (NAEP), *NAEP Trends in Academic Progress*, 1996 and 1999; and 2004 and 2008 NAEP Long-Term Trend Reading Assessments, retrieved June 24, 2009, from the Long-Term Trend NAEP Data Explorer (http://nces.ed.gov/nationsreportcard/naepdata/). (This table was prepared June 2009.)

Percentage of students at or above selected reading score levels, by age, sex, and race/ethnicity: Selected years, 1971 through 2008

Selected characteristic	1971		1975		1980		1984		1988		1990		1992		1994		1996		1999		2004		2008	
1	2		3		4		5		6		7		8		9		10		11		12		13	
9-year-olds																								
Total																								
Level 150	91	(0.5)	93	(0.4)	95	(0.4)	92	(0.4)	93	(0.7)	90	(0.9)	92	(0.4)	92	(0.7)	93	(0.6)	93	(0.7)	94	(0.5)	96	(0.4)
Level 200	59	(1.0)	62	(0.8)	68	(1.0)	62	(0.8)	63	(1.3)	59	(1.3)	62	(1.1)	63	(1.4)	64	(1.3)	64	(1.4)	69	(1.0)	73	(0.9)
Level 250	16	(0.6)	15	(0.6)	18	(0.8)	17	(0.7)	17	(1.1)	18	(1.0)	16	(0.8)	17	(1.2)	17	(0.8)	16	(1.0)	19	(0.7)	21	(0.8)
Male																								
Level 150	88	(0.7)	91	(0.5)	93	(0.5)	90	(0.5)	90	(0.9)	88	(1.4)	90	(0.8)	90	(1.0)	92	(0.8)	91	(1.1)	92	(0.6)	94	(0.6)
Level 200	53	(1.2)	56	(1.0)	63	(1.1)	58	(1.0)	58	(1.8)	54	(1.9)	57	(1.6)	59	(1.5)	58	(2.0)	61	(1.8)	64	(1.3)	70	(1.2)
Level 250	12	(0.6)	12	(0.6)	15	(0.9)	16	(0.8)	16	(1.4)	16	(1.2)	14	(1.0)	15	(1.2)	14	(1.3)	15	(1.3)	17	(0.8)	19	(1.0)
Female																								
Level 150	93	(0.5)	95	(0.3)	96	(0.4)	94	(0.5)	95	(1.0)	92	(1.1)	94	(0.6)	94	(0.8)	95	(0.6)	95	(0.8)	96	(0.5)	97	(0.4)
Level 200	65	(1.1)	68	(0.8)	73	(1.0)	65	(1.0)	67	(1.4)	64	(1.2)	67	(1.2)	67	(1.9)	70	(1.6)	67	(1.6)	73	(1.2)	77	(1.1)
Level 250	19	(0.8)	18	(0.8)	21	(1.0)	18	(0.8)	19	(1.2)	21	(1.2)	18	(1.1)	18	(1.5)	18	(1.3)	17	(1.3)	20	(1.0)	22	(1.0)
White																								
Level 150	94 [1]	(0.4)	96	(0.3)	97	(0.2)	95	(0.3)	95	(0.7)	94	(0.9)	96	(0.5)	96	(0.5)	96	(0.6)	97	(0.4)	97	(0.4)	98	(0.4)
Level 200	65 [1]	(1.0)	69	(0.8)	74	(0.7)	69	(0.9)	68	(1.6)	66	(1.4)	69	(1.2)	70	(1.5)	71	(1.5)	73	(1.6)	77	(1.0)	81	(1.0)
Level 250	18 [1]	(0.7)	17	(0.7)	21	(0.9)	21	(0.8)	20	(1.5)	23	(1.2)	20	(1.0)	20	(1.5)	20	(1.1)	20	(1.4)	24	(0.8)	27	(1.1)
Black																								
Level 150	70 [1]	(1.7)	81	(1.1)	85	(1.4)	81	(1.2)	83	(2.4)	77	(2.7)	80	(2.2)	79	(2.4)	84	(1.9)	82	(2.5)	88	(1.7)	91	(1.1)
Level 200	22 [1]	(1.5)	32	(1.5)	41	(1.9)	37	(1.5)	39	(2.9)	34	(3.4)	37	(2.2)	38	(2.8)	42	(3.2)	36	(3.0)	50	(2.3)	58	(2.3)
Level 250	2 [1]	(0.5)	2	(0.3)	4	(0.6)	5	(0.5)	6	(1.2)	5	(1.5)	5	(0.8)	4	(1.5)	6	(1.1)	4	(1.1)	7	(0.8)	9	(0.9)
Hispanic																								
Level 150	[2]	(†)	81	(2.5)	84	(1.8)	82	(3.0)	86	(3.5)	84	(1.8)	83	(2.6)	80	(4.6)	86	(2.4)	87	(3.3)	89	(1.3)	93	(0.8)
Level 200	[2]	(†)	35	(3.0)	42	(2.6)	40	(2.7)	46	(3.3)	41	(2.7)	43	(3.5)	37	(4.6)	48	(3.8)	44	(3.4)	53	(1.7)	62	(1.7)
Level 250	[2]	(†)	3	(0.5)	5	(1.4)	4	(0.6)	9	(2.3)	6	(2.0)	7	(2.3)	6	(1.6)	7	(3.2)	6	(1.7)	7	(0.8)	10	(1.2)
13-year-olds																								
Total																								
Level 200	93	(0.5)	93	(0.4)	95	(0.4)	94	(0.3)	95	(0.6)	94	(0.6)	93	(0.7)	92	(0.6)	92	(0.7)	93	(0.7)	92	(0.6)	94	(0.4)
Level 250	58	(1.1)	59	(1.0)	61	(1.1)	59	(0.8)	59	(1.3)	59	(1.0)	62	(1.4)	60	(1.2)	60	(1.3)	61	(1.5)	59	(1.1)	63	(0.8)
Level 300	10	(0.5)	10	(0.5)	11	(0.5)	11	(0.4)	11	(0.8)	11	(0.8)	15	(0.9)	14	(0.8)	14	(1.0)	15	(1.1)	12	(0.8)	13	(0.5)
Male																								
Level 200	91	(0.7)	91	(0.5)	93	(0.6)	92	(0.4)	93	(1.0)	91	(0.9)	90	(1.1)	89	(1.1)	89	(1.2)	91	(0.9)	89	(0.8)	92	(0.6)
Level 250	52	(1.2)	52	(1.1)	56	(1.2)	54	(0.9)	52	(1.9)	52	(1.5)	55	(2.0)	53	(1.9)	53	(1.6)	55	(1.9)	55	(1.3)	59	(1.2)
Level 300	7	(0.5)	7	(0.4)	9	(0.7)	9	(0.5)	9	(0.9)	8	(0.8)	13	(1.1)	10	(0.7)	11	(1.1)	11	(1.1)	11	(0.9)	11	(0.7)
Female																								
Level 200	95	(0.4)	96	(0.4)	96	(0.4)	96	(0.3)	97	(0.6)	96	(0.6)	95	(0.7)	95	(0.6)	95	(0.6)	96	(0.7)	95	(0.6)	96	(0.5)
Level 250	64	(1.1)	65	(1.2)	65	(1.1)	64	(0.8)	65	(1.4)	65	(1.5)	68	(1.4)	68	(1.7)	66	(1.6)	66	(1.9)	65	(1.3)	66	(1.0)
Level 300	12	(0.6)	13	(0.7)	13	(0.6)	13	(0.6)	13	(0.9)	14	(0.9)	18	(1.1)	18	(1.1)	17	(1.3)	18	(1.7)	14	(1.0)	16	(0.9)
White																								
Level 200	96 [1]	(0.3)	96	(0.2)	97	(0.2)	96	(0.2)	96	(0.6)	96	(0.6)	96	(0.6)	95	(0.7)	95	(0.5)	96	(0.6)	95	(0.5)	96	(0.4)
Level 250	64 [1]	(0.9)	65	(0.9)	68	(0.8)	65	(0.8)	64	(1.5)	65	(1.2)	68	(1.4)	68	(1.3)	69	(1.4)	69	(1.7)	68	(1.1)	72	(1.2)
Level 300	11 [1]	(0.5)	12	(0.5)	14	(0.6)	13	(0.6)	12	(0.9)	13	(0.9)	18	(1.1)	17	(1.0)	17	(1.3)	18	(1.4)	16	(0.9)	18	(0.8)
Black																								
Level 200	74 [1]	(1.7)	77	(1.3)	84	(1.7)	85	(1.2)	91	(2.2)	88	(2.3)	82	(2.7)	81	(2.3)	82	(3.2)	85	(2.3)	86	(1.5)	91	(1.1)
Level 250	21 [1]	(1.2)	25	(1.6)	30	(2.0)	35	(1.3)	40	(2.3)	42	(3.5)	38	(2.7)	36	(3.5)	34	(3.9)	38	(2.7)	40	(2.3)	48	(2.3)
Level 300	1 [1]	(0.2)	2	(0.3)	2	(0.5)	3	(0.6)	5	(1.2)	5	(0.8)	6	(1.4)	4	(1.2)	3	(0.9)	5	(1.4)	4	(0.7)	6	(0.8)
Hispanic																								
Level 200	[2]	(†)	81	(2.3)	87	(2.4)	86	(1.7)	87	(2.6)	86	(2.4)	83	(3.5)	82	(2.7)	85	(3.2)	89	(2.8)	85	(1.9)	87	(1.3)
Level 250	[2]	(†)	32	(3.6)	35	(2.6)	39	(2.3)	38	(4.4)	37	(2.9)	41	(5.1)	34	(3.9)	38	(3.7)	43	(3.8)	44	(2.3)	44	(1.8)
Level 300	[2]	(†)	2	(1.0)	2	(0.6)	4	(1.0)	4	(1.9)	4	(1.2)	6	(1.9)	4	(1.8)	5	(1.7)	6	(1.8)	5	(1.2)	5	(0.6)
17-year-olds																								
Total																								
Level 250	79	(0.9)	80	(0.7)	81	(0.9)	83	(0.6)	86	(0.8)	84	(1.0)	83	(0.8)	81	(1.0)	82	(0.8)	82	(1.0)	79	(0.9)	80	(0.6)
Level 300	39	(1.0)	39	(0.8)	38	(1.1)	40	(1.0)	41	(1.5)	41	(1.0)	43	(1.1)	41	(1.2)	39	(1.4)	40	(1.4)	36	(1.2)	39	(0.8)
Male																								
Level 250	74	(1.0)	76	(0.8)	78	(1.0)	80	(0.7)	83	(1.4)	80	(1.4)	78	(1.2)	76	(1.5)	77	(1.2)	77	(1.5)	73	(1.2)	76	(0.8)
Level 300	34	(1.1)	34	(1.0)	35	(1.3)	36	(1.0)	37	(2.3)	36	(1.5)	38	(1.6)	36	(1.9)	34	(1.9)	34	(1.7)	32	(1.2)	35	(0.9)
Female																								
Level 250	83	(1.0)	84	(0.9)	84	(1.0)	87	(0.6)	88	(1.1)	89	(1.0)	87	(1.1)	86	(1.2)	87	(1.0)	87	(1.0)	84	(0.9)	84	(0.8)
Level 300	44	(1.2)	44	(0.9)	41	(1.2)	45	(1.1)	44	(2.0)	47	(1.3)	48	(1.5)	46	(1.5)	45	(1.7)	45	(1.8)	41	(1.6)	43	(1.0)
White																								
Level 250	84 [1]	(0.7)	86	(0.6)	87	(0.6)	88	(0.5)	89	(0.9)	88	(1.1)	88	(0.9)	86	(1.1)	87	(0.8)	87	(1.3)	83	(0.9)	87	(0.6)
Level 300	43 [1]	(0.9)	44	(0.8)	43	(1.1)	47	(1.1)	45	(1.6)	48	(1.2)	50	(1.4)	48	(1.4)	46	(1.5)	46	(1.5)	42	(1.3)	47	(1.0)
Black																								
Level 250	40 [1]	(1.6)	43	(1.6)	44	(2.0)	65	(1.5)	76	(2.4)	69	(2.8)	61	(2.3)	66	(4.1)	68	(4.0)	66	(2.5)	64	(2.2)	67	(2.4)
Level 300	8 [1]	(0.9)	8	(0.7)	7	(0.8)	16	(1.0)	25	(3.1)	20	(1.8)	17	(2.5)	22	(3.7)	18	(2.2)	17	(1.7)	16	(1.8)	21	(1.5)
Hispanic																								
Level 250	[2]	(†)	53	(4.1)	62	(3.1)	68	(2.4)	71	(4.8)	75	(4.7)	69	(4.0)	63	(4.4)	65	(4.2)	68	(4.3)	67	(2.4)	70	(1.5)
Level 300	[2]	(†)	13	(2.7)	17	(2.1)	21	(3.0)	23	(3.7)	27	(3.3)	27	(3.2)	20	(3.0)	20	(4.8)	24	(3.8)	23	(2.1)	22	(1.0)

†Not applicable.

[1] Data for 1971 include persons of Hispanic ethnicity.

[2] Test scores of Hispanics were not tabulated separately.

NOTE: The NAEP reading scores have been evaluated at certain performance levels. Scale ranges from 0 to 500. Students scoring 150 (or higher) are able to follow brief written directions and carry out simple, discrete reading tasks. Students scoring 200 are able to understand, combine ideas, and make inferences based on short uncomplicated passages about specific or sequentially related information. Students scoring 250 are able to search for specific information, interrelate ideas, and make generalizations about literature, science, and social studies materials. Students scoring 300 are able to find, understand, summarize, and explain relatively complicated literary and informational material. Includes

public and private schools. Excludes persons not enrolled in school and students who were unable to be tested due to limited proficiency in English or due to a disability. Beginning in 2004, data are for a revised assessment format that provides accommodations for students with disabilities and English language learners. Race categories exclude persons of Hispanic ethnicity, except where noted. Standard errors appear in parentheses.

SOURCE: U.S. Department of Education, National Center for Education Statistics, National Assessment of Educational Progress (NAEP), *NAEP 1999 Trends in Academic Progress*; and 2004 and 2008 Long-Term Trend Reading Assessments, retrieved May 12, 2009, from the Long-Term Trend NAEP Data Explorer (http://nces.ed.gov/nationsreportcard/naepdata/). (This table was prepared May 2009.)

Average reading scale score and percentage of 4th-graders in public schools attaining reading achievement levels, by race/ethnicity and state or jurisdiction: Selected years, 1992 through 2007

State or jurisdiction	Average scale score[1] 1992	1994	1998	2002	2003	2005	2007	Average scale score[1] by race/ethnicity,[2] 2007 — White	Black	Hispanic	Asian/Pacific Islander	American Indian/Alaska Native	Percent attaining reading achievement levels, 2007 — At or above Basic[3]	At or above Proficient[4]	At Advanced[5]
	2	3	4	5	6	7	8	9	10	11	12	13	14	15	16
United States	215 (1.0)	212 (1.1)	213 (1.2)	217 (0.5)	216 (0.3)	217 (0.2)	220 (0.3)	230 (0.2)	203 (0.4)	204 (0.5)	231 (1.0)	206 (1.2)	66 (0.3)	32 (0.3)	7 (0.1)
Alabama	207 (1.7)	208 (1.5)	211 (1.9)	207 (1.4)	207 (1.7)	208 (1.2)	216 (1.3)	227 (1.4)	201 (1.6)	197 (6.7)	‡ (†)	‡ (†)	62 (1.4)	29 (1.4)	7 (0.9)
Alaska	— (†)	— (†)	— (†)	— (†)	212 (1.6)	211 (1.4)	214 (1.0)	228 (1.2)	207 (3.2)	206 (4.4)	217 (3.1)	188 (1.9)	62 (1.2)	29 (1.0)	6 (0.8)
Arizona	209 (1.2)	206 (1.9)	206 (1.4)	205 (1.5)	209 (1.2)	207 (1.6)	210 (1.6)	224 (1.3)	206 (3.5)	197 (2.4)	229 (6.3)	187 (3.4)	56 (1.7)	24 (1.5)	5 (0.6)
Arkansas	211 (1.2)	209 (1.7)	209 (1.6)	213 (1.4)	214 (1.4)	217 (1.1)	217 (1.2)	226 (1.1)	195 (1.3)	202 (4.0)	‡ (†)	‡ (†)	64 (1.3)	29 (1.3)	5 (0.6)
California[6,7]	202 (2.0)	197 (1.8)	202 (2.5)	206 (2.5)	206 (1.2)	207 (0.7)	209 (1.0)	227 (1.2)	200 (2.4)	195 (0.9)	228 (2.6)	‡ (†)	53 (1.0)	23 (0.9)	5 (0.4)
Colorado	217 (1.1)	213 (1.3)	220 (1.4)	— (†)	224 (1.2)	224 (1.1)	224 (1.1)	234 (1.0)	210 (3.2)	204 (1.7)	233 (3.6)	‡ (†)	70 (1.3)	36 (1.4)	9 (1.0)
Connecticut	222 (1.3)	222 (1.6)	230 (1.6)	229 (1.1)	228 (1.1)	226 (1.0)	227 (1.3)	238 (1.3)	203 (3.0)	203 (2.7)	244 (3.6)	‡ (†)	73 (1.4)	41 (1.6)	12 (1.2)
Delaware	213 (0.6)	206 (1.1)	207 (1.7)	224 (0.6)	224 (0.7)	226 (0.8)	225 (0.7)	233 (0.9)	213 (1.0)	218 (2.3)	246 (3.6)	‡ (†)	73 (1.2)	34 (1.4)	7 (0.6)
District of Columbia	188 (0.8)	— (†)	179 (1.4)	191 (0.9)	188 (0.9)	191 (1.0)	197 (0.9)	258 (3.9)	192 (1.0)	206 (3.6)	‡ (†)	‡ (†)	39 (1.1)	14 (0.8)	4 (0.5)
Florida	208 (1.2)	205 (1.7)	206 (1.4)	214 (1.4)	218 (1.1)	220 (0.9)	224 (0.8)	232 (1.0)	208 (1.5)	218 (1.2)	241 (3.2)	‡ (†)	70 (1.0)	34 (1.0)	8 (0.6)
Georgia	212 (1.5)	207 (2.4)	209 (1.4)	215 (1.0)	214 (1.3)	214 (1.2)	219 (0.9)	230 (1.1)	205 (1.4)	212 (3.3)	232 (6.1)	‡ (†)	66 (1.3)	28 (1.5)	5 (0.7)
Hawaii	203 (1.7)	201 (1.7)	200 (1.5)	208 (0.9)	208 (1.4)	210 (1.0)	213 (1.1)	227 (2.2)	212 (4.6)	205 (4.1)	210 (1.2)	‡ (†)	59 (1.4)	26 (1.4)	5 (0.6)
Idaho	219 (0.9)	— (†)	— (†)	220 (1.1)	218 (1.0)	222 (0.9)	223 (0.8)	227 (0.7)	‡ (†)	204 (2.5)	‡ (†)	202 (10.9)	70 (1.0)	35 (1.2)	8 (0.6)
Illinois	— (†)	— (†)	— (†)	207 (1.7)	216 (1.6)	217 (1.2)	219 (1.2)	230 (1.7)	201 (2.4)	205 (1.2)	240 (4.2)	‡ (†)	65 (1.6)	32 (1.3)	8 (0.9)
Indiana	221 (1.3)	220 (1.3)	— (†)	222 (1.4)	220 (1.0)	218 (1.1)	222 (0.9)	226 (1.0)	201 (2.4)	207 (2.5)	‡ (†)	‡ (†)	68 (1.2)	33 (1.3)	7 (0.7)
Iowa[6,7]	225 (1.1)	223 (1.3)	220 (1.6)	223 (1.1)	223 (1.1)	221 (0.9)	225 (1.1)	227 (1.1)	205 (4.0)	208 (3.1)	235 (6.9)	‡ (†)	74 (1.6)	36 (1.4)	7 (0.8)
Kansas[6,7]	— (†)	— (†)	221 (1.4)	222 (1.4)	220 (1.2)	225 (1.3)	225 (1.1)	229 (1.1)	208 (2.6)	209 (2.4)	229 (5.4)	204 (3.1)	72 (1.2)	36 (1.5)	8 (0.9)
Kentucky	213 (1.3)	212 (1.6)	218 (1.5)	219 (1.1)	219 (1.3)	220 (1.1)	222 (1.1)	225 (1.1)	203 (2.2)	‡ (†)	‡ (†)	‡ (†)	68 (1.4)	33 (1.4)	8 (0.7)
Louisiana	204 (1.2)	197 (1.4)	200 (1.6)	207 (1.7)	205 (1.4)	209 (1.3)	207 (1.6)	220 (1.8)	194 (1.7)	213 (5.5)	218 (3.6)	205 (5.5)	52 (2.0)	20 (1.4)	3 (0.6)
Maine	227 (1.1)	228 (1.3)	225 (1.4)	225 (1.1)	224 (0.9)	225 (0.9)	226 (0.9)	226 (0.9)	‡ (†)	‡ (†)	‡ (†)	‡ (†)	73 (1.1)	36 (1.3)	7 (0.8)
Maryland	211 (1.6)	210 (1.5)	212 (1.6)	217 (1.5)	219 (1.4)	220 (1.3)	225 (1.1)	236 (1.5)	208 (1.2)	213 (2.4)	243 (2.8)	‡ (†)	69 (1.3)	36 (1.5)	10 (0.7)
Massachusetts[6]	226 (0.9)	223 (1.3)	223 (1.4)	234 (1.1)	228 (1.2)	231 (0.9)	236 (1.0)	241 (1.1)	211 (2.1)	209 (2.0)	241 (3.5)	‡ (†)	81 (1.1)	49 (1.7)	16 (1.3)
Michigan	216 (1.5)	— (†)	216 (1.5)	219 (1.1)	219 (1.2)	218 (1.5)	220 (1.4)	227 (1.2)	197 (2.7)	210 (4.2)	233 (4.6)	‡ (†)	66 (1.7)	32 (1.6)	8 (0.7)
Minnesota[6,7]	221 (1.2)	218 (1.4)	219 (1.7)	225 (1.2)	223 (1.1)	225 (1.3)	225 (1.2)	231 (1.1)	198 (2.5)	200 (3.8)	218 (3.6)	205 (5.5)	73 (1.3)	37 (1.5)	9 (0.8)
Mississippi	199 (1.3)	202 (1.6)	203 (1.3)	203 (1.3)	205 (1.3)	204 (1.4)	208 (1.0)	222 (0.9)	195 (0.9)	‡ (†)	235 (4.3)	‡ (†)	51 (1.4)	19 (1.0)	3 (0.4)
Missouri[6,7]	220 (1.2)	217 (1.5)	216 (1.3)	220 (1.3)	222 (1.2)	221 (0.9)	221 (1.1)	226 (1.2)	200 (2.1)	213 (4.1)	‡ (†)	‡ (†)	67 (1.3)	32 (1.3)	7 (0.6)
Montana[6,7]	— (†)	222 (1.4)	225 (1.5)	224 (1.8)	223 (1.2)	225 (1.1)	227 (1.0)	230 (0.9)	‡ (†)	220 (4.2)	‡ (†)	204 (3.1)	75 (1.0)	39 (1.8)	8 (0.9)
Nebraska[8]	221 (1.1)	220 (1.5)	— (†)	222 (1.5)	221 (1.0)	223 (1.2)	223 (1.3)	230 (0.9)	194 (3.7)	203 (2.8)	‡ (†)	‡ (†)	71 (1.4)	35 (1.5)	8 (0.8)
Nevada	— (†)	— (†)	206 (1.8)	209 (1.2)	207 (1.2)	207 (1.2)	211 (1.2)	224 (1.5)	202 (3.1)	196 (1.6)	220 (2.5)	205 (5.5)	57 (1.3)	24 (1.3)	5 (0.5)
New Hampshire[6]	228 (1.2)	223 (1.5)	226 (1.7)	— (†)	228 (1.0)	227 (0.9)	229 (0.9)	230 (0.9)	215 (5.0)	209 (3.9)	235 (4.3)	‡ (†)	76 (0.9)	41 (1.5)	11 (0.9)
New Jersey	223 (1.4)	219 (1.2)	— (†)	217 (1.5)	225 (1.2)	223 (1.3)	231 (1.2)	238 (1.1)	212 (2.7)	214 (2.5)	245 (2.5)	‡ (†)	77 (1.3)	43 (1.5)	12 (0.9)
New Mexico[6,7]	211 (1.5)	205 (1.7)	205 (1.4)	208 (1.6)	203 (1.5)	207 (1.3)	212 (1.3)	228 (1.9)	208 (4.0)	204 (1.4)	‡ (†)	197 (3.7)	58 (1.5)	24 (1.6)	5 (0.7)
New York[6,7]	215 (1.4)	212 (1.4)	215 (1.6)	222 (1.5)	222 (1.1)	223 (1.1)	224 (1.0)	234 (1.5)	208 (1.5)	206 (1.7)	236 (2.8)	‡ (†)	69 (1.2)	36 (1.3)	8 (0.8)
North Carolina	212 (1.1)	214 (1.5)	213 (1.6)	222 (1.0)	221 (1.0)	217 (1.0)	218 (0.9)	228 (1.1)	202 (1.1)	205 (2.2)	228 (5.0)	202 (4.3)	64 (1.2)	29 (1.1)	6 (0.5)
North Dakota[7]	226 (1.1)	225 (1.2)	— (†)	224 (1.0)	222 (0.9)	225 (0.7)	226 (0.9)	229 (0.7)	‡ (†)	‡ (†)	‡ (†)	204 (3.5)	75 (1.2)	35 (1.4)	6 (0.6)

See notes at end of table.

Average reading scale score and percentage of 4th-graders in public schools attaining reading achievement levels, by race/ethnicity and state or jurisdiction: Selected years, 1992 through 2007—Continued

State or jurisdiction	Average scale score[1]							Average scale score[1] by race/ethnicity[2] 2007					Percent attaining reading achievement levels, 2007		
	1992	1994	1998	2002	2003	2005	2007	White	Black	Hispanic	Asian/Pacific Islander	American Indian/ Alaska Native	At or above Basic[3]	At or above Proficient[4]	At Advanced[5]
1	2	3	4	5	6	7	8	9	10	11	12	13	14	15	16
Ohio	217 (1.3)	— (†)	—	222 (1.3)	222 (1.2)	223 (1.4)	226 (1.1)	231 (1.1)	204 (2.1)	214 (4.5)	‡ (†)	‡ (†)	73 (1.5)	36 (1.6)	8 (1.0)
Oklahoma	220 (0.9)	— (†)	219 (1.2)	213 (1.2)	214 (1.2)	214 (1.1)	217 (1.1)	223 (1.1)	204 (2.2)	198 (3.9)	221 (7.6)	213 (1.8)	65 (1.5)	27 (1.2)	4 (0.5)
Oregon	— (†)	— (†)	212 (1.8)	220 (1.4)	218 (1.3)	217 (1.4)	215 (1.4)	222 (1.3)	198 (3.8)	190 (2.3)	218 (6.3)	206 (7.2)	62 (1.5)	28 (1.5)	6 (0.7)
Pennsylvania[8]	221 (1.3)	215 (1.6)	—	221 (1.2)	219 (1.3)	223 (1.3)	226 (1.0)	233 (0.8)	200 (2.9)	200 (5.0)	228 (3.7)	‡ (†)	73 (1.3)	40 (1.1)	11 (0.8)
Rhode Island[8]	217 (1.8)	220 (1.3)	218 (1.4)	220 (1.2)	216 (1.3)	216 (1.2)	219 (1.0)	227 (1.1)	198 (2.3)	198 (2.1)	219 (4.2)	‡ (†)	65 (1.2)	31 (1.2)	7 (0.7)
South Carolina	210 (1.3)	203 (1.4)	209 (1.4)	214 (1.3)	215 (1.3)	213 (1.3)	214 (1.2)	224 (1.2)	199 (1.5)	205 (3.5)	‡ (†)	‡ (†)	59 (1.5)	26 (1.3)	5 (0.5)
South Dakota[7,8]	— (†)	— (†)	— (†)	—	222 (1.2)	222 (0.5)	223 (1.0)	228 (0.9)	‡ (†)	209 (5.2)	‡ (†)	196 (2.6)	71 (1.2)	34 (1.6)	7 (0.8)
Tennessee[7,8]	212 (1.4)	213 (1.7)	212 (1.4)	214 (1.2)	212 (1.6)	214 (1.4)	216 (1.2)	224 (1.3)	192 (1.6)	208 (4.0)	‡ (†)	‡ (†)	61 (1.6)	27 (1.2)	6 (0.8)
Texas	213 (1.6)	212 (1.9)	214 (1.9)	217 (1.7)	215 (1.0)	219 (0.8)	220 (0.9)	232 (1.1)	207 (1.6)	212 (1.2)	236 (3.2)	‡ (†)	66 (1.1)	30 (1.1)	6 (0.5)
Utah	220 (1.1)	217 (1.3)	216 (1.2)	222 (1.0)	219 (1.0)	221 (1.1)	221 (1.2)	226 (1.0)	‡ (†)	201 (2.8)	217 (3.9)	‡ (†)	69 (1.4)	34 (1.4)	8 (0.5)
Vermont	—	— (†)	— (†)	227 (1.1)	226 (0.9)	227 (0.9)	228 (0.8)	229 (0.9)	‡ (†)	216 (†)	‡ (†)	‡ (†)	74 (1.2)	41 (1.2)	11 (0.7)
Virginia	221 (1.4)	213 (1.5)	217 (1.2)	225 (1.3)	223 (1.5)	226 (0.8)	227 (1.1)	233 (1.3)	213 (1.4)	216 (2.8)	237 (2.7)	‡ (†)	74 (1.5)	38 (1.4)	9 (1.0)
Washington[7]	—	213 (1.5)	218 (1.4)	224 (1.2)	221 (1.1)	224 (1.1)	224 (1.4)	229 (1.4)	206 (3.5)	206 (2.3)	232 (3.6)	205 (5.0)	70 (1.5)	36 (1.7)	10 (1.1)
West Virginia	216 (1.3)	213 (1.1)	216 (1.7)	219 (1.2)	219 (1.0)	215 (0.8)	215 (1.1)	216 (1.1)	202 (2.9)	‡ (†)	‡ (†)	‡ (†)	63 (1.2)	28 (1.1)	5 (0.6)
Wisconsin[6,7,8]	224 (1.0)	224 (1.1)	222 (1.1)	— (†)	221 (0.8)	221 (1.0)	223 (1.2)	229 (1.2)	191 (4.2)	208 (2.8)	222 (4.4)	‡ (†)	70 (1.4)	36 (1.4)	8 (0.7)
Wyoming	223 (1.1)	221 (1.2)	218 (1.5)	221 (1.0)	222 (0.8)	223 (0.7)	225 (0.5)	228 (0.6)	‡ (†)	210 (2.4)	‡ (†)	200 (3.6)	73 (1.0)	36 (1.0)	8 (0.9)
Department of Defense dependents schools[9]	—	—	220 (0.7)	224 (0.4)	224 (0.5)	226 (0.6)	229 (0.5)	235 (0.8)	218 (1.6)	223 (1.4)	228 (2.1)	‡ (†)	78 (0.9)	40 (1.0)	8 (0.5)
Other jurisdictions															
Guam	182 (1.4)	181 (1.2)	— (†)	185 (1.3)	— (†)	— (†)	— (†)	— (†)	— (†)	— (†)	— (†)	— (†)	— (†)	— (†)	— (†)
U.S. Virgin Islands	171 (1.7)	— (†)	174 (2.2)	179 (1.9)	— (†)	— (†)	— (†)	— (†)	— (†)	— (†)	— (†)	— (†)	— (†)	— (†)	— (†)

—Not available.
†Not applicable.
‡Reporting standards not met.
[1]Scale ranges from 0 to 500.
[2]Race/ethnicity based on school records.
[3]Basic denotes partial mastery of the knowledge and skills that are fundamental for proficient work at the 4th-grade level.
[4]Proficient represents solid academic performance for 4th-graders. Students reaching this level have demonstrated competency over challenging subject matter.
[5]Advanced signifies superior performance.
[6]Did not satisfy one or more of the guidelines for school participation in 1998. Data are subject to appreciable nonresponse bias.

[7]Did not satisfy one or more of the guidelines for school participation in 2002. Data are subject to appreciable nonresponse bias.
[8]Did not satisfy one or more of the guidelines for school participation in 1994. Data are subject to appreciable nonresponse bias.
[9]Prior to 2005, NAEP divided the Department of Defense (DoD) schools into two jurisdictions, domestic and overseas. In 2005, NAEP began combining the DoD domestic and overseas schools into a single jurisdiction. Data shown in this table for years prior to 2005 were recalculated for comparability.
NOTE: The reading data include students for whom accommodations were permitted except for the 1992 and 1994 data. Race categories exclude persons of Hispanic ethnicity. Standard errors appear in parentheses.
SOURCE: U.S. Department of Education, National Center for Education Statistics, National Assessment of Educational Progress (NAEP), 1992, 1994, 1998, 2002, 2003, 2005, and 2007 Reading Assessments, retrieved May 16, 2008, from the NAEP Data Explorer (http://nces.ed.gov/nationsreportcard/nde/). (This table was prepared May 2008.)

Average reading scale score and percentage of 8th-graders in public schools attaining reading achievement levels, by locale and state or jurisdiction: Selected years, 1998 through 2007

State or jurisdiction	Average scale score[1]					Percent attaining reading achievement levels, 2007				Average scale score[1] by locale,[2] 2005		
	1998	2002	2003	2005	2007	Below Basic[3]	At or above Basic[3]	At or above Proficient[4]	At Advanced[5]	Central city	Urban fringe/ large town	Rural/ small town
1	2	3	4	5	6	7	8	9	10	11	12	13
United States	261 (0.8)	263 (0.5)	261 (0.2)	260 (0.2)	261 (0.2)	27 (0.3)	73 (0.3)	29 (0.2)	2 (0.1)	254 (0.4)	264 (0.3)	262 (0.4)
Alabama	255 (1.4)	253 (1.3)	253 (1.5)	252 (1.4)	252 (1.0)	38 (1.2)	62 (1.2)	21 (1.3)	1 (0.4)	246 (2.8)	260 (3.1)	250 (1.6)
Alaska	— (†)	— (†)	256 (1.1)	259 (0.9)	259 (1.0)	29 (1.2)	71 (1.2)	27 (1.2)	2 (0.4)	‡ (†)	‡ (†)	‡ (†)
Arizona	260 (1.1)	257 (1.3)	255 (1.4)	255 (1.0)	255 (1.2)	35 (1.6)	65 (1.6)	24 (1.4)	2 (0.5)	253 (1.5)	258 (2.2)	253 (4.5)
Arkansas	256 (1.3)	260 (1.1)	258 (1.3)	258 (1.1)	258 (1.0)	30 (1.3)	70 (1.3)	25 (1.1)	1 (0.4)	257 (2.8)	261 (2.0)	257 (1.3)
California[6,7,8]	252 (1.6)	250 (1.8)	251 (1.3)	250 (0.6)	251 (0.8)	38 (0.8)	62 (0.8)	21 (0.8)	2 (0.3)	249 (0.9)	251 (0.9)	257 (3.6)
Colorado	264 (1.0)	— (†)	268 (1.2)	265 (1.1)	266 (1.0)	21 (1.2)	79 (1.2)	35 (1.5)	2 (0.5)	260 (2.1)	268 (1.5)	266 (2.0)
Connecticut	270 (1.0)	267 (1.2)	267 (1.1)	264 (1.3)	267 (1.6)	23 (1.7)	77 (1.7)	37 (1.7)	5 (0.4)	245 (3.0)	270 (1.5)	269 (1.8)
Delaware	254 (1.3)	267 (0.5)	265 (0.7)	266 (0.6)	265 (0.6)	23 (0.8)	77 (0.8)	31 (1.2)	2 (0.4)	266 (2.4)	265 (0.7)	269 (1.4)
District of Columbia	236 (2.1)	240 (0.9)	239 (0.8)	238 (0.9)	241 (0.7)	52 (1.1)	48 (1.1)	12 (1.0)	1 (0.3)	238 (0.9)	‡ (†)	‡ (†)
Florida	255 (1.4)	261 (1.6)	257 (1.3)	256 (1.2)	260 (1.2)	29 (1.3)	71 (1.3)	28 (1.3)	2 (0.4)	252 (2.4)	257 (1.5)	257 (2.6)
Georgia	257 (1.4)	258 (1.0)	258 (1.1)	257 (1.3)	259 (1.0)	30 (1.4)	70 (1.4)	26 (1.4)	2 (0.5)	245 (2.8)	261 (2.1)	257 (2.1)
Hawaii	249 (1.0)	252 (0.9)	251 (0.9)	249 (0.9)	251 (0.8)	38 (1.0)	62 (1.0)	20 (0.9)	1 (0.3)	255 (1.6)	249 (1.4)	243 (1.5)
Idaho	— (†)	266 (1.1)	264 (0.9)	264 (1.1)	265 (0.9)	22 (0.8)	78 (0.8)	32 (1.3)	2 (0.4)	266 (1.3)	264 (1.4)	263 (2.0)
Illinois	— (†)	— (†)	266 (1.0)	264 (1.0)	263 (1.0)	25 (1.1)	75 (1.1)	30 (1.5)	2 (0.4)	256 (1.9)	268 (1.5)	266 (2.1)
Indiana	— (†)	265 (1.3)	265 (1.0)	261 (1.1)	264 (1.1)	24 (1.1)	76 (1.1)	31 (1.5)	2 (0.5)	254 (2.1)	265 (2.0)	263 (1.6)
Iowa	— (†)	— (†)	268 (0.8)	267 (0.9)	267 (0.9)	20 (1.0)	80 (1.0)	36 (1.4)	2 (0.6)	262 (1.5)	272 (2.3)	268 (1.4)
Kansas[6,7,8]	268 (1.4)	269 (1.3)	266 (1.5)	267 (1.0)	267 (0.8)	19 (1.0)	81 (1.0)	35 (1.2)	2 (0.4)	262 (2.6)	270 (1.7)	267 (1.1)
Kentucky	262 (1.4)	265 (1.0)	266 (1.3)	264 (1.1)	262 (1.0)	27 (1.2)	73 (1.2)	28 (1.2)	3 (0.5)	271 (2.3)	262 (2.1)	263 (1.6)
Louisiana	252 (1.4)	256 (1.5)	253 (1.6)	253 (1.6)	253 (1.1)	36 (1.6)	64 (1.6)	19 (1.2)	1 (0.5)	247 (2.8)	255 (2.8)	255 (1.9)
Maine	271 (1.2)	270 (0.9)	268 (1.0)	270 (1.0)	270 (0.8)	17 (1.0)	83 (1.0)	37 (1.5)	3 (0.5)	269 (2.1)	277 (2.1)	269 (1.1)
Maryland[6,7]	261 (1.8)	263 (1.7)	262 (1.4)	261 (1.2)	265 (1.2)	24 (1.3)	76 (1.3)	33 (1.5)	3 (0.4)	251 (3.6)	262 (1.5)	266 (2.7)
Massachusetts	269 (1.4)	271 (1.3)	273 (1.0)	274 (1.0)	273 (1.0)	16 (0.9)	84 (0.9)	43 (1.5)	4 (0.7)	258 (1.4)	280 (1.3)	282 (3.1)
Michigan[6,7]	— (†)	265 (1.6)	264 (1.8)	261 (1.2)	260 (1.2)	28 (1.5)	72 (1.5)	28 (1.3)	2 (0.4)	251 (2.9)	265 (2.1)	266 (2.2)
Minnesota[6,7]	265 (1.4)	— (†)	268 (1.1)	268 (1.2)	268 (0.9)	20 (1.2)	80 (1.2)	37 (1.2)	3 (0.5)	264 (3.2)	272 (1.6)	267 (1.6)
Mississippi	251 (1.2)	255 (0.9)	255 (1.4)	251 (1.3)	250 (1.1)	40 (1.4)	60 (1.4)	17 (1.4)	1 (0.3)	246 (2.9)	254 (2.2)	250 (1.8)
Missouri	262 (1.3)	268 (1.0)	267 (1.0)	265 (1.0)	263 (1.0)	25 (1.1)	75 (1.1)	31 (1.2)	3 (0.3)	258 (3.0)	267 (1.3)	266 (1.6)
Montana[6,7]	271 (1.3)	270 (1.0)	270 (1.0)	269 (0.7)	271 (0.8)	15 (1.0)	85 (1.0)	39 (1.4)	2 (0.4)	270 (1.6)	271 (1.8)	268 (0.9)
Nebraska	— (†)	270 (0.9)	266 (0.9)	267 (0.9)	267 (0.9)	21 (1.2)	79 (1.2)	35 (1.3)	3 (0.5)	266 (1.6)	268 (1.6)	268 (1.4)
Nevada	258 (1.0)	251 (0.8)	252 (0.8)	253 (0.9)	252 (0.8)	37 (0.9)	63 (0.9)	22 (1.0)	2 (0.4)	253 (1.4)	251 (1.4)	256 (1.5)
New Hampshire	— (†)	— (†)	271 (0.9)	270 (1.2)	270 (1.1)	18 (1.2)	82 (1.2)	37 (1.3)	3 (0.4)	264 (2.1)	270 (2.0)	272 (1.9)
New Jersey[6,7]	— (†)	268 (1.2)	268 (1.2)	269 (1.2)	270 (1.1)	19 (1.0)	81 (1.0)	39 (1.5)	4 (0.6)	‡ (†)	270 (1.2)	278 (3.0)
New Mexico	258 (1.2)	254 (1.0)	252 (0.9)	251 (1.0)	251 (0.8)	38 (1.3)	62 (1.3)	17 (0.9)	1 (0.3)	256 (1.9)	249 (1.9)	248 (1.7)
New York[6,7]	265 (1.5)	264 (1.5)	265 (1.3)	265 (1.0)	264 (1.1)	25 (1.3)	75 (1.3)	32 (1.4)	3 (0.3)	252 (1.5)	275 (1.4)	272 (1.4)
North Carolina	262 (1.1)	265 (1.1)	262 (1.0)	258 (0.9)	259 (1.1)	29 (1.3)	71 (1.3)	28 (1.1)	2 (0.4)	257 (1.6)	261 (1.9)	258 (1.5)
North Dakota[7]	— (†)	268 (0.8)	270 (0.8)	270 (0.6)	268 (0.7)	16 (1.0)	84 (1.0)	32 (1.3)	1 (0.5)	271 (1.5)	270 (1.8)	270 (0.8)

See notes at end of table.

Average reading scale score and percentage of 8th-graders in public schools attaining reading achievement levels, by locale and state or jurisdiction: Selected years, 1998 through 2007—Continued

State or jurisdiction	Average scale score[1]					Percent attaining reading achievement levels, 2007				Average scale score[1] by locale,[2] 2005		
	1998	2002	2003	2005	2007	Below Basic	At or above Basic[3]	At or above Proficient[4]	At Advanced[5]	Central city	Urban fringe/large town	Rural/small town
1	2	3	4	5	6	7	8	9	10	11	12	13
Ohio	— (†)	268 (1.6)	267 (1.3)	267 (1.3)	268 (1.2)	21 (1.2)	79 (1.2)	36 (1.6)	3 (0.6)	248 (3.1)	272 (1.6)	272 (2.2)
Oklahoma	265 (1.2)	262 (0.8)	262 (0.9)	260 (1.1)	260 (0.8)	28 (1.0)	72 (1.0)	26 (1.2)	1 (0.3)	252 (4.0)	264 (1.3)	259 (1.4)
Oregon[7]	266 (1.5)	268 (1.3)	264 (1.2)	263 (1.1)	266 (0.9)	23 (1.2)	77 (1.2)	34 (1.7)	3 (0.4)	264 (2.2)	264 (1.7)	261 (1.9)
Pennsylvania	— (†)	265 (1.0)	264 (1.2)	267 (1.3)	268 (1.2)	21 (1.4)	79 (1.4)	36 (1.5)	3 (0.6)	247 (3.9)	273 (1.9)	268 (1.4)
Rhode Island	264 (0.9)	262 (0.8)	261 (0.7)	261 (0.7)	258 (0.9)	31 (1.2)	69 (1.2)	27 (1.1)	2 (0.3)	245 (1.4)	267 (1.0)	275 (1.8)
South Carolina	255 (1.1)	258 (1.1)	258 (1.3)	257 (1.1)	257 (0.9)	31 (1.2)	69 (1.2)	25 (1.4)	2 (0.3)	259 (2.5)	262 (1.6)	253 (1.5)
South Dakota	— (†)	— (†)	270 (0.8)	269 (0.6)	270 (0.7)	17 (0.9)	83 (0.9)	37 (1.9)	2 (0.4)	267 (1.1)	271 (2.4)	269 (0.7)
Tennessee[7]	258 (1.2)	260 (1.4)	258 (1.2)	259 (0.9)	259 (1.0)	29 (1.3)	71 (1.3)	26 (1.1)	2 (0.4)	252 (1.7)	264 (2.3)	260 (1.6)
Texas	261 (1.4)	262 (1.4)	259 (1.1)	258 (0.6)	261 (0.9)	27 (1.0)	73 (1.0)	28 (1.2)	2 (0.3)	256 (1.1)	261 (1.1)	259 (1.6)
Utah	263 (1.0)	263 (1.1)	264 (0.8)	262 (0.8)	262 (1.0)	25 (1.1)	75 (1.1)	30 (1.2)	2 (0.4)	261 (1.4)	262 (1.0)	264 (3.0)
Vermont	— (†)	272 (0.9)	271 (0.8)	269 (0.7)	273 (0.8)	16 (1.1)	84 (1.1)	42 (1.3)	4 (0.6)	‡ (†)	‡ (†)	266 (2.1)
Virginia[7]	266 (1.1)	269 (1.0)	268 (1.1)	268 (1.0)	267 (1.1)	21 (1.2)	79 (1.2)	34 (1.6)	3 (0.4)	260 (1.7)	273 (1.6)	266 (2.1)
Washington[7]	264 (1.2)	268 (1.2)	264 (0.9)	265 (1.3)	265 (0.9)	23 (1.1)	77 (1.1)	34 (1.3)	3 (0.4)	264 (2.4)	265 (1.5)	265 (2.3)
West Virginia	262 (1.0)	264 (1.0)	260 (1.0)	255 (1.2)	255 (1.0)	32 (1.2)	68 (1.2)	23 (1.1)	1 (0.3)	261 (2.0)	259 (2.7)	252 (1.3)
Wisconsin[6,7]	265 (1.8)	— (†)	266 (1.3)	266 (1.1)	264 (1.0)	24 (1.3)	76 (1.3)	33 (1.7)	3 (0.4)	255 (2.6)	276 (1.6)	266 (1.6)
Wyoming	263 (1.3)	265 (0.7)	267 (0.5)	268 (0.7)	266 (0.7)	20 (1.1)	80 (1.1)	33 (1.0)	2 (0.5)	267 (1.6)	270 (3.7)	269 (0.8)
Department of Defense dependents schools[9]	269 (1.3)	273 (0.5)	272 (0.6)	271 (0.7)	273 (1.0)	13 (1.3)	87 (1.3)	39 (1.6)	2 (0.5)	‡ (†)	‡ (†)	‡ (†)
Other jurisdictions												
American Samoa	— (†)	198 (1.7)	— (†)	— (†)	— (†)	—	—	—	— (†)	— (†)	— (†)	— (†)
Guam	— (†)	240 (1.2)	— (†)	— (†)	— (†)	—	—	—	— (†)	— (†)	— (†)	— (†)
U.S. Virgin Islands	231 (2.1)	241 (1.3)	— (†)	— (†)	— (†)	—	—	—	— (†)	— (†)	— (†)	— (†)

—Not available.
†Not applicable.
‡Reporting standards not met.
[1]Scale ranges from 0 to 500.
[2]Central city is a large or mid-size central city of a Metropolitan Statistical Area (MSA). Urban fringe/large town includes places that are within an MSA of a central city but not primarily within its central city, as well as towns that are incorporated places not within an MSA and have a population greater than or equal to 25,000. Rural/small town includes places that are defined as rural by the U.S. Census Bureau and have a population less than 2,500 and/or a population density of less than 1,000 per square mile, as well as towns that are incorporated places not within an MSA and have a population less than 25,000 but greater than or equal to 2,500.
[3]Basic denotes partial mastery of the knowledge and skills that are fundamental for proficient work at the 8th-grade level.
[4]Proficient represents solid academic performance for 8th-graders. Students reaching this level have demonstrated competency over challenging subject matter.

[5]Advanced signifies superior performance.
[6]Did not satisfy one or more of the guidelines for school participation in 1998. Data are subject to appreciable nonresponse bias.
[7]Did not satisfy one or more of the guidelines for school participation in 2002. Data are subject to appreciable nonresponse bias.
[8]Did not satisfy one or more of the guidelines for school participation in 2003. Data are subject to appreciable nonresponse bias.
[9]Prior to 2005, NAEP divided the Department of Defense (DoD) schools into two jurisdictions, domestic and overseas. In 2005, NAEP began combining the DoD domestic and overseas schools into a single jurisdiction. Data shown in this table for years prior to 2005 were recalculated for comparability.
NOTE: The reading data include students for whom accommodations were permitted. Standard errors appear in parentheses.
SOURCE: U.S. Department of Education, National Center for Education Statistics, National Assessment of Educational Progress (NAEP), 1998, 2002, 2003, 2005, and 2007 Reading Assessments, retrieved May 19, 2008, from the NAEP Data Explorer (http://nces.ed.gov/nationsreportcard/nde/). (This table was prepared May 2008.)

Average scores and achievement-level results in NAEP writing for eighth-grade public school students, by state: 2007

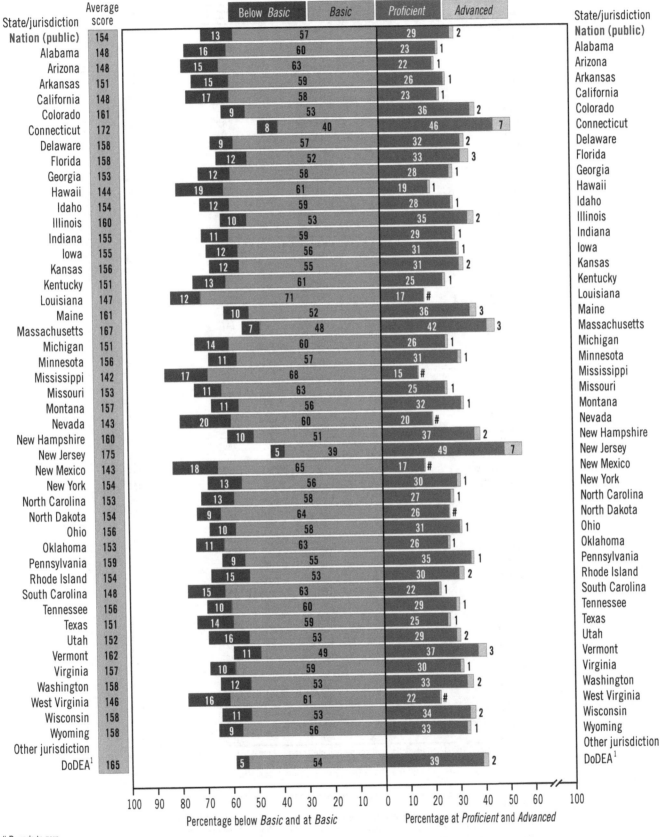

State/jurisdiction	Average score	Below Basic	Basic	Proficient	Advanced	State/jurisdiction
Nation (public)	154	13	57	29	2	Nation (public)
Alabama	148	16	60	23	1	Alabama
Arizona	148	15	63	22	1	Arizona
Arkansas	151	15	59	26	1	Arkansas
California	148	17	58	23	1	California
Colorado	161	9	53	36	2	Colorado
Connecticut	172	8	40	46	7	Connecticut
Delaware	158	9	57	32	2	Delaware
Florida	158	12	52	33	3	Florida
Georgia	153	12	58	28	1	Georgia
Hawaii	144	19	61	19	1	Hawaii
Idaho	154	12	59	28	1	Idaho
Illinois	160	10	53	35	2	Illinois
Indiana	155	11	59	29	1	Indiana
Iowa	155	12	56	31	1	Iowa
Kansas	156	12	55	31	2	Kansas
Kentucky	151	13	61	25	1	Kentucky
Louisiana	147	12	71	17	#	Louisiana
Maine	161	10	52	36	3	Maine
Massachusetts	167	7	48	42	3	Massachusetts
Michigan	151	14	60	26	1	Michigan
Minnesota	156	11	57	31	1	Minnesota
Mississippi	142	17	68	15	#	Mississippi
Missouri	153	11	63	25	1	Missouri
Montana	157	11	56	32	1	Montana
Nevada	143	20	60	20	#	Nevada
New Hampshire	160	10	51	37	2	New Hampshire
New Jersey	175	5	39	49	7	New Jersey
New Mexico	143	18	65	17	#	New Mexico
New York	154	13	56	30	1	New York
North Carolina	153	13	58	27	1	North Carolina
North Dakota	154	9	64	26	#	North Dakota
Ohio	156	10	58	31	1	Ohio
Oklahoma	153	11	63	26	1	Oklahoma
Pennsylvania	159	9	55	35	1	Pennsylvania
Rhode Island	154	15	53	30	2	Rhode Island
South Carolina	148	15	63	22	1	South Carolina
Tennessee	156	10	60	29	1	Tennessee
Texas	151	14	59	25	1	Texas
Utah	152	16	53	29	2	Utah
Vermont	162	11	49	37	3	Vermont
Virginia	157	10	59	30	1	Virginia
Washington	158	12	53	33	2	Washington
West Virginia	146	16	61	22	#	West Virginia
Wisconsin	158	11	53	34	2	Wisconsin
Wyoming	158	9	56	33	1	Wyoming
Other jurisdiction						Other jurisdiction
DoDEA[1]	165	5	54	39	2	DoDEA[1]

Percentage below *Basic* and at *Basic*   Percentage at *Proficient* and *Advanced*

Rounds to zero.
[1] Department of Defense Education Activity (overseas and domestic schools).
NOTE: The shaded bars are graphed using unrounded numbers. Alaska, the District of Columbia, Maryland, Nebraska, Oregon, and South Dakota did not participate in 2007. Detail may not sum to totals because of rounding.
SOURCE: U.S. Department of Education, Institute of Education Sciences, National Center for Education Statistics, National Assessment of Educational Progress (NAEP), 2007 Writing Assessment.

369

Average scores in NAEP writing for eighth-grade public school students, by state: 1998, 2002, and 2007

State/jurisdiction	1998	2002	2007
Nation (public)[1]	**148***	**152***	**154**
Alabama	144*	142*	148
Alaska	—	—	—
Arizona	143*	141*	148
Arkansas	137*	142*	151
California	141*	144	148
Colorado	151*	—	161
Connecticut	165*	164*	172
Delaware	144*	159	158
Florida	142*	154*	158
Georgia	146*	147*	153
Hawaii	135*	138*	144
Idaho	—	151*	154
Illinois	—	—	160
Indiana	—	150*	155
Iowa	—	—	155
Kansas	—	155	156
Kentucky	146*	149	151
Louisiana	136*	142*	147
Maine	155*	157*	161
Maryland	147	157	—
Massachusetts	155*	163	167
Michigan	—	147	151
Minnesota	148*	—	156
Mississippi	134*	141	142
Missouri	142*	151	153
Montana	150*	152*	157
Nebraska	—	156	—
Nevada	140*	137*	143
New Hampshire	—	—	160
New Jersey	—	—	175
New Mexico	141	140	143
New York	146*	151	154
North Carolina	150	157*	153
North Dakota	—	147*	154
Ohio	—	160	156
Oklahoma	152	150	153
Oregon	149	155	—
Pennsylvania	—	154*	159
Rhode Island	148*	151*	154
South Carolina	140*	146	148
South Dakota	—	—	—
Tennessee	148*	148*	156
Texas	154	152	151
Utah	143*	143*	152
Vermont	—	163	162
Virginia	153*	157	157
Washington	148*	155	158
West Virginia	144	144	146
Wisconsin	153*	—	158
Wyoming	146*	151*	158
Other jurisdictions			
District of Columbia	126	128	—
DoDEA[2]	157*	162*	165

— Not available. The state/jurisdiction did not participate or did not meet minimum participation guidelines for reporting.

* Significantly different ($p < .05$) from 2007 when only one state/jurisdiction or the nation is being examined.

[1] National results for assessments prior to 2002 are based on the national sample, not on aggregated state samples.

[2] Department of Defense Education Activity (overseas and domestic schools). Before 2005, DoDEA overseas and domestic schools were separate jurisdictions in NAEP. Pre-2005 data presented here were recalculated for comparability.

SOURCE: U.S. Department of Education, Institute of Education Sciences, National Center for Education Statistics, National Assessment of Educational Progress (NAEP), 1998, 2002, and 2007 Writing Assessments.

Percentage of eighth-grade public school students and average scores in NAEP writing for selected student groups, by state: 2007

	Race/ethnicity									
	White		Black		Hispanic		Asian/Pacific Islander		American Indian/ Alaska Native	
State/jurisdiction	Percentage of students	Average scale score	Percentage of students	Average scale score	Percentage of students	Average scale score	Percentage of students	Average scale score	Percentage of students	Average scale score
Nation (public)	**58**	**162**	**17**	**140**	**19**	**141**	**5**	**166**	**1**	**143**
Alabama	61	157	36	132	2	‡	1	‡	#	‡
Alaska	—	—	—	—	—	—	—	—	—	—
Arizona	46	160	6	143	39	136	3	169	7	133
Arkansas	67	156	24	138	7	141	1	‡	#	‡
California	31	161	7	138	48	137	12	164	1	136
Colorado	62	170	7	145	27	142	3	173	1	‡
Connecticut	69	181	12	150	15	147	3	173	#	‡
Delaware	55	167	35	147	8	142	3	177	#	‡
Florida	49	167	22	144	23	150	2	170	#	‡
Georgia	48	162	43	144	6	142	2	‡	#	‡
Hawaii	14	150	2	140	3	137	69	143	1	‡
Idaho	83	157	1	‡	13	136	1	‡	2	‡
Illinois	58	169	19	142	18	143	4	180	#	‡
Indiana	78	158	12	140	6	139	1	‡	#	‡
Iowa	87	157	5	134	5	133	2	173	#	‡
Kansas	76	160	8	140	11	138	2	‡	1	‡
Kentucky	86	153	10	141	2	‡	1	‡	#	‡
Louisiana	52	153	44	139	2	‡	1	‡	1	‡
Maine	96	161	2	‡	1	‡	1	‡	#	‡
Maryland	—	—	—	—	—	—	—	—	—	—
Massachusetts	74	173	9	146	10	138	5	175	#	‡
Michigan	75	156	19	132	3	135	2	‡	1	‡
Minnesota	80	160	7	133	4	140	6	153	2	135
Mississippi	46	151	52	134	1	‡	1	‡	#	‡
Missouri	77	156	19	140	3	142	2	‡	#	‡
Montana	85	160	1	‡	2	‡	1	‡	11	133
Nebraska	—	—	—	—	—	—	—	—	—	—
Nevada	45	152	11	134	35	132	8	151	2	‡
New Hampshire	94	161	1	‡	3	140	2	‡	#	‡
New Jersey	58	184	16	152	18	162	8	191	#	‡
New Mexico	31	153	2	‡	53	138	2	‡	12	136
New York	56	161	19	140	18	140	7	170	#	‡
North Carolina	57	162	29	138	7	138	2	164	1	145
North Dakota	89	155	1	‡	1	‡	1	‡	8	135
Ohio	76	160	19	138	2	141	1	‡	#	‡
Oklahoma	60	156	9	141	8	143	2	‡	20	151
Oregon	—	—	—	—	—	—	—	—	—	—
Pennsylvania	76	164	15	138	6	145	3	170	#	‡
Rhode Island	71	162	8	136	17	128	3	160	#	‡
South Carolina	55	156	39	137	4	140	1	‡	#	‡
South Dakota	—	—	—	—	—	—	—	—	—	—
Tennessee	68	161	26	144	5	147	1	‡	#	‡
Texas	37	165	16	142	44	142	3	167	#	‡
Utah	81	156	1	‡	13	128	3	157	2	‡
Vermont	95	162	2	‡	1	‡	1	‡	1	‡
Virginia	61	163	27	142	6	145	4	173	#	‡
Washington	69	162	6	150	13	139	10	162	2	138
West Virginia	93	147	5	136	1	‡	1	‡	#	‡
Wisconsin	80	162	10	131	6	149	3	167	1	‡
Wyoming	85	160	1	‡	10	153	1	‡	4	127
Other jurisdictions										
District of Columbia	—	—	—	—	—	—	—	—	—	—
DoDEA[1]	47	167	18	155	14	165	8	172	1	‡

See notes at end of table.

Percentage of eighth-grade public school students and average scores in NAEP writing for selected student groups, by state: 2007 Continued

| State/jurisdiction | Eligibility for free/reduced-price school lunch | | | | Gender | | | |
| | Eligible | | Not eligible | | Male | | Female | |
	Percentage of students	Average scale score	Percentage of students	Average scale score	Percentage of students	Average scale score	Percentage of students	Average scale score
Nation (public)	**41**	**141**	**58**	**164**	**51**	**144**	**49**	**164**
Alabama	50	135	50	160	50	138	50	157
Alaska	—	—	—	—	—	—	—	—
Arizona	44	136	53	157	51	139	49	157
Arkansas	53	141	47	161	52	139	48	164
California	47	136	49	159	52	139	48	157
Colorado	36	143	64	171	50	152	50	169
Connecticut	27	149	73	181	51	163	49	181
Delaware	32	146	67	165	49	151	51	166
Florida	43	146	57	167	50	147	50	169
Georgia	47	141	53	165	48	143	52	164
Hawaii	41	132	59	151	53	134	47	155
Idaho	38	144	60	160	53	143	47	167
Illinois	40	142	60	172	51	150	49	170
Indiana	35	142	65	161	50	144	50	165
Iowa	31	140	69	161	52	143	48	167
Kansas	36	142	64	164	50	144	50	168
Kentucky	47	141	53	160	50	142	50	161
Louisiana	60	140	40	157	52	138	48	156
Maine	34	150	66	167	51	149	49	174
Maryland	—	—	—	—	—	—	—	—
Massachusetts	27	146	73	174	52	157	48	178
Michigan	32	137	68	158	50	140	50	162
Minnesota	28	140	71	162	50	144	50	168
Mississippi	66	136	32	153	49	132	51	152
Missouri	37	141	62	160	51	143	49	163
Montana	35	143	64	164	52	145	48	169
Nebraska	—	—	—	—	—	—	—	—
Nevada	37	132	60	151	51	131	49	156
New Hampshire	17	143	80	164	52	149	48	173
New Jersey	26	155	72	183	50	168	50	183
New Mexico	62	137	37	153	48	133	52	152
New York	47	145	51	164	50	145	50	163
North Carolina	44	141	55	163	51	142	49	164
North Dakota	27	145	73	157	51	142	49	166
Ohio	32	140	66	163	52	147	48	166
Oklahoma	48	146	52	159	51	143	49	162
Oregon	—	—	—	—	—	—	—	—
Pennsylvania	30	144	70	166	51	151	49	168
Rhode Island	31	136	69	162	50	143	50	165
South Carolina	50	139	50	157	49	137	51	159
South Dakota	—	—	—	—	—	—	—	—
Tennessee	45	146	55	165	51	146	49	167
Texas	50	140	50	162	51	142	49	160
Utah	32	139	67	158	52	140	48	165
Vermont	28	144	72	168	53	149	47	176
Virginia	27	141	73	163	51	146	49	168
Washington	34	144	64	166	52	146	48	170
West Virginia	47	137	53	155	50	133	50	159
Wisconsin	29	142	69	164	51	146	49	170
Wyoming	29	145	71	163	52	146	48	171
Other jurisdictions								
District of Columbia	—	—	—	—	—	—	—	—
DoDEA[1]	#	‡	#	‡	53	156	47	175

— Not available. The state/jurisdiction did not participate.

\# Rounds to zero.

‡ Reporting standards not met. Sample size is insufficient to permit a reliable estimate.

[1] Department of Defense Education Activity (overseas and domestic schools).

NOTE: Black includes African American, Hispanic includes Latino, and Pacific Islander includes Native Hawaiian. Race categories exclude Hispanic origin. Results are not shown for students whose race/ethnicity was unclassified and for students whose eligibility for free/reduced-price school lunch was not available. Detail may not sum to totals because of rounding.

SOURCE: U.S. Department of Education, Institute of Education Sciences, National Center for Education Statistics, National Assessment of Educational Progress (NAEP), 2007 Writing Assessment.

Average writing scale score and percentage of students attaining writing achievement levels, by selected student characteristics and grade level: 2002 and 2007

Grade, year, and achievement level	All students	Sex		Race/ethnicity					Parents' highest level of education				Free/reduced-price lunch eligibility		
		Male	Female	White	Black	Hispanic	Asian/ Pacific Islander	American Indian/ Alaska Native	Did not finish high school	Graduated high school	Some education after high school	Graduated college	Eligible	Not eligible	Information not available
1	2	3	4	5	6	7	8	9	10	11	12	13	14	15	16
Average scale score[1]															
4th-graders, 2002	154 (0.4)	146 (0.6)	163 (0.4)	161 (0.3)	140 (0.7)	141 (1.6)	167 (1.5)	139 (1.9)	— (†)	— (†)	— (†)	— (†)	141 (0.8)	163 (0.5)	161 (1.5)
8th-graders															
2002	153 (0.5)	143 (0.6)	164 (0.6)	161 (0.6)	135 (0.7)	137 (0.9)	161 (2.0)	137 (2.9)	136 (0.9)	144 (0.6)	156 (0.6)	165 (0.6)	136 (0.5)	162 (0.7)	161 (1.5)
2007	156 (0.2)	146 (0.3)	166 (0.3)	164 (0.2)	141 (0.4)	142 (0.6)	167 (1.2)	143 (1.3)	139 (0.6)	147 (0.5)	158 (0.4)	166 (0.3)	141 (0.3)	164 (0.3)	170 (1.2)
12th-graders															
2002	148 (0.8)	136 (0.8)	160 (0.9)	154 (0.8)	130 (1.3)	136 (1.5)	151 (2.4)	‡ (†)	129 (1.7)	139 (1.1)	149 (0.9)	158 (1.0)	132 (1.4)	152 (1.0)	156 (1.5)
2007	153 (0.6)	144 (0.6)	162 (0.7)	159 (0.6)	137 (1.0)	139 (1.0)	160 (1.7)	140 (3.9)	134 (1.0)	141 (0.8)	152 (0.7)	163 (0.6)	138 (0.7)	157 (0.6)	165 (1.5)
Percent attaining achievement levels															
4th-graders, 2002															
Below Basic	14 (0.4)	19 (0.5)	9 (0.3)	10 (0.2)	23 (0.8)	23 (1.6)	7 (1.1)	25 (2.6)	— (†)	— (†)	— (†)	— (†)	22 (0.8)	8 (0.3)	10 (1.1)
At or above Basic[2]	86 (0.4)	81 (0.5)	91 (0.3)	90 (0.2)	77 (0.8)	77 (1.6)	93 (1.1)	75 (2.6)	— (†)	— (†)	— (†)	— (†)	78 (0.8)	92 (0.3)	90 (1.1)
At or above Proficient[3]	28 (0.4)	20 (0.5)	36 (0.6)	34 (0.4)	14 (0.7)	17 (0.9)	41 (2.1)	15 (1.7)	— (†)	— (†)	— (†)	— (†)	15 (0.5)	36 (0.6)	34 (1.6)
At Advanced[4]	2 (0.1)	1 (0.1)	3 (0.1)	3 (0.2)	1 (0.2)	1 (0.2)	4 (0.6)	1 (0.5)	— (†)	— (†)	— (†)	— (†)	1 (0.1)	3 (0.2)	3 (0.3)
8th-graders															
2002															
Below Basic	15 (0.4)	21 (0.6)	9 (0.3)	10 (0.4)	26 (1.0)	27 (1.0)	12 (1.3)	27 (3.9)	26 (1.3)	19 (0.7)	11 (0.6)	9 (0.4)	26 (0.6)	9 (0.4)	11 (0.7)
At or above Basic[2]	85 (0.4)	79 (0.6)	91 (0.3)	90 (0.4)	74 (1.0)	73 (1.0)	88 (1.3)	73 (3.9)	74 (1.3)	81 (0.7)	89 (0.6)	91 (0.4)	74 (0.6)	91 (0.4)	89 (0.7)
At or above Proficient[3]	31 (0.6)	21 (0.6)	42 (0.8)	38 (0.6)	13 (0.6)	16 (1.1)	40 (2.6)	16 (2.5)	14 (1.0)	20 (0.6)	31 (0.8)	43 (0.8)	16 (0.6)	39 (0.8)	39 (1.7)
At Advanced[4]	2 (0.1)	1 (0.1)	3 (0.2)	3 (0.2)	# (†)	1 (0.2)	4 (0.8)	1 (#)	# (†)	1 (#)	1 (0.1)	4 (0.2)	1 (0.1)	3 (0.2)	4 (0.6)
2007															
Below Basic	12 (0.2)	17 (0.3)	7 (0.2)	7 (0.2)	19 (0.5)	20 (0.6)	8 (0.8)	21 (1.3)	21 (1.0)	16 (0.5)	9 (0.4)	7 (0.2)	20 (0.3)	7 (0.2)	5 (0.6)
At or above Basic[2]	88 (0.2)	83 (0.3)	93 (0.2)	93 (0.2)	81 (0.5)	80 (0.6)	92 (0.8)	79 (1.3)	79 (1.0)	84 (0.5)	91 (0.4)	93 (0.2)	80 (0.3)	93 (0.2)	95 (0.6)
At or above Proficient[3]	33 (0.3)	22 (0.3)	43 (0.4)	41 (0.3)	16 (0.6)	18 (0.5)	46 (1.4)	20 (1.6)	14 (0.6)	21 (0.6)	33 (0.5)	44 (0.4)	17 (0.3)	41 (0.4)	49 (1.8)
At Advanced[4]	2 (0.1)	1 (0.1)	3 (0.1)	3 (0.1)	# (†)	1 (0.1)	5 (0.5)	1 (0.4)	# (†)	# (†)	1 (0.1)	3 (0.1)	# (†)	3 (0.1)	4 (0.5)
12th-graders															
2002															
Below Basic	26 (0.7)	37 (1.0)	15 (0.7)	21 (0.7)	41 (1.7)	36 (1.8)	24 (2.3)	‡ (†)	43 (2.1)	32 (1.2)	23 (1.0)	18 (0.9)	40 (1.5)	23 (0.8)	19 (1.3)
At or above Basic[2]	74 (0.7)	63 (1.0)	85 (0.7)	79 (0.7)	59 (1.7)	64 (1.8)	76 (2.3)	‡ (†)	57 (2.1)	68 (1.2)	77 (1.0)	82 (0.9)	60 (1.5)	77 (0.8)	81 (1.3)
At or above Proficient[3]	24 (0.8)	14 (0.8)	33 (1.0)	28 (0.9)	9 (1.0)	13 (1.4)	25 (2.8)	‡ (†)	8 (1.4)	14 (1.1)	22 (1.3)	32 (1.0)	11 (1.0)	26 (1.0)	29 (1.6)
At Advanced[4]	2 (0.2)	1 (0.1)	3 (0.3)	2 (0.3)	# (†)	1 (0.2)	3 (1.1)	‡ (†)	# (†)	1 (0.2)	1 (0.2)	3 (0.4)	1 (0.2)	2 (0.2)	2 (0.4)
2007															
Below Basic	18 (0.5)	26 (0.6)	11 (0.5)	14 (0.5)	31 (1.2)	29 (1.1)	14 (1.5)	30 (5.3)	34 (1.5)	27 (1.1)	16 (0.7)	12 (0.4)	31 (1.0)	15 (0.5)	10 (1.0)
At or above Basic[2]	82 (0.5)	74 (0.6)	89 (0.5)	86 (0.5)	69 (1.2)	71 (1.1)	86 (1.5)	70 (5.3)	66 (1.5)	73 (1.1)	84 (0.7)	88 (0.4)	69 (1.0)	85 (0.5)	90 (1.0)
At or above Proficient[3]	24 (0.6)	16 (0.6)	32 (0.8)	30 (0.6)	9 (0.8)	11 (0.9)	30 (2.2)	12 (2.6)	8 (1.0)	13 (0.6)	20 (0.7)	34 (0.8)	11 (0.5)	27 (0.7)	36 (2.1)
At Advanced[4]	1 (0.1)	# (†)	1 (0.2)	1 (0.2)	# (†)	# (†)	1 (0.6)	1 (0.4)	# (†)	# (†)	# (†)	2 (0.2)	# (†)	1 (0.2)	3 (0.4)

—Not available.
†Not applicable.
‡Reporting standards not met.
#Rounds to zero.

[1]Scale ranges from 1 to 300 for all three grades, but scores cannot be compared across grades. For example, a score of 156 at grade 8 does not denote higher performance than a score of 153 at grade 12.
[2]Basic denotes partial mastery of the knowledge and skills that are fundamental for proficient work at a given grade.
[3]Proficient represents solid academic performance. Students reaching this level have demonstrated competency over challenging subject matter.
[4]Advanced signifies superior performance for a given grade.

NOTE: Includes public and private schools. Excludes persons unable to be tested due to limited proficiency in English or due to a disability (if the accommodations provided were not sufficient to enable the test to properly reflect the students' writing proficiency). In 2002, the NAEP national samples of 4th- and 8th-graders were obtained by aggregating the samples from each state, rather than by independently selecting national samples for grades 4 and 8. As a consequence, the size of the national samples increased for these grade levels, and smaller differences were found to be statistically significant than would have been detected in previous assessments. Grade 4 was not included in the 2007 assessment. Race categories exclude persons of Hispanic ethnicity. Some data have been revised from previously published figures. Detail may not sum to totals because of rounding. Standard errors appear in parentheses.

SOURCE: U.S. Department of Education, National Center for Education Statistics, National Assessment of Educational Progress (NAEP), 2002 and 2007 Writing Assessments, retrieved May 6, 2008, from the NAEP Data Explorer (http://nces.ed.gov/nationsreportcard/nde/). (This table was prepared May 2008.)

Average scores and achievement-level results in NAEP mathematics for public school students at grade 4, by state/jurisdiction: 2009

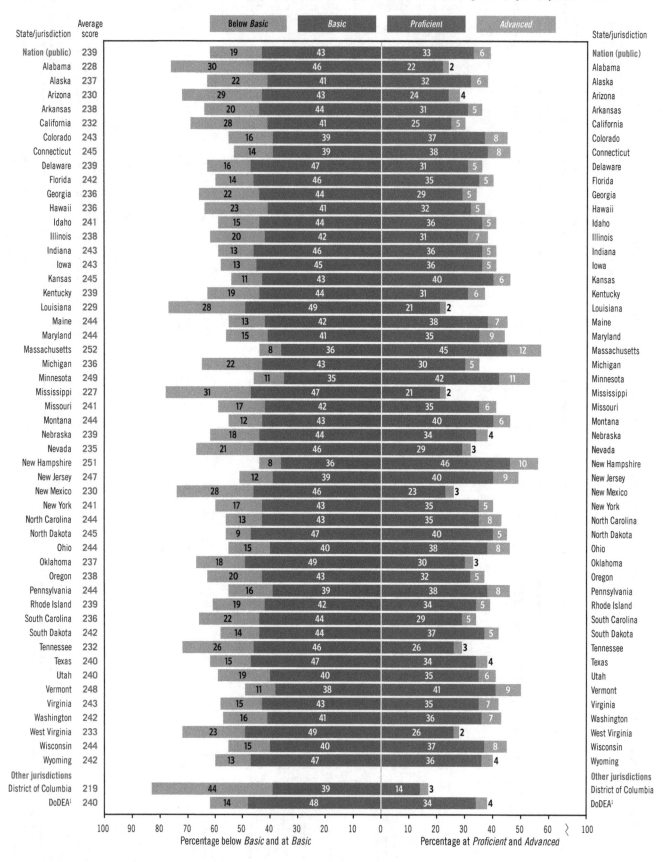

State/jurisdiction	Average score	Below Basic	Basic	Proficient	Advanced
Nation (public)	239	19	43	33	6
Alabama	228	30	46	22	2
Alaska	237	22	41	32	6
Arizona	230	29	43	24	4
Arkansas	238	20	44	31	5
California	232	28	41	25	5
Colorado	243	16	39	37	8
Connecticut	245	14	39	38	8
Delaware	239	16	47	31	5
Florida	242	14	46	35	5
Georgia	236	22	44	29	5
Hawaii	236	23	41	32	5
Idaho	241	15	44	36	5
Illinois	238	20	42	31	7
Indiana	243	13	46	36	5
Iowa	243	13	45	36	5
Kansas	245	11	43	40	6
Kentucky	239	19	44	31	6
Louisiana	229	28	49	21	2
Maine	244	13	42	38	7
Maryland	244	15	41	35	9
Massachusetts	252	8	36	45	12
Michigan	236	22	43	30	5
Minnesota	249	11	35	42	11
Mississippi	227	31	47	21	2
Missouri	241	17	42	35	6
Montana	244	12	43	40	6
Nebraska	239	18	44	34	4
Nevada	235	21	46	29	3
New Hampshire	251	8	36	46	10
New Jersey	247	12	39	40	9
New Mexico	230	28	46	23	3
New York	241	17	43	35	5
North Carolina	244	13	43	35	8
North Dakota	245	9	47	40	5
Ohio	244	15	40	38	8
Oklahoma	237	18	49	30	3
Oregon	238	20	43	32	5
Pennsylvania	244	16	39	38	8
Rhode Island	239	19	42	34	5
South Carolina	236	22	44	29	5
South Dakota	242	14	44	37	5
Tennessee	232	26	46	26	3
Texas	240	15	47	34	4
Utah	240	19	40	35	6
Vermont	248	11	38	41	9
Virginia	243	15	43	35	7
Washington	242	16	41	36	7
West Virginia	233	23	49	26	2
Wisconsin	244	15	40	37	8
Wyoming	242	13	47	36	4
Other jurisdictions					
District of Columbia	219	44	39	14	3
DoDEA[1]	240	14	48	34	4

Percentage below *Basic* and at *Basic* — Percentage at *Proficient* and *Advanced*

[1] Department of Defense Education Activity (overseas and domestic schools).
NOTE: The shaded bars are graphed using unrounded numbers. Detail may not sum to totals because of rounding.
SOURCE: U.S. Department of Education, Institute of Education Sciences, National Center for Education Statistics, National Assessment of Educational Progress (NAEP), 2009 Mathematics Assessment.

Average scores and achievement-level results in NAEP mathematics for fourth-grade public school students, by race/ethnicity and state/jurisdiction: 2009

State/jurisdiction	White					Black					Hispanic				
	Average scale score	Below Basic	At or above Basic	At or above Proficient	At Advanced	Average scale score	Below Basic	At or above Basic	At or above Proficient	At Advanced	Average scale score	Below Basic	At or above Basic	At or above Proficient	At Advanced
Nation (public)	**248**	**10**	**90**	**50**	**8**	**222**	**37**	**63**	**15**	**1**	**227**	**30**	**70**	**21**	**1**
Alabama	237	18	82	34	4	211	51	49	7	#	220	39	61	11	1
Alaska	249	9	91	52	9	225	30	70	17	#	232	23	77	27	2
Arizona	243	14	86	44	7	222	41	59	19	3	220	40	60	15	1
Arkansas	245	12	88	46	7	217	44	56	12	#	233	21	79	26	2
California	247	11	89	51	9	217	44	56	13	1	219	41	59	14	1
Colorado	252	7	93	57	11	225	33	67	23	2	228	31	69	24	3
Connecticut	253	7	93	58	11	222	38	62	14	1	227	30	70	18	2
Delaware	249	7	93	50	8	226	30	70	17	#	231	23	77	22	2
Florida	250	7	93	53	9	228	27	73	20	1	238	16	84	33	2
Georgia	247	10	90	48	8	221	38	62	15	#	231	25	75	26	2
Hawaii	247	11	89	51	7	232	24	76	33	2	230	26	74	28	2
Idaho	244	12	88	44	5	‡	‡	‡	‡	‡	225	34	66	18	1
Illinois	249	10	90	52	10	216	46	54	11	1	227	28	72	20	1
Indiana	247	9	91	48	6	222	34	66	13	#	230	23	77	23	1
Iowa	245	10	90	45	6	226	31	69	17	1	223	36	64	17	1
Kansas	251	6	94	55	8	224	34	66	18	2	233	19	81	24	2
Kentucky	241	16	84	39	6	220	41	59	14	1	227	33	67	22	1
Louisiana	241	13	87	37	3	218	43	57	8	1	230	25	75	23	1
Maine	245	12	88	46	7	228	31	69	28	2	‡	‡	‡	‡	‡
Maryland	255	6	94	60	15	228	28	72	21	1	238	17	83	32	4
Massachusetts	258	3	97	67	14	236	16	84	30	2	232	22	78	25	2
Michigan	243	14	86	43	6	212	52	48	9	#	227	29	71	20	1
Minnesota	255	6	94	61	14	227	34	66	25	2	232	27	73	29	2
Mississippi	241	13	87	37	3	215	47	53	8	#	‡	‡	‡	‡	‡
Missouri	245	12	88	46	7	221	40	60	17	1	237	22	78	37	4
Montana	247	9	91	49	6	‡	‡	‡	‡	‡	241	14	86	41	4
Nebraska	245	11	89	45	5	213	52	48	10	#	224	34	66	16	1
Nevada	245	10	90	46	5	218	43	57	12	#	227	30	70	19	1
New Hampshire	252	7	93	57	10	‡	‡	‡	‡	‡	234	21	79	31	2
New Jersey	255	5	95	63	12	228	27	73	19	2	232	23	77	25	2
New Mexico	245	12	88	47	7	225	33	67	19	2	224	34	66	18	1
New York	248	9	91	50	7	225	33	67	19	1	231	25	75	25	2
North Carolina	254	5	95	59	13	226	29	71	18	1	236	16	84	27	2
North Dakota	248	6	94	49	6	‡	‡	‡	‡	‡	233	21	79	25	2
Ohio	249	9	91	54	9	222	36	64	14	1	229	25	75	20	2
Oklahoma	241	13	87	40	4	222	36	64	14	1	221	39	61	16	1
Oregon	243	14	86	43	6	223	37	63	18	#	227	32	68	23	1
Pennsylvania	249	9	91	53	9	223	36	64	17	2	219	41	59	14	1
Rhode Island	247	11	89	50	7	221	37	63	15	#	232	23	77	28	2
South Carolina	245	12	88	46	7	220	40	60	14	1	233	25	75	27	4
South Dakota	247	9	91	47	6	225	35	65	17	#	233	25	75	27	4
Tennessee	239	17	83	36	3	213	51	49	7	#	225	34	66	19	2
Texas	254	5	95	61	9	231	21	79	23	1	233	20	80	26	1
Utah	246	13	87	48	8	221	39	61	15	1	219	43	57	16	1
Vermont	248	11	89	51	9	‡	‡	‡	‡	‡	‡	‡	‡	‡	‡
Virginia	251	7	93	54	9	225	31	69	16	1	234	20	80	28	2
Washington	247	11	89	51	8	227	29	71	24	3	227	31	69	20	1
West Virginia	233	22	78	28	2	225	34	66	20	1	‡	‡	‡	‡	‡
Wisconsin	250	9	91	53	9	217	45	55	11	#	228	29	71	22	1
Wyoming	244	10	90	44	5	‡	‡	‡	‡	‡	231	23	77	22	#
Other jurisdictions															
District of Columbia	270	1	99	81	33	213	50	50	9	#	227	30	70	24	1
DoDEA[1]	245	10	90	45	5	229	26	74	19	1	235	20	80	30	2

See notes at end of table.

Average scores and achievement-level results in NAEP mathematics for fourth-grade public school students, by race/ethnicity and state/jurisdiction: 2009—Continued

State/jurisdiction	Asian/Pacific Islander					American Indian/Alaska Native				
	Average scale score	Percentage of students				Average scale score	Percentage of students			
		Below Basic	At or above Basic	At or above Proficient	At Advanced		Below Basic	At or above Basic	At or above Proficient	At Advanced
Nation (public)	**255**	**9**	**91**	**61**	**18**	**227**	**32**	**68**	**23**	**2**
Alabama	‡	‡	‡	‡	‡	‡	‡	‡	‡	‡
Alaska	236	22	78	35	4	216	47	53	14	2
Arizona	245	13	87	45	12	215	49	51	13	1
Arkansas	‡	‡	‡	‡	‡	‡	‡	‡	‡	‡
California	257	7	93	61	20	‡	‡	‡	‡	‡
Colorado	246	15	85	51	11	‡	‡	‡	‡	‡
Connecticut	257	7	93	65	15	‡	‡	‡	‡	‡
Delaware	258	6	94	66	19	‡	‡	‡	‡	‡
Florida	261	7	93	73	21	‡	‡	‡	‡	‡
Georgia	256	7	93	60	18	‡	‡	‡	‡	‡
Hawaii	235	23	77	35	5	‡	‡	‡	‡	‡
Idaho	‡	‡	‡	‡	‡	‡	‡	‡	‡	‡
Illinois	265	3	97	73	25	‡	‡	‡	‡	‡
Indiana	‡	‡	‡	‡	‡	‡	‡	‡	‡	‡
Iowa	259	6	94	66	23	‡	‡	‡	‡	‡
Kansas	258	6	94	64	16	‡	‡	‡	‡	‡
Kentucky	265	7	93	69	35	‡	‡	‡	‡	‡
Louisiana	‡	‡	‡	‡	‡	‡	‡	‡	‡	‡
Maine	‡	‡	‡	‡	‡	‡	‡	‡	‡	‡
Maryland	259	5	95	67	18	‡	‡	‡	‡	‡
Massachusetts	264	4	96	70	28	‡	‡	‡	‡	‡
Michigan	252	13	87	55	19	‡	‡	‡	‡	‡
Minnesota	243	18	82	44	11	233	26	74	27	5
Mississippi	‡	‡	‡	‡	‡	‡	‡	‡	‡	‡
Missouri	255	11	89	62	22	‡	‡	‡	‡	‡
Montana	‡	‡	‡	‡	‡	228	32	68	23	2
Nebraska	251	10	90	55	11	‡	‡	‡	‡	‡
Nevada	245	12	88	45	7	‡	‡	‡	‡	‡
New Hampshire	257	9	91	67	16	‡	‡	‡	‡	‡
New Jersey	261	5	95	72	22	‡	‡	‡	‡	‡
New Mexico	‡	‡	‡	‡	‡	217	43	57	14	#
New York	257	8	92	67	16	‡	‡	‡	‡	‡
North Carolina	259	7	93	62	25	232	23	77	30	2
North Dakota	‡	‡	‡	‡	‡	226	29	71	17	2
Ohio	‡	‡	‡	‡	‡	‡	‡	‡	‡	‡
Oklahoma	‡	‡	‡	‡	‡	234	21	79	29	2
Oregon	245	18	82	48	12	223	37	63	15	3
Pennsylvania	258	9	91	62	22	‡	‡	‡	‡	‡
Rhode Island	242	14	86	40	10	‡	‡	‡	‡	‡
South Carolina	‡	‡	‡	‡	‡	‡	‡	‡	‡	‡
South Dakota	‡	‡	‡	‡	‡	220	40	60	15	#
Tennessee	‡	‡	‡	‡	‡	‡	‡	‡	‡	‡
Texas	259	4	96	71	17	‡	‡	‡	‡	‡
Utah	241	17	83	39	7	219	46	54	17	#
Vermont	‡	‡	‡	‡	‡	‡	‡	‡	‡	‡
Virginia	258	5	95	64	18	‡	‡	‡	‡	‡
Washington	253	9	91	56	16	227	31	69	21	3
West Virginia	‡	‡	‡	‡	‡	‡	‡	‡	‡	‡
Wisconsin	240	21	79	39	12	228	29	71	21	1
Wyoming	‡	‡	‡	‡	‡	‡	‡	‡	‡	‡
Other jurisdictions										
District of Columbia	‡	‡	‡	‡	‡	‡	‡	‡	‡	‡
DoDEA[1]	244	9	91	42	5	‡	‡	‡	‡	‡

\# Rounds to zero.

‡ Reporting standards not met. Sample size insufficient to permit a reliable estimate.

[1] Department of Defense Education Activity (overseas and domestic schools).

NOTE: Black includes African American, Hispanic includes Latino, and Pacific Islander includes Native Hawaiian. Race categories exclude Hispanic origin. Results are not shown for students whose race/ethnicity was unclassified. Detail may not sum to totals because of rounding.

SOURCE: U.S. Department of Education, Institute of Education Sciences, National Center for Education Statistics, National Assessment of Educational Progress (NAEP), 2009 Mathematics Assessment.

Average scores and achievement-level results in NAEP mathematics for fourth-grade public school students, by gender and state/jurisdiction: 2009

State/jurisdiction	Male Average scale score	Below Basic	At or above Basic	At or above Proficient	At Advanced	Female Average scale score	Below Basic	At or above Basic	At or above Proficient	At Advanced
Nation (public)	**240**	**19**	**81**	**40**	**7**	**238**	**19**	**81**	**37**	**5**
Alabama	228	30	70	25	3	228	29	71	24	2
Alaska	238	21	79	40	7	236	22	78	36	5
Arizona	230	30	70	30	4	230	29	71	26	3
Arkansas	239	20	80	39	6	236	20	80	34	4
California	233	28	72	32	6	231	29	71	29	5
Colorado	244	16	84	46	9	242	16	84	44	7
Connecticut	246	14	86	49	11	243	15	85	44	6
Delaware	241	16	84	40	6	238	17	83	33	4
Florida	243	14	86	42	6	241	14	86	39	5
Georgia	237	23	77	35	5	236	21	79	32	4
Hawaii	235	23	77	37	6	236	22	78	37	4
Idaho	242	15	85	42	5	240	15	85	39	4
Illinois	240	20	80	41	7	237	21	79	35	6
Indiana	243	13	87	42	6	242	12	88	41	4
Iowa	243	13	87	43	6	242	13	87	40	5
Kansas	246	11	89	48	7	244	11	89	44	6
Kentucky	240	18	82	39	7	238	20	80	34	5
Louisiana	230	27	73	24	2	229	28	72	21	1
Maine	247	11	89	48	9	242	14	86	42	5
Maryland	244	16	84	44	11	243	14	86	43	7
Massachusetts	253	8	92	59	14	251	7	93	55	10
Michigan	238	22	78	37	7	235	22	78	33	4
Minnesota	251	11	89	56	14	248	12	88	51	9
Mississippi	227	33	67	23	2	228	29	71	21	1
Missouri	241	17	83	43	7	240	17	83	39	5
Montana	247	10	90	49	7	242	14	86	41	5
Nebraska	239	19	81	39	4	239	17	83	37	4
Nevada	236	21	79	34	4	234	22	78	30	3
New Hampshire	252	8	92	58	11	250	8	92	54	9
New Jersey	248	12	88	51	11	245	13	87	46	7
New Mexico	231	28	72	27	4	229	29	71	25	2
New York	242	16	84	43	6	239	17	83	37	5
North Carolina	244	14	86	44	8	244	13	87	42	8
North Dakota	247	8	92	47	7	244	10	90	42	3
Ohio	245	13	87	48	9	242	16	84	43	6
Oklahoma	238	18	82	35	4	236	19	81	30	2
Oregon	240	19	81	40	7	236	21	79	34	4
Pennsylvania	245	15	85	48	9	242	16	84	43	6
Rhode Island	240	18	82	43	6	237	21	79	36	4
South Carolina	236	23	77	36	5	235	22	78	32	4
South Dakota	243	13	87	44	6	241	14	86	39	3
Tennessee	232	26	74	29	3	231	26	74	28	2
Texas	241	15	85	39	5	240	14	86	37	3
Utah	241	18	82	42	7	239	19	81	40	5
Vermont	249	11	89	53	11	247	11	89	49	8
Virginia	245	15	85	46	9	241	14	86	39	6
Washington	242	17	83	45	8	242	15	85	42	6
West Virginia	234	22	78	30	3	232	24	76	26	1
Wisconsin	245	15	85	47	9	242	15	85	43	7
Wyoming	243	12	88	43	4	241	14	86	38	4
Other jurisdictions										
District of Columbia	218	45	55	17	4	221	42	58	17	3
DoDEA[1]	242	13	87	42	4	238	16	84	33	3

[1] Department of Defense Education Activity (overseas and domestic schools).
NOTE: Detail may not sum to totals because of rounding.
SOURCE: U.S. Department of Education, Institute of Education Sciences, National Center for Education Statistics, National Assessment of Educational Progress (NAEP), 2009 Mathematics Assessment.

Average scores and achievement-level results in NAEP mathematics for public school students at grade 8, by state/jurisdiction: 2009

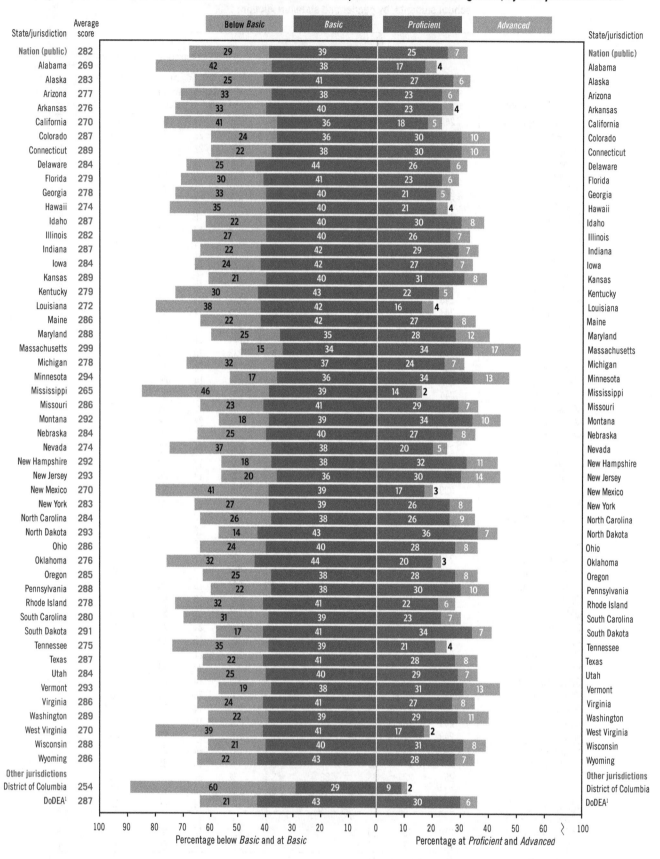

State/jurisdiction	Average score	Below *Basic*	*Basic*	*Proficient*	*Advanced*
Nation (public)	282	29	39	25	7
Alabama	269	42	38	17	4
Alaska	283	25	41	27	6
Arizona	277	33	38	23	6
Arkansas	276	33	40	23	4
California	270	41	36	18	5
Colorado	287	24	36	30	10
Connecticut	289	22	38	30	10
Delaware	284	25	44	26	6
Florida	279	30	41	23	6
Georgia	278	33	40	21	5
Hawaii	274	35	40	21	4
Idaho	287	22	40	30	8
Illinois	282	27	40	26	7
Indiana	287	22	42	29	7
Iowa	284	24	42	27	7
Kansas	289	21	40	31	8
Kentucky	279	30	43	22	5
Louisiana	272	38	42	16	4
Maine	286	22	42	27	8
Maryland	288	25	35	28	12
Massachusetts	299	15	34	34	17
Michigan	278	32	37	24	7
Minnesota	294	17	36	34	13
Mississippi	265	46	39	14	2
Missouri	286	23	41	29	7
Montana	292	18	39	34	10
Nebraska	284	25	40	27	8
Nevada	274	37	38	20	5
New Hampshire	292	18	38	32	11
New Jersey	293	20	36	30	14
New Mexico	270	41	39	17	3
New York	283	27	39	26	8
North Carolina	284	26	38	26	9
North Dakota	293	14	43	36	7
Ohio	286	24	40	28	8
Oklahoma	276	32	44	20	3
Oregon	285	25	38	28	8
Pennsylvania	288	22	38	30	10
Rhode Island	278	32	41	22	6
South Carolina	280	31	39	23	7
South Dakota	291	17	41	34	7
Tennessee	275	35	39	21	4
Texas	287	22	41	28	8
Utah	284	25	40	29	7
Vermont	293	19	38	31	13
Virginia	286	24	41	27	8
Washington	289	22	39	29	11
West Virginia	270	39	41	17	2
Wisconsin	288	21	40	31	8
Wyoming	286	22	43	28	7
Other jurisdictions					
District of Columbia	254	60	29	9	2
DoDEA[1]	287	21	43	30	6

Percentage below *Basic* and at *Basic*   Percentage at *Proficient* and *Advanced*

[1] Department of Defense Education Activity (overseas and domestic schools).
NOTE: The shaded bars are graphed using unrounded numbers. Detail may not sum to totals because of rounding.
SOURCE: U.S. Department of Education, Institute of Education Sciences, National Center for Education Statistics, National Assessment of Educational Progress (NAEP), 2009 Mathematics Assessment.

Average scores and achievement-level results in NAEP mathematics for eighth-grade public school students, by race/ethnicity and state/jurisdiction: 2009

State/jurisdiction	White					Black					Hispanic				
		Percentage of students					Percentage of students					Percentage of students			
	Average scale score	Below Basic	At or above Basic	At or above Proficient	At Advanced	Average scale score	Below Basic	At or above Basic	At or above Proficient	At Advanced	Average scale score	Below Basic	At or above Basic	At or above Proficient	At Advanced
Nation (public)	**292**	**18**	**82**	**43**	**10**	**260**	**51**	**49**	**12**	**1**	**266**	**44**	**56**	**17**	**2**
Alabama	280	28	72	29	5	248	66	34	6	1	260	51	49	10	#
Alaska	293	14	86	44	8	268	42	58	17	1	275	31	69	23	5
Arizona	292	19	81	42	11	269	42	58	23	5	265	44	56	16	1
Arkansas	284	24	76	34	6	251	64	36	8	#	269	37	63	15	1
California	289	22	78	39	10	250	60	40	10	1	256	55	45	11	1
Colorado	299	13	87	51	14	263	47	53	16	1	267	45	55	18	2
Connecticut	298	13	87	49	13	261	50	50	10	1	263	45	55	14	1
Delaware	294	14	86	43	9	267	42	58	13	1	278	28	72	22	2
Florida	289	20	80	39	9	264	47	53	13	1	274	34	66	22	3
Georgia	289	20	80	39	9	262	50	50	11	1	270	41	59	18	2
Hawaii	282	26	74	31	6	271	40	60	21	4	276	30	70	26	4
Idaho	292	17	83	43	9	‡	‡	‡	‡	‡	264	46	54	15	1
Illinois	294	15	85	44	10	255	59	41	9	1	269	41	59	17	1
Indiana	291	17	83	41	8	266	46	54	14	1	273	36	64	19	2
Iowa	287	21	79	37	7	259	50	50	9	2	266	43	57	15	1
Kansas	294	15	85	45	10	264	48	52	15	1	274	35	65	22	3
Kentucky	282	27	73	29	5	258	55	45	8	#	272	37	63	22	3
Louisiana	283	23	77	29	6	257	57	43	7	1	‡	‡	‡	‡	‡
Maine	287	21	79	36	8	261	54	46	14	5	‡	‡	‡	‡	‡
Maryland	303	11	89	56	18	266	45	55	15	1	275	36	64	26	4
Massachusetts	305	9	91	59	20	272	38	62	23	3	271	38	62	21	4
Michigan	286	23	77	37	8	246	68	32	5	1	269	38	62	17	2
Minnesota	300	11	89	53	15	264	47	53	13	2	269	45	55	21	4
Mississippi	279	26	74	25	3	251	64	36	5	#	‡	‡	‡	‡	‡
Missouri	290	18	82	39	7	260	54	46	11	2	284	24	76	37	4
Montana	296	13	87	47	11	‡	‡	‡	‡	‡	278	30	70	27	5
Nebraska	291	17	83	41	9	253	60	40	10	2	262	50	50	10	1
Nevada	287	22	78	36	8	256	59	41	10	1	262	50	50	13	2
New Hampshire	293	17	83	44	11	‡	‡	‡	‡	‡	270	45	55	22	6
New Jersey	302	11	89	54	17	267	42	58	17	2	272	37	63	22	3
New Mexico	288	19	81	39	7	259	45	55	13	2	262	50	50	12	1
New York	294	14	86	44	10	262	49	51	13	1	262	48	52	15	2
North Carolina	297	15	85	49	14	262	47	53	12	1	274	33	67	24	2
North Dakota	296	10	90	46	8	‡	‡	‡	‡	‡	‡	‡	‡	‡	‡
Ohio	291	17	83	41	9	260	55	45	11	1	267	42	58	16	#
Oklahoma	282	24	76	29	4	261	49	51	10	1	263	50	50	12	1
Oregon	290	19	81	41	9	264	47	53	12	1	264	46	54	15	1
Pennsylvania	294	16	84	45	11	260	51	49	13	1	266	45	55	18	3
Rhode Island	286	23	77	35	7	256	55	45	8	1	255	57	43	8	1
South Carolina	293	17	83	43	11	263	48	52	12	1	269	43	57	16	3
South Dakota	295	13	87	46	8	‡	‡	‡	‡	‡	268	38	62	13	1
Tennessee	282	27	73	30	6	254	60	40	10	1	270	39	61	19	2
Texas	301	11	89	54	16	272	34	66	17	2	277	30	70	25	2
Utah	289	19	81	40	8	‡	‡	‡	‡	‡	259	54	46	11	1
Vermont	293	18	82	44	13	‡	‡	‡	‡	‡	‡	‡	‡	‡	‡
Virginia	294	16	84	44	10	268	41	59	14	1	274	35	65	23	3
Washington	295	15	85	46	12	269	40	60	16	4	264	47	53	13	2
West Virginia	271	39	61	20	2	263	47	53	11	1	‡	‡	‡	‡	‡
Wisconsin	294	14	86	45	10	254	62	38	11	2	268	44	56	20	3
Wyoming	289	18	82	38	8	‡	‡	‡	‡	‡	269	40	60	15	3
Other jurisdictions															
District of Columbia	‡	‡	‡	‡	‡	249	64	36	8	#	265	42	58	18	2
DoDEA[1]	294	13	87	44	9	269	40	60	14	1	281	28	72	28	4

See notes at end of table.

Average scores and achievement-level results in NAEP mathematics for eighth-grade public school students, by race/ethnicity and state/jurisdiction: 2009—Continued

State/jurisdiction	Asian/Pacific Islander					American Indian/Alaska Native				
		Percentage of students					Percentage of students			
	Average scale score	Below *Basic*	At or above *Basic*	At or above *Proficient*	At *Advanced*	Average scale score	Below *Basic*	At or above *Basic*	At or above *Proficient*	At *Advanced*
Nation (public)	**300**	**16**	**84**	**53**	**20**	**267**	**43**	**57**	**20**	**3**
Alabama	‡	‡	‡	‡	‡	‡	‡	‡	‡	‡
Alaska	282	28	72	31	7	262	49	51	15	2
Arizona	295	19	81	52	18	254	57	43	12	2
Arkansas	‡	‡	‡	‡	‡	‡	‡	‡	‡	‡
California	294	18	82	46	13	‡	‡	‡	‡	‡
Colorado	301	14	86	55	18	‡	‡	‡	‡	‡
Connecticut	305	10	90	61	18	‡	‡	‡	‡	‡
Delaware	312	8	92	69	27	‡	‡	‡	‡	‡
Florida	302	13	87	55	19	‡	‡	‡	‡	‡
Georgia	300	14	86	49	20	‡	‡	‡	‡	‡
Hawaii	274	36	64	25	4	‡	‡	‡	‡	‡
Idaho	‡	‡	‡	‡	‡	‡	‡	‡	‡	‡
Illinois	304	11	89	60	19	‡	‡	‡	‡	‡
Indiana	‡	‡	‡	‡	‡	‡	‡	‡	‡	‡
Iowa	‡	‡	‡	‡	‡	‡	‡	‡	‡	‡
Kansas	‡	‡	‡	‡	‡	‡	‡	‡	‡	‡
Kentucky	‡	‡	‡	‡	‡	‡	‡	‡	‡	‡
Louisiana	‡	‡	‡	‡	‡	‡	‡	‡	‡	‡
Maine	‡	‡	‡	‡	‡	‡	‡	‡	‡	‡
Maryland	320	5	95	76	35	‡	‡	‡	‡	‡
Massachusetts	314	10	90	66	35	‡	‡	‡	‡	‡
Michigan	309	11	89	59	28	‡	‡	‡	‡	‡
Minnesota	283	32	68	35	11	277	26	74	21	4
Mississippi	‡	‡	‡	‡	‡	‡	‡	‡	‡	‡
Missouri	‡	‡	‡	‡	‡	‡	‡	‡	‡	‡
Montana	‡	‡	‡	‡	‡	260	49	51	16	2
Nebraska	‡	‡	‡	‡	‡	‡	‡	‡	‡	‡
Nevada	283	30	70	33	7	‡	‡	‡	‡	‡
New Hampshire	308	9	91	62	26	‡	‡	‡	‡	‡
New Jersey	323	5	95	77	43	‡	‡	‡	‡	‡
New Mexico	‡	‡	‡	‡	‡	256	54	46	10	1
New York	309	10	90	63	26	‡	‡	‡	‡	‡
North Carolina	311	13	87	65	36	256	55	45	14	2
North Dakota	‡	‡	‡	‡	‡	263	48	52	16	2
Ohio	‡	‡	‡	‡	‡	‡	‡	‡	‡	‡
Oklahoma	289	20	80	38	8	269	40	60	19	2
Oregon	296	20	80	50	18	273	36	64	25	6
Pennsylvania	305	13	87	60	25	‡	‡	‡	‡	‡
Rhode Island	292	15	85	40	10	‡	‡	‡	‡	‡
South Carolina	‡	‡	‡	‡	‡	‡	‡	‡	‡	‡
South Dakota	‡	‡	‡	‡	‡	266	45	55	17	1
Tennessee	‡	‡	‡	‡	‡	‡	‡	‡	‡	‡
Texas	313	8	92	67	31	‡	‡	‡	‡	‡
Utah	276	36	64	27	7	263	49	51	18	1
Vermont	‡	‡	‡	‡	‡	‡	‡	‡	‡	‡
Virginia	304	11	89	55	24	‡	‡	‡	‡	‡
Washington	302	15	85	53	22	269	42	58	23	8
West Virginia	‡	‡	‡	‡	‡	‡	‡	‡	‡	‡
Wisconsin	289	18	82	40	7	‡	‡	‡	‡	‡
Wyoming	‡	‡	‡	‡	‡	‡	‡	‡	‡	‡
Other jurisdictions										
District of Columbia	‡	‡	‡	‡	‡	‡	‡	‡	‡	‡
DoDEA[1]	292	17	83	44	8	‡	‡	‡	‡	‡

\# Rounds to zero.

‡ Reporting standards not met. Sample size insufficient to permit a reliable estimate.

[1] Department of Defense Education Activity (overseas and domestic schools).

NOTE: Black includes African American, Hispanic includes Latino, and Pacific Islander includes Native Hawaiian. Race categories exclude Hispanic origin. Results are not shown for students whose race/ethnicity was unclassified. Detail may not sum to totals because of rounding.

SOURCE: U.S. Department of Education, Institute of Education Sciences, National Center for Education Statistics, National Assessment of Educational Progress (NAEP), 2009 Mathematics Assessment.

Average scores and achievement-level results in NAEP mathematics for eighth-grade public school students, by gender and state/jurisdiction: 2009

State/jurisdiction	Male					Female				
	Average scale score	Percentage of students				Average scale score	Percentage of students			
		Below Basic	At or above Basic	At or above Proficient	At Advanced		Below Basic	At or above Basic	At or above Proficient	At Advanced
Nation (public)	**283**	**28**	**72**	**34**	**8**	**281**	**29**	**71**	**31**	**7**
Alabama	268	42	58	21	4	269	42	58	20	3
Alaska	283	26	74	34	7	283	25	75	33	5
Arizona	279	32	68	31	7	276	33	67	27	5
Arkansas	275	34	66	27	4	277	32	68	27	5
California	272	39	61	26	6	268	42	58	21	4
Colorado	289	24	76	41	11	286	25	75	38	9
Connecticut	288	23	77	39	11	289	21	79	41	10
Delaware	284	24	76	32	7	283	25	75	31	6
Florida	281	29	71	31	7	278	31	69	27	5
Georgia	277	35	65	27	6	278	32	68	27	5
Hawaii	271	38	62	24	5	276	32	68	27	4
Idaho	288	21	79	39	9	286	22	78	37	7
Illinois	284	26	74	35	9	280	29	71	31	6
Indiana	288	21	79	39	8	285	24	76	34	7
Iowa	285	24	76	35	8	284	24	76	33	5
Kansas	290	21	79	43	9	287	21	79	36	7
Kentucky	281	29	71	30	6	278	30	70	25	4
Louisiana	272	39	61	21	5	273	37	63	20	3
Maine	288	22	78	38	10	284	23	77	32	6
Maryland	290	24	76	42	14	287	25	75	38	11
Massachusetts	300	14	86	53	18	298	15	85	50	16
Michigan	280	31	69	32	8	277	33	67	29	5
Minnesota	296	17	83	49	15	293	18	82	45	11
Mississippi	265	45	55	15	2	265	46	54	15	1
Missouri	287	23	77	37	8	285	23	77	34	5
Montana	292	18	82	45	11	291	17	83	42	9
Nebraska	286	24	76	37	9	283	26	74	32	7
Nevada	275	36	64	26	5	273	38	62	24	4
New Hampshire	293	19	81	45	13	292	18	82	42	10
New Jersey	295	19	81	47	16	290	20	80	42	12
New Mexico	271	39	61	21	4	269	42	58	19	3
New York	283	27	73	36	8	282	28	72	32	7
North Carolina	284	27	73	37	9	284	25	75	34	9
North Dakota	294	13	87	45	10	291	14	86	42	5
Ohio	287	23	77	38	9	284	25	75	34	7
Oklahoma	278	31	69	26	4	274	34	66	21	3
Oregon	287	24	76	40	10	283	26	74	33	7
Pennsylvania	290	22	78	42	12	287	22	78	37	8
Rhode Island	278	32	68	29	6	278	31	69	26	5
South Carolina	281	31	69	31	8	280	31	69	29	6
South Dakota	292	17	83	44	9	289	18	82	39	5
Tennessee	275	36	64	26	4	275	35	65	25	4
Texas	287	22	78	38	8	286	23	77	35	9
Utah	285	25	75	37	7	283	25	75	33	6
Vermont	294	19	81	45	14	292	19	81	42	11
Virginia	287	23	77	38	9	285	24	76	33	7
Washington	290	21	79	41	12	288	23	77	38	10
West Virginia	271	40	60	21	3	270	39	61	18	2
Wisconsin	289	20	80	41	10	287	22	78	38	7
Wyoming	288	20	80	38	8	284	24	76	31	6
Other jurisdictions										
District of Columbia	252	61	39	12	2	255	59	41	11	2
DoDEA[1]	288	19	81	38	6	286	22	78	34	6

[1] Department of Defense Education Activity (overseas and domestic schools).

NOTE: Detail may not sum to totals because of rounding.

SOURCE: U.S. Department of Education, Institute of Education Sciences, National Center for Education Statistics, National Assessment of Educational Progress (NAEP), 2009 Mathematics Assessment.

Average mathematics scale score, by age and selected student and school characteristics: Selected years, 1973 through 2008

Selected student and school characteristic	1973		1978		1982		1986		1990		1992		1994		1996		1999		2004		2008	
1	2		3		4		5		6		7		8		9		10		11		12	
9-year-olds																						
All students	219	(0.8)	219	(0.8)	219	(1.1)	222	(1.0)	230	(0.8)	230	(0.8)	231	(0.8)	231	(0.8)	232	(0.8)	239	(0.9)	243	(0.8)
Sex																						
Male	218	(0.7)	217	(0.7)	217	(1.2)	222	(1.1)	229	(0.9)	231	(1.0)	232	(1.0)	233	(1.2)	233	(1.0)	239	(1.0)	242	(0.9)
Female	220	(1.1)	220	(1.0)	221	(1.2)	222	(1.2)	230	(1.1)	228	(1.0)	230	(0.9)	229	(0.7)	231	(0.9)	240	(1.0)	243	(1.0)
Race/ethnicity																						
White	225	(1.0)	224	(0.9)	224	(1.1)	227	(1.1)	235	(0.8)	235	(0.8)	237	(1.0)	237	(1.0)	239	(0.9)	245	(0.8)	250	(0.8)
Black	190	(1.8)	192	(1.1)	195	(1.6)	202	(1.6)	208	(2.2)	208	(2.0)	212	(1.6)	212	(1.4)	211	(1.6)	221	(2.1)	224	(1.9)
Hispanic	202	(2.4)	203	(2.2)	204	(1.3)	205	(2.1)	214	(2.1)	212	(2.3)	210	(2.3)	215	(1.7)	213	(1.9)	229	(2.0)	234	(1.2)
Region																						
Northeast	227	(1.9)	227	(1.9)	226	(1.8)	226	(2.7)	236	(2.1)	235	(1.9)	238	(2.2)	236	(2.0)	242	(1.7)	243	(2.5)	248	(1.5)
Southeast	208	(1.3)	209	(1.2)	210	(2.5)	218	(2.5)	224	(2.4)	221	(1.7)	229	(1.4)	227	(2.0)	226	(2.6)	236	(1.7)	237	(1.9)
Central	224	(1.5)	224	(1.5)	221	(2.7)	226	(2.3)	231	(1.3)	234	(1.6)	233	(1.8)	233	(2.3)	233	(1.4)	240	(1.9)	244	(1.6)
West	216	(2.2)	213	(1.3)	219	(1.8)	217	(2.4)	228	(1.8)	229	(2.3)	226	(1.6)	229	(1.3)	228	(1.7)	239	(1.7)	243	(1.1)
13-year-olds																						
All students	266	(1.1)	264	(1.1)	269	(1.1)	269	(1.2)	270	(0.9)	273	(0.9)	274	(1.0)	274	(0.8)	276	(0.8)	279	(1.0)	281	(0.9)
Sex																						
Male	265	(1.3)	264	(1.3)	269	(1.4)	270	(1.1)	271	(1.2)	274	(1.1)	276	(1.3)	276	(0.9)	277	(0.9)	279	(1.0)	284	(1.0)
Female	267	(1.1)	265	(1.1)	268	(1.1)	268	(1.5)	270	(0.9)	272	(1.0)	273	(1.0)	272	(1.0)	274	(1.1)	278	(1.2)	279	(1.0)
Race/ethnicity																						
White	274	(0.9)	272	(0.8)	274	(1.0)	274	(1.3)	276	(1.1)	279	(0.9)	281	(0.9)	281	(0.9)	283	(0.8)	287	(0.9)	290	(1.2)
Black	228	(1.9)	230	(1.9)	240	(1.6)	249	(2.3)	249	(2.3)	250	(1.9)	252	(3.5)	252	(1.3)	251	(2.6)	257	(1.8)	262	(1.2)
Hispanic	239	(2.2)	238	(2.0)	252	(1.7)	254	(2.9)	255	(1.8)	259	(1.8)	256	(1.9)	256	(1.6)	259	(1.7)	264	(1.5)	268	(1.2)
Parents' highest level of education																						
Did not finish high school	—	(†)	245	(1.2)	251	(1.4)	252	(2.3)	253	(1.8)	256	(1.0)	255	(2.1)	254	(2.4)	256	(2.8)	263	(1.9)	268	(1.3)
Graduated high school	—	(†)	263	(1.0)	263	(0.8)	263	(1.2)	263	(1.2)	263	(1.2)	266	(1.1)	267	(1.1)	264	(1.1)	270	(1.3)	272	(1.1)
Some education after high school	—	(†)	273	(1.2)	275	(0.9)	274	(0.8)	277	(1.0)	278	(1.0)	277	(1.6)	277	(1.4)	279	(0.9)	282	(1.4)	285	(1.1)
Graduated college	—	(†)	284	(1.2)	282	(1.5)	280	(1.4)	280	(1.0)	283	(1.0)	285	(1.2)	283	(1.2)	286	(1.0)	289	(1.1)	291	(1.0)
Region																						
Northeast	275	(2.4)	273	(2.4)	277	(2.0)	277	(2.2)	275	(2.3)	274	(2.2)	284	(1.5)	275	(2.1)	279	(2.7)	282	(2.5)	285	(1.6)
Southeast	255	(3.2)	253	(3.3)	258	(2.2)	263	(1.4)	266	(1.9)	271	(2.5)	269	(2.0)	270	(1.8)	270	(2.3)	276	(2.4)	277	(1.8)
Central	271	(1.8)	269	(1.8)	273	(2.1)	266	(4.5)	272	(2.4)	275	(1.5)	275	(3.4)	280	(1.3)	278	(1.8)	281	(1.7)	284	(2.2)
West	262	(1.9)	260	(1.9)	266	(2.4)	270	(2.1)	269	(1.6)	272	(1.4)	272	(1.7)	273	(1.9)	276	(1.4)	278	(1.5)	281	(1.3)
17-year-olds																						
All students	304	(1.1)	300	(1.0)	298	(0.9)	302	(0.9)	305	(0.9)	307	(0.9)	306	(1.0)	307	(1.2)	308	(1.0)	305	(0.7)	306	(0.6)
Sex																						
Male	309	(1.2)	304	(1.0)	301	(1.0)	305	(1.2)	306	(1.1)	309	(1.1)	309	(1.4)	310	(1.3)	310	(1.4)	307	(0.9)	309	(0.7)
Female	301	(1.1)	297	(1.0)	296	(1.0)	299	(1.0)	303	(1.1)	305	(1.1)	304	(1.1)	305	(1.4)	307	(1.0)	304	(0.8)	303	(0.8)
Race/ethnicity																						
White	310	(1.1)	306	(0.9)	304	(0.9)	308	(1.0)	309	(1.0)	312	(0.8)	312	(1.1)	313	(1.4)	315	(1.1)	311	(0.7)	314	(0.7)
Black	270	(1.3)	268	(1.3)	272	(1.2)	279	(2.1)	289	(2.8)	286	(2.2)	286	(1.8)	286	(1.7)	283	(1.5)	284	(1.4)	287	(1.2)
Hispanic	277	(2.2)	276	(2.3)	277	(1.8)	283	(2.9)	284	(2.9)	292	(2.6)	291	(3.7)	292	(2.1)	293	(2.5)	292	(1.2)	293	(1.1)
Parents' highest level of education																						
Did not finish high school	—	(†)	280	(1.2)	279	(1.0)	279	(2.3)	285	(2.2)	285	(2.3)	284	(2.4)	281	(2.4)	289	(1.8)	287	(1.2)	292	(1.3)
Graduated high school	—	(†)	294	(0.8)	293	(0.8)	293	(1.0)	294	(0.9)	298	(1.7)	295	(1.1)	297	(2.4)	299	(1.6)	294	(0.9)	296	(1.2)
Some education after high school	—	(†)	305	(0.9)	304	(0.9)	305	(1.2)	308	(1.0)	308	(1.1)	305	(1.3)	307	(1.5)	308	(1.6)	305	(0.9)	306	(0.8)
Graduated college	—	(†)	317	(1.0)	312	(1.0)	314	(1.4)	316	(1.3)	316	(1.0)	318	(1.4)	317	(1.3)	317	(1.2)	315	(0.9)	316	(0.7)
Region																						
Northeast	312	(1.8)	307	(1.8)	304	(2.0)	307	(1.9)	304	(2.1)	311	(2.0)	313	(2.9)	309	(3.0)	313	(2.4)	306	(1.6)	308	(1.4)
Southeast	296	(1.8)	292	(1.7)	292	(2.1)	297	(1.4)	301	(2.3)	301	(1.9)	301	(1.6)	303	(2.1)	300	(1.4)	300	(1.2)	303	(1.5)
Central	306	(1.8)	305	(1.9)	302	(1.4)	304	(1.9)	311	(2.1)	312	(2.0)	307	(2.2)	314	(2.0)	310	(2.0)	310	(1.3)	309	(1.6)
West	303	(2.0)	295	(1.8)	294	(1.9)	299	(2.7)	302	(1.5)	303	(2.3)	305	(2.4)	304	(2.3)	310	(2.0)	305	(1.6)	305	(1.1)

—Not available.
†Not applicable.
NOTE: Scale ranges from 0 to 500. Students scoring 150 (or higher) know some basic addition and subtraction facts. Students scoring 200 have considerable understanding of two-digit numbers and know some basic multiplication and division facts. Students scoring 250 have an initial understanding of the four basic operations and are developing an ability to analyze simple logical relations. Students scoring 300 can perform reasoning and problem solving involving fractions, decimals, percents, elementary geometry, and simple algebra. Students scoring 350 can perform reasoning and problem solving involving geometry, algebra, and beginning statistics and probability. Includes public and private schools. Excludes persons not enrolled in school and students who were unable to be tested due to limited proficiency in English or due to a disability. Beginning in 2004, data are for a revised assessment format that provides accommodations for students with disabilities and English language learners. Race categories exclude persons of Hispanic ethnicity. Totals include other racial/ethnic groups not shown separately. Some data have been revised from previously published figures. Standard errors appear in parentheses.
SOURCE: U.S. Department of Education, National Center for Education Statistics, National Assessment of Educational Progress (NAEP), *NAEP 2004 Trends in Academic Progress*; and 2008 NAEP Long-Term Trend Mathematics Assessment, retrieved May 4, 2009, from the Long-Term Trend NAEP Data Explorer (http://nces.ed.gov/nationsreportcard/naepdata/). (This table was prepared May 2009.)

Percentage of students at or above selected mathematics proficiency levels, by age, sex, and race/ethnicity: Selected years, 1978 through 2008

Selected characteristic	9-year-olds Simple arithmetic facts[1]		Beginning skills and understanding[2]		Numerical operations and beginning problem solving[3]		13-year-olds Beginning skills and understanding[2]		Numerical operations and beginning problem solving[3]		Moderately complex procedures and reasoning[4]		17-year-olds Numerical operations and beginning problem solving[3]		Moderately complex procedures and reasoning[4]		Multistep problem solving and algebra[5]	
1	2		3		4		5		6		7		8		9		10	
Total																		
1978	96.7	(0.25)	70.4	(0.92)	19.6	(0.73)	94.6	(0.46)	64.9	(1.18)	18.0	(0.73)	92.0	(0.50)	51.5	(1.14)	7.3	(0.44)
1982	97.1	(0.35)	71.4	(1.18)	18.8	(0.96)	97.7	(0.37)	71.4	(1.18)	17.4	(0.95)	93.0	(0.50)	48.5	(1.28)	5.5	(0.43)
1986	97.9	(0.29)	74.1	(1.24)	20.7	(0.88)	98.6	(0.25)	73.3	(1.59)	15.8	(1.01)	95.6	(0.48)	51.7	(1.43)	6.5	(0.52)
1990	99.1	(0.21)	81.5	(0.96)	27.7	(0.86)	98.5	(0.21)	74.7	(1.03)	17.3	(0.99)	96.0	(0.52)	56.1	(1.43)	7.2	(0.63)
1992	99.0	(0.24)	81.4	(0.80)	27.8	(0.90)	98.7	(0.25)	77.9	(1.06)	18.9	(1.01)	96.6	(0.52)	59.1	(1.26)	7.2	(0.63)
1994	99.0	(0.24)	82.0	(0.66)	29.9	(1.12)	98.5	(0.33)	78.1	(1.07)	21.3	(1.35)	96.5	(0.50)	58.6	(1.35)	7.4	(0.76)
1996	99.1	(0.18)	81.5	(0.76)	29.7	(1.02)	98.8	(0.20)	78.6	(0.87)	20.6	(1.24)	96.8	(0.42)	60.1	(1.72)	7.4	(0.77)
1999	98.9	(0.17)	82.5	(0.84)	30.9	(1.07)	98.7	(0.25)	78.8	(1.02)	23.2	(0.95)	96.8	(0.45)	60.7	(1.63)	8.4	(0.83)
2004	98.7	(0.19)	87.0	(0.77)	40.9	(0.89)	98.1	(0.19)	81.1	(0.98)	27.8	(1.09)	95.8	(0.40)	58.3	(1.12)	6.1	(0.47)
2008	99.0	(0.18)	89.1	(0.69)	44.5	(1.01)	98.2	(0.19)	83.4	(0.63)	30.0	(1.08)	96.0	(0.37)	59.4	(0.87)	6.2	(0.40)
Male																		
1978	96.2	(0.48)	68.9	(0.98)	19.2	(0.64)	93.9	(0.49)	63.9	(1.32)	18.4	(0.85)	93.0	(0.52)	55.1	(1.21)	9.5	(0.57)
1982	96.5	(0.55)	68.8	(1.29)	18.1	(1.06)	97.5	(0.55)	71.3	(1.44)	18.9	(1.18)	93.9	(0.58)	51.9	(1.51)	6.9	(0.70)
1986	98.0	(0.51)	74.0	(1.45)	20.9	(1.10)	98.5	(0.32)	73.8	(1.76)	17.6	(1.12)	96.1	(0.63)	54.6	(1.78)	8.4	(0.91)
1990	99.0	(0.26)	80.6	(1.05)	27.5	(0.96)	98.2	(0.34)	75.1	(1.75)	19.0	(1.24)	95.8	(0.77)	57.6	(1.42)	8.8	(0.76)
1992	99.0	(0.29)	81.9	(1.05)	29.4	(1.21)	98.8	(0.42)	78.1	(1.60)	20.7	(1.13)	96.9	(0.56)	60.5	(1.80)	9.1	(0.73)
1994	99.1	(0.27)	82.3	(0.87)	31.5	(1.59)	98.3	(0.45)	78.9	(1.49)	23.9	(1.59)	97.3	(0.47)	60.2	(2.08)	9.3	(1.04)
1996	99.1	(0.20)	82.5	(1.10)	32.7	(1.74)	98.7	(0.25)	79.8	(1.43)	23.0	(1.64)	97.0	(0.66)	62.7	(1.77)	9.5	(1.32)
1999	98.8	(0.28)	82.6	(0.92)	32.4	(1.25)	98.5	(0.27)	79.3	(1.12)	25.4	(1.19)	96.5	(0.81)	63.1	(2.12)	9.8	(1.09)
2004	98.3	(0.27)	86.1	(0.89)	40.7	(1.03)	97.7	(0.29)	80.5	(1.08)	29.9	(1.27)	95.6	(0.45)	60.8	(1.31)	7.3	(0.68)
2008	99.0	(0.27)	88.4	(0.87)	44.4	(1.18)	98.2	(0.28)	84.3	(0.75)	33.4	(1.29)	96.2	(0.47)	62.9	(0.96)	7.6	(0.61)
Female																		
1978	97.2	(0.27)	72.0	(1.05)	19.9	(1.00)	95.2	(0.49)	65.9	(1.17)	17.5	(0.75)	91.0	(0.57)	48.2	(1.29)	5.2	(0.66)
1982	97.6	(0.33)	74.0	(1.30)	19.6	(1.11)	98.0	(0.27)	71.4	(1.29)	15.9	(1.00)	92.1	(0.56)	45.3	(1.37)	4.1	(0.42)
1986	97.8	(0.38)	74.3	(1.32)	20.6	(1.28)	98.6	(0.31)	72.7	(1.95)	14.1	(1.31)	95.1	(0.65)	48.9	(1.73)	4.7	(0.59)
1990	99.1	(0.26)	82.3	(1.26)	27.9	(1.31)	98.9	(0.18)	74.4	(1.32)	15.7	(1.00)	96.2	(0.84)	54.7	(1.84)	5.6	(0.79)
1992	99.0	(0.33)	80.9	(1.15)	26.3	(1.52)	98.6	(0.23)	77.7	(1.06)	17.2	(1.39)	96.3	(0.82)	57.7	(1.63)	5.2	(0.75)
1994	98.9	(0.31)	81.7	(0.91)	28.3	(1.28)	98.7	(0.31)	77.3	(0.99)	18.7	(1.39)	96.0	(0.65)	57.2	(1.40)	5.5	(0.87)
1996	99.1	(0.36)	80.7	(0.93)	26.7	(1.07)	98.8	(0.27)	77.4	(1.09)	18.4	(1.48)	96.7	(0.57)	57.6	(2.21)	5.3	(0.80)
1999	99.0	(0.19)	82.5	(1.15)	29.4	(1.36)	99.0	(0.40)	78.4	(1.22)	21.0	(1.38)	97.2	(0.40)	58.5	(1.89)	7.1	(1.06)
2004	99.0	(0.22)	87.8	(0.96)	41.1	(1.13)	98.4	(0.25)	81.7	(1.10)	25.7	(1.24)	95.9	(0.58)	55.9	(1.18)	4.9	(0.48)
2008	99.0	(0.21)	89.9	(0.78)	44.6	(1.18)	98.2	(0.25)	82.5	(0.86)	26.7	(1.13)	95.7	(0.43)	55.8	(1.25)	4.6	(0.34)
White																		
1978	98.3	(0.19)	76.3	(1.00)	22.9	(0.87)	97.6	(0.27)	72.9	(0.85)	21.4	(0.73)	95.6	(0.30)	57.6	(1.14)	8.5	(0.48)
1982	98.5	(0.25)	76.8	(1.22)	21.8	(1.13)	99.1	(0.14)	78.3	(0.94)	20.5	(1.00)	96.2	(0.33)	54.7	(1.41)	6.4	(0.54)
1986	98.8	(0.24)	79.6	(1.33)	24.6	(1.03)	99.3	(0.27)	78.9	(1.69)	18.6	(1.17)	98.0	(0.36)	59.1	(1.69)	7.9	(0.68)
1990	99.6	(0.16)	86.9	(0.86)	32.7	(1.04)	99.4	(0.14)	82.0	(1.01)	21.0	(1.23)	97.6	(0.28)	63.2	(1.59)	8.3	(0.73)
1992	99.6	(0.14)	86.9	(0.68)	32.4	(1.01)	99.6	(0.18)	84.9	(1.10)	22.8	(1.28)	98.3	(0.36)	66.4	(1.40)	8.7	(0.87)
1994	99.6	(0.16)	87.0	(0.84)	35.3	(1.33)	99.3	(0.22)	85.5	(0.93)	25.6	(1.64)	98.4	(0.36)	67.0	(1.40)	9.4	(1.06)
1996	99.6	(0.15)	86.6	(0.80)	35.7	(1.38)	99.6	(0.16)	86.4	(1.02)	25.4	(1.50)	98.7	(0.37)	68.7	(2.18)	9.2	(1.02)
1999	99.6	(0.12)	88.6	(0.78)	37.1	(1.35)	99.4	(0.29)	86.7	(0.92)	29.0	(1.26)	98.7	(0.40)	69.9	(1.96)	10.4	(1.07)
2004	99.2	(0.18)	91.9	(0.61)	47.2	(0.97)	99.1	(0.16)	89.3	(0.82)	35.1	(1.21)	97.5	(0.28)	66.8	(1.08)	7.6	(0.63)
2008	99.6	(0.12)	94.0	(0.52)	52.9	(1.29)	98.9	(0.17)	90.4	(0.83)	39.2	(1.60)	98.2	(0.26)	70.5	(1.09)	8.1	(0.55)
Black																		
1978	88.4	(1.01)	42.0	(1.44)	4.1	(0.64)	79.7	(1.48)	28.7	(2.06)	2.3	(0.48)	70.7	(1.73)	16.8	(1.57)	0.5	(—)
1982	90.2	(0.97)	46.1	(2.35)	4.4	(0.81)	90.2	(1.60)	37.9	(2.51)	2.9	(0.96)	76.4	(1.47)	17.1	(1.51)	0.5	(—)
1986	93.9	(1.37)	53.4	(2.47)	5.6	(0.92)	95.4	(0.95)	49.0	(3.70)	4.0	(1.42)	85.6	(2.53)	20.8	(2.83)	0.2	(—)
1990	96.9	(0.88)	60.0	(2.76)	9.4	(1.72)	95.4	(1.10)	48.7	(3.56)	3.9	(1.61)	92.4	(2.20)	32.8	(4.49)	2.0	(1.04)
1992	96.6	(1.12)	59.8	(2.82)	9.6	(1.42)	95.0	(1.35)	51.0	(2.73)	4.0	(0.69)	89.6	(2.53)	29.8	(3.94)	0.9	(—)
1994	97.4	(0.98)	65.9	(2.56)	11.1	(1.71)	95.6	(1.60)	51.0	(3.91)	6.4	(2.37)	90.6	(1.79)	29.8	(3.38)	0.4	(—)
1996	97.3	(0.84)	65.3	(2.38)	10.0	(1.24)	96.2	(1.27)	53.7	(2.56)	4.8	(1.08)	90.6	(1.33)	31.2	(2.51)	0.9	(—)
1999	96.4	(0.64)	63.3	(2.11)	12.3	(1.48)	96.5	(1.06)	50.8	(4.01)	4.4	(1.37)	88.6	(1.95)	26.6	(2.70)	1.0	(—)
2004	97.1	(0.65)	74.3	(2.61)	22.0	(1.72)	95.3	(0.78)	61.5	(2.47)	9.7	(1.35)	89.1	(1.63)	29.4	(2.07)	0.4	(—)
2008	96.9	(0.86)	75.6	(2.31)	24.6	(1.67)	96.6	(0.68)	67.6	(1.69)	10.2	(1.17)	90.6	(1.42)	31.8	(1.60)	0.8	(0.23)
Hispanic																		
1978	93.0	(1.20)	54.2	(2.80)	9.2	(2.49)	86.4	(0.94)	36.0	(2.92)	4.0	(0.95)	78.3	(2.29)	23.4	(2.67)	1.4	(0.58)
1982	94.3	(1.19)	55.7	(2.26)	7.8	(1.74)	95.9	(0.95)	52.2	(2.48)	6.3	(0.97)	81.4	(1.86)	21.6	(2.16)	0.7	(0.36)
1986	96.4	(1.29)	57.6	(2.95)	7.3	(2.81)	96.9	(1.43)	56.0	(5.01)	5.5	(1.15)	89.3	(2.52)	26.5	(4.48)	1.1	(—)
1990	98.0	(0.76)	68.4	(3.03)	11.3	(3.49)	96.8	(1.06)	56.7	(3.32)	6.4	(1.70)	85.8	(4.18)	30.1	(3.09)	1.9	(0.78)
1992	97.2	(1.29)	65.0	(2.94)	11.7	(2.53)	98.1	(0.70)	63.3	(2.67)	7.0	(1.15)	94.1	(2.21)	39.2	(4.86)	1.2	(—)
1994	97.2	(1.15)	63.5	(3.08)	9.7	(1.82)	96.2	(0.78)	59.2	(2.17)	6.4	(1.78)	91.8	(3.57)	38.3	(5.50)	1.4	(—)
1996	98.1	(0.73)	67.1	(2.14)	13.8	(2.26)	97.2	(0.60)	58.3	(2.28)	6.7	(1.17)	92.2	(2.24)	40.1	(3.47)	1.8	(—)
1999	98.1	(0.71)	67.5	(2.47)	10.5	(1.63)	96.4	(0.66)	62.9	(2.50)	8.2	(1.37)	93.6	(2.21)	37.7	(4.15)	3.1	(1.12)
2004	98.0	(0.46)	80.5	(2.03)	30.2	(2.17)	97.0	(0.44)	68.5	(1.86)	13.7	(1.44)	92.3	(1.05)	38.1	(2.12)	1.9	(0.60)
2008	98.9	(0.28)	85.1	(1.25)	33.5	(1.46)			73.3	(1.71)	14.4	(1.09)	92.2	(1.10)	41.1	(1.69)	1.5	(0.41)

—Not available.

[1]Scale score of 150 or above.
[2]Scale score of 200 or above.
[3]Scale score of 250 or above.
[4]Scale score of 300 or above.
[5]Scale score of 350 or above.

NOTE: Excludes persons not enrolled in school and students who were unable to be tested due to limited proficiency in English or due to a disability. Beginning in 2004, data are for a revised assessment format that provides accommodations for students with disabilities and English language learners. Totals include other racial/ethnic groups not shown separately. Race categories exclude persons of Hispanic ethnicity. Standard errors appear in parentheses. SOURCE: U.S. Department of Education, National Center for Education Statistics, National Assessment of Educational Progress (NAEP), *NAEP 1999 Trends in Academic Progress*; and 2004 and 2008 Long-Term Trend Mathematics Assessments, retrieved May 4, 2009, from the Long-Term Trend NAEP Data Explorer (http://nces.ed.gov/nationsreportcard/naepdata/). (This table was prepared June 2009.)

Average mathematics scale score of 4th-grade public school students and percentages attaining mathematics achievement levels and having 5 or more hours of mathematics instruction per week, by state or jurisdiction: Selected years, 1992 through 2009

State or jurisdiction	Average scale score[1]												Percent of students, 2009								
													Attaining mathematics achievement levels								Having 5 or more hours of math instruction each week
	1992		2000		2003		2005		2007		2009		Below *Basic*		At or above *Basic*[2]		At or above *Proficient*[3]		At *Advanced*[4]		
1	2		3		4		5		6		7		8		9		10		11		12
United States	**219**	**(0.8)**	**224**	**(1.0)**	**234**	**(0.2)**	**237**	**(0.2)**	**239**	**(0.2)**	**239**	**(0.2)**	**19**	**(0.3)**	**81**	**(0.3)**	**38**	**(0.3)**	**6**	**(0.2)**	**88**	**(0.4)**
Alabama	208	(1.6)	217	(1.2)	223	(1.2)	225	(0.9)	229	(1.3)	228	(1.1)	30	(1.5)	70	(1.5)	24	(1.5)	2	(0.5)	91	(2.1)
Alaska	—	(†)	—	(†)	233	(0.8)	236	(1.0)	237	(1.0)	237	(0.9)	22	(1.1)	78	(1.1)	38	(1.3)	6	(0.8)	88	(2.2)
Arizona	215	(1.1)	219	(1.3)	229	(1.1)	230	(1.1)	232	(1.0)	230	(1.1)	29	(1.4)	71	(1.4)	28	(1.6)	4	(0.6)	84	(2.1)
Arkansas	210	(0.9)	216	(1.1)	229	(0.9)	236	(0.9)	238	(1.1)	238	(0.9)	20	(1.0)	80	(1.0)	36	(1.4)	5	(0.5)	92	(1.7)
California[5]	208	(1.6)	213	(1.6)	227	(0.9)	230	(0.6)	230	(0.7)	232	(1.2)	28	(1.4)	72	(1.4)	30	(1.6)	5	(0.7)	89	(1.6)
Colorado	221	(1.0)	—	(†)	235	(1.0)	239	(1.1)	240	(1.0)	243	(0.8)	16	(1.2)	84	(1.2)	45	(1.6)	8	(0.9)	89	(1.6)
Connecticut	227	(1.1)	234	(1.1)	241	(0.8)	242	(0.8)	243	(1.1)	245	(1.0)	14	(1.1)	86	(1.1)	46	(1.6)	8	(0.8)	92	(1.6)
Delaware	218	(0.8)	—	(†)	236	(0.5)	240	(0.5)	242	(0.4)	239	(0.5)	16	(0.9)	84	(0.9)	36	(1.1)	5	(0.5)	86	(0.4)
District of Columbia	193	(0.5)	192	(1.1)	205	(0.7)	211	(0.8)	214	(0.8)	219	(0.7)	44	(1.3)	56	(1.3)	17	(0.8)	3	(0.4)	93	(0.5)
Florida	214	(1.5)	—	(†)	234	(1.1)	239	(0.7)	242	(0.8)	242	(1.0)	14	(1.2)	86	(1.2)	40	(1.5)	5	(0.5)	88	(1.7)
Georgia	216	(1.2)	219	(1.1)	230	(1.0)	234	(1.0)	235	(0.8)	236	(0.9)	22	(1.2)	78	(1.2)	34	(1.5)	5	(0.6)	91	(1.6)
Hawaii	214	(1.3)	216	(1.0)	227	(1.0)	230	(0.8)	234	(0.8)	236	(1.1)	23	(1.4)	77	(1.4)	37	(1.5)	5	(0.6)	92	(1.5)
Idaho[5]	222	(1.0)	224	(1.4)	235	(0.7)	242	(0.7)	241	(0.7)	241	(0.8)	15	(1.0)	85	(1.0)	41	(1.4)	5	(0.5)	89	(1.9)
Illinois[5]	—	(†)	223	(1.9)	233	(1.1)	233	(1.0)	237	(1.1)	238	(1.0)	20	(1.2)	80	(1.2)	38	(1.5)	7	(0.7)	83	(2.2)
Indiana[5]	221	(1.0)	233	(1.1)	238	(0.9)	240	(0.9)	245	(0.8)	243	(0.9)	13	(1.0)	87	(1.0)	42	(1.4)	5	(0.9)	83	(2.5)
Iowa[5]	230	(1.0)	231	(1.2)	238	(0.7)	240	(0.7)	243	(0.8)	243	(0.8)	13	(0.8)	87	(0.8)	41	(1.8)	5	(0.5)	76	(2.7)
Kansas[5]	—	(†)	232	(1.6)	242	(1.0)	246	(1.0)	248	(1.0)	245	(1.0)	11	(1.1)	89	(1.1)	46	(1.9)	6	(0.7)	93	(1.6)
Kentucky	215	(1.0)	219	(1.4)	229	(1.1)	232	(0.9)	235	(0.9)	239	(1.1)	19	(1.0)	81	(1.0)	37	(1.7)	6	(0.8)	85	(2.3)
Louisiana	204	(1.4)	218	(1.4)	226	(1.0)	230	(0.9)	230	(1.0)	229	(1.0)	28	(1.3)	72	(1.3)	23	(1.4)	2	(0.4)	91	(1.9)
Maine[5]	232	(1.0)	230	(1.0)	238	(0.7)	241	(0.8)	242	(0.8)	244	(0.8)	13	(0.8)	87	(0.8)	45	(1.4)	7	(0.7)	89	(1.9)
Maryland	217	(1.3)	222	(1.2)	233	(1.3)	238	(1.0)	240	(0.9)	244	(0.9)	15	(1.0)	85	(1.0)	44	(1.5)	9	(0.8)	96	(1.2)
Massachusetts	227	(1.2)	233	(1.2)	242	(0.8)	247	(0.8)	252	(0.8)	252	(0.9)	8	(0.8)	92	(0.8)	57	(1.4)	12	(1.0)	96	(1.3)
Michigan[5]	220	(1.7)	229	(1.6)	236	(0.9)	238	(1.2)	238	(1.3)	236	(1.0)	22	(1.2)	78	(1.2)	35	(1.3)	5	(0.7)	83	(2.6)
Minnesota[5]	228	(0.9)	234	(1.3)	242	(0.9)	246	(1.0)	247	(1.0)	249	(1.1)	11	(1.0)	89	(1.0)	54	(1.8)	11	(1.0)	91	(1.6)
Mississippi	202	(1.1)	211	(1.1)	223	(1.0)	227	(0.9)	228	(1.0)	227	(1.0)	31	(1.3)	69	(1.3)	22	(1.4)	2	(0.3)	92	(1.7)
Missouri	222	(1.2)	228	(1.2)	235	(0.9)	235	(0.9)	239	(0.9)	241	(1.2)	17	(1.2)	83	(1.2)	41	(1.8)	6	(0.7)	88	(2.3)
Montana[5]	—	(†)	228	(1.7)	236	(0.8)	241	(0.8)	244	(0.8)	244	(0.7)	12	(0.9)	88	(0.9)	45	(1.3)	6	(0.5)	91	(1.4)
Nebraska	225	(1.2)	225	(1.8)	236	(0.8)	238	(0.9)	238	(1.1)	239	(1.0)	18	(1.3)	82	(1.3)	38	(1.5)	4	(0.5)	84	(2.6)
Nevada	—	(†)	220	(1.0)	228	(0.8)	230	(0.8)	232	(0.9)	235	(0.9)	21	(1.1)	79	(1.1)	32	(1.4)	3	(0.4)	95	(1.3)
New Hampshire	230	(1.2)	—	(†)	243	(0.9)	246	(0.9)	249	(0.9)	251	(0.8)	8	(0.8)	92	(0.8)	56	(1.7)	10	(0.7)	89	(1.5)
New Jersey	227	(1.5)	—	(†)	239	(1.1)	244	(1.1)	249	(1.1)	247	(1.0)	12	(1.1)	88	(1.1)	49	(1.5)	9	(0.8)	88	(2.0)
New Mexico[5]	213	(1.4)	213	(1.5)	223	(1.1)	224	(0.8)	228	(0.9)	230	(1.0)	28	(1.6)	72	(1.6)	26	(1.4)	3	(0.5)	91	(1.4)
New York[5]	218	(1.2)	225	(1.4)	236	(0.9)	238	(0.9)	243	(0.8)	241	(0.7)	17	(0.8)	83	(0.8)	40	(1.3)	5	(0.7)	78	(2.5)
North Carolina	213	(1.1)	230	(1.1)	242	(0.8)	241	(0.9)	242	(0.8)	244	(0.8)	13	(1.0)	87	(1.0)	43	(1.4)	8	(0.8)	91	(1.6)
North Dakota	229	(0.8)	230	(1.2)	238	(0.7)	243	(0.5)	245	(0.5)	245	(0.6)	9	(0.6)	91	(0.6)	45	(1.3)	5	(0.7)	78	(0.5)
Ohio[5]	219	(1.2)	230	(1.5)	238	(1.0)	242	(1.0)	245	(1.0)	244	(1.1)	15	(1.0)	85	(1.0)	45	(1.9)	8	(0.8)	81	(3.4)
Oklahoma	220	(1.0)	224	(1.0)	229	(1.0)	234	(1.0)	237	(0.8)	237	(0.9)	18	(1.2)	82	(1.2)	33	(1.6)	3	(0.4)	86	(2.2)
Oregon[5]	—	(†)	224	(1.8)	236	(0.9)	238	(0.9)	236	(1.0)	238	(0.9)	20	(1.0)	80	(1.0)	37	(1.5)	5	(0.6)	79	(2.5)
Pennsylvania	224	(1.3)	—	(†)	236	(1.1)	241	(1.2)	244	(0.8)	244	(1.1)	16	(1.0)	84	(1.0)	46	(1.6)	8	(0.8)	90	(2.1)
Rhode Island	215	(1.5)	224	(1.1)	230	(1.0)	233	(0.9)	236	(0.9)	239	(0.8)	19	(1.0)	81	(1.0)	39	(1.3)	5	(0.6)	93	(1.2)
South Carolina	212	(1.1)	220	(1.4)	236	(0.9)	238	(0.9)	237	(0.8)	236	(0.9)	22	(1.2)	78	(1.2)	34	(1.3)	5	(0.6)	87	(2.0)
South Dakota	—	(†)	—	(†)	237	(0.7)	242	(0.5)	241	(0.7)	242	(0.5)	14	(0.9)	86	(0.9)	42	(1.1)	5	(0.5)	86	(0.5)
Tennessee	211	(1.4)	220	(1.4)	228	(1.0)	232	(1.2)	233	(0.9)	232	(1.1)	26	(1.4)	74	(1.4)	28	(1.5)	3	(0.5)	88	(2.5)
Texas	218	(1.2)	231	(1.1)	237	(0.9)	242	(0.6)	242	(0.7)	240	(0.7)	15	(0.9)	85	(0.9)	38	(1.4)	4	(0.5)	92	(1.8)
Utah	224	(1.0)	227	(1.3)	235	(0.8)	239	(0.8)	239	(0.8)	240	(1.0)	19	(1.0)	81	(1.0)	41	(1.4)	6	(0.7)	87	(1.8)
Vermont[5]	—	(†)	232	(1.6)	242	(0.8)	244	(0.5)	246	(0.5)	248	(0.4)	11	(0.8)	89	(0.8)	51	(1.0)	9	(0.8)	91	(0.3)
Virginia	221	(1.3)	230	(1.0)	239	(1.1)	241	(0.9)	244	(0.9)	243	(1.0)	15	(1.2)	85	(1.2)	43	(1.6)	7	(0.8)	91	(1.7)
Washington	—	(†)	—	(†)	238	(1.0)	242	(0.9)	243	(1.0)	242	(0.8)	16	(1.0)	84	(1.0)	43	(1.2)	7	(1.0)	93	(1.5)
West Virginia	215	(1.1)	223	(1.3)	231	(0.8)	231	(0.8)	236	(0.9)	233	(0.8)	23	(1.3)	77	(1.3)	28	(1.2)	2	(0.3)	97	(0.9)
Wisconsin[5]	229	(1.1)	—	(†)	237	(0.9)	241	(0.9)	244	(0.9)	244	(0.9)	15	(1.0)	85	(1.0)	45	(1.6)	8	(0.8)	88	(1.9)
Wyoming	225	(0.9)	229	(1.1)	241	(0.6)	243	(0.6)	244	(0.5)	242	(0.6)	13	(0.9)	87	(0.9)	40	(1.2)	4	(0.5)	91	(0.5)
Department of Defense dependents schools[6]	—	(†)	227	(0.6)	237	(0.4)	239	(0.5)	240	(0.4)	240	(0.5)	14	(0.8)	86	(0.8)	38	(1.1)	4	(0.5)	86	(0.4)
Other jurisdictions																						
American Samoa	—	(†)	152	(2.5)	—	(†)	—	(†)	—	(†)	—	(†)	—	(†)	—	(†)	—	(†)	—	(†)	—	(†)
Guam	193	(0.8)	184	(1.7)	—	(†)	—	(†)	—	(†)	—	(†)	—	(†)	—	(†)	—	(†)	—	(†)	—	(†)
Puerto Rico[7]	—	(†)	—	(†)	179	(1.0)	183	(0.9)	—	(†)	—	(†)	—	(†)	—	(†)	—	(†)	—	(†)	—	(†)
U.S. Virgin Islands	—	(†)	181	(1.8)	—	(†)	—	(†)	—	(†)	—	(†)	—	(†)	—	(†)	—	(†)	—	(†)	—	(†)

—Not available.

†Not applicable.

[1]Scale ranges from 0 to 500.

[2]*Basic* denotes partial mastery of prerequisite knowledge and skills that are fundamental for proficient work at the 4th-grade level.

[3]*Proficient* represents solid academic performance for 4th-graders. Students reaching this level have demonstrated competency over challenging subject matter.

[4]*Advanced* signifies superior performance.

[5]Did not meet one or more of the guidelines for school participation in 2000. Data are subject to appreciable nonresponse bias.

[6]Prior to 2005, NAEP divided the Department of Defense (DoD) schools into two jurisdictions, domestic and overseas. In 2005, NAEP began combining the DoD domestic and overseas schools into a single jurisdiction. Data shown in this table for years prior to 2005 were recalculated for comparability.

[7]Because of modifications to the 2005 Puerto Rico administration, results from 2003 should not be compared to results from 2005. Although parallel changes were not made in the nation in 2005, within-year comparisons between Puerto Rico and the nation are valid.

NOTE: With the exception of 1992, includes students for whom accommodations were permitted. Excludes students unable to be tested (even with accommodations) due to limited proficiency in English or due to a disability. Some data have been revised from previously published figures. Detail may not sum to totals because of rounding. Standard errors appear in parentheses.

SOURCE: U.S. Department of Education, National Center for Education Statistics, National Assessment of Educational Progress (NAEP), 1992, 2000, 2003, 2005, 2007, and 2009 Mathematics Assessments, retrieved November 19, 2009, from the Main NAEP Data Explorer (http://nces.ed.gov/nationsreportcard/naepdata). (This table was prepared November 2009.)

Average mathematics scale score of 8th-grade public school students and percentage attaining mathematics achievement levels, by level of parental education and state or jurisdiction: Selected years, 1990 through 2009

State or jurisdiction	Average scale score[1]							Percent attaining mathematics achievement levels, 2009				Average scale score, by highest level of education attained by parents, 2009[2]			
	1990	1996	2000	2003	2005	2007	2009	Below Basic	At or above Basic[3]	At or above Proficient[4]	At Advanced[5]	Did not finish high school	Graduated high school	Some education after high school	Graduated college
1	2	3	4	5	6	7	8	9	10	11	12	13	14	15	16
United States	262 (1.4)	271 (1.2)	272 (0.9)	276 (0.3)	278 (0.2)	280 (0.3)	282 (0.3)	29 (0.3)	71 (0.3)	33 (0.3)	7 (0.1)	265 (0.6)	270 (0.4)	283 (0.4)	294 (0.3)
Alabama	253 (1.1)	257 (2.1)	264 (1.8)	262 (1.5)	262 (1.5)	266 (1.5)	269 (1.2)	42 (1.5)	58 (1.5)	20 (1.3)	4 (0.5)	255 (2.3)	257 (1.7)	273 (2.1)	278 (1.5)
Alaska	—	278 (1.8)	— (†)	279 (0.9)	279 (0.8)	283 (1.1)	283 (1.0)	25 (1.5)	75 (1.5)	33 (1.3)	6 (0.6)	‡ (†)	‡ (†)	‡ (†)	‡ (†)
Arizona[6]	260 (1.3)	268 (1.6)	269 (1.8)	271 (1.2)	274 (1.1)	276 (1.2)	277 (1.4)	33 (1.5)	67 (1.5)	29 (1.6)	6 (0.8)	263 (2.7)	267 (2.0)	282 (2.1)	292 (1.8)
Arkansas	256 (0.9)	262 (1.5)	257 (1.5)	266 (1.2)	272 (1.2)	274 (1.1)	276 (1.1)	33 (1.5)	67 (1.5)	27 (1.2)	4 (0.5)	264 (2.4)	267 (1.7)	282 (1.7)	285 (1.6)
California[6]	256 (1.3)	263 (1.9)	260 (2.1)	267 (1.2)	269 (0.7)	270 (0.8)	270 (1.3)	41 (1.5)	59 (1.5)	23 (1.4)	5 (0.7)	258 (2.0)	261 (1.9)	278 (2.1)	287 (1.8)
Colorado	267 (0.9)	276 (1.1)	— (†)	283 (1.1)	281 (1.2)	286 (0.9)	287 (1.4)	24 (1.5)	76 (1.5)	40 (1.4)	10 (0.8)	265 (2.8)	272 (2.3)	286 (1.9)	301 (1.5)
Connecticut	270 (1.0)	280 (1.1)	281 (1.3)	284 (1.2)	281 (1.4)	282 (1.5)	289 (1.0)	22 (1.2)	78 (1.2)	40 (1.4)	10 (0.7)	263 (2.5)	270 (1.9)	284 (1.7)	300 (0.9)
Delaware	261 (0.9)	267 (0.9)	— (†)	277 (0.7)	281 (0.6)	283 (0.6)	284 (0.5)	25 (0.8)	75 (0.8)	32 (0.8)	6 (0.6)	276 (2.4)	276 (1.3)	284 (1.7)	292 (0.9)
District of Columbia	231 (0.9)	233 (1.3)	235 (1.1)	243 (0.8)	245 (0.9)	248 (0.9)	254 (0.9)	60 (1.4)	40 (1.4)	11 (0.8)	2 (0.4)	249 (3.3)	247 (2.1)	260 (2.2)	259 (1.7)
Florida	255 (1.2)	264 (1.8)	— (†)	271 (1.5)	274 (1.1)	277 (1.3)	279 (1.1)	30 (1.1)	70 (1.1)	29 (1.4)	6 (0.6)	266 (2.2)	272 (1.5)	285 (1.4)	287 (1.5)
Georgia	259 (1.3)	262 (1.6)	265 (1.2)	270 (1.2)	272 (1.1)	275 (1.0)	278 (0.9)	33 (1.2)	67 (1.2)	27 (1.2)	5 (0.5)	261 (2.2)	267 (1.8)	280 (1.7)	288 (1.2)
Hawaii	251 (0.8)	262 (1.0)	262 (1.4)	266 (0.8)	266 (0.7)	269 (0.8)	274 (0.7)	35 (1.0)	65 (1.0)	25 (1.0)	4 (0.6)	258 (3.4)	264 (1.8)	278 (1.8)	284 (1.1)
Idaho[6]	271 (0.8)	— (†)	277 (1.0)	280 (0.9)	281 (0.9)	284 (0.9)	287 (0.8)	22 (1.0)	78 (1.0)	38 (0.9)	8 (0.5)	267 (2.9)	274 (1.7)	290 (1.5)	297 (0.8)
Illinois[6]	261 (1.7)	— (†)	275 (1.7)	277 (1.2)	278 (1.1)	280 (1.1)	282 (1.2)	27 (1.4)	73 (1.4)	33 (1.5)	7 (0.7)	266 (2.1)	269 (1.6)	280 (1.7)	294 (1.3)
Indiana[6]	267 (1.2)	276 (1.4)	281 (1.4)	281 (1.1)	282 (1.0)	285 (1.1)	287 (0.9)	22 (1.1)	78 (1.1)	36 (1.1)	7 (0.6)	275 (4.2)	278 (1.8)	286 (1.6)	295 (1.2)
Iowa[6]	278 (1.1)	284 (1.3)	— (†)	284 (0.8)	284 (0.9)	285 (0.9)	284 (1.0)	24 (1.0)	76 (1.0)	34 (1.4)	7 (0.9)	264 (3.0)	274 (1.8)	285 (1.8)	293 (1.2)
Kansas[6]	— (†)	— (†)	283 (1.7)	284 (1.3)	284 (1.0)	290 (1.1)	289 (1.0)	21 (1.3)	79 (1.3)	39 (1.4)	8 (0.8)	272 (2.5)	280 (2.0)	290 (1.8)	298 (1.1)
Kentucky	257 (1.2)	267 (1.1)	270 (1.3)	274 (1.2)	274 (1.2)	279 (1.1)	279 (1.1)	30 (1.2)	70 (1.2)	27 (1.4)	5 (0.6)	262 (2.2)	271 (1.8)	283 (1.3)	289 (1.3)
Louisiana	246 (1.2)	252 (1.6)	259 (1.5)	266 (1.5)	268 (1.4)	272 (1.1)	272 (1.6)	38 (1.6)	62 (1.6)	20 (1.8)	4 (1.1)	265 (2.3)	265 (1.7)	277 (1.9)	281 (2.6)
Maine[6]	— (†)	284 (1.4)	281 (1.1)	282 (0.9)	281 (1.0)	286 (0.8)	286 (0.7)	22 (1.1)	78 (1.1)	35 (1.1)	8 (0.6)	268 (3.1)	278 (1.8)	286 (1.6)	295 (1.0)
Maryland	261 (1.4)	270 (2.1)	272 (1.7)	278 (1.0)	278 (1.1)	286 (1.2)	288 (1.1)	25 (1.2)	75 (1.2)	40 (1.6)	12 (0.9)	271 (2.8)	272 (1.9)	286 (1.9)	299 (1.5)
Massachusetts[6]	— (†)	278 (1.7)	279 (1.5)	287 (0.9)	292 (0.9)	298 (1.3)	299 (1.3)	15 (1.2)	85 (1.2)	52 (1.6)	17 (1.3)	275 (3.6)	285 (2.1)	290 (2.1)	310 (1.1)
Michigan[6]	264 (1.2)	277 (1.8)	277 (1.9)	276 (2.0)	277 (1.5)	277 (1.4)	278 (1.6)	32 (1.8)	68 (1.8)	31 (1.6)	8 (0.7)	253 (3.6)	263 (2.2)	277 (2.4)	290 (1.7)
Minnesota	275 (0.9)	284 (1.3)	287 (1.4)	291 (1.1)	290 (1.2)	292 (1.0)	294 (1.0)	17 (1.0)	83 (1.0)	47 (1.3)	13 (1.0)	265 (3.4)	276 (2.2)	294 (1.9)	304 (1.3)
Mississippi	—	250 (1.2)	254 (1.1)	261 (1.1)	263 (1.2)	265 (0.8)	265 (1.2)	46 (1.8)	54 (1.8)	15 (1.0)	2 (0.4)	252 (2.5)	256 (1.7)	273 (1.6)	271 (1.4)
Missouri	— (†)	273 (1.4)	271 (1.5)	279 (1.1)	276 (1.3)	281 (1.0)	286 (1.0)	23 (1.3)	77 (1.3)	35 (1.2)	7 (0.6)	269 (2.9)	275 (1.7)	287 (1.5)	294 (1.2)
Montana[6]	280 (0.9)	283 (1.3)	285 (1.4)	286 (0.8)	286 (0.7)	287 (0.7)	292 (0.9)	18 (0.9)	82 (0.9)	44 (1.2)	10 (0.9)	268 (4.3)	280 (1.9)	294 (2.1)	300 (1.0)
Nebraska	276 (1.0)	283 (1.0)	280 (1.2)	282 (0.9)	284 (1.0)	284 (1.0)	284 (1.1)	25 (1.3)	75 (1.3)	35 (1.3)	8 (0.7)	265 (2.6)	272 (2.0)	283 (1.8)	294 (1.2)
Nevada[6]	— (†)	—	265 (0.8)	268 (0.8)	270 (0.8)	271 (0.8)	274 (1.0)	37 (1.4)	63 (1.4)	25 (0.9)	5 (0.5)	260 (1.7)	266 (1.6)	280 (1.6)	287 (1.3)
New Hampshire	273 (0.9)	— (†)	—	286 (0.8)	285 (0.8)	288 (0.7)	292 (0.9)	18 (1.3)	82 (1.3)	43 (1.3)	11 (0.7)	275 (3.5)	280 (1.6)	289 (1.5)	301 (1.0)
New Jersey	270 (1.1)	— (†)	— (†)	281 (1.1)	284 (1.4)	289 (1.2)	293 (1.3)	20 (1.4)	80 (1.4)	44 (1.7)	14 (0.9)	270 (3.3)	277 (2.3)	292 (1.8)	302 (1.6)
New Mexico	256 (0.7)	262 (1.2)	259 (1.3)	263 (1.0)	263 (0.9)	268 (0.9)	270 (1.1)	41 (1.3)	59 (1.3)	20 (1.4)	3 (0.4)	260 (1.9)	261 (2.0)	273 (1.8)	284 (1.4)
New York[6]	261 (1.4)	270 (1.7)	271 (2.2)	280 (1.1)	280 (0.9)	280 (1.0)	283 (1.1)	27 (1.3)	73 (1.4)	34 (1.3)	8 (0.7)	268 (2.8)	272 (2.0)	280 (1.6)	294 (1.3)
North Carolina	250 (1.1)	268 (1.4)	276 (1.3)	281 (1.0)	282 (0.9)	284 (1.1)	284 (1.3)	26 (1.3)	74 (1.3)	36 (1.5)	9 (0.8)	267 (2.3)	272 (1.7)	284 (1.7)	296 (1.4)
North Dakota	281 (1.2)	284 (0.9)	282 (1.1)	287 (0.8)	287 (0.6)	292 (0.7)	293 (0.7)	14 (0.8)	86 (0.8)	43 (1.1)	7 (0.9)	275 (5.2)	281 (1.9)	292 (1.9)	298 (0.8)

See notes at end of table.

Average mathematics scale score of 8th-grade public school students and percentage attaining mathematics achievement levels, by level of parental education and state or jurisdiction: Selected years, 1990 through 2009—Continued

State or jurisdiction	Average scale score[1]							Percent attaining mathematics achievement levels, 2009				Average scale score, by highest level of education attained by parents, 2009[2]			
	1990	1996	2000	2003	2005	2007	2009	Below *Basic*	At or above *Basic*[3]	At or above *Proficient*[4]	At *Advanced*[5]	Did not finish high school	Graduated high school	Some education after high school	Graduated college
1	2	3	4	5	6	7	8	9	10	11	12	13	14	15	16
Ohio	264 (1.0)	— (†)	281 (1.6)	282 (1.3)	283 (1.1)	285 (1.2)	286 (1.0)	24 (1.4)	76 (1.4)	36 (1.3)	8 (0.6)	270 (2.5)	276 (1.5)	285 (1.7)	295 (1.1)
Oklahoma	263 (1.3)	— (†)	270 (1.3)	272 (1.1)	271 (1.0)	275 (0.9)	276 (1.0)	32 (1.3)	68 (1.3)	24 (1.3)	3 (0.6)	259 (2.7)	267 (1.9)	279 (1.5)	284 (1.5)
Oregon[6]	271 (1.0)	276 (1.5)	280 (1.5)	281 (1.3)	282 (1.0)	284 (1.1)	285 (1.0)	25 (1.0)	75 (1.0)	37 (1.3)	8 (0.9)	268 (1.8)	273 (1.7)	289 (1.7)	299 (1.4)
Pennsylvania	266 (1.6)	— (†)	— (†)	279 (1.1)	281 (1.5)	286 (1.1)	288 (1.3)	22 (1.1)	78 (1.1)	40 (1.8)	10 (1.0)	268 (3.3)	274 (1.6)	289 (2.0)	300 (1.5)
Rhode Island	260 (0.6)	269 (0.9)	269 (1.3)	272 (0.7)	272 (0.8)	275 (0.7)	278 (0.8)	32 (1.3)	68 (1.3)	28 (1.0)	6 (0.6)	257 (2.8)	268 (1.7)	279 (1.8)	289 (1.2)
South Carolina	— (†)	261 (1.5)	265 (1.5)	277 (1.3)	281 (0.9)	282 (1.0)	280 (1.3)	31 (1.6)	69 (1.6)	30 (1.3)	7 (0.7)	266 (2.5)	269 (2.0)	283 (1.5)	290 (1.5)
South Dakota	— (†)	— (†)	— (†)	285 (0.8)	287 (0.6)	288 (0.8)	291 (0.5)	17 (0.7)	83 (0.7)	42 (1.1)	7 (0.5)	271 (2.8)	280 (1.7)	292 (1.3)	298 (0.7)
Tennessee	— (†)	263 (1.4)	262 (1.5)	268 (1.8)	271 (1.1)	274 (1.1)	275 (1.4)	35 (1.7)	65 (1.7)	25 (1.5)	4 (0.6)	264 (2.1)	262 (1.6)	280 (1.7)	284 (1.8)
Texas	258 (1.4)	270 (1.4)	273 (1.6)	277 (1.1)	281 (0.6)	286 (1.0)	287 (1.3)	22 (1.5)	78 (1.5)	36 (1.5)	8 (0.9)	273 (1.8)	278 (1.7)	289 (1.8)	300 (1.7)
Utah	— (†)	277 (1.0)	274 (1.2)	281 (1.0)	279 (0.7)	281 (0.9)	284 (0.9)	25 (1.0)	75 (1.0)	35 (1.2)	7 (0.8)	258 (3.2)	270 (2.3)	283 (1.7)	294 (1.1)
Vermont[6]	— (†)	279 (1.0)	281 (1.5)	286 (0.8)	287 (0.8)	291 (0.7)	293 (0.6)	19 (0.8)	81 (0.8)	43 (0.9)	13 (0.8)	271 (3.4)	276 (1.4)	288 (1.6)	304 (0.8)
Virginia[6]	264 (1.5)	270 (1.6)	275 (1.3)	282 (1.3)	284 (1.1)	288 (1.1)	286 (1.1)	24 (1.2)	76 (1.2)	36 (1.4)	8 (0.8)	269 (2.9)	271 (1.7)	284 (1.8)	296 (1.5)
Washington	— (†)	276 (1.3)	— (†)	281 (0.9)	285 (1.0)	285 (1.0)	289 (1.0)	22 (1.1)	78 (1.1)	39 (1.2)	11 (0.8)	262 (2.1)	277 (1.7)	290 (2.0)	301 (1.2)
West Virginia	256 (1.0)	265 (1.0)	266 (1.2)	271 (1.2)	269 (1.0)	270 (1.0)	270 (1.0)	39 (1.3)	61 (1.3)	19 (0.9)	2 (0.4)	253 (3.1)	260 (1.8)	277 (1.5)	281 (1.3)
Wisconsin	274 (1.3)	283 (1.5)	— (†)	284 (1.3)	285 (1.2)	286 (1.1)	288 (0.9)	21 (1.0)	79 (1.0)	39 (1.2)	8 (0.8)	262 (3.0)	279 (1.7)	289 (1.6)	298 (1.2)
Wyoming	272 (0.7)	275 (0.9)	276 (1.0)	284 (0.7)	282 (0.8)	287 (0.7)	286 (0.6)	22 (1.2)	78 (1.2)	35 (1.1)	7 (0.6)	270 (3.4)	275 (1.8)	288 (1.6)	295 (1.1)
Department of Defense dependents schools[7]	— (†)	274 (0.9)	277 (1.1)	285 (0.7)	284 (0.7)	285 (0.8)	287 (0.9)	21 (1.0)	79 (1.0)	36 (1.4)	6 (0.8)	‡ (†)	272 (2.7)	286 (1.5)	293 (1.2)
Other jurisdictions															
American Samoa	— (†)	— (†)	192 (5.5)	— (†)	— (†)	— (†)	— (†)	— (†)	— (†)	— (†)	— (†)	— (†)	— (†)	— (†)	— (†)
Guam	232 (0.7)	239 (1.7)	234 (2.6)	— (†)	— (†)	— (†)	— (†)	— (†)	— (†)	— (†)	— (†)	— (†)	— (†)	— (†)	— (†)
Puerto Rico[8]	— (†)	— (†)	— (†)	212 (1.0)	218 (1.0)	— (†)	— (†)	— (†)	— (†)	— (†)	— (†)	— (†)	— (†)	— (†)	— (†)
U.S. Virgin Islands	219 (0.9)	— (†)	— (†)	— (†)	— (†)	— (†)	— (†)	— (†)	— (†)	— (†)	— (†)	— (†)	— (†)	— (†)	— (†)

—Not available.
†Not applicable.
‡Reporting standards not met.
[1]Scale ranges from 0 to 500.
[2]Excludes students who responded "I don't know" to the question about educational level of parents.
[3]*Basic* denotes partial mastery of prerequisite knowledge and skills that are fundamental for proficient work at the 8th-grade level.
[4]*Proficient* represents solid academic performance for 8th-graders. Students reaching this level have demonstrated competency over challenging subject matter.
[5]*Advanced* signifies superior performance.
[6]Did not meet one or more of the guidelines for school participation in 2000. Data are subject to appreciable nonresponse bias.
[7]Prior to 2005, NAEP divided the Department of Defense (DoD) schools into two jurisdictions, domestic and overseas. In 2005, NAEP began combining the DoD domestic and overseas schools into a single jurisdiction. Data shown in this table for years prior to 2005 were recalculated for comparability.
[8]Because of modifications to the 2005 Puerto Rico administration, results from 2003 should not be compared to results from 2005. Although parallel changes were not made in the nation in 2005, within-year comparisons between Puerto Rico and the nation are valid.

NOTE: Excludes persons not enrolled in school and those who were unable to be tested due to limited proficiency in English or due to a disability. Data for 2000, 2003, 2005, 2007, and 2009 include students for whom accommodations were permitted. Detail may not sum to totals because of rounding. Standard errors appear in parentheses.

SOURCE: U.S. Department of Education, National Center for Education Statistics, National Assessment of Educational Progress (NAEP), 1990, 1996, 2000, 2003, 2005, 2007, and 2009 Mathematics Assessments, retrieved November 18, 2008, from the Main NAEP Data Explorer (http://nces.ed.gov/nationsreportcard/naepdata). (This table was prepared November 2009.)

Average mathematics scale scores of 4th-, 8th-, and 12th-graders, by selected student and school characteristics: Selected years, 1990 through 2009

Selected student or school characteristic	1990[1]		1992[1]		1996		2000		2003		2005		2007		2009	
1	2		3		4		5		6		7		8		9	
4th-graders, all students	213	(0.9)	220	(0.7)	224	(1.0)	226	(0.9)	235	(0.2)	238	(0.1)	240	(0.2)	240	(0.2)
Sex																
Male	214	(1.2)	221	(0.8)	224	(1.1)	227	(1.0)	236	(0.3)	239	(0.2)	241	(0.2)	241	(0.3)
Female	213	(1.1)	219	(1.0)	223	(1.1)	224	(0.9)	233	(0.2)	237	(0.2)	239	(0.2)	239	(0.3)
Race/ethnicity																
White	220	(1.0)	227	(0.8)	232	(1.0)	234	(0.8)	243	(0.2)	246	(0.1)	248	(0.2)	248	(0.2)
Black	188	(1.8)	193	(1.4)	198	(1.6)	203	(1.2)	216	(0.4)	220	(0.3)	222	(0.3)	222	(0.3)
Hispanic	200	(2.2)	202	(1.5)	207	(1.9)	208	(1.5)	222	(0.4)	226	(0.3)	227	(0.3)	227	(0.4)
Asian/Pacific Islander	225	(4.1)	231	(2.1)	229	(4.2)	‡	(†)	246	(1.1)	251	(0.7)	253	(0.8)	255	(1.0)
American Indian/Alaska Native	‡	(†)	‡	(†)	217	(5.6)	208	(3.5)	223	(1.0)	226	(0.9)	228	(0.7)	225	(0.9)
Eligibility for free or reduced-price lunch																
Eligible	—	(†)	—	(†)	207	(1.3)	208	(0.9)	222	(0.3)	225	(0.2)	227	(0.2)	227	(0.2)
Not eligible	—	(†)	—	(†)	232	(0.8)	235	(1.1)	244	(0.3)	248	(0.2)	249	(0.2)	250	(0.3)
Unknown	—	(†)	—	(†)	231	(2.8)	237	(1.6)	241	(0.7)	244	(0.7)	246	(0.9)	246	(1.1)
Control of school																
Public	212	(1.1)	219	(0.8)	222	(1.1)	224	(1.0)	234	(0.2)	237	(0.2)	239	(0.2)	239	(0.2)
Private	224	(2.6)	228	(1.1)	235	(1.9)	238	(0.8)	244	(0.7)	246	(0.8)	‡	(†)	246	(0.8)
Amount of math homework assigned per day																
None	—	(†)	—	(†)	227	(5.4)	227	(2.4)	234	(1.0)	—	(†)	236	(0.9)	236	(0.9)
15 minutes	—	(†)	—	(†)	227	(1.6)	229	(1.2)	237	(0.4)	—	(†)	242	(0.2)	242	(0.3)
30 minutes	—	(†)	—	(†)	223	(1.9)	225	(1.4)	234	(0.4)	—	(†)	239	(0.3)	239	(0.4)
45 minutes	—	(†)	—	(†)	217	(4.7)	214	(2.7)	229	(1.2)	—	(†)	233	(0.9)	235	(1.0)
1 hour	—	(†)	—	(†)	‡	(†)	225	(4.7)	225	(2.2)	—	(†)	233	(2.5)	228	(3.0)
More than 1 hour	—	(†)	—	(†)	‡	(†)	‡	(†)	217	(3.0)	—	(†)	233	(4.4)	222	(5.9)
8th-graders, all students	263	(1.3)	268	(0.9)	270	(0.9)	273	(0.8)	278	(0.3)	279	(0.2)	281	(0.3)	283	(0.3)
Sex																
Male	263	(1.6)	268	(1.1)	271	(1.1)	274	(0.9)	278	(0.3)	280	(0.2)	282	(0.3)	284	(0.3)
Female	262	(1.3)	269	(1.0)	269	(1.1)	272	(0.9)	277	(0.3)	278	(0.2)	280	(0.3)	282	(0.4)
Race/ethnicity																
White	270	(1.3)	277	(1.0)	281	(1.1)	284	(0.8)	288	(0.3)	289	(0.2)	291	(0.3)	293	(0.3)
Black	237	(2.7)	237	(1.3)	240	(1.9)	244	(1.2)	252	(0.5)	255	(0.4)	260	(0.4)	261	(0.5)
Hispanic	246	(4.3)	249	(1.2)	251	(1.7)	253	(1.3)	259	(0.6)	262	(0.4)	265	(0.4)	266	(0.6)
Asian/Pacific Islander	275	(5.0)	290	(5.9)	‡	(†)	288	(3.5)	291	(1.3)	295	(0.9)	297	(0.9)	301	(1.2)
American Indian/Alaska Native	‡	(†)	‡	(†)	‡	(†)	259	(7.5)	263	(1.8)	264	(0.9)	264	(1.2)	266	(1.1)
Eligibility for free or reduced-price lunch																
Eligible	—	(†)	—	(†)	250	(1.7)	253	(1.1)	259	(0.4)	262	(0.2)	265	(0.3)	266	(0.3)
Not eligible	—	(†)	—	(†)	277	(1.3)	283	(1.1)	287	(0.3)	288	(0.2)	291	(0.3)	294	(0.3)
Unknown	—	(†)	—	(†)	279	(2.3)	276	(1.6)	285	(1.0)	289	(1.2)	291	(1.7)	295	(1.4)
Parents' highest level of education																
Did not finish high school	242	(2.0)	249	(1.7)	250	(2.0)	253	(1.4)	257	(0.6)	259	(0.5)	263	(0.5)	265	(0.6)
Graduated high school	255	(1.6)	257	(1.2)	260	(1.3)	261	(1.0)	267	(0.4)	267	(0.3)	270	(0.4)	270	(0.5)
Some education after high school	267	(1.6)	271	(1.1)	277	(1.2)	277	(1.1)	280	(0.4)	280	(0.3)	283	(0.4)	284	(0.4)
Graduated college	274	(1.5)	281	(1.2)	281	(1.2)	286	(1.0)	288	(0.3)	290	(0.2)	292	(0.3)	295	(0.3)
Control of school																
Public	262	(1.4)	267	(1.0)	269	(1.0)	272	(0.9)	276	(0.3)	278	(0.2)	280	(0.3)	282	(0.3)
Private	271	(2.5)	281	(2.2)	285	(1.8)	286	(1.2)	292	(1.2)	‡	(†)	293	(1.3)	296	(1.2)
Amount of math homework assigned per day																
None	—	(†)	—	(†)	—	(†)	—	(†)	—	(†)	—	(†)	—	(†)	263	(2.0)
Less than 1 hour	—	(†)	—	(†)	—	(†)	—	(†)	—	(†)	—	(†)	—	(†)	284	(0.3)
About 1 hour	—	(†)	—	(†)	—	(†)	—	(†)	—	(†)	—	(†)	—	(†)	284	(0.8)
About 2–3 hours	—	(†)	—	(†)	—	(†)	—	(†)	—	(†)	—	(†)	—	(†)	274	(3.0)
More than 3 hours	—	(†)	—	(†)	—	(†)	—	(†)	—	(†)	—	(†)	—	(†)	269	(5.0)
12th-graders, all students	294	(1.1)	299	(0.9)	302	(1.0)	300	(1.0)	—	(†)	—	(†)	—	(†)	—	(†)
Sex																
Male	297	(1.4)	301	(1.1)	303	(1.2)	302	(1.2)	—	(†)	—	(†)	—	(†)	—	(†)
Female	291	(1.3)	298	(1.0)	300	(1.2)	299	(1.0)	—	(†)	—	(†)	—	(†)	—	(†)
Race/ethnicity																
White	300	(1.2)	305	(0.9)	309	(1.2)	307	(1.1)	—	(†)	—	(†)	—	(†)	—	(†)
Black	268	(2.0)	275	(1.8)	275	(1.6)	273	(2.0)	—	(†)	—	(†)	—	(†)	—	(†)
Hispanic	276	(3.8)	286	(1.6)	284	(2.2)	282	(2.0)	—	(†)	—	(†)	—	(†)	—	(†)
Asian/Pacific Islander	311	(5.2)	312	(4.2)	305	(2.7)	315	(4.2)	—	(†)	—	(†)	—	(†)	—	(†)
American Indian/Alaska Native	‡	(†)	‡	(†)	‡	(†)	294	(5.0)	—	(†)	—	(†)	—	(†)	—	(†)
Eligibility for free or reduced-price lunch																
Eligible	—	(†)	—	(†)	280	(1.7)	279	(1.7)	—	(†)	—	(†)	—	(†)	—	(†)
Not eligible	—	(†)	—	(†)	306	(1.2)	304	(1.5)	—	(†)	—	(†)	—	(†)	—	(†)
Unknown	—	(†)	—	(†)	303	(2.4)	303	(1.7)	—	(†)	—	(†)	—	(†)	—	(†)
Parents' highest level of education																
Did not finish high school	272	(2.1)	278	(1.7)	280	(2.0)	278	(1.6)	—	(†)	—	(†)	—	(†)	—	(†)
Graduated high school	283	(2.0)	288	(1.4)	290	(1.0)	287	(1.3)	—	(†)	—	(†)	—	(†)	—	(†)
Some education after high school	297	(1.2)	299	(1.0)	302	(0.9)	299	(1.2)	—	(†)	—	(†)	—	(†)	—	(†)
Graduated college	306	(1.6)	311	(1.2)	313	(1.3)	312	(1.3)	—	(†)	—	(†)	—	(†)	—	(†)
Control of school																
Public	294	(1.2)	297	(1.0)	301	(1.1)	299	(1.1)	—	(†)	—	(†)	—	(†)	—	(†)
Private	300	(3.6)	314	(2.3)	310	(2.6)	315	(1.1)	—	(†)	—	(†)	—	(†)	—	(†)

—Not available.
†Not applicable.
‡Reporting standards not met.
[1]Accommodations were not permitted for this assessment.
NOTE: Scale ranges from 0 to 500. Includes public and private schools. Excludes persons not enrolled in school and students who were unable to be tested due to limited proficiency in English or due to a disability. Race categories exclude persons of Hispanic ethnicity.

Some data have been revised from previously published figures. Standard errors appear in parentheses.
SOURCE: U.S. Department of Education, National Center for Education Statistics, National Assessment of Educational Progress (NAEP), 1990, 1992, 1996, 2000, 2003, 2005, 2007, and 2009 Mathematics Assessments, retrieved September 2, 2009 and November 18, 2009, from the Main NAEP Data Explorer (http://nces.ed.gov/nationsreportcard/naepdata/). (This table was prepared November 2009.)

Average scores and achievement-level results in NAEP science for public school students at grade 4, by state/jurisdiction: 2009

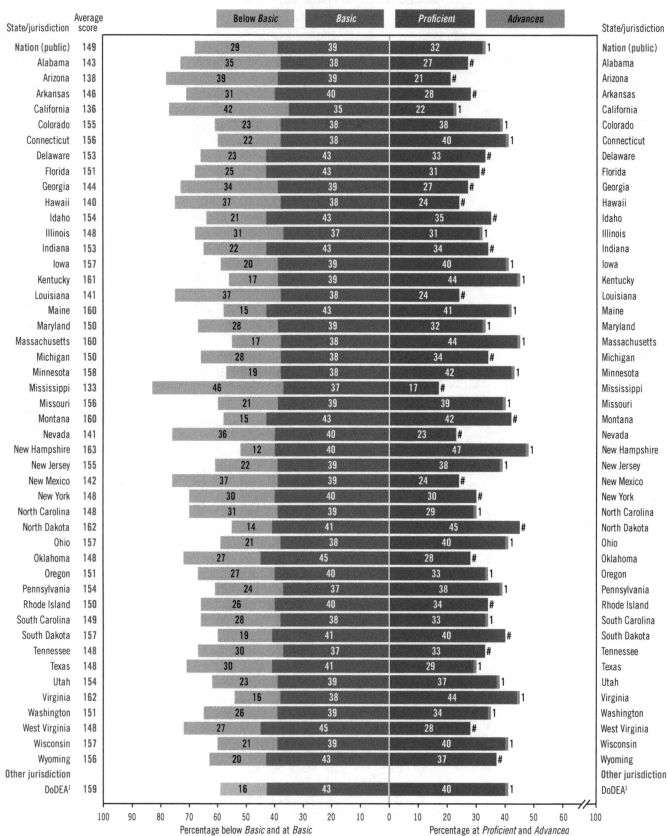

State/jurisdiction	Average score	Below Basic	Basic	Proficient	Advanced
Nation (public)	149	29	39	32	1
Alabama	143	35	38	27	#
Arizona	138	39	39	21	#
Arkansas	146	31	40	28	#
California	136	42	35	22	1
Colorado	155	23	38	38	1
Connecticut	156	22	38	40	1
Delaware	153	23	43	33	#
Florida	151	25	43	31	#
Georgia	144	34	39	27	#
Hawaii	140	37	38	24	#
Idaho	154	21	43	35	#
Illinois	148	31	37	31	1
Indiana	153	22	43	34	#
Iowa	157	20	39	40	1
Kentucky	161	17	39	44	1
Louisiana	141	37	38	24	#
Maine	160	15	43	41	1
Maryland	150	28	39	32	1
Massachusetts	160	17	38	44	1
Michigan	150	28	38	34	#
Minnesota	158	19	38	42	1
Mississippi	133	46	37	17	#
Missouri	156	21	39	39	1
Montana	160	15	43	42	#
Nevada	141	36	40	23	#
New Hampshire	163	12	40	47	1
New Jersey	155	22	39	38	1
New Mexico	142	37	39	24	#
New York	148	30	40	30	#
North Carolina	148	31	39	29	1
North Dakota	162	14	41	45	#
Ohio	157	21	38	40	1
Oklahoma	148	27	45	28	#
Oregon	151	27	40	33	1
Pennsylvania	154	24	37	38	1
Rhode Island	150	26	40	34	#
South Carolina	149	28	38	33	1
South Dakota	157	19	41	40	#
Tennessee	148	30	37	33	#
Texas	148	30	41	29	1
Utah	154	23	39	37	1
Virginia	162	16	38	44	1
Washington	151	26	39	34	1
West Virginia	148	27	45	28	#
Wisconsin	157	21	39	40	1
Wyoming	156	20	43	37	#
Other jurisdiction					
DoDEA[1]	159	16	43	40	1

Percentage below *Basic* and at *Basic*   Percentage at *Proficient* and *Advanced*

Rounds to zero.

[1] Department of Defense Education Activity (overseas and domestic schools).

NOTE: Alaska, the District of Columbia, Kansas, Nebraska, and Vermont did not participate in the 2009 science assessment at the state level. The shaded bars are graphed using unrounded numbers. Detail may not sum to totals because of rounding.

SOURCE: U.S. Department of Education, Institute of Education Sciences, National Center for Education Statistics, National Assessment of Educational Progress (NAEP), 2009 Science Assessment.

Average scores and achievement-level results in NAEP science for fourth-grade public school students, by race/ethnicity and state/jurisdiction: 2009

State/jurisdiction	White					Black					Hispanic				
	Average scale score	Percentage of students				Average scale score	Percentage of students				Average scale score	Percentage of students			
		Below Basic	At or above Basic	At or above Proficient	At Advanced		Below Basic	At or above Basic	At or above Proficient	At Advanced		Below Basic	At or above Basic	At or above Proficient	At Advanced
Nation (public)	162	14	86	46	1	127	54	46	10	#	130	48	52	13	#
Alabama	155	20	80	39	#	121	61	39	6	#	125	55	45	9	#
Alaska	—	—	—	—	—	—	—	—	—	—	—	—	—	—	—
Arizona	155	19	81	37	1	129	48	52	13	#	124	55	45	9	#
Arkansas	157	18	82	38	#	117	66	34	6	#	136	42	58	15	#
California	157	19	81	41	1	122	59	41	9	#	121	58	42	8	#
Colorado	166	11	89	53	1	128	48	52	12	#	134	44	56	15	#
Connecticut	167	10	90	53	1	129	51	49	9	#	128	52	48	11	#
Delaware	166	9	91	50	#	135	43	57	11	#	142	34	66	20	#
Florida	163	12	88	46	#	131	49	51	10	#	144	30	70	23	#
Georgia	159	16	84	42	#	126	55	45	10	#	133	47	53	15	#
Hawaii	159	18	82	43	1	134	43	57	16	#	134	42	58	22	#
Idaho	159	16	84	40	#	‡	‡	‡	‡	‡	128	53	47	10	#
Illinois	164	13	87	48	1	120	63	37	9	#	129	49	51	10	#
Indiana	158	16	84	41	1	129	50	50	9	#	136	41	59	15	#
Iowa	161	15	85	45	1	130	50	50	14	#	134	40	60	15	#
Kansas	—	—	—	—	—	—	—	—	—	—	—	—	—	—	—
Kentucky	164	13	87	49	1	135	43	57	15	#	150	27	73	31	2
Louisiana	159	15	85	42	1	123	60	40	8	#	144	31	69	23	1
Maine	161	14	86	43	1	139	38	62	26	1	‡	‡	‡	‡	‡
Maryland	164	13	87	48	1	131	50	50	12	#	143	34	66	21	#
Massachusetts	169	8	92	56	1	138	39	61	17	#	132	44	56	12	#
Michigan	160	17	83	43	1	118	66	34	6	#	138	40	60	20	#
Minnesota	166	11	89	51	1	129	50	50	12	#	134	45	55	16	#
Mississippi	152	22	78	31	#	116	68	32	4	#	142	34	66	21	#
Missouri	164	13	87	47	1	127	54	46	12	#	141	34	66	21	#
Montana	164	10	90	47	1	‡	‡	‡	‡	‡	149	27	73	26	#
Nebraska	—	—	—	—	—	—	—	—	—	—	—	—	—	—	—
Nevada	156	19	81	37	#	122	59	41	8	#	128	51	49	12	#
New Hampshire	165	11	89	49	1	‡	‡	‡	‡	‡	139	39	61	20	#
New Jersey	166	10	90	52	1	133	46	54	12	#	136	42	58	15	#
New Mexico	163	14	86	48	1	134	44	56	16	#	134	45	55	15	#
New York	161	14	86	44	1	127	55	45	9	#	130	49	51	13	#
North Carolina	162	14	86	45	1	126	56	44	9	#	132	49	51	11	#
North Dakota	165	10	90	49	1	‡	‡	‡	‡	‡	‡	‡	‡	‡	‡
Ohio	165	11	89	50	1	129	53	47	10	#	140	42	58	26	1
Oklahoma	156	17	83	37	#	125	56	44	8	#	131	47	53	12	#
Oregon	157	20	80	40	1	131	47	53	12	#	128	53	47	12	#
Pennsylvania	164	13	87	48	1	121	61	39	7	#	125	54	46	12	#
Rhode Island	161	14	86	44	#	126	54	46	10	#	124	56	44	9	#
South Carolina	163	13	87	49	1	128	53	47	10	#	140	35	65	23	#
South Dakota	162	13	87	46	1	‡	‡	‡	‡	‡	145	28	72	23	#
Tennessee	159	19	81	43	1	121	61	39	8	#	134	44	56	17	#
Texas	168	10	90	53	2	139	38	62	18	#	136	42	58	16	#
Utah	161	16	84	45	1	‡	‡	‡	‡	‡	129	50	50	12	#
Vermont	—	—	—	—	—	—	—	—	—	—	—	—	—	—	—
Virginia	172	7	93	59	2	141	36	64	18	#	152	20	80	32	#
Washington	160	15	85	44	1	127	51	49	8	#	125	56	44	10	#
West Virginia	150	25	75	29	#	130	50	50	11	#	‡	‡	‡	‡	‡
Wisconsin	164	12	88	49	1	121	62	38	8	#	138	40	60	17	#
Wyoming	159	16	84	41	#	‡	‡	‡	‡	‡	140	38	62	18	#
Other jurisdictions															
District of Columbia	—	—	—	—	—	—	—	—	—	—	—	—	—	—	—
DoDEA[1]	166	9	91	51	1	141	35	65	16	#	153	22	78	32	#

See notes at end of table.

Average scores and achievement-level results in NAEP science for fourth-grade public school students, by race/ethnicity and state/jurisdiction: 2009—Continued

State/jurisdiction	Asian/Pacific Islander					American Indian/Alaska Native				
	Average scale score	Percentage of students				Average scale score	Percentage of students			
		Below *Basic*	At or above *Basic*	At or above *Proficient*	At *Advanced*		Below *Basic*	At or above *Basic*	At or above *Proficient*	At *Advanced*
Nation (public)	**160**	**20**	**80**	**45**	**2**	**137**	**40**	**60**	**19**	**#**
Alabama	‡	‡	‡	‡	‡	‡	‡	‡	‡	‡
Alaska	—	—	—	—	—	—	—	—	—	—
Arizona	156	22	78	43	#	123	57	43	9	#
Arkansas	152	23	77	34	1	‡	‡	‡	‡	‡
California	160	19	81	45	3	‡	‡	‡	‡	‡
Colorado	162	15	85	48	1	‡	‡	‡	‡	‡
Connecticut	164	14	86	48	#	‡	‡	‡	‡	‡
Delaware	169	11	89	53	5	‡	‡	‡	‡	‡
Florida	158	19	81	44	2	‡	‡	‡	‡	‡
Georgia	167	11	89	50	1	‡	‡	‡	‡	‡
Hawaii	138	40	60	21	#	‡	‡	‡	‡	‡
Idaho	156	23	77	39	3	‡	‡	‡	‡	‡
Illinois	166	14	86	51	3	‡	‡	‡	‡	‡
Indiana	‡	‡	‡	‡	‡	‡	‡	‡	‡	‡
Iowa	156	24	76	43	1	‡	‡	‡	‡	‡
Kansas	—	—	—	—	—	—	—	—	—	—
Kentucky	172	11	89	65	3	‡	‡	‡	‡	‡
Louisiana	‡	‡	‡	‡	‡	‡	‡	‡	‡	‡
Maine	‡	‡	‡	‡	‡	‡	‡	‡	‡	‡
Maryland	164	14	86	47	1	‡	‡	‡	‡	‡
Massachusetts	167	14	86	53	4	‡	‡	‡	‡	‡
Michigan	162	21	79	49	2	‡	‡	‡	‡	‡
Minnesota	147	33	67	31	#	134	42	58	12	#
Mississippi	‡	‡	‡	‡	‡	‡	‡	‡	‡	‡
Missouri	‡	‡	‡	‡	‡	‡	‡	‡	‡	‡
Montana	‡	‡	‡	‡	‡	137	39	61	16	#
Nebraska	—	—	—	—	—	—	—	—	—	—
Nevada	151	25	75	32	#	‡	‡	‡	‡	‡
New Hampshire	171	8	92	57	2	‡	‡	‡	‡	‡
New Jersey	173	10	90	63	4	‡	‡	‡	‡	‡
New Mexico	‡	‡	‡	‡	‡	126	56	44	8	#
New York	156	20	80	38	1	‡	‡	‡	‡	‡
North Carolina	163	17	83	52	#	128	54	46	10	#
North Dakota	‡	‡	‡	‡	‡	135	45	55	15	#
Ohio	‡	‡	‡	‡	‡	‡	‡	‡	‡	‡
Oklahoma	‡	‡	‡	‡	‡	145	29	71	23	#
Oregon	159	20	80	44	3	143	35	65	25	#
Pennsylvania	166	16	84	53	2	‡	‡	‡	‡	‡
Rhode Island	152	29	71	37	1	‡	‡	‡	‡	‡
South Carolina	‡	‡	‡	‡	‡	‡	‡	‡	‡	‡
South Dakota	‡	‡	‡	‡	‡	128	52	48	11	#
Tennessee	‡	‡	‡	‡	‡	‡	‡	‡	‡	‡
Texas	163	16	84	47	2	‡	‡	‡	‡	‡
Utah	147	30	70	28	1	124	64	36	9	#
Vermont	—	—	—	—	—	—	—	—	—	—
Virginia	174	7	93	61	4	‡	‡	‡	‡	‡
Washington	156	22	78	41	1	137	37	63	18	#
West Virginia	‡	‡	‡	‡	‡	‡	‡	‡	‡	‡
Wisconsin	153	27	73	37	#	145	29	71	20	#
Wyoming	‡	‡	‡	‡	‡	134	43	57	9	#
Other jurisdictions										
District of Columbia	—	—	—	—	—	—	—	—	—	—
DoDEA[1]	161	15	85	44	#	‡	‡	‡	‡	‡

— Not available.

\# Rounds to zero.

‡ Reporting standards not met. Sample size insufficient to permit a reliable estimate.

[1] Department of Defense Education Activity (overseas and domestic schools).

NOTE: Black includes African American, Hispanic includes Latino, and Pacific Islander includes Native Hawaiian. Race categories exclude Hispanic origin. Results are not shown for students whose race/ethnicity was unclassified. Detail may not sum to totals because of rounding.

SOURCE: U.S. Department of Education, Institute of Education Sciences, National Center for Education Statistics, National Assessment of Educational Progress (NAEP), 2009 Science Assessment.

Average scores and achievement-level results in NAEP science for fourth-grade public school students, by gender and state/jurisdiction: 2009

State/jurisdiction	Male					Female				
	Average scale score	Percentage of students				Average scale score	Percentage of students			
		Below Basic	At or above Basic	At or above Proficient	At Advanced		Below Basic	At or above Basic	At or above Proficient	At Advanced
Nation (public)	**149**	**29**	**71**	**34**	**1**	**148**	**29**	**71**	**31**	**#**
Alabama	144	34	66	29	#	142	36	64	25	#
Alaska	—	—	—	—	—	—	—	—	—	—
Arizona	137	40	60	23	#	138	39	61	21	#
Arkansas	146	31	69	30	#	146	31	69	27	#
California	136	43	57	22	#	137	42	58	22	1
Colorado	156	22	78	40	1	153	24	76	37	1
Connecticut	156	22	78	42	1	155	22	78	38	1
Delaware	153	24	76	35	1	152	23	77	32	#
Florida	151	25	75	33	#	150	25	75	31	#
Georgia	145	33	67	29	#	143	35	65	25	#
Hawaii	137	41	59	24	1	143	33	67	25	#
Idaho	154	21	79	37	#	153	22	78	34	#
Illinois	148	31	69	34	1	147	31	69	30	1
Indiana	153	22	78	36	1	152	23	77	34	#
Iowa	158	20	80	42	1	157	20	80	40	1
Kansas	—	—	—	—	—	—	—	—	—	—
Kentucky	161	16	84	46	1	160	17	83	43	1
Louisiana	141	37	63	26	1	141	37	63	24	#
Maine	161	14	86	44	1	158	16	84	39	#
Maryland	151	27	73	33	1	149	30	70	32	#
Massachusetts	162	16	84	47	1	159	18	82	43	1
Michigan	151	27	73	37	#	149	28	72	32	1
Minnesota	159	19	81	45	1	158	18	82	41	1
Mississippi	134	45	55	18	#	132	48	52	16	#
Missouri	155	22	78	40	1	158	19	81	40	1
Montana	160	15	85	43	#	160	14	86	42	#
Nebraska	—	—	—	—	—	—	—	—	—	—
Nevada	142	35	65	26	#	139	38	62	21	#
New Hampshire	163	12	88	47	1	163	13	87	48	1
New Jersey	156	22	78	41	1	154	23	77	37	#
New Mexico	142	36	64	25	#	141	37	63	23	#
New York	148	29	71	31	1	147	30	70	29	#
North Carolina	149	30	70	33	1	146	32	68	27	#
North Dakota	164	13	87	49	1	160	14	86	42	#
Ohio	159	19	81	45	1	155	22	78	38	1
Oklahoma	148	28	72	29	#	148	26	74	28	#
Oregon	151	27	73	34	1	151	26	74	34	#
Pennsylvania	156	23	77	41	1	151	26	74	36	#
Rhode Island	151	26	74	36	#	149	27	73	32	#
South Carolina	150	28	72	34	1	149	29	71	33	#
South Dakota	158	18	82	42	1	156	20	80	38	#
Tennessee	149	30	70	33	1	148	31	69	33	#
Texas	148	30	70	30	1	147	31	69	28	1
Utah	155	22	78	39	1	153	24	76	36	1
Vermont	—	—	—	—	—	—	—	—	—	—
Virginia	161	17	83	45	1	162	16	84	47	1
Washington	151	26	74	34	1	151	26	74	35	1
West Virginia	149	27	73	30	#	147	28	72	26	#
Wisconsin	157	21	79	41	1	156	20	80	40	1
Wyoming	157	18	82	38	#	154	21	79	36	#
Other jurisdictions										
District of Columbia	—	—	—	—	—	—	—	—	—	—
DoDEA[1]	158	18	82	40	1	159	15	85	41	#

— Not available.
Rounds to zero.
[1] Department of Defense Education Activity (overseas and domestic schools).
NOTE: Detail may not sum to totals because of rounding.
SOURCE: U.S. Department of Education, Institute of Education Sciences, National Center for Education Statistics, National Assessment of Educational Progress (NAEP), 2009 Science Assessment.

Average scores and achievement-level results in NAEP science for public school students at grade 8, by state/jurisdiction: 2009

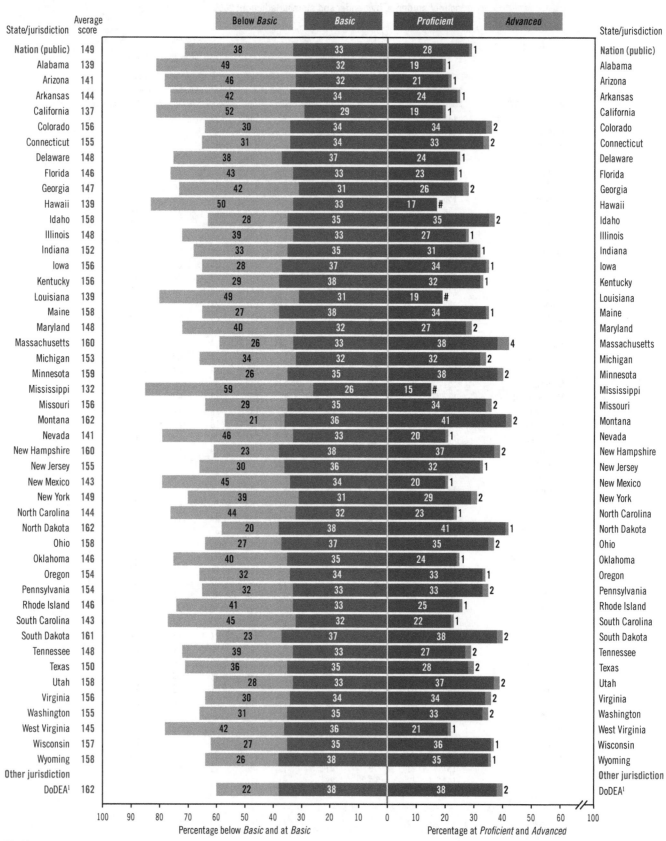

State/jurisdiction	Average score	Below Basic	Basic	Proficient	Advanced
Nation (public)	149	38	33	28	1
Alabama	139	49	32	19	1
Arizona	141	46	32	21	1
Arkansas	144	42	34	24	1
California	137	52	29	19	1
Colorado	156	30	34	34	2
Connecticut	155	31	34	33	2
Delaware	148	38	37	24	1
Florida	146	43	33	23	1
Georgia	147	42	31	26	2
Hawaii	139	50	33	17	#
Idaho	158	28	35	35	2
Illinois	148	39	33	27	1
Indiana	152	33	35	31	1
Iowa	156	28	37	34	1
Kentucky	156	29	38	32	1
Louisiana	139	49	31	19	#
Maine	158	27	38	34	1
Maryland	148	40	32	27	2
Massachusetts	160	26	33	38	4
Michigan	153	34	32	32	2
Minnesota	159	26	35	38	2
Mississippi	132	59	26	15	#
Missouri	156	29	35	34	2
Montana	162	21	36	41	2
Nevada	141	46	33	20	1
New Hampshire	160	23	38	37	2
New Jersey	155	30	36	32	1
New Mexico	143	45	34	20	1
New York	149	39	31	29	2
North Carolina	144	44	32	23	1
North Dakota	162	20	38	41	1
Ohio	158	27	37	35	2
Oklahoma	146	40	35	24	1
Oregon	154	32	34	33	1
Pennsylvania	154	32	33	33	2
Rhode Island	146	41	33	25	1
South Carolina	143	45	32	22	1
South Dakota	161	23	37	38	2
Tennessee	148	39	33	27	2
Texas	150	36	35	28	2
Utah	158	28	33	37	2
Virginia	156	30	34	34	2
Washington	155	31	35	33	2
West Virginia	145	42	36	21	1
Wisconsin	157	27	35	36	1
Wyoming	158	26	38	35	1
Other jurisdiction					
DoDEA[1]	162	22	38	38	2

Percentage below *Basic* and at *Basic*   Percentage at *Proficient* and *Advanced*

Rounds to zero.

[1] Department of Defense Education Activity (overseas and domestic schools).

NOTE: Alaska, the District of Columbia, Kansas, Nebraska, and Vermont did not participate in the 2009 science assessment at the state level. The shaded bars are graphed using unrounded numbers. Detail may not sum to totals because of rounding.

SOURCE: U.S. Department of Education, Institute of Education Sciences, National Center for Education Statistics, National Assessment of Educational Progress (NAEP), 2009 Science Assessment.

Average scores and achievement-level results in NAEP science for eighth-grade public school students, by race/ethnicity and state/jurisdiction: 2009

State/jurisdiction	White					Black					Hispanic				
	Average scale score	Percentage of students				Average scale score	Percentage of students				Average scale score	Percentage of students			
		Below Basic	At or above Basic	At or above Proficient	At Advanced		Below Basic	At or above Basic	At or above Proficient	At Advanced		Below Basic	At or above Basic	At or above Proficient	At Advanced
Nation (public)	**161**	**23**	**77**	**41**	**2**	**125**	**68**	**32**	**8**	**#**	**131**	**59**	**41**	**12**	**#**
Alabama	152	32	68	28	1	115	77	23	4	#	129	66	34	10	#
Alaska	—	—	—	—	—	—	—	—	—	—	—	—	—	—	—
Arizona	157	26	74	35	1	126	63	37	8	#	127	64	36	10	#
Arkansas	154	29	71	32	1	111	81	19	4	#	134	54	46	12	#
California	157	29	71	38	2	122	69	31	8	#	122	67	33	7	#
Colorado	166	17	83	48	2	135	56	44	13	#	137	52	48	14	#
Connecticut	164	18	82	44	2	126	65	35	9	#	128	65	35	9	#
Delaware	159	23	77	35	1	133	59	41	10	#	141	51	49	16	#
Florida	158	28	72	36	2	126	68	32	7	#	139	49	51	17	#
Georgia	161	25	75	41	3	129	64	36	10	#	137	49	51	15	#
Hawaii	153	32	68	30	#	133	55	45	15	#	148	38	62	25	1
Idaho	162	23	77	42	2	‡	‡	‡	‡	‡	137	53	47	14	#
Illinois	162	21	79	41	2	118	77	23	4	#	131	60	40	10	#
Indiana	159	25	75	38	2	126	66	34	8	#	135	54	46	16	#
Iowa	160	24	76	38	1	127	62	38	9	#	133	55	45	12	#
Kansas	—	—	—	—	—	—	—	—	—	—	—	—	—	—	—
Kentucky	159	25	75	36	2	137	54	46	16	#	145	42	58	24	2
Louisiana	155	30	70	31	1	120	73	27	5	#	‡	‡	‡	‡	‡
Maine	159	26	74	36	1	126	67	33	11	#	‡	‡	‡	‡	‡
Maryland	164	20	80	44	2	127	66	34	8	#	136	54	46	12	1
Massachusetts	167	18	82	48	4	132	58	42	13	1	131	57	43	14	#
Michigan	162	23	77	42	3	121	73	27	6	#	139	50	50	20	1
Minnesota	166	17	83	46	2	128	64	36	11	#	132	60	40	14	#
Mississippi	150	35	65	27	#	114	81	19	3	#	‡	‡	‡	‡	‡
Missouri	161	23	77	40	2	129	62	38	9	#	150	38	62	29	2
Montana	166	17	83	46	2	‡	‡	‡	‡	‡	155	29	71	33	1
Nebraska	—	—	—	—	—	—	—	—	—	—	—	—	—	—	—
Nevada	153	32	68	30	1	127	66	34	9	#	129	61	39	10	#
New Hampshire	161	22	78	40	2	‡	‡	‡	‡	‡	131	59	41	12	#
New Jersey	165	17	83	44	2	127	65	35	8	#	138	51	49	13	#
New Mexico	163	19	81	39	2	‡	‡	‡	‡	‡	135	56	44	14	#
New York	164	20	80	45	3	123	70	30	7	#	125	66	34	11	#
North Carolina	158	27	73	36	2	121	75	25	5	#	132	59	41	11	#
North Dakota	166	16	84	46	1	‡	‡	‡	‡	‡	‡	‡	‡	‡	‡
Ohio	164	18	82	43	2	126	68	32	6	#	140	52	48	18	#
Oklahoma	155	30	70	33	1	124	68	32	7	#	127	63	37	9	#
Oregon	160	25	75	40	2	135	52	48	13	#	130	60	40	12	#
Pennsylvania	162	22	78	42	2	123	70	30	7	#	121	73	27	7	#
Rhode Island	155	30	70	33	2	125	68	32	8	#	119	74	26	5	#
South Carolina	158	26	74	35	2	124	70	30	6	#	129	58	42	13	#
South Dakota	165	17	83	45	2	141	45	55	24	1	135	55	45	10	1
Tennessee	157	28	72	36	2	122	70	30	6	#	139	52	48	21	1
Texas	167	17	83	47	3	133	57	43	13	#	141	47	53	17	#
Utah	164	21	79	45	2	‡	‡	‡	‡	‡	129	60	40	13	#
Vermont	—	—	—	—	—	—	—	—	—	—	—	—	—	—	—
Virginia	166	18	82	48	2	135	57	43	11	#	144	41	59	20	#
Washington	161	23	77	41	2	135	54	46	16	#	132	57	43	9	#
West Virginia	146	41	59	23	1	127	65	35	10	#	‡	‡	‡	‡	‡
Wisconsin	165	18	82	44	2	120	74	26	6	#	134	54	46	15	#
Wyoming	162	21	79	40	2	‡	‡	‡	‡	‡	137	51	49	12	#
Other jurisdictions															
District of Columbia	—	—	—	—	—	—	—	—	—	—	—	—	—	—	—
DoDEA[1]	170	13	87	53	3	144	45	55	14	#	155	28	72	28	1

See notes at end of table.

Average scores and achievement-level results in NAEP science for eighth-grade public school students, by race/ethnicity and state/jurisdiction: 2009—Continued

State/jurisdiction	Asian/Pacific Islander					American Indian/Alaska Native				
	Average scale score	Percentage of students				Average scale score	Percentage of students			
		Below *Basic*	At or above *Basic*	At or above *Proficient*	At *Advanced*		Below *Basic*	At or above *Basic*	At or above *Proficient*	At *Advanced*
Nation (public)	**159**	**28**	**72**	**40**	**3**	**138**	**51**	**49**	**18**	**#**
Alabama	‡	‡	‡	‡	‡	‡	‡	‡	‡	‡
Alaska	—	—	—	—	—	—	—	—	‡	—
Arizona	159	32	68	43	5	126	65	35	7	#
Arkansas	‡	‡	‡	‡	‡	‡	‡	‡	‡	‡
California	154	31	69	34	2	‡	‡	‡	‡	‡
Colorado	161	21	79	41	2	‡	‡	‡	‡	‡
Connecticut	169	22	78	52	7	‡	‡	‡	‡	‡
Delaware	160	25	75	40	3	‡	‡	‡	‡	‡
Florida	163	21	79	40	4	‡	‡	‡	‡	‡
Georgia	172	15	85	58	6	‡	‡	‡	‡	‡
Hawaii	136	54	46	14	#	‡	‡	‡	‡	‡
Idaho	‡	‡	‡	‡	‡	‡	‡	‡	‡	‡
Illinois	167	20	80	48	5	‡	‡	‡	‡	‡
Indiana	‡	‡	‡	‡	‡	‡	‡	‡	‡	‡
Iowa	‡	‡	‡	‡	‡	‡	‡	‡	‡	‡
Kansas	—	—	—	—	—	—	—	—	—	—
Kentucky	‡	‡	‡	‡	‡	‡	‡	‡	‡	‡
Louisiana	‡	‡	‡	‡	‡	‡	‡	‡	‡	‡
Maine	‡	‡	‡	‡	‡	‡	‡	‡	‡	‡
Maryland	169	14	86	51	5	‡	‡	‡	‡	‡
Massachusetts	168	22	78	49	10	‡	‡	‡	‡	‡
Michigan	‡	‡	‡	‡	‡	‡	‡	‡	‡	‡
Minnesota	141	50	50	23	2	141	44	56	14	#
Mississippi	‡	‡	‡	‡	‡	‡	‡	‡	‡	‡
Missouri	167	22	78	48	7	‡	‡	‡	‡	‡
Montana	‡	‡	‡	‡	‡	138	51	49	18	#
Nebraska	—	—	—	—	—	—	—	—	—	—
Nevada	148	37	63	26	1	‡	‡	‡	‡	‡
New Hampshire	‡	‡	‡	‡	‡	‡	‡	‡	‡	‡
New Jersey	174	10	90	58	4	‡	‡	‡	‡	‡
New Mexico	‡	‡	‡	‡	‡	130	64	36	10	#
New York	161	25	75	43	4	‡	‡	‡	‡	‡
North Carolina	165	21	79	44	5	119	70	30	6	#
North Dakota	‡	‡	‡	‡	‡	135	56	44	11	#
Ohio	‡	‡	‡	‡	‡	‡	‡	‡	‡	‡
Oklahoma	‡	‡	‡	‡	‡	142	47	53	19	#
Oregon	160	26	74	45	2	153	34	66	35	#
Pennsylvania	159	26	74	41	2	‡	‡	‡	‡	‡
Rhode Island	146	41	59	21	2	‡	‡	‡	‡	‡
South Carolina	‡	‡	‡	‡	‡	‡	‡	‡	‡	‡
South Dakota	‡	‡	‡	‡	‡	137	52	48	16	#
Tennessee	‡	‡	‡	‡	‡	‡	‡	‡	‡	‡
Texas	170	18	82	55	5	‡	‡	‡	‡	‡
Utah	147	43	57	31	2	130	59	41	10	#
Vermont	—	—	—	—	—	—	—	—	—	—
Virginia	168	17	83	49	4	‡	‡	‡	‡	‡
Washington	157	31	69	39	3	142	47	53	20	#
West Virginia	‡	‡	‡	‡	‡	‡	‡	‡	‡	‡
Wisconsin	152	35	65	28	2	‡	‡	‡	‡	‡
Wyoming	‡	‡	‡	‡	‡	‡	‡	‡	‡	‡
Other jurisdictions										
District of Columbia	—	—	—	—	—	—	—	—	—	—
DoDEA[1]	160	23	77	41	1	‡	‡	‡	‡	‡

— Not available.

Rounds to zero.

‡ Reporting standards not met. Sample size insufficient to permit a reliable estimate.

[1] Department of Defense Education Activity (overseas and domestic schools).

NOTE: Black includes African American, Hispanic includes Latino, and Pacific Islander includes Native Hawaiian. Race categories exclude Hispanic origin. Results are not shown for students whose race/ethnicity was unclassified. Detail may not sum to totals because of rounding.

SOURCE: U.S. Department of Education, Institute of Education Sciences, National Center for Education Statistics, National Assessment of Educational Progress (NAEP), 2009 Science Assessment.

Average scores and achievement-level results in NAEP science for eighth-grade public school students, by gender and state/jurisdiction: 2009

State/jurisdiction	Male					Female				
		Percentage of students					Percentage of students			
	Average scale score	Below Basic	At or above Basic	At or above Proficient	At Advanced	Average scale score	Below Basic	At or above Basic	At or above Proficient	At Advanced
Nation (public)	**151**	**36**	**64**	**32**	**2**	**147**	**40**	**60**	**26**	**1**
Alabama	142	46	54	24	1	136	52	48	15	#
Alaska	—	—	—	—	—	—	—	—	—	—
Arizona	143	44	56	26	1	139	49	51	18	#
Arkansas	145	41	59	28	1	142	44	56	20	#
California	138	50	50	22	1	135	53	47	17	1
Colorado	158	28	72	39	2	153	32	68	32	1
Connecticut	157	29	71	38	2	153	32	68	32	1
Delaware	151	35	65	29	1	146	41	59	21	#
Florida	148	41	59	28	2	144	44	56	21	1
Georgia	150	39	61	30	2	144	45	55	24	1
Hawaii	140	47	53	19	1	137	52	48	15	#
Idaho	160	26	74	42	3	155	29	71	33	1
Illinois	150	36	64	32	2	146	42	58	25	1
Indiana	155	30	70	35	2	150	35	65	28	1
Iowa	158	26	74	38	2	154	30	70	31	#
Kansas	—	—	—	—	—	—	—	—	—	—
Kentucky	159	26	74	37	2	154	31	69	30	1
Louisiana	141	47	53	22	1	138	51	49	18	#
Maine	160	25	75	38	2	156	28	72	33	1
Maryland	150	38	62	32	2	146	41	59	25	1
Massachusetts	162	26	74	44	5	158	26	74	38	2
Michigan	155	32	68	38	2	152	35	65	31	2
Minnesota	161	25	75	43	3	157	26	74	36	1
Mississippi	134	56	44	17	#	130	61	39	13	#
Missouri	158	28	72	38	2	154	31	69	33	1
Montana	165	18	82	47	2	159	24	76	38	1
Nebraska	—	—	—	—	—	140	48	52	19	#
Nevada	142	45	55	21	1	157	25	75	33	1
New Hampshire	164	21	79	44	2	153	32	68	31	1
New Jersey	156	29	71	37	2	140	50	50	18	#
New Mexico	147	40	60	24	1	147	40	60	27	1
New York	150	38	62	34	2	143	45	55	22	1
North Carolina	145	43	57	25	2	159	23	77	37	1
North Dakota	166	17	83	47	2	154	29	71	32	1
Ohio	161	24	76	41	3	144	43	57	22	#
Oklahoma	149	37	63	28	1	152	34	66	32	1
Oregon	156	29	71	37	2	151	35	65	31	1
Pennsylvania	157	30	70	39	2	143	45	55	22	1
Rhode Island	149	38	62	30	1	142	46	54	22	1
South Carolina	144	44	56	24	1	157	25	75	35	1
South Dakota	164	20	80	45	2	146	42	58	24	1
Tennessee	149	37	63	32	2	148	39	61	26	1
Texas	152	33	67	32	2	156	28	72	36	1
Utah	159	27	73	43	3	—	—	—	—	—
Vermont	—	—	—	—	—	155	30	70	33	1
Virginia	157	29	71	39	2	153	32	68	30	1
Washington	156	30	70	38	2	142	46	54	18	#
West Virginia	148	39	61	26	1	155	29	71	33	1
Wisconsin	160	25	75	43	2	154	29	71	30	1
Wyoming	162	22	78	42	2					
Other jurisdictions										
District of Columbia	—	—	—	—	—	—	—	—	—	—
DoDEA[1]	164	21	79	44	2	159	24	76	36	1

— Not available.

\# Rounds to zero.

[1] Department of Defense Education Activity (overseas and domestic schools).

NOTE: Detail may not sum to totals because of rounding.

SOURCE: U.S. Department of Education, Institute of Education Sciences, National Center for Education Statistics, National Assessment of Educational Progress (NAEP), 2009 Science Assessment.

Average science scale scores and percentage of 4th-, 8th-, and 12th-graders attaining science achievement levels, by selected student characteristics and percentile: 1996, 2000, and 2005

Selected characteristic, percentile, and achievement level	4th-graders 1996[1]	4th-graders 2000	4th-graders 2005	8th-graders 1996[1]	8th-graders 2000	8th-graders 2005	12th-graders 1996[1]	12th-graders 2000	12th-graders 2005
	2	3	4	5	6	7	8	9	10
All students	**147** (1.1)	**147** (0.9)	**151** (0.3)	**149** (0.8)	**149** (1.0)	**149** (0.3)	**150** (0.7)	**146** (0.9)	**147** (0.6)
Sex									
Male	148 (1.3)	149 (1.1)	153 (0.3)	150 (0.9)	153 (1.1)	150 (0.4)	154 (1.0)	148 (1.1)	149 (0.7)
Female	146 (1.1)	145 (1.0)	149 (0.3)	148 (0.9)	146 (1.1)	147 (0.3)	147 (0.8)	145 (1.0)	145 (0.6)
Race/ethnicity									
White	158 (0.9)	159 (0.7)	162 (0.3)	159 (0.8)	161 (0.8)	160 (0.2)	159 (0.9)	153 (1.2)	156 (0.6)
Black	120 (1.3)	122 (1.0)	129 (0.6)	121 (0.9)	121 (1.4)	124 (0.4)	123 (1.1)	122 (1.7)	120 (0.9)
Hispanic	124 (3.0)	122 (2.3)	133 (0.5)	128 (2.7)	127 (1.4)	129 (0.5)	131 (2.2)	128 (1.7)	128 (1.3)
Asian/Pacific Islander	144 (3.7)	‡ (†)	158 (1.0)	151 (4.2)	153 (2.9)	156 (0.9)	147 (3.3)	149 (3.6)	153 (1.7)
American Indian	129 (11.9)	135 (6.9)	138 (1.9)	148 (3.5)	147 (6.7)	128 (4.0)	144 (7.5)	151 (3.6)	139 (5.3)
Parents' education									
Less than high school	— (†)	— (†)	— (†)	— (†)	— (†)	128 (0.5)	— (†)	— (†)	125 (1.4)
High school diploma or equivalent	— (†)	— (†)	— (†)	— (†)	— (†)	138 (0.5)	— (†)	— (†)	136 (0.9)
Some college	— (†)	— (†)	— (†)	— (†)	— (†)	151 (0.4)	— (†)	— (†)	148 (0.7)
Bachelor's degree or higher	— (†)	— (†)	— (†)	— (†)	— (†)	159 (0.3)	— (†)	— (†)	157 (0.6)
Eligible for free or reduced-price lunch									
Eligible	129 (1.7)	127 (1.3)	135 (0.3)	129 (1.6)	127 (1.1)	130 (0.3)	— (†)	— (†)	— (†)
Not eligible	159 (0.9)	158 (1.1)	162 (0.3)	156 (0.9)	159 (1.0)	159 (0.3)	— (†)	— (†)	— (†)
Information not available	151 (3.9)	160 (1.5)	160 (0.9)	157 (2.3)	155 (1.7)	160 (1.5)	— (†)	— (†)	— (†)
Percentile[2]									
10th	99 (2.1)	99 (1.7)	109 (0.5)	103 (1.5)	101 (1.2)	101 (0.6)	105 (1.4)	101 (1.4)	101 (1.2)
25th	125 (1.6)	125 (1.4)	130 (0.4)	127 (1.2)	126 (1.3)	126 (0.4)	128 (1.1)	124 (1.0)	125 (0.8)
50th	150 (1.2)	150 (0.9)	153 (0.4)	152 (0.7)	152 (0.9)	151 (0.3)	152 (1.2)	148 (1.0)	149 (0.8)
75th	172 (1.0)	172 (0.7)	173 (0.3)	174 (0.8)	175 (0.8)	174 (0.3)	174 (0.8)	170 (1.2)	171 (0.8)
90th	190 (0.8)	190 (1.0)	189 (0.3)	192 (0.8)	194 (1.0)	192 (0.3)	192 (0.9)	189 (1.2)	189 (1.2)
Percent attaining science achievement levels									
Achievement level									
Below Basic[3]	37 (1.4)	37 (1.2)	32 (0.4)	40 (1.0)	41 (1.2)	41 (0.4)	43 (1.0)	48 (1.2)	46 (0.8)
At or above Basic[3]	63 (1.4)	63 (1.2)	68 (0.4)	60 (1.0)	59 (1.2)	59 (0.4)	57 (1.0)	52 (1.2)	54 (0.8)
At or above Proficient[4]	28 (1.0)	27 (0.9)	29 (0.4)	29 (0.9)	30 (1.0)	29 (0.3)	21 (0.8)	18 (0.9)	18 (0.6)
At Advanced[5]	3 (0.3)	3 (0.4)	3 (0.1)	3 (0.3)	4 (0.3)	4 (0.1)	3 (0.3)	2 (0.3)	2 (0.2)

—Not available.

†Not applicable.

‡Reporting standards not met.

[1]Testing accommodations (e.g., extended time, small group testing) for children with disabilities and limited-English-proficient students were not permitted on the 1996 science assessment.

[2]The percentile represents a specific point on the percentage distribution of all students ranked by their science score from low to high. For example, 10 percent of students scored at or below the 10th percentile score, while 90 percent of students scored above it.

[3]Basic denotes partial mastery of the knowledge and skills that are fundamental for proficient work.

[4]Proficient represents solid academic performance. Students reaching this level have demonstrated competency over challenging subject matter.

[5]Advanced signifies superior performance.

NOTE: The NAEP science scale ranges from 0 to 300. Race categories exclude persons of Hispanic ethnicity. Standard errors appear in parentheses.

SOURCE: U.S. Department of Education, National Center for Education Statistics, National Assessment of Educational Progress (NAEP), NAEP Data Explorer (http://nces.ed.gov/nationsreportcard/nde/), retrieved November 2006. (This table was prepared November 2006.)

Average science scale score for 8th-graders in public schools, by selected student characteristics and state or jurisdiction: 1996, 2000, and 2005

State or jurisdiction	Average scale score 1996[1]	2000	2005	Sex, 2005 Male	Female	Race/ethnicity, 2005 White	Black	Hispanic	Asian/Pacific Islander	American Indian/Alaska Native	National School Lunch Program eligibility, 2005 Eligible	Not eligible
1	2	3	4	5	6	7	8	9	10	11	12	13
United States	148 (0.9)	148 (1.1)	147 (0.3)	149 (0.4)	145 (0.4)	159 (0.3)	123 (0.4)	127 (0.5)	155 (0.9)	134 (1.5)	130 (0.3)	158 (0.3)
Alabama	139 (1.6)	143[2] (1.7)	138 (1.3)	138 (1.6)	137 (1.4)	152 (1.3)	114 (1.5)	‡ (†)	‡ (†)	‡ (†)	123 (1.5)	152 (1.4)
Alaska	153[3] (1.3)	— (†)	— (†)	— (†)	— (†)	— (†)	— (†)	— (†)	‡ (†)	— (†)	— (†)	— (†)
Arizona	145[2] (1.6)	145[2,4] (1.3)	140 (0.9)	141 (1.1)	139 (1.2)	156 (1.0)	125 (3.5)	123 (1.2)	‡ (†)	121 (3.0)	124 (1.2)	152 (1.4)
Arkansas	144[3] (1.3)	142 (1.2)	144 (1.0)	146 (1.3)	142 (1.1)	155 (0.9)	113 (1.3)	136 (4.0)	‡ (†)	‡ (†)	131 (1.3)	157 (0.9)
California	138 (1.7)	129[2,4] (1.8)	136 (0.7)	138 (0.8)	135 (0.8)	154 (0.9)	120 (1.5)	122 (0.8)	152 (1.8)	132 (5.2)	121 (0.9)	150 (0.7)
Colorado	155 (0.9)	— (†)	155 (1.3)	158 (1.4)	152 (1.6)	166 (1.1)	133 (3.7)	134 (2.0)	158 (4.4)	‡ (†)	135 (1.9)	164 (1.2)
Connecticut	155 (1.3)	153 (1.6)	152 (1.0)	153 (1.6)	151 (1.1)	163 (0.9)	124 (2.2)	123 (2.7)	163 (3.6)	‡ (†)	127 (1.7)	161 (1.0)
Delaware	142[2] (0.8)	— (†)	152 (0.6)	154 (0.7)	150 (1.0)	162 (0.6)	134 (1.1)	136 (2.4)	165 (3.4)	‡ (†)	136 (1.0)	158 (0.7)
District of Columbia	113 (0.7)	— (†)	— (†)	— (†)	— (†)	— (†)	— (†)	— (†)	— (†)	— (†)	— (†)	— (†)
Florida	142 (1.6)	— (†)	141 (1.2)	142 (1.2)	140 (1.4)	155 (1.1)	118 (1.5)	131 (2.0)	149 (4.2)	‡ (†)	128 (1.2)	152 (1.2)
Georgia	142 (1.4)	142 (1.6)	144 (1.1)	145 (1.4)	142 (1.2)	159 (1.4)	125 (1.3)	127 (3.6)	163 (5.9)	‡ (†)	127 (1.0)	158 (1.3)
Hawaii	135 (0.7)	130[2] (1.4)	136 (0.8)	138 (1.4)	135 (0.9)	152 (1.7)	‡ (†)	131 (3.9)	133 (1.0)	‡ (†)	124 (1.2)	146 (0.9)
Idaho	— (†)	158[4] (1.0)	158 (1.0)	161 (1.4)	154 (1.0)	161 (0.9)	‡ (†)	131 (2.2)	‡ (†)	‡ (†)	147 (1.2)	164 (1.1)
Illinois	— (†)	148[4] (1.7)	148 (1.1)	150 (1.4)	146 (1.2)	161 (1.2)	120 (1.5)	130 (1.7)	164 (3.7)	‡ (†)	128 (1.2)	161 (1.2)
Indiana	153 (1.4)	154[2,4] (1.4)	150 (1.3)	154 (1.4)	147 (1.7)	156 (1.3)	119 (2.1)	131 (3.1)	‡ (†)	‡ (†)	135 (2.0)	159 (1.4)
Iowa	158[3] (1.2)	— (†)	— (†)	— (†)	— (†)	— (†)	— (†)	— (†)	— (†)	— (†)	— (†)	— (†)
Kansas	— (†)	— (†)	— (†)	— (†)	— (†)	— (†)	— (†)	— (†)	— (†)	— (†)	— (†)	— (†)
Kentucky	147[2] (1.2)	150[2] (1.2)	153 (0.9)	154 (1.3)	151 (1.0)	155 (0.9)	130 (2.4)	‡ (†)	‡ (†)	‡ (†)	145 (1.4)	159 (1.2)
Louisiana	132[2] (1.6)	134[2] (1.5)	138 (1.5)	141 (1.7)	136 (1.6)	153 (1.3)	120 (1.5)	‡ (†)	‡ (†)	‡ (†)	127 (1.4)	153 (1.4)
Maine	163[2] (1.0)	158[4] (0.9)	158 (0.7)	159 (1.0)	156 (1.1)	158 (0.8)	‡ (†)	‡ (†)	‡ (†)	‡ (†)	150 (1.2)	161 (0.8)
Maryland	145[3] (1.5)	146 (1.4)	145 (1.4)	145 (1.7)	144 (1.6)	160 (1.3)	123 (1.8)	132 (6.1)	165 (3.5)	‡ (†)	122 (2.4)	155 (1.3)
Massachusetts	157[2] (1.4)	158[2] (1.1)	161 (1.0)	162 (1.2)	160 (1.2)	168 (1.0)	133 (2.2)	133 (2.2)	166 (3.4)	‡ (†)	142 (2.1)	168 (1.2)
Michigan	153[3] (1.4)	155[4] (1.8)	155 (1.2)	156 (1.6)	154 (1.4)	163 (1.2)	128 (2.3)	132 (3.8)	‡ (†)	‡ (†)	140 (1.9)	161 (1.3)
Minnesota	159 (1.3)	159[4] (1.2)	158 (1.1)	161 (1.5)	155 (1.3)	166 (0.9)	120 (2.6)	133 (4.3)	137 (2.7)	‡ (†)	139 (1.5)	166 (1.1)
Mississippi	133 (1.4)	134 (1.2)	132 (1.3)	135 (1.5)	130 (1.3)	150 (1.0)	114 (1.5)	‡ (†)	‡ (†)	‡ (†)	121 (1.3)	151 (1.1)
Missouri	151 (1.2)	154 (1.5)	154 (1.2)	157 (1.3)	151 (1.4)	161 (0.9)	124 (2.8)	150 (4.9)	‡ (†)	‡ (†)	140 (2.1)	162 (1.3)
Montana	162[3] (1.2)	164[4] (1.4)	162 (0.8)	162 (1.2)	161 (1.0)	165 (0.7)	‡ (†)	‡ (†)	‡ (†)	135 (2.6)	149 (1.4)	168 (0.7)
Nebraska	157 (1.0)	158 (1.4)	— (†)	— (†)	— (†)	— (†)	— (†)	— (†)	— (†)	— (†)	— (†)	— (†)
Nevada	‡ (†)	141[2] (1.0)	138 (0.9)	139 (1.1)	138 (1.3)	150 (1.0)	115 (2.4)	122 (1.3)	150 (3.4)	‡ (†)	124 (1.3)	146 (1.0)
New Hampshire	‡ (†)	— (†)	162 (0.9)	163 (1.1)	161 (1.1)	163 (0.8)	‡ (†)	‡ (†)	‡ (†)	‡ (†)	149 (1.7)	165 (0.9)
New Jersey	‡ (†)	— (†)	153 (1.2)	157 (1.6)	150 (1.3)	165 (1.1)	131 (2.6)	133 (1.9)	172 (2.4)	‡ (†)	131 (1.9)	162 (1.2)
New Mexico	141[2] (1.0)	139 (1.5)	138 (0.9)	141 (1.2)	135 (1.3)	157 (1.3)	129 (4.5)	129 (1.1)	‡ (†)	124 (1.5)	129 (1.0)	153 (1.4)
New York	146[3] (1.6)	145[4] (2.1)	— (†)	— (†)	— (†)	— (†)	— (†)	— (†)	— (†)	— (†)	— (†)	— (†)
North Carolina	147 (1.2)	145 (1.4)	144 (1.0)	145 (1.3)	143 (1.1)	155 (0.8)	122 (1.6)	132 (3.2)	157 (9.9)	‡ (†)	129 (1.3)	154 (1.0)
North Dakota	162 (0.8)	159[2] (1.1)	163 (0.6)	165 (0.9)	161 (0.9)	166 (0.6)	‡ (†)	‡ (†)	‡ (†)	137 (3.2)	151 (1.5)	168 (0.6)
Ohio	— (†)	159 (1.5)	155 (1.2)	157 (1.7)	154 (1.3)	162 (1.0)	124 (3.3)	142 (5.6)	‡ (†)	‡ (†)	134 (1.8)	165 (1.0)
Oklahoma	— (†)	149 (1.1)	147 (1.3)	149 (1.4)	144 (1.5)	155 (1.1)	120 (2.7)	132 (3.1)	‡ (†)	139 (2.2)	137 (1.5)	156 (1.5)
Oregon	155 (1.6)	154[4] (1.3)	153 (1.0)	155 (1.4)	152 (1.3)	159 (0.9)	127 (5.5)	129 (3.1)	154 (4.6)	‡ (†)	141 (1.8)	160 (1.2)
Pennsylvania	— (†)	— (†)	— (†)	— (†)	— (†)	— (†)	— (†)	— (†)	— (†)	— (†)	— (†)	— (†)
Rhode Island	149[2] (0.8)	148 (0.9)	146 (0.7)	149 (0.9)	144 (0.9)	156 (0.7)	122 (2.2)	115 (1.8)	141 (4.7)	‡ (†)	127 (1.3)	155 (0.8)

See notes at end of table.

Average science scale score for 8th-graders in public schools, by selected student characteristics and state or jurisdiction: 1996, 2000, and 2005—Continued

State or jurisdiction	Average scale score			Sex, 2005		Race/ethnicity, 2005					National School Lunch Program eligibility, 2005	
	1996[1]	2000	2005	Male	Female	White	Black	Hispanic	Asian/ Pacific Islander	American Indian/ Alaska Native	Eligible	Not eligible
1	2	3	4	5	6	7	8	9	10	11	12	13
South Carolina	139[2,3] (1.5)	140[2] (1.4)	145 (1.1)	146 (1.5)	144 (1.2)	159 (1.3)	127 (1.4)	130 (5.9)	‡ (†)	‡ (†)	131 (1.2)	158 (1.2)
South Dakota	— (†)	— (†)	161 (0.7)	164 (1.0)	158 (0.9)	165 (0.7)	‡ (†)	‡ (†)	‡ (†)	133 (2.7)	149 (1.3)	168 (0.8)
Tennessee	143 (1.8)	145 (1.5)	145 (1.2)	146 (1.5)	144 (1.4)	153 (1.0)	119 (2.2)	‡ (†)	‡ (†)	‡ (†)	131 (1.5)	156 (1.3)
Texas	145 (1.8)	143 (1.7)	143 (0.8)	145 (1.1)	141 (0.9)	160 (0.9)	125 (1.5)	131 (1.1)	161 (3.8)	‡ (†)	129 (1.0)	156 (1.0)
Utah	156[2] (0.8)	154 (1.0)	154 (0.7)	155 (1.1)	152 (0.9)	158 (0.7)	‡ (†)	130 (2.4)	139 (3.9)	‡ (†)	142 (1.2)	160 (0.9)
Vermont	157[2,3] (1.0)	159[2,4] (1.0)	162 (0.6)	163 (0.9)	161 (0.8)	162 (0.6)	‡ (†)	‡ (†)	‡ (†)	‡ (†)	150 (1.3)	166 (0.6)
Virginia	149[2] (1.6)	151[2] (1.0)	155 (1.1)	157 (1.3)	153 (1.2)	165 (1.1)	133 (1.6)	141 (2.7)	161 (3.0)	‡ (†)	136 (1.4)	163 (1.1)
Washington	150[2] (1.3)	— (†)	154 (0.8)	155 (1.2)	153 (1.0)	160 (0.8)	137 (3.1)	128 (3.2)	149 (2.6)	135 (5.8)	140 (1.4)	161 (0.9)
West Virginia	147 (0.9)	146 (1.1)	147 (0.8)	150 (1.0)	144 (0.9)	148 (0.7)	128 (3.3)	‡ (†)	‡ (†)	‡ (†)	137 (0.9)	156 (0.9)
Wisconsin	160[3] (1.7)	‡ (†)	158 (1.0)	160 (1.3)	156 (1.2)	165 (0.8)	120 (3.1)	133 (3.1)	153 (4.1)	‡ (†)	137 (2.1)	165 (0.9)
Wyoming	158 (0.6)	156[2] (1.0)	159 (0.6)	161 (1.0)	157 (0.9)	161 (0.6)	‡ (†)	145 (2.3)	‡ (†)	145 (4.5)	148 (1.2)	164 (0.7)
Department of Defense dependents schools[5]	155[2] (0.6)	158[2] (0.7)	160 (0.7)	162 (1.1)	158 (1.0)	168 (0.9)	143 (0.7)	160 (1.9)	161 (2.6)	‡ (†)	‡ (†)	‡ (†)
Other jurisdictions												
American Samoa	— (†)	74 (4.2)	— (†)	— (†)	— (†)	— (†)	— (†)	— (†)	— (†)	— (†)	— (†)	— (†)
Guam	120 (1.1)	114 (1.8)	— (†)	— (†)	— (†)	— (†)	— (†)	— (†)	— (†)	— (†)	— (†)	— (†)

—Not available.
†Not applicable.
‡Reporting standards not met.
[1]Accommodations were not permitted for this assessment.
[2]Significantly different from 2005 when only one jurisdiction or the nation is being examined.
[3]Did not satisfy one or more of the guidelines for school participation in 1996. Data are subject to appreciable nonresponse bias.
[4]Did not satisfy one or more of the guidelines for school participation in 2000. Data are subject to appreciable nonresponse bias.
[5]Before 2005, Department of Defense domestic and overseas schools were separate jurisdictions in NAEP. Data for 1996 and 2000 were recalculated for comparability.

NOTE: Excludes persons not enrolled in school and those who were unable to be tested due to limited proficiency in English or due to a disability (if sample not tested with accommodations or if the accommodations provided in 2000 and 2005 were not sufficient to enable the test to properly reflect the students' science proficiency). Scale ranges from 0 to 300. Race categories exclude persons of Hispanic ethnicity. Standard errors appear in parentheses. Some data have been revised from previously published figures.

SOURCE: U.S. Department of Education, National Center for Education Statistics, National Assessment of Educational Progress (NAEP), NAEP 1996 Science Report Card for the Nation and the States, The Nation's Report Card: Science 2005, and the NAEP Data Explorer (http://nces.ed.gov/nationsreportcard/nde/, retrieved on December 4, 2006). (This table was prepared December 2006.)

Average arts scale score of 8th-graders, percentage distribution by frequency of instruction, and percentage participating in selected activities, by subject and selected student and school characteristics: 2008

Selected student or school characteristic	Average score — Music,[1] responding scale score (0 to 300)	Average score — Visual arts[2] Responding scale score (0 to 300)	Average score — Visual arts[2] Creating task score (0 to 100)	Music — Subject not offered	Music — Less than once a week	Music — Once or twice a week	Music — At least 3 or 4 times a week	Visual arts — Subject not offered	Visual arts — Less than once a week	Visual arts — Once or twice a week	Visual arts — At least 3 or 4 times a week	Play in band	Play in orchestra	Sing in chorus or choir
	2	3	4	5	6	7	8	9	10	11	12	13	14	15
All students	150 (1.2)	150 (1.2)	52 (0.6)	8 (2.0)	8 (2.0)	27 (3.1)	57 (3.2)	14 (2.4)	10 (2.5)	30 (3.5)	47 (3.9)	16 (0.9)	5 (0.5)	17 (1.2)
Sex														
Male	145 (1.3)	145 (1.4)	49 (0.7)	9 (2.1)	8 (2.1)	27 (3.1)	56 (3.2)	14 (2.6)	10 (2.5)	30 (3.6)	46 (4.1)	18 (1.0)	3 (0.5)	9 (1.2)
Female	155 (1.4)	155 (1.2)	54 (0.7)	8 (2.0)	7 (1.9)	28 (3.2)	57 (3.2)	13 (2.3)	10 (2.5)	29 (3.3)	48 (3.8)	14 (1.0)	6 (0.6)	26 (1.8)
Race/ethnicity														
White	161 (1.3)	160 (1.2)	55 (0.5)	6 (2.5)	8 (2.5)	29 (4.0)	57 (3.6)	11 (2.6)	11 (3.4)	34 (4.4)	44 (4.6)	19 (1.2)	5 (0.6)	19 (1.6)
Black	130 (2.0)	129 (2.4)	43 (1.5)	8 (2.9)	8 (4.5)	26 (5.5)	56 (7.0)	18 (4.9)	10 (4.9)	24 (4.5)	49 (5.7)	13 (1.2)	4 (1.0)	21 (1.9)
Hispanic	129 (1.9)	134 (1.9)	46 (1.1)	14 (4.3)	6 (2.3)	21 (4.1)	59 (4.5)	17 (4.5)	5 (2.0)	23 (4.7)	56 (6.0)	8 (1.2)	3 (0.6)	10 (1.6)
Asian/Pacific Islander	159 (4.7)	156 (4.2)	54 (2.0)	7 (4.1)	8 (3.4)	25 (6.6)	60 (8.7)	5 (2.5)	11 (4.6)	29 (6.0)	54 (8.4)	21 (3.5)	6 (2.1)	16 (2.9)
Free or reduced-price lunch eligibility														
Eligible	132 (1.3)	132 (1.4)	46 (1.0)	10 (2.1)	6 (2.1)	26 (3.4)	58 (3.9)	18 (3.4)	9 (3.2)	26 (3.7)	47 (4.7)	12 (1.2)	3 (0.6)	15 (1.4)
Not eligible	161 (1.4)	161 (1.2)	55 (0.6)	8 (2.6)	8 (2.6)	26 (4.0)	59 (4.0)	10 (2.4)	10 (3.2)	30 (4.1)	50 (4.6)	19 (1.0)	5 (0.6)	19 (1.6)
Unknown	156 (5.6)	156 (5.9)	57 (2.6)	4 (†)	19 (8.7)	54 (11.5)	23 (10.5)	16 (10.3)	13 (8.4)	47 (13.6)	24 (10.6)	14 (6.3)	5 (2.3)	13 (2.0)
Control of school														
Public	149 (1.3)	149 (1.2)	51 (0.7)	8 (2.1)	7 (2.1)	24 (3.2)	61 (3.5)	13 (2.4)	10 (2.7)	26 (3.5)	51 (4.2)	17 (0.9)	5 (0.5)	18 (1.3)
Private	163 (2.8)	159 (5.2)	60 (1.3)	10 (6.0)	15 (6.9)	71 (8.8)	3 (†)	17 (8.2)	10 (6.1)	70 (10.2)	3 (0.9)	9 (1.9)	1 (0.4)	13 (2.1)
School location														
City	142 (2.0)	144 (2.1)	49 (1.2)	13 (4.0)	10 (3.8)	24 (5.7)	52 (5.6)	12 (2.6)	9 (3.5)	24 (4.9)	55 (5.4)	14 (1.0)	4 (0.6)	13 (1.3)
Suburban	155 (1.9)	155 (1.8)	54 (0.7)	3 (2.2)	7 (3.5)	32 (5.6)	57 (6.3)	10 (3.1)	10 (4.6)	33 (6.4)	46 (6.1)	14 (1.5)	6 (1.0)	16 (1.6)
Town	156 (3.5)	149 (2.8)	50 (1.2)	4 (1.0)	# (†)	18 (9.0)	78 (9.0)	16 (8.4)	# (†)	23 (9.2)	60 (10.5)	23 (3.0)	4 (1.3)	23 (3.4)
Rural	150 (2.6)	151 (3.0)	52 (1.5)	13 (5.0)	8 (4.8)	29 (5.7)	50 (7.7)	20 (7.3)	17 (6.8)	35 (7.8)	28 (6.7)	18 (2.5)	3 (1.0)	21 (3.4)
Region														
Northeast	154 (3.1)	160 (2.3)	52 (0.9)	10 (5.3)	13 (5.8)	40 (9.0)	37 (8.6)	5 (3.3)	5 (†)	50 (6.2)	39 (9.3)	16 (2.7)	6 (0.9)	17 (2.6)
Midwest	158 (2.9)	155 (2.3)	53 (1.3)	12 (6.6)	# (†)	25 (7.2)	63 (5.8)	9 (2.0)	15 (7.7)	26 (6.7)	50 (7.3)	22 (2.1)	6 (1.3)	24 (3.1)
South	147 (1.9)	147 (2.2)	51 (1.0)	6 (1.8)	10 (4.0)	25 (3.9)	59 (5.7)	19 (5.3)	9 (3.8)	26 (5.0)	46 (6.4)	16 (1.2)	4 (0.6)	16 (2.0)
West	144 (2.0)	143 (2.1)	51 (1.1)	8 (3.7)	8 (3.5)	24 (6.9)	60 (5.4)	15 (4.9)	9 (4.0)	25 (9.0)	51 (8.2)	9 (1.2)	3 (0.6)	12 (1.7)
Frequency of instruction														
Subject not offered	139 (6.3)	138 (4.2)	‡ (†)	‡ (†)	‡ (†)	‡ (†)	‡ (†)	‡ (†)	‡ (†)	‡ (†)	‡ (†)	17 (4.0)	4 (1.5)	11 (2.1)
Less than once a week	149 (6.4)	154 (5.3)	‡ (†)	‡ (†)	‡ (†)	‡ (†)	‡ (†)	‡ (†)	‡ (†)	‡ (†)	‡ (†)	11 (2.4)	4 (1.5)	10 (2.0)
Once or twice a week	152 (2.8)	154 (2.6)	‡ (†)	‡ (†)	‡ (†)	‡ (†)	‡ (†)	‡ (†)	‡ (†)	‡ (†)	‡ (†)	12 (1.7)	3 (0.8)	17 (2.2)
At least 3 or 4 times a week	149 (1.8)	149 (1.8)	‡ (†)	‡ (†)	‡ (†)	‡ (†)	‡ (†)	‡ (†)	‡ (†)	‡ (†)	‡ (†)	17 (1.4)	5 (0.7)	20 (1.6)

†Not applicable.
#Rounds to zero.
‡Reporting standards not met.
[1]Students were asked to analyze and describe aspects of music they heard, critique instrumental and vocal performances, and demonstrate their knowledge of standard musical notation and music's role in society.
[2]Responding questions asked students to analyze and describe works of art and design, while creating questions required students to create works of art and design of their own.

NOTE: Excludes students unable to be tested due to limited proficiency in English or due to a disability (if the accommodations provided were not sufficient to enable the test to properly reflect the students' music or visual arts proficiency). Detail may not sum to totals because of rounding. Race categories exclude persons of Hispanic ethnicity. Totals include other racial/ethnic groups not shown separately. Standard errors appear in parentheses.
SOURCE: U.S. Department of Education, National Center for Education Statistics, National Assessment of Educational Progress (NAEP), 2008 Arts Assessment, retrieved June 30, 2009, from the Main NAEP Data Explorer (http://nces.ed.gov/nationsreportcard/naepdata/). (This table was prepared June 2009.)

Percentage of students attaining U.S. history achievement levels, by grade level and selected student characteristics: 2001 and 2006

Selected student characteristic	Percent of 4th-graders					Percent of 8th-graders					Percent of 12th-graders				
	2001, At or above Basic[1]	2006				2001, At or above Basic[1]	2006				2001, At or above Basic[1]	2006			
		Below Basic	At or above Basic[1]	At or above Proficient[2]	At Advanced[3]		Below Basic	At or above Basic[1]	At or above Proficient[2]	At Advanced[3]		Below Basic	At or above Basic[1]	At or above Proficient[2]	At Advanced[3]
1	2	3	4	5	6	7	8	9	10	11	12	13	14	15	16
All students	66 (1.2)	30 (1.3)	70 (1.3)	18 (1.0)	2 (0.3)	62 (1.0)	35 (1.0)	65 (1.0)	17 (0.8)	1 (0.1)	43 (1.2)	53 (1.1)	47 (1.1)	13 (0.7)	1 (0.2)
Sex															
Male	65 (1.3)	31 (1.5)	69 (1.5)	20 (1.3)	2 (0.4)	62 (1.1)	33 (1.3)	67 (1.3)	19 (1.0)	2 (0.2)	45 (1.6)	50 (1.2)	50 (1.2)	15 (0.8)	1 (0.2)
Female	67 (1.4)	30 (1.2)	70 (1.2)	16 (1.0)	1 (0.3)	61 (1.2)	36 (1.0)	64 (1.0)	14 (0.7)	1 (0.2)	40 (1.2)	56 (1.2)	44 (1.2)	11 (0.7)	1 (0.2)
Race/ethnicity															
White	76 (1.5)	16 (1.2)	84 (1.2)	26 (1.5)	2 (0.4)	71 (1.1)	21 (0.8)	79 (0.8)	23 (1.1)	2 (0.2)	49 (1.3)	44 (1.3)	56 (1.3)	16 (0.8)	1 (0.2)
Black	41 (2.3)	54 (2.5)	46 (2.5)	5 (1.0)	# (†)	35 (2.1)	60 (1.7)	40 (1.7)	4 (0.5)	# (†)	19 (1.5)	80 (1.3)	20 (1.6)	2 (0.5)	# (†)
Hispanic	40 (2.8)	51 (2.7)	49 (2.7)	6 (0.7)	1 (0.2)	36 (2.6)	54 (2.2)	46 (2.2)	6 (0.8)	# (0.1)	24 (2.3)	73 (1.4)	27 (1.4)	4 (0.6)	# (†)
Asian/Pacific Islander	74 (4.5)	29 (4.8)	71 (4.8)	22 (4.3)	2 (—)	65 (3.0)	25 (4.4)	75 (4.4)	22 (3.0)	1 (0.6)	51 (6.7)	46 (3.5)	54 (3.5)	20 (3.1)	3 (0.7)
American Indian/Alaska Native	‡ (†)	59 (7.7)	41 (7.7)	6 (3.2)	# (†)	57 (6.5)	57 (6.1)	43 (6.1)	5 (—)	# (†)	37 (7.8)	68 (7.3)	32 (7.3)	4 (2.9)	# (†)
Parents' highest level of education															
Not high school graduate	—	— (†)	— (†)	— (†)	— (†)	38 (4.1)	60 (2.2)	40 (2.2)	3 (0.9)	# (†)	19 (2.1)	82 (1.7)	18 (1.7)	3 (0.8)	# (†)
Graduated high school	—	— (†)	— (†)	— (†)	— (†)	50 (1.8)	48 (2.2)	52 (2.2)	7 (0.7)	# (†)	25 (1.6)	69 (1.4)	31 (1.4)	5 (0.7)	# (†)
Some college	—	— (†)	— (†)	— (†)	— (†)	69 (1.5)	30 (1.3)	70 (1.3)	14 (1.2)	1 (0.3)	39 (1.3)	55 (1.4)	45 (1.4)	9 (0.8)	# (†)
Graduated college	—	— (†)	— (†)	— (†)	— (†)	77 (1.0)	21 (1.1)	79 (1.1)	27 (1.1)	2 (0.3)	58 (1.5)	40 (1.4)	60 (1.4)	20 (1.1)	2 (0.3)
Free/reduced-price lunch eligibility															
Eligible	45 (1.7)	49 (1.6)	51 (1.6)	6 (0.5)	# (†)	38 (1.7)	56 (1.6)	44 (1.6)	5 (0.5)	# (†)	22 (1.9)	76 (1.3)	24 (1.3)	3 (0.5)	# (†)
Not eligible	79 (1.6)	16 (1.1)	84 (1.1)	27 (1.5)	3 (0.4)	71 (1.6)	22 (0.8)	78 (0.8)	23 (1.0)	2 (0.2)	44 (1.5)	48 (1.2)	52 (1.2)	15 (0.9)	1 (0.2)
Not available	74 (2.8)	15 (4.0)	85 (4.0)	33 (4.7)	5 (1.7)	68 (2.2)	14 (3.2)	86 (3.2)	33 (3.8)	4 (1.1)	52 (2.9)	38 (3.7)	62 (3.7)	19 (2.6)	1 (0.5)
Region															
Northeast	— (†)	25 (2.5)	75 (2.5)	19 (1.5)	2 (0.5)	— (†)	31 (2.4)	69 (2.4)	21 (2.1)	2 (0.4)	— (†)	44 (3.0)	56 (3.0)	19 (1.9)	2 (0.5)
Midwest	— (†)	20 (2.1)	80 (2.1)	25 (2.8)	2 (0.7)	— (†)	27 (1.8)	73 (1.8)	21 (1.7)	1 (0.3)	— (†)	50 (1.3)	50 (1.3)	14 (1.0)	1 (0.2)
South	— (†)	29 (2.1)	71 (2.1)	18 (2.0)	2 (0.5)	— (†)	36 (1.5)	64 (1.5)	15 (1.0)	1 (0.2)	— (†)	59 (2.0)	41 (2.0)	11 (1.0)	1 (0.2)
West	— (†)	45 (3.8)	55 (3.8)	11 (1.6)	1 (0.3)	— (†)	44 (2.6)	56 (2.6)	11 (1.3)	1 (0.2)	— (†)	‡ (†)	‡ (†)	‡ (†)	‡ (†)

—Not available.
†Not applicable.
#Rounds to zero.
‡Reporting standards not met.
[1]Basic denotes partial mastery of the knowledge and skills that are fundamental for proficient work at a given grade.
[2]Proficient represents solid academic performance. Students reaching this level have demonstrated competency over challenging subject matter.
[3]Advanced signifies superior performance for a given grade.

NOTE: Includes public and private schools. Excludes students unable to be tested due to limited proficiency in English or due to a disability (if the accommodations provided were not sufficient to enable the test to properly reflect the students' U.S. history proficiency). Race categories exclude persons of Hispanic ethnicity. Totals include other racial/ethnic groups not shown separately. Standard errors appear in parentheses. Some data have been revised from previously published figures.
SOURCE: U.S. Department of Education, National Center for Education Statistics, National Assessment of Educational Progress (NAEP), 2001 and 2006 U.S. History Assessments, retrieved May 22, 2007, from the NAEP Data Explorer (http://nces.ed.gov/nationsreportcard/nde/). (This table was prepared May 2007.)

Average U.S. history scale score, by grade level and selected student characteristics, and percentage distribution of 12th-graders, by selected student characteristics: 1994, 2001, and 2006

Selected student characteristic	4th-graders			8th-graders			12th-graders			Percentage distribution of 12th-graders		
	1994[1]	2001	2006	1994[1]	2001	2006	1994[1]	2001	2006	1994[1]	2001	2006
1	2	3	4	5	6	7	8	9	10	11	12	13
All students	205 (1.0)	208 (0.9)	211 (1.1)	259 (0.6)	260 (0.8)	263 (0.8)	286 (0.8)	287 (0.9)	290 (0.7)	100 (†)	100 (†)	100 (†)
Sex												
Male	203 (1.5)	207 (1.1)	211 (1.2)	259 (0.8)	261 (0.9)	264 (0.9)	288 (0.8)	288 (1.1)	292 (0.9)	50 (0.8)	50 (0.7)	50 (0.4)
Female	206 (1.1)	209 (1.2)	211 (1.1)	259 (0.7)	260 (0.9)	261 (0.8)	285 (0.9)	286 (0.9)	288 (0.8)	50 (0.8)	50 (0.7)	50 (0.4)
Race/ethnicity												
White	214 (1.3)	217 (1.3)	223 (1.1)	266 (0.8)	268 (0.9)	273 (0.6)	292 (0.8)	292 (1.0)	297 (0.8)	75 (0.5)	72 (0.5)	66 (1.3)
Black	176 (1.6)	186 (2.0)	191 (1.9)	238 (1.6)	240 (1.9)	244 (1.2)	265 (1.5)	267 (1.4)	270 (1.3)	13 (0.3)	13 (0.2)	13 (0.9)
Hispanic	175 (2.6)	184 (2.6)	194 (1.9)	243 (1.4)	240 (2.0)	248 (1.2)	267 (1.7)	271 (1.9)	275 (1.0)	7 (0.5)	9 (0.4)	13 (1.2)
Asian/Pacific Islander	204 (3.6)	216 (3.7)	214 (5.1)	261 (5.0)	264 (2.8)	270 (3.0)	283 (3.5)	294 (6.0)	296 (2.6)	4 (0.3)	4 (0.3)	6 (0.6)
American Indian/Alaska Native	‡ (†)	‡ (†)	190 (5.9)	245 (3.4)	255 (4.4)	244 (6.3)	272 (3.0)	283 (4.2)	278 (4.1)	1 (0.3)	1 (0.2)	2 (0.7)
Parents' highest level of education												
Not high school graduate	— (†)	— (†)	†	241 (1.3)	241 (2.8)	244 (1.2)	263 (1.4)	266 (1.6)	268 (1.3)	7 (0.4)	7 (0.4)	8 (0.4)
Graduated high school	— (†)	— (†)	†	251 (0.8)	251 (1.0)	252 (1.3)	276 (1.1)	274 (1.1)	278 (1.0)	20 (0.7)	19 (0.6)	18 (0.6)
Some college	— (†)	— (†)	†	264 (0.8)	264 (1.0)	265 (0.9)	287 (1.2)	286 (0.8)	290 (0.8)	25 (0.5)	24 (0.7)	23 (0.6)
Graduated college	— (†)	— (†)	†	270 (0.8)	273 (0.9)	274 (0.8)	296 (0.9)	298 (1.2)	300 (0.8)	45 (1.0)	46 (1.1)	49 (1.0)
Free/reduced-price lunch eligibility												
Eligible	— (†)	188 (1.4)	195 (1.1)	— (†)	242 (1.3)	247 (1.1)	— (†)	269 (1.4)	273 (1.0)	— (†)	15 (0.9)	22 (1.0)
Not eligible	— (†)	219 (1.4)	224 (1.0)	— (†)	267 (1.1)	273 (0.7)	— (†)	289 (1.2)	295 (0.8)	— (†)	64 (2.2)	67 (1.4)
Not available	— (†)	217 (2.8)	227 (3.9)	— (†)	266 (2.0)	281 (2.7)	— (†)	294 (2.1)	300 (2.4)	— (†)	21 (2.5)	11 (1.3)
Region												
Northeast	— (†)	— (†)	215 (1.7)	— (†)	— (†)	267 (1.8)	— (†)	— (†)	297 (2.2)	— (†)	— (†)	20 (0.8)
Midwest	— (†)	— (†)	220 (2.2)	— (†)	— (†)	269 (1.4)	— (†)	— (†)	292 (1.1)	— (†)	— (†)	23 (0.7)
South	— (†)	— (†)	213 (2.0)	— (†)	— (†)	262 (1.2)	— (†)	— (†)	286 (1.4)	— (†)	— (†)	33 (0.8)
West	— (†)	— (†)	199 (2.9)	— (†)	— (†)	255 (1.9)	— (†)	— (†)	‡ (†)	— (†)	— (†)	‡ (†)

—Not available.
†Not applicable.
‡Reporting standards not met.
[1]Accommodations were not permitted for this assessment.
NOTE: Scale ranges from 0 to 500. Includes public and private schools. Excludes students unable to be tested due to limited proficiency in English or due to a disability (if the accommodations provided were not sufficient to enable the test to properly reflect the students' proficiency in U.S. history). Race categories exclude persons of Hispanic ethnicity. Totals include other racial/ethnic groups not shown separately. Detail may not sum to totals because of rounding. Standard errors appear in parentheses. Some data have been modified from previously published figures.
SOURCE: U.S. Department of Education, National Center for Education Statistics, National Assessment of Educational Progress (NAEP), 1994, 2001, and 2006 U.S. History Assessments, retrieved June 6, 2007, from the NAEP Data Explorer (http://nces.ed.gov/nationsreportcard/nde/). (This table was prepared June 2007.)

Average civics scale score and percentage of students attaining civics achievement levels, by grade level and selected student characteristics: 1998 and 2006

Selected student characteristic	Average scale score[1]				At or above Basic[2]				At or above Proficient[3]				At Advanced[4]			
	1998[5]		2006		1998[5]		2006		1998[5]		2006		1998[5]		2006	
1	2		3		4		5		6		7		8		9	
4th-graders	**150**	**(0.7)**	**154**	**(1.0)**	**69**	**(1.0)**	**73**	**(1.2)**	**23**	**(0.9)**	**24**	**(1.0)**	**2**	**(0.3)**	**1**	**(0.2)**
Sex																
Male	149	(1.0)	153	(1.1)	68	(1.2)	72	(1.3)	22	(1.2)	24	(1.2)	2	(0.4)	1	(0.3)
Female	151	(0.9)	155	(1.1)	70	(1.0)	75	(1.4)	23	(1.2)	24	(1.2)	1	(0.4)	1	(0.2)
Race/ethnicity																
White	158	(0.9)	164	(0.9)	78	(1.3)	85	(1.0)	29	(1.2)	34	(1.4)	2	(0.4)	2	(0.3)
Black	130	(1.1)	140	(1.5)	45	(1.7)	57	(2.3)	7	(1.1)	10	(1.2)	1	(0.3)	#	(†)
Hispanic	123	(2.2)	138	(1.3)	40	(2.8)	55	(2.0)	6	(1.1)	10	(1.1)	#	(†)	#	(0.1)
Asian/Pacific Islander	147	(4.0)	154	(3.8)	66	(5.5)	75	(4.5)	20	(3.5)	24	(4.0)	2	(0.9)	1	(0.6)
American Indian/Alaska Native	‡	(†)	124	(7.6)	‡	(†)	38	(11.3)	‡	(†)	7	(3.9)	‡	(†)	#	(†)
Free/reduced-price lunch eligibility																
Eligible	132	(0.9)	139	(1.1)	49	(1.3)	56	(1.6)	9	(0.9)	9	(0.8)	#	(†)	#	(†)
Not eligible	160	(1.1)	166	(0.8)	80	(1.4)	87	(0.9)	30	(1.3)	36	(1.4)	2	(0.5)	2	(0.3)
Not available	154	(2.2)	167	(2.1)	72	(3.1)	88	(2.2)	27	(2.5)	37	(4.0)	2	(0.9)	3	(1.4)
8th-graders	**150**	**(0.7)**	**150**	**(0.8)**	**70**	**(0.9)**	**70**	**(1.1)**	**22**	**(0.8)**	**22**	**(0.8)**	**2**	**(0.2)**	**2**	**(0.2)**
Sex																
Male	148	(0.9)	149	(1.0)	67	(1.1)	68	(1.3)	22	(1.0)	23	(0.9)	2	(0.3)	2	(0.3)
Female	152	(0.8)	151	(0.8)	73	(1.2)	72	(1.2)	22	(1.1)	21	(0.9)	1	(0.3)	1	(0.2)
Race/ethnicity																
White	158	(0.9)	161	(0.8)	78	(1.1)	82	(0.9)	28	(1.0)	30	(1.0)	2	(0.3)	2	(0.3)
Black	131	(1.2)	133	(1.5)	49	(1.7)	50	(2.0)	7	(1.0)	9	(1.1)	#	(†)	#	(0.2)
Hispanic	127	(1.3)	131	(1.1)	44	(2.3)	50	(2.2)	7	(1.0)	8	(1.0)	#	(0.2)	#	(†)
Asian/Pacific Islander	151	(8.9)	154	(3.2)	69	(9.5)	73	(4.0)	25	(5.8)	27	(3.2)	3	(1.3)	3	(0.9)
American Indian/Alaska Native	‡	(†)	127	(7.3)	‡	(†)	46	(9.5)	‡	(†)	7	(2.9)	‡	(†)	#	(†)
Parents' highest level of education																
Not high school graduate	—	(†)	129	(1.6)	—	(†)	47	(3.3)	—	(†)	6	(1.0)	—	(†)	#	(†)
Graduated high school	—	(†)	140	(1.3)	—	(†)	59	(1.8)	—	(†)	11	(1.0)	—	(†)	#	(0.2)
Some college	—	(†)	153	(1.0)	—	(†)	75	(1.7)	—	(†)	20	(1.3)	—	(†)	1	(0.3)
Graduated college	—	(†)	162	(0.9)	—	(†)	82	(0.9)	—	(†)	33	(1.2)	—	(†)	3	(0.4)
Free/reduced-price lunch eligibility																
Eligible	131	(1.1)	132	(1.0)	48	(1.6)	51	(1.5)	8	(0.8)	8	(0.5)	#	(0.2)	#	(0.1)
Not eligible	157	(1.0)	160	(0.8)	78	(1.2)	82	(1.0)	27	(1.2)	29	(0.9)	2	(0.3)	2	(0.3)
Not available	156	(2.2)	171	(2.4)	76	(2.7)	90	(2.2)	29	(2.1)	44	(4.1)	3	(0.6)	5	(1.8)
12th-graders	**150**	**(0.8)**	**151**	**(0.9)**	**65**	**(0.9)**	**66**	**(1.1)**	**26**	**(0.9)**	**27**	**(1.0)**	**4**	**(0.4)**	**5**	**(0.4)**
Sex																
Male	148	(1.1)	150	(1.1)	62	(1.2)	64	(1.5)	27	(1.2)	28	(1.2)	5	(0.6)	5	(0.5)
Female	152	(0.8)	152	(1.0)	68	(1.2)	67	(1.2)	26	(1.1)	26	(1.2)	3	(0.4)	4	(0.5)
Race/ethnicity																
White	157	(1.0)	158	(1.0)	73	(1.1)	74	(1.2)	32	(1.3)	34	(1.2)	5	(0.6)	6	(0.6)
Black	130	(1.6)	131	(1.4)	41	(2.0)	42	(1.9)	9	(1.3)	9	(1.1)	1	(0.3)	1	(0.3)
Hispanic	132	(1.1)	134	(1.1)	45	(1.9)	46	(1.7)	10	(1.2)	12	(1.2)	1	(0.3)	1	(0.3)
Asian/Pacific Islander	149	(5.2)	155	(3.1)	63	(4.8)	68	(3.7)	27	(6.6)	33	(3.9)	5	(2.3)	8	(1.6)
American Indian/Alaska Native	‡	(†)	131	(3.5)	‡	(†)	42	(8.0)	‡	(†)	9	(3.0)	‡	(†)	#	(†)
Parents' highest level of education																
Not high school graduate	—	(†)	126	(1.8)	—	(†)	35	(3.0)	—	(†)	8	(1.4)	—	(†)	1	(0.5)
Graduated high school	—	(†)	138	(1.0)	—	(†)	52	(1.6)	—	(†)	13	(1.2)	—	(†)	1	(0.3)
Some college	—	(†)	150	(0.9)	—	(†)	66	(1.4)	—	(†)	23	(1.2)	—	(†)	3	(0.5)
Graduated college	—	(†)	162	(1.1)	—	(†)	77	(1.2)	—	(†)	39	(1.4)	—	(†)	8	(0.7)
Free/reduced-price lunch eligibility																
Eligible	130	(1.4)	133	(1.0)	42	(2.1)	45	(1.5)	10	(1.7)	11	(1.1)	1	(0.4)	1	(0.4)
Not eligible	153	(1.0)	156	(1.0)	69	(1.1)	71	(1.2)	29	(1.3)	31	(1.2)	5	(0.5)	6	(0.5)
Not available	153	(1.3)	160	(2.4)	68	(1.6)	76	(3.1)	29	(1.5)	34	(2.8)	5	(0.7)	7	(1.3)

—Not available.

\#Rounds to zero.

†Not applicable.

‡Reporting standards not met.

[1]Scale ranges from 0 to 300.

[2]Basic denotes partial mastery of the knowledge and skills that are fundamental for proficient work at a given grade.

[3]Proficient represents solid academic performance. Students reaching this level have demonstrated competency over challenging subject matter.

[4]Advanced signifies superior performance for a given grade.

[5]Accommodations were not permitted for this assessment.

NOTE: Includes public and private schools. Excludes students unable to be tested due to limited proficiency in English or due to a disability (if the accommodations provided were not sufficient to enable the test to properly reflect the students' proficiency in civics). Race categories exclude persons of Hispanic ethnicity. Totals include other racial/ethnic groups not shown separately. Standard errors appear in parentheses.

SOURCE: U.S. Department of Education, National Center for Education Statistics, National Assessment of Educational Progress (NAEP), 1998 and 2006 Civics Assessments, retrieved July 3, 2007, from the NAEP Data Explorer (http://nces.ed.gov/nationsreportcard/nde/). (This table was prepared July 2007.)

Average economics scale score of 12th-graders, percentage attaining economics achievement levels, and percentage with different levels of economics coursework, by selected student and school characteristics: 2006

Selected student or school characteristic	Average scale score[1]		Percent of students attaining achievement levels								Percentage distribution of students by highest level of economics coursework taken									
			Below Basic		At or above Basic[2]		At or above Proficient[3]		At Advanced[4]		No economics courses		Combined course		Consumer economics/business		General economics		Advanced economics[5]	
1	2		3		4		5		6		7		8		9		10		11	
All students	**150**	**(0.9)**	**21**	**(0.8)**	**79**	**(0.8)**	**42**	**(1.1)**	**3**	**(0.3)**	**13**	**(0.9)**	**12**	**(0.7)**	**11**	**(0.7)**	**49**	**(1.4)**	**16**	**(0.7)**
Sex																				
Male	152	(1.0)	21	(0.8)	79	(0.8)	45	(1.3)	4	(0.5)	13	(1.0)	10	(0.6)	10	(0.7)	50	(1.4)	16	(0.8)
Female	148	(0.9)	21	(0.9)	79	(0.9)	38	(1.3)	2	(0.3)	12	(0.9)	13	(0.9)	11	(0.8)	48	(1.6)	15	(0.8)
Race/ethnicity																				
White	158	(0.8)	13	(0.7)	87	(0.7)	51	(1.2)	4	(0.4)	15	(1.1)	12	(0.8)	11	(0.8)	49	(1.6)	13	(0.9)
Black	127	(1.2)	43	(1.9)	57	(1.9)	16	(1.3)	#	(†)	8	(0.8)	11	(0.9)	11	(1.2)	49	(1.7)	21	(1.1)
Hispanic	133	(1.2)	36	(1.6)	64	(1.6)	21	(1.2)	#	(†)	8	(1.7)	13	(1.1)	7	(0.9)	55	(2.6)	18	(1.2)
Asian/Pacific Islander	153	(3.5)	20	(4.0)	80	(4.0)	44	(4.5)	4	(1.4)	13	(1.8)	10	(1.8)	10	(1.4)	45	(4.1)	22	(1.9)
American Indian/Alaska Native	137	(4.1)	28	(5.6)	72	(5.6)	26	(4.8)	2	(—)	11	(3.9)	18	(2.7)	17	(3.2)	41	(4.9)	13	(3.1)
Parents' highest level of education																				
Not high school graduate	129	(1.4)	41	(2.1)	59	(2.1)	17	(1.7)	#	(†)	10	(1.7)	13	(1.4)	10	(1.4)	53	(3.2)	14	(1.3)
Graduated high school	138	(1.2)	31	(1.5)	69	(1.5)	27	(1.4)	1	(0.3)	11	(1.2)	12	(1.0)	12	(1.0)	52	(1.7)	13	(0.9)
Some college	150	(0.8)	18	(1.1)	82	(1.1)	39	(1.4)	1	(0.4)	11	(1.0)	13	(0.9)	12	(1.0)	51	(1.9)	14	(1.0)
Graduated college	160	(0.9)	13	(0.8)	87	(0.8)	54	(1.3)	5	(0.6)	14	(1.0)	11	(0.8)	10	(0.7)	47	(1.5)	17	(1.0)
Free/reduced-price lunch eligibility																				
Eligible	132	(0.9)	38	(1.1)	62	(1.1)	20	(1.1)	1	(0.2)	9	(0.7)	13	(1.1)	10	(0.9)	50	(1.6)	18	(0.8)
Not eligible	155	(0.9)	16	(0.8)	84	(0.8)	48	(1.2)	4	(0.4)	13	(1.1)	12	(0.8)	12	(0.9)	48	(1.6)	16	(0.9)
Not available	157	(1.9)	14	(1.7)	86	(1.7)	50	(2.8)	4	(1.1)	16	(3.0)	12	(1.6)	7	(1.1)	54	(3.1)	11	(1.4)
School location																				
Central city	148	(1.4)	24	(1.3)	76	(1.3)	39	(1.8)	3	(0.7)	10	(1.3)	12	(1.2)	9	(1.0)	51	(2.7)	18	(1.3)
Urban fringe	152	(1.2)	20	(1.1)	80	(1.1)	44	(1.6)	3	(0.5)	14	(1.5)	12	(0.9)	11	(0.9)	47	(1.8)	17	(1.2)
Rural	149	(1.3)	20	(1.5)	80	(1.5)	40	(1.7)	2	(0.4)	12	(1.9)	12	(1.3)	13	(1.3)	51	(2.6)	12	(1.2)
Region																				
Northeast	153	(2.0)	19	(1.7)	81	(1.7)	46	(2.6)	4	(0.9)	26	(2.6)	7	(1.1)	11	(1.3)	43	(3.2)	13	(1.4)
Midwest	153	(1.5)	17	(1.4)	83	(1.4)	45	(2.0)	3	(0.6)	12	(2.2)	12	(1.6)	15	(1.5)	51	(2.6)	10	(1.0)
South	147	(1.4)	23	(1.4)	77	(1.4)	37	(1.7)	2	(0.5)	6	(1.1)	14	(1.2)	9	(1.3)	49	(2.0)	22	(1.5)
West	‡	(†)	‡	(†)	‡	(†)	‡	(†)	‡	(†)	‡	(†)	‡	(†)	‡	(†)	‡	(†)	‡	(†)

—Not available.

†Not applicable.

#Rounds to zero.

‡Reporting standards not met.

[1]Scale ranges from 0 to 300.

[2]Basic denotes partial mastery of the knowledge and skills that are fundamental for proficient work at a given grade.

[3]Proficient represents solid academic performance. Students reaching this level have demonstrated competency over challenging subject matter.

[4]Advanced signifies superior performance for a given grade.

[5]Advanced economics includes Advanced Placement, International Baccalaureate, and honors courses.

NOTE: Includes public and private schools. Excludes persons unable to be tested due to limited proficiency in English or due to a disability (if the accommodations provided were not sufficient to enable the test to properly reflect the students' economics proficiency). Detail may not sum to totals due to rounding. Race categories exclude persons of Hispanic ethnicity. Totals include other racial/ethnic groups not shown separately. Standard errors appear in parentheses.

SOURCE: U.S. Department of Education, National Center for Education Statistics, National Assessment of Educational Progress (NAEP), 2006 Economics Assessment, retrieved August 23, 2007, from the NAEP Data Explorer (http://nces.ed.gov/nationsreportcard/ndel). (This table was prepared August 2007.)

Percentage of students attaining geography achievement levels, by grade level and selected student characteristics: 2001

Selected student characteristic	Percent of 4th-graders				Percent of 8th-graders				Percent of 12th-graders			
	Below Basic	At or above Basic	At or above Proficient	At Advanced	Below Basic	At or above Basic	At or above Proficient	At Advanced	Below Basic	At or above Basic	At or above Proficient	At Advanced
1	2	3	4	5	6	7	8	9	10	11	12	13
All students	26 (1.2)	74 (1.2)	21 (1.0)	2 (0.3)	26 (0.9)	74 (0.9)	30 (1.2)	4 (0.6)	29 (0.9)	71 (0.9)	25 (1.1)	1 (0.3)
Sex												
Male....................	25 (1.3)	75 (1.3)	24 (1.4)	3 (0.5)	25 (1.0)	75 (1.0)	33 (1.5)	5 (0.7)	27 (1.1)	73 (1.1)	28 (1.5)	2 (0.4)
Female.................	28 (1.6)	72 (1.6)	18 (1.1)	1 (0.4)	27 (1.2)	73 (1.2)	26 (1.4)	3 (0.6)	30 (1.0)	70 (1.0)	21 (1.0)	1 (0.3)
Race/ethnicity												
White....................	13 (1.3)	87 (1.3)	29 (1.5)	3 (0.5)	14 (0.9)	86 (0.9)	39 (1.7)	5 (0.8)	19 (0.9)	81 (0.9)	31 (1.4)	2 (0.4)
Black....................	56 (2.1)	44 (2.1)	5 (0.9)	# (†)	60 (2.3)	40 (2.3)	6 (0.8)	# (†)	65 (2.3)	35 (2.3)	4 (0.7)	# (†)
Hispanic...............	51 (3.0)	49 (3.0)	6 (1.0)	# (†)	52 (1.9)	48 (1.9)	10 (1.0)	1 (0.2)	48 (2.6)	52 (2.6)	10 (1.4)	# (†)
Asian/Pacific Islander......	23 (3.4)	77 (3.4)	25 (3.0)	1 (0.9)	21 (3.4)	79 (3.4)	32 (3.2)	4 (1.8)	28 (4.3)	72 (4.3)	26 (4.7)	1 (0.7)
Free/reduced-price lunch eligibility												
Eligible.................	49 (2.2)	51 (2.2)	6 (0.9)	# (†)	50 (1.8)	50 (1.8)	11 (1.2)	1 (0.3)	49 (2.3)	51 (2.3)	11 (1.6)	# (†)
Not eligible...........	14 (1.1)	86 (1.1)	29 (1.5)	3 (0.6)	17 (0.9)	83 (0.9)	37 (1.7)	5 (0.8)	25 (1.2)	75 (1.2)	26 (1.6)	1 (0.4)
Not available.........	16 (2.5)	84 (2.5)	27 (3.2)	3 (0.8)	21 (2.1)	79 (2.1)	33 (2.5)	4 (0.9)	24 (2.0)	76 (2.0)	31 (2.1)	2 (0.4)
Region												
Northeast.............	22 (3.7)	78 (3.7)	24 (2.2)	3 (0.9)	22 (2.5)	78 (2.5)	34 (3.3)	4 (1.3)	29 (2.3)	71 (2.3)	26 (4.1)	2 (1.1)
Southeast.............	28 (2.5)	72 (2.5)	18 (1.9)	1 (0.6)	27 (2.4)	73 (2.4)	26 (1.6)	3 (0.6)	33 (1.6)	67 (1.6)	21 (1.3)	1 (0.3)
Central.................	18 (1.7)	82 (1.7)	30 (2.5)	3 (0.7)	18 (2.3)	82 (2.3)	38 (3.7)	6 (1.3)	24 (1.8)	76 (1.8)	28 (1.9)	1 (0.5)
West....................	34 (2.7)	66 (2.7)	14 (1.7)	1 (0.3)	34 (1.7)	66 (1.7)	23 (1.7)	2 (0.6)	30 (1.9)	70 (1.9)	23 (1.8)	1 (0.4)

†Not applicable.

#Rounds to zero.

NOTE: Includes public and private schools. Excludes students unable to be tested due to limited proficiency in English or due to a disability (if the accommodations provided were not sufficient to enable the test to properly reflect the students' proficiency in geography). Race categories exclude persons of Hispanic ethnicity. Totals include other racial/ethnic groups not shown separately. Detail may not sum to totals because of rounding. Standard errors appear in parentheses.

SOURCE: U.S. Department of Education, National Center for Education Statistics, National Assessment of Educational Progress (NAEP), *The Nation's Report Card: Geography 2001*. (This table was prepared July 2002.)

SAT mean scores of college-bound seniors, by race/ethnicity: Selected years, 1986–87 through 2008–09

Race/ethnicity	1986–87	1990–91	1996–97	1998–99	1999–2000	2000–01	2001–02	2002–03	2003–04	2004–05	2005–06	2006–07	2007–08	2008–09	Score change			
															1986–87 to 1996–97	1998–99 to 2008–09	2003–04 to 2008–09	2007–08 to 2008–09
1	2	3	4	5	6	7	8	9	10	11	12	13	14	15	16	17	18	19
SAT—Critical reading																		
All students	**507**	**499**	**505**	**505**	**505**	**506**	**504**	**507**	**508**	**508**	**503**	**502**	**502**	**501**	**-2**	**-4**	**-7**	**-1**
White	524	518	526	527	528	529	527	529	528	532	527	527	528	528	2	1	0	0
Black	428	427	434	434	434	433	430	431	430	433	434	429	430	429	6	-5	-1	-1
Mexican American	457	454	451	453	453	451	446	448	451	453	454	455	454	453	-6	0	2	-1
Puerto Rican	436	436	454	455	456	457	455	456	457	460	459	459	456	452	18	-3	-5	-4
Other Hispanic	464	458	466	463	461	460	458	457	461	463	458	459	455	455	2	-8	-6	0
Asian/Pacific Islander	479	485	496	498	499	501	501	508	507	511	510	514	513	516	17	18	9	3
American Indian/Alaska Native	471	470	475	484	482	481	479	480	483	489	487	487	485	486	4	2	3	1
Other	480	486	512	511	508	503	502	501	494	495	494	497	496	494	32	-17	0	-2
SAT—Mathematics																		
All students	**501**	**500**	**511**	**511**	**514**	**514**	**516**	**519**	**518**	**520**	**518**	**515**	**515**	**515**	**10**	**4**	**-3**	**0**
White	514	513	526	528	530	531	533	534	531	536	536	534	537	536	12	8	5	-1
Black	411	419	423	422	426	426	427	426	427	431	429	429	426	426	12	4	-1	0
Mexican American	455	459	458	456	460	458	457	457	458	463	465	466	463	463	3	7	5	0
Puerto Rican	432	439	447	448	451	451	451	453	452	457	456	454	453	450	15	2	-2	-3
Other Hispanic	462	462	468	464	467	465	464	464	465	469	463	463	461	461	6	-3	-4	0
Asian/Pacific Islander	541	548	560	560	565	566	569	575	577	580	578	578	581	587	19	27	10	6
American Indian/Alaska Native	463	468	475	481	481	479	483	482	488	493	494	494	491	493	12	12	5	2
Other	482	492	514	513	515	512	514	513	508	513	513	512	512	514	32	1	6	2
SAT—Writing																		
All students	†	†	†	†	†	†	†	†	†	†	**497**	**494**	**494**	**493**	**†**	**†**	**†**	**-1**
White	†	†	†	†	†	†	†	†	†	†	519	518	518	517	†	†	†	-1
Black	†	†	†	†	†	†	†	†	†	†	428	425	424	421	†	†	†	-3
Mexican American	†	†	†	†	†	†	†	†	†	†	452	450	447	446	†	†	†	-1
Puerto Rican	†	†	†	†	†	†	†	†	†	†	448	447	445	443	†	†	†	-2
Other Hispanic	†	†	†	†	†	†	†	†	†	†	450	450	448	448	†	†	†	0
Asian/Pacific Islander	†	†	†	†	†	†	†	†	†	†	512	513	516	520	†	†	†	4
American Indian/Alaska Native	†	†	†	†	†	†	†	†	†	†	474	473	470	469	†	†	†	-1
Other	†	†	†	†	†	†	†	†	†	†	493	493	494	493	†	†	†	-1

†Not applicable.

NOTE: Data are for seniors who took the SAT any time during their high school years through March of their senior year. If a student took a test more than once, the most recent score was used. The SAT was formerly known as the Scholastic Assessment Test and the Scholastic Aptitude Test. Possible scores on each part of the SAT range from 200 to 800. The critical reading section was formerly known as the verbal section. The writing section was introduced in March 2005.

SOURCE: College Entrance Examination Board, *College-Bound Seniors: Total Group Profile [National] Report*, selected years, 1986–87 through 2008–09, retrieved August 25, 2009, from http://professionals.collegeboard.com/data-reports/research/sat/cb-seniors-2009. (This table was prepared August 2009.)

SAT mean scores of college-bound seniors, by sex: 1966–67 through 2008–09

School year	SAT[1]									Scholastic Aptitude Test (old scale)					
	Critical reading score			Mathematics score			Writing score[2]			Verbal score			Mathematics score		
	Total	Male	Female	Total	Male	Female	Total	Male	Female	Total	Male	Female	Total	Male	Female
1	2	3	4	5	6	7	8	9	10	11	12	13	14	15	16
1966–67	543	540	545	516	535	495	†	†	†	466	463	468	492	514	467
1967–68	543	541	543	516	533	497	†	†	†	466	464	466	492	512	470
1968–69	540	536	543	517	534	498	†	†	†	463	459	466	493	513	470
1969–70	537	536	538	512	531	493	†	†	†	460	459	461	488	509	465
1970–71	532	531	534	513	529	494	†	†	†	455	454	457	488	507	466
1971–72	530	531	529	509	527	489	†	†	†	453	454	452	484	505	461
1972–73	523	523	521	506	525	489	†	†	†	445	446	443	481	502	460
1973–74	521	524	520	505	524	488	†	†	†	444	447	442	480	501	459
1974–75	512	515	509	498	518	479	†	†	†	434	437	431	472	495	449
1975–76	509	511	508	497	520	475	†	†	†	431	433	430	472	497	446
1976–77	507	509	505	496	520	474	†	†	†	429	431	427	470	497	445
1977–78	507	511	503	494	517	474	†	†	†	429	433	425	468	494	444
1978–79	505	509	501	493	516	473	†	†	†	427	431	423	467	493	443
1979–80	502	506	498	492	515	473	†	†	†	424	428	420	466	491	443
1980–81	502	508	496	492	516	473	†	†	†	424	430	418	466	492	443
1981–82	504	509	499	493	516	473	†	†	†	426	431	421	467	493	443
1982–83	503	508	498	494	516	474	†	†	†	425	430	420	468	493	445
1983–84	504	511	498	497	518	478	†	†	†	426	433	420	471	495	449
1984–85	509	514	503	500	522	480	†	†	†	431	437	425	475	499	452
1985–86	509	515	504	500	523	479	†	†	†	431	437	426	475	501	451
1986–87	507	512	502	501	523	481	†	†	†	430	435	425	476	500	453
1987–88	505	512	499	501	521	483	†	†	†	428	435	422	476	498	455
1988–89	504	510	498	502	523	482	†	†	†	427	434	421	476	500	454
1989–90	500	505	496	501	521	483	†	†	†	424	429	419	476	499	455
1990–91	499	503	495	500	520	482	†	†	†	422	426	418	474	497	453
1991–92	500	504	496	501	521	484	†	†	†	423	428	419	476	499	456
1992–93	500	504	497	503	524	484	†	†	†	424	428	420	478	502	457
1993–94	499	501	497	504	523	487	†	†	†	423	425	421	479	501	460
1994–95	504	505	502	506	525	490	†	†	†	428	429	426	482	503	463
1995–96	505	507	503	508	527	492	†	†	†	—	—	—	—	—	—
1996–97	505	507	503	511	530	494	†	†	†	—	—	—	—	—	—
1997–98	505	509	502	512	531	496	†	†	†	—	—	—	—	—	—
1998–99	505	509	502	511	531	495	†	†	†	—	—	—	—	—	—
1999–2000	505	507	504	514	533	498	†	†	†	†	†	†	†	†	†
2000–01	506	509	502	514	533	498	†	†	†	†	†	†	†	†	†
2001–02	504	507	502	516	534	500	†	†	†	†	†	†	†	†	†
2002–03	507	512	503	519	537	503	†	†	†	†	†	†	†	†	†
2003–04	508	512	504	518	537	501	†	†	†	†	†	†	†	†	†
2004–05	508	513	505	520	538	504	†	†	†	†	†	†	†	†	†
2005–06	503	505	502	518	536	502	497	491	502	†	†	†	†	†	†
2006–07	502	504	502	515	533	499	494	489	500	†	†	†	†	†	†
2007–08	502	504	500	515	533	500	494	488	501	†	†	†	†	†	†
2008–09	501	503	498	515	534	499	493	486	499	†	†	†	†	†	†

—Not available.

†Not applicable.

[1]Data for 1966–67 to 1985–86 were converted to the recentered scale by using a formula applied to the original mean and standard deviation. For 1986–87 to 1994–95, individual student scores were converted to the recentered scale and then the mean was recomputed. For 1995–96 to 1998–99, nearly all students received scores on the recentered scale; any score on the original scale was converted to the recentered scale prior to recomputing the mean. From 1999–2000 on, all scores have been reported on the recentered scale.

[2]Writing data are based on students who took the SAT writing section, which was introduced in March 2005.

NOTE: Data for 1966–67 through 1970–71 are estimates derived from the test scores of all participants. Data for 1971–72 and later are for seniors who took the SAT any time during their high school years through March of their senior year. If a student took a test more than once, the most recent score was used. The SAT was formerly known as the Scholastic Assessment Test and the Scholastic Aptitude Test. Possible scores on each part of the SAT range from 200 to 800. The critical reading section was formerly known as the verbal section. SOURCE: College Entrance Examination Board, *College-Bound Seniors: Total Group Profile [National] Report*, 1966–67 through 2008–09, retrieved August 25, 2009, from http://professionals .collegeboard.com/data-reports-research/sat/cb-seniors-2009. (This table was prepared August 2009.)

SAT mean scores of college-bound seniors, by selected student characteristics: Selected years, 1995–96 through 2008–09

Selected student characteristic	1995–96			2000–01			2006–07				2007–08				2008–09			
	Critical reading score[1]	Mathematics score	Percentage distribution	Critical reading score[1]	Mathematics score	Percentage distribution	Critical reading score[1]	Mathematics score	Writing score[2]	Percentage distribution	Critical reading score[1]	Mathematics score	Writing score[2]	Percentage distribution	Critical reading score[1]	Mathematics score	Writing score[2]	Percentage distribution
1	2	3	4	5	6	7	8	9	10	11	12	13	14	15	16	17	18	19
All students	**505**	**508**	**100**	**506**	**514**	**100**	**502**	**515**	**494**	**100**	**502**	**515**	**494**	**100**	**501**	**515**	**493**	**100**
High school rank																		
Top decile	591	606	22	588	607	24	580	602	575	32	573	598	569	31	576	603	573	33
Second decile	530	539	22	526	540	23	516	534	508	26	511	531	505	27	512	534	505	27
Second quintile	494	496	28	490	497	26	484	497	474	20	481	495	472	20	482	497	471	19
Third quintile	455	448	24	454	452	22	—	—	—	—	—	—	—	—	—	—	—	—
Fourth quintile	429	418	4	423	417	4	—	—	—	—	—	—	—	—	—	—	—	—
Fifth quintile	411	401	1	407	401	1	—	—	—	—	—	—	—	—	—	—	—	—
Bottom three quintiles[3]	—	—	—	—	—	—	444	450	434	22	441	447	431	22	441	448	430	20
High school grade point average																		
A+ (97–100)	617	632	6	609	626	7	604	620	599	7	595	615	592	6	599	621	597	6
A (93–96)	573	583	14	566	581	17	565	581	559	18	559	578	555	18	563	583	559	19
A– (90–92)	545	554	15	540	552	17	534	550	528	18	529	547	523	19	532	551	526	19
B (80–89)	486	485	49	482	486	47	478	486	469	45	474	484	465	47	474	484	464	46
C (70–79)	432	426	15	428	425	12	424	427	411	11	421	423	408	11	420	422	406	11
D, E, or F (below 70)	414	408	#	403	404	#	403	412	388	#	402	411	390	#	399	412	387	#
High school type																		
Public	502	506	83	502	510	83	498	509	488	84	497	510	488	84	496	510	487	84
Private, religiously affiliated	525	510	12	530	523	12	531	526	527	11	532	531	529	11	533	533	530	11
Private, independent	547	556	5	549	567	5	546	569	548	5	550	574	553	5	550	578	555	6
Intended college major[4]																		
Agriculture/natural resources	491	484	2	487	484	1	476	480	463	1	478	481	465	1	478	485	465	1
Architecture/environmental design	492	519	3	493	521	2	492	535	486	3	488	532	483	2	491	534	485	2
Area, ethnic, cultural and gender studies	†	†	†	†	†	†	547	514	533	#	554	521	541	#	551	515	536	#
Arts: visual/performing	520	497	6	518	501	8	517	503	507	9	516	502	506	8	516	503	506	8
Biological sciences	546	545	6	545	549	5	540	552	531	6	537	551	528	5	541	557	533	6
Business and commerce	483	500	13	489	511	14	485	510	479	15	481	509	477	15	486	516	481	14
Communications	527	497	4	527	506	4	523	501	519	4	522	502	519	4	522	502	518	4
Computer or information sciences	497	522	3	501	533	7	505	533	481	3	502	529	477	3	506	533	481	3
Construction trades	†	†	†	†	†	†	415	447	402	#	424	460	409	#	423	458	404	#
Education	487	477	8	483	481	9	480	483	476	8	478	482	475	7	478	483	475	7
Engineering	525	569	8	523	572	9	524	579	510	8	522	579	508	8	526	582	511	8
Engineering technologies/techniques	†	†	†	†	†	†	451	491	435	1	462	508	447	1	464	511	448	1
Foreign/classical languages	556	534	#	557	540	1	581	549	569	1	576	545	564	1	574	545	563	1
General/interdisciplinary	576	553	#	554	539	#	†	†	†	#	†	†	†	†	†	†	†	†
Health and allied services	500	505	19	494	502	15	487	498	484	19	486	498	483	19	488	501	485	19
History	†	†	†	†	†	†	556	518	528	1	548	515	518	1	548	517	518	1
Home economics[5]	458	452	#	459	458	#	463	464	458	#	466	467	462	#	467	468	462	#
Language and literature	605	545	1	606	549	1	596	536	581	2	592	533	577	2	589	530	572	2
Legal professions and studies	†	†	†	†	†	†	516	505	504	2	509	505	500	3	510	506	500	3
Liberal arts and sciences, general studies, and humanities	554	512	†	574	504	†	531	509	516	1	554	532	544	1	553	532	541	1
Library and archival sciences	552	628	†	549	625	#	592	517	544	#	587	517	537	#	576	510	534	#
Mathematics	†	†	†	†	†	†	533	614	529	1	525	609	532	1	528	613	527	1
Mechanic and repair technologies/technician	†	†	†	†	†	†	423	449	405	#	420	449	403	#	418	447	401	#
Military sciences	503	505	†	507	511	†	517	524	492	#	516	518	486	#	518	520	483	#
Multi/interdisciplinary studies	†	†	†	†	†	†	582	584	570	#	598	586	586	#	604	594	590	#
Natural resources and conservation	†	†	†	†	†	†	499	502	481	1	522	519	503	1	521	521	504	1

See notes at end of table.

SAT mean scores of college-bound seniors, by selected student characteristics: Selected years, 1995–96 through 2008–09—Continued

Selected student characteristic	1995–96 Critical reading score[1]	1995–96 Mathematics score	1995–96 Percentage distribution	2000–01 Critical reading score[1]	2000–01 Mathematics score	2000–01 Percentage distribution	2006–07 Critical reading score[1]	2006–07 Mathematics score	2006–07 Writing score[2]	2006–07 Percentage distribution	2007–08 Critical reading score[1]	2007–08 Mathematics score	2007–08 Writing score[2]	2007–08 Percentage distribution	2008–09 Critical reading score[1]	2008–09 Mathematics score	2008–09 Writing score[2]	2008–09 Percentage distribution
1	2	3	4	5	6	7	8	9	10	11	12	13	14	15	16	17	18	19
Parks, recreation, leisure, and fitness studies	†	†	†	†	†	†	449	462	437	#	455	478	448	1	452	476	442	1
Personal and culinary services	†	†	†	†	†	†	444	440	432	#	459	459	446	#	460	458	445	#
Philosophy/religion/theology	560	536	#	561	539	1	563	538	541	#	569	548	546	#	567	543	543	#
Physical sciences	575	595	#	568	588	1	560	589	545	2	556	586	539	1	561	592	544	1
Precision production	†	†	†	†	†	†	442	462	409	#	436	462	412	#	441	468	411	#
Psychology	†	†	†	†	†	†	506	488	496	4	503	488	496	5	501	488	494	5
Public affairs and services	458	448	3	461	455	2	497	480	488	1	467	452	461	#	466	451	458	#
Security and protective services	†	†	†	†	†	†	455	457	444	2	451	458	440	2	449	458	438	2
Social sciences and history	532	509	11	531	512	10	†	†	†	†	†	†	†	†	†	†	†	†
Social sciences	†	†	†	†	†	†	569	544	551	3	567	546	551	3	568	550	552	2
Technical and vocational	435	441	1	444	451	1	†	†	†	†	†	†	†	†	†	†	†	†
Theology and religious vocations	†	†	†	†	†	†	541	524	521	#	544	525	522	#	542	527	521	#
Transportation and materials moving	†	†	†	†	†	†	476	495	461	#	461	490	445	#	460	486	445	#
Other	†	†	†	†	†	†	443	445	430	#	466	472	456	1	467	474	456	1
Undecided	500	507	7	515	524	7	519	535	508	3	525	540	516	3	532	549	523	4
Degree-level goal																		
Certificate program	434	439	1	443	455	1	442	461	434	1	438	455	430	1	441	461	432	1
Associate's degree	422	415	2	419	416	2	415	419	407	1	416	419	407	1	415	418	404	1
Bachelor's degree	476	476	23	478	483	25	476	485	467	26	475	485	466	27	476	486	465	26
Master's degree	514	518	29	516	526	31	510	522	502	30	505	519	498	31	507	522	500	31
Doctor's or related degree	548	552	24	547	554	21	540	550	531	20	531	542	524	19	534	548	528	20
Other	430	438	1	438	449	1	436	452	432	1	433	449	430	#	433	452	429	#
Undecided	502	503	20	511	517	19	517	527	508	22	512	523	504	21	516	529	508	20
Family income																		
Less than $20,000	—	—	—	—	—	—	—	—	—	—	434	456	430	10	434	457	430	10
$20,000, but less than $40,000	—	—	—	—	—	—	—	—	—	—	462	473	453	15	462	475	453	15
$40,000, but less than $60,000	—	—	—	—	—	—	—	—	—	—	488	496	477	16	488	497	476	15
$60,000, but less than $80,000	—	—	—	—	—	—	—	—	—	—	502	510	490	16	503	512	491	15
$80,000, but less than $100,000	—	—	—	—	—	—	—	—	—	—	514	525	504	13	517	528	505	13
$100,000, but less than $120,000	—	—	—	—	—	—	—	—	—	—	522	534	512	11	525	538	516	11
$120,000, but less than $140,000	—	—	—	—	—	—	—	—	—	—	526	537	517	5	529	542	520	5
$140,000, but less than $160,000	—	—	—	—	—	—	—	—	—	—	533	546	525	4	536	550	527	4
$160,000, but less than $200,000	—	—	—	—	—	—	—	—	—	—	535	548	529	4	542	554	535	5
More than $200,000	—	—	—	—	—	—	—	—	—	—	554	570	552	6	563	579	560	7
Highest level of parental education																		
No high school diploma	414	439	4	411	438	4	421	445	418	4	419	441	417	5	420	443	418	5
High school diploma	475	474	35	472	476	32	466	476	457	31	464	474	455	32	464	474	454	31
Associate's degree	489	487	8	489	491	9	484	492	473	9	482	490	471	9	482	491	469	9
Bachelor's degree	525	529	28	525	533	29	522	533	513	30	518	531	510	30	521	535	512	30
Graduate degree	556	558	25	559	567	26	560	569	552	26	553	565	546	25	559	572	552	25

—Not available.
†Not applicable.
#Rounds to zero.
[1] Prior to 2006, the critical reading section was known as the verbal section.
[2] Writing data are based on students who took the SAT writing section, which was introduced in March 2005.
[3] Beginning in 2005–06, the College Board has reported third, fourth, and fifth quintiles as the bottom three quintiles instead of reporting them separately as in previous years.
[4] Data may not be comparable over time because of additions to the list of majors and changes in subspecialties within majors.
[5] Home economics was changed to Family and consumer sciences/human sciences as of 2006–07.

NOTE: Data are for seniors who took the SAT any time during their high school years through March of their senior year. If a student took a test more than once, the most recent score was used. The SAT was formerly known as the Scholastic Assessment Test and the Scholastic Aptitude Test. Possible scores on each part of the SAT range from 200 to 800. Detail may not sum to totals because of rounding and survey item nonresponse.

SOURCE: College Entrance Examination Board, College-Bound Seniors: Total Group Profile [National] Report, selected years, 1995–96 through 2008–09, retrieved August 25, 2009, from http://professionals.collegeboard.com/data-reports-research/sat/cb-seniors-2009. (This table was prepared August 2009.)

SAT mean scores of college-bound seniors and percentage of graduates taking SAT, by state or jurisdiction:
Selected years, 1987–88 through 2008–09

State or jurisdiction	1987–88 Critical reading	1987–88 Mathematics	1995–96 Critical reading	1995–96 Mathematics	2000–01 Critical reading	2000–01 Mathematics	2005–06 Critical reading	2005–06 Mathematics	2005–06 Writing[2]	2007–08 Critical reading	2007–08 Mathematics	2007–08 Writing[2]	2008–09 Critical reading	2008–09 Mathematics	2008–09 Writing[2]	Percent of graduates taking SAT, 2007–08[1]	Percent of graduates taking SAT, 2008–09[1]
1	2	3	4	5	6	7	8	9	10	11	12	13	14	15	16	17	18
United States	505	501	505	508	506	514	503	518	497	502	515	494	501	515	493	45	46
Alabama	554	540	565	558	559	554	565	561	565	565	557	554	557	552	549	8	7
Alaska	518	501	521	513	514	510	517	517	493	520	520	493	520	516	492	45	46
Arizona	531	523	525	521	523	525	521	528	507	516	522	500	516	521	497	26	26
Arkansas	554	536	566	550	562	550	574	568	567	575	567	559	572	572	556	5	5
California	500	508	495	511	498	517	501	518	501	499	515	498	500	513	498	48	49
Colorado	537	532	536	538	539	542	558	564	548	564	570	553	568	575	555	21	20
Connecticut	513	498	507	504	509	510	512	516	511	509	513	513	509	513	512	83	83
Delaware	510	493	508	495	501	499	495	500	484	499	498	490	495	498	484	70	71
District of Columbia	479	461	489	473	482	474	487	472	482	470	455	465	466	451	461	84	79
Florida	499	495	498	496	498	499	496	497	480	496	497	481	497	498	480	54	59
Georgia	480	473	484	477	491	489	494	496	487	491	493	482	490	491	479	70	71
Hawaii	484	505	485	510	486	515	482	509	472	481	502	470	479	502	469	58	58
Idaho	543	523	543	536	543	542	543	545	525	540	540	517	541	540	520	18	18
Illinois	540	540	564	575	576	589	591	609	586	583	601	578	588	604	583	7	6
Indiana	490	486	494	494	499	501	498	509	486	496	508	481	496	507	480	62	63
Iowa	587	588	590	600	593	603	602	613	591	603	612	582	610	615	588	3	3
Kansas	568	557	579	571	577	580	582	590	566	580	589	564	581	589	564	7	7
Kentucky	551	535	549	544	550	550	562	562	555	568	570	554	573	573	561	8	7
Louisiana	551	533	559	550	564	562	570	571	571	566	564	558	563	558	555	7	7
Maine[3]	508	493	504	498	506	500	501	501	491	469	466	461	468	467	455	87	90
Maryland	509	501	507	504	508	510	503	509	499	499	502	497	500	502	495	69	69
Massachusetts	508	499	507	504	511	515	513	524	510	514	525	513	514	526	510	83	84
Michigan	532	533	557	565	561	572	568	583	555	581	598	572	584	603	575	6	5
Minnesota	546	549	582	593	580	589	591	600	574	596	609	579	595	609	578	8	7
Mississippi	557	539	569	557	566	551	556	541	562	574	556	566	567	554	559	3	4
Missouri	547	539	570	569	577	577	587	591	582	594	597	584	595	600	584	5	5
Montana	547	547	546	547	539	539	538	545	524	541	548	523	541	542	519	24	22
Nebraska	562	561	567	568	562	568	576	583	566	581	585	567	587	594	572	5	4
Nevada	517	510	508	507	509	515	498	508	481	498	506	478	501	505	479	40	42
New Hampshire	523	511	520	514	520	516	520	524	509	521	523	511	523	523	510	74	75
New Jersey	500	495	498	505	499	513	496	515	496	495	513	496	496	513	496	76	76
New Mexico	553	543	554	548	551	542	557	549	543	557	548	540	553	546	534	12	11
New York	497	495	497	499	495	505	493	510	483	488	504	481	485	502	478	84	85
North Carolina	478	470	490	486	493	499	495	513	485	496	511	482	495	511	480	63	63
North Dakota	572	569	596	599	592	599	610	617	588	594	604	568	590	593	566	3	3
Ohio	529	521	536	535	534	539	535	544	521	534	544	521	537	546	523	24	22
Oklahoma	558	542	566	557	567	561	576	574	563	572	572	557	575	571	557	6	5
Oregon	517	507	523	521	526	526	523	529	503	523	527	502	523	525	499	53	52
Pennsylvania	502	489	498	492	500	499	493	500	483	494	501	483	493	501	483	71	71
Rhode Island	508	496	501	491	501	499	495	502	490	495	498	493	498	496	494	66	66
South Carolina	477	468	480	474	486	488	487	498	480	488	497	476	486	496	470	61	67
South Dakota	585	573	574	566	577	582	590	604	578	595	596	575	589	600	569	3	3
Tennessee	560	548	543	552	562	553	573	569	572	571	570	566	571	565	565	11	10
Texas	494	490	495	500	493	499	491	506	487	488	505	480	486	506	475	50	51
Utah	572	553	583	575	575	570	560	557	550	561	557	543	559	558	540	6	6
Vermont	514	499	506	500	511	506	513	519	502	519	523	507	518	518	506	64	64
Virginia	507	498	507	496	510	501	512	513	500	511	512	499	511	512	498	68	68
Washington	525	517	519	519	527	527	527	532	511	526	533	509	524	531	507	52	53
West Virginia	528	519	526	506	527	512	519	510	515	512	501	498	511	501	499	19	18
Wisconsin	549	551	577	586	584	596	588	600	577	587	604	577	594	608	582	5	5
Wyoming	550	545	544	544	547	545	548	555	537	562	574	541	567	568	550	6	5

[1]Participation rate is based on the projection of high school graduates by the Western Interstate Commission for Higher Education (WICHE), and the number of seniors who took the SAT in each state.

[2]Writing data are based on students who took the SAT writing section, which was introduced in March 2005.

[3]Beginning with the spring SAT administration in 2006, all Maine high school juniors, including all students in their third year of high school, are required to take SAT tests in critical reading, writing, and mathematics.

NOTE: Data are for seniors who took the SAT any time during their high school years through March of their senior year. If a student took a test more than once, the most recent score was used. The SAT was formerly known as the Scholastic Assessment Test and the Scholastic Aptitude Test. Possible scores on each part of the SAT range from 200 to 800. The critical reading section was formerly known as the verbal section.
SOURCE: College Entrance Examination Board, College-Bound Seniors Tables and Related Items, selected years, 1987–88 through 2008–09, retrieved August 25, 2009, from http://professionals.collegeboard.com/data-reports-research/sat/cb-seniors-2009. (This table was prepared August 2009.)

ACT score averages and standard deviations, by sex and race/ethnicity, and percentage of ACT test takers, by selected composite score ranges and planned fields of study: Selected years, 1995 through 2009

Score type and test-taker characteristic	1995	1998	1999	2000	2001	2002	2003	2004	2005	2006	2007	2008	2009
1	2	3	4	5	6	7	8	9	10	11	12	13	14
Total test takers													
Number (in thousands) ...	945	995	1,019	1,065	1,070	1,116	1,175	1,171	1,186	1,206	1,301	1,422	1,480
Percent of graduates	37.5	36.8	36.9	37.6	37.6	38.4	39.0	38.4	38.2	38.6	39.9	42.5	44.5
Average test score[1]													
Composite score, total ...	20.8	21.0	21.0	21.0	21.0	20.8	20.8	20.9	20.9	21.1	21.2	21.1	21.1
Sex													
Male	21.0	21.2	21.1	21.2	21.1	20.9	21.0	21.0	21.1	21.2	21.2	21.2	21.3
Female	20.7	20.9	20.9	20.9	20.9	20.7	20.8	20.9	20.9	21.0	21.0	21.0	20.9
Race/ethnicity													
White	—	22.7	22.7	22.7	21.8	21.7	21.7	21.8	21.9	22.0	22.1	22.1	22.2
Black	—	17.9	17.9	17.8	16.9	16.8	16.9	17.1	17.0	17.1	17.0	16.9	16.9
Mexican American	—	19.6	19.6	19.5	18.5	18.2	18.3	18.4	18.4	—	—	—	—
Other Hispanic	—	20.7	20.7	20.5	19.4	18.8	19.0	18.8	18.9	—	—	—	—
Hispanic	—	—	—	—	—	18.4	18.5	18.5	18.6	18.6	18.7	18.7	18.7
Asian American or Pacific Islander	—	22.6	22.3	22.4	21.7	21.6	21.8	21.9	22.1	22.3	22.6	22.9	23.2
American Indian/Alaska Native	—	20.4	20.4	20.4	18.8	18.6	18.7	18.8	18.7	18.8	18.9	19.0	18.9
Subject-area scores													
English	20.2	20.4	20.5	20.5	20.5	20.2	20.3	20.4	20.4	20.6	20.7	20.6	20.6
Male	19.8	19.9	20.0	20.0	20.0	19.7	19.8	19.9	20.0	20.1	20.2	20.1	20.2
Female	20.6	20.8	20.9	20.9	20.8	20.6	20.7	20.8	20.8	21.0	21.0	21.0	20.9
Mathematics	20.2	20.8	20.7	20.7	20.7	20.6	20.6	20.7	20.7	20.8	21.0	21.0	21.0
Male	20.9	21.5	21.4	21.4	21.4	21.2	21.2	21.3	21.3	21.5	21.6	21.6	21.6
Female	19.7	20.2	20.2	20.2	20.2	20.1	20.1	20.2	20.2	20.3	20.4	20.4	20.4
Reading	21.3	21.4	21.4	21.4	21.3	21.1	21.2	21.3	21.3	21.4	21.5	21.4	21.4
Male	21.1	21.1	21.1	21.2	21.1	20.9	21.0	21.1	21.0	21.1	21.2	21.2	21.3
Female	21.4	21.6	21.6	21.5	21.5	21.3	21.4	21.5	21.5	21.6	21.6	21.5	21.4
Science reasoning	21.0	21.1	21.0	21.0	21.0	20.8	20.8	20.9	20.9	20.9	21.0	20.8	20.9
Male	21.6	21.8	21.5	21.6	21.6	21.3	21.3	21.3	21.4	21.4	21.4	21.3	21.4
Female	20.5	20.6	20.6	20.6	20.6	20.4	20.4	20.5	20.5	20.5	20.5	20.4	20.4
Standard deviation[2]													
Composite score, total ...	—	4.7	4.7	4.7	4.7	4.8	4.8	4.8	—	4.8	5.0	5.0	5.1
Sex													
Male	—	4.9	4.9	4.9	4.9	5.0	5.0	5.0	5.0	—	—	—	—
Female	—	4.6	4.6	4.6	4.6	4.7	4.7	4.7	4.7	—	—	—	—
Subject-area scores													
English	—	5.4	5.5	5.5	5.6	5.8	5.8	5.9	—	5.9	6.0	6.1	6.3
Male	—	5.4	5.5	5.6	5.6	5.8	5.8	5.9	6.0	—	—	—	—
Female	—	5.4	5.5	5.5	5.6	5.7	5.8	5.8	5.9	—	—	—	—
Mathematics	—	5.1	5.0	5.0	5.0	5.0	5.1	5.0	—	5.0	5.1	5.2	5.3
Male	—	5.3	5.2	5.2	5.2	5.3	4.8	5.3	5.3	—	—	—	—
Female	—	4.8	4.7	4.8	4.7	4.8	5.3	4.8	4.8	—	—	—	—
Reading	—	6.0	6.0	6.1	6.0	6.1	6.1	6.0	—	6.0	6.1	6.1	6.2
Male	—	6.2	6.1	6.1	6.1	6.3	5.3	6.1	6.1	—	—	—	—
Female	—	5.9	5.9	6.0	6.0	6.1	4.8	5.9	6.0	—	—	—	—
Science reasoning	—	4.6	4.5	4.5	4.6	4.6	4.6	4.6	—	4.6	4.9	4.9	5.0
Male	—	4.9	4.8	4.8	4.9	4.9	4.9	4.9	4.9	—	—	—	—
Female	—	4.3	4.2	4.3	4.3	4.3	4.3	4.3	4.3	—	—	—	—
Percent of ACT test takers													
Obtaining composite scores of—													
28 or above	—	10	10	10	10	10	10	10	10	11	11	12	12
17 or below	—	25	25	25	25	27	27	26	26	25	25	26	27
Percent of ACT test takers													
Planned major field of study													
Business[3]	13	12	12	11	11	10	10	9	9	9	8	11	12
Engineering[4]	8	8	8	8	7	7	7	6	6	6	5	7	8
Social science[5]	9	9	9	9	9	8	8	7	7	6	5	6	7
Education[6]	8	9	9	9	8	8	7	7	7	6	5	6	7

—Not available.

[1]Minimum score is 1 and maximum score is 36.

[2]Standard deviations not available for racial/ethnic groups.

[3]Includes business and management, business and office, and marketing and distribution.

[4]Includes engineering and engineering-related technologies.

[5]Includes social science and philosophy, religion, and theology.

[6]Includes education and teacher education.

NOTE: Data are for high school graduates who took the ACT during their sophomore, junior, or senior year. If a student took a test more than once, the most recent score was used. Race categories exclude persons of Hispanic ethnicity. Some data have been revised from previously published figures.

SOURCE: ACT, *High School Profile Report*, selected years, 1995 through 2009. U.S. Department of Education, National Center for Education Statistics, Common Core of Data (CCD), "State Nonfiscal Survey of Public Elementary/Secondary Education," 1995–96 through 2006–07; Private School Universe Survey (PSS), 1995 through 2005; and *Projections of Education Statistics to 2017*. (This table was prepared August 2009.)

Enrollment in public elementary and secondary schools, by state or jurisdiction: Selected years, fall 1990 through fall 2009

| State or jurisdiction | Total | | | | | | | | | | | | | Fall 2006 | | | Fall 2007 | | | Projected fall 2008 enrollment | Projected fall 2009 enrollment |
| | Fall 1990 | Fall 1994 | Fall 1995 | Fall 1996 | Fall 1997 | Fall 1998 | Fall 1999 | Fall 2000 | Fall 2001 | Fall 2002 | Fall 2003 | Fall 2004 | Fall 2005 | Total | Prekindergarten to grade 8[1] | Grades 9 to 12[2] | Total | Prekindergarten to grade 8[1] | Grades 9 to 12[2] | | |
1	2	3	4	5	6	7	8	9	10	11	12	13	14	15	16	17	18	19	20	21	22
United States	41,216,683	44,111,482	44,840,481	45,611,046	46,126,897	46,538,585	46,857,149	47,203,539	47,671,870	48,183,086	48,540,215	48,795,465	49,113,298	49,315,842	34,234,751	15,081,091	49,292,507	34,205,362	15,087,145	49,623,000	49,788,000
Alabama	721,806	736,531	746,149	747,932	749,207	747,980	740,732	739,992	737,190	739,366	731,220	730,140	741,761	743,632	528,664	214,968	744,865	527,259	217,606	748,000	748,000
Alaska	113,903	127,057	127,618	129,919	132,123	135,373	134,391	133,356	134,364	134,364	133,933	132,970	133,288	132,608	90,167	42,441	131,029	88,980	42,049	129,000	129,000
Arizona	639,853	737,424	743,566	799,250	814,113	848,262	852,612	877,696	922,180	937,755	1,012,068	1,043,298	1,094,454	1,068,249	759,656	308,593	1,087,447	771,056	316,391	1,126,000	1,161,000
Arkansas	436,286	447,565	453,257	457,349	456,497	452,256	451,034	449,959	449,805	450,985	454,523	463,115	474,206	476,409	336,552	139,857	479,016	339,920	139,096	483,000	487,000
California	4,950,474	5,407,475	5,536,406	5,686,198	5,803,887	5,926,037	6,038,590	6,140,814	6,247,726	6,353,667	6,413,862	6,441,557	6,437,202	6,406,750	4,410,105	1,996,645	6,343,471	4,328,968	2,014,503	6,431,000	6,435,000
Colorado	574,213	640,521	656,279	673,438	687,167	699,135	708,109	724,508	742,145	751,862	757,693	765,976	779,826	794,026	559,041	234,985	801,867	565,726	236,141	816,000	827,000
Connecticut	469,123	506,824	517,935	527,129	535,164	544,698	553,993	562,179	570,228	570,023	577,203	577,390	575,059	575,100	398,063	177,037	570,626	394,034	176,592	564,000	559,000
Delaware	99,658	106,813	108,461	110,549	111,960	113,262	112,836	114,676	115,555	116,342	117,668	119,091	120,937	122,254	84,996	37,258	122,574	85,019	37,555	125,000	125,000
District of Columbia	80,694	80,450	79,802	78,648	77,111	71,889	77,194	68,925	75,392	76,166	78,057	76,714	76,876	72,850	52,391	20,459	78,422	55,836	22,586	69,000	70,000
Florida	1,861,592	2,111,188	2,176,222	2,242,212	2,294,077	2,337,633	2,381,396	2,434,821	2,500,478	2,539,929	2,587,628	2,639,336	2,675,024	2,671,513	1,866,562	804,951	2,666,811	1,855,859	810,952	2,736,000	2,771,000
Georgia	1,151,687	1,270,948	1,311,126	1,346,761	1,375,980	1,401,291	1,422,762	1,444,937	1,470,634	1,496,012	1,522,611	1,553,437	1,598,461	1,629,157	1,166,508	462,649	1,649,589	1,178,577	471,012	1,705,000	1,735,000
Hawaii	171,708	183,795	187,180	187,653	189,887	188,069	185,860	184,360	184,546	183,829	183,609	183,185	182,818	180,728	126,008	54,720	179,897	125,556	54,341	176,000	174,000
Idaho	220,840	240,448	243,097	245,252	244,403	244,722	245,136	245,117	246,521	248,604	252,120	256,084	261,982	267,380	187,005	80,375	272,119	191,171	80,948	278,000	283,000
Illinois	1,821,407	1,916,172	1,943,623	1,973,040	1,998,289	2,011,530	2,027,600	2,048,792	2,071,391	2,084,187	2,100,961	2,097,503	2,111,706	2,118,276	1,477,679	640,597	2,112,805	1,472,909	639,896	2,119,000	2,117,000
Indiana	954,525	969,022	977,263	982,876	986,836	989,001	988,702	989,267	996,133	1,003,875	1,011,130	1,021,348	1,035,074	1,045,940	730,108	315,832	1,046,766	729,550	317,216	1,049,000	1,049,000
Iowa	483,652	500,440	502,343	502,941	501,054	498,214	497,301	495,080	485,932	482,210	481,226	478,319	483,482	483,122	326,218	156,904	485,115	329,504	155,611	481,000	480,000
Kansas	437,034	460,838	463,008	466,293	468,687	472,353	472,188	470,610	470,205	470,957	470,490	469,136	467,525	469,506	326,201	143,305	468,295	326,771	141,524	467,000	467,000
Kentucky	636,401	657,642	659,821	656,089	669,322	655,687	648,180	665,850	654,363	660,782	663,885	674,796	679,878	683,152	487,165	195,987	666,225	469,373	196,852	690,000	692,000
Louisiana	784,757	797,933	797,366	793,296	776,813	768,734	756,579	743,089	731,328	730,464	727,709	724,281	654,526	675,851	492,116	183,735	681,038	499,549	181,489	664,000	661,000
Maine	215,149	212,601	213,569	213,593	212,579	211,051	209,253	207,037	205,586	204,337	202,084	198,820	195,498	193,986	132,338	61,648	196,245	130,742	65,503	188,000	185,000
Maryland	715,176	790,938	805,544	818,583	830,744	841,671	846,582	852,920	860,640	866,743	869,113	865,561	860,020	851,640	579,065	272,575	845,700	576,479	269,221	835,000	828,000
Massachusetts	834,314	893,727	915,007	933,898	949,006	962,317	971,425	975,150	973,139	982,989	980,459	975,574	971,909	968,661	670,628	298,033	962,958	666,926	296,032	949,000	941,000
Michigan	1,584,431	1,614,784	1,641,456	1,685,714	1,702,717	1,720,287	1,725,639	1,720,626	1,730,669	1,785,160	1,757,604	1,751,290	1,742,282	1,722,656	1,170,558	552,098	1,692,739	1,136,823	555,916	1,662,000	1,635,000
Minnesota	756,374	821,693	835,166	847,204	853,621	856,455	854,034	854,340	851,384	846,891	842,854	838,503	839,243	840,565	558,445	282,120	837,578	558,180	279,398	832,000	830,000
Mississippi	502,417	505,962	506,272	503,967	504,792	502,379	500,716	497,871	493,507	492,645	493,540	495,376	494,954	495,026	356,382	138,644	494,122	353,512	140,610	496,000	496,000
Missouri	816,558	878,541	889,881	900,517	910,613	913,494	914,110	912,744	909,792	906,499	905,941	905,449	917,705	920,353	634,275	286,078	917,188	631,746	285,442	919,000	919,000
Montana	152,974	164,341	165,547	164,627	162,335	159,988	157,556	154,875	151,947	149,995	148,356	146,705	145,416	144,418	97,021	47,397	142,823	96,354	46,469	142,000	142,000
Nebraska	274,081	287,100	289,744	291,967	292,681	291,140	288,261	286,199	285,095	285,402	285,542	285,761	286,646	287,580	195,769	91,811	291,244	200,095	91,149	289,000	290,000
Nevada	201,316	250,747	265,041	282,131	296,621	311,061	325,610	340,706	356,814	369,498	385,401	400,083	412,395	424,766	302,953	121,813	429,362	307,573	121,789	451,000	463,000
New Hampshire	172,785	189,319	194,171	198,308	201,629	204,713	206,783	208,461	206,847	207,417	207,417	206,852	205,767	203,572	136,188	67,384	200,772	134,359	66,413	199,000	198,000
New Jersey	1,089,646	1,174,206	1,197,381	1,227,832	1,250,276	1,268,996	1,289,256	1,313,405	1,341,656	1,367,438	1,380,753	1,393,347	1,395,602	1,388,850	963,418	425,432	1,382,348	954,418	427,930	1,368,000	1,362,000
New Mexico	301,881	327,248	329,640	332,632	331,673	328,753	324,495	320,306	320,260	320,234	323,066	326,102	326,758	328,220	230,091	98,129	329,040	229,718	99,322	330,000	331,000
New York	2,598,337	2,766,208	2,813,230	2,843,131	2,861,823	2,877,143	2,887,776	2,882,188	2,872,132	2,888,233	2,864,775	2,836,337	2,815,581	2,809,649	1,887,284	922,365	2,765,435	1,856,315	909,120	2,707,000	2,669,000
North Carolina	1,086,871	1,156,767	1,183,090	1,210,108	1,236,083	1,254,821	1,275,925	1,293,638	1,315,363	1,335,954	1,360,209	1,385,754	1,416,436	1,444,481	1,027,067	417,414	1,489,492	1,072,324	417,168	1,496,000	1,520,000
North Dakota	117,825	119,288	119,100	120,123	118,572	114,927	112,751	109,201	106,047	104,225	102,233	100,513	98,283	96,670	64,395	32,275	95,059	63,492	31,567	93,000	92,000

See notes at end of table.

Enrollment in public elementary and secondary schools, by state or jurisdiction: Selected years, fall 1990 through fall 2009—Continued

State or jurisdiction	Total Fall 1990	Fall 1994	Fall 1995	Fall 1996	Fall 1997	Fall 1998	Fall 1999	Fall 2000	Fall 2001	Fall 2002	Fall 2003	Fall 2004	Fall 2005	Fall 2006 Total	Fall 2006 Prekindergarten to grade 8[1]	Fall 2006 Grades 9 to 12[2]	Fall 2007 Total	Fall 2007 Prekindergarten to grade 8[1]	Fall 2007 Grades 9 to 12[2]	Projected fall 2008 enrollment	Projected fall 2009 enrollment
1	2	3	4	5	6	7	8	9	10	11	12	13	14	15	16	17	18	19	20	21	22
Ohio	1,771,089	1,814,290	1,836,015	1,844,698	1,847,114	1,842,163	1,836,554	1,835,049	1,830,985	1,838,285	1,845,428	1,840,032	1,839,683	1,836,722	1,253,193	583,529	1,827,184	1,241,322	585,862	1,814,000	1,802,000
Oklahoma	579,087	609,718	616,393	620,695	623,681	628,492	627,032	623,110	622,139	624,548	626,160	629,476	634,739	639,391	459,944	179,447	642,065	462,629	179,436	646,000	649,000
Oregon	472,394	521,945	527,914	537,854	541,346	542,809	545,033	546,231	551,480	554,071	551,273	552,505	552,194	562,574	380,576	181,998	565,586	383,598	181,988	564,000	565,000
Pennsylvania	1,667,834	1,764,946	1,787,533	1,804,256	1,815,151	1,816,414	1,816,716	1,814,311	1,821,627	1,816,747	1,821,146	1,828,089	1,830,684	1,871,060	1,220,074	650,986	1,801,971	1,205,351	596,620	1,844,000	1,824,000
Rhode Island	138,813	147,487	149,799	151,324	153,321	154,785	156,454	157,347	158,046	159,205	159,375	156,498	153,422	151,612	101,996	49,616	147,629	99,159	48,470	145,000	142,000
South Carolina	622,112	648,725	645,586	652,816	659,273	664,600	666,780	677,411	676,198	694,389	699,198	703,736	701,544	708,021	501,273	206,748	712,317	504,566	207,751	707,000	706,000
South Dakota	129,164	143,482	144,685	143,331	142,443	132,495	131,037	128,603	127,542	130,048	125,537	122,798	122,012	121,158	83,137	38,021	121,606	83,424	38,182	120,000	119,000
Tennessee	824,595	881,425	893,770	904,818	893,044	905,454	916,202	909,161	924,899	927,608	936,681	941,091	953,928	978,368	691,971	286,397	964,259	681,751	282,508	997,000	1,006,000
Texas	3,382,887	3,677,171	3,748,167	3,828,975	3,891,877	3,945,367	3,991,783	4,059,619	4,163,447	4,259,823	4,331,751	4,405,215	4,525,394	4,599,509	3,319,782	1,279,727	4,674,832	3,374,684	1,300,148	4,834,000	4,949,000
Utah	446,652	474,675	477,121	481,812	482,957	481,176	480,255	481,485	484,684	489,262	495,981	503,607	508,430	523,386	371,272	152,114	576,244	410,258	165,986	559,000	573,000
Vermont	95,762	104,533	105,565	106,341	105,984	105,120	104,559	102,049	101,179	99,978	99,103	98,352	96,638	95,399	63,740	31,659	94,038	63,096	30,942	91,000	89,000
Virginia	998,601	1,060,809	1,079,854	1,096,093	1,110,815	1,124,022	1,133,994	1,144,915	1,163,091	1,177,229	1,192,092	1,204,739	1,213,616	1,220,440	841,685	378,755	1,230,857	850,444	380,413	1,233,000	1,238,000
Washington	839,709	938,314	956,572	974,504	991,235	998,053	1,003,714	1,004,770	1,009,200	1,014,798	1,021,349	1,020,005	1,031,985	1,026,774	694,858	331,916	1,030,247	697,407	332,840	1,026,000	1,026,000
West Virginia	322,389	310,511	307,112	304,052	301,419	297,530	291,811	286,367	282,885	282,455	281,215	280,129	280,866	281,939	197,573	84,366	282,535	198,545	83,990	281,000	281,000
Wisconsin	797,621	860,581	870,175	879,259	881,780	879,542	877,753	879,476	879,361	881,231	880,031	864,757	875,174	876,700	584,600	292,100	874,633	585,212	289,421	864,000	861,000
Wyoming	98,226	100,314	99,859	99,058	97,115	95,241	92,105	89,940	88,128	88,116	87,462	84,733	84,409	85,193	57,995	27,198	86,422	59,243	27,179	86,000	87,000
Bureau of Indian Education	—	—	—	—	—	—	—	—	—	—	—	—	—	—	—	—	—	—	—	—	—
DoD, overseas	—	—	—	—	—	50,125	49,076	46,938	46,476	46,126	45,828	45,828	50,938	—	—	—	—	—	—	—	—
DoD, domestic	—	—	—	80,715	78,254	78,170	108,035[3]	73,581	73,212	72,889	71,053	68,327	62,543	60,891	47,589	13,302	57,247	44,418	12,829	—	—
Other jurisdictions																					
American Samoa	12,463	14,445	14,576	14,766	15,214	15,372	15,477	15,702	15,897	15,984	15,893	16,126	16,438	16,400	11,763	4,637	—	—	—	—	—
Guam	26,391	32,185	32,960	33,393	32,444	32,222	32,951	32,473	31,992	—	31,572	30,605	30,986	26,631	24,052	2,579	27,548	24,807	2,741	—	—
Northern Marianas	6,449	8,429	8,800	9,041	9,246	9,498	9,732	10,004	10,479	11,251	11,244	11,601	11,718	11,695	8,504	3,191	11,299	8,140	3,159	—	—
Puerto Rico	644,734	621,121	627,620	618,861	617,157	613,862	613,019	612,725	604,177	596,502	584,916	575,648	563,490	544,138	382,647	161,491	526,565	372,514	154,051	—	—
U.S. Virgin Islands	21,750	23,126	22,737	22,385	22,136	20,976	20,866	19,459	18,780	18,333	17,716	16,429	16,750	16,284	11,237	5,047	15,903	10,770	5,133	—	—

—Not available.
[1] Includes elementary unclassified.
[2] Includes secondary unclassified.
[3] Includes both overseas and domestic schools.

NOTE: DoD = Department of Defense. Some data have been revised from previously published figures.
SOURCE: U.S. Department of Education, National Center for Education Statistics, Common Core of Data (CCD), "State Non-fiscal Survey of Public Elementary/Secondary Education," 1990–91 through 2007–08, and Projections of Education Statistics to 2018. (This table was prepared September 2009.)

Number and percentage of homeschooled students ages 5 through 17 with a grade equivalent of kindergarten through 12th grade, by selected child, parent, and household characteristics: 1999, 2003, and 2007

Selected characteristic	1999 Number of students[1] (in thousands)	1999 Number homeschooled (in thousands)	1999 Percent homeschooled	2003 Number of students[1] (in thousands)	2003 Number homeschooled (in thousands)	2003 Percent homeschooled	2007 Number of students[1] (in thousands)	2007 Number homeschooled (in thousands)	2007 Percent homeschooled
1	2	3	4	5	6	7	8	9	10
Total	**50,188 (72.7)**	**850 (71.1)**	**1.7 (0.14)**	**50,707 (89.3)**	**1,096 (92.3)**	**2.2 (0.18)**	**51,135 (155.3)**	**1,508 (117.9)**	**2.9 (0.23)**
Sex of child									
Male	25,515 (233.9)	417 (43.9)	1.6 (0.17)	25,819 (286.8)	569 (61.9)	2.2 (0.24)	26,286 (355.6)	633 (75.2)	2.4 (0.28)
Female	24,673 (238.7)	434 (46.1)	1.8 (0.19)	24,888 (277.7)	527 (58.2)	2.1 (0.23)	24,849 (386.9)	875 (97.7)	3.5 (0.39)
Race/ethnicity of child									
White	32,474 (168.2)	640 (62.3)	2.0 (0.19)	31,584 (187.2)	843 (77.5)	2.7 (0.25)	29,815 (197.9)	1159 (101.6)	3.9 (0.34)
Black	8,047 (102.3)	84 (24.8)	1.0 (0.31)	7,985 (45.7)	103 ! (33.9)	1.3 ! (0.42)	7,523 (114.0)	61 ! (21.2)	0.8 ! (0.28)
Hispanic	7,043 (85.5)	77 (17.7)	1.1 (0.25)	8,075 (35.1)	59 ! (21.0)	0.7 ! (0.26)	9,589 (84.8)	147 (27.5)	1.5 (0.29)
Other	2,623 (114.2)	49 ! (17.2)	1.9 ! (0.65)	3,063 (161.1)	91 ! (31.5)	3.0 ! (1.02)	4,208 (170.6)	141 (36.1)	3.3 (0.86)
Grade equivalent[2]									
Kindergarten through 5th grade	24,428 (20.5)	428 (48.1)	1.8 (0.20)	24,269 (24.7)	472 (55.3)	1.9 (0.23)	23,529 (68.1)	717 (83.8)	3.0 (0.36)
Kindergarten	3,790 (20.0)	92 (19.7)	2.4 (0.52)	3,643 (24.7)	98 (23.5)	2.7 (0.64)	3,669 (67.9)	114 ! (35.4)	3.1 ! (0.96)
Grades 1 through 3	12,692 (6.2)	199 (36.7)	1.6 (0.29)	12,098 (#)	214 (33.3)	1.8 (0.28)	11,965 (2.4)	406 (64.5)	3.4 ! (0.54)
Grades 4 through 5	7,946 (1.3)	136 (22.5)	1.7 (0.28)	8,528 (#)	160 (30.1)	1.9 (0.35)	7,895 (2.1)	197 (41.4)	2.5 (0.52)
Grades 6 through 8	11,788 (3.4)	186 (28.0)	1.6 (0.24)	12,472 (6.5)	302 (44.9)	2.4 (0.36)	12,435 (0.7)	359 (64.9)	2.9 (0.52)
Grades 9 through 12	13,954 (70.5)	235 (33.2)	1.7 (0.24)	13,958 (81.8)	315 (47.0)	2.3 (0.33)	15,161 (129.3)	422 (58.2)	2.8 (0.38)
Number of children in the household									
One child	8,226 (153.8)	120 (20.3)	1.5 (0.24)	8,033 (218.1)	110 (22.3)	1.4 (0.27)	8,463 (227.1)	187 (31.4)	2.2 (0.37)
Two children	19,883 (211.4)	207 (27.1)	1.0 (0.14)	20,530 (319.4)	306 (45.1)	1.5 (0.22)	20,694 (295.3)	412 (67.3)	2.0 (0.33)
Three or more children	22,078 (241.2)	523 (65.2)	2.4 (0.30)	22,144 (362.8)	679 (80.2)	3.1 (0.36)	21,979 (331.0)	909 (102.4)	4.1 (0.46)
Number of parents in the household									
Two parents	33,007 (203.8)	683 (68.3)	2.1 (0.21)	35,936 (315.1)	886 (82.7)	2.5 (0.23)	37,262 (302.1)	1348 (111.5)	3.6 (0.30)
One parent	15,454 (209.4)	142 (25.0)	0.9 (0.16)	13,260 (319.2)	196 (42.6)	1.5 (0.32)	11,734 (299.2)	115 (28.4)	1.0 (0.24)
Nonparental guardians	1,727 (86.0)	25 ! (14.4)	1.4 ! (0.82)	1,511 (100.1)	14 ! (11.1)	0.9 ! (0.74)	2,139 (203.2)	45 ! (17.3)	2.1 ! (0.81)
Parent participation in the labor force									
Two parents—both in labor force	22,880 (241.5)	237 (39.8)	1.0 (0.17)	25,108 (373.1)	274 (44.1)	1.1 (0.18)	26,075 (318.9)	509 (76.8)	2.0 (0.30)
Two parents—one in labor force	9,628 (194.4)	444 (53.8)	4.6 (0.55)	10,545 (297.2)	594 (73.7)	5.6 (0.67)	10,776 (284.8)	808 (94.3)	7.5 (0.82)
One parent—in labor force	13,907 (220.0)	98 (21.8)	0.7 (0.16)	12,045 (267.9)	174 (39.8)	1.4 (0.33)	9,989 (277.2)	127 (29.5)	1.3 (0.30)
No parent participation in labor force	3,773 (162.3)	71 (18.8)	1.9 (0.48)	3,008 (171.4)	54 ! (23.7)	1.8 ! (0.78)	4,296 (228.0)	64 ! (20.6)	1.5 ! (0.48)
Highest education level of parents									
High school diploma or less	18,334 (217.3)	160 (26.5)	0.9 (0.15)	16,106 (272.3)	269 (51.6)	1.7 (0.32)	14,303 (292.6)	206 (35.6)	1.4 (0.24)
Vocational/technical or some college	15,177 (215.2)	287 (37.3)	1.9 (0.24)	16,068 (323.4)	338 (57.7)	2.1 (0.36)	14,584 (326.3)	549 (77.3)	3.8 (0.52)
Bachelor's degree/some graduate school	9,412 (179.0)	230 (36.3)	2.4 (0.37)	10,849 (275.0)	309 (48.5)	2.8 (0.45)	12,321 (281.6)	502 (70.1)	4.1 (0.57)
Graduate/professional degree	7,264 (179.9)	173 (39.9)	2.4 (0.54)	7,683 (239.5)	180 (41.6)	2.3 (0.55)	9,927 (242.9)	251 (41.0)	2.5 (0.41)
Household income									
$25,000 or less	16,776 (116.9)	262 (45.0)	1.6 (0.27)	12,375 (53.6)	283 (56.0)	2.3 (0.45)	11,544 (123.8)	239 (49.9)	2.1 (0.43)
$25,001 to $50,000	15,220 (232.7)	278 (36.7)	1.8 (0.24)	13,220 (270.2)	311 (49.9)	2.4 (0.37)	10,592 (236.4)	364 (56.9)	3.4 (0.52)
$50,001 to $75,000	8,576 (189.3)	162 (25.5)	1.9 (0.30)	10,961 (282.2)	264 (51.1)	2.4 (0.46)	10,289 (232.9)	405 (57.9)	3.9 (0.56)
Over $75,000	9,615 (211.2)	148 (26.5)	1.5 (0.28)	14,150 (261.7)	238 (45.8)	1.7 (0.33)	18,710 (232.6)	501 (74.9)	2.7 (0.40)
Urbanicity[3]									
Urban	37,415 (129.2)	575 (57.3)	1.5 (0.15)	40,180 (82.3)	794 (87.2)	2.0 (0.22)	40,560 (151.9)	995 (94.5)	2.5 (0.23)
Rural	12,773 (112.6)	275 (39.8)	2.2 (0.31)	10,527 (56.3)	302 (58.0)	2.9 (0.55)	10,576 (110.9)	513 (75.5)	4.9 (0.71)

\# Rounds to zero.

! Interpret data with caution.

[1] Refers to all students in public and private schools and homeschooled students.

[2] Students whose grade-equivalent was "ungraded" were excluded from the grade analysis. The percentage of students with an "ungraded" grade-equivalent was 0.03 percent in 1999 and 0.02 percent in 2003 and 2007.

[3] Urbanicity is based on a U.S. Census Bureau classification of places. Urban is a place with at least 50,000 people. Rural is a place not classified as urban.

NOTE: The number and percentage of homeschoolers exclude students who were enrolled in school for more than 25 hours a week; also excluded in 1999 and 2003 are students who were homeschooled only due to a temporary illness and, in 2007, students who were homeschooled primarily due to a temporary illness. Some data have been revised from previously published figures. Race categories exclude persons of Hispanic ethnicity. Standard errors appear in parentheses.

SOURCE: U.S. Department of Education, National Center for Education Statistics, *Homeschooling in the United States: 2003*, and Parent Survey (Parent:1999) and Parent and Family Involvement in Education Survey (PFI:2003 and PFI:2007) of the National Household Education Surveys Program. (This table was prepared August 2009.)

Number and percentage of public school students eligible for free or reduced-price lunch, by state: 2000–01, 2005–06, 2006–07, and 2007–08

State or jurisdiction	Number of students				Number of students eligible for free/reduced-price lunch				Percent of students eligible for free/reduced-price lunch			
	2000–01	2005–06	2006–07	2007–08	2000–01	2005–06	2006–07	2007–08	2000–01	2005–06	2006–07	2007–08
1	2	3	4	5	6	7	8	9	10	11	12	13
United States	—	48,403,390	48,357,258 [1]	47,768,533 [1]	—	20,333,474	20,485,664 [1]	20,516,584 [1]	—	42.0	42.4 [1]	42.9 [1]
Alabama	728,351	741,544	743,469	738,382	335,143	383,219	379,537	377,454	46.0	51.7	51.0	51.1
Alaska	105,333	103,498	116,682	131,029	32,468	41,872	45,028	44,043	30.8	40.5	38.6	33.6
Arizona	—	955,320	1,014,149	1,010,604	—	492,450	434,432	412,305	—	51.5	42.8	40.8
Arkansas	449,959	474,206	476,132	479,016	205,058	250,641	279,400	269,355	45.6	52.9	58.7	56.2
California	6,050,753	6,311,900	6,210,343	5,953,047	2,820,611	3,063,627	3,119,120	3,099,565	46.6	48.5	50.2	52.1
Colorado	724,349	779,825	789,014	791,996	195,148	258,264	269,926	275,475	26.9	33.1	34.2	34.8
Connecticut	—	575,051	558,532	568,405	—	152,669	156,735	168,586	—	26.5	28.1	29.7
Delaware	114,676	120,937	121,886	119,256	37,766	43,682	45,163	44,185	32.9	36.1	37.1	37.1
District of Columbia	68,380	66,498	61,922	61,184	47,839	41,050	38,425	38,309	70.0	61.7	62.1	62.6
Florida	2,434,755	2,674,998	2,670,482	2,666,811	1,079,009	1,224,228	1,207,511	1,215,459	44.3	45.8	45.2	45.6
Georgia	1,444,937	1,598,461	1,628,309	1,649,589	624,511	795,394	819,824	840,921	43.2	49.8	50.3	51.0
Hawaii	184,357	184,925	179,730	179,897	80,657	74,926	73,650	67,747	43.8	40.5	41.0	37.7
Idaho	244,755	260,343	265,045	271,976	85,824	99,093	99,639	101,202	35.1	38.1	37.6	37.2
Illinois	—	1,976,077	1,944,728	1,955,299	—	785,715	794,322	810,398	—	39.8	40.8	41.4
Indiana	977,219	1,034,719	1,044,175	1,044,593	285,267	373,433	392,272	410,324	29.2	36.1	37.6	39.3
Iowa	492,021	481,094	481,181	482,204	131,553	154,416	155,065	161,551	26.7	32.1	32.2	33.5
Kansas	462,594	466,263	459,171	468,014	154,693	180,919	182,860	186,948	33.4	38.8	39.8	39.9
Kentucky	626,723	641,682	646,461	665,066	298,334	336,287	331,361	340,413	47.6	52.4	51.3	51.2
Louisiana	741,162	654,388	675,381	680,499	433,068	400,596	416,402	430,263	58.4	61.2	61.7	63.2
Maine	198,532	189,572	192,078	190,737	60,162	65,877	67,289	68,814	30.3	34.8	35.0	36.1
Maryland	852,911	860,018	850,026	841,948	255,872	272,069	274,539	282,129	30.0	31.6	32.3	33.5
Massachusetts	979,590	971,907	958,858	962,806	237,871	274,515	280,165	283,819	24.3	28.2	29.2	29.5
Michigan	1,703,260	1,711,532	1,713,777	1,665,559	504,044	609,754	619,879	627,239	29.6	35.6	36.2	37.7
Minnesota	854,154	838,998	838,453	833,547	218,867	253,938	259,532	264,646	25.6	30.3	31.0	31.7
Mississippi	497,421	494,744	494,686	494,013	319,670	344,107	334,359	330,635	64.3	69.6	67.6	66.9
Missouri	912,247	915,844	919,668	917,188	315,608	358,428	359,193	362,385	34.6	39.1	39.1	39.5
Montana	154,438	143,093	142,137	140,715	47,415	50,172	50,656	50,936	30.7	35.1	35.6	36.2
Nebraska	286,138	286,610	286,823	291,238	87,045	99,387	104,783	108,986	30.4	34.7	36.5	37.4
Nevada	282,621	410,531	424,766 [2]	423,309	92,978	170,039	172,430 [2]	169,144	32.9	41.4	40.6 [2]	40.0
New Hampshire	206,919	203,998	201,108	200,772	31,212	35,087	35,945	36,416	15.1	17.2	17.9	18.1
New Jersey	1,312,983	1,395,600	1,333,110	1,341,122	357,728	373,946	378,927	387,965	27.2	26.8	28.4	28.9
New Mexico	320,303	326,755	326,113	321,544	174,939	181,916	198,304	199,302	54.6	55.7	60.8	62.0
New York	2,859,927	2,812,964	2,753,057	2,765,435	1,236,945	1,260,933	1,229,063	1,220,052	43.3	44.8	44.6	44.1
North Carolina	1,194,371	1,356,570	1,422,787	1,003,293	470,316	603,316	624,349	456,210	39.4	44.5	43.9	45.5
North Dakota	109,201	98,284	96,587	95,052	31,840	29,064	29,246	29,687	29.2	29.6	30.3	31.2
Ohio	1,745,237	1,836,982	1,832,100	1,822,586 [2]	494,829	597,517	619,247	616,031 [2]	28.4	32.5	33.8	33.8 [2]
Oklahoma	623,110	632,812	638,736	640,515	300,179	346,070	352,841	354,139	48.2	54.7	55.2	55.3
Oregon	535,617	534,814	553,054	558,791	186,203	230,737	232,435	235,632	34.8	43.1	42.0	42.2
Pennsylvania	1,798,977	1,813,760	1,757,776	1,635,217	510,121	574,951	556,645	560,384	28.4	31.7	31.7	34.3
Rhode Island	157,347	151,686	149,441	146,228	52,209	53,521	49,558	55,596	33.2	35.3	33.2	38.0
South Carolina	677,411	700,397	702,851	711,552	320,254	361,567	360,907	366,883	47.3	51.6	51.3	51.6
South Dakota	128,598	121,999	115,450	114,885	37,857	39,059	34,996	34,309	29.4	32.0	30.3	29.9
Tennessee	—	934,444	958,352	948,934	—	448,431	466,781	475,202	—	48.0	48.7	50.1
Texas	4,059,353	4,523,575	4,566,432	4,673,455	1,823,029	2,181,697	2,172,930	2,230,688	44.9	48.2	47.6	47.7
Utah	470,265	508,399	520,331	526,542	135,428	164,255	160,559	172,576	28.8	32.3	30.9	32.8
Vermont	102,049	96,638	91,238	87,038	23,986	25,487	24,467	25,767	23.5	26.4	26.8	29.6
Virginia	1,067,710	1,167,860	1,172,057	1,224,044	320,233	377,725	383,298	386,805	30.0	32.3	32.7	31.6
Washington	—	1,031,967	1,021,710	1,030,247	—	376,198	375,159	383,802	—	36.5	36.7	37.3
West Virginia	286,285	280,699	281,070	282,512	143,446	137,878	139,804	138,931	50.1	49.1	49.7	49.2
Wisconsin	859,276	864,207	870,647	874,478	219,276	256,645	271,422	281,027	25.5	29.7	31.2	32.1
Wyoming	89,895	84,402	85,187	86,364	43,483	26,707	25,284	25,944	48.4	31.6	29.7	30.0

—Not available.
[1] U.S. total includes imputation for nonreporting state.
[2] Imputation for survey nonresponse.
NOTE: Table reflects counts of students enrolled in schools for which both enrollment data and free/reduced price lunch eligibility data were reported.

SOURCE: U.S. Department of Education, National Center for Education Statistics, Common Core of Data (CCD), "Public Elementary/Secondary School Universe Survey," 2000–01, 2005–06, 2006–07, and 2007–08. (This table was prepared September 2009.)

Enrollment of 3-, 4-, and 5-year-old children in preprimary programs, by level of program, control of program, and attendance status: Selected years, 1965 through 2008

[Numbers in thousands]

Year and age	Total population, 3 to 5 years old		Enrollment by level and control								Enrollment by attendance					
			Total		Percent enrolled		Nursery school				Kindergarten				Full-day		Part-day		Percent full-day	
							Public		Private		Public		Private							
1	2		3		4		5		6		7		8		9		10		11	
Total, 3 to 5 years old																				
1965	12,549	(144.5)	3,407	(87.1)	27.1	(0.69)	127	(19.6)	393	(34.1)	2,291	(75.6)	596	(41.6)	—	(†)	—	(†)	—	(†)
1970	10,949	(109.4)	4,104	(71.5)	37.5	(0.65)	332	(25.3)	762	(37.6)	2,498	(62.0)	511	(31.1)	698	(36.1)	3,405	(68.3)	17.0	(0.83)
1975	10,185	(105.8)	4,955	(71.2)	48.7	(0.70)	570	(32.7)	1,174	(45.5)	2,682	(62.7)	528	(31.6)	1,295	(47.4)	3,659	(68.3)	26.1	(0.88)
1980	9,284	(102.6)	4,878	(68.8)	52.5	(0.74)	628	(34.6)	1,353	(48.6)	2,438	(60.6)	459	(29.9)	1,551	(51.4)	3,327	(66.1)	31.8	(0.95)
1985	10,733	(115.6)	5,865	(77.6)	54.6	(0.72)	846	(42.0)	1,631	(56.0)	2,847	(68.8)	541	(34.1)	2,144	(62.3)	3,722	(74.2)	36.6	(0.95)
1990	11,207	(124.2)	6,659	(82.3)	59.4	(0.73)	1,199	(51.8)	2,180	(66.4)	2,772	(72.3)	509	(34.9)	2,577	(70.6)	4,082	(80.7)	38.7	(0.95)
1995[1]	12,518	(131.5)	7,739	(86.6)	61.8	(0.69)	1,950	(64.6)	2,381	(69.9)	2,800	(74.2)	608	(38.3)	3,689	(81.2)	4,051	(83.4)	47.7	(0.90)
2000[1]	11,858	(133.0)	7,592	(86.3)	64.0	(0.70)	2,146	(69.2)	2,180	(69.7)	2,701	(75.4)	565	(38.3)	4,008	(85.1)	3,584	(82.6)	52.8	(0.95)
2004[1]	12,362	(145.9)	7,969	(83.3)	64.5	(0.67)	2,428	(69.2)	2,243	(67.1)	2,812	(73.0)	484	(33.8)	4,507	(83.8)	3,461	(78.2)	56.6	(0.87)
2005[1]	12,134	(144.6)	7,801	(82.7)	64.3	(0.68)	2,409	(68.8)	2,120	(65.5)	2,804	(72.7)	468	(33.2)	4,548	(83.5)	3,253	(76.4)	58.3	(0.87)
2006[1]	12,186	(144.9)	8,010	(82.1)	65.7	(0.67)	2,481	(69.6)	2,156	(66.0)	2,960	(74.1)	413	(31.3)	4,723	(84.2)	3,286	(76.7)	59.0	(0.86)
2007[1]	12,326	(145.7)	8,056	(82.7)	65.4	(0.67)	2,532	(70.2)	2,037	(64.6)	3,088	(75.3)	400	(30.8)	4,578	(84.0)	3,478	(78.3)	56.8	(0.86)
2008[1]	12,583	(147.1)	7,928	(84.8)	63.0	(0.67)	2,609	(71.2)	1,961	(63.7)	2,982	(74.7)	376	(29.9)	4,615	(84.7)	3,313	(77.4)	58.2	(0.87)
3 years old																				
1965	4,149	(84.9)	203	(24.3)	4.9	(0.59)	41	(11.1)	153	(21.2)	5	(3.9)	4	(3.5)	—	(†)	—	(†)	—	(†)
1970	3,516	(63.2)	454	(28.1)	12.9	(0.80)	110	(14.6)	322	(24.1)	12	(4.9)	10	(4.5)	142	(16.5)	312	(23.8)	31.3	(3.07)
1975	3,177	(60.2)	683	(32.7)	21.5	(1.03)	179	(18.3)	474	(28.3)	11	(4.7)	18	(6.0)	259	(21.8)	423	(27.0)	37.9	(2.62)
1980	3,143	(60.7)	857	(35.7)	27.3	(1.14)	221	(20.5)	604	(31.6)	16	(5.7)	17	(5.9)	321	(24.3)	536	(30.2)	37.5	(2.36)
1985	3,594	(68.2)	1,035	(40.8)	28.8	(1.14)	278	(24.1)	679	(35.3)	52	(10.8)	26	(7.6)	350	(26.7)	685	(35.4)	33.8	(2.21)
1990	3,692	(72.7)	1,205	(45.1)	32.6	(1.22)	347	(28.1)	840	(40.3)	11	(5.4)	7	(4.2)	447	(31.4)	758	(38.9)	37.1	(2.20)
1995[1]	4,148	(77.4)	1,489	(49.2)	35.9	(1.19)	511	(33.7)	947	(43.0)	15	(6.1)	17	(6.5)	754	(39.6)	736	(39.2)	50.6	(2.06)
2000[1]	3,929	(78.2)	1,541	(50.5)	39.2	(1.29)	644	(38.3)	854	(42.7)	27	(8.5)	16	(6.7)	761	(40.9)	779	(41.3)	49.4	(2.10)
2004[1]	4,089	(85.7)	1,583	(48.8)	38.7	(1.19)	674	(37.2)	849	(40.6)	40	(9.9)	20	(7.0)	808	(39.9)	775	(39.3)	51.0	(1.97)
2005[1]	4,151	(86.3)	1,715	(49.7)	41.3	(1.20)	777	(39.4)	869	(41.1)	54	(11.4)	15	(6.0)	901	(41.6)	814	(40.1)	52.5	(1.89)
2006[1]	4,043	(85.2)	1,716	(49.2)	42.4	(1.22)	733	(38.4)	912	(41.6)	54	(11.5)	17	(6.4)	884	(41.2)	833	(40.3)	51.5	(1.89)
2007[1]	4,142	(86.2)	1,717	(49.7)	41.5	(1.20)	766	(39.1)	832	(40.4)	106	(15.9)	13	(5.7)	883	(41.3)	834	(40.4)	51.4	(1.89)
2008[1]	4,204	(86.9)	1,655	(49.6)	39.4	(1.18)	755	(39.0)	802	(39.9)	90	(14.7)	7	(4.1)	852	(40.8)	803	(39.9)	51.5	(1.92)
4 years old																				
1965	4,238	(85.8)	683	(41.8)	16.1	(0.99)	68	(14.3)	213	(24.9)	284	(28.4)	118	(18.7)	—	(†)	—	(†)	—	(†)
1970	3,620	(64.1)	1,007	(38.0)	27.8	(1.05)	176	(18.3)	395	(26.5)	318	(24.0)	117	(15.0)	230	(20.7)	776	(34.8)	22.8	(1.87)
1975	3,499	(63.1)	1,418	(41.0)	40.5	(1.17)	332	(24.5)	644	(32.3)	313	(23.8)	129	(15.7)	411	(26.9)	1,008	(37.8)	29.0	(1.70)
1980	3,072	(60.0)	1,423	(39.5)	46.3	(1.29)	363	(25.6)	701	(33.3)	239	(21.2)	120	(15.4)	467	(28.5)	956	(36.7)	32.8	(1.78)
1985	3,598	(68.2)	1,766	(45.1)	49.1	(1.25)	496	(31.1)	859	(38.5)	276	(24.0)	135	(17.1)	643	(34.6)	1,123	(41.8)	36.4	(1.72)
1990	3,723	(73.0)	2,087	(48.0)	56.1	(1.29)	695	(37.7)	1,144	(44.6)	157	(19.4)	91	(14.9)	716	(38.1)	1,371	(46.6)	34.3	(1.65)
1995[1]	4,145	(77.4)	2,553	(49.9)	61.6	(1.20)	1,054	(44.6)	1,208	(46.6)	207	(22.3)	84	(14.5)	1,104	(45.3)	1,449	(48.9)	43.3	(1.56)
2000[1]	3,940	(78.3)	2,556	(49.5)	64.9	(1.26)	1,144	(47.0)	1,121	(46.8)	227	(24.2)	65	(13.2)	1,182	(47.5)	1,374	(49.4)	46.2	(1.63)
2004[1]	4,339	(88.2)	2,969	(48.0)	68.4	(1.11)	1,462	(48.8)	1,213	(46.3)	208	(22.1)	85	(14.3)	1,484	(48.9)	1,485	(48.9)	50.0	(1.44)
2005[1]	4,028	(85.1)	2,668	(47.0)	66.2	(1.17)	1,295	(46.4)	1,083	(44.1)	215	(22.3)	75	(13.5)	1,332	(46.8)	1,336	(46.8)	49.9	(1.52)
2006[1]	4,095	(85.8)	2,817	(46.4)	68.8	(1.13)	1,401	(47.5)	1,067	(44.0)	306	(26.4)	43	(10.3)	1,418	(47.7)	1,399	(47.5)	50.3	(1.48)
2007[1]	4,092	(85.7)	2,774	(46.8)	67.8	(1.14)	1,417	(47.7)	993	(42.9)	295	(25.9)	69	(12.9)	1,297	(46.6)	1,476	(48.1)	46.8	(1.48)
2008[1]	4,241	(87.2)	2,804	(48.3)	66.1	(1.14)	1,525	(48.9)	995	(43.2)	234	(23.3)	49	(10.9)	1,332	(47.3)	1,472	(48.6)	47.5	(1.48)
5 years old[2]																				
1965	4,162	(85.1)	2,521	(55.1)	60.6	(1.32)	18	(7.4)	27	(9.1)	2,002	(56.3)	474	(35.8)	—	(†)	—	(†)	—	(†)
1970	3,814	(65.8)	2,643	(40.2)	69.3	(1.05)	45	(9.4)	45	(9.4)	2,168	(43.2)	384	(26.2)	326	(24.4)	2,317	(42.5)	12.3	(0.90)
1975	3,509	(63.2)	2,854	(32.6)	81.3	(0.93)	59	(10.7)	57	(10.6)	2,358	(39.2)	381	(26.0)	625	(32.0)	2,228	(40.2)	21.9	(1.09)
1980	3,069	(60.0)	2,598	(28.6)	84.7	(0.93)	44	(9.4)	48	(9.8)	2,183	(35.9)	322	(24.3)	763	(34.2)	1,835	(38.8)	29.4	(1.28)
1985	3,542	(67.7)	3,065	(30.6)	86.5	(0.86)	73	(12.7)	94	(14.4)	2,519	(40.6)	379	(27.7)	1,151	(41.9)	1,914	(44.6)	37.6	(1.32)
1990	3,792	(73.7)	3,367	(30.8)	88.8	(0.81)	157	(19.4)	196	(21.6)	2,604	(45.2)	411	(30.3)	1,414	(47.2)	1,953	(48.7)	42.0	(1.35)
1995[1]	4,224	(78.1)	3,697	(34.2)	87.5	(0.81)	385	(29.8)	226	(23.3)	2,578	(50.5)	507	(33.7)	1,830	(51.3)	1,867	(51.4)	49.5	(1.31)
2000[1]	3,989	(78.7)	3,495	(34.3)	87.6	(0.86)	359	(29.8)	206	(23.1)	2,447	(50.8)	484	(34.1)	2,065	(52.1)	1,431	(50.0)	59.1	(1.37)
2004[1]	3,934	(84.1)	3,417	(33.2)	86.9	(0.84)	293	(25.8)	181	(20.6)	2,564	(46.8)	380	(29.0)	2,215	(48.7)	1,201	(45.2)	64.8	(1.28)
2005[1]	3,955	(84.3)	3,418	(33.7)	86.4	(0.85)	337	(27.5)	168	(19.9)	2,535	(47.3)	378	(29.0)	2,316	(48.5)	1,102	(44.2)	67.7	(1.25)
2006[1]	4,049	(85.3)	3,476	(34.7)	85.9	(0.86)	346	(27.9)	178	(20.4)	2,599	(47.8)	353	(28.1)	2,422	(48.9)	1,054	(43.7)	69.7	(1.22)
2007[1]	4,091	(85.7)	3,565	(33.5)	87.1	(0.82)	349	(28.0)	212	(22.2)	2,687	(47.6)	317	(26.8)	2,397	(49.3)	1,168	(45.2)	67.2	(1.23)
2008[1]	4,137	(86.2)	3,470	(37.1)	83.9	(0.90)	329	(27.2)	163	(19.6)	2,659	(48.3)	320	(26.9)	2,432	(49.6)	1,038	(43.7)	70.1	(1.22)

—Not available.
†Not applicable.
[1]Data collected using new procedures. Data may not be comparable with figures prior to 1994.
[2]Enrollment data include only those students in preprimary programs.
NOTE: Data are based on sample surveys of the civilian noninstitutional population. Although cells with fewer than 75,000 children are subject to wide sampling variation, they are included in the table to permit various types of aggregations. Detail may not sum to totals because of rounding. Standard errors appear in parentheses.
SOURCE: U.S. Department of Education, National Center for Education Statistics, *Preprimary Enrollment*, 1965, 1970, and 1975. U.S. Department of Commerce, Census Bureau, Current Population Survey (CPS), October, 1980 through 2008. (This table was prepared August 2009.)

Children 3 to 21 years old served under Individuals with Disabilities Education Act, Part B, by type of disability: Selected years, 1976–77 through 2007–08

Type of disability	1976–77	1980–81	1990–91	1995–96	1997–98	1998–99	1999–2000	2000–01	2001–02	2002–03	2003–04	2004–05	2005–06	2006–07	2007–08[1]
1	2	3	4	5	6	7	8	9	10	11	12	13	14	15	16
						Number served (in thousands)									
All disabilities	**3,694**	**4,144**	**4,710**	**5,572**	**5,908**	**6,056**	**6,195**	**6,296**	**6,407**	**6,523**	**6,634**	**6,719**	**6,713**	**6,686**	**6,606**
Specific learning disabilities	796	1,462	2,129	2,578	2,727	2,790	2,834	2,868	2,861	2,848	2,831	2,798	2,735	2,665	2,573
Speech or language impairments	1,302	1,168	985	1,022	1,060	1,068	1,080	1,409	1,391	1,412	1,441	1,463	1,468	1,475	1,456
Mental retardation	961	830	534	571	589	597	600	624	616	602	593	578	556	534	500
Emotional disturbance	283	347	389	437	454	462	469	481	483	485	489	489	477	464	442
Hearing impairments	88	79	58	67	69	70	71	78	78	78	79	79	79	80	79
Orthopedic impairments	87	58	49	63	67	69	71	83	83	83	77	73	71	69	67
Other health impairments[2]	141	98	55	133	190	220	253	303	350	403	464	521	570	611	641
Visual impairments	38	31	23	25	26	26	26	29	28	29	28	29	29	29	29
Multiple disabilities	—	68	96	93	106	106	111	133	136	138	140	140	141	142	138
Deaf-blindness	—	3	1	1	1	2	2	1	2	2	2	2	2	2	2
Autism	—	—	—	28	42	53	65	94	114	137	163	191	223	258	296
Traumatic brain injury	—	—	—	9	12	13	14	16	22	22	23	24	24	25	25
Developmental delay	—	—	—	—	2	12	19	178	242	283	305	332	339	333	358
Preschool disabled[3]	†	†	390	544	565	568	581	†	†	†	†	†	†	†	†
						Percentage distribution of children served									
All disabilities	**100.0**	**100.0**	**100.0**	**100.0**	**100.0**	**100.0**	**100.0**	**100.0**	**100.0**	**100.0**	**100.0**	**100.0**	**100.0**	**100.0**	**100.0**
Specific learning disabilities	21.5	35.3	45.2	46.3	46.2	46.1	45.7	45.5	44.7	43.7	42.7	41.6	40.7	39.9	39.0
Speech or language impairments	35.2	28.2	20.9	18.3	17.9	17.6	17.4	22.4	21.7	21.6	21.7	21.8	21.9	22.1	22.0
Mental retardation	26.0	20.0	11.3	10.2	10.0	9.9	9.7	9.9	9.6	9.2	8.9	8.6	8.3	8.0	7.6
Emotional disturbance	7.7	8.4	8.3	7.8	7.7	7.6	7.6	7.6	7.5	7.4	7.4	7.3	7.1	6.9	6.7
Hearing impairments	2.4	1.9	1.2	1.2	1.2	1.2	1.1	1.2	1.2	1.2	1.2	1.2	1.2	1.2	1.2
Orthopedic impairments	2.4	1.4	1.0	1.1	1.1	1.1	1.1	1.3	1.3	1.3	1.2	1.1	1.1	1.0	1.0
Other health impairments[2]	3.8	2.4	1.2	2.4	3.2	3.6	4.1	4.8	5.5	6.2	7.0	7.7	8.5	9.1	9.7
Visual impairments	1.0	0.7	0.5	0.4	0.4	0.4	0.4	0.5	0.4	0.4	0.4	0.4	0.4	0.4	0.4
Multiple disabilities	—	1.6	2.0	1.7	1.8	1.8	1.8	2.1	2.1	2.1	2.1	2.1	2.1	2.1	2.1
Deaf-blindness	—	0.1	#	#	#	#	#	#	#	#	#	#	#	#	#
Autism	—	—	—	0.5	0.7	0.9	1.0	1.5	1.8	2.1	2.5	2.8	3.3	3.9	4.5
Traumatic brain injury	—	—	—	0.2	0.2	0.2	0.2	0.3	0.3	0.3	0.4	0.4	0.4	0.4	0.4
Developmental delay	—	—	—	—	0.0	0.2	0.3	2.8	3.8	4.3	4.6	4.9	5.1	5.0	5.4
Preschool disabled[3]	†	†	8.3	9.8	9.6	9.4	9.4	†	†	†	†	†	†	†	†
						Number served as a percent of total enrollment[4]									
All disabilities	**8.3**	**10.1**	**11.4**	**12.4**	**12.8**	**13.0**	**13.2**	**13.3**	**13.4**	**13.5**	**13.7**	**13.8**	**13.7**	**13.6**	**13.4**
Specific learning disabilities	1.8	3.6	5.2	5.8	5.9	6.0	6.0	6.1	6.0	5.9	5.8	5.7	5.6	5.4	5.2
Speech or language impairments	2.9	2.9	2.4	2.3	2.3	2.3	2.3	3.0	2.9	2.9	3.0	3.0	3.0	3.0	3.0
Mental retardation	2.2	2.0	1.3	1.3	1.3	1.3	1.3	1.3	1.3	1.2	1.2	1.2	1.1	1.1	1.0
Emotional disturbance	0.6	0.8	0.9	1.0	1.0	1.0	1.0	1.0	1.0	1.0	1.0	1.0	1.0	0.9	0.9
Hearing impairments	0.2	0.2	0.1	0.1	0.1	0.2	0.2	0.2	0.2	0.2	0.2	0.2	0.2	0.2	0.2
Orthopedic impairments	0.2	0.1	0.1	0.1	0.1	0.1	0.2	0.2	0.2	0.2	0.2	0.2	0.1	0.1	0.1
Other health impairments[2]	0.3	0.2	0.1	0.3	0.4	0.5	0.5	0.6	0.7	0.8	1.0	1.1	1.2	1.2	1.3
Visual impairments	0.1	0.1	0.1	0.1	0.1	0.1	0.1	0.1	0.1	0.1	0.1	0.1	0.1	0.1	0.1
Multiple disabilities	—	0.2	0.2	0.2	0.2	0.2	0.2	0.3	0.3	0.3	0.3	0.3	0.3	0.3	0.3
Deaf-blindness	—	#	#	#	#	#	#	#	#	#	#	#	#	#	#
Autism	—	—	—	0.1	0.1	0.1	0.1	0.2	0.2	0.3	0.3	0.4	0.5	0.5	0.6
Traumatic brain injury	—	—	—	#	#	#	#	#	#	#	#	#	#	0.1	0.1
Developmental delay	—	—	—	#	#	#	0.4	0.5	0.6	0.6	0.7	0.7	0.7	0.7	0.7
Preschool disabled[3]	†	†	0.9	1.2	1.2	1.2	1.2	†	†	†	†	†	†	†	†

—Not available.
†Not applicable.
#Rounds to zero.
[1]Data do not include Vermont, for which 2007–08 data were not available. In 2006–07, the total number of 3- to 21-year-olds served in Vermont was 14,010.
[2]Other health impairments include having limited strength, vitality, or alertness due to chronic or acute health problems such as a heart condition, tuberculosis, rheumatic fever, nephritis, asthma, sickle cell anemia, hemophilia, epilepsy, lead poisoning, leukemia, or diabetes.
[3]Prior to 1990–91 and after 1999–2000, preschool children are included in the counts by disability condition. For other years, preschool children are not included in the counts by disability condition, but are separately reported.
[4]Based on the total enrollment in public schools, prekindergarten through 12th grade.
NOTE: Prior to October 1994, children and youth with disabilities were served under Chapter 1 of the Elementary and Secondary Education Act as well as under the Individuals with Disabilities

Education Act (IDEA), Part B. Data reported in this table for years prior to 1994–95 include children ages 0–21 served under Chapter 1. Data are for the 50 states and the District of Columbia only. Increases since 1987–88 are due in part to new legislation enacted in fall 1986, which added a mandate for public school special education services for 3- to 5-year-old disabled children. Some data have been revised from previously published figures. Detail may not sum to totals because of rounding.
SOURCE: U.S. Department of Education, Office of Special Education Programs, *Annual Report to Congress on the Implementation of the Individuals with Disabilities Education Act*, selected years, 1979 through 2007; and Individuals with Disabilities Education Act (IDEA) database, retrieved April 14, 2009, from http://www.ideadata.org/PartBdata.asp. National Center for Education Statistics, *Statistics of Public Elementary and Secondary School Systems*, 1977 and 1980; Common Core of Data (CCD), "State Nonfiscal Survey of Public Elementary/Secondary Education," 1990–91 through 2007–08. (This table was prepared September 2009.)

Percentage distribution of students 6 to 21 years old served under Individuals with Disabilities Education Act, Part B, by educational environment and type of disability: Selected years, fall 1989 through fall 2007

Type of disability	All environments	Regular school, time outside regular class			Separate school for students with disabilities		Separate residential facility		Parentally placed in regular private schools	Homebound /hospital placement	Correctional facility
		Less than 21 percent	21–60 percent	More than 60 percent	Public	Private	Public	Private			
1	2	3	4	5	6	7	8	9	10	11	12
All students with disabilities											
1989	100.0	31.7	37.5	24.9	3.2	1.3	0.7	0.3	—	0.6	—
1990	100.0	33.1	36.4	25.0	2.9	1.3	0.6	0.3	—	0.5	—
1994	100.0	44.8	28.5	22.4	2.0	1.0	0.5	0.3	—	0.6	—
1995	100.0	45.7	28.5	21.5	2.1	1.0	0.4	0.3	—	0.5	—
1996	100.0	46.1	28.3	21.4	2.0	1.0	0.4	0.3	—	0.5	—
1997	100.0	46.8	28.8	20.4	1.8	1.0	0.4	0.3	—	0.5	—
1998	100.0	46.0	29.9	20.0	1.8	1.1	0.4	0.3	—	0.5	—
1999	100.0	45.9	29.8	20.3	1.9	1.0	0.4	0.3	—	0.5	—
2000	100.0	46.5	29.8	19.5	1.9	1.1	0.4	0.3	—	0.5	—
2001	100.0	48.2	28.5	19.2	1.7	1.2	0.4	0.4	—	0.4	—
2002	100.0	48.2	28.7	19.0	1.7	1.2	0.3	0.4	—	0.5	—
2003	100.0	49.9	27.7	18.5	1.7	1.1	0.3	0.4	—	0.5	—
2004	100.0	51.9	26.5	17.6	1.8	1.2	0.3	0.3	—	0.4	—
2005											
All students with disabilities	100.0	54.2	25.1	16.7	1.8	1.2	0.3	0.3	—	0.5	—
Specific learning disabilities	100.0	54.5	33.7	10.9	0.3	0.3	0.1	0.1	—	0.2	—
Speech or language impairments	100.0	88.7	6.2	4.6	0.1	0.3	#	#	—	0.1	—
Mental retardation	100.0	14.1	29.1	50.2	4.6	1.0	0.2	0.3	—	0.5	—
Emotional disturbance	100.0	34.7	21.6	26.8	6.9	5.7	1.2	1.8	—	1.3	—
Multiple disabilities	100.0	13.3	16.9	45.1	12.2	8.0	0.9	1.3	—	2.3	—
Hearing impairments	100.0	48.8	18.3	19.5	4.8	2.3	5.8	0.4	—	0.2	—
Orthopedic impairments	100.0	49.5	18.1	25.7	4.1	0.8	0.1	0.1	—	1.6	—
Other health impairments[1]	100.0	56.0	28.0	12.8	0.8	0.8	0.1	0.2	—	1.3	—
Visual impairments	100.0	58.2	15.2	14.2	4.1	1.6	5.4	0.7	—	0.6	—
Autism	100.0	31.4	18.2	39.8	5.1	4.4	0.1	0.6	—	0.4	—
Deaf-blindness	100.0	22.8	15.1	33.6	10.1	7.3	6.6	3.2	—	1.4	—
Traumatic brain injury	100.0	40.0	27.5	24.5	2.8	3.0	0.2	0.5	—	1.5	—
Developmental delay	100.0	59.5	23.4	15.8	0.7	0.3	0.1	#	—	0.2	—
2006											
All students with disabilities	100.0	53.7	23.7	17.6	2.9 [2]	(2)	0.4 [2]	(2)	1.0 [3]	0.4	0.4
Specific learning disabilities	100.0	54.8	31.4	11.8	0.7 [2]	(2)	0.1 [2]	(2)	0.7 [3]	0.2	0.4
Speech or language impairments	100.0	84.2	6.1	6.8	0.3 [2]	(2)	# [2]	(2)	2.5 [3]	0.1	#
Mental retardation	100.0	16.0	28.7	48.4	5.6 [2]	(2)	0.4 [2]	(2)	0.2 [3]	0.5	0.3
Emotional disturbance	100.0	35.1	20.8	26.6	12.3 [2]	(2)	2.1 [2]	(2)	0.2 [3]	1.2	1.7
Multiple disabilities	100.0	13.4	16.7	44.4	20.5 [2]	(2)	2.0 [2]	(2)	0.4 [3]	2.3	0.3
Hearing impairments	100.0	48.8	17.8	19.8	8.2 [2]	(2)	4.2 [2]	(2)	1.0 [3]	0.2	0.1
Orthopedic impairments	100.0	47.0	19.0	26.3	5.3 [2]	(2)	0.2 [2]	(2)	0.7 [3]	1.4	#
Other health impairments[1]	100.0	54.8	26.5	14.9	1.6 [2]	(2)	0.2 [2]	(2)	0.8 [3]	1.0	0.2
Visual impairments	100.0	57.2	14.7	15.9	6.4 [2]	(2)	4.4 [2]	(2)	0.9 [3]	0.5	0.1
Autism	100.0	32.3	18.4	38.7	9.0 [2]	(2)	0.7 [2]	(2)	0.5 [3]	0.3	#
Deaf-blindness	100.0	21.0	13.5	34.8	20.7 [2]	(2)	7.6 [2]	(2)	0.6 [3]	1.8	#
Traumatic brain injury	100.0	41.7	26.1	23.7	5.7 [2]	(2)	0.6 [2]	(2)	0.6 [3]	1.4	0.2
Developmental delay	100.0	58.8	21.3	18.4	0.8 [2]	(2)	0.1 [2]	(2)	0.4 [3]	0.2	#
2007											
All students with disabilities	100.0	56.8	22.4	15.4	3.0 [2]	(2)	0.4 [2]	(2)	1.1 [3]	0.4	0.4
Specific learning disabilities	100.0	59.0	29.7	9.2	0.6 [2]	(2)	0.1 [2]	(2)	0.9 [3]	0.2	0.4
Speech or language impairments	100.0	86.7	5.7	4.5	0.3 [2]	(2)	0.0 [2]	(2)	2.8 [3]	0.1	#
Mental retardation	100.0	15.8	27.6	49.0	6.0 [2]	(2)	0.4 [2]	(2)	0.3 [3]	0.5	0.3
Emotional disturbance	100.0	37.3	19.7	24.1	13.1 [2]	(2)	2.1 [2]	(2)	0.4 [3]	1.2	2.0
Multiple disabilities	100.0	12.9	16.1	45.2	20.6 [2]	(2)	1.9 [2]	(2)	0.5 [3]	2.5	0.3
Hearing impairments	100.0	51.9	17.6	16.8	8.0 [2]	(2)	4.3 [2]	(2)	1.1 [3]	0.2	0.1
Orthopedic impairments	100.0	50.0	17.4	24.5	5.5 [2]	(2)	0.2 [2]	(2)	0.9 [3]	1.5	0.1
Other health impairments[1]	100.0	59.0	25.4	11.7	1.6 [2]	(2)	0.2 [2]	(2)	1.0 [3]	1.0	0.3
Visual impairments	100.0	60.1	14.3	12.9	6.3 [2]	(2)	4.5 [2]	(2)	1.3 [3]	0.6	0.1
Autism	100.0	34.6	18.2	36.9	8.7 [2]	(2)	0.7 [2]	(2)	0.6 [3]	0.3	#
Deaf-blindness	100.0	20.8	13.8	32.4	21.2 [2]	(2)	9.3 [2]	(2)	0.3 [3]	2.0	0.2
Traumatic brain injury	100.0	43.9	24.8	22.5	5.7 [2]	(2)	0.7 [2]	(2)	0.7 [3]	1.6	0.2
Developmental delay	100.0	61.6	20.8	16.2	0.7 [2]	(2)	0.1 [2]	(2)	0.5 [3]	0.2	#

—Not available.
#Rounds to zero.

[1]Other health impairments include having limited strength, vitality, or alertness due to chronic or acute health problems such as a heart condition, tuberculosis, rheumatic fever, nephritis, asthma, sickle cell anemia, hemophilia, epilepsy, lead poisoning, leukemia, or diabetes.

[2]Data for 2006 and 2007 combine public and private schools and combine public and private residential facilities.

[3]Students who are enrolled by their parents or guardians in regular private schools and have their basic education paid through private resources, but receive special education services at public expense. These students are not included under "Regular school, time outside general class" (columns 3 through 5).

NOTE: Data are for the 50 United States, the District of Columbia, and the Bureau of Indian Education schools. Detail may not sum to totals because of rounding.

SOURCE: U.S. Department of Education, Office of Special Education Programs, Individuals with Disabilities Education Act (IDEA) database. Retrieved April 21, 2009, from https://www.ideadata.org/arc_toc9.asp#partbLRE. (This table was prepared April 2009.)

Number and percentage of children served under Individuals with Disabilities Education Act, Part B, by age group and state or jurisdiction: Selected years, 1990–91 through 2007–08

State or jurisdiction	3- to 21-year-olds served							As a percent of public school enrollment, 2007–08[1]	Percent change in number served, 2000–01 to 2007–08	3- to 5-year-olds served				
	1990–91	2000–01	2003–04	2004–05	2005–06	2006–07	2007–08			1990–91	2000–01	2005–06	2006–07	2007–08
1	2	3	4	5	6	7	8	9	10	11	12	13	14	15
United States	4,710,089	6,295,816	6,633,902	6,718,619	6,712,605	6,686,361	6,605,695	13.4	4.9	389,751	592,087	698,608	706,401	699,841
Alabama.........................	94,601	99,828	93,056	93,402	92,635	89,013	84,772	11.4	-15.1	7,154	7,554	8,218	8,026	7,111
Alaska...........................	14,390	17,691	17,959	18,134	17,997	17,760	17,535	13.4	-0.9	1,458	1,637	2,082	1,987	1,954
Arizona.........................	56,629	96,442	112,125	119,841	124,504	126,654	131,136	12.1	36.0	4,330	9,144	14,062	14,040	14,097
Arkansas.......................	47,187	62,222	66,793	68,088	67,314	68,133	65,965	13.8	6.0	4,626	9,376	10,286	11,689	11,795
California.......................	468,420	645,287	675,763	675,417	676,318	672,737	670,904	10.6	4.0	39,627	57,651	66,653	67,052	68,002
Colorado.......................	56,336	78,715	82,447	83,249	83,498	83,559	83,077	10.4	5.5	4,128	8,202	10,540	10,939	10,802
Connecticut...................	63,886	73,886	73,952	73,028	71,968	69,127	68,987	12.1	-6.6	5,466	7,172	7,881	6,833	7,660
Delaware.......................	14,208	16,760	18,417	18,698	18,857	19,366	19,435	15.9	16.0	1,493	1,652	2,073	2,213	2,264
District of Columbia	6,290	10,559	13,242	13,424	11,738	11,113	10,863	13.9	2.9	411	374	507	754	567
Florida..........................	234,509	367,335	397,758	400,001	398,916	398,289	391,092	14.7	6.5	14,883	30,660	34,350	33,644	32,819
Georgia.........................	101,762	171,292	190,948	195,928	197,596	196,810	189,424	11.5	10.6	7,098	16,560	20,728	20,410	18,454
Hawaii...........................	12,705	23,951	23,266	22,711	21,963	21,099	20,441	11.4	-14.7	809	1,919	2,423	2,459	2,477
Idaho............................	21,703	29,174	29,092	28,880	29,021	28,439	27,989	10.3	-4.1	2,815	3,591	4,043	3,889	3,976
Illinois..........................	236,060	297,316	318,111	322,982	323,444	326,763	321,668	15.2	8.2	22,997	28,787	35,454	37,152	36,957
Indiana..........................	112,949	156,320	171,896	175,205	177,826	179,043	179,076	17.1	14.6	7,243	15,101	19,228	19,364	19,530
Iowa.............................	59,787	72,461	73,717	73,637	72,457	71,394	69,204	14.3	-4.5	5,421	5,580	6,118	6,199	5,872
Kansas..........................	44,785	61,267	65,139	65,290	65,595	65,831	65,712	14.0	7.3	3,881	7,728	9,267	9,524	9,608
Kentucky.......................	78,853	94,572	103,783	106,916	108,798	109,354	109,187	16.4	15.5	10,440	16,372	21,317	21,007	20,591
Louisiana.......................	72,825	97,938	101,933	102,498	90,453	89,422	88,153	12.9	-10.0	6,703	9,957	10,597	10,503	10,151
Maine............................	27,987	35,633	37,784	37,573	36,522	35,564	34,425	17.5	-3.4	2,895	3,978	4,348	4,145	3,889
Maryland........................	88,017	112,077	113,865	112,404	110,959	106,739	104,585	12.4	-6.7	7,163	10,003	12,148	11,590	11,752
Massachusetts...............	149,743	162,216	159,042	161,993	162,654	165,959	166,747	17.3	2.8	12,141	14,328	15,195	15,813	15,920
Michigan........................	166,511	221,456	238,292	242,083	243,607	241,941	236,576	14.0	6.8	14,547	19,937	24,290	24,268	24,097
Minnesota......................	79,013	109,880	114,193	115,491	116,511	117,924	119,332	14.2	8.6	8,646	11,522	13,402	13,989	14,286
Mississippi.....................	60,872	62,281	66,848	68,883	68,099	67,590	65,717	13.3	5.5	5,642	6,944	8,319	8,430	8,422
Missouri.........................	101,166	137,381	143,593	142,872	143,204	141,406	138,292	15.1	0.7	4,100	11,307	15,268	15,415	15,629
Montana.........................	16,955	19,313	19,435	19,515	19,259	18,557	18,158	12.7	-6.0	1,751	1,635	1,925	1,941	1,971
Nebraska.......................	32,312	42,793	44,561	45,712	45,239	44,833	45,687	15.7	6.8	2,512	3,724	4,665	4,886	5,179
Nevada..........................	18,099	38,160	45,201	47,015	47,794	48,230	48,332	11.3	26.7	1,401	3,676	5,492	5,669	5,715
New Hampshire...............	19,049	30,077	31,311	31,675	31,782	31,399	32,274	16.1	7.3	1,468	2,387	2,902	2,905	2,523
New Jersey.....................	178,870	221,715	241,272	245,878	249,385	250,109	250,099	18.1	12.8	14,741	16,361	19,329	19,782	19,580
New Mexico....................	36,000	52,256	51,814	51,464	50,322	47,917	46,384	14.1	-11.2	2,210	4,970	6,441	6,300	6,337
New York........................	307,366	441,333	442,665	452,312	447,422	451,929	453,715	16.4	2.8	26,266	51,665	58,297	60,156	63,040
North Carolina	122,942	173,067	193,956	193,377	192,820	192,451	191,668	12.9	10.7	10,516	17,361	20,543	20,433	19,914
North Dakota	12,294	13,652	14,044	14,681	13,883	13,825	13,616	14.3	-0.3	1,164	1,247	1,520	1,567	1,560
Ohio.............................	205,440	237,643	253,878	260,710	266,447	269,133	269,742	14.8	13.5	12,487	18,664	22,702	23,455	23,137
Oklahoma......................	65,457	85,577	93,045	95,022	96,601	95,860	95,323	14.8	11.4	5,163	6,393	8,149	7,625	7,617
Oregon..........................	54,422	75,204	76,083	77,094	77,376	77,832	78,264	13.8	4.1	2,854	6,926	8,167	8,311	8,572
Pennsylvania..................	214,254	242,655	273,259	282,356	288,733	292,798	293,865	16.3	21.1	17,982	21,477	25,964	27,599	28,145
Rhode Island	20,646	30,727	32,223	31,532	30,681	30,243	29,033	19.7	-5.5	1,682	2,614	2,815	2,982	2,967
South Carolina...............	77,367	105,922	111,077	111,509	110,219	107,353	103,731	14.6	-2.1	7,948	11,775	11,603	13,864	10,472
South Dakota.................	14,726	16,825	17,760	17,921	17,631	17,824	17,971	14.8	6.8	2,105	2,286	2,747	2,624	2,683
Tennessee.....................	104,853	125,863	122,627	122,643	120,122	120,263	120,925	12.5	-3.9	7,487	10,699	12,008	11,967	12,264
Texas............................	344,529	491,642	506,771	514,236	507,405	494,302	472,749	10.1	-3.8	24,848	36,442	40,236	39,351	37,528
Utah..............................	46,606	53,921	57,745	59,840	60,526	61,166	63,066	10.9	17.0	3,424	5,785	7,462	7,597	8,023
Vermont.........................	12,160	13,623	13,670	13,894	13,917	14,010	—	—	—	1,097	1,237	1,556	1,602	—
Virginia..........................	112,072	162,212	172,788	174,417	174,640	170,794	168,496	13.7	3.9	9,892	14,444	17,480	16,968	16,845
Washington....................	83,545	118,851	123,673	124,067	124,999	122,979	123,698	12.0	4.1	9,558	11,760	13,429	13,174	13,529
West Virginia..................	42,428	50,333	50,772	50,377	49,677	49,054	47,855	16.9	-4.9	2,923	5,445	5,833	6,013	5,849
Wisconsin......................	85,651	125,358	127,828	129,179	130,076	128,526	126,496	14.5	0.9	10,934	14,383	16,077	15,591	14,867
Wyoming........................	10,852	13,154	13,430	13,565	13,696	13,945	14,254	16.5	8.4	1,221	1,695	2,469	2,645	2,842
Bureau of Indian Education	6,997	8,448	8,343	8,051	7,795	6,918	7,057	—	-16.5	1,092	338	330	234	325
Other jurisdictions ...	38,986	70,670	83,948	93,716	93,256	102,995	105,451	—	49.2	3,892	8,168	5,149	7,749	10,205
American Samoa..............	363	697	1,135	1,239	1,211	1,146	1,171	—	68.0	48	48	80	78	169
Guam............................	1,750	2,267	2,460	2,485	2,480	2,380	2,259	—	-0.4	198	205	171	152	162
Northern Marianas	411	569	669	751	750	774	784	6.9	37.8	211	53	70	76	78
Palau............................	—	131	—	—	—	—	—	—	—	—	10	—	—	—
Puerto Rico....................	35,129	65,504	77,932	87,485	87,125	97,129	99,680	18.9	52.2	3,345	7,746	4,677	7,314	9,644
U.S. Virgin Islands	1,333	1,502	1,752	1,756	1,690	1,566	1,557	9.8	3.7	90	106	151	129	152

—Not available.
[1]Percentage of students with disabilities is based on the total enrollment in public schools, prekindergarten through 12th grade.
NOTE: Prior to October 1994, children and youth with disabilities were served under Chapter 1 of the Elementary and Secondary Education Act as well as under the Individuals with Disabilities Education Act (IDEA), Part B. Data reported in this table for 1990–91 include children ages 0–21 served under Chapter 1. Some data have been revised from previously published figures. U.S. totals for 2007–08 do not include data for Vermont.

SOURCE: U.S. Department of Education, Office of Special Education Programs, *Annual Report to Congress on the Implementation of the Individuals with Disabilities Education Act,* selected years, 1992 through 2007, and Individuals with Disabilities Education Act (IDEA) database, retrieved April 21, 2009, from http://www.ideadata.org/PartBdata.asp. National Center for Education Statistics, Common Core of Data (CCD), "State Nonfiscal Survey of Public Elementary/ Secondary Education," 2007–08. (This table was prepared September 2009.)

Number of gifted and talented students in public elementary and secondary schools, by sex, race/ethnicity, and state: 2004 and 2006

				2006					
			Sex		Race/ethnicity				
State	2004, total	Total	Male	Female	White	Black	Hispanic	Asian/Pacific Islander	American Indian/Alaska Native
1	2	3	4	5	6	7	8	9	10
United States	3,202,760 (24,248)	3,236,990 (21,177)	1,579,000 (10,460)	1,657,990 (10,859)	2,191,210 (15,896)	296,150 (3,375)	414,060 (3,350)	304,220 (6,195)	31,360 (1,179)
Alabama	35,680 (798)	40,610 (361)	20,650 (184)	19,970 (184)	31,450 (338)	7,260 (109)	660 (14)	820 (6)	420 (6)
Alaska	5,390 (166)	5,620 (192)	2,810 (102)	2,810 (91)	4,390 (143)	160 (#)	160 (5)	490 (31)	420 (29)
Arizona	57,570 (1,275)	60,060 (711)	29,290 (412)	30,770 (306)	38,830 (544)	1,730 (20)	13,940 (178)	3,620 (29)	1,940 (394)
Arkansas	50,340 (3,219)	45,600 (1,870)	24,290 (924)	21,110 (967)	34,900 (1,253)	7,470 (677)	2,200 (860)	760 (26)	270 (41)
California	527,370 (10,256)	523,450 (13,209)	263,440 (6,688)	260,010 (6,567)	230,220 (7,405)	21,150 (559)	147,040 (2,827)	121,410 (5,930)	3,630 (276)
Colorado	50,350 (747)	54,000 (620)	27,770 (314)	26,240 (319)	40,420 (543)	2,280 (6)	8,190 (93)	2,730 (11)	400 (11)
Connecticut[1]	15,980 (1,572)	20,170 (2,183)	9,660 (1,094)	10,510 (1,097)	15,470 (1,515)	1,710 (404)	1,350 (295)	1,560 (192)	90 ! (46)
Delaware[1]	5,260 (†)	6,240 (†)	2,830 (†)	3,410 (†)	4,120 (†)	1,290 (†)	390 (†)	430 (†)	10 (†)
District of Columbia	—	—	—	—	—	—	—	—	—
Florida	114,400 (1,095)	132,440 (893)	66,740 (462)	65,700 (438)	81,710 (761)	13,170 (92)	31,020 (106)	6,130 (23)	400 (6)
Georgia	136,620 (3,954)	150,680 (5,291)	71,110 (2,572)	79,560 (2,725)	110,350 (4,419)	26,370 (796)	4,470 (187)	9,250 (265)	240 (14)
Hawaii[2]	10,290 (993)	11,140 (993)	4,680 (242)	6,460 (237)	2,570 (425)	120 (3)	450 (38)	8,180 (18)	50 (8)
Idaho	9,920 (528)	10,650 (475)	5,570 (242)	5,070 (237)	9,850 (425)	50 (3)	450 (38)	240 (18)	40 (6)
Illinois	112,570 (4,554)	118,480 (5,016)	56,230 (2,375)	62,250 (2,674)	76,680 (3,996)	18,240 (1,697)	12,720 (225)	10,610 (667)	230 (24)
Indiana	74,780 (5,219)	82,830 (4,222)	37,930 (1,896)	44,900 (2,350)	72,400 (3,820)	5,320 (644)	2,560 (222)	2,450 (272)	110 (14)
Iowa	41,460 (1,657)	39,300 (1,030)	19,490 (516)	19,820 (533)	36,060 (970)	1,000 (21)	910 (86)	1,250 (71)	80 (6)
Kansas	15,150 (389)	14,430 (487)	7,810 (280)	6,610 (218)	12,760 (445)	390 (17)	500 (20)	650 (25)	120 (11)
Kentucky	85,660 (3,179)	96,600 (2,885)	45,310 (1,384)	51,290 (1,528)	89,170 (2,781)	5,510 (394)	890 (43)	1,310 (54)	70 (8)
Louisiana	28,020 (2,300)	22,010 (721)	10,710 (362)	11,300 (369)	15,740 (591)	4,590 (107)	510 (15)	1,010 (18)	160 (30)
Maine	5,640 (619)	6,030 (304)	2,960 (147)	3,060 (168)	5,750 (297)	50 (5)	50 (10)	160 (15)	20 (9)
Maryland[1]	117,010 (1,190)	137,410 (908)	65,760 (348)	71,650 (631)	86,470 (820)	22,510 (30)	10,480 (86)	17,520 (106)	430 (6)
Massachusetts	7,440 (401)	6,130 (251)	3,580 (133)	2,550 (125)	4,240 (235)	540 (30)	510 (20)	820 (25)	30 (31)
Michigan	65,970 (6,408)	54,950 (4,750)	26,470 (2,312)	28,480 (2,467)	44,610 (3,918)	5,510 (1,255)	1,050 (117)	3,600 (507)	190 (21)
Minnesota	73,940 (2,585)	72,280 (2,154)	35,550 (1,043)	36,740 (1,120)	56,970 (2,047)	4,590 (24)	2,460 (43)	7,560 (62)	710 (54)
Mississippi	30,510 (837)	31,070 (1,015)	15,110 (496)	15,970 (534)	22,580 (806)	7,520 (253)	410 (23)	530 (51)	40 (6)
Missouri	34,470 (898)	33,070 (831)	16,960 (424)	16,110 (422)	28,780 (767)	2,350 (93)	510 (18)	1,420 (47)	80 (6)
Montana	8,760 (401)	7,490 (251)	3,770 (133)	3,720 (125)	6,800 (235)	30 (93)	140 (10)	130 (9)	390 (31)
Nebraska	32,160 (824)	32,650 (604)	16,200 (307)	16,450 (305)	29,100 (581)	1,080 (11)	1,390 (57)	960 (12)	130 (7)
Nevada[2]	7,640 (23)	8,270 (23)	4,220 (540)	4,050 (469)	5,570 (969)	410 (24)	1,210 (6)	1,010 (39)	70 (7)
New Hampshire	4,450 (1,089)	4,700 (1,005)	2,350 (540)	2,350 (469)	4,380 (969)	40 (7)	50 (6)	220 (39)	10 ! (7)
New Jersey	88,960 (4,851)	97,260 (4,904)	43,920 (2,190)	53,350 (2,764)	64,810 (3,890)	8,620 (808)	9,360 (787)	14,390 (1,327)	90 (9)
New Mexico	36,410 (404)	12,950 (399)	6,890 (219)	6,050 (185)	7,180 (256)	240 (8)	4,280 (137)	510 (53)	740 (36)
New York	61,350 (5,223)	81,520 (3,741)	38,090 (1,799)	43,440 (1,955)	49,010 (3,322)	12,090 (358)	8,480 (177)	10,900 (342)	230 (24)
North Carolina	155,330 (10,613)	149,700 (4,678)	72,600 (2,261)	77,100 (2,429)	120,700 (3,981)	18,000 (639)	4,040 (168)	5,150 (155)	1,710 ! (777)
North Dakota	3,320 (305)	2,770 (162)	1,450 (87)	1,320 (76)	2,370 (100)	30 (1)	20 (#)	50 (2)	300 ! (123)
Ohio	133,690 (7,411)	127,610 (5,925)	64,720 (3,150)	62,900 (2,829)	108,200 (5,477)	13,890 (949)	1,540 (70)	3,860 (386)	130 (13)
Oklahoma	87,620 (2,447)	87,320 (2,151)	42,520 (990)	44,760 (1,192)	61,980 (1,581)	5,050 (93)	4,010 (94)	2,460 (46)	13,820 (692)
Oregon	39,440 (903)	38,570 (666)	20,600 (357)	17,970 (318)	32,590 (603)	640 (10)	1,750 (63)	3,110 (26)	480 (33)
Pennsylvania	85,070 (3,170)	75,930 (2,681)	38,830 (1,414)	37,090 (1,297)	63,480 (2,415)	6,680 (292)	1,370 (60)	4,350 (362)	50 (9)
Rhode Island	2,780 (531)	2,060 (300)	920 (134)	1,150 (168)	1,560 (252)	230 (41)	230 (30)	110 (13)	# (†)
South Carolina	88,070 (6,564)	77,520 (3,781)	36,580 (1,772)	40,940 (2,022)	59,580 (2,832)	14,660 (964)	1,510 (118)	1,620 (164)	160 (31)
South Dakota	2,940 (241)	3,070 (175)	1,680 (92)	1,390 (87)	2,790 (139)	20 (#)	20 (1)	50 (3)	190 (93)
Tennessee	32,530 (1,451)	17,100 (904)	8,810 (493)	8,290 (416)	14,540 (827)	1,650 (63)	260 (15)	620 (43)	30 (4)
Texas	344,500 (3,483)	344,640 (2,413)	167,640 (1,243)	177,000 (1,234)	175,730 (1,923)	28,320 (618)	115,950 (1,189)	23,630 (134)	1,070 (30)
Utah	23,510 (1,218)	25,660 (170)	12,090 (79)	13,570 (91)	20,380 (152)	20 (3)	2,880 (19)	1,890 (#)	190 (#)
Vermont	740 (151)	730 (129)	390 (70)	340 (61)	690 (121)	10 (3)	10 (5)	20 (6)	# (†)
Virginia	142,140 (3,772)	160,140 (3,319)	77,980 (1,608)	82,160 (1,732)	116,360 (2,709)	18,410 (1,070)	7,310 (117)	17,510 (165)	560 (107)
Washington	38,520 (843)	39,010 (1,289)	19,050 (573)	19,960 (726)	30,390 (1,170)	850 (12)	2,430 (89)	4,970 (90)	380 (17)
West Virginia	6,040 (493)	6,630 (559)	3,500 (305)	3,130 (262)	6,120 (504)	230 (35)	30 (4)	240 (40)	10 ! (3)
Wisconsin	62,000 (4,348)	56,450 (3,095)	27,340 (1,478)	29,100 (1,628)	48,560 (2,821)	3,370 (210)	2,180 (125)	1,900 (129)	440 (151)
Wyoming	2,910 ! (944)	2,030 (314)	990 (152)	1,040 (164)	1,830 (295)	30 (2)	80 (8)	70 (13)	30 (#)

—Not available.
†Not applicable.
#Rounds to zero.
! Interpret data with caution.
[1]Data are based on universe counts of schools and school districts; therefore, these figures do not have standard errors.

[2]Data for 2006 are based on universe counts of schools and school districts; therefore, these figures do not have standard errors.
NOTE: Race categories exclude persons of Hispanic ethnicity. Standard errors appear in parentheses. Detail may not sum to totals because of rounding.
SOURCE: U.S. Department of Education, Office for Civil Rights, Civil Rights Data Collection: 2004 and 2006. (This table was revised May 2008.)

Percentage of gifted and talented students in public elementary and secondary schools, by sex, race/ethnicity, and state: 2004 and 2006

State	Total		Sex				Race/ethnicity									
			Male		Female		White		Black		Hispanic		Asian/Pacific Islander		American Indian/Alaska Native	
	2004	2006	2004	2006	2004	2006	2004	2006	2004	2006	2004	2006	2004	2006	2004	2006
1	2	3	4	5	6	7	8	9	10	11	12	13	14	15	16	17
United States	**6.7 (0.05)**	**6.7 (0.04)**	**6.3 (0.05)**	**6.3 (0.04)**	**7.0 (0.06)**	**7.0 (0.05)**	**7.9 (0.07)**	**8.0 (0.07)**	**3.5 (0.05)**	**3.6 (0.05)**	**4.3 (0.05)**	**4.2 (0.04)**	**11.9 (0.20)**	**13.1 (0.29)**	**5.2 (0.20)**	**5.2 (0.24)**
Alabama	4.8 (0.11)	5.5 (0.06)	4.6 (0.11)	5.2 (0.06)	4.9 (0.11)	5.7 (0.07)	6.3 (0.16)	7.1 (0.11)	2.4 (0.09)	2.8 (0.06)	2.3 (0.17)	2.9 (0.09)	9.4 (0.50)	10.2 (0.45)	4.9 (0.54)	6.1 (0.43)
Alaska	4.1 (0.19)	4.1 (0.19)	3.9 (0.19)	4.0 (0.19)	4.2 (0.19)	4.3 (0.19)	5.8 (0.22)	5.8 (0.22)	2.1 (0.03)	2.5 (0.02)	2.3 (0.11)	2.5 (0.13)	4.5 (0.45)	5.0 (0.52)	1.0 (0.08)	1.1 (0.12)
Arizona	5.9 (0.17)	6.3 (0.11)	5.9 (0.17)	6.3 (0.12)	5.9 (0.17)	6.3 (0.11)	8.4 (0.26)	9.1 (0.21)	3.5 (0.14)	3.4 (0.06)	3.3 (0.13)	3.5 (0.07)	13.9 (0.54)	14.2 (0.21)	4.0 (1.09)	3.7 (0.92)
Arkansas	9.9 (0.65)	9.5 (0.43)	8.8 (0.63)	8.6 (0.41)	11.0 (0.67)	10.5 (0.50)	11.2 (0.80)	10.7 (0.53)	7.1 (0.90)	7.3 (0.73)	5.8 ! (2.39)	5.8 ! (2.29)	10.6 (0.78)	10.3 (0.62)	4.7 (1.21)	8.2 (1.35)
California	8.4 (0.18)	8.3 (0.21)	8.0 (0.16)	8.0 (0.21)	8.8 (0.20)	8.6 (0.23)	12.0 (0.36)	11.9 (0.42)	4.6 (0.16)	4.3 (0.16)	5.1 (0.13)	4.8 (0.11)	14.6 (0.56)	16.1 (0.89)	6.5 (0.56)	5.8 (0.62)
Colorado	6.7 (0.11)	6.8 (0.11)	6.6 (0.11)	6.9 (0.11)	6.8 (0.12)	6.8 (0.11)	7.9 (0.14)	8.2 (0.16)	5.2 (0.03)	5.0 (0.02)	3.9 (0.14)	3.8 (0.07)	9.6 (0.11)	10.4 (0.09)	4.5 (0.39)	4.3 (0.29)
Connecticut	3.0 (0.32)	3.8 (0.41)	2.9 (0.31)	3.5 (0.40)	3.2 (0.34)	4.0 (0.44)	3.5 (0.38)	4.3 (0.44)	1.7 (0.44)	2.3 (0.59)	1.4 (0.33)	1.8 (0.42)	5.7 (0.68)	7.3 (0.95)	1.7 (0.44)	4.3 ! (2.37)
Delaware[1]	4.6 (†)	5.6 (†)	4.0 (†)	4.9 (†)	5.3 (†)	6.3 (†)	6.1 (†)	6.8 (†)	2.2 (†)	3.6 (†)	1.7 (†)	3.5 (†)	11.5 (†)	13.2 (†)	3.4 (†)	3.7 (†)
District of Columbia	— (†)	— (†)	— (†)	— (†)	— (†)	— (†)	— (†)	— (†)	— (†)	— (†)	— (†)	— (†)	— (†)	— (†)	— (†)	— (†)
Florida	4.5 (0.06)	4.7 (0.05)	4.5 (0.06)	4.7 (0.05)	4.5 (0.05)	4.8 (0.05)	5.7 (0.11)	6.1 (0.10)	2.0 (0.02)	2.0 (0.02)	4.0 (0.02)	4.4 (0.03)	8.8 (0.08)	9.3 (0.06)	4.6 (0.12)	5.0 (0.15)
Georgia	8.9 (0.30)	9.3 (0.35)	8.3 (0.29)	8.6 (0.33)	9.5 (0.31)	10.0 (0.39)	13.6 (0.59)	14.1 (0.69)	3.7 (0.15)	4.1 (0.15)	2.6 (0.25)	3.1 (0.17)	18.8 (0.41)	19.3 (0.71)	7.6 (0.49)	9.6 (0.65)
Hawaii[2]	5.7 (0.57)	6.2 (†)	4.4 (0.42)	5.1 (†)	7.0 (0.74)	7.5 (†)	7.7 (0.95)	9.7 (†)	2.9 (0.53)	2.9 (†)	2.6 (0.36)	3.9 (†)	5.5 (0.59)	5.8 (†)	4.3 (0.76)	4.8 (†)
Idaho	3.9 (0.23)	4.2 (0.20)	3.9 (0.21)	4.3 (0.20)	3.9 (0.24)	4.1 (0.21)	4.4 (0.26)	4.7 (0.23)	1.7 (0.20)	2.0 (0.14)	0.9 (0.13)	1.3 (0.12)	6.9 (0.38)	6.1 (0.46)	1.2 (0.28)	1.0 (0.23)
Illinois	5.4 (0.22)	5.8 (0.24)	5.0 (0.20)	5.4 (0.23)	5.8 (0.24)	6.3 (0.28)	6.7 (0.33)	7.0 (0.39)	2.5 (0.18)	4.2 (0.40)	2.8 (0.13)	3.1 (0.08)	13.1 (0.98)	13.3 (0.97)	5.4 (1.15)	5.1 (0.83)
Indiana	7.1 (0.49)	7.9 (0.40)	6.3 (0.44)	7.0 (0.36)	7.9 (0.55)	8.8 (0.49)	7.7 (0.52)	8.7 (0.50)	3.8 (0.78)	4.1 (0.54)	3.8 (0.66)	3.9 (0.39)	15.5 (2.71)	14.1 (2.08)	6.7 (1.64)	3.9 (0.56)
Iowa	8.5 (0.38)	8.2 (0.26)	8.2 (0.37)	7.9 (0.25)	8.9 (0.40)	8.5 (0.29)	9.0 (0.41)	8.8 (0.30)	4.6 (0.33)	3.9 (0.11)	3.7 (0.61)	3.1 (0.38)	13.5 (1.10)	12.2 (0.97)	3.6 (0.35)	2.9 (0.25)
Kansas	3.3 (0.11)	3.0 (0.12)	3.5 (0.11)	3.2 (0.13)	3.1 (0.11)	2.9 (0.12)	3.9 (0.15)	3.6 (0.16)	1.1 (0.05)	1.0 (0.04)	1.0 (0.08)	0.8 (0.04)	5.5 (0.17)	5.4 (0.25)	1.5 (0.19)	1.8 (0.20)
Kentucky	13.0 (0.54)	14.6 (0.50)	11.9 (0.51)	13.2 (0.47)	14.2 (0.57)	16.1 (0.60)	14.2 (0.62)	15.8 (0.64)	5.2 (0.54)	7.0 (0.60)	4.6 (0.46)	5.7 (0.38)	20.2 (1.48)	21.3 (1.14)	6.6 (1.24)	7.2 (0.96)
Louisiana	3.9 (0.32)	3.4 (0.13)	3.8 (0.31)	3.2 (0.13)	4.0 (0.34)	3.5 (0.14)	5.5 (0.60)	4.8 (0.26)	1.9 (0.07)	1.6 (0.04)	4.2 (0.34)	3.3 (0.12)	11.7 (0.91)	11.7 (0.34)	2.6 ! (1.04)	2.7 (0.78)
Maine	3.0 (0.36)	3.2 (0.19)	2.9 (0.33)	3.1 (0.18)	3.2 (0.39)	3.4 (0.22)	3.1 (0.37)	3.3 (0.20)	1.3 (0.22)	1.1 (0.12)	1.2 (0.27)	2.3 (0.54)	3.8 (0.80)	5.6 (0.60)	0.8 ! (0.35)	3.1 ! (1.29)
Maryland[1]	13.8 (†)	16.1 (†)	12.9 (†)	15.0 (†)	14.7 (†)	17.2 (†)	17.0 (†)	21.1 (†)	6.7 (†)	7.0 (†)	14.5 (†)	14.7 (†)	33.8 (†)	37.8 (†)	9.8 (†)	12.6 (†)
Massachusetts	0.8 (0.13)	0.7 (0.10)	0.7 (0.12)	0.6 (0.08)	0.9 (0.14)	0.8 (0.15)	0.8 (0.14)	0.6 (0.12)	0.7 (0.13)	0.7 (0.05)	0.8 ! (0.21)	0.5 (0.04)	1.9 (0.30)	1.7 (0.24)	0.9 ! (0.25)	0.5 (0.13)
Michigan	3.9 (0.37)	3.4 (0.29)	3.6 (0.35)	3.2 (0.28)	4.3 (0.40)	3.7 (0.32)	4.1 (0.41)	3.8 (0.34)	3.0 (0.62)	1.9 (0.44)	2.7 (0.54)	1.4 (0.18)	10.1 (1.56)	8.1 (1.30)	1.4 (0.25)	1.2 (0.19)
Minnesota	8.1 (0.37)	8.8 (0.28)	7.7 (0.36)	8.4 (0.26)	8.6 (0.38)	9.2 (0.32)	8.3 (0.44)	8.8 (0.36)	5.2 (0.34)	6.7 (0.11)	4.5 (0.20)	5.4 (0.18)	13.7 (0.33)	16.5 (0.25)	3.8 (0.57)	4.6 (0.54)
Mississippi	6.0 (0.19)	6.1 (0.20)	5.7 (0.18)	5.8 (0.19)	6.3 (0.22)	6.4 (0.22)	9.1 (0.38)	9.6 (0.41)	3.3 (0.21)	2.9 (0.11)	5.0 (0.43)	4.5 (0.37)	10.7 (0.48)	13.5 (1.47)	3.7 (0.93)	3.7 (0.64)
Missouri	3.8 (0.12)	3.6 (0.11)	3.8 (0.12)	3.5 (0.11)	3.8 (0.13)	3.6 (0.11)	4.3 (0.15)	4.0 (0.14)	1.7 (0.05)	1.5 (0.08)	1.4 (0.10)	1.3 (0.09)	9.0 (0.33)	9.1 (0.36)	2.0 (0.22)	2.4 (0.20)
Montana	5.6 (0.28)	5.2 (0.20)	5.4 (0.26)	5.0 (0.20)	5.9 (0.31)	5.3 (0.21)	6.0 (0.31)	5.7 (0.24)	2.8 (0.21)	2.2 (0.22)	3.3 (0.22)	3.9 (0.29)	9.9 (0.77)	8.2 (0.62)	2.9 (0.38)	2.1 (0.23)
Nebraska	11.4 (0.31)	11.4 (0.24)	10.9 (0.30)	11.0 (0.24)	11.9 (0.32)	11.8 (0.27)	12.8 (0.38)	13.3 (0.33)	6.4 (0.06)	4.8 (0.05)	4.5 (0.32)	3.9 (0.24)	17.0 (0.25)	18.2 (0.28)	4.6 (0.94)	3.1 (0.36)
Nevada[2]	1.9 (0.01)	1.9 (†)	2.1 (0.01)	1.9 (†)	1.8 (0.01)	1.9 (†)	2.8 (0.01)	3.0 (†)	0.8 (#)	0.9 (†)	0.8 (0.01)	0.8 (†)	2.8 (0.02)	3.1 (†)	1.0 (0.07)	1.1 (†)
New Hampshire	2.3 (0.55)	2.6 (0.54)	2.1 (0.49)	2.5 (0.56)	2.5 ! (0.62)	2.7 (0.54)	2.3 (0.56)	2.6 (0.58)	0.6 (0.11)	1.1 (0.19)	1.0 (0.20)	0.9 (0.10)	5.8 (1.25)	5.9 (1.07)	0.9 (0.09)	2.1 ! (1.20)
New Jersey	6.9 (0.38)	7.0 (0.35)	6.2 (0.34)	6.1 (0.31)	7.7 (0.42)	7.9 (0.43)	8.4 (0.53)	8.4 (0.55)	3.3 (0.35)	3.5 (0.36)	3.4 (0.39)	3.5 (0.33)	12.2 (1.13)	13.9 (1.50)	3.3 (0.59)	4.8 (0.61)
New Mexico	10.7 (0.26)	4.0 (0.14)	10.9 (0.27)	4.1 (0.15)	10.5 (0.26)	3.8 (0.14)	12.6 (0.42)	7.1 (0.31)	9.6 (0.18)	2.8 (0.11)	11.4 (0.37)	2.4 (0.11)	13.6 (1.09)	12.0 (1.34)	2.2 (0.17)	2.1 (0.15)
New York	2.2 (0.18)	2.9 (0.13)	2.0 (0.17)	2.6 (0.12)	2.3 (0.19)	3.2 (0.15)	3.4 (0.31)	3.3 (0.23)	0.8 (0.07)	2.4 (0.09)	0.4 (0.04)	1.5 (0.04)	1.7 (0.18)	5.5 (0.19)	1.4 (0.29)	1.5 (0.25)
North Carolina	10.9 (0.83)	10.8 (0.42)	10.3 (0.81)	10.2 (0.40)	11.6 (0.85)	11.3 (0.47)	15.7 (1.17)	15.4 (0.68)	3.9 (0.27)	4.3 (0.20)	3.0 (0.29)	3.1 (0.18)	16.5 (2.76)	17.3 (0.98)	6.3 (1.39)	6.2 ! (3.81)
North Dakota	3.1 (0.30)	2.8 (0.18)	3.0 (0.30)	2.9 (0.19)	3.2 (0.32)	2.8 (0.18)	2.8 (0.23)	2.8 (0.15)	2.3 (0.05)	1.7 (0.09)	1.5 (0.23)	1.4 (0.13)	8.1 (0.38)	5.4 (0.26)	7.0 ! (3.34)	3.3 ! (1.46)
Ohio	7.4 (0.40)	7.3 (0.33)	7.3 (0.40)	7.2 (0.34)	7.6 (0.40)	7.4 (0.35)	7.6 (0.48)	7.8 (0.42)	6.5 (0.37)	4.7 (0.37)	3.5 (0.26)	3.3 (0.28)	13.6 (1.44)	14.0 (1.64)	5.6 (0.62)	5.4 (0.60)
Oklahoma	14.0 (0.45)	13.7 (0.39)	13.1 (0.41)	13.0 (0.36)	15.0 (0.50)	14.4 (0.47)	16.6 (0.56)	16.2 (0.55)	7.7 (0.22)	7.4 (0.23)	7.0 (0.27)	6.8 (0.23)	23.6 (0.56)	21.5 (0.60)	11.3 (0.67)	11.8 (0.72)
Oregon	7.1 (0.20)	6.9 (0.16)	7.3 (0.20)	7.2 (0.17)	6.9 (0.21)	6.6 (0.16)	8.0 (0.24)	8.0 (0.22)	3.6 (0.05)	3.5 (0.09)	1.8 (0.10)	2.0 (0.09)	11.6 (0.14)	11.1 (0.21)	3.6 (0.42)	3.9 (0.31)
Pennsylvania	4.8 (0.19)	4.5 (0.17)	4.9 (0.20)	4.5 (0.17)	4.8 (0.19)	4.5 (0.18)	5.3 (0.23)	5.0 (0.22)	2.7 (0.16)	2.4 (0.15)	1.8 (0.38)	1.7 (0.12)	9.5 (0.87)	9.7 (0.96)	2.2 (0.35)	1.9 (0.36)
Rhode Island	1.8 (0.38)	1.4 (0.21)	1.6 (0.35)	1.2 (0.18)	2.1 (0.41)	1.6 (0.24)	2.0 (0.44)	1.5 (0.25)	1.5 (0.47)	1.2 ! (0.34)	1.2 (0.48)	1.0 (0.13)	2.2 (0.60)	2.3 (0.30)	0.9 ! (0.34)	0.3 ! (0.10)
South Carolina	12.7 (0.98)	11.0 (0.57)	11.7 (0.89)	10.1 (0.52)	13.9 (1.07)	11.9 (0.68)	17.8 (1.29)	15.9 (0.95)	5.9 (0.70)	5.1 (0.39)	5.1 (0.93)	4.6 (0.56)	21.6 (3.32)	19.3 (2.33)	8.3 (1.29)	8.2 (2.52)
South Dakota	2.2 (0.20)	2.7 (0.17)	2.3 (0.20)	2.8 (0.18)	2.1 (0.20)	2.5 (0.18)	2.4 (0.21)	2.9 (0.19)	1.2 (0.16)	0.9 (0.03)	0.6 (0.12)	0.7 (0.04)	3.3 (0.37)	4.2 (0.31)	1.3 ! (0.67)	1.4 ! (0.70)
Tennessee	3.3 (0.18)	1.7 (0.10)	3.1 (0.18)	1.7 (0.10)	3.5 (0.18)	1.7 (0.09)	2.9 (0.21)	2.0 (0.13)	4.5 (0.15)	0.7 (0.03)	1.6 (0.15)	0.6 (0.04)	7.9 (0.77)	4.2 (0.37)	2.9 (0.41)	1.4 (0.20)
Texas	8.0 (0.10)	7.6 (0.07)	7.5 (0.10)	7.2 (0.07)	8.5 (0.11)	8.0 (0.08)	11.2 (0.21)	10.8 (0.17)	4.9 (0.14)	4.4 (0.11)	5.6 (0.12)	5.5 (0.07)	16.4 (0.28)	16.0 (0.13)	7.1 (0.27)	7.1 (0.24)
Utah	4.6 (0.29)	5.0 (0.05)	4.3 (0.28)	4.6 (0.05)	5.0 (0.29)	5.5 (0.06)	4.5 (0.29)	4.9 (0.06)	5.1 (0.26)	4.6 (0.03)	4.4 (0.37)	4.1 (0.05)	11.7 (0.81)	12.0 (0.06)	2.6 (0.36)	2.7 (0.03)
Vermont	0.8 (0.17)	0.8 (0.15)	0.8 (0.17)	0.9 (0.16)	0.9 (0.17)	0.8 (0.15)	0.8 (0.17)	0.8 (0.15)	0.4 ! (0.16)	0.5 ! (0.16)	# (†)	1.3 ! (0.57)	0.2 ! (0.10)	1.4 ! (0.41)	# (†)	# (†)
Virginia	12.1 (0.38)	12.6 (0.32)	11.5 (0.36)	12.0 (0.30)	12.8 (0.40)	13.3 (0.37)	14.9 (0.55)	15.6 (0.50)	4.6 (0.21)	5.2 (0.35)	6.7 (0.65)	7.5 (0.23)	24.5 (0.83)	26.4 (0.46)	8.3 (2.41)	13.3 (2.61)
Washington	3.8 (0.10)	3.9 (0.13)	3.6 (0.10)	3.7 (0.12)	3.9 (0.10)	4.1 (0.16)	4.2 (0.14)	4.4 (0.19)	1.4 (0.02)	1.4 (0.02)	1.8 (0.12)	1.7 (0.09)	5.0 (0.09)	5.8 (0.12)	1.6 (0.28)	1.4 (0.10)
West Virginia	2.2 (0.19)	2.2 (0.21)	2.3 (0.20)	2.2 (0.22)	2.0 (0.18)	2.1 (0.21)	2.2 (0.19)	2.2 (0.21)	1.4 (0.17)	1.6 (0.32)	1.6 (0.37)	0.9 (0.23)	9.3 (1.90)	10.9 (2.21)	3.9 ! (1.25)	2.9 ! (0.82)
Wisconsin	6.8 (0.47)	6.4 (0.35)	6.4 (0.44)	6.1 (0.33)	7.3 (0.51)	6.8 (0.41)	7.8 (0.55)	7.1 (0.45)	2.0 (0.21)	3.7 (0.25)	2.4 (0.23)	3.5 (0.21)	6.7 (0.55)	6.1 (0.44)	4.6 ! (2.04)	3.2 ! (1.23)
Wyoming	3.2 ! (1.04)	2.2 (0.35)	2.8 ! (0.90)	2.0 (0.32)	3.7 ! (1.19)	2.3 (0.39)	3.5 ! (1.14)	2.3 (0.39)	1.5 ! (0.47)	2.0 (0.19)	1.2 (0.29)	0.9 (0.11)	3.6 (0.31)	6.7 (1.35)	0.7 ! (0.53)	1.0 (0.16)

—Not available.
†Not applicable.
#Rounds to zero.
!Interpret data with caution.
[1]Data are based on universe counts of schools and school districts; therefore, these figures do not have standard errors.
[2]Data for 2006 are based on universe counts of schools and school districts; therefore, these figures do not have standard errors.
NOTE: Race categories exclude persons of Hispanic ethnicity. Standard errors appear in parentheses.
SOURCE: U.S. Department of Education, Office for Civil Rights, Civil Rights Data Collection: 2004 and 2006. (This table was prepared June 2008.)

High school graduates, by sex and control of school: Selected years, 1869–70 through 2018–19

School year	High school graduates					Averaged freshman graduation rate for public schools[3]	Population 17 years old[4]	Graduates as a ratio of 17-year-old population
	Total[1]	Sex		Control				
		Males	Females	Public[2]	Private			
1	2	3	4	5	6	7	8	9
1869–70	16,000	7,064	8,936	—	—	—	815,000	2.0
1879–80	23,634	10,605	13,029	—	—	—	946,026	2.5
1889–90	43,731	18,549	25,182	21,882	21,849 [5]	—	1,259,177	3.5
1899–1900	94,883	38,075	56,808	61,737	33,000 [5]	—	1,489,146	6.4
1909–10	156,429	63,676	92,753	111,363	45,066 [5]	—	1,786,240	8.8
1919–20	311,266	123,684	187,582	230,902	80,364 [5]	—	1,855,173	16.8
1929–30	666,904	300,376	366,528	591,719	75,185 [5]	—	2,295,822	29.0
1939–40	1,221,475	578,718	642,757	1,143,246	78,229 [5]	—	2,403,074	50.8
1949–50	1,199,700	570,700	629,000	1,063,444	136,256 [5]	—	2,034,450	59.0
1959–60	1,858,023	895,000	963,000	1,627,050	230,973	—	2,672,000	69.5
1969–70	2,888,639	1,430,000	1,459,000	2,588,639	300,000 [5]	78.7	3,757,000	76.9
1970–71	2,937,642	1,454,000	1,484,000	2,637,642	300,000 [5]	78.0	3,872,000	75.9
1971–72	3,001,553	1,487,000	1,515,000	2,699,553	302,000 [5]	77.4	3,973,000	75.5
1972–73	3,034,822	1,500,000	1,535,000	2,728,822	306,000 [5]	76.8	4,049,000	75.0
1973–74	3,073,317	1,512,000	1,561,000	2,763,317	310,000 [5]	75.4	4,132,000	74.4
1974–75	3,132,502	1,542,000	1,591,000	2,822,502	310,000 [5]	74.9	4,256,000	73.6
1975–76	3,142,120	1,552,000	1,596,000	2,837,129	304,991	74.9	4,272,000	73.6
1976–77	3,139,536	1,548,000	1,604,000	2,837,340	302,196	74.4	4,272,000	73.5
1977–78	3,128,824	1,531,000	1,596,000	2,824,636	304,188	73.2	4,286,000	73.0
1978–79	3,101,152	1,517,000	1,584,000	2,801,152	300,000 [5]	71.9	4,327,000	71.7
1979–80	3,042,214	1,491,000	1,552,000	2,747,678	294,536	71.5	4,262,000	71.4
1980–81	3,020,285	1,483,000	1,537,000	2,725,285	295,000 [5]	72.2	4,212,000	71.7
1981–82	2,994,758	1,471,000	1,524,000	2,704,758	290,000 [5]	72.9	4,134,000	72.4
1982–83	2,887,604	1,437,000	1,451,000	2,597,604	290,000 [5]	73.8	3,962,000	72.9
1983–84	2,766,797	—	—	2,494,797	272,000 [5]	74.5	3,784,000	73.1
1984–85	2,676,917	—	—	2,413,917	263,000 [5]	74.2	3,699,000	72.4
1985–86	2,642,616	—	—	2,382,616	260,000 [5]	74.3	3,670,000	72.0
1986–87	2,693,803	—	—	2,428,803	265,000 [5]	74.3	3,754,000	71.8
1987–88	2,773,020	—	—	2,500,020	273,000 [5]	74.2	3,849,000	72.0
1988–89	2,743,743	—	—	2,458,800	284,943	73.4	3,842,000	71.4
1989–90	2,574,162	—	—	2,320,337	253,825 [6]	73.6	3,505,000	73.4
1990–91	2,492,988	—	—	2,234,893	258,095	73.7	3,417,913	72.9
1991–92	2,480,399	—	—	2,226,016	254,383 [6]	74.2	3,398,884	73.0
1992–93	2,480,519	—	—	2,233,241	247,278	73.8	3,449,143	71.9
1993–94	2,463,849	—	—	2,220,849	243,000 [5]	73.1	3,442,521	71.6
1994–95	2,519,084	—	—	2,273,541	245,543	71.8	3,635,803	69.3
1995–96	2,518,109	—	—	2,273,109	245,000 [5]	71.0	3,640,132	69.2
1996–97	2,611,988	—	—	2,358,403	253,585	71.3	3,792,207	68.9
1997–98	2,704,050	—	—	2,439,050	265,000 [5]	71.3	4,008,416	67.5
1998–99	2,758,655	—	—	2,485,630	273,025	71.1	3,917,885	70.4
1999–2000	2,832,844	—	—	2,553,844	279,000 [5]	71.7	4,056,639	69.8
2000–01	2,847,973	—	—	2,569,200	278,773	71.7	4,016,555	70.9
2001–02	2,906,534	—	—	2,621,534	285,000 [5]	72.6	4,005,471	72.6
2002–03	3,015,702	—	—	2,719,947	295,755	73.9	4,099,928	73.6
2003–04[7]	3,054,438	—	—	2,753,438	301,000 [5]	74.3	4,086,606	74.7
2004–05	3,106,499	—	—	2,799,250	307,249	74.7	4,094,794	75.9
2005–06	3,122,544	—	—	2,815,544	307,000 [5]	73.4	4,177,009	74.8
2006–07	3,198,956	—	—	2,892,351	306,605	73.9	4,274,536	74.8
2007–08[8]	3,321,500	—	—	3,010,900	310,600	75.0	4,414,699	75.2
2008–09[8]	3,329,200	—	—	3,018,700	310,500	75.0	4,315,640	77.1
2009–10[8]	3,294,600	—	—	2,983,400	311,200	—	—	—
2010–11[8]	3,273,300	—	—	2,962,400	310,900	—	—	—
2011–12[8]	3,224,700	—	—	2,912,400	312,300	—	—	—
2012–13[8]	3,210,500	—	—	2,904,800	305,800	—	—	—
2013–14[8]	3,193,500	—	—	2,888,900	304,600	—	—	—
2014–15[8]	3,186,900	—	—	2,892,300	294,600	—	—	—
2015–16[8]	3,217,400	—	—	2,926,100	291,300	—	—	—
2016–17[8]	3,244,900	—	—	2,958,500	286,400	—	—	—
2017–18[8]	3,285,800	—	—	3,004,200	281,700	—	—	—
2018–19[8]	3,410,200	—	—	3,133,100	277,200	—	—	—

—Not available.

[1]Includes graduates of public and private schools.

[2]Data for 1929–30 and preceding years are from *Statistics of Public High Schools* and exclude graduates from high schools that failed to report to the Office of Education.

[3]The averaged freshman graduation rate provides an estimate of the percentage of students who receive a regular diploma within 4 years of entering ninth grade. The rate uses aggregate student enrollment data to estimate the size of an incoming freshman class and aggregate counts of the number of diplomas awarded 4 years later. Averaged freshman graduation rates in this table are based on reported totals of enrollment by grade and high school graduates, rather than on details reported by race/ethnicity.

[4]Derived from Current Population Reports, Series P-25. For years 1869–70 through 1989–90, 17-year-old population is an estimate of the October 17-year-old population based on July data. Data for 1990–91 and later years are October resident population estimates prepared by the Census Bureau.

[5]Estimated.

[6]Projected by private schools.

[7]Includes estimates for New York and Wisconsin. Without estimates for these two states, the averaged freshman graduation rate for the remaining 48 states and the District of Columbia is 75.0 percent.

[8]Projected by NCES.

NOTE: Includes graduates of regular day school programs. Excludes graduates of other programs, when separately reported, and recipients of high school equivalency certificates. Some data have been revised from previously published figures. Detail may not sum to totals because of rounding.

SOURCE: U.S. Department of Education, National Center for Education Statistics, *Annual Report of the Commissioner of Education*, 1870 through 1910; *Biennial Survey of Education in the United States*, 1919–20 through 1949–50; *Statistics of State School Systems*, 1951–52 through 1957–58; *Statistics of Public Elementary and Secondary School Systems*, 1958–59 through 1980–81; *Statistics of Nonpublic Elementary and Secondary Schools*, 1959 through 1980; Common Core of Data (CCD), "State Nonfiscal Survey of Public Elementary/Secondary Education," 1981–82 through 2007–08; Private School Universe Survey (PSS), 1989 through 2007; and *Projections of Education Statistics to 2018*. U.S. Department of Commerce, Census Bureau, Population Estimates, retrieved September 17, 2009, from http://www.census.gov/popest/related.html. (This table was prepared September 2009.)

Public high school graduates, by state or jurisdiction: Selected years, 1980–81 through 2007–08

State or jurisdiction	1980–81	1989–90	1999–2000	2001–02	2002–03	2003–04	2004–05	2005–06	2006–07	Projected 2007–08 graduates	Percent change, 1999–2000 to 2007–08
1	2	3	4	5	6	7	8	9	10	11	12
United States	**2,725,285**	**2,320,337** [1]	**2,553,844**	**2,621,534**	**2,719,947**	**2,753,438** [1]	**2,799,250**	**2,815,544** [1]	**2,892,351**	**3,010,890**	**17.9**
Alabama	44,894	40,485	37,819	35,887	36,741	36,464	37,453	37,918	38,912	39,440	4.3
Alaska	5,343	5,386	6,615	6,945	7,297	7,236	6,909	7,361	7,666	7,980	20.6
Arizona	28,416	32,103	38,304	47,175	49,986	45,508	59,498	54,091	55,954	52,060	35.9
Arkansas	29,577	26,475	27,335	26,984	27,555	27,181	26,621	28,790	27,166	29,480	7.8
California	242,172	236,291	309,866	325,895	341,097	343,480	355,217	343,515	356,641	385,290	24.3
Colorado	35,897	32,967	38,924	40,760	42,379	44,777	44,532	44,424	45,628	48,040	23.4
Connecticut	38,369	27,878	31,562	32,327	33,667	34,573	35,515	36,222	37,541	38,400	21.7
Delaware	7,349	5,550	6,108	6,482	6,817	6,951	6,934	7,275	7,205	7,480	22.5
District of Columbia[2]	4,848	3,626	2,695	3,090	2,725	3,031	2,781	3,150 [3]	2,944	3,320	23.2
Florida	88,755	88,934	106,708	119,537	127,484	131,418	133,318	134,686	142,284	148,170	38.9
Georgia	62,963	56,605	62,563	65,983	66,890	68,550	70,834	73,498	77,829	79,740	27.5
Hawaii	11,472	10,325	10,437	10,452	10,013	10,324	10,813	10,922	11,063	11,000	5.4
Idaho	12,679	11,971	16,170	15,874	15,858	15,547	15,768	16,096	16,242	16,760	3.6
Illinois	136,795	108,119	111,835	116,657	117,507	124,763	123,615	126,817	130,220	133,060	19.0
Indiana	73,381	60,012	57,012	56,722	57,897	56,008	55,444	57,920	59,887	62,960	10.4
Iowa	42,635	31,796	33,926	33,789	34,860	34,339	33,547	33,693	34,127	35,280	4.0
Kansas	29,397	25,367	29,102	29,541	29,963	30,155	30,355	29,818	30,139	29,990	3.1
Kentucky	41,714	38,005	36,830	36,337	37,654	37,787	38,399	38,449	39,099	40,650	10.4
Louisiana	46,199	36,053	38,430	37,905	37,610	37,019	36,009	33,275	34,274	34,130	-11.2
Maine	15,554	13,839	12,211	12,593	12,947	13,278	13,077	12,950	13,151	13,210	8.2
Maryland	54,050	41,566	47,849	50,881	51,864	52,870	54,170	55,536	57,564	58,270	21.8
Massachusetts	74,831	55,941 [4]	52,950	55,272	55,987	58,326	59,665	61,272	63,903	63,850	20.6
Michigan	124,372	93,807	97,679	95,001	100,301	98,823	101,582	102,582	111,838	109,390	12.0
Minnesota	64,166	49,087	57,372	57,440	59,432	59,096	58,391	58,898	59,497	60,900	6.1
Mississippi	28,083	25,182	24,232	23,740	23,810	23,735	23,523	23,848	24,186	24,890	2.7
Missouri	60,359	48,957	52,848	54,487	56,925	57,983	57,841	58,417	60,275	60,460	14.4
Montana	11,634	9,370	10,903	10,554	10,657	10,500	10,335	10,283	10,122	10,320	-5.3
Nebraska	21,411	17,664	20,149	19,910	20,161	20,309	19,940	19,764	19,873	20,740	2.9
Nevada	9,069	9,477	14,551	16,270	16,378	15,201	15,740	16,455	16,455	18,230	25.3
New Hampshire	11,552	10,766	11,829	12,452	13,210	13,309	13,775	13,988	14,452	14,590	23.3
New Jersey	93,168	69,824	74,420	77,664	81,391	83,826	86,502	90,049	93,013	95,110	27.8
New Mexico	17,915	14,884	18,031	18,094	16,923	17,892	17,353	17,822	16,131	17,750	-1.6
New York	198,465	143,318	141,731	140,139	143,818	142,526 [5]	153,203	161,817	168,333	169,690	19.7
North Carolina	69,395	64,782	62,140	65,955	69,696	72,126	75,010	76,710	76,031	81,210	30.7
North Dakota	9,924	7,690	8,606	8,114	8,169	7,888	7,555	7,192	7,159	7,150	-16.9
Ohio	143,503	114,513	111,668	110,608	115,762	119,029	116,702	117,356	117,658	122,580	9.8
Oklahoma	38,875	35,606	37,646	36,852	36,694	36,799	36,227	36,497	37,100	37,340	-0.8
Oregon	28,729	25,473	30,151	31,153	32,587	32,958	32,602	32,394	33,446	36,400	20.7
Pennsylvania	144,645	110,527	113,959	114,943	119,933	123,474	124,758	127,830 [3]	128,603	151,670	33.1
Rhode Island	10,719	7,825	8,477	9,006	9,318	9,258	9,881	10,108	10,384	10,340	22.0
South Carolina	38,347	32,483	31,617	31,302	32,482	33,235	33,439	34,970 [3]	35,140	35,140	11.1
South Dakota	10,385	7,650	9,278	8,796	8,999	9,001	8,585	8,589	8,346	8,210	-11.5
Tennessee	50,648	46,094	41,568	40,894	44,113	46,096	47,967	50,880	54,502	54,220	30.4
Texas	171,665	172,480	212,925	225,167	238,111	244,165	239,717	240,485	241,193	259,500	21.9
Utah	19,886	21,196	32,501	30,183	29,527	30,252	30,253	29,050	28,276	30,840	-5.1
Vermont	6,424	6,127	6,675	7,083	6,970	7,100	7,152	6,779	7,317	7,080	6.1
Virginia	67,126	60,605	65,596	66,519	72,943	72,042	73,667	69,597	73,997	77,080	17.5
Washington	50,046	45,941	57,597	58,311	60,435	61,274	61,094	60,213	62,801	62,590	8.7
West Virginia	23,580	21,854	19,437	17,128	17,287	17,339	17,137	16,763	17,407	17,500	-10.0
Wisconsin	67,743	52,038	58,545	60,575	63,272	62,784 [5]	63,229	63,003	63,968	66,020	12.8
Wyoming	6,161	5,823	6,462	6,106	5,845	5,833	5,616	5,527	5,441	5,420	-16.1
Bureau of Indian Education	—	—	—	—	—	—	—	—	—	—	—
DoD, overseas	—	—	2,642	2,554	2,641	2,766	—	—	—	—	—
DoD, domestic	—	—	560	565	590	584	—	—	—	—	—
Other jurisdictions											
American Samoa	—	703	698	823	832	852	905	879	954	—	—
Guam	—	1,033	1,406	—	1,502	1,346	1,179	—	—	—	—
Northern Marianas	—	227	360	416	422	575	614	670	643	—	—
Puerto Rico	—	29,049	30,856	30,278	31,408	30,083	29,071	31,896	31,718	—	—
U.S. Virgin Islands	—	1,260	1,060	883	886	816	940	—	820	—	—

—Not available.
[1] U.S. total includes estimates for nonreporting states.
[2] Beginning in 1989–90, graduates from adult programs are excluded.
[3] Data from NCES 2009-062, *Projections of Education Statistics to 2018*.
[4] Projected data from NCES 91-490, *Projections of Education Statistics to 2002*.
[5] Estimated high school graduates from NCES 2006-606rev, *The Averaged Freshman Graduation Rate for Public High Schools From the Common Core of Data: School Years 2002–03 and 2003–04*.

NOTE: Data include regular diploma recipients, but exclude students receiving a certificate of attendance and persons receiving high school equivalency certificates. DoD = Department of Defense. Detail may not sum to totals because of rounding.
SOURCE: U.S. Department of Education, National Center for Education Statistics; *Projections of Education Statistics to 2018*; Common Core of Data (CCD), "State Nonfiscal Survey of Public Elementary/Secondary Education," 1981–82 through 2007–08; and *The Averaged Freshman Graduation Rate for Public High Schools From the Common Core of Data: School Years 2002–03 and 2003–04*. (This table was prepared September 2009.)

Averaged freshman graduation rates for public secondary schools, by state or jurisdiction: Selected years, 1990–91 through 2006–07

State or jurisdiction	1990–91	1993–94	1994–95	1995–96	1996–97	1997–98	1998–99	1999–2000	2000–01	2001–02	2002–03	2003–04	2004–05	2005–06	2006–07
1	2	3	4	5	6	7	8	9	10	11	12	13	14	15	16
United States	**73.7**	**73.1**	**71.8**	**71.0**	**71.3**	**71.3**	**71.1**	**71.7**	**71.7**	**72.6**	**73.9**	**74.3** [1]	**74.7**	**73.4** [2]	**73.9**
Alabama	69.8	64.3	64.8	62.7	62.4	64.4	61.3	64.1	63.7	62.1	64.7	65.0	65.9	66.2	67.1
Alaska	74.6	73.8	71.2	68.3	67.9	68.9	70.0	66.7	68.0	65.9	68.0	67.2	64.1	66.5	69.0
Arizona	76.7	71.7	65.1	60.8	65.3	65.6	62.3	63.6	74.2	74.7	75.9	66.8	84.7	70.5	69.6
Arkansas	76.6	76.1	72.7	74.2	70.6	73.9	73.7	74.6	73.9	74.8	76.6	76.8	75.7	80.4	74.4
California	69.6	68.6	66.8	67.6	68.8	69.6	71.1	71.7	71.6	72.7	74.1	73.9	74.6	69.2	70.7
Colorado	76.3	77.3	76.0	74.8	74.7	73.9	73.4	74.1	73.2	74.7	76.4	78.7	76.7	75.5	76.6
Connecticut	80.2	79.9	77.2	76.1	76.7	76.9	76.0	81.9	77.5	79.7	80.9	80.7	80.9	80.9	81.8
Delaware	72.5	70.8	68.7	70.4	71.7	74.1	70.4	66.8	71.0	69.5	73.0	72.9	73.0	76.3	71.9
District of Columbia	54.5	58.7	54.6	49.7	54.6	53.9	52.0	54.5	60.2	68.4	59.6	68.2	66.3	65.4 [3]	54.8
Florida	65.6	64.2	63.5	62.3	62.7	62.1	61.4	61.0	61.2	63.4	66.7	66.4	64.6	63.6	65.0
Georgia	70.3	66.3	63.5	61.9	62.0	58.2	57.5	59.7	58.7	61.1	60.8	61.2	61.7	62.4	64.1
Hawaii	75.9	75.7	74.8	74.5	69.1	68.8	67.5	70.9	68.3	72.1	71.3	72.6	75.1	75.5	75.4
Idaho	79.6	79.9	80.2	80.5	80.1	79.7	79.5	79.4	79.6	79.3	81.4	81.5	81.0	80.5	80.4
Illinois	76.6	76.3	74.8	75.2	76.1	76.8	76.0	76.3	75.6	77.1	75.9	80.3	79.4	79.7	79.5
Indiana	76.9	74.7	73.8	73.6	74.0	73.8	74.3	71.8	72.1	73.1	75.5	73.5	73.2	73.3	73.9
Iowa	84.4	86.1	84.5	84.3	84.6	83.9	83.3	83.1	82.8	84.1	85.3	85.8	86.6	86.9	86.5
Kansas	80.8	80.2	78.8	77.1	76.9	76.0	76.7	77.1	76.5	77.1	76.9	77.9	79.2	77.5	78.8
Kentucky	72.9	79.2	73.8	71.3	71.1	70.2	70.0	69.7	69.8	69.8	71.7	73.0	75.9	77.2	76.4
Louisiana	57.5	61.5	62.4	61.7	59.3	61.3	61.1	62.2	63.7	64.4	64.1	69.4	63.9	59.5	61.3
Maine	80.7	74.0	73.6	73.7	75.2	78.5	74.7	75.9	76.4	75.6	76.3	77.6	78.6	76.3	78.5
Maryland	77.5	78.9	78.2	78.3	76.6	76.2	76.6	77.6	78.7	79.7	79.2	79.5	79.3	79.9	80.0
Massachusetts	79.1	79.7	78.1	78.0	78.4	78.3	77.9	78.0	78.9	77.6	75.7	79.3	78.7	79.5	80.8
Michigan	72.1	72.4	71.3	71.4	73.5	74.6	73.9	75.3	75.4	72.9	74.0	72.5	73.0	72.2	77.0
Minnesota	90.8	88.8	87.7	86.1	78.6	85.0	86.0	84.9	83.6	83.9	84.8	84.7	85.9	86.2	86.5
Mississippi	63.3	63.8	62.0	59.7	59.6	59.8	59.2	59.4	59.7	61.2	62.7	62.7	63.3	63.5	63.5
Missouri	76.0	76.8	76.0	75.0	74.7	75.2	75.8	76.3	75.5	76.8	78.3	80.4	80.6	81.0	81.9
Montana	84.4	85.5	86.5	83.9	83.2	82.2	81.3	80.8	80.0	79.8	81.0	80.4	81.5	81.9	81.5
Nebraska	86.7	87.2	86.9	85.6	84.8	85.6	87.3	85.7	83.8	83.9	85.2	87.6	87.8	87.0	86.3
Nevada	77.0	68.2	65.8	65.8	73.2	70.6	71.0	69.7	70.0	71.9	72.3	57.4	55.8	55.8	52.0
New Hampshire	78.6	80.5	78.4	77.5	77.3	76.7	75.3	76.1	77.8	77.8	78.2	78.7	80.1	81.1	81.7
New Jersey	81.4	83.4	82.1	82.8	83.9	76.3	77.5	83.6	85.4	85.8	87.0	86.3	85.1	84.8	84.4
New Mexico	70.1	66.9	64.4	63.7	62.5	61.6	63.3	64.7	65.9	67.4	63.1	67.0	65.4	67.3	59.1
New York	66.1	66.2	63.7	63.6	65.3	63.4	62.5	61.8	61.5	60.5	60.9	60.9 [4]	65.3	67.4	68.9
North Carolina	71.3	69.7	69.1	66.5	65.5	65.6	65.4	65.8	66.5	68.2	70.1	71.4	72.6	71.8	68.6
North Dakota	87.6	88.4	87.5	89.5	87.8	86.7	85.6	86.0	85.4	85.0	86.4	86.1	86.3	82.2	83.1
Ohio	77.5	81.1	79.9	74.5	76.4	77.0	75.0	75.2	76.5	77.5	79.0	81.3	80.2	79.2	78.7
Oklahoma	76.5	77.6	77.4	75.6	74.8	75.1	76.4	75.8	75.8	76.0	76.0	77.0	76.9	77.8	77.8
Oregon	72.7	72.9	71.2	68.3	69.1	69.0	68.2	69.6	68.3	71.0	73.7	74.2	74.2	73.0	73.8
Pennsylvania	79.7	81.0	80.1	80.0	79.8	79.4	79.1	78.7	79.0	80.2	81.7	82.2	82.5	83.5 [3]	83.0
Rhode Island	75.0	73.9	74.3	72.7	72.9	72.5	72.2	72.8	73.5	75.7	77.7	75.9	78.4	77.8	78.4
South Carolina	66.6	64.3	61.6	60.9	59.6	59.3	59.1	58.6	56.5	57.9	59.7	60.6	60.1	61.0 [3]	58.9
South Dakota	83.8	90.8	86.9	84.5	84.2	77.7	74.2	77.6	77.4	79.0	83.0	83.7	82.3	84.5	82.5
Tennessee	69.8	65.7	66.7	66.6	61.6	58.4	58.5	59.5	59.0	59.6	63.4	66.1	68.5	70.7	72.6
Texas	72.2	66.2	66.8	66.1	67.0	69.4	69.2	71.0	70.8	73.5	75.5	76.7	74.0	72.5	71.9
Utah	77.5	78.7	77.7	76.9	81.1	80.7	81.6	82.5	81.6	80.5	80.2	83.0	84.4	78.6	76.6
Vermont	79.5	83.5	88.9	85.3	83.6	83.9	81.9	81.0	80.2	82.0	83.6	85.4	86.5	82.3	88.5
Virginia	76.2	75.7	75.0	76.2	76.6	76.6	76.3	76.9	77.5	76.7	80.6	79.3	79.6	74.5	75.5
Washington	75.7	79.5	76.4	75.5	74.0	73.3	73.2	73.7	69.2	72.2	74.2	74.6	75.0	72.9	74.8
West Virginia	76.6	77.7	75.7	77.0	76.7	77.4	77.9	76.7	75.9	74.2	75.7	76.9	77.3	76.9	78.2
Wisconsin	85.2	84.7	84.0	83.6	83.7	83.1	82.6	82.7	83.3	84.8	85.8	85.8 [4]	86.7	87.5	88.5
Wyoming	81.1	84.0	78.8	77.7	78.4	77.1	76.6	76.3	73.4	74.4	73.9	76.0	76.7	76.1	75.8
Other jurisdictions															
American Samoa	85.3	83.7	78.7	79.7	79.7	76.6	80.4	71.9	77.0	82.9	81.0	80.2	81.1	81.0	84.6
Guam	48.2	45.4	45.2	44.6	45.4	39.5	54.7	52.9	51.7	—	56.3	48.4	—	—	—
Northern Marianas	—	78.9	62.9	62.9	68.4	63.4	63.5	61.1	62.7	65.2	65.2	75.3	75.4	80.3	73.6
Puerto Rico	60.9	57.1	60.4	60.8	61.5	61.9	63.6	64.7	65.7	66.2	67.8	64.8	61.7	68.6	66.7
U.S. Virgin Islands	53.2	59.2	59.7	54.2	62.0	58.6	58.6	53.8	57.3	48.7	53.5	—	—	—	57.8

—Not available.

[1] Includes estimates for New York and Wisconsin. Without estimates for these two states, the averaged freshman graduation rate for the remaining 48 states and the District of Columbia is 75.0 percent.

[2] U.S. total includes estimates for nonreporting states.

[3] Projected high school graduates from NCES 2008-078, *Projections of Education Statistics to 2017*.

[4] Estimated high school graduates from NCES 2006-606rev, *The Averaged Freshman Graduation Rate for Public High Schools From the Common Core of Data: School Years 2002–03 and 2003–04.*

NOTE: The averaged freshman graduation rate provides an estimate of the percentage of students who receive a regular diploma within 4 years of entering ninth grade. The rate uses aggregate student enrollment data to estimate the size of an incoming freshman class and aggregate counts of the number of diplomas awarded 4 years later. Averaged freshman graduation rates in this table are based on reported totals of enrollment by grade and high school graduates, rather than on details reported by race/ethnicity. Some data have been revised from previously published figures.

SOURCE: U.S. Department of Education, National Center for Education Statistics, Common Core of Data (CCD), "State Nonfiscal Survey of Public Elementary/Secondary Education," 1986–87 through 2007–08; *The Averaged Freshman Graduation Rate for Public High Schools From the Common Core of Data: School Years 2002–03 and 2003–04*; and *Projections of Education Statistics to 2017.* (This table was prepared September 2009.)

Public high school graduates and dropouts, by race/ethnicity and state or jurisdiction: 2006–07

State or other jurisdiction	High school graduates, by race/ethnicity, 2006–07[1]						Event dropout rates (percent of 9th- to 12th-graders who dropped out) during 2006–07, by race/ethnicity					
	Total	White	Black	Hispanic	Asian/ Pacific Islander	American Indian/ Alaska Native	Total	White	Black	Hispanic	Asian/ Pacific Islander	American Indian/ Alaska Native
1	2	3	4	5	6	7	8	9	10	11	12	13
United States[2]	**2,871,129**	**1,872,632**	**408,759**	**404,223**	**153,261**	**30,656**	**4.4**	**3.0**	**6.8**	**6.5**	**2.6**	**7.6**
Alabama	38,883	25,004	12,546	580	411	342	2.3	2.1	2.8	2.5	0.7	1.0
Alaska	7,666	4,921	282	250	520	1,693	7.3	5.2	10.0	9.0	6.7	9.5
Arizona	55,954	30,578	2,930	17,593	1,699	3,154	7.6	6.3	7.9	8.5	4.1	13.2
Arkansas	26,707	19,449	5,534	1,121	449	154	4.6	4.0	6.5	5.5	2.9	4.5
California	347,912	138,595	25,737	128,462	52,252	2,866	5.5	3.5	10.0	6.8	2.7	7.7
Colorado	45,628	33,031	2,417	8,100	1,635	445	6.9	4.3	10.0	13.8	4.0	12.5
Connecticut	37,541	27,384	4,689	4,139	1,227	102	2.1	1.3	3.6	4.7	1.1	3.4
Delaware	7,205	4,483	2,034	424	237	27	5.5	4.4	7.1	8.6	2.3	2.3
District of Columbia	2,944	—	—	—	—	—	7.1	1.6	6.9	11.0	6.1	0.0
Florida	140,012	78,413	28,099	28,861	4,234	405	3.8	2.7	5.8	4.5	1.8	3.1
Georgia	76,538	43,936	26,195	3,515	2,798	94	4.6	4.3	4.9	5.8	1.7	5.2
Hawaii	11,063	2,071	197	450	8,301	44	5.4	5.9	6.6	6.6	5.1	10.8
Idaho	16,242	14,186	129	1,446	279	202	2.6	2.3	2.7	5.2	2.0	3.7
Illinois	129,181	85,552	21,116	16,128	5,963	422	4.0	2.2	7.7	6.9	1.5	3.5
Indiana	58,962	50,578	5,279	2,161	821	123	2.7	2.3	5.2	4.4	1.4	4.3
Iowa	34,127	31,019	1,190	1,156	610	152	2.3	2.0	5.6	5.5	2.1	5.9
Kansas	29,377	23,858	2,236	2,283	662	338	2.7	2.2	3.8	4.3	2.3	4.6
Kentucky	39,099	—	—	—	—	—	3.0	2.8	4.6	5.3	1.3	2.4
Louisiana	34,274	19,767	13,051	556	658	242	7.4	5.2	10.1	8.1	4.4	7.3
Maine	13,151	12,561	227	103	184	76	5.3	5.2	6.6	6.5	5.0	13.0
Maryland	57,564	31,165	19,779	3,130	3,311	179	3.8	—	—	—	—	—
Massachusetts	63,141	49,287	4,791	5,918	3,004	141	3.8	2.7	6.4	9.1	2.6	5.0
Michigan	111,313	86,495	17,945	3,213	2,711	949	7.4	4.7	16.6	11.8	6.0	10.2
Minnesota	59,497	50,534	3,323	1,690	3,060	890	3.0	1.9	8.0	9.6	3.2	10.0
Mississippi	24,186	12,240	11,437	227	243	39	4.3	3.4	5.2	4.8	3.0	6.3
Missouri	60,275	48,677	8,970	1,371	1,035	222	3.7	3.0	6.5	6.8	2.4	4.6
Montana	10,122	8,937	49	206	144	786	3.7	3.2	5.3	6.8	1.5	7.5
Nebraska	19,873	16,800	1,226	1,290	346	211	2.8	1.9	8.3	5.9	1.9	8.2
Nevada	16,455	9,902	1,385	3,421	1,516	231	4.5	3.6	5.6	6.1	3.0	4.3
New Hampshire	13,988	13,739	257	188	237	31	3.2	3.2	5.6	4.6	0.8	11.8
New Jersey	92,722	57,416	14,359	13,507	7,243	197	2.0	1.2	3.2	3.7	0.6	3.6
New Mexico	16,131	6,253	386	7,395	258	1,839	6.1	3.9	6.7	6.4	3.1	8.1
New York	168,333	—	—	—	—	—	5.3	—	—	—	—	—
North Carolina	76,710	48,226	20,526	3,364	1,824	861	5.7	—	—	—	2.6	8.7
North Dakota	7,159	6,542	74	68	62	413	2.3	1.8	3.8	3.9	0.0	7.9
Ohio	116,136	98,390	14,058	1,899	1,652	137	4.5	3.0	9.5	19.6	2.0	9.1
Oklahoma	37,100	23,530	3,599	2,385	856	6,730	3.5	3.1	4.5	5.3	2.8	3.7
Oregon	32,643	26,227	806	3,242	1,687	681	4.6	3.8	7.9	8.3	3.2	7.4
Pennsylvania	127,830	104,217	15,515	5,566	3,173	132	—	—	5.1	6.5	—	—
Rhode Island	10,384	7,663	871	1,485	322	43	5.8	4.1	8.3	11.5	6.9	9.6
South Carolina	34,970	21,062	12,643	631	462	44	3.9	3.6	4.4	4.6	2.1	6.0
South Dakota	8,346	7,535	93	116	111	491	3.9	2.7	4.3	9.3	2.2	15.5
Tennessee	54,502	40,140	12,188	1,146	934	94	3.1	2.2	5.7	5.4	2.3	3.8
Texas	241,193	112,215	32,139	86,332	9,625	882	4.0	1.9	5.8	5.6	1.5	2.9
Utah	28,276	24,679	231	2,100	876	390	3.1	2.7	4.4	6.0	2.8	6.0
Vermont	6,667	6,325	91	63	92	96	—	—	—	—	—	—
Virginia	73,193	47,804	16,982	3,916	4,310	181	2.6	1.9	3.8	5.7	1.5	3.0
Washington	62,339	46,996	2,749	5,625	5,696	1,273	5.1	4.4	7.8	7.8	3.5	10.1
West Virginia	17,407	16,475	715	87	114	16	4.0	3.9	5.0	4.1	1.1	3.4
Wisconsin	63,968	54,078	4,332	2,580	2,202	776	2.2	1.3	7.8	5.2	1.9	5.1
Wyoming	5,441	4,882	53	328	59	119	5.1	4.5	7.9	8.0	2.1	12.3
Bureau of Indian Education	—	—	—	—	—	—	—	—	—	—	—	—
DoD, overseas	—	—	—	—	—	—	—	—	—	—	—	—
DoD, domestic	—	—	—	—	—	—	—	—	—	—	—	—
Other jurisdictions												
American Samoa	954	0	0	0	954	0	—	—	—	—	—	—
Guam	—	—	—	—	—	—	—	—	—	—	—	—
Northern Marianas	643	2	0	0	641	0	3.1	—	—	—	—	—
Puerto Rico	31,718	0	0	31,718	0	0	—	—	—	—	—	—
U.S. Virgin Islands	820	7	720	88	1	4	5.4	10.3	5.7	2.6	0.0	0.0

—Not available.

[1] Data differ slightly from figures reported in other tables due to varying reporting practices for racial/ethnic survey data.

[2] High school graduate counts include estimates for nonreporting states, based on 2006 12th-grade enrollment racial/ethnic distribution reported by state. Event dropout rate totals are totals for reporting states only.

NOTE: Includes only graduates for whom race/ethnicity was reported. Race categories exclude persons of Hispanic ethnicity. Event dropout rates measure the percentage of public school stu-dents in grades 9 through 12 who dropped out of school between one October and the next. DoD = Department of Defense.

SOURCE: U.S. Department of Education, National Center for Education Statistics, Common Core of Data (CCD), "State Nonfiscal Survey of Public Elementary/Secondary Education," 2006–07 and 2007–08, and "NCES Common Core of Data State Dropout and Completion Data File," 2006–07; and unpublished tabulations. (This table was prepared November 2009.)

General Educational Development (GED) test takers and test passers, by age: 1971 through 2008

Year	Number of test takers (in thousands)			Percentage distribution of test passers, by age[1]				
	Total[2]	Completing test battery[3]	Passing tests[4]	19 years old or less	20 to 24 years old	25 to 29 years old	30 to 34 years old	35 years old or over
1	2	3	4	5	6	7	8	9
1971[5]	377	—	227	—	—	—	—	—
1972[5]	419	—	245	—	—	—	—	—
1973[5]	423	—	249	—	—	—	—	—
1974	—	—	294	35	27	13	9	17
1975	—	—	340	33	26	14	9	18
1976	—	—	333	31	28	14	10	17
1977	—	—	330	40	24	13	8	14
1978	—	—	381	31	27	13	10	18
1979	—	—	426	37	28	12	13	11
1980	—	—	479	37	27	13	8	15
1981	—	—	489	37	27	13	8	14
1982	—	—	486	37	28	13	8	15
1983	—	—	465	34	29	14	8	15
1984	—	—	427	32	28	15	9	16
1985	—	—	413	32	26	15	10	16
1986	—	—	428	32	26	15	10	17
1987	—	—	444	33	24	15	10	18
1988	—	—	410	35	22	14	10	18
1989	632	541	357	35	24	13	—	—
1990	714	615	410	36	25	13	10	15
1991	755	657	462	33	28	13	10	16
1992	739	639	457	33	28	13	9	17
1993	746	651	469	33	27	13	10	16
1994	774	668	491	36	25	13	9	15
1995	787	682	504	38	25	13	9	15
1996	824	716	488	39	25	13	9	14
1997	785	681	460	43	24	12	8	13
1998	776	673	481	44	24	11	7	13
1999	808	702	498	44	25	11	7	13
2000	811	699	487	45	25	11	7	13
2001	1,016	928	648	41	26	11	8	14
2002	557	467	330	49	25	10	6	11
2003	657	552	387	47	26	10	7	11
2004	666	570	406	46	26	11	6	10
2005	681	588	424	45	26	12	7	11
2006	676	580	398	46	25	12	6	11
2007	692	600	429	46	24	12	7	11
2008	737	642	469	41	24	13	8	14

—Not available.

[1]People who did not report their age were excluded from this calculation. Age data for 1988 and prior years are for all test takers and may not be comparable to data for later years.
[2]All people taking the GED tests (one or more subtests).
[3]People completing the entire GED battery of five tests.
[4]Data for 2002 and later years are for people passing the GED tests (i.e., earning both a passing total score on the test battery and a passing score on each individual test). Data for 2001 and prior years are for high school equivalency credentials issued by the states to GED test passers. In order to receive high school equivalency credentials in some states, GED test passers must meet additional state requirements (e.g., complete an approved course in civics or government).

[5]Includes other jurisdictions, such as Puerto Rico, Guam, and American Samoa.
NOTE: Data are for the United States only and exclude other jurisdictions, except where noted. Detail may not sum to totals because of rounding. Some data have been revised from previously published figures.
SOURCE: American Council on Education, General Educational Development Testing Service, the GED annual Statistical Report, 1971 through 1992; *Who Took the GED?* 1993 through 2001; *Who Passed the GED Tests?* 2002 through 2005; and *GED Testing Program Statistical Report,* 2006, 2007, and 2008. Retrieved November 18, 2009, from http://www.acenet.edu/Content/NavigationMenu/ged/pubs/GED_ASR_2008.pdf. (This table was prepared November 2009.)

Percentage of high school dropouts among persons 16 through 24 years old (status dropout rate), by sex and race/ethnicity: Selected years, 1960 through 2008

Year	Total status dropout rate				Male status dropout rate				Female status dropout rate			
	All races[1]	White	Black	Hispanic	All races[1]	White	Black	Hispanic	All races[1]	White	Black	Hispanic
1	2	3	4	5	6	7	8	9	10	11	12	13
1960[2]	27.2 (—)	— (†)	— (†)	— (†)	27.8 (—)	— (†)	— (†)	— (†)	26.7 (—)	— (†)	— (†)	— (†)
1967[3]	17.0 (—)	15.4 (—)	28.6 (—)	— (†)	16.5 (—)	14.7 (—)	30.6 (—)	— (†)	17.3 (—)	16.1 (—)	26.9 (—)	— (†)
1968[3]	16.2 (—)	14.7 (—)	27.4 (—)	— (†)	15.8 (—)	14.4 (—)	27.1 (—)	— (†)	16.5 (—)	15.0 (—)	27.6 (—)	— (†)
1969[3]	15.2 (—)	13.6 (—)	26.7 (—)	— (†)	14.3 (—)	12.6 (—)	26.9 (—)	— (†)	16.0 (—)	14.6 (—)	26.7 (—)	— (†)
1970[3]	15.0 (0.29)	13.2 (0.30)	27.9 (1.22)	— (†)	14.2 (0.42)	12.2 (0.42)	29.4 (1.82)	— (†)	15.7 (0.41)	14.1 (0.42)	26.6 (1.65)	— (†)
1971[3]	14.7 (0.28)	13.4 (0.29)	24.0 (1.14)	— (†)	14.2 (0.41)	12.6 (0.41)	25.5 (1.70)	— (†)	15.2 (0.40)	14.2 (0.42)	22.6 (1.54)	— (†)
1972	14.6 (0.28)	12.3 (0.29)	21.3 (1.07)	34.3 (2.22)	14.1 (0.40)	11.6 (0.40)	22.3 (1.59)	33.7 (3.23)	15.1 (0.39)	12.8 (0.41)	20.5 (1.44)	34.8 (3.05)
1973	14.1 (0.27)	11.6 (0.28)	22.2 (1.06)	33.5 (2.24)	13.7 (0.38)	11.5 (0.39)	21.5 (1.53)	30.4 (3.16)	14.5 (0.38)	11.8 (0.39)	22.8 (1.47)	36.4 (3.16)
1974	14.3 (0.27)	11.9 (0.28)	21.2 (1.05)	33.0 (2.08)	14.2 (0.39)	12.0 (0.40)	20.1 (1.51)	33.8 (2.99)	14.3 (0.38)	11.8 (0.39)	22.1 (1.45)	32.2 (2.90)
1975	13.9 (0.27)	11.4 (0.27)	22.9 (1.06)	29.2 (2.02)	13.3 (0.37)	11.0 (0.38)	23.0 (1.56)	26.7 (2.84)	14.5 (0.38)	11.8 (0.39)	22.9 (1.44)	31.6 (2.86)
1976	14.1 (0.27)	12.0 (0.28)	20.5 (1.00)	31.4 (2.01)	14.1 (0.38)	12.1 (0.39)	21.2 (1.49)	30.3 (2.94)	14.2 (0.37)	11.8 (0.39)	19.9 (1.35)	32.3 (2.76)
1977	14.1 (0.27)	11.9 (0.28)	19.8 (0.99)	33.0 (2.02)	14.5 (0.38)	12.6 (0.40)	19.5 (1.45)	31.6 (2.89)	13.8 (0.37)	11.2 (0.38)	20.0 (1.36)	34.3 (2.83)
1978	14.2 (0.27)	11.9 (0.28)	20.2 (1.00)	33.3 (2.00)	14.6 (0.38)	12.2 (0.40)	22.5 (1.52)	33.6 (2.88)	13.9 (0.37)	11.6 (0.39)	18.3 (1.31)	33.1 (2.78)
1979	14.6 (0.27)	12.0 (0.28)	21.1 (1.01)	33.8 (1.98)	15.0 (0.39)	12.6 (0.40)	22.4 (1.52)	33.0 (2.83)	14.2 (0.37)	11.5 (0.38)	20.0 (1.35)	34.5 (2.77)
1980	14.1 (0.26)	11.4 (0.27)	19.1 (0.97)	35.2 (1.89)	15.1 (0.39)	12.3 (0.40)	20.8 (1.47)	37.2 (2.72)	13.1 (0.36)	10.5 (0.37)	17.7 (1.28)	33.2 (2.61)
1981	13.9 (0.26)	11.3 (0.27)	18.4 (0.93)	33.2 (1.80)	15.1 (0.38)	12.5 (0.40)	19.9 (1.40)	36.0 (2.61)	12.8 (0.35)	10.2 (0.36)	17.1 (1.24)	30.4 (2.48)
1982	13.9 (0.27)	11.4 (0.29)	18.4 (0.97)	31.7 (1.93)	14.5 (0.40)	12.0 (0.42)	21.2 (1.50)	30.5 (2.73)	13.3 (0.38)	10.8 (0.40)	15.9 (1.26)	32.8 (2.71)
1983	13.7 (0.27)	11.1 (0.29)	18.0 (0.97)	31.6 (1.93)	14.9 (0.41)	12.2 (0.43)	19.9 (1.46)	34.3 (2.84)	12.5 (0.37)	10.1 (0.39)	16.2 (1.28)	29.1 (2.61)
1984	13.1 (0.27)	11.0 (0.29)	15.5 (0.91)	29.8 (1.91)	14.0 (0.40)	11.9 (0.43)	16.8 (1.37)	30.6 (2.78)	12.3 (0.37)	10.1 (0.39)	14.3 (1.22)	29.0 (2.63)
1985	12.6 (0.27)	10.4 (0.29)	15.2 (0.92)	27.6 (1.93)	13.4 (0.40)	11.1 (0.42)	16.1 (1.37)	29.9 (2.76)	11.8 (0.37)	9.8 (0.39)	14.3 (1.23)	25.2 (2.68)
1986	12.2 (0.27)	9.7 (0.28)	14.2 (0.90)	30.1 (1.88)	13.1 (0.40)	10.3 (0.42)	15.0 (1.33)	32.8 (2.66)	11.4 (0.37)	9.1 (0.39)	13.5 (1.21)	27.2 (2.63)
1987	12.6 (0.28)	10.4 (0.30)	14.1 (0.90)	28.6 (1.84)	13.2 (0.40)	10.8 (0.43)	15.0 (1.35)	29.1 (2.57)	12.1 (0.38)	10.0 (0.41)	13.3 (1.21)	28.1 (2.64)
1988	12.9 (0.30)	9.6 (0.31)	14.5 (1.00)	35.8 (2.30)	13.5 (0.44)	10.3 (0.46)	15.0 (1.48)	36.0 (3.19)	12.2 (0.42)	8.9 (0.43)	14.0 (1.36)	35.4 (3.31)
1989	12.6 (0.31)	9.4 (0.32)	13.9 (0.98)	33.0 (2.19)	13.6 (0.45)	10.3 (0.47)	14.9 (1.46)	34.4 (3.08)	11.7 (0.42)	8.5 (0.43)	13.0 (1.32)	31.6 (3.11)
1990	12.1 (0.29)	9.0 (0.30)	13.2 (0.94)	32.4 (1.91)	12.3 (0.42)	9.3 (0.44)	11.9 (1.30)	34.3 (2.71)	11.8 (0.41)	8.7 (0.42)	14.4 (1.34)	30.3 (2.70)
1991	12.5 (0.30)	8.9 (0.31)	13.6 (0.95)	35.3 (1.93)	13.0 (0.43)	8.9 (0.44)	13.5 (1.37)	39.2 (2.74)	11.9 (0.41)	8.9 (0.43)	13.7 (1.31)	31.1 (2.70)
1992[4]	11.0 (0.28)	7.7 (0.29)	13.7 (0.95)	29.4 (1.86)	11.3 (0.41)	8.0 (0.42)	12.5 (1.32)	32.1 (2.67)	10.7 (0.39)	7.4 (0.40)	14.8 (1.36)	26.6 (2.56)
1993[4]	11.0 (0.28)	7.9 (0.29)	13.6 (0.94)	27.5 (1.79)	11.2 (0.40)	8.2 (0.42)	12.6 (1.32)	28.1 (2.54)	10.9 (0.40)	7.6 (0.41)	14.4 (1.34)	26.9 (2.52)
1994[4]	11.4 (0.26)	7.7 (0.27)	12.6 (0.75)	30.0 (1.16)	12.3 (0.38)	8.0 (0.38)	14.1 (1.14)	31.6 (1.60)	10.6 (0.36)	7.5 (0.37)	11.3 (0.99)	28.1 (1.66)
1995[4]	12.0 (0.27)	8.6 (0.28)	12.1 (0.74)	30.0 (1.15)	12.2 (0.38)	9.0 (0.40)	11.1 (1.05)	30.0 (1.59)	11.7 (0.37)	8.2 (0.39)	12.9 (1.05)	30.0 (1.66)
1996[4]	11.1 (0.27)	7.3 (0.27)	13.0 (0.80)	29.4 (1.19)	11.4 (0.38)	7.3 (0.38)	13.5 (1.18)	30.3 (1.67)	10.9 (0.38)	7.3 (0.39)	12.5 (1.08)	28.3 (1.69)
1997[4]	11.0 (0.27)	7.6 (0.28)	13.4 (0.80)	25.3 (1.11)	11.9 (0.39)	8.5 (0.41)	13.3 (1.16)	27.0 (1.55)	10.1 (0.36)	6.7 (0.37)	13.5 (1.11)	23.4 (1.59)
1998[4]	11.8 (0.27)	7.7 (0.28)	13.8 (0.81)	29.5 (1.12)	13.3 (0.40)	8.6 (0.41)	15.5 (1.24)	33.5 (1.59)	10.3 (0.36)	6.9 (0.37)	12.2 (1.05)	25.0 (1.56)
1999[4]	11.2 (0.26)	7.3 (0.27)	12.6 (0.77)	28.6 (1.11)	11.9 (0.38)	7.7 (0.39)	12.1 (1.10)	31.0 (1.58)	10.5 (0.36)	6.9 (0.37)	13.0 (1.08)	26.0 (1.54)
2000[4]	10.9 (0.26)	6.9 (0.26)	13.1 (0.78)	27.8 (1.08)	12.0 (0.38)	7.0 (0.37)	15.3 (1.20)	31.8 (1.56)	9.9 (0.35)	6.9 (0.37)	11.1 (1.00)	23.5 (1.48)
2001[4]	10.7 (0.25)	7.3 (0.26)	10.9 (0.71)	27.0 (1.06)	12.2 (0.38)	7.9 (0.39)	13.0 (1.12)	31.6 (1.55)	9.3 (0.34)	6.7 (0.36)	9.0 (0.90)	22.1 (1.42)
2002[4]	10.5 (0.24)	6.5 (0.24)	11.3 (0.70)	25.7 (0.93)	11.8 (0.35)	6.7 (0.35)	12.8 (1.07)	29.6 (1.32)	9.2 (0.32)	6.3 (0.34)	9.9 (0.91)	21.2 (1.27)
2003[4,5]	9.9 (0.23)	6.3 (0.24)	10.9 (0.69)	23.5 (0.90)	11.3 (0.34)	7.1 (0.35)	12.5 (1.05)	26.7 (1.29)	8.4 (0.30)	5.6 (0.32)	9.5 (0.89)	20.1 (1.23)
2004[4,5]	10.3 (0.23)	6.8 (0.24)	11.8 (0.70)	23.8 (0.89)	11.6 (0.34)	7.1 (0.35)	13.5 (1.08)	28.5 (1.30)	9.0 (0.31)	6.4 (0.34)	10.2 (0.92)	18.5 (1.18)
2005[4,5]	9.4 (0.22)	6.0 (0.23)	10.4 (0.66)	22.4 (0.87)	10.8 (0.33)	6.6 (0.34)	12.0 (1.02)	26.4 (1.26)	8.0 (0.29)	5.3 (0.31)	9.0 (0.86)	18.1 (1.16)
2006[4,5]	9.3 (0.22)	5.8 (0.23)	10.7 (0.66)	22.1 (0.86)	10.3 (0.33)	6.4 (0.33)	9.7 (0.91)	25.7 (1.25)	8.3 (0.30)	5.3 (0.31)	11.7 (0.96)	18.1 (1.15)
2007[4,5]	8.7 (0.21)	5.3 (0.22)	8.4 (0.59)	21.4 (0.83)	9.8 (0.32)	6.0 (0.32)	8.0 (0.82)	24.7 (1.22)	7.7 (0.29)	4.5 (0.28)	8.8 (0.84)	18.0 (1.13)
2008[4,5]	8.0 (0.20)	4.8 (0.21)	9.9 (0.63)	18.3 (0.78)	8.5 (0.30)	5.4 (0.30)	8.7 (0.85)	19.9 (1.12)	7.5 (0.28)	4.2 (0.28)	11.1 (0.93)	16.7 (1.08)

—Not available.
†Not applicable.
[1] Includes other racial/ethnic categories not separately shown.
[2] Based on the April 1960 decennial census.
[3] White and Black include persons of Hispanic ethnicity.
[4] Because of changes in data collection procedures, data may not be comparable with figures for years prior to 1992.
[5] White and Black exclude persons identifying themselves as two or more races.

NOTE: "Status" dropouts are 16- to 24-year-olds who are not enrolled in school and who have not completed a high school program, regardless of when they left school. People who have received GED credentials are counted as high school completers. All data except for 1960 are based on October counts. Data are based on sample surveys of the civilian noninstitutionalized population, which excludes persons in prisons, persons in the military, and other persons not living in households. Race categories exclude persons of Hispanic ethnicity except where otherwise noted. Standard errors appear in parentheses.
SOURCE: U.S. Department of Commerce, Census Bureau, Current Population Survey (CPS), October 1967 through October 2008. (This table was prepared August 2009.)

Number of 14- through 21-year-old students served under Individuals with Disabilities Education Act, Part B, who exited school, by exit reason, age, and type of disability: United States and other jurisdictions, 2005–06 and 2006–07

Age and type of disability	Total	Exiting school					Transferred to regular education[3]	Moved, known to be continuing
		Graduated with diploma	Received a certificate of attendance	Reached maximum age[1]	Dropped out[2]	Died		
1	2	3	4	5	6	7	8	9
2005-06								
Total..........................	396,857	224,343	60,864	5,424	104,101	2,125	71,397	210,984
Age								
14...........................	5,935	93	23	†	5,490	329	19,591	45,635
15...........................	11,067	75	54	†	10,567	371	17,111	49,035
16...........................	27,713	4,810	623	†	21,885	395	15,526	48,667
17...........................	142,510	94,529	17,466	†	30,103	412	11,478	39,079
18...........................	141,364	91,785	25,028	749	23,517	285	5,576	19,859
19...........................	42,605	23,694	9,857	372	8,509	173	1,489	5,923
20...........................	15,397	6,585	4,272	1,471	2,969	100	422	1,971
21...........................	10,266	2,772	3,541	2,832	1,061	60	204	815
Type of disability								
Specific learning disabilities......................	236,135	145,558	29,491	1,184	59,221	681	39,634	109,527
Mental retardation......................	46,588	17,111	16,562	2,125	10,409	381	2,301	21,050
Emotional disturbance......................	47,519	20,634	4,728	592	21,331	234	8,080	46,908
Speech or language impairments..............	8,923	6,005	825	43	2,028	22	10,512	5,139
Multiple disabilities......................	8,251	3,615	2,110	682	1,544	300	379	4,556
Other health impairment[4]......................	32,274	20,464	3,781	178	7,545	306	8,251	17,389
Hearing impairments......................	4,674	3,211	770	55	626	12	672	1,738
Orthopedic impairments......................	3,455	2,131	663	133	405	123	707	1,203
Visual impairmets......................	1,766	1,273	245	28	201	19	217	581
Autism......................	4,876	2,783	1,297	326	446	24	409	2,038
Deaf-blindness......................	150	98	21	13	13	5	14	56
Traumatic brain injury......................	2,246	1,460	371	65	332	18	221	799
2006-07								
Total..........................	394,786	221,306	64,918	5,925	100,831	1,806	66,840	213,544
Age								
14...........................	4,924	4	10	†	4,668	242	17,819	43,865
15...........................	9,880	38	29	†	9,523	290	15,213	49,041
16...........................	23,823	2,089	722	†	20,643	369	14,676	49,796
17...........................	147,595	94,994	21,751	†	30,475	375	11,521	41,104
18...........................	143,386	93,163	25,681	988	23,295	259	5,692	20,887
19...........................	40,763	22,314	8,900	786	8,622	141	1,314	6,216
20...........................	14,677	6,288	4,260	1,366	2,671	92	401	1,879
21...........................	9,738	2,416	3,565	2,785	934	38	204	756
Type of disability								
Specific learning disabilities......................	232,114	140,795	32,852	1,283	56,614	570	36,183	110,023
Mental retardation......................	45,288	16,987	15,625	2,303	10,039	334	2,447	20,386
Emotional disturbance......................	46,016	19,733	5,021	633	20,458	171	6,984	46,704
Speech or language impairments..............	9,048	6,028	1,088	50	1,852	30	10,009	5,147
Multiple disabilities......................	8,328	3,780	1,990	708	1,591	259	316	4,752
Other health impairment[4]......................	35,970	22,637	4,551	235	8,280	267	8,817	19,822
Hearing impairments......................	4,392	2,927	827	58	563	17	614	1,697
Orthopedic impairments......................	3,546	2,113	738	128	476	91	532	1,120
Visual impairmets......................	1,644	1,174	247	32	176	15	205	574
Autism......................	5,958	3,536	1,567	405	420	30	557	2,441
Deaf-blindness......................	181	136	12	11	14	8	5	58
Traumatic brain injury......................	2,301	1,460	400	79	348	14	171	820

†Not applicable.

[1]Students may exit special education services due to maximum age beginning at age 18 depending on state law or practice or order of any court.

[2]"Dropped out" is defined as the total who were enrolled at some point in the reporting year, were not enrolled at the end of the reporting year, and did not exit through any of the other bases described. Includes students previously categorized as "moved, not known to continue."

[3]"Transferred to regular education" was previously labeled "no longer receives special education."

[4]Other health impairments include having limited strength, vitality, or alertness due to chronic or acute health problems such as a heart condition, tuberculosis, rheumatic fever, nephritis, asthma, sickle cell anemia, hemophilia, epilepsy, lead poisoning, leukemia, or diabetes.

SOURCE: U.S. Department of Education, Office of Special Education Programs, Individuals with Disabilities Education Act (IDEA) database. Retrieved March 9, 2009, from https://www.ideadata.org/PartBData.asp. (This table was prepared March 2009.)

Private elementary and secondary enrollment, number of schools, and average tuition, by school level, orientation, and tuition: 1999–2000, 2003–04, and 2007–08

School orientation and tuition	Kindergarten through 12th-grade enrollment[1]				Schools				Average tuition charged to students[2] (in current dollars)			
	Total	Elementary	Secondary	Combined	Total	Elementary	Secondary	Combined	Total	Elementary	Secondary	Combined
1	2	3	4	5	6	7	8	9	10	11	12	13
1999–2000												
Total	5,262,850 (131,001)	2,920,680 (55,056)	818,920 (34,102)	1,523,240 (88,816)	27,220 (239)	16,560 (278)	2,580 (126)	8,080 (276)	$4,689 (254.3)	$3,267 (128.3)	$6,053 (1,529.3)	$6,779 (798.1)
Catholic	2,548,710 (23,352)	1,810,330 (18,134)	616,190 (25,935)	122,190 (15,613)	7,930 (41)	6,530 (68)	1,100 (56)	300 (28)	3,236 (439.8)	2,451 (109.4)	4,845 (253.7)	6,780 (1,159.7)
Other religious	1,871,850 (86,781)	831,060 (41,035)	115,010 (10,980)	925,780 (66,926)	12,520 (271)	6,610 (231)	720 (76)	5,190 (243)	4,063 (936.7)	3,503 (609.1)	6,536 (787.7)	4,260 (1,240.4)
Nonsectarian	842,290 (61,373)	279,290 (28,987)	87,720 (11,774)	475,270 (43,377)	5,130 (156)	2,780 (153)	590 (90)	1,770 (151)	10,992 (928.4)	7,884 (1,727.8)	14,638 (1,279.2)	12,363 (3,043.5)
2003–04												
Total	5,059,450 (104,287)	2,675,960 (55,714)	832,320 (54,051)	1,551,170 (82,059)	28,380 (262)	17,330 (262)	2,660 (206)	8,400 (217)	$6,600 (144.5)	$5,049 (119.5)	$8,412 (433.4)	$8,302 (289.7)
Catholic	2,320,040 (49,156)	1,645,680 (41,231)	584,250 (32,236)	90,110 (14,746)	7,920 (35)	6,530 (50)	1,060 (39)	320 (39)	4,254 (95.9)	3,533 (105.9)	6,046 (130.6)	5,801 (883.0)
Other religious	1,746,460 (63,090)	714,860 (28,935)	107,980 (33,776)	923,630 (48,379)	13,660 (203)	7,280 (200)	640 (175)	5,740 (182)	5,839 (143.9)	5,398 (161.4)	9,537 (962.6)	5,748 (230.3)
Nonsectarian	992,940 (71,519)	315,430 (30,820)	140,080 (27,556)	537,440 (59,332)	6,810 (136)	3,510 (141)	960 (108)	2,340 (144)	13,419 (379.1)	12,169 (468.5)	17,413 (1,987.6)	13,112 (480.4)
2007–08												
Total	5,165,280 (104,435)	2,462,980 (58,830)	850,750 (38,553)	1,851,550 (91,348)	28,220 (328)	16,370 (291)	3,040 (149)	8,810 (254)	$8,549 (176.0)	$6,733 (180.6)	$10,549 (355.5)	$10,045 (371.6)
Less than $2,499	455,850 (33,102)	271,960 (21,952)	‡	173,660 (24,693)	6,100 (347)	3,450 (229)	‡	2,370 (226)	1,670 (80.6)	1,938 (42.7)	‡	1,313 (175.7)
$2,500 to $3,499	666,450 (42,950)	478,050 (33,038)	‡	168,440 (26,113)	3,930 (257)	2,820 (225)	‡	1,020 (119)	3,428 (41.0)	3,453 (43.2)	‡	3,416 (116.5)
$3,500 to $5,999	1,790,410 (77,850)	1,066,750 (45,444)	143,510 (19,815)	580,150 (53,528)	9,110 (341)	6,100 (263)	550 (76)	2,460 (192)	5,206 (41.6)	5,218 (49.3)	5,081 (80.0)	5,214 (89.0)
$6,000 to $9,999	1,155,290 (60,342)	366,470 (37,396)	455,840 (33,376)	332,980 (36,574)	4,460 (232)	2,390 (188)	1,050 (85)	1,020 (114)	8,264 (100.6)	9,231 (286.7)	7,657 (104.7)	8,031 (191.9)
$10,000 or more	1,097,280 (67,145)	279,740 (31,540)	221,210 (23,837)	596,320 (60,614)	4,630 (232)	1,620 (156)	1,070 (96)	1,940 (150)	20,272 (513.4)	19,510 (1,006.4)	21,202 (1,081.1)	20,285 (712.1)
Catholic	2,224,470 (49,385)	1,457,960 (32,114)	620,840 (32,581)	145,680 (25,445)	7,400 (34)	5,950 (57)	1,080 (46)	370 (39)	6,018 (180.3)	4,944 (211.6)	7,826 (231.8)	9,066 (964.2)
Less than $2,499	190,800 (20,946)	174,580 (20,080)	‡	‡	1,130 (102)	1,050 (96)	‡	‡	2,144 (75.7)	2,166 (74.7)	‡	‡
$2,500 to $3,499	428,610 (35,795)	396,980 (32,130)	‡	‡	1,680 (131)	1,630 (126)	‡	‡	3,352 (42.8)	3,385 (45.8)	‡	‡
$3,500 to $5,999	826,120 (37,974)	683,980 (32,576)	‡	‡	3,040 (131)	2,680 (117)	‡	‡	4,896 (48.8)	4,864 (56.7)	‡	‡
$6,000 to $9,999	607,980 (49,329)	165,120 (28,123)	111,770 (16,043)	‡	1,170 (102)	470 (72)	280 (43)	‡	7,682 (116.3)	7,785 (240.4)	5,150 (80.2)	‡
$10,000 or more	170,960 (27,585)	‡	395,900 (30,158)	‡	380 (62)	‡	630 (49)	‡	16,536 (1,704.9)	‡	7,650 (116.7)	‡
Other religious	1,975,980 (81,216)	709,730 (36,666)	128,550 (15,136)	1,137,700 (75,038)	13,950 (282)	7,170 (228)	960 (85)	5,820 (192)	7,117 (237.1)	6,576 (241.5)	10,493 (1,336.5)	7,073 (358.7)
Less than $2,499	221,810 (25,272)	94,820 (10,131)	‡	122,890 (21,602)	4,160 (294)	2,320 (215)	‡	1,780 (185)	1,577 (129.3)	1,552 (178.6)	‡	1,601 (185.7)
$2,500 to $3,499	208,200 (24,333)	77,840 (11,714)	‡	129,590 (23,401)	2,020 (208)	1,120 (175)	‡	880 (115)	3,520 (84.3)	3,758 (170.4)	‡	3,380 (74.7)
$3,500 to $5,999	860,370 (59,588)	340,150 (27,800)	‡	489,390 (49,116)	5,030 (257)	2,640 (170)	‡	2,160 (175)	5,372 (74.8)	5,568 (110.6)	‡	5,269 (100.8)
$6,000 to $9,999	384,850 (39,687)	103,280 (15,561)	57,150 (10,809)	224,420 (33,273)	1,640 (137)	680 (94)	370 (65)	600 (72)	8,045 (155.1)	8,807 (429.9)	7,683 (187.6)	7,787 (163.8)
$10,000 or more	300,750 (34,146)	93,640 (19,216)	‡	171,400 (31,330)	1,100 (114)	420 (72)	‡	420 (81)	17,497 (759.9)	15,209 (632.4)	‡	18,008 (1,196.0)
Nonsectarian	964,830 (55,074)	295,280 (25,191)	101,370 (12,739)	568,180 (48,321)	6,860 (119)	3,240 (143)	1,010 (87)	2,620 (138)	17,316 (555.2)	15,945 (702.2)	27,302 (1,506.3)	16,247 (795.3)
Less than $2,499	43,250 (6,840)	‡	‡	‡	800 (113)	‡	‡	‡	54 (33.2)	‡	‡	‡
$2,500 to $3,499	‡	‡	‡	‡	‡	‡	‡	‡	‡	‡	‡	‡
$3,500 to $5,999	103,930 (18,494)	42,610 (7,809)	‡	1,040 (143)	770 (139)	‡	‡	6,289 (352.1)	8,094 (687.4)	‡	‡	
$6,000 to $9,999	162,450 (24,872)	98,070 (16,434)	‡	1,650 (168)	1,250 (151)	‡	‡	10,963 (530.4)	12,111 (792.2)	‡	‡	
$10,000 or more	625,570 (45,837)	148,810 (20,542)	90,480 (12,896)	386,280 (43,701)	3,150 (177)	1,070 (129)	660 (77)	1,410 (131)	22,628 (703.0)	21,232 (1,046.6)	30,265 (1,589.3)	21,377 (983.4)

†Not applicable.

‡Reporting standards not met.

[1]Only includes kindergarten students who attend schools that offer first or higher grade.

[2]Tuition weighted by the number of students enrolled in schools.

NOTE: Excludes schools not offering first or higher grade. Elementary schools have grade 6 or lower and no grade higher than 8. Secondary schools have no grade lower than 7. Combined schools have grades lower than 7 and higher than 8.

Excludes prekindergarten students. Includes schools reporting tuition of 0. Detail may not sum to totals because of rounding and cell suppression. Standard errors appear in parentheses.

SOURCE: U.S. Department of Education, National Center for Education Statistics, Schools and Staffing Survey (SASS), "Private School Questionnaire," 1999–2000, 2003–04, and 2007–08. (This table was prepared in October 2009.)

Enrollment and instructional staff in Catholic elementary and secondary schools, by level: Selected years, 1919–20 through 2008–09

School year	Number of schools			Enrollment[1]				Instructional staff[2]		
	Total	Elementary[3]	Secondary	Total	Pre-kindergarten	Elementary	Secondary	Total	Elementary[3]	Secondary
1	2	3	4	5	6		7	8	9	10
1919–20	8,103	6,551	1,552	1,925,521	(4)	1,795,673	129,848	49,516	41,592	7,924
1929–30	10,046	7,923	2,123	2,464,467	(4)	2,222,598	241,869	72,552	58,245	14,307
1939–40	10,049	7,944	2,105	2,396,305	(4)	2,035,182	361,123	81,057	60,081	20,976
1949–50	10,778	8,589	2,189	3,066,387	(4)	2,560,815	505,572	94,295	66,525	27,770
Fall 1960	12,893	10,501	2,392	5,253,791	(4)	4,373,422	880,369	151,902	108,169	43,733
1969–70	11,352	9,366	1,986	4,367,000	(4)	3,359,000	1,008,000	195,400 [5]	133,200 [5]	62,200 [5]
1970–71	11,350	9,370	1,980	4,363,566	(4)	3,355,478	1,008,088	166,208	112,750	53,458
1974–75	10,127	8,437	1,690	3,504,000	(4)	2,602,000	902,000	150,179	100,011	50,168
1975–76	9,993	8,340	1,653	3,415,000	(4)	2,525,000	890,000	149,276	99,319	49,957
1979–80	9,640	8,100	1,540	3,139,000	(4)	2,293,000	846,000	147,294	97,724	49,570
1980–81	9,559	8,043	1,516	3,106,000	(4)	2,269,000	837,000	145,777	96,739	49,038
1981–82	9,494	7,996	1,498	3,094,000	(4)	2,266,000	828,000	146,172	96,847	49,325
1982–83	9,432	7,950	1,482	3,007,189	(4)	2,211,412	795,777	146,460	97,337	49,123
1983–84	9,401	7,937	1,464	2,969,000	(4)	2,179,000	790,000	146,913	98,591	48,322
1984–85	9,325	7,876	1,449	2,903,000	(4)	2,119,000	784,000	149,888	99,820	50,068
1985–86	9,220	7,790	1,430	2,821,000	(4)	2,061,000	760,000	146,594	96,741	49,853
1986–87	9,102	7,693	1,409	2,726,000	(4)	1,998,000	728,000	141,930	93,554	48,376
1987–88	8,992	7,601	1,391	2,690,668	67,637	1,942,148	680,883	139,887	93,199	46,688
1988–89	8,867	7,505	1,362	2,627,745	76,626	1,911,911	639,208	137,700	93,154	44,546
1989–90	8,719	7,395	1,324	2,588,893	90,023	1,892,913	605,957	136,900	94,197	42,703
1990–91	8,587	7,291	1,296	2,575,815	100,376	1,883,906	591,533	131,198	91,039	40,159
1991–92	8,508	7,239	1,269	2,550,863	107,939	1,856,302	586,622	153,334	109,084	44,250
1992–93	8,423	7,174	1,249	2,567,630	122,788	1,860,937	583,905	154,816	109,825	44,991
1993–94	8,345	7,114	1,231	2,576,845	132,236	1,859,947	584,662	157,201	112,199	45,002
1994–95	8,293	7,055	1,238	2,618,567	143,360	1,877,782	597,425	164,219	117,620	46,599
1995–96	8,250	7,022	1,228	2,635,210	144,099	1,884,461	606,650	166,759	118,753	48,006
1996–97	8,231	7,005	1,226	2,645,462	148,264	1,885,037	612,161	153,276	107,548	45,728
1997–98	8,223	7,004	1,219	2,648,859	150,965	1,879,737	618,157	152,259	105,717	46,542
1998–99	8,217	6,990	1,227	2,648,844	152,356	1,876,211	620,277	153,081	105,943	47,138
1999–2000	8,144	6,923	1,221	2,653,038	152,622	1,877,236	623,180	157,134	109,404	47,730
2000–01	8,146	6,920	1,226	2,647,301	155,742	1,863,682	627,877	160,731	111,937	48,794
2001–02	8,114	6,886	1,228	2,616,330	159,869	1,827,319	629,142	155,658	108,485	47,173
2002–03	8,000	6,785	1,215	2,553,277	157,250	1,765,893	630,134	163,004	112,884	50,120
2003–04	7,955	6,727	1,228	2,484,252	150,422	1,708,501	625,329	162,337	112,303	50,034
2004–05	7,799	6,574	1,225	2,420,590	150,905	1,642,868	626,817	160,153	107,764	52,389
2005–06	7,589	6,386	1,203	2,325,220	146,327	1,568,687	610,206	152,502 [6]	103,481 [6]	49,021 [6]
2006–07	7,498	6,288	1,210	2,320,651	152,429	1,544,695	623,527	159,135	107,682	51,453
2007–08	7,378	6,165	1,213	2,270,913	152,980	1,494,979	622,954	160,075	107,217	52,858
2008–09	7,248	6,028	1,220	2,192,531	153,325	1,434,949	604,257	157,615	105,518	52,097

[1]Elementary enrollment is for kindergarten through grade 8, and secondary enrollment is for grades 9 through 12.
[2]From 1919-20 through fall 1960, includes part-time teachers. From 1969-70 through 1993-94, excludes part-time teachers. Beginning in 1994-95, reported in full-time equivalents (FTE). Prekindergarten teachers not counted separately, but may be included with elementary teachers.
[3]Includes middle schools.
[4]Prekindergarten enrollment was not reported separately, but may be included in elementary enrollment.
[5]Includes estimates for the nonreporting schools.

[6]Excludes the Archdiocese of New Orleans.
NOTE: Data collected by the National Catholic Educational Association and data collected by the National Center for Education Statistics are not directly comparable because survey procedures and definitions differ. Some data have been revised from previously published figures.
SOURCE: National Catholic Educational Association, A *Statistical Report on Catholic Elementary and Secondary Schools for the Years 1967–68 to 1969–70; A Report on Catholic Schools*, 1970–71 through 1973–74; *A Statistical Report on U.S. Catholic Schools*, 1974–75 through 1980–81; and *United States Catholic Elementary and Secondary Schools*, 1981–82 through 2008–09. (This table was prepared April 2009.)

Private elementary and secondary schools, enrollment, teachers, and high school graduates, by state: Selected years, 1997 through 2007

State	Schools, fall 2007		Enrollment in prekindergarten through grade 12												Teachers,[1] fall 2007		High school graduates, 2006–07	
			Fall 1997		Fall 1999		Fall 2001		Fall 2003		Fall 2005		Fall 2007					
1	2		3		4		5		6		7		8		9		10	
United States	33,740	(370)	5,944,320	(18,543)	6,018,280	(30,179)	6,319,650	(40,272)	6,099,220	(41,219)	6,073,240	(42,446)	5,910,210	(28,363)	456,270	(2,897)	306,610	(2,488)
Alabama	420	(17)	82,060	(†)	81,040	(†)	92,380	(3,926)	99,580	(12,130)	92,280	(5,892)	83,840	(103)	6,400	(17)	4,580	(†)
Alaska	60	(†)	7,230	(†)	6,980	(†)	7,420	(†)	7,370	(424)	7,500	(1,028)	4,990	(†)	460	(†)	200	(†)
Arizona	360	(†)	59,730	(261)	58,740	(2,591)	78,660	(18,218)	75,360	(16,426)	66,840	(†)	64,910	(†)	4,220	(†)	2,590	(†)
Arkansas	300 !	(136)	30,410	(†)	29,400	(†)	32,570	(†)	31,300	(†)	35,390	(5,858)	40,120 !	(11,961)	3,150 !	(948)	1,380	(†)
California	4,010	(44)	721,210	(2,146)	724,010	(1,403)	757,750	(8,415)	740,460	(8,703)	737,490	(15,529)	703,810	(6,129)	50,150	(495)	34,880	(465)
Colorado	420	(†)	65,410	(†)	65,690	(†)	64,700	(†)	62,080	(476)	70,770	(1,160)	64,740	(†)	4,830	(†)	2,520	(†)
Connecticut	420	(17)	76,740	(785)	80,060	(391)	82,320	(†)	102,960	(25,024)	76,220	(1,619)	85,150	(9,241)	8,240	(705)	7,990	(1,925)
Delaware	210 !	(68)	36,730	(7,525)	26,940	(†)	31,690	(1,023)	33,020	(2,649)	29,830	(†)	32,520	(2,701)	2,440	(124)	1,800	(†)
District of Columbia	90	(†)	17,480	(†)	17,000	(†)	33,660	(14,373)	23,510	(6,121)	19,880	(†)	19,640	(†)	2,190	(†)	1,660	(†)
Florida	1,940	(82)	329,770	(2,120)	349,180	(4,957)	365,890	(8,301)	398,720	(14,590)	396,790	(7,429)	391,660	(6,123)	29,790	(653)	18,580	(291)
Georgia	910	(169)	126,520	(5,983)	137,420	(9,460)	137,060	(4,550)	144,850	(6,527)	152,600	(10,394)	157,430	(9,185)	14,010	(902)	7,570	(106)
Hawaii	140	(4)	35,530	(†)	35,550	(746)	42,980	(220)	39,940	(†)	32,810	(†)	37,300	(290)	2,880	(24)	2,390	(†)
Idaho	190 !	(71)	11,140	(†)	12,720	(†)	12,050	(†)	12,570	(†)	15,320	(2,518)	24,700 !	(11,608)	1,680 !	(758)	910 !	(405)
Illinois	1,920	(194)	345,250	(720)	347,750	(700)	357,390	(19,293)	316,430	(1,698)	317,940	(4,263)	312,270	(6,638)	20,750	(535)	15,110	(113)
Indiana	810	(27)	122,430	(1,222)	121,960	(†)	129,240	(326)	124,500	(455)	139,370	(17,870)	119,910	(2,284)	8,100	(231)	4,790	(101)
Iowa	240	(†)	64,320	(9,269)	54,640	(844)	51,540	(†)	53,850	(4,634)	60,960	(8,311)	47,820	(†)	3,410	(†)	2,260	(†)
Kansas	250	(32)	45,430	(1,964)	56,840	(12,716)	51,540	(8,341)	47,710	(2,151)	47,130	(1,654)	47,780	(2,414)	3,500	(178)	2,380	(†)
Kentucky	400	(57)	81,770	(1,078)	89,300	(6,657)	85,230	(3,227)	82,100	(1,525)	78,880	(1,228)	76,140	(2,074)	5,640	(174)	4,030	(†)
Louisiana	390	(†)	153,710	(1,198)	148,020	(†)	159,910	(11,381)	155,780	(3,515)	138,270	(525)	137,460	(†)	9,080	(†)	7,530	(†)
Maine	200	(24)	18,260	(†)	19,820	(261)	20,820	(174)	24,740	(3,629)	20,680	(337)	21,260	(143)	2,140	(24)	2,620	(†)
Maryland	820	(20)	154,920	(1,725)	166,570	(1,030)	175,740	(†)	172,360	(†)	170,350	(4,201)	165,760	(1,160)	14,290	(101)	9,450	(†)
Massachusetts	950	(57)	151,300	(†)	154,060	(147)	177,490	(9,836)	164,390	(6,636)	157,770	(3,273)	151,640	(2,516)	15,040	(295)	10,430	(85)
Michigan	910	(11)	211,950	(3,152)	208,470	(4,965)	198,380	(†)	180,080	(†)	166,950	(407)	159,100	(2,047)	10,870	(134)	8,520	(†)
Minnesota	580	(16)	97,470	(†)	101,360	(†)	112,310	(2,993)	106,010	(3,011)	104,730	(3,467)	101,740	(3,903)	7,180	(218)	4,930	(442)
Mississippi	220	(†)	57,150	(416)	67,200	(14,096)	67,380	(10,106)	57,110	(2,981)	57,930	(4,104)	55,270	(†)	4,150	(†)	3,350	(†)
Missouri	690	(73)	138,460	(6,478)	131,750	(†)	138,140	(4,321)	141,530	(9,966)	137,810	(10,580)	125,610	(3,685)	9,720	(390)	7,330	(87)
Montana	140 !	(40)	9,050	(†)	10,170	(487)	12,930	(1,895)	12,510	(2,091)	35,980 !	(22,655)	15,030 !	(5,465)	1,200 !	(364)	1,700 !	(1,214)
Nebraska	220	(†)	43,210	(†)	44,560	(†)	45,590	(618)	41,650	(†)	42,420	(†)	40,320	(†)	2,820	(†)	2,160	(†)
Nevada	160	(10)	15,360	(†)	17,350	(†)	20,370	(385)	23,930	(†)	29,120	(†)	29,820	(2,009)	1,550	(123)	700	(†)
New Hampshire	310	(†)	31,670	(1,565)	36,480	(†)	38,650	(†)	33,780	(†)	33,220	(†)	30,920	(†)	2,970	(†)	2,290	(†)
New Jersey	1,440	(86)	248,110	(8,025)	237,540	(2,316)	282,450	(4,182)	269,530	(7,577)	256,160	(8,439)	253,250	(5,016)	19,510	(301)	13,340	(†)
New Mexico	210	(31)	23,580	(84)	28,570	(220)	26,510	(†)	29,310	(3,928)	25,030	(141)	27,290	(1,388)	2,170	(123)	1,500	(65)
New York	2,130	(65)	531,510	(2,416)	542,520	(4,368)	559,670	(1,669)	515,620	(4,071)	510,750	(3,596)	518,850	(7,196)	42,840	(953)	29,890	(117)
North Carolina	660	(33)	105,450	(8,920)	104,370	(1,403)	116,500	(4,112)	126,230	(11,439)	117,280	(11,681)	121,660	(2,226)	10,850	(430)	5,590	(†)
North Dakota	50	(†)	7,970	(†)	7,730	(†)	7,180	(†)	6,840	(†)	7,290	(†)	7,430	(†)	560	(†)	‡	(†)
Ohio	1,190	(136)	285,150	(3,088)	280,930	(1,730)	290,370	(7,180)	270,660	(7,094)	254,530	(9,821)	239,520	(2,741)	16,370	(442)	13,060	(61)
Oklahoma	300 !	(90)	39,580	(7,068)	45,660	(7,770)	46,570	(8,723)	34,300	(2,013)	35,350	(1,194)	40,320	(5,032)	3,900	(880)	2,030	(293)
Oregon	560	(69)	58,290	(4,441)	61,000	(5,195)	71,500	(15,519)	54,320	(†)	69,620	(14,139)	66,260	(5,188)	4,740	(480)	2,810	(†)
Pennsylvania	2,500	(117)	395,940	(5,960)	392,060	(6,679)	374,490	(†)	357,580	(3,364)	332,740	(3,918)	324,020	(6,253)	24,640	(729)	17,480	(321)
Rhode Island	230	(50)	30,310	(†)	29,570	(†)	30,970	(†)	31,960	(†)	30,600	(†)	28,260	(1,096)	2,530	(57)	1,580	(†)
South Carolina	410	(20)	82,390	(7,965)	86,810	(18,537)	70,950	(†)	73,800	(†)	70,240	(1,797)	71,430	(1,043)	5,550	(20)	3,210	(†)
South Dakota	80	(†)	10,350	(†)	10,120	(†)	11,740	(†)	11,980	(†)	12,700	(†)	12,280	(†)	930	(†)	560	(†)
Tennessee	560	(32)	91,880	(†)	104,150	(5,281)	98,790	(†)	93,390	(†)	105,240	(2,531)	117,540	(12,851)	10,110	(1,518)	5,890	(†)
Texas	1,650	(115)	283,120	(7,997)	277,770	(2,338)	314,210	(12,244)	271,380	(2,758)	304,170	(20,453)	296,540	(4,132)	23,620	(367)	11,920	(†)
Utah	150	(†)	18,250	(†)	15,900	(†)	20,040	(†)	19,990	(†)	21,220	(†)	20,860	(†)	1,720	(†)	1,350	(†)
Vermont	150	(23)	12,230	(398)	15,010	(1,829)	14,090	(†)	12,730	(†)	11,530	(†)	12,600	(232)	1,550	(23)	1,760	(325)
Virginia	870	(104)	115,560	(443)	116,110	(215)	129,470	(†)	131,160	(6,936)	155,220	(14,290)	143,140	(7,988)	12,920	(874)	6,910	(270)
Washington	730	(93)	88,160	(1,870)	88,080	(1,493)	91,150	(2,028)	101,130	(7,935)	119,640	(13,187)	104,070	(3,054)	7,460	(225)	4,570	(9)
West Virginia	140	(†)	15,260	(†)	16,370	(†)	16,560	(†)	15,300	(†)	16,120	(†)	14,980	(†)	1,260	(†)	600	(†)
Wisconsin	990	(48)	156,330	(†)	154,340	(1,581)	162,220	(9,080)	159,240	(11,743)	142,280	(137)	138,290	(1,597)	9,910	(100)	5,430	(†)
Wyoming	40	(†)	3,200	(†)	2,640	(†)	2,430	(†)	2,600	(†)	2,310	(†)	2,930	(†)	260	(†)	‡	(†)

†Not applicable.
!Interpret data with caution.
‡Reporting standards not met.
[1]Reported in full-time equivalents (FTE). Excludes teachers who teach only prekindergarten students.
NOTE: Includes special education, vocational/technical education, and alternative schools. Tabulation includes schools that offer kindergarten or higher grade. Includes enrollment of students in prekindergarten though grade 12 in schools that offer kindergarten or higher grade. Some data have been revised from previously published figures. Detail may not sum to totals because of rounding. Standard errors appear in parentheses.
SOURCE: U.S. Department of Education, National Center for Education Statistics, Private School Universe Survey (PSS), various years, 1997–98 through 2007–08. (This table was prepared June 2009.)

Public and private elementary and secondary teachers, enrollment, and pupil/teacher ratios: Selected years, fall 1955 through fall 2018

Year	Teachers (in thousands)			Enrollment (in thousands)			Pupil/teacher ratio		
	Total	Public	Private	Total	Public	Private	Total	Public	Private
1	2	3	4	5	6	7	8	9	10
1955	1,286	1,141	145 [1]	35,280	30,680	4,600 [1]	27.4	26.9	31.7 [1]
1960	1,600	1,408	192 [1]	42,181	36,281	5,900 [1]	26.4	25.8	30.7 [1]
1965	1,933	1,710	223	48,473	42,173	6,300	25.1	24.7	28.3
1970	2,292	2,059	233	51,257	45,894	5,363	22.4	22.3	23.0
1971	2,293	2,063	230 [1]	51,271	46,071	5,200 [1]	22.4	22.3	22.6 [1]
1972	2,337	2,106	231 [1]	50,726	45,726	5,000 [1]	21.7	21.7	21.6 [1]
1973	2,372	2,136	236 [1]	50,445	45,445	5,000 [1]	21.3	21.3	21.2 [1]
1974	2,410	2,165	245 [1]	50,073	45,073	5,000 [1]	20.8	20.8	20.4 [1]
1975	2,453	2,198	255 [1]	49,819	44,819	5,000 [1]	20.3	20.4	19.6 [1]
1976	2,457	2,189	268	49,478	44,311	5,167	20.1	20.2	19.3
1977	2,488	2,209	279	48,717	43,577	5,140	19.6	19.7	18.4
1978	2,479	2,207	272	47,637	42,551	5,086	19.2	19.3	18.7
1979	2,461	2,185	276 [1]	46,651	41,651	5,000 [1]	19.0	19.1	18.1 [1]
1980	2,485	2,184	301	46,208	40,877	5,331	18.6	18.7	17.7
1981	2,440	2,127	313 [1]	45,544	40,044	5,500 [1]	18.7	18.8	17.6 [1]
1982	2,458	2,133	325 [1]	45,166	39,566	5,600 [1]	18.4	18.6	17.2 [1]
1983	2,476	2,139	337	44,967	39,252	5,715	18.2	18.4	17.0
1984	2,508	2,168	340 [1]	44,908	39,208	5,700 [1]	17.9	18.1	16.8 [1]
1985	2,549	2,206	343	44,979	39,422	5,557	17.6	17.9	16.2
1986	2,592	2,244	348 [1]	45,205	39,753	5,452 [1]	17.4	17.7	15.7 [1]
1987	2,631	2,279	352	45,488	40,008	5,479	17.3	17.6	15.6
1988	2,668	2,323	345	45,430	40,189	5,242 [1]	17.0	17.3	15.2 [1]
1989	2,713	2,357	356	46,141	40,543	5,599	17.0	17.2	15.7
1990	2,759	2,398	361 [1]	46,864	41,217	5,648 [1]	17.0	17.2	15.6 [1]
1991	2,797	2,432	365	47,728	42,047	5,681	17.1	17.3	15.6
1992	2,823	2,459	364 [1]	48,694	42,823	5,870 [1]	17.2	17.4	16.1 [1]
1993	2,868	2,504	364	49,532	43,465	6,067	17.3	17.4	16.7
1994	2,922	2,552	370 [1]	50,106	44,111	5,994 [1]	17.1	17.3	16.2 [1]
1995	2,974	2,598	376	50,759	44,840	5,918	17.1	17.3	15.7
1996	3,051	2,667	384 [1]	51,544	45,611	5,933 [1]	16.9	17.1	15.5 [1]
1997	3,138	2,746	391	52,071	46,127	5,944	16.6	16.8	15.2
1998	3,230	2,830	400 [1]	52,526	46,539	5,988 [1]	16.3	16.4	15.0 [1]
1999	3,319	2,911	408	52,875	46,857	6,018	15.9	16.1	14.7
2000	3,366	2,941	424 [1]	53,373	47,204	6,169 [1]	15.9	16.0	14.5 [1]
2001	3,440	3,000	441	53,992	47,672	6,320	15.7	15.9	14.3
2002	3,476	3,034	442 [1]	54,403	48,183	6,220 [1]	15.7	15.9	14.1 [1]
2003	3,490	3,049	441	54,639	48,540	6,099	15.7	15.9	13.8
2004	3,538	3,091	447 [1]	54,882	48,795	6,087 [1]	15.5	15.8	13.6 [1]
2005	3,593	3,143	450	55,187	49,113	6,073	15.4	15.6	13.5
2006	3,622	3,166	456 [1]	55,307	49,316	5,991 [1]	15.3	15.6	13.2 [1]
2007	3,634	3,178	456	55,203	49,293	5,910	15.2	15.5	13.0
2008 [2]	3,689	3,233	456	55,500	49,623	5,878	15.0	15.3	12.9
2009 [2]	3,705	3,249	456	55,632	49,788	5,845	15.0	15.3	12.8
2010 [2]	3,725	3,271	454	55,850	50,034	5,817	15.0	15.3	12.8
2011 [2]	3,763	3,310	453	56,144	50,349	5,795	14.9	15.2	12.8
2012 [2]	3,812	3,358	454	56,545	50,767	5,778	14.8	15.1	12.7
2013 [2]	3,867	3,410	457	57,012	51,239	5,773	14.7	15.0	12.6
2014 [2]	3,933	3,473	460	57,544	51,769	5,775	14.6	14.9	12.6
2015 [2]	4,001	3,536	465	58,137	52,346	5,791	14.5	14.8	12.5
2016 [2]	4,069	3,599	470	58,706	52,892	5,814	14.4	14.7	12.4
2017 [2]	4,141	3,665	476	59,270	53,426	5,843	14.3	14.6	12.3
2018 [2]	4,205	3,722	483	59,813	53,933	5,879	14.2	14.5	12.2

[1]Estimated.
[2]Projected.
NOTE: Data for teachers are expressed in full-time equivalents (FTE). Counts of private school teachers and enrollment include prekindergarten through grade 12 in schools offering kindergarten or higher grades. Counts of public school teachers and enrollment include prekindergarten through grade 12. The pupil/teacher ratio includes teachers for students with disabilities and other special teachers, while these teachers are generally excluded from class size calculations. Ratios for public schools reflect totals reported by states and differ from totals reported for schools or school districts. Some data have been revised from previously published figures. Detail may not sum to totals because of rounding. SOURCE: U.S. Department of Education, National Center for Education Statistics, *Statistics of Public Elementary and Secondary Day Schools*, 1955–56 through 1984–85; Common Core of Data (CCD), "State Nonfiscal Survey of Public Elementary/Secondary Education," 1985–86 through 2007–08; Private School Universe Survey (PSS), 1989–90 through 2007–08; *Projections of Education Statistics to 2018*; and unpublished data. (This table was prepared September 2009.)

Public elementary and secondary teachers, by level and state or jurisdiction: Selected years, fall 2000 through fall 2007

State or jurisdiction	Fall 2000	Fall 2003	Fall 2004	Fall 2005	Fall 2006[1] Total	Elementary	Secondary	Ungraded	Fall 2007 Total	Elementary	Secondary	Ungraded
1	2	3	4	5	6	7	8	9	10	11	12	13
United States	2,941,461[2]	3,048,652[2]	3,090,925[2]	3,143,003[2]	3,166,391[2]	1,666,282[2]	1,247,403[2]	252,706[2]	3,178,142[2]	1,688,240[2]	1,258,069	231,833
Alabama	48,194[3]	58,070	51,594	57,757	56,134	34,385	21,749	0	50,420	29,086	21,334	0
Alaska	7,880	7,808	7,756	7,912	7,903	4,127	3,776	0	7,613	3,897	3,716	0
Arizona	44,438	47,507	48,935	51,376	52,625	37,793	14,832	0	54,032	38,807	15,225	0
Arkansas	31,947	30,876	31,234	32,997	35,089	16,315	15,983	2,791	33,882	17,942	13,520	2,420
California	298,021[3]	304,311[3]	305,969[3]	309,222[3]	307,366[3]	213,380[3]	85,106	8,880	305,230[3]	209,146[3]	86,030	10,054
Colorado	41,983	44,904	45,165	45,841	46,973	23,798	23,175	0	47,761	26,947	20,814	0
Connecticut	41,044	42,370	38,808	39,687	39,115	25,945	12,126	1,044	39,304	26,005	12,259	1,040
Delaware	7,469	7,749	7,856	7,998	8,038	3,981	4,057	0	8,198	4,110	4,088	0
District of Columbia	4,949	5,676	5,387	5,481[4]	5,383[4]	2,828[4]	2,271[4]	284[4]	6,347	3,238	2,619	490
Florida	132,030	144,955	154,864	158,962	162,851	72,116	64,334	26,401	168,737	75,670	67,019	26,048
Georgia	91,043	97,150	104,987	108,535	113,597	68,690	44,907	0	116,857	71,109	45,681	67
Hawaii	10,927	11,129	11,146	11,226	11,271	5,943	5,289	39	11,397	6,075	5,280	42
Idaho	13,714	14,049	14,269	14,521	14,770	7,690	7,080	0	15,013	7,874	7,139	0
Illinois	127,620	127,669	131,047	133,857	140,988	57,332	62,187	21,469	136,571	56,585	58,489	21,497
Indiana	59,226	59,924	60,563	60,592	61,346	33,470	27,855	21	62,334	33,870	28,074	390
Iowa	34,636	34,791	34,697	35,181	35,653	19,128	16,525	0	36,089	19,608	16,481	0
Kansas	32,742	32,589	32,932	33,608	35,297	16,418	18,713	166	35,359	16,604	18,572	183
Kentucky	39,589	41,246	41,463	42,413	43,371	21,615	10,101	11,655	43,536	21,699	10,168	11,669
Louisiana	49,915	50,495	49,192	44,660	45,951	32,186	13,765	0	48,610	34,042	14,568	0
Maine	16,559	17,621	16,656	16,684	16,826	11,432	5,159	235	16,558	11,351	5,207	0
Maryland	52,433	55,198	55,101	56,685	58,443	33,898	24,545	0	59,320	34,449	24,871	0
Massachusetts	67,432	72,062	73,399	73,596	73,157	41,984	20,793	10,380	70,719	47,026	23,693	0
Michigan	97,031	97,014	100,638	98,069	98,037	38,666	39,265	20,106	96,204	38,063	38,343	19,798
Minnesota	53,457	51,611	52,152	51,107	51,880	25,905	24,387	1,588	52,975	27,012	24,483	1,480
Mississippi	31,006	32,591	31,321	31,433	32,351	15,669	12,408	4,274	33,560	16,149	13,103	4,308
Missouri	64,735	65,169	65,847	67,076	67,521	34,983	32,538	0	68,430	35,420	33,010	0
Montana	10,411	10,301	10,224	10,369	10,398	6,944	3,454	0	10,519	7,082	3,437	0
Nebraska	20,983	20,921	21,236	21,359	21,459	13,588	7,755	116	21,930	13,996	7,847	87
Nevada	18,293	20,234	20,950	21,744	22,908	11,763	7,866	3,279	23,423	12,003	8,067	3,353
New Hampshire	14,341	15,112	15,298	15,536	15,515	10,582	4,933	0	15,484	10,576	4,908	0
New Jersey	99,061	109,077	114,875	112,673	112,301	45,494	48,157	18,650	111,500	47,442	46,343	17,715
New Mexico	21,042	21,569	21,730	22,021	22,016	15,628	6,388	0	22,300	15,589	6,629	82
New York	206,961	216,116	218,612[4]	218,989	218,879	106,391	76,693	35,795	211,854	102,626	71,116	38,112
North Carolina	83,680	89,988	92,550	95,664	112,304	62,958	47,713	1,633	106,562	56,192	48,685	1,685
North Dakota	8,141	8,037	8,070	8,003	8,007	4,908	3,099	0	8,068	4,970	3,098	0
Ohio	118,361	121,735	118,060	117,982	110,459	52,136	52,596	5,727	109,766	52,616	52,498	4,652
Oklahoma	41,318	39,253	40,416	41,833	42,206	20,668	17,059	4,479	46,735	22,276	19,974	4,485
Oregon	28,094	26,732	27,431	28,346	29,940	20,175	8,875	890	30,013	20,677	9,120	216
Pennsylvania	116,963	119,889	121,167	122,397	123,114	50,218	53,175	19,721	135,234	62,770	63,313	9,151
Rhode Island	10,645	11,918	11,781	14,180[3]	11,381	5,407	5,974	0	11,271	5,383	5,888	0
South Carolina	45,380	45,830	46,914	48,212	49,284	14,980	31,882	2,422	47,382	14,200	30,757	2,425
South Dakota	9,397	9,245	9,064	9,129	9,070	5,721	2,547	802	9,416	5,729	2,533	1,154
Tennessee	57,164	59,584	60,022	59,596	62,176	43,484	18,210	482	64,659	44,454	18,626	1,579
Texas	274,826	289,481	294,547	302,425	311,649	155,549	119,809	36,291	321,929	159,819	123,974	38,136
Utah	22,008	22,147	22,287[3]	22,993	23,640	11,569	9,642	2,429	24,336	12,165	9,711	2,460
Vermont	8,414	8,749	8,720	8,851	8,859	3,413	3,614	1,832	8,749	3,399	3,601	1,749
Virginia	86,977[3]	90,573	93,732	103,944	79,688	39,061	40,627	0	71,861	34,907	36,954	0
Washington	51,098	52,824	53,125	53,508	53,743	26,319	22,181	5,243	53,960	26,518	22,264	5,178
West Virginia	20,930	20,020	19,958	19,940	19,633	8,441	7,788	3,404	20,306	9,493	10,813	0
Wisconsin	60,165	58,216	60,521	60,127	59,089	27,921	31,003	165	58,914	28,023	30,763	128
Wyoming	6,783	6,567	6,657	6,706	6,737	3,287	3,437	13	6,915	3,551	3,364	0
Bureau of Indian Education	—	—	—	—	—	—	—	—	—	—	—	—
DoD, overseas	5,105	4,728	4,885	5,726	5,204	1,762	1,603	1,839	4,147	1,610	1,519	1,018
DoD, domestic	2,399	2,301	2,002	2,033	2,033	1,053	446	534	2,243	992	433	818
Other jurisdictions												
American Samoa	820	988	945	989	971	684	267	20	—	—	—	—
Guam	1,975	1,760	1,672	1,804	—	—	—	—	—	—	—	—
Northern Marianas	526	550	579	614	579	322	253	4	550	310	236	4
Puerto Rico	37,620	42,444	43,054	42,036	40,163	21,970	13,486	4,707	40,826	21,357	14,017	5,452
U.S. Virgin Islands	1,511	1,512	1,545	1,434	1,531	698	810	23	1,518	643	588	287

—Not available.
[1] Data have been revised from previously published figures.
[2] Includes imputed values for states.
[3] Includes imputations for underreporting of prekindergarten teachers.
[4] Imputed.

NOTE: Distribution of elementary and secondary teachers determined by reporting units. Teachers reported in full-time equivalents (FTE). DoD = Department of Defense. SOURCE: U.S. Department of Education, National Center for Education Statistics, Common Core of Data (CCD), "State Nonfiscal Survey of Public Elementary/Secondary Education," 2000–01 through 2007–08. (This table was prepared September 2009.)

Teachers, enrollment, and pupil/teacher ratios in public elementary and secondary schools, by state or jurisdiction: Selected years, fall 2000 through fall 2007

State or jurisdiction	Pupil/teacher ratio				Fall 2005			Fall 2006[1]			Fall 2007		
	Fall 2000	Fall 2002	Fall 2003	Fall 2004[1]	Teachers	Enrollment	Pupil/teacher ratio	Teachers	Enrollment	Pupil/teacher ratio	Teachers	Enrollment	Pupil/teacher ratio
1	2	3	4	5	6	7	8	9	10	11	12	13	14
United States	16.0 [2]	15.9 [2]	15.9 [2]	15.8 [2]	3,143,003 [2]	49,113,298 [2]	15.6 [2]	3,166,391 [2]	49,315,842 [2]	15.6 [2]	3,178,142 [2]	49,292,507 [2]	15.5 [2]
Alabama	15.4 [3]	15.7 [3]	12.6	14.2	57,757	741,761	12.8	56,134	743,632	13.2	50,420	744,865	14.8
Alaska	16.9	16.6	17.2	17.1	7,912	133,288	16.8	7,903	132,608	16.8	7,613	131,029	17.2
Arizona	19.8	19.9	21.3	21.3	51,376	1,094,454	21.3	52,625	1,068,249	20.3	54,032	1,087,447	20.1
Arkansas	14.1	14.9	14.7	14.8	32,997	474,206	14.4	35,089	476,409	13.6	33,882	479,016	14.1
California	20.6 [3]	20.6 [3]	21.1 [3]	21.1 [3]	309,222 [3]	6,437,202 [3]	20.8 [3]	307,366 [3]	6,406,750 [3]	20.8 [3]	305,230 [3]	6,343,471 [3]	20.8 [3]
Colorado	17.3	16.6	16.9	17.0	45,841	779,826	17.0	46,973	794,026	16.9	47,761	801,867	16.8
Connecticut	13.7	13.5	13.6	14.9	39,687	575,059	14.5	39,115	575,100	14.7	39,304	570,626	14.5
Delaware	15.4	15.1	15.2	15.2	7,998	120,937	15.1	8,038	122,254	15.2	8,198	122,574	15.0
District of Columbia	13.9	13.9	13.8	14.2	5,481 [4]	76,876	14.0 [4]	5,383 [4]	72,850	13.5 [4]	6,347	78,422	12.4
Florida	18.4	18.4	17.9	17.0	158,962	2,675,024	16.8	162,851	2,671,513	16.4	168,737	2,666,811	15.8
Georgia	15.9	15.6	15.7	14.8	108,535	1,598,461	14.7	113,597	1,629,157	14.3	116,857	1,649,589	14.1
Hawaii	16.9	16.8	16.5	16.4	11,226	182,818	16.3	11,271	180,728	16.0	11,397	179,897	15.8
Idaho	17.9	17.9	17.9	17.9	14,521	261,982	18.0	14,770	267,380	18.1	15,013	272,119	18.1
Illinois	16.1	15.9	16.5	16.0	133,857	2,111,706	15.8	140,988	2,118,276	15.0	136,571	2,112,805	15.5
Indiana	16.7	16.7	16.9	16.9	60,592	1,035,074	17.1	61,346	1,045,940	17.0	62,334	1,046,766	16.8
Iowa	14.3	13.9	13.8	13.8	35,181	483,482	13.7	35,653	483,122	13.6	36,089	485,115	13.4
Kansas	14.4	14.4	14.4	14.2	33,608	467,525	13.9	35,297	469,506	13.3	35,359	468,295	13.2
Kentucky	16.8	16.3	16.1	16.3	42,413	679,878	16.0	43,371	683,152	15.8	43,536	666,225	15.3
Louisiana	16.6	16.6	16.6	16.6	44,660	654,526	16.6	45,951	675,851	16.6	48,610	681,038	16.6
Maine	12.5	12.1	11.5	11.9	16,684	195,498	11.7	16,826	193,986	11.5	16,558	196,245	11.9
Maryland	16.3	15.7	15.7	15.7	56,685	860,020	15.2	58,443	851,640	14.6	59,320	845,700	14.3
Massachusetts	14.5	13.2	13.6	13.3	73,596	971,909	13.2	73,157	968,661	13.2	70,719	962,958	13.6
Michigan	17.7 [3]	19.9	18.1	17.4	98,069	1,742,282	17.8	98,037	1,722,656	17.6	96,204	1,692,739	17.6
Minnesota	16.0	16.0	16.3	16.1	51,107	839,243	16.4	51,880	840,565	16.2	52,975	837,578	15.8
Mississippi	16.1	15.6	15.1	15.8	31,433	494,954	15.7	32,351	495,026	15.3	33,560	494,122	14.7
Missouri	14.1	13.6	13.9	13.8	67,076	917,705	13.7	67,521	920,353	13.6	68,430	917,188	13.4
Montana	14.9	14.5	14.4	14.3	10,369	145,416	14.0	10,398	144,418	13.9	10,519	142,823	13.6
Nebraska	13.6	13.6	13.6	13.5	21,359	286,646	13.4	21,459	287,580	13.4	21,930	291,244	13.3
Nevada	18.6	18.4	19.0	19.1	21,744	412,395	19.0	22,908	424,766	18.5	23,423	429,362	18.3
New Hampshire	14.5	13.9	13.7	13.5	15,536	205,767	13.2	15,515	203,572	13.1	15,484	200,772	13.0
New Jersey	13.3	12.8	12.7	12.1	112,673	1,395,602	12.4	112,301	1,388,850	12.4	111,500	1,382,348	12.4
New Mexico	15.2	15.1	15.0	15.0	22,021	326,758	14.8	22,016	328,220	14.9	22,300	329,040	14.8
New York	13.9	13.7	13.3	13.0	218,989	2,815,581	12.9	218,879	2,809,649	12.8	211,854	2,765,435	13.1
North Carolina	15.5	15.2	15.1	15.0	95,664	1,416,436	14.8	112,304	1,444,481	12.9	106,562	1,489,492	14.0
North Dakota	13.4	12.9	12.7	12.5	8,003	98,283	12.3	8,007	96,670	12.1	8,068	95,059	11.8
Ohio	15.5	14.7	15.2	15.6	117,982	1,839,683	15.6	110,459	1,836,722	16.6	109,766	1,827,184	16.6
Oklahoma	15.1	15.4	16.0	15.6	41,833	634,739	15.2	42,206	639,391	15.1	46,735	642,065	13.7
Oregon	19.4	20.4	20.6	20.1	28,346	552,194	19.5	29,940	562,574	18.8	30,013	565,586	18.8
Pennsylvania	15.5	15.4	15.2	15.1	122,397	1,830,684	15.0	123,114	1,871,060	15.2	135,234	1,801,971	13.3
Rhode Island	14.8	14.2	13.4	13.3	14,180 [3]	153,422	10.8	11,381	151,612	13.3	11,271	147,629	13.1
South Carolina	14.9	14.9	15.3	15.0	48,212	701,544	14.6	49,284	708,021	14.4	47,382	712,317	15.0
South Dakota	13.7	14.0	13.6	13.5	9,129	122,012	13.4	9,070	121,158	13.4	9,416	121,606	12.9
Tennessee	15.9 [3]	15.8 [3]	15.7 [3]	15.7 [3]	59,596	953,928	16.0	62,176	978,368	15.7	64,659	964,259	14.9
Texas	14.8	14.8	15.0	15.0	302,425	4,525,394	15.0	311,649	4,599,509	14.8	321,929	4,674,832	14.5
Utah	21.9	21.8	22.4	22.6 [3]	22,993	508,430	22.1	23,640	523,386	22.1	24,336	576,244	23.7
Vermont	12.1	11.7	11.3	11.3	8,851	96,638	10.9	8,859	95,399	10.8	8,749	94,038	10.7
Virginia	13.2 [3]	11.8	13.2	12.9	103,944	1,213,616	11.7	79,688	1,220,440	15.3	71,861	1,230,857	17.1
Washington	19.7	19.2	19.3	19.2	53,508	1,031,985	19.3	53,743	1,026,774	19.1	53,960	1,030,247	19.1
West Virginia	13.7	14.0	14.0	14.0	19,940	280,866	14.1	19,633	281,939	14.4	20,306	282,535	13.9
Wisconsin	14.6	14.6	15.1	14.3	60,127	875,174	14.6	59,089	876,700	14.8	58,914	874,633	14.8
Wyoming	13.3	13.0 [3]	13.3	12.7	6,706	84,409	12.6	6,737	85,193	12.6	6,915	86,422	12.5
Bureau of Indian Education	—	—	—	—		50,938	—	—	—	—	—	—	—
DoD, overseas	14.4	15.2	15.0	14.0	5,726	62,543	10.9	5,204	60,891	11.7	4,147	57,247	13.8
DoD, domestic	14.2	13.2	13.3	14.6	2,033	28,329	13.9	2,033	26,631	13.1	2,243	27,548	12.3
Other jurisdictions													
American Samoa	19.1	17.0	16.1	17.1	989	16,438	16.6	971	16,400	16.9	—	—	—
Guam	16.4	—	17.9	18.3	1,804	30,986	17.2	—	—	—	—	—	—
Northern Marianas	19.0	20.6	20.4	20.0	614	11,718	19.1	579	11,695	20.2	550	11,299	20.5
Puerto Rico	16.3	14.1	13.8	13.4	42,036	563,490	13.4	40,163	544,138	13.5	40,826	526,565	12.9
U.S. Virgin Islands	12.9	12.2	11.7	10.6	1,434	16,750	11.7	1,531	16,284	10.6	1,518	15,903	10.5

—Not available.
[1] Data have been revised from previously published figures.
[2] Includes imputed values for states.
[3] Includes imputations for underreporting of prekindergarten teachers/enrollment.
[4] Imputed.

NOTE: Teachers reported in full-time equivalents (FTE). DoD = Department of Defense.
SOURCE: U.S. Department of Education, National Center for Education Statistics, Common Core of Data (CCD), "State Nonfiscal Survey of Public Elementary/Secondary Education," 2000–01 through 2007–08. (This table was prepared September 2009.)

Teachers' perceptions about teaching and school conditions, by control and level of school: Selected years, 1993–94 through 2007–08

Statement about conditions	Public school teachers							Private school teachers						
	1993–94 total	1999–2000 total	2003–04 total	2007–08				1993–94 total	1999–2000 total	2003–04 total	2007–08			
				Total	Elementary schools	Secondary schools	Combined schools				Total	Elementary schools	Secondary schools	Combined schools
1	2	3	4	5	6	7	8	9	10	11	12	13	14	15
	Percent of teachers somewhat agreeing or strongly agreeing with statement													
The school administration's behavior toward the staff is supportive	79.2 (0.36)	78.8 (0.38)	85.2 (0.33)	87.7 (0.39)	88.1 (0.51)	87.1 (0.47)	86.3 (1.25)	88.2 (0.42)	87.3 (0.45)	91.1 (0.74)	93.1 (0.43)	92.6 (0.49)	92.3 (1.15)	93.9 (0.74)
My principal enforces school rules for student conduct and backs me up when I need it	80.8 (0.35)	82.2 (0.33)	87.2 (0.35)	88.0 (0.37)	89.3 (0.48)	85.9 (0.51)	86.0 (1.12)	88.4 (0.41)	88.3 (0.39)	92.2 (0.62)	92.2 (0.58)	91.8 (0.71)	91.8 (1.17)	92.8 (0.97)
The principal lets staff members know what is expected of them	85.6 (0.30)	87.7 (0.26)	91.8 (0.23)	— (†)	— (†)	— (†)	— (†)	88.2 (0.34)	89.8 (0.35)	93.8 (0.55)	— (†)	— (†)	— (†)	— (†)
Principal talks to me frequently about my instructional practices	44.3 (0.46)	45.6 (0.43)	— (†)	— (†)	— (†)	— (†)	— (†)	54.0 (0.64)	50.4 (0.64)	— (†)	— (†)	— (†)	— (†)	— (†)
In this school, staff members are recognized for a job well done	67.9 (0.39)	68.3 (0.42)	75.4 (0.38)	76.7 (0.56)	78.3 (0.77)	74.2 (0.63)	72.4 (1.41)	81.1 (0.40)	78.9 (0.50)	83.8 (1.09)	84.1 (0.67)	84.0 (0.78)	83.0 (1.71)	84.6 (1.05)
Principal knows what kind of school he/she wants and has communicated it to the staff	80.5 (0.36)	83.2 (0.28)	87.3 (0.30)	88.4 (0.33)	89.6 (0.44)	86.6 (0.51)	84.4 (1.20)	88.6 (0.38)	88.4 (0.43)	91.9 (0.68)	91.7 (0.53)	91.3 (0.65)	90.7 (1.20)	92.5 (0.82)
Most of my colleagues share my beliefs and values about what the central mission of the school should be	84.2 (0.22)	84.7 (0.26)	88.1 (0.26)	88.3 (0.35)	90.7 (0.52)	83.8 (0.53)	87.4 (0.86)	93.2 (0.37)	92.2 (0.31)	93.8 (0.50)	93.7 (0.44)	94.9 (0.47)	90.5 (1.36)	93.7 (0.79)
There is a great deal of cooperative effort among staff	77.5 (0.31)	78.4 (0.32)	83.2 (0.36)	84.3 (0.33)	86.1 (0.47)	81.0 (0.51)	81.9 (1.19)	90.5 (0.29)	89.0 (0.42)	91.1 (0.75)	91.8 (0.63)	92.3 (0.53)	88.3 (1.43)	92.5 (1.08)
I receive a great deal of support from parents for the work I do	52.5 (0.38)	57.9 (0.40)	61.1 (0.50)	64.3 (0.52)	66.5 (0.78)	60.4 (0.66)	62.5 (1.45)	84.6 (0.41)	84.0 (0.49)	86.0 (2.39)	87.7 (0.60)	89.4 (0.69)	85.1 (1.79)	86.9 (1.01)
I make a conscious effort to coordinate the content of my courses with that of other teachers	85.0 (0.25)	84.1 (0.24)	86.3 (0.31)	— (†)	— (†)	— (†)	— (†)	85.2 (0.44)	81.4 (0.55)	84.5 (1.20)	— (†)	— (†)	— (†)	— (†)
Routine duties and paperwork interfere with my job of teaching	70.8 (0.38)	71.1 (0.30)	70.8 (0.44)	69.0 (0.54)	69.4 (0.82)	68.7 (0.69)	64.4 (1.32)	40.1 (0.65)	44.5 (0.57)	40.8 (2.51)	42.7 (0.98)	44.8 (1.26)	46.2 (2.27)	39.3 (1.75)
Level of student misbehavior in this school interferes with my teaching	44.1 (0.40)	40.8 (0.42)	37.2 (0.53)	36.1 (0.57)	33.8 (0.80)	40.2 (0.79)	38.9 (1.37)	22.4 (0.43)	24.1 (0.61)	20.8 (2.55)	20.6 (0.73)	20.8 (0.97)	19.5 (1.71)	20.7 (1.38)
Amount of student tardiness and class cutting in this school interferes with my teaching	27.9 (0.32)	31.5 (0.35)	33.4 (0.45)	33.4 (0.65)	26.4 (0.86)	47.2 (0.86)	32.8 (1.35)	16.9 (0.75)	15.0 (0.43)	16.9 (1.01)	17.8 (0.71)	17.1 (0.78)	20.4 (1.76)	17.6 (1.63)
Rules for student behavior are consistently enforced by teachers in this school, even for students who are not in their classes	61.8 (0.42)	62.6 (0.39)	71.1 (0.46)	70.6 (0.55)	78.8 (0.68)	55.1 (0.66)	68.1 (1.38)	77.6 (0.50)	75.9 (0.51)	80.9 (1.51)	80.0 (0.81)	85.3 (0.87)	69.8 (2.00)	78.5 (1.49)
I am satisfied with my class sizes	64.9 (0.38)	67.7 (0.36)	69.1 (0.43)	— (†)	— (†)	— (†)	— (†)	84.4 (0.40)	85.7 (0.45)	87.6 (0.92)	— (†)	— (†)	— (†)	— (†)
I am satisfied with my teaching salary	44.9 (0.45)	39.4 (0.36)	45.9 (0.46)	50.9 (0.65)	48.9 (0.91)	55.2 (0.73)	47.9 (1.27)	41.6 (0.59)	42.6 (0.73)	50.6 (1.67)	51.7 (0.88)	44.5 (1.13)	55.8 (2.63)	57.6 (2.06)
I sometimes feel it is a waste of time to try to do my best as a teacher	26.8 (0.35)	20.3 (0.29)	16.7 (0.32)	— (†)	— (†)	— (†)	— (†)	10.2 (0.65)	10.5 (0.38)	8.7 (0.71)	— (†)	— (†)	— (†)	— (†)
I plan with the librarian/media specialist for the integration of services into my teaching	66.9 (0.42)	58.6 (0.38)	— (†)	— (†)	— (†)	— (†)	— (†)	60.6 (0.71)	48.7 (0.74)	— (†)	— (†)	— (†)	— (†)	— (†)
Necessary materials are available as needed by staff	73.1 (0.42)	75.0 (0.32)	79.0 (0.42)	82.2 (0.55)	82.5 (0.77)	81.5 (0.51)	82.1 (1.06)	85.7 (0.44)	89.0 (0.38)	91.8 (0.71)	92.1 (0.54)	92.3 (0.59)	91.2 (1.33)	92.2 (1.02)
I worry about the security of my job because of the performance of my students on state or local tests	— (†)	28.8 (0.37)	31.2 (0.43)	30.9 (0.58)	32.3 (0.81)	28.3 (0.54)	30.5 (1.32)	— (†)	6.7 (0.29)	7.8 (0.65)	7.7 (0.47)	8.2 (0.57)	6.4 (1.06)	7.6 (0.82)
State or district content standards have had a positive influence on my satisfaction with teaching	— (†)	— (†)	— (†)	49.3 (0.62)	52.1 (0.95)	44.1 (0.57)	48.5 (1.29)	— (†)	— (†)	— (†)	41.0 (0.81)	49.1 (1.20)	34.1 (2.01)	35.2 (1.52)
I am given the support I need to teach students with special needs	— (†)	60.9 (0.33)	64.4 (0.46)	67.2 (0.57)	66.2 (0.74)	68.3 (0.69)	72.7 (1.18)	— (†)	67.1 (0.58)	71.8 (2.05)	68.5 (0.84)	66.5 (1.17)	69.5 (1.81)	70.2 (1.55)
I am generally satisfied with being a teacher at this school	— (†)	89.7 (0.24)	90.9 (0.28)	92.9 (0.31)	93.1 (0.42)	92.4 (0.37)	93.1 (0.59)	— (†)	93.3 (0.26)	95.2 (0.55)	95.7 (0.43)	95.2 (0.52)	95.5 (0.92)	96.2 (0.65)

—Not available.
†Not applicable.
NOTE: Standard errors appear in parentheses.

SOURCE: U.S. Department of Education, National Center for Education Statistics, Schools and Staffing Survey (SASS), "Public Teacher Questionnaire," selected years 1993–94 through 2007–08; "Private Teacher Questionnaire," selected years 1993–94 through 2007–08; and "Charter Teacher Questionnaire," 1999–2000. (This table was prepared September 2009.)

Estimated average annual salary of teachers in public elementary and secondary schools: Selected years, 1959–60 through 2008–09

	Current dollars					Average public school teachers' salary in constant 2007–08 dollars[2]		
	Average public school teachers' salary			Wage and salary accruals per full-time-equivalent (FTE) employee[1]	Ratio of average teachers' salary to accruals per FTE employee			
School year	All teachers	Elementary teachers	Secondary teachers			All teachers	Elementary teachers	Secondary teachers
1	2	3	4	5	6	7	8	9
1959–60	$4,995	$4,815	$5,276	$4,749	1.05	$35,989	$34,692	$38,013
1961–62	5,515	5,340	5,775	5,063	1.09	38,843	37,610	40,674
1963–64	5,995	5,805	6,266	5,478	1.09	41,150	39,846	43,010
1965–66	6,485	6,279	6,761	5,934	1.09	43,026	41,660	44,858
1967–68	7,423	7,208	7,692	6,533	1.14	46,209	44,870	47,883
1969–70	8,626	8,412	8,891	7,486	1.15	48,343	47,143	49,828
1970–71	9,268	9,021	9,568	7,998	1.16	49,391	48,075	50,990
1971–72	9,705	9,424	10,031	8,521	1.14	49,929	48,483	51,606
1972–73	10,174	9,893	10,507	9,056	1.12	50,314	48,925	51,961
1973–74	10,770	10,507	11,077	9,667	1.11	48,901	47,707	50,295
1974–75	11,641	11,334	12,000	10,411	1.12	47,583	46,328	49,051
1975–76	12,600	12,280	12,937	11,194	1.13	48,099	46,877	49,385
1976–77	13,354	12,989	13,776	11,971	1.12	48,168	46,851	49,690
1977–78	14,198	13,845	14,602	12,811	1.11	47,990	46,797	49,355
1978–79	15,032	14,681	15,450	13,807	1.09	46,457	45,372	47,749
1979–80	15,970	15,569	16,459	15,050	1.06	43,549	42,456	44,883
1980–81	17,644	17,230	18,142	16,461	1.07	43,120	42,108	44,337
1981–82	19,274	18,853	19,805	17,795	1.08	43,358	42,411	44,553
1982–83	20,695	20,227	21,291	18,873	1.10	44,638	43,628	45,923
1983–84	21,935	21,487	22,554	19,781	1.11	45,623	44,692	46,911
1984–85	23,600	23,200	24,187	20,694	1.14	47,238	46,437	48,412
1985–86	25,199	24,718	25,846	21,685	1.16	49,024	48,089	50,283
1986–87	26,569	26,057	27,244	22,700	1.17	50,567	49,593	51,852
1987–88	28,034	27,519	28,798	23,777	1.18	51,232	50,291	52,629
1988–89	29,564	29,022	30,218	24,752	1.19	51,643	50,697	52,786
1989–90	31,367	30,832	32,049	25,762	1.22	52,297	51,405	53,434
1990–91	33,084	32,490	33,896	26,935	1.23	52,301	51,362	53,584
1991–92	34,063	33,479	34,827	28,169	1.21	52,177	51,282	53,347
1992–93	35,029	34,350	35,880	29,245	1.20	52,031	51,022	53,295
1993–94	35,737	35,233	36,566	30,030	1.19	51,742	51,013	52,943
1994–95	36,675	36,088	37,523	30,857	1.19	51,621	50,795	52,814
1995–96	37,642	37,138	38,397	31,822	1.18	51,579	50,888	52,613
1996–97	38,443	38,039	39,184	33,058	1.16	51,215	50,677	52,202
1997–98	39,350	39,002	39,944	34,635	1.14	51,505	51,049	52,282
1998–99	40,544	40,165	41,203	36,306	1.12	52,165	51,677	53,012
1999–2000	41,807	41,306	42,546	38,176	1.10	52,280	51,654	53,204
2000–01	43,378	42,910	44,053	39,722	1.09	52,448	51,882	53,264
2001–02	44,655	44,177	45,310	40,579	1.10	53,053	52,485	53,831
2002–03	45,686	45,408	46,106	41,704	1.10	53,110	52,787	53,599
2003–04	46,542	46,187	46,976	43,301	1.07	52,947	52,543	53,441
2004–05	47,516	47,122	47,688	44,941	1.06	52,476	52,041	52,666
2005–06	48,804	48,420	49,041	46,755	1.04	51,921	51,513	52,173
2006–07	50,758	50,699	50,829	48,812	1.04	52,639	52,578	52,712
2007–08	52,308	52,149	52,367	50,476	1.04	52,308	52,149	52,367
2008–09	53,910	54,037	53,724	—	—	53,168	53,293	52,984

—Not available.
[1]The average monetary remuneration earned by FTE employees across all industries in a given year, including wages, salaries, commissions, tips, bonuses, voluntary employee contributions to certain deferred compensation plans, and receipts in kind that represent income. Calendar-year data from the U.S. Department of Commerce, Bureau of Economic Analysis, have been converted to a school-year basis by averaging the two appropriate calendar years in each case.
[2]Constant dollars based on the Consumer Price Index, prepared by the Bureau of Labor Statistics, U.S. Department of Labor, adjusted to a school-year basis.

NOTE: Some data have been revised from previously published figures. Standard errors are not available for these estimates, which are based on state reports.
SOURCE: National Education Association, *Estimates of School Statistics*, 1959–60 through 2008–09; and unpublished tabulations. U.S. Department of Commerce, Bureau of Economic Analysis, National Income and Product Accounts, tables 6.6B-D, retrieved August 25, 2009, from http://www.bea.gov/national/nipaweb/SelectTable.asp. (This table was prepared August 2009.)

Estimated average annual salary of teachers in public elementary and secondary schools, by state or jurisdiction: Selected years, 1969–70 through 2008–09

State	Current dollars							Constant 2007–08 dollars[1]							Percent change, 1999–2000 to 2008–09
	1969–70	1979–80	1989–90	1999–2000	2005–06	2007–08	2008–09	1969–70	1979–80	1989–90	1999–2000	2005–06	2007–08	2008–09	
1	2	3	4	5	6	7	8	9	10	11	12	13	14	15	16
United States...	$8,626	$15,970	$31,367	$41,807	$48,804	$52,308	$53,910	$48,343	$43,549	$52,297	$52,280	$51,921	$52,308	$53,168	1.7
Alabama	6,818	13,060	24,828	36,689	40,347	46,604	48,906	38,210	35,614	41,395	45,880	42,924	46,604	48,233	5.1
Alaska	10,560	27,210	43,153	46,462	53,553	56,758	58,916	59,181	74,200	71,948	58,102	56,974	56,758	58,105	#
Arizona	8,711	15,054	29,402	36,902	44,672	45,772	47,937	48,819	41,051	49,021	46,147	47,525	45,772	47,277	2.4
Arkansas	6,307	12,299	22,352	33,386	42,768	45,773	47,472	35,346	33,539	37,267	41,750	45,500	45,773	46,818	12.1
California	10,315	18,020	37,998	47,680	59,825	64,424	66,986	57,808	49,140	63,353	59,625	63,646	64,424	66,064	10.8
Colorado	7,761	16,205	30,758	38,163	44,439	47,248	48,707	43,495	44,190	51,282	47,723	47,278	47,248	48,036	0.7
Connecticut	9,262	16,229	40,461	51,780	59,304	61,976	63,976	51,907	44,256	67,460	64,752	63,092	61,976	63,095	-2.6
Delaware	9,015	16,148	33,377	44,435	54,264	55,994	55,994	50,523	44,035	55,649	55,567	57,730	55,994	55,223	-0.6
District of Columbia..	10,285	22,190	38,402	47,076	59,000	60,628	62,557	57,640	60,511	64,027	58,869	62,769	60,628	61,696	4.8
Florida	8,412	14,149	28,803	36,722	43,302	46,930	48,126	47,143	38,584	48,023	45,921	46,068	46,930	47,463	3.4
Georgia	7,276	13,853	28,006	41,023	48,300	51,560	53,270	40,777	37,776	46,694	51,300	51,385	51,560	52,537	2.4
Hawaii	9,453	19,920	32,047	40,578	49,292	53,400	55,733	52,977	54,321	53,431	50,743	52,441	53,400	54,966	8.3
Idaho	6,890	13,611	23,861	35,547	41,150	44,099	45,439	38,614	37,117	39,783	44,452	43,778	44,099	44,813	0.8
Illinois	9,569	17,601	32,794	46,486	58,686	60,474	62,787	53,627	47,997	54,677	58,132	62,435	60,474	61,922	6.5
Indiana	8,833	15,599	30,902	41,850	47,255	48,508	49,198	49,503	42,538	51,522	52,334	50,273	48,508	48,521	-7.3
Iowa	8,355	15,203	26,747	35,678	41,083	46,664	48,969	46,824	41,458	44,595	44,616	43,707	46,664	48,295	8.2
Kansas	7,612	13,690	28,744	34,981	41,467	45,136	46,987	42,660	37,332	47,924	43,744	44,116	45,136	46,340	5.9
Kentucky	6,953	14,520	26,292	36,380	42,592	47,207	49,539	38,967	39,595	43,836	45,494	45,313	47,207	48,857	7.4
Louisiana	7,028	13,760	24,300	33,109	40,029	46,964	49,284	39,387	37,523	40,515	41,403	42,586	46,964	48,605	17.4
Maine	7,572	13,071	26,881	35,561	40,737	43,397	44,731	42,436	35,644	44,818	44,470	43,339	43,397	44,115	-0.8
Maryland	9,383	17,558	36,319	44,048	54,333	60,069	60,844	52,585	47,880	60,554	55,083	57,803	60,069	60,006	8.9
Massachusetts	8,764	17,253	34,712	46,580	56,369	60,471	62,769	49,116	47,048	57,874	58,249	59,970	60,471	61,905	6.3
Michigan	9,826	19,663	37,072	49,044	54,739	56,096	57,327	55,068	53,620	61,809	61,330	58,235	56,096	56,538	-7.8
Minnesota	8,658	15,912	32,190	39,802	48,489	50,582	51,938	48,522	43,391	53,670	49,773	51,586	50,582	51,223	2.9
Mississippi	5,798	11,850	24,292	31,857	40,576	42,403	44,498	32,494	32,314	40,501	39,838	43,168	42,403	43,885	10.2
Missouri	7,799	13,682	27,094	35,656	40,462	43,206	44,712	43,708	37,310	45,173	44,588	43,046	43,206	44,096	-1.1
Montana	7,606	14,537	25,081	32,121	39,832	42,874	44,426	42,626	39,642	41,817	40,168	42,376	42,874	43,814	9.1
Nebraska	7,375	13,516	25,522	33,237	40,382	42,885	44,120	41,332	36,857	42,552	41,563	42,961	42,885	43,513	4.7
Nevada	9,215	16,295	30,590	39,390	44,426	47,710	50,067	51,644	44,436	51,002	49,258	47,264	47,710	49,378	0.2
New Hampshire	7,771	13,017	28,986	37,734	45,263	47,609	48,934	43,551	35,497	48,328	47,187	48,154	47,609	48,260	2.3
New Jersey	9,130	17,161	35,676	52,015	58,156	61,277	63,018	51,167	46,797	59,482	65,046	61,871	61,277	62,150	-4.5
New Mexico	7,796	14,887	24,756	32,554	41,637	45,112	47,341	43,691	40,596	41,275	40,709	44,297	45,112	46,689	14.7
New York	10,336	19,812	38,925	51,020	57,354	62,332	65,234	57,926	54,026	64,899	63,801	61,017	62,332	64,336	0.8
North Carolina	7,494	14,117	27,883	39,404	43,922	47,354	48,603	41,999	38,496	46,489	49,275	46,727	47,354	47,934	-2.7
North Dakota	6,696	13,263	23,016	29,863	37,764	40,279	41,534	37,526	36,168	38,374	37,344	40,176	40,279	40,962	9.7
Ohio	8,300	15,269	31,218	41,436	50,314	53,410	54,925	46,516	41,638	52,049	51,816	53,528	53,410	54,169	4.5
Oklahoma	6,882	13,107	23,070	31,298	38,772	43,551	45,702	38,569	35,742	38,464	39,139	41,249	43,551	45,073	15.2
Oregon	8,818	16,266	30,840	42,336	50,044	51,811	52,950	49,419	44,357	51,419	52,942	53,241	51,811	52,221	-1.4
Pennsylvania	8,858	16,515	33,338	48,321	54,027	55,833	56,906	49,643	45,036	55,589	60,426	57,478	55,833	56,122	-7.1
Rhode Island	8,776	18,002	36,057	47,041	54,730	57,168	58,491	49,183	49,091	60,117	58,826	58,226	57,168	57,686	-1.9
South Carolina	6,927	13,063	27,217	36,081	43,011	45,758	47,704	38,821	35,622	45,378	45,120	45,758	45,758	47,047	4.3
South Dakota	6,403	12,348	21,300	29,071	34,709	36,674	38,017	35,884	33,672	35,513	36,354	36,926	36,674	37,494	3.1
Tennessee	7,050	13,972	27,052	36,328	42,537	45,030	46,278	39,510	38,101	45,103	45,429	45,254	45,030	45,641	0.5
Texas	7,255	14,132	27,496	37,567	41,744	46,179	46,179	40,659	38,537	45,843	46,978	44,410	46,179	45,543	-3.1
Utah	7,644	14,909	23,686	34,946	40,007	41,615	42,335	42,839	40,656	39,491	43,701	42,562	41,615	41,752	-4.5
Vermont	7,968	12,484	29,012	37,758	46,622	46,593	47,697	44,655	34,043	48,371	47,217	49,600	46,593	47,040	-0.4
Virginia	8,070	14,060	30,938	38,744	43,823	46,796	48,554	45,227	38,341	51,582	48,450	46,622	46,796	47,885	-1.2
Washington	9,225	18,820	30,457	41,043	46,326	49,884	51,970	51,700	51,321	50,780	51,325	49,285	49,884	51,254	-0.1
West Virginia	7,650	13,710	22,842	35,009	38,284	42,529	44,625	42,873	37,386	38,084	43,779	40,729	42,529	44,011	0.5
Wisconsin	8,963	16,006	31,921	41,153	46,390	49,051	50,424	50,231	43,648	53,221	51,463	49,353	49,051	49,730	-3.4
Wyoming	8,232	16,012	28,141	34,127	43,225	53,074	55,696	46,135	43,664	46,919	42,676	45,986	53,074	54,929	28.7

#Rounds to zero.
[1]Constant dollars based on the Consumer Price Index (CPI), prepared by the Bureau of Labor Statistics, U.S. Department of Labor, adjusted to a school-year basis. The CPI does not account for differences in inflation rates from state to state.

NOTE: Some data have been revised from previously published figures. Standard errors are not available for these estimates, which are based on state reports.
SOURCE: National Education Association, *Estimates of School Statistics*, 1969–70 through 2008–09. (This table was prepared July 2009.)

Revenues for public elementary and secondary schools, by source of funds: Selected years, 1919–20 through 2006–07

School year	Total (in thousands)	Federal (in thousands)	Federal revenue per student — Current dollars	Federal revenue per student — Constant 2007–08 dollars	State (in thousands)	Local (including intermediate)[1] (in thousands)	Percentage distribution — Total	Percentage distribution — Federal	Percentage distribution — State	Percentage distribution — Local (including intermediate)[1]
1	2	3	4	5	6	7	8	9	10	11
1919–20	$970,121	$2,475	#	$1	$160,085	$807,561	100.0	0.3	16.5	83.2
1929–30	2,088,557	7,334	#	4	353,670	1,727,553	100.0	0.4	16.9	82.7
1939–40	2,260,527	39,810	$2	24	684,354	1,536,363	100.0	1.8	30.3	68.0
1941–42	2,416,580	34,305	1	19	759,993	1,622,281	100.0	1.4	31.4	67.1
1943–44	2,604,322	35,886	2	19	859,183	1,709,253	100.0	1.4	33.0	65.6
1945–46	3,059,845	41,378	2	21	1,062,057	1,956,409	100.0	1.4	34.7	63.9
1947–48	4,311,534	120,270	5	46	1,676,362	2,514,902	100.0	2.8	38.9	58.3
1949–50	5,437,044	155,848	6	55	2,165,689	3,115,507	100.0	2.9	39.8	57.3
1951–52	6,423,816	227,711	9	69	2,478,596	3,717,507	100.0	3.5	38.6	57.9
1953–54	7,866,852	355,237	12	97	2,944,103	4,567,512	100.0	4.5	37.4	58.1
1955–56	9,686,677	441,442	14	113	3,828,886	5,416,350	100.0	4.6	39.5	55.9
1957–58	12,181,513	486,484	15	109	4,800,368	6,894,661	100.0	4.0	39.4	56.6
1959–60	14,746,618	651,639	19	133	5,768,047	8,326,932	100.0	4.4	39.1	56.5
1961–62	17,527,707	760,975	20	143	6,789,190	9,977,542	100.0	4.3	38.7	56.9
1963–64	20,544,182	896,956	22	153	8,078,014	11,569,213	100.0	4.4	39.3	56.3
1965–66	25,356,858	1,996,954	47	314	9,920,219	13,439,686	100.0	7.9	39.1	53.0
1967–68	31,903,064	2,806,469	64	398	12,275,536	16,821,063	100.0	8.8	38.5	52.7
1969–70	40,266,923	3,219,557	71	396	16,062,776	20,984,589	100.0	8.0	39.9	52.1
1970–71	44,511,292	3,753,461	82	435	17,409,086	23,348,745	100.0	8.4	39.1	52.5
1971–72	50,003,645	4,467,969	97	498	19,133,256	26,402,420	100.0	8.9	38.3	52.8
1972–73	52,117,930	4,525,000	99	489	20,699,752	26,893,180	100.0	8.7	39.7	51.6
1973–74	58,230,892	4,930,351	108	492	24,113,409	29,187,132	100.0	8.5	41.4	50.1
1974–75	64,445,239	5,811,595	129	527	27,060,563	31,573,079	100.0	9.0	42.0	49.0
1975–76	71,206,073	6,318,345	141	538	31,602,885	33,284,840	100.0	8.9	44.4	46.7
1976–77	75,332,532	6,629,498	150	539	32,526,018	36,177,019	100.0	8.8	43.2	48.0
1977–78	81,443,160	7,694,194	177	596	35,013,266	38,735,700	100.0	9.4	43.0	47.6
1978–79	87,994,143	8,600,116	202	624	40,132,136	39,261,891	100.0	9.8	45.6	44.6
1979–80	96,881,165	9,503,537	228	622	45,348,814	42,028,813	100.0	9.8	46.8	43.4
1980–81	105,949,087	9,768,262	239	583	50,182,659	45,998,166	100.0	9.2	47.4	43.4
1981–82	110,191,257	8,186,466	204	459	52,436,435	49,568,356	100.0	7.4	47.6	45.0
1982–83	117,497,502	8,339,990	211	454	56,282,157	52,875,354	100.0	7.1	47.9	45.0
1983–84	126,055,419	8,576,547	218	454	60,232,981	57,245,892	100.0	6.8	47.8	45.4
1984–85	137,294,678	9,105,569	232	464	67,168,684	61,020,425	100.0	6.6	48.9	44.4
1985–86	149,127,779	9,975,622	253	492	73,619,575	65,532,582	100.0	6.7	49.4	43.9
1986–87	158,523,693	10,146,013	255	485	78,830,437	69,547,243	100.0	6.4	49.7	43.9
1987–88	169,561,974	10,716,687	268	489	84,004,415	74,840,873	100.0	6.3	49.5	44.1
1988–89	192,016,374	11,902,001	296	517	91,768,911	88,345,462	100.0	6.2	47.8	46.0
1989–90	208,547,573	12,700,784	313	522	98,238,633	97,608,157	100.0	6.1	47.1	46.8
1990–91	223,340,537	13,776,066	334	528	105,324,533	104,239,939	100.0	6.2	47.2	46.7
1991–92	234,581,384	15,493,330	368	564	108,783,449	110,304,605	100.0	6.6	46.4	47.0
1992–93	247,626,168	17,261,252	403	598	113,403,436	116,961,481	100.0	7.0	45.8	47.2
1993–94	260,159,468	18,341,483	422	610	117,474,209	124,343,776	100.0	7.1	45.2	47.8
1994–95	273,149,449	18,582,157	421	592	127,729,576	126,837,717	100.0	6.8	46.8	46.4
1995–96	287,702,844	19,104,019	426	583	136,670,754	131,928,071	100.0	6.6	47.5	45.9
1996–97	305,065,192	20,081,287	440	586	146,435,584	138,548,321	100.0	6.6	48.0	45.4
1997–98	325,925,708	22,201,965	481	629	157,645,372	146,078,370	100.0	6.8	48.4	44.8
1998–99	347,377,993	24,521,817	527	677	169,298,232	153,557,944	100.0	7.1	48.7	44.2
1999–2000	372,943,802	27,097,866	578	722	184,613,352	161,232,584	100.0	7.3	49.5	43.2
2000–01	401,356,120	29,100,183	616	745	199,583,097	172,672,840	100.0	7.3	49.7	43.0
2001–02	419,501,976	33,144,633	695	825	206,541,793	179,815,551	100.0	7.9	49.2	42.9
2002–03	440,111,653	37,515,909	779	904	214,277,407	188,318,337	100.0	8.5	48.7	42.8
2003–04	462,026,099	41,923,435	864	982	217,384,191	202,718,474	100.0	9.1	47.1	43.9
2004–05	487,753,525	44,809,532	918	1,013	228,553,579	214,390,414	100.0	9.2	46.9	44.0
2005–06[2]	520,621,788	47,553,778	968	1,068	242,151,076	230,916,934	100.0	9.1	46.5	44.4
2006–07	555,337,583	47,041,419	955	1,015	264,226,896	244,069,269	100.0	8.5	47.6	43.9

Revenues for public elementary and secondary schools, by source and state or jurisdiction: 2006–07

State or jurisdiction	Total (in thousands)	Federal Amount (in thousands)	Per student	Percent of total	State Amount (in thousands)	Percent of total	Local and intermediate Amount (in thousands)	Percent of total	Private[1] Amount (in thousands)	Percent of total
1	2	3	4	5	6	7	8	9	10	11
United States	$555,337,583	$47,041,419	$955	8.5	$264,226,896	47.6	$232,211,575	41.8	$11,857,694	2.1
Alabama	7,100,169	720,476	969	10.1	4,070,907	57.3	2,001,570	28.2	307,215	4.3
Alaska	1,896,849	284,203	2,143	15.0	1,146,630	60.4	446,188	23.5	19,828	1.0
Arizona	9,638,544	1,076,040	1,010	11.2	4,958,859	51.4	3,362,821	34.9	240,824	2.5
Arkansas	4,459,921	500,105	1,050	11.2	2,556,917	57.3	1,259,981	28.3	142,919	3.2
California	69,557,257	6,710,418	1,047	9.6	42,754,127	61.5	19,497,640	28.0	595,072	0.9
Colorado	7,717,989	541,519	682	7.0	3,323,182	43.1	3,543,206	45.9	310,083	4.0
Connecticut	9,050,539	419,906	730	4.6	3,509,495	38.8	5,001,042	55.3	120,096	1.3
Delaware	1,631,426	122,161	999	7.5	1,029,607	63.1	461,528	28.3	18,130	1.1
District of Columbia	1,282,317	155,019	2,128	12.1	†	†	1,119,711	87.3	7,587	0.6
Florida	27,372,359	2,533,503	948	9.3	11,133,826	40.7	12,766,986	46.6	938,044	3.4
Georgia	17,714,805	1,509,809	927	8.5	7,941,066	44.8	7,779,258	43.9	484,672	2.7
Hawaii	2,950,803	255,035	1,411	8.6	2,646,792	89.7	27,721	0.9	21,255	0.7
Idaho	2,039,338	209,685	784	10.3	1,371,187	67.2	420,405	20.6	38,061	1.9
Illinois	24,026,545	1,870,304	883	7.8	7,316,138	30.5	14,346,885	59.7	493,219	2.1
Indiana	10,062,766	805,079	770	8.0	5,354,404	53.2	3,602,508	35.8	300,775	3.0
Iowa	5,009,516	401,282	831	8.0	2,279,210	45.5	2,192,775	43.8	136,249	2.7
Kansas	5,259,228	445,010	948	8.5	2,980,534	56.7	1,716,551	32.6	117,133	2.2
Kentucky	6,141,245	687,706	1,007	11.2	3,483,546	56.7	1,856,212	30.2	113,782	1.9
Louisiana	7,142,552	1,233,167	1,825	17.3	3,043,752	42.6	2,801,766	39.2	63,867	0.9
Maine	2,537,228	231,870	1,195	9.1	1,147,116	45.2	1,114,825	43.9	43,417	1.7
Maryland	11,612,299	675,852	794	5.8	4,684,823	40.3	5,930,388	51.1	321,236	2.8
Massachusetts	14,179,328	763,031	788	5.4	6,641,467	46.8	6,574,725	46.4	200,104	1.4
Michigan	19,584,946	1,576,501	919	8.0	11,484,249	58.6	6,186,757	31.6	337,439	1.7
Minnesota	9,715,233	588,282	700	6.1	6,488,998	66.8	2,333,335	24.0	304,618	3.1
Mississippi	4,157,666	712,855	1,440	17.1	2,214,691	53.3	1,115,555	26.8	114,565	2.8
Missouri	9,345,716	787,309	875	8.4	3,111,235	33.3	5,099,403	54.6	347,769	3.7
Montana	1,474,331	192,940	1,343	13.1	709,781	48.1	515,189	34.9	56,422	3.8
Nebraska	3,123,329	293,223	1,045	9.4	990,277	31.7	1,696,805	54.3	143,024	4.6
Nevada	4,008,036	280,453	661	7.0	1,077,524	26.9	2,520,482	62.9	129,577	3.2
New Hampshire	2,502,258	137,549	676	5.5	937,660	37.5	1,376,859	55.0	50,190	2.0
New Jersey	24,190,490	1,055,816	760	4.4	10,194,361	42.1	12,427,778	51.4	512,535	2.1
New Mexico	3,352,094	468,393	1,427	14.0	2,399,420	71.6	434,203	13.0	50,078	1.5
New York	49,749,322	3,320,153	1,182	6.7	21,632,213	43.5	24,441,606	49.1	355,349	0.7
North Carolina	11,991,073	1,196,942	838	10.0	7,613,227	63.5	2,915,797	24.3	265,107	2.2
North Dakota	995,395	150,169	1,553	15.1	353,519	35.5	446,663	44.9	45,043	4.5
Ohio	22,242,577	1,589,201	866	7.1	9,888,710	44.5	10,074,699	45.3	689,966	3.1
Oklahoma	5,233,050	649,871	1,016	12.4	2,820,218	53.9	1,519,262	29.0	243,700	4.7
Oregon	5,661,558	547,425	973	9.7	2,908,103	51.4	2,061,087	36.4	144,943	2.6
Pennsylvania	23,988,602	1,762,026	942	7.3	8,675,316	36.2	13,132,108	54.7	419,153	1.7
Rhode Island	2,145,821	173,402	1,144	8.1	865,044	40.3	1,084,329	50.5	23,047	1.1
South Carolina	7,130,019	699,132	994	9.8	3,147,685	44.1	3,038,522	42.6	244,680	3.4
South Dakota	1,138,701	177,130	1,462	15.6	374,228	32.9	553,472	48.6	33,871	3.0
Tennessee	7,725,838	827,929	846	10.7	3,349,705	43.4	3,108,172	40.2	440,031	5.7
Texas	43,282,278	4,466,298	971	10.3	16,349,077	37.8	21,578,442	49.9	888,461	2.1
Utah	3,777,931	335,684	641	8.9	2,104,005	55.7	1,258,955	33.3	79,287	2.1
Vermont	1,441,199	97,252	1,019	6.7	1,238,582	85.9	85,173	5.9	20,191	1.4
Virginia	13,962,224	890,128	729	6.4	5,813,437	41.6	6,977,648	50.0	281,010	2.0
Washington	10,450,101	870,261	848	8.3	6,383,843	61.1	2,877,317	27.5	318,681	3.0
West Virginia	3,039,383	354,772	1,258	11.7	1,808,685	59.5	847,074	27.9	28,852	0.9
Wisconsin	10,069,345	577,878	663	5.7	5,197,595	51.6	4,054,513	40.3	239,360	2.4
Wyoming	1,476,046	111,264	1,313	7.5	721,925	48.9	625,680	42.4	17,177	1.2
Other jurisdictions										
American Samoa	61,984	45,653	2,779	73.7	16,089	26.0	0	0.0	242	0.4
Guam	228,202	49,305	—	21.6	0	0.0	178,064	78.0	834	0.4
Northern Marianas	66,691	29,666	2,537	44.5	36,354	54.5	650	1.0	21	#
Puerto Rico	3,290,513	951,213	1,748	28.9	2,339,194	71.1	10	#	97	#
U.S. Virgin Islands	215,970	38,088	2,339	17.6	0	0.0	177,729	82.3	152	0.1

—Not available.
†Not applicable.
#Rounds to zero.
[1]Includes revenues from gifts, and tuition and fees from patrons.

NOTE: Excludes revenues for state education agencies. Detail may not sum to totals because of rounding.
SOURCE: U.S. Department of Education, National Center for Education Statistics, Common Core of Data (CCD), "National Public Education Financial Survey," 2006–07. (This table was prepared May 2009.)

Total expenditures for public elementary and secondary education, by function and state or jurisdiction: 2006–07

[In thousands of current dollars]

State or jurisdiction	Total	Elementary/ secondary current expenditures, total	Instruction	Total	Student support[4]	Instructional staff[5]	General administration	School administration	Operation and maintenance	Student transportation	Other support services	Food services	Enterprise operations[3]	Other current expenditures[1]	Capital outlay[2]	Interest on school debt
1	2	3	4	5	6	7	8	9	10	11	12	13	14	15	16	17
United States	$562,252,677	$476,825,866	$290,710,402	$166,881,038	$25,200,234	$23,152,421	$9,337,239	$26,875,252	$46,824,904	$19,979,044	$15,511,944	$18,149,847	$1,084,578	$7,804,253	$62,909,675	$14,712,882
Alabama	7,211,897	6,245,031	3,655,694	2,177,596	330,677	304,554	163,764	386,392	565,368	298,363	128,479	411,741	0	137,255	690,125	139,486
Alaska	1,940,429	1,634,316	931,068	649,395	105,339	91,130	23,733	97,485	216,326	55,388	59,994	47,234	6,620	7,754	258,666	39,694
Arizona	9,539,185	7,815,720	4,751,055	2,719,232	554,492	185,912	124,070	382,067	858,695	293,163	320,832	345,434	1,712	53,296	1,443,179	226,990
Arkansas	4,644,397	3,997,701	2,365,794	1,422,035	189,033	286,027	103,453	214,949	382,274	145,778	100,523	208,159	0	25,899	513,872	106,925
California	70,071,235	57,352,599	34,461,563	20,713,553	2,731,324	3,815,115	551,574	3,854,644	5,867,943	1,406,157	2,486,796	2,055,898	121,585	1,122,084	9,980,745	1,615,807
Colorado	8,067,005	6,579,053	3,805,179	2,532,062	297,656	350,385	112,912	446,154	662,343	195,041	467,572	211,915	29,898	53,486	1,089,558	344,908
Connecticut	9,300,606	7,855,459	4,934,292	2,654,233	476,950	256,306	156,888	441,701	759,693	381,894	180,800	198,102	68,832	140,237	1,151,074	153,836
Delaware	1,739,840	1,437,707	861,627	513,581	72,979	19,824	17,711	80,565	143,369	90,900	88,234	62,499	0	16,357	254,456	31,319
District of Columbia	1,389,995	1,130,006	586,076	520,716	72,726	77,707	26,199	61,519	150,811	84,513	57,242	23,214	0	19,260	240,729	0
Florida	30,107,621	22,887,024	13,646,302	8,239,301	1,061,831	1,533,846	221,442	1,298,584	2,529,738	953,468	640,393	1,001,420	0	497,754	5,993,351	729,492
Georgia	17,301,301	14,828,715	9,357,132	4,716,438	695,559	776,179	191,376	884,479	1,071,342	593,438	504,065	713,136	42,009	36,425	2,271,939	164,222
Hawaii	2,300,383	1,998,913	1,177,781	732,536	240,925	68,883	19,979	136,602	179,079	36,264	50,804	88,596	0	62,647	139,182	99,643
Idaho	2,148,752	1,777,491	1,091,113	603,197	98,815	79,857	40,927	99,321	164,263	84,942	34,071	83,102	79	4,324	316,782	50,155
Illinois	23,157,195	20,326,591	11,970,050	7,699,014	1,322,640	936,584	671,354	1,050,243	2,016,805	999,556	701,832	657,528	0	152,743	2,082,240	595,621
Indiana	10,869,170	9,497,077	5,695,474	3,392,704	421,863	294,478	181,104	545,143	1,038,664	538,166	373,286	408,900	0	59,077	865,693	447,323
Iowa	4,991,024	4,231,932	2,546,475	1,486,916	242,162	195,896	114,781	255,077	388,177	153,011	137,813	193,065	5,476	27,150	652,287	79,655
Kansas	4,868,048	4,339,477	2,632,373	1,512,390	244,480	197,802	135,041	251,410	411,569	167,225	104,861	194,715		4,762	378,570	145,239
Kentucky	6,386,594	5,424,621	3,223,881	1,880,491	232,617	295,214	117,992	297,284	502,287	311,954	123,143	308,031	12,218	81,339	749,959	130,676
Louisiana	6,828,819	6,040,368	3,506,624	2,190,038	260,297	313,162	145,060	325,955	635,211	338,661	171,693	343,605	102	56,749	629,297	102,405
Maine	2,420,878	2,258,764	1,476,962	708,213	89,734	84,861	45,140	119,223	232,016	100,192	37,046	73,589	0	24,061	93,624	44,429
Maryland	11,547,486	10,198,084	6,258,240	3,490,319	427,815	550,494	76,162	672,028	960,470	515,060	288,291	281,727	167,797	24,872	1,199,800	124,730
Massachusetts	13,409,188	12,453,611	8,029,462	4,050,678	698,998	587,974	226,248	528,583	1,135,606	531,815	341,452	373,471	0	51,117	618,046	286,414
Michigan	19,931,731	17,013,259	9,654,939	6,828,411	1,264,116	840,234	351,001	1,005,596	1,821,304	737,961	808,199	529,909	0	345,899	1,760,625	811,948
Minnesota	9,944,675	8,060,410	5,204,264	2,491,713	218,944	370,136	253,087	341,880	621,940	445,371	240,355	339,449	24,984	376,478	1,067,873	439,914
Mississippi	4,086,883	3,692,358	2,170,683	1,303,265	169,541	176,463	106,760	210,155	395,793	166,109	78,445	218,063	347	29,547	294,450	70,527
Missouri	9,345,921	7,957,705	4,810,938	2,790,190	380,342	364,015	249,544	439,403	793,260	402,797	160,827	356,577	1,925	174,707	926,684	286,825
Montana	1,447,251	1,320,112	799,471	466,006	73,700	50,516	39,455	72,094	137,672	61,070	31,498	52,709	79,701	7,220	106,772	13,148
Nebraska	3,242,741	2,825,608	1,796,902	838,066	121,838	92,147	97,860	143,789	247,602	70,084	64,746	110,939	0	2,785	347,950	66,399
Nevada	4,278,047	3,311,471	2,007,845	1,189,274	120,117	97,209	63,759	221,817	336,715	126,549	223,108	114,352	0	22,790	735,270	208,516
New Hampshire	2,512,692	2,246,692	1,447,806	733,980	153,969	69,587	75,800	122,699	195,303	95,517	21,105	64,906	0	5,949	208,009	52,043
New Jersey	24,911,786	22,448,262	13,348,606	8,412,743	2,053,895	739,436	529,342	1,505,887	2,269,591	1,210,611	103,981	501,335	185,577	197,857	1,911,004	354,663
New Mexico	3,240,023	2,904,474	1,644,674	1,137,815	283,957	90,003	66,447	215,911	300,457	105,601	75,440	120,529	1,454	2,701	332,677	171
New York	49,552,219	43,679,908	30,174,472	12,541,875	1,405,184	1,217,594	847,174	1,774,187	3,795,201	2,325,859	1,176,676	963,561	0	1,833,250	2,940,768	1,098,293
North Carolina	12,829,210	11,248,336	6,978,065	3,669,577	633,899	457,863	202,863	739,365	898,026	439,950	297,611	600,694	0	49,765	1,464,124	66,985
North Dakota	946,658	838,221	485,805	281,662	35,790	27,308	39,559	41,384	80,691	36,798	20,131	44,500	26,254	6,028	90,189	12,220
Ohio	21,729,555	18,251,361	10,469,978	7,180,598	1,094,606	1,158,781	535,318	1,058,825	1,690,145	842,722	800,200	599,289	1,496	453,159	2,578,930	446,105
Oklahoma	5,229,868	4,750,536	2,754,020	1,683,419	305,355	177,922	133,381	254,496	533,008	149,163	130,094	268,530	44,567	14,074	416,187	49,071
Oregon	5,573,769	5,039,632	2,955,718	1,904,409	352,399	208,073	70,180	320,778	423,681	219,730	309,567	177,492	2,013	19,703	293,279	221,154
Pennsylvania	24,459,545	20,404,304	12,476,672	7,138,482	1,000,133	785,630	628,455	892,492	2,126,330	991,896	713,547	696,475	92,674	581,392	2,575,259	898,591
Rhode Island	2,169,474	2,039,633	1,228,525	758,763	236,532	95,162	25,393	103,123	173,748	76,610	48,195	52,344	0	52,235	42,599	35,007
South Carolina	7,676,692	6,023,043	3,472,987	2,227,382	426,341	412,179	80,349	344,810	562,750	216,846	184,105	303,125	19,550	68,883	1,263,432	321,335
South Dakota	1,106,123	977,006	567,277	354,660	53,780	41,802	34,996	48,876	104,955	34,545	35,705	50,519	4,550	3,074	105,388	20,655
Tennessee	7,755,934	6,975,099	4,448,730	2,177,242	242,800	389,291	142,214	394,437	636,444	253,408	118,649	349,126	0	53,063	566,576	212,630
Texas	45,189,026	36,105,784	21,492,698	12,744,571	1,759,204	1,959,752	555,738	2,010,684	4,142,758	991,584	1,324,851	1,868,515	0	316,528	6,654,084	2,112,630
Utah	3,807,310	2,987,810	1,887,343	922,880	111,389	133,297	37,487	184,974	291,653	98,647	65,434	160,675	16,912	89,863	644,375	85,262

See notes at end of table.

Total expenditures for public elementary and secondary education, by function and state or jurisdiction: 2006–07—Continued
[In thousands of current dollars]

State or jurisdiction	Total	Elementary/ secondary current expenditures, total	Total expenditures — Current expenditures for elementary and secondary programs		Support services							Food services	Enterprise operations[3]	Other current expenditures[1]	Capital outlay[2]	Interest on school debt
			Instruction	Total	Student support[4]	Instructional staff[5]	General administration	School administration	Operation and maintenance	Student transportation	Other support services					
1	2	3	4	5	6	7	8	9	10	11	12	13	14	15	16	17
Vermont...............	1,393,637	1,300,149	822,122	443,624	95,756	50,706	30,532	88,162	106,618	42,028	29,822	33,919	484	7,525	70,716	15,247
Virginia...............	14,234,484	12,465,858	7,631,016	4,338,036	597,727	822,764	179,060	730,020	1,194,198	617,847	196,420	494,763	2,044	76,783	1,519,356	172,487
Washington............	10,814,992	8,752,007	5,196,114	3,137,088	569,081	399,392	169,590	513,166	810,733	357,227	317,899	295,883	122,922	49,955	1,630,529	382,500
West Virginia..........	2,845,230	2,742,344	1,628,022	960,129	98,081	110,776	69,944	145,928	291,828	198,240	45,331	154,193	0	37,156	54,208	11,521
Wisconsin.............	10,372,911	9,029,660	5,528,117	3,191,925	415,956	437,153	232,350	458,809	858,993	339,342	449,320	309,527	92	258,456	448,497	636,298
Wyoming..............	1,383,239	1,124,564	662,376	428,615	65,890	75,039	22,694	62,092	111,454	49,982	41,462	32,869	704	8,779	246,694	3,203
Other jurisdictions																
American Samoa......	67,085	57,093	28,615	15,552	1,519	3,321	981	6,198	1,483	1,047	1,003	12,926	0	4,227	5,764	0
Guam.................	224,611	219,881	128,234	80,129	24,317	6,702	4,051	11,678	26,575	1,245	5,561	10,723	794	0	3,948	782
Northern Marianas....	60,363	55,048	43,180	5,590	843	562	1,530	98	1,337	1,086	134	547	5,730	375	4,941	0
Puerto Rico...........	3,465,934	3,268,200	2,220,789	767,147	252,424	54,345	15,999	0	314,215	86,055	44,109	280,264	0	103,478	81,230	13,025
U.S. Virgin Islands....	180,028	157,446	95,816	56,908	10,022	5,006	7,348	9,304	10,405	11,439	3,384	3,965	756	1,670	20,912	0

[1] Includes expenditures for adult education, community colleges, private school programs funded by local and state education agencies, and community services.
[2] Includes expenditures for property and for buildings and alterations completed by school district staff or contractors.
[3] Includes expenditures for operations funded by sales of products or services (e.g., school bookstore or computer time). Also includes small amounts for direct program support made by state education agencies for local school districts.

[4] Includes expenditures for health, attendance, and speech pathology services.
[5] Includes expenditures for curriculum development, staff training, libraries, and media and computer centers.
NOTE: Excludes expenditures for state education agencies. Detail may not sum to totals because of rounding.
SOURCE: U.S. Department of Education, National Center for Education Statistics, Common Core of Data (CCD), "National Public Education Financial Survey," 2006–07. (This table was prepared May 2009.)

Total and current expenditures per pupil in public elementary and secondary schools: Selected years, 1919–20 through 2006–07

| | Expenditure per pupil in average daily attendance | | | | Expenditure per pupil in fall enrollment[1] | | | | |
| | Unadjusted dollars | | Constant 2007–08 dollars[2] | | Unadjusted dollars | | Constant 2007–08 dollars[2] | | |
School year	Total expenditure[3]	Current expenditure	Total expenditure[3]	Current expenditure	Total expenditure[3]	Current expenditure	Total expenditure[3]	Current expenditure	Annual percent change in current expenditure
1	2	3	4	5	6	7	8	9	10
1919–20	$64	$53	$710	$592	$48	$40	$532	$443	—
1929–30	108	87	1,342	1,072	90	72	1,111	888	—
1931–32	97	81	1,422	1,191	82	69	1,204	1,008	—
1933–34	76	67	1,219	1,079	65	57	1,035	917	—
1935–36	88	74	1,355	1,145	74	63	1,146	968	—
1937–38	100	84	1,473	1,239	86	72	1,265	1,064	—
1939–40	106	88	1,602	1,335	92	76	1,388	1,157	—
1941–42	110	98	1,494	1,335	94	84	1,279	1,143	—
1943–44	125	117	1,515	1,421	105	99	1,276	1,198	—
1945–46	146	136	1,693	1,583	124	116	1,442	1,349	—
1947–48	205	181	1,861	1,649	179	158	1,625	1,440	—
1949–50	260	210	2,327	1,880	231	187	2,065	1,669	—
1951–52	314	246	2,533	1,982	275	215	2,218	1,735	—
1953–54	351	265	2,763	2,085	312	236	2,457	1,854	—
1955–56	387	294	3,048	2,317	354	269	2,786	2,118	—
1957–58	447	341	3,317	2,529	408	311	3,025	2,306	—
1959–60	471	375	3,394	2,703	440	350	3,170	2,525	—
1961–62	517	419	3,642	2,951	485	393	3,418	2,769	—
1963–64	559	460	3,835	3,160	520	428	3,569	2,941	—
1965–66	654	538	4,338	3,567	607	499	4,027	3,312	—
1967–68	786	658	4,896	4,098	732	612	4,554	3,812	—
1969–70	955	816	5,352	4,573	879	751	4,927	4,210	—
1970–71	1,049	911	5,593	4,856	970	842	5,170	4,489	6.6
1971–72	1,128	990	5,802	5,091	1,034	908	5,321	4,670	4.0
1972–73	1,211	1,077	5,987	5,326	1,117	993	5,522	4,913	5.2
1973–74	1,364	1,207	6,193	5,481	1,244	1,101	5,647	4,998	1.7
1974–75	1,545	1,365	6,314	5,578	1,423	1,257	5,817	5,138	2.8
1975–76	1,697	1,504	6,479	5,740	1,563	1,385	5,966	5,285	2.9
1976–77	1,816	1,638	6,551	5,907	1,674	1,509	6,037	5,443	3.0
1977–78	2,002	1,823	6,768	6,161	1,842	1,677	6,225	5,667	4.1
1978–79	2,210	2,020	6,830	6,244	2,029	1,855	6,272	5,734	1.2
1979–80	2,491	2,272	6,792	6,195	2,290	2,088	6,244	5,695	-0.7
1980–81	2,742 [4]	2,502	6,702 [4]	6,114	2,529 [4]	2,307	6,182 [4]	5,639	-1.0
1981–82	2,973 [4]	2,726	6,689 [4]	6,132	2,754 [4]	2,525	6,196 [4]	5,680	0.7
1982–83	3,203 [4]	2,955	6,909 [4]	6,374	2,966 [4]	2,736	6,398 [4]	5,902	3.9
1983–84	3,471 [4]	3,173	7,220 [4]	6,600	3,216 [4]	2,940	6,689 [4]	6,115	3.6
1984–85	3,722 [4]	3,470	7,450 [4]	6,946	3,456 [4]	3,222	6,917 [4]	6,450	5.5
1985–86	4,020 [4]	3,756	7,821 [4]	7,306	3,724 [4]	3,479	7,245 [4]	6,769	5.0
1986–87	4,308 [4]	3,970	8,199 [4]	7,557	3,995 [4]	3,682	7,603 [4]	7,007	3.5
1987–88	4,654 [4]	4,240	8,505 [4]	7,749	4,310 [4]	3,927	7,877 [4]	7,176	2.4
1988–89	5,108	4,645	8,922	8,114	4,737	4,307	8,274	7,524	4.8
1989–90	5,547	4,980	9,248	8,303	5,172	4,643	8,623	7,741	2.9
1990–91	5,882	5,258	9,298	8,312	5,484	4,902	8,669	7,749	0.1
1991–92	6,072	5,421	9,301	8,304	5,626	5,023	8,618	7,694	-0.7
1992–93	6,279	5,584	9,327	8,294	5,802	5,160	8,619	7,664	-0.4
1993–94	6,489	5,767	9,395	8,350	5,994	5,327	8,678	7,713	0.6
1994–95	6,723	5,989	9,463	8,430	6,206	5,529	8,735	7,782	0.9
1995–96	6,959	6,147	9,536	8,423	6,441	5,689	8,826	7,796	0.2
1996–97	7,297	6,393	9,722	8,517	6,761	5,923	9,008	7,891	1.2
1997–98	7,701	6,676	10,079	8,738	7,139	6,189	9,345	8,101	2.7
1998–99	8,115	7,013	10,441	9,023	7,531	6,508	9,689	8,373	3.4
1999–2000	8,589	7,394	10,741	9,246	8,030	6,912	10,041	8,644	3.2
2000–01	9,180	7,904	11,099	9,556	8,572	7,380	10,364	8,923	3.2
2001–02	9,611	8,259	11,419	9,812	8,993	7,727	10,684	9,181	2.9
2002–03	9,950	8,610	11,567	10,009	9,296	8,044	10,807	9,351	1.9
2003–04	10,308	8,900	11,726	10,125	9,625	8,310	10,950	9,454	1.1
2004–05	10,779	9,316	11,904	10,288	10,078	8,711	11,130	9,620	1.8
2005–06	11,338	9,778	12,062	10,403	10,603	9,145	11,280	9,729	1.1
2006–07	12,018	10,337	12,463	10,720	11,257	9,683	11,674	10,041	3.2

—Not available.
[1]Data for 1919–20 to 1953–54 are based on school-year enrollment.
[2]Constant dollars based on the Consumer Price Index, prepared by the Bureau of Labor Statistics, U.S. Department of Labor, adjusted to a school-year basis.
[3]Excludes "Other current expenditures," such as community services, private school programs, adult education, and other programs not allocable to expenditures per student at public schools.
[4]Estimated.
NOTE: Beginning in 1980–81, state administration expenditures are excluded from both "total" and "current" expenditures. Current expenditures include instruction, student support services, food services, and enterprise operations. Total expenditures include current expenditures, capital outlay, and interest on debt. Beginning in 1988–89, extensive changes were made in the data collection procedures. Some data have been revised from previously published figures.
SOURCE: U.S. Department of Education, National Center for Education Statistics, *Biennial Survey of Education in the United States*, 1919–20 through 1955–56; *Statistics of State School Systems*, 1957–58 through 1969–70; *Revenues and Expenditures for Public Elementary and Secondary Education*, 1970–71 through 1986–87; and Common Core of Data (CCD), "National Public Education Financial Survey," 1987–88 through 2006–07. (This table was prepared May 2009.)

Total and current expenditures per pupil in fall enrollment in public elementary and secondary education, by function and state or jurisdiction: 2006–07

State or jurisdiction	Total[1]	Current expenditures, capital expenditures, and interest on school debt												Capital outlay[2]	Interest on school debt
		Current expenditures													
		Total	Instruction	Student services								Food services	Enterprise operations[3]		
				Total	Student support[4]	Instruc-tional staff[5]	General admini-stration	School admini-stration	Operation and mainte-nance	Student transpor-tation	Other support services				
1	2	3	4	5	6	7	8	9	10	11	12	13	14	15	16
United States	**$11,257**	**$9,683**	**$5,903**	**$3,389**	**$512**	**$470**	**$190**	**$546**	**$951**	**$406**	**$315**	**$369**	**$22**	**$1,277**	**$299**
Alabama	9,514	8,398	4,916	2,928	445	410	220	520	760	401	173	554	0	928	188
Alaska	14,574	12,324	7,021	4,897	794	687	179	735	1,631	418	452	356	50	1,951	299
Arizona	8,904	7,338	4,461	2,553	521	175	116	359	806	275	301	324	0	1,355	213
Arkansas	9,694	8,391	4,966	2,985	397	600	217	451	802	306	211	437	4	1,079	224
California	10,761	8,952	5,379	3,233	426	595	86	602	916	219	388	321	19	1,558	252
Colorado	10,092	8,286	4,792	3,189	375	441	142	562	834	246	589	267	38	1,372	434
Connecticut	15,925	13,659	8,580	4,615	829	446	273	768	1,321	664	314	344	120	2,002	267
Delaware	14,098	11,760	7,048	4,201	597	162	145	659	1,173	744	722	511	0	2,081	256
District of Columbia	18,791	15,511	8,045	7,148	861	1,067	360	844	2,070	1,160	786	319	0	3,304	0
Florida	11,077	8,567	5,108	3,084	397	574	83	486	947	357	240	375	0	2,243	273
Georgia	10,597	9,102	5,744	2,895	427	476	117	543	658	364	309	438	26	1,395	101
Hawaii	12,358	11,060	6,517	4,053	1,333	381	111	756	991	201	281	490	0	770	551
Idaho	8,020	6,648	4,081	2,256	373	299	153	371	614	318	127	311	0	1,185	188
Illinois	10,859	9,596	5,651	3,635	624	442	317	496	952	472	331	310	0	983	281
Indiana	10,334	9,080	5,445	3,244	403	282	173	521	993	515	357	391	0	828	428
Iowa	10,311	8,791	5,290	3,089	503	407	238	530	806	318	286	401	11	1,355	165
Kansas	10,358	9,243	5,607	3,221	521	421	288	535	877	356	223	415	0	806	309
Kentucky	9,228	7,940	4,719	2,753	340	432	173	435	735	457	180	451	18	1,098	191
Louisiana	10,020	8,937	5,188	3,240	385	463	215	482	940	501	254	508	0	931	152
Maine	12,355	11,644	7,614	3,651	463	437	233	615	1,196	516	191	379	0	483	229
Maryland	13,529	11,975	7,348	4,098	502	646	89	789	1,128	605	339	331	197	1,409	146
Massachusetts	13,790	12,857	8,289	4,182	722	607	234	546	1,172	549	352	386	0	638	296
Michigan	11,421	9,922	5,631	3,982	737	490	205	586	1,062	430	471	309	0	1,027	474
Minnesota	11,379	9,589	6,191	2,964	260	440	301	407	740	530	286	404	30	1,270	523
Mississippi	8,195	7,459	4,385	2,633	342	356	216	425	800	336	158	441	1	595	142
Missouri	10,195	8,848	5,349	3,102	423	405	277	489	882	448	179	396	0	1,030	319
Montana	10,026	9,191	5,566	3,245	513	352	275	502	959	425	219	367	13	743	92
Nebraska	11,544	10,068	6,403	2,986	434	328	349	512	882	250	231	395	284	1,240	237
Nevada	10,028	7,806	4,733	2,803	283	229	150	523	794	298	526	270	0	1,733	492
New Hampshire	12,312	11,037	7,113	3,606	756	342	372	603	959	469	104	319	0	1,022	256
New Jersey	17,794	16,163	9,611	6,057	1,479	532	381	1,084	1,634	872	75	361	134	1,376	255
New Mexico	9,863	8,849	5,011	3,467	865	274	202	658	915	322	230	367	4	1,014	1
New York	16,981	15,546	10,740	4,464	500	433	302	631	1,351	828	419	343	0	1,047	391
North Carolina	8,950	7,878	4,887	2,570	444	321	142	518	629	308	208	421	0	1,025	47
North Dakota	9,721	8,671	5,025	2,914	370	282	409	428	835	381	208	460	272	933	126
Ohio	11,573	9,940	5,702	3,911	596	631	292	577	921	459	436	326	1	1,405	243
Oklahoma	8,157	7,430	4,307	2,633	478	278	209	398	834	233	203	420	70	651	77
Oregon	9,872	8,958	5,254	3,385	626	370	125	570	753	391	550	316	4	521	393
Pennsylvania	12,759	10,905	6,668	3,815	535	420	336	477	1,136	530	381	372	50	1,376	480
Rhode Island	13,964	13,453	8,103	5,005	1,560	628	167	680	1,146	505	318	345	0	281	231
South Carolina	10,819	8,566	4,939	3,168	606	586	114	490	800	308	262	431	28	1,797	457
South Dakota	9,104	8,064	4,682	2,927	444	345	289	403	866	285	295	417	38	870	170
Tennessee	7,872	7,129	4,547	2,225	248	398	145	403	651	259	121	357	0	579	165
Texas	9,756	7,850	4,673	2,771	382	426	121	437	901	216	288	406	0	1,447	459
Utah	7,097	5,706	3,605	1,763	213	255	72	353	557	188	125	307	32	1,231	163
Vermont	14,528	13,629	8,618	4,650	1,004	532	320	924	1,118	441	313	356	5	741	160
Virginia	11,600	10,214	6,253	3,554	490	674	147	598	978	506	161	405	2	1,245	141
Washington	10,484	8,524	5,061	3,055	554	389	165	500	790	348	310	288	120	1,588	373
West Virginia	9,959	9,727	5,774	3,405	348	393	248	518	1,035	703	161	547	0	192	41
Wisconsin	11,608	10,367	6,347	3,665	478	502	267	527	986	390	516	355	0	515	731
Wyoming	16,183	13,266	7,814	5,056	777	885	268	732	1,315	590	489	388	8	2,910	38
Other jurisdictions															
American Samoa	3,826	3,476	1,742	947	92	202	60	377	90	64	61	787	0	351	0
Guam	—	—	—	—	—	—	—	—	—	—	—	—	—	—	—
Northern Marianas	5,129	4,707	3,692	478	72	48	131	8	114	93	11	47	490	422	0
Puerto Rico	6,177	6,006	4,081	1,410	464	100	29	0	577	158	81	515	0	149	24
U.S. Virgin Islands	10,953	9,669	5,884	3,495	615	307	451	571	639	702	208	244	46	1,284	0

—Not available.

[1]Excludes "Other current expenditures," such as community services, private school programs, adult education, and other programs not allocable to expenditures per pupil in public schools.
[2]Includes expenditures for property and for buildings and alterations completed by school district staff or contractors. Excludes capital outlay related to "Other current expenditures."
[3]Includes expenditures for operations funded by sales of products or services (e.g., school bookstore or computer time).

[4]Includes expenditures for health, attendance, and speech pathology services.
[5]Includes expenditures for curriculum development, staff training, libraries, and media and computer centers.
NOTE: Excludes expenditures for state education agencies. "0" indicates none or less than $0.50. Detail may not sum to totals because of rounding.
SOURCE: U.S. Department of Education, National Center for Education Statistics, Common Core of Data (CCD), "National Public Education Financial Survey," 2006–07. (This table was prepared May 2009.)

Number of public school districts and public and private elementary and secondary schools: Selected years, 1869–70 through 2007–08

School year	Regular public school districts[1]	Public schools[2]					Private schools[2,3]		
		Total, all schools[4]	Total, schools with reported grade spans[5]	Schools with elementary grades Total	One-teacher	Schools with secondary grades	Total[4]	Schools with elementary grades	Schools with secondary grades
1	2	3	4	5	6	7	8	9	10
1869–70	—	116,312	—	—	—	—	—	—	—
1879–80	—	178,122	—	—	—	—	—	—	—
1889–90	—	224,526	—	—	—	—	—	—	—
1899–1900	—	248,279	—	—	—	—	—	—	—
1909–10	—	265,474	—	—	212,448	—	—	—	—
1919–20	—	271,319	—	—	187,948	—	—	—	—
1929–30	—	248,117	—	238,306	148,712	23,930	—	9,275 [6]	3,258 [6]
1939–40	117,108 [7]	226,762	—	—	113,600	—	—	11,306 [6]	3,568 [6]
1949–50	83,718 [7]	—	—	128,225	59,652	24,542	—	10,375 [6]	3,331 [6]
1951–52	71,094 [7]	—	—	123,763	50,742	23,746	—	10,666 [6]	3,322 [6]
1959–60	40,520 [7]	—	—	91,853	20,213	25,784	—	13,574 [6]	4,061 [6]
1961–62	35,676 [7]	107,260	—	81,910	13,333	25,350	18,374	14,762 [6]	4,129 [6]
1963–64	31,705 [7]	104,015	—	77,584	9,895	26,431	—	—	4,451 [6]
1965–66	26,983 [7]	99,813	—	73,216	6,491	26,597	17,849 [6]	15,340 [6]	4,606 [6]
1967–68	22,010 [7]	—	94,197	70,879	4,146	27,011	—	—	—
1970–71	17,995 [7]	—	89,372	65,800	1,815	25,352	—	14,372 [6]	3,770 [6]
1973–74	16,730 [7]	—	88,655	65,070	1,365	25,906	—	—	—
1975–76	16,376 [7]	88,597	87,034	63,242	1,166	25,330	—	—	—
1976–77	16,271 [7]	—	86,501	62,644	1,111	25,378	19,910 [6]	16,385 [6]	5,904 [6]
1978–79	16,014 [7]	—	84,816	61,982	1,056	24,504	19,489 [6]	16,097 [6]	5,766 [6]
1979–80	15,944 [7]	87,004	—	—	—	—	—	—	—
1980–81	15,912 [7]	85,982	83,688	61,069	921	24,362	20,764 [6]	16,792 [6]	5,678 [6]
1982–83	15,824 [7]	84,740	82,039	59,656	798	23,988	—	—	—
1983–84	15,747 [7]	84,178	81,418	59,082	838	23,947	27,694	20,872	7,862
1984–85	—	84,007	81,147	58,827	825	23,916	—	—	—
1985–86	—	—	—	—	—	—	25,616	20,252	7,387
1986–87	15,713	83,455	82,190	60,784	763	23,389	—	—	—
1987–88	15,577	83,248	81,416	59,754	729	23,841	26,807	22,959	8,418
1988–89	15,376	83,165	81,579	60,176	583	23,638	—	—	—
1989–90	15,367	83,425	81,880	60,699	630	23,461	26,712	24,221	10,197
1990–91	15,358	84,538	82,475	61,340	617	23,460	24,690	22,223	8,989
1991–92	15,173	84,578	82,506	61,739	569	23,248	25,998	23,523	9,282
1992–93	15,025	84,497	82,896	62,225	430	23,220	—	—	—
1993–94	14,881	85,393	83,431	62,726	442	23,379	26,093	23,543	10,555
1994–95	14,772	86,221	84,476	63,572	458	23,668	—	—	—
1995–96	14,766	87,125	84,958	63,961	474	23,793	34,394	32,401	10,942
1996–97	14,841	88,223	86,092	64,785	487	24,287	—	—	—
1997–98	14,805	89,508	87,541	65,859	476	24,802	33,895	31,408	10,779
1998–99	14,891	90,874	89,259	67,183	463	25,797	—	—	—
1999–2000	14,928	92,012	90,538	68,173	423	26,407	32,995	30,457	10,693
2000–01	14,859	93,273	91,691	69,697	411	27,090	—	—	—
2001–02	14,559	94,112	92,696	70,516	408	27,468	35,895	33,191	11,846
2002–03	14,465	95,615	93,869	71,270	366	28,151	—	—	—
2003–04	14,383	95,726	93,977	71,195	376	28,219	34,681	31,988	11,188
2004–05	14,205	96,513	95,001	71,556	338	29,017	—	—	—
2005–06[8]	14,166	97,382	95,731	71,733	326	29,705	35,054	32,127	12,184
2006–07[8]	13,856	98,793	96,362	72,442	313	29,904	—	—	—
2007–08	13,924	98,916	97,680	73,254	288	30,648	33,740	30,808	11,870

Selected statistics on enrollment, teachers, dropouts, and graduates in public school districts enrolling more than 15,000 students: 1990, 2000, 2005–06, and 2007

Name of district	State	Enrollment, fall 1990	Enrollment, fall 2000	Enrollment, fall 2007	Percentage distribution of enrollment, by race, fall 2007					Teachers and staff, fall 2007					Dropouts and graduates, 2006				Number of schools, fall 2007
					White	Black	Hispanic	Asian/Pacific Islander	American Indian/Alaska Native	Number of classroom teachers	Pupil/teacher ratio	Total number of staff	Student/staff ratio	Teachers as a percentage of total staff	Percent dropouts from grades 9–12	Number of dropouts from grades 9–12	Averaged freshman graduation rate (AFGR)[1]	Number of high school graduates[2]	
1	2	3	4	5	6	7	8	9	10	11	12	13	14	15	16	17	18	19	20
Districts with more than 15,000 students	†	16,957,591	20,368,709	21,579,842	38.8	23.7	30.0	6.8	0.7	1,301,241	16.6	2,480,817	8.7	52.5	—	—	—	—	32,159
Baldwin County	AL	17,479	22,656	26,512	79.7	14.9	4.0	0.7	0.6	1,999	13.3	4,166	6.4	48.0	0.1	5	67.1	1,304	47
Birmingham City	AL	41,536	37,843	28,266	1.0	97.0	1.9	0.2	0.0	1,817	15.6	3,547	8.0	51.2	2.4	215	59.4	1,697	83
Huntsville City	AL	23,945	22,832	22,799	48.8	43.2	4.9	2.6	0.6	1,789	12.7	3,214	7.1	55.7	2.0	135	63.0	1,169	52
Jefferson County	AL	40,664	40,726	36,109	55.8	40.1	3.5	0.5	0.1	2,527	14.3	5,175	7.0	55.8	2.3	253	57.9	1,951	59
Madison County	AL	13,861	15,675	19,146	73.6	17.9	2.0	1.4	5.0	1,259	15.2	2,591	7.4	48.6	4.1	220	75.4	961	28
Mobile County	AL	67,203	64,976	64,375	45.1	50.4	1.3	2.2	1.0	4,049	15.9	9,131	7.0	44.3	1.7	302	60.4	2,995	115
Montgomery County	AL	35,956	33,267	31,618	16.3	78.9	2.3	2.4	0.1	1,964	16.1	4,113	7.7	47.8	4.5	363	48.8	1,170	61
Shelby County	AL	16,089	20,129	26,299	77.8	13.3	7.1	1.7	0.1	2,019	13.0	4,053	6.5	49.8	1.8	121	82.7	1,357	38
Tuscaloosa County	AL	14,426	15,666	16,968	71.0	26.3	2.0	0.6	0.1	1,044	16.3	2,296	7.4	45.5	3.7	170	65.1	801	33
Anchorage	AK	42,300	49,526	48,857	57.1	7.1	11.7	13.9	10.2	2,685	18.2	5,629	8.7	47.7	8.5	1,316	71.1	2,808	96
Matanuska-Susitna Borough	AK	9,892	13,008	16,159	82.5	1.3	2.6	1.5	12.0	897	18.0	1,613	10.0	55.6	7.2	359	75.8	912	41
Alhambra Elementary	AZ	8,166	14,290	15,242	8.2	7.0	79.7	2.5	2.5	797	19.1	1,784	8.5	44.6	†	†	†	†	15
Amphitheater Unified	AZ	13,835	16,857	16,404	53.7	4.6	36.6	3.3	1.9	981	16.7	1,941	8.5	50.5	2.6	140	(3)	1,022	20
Cartwright Elementary	AZ	14,369	17,746	20,454	4.6	3.7	90.3	0.4	0.9	1,108	18.5	2,357	8.7	47.0	†	†	†	†	23
Chandler Unified	AZ	11,038	21,703	36,064	56.6	6.5	28.0	7.4	1.4	1,883	19.2	3,540	10.2	53.2	2.4	208	78.4	1,617	38
Deer Valley Unified	AZ	15,898	27,158	36,875	77.1	3.4	14.8	3.9	0.9	1,877	19.6	3,266	11.3	57.5	3.7	374	†	1,840	37
Dysart Unified	AZ	3,805	5,459	23,401	48.7	9.8	37.3	3.1	1.1	1,139	20.5	1,940	12.1	58.7	4.4	180	89.6	568	21
Gilbert Unified	AZ	10,863	29,188	38,539	73.0	4.7	16.6	4.7	1.0	2,180	17.7	4,150	9.3	52.5	4.3	490	†	2,305	42
Glendale Union High	AZ	12,178	13,453	15,068	40.3	8.4	45.2	3.2	2.9	735	20.5	1,439	10.5	51.0	3.0	449	†	2,698	10
Kyrene Elementary	AZ	10,487	19,446	18,283	61.4	9.4	16.9	8.9	3.3	985	18.6	1,748	10.5	56.4	†	†	†	†	26
Mesa Unified	AZ	62,470	73,587	73,044	52.1	4.2	37.3	2.5	3.9	3,808	19.2	7,658	9.5	49.7	5.3	1,128	71.9	4,034	90
Paradise Valley Unified	AZ	26,698	34,882	34,114	69.3	3.4	22.5	3.6	1.2	1,949	17.5	3,297	10.3	59.1	2.1	224	82.8	2,214	47
Peoria Unified	AZ	20,846	32,608	39,143	63.5	5.7	26.2	3.3	1.3	2,038	19.2	3,559	11.0	57.3	2.8	336	81.1	2,411	39
Phoenix Union High	AZ	18,182	32,192	26,483	7.0	9.8	78.3	1.5	3.4	1,440	18.4	2,714	9.8	53.0	4.4	1,088	—	3,659	16
Scottsdale Unified	AZ	19,741	26,958	26,611	75.3	2.8	15.7	4.3	1.8	1,614	16.5	2,751	9.7	58.7	2.2	196	79.0	1,762	34
Sunnyside Unified	AZ	13,058	14,518	17,785	5.5	2.2	87.6	0.7	4.1	1,020	17.4	2,052	8.7	49.7	7.9	308	50.4	614	23
Tucson Unified	AZ	56,177	61,869	59,327	31.0	7.1	55.0	2.7	4.2	3,476	17.1	6,328	9.4	54.9	2.6	450	68.5	3,322	125
Washington Elementary	AZ	22,446	24,723	24,312	36.8	6.7	49.5	3.0	4.0	1,321	18.4	2,486	9.8	53.1	†	†	†	†	32
Little Rock	AR	25,813	25,502	27,084	22.5	68.6	6.8	1.8	0.3	2,054	13.2	3,729	7.3	55.1	3.6	262	68.0	1,279	49
Pulaski Co. Spec. School Dist.	AR	21,495	18,735	18,016	50.8	43.8	3.6	1.6	0.2	1,369	13.2	2,504	7.2	54.7	4.1	214	64.5	896	37
Springdale	AR	7,877	11,422	17,206	49.4	2.2	40.6	7.2	0.6	1,045	16.5	1,978	8.7	52.8	3.8	154	76.9	768	24
ABC Unified	CA	20,972	22,303	20,860	8.4	10.0	40.9	40.6	0.2	924	22.6	1,764	11.8	52.4	0.5	39	86.8	1,572	30
Alhambra Unified	CA	20,313	19,776	18,976	4.6	0.7	40.3	54.3	0.1	801	23.7	1,457	13.0	55.0	—	—	—	1,011	18
Alvord Unified	CA	14,853	17,664	19,987	15.7	4.5	73.8	5.6	0.4	879	22.7	1,549	12.9	56.7	9.8	559	70.1	—	22
Anaheim City	CA	14,972	22,275	19,332	5.6	1.7	85.7	6.8	0.3	942	20.5	1,684	11.5	55.9	†	†	†	†	24
Anaheim Union High	CA	23,086	29,363	33,343	17.5	2.9	62.4	17.0	0.2	1,407	23.7	2,604	12.8	54.0	0.2	51	61.8	3,459	22
Antelope Valley Union High	CA	10,937	19,056	26,453	27.6	21.2	47.8	2.7	0.5	1,151	23.0	2,122	12.5	54.2	2.3	594	89.9	3,553	14
Antioch Unified	CA	13,045	20,018	20,086	39.4	22.6	36.1	1.0	0.9	969	20.7	1,584	12.7	61.2	2.6	181	64.0	1,055	26
Apple Valley Unified	CA	11,265	13,292	15,789	49.2	10.9	35.1	3.5	0.5	657	24.0	1,306	12.1	50.3	5.0	265	82.0	1,028	18
Bakersfield City	CA	24,911	27,674	27,080	12.2	11.5	74.3	1.6	1.0	1,384	19.6	2,514	10.8	55.0	†	†	†	†	43
Baldwin Park Unified	CA	15,878	17,473	19,696	4.6	3.2	86.1	6.0	0.1	821	24.0	1,610	12.2	51.0	28.9	2,125	70.4	1,040	23
Burbank Unified	CA	12,057	17,473	16,640	48.5	2.8	38.2	10.3	0.2	799	20.8	1,405	11.8	56.9	9.7	649	69.2	1,076	21
Cajon Valley Union Elementary	CA	17,328	19,059	16,295	51.4	7.6	36.6	3.7	0.7	793	20.6	1,389	11.7	57.1	†	†	†	†	30
Capistrano Unified	CA	26,852	45,074	52,390	71.3	1.4	19.7	7.3	0.3	2,238	23.4	3,850	13.6	58.1	0.5	75	80.2	2,867	61
Chaffey Joint Union High	CA	13,505	19,851	25,108	24.0	10.7	58.0	7.0	0.2	996	25.2	1,728	14.5	57.6	2.6	658	74.5	4,123	11
Chino Valley Unified	CA	23,257	31,763	33,047	29.7	4.5	51.8	13.7	0.4	1,418	23.3	2,385	13.9	59.4	2.0	219		1,941	36
Chula Vista Elementary	CA	17,604	23,132	27,264	13.0	4.3	68.8	13.5	0.4	1,416	19.3	2,527	10.8	56.0	†	†	†	†	44
Clovis Unified	CA	23,224	32,717	36,810	54.4	3.7	24.8	16.0	1.1	1,762	20.9	3,128	11.8	56.3	1.6	183	80.0	2,282	46
Coachella Valley Unified	CA	9,091	12,636	18,203	1.3	0.4	97.6	0.3	0.3	866	20.9	1,751	10.4	49.5	2.5	105	63.9	669	23
Colton Joint Unified	CA	16,415	22,118	24,528	10.6	7.6	77.3	4.0	0.5	1,138	21.5	1,933	12.7	58.9	4.2	288	53.5	1,019	28
Compton Unified	CA	27,585	31,037	28,081	0.2	23.9	74.8	1.0	0.1	1,225	22.9	3,129	9.0	39.2	10.2	716	42.9	871	40

See notes at end of table.

Selected statistics on enrollment, teachers, dropouts, and graduates in public school districts enrolling more than 15,000 students: 1990, 2000, 2005–06, and 2007—Continued

Name of district	State	Enrollment, fall 1990	Enrollment, fall 2000	Enrollment, fall 2007	Percentage distribution of enrollment, by race, fall 2007					Teachers and staff, fall 2007					Dropouts and graduates, 2006				Number of schools, fall 2007
					White	Black	Hispanic	Asian/ Pacific Islander	American Indian/ Alaska Native	Number of classroom teachers	Pupil/ teacher ratio	Total number of staff	Student/ staff ratio	Teachers as a percentage of total staff	Percent dropouts from grades 9–12	Number of dropouts from grades 9–12	Averaged freshman graduation rate (AFGR)[1]	Number of high school graduates[2]	
1	2	3	4	5	6	7	8	9	10	11	12	13	14	15	16	17	18	19	20
Conejo Valley Unified	CA	17,209	20,999	21,209	68.6	1.6	18.7	10.4	0.7	996	21.3	1,750	12.1	56.9	0.8	62	82.8	1,411	29
Corona-Norco Unified	CA	23,036	37,487	51,322	34.3	6.1	50.6	8.6	0.3	2,387	21.5	3,995	12.8	59.7	1.8	260	84.2	2,646	50
Cupertino Union	CA	12,227	15,670	17,294	24.3	1.2	4.5	69.7	0.3	806	21.5	1,341	12.9	60.1	†	†	†	†	25
Desert Sands Unified	CA	16,058	23,500	28,775	27.8	2.2	67.2	2.4	0.4	1,298	22.2	2,199	13.1	59.0	4.6	390	77.7	1,568	33
Downey Unified	CA	15,418	21,474	22,358	9.7	3.6	81.6	4.6	0.4	998	22.4	1,651	13.5	60.5	0.2	15	71.3	1,391	20
East Side Union High	CA	21,973	24,282	26,280	10.5	4.0	49.1	36.0	0.4	1,186	22.2	2,039	12.9	58.2	7.0	1,793	—	4,900	22
Elk Grove Unified	CA	27,246	47,736	62,294	28.6	19.8	22.6	28.4	0.6	2,985	20.9	5,093	12.2	58.6	3.1	581	85.3	3,493	64
Escondido Union Elementary	CA	14,663	19,312	19,445	25.8	2.9	65.6	5.2	0.5	1,014	19.2	1,744	11.2	58.2	†	†	†	†	25
Fairfield-Suisun Unified	CA	20,227	22,263	22,774	26.6	22.8	32.5	17.0	1.0	1,097	20.8	1,960	11.6	56.0	1.8	133	69.9	1,250	31
Folsom-Cordova Unified	CA	12,656	16,277	19,029	62.2	7.8	15.7	13.4	0.9	889	21.4	1,568	12.1	56.7	2.1	116	73.3	1,016	35
Fontana Unified	CA	27,043	37,244	41,959	6.7	7.2	82.8	2.8	0.4	1,832	22.9	2,647	15.9	69.2	6.4	784	64.7	1,944	44
Fremont Unified	CA	27,172	31,078	31,948	23.9	5.1	16.1	54.6	0.3	1,514	21.1	2,240	14.3	67.6	0.5	51	73.1	1,884	41
Fresno Unified	CA	71,500	79,007	76,460	14.7	10.8	58.8	14.8	0.8	3,919	19.5	7,002	10.9	56.0	4.6	1,074	56.0	3,735	105
Fullerton Joint Union High	CA	12,729	15,165	16,321	25.3	2.3	49.8	22.4	0.2	590	27.7	1,107	14.7	53.3	0.7	111	74.7	2,781	8
Garden Grove Unified	CA	37,969	48,742	48,669	13.2	0.9	53.6	32.0	0.2	2,107	23.1	3,842	12.7	54.8	0.8	112	80.7	2,792	67
Glendale Unified	CA	25,459	30,329	27,035	56.8	1.2	22.2	19.7	0.2	1,285	21.0	2,156	12.5	59.6	1.2	120	89.3	1,975	32
Grossmont Union High	CA	18,647	23,639	24,195	54.6	8.8	29.1	5.9	1.7	1,000	24.2	1,531	15.8	65.3	2.1	504	61.3	4,117	19
Hacienda La Puente Unified	CA	23,267	24,205	21,997	5.1	1.4	77.5	15.6	0.4	1,045	21.1	1,777	12.4	58.8	4.9	368	58.7	1,363	38
Hayward Unified	CA	19,122	24,646	21,612	10.0	15.3	54.6	19.6	0.5	1,087	19.9	1,782	12.1	61.0	3.5	220	58.7	1,007	33
Hemet Unified	CA	12,811	17,451	23,567	42.8	7.2	45.2	3.4	1.4	1,112	21.2	1,967	12.0	56.5	3.7	255	65.9	1,044	29
Hesperia Unified	CA	13,113	15,360	22,481	31.5	7.3	58.0	2.4	0.7	991	22.7	1,831	12.3	54.1	6.2	404	79.6	1,034	30
Huntington Beach Union High	CA	14,039	14,359	16,052	46.2	1.3	21.1	30.6	0.7	634	25.3	1,207	13.3	52.5	1.0	151	52.3	3,096	9
Inglewood Unified	CA	16,355	17,295	15,234	0.4	39.7	58.8	1.0	0.1	654	23.3	1,136	13.4	57.5	2.4	97	98.4	597	20
Irvine Unified	CA	20,735	23,961	26,128	42.1	2.3	8.3	46.6	0.7	1,121	23.3	1,901	13.7	59.0	0.8	67	63.7	2,008	36
Jurupa Unified	CA	15,419	19,839	20,657	17.7	3.3	76.6	2.1	0.3	939	22.0	1,681	12.3	55.9	6.9	447	—	1,031	25
Kern Union High	CA	20,183	19,333	37,341	32.1	7.7	55.7	3.7	0.8	1,602	23.3	3,255	11.5	49.2	5.7	2,029	80.4	5,784	24
Lake Elsinore Unified	CA	11,000	17,178	22,109	38.5	5.0	51.3	4.4	0.8	997	22.2	1,666	13.3	59.9	1.1	67	64.7	1,171	27
Lancaster Elementary	CA	11,248	14,433	15,793	18.8	29.1	48.3	3.1	0.7	781	20.2	1,385	11.4	56.4	†	†	†	†	19
Lodi Unified	CA	23,954	27,339	31,609	29.6	9.1	37.3	23.3	0.7	1,606	19.7	2,847	11.1	56.4	8.4	788	66.3	1,457	54
Long Beach Unified	CA	71,342	93,694	88,186	16.5	17.6	51.7	13.9	0.3	4,210	20.9	7,842	11.2	53.7	5.4	1,539	47.4	4,896	93
Los Angeles Unified	CA	625,086	721,346	693,680	8.8	10.9	73.7	6.6	#	34,960	19.8	67,997	10.2	51.4	5.1	10,588	50.6	28,322	825
Lynwood Unified	CA	15,469	18,237	17,619	0.2	7.4	91.9	0.5	0.5	821	21.5	1,389	12.7	59.1	9.1	481	47.4	754	20
Madera Unified	CA	13,728	15,957	18,941	12.8	3.1	82.1	1.5	1.2	901	21.0	1,653	11.5	54.5	16.3	794	70.8	538	27
Manteca Unified	CA	13,356	19,746	23,654	29.3	10.3	45.7	13.6	1.0	1,094	21.6	1,821	13.0	60.1	1.1	79	—	1,183	29
Modesto City Elementary	CA	17,405	18,740	16,147	24.0	5.0	63.8	6.3	0.8	852	19.0	1,443	11.2	59.0	†	†	†	†	27
Modesto City High	CA	10,697	14,547	15,742	39.3	5.8	44.6	10.2	0.1	616	25.6	1,221	12.9	50.4	12.1	1,924	—	2,794	7
Montebello Unified	CA	32,938	34,794	33,493	2.1	0.4	94.0	3.0	0.5	1,439	23.3	2,672	12.5	53.8	0.1	7	61.4	1,756	29
Moreno Valley Unified	CA	29,064	32,730	37,126	13.1	19.8	61.7	4.9	0.6	1,668	22.3	2,976	12.5	56.0	7.0	798	61.0	1,757	38
Mount Diablo Unified	CA	32,840	36,648	35,355	49.7	5.6	31.1	13.0	0.5	1,735	20.4	2,886	12.2	60.1	3.6	397	78.6	2,194	55
Murrieta Valley Unified	CA	3,990	12,065	21,226	56.4	6.5	26.0	10.1	1.0	917	23.1	1,707	12.4	53.7	1.6	101	93.4	1,165	18
Napa Valley Unified	CA	13,705	16,392	17,552	41.8	2.3	47.5	7.4	1.0	920	19.1	1,548	11.3	59.4	1.7	92	73.4	991	37
Newport-Mesa Unified	CA	16,434	21,658	21,338	51.0	1.3	41.3	6.1	0.4	963	22.2	1,969	10.8	48.9	1.5	104	78.0	1,350	32
Norwalk-La Mirada Unified	CA	19,179	23,610	22,092	12.9	3.5	75.5	7.8	0.4	929	23.8	1,795	12.3	51.7	1.7	124	65.6	1,248	29
Oakland Unified	CA	52,095	54,863	46,431	6.5	38.1	38.5	16.4	0.4	2,627	17.7	4,451	10.4	59.0	7.2	941	48.6	1,889	143
Oceanside Unified	CA	17,034	22,354	21,222	28.5	3.4	54.7	8.1	0.6	1,065	19.9	1,803	11.8	59.1	1.8	108	66.3	1,041	30
Ontario-Montclair Elementary	CA	21,033	26,407	23,307	6.1	3.4	87.0	3.2	0.3	1,114	20.9	2,026	11.5	55.0	†	†	†	†	34
Orange Unified	CA	25,224	31,097	30,127	38.3	1.5	47.2	12.5	0.5	1,361	22.1	2,778	10.8	49.0	1.1	103	77.4	1,925	43
Oxnard Elementary	CA	12,212	16,249	15,281	5.7	2.1	88.7	3.3	0.2	680	22.5	1,159	13.2	58.7	†	†	†	†	21
Oxnard Union High	CA	11,512	14,552	16,868	18.7	3.1	70.2	7.3	0.6	670	25.2	1,206	14.0	55.6	2.5	402	61.4	2,574	9
Pajaro Valley Unified	CA	16,355	19,864	19,420	18.4	0.6	78.1	2.3	0.6	877	22.1	1,605	12.1	54.6	9.3	526	60.4	921	33
Palm Springs Unified	CA	14,427	20,847	24,400	19.3	5.2	71.2	3.6	0.7	1,109	22.0	1,836	13.3	60.4	6.8	472	—	1,049	25
Palmdale Elementary	CA	13,199	20,853	22,193	12.0	16.7	68.2	2.7	0.4	925	24.0	1,644	13.5	56.3	†	†	†	†	28
Panama-Buena Vista Union	CA	10,066	12,843	16,561	33.1	11.6	46.9	7.8	0.7	807	20.5	1,161	14.3	69.5	†	†	†	†	22
Paramount Unified	CA	12,855	16,862	15,952	2.4	10.7	83.8	2.7	0.4	748	21.3	1,332	12.0	56.2	4.3	205	53.5	630	19
Pasadena Unified	CA	21,802	23,559	20,905	16.6	22.3	56.2	4.7	0.2	1,015	20.6	2,275	9.2	44.6	4.1	252	52.1	933	33

See notes at end of table.

Selected statistics on enrollment, teachers, dropouts, and graduates in public school districts enrolling more than 15,000 students: 1990, 2000, 2005–06, and 2007—Continued

Name of district	State	Enrollment, fall 1990	Enrollment, fall 2000	Enrollment, fall 2007	White	Black	Hispanic	Asian/Pacific Islander	American Indian/Alaska Native	Number of classroom teachers	Pupil/teacher ratio	Total number of staff	Student/staff ratio	Teachers as a percentage of total staff	Percent dropouts from grades 9–12	Number of dropouts from grades 9–12	Averaged freshman graduation rate (AFGR)[1]	Number of high school graduates[2]	Number of schools, fall 2007
1	2	3	4	5	6	7	8	9	10	11	12	13	14	15	16	17	18	19	20
Placentia-Yorba Linda Unified	CA	21,438	26,046	26,243	53.3	1.9	33.2	11.4	0.2	1,098	23.9	2,031	12.9	54.1	0.4	34	84.8	1,773	32
Pomona Unified	CA	26,918	34,479	30,779	5.9	6.5	81.3	6.2	0.1	1,481	20.8	2,566	12.0	57.7	2.6	230	55.4	1,512	45
Poway Unified	CA	24,662	32,532	33,283	59.9	3.3	11.3	25.1	0.5	1,463	22.8	2,750	12.1	53.2	1.0	103	88.1	2,301	34
Redlands Unified	CA	16,002	19,411	21,482	40.5	7.6	39.1	12.1	0.7	982	21.9	1,642	13.1	59.8	1.7	123	83.5	1,437	23
Rialto Unified	CA	19,794	28,060	29,070	6.2	17.8	73.3	2.1	0.3	1,340	21.7	2,353	12.4	56.9	6.9	633	57.0	1,396	28
Riverside Unified	CA	31,326	38,124	43,560	31.3	9.2	53.9	5.2	0.5	1,789	24.3	3,388	12.9	52.8	1.9	274	72.4	2,563	49
Rowland Unified	CA	19,143	18,972	16,920	4.1	2.6	63.5	29.7	0.1	801	21.1	1,585	10.7	50.5	0.4	23	61.4	882	23
Sacramento City Unified	CA	49,557	52,734	48,446	21.2	21.1	32.7	23.9	1.2	2,404	20.2	4,175	11.6	57.6	2.9	429	56.9	2,375	91
Saddleback Valley Unified	CA	25,130	35,199	33,558	61.9	2.1	24.9	10.8	0.4	1,424	23.6	2,473	13.6	57.6	0.9	105	85.4	2,337	37
San Bernardino City Unified	CA	40,589	52,031	56,727	11.2	16.7	69.8	1.6	0.8	2,594	21.9	4,581	12.4	56.6	8.0	1,299	47.7	2,166	72
San Diego Unified	CA	121,152	141,804	131,577	25.3	13.5	44.4	16.3	0.5	6,986	18.8	14,726	8.9	47.4	3.6	1,389	63.6	6,588	214
San Francisco Unified	CA	61,688	59,979	55,069	10.8	13.1	24.1	51.3	0.7	3,114	17.7	4,694	11.7	66.3	1.7	325	76.4	3,828	111
San Jose Unified	CA	29,630	33,015	31,230	27.7	3.6	52.2	15.6	0.9	1,525	20.5	2,586	12.1	59.0	2.7	258	74.5	1,780	52
San Juan Unified	CA	47,690	50,266	47,400	67.3	7.4	16.5	6.8	2.0	2,240	21.2	4,457	10.6	50.2	5.6	989	85.4	3,766	77
San Marcos Unified	CA	9,108	12,804	17,380	39.8	3.2	48.1	8.2	0.3	752	23.1	1,411	12.3	53.3	2.0	85	79.5	735	19
San Ramon Valley Unified	CA	16,119	20,742	25,959	67.8	2.5	5.3	24.1	0.3	1,218	21.3	2,039	12.7	59.8	0.7	53	97.9	1,715	33
Santa Ana Unified	CA	45,964	60,643	57,061	3.3	0.7	92.8	3.1	0.1	2,593	22.0	4,489	12.7	57.8	3.2	500	49.9	2,253	59
Simi Valley Unified	CA	18,262	21,181	21,137	64.5	1.5	24.8	8.6	0.7	937	22.6	1,687	12.5	55.5	2.6	183	74.7	1,260	30
Stockton Unified	CA	32,687	37,573	38,408	9.1	12.4	56.6	17.6	4.3	1,759	21.8	3,526	10.9	49.9	3.1	323	67.5	2,145	55
Sweetwater Union High	CA	27,894	35,330	42,591	10.5	4.5	72.6	11.9	0.4	1,896	22.5	3,722	11.4	50.9	1.7	501	74.5	5,109	31
Temecula Valley Unified	CA	7,596	18,980	29,435	58.8	5.0	23.6	11.4	1.2	1,368	21.5	2,426	12.1	56.4	0.9	78	86.6	1,496	31
Torrance Unified	CA	19,645	24,118	24,972	37.2	3.8	19.9	38.5	0.6	1,105	22.6	2,044	12.2	54.1	0.3	26	98.0	2,101	31
Tracy Joint Unified	CA	7,626	13,816	17,333	31.7	8.7	42.1	16.8	0.8	836	20.7	1,427	12.1	58.6	0.3	20	78.1	1,043	24
Tustin Unified	CA	10,831	16,963	20,909	35.8	2.5	43.7	17.7	0.3	887	23.6	1,572	13.3	56.4	0.4	20	81.6	1,074	28
Val Verde Unified	CA	—	11,242	19,547	8.0	17.5	70.4	3.9	0.2	855	22.9	1,500	13.0	57.0	5.2	241	55.4	567	21
Vallejo City Unified	CA	19,049	20,270	17,408	11.7	33.2	29.4	25.0	0.7	843	20.6	1,557	11.2	54.2	7.0	421	69.6	988	29
Ventura Unified	CA	15,383	17,527	17,321	49.7	2.0	43.2	3.7	1.4	738	23.5	1,393	12.4	53.0	2.1	121	73.2	1,010	31
Visalia Unified	CA	21,309	23,989	26,722	31.7	3.0	56.9	6.4	2.0	1,140	23.4	2,070	12.9	55.1	7.3	594	74.5	1,424	36
Vista Unified	CA	18,489	27,651	27,002	32.4	5.6	55.9	5.5	0.6	1,250	21.6	2,361	11.4	53.0	19.4	1,740	(3)	2,210	33
Walnut Valley Unified	CA	12,613	14,849	15,316	13.7	3.3	19.5	63.5	0.1	660	23.2	1,105	13.9	59.8	0.2	10	(3)	1,516	15
West Contra Costa Unified	CA	31,292	34,499	30,830	11.6	24.3	47.3	16.6	0.3	1,569	19.6	2,813	11.0	55.8	2.7	270	57.7	1,546	65
William S. Hart Union High	CA	10,278	17,001	25,243	55.3	5.0	28.2	11.1	0.5	1,039	24.3	1,714	14.7	60.6	1.7	271	93.1	3,277	19
Academy, School District No. 20	CO	10,986	17,628	21,423	82.1	4.1	7.8	5.2	0.8	1,312	16.3	2,652	8.1	49.5	1.7	111	88.7	1,352	31
Aurora, Joint District No. 28	CO	25,897	30,453	33,563	24.6	20.0	50.5	4.0	0.9	1,886	17.8	4,118	8.2	45.8	18.5	1,647	52.6	1,316	52
Boulder Valley	CO	21,502	27,508	28,543	76.7	0.7	14.4	6.7	0.7	1,748	16.3	3,768	7.6	46.4	3.1	284	86.2	2,049	54
Cherry Creek	CO	29,210	42,320	50,601	64.1	14.3	13.1	8.0	0.5	2,942	17.2	6,125	8.3	48.0	2.9	435	89.9	3,182	56
Colorado Springs	CO	30,009	32,699	29,496	62.8	10.6	22.2	2.8	1.6	1,861	15.8	3,984	7.4	46.7	9.3	939	73.2	1,914	64
Denver	CO	59,013	70,847	73,053	21.4	17.9	56.5	3.2	1.1	4,142	17.6	8,582	8.5	48.3	21.4	3,885	50.4	2,664	148
Douglas County	CO	13,125	34,918	52,983	85.6	2.0	7.3	4.5	0.6	2,951	18.0	6,328	8.4	46.6	2.0	246	86.5	2,463	72
Greeley	CO	11,657	15,998	18,397	44.4	1.2	52.6	1.1	0.7	1,076	17.1	2,143	8.6	50.2	9.2	462	76.8	1,019	31
Jefferson County	CO	76,275	87,703	86,168	74.5	1.9	18.6	3.8	1.2	4,890	17.6	10,671	8.1	45.8	5.4	1,515	79.4	5,646	163
Littleton	CO	15,524	16,516	15,937	82.2	2.2	11.5	3.4	0.7	900	17.7	1,891	8.4	47.6	2.3	133	90.3	1,261	25
Mesa County Valley	CO	17,024	19,688	21,281	77.5	1.4	18.5	1.2	1.4	1,248	17.1	2,624	8.1	47.6	8.2	516	74.3	1,198	43
Northglenn-Thornton	CO	20,838	30,079	38,815	60.5	2.7	30.7	5.2	0.9	1,997	19.4	4,041	9.6	49.4	10.3	1,033	77.7	1,858	50
Poudre	CO	18,589	24,052	25,599	77.9	1.9	15.6	3.5	1.1	1,482	17.3	3,172	8.1	46.7	4.8	385	87.3	1,771	52
Pueblo	CO	18,364	17,636	18,289	33.5	2.8	61.8	0.7	1.2	1,078	17.0	2,223	8.2	48.5	10.8	543	64.2	917	39
Saint Vrain Valley	CO	15,070	19,620	24,582	67.5	1.2	26.9	3.5	0.9	1,358	18.1	2,589	9.5	52.4	5.6	387	82.7	1,327	43
Thompson	CO	12,019	14,766	15,304	81.3	1.1	15.2	1.5	0.9	883	17.3	1,879	8.1	47.0	4.1	201	85.4	1,047	30
Bridgeport	CT	19,687	22,432	20,824	9.0	41.6	46.4	2.9	0.2	1,302	16.0	2,758	7.5	47.2	8.1	442	56.0	834	39
Hartford	CT	25,481	22,543	22,359	6.2	40.2	52.1	1.1	0.2	1,528	14.6	2,978	7.5	51.3	6.5	352	45.9	732	42
New Haven	CT	17,881	19,549	19,863	12.5	51.4	34.4	1.5	0.2	1,418	14.0	3,137	6.3	45.2	4.3	233	62.9	948	46
Waterbury	CT	13,323	16,282	18,304	26.7	28.1	43.1	1.8	0.3	1,216	15.1	2,649	6.9	45.9	3.4	148	59.8	730	31

See notes at end of table.

Selected statistics on enrollment, teachers, dropouts, and graduates in public school districts enrolling more than 15,000 students: 1990, 2000, 2005–06, and 2007—Continued

Name of district	State	Enrollment, fall 1990	Enrollment, fall 2000	Enrollment, fall 2007	Percentage distribution of enrollment, by race, fall 2007					Number of classroom teachers	Pupil/ teacher ratio	Teachers and staff, fall 2007 Total number of staff	Student/ staff ratio	Teachers as a percentage of total staff	Percent dropouts from grades 9–12	Dropouts and graduates, 2006 Number of dropouts from grades 9–12	Averaged freshman graduation rate (AFGR)[1]	Number of high school graduates[2]	Number of schools, fall 2007
					White	Black	Hispanic	Asian/ Pacific Islander	American Indian/ Alaska Native										
1	2	3	4	5	6	7	8	9	10	11	12	13	14	15	16	17	18	19	20
Christina	DE	17,872	19,882	16,648	39.0	42.8	13.4	4.5	0.3	1,168	14.3	2,470	6.7	47.3	9.3	476	58.1	908	29
Red Clay Consolidated	DE	14,551	15,827	15,721	48.5	26.3	21.0	4.1	0.1	928	16.9	1,763	8.9	52.6	7.1	273	62.8	758	28
District of Columbia	DC	80,694	68,925	58,191	6.3	81.1	10.8	1.8	0.1	4,400	13.2	7,930	7.3	55.5	7.9	1,188	—	—	166
Alachua	FL	26,305	29,712	28,378	51.1	38.2	6.2	4.2	0.3	1,691	16.8	3,991	7.1	42.4	6.8	632	70.7	1,729	64
Bay	FL	21,827	25,755	26,236	77.4	16.1	3.9	2.1	0.4	1,711	15.3	3,417	7.7	50.1	2.4	199	70.2	1,482	45
Brevard	FL	56,503	70,597	74,369	73.5	15.5	8.6	2.2	0.3	4,623	16.1	9,058	8.2	51.0	1.0	223	75.1	4,522	124
Broward	FL	161,101	251,129	258,893	31.2	38.6	26.6	3.4	0.2	14,931	17.3	27,335	9.5	54.6	3.1	2,489	65.0	13,732	297
Charlotte	FL	13,030	17,170	17,795	80.2	9.5	8.3	1.7	0.3	1,061	16.8	2,406	7.4	44.1	2.9	179	84.0	1,321	22
Citrus	FL	11,697	15,199	16,170	88.5	4.6	4.9	1.6	0.4	1,066	15.2	2,308	7.0	46.2	5.3	268	68.9	951	23
Clay	FL	21,925	28,115	36,093	77.1	12.9	7.0	2.8	0.2	2,467	14.6	4,719	7.6	52.3	2.2	230	76.4	1,992	38
Collier	FL	20,850	34,203	42,723	44.0	11.7	42.8	1.2	0.3	2,792	15.3	5,755	7.4	48.5	2.4	305	71.6	2,269	66
Dade	FL	292,023	368,625	348,128	9.3	26.6	62.8	1.2	0.1	22,048	15.8	39,853	8.7	55.3	7.6	8,484	53.7	16,941	471
Duval	FL	111,142	125,846	124,740	42.7	46.1	7.0	4.0	0.2	7,848	15.9	12,967	9.6	60.5	8.0	2,772	56.2	5,750	177
Escambia	FL	42,950	45,012	41,854	55.2	38.0	3.4	2.7	0.8	2,886	14.5	5,615	7.5	51.4	4.1	517	58.4	2,089	76
Hernando	FL	12,831	17,215	22,837	78.9	7.2	12.3	1.3	0.2	1,652	13.8	3,123	7.3	52.9	4.6	310	69.3	1,134	26
Hillsborough	FL	124,337	164,311	193,180	44.3	23.3	29.1	3.1	0.3	12,759	15.1	24,692	7.8	51.7	2.5	1,331	65.6	9,642	285
Indian River	FL	11,683	14,979	17,646	65.8	15.9	16.8	1.2	0.2	1,033	17.1	2,107	8.4	49.0	1.2	63	70.3	941	27
Lake	FL	21,065	29,293	40,669	63.7	16.1	17.4	2.2	0.6	2,503	16.2	5,563	7.3	45.0	4.6	507	74.0	1,861	55
Lee	FL	43,240	58,401	80,541	53.3	14.7	30.0	1.6	0.4	4,953	16.3	9,619	8.4	51.5	4.4	944	68.6	3,525	110
Leon	FL	27,241	32,050	32,472	50.5	43.0	3.3	3.0	0.1	2,043	15.9	4,499	7.2	45.4	2.6	239	73.6	1,784	58
Manatee	FL	26,207	36,569	42,524	59.0	15.5	23.7	1.7	0.1	2,551	16.7	5,510	7.7	46.3	3.9	473	62.6	2,107	75
Marion	FL	29,577	38,562	42,577	62.2	20.3	15.3	1.6	0.6	2,688	15.8	6,135	6.9	43.8	4.9	636	67.0	2,195	62
Martin	FL	11,692	16,308	18,109	70.3	8.7	19.5	1.4	0.2	1,086	16.7	2,144	8.4	50.7	0.5	27	76.2	1,090	35
Okaloosa	FL	26,140	30,344	29,568	78.1	12.8	5.8	2.8	0.5	1,844	16.0	3,132	9.4	58.9	2.8	280	77.0	1,951	59
Orange	FL	102,672	150,681	174,142	35.0	28.1	32.0	4.4	0.4	11,117	15.7	22,866	7.6	48.6	2.2	1,165	66.1	8,772	233
Osceola	FL	19,514	34,566	52,742	32.5	11.3	53.2	2.6	0.3	3,054	17.3	6,784	7.8	45.0	5.1	783	70.6	2,411	60
Palm Beach	FL	105,712	153,871	170,883	41.8	30.1	24.8	2.8	0.5	10,737	15.9	19,550	8.7	54.9	3.2	1,709	59.5	8,493	258
Pasco	FL	33,891	49,704	66,314	77.7	5.8	14.0	2.2	0.3	4,378	15.1	9,026	7.3	48.5	5.0	928	64.1	3,019	100
Pinellas	FL	92,976	113,027	107,892	65.9	20.2	9.8	3.9	0.3	7,048	15.3	14,225	7.6	49.5	3.6	1,307	54.5	5,648	169
Polk	FL	64,579	79,477	93,980	53.2	22.4	22.7	1.5	0.3	6,707	14.0	13,027	7.2	51.5	4.9	1,218	63.1	3,992	152
Saint Johns	FL	12,080	20,090	27,863	84.0	8.7	4.6	2.5	0.3	1,636	17.0	3,263	8.5	50.1	2.3	185	82.5	1,496	39
Saint Lucie	FL	22,224	29,540	40,347	44.2	30.4	23.3	1.8	0.3	2,309	17.5	4,941	8.2	46.7	3.0	313	58.5	1,519	47
Santa Rosa	FL	15,708	22,633	25,711	89.0	5.5	3.1	1.9	0.6	1,621	15.9	2,605	9.9	62.2	2.8	219	76.0	1,571	38
Sarasota	FL	26,881	35,533	42,013	75.0	10.1	12.7	1.9	0.3	2,808	15.0	5,757	7.3	48.8	2.8	362	74.0	2,408	60
Seminole	FL	48,831	60,869	65,378	62.1	14.6	19.1	4.0	0.3	4,136	15.8	7,559	8.6	54.7	1.6	340	69.9	3,837	77
Volusia	FL	48,342	61,517	64,488	66.7	15.2	16.3	1.6	0.2	4,322	14.9	8,762	7.4	49.3	1.7	354	63.3	3,584	95
Atlanta	GA	60,714	58,230	49,991	9.7	85.0	4.6	0.7	0.1	3,766	13.3	6,947	7.2	54.2	8.4	1,084	47.5	1,895	113
Bibb County	GA	24,378	24,739	25,030	22.3	74.4	1.8	1.4	0.1	1,669	15.0	3,778	6.6	44.2	7.9	504	47.2	867	48
Carroll County	GA	10,664	12,321	15,080	74.1	20.0	5.0	0.7	0.3	1,054	14.3	2,239	6.7	47.1	7.3	304	56.6	585	25
Chatham County	GA	34,044	35,344	34,058	26.3	67.2	4.3	2.0	0.2	2,593	13.1	4,790	7.1	54.1	8.0	724	52.7	1,378	57
Cherokee County	GA	16,086	26,043	36,353	80.4	6.8	11.0	1.6	0.2	2,621	13.9	4,821	7.5	54.4	5.8	524	69.8	1,520	37
Clayton County	GA	34,754	46,930	52,717	5.2	76.2	14.1	4.4	0.1	3,630	14.5	7,671	6.9	47.3	1.2	180	51.3	2,038	64
Cobb County	GA	69,441	95,781	107,307	48.9	30.9	15.4	4.6	0.1	8,119	13.2	14,439	7.4	56.2	4.0	1,320	75.6	6,000	116
Columbia County	GA	14,096	18,756	22,464	75.8	17.0	3.5	3.5	0.2	1,464	15.3	3,073	7.3	47.7	4.1	265	77.2	1,218	29
Coweta County	GA	10,430	16,766	21,790	70.8	22.4	5.4	1.1	0.2	1,462	14.9	3,172	6.9	46.1	4.0	232	67.3	950	28
DeKalb County	GA	74,108	95,958	100,273	10.5	76.8	9.1	3.5	0.1	6,999	14.3	14,620	6.9	47.9	2.6	778	56.7	4,437	149
Dougherty County	GA	18,482	16,799	16,436	10.7	87.5	1.3	0.5	0.1	1,105	14.9	2,543	6.5	43.4	5.9	252	48.6	631	29
Douglas County	GA	14,000	17,489	24,730	41.1	48.7	8.7	1.4	0.1	1,727	14.3	3,384	7.3	51.0	5.0	328	70.3	1,024	35
Fayette County	GA	13,105	19,590	22,223	65.8	23.7	6.0	4.3	0.2	1,605	13.8	3,078	7.2	52.1	1.4	109	84.6	1,584	30
Forsyth County	GA	7,742	17,131	30,655	84.0	2.1	9.3	4.4	0.1	2,118	14.5	3,969	7.7	53.4	3.7	239	76.5	1,110	31
Fulton County	GA	41,195	68,583	86,225	37.5	43.4	10.5	8.5	0.1	6,211	13.9	11,874	7.3	52.3	3.7	872	74.7	4,132	99
Gwinnett County	GA	63,930	110,075	155,618	38.0	28.3	22.7	10.8	0.1	10,840	14.4	19,733	7.9	54.9	4.5	1,826	71.5	6,915	112
Hall County	GA	13,738	20,330	25,585	58.0	5.4	34.5	1.7	0.4	1,791	14.3	3,266	7.8	54.9	7.3	484	57.3	1,002	34

See notes at end of table.

Selected statistics on enrollment, teachers, dropouts, and graduates in public school districts enrolling more than 15,000 students: 1990, 2000, 2005–06, and 2007—Continued

Name of district	State	Enrollment, fall 1990	Enrollment, fall 2000	Enrollment, fall 2007	White	Black	Hispanic	Asian/Pacific Islander	American Indian/Alaska Native	Number of classroom teachers	Pupil/teacher ratio	Total number of staff	Student/staff ratio	Teachers as a percentage of total staff	Percent dropouts from grades 9–12	Number of dropouts from grades 9–12	Averaged freshman graduation rate (AFGR)[1]	Number of high school graduates[2]	Number of schools, fall 2007
1	2	3	4	5	6	7	8	9	10	11	12	13	14	15	16	17	18	19	20
Henry County	GA	10,929	23,601	39,000	47.7	43.9	5.6	2.5	0.2	2,623	14.9	4,929	7.9	53.2	6.2	646	71.9	1,636	45
Houston County	GA	16,249	21,529	25,921	56.5	36.2	5.0	2.1	0.2	1,872	13.8	3,804	6.8	49.2	4.6	339	72.8	1,327	39
Muscogee County	GA	30,038	32,916	32,763	31.9	62.0	4.1	1.9	0.2	2,339	14.0	5,173	6.3	45.2	5.2	503	58.4	1,551	63
Newton County	GA	8,054	11,734	19,111	42.9	51.5	4.5	1.0	0.2	1,288	14.8	2,616	7.3	49.2	3.2	146	50.7	576	22
Paulding County	GA	7,604	16,587	26,857	73.0	21.1	5.0	0.8	0.1	1,918	14.0	3,520	7.6	54.5	5.6	356	66.3	935	32
Richmond County	GA	33,660	35,424	32,906	22.0	74.4	2.4	1.1	0.1	2,300	14.3	4,732	7.0	48.6	6.5	635	51.6	1,439	62
Rockdale County	GA	10,942	13,519	15,614	31.9	56.1	10.2	1.6	0.1	1,047	14.9	2,217	7.0	47.2	4.6	219	63.5	825	20
Hawaii Department of Education	HI	171,309	184,360	179,897	19.4	2.3	4.6	73.0	0.6	11,396	15.8	21,652	8.3	52.6	4.7	2,608	75.5	10,922	287
Boise Independent	ID	23,394	26,598	25,614	83.7	2.8	9.0	4.0	0.5	1,483	17.3	2,684	9.5	55.2	2.4	195	83.2	1,744	55
Meridian Joint	ID	14,802	23,854	33,432	88.8	1.7	5.8	2.9	0.7	1,706	19.6	3,279	10.2	52.0	1.5	133	85.0	1,773	51
Nampa	ID	7,878	11,403	15,202	68.1	1.2	28.7	1.4	0.7	777	19.6	1,310	11.6	59.3	5.5	195	56.1	547	28
Carpentersville (CUSD 300)	IL	11,196	16,711	19,594	61.8	5.1	27.7	5.2	0.3	918	21.3	1,319	14.9	69.6	1.9	100	92.2	1,176	27
City of Chicago	IL	408,714	435,261	407,510	8.2	47.9	40.2	3.4	0.2	20,924	19.5	26,974	15.1	77.6	10.5	11,505	56.7	17,065	631
Elgin (SD U-46)	IL	27,726	36,767	40,708	40.5	7.1	44.2	8.0	0.2	2,023	20.1	2,778	14.7	72.8	5.5	598	79.3	2,243	58
Indian Prairie (CUSD 204)	IL	7,670	23,173	29,127	66.6	9.2	7.0	17.0	0.1	1,560	18.7	2,148	13.6	72.6	0.8	59	95.9	1,700	31
Naperville CUSD 203	IL	16,212	18,762	18,211	76.3	4.4	4.6	14.6	0.1	940	19.4	1,368	13.3	68.7	0.9	57	95.5	1,055	21
Plainfield (SD 202)	IL	3,324	11,986	28,456	65.1	9.0	20.5	5.2	0.1	1,420	20.0	2,013	14.1	70.5	1.2	70	97.7	1,371	28
Rockford (SD 205)	IL	27,255	27,399	29,353	41.2	32.2	23.2	3.2	0.2	1,525	19.2	2,168	13.5	70.4	3.9	313	63.0	807	51
Springfield (SD 186)	IL	15,813	15,387	15,363	56.5	38.9	2.2	2.1	0.3	871	17.6	1,260	12.2	69.1	1.9	79	67.8	868	35
Valley View (CUSD 365)	IL	11,781	13,558	18,008	33.4	25.0	35.2	6.2	0.1	895	20.1	1,316	13.7	68.0	3.0	155	74.0	711	20
Waukegan (CUSD 60)	IL	12,116	15,510	17,046	6.9	17.9	73.5	1.5	0.1	818	20.8	1,156	14.8	70.8	3.5	142	62.0	865	24
Carmel Clay Schools	IN	8,449	12,073	15,026	84.9	3.1	2.0	9.8	0.1	867	17.3	2,279	6.6	38.0	0.5	20	88.9	1,288	17
Evansville-Vanderburgh Sch. Corp.	IN	22,918	22,855	22,265	81.3	15.6	1.7	1.2	0.3	1,473	15.1	2,857	7.8	51.6	0.1	9	73.5	1,699	42
Fort Wayne	IN	31,611	31,843	31,561	57.2	26.9	12.5	2.9	0.6	1,885	16.7	3,864	8.2	48.8	3.2	302	69.1	634	54
Hamilton Southeastern	IN	3,113	8,777	16,196	84.9	6.8	3.1	5.1	0.2	856	18.9	1,822	8.9	47.0	0.4	13	88.9	1,260	18
Indianapolis	IN	48,140	41,008	35,257	24.7	60.3	14.4	0.3	0.2	2,559	13.8	5,568	6.3	46.0	9.9	947	40.4	1,003	78
MSD Lawrence Township	IN	11,066	15,692	16,153	48.7	40.1	9.4	1.8	0.1	920	17.6	2,304	7.0	39.9	2.7	143	78.0	1,051	18
South Bend Community Sch. Corp.	IN	21,425	21,536	21,579	43.8	38.1	16.4	1.2	0.5	1,266	17.0	3,198	6.7	39.6	8.0	529	60.0	891	38
Vigo County School Corp.	IN	16,982	16,545	16,203	91.3	6.3	0.9	1.4	0.1	985	16.4	1,995	8.1	49.4	3.5	169	70.8	1,104	29
Cedar Rapids	IA	16,988	17,780	16,838	79.5	14.6	3.0	2.3	0.6	1,111	15.2	2,337	7.2	47.5	3.7	206	78.6	979	35
Davenport	IA	17,841	16,874	16,275	64.8	22.0	9.5	2.8	0.8	1,075	15.1	2,049	7.9	52.5	7.0	351	78.4	1,848	35
Des Moines Independent	IA	30,514	32,435	32,043	60.1	18.1	16.1	5.0	0.6	2,207	14.5	4,417	7.3	50.0	4.8	421	74.5	1,410	61
Blue Valley	KS	9,432	17,111	20,904	85.2	3.7	2.4	8.3	0.3	1,378	15.2	2,075	10.1	66.4	0.5	31	99.8	989	32
Kansas City	KS	21,948	21,173	19,965	16.6	43.1	36.6	3.2	0.5	1,390	14.4	2,036	9.8	68.3	5.8	333	58.3	1,506	45
Olathe	KS	14,868	20,703	26,160	80.4	5.9	9.2	4.2	0.3	1,980	13.2	3,084	8.5	64.2	1.0	69	87.9	2,134	47
Shawnee Mission	KS	30,563	30,765	27,798	77.0	8.6	10.6	3.0	0.8	1,936	14.4	2,835	9.8	68.3	0.8	81	84.9	2,444	48
Wichita	KS	46,847	48,228	46,788	43.7	22.2	25.1	5.6	3.4	2,945	15.9	4,617	10.1	63.8	5.4	739	66.1	—	90
Boone County	KY	9,911	13,445	18,037	91.3	2.9	3.3	2.3	0.2	1,107	16.3	2,360	7.6	46.9	3.0	140	—	—	21
Fayette County	KY	32,083	33,130	35,416	63.0	24.6	8.6	3.6	0.2	2,569	13.8	5,186	6.8	49.5	3.0	359	—	—	65
Jefferson County	KY	91,450	96,860	95,871	55.2	37.4	4.7	2.5	0.2	6,057	15.8	13,980	6.9	43.3	6.6	1,862	—	—	173
Ascension Parish	LA	13,001	15,038	18,595	64.2	30.3	4.4	0.8	0.3	1,299	14.3	2,473	7.5	52.5	5.9	271	79.4	882	23
Bossier Parish	LA	17,804	18,797	19,526	63.2	30.1	4.7	1.7	0.3	1,259	15.5	2,590	6.5	48.6	4.6	237	73.3	1,086	34
Caddo Parish	LA	51,375	45,119	42,865	33.3	64.2	1.3	1.0	0.2	2,883	14.9	6,594	6.5	43.7	9.8	1,107	57.7	2,034	76
Calcasieu Parish	LA	32,917	32,261	32,522	61.3	36.0	1.6	0.9	0.2	2,359	13.8	4,886	6.7	48.3	4.0	336	66.1	1,640	60
East Baton Rouge Parish	LA	61,669	54,246	45,714	11.8	83.2	2.4	2.5	0.1	3,090	14.8	6,164	7.4	50.1	12.0	1,461	63.8	2,407	90
Jefferson Parish	LA	58,177	50,891	43,468	32.4	49.6	12.1	5.1	0.8	3,101	14.0	6,587	6.6	47.1	11.1	1,230	51.2	1,918	86
Lafayette Parish	LA	29,403	28,931	29,762	52.4	42.9	2.8	1.6	0.3	2,270	13.1	4,279	7.0	53.1	9.5	793	70.2	1,608	44
Livingston Parish	LA	16,310	19,723	23,263	91.2	6.5	1.8	0.3	0.2	1,528	15.2	3,051	7.6	50.1	3.5	195	69.6	1,060	41
Ouachita Parish	LA	17,667	17,479	19,050	66.6	31.5	1.2	0.8	0.0	1,318	14.5	2,949	6.5	44.7	6.7	341	68.0	972	35
Rapides Parish	LA	24,765	23,467	23,384	52.6	43.3	1.9	1.2	0.9	1,693	13.8	3,384	6.9	50.0	9.7	615	68.8	1,193	52
Saint Landry Parish	LA	17,213	15,457	15,231	41.4	57.4	0.7	0.5	0.1	1,074	14.2	2,185	7.0	49.2	7.6	292	64.8	752	39

See notes at end of table.

Selected statistics on enrollment, teachers, dropouts, and graduates in public school districts enrolling more than 15,000 students: 1990, 2000, 2005–06, and 2007—Continued

Name of district	State	Enrollment, fall 1990	Enrollment, fall 2000	Enrollment, fall 2007	Percentage distribution of enrollment, by race, fall 2007					Teachers and staff, fall 2007					Dropouts and graduates, 2006				Number of schools, fall 2007
					White	Black	Hispanic	Asian/Pacific Islander	American Indian/Alaska Native	Number of classroom teachers	Pupil/teacher ratio	Total number of staff	Student/staff ratio	Teachers as a percentage of total staff	Percent dropouts from grades 9–12	Number of dropouts from grades 9–12	Averaged freshman graduation rate (AFGR)[1]	Number of high school graduates[2]	
1	2	3	4	5	6	7	8	9	10	11	12	13	14	15	16	17	18	19	20
Saint Tammany Parish	LA	27,522	32,392	35,170	76.8	18.5	2.8	1.5	0.4	2,592	13.6	5,223	6.7	49.6	3.7	372	72.2	1,994	52
Tangipahoa Parish	LA	16,724	18,197	19,576	50.7	46.5	2.0	0.6	0.2	1,208	16.2	2,587	7.6	46.7	9.0	461	71.6	974	37
Terrebonne Parish	LA	21,116	19,774	19,027	59.0	28.8	2.2	1.2	8.9	1,408	13.5	2,659	7.2	53.0	8.1	417	62.6	945	41
Anne Arundel County	MD	65,011	74,491	73,400	67.1	22.7	6.0	3.8	0.5	5,000	14.7	9,263	7.9	54.0	2.1	503	78.8	4,755	123
Baltimore City	MD	108,663	99,859	81,284	7.6	88.9	2.5	0.7	0.3	5,877	13.8	11,710	6.9	50.2	11.9	2,898	56.4	4,108	195
Baltimore County	MD	86,737	106,898	104,283	49.9	40.0	4.3	5.4	0.5	7,374	14.1	14,202	7.3	51.9	4.6	1,560	82.8	7,326	171
Calvert County	MD	10,398	16,170	17,394	79.0	17.0	2.0	1.7	0.3	1,126	15.4	2,222	7.8	50.7	2.3	134	86.0	1,195	27
Carroll County	MD	21,835	27,528	28,320	91.6	4.0	2.3	1.8	0.4	1,941	14.6	3,541	8.0	54.8	1.4	139	92.9	2,218	46
Cecil County	MD	12,868	15,905	16,290	85.6	9.8	3.1	1.2	0.3	1,174	13.9	2,217	7.3	52.9	4.7	235	74.6	945	29
Charles County	MD	18,708	23,468	26,676	40.9	51.6	3.5	3.3	0.8	1,725	15.5	3,246	8.2	53.1	3.6	319	90.9	1,925	36
Frederick County	MD	26,848	36,885	40,487	75.3	12.0	7.9	4.4	0.6	2,695	15.0	5,282	7.7	51.0	0.8	102	91.5	2,724	64
Harford County	MD	31,500	39,520	39,172	73.2	19.9	3.4	2.9	0.6	2,772	14.1	5,228	7.5	53.0	3.5	442	85.7	2,662	54
Howard County	MD	29,949	44,946	49,542	58.6	20.9	5.3	14.9	0.3	3,757	13.2	7,342	6.7	51.2	1.5	231	90.0	3,486	73
Montgomery County	MD	103,757	134,180	137,717	40.1	22.9	21.5	15.2	0.4	9,639	14.3	18,454	6.8	47.8	2.2	990	87.4	9,799	205
Prince George's County	MD	108,868	133,723	129,752	5.1	74.2	17.4	2.9	0.4	9,005	14.4	20,172	7.0	48.8	4.5	1,870	71.6	7,814	214
Saint Mary's County	MD	12,549	15,151	16,890	73.1	20.6	2.9	2.8	0.6	1,014	16.7	1,969	8.6	51.5	4.1	217	72.6	969	27
Washington County	MD	17,778	19,782	21,703	80.8	12.9	4.3	1.7	0.3	1,503	14.4	2,800	7.8	53.7	2.4	155	86.3	1,387	44
Boston	MA	60,543	63,024	56,168	13.6	40.0	37.3	8.6	0.5	4,372	12.8	7,792	7.2	56.1	10.0	1,877	64.8	3,255	138
Brockton	MA	14,529	16,791	15,338	32.6	49.5	14.5	2.6	0.8	1,125	13.6	2,085	7.4	53.9	7.0	310	61.0	837	23
Springfield	MA	24,194	26,526	25,233	17.5	25.0	55.2	2.2	0.1	2,208	11.4	3,583	7.0	61.6	8.3	557	44.7	955	44
Worcester	MA	21,066	25,828	22,876	41.7	13.2	36.6	8.0	0.4	1,602	14.3	2,837	8.1	56.5	4.3	307	69.1	1,312	44
Ann Arbor	MI	14,199	16,539	16,742	63.8	15.7	4.9	15.2	0.5	983	17.0	3,221	5.2	30.5	1.4	83	92.8	1,327	33
Chippewa Valley	MI	9,350	12,329	15,533	88.6	6.5	2.1	2.5	0.2	734	21.2	1,345	11.5	54.5	0.9	42	85.5	896	19
Dearborn City	MI	13,380	17,129	18,277	92.4	4.3	2.2	0.8	0.3	1,117	16.4	2,168	8.4	51.5	2.0	112	73.6	1,094	36
Detroit City	MI	168,116	162,194	107,874	2.5	89.1	7.2	0.8	0.3	6,406	16.8	14,817	7.3	43.2	7.6	2,990	43.0	5,866	199
Flint City	MI	27,601	22,532	16,774	15.5	81.2	2.4	0.4	0.5	1,044	16.1	2,542	6.6	41.1	4.4	216	40.1	611	48
Grand Rapids	MI	26,250	25,625	20,300	22.4	44.7	30.3	1.3	1.2	1,363	14.9	2,849	7.1	47.9	7.1	458	35.8	693	77
Lansing	MI	21,350	17,610	15,545	32.1	46.6	15.8	4.3	1.2	922	16.9	1,943	8.0	47.5	6.1	294	49.7	700	37
Livonia	MI	16,373	18,347	17,058	88.9	6.3	1.7	2.9	0.4	962	17.7	2,086	8.2	46.1	3.2	202	83.6	1,368	28
Plymouth-Canton	MI	14,955	16,518	19,140	77.5	7.9	2.7	12.2	0.2	964	19.9	1,920	10.0	50.2	2.7	156	85.8	1,198	27
Rochester	MI	10,726	13,862	15,033	80.8	5.2	2.7	11.1	0.2	809	18.6	1,750	8.6	46.2	1.5	70	94.7	1,059	22
Utica	MI	23,960	27,786	29,605	91.8	3.8	1.5	2.7	0.1	1,449	20.4	3,011	9.8	48.1	1.4	133	90.2	2,040	43
Walled Lake Consolidated	MI	9,059	14,438	15,650	84.7	6.9	2.3	5.8	0.3	865	18.1	1,749	9.0	49.4	2.5	126	91.7	1,094	26
Warren Consolidated	MI	14,336	14,602	15,578	82.3	10.2	0.9	6.2	0.5	820	19.0	1,567	9.9	52.3	1.0	55	86.1	1,091	59
Anoka-Hennepin	MN	34,524	41,314	40,719	80.9	8.5	3.2	6.2	1.3	2,431	16.8	4,751	8.6	51.2	2.9	399	87.6	2,833	107
Minneapolis	MN	36,763	48,834	35,631	30.0	39.3	17.2	9.0	4.5	2,227	16.0	5,297	6.7	42.1	10.4	1,277	54.4	1,829	32
Osseo	MN	19,483	22,017	22,053	57.2	22.6	6.1	13.4	0.7	1,303	16.9	2,664	8.3	48.9	2.2	156	79.2	1,381	44
Robbinsdale	MN	13,897	15,929	16,203	72.4	11.2	6.6	9.4	0.4	978	16.6	1,990	8.1	49.2	2.3	127	84.5	1,170	36
Rosemount-Apple Valley-Eagan	MN	17,029	28,330	27,954	79.8	8.0	4.9	6.9	0.5	1,720	16.2	3,394	8.2	50.7	1.8	167	91.8	2,073	44
Saint Paul	MN	32,366	45,115	40,107	25.3	30.3	13.4	29.2	1.8	2,626	15.3	5,851	6.9	44.9	5.1	692	70.0	2,365	123
South Washington County	MN	11,260	14,953	17,137	78.3	7.2	5.1	8.9	0.6	1,008	17.0	1,890	9.1	53.4	1.8	88	91.6	1,085	24
Desoto County	MS	13,470	19,812	29,886	65.4	27.9	5.2	1.3	0.2	1,634	18.3	3,477	8.6	47.0	0.6	42	67.5	1,143	34
Jackson	MS	33,546	31,351	31,191	1.7	97.5	0.6	0.2	#	1,960	15.9	4,721	6.6	41.5	4.1	333	49.7	1,177	61
Rankin County	MS	12,824	15,013	17,876	75.5	21.8	1.4	1.2	0.1	1,218	14.7	2,183	8.2	55.8	1.2	54	65.9	788	25
Columbia 93	MO	12,786	16,178	17,186	67.5	22.6	4.2	5.4	0.3	1,347	12.8	2,562	6.7	52.6	3.8	198	91.4	1,115	31
Fort Zumwalt R-II	MO	10,110	16,521	18,742	89.5	6.1	2.1	2.0	0.2	1,169	16.0	2,397	7.8	48.8	2.3	136	84.8	1,254	24
Francis Howell R-III	MO	13,391	19,497	22,092	90.0	5.1	2.1	2.6	0.1	1,038	21.3	1,977	11.2	52.5	2.2	133	88.4	1,302	28
Hazelwood	MO	16,985	18,855	19,270	30.2	67.2	1.5	1.0	0.1	1,251	15.4	2,493	7.7	50.2	3.8	250	69.1	1,137	30
Kansas City 33	MO	34,486	37,298	25,094	14.1	62.3	21.3	2.0	0.3	1,980	12.7	4,078	6.2	48.6	12.4	1,011	59.1	1,560	69
Lee's Summit R-VII	MO	7,132	14,340	17,204	81.6	12.4	3.9	2.2	0.3	1,137	15.1	2,833	6.1	40.1	1.9	97	93.8	1,128	25
North Kansas City 74	MO	15,732	17,258	17,894	71.7	12.4	10.5	4.3	1.2	1,264	14.2	2,610	6.9	48.4	3.9	214	94.7	1,260	30
Parkway C-2	MO	21,542	20,433	17,927	70.0	16.7	2.2	10.9	0.2	1,182	15.2	2,505	7.2	47.2	1.7	107	88.6	1,427	28

See notes at end of table.

Selected statistics on enrollment, teachers, dropouts, and graduates in public school districts enrolling more than 15,000 students: 1990, 2000, 2005–06, and 2007—Continued

Name of district	State	Enrollment, fall 1990	Enrollment, fall 2000	Enrollment, fall 2007	White	Black	Hispanic	Asian/ Pacific Islander	American Indian/ Alaska Native	Number of classroom teachers	Pupil/ teacher ratio	Total number of staff	Student/ staff ratio	Teachers as a percentage of total staff	Percent dropouts from grades 9–12	Number of dropouts from grades 9–12	Averaged freshman graduation rate (AFGR)[1]	Number of high school graduates[2]	Number of schools, fall 2007
1	2	3	4	5	6	7	8	9	10	11	12	13	14	15	16	17	18	19	20
Rockwood R-VI	MO	15,608	21,203	22,721	82.4	11.1	1.8	4.6	0.2	1,432	15.9	3,166	7.2	45.2	1.3	96	89.2	1,659	31
Saint Louis City	MO	43,284	44,412	27,616	13.6	81.4	2.6	2.2	0.3	2,392	11.5	3,890	7.1	61.5	18.9	1,966	51.4	1,622	96
Springfield R-XII	MO	23,631	24,630	24,295	86.3	7.2	3.4	2.5	0.6	1,596	15.2	3,111	7.8	51.3	6.7	501	81.2	1,555	54
Lincoln	NE	27,986	31,354	33,466	77.5	9.5	7.3	4.1	1.6	2,439	13.7	4,553	7.4	53.6	4.2	421	87.4	1,989	64
Millard	NE	16,764	19,160	22,027	88.1	3.1	4.2	4.2	0.3	1,420	15.5	2,414	9.1	58.8	1.5	101	95.5	1,442	36
Omaha	NE	41,699	45,197	47,763	41.0	31.8	23.9	1.8	1.6	3,333	14.3	7,468	6.4	44.6	7.4	1,013	65.4	2,423	98
Clark County	NV	121,959	231,655	309,051	36.1	14.2	39.7	9.2	0.8	16,427	18.8	19,684	15.7	83.5	9.7	7,750	54.5	10,943	341
Washoe County	NV	38,466	56,268	65,663	54.5	3.8	32.8	6.4	2.5	3,641	18.0	4,267	15.4	85.3	3.1	590	54.0	2,725	104
Manchester	NH	14,604	17,407	16,309	76.7	7.8	12.1	3.0	0.5	1,135	14.4	1,907	8.6	59.5	5.3	373	—	—	22
Elizabeth	NJ	15,266	19,674	21,303	8.9	24.2	65.0	1.8	#	1,912	11.1	3,043	7.0	62.8	5.7	298	60.1	939	30
Jersey City	NJ	28,585	31,347	28,117	10.5	35.8	38.5	14.0	0.2	2,507	11.2	4,188	6.7	59.9	5.5	387	76.2	1,488	38
Newark	NJ	48,433	42,150	40,507	7.5	58.0	33.6	0.9	0.1	2,844	14.2	4,076	9.9	69.8	1.4	165	66.2	2,117	74
Paterson	NJ	22,109	24,629	24,087	5.7	34.5	57.1	2.6	0.2	2,250	10.7	3,424	7.0	65.7	2.2	134	40.7	818	39
Toms River Regional	NJ	16,002	17,621	17,097	84.8	4.3	7.3	3.5	0.1	991	17.3	1,304	13.1	76.0	3.0	178	86.2	1,312	18
Albuquerque	NM	88,295	85,276	95,965	31.8	4.0	56.6	2.4	5.2	6,335	15.1	13,210	7.3	48.0	8.5	2,313	63.7	4,643	171
Las Cruces	NM	19,216	22,185	24,384	24.4	2.4	71.3	1.1	0.8	1,633	14.9	3,287	7.4	49.7	2.6	184	66.2	1,268	38
Rio Rancho	NM	—	10,219	15,653	48.3	4.4	40.9	2.3	4.1	1,063	14.7	1,870	8.4	56.9	6.4	265	90.8	876	16
Brentwood Union Free	NY	11,749	15,565	15,874	10.5	17.7	69.5	2.0	0.3	1,230	12.9	2,456	6.5	50.1	5.7	281	69.1	844	17
Buffalo City	NY	47,235	45,721	35,677	24.6	57.2	14.9	1.7	1.5	2,988	11.9	5,268	6.8	56.7	9.6	945	46.9	1,623	61
New York City	NY	944,113	1,066,516	989,941	14.2	31.7	39.7	14.0	0.4	60,593	16.3	76,673	12.9	79.0	†	†	—	—	1,454
Rochester City	NY	32,705	36,294	32,924	11.3	65.4	21.2	1.8	0.3	2,969	11.1	5,713	5.8	52.0	12.8	1,190	40.9	1,178	60
Sachem Central	NY	15,187	14,948	15,182	85.6	1.7	8.1	4.5	0.2	1,122	13.5	2,056	7.4	54.6	2.0	99	88.5	1,110	18
Syracuse City	NY	22,432	23,015	20,645	30.6	54.3	10.7	2.9	1.4	1,819	11.3	4,084	5.1	44.5	7.7	467	38.8	694	34
Yonkers City	NY	18,621	26,237	24,153	18.1	26.2	49.5	6.0	0.2	1,762	13.7	3,570	6.8	49.4	7.1	496	59.6	1,159	39
Alamance-Burlington	NC	10,322	20,729	22,704	57.1	23.6	17.4	1.5	0.3	1,511	15.0	2,909	7.8	52.0	6.1	418	—	—	35
Buncombe County	NC	22,026	24,708	25,366	83.7	6.1	8.4	1.3	0.5	1,665	15.2	3,593	7.1	46.4	—	—	—	—	41
Cabarrus County	NC	12,853	19,115	27,096	69.1	17.4	11.3	1.9	0.4	1,837	14.8	3,478	7.8	52.8	4.6	318	—	—	34
Catawba County	NC	12,770	16,250	17,610	77.1	6.5	8.8	7.4	0.3	1,135	15.5	2,168	8.1	52.3	4.4	228	—	—	28
Charlotte-Mecklenburg	NC	77,069	103,336	131,176	35.8	43.7	15.4	4.6	0.5	9,147	14.3	17,945	7.3	51.0	—	—	—	—	161
Cleveland County	NC	8,131	9,663	16,675	67.4	28.5	3.0	0.9	0.2	1,198	13.9	2,436	6.8	49.2	7.5	391	—	—	28
Cumberland County	NC	44,612	50,850	53,295	38.8	49.7	7.5	2.0	2.0	3,692	14.4	7,547	7.1	48.9	—	—	—	—	89
Davidson County	NC	16,426	19,136	20,539	91.5	2.9	4.3	1.0	0.3	1,243	16.5	2,440	8.4	50.9	6.4	379	—	—	31
Durham Public	NC	18,517	29,728	32,473	23.6	55.9	17.6	2.7	0.2	2,272	14.3	4,500	7.2	50.5	—	—	—	—	50
Forsyth County	NC	37,625	44,769	51,738	47.5	33.5	16.9	1.9	0.2	3,847	13.5	7,335	7.1	52.4	—	—	—	—	77
Gaston County	NC	29,631	30,603	32,182	70.3	20.8	7.3	1.5	0.3	2,073	15.5	3,991	8.1	51.9	—	—	—	—	53
Guilford County	NC	24,575	63,417	72,389	41.9	42.9	9.1	5.6	0.5	5,023	14.4	10,083	7.2	49.8	—	—	—	—	120
Harnett County	NC	11,890	16,338	18,408	57.1	28.6	12.7	0.6	1.1	1,260	14.6	2,347	7.8	53.7	6.8	346	—	—	26
Iredell-Statesville	NC	10,610	17,235	21,272	73.5	14.8	8.8	2.7	0.4	1,443	14.7	2,768	7.7	52.1	5.0	294	—	—	35
Johnston County	NC	14,647	21,334	30,303	65.0	18.4	15.6	0.6	0.4	2,116	14.3	3,922	7.7	53.9	5.7	417	—	—	39
Nash-Rocky Mount	NC	11,653	18,342	18,027	37.2	53.9	7.1	1.3	0.5	1,157	15.6	2,371	7.6	48.8	7.2	390	—	—	28
New Hanover County	NC	19,090	21,605	23,712	66.6	25.6	5.9	1.5	0.4	1,670	14.2	3,586	6.6	46.6	4.5	336	—	—	39
Onslow County	NC	18,605	20,984	23,605	67.4	23.0	7.2	1.5	0.8	1,540	15.3	3,184	7.4	48.4	5.1	335	—	—	33
Pitt County	NC	17,629	20,040	22,835	40.6	50.7	7.2	1.4	0.2	1,654	13.8	3,186	7.2	51.9	6.9	454	—	—	35
Randolph County	NC	13,572	17,271	19,143	82.6	4.4	11.2	1.2	0.6	1,230	15.6	2,447	7.8	50.2	6.1	328	—	—	29
Robeson County	NC	23,251	23,911	24,140	17.9	28.5	8.3	0.6	44.7	1,597	15.1	3,280	7.4	48.7	8.4	564	—	—	43
Rowan-Salisbury	NC	16,403	20,472	20,980	68.7	20.6	9.2	0.9	0.3	1,452	14.4	2,901	7.2	50.1	5.0	329	—	—	34
Union County	NC	12,864	22,862	37,053	71.5	14.9	11.8	1.5	0.3	2,499	14.8	4,867	7.6	51.4	4.6	404	—	—	47
Wake County	NC	64,266	98,950	134,401	54.7	27.7	11.6	5.8	0.3	9,020	14.9	16,556	8.1	54.5	4.3	1,470	—	—	153
Wayne County	NC	13,653	19,279	19,401	46.9	40.1	11.5	1.2	0.2	1,350	14.4	2,656	7.3	50.8	6.1	347	—	—	33

See notes at end of table.

Selected statistics on enrollment, teachers, dropouts, and graduates in public school districts enrolling more than 15,000 students: 1990, 2000, 2005–06, and 2007—Continued

Name of district	State	Enrollment, fall 1990	Enrollment, fall 2000	Enrollment, fall 2007	Percentage distribution of enrollment, by race, fall 2007					Teachers and staff, fall 2007					Dropouts and graduates, 2006				Number of schools, fall 2007
					White	Black	Hispanic	Asian/ Pacific Islander	American Indian/ Alaska Native	Number of classroom teachers	Pupil/ teacher ratio	Total number of staff	Student/ staff ratio	Teachers as a percentage of total staff	Percent dropouts from grades 9–12	Number of dropouts from grades 9–12	Averaged freshman graduation rate (AFGR)[1]	Number of high school graduates[2]	
1	2	3	4	5	6	7	8	9	10	11	12	13	14	15	16	17	18	19	20
Akron City	OH	33,213	31,464	25,408	45.1	51.2	1.5	2.1	0.1	1,751	14.5	5,375	4.7	32.6	5.3	429	68.2	1,495	60
Cincinnati City	OH	50,394	46,562	35,435	25.0	72.3	1.7	0.9	0.1	1,930	18.4	4,446	8.0	43.4	4.5	498	49.8	1,725	64
Cleveland Municipal City	OH	68,924	75,684	52,954	15.9	71.5	11.7	0.6	0.3	3,512	15.1	7,713	6.9	45.5	9.7	1,644	43.8	2,451	106
Columbus City	OH	63,956	64,511	55,269	28.5	63.6	5.7	1.9	0.2	2,962	18.7	7,317	7.6	40.5	8.1	1,315	57.2	2,763	136
Dayton City	OH	28,000	23,522	15,920	25.7	71.0	2.8	0.4	#	889	17.9	2,453	6.5	36.2	2.2	109	46.5	778	34
Hilliard City	OH	6,533	12,423	15,149	84.3	6.1	3.8	5.6	0.2	869	17.4	1,672	9.1	52.0	1.3	55	97.0	952	21
Lakota Local	OH	9,356	14,659	18,261	82.1	9.2	3.4	5.1	0.1	879	20.8	1,818	10.0	48.4	0.9	45	91.9	1,072	21
South-Western City	OH	16,605	19,216	21,607	76.3	12.3	9.3	1.9	0.3	1,118	19.3	2,441	8.9	45.8	2.7	174	75.9	1,158	36
Toledo City	OH	40,126	37,738	28,251	42.4	48.5	8.3	0.7	0.1	1,922	14.7	3,790	7.5	50.7	1.8	162	53.3	1,591	65
Broken Arrow	OK	13,872	14,990	16,020	75.7	5.3	6.2	2.9	9.9	1,003	16.0	1,989	8.1	50.4	4.1	183	81.9	909	22
Edmond	OK	13,041	17,084	19,917	75.6	11.3	4.9	4.4	3.8	1,156	17.2	2,300	8.7	50.2	1.0	60	92.9	1,364	23
Lawton	OK	17,727	17,338	16,461	46.8	32.2	11.1	2.4	7.4	1,117	14.7	2,355	7.0	47.4	4.0	187	76.5	984	35
Moore	OK	16,630	18,101	20,923	65.8	7.2	9.4	5.1	12.5	1,222	17.1	2,281	9.2	53.6	2.1	123	78.3	1,123	28
Oklahoma City	OK	36,038	39,750	40,985	23.1	30.8	38.3	2.7	5.1	2,536	16.2	4,848	8.5	52.3	4.8	449	58.5	1,619	94
Putnam City	OK	18,071	19,506	18,774	52.3	24.8	14.3	4.4	4.2	1,206	15.6	2,193	8.6	55.0	2.8	161	70.3	1,181	26
Tulsa	OK	40,732	42,812	41,271	34.2	35.1	19.4	1.5	9.9	2,698	15.3	5,926	7.0	45.5	9.5	903	62.1	1,819	89
Beaverton	OR	24,874	33,600	37,821	63.0	3.1	18.9	14.4	0.6	2,158	17.5	4,016	9.4	53.7	3.6	415	75.7	2,023	52
Bend-Lapine Administrative	OR	9,481	13,128	15,843	87.5	0.8	8.9	1.7	1.0	756	20.9	1,574	10.1	48.0	2.3	115	84.8	914	26
Eugene	OR	17,904	18,432	18,025	80.0	2.9	8.4	6.1	2.5	848	21.3	1,899	9.5	44.7	2.4	140	81.4	1,264	43
Hillsboro	OR	10,396	18,315	20,246	58.9	2.3	30.9	7.2	0.7	983	20.6	2,048	9.9	48.0	3.6	205	85.1	1,146	35
North Clackamas	OR	12,403	14,876	17,651	76.1	2.5	12.3	7.8	1.2	881	20.0	1,845	9.6	47.8	3.5	179	67.6	883	32
Portland	OR	53,042	53,141	46,262	57.0	15.9	14.2	11.2	1.7	2,623	17.6	5,247	8.8	50.0	8.6	1,104	73.4	2,545	92
Salem-Keizer	OR	27,756	35,108	40,106	59.7	1.2	32.8	4.5	1.8	2,087	19.2	4,492	8.9	46.5	8.0	868	69.9	1,958	68
Allentown City	PA	13,519	16,424	17,892	19.6	17.2	61.6	1.5	0.2	954	18.7	1,994	9.0	47.9	8.2	460	—	—	22
Bethlehem Area	PA	12,220	14,165	15,306	54.9	9.5	32.3	3.1	0.2	1,047	14.6	1,951	7.8	53.7	4.1	207	—	—	22
Central Bucks	PA	10,286	17,305	20,357	91.8	1.7	2.2	4.2	0.1	1,229	16.6	2,398	8.5	51.3	0.8	48	—	—	23
Philadelphia	PA	190,978	201,190	172,704	13.4	63.4	16.9	6.1	0.2	10,665	16.2	21,593	8.0	49.4	9.2	5,164	—	—	272
Pittsburgh	PA	39,896	38,560	27,680	38.1	59.0	1.1	1.6	0.3	2,317	11.9	4,827	5.7	48.0	3.3	331	—	—	68
Reading	PA	11,965	15,487	17,464	11.7	12.9	74.6	0.8	#	1,197	14.6	2,215	7.9	54.1	7.3	320	—	—	21
Providence	RI	20,908	26,937	24,494	11.8	22.2	59.6	5.7	0.7	1,501	16.3	1,676	14.6	89.6	7.5	582	63.6	1,381	53
Aiken 01	SC	23,964	25,147	24,806	58.0	36.0	4.9	0.8	0.3	1,430	17.3	2,161	11.5	66.2	—	—	—	—	41
Beaufort 01	SC	12,525	16,721	19,521	44.1	36.2	18.3	1.2	0.3	1,219	16.0	1,520	12.8	80.2	—	—	—	—	28
Berkeley 01	SC	27,392	26,635	28,467	55.8	35.5	6.1	2.3	0.3	1,515	18.8	2,214	12.9	68.4	—	—	—	—	35
Charleston 01	SC	43,667	44,767	42,216	51.5	41.5	5.1	1.5	0.3	3,006	14.0	4,191	10.1	71.7	—	—	—	—	80
Dorchester 02	SC	13,737	16,678	21,201	62.3	30.6	3.9	2.7	0.6	1,249	17.0	1,516	14.0	82.4	—	—	—	—	19
Florence 01	SC	14,736	13,930	15,456	44.2	52.3	1.5	1.8	0.2	1,029	15.0	1,590	9.7	64.7	—	—	—	—	23
Greenville 01	SC	51,471	59,875	69,444	60.6	26.9	9.8	2.4	0.2	4,297	16.2	5,840	11.9	73.6	—	—	—	—	91
Horry 01	SC	24,085	29,894	37,200	67.8	23.5	6.7	1.4	0.6	2,135	17.4	3,265	11.4	65.4	—	—	—	—	48
Lexington 01	SC	11,204	17,285	20,995	83.4	9.6	4.3	2.2	0.5	1,358	15.5	1,811	11.6	75.0	—	—	—	—	24
Lexington 05	SC	11,688	15,064	16,895	65.9	29.2	2.2	2.6	0.2	1,106	15.3	1,450	11.6	76.2	—	—	—	—	19
Pickens 01	SC	14,298	15,938	16,658	88.2	9.6	3.5	1.3	0.4	1,073	15.5	1,454	11.5	73.8	—	—	—	—	25
Richland 01	SC	27,071	27,061	24,328	18.1	78.3	2.5	0.9	0.1	1,625	15.0	2,110	11.5	77.0	—	—	—	—	50
Richland 02	SC	12,792	17,409	23,854	32.4	59.5	5.1	2.8	0.1	1,606	14.9	1,950	12.2	82.3	—	—	—	—	26
York 03	SC	12,690	14,925	17,356	54.3	37.1	5.2	1.8	1.5	957	18.1	1,228	14.1	77.9	—	—	—	—	26
Sioux Falls	SD	16,120	19,097	19,947	81.0	6.9	5.4	2.4	4.4	1,499	13.3	2,463	8.1	60.9	5.8	355	80.9	1,226	48
Davidson County	TN	67,452	67,669	73,715	34.1	48.1	14.3	3.2	0.2	5,034	14.6	9,972	7.4	50.5	5.1	1,018	61.2	3,172	137
Hamilton County	TN	22,874	39,915	41,230	59.6	33.7	4.6	1.9	0.2	2,841	14.5	5,946	6.9	47.8	6.4	764	66.8	2,143	76
Knox County	TN	50,429	51,944	54,490	79.8	14.7	3.3	1.9	0.3	3,734	14.6	6,991	7.8	53.4	4.0	666	75.8	3,087	86
Memphis City	TN	106,223	113,790	115,342	7.1	86.2	5.3	1.2	0.1	7,208	16.0	13,135	8.8	54.9	4.9	1,694	65.2	5,740	190
Montgomery County	TN	17,532	23,339	28,505	62.0	27.6	7.3	2.6	0.6	1,862	15.3	3,597	7.9	51.8	2.5	192	72.2	1,341	32
Rutherford County	TN	18,228	25,356	35,595	72.8	15.6	7.6	3.8	0.2	2,324	15.3	3,657	9.7	63.5	2.0	219	83.3	2,188	42
Shelby County	TN	37,605	46,972	46,918	55.5	36.0	3.9	4.2	0.4	2,976	15.8	5,266	8.9	56.5	0.3	33	70.9	2,533	50

See notes at end of table.

Selected statistics on enrollment, teachers, dropouts, and graduates in public school districts enrolling more than 15,000 students: 1990, 2000, 2005–06, and 2007—Continued

Name of district	State	Enrollment, fall 1990	Enrollment, fall 2000	Enrollment, fall 2007	Percentage distribution of enrollment, by race, fall 2007					Teachers and staff, fall 2007					Dropouts and graduates, 2006				Number of schools, fall 2007
					White	Black	Hispanic	Asian/Pacific Islander	American Indian/Alaska Native	Number of classroom teachers	Pupil/teacher ratio	Total number of staff	Student/staff ratio	Teachers as a percentage of total staff	Percent dropouts from grades 9–12	Number of dropouts from grades 9–12	Averaged freshman graduation rate (AFGR)[1]	Number of high school graduates[2]	
1	2	3	4	5	6	7	8	9	10	11	12	13	14	15	16	17	18	19	20
Sumner County	TN	19,650	22,347	26,485	85.1	9.6	3.9	1.2	0.2	1,783	14.9	3,646	7.3	48.9	2.2	167	78.3	1,511	42
Williamson County	TN	11,502	19,545	28,556	88.9	4.3	3.0	3.7	0.1	1,819	15.7	3,369	8.5	54.0	1.4	117	(³)	1,934	37
Abilene ISD	TX	18,217	18,118	16,532	49.3	13.9	34.8	1.5	0.6	1,252	13.2	2,467	6.7	50.8	5.0	224	68.0	900	44
Aldine ISD	TX	41,372	52,520	60,083	3.6	30.5	64.0	1.8	0.1	4,011	15.0	8,140	7.4	49.3	6.1	857	55.4	2,245	70
Alief ISD	TX	29,774	42,151	45,183	3.9	35.9	47.6	12.4	0.1	3,066	14.7	5,942	7.6	51.6	6.1	758	61.1	2,113	45
Allen ISD	TX	4,859	10,604	17,102	65.7	10.8	12.3	10.6	0.7	1,117	15.3	1,953	8.8	57.2	0.5	24	(³)	982	21
Alvin ISD	TX	8,634	11,324	15,329	41.2	10.8	42.4	5.4	0.2	981	15.6	1,979	7.7	49.6	2.5	86	63.6	600	20
Amarillo ISD	TX	27,374	28,908	30,560	44.4	11.4	41.0	2.9	0.3	2,155	14.2	3,906	7.8	55.2	5.9	469	71.1	1,528	55
Arlington ISD	TX	44,958	58,866	62,863	31.4	23.9	37.2	7.1	0.5	4,069	15.5	8,126	7.7	50.1	3.8	661	66.4	3,259	76
Austin ISD	TX	65,797	77,816	82,564	26.4	12.1	58.1	3.3	0.2	5,836	14.1	11,100	7.4	52.6	5.2	1,068	65.4	3,862	119
Beaumont ISD	TX	18,684	20,696	19,292	17.3	64.5	14.8	3.2	0.2	1,439	13.4	2,897	6.7	49.7	7.6	422	60.4	978	36
Birdville ISD	TX	18,466	21,246	22,063	56.1	6.9	30.6	5.7	0.7	1,447	15.3	2,782	7.9	52.0	2.8	187	69.7	1,258	34
Brownsville ISD	TX	34,906	40,898	48,837	1.5	0.2	98.0	0.3	#	3,273	14.9	7,323	6.7	44.7	6.0	732	60.4	1,916	54
Carrollton-Farmers Branch ISD	TX	16,234	24,134	26,397	24.0	14.1	50.3	11.1	0.4	1,848	15.3	3,368	7.8	54.9	2.1	158	70.0	1,447	45
Clear Creek ISD	TX	22,372	29,875	36,351	61.1	8.9	19.5	10.2	0.3	2,363	15.4	4,402	8.2	53.7	0.8	83	84.4	2,183	41
Comal ISD	TX	5,450	10,695	15,151	67.4	2.2	28.9	1.1	0.3	995	15.2	1,967	7.7	50.6	1.6	65	88.8	890	18
Conroe ISD	TX	23,288	34,928	46,524	63.4	6.7	26.1	3.4	0.5	2,927	15.9	5,546	8.4	52.8	2.2	277	82.5	2,523	51
Corpus Christi ISD	TX	41,881	39,138	38,693	16.4	5.3	76.3	1.8	0.2	2,430	15.9	5,015	7.7	48.5	5.0	525	68.2	2,041	62
Cypress-Fairbanks ISD	TX	41,196	63,497	96,837	38.8	15.2	37.1	8.6	0.3	6,258	15.5	12,059	8.0	51.9	1.4	335	57.5	4,768	75
Dallas ISD	TX	135,320	161,548	157,804	4.8	28.7	65.3	1.0	0.2	11,392	13.9	20,830	7.6	54.7	7.9	3,133	52.3	6,343	249
Denton ISD	TX	10,690	13,645	20,892	54.7	12.2	29.9	2.5	0.7	1,631	12.8	2,949	7.1	55.3	1.8	85	67.9	768	33
Ector County ISD	TX	26,993	26,831	26,680	30.6	5.3	62.5	0.8	0.1	1,720	15.5	3,320	8.0	51.8	7.4	545	59.4	1,272	39
Edinburg CISD	TX	13,685	22,005	29,858	1.9	0.4	96.9	0.7	0.1	1,983	15.1	4,187	7.1	47.4	4.2	283	70.0	1,197	39
El Paso ISD	TX	64,092	62,325	62,123	12.2	4.8	81.3	1.4	0.3	4,405	14.1	8,714	7.1	50.6	3.9	731	68.8	3,328	93
Fort Bend ISD	TX	36,270	53,999	67,992	24.3	31.8	23.1	20.6	0.2	4,320	15.7	8,933	7.6	48.4	2.2	471	91.1	4,613	67
Fort Worth ISD	TX	69,163	79,661	78,857	14.3	25.6	58.2	1.6	0.3	5,003	15.8	10,318	7.6	48.5	6.0	1,201	59.1	3,556	148
Frisco ISD	TX	1,310	7,234	27,418	62.8	12.0	13.7	11.0	0.6	1,971	13.9	3,549	7.7	55.5	1.1	47	(³)	713	39
Galena Park ISD	TX	15,593	18,885	21,114	6.9	20.3	71.4	1.3	0.1	1,545	13.7	2,972	7.1	52.0	3.8	221	74.0	1,147	24
Garland ISD	TX	37,978	50,312	57,169	30.5	18.5	42.7	7.8	0.5	3,806	15.0	7,255	7.9	52.5	3.0	491	77.8	3,363	75
Goose Creek CISD	TX	17,654	18,003	20,354	29.4	19.3	49.8	1.2	0.2	1,356	15.0	2,642	7.7	51.3	5.6	307	65.3	914	28
Grand Prairie ISD	TX	16,482	20,257	25,317	17.4	17.0	61.3	3.7	0.6	1,649	15.4	3,049	8.3	54.1	6.3	400	62.3	1,108	38
Harlingen CISD	TX	13,805	15,857	17,894	8.6	0.7	89.8	0.8	0.1	1,161	15.4	2,532	7.1	45.9	5.6	272	66.1	868	29
Houston ISD	TX	194,435	208,462	199,534	8.0	28.4	60.3	3.2	0.1	11,971	16.7	24,294	8.2	49.3	8.1	4,012	53.4	7,853	294
Humble ISD	TX	19,560	24,684	32,970	54.3	17.4	24.6	3.4	0.4	2,330	14.2	4,360	7.6	53.4	2.7	241	84.7	1,773	43
Hurst-Euless-Bedford ISD	TX	18,733	19,203	20,392	51.2	15.0	23.2	9.7	0.9	1,299	15.7	2,423	8.4	53.6	2.0	113	82.7	1,204	32
Irving ISD	TX	23,509	29,097	32,746	16.0	12.2	67.3	4.1	0.4	2,270	14.4	3,304	9.9	68.7	4.2	355	65.2	1,502	39
Judson ISD	TX	13,145	16,603	20,634	22.3	27.3	47.6	2.5	0.3	1,447	14.3	2,858	7.2	50.6	4.3	221	68.8	942	25
Katy ISD	TX	19,507	34,503	54,402	50.8	9.6	29.7	9.7	0.2	3,674	14.8	6,788	8.0	54.1	1.4	204	93.4	2,941	53
Keller ISD	TX	8,212	17,083	29,458	68.2	7.6	16.2	7.1	0.9	1,817	16.2	3,258	9.0	55.8	2.1	148	91.4	1,424	34
Killeen ISD	TX	22,131	29,687	38,229	36.5	38.4	20.5	3.9	0.7	2,712	14.1	5,545	6.9	48.9	5.4	452	72.3	1,435	53
Klein ISD	TX	26,220	32,376	42,935	45.1	15.6	30.5	8.5	0.3	2,789	15.4	5,383	8.0	51.8	2.8	340	79.5	2,494	41
La Joya ISD	TX	8,523	17,641	26,109	0.2	0.0	99.7	0.0	#	1,771	14.7	3,725	7.0	47.6	7.5	428	63.2	872	33
Lamar CISD	TX	12,335	15,159	21,936	31.4	18.7	45.2	4.5	0.2	1,366	16.1	2,712	8.1	50.4	3.6	198	81.3	1,049	30
Laredo ISD	TX	23,304	22,547	25,148	0.3	0.1	99.5	0.1	#	1,583	15.9	3,858	6.5	41.0	5.4	307	58.1	959	30
Leander ISD	TX	5,419	14,499	26,551	69.9	5.3	19.7	4.5	0.5	1,877	14.1	3,387	7.8	55.4	2.7	154	85.8	1,052	32
Lewisville ISD	TX	20,776	39,096	49,636	61.1	8.9	20.4	9.1	0.5	3,578	13.9	5,896	8.4	60.7	4.1	181	85.1	2,684	63
Lubbock ISD	TX	30,786	29,026	28,601	34.3	14.9	48.7	1.8	0.3	2,062	13.9	3,725	7.7	55.4	4.1	324	78.3	1,647	60
Mansfield ISD	TX	7,570	14,888	29,696	47.1	26.3	20.3	5.8	0.5	1,839	16.1	3,448	8.6	53.3	1.9	138	91.4	1,373	36
McAllen ISD	TX	18,432	21,747	24,973	6.1	0.5	91.4	1.9	0.1	1,743	14.3	3,501	7.1	49.8	5.5	356	68.0	1,213	32
McKinney ISD	TX	4,703	12,000	22,426	62.3	12.1	22.0	3.1	0.5	1,587	14.1	2,452	9.1	64.7	1.7	79	85.9	939	31
Mesquite ISD	TX	25,920	32,334	36,640	31.0	24.7	40.5	3.2	0.6	2,377	15.4	4,372	8.4	54.4	2.8	295	75.6	2,159	46
Midland ISD	TX	21,082	20,522	21,056	36.7	9.5	52.5	0.9	0.5	1,402	15.0	2,673	7.9	52.4	6.3	379	69.4	1,152	37
Mission CISD	TX	9,664	12,464	15,595	1.5	0.2	98.2	0.1	#	987	15.8	2,167	7.2	45.5	2.9	109	68.6	625	20
North East ISD	TX	39,909	50,875	62,181	39.3	9.3	47.4	3.7	0.3	4,233	14.7	8,218	7.6	51.5	1.9	330	85.1	3,626	72
Northside ISD	TX	50,229	63,739	86,260	25.4	7.8	63.2	3.3	0.3	5,508	15.7	11,553	7.5	47.7	3.6	793	80.3	4,259	97

See notes at end of table.

Selected statistics on enrollment, teachers, dropouts, and graduates in public school districts enrolling more than 15,000 students: 1990, 2000, 2005–06, and 2007—Continued

Name of district	State	Enrollment, fall 1990	Enrollment, fall 2000	Enrollment, fall 2007	Percentage distribution of enrollment, by race, fall 2007					Number of classroom teachers	Pupil/ teacher ratio	Total number of staff	Student/ staff ratio	Teachers as a percentage of total staff	Percent dropouts from grades 9–12	Number of dropouts from grades 9–12	Averaged freshman graduation rate (AFGR)[1]	Number of high school graduates[2]	Number of schools, fall 2007
					White	Black	Hispanic	Asian/ Pacific Islander	American Indian/ Alaska Native										
1	2	3	4	5	6	7	8	9	10	11	12	13	14	15	16	17	18	19	20
Pasadena ISD	TX	37,643	42,577	50,757	12.6	7.4	76.6	3.2	0.2	3,333	15.2	6,893	7.4	48.3	5.5	692	64.5	2,093	64
Pearland ISD	TX	6,234	10,618	17,090	48.4	17.0	24.9	9.5	0.2	1,042	16.4	2,092	8.2	49.8	1.7	72	87.0	882	24
Pflugerville ISD	TX	6,482	14,545	20,807	31.9	22.8	36.2	8.9	0.0	1,382	15.1	2,340	8.9	59.1	2.3	124	77.7	964	28
Pharr-San Juan-Alamo ISD	TX	16,563	22,537	29,999	0.9	0.2	98.7	0.2	0.0	1,798	16.7	3,973	7.6	45.2	6.7	454	57.5	1,029	38
Plano ISD	TX	28,398	47,161	53,683	52.7	10.6	17.2	19.1	0.4	4,003	13.4	6,894	7.8	58.1	1.3	200	84.7	3,268	81
Richardson ISD	TX	32,555	35,138	34,180	32.9	25.8	33.3	7.5	0.4	2,467	13.9	4,656	7.3	53.0	3.2	318	72.2	1,985	58
Round Rock ISD	TX	19,636	31,536	40,493	53.1	10.4	25.3	10.8	0.4	2,775	14.6	5,035	8.0	55.1	3.1	327	81.7	2,158	47
San Antonio ISD	TX	60,161	57,273	54,779	2.9	7.8	88.9	0.2	0.1	3,388	16.2	7,564	7.2	44.8	9.4	1,295	55.6	2,249	105
Socorro ISD	TX	14,350	26,711	38,878	4.3	1.8	93.1	0.5	0.4	2,451	15.9	4,742	8.2	51.7	2.5	263	71.5	1,754	43
Spring Branch ISD	TX	23,661	31,659	32,040	32.3	6.7	54.6	6.2	0.2	2,294	14.0	4,514	7.1	50.8	3.5	315	72.8	1,810	51
Spring ISD	TX	18,537	23,034	33,249	18.7	38.9	37.7	4.6	0.2	2,199	15.1	4,471	7.4	49.2	1.6	137	78.8	1,595	33
Tyler ISD	TX	16,182	16,626	18,064	29.1	32.2	37.0	1.4	0.3	1,266	14.3	2,468	7.3	51.3	4.7	233	69.7	944	27
United ISD	TX	12,553	27,556	39,009	1.5	0.2	97.8	0.5	#	2,402	16.2	5,636	6.9	42.6	1.7	147	78.4	1,644	45
Waco ISD	TX	14,304	15,433	15,247	13.6	34.9	51.0	0.4	0.1	1,062	14.4	2,133	7.1	49.8	6.6	256	62.9	748	36
Weslaco ISD	TX	10,835	13,407	16,188	1.8	0.2	97.7	0.4	0.0	1,070	15.1	2,393	6.8	44.7	4.1	161	66.4	715	21
Ysleta ISD	TX	49,974	46,394	45,049	5.6	2.2	91.5	0.3	0.4	2,965	15.2	6,125	7.4	48.4	4.8	663	72.6	2,710	65
Alpine	UT	38,852	47,117	63,856	87.1	0.8	9.2	2.3	0.5	2,339	27.3	4,602	13.9	50.8	0.7	110	—	—	70
Cache	UT	12,280	13,026	15,085	89.8	0.6	8.0	1.1	0.5	620	24.3	1,359	11.1	45.6	1.2	47	—	—	26
Davis	UT	55,558	59,578	70,323	86.5	1.7	8.3	2.8	0.7	2,898	24.3	5,787	12.2	50.1	2.1	384	—	—	101
Granite	UT	78,554	71,328	75,982	60.1	2.6	28.6	7.1	1.5	3,192	23.8	6,110	12.4	52.2	2.4	500	—	—	114
Jordan	UT	64,991	73,158	85,651	85.1	1.2	9.9	3.3	0.6	3,314	25.8	6,508	13.2	50.9	5.7	1,347	—	—	97
Nebo	UT	16,393	21,094	28,606	87.1	0.8	10.0	1.3	0.8	1,119	25.6	2,341	12.2	47.8	0.8	53	—	—	46
Salt Lake	UT	24,766	25,367	24,908	43.5	5.1	40.1	9.1	2.1	1,134	22.0	2,515	9.9	45.1	7.0	456	—	—	44
Washington	UT	13,264	21,124	26,260	82.4	0.8	12.3	2.5	1.9	1,170	22.4	2,087	12.6	56.1	3.1	205	—	—	44
Weber	UT	25,425	27,783	31,637	85.4	1.4	10.5	2.0	0.7	1,332	23.7	2,493	12.7	53.4	2.3	206	—	—	49
Arlington County	VA	14,825	18,870	18,736	47.6	13.8	27.6	11.0	0.1	1,273	14.7	3,369	5.6	37.8	2.5	132	71.0	996	31
Chesapeake City	VA	29,533	37,645	40,003	57.2	36.3	3.0	3.2	0.3	2,152	18.6	6,218	6.4	34.6	2.8	375	79.6	2,562	46
Chesterfield County	VA	44,480	51,212	58,969	61.1	27.6	7.3	3.4	0.6	3,165	18.6	8,121	7.3	39.0	2.6	473	86.2	3,695	63
Fairfax County	VA	128,766	156,412	165,722	51.0	11.3	17.9	19.5	0.3	9,463	17.5	32,283	5.1	29.3	2.3	1,194	82.8	10,700	199
Hampton City	VA	21,383	23,290	22,329	31.1	63.1	3.4	2.1	0.4	1,314	17.0	3,916	5.7	33.5	3.6	255	71.5	1,399	35
Hanover County	VA	11,328	16,611	19,100	86.3	9.8	1.7	1.9	0.4	1,087	17.6	3,171	6.0	34.3	0.9	55	81.7	1,115	23
Henrico County	VA	32,638	41,655	48,620	50.8	38.4	4.5	6.0	0.3	2,696	18.0	6,370	7.6	42.3	4.3	624	76.0	2,671	70
Loudoun County	VA	14,485	31,804	53,961	65.2	8.3	13.3	12.9	0.3	3,192	16.9	9,888	5.5	32.3	1.3	161	94.1	2,505	70
Newport News City	VA	28,925	33,008	31,553	31.5	58.7	6.5	2.7	0.6	1,706	18.5	5,020	6.3	34.0	0.4	42	68.4	1,719	46
Norfolk City	VA	36,541	37,349	35,063	25.2	68.0	4.1	2.6	0.2	2,170	16.2	6,304	5.6	34.4	2.5	228	49.0	1,338	54
Portsmouth City	VA	18,405	16,473	15,405	24.1	73.1	1.8	0.8	0.2	808	19.1	2,316	6.7	34.9	5.3	243	56.1	703	22
Prince William County	VA	41,888	54,646	72,988	42.4	23.4	26.2	7.7	0.3	3,847	19.0	10,496	7.0	36.7	4.2	867	75.0	3,636	81
Richmond City	VA	27,021	27,237	23,754	7.4	87.9	4.0	0.6	0.1	1,200	19.8	4,092	5.8	29.3	3.0	243	51.5	917	53
Roanoke County	VA	13,421	13,869	15,105	88.4	6.2	1.9	3.4	0.1	809	18.7	2,663	5.7	30.4	1.2	60	86.2	954	28
Spotsylvania County	VA	12,227	18,876	24,304	68.5	20.2	8.3	2.6	0.3	1,443	16.8	3,435	7.1	42.0	0.9	64	80.7	1,380	32
Stafford County	VA	12,555	21,124	26,582	66.1	21.3	9.1	3.0	0.4	1,416	18.8	3,889	6.8	36.4	1.7	139	88.4	1,662	29
Virginia Beach City	VA	70,266	76,586	72,477	58.1	28.9	5.9	6.7	0.4	4,051	17.9	11,008	6.6	36.8	1.8	420	69.7	4,439	86
Bellevue	WA	14,748	15,431	16,772	60.0	2.8	8.7	28.2	0.3	971	17.3	1,811	9.3	53.6	2.2	124	90.4	1,142	30
Bethel	WA	11,669	16,029	18,006	65.5	11.5	10.8	8.9	3.3	875	20.6	1,735	10.4	50.4	4.8	280	81.4	1,118	34
Edmonds	WA	18,868	22,067	20,905	67.1	6.3	10.0	15.2	1.4	1,040	20.1	2,049	10.2	50.7	5.2	383	70.1	1,220	42
Everett	WA	15,343	18,683	18,935	70.2	4.7	10.7	13.1	1.4	931	20.3	1,727	11.0	53.9	4.6	271	64.9	996	33
Evergreen (Clark)	WA	14,810	21,650	25,396	77.3	3.9	8.6	9.0	1.2	1,351	18.8	2,466	10.3	54.8	5.6	444	73.9	1,247	36
Federal Way	WA	18,168	22,623	22,398	47.9	13.8	18.4	18.5	1.4	1,174	19.1	2,174	10.3	54.0	5.0	374	67.7	1,241	44
Highline	WA	16,208	18,024	17,331	35.3	14.5	27.1	21.2	2.0	958	18.1	1,952	8.9	49.1	5.5	307	52.8	809	49
Issaquah	WA	8,888	14,259	16,642	71.8	2.3	5.0	20.2	0.7	803	20.7	1,490	11.2	53.9	2.3	116	86.3	1,015	26
Kennewick	WA	11,422	13,629	15,087	67.2	2.4	27.1	2.5	0.8	746	20.2	1,435	10.5	52.0	5.4	255	76.0	887	25
Kent	WA	21,027	26,535	27,462	55.3	11.7	12.5	19.0	1.4	1,403	19.6	2,682	10.2	52.3	8.8	766	66.6	1,504	41
Lake Washington	WA	23,050	23,662	23,722	74.5	2.5	6.9	15.4	0.6	1,222	19.4	2,160	11.0	56.6	1.8	137	85.3	1,539	52
Northshore	WA	17,511	20,255	20,018	77.6	2.1	7.6	11.7	1.0	982	20.4	1,853	10.8	53.0	2.1	145	91.6	1,579	34

See notes at end of table.

Selected statistics on enrollment, teachers, dropouts, and graduates in public school districts enrolling more than 15,000 students: 1990, 2000, 2005–06, and 2007—Continued

Name of district	State	Enrollment, fall 1990	Enrollment, fall 2000	Enrollment, fall 2007	Percentage distribution of enrollment, by race, fall 2007					Teachers and staff, fall 2007					Dropouts and graduates, 2006				Number of schools, fall 2007
					White	Black	Hispanic	Asian/ Pacific Islander	American Indian/ Alaska Native	Number of classroom teachers	Pupil/ teacher ratio	Total number of staff	Student/ staff ratio	Teachers as a percentage of total staff	Percent dropouts from grades 9–12	Number of dropouts from grades 9–12	Averaged freshman graduation rate (AFGR)[1]	Number of high school graduates[2]	
1	2	3	4	5	6	7	8	9	10	11	12	13	14	15	16	17	18	19	20
Puyallup	WA	15,100	19,757	21,203	79.1	4.5	7.3	7.4	1.7	1,036	20.5	1,967	10.8	52.7	4.9	333	76.3	1,256	35
Seattle	WA	43,593	47,575	45,581	42.8	21.4	11.6	22.1	2.1	2,499	18.2	4,826	9.4	51.8	15.7	2,253	78.5	2,690	106
Spokane	WA	29,186	31,725	29,454	83.8	4.5	4.1	3.6	4.1	1,708	17.2	3,138	9.4	54.4	7.8	797	70.7	1,829	65
Tacoma	WA	30,169	34,093	29,677	48.8	23.2	13.0	13.0	2.0	1,642	18.1	3,144	9.4	52.2	7.2	688	48.9	1,414	65
Vancouver	WA	16,423	21,892	22,655	74.6	5.4	12.5	5.8	1.7	1,152	19.7	2,311	9.8	49.8	4.0	285	70.8	1,256	40
Berkeley County	WV	10,415	13,076	16,868	82.2	11.3	5.2	1.1	0.2	1,193	14.1	2,283	7.4	52.2	4.1	182	77.7	885	29
Kanawha County	WV	34,284	29,250	28,350	85.3	12.8	0.5	1.4	0.1	1,891	15.0	3,711	7.6	50.9	5.3	421	70.8	1,538	72
Appleton Area	WI	12,876	14,793	15,233	78.1	3.7	6.2	11.1	0.9	955	15.9	1,568	9.7	60.9	0.9	47	99.8	1,219	37
Green Bay Area	WI	18,048	20,104	19,534	63.7	6.7	17.0	7.8	4.9	1,426	13.7	2,436	8.0	58.5	5.0	331	81.4	1,267	37
Kenosha	WI	16,219	20,099	22,669	62.5	16.3	18.9	1.9	0.4	1,441	15.7	2,547	8.9	56.6	2.4	161	84.9	1,428	44
Madison Metropolitan	WI	23,214	25,087	24,670	52.2	23.0	13.7	10.4	0.7	1,758	14.0	3,428	7.2	51.3	3.2	263	88.0	1,889	53
Milwaukee	WI	92,784	97,985	86,819	15.6	57.3	21.9	4.5	0.8	4,798	18.1	9,640	9.0	49.8	8.5	2,201	56.5	4,312	214
Racine	WI	21,904	21,102	21,552	50.8	26.6	20.8	1.5	0.3	1,362	15.8	2,494	8.6	54.6	5.6	389	65.8	1,211	35

—Not available.

†Not applicable.

#Rounds to zero.

[1] The averaged freshman graduation rate provides an estimate of the percentage of students who receive a regular diploma within 4 years of entering ninth grade. The rate uses aggregate student enrollment data to estimate the size of an incoming freshman class and aggregate counts of the number of diplomas awarded 4 years later.

[2] Includes regular diplomas only.

[3] Reported data indicated an averaged freshman graduation rate of greater than 100.0 percent.

NOTE: Total enrollment, staff, and teacher data in this table reflect totals reported by school districts and may differ from data derived from summing school-level data to school district aggregates. ISD = independent school district. CISD = consolidated independent school district. Race categories exclude persons of Hispanic ethnicity. Detail may not sum to totals because of rounding.

SOURCE: U.S. Department of Education, National Center for Education Statistics, Common Core of Data (CCD), "Public Elementary/Secondary School Universe Survey," 2007–08; "Local Education Agency Universe Survey," 1990–91, 2000–01, and 2007–08; and "Local Education Agency-Level Public-Use Data File on Public School Dropouts: School Year 2005–06." (This table was prepared September 2009.)

Enrollment, poverty, and federal funds for the 100 largest school districts, by enrollment size in 2007: Fall 2007, 2006–07, and fiscal year 2009

Name of district	State	Rank order	Enrollment, fall 2007	5- to 17-year-old population, 2007	5- to 17-year-olds in poverty, 2007	Poverty rate of 5- to 17-year-olds, 2007[1]	Revenues by source of funds, 2006–07: Total (in thousands)	Federal (in thousands)	Federal as a percent of total	Federal revenue per student[3]	Revenue for selected federal programs 2006–07: Title I basic and concentration grants	School lunch	Vocational education	Drug-free schools	Eisenhower math and science	Special education	Title I allocations FY2009: Total	Basic grants	Concentration grants	Targeted grants	Education finance incentive grants[2]
1	2	3	4	5	6	7	8	9	10	11	12	13	14	15	16	17	18	19	20	21	22
New York City	NY	1	989,941	1,333,830	355,528	26.7	$19,368,571	$1,889,716	9.8	$1,901	$870,868	$240,943	—	$18,417	$32,185	$297,023	$1,581,698	$325,164	$82,492	$644,867	$529,176
Los Angeles Unified	CA	2	693,680	838,081	194,010	23.1	9,064,937	1,052,743	11.6	1,488	442,789	139,471	$56,261	5,201	12,065	216,684	774,056	141,892	35,411	284,774	311,979
City of Chicago	IL	3	407,510	503,932	135,343	26.9	4,702,647	702,909	14.9	1,699	286,008	81,721	22,514	3,546	8,589	147,408	604,271	125,729	31,780	219,464	227,298
Dade	FL	4	348,128	388,022	72,504	18.7	3,814,807	433,672	11.4	1,226	161,047	71,400	11,306	2,340	7,420	87,367	223,900	46,667	12,039	91,214	73,980
Clark County	NV	5	309,051	339,260	47,694	14.1	2,843,207	202,379	7.1	667	55,912	44,398	—	849	3,693	48,276	134,706	28,768	7,332	54,501	44,105
Broward	FL	6	258,893	301,128	39,933	13.3	2,709,902	229,713	8.5	874	50,390	48,203	11,874	1,210	4,003	45,383	114,811	25,254	6,437	45,896	37,224
Houston ISD	TX	7	199,534	258,340	71,349	27.6	2,057,191	273,906	13.3	1,350	95,927	34,505	20,056	1,436	3,065	70,340	222,634	46,633	11,788	84,599	79,614
Hillsborough	FL	8	193,180	206,940	28,444	13.7	2,129,937	252,566	11.9	1,305	57,114	41,436	8,645	1,225	3,374	46,406	81,485	18,550	4,728	32,140	26,067
Hawaii Dept. of Education	HI	9	179,897	199,004	18,364	9.2	2,985,593	256,696	8.6	1,420	57,755	36,629	776	1,563	2,873	38,591	76,230	17,744	3,939	27,381	27,166
Orange	FL	10	174,142	187,804	25,922	13.8	1,976,983	149,156	7.5	851	38,053	37,446	7,679	691	2,384	35,563	72,807	17,715	4,570	27,896	22,625
Philadelphia	PA	11	172,704	256,496	81,430	31.7	2,441,472	311,782	12.8	1,749	153,577	—	22,136	2,007	6,612	62,723	412,717	71,074	18,115	144,706	178,823
Palm Beach	FL	12	170,883	192,117	24,516	12.8	2,057,933	133,639	6.5	780	37,682	33,753	59	—	557	29,325	69,114	16,637	4,292	26,606	21,579
Fairfax County	VA	13	165,722	177,497	9,949	5.6	2,255,060	83,635	3.7	510	15,840	29,763	4,332	561	1,598	15,204	34,415	7,744	1,974	11,367	13,332
Dallas ISD	TX	14	157,804	196,138	57,748	29.4	1,587,549	213,494	13.4	1,342	83,091	27,280	12,935	1,272	2,110	56,274	171,139	34,032	8,674	66,166	62,267
Gwinnett County	GA	15	155,618	154,335	14,222	9.2	1,571,111	87,664	5.6	577	—	—	—	—	—	32,686	45,060	9,603	2,448	15,258	17,750
Montgomery County	MD	16	137,717	160,378	8,610	5.4	2,249,696	92,959	4.1	675	21,400	26,968	4,992	772	1,522	15,718	31,141	8,515	2,152	10,977	9,496
Wake County	NC	17	134,401	151,288	14,547	9.6	1,447,470	65,144	4.5	506	—	—	—	—	—	15,052	39,084	8,609	2,194	13,723	14,558
San Diego Unified	CA	18	131,577	157,229	26,672	17.0	1,617,096	144,726	8.9	1,105	47,492	24,816	9,394	1,170	1,243	31,777	81,824	17,648	4,498	30,408	29,270
Charlotte-Mecklenburg	NC	19	131,176	158,935	20,521	12.9	1,244,057	91,893	7.4	714	—	—	—	—	—	30,805	57,658	12,249	3,122	20,520	21,767
Prince George's County	MD	20	129,752	148,216	14,277	9.6	1,761,330	111,266	6.3	849	30,079	24,635	7,328	632	1,424	27,161	54,735	12,617	3,216	20,081	18,822
Duval	FL	21	124,740	155,148	25,604	16.5	1,218,342	117,295	9.6	937	33,032	33,910	7,122	686	1,399	24,252	70,463	16,172	4,122	27,701	22,467
Memphis City	TN	22	115,342	134,114	42,008	31.3	1,067,335	142,662	13.4	1,216	46,625	23,468	0	1,123	4,312	38,950	128,385	24,307	6,195	44,528	53,355
Pinellas	FL	23	107,892	128,701	17,952	13.9	1,160,215	101,691	8.8	925	32,166	26,355	5,983	502	2,118	18,650	48,826	11,505	2,932	18,988	15,400
Detroit City	MI	24	107,874	103,661	80,289	39.4	1,508,139	269,588	17.9	2,292	178,014	—	20,100	2,960	4,514	31,658	364,122	62,415	15,908	126,621	159,178
Cobb County	GA	25	107,307	117,595	10,569	9.0	1,190,519	68,721	5.8	641	—	—	—	—	—	14,823	32,398	7,300	1,861	10,959	12,278
Baltimore County	MD	26	104,283	129,316	10,673	8.3	1,328,911	92,367	7.0	873	22,713	23,121	4,410	516	1,151	14,843	40,335	9,756	2,487	14,741	13,351
DeKalb County	GA	27	100,273	115,932	21,590	18.6	1,193,406	94,124	7.9	928	—	—	—	—	—	30,783	72,749	14,640	3,731	24,661	29,717
Cypress-Fairbanks ISD	TX	28	96,837	73,538	8,729	11.9	751,839	37,840	5.0	411	4,790	11,924	1,377	229	466	13,638	20,657	5,169	1,318	7,300	6,870
Albuquerque	NM	29	95,965	109,303	19,289	17.6	909,023	87,631	9.6	918	25,748	20,498	8,616	746	1,055	0	59,861	12,237	3,119	20,370	24,135
Jefferson County	KY	30	95,871	121,298	22,404	18.5	1,026,965	107,923	10.5	1,165	—	—	—	—	—	24,472	72,793	14,841	3,783	25,115	29,055
Polk	FL	31	93,980	98,428	16,285	16.5	982,220	82,301	8.4	887	24,727	17,414	3,905	426	1,202	24,187	43,598	10,377	2,645	16,883	13,693
Long Beach Unified	CA	32	88,186	101,285	24,266	24.0	909,270	133,819	14.7	1,476	48,235	14,990	6,311	928	1,020	24,285	73,891	16,870	4,264	26,954	25,803
Milwaukee	WI	33	86,819	120,900	39,231	32.4	1,146,819	159,448	13.9	1,773	65,415	25,804	—	—	2,015	28,241	167,281	35,663	9,014	55,377	67,227
Northside ISD	TX	34	86,260	78,454	11,867	15.1	731,923	55,227	7.5	669	11,723	14,915	2,582	315	713	16,066	30,366	7,159	1,825	11,015	10,366
Fulton County	GA	35	86,225	100,226	12,912	12.9	997,880	45,745	4.6	545	—	—	—	—	—	14,957	40,427	8,761	2,233	13,685	15,748
Jefferson County	CO	36	86,168	89,891	8,428	9.4	825,158	41,486	5.0	482	8,956	17,667	2,948	253	487	7,044	22,392	5,441	1,387	7,657	7,908
Jordan	UT	37	85,651	87,133	5,284	6.1	552,931	39,461	7.1	504	4,457	12,923	1,712	179	684	8,723	11,939	3,167	—	4,097	4,675
Austin ISD	TX	38	82,564	105,418	19,830	18.8	960,995	82,135	8.5	1,000	24,485	14,972	4,464	413	954	20,551	52,876	11,773	3,001	19,629	18,473
Baltimore City	MD	39	81,284	108,700	27,171	25.0	1,246,552	122,920	9.9	1,454	52,655	20,244	11,950	1,114	2,162	24,619	122,988	26,175	6,671	45,393	44,749
Lee	FL	40	80,541	87,115	11,082	12.7	1,003,253	66,646	6.6	844	14,795	14,086	—	333	1,067	15,403	27,924	6,997	1,783	10,571	8,574

See notes at end of table.

Enrollment, poverty, and federal funds for the 100 largest school districts, by enrollment size in 2007: Fall 2007, 2006–07, and fiscal year 2009—Continued

Name of district	State	Rank order	Enrollment, fall 2007	5- to 17-year-old population, 2007	5- to 17-year-olds in poverty, 2007	Poverty rate of 5- to 17-year-olds, 2007[1]	Revenues by source of funds, 2006–07 — Total (in thousands)	Federal (in thousands)	Federal as a percent of total	Federal revenue per student[3]	Revenue for selected federal programs (in thousands), 2006–07 — Title I basic and concentration grants	School lunch	Vocational education	Drug-free schools	Eisenhower math and science	Special education	Title I allocations (in thousands), fiscal year 2009[2] — Total	Basic grants	Concentration grants	Targeted grants	Education finance incentive grants
1	2	3	4	5	6	7	8	9	10	11	12	13	14	15	16	17	18	19	20	21	22
Fort Worth ISD	TX	41	78,857	101,392	22,916	22.6	710,684	98,401	13.8	1,238	33,617	16,795	—	518	1,263	20,843	62,253	14,065	3,554	22,994	21,639
Fresno Unified	CA	42	76,460	86,474	27,980	32.4	821,413	120,670	14.7	1,556	58,951	14,522	6,542	644	1,620	25,812	86,425	19,448	4,677	31,716	30,583
Granite	UT	43	75,982	78,926	8,831	11.2	448,235	49,274	11.0	730	9,689	12,116	2,767	195	744	12,110	22,975	5,231	1,333	7,450	8,961
Brevard	FL	44	74,369	80,670	9,202	11.4	741,110	53,583	7.2	716	14,026	15,621	—	294	820	11,138	22,722	6,001	1,548	8,378	6,795
Davidson County	TN	45	73,715	100,670	20,190	20.1	720,591	72,974	10.1	990	19,991	16,792	—	—	1,808	20,091	56,557	11,743	2,993	19,608	22,213
Anne Arundel County	MD	46	73,400	89,886	5,037	5.6	931,352	45,134	4.8	618	9,596	16,760	2,237	278	643	6,173	15,869	4,441	1,080	5,683	4,665
Denver	CO	47	73,053	92,685	22,580	24.4	797,383	86,525	10.9	1,192	30,385	16,775	5,830	467	1,328	16,466	70,440	14,308	3,647	24,212	28,273
Mesa Unified	AZ	48	73,044	104,066	15,967	15.3	613,251	51,825	8.5	699	13,957	10,807	3,062	359	1,129	14,482	45,024	9,519	2,426	15,455	17,625
Prince William County	VA	49	72,998	72,252	4,335	6.0	847,608	35,176	4.2	496	8,011	11,037	952	250	610	8,939	12,041	3,364	0	4,180	4,497
Virginia Beach City	VA	50	72,477	80,961	6,910	8.5	807,157	61,259	7.6	845	11,320	16,181	2,652	347	1,085	8,693	21,911	5,397	1,376	7,216	7,922
Guilford County	NC	51	72,389	79,602	13,977	17.6	652,707	55,835	8.6	778	—	—	1,533	143	—	18,611	37,179	8,236	2,099	13,026	13,818
Davis	UT	52	70,323	65,142	4,590	7.0	418,693	34,790	8.3	559	2,754	10,490	—	—	761	8,389	9,914	2,692	0	3,387	3,835
Greenville 01	SC	53	69,444	77,118	10,626	13.8	637,541	52,331	8.2	775	14,819	16,324	2,685	297	1,127	12,880	32,679	6,994	1,783	10,523	13,380
Fort Bend ISD	TX	54	67,992	71,991	6,025	8.4	550,235	28,496	5.2	425	4,327	12,009	1,416	171	455	7,116	13,174	3,699	0	4,881	4,594
Pasco	FL	55	66,314	70,546	10,569	15.0	685,854	48,179	7.0	745	11,957	12,628	2,261	284	634	13,116	26,378	6,663	1,698	9,948	8,069
Washoe County	NV	56	65,663	69,823	7,401	10.6	580,576	34,882	6.0	537	8,764	8,956	1,813	428	1,193	8,633	16,192	4,616	1,176	6,297	4,103
Seminole	FL	57	65,378	69,832	6,586	9.4	633,727	42,441	6.7	640	8,594	14,086	2,450	252	585	11,522	15,160	4,140	1,055	5,502	4,463
Volusia	FL	58	64,488	72,195	13,732	19.0	701,777	51,455	7.3	781	15,763	14,009	3,183	287	1,213	12,096	35,831	8,702	2,218	13,755	11,156
Mobile County	AL	59	64,375	77,396	20,751	26.8	580,429	80,697	13.9	1,240	30,996	20,194	5,059	647	2,242	19,758	58,720	12,429	3,168	20,825	22,297
Alpine	UT	60	63,856	63,312	4,448	7.0	359,176	31,146	8.7	552	4,001	8,455	1,407	124	574	6,865	9,785	2,661	0	3,342	3,782
Arlington ISD	TX	61	62,863	74,266	11,296	15.2	518,791	44,809	8.6	710	12,050	11,189	1,923	275	662	14,433	28,015	6,677	1,702	10,116	9,520
Elk Grove Unified	CA	62	62,294	52,631	6,894	13.1	584,299	39,639	6.8	641	9,364	8,990	1,760	277	385	10,756	18,485	4,970	1,267	6,738	5,511
North East ISD	TX	63	62,181	64,634	9,186	14.2	581,418	32,159	5.5	525	5,523	10,551	1,685	189	488	10,027	22,221	5,490	1,399	7,898	7,433
El Paso ISD	TX	64	62,123	64,509	24,239	37.6	563,711	86,039	15.3	1,369	34,395	12,591	4,689	535	1,089	18,094	64,953	14,249	3,632	24,251	22,822
Aldine ISD	TX	65	60,083	57,604	14,873	25.8	536,158	68,261	12.7	1,160	16,613	11,280	3,605	250	727	24,065	39,087	9,302	2,400	14,108	13,277
Tucson Unified	AZ	66	59,327	82,274	16,084	19.5	527,757	63,504	12.0	1,053	22,373	10,569	4,197	980	1,799	13,434	46,486	9,788	2,495	15,959	18,245
Chesterfield County	VA	67	58,969	56,756	3,799	6.7	598,918	25,246	4.2	432	4,188	10,842	1,085	180	577	4,288	10,281	2,943	0	3,551	3,787
District of Columbia	DC	68	58,191	77,505	18,995	24.5	1,148,358	134,700	11.7	2,366	72,077	14,306	—	1,510	3,800	13,319	86,414	19,620	5,001	33,156	28,637
Garland ISD	TX	69	57,169	57,384	10,381	18.1	469,348	35,589	7.6	625	6,345	11,153	1,477	257	437	11,128	25,229	6,106	1,556	9,049	8,516
Santa Ana Unified	CA	70	57,061	64,115	11,542	18.0	566,980	73,721	13.0	1,287	29,003	10,670	2,633	296	589	17,914	32,273	8,576	2,168	11,370	10,160
San Bernardino City Unified	CA	71	56,727	60,267	14,782	24.5	619,398	78,412	12.7	1,366	36,212	10,391	4,615	578	758	19,070	45,792	12,368	3,118	15,750	14,556
Boston	MA	72	56,168	81,381	22,958	28.2	1,220,761	102,201	8.4	1,812	45,777	18,934	—	—	1,307	11,386	104,404	20,280	5,169	34,387	44,568
Columbus City	OH	73	55,269	79,001	24,778	31.4	907,767	100,819	11.1	1,800	—	15,183	—	456	2,872	17,221	100,553	19,200	4,894	32,857	43,602
San Francisco Unified	CA	74	55,069	69,616	9,216	13.2	655,003	74,706	11.4	1,330	23,792	—	6,579	338	397	11,272	24,335	6,336	1,555	8,832	7,613
San Antonio ISD	TX	75	54,779	70,385	21,846	31.0	543,509	97,844	18.0	1,766	32,086	12,745	5,127	542	1,117	23,689	61,873	15,026	3,797	22,178	20,872
Knox County	TN	76	54,490	67,969	9,828	14.5	478,390	42,000	8.8	704	12,514	12,889	—	304	917	9,513	24,970	5,858	1,493	8,620	8,999
Katy ISD	TX	77	54,402	39,618	3,712	9.4	462,280	16,553	3.6	323	915	6,571	546	100	219	5,292	7,475	2,237	0	2,699	2,540
Loudoun County	VA	78	53,961	57,633	1,467	2.5	684,499	9,462	1.4	188	404	2,628	667	91	323	2,453	1,151	1,151	0	0	0
Plano ISD	TX	79	53,683	80,867	4,331	5.4	648,715	20,962	3.2	396	2,213	8,950	1,167	146	451	4,688	8,768	2,569	0	3,194	3,006
Cumberland County	NC	80	53,295	56,218	12,182	21.7	423,987	55,700	13.1	1,039	—	—	—	—	—	15,118	32,095	7,239	1,845	11,166	11,845

See notes at end of table.

Enrollment, poverty, and federal funds for the 100 largest school districts, by enrollment size in 2007: Fall 2007, 2006–07, and fiscal year 2009—Continued

Name of district	State	Rank order	Enrollment, fall 2007	5- to 17-year-old population, 2007	5- to 17-year-olds in poverty, 2007	Poverty rate of 5- to 17-year-olds, 2007[1]	Revenues by source of funds, 2006–07 — Total (in thousands)	Federal (in thousands)	Federal as a percent of total	Federal revenue per student[3]	Title I basic and concentration grants	School lunch	Vocational education	Drug-free schools	Eisenhower math and science	Special education	Title I allocations FY2009[2] — Total	Basic grants	Concentration grants	Targeted grants	Education finance incentive grants[2]
1	2	3	4	5	6	7	8	9	10	11	12	13	14	15	16	17	18	19	20	21	22
Douglas County	CO	81	52,983	56,990	1,242	2.2	471,882	10,102	2.1	201	—	6,833	587	67	125	1,088	992	992	0	0	0
Cleveland Municipal City	OH	82	52,954	86,903	29,767	34.3	911,109	130,506	14.3	2,348	—	20,371	—	750	2,230	20,230	122,887	24,967	6,401	39,161	52,359
Osceola	FL	83	52,742	46,981	7,524	16.0	532,103	38,652	7.3	743	8,415	9,016	—	207	623	12,417	17,725	4,788	1,220	6,470	5,247
Clayton County	GA	84	52,717	58,190	11,023	18.9	556,161	58,860	10.6	1,120	—	—	—	—	—	18,470	33,031	7,416	1,890	11,174	12,552
Capistrano Unified	CA	85	52,390	56,887	3,222	5.7	444,583	22,214	5.0	431	3,775	8,124	1,141	173	223	3,258	6,375	2,080	0	2,412	1,884
Forsyth County	NC	86	51,738	58,820	11,769	20.0	463,122	44,643	9.6	870	—	7,376	—	133	—	12,032	30,491	6,925	1,765	10,579	11,222
Corona-Norco Unified	CA	87	51,322	47,063	4,676	9.9	522,274	23,394	4.5	469	4,107	—	1,177	133	205	8,105	10,211	3,104	0	3,942	3,164
Pasadena ISD	TX	88	50,757	50,372	10,936	21.7	434,863	45,102	10.4	905	11,759	11,895	2,475	247	419	14,232	27,891	7,143	1,841	9,740	9,166
Cherry Creek	CO	89	50,601	45,276	4,369	9.6	472,054	17,805	3.8	358	3,058	8,029	763	100	175	4,056	9,621	2,775	0	3,460	3,387
Atlanta	GA	90	49,991	81,872	22,726	27.8	814,744	88,422	10.9	1,746	—	—	—	—	—	17,010	79,048	16,883	4,268	26,210	31,687
Lewisville ISD	TX	91	49,636	59,552	2,676	4.5	467,179	23,471	5.0	478	1,841	7,677	779	108	312	4,814	1,609	1,609	0	0	0
Howard County	MD	92	49,542	52,535	2,066	3.9	754,403	18,529	2.5	378	2,133	8,991	1,586	88	441	2,634	1,836	1,836	0	0	0
Anchorage	AK	93	48,857	52,849	4,466	8.5	536,620	60,069	11.2	1,220	12,837	10,467	4,685	571	1,003	8,824	24,927	5,532	0	9,585	9,811
Brownsville ISD	TX	94	48,837	43,272	19,276	44.5	465,961	78,309	16.8	1,620	26,267	10,794	5,467	371	708	23,280	52,452	12,665	3,267	18,814	17,705
Garden Grove Unified	CA	95	48,669	54,916	8,870	16.2	456,133	43,375	9.5	889	14,803	8,226	2,727	218	415	12,947	23,043	5,726	2,242	8,149	6,927
Henrico County	VA	96	48,620	50,702	5,397	10.6	467,012	25,324	5.4	531	4,721	10,343	1,336	230	970	4,821	15,562	4,207	0	5,439	5,916
Sacramento City Unified	CA	97	48,446	64,994	12,439	19.1	550,875	75,511	13.7	1,530	25,878	11,688	3,562	492	723	13,636	37,129	9,458	2,391	13,241	12,039
Omaha	NE	98	47,763	61,143	11,409	18.7	496,376	78,550	15.8	1,670	21,502	11,901	5,972	381	1,070	13,294	46,207	9,253	2,358	14,325	20,272
San Juan Unified	CA	99	47,400	59,646	7,409	12.4	488,602	42,664	8.7	891	10,896	9,535	2,099	200	440	6,939	19,347	5,143	1,311	7,060	5,834
Shelby County	TN	100	46,918	44,375	4,363	9.8	344,040	19,178	5.6	407	2,459	7,454	—	—	396	5,140	9,908	2,837	0	3,604	3,467

—Not available.

[1] Poverty is defined based on the number of persons and related children in the family and their income. For information on poverty thresholds for 2007, see http://www.census.gov/hhes/www/poverty/threshld/thresh05.html.

[2] Fiscal year 2009 Department of Education funds available for spending by school districts in the 2009–10 school year.

[3] Federal revenue per student is based on fall enrollment collected through the "School District Finance Survey (Form F-33)."

NOTE: Detail may not sum to totals because of rounding. ISD = independent school district.
SOURCE: U.S. Department of Education, National Center for Education Statistics, Common Core of Data (CCD), "School District Finance Survey (Form F-33)," 2006–07, and "Local Education Agency Universe Survey," 2007–08; and unpublished Department of Education budget data. (This table was prepared September 2009.)

Public elementary and secondary schools, by type of school: Selected years, 1967–68 through 2007–08

Year	Total, all public schools	Schools with reported grade spans — Total	Elementary schools — Total[2]	Middle schools[3]	One-teacher schools	Other elementary schools	Secondary schools — Total[4]	Junior high[5]	3-year or 4-year high schools	5-year or 6-year high schools	Other secondary schools	Combined elementary/secondary schools[6]	Other schools[1]
1	2	3	4	5	6	7	8	9	10	11	12	13	14
1967–68	—	94,197	67,186	—	4,146	63,040	23,318	7,437	10,751	4,650	480	3,693	
1970–71	—	89,372	64,020	2,080	1,815	60,125	23,572	7,750	11,265	3,887	670	1,780	—
1972–73	—	88,864	62,942	2,308	1,475	59,159	23,919	7,878	11,550	3,962	529	2,003	—
1974–75	—	87,456	61,759	3,224	1,247	57,288	23,837	7,690	11,480	4,122	545	1,860	—
1975–76	88,597	87,034	61,704	3,916	1,166	56,622	23,792	7,521	11,572	4,113	586	1,538	1,563
1976–77	—	86,501	61,123	4,180	1,111	55,832	23,857	7,434	11,658	4,130	635	1,521	—
1978–79	—	84,816	60,312	5,879	1,056	53,377	22,834	6,282	11,410	4,429	713	1,670	—
1980–81	85,982	83,688	59,326	6,003	921	52,402	22,619	5,890	10,758	4,193	1,778	1,743	2,294
1982–83	84,740	82,039	58,051	6,875	798	50,378	22,383	5,948	11,678	4,067	690	1,605	2,701
1983–84	84,178	81,418	57,471	6,885	838	49,748	22,336	5,936	11,670	4,046	684	1,611	2,760
1984–85	84,007	81,147	57,231	6,893	825	49,513	22,320	5,916	11,671	4,021	712	1,596	2,860
1986–87	83,455	82,190	58,801	7,452	763	50,586	21,406	5,142	11,453	4,197	614	1,983	1,265 [7]
1987–88	83,248	81,416	57,575	7,641	729	49,205	21,662	4,900	11,279	4,048	1,435	2,179	1,832 [7]
1988–89	83,165	81,579	57,941	7,957	583	49,401	21,403	4,687	11,350	3,994	1,372	2,235	1,586 [7]
1989–90	83,425	81,880	58,419	8,272	630	49,517	21,181	4,512	11,492	3,812	1,365	2,280	1,545 [7]
1990–91	84,538	82,475	59,015	8,545	617	49,853	21,135	4,561	11,537	3,723	1,314	2,325	2,063
1991–92	84,578	82,506	59,258	8,829	569	49,860	20,767	4,298	11,528	3,699	1,242	2,481	2,072
1992–93	84,497	82,896	59,676	9,152	430	50,094	20,671	4,115	11,651	3,613	1,292	2,549	2,072
1993–94	85,393	83,431	60,052	9,573	442	50,037	20,705	3,970	11,858	3,595	1,282	2,674	1,601
1994–95	86,221	84,476	60,808	9,954	458	50,396	20,904	3,859	12,058	3,628	1,359	2,764	1,962
1995–96	87,125	84,958	61,165	10,205	474	50,486	20,997	3,743	12,168	3,621	1,465	2,796	1,745
1996–97	88,223	86,092	61,805	10,499	487	50,819	21,307	3,707	12,424	3,614	1,562	2,980	2,167
1997–98	89,508	87,541	62,739	10,944	476	51,319	21,682	3,599	12,734	3,611	1,738	3,120	2,131
1998–99	90,874	89,259	63,462	11,202	463	51,797	22,076	3,607	13,457	3,707	1,305	3,721	1,967
1999–2000	92,012	90,538	64,131	11,521	423	52,187	22,365	3,566	13,914	3,686	1,199	4,042	1,615
2000–01	93,273	91,691	64,601	11,696	411	52,494	21,994	3,318	13,793	3,974	909	5,096	1,474
2001–02	94,112	92,696	65,228	11,983	408	52,837	22,180	3,285	14,070	3,917	908	5,288	1,582
2002–03	95,615	93,869	65,718	12,174	366	53,178	22,599	3,263	14,330	4,017	989	5,552	1,416
2003–04	95,726	93,977	65,758	12,341	376	53,041	22,782	3,251	14,595	3,840	1,096	5,437	1,746
2004–05	96,513	95,001	65,984	12,530	338	53,116	23,445	3,250	14,854	3,945	1,396	5,572	1,749
2005–06[8]	97,382	95,731	66,026	12,545	326	53,155	23,998	3,249	15,103	3,910	1,736	5,707	1,512
2006–07[8]	98,793	96,362	66,458	12,773	313	53,372	23,920	3,112	15,043	4,048	1,717	5,984	1,651
2007–08	98,916	97,680	67,032	12,940	288	53,804	24,426	3,047	15,927	4,055	1,397	6,222	2,431

—Not available.

[1] Includes special education, alternative, and other schools not reported by grade span.
[2] Includes schools beginning with grade 6 or below and with no grade higher than 8.
[3] Includes schools with grade spans beginning with 4, 5, or 6 and ending with 6, 7, or 8.
[4] Includes schools with no grade lower than 7.
[5] Includes schools with grades 7 and 8 or grades 7 through 9.
[6] Includes schools beginning with grade 6 or lower and ending with grade 9 or above.

[7] Because of revision in data collection procedures, figures not comparable to data for other years.
[8] Some data have been revised from previously published figures.
SOURCE: U.S. Department of Education, National Center for Education Statistics, *Statistics of State School Systems*, 1967–68 and 1975–76; *Statistics of Public Elementary and Secondary Day Schools*, 1970–71, 1972–73, 1974–75, and 1976–77 through 1980–81; and Common Core of Data (CCD), "Public Elementary/Secondary School Universe Survey," 1982–83 through 2007–08. (This table was prepared September 2009.)

Public elementary and secondary schools, by type and state or jurisdiction: 1990–91, 2000–01, and 2007–08

| State or jurisdiction | Total, all schools, 1990–91 | Total, all schools, 2000–01 | Number of schools, 2007–08 | | | Combined elementary/secondary[3] | | | | | | | | |
| | | | Total | Elementary[1] | Secondary[2] | Total | Prekindergarten, kindergarten, or 1st grade to grade 12 | Other schools ending with grade 12 | Other combined schools | Other[4] | Alternative[5] | Special education[5] | Charter[5] | One-teacher schools[5] |
1	2	3	4	5	6	7	8	9	10	11	12	13	14	15
United States	**84,538**	**93,273**	**98,916**	**67,032**	**24,426**	**6,222**	**3,113**	**2,261**	**848**	**1,236**	**6,966**	**2,267**	**4,388**	**288**
Alabama	1,297	1,517	1,605	948	414	241	161	65	15	2	119	40	0	0
Alaska	498	515	501	185	84	232	211	15	6	0	49	1	23	10
Arizona	1,049	1,724	2,135	1,320	667	136	73	40	23	12	79	10	457	5
Arkansas	1,098	1,138	1,121	717	393	11	2	6	3	0	11	4	25	0
California	7,913	8,773	9,983	6,935	2,449	587	447	103	37	12	1,325	144	691	62
Colorado	1,344	1,632	1,757	1,250	410	97	37	49	11	0	93	9	141	1
Connecticut	985	1,248	1,117	822	261	34	10	8	16	0	45	36	16	0
Delaware	173	191	235	142	46	41	29	8	4	6	33	19	17	0
District of Columbia	181	198	244	166	38	28	8	10	10	12	14	15	77	0
Florida	2,516	3,316	3,935	2,605	668	508	155	331	22	154	457	159	364	7
Georgia	1,734	1,946	2,452	1,749	435	64	16	23	25	204	183	70	67	0
Hawaii	235	261	287	208	53	24	20	2	2	2	1	3	28	0
Idaho	582	673	727	432	231	64	39	16	9	0	83	11	32	15
Illinois	4,239	4,342	4,399	3,184	1,007	170	86	62	22	38	190	227	35	3
Indiana	1,915	1,976	1,970	1,422	439	108	68	29	11	1	21	37	40	0
Iowa	1,588	1,534	1,511	1,021	449	41	3	38	0	0	70	10	10	4
Kansas	1,477	1,430	1,422	966	392	59	33	21	5	5	1	14	29	1
Kentucky	1,400	1,526	1,528	982	465	75	27	42	6	6	161	10	0	0
Louisiana	1,533	1,530	1,470	972	310	188	120	60	8	0	156	41	51	0
Maine	747	714	670	504	153	13	9	4	0	0	0	3	0	1
Maryland	1,220	1,383	1,453	1,116	277	39	21	10	8	21	76	50	30	1
Massachusetts	1,842	1,905	1,878	1,463	370	43	19	17	7	2	22	27	61	1
Michigan	3,313	3,998	4,096	2,544	1,082	212	94	72	46	258	300	252	281	5
Minnesota	1,590	2,362	2,679	1,433	894	296	144	117	35	56	725	290	169	1
Mississippi	972	1,030	1,068	614	321	127	73	50	4	6	62	4	1	0
Missouri	2,199	2,368	2,417	1,561	684	172	84	79	9	0	99	65	39	1
Montana	900	879	831	479	352	0	0	0	0	0	5	2	0	62
Nebraska	1,506	1,326	1,143	750	329	64	60	2	2	0	3	38	0	23
Nevada	354	511	610	452	134	23	6	12	5	1	30	8	27	9
New Hampshire	439	526	488	382	106	0	0	0	0	0	0	0	12	1
New Jersey	2,272	2,410	2,591	1,941	503	80	14	64	2	67	119	74	57	0
New Mexico	681	765	851	598	230	23	11	10	2	0	40	6	67	5
New York	4,010	4,336	4,631	3,231	1,059	270	86	95	89	71	28	127	96	0
North Carolina	1,955	2,207	2,516	1,835	516	136	60	59	17	29	88	33	98	0
North Dakota	663	579	528	308	186	0	0	0	0	34	0	35	0	5
Ohio	3,731	3,916	3,924	2,640	1,015	219	58	65	96	50	20	75	329	1
Oklahoma	1,880	1,821	1,798	1,229	564	3	0	3	0	2	5	5	15	0
Oregon	1,199	1,273	1,295	920	302	67	40	22	5	6	45	3	80	14
Pennsylvania	3,260	3,252	3,246	2,299	815	126	58	39	29	6	13	13	125	1
Rhode Island	309	328	328	246	75	7	5	2	0	0	15	3	11	0
South Carolina	1,097	1,127	1,195	886	275	25	8	12	5	9	23	10	29	1
South Dakota	802	769	730	432	270	26	9	14	3	2	29	9	0	18
Tennessee	1,543	1,624	1,718	1,284	345	72	35	31	6	17	25	20	12	0
Texas	5,991	7,519	8,758	5,712	2,158	862	338	388	136	26	1,417	23	450	0
Utah	714	793	1,010	605	305	76	39	8	29	24	93	82	58	8
Vermont	397	393	329	240	72	17	11	6	0	0	1	0	0	1
Virginia	1,811	1,969	2,027	1,503	385	48	36	9	3	91	128	12	3	0
Washington	1,936	2,305	2,311	1,444	574	293	165	63	65	0	320	117	0	3
West Virginia	1,015	840	762	561	130	71	54	16	1	0	28	7	0	0
Wisconsin	2,018	2,182	2,268	1,553	631	80	20	56	4	4	92	9	232	8
Wyoming	415	393	368	241	103	24	11	8	5	0	24	5	3	10
Bureau of Indian Education	—	189	174	109	21	44	39	3	2	0	0	0	0	—
DoD, domestic	—	71	67	50	7	2	1	1	0	8	0	0	0	0
DoD, overseas	—	156	130	87	32	11	8	3	0	0	0	0	0	0
Other jurisdictions														
American Samoa	30	31	31	24	6	0	0	0	0	1	0	1	0	0
Guam	35	38	36	32	0	4	4	0	0	0	0	0	0	0
Northern Marianas	26	29	31	23	6	0	0	0	0	2	1	0	0	0
Puerto Rico	1,619	1,543	1,511	908	398	181	4	5	172	24	8	28	0	0
U.S. Virgin Islands	33	36	34	23	10	1	1	0	0	1	0	1	0	0

—Not available.
[1]Includes schools beginning with grade 6 or below and with no grade higher than 8.
[2]Includes schools with no grade lower than 7.
[3]Includes schools beginning with grade 6 or below and ending with grade 9 or above.
[4]Includes schools not reported by grade span.
[5]Schools are also included under elementary, secondary, combined, or other as appropriate.
NOTE: DoD = Department of Defense.
SOURCE: U.S. Department of Education, National Center for Education Statistics, Common Core of Data (CCD), "Public Elementary/Secondary School Universe Survey," 1990–91, 2000–01, and 2007–08. (This table was prepared September 2009.)

Public elementary schools, by grade span, average school size, and state or jurisdiction: 2007–08

State or jurisdiction	Total, all elementary schools	Total, all regular elementary schools[1]	Prekindergarten, kindergarten, or 1st grade to grades 3 or 4	Prekindergarten, kindergarten, or 1st grade to grade 5	Prekindergarten, kindergarten, or 1st grade to grade 6	Prekindergarten, kindergarten, or 1st grade to grade 8	Grade 4, 5, or 6 to grade 6, 7, or 8	Other grade spans	All elementary schools	Regular elementary schools[1]
1	2	3	4	5	6	7	8	9	10	11
United States	**67,032**	**65,658**	**4,958**	**24,753**	**12,020**	**6,049**	**12,940**	**6,312**	**469**	**475**
Alabama	948	934	82	307	171	66	218	104	477	480
Alaska	185	184	1	31	101	15	19	18	330	330
Arizona	1,320	1,296	55	261	337	417	185	65	536	540
Arkansas	717	714	122	149	184	7	150	105	414	415
California	6,935	6,704	164	2,437	2,176	883	1,050	225	542	558
Colorado	1,250	1,245	29	559	272	94	224	72	412	413
Connecticut	822	806	87	285	112	73	144	121	438	445
Delaware	142	139	22	61	11	7	32	9	544	553
District of Columbia	166	156	8	21	74	15	24	24	283	287
Florida	2,605	2,535	19	1,613	153	127	562	131	689	706
Georgia	1,749	1,744	33	1,053	26	14	451	172	665	666
Hawaii	208	207	0	76	98	5	26	3	532	534
Idaho	432	429	39	133	145	23	72	20	380	382
Illinois	3,184	3,092	312	798	353	691	575	455	439	446
Indiana	1,422	1,419	130	554	351	29	275	83	463	464
Iowa	1,021	1,016	125	330	190	14	228	134	297	298
Kansas	966	962	94	302	224	88	183	75	307	308
Kentucky	982	967	40	486	137	83	190	46	458	464
Louisiana	972	919	85	319	120	123	208	117	458	467
Maine	504	503	59	93	76	100	89	87	243	244
Maryland	1,116	1,091	17	630	131	45	221	72	502	508
Massachusetts	1,463	1,445	196	506	138	95	297	231	429	430
Michigan	2,544	2,527	242	949	322	188	507	336	405	407
Minnesota	1,433	1,129	106	358	403	136	243	187	398	436
Mississippi	614	612	73	121	123	43	137	117	499	500
Missouri	1,561	1,551	146	454	358	125	293	185	369	370
Montana	479	476	19	53	219	109	52	27	173	173
Nebraska	750	745	0	0	548	88	85	29	240	241
Nevada	452	446	11	237	86	10	86	22	648	657
New Hampshire	382	382	59	113	39	49	80	42	340	340
New Jersey	1,941	1,929	280	560	164	272	369	296	464	466
New Mexico	598	587	23	223	139	19	129	65	356	361
New York	3,231	3,211	267	1,282	401	180	705	396	527	529
North Carolina	1,835	1,828	76	1,046	62	123	440	88	554	556
North Dakota	308	306	10	55	144	60	25	14	183	184
Ohio	2,640	2,600	353	700	453	233	527	374	411	416
Oklahoma	1,229	1,225	69	375	117	308	237	123	359	360
Oregon	920	915	43	396	164	95	180	42	388	388
Pennsylvania	2,299	2,298	267	781	466	180	425	180	463	464
Rhode Island	246	244	24	102	40	4	43	33	381	383
South Carolina	886	883	40	446	56	29	225	90	550	552
South Dakota	432	430	15	120	90	101	87	19	182	182
Tennessee	1,284	1,274	172	490	85	185	279	73	502	505
Texas	5,712	5,536	584	2,466	585	126	1,298	653	551	562
Utah	605	570	11	97	372	23	40	62	554	578
Vermont	240	240	11	31	108	62	18	10	222	222
Virginia	1,503	1,501	50	843	149	9	312	140	542	543
Washington	1,444	1,364	47	564	401	71	237	124	429	444
West Virginia	561	558	83	236	62	39	110	31	335	336
Wisconsin	1,553	1,544	133	597	196	153	307	167	357	358
Wyoming	241	240	25	54	88	15	41	18	210	211
Bureau of Indian Education	109	109	6	5	24	66	3	5	—	—
DoD, domestic	50	50	12	14	6	1	7	10	413	413
DoD, overseas	87	87	6	21	33	9	15	3	442	442
Other jurisdictions										
American Samoa	24	24	1	0	0	21	1	1	—	—
Guam	32	32	0	24	0	7	0	1	—	—
Northern Marianas	23	23	0	2	10	0	2	9	297	297
Puerto Rico	908	906	59	6	793	3	26	21	268	268
U.S. Virgin Islands	23	23	1	0	21	0	1	0	368	368

—Not available.

[1]Excludes special education and alternative schools.

[2]Average for schools reporting enrollment data. Enrollment data were available for 66,476 out of 67,032 public elementary schools in 2007–08.

NOTE: Includes schools beginning with grade 6 or below and with no grade higher than 8. Excludes schools not reported by grade level, such as some special education schools for the disabled. DoD = Department of Defense.

SOURCE: U.S. Department of Education, National Center for Education Statistics, Common Core of Data (CCD), "Public Elementary/Secondary School Universe Survey," 2007–08. (This table was prepared September 2009.)

Public secondary schools, by grade span, average school size, and state or jurisdiction: 2007–08

State or jurisdiction	Total, all secondary schools	Total, all regular secondary schools[1]	Grades 7 to 8 and 7 to 9	Grades 7 to 12	Grades 8 to 12	Grades 9 to 12	Grades 10 to 12	Other spans ending with grade 12	Other grade spans	Vocational schools[2]	Average number of students per school[3] All secondary schools	Regular secondary schools[1]
1	2	3	4	5	6	7	8	9	10	11	12	13
United States	**24,426**	**19,264**	**3,047**	**3,278**	**777**	**15,179**	**748**	**378**	**1,019**	**1,409**	**706**	**816**
Alabama	414	314	34	96	19	226	28	3	8	73	681	709
Alaska	84	65	16	20	3	43	2	0	0	3	494	601
Arizona	667	470	76	36	7	527	10	3	8	166	696	729
Arkansas	393	360	59	134	8	127	42	1	22	24	484	494
California	2,449	1,495	342	321	42	1,679	25	13	27	76	901	1,355
Colorado	410	344	61	60	1	274	7	1	6	5	619	710
Connecticut	261	195	35	12	11	184	11	2	6	17	756	941
Delaware	46	34	7	1	27	10	0	0	1	6	952	1,008
District of Columbia	38	30	6	3	1	26	1	0	1	5	549	606
Florida	668	475	20	67	30	488	9	19	35	51	1,276	1,667
Georgia	435	392	11	14	8	350	7	2	43	3	1,137	1,201
Hawaii	53	52	11	9	0	33	0	0	0	0	1,191	1,210
Idaho	231	154	40	47	1	115	24	0	4	11	440	593
Illinois	1,007	802	150	67	19	634	11	57	69	55	745	847
Indiana	439	420	75	89	1	265	1	1	7	29	853	866
Iowa	449	381	48	80	1	302	9	4	5	0	392	450
Kansas	392	387	58	81	4	239	8	0	2	1	430	432
Kentucky	465	240	30	43	24	295	12	9	52	126	586	803
Louisiana	310	263	41	49	68	125	18	0	9	6	637	709
Maine	153	124	15	10	2	115	9	0	2	27	525	533
Maryland	277	208	20	6	8	213	2	6	22	24	1,065	1,270
Massachusetts	370	315	33	36	6	293	0	1	1	39	860	894
Michigan	1,082	745	102	96	37	664	64	39	80	55	569	749
Minnesota	894	482	63	298	40	391	57	32	13	11	405	625
Mississippi	321	226	29	60	8	188	26	2	8	89	652	658
Missouri	684	587	80	204	1	350	21	11	17	63	548	557
Montana	352	348	180	1	0	171	0	0	0	0	172	173
Nebraska	329	325	28	181	1	116	1	1	1	0	360	361
Nevada	134	111	23	7	8	87	2	5	2	1	998	1,158
New Hampshire	106	106	18	0	0	85	0	0	3	0	681	681
New Jersey	503	401	60	40	8	352	18	7	18	55	930	1,094
New Mexico	230	200	39	30	7	137	9	0	8	2	527	572
New York	1,059	980	89	132	10	722	24	3	79	29	862	878
North Carolina	516	486	26	10	7	439	6	5	23	10	830	867
North Dakota	186	179	11	105	2	56	3	1	8	6	215	216
Ohio	1,015	928	131	142	80	605	9	17	31	75	664	684
Oklahoma	564	560	84	0	0	417	45	3	15	0	354	355
Oregon	302	270	30	41	12	211	7	1	0	0	620	679
Pennsylvania	815	720	101	162	13	449	59	9	22	87	863	875
Rhode Island	75	52	9	4	0	59	2	0	1	12	795	906
South Carolina	275	222	24	14	5	210	14	3	5	40	974	983
South Dakota	270	257	80	1	1	188	0	0	0	0	164	166
Tennessee	345	308	24	27	18	248	13	10	5	22	868	924
Texas	2,158	1,482	316	215	109	1,185	37	47	249	1	702	948
Utah	305	219	85	45	23	68	48	12	24	8	715	934
Vermont	72	56	8	19	0	30	0	0	15	15	582	592
Virginia	385	343	33	6	36	272	3	0	35	31	1,183	1,197
Washington	574	388	83	67	53	327	24	9	11	11	652	885
West Virginia	130	116	10	19	1	93	2	3	2	31	657	715
Wisconsin	631	561	69	60	4	434	14	36	14	8	495	543
Wyoming	103	86	24	11	2	62	4	0	0	0	310	358
Bureau of Indian Education	21	21	2	5	0	14	0	0	0	0	—	—
DoD, domestic	7	7	2	0	0	5	0	0	0	0	476	476
DoD, overseas	32	32	2	13	0	17	0	0	0	0	453	453
Other jurisdictions												
American Samoa	6	5	0	0	0	5	1	0	0	1	—	—
Guam	0	0	0	0	0	0	0	0	0	0	—	—
Northern Marianas	6	6	1	1	0	4	0	0	0	0	727	727
Puerto Rico	398	368	191	28	1	3	158	0	17	27	529	518
U.S. Virgin Islands	10	8	5	0	0	5	0	0	0	1	803	896

—Not available.

[1] Excludes vocational, special education, and alternative schools.
[2] Vocational schools are also included under appropriate grade span.
[3] Average for schools reporting enrollment data. Enrollment data were available for 22,800 out of 24,426 public secondary schools in 2007–08.

NOTE: Includes schools with no grade lower than 7. Excludes schools not reported by grade level, such as some special education schools for the disabled. DoD = Department of Defense.
SOURCE: U.S. Department of Education, National Center for Education Statistics, Common Core of Data (CCD), "Public Elementary/Secondary School Universe Survey," 2007–08. (This table was prepared September 2009.)

Age range for compulsory school attendance and special education services, and policies on year-round schools and kindergarten programs, by state: Selected years, 1997 through 2008

State	Compulsory attendance						Compulsory special education services, 1997[1]	Year-round schools, 2008		Kindergarten education, 2008		
								Has policy on year-round schools	Has districts with year-round schools	School districts required to offer		Attendance required
	2000	2002	2004	2006	2007	2008				Program	Full-day program	
1	2	3	4	5	6	7	8	9	10	11	12	13
Alabama	7 to 16	7 to 16	7 to 16[2]	7 to 16	7 to 16	7 to 16	6 to 21		Yes		X	
Alaska	7 to 16	7 to 16	7 to 16[2]	7 to 16	7 to 16	7 to 16	3 to 22		Yes			
Arizona	6 to 16[2]	6 to 16[2]	6 to 16[2]	6 to 16[2]	6 to 16[2]	6 to 16[2]	3 to 22		—	X[3,4]		
Arkansas	5 to 17[2]	5 to 17[2]	5 to 17	5 to 17	5 to 17	5 to 17	5 to 21	X	Yes		X	
California	6 to 18[2]	6 to 18	6 to 18	6 to 18	6 to 18	6 to 18	Birth to 21	X	Yes	X		
Colorado	—	—	7 to 16	7 to 16	6 to 17	6 to 17	3 to 21		Yes	X		
Connecticut	7 to 16	7 to 18[2]	7 to 18[2]	5 to 18[5]	5 to 18[5]	5 to 18[5]	Under 21[6]		—	X		X
Delaware	5 to 16	5 to 16	5 to 16[2]	5 to 16	5 to 16	5 to 16	3 to 20		Yes	X	X[7]	X
District of Columbia	—	5 to 18	5 to 18	5 to 18	5 to 18	5 to 18	—			X		X
Florida	6 to 16[8]	6 to 16[8]	6 to 16[8]	6 to 16[8]	6 to 16[8]	6 to 16[8]		X	Yes	X		X
Georgia	6 to 16	6 to 16	6 to 16	6 to 16	6 to 16	6 to 16	Under 21[6]		Yes		X	
Hawaii	6 to 18	6 to 18	6 to 18	6 to 18	6 to 18	6 to 18	Under 20		(9)	X		
Idaho	7 to 16	7 to 16	7 to 16	7 to 16	7 to 16	7 to 16	3 to 21		Yes			
Illinois	7 to 16	7 to 16	7 to 17	7 to 17	7 to 17	7 to 17	3 to 21	X	Yes	X[3]		
Indiana	7 to 16	7 to 16	7 to 16	7 to 18[2]	7 to 18[2]	7 to 18[2]	3 to 22		Yes	X		
Iowa	6 to 16[2]	6 to 16[2]	6 to 16	6 to 16	6 to 16	6 to 16	Under 21	X	Yes	X		
Kansas	7 to 18[2]	7 to 18[2]	7 to 18[2]	7 to 18[2]	7 to 18[2]	7 to 18[2]	Under 21		(10)	X		
Kentucky	6 to 16	6 to 16	6 to 16[2]	6 to 16	6 to 16	6 to 16	Under 21		Yes	X		
Louisiana	7 to 17	7 to 17	7 to 17	7 to 18[2]	7 to 18[2]	7 to 18[2]	3 to 21		Yes	X	X	X
Maine	7 to 17	7 to 17	7 to 17[2]	7 to 17[2]	7 to 17[2]	7 to 17[2]	5 to 19[11]		—	X		
Maryland	5 to 16	5 to 16	5 to 16	5 to 16	5 to 16	5 to 16[5]	Under 21	X	—	X	X	X
Massachusetts	6 to 16	6 to 16	6 to 16	6 to 16[2]	6 to 16[2]	6 to 16[2]	3 to 21	(12)	—	X		
Michigan	6 to 16	6 to 16	6 to 16	6 to 16	6 to 16	6 to 16	Under 26	X	Yes	X[13]		
Minnesota	7 to 18[2]	7 to 16	7 to 16	7 to 16[2]	7 to 16[2]	7 to 16[2,5]	Under 22	X	Yes			
Mississippi	6 to 17	6 to 17	6 to 16	6 to 16	6 to 17	6 to 17	Birth to 20		—	X		
Missouri	7 to 16[2]	7 to 16[2]	7 to 16[2]	7 to 16[2]	7 to 16[2]	7 to 16	Under 21		Yes[14]	X		
Montana	7 to 16	7 to 16	7 to 16	7 to 16	7 to 16	7 to 16	3 to 18		—	X		
Nebraska	7 to 16	7 to 16	7 to 16	6 to 18	6 to 18	6 to 18	Birth to 21		Yes	X		
Nevada	7 to 17	7 to 17	7 to 17	7 to 17	7 to 18[2,5]	7 to 18[2,5]	Under 22		Yes	X		X
New Hampshire	6 to 16	6 to 16	6 to 16	6 to 16	6 to 16[15]	6 to 16[15]	3 to 21		—			
New Jersey	6 to 16	6 to 16	6 to 16	6 to 16	6 to 16	6 to 16	5 to 21		—		X[16]	
New Mexico	5 to 18	5 to 18	5 to 18[2]	5 to 18[2]	5 to 18[2]	5 to 18[2]	(17)	X	Yes	X		X
New York	6 to 16[2]	6 to 16	6 to 16	6 to 16[18]	6 to 16[18]	6 to 16[18]	Under 21		—			
North Carolina	7 to 16	7 to 16	7 to 16	7 to 16	7 to 16	7 to 16	5 to 20	X	Yes		X	
North Dakota	7 to 16	7 to 16	7 to 16	7 to 16	7 to 16	7 to 16	3 to 20[19]		No			
Ohio	6 to 18	6 to 18	6 to 18	6 to 18	6 to 18	6 to 18	Under 22	X		X[3]		X[20]
Oklahoma	5 to 18	5 to 18	5 to 18	5 to 18	5 to 18	5 to 18	3 and up[21]		Yes	X	(22)	X
Oregon	7 to 18	7 to 18	7 to 18[2]	7 to 18	7 to 18	7 to 18	3 to 21		Yes	X		
Pennsylvania	8 to 17	8 to 17	8 to 17[2]	8 to 17[2]	8 to 17[2]	8 to 17[2]	6 to 21	X[14]	—[14]	X		
Rhode Island	6 to 16	6 to 16	6 to 16	6 to 16	6 to 16	6 to 16	3 to 21		—	X		
South Carolina	5 to 16	5 to 16	5 to 16	5 to 17[5]	5 to 17[5]	5 to 17[5]	3 to 21		—		X[3,4]	X
South Dakota	6 to 16	6 to 16	6 to 16	6 to 16	6 to 16	6 to 16[5,23]	Under 21	X	Yes	X		X
Tennessee	6 to 17	6 to 17	6 to 17	6 to 17[5]	6 to 17[5]	6 to 18	3 to 21	X	Yes	X		X
Texas	6 to 18	6 to 18	6 to 18	6 to 18	6 to 18	6 to 18	3 to 21	X	Yes	X		
Utah	6 to 18	6 to 18	6 to 18	6 to 18	6 to 18	6 to 18	3 to 22		Yes	X		
Vermont	7 to 16	6 to 16	6 to 16	6 to 16[2]	6 to 16[2]	6 to 16[2]	3 to 21		—[14]	X		
Virginia	5 to 18	5 to 18	5 to 18	5 to 18[2]	5 to 18[2]	5 to 18[2,5]	2 to 21	X	Yes	X		X
Washington	8 to 17[2]	8 to 17[2]	8 to 17[2]	8 to 16[2]	8 to 18	8 to 18	3 to 21[24]	X	Yes	X		
West Virginia	6 to 16	6 to 16	6 to 16	6 to 16	6 to 16	6 to 16	5 to 21	X	Yes	X	X	X
Wisconsin	6 to 18	6 to 18	6 to 18	6 to 18	6 to 18	6 to 18	Under 21		Yes	X	X[25]	
Wyoming	6 to 16[2]	6 to 16[2]	7 to 16[2]	7 to 16[2]	7 to 16[2]	7 to 16[2]	3 to 21		—	X		

—Not available.

X Denotes that the state has a policy. A blank denotes that the state does not have a policy.

[1]Most states have a provision whereby education is provided up to a certain age or completion of secondary school, whichever comes first.

[2]Child may be exempted from compulsory attendance if he/she meets state requirements for early withdrawal with or without meeting conditions for a diploma or equivalency.

[3]State requires districts with full-day programs to offer half-day programs.

[4]Districts may apply for exemptions from the requirement.

[5]Parent/guardian may delay child's entry until a later age per state law/regulation.

[6]Under 21 or until child graduates from high school.

[7]Full-day requirement becomes effective upon each district's confirming vote and upon specific funding appropriation by the General Assembly.

[8]Attendance is compulsory until age 18 for Manatee County students, unless they earn a high school diploma prior to reaching their 18th birthday.

[9]Some districts operate on a multi-track system; the schools are open year-round, but different cohorts start and end at different times.

[10]To be determined by rules and regulations adopted by the state board.

[11]Must be age 5 before October 1, and not age 20 before start of school year.

[12]Policies about year-round schools are decided locally.

[13]State requires a "program," not necessarily a traditional kindergarten program.

[14]State did not participate in the 2008 online survey. Data shown are from 2006.

[15]Compulsory attendance age is 18 effective July 1, 2009.

[16]Abbott districts only (31). These are districts covered by New Jersey Supreme Court rulings requiring the state to implement comprehensive programs and reforms to improve the education of students in the poorest schools.

[17]School-age unless otherwise provided by law.

[18]New York City and Buffalo require school attendance until age 17 unless employed; Syracuse requires kindergarten attendance at age 5.

[19]Must not be age 21 by September 1.

[20]A child may skip kindergarten at the parent's request and if the child demonstrates that he or she possesses the social, emotional, and cognitive skills for first grade.

[21]Children from birth through age 2 are eligible for additional services. Eligibility for special education services ceases upon completion of a secondary education program; no age limit.

[22]Beginning in 2011–12, with the option for districts to transfer intradistrict, interdistrict, or to a licensed child care provider.

[23]Compulsory attendance until age 18 is effective July 1, 2009; compulsory attendance beginning at age 5 is effective July 1, 2010.

[24]Student may complete school year if 21st birthday occurs while attending school.

[25]Districts are required to provide full-day kindergarten for low-income students.

NOTE: The Education of the Handicapped Act (EHA) Amendments of 1986 make it mandatory for all states receiving EHA funds to serve all 3- to 18-year-old disabled children.

SOURCE: Council of Chief State School Officers, *Key State Education Policies on PK–12 Education,* 2000, 2002, 2004, and 2008 (prepublication copy); Education Commission of the States, ECS StateNotes, *Kindergarten: State Statutes Regarding Kindergarten* (prepublication copy of 2008 update) and *Attendance: Compulsory School Age Requirements,* retrieved July 1, 2009, from http://www.ecs.org/clearinghouse/80/44/8044.pdf; and supplemental information retrieved June 20, 2009, from School District of Manatee County Policy and Procedures (http://www.manatee.k12.fl.us/policy_procedure/pdfs/chapters/Chapter_5.pdf) and retrieved July 8, 2009, from the state websites for Florida (http://www.leg.state.fl.us/STATUTES/index.cfm?App-mode=Display_Statute&Search_String=&URL=Ch1003/Sec21.HTM), New Jersey (http://www.nj.gov/education/abbotts/about/), and Ohio (http://law.justia.com/ohio/codes/orc/jd_332101-8741.html). (This table was prepared July 2009.)

Minimum amount of instructional time per year and policy on textbook selection, by state: 2000, 2006, and 2008

State	Minimum amount of instructional time per year				State policy on textbook selection, 2008					State
	In days			In hours	State recommends or selects textbooks			Local decision	State standards used in recommendation or selection	
	2000	2006	2008	2008	Recommends	Selects	Either recommends or selects			State
1	2	3	4	5	6	7	8	9	10	11
Alabama	175	175	180	†			X		X	Alabama
Alaska	180	180	180[1]	740 (K–3); 900 (4–12)				X		Alaska
Arizona	175[2]	180	180[3]	†				X		Arizona
Arkansas	178	178	178[4]	†	X				X	Arkansas
California	175	180	180	†	X					California
Colorado	[5]	160	160	450/900 (K); 990 (1–5); 1,080 (6–12)				X		Colorado
Connecticut	180	180	180	450/900 (K); 900 (1–12)				X		Connecticut
Delaware	[5]	†	†	440 (K); 1,060 (1–11); 1,032 (12)				X		Delaware
District of Columbia	180[6]	180	180	†						District of Columbia
Florida	180	180	180	†	X				X	Florida
Georgia	180[6]	180	180	†	X				X	Georgia
Hawaii	184	179	180	†	X				X	Hawaii
Idaho	180	†	†	450[1] (K); 810[1] (1–3); 900[1] (4–8); 990[1,7] (9–12)	X				X	Idaho
Illinois	180[8]	176	176	†				X		Illinois
Indiana	180	180	180	†	X				X	Indiana
Iowa	180	180	180	†				X		Iowa
Kansas	186	186 (K–11); 181 (12)	186 (K–11); 181 (12)	465 (K); 1,116 (1–11); 1,086 (12)				X		Kansas
Kentucky	175	175	175[1]	†	X				X	Kentucky
Louisiana	175	177	177[4]	†			X			Louisiana
Maine	175	175	175[4]	†				X		Maine
Maryland	180	180	180	1,080				X		Maryland
Massachusetts	180	180	180	425 (K); 900 (1–8)[9]; 990 (6–12)[10]				X		Massachusetts
Michigan	180	†	†	1,098				X		Michigan
Minnesota	[5]	[5]	[5]	†				X		Minnesota
Mississippi	180	180	180	†		X				Mississippi
Missouri	174	174	174	1,044	—	—	—	—	—	Missouri
Montana	180	90 (K); 180 (K–12)	†	360/720 (K); 720 (1–3); 1,080[7] (4–12)				X		Montana
Nebraska	[5]	180	180	400 (K); 1,032 (1–8); 1,080 (9–12)				X		Nebraska
Nevada	180	180	180	†				X		Nevada
New Hampshire	180	180	180	945 (1–8)[11]; 990 (9–12)				X		New Hampshire
New Jersey	180	180	180	†				X		New Jersey
New Mexico	180	180	180	450/990[12] (K); 990[12] (1–6); 1,080 (7–12)		X		X	X	New Mexico
New York	180[6]	180	180	†				X		New York
North Carolina	180	180	180	1,000	X			X		North Carolina
North Dakota	173	173	173[13]	†				X		North Dakota
Ohio	182	182	182[1]	†				X		Ohio
Oklahoma	180	180	175[4]	†	X				X	Oklahoma
Oregon	[5]	†	†	405 (K); 810 (1–3); 900 (4–8); 990[7] (9–12)			X		X	Oregon
Pennsylvania	180	180	180	450 (K); 900 (1–6); 990 (7–12)	—	—	—	—	—	Pennsylvania
Rhode Island	180	180	180	†				X		Rhode Island
South Carolina	180	180	180[4]	†			X	X	X	South Carolina
South Dakota	—	†	†	437.5[14] (K); Board decision (1–3)[15]; 962.5[7] (4–12)						South Dakota
Tennessee	180	180	180[13]	†		X			X	Tennessee
Texas	187	180	180	†			X			Texas
Utah	180	180	180	450 (K); 810 (1); 990 (2–12)			X			Utah
Vermont	175	175	175	†	—	—	—	—	—	Vermont
Virginia	180	180	180	540 (K); 990 (1–12)	X			X	X	Virginia
Washington	180[8]	180	180	450 (K); 1,000 (1–12)				X	X	Washington
West Virginia	180	180	180	†			X			West Virginia
Wisconsin	180	180	180	437 (K); 1,050 (1–6); 1,137 (7–12)				X		Wisconsin
Wyoming	175	175	175	†				X		Wyoming

—Not available.

†Not applicable.

X Denotes that the state has a policy. A blank denotes that the state does not have a policy.

[1] Includes time for staff development.

[2] 1994 data.

[3] Or an equivalent number of minutes of instruction per year for districts on an alternate schedule.

[4] Does not include time for staff development.

[5] No statewide policy; varies by district.

[6] 1996 data.

[7] Instructional time for graduating seniors may be reduced.

[8] 1998 data.

[9] Instructional hours shown apply to schools with grades 1 through 5, 6, 7, or 8.

[10] Instructional hours shown apply to schools with any combination of grades within the given range.

[11] Middle schools (any combination of grades 4 through 8) are required to have the same hours as secondary schools (grades 9 through 12).

[12] Teachers may use 33 hours of the full-day kindergarten program and 22 hours of the grades 1 through 5 programs for home visits or parent-teacher conferences.

[13] Does not include time for staff development and parent-teacher conferences.

[14] Kindergarten instructional time is effective July 1, 2010.

[15] The Board of Education sets the minimum number of hours in the school term for grades 1 through 3.

NOTE: Minimum number of instructional days refers to the actual number of days that pupils have contact with a teacher. Some states allow for different types of school calendars by setting instructional time in both days and hours, while others use only days or only hours. For states in which the number of days or hours varies by grade, the relevant grade(s) appear in parentheses.

SOURCE: Council of Chief State School Officers, *Key State Education Policies on PK–12 Education*, 2000, 2006, and 2008 (prepublication copy); Education Commission of the States, StateNotes, *Scheduling/Length of School Year*, 2008, retrieved June 10, 2009, from http://ecs.org/clearinghouse/78/24/7824.pdf; and supplemental information retrieved June 10, 2009, from the Massachusetts Department of Elementary and Secondary School Education, http://www.doe.mass.edu/lawsregs/603cmr27.html?section=105; retrieved July 16, 2009, from the New Hampshire General Court, http://state.nh.us/rules/ed300.html; retrieved July 21, 2009, from the South Dakota Department of Education, http://doe.sd.gov/oatq/accreditation/exemptionSDCL.asp; and retrieved July 23, 2009, from the Pennsylvania Code, http://pacode.com/secure/data/022/Chapter11/s11.3.html. (This table was prepared July 2009.)

Credit requirements and exit exam requirements for a standard high school diploma and the use of other high school completion credentials, by state: 2008 and 2009

State	Total required credits for standard diploma, all courses	English/ language arts	Social studies	Science	Mathematics	Other credits	Exit exam required for standard diploma	Subjects tested[1]	Exam based on standards for 10th grade or higher	Appeals or alternative route to standard diploma if exam failed	Advanced recognition for exceeding standard requirements	Alternative credential for not meeting all standard requirements
1	2	3	4	5	6	7	8	9	10	11	12	13
Alabama	24.0	4.0	4.0	4.0	4.0	8.0	Yes	EMSH	Yes	Yes	Yes	Yes
Alaska	21.0	4.0	3.0	2.0	2.0	10.0	Yes	EM	Yes	Yes	No	Yes
Arizona	20.0	4.0	3.0	2.0	3.0	8.0	Yes	EM	Yes	Yes	Yes	No
Arkansas	22.0	4.0	3.0	3.0	4.0	8.0	No [2]	†	†	†	No	No
California	13.0	3.0	3.0	2.0	2.0	3.0	Yes	EM	Yes	Yes	Yes	Yes
Colorado	† [3]	† [3]	† [3]	† [3]	† [3]	† [3]	No	†	†	†	No	No
Connecticut	20.0	4.0	3.0	2.0	3.0	8.0	No	†	†	†	No	No
Delaware	22.0	4.0	3.0	3.0	3.0	9.0	No	†	†	†	No	Yes
District of Columbia	24.0	4.0	4.0	4.0	4.0	8.0	No	†	†	†	No	Yes
Florida	24.0 or 18.0 [4]	4.0	3.0	3.0	4.0 or 3.0 [4]	10.0 or 5.0 [4]	Yes	EM	Yes	Yes	Yes	Yes
Georgia	23.0	4.0	3.0	4.0	4.0	8.0	Yes	EMSH	Yes	Yes	Yes	Yes
Hawaii	22.0	4.0	4.0	3.0	3.0	8.0	No	†	†	†	Yes	Yes
Idaho	42.0 [5]	9.0 [5]	5.0 [5]	4.0 [5]	4.0 [5]	20.0 [5]	Yes	EM	Yes	Yes	No	No
Illinois	18.0	3.0	2.0	1.0	3.0	9.0	No	†	†	†	No	No
Indiana	40.0 [5]	8.0 [5]	6.0 [5]	6.0 [5]	6.0 [5]	14.0 [5]	Yes	EM	No	Yes	Yes	No
Iowa	† [3]	† [3]	1.5	† [3]	† [3]	† [3]	No	†	†	†	Yes	No
Kansas	21.0	4.0	3.0	3.0	3.0	8.0	No	†	†	†	No	No
Kentucky	22.0	4.0	3.0	3.0	3.0	9.0	No	†	†	†	Yes	Yes
Louisiana	23.0	4.0	3.0	3.0	3.0	10.0	Yes	EMSH	Yes	Yes	Yes	Yes
Maine	16.0	4.0	2.0	2.0	2.0	6.0	No	†	†	†	No	No
Maryland	21.0	4.0	3.0	3.0	3.0	8.0	Yes	EMSH	Yes	Yes	Yes	Yes
Massachusetts	† [3]	† [3]	† [3]	† [3]	† [3]	† [3]	Yes	EM	Yes	Yes	Yes	Yes
Michigan	† [3]	4.0	3.0	3.0	4.0	† [3]	No	†	†	†	No	Yes
Minnesota	21.5	4.0	3.5	3.0	3.0	8.0	Yes	EM	No	Yes	No	No
Mississippi	20.0	4.0	3.0	3.0	3.0	7.0	Yes	EMSH	Yes	Yes	No	Yes
Missouri	22.0 [6]	4.0 [6]	2.0 [6]	2.0 [6]	2.0 [6]	12.0 [6]	No	†	†	†	Yes	No
Montana	20.0	4.0	2.0	2.0	2.0	10.0	No	†	†	†	No	No
Nebraska	200.0 [7]	† [3]	† [3]	† [3]	† [3]	† [3]	No	†	†	†	No	No
Nevada	22.5	4.0	2.0	2.0	3.0	11.5	Yes	EMS	Yes	Yes	Yes	Yes
New Hampshire	20.0	4.0	2.5	2.0	3.0	8.5	No	†	†	†	Yes	Yes
New Jersey	22.0	4.0	3.0	3.0	3.0	9.0	Yes	EM	Yes	Yes	No	No
New Mexico	24.0	4.0	3.0	3.0	4.0	10.0	Yes	EMSH	No	Yes	No	Yes
New York	22.0	4.0	4.0	3.0	3.0	8.0	Yes	EMSH	Yes	Yes	Yes	Yes
North Carolina	20.0	4.0	3.0	3.0	4.0	6.0	Yes	EMT	No	Yes	Yes	Yes
North Dakota	21.0	† [3]	† [3]	† [3]	† [3]	† [3]	No	†	†	†	No	No
Ohio	20.0	4.0	3.0	3.0	3.0	7.0	Yes	EMSH	Yes	Yes	Yes	No
Oklahoma	23.0	4.0	3.0	3.0	3.0	10.0	No [2]	†	†	†	Yes	No
Oregon	22.0	3.0	3.0	2.0	2.0	12.0	No	†	†	†	No	Yes
Pennsylvania	† [3,6]	† [3,6]	† [3,6]	† [3,6]	† [3,6]	† [3,6]	No	†	†	†	Yes	No
Rhode Island	20.0	4.0	3.0	3.0	4.0	6.0	No	†	†	†	No	Yes
South Carolina	24.0	4.0	3.0	3.0	4.0	10.0	Yes	EM	Yes	No	No	No
South Dakota	22.0	4.0	3.0	3.0	3.0	9.0	No	†	†	†	Yes	No
Tennessee	20.0	4.0	3.0	3.0	3.0	7.0	Yes	EMS	Yes	No	No	Yes
Texas	24.0	4.0	5.0	3.0	3.0	9.0	Yes	EMSH	Yes	No	Yes	Yes
Utah	24.0	3.0	2.5	2.0	2.0	14.5	No	†	†	†	No	Yes
Vermont	20.0 [6]	4.0 [6]	3.0 [6]	3.0 [6]	3.0 [6]	7.0 [6]	No	†	†	†	No	No
Virginia	22.0	4.0	3.0	3.0	3.0	9.0	Yes	EMSH	Yes	Yes	Yes	Yes
Washington	19.0	3.0	2.5	2.0	2.0	9.5	Yes	E	Yes	Yes	No	No
West Virginia	24.0	4.0	4.0	3.0	4.0	9.0	No	†	†	†	No	Yes
Wisconsin	21.5 [8]	4.0	3.0	2.0	2.0	10.5	No	†	†	†	No	No
Wyoming	13.0	4.0	3.0	3.0	3.0	0.0	No	†	†	†	Yes	Yes

†Not applicable.

[1]Exit exam subjects tested: E = English (including writing), M = Mathematics, S = Science, H = History/social studies, and T = Technology.

[2]Requirement takes effect for class of 2010 in Arkansas and class of 2012 in Oklahoma.

[3]Graduation requirements are determined locally.

[4]Florida offers three graduation programs: one 4-year, 24-credit program, and two 3-year, 18-credit programs. The 4-year program requires 4 credits of mathematics, and both 3-year programs require 3 credits of mathematics.

[5]Expressed in semester credits instead of Carnegie units.

[6]State did not participate in the 2008 online survey; data are from 2006.

[7]Expressed in credit hours instead of Carnegie units.

[8]Determined locally, but state encourages school boards to adopt this requirement.

NOTE: Local school districts frequently have other graduation requirements in addition to state requirements. The Carnegie unit is a standard of measurement that represents one credit for the completion of a 1-year course.

SOURCE: Council of Chief State School Officers, *Key State Education Policies on PK–12 Education, 2008* (prepublication copy), table 7; *Education Week* and Editorial Projects in Education Research Center, *Diplomas Count 2009*, "Graduation Policies" table, retrieved July 20, 2009, from http://www.edweek.org/media/ew/dc/2009/33sos_2009policies.pdf. (This table was prepared July 2009.)

States that use criterion-referenced tests (CRTs) aligned to state standards, by subject area and level: 2006–07

State	Aligned to state standards		Off-the-shelf/ norm-referenced test (NRT)[1]	Criterion-referenced tests,[2] by subject area and level			
	Custom-developed test (CRT)[2]	Augmented or hybrid test[3]		English/ language arts	Mathematics	Science	Social studies/ history
1	2	3	4	5	6	7	8
Alabama	X		X	ES, MS, HS	ES, MS, HS	HS	HS
Alaska	X		X	ES, MS, HS	ES, MS, HS		
Arizona	X	X	X	ES, MS, HS	ES, MS, HS	ES, MS	
Arkansas	X		X	ES, MS, HS	ES, MS, HS	ES, MS, HS	MS, HS
California	X		X	ES, MS, HS	ES, MS, HS	ES, MS, HS	
Colorado	X			ES, MS, HS	ES, MS, HS	HS	
Connecticut	X			ES, MS, HS	ES, MS, HS		
Delaware		X		ES, MS, HS	ES, MS, HS	ES, MS, HS	ES, MS, HS
District of Columbia	X			ES, MS, HS	ES, MS, HS		
Florida	X		X	ES, MS, HS	ES, MS, HS	ES, MS, HS	
Georgia		X	X	ES, MS, HS	ES, MS, HS		
Hawaii		X		ES, MS, HS	ES, MS, HS		
Idaho	X	X		ES, MS, HS	ES, MS, HS		
Illinois	X			ES, MS, HS	ES, MS, HS	HS	
Indiana	X			ES, MS, HS	ES, MS, HS	ES, MS	
Iowa	X		X	ES, MS, HS	ES, MS, HS	ES, MS, HS	
Kansas	X			ES, MS, HS	ES, MS, HS		
Kentucky	X		X	ES, MS, HS	ES, MS, HS	ES, MS, HS	ES, MS, HS
Louisiana	X		X	ES, MS, HS	ES, MS, HS	ES, MS, HS	ES, MS, HS
Maine	X		X	ES, MS, HS	ES, MS, HS	ES, MS	
Maryland	X	X		ES, MS, HS	ES, MS, HS	HS	HS
Massachusetts	X			ES, MS, HS	ES, MS, HS	ES, MS, HS	
Michigan	X		X	ES, MS, HS	ES, MS, HS	ES, MS, HS	MS, HS
Minnesota	X			ES, MS, HS	ES, MS, HS		
Mississippi	X		X	ES, MS, HS	ES, MS, HS	ES, MS, HS	HS
Missouri		X	X	ES, MS, HS	ES, MS, HS		
Montana	X		X	ES, MS, HS			
Nebraska	X			ES, MS, HS	ES, MS, HS		
Nevada	X		X	ES, MS, HS	ES, MS, HS		
New Hampshire	X			ES, MS	ES, MS		
New Jersey	X			ES, MS, HS	ES, MS, HS	ES, MS	
New Mexico	X		X	ES, MS, HS	ES, MS, HS	ES, MS, HS	
New York	X			ES, MS, HS	ES, MS, HS	ES, MS, HS	ES, MS, HS
North Carolina	X			ES, MS, HS	ES, MS, HS	HS	HS
North Dakota	X			ES, MS, HS	ES, MS, HS	ES, MS, HS	
Ohio	X			ES, MS, HS	ES, MS, HS	ES, MS, HS	ES, MS, HS
Oklahoma	X			ES, MS, HS	ES, MS, HS	ES, MS, HS	ES, MS, HS
Oregon	X			ES, MS, HS	ES, MS, HS	MS, HS	
Pennsylvania	X			ES, MS, HS	ES, MS, HS		
Rhode Island	X		X	ES, MS, HS	ES, MS, HS		
South Carolina	X			ES, MS, HS	ES, MS, HS	ES, MS, HS	ES, MS, HS
South Dakota	X	X	X	ES, MS, HS	ES, MS, HS	ES, MS, HS	
Tennessee	X			ES, MS, HS	ES, MS, HS	ES, MS, HS	ES, MS, HS
Texas	X		X	ES, MS, HS	ES, MS, HS	ES, MS, HS	MS, HS
Utah	X			ES, MS, HS	ES, MS, HS	ES, MS, HS	
Vermont	X			ES, MS	ES, MS		
Virginia	X			ES, MS, HS	ES, MS, HS	ES, MS, HS	ES, MS, HS
Washington	X		X	ES, MS, HS	ES, MS, HS	ES, MS, HS	
West Virginia	X			ES, MS, HS	ES, MS, HS	ES, MS, HS	ES, MS
Wisconsin		X		ES, MS, HS	ES, MS, HS	ES, MS, HS	ES, MS, HS
Wyoming	X			ES, MS, HS	ES, MS, HS		

X State has a test.

[1] Off-the-shelf/norm-referenced tests (NRTs) are commercially developed tests that have not been modified to reflect state content standards.

[2] Custom-developed criterion-referenced tests (CRTs) are explicitly designed to measure state content standards.

[3] Augmented or hybrid tests incorporate elements of both NRTs and CRTs. These tests include NRTs that have been augmented or modified to reflect state standards.

NOTE: ES = elementary school, MS = middle school, and HS = high school.

SOURCE: Quality Counts 2007, Cradle to Career, *Education Week*, 2007. (This table was prepared September 2008.)

States requiring testing for initial certification of elementary and secondary teachers, by skills or knowledge assessment and state: 2008 and 2009

State	Assessment for certification, 2008				Assessment for certification, 2009			
	Basic skills exam	Subject-matter exam	Knowledge of teaching exam	Assessment of teaching performance	Basic skills exam	Subject-matter exam	Knowledge of teaching exam	Assessment of teaching performance
1	2	3	4	5	6	7	8	9
Alabama	X	X	X	X	X	X	X	X
Alaska	X				X			
Arizona		X	X			X	X	
Arkansas	X	X	X	X	X	X	X	X
California	X	—		X	X	—		X
Colorado		X				X		
Connecticut	X	X	X	X	X	X	X	X
Delaware	X	X			X	X		
District of Columbia	X	X	—	—	X	X	—	—
Florida	X			X	X			X
Georgia	X	X			X	X		
Hawaii	X	X	X	—	X	X	X	—
Idaho		X	X	X		X	X	X
Illinois	X	X	X		X	X	X	
Indiana	X	X		X	X	X		X
Iowa	—		—		—		—	
Kansas		X	X			X	X	
Kentucky	X	X	X	X	X	X	X	X
Louisiana	X	X	X	X	X	X	X	X
Maine	—	—	—	—	—	—	—	—
Maryland	X	X	X	X	X	X	X	X
Massachusetts	X	X		X	X	X		X
Michigan	X	X		X	X	X		X
Minnesota	X	X	X		X	X	X	
Mississippi	—	—	—	—	—	—	—	—
Missouri	X	X		X	X	X		X
Montana								
Nebraska	X				X			
Nevada	—	X	—	—	—	X	—	—
New Hampshire	X	X			X	X		
New Jersey	—	—	—	—	—	—	—	—
New Mexico	X	X	X	X	X	X	X	X
New York		X	X			X	X	
North Carolina	—	—	—	—	—	—	—	—
North Dakota	—	X	—	—	—	X	—	—
Ohio		X	X	X		X	X	X
Oklahoma	—	—	—		—	—	—	
Oregon	X	X	—	—	X	X	—	—
Pennsylvania	X	X	X	X	X	X	X	X
Rhode Island			X	X			X	X
South Carolina		X	X			X	X	
South Dakota	X	X	X	X	X	X	X	X
Tennessee	X	X	X		X	X	X	
Texas	—	—	—		—	—	—	
Utah		X		X		X		X
Vermont	X	X			X	X		
Virginia	X	X	X		X	X	X	
Washington	X	X		X	X	X		X
West Virginia	X	X	X	X	X	X	X	X
Wisconsin	X	X			X	X		
Wyoming	—		—	—	—		—	—

—Not available.
X State requires testing.

SOURCE: National Association of State Directors of Teacher Education and Certification, NASDTEC Knowledgebase, retrieved July 15, 2009, from https://www.nasdtec.info/. (This table was prepared July 2009.)

Percentage of students suspended and expelled from public elementary and secondary schools, by sex, race/ethnicity, and state: 2006

State	Percent suspended								Percent expelled							
		Sex		Race/ethnicity						Sex		Race/ethnicity				
	Total	Male	Female	White	Black	Hispanic	Asian/Pacific Islander	American Indian/Alaska Native	Total	Male	Female	White	Black	Hispanic	Asian/Pacific Islander	American Indian/Alaska Native
1	2	3	4	5	6	7	8	9	10	11	12	13	14	15	16	17
United States	**6.9 (0.04)**	**9.1 (0.06)**	**4.5 (0.03)**	**4.8 (0.04)**	**15.0 (0.14)**	**6.8 (0.07)**	**2.7 (0.04)**	**7.9 (0.49)**	**0.21 (0.003)**	**0.31 (0.004)**	**0.11 (0.002)**	**0.14 (0.002)**	**0.47 (0.011)**	**0.22 (0.004)**	**0.07 (0.002)**	**0.26 (0.013)**
Alabama	10.1 (0.11)	13.3 (0.15)	6.8 (#)	5.8 (0.10)	18.3 (0.32)	4.3 (0.10)	3.2 (0.14)	4.8 (0.49)	0.18 (0.003)	0.24 (0.006)	0.11 (0.002)	0.09 (0.002)	0.33 (0.009)	0.16 (0.003)	# (†)	0.01 (0.001)
Alaska	5.9 (0.35)	8.0 (0.47)	3.6 (0.21)	4.6 (0.13)	10.0 (0.10)	5.9 (0.29)	4.6 (0.50)	8.2 (1.18)	0.13 (0.005)	0.20 (0.007)	0.07 (0.006)	0.13 (0.004)	0.45 (0.003)	0.16 (0.006)	0.13 (0.011)	0.10 (0.009)
Arizona	5.9 (0.14)	8.4 (0.19)	3.3 (0.09)	4.5 (0.10)	11.8 (0.27)	6.4 (0.14)	2.6 (0.05)	10.0 (2.19)	0.07 (0.004)	0.11 (0.008)	0.03 (0.001)	0.06 (0.008)	0.12 (0.006)	0.08 (0.004)	0.03 (#)	0.08 (0.015)
Arkansas	7.3 (0.30)	10.2 (0.43)	4.3 (0.17)	5.0 (0.28)	15.9 (0.96)	4.9 (0.48)	3.5 (0.35)	4.7 (0.63)	0.10 (0.009)	0.15 (0.012)	0.06 (0.008)	0.10 (0.010)	0.14 (0.016)	0.09 ! (0.025)	0.07 ! (0.031)	0.03 (0.002)
California	7.5 (0.18)	10.5 (0.25)	4.4 (0.12)	6.0 (0.18)	17.1 (0.82)	7.9 (0.22)	3.3 (0.13)	12.2 (2.33)	0.31 (0.010)	0.48 (0.015)	0.13 (0.005)	0.28 (0.013)	0.61 (0.030)	0.32 (0.013)	0.11 (0.006)	0.46 (0.068)
Colorado	6.0 (0.09)	8.3 (0.13)	3.7 (0.06)	4.5 (0.09)	13.2 (0.05)	8.1 (0.14)	3.2 (0.03)	8.7 (0.89)	0.28 (0.008)	0.43 (0.012)	0.12 (0.007)	0.20 (0.007)	0.56 (0.005)	0.40 (0.022)	0.12 (0.003)	0.60 (0.138)
Connecticut	6.8 (0.52)	8.9 (0.65)	4.7 (0.39)	4.0 (0.37)	17.2 (2.39)	11.4 (1.39)	2.4 (0.22)	5.2 (0.95)	0.25 (0.026)	0.36 (0.034)	0.14 (0.022)	0.13 (0.016)	0.66 (0.126)	0.45 (0.079)	0.10 (0.017)	0.15 ! (0.069)
Delaware[1]	10.9 (†)	13.8 (†)	7.9 (†)	6.4 (†)	20.1 (†)	9.2 (†)	3.3 (†)	5.5 (†)	0.20 (†)	0.30 (†)	0.10 (†)	0.17 (†)	0.32 (†)	0.06 (†)	0.06 (†)	0.00 (†)
District of Columbia[1]	0.4 (†)	0.4 (†)	0.3 (†)	0.2 (†)	0.4 (†)	0.2 (†)	0.0 (†)	0.0 (†)	0.22 (†)	0.25 (†)	0.20 (†)	0.03 (†)	0.25 (†)	0.17 (†)	0.10 (†)	0.00 (†)
Florida	10.5 (0.14)	13.4 (0.17)	7.3 (0.11)	7.9 (0.16)	19.3 (0.34)	7.7 (0.08)	2.9 (0.03)	7.2 (0.59)	0.04 (0.003)	0.06 (0.004)	0.02 (0.001)	0.04 (0.003)	0.06 (0.005)	0.02 (0.001)	0.01 (#)	0.06 (0.012)
Georgia	8.8 (0.23)	11.4 (0.29)	6.1 (0.16)	4.8 (0.21)	15.0 (0.36)	5.4 (0.27)	2.1 (0.07)	3.7 (0.21)	0.23 (0.011)	0.33 (0.017)	0.12 (0.006)	0.18 (0.013)	0.32 (0.015)	0.11 (0.011)	0.04 (0.005)	0.08 ! (0.035)
Hawaii[1]	5.5 (†)	7.2 (†)	3.6 (†)	4.9 (†)	7.0 (†)	5.7 (†)	5.5 (†)	6.0 (†)	0.00 (†)	0.00 (†)	0.00 (†)	0.00 (†)	0.00 (†)	0.00 (†)	0.00 (†)	0.00 (†)
Idaho	3.6 (0.18)	5.3 (0.26)	1.7 (0.10)	3.3 (0.19)	3.5 (0.21)	5.1 (0.29)	1.6 (0.07)	8.6 ! (2.90)	0.09 (0.005)	0.14 (0.008)	0.03 (0.004)	0.07 (0.005)	# (†)	0.20 (0.018)	# (†)	0.37 (0.111)
Illinois	6.4 (0.15)	8.4 (0.20)	4.4 (0.10)	3.8 (0.17)	14.5 (0.53)	6.0 (0.19)	1.7 (0.08)	2.9 (0.41)	0.14 (0.007)	0.20 (0.008)	0.07 (0.006)	0.08 (0.011)	0.32 (0.011)	0.11 (0.004)	0.03 (0.005)	0.07 (0.008)
Indiana	7.4 (0.28)	9.9 (0.37)	4.7 (0.20)	6.0 (0.27)	17.3 (1.18)	7.4 (0.87)	1.8 (0.24)	6.1 (0.70)	0.63 (0.039)	0.85 (0.053)	0.40 (0.028)	0.54 (0.039)	1.24 (0.111)	0.70 (0.077)	0.19 (0.038)	0.60 ! (0.168)
Iowa	3.0 (0.11)	4.0 (0.14)	1.9 (0.08)	2.4 (0.11)	11.4 (0.31)	3.2 (0.27)	1.6 (0.18)	5.2 (0.25)	0.04 (0.008)	0.07 (0.013)	0.01 (0.004)	0.04 (0.008)	0.07 (0.012)	0.06 ! (0.022)	0.01 (0.001)	0.11 ! (0.074)
Kansas	5.1 (0.18)	6.9 (0.26)	3.1 (0.11)	3.8 (0.20)	14.6 (0.27)	6.6 (0.22)	2.9 (0.10)	5.8 (0.59)	0.18 (0.014)	0.25 (0.015)	0.10 (0.013)	0.12 (0.017)	0.68 (0.019)	0.19 (0.011)	0.12 (0.013)	0.20 ! (0.090)
Kentucky	6.6 (0.36)	8.7 (0.48)	4.3 (0.24)	5.8 (0.33)	13.3 (1.27)	4.0 (0.33)	1.5 (0.19)	3.8 (0.89)	0.08 (0.017)	0.11 (0.021)	0.05 ! (0.014)	0.07 (0.012)	0.18 ! (0.091)	0.01 ! (0.004)	0.03 ! (0.013)	# (†)
Louisiana	10.3 (0.41)	13.2 (0.51)	7.3 (0.31)	7.1 (0.56)	14.6 (0.48)	4.7 (0.16)	2.6 (0.14)	6.8 ! (2.24)	0.89 (0.037)	1.23 (0.054)	0.52 (0.021)	0.45 (0.039)	1.42 (0.056)	0.47 (0.020)	0.17 (0.011)	0.39 (0.109)
Maine	4.6 (0.28)	6.6 (0.41)	2.4 (0.15)	4.5 (0.28)	9.0 (0.38)	5.7 (1.11)	2.9 (0.18)	6.4 (1.13)	0.09 (0.012)	0.13 (0.015)	0.04 ! (0.011)	0.09 (0.012)	0.09 ! (0.022)	0.05 (0.002)	0.07 ! (0.038)	# (†)
Maryland[1]	7.1 (†)	8.9 (†)	5.2 (†)	5.8 (†)	8.2 (†)	12.9 (†)	2.2 (†)	8.5 (†)	0.18 (†)	0.27 (†)	0.09 (†)	0.08 (†)	0.31 (†)	0.27 (†)	0.03 (†)	0.09 (†)
Massachusetts	5.6 (0.28)	7.1 (0.35)	3.9 (0.22)	4.2 (0.25)	10.3 (0.50)	12.0 (1.18)	2.5 (0.25)	5.0 (0.63)	0.06 (0.004)	0.09 (0.006)	0.03 (0.003)	0.03 (0.005)	0.24 (0.013)	0.13 (0.009)	0.02 (0.003)	0.04 (0.003)
Michigan	8.2 (0.34)	10.8 (0.43)	5.4 (0.27)	6.1 (0.27)	17.8 (1.48)	7.4 (0.83)	2.2 (0.34)	6.8 (1.08)	0.13 (0.010)	0.19 (0.014)	0.07 (0.006)	0.09 (0.007)	0.32 (0.040)	0.15 (0.023)	0.06 (0.012)	0.12 ! (0.041)
Minnesota	3.7 (0.10)	5.0 (0.14)	2.4 (0.07)	2.4 (0.09)	14.4 (0.33)	5.4 (0.28)	2.5 (0.05)	10.0 (1.43)	0.03 (0.002)	0.05 (0.004)	0.01 (0.001)	0.02 (0.002)	0.08 (0.002)	0.04 (0.007)	0.01 (0.002)	0.14 ! (0.048)
Mississippi	10.2 (0.33)	13.3 (0.41)	7.0 (0.24)	5.5 (0.26)	14.8 (0.55)	4.3 (0.44)	3.0 (0.47)	12.7 ! (3.08)	0.29 (0.015)	0.42 (0.025)	0.16 (0.006)	0.12 (0.020)	0.46 (0.019)	0.07 (0.007)	0.08 (0.013)	0.09 (0.009)
Missouri	7.3 (0.24)	9.8 (0.32)	4.6 (0.16)	4.6 (0.19)	20.2 (1.07)	5.4 (0.32)	2.9 (0.10)	7.0 (0.51)	0.03 (0.004)	0.05 (0.005)	0.01 (0.003)	0.03 (0.005)	0.04 (0.003)	0.02 (0.001)	0.01 (#)	# (†)
Montana	4.5 (0.18)	6.1 (0.24)	2.7 (0.12)	3.7 (0.17)	4.9 (0.27)	3.5 (0.19)	2.3 (0.16)	9.6 (1.05)	0.07 (0.007)	0.12 (0.013)	0.02 (0.005)	0.05 (0.007)	# (†)	# (†)	# (†)	0.24 (0.040)
Nebraska	3.7 (0.08)	4.9 (0.11)	2.4 (0.05)	2.6 (0.06)	12.6 (0.05)	5.0 (0.30)	1.9 (0.04)	6.7 (0.89)	0.23 (0.005)	0.32 (0.008)	0.12 (0.002)	0.13 (0.004)	0.92 (0.004)	0.32 (0.018)	0.13 (0.001)	0.76 (0.121)
Nevada[1]	7.4 (†)	9.5 (†)	5.2 (†)	5.1 (†)	15.5 (†)	8.5 (†)	3.9 (†)	6.6 (†)	0.36 (†)	0.55 (†)	0.16 (†)	0.26 (†)	0.86 (†)	0.35 (†)	0.22 (†)	0.36 (†)
New Hampshire	5.6 (0.32)	7.2 (0.46)	3.9 (0.18)	5.4 (0.33)	8.7 (0.32)	12.1 (0.23)	2.2 (0.19)	4.8 (0.45)	0.06 ! (0.021)	0.08 ! (0.024)	0.04 ! (0.020)	0.06 ! (0.021)	0.28 (0.065)	0.07 (0.001)	0.03 (0.001)	0.17 (0.011)
New Jersey	5.7 (0.26)	7.5 (0.33)	3.7 (0.19)	3.7 (0.30)	12.4 (0.79)	6.9 (0.51)	1.4 (0.13)	3.7 (0.70)	0.02 ! (0.008)	0.03 ! (0.016)	# (†)	0.01 ! (0.006)	0.03 ! (0.009)	0.03 ! (0.015)	0.01 ! (0.008)	# (†)
New Mexico	5.3 (0.20)	6.9 (0.26)	3.5 (0.14)	4.0 (0.19)	7.0 (0.21)	5.4 (0.31)	2.5 (0.12)	8.3 (0.47)	0.07 (0.005)	0.12 (0.009)	0.03 (0.002)	0.03 (0.003)	0.13 (0.002)	0.06 (0.006)	0.17 (0.006)	0.22 (0.030)
New York	3.8 (0.14)	5.1 (0.17)	2.5 (0.11)	3.4 (0.14)	7.3 (0.45)	2.8 (0.15)	0.7 (0.05)	4.5 (0.97)	0.03 (0.006)	0.05 (0.010)	0.01 (0.003)	0.04 (0.010)	0.04 ! (0.014)	0.01 (0.002)	# (†)	0.07 ! (0.044)
North Carolina	10.8 (0.52)	14.3 (0.66)	7.0 (0.37)	6.5 (0.33)	20.0 (1.06)	7.2 (0.40)	2.7 (0.19)	14.9 ! (8.53)	0.14 ! (0.060)	0.21 ! (0.081)	0.07 ! (0.038)	0.04 (0.007)	0.37 ! (0.193)	0.05 (0.007)	0.03 (0.004)	0.09 ! (0.050)
North Dakota	2.2 (0.17)	2.9 (0.21)	1.4 (0.13)	1.5 (0.10)	5.0 (0.16)	3.1 (0.35)	2.0 (0.12)	8.0 (1.80)	0.02 (0.006)	0.05 (0.008)	# (†)	0.01 (0.002)	0.05 (0.001)	# (†)	# (†)	0.12 ! (0.061)
Ohio	6.2 (0.24)	8.2 (0.30)	4.2 (0.17)	4.6 (0.21)	14.6 (0.99)	6.0 (0.83)	2.1 (0.24)	3.7 (0.45)	0.47 (0.020)	0.61 (0.026)	0.32 (0.014)	0.20 (0.016)	1.69 (0.091)	0.72 (0.078)	0.09 (0.014)	0.21 ! (0.038)
Oklahoma	4.9 (0.17)	6.7 (0.24)	3.0 (0.11)	3.9 (0.18)	12.1 (0.60)	5.3 (0.18)	1.8 (0.07)	4.0 (0.24)	0.34 (0.013)	0.47 (0.019)	0.21 (0.008)	0.28 (0.014)	0.94 (0.039)	0.23 (0.014)	0.16 (0.039)	0.29 (0.021)
Oregon	4.9 (0.18)	7.1 (0.26)	2.7 (0.15)	4.8 (0.19)	8.8 (0.24)	5.5 (0.37)	2.1 (0.08)	7.2 (0.57)	0.34 (0.025)	0.52 (0.044)	0.15 (0.010)	0.32 (0.026)	0.58 (0.093)	0.41 (0.015)	0.18 (0.028)	0.47 (0.070)
Pennsylvania	6.8 (0.37)	8.7 (0.45)	4.8 (0.29)	4.2 (0.23)	18.9 (1.41)	8.7 (0.79)	2.7 (0.46)	3.4 (0.64)	0.16 (0.008)	0.22 (0.011)	0.10 (0.005)	0.09 (0.007)	0.52 (0.031)	0.21 (0.017)	0.06 (0.013)	0.04 (0.002)
Rhode Island	8.4 (0.74)	10.7 (1.00)	5.9 (0.47)	6.7 (0.83)	14.6 (2.07)	12.6 (0.65)	7.2 (0.73)	11.8 (2.92)	# (†)	# (†)	# (†)	# (†)	# (†)	# (†)	# (†)	# (†)
South Carolina	11.9 (0.44)	15.1 (0.56)	8.6 (0.33)	6.9 (0.36)	19.2 (0.89)	6.5 (1.05)	2.9 (0.31)	9.6 ! (4.26)	0.73 (0.043)	1.03 (0.063)	0.40 (0.026)	0.37 (0.029)	1.26 (0.091)	0.20 (0.035)	0.19 (0.047)	0.42 ! (0.169)
South Dakota	2.7 (0.16)	3.7 (0.22)	1.6 (0.11)	1.9 (0.12)	7.1 (0.24)	4.3 (0.16)	3.0 (0.19)	6.8 (1.19)	0.11 ! (0.045)	0.16 ! (0.066)	0.05 ! (0.024)	0.04 ! (0.025)	0.08 ! (0.038)	0.20 ! (0.107)	# (†)	0.55 ! (0.221)
Tennessee	7.2 (0.26)	9.6 (0.35)	4.8 (0.17)	5.5 (0.27)	12.8 (0.38)	5.4 (0.22)	2.7 (0.15)	3.4 (0.36)	0.32 (0.010)	0.47 (0.016)	0.15 (0.006)	0.19 (0.011)	0.70 (0.011)	0.29 (0.011)	0.17 (0.009)	0.29 (0.014)
Texas	5.6 (0.06)	7.4 (0.08)	3.6 (0.04)	2.9 (0.06)	12.7 (0.24)	5.7 (0.08)	1.6 (0.01)	3.1 (0.10)	0.26 (0.005)	0.39 (0.008)	0.13 (0.002)	0.16 (0.007)	0.58 (0.016)	0.26 (0.005)	0.08 (#)	0.20 (0.004)
Utah	3.2 (0.04)	4.5 (0.05)	1.9 (0.03)	2.4 (0.03)	7.8 (0.04)	6.7 (0.07)	4.2 (0.04)	6.9 (0.09)	0.05 (0.001)	0.07 (0.002)	0.02 (#)	0.04 (0.001)	0.22 (0.001)	0.06 (0.002)	0.09 (#)	0.19 (0.020)
Vermont	4.0 (0.18)	5.5 (0.25)	2.4 (0.12)	4.0 (0.18)	5.8 (0.50)	4.1 (0.55)	1.8 (0.23)	5.7 (0.77)	0.05 ! (0.019)	0.08 ! (0.031)	0.02 ! (0.006)	0.05 ! (0.020)	0.06 ! (0.033)	0.12 ! (0.069)	# (†)	# (†)
Virginia	7.2 (0.24)	9.4 (0.31)	4.9 (0.18)	4.7 (0.17)	13.9 (0.73)	5.6 (0.21)	2.1 (0.06)	4.0 (0.34)	0.09 (0.014)	0.15 (0.025)	0.03 (0.003)	0.08 ! (0.022)	0.12 (0.013)	0.09 (0.005)	0.06 (0.003)	0.10 ! (0.045)
Washington	5.9 (0.15)	8.6 (0.21)	3.2 (0.08)	5.3 (0.17)	12.0 (0.09)	7.2 (0.39)	3.7 (0.05)	11.3 (1.36)	0.34 (0.014)	0.53 (0.021)	0.14 (0.007)	0.31 (0.016)	0.48 (0.010)	0.50 (0.035)	0.16 (0.002)	0.69 (0.130)
West Virginia	10.2 (1.02)	13.8 (1.31)	6.4 (0.70)	9.7 (0.91)	21.5 (4.03)	11.2 (3.07)	2.4 (0.54)	8.2 (1.98)	0.07 (0.012)	0.09 (0.015)	0.04 (0.010)	0.07 (0.011)	0.09 ! (0.034)	0.07 ! (0.053)	# (†)	# (†)
Wisconsin	5.0 (0.16)	6.3 (0.20)	3.6 (0.13)	2.7 (0.12)	19.7 (0.60)	7.5 (0.18)	2.1 (0.07)	13.5 ! (5.23)	0.17 (0.008)	0.23 (0.012)	0.10 (0.006)	0.12 (0.009)	0.47 (0.016)	0.22 (0.020)	0.06 (0.008)	0.30 ! (0.105)
Wyoming	2.8 (0.34)	4.0 (0.33)	1.6 (0.88)	2.7 (0.34)	3.2 (0.26)	3.1 (0.43)	1.7 (0.26)	6.4 ! (1.37)	0.11 (0.018)	0.18 (0.027)	0.03 ! (0.010)	0.11 (0.021)	0.23 (0.006)	0.09 (0.005)	0.10 (0.007)	# (†)

†Not applicable.
#Rounds to zero.
!Interpret data with caution.
[1]Data are based on universe counts of schools and school districts; therefore, these figures do not have standard errors.

NOTE: Race categories exclude persons of Hispanic ethnicity. Detail may not sum to totals because of rounding. Standard errors appear in parentheses.
SOURCE: U.S. Department of Education, Office for Civil Rights, Civil Rights Data Collection: 2006. (This table was prepared May 2008.)

Percentage of students in grades 9 through 12 who reported experience with drugs and violence on school property, by race/ethnicity, grade, and sex: Selected years, 1997 through 2007

Type of violence or drug-related behavior	1997 total	1999 total	2003 total	2005 total	2007 Total	Race/ethnicity White	Race/ethnicity Black	Race/ethnicity Hispanic	Grade 9th	Grade 10th	Grade 11th	Grade 12th
1	2	3	4	5	6	7	8	9	10	11	12	13
Felt too unsafe to go to school[1]	4.0 (0.6)	5.2 (1.3)	5.4 (0.41)	6.0 (0.61)	5.5 (0.39)	4.0 (0.43)	6.5 (0.64)	9.6 (1.00)	6.5 (0.64)	5.4 (0.42)	4.7 (0.61)	4.8 (0.58)
Male	4.1 (0.8)	4.8 (1.6)	5.5 (0.51)	5.7 (0.56)	5.4 (0.44)	3.7 (0.44)	6.8 (1.07)	9.6 (1.09)	5.8 (0.66)	4.8 (0.58)	5.5 (0.93)	5.3 (0.72)
Female	3.9 (0.7)	5.7 (1.5)	5.3 (0.51)	6.3 (0.77)	5.6 (0.53)	4.2 (0.66)	6.3 (0.82)	9.7 (1.24)	7.4 (0.96)	6.0 (0.68)	3.9 (0.61)	4.3 (0.71)
Carried a weapon on school property[1,2]	8.5 (1.5)	6.9 (1.2)	6.1 (0.56)	6.5 (0.46)	5.9 (0.37)	5.3 (0.56)	6.0 (0.46)	7.3 (0.82)	6.0 (0.59)	5.8 (0.61)	5.5 (0.68)	6.0 (0.58)
Male	12.5 (2.9)	11.0 (2.1)	8.9 (0.77)	10.2 (0.82)	9.0 (0.65)	8.5 (0.97)	8.4 (0.64)	10.4 (1.18)	8.7 (0.95)	8.8 (1.04)	8.6 (1.25)	9.8 (1.14)
Female	3.7 (0.7)	2.8 (0.7)	3.1 (0.51)	2.6 (0.31)	2.7 (0.33)	2.1 (0.37)	3.5 (0.55)	4.1 (0.72)	3.1 (0.61)	2.6 (0.71)	2.4 (0.36)	2.3 (0.50)
Threatened or injured with a weapon on school property[3]	7.4 (0.9)	7.7 (0.8)	9.2 (0.77)	7.9 (0.36)	7.8 (0.44)	6.9 (0.52)	9.7 (0.87)	8.7 (0.60)	9.2 (0.69)	8.4 (0.51)	6.8 (0.57)	6.3 (0.64)
Male	10.2 (1.4)	9.5 (1.6)	11.6 (0.97)	9.7 (0.41)	10.2 (0.59)	9.2 (0.72)	11.2 (1.34)	12.0 (0.89)	11.4 (0.88)	10.4 (0.73)	10.5 (1.06)	8.1 (1.01)
Female	4.0 (0.6)	5.8 (1.2)	6.5 (0.61)	6.1 (0.41)	5.4 (0.41)	4.6 (0.52)	8.1 (0.86)	5.4 (0.69)	6.8 (0.80)	6.3 (0.71)	3.2 (0.45)	4.5 (0.75)
Engaged in a physical fight on school property[3]	14.8 (1.3)	14.2 (1.3)	12.8 (0.77)	13.6 (0.56)	12.4 (0.48)	10.2 (0.57)	17.6 (1.10)	15.5 (0.81)	17.0 (0.67)	11.7 (0.86)	11.0 (0.73)	8.6 (0.62)
Male	20.0 (2.0)	18.5 (1.4)	17.1 (0.92)	18.2 (0.92)	16.3 (0.60)	14.5 (0.76)	20.0 (1.66)	18.5 (1.22)	22.3 (1.25)	15.0 (1.06)	14.8 (1.13)	11.1 (0.77)
Female	8.6 (1.5)	9.8 (1.9)	8.0 (0.71)	8.8 (0.51)	8.5 (0.62)	5.9 (0.64)	15.2 (1.10)	12.4 (1.29)	11.4 (1.02)	8.3 (1.08)	7.3 (0.96)	6.2 (0.76)
Property stolen or deliberately damaged on school property[3]	32.9 (2.6)	— (†)	29.8 (0.71)	29.8 (0.77)	27.1 (0.69)	25.9 (0.81)	29.2 (1.25)	29.0 (1.34)	30.6 (1.36)	27.6 (1.19)	25.9 (0.97)	22.9 (1.29)
Male	36.1 (2.6)	— (†)	33.1 (0.87)	31.4 (0.82)	30.4 (0.99)	29.3 (1.08)	32.8 (1.74)	32.0 (1.79)	32.2 (1.70)	29.3 (1.70)	32.1 (1.37)	27.2 (1.86)
Female	29.0 (3.7)	— (†)	26.2 (0.82)	28.0 (1.07)	23.7 (0.73)	22.6 (0.94)	25.6 (1.75)	26.0 (1.70)	28.8 (1.63)	25.8 (1.30)	19.7 (1.14)	18.8 (1.19)
Cigarette use on school property[1]	14.6 (1.5)	14.0 (1.9)	8.0 (0.71)	6.8 (0.41)	5.7 (0.50)	6.4 (0.70)	3.4 (0.52)	4.9 (0.52)	4.2 (0.60)	5.4 (0.57)	5.9 (0.83)	7.4 (0.89)
Male	15.9 (1.7)	14.8 (2.0)	8.2 (0.66)	7.4 (0.41)	6.5 (0.53)	7.1 (0.72)	5.1 (0.92)	5.6 (0.66)	4.7 (0.88)	5.8 (0.85)	7.2 (0.99)	8.9 (0.97)
Female	13.0 (2.2)	13.2 (2.0)	7.6 (0.92)	6.2 (0.61)	4.8 (0.56)	5.6 (0.77)	1.7 (0.39)	4.2 (0.88)	3.7 (0.71)	5.0 (0.90)	4.7 (0.92)	5.9 (1.09)
Smokeless tobacco use on school property[4]	5.1 (1.4)	4.2 (1.8)	5.9 (1.53)	5.0 (0.61)	4.9 (0.71)	6.2 (0.94)	0.9 (0.22)	3.2 (0.56)	4.0 (0.90)	5.9 (0.86)	4.2 (0.74)	5.5 (0.93)
Male	9.0 (2.5)	8.1 (3.5)	8.5 (1.48)	9.2 (1.12)	8.9 (1.31)	11.3 (1.70)	1.5 (0.41)	4.9 (1.02)	6.9 (1.68)	10.4 (1.55)	7.9 (1.40)	10.2 (1.60)
Female	0.4 (0.2)	0.3 (0.2)	3.3 (1.68)	0.8 (0.15)	1.0 (0.20)	1.0 (0.26)	0.2 (0.16)	1.5 (0.40)	0.9 (0.31)	1.3 (0.44)	0.6 (0.21)	1.0 (0.54)
Alcohol use on school property[1]	5.6 (0.7)	4.9 (0.7)	5.2 (0.46)	4.3 (0.31)	4.1 (0.32)	3.2 (0.35)	3.4 (0.63)	7.5 (0.86)	3.4 (0.43)	4.1 (0.50)	4.2 (0.54)	4.9 (0.55)
Male	7.2 (1.3)	6.1 (1.1)	6.0 (0.61)	5.3 (0.41)	4.6 (0.35)	3.8 (0.47)	3.7 (0.70)	7.8 (0.93)	3.4 (0.45)	4.6 (0.68)	4.5 (0.64)	6.3 (0.73)
Female	3.6 (0.7)	3.6 (0.7)	4.2 (0.41)	3.3 (0.31)	3.6 (0.37)	2.6 (0.33)	2.8 (0.78)	7.1 (1.16)	3.4 (0.64)	3.6 (0.62)	3.9 (0.64)	3.4 (0.59)
Marijuana use on school property[1]	7.0 (1.0)	7.2 (1.4)	5.8 (0.66)	4.5 (0.31)	4.5 (0.46)	4.0 (0.61)	5.0 (0.73)	5.4 (0.80)	4.0 (0.52)	4.8 (0.60)	4.0 (0.68)	5.1 (0.73)
Male	9.0 (1.3)	10.1 (2.6)	7.6 (0.87)	6.0 (0.46)	5.9 (0.61)	5.2 (0.87)	7.4 (1.07)	6.9 (1.22)	5.2 (0.74)	6.5 (0.87)	5.3 (1.02)	6.6 (1.04)
Female	4.6 (1.1)	4.4 (0.8)	3.7 (0.46)	3.0 (0.31)	3.0 (0.39)	2.7 (0.43)	2.6 (0.66)	3.9 (0.71)	2.7 (0.65)	3.1 (0.62)	2.7 (0.54)	3.7 (0.72)
Offered, sold, or given an illegal drug on school property[3]	31.7 (1.8)	30.2 (2.4)	28.7 (1.94)	25.4 (1.07)	22.3 (1.04)	20.7 (1.23)	19.3 (1.36)	29.1 (1.94)	21.2 (1.24)	25.3 (1.29)	22.7 (1.41)	19.6 (1.26)
Male	37.4 (2.3)	34.7 (3.3)	31.9 (2.09)	28.8 (1.22)	25.7 (1.15)	24.0 (1.48)	25.1 (1.86)	30.9 (2.08)	25.0 (1.67)	29.5 (1.51)	25.7 (1.42)	22.4 (2.03)
Female	24.7 (2.4)	25.7 (2.4)	25.0 (1.94)	21.8 (1.02)	18.7 (1.16)	17.4 (1.37)	13.4 (1.52)	27.2 (2.32)	17.2 (1.52)	21.0 (1.73)	19.8 (2.12)	16.8 (1.24)

—Not available.

†Not applicable.

[1] One or more times during the 30 days preceding the survey.

[2] Such as a gun, knife, or club.

[3] One or more times during the 12 months preceding the survey.

[4] Used chewing tobacco or snuff one or more times during the 30 days preceding the survey.

NOTE: Totals include other racial/ethnic groups not shown separately. Race categories exclude persons of Hispanic ethnicity. Standard errors appear in parentheses.

SOURCE: U.S. Department of Health and Human Services, Centers for Disease Control and Prevention, Youth Risk Behavior Survey (YRBS), 2007 National YRBS Data Files, retrieved July 15, 2008, from http://www.cdc.gov/HealthyYouth/YRBS/data/index.htm. (This table was prepared July 2008.)

Percentage of 12- to 17-year-olds reporting use of illicit drugs, alcohol, and cigarettes during the past 30 days and the past year, by substance used, sex, and race/ethnicity: Selected years, 1982 through 2007

Year, sex, and race/ethnicity	Past 30 days — Illicit drugs Any[1]	Marijuana	Cocaine	Alcohol	Cigarettes	Past year — Illicit drugs Any[1]	Marijuana	Cocaine	Alcohol	Cigarettes
1	2	3	4	5	6	7	8	9	10	11
1982	— (†)	9.9 (—)	1.9 (—)	34.9 (—)	— (†)	(†)	17.7 (—)	3.7 (—)	46.1 (—)	(†)
1985	13.2 (—)	10.2 (—)	1.5 (—)	41.2 (—)	29.4 (—)	— (—)	16.7 (—)	3.4 (—)	52.7 (—)	29.9 (—)
1988	8.1 (—)	5.4 (—)	1.2 (—)	33.4 (—)	22.7 (—)	— (—)	10.7 (—)	2.5 (—)	45.5 (—)	26.8 (—)
1990	7.1 (—)	4.4 (—)	0.6 (—)	32.5 (—)	22.4 (—)	— (—)	9.6 (—)	1.9 (—)	41.8 (—)	26.2 (—)
1993	5.7 (—)	4.0 (—)	0.4 (—)	23.9 (—)	18.5 (—)	— (—)	8.5 (—)	0.7 (—)	35.9 (—)	22.5 (—)
1994	8.2 (—)	6.0 (—)	0.3 (—)	21.6 (—)	18.9 (—)	— (—)	11.4 (—)	1.1 (—)	36.2 (—)	24.5 (—)
1995	10.9 (—)	8.2 (—)	0.8 (—)	21.1 (—)	20.2 (—)	— (—)	14.2 (—)	1.7 (—)	35.1 (—)	26.6 (—)
1996	9.0 (—)	7.1 (—)	0.6 (—)	18.8 (—)	18.3 (—)	— (—)	13.0 (—)	1.4 (—)	32.7 (—)	24.2 (—)
1997	11.4 (—)	9.4 (—)	1.0 (—)	20.5 (—)	19.9 (—)	— (—)	15.8 (—)	2.2 (—)	34.0 (—)	26.4 (—)
1998	9.9 (—)	8.3 (—)	0.8 (—)	19.1 (—)	18.2 (—)	— (—)	14.1 (—)	1.7 (—)	31.8 (—)	23.8 (—)
1999	9.8 (0.23)	7.2 (0.20)	0.5 (0.06)	16.5 (0.30)	14.9 (0.31)	19.8 (0.32)	14.2 (0.29)	1.6 (0.10)	34.1 (0.41)	23.4 (0.37)
2000	9.7 (0.24)	7.2 (0.21)	0.6 (0.07)	16.4 (0.29)	13.4 (0.28)	18.6 (0.31)	13.4 (0.27)	1.7 (0.12)	33.0 (0.39)	20.8 (0.34)
2001	10.8 (0.26)	8.0 (0.24)	0.4 (0.06)	17.3 (0.33)	13.0 (0.28)	20.8 (0.36)	15.2 (0.32)	1.5 (0.10)	33.9 (0.39)	20.0 (0.35)
2002	11.6 (0.29)	8.2 (0.24)	0.6 (0.07)	17.6 (0.32)	13.0 (0.30)	22.2 (0.38)	15.8 (0.32)	2.1 (0.13)	34.6 (0.42)	20.3 (0.35)
2003	11.2 (0.27)	7.9 (0.24)	0.6 (0.06)	17.7 (0.33)	12.2 (0.29)	21.8 (0.36)	15.0 (0.31)	1.8 (0.11)	34.3 (0.42)	19.0 (0.36)
2004	10.6 (0.27)	7.6 (0.23)	0.5 (0.06)	17.6 (0.32)	11.9 (0.30)	21.0 (0.34)	14.5 (0.31)	1.6 (0.11)	33.9 (0.41)	18.4 (0.35)
2005	10.6 (0.27)	7.6 (0.23)	0.5 (0.06)	17.6 (0.32)	11.9 (0.30)	21.0 (0.34)	14.5 (0.31)	1.6 (0.11)	33.9 (0.41)	18.4 (0.35)
2006	9.8 (0.27)	6.7 (0.21)	0.4 (0.05)	16.6 (0.32)	10.4 (0.26)	19.6 (0.37)	13.2 (0.31)	1.6 (0.11)	32.9 (0.42)	17.0 (0.35)
Sex										
Male	9.8 (0.36)	6.8 (0.30)	0.4 (0.07)	16.3 (0.44)	10.0 (0.36)	19.5 (0.50)	13.4 (0.42)	1.4 (0.14)	32.2 (0.57)	16.7 (0.46)
Female	9.7 (0.36)	6.4 (0.29)	0.5 (0.08)	17.0 (0.47)	10.7 (0.37)	19.7 (0.49)	12.9 (0.41)	1.9 (0.16)	33.7 (0.58)	17.4 (0.48)
Race/ethnicity										
White	10.0 (0.31)	7.1 (0.26)	0.5 (0.07)	19.2 (0.42)	12.4 (0.35)	20.2 (0.42)	13.9 (0.35)	2.0 (0.15)	36.7 (0.50)	19.5 (0.42)
Black	10.2 (0.66)	6.5 (0.51)	0.2 (0.11)	10.5 (0.71)	6.0 (0.50)	18.6 (0.91)	12.2 (0.71)	0.4 (0.15)	24.1 (0.95)	10.8 (0.69)
Hispanic	8.9 (0.66)	5.8 (0.53)	0.5 (0.14)	15.3 (0.84)	8.2 (0.59)	18.8 (0.98)	12.3 (0.80)	1.7 (0.29)	31.3 (1.10)	15.1 (0.84)
Asian	6.7 (1.52)	3.2 (0.92)	0.1 (0.11)	7.6 (1.86)	5.2 (1.16)	13.7 (2.02)	7.3 (1.33)	0.6 (0.52)	20.2 (2.45)	11.0 (2.06)
Native Hawaiian/Pacific Islander	18.7 (4.38)	11.3 (2.47)	‡ (†)	20.5 (3.96)	21.2 (3.63)	‡ (†)	‡ (†)	2.2 (1.00)	33.2 (3.97)	‡ (†)
American Indian/Alaska Native	11.8 (1.96)	8.4 (1.74)	0.1 (0.10)	16.2 (2.36)	12.7 (1.90)	24.3 (3.09)	17.7 (2.91)	3.0 (1.25)	31.2 (2.74)	19.2 (2.32)
Two or more races	‡ (†)	‡ (†)	1.2 (0.73)	‡ (†)	‡ (†)	‡ (†)	‡ (†)	‡ (†)	‡ (†)	‡ (†)
2007	9.5 (0.27)	6.7 (0.22)	0.4 (0.05)	15.9 (0.34)	9.8 (0.26)	18.7 (0.35)	12.5 (0.30)	1.5 (0.11)	31.8 (0.42)	15.7 (0.34)
Sex										
Male	10.0 (0.41)	7.5 (0.34)	0.4 (0.07)	15.9 (0.47)	10.0 (0.37)	19.4 (0.52)	13.6 (0.44)	1.3 (0.14)	31.5 (0.58)	16.0 (0.47)
Female	9.1 (0.35)	5.8 (0.29)	0.5 (0.08)	16.0 (0.49)	9.7 (0.37)	18.0 (0.47)	11.3 (0.39)	1.7 (0.16)	32.1 (0.61)	15.3 (0.46)
Race/ethnicity										
White	10.2 (0.33)	7.3 (0.28)	0.5 (0.07)	18.2 (0.43)	12.2 (0.36)	19.9 (0.45)	13.7 (0.38)	1.7 (0.14)	34.8 (0.53)	18.7 (0.46)
Black	9.4 (0.64)	5.8 (0.52)	0.1 (0.09)	10.1 (0.74)	6.1 (0.62)	17.6 (0.84)	11.0 (0.69)	0.3 (0.14)	24.1 (1.04)	9.6 (0.72)
Hispanic	8.1 (0.63)	5.7 (0.50)	0.5 (0.14)	15.2 (0.80)	6.7 (0.58)	17.1 (0.83)	10.8 (0.69)	2.1 (0.30)	31.6 (1.07)	13.1 (0.74)
Asian	6.0 (1.30)	4.2 (1.40)	‡ (†)	8.1 (1.68)	3.4 (0.99)	10.9 (1.64)	6.4 (1.59)	0.2 (0.10)	17.2 (2.08)	6.1 (1.46)
Native Hawaiian/Pacific Islander	‡ (†)	‡ (†)	‡ (†)	‡ (†)	‡ (†)	‡ (†)	‡ (†)	‡ (†)	‡ (†)	‡ (†)
American Indian/Alaska Native	‡ (†)	‡ (†)	‡ (†)	‡ (†)	13.4 (3.91)	‡ (†)	‡ (†)	‡ (†)	19.3 (4.33)	19.3 (4.33)
Two or more races	9.2 (1.43)	6.9 (1.25)	0.1 (0.08)	12.5 (1.51)	8.9 (1.36)	18.9 (2.01)	14.3 (1.78)	1.1 (0.50)	27.7 (2.20)	14.5 (1.71)

—Not available.

†Not applicable.

‡Reporting standards not met.

[1]Includes other illegal drug use not shown separately.

NOTE: Marijuana includes hashish usage for 1996 and later years. Data for 1999 and later years were gathered using Computer Assisted Interviewing (CAI) and may not be directly comparable to previous years. Because of survey improvements in 2002, the 2002 data constitute a new baseline for tracking trends. Valid trend comparisons can be made for 1982 through 1998, 1999 through 2001, and 2002 through 2007. Race categories exclude persons of Hispanic ethnicity. Standard errors appear in parentheses.

SOURCE: U.S. Department of Health and Human Services, Substance Abuse and Mental Health Services Administration, *National Household Survey on Drug Abuse: Main Findings*, selected years, 1982 through 2001, and National Survey on Drug Use and Health, 2002 through 2007. Retrieved March 26, 2009, from http://www.oas.samhsa.gov/WebOnly.htm#NSDUHtabs. (This table was prepared March 2009.)

Percentage of high school seniors reporting drug use, by type of drug and reporting period: Selected years, 1975 through 2008

Type of drug	Class of 1975	Class of 1980	Class of 1985	Class of 1990	Class of 1995	Class of 2000	Class of 2001	Class of 2002	Class of 2003	Class of 2004	Class of 2005	Class of 2006	Class of 2007	Class of 2008
1	2	3	4	5	6	7	8	9	10	11	12	13	14	15
Percent reporting having ever used drugs														
Alcohol[1]	90.4 (0.69)	93.2 (0.46)	92.2 (0.48)	89.5 (0.57)	80.7 (0.73)	80.3 (0.80)	79.7 (0.81)	78.4 (0.83)	76.6 (0.80)	76.8 (0.80)	75.1 (0.81)	72.7 (0.85)	72.2 (0.83)	71.9 (0.85)
Any illicit drug	55.2 (1.68)	65.4 (1.23)	60.6 (1.26)	47.9 (1.33)	48.4 (1.32)	54.0 (1.44)	53.9 (1.44)	53.0 (1.44)	51.1 (1.35)	51.1 (1.35)	50.4 (1.35)	48.2 (1.37)	46.8 (1.33)	47.4 (1.35)
Marijuana only	19.0 (1.32)	26.7 (1.15)	20.9 (1.05)	18.5 (1.03)	20.3 (1.06)	25.0 (1.25)	23.2 (1.22)	23.5 (1.22)	23.4 (1.15)	22.4 (1.13)	23.0 (1.14)	21.3 (1.12)	21.3 (1.09)	22.5 (1.13)
Any illicit drug other than marijuana[2]	36.2 (1.33)	38.7 (1.04)	39.7 (1.04)	29.4 (0.99)	28.1 (0.97)	29.0 (1.08)	30.7 (1.09)	29.5 (1.08)	27.7 (0.99)	28.7 (1.00)	27.4 (0.99)	26.9 (1.00)	25.5 (0.95)	24.9 (0.96)
Use of selected drugs														
Cocaine	9.0 (0.73)	15.7 (0.72)	17.3 (0.74)	9.4 (0.59)	6.0 (0.48)	8.6 (0.62)	8.2 (0.60)	7.8 (0.59)	7.7 (0.55)	8.1 (0.56)	8.0 (0.56)	8.5 (0.58)	7.8 (0.54)	7.2 (0.53)
Heroin	2.2 (0.21)	1.1 (0.12)	1.2 (0.12)	1.3 (0.13)	1.6 (0.14)	2.4 (0.19)	1.8 (0.17)	1.7 (0.16)	1.5 (0.14)	1.5 (0.14)	1.5 (0.14)	1.4 (0.14)	1.5 (0.14)	1.3 (0.13)
LSD	11.3 (0.81)	9.3 (0.57)	7.5 (0.52)	8.7 (0.57)	11.7 (0.64)	11.1 (0.69)	10.9 (0.69)	8.4 (0.61)	5.9 (0.49)	4.6 (0.43)	3.5 (0.38)	3.3 (0.37)	3.4 (0.37)	4.0 (0.40)
Marijuana/hashish	47.3 (1.68)	60.3 (1.27)	54.2 (1.83)	40.7 (1.30)	41.7 (1.30)	48.8 (1.45)	49.0 (1.45)	47.8 (1.44)	46.1 (1.35)	45.7 (1.35)	44.8 (1.34)	42.3 (1.36)	41.8 (1.31)	42.6 (1.34)
PCP	— (†)	9.6 (0.33)	4.9 (0.24)	2.8 (0.19)	2.7 (0.18)	3.4 (0.23)	3.5 (0.23)	3.1 (0.22)	2.5 (0.18)	1.6 (0.15)	2.4 (0.18)	2.2 (0.17)	2.1 (0.17)	1.8 (0.16)
Percent reporting use of drugs in the past 12 months														
Alcohol[1]	84.8 (0.84)	87.9 (0.59)	85.6 (0.63)	80.6 (0.73)	73.7 (0.81)	73.2 (0.89)	73.3 (0.89)	71.5 (0.91)	70.1 (0.86)	70.6 (0.86)	68.6 (0.87)	66.5 (0.90)	66.4 (0.88)	65.5 (0.90)
Any illicit drug	45.0 (1.64)	53.1 (1.26)	46.3 (1.26)	32.5 (1.21)	39.0 (1.26)	40.9 (1.39)	41.4 (1.39)	41.0 (1.38)	39.3 (1.29)	38.8 (1.29)	38.4 (1.28)	36.5 (1.29)	35.9 (1.25)	36.6 (1.27)
Marijuana only	18.8 (1.29)	22.7 (1.06)	18.9 (0.99)	14.6 (0.91)	19.6 (1.02)	20.5 (1.14)	19.8 (1.12)	20.1 (1.13)	19.5 (1.05)	18.3 (1.02)	18.8 (1.03)	17.3 (1.01)	17.4 (0.99)	18.3 (1.02)
Any illicit drug other than marijuana[2]	26.2 (1.15)	30.4 (0.92)	27.4 (0.89)	17.9 (0.79)	19.4 (0.81)	20.4 (0.90)	21.6 (0.92)	20.9 (0.91)	19.8 (0.83)	20.5 (0.85)	19.7 (0.83)	19.2 (0.84)	18.5 (0.80)	18.3 (0.81)
Use of selected drugs														
Cocaine	5.6 (0.52)	12.3 (0.58)	13.1 (0.59)	5.3 (0.40)	4.0 (0.35)	5.0 (0.43)	4.8 (0.42)	5.0 (0.42)	4.8 (0.39)	5.3 (0.41)	5.1 (0.40)	5.7 (0.43)	5.2 (0.40)	4.4 (0.38)
Heroin	1.0 (0.13)	0.5 (0.07)	0.6 (0.07)	0.5 (0.07)	1.1 (0.10)	1.5 (0.13)	0.9 (0.10)	1.0 (0.11)	0.8 (0.09)	0.9 (0.10)	0.8 (0.09)	0.8 (0.09)	0.9 (0.09)	0.7 (0.08)
LSD	7.2 (0.59)	6.5 (0.43)	4.4 (0.36)	5.4 (0.41)	8.4 (0.49)	6.6 (0.49)	6.6 (0.49)	3.5 (0.36)	1.9 (0.25)	2.2 (0.27)	1.8 (0.24)	1.7 (0.24)	2.1 (0.26)	2.7 (0.30)
Marijuana/hashish	40.0 (1.61)	48.8 (1.27)	40.6 (1.24)	27.0 (1.15)	34.7 (1.23)	36.5 (1.36)	37.0 (1.36)	36.2 (1.35)	34.9 (1.26)	34.3 (1.25)	33.6 (1.24)	31.5 (1.24)	31.7 (1.21)	32.4 (1.24)
PCP	— (†)	4.4 (0.20)	2.9 (0.16)	1.2 (0.11)	1.8 (0.13)	2.3 (0.16)	1.8 (0.14)	1.1 (0.11)	1.3 (0.11)	0.7 (0.08)	1.3 (0.11)	0.7 (0.09)	0.9 (0.09)	1.1 (0.11)
Percent reporting use of drugs in the past 30 days														
Alcohol[1]	68.2 (1.10)	72.0 (0.81)	65.9 (0.85)	57.1 (0.92)	51.3 (0.92)	50.0 (1.01)	49.8 (1.01)	48.6 (1.00)	47.5 (0.94)	48.0 (0.94)	47.0 (0.94)	45.3 (0.95)	44.4 (0.92)	43.1 (0.93)
Any illicit drug	30.7 (1.35)	37.2 (1.09)	29.7 (1.03)	17.2 (0.87)	23.8 (0.98)	24.9 (1.09)	25.7 (1.10)	25.4 (1.09)	24.1 (1.01)	23.4 (1.00)	23.1 (0.99)	21.5 (0.98)	21.9 (0.96)	22.3 (0.98)
Marijuana only	15.3 (1.06)	18.8 (0.88)	14.8 (0.80)	9.2 (0.67)	13.8 (0.79)	14.5 (0.89)	14.7 (0.89)	14.1 (0.87)	13.7 (0.93)	12.8 (0.91)	12.8 (0.78)	11.7 (0.77)	12.4 (0.76)	13.0 (0.79)
Any illicit drug other than marijuana[2]	15.4 (0.80)	18.4 (0.66)	14.9 (0.60)	8.0 (0.47)	10.0 (0.52)	10.4 (0.58)	11.0 (0.59)	11.3 (0.60)	10.4 (0.54)	10.8 (0.55)	10.3 (0.54)	9.8 (0.54)	9.5 (0.51)	9.3 (0.52)
Use of selected drugs														
Cocaine	1.9 (0.25)	5.2 (0.31)	6.7 (0.35)	1.9 (0.20)	1.8 (0.19)	2.1 (0.23)	2.1 (0.23)	2.3 (0.24)	2.1 (0.21)	2.3 (0.22)	2.3 (0.22)	2.5 (0.23)	2.0 (0.20)	1.9 (0.20)
Heroin	0.4 (0.08)	0.2 (0.04)	0.3 (0.05)	0.2 (0.04)	0.6 (0.08)	0.7 (0.09)	0.4 (0.07)	0.5 (0.08)	0.4 (0.06)	0.5 (0.07)	0.5 (0.07)	0.4 (0.06)	0.4 (0.06)	0.4 (0.06)
LSD	2.3 (0.28)	2.3 (0.21)	1.6 (0.18)	1.9 (0.20)	4.0 (0.28)	1.6 (0.20)	2.3 (0.24)	0.7 (0.13)	0.6 (0.11)	0.7 (0.12)	0.7 (0.12)	0.6 (0.12)	0.6 (0.11)	1.1 (0.15)
Marijuana/hashish	27.1 (1.30)	33.7 (1.07)	25.7 (0.98)	14.0 (0.80)	21.2 (0.94)	21.6 (1.04)	22.4 (1.05)	21.5 (1.03)	21.2 (0.96)	19.9 (0.94)	19.8 (0.94)	18.3 (0.92)	18.8 (0.90)	19.4 (0.93)
PCP	— (†)	1.4 (0.11)	1.6 (0.12)	0.4 (0.06)	0.6 (0.08)	0.9 (0.10)	0.5 (0.08)	0.4 (0.07)	0.4 (0.06)	0.7 (0.06)	1.3 (0.11)	0.7 (0.06)	0.5 (0.07)	0.6 (0.08)

—Not available.

†Not applicable.

[1]Survey question changed in 1993; later data are not comparable to figures for earlier years.

[2]Other illicit drugs include any use of LSD or other hallucinogens, crack or other cocaine, or heroin, or any use of other narcotics, amphetamines, barbiturates, or tranquilizers not under a doctor's orders.

NOTE: Standard errors appear in parentheses. Standard errors were calculated from formulas to perform trend analysis over an interval greater than 1 year (for example, a comparison between 1975 and 1990). A revised questionnaire was used in 1982 and later years to reduce the inappropriate reporting of nonprescription stimulants. This slightly reduced the positive responses for some types of drug abuse.

SOURCE: University of Michigan, Institute for Social Research, Monitoring the Future, selected years, 1975 through 2008, retrieved June 2, 2009, from http://www.monitoringthefuture.org/pubs/monographs/overview2008.pdf. (This table was prepared June 2009.)

Public and private elementary and secondary teachers, enrollment, and pupil/teacher ratios: Selected years, fall 1955 through fall 2018

Year	Teachers (in thousands)			Enrollment (in thousands)			Pupil/teacher ratio		
	Total	Public	Private	Total	Public	Private	Total	Public	Private
1	2	3	4	5	6	7	8	9	10
1955........................	1,286	1,141	145 [1]	35,280	30,680	4,600 [1]	27.4	26.9	31.7 [1]
1960........................	1,600	1,408	192 [1]	42,181	36,281	5,900 [1]	26.4	25.8	30.7 [1]
1965........................	1,933	1,710	223	48,473	42,173	6,300	25.1	24.7	28.3
1970........................	2,292	2,059	233	51,257	45,894	5,363	22.4	22.3	23.0
1971........................	2,293	2,063	230 [1]	51,271	46,071	5,200 [1]	22.4	22.3	22.6 [1]
1972........................	2,337	2,106	231 [1]	50,726	45,726	5,000 [1]	21.7	21.7	21.6 [1]
1973........................	2,372	2,136	236 [1]	50,445	45,445	5,000 [1]	21.3	21.3	21.2 [1]
1974........................	2,410	2,165	245 [1]	50,073	45,073	5,000 [1]	20.8	20.8	20.4 [1]
1975........................	2,453	2,198	255 [1]	49,819	44,819	5,000 [1]	20.3	20.4	19.6 [1]
1976........................	2,457	2,189	268	49,478	44,311	5,167	20.1	20.2	19.3
1977........................	2,488	2,209	279	48,717	43,577	5,140	19.6	19.7	18.4
1978........................	2,479	2,207	272	47,637	42,551	5,086	19.2	19.3	18.7
1979........................	2,461	2,185	276 [1]	46,651	41,651	5,000 [1]	19.0	19.1	18.1 [1]
1980........................	2,485	2,184	301	46,208	40,877	5,331	18.6	18.7	17.7
1981........................	2,440	2,127	313 [1]	45,544	40,044	5,500 [1]	18.7	18.8	17.6 [1]
1982........................	2,458	2,133	325 [1]	45,166	39,566	5,600 [1]	18.4	18.6	17.2 [1]
1983........................	2,476	2,139	337	44,967	39,252	5,715	18.2	18.4	17.0
1984........................	2,508	2,168	340 [1]	44,908	39,208	5,700 [1]	17.9	18.1	16.8 [1]
1985........................	2,549	2,206	343	44,979	39,422	5,557	17.6	17.9	16.2
1986........................	2,592	2,244	348 [1]	45,205	39,753	5,452 [1]	17.4	17.7	15.7 [1]
1987........................	2,631	2,279	352	45,488	40,008	5,479	17.3	17.6	15.6
1988........................	2,668	2,323	345	45,430	40,189	5,242 [1]	17.0	17.3	15.2 [1]
1989........................	2,713	2,357	356	46,141	40,543	5,599	17.0	17.2	15.7
1990........................	2,759	2,398	361 [1]	46,864	41,217	5,648 [1]	17.0	17.2	15.6 [1]
1991........................	2,797	2,432	365	47,728	42,047	5,681	17.1	17.3	15.6
1992........................	2,823	2,459	364 [1]	48,694	42,823	5,870 [1]	17.2	17.4	16.1 [1]
1993........................	2,868	2,504	364	49,532	43,465	6,067	17.3	17.4	16.7
1994........................	2,922	2,552	370 [1]	50,106	44,111	5,994 [1]	17.1	17.3	16.2 [1]
1995........................	2,974	2,598	376	50,759	44,840	5,918	17.1	17.3	15.7
1996........................	3,051	2,667	384 [1]	51,544	45,611	5,933 [1]	16.9	17.1	15.5 [1]
1997........................	3,138	2,746	391	52,071	46,127	5,944	16.6	16.8	15.2
1998........................	3,230	2,830	400 [1]	52,526	46,539	5,988 [1]	16.3	16.4	15.0 [1]
1999........................	3,319	2,911	408	52,875	46,857	6,018	15.9	16.1	14.7
2000........................	3,366	2,941	424 [1]	53,373	47,204	6,169 [1]	15.9	16.0	14.5 [1]
2001........................	3,440	3,000	441	53,992	47,672	6,320	15.7	15.9	14.3
2002........................	3,476	3,034	442 [1]	54,403	48,183	6,220 [1]	15.7	15.9	14.1 [1]
2003........................	3,490	3,049	441	54,639	48,540	6,099	15.7	15.9	13.8
2004........................	3,538	3,091	447 [1]	54,882	48,795	6,087 [1]	15.5	15.8	13.6 [1]
2005........................	3,593	3,143	450	55,187	49,113	6,073	15.4	15.6	13.5
2006........................	3,622	3,166	456 [1]	55,307	49,316	5,991 [1]	15.3	15.6	13.2 [1]
2007........................	3,634	3,178	456	55,203	49,293	5,910	15.2	15.5	13.0
2008[2]........................	3,689	3,233	456	55,500	49,623	5,878	15.0	15.3	12.9
2009[2]........................	3,705	3,249	456	55,632	49,788	5,845	15.0	15.3	12.8
2010[2]........................	3,725	3,271	454	55,850	50,034	5,817	15.0	15.3	12.8
2011[2]........................	3,763	3,310	453	56,144	50,349	5,795	14.9	15.2	12.8
2012[2]........................	3,812	3,358	454	56,545	50,767	5,778	14.8	15.1	12.7
2013[2]........................	3,867	3,410	457	57,012	51,239	5,773	14.7	15.0	12.6
2014[2]........................	3,933	3,473	460	57,544	51,769	5,775	14.6	14.9	12.6
2015[2]........................	4,001	3,536	465	58,137	52,346	5,791	14.5	14.8	12.5
2016[2]........................	4,069	3,599	470	58,706	52,892	5,814	14.4	14.7	12.4
2017[2]........................	4,141	3,665	476	59,270	53,426	5,843	14.3	14.6	12.3
2018[2]........................	4,205	3,722	483	59,813	53,933	5,879	14.2	14.5	12.2

[1]Estimated.
[2]Projected.
NOTE: Data for teachers are expressed in full-time equivalents (FTE). Counts of private school teachers and enrollment include prekindergarten through grade 12 in schools offering kindergarten or higher grades. Counts of public school teachers and enrollment include prekindergarten through grade 12. The pupil/teacher ratio includes teachers for students with disabilities and other special teachers, while these teachers are generally excluded from class size calculations. Ratios for public schools reflect totals reported by states and differ from totals reported for schools or school districts. Some data have been revised from previously published figures. Detail may not sum to totals because of rounding.
SOURCE: U.S. Department of Education, National Center for Education Statistics, *Statistics of Public Elementary and Secondary Day Schools*, 1955–56 through 1984–85; Common Core of Data (CCD), "State Nonfiscal Survey of Public Elementary/Secondary Education," 1985–86 through 2007–08; Private School Universe Survey (PSS), 1989–90 through 2007–08; *Projections of Education Statistics to 2018*; and unpublished data. (This table was prepared September 2009.)

Public elementary and secondary teachers, by level and state or jurisdiction: Selected years, fall 2000 through fall 2007

State or jurisdiction	Fall 2000	Fall 2003	Fall 2004	Fall 2005	Fall 2006[1] Total	Fall 2006[1] Elementary	Fall 2006[1] Secondary	Fall 2006[1] Ungraded	Fall 2007 Total	Fall 2007 Elementary	Fall 2007 Secondary	Fall 2007 Ungraded
1	2	3	4	5	6	7	8	9	10	11	12	13
United States	2,941,461 [2]	3,048,652 [2]	3,090,925 [2]	3,143,003 [2]	3,166,391 [2]	1,666,282 [2]	1,247,403 [2]	252,706 [2]	3,178,142 [2]	1,688,240 [2]	1,258,069	231,833
Alabama	48,194 [3]	58,070	51,594	57,757	56,134	34,385	21,749	0	50,420	29,086	21,334	0
Alaska	7,880	7,808	7,756	7,912	7,903	4,127	3,776	0	7,613	3,897	3,716	0
Arizona	44,438	47,507	48,935	51,376	52,625	37,793	14,832	0	54,032	38,807	15,225	0
Arkansas....................	31,947	30,876	31,234	32,997	35,089	16,315	15,983	2,791	33,882	17,942	13,520	2,420
California	298,021 [3]	304,311 [3]	305,969 [3]	309,222 [3]	307,366 [3]	213,380 [3]	85,106	8,880	305,230 [3]	209,146 [3]	86,030	10,054
Colorado	41,983	44,904	45,165	45,841	46,973	23,798	23,175	0	47,761	26,947	20,814	0
Connecticut................	41,044	42,370	38,808	39,687	39,115	25,945	12,126	1,044	39,304	26,005	12,259	1,040
Delaware....................	7,469	7,749	7,856	7,998	8,038	3,981	4,057	0	8,198	4,110	4,088	0
District of Columbia	4,949	5,676	5,387	5,481 [4]	5,383 [4]	2,828 [4]	2,271 [4]	284 [4]	6,347	3,238	2,619	490
Florida.......................	132,030	144,955	154,864	158,962	162,851	72,116	64,334	26,401	168,737	75,670	67,019	26,048
Georgia......................	91,043	97,150	104,987	108,535	113,597	68,690	44,907	0	116,857	71,109	45,681	67
Hawaii	10,927	11,129	11,146	11,226	11,271	5,943	5,289	39	11,397	6,075	5,280	42
Idaho.........................	13,714	14,049	14,269	14,521	14,770	7,690	7,080	0	15,013	7,874	7,139	0
Illinois.......................	127,620	127,669	131,047	133,857	140,988	57,332	62,187	21,469	136,571	56,585	58,489	21,497
Indiana.......................	59,226	59,924	60,563	60,592	61,346	33,470	27,855	21	62,334	33,870	28,074	390
Iowa..........................	34,636	34,791	34,697	35,181	35,653	19,128	16,525	0	36,089	19,608	16,481	0
Kansas.......................	32,742	32,589	32,932	33,608	35,297	16,418	18,713	166	35,359	16,604	18,572	183
Kentucky	39,589	41,246	41,463	42,413	43,371	21,615	10,101	11,655	43,536	21,699	10,168	11,669
Louisiana	49,915	50,495	49,192	44,660	45,951	32,186	13,765	0	48,610	34,042	14,568	0
Maine........................	16,559	17,621	16,656	16,684	16,826	11,442	5,159	235	16,558	11,351	5,207	0
Maryland.....................	52,433	55,198	55,101	56,685	58,443	33,898	24,545	0	59,320	34,449	24,871	0
Massachusetts................	67,432	72,062	73,399	73,596	73,157	41,984	20,793	10,380	70,719	47,026	23,693	0
Michigan	97,031	97,014	100,638	98,069	98,037	38,666	39,265	20,106	96,204	38,063	38,343	19,798
Minnesota...................	53,457	51,611	52,152	51,107	51,880	25,905	24,387	1,588	52,975	27,012	24,483	1,480
Mississippi..................	31,006	32,591	31,321	31,433	32,351	15,669	12,408	4,274	33,560	16,149	13,103	4,308
Missouri.....................	64,735	65,169	65,847	67,076	67,521	34,983	32,538	0	68,430	35,420	33,010	0
Montana.....................	10,411	10,301	10,224	10,369	10,398	6,944	3,454	0	10,519	7,082	3,437	0
Nebraska....................	20,983	20,921	21,236	21,359	21,459	13,588	7,755	116	21,930	13,996	7,847	87
Nevada	18,293	20,234	20,950	21,744	22,908	11,763	7,866	3,279	23,423	12,003	8,067	3,353
New Hampshire	14,341	15,112	15,298	15,536	15,515	10,582	4,933	0	15,484	10,576	4,908	0
New Jersey..................	99,061	109,077	114,875	112,673	112,301	45,494	48,157	18,650	111,500	47,442	46,343	17,715
New Mexico.................	21,042	21,569	21,730	22,021	22,016	15,628	6,388	0	22,330	15,589	6,629	82
New York....................	206,961	216,116	218,612 [4]	218,989	218,879	106,391	76,693	35,795	211,854	102,626	71,116	38,112
North Carolina	83,680	89,988	92,550	95,664	112,304	62,958	47,713	1,633	106,562	56,192	48,685	1,685
North Dakota	8,141	8,037	8,070	8,003	8,007	4,908	3,099	0	8,068	4,970	3,098	0
Ohio..........................	118,361	121,735	118,060	117,982	110,459	52,136	52,596	5,727	109,766	52,616	52,498	4,652
Oklahoma...................	41,318	39,253	40,416	41,833	42,206	20,668	17,059	4,479	46,735	22,276	19,974	4,485
Oregon.......................	28,094	26,732	27,431	28,346	29,940	20,175	8,875	890	30,013	20,677	9,120	216
Pennsylvania................	116,963	119,889	121,167	122,397	123,114	50,218	53,175	19,721	135,234	62,770	63,313	9,151
Rhode Island	10,645	11,918	11,781	14,180 [3]	11,381	5,407	5,974	0	11,271	5,383	5,888	0
South Carolina.............	45,380	45,830	46,914	48,212	49,284	14,980	31,882	2,422	47,382	14,200	30,757	2,425
South Dakota...............	9,397	9,245	9,064	9,129	9,070	5,721	2,547	802	9,416	5,729	2,533	1,154
Tennessee	57,164	59,584	60,022	59,596	62,176	43,484	18,210	482	64,659	44,454	18,626	1,579
Texas........................	274,826	289,481	294,547	302,425	311,649	155,549	119,809	36,291	321,929	159,819	123,974	38,136
Utah..........................	22,008	22,147	22,287 [3]	22,993	23,640	11,569	9,642	2,429	24,336	12,165	9,711	2,460
Vermont	8,414	8,749	8,720	8,851	8,859	3,413	3,614	1,832	8,749	3,399	3,601	1,749
Virginia......................	86,977 [3]	90,573	93,732	103,944	79,688	39,061	40,627	0	71,861	34,907	36,954	0
Washington..................	51,098	52,824	53,125	53,508	53,743	26,319	22,181	5,243	53,960	26,518	22,264	5,178
West Virginia................	20,930	20,020	19,958	19,940	19,633	8,441	7,788	3,404	20,306	9,493	10,813	0
Wisconsin	60,165	58,216	60,521	60,127	59,089	27,921	31,003	165	58,914	28,023	30,763	128
Wyoming.....................	6,783	6,567	6,657	6,706	6,737	3,287	3,437	13	6,915	3,551	3,364	0
Bureau of Indian Education .	—	—	—	—	—	—	—	—	—	—	—	—
DoD, overseas	5,105	4,728	4,885	5,726	5,204	1,762	1,603	1,839	4,147	1,610	1,519	1,018
DoD, domestic	2,399	2,301	2,002	2,033	2,033	1,053	446	534	2,243	992	433	818
Other jurisdictions												
American Samoa	820	988	945	989	971	684	267	20	—	—	—	—
Guam	1,975	1,760	1,672	1,804	—	—	—	—	—	—	—	—
Northern Marianas........	526	550	579	614	579	322	253	4	550	310	236	4
Puerto Rico	37,620	42,444	43,054	42,036	40,163	21,970	13,486	4,707	40,826	21,357	14,017	5,452
U.S. Virgin Islands..........	1,511	1,512	1,545	1,434	1,531	698	810	23	1,518	643	588	287

—Not available.
[1]Data have been revised from previously published figures.
[2]Includes imputed values for states.
[3]Includes imputations for underreporting of prekindergarten teachers.
[4]Imputed.

NOTE: Distribution of elementary and secondary teachers determined by reporting units. Teachers reported in full-time equivalents (FTE). DoD = Department of Defense.
SOURCE: U.S. Department of Education, National Center for Education Statistics, Common Core of Data (CCD), "State Nonfiscal Survey of Public Elementary/Secondary Education," 2000–01 through 2007–08. (This table was prepared September 2009.)

Teachers, enrollment, and pupil/teacher ratios in public elementary and secondary schools, by state or jurisdiction: Selected years, fall 2000 through fall 2007

State or jurisdiction	Pupil/teacher ratio				Fall 2005			Fall 2006[1]			Fall 2007		
	Fall 2000	Fall 2002	Fall 2003	Fall 2004[1]	Teachers	Enrollment	Pupil/ teacher ratio	Teachers	Enrollment	Pupil/ teacher ratio	Teachers	Enrollment	Pupil/ teacher ratio
1	2	3	4	5	6	7	8	9	10	11	12	13	14
United States	16.0 [2]	15.9 [2]	15.9 [2]	15.8 [2]	3,143,003 [2]	49,113,298 [2]	15.6 [2]	3,166,391 [2]	49,315,842 [2]	15.6 [2]	3,178,142 [2]	49,292,507 [2]	15.5 [2]
Alabama	15.4 [3]	15.7 [3]	12.6	14.2	57,757	741,761	12.8	56,134	743,632	13.2	50,420	744,865	14.8
Alaska	16.9	16.6	17.2	17.1	7,912	133,288	16.8	7,903	132,608	16.8	7,613	131,029	17.2
Arizona	19.8	19.9	21.3	21.3	51,376	1,094,454	21.3	52,625	1,068,249	20.3	54,032	1,087,447	20.1
Arkansas....................	14.1	14.9	14.7	14.8	32,997	474,206	14.4	35,089	476,409	13.6	33,882	479,016	14.1
California	20.6 [3]	20.6 [3]	21.1 [3]	21.1 [3]	309,222 [3]	6,437,202 [3]	20.8 [3]	307,366 [3]	6,406,750 [3]	20.8 [3]	305,230 [3]	6,343,471 [3]	20.8 [3]
Colorado	17.3	16.6	16.9	17.0	45,841	779,826	17.0	46,973	794,026	16.9	47,761	801,867	16.8
Connecticut................	13.7	13.5	13.6	14.9	39,687	575,059	14.5	39,115	575,100	14.7	39,304	570,626	14.5
Delaware....................	15.4	15.1	15.2	15.2	7,998	120,937	15.1	8,038	122,254	15.2	8,198	122,574	15.0
District of Columbia	13.9	13.9	13.8	14.2	5,481 [4]	76,876	14.0 [4]	5,383 [4]	72,850	13.5 [4]	6,347	78,422	12.4
Florida.......................	18.4	18.4	17.9	17.0	158,962	2,675,024	16.8	162,851	2,671,513	16.4	168,737	2,666,811	15.8
Georgia......................	15.9	15.6	15.7	14.8	108,535	1,598,461	14.7	113,597	1,629,157	14.3	116,857	1,649,589	14.1
Hawaii	16.9	16.8	16.5	16.4	11,226	182,818	16.3	11,271	180,728	16.0	11,397	179,897	15.8
Idaho	17.9	17.9	17.9	17.9	14,521	261,982	18.0	14,770	267,380	18.1	15,013	272,119	18.1
Illinois.......................	16.1	15.9	16.5	16.0	133,857	2,111,706	15.8	140,988	2,118,276	15.0	136,571	2,112,805	15.5
Indiana......................	16.7	16.7	16.9	16.9	60,592	1,035,074	17.1	61,346	1,045,940	17.0	62,334	1,046,766	16.8
Iowa	14.3	13.9	13.8	13.8	35,181	483,482	13.7	35,653	483,122	13.6	36,089	485,115	13.4
Kansas......................	14.4	14.4	14.4	14.2	33,608	467,525	13.9	35,297	469,506	13.3	35,359	468,295	13.2
Kentucky....................	16.8	16.3	16.1	16.3	42,413	679,878	16.0	43,371	683,152	15.8	43,536	666,225	15.3
Louisiana...................	16.6	16.6	16.6	16.6	44,660	654,526	16.6	45,951	675,851	16.6	48,610	681,038	16.6
Maine........................	12.5	12.1	11.5	11.9	16,684	195,498	11.7	16,826	193,986	11.5	16,558	196,245	11.9
Maryland....................	16.3	15.7	15.7	15.7	56,685	860,020	15.2	58,443	851,640	14.6	59,320	845,700	14.3
Massachusetts............	14.5	13.2	13.6	13.3	73,596	971,909	13.2	73,157	968,661	13.2	70,719	962,958	13.6
Michigan....................	17.7 [3]	19.9	18.1	17.4	98,069	1,742,282	17.8	98,037	1,722,656	17.6	96,204	1,692,739	17.6
Minnesota..................	16.0	16.0	16.3	16.1	51,107	839,243	16.4	51,880	840,565	16.2	52,975	837,578	15.8
Mississippi	16.1	15.6	15.1	15.8	31,433	494,954	15.7	32,351	495,026	15.3	33,560	494,122	14.7
Missouri	14.1	13.6	13.9	13.8	67,076	917,705	13.7	67,521	920,353	13.6	68,430	917,188	13.4
Montana.....................	14.9	14.5	14.4	14.3	10,369	145,416	14.0	10,398	144,418	13.9	10,519	142,823	13.6
Nebraska....................	13.6	13.6	13.6	13.5	21,359	286,646	13.4	21,459	287,580	13.4	21,930	291,244	13.3
Nevada	18.6	18.4	19.0	19.1	21,744	412,395	19.0	22,908	424,766	18.5	23,423	429,362	18.3
New Hampshire	14.5	13.9	13.7	13.5	15,536	205,767	13.2	15,515	203,572	13.1	15,484	200,772	13.0
New Jersey.................	13.3	12.8	12.7	12.1	112,673	1,395,602	12.4	112,301	1,388,850	12.4	111,500	1,382,348	12.4
New Mexico	15.2	15.1	15.0	15.0	22,021	326,758	14.8	22,016	328,220	14.9	22,300	329,040	14.8
New York....................	13.9	13.7	13.3	13.0	218,989	2,815,581	12.9	218,879	2,809,649	12.8	211,854	2,765,435	13.1
North Carolina	15.5	15.2	15.1	15.0	95,664	1,416,436	14.8	112,304	1,444,481	12.9	106,562	1,489,492	14.0
North Dakota	13.4	12.9	12.7	12.5	8,003	98,283	12.3	8,007	96,670	12.1	8,068	95,059	11.8
Ohio	15.5	14.7	15.2	15.6	117,982	1,839,683	15.6	110,459	1,836,722	16.6	109,766	1,827,184	16.6
Oklahoma	15.1	15.4	16.0	15.6	41,833	634,739	15.2	42,206	639,391	15.1	46,735	642,065	13.7
Oregon	19.4	20.4	20.6	20.1	28,346	552,194	19.5	29,940	562,574	18.8	30,013	565,586	18.8
Pennsylvania..............	15.5	15.4	15.2	15.1	122,397	1,830,684	15.0	123,114	1,871,060	15.2	135,234	1,801,971	13.3
Rhode Island..............	14.8	14.2	13.4	13.3	14,180 [3]	153,422	10.8	11,381	151,612	13.3	11,271	147,629	13.1
South Carolina............	14.9	14.9	15.3	15.0	48,212	701,544	14.6	49,284	708,021	14.4	47,382	712,317	15.0
South Dakota..............	13.7	14.0	13.6	13.5	9,129	122,012	13.4	9,070	121,158	13.4	9,416	121,606	12.9
Tennessee	15.9 [3]	15.8 [3]	15.7 [3]	15.7 [3]	59,596	953,928	16.0	62,176	978,368	15.7	64,659	964,259	14.9
Texas	14.8	14.8	15.0	15.0	302,425	4,525,394	15.0	311,649	4,599,509	14.8	321,929	4,674,832	14.5
Utah	21.9	21.8	22.4	22.6 [3]	22,993	508,430	22.1	23,640	523,386	22.1	24,336	576,244	23.7
Vermont	12.1	11.7	11.3	11.3	8,851	96,638	10.9	8,859	95,399	10.8	8,749	94,038	10.7
Virginia......................	13.2 [3]	11.8	13.2	12.9	103,944	1,213,616	11.7	79,688	1,220,440	15.3	71,861	1,230,857	17.1
Washington.................	19.7	19.2	19.3	19.2	53,508	1,031,985	19.3	53,743	1,026,774	19.1	53,960	1,030,247	19.1
West Virginia...............	13.7	14.0	14.0	14.0	19,940	280,866	14.1	19,633	281,939	14.4	20,306	282,535	13.9
Wisconsin...................	14.6	14.6	15.1	14.3	60,127	875,174	14.6	59,089	876,700	14.8	58,914	874,633	14.8
Wyoming....................	13.3	13.0 [3]	13.3	12.7	6,706	84,409	12.6	6,737	85,193	12.6	6,915	86,422	12.5
Bureau of Indian Education.................	—	—	—	—	—	50,938	—	—	—	—	—	—	—
DoD, overseas	14.4	15.2	15.0	14.0	5,726	62,543	10.9	5,204	60,891	11.7	4,147	57,247	13.8
DoD, domestic	14.2	13.2	13.3	14.6	2,033	28,329	13.9	2,033	26,631	13.1	2,243	27,548	12.3
Other jurisdictions													
American Samoa	19.1	17.0	16.1	17.1	989	16,438	16.6	971	16,400	16.9	—	—	—
Guam	16.4	—	17.9	18.3	1,804	30,986	17.2	—	—	—	—	—	—
Northern Marianas......	19.0	20.6	20.4	20.0	614	11,718	19.1	579	11,695	20.2	550	11,299	20.5
Puerto Rico	16.3	14.1	13.8	13.4	42,036	563,490	13.4	40,163	544,138	13.5	40,826	526,565	12.9
U.S. Virgin Islands.......	12.9	12.2	11.7	10.6	1,434	16,750	11.7	1,531	16,284	10.6	1,518	15,903	10.5

—Not available.
[1]Data have been revised from previously published figures.
[2]Includes imputed values for states.
[3]Includes imputations for underreporting of prekindergarten teachers/enrollment.
[4]Imputed.

NOTE: Teachers reported in full-time equivalents (FTE). DoD = Department of Defense.
SOURCE: U.S. Department of Education, National Center for Education Statistics, Common Core of Data (CCD), "State Nonfiscal Survey of Public Elementary/Secondary Education," 2000–01 through 2007–08. (This table was prepared September 2009.)

Teachers' perceptions about teaching and school conditions, by control and level of school: Selected years, 1993–94 through 2007–08

Percent of teachers somewhat agreeing or strongly agreeing with statement

Statement about conditions	Public school teachers							Private school teachers						
	1993–94 total	1999–2000 total	2003–04 total	2007–08				1993–94 total	1999–2000 total	2003–04 total	2007–08			
				Total	Elementary schools	Secondary schools	Combined schools				Total	Elementary schools	Secondary schools	Combined schools
1	2	3	4	5	6	7	8	9	10	11	12	13	14	15
The school administration's behavior toward the staff is supportive	79.2 (0.36)	78.8 (0.38)	85.2 (0.33)	87.7 (0.39)	88.1 (0.51)	87.1 (0.47)	86.3 (1.25)	88.2 (0.42)	87.3 (0.45)	91.1 (0.74)	93.1 (0.43)	92.6 (0.49)	92.3 (1.15)	93.9 (0.74)
My principal enforces school rules for student conduct and backs me up when I need it	80.8 (0.35)	82.2 (0.33)	87.2 (0.35)	88.0 (0.37)	89.3 (0.48)	85.9 (0.51)	86.0 (1.12)	88.4 (0.41)	88.3 (0.39)	92.2 (0.62)	92.2 (0.58)	91.8 (0.71)	91.8 (1.17)	92.8 (0.97)
The principal lets staff members know what is expected of them	85.6 (0.30)	87.7 (0.26)	91.8 (0.23)	— (†)	— (†)	— (†)	— (†)	88.2 (0.34)	89.8 (0.35)	93.8 (0.55)	— (†)	— (†)	— (†)	— (†)
Principal talks to me frequently about my instructional practices	44.3 (0.46)	45.6 (0.43)	— (†)	— (†)	— (†)	— (†)	— (†)	54.0 (0.64)	50.4 (0.64)	— (†)	— (†)	— (†)	— (†)	— (†)
In this school, staff members are recognized for a job well done	67.9 (0.39)	68.3 (0.42)	75.4 (0.38)	76.7 (0.56)	78.3 (0.77)	74.2 (0.63)	72.4 (1.41)	81.1 (0.40)	78.9 (0.50)	83.8 (1.09)	84.1 (0.67)	84.0 (0.78)	83.0 (1.71)	84.6 (1.05)
Principal knows what kind of school he/she wants and has communicated it to the staff	80.5 (0.36)	83.2 (0.28)	87.3 (0.30)	88.4 (0.33)	89.6 (0.44)	86.6 (0.51)	84.4 (1.20)	88.6 (0.38)	88.4 (0.43)	91.9 (0.68)	91.7 (0.53)	91.3 (0.65)	90.7 (1.20)	92.5 (0.82)
Most of my colleagues share my beliefs and values about what the central mission of the school should be	84.2 (0.22)	84.7 (0.26)	88.1 (0.26)	88.3 (0.35)	90.7 (0.52)	83.8 (0.53)	87.4 (0.86)	93.2 (0.37)	92.2 (0.31)	93.8 (0.50)	93.7 (0.44)	94.9 (0.47)	90.5 (1.36)	93.7 (0.79)
There is a great deal of cooperative effort among staff	77.5 (0.31)	78.4 (0.32)	83.2 (0.36)	84.3 (0.33)	86.1 (0.47)	81.0 (0.51)	81.9 (1.19)	90.5 (0.29)	89.0 (0.42)	91.1 (0.75)	91.8 (0.63)	92.3 (0.53)	88.3 (1.43)	92.5 (1.08)
I receive a great deal of support from parents for the work I do	52.5 (0.38)	57.9 (0.40)	61.1 (0.50)	64.3 (0.52)	66.5 (0.78)	60.4 (0.66)	62.5 (1.45)	84.6 (0.41)	84.0 (0.49)	86.0 (2.39)	87.7 (0.60)	89.4 (0.69)	85.1 (1.79)	86.9 (1.01)
I make a conscious effort to coordinate the content of my courses with that of other teachers	85.0 (0.25)	84.1 (0.24)	86.3 (0.31)	— (†)	— (†)	— (†)	— (†)	85.2 (0.44)	81.4 (0.55)	84.5 (1.20)	— (†)	— (†)	— (†)	— (†)
Routine duties and paperwork interfere with my job of teaching	70.8 (0.38)	71.1 (0.30)	70.8 (0.44)	69.0 (0.54)	69.4 (0.82)	68.7 (0.69)	64.4 (1.32)	40.1 (0.65)	44.5 (0.57)	40.8 (2.51)	42.7 (0.98)	44.8 (1.26)	46.2 (2.27)	39.3 (1.75)
Level of student misbehavior in this school interferes with my teaching	44.1 (0.40)	40.8 (0.42)	37.2 (0.53)	36.1 (0.57)	33.8 (0.80)	40.2 (0.79)	38.9 (1.37)	22.4 (0.43)	24.1 (0.61)	20.8 (2.55)	20.6 (0.73)	20.8 (0.97)	19.5 (1.71)	20.7 (1.38)
Amount of student tardiness and class cutting in this school interferes with my teaching	27.9 (0.32)	31.5 (0.35)	33.4 (0.45)	33.4 (0.65)	26.4 (0.86)	47.2 (0.86)	32.8 (1.35)	16.9 (0.75)	15.0 (0.43)	16.9 (1.01)	17.8 (0.71)	17.1 (0.78)	20.4 (1.76)	17.6 (1.63)
Rules for student behavior are consistently enforced by teachers in this school, even for students who are not in their classes	61.8 (0.42)	62.6 (0.39)	71.1 (0.46)	70.6 (0.55)	78.8 (0.68)	55.1 (0.66)	68.1 (1.38)	77.6 (0.50)	75.9 (0.51)	80.9 (1.51)	80.0 (0.81)	85.3 (0.87)	69.8 (2.00)	78.5 (1.49)
I am satisfied with my class sizes	64.9 (0.38)	67.7 (0.36)	69.1 (0.43)	— (†)	— (†)	— (†)	— (†)	84.4 (0.40)	85.7 (0.45)	87.6 (0.92)	— (†)	— (†)	— (†)	— (†)
I am satisfied with my teaching salary	44.9 (0.45)	39.4 (0.36)	45.9 (0.46)	50.9 (0.65)	48.9 (0.91)	55.2 (0.73)	47.9 (1.27)	41.6 (0.59)	42.6 (0.73)	50.6 (1.67)	51.7 (0.88)	44.5 (1.13)	55.8 (2.63)	57.6 (2.06)
I sometimes feel it is a waste of time to try to do my best as a teacher	26.8 (0.35)	20.3 (0.29)	16.7 (0.32)	— (†)	— (†)	— (†)	— (†)	10.2 (0.65)	10.5 (0.38)	8.7 (0.71)	— (†)	— (†)	— (†)	— (†)
I plan with the librarian/media specialist for the integration of services into my teaching	66.9 (0.42)	58.6 (0.38)	— (†)	— (†)	— (†)	— (†)	— (†)	60.6 (0.71)	48.7 (0.74)	— (†)	— (†)	— (†)	— (†)	— (†)
Necessary materials are available as needed by staff	73.1 (0.42)	75.0 (0.32)	79.0 (0.42)	82.2 (0.55)	82.5 (0.77)	81.5 (0.51)	82.1 (1.06)	85.7 (0.44)	89.0 (0.38)	91.8 (0.71)	92.1 (0.54)	92.3 (0.59)	91.2 (1.33)	92.2 (1.02)
I worry about the security of my job because of the performance of my students on state or local tests	— (†)	28.8 (0.37)	31.2 (0.43)	30.9 (0.58)	32.3 (0.81)	28.3 (0.54)	30.5 (1.32)	— (†)	6.7 (0.29)	7.8 (0.65)	7.7 (0.47)	8.2 (0.57)	6.4 (1.06)	7.6 (0.82)
State or district content standards have had a positive influence on my satisfaction with teaching	— (†)	— (†)	— (†)	49.3 (0.62)	52.1 (0.95)	44.1 (0.57)	48.5 (1.29)	— (†)	— (†)	— (†)	41.0 (0.81)	49.1 (1.20)	34.1 (2.01)	35.2 (1.52)
I am given the support I need to teach students with special needs	— (†)	60.9 (0.33)	64.4 (0.46)	67.2 (0.57)	66.2 (0.74)	68.3 (0.69)	72.7 (1.18)	— (†)	67.1 (0.58)	71.8 (2.05)	68.5 (0.84)	66.5 (1.17)	69.5 (1.81)	70.2 (1.55)
I am generally satisfied with being a teacher at this school	— (†)	89.7 (0.24)	90.9 (0.28)	92.9 (0.31)	93.1 (0.42)	92.4 (0.37)	93.1 (0.59)	— (†)	93.3 (0.26)	95.2 (0.55)	95.7 (0.43)	95.2 (0.52)	95.5 (0.92)	96.2 (0.65)

—Not available.
†Not applicable.
NOTE: Standard errors appear in parentheses.

SOURCE: U.S. Department of Education, National Center for Education Statistics, Schools and Staffing Survey (SASS), "Public Teacher Questionnaire," selected years 1993–94 through 2007–08; "Private Teacher Questionnaire," selected years 1993–94 through 2007–08; and "Charter Teacher Questionnaire," 1999–2000. (This table was prepared September 2009.)

Estimated average annual salary of teachers in public elementary and secondary schools: Selected years, 1959–60 through 2008–09

School year	Current dollars					Average public school teachers' salary in constant 2007–08 dollars[2]		
	Average public school teachers' salary			Wage and salary accruals per full-time-equivalent (FTE) employee[1]	Ratio of average teachers' salary to accruals per FTE employee			
	All teachers	Elementary teachers	Secondary teachers			All teachers	Elementary teachers	Secondary teachers
1	2	3	4	5	6	7	8	9
1959–60	$4,995	$4,815	$5,276	$4,749	1.05	$35,989	$34,692	$38,013
1961–62	5,515	5,340	5,775	5,063	1.09	38,843	37,610	40,674
1963–64	5,995	5,805	6,266	5,478	1.09	41,150	39,846	43,010
1965–66	6,485	6,279	6,761	5,934	1.09	43,026	41,660	44,858
1967–68	7,423	7,208	7,692	6,533	1.14	46,209	44,870	47,883
1969–70	8,626	8,412	8,891	7,486	1.15	48,343	47,143	49,828
1970–71	9,268	9,021	9,568	7,998	1.16	49,391	48,075	50,990
1971–72	9,705	9,424	10,031	8,521	1.14	49,929	48,483	51,606
1972–73	10,174	9,893	10,507	9,056	1.12	50,314	48,925	51,961
1973–74	10,770	10,507	11,077	9,667	1.11	48,901	47,707	50,295
1974–75	11,641	11,334	12,000	10,411	1.12	47,583	46,328	49,051
1975–76	12,600	12,280	12,937	11,194	1.13	48,099	46,877	49,385
1976–77	13,354	12,989	13,776	11,971	1.12	48,168	46,851	49,690
1977–78	14,198	13,845	14,602	12,811	1.11	47,990	46,797	49,355
1978–79	15,032	14,681	15,450	13,807	1.09	46,457	45,372	47,749
1979–80	15,970	15,569	16,459	15,050	1.06	43,549	42,456	44,883
1980–81	17,644	17,230	18,142	16,461	1.07	43,120	42,108	44,337
1981–82	19,274	18,853	19,805	17,795	1.08	43,358	42,411	44,553
1982–83	20,695	20,227	21,291	18,873	1.10	44,638	43,628	45,923
1983–84	21,935	21,487	22,554	19,781	1.11	45,623	44,692	46,911
1984–85	23,600	23,200	24,187	20,694	1.14	47,238	46,437	48,412
1985–86	25,199	24,718	25,846	21,685	1.16	49,024	48,089	50,283
1986–87	26,569	26,057	27,244	22,700	1.17	50,567	49,593	51,852
1987–88	28,034	27,519	28,798	23,777	1.18	51,232	50,291	52,629
1988–89	29,564	29,022	30,218	24,752	1.19	51,643	50,697	52,786
1989–90	31,367	30,832	32,049	25,762	1.22	52,297	51,405	53,434
1990–91	33,084	32,490	33,896	26,935	1.23	52,301	51,362	53,584
1991–92	34,063	33,479	34,827	28,169	1.21	52,177	51,282	53,347
1992–93	35,029	34,350	35,880	29,245	1.20	52,031	51,022	53,295
1993–94	35,737	35,233	36,566	30,030	1.19	51,742	51,013	52,943
1994–95	36,675	36,088	37,523	30,857	1.19	51,621	50,795	52,814
1995–96	37,642	37,138	38,397	31,822	1.18	51,579	50,888	52,613
1996–97	38,443	38,039	39,184	33,058	1.16	51,215	50,677	52,202
1997–98	39,350	39,002	39,944	34,635	1.14	51,505	51,049	52,282
1998–99	40,544	40,165	41,203	36,306	1.12	52,165	51,677	53,012
1999–2000	41,807	41,306	42,546	38,176	1.10	52,280	51,654	53,204
2000–01	43,378	42,910	44,053	39,722	1.09	52,448	51,882	53,264
2001–02	44,655	44,177	45,310	40,579	1.10	53,053	52,485	53,831
2002–03	45,686	45,408	46,106	41,704	1.10	53,110	52,787	53,599
2003–04	46,542	46,187	46,976	43,301	1.07	52,947	52,543	53,441
2004–05	47,516	47,122	47,688	44,941	1.06	52,476	52,041	52,666
2005–06	48,804	48,420	49,041	46,755	1.04	51,921	51,513	52,173
2006–07	50,758	50,699	50,829	48,812	1.04	52,639	52,578	52,712
2007–08	52,308	52,149	52,367	50,476	1.04	52,308	52,149	52,367
2008–09	53,910	54,037	53,724	—	—	53,168	53,293	52,984

—Not available.

[1]The average monetary remuneration earned by FTE employees across all industries in a given year, including wages, salaries, commissions, tips, bonuses, voluntary employee contributions to certain deferred compensation plans, and receipts in kind that represent income. Calendar-year data from the U.S. Department of Commerce, Bureau of Economic Analysis, have been converted to a school-year basis by averaging the two appropriate calendar years in each case.
[2]Constant dollars based on the Consumer Price Index, prepared by the Bureau of Labor Statistics, U.S. Department of Labor, adjusted to a school-year basis.

NOTE: Some data have been revised from previously published figures. Standard errors are not available for these estimates, which are based on state reports.
SOURCE: National Education Association, *Estimates of School Statistics*, 1959–60 through 2008–09; and unpublished tabulations. U.S. Department of Commerce, Bureau of Economic Analysis, National Income and Product Accounts, tables 6.6B-D, retrieved August 25, 2009, from http://www.bea.gov/national/nipaweb/SelectTable.asp. (This table was prepared August 2009.)

Estimated average annual salary of teachers in public elementary and secondary schools, by state or jurisdiction: Selected years, 1969–70 through 2008–09

State	Current dollars							Constant 2007–08 dollars[1]							Percent change, 1999–2000 to 2008–09
	1969–70	1979–80	1989–90	1999–2000	2005–06	2007–08	2008–09	1969–70	1979–80	1989–90	1999–2000	2005–06	2007–08	2008–09	
1	2	3	4	5	6	7	8	9	10	11	12	13	14	15	16
United States...	$8,626	$15,970	$31,367	$41,807	$48,804	$52,308	$53,910	$48,343	$43,549	$52,297	$52,280	$51,921	$52,308	$53,168	1.7
Alabama	6,818	13,060	24,828	36,689	40,347	46,604	48,906	38,210	35,614	41,395	45,880	42,924	46,604	48,233	5.1
Alaska	10,560	27,210	43,153	46,462	53,553	56,758	58,916	59,181	74,200	71,948	58,102	56,974	56,758	58,105	#
Arizona	8,711	15,054	29,402	36,902	44,672	45,772	47,937	48,819	41,051	49,021	46,147	47,525	45,772	47,277	2.4
Arkansas	6,307	12,299	22,352	33,386	42,768	45,773	47,472	35,346	33,539	37,267	41,750	45,500	45,773	46,818	12.1
California	10,315	18,020	37,998	47,680	59,825	64,424	66,986	57,808	49,140	63,353	59,625	63,646	64,424	66,064	10.8
Colorado	7,761	16,205	30,758	38,163	44,439	47,248	48,707	43,495	44,190	51,282	47,723	47,278	47,248	48,036	0.7
Connecticut	9,262	16,229	40,461	51,780	59,304	61,976	63,976	51,907	44,256	67,460	64,752	63,092	61,976	63,095	-2.6
Delaware	9,015	16,148	33,377	44,435	54,264	55,994	55,994	50,523	44,035	55,649	55,567	57,730	55,994	55,223	-0.6
District of Columbia	10,285	22,190	38,402	47,076	59,000	60,628	62,557	57,640	60,511	64,027	58,869	62,769	60,628	61,696	4.8
Florida	8,412	14,149	28,803	36,722	43,302	46,930	48,126	47,143	38,584	48,023	45,921	46,068	46,930	47,463	3.4
Georgia	7,276	13,853	28,006	41,023	48,300	51,560	53,270	40,777	37,776	46,694	51,300	51,385	51,560	52,537	2.4
Hawaii	9,453	19,920	32,047	40,578	49,292	53,400	55,733	52,977	54,321	53,431	50,743	52,441	53,400	54,966	8.3
Idaho	6,890	13,611	23,861	35,547	41,150	44,099	45,439	38,614	37,117	39,783	44,452	43,778	44,099	44,813	0.8
Illinois	9,569	17,601	32,794	46,486	58,686	60,474	62,787	53,627	47,997	54,677	58,132	62,435	60,474	61,922	6.5
Indiana	8,833	15,599	30,902	41,850	47,255	48,508	49,198	49,503	42,538	51,522	52,334	50,273	48,508	48,521	-7.3
Iowa	8,355	15,203	26,747	35,678	41,083	46,664	48,969	46,824	41,458	44,595	44,616	43,707	46,664	48,295	8.2
Kansas	7,612	13,690	28,744	34,981	41,467	45,136	46,987	42,660	37,332	47,924	43,744	44,116	45,136	46,340	5.9
Kentucky	6,953	14,520	26,292	36,380	42,592	47,207	49,539	38,967	39,595	43,836	45,494	45,313	47,207	48,857	7.4
Louisiana	7,028	13,760	24,300	33,109	40,029	46,964	49,284	39,387	37,523	40,515	41,403	42,586	46,964	48,605	17.4
Maine	7,572	13,071	26,881	35,561	40,737	43,397	44,731	42,436	35,644	44,818	44,470	43,339	43,397	44,115	-0.8
Maryland	9,383	17,558	36,319	44,048	54,333	60,069	60,844	52,585	47,880	60,554	55,083	57,803	60,069	60,006	8.9
Massachusetts	8,764	17,253	34,712	46,580	56,369	60,471	62,769	49,116	47,048	57,874	58,249	59,970	60,471	61,905	6.3
Michigan	9,826	19,663	37,072	49,044	54,739	56,096	57,327	55,068	53,620	61,809	61,330	58,235	56,096	56,538	-7.8
Minnesota	8,658	15,912	32,190	39,802	48,489	50,582	51,938	48,522	43,391	53,670	49,773	51,586	50,582	51,223	2.9
Mississippi	5,798	11,850	24,292	31,857	40,576	42,403	44,498	32,494	32,314	40,501	39,838	43,168	42,403	43,885	10.2
Missouri	7,799	13,682	27,094	35,656	40,462	43,206	44,712	43,708	37,310	45,173	44,588	43,046	43,206	44,096	-1.1
Montana	7,606	14,537	25,081	32,121	39,832	42,874	44,426	42,626	39,642	41,817	40,168	42,376	42,874	43,814	9.1
Nebraska	7,375	13,516	25,522	33,237	40,382	42,885	44,120	41,332	36,857	42,552	41,563	42,961	42,885	43,513	4.7
Nevada	9,215	16,295	30,590	39,390	44,426	47,710	50,067	51,644	44,436	51,002	49,258	47,264	47,710	49,378	0.2
New Hampshire	7,771	13,017	28,986	37,734	45,263	47,609	48,934	43,551	35,497	48,328	47,187	48,154	47,609	48,260	2.3
New Jersey	9,130	17,161	35,676	52,015	58,156	61,277	63,018	51,167	46,797	59,482	65,046	61,871	61,277	62,150	-4.5
New Mexico	7,796	14,887	24,756	32,554	41,637	45,112	47,341	43,691	40,596	41,275	40,709	44,297	45,112	46,689	14.7
New York	10,336	19,812	38,925	51,020	57,354	62,332	65,234	57,926	54,026	64,899	63,801	61,017	62,332	64,336	0.8
North Carolina	7,494	14,117	27,883	39,404	43,922	47,354	48,603	41,999	38,496	46,489	49,275	46,727	47,354	47,934	-2.7
North Dakota	6,696	13,263	23,016	29,863	37,764	40,279	41,534	37,526	36,168	38,374	37,344	40,176	40,279	40,962	9.7
Ohio	8,300	15,269	31,218	41,436	50,314	53,410	54,925	46,516	41,638	52,049	51,816	53,528	53,410	54,169	4.5
Oklahoma	6,882	13,107	23,070	31,298	38,772	43,551	45,702	38,569	35,742	38,464	39,139	41,249	43,551	45,073	15.2
Oregon	8,818	16,266	30,840	42,336	50,044	51,811	52,950	49,419	44,357	51,419	52,942	53,241	51,811	52,221	-1.4
Pennsylvania	8,858	16,515	33,338	48,321	54,027	55,833	56,906	49,643	45,036	55,584	60,426	57,478	55,833	56,122	-7.1
Rhode Island	8,776	18,002	36,057	47,041	54,730	57,168	58,491	49,183	49,091	60,117	58,826	58,226	57,168	57,686	-1.9
South Carolina	6,927	13,063	27,217	36,081	43,011	45,758	47,704	38,821	35,622	45,378	45,120	45,758	45,758	47,047	4.3
South Dakota	6,403	12,348	21,300	29,071	34,709	36,674	38,017	35,884	33,672	35,513	36,354	36,926	36,674	37,494	3.1
Tennessee	7,050	13,972	27,052	36,328	42,537	45,030	46,278	39,510	38,101	45,103	45,429	45,254	45,030	45,641	0.5
Texas	7,255	14,132	27,496	37,567	41,744	46,179	46,179	40,659	38,537	45,843	46,978	44,410	46,179	45,543	-3.1
Utah	7,644	14,909	23,686	34,946	40,007	41,615	42,335	42,839	40,656	39,491	43,701	42,562	41,615	41,752	-4.5
Vermont	7,968	12,484	29,012	37,758	46,622	46,593	47,697	44,655	34,043	48,371	47,217	49,600	46,593	47,040	-0.4
Virginia	8,070	14,060	30,938	38,744	43,823	46,796	48,554	45,227	38,341	51,582	48,450	46,622	46,796	47,885	-1.2
Washington	9,225	18,820	30,457	41,043	46,326	49,884	51,970	51,700	51,321	50,780	51,325	49,285	49,884	51,254	-0.1
West Virginia	7,650	13,710	22,842	35,009	38,284	42,529	44,625	42,873	37,386	38,084	43,779	40,729	42,529	44,011	0.5
Wisconsin	8,963	16,006	31,921	41,153	46,390	49,051	50,424	50,231	43,648	53,221	51,463	49,353	49,051	49,730	-3.4
Wyoming	8,232	16,012	28,141	34,127	43,225	53,074	55,696	46,135	43,664	46,919	42,676	45,986	53,074	54,929	28.7

#Rounds to zero.
[1]Constant dollars based on the Consumer Price Index (CPI), prepared by the Bureau of Labor Statistics, U.S. Department of Labor, adjusted to a school-year basis. The CPI does not account for differences in inflation rates from state to state.

NOTE: Some data have been revised from previously published figures. Standard errors are not available for these estimates, which are based on state reports.
SOURCE: National Education Association, *Estimates of School Statistics*, 1969–70 through 2008–09. (This table was prepared July 2009.)

Federal support and estimated federal tax expenditures for education, by category: Selected fiscal years, 1965 through 2009

[In millions of dollars]

Fiscal year	Total on-budget support, off-budget support, and nonfederal funds generated by federal legislation	On-budget support[1]					Off-budget support and nonfederal funds generated by federal legislation									Estimated federal tax expenditures for education[2]
		Total	Elementary and secondary	Post-secondary	Other education[3]	Research at educational institutions	Off-budget support		Nonfederal funds							
							Total	Direct Loan Program[4]	Federal Family Education Loan Program[5]	Perkins Loans[6]	Income Contingent Loans[7]	Leveraging Educational Assistance Partnerships[8]	Supplemental Educational Opportunity Grants[9]	Work-Study Aid[10]	
1	2	3	4	5	6	7	8	9	10	11	12	13	14	15	16
						Current dollars									
1965	$5,354.7	$5,331.0	$1,942.6	$1,197.5	$374.7	$1,816.3	$23.7	†	†	$16.1	†	†	†	$7.6	—
1970	13,359.1	12,526.5	5,830.4	3,447.7	964.7	2,283.6	832.6	†	$770.0	21.0	†	†	†	41.6	—
1975	24,691.5	23,288.1	10,617.2	7,644.0	1,608.5	3,418.4	1,403.4	†	1,233.0	35.7	†	$20.0	†	114.7	$8,605.0
1980	39,349.5	34,493.5	16,027.7	11,115.9	1,548.7	5,801.2	4,856.0	†	4,598.0	31.8	†	76.8	†	149.4	13,320.0
1985	47,753.4	39,027.9	16,901.3	11,174.4	2,107.6	8,844.6	8,725.5	†	8,467.0	21.4	†	76.0	†	161.1	19,105.0
1986	48,357.3	39,962.9	17,049.9	11,283.6	2,620.0	9,009.4	8,394.4	†	8,142.0	20.2	†	72.7	†	159.5	20,425.0
1987	50,724.6	41,194.7	17,535.7	10,300.0	2,820.4	10,538.6	9,529.8	†	9,272.0	20.9	$0.6	76.0	†	160.4	20,830.0
1988	54,078.7	43,454.4	18,564.9	10,657.5	2,981.6	11,250.5	10,624.3	†	10,380.0	20.6	0.5	72.8	†	150.4	17,025.0
1989	59,537.4	48,269.6	19,809.5	13,269.9	3,180.3	12,009.8	11,267.8	†	10,938.0	20.4	0.5	71.9	$22.0	215.0	17,755.0
1990	62,811.5	51,624.3	21,984.4	13,650.9	3,383.0	12,606.0	11,187.2	†	10,826.0	15.0	0.5	59.2	48.8	237.7	19,040.0
1991	70,375.6	57,599.5	25,418.0	14,707.4	3,698.6	13,775.4	12,776.1	†	12,372.0	17.3	0.5	63.5	87.7	235.0	18,995.0
1992	74,481.1	60,483.1	27,926.9	14,387.4	3,992.0	14,176.9	13,998.0	†	13,568.0	17.3	0.5	72.0	97.2	242.9	19,950.0
1993	84,741.5	67,740.6	30,834.3	17,844.0	4,107.2	14,955.1	17,000.8	$813.0	16,524.0	29.3	†	72.4	184.6	190.5	21,010.0
1994	92,781.5	68,254.2	32,304.4	16,177.1	4,483.7	15,289.1	24,527.3	†	23,214.0	52.7	†	72.4	184.6	190.5	22,630.0
1995	95,810.8	71,639.5	33,623.8	17,618.1	4,719.7	15,677.9	24,171.2	5,161.0	18,519.0	52.7	†	63.4	184.6	190.5	24,600.0
1996	96,833.0	71,327.4	34,391.5	15,775.5	4,828.0	16,332.3	25,505.6	8,357.0	16,711.0	31.1	†	31.4	184.6	190.5	26,340.0
1997	103,259.8	73,731.8	35,478.9	15,959.4	5,021.2	17,272.4	29,528.0	9,838.0	19,163.0	52.7	†	50.0	184.6	239.7	28,125.0
1998	107,810.5	76,909.2	37,486.2	15,799.6	5,148.5	18,475.0	30,901.3	10,400.1	20,002.5	45.0	†	25.0	194.3	234.4	29,540.0
1999	113,417.2	82,863.6	39,937.9	17,651.2	5,318.0	19,956.5	30,553.6	9,953.0	20,107.0	33.3	†	25.0	195.9	239.4	37,360.0
2000	119,541.6	85,944.2	43,790.8	15,008.7	5,484.6	21,660.1	33,597.4	10,347.0	22,711.0	33.3	†	50.0	199.7	256.4	39,475.0
2001	130,668.5	94,846.5	48,530.1	14,938.3	5,880.0	25,498.1	35,822.0	10,635.0	24,694.0	25.0	†	80.0	184.0	204.0	41,460.0
2002	150,034.5	109,211.5	52,754.1	22,964.2	6,297.7	27,195.5	40,823.0	11,689.0	28,606.0	25.0	†	104.0	192.0	207.0	—
2003	170,671.5	124,374.5	59,274.2	29,499.7	6,532.5	29,068.1	46,297.0	11,969.0	33,791.0	33.0	†	103.0	202.0	199.0	—
2004	185,176.7	132,420.7	62,653.2	32,433.0	6,576.8	30,757.7	52,756.0	12,840.0	39,266.0	33.0	†	102.0	244.0	271.0	—
2005	203,036.0	146,207.0	68,957.7	38,587.3	6,908.5	31,753.5	56,829.0	12,930.0	43,284.0	0.0	†	101.0	246.0	268.0	—
2006	226,495.7	166,495.7	70,948.2	57,757.7	7,074.5	30,715.2	60,483.0	12,677.0	47,307.0	0.0	†	100.0	205.0	194.0	—
2007	211,915.7	147,077.7	70,604.2	37,465.3	7,214.9	31,793.3 [11]	64,838.0	13,022.0	51,320.0	0.0	†	100.0	205.0	191.0	—
2008	223,273.5	147,275.5	71,626.7	36,460.9	7,882.2	31,305.7 [11]	75,998.0	18,213.0	57,296.0	0.0	†	98.0	201.0	190.0	—
2009[1]	—	—	82,896.1	37,221.1	8,581.7	—	86,352.0	21,836.0	63,980.0	0.0	†	98.0	201.0	237.0	—

See notes at end of table.

Federal support and estimated federal tax expenditures for education, by category: Selected fiscal years, 1965 through 2009—Continued

[In millions of dollars]

[Constant fiscal year 2009 dollars[12]]

Fiscal year	Total on-budget support, off-budget support, and nonfederal funds generated by federal legislation	On-budget support[1] — Total	Elementary and secondary	Post-secondary	Other education[3]	Research at educational institutions	Off-budget support and nonfederal funds generated by federal legislation — Total	Off-budget support — Direct Loan Program[4]	Federal Family Education Loan Program[5]	Perkins Loans[6]	Nonfederal funds — Income Contingent Loans[7]	Leveraging Educational Assistance Partnerships[8]	Supplemental Educational Opportunity Grants[9]	Work-Study Aid[10]	Estimated federal tax expenditures for education[2]
1	2	3	4	5	6	7	8	9	10	11	12	13	14	15	16
1965	$35,508.4	$35,351.2	$12,881.7	$7,941.0	$2,484.4	$12,044.1	$157.2	†	†	$106.8	†	†	†	$50.4	—
1970	72,279.2	67,774.6	31,545.6	18,653.7	5,219.6	12,355.6	4,504.6	†	$4,166.1	113.5	†	†	†	225.1	—
1975	93,286.2	87,984.2	40,112.5	28,879.7	6,076.9	12,915.0	5,302.0	†	4,658.4	134.8	†	$75.6	†	433.3	$32,510.3
1980	100,036.4	87,691.3	40,746.5	28,259.4	3,937.3	14,748.1	12,345.1	†	11,689.3	80.8	†	195.2	†	379.8	33,862.8
1985	90,034.9	73,583.7	31,866.0	21,068.3	3,973.7	16,675.7	16,451.2	†	15,963.8	40.3	†	143.8	†	303.7	36,020.9
1986	88,995.0	73,546.2	31,378.1	20,765.9	4,821.8	16,580.5	15,448.7	†	14,984.2	37.2	†	133.8	†	293.5	37,589.4
1987	90,790.1	73,733.0	31,386.5	18,435.6	5,048.1	18,862.7	17,057.1	†	16,595.6	37.4	$1.0	136.0	†	287.1	37,282.9
1988	93,952.5	75,494.6	32,253.3	18,515.6	5,180.0	19,545.8	18,457.9	†	18,033.5	35.9	0.8	126.5	†	261.3	29,578.0
1989	99,749.2	80,871.0	33,188.9	22,232.4	5,328.3	20,121.3	18,878.2	†	18,325.6	34.2	0.9	120.5	$36.9	360.2	29,746.8
1990	101,883.5	83,737.3	35,659.7	22,142.5	5,487.4	20,447.6	18,146.2	†	17,560.3	24.4	0.8	96.0	79.2	385.6	30,883.8
1991	109,379.0	89,522.2	39,505.2	22,858.5	5,748.5	21,410.0	19,856.8	†	19,228.8	27.0	0.8	98.7	136.3	365.2	29,522.4
1992	111,923.1	90,888.1	41,965.8	21,620.0	5,998.7	21,303.6	21,034.9	†	20,388.7	26.0	0.8	108.2	146.1	365.0	29,978.9
1993	124,174.2	99,262.3	45,182.4	26,147.4	6,018.4	21,914.1	24,911.8	†	24,213.1	42.9	†	106.1	270.5	279.2	30,786.6
1994	133,252.2	98,026.3	46,395.3	23,233.4	6,439.5	21,958.1	35,225.9	$1,167.6	33,339.8	75.6	†	104.0	265.2	273.7	32,501.1
1995	134,313.6	100,428.9	47,136.0	24,698.2	6,616.6	21,978.3	33,884.8	7,235.0	25,961.1	73.8	†	88.9	258.8	267.1	34,485.4
1996	132,719.7	97,761.6	47,137.2	21,622.0	6,617.3	22,385.1	34,958.1	11,454.1	22,904.2	42.6	†	43.0	253.0	261.1	36,101.7
1997	138,849.1	99,144.1	47,707.0	21,460.0	6,751.7	23,225.4	39,705.0	13,228.7	25,767.7	70.9	†	67.2	248.2	322.3	37,818.5
1998	143,534.1	102,393.5	49,907.4	21,034.8	6,854.5	24,596.8	41,140.6	13,846.2	26,630.4	59.9	†	33.3	258.7	312.1	39,328.2
1999	148,752.4	108,679.8	52,380.6	23,150.4	6,974.9	26,173.9	40,072.6	13,053.9	26,371.4	43.7	†	32.8	256.9	314.0	48,999.5
2000	152,833.9	109,879.7	55,986.5	19,188.6	7,012.0	27,692.5	42,954.3	13,228.6	29,036.0	42.6	†	63.9	255.3	327.8	50,468.8
2001	163,239.8	118,488.6	60,627.0	18,661.9	7,345.7	31,854.0	44,751.2	13,286.0	30,849.4	31.2	†	99.9	229.9	254.9	51,794.6
2002	183,999.1	133,934.7	64,696.5	28,162.8	7,723.4	33,352.0	50,064.5	14,335.1	35,081.8	30.7	†	127.5	235.5	253.9	—
2003	203,871.3	148,568.4	70,804.5	35,238.1	7,803.2	34,722.5	55,302.9	14,297.3	40,364.2	39.4	†	123.0	241.3	237.7	—
2004	214,952.3	153,713.3	72,727.6	37,648.0	7,634.3	35,703.4	61,238.9	14,904.6	45,579.8	38.3	†	118.4	283.2	314.6	—
2005	227,364.0	163,725.7	77,220.3	43,210.9	7,736.3	35,558.0	63,638.3	14,479.3	48,470.3	0.0	†	113.1	275.5	300.1	—
2006	245,738.2	180,256.3	76,812.0	62,531.3	7,659.2	33,253.8	65,481.8	13,724.7	51,216.9	0.0	†	108.3	221.9	210.0	—
2007	224,264.7	155,648.4	74,718.6	39,648.5	7,635.3	33,646.0 [11]	68,616.3	13,780.8	54,310.6	0.0	†	105.8	216.9	202.1	—
2008	226,639.8	149,627.9	72,770.8	37,043.2	8,008.1	31,805.8 [11]	77,211.9	18,503.9	58,211.2	0.0	†	99.6	204.2	193.0	—
2009[11]	—	—	82,896.1	37,221.1	8,581.7	—	86,352.0	21,836.0	63,980.0	0.0	†	98.0	201.0	237.0	—

—Not available.
†Not applicable.

[1]On-budget support includes federal funds for education programs tied to appropriations.

[2]Losses of tax revenue attributable to provisions of the federal income tax laws that allow a special exclusion, exemption, or deduction from gross income or provide a special credit, preferential rate of tax, or a deferral of tax liability affecting individual or corporate income tax liabilities.

[3]Other education includes libraries, museums, cultural activities, and miscellaneous research.

[4]The William D. Ford Direct Program (commonly referred to as the Direct Loan Program) provides students with the same benefits they are currently eligible to receive under the Federal Family Education Loan (FFEL) program, but provides loans to students through federal capital rather than through private lenders.

[5]Formerly the Guaranteed Student Loan program. Includes new student loans guaranteed by the federal government and disbursed to borrowers.

[6]Student loans created from institutional matching funds (since 1993 one-third of federal capital contributions). Excludes repayments of outstanding loans.

[7]Student loans created from institutional matching funds (one-ninth of the federal contribution). This was a demonstration project that involved only 10 institutions and had unsubsidized interest rates. Program repealed in fiscal year 1992.

[8]Formerly the State Student Incentive Grant program. Starting in fiscal year 2000, amounts under $30.0 million have required dollar-for-dollar state matching contributions, while amounts over $30.0 million have required two-to-one state matching contributions.

[9]Institutions award grants to undergraduate students, and the federal share of such grants may not exceed 75 percent of the total grant.

[10]Employer contributions to student earnings are generally one-third of federal allocation.

[11]Estimated.

[12]Data adjusted by the federal funds composite deflator reported in the U.S. Office of Management and Budget, *Budget of the U.S. Government, Historical Tables, Fiscal Year 2010.*

NOTE: To the extent possible, federal education funds data represent outlays rather than obligations. Some data have been revised from previously published figures. Detail may not sum to totals because of rounding. Changes in postsecondary expenditures between 2005 and 2009 resulted primarily from changes in accounting procedures.

SOURCE: U.S. Department of Education, Budget Service, unpublished tabulations. U.S. Department of Education, National Center for Education Statistics, unpublished tabulations. U.S. Office of Management and Budget, *Budget of the U.S. Government, Appendix,* fiscal years 1967 through 2010. National Science Foundation, *Federal Funds for Research and Development,* fiscal years 1967 through 2008. (This table was prepared October 2009.)

Federal on-budget funds for education, by agency: Selected fiscal years, 1970 through 2008

[In thousands of current dollars]

Agency	1970	1980	1985	1990	1995	2000	2005	2006	2007	2008
1	2	3	4	5	6	7	8	9	10	11
Total	$12,526,499	$34,493,502	$39,027,876	$51,624,342	$71,639,520	$85,944,203	$146,206,999	$166,495,660	$147,077,686	$147,275,507
Department of Education	4,625,224	13,137,785	16,701,065	23,198,575	31,403,000	34,106,697	72,893,301	93,571,541	71,808,014	72,177,819
Department of Agriculture	960,910	4,562,467	4,782,274	6,260,843	9,092,089	11,080,031	13,817,553	14,677,672	15,634,477	16,266,919
Department of Commerce	13,990	135,561	55,114	53,835	88,929	114,575	243,948	249,962	168,407	199,635
Department of Defense	821,388	1,560,301	3,119,213	3,605,509	3,879,002	4,525,080	6,320,454	6,136,390	6,599,550	6,263,987
Department of Energy	551,527	1,605,558	2,247,822	2,561,950	2,692,314	3,577,004	4,339,879	4,283,520	4,633,462	4,631,149
Department of Health and Human Services	1,796,854	5,613,930	5,322,356	7,956,011	12,469,563	17,670,867	26,107,860	25,601,712	25,292,293	25,470,474
Department of Homeland Security	†	†	†	†	†	†	624,860	560,380	622,170	515,945
Department of Housing and Urban Development	114,709	5,314	438	118	1,613	1,400	1,100	600	600	700
Department of the Interior	190,975	440,547	549,479	630,537	702,796	959,802	1,254,533	1,146,750	952,273	901,769
Department of Justice	15,728	60,721	66,802	99,775	172,350	278,927	608,148	563,434	768,156	815,950
Department of Labor	424,494	1,862,738	1,948,685	2,511,380	3,967,914	4,696,100	5,764,500	5,414,500	5,370,800	5,186,600
Department of State	59,742	25,188	23,820	51,225	54,671	388,349	533,309	555,014	587,120	638,280
Department of Transportation	27,534	54,712	82,035	76,186	135,816	117,054	126,900	133,700	118,900	135,078
Department of the Treasury	18	1,247,463	290,276	41,715	49,496	83,000	0	0	200	0
Department of Veterans Affairs	1,032,918	2,351,233	1,289,849	757,476	1,324,382	1,577,374	4,293,624	4,547,560	5,256,399	4,624,991
Other agencies and programs										
ACTION	†	2,833	1,761	8,472	†	†	†	†	†	†
Agency for International Development	88,034	176,770	198,807	249,786	290,580	332,500	602,100	596,100	658,500	637,720
Appalachian Regional Commission	37,838	19,032	4,745	93	10,623	7,243	8,542	11,027	7,463	3,056
Barry Goldwater Scholarship and Excellence in Education Foundation	†	†	†	1,033	3,000	3,000	3,000	3,000	3,000	3,000
Corporation for National and Community Service	†	†	†	†	214,600	386,000	472,000	503,000	395,000	333,000
Environmental Protection Agency	19,446	41,083	60,521	87,481	125,721	98,900	83,400	64,600	57,500	56,100
Estimated education share of federal aid to the District of Columbia	33,019	81,847	107,340	104,940	78,796	127,127	154,962	140,997	168,156	149,722
Federal Emergency Management Agency	290	1,946	1,828	215	170,400	14,894	†	†	†	†
General Services Administration	14,775	34,800	†	†	†	†	†	†	†	†
Harry S Truman Scholarship fund	†	-1,895	1,332	2,883	3,000	3,000	3,000	3,000	3,000	3,000
Institute of American Indian and Alaska Native Culture and Arts Development	†	†	†	4,305	13,000	2,000	6,000	6,000	6,000	7,000
Institute of Museum and Library Services	†	†	†	†	†	166,000	250,000	241,000	258,000	253,000
James Madison Memorial Fellowship Foundation	†	†	†	191	2,000	7,000	2,000	2,000	2,000	2,000
Japanese-United States Friendship Commission	†	2,294	2,236	2,299	2,000	3,000	3,000	2,000	2,000	2,000
Library of Congress	29,478	151,871	169,310	189,827	241,000	299,000	430,000	435,000	463,000	434,000
National Aeronautics and Space Administration	258,366	255,511	487,624	1,093,303	1,757,900	2,077,830	2,763,120	2,386,342	2,389,743	2,404,213
National Archives and Records Administration	†	†	52,118	77,397	105,172	121,879	276,000	276,000	273,000	279,000
National Commission on Libraries and Information Science	†	2,090	723	3,281	1,000	2,000	1,000	1,000	1,000	1,000
National Endowment for the Arts	340	5,220	5,536	5,577	9,421	10,048	10,976	10,561	11,767	12,808
National Endowment for the Humanities	8,459	142,586	125,671	141,048	151,727	100,014	117,825	120,305	121,086	124,162
National Science Foundation	295,628	808,392	1,147,115	1,588,891	2,086,195	2,955,244	3,993,216	4,087,701	4,344,849	4,638,561
Nuclear Regulatory Commission	†	32,590	30,261	42,328	22,188	12,200	15,100	13,600	12,400	12,400
Office of Economic Opportunity	1,092,410	†	†	†	†	†	†	†	†	†
Smithsonian Institution	2,461	5,153	7,886	5,779	9,961	25,764	45,890	42,092	46,101	64,768
United States Arms Control Agency	100	661	395	25	†	†	†	†	†	†
United States Information Agency	8,423	66,210	143,007	201,547	294,800	†	†	†	†	†
United States Institute of Peace	†	†	†	7,621	12,000	13,000	28,000	101,000	32,000	17,000
Other agencies	1,421	990	432	885	500	300	7,900	6,600	9,300	8,700

†Not applicable.

NOTE: To the extent possible, amounts reported represent outlays, rather than obligations. Some data have been revised from previously published figures. Detail may not sum to totals because of rounding. Negative amounts occur when program receipts exceed outlays. Much of the fluctuation in Department of Education funds between 2005 and 2008 was due to changes in postsecondary expenditures that resulted primarily from changes in accounting procedures.

SOURCE: U.S. Department of Education, National Center for Education Statistics, unpublished tabulations. U.S. Office of Management and Budget, *Budget of the U.S. Government, Appendix,* fiscal years 1972 through 2010. National Science Foundation, *Federal Funds for Research and Development,* fiscal years 1970 to 2008. (This table was prepared October 2009.)

Federal on-budget funds for education, by level/educational purpose, agency, and program: Selected fiscal years, 1970 through 2009

[In thousands of current dollars]

Level/educational purpose, agency, and program	1970	1980	1990[1]	1995[1]	2000[1]	2005[1]	2006[1]	2007[1,2]	2008[1,2]	2009[1,2]
1	2	3	4	5	6	7	8	9	10	11
Total	$12,526,499	$34,493,502	$51,624,342	$71,639,520	$85,944,203	$146,206,999	$166,495,660	$147,077,686	$147,275,507	$82,896,059
Elementary/secondary education	5,830,442	16,027,686	21,984,361	33,623,809	43,790,783	68,957,711	70,948,229	70,604,233	71,626,709	82,896,059
Department of Education[3]	2,719,204	6,629,095	9,681,313	14,029,000	20,039,563	37,477,594	38,863,442	37,562,078	38,330,372	44,867,105
Education for the disadvantaged	1,339,014	3,204,664	4,494,111	6,808,000	8,529,111	14,635,566	14,695,815	14,486,936	14,872,535	15,924,213
Impact aid program[4]	656,372	690,170	816,366	808,000	877,101	1,262,174	1,141,455	1,162,814	1,247,691	1,569,385
School improvement programs[5]	288,304	788,918	1,189,158	1,397,000	2,549,971	7,918,091	7,463,468	7,083,651	7,077,721	12,475,387
Indian education	†	93,365	69,451	71,000	65,285	121,911	120,360	117,992	115,780	114,559
English Language Acquisition	21,250	169,540	188,919	225,000	362,662	667,485	616,075	728,703	700,395	730,000
Special education	79,090	821,777	1,616,623	3,177,000	4,948,977	10,940,312	11,836,477	11,777,258	12,280,101	11,734,079
Vocational and adult education	335,174	860,661	1,306,685	1,482,000	1,462,977	1,967,086	1,987,455	1,955,780	1,894,706	2,174,695
Education Reform—Goals 2000[6]	†	†	†	61,000	1,243,479	-35,031	16,540	†	†	†
Hurricane Education Recovery	†	†	†	†	†	†	985,797	248,944	141,443	144,787
Department of Agriculture[7]	760,477	4,064,497	5,528,950	8,201,294	10,051,278	12,577,265	13,412,550	14,245,994	15,139,602	16,592,100
Child nutrition programs[7]	299,131	3,377,056	4,977,075	7,644,789	9,554,028	11,901,943	12,660,758	13,081,994	13,932,120	15,552,100
McGovern-Dole International Food for Education and Child Nutrition Program[8]	†	†	†	†	†	86,000	98,000	98,000	89,000	194,000
Agricultural Marketing Service—commodities[9]	341,597	388,000	350,441	400,000	400,000	399,322	463,792	878,000	940,000	670,000
Special Milk Program	83,800	159,293	18,707	(2)	(2)	(2)	(2)	(2)	(2)	(2)
Estimated education share of Forest Service permanent appropriations	35,949	140,148	182,727	156,505	97,250	190,000	190,000	188,000	178,482	176,000
Department of Commerce	†	54,816	†	†	†	†	†	†	†	†
Local public works program—school facilities[10]	†	54,816	†	†	†	†	†	†	†	†
Department of Defense	143,100	370,846	1,097,876	1,295,547	1,485,611	1,786,253	1,755,924	1,772,293	1,863,835	1,918,386
Junior Reserve Officers Training Corps (JROTC)	12,100	32,000	39,300	155,600	210,432	315,122	308,208	324,917	352,821	370,743
Overseas dependents schools	131,000	338,846	864,958	855,772	904,829	1,060,920	1,063,908	1,062,367	1,110,108	1,137,613
Domestic schools[4]	†	†	193,618	284,175	370,350	410,211	383,808	385,009	400,906	410,030
Department of Energy	200	77,633	15,563	12,646	†	†	†	†	†	†
Energy conservation for school buildings[11]	200	77,240	15,213	10,746	†	†	†	†	†	†
Pre-engineering program	†	393	350	1,900	†	†	†	†	†	†
Department of Health and Human Services	167,333	1,077,000	2,396,793	5,116,559	6,011,036	8,003,348	8,118,935	7,901,700	8,003,300	9,731,800
Head Start[12]	†	735,000	1,447,758	3,534,000	5,267,000	6,842,348	6,851,235	6,888,000	6,877,000	8,502,000
Payments to states for Aid for Families with Dependent Children (AFDC) work programs[13]	†	†	459,221	953,000	15,000	†	†	†	†	†
Social Security student benefits[14]	167,333	342,000	489,814	629,559	729,036	1,161,000	1,267,700	1,013,700	1,126,300	1,229,800
Department of Homeland Security	†	†	†	†	†	500	511	500	2,600	2,900
Tuition assistance for educational accreditation—Coast Guard personnel[15]	†	†	†	†	†	500	511	500	2,600	2,900
Department of the Interior	140,705	318,170	445,267	493,124	725,423	938,506	928,637	728,078	679,171	696,846
Mineral Leasing Act and other funds										
Payments to states—estimated education share	12,294	62,636	123,811	18,750	24,610	60,290	56,806	52,030	50,913	50,000
Payments to counties—estimated education share	16,359	48,953	102,522	37,490	53,500	79,686	124,000	71,034	72,743	71,250
Indian Education										
Bureau of Indian Education schools	95,850	178,112	192,841	411,524	466,905	517,647	523,673	518,700	540,734	560,799
Johnson-O'Malley assistance[16]	16,080	28,081	25,556	24,359	17,387	16,510	16,371	12,000	13,782	13,797
Education construction	†	†	†	†	161,021	263,373	206,787	73,314	—	—
Education expenses for children of employees, Yellowstone National Park	122	388	538	1,000	2,000	1,000	1,000	1,000	1,000	1,000
Department of Justice	8,237	23,890	65,997	128,850	224,800	554,500	514,300	719,600	769,825	828,143
Vocational training expenses for prisoners in federal prisons	2,720	4,966	2,066	3,000	1,000	0	1,000	6,000	1,025	943
Inmate programs[17]	5,517	18,924	63,931	125,850	223,800	554,500	513,300	713,600	768,800	827,200
Department of Labor	420,927	1,849,800	2,505,487	3,957,800	4,683,200	5,654,000	5,355,000	5,226,000	5,070,000	6,321,000
Job Corps	†	469,800	739,376	1,029,000	1,256,000	1,521,000	1,599,000	1,605,000	763,000	1,664,000
Training programs—estimated funds for education programs[18]	420,927	1,380,000	1,766,111	2,928,800	3,427,200	4,133,000	3,756,000	3,621,000	4,307,000	4,657,000
Department of Transportation	45	60	46	62	188	†	†	†	†	†
Tuition assistance for educational accreditation—Coast Guard personnel[15]	45	60	46	62	188	†	†	†	†	†
Department of the Treasury	†	935,903	†	†	†	†	†	†	†	†
Estimated education share of general revenue sharing[19]										
State[20]	†	525,019	†	†	†	†	†	†	†	†
Local	†	410,884	†	†	†	†	†	†	†	†

See notes at end of table.

Federal on-budget funds for education, by level/educational purpose, agency, and program: Selected fiscal years, 1970 through 2009—Continued

[In thousands of current dollars]

Level/educational purpose, agency, and program	1970	1980	1990	1995[1]	2000[1]	2005[1]	2006[1]	2007[1,2]	2008[1,2]	2009[1,2]
1	2	3	4	5	6	7	8	9	10	11
Department of Veterans Affairs	338,910	545,786	155,351	311,768	445,052	1,815,000	1,866,000	2,300,564	1,628,100	1,789,200
Noncollegiate and job training programs[21]	281,640	439,993	12,848	†	†	†	†	†	†	†
Vocational rehabilitation for disabled veterans[22]	41,700	87,980	136,780	298,132	438,635	1,815,000	1,866,000	2,300,564	1,628,100	1,789,200
Dependents' education[23]	15,570	17,813	5,723	5,961	6,417	†	†	†	†	†
Service members occupational conversion training act of 1992	†	†	†	7,675	†	†	†	†	†	†
Other agencies										
Appalachian Regional Commission	33,161	9,157	93	2,173	2,588	2,962	1,218	1,110	0	900
National Endowment for the Arts	†	4,989	4,641	7,117	6,002	8,470	8,058	8,825	9,606	9,775
Arts in education	†	4,989	4,641	7,117	6,002	8,470	8,058	8,825	9,606	9,775
National Endowment for the Humanities	20	330	404	997	812	603	†	75	0	0
Office of Economic Opportunity	1,072,375	†	†	†	†	†	†	†	†	†
Head Start[24]	325,700	†	†	†	†	†	†	†	†	†
Other elementary and secondary programs[25]	42,809	†	†	†	†	†	†	†	†	†
Job Corps[26]	144,000	†	†	†	†	†	†	†	†	†
Youth Corps and other training programs[26]	553,368	†	†	†	†	†	†	†	†	†
Volunteers in Service to America (VISTA)[27]	6,498	†	†	†	†	†	†	†	†	†
Other programs										
Estimated education share of federal aid to the District of Columbia	25,748	65,714	86,579	66,871	115,230	138,710	123,653	137,416	130,298	137,904
Postsecondary education	**$3,447,697**	**$11,115,882**	**$13,650,915**	**$17,618,137**	**$15,008,715**	**$38,587,287**	**$57,757,738**	**$37,465,287**	**$36,460,850**	**$37,221,063**
Department of Education[3]	1,187,962	5,682,242	11,175,978	14,234,000	10,727,315	31,420,023	50,624,621	30,052,007	28,838,752	27,712,869
Student financial assistance	†	3,682,328	5,920,328	7,047,000	9,060,317	15,209,515	14,864,129	15,355,736	17,751,084	23,172,078
Federal Direct Student Loan Program	†	†	†	840,000	-2,862,240	3,020,992	6,842,092	5,391,146	5,333,920	1,420,746
Federal Family Education Loan Program	2,323	1,407,977	4,372,446	5,190,000	2,707,473	10,777,470	26,336,661	6,033,322	3,288,531	352,119
Higher education	1,029,131	399,787	659,492	871,000	1,530,779	2,053,288	2,058,920	2,399,892	2,029,379	2,340,146
Facilities—loans and insurance	114,199	-19,031	19,219	-6,000	-2,174	-1,464	-1,304	-1,671	-1,688	-1,872
College housing loans[28]	774	14,082	-57,167	-46,000	-41,886	-33,521	-27,229	-20,722	-17,529	-17,330
Educational activities overseas	†	3,561	82	†	150	169	165	†	†	†
Historically Black Colleges and Universities Capital Financing, Program Account	†	†	†	†	†	†	†	318,840	18,222	11,491
Gallaudet College and Howard University	38,559	176,829	230,327	292,000	291,060	339,823	340,664	351,665	343,164	339,389
National Technical Institute for the Deaf	2,976	16,248	31,251	46,000	43,836	53,751	56,670	57,836	58,308	59,905
Hurricane Katrina, aid to institutions	†	†	†	†	†	†	153,853	165,963	35,361	36,197
Department of Agriculture	†	10,453	31,273	33,373	30,676	61,957	62,327	64,357	66,709	73,150
Agriculture Extension Service, Second Morrill Act payments to agricultural and mechanical colleges and Tuskegee Institute	†	10,453	31,273	33,373	30,676	61,957	62,327	64,357	66,709	73,150
Department of Commerce	8,277	29,971	3,312	3,487	3,800	†	†	†	†	†
Sea Grant Program[29]	†	3,123	3,312	3,487	3,800	†	†	†	†	†
Merchant Marine Academy[30]	6,160	14,809	†	†	†	†	†	†	†	†
State marine schools[30]	2,117	12,039	†	†	†	†	†	†	†	†
Department of Defense	322,500	545,000	635,769	729,500	1,147,759	1,858,301	1,833,446	1,846,850	1,946,352	2,180,437
Tuition assistance for military personnel	57,500	106,100	95,300	127,000	263,303	608,109	563,961	607,515	603,610	678,609
Service academies	78,700	†	120,613	163,300	212,678	300,760	321,920	354,528	330,156	352,707
Senior Reserve Officers Training Corps (SROTC)[31]	108,100	†	193,056	219,400	363,461	537,525	498,165	434,687	549,633	646,796
Professional development education[31]	77,800	†	226,800	219,800	308,317	411,907	449,400	450,120	462,953	502,325
Department of Energy	3,000	57,701	25,502	28,027	†	†	†	†	†	†
University laboratory cooperative program	3,000	2,800	9,402	8,552	†	†	†	†	†	†
Teacher development projects	†	1,400	7,459	7,381	†	†	†	†	†	†
Energy conservation for buildings—higher education[11]	†	53,501	†	†	†	†	†	†	†	†
Minority honors vocational training	†	†	6,472	2,221	†	†	†	†	†	†
Honors research program	†	†	2,169	9,873	†	†	†	†	†	†
Students and teachers	†	†	†	†	†	†	†	†	†	†
Department of Health and Human Services	981,483	2,412,058	578,542	796,035	954,190	1,433,516	1,264,585	1,159,279	1,184,856	1,250,128
Health professions training programs[32]	353,029	460,736	230,600	298,302	340,361	581,661	420,115	302,081	318,225	354,332
Indian health manpower	†	7,187	†	27,000	16,000	27,000	32,000	32,000	29,000	37,000
National Health Service Corps scholarships[33]	†	70,667	9,508	78,206	33,300	45,000	40,000	40,000	40,000	40,000
National Institute of Health training grants[33]	†	176,388	241,356	380,502	550,220	756,014	748,642	761,034	770,481	790,246
National Institute of Occupational Safety and Health training grants[34]	†	12,899	4,759	11,660	14,198	23,841	23,828	24,164	27,150	28,550
Alcohol, drug abuse, and mental health training programs[34]	8,088	122,103	10,461	†	†	†	†	†	†	†
Health teaching facilities[35]	118,366	3,078	81,353	†	†	†	†	†	†	†
Social Security postsecondary students' benefits[36]	502,000	1,559,000	505	365	110	†	†	†	†	†

See notes at end of table.

Federal on-budget funds for education, by level/educational purpose, agency, and program: Selected fiscal years, 1970 through 2009—Continued

[In thousands of current dollars]

Level/educational purpose, agency, and program	1970	1980	1990[1]	1995[1]	2000[1]	2005[1]	2006[1]	2007[1,2]	2008[1,2]	2009[1,2]
1	2	3	4	5	6	7	8	9	10	11
Department of Homeland Security	†	†	†	†	†	36,400	44,000	48,900	52,400	55,700
Coast Guard Academy[15]	†	†	†	†	†	16,400	22,800	23,000	21,500	22,000
Postgraduate training for Coast Guard officers[37]	†	†	†	†	†	8,700	11,400	12,800	17,000	18,500
Tuition assistance to Coast Guard military personnel[15]	†	†	†	†	†	11,300	9,800	12,700	13,900	15,200
Department of Housing and Urban Development[28]	114,199	†	†	†	†	†	†	†	†	†
College housing loans[28]	114,199	†	†	†	†	†	†	†	†	†
Department of the Interior	31,749	80,202	135,480	159,054	187,179	249,227	165,313	176,695	180,497	183,374
Shared revenues, Mineral Leasing Act and other receipts—estimated education share	6,949	35,403	69,980	82,810	98,740	146,235	59,579	52,400	52,743	51,250
Indian programs										
Continuing education	9,380	16,909	34,911	43,907	57,576	76,271	79,061	98,463	101,795	106,029
Higher education scholarships	15,420	27,880	30,589	32,337	30,863	26,721	26,124	25,832	25,959	26,095
Department of State	30,850	†	2,167	3,000	319,000	424,000	443,000	473,000	522,000	538,000
Educational exchange[38]	30,850	†			319,000	424,000	443,000	473,000	522,000	538,000
Mutual educational and cultural exchange activities	30,454	†			303,000	402,000	423,000	453,000	503,000	517,000
International educational exchange activities	396	†	2,167	3,000	16,000	22,000	20,000	20,000	19,000	21,000
Russian, Eurasian, and East European Research and Training										
Department of Transportation	11,197	12,530	46,025	59,257	60,300	73,000	71,000	74,000	72,000	83,000
Merchant Marine Academy[30]			20,926	30,850	34,000	61,000	63,000	61,000	59,000	66,000
State marine schools[30]			8,269	8,980	7,000	12,000	8,000	13,000	13,000	17,000
Coast Guard Academy[15]	9,342	10,000	12,074	13,500	15,500	†	†	†	†	†
Postgraduate training for Coast Guard officers[37]	1,655	2,230	4,173	5,513	2,500	†	†	†	†	†
Tuition assistance to Coast Guard military personnel[15]	200	300	582	414	1,300	†	†	†	†	†
Department of the Treasury	†	296,750	†	†	†	†	†	†	†	†
General revenue sharing—estimated state share to higher education[19,20]	†	296,750	†	†	†	†	†	†	†	†
Department of Veterans Affairs	693,490	1,803,847	599,825	1,010,114	1,132,322	2,478,624	2,681,560	2,955,835	2,996,891	4,290,800
Vietnam-era veterans	638,260	1,579,974	46,998							†
College student support		1,560,081	39,458							†
Work-study		19,893	7,540							†
Service persons college support	18,900	46,617	8,911							†
Post-Vietnam veterans		922	161,475	33,596	3,958	1,136	1,275	914	891	800
All-volunteer-force educational assistance			269,947	868,394	984,068	2,070,996	2,230,022	2,227,531	2,166,000	3,452,000
Veterans			183,765	760,390	876,434	1,887,239	1,956,747	2,081,097	2,017,000	3,391,000
Reservists			86,182	108,004	107,634	183,757	273,275	146,434	149,000	61,000
Veteran dependents' education	36,330	176,334	100,494	95,124	131,296	388,719	413,136	511,793	434,000	464,000
Payments to state education agencies	†	†	12,000	13,000	13,000	17,773	17,657	†	†	†
Reserve Education Assistance Program (REAP)[39]	†	†	3				19,470	215,597	396,000	374,000
Other agencies										
Appalachian Regional Commission	4,105	1,751	—	2,741	2,286	4,407	7,876	3,498	0	0
National Endowment for the Humanities	3,349	56,451	50,938	56,481	28,395	29,253	34,055	40,446	36,472	36,000
National Science Foundation	42,000	64,583	161,884	211,800	389,000	490,000	496,000	527,000	531,000	776,000
Science and engineering education programs	37,000	64,583	161,884	211,800	389,000	490,000	496,000	527,000	531,000	776,000
Sea Grant Program[29]	5,000									†
United States Information Agency[40]	8,423	51,095	181,172	260,800						†
Educational and cultural affairs[38]		49,546	35,862	13,600						†
Educational exchange activities, international	8,423	1,549	145,307	247,200						†
Information center and library activities		†	3							†
Other programs										
Barry Goldwater Scholarship and Excellence in Education Foundation	5,513	13,143	1,033	3,000	3,000	3,000	3,000	3,000	3,000	4,000
Estimated education share of federal aid to the District of Columbia	†		14,637	9,468	11,493	14,578	15,954	29,418	17,920	24,605
Harry S Truman Scholarship fund	†	-1,895	2,883	3,000	3,000	3,000	3,000	3,000	3,000	3,000
Institute of American Indian and Alaska Native Culture and Arts Development	†	†	4,305	13,000	2,000	6,000	6,000	6,000	7,000	8,000
James Madison Memorial Fellowship Foundation	†	†	191	2,000	7,000	2,000	2,000	2,000	2,000	2,000

See notes at end of table.

Federal on-budget funds for education, by level/educational purpose, agency, and program: Selected fiscal years, 1970 through 2009—Continued

[In thousands of current dollars]

Level/educational purpose, agency, and program	1970	1980	1990[1]	1995[1]	2000[1]	2005[1]	2006[1]	2007[1,2]	2008[1,2]	2009[1,2]
1	2	3	4	5	6	7	8	9	10	11
Other education	**$964,719**	**$1,548,730**	**$3,383,031**	**$4,719,655**	**$5,484,571**	**$6,908,504**	**$7,074,484**	**$7,214,906**	**$7,882,220**	**$8,581,717**
Department of Education[3]	630,235	747,706	2,251,801	2,861,000	3,223,355	3,538,862	3,692,930	3,756,445	4,544,966	5,255,099
Administration	47,456	187,317	328,293	404,000	458,054	548,842	557,837	539,378	1,252,527	1,314,798
Libraries[42]	108,284	129,127	137,264	117,000	†	†	†	†	†	†
Rehabilitative services and disability research	473,091	426,886	1,780,360	2,333,000	2,755,468	2,973,346	3,115,842	3,177,031	3,242,297	3,914,004
American Printing House for the Blind	1,404	4,349	5,736	7,000	9,368	16,538	18,901	18,359	19,522	26,297
Trust funds and contributions	0	27	148	0	465	136	350	21,677	30,620	0
Department of Agriculture	135,637	271,112	352,511	422,878	444,477	468,631	475,395	515,026	517,208	541,754
Extension Service	131,734	263,584	337,907	405,371	424,174	445,631	451,395	491,026	494,208	519,754
National Agricultural Library	3,903	7,528	14,604	17,507	20,303	23,000	24,000	24,000	23,000	22,000
Department of Commerce	1,226	2,479	†	†	†	†	†	†	†	†
Maritime Administration										
Training for private sector employees[30]	1,226	2,479	†	†	†	†	†	†	†	†
Department of Health and Human Services	24,273	37,819	77,962	138,000	214,000	313,000	312,000	307,000	323,000	331,000
National Library of Medicine	24,273	37,819	77,962	138,000	214,000	313,000	312,000	307,000	323,000	331,000
Department of Homeland Security	†	†	†	†	†	278,243	194,744	307,076	264,523	277,000
Federal Law Enforcement Training Center[43]	†	†	†	†	†	159,000	180,000	280,000	245,000	262,000
Estimated disaster relief[44]	†	†	†	†	†	119,243	14,744	27,076	19,523	15,000
Department of Justice	5,546	27,642	26,920	36,296	34,727	26,148	26,734	28,056	28,425	30,046
Federal Bureau of Investigation National Academy	2,066	7,234	6,028	12,831	22,479	15,619	15,931	16,727	17,062	17,915
Federal Bureau of Investigation Field Police Academy	2,500	7,715	10,548	11,140	11,962	10,456	10,770	11,308	11,343	12,111
Narcotics and dangerous drug training	980	2,416	850	325	286	73	33	20	20	20
National Institute of Corrections		10,277	9,494	12,000						
Department of State	20,672	25,000	47,539	51,648	69,349	109,309	112,014	114,120	116,280	117,000
Foreign Service Institute	15,857	25,000	47,539	51,648	69,349	109,309	112,014	114,120	116,280	117,000
Center for Cultural and Technical Interchange[38]	4,815	†	†	†	†	†	†	†	†	†
Department of Transportation	3,964	10,212	1,507	650	700	1,100	700	200	178	180
Highways training and education grants	2,418	3,412								
Maritime Administration										
Training for private sector employees[30]	1,546	500	1,507	650	700	1,100	700	200	178	180
Urban mass transportation—managerial training grants	—	—	—	—	—	—	—	—	—	—
Federal Aviation Administration										
Air traffic controllers second career program		6,300								
Department of the Treasury	18	14,584	41,488	48,000	83,000	†	—	—	—	†
Federal Law Enforcement Training Center[43]	18	14,584	41,488	48,000	83,000	†	—	—	—	†
Other agencies										
ACTION[45]	†	†	†	†	†	†	†	†	†	†
Estimated education funds	†	†	†	†	†	†	†	†	†	†
Agency for International Development	88,034	99,707	170,371	260,408	299,000	574,000	566,800	629,200	608,420	620,000
Education and human resources	61,570	80,518	142,801	248,408	299,000	574,000	566,800	629,200	608,420	620,000
American schools and hospitals abroad	26,464	19,189	27,570	12,000	†	†	†	†	†	†
Appalachian Regional Commission	572	8,124	†	5,709	2,369	1,173	1,933	2,855	3,056	3,100
Corporation for National and Community Service[45]				214,600	386,000	472,000	503,000	395,000	333,000	198,000
Estimated education funds				214,600	386,000	472,000	503,000	395,000	333,000	198,000
Federal Emergency Management Agency[46]	290	281	215	170,400	14,894	†	†	†	†	†
Estimated architect/engineer student development program	40	31	200	—	—					
Estimated other training programs[47]	250	250	15	—	—					
Estimated disaster relief[44]	—	—	—	170,400	14,894					
General Services Administration										
Libraries and other archival activities[48]	14,775	34,800	†	†	†	†	†	†	†	†
Institute of Museum and Library Services[42]	†	†	†	†	166,000	250,000	241,000	258,000	253,000	254,000
Japanese-United States Friendship Commission	†	2,294	2,299	2,000	3,000	3,000	2,000	2,000	2,000	3,000

See notes at end of table.

Federal on-budget funds for education, by level/educational purpose, agency, and program: Selected fiscal years, 1970 through 2009—Continued

[In thousands of current dollars]

Level/educational purpose, agency, and program	1970	1980	1990[1]	1995[1]	2000[1]	2005[1]	2006[1]	2007[1,2]	2008[1,2]	2009[1,2]
1	2	3	4	5	6	7	8	9	10	11
Library of Congress	29,478	151,871	189,827	241,000	299,000	430,000	435,000	463,000	434,000	439,000
Salaries and expenses	20,700	102,364	148,985	198,000	247,000	383,000	381,000	413,000	395,000	372,000
Books for the blind and the physically handicapped	6,195	31,436	37,473	39,000	46,000	47,000	54,000	50,000	39,000	67,000
Special foreign currency program	2,273	3,492	10	†	†	†	†	†	†	†
Furniture and furnishings	310	14,579	3,359	4,000	6,000	—	—	—	—	—
National Aeronautics and Space Administration										
Aerospace education services project	350	882	3,300	5,923	6,800	—	—	—	—	—
National Archives and Records Administration										
Libraries and other archival activities[48]	†	†	77,397	105,172	121,879	276,000	276,000	273,000	279,000	317,000
National Commission on Libraries and Information Science[49]	†	2,090	3,281	1,000	2,000	1,000	1,000	1,000	1,000	†
National Endowment for the Arts	340	231	936	2,304	4,046	2,506	2,503	2,942	3,202	3,258
National Endowment for the Humanities	5,090	85,805	89,706	94,249	70,807	87,969	86,250	80,564	87,690	89,000
Smithsonian Institution	2,461	5,153	5,779	9,961	25,764	45,890	42,092	46,101	64,768	71,772
Museum programs and related research	2,261	3,254	690	3,190	18,000	32,000	33,000	37,000	55,600	61,600
National Gallery of Art extension service	200	426	474	771	764	890	92	101	168	172
Woodrow Wilson International Center for Scholars	†	1,473	4,615	6,000	7,000	13,000	9,000	9,000	9,000	10,000
U.S. Information Agency—Center for Cultural and Technical Interchange[38]	†	15,115	20,375	34,000	†	†	†	†	†	†
U.S. Institute of Peace	†	†	7,621	12,000	13,000	28,000	101,000	32,000	17,000	30,000
Other programs										
Estimated education share of federal aid for the District of Columbia[50]	1,758	2,990	3,724	2,457	404	1,674	1,389	1,321	1,504	1,508
Research programs at universities and related institutions[50]	**$2,283,641**	**$5,801,204**	**$12,606,035**	**$15,677,919**	**$21,660,134**	**$31,753,498**	**$30,715,210**	**$31,793,260**	**$31,305,727**	**—**
Department of Education[51]	87,823	78,742	89,483	279,000	116,464	456,822	390,548	437,484	463,729	658,224
Department of Agriculture	64,796	216,405	348,109	434,544	553,600	709,700	727,400	809,100	543,400	—
Department of Commerce	4,487	48,295	50,523	85,442	110,775	243,948	249,962	168,407	199,635	—
Department of Defense	356,188	644,455	1,871,864	1,853,955	1,891,710	2,675,900	2,547,020	2,980,407	2,453,800	—
Department of Energy	548,327	1,470,224	2,520,885	2,651,641	3,577,004	4,339,879	4,283,520	4,633,462	4,631,149	—
Department of Health and Human Services	623,765	2,087,053	4,902,714	6,418,984	10,491,641	16,357,996	15,906,192	15,924,314	15,959,318	—
Department of Homeland Security	—	—	—	—	—	309,717	321,125	265,694	196,422	—
Department of Housing and Urban Development	510	5,314	118	1,613	1,400	1,100	600	600	700	—
Department of the Interior	18,521	42,175	49,790	50,618	47,200	66,800	52,800	47,500	42,100	—
Department of Justice	1,945	9,189	6,858	7,204	19,400	27,500	22,400	20,500	17,700	—
Department of Labor	3,567	12,938	5,893	10,114	12,900	110,500	59,500	144,800	116,600	—
Department of State	8,220	188	1,519	23	†	†	†	†	†	—
Department of Transportation	12,328	31,910	28,608	75,847	55,866	52,800	62,000	44,700	62,900	—
Department of the Treasury	†	226	227	1,496	†	†	†	200	†	—
Department of Veterans Affairs	518	1,600	2,300	2,500	†	†	†	†	†	—
Agency for International Development	19,446	77,063	79,415	30,172	33,500	28,100	29,300	29,300	29,300	—
Environmental Protection Agency	†	41,083	87,481	125,721	98,900	83,400	64,600	57,500	56,100	—
Federal Emergency Management Agency	†	1,665	†	†	†	†	†	†	†	—
National Aeronautics and Space Administration	258,016	254,059	1,090,003	1,751,977	2,071,030	2,763,120	2,386,342	2,389,743	2,404,213	—
National Science Foundation	253,628	743,809	1,427,007	1,874,395	2,566,244	3,503,216	3,591,701	3,817,849	4,107,561	—
Nuclear Regulatory Commission	†	32,590	42,328	22,188	12,200	15,100	13,600	12,400	12,400	—
Office of Economic Opportunity	20,035	†	†	†	†	†	†	†	†	—
US Arms Control and Disarmament Agency	100	661	25	†	†	†	†	†	†	—
Other agencies	1,421	990	885	500	300	7,900	6,600	9,300	8,700	—

—Not available.

†Not applicable.

[1]Excludes federal support for medical education benefits under Medicare in the U.S. Department of Health and Human Services. Benefits excluded from total because data before fiscal year (FY) 1990 are not available. This program existed since Medicare began, but was not available as a separate budget item until FY 1990. Excluded amounts are as follows: $4,440,000,000 in FY 1990, $7,510,000,000 in FY 1995, $8,020,000,000 in FY 2000, $8,400,000,000 in FY 2005, $8,400,000,000 in FY 2006, $8,500,000,000 in FY 2007, $8,610,000,000 in FY 2008, and an estimated $9,005,000,000 in FY 2009.

[2]Estimated.

[3]The U.S. Department of Education was created in May 1980. It formerly was the Office of Education in the U.S. Department of Health, Education, and Welfare.

[4]Arranges for the education of children who reside on federal property when no suitable local school district can or will provide for the education of these children.

[5]Includes many programs, such as No Child Left Behind, 21st Century Community Learning Centers, Class Size Reduction, Charter Schools, Safe and Drug-Free Schools, and Innovative programs.

[6]Included the School-To-Work Opportunities program, which initiated a national system to be administered jointly by the U.S. Departments of Education and Labor. Programs in the Education Reform program were transferred to the school improvement programs or discontinued in FY 2002. Amounts after FY 2002 reflect balances that are spending out from prior-year appropriations.

[7] Starting in FY 1994, the Special Milk Program has been included in the child nutrition programs.

[8] The Farm Security and Rural Investment Act of 2002 (Public Law 107-171) carries out preschool and school feeding programs in foreign countries to help reduce the incidence of hunger and malnutrition, and improve literacy and primary education.

[9] These commodities are purchased under Section 32 of the Act of August 24, 1935, for use in the child nutrition programs.

[10] Assisted in the construction of public facilities, such as vocational schools, through grants or loans. No funds have been appropriated for this program since FY 1977, and it was completely phased out in FY 1980.

[11] Established in 1979, with funds first appropriated in FY 1980.

[12] Formerly in the Office of Economic Opportunity. In FY 1972, funds were transferred to the U.S. Department of Health, Education, and Welfare, Office of Child Development.

[13] Created by the Family Support Act of 1988 to provide funds for the Job Opportunities and Basic Skills Training program. Replaced by Temporary Assistance for Needy Families program.

[14] After age 18, benefits terminate at the end of the school term or in 3 months, whichever comes first.

[15] Transferred from the U.S. Department of Transportation to the U.S. Department of Homeland Security in March of 2003.

[16] Provides funding for supplemental programs for eligible American Indian students in public schools.

[17] Finances the cost of academic, social, and occupational education courses for inmates in federal prisons.

[18] Some of the work and training programs were in the Office of Economic Opportunity and were transferred to the U.S. Department of Labor in FYs 1971 and 1972. From FY 1994 through FY 2001, included the School-to-Work Opportunities program, which was administered jointly by the U.S. Departments of Education and Labor.

[19] Established in FY 1972 and closed in FY 1986.

[20] The states' share of revenue-sharing funds could not be spent on education in FYs 1981 through 1986.

[21] Provided educational assistance allowances in order to restore lost educational opportunities to those individuals whose careers were interrupted or impeded by reason of active military service between January 31, 1955, and January 1, 1977.

[22] This program is in "Readjustment Benefits" program, Chapter 31, and covers the costs of subsistence, tuition, books, supplies, and equipment for disabled veterans requiring vocational rehabilitation.

[23] This program is in "Readjustment Benefits" program, Chapter 35, and provides benefits to children and spouses of veterans.

[24] Head Start program funds were transferred to the U.S. Department of Health, Education, and Welfare, Office of Child Development, in FY 1972.

[25] Most of these programs were transferred to the U.S. Department of Health, Education, and Welfare, Office of Education, in FY 1972.

[26] Transferred to the U.S. Department of Labor in FYs 1971 and 1972.

[27] Transferred to the ACTION Agency in FY 1972.

[28] Transferred from the U.S. Department of Housing and Urban Development to the U.S. Department of Health, Education, and Welfare, Office of Education, in FY 1979.

[29] Transferred from the National Science Foundation to the U.S. Department of Commerce in October 1970.

[30] Transferred from the U.S. Department of Commerce to the U.S. Department of Transportation in FY 1981.

[31] Includes special education programs (military and civilian); legal education program; flight training; advanced degree program; college degree program (officers); and "Armed Forces Health Professions Scholarship" program.

[32] Does not include higher education assistance loans.

[33] Alcohol, drug abuse, and mental health training programs are included starting in FY 1992.

[34] Beginning in FY 1992, data were included in the National Institutes of Health training grants program.

[35] This program closed in FY 2004.

[36] Postsecondary student benefits were ended by the Omnibus Budget Reconciliation Act of 1981 (Public Law 97-35) and were completely phased out by August 1985.

[37] Includes flight training. Transferred to the U.S. Department of Homeland Security in March of 2003.

[38] Transferred from the U.S. Department of State to the United States Information Agency in 1977, then transferred back to the U.S. Department of State in FY 1998.

[39] Part of the Ronald W. Reagan National Defense Authorization Act for FY 2005 (Public Law 108-375), enacted October 28, 2004. The Reserve Education Assistance Program (REAP) provides educational assistance to members of the National Guard and Reserves who serve on active duty in support of a contingency operation under federal authority on or after September 11, 2001.

[40] Abolished in FY 1998, with functions transferred to the U.S. Department of State and the newly created Broadcasting Board of Governors.

[41] Included in the "Educational and Cultural Affairs" program in FYs 1980 through 1983, and became an independent program in FY 1984.

[42] Transferred from U.S. Department of Education to the Institute of Museum and Library Services in FY 1997.

[43] Transferred to the U.S. Department of Homeland Security in FY 2003.

[44] The disaster relief program repairs and replaces damaged and destroyed school buildings. In FY 1995, funds were for repairs due to the Northridge Earthquake in California. In FY 1995, $74.4 million was spent on school districts, $8.4 million on community colleges, and $87.6 million on colleges and universities. This program was transferred from the Federal Emergency Management Agency to the U.S. Department of Homeland Security in FY 2003.

[45] The National Service Trust Act of 1993 established the Corporation for National and Community Service. In 1993, ACTION became part of this agency.

[46] The Federal Emergency Management Agency was created in 1979, representing a combination of five existing agencies. The funds for the Federal Emergency Management Agency in FY 1970 to FY 1975 were in other agencies. This agency was transferred to the U.S. Department of Homeland Security in March of 2003.

[47] These programs include the Fall-Out Shelter Analysis, Blast Protection Design through FY 1992. Starting in FY 1993, earthquake training and safety for teachers and administrators for grades 1 through 12 are included.

[48] Transferred from the General Services Administration to the National Archives and Records Administration in April 1985.

[49] Public Law 110-161 transferred the National Commission on Libraries and Information Science to the Institute of Museum and Library Services starting in FY 2008.

[50] Includes federal obligations for research and development centers and R & D plant administered by colleges and universities. FY 2007 and FY 2008 data are estimated, except the U.S Department of Education data, which are actual numbers.

[51] FY 1970 includes outlays for the "Research and Training" program. FY 1975 includes the "National Institute of Education" program. FYs 1990 through 2009 include outlays for the Office of Educational Research and Improvement and the Institute for Education Sciences.

NOTE: Some data have been revised from previously published figures. To the extent possible, amounts reported represent outlays rather than obligations. Detail may not sum to totals because of rounding. Negative amounts occur when program receipts exceed outlays. Changes in total postsecondary expenditures between 2005 and 2009 resulted primarily from changes in accounting procedures in the Federal Family Education Loan Program.

SOURCE: U.S. Department of Education, Budget Service, unpublished tabulations. U.S. Office of Management and Budget, *Budget of the U.S. Government, Appendix,* fiscal years 1972 through 2010. National Science Foundation, *Federal Funds for Research and Development,* fiscal years 1970 through 2008. (This table was prepared October 2009.)

U.S. Department of Education outlays, by type of recipient and level of education: Selected fiscal years, 1980 through 2009

[In millions of current dollars]

Year and level of education	Total	Local education agencies	State education agencies	Postsecondary students	Postsecondary institutions	Federal institutions	Other education organizations[1]	Other recipients[2]
1	2	3	4	5	6	7	8	9
1980 total	$13,137.8	$5,313.7	$1,103.2	$2,137.4	$2,267.2	$249.8	$693.8	$1,372.7
Elementary/secondary	6,629.1	5,309.4	662.2	34.2	22.0	62.5	513.4	25.5
Postsecondary	5,682.2	†	99.5	2,103.2	2,166.5	†	†	1,313.0
Other programs	747.7	4.3	341.5	†	†	187.3	180.4	34.2
Education research and statistics	78.7	†	†	†	78.7	†	†	†
1985 total	16,701.1	6,225.0	1,502.9	2,434.7	2,362.3	287.3	503.9	3,385.0
Elementary/secondary	7,296.7	6,220.8	636.0	58.0	25.2	2.4	322.4	31.9
Postsecondary	8,202.5	†	228.3	2,376.7	2,308.3	†	†	3,289.2
Other programs	1,173.1	4.2	638.6	†	†	284.9	181.5	63.9
Education research and statistics	28.8	†	†	†	28.8	†	†	†
1990 total	23,198.6	8,000.7	2,490.3	3,859.6	3,649.8	441.4	912.2	3,844.4
Elementary/secondary	9,681.3	7,995.0	700.3	80.5	85.4	113.1	650.7	56.3
Postsecondary	11,176.0	†	261.6	3,779.1	3,475.0	†	†	3,660.4
Other programs	2,251.8	5.7	1,528.5	†	†	328.3	261.5	127.8
Education research and statistics	89.5	†	†	†	89.5	†	†	†
1995 total	31,403.0	11,210.7	3,584.0	4,964.7	5,016.1	485.4	1,349.2	4,792.9
Elementary/secondary	14,029.0	11,203.3	1,410.0	190.5	170.1	70.3	946.9	37.9
Postsecondary	14,234.0	†	250.8	4,774.2	4,567.0	†	†	4,642.0
Other programs	2,861.0	7.4	1,923.2	†	†	415.1	402.3	113.0
Education research and statistics	279.0	†	†	†	279.0	†	†	†
2000 total	34,106.7	16,016.0	4,316.5	4,711.7	5,005.7	506.6	1,820.2	1,730.1
Elementary/secondary	20,039.6	16,003.5	1,989.6	260.5	198.9	48.5	1,461.8	76.8
Postsecondary	10,727.3	†	55.2	4,451.2	4,690.3	†	†	1,530.6
Other programs	3,223.4	12.5	2,271.7	†	†	458.1	358.4	122.7
Education research and statistics	116.5	†	†	†	116.5	†	†	†
2001 total	36,562.0	18,027.4	4,336.7	4,525.6	5,793.3	600.4	2,149.1	1,129.7
Elementary/secondary	22,862.4	18,014.5	1,999.8	392.5	405.9	69.8	1,780.6	199.4
Postsecondary	9,840.7	†	98.5	4,133.1	4,821.9	†	†	787.2
Other programs	3,293.4	12.9	2,238.4	†	†	530.6	368.5	143.1
Education research and statistics	565.5	†	†	†	565.5	†	†	†
2002 total	46,324.4	19,742.1	4,967.8	8,306.0	8,668.2	608.9	2,200.3	1,831.3
Elementary/secondary	25,246.2	19,729.2	2,429.8	490.0	454.9	77.6	1,829.5	235.3
Postsecondary	17,056.2	†	199.2	7,816.0	7,588.1	†	†	1,452.9
Other programs	3,396.8	12.9	2,338.8	†	†	531.3	370.8	143.1
Education research and statistics	625.2	†	†	†	625.2	†	†	†
2003 total	57,442.9	23,837.7	6,164.6	11,032.5	10,731.8	657.8	2,478.9	2,539.6
Elementary/secondary	30,749.3	23,882.8	3,141.1	594.3	637.4	109.5	2,105.6	338.6
Postsecondary	22,706.4	†	668.6	10,438.2	9,542.5	†	†	2,057.2
Other programs	3,435.2	14.9	2,354.9	†	†	548.3	373.3	143.8
Education research and statistics	551.9	†	†	†	551.9	†	†	†
2004 total	62,903.4	26,012.4	6,334.5	12,005.0	10,977.0	648.9	2,730.1	4,195.4
Elementary/secondary	33,689.4	25,990.0	3,611.7	606.2	642.5	126.4	2,300.0	412.6
Postsecondary	25,341.0	†	420.9	11,398.8	9,899.3	†	†	3,621.9
Other programs	3,437.8	22.4	2,301.9	†	†	522.5	430.1	160.9
Education research and statistics	435.2	†	†	†	435.2	†	†	†
2005 total	72,893.3	28,900.2	7,126.3	14,708.2	13,362.4	669.8	3,023.0	5,103.4
Elementary/secondary	37,477.6	28,878.6	3,971.6	698.1	790.0	145.9	2,578.4	415.0
Postsecondary	31,420.0	†	777.1	14,010.1	12,115.6	†	†	4,517.2
Other programs	3,538.9	21.6	2,377.6	†	†	523.9	444.6	171.2
Education research and statistics	456.8	†	†	†	456.8	†	†	†
2006 total	93,571.5	30,236.6	8,331.3	22,955.1	21,376.1	693.2	2,902.3	7,076.8
Elementary/secondary	38,863.4	30,214.8	4,098.7	741.5	775.1	168.6	2,455.5	409.2
Postsecondary	50,624.6	†	1,702.4	22,213.6	20,210.5	†	†	6,498.1
Other programs	3,692.9	21.8	2,530.2	†	†	524.6	446.8	169.5
Education research and statistics	390.5	†	†	†	390.5	†	†	†
2007 total	71,808.0	29,008.8	7,429.4	14,269.9	13,877.6	613.2	2,931.5	3,677.7
Elementary/secondary	37,562.1	28,990.4	4,018.7	824.4	781.5	73.8	2,460.7	412.6
Postsecondary	30,052.0	†	805.5	13,445.5	12,658.6	†	†	3,084.6
Other programs	3,756.4	18.4	2,605.2	†	†	539.4	413.0	180.5
Education research and statistics	437.5	†	†	†	437.5	†	†	†
2008 total	72,177.8	29,553.0	7,377.7	14,371.2	13,585.9	1,348.8	2,997.9	2,943.3
Elementary/secondary	38,330.4	29,533.5	4,100.2	859.6	800.2	96.3	2,518.1	422.5
Postsecondary	28,838.8	†	618.8	13,511.6	12,322.0	†	†	2,328.1
Other programs	4,545.0	19.5	2,658.7	†	†	1,252.5	421.5	192.7
Education research and statistics	463.7	†	†	†	463.7	†	†	†
2009 total	75,080.6	29,660.0	8,259.4	14,331.0	14,128.2	1,388.6	3,401.1	3,912.4
Elementary/secondary	38,900.3	29,633.7	4,201.9	835.5	798.6	73.8	2,871.9	484.9
Postsecondary	30,267.1	†	808.9	13,495.5	12,671.4	†	†	3,231.8
Other programs	5,255.1	26.3	3,248.6	†	†	1,314.8	469.7	195.7
Education research and statistics	658.2	†	†	†	658.2	†	†	†

†Not applicable.

[1]Includes funds for vocational education and for federal programs at libraries and museums.

[2]Other recipients include American Indian tribes, private nonprofit agencies, and banks.

NOTE: Outlays by type of recipient are estimated based on obligation data. Changes in postsecondary expenditures between 2005 and 2009 resulted primarily from changes in accounting procedures. Some data have been revised from previously published figures. Detail may not sum to totals because of rounding.

SOURCE: U.S. Office of Management and Budget, *Budget of the U.S. Government*, fiscal years 1982 through 2010. U.S. Department of Education, Budget Service, unpublished tabulations. (This table was prepared October 2009.)

U.S. Department of Education appropriations for major programs, by state or jurisdiction: Fiscal year 2008

[In thousands of current dollars]

State or jurisdiction	Total	Grants for the disadvantaged[1]	Block grants to states for school improvement[2]	School assistance in federally affected areas[3]	Career/ technical and adult education[4]	Special education[5]	Language assistance[6]	American Indian education	Degreegranting institutions[7]	Student financial assistance[8]	Rehabilitation services[9]
1	2	3	4	5	6	7	8	9	10	11	12
Total, 50 states and D.C.[10]	$62,423,917	$14,081,958	$5,604,314	$1,067,636	$1,778,110	$11,490,859	$643,135	$96,613	$2,409,349	$22,284,886	$2,967,057
Total, 50 states, D.C., other activities, and other jurisdictions......................	65,032,137	14,788,645	5,893,564	1,171,645	1,840,329	11,757,265	700,395	96,613	2,468,001	23,227,946	3,087,734
Alabama............................	1,105,578	226,216	94,601	3,059	30,786	184,411	3,663	1,684	81,938	419,045	60,175
Alaska................................	289,156	47,060	28,371	108,412	5,584	37,747	1,069	9,609	17,868	21,618	11,817
Arizona..............................	1,916,853	292,408	104,404	161,093	36,967	188,135	22,008	10,611	24,266	1,015,229	61,732
Arkansas...........................	680,128	155,066	62,040	431	19,029	115,841	2,993	293	31,218	254,513	38,704
California...........................	7,244,200	1,884,206	662,303	55,822	220,086	1,256,934	164,463	5,864	250,128	2,448,743	295,651
Colorado...........................	826,770	147,871	65,281	13,024	23,646	155,898	10,347	766	31,908	339,052	38,977
Connecticut.......................	551,572	120,857	52,901	5,252	17,061	135,272	5,702	0	15,462	176,451	22,614
Delaware...........................	169,627	40,431	28,211	66	6,750	35,051	1,220	0	7,795	38,301	11,802
District of Columbia..........	484,070	48,772	28,110	1,274	5,879	18,305	1,027	0	254,899	110,880	14,925
Florida...............................	3,272,904	703,289	262,788	9,368	101,003	639,636	42,406	43	70,363	1,277,132	166,876
Georgia.............................	1,982,714	470,216	169,616	21,005	58,299	328,223	15,945	0	72,606	749,589	97,215
Hawaii...............................	255,123	46,631	28,593	38,421	8,424	41,055	2,763	0	25,660	50,164	13,411
Idaho.................................	301,080	52,483	30,367	7,482	9,479	56,093	1,885	395	8,421	116,240	18,235
Illinois...............................	2,610,611	613,760	235,568	19,600	72,052	516,188	27,696	103	77,242	935,750	112,651
Indiana..............................	1,235,959	261,282	100,552	140	38,242	260,350	6,846	0	25,277	472,882	70,388
Iowa..................................	679,607	77,502	45,123	416	17,729	123,819	3,039	213	26,623	350,637	34,505
Kansas..............................	576,814	109,703	48,444	21,330	16,177	109,690	3,580	1,095	25,165	212,336	29,293
Kentucky...........................	964,714	223,671	91,200	668	28,589	165,508	2,901	0	38,818	358,894	54,463
Louisiana...........................	1,164,313	309,247	125,649	7,807	33,192	192,074	2,401	768	62,967	384,370	45,839
Maine................................	281,069	54,303	32,605	2,658	8,271	56,614	826	130	11,898	96,286	17,478
Maryland............................	888,039	198,701	81,261	4,991	27,408	204,347	8,539	74	42,475	277,229	43,012
Massachusetts...................	1,158,608	243,368	99,137	832	30,661	286,869	11,646	77	34,034	402,304	49,680
Michigan............................	2,176,590	552,163	212,325	4,083	59,927	405,376	9,808	3,202	42,331	783,942	103,433
Minnesota..........................	916,472	133,071	71,159	15,191	26,433	194,715	8,213	3,399	32,341	385,676	46,275
Mississippi........................	857,091	195,755	85,143	1,894	21,342	121,633	1,388	346	47,101	338,483	44,008
Missouri............................	1,197,330	236,293	105,017	21,810	35,301	229,561	4,153	95	28,782	470,565	65,752
Montana............................	284,698	46,043	33,327	42,296	7,372	38,419	500	2,929	27,188	73,199	13,425
Nebraska...........................	363,371	67,535	34,496	20,149	10,404	75,744	2,846	786	13,211	118,032	20,169
Nevada..............................	309,704	84,158	34,588	3,691	12,790	71,124	7,276	693	14,630	62,142	18,613
New Hampshire..................	218,095	40,008	30,448	13	7,938	48,771	751	0	3,899	73,173	13,094
New Jersey........................	1,388,475	299,630	123,597	13,926	43,225	365,502	18,603	59	30,395	433,255	60,284
New Mexico........................	611,968	118,272	47,971	92,990	13,479	92,652	5,798	8,065	40,389	167,208	25,085
New York............................	4,578,885	1,269,390	448,515	15,730	105,299	778,319	51,902	1,739	95,535	1,653,418	159,038
North Carolina...................	1,700,578	379,147	142,382	14,108	53,924	328,440	14,757	3,393	88,431	578,064	97,933
North Dakota......................	218,728	35,285	28,303	27,649	5,764	28,654	517	1,674	14,999	64,138	11,745
Ohio..................................	2,319,683	532,641	207,121	2,256	67,960	442,684	7,815	0	51,001	882,915	125,290
Oklahoma..........................	857,703	155,445	75,387	39,017	23,137	149,415	3,490	23,870	43,257	301,111	43,574
Oregon..............................	691,765	155,418	60,304	2,713	20,824	131,060	7,609	2,190	18,761	254,992	37,894
Pennsylvania.....................	2,450,108	591,020	221,022	1,215	70,166	433,935	11,326	0	50,876	939,709	130,840
Rhode Island......................	261,210	55,164	28,752	2,343	8,393	45,341	1,659	0	9,138	97,712	12,708
South Carolina...................	934,254	214,929	82,116	2,204	29,022	179,373	4,112	5	51,768	317,057	53,667
South Dakota.....................	268,139	43,805	29,191	46,559	6,131	34,222	521	3,555	16,523	75,823	11,809
Tennessee.........................	1,214,235	249,391	102,419	3,581	37,291	236,500	5,122	0	51,052	459,721	69,159
Texas................................	5,343,497	1,406,346	498,911	91,193	149,577	977,912	93,022	313	197,595	1,697,779	230,848
Utah..................................	522,159	64,895	36,536	8,686	17,032	110,830	4,719	1,218	15,544	232,310	30,390
Vermont.............................	170,798	35,190	27,660	5	5,503	27,783	500	172	9,657	52,534	11,794
Virginia..............................	1,258,031	235,811	101,300	37,684	40,782	286,911	11,993	12	51,159	424,575	67,804
Washington........................	1,073,892	214,593	92,979	49,383	33,178	226,827	14,234	4,332	54,379	329,095	54,890
West Virginia......................	462,056	103,426	47,387	25	13,256	77,742	640	0	38,864	152,951	27,764
Wisconsin..........................	975,393	206,529	91,260	12,978	31,961	214,161	6,396	2,277	25,425	325,410	58,997
Wyoming............................	159,563	33,562	27,573	11,112	5,382	29,194	500	566	8,086	32,255	11,333
Other activities/jurisdictions											
Indian Tribe (Set-Aside)	284,035	99,607	35,782	0	14,511	94,146	5,000	0	0	0	34,990
Other..................................	276,200	54,073	41,733	103,801	12,718	15,000	45,526	0	0	0	3,338
American Samoa	34,641	10,230	7,170		562	6,879	1,174	0	1,575	5,577	1,473
Guam................................	57,970	12,132	10,444	41	1,022	15,387	1,142	0	3,055	12,215	2,532
Marshall Islands.................	309	0	0	0				0	309	0	0
Federated States of Micronesia....	53,260	0	0	0	194	6,579		0	1,663	44,824	0
Northern Marianas..............	20,083	3,716	3,980	0	622	5,232	1,133	0	1,424	2,336	1,639
Palau.................................	1,336	0	0	0	0				1,336	0	
Puerto Rico........................	1,837,151	513,462	180,994	0	31,513	113,550	3,232	0	46,304	874,003	74,093
U.S. Virgin Islands..............	43,235	13,467	9,147	166	1,067	9,634	52	0	2,985	4,104	2,612

[1]Title I includes Grants to Local Education Agencies (Basic, Concentration, Targeted, and Education Finance Incentive Grants); Reading First State Grants; Even Start; Migrant Education Grants; Neglected and Delinquent Children Grants; and Comprehensive School Reform Grants.
[2]Title VI includes Teacher Quality State Grants; 21st Century Community Learning Centers; Educational Technology State Grants; State Grants for Innovative Programs; State Assessments, including No Child Left Behind; Education for the Homeless Children and Youth; Rural and Low-Income Schools Program; Small, Rural School Achievement Program; Safe and Drug Free Schools and Communities State Grants; Mathematics and Science Partnerships; and School Improvement Grants.
[3]Includes Impact Aid—Basic Support Payments; Impact Aid—Payments for Children with Disabilities; and Impact Aid—Construction.
[4]Includes Career and Technical Education State Grants; English Literacy and Civics Education State Grants; Tech-Prep Education; State Grants for Incarcerated Youth Offenders; and Adult Basic and Literacy Education State Grants.
[5]Includes Special Education—Grants to States; Preschool Grants; and Grants for Infants and Families.
[6]Includes Language Acquisition State Grants.

[7]Includes Institutional Aid to Strengthen Higher Education Institutions serving significant numbers of low-income students; Other Special Programs for the Disadvantaged; Cooperative Education; Fund for the Improvement of Postsecondary Education; Fellowships and Scholarships; and annual interest subsidy grants for lenders.
[8]Includes Pell Grants; Leveraging Educational Assistance Partnership; Federal Supplemental Educational Opportunity Grants; Federal Work-Study; Special Allowances; College Access Challenge; and Federal Family Education Loan Program interest subsidies.
[9]Includes Vocational Rehabilitation State Grants; Supported Employment State Grants; Client Assistance State Grants; Independent Living State Grants; Services for Older Blind Individuals; Protection and Advocacy for Assistive Technology; Assistive Technology State Grant Program; and Protection and Advocacy of Individual Rights.
[10]Total excludes other activities and other jurisdictions.
NOTE: Data reflect revisions to figures in the *Budget of the United States Government, Fiscal Year 2010*. Detail may not sum to totals because of rounding.
SOURCE: U.S. Department of Education, Budget Service, unpublished tabulations. (This table was prepared October 2009.)

Appropriations for Title I and selected other programs under the No Child Left Behind Act of 2001, by program and state or jurisdiction: Fiscal years 2008 and 2009

[In thousands of current dollars]

State or jurisdiction	Title I total, 2008	Title I, 2009						Improving Teacher Quality State Grants, 2009
		Total	Grants to local education agencies[1]	State agency programs		Even Start	State Assessments, 2009	
				Neglected and Delinquent	Migrant			
1	2	3	4	5	6	7	8	9
Total, 50 states and D.C.[2]	$14,081,595	$14,301,514	$13,809,281	$48,633	$384,771	$58,829	$389,678	$2,798,849
Total, 50 states, D.C., other activities, and other jurisdictions	14,787,039	15,004,053	14,492,401	50,427	394,771	66,454	410,732	2,947,749
Alabama	226,337	242,060	238,216	745	2,096	1,002	6,628	47,444
Alaska	47,060	46,044	38,215	242	7,281	306	3,571	13,986
Arizona	292,505	300,152	290,541	1,377	7,040	1,195	8,326	49,362
Arkansas	155,015	170,408	163,674	405	5,645	684	5,237	29,165
California	1,883,812	1,800,558	1,651,553	2,376	139,756	6,873	32,776	327,107
Colorado	147,827	166,968	159,990	551	5,752	675	6,795	33,921
Connecticut	120,892	115,601	112,784	1,285	1,090	443	5,685	26,558
Delaware	40,431	42,313	41,031	694	282	306	3,657	13,986
District of Columbia	48,785	49,535	48,889	341	0	306	3,338	13,986
Florida	703,197	702,690	674,794	1,950	23,048	2,899	15,804	132,561
Georgia	470,040	506,877	496,479	1,237	7,044	2,117	11,085	80,809
Hawaii	46,618	44,783	43,230	289	958	306	3,885	13,986
Idaho	52,499	53,409	50,102	438	2,563	306	4,301	13,986
Illinois	613,591	640,580	635,103	1,003	1,929	2,544	13,216	118,574
Indiana	261,215	269,669	261,306	887	6,428	1,049	8,104	50,643
Iowa	77,472	80,164	78,077	435	1,330	321	5,286	22,459
Kansas	109,774	115,985	103,935	388	11,663	0	5,226	22,861
Kentucky	223,604	235,930	226,000	975	8,005	951	6,235	45,509
Louisiana	309,163	315,407	309,973	1,625	2,642	1,166	6,565	64,041
Maine	54,329	54,832	52,874	198	1,454	306	3,909	13,986
Maryland	198,786	194,194	191,811	1,129	437	818	7,332	41,151
Massachusetts	243,726	248,911	244,146	2,143	1,611	1,010	7,665	51,825
Michigan	551,994	566,379	554,960	395	8,681	2,344	10,890	112,425
Minnesota	133,032	144,364	140,234	248	3,295	587	7,007	38,884
Mississippi	195,828	201,042	198,545	745	936	816	5,441	42,810
Missouri	236,207	238,468	234,624	1,379	1,530	935	7,569	50,700
Montana	46,039	47,250	45,701	106	1,137	306	3,712	13,986
Nebraska	67,513	73,880	68,008	471	5,095	306	4,408	14,263
Nevada	84,215	93,546	92,553	320	267	406	5,095	15,836
New Hampshire	40,008	40,758	39,848	448	156	306	3,975	13,986
New Jersey	299,771	291,371	285,749	2,629	1,845	1,148	9,663	64,928
New Mexico	118,239	119,878	118,077	253	1,055	493	4,583	22,958
New York	1,269,809	1,264,435	1,245,206	2,954	10,940	5,335	17,305	227,449
North Carolina	379,106	378,758	371,118	1,037	5,035	1,568	10,113	67,951
North Dakota	35,285	36,283	35,642	70	265	306	3,452	13,986
Ohio	532,497	555,749	548,168	2,192	3,098	2,291	11,882	108,260
Oklahoma	155,535	164,244	161,384	301	1,885	673	5,859	34,252
Oregon	155,357	148,129	138,639	1,021	7,891	577	5,790	28,646
Pennsylvania	590,980	589,777	576,938	1,315	9,096	2,429	12,052	114,956
Rhode Island	55,184	53,545	52,239	728	272	306	3,749	13,986
South Carolina	214,862	213,873	210,587	1,784	623	879	6,412	37,806
South Dakota	43,805	45,102	43,747	157	892	306	3,625	13,986
Tennessee	249,559	278,045	275,730	460	680	1,176	7,749	52,244
Texas	1,406,279	1,437,805	1,366,709	2,433	62,950	5,713	24,007	248,187
Utah	64,928	72,333	69,138	783	2,107	306	5,596	19,513
Vermont	35,190	34,913	33,494	416	697	306	3,431	13,986
Virginia	235,732	251,482	247,926	1,720	801	1,035	8,815	52,705
Washington	214,539	215,768	199,417	1,065	14,451	834	7,954	48,044
West Virginia	103,392	94,877	93,698	722	78	379	4,255	23,377
Wisconsin	206,485	217,408	214,714	1,127	688	878	7,257	46,847
Wyoming	33,545	34,981	33,766	640	270	306	3,403	13,986
Other activities/jurisdictions								
Indian Tribe Set-Aside	99,607	102,123	101,126	0	0	997	2,000	14,665
Other nonstate allocations	52,468	24,248	9,000	1,261	10,000	3,987	10,732	27,239
American Samoa	10,230	9,921	9,837	0	0	84	379	3,498
Guam	12,132	12,234	12,130	0	0	104	815	5,155
Northern Marianas	3,716	3,604	3,573	0	0	31	256	1,646
Puerto Rico	513,825	537,078	534,236	533	0	2,309	6,322	92,331
U.S. Virgin Islands	13,467	13,331	13,218	0	0	113	551	4,365

[1]Includes Basic, Concentration, Targeted, and Education Finance Incentive Grants.
[2]Total excludes other activities and other jurisdictions.
NOTE: Detail may not sum to totals because of rounding. These are preliminary estimates for fiscal year 2009. Reading First State Grants has no allocations for fiscal year 2009.

SOURCE: U.S. Department of Education, Budget Service, Elementary, Secondary, and Vocational Education Analysis Division, unpublished tabulations. (This table was prepared August 2009.)

Selected population and enrollment statistics for countries with populations over 10 million, by continent: Selected years, 1990 through 2007

Country[1]	Midyear population (in millions)			Persons per square kilometer, 2007	First level[2]						Second level[3]						Third level[4]					
					Enrollment (in thousands)			Gross enrollment ratio[5]			Enrollment (in thousands)			Gross enrollment ratio[5]			Enrollment (in thousands)			Gross enrollment ratio[5]		
	1990	2000	2007		1989–90	1999–2000	2006–07	1989–90	1999–2000	2006–07	1989–90	1999–2000	2006–07	1989–90	1999–2000	2006–07	1989–90	1999–2000	2006–07	1989–90	1999–2000	2006–07
	2	3	4	5	6	7	8	9	10	11	12	13	14	15	16	17	18	19	20	21	22	23
World total[6]	5,282	6,085	6,632	51	596,853	652,799[7]	694,294[7]	99	99[7]	106[7]	315,008	451,014	519,229[7]	52	60	66[7]	68,613	98,304	150,656[7]	14	19	26[7]
Africa																						
Algeria[8]	25	30	33	14	4,189	4,843	4,079	100	108	110	2,176	—	—	61	—	—	286	—	902	11	—	24
Angola	9	13	12	10	990[9]	—	1,561	92	44	65	186	355	352	12	15	16	7	11[7]	33	1	—	3
Burkina Faso	9	11	15	54	504	852	—	33	44	—	99	190	—	7	10	—	5	11[7]	—	1	1[7]	3
Cameroon	11	15	18	39	1,964	2,237[10]	3,120	101	86[10]	110	500	700	875	28	27	—	33	66[7]	132	3	4[7]	7
Cote d'Ivoire	12	16	20	62	1,415	1,944	2,180	67	69	72	361	620[7]	2,815	22	22[7]	25[11]	30[12]	104[7]	157	2	7[7]	8
Democratic Rep. of the Congo	37	51	64	28	4,562	7,947[7]	8,840	70	101[7]	85	1,097[12]	—	3,430	21[12]	—	33	80	—	238	2	—	4
Egypt[8]	56	64	80	81	6,964	5,847	9,988	94	101[7]	105	5,507	8,028[7]	—	76	85[7]	30	628[13,14]	68	210	16	—	3
Ethiopia	48	64	80	71	2,466	2,561	12,175	33	52	91	866	1,195	3,430	14	13	49[7]	34	55	140	1	1	3
Ghana[8]	15	19	23	99	1,945	5,035	3,366	75	80	98	618[16]	1,057	1,581[7]	36	38	53	10[15]	89	140	1	3	6
Kenya[8]	23	30	37	65	5,392	2,208	6,688	95	97	113	323[16]	1,909	2,729	24	39	48	35[15]	32	58	2	2	3
Madagascar	13	16	19	33	1,571	2,695	3,837	103	99	141	61	487	836[7]	18	31	26[7]	36	4[11]	6	1	2	3
Malawi	9	11	14	145	1,401	1,017	2,943	68	137	116	84	258[7]	574	8	38	28	5	20	51	1	2	4
Mali	8	11	12	10	395	3,670	1,717	26	61	83	—	1,541	534	7	19[7]	32	5[17]	276	369	1	9	11
Morocco[8]	24	29	34	76	2,484	2,544	3,939	67	92	107	1,194	124	2,173	35	6	56	256	12	—	11	1	1
Mozambique[8]	14	18	21	27	1,260	579	4,564	67	75	111	160	106[7]	445	8	7[7]	18	5[17]	—	11	#	—	—
Niger	8	11	14	11	369	—	1,235	29	33	53	77	—	214	7	7	11	—	—	—	—	—	—
Nigeria[8]	96	127	143	157	13,607	19,151	—	91	92	84	2,908	4,104	505[7]	25	24	26[7]	208[15,18]	—	77[7]	4[17,18]	—	7[7]
Senegal	8	10	13	68	708	1,108	1,572	59	67	103	—	250	4,780[7]	16	16	97[7]	19	645	—	3	14	7
South Africa	37	43	48	40	6,952	7,445	7,312	122	108	66	2,742	4,142	1,463	74	86	33	439[19]	204[7]	326	13	6[7]	31
Sudan[7]	24	34	39	17	2,043	2,567	3,959	53	49	66	732	980	1,268	24	26	88	60[13]	180	—	3	19	—
Tunisia	8	10	10	66	1,406	1,414	1,069	113	113	105	565	1,104[7]	1,001[7]	45	75[7]	23[7]	69	56	55	9	3	1
Uganda	17	22	30	152	2,470[20,21]	6,559	7,538	70	69	116	245[16,21]	547	—	13	16	—	18	—	—	1	—	—
United Republic of Tanzania.	25	34	39	44	3,379	4,382	8,317	74	100	112	167	276	607	5	23	43	7[12]	25[7]	55	#	2[7]	1
Zambia	8	10	11	16	1,461	1,590	2,790	99	80	119	190	844	—	24	43	—	15	49[7]	—	#	4[7]	—
Zimbabwe	10	12	11	30	2,116	2,461	—	116	100	—	661	—	—	50	—	—	49	—	—	5	—	—
Asia																						
Afghanistan[8]	15	24	32	49	623	749	4,718	27	22	103	182	—	1,036	9	—	28	24	—	1,145	2	—	7
Bangladesh	110	130	152	1,135	11,940	—	16,313	72	—	91	3,593	10,329	10,445	19	46	43	434	727	92	4	5	7
Cambodia	9	12	14	79	1,330	2,248	2,480	121	102	119	264	351	875	32	18	40	7	22	—	1	2	5
China[8]	1,155	1,261	1,322	142	122,414	113,613	107,395	125	94	112	52,386	81,488	101,831	49	63	77	3,822	7,364	25,346	3	8	23
India	851	1,016	1,130	380	99,118	28,202[7]	29,797	97	109[7]	117	54,180[16]	71,031	18,717	44	46	73	4,951	9,404	3,755	6	10	17
Indonesia	183	210	235	129	29,754	8,288	7,152	115	94	121	10,965	14,264[7]	9,145	44	55[7]	83	1,773[12]	1,405	2,829	9	19	31
Iran, Islamic Republic of	59	64	65	40	9,370	3,639	7,220	112	91	109	5,085	9,955	6,366	55	86	94	312[13]	289	4,033	10[22]	12	58
Iraq	18	23	27	64	3,328	7,529	3,174	111	101	98	1,024[16]	1,224	2,826	47	36	—	170[12]	404	773	12[22]	—	51
Japan	124	127	127	340	9,373	1,208	1,622	100	100	99	11,026	8,782	7,427	97	102	101	2,899[12]	3,982	3,209	30	47	—
Kazakhstan	17	15	15	6	1,197	—	948	87	97	105	2,144	2,003	1,874	98	93	93	537	370	—	40	28	—
Korea, North (DPR)	20	22	22	187	—	—	—	105	100	107	4,560	3,959	3,917	90	94	98	1,691	3,003	—	39	78	95
Korea, South (Republic of)	43	47	48	491	4,869	4,030	3,838	94	97	—	1,456	2,205	—	56	65	—	121	549	—	7	26	—
Malaysia	18	23	25	76	2,456	3,026	5,014	106	100	126	1,281	2,268	2,686	23	94	43[7]	196[12]	—	508	4	—	11
Myanmar[8]	41	46	47	72	5,385	4,858	4,515	108	117[10]	92	709	1,348	1,999[7]	33	35	33	94	94	321	5	4	5[11]
Nepal[8]	19	24	28	194	2,789	3,780[10]	17,979	61	69[11]	109	4,345	—	9,145	23	—	94	—	—	955[11]	3	—	—
Pakistan	119	138	169	218	11,451[23]	13,987[11]	13,145	111	—	98	4,034	6,366	2,826	73	—	—	1,709	404	—	28	22	—
Philippines	61	76	94	316	10,427	—	3,174	111	—	109	893	1,224	—	44	—	83	154	289	—	12	—	—
Saudi Arabia	16	21	28	13	1,877	—	1,622	73	—	98	2,082	—	2,549	74	102	94	55[12,24]	—	—	5	—	—
Sri Lanka[8]	17	19	21	323	2,112	—	2,310	106	—	126	914	1,069	—	52	41	72	222	—	—	18	—	—
Syrian Arab Republic	12	16	19	105	2,452	2,775	—	108	104	—	—	—	—	—	—	—	—	—	—	—	—	—
Taiwan	20	22	23	709	6,957	6,101	5,704	99	106	106	2,230	—	4,789	30	—	83	1,156[17]	1,900	2,504	19[17]	35	50
Thailand	56	61	65	127	6,862	7,850[10]	8,065[7]	99	95[7]	96[7]	3,808	3,566	5,527[7]	47	88	80[7]	750	1,588[7]	2,454	13	23[7]	36
Turkey	56	65	75	97	6,882	2,602	2,165	99	99	95	3,295	7,926	4,598	99	99	102	603	305	289	13	13	10
Uzbekistan	21	25	27	64	1,778	—	—	81	99	—	3,236	—	9,845	32[18]	88	—	130	732	1,588	30	9	—
Vietnam	67	79	85	262	8,862	10,063	7,041	103[18]	106	—	212[18]	—	—	23[18]	65	—	53[12]	173[7]	—	2	7[7]	—
Yemen	12	18	22	42	2,679[18]	2,464[7]	—	79[18]	74[7]	—	212[18]	1,151[7]	—	23[18]	43[7]	—	53[12]	173[7]	—	4[12]	10[7]	—

See notes at end of table.

Selected population and enrollment statistics for countries with populations over 10 million, by continent: Selected years, 1990 through 2007—Continued

Country[1]	Midyear population (in millions)			Persons per square kilometer, 2007	First level[2] Enrollment (in thousands)			First level[2] Gross enrollment ratio[5]			Second level[3] Enrollment (in thousands)			Second level[3] Gross enrollment ratio[5]			Third level[4] Enrollment (in thousands)			Third level[4] Gross enrollment ratio[5]		
	1990	2000	2007	2007	1989-90	1999-2000	2006-07	1989-90	1999-2000	2006-07	1989-90	1999-2000	2006-07	1989-90	1999-2000	2006-07	1989-90	1999-2000	2006-07	1989-90	1999-2000	2006-07
1	2	3	4	5	6	7	8	9	10	11	12	13	14	15	16	17	18	19	20	21	22	23
Europe																						
Belgium	10	10	10	343	719	774	732	101	106	103	769	1,058	825	103	146	110	276	356	394	40	58	62
Czech Republic	10	10	10	132	546	645	463	96	103	101	1,268	958	937	91	88	96	118[25]	254	363	16	29	55
France	57	59	64	100	4,149	3,885	4,106	108	107	110	5,522	5,929	5,940	99	110	113	1,699	2,015	2,180	40	53	56
Germany[28]	79	82	82	236	3,431	3,656	3,311	101	105	104	7,398	8,307	7,982	98	98	100	2,049	—	—	34	—	—
Greece	10	11	11	82	813	645	639	98	96	101	851	739	682	83	89	102	283	422	603	36	51	91
Italy[2]	57	58	58	198	3,056	2,836	2,820	103	101	105	5,118	4,404	4,553	120	93	101	1,452	1,770	2,034	32	49	68
Netherlands[6]	15	16	17	489	1,082	1,279	1,281	102	108	107	1,402	1,379	1,444	81	123	120	479	488	590	40	52	60
Poland[6]	38	39	39	127	5,189	3,319	2,485	98	99	97	1,888	3,988	3,206	67	100	100	545	1,580	2,147	22	50	67
Portugal[6]	10	10	11	116	1,020	811	754	123	124	115	670	831	680	92	108	101	186	374	367	23	48	56
Romania[6]	23	22	22	97	1,253	1,189	918	91	103	105	2,838	2,226	1,954	93	81	87	193	453	928	10	24	58
Russian Federation	148	146	141	8	7,596	6,138	5,010	109	107	96	13,956	—	10,798	—	—	84	5,100	—	9,370	52	—	75
Spain[6]	39	39	40	81	2,820	2,540	2,556	109	106	106	4,755	3,246	3,080	104	111	120	1,222	1,829	1,777	37	59	69
Ukraine[6]	52	50	46	77	3,991	2,079	1,648	89	109	100	3,408	5,204	3,709	93	99	94	1,652	1,812	2,819	47	49	76
United Kingdom[6]	58	60	61	252	4,533	4,632	4,409	104	101	104	4,336	5,304	5,306	85	102	97	1,258	2,024	2,363	30	58	59
North America																						
Canada	28	31	33	4	2,376	2,456	—	103	99	—	2,292	2,621	—	101	107	—	1,917	1,212	—	95	59	—
Cuba	11	11	11	103	888	1,046	883	98	111	102	1,002	790	899	89	79	93	242	159	865	21	22	109
Guatemala	9	11	13	117	1,165	1,909	2,449	78	104	113	295[12]	504	864	23[12]	38	56	70[17]	—	234	8[17]	—	18
Mexico	83	98	109	57	14,402	14,766	14,631	114	110	114	6,704	9,094	11,122	53	72	89	1,311	1,963	2,529	15	20	27
United States	254	282	301	33	22,429	24,973	24,492	102	100	99	19,270	22,594	24,731	93	94	94	13,819	13,203	17,759	75	69	82
South America																						
Argentina	33	37	40	15	4,965	4,728	—	106	114	—	2,160	3,428	—	71	86	—	1,008[12]	1,767[8]	—	38[12]	53[7]	—
Brazil	148	170	194	23	28,944	20,212	17,996	106	150	130	3,499	26,097	23,424	38	104	100	1,540[27]	2,781	5,273	11	16	30
Chile	13	15	16	22	1,991	1,799	1,679	100	100	106	720	1,391	1,612	73	83	91	262[12]	452	753	21[12]	37	52
Colombia	33	42	44	43	4,247	5,221	5,299	102	115	116	2,378[12]	3,569	4,657	50	69	85	487	934	1,373	13	23	32
Ecuador	10	13	14	51	1,846	1,925	2,039	116	115	118	786[16,28]	917	1,142	55	57	70	207	—	444	20	—	35
Peru	22	26	29	23	3,865	4,338	3,994	118	121	117	1,698	2,374	2,861	67	87	98	678	—	—	30	—	—
Venezuela	20	24	26	30	4,053	3,328	3,521	96	102	106	281	1,543	2,175	35	59	79	550	668	—	29	28	—
Oceania																						
Australia[6]	17	19	21	3	1,583	1,906	1,973	108	101	107	1,278	2,589	2,511	82	162	149	485[29]	845	1,084	36	66	75

—Not available.

#Rounds to zero.

[1]Selection based on total population for midyear 2007.

[2]First-level enrollment consists of elementary school, typically corresponding to grades 1-6 in the United States.

[3]Second-level enrollment includes general education, teacher training (at the second level), and technical and vocational education.

[4]Third-level enrollment includes college and university enrollment, and technical and vocational education beyond the secondary school level.

[5]Data represent the total enrollment of all ages in the school level divided by the population of the specific age groups that correspond to the school level. Adjustments have been made for the varying lengths of first and second level programs. Ratios may exceed 100 because some countries have many students from outside the normal age range.

[6]Enrollment totals and ratios exclude Democratic People's Republic of Korea. Data do not include adult education or special education provided outside regular schools.

[7]Estimated by the UNESCO Institute for Statistics.

[8]Data for 1994-95.

[9]Classification or data coverage of levels has been revised. Data by level may not be comparable over time.

[10]Policy change in 1999-2000: introduction of free universal primary education.

[11]National estimation.

[12]Data for 1991-92.

[13]Excludes private institutions.

[14]Data refer to universities and exclude Al Azhar.

[15]Excludes nonuniversity institutions (such as teacher training colleges and technical colleges) and excludes distance-learning universities.

[16]General education enrollment only. Excludes teacher training and vocational education enrollments.

[17]Data for 1992-93.

[18]Data for 1993-94.

[19]Not including the former Independent States of Transke, Bophuthatswana, Venda, and Ciskei.

[20]Estimated.

[21]Data refer to government aided and maintained schools only.

[22]Data for 1985-86.

[23]Includes preprimary education.

[24]Excludes some nonuniversity institutions.

[25]Excludes full-time students only.

[26]Data include both former East and West Germany.

[27]Not including former ISCED level 7.

[28]Including vocational education.

NOTE: Some data have been revised from previously published figures. Detail may not sum to totals because of rounding.

SOURCE: United Nations Educational, Scientific, and Cultural Organization (UNESCO), Statistical Yearbook, 1999; Global Education Digest, 2003 and 2007; unpublished tabulations; and tables 3B, 5, and 14, retrieved June 17, 2009, from http://stats.uis.unesco.org/unesco/ReportFolders/ReportFolders.aspx. World Bank, World Development Indicators, 2000 and World Development Report, 2002. U.S. Department of Commerce, Census Bureau, International Data Base, retrieved June 22, 2009, from http://www.census.gov/ipc/www/idb/tables.html. (This table was prepared July 2009.)

Pupils per teacher in public and private elementary and secondary schools, by level of education and country: Selected years, 1985 through 2007

Elementary

Country	1985	1990	2000	2003	2004	2005	2006	2007
	2	3	4	5	6	7	8	9
OECD average	—	—	17.7	16.5	16.9	16.7	16.2	16.0
Australia	13.8[1]	—	17.3	16.6	16.4	16.2	16.0	15.9
Austria	11.3	11.6	—	14.4	15.1	14.1	13.9	13.6
Belgium	—	—	15.0[4]	13.1	12.9	12.8	12.6	12.6[5]
Canada	18.1	17.1	18.1	—	—	—	—	—
Czech Republic	[8]	[8]	19.7	18.3	17.9	17.5	17.3	18.7
Denmark	12.7	11.2	10.4	—	—	—	—	—
Finland	—	—	16.9	16.6	16.3	15.9	15.0	15.0
France	20.7	20.3	19.8	19.4	19.4	19.4	19.3[5]	19.7[5]
Germany[10]	—	[8]	19.8	18.7	18.8	18.8	18.7	18.3
Greece	—	—	10.9	10.6	10.7	10.6	10.4	10.1
Hungary	—	—	10.9	10.8	10.7	10.6	10.4	10.2
Iceland	—	—	11.0	10.9	11.1	11.1	10.6	—
Ireland	12.8	10.7	21.5	18.7	18.3	17.9	19.4	17.9[7]
Italy	—	10.8[1]	11.0	10.9	10.7	10.6	10.7	10.5
Japan	—	20.8[1]	20.9	19.9	19.6	19.4	19.2	19.0
Korea, Republic of	—	—	32.1	30.2	29.1	28.0	26.7	25.6
Luxembourg	—	—	15.9[1]	10.8[1]	11.9[1]	11.7	11.3[1]	11.2[1]
Mexico	20.2	19.2	27.2	26.7	28.5	28.3	28.0	28.0
Netherlands	20.1	—	16.8[4]	16.0[4]	15.9[4]	15.9[4]	15.3[4]	15.6[4]
New Zealand	26.8	—	20.6	19.9	16.7	18.1	17.7	17.5
Norway	—	—	12.4	11.7[1]	11.9[1]	11.7	10.9[1]	11.0[1]
Poland	—	—	12.7	11.9	11.1	10.8	11.5	11.0
Portugal	[8]	[8]	12.1	12.3	11.1	10.8	10.6	11.8
Slovak Republic	[8]	[8]	18.3	19.4	18.9	18.9	18.6	13.6
Spain	11.6	10.6	12.8	12.3	12.1	12.2	12.1	12.3
Sweden	—	—	12.8	12.3	14.3[1]	14.6[1]	15.1[1]	14.8[1]
Switzerland	—	—	30.5	25.9	26.5	25.8	26.7	26.2
Turkey	31.1	30.6	21.2	20.0	21.1	20.7	19.8	19.4
United Kingdom	19.7	22.0	15.8	15.5	15.0	14.9	14.6	14.6
United States	17.0	15.6	—	—	—	—	—	—
Reporting partner countries								
Brazil	[8]	[8]	—	—	23.5	22.9	22.5	25.8
Chile	[8]	[8]	—	33.9	27.1	25.9	25.5	24.7
Estonia	—	[8]	—	—	—	—	14.1	14.4
Israel	[8]	[8]	—	20.9	16.9	17.3	17.2	16.4
Russian Federation	[8]	[8]	—	17.0	17.0	—	14.9	17.0[1]
Slovenia	[8]	[8]	—	15.5	15.0	15.0	14.6	15.2

Junior high school (lower secondary)

Country	1985	1990	2000	2003	2004	2005	2006	2007
	10	11	12	13	14	15	16	17
OECD average	—	—	15.0	14.3	13.7	13.7	13.3	13.2
Australia	—	—	—	10.0	10.4	10.6	10.4	10.3
Austria	9.2	7.7	—	10.6	10.6	9.4	9.4	9.2[5]
Belgium	—	15.5	18.1	14.7	13.5	13.5	12.3	12.3
Canada	16.0	—	—	—	—	—	—	—
Czech Republic	[8]	[8]	—	10.8[7]	11.3[7]	11.7[7]	11.4[7]	11.2[7]
Denmark	10.2	9.3	11.4	10.8[7]	11.3[7]	11.9[7]	11.5[7]	11.2[7]
Finland	—	—	10.7	9.8	10.0	10.0	9.7	9.9
France	16.9	14.6	14.7	13.7	14.1	14.2	14.1[5]	14.3[5]
Germany[10]	—	[8]	15.7	15.6	15.6	15.5	15.5	15.2
Greece	—	—	10.8	8.7	8.2	7.9	8.0	7.7
Hungary	—	—	12.7	11.3[7]	11.4[7]	11.3[7]	10.6[7]	10.2
Iceland	—	8.5	10.4	10.3	10.3	10.1	10.3	10.4[7]
Ireland	9.6	—	10.4	15.7	15.3	15.1	14.9	9.4
Italy	9.6	18.6	16.8	18.8	17.3	16.8	16.6	14.8
Japan	—	—	21.5	19.9	20.4	20.8	20.8	20.5
Korea, Republic of	12.7	—	34.8	32.4	33.7	33.7	33.4	33.3
Luxembourg	—	—	27.2	18.8	15.8[3]	16.8	16.6	16.2
Mexico	—	12.4	19.9	18.8	17.3	18.1	14.2	—
Netherlands	—	—	9.9	10.4[1]	10.5[1]	—	10.9[1]	11.0[1]
New Zealand	—	—	11.5	12.6	10.0	11.7	11.5	11.0
Norway	—	—	10.4	13.9	13.9	14.1	13.7	11.8
Poland	—	—	13.5	13.3	12.9	12.5	14.2	12.4
Portugal	—	10.2	12.8	12.1	11.9	12.0	11.4	7.9
Slovak Republic	10.8	10.6	12.1	—	11.2[1]	11.7[1]	12.3[1]	13.9
Spain	41.3	48.4	17.6[2]	17.4	17.1	17.0	16.7	11.7
Sweden	16.5	15.9	16.3	15.5	15.2	15.1	14.7	11.5
Switzerland	—	—	—	—	—	—	—	12.3[1]
Turkey	41.3	48.4	17.6[2]	17.4	17.1	17.0	16.7	16.7
United Kingdom	16.5	15.9	16.3	15.5	15.2	15.1	14.7	14.7
United States	—	—	—	—	—	—	—	—
Reporting partner countries								
Brazil	[8]	[8]	[8]	33.5	18.8	18.1	17.6	22.3
Chile	[8]	[8]	[8]	—	44.3	25.9	25.5	24.7
Estonia	[8]	[8]	[8]	13.4	14.1	13.4	12.3	11.4
Israel	[8]	[8]	[8]	13.4	14.1	—	14.1	12.4
Russian Federation	[8]	[8]	[8]	—	—	11.1	10.2	9.5
Slovenia	[8]	[8]	[8]	—	—	—	—	—

Senior high school (upper secondary)

Country	1985	1990	2000	2003	2004	2005	2006	2007
	18	19	20	21	22	23	24	25
OECD average	—	—	13.9	13.0	12.7	13.0	12.4	12.5
Australia	3.2	12.4	—	12.4[2,3]	12.3[2,3]	12.1[2,3]	12.2[2,3]	12.1[2,3]
Austria	15.2	—	9.7[3,6]	10.2	11.0	11.3	11.3	11.0
Belgium	—	15.3	19.5	9.6[6]	9.2[6]	9.9[6]	10.2[6]	10.2[5,6]
Canada	16.0	—	11.5	12.6	12.6	12.8	—	16.4[1,3,4,7]
Czech Republic	14.8	13.3	14.4	13.4	13.5	13.6	12.5	12.3
Denmark	14.8	13.3	14.4	15.9[6,9]	16.2[6,9]	18.0[6,9]	15.8[6,9]	15.9[6]
Finland	—	—	10.4	10.6	10.3	10.3	9.7	9.6[5]
France	23.7	21.0	13.9	13.7	13.9	14.0	14.3	14.3
Germany[10]	—	[8]	14.0	13.5	13.2	13.0	12.7	7.3
Greece	—	—	11.4[6]	13.2	12.3	12.2	12.3	12.1
Hungary	7.2	8.3	9.7	10.7[6]	11.1	11.3[7]	10.8[6]	10.2[6]
Iceland	10.8	10.7	14.0	13.7[3,6]	14.3[3,6]	15.5[3,6]	14.6[3,6]	13.2[1,3,6]
Ireland	—	16.2	14.0	10.8	11.5	11.0	11.0	10.8
Italy	—	16.2	14.0	13.5[6]	13.2[6]	13.0[6]	12.7[6]	12.5[6]
Japan	—	—	20.9	16.0	15.9	16.0	15.9	16.2
Korea, Republic of	—	—	26.5	24.0	25.2	25.8	25.4	25.7
Luxembourg	—	14.8	17.1[3]	15.7[3]	15.8[3]	16.2[3]	15.8[3,6]	15.7[3,6]
Mexico	—	15.3	13.1	10.9	12.5	12.9	12.7	13.3
Netherlands	—	16.2	13.1	10.9	12.5	12.9	12.7	13.3
New Zealand	—	—	9.7	9.2[1,6]	9.6[1,6]	—	9.7[1,6]	9.8[1,6]
Norway	—	16.9	16.9	13.5	7.3	12.9	12.8	12.2
Poland	—	7.9	7.9	—	7.3	8.0	7.5[6]	8.4[6]
Portugal	15.3	14.8	12.8	14.0	14.2	14.3	14.2	14.1
Slovak Republic	15.3	14.8	11.9[3]	7.9	8.0	8.1	7.8	7.7
Spain	13.1	11.9	15.2	14.1	14.0	14.0	13.8	13.6
Sweden	11.0	12.1	14.0	18.0	11.1	10.5[1,2]	10.5[1,2]	10.6[1,2]
Switzerland	11.1	13.9	12.5[2]	12.6[2]	16.9	16.2[2]	15.8[3,6]	16.2
Turkey	16.7	15.8	14.1	15.6	12.3[2,6]	11.8[2,6]	11.6[2,6]	11.3[2,6]
United Kingdom	16.2	15.8	14.1	15.6	16.0	16.0	15.7	15.6
United States	—	—	—	—	—	—	—	—
Reporting partner countries								
Brazil	[8]	[8]	[8]	32.3	18.3	17.6	17.0	20.2
Chile	[8]	[8]	[8]	—	26.8	26.6	26.3	25.7
Estonia	[8]	[8]	[8]	12.9	12.2	13.4	13.2	11.8
Israel	[8]	[8]	[8]	8.5[3]	10.3[3,6]	11.2[6,11]	9.9[3,6,11]	8.8[3,6,11,12]
Russian Federation	[8]	[8]	[8]	—	14.0[6]	14.6	14.0[6]	13.9[6]
Slovenia	[8]	[8]	[8]	—	—	—	—	—

—Not available.
†Not applicable.
[1]Public schools only.
[2]Includes only general programs.
[3]Includes junior high school data.
[4]Includes preprimary data.
[5]Excludes independent private institutions.
[6]Includes postsecondary non-higher education.
[7]Includes elementary school data.
[8]Country did not exist in its current form in the given year.

[9]Includes tertiary type B education (i.e., occupation-specific education corresponding to that offered at the associate's degree level in the United States).
[10]Data for 1985 are for the former West Germany.
[11]Excludes general programs.
[12]Excludes part-time personnel in public institutions.
NOTE: In the U.S. data in this table, elementary corresponds to grades 1 through 6, junior high school corresponds to grades 7 through 9, and senior high school corresponds to grades 10 through 12.
SOURCE: Organization for Economic Cooperation and Development (OECD), Online Education Database; *Annual National Accounts, Vol. 1, 1997*; and *Education at a Glance, 2002 through 2008*. (This table was prepared July 2009.)

Average mathematics literacy, reading literacy, and science literacy scores of 15-year-old students, by sex and country: 2006

Country or other jurisdiction	Mathematics literacy Total		Male		Female		Reading literacy Total		Male		Female		Science literacy Total		Male		Female	
1	2		3		4		5		6		7		8		9		10	
OECD total[1]	484	(1.2)	489	(1.3)	478	(1.3)	484	(1.0)	466	(1.2)	502	(1.3)	491	(1.2)	492	(1.4)	490	(1.3)
OECD average[2]	498	(0.5)	503	(0.7)	492	(0.6)	492	(0.6)	473	(0.7)	511	(0.7)	500	(0.5)	501	(0.7)	499	(0.6)
Australia	520	(2.2)	527	(3.2)	513	(2.4)	513	(2.1)	495	(3.0)	532	(2.2)	527	(2.3)	527	(3.2)	527	(2.7)
Austria	505	(3.7)	517	(4.4)	494	(4.1)	490	(4.1)	468	(4.9)	513	(5.5)	511	(3.9)	515	(4.2)	507	(4.9)
Belgium	520	(3.0)	524	(4.1)	517	(3.4)	501	(3.0)	482	(4.1)	522	(3.5)	510	(2.5)	511	(3.3)	510	(3.2)
Canada	527	(2.0)	534	(2.4)	520	(2.0)	527	(2.4)	511	(2.8)	543	(2.5)	534	(2.0)	536	(2.5)	532	(2.1)
Czech Republic	510	(3.6)	514	(4.2)	504	(4.8)	483	(4.2)	463	(5.0)	509	(5.4)	513	(3.5)	515	(4.2)	510	(4.8)
Denmark	513	(2.6)	518	(2.9)	508	(3.0)	494	(3.2)	480	(3.6)	509	(3.5)	496	(3.1)	500	(3.6)	491	(3.4)
Finland	548	(2.3)	554	(2.7)	543	(2.6)	547	(2.1)	521	(2.7)	572	(2.3)	563	(2.0)	562	(2.6)	565	(2.4)
France	496	(3.2)	499	(4.0)	492	(3.3)	488	(4.1)	470	(5.2)	505	(3.9)	495	(3.4)	497	(4.3)	494	(3.6)
Germany	504	(3.9)	513	(4.6)	494	(3.9)	495	(4.4)	475	(5.3)	517	(4.4)	516	(3.8)	519	(4.6)	512	(3.8)
Greece	459	(3.0)	462	(4.3)	457	(3.0)	460	(4.0)	432	(5.7)	488	(3.5)	473	(3.2)	468	(4.5)	479	(3.4)
Hungary	491	(2.9)	496	(3.5)	486	(3.7)	482	(3.3)	463	(3.7)	503	(3.9)	504	(2.7)	507	(3.3)	501	(3.5)
Iceland	506	(1.8)	503	(2.6)	508	(2.2)	484	(1.9)	460	(2.8)	509	(2.3)	491	(1.6)	488	(2.6)	494	(2.1)
Ireland	501	(2.8)	507	(3.7)	496	(3.2)	517	(3.5)	500	(4.5)	534	(3.8)	508	(3.2)	508	(4.3)	509	(3.3)
Italy	462	(2.3)	470	(2.9)	453	(2.7)	469	(2.4)	448	(3.4)	489	(2.8)	475	(2.0)	477	(2.8)	474	(2.5)
Japan	523	(3.3)	533	(4.8)	513	(4.9)	498	(3.6)	483	(5.4)	513	(5.2)	531	(3.4)	533	(4.9)	530	(5.1)
Korea, Republic of	547	(3.8)	552	(5.3)	543	(4.5)	556	(3.8)	539	(4.6)	574	(4.5)	522	(3.4)	521	(4.8)	523	(3.9)
Luxembourg	490	(1.1)	498	(1.7)	482	(1.8)	479	(1.3)	464	(2.0)	495	(2.1)	486	(1.1)	491	(1.8)	482	(1.8)
Mexico	406	(2.9)	410	(3.4)	401	(3.1)	410	(3.1)	393	(3.5)	427	(3.0)	410	(2.7)	413	(3.2)	406	(2.6)
Netherlands	531	(2.6)	537	(3.1)	524	(2.8)	507	(2.9)	495	(3.7)	519	(3.0)	525	(2.7)	528	(3.2)	521	(3.1)
New Zealand	522	(2.4)	527	(3.1)	517	(3.6)	521	(3.0)	502	(3.6)	539	(3.6)	530	(2.7)	528	(3.9)	532	(3.6)
Norway	490	(2.6)	493	(3.3)	487	(2.8)	484	(3.2)	462	(3.8)	508	(3.3)	487	(3.1)	484	(3.8)	489	(3.2)
Poland	495	(2.4)	500	(2.8)	491	(2.7)	508	(2.8)	487	(3.4)	528	(2.8)	498	(2.3)	500	(2.7)	496	(2.6)
Portugal	466	(3.1)	474	(3.7)	459	(3.2)	472	(3.6)	455	(4.4)	488	(3.5)	474	(3.0)	477	(3.7)	472	(3.2)
Slovak Republic	492	(2.8)	499	(3.7)	485	(3.5)	466	(3.1)	446	(4.2)	488	(3.8)	488	(2.6)	491	(3.9)	485	(3.0)
Spain	480	(2.3)	484	(2.6)	476	(2.6)	461	(2.2)	443	(2.6)	479	(2.3)	488	(2.6)	491	(2.9)	486	(2.7)
Sweden	502	(2.4)	505	(2.7)	500	(3.0)	507	(3.4)	488	(4.0)	528	(3.5)	503	(2.4)	504	(2.7)	503	(2.9)
Switzerland	530	(3.2)	536	(3.3)	523	(3.6)	499	(3.1)	484	(3.2)	515	(3.3)	512	(3.2)	514	(3.3)	509	(3.6)
Turkey	424	(4.9)	427	(5.6)	421	(5.1)	447	(4.2)	427	(5.1)	471	(4.3)	424	(3.8)	418	(4.6)	430	(4.1)
United Kingdom	495	(2.1)	504	(2.6)	487	(2.6)	495	(2.3)	480	(3.0)	510	(2.6)	515	(2.3)	520	(3.0)	510	(2.8)
United States[3]	474	(4.0)	479	(4.6)	470	(3.9)	—	(†)	—	(†)	—	(†)	489	(4.2)	489	(5.1)	489	(4.0)
Reporting partner countries																		
Argentina	381	(6.2)	388	(6.5)	375	(7.2)	374	(7.2)	345	(8.3)	399	(7.4)	391	(6.1)	384	(6.5)	397	(6.8)
Azerbaijan	476	(2.3)	475	(2.4)	477	(2.6)	353	(3.1)	343	(3.5)	363	(3.3)	382	(2.8)	379	(3.1)	386	(2.7)
Brazil	370	(2.9)	380	(3.4)	361	(3.0)	393	(3.7)	376	(4.3)	408	(3.7)	390	(2.8)	395	(3.2)	386	(2.9)
Bulgaria	413	(6.1)	412	(6.7)	415	(6.5)	402	(6.9)	374	(7.7)	432	(6.9)	434	(6.1)	426	(6.6)	443	(6.9)
Chile	411	(4.6)	424	(5.5)	396	(4.7)	442	(5.0)	434	(6.0)	451	(5.4)	438	(4.3)	448	(5.4)	426	(4.4)
Colombia	370	(3.8)	382	(4.1)	360	(5.0)	385	(5.1)	375	(5.6)	394	(5.6)	388	(3.4)	393	(4.1)	384	(4.1)
Croatia	467	(2.4)	474	(3.2)	461	(2.8)	477	(2.8)	452	(3.8)	502	(3.3)	493	(2.4)	492	(3.3)	494	(3.1)
Estonia	515	(2.7)	515	(3.3)	514	(3.0)	501	(2.9)	478	(3.2)	524	(3.1)	531	(2.5)	530	(3.1)	533	(2.9)
Hong Kong-China	547	(2.7)	555	(3.9)	540	(3.7)	536	(2.4)	520	(3.5)	551	(3.0)	542	(2.5)	546	(3.5)	539	(3.5)
Indonesia	391	(5.6)	399	(8.3)	382	(4.0)	393	(5.9)	384	(8.7)	402	(4.2)	393	(5.7)	399	(8.2)	387	(3.7)
Israel	442	(4.3)	448	(6.6)	436	(4.3)	439	(4.6)	417	(6.5)	460	(4.6)	454	(3.7)	456	(5.6)	452	(4.2)
Jordan	384	(3.3)	381	(5.3)	388	(3.9)	401	(3.3)	373	(5.6)	428	(3.4)	422	(2.8)	408	(4.5)	436	(3.3)
Kyrgyzstan	311	(3.4)	311	(4.0)	310	(3.4)	285	(3.5)	257	(4.4)	308	(3.3)	322	(2.9)	319	(3.6)	325	(3.0)
Latvia	486	(3.0)	489	(3.5)	484	(3.2)	479	(3.7)	454	(4.3)	504	(3.5)	490	(3.0)	486	(3.5)	493	(3.2)
Liechtenstein	525	(4.2)	525	(7.4)	525	(7.0)	510	(3.9)	486	(7.7)	531	(6.3)	522	(4.1)	516	(7.6)	527	(6.3)
Lithuania	486	(2.9)	487	(3.3)	485	(3.3)	470	(3.0)	445	(3.5)	496	(3.2)	488	(2.8)	483	(3.1)	493	(3.1)
Macao-China	525	(1.3)	530	(2.1)	520	(1.7)	492	(1.1)	479	(1.8)	505	(1.5)	511	(1.1)	513	(1.8)	509	(1.6)
Montenegro	399	(1.4)	405	(2.3)	393	(1.9)	392	(1.2)	370	(2.0)	415	(1.8)	412	(1.1)	411	(1.7)	413	(1.7)
Qatar	318	(1.0)	311	(1.6)	325	(1.3)	312	(1.2)	280	(1.9)	346	(1.6)	349	(0.9)	334	(1.2)	365	(1.3)
Romania	415	(4.2)	418	(4.2)	412	(4.9)	396	(4.7)	374	(4.5)	418	(5.2)	418	(4.2)	417	(4.1)	419	(4.8)
Russian Federation	476	(3.9)	479	(4.6)	473	(3.9)	440	(4.3)	420	(4.8)	458	(4.3)	479	(3.7)	481	(4.1)	478	(3.7)
Serbia	435	(3.5)	438	(4.0)	433	(4.4)	401	(3.5)	381	(3.4)	422	(4.2)	436	(3.0)	433	(3.3)	438	(3.8)
Slovenia	504	(1.0)	507	(1.8)	502	(1.8)	494	(1.0)	467	(1.9)	521	(1.4)	519	(1.1)	515	(2.0)	523	(1.9)
Chinese Taipei	549	(4.1)	556	(4.7)	543	(5.9)	496	(3.4)	486	(4.4)	507	(4.2)	532	(3.6)	536	(4.3)	529	(5.1)
Thailand	417	(2.3)	413	(3.8)	420	(2.6)	417	(2.6)	386	(4.0)	440	(3.0)	421	(2.1)	411	(3.4)	428	(2.5)
Tunisia	365	(4.0)	373	(4.4)	358	(4.4)	380	(4.0)	361	(4.6)	398	(3.9)	386	(3.0)	383	(3.2)	388	(3.5)
Uruguay	427	(2.6)	433	(3.6)	420	(3.1)	413	(3.4)	389	(4.4)	435	(3.8)	428	(2.7)	427	(4.0)	430	(2.7)

—Not available.

†Not applicable.

[1]Illustrates how a country compares with the OECD area as a whole. Computed taking the OECD countries as a single entity, to which each country contributes in proportion to the number of 15-year-olds enrolled in its schools.

[2]Refers to the mean of the data values for all OECD countries, to which each country contributes equally, regardless of the absolute size of the student population of each country.

[3]PISA 2006 reading literacy results are not reported for the United States because of an error in printing the test booklets. In several areas of the reading literacy assessment, students were incorrectly instructed to refer to the passage on the "opposite page" when, in fact, the necessary passage appeared on the previous page. Because of the small number of items used in assessing reading literacy, it was not possible to recalibrate the score to exclude the affected items. Also, as a result of the printing error, the mean performance in mathematics and science may be misestimated by approximately 1 score point. The impact is below one standard error.

NOTE: PISA scores are reported on a scale from 0 to 1,000. Standard errors appear in parentheses.

SOURCE: Organization for Economic Cooperation and Development (OECD), Program for International Student Assessment (PISA), 2006, *PISA 2006: Science Competencies for Tomorrow's World.* (This table was prepared July 2008.)

Mean scores and percentage distribution of 15-year-old students scoring at each mathematics literacy proficiency level, by country: 2006

Country or other jurisdiction	Mean score		Percentage distribution at levels of proficiency[1]												
			Below level 1		Level 1		Level 2		Level 3		Level 4		Level 5		Level 6	
1		2		3		4		5		6		7		8		9
OECD total[2]	484	(1.2)	10.2	(0.35)	16.2	(0.31)	23.2	(0.40)	22.8	(0.40)	16.7	(0.29)	8.3	(0.21)	2.6	(0.10)
OECD average[3]	498	(0.5)	7.7	(0.14)	13.6	(0.15)	21.9	(0.17)	24.3	(0.16)	19.1	(0.16)	10.0	(0.12)	3.3	(0.09)
Australia	520	(2.2)	3.3	(0.28)	9.7	(0.41)	20.5	(0.62)	26.9	(0.57)	23.2	(0.54)	12.1	(0.48)	4.3	(0.47)
Austria	505	(3.7)	7.5	(0.95)	12.5	(1.09)	19.5	(1.06)	23.3	(0.90)	21.3	(1.12)	12.3	(0.79)	3.5	(0.50)
Belgium	520	(3.0)	7.1	(0.85)	10.2	(0.71)	17.0	(0.69)	21.4	(0.67)	21.9	(0.79)	16.0	(0.68)	6.4	(0.40)
Canada	527	(2.0)	2.8	(0.29)	8.0	(0.52)	18.6	(0.65)	27.5	(0.73)	25.1	(0.66)	13.6	(0.58)	4.4	(0.37)
Czech Republic	510	(3.6)	7.2	(0.72)	11.9	(0.84)	20.5	(0.99)	23.0	(0.92)	19.1	(1.06)	12.3	(0.75)	6.0	(0.67)
Denmark	513	(2.6)	3.6	(0.54)	10.0	(0.67)	21.4	(0.78)	28.8	(0.88)	22.5	(0.85)	10.9	(0.58)	2.8	(0.39)
Finland	548	(2.3)	1.1	(0.21)	4.8	(0.53)	14.4	(0.70)	27.2	(0.73)	28.1	(0.83)	18.1	(0.76)	6.3	(0.50)
France	496	(3.2)	8.4	(0.82)	13.9	(1.00)	21.4	(1.16)	24.2	(1.01)	19.6	(0.95)	9.9	(0.67)	2.6	(0.47)
Germany	504	(3.9)	7.3	(1.01)	12.5	(0.80)	21.2	(1.13)	24.0	(1.07)	19.4	(0.90)	11.0	(0.78)	4.5	(0.50)
Greece	459	(3.0)	13.3	(1.10)	19.0	(1.19)	26.8	(0.94)	23.2	(1.12)	12.6	(1.05)	4.2	(0.47)	0.9	(0.17)
Hungary	491	(2.9)	6.7	(0.56)	14.5	(0.80)	25.1	(1.01)	26.5	(0.94)	16.9	(1.07)	7.7	(0.72)	2.6	(0.47)
Iceland	506	(1.8)	5.1	(0.41)	11.7	(0.68)	22.3	(0.88)	26.6	(1.00)	21.7	(0.88)	10.1	(0.65)	2.5	(0.32)
Ireland	501	(2.8)	4.1	(0.50)	12.3	(0.93)	24.1	(1.00)	28.6	(0.90)	20.6	(0.94)	8.6	(0.67)	1.6	(0.25)
Italy	462	(2.3)	13.5	(0.72)	19.3	(0.69)	25.5	(0.75)	22.1	(0.67)	13.3	(0.56)	5.0	(0.36)	1.3	(0.27)
Japan	523	(3.3)	3.9	(0.59)	9.1	(0.71)	18.9	(0.89)	26.1	(1.00)	23.7	(1.03)	13.5	(0.79)	4.8	(0.51)
Korea, Republic of	547	(3.8)	2.3	(0.52)	6.5	(0.71)	15.2	(0.69)	23.5	(1.07)	25.5	(0.99)	18.0	(0.78)	9.1	(1.29)
Luxembourg	490	(1.1)	8.3	(0.55)	14.5	(0.67)	23.2	(0.72)	25.2	(0.83)	18.2	(1.02)	8.2	(0.54)	2.3	(0.28)
Mexico	406	(2.9)	28.4	(1.37)	28.1	(0.88)	25.2	(0.85)	13.1	(0.64)	4.3	(0.40)	0.8	(0.19)	0.1	(0.04)
Netherlands	531	(2.6)	2.4	(0.61)	9.1	(0.82)	18.9	(0.94)	24.3	(0.88)	24.1	(1.06)	15.8	(0.76)	5.4	(0.64)
New Zealand	522	(2.4)	4.0	(0.32)	10.0	(0.79)	19.5	(0.99)	25.5	(1.13)	22.1	(1.02)	13.2	(0.75)	5.7	(0.50)
Norway	490	(2.6)	7.3	(0.73)	14.9	(0.97)	24.3	(0.81)	25.6	(1.01)	17.4	(0.85)	8.3	(0.74)	2.1	(0.25)
Poland	495	(2.4)	5.7	(0.42)	14.2	(0.70)	24.7	(0.80)	26.2	(0.69)	18.6	(0.78)	8.6	(0.67)	2.0	(0.29)
Portugal	466	(3.1)	12.0	(1.05)	18.7	(0.87)	25.1	(0.90)	24.0	(0.92)	14.4	(0.81)	4.9	(0.45)	0.8	(0.20)
Slovak Republic	492	(2.8)	8.1	(0.72)	12.8	(0.86)	24.1	(1.03)	25.3	(0.97)	18.8	(0.87)	8.6	(0.69)	2.4	(0.41)
Spain	480	(2.3)	8.6	(0.52)	16.1	(0.85)	25.2	(0.94)	26.2	(0.61)	16.8	(0.54)	6.1	(0.43)	1.2	(0.18)
Sweden	502	(2.4)	5.4	(0.60)	12.9	(0.83)	23.0	(0.82)	26.0	(0.97)	20.1	(0.89)	9.7	(0.61)	2.9	(0.37)
Switzerland	530	(3.2)	4.6	(0.49)	9.0	(0.60)	17.4	(0.96)	23.2	(0.82)	23.2	(0.91)	15.9	(0.72)	6.8	(0.63)
Turkey	424	(4.9)	24.0	(1.37)	28.1	(1.35)	24.3	(1.25)	12.8	(0.80)	6.7	(0.95)	3.0	(0.77)	1.2	(0.55)
United Kingdom	495	(2.1)	5.9	(0.60)	13.8	(0.70)	24.7	(0.79)	26.3	(0.71)	18.1	(0.60)	8.7	(0.48)	2.5	(0.27)
United States[4]	474	(4.0)	9.9	(1.15)	18.2	(0.91)	26.1	(1.21)	23.1	(1.09)	15.1	(0.99)	6.4	(0.66)	1.3	(0.24)
Reporting partner countries															
Argentina	381	(6.2)	39.4	(2.72)	24.7	(1.46)	20.4	(1.66)	10.6	(1.05)	3.8	(0.56)	0.9	(0.31)	0.1	(0.11)
Azerbaijan	476	(2.3)	0.2	(0.10)	10.4	(0.99)	47.6	(1.64)	34.4	(1.59)	6.6	(0.86)	0.6	(0.26)	0.2	(0.13)
Brazil	370	(2.9)	46.6	(1.40)	25.9	(1.25)	16.6	(0.90)	7.1	(0.58)	2.8	(0.42)	0.8	(0.25)	0.2	(0.10)
Bulgaria	413	(6.1)	29.4	(2.18)	23.9	(1.12)	22.0	(1.04)	14.9	(1.08)	6.7	(0.82)	2.5	(0.57)	0.6	(0.28)
Chile	411	(4.6)	28.2	(1.94)	26.9	(1.20)	23.9	(1.14)	13.9	(1.03)	5.6	(0.71)	1.3	(0.34)	0.1	(0.07)
Colombia	370	(3.8)	44.6	(1.76)	27.3	(1.13)	18.2	(1.27)	7.6	(0.67)	1.9	(0.44)	0.4	(0.18)	#	(†)
Croatia	467	(2.4)	9.3	(0.69)	19.3	(0.92)	28.9	(1.06)	24.3	(0.86)	13.6	(0.67)	4.0	(0.47)	0.8	(0.21)
Estonia	515	(2.7)	2.7	(0.46)	9.4	(0.82)	21.9	(0.91)	30.2	(1.01)	23.3	(1.11)	10.0	(0.63)	2.6	(0.36)
Hong Kong-China	547	(2.7)	2.9	(0.45)	6.6	(0.63)	14.4	(0.84)	22.7	(1.07)	25.6	(0.90)	18.7	(0.78)	9.0	(0.82)
Indonesia	391	(5.6)	35.2	(2.21)	30.5	(1.58)	20.4	(0.99)	10.6	(2.04)	2.8	(0.74)	0.4	(0.16)	#	(†)
Israel	442	(4.3)	22.2	(1.54)	19.8	(1.01)	21.8	(1.03)	18.4	(0.93)	11.8	(0.76)	4.8	(0.54)	1.3	(0.24)
Jordan	384	(3.3)	36.9	(1.44)	29.4	(1.00)	21.9	(0.91)	9.3	(0.79)	2.2	(0.41)	0.2	(0.13)	#	(†)
Kyrgyzstan	311	(3.4)	72.9	(1.54)	16.5	(1.01)	7.1	(0.65)	2.8	(0.46)	0.7	(0.22)	#	(†)	#	(†)
Latvia	486	(3.0)	6.4	(0.62)	14.3	(0.92)	26.3	(0.90)	29.0	(0.96)	17.4	(1.05)	5.5	(0.49)	1.1	(0.28)
Liechtenstein	525	(4.2)	4.0	(1.10)	9.2	(1.98)	18.2	(2.97)	26.4	(3.78)	23.7	(2.92)	12.6	(2.05)	5.8	(1.21)
Lithuania	486	(2.9)	7.8	(0.64)	15.2	(0.77)	25.1	(0.97)	25.1	(1.06)	17.8	(0.83)	7.3	(0.84)	1.8	(0.37)
Macao-China	525	(1.3)	2.6	(0.26)	8.3	(0.63)	20.0	(0.92)	27.3	(0.89)	24.4	(0.76)	13.6	(0.56)	3.8	(0.41)
Montenegro	399	(1.4)	31.6	(0.85)	28.4	(0.80)	23.3	(0.85)	11.8	(0.62)	4.0	(0.38)	0.8	(0.18)	0.1	(0.07)
Qatar	318	(1.0)	71.7	(0.53)	15.5	(0.50)	7.5	(0.59)	3.3	(0.29)	1.4	(0.18)	0.5	(0.10)	0.1	(0.05)
Romania	415	(4.2)	24.7	(2.17)	28.0	(1.88)	26.5	(1.77)	14.1	(1.09)	5.4	(0.83)	1.1	(0.29)	0.1	(0.06)
Russian Federation	476	(3.9)	9.1	(0.94)	17.6	(1.15)	27.0	(1.42)	26.0	(0.93)	14.7	(1.02)	5.7	(0.63)	1.7	(0.30)
Serbia	435	(3.5)	19.6	(1.31)	23.0	(1.06)	26.8	(0.86)	18.7	(0.98)	9.1	(0.66)	2.4	(0.36)	0.4	(0.14)
Slovenia	504	(1.0)	4.6	(0.31)	13.1	(0.75)	23.5	(0.77)	26.0	(0.78)	19.2	(0.79)	10.3	(0.82)	3.4	(0.45)
Chinese Taipei	549	(4.1)	3.6	(0.58)	8.3	(0.73)	14.3	(0.86)	19.4	(0.70)	22.4	(0.84)	20.1	(0.89)	11.8	(0.83)
Thailand	417	(2.3)	23.3	(1.26)	29.7	(1.39)	26.4	(0.92)	14.0	(0.70)	5.3	(0.43)	1.1	(0.22)	0.2	(0.07)
Tunisia	365	(4.0)	48.5	(1.75)	24.0	(1.12)	16.5	(1.06)	8.1	(0.94)	2.4	(0.56)	0.5	(0.23)	#	(†)
Uruguay	427	(2.6)	24.4	(1.05)	21.7	(0.98)	24.3	(0.84)	18.3	(1.08)	8.2	(0.69)	2.6	(0.36)	0.6	(0.16)

†Not applicable.
#Rounds to zero.

[1]Level 1: Able to answer questions involving familiar contexts where all relevant information is present and the questions are clearly defined. Level 2: Able to interpret and recognize situations in contexts that require no more than direct inference, extract relevant information from a single source, and employ direct reasoning for literal interpretations of results. Level 3: Able to execute clearly described procedures, interpret and use representations based on different information sources, and develop short communications reporting their interpretations, results, and reasoning. Level 4: Able to work effectively with explicit models for complex concrete situations that may involve constraints or call for making assumptions, select and integrate different representations, reason with some insight, and construct and communicate explanations and arguments based on their interpretations and actions. Level 5: Able to develop and work with models for complex situations, work strategically using broad, well-developed thinking and reasoning skills, and communicate their interpretations and reasoning. Level 6: Able to conceptualize, generalize,

and utilize information, link different information sources and representations, and formulate and precisely communicate actions and reflections regarding findings and interpretations.
[2]Illustrates how a country compares with the OECD area as a whole. Computed by taking the OECD countries as a single entity to which each country contributes in proportion to the number of 15-year-olds enrolled in its schools.
[3]Refers to the mean of the data values for all OECD countries, to which each country contributes equally, regardless of the absolute size of the student population of each country.
[4]As a result of an error in printing the test booklets, the mean performance in mathematics may be misestimated by approximately 1 score point. The impact is below one standard error.
NOTE: PISA scores are reported on a scale from 0 to 1,000. Detail may not sum to totals because of rounding. Standard errors appear in parentheses.
SOURCE: Organization for Economic Cooperation and Development (OECD), Program for International Student Assessment (PISA), 2006, *PISA 2006: Science Competencies for Tomorrow's World*. (This table was prepared July 2008.)

Mean scores and percentage distribution of 15-year-old students scoring at each science literacy proficiency level, by country: 2006

Country or other jurisdiction	Mean score		Percentage distribution at levels of proficiency[1]												
			Below Level 1		Level 1		Level 2		Level 3		Level 4		Level 5		Level 6	
1		2		3		4		5		6		7		8		9
OECD total[2]	491	(1.2)	6.9	(0.28)	16.3	(0.30)	24.2	(0.35)	25.1	(0.27)	18.7	(0.30)	7.4	(0.18)	1.4	(0.08)
OECD average[3]	500	(0.5)	5.2	(0.11)	14.1	(0.15)	24.0	(0.17)	27.4	(0.17)	20.3	(0.16)	7.7	(0.10)	1.3	(0.04)
Australia	527	(2.3)	3.0	(0.25)	9.8	(0.46)	20.2	(0.63)	27.7	(0.51)	24.6	(0.53)	11.8	(0.53)	2.8	(0.26)
Austria	511	(3.9)	4.3	(0.88)	12.0	(0.98)	21.8	(1.05)	28.3	(1.05)	23.6	(1.12)	8.8	(0.69)	1.2	(0.20)
Belgium	510	(2.5)	4.8	(0.72)	12.2	(0.62)	20.8	(0.84)	27.6	(0.84)	24.5	(0.77)	9.1	(0.47)	1.0	(0.17)
Canada	534	(2.0)	2.2	(0.27)	7.8	(0.47)	19.1	(0.64)	28.8	(0.58)	27.7	(0.65)	12.0	(0.52)	2.4	(0.25)
Czech Republic	513	(3.5)	3.5	(0.57)	12.1	(0.84)	23.4	(1.17)	27.8	(1.09)	21.7	(0.92)	9.8	(0.86)	1.8	(0.32)
Denmark	496	(3.1)	4.3	(0.64)	14.1	(0.75)	26.0	(1.07)	29.3	(1.04)	19.5	(0.91)	6.1	(0.66)	0.7	(0.18)
Finland	563	(2.0)	0.5	(0.13)	3.6	(0.45)	13.6	(0.68)	29.1	(1.07)	32.2	(0.89)	17.0	(0.72)	3.9	(0.35)
France	495	(3.4)	6.6	(0.71)	14.5	(1.05)	22.8	(1.12)	27.2	(1.09)	20.9	(1.00)	7.2	(0.60)	0.8	(0.17)
Germany	516	(3.8)	4.1	(0.68)	11.3	(0.96)	21.4	(1.06)	27.9	(1.08)	23.6	(0.95)	10.0	(0.62)	1.8	(0.24)
Greece	473	(3.2)	7.2	(0.86)	16.9	(0.88)	28.9	(1.19)	29.4	(1.01)	14.2	(0.83)	3.2	(0.33)	0.2	(0.09)
Hungary	504	(2.7)	2.7	(0.33)	12.3	(0.83)	26.0	(1.15)	31.1	(1.07)	21.0	(0.87)	6.2	(0.57)	0.6	(0.16)
Iceland	491	(1.6)	5.8	(0.50)	14.7	(0.84)	25.9	(0.71)	28.3	(0.92)	19.0	(0.74)	5.6	(0.49)	0.7	(0.18)
Ireland	508	(3.2)	3.5	(0.47)	12.0	(0.82)	24.0	(0.91)	29.7	(0.98)	21.4	(0.87)	8.3	(0.62)	1.1	(0.19)
Italy	475	(2.0)	7.3	(0.46)	18.0	(0.62)	27.6	(0.78)	27.4	(0.61)	15.1	(0.58)	4.2	(0.31)	0.4	(0.09)
Japan	531	(3.4)	3.2	(0.45)	8.9	(0.73)	18.5	(0.86)	27.5	(0.85)	27.0	(1.14)	12.4	(0.63)	2.6	(0.33)
Korea, Republic of	522	(3.4)	2.5	(0.49)	8.7	(0.77)	21.2	(1.05)	31.8	(1.17)	25.5	(0.91)	9.2	(0.83)	1.1	(0.29)
Luxembourg	486	(1.1)	6.5	(0.39)	15.6	(0.65)	25.4	(0.66)	28.6	(0.93)	18.1	(0.71)	5.4	(0.34)	0.5	(0.11)
Mexico	410	(2.7)	18.2	(1.22)	32.8	(0.89)	30.8	(0.95)	14.8	(0.66)	3.2	(0.34)	0.3	(0.09)	#	(†)
Netherlands	525	(2.7)	2.3	(0.38)	10.7	(0.88)	21.1	(0.98)	26.9	(0.87)	25.8	(1.04)	11.5	(0.81)	1.7	(0.24)
New Zealand	530	(2.7)	4.0	(0.43)	9.7	(0.58)	19.7	(0.80)	25.1	(0.71)	23.9	(0.81)	13.6	(0.74)	4.0	(0.37)
Norway	487	(3.1)	5.9	(0.84)	15.2	(0.84)	27.3	(0.79)	28.5	(0.99)	17.1	(0.72)	5.5	(0.44)	0.6	(0.13)
Poland	498	(2.3)	3.2	(0.36)	13.8	(0.63)	27.5	(0.94)	29.4	(1.02)	19.3	(0.80)	6.1	(0.44)	0.7	(0.14)
Portugal	474	(3.0)	5.8	(0.76)	18.7	(1.05)	28.8	(0.92)	28.8	(1.22)	14.7	(0.88)	3.0	(0.35)	0.1	(0.05)
Slovak Republic	488	(2.6)	5.2	(0.60)	15.0	(0.87)	28.0	(0.96)	28.1	(0.99)	17.9	(1.02)	5.2	(0.49)	0.6	(0.14)
Spain	488	(2.6)	4.7	(0.44)	14.9	(0.69)	27.4	(0.77)	30.2	(0.68)	17.9	(0.75)	4.5	(0.38)	0.3	(0.10)
Sweden	503	(2.4)	3.8	(0.44)	12.6	(0.64)	25.2	(0.88)	29.5	(0.90)	21.1	(0.90)	6.8	(0.47)	1.1	(0.21)
Switzerland	512	(3.2)	4.5	(0.52)	11.6	(0.56)	21.8	(0.87)	28.2	(0.81)	23.5	(1.07)	9.1	(0.78)	1.4	(0.27)
Turkey	424	(3.8)	12.9	(0.83)	33.7	(1.31)	31.3	(1.42)	15.1	(1.06)	6.2	(1.15)	0.9	(0.32)	#	(†)
United Kingdom	515	(2.3)	4.8	(0.49)	11.9	(0.61)	21.8	(0.71)	25.9	(0.68)	21.8	(0.62)	10.9	(0.53)	2.9	(0.31)
United States[4]	489	(4.2)	7.6	(0.94)	16.8	(0.88)	24.2	(0.94)	24.0	(0.79)	18.3	(0.97)	7.5	(0.62)	1.5	(0.25)
Reporting partner countries																
Argentina	391	(6.1)	28.3	(2.34)	27.9	(1.39)	25.6	(1.27)	13.6	(1.29)	4.1	(0.63)	0.4	(0.14)	#	(†)
Azerbaijan	382	(2.8)	19.4	(1.50)	53.1	(1.57)	22.4	(1.41)	4.7	(0.86)	0.4	(0.15)	#	(†)	#	(†)
Brazil	390	(2.8)	27.9	(0.99)	33.1	(0.96)	23.8	(0.93)	11.3	(0.88)	3.4	(0.42)	0.5	(0.21)	#	(†)
Bulgaria	434	(6.1)	18.3	(1.72)	24.3	(1.32)	25.2	(1.23)	18.8	(1.14)	10.3	(1.13)	2.6	(0.51)	0.4	(0.18)
Chile	438	(4.3)	13.1	(1.12)	26.7	(1.54)	29.9	(1.18)	20.1	(1.44)	8.4	(1.01)	1.8	(0.32)	0.1	(0.06)
Colombia	388	(3.4)	26.2	(1.71)	34.0	(1.55)	27.2	(1.53)	10.6	(1.04)	1.9	(0.35)	0.2	(0.05)	#	(†)
Croatia	493	(2.4)	3.0	(0.43)	14.0	(0.71)	29.3	(0.91)	31.0	(0.99)	17.7	(0.86)	4.6	(0.44)	0.5	(0.12)
Estonia	531	(2.5)	1.0	(0.23)	6.7	(0.57)	21.0	(0.88)	33.7	(0.96)	26.2	(0.94)	10.1	(0.71)	1.4	(0.27)
Hong Kong-China	542	(2.5)	1.7	(0.36)	7.0	(0.68)	16.9	(0.81)	28.7	(0.95)	29.7	(0.95)	13.9	(0.80)	2.1	(0.30)
Indonesia	393	(5.7)	20.3	(1.71)	41.3	(2.23)	27.5	(1.46)	9.5	(1.99)	1.4	(0.53)	#	(†)	#	(†)
Israel	454	(3.7)	14.9	(1.18)	21.2	(1.01)	24.0	(0.95)	20.8	(0.96)	13.8	(0.80)	4.4	(0.49)	0.8	(0.18)
Jordan	422	(2.8)	16.2	(0.86)	28.2	(0.86)	30.8	(0.83)	18.7	(0.81)	5.6	(0.66)	0.6	(0.20)	#	(†)
Kyrgyzstan	322	(2.9)	58.2	(1.56)	28.2	(1.13)	10.0	(0.81)	2.9	(0.39)	0.7	(0.18)	#	(†)	#	(†)
Latvia	490	(3.0)	3.6	(0.49)	13.8	(0.98)	29.0	(1.19)	32.9	(0.95)	16.6	(0.96)	3.8	(0.39)	0.3	(0.09)
Liechtenstein	522	(4.1)	2.6	(0.99)	10.3	(2.11)	21.0	(2.84)	28.7	(2.58)	25.2	(2.54)	10.0	(1.77)	2.2	(0.84)
Lithuania	488	(2.8)	4.3	(0.44)	16.0	(0.83)	27.4	(0.91)	29.8	(0.85)	17.5	(0.85)	4.5	(0.60)	0.4	(0.15)
Macao-China	511	(1.1)	1.4	(0.24)	8.9	(0.50)	26.0	(0.97)	35.7	(1.14)	22.8	(0.73)	5.0	(0.34)	0.3	(0.09)
Montenegro	412	(1.1)	17.3	(0.79)	33.0	(1.20)	31.0	(0.91)	14.9	(0.65)	3.6	(0.37)	0.3	(0.11)	#	(†)
Qatar	349	(0.9)	47.6	(0.62)	31.5	(0.63)	13.9	(0.49)	5.0	(0.35)	1.6	(0.14)	0.3	(0.09)	#	(†)
Romania	418	(4.2)	16.0	(1.53)	30.9	(1.55)	31.8	(1.62)	16.6	(1.24)	4.2	(0.77)	0.5	(0.14)	#	(†)
Russian Federation	479	(3.7)	5.2	(0.65)	17.0	(1.08)	30.2	(0.93)	28.3	(1.32)	15.1	(1.09)	3.7	(0.46)	0.5	(0.13)
Serbia	436	(3.0)	11.9	(0.91)	26.6	(1.18)	32.3	(1.26)	21.8	(1.18)	6.6	(0.57)	0.8	(0.18)	#	(†)
Slovenia	519	(1.1)	2.8	(0.34)	11.1	(0.72)	23.1	(0.68)	27.6	(1.08)	22.5	(1.13)	10.7	(0.57)	2.2	(0.29)
Chinese Taipei	532	(3.6)	1.9	(0.29)	9.7	(0.82)	18.6	(0.86)	27.3	(0.80)	27.9	(1.03)	12.9	(0.77)	1.7	(0.24)
Thailand	421	(2.1)	12.6	(0.80)	33.5	(1.03)	33.2	(0.88)	16.3	(0.80)	4.0	(0.42)	0.4	(0.12)	#	(†)
Tunisia	386	(3.0)	27.7	(1.12)	35.1	(0.94)	25.0	(0.97)	10.2	(0.98)	1.9	(0.45)	0.1	(0.06)	#	(†)
Uruguay	428	(2.7)	16.7	(1.25)	25.4	(1.09)	29.8	(1.50)	19.7	(1.07)	6.9	(0.54)	1.3	(0.21)	0.1	(0.07)

†Not applicable.
#Rounds to zero.

[1]Level 1: Able to present scientific explanations that are obvious and that follow explicitly from given evidence. Level 2: Able to provide possible explanations in familiar contexts, draw conclusions based on simple investigations, and make literal interpretations of the results of scientific inquiry or technological problem solving. Level 3: Able to select facts to explain phenomena and apply simple models or inquiry strategies, develop short statements using facts, and make decisions based on scientific knowledge. Level 4: Able to select and integrate explanations from different disciplines of science or technology, link those explanations directly to aspects of life situations, and communicate decisions using scientific knowledge and evidence. Level 5: Able to apply scientific concepts and knowledge to many complex life situations, select and evaluate appropriate scientific evidence, bring critical insights to situations, and construct explanations based on evidence and arguments based on critical analysis. Level 6: Able to consistently explain and apply scientific knowledge in a variety of complex life situations, use evidence from different sources to justify decisions, clearly and consistently demonstrate advanced scientific thinking and reasoning, and develop arguments in support of recommendations and decisions that center on personal, social, or global situations.

[2]Illustrates how a country compares with the OECD area as a whole. Computed by taking the OECD countries as a single entity to which each country contributes in proportion to the number of 15-year-olds enrolled in its schools.

[3]Refers to the mean of the data values for all OECD countries, to which each country contributes equally, regardless of the absolute size of the student population of each country.

[4]As a result of an error in printing the test booklets, the mean performance in science may be misestimated by approximately 1 score point. The impact is below one standard error.

NOTE: PISA scores are reported on a scale from 0 to 1,000. Detail may not sum to totals because of rounding. Standard errors appear in parentheses.

SOURCE: Organization for Economic Cooperation and Development (OECD), Program for International Student Assessment (PISA), 2006, *PISA 2006: Science Competencies for Tomorrow's World*. (This table was prepared July 2008.)

Average fourth-grade mathematics scores, by content and cognitive domain, index of time spent doing mathematics homework, and country: 2007

Country or other jurisdiction	Mathematics overall	Content domain[1]: Number	Content domain[1]: Geometric shapes and measures	Content domain[1]: Data display	Cognitive domain[2]: Knowing	Cognitive domain[2]: Applying	Cognitive domain[2]: Reasoning	High TMH: Percent of students	High TMH: Average score	Medium TMH: Percent of students	Medium TMH: Average score	Low TMH: Percent of students	Low TMH: Average score
1	2	3	4	5	6	7	8	9	10	11	12	13	14
International average	— (†)	— (†)	— (†)	— (†)	— (†)	— (†)	— (†)	21 (0.2)	469 (1.0)	58 (0.2)	479 (0.7)	21 (0.2)	468 (1.5)
Algeria[4]	378 (5.2)	391 (5.0)	383 (4.5)	361 (5.2)	384 (5.4)	376 (5.2)	387 (4.7)	35 (1.7)	397 (6.6)	54 (1.5)	385 (6.0)	11 (1.0)	373 (9.1)
Armenia[4]	500 (4.3)	522 (4.0)	483 (4.7)	458 (4.3)	518 (4.8)	493 (4.1)	489 (4.7)	31 (1.5)	510 (5.3)	64 (1.4)	503 (3.7)	5 (0.7)	509 (24.8)
Australia	516 (3.5)	496 (3.7)	536 (3.1)	534 (3.1)	509 (4.2)	523 (3.5)	516 (3.4)	7 (0.8)	508 (10.6)	42 (1.5)	517 (3.9)	51 (1.8)	525 (4.4)
Austria	505 (2.0)	502 (2.2)	509 (2.4)	508 (2.6)	505 (2.0)	507 (1.8)	506 (2.1)	16 (0.8)	493 (3.9)	76 (1.0)	511 (2.1)	8 (0.8)	501 (5.0)
Chinese Taipei	576 (1.7)	581 (1.9)	556 (2.2)	567 (2.0)	584 (1.7)	569 (1.7)	566 (1.9)	17 (0.9)	568 (4.0)	63 (1.4)	584 (1.7)	20 (1.3)	569 (3.8)
Colombia[4]	355 (5.0)	360 (4.3)	361 (4.8)	363 (5.9)	360 (5.2)	357 (5.1)	372 (4.9)	29 (1.5)	384 (5.5)	58 (1.4)	369 (4.8)	13 (1.4)	354 (6.9)
Czech Republic	486 (2.8)	482 (2.8)	494 (2.8)	493 (3.3)	473 (2.4)	496 (2.7)	493 (3.4)	8 (0.6)	473 (4.7)	65 (2.0)	489 (2.9)	28 (1.9)	491 (4.6)
Denmark[4]	523 (2.4)	509 (2.9)	544 (2.6)	529 (3.4)	513 (2.7)	528 (2.5)	524 (2.1)	23 (1.2)	514 (3.3)	52 (1.2)	524 (2.7)	25 (1.4)	538 (3.8)
El Salvador[4]	330 (4.1)	317 (3.9)	333 (4.3)	367 (3.5)	312 (4.1)	339 (3.7)	356 (4.0)	24 (1.2)	345 (6.3)	62 (1.2)	340 (4.6)	14 (1.1)	346 (6.5)
England	541 (2.9)	531 (3.2)	548 (2.7)	547 (2.5)	544 (3.6)	540 (3.1)	537 (3.1)	3 (0.4)	525 (11.2)	31 (1.6)	547 (5.0)	66 (1.6)	544 (2.9)
Georgia[4,6]	438 (4.2)	464 (3.8)	415 (4.8)	414 (4.6)	450 (4.0)	433 (4.5)	437 (4.2)	27 (1.5)	451 (5.6)	71 (1.5)	449 (4.4)	2 (0.4)	‡ (†)
Germany[4]	525 (2.3)	521 (2.3)	528 (2.0)	534 (3.1)	514 (2.0)	531 (2.2)	528 (2.5)	19 (0.8)	517 (5.3)	76 (0.9)	534 (3.5)	5 (0.6)	496 (10.0)
Hong Kong SAR[7]	607 (3.6)	606 (3.7)	599 (3.1)	585 (2.7)	617 (3.5)	599 (3.4)	589 (3.5)	18 (1.1)	599 (6.2)	78 (1.1)	613 (3.5)	4 (0.5)	562 (6.2)
Hungary	510 (3.5)	510 (3.8)	510 (3.3)	504 (3.5)	511 (3.4)	507 (3.5)	509 (3.8)	21 (1.0)	517 (4.3)	75 (1.1)	518 (3.8)	4 (0.7)	493 (16.6)
Iran, Islamic Republic of	402 (4.1)	398 (3.6)	429 (3.3)	400 (4.0)	410 (3.6)	405 (3.7)	410 (3.8)	34 (1.7)	424 (5.8)	51 (1.6)	401 (4.5)	15 (1.4)	386 (6.9)
Italy	507 (3.1)	505 (3.2)	509 (3.0)	506 (3.4)	514 (3.2)	501 (2.9)	509 (3.1)	18 (1.3)	498 (4.7)	62 (1.6)	508 (3.8)	19 (1.8)	515 (3.9)
Japan	568 (2.1)	561 (2.2)	566 (2.2)	578 (2.8)	565 (2.1)	566 (2.0)	563 (2.1)	11 (0.9)	542 (4.6)	64 (1.9)	573 (2.4)	25 (1.9)	572 (3.5)
Kazakhstan[8]	549 (7.1)	556 (6.6)	542 (7.4)	522 (5.8)	559 (7.3)	547 (7.2)	539 (6.1)	42 (2.0)	549 (9.3)	56 (1.9)	552 (7.3)	2 (0.3)	‡ (†)
Kuwait[4,8]	316 (3.6)	321 (3.5)	316 (3.6)	318 (4.7)	326 (4.6)	305 (4.1)	— (†)	17 (0.9)	313 (6.4)	63 (1.7)	336 (3.8)	20 (1.4)	350 (6.9)
Latvia[6]	537 (2.3)	536 (2.1)	532 (2.6)	536 (3.0)	530 (2.2)	540 (2.5)	537 (2.5)	34 (1.3)	534 (3.2)	65 (1.3)	545 (2.6)	1 (0.2)	‡ (†)
Lithuania[6]	530 (2.4)	533 (2.3)	518 (2.4)	530 (2.9)	520 (2.8)	539 (2.4)	526 (2.5)	29 (1.3)	526 (3.5)	68 (1.3)	537 (2.5)	3 (0.5)	530 (10.7)
Morocco[10]	341 (4.7)	353 (4.7)	365 (4.3)	316 (6.1)	354 (4.8)	346 (4.7)	— (†)	24 (1.6)	360 (9.1)	61 (1.9)	352 (5.3)	16 (1.7)	350 (12.7)
Netherlands[9]	535 (2.1)	535 (2.1)	522 (2.3)	543 (2.6)	525 (2.2)	540 (2.0)	534 (2.4)	1 (0.2)	‡ (†)	10 (0.9)	507 (5.3)	89 (0.9)	541 (2.3)
New Zealand	492 (2.3)	478 (2.7)	502 (2.3)	513 (2.6)	482 (2.5)	495 (2.3)	503 (2.8)	8 (0.5)	469 (5.3)	38 (1.1)	487 (3.7)	54 (1.4)	509 (2.4)
Norway	473 (2.5)	461 (2.8)	490 (3.0)	487 (2.6)	461 (2.9)	479 (2.8)	489 (2.7)	12 (1.0)	465 (7.4)	53 (1.8)	478 (2.9)	35 (2.1)	487 (3.4)
Qatar[10]	296 (1.0)	292 (1.2)	296 (1.4)	326 (1.6)	293 (1.3)	296 (1.2)	— (†)	20 (0.6)	301 (3.1)	61 (0.7)	315 (2.3)	19 (0.5)	311 (3.3)
Russian Federation	544 (4.9)	546 (4.4)	538 (5.1)	530 (4.9)	538 (4.5)	547 (4.8)	540 (4.8)	37 (1.4)	541 (5.7)	61 (1.3)	550 (5.0)	1 (0.3)	‡ (†)
Scotland[5]	494 (2.2)	481 (2.6)	503 (2.6)	516 (2.2)	489 (2.6)	500 (2.4)	497 (2.2)	3 (0.3)	453 (10.7)	30 (1.7)	484 (3.1)	67 (1.8)	505 (2.9)
Singapore	599 (3.7)	611 (4.3)	570 (3.7)	583 (3.2)	620 (4.0)	590 (3.7)	578 (3.8)	34 (0.9)	607 (4.4)	52 (0.9)	603 (3.1)	15 (0.8)	581 (5.6)
Slovak Republic	496 (4.5)	495 (3.9)	499 (4.3)	492 (4.2)	492 (3.9)	498 (4.0)	499 (4.0)	10 (0.6)	481 (4.0)	79 (1.2)	508 (3.2)	11 (1.0)	496 (9.1)
Slovenia	502 (1.8)	485 (1.9)	522 (1.8)	518 (2.5)	497 (1.8)	504 (1.9)	505 (2.1)	19 (0.9)	487 (3.2)	79 (1.0)	510 (2.1)	3 (0.3)	479 (9.0)
Sweden	503 (2.5)	490 (2.5)	508 (2.3)	529 (2.7)	482 (2.5)	508 (2.2)	519 (2.5)	5 (0.6)	472 (6.4)	34 (1.2)	493 (2.9)	60 (1.4)	513 (3.0)
Tunisia[4]	327 (4.5)	352 (4.5)	307 (4.5)	307 (4.8)	343 (4.9)	329 (4.8)	— (†)	33 (1.7)	362 (5.5)	53 (1.4)	352 (4.8)	14 (1.2)	342 (7.7)
Ukraine[4]	469 (2.9)	480 (2.9)	457 (2.8)	462 (3.2)	472 (3.0)	466 (3.1)	474 (3.2)	37 (1.3)	475 (3.3)	61 (1.3)	475 (3.4)	2 (0.?)	‡ (†)
United States[5,11]	529 (2.4)	524 (2.7)	522 (2.5)	543 (2.4)	541 (2.6)	524 (2.6)	523 (2.2)	12 (0.5)	522 (3.6)	65 (1.2)	535 (2.8)	23 (1.3)	528 (3.2)
Yemen	224 (6.0)	— (†)	— (†)	— (†)	— (†)	— (†)	— (†)	30 (2.4)	243 (9.7)	64 (2.5)	245 (6.6)	6 (1.0)	218 (11.8)

—Not available.

†Not applicable.

‡Reporting standards not met.

[1] *Number* includes whole numbers, fractions and decimals, number sentences, and patterns and relationships. *Geometric shapes and measures* includes lines and angles, two- and three-dimensional shapes, and location and movement. *Data display* includes reading and interpreting, and organizing and representing.

[2] *Knowing* addresses the facts, procedures, and concepts that students need to know to function mathematically. *Applying* focuses on students' ability to apply knowledge and conceptual understanding in order to solve problems or answer questions. *Reasoning* goes beyond the cognitive processes involved in solving routine problems to include unfamiliar situations, complex contexts, and multistep problems.

[3] *High TMH* indicates more than 30 minutes of mathematics homework assigned 3–4 times per week. *Medium TMH* includes all possible combinations of responses not included in the high or low categories. *Low TMH* indicates no more than 30 minutes of mathematics homework assigned no more than 2 times per week. TMH index data are provided by students.

[4] For the TMH index, data are available for for at least 70 percent but less than 85 percent of the students.

[5] Met guidelines for sample participation rates only after substitute schools were included.

[6] National Target Population does not include all of the International Target Population defined by the Trends in International Mathematics and Science Study (TIMSS).

[7] Hong Kong is a Special Administrative Region (SAR) of the People's Republic of China.

[8] Kuwait tested the same cohort of students as other countries, but later in 2007, at the beginning of the next school year.

[9] Nearly satisfied guidelines for sample participation rates only after substitute schools were included.

[10] For the TMH index, data are available for at least 50 percent but less than 70 percent of the students.

[11] National Defined Population covers 90 to 95 percent of National Target Population.

NOTE: TIMSS scores are reported on a scale from 0 to 1,000, with the scale average fixed at 500 and the standard deviation fixed at 100. Countries were required to sample students in the grade that corresponded to the end of 4 years of formal schooling, providing that the mean age at the time of testing was at least 9.5 years. Detail may not sum to totals because of rounding. Standard errors appear in parentheses.

SOURCE: International Association for the Evaluation of Educational Achievement (IEA), Trends in International Mathematics and Science Study (TIMSS), 2007, *TIMSS 2007 International Mathematics Report*, by Ina V.S. Mullis et al. (This table was prepared May 2009.)

International Comparisons of Education

Average eighth-grade mathematics scores overall and in content and cognitive domains, by country: 2007

Country or other jurisdiction	Mathematics overall		Content domain[1] Number		Algebra		Geometry		Data and chance		Cognitive domain[2] Knowing		Applying		Reasoning	
1	2		3		4		5		6		7		8		9	
Algeria	387	(2.1)	403	(1.7)	349	(2.4)	432	(2.1)	371	(1.7)	371	(1.9)	412	(2.0)	—	(†)
Armenia	499	(3.5)	492	(3.1)	532	(2.5)	493	(4.1)	427	(3.9)	507	(3.1)	493	(3.8)	489	(3.8)
Australia	496	(3.9)	503	(3.7)	471	(3.7)	487	(3.6)	525	(3.2)	487	(3.3)	500	(3.4)	502	(3.3)
Bahrain	398	(1.6)	388	(2.0)	403	(1.8)	412	(2.1)	418	(2.1)	395	(1.7)	403	(1.9)	413	(2.1)
Bosnia and Herzegovina	456	(2.7)	451	(3.0)	475	(3.2)	451	(3.5)	437	(2.3)	478	(2.9)	440	(2.6)	452	(2.9)
Botswana	364	(2.3)	366	(2.9)	394	(2.2)	325	(3.2)	384	(2.6)	376	(2.1)	351	(2.6)	—	(†)
Bulgaria	464	(5.0)	458	(4.7)	476	(5.1)	468	(5.0)	440	(4.7)	477	(4.7)	458	(4.8)	455	(4.7)
Chinese Taipei	598	(4.5)	577	(4.2)	617	(5.4)	592	(4.6)	566	(3.6)	594	(4.5)	592	(4.2)	591	(4.1)
Colombia	380	(3.6)	369	(3.5)	390	(3.1)	371	(3.3)	405	(3.8)	364	(3.4)	384	(3.7)	416	(3.3)
Cyprus	465	(1.6)	464	(1.6)	468	(2.0)	458	(2.7)	464	(1.6)	468	(1.6)	465	(1.8)	461	(2.1)
Czech Republic	504	(2.4)	511	(2.5)	484	(2.4)	498	(2.7)	512	(2.8)	502	(2.5)	504	(2.7)	500	(2.6)
Egypt	391	(3.6)	393	(3.1)	409	(3.3)	406	(3.4)	384	(3.1)	392	(3.6)	393	(3.6)	396	(3.4)
El Salvador	340	(2.8)	355	(3.0)	331	(3.7)	318	(3.7)	362	(3.0)	336	(3.1)	347	(3.3)	—	(†)
England[3]	513	(4.8)	510	(5.0)	492	(4.6)	510	(4.4)	547	(5.0)	503	(4.0)	514	(4.9)	518	(4.3)
Georgia[4]	410	(5.9)	421	(5.6)	421	(6.6)	409	(6.7)	373	(4.3)	427	(5.8)	401	(5.5)	389	(5.8)
Ghana	309	(4.4)	310	(3.9)	358	(3.6)	275	(4.9)	321	(3.6)	313	(4.6)	297	(4.2)	—	(†)
Hong Kong SAR[3,5]	572	(5.8)	567	(5.6)	565	(5.6)	570	(5.5)	549	(4.7)	574	(5.4)	569	(5.9)	557	(5.6)
Hungary	517	(3.5)	517	(3.6)	503	(3.6)	508	(3.6)	524	(3.3)	518	(3.3)	513	(3.1)	513	(3.2)
Indonesia	397	(3.8)	399	(3.7)	405	(3.5)	395	(4.5)	402	(3.6)	397	(4.0)	398	(3.7)	405	(3.3)
Iran, Islamic Republic of	403	(4.1)	395	(3.9)	408	(3.9)	423	(4.4)	415	(3.5)	403	(4.1)	402	(4.2)	427	(3.5)
Israel[6]	463	(3.9)	469	(3.2)	470	(3.9)	436	(4.3)	465	(4.4)	473	(3.7)	456	(4.1)	462	(4.1)
Italy	480	(3.0)	478	(2.8)	460	(3.2)	490	(3.1)	491	(3.1)	476	(3.0)	483	(2.9)	483	(2.8)
Japan	570	(2.4)	551	(2.3)	559	(2.5)	573	(2.2)	573	(2.2)	560	(2.2)	565	(2.2)	568	(2.4)
Jordan	427	(4.1)	416	(4.3)	448	(4.1)	436	(3.9)	425	(3.8)	432	(4.2)	422	(4.1)	440	(3.6)
Korea, Republic of	597	(2.7)	583	(2.4)	596	(3.0)	587	(2.3)	580	(2.0)	596	(2.5)	595	(2.8)	579	(2.3)
Kuwait[7]	354	(2.3)	347	(3.1)	354	(3.0)	385	(2.8)	366	(3.5)	347	(3.1)	361	(2.7)	—	(†)
Lebanon	449	(4.0)	454	(3.4)	465	(3.2)	462	(4.0)	407	(4.4)	464	(3.9)	448	(4.6)	429	(4.0)
Lithuania[4]	506	(2.3)	506	(2.7)	483	(2.7)	507	(2.6)	523	(2.3)	508	(2.5)	511	(2.4)	486	(2.5)
Malaysia	474	(5.0)	491	(5.1)	454	(4.3)	477	(5.6)	469	(4.1)	477	(4.8)	478	(4.9)	468	(3.8)
Malta	488	(1.2)	496	(1.3)	473	(1.4)	495	(1.1)	487	(1.4)	490	(1.6)	492	(1.0)	475	(1.3)
Norway	469	(2.0)	488	(2.0)	425	(2.8)	459	(2.3)	505	(2.5)	458	(1.8)	477	(2.2)	475	(2.3)
Oman	372	(3.4)	363	(2.7)	391	(3.2)	387	(3.0)	389	(3.0)	372	(3.5)	368	(3.0)	397	(3.3)
Palestinian National Authority	367	(3.5)	366	(3.2)	382	(3.4)	388	(3.8)	371	(2.9)	365	(3.8)	371	(3.4)	381	(3.5)
Qatar	307	(1.4)	334	(1.6)	312	(1.5)	301	(1.8)	305	(1.6)	307	(1.4)	305	(1.4)	—	(†)
Romania	461	(4.1)	457	(3.5)	478	(4.6)	466	(4.0)	429	(3.7)	470	(4.2)	462	(4.0)	449	(4.6)
Russian Federation	512	(4.1)	507	(3.8)	518	(4.5)	510	(4.1)	487	(3.8)	521	(3.9)	510	(3.7)	497	(3.6)
Saudi Arabia	329	(2.9)	309	(3.3)	344	(2.8)	359	(2.6)	348	(2.2)	308	(2.6)	335	(2.3)	—	(†)
Scotland[3]	487	(3.7)	489	(3.7)	467	(3.7)	485	(3.9)	517	(3.5)	481	(3.3)	489	(3.7)	495	(3.3)
Serbia[4,8]	486	(3.3)	478	(2.9)	500	(3.2)	486	(3.6)	458	(3.0)	500	(3.2)	478	(3.3)	474	(3.3)
Singapore	593	(3.8)	597	(3.5)	579	(3.7)	578	(3.4)	574	(3.9)	581	(3.4)	593	(3.6)	579	(4.1)
Slovenia	501	(2.1)	502	(2.3)	488	(2.4)	499	(2.4)	511	(2.3)	500	(2.2)	503	(2.0)	496	(2.5)
Sweden	491	(2.3)	507	(1.8)	456	(2.4)	472	(2.5)	526	(3.0)	478	(2.0)	497	(2.0)	490	(2.6)
Syrian Arab Republic	395	(3.8)	393	(3.4)	406	(3.7)	417	(3.4)	387	(2.7)	393	(4.2)	401	(3.4)	396	(3.4)
Thailand	441	(5.0)	444	(4.8)	433	(5.0)	442	(5.3)	453	(4.1)	436	(4.8)	446	(4.7)	456	(4.4)
Tunisia	420	(2.4)	425	(2.6)	423	(2.6)	437	(2.6)	411	(2.3)	421	(2.6)	423	(2.4)	425	(2.3)
Turkey	432	(4.8)	429	(4.0)	440	(5.1)	411	(5.1)	445	(4.4)	439	(4.8)	425	(4.5)	441	(4.2)
Ukraine	462	(3.6)	460	(3.7)	464	(3.9)	467	(3.6)	458	(3.5)	471	(3.5)	464	(3.5)	445	(3.8)
United States[3,8]	508	(2.8)	510	(2.7)	501	(2.7)	480	(2.5)	531	(2.8)	514	(2.6)	503	(2.9)	505	(2.4)

—Not available.

†Not applicable.

[1] *Number* includes whole numbers; fractions and decimals; integers; and ratio, proportion, and percent. *Algebra* includes patterns; algebraic expressions; and equations/formulas and functions. *Geometry* includes geometric shapes; geometric measurement; and location and movement. *Data and chance* includes data organization and representation; data interpretation; and chance.

[2] *Knowing* addresses the facts, procedures, and concepts that students need to know to function mathematically. *Applying* focuses on students' ability to apply knowledge and conceptual understanding in order to solve problems or answer questions. *Reasoning* goes beyond the cognitive processes involved in solving routine problems to include unfamiliar situations, complex contexts, and multistep problems.

[3] Met guidelines for sample participation rates only after substitute schools were included.

[4] National Target Population does not include all of the International Target Population defined by the Trends in International Mathematics and Science Study (TIMSS).

[5] Hong Kong is a Special Administrative Region (SAR) of the People's Republic of China.

[6] National Defined Population covers less than 90 percent of National Target Population (but at least 77 percent).

[7] Kuwait tested the same cohort of students as other countries, but later in 2007, at the beginning of the next school year.

[8] National Defined Population covers 90 to 95 percent of National Target Population.

NOTE: TIMSS scores are reported on a scale from 0 to 1,000, with the scale average fixed at 500 and the standard deviation fixed at 100. Countries were required to sample students in the grade that corresponded to the end of 8 years of formal schooling, providing that the mean age at the time of testing was at least 13.5 years. Standard errors appear in parentheses.

SOURCE: International Association for the Evaluation of Educational Achievement (IEA), Trends in International Mathematics and Science Study (TIMSS), 2007, *TIMSS 2007 International Mathematics Report*, by Ina V.S. Mullis et al. (This table was prepared April 2009.)

Percentage distribution of mathematics lesson time spent by eighth-grade students on various activities in a typical week, by country: 2007

Country or other jurisdiction	Reviewing homework		Listening to lecture-style presentations		Working problems with teacher's guidance		Working problems on their own without teacher's guidance		Listening to teacher re-teach and clarify content/ procedures		Taking tests or quizzes		Participating in classroom management tasks not related to the lesson's content/purpose		Other student activities	
1	2		3		4		5		6		7		8		9	
International average	11	(0.1)	20	(0.1)	21	(0.1)	16	(0.1)	12	(0.1)	10	(0.1)	5	(0.1)	5	(0.1)
Algeria[1]	11	(0.6)	15	(1.2)	21	(1.2)	15	(1.0)	18	(1.0)	10	(0.8)	5	(0.4)	5	(0.6)
Armenia	10	(0.4)	23	(0.9)	19	(0.6)	16	(0.6)	11	(0.4)	10	(0.4)	5	(0.3)	5	(0.7)
Australia	7	(0.3)	17	(0.8)	23	(1.0)	24	(1.2)	10	(0.5)	7	(0.3)	8	(0.5)	4	(0.4)
Bahrain[2]	11	(0.3)	23	(0.6)	18	(0.7)	12	(0.3)	15	(0.8)	11	(0.3)	6	(0.2)	6	(0.3)
Bosnia and Herzegovina[2]	7	(0.4)	29	(1.5)	24	(1.0)	15	(0.7)	11	(0.6)	7	(0.5)	3	(0.3)	4	(0.5)
Botswana[2]	13	(0.9)	13	(0.8)	20	(1.0)	21	(1.2)	10	(0.6)	10	(0.8)	6	(0.4)	6	(0.7)
Bulgaria	8	(0.4)	19	(1.1)	26	(1.0)	17	(0.7)	9	(0.4)	14	(0.6)	3	(0.3)	3	(0.3)
Chinese Taipei	13	(0.6)	41	(1.3)	13	(0.6)	7	(0.4)	10	(0.7)	8	(0.3)	5	(0.5)	3	(0.3)
Colombia	10	(0.3)	17	(0.9)	21	(0.8)	17	(0.7)	12	(0.7)	12	(0.5)	6	(0.4)	5	(0.5)
Cyprus[2]	20	(0.6)	17	(0.6)	23	(0.6)	12	(0.4)	10	(0.3)	9	(0.2)	7	(0.2)	4	(0.3)
Czech Republic	6	(0.3)	20	(0.6)	25	(0.8)	21	(0.7)	9	(0.3)	11	(0.4)	4	(0.3)	4	(0.3)
Egypt[2]	10	(0.4)	25	(1.2)	17	(0.7)	14	(0.8)	11	(0.5)	9	(0.4)	6	(0.4)	7	(0.4)
El Salvador	10	(0.5)	13	(0.8)	22	(0.8)	20	(0.8)	14	(0.6)	10	(0.5)	6	(0.4)	5	(0.3)
England[3]	6	(0.3)	17	(0.6)	28	(1.2)	23	(1.2)	11	(0.7)	4	(0.3)	7	(0.5)	4	(0.5)
Georgia[4]	11	(0.5)	21	(1.0)	19	(0.6)	15	(0.7)	11	(0.4)	12	(0.5)	5	(0.4)	6	(0.4)
Ghana[2]	12	(0.6)	16	(1.0)	18	(0.7)	15	(0.7)	11	(0.6)	15	(0.7)	8	(0.5)	6	(0.4)
Hong Kong SAR[3,5]	11	(0.7)	35	(1.6)	16	(0.9)	13	(0.8)	10	(0.4)	8	(0.4)	4	(0.4)	3	(0.4)
Hungary	11	(0.4)	12	(0.7)	27	(0.9)	22	(0.8)	9	(0.5)	11	(0.3)	4	(0.3)	4	(0.4)
Indonesia[1]	11	(0.5)	20	(1.0)	19	(0.9)	15	(0.8)	11	(0.6)	14	(0.7)	6	(0.3)	6	(0.5)
Iran, Islamic Republic of	11	(0.5)	16	(0.8)	19	(0.8)	14	(0.7)	16	(0.8)	11	(0.5)	7	(0.5)	7	(0.4)
Israel[1,6]	14	(0.5)	16	(1.0)	22	(0.7)	19	(0.8)	11	(0.4)	10	(0.6)	5	(0.3)	3	(0.5)
Italy	16	(0.6)	22	(0.6)	18	(0.6)	12	(0.4)	14	(0.5)	11	(0.5)	5	(0.3)	3	(0.3)
Japan	7	(0.4)	30	(0.8)	26	(0.9)	12	(0.9)	14	(0.5)	7	(0.4)	2	(0.3)	2	(0.4)
Jordan	12	(0.4)	19	(0.7)	18	(0.6)	15	(0.4)	14	(0.5)	11	(0.4)	6	(0.3)	6	(0.3)
Korea, Republic of	6	(0.2)	33	(1.1)	18	(0.6)	17	(0.6)	11	(0.5)	7	(0.4)	5	(0.3)	4	(0.3)
Kuwait[1,7]	11	(0.6)	21	(1.6)	18	(0.9)	14	(0.8)	16	(1.1)	9	(0.6)	7	(0.6)	5	(0.5)
Lebanon[1]	22	(1.2)	16	(1.0)	20	(1.2)	10	(1.0)	12	(0.6)	11	(0.5)	5	(0.5)	4	(0.4)
Lithuania[4]	9	(0.3)	9	(0.6)	26	(0.8)	25	(0.8)	11	(0.4)	14	(0.7)	3	(0.2)	3	(0.3)
Malaysia[2]	13	(0.8)	22	(1.3)	18	(0.8)	13	(0.7)	12	(0.6)	9	(0.4)	7	(0.5)	5	(0.4)
Malta	18	(#)	19	(#)	20	(#)	15	(#)	12	(#)	5	(#)	8	(#)	3	(#)
Norway	8	(0.4)	22	(0.7)	22	(0.9)	25	(1.0)	11	(0.4)	6	(0.2)	4	(0.3)	3	(0.3)
Oman[2]	11	(0.5)	18	(1.1)	20	(0.8)	14	(0.6)	15	(0.9)	11	(0.6)	6	(0.3)	6	(0.4)
Palestinian National Authority[2]	13	(0.7)	20	(0.9)	18	(0.7)	14	(0.8)	13	(0.6)	9	(0.5)	6	(0.4)	6	(0.5)
Qatar[2]	11	(#)	21	(#)	20	(#)	13	(#)	14	(#)	10	(#)	6	(#)	6	(#)
Romania	9	(0.4)	18	(0.8)	29	(0.8)	14	(0.5)	9	(0.3)	14	(0.7)	3	(0.2)	3	(0.3)
Russian Federation	10	(0.2)	18	(0.5)	22	(0.6)	20	(0.5)	9	(0.2)	16	(0.4)	1	(0.1)	4	(0.4)
Saudi Arabia[2]	12	(0.5)	22	(1.2)	17	(0.9)	11	(0.5)	15	(0.9)	10	(0.5)	7	(0.4)	7	(0.4)
Scotland[3]	8	(0.4)	21	(0.6)	25	(1.2)	24	(1.1)	8	(0.3)	3	(0.2)	6	(0.4)	4	(0.5)
Serbia[4,8]	6	(0.3)	24	(1.2)	26	(1.1)	20	(1.0)	10	(0.6)	8	(0.5)	3	(0.4)	3	(0.4)
Singapore	12	(0.4)	26	(0.8)	19	(0.5)	13	(0.4)	10	(0.3)	8	(0.3)	8	(0.4)	5	(0.4)
Slovenia	10	(0.3)	21	(0.5)	23	(0.6)	21	(0.6)	11	(0.4)	5	(0.3)	4	(0.2)	4	(0.4)
Sweden[2]	4	(0.2)	15	(0.6)	33	(1.3)	28	(1.6)	9	(0.3)	6	(0.2)	3	(0.2)	4	(0.5)
Syrian Arab Republic[2]	12	(0.6)	24	(1.3)	16	(0.8)	10	(0.5)	15	(0.6)	12	(0.6)	6	(0.4)	6	(0.6)
Thailand	12	(0.6)	21	(1.0)	15	(0.7)	12	(0.5)	15	(0.6)	10	(0.5)	8	(0.4)	7	(0.5)
Tunisia[1]	15	(1.0)	13	(1.2)	25	(1.4)	16	(1.3)	17	(1.0)	8	(0.7)	4	(0.4)	3	(0.3)
Turkey	8	(0.6)	20	(1.2)	19	(1.0)	13	(0.7)	14	(0.9)	8	(0.6)	10	(1.1)	8	(0.9)
Ukraine	11	(0.4)	14	(0.7)	19	(0.6)	18	(0.6)	17	(0.9)	14	(0.6)	2	(0.3)	4	(0.4)
United States[3,8]	13	(0.4)	21	(0.6)	19	(0.5)	17	(0.5)	10	(0.3)	11	(0.3)	5	(0.3)	5	(0.4)

#Rounds to zero.
[1]Data are available for at least 50 percent but less than 70 percent of students.
[2]Data are available for at least 70 percent but less than 85 percent of students.
[3]Met guidelines for sample participation rates only after replacement schools were included.
[4]National Target Population does not include all of the International Target Population defined by the Trends in International Mathematics and Science Study (TIMSS).
[5]Hong Kong is a Special Administrative Region (SAR) of the People's Republic of China.
[6]National Defined Population covers less than 90 percent of National Target Population (but at least 77 percent).

[7]Kuwait tested the same cohort of students as other countries, but later in 2007, at the beginning of the next school year.
[8]National Defined Population covers 90 to 95 percent of National Target Population.
NOTE: Data provided by teachers. Countries were required to sample students in the grade that corresponded to the end of 8 years of formal schooling, providing that the mean age at the time of testing was at least 13.5 years. Detail may not sum to totals because of rounding. Standard errors appear in parentheses.
SOURCE: International Association for the Evaluation of Educational Achievement (IEA), Trends in International Mathematics and Science Study (TIMSS), 2007, *TIMSS 2007 International Mathematics Report*, by Ina V.S. Mullis et al. (This table was prepared May 2009.)

Mathematics class sizes and average scores of eighth-grade students, yearly mathematics instructional time, and mathematics instructional time as a percentage of total instructional time, by country: 2007

Country or other jurisdiction	Overall average class size	Percentage distribution and average scores of students, by class size						Students' average hours per year of mathematics instructional time	Mathematics instructional time as a percent of total instructional time
		1 to 24 students		25 to 40 students		41 or more students			
		Percent of students	Average score	Percent of students	Average score	Percent of students	Average score		
1	2	3	4	5	6	7	8	9	10
International average	29 (0.1)	30 (0.4)	439 (1.6)	59 (0.5)	456 (0.9)	11 (0.3)	449 (2.9)	120 (0.4)	12 (#)
Algeria	37[1] (0.7)	5[1] (2.1)	370[1] (10.8)	64[1] (4.2)	388[1] (2.8)	31[1] (3.9)	389[1] (3.2)	‡ (†)	13[2] (0.4)
Armenia	25 (0.4)	40 (4.0)	502 (6.2)	60 (3.9)	497 (4.2)	# (†)	‡ (†)	110 (3.9)	11 (0.4)
Australia	26 (0.3)	30 (2.8)	471 (6.3)	70 (2.9)	511 (5.3)	# (†)	‡ (†)	131[1] (2.0)	13[1] (0.2)
Bahrain	31 (0.1)	6 (0.7)	449 (6.3)	94 (0.7)	393 (1.8)	# (†)	‡ (†)	96[2] (2.8)	9[1] (0.3)
Bosnia and Herzegovina	24 (0.4)	48 (3.6)	454 (3.9)	52 (3.6)	458 (4.4)	# (†)	‡ (†)	102[1] (0.9)	11 (0.3)
Botswana	38 (0.4)	1 (0.6)	‡ (†)	73 (3.8)	367 (3.1)	26 (3.7)	355 (5.3)	138[1] (1.5)	13[1] (0.3)
Bulgaria	22 (0.3)	59 (3.5)	441 (7.2)	41 (3.5)	507 (7.1)	# (†)	‡ (†)	93[1] (2.0)	12[1] (0.3)
Chinese Taipei	35 (0.5)	4 (1.8)	549 (29.9)	85 (3.3)	593 (4.6)	11 (2.7)	660 (11.0)	158 (3.5)	14 (0.2)
Colombia	35 (0.6)	13 (2.5)	357 (16.1)	66 (4.6)	386 (5.1)	21 (3.9)	383 (5.9)	151[1] (4.7)	12[1] (0.7)
Cyprus	24 (0.2)	54 (2.7)	466 (2.4)	45 (2.7)	462 (2.6)	1 (#)	‡ (†)	72[2] (0.3)	8[2] (#)
Czech Republic	24 (0.3)	49 (4.3)	494 (3.8)	51 (4.3)	514 (3.8)	# (†)	‡ (†)	128 (2.1)	14[1] (0.2)
Egypt	39 (0.6)	4 (1.5)	410 (12.8)	53 (3.6)	395 (4.9)	43 (3.7)	386 (5.6)	93[1] (4.3)	8 (0.4)
El Salvador	29 (0.8)	35 (3.7)	323 (5.7)	51 (4.0)	348 (3.8)	14 (3.2)	348 (10.0)	142 (2.6)	17 (0.5)
England[3]	26 (0.6)	30 (3.8)	469 (8.6)	69 (3.7)	533 (5.8)	1 (1.0)	‡ (†)	113 (1.7)	12 (0.2)
Georgia[4]	23 (0.6)	52 (5.2)	412 (7.4)	47 (5.3)	408 (9.2)	1 (0.6)	‡ (†)	110 (0.8)	13 (0.2)
Ghana	46 (1.9)	13 (2.4)	299 (11.3)	40 (4.2)	299 (7.9)	47 (4.3)	321 (7.7)	146[1] (5.0)	13 (0.5)
Hong Kong SAR[3,5]	37 (0.5)	10 (1.9)	513 (23.5)	44 (4.3)	555 (10.1)	46 (4.1)	604 (7.2)	148[2] (3.8)	14[2] (0.4)
Hungary	21 (0.5)	72 (3.4)	510 (4.7)	27 (3.3)	533 (8.3)	1 (0.9)	‡ (†)	99[2] (1.3)	13[2] (0.2)
Indonesia	38 (0.9)	6 (1.7)	374 (13.7)	61 (4.2)	400 (5.1)	33 (4.1)	396 (8.6)	136[2] (4.7)	11[2] (0.3)
Iran, Islamic Republic of	26 (0.5)	35 (3.2)	386 (5.5)	64 (3.3)	411 (5.7)	1 (1.1)	‡ (†)	99[2] (2.3)	11[2] (0.3)
Israel[6]	33[2] (0.4)	5[2] (1.2)	473[2] (22.6)	92[2] (2.2)	467[2] (4.7)	3[2] (1.8)	496[2] (42.7)	‡ (†)	12[2] (0.3)
Italy	22 (0.2)	73 (2.9)	475 (3.4)	27 (2.9)	493 (5.7)	# (†)	‡ (†)	136[1] (1.5)	13[1] (0.2)
Japan	34 (0.5)	10 (2.1)	555 (5.9)	85 (2.7)	567 (2.9)	5 (1.6)	645 (24.7)	105 (1.6)	10 (0.1)
Jordan	35 (0.7)	13 (2.5)	431 (17.4)	58 (4.4)	427 (6.2)	29 (4.1)	425 (7.8)	141 (1.1)	14 (0.2)
Korea, Republic of	37 (0.4)	4 (1.4)	558 (15.6)	78 (2.6)	596 (3.1)	18 (2.3)	607 (7.2)	104[2] (0.7)	11[2] (0.2)
Kuwait[7]	30[2] (0.5)	12[2] (3.3)	356[2] (9.9)	87[2] (3.2)	357[2] (2.8)	1[2] (#)	‡ (†)	‡ (†)	6[2] (0.6)
Lebanon	26 (0.6)	38 (4.3)	426 (6.3)	58 (4.5)	464 (7.1)	4 (1.2)	423 (14.4)	‡ (†)	‡ (†)
Lithuania[4]	25 (0.3)	35 (3.2)	480 (4.1)	65 (3.2)	520 (3.6)	# (†)	‡ (†)	116[1] (0.9)	13[1] (0.2)
Malaysia	36 (0.4)	1 (0.8)	‡ (†)	80 (3.2)	470 (5.8)	19 (3.1)	486 (10.9)	123 (1.0)	11 (0.1)
Malta	22 (#)	71 (0.2)	472 (1.4)	29 (0.2)	523 (1.9)	# (†)	‡ (†)	128 (0.1)	13 (#)
Norway	25 (0.4)	47 (3.9)	468 (3.4)	51 (4.0)	471 (2.4)	1 (1.0)	‡ (†)	113 (1.6)	13 (0.2)
Oman	32 (0.4)	10 (2.2)	363 (8.8)	90 (2.2)	373 (3.6)	# (†)	‡ (†)	150[2] (4.5)	15 (0.5)
Palestinian National Authority	38 (0.5)	8 (1.6)	383 (11.7)	51 (4.0)	367 (5.2)	41 (3.6)	364 (6.0)	100[2] (4.0)	11[2] (0.4)
Qatar	27 (#)	20 (0.1)	300 (3.5)	77 (0.2)	309 (1.8)	2 (#)	‡ (†)	138[2] (0.1)	13[2] (#)
Romania	21 (0.3)	76 (2.9)	450 (4.5)	24 (2.9)	500 (8.8)	# (†)	‡ (†)	122[1] (1.9)	14[1] (0.3)
Russian Federation	21 (0.3)	63 (2.8)	499 (4.6)	37 (2.8)	533 (6.0)	# (†)	‡ (†)	131[1] (1.4)	15[1] (0.2)
Saudi Arabia	30 (0.8)	28 (3.6)	330 (5.1)	61 (4.0)	329 (4.2)	11 (2.6)	322 (11.4)	107[2] (3.2)	11[2] (0.3)
Scotland[3]	25 (0.5)	43 (3.2)	449 (6.3)	56 (3.1)	517 (4.8)	1 (0.8)	‡ (†)	135[2] (2.2)	13[2] (0.2)
Serbia[4,8]	24 (0.4)	53 (3.9)	480 (4.8)	47 (3.9)	490 (5.1)	# (†)	‡ (†)	103[2] (0.8)	13[2] (0.2)
Singapore	38 (0.2)	2 (0.6)	‡ (†)	76 (2.5)	593 (5.2)	22 (2.5)	592 (7.2)	124 (1.0)	13 (0.1)
Slovenia	16 (0.2)	94 (1.0)	500 (2.3)	6 (1.0)	513 (8.2)	# (†)	‡ (†)	113 (0.4)	13 (0.1)
Sweden	23 (0.5)	63 (3.6)	488 (2.9)	35 (3.4)	499 (3.7)	2 (1.1)	‡ (†)	113 (0.4)	13 (0.1)
Syrian Arab Republic	31 (0.6)	24 (3.6)	405 (8.7)	65 (4.2)	391 (4.7)	11 (2.6)	392 (11.3)	93[1] (1.4)	10[1] (0.2)
Thailand	38 (0.6)	11 (2.4)	406 (11.2)	47 (3.7)	416 (5.7)	42 (3.1)	479 (9.3)	76[1] (3.4)	10 (0.4)
Tunisia	32 (0.4)	3 (1.2)	398 (6.9)	96 (1.6)	421 (2.4)	1 (1.0)	‡ (†)	126[2] (2.1)	10[1] (0.2)
Turkey	33 (0.7)	18 (3.4)	423 (11.7)	61 (3.9)	434 (6.5)	20 (2.7)	436 (11.3)	95 (0.4)	11 (0.3)
Ukraine	25 (0.4)	36 (3.2)	447 (6.4)	63 (3.1)	471 (4.8)	1 (0.8)	‡ (†)	130 (2.0)	15 (0.2)
United States[3,8]	24 (0.4)	57 (2.3)	511 (4.0)	41 (2.3)	506 (5.0)	2 (0.9)	‡ (†)	148[2] (2.3)	13[2] (0.2)

†Not applicable.
#Rounds to zero.
‡Reporting standards not met.
[1]Data are available for at least 70 percent but less than 85 percent of students.
[2]Data are available for at least 50 percent but less than 70 percent of students.
[3]Met guidelines for sample participation rates only after substitute schools were included.
[4]National Target Population does not include all of the International Target Population defined by the Trends in International Mathematics and Science Study (TIMSS).
[5]Hong Kong is a Special Administrative Region (SAR) of the People's Republic of China.
[6]National Defined Population covers less than 90 percent of National Target Population (but at least 77 percent).

[7]Kuwait tested the same cohort of students as other countries, but later in 2007, at the beginning of the next school year.
[8]National Defined Population covers 90 to 95 percent of National Target Population.
NOTE: Class size and implemented instructional time for mathematics provided by teachers; total instructional time provided by schools. TIMSS scores are reported on a scale from 0 to 1,000, with the scale average fixed at 500 and the standard deviation fixed at 100. Countries were required to sample students in the grade that corresponded to the end of 8 years of formal schooling, providing that the mean age at the time of testing was at least 13.5 years. Detail may not sum to totals because of rounding. Standard errors appear in parentheses.
SOURCE: International Association for the Evaluation of Educational Achievement (IEA), Trends in International Mathematics and Science Study (TIMSS), 2007, *TIMSS 2007 International Mathematics Report*, by Ina V.S. Mullis et al. (This table was prepared June 2009.)

Average mathematics scores and percentage distribution of eighth-graders, by index of self-confidence in learning mathematics, index of time spent doing mathematics homework, and country: 2007

Country or other jurisdiction	High SCM — Percent of students	High SCM — Average score	Medium SCM — Percent of students	Medium SCM — Average score	Low SCM — Percent of students	Low SCM — Average score	High TMH — Percent of students	High TMH — Average score	Medium TMH — Percent of students	Medium TMH — Average score	Low TMH — Percent of students	Low TMH — Average score
1	2	3	4	5	6	7	8	9	10	11	12	13
International average	43 (0.2)	492 (0.6)	37 (0.1)	433 (0.6)	20 (0.1)	412 (0.7)	27 (0.2)	458 (0.9)	53 (0.2)	457 (0.7)	20 (0.2)	441 (1.1)
Algeria	46 (1.0)	412 (2.2)	41 (0.9)	372 (2.7)	12 (0.6)	358 (2.7)	— (†)	— (†)	— (†)	— (†)	— (†)	— (†)
Armenia[3]	37 (0.9)	521 (4.0)	38 (1.1)	496 (4.6)	26 (1.0)	485 (4.7)	32 (1.2)	501 (4.6)	64 (1.2)	502 (4.4)	4 (0.5)	499 (12.7)
Australia	45 (1.2)	539 (4.8)	35 (0.8)	472 (4.1)	19 (0.9)	445 (3.7)	15 (1.1)	523 (6.6)	44 (1.5)	511 (5.2)	42 (2.0)	481 (4.6)
Bahrain	53 (0.8)	435 (2.1)	33 (0.7)	366 (2.4)	15 (0.6)	350 (3.0)	15 (0.7)	391 (4.0)	67 (1.1)	404 (1.8)	18 (1.0)	405 (5.2)
Bosnia and Herzegovina	41 (1.2)	502 (2.6)	27 (0.8)	441 (3.2)	32 (1.1)	422 (3.5)	24 (1.2)	466 (4.0)	51 (1.2)	458 (3.2)	25 (1.4)	459 (3.8)
Botswana	42 (1.0)	385 (3.0)	41 (0.9)	355 (2.6)	17 (0.7)	354 (3.6)	29 (0.9)	383 (3.0)	50 (0.9)	365 (2.8)	20 (1.0)	356 (3.4)
Bulgaria	37 (1.3)	516 (5.5)	38 (1.1)	452 (5.8)	25 (1.1)	430 (7.6)	36 (1.4)	475 (6.4)	48 (1.2)	472 (5.4)	15 (1.5)	458 (8.1)
Chinese Taipei	27 (1.1)	674 (3.7)	27 (0.7)	610 (5.0)	46 (1.2)	547 (4.4)	31 (1.9)	628 (4.0)	46 (1.3)	613 (4.1)	23 (1.7)	563 (8.7)
Colombia	46 (1.3)	409 (3.6)	40 (1.2)	363 (3.8)	13 (0.7)	351 (4.5)	36 (1.3)	386 (4.5)	48 (0.9)	379 (3.8)	16 (1.0)	378 (6.0)
Cyprus	50 (1.0)	508 (1.7)	30 (0.8)	437 (2.5)	20 (0.7)	411 (3.3)	20 (0.9)	463 (4.1)	70 (0.9)	480 (1.8)	11 (0.7)	451 (4.8)
Czech Republic	43 (0.9)	542 (2.6)	31 (0.7)	490 (2.8)	25 (0.8)	456 (3.1)	5 (0.6)	473 (6.4)	46 (2.1)	504 (4.1)	49 (2.4)	511 (3.4)
Egypt	55 (1.5)	422 (3.7)	38 (1.4)	368 (3.8)	7 (0.4)	356 (8.0)	30 (1.1)	381 (4.6)	58 (1.1)	404 (3.6)	13 (1.0)	416 (6.8)
El Salvador	35 (1.1)	377 (3.2)	52 (1.1)	327 (2.7)	13 (0.8)	323 (4.5)	46 (1.4)	351 (3.2)	45 (1.0)	337 (3.3)	9 (0.7)	337 (5.2)
England[4]	53 (1.4)	543 (4.9)	32 (1.0)	494 (4.7)	15 (0.8)	457 (5.5)	5 (0.6)	518 (11.0)	31 (1.3)	530 (6.8)	65 (1.7)	513 (4.9)
Georgia[5]	44 (1.8)	455 (4.9)	37 (1.5)	401 (7.5)	19 (1.0)	379 (7.0)	34[3] (1.5)	432[3] (5.1)	62[3] (1.6)	414[3] (7.0)	4[3] (0.5)	372[3] (14.2)
Ghana	44 (1.3)	341 (4.8)	46 (0.9)	292 (4.8)	11 (0.8)	285 (7.4)	28 (1.2)	332 (5.2)	55 (1.0)	307 (4.8)	16 (1.0)	313 (5.4)
Hong Kong SAR[4,6]	30 (1.1)	622 (5.1)	40 (1.0)	562 (6.7)	30 (0.7)	539 (5.8)	34 (1.6)	589 (4.9)	48 (1.2)	576 (5.9)	18 (1.4)	555 (9.0)
Hungary	42 (1.0)	566 (3.5)	32 (0.9)	499 (4.2)	26 (1.0)	464 (3.7)	16 (0.9)	517 (5.6)	78 (1.2)	524 (3.4)	6 (1.0)	488 (8.0)
Indonesia	28 (1.0)	405 (5.4)	58 (1.0)	394 (3.8)	14 (0.8)	401 (5.0)	29 (1.1)	417 (5.0)	53 (0.9)	397 (4.0)	18 (0.8)	384 (5.1)
Iran, Islamic Republic of	45 (1.2)	443 (5.0)	40 (1.1)	380 (3.7)	14 (0.9)	368 (6.1)	19 (1.4)	440 (7.7)	55 (1.6)	404 (3.8)	26 (1.5)	378 (5.0)
Israel[7]	59 (1.0)	495 (4.1)	29 (0.9)	432 (5.3)	12 (0.7)	417 (7.2)	34 (1.5)	485 (4.9)	53 (1.4)	472 (4.1)	13 (0.9)	448 (9.0)
Italy	48 (1.0)	514 (3.1)	28 (0.7)	462 (3.6)	24 (0.9)	434 (3.7)	45 (1.3)	475 (3.1)	47 (1.2)	488 (4.1)	7 (0.6)	483 (5.5)
Japan	17 (0.6)	638 (3.9)	35 (0.8)	586 (2.9)	48 (0.9)	535 (2.6)	8 (1.1)	566 (10.0)	36 (1.3)	569 (3.3)	57 (2.0)	574 (3.3)
Jordan	58 (1.5)	468 (3.7)	34 (1.2)	388 (4.2)	9 (0.6)	361 (6.6)	26 (1.2)	424 (5.0)	62 (1.1)	439 (4.4)	12 (0.9)	422 (7.1)
Korea, Republic of	29 (0.8)	668 (2.6)	34 (0.7)	606 (3.1)	38 (0.8)	536 (2.8)	6 (0.7)	591 (5.8)	31 (1.5)	595 (3.7)	62 (1.7)	605 (3.1)
Kuwait[8]	54 (0.9)	381 (2.5)	35 (0.9)	331 (2.6)	11 (0.6)	319 (5.7)	14 (0.7)	334 (5.1)	58 (1.3)	358 (2.7)	27 (1.5)	373 (3.9)
Lebanon	49 (1.2)	483 (4.1)	39 (1.3)	425 (4.2)	12 (0.9)	416 (4.9)	25[3] (1.3)	445[3] (6.0)	67[3] (1.4)	460[3] (3.9)	8[3] (0.9)	434[3] (9.0)
Lithuania[5]	41 (1.0)	556 (2.7)	34 (0.9)	481 (2.9)	25 (0.9)	461 (3.1)	27 (1.1)	498 (2.8)	69 (1.1)	515 (2.7)	4 (0.8)	481 (8.8)
Malaysia	27 (1.4)	521 (5.3)	50 (1.2)	458 (5.1)	23 (0.8)	453 (4.5)	41 (1.1)	486 (5.1)	47 (1.0)	473 (5.1)	12 (0.9)	446 (9.1)
Malta	38 (0.7)	536 (2.1)	35 (0.7)	467 (2.0)	27 (0.6)	449 (2.2)	24 (0.7)	508 (2.8)	71 (0.7)	498 (1.7)	5 (0.3)	402 (7.4)
Norway	50 (0.8)	505 (2.1)	31 (0.7)	450 (2.1)	19 (0.7)	415 (2.2)	25 (1.5)	466 (2.6)	53 (1.3)	474 (2.0)	22 (1.6)	473 (3.5)
Oman	45 (1.1)	415 (3.4)	47 (1.1)	346 (3.7)	8 (0.5)	327 (5.6)	12 (0.7)	374 (5.2)	73 (1.3)	383 (3.1)	15 (1.4)	367 (7.9)
Palestinian National Authority	44 (1.1)	414 (3.6)	44 (1.0)	341 (4.3)	13 (0.7)	333 (5.0)	24 (1.1)	374 (4.4)	68 (1.2)	378 (3.8)	7 (0.8)	345 (9.1)
Qatar	55 (0.6)	339 (2.3)	34 (0.6)	279 (2.3)	11 (0.3)	267 (3.4)	16 (0.4)	300 (3.2)	67 (0.5)	319 (1.5)	17 (0.4)	308 (4.0)
Romania	33 (1.2)	517 (5.3)	41 (1.1)	449 (4.6)	27 (1.2)	426 (4.4)	66 (1.3)	488 (4.0)	29 (1.3)	433 (5.1)	5 (0.5)	432 (11.4)
Russian Federation	41 (1.1)	560 (4.3)	31 (0.8)	496 (4.9)	28 (0.8)	466 (4.1)	50 (1.3)	510 (4.4)	49 (1.2)	520 (4.2)	2 (0.3)	‡ (†)
Saudi Arabia	47 (1.2)	361 (3.2)	42 (1.0)	310 (3.5)	11 (0.7)	294 (4.9)	13 (0.8)	316 (4.8)	61 (1.8)	339 (3.3)	26 (1.8)	334 (4.4)
Scotland[4]	53 (1.3)	515 (4.0)	33 (1.0)	465 (3.6)	14 (0.7)	442 (4.6)	8 (0.7)	519 (7.2)	41 (1.8)	505 (4.4)	51 (2.1)	478 (4.3)
Serbia[5,9]	48 (1.3)	539 (3.4)	25 (0.8)	464 (3.6)	27 (1.1)	426 (3.9)	31 (1.4)	490 (5.0)	40 (1.3)	496 (4.3)	28 (1.4)	481 (4.3)
Singapore	41 (1.0)	638 (3.3)	34 (0.9)	572 (4.6)	25 (0.8)	547 (4.7)	42 (1.0)	616 (3.2)	43 (0.9)	595 (4.3)	16 (0.9)	547 (6.9)
Slovenia	40 (1.1)	541 (2.9)	41 (0.9)	485 (2.2)	19 (0.8)	458 (3.2)	20 (1.1)	503 (2.6)	64 (1.3)	505 (2.4)	16 (1.0)	498 (4.1)
Sweden	49 (1.0)	528 (2.6)	35 (0.7)	468 (2.4)	16 (0.6)	438 (3.6)	3[3] (0.4)	461[3] (7.7)	35[3] (1.2)	490[3] (3.1)	62[3] (1.3)	498[3] (2.4)
Syrian Arab Republic	47 (1.1)	429 (3.5)	40 (0.9)	378 (4.2)	13 (0.7)	361 (4.7)	44[3] (1.1)	408[3] (3.9)	48[3] (0.9)	399[3] (3.8)	8[3] (0.6)	409[3] (6.8)
Thailand	22 (1.1)	489 (6.9)	60 (0.9)	428 (4.6)	18 (0.7)	430 (5.6)	39 (1.4)	461 (5.6)	45 (1.1)	435 (5.4)	15 (1.0)	419 (6.7)
Tunisia	45 (1.3)	452 (2.8)	34 (0.8)	400 (2.6)	21 (1.0)	391 (2.7)	45 (1.3)	425 (2.8)	44 (1.0)	419 (2.9)	11 (0.9)	417 (4.1)
Turkey	39 (1.1)	494 (6.1)	36 (0.8)	403 (4.7)	24 (1.0)	384 (4.3)	22 (1.1)	428 (5.8)	49 (1.0)	433 (5.0)	29 (1.2)	443 (5.9)
Ukraine	36 (1.2)	523 (3.8)	36 (0.9)	448 (3.5)	28 (1.1)	423 (3.2)	40 (1.2)	468 (4.5)	53 (1.1)	467 (3.5)	7 (0.7)	466 (6.8)
United States[4,9]	53 (1.0)	537 (2.5)	28 (0.7)	487 (3.2)	19 (0.7)	462 (3.0)	26 (1.1)	522 (3.8)	62 (1.2)	510 (3.0)	12 (1.2)	484 (4.3)

—Not available.

†Not applicable.

‡Reporting standards not met.

[1]Index based on students' responses to four statements: 1) I usually do well in mathematics; 2) Mathematics is more difficult for me than for many of my classmates (reverse scored); 3) Mathematics is not one of my strengths (reverse scored); 4) I learn things quickly in mathematics. Average is computed across the four items based on a 4-point scale: 1. Agree a lot; 2. Agree a little; 3. Disagree a little; 4. Disagree a lot. High SCM indicates agreeing a little or a lot on average across the four statements. Low SCM indicates disagreeing a little or a lot on average across the four statements. Medium SCM indicates mixed attitudes across the four statements.

[2]Index based on students' reports on frequency of and amount of time spent on homework. High TMH indicates more than 30 minutes of mathematics homework assigned 3–4 times per week. Medium TMH includes all possible combinations of responses not included in the high or low categories. Low TMH indicates no more than 30 minutes of mathematics homework assigned no more than 2 times per week.

[3]Data are available for at least 70 percent but less than 85 percent of students.

[4]Met guidelines for sample participation rates only after substitute schools were included.

[5]National Target Population does not include all of the International Target Population defined by the Trends in International Mathematics and Science Study (TIMSS).

[6]Hong Kong is a Special Administrative Region (SAR) of the People's Republic of China.

[7]National Defined Population covers less than 90 percent of National Target Population (but at least 77 percent).

[8]Kuwait tested the same cohort of students as other countries, but later in 2007, at the beginning of the next school year.

[9]National Defined Population covers 90 to 95 percent of National Target Population.

NOTE: TIMSS scores are reported on a scale from 0 to 1,000, with the scale average fixed at 500 and the standard deviation fixed at 100. Countries were required to sample students in the grade that corresponded to the end of 8 years of formal schooling, providing that the mean age at the time of testing was at least 13.5 years. Detail may not sum to totals because of rounding. Standard errors appear in parentheses.

SOURCE: International Association for the Evaluation of Educational Achievement (IEA), Trends in International Mathematics and Science Study (TIMSS), 2007, TIMSS 2007 International Mathematics Report, by Ina V. S. Mullis et al. (This table was prepared July 2009.)

Average fourth-grade science scores overall and in content and cognitive domains, yearly science instructional time, and science instructional time as a percentage of total instructional time, by country: 2007

Country or other jurisdiction	Science overall		Content domain[1]						Cognitive domain[2]						Students' average hours per year of science instructional time		Science instructional time as a percent of total instructional time	
			Life science		Physical science		Earth science		Knowing		Applying		Reasoning					
1	2		3		4		5		6		7		8		9		10	
International average	—	(†)	—	(†)	—	(†)	—	(†)	—	(†)	—	(†)	—	(†)	67	(0.4)	8	(#)
Algeria	354	(6.0)	351	(6.2)	377	(5.3)	365	(5.7)	350	(5.8)	379	(5.7)	357	(5.8)	67 [3]	(4.7)	6 [4]	(0.4)
Armenia	484	(5.7)	489	(5.9)	492	(5.1)	479	(5.5)	486	(5.2)	487	(5.6)	484	(5.3)	81	(4.0)	9	(0.4)
Australia	527	(3.3)	528	(3.4)	522	(3.1)	534	(3.2)	529	(3.1)	523	(3.3)	530	(3.4)	46 [3]	(2.2)	5 [3]	(0.2)
Austria	526	(2.5)	526	(2.0)	514	(2.4)	532	(1.9)	529	(2.0)	526	(2.2)	513	(2.3)	92	(1.0)	12	(0.1)
Chinese Taipei	557	(2.0)	541	(2.1)	559	(2.5)	553	(1.9)	536	(2.5)	556	(2.1)	571	(2.4)	79 [3]	(1.5)	9 [4]	(0.4)
Colombia	400	(5.4)	408	(5.2)	411	(4.9)	401	(5.6)	409	(5.5)	404	(5.4)	409	(5.1)	139 [4]	(3.9)	13 [4]	(0.4)
Czech Republic	515	(3.1)	520	(2.9)	511	(2.8)	518	(2.6)	520	(2.7)	516	(3.1)	510	(2.9)	41 [4]	(1.3)	5	(0.2)
Denmark[5]	517	(2.9)	527	(2.4)	502	(2.5)	522	(2.7)	516	(2.9)	515	(2.6)	525	(3.8)	59 [4]	(0.9)	7 [3]	(0.1)
El Salvador	390	(3.4)	410	(3.6)	392	(3.8)	393	(3.3)	410	(3.9)	393	(3.6)	376	(4.0)	135	(3.2)	15	(0.5)
England	542	(2.9)	532	(2.7)	543	(2.7)	538	(2.9)	543	(2.9)	536	(2.7)	537	(2.7)	70 [4]	(1.7)	7	(0.1)
Georgia[6]	418	(4.6)	427	(3.5)	414	(4.0)	432	(5.0)	434	(3.8)	424	(4.1)	388	(4.9)	35 [4]	(2.8)	5 [3]	(0.5)
Germany	528	(2.4)	529	(2.0)	524	(2.5)	524	(2.4)	527	(2.2)	526	(2.2)	525	(2.3)	106 [4]	(2.1)	13 [4]	(0.2)
Hong Kong SAR[7]	554	(3.5)	532	(3.5)	558	(3.5)	560	(3.2)	546	(3.2)	549	(3.0)	561	(4.4)	72 [3]	(5.2)	7 [3]	(0.5)
Hungary	536	(3.3)	548	(2.8)	529	(3.3)	517	(3.5)	540	(3.0)	531	(3.2)	529	(3.7)	54 [3]	(1.5)	8 [3]	(0.2)
Iran, Islamic Republic of	436	(4.3)	442	(4.4)	454	(4.2)	433	(4.1)	437	(4.3)	451	(4.3)	436	(4.3)	83	(4.2)	12	(0.4)
Italy	535	(3.2)	549	(3.0)	521	(3.1)	526	(3.0)	530	(3.9)	539	(3.1)	526	(3.8)	68 [4]	(1.4)	6 [4]	(0.1)
Japan	548	(2.1)	530	(2.0)	564	(2.3)	529	(2.7)	528	(2.2)	542	(2.7)	567	(2.1)	82	(1.2)	9	(0.1)
Kazakhstan[6]	533	(5.6)	528	(5.0)	528	(5.8)	534	(5.2)	534	(5.8)	536	(4.9)	519	(5.3)	52	(1.3)	7	(0.2)
Kuwait[8]	348	(4.4)	353	(4.9)	345	(5.2)	363	(3.8)	360	(3.9)	338	(4.3)	331	(5.4)	‡	(†)	‡	(†)
Latvia[6]	542	(2.3)	535	(2.1)	544	(2.4)	536	(2.2)	540	(2.2)	535	(2.4)	551	(2.7)	48 [4]	(1.2)	7 [4]	(0.2)
Lithuania[6]	514	(2.4)	516	(1.8)	514	(1.4)	511	(2.5)	511	(1.7)	515	(2.8)	524	(2.4)	51 [4]	(0.6)	8	(0.1)
Morocco	297	(5.9)	292	(6.8)	324	(5.5)	293	(6.2)	291	(5.8)	311	(6.3)	318	(5.4)	54 [3]	(4.2)	5 [3]	(0.3)
Netherlands[9]	523	(2.6)	536	(2.2)	503	(2.3)	524	(2.5)	518	(2.5)	525	(2.2)	525	(2.3)	33 [3]	(1.5)	3 [3]	(0.1)
New Zealand	504	(2.6)	506	(2.5)	498	(2.5)	515	(2.6)	511	(2.5)	500	(2.4)	505	(2.9)	45 [3]	(2.5)	5 [3]	(0.3)
Norway	477	(3.5)	487	(2.5)	469	(2.7)	497	(2.9)	485	(2.4)	478	(2.8)	480	(3.2)	44 [4]	(1.9)	5 [4]	(0.2)
Qatar	294	(2.6)	291	(1.4)	303	(2.1)	305	(2.2)	304	(2.3)	283	(2.7)	293	(2.9)	‡	(†)	‡	(†)
Russian Federation	546	(4.8)	539	(4.1)	547	(4.6)	536	(4.3)	542	(4.8)	546	(4.7)	542	(4.6)	40 [3]	(1.1)	6 [3]	(0.2)
Scotland[5]	500	(2.3)	504	(2.2)	499	(1.9)	508	(2.5)	511	(2.0)	494	(2.4)	501	(2.2)	51 [3]	(3.1)	5 [4]	(0.3)
Singapore	587	(4.1)	582	(4.1)	585	(3.9)	554	(3.3)	587	(4.1)	579	(3.7)	568	(3.7)	82	(0.9)	9	(0.1)
Slovak Republic	526	(4.8)	532	(4.0)	513	(4.6)	530	(4.8)	527	(4.4)	527	(4.4)	513	(4.9)	59 [4]	(0.7)	7	(0.1)
Slovenia	518	(1.9)	511	(2.2)	530	(1.6)	517	(2.5)	511	(1.6)	525	(2.1)	527	(1.8)	84 [4]	(0.8)	12 [4]	(0.1)
Sweden	525	(2.5)	531	(2.5)	508	(2.7)	535	(2.7)	526	(2.5)	521	(2.9)	527	(3.5)	56 [4]	(2.5)	6 [4]	(0.3)
Tunisia	318	(5.9)	323	(5.6)	340	(6.4)	325	(5.8)	316	(5.9)	329	(6.3)	349	(5.3)	71 [3]	(2.7)	8 [3]	(0.3)
Ukraine	474	(3.1)	482	(2.5)	475	(2.7)	474	(3.1)	476	(2.4)	477	(3.2)	478	(3.0)	33	(1.1)	5	(0.2)
United States[5,10]	539	(2.7)	540	(2.5)	534	(2.3)	533	(2.6)	541	(2.3)	533	(2.8)	535	(2.6)	89 [4]	(2.5)	8 [4]	(0.2)
Yemen	197	(7.2)	—	(†)	—	(†)	—	(†)	—	(†)	—	(†)	—	(†)	83 [3]	(5.7)	10 [4]	(0.5)

—Not available.
†Not applicable.
#Rounds to zero.
‡Reporting standards not met.

[1] *Life science* includes characteristics and life processes of living things; life cycles, reproduction, and heredity; interaction with the environment; ecosystems; and human health. *Physical science* includes classification and properties of matter; physical states and changes in matter; energy sources, heat, and temperature; light and sound; electricity and magnetism; and forces and motion. *Earth science* includes Earth's structure, physical characteristics, and resources; Earth's processes, cycles, and history; and Earth in the solar system.
[2] *Knowing* addresses the facts, information, concepts, tools, and procedures that students need to know to function scientifically. *Applying* focuses on students' ability to apply knowledge and conceptual understanding to solve problems or answer questions. *Reasoning* goes beyond the cognitive processes involved in solving routine problems to include more complex tasks.
[3] Data are available for at least 50 percent but less than 70 percent of the students.
[4] Data are available for at least 70 percent but less than 85 percent of the students.

[5] Met guidelines for sample participation rates only after replacement schools were included.
[6] National Target Population does not include all of the International Target Population defined by the Trends in International Mathematics and Science Study (TIMSS).
[7] Hong Kong is a Special Administrative Region (SAR) of the People's Republic of China.
[8] Kuwait tested the same cohort of students as other countries, but later in 2007, at the beginning of the next school year.
[9] Nearly satisfied guidelines for sample participation rates only after replacement schools were included.
[10] National Defined Population covers 90 to 95 percent of National Target Population.
NOTE: Implemented instructional time for science provided by teachers; total instructional time provided by schools. TIMSS scores are reported on a scale from 0 to 1,000, with the scale average fixed at 500 and the standard deviation fixed at 100. Countries were required to sample students in the grade that corresponded to the end of 4 years of formal schooling, providing that the mean age at the time of testing was at least 9.5 years. Standard errors appear in parentheses.
SOURCE: International Association for the Evaluation of Educational Achievement (IEA), Trends in International Mathematics and Science Study (TIMSS), 2007, *TIMSS 2007 International Science Report*, by Michael O. Martin et al. (This table was prepared June 2009.)

Average eighth-grade science scores overall and in content and cognitive domains, by country: 2007

Country or other jurisdiction	Science overall		Content domain[1] Biology		Chemistry		Physics		Earth science		Cognitive domain[2] Knowing		Applying		Reasoning	
1		2		3		4		5		6		7		8		9
Algeria	408	(1.7)	411	(1.9)	414	(1.7)	397	(2.2)	413	(1.6)	409	(1.9)	410	(2.4)	414	(1.9)
Armenia	488	(5.8)	490	(5.9)	478	(6.3)	503	(5.6)	475	(5.8)	493	(6.4)	502	(5.4)	459	(6.5)
Australia	515	(3.6)	518	(3.4)	505	(3.6)	508	(4.2)	519	(3.8)	501	(3.1)	510	(3.2)	530	(3.6)
Bahrain	467	(1.7)	473	(2.0)	468	(2.4)	466	(1.5)	465	(2.4)	469	(2.1)	468	(2.1)	469	(2.0)
Bosnia and Herzegovina	466	(2.8)	464	(3.0)	468	(2.9)	463	(3.1)	469	(3.4)	486	(3.7)	463	(2.8)	452	(3.1)
Botswana	355	(3.1)	359	(2.9)	371	(2.4)	351	(3.2)	361	(4.0)	361	(2.9)	358	(3.2)	362	(2.7)
Bulgaria[3]	470	(5.9)	467	(6.0)	472	(6.1)	466	(5.6)	480	(5.5)	489	(5.8)	471	(6.1)	448	(6.1)
Chinese Taipei	561	(3.7)	549	(3.4)	573	(4.2)	554	(3.7)	545	(2.9)	565	(3.5)	560	(3.4)	541	(3.5)
Colombia	417	(3.5)	434	(3.7)	420	(3.1)	407	(3.5)	407	(3.9)	418	(4.0)	417	(3.1)	428	(2.7)
Cyprus	452	(2.0)	447	(1.9)	452	(2.5)	458	(2.8)	457	(2.3)	438	(2.6)	456	(2.0)	460	(2.3)
Czech Republic	539	(1.9)	531	(2.1)	535	(2.7)	537	(2.1)	534	(2.0)	533	(2.1)	539	(1.9)	534	(2.3)
Egypt	408	(3.6)	406	(3.4)	413	(4.0)	413	(3.3)	426	(3.8)	434	(3.9)	404	(3.6)	395	(3.4)
El Salvador	387	(2.9)	398	(3.0)	377	(3.2)	380	(3.5)	400	(2.9)	394	(3.2)	388	(3.2)	384	(3.4)
England[4]	542	(4.5)	541	(4.4)	534	(4.0)	545	(4.0)	529	(4.3)	530	(4.9)	538	(4.0)	547	(4.0)
Georgia[5]	421	(4.8)	423	(3.9)	418	(4.6)	416	(5.8)	425	(4.1)	440	(5.1)	422	(4.5)	394	(4.6)
Ghana	303	(5.4)	304	(4.9)	342	(4.9)	276	(5.8)	294	(5.8)	316	(5.7)	291	(5.5)	—	(†)
Hong Kong SAR[4,6]	530	(4.9)	527	(4.6)	517	(4.6)	528	(4.8)	532	(4.5)	532	(4.5)	522	(4.9)	533	(5.0)
Hungary	539	(2.9)	534	(2.7)	536	(3.5)	541	(3.2)	531	(2.9)	524	(3.0)	549	(3.0)	530	(3.0)
Indonesia	427	(3.4)	428	(3.1)	421	(3.4)	432	(3.1)	442	(3.3)	426	(3.6)	425	(3.1)	438	(3.2)
Iran, Islamic Republic of	459	(3.6)	449	(3.6)	463	(3.5)	470	(3.6)	476	(3.7)	468	(3.9)	454	(3.8)	462	(3.8)
Israel[3]	468	(4.3)	472	(4.2)	467	(4.6)	472	(4.6)	462	(4.1)	456	(5.0)	472	(4.2)	481	(4.2)
Italy	495	(2.8)	502	(3.0)	481	(2.9)	489	(3.1)	503	(3.1)	494	(3.3)	498	(2.9)	493	(2.6)
Japan	554	(1.9)	553	(1.9)	551	(1.9)	558	(1.9)	533	(2.5)	534	(2.2)	555	(2.0)	560	(2.0)
Jordan	482	(4.0)	478	(3.8)	491	(4.1)	479	(4.2)	484	(3.6)	491	(4.5)	485	(4.1)	471	(4.1)
Korea, Republic of	553	(2.0)	548	(1.9)	536	(2.4)	571	(2.4)	538	(2.2)	543	(2.0)	547	(2.0)	558	(2.0)
Kuwait[7]	418	(2.8)	419	(2.6)	418	(3.8)	438	(2.8)	410	(3.0)	430	(2.5)	417	(2.9)	411	(2.9)
Lebanon	414	(5.9)	405	(6.2)	447	(5.5)	431	(5.1)	389	(6.4)	403	(5.9)	422	(5.8)	420	(5.6)
Lithuania[5]	519	(2.5)	527	(2.3)	507	(2.3)	505	(2.9)	515	(2.5)	513	(2.4)	512	(2.2)	527	(2.5)
Malaysia	471	(6.0)	469	(5.8)	479	(5.0)	484	(5.7)	463	(5.4)	458	(6.5)	473	(5.9)	487	(4.9)
Malta	457	(1.4)	453	(1.7)	461	(2.1)	470	(1.7)	456	(1.5)	436	(1.5)	462	(1.6)	473	(1.4)
Norway	487	(2.2)	487	(2.3)	483	(2.2)	475	(3.0)	502	(2.5)	486	(2.0)	486	(2.3)	491	(2.8)
Oman	423	(3.0)	414	(3.1)	416	(3.6)	443	(2.9)	439	(2.5)	428	(3.5)	423	(3.2)	428	(3.5)
Palestinian National Authority	404	(3.5)	402	(4.1)	413	(4.2)	414	(3.7)	408	(3.7)	407	(3.5)	412	(4.0)	396	(3.8)
Qatar	319	(1.7)	318	(1.7)	322	(1.8)	347	(2.1)	312	(1.9)	325	(1.7)	322	(1.5)	—	(†)
Romania	462	(3.9)	459	(3.2)	463	(4.0)	458	(3.4)	471	(3.3)	451	(4.2)	470	(3.5)	460	(3.5)
Russian Federation	530	(3.9)	525	(3.6)	535	(3.7)	519	(4.0)	525	(3.4)	534	(4.3)	527	(3.8)	520	(3.7)
Saudi Arabia	403	(2.4)	407	(2.4)	390	(2.5)	408	(2.3)	423	(2.3)	417	(2.1)	403	(2.7)	395	(2.5)
Scotland[4]	496	(3.4)	495	(3.2)	497	(3.2)	494	(3.7)	498	(3.2)	480	(3.9)	495	(3.1)	511	(3.6)
Serbia[5,8]	470	(3.2)	474	(3.2)	467	(3.7)	467	(3.0)	466	(3.8)	485	(2.8)	469	(3.6)	455	(3.5)
Singapore	567	(4.4)	564	(4.2)	560	(4.1)	575	(3.9)	541	(4.1)	554	(4.5)	567	(4.2)	564	(4.1)
Slovenia	538	(2.2)	530	(2.3)	539	(2.5)	524	(2.0)	542	(2.2)	533	(2.0)	533	(2.2)	538	(2.2)
Sweden	511	(2.6)	515	(2.4)	499	(2.4)	506	(2.7)	510	(3.0)	505	(2.3)	509	(2.7)	517	(2.6)
Syrian Arab Republic	452	(2.9)	459	(2.7)	450	(2.9)	447	(2.7)	448	(3.2)	474	(2.9)	445	(3.0)	440	(2.7)
Thailand	471	(4.3)	478	(4.5)	462	(4.1)	458	(4.2)	488	(3.8)	473	(4.4)	472	(4.1)	473	(4.0)
Tunisia	445	(2.1)	452	(2.2)	458	(2.5)	432	(2.5)	447	(1.8)	441	(2.0)	445	(2.3)	458	(2.9)
Turkey	454	(3.7)	462	(3.4)	435	(5.2)	445	(4.3)	466	(3.3)	462	(3.6)	450	(3.6)	462	(3.4)
Ukraine	485	(3.5)	477	(3.4)	490	(3.3)	492	(3.9)	482	(4.0)	477	(3.8)	488	(3.7)	488	(3.9)
United States[4,8]	520	(2.9)	530	(2.8)	510	(2.7)	503	(2.7)	525	(3.1)	512	(2.9)	516	(2.7)	529	(2.9)

—Not available.
†Not applicable.

[1] *Biology* includes characteristics, classification, and life processes of organisms; cells and their functions; life cycles, reproduction, and heredity; diversity, adaptation, and natural selection; ecosystems; and human health. *Chemistry* includes classification and composition of matter; properties of matter; and chemical change. *Physics* includes physical states and changes in matter; energy transformations, heat, and temperature; light; sound; electricity and magnetism; and forces and motion. *Earth science* includes Earth's structure and physical features; Earth's processes, cycles, and history; Earth's resources and their use and conservation; and Earth in the solar system and the universe.

[2] *Knowing* addresses the facts, information, concepts, tools, and procedures that students need to know to function scientifically. *Applying* focuses on students' ability to apply knowledge and conceptual understanding to solve problems or answer questions. *Reasoning* goes beyond the cognitive processes involved in solving routine problems to include more complex tasks.

[3] National Defined Population covers less than 90 percent of National Target Population (but at least 77 percent).

[4] Met guidelines for sample participation rates only after substitute schools were included.
[5] National Target Population does not include all of the International Target Population defined by the Trends in International Mathematics and Science Study (TIMSS).
[6] Hong Kong is a Special Administrative Region (SAR) of the People's Republic of China.
[7] Kuwait tested the same cohort of students as other countries, but later in 2007, at the beginning of the next school year.
[8] National Defined Population covers 90 to 95 percent of National Target Population.
NOTE: TIMSS scores are reported on a scale from 0 to 1,000, with the scale average fixed at 500 and the standard deviation fixed at 100. Countries were required to sample students in the grade that corresponded to the end of 8 years of formal schooling, providing that the mean age at the time of testing was at least 13.5 years. Standard errors appear in parentheses.
SOURCE: International Association for the Evaluation of Educational Achievement (IEA), Trends in International Mathematics and Science Study (TIMSS), 2007, *TIMSS 2007 International Science Report*, by Michael O. Martin et al. (This table was prepared June 2009.)

Percentage distribution of science lesson time spent by eighth-grade students on various activities in a typical week, by country: 2007

Country or other jurisdiction [1]	Reviewing homework [2]	Listening to lecture-style presentations [3]	Working problems with teacher's guidance [4]	Working problems on their own without teacher's guidance [5]	Listening to teacher re-teach and clarify content/procedures [6]	Taking tests or quizzes [7]	Participating in classroom management tasks not related to the lesson's content/purpose [8]	Other student activities [9]
International average	9 (0.1)	25 (0.2)	17 (0.1)	13 (0.1)	13 (0.1)	10 (0.1)	6 (0.1)	7 (0.1)
Algeria[1]	10 (0.4)	22 (1.5)	14 (0.7)	12 (0.7)	20 (1.3)	10 (0.7)	5 (0.3)	7 (0.6)
Armenia	12 (0.5)	24 (0.6)	15 (0.4)	13 (0.4)	13 (0.4)	11 (0.3)	5 (0.3)	7 (0.6)
Australia	7 (0.3)	19 (0.8)	20 (0.8)	15 (0.7)	11 (0.5)	7 (0.3)	6 (0.2)	5 (0.3)
Bahrain[2]	10 (0.3)	24 (0.9)	16 (0.4)	10 (0.3)	13 (0.4)	12 (0.5)	10 (0.7)	12 (1.1)
Bosnia and Herzegovina[1]	6 (0.2)	34 (1.1)	20 (0.6)	13 (0.5)	11 (0.4)	8 (0.3)	4 (0.2)	5 (0.4)
Botswana[2,3]	11 (0.5)	20 (1.3)	17 (1.0)	15 (0.9)	13 (0.8)	11 (0.7)	6 (0.4)	7 (0.7)
Bulgaria[2,3]	6 (0.3)	30 (1.0)	17 (0.6)	13 (0.5)	8 (0.3)	17 (0.6)	4 (0.4)	4 (0.7)
Chinese Taipei	10 (0.5)	48 (1.5)	11 (0.6)	5 (0.4)	9 (0.8)	8 (0.6)	4 (0.3)	3 (0.4)
Colombia	11 (0.6)	17 (1.0)	18 (1.3)	18 (1.1)	11 (0.6)	11 (0.6)	7 (0.5)	6 (0.5)
Cyprus[1]	12 (0.2)	23 (0.4)	18 (0.2)	10 (0.2)	14 (0.2)	10 (0.1)	7 (0.2)	6 (0.2)
Czech Republic	5 (0.2)	31 (0.6)	18 (0.3)	15 (0.4)	10 (0.3)	10 (0.2)	5 (0.3)	6 (0.3)
Egypt[1]	11 (0.7)	28 (1.4)	13 (0.8)	11 (0.6)	14 (0.8)	10 (0.5)	5 (0.3)	6 (0.3)
El Salvador	12 (0.5)	16 (0.7)	16 (0.7)	14 (0.7)	16 (0.7)	11 (0.5)	8 (0.4)	7 (0.5)
England[2,4]	7 (0.3)	16 (0.9)	28 (1.0)	20 (0.8)	10 (0.4)	5 (0.2)	7 (0.4)	8 (0.6)
Georgia[2,5]	12 (0.4)	23 (1.4)	12 (0.4)	9 (0.4)	9 (0.4)	18 (0.6)	6 (0.4)	10 (1.2)
Ghana[2]	11 (0.7)	16 (0.9)	17 (0.8)	14 (0.6)	12 (0.7)	15 (0.6)	8 (0.5)	7 (0.4)
Hong Kong SAR[4,6]	9 (0.6)	39 (1.6)	15 (1.0)	8 (0.9)	8 (0.4)	8 (0.9)	5 (0.4)	7 (0.4)
Hungary[2]	8 (0.2)	20 (0.7)	19 (0.5)	16 (0.4)	13 (0.4)	14 (0.3)	4 (0.2)	8 (1.0)
Indonesia[1]	12 (0.5)	24 (1.1)	15 (0.8)	11 (0.5)	12 (0.5)	13 (0.7)	7 (0.3)	7 (0.4)
Iran, Islamic Republic of	9 (0.3)	17 (0.7)	15 (0.6)	12 (0.5)	15 (0.6)	14 (0.6)	8 (0.5)	9 (0.4)
Israel[3]	‡ (†)	‡ (†)	‡ (†)	‡ (†)	‡ (†)	‡ (†)	‡ (†)	‡ (†)
Italy	12 (0.4)	29 (0.7)	13 (0.4)	10 (0.4)	16 (0.6)	10 (0.4)	5 (0.3)	5 (0.4)
Japan[2]	3 (0.3)	47 (1.5)	15 (1.0)	5 (0.8)	14 (0.7)	5 (0.5)	2 (0.3)	8 (1.3)
Jordan	13 (0.5)	20 (1.1)	17 (0.5)	12 (0.5)	14 (0.5)	12 (0.5)	6 (0.3)	6 (0.4)
Korea, Republic of[2]	5 (0.3)	49 (1.6)	9 (0.4)	8 (0.4)	13 (0.8)	6 (0.4)	6 (0.5)	5 (0.5)
Kuwait[7]	‡ (†)	‡ (†)	‡ (†)	‡ (†)	‡ (†)	‡ (†)	‡ (†)	‡ (†)
Lebanon[1]	16 (0.8)	18 (1.2)	19 (0.8)	8 (0.7)	14 (0.9)	14 (0.6)	6 (0.4)	6 (0.4)
Lithuania[5]	8 (0.2)	12 (0.5)	22 (0.5)	23 (0.5)	14 (0.4)	14 (0.5)	6 (0.4)	6 (0.4)
Malaysia[2]	13 (0.6)	24 (1.4)	15 (0.7)	11 (0.6)	13 (0.8)	10 (0.5)	3 (0.2)	6 (0.3)
Malta	10 (#)	31 (0.1)	15 (#)	10 (0.1)	13 (0.1)	5 (#)	9 (0.1)	7 (#)
Norway	8 (0.4)	27 (0.8)	18 (0.9)	16 (0.7)	12 (0.4)	6 (0.3)	4 (0.3)	9 (0.8)
Oman[2]	10 (0.7)	21 (1.5)	16 (0.8)	13 (0.6)	14 (0.8)	11 (0.7)	5 (0.3)	9 (0.9)
Palestinian National Authority[1]	11 (0.5)	25 (1.3)	16 (0.7)	11 (0.5)	14 (0.8)	10 (0.4)	6 (0.4)	7 (0.4)
Qatar[1]	11 (#)	25 (0.1)	13 (#)	12 (#)	12 (#)	10 (#)	7 (#)	11 (#)
Romania	9 (0.3)	24 (0.8)	19 (0.5)	13 (0.4)	11 (0.5)	14 (0.5)	5 (0.2)	5 (0.2)
Russian Federation	12 (0.3)	23 (0.5)	19 (0.4)	16 (0.4)	9 (0.2)	15 (0.4)	1 (0.1)	4 (0.2)
Saudi Arabia[2,4]	‡ (†)	‡ (†)	‡ (†)	‡ (†)	‡ (†)	‡ (†)	‡ (†)	‡ (†)
Scotland[2,4]	‡ (†)	23 (0.6)	28 (0.7)	18 (0.8)	9 (0.3)	4 (0.2)	‡ (†)	‡ (†)
Serbia[2,5,8]	5 (0.2)	39 (0.8)	19 (0.6)	11 (0.4)	11 (0.3)	8 (0.3)	7 (0.3)	5 (0.3)
Singapore	12 (0.3)	34 (0.8)	14 (0.5)	10 (0.3)	9 (0.3)	8 (0.3)	7 (0.4)	5 (0.4)
Slovenia	6 (0.2)	28 (0.7)	22 (0.6)	16 (0.4)	13 (0.4)	5 (0.3)	4 (0.2)	7 (0.5)
Sweden[2]	5 (0.3)	25 (0.7)	29 (0.8)	15 (0.9)	11 (0.3)	7 (0.2)	4 (0.2)	5 (0.6)
Syrian Arab Republic[1]	12 (0.6)	28 (1.4)	14 (0.6)	10 (0.5)	14 (0.8)	11 (0.5)	6 (0.3)	5 (0.6)
Thailand	11 (0.6)	21 (1.2)	14 (0.7)	11 (0.6)	18 (0.8)	11 (0.5)	6 (0.3)	6 (0.3)
Tunisia[2]	9 (0.7)	14 (1.2)	26 (1.5)	14 (1.0)	18 (1.0)	11 (0.9)	5 (0.4)	7 (0.5)
Turkey	8 (0.3)	18 (0.8)	19 (0.9)	12 (0.6)	15 (0.8)	9 (0.6)	9 (0.6)	8 (0.4)
Ukraine	12 (0.3)	16 (0.8)	15 (0.4)	15 (0.4)	20 (0.8)	14 (0.4)	9 (0.6)	8 (0.4)
United States[4,8]	9 (0.4)	20 (0.8)	18 (0.6)	15 (0.6)	11 (0.4)	9 (0.3)	3 (0.1)	12 (0.9)

†Not applicable.
#Rounds to zero.
‡Reporting standards not met.
[1] Data are available for at least 50 percent but less than 70 percent of students.
[2] Data are available for at least 70 percent but less than 85 percent of students.
[3] National Defined Population covers less than 90 percent of National Target Population (but at least 77 percent).
[4] Met guidelines for sample participation rates only after substitute schools were included.
[5] National Target Population does not include all of the International Target Population defined by the Trends in International Mathematics and Science Study (TIMSS).
[6] Hong Kong is a Special Administrative Region (SAR) of the People's Republic of China.
[7] Kuwait tested the same cohort of students as other countries, but later in 2007, at the beginning of the next school year.
[8] National Defined Population covers 90 to 95 percent of National Target Population.
NOTE: Data provided by teachers. Countries were required to sample students in the grade that corresponded to the end of 8 years of formal schooling, providing that the mean age at the time of testing was at least 13.5 years. Detail may not sum to totals because of rounding. Standard errors appear in parentheses.
SOURCE: International Association for the Evaluation of Educational Achievement (IEA), Trends in International Mathematics and Science Study (TIMSS), 2007, *TIMSS 2007 International Science Report*, by Michael O. Martin et al. (This table was prepared July 2009.)

Number of bachelor's degree recipients per 100 persons of the typical age of graduation, by sex and country: 2002 through 2006

Country	Typical age of graduation	Total					Male					Female				
		2002	2003	2004	2005	2006	2002	2003	2004	2005	2006	2002	2003	2004	2005	2006
1	2	3	4	5	6	7	8	9	10	11	12	13	14	15	16	17
OECD average[1]	—	31.8	—	34.3	36.3	37.8	26.9	—	27.8	29.0	30.3	36.9	—	40.9	43.9	45.8
Australia	20–24	50.7	54.8	46.9	59.9	59.6	43.0	46.7	37.4	47.9	47.4	58.8	63.4	57.0	72.5	72.5
Austria	22–26	18.0	19.0	19.6	20.4	21.7	17.9	18.7	19.0	19.0	20.4	18.1	19.4	20.3	21.8	22.9
Belgium (Flemish)	22–24	19.2	—	18.3	18.4	19.0	18.7	—	17.5	17.0	17.9	19.7	—	19.0	19.8	20.2
Canada	22–24	—	—	31.5	33.6	39.3	—	—	24.3	25.2	29.5	—	—	39.1	42.2	49.7
Czech Republic	22–25	15.4	17.3	21.0	26.0	30.7	14.3	15.9	18.8	22.6	26.5	16.6	18.8	23.4	29.5	35.2
Denmark	22–26	34.4	38.6	49.9	52.9	50.3	23.4	25.1	35.6	37.2	37.0	45.7	52.3	64.4	69.2	63.7
Finland	22–28	51.8	55.8	54.7	53.8	57.3	37.7	40.4	39.5	38.8	40.6	66.4	72.2	70.5	69.7	74.5
France	20–25	39.0	41.5	40.0	—	34.2	32.9	34.9	33.4	—	30.6	45.3	48.4	46.9	—	37.9
Germany	24–27	19.2	19.5	20.6	20.5	21.0	19.3	19.3	20.3	20.0	20.0	19.1	19.7	20.9	21.1	22.0
Greece	(2)	—	—	19.1	23.9	23.5	—	—	13.3	16.3	16.1	—	—	25.4	32.2	31.7
Hungary	23–24	31.1	33.6	37.3	41.5	38.2	23.2	24.6	26.6	29.0	26.1	39.3	43.2	48.4	54.5	51.0
Iceland	23–26	40.0	44.2	50.5	56.3	62.8	27.2	29.4	31.4	33.6	37.7	53.1	59.1	70.3	80.5	89.6
Ireland	21–24	39.0	36.8	38.6	40.7	42.8	25.6	29.7	31.9	33.3	33.4	36.2	44.0	45.3	48.0	52.5
Italy	22–25	22.4	27.8	40.1	44.8	42.7	19.2	24.0	33.3	37.3	35.1	25.6	31.6	47.2	52.7	50.6
Japan	22–24	34.1	34.4	36.3	36.9	38.7	40.2	40.1	41.4	41.3	42.8	27.6	28.5	31.0	32.2	34.3
Korea, Republic of	21–23	31.5	31.7	32.3	35.5	41.0	31.6	32.1	31.5	34.8	40.2	31.3	31.2	33.2	36.2	41.7
Mexico	(2)	16.5	14.3	13.8	15.2	18.1	15.6	13.3	13.1	14.5	16.7	17.4	15.3	14.4	15.9	19.5
Netherlands	21–24	38.6	42.5	42.9	47.2	49.2	34.4	36.4	37.2	40.2	42.9	42.9	48.7	48.6	54.3	55.7
New Zealand	21–24	41.6	39.0	47.6	49.0	53.5	31.8	29.1	34.9	36.6	40.6	51.3	49.1	61.0	62.0	67.0
Norway	22–25	41.1	42.0	43.3	42.1	45.1	29.7	30.0	31.5	28.8	31.9	52.8	54.2	55.3	55.8	58.8
Poland	23–25	—	—	44.4	45.0	44.8	—	—	32.6	32.8	32.9	—	—	56.6	57.6	57.1
Portugal	22–24	—	—	32.9	33.7	34.9	—	—	20.4	21.7	22.7	—	—	45.6	46.0	47.4
Slovak Republic	21–24	—	—	28.3	30.1	33.7	—	—	24.4	25.6	26.0	—	—	32.4	34.8	41.8
Spain	20–22	33.1	32.0	35.2	35.0	35.3	26.4	25.5	27.5	27.1	27.1	40.0	38.9	43.2	43.3	43.8
Sweden	23–26	35.2	38.4	39.9	44.0	43.3	26.5	28.6	29.7	30.8	29.8	44.1	48.5	50.5	57.6	57.2
Switzerland	23–27	20.8	20.9	22.4	25.0	27.0	23.3	23.5	24.0	26.1	26.8	18.3	18.4	20.9	23.9	27.1
Turkey	22–28	—	—	14.0	11.3	15.4	—	—	15.2	11.8	16.3	—	—	12.7	10.7	14.5
United Kingdom	20–24	—	—	39.2	39.8	39.0	—	—	34.2	34.1	33.0	—	—	44.3	45.7	45.2
United States	22–24	36.1	33.4	33.2	34.2	35.5	29.7	27.6	27.5	28.1	29.1	42.9	39.4	39.2	40.7	42.4
Reporting partner countries																
Brazil	(2)	—	—	15.6	17.5	21.3	—	—	11.8	13.3	16.2	—	—	19.4	21.6	26.4
Chile	22–24	—	—	25.1	11.5	15.0	—	—	22.9	9.7	13.0	—	—	27.5	13.4	17.0
Estonia	22–24	—	—	—	28.5	26.4	—	—	—	17.6	15.4	—	—	—	39.5	37.8
Israel	(2)	—	—	32.3	32.9	33.4	—	—	25.3	25.7	26.8	—	—	39.6	40.2	40.3
Russian Federation	19–25	—	—	—	45.9	43.7	—	—	—	—	—	—	—	—	—	—
Slovenia	25–26	—	—	—	21.6	21.6	—	—	—	14.3	14.2	—	—	—	29.4	29.3

—Not available.

[1]Refers to the mean of the data values for all reporting OECD countries, to which each country reporting data contributes equally. The average is omitted for years in which less than 75 percent of the countries reported data.

[2]Typical age of graduation data not available. Estimates calculated using the age range 22–24.

NOTE: Data in this table refer to degrees classified by the Organization for Economic Cooperation and Development (OECD) as International Standard Classification of Education (ISCED) level 5A, first award. This level corresponds to the bachelor's degree in the United States. The recipients per 100 persons ratio relates the number of people of all ages earning bachelor's degrees in a particular year to the number of people in the population at the typical age of graduation. The typical age is based on full-time attendance and normal progression through the education system (without repeating a year, taking a year off, etc.); this age varies across countries because of differences in their education systems and differences in program duration. Data for Luxembourg are not shown because tertiary students study for only 1 year in Luxembourg. Some data have been revised from previously published figures.

SOURCE: Organization for Economic Cooperation and Development (OECD), *Education at a Glance*, 2004 through 2008; and Online Education Database, retrieved July 6, 2009, from http://stats.oecd.org/default.aspx. (This table was prepared July 2009.)

Percentage of bachelor's degrees awarded in mathematics and science, by field and country: Selected years, 1985 through 2006

Country	All mathematics and science degrees[1]						Natural sciences[2]						Mathematics and computer science[3]						Engineering					
	1985	1990	1995	2000	2005	2006	1985	1990	1995	2000	2005	2006	1985	1990	1995	2000	2005	2006	1985	1990	1995	2000	2005	2006
	2	3	4	5	6	7	8	9	10	11	12	13	14	15	16	17	18	19	20	21	22	23	24	25
OECD average[4]	—	—	—	**22.9**	**22.8**	**22.3**	—	—	—	**5.8**	**4.8**	**4.6**	—	—	—	**4.0**	**5.4**	**5.3**	—	—	—	**13.3**	**12.7**	**12.4**
Australia	—	—	19.3	21.1	21.1	21.3	—	—	9.9	7.6	5.9	6.4	—	—	3.8	5.1	8.2	7.7	—	—	5.6	8.5	7.0	7.2
Austria	16.8	19.6	21.1	25.7	26.8	29.2	5.0	5.3	6.0	5.0	5.4	6.1	4.1	5.2	5.3	3.4	7.2	8.8	—	9.0	9.9	17.3	14.2	14.3
Belgium (Flemish)	—	—	—	23.6	24.7	24.9	4.6	—	—	6.4	5.7	5.5	1.7	—	—	2.3	5.2	5.1	7.7	—	—	14.9	13.8	14.3
Canada	17.1	16.4	16.7	20.0	20.7	17.0	4.9	6.0	6.5	8.1	6.5	5.5	4.5	4.2	3.8	4.3	5.9	4.5	7.7	6.2	6.4	7.6	8.2	7.0
Czech Republic	(5)	(5)	—	29.5	26.7	27.0	(5)	(5)	—	4.2	3.9	3.5	(5)	(5)	—	8.4	3.8	4.7	(5)	(5)	—	16.9	19.0	18.8
Denmark	39.3	33.5	—	10.5	16.3	16.2	6.3	4.4	2.5	6.8	2.4	2.3	—	—	—	3.1	3.1	2.6	16.2	21.7	17.0	0.6	10.8	11.2
Finland	—	—	37.2	32.2	30.0	29.1	7.7	4.1	4.0	3.9	2.7	2.8	6.3	5.9	6.9	3.3	5.6	5.3	25.3	23.4	26.3	24.9	21.7	20.9
France	23.8	31.3	31.6	30.1	26.0	26.2	5.0	7.2	6.7	12.2	6.5	6.7	2.3	3.5	5.2	5.5	5.5	5.7	16.5	20.5	19.7	12.5	14.0	13.8
Germany[6]	—	—	—	31.7	31.3	27.2	—	—	—	6.4	6.3	6.3	(5)	(5)	—	4.9	8.1	8.1	—	—	—	20.3	16.9	12.8
Greece	—	—	—	—	25.9	—	—	—	—	—	8.3	—	—	—	—	—	8.4	—	—	—	—	—	9.2	—
Hungary	28.8	34.1	32.3	12.6	11.0	13.9	12.8	14.1	16.9	1.1	1.2	1.3	4.0	6.3	4.7	4.0	2.4	5.5	12.0	13.7	10.7	7.5	7.4	7.1
Iceland	—	—	—	16.5	14.1	14.6	—	—	—	6.0	5.0	4.7	—	—	—	4.0	3.5	3.0	—	—	—	6.5	5.5	6.9
Ireland	—	—	—	29.3	17.7	—	—	—	—	11.5	3.5	4.8	—	—	—	7.2	4.4	2.2	—	—	—	10.6	9.9	8.9
Italy	19.5	19.7	19.5	27.5	23.9	23.2	8.1	7.6	6.8	5.9	4.8	4.8	3.1	3.9	3.8	3.2	2.2	2.2	8.3	8.2	8.9	18.4	16.9	16.2
Japan	—	—	—	23.0	22.9	22.1	2.4	2.4	3.4	0.7	0.8	1.4	1.8	0.6	0.5	3.4	4.7	3.8	—	—	—	18.9	17.4	16.9
Korea, Republic of	—	—	—	36.9	37.0	36.3	—	—	—	6.3	5.2	5.3	—	—	1.6	4.3	5.4	5.7	—	—	—	26.3	26.3	25.4
Mexico	—	—	15.0	23.0	27.3	26.9	—	—	—	2.2	2.6	2.6	—	—	—	6.7	9.3	8.9	—	—	—	14.1	15.3	15.4
Netherlands	21.8	21.1	—	16.2	14.9	14.6	8.5	7.1	—	3.2	2.5	1.4	1.2	1.6	—	1.9	4.6	5.1	12.1	12.4	—	11.1	7.7	8.1
New Zealand	20.5	19.5	—	17.8	19.9	19.4	11.7	8.2	—	11.2	6.7	6.6	5.5	5.5	—	1.9	7.6	6.7	3.3	5.8	3.2	4.7	5.6	6.1
Norway	15.4	12.9	16.8	11.6	13.7	13.2	2.5	2.1	3.1	0.7	0.8	1.4	1.8	0.6	0.5	3.4	4.7	3.8	11.3	10.2	13.2	7.5	8.2	7.9
Poland	(5)	(5)	—	16.7	17.7	21.6	—	—	—	2.7	2.3	4.0	—	—	—	2.0	5.3	6.0	(5)	(5)	—	12.0	10.1	11.6
Portugal	—	15.0	15.0	17.5	25.6	25.5	—	1.7	2.2	1.7	6.0	4.9	—	2.8	—	3.6	6.2	6.5	—	10.5	—	12.2	13.4	14.1
Slovak Republic	13.9	15.0	18.2	21.9	24.6	21.1	(5)	(5)	5.5	2.0	3.7	3.5	(5)	(5)	4.5	4.6	4.4	4.0	(5)	(5)	9.4	15.3	16.5	13.7
Spain	—	18.2	22.7	22.7	24.1	24.4	—	6.7	4.3	5.3	4.2	4.0	—	4.7	4.5	4.3	5.2	5.5	—	6.7	9.4	13.1	14.7	14.8
Sweden	20.2	24.0	26.4	27.7	26.9	26.2	2.6	4.1	3.9	3.7	4.0	3.6	1.6	5.5	5.5	3.7	3.7	3.9	11.3	15.2	17.0	20.3	19.2	18.7
Switzerland	20.2	23.0	22.3	25.1	24.2	22.7	10.3	11.2	10.4	6.0	6.9	6.2	2.1	3.6	3.7	3.7	4.7	4.3	7.9	8.1	8.3	11.0	12.7	12.1
Turkey	23.0	20.6	20.9	24.1	22.3	17.1	3.6	4.6	5.1	7.4	6.1	4.9	1.6	2.1	2.7	3.6	3.6	3.2	17.8	13.8	13.1	13.1	12.4	9.0
United Kingdom	—	—	—	28.5	26.0	25.2	—	—	—	12.5	9.2	9.0	—	—	—	5.8	8.3	7.7	—	13.8	13.1	10.2	8.4	8.5
United States	21.7	16.9	—	17.1	16.7	16.4	6.3	5.1	—	6.6	5.8	6.0	5.5	4.0	—	3.9	4.8	4.2	9.8	7.8	—	6.6	6.2	6.1
Reporting partner countries																								
Brazil	—	—	—	—	11.4	11.3	—	—	—	—	3.2	3.2	—	—	—	—	3.5	3.3	—	—	—	—	4.8	4.7
Chile	—	—	—	—	22.9	24.0	—	—	—	—	3.2	2.5	—	—	—	—	2.6	3.8	—	—	—	—	17.2	17.7
Estonia	—	—	—	—	23.8	21.1	—	—	—	—	6.3	4.7	—	—	—	—	6.2	5.9	—	—	—	—	11.3	10.5
Israel	—	—	—	19.0	26.7	24.1	—	—	—	3.1	5.1	5.4	—	—	—	6.8	7.5	5.4	—	—	—	9.1	14.1	13.3
Russian Federation	—	—	—	—	—	—	—	—	—	—	—	—	—	—	—	—	—	—	—	—	—	—	—	—
Slovenia	—	—	—	—	17.7	15.0	—	—	—	—	4.1	2.8	—	—	—	—	2.0	2.1	—	—	—	—	11.7	10.1

—Not available.

[1] Includes life sciences, physical sciences, mathematics/statistics, computer science, and engineering.
[2] Includes life sciences and physical sciences.
[3] Includes mathematics/statistics and computer science.
[4] Refers to the mean of the data values for all reporting OECD countries, to which each country reporting data contributes equally. The average is omitted for years in which less than 75 percent of the countries reported data.
[5] Country did not exist in its current form in the given year.
[6] Data for 1985 are for the former West Germany.

NOTE: Data in this table refer to degrees classified by the Organization for Economic Cooperation and Development (OECD) as International Standard Classification of Education (ISCED) level 5A, first award. This level corresponds to the bachelor's degree in the United States. Data for Luxembourg are not shown because tertiary students study for only 1 year in Luxembourg. Some data have been revised from previously published figures.

SOURCE: Organization for Economic Cooperation and Development (OECD), Online Education Database. Retrieved July 23, 2009, from http://stats.oecd.org/index.aspx. (This table was prepared July 2009.)

Percentage of graduate degrees awarded in mathematics and science, by field and country: Selected years, 1985 through 2006

Country	All mathematics and science degrees[1]						Natural sciences[2]						Mathematics and computer science[3]						Engineering					
1	1985	1990	1996	2000	2005	2006	1985	1990	1996	2000	2005	2006	1985	1990	1996	2000	2005	2006	1985	1990	1996	2000	2005	2006
	2	3	4	5	6	7	8	9	10	11	12	13	14	15	16	17	18	19	20	21	22	23	24	25
OECD average[4]	—	—	—	**27.5**	**24.5**	**23.5**	—	—	—	**10.8**	**8.7**	**7.9**	—	—	—	**5.1**	**5.0**	**4.9**	—	—	—	**12.2**	**11.8**	**11.5**
Australia	43.3	—	14.0	15.2	20.0	21.4	—	—	5.4	4.0	3.1	2.7	—	—	3.8	4.9	8.7	10.6	—	—	4.7	6.3	8.1	8.0
Austria	—	37.7	38.8	39.2	38.6	43.0	14.2	12.3	17.5	16.7	15.0	14.4	7.3	4.6	4.7	4.7	6.6	12.0	21.7	20.8	16.6	17.7	16.9	16.6
Belgium (Flemish)	—	20.0	—	22.4	18.7	19.7	—	7.8	—	12.7	9.3	9.6	—	3.4	—	4.1	3.3	3.7	—	8.8	—	7.0	6.2	6.4
Canada	19.7	20.0	22.3	22.4	18.8	25.3	7.5	7.8	7.7	7.4	5.0	6.5	2.8	3.4	3.5	4.1	4.0	4.9	9.4	8.8	11.2	10.9	9.8	13.9
Czech Republic	(⁵)	(⁵)	—	21.0	26.1	16.4	(⁵)	(⁵)	—	5.3	8.3	4.3	(⁵)	(⁵)	—	7.9	5.6	3.3	(⁵)	(⁵)	—	7.7	12.3	8.7
Denmark	16.0	22.2	12.3	27.8	23.4	22.2	4.1	5.8	3.1	9.8	7.5	6.9	2.7	4.8	1.5	2.5	9.2	8.0	9.2	11.6	7.8	15.4	6.7	7.2
Finland	47.6	30.6	28.3	28.7	30.5	33.8	24.0	14.7	11.6	11.3	11.6	12.4	6.3	5.4	4.0	2.4	4.1	4.5	17.2	10.5	12.7	14.9	14.8	16.9
France	27.7	33.2	38.6	26.4	28.4	26.6	18.7	23.5	25.5	13.5	12.5	10.1	1.8	2.3	3.5	5.6	7.0	6.5	7.2	7.4	9.5	7.3	8.9	10.1
Germany[6]	—	—	—	38.1	30.9	31.3	—	—	—	24.9	14.8	14.0	—	—	—	3.7	4.8	5.7	—	—	—	9.5	11.3	11.7
Greece	—	—	—	—	42.8	—	—	—	—	—	22.3	—	—	—	—	—	5.3	—	—	—	—	—	15.2	—
Hungary	—	—	—	9.9	6.4	6.1	—	—	—	1.7	1.8	1.7	—	—	—	0.7	1.7	1.2	—	—	—	7.5	2.9	3.2
Iceland	—	—	—	35.9	23.0	14.8	—	—	—	19.4	9.5	7.0	—	—	—	#	3.0	1.9	—	—	—	16.5	10.5	5.9
Ireland	31.4	34.5	23.1	28.1	16.8	12.9	18.9	19.4	10.9	6.9	4.1	4.8	2.6	—	3.0	15.2	6.3	2.0	9.9	—	9.2	6.0	6.4	6.1
Italy	—	—	—	11.7	15.9	18.2	9.5	9.5	10.2	0.3	3.5	4.8	—	—	—	5.8	3.5	2.0	40.5	45.1	44.4	41.9	38.0	36.9
Japan	—	—	—	22.0	25.8	26.1	—	—	—	14.9	7.8	8.2	—	—	—	4.6	11.9	11.7	—	—	—	2.5	6.1	6.2
Korea, Republic of	—	—	—	48.4	43.9	41.6	—	—	—	8.5	9.5	9.2	—	—	—	5.7	2.0	1.8	—	—	—	34.3	32.4	30.6
Mexico	—	—	18.6	31.4	14.7	14.0	—	—	4.4	18.9	3.3	3.2	—	—	3.7	4.1	3.2	3.6	—	—	10.6	8.4	8.2	7.2
Netherlands	—	28.9	16.7	20.5	18.2	14.7	—	13.8	2.4	11.6	3.6	3.2	—	4.7	3.7	1.4	2.3	2.5	—	9.7	10.6	7.5	11.9	8.9
New Zealand	45.1	22.6	—	22.0	16.6	15.0	24.6	8.0	—	14.7	7.2	7.7	5.4	4.7	—	2.1	5.2	4.0	15.1	9.9	—	5.2	4.2	3.3
Norway	40.1	33.4	38.3	—	23.7	26.1	17.9	8.0	8.7	—	7.8	8.2	3.5	2.1	1.9	—	4.1	4.1	18.7	23.3	27.7	—	11.8	13.8
Poland	—	—	—	3.3	8.7	9.8	—	—	—	0.7	1.5	2.6	—	—	—	0.7	3.7	3.1	—	—	—	1.9	3.5	4.1
Portugal	(⁵)	(⁵)	—	39.3	33.8	35.8	(⁵)	(⁵)	—	11.7	12.9	9.8	(⁵)	(⁵)	—	9.4	10.0	10.4	(⁵)	(⁵)	—	18.2	11.9	12.5
Slovak Republic	(⁵)	(⁵)	36.1	38.1	36.8	34.3	(⁵)	(⁵)	—	12.6	10.8	9.2	(⁵)	(⁵)	4.1	4.7	4.2	4.2	(⁵)	(⁵)	—	20.9	21.8	21.0
Spain	35.6	26.9	36.0	36.1	37.5	34.3	—	—	—	23.9	23.8	26.1	—	1.8	4.1	5.4	4.6	4.2	5.1	5.7	7.1	6.8	9.1	4.1
Sweden	48.0	48.5	32.3	40.5	23.7	30.3	21.2	19.4	9.2	14.3	8.0	8.5	6.8	9.2	5.9	4.0	2.8	4.1	20.0	19.9	17.1	22.2	12.9	17.7
Switzerland	30.7	30.2	40.1	42.7	32.0	31.0	20.3	22.0	25.8	11.7	11.7	12.9	2.8	1.7	4.1	19.5	3.4	3.2	7.6	6.5	10.1	11.6	16.9	14.9
Turkey	35.8	24.0	—	25.7	21.4	20.1	6.6	7.6	—	7.6	6.7	5.9	2.8	3.3	—	3.0	3.4	3.2	26.3	13.2	—	15.2	11.2	11.0
United Kingdom	—	—	—	21.7	20.3	20.1	—	—	—	7.4	5.5	5.5	—	—	—	5.0	5.7	5.3	—	—	—	9.2	9.1	9.3
United States	13.5	14.5	13.8	13.0	13.5	13.1	4.5	4.2	4.0	3.4	3.3	3.4	2.8	3.4	3.2	3.4	3.5	3.3	6.3	6.9	6.7	6.2	6.7	6.4
Reporting partner countries																								
Brazil	—	—	—	—	8.5	8.7	—	—	—	—	2.2	3.2	—	—	—	—	1.6	1.2	—	—	—	—	4.6	4.2
Chile	—	—	—	—	23.9	22.3	—	—	—	—	10.0	10.3	—	—	—	—	5.0	5.0	—	—	—	—	8.9	7.0
Estonia	(⁵)	(⁵)	—	18.1	17.9	19.5	(⁵)	(⁵)	—	9.2	8.9	9.6	(⁵)	(⁵)	—	2.8	3.2	3.5	(⁵)	(⁵)	—	6.1	5.9	6.5
Israel	(⁵)	(⁵)	—	—	—	—	(⁵)	(⁵)	—	—	—	—	(⁵)	(⁵)	—	—	—	—	(⁵)	(⁵)	—	—	—	—
Russian Federation	(⁵)	(⁵)	—	—	24.2	20.4	(⁵)	(⁵)	—	—	6.4	5.6	(⁵)	(⁵)	—	—	4.2	4.4	(⁵)	(⁵)	—	—	13.6	10.5

— Not available.
Rounds to zero.
[1] Includes life sciences, physical sciences, mathematics/statistics, computer science, and engineering.
[2] Includes life sciences and physical sciences.
[3] Includes mathematics/statistics and computer science.
[4] Refers to the mean of the data values for all reporting OECD countries, to which each country reporting data contributes equally. The average is omitted for years in which less than 75 percent of the countries reported data.
[5] Country did not exist in its current form in the given year.
[6] Data for 1985 are for the former West Germany.

NOTE: Data in this table refer to degrees classified by the Organization for Economic Cooperation and Development (OECD) as International Standard Classification of Education (ISCED) level 5A, second award, and as ISCED 6. ISCED 5A, second award, corresponds to master's and first-professional degrees in the United States, and ISCED 6 corresponds to doctor's degrees. Data for Luxembourg are not shown because tertiary students study for only 1 year in Luxembourg. Some data have been revised from previously published figures.

SOURCE: Organization for Economic Cooperation and Development (OECD), Online Education Database. Retrieved July 27, 2009, from http://stats.oecd.org/Index.aspx. (This table was prepared July 2009.)

Public and private education expenditures per student, by level of education and country: Selected years, 2000 through 2006

Country	Elementary education				Secondary education				Higher education			
	2000	2004	2005	2006	2000	2004	2005	2006	2000	2004	2005	2006
1	2	3	4	5	6	7	8	9	10	11	12	13
Current dollars												
OECD average[1]	$4,393	$5,832	$6,252	$6,437	$5,934	$7,294	$7,802	$8,015	$9,509	$11,100	$11,512	$12,336
Australia	4,967	5,776	5,992	6,311	6,894	8,160	8,408	8,700	12,854	14,036	14,579	15,016
Austria	6,560	7,669	8,259	8,516	8,578	9,446	9,751	10,577	10,851	13,959	14,775	15,148
Belgium	4,310	6,636	6,648	7,072	6,889 [2]	7,751 [2]	7,731 [2]	8,601 [2]	10,771	11,842	11,960	13,244
Canada	—	—	—	—	5,947 [3]	7,837 [3,4]	7,774 [3,4]	—	14,983	—	—	—
Czech Republic	1,827	2,791	2,812	3,217	3,239	4,779	4,847	5,307	5,431	6,752	6,649	7,989
Denmark	7,074	8,081	8,513	8,798	7,726 [5]	8,849 [5]	9,407 [5]	9,662 [5]	11,981 [5]	15,225 [5]	14,959 [5]	15,391 [5]
Finland	4,317	5,581	5,557	5,899	6,094 [2]	7,441 [2]	7,324 [2]	7,533 [2]	8,244	12,505	12,285	12,845
France	4,486	5,082	5,365	5,482	7,636	8,737	8,927	9,303	8,373	10,668	10,995	11,568
Germany	4,198	4,948	5,014	5,362	6,826	7,576	7,636	7,548	10,898	12,255	12,446	13,016
Greece	3,318 [4,6]	4,595 [4]	5,146 [4]	—	3,859 [6]	5,213	8,423	—	3,402 [6]	5,593	6,130	—
Hungary[6]	2,245	3,841	4,438	4,599	2,446	3,692	3,806	3,978	7,024	7,095	6,244	6,367
Iceland	5,854 [6]	8,434	9,254	9,299	6,518 [6]	7,721 [5]	8,411 [5]	8,493 [2]	7,994 [6]	8,881 [5]	9,474 [5]	8,579
Ireland	3,385	5,422	5,732	6,337	4,638	7,110	7,500	8,991	11,083	10,211	10,468	11,832
Italy	5,973 [6]	7,390 [6]	6,835 [6]	7,716 [6]	7,218 [6]	7,843 [6]	7,648 [6]	8,495 [6]	8,065 [6]	7,723 [6]	8,026 [6]	8,725
Japan	5,507	6,551	6,744	6,989	6,266 [5]	7,615 [5]	7,908 [5]	8,305 [5]	10,914 [5]	12,193 [5]	12,326 [5]	13,418 [5]
Korea, Republic of	3,155	4,490	4,691	4,935	4,069	6,761	6,645	7,261	6,118	7,068	7,606	8,564
Luxembourg	—	13,458 [4,6]	14,079 [4,6]	13,676 [4,6]	—	17,876 [6]	18,845 [6]	18,144 [6]	—	—	—	—
Mexico	1,291	1,694	1,913	2,003	1,615	1,922	2,180	2,165	4,688	5,778	6,402	6,462
Netherlands	4,325	6,222	6,266	6,425	5,912	7,541	7,741	9,516	11,934	13,846	13,883	15,196
New Zealand	—	5,190	4,780	4,952	—	6,299	6,278	6,043	—	8,866	10,262	9,288
Norway	6,550	8,533	9,001	9,486	8,476 [2,6]	11,109 [2]	10,995 [2]	11,435 [2]	13,353 [6]	14,997	15,552	16,235
Poland[6]	2,105	3,130	3,312	3,770	—	2,889	3,055	3,411	3,222	4,412	5,593	5,224
Portugal	3,672	4,681 [6]	4,871 [6]	5,138 [6]	5,349	6,168 [6]	6,473 [6]	6,846 [6]	4,766	7,741 [6]	8,787 [6]	9,724 [6]
Slovak Republic	1,308	2,073	2,806	3,221	1,927 [2]	2,744 [2]	2,716 [2]	2,963 [2]	4,949	6,535	5,783	6,056
Spain	3,941	4,965	5,502	5,970	5,185 [2]	6,701	7,211	7,955	6,666	9,378	10,089	11,087
Sweden	6,336	7,469	7,532	7,699	6,339	8,039	8,198	8,496	15,097	16,218	15,946	16,991
Switzerland[6]	6,631	8,570	8,469	8,793	9,780	12,176	12,861	13,268	18,450	21,966	21,734	22,230
Turkey[6]	—	1,120	—	1,130	—	1,808	—	1,834	4,121	—	—	—
United Kingdom	3,877	5,941	6,361	7,732	5,991 [2]	7,090 [2]	7,167 [2]	8,763 [2]	9,657	11,484	13,506	15,447
United States	6,995	8,805	9,156	9,709	8,855	9,938	10,390	10,821	20,358 [2]	22,476	24,370	25,109
Constant 2008 dollars												
OECD average[1]	$5,492	$6,648	$6,892	$6,875	$7,419	$8,315	$8,601	$8,560	$11,889	$12,653	$12,692	$13,176
Australia	6,210	6,584	6,606	6,740	8,620	9,301	9,270	9,291	16,071	15,999	16,073	16,037
Austria	8,202	8,742	9,105	9,096	10,725	10,767	10,751	11,296	13,567	15,911	16,289	16,178
Belgium	5,389	7,564	7,329	7,553	8,613 [2]	8,835 [2]	8,523 [2]	9,186 [2]	13,467	13,498	13,186	14,144
Canada	—	—	—	—	7,436 [3]	8,933 [3,4]	8,571 [3,4]	—	18,733	—	—	—
Czech Republic	2,284	3,181	3,100	3,436	4,050	5,447	5,344	5,668	6,790	7,696	7,330	8,532
Denmark	8,845	9,211	9,386	9,396	9,660 [5]	10,087 [5]	10,371 [5]	10,319 [5]	14,980 [5]	17,355 [5]	16,492 [5]	16,438 [5]
Finland	5,398	6,362	6,127	6,300	7,619 [2]	8,482 [2]	8,074 [2]	8,045 [2]	10,308	14,254	13,544	13,719
France	5,609	5,793	5,915	5,855	9,547	9,959	9,841	9,936	10,469	12,160	12,122	12,355
Germany	5,249	5,640	5,528	5,727	8,535	8,636	8,418	8,061	13,626	13,969	13,721	13,901
Greece	4,149 [4,6]	5,238 [4]	5,673 [4]	—	4,825 [6]	5,942	9,286	—	4,254 [6]	6,375	6,759	—
Hungary[6]	2,807	4,378	4,893	4,912	3,058	4,208	4,196	4,248	8,782	8,087	6,884	6,800
Iceland	7,319 [6]	9,614	10,202	9,932	8,149 [6]	8,801 [5]	9,273 [5]	9,070 [2]	9,995 [6]	10,123 [5]	10,445 [5]	9,162
Ireland	4,232	6,180	6,320	6,768	5,799	8,104	8,269	9,602	13,857	11,639	11,541	12,636
Italy	7,468 [6]	8,424 [6]	7,535 [6]	8,241 [6]	9,025 [6]	8,940 [6]	8,432 [6]	9,073 [6]	10,084 [6]	8,803 [6]	8,848 [6]	9,318
Japan	6,885	7,467	7,435	7,465	7,834 [5]	8,680 [5]	8,718 [5]	8,870 [5]	13,646 [5]	13,898 [5]	13,589 [5]	14,331 [5]
Korea, Republic of	3,945	5,118	5,171	5,271	5,087	7,707	7,326	7,755	7,649	8,057	8,385	9,147
Luxembourg	—	15,340 [4,6]	15,522 [4,6]	14,606 [4,6]	—	20,376 [6]	20,776 [6]	19,378 [6]	—	—	—	—
Mexico	1,614	1,931	2,109	2,139	2,019	2,191	2,403	2,312	5,861	6,586	7,058	6,901
Netherlands	5,408	7,092	6,909	6,862	7,392	8,596	8,534	10,163	14,921	15,783	15,305	16,229
New Zealand	—	5,916	5,270	5,289	—	7,180	6,922	6,454	—	10,106	11,313	9,919
Norway	8,189	9,727	9,923	10,131	10,598 [2,6]	12,663 [2]	12,121 [2]	12,213 [2]	16,695 [6]	17,095	17,146	17,339
Poland[6]	2,632	3,568	3,651	4,026	—	3,293	3,368	3,643	4,028	5,029	6,166	5,579
Portugal	4,591	5,336 [6]	5,370 [6]	5,488 [6]	6,688	7,031 [6]	7,137 [6]	7,312 [6]	5,959	8,824 [6]	9,688 [6]	10,385 [6]
Slovak Republic	1,635	2,363	3,094	3,440	2,409 [2]	3,128 [2]	2,994 [2]	3,164 [2]	6,188	7,449	6,376	6,468
Spain	4,927	5,659	6,066	6,376	6,483 [2]	7,638	7,950	8,496	8,335	10,690	11,123	11,841
Sweden	7,922	8,514	8,304	8,222	7,926	9,163	9,038	9,074	18,876	18,486	17,580	18,146
Switzerland[6]	8,291	9,769	9,337	9,391	12,228	13,879	14,179	14,170	23,068	25,038	23,961	23,742
Turkey[6]	—	1,277	—	1,207	—	2,061	—	1,959	5,153	—	—	—
United Kingdom	4,847	6,772	7,013	8,258	7,491 [2]	8,082 [2]	7,901 [2]	9,359 [2]	12,074	13,090	14,890	16,498
United States	8,746	10,037	10,094	10,369	11,071	11,328	11,454	11,557	25,454 [2]	25,620	26,867	26,816

—Not available.

[1]Refers to the mean of the data values for all reporting OECD countries, to which each country reporting data contributes equally. The average is omitted for years in which less than 75 percent of the countries reported data.

[2]Includes postsecondary non-higher-education.

[3]Includes elementary education.

[4]Includes preprimary education.

[5]Postsecondary non-higher-education included in both secondary and higher education.

[6]Public institutions only.

NOTE: Data adjusted to U.S. dollars using the purchasing-power-parity (PPP) index. Constant dollars based on the Consumer Price Index, prepared by the Bureau of Labor Statistics, U.S. Department of Labor.

SOURCE: Organization for Economic Cooperation and Development (OECD), *Education at a Glance*, 2002 through 2009. (This table was prepared June 2009.)

Total public direct expenditures on education as a percentage of the gross domestic product, by level of education and country: Selected years, 1985 through 2006

Country	All institutions							Primary and secondary institutions							Higher education institutions						
	1985	1990	1995	2000[1]	2004[1]	2005[1]	2006[1]	1985	1990	1995	2000[1]	2004[1]	2005[1]	2006[1]	1985	1990	1995	2000[1]	2004[1]	2005[1]	2006[1]
1	2	3	4	5	6	7	8	9	10	11	12	13	14	15	16	17	18	19	20	21	22
OECD average²	—	4.9	4.9	5.2	5.0	5.0	4.9	—	3.5	3.5	3.5	3.5	3.5	3.4	—	1.0	0.9	1.2	1.1	1.1	1.0
Australia	5.4	4.3	4.5	5.1	4.3	4.3	4.1	3.5	3.2	3.2	3.9	3.5	3.4	3.3	1.7	1.0	1.2	1.2	0.8	0.8	0.8
Austria	5.6	5.2	5.3	5.8	5.0	5.2	5.2	3.7	3.6	3.8	3.8[3]	3.6	3.5	3.5	1.0	1.0	0.9	1.4[3]	1.1	1.2	1.2
Belgium (Flemish)	6.3	4.8	5.0	5.2	5.8	5.8	5.9	4.0	3.4	3.4	3.4[4]	4.0	3.9	3.9	1.0	0.8	0.9	1.3[4]	1.2	1.2	1.2
Canada	6.1	5.4	5.8	5.5	4.7	4.8	—	4.1	3.7	4.0	3.3[5]	3.2[5,6]	3.3[5,6]	—	2.0	1.5	1.5	2.0[5]	1.4[5]	1.5[5]	—
Czech Republic	†	†	4.8	4.4	4.2	4.1	4.2	†	†	3.4	3.0[4]	2.8	2.7	2.7	†	†	0.7	0.8[4]	0.9	0.8	1.0
Denmark	6.2	6.2	6.5	8.4	6.9	6.8	6.7	4.7	4.4	4.2	4.8[3,8]	4.2[8]	4.4[8]	4.3[8]	1.2	1.3	1.3	2.5[3,8]	1.8[8]	1.6[8]	1.6[8]
Finland	5.8	6.4	6.6	6.0	6.0	5.9	5.7	—	4.3	4.2	3.6	3.9	3.8	3.7	—	1.2	1.7	2.0	1.7	1.7	1.6
France	—	5.1	5.8	5.8	5.7	5.6	5.5	—	3.7	4.1	4.1	3.9	3.8	3.7	—	0.8	1.0	1.0	1.2	1.1	1.1
Germany⁹	4.6	—	4.5	4.5	4.3	4.2	4.1	2.8	—	2.9	3.0	2.8	2.8	2.7	1.0	—	1.0	1.1	1.0	0.9	0.9
Greece	—	—	3.7	3.8	3.3	4.0	4.1	—	—	2.8	2.7[3,6]	2.1[6]	2.5[6]	2.7	—	—	0.8	0.9[3]	1.1	1.4	—
Hungary	—	5.0	4.9	4.9	5.1	5.1	5.1	—	3.5	3.3	3.1	3.3	3.3	3.2	—	0.8	0.8	1.0	0.9	0.9	0.9
Iceland	—	4.3	4.5	6.0	7.2	7.2	7.2	—	3.3	3.4	4.7[3]	5.2[8]	5.2[8]	5.1	—	0.6	0.7	1.1[3]	1.1[8]	1.1[8]	1.0
Ireland	5.6	4.7	4.7	4.4	4.3	4.3	5.1	4.0	3.3	3.3	3.0[4]	3.3	3.3	3.4	0.9	0.9	0.9	1.3[4]	1.0	1.0	1.0
Italy	4.7	5.8	4.5	4.6	4.4	4.3	4.6	3.2	4.1	3.2	3.2	3.3	3.2	3.4	0.6	1.0	0.7	0.8	0.7	0.6	0.7
Japan	3.6	3.6	3.6	3.6	3.5	3.4	3.3	—	2.9	2.8	2.7[8]	2.7[8]	2.6[8]	2.6[8]	—	0.4	0.4	0.5[8]	0.5[8]	0.5[8]	0.5[8]
Korea, Republic of	—	—	3.6	4.3	4.4	4.3	4.5	—	—	3.0	3.3	3.5	3.4	3.4	—	—	0.3	0.7	0.5	0.6	0.6
Luxembourg	—	—	4.3	—	—	—	—	—	—	4.2	—	3.8[6]	3.7[6]	3.3[6]	—	—	0.1	—	—	—	—
Mexico	—	3.2	4.6	4.9	5.2	5.3	4.6	—	2.2	3.4	3.4	3.6	3.7	3.2	—	0.7	0.8	0.9	0.9	0.9	0.8
Netherlands	6.2	5.7	4.6	4.8	4.6	4.6	4.8	4.1	3.6	3.0	3.2	3.3	3.3	3.3	1.5	1.6	1.1	1.3	1.0	1.0	1.1
New Zealand	—	5.5	5.3	7.0	5.6	5.2	5.0	—	3.9	3.8	4.9	4.4	4.0	3.8	—	1.2	1.1	1.7	0.9	0.9	0.9
Norway	5.1	6.2	6.8	6.7	6.2	5.7	5.4	4.0	4.1	4.1	3.9	4.2	3.8	3.7	0.7	1.1	1.5	1.7	1.4	1.3	1.2
Poland	—	—	5.2	5.2	5.4	5.4	5.2	—	—	3.3	3.8[3]	3.7	3.7	3.5	—	—	0.8	0.8[3]	1.1	1.2	0.9
Portugal	—	—	5.4	5.7	5.3	5.3	5.1	—	—	4.1	4.2[3]	3.8	3.8	3.6	—	—	1.0	1.0[3]	0.9	0.9	0.9
Slovak Republic	†	†	4.6	4.2	4.0	3.7	3.6	†	†	—	2.7[3,4]	2.6[10]	2.5[10]	2.4[10]	†	†	—	0.7[3,4]	0.9[10]	0.7[10]	0.8[10]
Spain	3.6	4.2	4.8	4.4	4.2	4.1	4.2	2.9	3.2	3.5	3.1	2.8	2.7	2.7	0.4	0.7	0.8	1.0	0.9	0.9	0.9
Sweden	4.9	5.3	6.6	7.4	6.5	6.2	6.2	4.0	3.7	4.4	4.9[4]	4.5	4.2	4.1	0.9	1.0	1.6	2.0[4]	1.6	1.5	1.4
Switzerland	—	5.0	5.5	5.4	5.9	5.6	5.4	—	3.7	4.1	3.9	3.9	3.9	3.7	—	1.0	1.1	1.2	1.6	1.4	1.4
Turkey	—	3.2	2.2	3.5	3.8	—	2.7	—	2.3	1.4	2.4[3]	2.9	—	1.9	—	0.9	0.8	1.1[3]	0.9	—	0.8
United Kingdom	4.9	4.3	4.6	4.8	5.0	5.0	5.2	3.1	3.5	3.8	3.4	3.8	3.8	3.9	1.0	0.7	0.7	1.0	0.9	0.9	0.9
United States	4.7	5.3	5.0	5.0	5.1	4.8	5.0	3.2	3.8	3.5	3.5[5]	3.7	3.5	3.7	1.3	1.4	1.1	1.5[5]	1.0	1.0	0.9
Reporting partner countries																					
Brazil	†	†	—	—	3.9	4.4	4.9	†	†	—	—	2.9[10]	3.3	3.8	†	†	—	—	0.7[10]	0.8	0.8
Chile	†	†	—	—	3.5	3.3	3.0	†	†	—	—	2.8	2.7	2.4	†	†	—	—	0.3	0.3	0.3
Estonia	†	†	—	—	4.9	4.7	4.6	†	†	—	—	3.7	3.5	3.4	†	†	—	—	0.9	0.9	0.9
Israel	†	†	—	—	6.6	6.2	6.2	†	†	—	—	4.4	4.2	4.1	†	†	—	—	1.1	1.0	1.0
Russian Federation	†	3.4	—	3.0	3.6	3.8	3.9	†	1.9	—	1.7	2.0	1.9	2.0	†	0.7	—	0.5	0.7	0.8	0.8
Slovenia	†	†	—	—	5.4	5.3	5.3	†	†	—	—	3.9	3.9	3.8	†	†	—	—	1.1	1.0	1.0

—Not available.
†Country did not exist in its current form in the given year.
[1]Includes public subsidies to households attributable for educational institutions and direct expenditure on educational institutions from international sources, except where noted.
²Refers to the mean of the data values for all reporting OECD countries, to which each country reporting data contributes equally. The average is omitted for years in which less than 75 percent of the countries reported data.
³Public subsidies to households not included in public expenditure.
⁴Direct expenditure on education institutions from international sources exceeds 1.5 percent of all public expenditure.
⁵Postsecondary non-higher-education included in higher education.
⁶Primary education (for children age 3 and older) is included in primary and secondary education.
⁷Country did not exist in its current form in the given year.
⁸Postsecondary non-higher-education included in both secondary and higher education.
⁹Data for 1985 are for the former West Germany.
¹⁰Occupation-specific education corresponding to that offered at the associate's degree level in the United States is included in primary and secondary education.
NOTE: Direct public expenditure on educational services includes both amounts spent directly by governments to hire educational personnel and to procure other resources, and amounts provided by governments to public or private institutions, or households. Figures for 1985 also include transfers and payments to private entities, and thus are not strictly comparable with later figures. Postsecondary non-higher-education is included in primary and secondary education unless otherwise noted. Some data have been revised from previously published figures.
SOURCE: Organization for Economic Cooperation and Development (OECD), Online Education Database; Annual National Accounts, Vol. 1, 1997; and Education at a Glance, 2007 through 2009. (This table was prepared August 2009.)

Foreign students enrolled in institutions of higher education in the United States, by continent, region, and selected countries of origin: Selected years, 1980–81 through 2007–08

Continent, region, and country of origin	1980–81 Number	Percent	1985–86 Number	Percent	1990–91 Number	Percent	1995–96 Number	Percent	2000–01 Number	Percent	2003–04 Number	Percent	2004–05 Number	Percent	2005–06 Number	Percent	2006–07 Number	Percent	2007–08 Number	Percent
1	2	3	4	5	6	7	8	9	10	11	12	13	14	15	16	17	18	19	20	21
Total	311,880	100.0	343,780	100.0	407,280	100.0	453,787	100.00	547,873	100.0	572,509	100.0	563,308	100.0	564,766	100.0	582,984	100.0	623,805	100.0
Africa	38,180	12.2	34,190	9.9	23,803	5.8	20,844	4.6	34,217	6.2	38,150	6.7	36,100	6.4	36,308	6.4	35,802	6.1	35,654	5.7
East Africa	6,260	2.0	6,730	2.0	7,592	1.9	7,596	1.7	13,516	2.5	14,831	2.6	13,675	2.4	13,635	2.4	13,374	2.3	12,664	2.0
Kenya	1,930	0.6	1,720	0.5	2,357	0.6	2,934	0.6	6,229	1.1	6,728	1.2	6,728	1.2	6,559	1.2	6,349	1.1	5,838	0.9
Central Africa	1,130	0.4	1,540	0.4	1,647	0.4	1,346	0.3	1,859	0.3	2,331	0.4	2,505	0.4	2,825	0.5	3,257	0.6	3,405	0.5
North Africa	7,310	2.3	5,980	1.7	4,541	1.1	3,422	0.8	5,184	0.9	4,487	0.8	3,898	0.7	3,770	0.7	3,700	0.6	3,858	0.6
Southern Africa	1,480	0.5	2,360	0.7	2,835	0.7	2,657	0.6	3,304	0.6	2,679	0.5	2,240	0.4	2,232	0.4	2,124	0.4	2,095	0.3
West Africa	22,000	7.1	17,580	5.1	7,178	1.8	5,818	1.3	10,346	1.9	13,821	2.4	13,782	2.4	13,846	2.5	13,344	2.3	13,632	2.2
Nigeria	17,350	5.6	13,710	4.0	3,714	0.9	2,093	0.5	3,820	0.7	6,140	1.1	6,335	1.1	6,192	1.1	5,943	1.0	6,222	1.0
Asia	94,640	30.3	156,830	45.6	229,825	56.4	259,893	57.3	302,058	55.1	324,006	56.6	325,112	57.7	327,785	58.0	344,495	59.1	380,465	61.0
East Asia	51,650	16.6	80,720	23.5	146,017	35.9	166,717	36.7	189,371	34.6	189,874	33.2	192,561	34.2	189,576	35.0	204,023	35.0	223,306	35.8
China	2,770	0.9	13,980	4.1	39,597	9.7	39,613	8.7	59,939	10.9	61,765	10.8	62,523	11.1	62,582	11.1	67,723	11.6	81,127	13.0
Hong Kong	9,660	3.1	10,710	3.1	12,625	3.1	12,018	2.6	7,627	1.4	7,353	1.3	7,180	1.3	7,849	1.4	7,722	1.3	8,286	1.3
Japan	13,500	4.3	13,360	3.9	36,611	9.0	45,531	10.0	46,497	8.5	40,835	7.1	42,215	7.5	38,712	6.9	35,282	6.1	33,974	5.4
South Korea	6,150	2.0	18,660	5.4	23,362	5.7	36,231	8.0	45,685	8.3	52,484	9.2	53,358	9.5	59,022	10.5	62,392	10.7	69,124	11.1
Taiwan	19,460	6.2	23,770	6.9	33,531	8.2	32,702	7.0	28,566	5.2	26,178	4.6	25,914	4.6	27,876	4.9	29,094	5.0	29,001	4.6
South and Central Asia	14,540	4.7	25,800	7.5	42,366	10.4	45,401	10.0	71,765	13.1	98,138	17.1	97,961	17.4	94,965	16.8	104,457	17.9	117,001	18.8
India	9,250	3.0	16,070	4.7	28,857	7.1	31,743	7.0	54,664	10.0	79,736	13.9	80,466	14.3	76,503	13.5	83,833	14.4	94,563	15.2
Nepal	250	0.1	390	0.1	670	0.2	1,219	0.3	2,618	0.5	4,384	0.8	4,861	0.9	6,061	1.1	7,754	1.3	8,936	1.4
Pakistan	2,990	1.0	5,440	1.6	7,725	1.9	6,427	1.4	6,948	1.3	7,325	1.3	6,296	1.1	5,759	1.0	5,401	0.9	5,345	0.9
Southeast Asia	28,450	9.1	50,310	14.6	41,441	10.2	47,774	10.5	40,916	7.5	35,994	6.3	34,590	6.1	35,244	6.2	36,015	6.2	40,152	6.4
Indonesia	3,250	1.0	8,210	2.4	9,524	2.3	12,820	2.8	11,625	2.1	8,880	1.6	7,760	1.4	7,575	1.3	7,338	1.3	7,692	1.2
Malaysia	6,010	1.9	23,020	6.7	13,606	3.3	14,015	3.1	7,795	1.4	6,483	1.1	6,142	1.1	5,515	1.0	5,281	0.9	5,428	0.9
Philippines	3,390	1.1	3,920	1.1	4,273	1.0	3,127	0.7	3,139	0.6	3,467	0.6	3,531	0.6	3,730	0.7	3,730	0.6	4,170	0.7
Singapore	1,320	0.4	3,930	1.1	4,495	1.1	4,098	0.9	4,166	0.8	3,955	0.7	3,769	0.7	3,758	0.7	3,705	0.6	3,976	0.6
Thailand	6,550	2.1	6,940	2.0	7,092	1.7	12,165	2.7	11,187	2.0	8,937	1.6	8,637	1.5	8,765	1.6	8,886	1.5	9,004	1.4
Vietnam	6,490	2.1	3,270	1.0	1,396	0.3	922	0.2	2,022	0.4	3,165	0.6	3,670	0.7	4,597	0.8	6,036	1.0	8,769	1.4
Europe[1]	28,650	9.2	38,910	11.3	55,422	13.6	76,855	16.9	93,784	17.1	87,094	15.2	85,409	15.2	84,697	15.0	82,731	14.2	83,981	13.5
Cyprus[1]	720	0.2	2,140	0.6	1,710	0.4	1,819	0.4	2,217	0.4	1,562	0.3	1,326	0.2	1,111	0.2	877	0.2	782	0.1
France	2,570	0.8	3,680	1.1	5,633	1.4	5,710	1.3	7,273	1.3	6,818	1.2	6,555	1.2	6,640	1.2	6,704	1.1	7,050	1.1
Germany[2]	3,310	1.1	4,730	1.4	7,003	1.7	9,017	2.0	10,128	1.8	8,745	1.5	8,640	1.5	8,829	1.6	8,656	1.5	8,907	1.4
Greece	3,750	1.2	4,740	1.3	4,357	1.1	3,365	0.7	2,768	0.5	2,126	0.4	2,035	0.4	2,088	0.4	1,986	0.3	1,981	0.3
Spain	950	0.3	1,740	0.5	4,304	1.1	4,809	1.1	4,156	0.8	3,631	0.6	3,512	0.6	3,455	0.6	3,575	0.6	3,660	0.6
Turkey[1]	2,600	0.8	2,460	0.7	4,078	1.0	7,678	1.7	10,983	2.0	11,398	2.0	12,474	2.2	11,622	2.1	11,506	2.0	12,030	1.9
United Kingdom	4,440	1.4	5,940	1.7	7,298	1.8	7,799	1.7	8,139	1.5	8,439	1.5	8,236	1.5	8,274	1.5	8,438	1.4	8,367	1.3
Latin America	49,810	16.0	45,480	13.2	47,318	11.6	47,253	10.4	63,634	11.6	69,658	12.2	66,087	11.7	64,769	11.5	64,579	11.1	64,473	10.3
Caribbean	10,650	3.4	11,100	3.2	12,349	3.0	10,737	2.4	14,423	2.6	15,606	2.7	13,898	2.5	13,855	2.5	13,854	2.4	12,739	2.0
Central America	12,970	4.2	12,740	3.7	15,949	3.9	14,220	3.1	16,764	3.1	19,264	3.4	19,227	3.4	19,709	3.5	19,743	3.4	20,800	3.3
Mexico	6,730	2.2	5,460	1.6	6,739	1.7	8,687	1.9	10,670	1.9	13,329	2.3	13,063	2.3	13,931	2.5	13,826	2.4	14,837	2.4
South America	26,190	8.4	21,640	6.3	19,010	4.7	22,296	4.9	32,447	5.9	34,788	6.1	32,962	5.9	31,205	5.5	30,982	5.3	30,932	5.0
Brazil	2,870	0.9	2,840	0.8	3,898	1.0	5,497	1.2	8,846	1.6	7,799	1.4	7,244	1.3	7,009	1.2	7,126	1.2	7,578	1.2
Colombia	3,930	1.3	4,010	1.2	3,183	0.8	3,462	0.8	6,765	1.2	7,533	1.3	7,334	1.3	6,835	1.2	6,750	1.2	6,662	1.1
Venezuela	11,750	3.8	7,040	2.0	2,894	0.7	4,456	1.0	5,217	1.0	5,575	1.0	5,279	0.9	4,597	0.8	4,523	0.8	4,446	0.7
Middle East[1]	81,390	26.1	48,120	14.0	27,636	6.8	21,066	4.6	23,658	4.3	18,892	3.3	17,448	3.1	17,806	3.2	22,321	3.8	24,755	4.0
Iran	47,550	15.2	14,210	4.1	6,262	1.5	2,628	0.6	1,844	0.3	2,321	0.4	2,251	0.4	2,420	0.4	2,795	0.5	3,060	0.5
Israel	2,710	0.9	2,600	0.8	2,977	0.7	2,637	0.6	3,402	0.6	3,474	0.6	3,323	0.6	3,419	0.6	3,269	0.6	3,004	0.5
Jordan	6,140	2.0	6,590	1.9	4,321	1.1	2,222	0.5	2,187	0.4	1,853	0.3	1,754	0.3	1,733	0.3	1,726	0.3	1,799	0.3
Kuwait	2,990	1.0	3,810	1.1	1,624	0.4	3,035	0.7	3,045	0.6	1,846	0.3	1,720	0.3	1,703	0.3	1,633	0.3	1,823	0.3
Lebanon	6,770	2.2	7,090	2.1	3,899	0.9	1,554	0.3	2,005	0.4	2,179	0.4	2,040	0.4	1,950	0.3	1,852	0.3	1,807	0.3
Saudi Arabia	10,440	3.3	6,900	2.0	3,584	0.9	4,191	0.9	5,273	1.0	3,521	0.6	3,035	0.5	3,448	0.6	7,886	1.4	9,873	1.6
North America[3]	14,790	4.7	16,030	4.7	18,949	4.7	23,644	5.2	25,888	4.7	27,650	4.8	28,634	5.1	28,699	5.1	28,756	4.9	29,472	4.7
Canada	14,320	4.6	15,410	4.5	18,350	4.5	23,005	5.1	25,279	4.6	27,017	4.7	28,140	5.0	28,202	5.0	28,280	4.9	29,051	4.7
Oceania	4,180	1.3	4,030	1.2	4,230	1.0	4,202	0.9	4,624	0.8	4,534	0.8	4,481	0.8	4,702	0.8	4,300	0.7	5,005	0.8
Australia	1,530	0.5	1,530	0.4	1,906	0.5	2,244	0.5	2,645	0.5	2,706	0.5	2,659	0.5	2,806	0.5	2,797	0.5	3,088	0.5
Unidentified[4]	240	0.1	190	0.1	89	#	30	#	10	#	19	#	37	#	#	#	#	#	#	#

Selected statistics on public school libraries/media centers, by level of school: 1999–2000, 2003–04, and 2007–08

Selected statistic	1999–2000	2003–04				2007–08			
		Total	Elementary	Secondary	Combined elementary/ secondary	Total	Elementary	Secondary	Combined elementary/ secondary
1	2	3	4	5	6	7	8	9	10
Number of schools with libraries/media centers	77,300 (421)	78,300 (548)	57,400 (440)	16,300 (313)	4,600 (201)	81,900 (634)	59,700 (492)	17,800 (414)	4,400 (239)
Average number of staff per library/media center	1.89 (0.018)	1.76 (0.014)	1.66 (0.018)	2.09 (0.025)	1.74 (0.116)	1.72 (0.017)	1.65 (0.019)	2.04 (0.039)	1.42 (0.057)
Certified library/media specialists	0.81 (0.007)	0.79 (0.009)	0.73 (0.012)	1.03 (0.018)	0.55 (0.023)	0.78 (0.011)	0.73 (0.012)	0.98 (0.019)	0.66 (0.033)
Full-time	0.65 (0.007)	0.65 (0.009)	0.58 (0.010)	0.92 (0.018)	0.37 (0.027)	0.66 (0.010)	0.61 (0.012)	0.88 (0.018)	0.49 (0.032)
Part-time	0.16 (0.006)	0.14 (0.007)	0.15 (0.009)	0.11 (0.009)	0.18 (0.020)	0.13 (0.007)	0.13 (0.010)	0.10 (0.009)	0.18 (0.020)
Other professional staff	0.17 (0.007)	0.19 (0.008)	0.19 (0.011)	0.14 (0.010)	0.28 (0.036)	0.22 (0.010)	0.22 (0.013)	0.21 (0.021)	0.24 (0.027)
Full-time	0.12 (0.005)	0.13 (0.007)	0.14 (0.009)	0.11 (0.009)	0.16 (0.022)	0.13 (0.008)	0.13 (0.010)	0.14 (0.017)	0.15 (0.022)
Part-time	0.06 (0.004)	0.05 (0.005)	0.05 (0.006)	0.03 (0.004)	0.11 (0.031)	0.08 (0.007)	0.08 (0.009)	0.07 (0.013)	0.08 (0.017)
Other paid employees	0.91 (0.014)	0.78 (0.011)	0.75 (0.013)	0.93 (0.017)	0.73 (0.085)	0.72 (0.013)	0.70 (0.016)	0.86 (0.027)	0.51 (0.017)
Full-time	0.49 (0.008)	0.46 (0.009)	0.41 (0.011)	0.65 (0.017)	0.35 (0.028)	0.43 (0.013)	0.39 (0.016)	0.60 (0.022)	0.27 (0.036)
Part-time	0.41 (0.014)	0.33 (0.012)	0.34 (0.014)	0.28 (0.014)	0.38 (0.085)	0.29 (0.011)	0.31 (0.014)	0.26 (0.018)	0.24 (0.028)
Percent of libraries/media centers with certain media equipment									
Automated catalog	72.8 (0.69)	82.7 (0.66)	81.9 (0.89)	90.6 (0.76)	63.7 (2.59)	87.2 (0.71)	87.5 (0.94)	90.6 (1.08)	69.8 (2.88)
Automated circulation system[1]	74.4 (0.65)	86.9 (0.61)	86.7 (0.82)	92.8 (0.80)	68.8 (2.45)	89.5 (0.68)	89.9 (0.87)	92.6 (0.98)	72.4 (3.15)
Media retrieval system[1]	— (†)	— (†)	— (†)	— (†)	— (†)	34.9 (1.05)	35.9 (1.33)	35.1 (1.66)	20.6 (2.32)
Connection to Internet	90.1 (0.57)	95.1 (0.35)	94.1 (0.48)	99.2 (0.22)	92.6 (1.40)	96.7 (0.40)	96.5 (0.51)	98.6 (0.51)	91.6 (1.90)
Digital video disc (DVD) player/video cassette recorder (VCR)	— (†)	87.8 (0.60)	87.0 (0.70)	90.4 (1.19)	89.1 (1.53)	87.2 (0.77)	86.7 (1.02)	89.6 (1.00)	84.5 (2.20)
Disability assistance technologies, such as TDD	— (†)	11.9 (0.50)	10.2 (0.61)	18.0 (0.79)	11.7 (1.34)	23.9 (1.05)	23.0 (1.33)	26.4 (1.34)	25.9 (2.76)
Percent of libraries/media centers with certain services									
Students permitted to check out laptops	— (†)	— (†)	— (†)	— (†)	— (†)	27.5 (1.02)	26.9 (1.27)	29.8 (1.34)	26.1 (2.57)
Staff permitted to check out laptops	— (†)	— (†)	— (†)	— (†)	— (†)	45.9 (1.07)	45.2 (1.35)	50.1 (1.50)	38.5 (2.85)
Number of library computer workstations per 100 students	— (†)	2.3 (0.04)	2.2 (0.05)	2.5 (0.05)	2.7 (0.17)	2.6 (0.05)	2.5 (0.07)	2.9 (0.06)	3.0 (0.17)
Average holdings per 100 students at the end of the school year[2]									
Books (number of volumes)	1,803 (19.7)	1,891 (45.1)	2,127 (70.2)	1,376 (20.0)	2,407 (117.7)	2,015 (30.5)	2,316 (40.2)	1,432 (36.6)	2,439 (132.3)
Audio and video materials	59 (0.9)	80 (3.7)	86 (5.7)	65 (2.2)	97 (13.6)	90 (3.8)	93 (5.6)	81 (5.2)	107 (13.3)
Average additions per 100 students during the school year[2]									
Books (number of volumes)	— (†)	99.3 (2.08)	118.4 (3.13)	61.2 (1.75)	109.2 (8.40)	95.3 (2.21)	113.3 (3.26)	62.1 (2.67)	103.4 (7.41)
Audio and video materials	— (†)	5.1 (0.19)	5.3 (0.28)	4.4 (0.20)	6.9 (0.83)	5.4 (0.49)	5.9 (0.77)	4.5 (0.41)	5.7 (0.84)
Total expenditures for library/media materials per pupil[2][3]	$23.37 (0.438)	$16.24 (0.322)	$16.00 (0.469)	$16.11 (0.320)	$21.24 (2.498)	$16.11 (0.461)	$16.18 (0.591)	$15.90 (0.647)	$17.00 (1.216)
Books	9.97 (0.153)	10.99 (0.299)	11.72 (0.452)	9.68 (0.275)	10.19 (0.631)	11.40 (0.291)	11.99 (0.389)	10.26 (0.504)	12.10 (1.094)
Audio and video materials	1.66 (0.032)	1.14 (0.045)	1.11 (0.053)	1.11 (0.062)	1.96 (0.619)	1.08 (0.055)	1.06 (0.088)	1.11 (0.054)	1.16 (0.152)
Current serial subscriptions	1.26 (0.016)	1.38 (0.025)	1.06 (0.031)	1.87 (0.049)	2.50 (0.148)	— (†)	— (†)	— (†)	— (†)
Electronic subscriptions	0.81 (0.018)	0.88 (0.033)	0.39 (0.042)	1.79 (0.061)	1.25 (0.249)	— (†)	— (†)	— (†)	— (†)

—Not available.

†Not applicable.

[1] Centralized video distribution equipment with a scheduling and control server that telecasts video to classrooms.

[2] Average holdings, acquisitions, and expenditures are from the prior school year, while enrollment counts are from the current school year.

[3] Includes other expenditures not separately shown.

NOTE: Detail may not sum to totals because of rounding. Standard errors appear in parentheses.

SOURCE: U.S. Department of Education, National Center for Education Statistics, Schools and Staffing Survey (SASS), "Public School Library Media Center Questionnaire," 1999–2000, 2003–04, and 2007–08; and "Charter School Questionnaire," 1999–2000. (This table was prepared November 2009.)

Collections, staff, and operating expenditures of the 60 largest college and university libraries: 2005–06

Institution	Rank order, by number of volumes	Number of volumes at end of year (in thousands)	Number of e-books at end of year	Number of serials at end of year	Full-time-equivalent staff		Operating expenditures (in thousands)		Public service hours per week	Gate count per week	Reference transactions per week
					Total	Librarians	Total	Salaries and wages			
1	2	3	4	5	6	7	8	9	10	11	12
Harvard University (MA)	1	15,827	867	98,988	1,265	420	$105,809	$58,047	168	38,945	5,554
Yale University (CT)	2	12,369	167,205	73,953	706	170	74,938	31,304	111	14,599	1,958
University of Illinois at Urbana-Champaign	3	10,371	247,242	63,413	503	99	35,602	19,151	119	84,639	5,264
University of California, Berkeley	4	10,094	—	114,860	531	96	50,253	26,035	98	27,000	3,300
University of Texas at Austin	5	9,022	—	53,125	536	100	41,586	19,810	107	71,992	6,149
Columbia University in the City of NY	6	8,832	342,573	102,901	618	139	51,901	26,064	107	72,484	3,579
Stanford University (CA)	7	8,402	365,000	30,850	697	149	74,233	40,958	105	19,500	2,203
University of Michigan, Ann Arbor	8	8,273	1,028,674	118,654	574	158	49,053	23,204	168	72,696	2,711
University of California, Los Angeles	9	8,157	24,299	77,509	622	125	50,894	26,271	97	69,736	1,975
University of Wisconsin, Madison	10	8,015	502,514	68,560	577	233	40,962	22,381	148	108,354	—
Cornell University (NY)	11	7,521	298,767	77,392	552	116	42,156	21,197	144	101,159	2,047
University of Chicago (IL)	12	7,462	304,016	86,239	318	66	32,301	11,635	144	25,062	802
Indiana University, Bloomington	13	7,242	237,835	71,330	486	97	32,453	14,313	168	87,561	2,346
University of Washington, Seattle Campus	14	6,677	280,140	60,629	463	135	35,218	18,234	142	136,000	2,056
Princeton University (NJ)	15	6,618	222,911	41,775	397	97	41,714	17,639	115	11,777	910
University of Minnesota, Twin Cities	16	6,587	126,892	88,309	408	93	38,322	17,470	100	41,521	3,024
University of North Carolina at Chapel Hill	17	5,817	236	54,591	436	139	34,489	16,203	145	77,538	2,489
Ohio State University, Main Campus	18	5,765	188,722	36,813	435	82	32,966	15,155	168	52,357	6,312
Duke University (NC)	19	5,665	26,000	57,223	359	113	33,532	14,598	137	62,999	2,635
University of Pennsylvania	20	5,571	309,277	47,787	393	120	34,369	15,215	111	36,300	5,000
New York University	21	5,145	769,197	62,537	451	125	41,004	18,186	119	42,795	2,676
University of Virginia, Main Campus	22	5,103	270,603	71,832	373	97	30,273	15,703	149	78,134	3,225
Pennsylvania State U., Penn State Main Campus	23	5,070	18,200	71,230	611	124	48,878	23,496	168	40,417	3,830
University of Arizona	24	5,050	441,889	23,288	237	61	22,547	8,931	168	42,133	659
Rutgers University, New Brunswick/Piscataway	25	5,003	176,995	40,848	321	68	23,161	12,831	105	47,280	1,408
University of Pittsburgh, Main Campus (PA)	26	4,909	224,216	50,232	362	120	30,357	11,869	118	83,242	3,565
University of Kansas, Main Campus	27	4,756	109,272	40,989	258	61	18,300	8,667	140	34,433	1,996
Michigan State University	28	4,736	53,101	35,994	271	69	22,260	10,046	138	41,594	773
Northwestern University (IL)	29	4,688	39,035	45,259	339	94	26,335	12,068	119	26,058	1,638
University of Iowa	30	4,551	324,934	51,374	278	79	25,666	11,335	115	36,630	1,647
University of Oklahoma, Norman Campus	31	4,346	363,116	34,404	153	37	14,444	4,048	117	21,015	640
University of Georgia	32	4,346	84,423	37,226	294	71	23,014	9,487	110	17,735	1,910
University of Florida	33	4,168	273,671	85,169	431	99	27,435	12,339	111	28,421	5,736
University of Southern California	34	3,969	287,712	60,718	375	68	31,894	14,534	159	55,000	1,100
Arizona State University at the Tempe Campus	35	3,896	281,588	30,925	274	72	22,044	9,742	149	73,892	2,317
Johns Hopkins University (MD)	36	3,773	1,488,106	60,858	342	78	31,560	13,369	120	18,982	1,593
Washington University in St. Louis (MO)	37	3,750	197,298	41,339	311	105	37,908	12,923	120	35,000	1,632
University of Tennessee	38	3,735	266,279	35,265	354	123	29,754	11,944	138	39,332	1,743
University of Maryland, College Park	39	3,690	200,000	32,777	304	145	25,284	11,195	162	54,935	4,550
University of Colorado at Boulder	40	3,641	40,677	30,221	212	52	19,210	8,252	104	2,051	2,391
University of Rochester (NY)	41	3,607	13,056	26,760	214	91	18,122	8,231	119	4,196	922
Brigham Young University (UT)	42	3,594	144,910	30,895	380	84	23,943	11,177	105	82,860	3,580
Brown University (RI)	43	3,569	743,698	40,082	208	53	18,945	8,648	154	17,301	466
University of South Carolina, Columbia	44	3,533	691	58,855	277	68	20,422	7,837	152	20,000	3,350
University of Delaware	45	3,471	317,560	12,532	207	52	16,937	7,199	100	19,138	2,052
Louisiana State U. and A&M College	46	3,468	191,428	13,225	212	54	13,454	5,250	100	41,900	896
Wayne State University (MI)	47	3,443	55,429	23,693	267	55	19,054	8,812	168	39,134	1,052
SUNY at Buffalo	48	3,423	103,905	37,288	249	67	19,454	9,965	141	25,000	977
University of Hawaii at Manoa	49	3,413	87,557	156,425	230	66	18,181	8,521	94	27,714	1,732
University of Kentucky	50	3,406	226,680	31,897	263	85	19,569	8,009	140	60,367	1,955
University of California, Santa Barbara	51	3,353	102,925	42,219	238	45	17,131	7,731	103	37,632	1,946
University of New Mexico, Main Campus	52	3,340	195,522	18,143	299	72	21,484	—	103	39,631	1,783
North Carolina State University at Raleigh	53	3,301	278,271	49,480	276	94	22,409	10,033	146	33,325	1,103
Texas A&M University	54	3,300	280,779	45,806	367	91	28,372	11,077	142	47,114	866
University of Missouri, Columbia	55	3,295	25,386	36,244	211	57	14,414	6,051	110	42,000	1,730
University of California, Davis	56	3,258	402,112	41,921	254	54	18,509	8,776	95	33,245	1,289
University of Oregon	57	3,255	230,970	23,186	208	42	13,739	6,921	107	40,581	2,123
University of Notre Dame (IN)	58	3,247	7,443	21,622	261	59	21,694	9,540	126	18,853	574
University of California, San Diego	59	3,236	142,804	24,438	337	58	25,400	13,571	113	65,659	1,477
University of Cincinnati, Main Campus	60	3,209	155,744	42,265	213	51	24,203	10,072	105	29,876	2,241

—Not available.

SOURCE: U.S. Department of Education, National Center for Education Statistics, Academic Libraries Survey (ALS), 2006. (This table was prepared July 2008.)

Public libraries, books and serial volumes, library visits, circulation, and reference transactions, by state: Fiscal years 2006 and 2007

State	Number of public libraries		Number of books and serial volumes				Library visits per capita[1]		Circulation per capita		Reference transactions per capita[2]	
			In thousands		Per capita							
	2006	2007	2006	2007	2006	2007	2006	2007	2006	2007	2006	2007
1	2	3	4	5	6	7	8	9	10	11	12	13
United States	9,208 [3]	9,214 [3]	807,246	812,483	2.8	2.8	4.8	4.9	7.3	7.4	1.0	1.0
Alabama	206	208	9,357	9,495	2.1	2.2	3.3	3.6	4.2	4.4	0.8	0.8
Alaska	90	87	2,387	2,445	3.6	3.6	5.2	5.1	6.2	6.3	0.6	0.5
Arizona	89	83	8,930	9,145	1.5	1.5	3.8	3.9	6.8	7.1	0.9	0.7
Arkansas	48	48	6,170	6,224	2.3	2.3	3.4	3.5	4.6	4.7	0.7	0.7
California	179	181	73,706	74,961	2.0	2.0	4.1	4.2	5.3	5.4	0.9	0.8
Colorado	115	115	11,719	11,728	2.5	2.5	6.2	6.2	11.2	11.4	1.2	1.2
Connecticut	194	195	15,658	15,528	4.5	4.4	6.5	6.5	9.0	9.0	1.3	1.3
Delaware	21	21	1,933	1,921	2.5	2.5	5.5	5.6	9.7	10.0	0.7	0.7
District of Columbia	1	1	2,172	2,097	3.7	3.6	3.1	3.7	2.1	2.5	1.7	1.4
Florida	78	79	32,554	31,995	1.8	1.7	4.1	4.2	5.6	5.9	1.3	1.5
Georgia	58	58	15,185	15,664	1.7	1.7	3.6	3.9	4.6	4.5	1.0	1.0
Hawaii	1	1	3,308	3,376	2.6	2.6	4.1	4.5	5.2	5.3	0.7	0.7
Idaho	104	104	4,006	4,100	3.1	3.1	6.0	6.1	8.3	8.6	0.7	0.8
Illinois	622	623	43,305	43,155	3.8	3.7	5.9	6.5	8.7	8.8	1.4	1.2
Indiana	239	239	24,576	25,360	4.3	4.5	6.8	6.9	12.8	13.0	1.0	0.9
Iowa	539	539	12,200	12,297	4.3	4.3	6.0	6.3	9.7	10.0	0.7	0.6
Kansas	325	326	11,024	11,106	4.8	4.7	6.6	6.4	11.1	11.1	1.2	1.2
Kentucky	116	116	8,582	8,602	2.1	2.1	4.0	4.3	6.2	6.4	0.7	0.8
Louisiana	66	67	11,036	11,450	2.6	2.7	3.1	3.4	4.1	4.1	1.0	1.2
Maine	272	272	6,411	6,495	5.4	5.5	5.7	5.9	7.6	7.5	0.7	0.7
Maryland	24	24	14,554	14,550	2.6	2.6	5.2	5.2	9.5	9.6	1.4	1.2
Massachusetts	370	370	32,319	32,436	5.1	5.0	6.1	6.1	8.0	8.1	0.8	0.8
Michigan	384	386	33,921	34,388	3.4	3.5	5.0	5.2	7.0	7.6	0.9	0.9
Minnesota	139	139	15,722	15,836	3.0	3.0	5.3	5.4	10.2	10.3	0.8	0.9
Mississippi	50	50	5,630	5,703	1.9	2.0	2.7	2.8	2.8	2.8	0.5	0.5
Missouri	151	152	18,049	18,433	3.5	3.6	5.0	5.3	9.0	9.3	1.1	1.1
Montana	80	80	2,803	2,781	3.1	3.1	4.5	4.4	6.1	6.2	0.4	0.4
Nebraska	269	271	6,745	6,735	4.7	5.2	6.5	7.4	9.4	10.2	0.9	0.9
Nevada	22	22	4,472	4,633	1.7	1.7	3.9	3.8	5.9	5.9	0.6	0.6
New Hampshire	230	230	6,064	6,116	4.7	4.7	5.1	5.2	7.9	8.1	0.6	0.6
New Jersey	304	303	30,738	30,673	3.7	3.7	5.5	5.6	6.5	6.8	1.0	1.0
New Mexico	90	91	4,444	4,582	3.0	3.0	4.7	4.7	6.4	6.1	0.9	0.9
New York	754	753	74,403	72,956	3.9	3.9	5.8	6.0	7.6	7.8	1.4	1.5
North Carolina	75	77	16,086	16,536	1.9	1.9	3.9	4.1	5.5	5.6	1.3	1.4
North Dakota	83	80	2,332	2,368	4.2	4.3	4.9	4.8	7.2	7.2	0.7	0.7
Ohio	251	251	46,896	46,974	4.1	4.1	7.5	7.6	15.5	15.9	1.6	1.7
Oklahoma	112	113	7,009	7,144	2.4	2.4	4.7	4.8	7.0	6.9	0.8	0.8
Oregon	128	128	9,209	9,505	2.8	2.8	6.2	6.3	15.0	14.9	0.8	0.8
Pennsylvania	457	457	29,706	30,114	2.5	2.5	3.8	3.9	5.5	5.6	0.7	0.7
Rhode Island	49	49	4,394	4,376	4.1	4.1	5.9	5.8	6.9	6.7	0.9	0.8
South Carolina	42	42	9,056	9,176	2.1	2.1	3.6	3.6	5.1	5.2	1.1	1.1
South Dakota	124	123	3,205	3,131	4.7	4.6	5.5	5.9	8.1	7.9	0.8	0.7
Tennessee	186	187	11,144	11,439	1.9	1.9	3.2	3.3	4.2	4.1	0.8	0.7
Texas	561	562	41,863	41,799	2.0	1.9	3.3	3.3	4.8	4.8	0.8	0.7
Utah	70	70	6,466	6,587	2.6	2.6	7.0	6.5	12.9	12.5	1.6	1.6
Vermont	183	183	2,845	2,865	4.7	4.8	6.3	6.4	7.4	7.5	0.8	0.8
Virginia	90	90	18,420	19,002	2.5	2.5	4.8	4.9	8.5	8.6	1.0	0.9
Washington	65	66	17,317	17,458	2.8	2.7	6.3	6.2	11.3	11.7	1.0	1.0
West Virginia	97	97	4,935	5,023	2.7	2.8	3.4	3.3	4.2	4.2	0.6	0.5
Wisconsin	382	382	19,947	19,596	3.6	3.5	6.0	6.1	10.6	10.6	0.9	0.9
Wyoming	23	23	2,334	2,429	4.6	4.7	6.4	6.4	8.7	8.4	1.1	1.1

[1]The total number of persons entering the library for any purpose during the year.

[2]A reference transaction is an information contact that involves the knowledge, use, recommendations, interpretation, or instructions in the use of one or more information sources by a member of the library staff.

[3]In 2006, of the 9,208 public libraries in the 50 states and the District of Columbia, 7,449 were single-outlet libraries and 1,759 were multiple-outlet libraries. In 2007, of the 9,214 public libraries in the 50 states and the District of Columbia, 7,463 were single-outlet libraries and 1,751 were multiple-outlet libraries. Single-outlet libraries consist of a central library, bookmobile, or books-by-mail-only outlet. Multiple-outlet libraries have two or more direct service outlets, including some combination of one central library, branch(es), bookmobile(s), and/or books-by-mail-only outlets.

NOTE: Data include imputations for nonresponse. Detail may not sum to totals because of rounding.

SOURCE: U.S. Census Bureau, Institute of Museum and Library Services, *Public Libraries in the United States*, fiscal years 2006 and 2007, retrieved July 14, 2009, from http://harvester.census.gov/imls/publib.asp. (This table was prepared July 2009.)

Public schools and instructional rooms with internet access, by selected school characteristics: Selected years, 1994 through 2005

Schools, computers, instructional rooms, and access	All public schools	Instructional level[1] Elementary	Instructional level[1] Secondary	Size of school enrollment Less than 300	Size of school enrollment 300 to 999	Size of school enrollment 1,000 or more	Metropolitan status City	Metropolitan status Urban fringe	Metropolitan status Town	Metropolitan status Rural	Percent of students eligible for free or reduced-price lunch[2] Less than 35 percent	35 to 49 percent	50 to 74 percent	75 percent or more
1	2	3	4	5	6	7	8	9	10	11	12	13	14	15
Estimated total number of schools														
1995	77,850 (—)	57,710 (—)	18,080 (—)	20,670 (—)	50,040 (—)	7,140 (—)	17,910 (—)	18,460 (—)	19,540 (—)	21,940 (—)	37,450 (—)	13,630 (—)	12,810 (—)	13,170 (—)
1998	78,790 (333)	59,170 (293)	19,190 (220)	20,100 (479)	50,660 (467)	8,040 (165)	20,700 (88)	26,270 (98)	11,240 (182)	20,520 (273)	38,160 (1,530)	12,090 (1,185)	13,970 (991)	14,540 (1,263)
1999	78,400 (665)	59,580 (722)	19,110 (521)	20,070 (1,263)	50,390 (681)	7,990 (291)	21,030 (605)	26,250 (514)	11,240 (343)	19,890 (506)	35,650 (1,211)	13,910 (977)	16,100 (1,067)	11,990 (949)
2000	78,400 (650)	59,780 (569)	18,410 (359)	20,670 (697)	50,390 (206)	7,990 (217)	21,120 (1,380)	26,250 (1,746)	11,880 (1,323)	20,550 (1,478)	36,560 (1,215)	12,410 (792)	17,030 (1,071)	13,910 (923)
2001	80,130 (492)	61,640 (527)	17,630 (414)	20,670 (589)	51,970 (274)	8,430 (139)	18,000 (1,416)	26,580 (1,002)	10,180 (746)	26,280 (1,087)	34,930 (1,191)	14,750 (1,203)	16,630 (995)	14,710 (814)
2002	81,070 (780)	62,130 (647)	17,610 (371)	21,430 (761)	51,880 (253)	8,730 (145)	18,550 (963)	26,260 (922)	10,770 (1,080)	26,630 (1,289)	34,990 (1,194)	13,240 (1,050)	19,040 (1,134)	14,770 (862)
2003	82,040 (763)	62,300 (759)	17,890 (396)	21,620 (697)	51,950 (448)	8,660 (154)	18,800 (1,160)	26,430 (1,060)	10,600 (1,098)	26,350 (1,422)	32,500 (1,381)	14,870 (1,111)	18,580 (1,095)	16,290 (999)
2005	82,480 (484)	61,920 (457)	18,910 (332)	20,960 (534)	53,420 (599)	8,100 (398)	19,010 (1,094)	23,820 (1,546)	11,810 (939)	27,850 (1,288)	32,280 (1,158)	14,350 (924)	18,290 (1,268)	17,570 (956)
Percent of schools with internet access[3]														
1994	35 (1.5)	30 (1.9)	49 (2.4)	30 (3.4)	35 (2.0)	58 (3.0)	40 (3.1)	38 (2.9)	29 (2.3)	35 (2.7)	39 (2.3)	35 (4.6)	32 (5.0)	18 (4.6)
1995	50 (1.8)	46 (2.4)	65 (2.7)	39 (3.9)	52 (2.2)	69 (4.1)	47 (4.3)	59 (3.8)	47 (3.7)	48 (3.8)	60 (2.4)	48 (3.9)	41 (4.6)	31 (4.4)
1996	65 (1.8)	61 (2.1)	77 (1.8)	57 (4.4)	66 (2.0)	80 (3.4)	64 (4.5)	75 (3.3)	61 (4.0)	60 (3.3)	74 (2.0)	59 (4.8)	53 (5.1)	53 (5.4)
1998	89 (1.3)	88 (1.6)	94 (2.1)	87 (3.4)	89 (1.4)	95 (2.4)	92 (2.1)	85 (2.8)	90 (4.0)	92 (3.4)	92 (1.1)	93 (2.2)	88 (3.0)	79 (3.7)
1999	95 (0.8)	94 (1.0)	98 (0.8)	96 (1.5)	94 (1.0)	96 (1.7)	93 (1.5)	96 (1.2)	94 (2.5)	96 (1.4)	95 (0.7)	98 (0.9)	96 (1.3)	89 (3.1)
2000	98 (0.6)	97 (0.7)	100[4] (†)	96 (1.7)	98 (0.5)	99 (0.6)	96 (1.1)	98 (0.9)	98 (1.2)	99 (0.9)	99 (1.0)	99 (0.7)	97 (0.5)	94 (1.7)
2001	99 (0.3)	99 (0.4)	100[4] (†)	99 (1.0)	99 (0.4)	100 (†)	97 (1.4)	99 (0.5)	100 (†)	100[4] (†)	99 (1.0)	100 (†)	99 (†)	97 (1.1)
2002	99 (0.5)	99 (0.6)	100[4] (†)	96 (1.7)	100[4] (†)	100 (†)	99 (0.7)	100[4] (†)	98 (2.2)	98 (1.0)	98 (1.0)	100 (†)	100 (†)	99 (0.9)
2003	100[4] (†)	100[4] (†)	100 (†)	100 (†)	100[4] (†)	100 (†)	100 (†)	100[4] (†)	100 (†)	100 (†)	100 (†)	100 (†)	100 (†)	99 (0.8)
2005	100[4] (†)	100[4] (†)	100 (†)	100 (†)	99 (0.4)	100 (†)	99 (0.6)	99 (0.6)	100 (†)	100 (†)	99 (0.5)	100 (†)	100 (†)	99 (0.7)
Number of computers for instructional purposes (in thousands)														
1995	5,621 (—)	3,453 (145)	2,021 (94)	850 (53)	3,600 (136)	1,171 (106)	1,497 (74)	1,526 (129)	1,404 (58)	1,195 (77)	2,905 (198)	806 (114)	950 (89)	882 (155)
1998	7,111 (183)	4,519 (114)	2,549 (103)	952 (76)	4,414 (127)	1,744 (127)	2,148 (113)	2,606 (121)	1,047 (125)	1,311 (75)	3,630 (152)	1,105 (115)	1,127 (116)	1,235 (98)
1999	7,806 (147)	4,923 (149)	2,728 (113)	1,021 (73)	4,952 (121)	1,834 (103)	2,320 (179)	2,975 (213)	1,022 (132)	1,489 (131)	3,900 (147)	1,245 (93)	1,429 (132)	1,170 (107)
2000	8,776 (174)	5,296 (165)	3,271 (98)	1,135 (57)	5,524 (140)	2,117 (103)	2,537 (192)	3,396 (168)	1,155 (124)	1,689 (142)	4,394 (206)	1,373 (147)	1,606 (132)	1,384 (117)
2001	10,058 (180)	6,165 (187)	3,654 (105)	1,085 (77)	6,273 (181)	2,700 (85)	2,685 (158)	3,791 (173)	1,134 (78)	2,448 (164)	4,781 (170)	1,707 (172)	1,862 (137)	1,698 (136)
2002	10,711 (237)	6,775 (234)	3,705 (115)	1,347 (101)	6,533 (179)	2,831 (101)	2,662 (163)	4,043 (177)	1,320 (82)	2,686 (220)	4,982 (252)	1,673 (172)	2,265 (137)	1,792 (110)
2003	11,180 (265)	6,879 (251)	4,087 (105)	1,275 (77)	6,709 (186)	3,196 (118)	2,825 (177)	4,188 (242)	1,357 (139)	2,810 (255)	5,049 (261)	1,923 (165)	2,248 (165)	1,960 (152)
2005	12,672 (281)	7,701	4,783 (148)	1,566 (98)	7,966 (243)	3,139 (163)	3,132	4,058	1,819 (193)	3,663	5,352	2,193 (185)	2,687 (244)	2,440
Average number of instructional computers per school														
1995	72 (—)	60 (—)	112 (—)	41 (—)	72 (—)	164 (—)	84 (—)	83 (—)	72 (—)	54 (—)	78 (—)	59 (6.1)	74 (—)	67 (7.7)
1998	90 (2.3)	76 (2.4)	133 (4.9)	47 (2.6)	87 (2.5)	217 (13.0)	104 (3.6)	99 (4.9)	93 (5.2)	64 (3.6)	95 (3.7)	91 (6.8)	81 (4.5)	85 (5.2)
1999	100 (2.2)	83 (2.4)	159 (6.4)	51 (2.5)	98 (2.3)	229 (10.7)	110 (4.7)	113 (4.2)	91 (4.2)	75 (3.6)	109 (2.8)	90 (5.9)	89 (5.6)	98 (5.5)
2000	110 (2.0)	89 (2.7)	178 (5.3)	57 (3.1)	106 (2.6)	259 (9.0)	120 (6.4)	128 (4.3)	97 (5.6)	82 (4.0)	120 (3.4)	111 (5.8)	94 (5.7)	99 (5.0)
2001	124 (2.3)	100 (2.9)	207 (6.2)	52 (2.5)	121 (3.5)	320 (10.1)	149 (6.4)	144 (4.7)	111 (6.0)	92 (4.5)	137 (4.9)	116 (8.5)	112 (6.0)	115 (5.9)
2002	131 (2.8)	109 (2.9)	210 (6.4)	63 (4.1)	126 (3.2)	324 (11.0)	144 (6.1)	153 (5.2)	123 (9.3)	102 (4.9)	142 (4.7)	126 (7.0)	119 (5.6)	120 (5.1)
2003	136 (2.6)	110 (3.1)	228 (4.9)	59 (2.9)	129 (3.2)	369 (11.0)	150 (7.2)	158 (5.6)	128 (6.7)	107 (5.9)	155 (5.9)	129 (9.3)	121 (6.9)	139 (7.4)
2005	154 (3.4)	124 (3.8)	253 (6.8)	75 (4.2)	149 (4.2)	388 (13.5)	165	170 (6.3)	154 (13.4)	132	166 (5.5)	153	147	
Number of instructional computers with internet access (in thousands)														
1995	447 (—)	232 (148)	187 (79)	59 (38)	315 (140)	73 (73)	96 (87)	131 (105)	126 (46)	94 (73)	286 (151)	46 (79)	57 (48)	36 (78)
1998	3,569 (173)	2,100 (111)	1,450 (89)	407 (60)	2,276 (132)	887 (68)	1,026 (94)	1,334 (93)	481 (50)	727 (70)	2,064 (140)	608 (59)	439 (79)	458 (55)
1999	4,809 (145)	2,773 (111)	1,945 (113)	663 (69)	2,988 (114)	1,158 (89)	1,265 (148)	1,887 (178)	691 (111)	966 (91)	2,762 (139)	778 (80)	810 (93)	858 (87)
2000	6,759 (174)	3,813 (144)	2,779 (95)	882 (61)	4,191 (139)	1,686 (102)	1,782 (164)	2,688 (150)	955 (74)	1,335 (137)	3,608 (196)	1,064 (105)	1,215 (114)	1,289 (101)
2001	8,500 (176)	4,936 (183)	3,357 (117)	874 (97)	5,229 (183)	2,396 (122)	2,175 (145)	3,178 (160)	1,008 (162)	2,139 (148)	4,225 (167)	1,447 (158)	1,529 (129)	1,549 (122)
2002	9,658 (236)	5,912 (237)	3,525 (151)	1,214 (71)	5,827 (186)	2,618 (122)	2,329 (163)	3,677 (168)	1,222 (128)	2,431 (217)	4,586 (244)	1,474 (158)	2,049 (134)	1,726 (107)
2003	10,361 (270)	6,225 (246)	3,935	1,156	6,169	3,036	2,593	3,887	1,264	2,616	4,751	1,724	2,121	2,332
2005	12,245 (274)	7,361	4,706	1,515	7,642	3,089	3,009	3,912	1,784	3,541	5,239	2,090	2,583	

See notes at end of table.

Public schools and instructional rooms with internet access, by selected school characteristics: Selected years, 1994 through 2005—Continued

Schools, computers, instructional rooms, and access	All public schools	Instructional level[1]		Size of school enrollment			Metropolitan status				Percent of students eligible for free or reduced-price lunch[2]			
		Elementary	Secondary	Less than 300	300 to 999	1,000 or more	City	Urban fringe	Town	Rural	Less than 35 percent	35 to 49 percent	50 to 74 percent	75 percent or more
1	2	3	4	5	6	7	8	9	10	11	12	13	14	15
Percent of instructional computers with internet access														
1995[5]	8 (—)	7 (—)	9 (—)	7 (—)	9 (—)	6 (—)	6 (—)	9 (—)	9 (—)	8 (—)	10 (—)	6 (—)	6 (—)	4 (—)
1998	50 (1.7)	46 (2.5)	57 (2.1)	43 (3.4)	52 (2.2)	51 (3.4)	48 (3.0)	51 (2.8)	46 (4.1)	55 (3.4)	57 (2.0)	55 (4.2)	39 (2.9)	37 (4.6)
1999	62 (1.4)	56 (1.6)	71 (2.4)	65 (3.0)	60 (1.7)	63 (3.6)	55 (2.6)	63 (2.4)	68 (3.1)	65 (2.7)	71 (2.2)	62 (3.6)	57 (2.8)	37 (3.6)
2000	77 (1.1)	72 (1.5)	85 (1.2)	78 (2.6)	76 (1.3)	80 (1.8)	70 (2.1)	79 (1.7)	83 (2.5)	79 (2.1)	82 (1.2)	77 (2.9)	76 (2.6)	62 (3.1)
2001	85 (0.8)	80 (1.2)	92 (0.8)	81 (2.8)	83 (1.2)	89 (1.4)	81 (2.1)	84 (1.5)	89 (2.1)	87 (1.3)	88 (1.2)	85 (2.0)	82 (2.5)	76 (2.2)
2002	90 (0.8)	87 (1.1)	95 (0.6)	90 (1.8)	89 (0.9)	92 (1.3)	87 (1.6)	91 (1.2)	93 (1.9)	93 (1.4)	92 (1.1)	88 (2.0)	90 (1.5)	86 (1.6)
2003	93 (0.6)	90 (0.8)	96 (0.8)	91 (1.9)	92 (0.8)	95 (1.0)	92 (1.0)	93 (1.1)	93 (1.6)	93 (1.3)	95 (0.8)	90 (2.3)	94 (1.0)	88 (1.5)
2005	97 (0.4)	96 (0.5)	98 (0.4)	97 (0.7)	96 (0.5)	98 (0.5)	96 (0.7)	96 (1.1)	98 (0.6)	97 (0.7)	98 (0.6)	95 (1.0)	96 (1.0)	96 (0.8)
Number of public school students per instructional computer with internet access														
1998	12.1 (0.6)	13.6 (0.9)	9.9 (0.4)	9.1 (0.7)	12.3 (0.7)	13.0 (1.0)	14.1 (1.2)	12.4 (0.9)	12.2 (1.2)	8.6 (0.8)	10.6 (0.6)	10.9 (1.2)	15.8 (1.4)	16.8 (2.5)
1999	9.1 (0.3)	10.6 (0.4)	7.0 (0.3)	5.7 (0.4)	9.4 (0.4)	10.0 (0.6)	11.4 (0.8)	9.1 (0.4)	8.2 (0.6)	6.6 (0.4)	7.6 (0.3)	9.0 (0.4)	10.0 (0.8)	16.8 (2.2)
2000	6.6 (0.1)	7.8 (0.2)	5.2 (0.2)	3.9 (0.3)	7.0 (0.1)	7.2 (0.2)	8.2 (0.4)	6.6 (0.2)	6.2 (0.3)	5.0 (0.3)	6.0 (0.2)	6.3 (0.4)	7.2 (0.4)	9.1 (0.7)
2001	5.4 (0.1)	6.1 (0.2)	4.3 (0.1)	4.1 (0.3)	5.6 (0.1)	5.4 (0.2)	5.9 (0.2)	5.7 (0.2)	5.0 (0.3)	4.6 (0.1)	4.9 (0.1)	5.2 (0.3)	5.6 (0.3)	6.8 (0.3)
2002	4.8 (0.1)	5.2 (0.2)	4.1 (0.1)	3.1 (0.2)	5.0 (0.1)	5.1 (0.2)	5.5 (0.2)	4.9 (0.2)	4.4 (0.2)	4.0 (0.2)	4.6 (0.1)	4.5 (0.3)	4.7 (0.2)	5.5 (0.3)
2003	4.4 (0.1)	4.9 (0.2)	3.8 (0.1)	3.2 (0.2)	4.7 (0.1)	4.3 (0.2)	5.0 (0.2)	4.6 (0.2)	4.1 (0.2)	3.8 (0.2)	4.2 (0.1)	4.4 (0.3)	4.4 (0.2)	5.1 (0.3)
2005	3.8 (0.1)	4.1 (0.1)	3.3 (0.1)	2.4 (0.1)	3.9 (0.1)	4.0 (0.1)	4.2 (0.2)	4.1 (0.1)	3.4 (0.2)	3.0 (0.1)	3.8 (0.1)	3.4 (0.2)	3.6 (0.2)	4.0 (0.2)
Number of instructional rooms[6] (in thousands)														
1998	2,709 (41)	1,772 (29)	916 (25)	349 (15)	1,740 (34)	620 (21)	839 (22)	981 (24)	390 (14)	498 (17)	1,372 (60)	413 (39)	451 (29)	471 (42)
1999	2,811 (36)	1,830 (28)	926 (29)	360 (26)	1,805 (39)	645 (30)	857 (29)	1,049 (33)	375 (16)	530 (23)	1,325 (46)	477 (34)	541 (42)	437 (34)
2000	2,905 (35)	1,864 (28)	972 (24)	377 (22)	1,871 (47)	657 (23)	866 (56)	1,086 (61)	413 (47)	541 (39)	1,380 (46)	465 (28)	570 (36)	482 (29)
2001	2,851 (31)	1,854 (30)	929 (18)	332 (17)	1,829 (23)	690 (15)	726 (49)	1,068 (46)	339 (24)	718 (36)	1,299 (48)	486 (34)	551 (35)	510 (29)
2002	2,988 (37)	2,006 (30)	919 (19)	396 (25)	1,896 (20)	696 (16)	748 (36)	1,101 (39)	378 (40)	761 (48)	1,368 (45)	451 (38)	648 (38)	520 (33)
2003	3,004 (47)	1,998 (44)	952 (20)	378 (18)	1,919 (33)	707 (16)	777 (45)	1,104 (51)	375 (38)	748 (54)	1,281 (51)	524 (39)	626 (38)	512 (34)
2005	3,283 (71)	2,152 (70)	1,078 (27)	426 (23)	2,152 (70)	705 (30)	849 (62)	1,050 (61)	439 (41)	945 (67)	1,339 (50)	593 (51)	695 (56)	655 (39)
Percent of instructional rooms[6] with internet access[3]														
1994	3 (0.3)	3 (0.4)	4 (0.6)	3 (0.7)	3 (0.5)	3 (0.6)	4 (0.8)	4 (0.8)	3 (0.6)	3 (0.4)	3 (0.5)	2 (0.4)	4 (1.8)	2 (0.9)
1995	8 (0.7)	8 (1.0)	8 (1.0)	9 (1.6)	8 (1.0)	4 (1.0)	6 (1.3)	8 (1.4)	8 (2.0)	8 (1.5)	10 (1.2)	6 (1.4)	6 (1.9)	3 (1.0)
1996	14 (1.0)	13 (1.5)	16 (1.5)	15 (2.9)	13 (1.2)	16 (2.1)	12 (1.6)	16 (2.9)	14 (1.9)	14 (2.2)	17 (1.6)	12 (2.2)	11 (2.8)	5 (1.8)
1998	51 (1.8)	51 (2.3)	52 (2.1)	54 (3.7)	53 (2.2)	45 (3.0)	47 (3.2)	50 (2.5)	55 (4.0)	57 (3.6)	57 (2.4)	60 (5.1)	41 (3.9)	38 (4.3)
1999	64 (1.6)	62 (1.8)	67 (2.6)	71 (3.2)	64 (1.9)	58 (2.2)	52 (2.6)	67 (2.0)	72 (3.4)	71 (3.0)	73 (2.3)	69 (3.4)	61 (3.1)	38 (4.4)
2000	77 (1.1)	76 (1.5)	79 (1.6)	83 (2.8)	78 (1.5)	70 (1.5)	66 (2.1)	78 (1.3)	87 (2.6)	85 (1.7)	82 (1.5)	81 (2.9)	77 (2.8)	60 (3.3)
2001	87 (0.9)	86 (1.1)	88 (1.2)	87 (2.1)	87 (1.1)	86 (1.1)	82 (2.1)	87 (1.0)	91 (2.2)	89 (1.0)	90 (1.2)	89 (2.2)	87 (2.4)	79 (2.4)
2002	92 (0.6)	92 (0.8)	91 (1.0)	91 (1.9)	93 (0.7)	89 (0.7)	88 (1.6)	92 (0.9)	96 (1.1)	93 (1.0)	93 (0.8)	90 (2.1)	91 (1.4)	89 (2.9)
2003	93 (0.5)	92 (0.7)	94 (0.9)	93 (1.6)	93 (0.7)	94 (1.1)	90 (1.6)	94 (0.9)	97 (0.9)	94 (1.2)	95 (1.0)	93 (1.4)	94 (1.1)	90 (1.5)
2005	94 (1.3)	93 (1.9)	95 (0.9)	92 (1.9)	94 (1.9)	94 (1.5)	88 (3.7)	96 (0.8)	98 (0.7)	95 (1.8)	96 (0.8)	88 (4.3)	96 (0.8)	91 (2.5)

—Not available.

†Not applicable.

[1] Data for combined schools are included in the totals and in analyses by other school characteristics, but are not shown separately.

[2] Percent of students eligible for free or reduced-price lunch was not available for some schools. In the 1994 survey, free and reduced-price lunch data came from the Common Core of Data (CCD) only and were missing for 430 schools (percentages presented in this table are based on cases for which data were available). In subsequent years, free and reduced-price lunch information was obtained on the questionnaire, supplemented, if necessary, with CCD data. Missing data ranged from 0 schools (2002, 2003, and 2005) to 10 schools (1999).

[3] Some data differ slightly (e.g., by 1 percent) from previously published figures.

[4] This estimate fell between 99.5 percent and 100.0 percent and therefore was rounded to 100 percent.

[5] Includes computers used for instructional or administrative purposes.

[6] Includes all classrooms, computer labs, and library/media centers.

NOTE: For estimates that are 100 percent, the event defined could have been reported by fewer schools had a different sample been drawn. Detail may not sum to totals because of rounding. Standard errors appear in parentheses.

SOURCE: U.S. Department of Education, National Center for Education Statistics, Fast Response Survey System (FRSS), *Internet Access in U.S. Public Schools and Classrooms: 1994–2005*; and unpublished tabulations. (This table was prepared July 2007.)

Average grade that the public would give the public schools in their community and in the nation at large: 1974 through 2009

Year	All adults		No children in school		Public school parents		Private school parents	
	Nation	Local community	Nation	Local community	Nation	Local community	Nation	Local community
1	2	3	4	5	6	7	8	9
1974	—	2.63	—	2.57	—	2.80	—	2.15
1975	—	2.38	—	2.31	—	2.49	—	1.81
1976	—	2.38	—	2.34	—	2.48	—	2.22
1977	—	2.33	—	2.25	—	2.59	—	2.05
1978	—	2.21	—	2.11	—	2.47	—	1.69
1979	—	2.21	—	2.15	—	2.38	—	1.88
1980	—	2.26	—	—	—	—	—	—
1981	1.94	2.20	—	2.12	—	2.36	—	1.88
1982	2.01	2.24	2.04	2.18	2.01	2.35	2.02	2.20
1983	1.91	2.12	1.92	2.10	1.92	2.31	1.82	1.89
1984	2.09	2.36	2.11	2.30	2.11	2.49	2.04	2.17
1985	2.14	2.39	2.16	2.36	2.20	2.44	1.93	2.00
1986	2.13	2.36	—	2.29	—	2.55	—	2.14
1987	2.18	2.44	2.20	2.38	2.22	2.61	2.03	2.01
1988	2.08	2.35	2.02	2.32	2.13	2.48	2.00	2.13
1989	2.01	2.35	1.99	2.27	2.06	2.56	1.93	2.12
1990	1.99	2.29	1.98	2.27	2.03	2.44	1.85	2.09
1991	2.00	2.36	—	—	—	—	—	—
1992	1.93	2.30	1.92	—	1.94	2.73	1.85	—
1993	1.95	2.41	1.97	2.40	1.97	2.48	1.80	2.11
1994	1.95	2.26	1.95	2.16	1.90	2.55	1.86	1.90
1995	1.97	2.28	1.98	2.25	1.93	2.41	1.81	1.85
1996	1.93	2.30	1.91	2.22	2.00	2.56	1.80	1.86
1997	1.97	2.35	1.99	2.27	2.01	2.56	1.99	1.87
1998	1.93	2.41	1.91	2.36	1.96	2.51	1.81	2.20
1999	2.02	2.44	2.03	2.42	1.97	2.56	—	—
2000	1.98	2.47	1.94	2.44	2.05	2.59	—	—
2001	2.01	2.47	2.00	2.42	2.04	2.66	—	—
2002	2.08	2.44	2.08	2.40	2.06	2.61	—	—
2003	2.11	2.41	2.09	2.32	2.16	2.57	—	—
2004	2.08	2.56	2.15	2.42	2.00	2.58	—	—
2005	2.06	2.45	2.07	2.43	2.11	2.60	—	—
2006	2.03	2.45	2.00	2.41	2.07	2.60	—	—
2007	1.90	2.31	1.89	2.27	1.96	2.54	—	—
2008	2.02	2.40	—	—	—	—	—	—
2009	1.89	2.45	—	—	—	—	—	—

—Not available.
NOTE: Average based on a scale where A = 4, B = 3, C = 2, D = 1, and F = 0.

SOURCE: Phi Delta Kappa, Phi Delta Kappan, "The Annual Gallup Poll of the Public's Attitudes Toward the Public Schools," 1974 through 2009. (This table was prepared September 2009.)

Percentage of elementary and secondary school children whose parents were involved in school activities, by selected child, parent, and school characteristics: 1999, 2003, and 2007

Percent of children whose parents report the following types of involvement in school activities

Child, parent, and school characteristic	1999 Attended a general school meeting	1999 Attended a parent-teacher conference	1999 Attended a class event	1999 Volunteered at school	2003 Attended a general school meeting	2003 Attended a parent-teacher conference	2003 Attended a class event	2003 Volunteered at school	2007 Attended a general school meeting	2007 Attended a parent-teacher conference	2007 Attended a class event	2007 Volunteered at school
	2	3	4	5	6	7	8	9	10	11	12	13
Total	78.3 (0.49)	72.8 (0.45)	65.4 (0.44)	36.8 (0.40)	87.7 (0.37)	77.1 (0.42)	69.9 (0.42)	41.8 (0.60)	89.4 (0.48)	78.1 (0.52)	74.5 (0.57)	46.4 (0.63)
Sex of child												
Male	78.0 (0.62)	74.0 (0.60)	63.4 (0.62)	36.7 (0.65)	87.4 (0.49)	77.7 (0.63)	67.4 (0.75)	41.2 (0.87)	89.3 (0.70)	79.2 (0.65)	71.5 (0.90)	44.8 (0.95)
Female	78.6 (0.69)	71.5 (0.56)	67.4 (0.59)	37.0 (0.61)	87.9 (0.55)	76.5 (0.63)	72.6 (0.63)	42.4 (0.83)	89.6 (0.59)	76.8 (0.94)	77.7 (0.82)	48.1 (1.01)
Race/ethnicity of child												
White	80.5 (0.54)	73.6 (0.48)	71.6 (0.53)	42.7 (0.51)	88.7 (0.51)	76.4 (0.62)	74.1 (0.65)	48.4 (0.82)	90.9 (0.52)	77.8 (0.64)	80.1 (0.68)	54.2 (0.85)
Black	74.5 (1.12)	71.1 (1.23)	53.8 (1.29)	26.2 (1.21)	88.7 (0.85)	78.7 (1.35)	63.3 (1.54)	32.0 (1.65)	86.7 (1.77)	77.3 (1.98)	64.7 (2.31)	35.0 (1.89)
Hispanic	73.1 (1.18)	71.0 (1.05)	51.5 (1.02)	24.5 (0.90)	82.6 (1.05)	78.1 (1.10)	60.9 (1.36)	27.7 (1.23)	86.7 (1.14)	80.2 (1.05)	65.0 (1.46)	31.8 (1.34)
Asian[1]	— (†)	— (†)	— (†)	— (†)	— (†)	— (†)	— (†)	— (†)	91.0 (2.06)	79.9 (2.87)	71.4 (2.89)	45.8 (3.78)
Pacific Islander[1]	— (†)	— (†)	— (†)	— (†)	— (†)	— (†)	— (†)	— (†)	‡ (†)	‡ (†)	‡ (†)	‡ (†)
American Indian/Alaska Native[1]	— (†)	— (†)	— (†)	— (†)	— (†)	— (†)	— (†)	— (†)	94.2 (2.96)	79.7 (7.16)	80.8 (9.63)	58.4 (12.64)
Other[2]	76.7 (2.00)	73.2 (1.94)	62.4 (2.01)	30.7 (1.94)	87.5 (1.63)	77.6 (2.25)	68.5 (2.32)	37.2 (2.16)	89.2 (1.76)	73.6 (3.48)	75.7 (2.83)	44.8 (3.13)
Highest education level of parents/guardians in the household												
Less than high school	57.4 (1.77)	60.0 (1.78)	37.8 (1.68)	12.9 (1.05)	69.8 (2.04)	67.8 (2.50)	42.4 (2.42)	15.6 (2.04)	75.2 (2.37)	69.7 (2.65)	48.1 (3.06)	19.5 (3.37)
High school/GED[3]	72.7 (1.00)	69.7 (0.87)	58.7 (0.93)	26.0 (0.88)	83.8 (0.91)	75.4 (0.93)	62.1 (1.28)	30.3 (1.27)	84.5 (1.15)	74.3 (1.16)	65.1 (1.52)	33.0 (1.56)
Vocational/technical or some college	78.0 (1.04)	72.8 (0.97)	66.0 (1.05)	35.7 (1.07)	88.5 (0.67)	78.0 (1.02)	69.1 (0.93)	38.8 (1.26)	87.5 (1.56)	75.7 (1.48)	69.3 (1.60)	40.2 (1.66)
Associate's degree	81.7 (1.14)	75.8 (1.39)	68.7 (1.57)	41.5 (1.53)	88.6 (1.27)	76.6 (1.68)	73.0 (1.76)	39.7 (1.67)	91.9 (1.18)	80.2 (1.75)	76.9 (2.14)	45.3 (2.32)
Bachelor's degree/some graduate school	87.0 (0.73)	79.6 (0.84)	75.8 (0.93)	49.6 (1.10)	92.0 (0.75)	79.8 (0.89)	80.1 (0.95)	53.9 (1.29)	93.6 (0.75)	81.4 (1.00)	83.2 (0.95)	57.1 (1.44)
Graduate/professional degree	89.4 (0.70)	76.2 (1.09)	79.2 (0.98)	55.1 (1.21)	94.6 (0.74)	79.4 (0.99)	80.8 (1.09)	61.8 (1.57)	95.6 (0.64)	82.3 (1.13)	87.3 (0.95)	64.1 (1.33)
Family income (in current dollars)												
$5,000 or less	67.0 (2.83)	66.7 (3.14)	47.4 (2.87)	17.6 (2.09)	77.7 (2.84)	72.4 (4.15)	55.6 (3.91)	27.3 (4.09)	76.3 (4.85)	66.1 (5.32)	44.7 (6.01)	27.8 (5.24)
$5,001 to 10,000	66.8 (2.13)	67.6 (2.25)	50.7 (2.23)	23.3 (1.91)	79.3 (3.26)	75.7 (3.28)	59.9 (3.60)	30.4 (3.35)	80.0 (3.45)	76.0 (3.81)	56.2 (4.56)	26.3 (4.53)
$10,001 to 15,000	67.1 (1.64)	70.0 (1.62)	49.9 (2.15)	20.4 (1.40)	80.0 (2.41)	75.6 (2.35)	53.4 (2.99)	22.5 (2.44)	76.7 (4.46)	73.0 (4.57)	56.8 (4.12)	28.8 (3.69)
$15,001 to 20,000	71.1 (1.76)	70.4 (1.52)	55.1 (1.89)	25.3 (1.70)	81.1 (2.60)	74.2 (2.23)	57.5 (2.28)	25.6 (2.84)	81.9 (3.07)	83.0 (4.57)	58.9 (4.17)	17.4 (2.12)
$20,001 to 25,000	70.6 (1.90)	67.0 (1.62)	53.4 (1.76)	26.2 (1.63)	83.5 (1.64)	79.1 (1.89)	62.4 (1.99)	27.0 (2.39)	84.8 (2.26)	78.9 (2.38)	64.7 (2.96)	29.9 (3.18)
$25,001 to 30,000	74.3 (1.35)	71.6 (1.31)	59.1 (1.71)	30.9 (1.69)	85.7 (1.46)	75.9 (2.41)	64.2 (2.23)	33.8 (2.86)	85.5 (3.09)	76.6 (3.20)	63.4 (3.20)	35.9 (3.53)
$30,001 to 35,000	79.0 (1.60)	73.8 (1.72)	67.6 (1.64)	37.9 (1.84)	84.5 (1.59)	76.3 (1.94)	64.7 (2.32)	33.5 (2.51)	85.6 (2.75)	72.4 (3.23)	67.6 (2.59)	31.5 (2.80)
$35,001 to 40,000	79.4 (1.38)	73.7 (1.38)	68.4 (1.64)	36.1 (1.84)	83.4 (2.50)	74.7 (2.10)	70.9 (2.41)	37.3 (3.50)	88.0 (1.65)	74.9 (2.85)	69.9 (2.57)	32.8 (2.52)
$40,001 to 50,000	81.6 (1.07)	75.1 (1.13)	72.8 (1.25)	40.1 (1.26)	87.5 (1.18)	79.3 (1.42)	68.5 (2.11)	40.0 (1.89)	88.8 (1.57)	79.4 (2.05)	74.3 (2.09)	40.8 (2.36)
$50,001 to 75,000	84.6 (0.78)	74.8 (0.91)	72.6 (0.90)	43.8 (1.05)	89.9 (0.79)	76.9 (0.96)	74.5 (1.04)	46.0 (1.27)	92.0 (0.73)	78.6 (0.96)	79.0 (1.15)	51.7 (1.18)
Over $75,000	88.5 (0.68)	77.3 (0.74)	79.3 (0.80)	54.9 (1.02)	93.9 (0.57)	78.6 (0.89)	79.3 (0.73)	56.8 (1.01)	95.0 (0.40)	79.9 (0.87)	85.4 (0.66)	62.0 (1.10)
Child attending public school	76.8 (0.54)	71.4 (0.50)	63.5 (0.48)	33.8 (0.41)	86.7 (0.40)	75.9 (0.45)	68.0 (0.47)	38.5 (0.64)	88.5 (0.53)	76.9 (0.59)	72.6 (0.66)	42.7 (0.69)
Elementary (kindergarten to grade 8)	81.7 (0.57)	80.9 (0.45)	66.9 (0.55)	38.1 (0.48)	90.9 (0.40)	85.1 (0.42)	71.7 (0.57)	42.8 (0.74)	91.7 (0.59)	85.1 (0.69)	76.1 (0.79)	48.5 (1.00)
Secondary (grades 9 to 12)	65.8 (0.99)	50.1 (1.10)	55.9 (0.97)	24.0 (0.77)	76.9 (1.06)	54.8 (1.02)	59.4 (1.06)	28.5 (0.98)	82.0 (1.12)	59.9 (1.14)	65.5 (1.20)	30.6 (1.05)
Child attending private school	91.4 (0.80)	85.0 (0.95)	81.7 (1.09)	63.8 (1.35)	95.7 (0.61)	86.6 (1.03)	85.6 (1.23)	68.7 (1.57)	96.3 (1.08)	86.5 (1.84)	88.1 (1.27)	74.1 (1.75)
Elementary (kindergarten to grade 8)	93.0 (0.73)	90.2 (0.81)	84.2 (1.11)	68.8 (1.37)	96.6 (0.69)	91.6 (0.92)	88.4 (1.22)	73.4 (1.90)	96.8 (1.46)	92.5 (1.61)	89.2 (1.65)	80.3 (1.87)
Secondary (grades 9 to 12)	85.9 (2.09)	66.9 (2.74)	73.0 (2.62)	46.3 (3.23)	93.0 (1.56)	72.2 (2.54)	76.6 (2.93)	55.2 (2.78)	95.2 (1.11)	71.2 (4.05)	85.2 (2.21)	58.6 (3.50)

—Not available.
†Not applicable.
‡Reporting standards not met.
[1]Included in "Other" in 1999 and 2003 data.
[2]Includes all other races or two or more races.
[3]GED—General Educational Development.
NOTE: Includes children enrolled in kindergarten through grade 12 and ungraded students. Excludes homeschooled children. The respondent was the parent most knowledgeable about the child's education. Responding parents reported on their own and their spouse's, or other household adults', activities. Race categories exclude persons of Hispanic ethnicity. Standard errors appear in parentheses.

SOURCE: U.S. Department of Education, National Center for Education Statistics, *Parent and Family Involvement in Education: 2002–03*; and Parent Survey (Parent:1999) and Parent and Family Involvement in Education Survey (PFI:2003 and 2007) of the National Household Education Surveys Program, unpublished tabulations. (This table was prepared August 2008.)

Percentage of kindergartners through fifth-graders whose parents reported doing education-related activities with their children in the past month, by selected child, parent, and school characteristics: 1999, 2003, and 2007

Child, parent, and school characteristic	Visited a library			Went to a play, concert, or other live show			Visited an art gallery, museum, or historical site			Visited a zoo or aquarium			Attended an event sponsored by a community, religious, or ethnic group[1]		
	1999	2003	2007	1999	2003	2007	1999	2003	2007	1999	2003	2007	1999	2003	2007
1	2	3	4	5	6	7	8	9	10	11	12	13	14	15	16
Total	48.6 (0.64)	50.2 (0.80)	48.8 (1.12)	32.1 (0.55)	35.5 (0.87)	31.4 (0.87)	22.2 (0.67)	22.2 (0.83)	26.3 (1.09)	14.1 (0.47)	16.5 (0.69)	19.0 (0.80)	52.8 (0.63)	62.0 (0.80)	58.9 (1.14)
Sex of child															
Male	47.2 (0.91)	47.3 (1.08)	46.8 (1.66)	30.5 (0.84)	33.6 (1.09)	28.7 (1.06)	22.3 (0.93)	23.1 (1.12)	27.1 (1.80)	13.9 (0.70)	16.3 (0.88)	18.5 (0.95)	50.9 (0.89)	61.0 (1.08)	57.3 (1.48)
Female	50.1 (1.02)	53.1 (1.11)	50.9 (1.52)	33.7 (0.81)	37.5 (1.09)	34.5 (1.57)	22.1 (0.89)	21.2 (1.07)	25.4 (1.30)	14.3 (0.70)	16.7 (0.87)	19.6 (1.41)	54.8 (0.95)	63.0 (1.09)	60.6 (1.49)
Race/ethnicity of child															
White	48.9 (0.85)	49.1 (1.03)	48.5 (1.22)	33.9 (0.72)	37.2 (1.26)	32.8 (1.13)	22.3 (0.76)	21.2 (1.09)	25.4 (1.18)	12.0 (0.54)	13.6 (0.85)	15.3 (0.85)	54.6 (0.81)	64.6 (1.12)	63.1 (1.19)
Black	47.8 (1.76)	52.3 (2.50)	56.1 (3.95)	31.3 (1.60)	36.7 (2.23)	34.5 (3.02)	21.0 (1.52)	24.4 (1.97)	32.7 (5.13)	15.7 (1.24)	18.9 (1.55)	24.2 (2.72)	53.0 (1.40)	66.3 (2.35)	61.7 (4.59)
Hispanic	43.9 (1.65)	48.2 (1.77)	44.6 (2.14)	24.4 (1.10)	28.0 (1.53)	25.1 (1.67)	20.6 (1.26)	20.8 (1.38)	23.5 (2.13)	19.7 (1.02)	23.7 (1.32)	25.4 (1.97)	45.8 (1.32)	49.3 (1.75)	44.9 (2.17)
Asian	— (†)	— (†)	60.3 (5.29)	— (†)	— (†)	29.2 (4.76)	— (†)	— (†)	27.9 (4.22)	— (†)	— (†)	23.7 (3.61)	— (†)	—	58.6 (5.15)
Highest education level of parents/guardians in the household															
Less than high school	34.5 (2.33)	36.1 (3.39)	37.3 (3.49)	17.5 (1.63)	20.0 (3.10)	20.2 (2.66)	12.1 (1.64)	9.3 (1.75)	17.8 (2.25)	15.2 (1.65)	15.3 (2.05)	17.3 (2.22)	36.7 (2.32)	34.3 (3.06)	35.5 (3.86)
High school/GED[2]	40.3 (1.42)	44.5 (1.64)	41.5 (3.52)	25.9 (1.13)	28.6 (1.83)	22.0 (2.31)	16.0 (1.04)	17.8 (1.73)	22.2 (3.58)	12.8 (0.98)	16.5 (1.18)	17.6 (2.21)	42.6 (1.23)	50.5 (1.81)	46.0 (3.23)
Vocational/technical or some college	47.2 (1.41)	44.3 (2.04)	43.5 (2.46)	30.2 (1.30)	32.8 (1.89)	29.6 (2.15)	20.4 (1.21)	19.1 (1.32)	18.6 (2.00)	11.9 (0.90)	15.2 (1.29)	16.4 (1.95)	53.7 (1.43)	62.1 (1.64)	58.2 (2.61)
Associate's degree	50.4 (2.12)	47.4 (3.04)	46.6 (2.74)	35.5 (2.10)	41.1 (3.24)	31.0 (2.46)	22.0 (1.77)	22.0 (2.40)	22.3 (2.72)	14.3 (1.42)	15.4 (2.09)	19.3 (2.56)	53.6 (2.26)	67.0 (2.85)	58.7 (2.84)
Bachelor's degree/some graduate school	57.6 (1.52)	57.7 (1.74)	51.9 (1.89)	40.0 (1.24)	40.1 (1.61)	37.1 (1.85)	29.1 (1.37)	27.6 (1.70)	32.1 (2.07)	15.2 (1.03)	16.0 (1.32)	21.1 (1.79)	64.6 (1.22)	71.3 (1.63)	66.7 (2.07)
Graduate/professional degree	62.9 (1.53)	65.2 (2.04)	62.2 (1.86)	43.3 (1.77)	47.2 (2.53)	40.0 (2.20)	34.7 (1.73)	31.7 (2.02)	34.7 (1.96)	17.9 (1.33)	20.7 (1.82)	20.3 (1.61)	65.3 (1.68)	75.6 (1.55)	72.3 (1.63)
Family income (in current dollars)															
$5,000 or less	42.7 (4.27)	38.2 (5.63)	46.5 (8.03)	24.9 (2.73)	25.7 (4.94)	18.6 (6.08)	16.5 (2.76)	13.2 (3.10)	21.4 (7.05)	16.6 (2.77)	18.7 (3.99)	12.3 (4.18)	37.3 (3.55)	52.9 (4.65)	43.5 (8.42)
$5,001 to 10,000	43.8 (2.86)	42.2 (4.99)	34.9 (5.37)	21.1 (2.34)	28.5 (4.74)	23.5 (5.99)	17.7 (2.07)	22.8 (4.79)	23.6 (5.63)	14.5 (1.65)	23.8 (4.05)	22.7 (5.16)	38.9 (2.62)	51.6 (4.74)	44.5 (6.75)
$10,001 to 15,000	44.8 (2.51)	49.1 (4.27)	35.6 (4.75)	24.5 (2.32)	27.3 (3.26)	21.0 (4.00)	18.2 (1.99)	20.7 (4.22)	10.6 (2.93)	15.3 (2.06)	20.9 (3.46)	17.6 (4.18)	45.5 (2.83)	49.1 (4.19)	51.0 (6.68)
$15,001 to 20,000	43.0 (3.07)	44.4 (3.95)	52.1 (9.98)	25.9 (2.37)	32.9 (3.75)	18.6 (3.76)	13.3 (1.74)	18.9 (2.83)	26.2 (11.91)	13.7 (1.61)	17.1 (2.61)	14.6 (3.78)	47.2 (2.78)	52.1 (4.19)	39.0 (7.73)
$20,001 to 25,000	38.9 (2.10)	48.4 (3.57)	45.3 (5.05)	26.3 (2.05)	26.0 (3.39)	30.1 (4.13)	18.7 (1.85)	16.3 (2.22)	21.2 (3.97)	14.7 (1.50)	16.4 (2.35)	20.4 (3.84)	47.7 (2.53)	57.8 (3.76)	52.6 (5.02)
$25,001 to 30,000	45.3 (2.27)	51.0 (3.71)	45.4 (5.59)	30.4 (2.35)	27.1 (3.35)	23.0 (3.90)	20.7 (1.97)	20.8 (3.12)	20.5 (5.61)	14.4 (1.70)	15.9 (2.50)	24.0 (6.29)	50.0 (2.30)	56.7 (3.96)	50.2 (5.60)
$30,001 to 35,000	49.2 (2.55)	44.9 (3.17)	45.9 (5.09)	31.3 (2.66)	33.2 (3.22)	30.4 (4.59)	21.4 (1.97)	18.3 (2.72)	23.7 (4.51)	11.9 (1.42)	17.1 (2.32)	20.4 (4.15)	53.7 (2.48)	59.7 (3.10)	65.5 (3.80)
$35,001 to 40,000	51.9 (2.30)	45.6 (4.30)	49.0 (3.80)	34.4 (2.60)	31.4 (3.79)	31.9 (3.85)	23.5 (2.18)	16.8 (2.99)	19.9 (4.22)	13.2 (1.48)	11.6 (2.92)	19.2 (3.80)	59.1 (2.45)	70.7 (3.70)	70.7 (4.46)
$40,001 to 50,000	52.1 (2.03)	52.2 (3.00)	47.0 (3.92)	32.5 (1.71)	35.8 (2.99)	31.8 (3.28)	22.5 (1.51)	20.9 (2.41)	26.9 (3.75)	13.1 (1.24)	14.8 (2.05)	20.9 (4.10)	58.5 (2.01)	63.1 (2.54)	56.4 (3.28)
$50,001 to 75,000	51.5 (1.67)	50.0 (1.65)	49.2 (2.28)	34.5 (1.47)	39.0 (1.59)	31.9 (1.80)	23.1 (1.37)	23.1 (1.42)	23.9 (1.64)	12.2 (0.86)	14.9 (1.27)	15.8 (1.50)	57.6 (1.72)	64.5 (1.42)	61.2 (2.02)
Over $75,000	55.5 (1.61)	55.8 (1.69)	53.5 (1.66)	44.5 (1.45)	42.6 (1.66)	38.1 (1.42)	31.6 (1.75)	27.3 (1.43)	33.1 (1.48)	15.8 (0.86)	16.9 (1.31)	20.3 (1.17)	61.9 (1.33)	67.9 (1.42)	67.6 (1.51)
Child attending public school	47.5 (0.68)	49.2 (0.87)	47.6 (1.22)	30.4 (0.58)	34.9 (0.88)	31.0 (0.93)	21.0 (0.70)	21.2 (0.92)	24.9 (1.12)	13.7 (0.49)	16.3 (0.71)	19.1 (0.88)	51.2 (0.68)	60.6 (0.85)	56.9 (1.25)
Child attending private school	56.4 (1.78)	57.0 (2.31)	57.0 (2.86)	44.3 (1.80)	40.0 (2.55)	34.3 (2.65)	31.0 (1.55)	29.0 (2.04)	35.6 (2.82)	17.1 (1.28)	17.9 (1.85)	18.5 (2.05)	64.8 (1.92)	72.2 (2.15)	71.8 (2.77)

—Not available.

†Not applicable.

[1]In 1999 and 2007, a single item asked parents if they had attended an event sponsored by a community, ethnic, or religious group. In 2003, attendance at an event sponsored by a religious group was asked about separately from attendance at an event sponsored by a community or ethnic group.

[2]GED = General Educational Development.

NOTE: The respondent was the parent most knowledgeable about the child's education. Responding parents reported on their own activities and the activities of their spouse/other adults in the household. Excludes homeschooled children. Totals include other racial/ethnic groups not separately shown. Race categories exclude persons of Hispanic ethnicity. Standard errors appear in parentheses.
SOURCE: U.S. Department of Education, National Center for Education Statistics, Parent Survey (Parent:1999) and Parent and Family Involvement in Education Survey (PFI:2003 and 2007) of the National Household Education Surveys Program. (This table was prepared July 2009.)

Labor force participation rates and employment to population ratios of persons 16 to 64 years old, by highest level of education, age, sex, and race/ethnicity: 2008

Age, sex, and race/ethnicity	Labor force participation rate[1]			College			Employment to population ratio[2]			College		
	Total	Less than high school completion[3]	High school completion	Some college, no degree	Associate's degree	Bachelor's or higher degree	Total	Less than high school completion[3]	High school completion	Some college, no degree	Associate's degree	Bachelor's or higher degree
1	2	3	4	5	6	7	8	9	10	11	12	13
16 to 19 years old[4]	**40.2** (0.38)	**31.2** (0.44)	**60.9** (0.88)	**54.3** (1.00)	**‡** (†)	**‡** (†)	**32.6** (0.36)	**24.3** (0.40)	**49.6** (0.90)	**48.8** (1.01)	**‡** (†)	**‡** (†)
Male	40.1 (0.53)	31.1 (0.60)	63.4 (1.20)	52.8 (1.51)	‡ (†)	‡ (†)	31.6 (0.50)	23.5 (0.55)	49.9 (1.24)	46.4 (1.51)	‡ (†)	‡ (†)
Female	40.2 (0.54)	31.3 (0.63)	58.2 (1.28)	55.6 (1.34)	‡ (†)	‡ (†)	33.7 (0.52)	25.0 (0.59)	49.2 (1.30)	50.7 (1.35)	‡ (†)	‡ (†)
White	44.9 (0.49)	35.9 (0.59)	64.0 (1.10)	57.7 (1.22)	‡ (†)	‡ (†)	37.9 (0.48)	29.4 (0.56)	53.3 (1.14)	53.1 (1.24)	‡ (†)	‡ (†)
Black	29.1 (0.88)	21.0 (0.94)	52.1 (2.28)	43.0 (2.94)	‡ (†)	‡ (†)	20.0 (0.78)	13.2 (0.78)	38.2 (2.22)	33.7 (2.80)	‡ (†)	‡ (†)
Hispanic	36.9 (0.81)	27.7 (0.90)	59.8 (1.95)	56.0 (2.48)	‡ (†)	‡ (†)	28.6 (0.76)	20.1 (0.81)	48.2 (1.98)	49.1 (2.49)	‡ (†)	‡ (†)
Asian	24.3 (1.77)	17.3 (1.97)	40.0 (5.73)	32.8 (3.96)	‡ (†)	‡ (†)	20.8 (1.68)	14.3 (1.83)	33.5 (5.52)	29.4 (3.84)	‡ (†)	‡ (†)
20 to 24 years old[4]	**74.4** (0.35)	**65.3** (1.14)	**78.2** (0.61)	**69.7** (0.60)	**82.3** (1.18)	**82.2** (0.83)	**66.8** (0.38)	**51.5** (1.20)	**68.1** (0.69)	**64.5** (0.63)	**77.4** (1.30)	**77.5** (0.91)
Male	78.7 (0.46)	78.5 (1.29)	84.9 (0.70)	70.5 (0.85)	84.5 (1.64)	83.6 (1.23)	69.7 (0.52)	62.9 (1.52)	73.5 (0.86)	64.4 (0.89)	79.5 (1.83)	78.1 (1.38)
Female	70.0 (0.50)	48.1 (1.73)	69.8 (0.97)	69.0 (0.80)	80.6 (1.57)	81.3 (1.05)	63.8 (0.52)	36.7 (1.66)	61.5 (1.03)	64.5 (0.83)	75.6 (1.71)	77.0 (1.14)
White	77.0 (0.43)	65.5 (1.89)	81.4 (0.76)	71.5 (0.72)	85.5 (1.31)	84.3 (0.91)	70.5 (0.47)	50.6 (1.99)	72.2 (0.87)	66.8 (0.76)	82.0 (1.43)	79.5 (1.01)
Black	67.9 (1.09)	55.4 (3.08)	70.1 (1.75)	66.9 (1.84)	75.5 (4.38)	79.5 (3.34)	55.7 (1.16)	36.3 (2.98)	55.8 (1.89)	58.4 (1.92)	63.3 (4.91)	73.0 (3.67)
Hispanic	73.7 (0.87)	70.1 (1.73)	77.1 (1.40)	70.1 (1.74)	80.0 (3.46)	82.6 (3.32)	65.2 (0.94)	59.3 (1.86)	67.6 (1.56)	64.2 (1.83)	73.1 (3.84)	77.7 (3.64)
Asian	59.7 (1.75)	61.4 (7.70)	69.5 (4.43)	51.4 (2.65)	63.7 (6.19)	66.9 (3.15)	56.4 (1.77)	53.8 (7.89)	62.9 (4.65)	49.5 (2.65)	60.2 (6.30)	63.8 (3.22)
25 to 64 years old	**79.2** (0.12)	**63.5** (0.42)	**76.3** (0.23)	**79.5** (0.28)	**83.8** (0.34)	**85.9** (0.18)	**75.5** (0.12)	**57.6** (0.43)	**71.9** (0.24)	**75.5** (0.30)	**80.7** (0.37)	**83.7** (0.19)
Male	86.4 (0.14)	76.8 (0.49)	84.3 (0.27)	85.9 (0.34)	89.0 (0.43)	91.7 (0.20)	82.3 (0.16)	69.9 (0.53)	79.2 (0.30)	81.6 (0.38)	85.7 (0.48)	89.5 (0.22)
Female	72.2 (0.17)	48.3 (0.60)	68.0 (0.34)	73.7 (0.40)	79.8 (0.47)	80.4 (0.27)	69.0 (0.18)	43.6 (0.60)	64.3 (0.35)	69.9 (0.42)	76.9 (0.50)	78.3 (0.28)
White	80.1 (0.14)	58.0 (0.71)	76.5 (0.28)	79.4 (0.34)	84.3 (0.39)	86.1 (0.20)	77.1 (0.15)	52.8 (0.71)	72.8 (0.29)	75.9 (0.35)	81.6 (0.42)	84.1 (0.22)
Black	75.9 (0.39)	54.3 (1.28)	73.2 (0.67)	79.3 (0.80)	82.4 (1.11)	87.2 (0.66)	69.9 (0.41)	45.9 (1.28)	66.4 (0.71)	72.8 (0.88)	77.3 (1.22)	83.9 (0.73)
Hispanic	77.9 (0.33)	70.9 (0.60)	79.1 (0.58)	81.6 (0.82)	83.8 (1.13)	86.7 (0.72)	73.2 (0.35)	65.2 (0.63)	74.2 (0.63)	77.2 (0.89)	80.5 (1.21)	83.8 (0.78)
Asian	79.0 (0.48)	63.2 (1.91)	76.3 (1.16)	78.5 (1.56)	80.5 (1.75)	82.3 (0.60)	76.3 (0.50)	59.0 (1.95)	73.0 (1.21)	75.7 (1.62)	77.6 (1.84)	80.0 (0.63)

†Not applicable.
‡Reporting standards not met.
[1]Percentage of the civilian population who are employed or seeking employment.
[2]Percentage of persons employed as a percentage of the civilian population.
[3]Includes persons reporting no school years completed.
[4]Excludes persons enrolled in school.

NOTE: Race categories exclude persons of Hispanic ethnicity. Standard errors appear in parentheses.
SOURCE: U.S. Department of Labor, Bureau of Labor Statistics, Office of Employment and Unemployment Statistics, unpublished 2008 annual average data from the Current Population Survey (CPS). (This table was prepared August 2009.)

Table. Unemployment rate of persons 16 years old and over, by age, sex, race/ethnicity, and educational attainment: 2006, 2007, and 2008

Sex, race/ethnicity, and educational attainment	Unemployment rate, 2006 — 16- to 24-year-olds[1] Total	16 to 19 years	20 to 24 years	25 years old and over	Unemployment rate, 2007 — 16- to 24-year-olds[1] Total	16 to 19 years	20 to 24 years	25 years old and over	Unemployment rate, 2008 — 16- to 24-year-olds[1] Total	16 to 19 years	20 to 24 years	25 years old and over
1	2	3	4	5	6	7	8	9	10	11	12	13
All persons, all education levels	**10.5 (0.16)**	**15.4 (0.29)**	**8.2 (0.17)**	**3.6 (0.04)**	**10.5 (0.16)**	**15.7 (0.30)**	**8.2 (0.17)**	**3.6 (0.04)**	**12.8 (0.17)**	**18.7 (0.32)**	**10.2 (0.19)**	**4.6 (0.04)**
Less than high school completion	16.6 (0.38)	17.5 (0.41)	14.3 (0.64)	6.8 (0.17)	17.3 (0.39)	18.3 (0.43)	15.3 (0.67)	7.1 (0.18)	21.9 (0.45)	22.2 (0.48)	21.1 (0.81)	9.0 (0.20)
High school completion, no college	12.0 (0.31)	15.7 (0.57)	10.5 (0.34)	4.3 (0.08)	11.6 (0.30)	15.5 (0.57)	10.1 (0.34)	4.4 (0.08)	14.5 (0.33)	18.6 (0.61)	12.9 (0.38)	5.7 (0.09)
Some college, no degree	6.3 (0.23)	8.1 (0.53)	5.9 (0.25)	3.9 (0.10)	6.5 (0.24)	8.4 (0.54)	6.1 (0.25)	3.8 (0.10)	8.1 (0.26)	10.2 (0.57)	7.5 (0.28)	5.1 (0.11)
Associate's degree	5.2 (0.50)	‡ (†)	5.1 (0.50)	3.0 (0.12)	4.5 (0.46)	‡ (†)	4.4 (0.47)	3.0 (0.12)	6.3 (0.55)	‡ (†)	6.0 (0.54)	3.7 (0.13)
Bachelor's or higher degree	5.1 (0.37)	‡ (†)	5.1 (0.37)	2.0 (0.05)	5.5 (0.37)	‡ (†)	5.4 (0.37)	2.0 (0.05)	5.8 (0.37)	‡ (†)	5.8 (0.38)	2.6 (0.06)
Male, all education levels	**11.2 (0.22)**	**16.9 (0.42)**	**8.7 (0.24)**	**3.5 (0.05)**	**11.6 (0.22)**	**17.6 (0.44)**	**8.9 (0.24)**	**3.6 (0.05)**	**14.4 (0.25)**	**21.2 (0.48)**	**11.4 (0.27)**	**4.8 (0.06)**
Less than high school completion	16.4 (0.48)	18.7 (0.58)	12.3 (0.71)	6.1 (0.20)	17.7 (0.52)	19.9 (0.61)	13.8 (0.77)	6.6 (0.21)	22.7 (0.59)	24.3 (0.69)	19.9 (0.94)	8.8 (0.24)
High school completion, no college	12.3 (0.40)	17.0 (0.81)	10.6 (0.43)	4.3 (0.11)	12.2 (0.40)	17.6 (0.83)	10.3 (0.43)	4.4 (0.11)	15.5 (0.44)	21.2 (0.87)	13.5 (0.48)	5.9 (0.12)
Some college, no degree	6.8 (0.34)	9.5 (0.88)	6.3 (0.36)	3.5 (0.13)	7.3 (0.35)	9.5 (0.88)	6.9 (0.38)	3.6 (0.13)	9.3 (0.39)	12.1 (0.93)	8.7 (0.42)	5.0 (0.15)
Associate's degree	6.4 (0.79)	‡ (†)	6.5 (0.81)	3.0 (0.17)	4.9 (0.70)	‡ (†)	4.8 (0.70)	3.0 (0.17)	6.2 (0.78)	‡ (†)	5.9 (0.78)	3.8 (0.18)
Bachelor's or higher degree	5.7 (0.60)	‡ (†)	5.7 (0.60)	1.9 (0.07)	6.4 (0.60)	‡ (†)	6.4 (0.61)	1.9 (0.07)	6.6 (0.60)	‡ (†)	6.7 (0.61)	2.5 (0.08)
Female, all education levels	**9.7 (0.21)**	**13.8 (0.40)**	**7.6 (0.23)**	**3.7 (0.06)**	**9.4 (0.21)**	**13.8 (0.40)**	**7.3 (0.23)**	**3.6 (0.06)**	**11.2 (0.23)**	**16.2 (0.43)**	**8.8 (0.25)**	**4.4 (0.06)**
Less than high school completion	16.8 (0.55)	16.3 (0.58)	18.7 (1.19)	7.9 (0.29)	16.9 (0.56)	16.5 (0.60)	18.5 (1.21)	8.2 (0.30)	20.0 (0.63)	20.7 (0.66)	23.6 (1.41)	9.4 (0.32)
High school completion, no college	11.5 (0.45)	14.2 (0.80)	10.3 (0.52)	4.3 (0.11)	10.9 (0.43)	13.2 (0.78)	9.8 (0.50)	4.3 (0.11)	13.0 (0.47)	15.4 (0.84)	11.9 (0.55)	5.3 (0.13)
Some college, no degree	5.9 (0.29)	7.1 (0.65)	5.5 (0.32)	4.3 (0.14)	5.9 (0.29)	7.6 (0.67)	5.4 (0.32)	4.1 (0.14)	6.9 (0.31)	8.7 (0.70)	6.4 (0.34)	5.1 (0.15)
Associate's degree	4.1 (0.58)	‡ (†)	3.9 (0.58)	3.1 (0.15)	4.0 (0.57)	‡ (†)	4.0 (0.58)	3.1 (0.15)	6.4 (0.71)	‡ (†)	6.1 (0.71)	3.7 (0.16)
Bachelor's or higher degree	4.7 (0.44)	‡ (†)	4.6 (0.44)	2.1 (0.07)	4.8 (0.43)	‡ (†)	4.6 (0.42)	2.1 (0.07)	5.2 (0.44)	‡ (†)	5.2 (0.44)	2.7 (0.08)
White, all education levels	**8.9 (0.18)**	**12.8 (0.32)**	**6.8 (0.20)**	**3.0 (0.04)**	**8.9 (0.18)**	**13.1 (0.33)**	**6.9 (0.20)**	**3.0 (0.04)**	**10.8 (0.20)**	**15.6 (0.37)**	**8.5 (0.22)**	**3.8 (0.05)**
Less than high school completion	14.9 (0.47)	14.7 (0.46)	15.5 (1.09)	6.5 (0.28)	15.7 (0.49)	15.4 (0.48)	17.0 (1.16)	7.3 (0.30)	19.0 (0.56)	18.1 (0.54)	22.7 (1.38)	8.3 (0.33)
High school completion, no college	10.3 (0.37)	12.9 (0.65)	9.2 (0.42)	3.7 (0.09)	9.8 (0.36)	12.5 (0.64)	8.6 (0.41)	3.8 (0.09)	12.9 (0.41)	16.7 (0.73)	11.3 (0.46)	4.9 (0.10)
Some college, no degree	5.4 (0.26)	6.9 (0.57)	5.0 (0.28)	3.3 (0.11)	5.8 (0.27)	7.4 (0.60)	5.4 (0.29)	3.3 (0.11)	6.9 (0.29)	8.1 (0.61)	6.6 (0.31)	4.4 (0.12)
Associate's degree	4.0 (0.51)	‡ (†)	3.9 (0.51)	2.7 (0.13)	3.7 (0.50)	‡ (†)	3.7 (0.50)	2.6 (0.13)	4.5 (0.55)	‡ (†)	4.1 (0.54)	3.3 (0.14)
Bachelor's or higher degree	4.9 (0.42)	‡ (†)	4.8 (0.42)	1.9 (0.06)	5.0 (0.40)	‡ (†)	5.0 (0.41)	1.9 (0.06)	5.7 (0.42)	‡ (†)	5.7 (0.42)	2.3 (0.06)
Black, all education levels	**20.5 (0.63)**	**29.9 (1.15)**	**16.4 (0.70)**	**6.8 (0.17)**	**19.4 (0.63)**	**29.7 (1.20)**	**15.3 (0.67)**	**6.2 (0.17)**	**21.7 (0.66)**	**31.2 (1.23)**	**17.9 (0.72)**	**7.9 (0.18)**
Less than high school completion	32.2 (1.46)	33.6 (1.61)	29.5 (2.44)	13.0 (0.72)	32.2 (1.54)	32.9 (1.70)	31.4 (2.59)	12.4 (0.73)	36.0 (1.61)	37.0 (1.80)	34.5 (2.63)	14.9 (0.79)
High school completion, no college	22.2 (1.09)	31.5 (2.18)	19.1 (1.19)	8.0 (0.32)	20.8 (1.05)	29.3 (2.09)	18.1 (1.15)	7.4 (0.30)	21.9 (1.09)	26.8 (2.06)	20.3 (1.22)	9.3 (0.34)
Some college, no degree	11.7 (0.94)	14.1 (2.26)	11.2 (1.01)	6.7 (0.38)	10.8 (0.92)	17.3 (2.73)	10.0 (0.95)	5.9 (0.35)	14.1 (1.02)	21.8 (2.75)	12.7 (1.06)	8.1 (0.40)
Associate's degree	15.3 (2.80)	‡ (†)	14.2 (2.78)	5.3 (0.49)	8.0 (2.22)	‡ (†)	7.6 (2.19)	4.9 (0.47)	16.8 (2.88)	‡ (†)	16.1 (2.88)	6.1 (0.51)
Bachelor's or higher degree	8.7 (1.76)	‡ (†)	8.4 (1.75)	2.8 (0.23)	8.8 (1.77)	‡ (†)	8.1 (1.71)	2.9 (0.24)	8.0 (1.67)	‡ (†)	8.2 (1.70)	3.9 (0.27)
Hispanic, all education levels	**9.7 (0.40)**	**15.9 (0.81)**	**7.2 (0.41)**	**4.2 (0.13)**	**10.7 (0.41)**	**18.1 (0.84)**	**7.8 (0.42)**	**4.6 (0.13)**	**14.7 (0.47)**	**22.4 (0.90)**	**11.5 (0.51)**	**6.1 (0.15)**
Less than high school completion	13.1 (0.73)	18.4 (1.14)	9.3 (0.82)	5.5 (0.24)	14.5 (0.77)	21.1 (1.21)	9.5 (0.84)	6.0 (0.25)	21.0 (0.93)	27.5 (1.33)	15.4 (1.12)	8.2 (0.29)
High school completion, no college	9.2 (0.67)	13.9 (1.43)	7.7 (0.71)	4.1 (0.23)	10.2 (0.69)	17.3 (1.57)	8.0 (0.71)	4.4 (0.23)	14.1 (0.78)	19.4 (1.58)	12.2 (0.85)	6.2 (0.26)
Some college, no degree	6.2 (0.70)	10.3 (1.81)	5.2 (0.71)	3.9 (0.32)	6.9 (0.72)	8.8 (1.55)	6.5 (0.79)	4.4 (0.34)	9.2 (0.80)	12.3 (1.71)	8.4 (0.87)	5.4 (0.36)
Associate's degree	4.5 (1.46)	‡ (†)	4.5 (1.49)	2.9 (0.41)	5.7 (1.52)	‡ (†)	5.7 (1.54)	3.5 (0.43)	8.9 (1.85)	‡ (†)	8.6 (1.87)	5.4 (0.45)
Bachelor's or higher degree	3.7 (1.33)	‡ (†)	4.1 (1.41)	2.2 (0.24)	6.5 (1.63)	‡ (†)	5.3 (1.50)	2.3 (0.24)	5.8 (1.54)	‡ (†)	5.9 (1.56)	3.4 (0.28)
Asian, all education levels	**7.4 (0.81)**	**13.7 (2.21)**	**5.6 (0.81)**	**2.6 (0.16)**	**7.0 (0.78)**	**11.9 (2.08)**	**5.6 (0.79)**	**2.8 (0.16)**	**7.6 (0.82)**	**14.7 (2.29)**	**5.5 (0.80)**	**3.5 (0.18)**
Less than high school completion	13.5 (2.85)	‡ (†)	‡ (†)	3.8 (0.71)	16.9 (3.12)	‡ (†)	‡ (†)	3.0 (0.65)	16.3 (3.03)	‡ (†)	‡ (†)	6.3 (0.89)
High school completion, no college	8.8 (1.90)	‡ (†)	5.4 (1.81)	3.1 (0.42)	5.7 (1.66)	‡ (†)	4.1 (1.63)	3.2 (0.41)	11.8 (2.42)	‡ (†)	9.5 (2.58)	4.2 (0.46)
Some college, no degree	5.9 (1.20)	‡ (†)	5.4 (1.26)	3.8 (0.63)	5.6 (1.14)	‡ (†)	5.0 (1.20)	3.6 (0.58)	4.9 (1.08)	‡ (†)	3.6 (1.04)	3.7 (0.61)
Associate's degree	‡ (†)	‡ (†)	6.7 (3.53)	2.3 (0.56)	‡ (†)	‡ (†)	‡ (†)	4.0 (0.74)	‡ (†)	‡ (†)	‡ (†)	3.7 (0.69)
Bachelor's or higher degree	‡ (†)	‡ (†)	5.1 (1.43)	2.1 (0.19)	6.7 (1.54)	‡ (†)	6.1 (1.49)	2.3 (0.20)	4.3 (1.24)	‡ (†)	4.6 (1.30)	2.8 (0.21)

†Not applicable.
‡Reporting standards not met.
[1]Excludes persons enrolled in school.

NOTE: The unemployment rate is the percentage of individuals in the labor force who are not working and who made specific efforts to find employment sometime during the prior 4 weeks. The labor force includes both employed and unemployed persons. Race categories exclude persons of Hispanic ethnicity. Standard errors appear in parentheses.
SOURCE: U.S. Department of Labor, Bureau of Labor Statistics, Office of Employment and Unemployment Statistics, unpublished 2006, 2007, and 2008 annual average data from the Current Population Survey (CPS). (This table was prepared August 2009.)

Occupation of employed persons 25 years old and over, by educational attainment and sex: 2008

Occupation and sex	Total employed (in thousands)	Total	Percentage distribution, by highest level of educational attainment						
			High school				College		
			Less than 1 year of high school	1–4 years of high school, no completion	High school completion	Some college, no degree	Associate's degree	Bachelor's degree	Master's or higher degree
1	2	3	4	5	6	7	8	9	10
All persons	**126,161** (229.8)	**100.0**	**3.3** (0.06)	**5.5** (0.07)	**28.6** (0.15)	**17.5** (0.12)	**10.3** (0.10)	**22.6** (0.14)	**12.3** (0.11)
Management, professional, and related	49,629 (220.0)	100.0	0.4 (0.03)	1.0 (0.05)	11.6 (0.17)	12.6 (0.17)	10.5 (0.16)	36.6 (0.25)	27.3 (0.23)
Management, business, and financial operations	21,181 (158.2)	100.0	0.7 (0.07)	1.7 (0.10)	17.1 (0.30)	16.2 (0.29)	9.0 (0.23)	36.9 (0.38)	18.3 (0.31)
Professional and related	28,448 (179.2)	100.0	0.2 (0.03)	0.5 (0.05)	7.5 (0.18)	10.0 (0.21)	11.5 (0.22)	36.3 (0.33)	34.0 (0.32)
Education, training, and library	7,908 (100.6)	100.0	0.1 (0.04)	0.4 (0.09)	6.9 (0.33)	7.5 (0.34)	5.1 (0.29)	36.7 (0.63)	43.2 (0.64)
Preschool and kindergarten teachers	606 (28.4)	100.0	# (†)	1.2 (0.50)	13.9 (1.62)	16.0 (1.72)	10.6 (1.44)	41.2 (2.31)	17.2 (1.77)
Elementary and middle school teachers	2,804 (60.7)	100.0	0.1 (0.07)	0.2 (0.10)	2.1 (0.32)	3.0 (0.37)	1.9 (0.30)	46.8 (1.09)	45.8 (1.09)
Secondary school teachers	1,155 (39.2)	100.0	0.1 (0.10)	# (†)	1.0 (0.35)	1.5 (0.41)	1.6 (0.42)	45.0 (1.69)	50.9 (1.70)
Special education teachers	369 (22.2)	100.0	— (†)	— (†)	2.2 (0.88)	2.4 (0.93)	2.7 (0.98)	39.8 (2.95)	52.8 (3.00)
Postsecondary teachers	1,117 (38.5)	100.0	— (†)	# (†)	0.9 (0.33)	1.5 (0.42)	2.3 (0.52)	15.6 (1.25)	79.7 (1.39)
Other education, training, and library workers	1,857 (49.6)	100.0	0.3 (0.14)	1.1 (0.28)	20.2 (1.08)	19.9 (1.07)	12.5 (0.89)	27.1 (1.19)	19.0 (1.05)
Service occupations	18,647 (149.6)	100.0	7.2 (0.22)	10.6 (0.26)	39.0 (0.41)	19.3 (0.33)	10.2 (0.26)	11.5 (0.27)	2.1 (0.12)
Sales and office occupations	29,353 (181.5)	100.0	1.1 (0.07)	3.7 (0.13)	33.7 (0.32)	24.9 (0.29)	11.3 (0.21)	21.2 (0.28)	4.1 (0.13)
Natural resources, construction, and maintenance	12,878 (126.5)	100.0	9.1 (0.29)	11.9 (0.33)	43.7 (0.51)	16.9 (0.38)	10.5 (0.31)	6.8 (0.26)	1.1 (0.11)
Production, transportation, and material moving	15,654 (138.3)	100.0	7.0 (0.24)	11.6 (0.30)	48.2 (0.46)	17.5 (0.35)	7.4 (0.24)	6.9 (0.23)	1.4 (0.11)
Males	**67,605** (153.5)	**100.0**	**4.1** (0.09)	**6.4** (0.34)	**29.7** (0.20)	**16.8** (0.16)	**8.9** (0.12)	**22.0** (0.18)	**12.1** (0.14)
Management, professional, and related	24,572 (152.8)	100.0	0.6 (0.05)	1.3 (0.26)	11.7 (0.23)	12.6 (0.24)	8.1 (0.20)	37.1 (0.35)	28.8 (0.33)
Management, business, and financial operations	12,208 (117.1)	100.0	1.0 (0.10)	2.0 (0.46)	17.4 (0.39)	15.4 (0.37)	7.6 (0.27)	37.5 (0.50)	19.1 (0.40)
Professional and related	12,364 (117.7)	100.0	0.2 (0.04)	0.5 (0.22)	6.1 (0.24)	9.8 (0.30)	8.5 (0.29)	36.6 (0.49)	38.3 (0.50)
Education, training, and library	2,042 (50.8)	100.0	# (†)	# (†)	2.6 (0.40)	4.1 (0.50)	3.3 (0.45)	34.5 (1.20)	55.4 (1.25)
Service occupations	7,919 (96.8)	100.0	8.0 (0.35)	9.6 (1.19)	36.4 (0.62)	19.7 (0.51)	9.9 (0.38)	13.8 (0.44)	2.6 (0.20)
Sales and office occupations	10,690 (110.6)	100.0	1.4 (0.13)	3.7 (0.65)	28.7 (0.50)	22.9 (0.46)	9.5 (0.32)	28.0 (0.49)	5.8 (0.26)
Natural resources, construction, and maintenance	12,348 (117.7)	100.0	9.0 (0.29)	12.0 (1.05)	44.1 (0.51)	16.7 (0.38)	10.6 (0.32)	6.6 (0.25)	1.0 (0.10)
Production, transportation, and material moving	12,077 (116.6)	100.0	6.2 (0.25)	11.4 (1.04)	48.1 (0.52)	18.1 (0.40)	7.7 (0.28)	7.0 (0.26)	1.3 (0.12)
Females	**58,555** (159.9)	**100.0**	**2.3** (0.07)	**4.5** (0.09)	**27.3** (0.20)	**18.3** (0.18)	**11.8** (0.15)	**23.2** (0.19)	**12.5** (0.15)
Management, professional, and related	25,057 (148.5)	100.0	0.2 (0.03)	0.8 (0.06)	11.4 (0.22)	12.7 (0.23)	12.8 (0.23)	36.1 (0.33)	25.9 (0.30)
Management, business, and financial operations	8,973 (99.0)	100.0	0.4 (0.07)	1.3 (0.13)	16.6 (0.43)	17.4 (0.44)	10.9 (0.44)	36.1 (0.56)	17.3 (0.44)
Professional and related	16,084 (126.8)	100.0	0.1 (0.03)	0.6 (0.07)	8.5 (0.24)	10.1 (0.26)	13.9 (0.30)	36.1 (0.42)	30.6 (0.40)
Education, training, and library	5,866 (81.6)	100.0	0.2 (0.06)	0.5 (0.11)	8.4 (0.40)	8.7 (0.40)	5.8 (0.33)	37.5 (0.70)	38.9 (0.70)
Service occupations	10,728 (107.1)	100.0	6.6 (0.26)	11.4 (0.34)	40.9 (0.52)	19.0 (0.42)	10.5 (0.33)	9.8 (0.32)	1.8 (0.14)
Sales and office occupations	18,663 (134.2)	100.0	0.9 (0.08)	3.7 (0.15)	36.6 (0.39)	26.0 (0.35)	12.4 (0.27)	17.3 (0.30)	3.1 (0.14)
Natural resources, construction, and maintenance	530 (25.3)	100.0	11.5 (1.53)	8.9 (1.36)	34.7 (2.28)	20.6 (1.93)	9.2 (1.39)	12.6 (1.59)	2.5 (0.74)
Production, transportation, and material moving	3,577 (64.5)	100.0	9.8 (0.55)	12.3 (0.61)	48.5 (0.92)	15.1 (0.66)	6.4 (0.45)	6.4 (0.45)	1.5 (0.22)

—Not available.
†Not applicable.
#Rounds to zero.

NOTE: Detail may not sum to totals because of rounding. Standard errors appear in parentheses.
SOURCE: U.S. Department of Labor, Bureau of Labor Statistics, Office of Employment and Unemployment Statistics, unpublished 2008 annual average data from the Current Population Survey (CPS). (This table was prepared August 2009.)

Median annual earnings of year-round, full-time workers 25 years old and over, by highest level of educational attainment and sex: 1990 through 2008

Current dollars

Sex and year	Total	Elementary/secondary			College						
		Less than 9th grade	Some high school, no completion[1]	High school completion (includes equivalency)[2]	Some college, no degree[3]	Associate's degree[6]	Bachelor's or higher degree[4] — Total	Bachelor's degree[5]	Master's degree[6]	Professional degree[6]	Doctor's degree[6]
	2	3	4	5	6	7	8	9	10	11	12
Males											
1990	$30,730 (—)	$17,390 (—)	$20,900 (—)	$26,650 (—)	$31,730 (—)	(†)	$42,670 (—)	$39,240 (—)	(†)	(†)	(†)
1991	31,610 (—)	17,620 (—)	21,400 (—)	26,780 (—)	31,660 (—)	$33,820 (—)	45,140 (—)	40,910 (—)	$49,730 (—)	$74,000 (—)	$57,190 (—)
1992	32,060 (120)	17,290 (—)	21,270 (—)	27,280 (175)	32,100 (—)	33,430 (—)	45,800 (—)	41,360 (304)	49,970 (—)	76,220 (—)	57,420 (—)
1993	32,360 (124)	16,860 (—)	21,750 (319)	27,370 (204)	32,080 (300)	33,690 (430)	47,740 (707)	42,760 (536)	51,870 (854)	80,550 (3,040)	63,150 (1,619)
1994	33,440 (246)	17,530 (453)	22,050 (342)	28,040 (322)	32,280 (517)	35,790 (535)	49,230 (312)	43,660 (633)	53,500 (973)	75,010 (2,582)	61,920 (2,188)
1995	34,550 (275)	18,350 (545)	22,190 (414)	29,510 (358)	33,880 (456)	35,200 (435)	50,480 (303)	45,270 (510)	55,220 (945)	79,670 (3,317)	65,340 (3,362)
1996	35,620 (150)	17,960 (594)	22,720 (466)	30,710 (184)	34,850 (293)	37,130 (774)	51,440 (755)	45,850 (458)	60,510 (771)	85,960 (4,253)	71,230 (3,611)
1997	36,680 (149)	19,290 (629)	24,730 (547)	31,220 (171)	35,950 (291)	38,020 (539)	53,450 (421)	48,620 (851)	61,690 (847)	85,010 (12,105)	76,230 (2,507)
1998	37,910 (291)	19,380 (600)	23,960 (535)	31,480 (169)	36,930 (581)	40,270 (459)	56,520 (439)	51,410 (349)	62,240 (690)	94,740 (37,836)	75,080 (3,953)
1999	40,330 (144)	19,430 (444)	25,040 (436)	33,180 (388)	39,220 (312)	41,640 (460)	60,200 (303)	52,990 (722)	66,240 (1,506)	100,000 (20,832)	81,690 (2,446)
2000	41,060 (156)	20,430 (376)	25,100 (251)	34,300 (457)	40,340 (214)	41,950 (561)	61,870 (279)	56,330 (573)	68,320 (687)	99,410 (—)	80,250 (3,013)
2001	41,620 (104)	20,790 (235)	26,210 (207)	34,720 (299)	41,050 (195)	42,780 (673)	62,220 (201)	55,930 (335)	70,900 (1,294)	100,000 (—)	86,970 (2,076)
2002	41,150 (100)	21,360 (213)	25,900 (280)	33,210 (311)	40,850 (182)	42,860 (719)	61,700 (187)	56,080 (385)	67,280 (562)	100,000 (—)	83,310 (2,528)
2003	41,940 (90)	20,920 (227)	26,470 (234)	35,410 (168)	41,350 (175)	42,870 (931)	62,080 (798)	56,500 (365)	70,640 (490)	100,000 (—)	87,130 (2,423)
2004	42,090 (89)	21,220 (191)	26,280 (237)	35,730 (148)	41,900 (323)	44,400 (367)	62,800 (356)	57,220 (393)	71,530 (1,229)	100,000 (—)	82,400 (3,061)
2005	43,320 (367)	21,660 (220)	27,190 (573)	36,300 (141)	42,420 (812)	47,180 (390)	66,170 (346)	60,020 (653)	75,030 (859)	100,000 (—)	85,860 (—)
2006	45,760 (134)	22,330 (398)	27,650 (590)	37,030 (164)	43,830 (585)	47,070 (801)	66,930 (241)	60,910 (235)	75,430 (416)	100,000 (—)	100,000 (—)
2007	47,000 (130)	22,710 (544)	29,320 (458)	37,880 (406)	44,900 (276)	49,040 (344)	70,400 (236)	62,090 (236)	76,280 (468)	100,000 (—)	92,090 (1,894)
2008	49,000 (339)	23,380 (631)	29,680 (—)	39,010 (399)	45,820 (—)	50,150 (—)	72,220 (—)	65,800 (388)	80,960 (—)	100,000 (—)	100,000 (—)
Females											
1990	21,370 (—)	12,250 (—)	14,430 (—)	18,320 (—)	22,230 (—)	(†)	30,380 (—)	28,020 (—)	(†)	(†)	(†)
1991	22,040 (—)	12,070 (—)	14,460 (—)	18,840 (—)	22,140 (—)	25,000 (—)	31,310 (—)	29,080 (—)	34,950 (—)	46,740 (—)	43,300 (—)
1992	23,140 (159)	12,960 (—)	14,560 (—)	19,430 (176)	23,160 (—)	25,620 (—)	32,300 (280)	30,330 (294)	36,040 (606)	46,260 (2,154)	45,790 (2,888)
1993	23,630 (166)	12,420 (427)	15,390 (328)	19,960 (173)	23,060 (327)	25,880 (295)	34,310 (313)	31,200 (310)	38,610 (556)	50,210 (2,532)	47,250 (2,373)
1994	24,400 (165)	12,430 (490)	15,130 (293)	20,370 (158)	23,510 (274)	25,940 (428)	35,380 (296)	31,740 (314)	39,460 (564)	50,620 (3,635)	51,120 (3,300)
1995	24,880 (160)	13,580 (559)	15,830 (333)	20,460 (162)	24,000 (267)	27,310 (526)	35,260 (481)	32,050 (273)	40,260 (837)	50,000 (4,737)	48,140 (3,626)
1996	25,810 (131)	14,410 (492)	16,950 (335)	21,180 (143)	25,170 (291)	28,080 (660)	36,460 (408)	33,530 (437)	41,900 (760)	57,620 (1,705)	56,270 (1,881)
1997	26,970 (134)	14,160 (429)	16,700 (322)	22,070 (148)	26,340 (271)	28,810 (513)	38,040 (275)	35,380 (295)	44,950 (862)	61,050 (4,479)	53,040 (3,130)
1998	27,960 (199)	14,470 (492)	16,480 (298)	22,780 (254)	27,420 (369)	29,920 (318)	39,790 (439)	36,560 (305)	45,280 (735)	57,570 (3,552)	57,800 (2,999)
1999	28,840 (216)	15,100 (327)	17,020 (434)	23,060 (279)	27,760 (364)	30,920 (307)	41,750 (367)	37,990 (614)	48,100 (328)	59,900 (3,976)	60,080 (2,228)
2000	30,330 (138)	15,800 (255)	17,920 (359)	24,970 (236)	28,700 (186)	31,070 (231)	42,710 (568)	40,420 (284)	50,140 (595)	58,960 (2,421)	57,080 (2,268)
2001	31,360 (91)	16,690 (297)	19,160 (360)	25,300 (132)	30,420 (299)	32,150 (211)	44,780 (291)	40,990 (231)	50,670 (454)	61,750 (3,469)	62,120 (2,462)
2002	31,010 (83)	16,510 (256)	19,310 (327)	25,180 (121)	29,400 (176)	31,630 (241)	43,250 (229)	40,850 (173)	48,890 (263)	57,020 (2,436)	65,720 (2,450)
2003	31,570 (85)	16,910 (241)	18,940 (319)	26,070 (118)	30,140 (135)	32,250 (489)	45,120 (232)	41,330 (204)	50,160 (283)	66,490 (2,774)	67,210 (2,490)
2004	31,990 (80)	17,020 (250)	19,160 (274)	26,030 (116)	30,820 (165)	33,480 (497)	45,910 (441)	41,680 (172)	51,320 (561)	75,040 (2,488)	68,880 (1,779)
2005	33,080 (242)	16,140 (408)	20,130 (270)	26,290 (134)	31,400 (165)	33,940 (376)	46,950 (158)	42,170 (179)	51,410 (412)	80,460 (910)	66,850 (2,155)
2006	35,100 (113)	18,130 (461)	20,130 (292)	26,740 (136)	31,950 (415)	35,160 (283)	49,570 (145)	45,410 (259)	52,440 (745)	76,240 (2,859)	70,520 (2,144)
2007	36,090 (105)	18,260 (494)	20,400 (295)	27,240 (133)	32,840 (355)	36,330 (243)	50,400 (—)	45,770 (262)	55,430 (—)	71,100 (—)	68,990 (—)
2008	36,700 (109)	18,630 (—)	20,410 (—)	28,380 (283)	32,630 (—)	36,760 (—)	51,410 (—)	47,030 (237)	57,510 (—)	71,300 (—)	74,030 (—)

See notes at end of table.

Median annual earnings of year-round, full-time workers 25 years old and over, by highest level of educational attainment and sex: 1990 through 2008—Continued

[Constant 2008 dollars[7]]

| | | Elementary/secondary | | | | College | | Bachelor's or higher degree[4] | | | | |
Sex and year	Total	Less than 9th grade	Some high school, no completion[1]	High school completion (includes equivalency)[2]	Some college, no degree[3]	Associate's degree	Total	Bachelor's degree[5]	Master's degree	Professional degree	Doctor's degree
Males											
1990	$50,630 (—)	$28,650 (—)	$34,430 (—)	$43,910 (—)	$52,280 (—)	$53,460 [6] (†)	$70,290 (—)	$64,640 (—)	$78,620 [6] (†)	$116,970 [6] (†)	$90,400 [6] (†)
1991	49,970 (—)	27,860 (—)	33,830 (—)	42,330 (269)	50,050 (—)	51,310 (—)	71,350 (—)	64,660 (467)	76,690 (—)	116,970 (—)	88,110 (—)
1992	49,190 (184)	26,540 (—)	32,650 (—)	41,860 (304)	49,260 (—)	50,200 (—)	70,290 (—)	63,460 (799)	77,280 (—)	120,020 (—)	94,090 (—)
1993	48,210 (185)	25,130 (658)	32,410 (463)	40,780 (468)	47,790 (436)	52,000 (625)	71,130 (1,027)	63,710 (920)	77,720 (1,241)	108,970 (4,416)	89,960 (2,352)
1994	48,580 (357)	25,470 (770)	32,030 (483)	40,730 (506)	46,890 (730)	49,730 (756)	71,520 (441)	63,430 (721)	78,010 (1,375)	112,550 (3,648)	92,300 (3,091)
1995	48,810 (389)	25,930 (815)	31,340 (568)	41,690 (252)	47,870 (626)	50,950 (597)	71,320 (416)	63,950 (628)	83,030 (1,297)	117,960 (4,552)	97,740 (4,613)
1996	48,880 (206)	24,650 (844)	31,170 (625)	42,140 (229)	47,820 (393)	51,000 (1,038)	70,580 (1,013)	62,910 (1,142)	82,750 (1,034)	114,040 (5,705)	102,260 (4,884)
1997	49,200 (200)	25,880 (793)	33,170 (723)	41,870 (223)	48,220 (384)	53,200 (712)	71,700 (556)	65,220 (461)	82,220 (1,119)	125,140 (15,989)	99,170 (3,311)
1998	50,070 (384)	25,600 (574)	31,650 (691)	41,580 (501)	48,790 (751)	53,810 (593)	74,660 (567)	67,900 (933)	85,610 (892)	129,230 (48,897)	105,570 (5,109)
1999	52,120 (186)	26,400 (470)	32,350 (545)	42,880 (571)	50,690 (390)	52,450 (575)	77,800 (379)	68,470 (716)	85,420 (1,883)	124,290 (26,046)	100,340 (3,058)
2000	51,340 (195)	25,990 (286)	31,380 (305)	42,890 (363)	50,430 (260)	52,000 (682)	77,350 (339)	67,990 (407)	86,190 (835)	119,680 (—)	105,720 (3,663)
2001	50,590 (126)	25,970 (255)	31,860 (248)	42,210 (372)	49,900 (233)	51,290 (805)	75,650 (241)	67,110 (461)	80,520 (1,549)	117,010 (—)	99,700 (2,485)
2002	49,250 (120)	25,040 (266)	31,000 (328)	39,740 (197)	48,890 (213)	50,160 (841)	73,840 (219)	66,110 (427)	82,660 (658)	113,980 (—)	101,950 (2,958)
2003	49,070 (105)	24,830 (218)	30,970 (267)	41,440 (169)	48,380 (199)	50,610 (1,061)	72,640 (910)	65,220 (448)	81,530 (558)	110,240 (—)	93,920 (2,762)
2004	47,970 (101)	24,690 (243)	29,950 (261)	40,720 (155)	47,750 (356)	52,010 (405)	71,570 (392)	66,170 (720)	82,710 (1,355)	106,800 (—)	94,660 (3,375)
2005	47,750 (405)	24,620 (405)	29,970 (261)	40,020 (175)	46,760 (867)	50,270 (417)	72,940 (370)	65,050 (251)	80,560 (917)	103,840 (—)	106,800 (—)
2006	48,870 (143)	24,250 (143)	29,530 (612)	39,550 (422)	46,810 (607)	50,920 (832)	71,480 (250)	64,470 (245)	79,210 (432)	100,000 (—)	95,620 (1,967)
2007	48,810 (135)	24,270 (565)	30,440 (613)	39,310 (399)	46,620 (276)	50,150 (344)	73,100 (236)	65,800 (388)	80,960 (468)	100,000 (—)	100,000 (—)
2008	49,000 (339)	24,260 (631)	29,680 (458)	39,010 (—)	45,820 (276)	50,150 (344)	72,220 (236)	65,800 (388)	80,960 (468)	100,000 (—)	100,000 (—)
Females											
1990	35,210 (—)	20,180 (—)	23,770 (—)	30,180 (—)	36,610 (—)	39,520 [6] (†)	50,040 (—)	46,150 (—)	55,250 [6] (†)	73,890 [6] (†)	68,450 [6] (†)
1991	34,850 (—)	19,070 (—)	22,850 (—)	29,780 (270)	35,000 (—)	39,320 (—)	49,490 (—)	45,970 (451)	55,300 (—)	70,990 (—)	70,270 (—)
1992	35,510 (244)	19,890 (—)	22,340 (—)	29,810 (258)	35,540 (—)	38,570 (—)	49,570 (—)	46,540 (462)	57,530 (—)	74,810 (—)	70,400 (—)
1993	35,210 (247)	18,500 (620)	22,920 (477)	29,740 (230)	34,350 (475)	37,690 (429)	51,120 (407)	46,480 (456)	57,320 (1,123)	73,530 (3,129)	74,260 (4,196)
1994	35,450 (240)	18,060 (692)	21,980 (414)	29,600 (229)	34,160 (387)	38,580 (605)	51,400 (442)	46,110 (386)	56,880 (1,004)	70,640 (3,577)	68,010 (3,352)
1995	35,140 (226)	19,180 (767)	22,360 (457)	28,910 (196)	33,960 (366)	38,540 (722)	49,810 (406)	45,280 (600)	57,500 (1,114)	79,070 (4,988)	77,210 (4,528)
1996	35,410 (180)	19,780 (660)	23,260 (449)	29,060 (199)	34,530 (390)	38,650 (885)	50,030 (645)	46,000 (396)	60,300 (919)	81,900 (6,354)	71,150 (4,864)
1997	36,180 (180)	19,000 (567)	22,400 (425)	29,600 (199)	35,330 (358)	39,530 (678)	51,030 (539)	47,460 (403)	59,810 (712)	76,040 (2,252)	76,340 (2,485)
1998	36,930 (263)	19,110 (636)	21,770 (385)	30,090 (336)	36,220 (477)	39,960 (411)	52,550 (678)	48,290 (793)	62,160 (531)	77,420 (5,788)	77,640 (4,045)
1999	37,280 (279)	19,510 (409)	21,990 (543)	29,800 (361)	35,870 (455)	38,850 (384)	53,950 (355)	49,100 (355)	62,690 (300)	73,710 (4,441)	71,370 (3,750)
2000	37,920 (173)	19,750 (310)	22,400 (436)	31,220 (295)	35,880 (226)	39,090 (281)	53,400 (549)	50,530 (281)	61,600 (312)	75,070 (4,834)	75,520 (2,709)
2001	38,120 (111)	20,290 (355)	23,290 (431)	30,760 (160)	36,980 (358)	37,850 (253)	54,430 (446)	49,840 (207)	60,510 (599)	68,240 (2,897)	78,650 (2,714)
2002	37,110 (99)	19,760 (300)	23,110 (383)	30,140 (145)	35,190 (206)	37,740 (282)	51,760 (680)	48,890 (239)	58,700 (428)	77,800 (4,059)	78,650 (2,881)
2003	36,930 (99)	19,780 (275)	22,160 (364)	30,510 (138)	35,270 (154)	38,160 (557)	52,790 (341)	48,360 (196)	58,490 (745)	85,520 (2,776)	78,500 (2,792)
2004	36,460 (91)	19,400 (276)	21,840 (302)	29,670 (132)	35,120 (182)	37,420 (548)	52,330 (261)	47,510 (197)	56,680 (300)	88,700 (3,058)	73,700 (2,745)
2005	36,460 (267)	17,800 (436)	22,190 (288)	28,980 (148)	34,610 (176)	37,550 (402)	51,760 (256)	46,490 (277)	56,000 (312)	81,420 (2,657)	75,310 (1,900)
2006	37,480 (121)	19,370 (479)	21,500 (303)	28,550 (145)	34,130 (431)	37,730 (294)	52,940 (471)	48,490 (599)	57,550 (599)	73,830 (945)	71,640 (2,238)
2007	37,470 (109)	18,960 (494)	21,180 (295)	28,290 (138)	34,100 (355)	36,760 (243)	52,330 (164)	47,530 (272)	57,510 (428)	71,300 (2,859)	74,030 (2,144)
2008	36,700 (109)	18,630 (494)	20,410 (295)	28,380 (283)	32,630 (355)	36,760 (243)	51,410 (145)	47,030 (237)	57,510 (745)	71,300 (2,859)	74,030 (2,144)

See notes at end of table.

Median annual earnings of year-round, full-time workers 25 years old and over, by highest level of educational attainment and sex: 1990 through 2008—Continued

Number of persons with earnings (in thousands)

Sex and year	Total	Elementary/secondary					College — Bachelor's or higher degree[4]				
		Less than 9th grade	Some high school, no completion[1]	High school completion (includes equivalency)[2]	Some college, no degree[3]	Associate's degree	Total	Bachelor's degree[5]	Master's degree	Professional degree	Doctor's degree
1	2	3	4	5	6	7	8	9	10	11	12
Males											
1990	44,406 (268.6)	2,250 (73.9)	3,315 (89.3)	16,394 (188.0)	9,113 (144.6)	(6) (†)	13,334 (171.8)	7,569 (132.6)	(6) (†)	(6) (†)	(6) (†)
1991	44,199 (268.3)	1,807 (66.3)	3,083 (86.2)	15,025 (181.1)	8,034 (136.4)	2,899 (83.6)	13,350 (171.9)	8,456 (139.7)	3,073 (86.6)	1,147 (53.0)	674 (40.7)
1992	44,752 (269.1)	1,815 (66.5)	3,009 (85.2)	14,722 (179.5)	8,067 (136.6)	3,203 (87.8)	13,937 (175.2)	8,719 (141.7)	3,178 (87.5)	1,295 (56.3)	745 (42.8)
1993	45,873 (270.6)	1,790 (66.0)	3,083 (86.2)	14,604 (178.9)	8,493 (140.0)	3,557 (92.4)	14,346 (177.5)	9,178 (145.1)	3,131 (86.8)	1,231 (54.9)	808 (44.5)
1994	47,566 (303.0)	1,895 (69.2)	3,057 (87.6)	15,109 (188.5)	8,783 (146.2)	3,735 (96.6)	14,987 (187.8)	9,636 (152.8)	3,225 (89.9)	1,258 (56.4)	868 (46.9)
1995	48,500 (306.1)	1,946 (72.8)	3,335 (94.9)	15,331 (195.6)	8,908 (152.3)	3,926 (102.8)	15,054 (194.0)	9,597 (157.8)	3,395 (95.7)	1,208 (57.5)	853 (48.4)
1996	49,764 (301.1)	2,041 (69.2)	3,441 (89.6)	15,840 (186.5)	9,173 (144.2)	3,931 (95.6)	15,339 (183.7)	9,898 (149.6)	3,272 (87.4)	1,277 (54.8)	893 (45.9)
1997	50,807 (299.0)	1,914 (67.0)	3,548 (90.9)	16,225 (187.8)	9,170 (143.9)	4,086 (97.4)	15,864 (185.9)	10,349 (152.4)	3,228 (86.7)	1,321 (55.8)	966 (47.7)
1998	52,381 (306.4)	1,870 (66.3)	3,613 (91.7)	16,442 (189.7)	9,375 (145.7)	4,347 (100.4)	16,733 (191.2)	11,058 (157.6)	3,414 (89.2)	1,264 (54.6)	998 (48.5)
1999	53,062 (307.8)	1,993 (68.4)	3,295 (87.7)	16,589 (190.5)	9,684 (148.0)	4,359 (100.6)	17,142 (193.3)	11,142 (158.2)	3,725 (93.1)	1,267 (54.8)	1,008 (48.8)
2000	54,065 (309.7)	1,968 (68.0)	3,354 (88.4)	16,834 (191.7)	9,792 (148.8)	4,729 (104.7)	17,387 (194.6)	11,395 (159.9)	3,680 (92.6)	1,274 (54.8)	1,038 (49.5)
2001	54,013 (304.8)	2,207 (51.4)	3,503 (64.5)	16,314 (135.4)	9,494 (104.9)	4,714 (74.7)	17,780 (142.7)	11,479 (116.3)	3,961 (68.5)	1,298 (39.5)	1,041 (35.4)
2002	54,108 (225.0)	2,154 (50.7)	3,680 (66.1)	16,005 (134.2)	9,603 (105.5)	4,399 (72.2)	18,267 (143.0)	11,829 (116.5)	4,065 (69.4)	1,308 (39.6)	1,065 (35.8)
2003	54,253 (225.2)	2,209 (51.4)	3,369 (63.3)	16,285 (135.3)	9,340 (104.1)	4,696 (74.5)	18,354 (142.9)	11,846 (116.6)	4,124 (69.9)	1,348 (40.2)	1,037 (35.3)
2004	55,469 (227.0)	2,427 (53.8)	3,468 (64.2)	17,067 (138.3)	9,257 (103.6)	4,913 (76.2)	18,338 (144.7)	11,701 (115.9)	4,243 (70.9)	1,305 (39.6)	1,088 (36.1)
2005	56,717 (228.7)	2,425 (53.8)	3,652 (65.9)	17,266 (139.0)	9,532 (105.1)	5,022 (77.0)	18,820 (144.7)	12,032 (117.4)	4,275 (71.2)	1,369 (40.5)	1,144 (37.1)
2006	58,109 (230.6)	2,361 (53.1)	3,872 (67.8)	17,369 (139.4)	9,493 (104.9)	5,110 (77.7)	19,903 (148.4)	12,764 (120.7)	4,542 (73.3)	1,425 (41.3)	1,172 (37.5)
2007	58,147 (230.7)	2,142 (50.6)	3,451 (64.0)	17,224 (138.9)	9,867 (106.8)	5,244 (78.7)	20,218 (149.5)	12,962 (121.6)	4,800 (75.3)	1,332 (40.0)	1,125 (36.7)
2008	55,655 (227.2)	1,982 (48.7)	3,118 (60.9)	16,195 (135.0)	9,515 (105.0)	5,020 (77.0)	19,825 (148.1)	12,609 (120.0)	4,709 (74.6)	1,388 (40.8)	1,119 (36.7)
Females											
1990	28,636 (234.7)	847 (45.6)	1,861 (67.3)	11,810 (162.8)	6,462 (123.1)	(6) (†)	7,655 (133.3)	4,704 (105.8)	(6) (†)	(6) (†)	(6) (†)
1991	29,474 (237.1)	733 (42.4)	1,819 (66.5)	10,959 (157.4)	5,633 (115.3)	2,523 (78.1)	7,807 (134.6)	5,263 (111.6)	2,025 (70.1)	312 (27.7)	206 (22.5)
1992	30,346 (239.6)	734 (42.4)	1,659 (63.6)	11,039 (157.9)	5,904 (117.9)	2,655 (80.1)	8,355 (138.9)	5,604 (116.3)	2,192 (72.9)	334 (28.7)	225 (23.5)
1993	30,683 (240.5)	765 (43.3)	1,576 (62.0)	10,513 (154.4)	6,279 (121.4)	3,067 (86.0)	8,483 (139.9)	5,735 (116.3)	2,166 (72.5)	323 (28.2)	260 (25.3)
1994	31,379 (259.2)	696 (42.0)	1,675 (65.1)	10,785 (161.2)	6,256 (124.2)	3,210 (89.7)	8,756 (146.0)	5,901 (120.8)	2,174 (74.0)	398 (31.8)	283 (26.8)
1995	32,673 (268.2)	774 (46.1)	1,763 (69.3)	11,064 (168.6)	6,329 (129.5)	3,336 (94.9)	9,406 (156.3)	6,434 (130.5)	2,268 (78.5)	421 (34.0)	283 (27.9)
1996	33,549 (259.0)	750 (42.1)	1,751 (64.1)	11,363 (159.7)	6,582 (122.9)	3,468 (89.9)	9,636 (147.7)	6,689 (123.9)	2,213 (72.0)	413 (31.2)	322 (27.6)
1997	34,624 (260.1)	791 (43.2)	1,765 (64.4)	11,475 (160.0)	6,628 (123.2)	3,538 (90.7)	10,427 (153.0)	7,173 (128.0)	2,448 (75.7)	488 (34.0)	318 (27.4)
1998	35,628 (265.4)	814 (43.8)	1,878 (66.4)	11,613 (161.3)	7,070 (127.3)	3,527 (90.7)	10,725 (155.4)	7,288 (129.2)	2,639 (78.6)	468 (33.3)	329 (27.9)
1999	37,091 (269.7)	886 (45.7)	1,883 (66.5)	11,824 (162.7)	7,453 (130.6)	3,804 (94.1)	11,242 (158.9)	7,607 (131.9)	2,818 (81.2)	470 (33.3)	346 (28.6)
2000	37,762 (271.6)	930 (46.8)	1,950 (67.7)	11,789 (162.5)	7,391 (130.0)	4,118 (97.8)	11,584 (161.1)	7,899 (134.3)	2,823 (81.2)	509 (34.7)	353 (28.9)
2001	38,228 (197.0)	927 (33.4)	1,869 (47.3)	11,690 (115.8)	7,283 (92.3)	4,190 (70.5)	12,269 (118.5)	8,257 (98.1)	3,089 (60.6)	531 (25.3)	392 (21.7)
2002	38,510 (197.6)	858 (32.1)	1,841 (46.9)	11,687 (115.8)	7,354 (92.7)	4,285 (71.2)	12,484 (119.6)	8,229 (97.9)	3,281 (62.5)	572 (26.2)	402 (22.0)
2003	38,681 (197.9)	882 (32.6)	1,739 (45.6)	11,587 (115.3)	7,341 (92.6)	4,397 (72.2)	12,735 (120.6)	8,330 (98.5)	3,376 (63.4)	567 (26.1)	462 (23.6)
2004	39,072 (198.7)	917 (33.2)	1,797 (46.4)	11,392 (114.4)	7,330 (92.6)	4,505 (73.0)	13,131 (122.4)	8,664 (100.4)	3,451 (64.0)	564 (26.0)	452 (23.3)
2005	40,021 (200.6)	902 (32.9)	1,740 (45.6)	11,419 (114.5)	7,452 (93.3)	4,751 (74.9)	13,758 (125.1)	9,074 (102.6)	3,591 (65.3)	657 (28.1)	437 (22.9)
2006	41,311 (203.2)	934 (33.5)	1,802 (46.4)	11,652 (115.6)	7,613 (94.3)	4,760 (75.0)	14,549 (128.4)	9,645 (105.7)	3,746 (66.7)	662 (28.2)	497 (24.5)
2007	42,196 (204.9)	823 (31.5)	1,649 (44.4)	11,447 (114.7)	7,916 (96.1)	4,891 (76.0)	15,469 (132.1)	9,931 (107.2)	4,389 (72.1)	666 (28.3)	484 (24.1)
2008	40,979 (202.5)	814 (31.3)	1,568 (43.3)	10,851 (111.8)	7,456 (93.3)	4,955 (76.5)	15,335 (131.6)	9,856 (106.8)	4,176 (70.3)	753 (30.1)	550 (25.7)

—Not available.
†Not applicable.
[1] Includes 1 to 3 years of high school for 1990.
[2] Includes 4 years of high school for 1990.
[3] Includes 1 to 3 years of college and associate's degrees for 1990.
[4] Includes 4 or more years of college for 1990.
[5] Includes 4 years of college for 1990.
[6] Not reported separately for 1990.
[7] Constant dollars based on the Consumer Price Index, prepared by the Bureau of Labor Statistics, U.S. Department of Labor.

NOTE: Detail may not sum to totals because of rounding. Standard errors appear in parentheses.

SOURCE: U.S. Department of Commerce, Census Bureau, Current Population Reports, Series P-60, Money Income of Households, Families, and Persons in the United States and Income, Poverty, and Valuation of Noncash Benefits, 1990 through 1994; Series P-60, Money Income in the United States, 1995 through 2002; and Detailed Income Tabulations from the CPS, 2003 through 2008. Retrieved September 10, 2009, from http://www.census.gov/hhes/www/income/dinctabs.html. (This table was prepared September 2009.)

Distribution of earnings and median earnings of persons 25 years old and over, by highest level of educational attainment and sex: 2008

Sex and earnings	Total	Elementary/secondary — Less than 9th grade	Elementary/secondary — Some high school (no completion)	Elementary/secondary — High school completion (includes equivalency)	College — Some college, no degree	College — Associate's degree	College — Total	College — Bachelor's or higher degree — Bachelor's degree	College — Bachelor's or higher degree — Master's degree	College — Bachelor's or higher degree — Professional degree	College — Bachelor's or higher degree — Doctor's degree
1	2	3	4	5	6	7	8	9	10	11	12
Total males and females (in thousands)	**198,285** (226.0)	**10,828** (113.7)	**15,587** (135.1)	**61,626** (240.8)	**33,832** (191.1)	**17,838** (143.8)	**58,574** (236.7)	**37,635** (199.8)	**15,118** (133.2)	**3,206** (62.9)	**2,614** (56.8)
With earnings	135,895 (278.2)	4,567 (74.8)	7,798 (97.1)	39,093 (202.9)	23,969 (164.5)	13,894 (128.0)	46,573 (217.5)	29,678 (180.7)	12,061 (119.7)	2,701 (57.8)	2,133 (51.4)
Distribution of total persons with earnings, by total annual earnings	100.0	100.0	100.0	100.0	100.0	100.0	100.0	100.0	100.0	100.0	100.0
$1 to $4,999 or loss	5.7 (0.07)	9.9 (0.49)	10.7 (0.39)	6.1 (0.14)	6.3 (0.18)	5.1 (0.21)	3.9 (0.10)	4.0 (0.13)	4.4 (0.21)	2.1 (0.31)	2.4 (0.37)
$5,000 to $9,999	5.3 (0.07)	10.5 (0.51)	11.7 (0.41)	6.3 (0.14)	5.6 (0.17)	4.3 (0.19)	3.1 (0.09)	3.6 (0.12)	2.6 (0.16)	1.7 (0.28)	1.9 (0.33)
$10,000 to $14,999	6.9 (0.08)	17.5 (0.63)	13.1 (0.43)	8.8 (0.16)	6.9 (0.18)	6.3 (0.23)	3.5 (0.10)	3.9 (0.13)	3.0 (0.17)	1.9 (0.29)	2.3 (0.37)
$15,000 to $19,999	7.2 (0.08)	16.5 (0.61)	13.6 (0.43)	10.2 (0.17)	6.9 (0.18)	5.3 (0.21)	3.4 (0.09)	4.1 (0.13)	2.6 (0.16)	1.9 (0.29)	1.4 (0.28)
$20,000 to $24,999	8.6 (0.08)	15.5 (0.60)	13.6 (0.43)	11.6 (0.18)	9.4 (0.21)	8.4 (0.26)	4.1 (0.10)	4.9 (0.14)	3.0 (0.17)	2.6 (0.34)	2.3 (0.36)
$25,000 to $29,999	7.4 (0.08)	7.9 (0.45)	9.0 (0.36)	9.7 (0.17)	9.3 (0.21)	7.8 (0.25)	4.2 (0.10)	5.1 (0.14)	3.0 (0.17)	1.9 (0.29)	1.5 (0.30)
$30,000 to $34,999	8.1 (0.08)	8.1 (0.45)	8.4 (0.35)	9.8 (0.17)	9.5 (0.21)	9.4 (0.28)	5.4 (0.12)	6.6 (0.16)	4.0 (0.20)	2.1 (0.31)	2.1 (0.34)
$35,000 to $39,999	6.8 (0.08)	4.2 (0.33)	4.8 (0.27)	8.1 (0.15)	7.7 (0.19)	8.3 (0.26)	5.4 (0.12)	6.4 (0.16)	4.1 (0.20)	1.7 (0.28)	3.0 (0.42)
$40,000 to $49,999	11.4 (0.10)	4.6 (0.35)	6.6 (0.31)	10.8 (0.18)	12.5 (0.24)	14.3 (0.33)	11.9 (0.17)	12.8 (0.22)	11.4 (0.32)	8.0 (0.58)	8.8 (0.69)
$50,000 to $74,999	17.5 (0.12)	3.6 (0.31)	5.9 (0.30)	12.9 (0.19)	16.7 (0.27)	20.7 (0.38)	24.2 (0.22)	23.8 (0.28)	27.4 (0.45)	19.0 (0.84)	19.5 (0.96)
$75,000 to $99,999	6.8 (0.08)	0.7 (0.14)	1.7 (0.16)	3.1 (0.10)	5.3 (0.16)	6.7 (0.24)	12.1 (0.17)	11.1 (0.20)	14.3 (0.36)	10.8 (0.67)	16.0 (0.89)
$100,000 or more	8.2 (0.08)	0.9 (0.16)	1.0 (0.13)	2.5 (0.09)	3.9 (0.14)	3.4 (0.17)	18.6 (0.20)	13.9 (0.22)	20.3 (0.41)	46.4 (1.07)	38.7 (1.18)
Median earnings[1]	$35,380 (78)	$18,180 (339)	$20,250 (174)	$27,960 (213)	$31,950 (125)	$36,400 (193)	$52,120 (111)	$48,100 (488)	$58,520 (1,029)	$87,780 (2,987)	$80,780 (1,072)
Number of males (in thousands)	**95,518** (137.6)	**5,399** (80.1)	**7,754** (95.0)	**30,025** (166.1)	**16,093** (131.3)	**7,541** (93.8)	**28,706** (163.7)	**18,101** (137.9)	**7,009** (90.6)	**1,953** (49.0)	**1,643** (45.0)
With earnings	72,297 (181.1)	2,989 (60.3)	4,826 (76.0)	21,712 (148.1)	12,445 (117.6)	6,325 (86.4)	23,999 (153.8)	15,150 (128.1)	5,819 (83.0)	1,684 (45.5)	1,347 (40.8)
Distribution of males with earnings, by total annual earnings	100.0	100.0	100.0	100.0	100.0	100.0	100.0	100.0	100.0	100.0	100.0
$1 to $4,999 or loss	4.0 (0.08)	6.4 (0.50)	7.1 (0.41)	4.5 (0.16)	4.3 (0.20)	3.7 (0.26)	2.6 (0.11)	2.6 (0.14)	3.2 (0.26)	1.7 (0.35)	1.2 (0.33)
$5,000 to $9,999	3.9 (0.08)	8.5 (0.57)	8.8 (0.46)	4.1 (0.15)	4.1 (0.20)	3.0 (0.24)	2.3 (0.11)	2.6 (0.14)	2.0 (0.20)	1.6 (0.34)	1.7 (0.39)
$10,000 to $14,999	5.1 (0.09)	14.2 (0.71)	10.2 (0.49)	6.3 (0.18)	4.8 (0.21)	3.8 (0.27)	2.3 (0.11)	2.5 (0.14)	2.0 (0.20)	1.5 (0.34)	2.7 (0.49)
$15,000 to $19,999	5.8 (0.10)	15.9 (0.75)	11.4 (0.51)	7.8 (0.20)	5.1 (0.22)	3.2 (0.25)	2.6 (0.11)	3.0 (0.16)	1.9 (0.20)	1.7 (0.35)	1.1 (0.32)
$20,000 to $24,999	7.3 (0.11)	17.0 (0.77)	14.8 (0.57)	9.9 (0.23)	6.9 (0.25)	5.3 (0.32)	3.0 (0.12)	3.3 (0.16)	2.6 (0.24)	2.7 (0.44)	1.2 (0.33)
$25,000 to $29,999	6.6 (0.11)	9.0 (0.59)	10.1 (0.49)	8.9 (0.22)	7.5 (0.26)	6.1 (0.34)	3.2 (0.13)	3.9 (0.18)	2.4 (0.22)	1.5 (0.33)	1.0 (0.30)
$30,000 to $34,999	7.6 (0.11)	10.4 (0.63)	9.8 (0.48)	9.5 (0.22)	9.2 (0.29)	7.9 (0.38)	4.2 (0.15)	5.2 (0.20)	3.0 (0.25)	1.3 (0.31)	1.9 (0.41)
$35,000 to $39,999	6.6 (0.10)	5.7 (0.47)	6.4 (0.39)	8.8 (0.22)	7.4 (0.26)	8.0 (0.38)	4.0 (0.14)	4.9 (0.20)	3.0 (0.25)	1.1 (0.28)	3.0 (0.52)
$40,000 to $49,999	11.8 (0.13)	6.2 (0.49)	9.3 (0.47)	13.6 (0.26)	14.2 (0.35)	15.6 (0.51)	9.2 (0.21)	10.4 (0.28)	7.8 (0.39)	5.3 (0.61)	7.9 (0.82)
$50,000 to $74,999	20.3 (0.17)	4.9 (0.44)	8.4 (0.45)	18.3 (0.29)	22.2 (0.42)	26.6 (0.62)	23.7 (0.31)	25.4 (0.40)	24.0 (0.63)	14.7 (0.96)	14.8 (1.08)
$75,000 to $99,999	8.9 (0.12)	0.7 (0.17)	2.3 (0.24)	4.8 (0.16)	7.9 (0.27)	10.9 (0.44)	15.0 (0.26)	15.1 (0.32)	16.2 (0.54)	10.1 (0.82)	14.9 (1.08)
$100,000 or more	12.0 (0.14)	1.1 (0.21)	1.4 (0.19)	3.5 (0.14)	6.3 (0.24)	5.8 (0.33)	27.9 (0.32)	21.2 (0.37)	32.0 (0.68)	56.8 (1.35)	48.6 (1.52)
Median earnings[1]	$41,400 (95)	$20,970 (196)	$23,830 (399)	$33,940 (420)	$40,260 (200)	$45,080 (626)	$65,950 (346)	$60,290 (240)	$71,880 (471)	$100,000 (—)	$95,880 (4,644)

See notes at end of table.

Distribution of earnings and median earnings of persons 25 years old and over, by highest level of educational attainment and sex: 2008—Continued

Sex and earnings	Total	Elementary/secondary			Some college, no degree	College					
		Less than 9th grade	Some high school (no completion)	High school completion (includes equivalency)		Associate's degree	Bachelor's or higher degree				
							Total	Bachelor's degree	Master's degree	Professional degree	Doctor's degree
1	2	3	4	5	6	7	8	9	10	11	12
Number of females (in thousands)	**102,767** (150.8)	**5,429** (80.5)	**7,833** (95.8)	**31,601** (171.7)	**17,739** (137.9)	**10,297** (108.6)	**29,868** (168.5)	**19,534** (143.5)	**8,110** (97.3)	**1,253** (39.4)	**971** (34.7)
With earnings	63,598 (197.5)	1,578 (44.1)	2,972 (60.2)	17,382 (136.7)	11,524 (114.3)	7,569 (94.2)	22,574 (152.0)	14,529 (126.6)	6,242 (86.1)	1,017 (35.5)	786 (31.2)
Distribution of females with earnings, by total annual earnings											
earnings	100.0 (†)	100.0 (†)	100.0 (†)	100.0 (†)	100.0 (†)	100.0 (†)	100.0 (†)	100.0 (†)	100.0 (†)	100.0 (†)	100.0 (†)
$1 to $4,999 or loss	7.6 (0.12)	16.6 (1.05)	16.6 (0.76)	8.1 (0.23)	8.4 (0.29)	6.3 (0.31)	5.3 (0.17)	5.4 (0.21)	5.6 (0.32)	2.8 (0.57)	4.5 (0.82)
$5,000 to $9,999	6.9 (0.11)	14.3 (0.99)	16.3 (0.76)	8.9 (0.24)	7.3 (0.27)	5.4 (0.29)	4.0 (0.15)	4.6 (0.19)	3.2 (0.25)	1.9 (0.47)	2.3 (0.60)
$10,000 to $14,999	9.1 (0.13)	23.8 (1.20)	18.0 (0.79)	12.1 (0.28)	9.1 (0.30)	8.3 (0.36)	4.7 (0.16)	5.4 (0.21)	3.9 (0.28)	2.3 (0.52)	2.0 (0.56)
$15,000 to $19,999	8.8 (0.13)	17.7 (1.07)	17.1 (0.77)	13.2 (0.29)	8.8 (0.29)	7.0 (0.33)	4.4 (0.15)	5.2 (0.21)	3.2 (0.25)	2.1 (0.50)	1.9 (0.55)
$20,000 to $24,999	10.1 (0.13)	12.6 (0.93)	11.4 (0.65)	13.9 (0.29)	12.2 (0.34)	11.0 (0.40)	5.4 (0.17)	6.5 (0.23)	3.4 (0.26)	2.5 (0.54)	3.9 (0.78)
$25,000 to $29,999	8.4 (0.12)	5.8 (0.66)	7.1 (0.53)	10.6 (0.26)	11.2 (0.33)	9.3 (0.37)	5.3 (0.17)	6.3 (0.23)	3.6 (0.26)	2.5 (0.54)	2.7 (0.64)
$30,000 to $34,999	8.6 (0.12)	3.7 (0.53)	6.2 (0.49)	10.2 (0.26)	9.8 (0.31)	10.6 (0.39)	6.7 (0.19)	7.9 (0.25)	4.9 (0.31)	3.3 (0.63)	2.4 (0.61)
$35,000 to $39,999	7.0 (0.11)	1.3 (0.32)	2.1 (0.30)	7.2 (0.22)	8.0 (0.28)	8.5 (0.36)	6.8 (0.19)	7.9 (0.25)	5.1 (0.31)	2.9 (0.58)	3.1 (0.69)
$40,000 to $49,999	10.9 (0.14)	1.6 (0.35)	2.3 (0.30)	7.3 (0.22)	10.8 (0.32)	13.3 (0.44)	14.8 (0.26)	15.3 (0.33)	14.7 (0.50)	12.4 (1.15)	10.3 (1.21)
$50,000 to $74,999	14.4 (0.16)	1.3 (0.31)	2.0 (0.29)	6.3 (0.21)	10.6 (0.32)	15.8 (0.47)	24.8 (0.32)	22.1 (0.38)	30.5 (0.65)	26.3 (1.54)	27.4 (1.78)
$75,000 to $99,999	4.4 (0.09)	0.6 (0.22)	0.7 (0.17)	1.0 (0.08)	2.6 (0.16)	3.3 (0.23)	9.1 (0.21)	7.0 (0.24)	12.5 (0.47)	12.1 (1.14)	17.7 (1.52)
$100,000 or more	3.8 (0.08)	0.6 (0.21)	0.3 (0.11)	1.1 (0.09)	1.3 (0.12)	1.3 (0.15)	8.7 (0.21)	6.3 (0.22)	9.4 (0.41)	29.0 (1.59)	21.9 (1.65)
Median earnings[1]	$29,270 (192)	$13,590 (422)	$14,710 (353)	$22,300 (126)	$26,440 (179)	$30,870 (205)	$44,370 (530)	$40,230 (173)	$50,840 (247)	$62,120 (1,518)	$64,080 (2,423)

—Not available.
†Not applicable.
[1]Excludes persons without earnings.
NOTE: Detail may not sum to totals because of rounding. Standard errors appear in parentheses.

SOURCE: U.S. Department of Commerce, Census Bureau, Current Population Survey, March 2009. Retrieved September 15, 2009, from http://www.census.gov/hhes/www/cpstables/032009/perinc/new03_000.htm. (This table was prepared September 2009.)

College enrollment and labor force status of 2006, 2007, and 2008 high school completers, by sex and race/ethnicity: 2006, 2007, and 2008

Selected characteristic	Civilian noninstitutional population — Number (in thousands)	Percent	Percent of high school completers	Percentage distribution of population — Employed	Unemployed (seeking employment)	Not in labor force	Labor force participation rate of population[1]	Civilian labor force[2] — Number (in thousands) — Total	Employed	Unemployed (seeking employment)	Unemployment rate	Population not in labor force (in thousands)
1	2	3	4	5	6	7	8	9	10	11	12	13
2006 high school completers[3]												
Total	2,692 (108.2)	100.0 (†)	100.0 (†)	46.2 (1.68)	9.0 (0.97)	44.8 (1.30)	55.2 (1.68)	1,484 (67.2)	1,244 (61.6)	241 (27.3)	16.2 (1.68)	1,207 (46.9)
Male	1,328 (76.1)	49.4 (2.09)	49.4 (2.09)	42.8 (2.34)	9.8 (1.41)	47.4 (2.36)	52.6 (2.36)	699 (45.4)	569 (41.0)	130 (19.7)	18.7 (2.54)	629 (43.1)
Female	1,363 (76.9)	50.6 (2.09)	50.6 (2.09)	49.5 (2.26)	8.1 (1.23)	42.4 (2.23)	57.6 (2.23)	785 (46.5)	675 (43.2)	111 (17.5)	14.1 (2.07)	578 (40.0)
White	1,805 (88.3)	67.1 (1.96)	67.1 (1.96)	49.6 (2.06)	8.2 (1.14)	42.2 (1.57)	57.8 (2.04)	1,044 (56.4)	896 (52.3)	149 (21.4)	14.2 (1.90)	761 (37.3)
Black	318 (44.9)	11.8 (1.61)	11.8 (1.61)	29.7 (4.76)	18.2 (4.02)	52.1 (5.21)	47.9 (5.21)	153 (22.9)	95 (18.0)	58 (14.1)	38.0 (7.31)	166 (23.8)
Hispanic	382 (63.9)	14.2 (2.27)	14.2 (2.27)	48.9 (4.75)	7.8 ! (2.55)	43.3 (4.71)	56.7 (4.71)	217 (27.2)	187 (25.3)	30 ! (10.1)	13.8 ! (4.35)	166 (23.8)
Enrolled in college, 2006	1,776 (60.0)	66.0 (1.33)	66.0 (1.33)	40.5 (2.04)	3.8 (0.80)	55.8 (1.60)	44.2 (2.06)	786 (49.0)	718 (46.9)	67 (14.4)	8.6 (1.76)	990 (42.5)
Male	875 (42.1)	49.2 (1.73)	32.5 (1.32)	35.1 (2.78)	3.8 (1.11)	61.1 (2.84)	38.9 (2.84)	340 (31.7)	307 (30.2)	33 ! (9.9)	9.7 (2.76)	535 (39.7)
Female	901 (42.7)	50.8 (1.73)	33.5 (1.33)	45.7 (2.77)	3.8 (1.06)	50.5 (2.78)	49.5 (2.78)	446 (35.1)	411 (33.8)	34 (9.8)	7.7 (2.11)	456 (35.5)
2-year	665 (37.3)	37.4 (1.68)	24.7 (1.21)	52.5 (3.39)	6.9 (1.73)	40.6 (2.58)	59.4 (3.34)	395 (34.8)	349 (32.7)	46 (11.9)	11.6 (2.84)	270 (22.2)
4-year	1,111 (47.9)	62.6 (1.68)	41.3 (1.39)	33.2 (2.48)	1.9 ! (0.73)	64.8 (1.94)	35.2 (2.51)	391 (34.6)	369 (33.6)	21 ! (8.1)	5.5 ! (2.03)	720 (36.3)
Full-time students	1,639 (57.8)	92.3 (0.93)	60.9 (1.37)	37.9 (2.10)	3.2 (0.77)	58.8 (1.65)	41.2 (2.13)	675 (45.4)	622 (43.6)	53 (12.8)	7.9 (1.82)	964 (41.9)
Part-time students	137 (17.1)	7.7 (0.93)	5.1 (0.62)	70.4 (6.82)	10.3 ! (4.57)	19.3 (4.56)	80.7 (5.89)	111 (18.4)	97 (17.2)	14 ! (6.6)	12.8 ! (5.58)	26 (7.0)
White	1,237 (49.9)	69.6 (1.59)	46.0 (1.40)	43.4 (2.47)	2.9 (0.84)	53.7 (1.92)	46.3 (2.48)	573 (41.9)	536 (40.5)	36 (10.6)	6.3 (1.79)	664 (34.8)
Black	177 (20.3)	9.9 (1.10)	6.6 (0.74)	27.6 (6.25)	9.9 ! (4.19)	62.5 (6.77)	37.5 (6.77)	66 (15.1)	49 (13.0)	18 ! (7.8)	‡ (†)	110 (19.5)
Hispanic	222 (24.2)	12.5 (1.30)	8.2 (0.88)	40.6 (6.13)	4.5 ! (2.59)	54.9 (6.21)	45.1 (6.21)	100 (18.6)	90 (17.6)	10 ! (5.9)	10.0 ! (5.57)	122 (20.4)
Not enrolled in college, 2006	916 (43.6)	34.0 (1.33)	34.0 (1.33)	57.3 (2.86)	19.0 (2.28)	23.7 (1.90)	76.3 (2.46)	699 (46.2)	525 (40.1)	174 (23.2)	24.9 (2.88)	217 (19.9)
Male	454 (30.7)	49.6 (2.41)	16.9 (1.05)	57.7 (4.00)	21.5 (3.32)	20.9 (3.29)	79.1 (3.29)	359 (32.6)	262 (27.8)	98 (17.0)	27.2 (4.04)	95 (16.8)
Female	462 (31.0)	50.4 (2.41)	17.2 (1.06)	57.0 (3.84)	16.5 (2.88)	26.5 (3.42)	73.5 (3.42)	340 (30.7)	263 (27.0)	76 (14.6)	22.4 (3.78)	122 (18.4)
White	568 (34.4)	62.1 (2.34)	21.1 (1.15)	63.2 (3.54)	19.8 (2.94)	17.0 (2.14)	83.0 (2.76)	472 (38.0)	359 (33.2)	112 (18.6)	23.8 (3.45)	97 (13.3)
Black	142 (18.2)	15.5 (1.86)	5.3 (0.67)	32.4 (7.31)	28.6 (7.06)	39.1 (7.62)	60.9 (7.62)	86 (17.2)	46 (12.6)	40 (11.8)	46.9 (9.99)	55 (13.8)
Hispanic	161 (20.7)	17.6 (2.08)	6.0 (0.76)	60.2 (7.17)	12.4 ! (4.82)	27.4 (6.54)	72.6 (6.54)	117 (20.0)	97 (18.3)	20 ! (8.3)	17.0 ! (6.47)	44 (12.3)
2007 high school completers[3]												
Total	2,955 (113.0)	100.0 (†)	100.0 (†)	44.2 (1.60)	7.6 (0.86)	48.2 (1.24)	51.8 (1.61)	1,531 (68.3)	1,307 (63.1)	224 (26.3)	14.7 (1.59)	1,424 (50.9)
Male	1,511 (80.7)	51.1 (1.99)	51.1 (1.99)	44.5 (2.20)	8.5 (1.23)	47.1 (2.21)	52.9 (2.21)	800 (48.5)	672 (44.5)	128 (19.5)	16.0 (2.23)	711 (45.8)
Female	1,444 (79.0)	48.9 (1.99)	48.9 (1.99)	44.0 (2.18)	6.7 (1.10)	49.4 (2.19)	50.6 (2.19)	731 (44.9)	635 (41.9)	96 (16.4)	13.2 (2.09)	713 (44.4)
White	2,043 (93.4)	69.1 (1.84)	69.1 (1.84)	47.2 (1.93)	5.5 (0.89)	47.3 (1.50)	52.7 (1.93)	1,077 (57.3)	964 (54.2)	113 (18.7)	10.5 (1.64)	967 (42.0)
Black	416 (50.8)	14.1 (1.66)	14.1 (1.66)	36.2 (4.38)	18.4 (3.53)	45.4 (4.54)	54.6 (4.54)	227 (27.9)	151 (22.7)	77 (16.2)	33.7 (5.83)	189 (25.4)
Hispanic	355 (61.8)	12.0 (2.02)	12.0 (2.02)	37.6 (4.78)	6.6 ! (2.44)	55.8 (4.90)	44.2 (4.90)	157 (23.2)	134 (21.4)	23 ! (9.0)	14.9 ! (5.28)	198 (26.0)
Enrolled in college, 2007	1,986 (63.3)	67.2 (1.26)	67.2 (1.26)	35.9 (1.89)	3.9 (0.76)	60.3 (1.49)	39.7 (1.92)	789 (49.1)	712 (46.7)	77 (15.4)	9.8 (1.86)	1,197 (46.7)
Male	999 (44.9)	50.3 (1.64)	33.8 (1.27)	35.9 (2.62)	2.8 ! (0.90)	61.2 (2.66)	38.8 (2.66)	387 (33.9)	359 (32.6)	28 ! (9.2)	7.3 ! (2.28)	612 (42.5)
Female	986 (44.6)	49.7 (1.64)	33.4 (1.27)	35.8 (2.55)	4.9 (1.15)	59.3 (2.61)	40.7 (2.61)	402 (33.4)	353 (31.3)	49 (11.6)	12.1 (2.72)	585 (40.2)
2-year	711 (38.6)	35.8 (1.57)	24.1 (1.15)	49.0 (3.28)	5.7 (1.53)	45.3 (2.53)	54.7 (3.27)	389 (34.5)	349 (32.7)	41 (11.2)	10.4 (2.73)	322 (24.3)
4-year	1,274 (51.2)	64.2 (1.57)	43.1 (1.33)	28.5 (2.22)	2.9 (0.82)	68.6 (1.76)	31.4 (2.28)	400 (35.0)	363 (33.4)	36 (10.6)	9.1 (2.53)	875 (40.0)
Full-time students	1,851 (61.2)	93.2 (0.82)	62.6 (1.30)	33.5 (1.92)	3.8 (0.78)	62.7 (1.52)	37.3 (1.97)	691 (46.0)	621 (43.6)	70 (14.8)	10.2 (2.02)	1,160 (46.0)
Part-time students	135 (16.9)	6.8 (0.82)	4.6 (0.56)	67.7 (7.05)	4.9 ! (3.28)	27.3 (5.19)	72.7 (6.72)	98 (17.3)	91 (16.7)	7 ! (4.5)	6.8 ! (4.47)	37 (8.2)

See notes at end of table.

College enrollment and labor force status of 2006, 2007, and 2008 high school completers, by sex and race/ethnicity: 2006, 2007, and 2008—Continued

	Civilian noninstitutional population		Percentage distribution of population					Civilian labor force[2]				Population not in labor force (in thousands)
	Number (in thousands)	Percent	Percent of high school completers	Employed	Unemployed (seeking employment)	Not in labor force	Labor force participation rate of population[1]	Number (in thousands)			Unemployment rate	
Selected characteristic								Total	Employed	Unemployed (seeking employment)		
1	2	3	4	5	6	7	8	9	10	11	12	13
White	1,421 (53.3)	71.5 (1.48)	48.1 (1.34)	37.2 (2.25)	3.7 (0.88)	59.2 (1.77)	40.8 (2.28)	580 (42.1)	528 (40.2)	52 (12.7)	9.0 (2.09)	841 (39.2)
Black	232 (23.1)	11.7 (1.12)	7.9 (0.77)	32.0 (5.69)	5.4 ! (2.76)	62.6 (5.90)	37.4 (5.90)	87 (17.3)	74 (16.0)	13 ! (6.6)	14.5 ! (7.02)	145 (22.3)
Hispanic	227 (24.5)	11.4 (1.18)	7.7 (0.81)	34.5 (5.86)	1.4 ! (1.46)	64.1 (5.92)	35.9 (5.92)	82 (16.8)	78 (16.4)	3 ! (3.3)	3.9 ! (4.01)	146 (22.4)
Not enrolled in college, 2007	970 (34.6)	100.0 (†)	32.8 (1.26)	61.3 (2.74)	15.2 (2.03)	23.4 (1.84)	76.6 (2.38)	742 (47.6)	595 (42.7)	147 (21.4)	19.9 (2.58)	227 (20.4)
Male	512 (32.6)	52.8 (2.34)	17.3 (1.02)	61.1 (3.71)	19.5 (3.02)	19.4 (3.01)	80.6 (3.01)	413 (34.9)	313 (30.4)	100 (17.2)	24.1 (3.63)	99 (17.2)
Female	458 (30.8)	47.2 (2.34)	15.5 (0.97)	61.6 (3.79)	10.4 (2.38)	28.0 (3.50)	72.0 (3.50)	330 (30.2)	282 (28.0)	48 (11.5)	14.5 (3.23)	128 (18.9)
White	623 (35.9)	64.2 (2.25)	21.1 (1.10)	70.0 (3.22)	9.7 (2.09)	20.2 (2.18)	79.8 (2.82)	497 (39.0)	436 (36.5)	61 (13.7)	12.2 (2.58)	126 (15.2)
Black	184 (20.7)	19.0 (1.96)	6.2 (0.69)	41.5 (6.75)	34.8 (6.52)	23.7 (5.82)	76.3 (5.82)	141 (22.0)	76 (16.2)	64 (14.9)	45.6 (7.81)	44 (12.3)
Hispanic	128 (18.6)	13.2 (1.80)	4.3 (0.62)	43.2 (8.14)	15.7 ! (5.98)	41.1 (8.08)	58.9 (8.08)	75 (16.1)	55 (13.8)	20 ! (8.3)	26.7 ! (9.47)	53 (13.5)
2008 high school completers[3]												
Total	3,151 (116.3)	100.0 (†)	100.0 (†)	41.6 (1.54)	10.6 (0.96)	47.8 (1.20)	52.2 (1.56)	1,644 (70.7)	1,310 (63.2)	334 (32.1)	20.3 (1.75)	1,507 (52.4)
Male	1,640 (83.8)	52.1 (1.93)	52.1 (1.93)	39.1 (2.08)	11.3 (1.35)	49.6 (2.13)	50.4 (2.13)	827 (49.3)	641 (43.5)	186 (23.5)	22.5 (2.50)	813 (48.9)
Female	1,511 (80.6)	47.9 (1.93)	47.9 (1.93)	44.2 (2.13)	9.8 (1.28)	45.9 (2.14)	54.1 (2.14)	817 (47.4)	668 (43.0)	148 (20.3)	18.2 (2.25)	694 (43.8)
White	2,091 (94.4)	66.3 (1.82)	66.3 (1.82)	44.7 (1.90)	9.9 (1.15)	45.4 (1.47)	54.6 (1.91)	1,141 (59.0)	934 (53.4)	207 (25.3)	18.2 (2.01)	949 (41.6)
Black	416 (50.8)	13.2 (1.56)	13.2 (1.56)	34.8 (4.34)	12.7 (3.03)	52.5 (4.55)	47.5 (4.55)	198 (26.0)	145 (22.3)	53 (13.5)	26.7 (5.85)	218 (27.3)
Hispanic	458 (69.5)	14.5 (2.11)	14.5 (2.11)	40.4 (4.26)	13.3 (2.95)	46.3 (4.33)	53.7 (4.33)	246 (28.9)	185 (25.1)	61 (14.5)	24.8 (5.12)	212 (26.9)
Enrolled in college, 2008	2,161 (65.9)	100.0 (†)	68.6 (1.21)	35.0 (1.80)	6.1 (0.91)	58.9 (1.43)	41.1 (1.85)	888 (52.1)	756 (48.1)	132 (20.2)	14.9 (2.10)	1,274 (48.2)
Male	1,080 (46.6)	50.0 (1.57)	34.3 (1.23)	30.3 (2.41)	5.7 (1.22)	64.0 (2.52)	36.0 (2.52)	389 (33.9)	327 (31.1)	62 (13.6)	15.9 (3.20)	691 (45.1)
Female	1,081 (46.6)	50.0 (1.57)	34.3 (1.23)	39.6 (2.48)	6.5 (1.25)	53.9 (2.53)	46.1 (2.53)	499 (37.1)	428 (34.4)	70 (14.0)	14.1 (2.60)	583 (40.1)
2-year	871 (42.6)	40.3 (1.54)	27.7 (1.16)	48.1 (2.96)	7.9 (1.60)	44.1 (2.28)	55.9 (2.95)	488 (38.6)	419 (35.8)	69 (14.6)	14.1 (2.77)	384 (26.5)
4-year	1,290 (51.5)	59.7 (1.54)	40.9 (1.28)	26.1 (2.14)	4.9 (1.06)	69.0 (1.74)	31.0 (2.26)	400 (35.0)	337 (32.1)	64 (14.0)	15.9 (3.22)	890 (40.3)
Full-time students	2,013 (63.7)	93.1 (0.79)	63.9 (1.25)	32.9 (1.83)	5.6 (0.90)	61.5 (1.47)	38.5 (1.90)	775 (48.7)	662 (45.0)	113 (18.7)	14.5 (2.23)	1,238 (47.5)
Part-time students	149 (17.8)	6.9 (0.79)	4.7 (0.55)	62.8 (6.94)	13.2 ! (4.88)	24.1 (4.75)	75.9 (6.14)	113 (18.6)	93 (16.9)	20 ! (7.8)	17.3 ! (6.27)	36 (8.1)
White	1,499 (54.6)	69.3 (1.45)	47.6 (1.30)	37.6 (2.19)	5.8 (1.06)	56.7 (1.73)	43.3 (2.24)	649 (44.6)	563 (41.5)	86 (16.3)	13.3 (2.34)	850 (39.4)
Black	232 (23.1)	10.7 (1.03)	7.4 (0.72)	27.3 (5.44)	5.8 ! (2.84)	66.9 (5.75)	33.1 (5.75)	77 (16.2)	63 (14.8)	13 ! (6.8)	17.4 ! (8.05)	155 (23.1)
Hispanic	292 (27.7)	13.5 (1.22)	9.3 (0.86)	34.7 (5.17)	9.9 ! (3.25)	55.4 (5.40)	44.6 (5.40)	130 (21.2)	101 (18.7)	29 ! (10.0)	22.2 ! (6.77)	162 (23.6)
Not enrolled in college, 2008	989 (45.3)	100.0 (†)	31.4 (1.21)	56.0 (2.76)	20.4 (2.25)	23.6 (1.83)	76.4 (2.37)	756 (48.1)	554 (41.2)	202 (25.0)	26.7 (2.83)	234 (20.7)
Male	560 (34.0)	56.6 (2.30)	17.8 (0.99)	56.1 (3.62)	22.1 (3.02)	21.9 (3.01)	78.1 (3.01)	438 (36.0)	314 (30.5)	124 (19.1)	28.2 (3.71)	122 (19.1)
Female	430 (29.9)	43.4 (2.30)	13.6 (0.89)	55.9 (4.00)	18.2 (3.11)	25.9 (3.53)	74.1 (3.53)	318 (29.7)	240 (25.8)	78 (14.7)	24.6 (4.03)	111 (17.6)
White	592 (35.1)	59.8 (2.28)	18.8 (1.02)	62.7 (3.48)	20.5 (2.92)	16.9 (2.08)	83.1 (2.70)	492 (38.8)	371 (33.7)	121 (19.4)	24.6 (3.42)	100 (13.5)
Black	184 (20.7)	18.6 (1.92)	5.9 (0.65)	44.2 (6.80)	21.4 (5.61)	34.4 (6.50)	65.6 (6.50)	121 (20.4)	81 (16.7)	39 (11.7)	32.6 (7.92)	63 (14.8)
Hispanic	165 (21.0)	16.7 (1.96)	5.2 (0.66)	50.5 (7.23)	19.4 (5.72)	30.1 (6.63)	69.9 (6.63)	115 (19.9)	83 (16.9)	32 ! (10.5)	27.7 (7.74)	50 (13.1)

†Not applicable.
!Interpret data with caution.
‡Reporting standards not met.
[1]The labor force participation rate is the percentage of persons who are either employed or seeking employment.
[2]The labor force includes all employed persons plus those seeking employment. The unemployment rate is the percentage of persons in the labor force who are not working and who made specific efforts to find employment sometime during the prior 4 weeks.

[3]Includes 16- to 24-year-olds who completed high school between October of the previous year and October of the given year.
NOTE: Enrollment data are for October of given year. Data are based on sample surveys of the civilian noninstitutional population. Percentages are only shown when the base is 75,000 or greater. Totals include race categories not separately shown. Race categories exclude persons of Hispanic ethnicity. Detail may not sum to totals because of rounding. Standard errors appear in parentheses.
SOURCE: U.S. Department of Commerce, Census Bureau, Current Population Survey (CPS), October 2006, 2007, and 2008. (This table was prepared August 2009.)

Labor force status of high school dropouts, by sex and race/ethnicity: Selected years, 1980 through 2008

Year, sex, and race/ethnicity	Number of dropouts (in thousands)	Percent of all dropouts	Percentage distribution of dropouts — Employed	Percentage distribution of dropouts — Unemployed (seeking employment)	Percentage distribution of dropouts — Not in labor force	Labor force participation rate of dropouts[1]	Dropouts in civilian labor force[2] — Number (in thousands) — Total	Dropouts in civilian labor force[2] — Number (in thousands) — Unemployed (seeking employment)	Dropouts in civilian labor force[2] — Unemployment rate	Dropouts not in labor force (in thousands)
1	2	3	4	5	6	7	8	9	10	11
All dropouts										
1980	738 (44.0)	100.0 (†)	43.8 (2.97)	20.0 (2.37)	36.2 (2.87)	63.8 (2.87)	471 (35.2)	148 (19.5)	31.4 (3.44)	267 (26.5)
1985	610 (42.3)	100.0 (†)	43.5 (3.45)	24.0 (2.94)	32.5 (3.25)	67.5 (3.25)	412 (34.8)	147 (20.6)	35.6 (4.01)	198 (24.1)
1990	412 (36.0)	100.0 (†)	46.3 (4.37)	21.6 (3.57)	32.2 (4.09)	67.8 (4.09)	279 (29.7)	89 (16.6)	31.8 (4.90)	132 (20.4)
1995	604 (43.6)	100.0 (†)	47.7 (3.61)	20.0 (2.86)	32.3 (3.38)	67.7 (3.38)	409 (35.9)	121 (19.3)	29.6 (3.97)	195 (24.8)
2000	515 (28.5)	100.0 (†)	48.7 (2.77)	19.2 (3.01)	32.0 (2.59)	68.0 (2.59)	350 (23.5)	99 (17.2)	28.1 (4.16)	165 (16.2)
2003	457 (26.9)	100.0 (†)	40.9 (2.90)	18.4 (3.14)	40.7 (2.89)	59.3 (2.89)	271 (20.7)	84 (15.9)	30.8 (4.86)	186 (17.2)
2004	496 (39.0)	100.0 (†)	32.5 (3.68)	21.4 (3.19)	46.3 (3.03)	53.7 (3.92)	267 (28.6)	106 (17.8)	39.9 (5.20)	229 (20.5)
2005	407 (35.3)	100.0 (†)	38.3 (4.22)	18.9 (3.42)	42.8 (3.32)	57.2 (4.30)	233 (26.7)	77 (15.4)	32.9 (5.42)	174 (17.9)
2006	445 (36.9)	100.0 (†)	40.3 (4.07)	12.5 (2.75)	47.2 (3.20)	52.8 (4.15)	235 (26.8)	55 (13.1)	23.6 (4.87)	210 (19.6)
2007	426 (36.1)	100.0 (†)	41.1 (4.17)	15.1 (3.05)	43.8 (3.25)	56.2 (4.21)	239 (27.1)	64 (14.1)	26.9 (5.04)	187 (18.5)
2008	400 (35.0)	100.0 (†)	29.3 (3.98)	19.1 (3.46)	51.6 (3.38)	48.4 (4.38)	194 (24.4)	77 (15.4)	39.5 (6.18)	206 (19.4)
Male										
1980	422 (32.5)	57.2 (2.89)	50.3 (3.86)	22.0 (3.20)	27.7 (3.45)	72.3 (3.45)	305 (27.7)	93 (15.3)	30.5 (4.18)	117 (17.1)
1985	319 (29.9)	52.3 (3.39)	50.8 (4.69)	30.6 (4.32)	18.6 (3.65)	81.4 (3.65)	260 (27.0)	98 (16.6)	37.6 (5.04)	59 (12.9)
1990	217 (25.6)	52.8 (4.27)	51.3 (5.89)	28.0 (5.29)	20.7 (4.77)	79.3 (4.77)	172 (22.8)	61 (13.5)	35.3 (6.32)	45 (11.6)
1995	339 (31.5)	56.2 (3.45)	52.8 (4.64)	21.3 (3.80)	26.0 (4.07)	74.0 (4.07)	251 (27.1)	72 (14.5)	28.7 (4.88)	88 (16.1)
2000	295 (29.3)	57.3 (3.73)	56.3 (4.94)	18.3 (3.85)	25.6 (4.35)	74.4 (4.35)	220 (25.3)	54 (12.6)	24.5 (4.96)	76 (14.9)
2003	242 (26.6)	53.0 (3.99)	43.8 (5.46)	21.9 (4.55)	34.4 (5.22)	65.6 (5.22)	159 (21.6)	53 (12.5)	33.2 (6.39)	83 (15.6)
2004	278 (28.7)	56.0 (3.84)	35.6 (4.95)	24.1 (4.42)	40.1 (5.07)	59.9 (5.07)	166 (22.2)	67 (14.1)	40.4 (6.56)	112 (18.2)
2005	227 (25.9)	55.8 (4.24)	38.3 (5.56)	21.6 (4.71)	40.3 (5.61)	59.7 (5.61)	136 (20.1)	49 (12.1)	35.9 (7.09)	91 (16.4)
2006	256 (27.6)	57.6 (4.04)	46.3 (5.37)	11.2 ! (3.39)	42.5 (5.32)	57.5 (5.32)	147 (20.9)	29 ! (9.2)	19.4 (5.62)	109 (18.0)
2007	233 (26.3)	54.6 (4.16)	41.4 (5.57)	19.0 (4.43)	39.6 (5.53)	60.4 (5.53)	141 (20.4)	44 (11.5)	31.5 (6.75)	92 (16.5)
2008	191 (23.8)	47.6 (4.30)	29.3 (5.69)	24.6 (5.38)	46.1 (6.22)	53.9 (6.22)	103 (17.5)	47 (11.8)	45.6 (8.47)	88 (16.1)
Female										
1980	316 (27.0)	42.8 (2.77)	35.0 (4.08)	17.4 (3.24)	47.6 (4.28)	52.4 (4.28)	165 (19.6)	55 (11.3)	33.2 (5.57)	150 (18.7)
1985	291 (27.4)	47.7 (3.25)	35.5 (4.51)	16.8 (3.52)	47.8 (4.71)	52.2 (4.71)	152 (19.8)	49 (11.2)	32.1 (6.09)	138 (18.9)
1990	194 (23.2)	47.2 (4.10)	40.6 (5.87)	14.4 (4.19)	45.0 (5.94)	55.0 (5.94)	107 (17.2)	28 ! (8.8)	26.1 (7.08)	87 (15.6)
1995	265 (26.6)	43.8 (3.31)	41.1 (4.96)	18.4 (3.91)	40.5 (4.95)	59.5 (4.95)	157 (20.6)	49 (11.5)	30.9 (6.05)	107 (17.0)
2000	220 (24.3)	42.7 (3.58)	39.1 (5.40)	20.5 (4.46)	40.6 (5.43)	59.4 (5.43)	131 (18.8)	45 (11.0)	34.2 (6.80)	90 (15.6)
2003	215 (24.0)	47.0 (3.83)	37.7 (5.42)	14.4 (3.93)	47.9 (5.59)	52.1 (5.59)	112 (17.4)	31 (9.1)	27.6 (6.93)	103 (16.6)
2004	218 (24.6)	44.0 (3.72)	28.0 (5.07)	17.9 (4.33)	54.1 (5.63)	45.9 (5.63)	100 (16.7)	39 (10.4)	38.9 (8.13)	118 (18.1)
2005	180 (22.4)	44.2 (4.11)	38.3 (6.04)	15.6 (4.51)	46.0 (6.20)	54.0 (6.20)	97 (16.4)	28 ! (8.8)	28.8 (7.67)	83 (15.2)
2006	189 (22.9)	42.4 (3.91)	32.3 (5.68)	14.2 (4.24)	53.5 (6.06)	46.5 (6.06)	88 (15.6)	27 ! (8.6)	30.6 (8.21)	101 (16.8)
2007	193 (23.2)	45.4 (4.02)	40.6 (5.89)	10.4 ! (3.66)	48.9 (5.99)	51.1 (5.99)	99 (16.6)	20 ! (7.5)	20.4 ! (6.76)	95 (16.2)
2008	210 (24.1)	52.4 (4.16)	29.2 (5.24)	14.2 (4.02)	56.6 (5.71)	43.4 (5.71)	91 (15.9)	30 ! (9.1)	32.7 (8.20)	119 (18.2)
White										
1980	489 (35.9)	66.2 (2.83)	50.3 (3.67)	18.0 (2.79)	31.7 (3.42)	68.3 (3.42)	334 (29.7)	88 (15.1)	26.3 (3.87)	155 (20.2)
1985	354 (32.3)	58.1 (3.43)	49.2 (4.56)	23.3 (3.82)	27.5 (4.07)	72.5 (4.07)	257 (27.5)	83 (15.4)	32.2 (4.95)	98 (16.9)
1990	242 (27.6)	58.8 (4.31)	56.3 (5.67)	18.7 (4.41)	25.0 (4.95)	75.0 (4.95)	181 (23.9)	45 (11.8)	25.0 (5.65)	60 (13.8)
1995	316 (31.6)	52.3 (3.61)	51.6 (5.00)	18.3 (3.83)	30.1 (4.59)	69.9 (4.59)	221 (26.4)	58 (13.4)	26.2 (5.21)	95 (17.3)
2000	288 (21.4)	55.9 (2.76)	60.2 (3.63)	16.5 (3.79)	23.4 (3.14)	76.6 (3.14)	221 (18.7)	47 (11.9)	21.5 (4.79)	67 (10.3)
2003	226 (18.9)	49.4 (2.95)	48.0 (4.19)	18.2 (4.45)	33.8 (3.97)	66.2 (3.97)	149 (15.4)	41 (11.1)	27.4 (6.33)	76 (11.0)
2004	239 (27.1)	48.2 (3.93)	36.1 (5.44)	14.9 (4.05)	49.0 (5.66)	51.0 (5.66)	122 (19.3)	36 (10.5)	29.2 (7.25)	117 (18.9)
2005	194 (24.4)	47.6 (4.34)	40.3 (6.17)	20.0 (5.05)	39.7 (6.16)	60.3 (6.16)	117 (18.9)	39 (10.9)	33.2 (7.67)	77 (15.4)
2006	214 (25.6)	48.0 (4.15)	48.9 (5.99)	8.2 ! (3.31)	42.8 (5.93)	57.2 (5.93)	122 (19.4)	18 ! (7.4)	14.4 ! (5.59)	92 (16.8)
2007	178 (23.4)	41.8 (4.18)	40.8 (6.45)	11.4 ! (4.19)	47.7 (6.56)	52.3 (6.56)	93 (16.9)	20 ! (7.9)	21.8 ! (7.54)	85 (16.1)
2008	152 (21.6)	38.1 (4.25)	38.6 (6.90)	20.6 (5.76)	40.9 (6.97)	59.1 (6.97)	90 (16.6)	31 ! (9.8)	34.8 (8.83)	62 (13.8)
Black										
1980	141 (19.9)	19.1 (2.43)	20.9 (5.77)	28.4 (6.40)	50.7 (7.09)	49.3 (7.09)	69 (14.0)	40 (10.6)	‡ (†)	71 (14.2)
1985	130 (20.2)	21.4 (2.95)	29.9 (7.13)	22.7 (6.52)	47.5 (7.78)	52.5 (7.78)	68 (14.7)	30 ! (9.7)	‡ (†)	62 (14.0)
1990	82 (16.6)	19.9 (3.62)	30.9 ! (9.42)	35.2 (9.74)	33.9 (9.64)	66.1 (9.64)	54 (13.5)	29 ! (9.9)	‡ (†)	28 ! (9.7)
1995	104 (18.5)	17.2 (2.79)	33.5 (8.40)	25.8 ! (7.78)	40.8 (8.75)	59.2 (8.75)	62 (14.2)	27 ! (9.4)	‡ (†)	42 (11.8)
2000	106 (18.7)	20.6 (3.24)	26.7 (7.79)	25.5 ! (7.68)	47.8 (8.80)	52.2 (8.80)	55 (13.5)	27 ! (9.4)	‡ (†)	51 (12.9)
2003	81 (16.3)	17.8 (3.25)	29.1 ! (9.15)	22.9 ! (8.46)	48.0 (10.06)	52.0 (10.06)	42 (11.8)	19 ! (7.8)	‡ (†)	39 (11.3)
2004	86 (17.2)	17.3 (3.16)	9.9 ! (5.99)	44.9 (9.97)	45.2 (9.98)	54.8 (9.98)	47 (12.7)	39 (11.5)	‡ (†)	39 (11.6)
2005	108 (19.3)	26.5 (4.07)	26.5 (7.89)	16.0 ! (6.56)	57.5 (8.84)	42.5 (8.84)	46 (12.6)	17 ! (7.7)	‡ (†)	62 (14.6)
2006	69 (15.4)	15.5 (3.19)	‡ (†)	‡ (†)	‡ (†)	‡ (†)	36 ! (11.2)	17 ! (7.6)	‡ (†)	33 ! (10.6)
2007	73 (15.9)	17.2 (3.40)	‡ (†)	‡ (†)	‡ (†)	‡ (†)	43 (12.2)	17 ! (7.6)	‡ (†)	30 ! (10.2)
2008	109 (19.4)	27.3 (4.14)	18.1 ! (6.84)	15.0 ! (6.34)	67.0 (8.36)	33.0 (8.36)	36 ! (11.2)	16 ! (7.5)	‡ (†)	73 (15.9)
Hispanic										
1980	91 (18.9)	12.3 (2.41)	47.2 (10.42)	17.9 ! (8.00)	34.8 (9.94)	65.2 (9.94)	59 (15.3)	16 ! (8.0)	‡ (†)	32 ! (11.2)
1985	105 (18.2)	17.3 (2.72)	37.9 (8.41)	32.0 (8.09)	30.1 (7.95)	69.9 (7.95)	74 (15.2)	34 ! (10.3)	‡ (†)	32 ! (10.0)
1990	72 (15.6)	17.4 (3.44)	‡ (†)	‡ (†)	‡ (†)	‡ (†)	32 ! (10.5)	10 ! (5.9)	‡ (†)	39 (11.5)
1995	174 (23.8)	28.8 (3.34)	48.5 (6.88)	20.1 (5.52)	31.4 (6.40)	68.6 (6.40)	119 (19.7)	35 ! (10.7)	29.3 (7.57)	55 (13.4)
2000	101 (18.2)	19.6 (3.18)	39.0 (8.83)	22.2 ! (7.52)	38.9 (8.82)	61.1 (8.82)	62 (14.2)	22 ! (8.6)	‡ (†)	39 (11.3)
2003	124 (20.2)	27.1 (3.77)	40.7 (8.00)	13.8 ! (5.62)	45.5 (8.11)	54.5 (8.11)	68 (14.9)	17 ! (7.5)	‡ (†)	57 (13.6)
2004	154 (23.0)	31.0 (3.86)	39.3 (7.32)	17.4 ! (5.68)	43.2 (7.42)	56.8 (7.42)	87 (17.3)	27 ! (9.6)	30.7 (9.17)	67 (15.1)
2005	86 (17.2)	21.1 (3.76)	45.1 (9.96)	19.2 ! (7.89)	35.7 (9.59)	64.3 (9.59)	55 (13.8)	17 ! (7.6)	‡ (†)	31 ! (10.3)
2006	136 (21.6)	30.5 (4.06)	35.3 (7.62)	12.6 ! (5.29)	52.2 (7.97)	47.8 (7.97)	65 (15.0)	17 ! (7.7)	‡ (†)	71 (15.6)
2007	119 (20.3)	28.0 (4.04)	37.6 (8.24)	23.0 ! (7.16)	39.5 (8.32)	60.5 (8.32)	72 (15.8)	27 ! (9.7)	‡ (†)	47 (12.7)
2008	111 (19.6)	27.8 (4.16)	31.9 (8.21)	24.5 ! (7.58)	43.7 (8.74)	56.3 (8.74)	63 (14.7)	27 ! (9.7)	‡ (†)	49 (12.9)

†Not applicable.

!Interpret data with caution.

‡Reporting standards not met.

[1]The labor force participation rate is the percentage of persons who are either employed or seeking employment.

[2]The labor force includes all employed persons plus those seeking employment. The unemployment rate is the percentage of persons in the labor force who are not working and who made specific efforts to find employment sometime during the prior 4 weeks.

NOTE: Data are based on sample surveys of the civilian noninstitutional population. Dropouts are considered persons 16 to 24 years old who dropped out of school in the 12-month period ending in October of years shown. Includes dropouts from any grade, including a small number from elementary and middle schools. Percentages are only shown when the base is 75,000 or greater. Totals include race categories not separately shown. Race categories exclude persons of Hispanic ethnicity. Detail may not sum to totals because of rounding. Standard errors appear in parentheses. Some data have been revised from previously published figures.

SOURCE: U.S. Department of Commerce, Census Bureau, Current Population Survey (CPS), October, selected years, 1980 through 2008. (This table was prepared September 2009.)

Participants in state-administered adult basic education, secondary education, and English as a second language programs, by type of program and state or jurisdiction: Selected fiscal years, 1990 through 2007

State or jurisdiction	1990	2000	2005	2006 Total	2006 Adult basic education	2006 Adult secondary education	2006 English as a second language	2007 Total	2007 Adult basic education	2007 Adult secondary education	2007 English as a second language
1	2	3	4	5	6	7	8	9	10	11	12
United States	3,535,970	2,629,643	2,543,953	2,308,380	919,819	292,144	1,096,417	2,302,827	941,659	297,838	1,063,330
Alabama	40,177	23,666	19,827	18,742	12,694	4,319	1,729	19,809	13,590	4,301	1,918
Alaska	5,067	5,312	3,791	3,244	2,005	656	583	2,877	2,043	299	535
Arizona	33,805	31,136	26,881	24,861	9,183	1,037	14,641	18,704	10,702	1,378	6,624
Arkansas	29,065	38,867	37,102	31,912	19,492	6,911	5,509	31,010	19,275	6,841	4,894
California	1,021,227	473,050	591,893	586,632	107,746	64,318	414,568	602,837	122,601	71,579	408,657
Colorado	12,183	13,818	15,011	14,530	3,763	1,164	9,603	14,683	3,770	1,180	9,733
Connecticut	46,434	30,844	31,958	26,686	6,623	7,949	12,114	27,549	7,312	7,593	12,644
Delaware	2,662	4,342	6,329	4,863	2,511	854	1,498	4,399	2,635	514	1,250
District of Columbia	19,586	3,667	3,646	3,384	1,236	500	1,648	3,694	1,908	428	1,358
Florida	419,429	404,912	348,119	239,648	92,630	31,656	115,362	264,670	107,093	33,098	124,479
Georgia	69,580	108,004	95,434	68,557	43,293	5,919	19,345	72,390	45,839	6,253	20,298
Hawaii	52,012	10,525	7,461	7,772	2,884	1,399	3,489	8,135	3,452	1,573	3,110
Idaho	11,171	10,506	7,744	7,961	4,279	656	3,026	6,953	3,795	537	2,621
Illinois	87,121	122,043	118,296	109,743	26,655	13,087	70,001	107,120	26,803	13,739	66,578
Indiana	44,166	42,135	43,498	40,771	23,026	9,714	8,031	38,468	22,737	8,766	6,965
Iowa	41,507	20,161	11,989	9,664	3,702	2,070	3,892	9,271	3,951	2,210	3,110
Kansas	10,274	11,248	9,475	9,323	4,134	1,387	3,802	8,611	4,009	1,092	3,510
Kentucky	28,090	31,050	30,931	31,458	22,433	5,677	3,348	31,456	22,728	5,338	3,390
Louisiana	40,039	30,929	29,367	23,601	18,002	3,598	2,001	23,642	17,896	3,603	2,143
Maine	14,964	12,430	8,151	8,215	3,774	2,767	1,674	7,878	3,689	2,643	1,546
Maryland	41,230	22,702	27,055	32,535	14,294	4,477	13,764	30,882	13,622	4,192	13,068
Massachusetts	34,220	24,053	21,448	23,957	5,517	3,333	15,107	21,706	4,917	3,525	13,264
Michigan	194,178	56,096	34,768	32,856	18,739	3,132	10,985	30,571	18,102	3,389	9,080
Minnesota	45,648	42,039	47,174	45,407	14,813	5,736	24,858	45,805	14,610	7,206	23,989
Mississippi	18,957	37,947	25,675	21,775	17,776	3,391	608	20,372	16,825	2,982	565
Missouri	31,815	41,089	37,052	34,374	22,194	5,097	7,083	33,497	22,061	4,775	6,661
Montana	6,071	4,892	3,291	2,697	1,813	694	190	2,930	2,176	539	215
Nebraska	6,158	7,917	10,226	8,699	4,019	928	3,752	8,503	3,801	1,096	3,606
Nevada	17,262	22,992	9,981	9,483	1,056	516	7,911	9,526	1,140	466	7,920
New Hampshire	7,198	5,962	5,804	5,797	1,794	2,255	1,748	5,592	1,662	2,217	1,713
New Jersey	64,080	44,317	40,889	35,374	11,301	2,437	21,636	34,198	11,372	2,152	20,674
New Mexico	30,236	23,243	24,132	20,040	10,467	1,972	7,601	20,063	10,623	2,015	7,425
New York	156,611	176,239	157,486	147,631	60,375	9,929	77,327	133,852	51,463	8,666	73,723
North Carolina	109,740	107,504	109,047	108,745	58,509	18,774	31,462	110,126	60,450	18,785	30,891
North Dakota	3,587	2,124	2,063	1,776	1,083	442	251	1,693	956	497	240
Ohio	95,476	65,579	50,869	47,462	31,881	8,322	7,259	48,209	32,526	8,479	7,204
Oklahoma	24,307	20,101	20,447	19,146	12,212	2,824	4,110	17,672	12,208	2,033	3,431
Oregon	37,075	25,228	21,668	21,713	9,224	1,818	10,671	21,690	9,507	1,631	10,552
Pennsylvania	52,444	49,369	54,274	53,557	28,751	9,989	14,817	50,996	26,860	10,238	13,898
Rhode Island	7,347	5,592	6,697	6,787	2,800	642	3,345	6,697	3,017	646	3,034
South Carolina	81,200	94,452	65,901	58,916	44,235	7,997	6,684	59,077	44,687	8,585	5,805
South Dakota	3,184	5,637	3,517	2,977	2,012	569	396	2,629	1,674	578	377
Tennessee	41,721	40,615	48,924	43,179	31,173	5,273	6,733	41,439	29,629	5,333	6,477
Texas	218,747	111,585	119,867	102,365	38,371	4,820	59,174	93,242	36,358	4,308	52,576
Utah	24,841	30,714	29,320	24,869	11,883	3,650	9,336	21,764	11,347	2,561	7,856
Vermont	4,808	1,146	2,015	2,404	1,533	713	158	1,756	1,189	446	121
Virginia	31,649	35,261	29,222	32,502	11,797	4,359	16,346	30,940	11,354	4,574	15,012
Washington	31,776	53,460	50,386	52,810	19,480	3,552	29,778	57,474	21,624	4,011	31,839
West Virginia	21,186	13,072	9,444	8,872	6,783	1,925	164	9,083	6,931	1,983	169
Wisconsin	61,081	27,304	26,029	25,792	12,730	6,154	6,908	24,302	11,938	6,257	6,107
Wyoming	3,578	2,767	2,379	2,316	1,139	786	391	2,385	1,202	708	475
Other jurisdictions	31,400	44,785	37,328	38,333	8,908	27,171	2,254	34,079	6,664	26,040	1,375
American Samoa	—	662	838	772	235	121	416	226	116	34	76
Federated States of Micronesia	—	0	0	0	0	0	0	0	0	0	0
Guam	1,311	1,092	1,062	1,113	604	327	182	1,079	593	365	121
Marshall Islands	—	335	0	0	0	0	0	0	0	0	0
Northern Marianas	—	680	740	530	41	316	173	613	82	304	227
Palau	—	132	206	73	13	60	0	55	0	55	0
Puerto Rico	28,436	41,043	33,463	34,903	7,606	25,985	1,312	31,924	5,756	25,276	892
U.S. Virgin Islands	1,653	841	1,019	942	409	362	171	182	117	6	59

—Not available.

NOTE: Adult basic education provides instruction in basic skills for adults 16 and over functioning at literacy levels below the secondary level. Adult secondary education provides instruction at the high school level for adults who are seeking to pass the GED or obtain an adult high school credential. English as a second language instruction is for adults who lack proficiency in English and who seek to improve their literacy and competence in English. Some data have been revised from previously published figures.
SOURCE: U.S. Department of Education, Office of Vocational and Adult Education (OVAE), Division of Adult Education and Literacy, "Adult Education Program Facts, Program Year 1990–1991"; and OVAE National Reporting System, retrieved July 9, 2009, from http://wdcrobcolp01.ed.gov/CFAPPS/OVAE/NRS/. (This table was prepared July 2009.)

Participation of employed persons, 17 years old and over, in career-related adult education during the previous 12 months, by selected characteristics of participants: Various years, 1995 through 2005

Characteristic of employed person	1995 — Percent of adults participating in career or job-related courses	1995 — Number of career or job-related courses taken, per employee	1999 — Percent of adults participating in career or job-related courses	1999 — Number of career or job-related courses taken, per employee	2003 — Percent of adults participating in career or job-related courses	2003 — Number of career or job-related courses taken, per employee[1]	2005 — Employed persons, in thousands[1]	2005 — Percent participating: In career or job-related courses	2005 — Percent participating: In apprentice programs	2005 — Percent participating: In personal interest courses	2005 — Percent participating: In informal learning activities for personal interest	2005 — Number of career or job-related courses taken (in thousands)	2005 — Number of career or job-related courses taken, per employee
1	2	3	4	5	6	7	8	9	10	11	12	13	14
Total	31.1	0.8	30.5 (1.14)	0.7 (0.03)	46.0 (0.70)	0.9 (0.02)	133,386 (1,508.1)	38.8 (0.83)	1.4 (0.24)	21.8 (0.94)	73.5 (1.01)	108,443	0.8 (0.03)
Sex													
Male	29.0	0.7	28.3 (1.15)	0.6 (0.03)	42.7 (1.15)	0.8 (0.03)	71,754 (934.7)	31.7 (1.22)	2.0 (0.37)	18.5 (1.30)	73.4 (1.52)	44,512	0.6 (0.03)
Female	33.4	0.9	32.9 (1.14)	0.8 (0.03)	49.4 (0.99)	1.0 (0.03)	61,632 (1,219.3)	47.1 (1.43)	0.8 (0.23)	25.8 (1.23)	73.6 (1.37)	63,931	1.0 (0.05)
Age													
17 through 24 years	18.6	0.4	19.1 (1.91)	0.4 (0.06)	33.9 (2.31)	0.5 (0.06)	15,027 (1,030.4)	26.4 (3.01)	3.0 (1.03)	25.2 (3.37)	71.4 (3.15)	8,024	0.5 (0.09)
25 through 29 years	31.2	0.8	34.3 (2.44)	0.8 (0.08)	49.7 (2.62)	0.9 (0.05)	14,555 (918.4)	36.1 (2.94)	3.1 (1.12)	24.5 (3.66)	70.9 (4.49)	9,493	0.7 (0.06)
30 through 34 years	31.6	0.8	34.4 (2.50)	0.8 (0.08)	48.4 (2.50)	0.9 (0.06)	15,250 (977.2)	41.0 (3.06)	2.7 (1.10)	23.7 (2.63)	74.0 (2.54)	12,681	0.8 (0.07)
35 through 39 years	35.1	0.9	29.2 (2.15)	0.7 (0.07)	48.8 (2.32)	1.0 (0.06)	15,286 (922.4)	41.7 (4.16)	1.0 (0.46)	21.6 (3.15)	77.7 (3.00)	13,807	0.9 (0.14)
40 through 44 years	36.6	0.9	36.4 (2.44)	0.8 (0.07)	46.1 (2.23)	0.9 (0.06)	18,141 (946.3)	39.8 (2.73)	0.9 (0.48)	23.3 (3.15)	71.2 (3.68)	15,586	0.9 (0.07)
45 through 49 years	39.6	1.0	30.4 (2.42)	0.7 (0.06)	50.8 (2.15)	1.1 (0.06)	18,149 (842.5)	45.0 (2.15)	0.7 (0.29)	19.0 (2.09)	73.5 (2.68)	16,809	0.9 (0.06)
50 through 54 years	34.4	0.9	34.7 (2.57)	0.8 (0.07)	52.5 (2.21)	1.2 (0.08)	14,624 (732.1)	42.6 (2.49)	0.7 (0.32)	19.5 (2.27)	76.3 (2.27)	14,881	1.0 (0.10)
55 through 59 years	26.7	0.7	30.3 (2.83)	0.6 (0.08)	46.3 (2.49)	1.0 (0.08)	10,522 (676.0)	44.7 (2.98)	0.2 (0.12)	18.3 (1.93)	73.0 (2.95)	9,901	0.9 (0.09)
60 through 64 years	21.1	0.5	27.2 (3.80)	0.7 (0.15)	37.8 (2.63)	0.8 (0.06)	6,021 (498.8)	38.9 (3.97)	0.6 (0.43)	23.4 (3.52)	73.0 (4.22)	4,919	0.8 (0.10)
65 and over	13.7	0.4	20.3 (4.21)	0.4 (0.08)	— (†)	— (†)	5,812 (493.3)	21.6 (3.48)	# (†)	17.4 (3.13)	74.2 (3.75)	2,343	0.4 (0.07)
65 through 69 years	—	—	— (†)	— (†)	33.5 (3.42)	0.7 (†)	3,385 (415.5)	19.1 (4.05)	# (†)	20.9 (4.88)	75.4 (5.18)	1,102	0.3 (0.08)
70 years and over	—	—	— (†)	— (†)	22.3 (3.35)	0.5 (0.09)	2,427 (282.3)	25.1 (5.81)	# (†)	12.6 (2.93)	72.6 (6.11)	1,241	0.5 (0.14)
Race/ethnicity													
White	33.2	0.8	32.8 (0.98)	0.6 (0.03)	48.5 (0.85)	1.0 (0.02)	94,881 (1,538.6)	41.3 (0.93)	1.2 (0.25)	22.2 (1.11)	75.3 (1.17)	82,511	0.9 (0.03)
Black	26.2	0.7	28.1 (2.34)	1.0 (0.07)	43.4 (2.19)	0.9 (0.06)	13,773 (533.2)	39.2 (3.82)	1.7 (0.83)	23.5 (3.04)	66.9 (3.02)	10,311	0.7 (0.11)
Hispanic	18.1	0.4	16.4 (1.83)	0.5 (0.05)	31.8 (2.32)	0.6 (0.06)	15,741 (681.0)	25.0 (2.66)	2.9 (0.85)	16.2 (2.31)	65.8 (3.39)	8,786	0.6 (0.11)
Asian	—	—	— (†)	— (†)	— (†)	— (†)	3,770 (520.7)	36.9 (7.00)	0.9 (0.90)	32.3 (7.26)	81.1 (5.88)	2,207	0.6 (0.12)
Pacific Islander	—	—	— (†)	— (†)	— (†)	— (†)	‡ (†)	‡ (†)	‡ (†)	‡ (†)	‡ (†)	‡	‡ (†)
Asian/Pacific Islander	25.5	0.6	32.8 (4.84)	0.4 (0.15)	50.4 (4.77)	0.8 (0.09)	‡ (†)	‡ (†)	‡ (†)	‡ (†)	‡ (†)	‡	‡ (†)
American Indian/Alaska Native	34.0	0.9	29.5 (11.52)	0.7 (0.52)	40.0 (15.14)	0.7 (0.25)	3,786 (562.7)	39.1 (6.85)	1.4 (0.85)	22.6 (6.34)	77.6 (8.40)	3,083	0.8 (0.15)
Two or more races	—	—	— (†)	— (†)	— (†)	— (†)	‡ (†)	‡ (†)	‡ (†)	‡ (†)	‡ (†)	‡	‡ (†)
Other races	—	—	— (†)	— (†)	— (†)	— (†)	‡ (†)	‡ (†)	‡ (†)	‡ (†)	‡ (†)	‡	‡ (†)
Highest level of education completed													
Less than high school completion	8.8	0.1	7.9 (2.29)	0.4 (0.05)	9.9 (3.11)	0.1 (0.05)	16,627 (838.2)	10.4 (2.11)	2.4 (0.90)	8.8 (1.54)	57.0 (3.76)	2,592	0.2 (0.03)
Eighth grade or less	—	—	— (†)	— (†)	— (†)	— (†)	5,016 (599.7)	2.7 (1.12)	4.4 (2.43)	3.8 (1.71)	46.7 (7.11)	197	# (†)
9th through 12th grade, no completion	—	—	— (†)	— (†)	16.3 (2.32)	0.2 (0.04)	11,610 (792.8)	13.7 (2.99)	1.5 (0.78)	11.0 (2.06)	61.5 (4.05)	2,396	0.2 (0.04)
High school completion	20.9	0.4	21.4 (1.45)	0.8 (0.03)	33.2 (1.39)	0.6 (0.03)	34,121 (1,147.2)	24.7 (1.76)	1.3 (0.46)	17.1 (1.89)	63.4 (2.55)	16,640	0.5 (0.05)
Some vocational/technical	32.3	0.8	28.7 (5.76)	0.9 (0.17)	41.7 (3.26)	1.0 (0.11)	3,744 (393.1)	48.2 (5.92)	2.0 (1.56)	25.5 (4.61)	74.0 (5.54)	3,802	1.0 (0.17)
Some college	29.9	0.7	29.0 (1.78)	0.7 (0.06)	45.6 (1.83)	0.9 (0.05)	24,479 (1,067.7)	39.9 (2.36)	1.9 (0.69)	25.2 (2.50)	79.8 (2.04)	18,437	0.8 (0.05)
Associate's degree	39.2	0.9	39.7 (3.07)	0.9 (0.09)	54.5 (2.74)	1.1 (0.07)	9,943 (730.7)	50.4 (3.71)	2.3 (0.84)	19.1 (2.86)	78.4 (3.88)	14,224	1.4 (0.21)
Bachelor's degree	44.6	1.2	43.8 (2.01)	1.0 (0.06)	64.2 (1.42)	1.3 (0.05)	26,475 (902.7)	53.1 (1.88)	0.2 (0.12)	29.0 (1.77)	78.7 (1.94)	28,099	1.1 (0.06)
Some graduate work (or study)	50.2	1.4	46.8 (4.17)	1.2 (0.14)	71.5 (1.87)	1.7 (0.07)	17,998 (735.4)	61.1 (2.16)	1.5 (0.80)	28.6 (2.01)	88.8 (1.16)	24,649	1.1 (0.07)
No degree	44.3	1.2	54.2 (4.94)	1.2 (0.11)	68.3 (4.90)	1.6 (0.15)	2,125 (227.9)	53.8 (5.79)	‡ (†)	39.3 (6.05)	75.0 (5.64)	2,412	1.1 (0.16)
Master's	50.5	1.4	45.3 (2.97)	1.1 (0.11)	73.4 (2.44)	1.7 (0.09)	11,330 (614.7)	62.7 (2.98)	‡ (†)	28.2 (2.27)	90.5 (1.40)	15,394	1.4 (0.09)
Doctor's	40.4	1.0	34.4 (4.79)	0.7 (0.12)	58.9 (6.15)	1.4 (0.25)	1,600 (227.2)	49.0 (5.80)	‡ (†)	28.8 (4.76)	87.8 (4.35)	2,204	1.4 (0.36)
Professional	67.6	2.0	67.6 (6.98)	1.9 (0.31)	75.3 (4.63)	1.6 (0.16)	2,943 (382.7)	66.5 (6.39)	‡ (†)	22.1 (5.05)	92.9 (2.21)	4,639	1.6 (0.21)

See notes at end of table.

Participation of employed persons, 17 years old and over, in career-related adult education during the previous 12 months, by selected characteristics of participants: Various years, 1995 through 2005—Continued

Characteristic of employed person	1995 Percent of adults participating in career or job-related courses	1995 Number of career or job-related courses taken, per employee	1999 Percent of adults participating in career or job-related courses	1999 Number of career or job-related courses taken, per employee	2003 Percent of adults participating in career or job-related courses[1]	2003 Number of career or job-related courses taken, per employee[1]	2005 Employed persons, in thousands	2005 In career or job-related courses	2005 In apprentice programs	2005 In personal interest courses	2005 In informal learning activities for personal interest	2005 Number of career or job-related courses taken (in thousands)	2005 Number of career or job-related courses taken, per employee
1	2	3	4	5	6	7	8	9	10	11	12	13	14
Urbanicity													
Urban	32.4	0.8	31.5 (1.67)	0.7 (0.05)	48.0 (0.75)	1.0 (0.02)	105,542 (1,279.1)	39.8 (1.06)	1.4 (0.27)	22.6 (0.94)	74.0 (1.13)	88,140	0.8 (0.03)
Urban, inside urbanized area	33.3	0.8	31.2 (0.99)	0.7 (0.03)	47.7 (0.88)	1.0 (0.02)	— (†)	— (†)	— (†)	— (†)	— (†)	—	— (†)
Urban, outside urbanized area	27.9	0.7	32.9 (2.48)	0.8 (0.08)	49.5 (2.19)	1.0 (0.06)	— (†)	— (†)	— (†)	— (†)	— (†)	—	— (†)
Rural	26.9	0.7	27.1 (1.74)	0.6 (0.05)	38.2 (2.08)	0.8 (0.05)	27,845 (849.4)	34.9 (2.18)	1.4 (0.58)	19.1 (2.17)	71.7 (2.30)	20,303	0.7 (0.06)
Occupation													
Executive, administrative, or managerial occupations	42.9	1.2	40.6 (2.06)	1.0 (0.07)	61.7 (2.13)	1.3 (0.06)	14,596 (707.6)	53.6 (2.79)	0.4 (0.25)	29.5 (2.89)	77.7 (2.87)	16,567	1.1 (0.09)
Engineers, surveyors, and architects	44.2	1.1	52.1 (6.96)	1.0 (0.16)	66.8 (4.60)	1.3 (0.13)	1,987 (244.9)	56.3 (5.68)	‡ (†)	30.5 (6.36)	81.0 (4.73)	2,323	1.2 (0.16)
Natural scientists and mathematicians	59.7	1.7	46.0 (6.61)	0.8 (0.14)	60.7 (5.89)	1.2 (0.13)	4,130 (445.4)	51.5 (5.64)	2.1 (1.55)	31.2 (4.83)	85.3 (5.44)	3,693	0.9 (0.11)
Social scientists and workers, religious workers, and lawyers	59.5	1.8	56.9 (5.66)	1.7 (0.24)	77.7 (3.90)	1.9 (0.15)	4,697 (480.9)	66.8 (4.48)	‡ (†)	28.3 (3.81)	88.6 (2.95)	7,822	1.7 (0.29)
Teachers, elementary/ secondary	53.9	1.5	52.1 (3.53)	1.2 (0.11)	76.5 (2.43)	1.5 (0.19)	7,085 (568.5)	67.7 (4.16)	0.6 (0.37)	31.5 (3.93)	83.0 (2.79)	12,233	1.7 (0.13)
Teachers, postsecondary and counselors, librarians, and archivists	41.6	1.0	35.6 (5.85)	0.7 (0.14)	65.7 (5.63)	1.8 (0.09)	2,393 (420.9)	53.1 (8.63)	‡ (†)	17.7 (4.91)	90.9 (3.97)	2,122	0.9 (0.09)
Health diagnosing and treating practitioners	68.6	2.0	65.2 (11.99)	1.5 (0.50)	88.5 (4.11)	2.0 (0.24)	978 (208.8)	78.9 (7.10)	‡ (†)	27.4 (9.60)	86.6 (5.37)	1,951	2.0 (0.25)
Registered nurses, pharmacists, dieticians, therapists, and physician's assistants	72.8	2.2	72.2 (5.04)	1.8 (0.21)	84.9 (2.80)	1.9 (0.11)	2,794 (238.8)	79.7 (4.60)	‡ (†)	29.4 (4.17)	84.3 (3.70)	4,984	1.8 (0.15)
Writers, artists, entertainers, and athletes	23.4	0.5	30.6 (6.21)	0.6 (0.18)	35.1 (4.84)	0.6 (0.11)	2,969 (405.2)	29.9 (5.69)	‡ (†)	31.8 (6.15)	88.9 (4.39)	1,865	0.6 (0.15)
Health technologists and technicians	50.0	1.4	41.8 (6.00)	1.0 (0.19)	59.4 (6.12)	1.4 (0.21)	3,060 (436.7)	70.6 (7.31)	2.0 (1.50)	27.8 (6.48)	77.5 (6.40)	4,473	1.5 (0.18)
Technologists and technicians, except health	43.8	1.1	37.6 (4.87)	1.0 (0.15)	51.9 (3.47)	1.2 (0.14)	1,774 (336.5)	29.4 (8.10)	‡ (†)	5.3 (2.02)	75.2 (8.98)	1,015	0.6 (0.17)
Marketing and sales occupations	25.2	0.6	21.1 (2.27)	0.4 (0.06)	38.7 (2.36)	0.6 (0.05)	14,845 (971.9)	32.3 (3.17)	1.3 (0.92)	20.8 (2.64)	70.5 (3.53)	7,724	0.5 (0.05)
Administrative support occupations, including clerical	30.8	0.7	27.4 (2.02)	0.6 (0.05)	45.1 (2.20)	0.8 (0.04)	21,167 (1,179.4)	36.1 (2.95)	0.8 (0.40)	28.2 (2.28)	72.9 (2.37)	15,443	0.7 (0.10)
Service occupations	22.6	0.6	21.0 (2.15)	0.5 (0.07)	37.2 (2.04)	0.8 (0.06)	17,180 (1,033.7)	33.7 (3.13)	1.1 (0.36)	16.2 (2.31)	69.0 (2.74)	13,029	0.8 (0.10)

See notes at end of table.

Participation of employed persons, 17 years old and over, in career-related adult education during the previous 12 months, by selected characteristics of participants: Various years, 1995 through 2005—Continued

Characteristic of employed person	1995 Percent of adults participating in career or job-related courses	1995 Number of career or job-related courses taken, per employee	1999 Percent of adults participating in career or job-related courses	1999 Number of career or job-related courses taken, per employee	2003 Percent of adults participating in career or job-related courses[1]	2003 Number of career or job-related courses taken, per employee[1]	2005 Employed persons, in thousands	2005 Percent of adults participating — In career or job-related courses	2005 — In apprentice programs	2005 — In personal interest courses	2005 — In informal learning activities for personal interest	2005 Number of career or job-related courses taken (in thousands)	2005 Number of career or job-related courses taken, per employee
1	2	3	4	5	6	7	8	9	10	11	12	13	14
Agriculture, forestry, and fishing occupations	12.4	0.3	12.2 (4.09)	0.2 (0.07)	33.9 (6.19)	0.5 (0.09)	2,522 (423.8)	22.4 (7.61)	2.4 (1.69)	23.0 (11.03)	62.9 (11.04)	960	0.4 (0.12)
Mechanics and repairers	29.1	0.7	15.0 (3.40)	0.3 (0.09)	32.1 (3.84)	0.7 (0.11)	5,241 (521.6)	28.3 (4.47)	4.0 (1.44)	12.6 (3.24)	69.3 (4.36)	2,669	0.5 (0.09)
Construction and extractive occupations	18.6	0.3	13.2 (3.16)	0.2 (0.06)	22.1 (2.87)	0.4 (0.06)	6,827 (647.1)	12.4 (3.04)	5.3 (2.26)	7.8 (1.88)	69.0 (5.25)	2,323	0.3 (0.13)
Precision production[2]	25.6	0.6	18.3 (6.52)	0.4 (0.12)	22.5 (6.15)	0.5 (0.13)	10,483 (839.3)	23.5 (3.79)	1.6 (0.90)	14.0 (3.34)	64.9 (3.74)	4,904	0.5 (0.07)
Production workers	14.8	0.3	23.0 (3.17)	0.5 (0.08)	27.6 (3.04)	0.5 (0.07)	— (†)	—	— (†)	—	—	—	— (†)
Transportation and material moving	15.8	0.3	18.4 (3.62)	0.3 (0.06)	25.8 (3.39)	0.4 (0.05)	7,858 (742.5)	15.2 (2.81)	3.4 (1.77)	10.5 (3.10)	62.5 (5.32)	1,935	0.2 (0.05)
Handlers, equipment cleaners, helpers, and laborers	11.7	0.2	6.8 (3.45)	0.2 (0.12)	15.9 (4.27)	0.3 (0.11)	— (†)	— (†)	‡ (†)	— (†)	— (†)	—	— (†)
Miscellaneous occupations	38.8	1.0	14.2 (4.62)	0.3 (0.08)	63.0 (21.53)	1.5 (0.61)	801 (189.4)	17.2 (6.87)	‡ (†)	8.7 (4.31)	48.3 (13.96)	409	0.5 (0.28)
Annual household income													
$10,000 or less	12.6	0.2	9.5 (3.09)	0.2 (0.05)	— (†)	— (†)	4,425 (444.8)	16.7 (4.35)	0.6 (0.48)	26.2 (7.96)	69.7 (5.72)	1,556	0.4 (0.12)
$5,000 or less	—	—	— (†)	— (†)	19.4 (4.50)	0.3 (0.09)	1,635 (252.7)	19.1 (6.52)	‡ (†)	22.9 (7.91)	60.9 (8.84)	850	0.5 (0.26)
$5,001 to $10,000	—	—	— (†)	— (†)	17.5 (2.85)	0.3 (0.04)	2,791 (454.1)	15.3 (5.68)	‡ (†)	28.1 (12.27)	74.8 (6.88)	706	0.3 (0.10)
$10,001 to $15,000	15.1	0.4	8.3 (1.88)	0.1 (0.03)	20.1 (3.00)	0.3 (0.05)	4,814 (633.4)	22.2 (5.77)	‡ (†)	17.3 (5.25)	64.5 (7.57)	2,189	0.5 (0.12)
$15,001 to $20,000	20.1	0.4	16.3 (2.75)	0.3 (0.05)	22.7 (3.44)	0.4 (0.07)	4,515 (398.8)	18.2 (3.09)	5.7 (2.71)	11.5 (1.96)	60.4 (5.11)	1,322	0.3 (0.05)
$20,001 to $25,000	20.4	0.5	18.8 (2.79)	0.4 (0.08)	29.4 (2.73)	0.5 (0.07)	5,593 (490.2)	23.8 (4.02)	1.1 (0.51)	13.3 (3.21)	71.5 (4.11)	2,817	0.5 (0.10)
$25,001 to $30,000	24.7	0.5	22.2 (2.73)	0.5 (0.07)	27.7 (2.60)	0.5 (0.07)	7,444 (680.4)	31.4 (4.88)	0.7 (0.44)	16.7 (3.77)	73.5 (3.91)	4,322	0.6 (0.11)
$30,001 to $40,000	30.2	0.8	26.6 (2.82)	0.6 (0.07)	40.4 (2.43)	0.8 (0.06)	13,123 (928.5)	35.1 (3.45)	1.5 (0.65)	21.7 (3.71)	69.1 (3.55)	8,224	0.6 (0.06)
$40,001 to $50,000	34.7	0.8	32.3 (2.34)	0.7 (0.07)	47.9 (2.50)	1.0 (0.07)	13,647 (1,058.4)	31.5 (3.01)	1.8 (0.72)	20.1 (3.32)	73.5 (2.78)	10,072	0.7 (0.10)
$50,001 to $75,000	40.0	1.0	36.6 (1.86)	0.9 (0.06)	49.3 (1.57)	1.0 (0.04)	33,665 (1,430.4)	42.7 (1.80)	1.2 (0.51)	20.9 (2.10)	71.3 (2.55)	28,991	0.9 (0.06)
More than $75,000	45.2	1.3	42.5 (1.79)	1.0 (0.06)	60.5 (1.36)	1.3 (0.04)	46,160 (1,263.3)	48.1 (1.57)	1.3 (0.39)	26.0 (1.37)	79.2 (1.55)	48,951	1.1 (0.05)

—Not available.
†Not applicable.
#Rounds to zero.
‡Reporting standards not met.
[1]Estimates are not directly comparable to 1995, 1999, or 2005 estimates due to wording in questionnaire.
[2]For 2005, figures include "Production workers" occupations data.

NOTE: Data do not include persons enrolled in high school or below. Race categories exclude persons of Hispanic ethnicity. Detail may not sum to totals because of rounding. Standard errors appear in parentheses. SOURCE: U.S. Department of Education, National Center for Education Statistics, Adult Education Survey (AE-NHES:1995, AE-NHES:1999, and AE-NHES:2005) and Adult Education for Work-Related Reasons Survey (AEWR-NHES:2003) of the National Household Education Surveys Program. (This table was prepared August 2006.)

Participation rate of persons, 17 years old and over, in adult education during the previous 12 months, by selected characteristics of participants: Selected years, 1991 through 2005

Characteristic of participant	Percent taking any program, class, or course					Percent taking specific programs, classes, or courses, 2005						Percent doing informal learning activities for personal interest, 2005
	1991	1995	1999	2001	2005	Basic skills/General Educational Development (GED) classes	English as a second language (ESL) classes	Part-time postsecondary education[1]	Career or job-related courses	Apprentice programs	Personal-interest courses	
1	2	3	4	5	6	7	8	9	10	11	12	13
Total	**33.0**	**40.2 (0.48)**	**44.5 (0.77)**	**46.4 (0.55)**	**44.4 (0.74)**	**1.3 (0.22)**	**0.9 (0.17)**	**5.0 (0.29)**	**27.0 (0.63)**	**1.2 (0.18)**	**21.4 (0.71)**	**70.5 (0.79)**
Sex												
Male	32.6	38.2 (0.65)	41.7 (1.15)	43.1 (0.83)	41.0 (1.20)	1.4 (0.41)	0.9 (0.29)	5.0 (0.44)	24.5 (0.99)	1.7 (0.31)	18.3 (1.08)	70.8 (1.10)
Female	33.2	42.1 (0.59)	47.1 (1.02)	49.5 (0.78)	47.5 (1.01)	1.2 (0.19)	0.9 (0.15)	5.1 (0.37)	29.2 (0.95)	0.7 (0.15)	24.2 (0.88)	70.2 (1.03)
Age												
17 to 24 years	37.8	47.0 (1.12)	49.9 (2.34)	52.8 (2.04)	52.8 (2.79)	6.0 (1.48)	1.7 (0.61)	11.5 (1.34)	21.3 (2.22)	2.7 (0.76)	26.3 (2.60)	69.2 (2.54)
25 to 29 years	40.0	49.6 (1.31)	56.5 (2.53)	52.9 (2.60)	51.6 (3.82)	1.8 (0.48)	3.3 (1.48)	9.1 (1.50)	29.5 (2.48)	3.2 (1.06)	20.9 (2.78)	66.8 (3.75)
30 to 34 years	37.6	47.3 (1.41)	56.2 (2.57)	53.7 (2.18)	52.7 (2.52)	1.9 (0.66)	1.6 (0.64)	8.4 (1.28)	33.8 (2.71)	2.5 (0.89)	23.2 (2.23)	73.8 (2.22)
35 to 39 years	42.1	47.7 (1.15)	50.1 (2.43)	54.0 (1.71)	48.6 (3.21)	0.4 (0.16)	0.7 (0.26)	6.1 (0.90)	32.6 (3.29)	0.9 (0.36)	20.7 (2.67)	75.5 (2.69)
40 to 44 years	49.2	50.9 (1.66)	50.5 (2.69)	53.5 (1.88)	48.9 (2.43)	0.8 (0.31)	0.6 (0.23)	4.7 (0.77)	34.8 (2.30)	0.9 (0.42)	23.4 (2.29)	71.5 (2.62)
45 to 49 years	40.0	48.7 (1.66)	49.8 (2.69)	55.4 (2.02)	49.0 (2.09)	0.6 (0.30)	0.3 (0.25)	3.2 (0.48)	37.7 (1.83)	0.5 (0.23)	19.3 (1.88)	71.6 (2.52)
50 to 54 years	26.8	42.5 (1.38)	47.2 (2.51)	51.1 (2.22)	46.6 (2.09)	0.6 (0.30)	0.4 (0.15)	3.2 (0.48)	35.2 (2.25)	0.6 (0.28)	20.3 (1.64)	75.6 (1.89)
55 to 59 years	29.0	32.2 (1.66)	38.0 (2.60)	44.1 (1.98)	42.2 (2.36)	0.4 (0.11)	‡	1.9 (0.43)	31.9 (2.39)	0.3 (0.17)	18.0 (1.63)	69.5 (2.56)
60 to 64 years	17.4	23.7 (1.89)	31.4 (2.83)	30.8 (2.18)	37.9 (3.00)	‡	0.4 (0.29)	0.9 (0.36)	20.9 (2.07)	0.3 (0.20)	24.1 (2.40)	71.4 (3.04)
65 to 69 years	14.2	18.1 (1.46)	25.4 (2.54)	20.5 (1.74)	26.2 (2.67)	‡	†	0.5 (0.22)	8.1 (1.36)	‡	20.9 (2.41)	67.6 (2.52)
70 years and over	8.6	13.8 (1.09)	15.0 (1.38)	21.7 (1.37)	21.5 (1.44)	0.2 (0.10)	†	0.3 (0.23)	4.0 (0.78)	†	17.9 (1.33)	62.9 (1.82)
Racial/ethnic group												
White	34.1	41.5 (0.54)	44.4 (0.89)	47.4 (0.59)	45.6 (0.84)	0.9 (0.23)	0.2 (0.08)	4.9 (0.35)	29.1 (0.70)	0.9 (0.17)	22.1 (0.87)	73.0 (0.92)
Black	25.9	37.0 (1.45)	46.3 (2.30)	43.3 (1.50)	46.4 (2.81)	1.9 (0.49)	†	5.4 (0.97)	27.0 (2.53)	1.5 (0.73)	23.7 (2.11)	65.3 (2.02)
Hispanic	31.4	33.7 (1.18)	41.3 (2.51)	41.7 (2.28)	37.8 (2.43)	2.6 (0.72)	5.6 (1.22)	5.7 (1.55)	16.9 (1.72)	2.2 (0.63)	15.4 (1.75)	57.5 (2.86)
Asian	—	— (†)	— (†)	— (†)	48.3 (5.39)	1.2 (0.65)	2.6 (1.03)	7.6 (2.62)	27.2 (4.70)	‡	26.5 (5.06)	81.1 (4.10)
Pacific Islander	—	— (†)	— (†)	— (†)	‡ (†)	‡	‡	3.5 (3.71)	‡	‡	‡	‡
Asian/Pacific Islander	35.9	39.7 (2.92)	51.1 (4.63)	49.5 (3.81)	36.3	‡	‡	5.9 (3.05)	23.0 (8.51)	‡	13.0 (6.16)	70.6 (9.18)
American Indian/Alaska Native	29.3	38.8 (4.85)	36.3 (9.16)	50.2	39.4 (4.94)	5.1 (2.17)	‡	4.4 (1.82)	23.8 (4.06)	1.3 (0.59)	21.0 (4.13)	77.6 (5.28)
Two or more races	—	— (†)	—	—	36.3 (10.17)	5.1 (2.17)	‡	3.2 (1.07)	23.8 (4.06)	1.3 (0.59)	21.0 (4.13)	77.6 (5.28)
Highest level of education completed												
8th grade or less	7.7	10.0 (1.10)	14.7 (2.92)	19.7 (2.84)	15.5 (2.47)	1.9 (0.57)	4.3 (1.70)	0.4 (0.23)	1.7 (0.55)	1.7 (0.91)	7.3 (1.24)	38.1 (3.27)
9th through 12th grade, no completion	15.8	20.2 (1.38)	25.6 (2.55)	25.5 (1.53)	27.2 (2.40)	7.9 (1.69)	1.1 (0.41)	2.1 (0.57)	7.6 (1.44)	1.5 (0.61)	12.5 (1.53)	55.7 (2.52)
High school completion	24.1	30.7 (0.84)	34.8 (1.37)	33.9 (1.07)	33.0 (1.62)	0.5 (0.24)	0.7 (0.24)	2.5 (0.36)	17.2 (1.18)	1.1 (0.35)	16.8 (1.27)	63.6 (1.93)
Some vocational/technical	34.2	41.9 (2.16)	41.1 (3.97)	50.7 (3.51)	43.3 (4.30)	0.5 (0.55)	†	4.5 (1.42)	28.3 (3.71)	†	23.2 (3.09)	77.6 (3.98)
Some college	41.4	49.3 (0.92)	51.1 (1.76)	57.4 (1.29)	51.1 (1.79)	0.3 (0.18)	0.8 (0.52)	8.6 (1.06)	28.8 (1.54)	1.4 (0.47)	26.8 (1.80)	79.8 (1.52)
Associate's degree	49.2	56.1 (1.85)	56.6 (2.93)	62.5 (2.15)	56.5 (3.64)	0.5 (0.40)	1.1 (0.51)	6.6 (1.42)	40.8 (3.27)	1.9 (0.66)	20.1 (2.48)	75.9 (3.70)
Bachelor's degree	51.1	56.9 (1.20)	60.3 (1.84)	64.5 (1.39)	59.8 (1.56)	‡	0.4 (0.17)	6.3 (0.82)	44.1 (1.61)	0.4 (0.17)	28.6 (1.55)	88.0 (1.06)
Some graduate work (or study)	55.1	59.9 (1.55)	63.6 (1.96)	68.9 (1.64)	66.5 (1.99)	‡	0.5 (0.32)	8.7 (0.86)	49.3 (2.15)	1.2 (0.61)	30.7 (1.77)	79.3 (1.72)
No degree	—	62.2 (2.67)	64.7 (4.39)	64.2 (3.54)	65.3 (4.84)	‡	‡	14.5 (2.55)	40.5 (4.68)	‡	38.7 (4.81)	88.2 (4.34)
Master's	—	59.1 (1.88)	65.7 (2.64)	70.7 (2.10)	67.5 (2.59)	‡	0.9 (0.52)	8.9 (1.31)	51.4 (2.81)	1.4 (0.97)	30.6 (2.04)	88.8 (1.33)
Doctor's	—	54.0 (6.99)	53.1 (4.73)	63.7 (3.98)	58.0 (4.94)	‡	‡	10.1 (3.14)	34.0 (4.53)	‡	31.4 (3.95)	90.3 (3.26)
Professional	—	65.9 (3.91)	72.5 (5.75)	72.8 (3.79)	68.2 (5.77)	5.1	‡	1.9 (1.01)	59.0 (6.35)	‡	23.9 (4.35)	91.6 (2.15)
Urbanicity												
Urban	34.5	41.8 (0.59)	46.0 (0.88)	48.0 (0.70)	45.7 (0.87)	1.4 (0.28)	1.1 (0.21)	5.5 (0.34)	27.8 (0.79)	1.2 (0.20)	22.2 (0.72)	71.4 (0.86)
Urban, inside urbanized area	—	42.3 (0.64)	46.5 (0.95)	49.3 (0.78)	— (†)	†	—	—	—	—	— (†)	— (†)
Urban, outside urbanized area	—	39.5 (1.12)	43.4 (2.23)	41.6 (1.70)	— (†)	†	—	—	—	—	— (†)	— (†)
Rural	28.3	35.4 (0.98)	39.9 (1.58)	41.6 (1.17)	39.2 (2.06)	0.8 (0.22)	0.3 (0.15)	3.5 (0.62)	23.7 (1.39)	1.1 (0.40)	18.5 (1.76)	67.2 (1.77)
Labor force status												
In labor force	40.7	49.8 (0.69)	52.1 (0.94)	— (†)	52.3 (0.93)	1.4 (0.32)	0.8 (0.19)	6.4 (0.39)	37.1 (0.83)	1.5 (0.24)	21.9 (0.91)	73.0 (0.94)
Employed	42.0	50.7 (0.53)	52.5 (0.96)	— (†)	53.4 (0.94)	1.1 (0.31)	0.7 (0.20)	6.5 (0.39)	38.8 (0.83)	1.4 (0.24)	21.8 (0.94)	73.5 (1.01)
Unemployed	26.0	36.6 (1.91)	44.9 (4.60)	— (†)	37.8 (4.26)	5.8 (1.60)	1.9 (0.79)	5.2 (1.37)	13.5 (2.16)	2.1 (1.23)	22.1 (3.99)	66.7 (3.80)
Not in labor force	15.7	21.3 (0.69)	24.9 (1.17)	— (†)	27.6 (1.18)	1.1 (0.24)	1.3 (0.36)	2.3 (0.45)	5.7 (0.55)	0.6 (0.22)	20.5 (0.97)	65.2 (1.27)
Occupation												
Executive, administrative, or managerial occupations	49.3	55.8 (1.92)	57.0 (2.11)	66.2 (1.61)	64.1 (2.73)	0.2 (0.24)	‡	6.0 (1.10)	51.8 (2.82)	0.4 (0.24)	28.8 (2.89)	78.6 (2.71)
Engineers, surveyors, and architects	62.6	65.5 (4.18)	79.8 (6.01)	68.1	71.2 (5.68)	‡	‡	9.3 (3.21)	55.6 (5.60)	‡	31.4 (6.19)	81.1 (4.63)

See notes at end of table.

Participation rate of persons, 17 years old and over, in adult education during the previous 12 months, by selected characteristics of participants: Selected years, 1991 through 2005—Continued

Characteristic of participant	Percent taking any program, class, or course					Percent taking specific programs, classes, or courses, 2005						Percent doing informal learning activities for personal interest, 2005
	1991	1995	1999	2001	2005	Basic skills/General Educational Development (GED) classes	English as a second language (ESL) classes	Part-time post-secondary education[1]	Career or job-related courses	Apprentice programs	Personal-interest courses	
1	2	3	4	5	6	7	8	9	10	11	12	13
Natural scientists and mathematicians	48.2	72.3 (3.52)	60.5 (6.74)	74.0 (4.46)	69.1 (4.63)	‡ (†)	‡ (†)	9.2 (2.49)	49.6 (5.27)	2.0 (1.47)	30.2 (4.53)	85.5 (5.16)
Social scientists and workers, religious workers, and lawyers	55.6	76.6 (2.61)	79.3 (4.35)	83.5 (3.05)	77.7 (4.11)	‡ (†)	‡ (†)	12.8 (3.16)	64.3 (4.42)	‡ (†)	29.2 (3.52)	89.4 (2.78)
Teachers, elementary/secondary	55.0	54.8 (4.64)	66.5 (5.61)	79.9 (2.95)	79.7 (2.59)	‡ (†)	1.6 (1.00)	8.3 (3.16)	65.0 (3.99)	0.6 (0.34)	31.7 (3.78)	83.8 (2.62)
Teachers, postsecondary and counselors, librarians, and archivists	45.5	76.7 (1.98)	78.4 (3.11)	69.4 (4.60)	61.3 (6.96)	‡ (†)	‡ (†)	4.7 (3.22)	49.0 (8.50)	‡ (†)	19.5 (4.98)	91.7 (3.58)
Health diagnosing and treating practitioners	67.1	71.1 (5.78)	79.8 (9.02)	78.5 (6.38)	88.8 (5.59)	0.6 (0.55)	‡ (†)	15.4 (2.47)	79.5 (6.59)	‡ (†)	31.9 (9.15)	84.5 (5.63)
Registered nurses, pharmacists, dieticians, therapists, and physician's assistants	59.6	86.7 (2.47)	85.4 (4.10)	82.7 (3.83)	85.4 (4.05)	‡ (†)	‡ (†)	7.9 (2.17)	78.2 (4.89)	‡ (†)	27.4 (3.73)	83.1 (3.92)
Writers, artists, entertainers, and athletes	42.9	49.9 (4.37)	50.0 (6.93)	46.8 (6.03)	52.5 (6.59)	0.2 (0.23)	‡ (†)	5.4 (2.16)	27.8 (5.02)	2.2 (1.53)	35.3 (6.42)	88.2 (3.89)
Health technologists and technicians	68.6	74.8 (3.64)	66.9 (6.16)	85.6 (3.25)	72.1 (8.37)	0.2 (0.16)	‡ (†)	6.0 (2.11)	63.2 (8.67)	1.7 (1.23)	24.6 (5.91)	75.6 (7.26)
Technologists and technicians, except health	55.4	64.3 (2.84)	59.6 (5.07)	70.2 (3.32)	33.8 (8.53)	‡ (†)	0.4 (0.26)	7.1 (3.19)	29.1 (7.68)	1.4 (0.80)	6.2 (2.14)	76.0 (8.80)
Marketing and sales occupations	34.4	44.2 (1.34)	44.4 (2.73)	51.1 (2.10)	45.7 (3.00)	1.7 (0.59)	‡ (0.88)	4.5 (0.88)	30.2 (2.77)	1.3 (0.63)	21.5 (2.43)	68.9 (3.37)
Administrative support occupations, including clerical	29.9	51.7 (1.25)	50.1 (2.29)	58.7 (1.72)	54.6 (2.70)	1.1 (0.53)	1.9 (0.88)	6.6 (0.98)	33.5 (2.70)	1.4 (0.57)	27.7 (2.18)	73.8 (2.33)
Service occupations	25.2	46.5 (1.38)	50.9 (2.74)	49.3 (2.24)	44.7 (2.47)	1.6 (0.39)	5.7 (4.02)	6.8 (1.42)	28.5 (2.64)	1.4 (1.53)	17.5 (2.10)	65.4 (2.71)
Agriculture, forestry, and fishing occupations	14.3	26.4 (3.55)	34.3 (7.16)	46.4 (6.80)	44.4 (9.02)	3.9 (3.49)	‡ (†)	1.1 (0.89)	20.3 (6.92)	2.3 (1.38)	21.6 (10.05)	64.0 (10.03)
Mechanics and repairers	32.1	47.6 (2.70)	42.2 (5.44)	35.1 (3.40)	40.1 (5.10)	0.5 (0.40)	‡ (†)	6.0 (1.89)	27.4 (4.26)	3.8 (1.38)	12.7 (3.18)	69.3 (4.27)
Construction and extractive occupations	21.9	38.0 (2.45)	34.5 (4.78)	32.3 (3.19)	27.6 (3.73)	1.2 (0.68)	1.1 (0.49)	3.2 (1.08)	12.3 (2.54)	5.2 (1.89)	11.4 (2.72)	72.3 (4.48)
Precision production[2]	31.2	43.0 (4.32)	38.3 (8.48)	35.1 (6.19)	33.0 (3.98)	0.5 (0.37)	0.4 (0.16)	4.2 (1.42)	22.2 (3.41)	1.5 (0.81)	13.3 (2.99)	63.9 (3.46)
Production workers	21.1	30.7 (1.29)	38.0 (3.47)	39.4 (2.82)	— (†)	— (†)	— (†)	1.3 (0.76)	— (†)	‡ (†)	11.2 (2.85)	60.8 (4.98)
Transportation, material moving, Handler, equipment, cleaners, helpers, and laborers	20.7 / 20.8	28.4 (2.32) / 25.1 (2.70)	33.3 (4.25) / 19.6 (4.56)	30.4 (3.29) / 18.2 (3.20)	34.6 (5.27) / — (†)	4.7 (3.29)	3.3 (2.35)	‡ (†)	14.7 (2.63)	3.2 (1.57)	7.8 (3.63)	52.2 (12.32)
Miscellaneous occupations	—	56.6 (3.61)	43.0 (7.98)	64.9 (7.07)	39.2 (11.25)	‡ (†)	‡ (†)	‡ (†)	15.7 (5.81)	— (†)	— (†)	— (†)
Annual household income												
$5,000 or less	13.6	21.3 (1.59)	21.0 (3.22)	25.1 (2.92)	35.9 (4.83)	3.3 (2.17)	1.8 (1.04)	3.6 (1.52)	13.7 (4.00)	2.3 (1.89)	17.2 (3.59)	52.9 (4.97)
$5,001 to $10,000	17.5	23.9 (1.37)	24.5 (3.39)	28.0 (2.74)	29.6 (4.49)	2.4 (0.92)	1.5 (0.71)	1.7 (0.81)	8.4 (2.11)	‡ (†)	21.8 (4.75)	61.0 (3.75)
$10,001 to $15,000	22.8	26.7 (1.61)	22.8 (2.45)	28.6 (2.30)	25.0 (3.41)	2.4 (0.69)	0.8 (0.33)	3.3 (1.17)	11.3 (2.52)	0.9 (0.66)	15.5 (3.14)	58.6 (4.43)
$15,001 to $20,000	21.9	31.8 (1.55)	31.4 (2.75)	30.2 (2.48)	24.3 (2.54)	1.0 (0.38)	0.5 (0.30)	3.3 (1.19)	10.1 (1.37)	2.6 (1.20)	12.9 (2.00)	61.1 (3.17)
$20,001 to $25,000	26.7	31.4 (1.27)	35.8 (2.81)	35.2 (2.27)	28.2 (2.51)	1.7 (0.78)	1.9 (0.62)	4.4 (1.26)	12.8 (2.04)	0.7 (0.50)	13.6 (1.88)	63.2 (3.11)
$25,001 to $30,000	32.1	37.9 (1.47)	36.7 (2.61)	38.3 (2.43)	28.6 (3.63)	1.4 (0.72)	1.0 (0.61)	6.8 (2.09)	20.2 (3.37)	1.1 (0.39)	18.4 (2.52)	71.0 (3.38)
$30,001 to $40,000	35.6	42.7 (0.86)	45.2 (2.05)	44.6 (1.54)	42.7 (2.65)	1.9 (0.65)	1.0 (0.49)	3.7 (0.68)	22.8 (2.27)	1.5 (0.56)	23.0 (2.49)	68.7 (2.36)
$40,001 to $50,000	44.8	46.8 (1.39)	47.9 (2.31)	49.1 (1.93)	41.4 (2.92)	1.6 (0.53)	2.4 (1.25)	2.9 (0.55)	22.4 (2.00)	0.9 (0.36)	20.5 (2.47)	71.9 (2.62)
$50,001 to $75,000	46.6	52.0 (0.94)	55.1 (1.80)	55.7 (1.48)	47.7 (1.74)	0.4 (0.19)	0.3 (0.17)	5.8 (0.69)	33.0 (1.37)	1.3 (0.38)	20.5 (1.67)	70.6 (2.15)
More than $75,000	48.7	58.0 (1.27)	56.9 (1.66)	59.5 (1.29)	57.5 (1.49)	1.1 (0.53)	0.5 (0.23)	6.7 (0.58)	39.1 (1.35)	1.3 (0.38)?	26.9 (1.13)	78.5 (1.34)

—Not available.
†Not applicable.
‡Reporting standards not met.
[1]Includes college and university degree programs, post-degree certificate programs, and vocational certificate programs.
[2]For 2005, figures include "Production workers" occupations data.

NOTE: Adult education is defined as all education activities, except full-time enrollment in higher education credential programs. Data do not include persons enrolled in high school or below. Race categories exclude persons of Hispanic ethnicity. Standard errors appear in parentheses.
SOURCE: U.S. Department of Education, National Center for Education Statistics, Adult Education Survey (AE-NHES:1991, AE-NHES:1995, AE-NHES:1999, and AE-NHES:2005) and Adult Education and Lifelong Learning Survey (AELL-NHES:2001) of the National Household Education Surveys Program. (This table was prepared May 2008.)

Degrees conferred by degree-granting institutions, by level of degree and sex of student: Selected years, 1869–70 through 2018–19

Year	Associate's degrees			Bachelor's degrees			Master's degrees			First-professional degrees			Doctor's degrees[1]		
	Total	Males	Females	Total	Males	Females	Total	Males	Females	Total	Males	Females	Total	Males	Females
1	2	3	4	5	6	7	8	9	10	11	12	13	14	15	16
1869–70	—	—	—	9,371[2]	7,993[2]	1,378[2]	0	0	0	(3)	(3)	(3)	1	1	0
1879–80	—	—	—	12,896[2]	10,411[2]	2,485[2]	879	868	11	(3)	(3)	(3)	54	51	3
1889–90	—	—	—	15,539[2]	12,857[2]	2,682[2]	1,015	821	194	(3)	(3)	(3)	149	147	2
1899–1900	—	—	—	27,410[2]	22,173[2]	5,237[2]	1,583	1,280	303	(3)	(3)	(3)	382	359	23
1909–10	—	—	—	37,199[2]	28,762[2]	8,437[2]	2,113	1,555	558	(3)	(3)	(3)	443	399	44
1919–20	—	—	—	48,622[2]	31,980[2]	16,642[2]	4,279	2,985	1,294	(3)	(3)	(3)	615	522	93
1929–30	—	—	—	122,484[2]	73,615[2]	48,869[2]	14,969	8,925	6,044	(3)	(3)	(3)	2,299	1,946	353
1939–40	—	—	—	186,500[2]	109,546[2]	76,954[2]	26,731	16,508	10,223	(3)	(3)	(3)	3,290	2,861	429
1949–50	—	—	—	432,058[2]	328,841[2]	103,217[2]	58,183	41,220	16,963	(3)	(3)	(3)	6,420	5,804	616
1959–60	—	—	—	392,440[2]	254,063[2]	138,377[2]	74,435	50,898	23,537	(3)	(3)	(3)	9,829	8,801	1,028
1969–70	206,023	117,432	88,591	792,316	451,097	341,219	208,291	125,624	82,667	34,918	33,077	1,841	29,866	25,890	3,976
1970–71	252,311	144,144	108,167	839,730	475,594	364,136	230,509	138,146	92,363	37,946	35,544	2,402	32,107	27,530	4,577
1971–72	292,014	166,227	125,787	887,273	500,590	386,683	251,633	149,550	102,083	43,411	40,723	2,688	33,363	28,090	5,273
1972–73	316,174	175,413	140,761	922,362	518,191	404,171	263,371	154,468	108,903	50,018	46,489	3,529	34,777	28,571	6,206
1973–74	343,924	188,591	155,333	945,776	527,313	418,463	277,033	157,842	119,191	53,816	48,530	5,286	33,816	27,365	6,451
1974–75	360,171	191,017	169,154	922,933	504,841	418,092	292,450	161,570	130,880	55,916	48,956	6,960	34,083	26,817	7,266
1975–76	391,454	209,996	181,458	925,746	504,925	420,821	311,771	167,248	144,523	62,649	52,892	9,757	34,064	26,267	7,797
1976–77	406,377	210,842	195,535	919,549	495,545	424,004	317,164	167,783	149,381	64,359	52,374	11,985	33,232	25,142	8,090
1977–78	412,246	204,718	207,528	921,204	487,347	433,857	311,620	161,212	150,408	66,581	52,270	14,311	32,131	23,658	8,473
1978–79	402,702	192,091	210,611	921,390	477,344	444,046	301,079	153,370	147,709	68,848	52,652	16,196	32,730	23,541	9,189
1979–80	400,910	183,737	217,173	929,417	473,611	455,806	298,081	150,749	147,332	70,131	52,716	17,415	32,615	22,943	9,672
1980–81	416,377	188,638	227,739	935,140	469,883	465,257	295,739	147,043	148,696	71,956	52,792	19,164	32,958	22,711	10,247
1981–82	434,526	196,944	237,582	952,998	473,364	479,634	295,546	145,532	150,014	72,032	52,223	19,809	32,707	22,224	10,483
1982–83	449,620	203,991	245,629	969,510	479,140	490,370	289,921	144,697	145,224	73,054	51,250	21,804	32,775	21,902	10,873
1983–84	452,240	202,704	249,536	974,309	482,319	491,990	284,263	143,595	140,668	74,468	51,378	23,090	33,209	22,064	11,145
1984–85	454,712	202,932	251,780	979,477	482,528	496,949	286,251	143,390	142,861	75,063	50,455	24,608	32,943	21,700	11,243
1985–86	446,047	196,166	249,881	987,823	485,923	501,900	288,567	143,508	145,059	73,910	49,261	24,649	33,653	21,819	11,834
1986–87	436,304	190,839	245,465	991,264	480,782	510,482	289,349	141,269	148,080	71,617	46,523	25,094	34,041	22,061	11,980
1987–88	435,085	190,047	245,038	994,829	477,203	517,626	299,317	145,163	154,154	70,735	45,484	25,251	34,870	22,615	12,255
1988–89	436,764	186,316	250,448	1,018,755	483,346	535,409	310,621	149,354	161,267	70,856	45,046	25,810	35,720	22,648	13,072
1989–90	455,102	191,195	263,907	1,051,344	491,696	559,648	324,301	153,653	170,648	70,988	43,961	27,027	38,371	24,401	13,970
1990–91	481,720	198,634	283,086	1,094,538	504,045	590,493	337,168	156,482	180,686	71,948	43,846	28,102	39,294	24,756	14,538
1991–92	504,231	207,481	296,750	1,136,553	520,811	615,742	352,838	161,842	190,996	74,146	45,071	29,075	40,659	25,557	15,102
1992–93	514,756	211,964	302,792	1,165,178	532,881	632,297	369,585	169,258	200,327	75,387	45,153	30,234	42,132	26,073	16,059
1993–94	530,632	215,261	315,371	1,169,275	532,422	636,853	387,070	176,085	210,985	75,418	44,707	30,711	43,185	26,552	16,633
1994–95	539,691	218,352	321,339	1,160,134	526,131	634,003	397,629	178,598	219,031	75,800	44,853	30,947	44,446	26,916	17,530
1995–96	555,216	219,514	335,702	1,164,792	522,454	642,338	406,301	179,081	227,220	76,734	44,748	31,986	44,652	26,841	17,811
1996–97	571,226	223,948	347,278	1,172,879	520,515	652,364	419,401	180,947	238,454	78,730	45,564	33,166	45,876	27,146	18,730
1997–98	558,555	217,613	340,942	1,184,406	519,956	664,450	430,164	184,375	245,789	78,598	44,911	33,687	46,010	26,664	19,346
1998–99	559,954	218,417	341,537	1,200,303	518,746	681,557	439,986	186,148	253,838	78,439	44,339	34,100	44,077	25,146	18,931
1999–2000	564,933	224,721	340,212	1,237,875	530,367	707,508	457,056	191,792	265,264	80,057	44,239	35,818	44,808	25,028	19,780
2000–01	578,865	231,645	347,220	1,244,171	531,840	712,331	468,476	194,351	274,125	79,707	42,862	36,845	44,904	24,728	20,176
2001–02	595,133	238,109	357,024	1,291,900	549,816	742,084	482,118	199,120	282,998	80,698	42,507	38,191	44,160	23,708	20,452
2002–03	634,016	253,451	380,565	1,348,811	573,258	775,553	513,339	211,664	301,675	80,897	41,887	39,010	46,042	24,351	21,691
2003–04	665,301	260,033	405,268	1,399,542	595,425	804,117	558,940	229,545	329,395	83,041	42,169	40,872	48,378	25,323	23,055
2004–05	696,660	267,536	429,124	1,439,264	613,000	826,264	574,618	233,590	341,028	87,289	43,849	43,440	52,631	26,973	25,658
2005–06	713,066	270,095	442,971	1,485,242	630,600	854,642	594,065	237,896	356,169	87,655	44,038	43,617	56,067	28,634	27,433
2006–07	728,114	275,187	452,927	1,524,092	649,570	874,522	604,607	238,189	366,418	90,064	45,057	45,007	60,616	30,251	30,365
2007–08	750,164	282,521	467,643	1,563,069	667,928	895,141	625,023	246,491	378,532	91,309	45,916	45,393	63,712	31,215	32,497
2008–09[4]	755,000	286,000	470,000	1,599,000	681,000	918,000	631,000	250,000	381,000	93,300	46,800	46,400	64,400	31,500	32,900
2009–10[4]	778,000	293,000	486,000	1,648,000	702,000	946,000	648,000	257,000	391,000	94,900	48,000	46,900	67,000	32,400	34,600
2010–11[4]	798,000	298,000	500,000	1,669,000	713,000	956,000	659,000	261,000	398,000	96,500	49,100	47,400	69,600	33,400	36,300
2011–12[4]	813,000	302,000	511,000	1,706,000	727,000	979,000	670,000	263,000	407,000	98,100	49,700	48,400	72,200	34,300	37,900
2012–13[4]	823,000	304,000	519,000	1,719,000	731,000	989,000	684,000	266,000	418,000	99,200	50,200	49,100	74,800	35,200	39,600
2013–14[4]	837,000	306,000	531,000	1,737,000	734,000	1,004,000	702,000	271,000	431,000	101,100	50,800	50,300	77,400	36,100	41,300
2014–15[4]	852,000	309,000	543,000	1,753,000	735,000	1,017,000	717,000	277,000	440,000	103,800	51,700	52,100	80,000	37,100	42,900
2015–16[4]	867,000	311,000	556,000	1,772,000	737,000	1,034,000	732,000	282,000	450,000	106,400	52,600	53,800	82,600	38,000	44,600
2016–17[4]	881,000	314,000	568,000	1,790,000	740,000	1,050,000	746,000	286,000	460,000	108,400	53,500	54,900	85,200	38,900	46,300
2017–18[4]	897,000	316,000	580,000	1,806,000	741,000	1,065,000	760,000	290,000	471,000	110,200	54,200	56,000	87,800	39,900	48,000
2018–19[4]	913,000	319,000	593,000	1,821,000	743,000	1,078,000	773,000	293,000	480,000	112,000	54,900	57,100	90,400	40,800	49,600

—Not available.

[1] Includes Ph.D., Ed.D., and comparable degrees at the doctoral level. Excludes first-professional, such as M.D., D.D.S., and law degrees.

[2] Includes first-professional degrees.

[3] First-professional degrees are included with bachelor's degrees.

[4] Projected.

NOTE: Data through 1994–95 are for institutions of higher education, while later data are for degree-granting institutions. Degree-granting institutions grant associate's or higher degrees and participate in Title IV federal financial aid programs. The degree-granting classification is very similar to the earlier higher education classification, but it includes more 2-year colleges and excludes a few higher education institutions that did not grant degrees. (See Appendix A: Guide to Sources for details.) Some data have been revised from previously published figures. Detail may not sum to totals because of rounding.

SOURCE: U.S. Department of Education, National Center for Education Statistics, *Earned Degrees Conferred*, 1869–70 through 1964–65; *Projections of Education Statistics to 2018*; Higher Education General Information Survey (HEGIS), "Degrees and Other Formal Awards Conferred" surveys, 1965–66 through 1985–86; and 1986–87 through 2007–08 Integrated Postsecondary Education Data System, "Completions Survey" (IPEDS-C:87–99), and Fall 2000 through Fall 2008. (This table was prepared July 2009.)

Degrees conferred by degree-granting institutions, by control of institution, level of degree, and field of study: 2007–08

Field of study	Public institutions				Private institutions			
	Associate's degrees	Bachelor's degrees	Master's degrees	Doctor's degrees[1]	Associate's degrees	Bachelor's degrees	Master's degrees	Doctor's degrees[1]
1	2	3	4	5	6	7	8	9
All fields, total	578,520	996,435	299,923	38,315	171,644	566,634	325,100	25,397
Agriculture and natural resources	5,518	20,974	3,853	1,163	220	3,139	831	94
Architecture and related services	525	7,211	3,791	135	43	2,594	2,274	64
Area, ethnic, cultural, and gender studies	149	5,319	1,035	144	20	3,135	743	126
Biological and biomedical sciences	2,156	53,114	5,998	4,724	44	24,740	3,567	2,194
Business	68,455	185,378	54,904	901	52,703	149,876	100,733	1,183
Communications, journalism, and related programs	2,165	52,949	3,519	372	455	23,433	3,396	117
Communications technologies	2,344	1,083	81	0	1,893	3,583	550	7
Computer and information sciences	13,217	18,184	8,507	1,169	15,079	20,292	8,580	529
Construction trades	3,138	161	0	0	1,171	19	0	0
Education	11,991	72,585	84,023	5,066	1,117	29,997	91,857	3,425
Engineering	1,880	52,356	21,624	5,962	406	16,320	10,095	2,150
Engineering technologies[2]	19,404	11,583	1,518	25	9,930	3,182	1,355	30
English language and literature/letters	1,391	38,365	6,130	946	11	16,673	3,031	316
Family and consumer sciences	7,925	18,647	1,522	243	688	3,223	677	80
Foreign languages, literatures, and linguistics	1,244	14,395	2,497	709	14	6,582	1,068	369
Health professions and related clinical sciences	109,359	67,584	28,318	4,731	46,457	43,894	29,802	5,155
Legal professions and studies	5,164	2,065	1,178	46	4,301	1,706	3,576	126
Liberal arts and sciences, general studies, and humanities	243,253	32,325	1,593	20	10,759	14,615	2,204	56
Library science	117	67	5,703	63	0	1	1,459	1
Mathematics and statistics	814	9,993	3,680	998	41	5,199	1,300	362
Mechanics and repair technologies	9,339	189	0	0	5,958	43	0	0
Military technologies	787	30	0	0	64	9	0	0
Multi/interdisciplinary studies	15,925	25,084	3,202	692	330	11,065	2,087	450
Parks, recreation, leisure and fitness studies	976	22,461	3,568	222	368	7,470	872	6
Philosophy and religious studies	95	5,469	654	273	363	6,788	1,225	362
Physical sciences and science technologies	3,298	14,932	4,350	3,359	90	7,002	1,549	1,445
Precision production	1,809	4	0	0	159	29	3	0
Psychology	2,254	62,278	7,915	2,251	158	30,309	13,516	3,045
Public administration and social service professions	3,882	14,986	20,762	458	310	8,507	12,267	302
Security and protective services	20,813	25,497	2,647	83	8,777	14,738	3,113	5
Social sciences and history	7,736	112,807	10,470	2,561	76	54,556	8,025	1,498
Social sciences	7,292	89,839	8,056	2,056	66	43,083	7,036	1,143
History	444	22,968	2,414	505	10	11,473	989	355
Theology and religious vocations	1	0	0	0	581	8,992	6,996	1,446
Transportation and materials moving	942	2,135	58	0	608	3,068	924	0
Visual and performing arts	10,454	46,225	6,823	999	8,436	41,478	7,341	454
Other and unclassified	0	0	0	0	14	377	84	0

[1]Includes Ph.D., Ed.D., and comparable degrees at the doctoral level. Excludes first-professional degrees, such as M.D., D.D.S., and law degrees.
[2]Excludes "Construction trades" and "Mechanics and repair technologies," which are listed separately.
NOTE: Degree-granting institutions grant associate's or higher degrees and participate in Title IV federal financial aid programs. To facilitate trend comparisons, certain aggregations have been made of the degree fields as reported in the IPEDS Fall survey: "Agriculture and natural resources" includes Agriculture, agriculture operations, and related sciences and Natural resources and conservation; and "Business" includes Business management, marketing, and related support services and Personal and culinary services.
SOURCE: U.S. Department of Education, National Center for Education Statistics, 2007–08 Integrated Postsecondary Education Data System (IPEDS), Fall 2008. (This table was prepared June 2009.)

First-professional degrees conferred by degree-granting institutions, by sex of student, control of institution, and field of study: Selected years, 1985–86 through 2007–08

Control of institution and field of study	1985–86	1990–91	1995–96	1998–99	1999–2000	2000–01	2001–02	2002–03	2003–04	2004–05	2005–06 Total	2005–06 Males	2005–06 Females	2006–07 Total	2006–07 Males	2006–07 Females	2007–08 Total	2007–08 Males	2007–08 Females
1	2	3	4	5	6	7	8	9	10	11	12	13	14	15	16	17	18	19	20
Total, all institutions	73,910	71,948	76,734	78,439	80,057	79,707	80,698	80,897	83,041	87,289	87,655	44,038	43,617	90,064	45,057	45,007	91,309	45,916	45,393
Dentistry (D.D.S. or D.M.D.)	5,046	3,699	3,697	4,144	4,250	4,391	4,239	4,345	4,335	4,454	4,389	2,435	1,954	4,596	2,548	2,048	4,795	2,661	2,134
Medicine (M.D.)	15,938	15,043	15,341	15,562	15,286	15,403	15,237	15,034	15,442	15,461	15,455	7,900	7,555	15,730	7,987	7,743	15,646	7,935	7,711
Optometry (O.D.)	1,029	1,115	1,231	1,285	1,293	1,289	1,280	1,281	1,275	1,252	1,198	490	708	1,311	493	818	1,304	445	859
Osteopathic medicine (D.O.)	1,547	1,459	1,895	2,135	2,236	2,450	2,416	2,596	2,722	2,762	2,718	1,434	1,284	2,992	1,475	1,517	3,232	1,581	1,651
Pharmacy (Pharm.D.)	903	1,244	2,555	3,992	5,669	6,324	7,076	7,474	8,221	8,885	9,292	3,032	6,260	10,439	3,394	7,045	10,932	3,716	7,216
Podiatry (Pod.D. or D.P.) or podiatric medicine (D.P.M.)	612	589	650	578	569	528	474	439	382	343	347	191	156	331	173	158	555	305	250
Veterinary medicine (D.V.M.)	2,270	2,032	2,109	2,226	2,251	2,248	2,289	2,354	2,228	2,354	2,370	535	1,835	2,443	537	1,906	2,504	580	1,924
Chiropractic (D.C. or D.C.M.)	3,395	2,640	3,379	3,639	3,809	3,796	3,284	2,718	2,730	2,560	2,564	1,615	949	2,525	1,617	908	2,639	1,683	956
Law (LL.B. or J.D.)	35,844	37,945	39,828	39,167	38,152	37,904	38,981	39,067	40,209	43,423	43,440	22,597	20,843	43,486	22,777	20,709	43,769	23,197	20,572
Theology (M. Div., M.H.L., B.D., or Ord. and M.H.L./Rav.)	7,283	5,695	5,879	5,558	6,129	5,026	5,195	5,360	5,332	5,533	5,666	3,760	1,906	5,990	4,000	1,990	5,751	3,777	1,974
Other	43	487	170	153	413	348	227	229	165	262	216	49	167	221	56	165	182	36	146
Total, public institutions	29,568	29,554	29,882	31,693	32,247	32,633	33,439	33,549	34,499	35,768	36,269	17,268	19,001	36,855	17,471	19,384	37,278	17,912	19,366
Dentistry (D.D.S. or D.M.D.)	2,827	2,308	2,198	2,479	2,512	2,477	2,525	2,493	2,498	2,577	2,669	1,515	1,154	2,769	1,586	1,183	2,760	1,577	1,183
Medicine (M.D.)	9,991	9,364	9,370	9,515	9,389	9,408	9,390	9,276	9,418	9,536	9,650	4,944	4,706	9,733	4,993	4,740	9,646	4,976	4,670
Optometry (O.D.)	441	477	499	488	493	497	503	481	476	477	462	185	277	518	198	320	492	147	345
Osteopathic medicine (D.O.)	486	493	528	548	535	562	538	571	586	568	585	284	301	637	301	336	634	306	328
Pharmacy (Pharm.D.)	473	808	1,557	2,503	3,485	3,876	4,382	4,558	4,930	5,352	5,523	1,861	3,662	5,903	1,966	3,937	6,218	2,129	4,089
Podiatry (Pod.D. or D.P.) or podiatric medicine (D.P.M.)	0	0	0	97	84	84	75	81	64	64	65	31	34	66	32	34	73	36	37
Veterinary medicine (D.V.M.)	1,931	1,814	1,889	1,989	2,021	2,017	2,052	2,023	1,912	2,033	2,048	482	1,566	2,116	474	1,642	2,123	507	1,616
Chiropractic (D.C. or D.C.M.)	0	0	0	0	0	0	0	0	0	0	0	0	0	0	0	0	0	0	0
Law (LL.B. or J.D.)	13,419	14,290	13,841	14,074	13,728	13,712	13,974	14,066	14,615	15,161	15,267	7,966	7,301	15,113	7,921	7,192	15,332	8,234	7,098
Theology (M. Div., M.H.L., B.D., or Ord. and M.H.L./Rav.)	0	0	0	0	0	0	0	0	0	0	0	0	0	0	0	0	0	0	0
Other	0	0	0	0	0	0	0	0	0	0	0	0	0	0	0	0	0	0	0
Total, private institutions	44,342	42,394	46,852	46,746	47,810	47,074	47,259	47,348	48,542	51,521	51,386	26,770	24,616	53,209	27,586	25,623	54,031	28,004	26,027
Dentistry (D.D.S. or D.M.D.)	2,219	1,391	1,499	1,665	1,738	1,914	1,714	1,852	1,837	1,877	1,720	920	800	1,827	962	865	2,035	1,084	951
Medicine (M.D.)	5,947	5,679	5,971	6,047	5,897	5,995	5,847	5,758	6,024	5,925	5,805	2,956	2,849	5,997	2,994	3,003	6,000	2,959	3,041
Optometry (O.D.)	588	638	732	797	800	792	777	800	799	775	736	305	431	793	295	498	812	298	514
Osteopathic medicine (D.O.)	1,061	966	1,367	1,587	1,701	1,888	1,878	2,025	2,136	2,194	2,133	1,150	983	2,355	1,174	1,181	2,598	1,275	1,323
Pharmacy (Pharm.D.)	430	436	998	1,489	2,184	2,448	2,694	2,916	3,291	3,533	3,769	1,171	2,598	4,536	1,428	3,108	4,714	1,587	3,127
Podiatry (Pod.D. or D.P.) or podiatric medicine (D.P.M.)	612	589	650	481	485	444	399	358	318	279	282	160	122	265	141	124	482	269	213
Veterinary medicine (D.V.M.)	339	218	220	237	230	231	237	331	316	321	322	53	269	327	63	264	381	73	308
Chiropractic (D.C. or D.C.M.)	3,395	2,640	3,379	3,639	3,809	3,796	3,284	2,718	2,730	2,560	2,564	1,615	949	2,525	1,617	908	2,639	1,683	956
Law (LL.B. or J.D.)	22,425	23,655	25,987	25,093	24,424	24,192	25,007	25,001	25,594	28,262	28,173	14,631	13,542	28,373	14,856	13,517	28,437	14,963	13,474
Theology (M. Div., M.H.L., B.D., or Ord. and M.H.L./Rav.)	7,283	5,695	5,879	5,558	6,129	5,026	5,195	5,360	5,332	5,533	5,666	3,760	1,906	5,990	4,000	1,990	5,751	3,777	1,974
Other	43	487	170	153	413	348	227	229	165	262	216	49	167	221	56	165	182	36	146

NOTE: Degree-granting institutions grant associate's or higher degrees and participate in Title IV federal financial aid programs. Includes degrees that require at least 6 years of college work for completion (including at least 2 years of preprofessional training).

SOURCE: U.S. Department of Education, National Center for Education Statistics, Higher Education General Information Survey (HEGIS), "Degrees and Other Formal Awards Conferred," 1985–86; and 1990–91 through 2007–08 Integrated Postsecondary Education Data System, "Completions Survey" (IPEDS-C:91–99), and Fall 2000 through Fall 2008. (This table was prepared June 2009.)

Associate's degrees conferred by degree-granting institutions, by race/ethnicity and sex of student: Selected years, 1976–77 through 2007–08

Year and sex	Number of degrees conferred							Percentage distribution of degrees conferred						
	Total	White	Black	Hispanic	Asian/ Pacific Islander	American Indian/ Alaska Native	Non-resident alien	Total	White	Black	Hispanic	Asian/ Pacific Islander	American Indian/ Alaska Native	Non-resident alien
1	2	3	4	5	6	7	8	9	10	11	12	13	14	15
Total														
1976–77[1]	404,956	342,290	33,159	16,636	7,044	2,498	3,329	100.0	84.5	8.2	4.1	1.7	0.6	0.8
1980–81[2]	410,174	339,167	35,330	17,800	8,650	2,584	6,643	100.0	82.7	8.6	4.3	2.1	0.6	1.6
1989–90	455,102	376,816	34,326	21,504	13,066	3,430	5,960	100.0	82.8	7.5	4.7	2.9	0.8	1.3
1990–91	481,720	391,264	38,835	25,540	15,257	3,871	6,953	100.0	81.2	8.1	5.3	3.2	0.8	1.4
1992–93	514,756	411,435	42,886	30,283	16,763	4,408	8,981	100.0	79.9	8.3	5.9	3.3	0.9	1.7
1993–94	530,632	419,694	45,523	32,118	18,444	4,876	9,977	100.0	79.1	8.6	6.1	3.5	0.9	1.9
1994–95	539,691	420,656	47,067	35,962	20,677	5,482	9,847	100.0	77.9	8.7	6.7	3.8	1.0	1.8
1995–96	555,216	426,106	52,014	38,254	23,138	5,573	10,131	100.0	76.7	9.4	6.9	4.2	1.0	1.8
1996–97	571,226	429,464	56,306	43,549	25,159	5,984	10,764	100.0	75.2	9.9	7.6	4.4	1.0	1.9
1997–98	558,555	413,561	55,314	45,876	25,196	6,246	12,362	100.0	74.0	9.9	8.2	4.5	1.1	2.2
1998–99	559,954	409,086	57,439	48,670	27,586	6,424	10,749	100.0	73.1	10.3	8.7	4.9	1.1	1.9
1999–2000	564,933	408,772	60,221	51,573	27,782	6,497	10,088	100.0	72.4	10.7	9.1	4.9	1.2	1.8
2000–01	578,865	411,075	63,855	57,288	28,463	6,623	11,561	100.0	71.0	11.0	9.9	4.9	1.1	2.0
2001–02	595,133	417,733	67,343	60,003	30,945	6,832	12,277	100.0	70.2	11.3	10.1	5.2	1.1	2.1
2002–03	634,016	438,261	75,609	66,673	32,629	7,461	13,383	100.0	69.1	11.9	10.5	5.1	1.2	2.1
2003–04	665,301	456,047	81,183	72,270	33,149	8,119	14,533	100.0	68.5	12.2	10.9	5.0	1.2	2.2
2004–05	696,660	475,513	86,402	78,557	33,669	8,435	14,084	100.0	68.3	12.4	11.3	4.8	1.2	2.0
2005–06	713,066	485,297	89,784	80,854	35,201	8,552	13,378	100.0	68.1	12.6	11.3	4.9	1.2	1.9
2006–07	728,114	491,572	91,529	85,410	37,266	8,583	13,754	100.0	67.5	12.6	11.7	5.1	1.2	1.9
2007–08	750,164	501,079	95,702	91,274	38,843	8,849	14,417	100.0	66.8	12.8	12.2	5.2	1.2	1.9
Males														
1976–77[1]	209,672	178,236	15,330	9,105	3,630	1,216	2,155	100.0	85.0	7.3	4.3	1.7	0.6	1.0
1980–81[2]	183,819	151,242	14,290	8,327	4,557	1,108	4,295	100.0	82.3	7.8	4.5	2.5	0.6	2.3
1989–90	191,195	158,954	12,502	9,370	6,170	1,364	2,835	100.0	83.1	6.5	4.9	3.2	0.7	1.5
1990–91	198,634	161,858	14,143	10,738	7,164	1,439	3,292	100.0	81.5	7.1	5.4	3.6	0.7	1.7
1992–93	211,964	169,841	15,689	13,014	7,937	1,680	3,803	100.0	80.1	7.4	6.1	3.7	0.8	1.8
1993–94	215,261	170,905	16,931	13,214	8,289	1,837	4,085	100.0	79.4	7.9	6.1	3.9	0.9	1.9
1994–95	218,352	170,251	16,727	15,670	9,252	2,098	4,354	100.0	78.0	7.7	7.2	4.2	1.0	2.0
1995–96	219,514	169,230	17,941	15,740	10,229	1,993	4,381	100.0	77.1	8.2	7.2	4.7	0.9	2.0
1996–97	223,948	168,882	19,394	17,990	10,937	2,068	4,677	100.0	75.4	8.7	8.0	4.9	0.9	2.1
1997–98	217,613	161,212	18,686	19,108	10,953	2,252	5,402	100.0	74.1	8.6	8.8	5.0	1.0	2.5
1998–99	218,417	160,794	19,402	19,379	11,671	2,241	4,930	100.0	73.6	8.9	8.9	5.3	1.0	2.3
1999–2000	224,721	164,315	20,967	20,946	12,010	2,225	4,258	100.0	73.1	9.3	9.3	5.3	1.0	1.9
2000–01	231,645	166,322	22,147	23,350	12,339	2,294	5,193	100.0	71.8	9.6	10.1	5.3	1.0	2.2
2001–02	238,109	170,622	22,806	23,963	13,256	2,308	5,154	100.0	71.7	9.6	10.1	5.6	1.0	2.2
2002–03	253,451	179,163	25,591	26,461	14,057	2,618	5,561	100.0	70.7	10.1	10.4	5.5	1.0	2.2
2003–04	260,033	183,819	25,961	27,828	13,907	2,740	5,778	100.0	70.7	10.0	10.7	5.3	1.1	2.2
2004–05	267,536	188,569	27,151	29,658	13,802	2,774	5,582	100.0	70.5	10.1	11.1	5.2	1.0	2.1
2005–06	270,095	190,139	27,619	30,040	14,224	2,774	5,299	100.0	70.4	10.2	11.1	5.3	1.0	2.0
2006–07	275,187	191,565	28,273	31,646	15,510	2,873	5,320	100.0	69.6	10.3	11.5	5.6	1.0	1.9
2007–08	282,521	194,099	30,016	33,817	15,936	3,003	5,650	100.0	68.7	10.6	12.0	5.6	1.1	2.0
Females														
1976–77[1]	195,284	164,054	17,829	7,531	3,414	1,282	1,174	100.0	84.0	9.1	3.9	1.7	0.7	0.6
1980–81[2]	226,355	187,925	21,040	9,473	4,093	1,476	2,348	100.0	83.0	9.3	4.2	1.8	0.7	1.0
1989–90	263,907	217,862	21,824	12,134	6,896	2,066	3,125	100.0	82.6	8.3	4.6	2.6	0.8	1.2
1990–91	283,086	229,406	24,692	14,802	8,093	2,432	3,661	100.0	81.0	8.7	5.2	2.9	0.9	1.3
1992–93	302,792	241,594	27,197	17,269	8,826	2,728	5,178	100.0	79.8	9.0	5.7	2.9	0.9	1.7
1993–94	315,371	248,789	28,592	18,904	10,155	3,039	5,892	100.0	78.9	9.1	6.0	3.2	1.0	1.9
1994–95	321,339	250,405	30,340	20,292	11,425	3,384	5,493	100.0	77.9	9.4	6.3	3.6	1.1	1.7
1995–96	335,702	256,876	34,073	22,514	12,909	3,580	5,750	100.0	76.5	10.1	6.7	3.8	1.1	1.7
1996–97	347,278	260,582	36,912	25,559	14,222	3,916	6,087	100.0	75.0	10.6	7.4	4.1	1.1	1.8
1997–98	340,942	252,349	36,628	26,768	14,243	3,994	6,960	100.0	74.0	10.7	7.9	4.2	1.2	2.0
1998–99	341,537	248,292	38,037	29,291	15,915	4,183	5,819	100.0	72.7	11.1	8.6	4.7	1.2	1.7
1999–2000	340,212	244,457	39,254	30,627	15,772	4,272	5,830	100.0	71.9	11.5	9.0	4.6	1.3	1.7
2000–01	347,220	244,753	41,708	33,938	16,124	4,329	6,368	100.0	70.5	12.0	9.8	4.6	1.2	1.8
2001–02	357,024	247,111	44,537	36,040	17,689	4,524	7,123	100.0	69.2	12.5	10.1	5.0	1.3	2.0
2002–03	380,565	259,098	50,018	40,212	18,572	4,843	7,822	100.0	68.1	13.1	10.6	4.9	1.3	2.1
2003–04	405,268	272,228	55,222	44,442	19,242	5,379	8,755	100.0	67.2	13.6	11.0	4.7	1.3	2.2
2004–05	429,124	286,944	59,251	48,899	19,867	5,661	8,502	100.0	66.9	13.8	11.4	4.6	1.3	2.0
2005–06	442,971	295,158	62,165	50,814	20,977	5,778	8,079	100.0	66.6	14.0	11.5	4.7	1.3	1.8
2006–07	452,927	300,007	63,256	53,764	21,756	5,710	8,434	100.0	66.2	14.0	11.9	4.8	1.3	1.9
2007–08	467,643	306,980	65,686	57,457	22,907	5,846	8,767	100.0	65.6	14.0	12.3	4.9	1.3	1.9

[1]Excludes 1,170 males and 251 females whose racial/ethnic group was not available.
[2]Excludes 4,819 males and 1,384 females whose racial/ethnic group was not available.
NOTE: Degree-granting institutions grant associate's or higher degrees and participate in Title IV federal financial aid programs. Race categories exclude persons of Hispanic ethnicity. For 1989–90 and later years, reported racial/ethnic distributions of students by level of degree, field of degree, and sex were used to estimate race/ethnicity for students whose race/ethnicity was not reported. (See Appendix A: Guide to Sources for details.) Detail may not sum to totals because of rounding.
SOURCE: U.S. Department of Education, National Center for Education Statistics, Higher Education General Information Survey (HEGIS), "Degrees and Other Formal Awards Conferred" surveys, 1976–77 and 1980–81; and 1989–90 through 2007–08 Integrated Postsecondary Education Data System, "Completions Survey" (IPEDS-C:90–99), and Fall 2000 through Fall 2008. (This table was prepared June 2009.)

Associate's degrees conferred by degree-granting institutions, by sex, race/ethnicity, and field of study: 2007–08

Field of study	Total							Males							Females						
	Total	White	Black	Hispanic	Asian/Pacific Islander	American Indian/Alaska Native	Non-resident alien	Total	White	Black	Hispanic	Asian/Pacific Islander	American Indian/Alaska Native	Non-resident alien	Total	White	Black	Hispanic	Asian/Pacific Islander	American Indian/Alaska Native	Non-resident alien
1	2	3	4	5	6	7	8	9	10	11	12	13	14	15	16	17	18	19	20	21	22
All fields, total	**750,164**	**501,079**	**95,702**	**91,274**	**38,843**	**8,849**	**14,417**	**282,521**	**194,099**	**30,016**	**33,817**	**15,936**	**3,003**	**5,650**	**467,643**	**306,980**	**65,686**	**57,457**	**22,907**	**5,846**	**8,767**
Agriculture and natural resources	5,738	5,364	70	146	38	93	27	3,598	3,370	52	87	16	62	11	2,140	1,994	18	59	22	31	16
Architecture and related services	568	320	46	115	48	9	30	260	126	31	58	33	4	8	308	194	15	57	15	5	22
Area, ethnic, cultural, and gender studies	169	27	28	32	2	78	2	59	14	10	12	0	23	0	110	13	18	20	2	55	2
Biological and biomedical sciences	2,200	1,201	168	372	323	60	76	667	360	56	116	97	14	24	1,533	841	112	256	226	46	52
Business	121,158	77,175	18,739	13,509	6,951	1,469	3,315	43,245	28,504	5,473	4,827	2,759	426	1,256	77,913	48,671	13,266	8,682	4,192	1,043	2,059
Communications, journalism, and related programs	2,620	1,840	253	317	91	33	86	1,271	933	106	141	50	15	26	1,349	907	147	176	41	18	60
Communications technologies	4,237	3,099	501	377	141	34	85	2,968	2,153	369	264	98	23	61	1,269	946	132	113	43	11	24
Computer and information sciences	28,296	18,774	4,582	2,928	1,286	326	400	21,191	14,523	2,862	2,307	997	202	300	7,105	4,251	1,720	621	289	124	100
Construction trades	4,309	3,572	287	284	86	72	8	4,106	3,415	267	269	79	68	8	203	157	20	15	7	4	0
Education	13,108	8,660	2,163	1,412	279	427	167	1,914	1,301	272	173	55	85	28	11,194	7,359	1,891	1,239	224	342	139
Engineering	2,286	1,478	238	306	146	30	88	1,986	1,307	208	251	121	21	78	300	171	30	55	25	9	10
Engineering technologies[1]	29,334	21,032	3,160	3,323	1,233	315	271	25,261	18,421	2,551	2,776	1,046	252	215	4,073	2,611	609	547	187	63	56
English language and literature/letters	1,402	726	122	354	155	13	32	484	235	38	133	63	4	11	918	491	84	221	92	9	21
Family and consumer sciences	8,613	4,614	1,871	1,561	304	120	143	344	191	64	53	23	2	11	8,269	4,423	1,807	1,508	281	118	132
Foreign languages, literatures, and linguistics	1,258	819	81	277	43	9	29	216	120	8	63	12	3	10	1,042	699	73	214	31	6	19
Health professions and related clinical sciences	155,816	110,963	20,427	13,370	7,749	1,589	1,718	22,934	15,166	2,664	2,525	1,962	224	393	132,882	95,797	17,763	10,845	5,787	1,365	1,325
Legal professions and studies	9,465	6,238	1,662	1,225	205	84	51	1,010	622	190	140	31	18	9	8,455	5,616	1,472	1,085	174	66	42
Liberal arts and sciences, general studies, and humanities	254,012	166,565	28,916	35,871	14,071	2,670	5,919	95,438	64,386	9,613	12,486	5,655	879	2,419	158,574	102,179	19,303	23,385	8,416	1,791	3,500
Library science	117	92	3	17	2	3	0	26	18	0	7	1	0	0	91	74	3	10	1	3	0
Mathematics and statistics	855	436	47	183	128	16	45	575	298	23	137	80	5	32	280	138	24	46	48	11	13
Mechanics and repair technologies	15,297	11,361	1,312	1,685	646	215	78	14,534	10,823	1,219	1,616	612	188	76	763	538	93	69	34	27	2
Military technologies	851	559	159	80	45	8	0	694	465	126	66	31	6	0	157	94	33	14	14	2	0
Multi/interdisciplinary studies	16,255	9,175	1,801	2,987	1,753	142	397	6,549	3,898	749	944	724	61	173	9,706	5,277	1,052	2,043	1,029	81	224
Parks, recreation, leisure and fitness studies	1,344	939	179	137	33	22	34	809	557	121	85	25	9	12	535	382	58	52	8	13	22
Philosophy and religious studies	458	376	17	25	7	1	32	137	104	7	13	2	1	10	321	272	10	12	5	0	22
Physical sciences and science technologies	3,388	2,121	275	393	381	55	163	1,954	1,244	159	237	191	25	98	1,434	877	116	156	190	30	65
Precision production	1,968	1,712	69	100	56	26	5	1,838	1,603	61	92	53	24	5	130	109	8	8	3	2	0
Psychology	2,412	1,440	228	523	120	71	30	554	336	39	120	33	19	7	1,858	1,104	189	403	87	52	23
Public administration and social service professions	4,192	2,268	1,141	580	73	96	34	569	311	149	74	9	18	8	3,623	1,957	992	506	64	78	26
Security and protective services	29,590	19,410	4,540	4,563	618	343	116	16,051	11,866	1,406	2,126	414	171	68	13,539	7,544	3,134	2,437	204	172	48
Social sciences and history	7,812	4,224	777	1,779	685	204	143	2,759	1,588	237	566	257	62	49	5,053	2,636	540	1,213	428	142	94
Social sciences	7,358	3,909	759	1,683	669	196	142	2,499	1,407	228	511	246	58	49	4,859	2,502	531	1,172	423	138	93
History	454	315	18	96	16	7	1	260	181	9	55	11	4	0	194	134	9	41	5	4	1
Theology and religious vocations	582	401	139	22	7	7	6	282	180	85	6	2	5	4	300	221	54	16	5	2	2
Transportation and materials moving	1,550	1,139	123	155	83	17	33	1,308	981	105	126	68	15	13	242	158	18	29	15	2	20
Visual and performing arts	18,890	12,959	1,564	2,266	1,055	192	854	6,927	4,680	693	921	337	69	227	11,963	8,279	871	1,345	718	123	627
Other and not classified	14	0	14	0	0	0	0	3	0	3	0	0	0	0	11	0	11	0	0	0	0

[1] Excludes "Construction trades" and "Mechanics and repair technologies," which are listed separately.

NOTE: Degree-granting institutions grant associate's or higher degrees and participate in Title IV federal financial aid programs. Race categories exclude persons of Hispanic ethnicity. Reported racial/ethnic distributions of students by level of degree, field of degree, and sex were used to estimate race/ethnicity for students whose race/ethnicity was not reported. To facilitate trend comparisons, certain aggregations have been made of the degree fields as reported in the IPEDS Fall survey: "Agriculture and natural resources" includes Agriculture, agriculture operations, and related sciences and Natural resources and conservation; and "Business" includes Business management, marketing, and related support services and Personal and culinary services.

SOURCE: U.S. Department of Education, National Center for Education Statistics, 2007–08 Integrated Postsecondary Education Data System (IPEDS), Fall 2008. (This table was prepared June 2009.)

Bachelor's degrees conferred by degree-granting institutions, by race/ethnicity and sex of student: Selected years, 1976–77 through 2007–08

Year and sex	Number of degrees conferred							Percentage distribution of degrees conferred						
	Total	White	Black	Hispanic	Asian/ Pacific Islander	American Indian/ Alaska Native	Non-resident alien	Total	White	Black	Hispanic	Asian/ Pacific Islander	American Indian/ Alaska Native	Non-resident alien
1	2	3	4	5	6	7	8	9	10	11	12	13	14	15
Total														
1976–77[1]	917,900	807,688	58,636	18,743	13,793	3,326	15,714	100.0	88.0	6.4	2.0	1.5	0.4	1.7
1980–81[2]	934,800	807,319	60,673	21,832	18,794	3,593	22,589	100.0	86.4	6.5	2.3	2.0	0.4	2.4
1989–90	1,051,344	887,151	61,046	32,829	39,230	4,390	26,698	100.0	84.4	5.8	3.1	3.7	0.4	2.5
1990–91	1,094,538	914,093	66,375	37,342	42,529	4,583	29,616	100.0	83.5	6.1	3.4	3.9	0.4	2.7
1992–93	1,165,178	952,194	78,099	45,417	51,481	5,683	32,304	100.0	81.7	6.7	3.9	4.4	0.5	2.8
1993–94	1,169,275	939,008	83,909	50,299	55,689	6,192	34,178	100.0	80.3	7.2	4.3	4.8	0.5	2.9
1994–95	1,160,134	914,610	87,236	54,230	60,502	6,610	36,946	100.0	78.8	7.5	4.7	5.2	0.6	3.2
1995–96	1,164,792	905,846	91,496	58,351	64,433	6,976	37,690	100.0	77.8	7.9	5.0	5.5	0.6	3.2
1996–97	1,172,879	900,809	94,349	62,509	68,859	7,425	38,928	100.0	76.8	8.0	5.3	5.9	0.6	3.3
1997–98	1,184,406	901,344	98,251	66,005	71,678	7,903	39,225	100.0	76.1	8.3	5.6	6.1	0.7	3.3
1998–99	1,200,303	907,245	102,214	70,085	74,197	8,423	38,139	100.0	75.6	8.5	5.8	6.2	0.7	3.2
1999–2000	1,237,875	929,106	108,013	75,059	77,912	8,719	39,066	100.0	75.1	8.7	6.1	6.3	0.7	3.2
2000–01	1,244,171	927,357	111,307	77,745	78,902	9,049	39,811	100.0	74.5	8.9	6.2	6.3	0.7	3.2
2001–02	1,291,900	958,597	116,623	82,966	83,093	9,165	41,456	100.0	74.2	9.0	6.4	6.4	0.7	3.2
2002–03	1,348,811	994,616	124,253	89,029	87,964	9,875	43,074	100.0	73.7	9.2	6.6	6.5	0.7	3.2
2003–04	1,399,542	1,026,114	131,241	94,644	92,073	10,638	44,832	100.0	73.3	9.4	6.8	6.6	0.8	3.2
2004–05	1,439,264	1,049,141	136,122	101,124	97,209	10,307	45,361	100.0	72.9	9.5	7.0	6.8	0.7	3.2
2005–06	1,485,242	1,075,561	142,420	107,588	102,376	10,940	46,357	100.0	72.4	9.6	7.2	6.9	0.7	3.1
2006–07	1,524,092	1,099,850	146,653	114,936	105,297	11,455	45,901	100.0	72.2	9.6	7.5	6.9	0.8	3.0
2007–08	1,563,069	1,122,675	152,457	123,048	109,058	11,509	44,322	100.0	71.8	9.8	7.9	7.0	0.7	2.8
Males														
1976–77[1]	494,424	438,161	25,147	10,318	7,638	1,804	11,356	100.0	88.6	5.1	2.1	1.5	0.4	2.3
1980–81[2]	469,625	406,173	24,511	10,810	10,107	1,700	16,324	100.0	86.5	5.2	2.3	2.2	0.4	3.5
1989–90	491,696	414,982	23,257	14,932	19,711	1,860	16,954	100.0	84.4	4.7	3.0	4.0	0.4	3.4
1990–91	504,045	421,290	24,800	16,598	21,203	1,938	18,216	100.0	83.6	4.9	3.3	4.2	0.4	3.6
1992–93	532,881	437,262	28,962	19,883	25,303	2,450	19,021	100.0	82.1	5.4	3.7	4.7	0.5	3.6
1993–94	532,422	430,526	30,766	21,834	26,952	2,620	19,724	100.0	80.9	5.8	4.1	5.1	0.5	3.7
1994–95	526,131	417,878	31,793	23,626	28,992	2,739	21,103	100.0	79.4	6.0	4.5	5.5	0.5	4.0
1995–96	522,454	409,565	32,974	25,029	30,669	2,885	21,332	100.0	78.4	6.3	4.8	5.9	0.6	4.1
1996–97	520,515	403,366	33,616	26,318	32,521	2,996	21,698	100.0	77.5	6.5	5.1	6.2	0.6	4.2
1997–98	519,956	399,553	34,510	27,677	33,445	3,151	21,620	100.0	76.8	6.6	5.3	6.4	0.6	4.2
1998–99	518,746	396,996	34,876	28,662	34,225	3,323	20,664	100.0	76.5	6.7	5.5	6.6	0.6	4.0
1999–2000	530,367	402,961	37,024	30,301	35,853	3,464	20,764	100.0	76.0	7.0	5.7	6.8	0.7	3.9
2000–01	531,840	401,780	38,103	31,368	35,865	3,700	21,024	100.0	75.5	7.2	5.9	6.7	0.7	4.0
2001–02	549,816	414,892	39,196	32,951	37,660	3,624	21,493	100.0	75.5	7.1	6.0	6.8	0.7	3.9
2002–03	573,258	430,248	41,494	35,101	40,230	3,870	22,315	100.0	75.1	7.2	6.1	7.0	0.7	3.9
2003–04	595,425	445,483	43,851	37,288	41,360	4,244	23,199	100.0	74.8	7.4	6.3	6.9	0.7	3.9
2004–05	613,000	456,592	45,810	39,490	43,711	4,143	23,254	100.0	74.5	7.5	6.4	7.1	0.7	3.8
2005–06	630,600	467,467	48,079	41,814	45,809	4,203	23,228	100.0	74.1	7.6	6.6	7.3	0.7	3.7
2006–07	649,570	480,558	49,685	44,750	47,582	4,505	22,490	100.0	74.0	7.6	6.9	7.3	0.7	3.5
2007–08	667,928	492,137	52,247	47,884	49,485	4,523	21,652	100.0	73.7	7.8	7.2	7.4	0.7	3.2
Females														
1976–77[1]	423,476	369,527	33,489	8,425	6,155	1,522	4,358	100.0	87.3	7.9	2.0	1.5	0.4	1.0
1980–81[2]	465,175	401,146	36,162	11,022	8,687	1,893	6,265	100.0	86.2	7.8	2.4	1.9	0.4	1.3
1989–90	559,648	472,169	37,789	17,897	19,519	2,530	9,744	100.0	84.4	6.8	3.2	3.5	0.5	1.7
1990–91	590,493	492,803	41,575	20,744	21,326	2,645	11,400	100.0	83.5	7.0	3.5	3.6	0.4	1.9
1992–93	632,297	514,932	49,137	25,534	26,178	3,233	13,283	100.0	81.4	7.8	4.0	4.1	0.5	2.1
1993–94	636,853	508,482	53,143	28,465	28,737	3,572	14,454	100.0	79.8	8.3	4.5	4.5	0.6	2.3
1994–95	634,003	496,732	55,443	30,604	31,510	3,871	15,843	100.0	78.3	8.7	4.8	5.0	0.6	2.5
1995–96	642,338	496,281	58,522	33,322	33,764	4,091	16,358	100.0	77.3	9.1	5.2	5.3	0.6	2.5
1996–97	652,364	497,443	60,733	36,191	36,338	4,429	17,230	100.0	76.3	9.3	5.5	5.6	0.7	2.6
1997–98	664,450	501,791	63,741	38,328	38,233	4,752	17,605	100.0	75.5	9.6	5.8	5.8	0.7	2.6
1998–99	681,557	510,249	67,338	41,423	39,972	5,100	17,475	100.0	74.9	9.9	6.1	5.9	0.7	2.6
1999–2000	707,508	526,145	70,989	44,758	42,059	5,255	18,302	100.0	74.4	10.0	6.3	5.9	0.7	2.6
2000–01	712,331	525,577	73,204	46,377	43,037	5,349	18,787	100.0	73.8	10.3	6.5	6.0	0.8	2.6
2001–02	742,084	543,705	77,427	50,015	45,433	5,541	19,963	100.0	73.3	10.4	6.7	6.1	0.7	2.7
2002–03	775,553	564,368	82,759	53,928	47,734	6,005	20,759	100.0	72.8	10.7	7.0	6.2	0.8	2.7
2003–04	804,117	580,631	87,390	57,356	50,713	6,394	21,633	100.0	72.2	10.9	7.1	6.3	0.8	2.7
2004–05	826,264	592,549	90,312	61,634	53,498	6,164	22,107	100.0	71.7	10.9	7.5	6.5	0.7	2.7
2005–06	854,642	608,094	94,341	65,774	56,567	6,737	23,129	100.0	71.2	11.0	7.7	6.6	0.8	2.7
2006–07	874,522	619,292	96,968	70,186	57,715	6,950	23,411	100.0	70.8	11.1	8.0	6.6	0.8	2.7
2007–08	895,141	630,538	100,210	75,164	59,573	6,986	22,670	100.0	70.4	11.2	8.4	6.7	0.8	2.5

[1]Excludes 1,121 males and 528 females whose racial/ethnic group was not available.
[2]Excludes 258 males and 82 females whose racial/ethnic group was not available.
NOTE: Degree-granting institutions grant associate's or higher degrees and participate in Title IV federal financial aid programs. Race categories exclude persons of Hispanic ethnicity. For 1989–90 and later years, reported racial/ethnic distributions of students by level of degree, field of degree, and sex were used to estimate race/ethnicity for students whose race/ethnicity was not reported. (See Appendix A: Guide to Sources for details.) Detail may not sum to totals because of rounding.
SOURCE: U.S. Department of Education, National Center for Education Statistics, Higher Education General Information Survey (HEGIS), "Degrees and Other Formal Awards Conferred" surveys, 1976–77 and 1980–81; and 1989–90 through 2007–08 Integrated Postsecondary Education Data System, "Completions Survey" (IPEDS-C:90–99), and Fall 2000 through Fall 2008. (This table was prepared June 2009.)

Bachelor's degrees conferred by degree-granting institutions, by sex, race/ethnicity, and field of study: 2007–08

Field of study	Total							Males							Females						
	Total	White	Black	Hispanic	Asian/ Pacific Islander	American Indian/ Alaska Native	Non-resident alien	Total	White	Black	Hispanic	Asian/ Pacific Islander	American Indian/ Alaska Native	Non-resident alien	Total	White	Black	Hispanic	Asian/ Pacific Islander	American Indian/ Alaska Native	Non-resident alien
1	2	3	4	5	6	7	8	9	10	11	12	13	14	15	16	17	18	19	20	21	22
All fields, total	1,563,069	1,122,675	152,457	123,048	109,058	11,509	44,322	667,928	492,137	52,247	47,884	49,485	4,523	21,652	895,141	630,538	100,210	75,164	59,573	6,986	22,670
Agriculture and natural resources	24,113	20,733	761	1,174	916	217	312	12,634	11,130	353	483	406	108	154	11,479	9,603	408	691	510	109	158
Architecture and related services	9,805	6,968	490	1,052	818	60	417	5,579	4,071	280	620	379	28	201	4,226	2,897	210	432	439	32	216
Area, ethnic, cultural, and gender studies	8,454	4,654	1,227	1,196	1,017	192	168	2,641	1,468	387	349	310	70	57	5,813	3,186	840	847	707	122	111
Biological and biomedical sciences	77,854	50,875	6,113	5,180	12,961	522	2,203	31,637	21,353	1,639	2,031	5,520	223	871	46,217	29,522	4,474	3,149	7,441	299	1,332
Business	335,254	229,211	37,981	26,099	24,701	2,226	15,036	170,978	123,780	14,512	11,789	12,213	1,010	7,674	164,276	105,431	23,469	14,310	12,488	1,216	7,362
Communications, journalism, and related programs	76,382	58,104	7,563	5,392	3,378	434	1,511	27,043	21,052	2,567	1,728	1,064	133	499	49,339	37,052	4,996	3,664	2,314	301	1,012
Communications technologies	4,666	3,328	456	430	285	26	141	3,341	2,434	274	323	200	18	92	1,325	894	182	107	85	8	49
Computer and information sciences	38,476	25,734	4,461	2,764	3,470	246	1,801	31,694	22,100	2,960	2,258	2,801	184	1,391	6,782	3,634	1,501	506	669	62	410
Construction trades	180	161	7	6	6	0	0	172	157	6	3	6	0	0	8	4	1	3	0	0	0
Education	102,582	86,545	6,595	5,436	2,122	909	975	21,828	18,359	1,621	998	377	204	269	80,754	68,186	4,974	4,438	1,745	705	706
Engineering	68,676	47,617	3,252	4,419	8,850	360	4,178	56,067	39,774	2,309	3,451	6,861	307	3,365	12,609	7,843	943	968	1,989	53	813
Engineering technologies[1]	14,765	11,193	1,397	996	691	118	370	13,266	10,238	1,132	860	631	102	303	1,499	955	265	136	60	16	67
English language and literature/letters	55,038	43,421	4,223	3,871	2,630	367	526	17,681	14,332	1,079	1,190	816	126	138	37,357	29,089	3,144	2,681	1,814	241	388
Family and consumer sciences	21,870	16,540	2,396	1,400	1,081	201	252	2,659	1,915	365	166	153	20	40	19,211	14,625	2,031	1,234	928	181	212
Foreign languages, literatures, and linguistics	20,977	14,865	874	3,484	1,161	120	473	6,254	4,552	238	951	353	34	126	14,723	10,313	636	2,533	808	86	347
Health professions and related clinical sciences	111,478	82,201	12,842	6,749	7,041	834	1,811	16,286	11,314	1,807	1,173	1,494	126	372	95,192	70,887	11,035	5,576	5,547	708	1,439
Legal professions and studies	3,771	2,422	643	403	245	30	28	1,089	759	115	96	101	8	10	2,682	1,663	528	307	144	22	18
Liberal arts and sciences, general studies, and humanities	46,940	31,585	6,533	4,999	1,944	515	1,364	15,876	11,283	2,138	1,206	592	169	488	31,064	20,302	4,395	3,793	1,352	346	876
Library science	68	67	1	0	0	0	0	6	6	0	0	0	0	0	62	61	1	0	0	0	1
Mathematics and statistics	15,192	11,139	818	943	1,531	77	684	8,490	6,224	416	510	882	51	407	6,702	4,915	402	433	649	26	277
Mechanics and repair technologies	232	186	11	11	7	5	12	219	174	10	11	7	5	12	13	12	1	0	0	0	0
Military technologies	39	31	4	3	0	1	0	35	29	2	3	0	1	0	4	2	2	0	0	0	0
Multi/interdisciplinary studies	36,149	24,739	3,239	4,352	2,651	249	919	11,279	7,990	973	972	927	80	337	24,870	16,749	2,266	3,380	1,724	169	582
Parks, recreation, leisure and fitness studies	29,931	23,204	2,937	2,044	1,023	230	493	15,615	11,868	1,712	1,156	527	116	236	14,316	11,336	1,225	888	496	114	257
Philosophy and religious studies	12,257	9,893	665	769	701	77	152	7,696	6,255	364	502	425	50	100	4,561	3,638	301	267	276	27	52
Physical sciences and science technologies	21,934	16,307	1,264	1,138	2,225	149	851	12,959	10,057	536	636	1,163	70	497	8,975	6,250	728	502	1,062	79	354
Precision production	33	25	2	4	0	0	2	22	18	1	1	0	0	1	11	7	1	3	0	0	1
Psychology	92,587	64,401	10,940	8,816	6,274	676	1,471	21,202	14,946	2,096	1,921	1,754	160	325	71,385	49,464	8,844	6,895	4,520	516	1,146
Public administration and social service professions	23,493	13,726	5,447	2,915	848	256	301	4,202	2,553	829	501	195	55	69	19,291	11,173	4,618	2,414	653	201	232
Security and protective services	40,235	25,359	7,599	5,269	1,253	348	407	20,149	14,149	2,695	2,274	698	142	191	20,086	11,210	4,904	2,995	555	206	216
Social sciences and history	167,363	118,552	15,290	14,646	13,051	1,376	4,448	84,868	63,521	5,821	6,451	6,218	637	2,220	82,495	55,031	9,469	8,195	6,833	739	2,228
Social sciences	132,922	90,112	13,545	12,222	11,736	1,088	4,219	64,512	46,324	5,009	5,081	5,530	468	2,100	68,410	43,788	8,536	7,141	6,206	620	2,119
History	34,441	28,440	1,745	2,424	1,315	288	229	20,356	17,197	812	1,370	688	169	120	14,085	11,243	933	1,054	627	119	109
Theology and religious vocations	8,992	7,646	599	323	197	31	196	5,873	5,089	294	202	127	15	146	3,119	2,557	305	121	70	16	50
Transportation and materials moving	5,203	4,159	347	345	194	44	114	4,604	3,688	305	311	170	34	95	599	471	42	34	24	9	19
Visual and performing arts	87,703	67,039	5,155	6,416	5,782	613	2,698	33,862	25,488	2,306	2,756	2,113	236	963	53,841	41,551	2,849	3,660	3,669	377	1,735
Other and not classified	377	36	325	4	3	0	9	122	11	104	2	1	0	4	255	25	221	2	2	0	5

[1]Excludes "Construction trades" and "Mechanics and repair technologies," which are listed separately.

NOTE: Degree-granting institutions grant associate's or higher degrees and participate in Title IV federal financial aid programs. Race categories exclude persons of Hispanic ethnicity. Reported racial/ethnic distributions of students by level of degree, field of degree, and sex were used to estimate race/ethnicity for students whose race/ethnicity was not reported. To facilitate trend comparisons, certain aggregations have been made of the degree fields as reported in the IPEDS Fall survey: "Agriculture and natural resources" includes Agriculture, agriculture operations, and related sciences and Natural resources and conservation; and "Business" includes Business management, marketing, and related support services and Personal and culinary services.

SOURCE: U.S. Department of Education, National Center for Education Statistics, 2007–08 Integrated Postsecondary Education Data System (IPEDS), Fall 2008. (This table was prepared June 2009.)

Master's degrees conferred by degree-granting institutions, by race/ethnicity and sex of student: Selected years, 1976–77 through 2007–08

Year and sex	Number of degrees conferred							Percentage distribution of degrees conferred						
	Total	White	Black	Hispanic	Asian/ Pacific Islander	American Indian/ Alaska Native	Non-resident alien	Total	White	Black	Hispanic	Asian/ Pacific Islander	American Indian/ Alaska Native	Non-resident alien
1	2	3	4	5	6	7	8	9	10	11	12	13	14	15
Total														
1976–77[1]	316,602	266,061	21,037	6,071	5,122	967	17,344	100.0	84.0	6.6	1.9	1.6	0.3	5.5
1980–81[2]	294,183	241,216	17,133	6,461	6,282	1,034	22,057	100.0	82.0	5.8	2.2	2.1	0.4	7.5
1989–90	324,301	254,299	15,336	7,892	10,439	1,090	35,245	100.0	78.4	4.7	2.4	3.2	0.3	10.9
1990–91	337,168	261,232	16,616	8,887	11,650	1,178	37,605	100.0	77.5	4.9	2.6	3.5	0.3	11.2
1992–93	369,585	279,827	19,744	10,638	13,863	1,405	44,108	100.0	75.7	5.3	2.9	3.8	0.4	11.9
1993–94	387,070	289,536	21,986	11,933	15,411	1,699	46,505	100.0	74.8	5.7	3.1	4.0	0.4	12.0
1994–95	397,629	293,345	24,166	12,905	16,847	1,621	48,745	100.0	73.8	6.1	3.2	4.2	0.4	12.3
1995–96	406,301	298,133	25,822	14,442	18,216	1,778	47,910	100.0	73.4	6.4	3.6	4.5	0.4	11.8
1996–97	419,401	305,005	28,403	15,440	19,061	1,940	49,552	100.0	72.7	6.8	3.7	4.5	0.5	11.8
1997–98	430,164	308,196	30,155	16,248	21,133	2,053	52,379	100.0	71.6	7.0	3.8	4.9	0.5	12.2
1998–99	439,986	313,487	32,541	17,838	22,072	2,016	52,032	100.0	71.2	7.4	4.1	5.0	0.5	11.8
1999–2000	457,056	320,485	35,874	19,253	23,218	2,246	55,980	100.0	70.1	7.8	4.2	5.1	0.5	12.2
2000–01	468,476	320,480	38,265	21,543	24,283	2,481	61,424	100.0	68.4	8.2	4.6	5.2	0.5	13.1
2001–02	482,118	327,645	40,370	22,385	25,411	2,624	63,683	100.0	68.0	8.4	4.6	5.3	0.5	13.2
2002–03	513,339	342,131	44,438	25,047	27,264	2,858	71,601	100.0	66.6	8.7	4.9	5.3	0.6	13.9
2003–04	558,940	369,582	50,657	29,666	30,952	3,192	74,891	100.0	66.1	9.1	5.3	5.5	0.6	13.4
2004–05	574,618	379,350	54,482	31,485	32,783	3,295	73,223	100.0	66.0	9.5	5.5	5.7	0.6	12.7
2005–06	594,065	393,357	58,976	32,438	34,029	3,504	71,761	100.0	66.2	9.9	5.5	5.7	0.6	12.1
2006–07	604,607	399,267	62,574	34,822	36,134	3,575	68,235	100.0	66.0	10.3	5.8	6.0	0.6	11.3
2007–08	625,023	409,312	65,062	36,801	37,408	3,758	72,682	100.0	65.5	10.4	5.9	6.0	0.6	11.6
Males														
1976–77[1]	167,396	139,210	7,781	3,268	3,123	521	13,493	100.0	83.2	4.6	2.0	1.9	0.3	8.1
1980–81[2]	145,666	115,562	6,158	3,085	3,773	501	16,587	100.0	79.3	4.2	2.1	2.6	0.3	11.4
1989–90	153,653	114,203	5,474	3,548	5,896	455	24,077	100.0	74.3	3.6	2.3	3.8	0.3	15.7
1990–91	156,482	114,419	5,916	3,936	6,575	488	25,148	100.0	73.1	3.8	2.5	4.2	0.3	16.1
1992–93	169,258	120,783	6,803	4,722	7,545	584	28,821	100.0	71.4	4.0	2.8	4.5	0.3	17.0
1993–94	176,085	124,409	7,424	5,122	8,298	692	30,140	100.0	70.7	4.2	2.9	4.7	0.4	17.1
1994–95	178,598	124,277	8,097	5,487	8,923	659	31,155	100.0	69.6	4.5	3.1	5.0	0.4	17.4
1995–96	179,081	124,847	8,445	5,843	9,400	705	29,841	100.0	69.7	4.7	3.3	5.2	0.4	16.7
1996–97	180,947	125,552	8,960	6,246	9,218	734	30,237	100.0	69.4	5.0	3.5	5.1	0.4	16.7
1997–98	184,375	125,605	9,652	6,512	10,262	782	31,562	100.0	68.1	5.2	3.5	5.6	0.4	17.1
1998–99	186,148	126,674	10,058	7,032	10,491	771	31,122	100.0	68.1	5.4	3.8	5.6	0.4	16.7
1999–2000	191,792	128,046	11,212	7,635	11,047	836	33,016	100.0	66.8	5.8	4.0	5.8	0.4	17.2
2000–01	194,351	125,993	11,568	8,271	11,349	917	36,253	100.0	64.8	6.0	4.3	5.8	0.5	18.7
2001–02	199,120	128,776	11,795	8,430	11,746	993	37,380	100.0	64.7	5.9	4.2	5.9	0.5	18.8
2002–03	211,664	133,398	12,869	9,270	12,518	1,027	42,582	100.0	63.0	6.1	4.4	5.9	0.5	20.1
2003–04	229,545	143,827	14,653	10,813	14,347	1,127	44,778	100.0	62.7	6.4	4.7	6.3	0.5	19.5
2004–05	233,590	147,546	15,733	11,385	15,031	1,160	42,735	100.0	63.2	6.7	4.9	6.4	0.5	18.3
2005–06	237,896	150,954	16,959	11,637	15,803	1,244	41,299	100.0	63.5	7.1	4.9	6.6	0.5	17.4
2006–07	238,189	151,358	17,907	12,362	16,451	1,264	38,847	100.0	63.5	7.5	5.2	6.9	0.5	16.3
2007–08	246,491	155,035	18,357	13,057	17,227	1,280	41,535	100.0	62.9	7.4	5.3	7.0	0.5	16.9
Females														
1976–77[1]	149,206	126,851	13,256	2,803	1,999	446	3,851	100.0	85.0	8.9	1.9	1.3	0.3	2.6
1980–81[2]	148,517	125,654	10,975	3,376	2,509	533	5,470	100.0	84.6	7.4	2.3	1.7	0.4	3.7
1989–90	170,648	140,096	9,862	4,344	4,543	635	11,168	100.0	82.1	5.8	2.5	2.7	0.4	6.5
1990–91	180,686	146,813	10,700	4,951	5,075	690	12,457	100.0	81.3	5.9	2.7	2.8	0.4	6.9
1992–93	200,327	159,044	12,941	5,916	6,318	821	15,287	100.0	79.4	6.5	3.0	3.2	0.4	7.6
1993–94	210,985	165,127	14,562	6,811	7,113	1,007	16,365	100.0	78.3	6.9	3.2	3.4	0.5	7.8
1994–95	219,031	169,068	16,069	7,418	7,924	962	17,590	100.0	77.2	7.3	3.4	3.6	0.4	8.0
1995–96	227,220	173,286	17,377	8,599	8,816	1,073	18,069	100.0	76.3	7.6	3.8	3.9	0.5	8.0
1996–97	238,454	179,453	19,443	9,194	9,843	1,206	19,315	100.0	75.3	8.2	3.9	4.1	0.5	8.1
1997–98	245,789	182,591	20,503	9,736	10,871	1,271	20,817	100.0	74.3	8.3	4.0	4.4	0.5	8.5
1998–99	253,838	186,813	22,483	10,806	11,581	1,245	20,910	100.0	73.6	8.9	4.3	4.6	0.5	8.2
1999–2000	265,264	192,439	24,662	11,618	12,171	1,410	22,964	100.0	72.5	9.3	4.4	4.6	0.5	8.7
2000–01	274,125	194,487	26,697	13,272	12,934	1,564	25,171	100.0	70.9	9.7	4.8	4.7	0.6	9.2
2001–02	282,998	198,869	28,575	13,955	13,665	1,631	26,303	100.0	70.3	10.1	4.9	4.8	0.6	9.3
2002–03	301,675	208,733	31,569	15,777	14,746	1,831	29,019	100.0	69.2	10.5	5.2	4.9	0.6	9.6
2003–04	329,395	225,755	36,004	18,853	16,605	2,065	30,113	100.0	68.5	10.9	5.7	5.0	0.6	9.1
2004–05	341,028	231,804	38,749	20,100	17,752	2,135	30,488	100.0	68.0	11.4	5.9	5.2	0.6	8.9
2005–06	356,169	242,403	42,017	20,801	18,226	2,260	30,462	100.0	68.1	11.8	5.8	5.1	0.6	8.6
2006–07	366,418	247,909	44,667	22,460	19,683	2,311	29,388	100.0	67.7	12.2	6.1	5.4	0.6	8.0
2007–08	378,532	254,277	46,705	23,744	20,181	2,478	31,147	100.0	67.2	12.3	6.3	5.3	0.7	8.2

[1]Excludes 387 males and 175 females whose racial/ethnic group was not available.
[2]Excludes 1,377 males and 179 females whose racial/ethnic group was not available.
NOTE: Degree-granting institutions grant associate's or higher degrees and participate in Title IV federal financial aid programs. Race categories exclude persons of Hispanic ethnicity. For 1989–90 and later years, reported racial/ethnic distributions of students by level of degree, field of degree, and sex were used to estimate race/ethnicity for students whose race/ethnicity was not reported. (See Appendix A: Guide to Sources for details.) Detail may not sum to totals because of rounding.

SOURCE: U.S. Department of Education, National Center for Education Statistics, Higher Education General Information Survey (HEGIS), "Degrees and Other Formal Awards Conferred" surveys, 1976–77 and 1980–81; and 1989–90 through 2007–08 Integrated Postsecondary Education Data System, "Completions Survey" (IPEDS-C:90–99), and Fall 2000 through Fall 2008. (This table was prepared June 2009.)

Master's degrees conferred by degree-granting institutions, by sex, race/ethnicity, and field of study: 2007–08

Field of study	Total							Males							Females						
	Total	White	Black	Hispanic	Asian/ Pacific Islander	American Indian/ Alaska Native	Non-resident alien	Total	White	Black	Hispanic	Asian/ Pacific Islander	American Indian/ Alaska Native	Non-resident alien	Total	White	Black	Hispanic	Asian/ Pacific Islander	American Indian/ Alaska Native	Non-resident alien
1	2	3	4	5	6	7	8	9	10	11	12	13	14	15	16	17	18	19	20	21	22
All fields, total	625,023	409,312	65,062	36,801	37,408	3,758	72,662	246,491	155,035	18,357	13,057	17,227	1,280	41,535	378,532	254,277	46,705	23,744	20,181	2,478	31,147
Agriculture and natural resources	4,684	3,546	124	128	113	36	737	2,180	1,651	46	56	46	12	369	2,504	1,895	78	72	67	24	368
Architecture and related services	6,065	4,063	253	357	405	31	956	3,252	2,277	121	191	170	16	477	2,813	1,786	132	166	235	15	479
Area, ethnic, cultural, and gender studies	1,778	960	196	198	132	36	256	642	366	53	72	44	18	89	1,136	594	143	126	88	18	167
Biological and biomedical sciences	9,565	5,797	597	494	1,120	65	1,492	4,041	2,544	188	188	483	31	607	5,524	3,253	409	306	637	34	885
Business	155,637	90,269	20,569	8,553	13,604	851	21,791	86,258	53,301	7,277	4,443	7,835	415	12,987	69,379	36,968	13,292	4,110	5,769	436	8,804
Communications, journalism, and related programs	6,915	4,407	738	387	367	45	971	2,216	1,489	187	111	106	10	313	4,699	2,918	551	276	261	35	658
Communications technologies	631	282	49	39	50	0	211	364	185	25	19	26	0	109	267	97	24	20	24	0	102
Computer and information sciences	17,087	6,108	1,120	484	1,919	52	7,404	12,513	4,802	668	370	1,289	41	5,343	4,574	1,306	452	114	630	11	2,061
Construction trades	0	0	0	0	0	0	0	0	0	0	0	0	0	0	0	0	0	0	0	0	0
Education	175,880	134,870	18,001	12,028	4,553	1,209	5,219	40,055	31,104	3,710	2,679	930	291	1,341	135,825	103,766	14,291	9,349	3,623	918	3,878
Engineering	31,719	12,685	993	1,145	3,700	83	13,113	24,446	10,205	705	828	2,607	64	10,037	7,273	2,480	288	317	1,093	19	3,076
Engineering technologies[1]	2,873	1,379	228	151	261	18	836	2,128	1,082	134	102	188	8	614	745	297	94	49	73	10	222
English language and literature/letters	9,161	7,425	499	441	347	58	391	3,027	2,510	125	135	120	33	104	6,134	4,915	374	306	227	25	287
Family and consumer sciences	2,199	1,569	247	93	83	18	189	316	224	31	18	12	2	29	1,883	1,345	216	75	71	16	160
Foreign languages, literatures, and linguistics	3,565	2,082	86	531	162	13	691	1,128	701	26	151	46	6	198	2,437	1,381	60	380	116	7	493
Health professions and related clinical sciences	58,120	41,373	6,143	3,266	4,141	404	2,793	11,010	7,091	972	721	1,050	78	1,098	47,110	34,282	5,171	2,545	3,091	326	1,695
Legal professions and studies	4,754	1,575	208	164	284	16	2,507	2,394	818	75	98	123	9	1,271	2,360	757	133	66	161	7	1,236
Liberal arts and sciences, general studies, and humanities	3,797	2,851	348	177	171	32	218	1,443	1,075	115	69	82	13	89	2,354	1,776	233	108	89	19	129
Library science	7,162	6,043	387	350	230	44	108	1,429	1,202	66	75	47	10	29	5,733	4,841	321	275	183	34	79
Mathematics and statistics	4,980	2,393	169	175	431	12	1,800	2,860	1,420	81	104	222	4	1,029	2,120	973	88	71	209	8	771
Mechanics and repair technologies	0	0	0	0	0	0	0	0	0	0	0	0	0	0	0	0	0	0	0	0	0
Military technologies	0	0	0	0	0	0	0	0	0	0	0	0	0	0	0	0	0	0	0	0	0
Multi/interdisciplinary studies	5,289	3,637	424	332	285	42	569	1,807	1,213	123	100	88	17	266	3,482	2,424	301	232	197	25	303
Parks, recreation, leisure and fitness studies	4,440	3,460	394	178	98	26	284	2,313	1,788	202	93	51	13	166	2,127	1,672	192	85	47	13	118
Philosophy and religious studies	1,879	1,488	80	79	80	8	144	1,228	980	40	57	57	6	88	651	508	40	22	23	2	56
Physical sciences and science technologies	5,899	3,551	192	214	302	23	1,617	3,649	2,227	93	127	148	8	1,046	2,250	1,324	99	87	154	15	571
Precision production	3	3	0	0	0	0	0	2	2	0	0	0	0	0	1	1	0	0	0	0	1
Psychology	21,431	15,097	2,920	1,680	893	128	713	4,356	3,211	421	383	177	21	143	17,075	11,886	2,499	1,297	716	107	570
Public administration and social service professions	33,029	20,774	6,168	2,772	1,407	293	1,615	8,140	5,075	1,271	636	337	59	762	24,889	15,699	4,897	2,136	1,070	234	853
Security and protective services	5,760	3,819	1,141	505	152	36	107	2,653	1,892	373	248	74	13	53	3,107	1,927	768	257	78	23	54
Social sciences and history	18,495	11,951	1,330	952	938	89	3,235	9,349	6,235	520	469	412	35	1,678	9,146	5,716	810	483	526	54	1,557
Social sciences	15,092	9,044	1,186	820	860	71	3,111	7,393	4,536	453	388	370	28	1,618	7,699	4,508	733	432	490	43	1,493
History	3,403	2,907	144	132	78	18	124	1,956	1,699	67	81	42	7	60	1,447	1,208	77	51	36	11	64
Theology and religious vocations	6,996	5,163	662	198	304	26	643	4,443	3,292	346	131	180	16	478	2,553	1,871	316	67	124	10	165
Transportation and materials moving	982	788	71	66	27	10	20	829	674	56	53	19	9	18	153	114	15	13	8	1	2
Visual and performing arts	14,164	9,892	656	664	848	54	2,050	5,998	4,395	290	330	258	22	703	8,166	5,497	366	334	590	32	1,347
Other and not classified	84	13	69	0	1	0	1	22	4	17	0	0	0	1	62	9	52	0	1	0	0

[1]Excludes "Construction trades" and "Mechanics and repair technologies," which are listed separately.

NOTE: Degree-granting institutions grant associate's or higher degrees and participate in Title IV federal financial aid programs. Race categories exclude persons of Hispanic ethnicity. Reported racial/ethnic distributions of students by level of degree, field of degree, and sex were used to estimate race/ethnicity for students whose race/ethnicity was not reported. To facilitate trend comparisons, certain aggregations have been made of the degree fields as reported in the IPEDS Fall survey. "Agriculture and natural resources" includes Agriculture, agriculture operations, and related sciences and Natural resources and conservation; and "Business" includes Business management, marketing, and related support services and Personal and culinary services.

SOURCE: U.S. Department of Education, National Center for Education Statistics, 2007–08 Integrated Postsecondary Education Data System (IPEDS), Fall 2008. (This table was prepared June 2009.)

Doctor's degrees conferred by degree-granting institutions, by race/ethnicity and sex of student: Selected years, 1976–77 through 2007–08

Year and sex	Number of degrees conferred[1]							Percentage distribution of degrees conferred[1]						
	Total	White	Black	Hispanic	Asian/ Pacific Islander	American Indian/ Alaska Native	Non-resident alien	Total	White	Black	Hispanic	Asian/ Pacific Islander	American Indian/ Alaska Native	Non-resident alien
1	2	3	4	5	6	7	8	9	10	11	12	13	14	15
Total														
1976–77[2]	33,126	26,851	1,253	522	658	95	3,747	100.0	81.1	3.8	1.6	2.0	0.3	11.3
1980–81[3]	32,839	25,908	1,265	456	877	130	4,203	100.0	78.9	3.9	1.4	2.7	0.4	12.8
1989–90	38,371	26,221	1,149	780	1,225	98	8,898	100.0	68.3	3.0	2.0	3.2	0.3	23.2
1990–91	39,294	25,855	1,248	757	1,504	106	9,824	100.0	65.8	3.2	1.9	3.8	0.3	25.0
1992–93	42,132	26,816	1,350	824	1,578	107	11,457	100.0	63.6	3.2	2.0	3.7	0.3	27.2
1993–94	43,185	27,212	1,385	900	2,024	134	11,530	100.0	63.0	3.2	2.1	4.7	0.3	26.7
1994–95	44,446	27,846	1,667	984	2,689	130	11,130	100.0	62.7	3.8	2.2	6.1	0.3	25.0
1995–96	44,652	27,773	1,632	997	2,641	159	11,450	100.0	62.2	3.7	2.2	5.9	0.4	25.6
1996–97	45,876	28,596	1,865	1,120	2,667	175	11,453	100.0	62.3	4.1	2.4	5.8	0.4	25.0
1997–98	46,010	28,803	2,067	1,275	2,339	186	11,340	100.0	62.6	4.5	2.8	5.1	0.4	24.6
1998–99	44,077	27,838	2,136	1,302	2,299	194	10,308	100.0	63.2	4.8	3.0	5.2	0.4	23.4
1999–2000	44,808	27,843	2,246	1,305	2,420	160	10,834	100.0	62.1	5.0	2.9	5.4	0.4	24.2
2000–01	44,904	27,454	2,207	1,516	2,587	177	10,963	100.0	61.1	4.9	3.4	5.8	0.4	24.4
2001–02	44,160	26,903	2,395	1,434	2,319	180	10,929	100.0	60.9	5.4	3.2	5.3	0.4	24.7
2002–03	46,042	27,709	2,522	1,562	2,424	196	11,629	100.0	60.2	5.5	3.4	5.3	0.4	25.3
2003–04	48,378	28,214	2,900	1,662	2,632	217	12,753	100.0	58.3	6.0	3.4	5.4	0.4	26.4
2004–05	52,631	30,261	3,056	1,824	2,911	237	14,342	100.0	57.5	5.8	3.5	5.5	0.5	27.3
2005–06	56,067	31,601	3,122	1,882	3,257	230	15,975	100.0	56.4	5.6	3.4	5.8	0.4	28.5
2006–07	60,616	34,071	3,727	2,034	3,541	249	16,994	100.0	56.2	6.1	3.4	5.8	0.4	28.0
2007–08	63,712	36,390	3,906	2,279	3,618	272	17,247	100.0	57.1	6.1	3.6	5.7	0.4	27.1
Males														
1976–77[2]	25,036	20,032	766	383	540	67	3,248	100.0	80.0	3.1	1.5	2.2	0.3	13.0
1980–81[3]	22,595	17,310	694	277	655	95	3,564	100.0	76.6	3.1	1.2	2.9	0.4	15.8
1989–90	24,401	15,314	531	419	865	49	7,223	100.0	62.8	2.2	1.7	3.5	0.2	29.6
1990–91	24,756	14,853	597	399	1,017	59	7,831	100.0	60.0	2.4	1.6	4.1	0.2	31.6
1992–93	26,073	14,991	617	437	1,040	52	8,936	100.0	57.5	2.4	1.7	4.0	0.2	34.3
1993–94	26,552	15,159	627	463	1,373	66	8,864	100.0	57.1	2.4	1.7	5.2	0.2	33.4
1994–95	26,916	15,375	730	488	1,756	58	8,509	100.0	57.1	2.7	1.8	6.5	0.2	31.6
1995–96	26,841	15,112	727	514	1,692	80	8,716	100.0	56.3	2.7	1.9	6.3	0.3	32.5
1996–97	27,146	15,499	795	585	1,645	87	8,535	100.0	57.1	2.9	2.2	6.1	0.3	31.4
1997–98	26,664	15,399	824	652	1,392	83	8,314	100.0	57.8	3.1	2.4	5.2	0.3	31.2
1998–99	25,146	14,726	873	625	1,337	92	7,493	100.0	58.6	3.5	2.5	5.3	0.4	29.8
1999–2000	25,028	14,472	876	611	1,356	57	7,656	100.0	57.8	3.5	2.4	5.4	0.2	30.6
2000–01	24,728	13,937	855	687	1,453	76	7,720	100.0	56.4	3.5	2.8	5.9	0.3	31.2
2001–02	23,708	13,330	922	650	1,242	67	7,497	100.0	56.2	3.9	2.7	5.2	0.3	31.6
2002–03	24,351	13,478	915	741	1,243	76	7,898	100.0	55.3	3.8	3.0	5.1	0.3	32.4
2003–04	25,323	13,567	1,015	766	1,293	90	8,592	100.0	53.6	4.0	3.0	5.1	0.4	33.9
2004–05	26,973	14,023	1,049	764	1,403	87	9,647	100.0	52.0	3.9	2.8	5.2	0.3	35.8
2005–06	28,634	14,659	1,081	826	1,555	105	10,408	100.0	51.2	3.8	2.9	5.4	0.4	36.3
2006–07	30,251	15,268	1,282	892	1,703	96	11,010	100.0	50.5	4.2	2.9	5.6	0.3	36.4
2007–08	31,215	16,168	1,312	977	1,628	115	11,015	100.0	51.8	4.2	3.1	5.2	0.4	35.3
Females														
1976–77	8,090	6,819	487	139	118	28	499	100.0	84.3	6.0	1.7	1.5	0.3	6.2
1980–81[3]	10,244	8,598	571	179	222	35	639	100.0	83.9	5.6	1.7	2.2	0.3	6.2
1989–90	13,970	10,907	618	361	360	49	1,675	100.0	78.1	4.4	2.6	2.6	0.4	12.0
1990–91	14,538	11,002	651	358	487	47	1,993	100.0	75.7	4.5	2.5	3.3	0.3	13.7
1992–93	16,059	11,825	733	387	538	55	2,521	100.0	73.6	4.6	2.4	3.4	0.3	15.7
1993–94	16,633	12,053	758	437	651	68	2,666	100.0	72.5	4.6	2.6	3.9	0.4	16.0
1994–95	17,530	12,471	937	496	933	72	2,621	100.0	71.1	5.3	2.8	5.3	0.4	15.0
1995–96	17,811	12,661	905	483	949	79	2,734	100.0	71.1	5.1	2.7	5.3	0.4	15.4
1996–97	18,730	13,097	1,070	535	1,022	88	2,918	100.0	69.9	5.7	2.9	5.5	0.5	15.6
1997–98	19,346	13,404	1,243	623	947	103	3,026	100.0	69.3	6.4	3.2	4.9	0.5	15.6
1998–99	18,931	13,112	1,263	677	962	102	2,815	100.0	69.3	6.7	3.6	5.1	0.5	14.9
1999–2000	19,780	13,371	1,370	694	1,064	103	3,178	100.0	67.6	6.9	3.5	5.4	0.5	16.1
2000–01	20,176	13,517	1,352	829	1,134	101	3,243	100.0	67.0	6.7	4.1	5.6	0.5	16.1
2001–02	20,452	13,573	1,473	784	1,077	113	3,432	100.0	66.4	7.2	3.8	5.3	0.6	16.8
2002–03	21,691	14,231	1,607	821	1,181	120	3,731	100.0	65.6	7.4	3.8	5.4	0.6	17.2
2003–04	23,055	14,647	1,885	896	1,339	127	4,161	100.0	63.5	8.2	3.9	5.8	0.6	18.0
2004–05	25,658	16,238	2,007	1,060	1,508	150	4,695	100.0	63.3	7.8	4.1	5.9	0.6	18.3
2005–06	27,433	16,942	2,041	1,056	1,702	125	5,567	100.0	61.8	7.4	3.8	6.2	0.5	20.3
2006–07	30,365	18,803	2,445	1,142	1,838	153	5,984	100.0	61.9	8.1	3.8	6.1	0.5	19.7
2007–08	32,497	20,222	2,594	1,302	1,990	157	6,232	100.0	62.2	8.0	4.0	6.1	0.5	19.2

[1]Includes Ph.D., Ed.D, and comparable degrees at the doctoral level. Excludes first-professional degrees, such as M.D., D.D.S., and law degrees.
[2]Excludes 106 males whose racial/ethnic group was not available.
[3]Excludes 116 males and 3 females whose racial/ethnic group was not available.
NOTE: Degree-granting institutions grant associate's or higher degrees and participate in Title IV federal financial aid programs. Race categories exclude persons of Hispanic ethnicity. For 1989–90 and later years, reported racial/ethnic distributions of students by level of degree, field of degree, and sex were used to estimate race/ethnicity for students whose race/ethnicity was not reported. (See Appendix A: Guide to Sources for details.) Detail may not sum to totals because of rounding.
SOURCE: U.S. Department of Education, National Center for Education Statistics, Higher Education General Information Survey (HEGIS), "Degrees and Other Formal Awards Conferred" surveys, 1976–77 and 1980–81; and 1989–90 through 2007–08 Integrated Postsecondary Education Data System, "Completions Survey" (IPEDS-C:90–99), and Fall 2000 through Fall 2008. (This table was prepared June 2009.)

Doctor's degrees conferred by degree-granting institutions, by sex, race/ethnicity, and field of study: 2007–08

Field of study	Total							Males							Females						
	Total	White	Black	Hispanic	Asian/ Pacific Islander	American Indian/ Alaska Native	Non-resident alien	Total	White	Black	Hispanic	Asian/ Pacific Islander	American Indian/ Alaska Native	Non-resident alien	Total	White	Black	Hispanic	Asian/ Pacific Islander	American Indian/ Alaska Native	Non-resident alien
1	2	3	4	5	6	7	8	9	10	11	12	13	14	15	16	17	18	19	20	21	22
All fields, total	63,712	36,390	3,906	2,279	3,618	272	17,247	31,215	16,168	1,312	977	1,628	115	11,015	32,497	20,222	2,594	1,302	1,990	157	6,232
Agriculture and natural resources	1,257	633	31	22	41	8	522	742	389	10	13	17	5	308	515	244	21	9	24	3	214
Architecture and related services	199	66	10	5	26	0	92	103	31	4	4	12	0	52	96	35	6	1	14	0	40
Area, ethnic, cultural, and gender studies	270	132	41	14	12	7	64	103	50	20	6	2	3	22	167	82	21	8	10	4	42
Biological and biomedical sciences	6,918	3,690	241	253	595	17	2,122	3,403	1,873	91	118	271	5	1,045	3,515	1,817	150	135	324	12	1,077
Business	2,084	1,004	228	60	114	15	663	1,250	624	110	39	64	12	401	834	380	118	21	50	3	262
Communications, journalism, and related programs	489	275	47	18	18	3	128	206	121	8	7	11	0	59	283	154	39	11	7	3	69
Communications technologies	7	2	2	0	0	0	3	3	2	0	0	0	0	1	4	0	2	0	0	0	2
Computer and information sciences	1,698	526	30	14	102	0	1,026	1,323	410	15	11	80	0	807	375	116	15	3	22	0	219
Construction trades	0	0	0	0	0	0	0	0	0	0	0	0	0	0	0	0	0	0	0	0	0
Education	8,491	5,589	1,437	442	283	61	679	2,773	1,906	383	149	58	24	253	5,718	3,683	1,054	293	225	37	426
Engineering	8,112	2,324	140	140	552	16	4,940	6,368	1,788	88	99	385	11	3,997	1,744	536	52	41	167	5	943
Engineering technologies[1]	55	25	2	0	2	0	26	45	21	1	0	2	0	21	10	4	1	0	0	0	5
English language and literature/letters	1,262	977	52	42	65	2	124	453	366	12	22	18	2	33	809	611	40	20	47	0	91
Family and consumer sciences	323	163	44	12	9	1	94	84	46	6	3	1	1	28	239	117	38	9	8	1	66
Foreign languages, literatures, and linguistics	1,078	541	23	84	47	4	379	431	231	7	27	15	3	148	647	310	16	57	32	1	231
Health professions and related clinical sciences	9,886	7,738	456	359	577	45	711	2,674	1,941	101	125	180	11	316	7,212	5,797	355	234	397	34	395
Legal professions and studies	172	30	4	1	5	0	132	104	18	3	0	2	0	81	68	12	1	1	3	0	51
Liberal arts and sciences, general studies, and humanities	76	59	9	2	0	1	5	30	24	4	1	0	0	1	46	35	5	1	0	1	4
Library science	64	34	4	2	3	0	21	21	12	4	2	0	0	5	43	22	0	2	3	0	16
Mathematics and statistics	1,360	550	25	33	59	2	691	938	376	13	28	33	2	486	422	174	12	5	26	0	205
Mechanics and repair technologies	0	0	0	0	0	0	0	0	0	0	0	0	0	0	0	0	0	0	0	0	0
Military technologies	0	0	0	0	0	0	0	0	0	0	0	0	0	0	0	0	0	0	0	0	0
Multi/interdisciplinary studies	1,142	683	67	50	79	7	256	506	297	24	27	35	2	121	636	386	43	23	44	5	135
Parks, recreation, leisure and fitness studies	228	151	6	6	6	1	58	126	82	2	4	2	1	33	102	69	4	2	2	0	25
Philosophy and religious studies	635	449	34	12	39	4	97	442	321	21	10	26	3	61	193	128	13	2	13	1	36
Physical sciences and science technologies	4,804	2,228	92	120	243	8	2,113	3,363	1,579	50	73	146	6	1,509	1,441	649	42	47	97	2	604
Precision production	0	0	0	0	0	0	0	0	0	0	0	0	0	0	0	0	0	0	0	0	0
Psychology	5,296	3,935	358	325	317	44	317	1,440	1,112	83	80	68	13	84	3,856	2,823	275	245	249	31	233
Public administration and social service professions	760	446	103	39	40	4	128	269	155	22	13	14	1	64	491	291	81	26	26	3	64
Security and protective services	88	55	11	2	4	1	15	39	20	6	0	3	0	9	49	35	5	1	1	0	6
Social sciences and history	4,059	2,254	185	162	205	15	1,238	2,194	1,191	85	75	84	9	750	1,865	1,063	100	87	121	6	488
Social sciences	3,199	1,619	128	121	177	9	1,145	1,705	818	60	54	75	5	693	1,494	801	68	67	102	4	452
History	860	635	57	41	28	6	93	489	373	25	21	9	4	57	371	262	32	20	19	2	36
Theology and religious vocations	1,446	886	182	25	87	1	265	1,107	686	117	21	71	0	212	339	200	65	4	16	1	53
Transportation and materials moving	0	0	0	0	0	0	0	0	0	0	0	0	0	0	0	0	0	0	0	0	0
Visual and performing arts	1,453	945	42	35	88	5	338	675	496	22	21	26	2	108	778	449	20	14	62	3	230

[1]Excludes "Construction trades" and "Mechanics and repair technologies," which are listed separately.

NOTE: Degree-granting institutions grant associate's or higher degrees and participate in Title IV federal financial aid programs. Race categories exclude persons of Hispanic ethnicity. Reported racial/ethnic distributions of students by level of degree, field of degree, and sex were used to estimate race/ethnicity for students whose race/ethnicity was not reported. To facilitate trend comparisons, certain aggregations have been made of the degree fields as reported in the IPEDS Fall survey. "Agriculture and natural resources" includes Agriculture, agriculture operations, and related sciences and Natural resources and con-

servation; and "Business" includes Business management, marketing, and related support services and Personal and culinary services. Includes Ph.D., Ed.D., and comparable degrees at the doctoral level. Excludes first-professional, such as M.D., D.D.S., and law degrees.

SOURCE: U.S. Department of Education, National Center for Education Statistics, 2007–08 Integrated Postsecondary Education Data System (IPEDS), Fall 2008. (This table was prepared June 2009.)

First-professional degrees conferred by degree-granting institutions, by race/ethnicity and sex of student: Selected years, 1976–77 through 2007–08

Year and sex	Number of degrees conferred							Percentage distribution of degrees conferred						
	Total	White	Black	Hispanic	Asian/ Pacific Islander	American Indian/ Alaska Native	Non-resident alien	Total	White	Black	Hispanic	Asian/ Pacific Islander	American Indian/ Alaska Native	Non-resident alien
1	2	3	4	5	6	7	8	9	10	11	12	13	14	15
Total														
1976–77[1]	63,953	58,422	2,537	1,076	1,021	196	701	100.0	91.4	4.0	1.7	1.6	0.3	1.1
1980–81[2]	71,340	64,551	2,931	1,541	1,456	192	669	100.0	90.5	4.1	2.2	2.0	0.3	0.9
1989–90	70,988	60,487	3,409	2,425	3,362	257	1,048	100.0	85.2	4.8	3.4	4.7	0.4	1.5
1990–91	71,948	60,631	3,588	2,547	3,835	261	1,086	100.0	84.3	5.0	3.5	5.3	0.4	1.5
1992–93	75,387	61,165	4,132	2,996	5,176	370	1,548	100.0	81.1	5.5	4.0	6.9	0.5	2.1
1993–94	75,418	60,143	4,444	3,131	5,892	371	1,437	100.0	79.7	5.9	4.2	7.8	0.5	1.9
1994–95	75,800	59,402	4,747	3,231	6,396	413	1,611	100.0	78.4	6.3	4.3	8.4	0.5	2.1
1995–96	76,734	59,525	5,022	3,475	6,627	463	1,622	100.0	77.6	6.5	4.5	8.6	0.6	2.1
1996–97	78,730	60,280	5,301	3,615	7,374	514	1,646	100.0	76.6	6.7	4.6	9.4	0.7	2.1
1997–98	78,598	59,443	5,499	3,552	7,757	561	1,786	100.0	75.6	7.0	4.5	9.9	0.7	2.3
1998–99	78,439	58,720	5,333	3,864	8,152	612	1,758	100.0	74.9	6.8	4.9	10.4	0.8	2.2
1999–2000	80,057	59,637	5,555	3,865	8,584	564	1,852	100.0	74.5	6.9	4.8	10.7	0.7	2.3
2000–01	79,707	58,598	5,416	3,806	9,261	543	2,083	100.0	73.5	6.8	4.8	11.6	0.7	2.6
2001–02	80,698	58,874	5,811	3,965	9,584	581	1,883	100.0	73.0	7.2	4.9	11.9	0.7	2.3
2002–03	80,897	58,740	5,719	4,093	9,798	586	1,961	100.0	72.6	7.1	5.1	12.1	0.7	2.4
2003–04	83,041	60,379	5,930	4,273	9,964	565	1,930	100.0	72.7	7.1	5.1	12.0	0.7	2.3
2004–05	87,289	63,429	6,313	4,445	10,501	564	2,037	100.0	72.7	7.2	5.1	12.0	0.6	2.3
2005–06	87,655	63,590	6,223	4,446	10,645	710	2,041	100.0	72.5	7.1	5.1	12.1	0.8	2.3
2006–07	90,064	64,546	6,474	4,700	11,686	681	1,977	100.0	71.7	7.2	5.2	13.0	0.8	2.2
2007–08	91,309	65,383	6,400	4,840	11,846	675	2,165	100.0	71.6	7.0	5.3	13.0	0.7	2.4
Males														
1976–77[1]	51,980	47,777	1,761	893	776	159	614	100.0	91.9	3.4	1.7	1.5	0.3	1.2
1980–81[2]	52,194	47,629	1,772	1,131	991	134	537	100.0	91.3	3.4	2.2	1.9	0.3	1.0
1989–90	43,961	38,036	1,671	1,449	1,962	135	708	100.0	86.5	3.8	3.3	4.5	0.3	1.6
1990–91	43,846	37,533	1,679	1,517	2,211	144	762	100.0	85.6	3.8	3.5	5.0	0.3	1.7
1992–93	45,153	37,415	1,801	1,771	2,871	192	1,103	100.0	82.9	4.0	3.9	6.4	0.4	2.4
1993–94	44,707	36,574	1,902	1,780	3,214	222	1,015	100.0	81.8	4.3	4.0	7.2	0.5	2.3
1994–95	44,853	36,147	2,077	1,835	3,490	223	1,081	100.0	80.6	4.6	4.1	7.8	0.5	2.4
1995–96	44,748	35,786	2,112	1,947	3,539	256	1,108	100.0	80.0	4.7	4.4	7.9	0.6	2.5
1996–97	45,564	36,008	2,201	1,985	3,959	290	1,121	100.0	79.0	4.8	4.4	8.7	0.6	2.5
1997–98	44,911	35,172	2,310	1,973	4,017	291	1,148	100.0	78.3	5.1	4.4	8.9	0.6	2.6
1998–99	44,339	34,271	2,197	2,064	4,333	333	1,141	100.0	77.3	5.0	4.7	9.8	0.8	2.6
1999–2000	44,239	34,004	2,313	2,095	4,372	285	1,170	100.0	76.9	5.2	4.7	9.9	0.6	2.6
2000–01	42,862	32,717	2,110	1,977	4,518	278	1,262	100.0	76.3	4.9	4.6	10.5	0.6	2.9
2001–02	42,507	32,224	2,223	2,045	4,613	292	1,110	100.0	75.8	5.2	4.8	10.9	0.7	2.6
2002–03	41,887	31,635	2,174	2,050	4,624	296	1,108	100.0	75.5	5.2	4.9	11.0	0.7	2.6
2003–04	42,169	31,994	2,248	2,080	4,528	275	1,044	100.0	75.9	5.3	4.9	10.7	0.7	2.5
2004–05	43,849	33,268	2,257	2,214	4,709	288	1,113	100.0	75.9	5.1	5.0	10.7	0.7	2.5
2005–06	44,038	33,544	2,290	2,123	4,641	332	1,108	100.0	76.2	5.2	4.8	10.5	0.8	2.5
2006–07	45,057	33,866	2,368	2,266	5,152	335	1,070	100.0	75.2	5.3	5.0	11.4	0.7	2.4
2007–08	45,916	34,618	2,389	2,301	5,135	343	1,130	100.0	75.4	5.2	5.0	11.2	0.7	2.5
Females														
1976–77[1]	11,973	10,645	776	183	245	37	87	100.0	88.9	6.5	1.5	2.0	0.3	0.7
1980–81[2]	19,146	16,922	1,159	410	465	58	132	100.0	88.4	6.1	2.1	2.4	0.3	0.7
1989–90	27,027	22,451	1,738	976	1,400	122	340	100.0	83.1	6.4	3.6	5.2	0.5	1.3
1990–91	28,102	23,098	1,909	1,030	1,624	117	324	100.0	82.2	6.8	3.7	5.8	0.4	1.2
1992–93	30,234	23,750	2,331	1,225	2,305	178	445	100.0	78.6	7.7	4.1	7.6	0.6	1.5
1993–94	30,711	23,569	2,542	1,351	2,678	149	422	100.0	76.7	8.3	4.4	8.7	0.5	1.4
1994–95	30,947	23,255	2,670	1,396	2,906	190	530	100.0	75.1	8.6	4.5	9.4	0.6	1.7
1995–96	31,986	23,739	2,910	1,528	3,088	207	514	100.0	74.2	9.1	4.8	9.7	0.6	1.6
1996–97	33,166	24,272	3,100	1,630	3,415	224	525	100.0	73.2	9.3	4.9	10.3	0.7	1.6
1997–98	33,687	24,271	3,189	1,579	3,740	270	638	100.0	72.0	9.5	4.7	11.1	0.8	1.9
1998–99	34,100	24,449	3,136	1,800	3,819	279	617	100.0	71.7	9.2	5.3	11.2	0.8	1.8
1999–2000	35,818	25,633	3,242	1,770	4,212	279	682	100.0	71.6	9.1	4.9	11.8	0.8	1.9
2000–01	36,845	25,881	3,306	1,829	4,743	265	821	100.0	70.2	9.0	5.0	12.9	0.7	2.2
2001–02	38,191	26,650	3,588	1,920	4,971	289	773	100.0	69.8	9.4	5.0	13.0	0.8	2.0
2002–03	39,010	27,105	3,545	2,043	5,174	290	853	100.0	69.5	9.1	5.2	13.3	0.7	2.2
2003–04	40,872	28,385	3,682	2,193	5,436	290	886	100.0	69.4	9.0	5.4	13.3	0.7	2.2
2004–05	43,440	30,161	4,056	2,231	5,792	276	924	100.0	69.4	9.3	5.1	13.3	0.6	2.1
2005–06	43,617	30,046	3,933	2,323	6,004	378	933	100.0	68.9	9.0	5.3	13.8	0.9	2.1
2006–07	45,007	30,680	4,106	2,434	6,534	346	907	100.0	68.2	9.1	5.4	14.5	0.8	2.0
2007–08	45,393	30,765	4,011	2,539	6,711	332	1,035	100.0	67.8	8.8	5.6	14.8	0.7	2.3

[1]Excludes 394 males and 12 females whose racial/ethnic group was not available.
[2]Excludes 598 males and 18 females whose racial/ethnic group was not available.
NOTE: Degree-granting institutions grant associate's or higher degrees and participate in Title IV federal financial aid programs. Includes degrees that require at least 6 years of college work for completion (including at least 2 years of preprofessional training). Race categories exclude persons of Hispanic ethnicity. For 1989–90 and later years, reported racial/ethnic distributions of students by level of degree, field of degree, and sex were used to estimate race/ethnicity for students whose race/ethnicity was not reported. (See Appendix A: Guide to Sources for details.) Detail may not sum to totals because of rounding.
SOURCE: U.S. Department of Education, National Center for Education Statistics, Higher Education General Information Survey (HEGIS), "Degrees and Other Formal Awards Conferred" surveys, 1976–77 and 1980–81; and 1989–90 through 2007–08 Integrated Postsecondary Education Data System, "Completions Survey" (IPEDS-C:90–99), and Fall 2000 through Fall 2008. (This table was prepared June 2009.)

First-professional degrees conferred by degree-granting institutions, by sex, race/ethnicity, and field of study: 2007–08

Field of study	Total							Males							Females						
	Total	White	Black	Hispanic	Asian/ Pacific Islander	American Indian/ Alaska Native	Non-resident alien	Total	White	Black	Hispanic	Asian/ Pacific Islander	American Indian/ Alaska Native	Non-resident alien	Total	White	Black	Hispanic	Asian/ Pacific Islander	American Indian/ Alaska Native	Non-resident alien
1	2	3	4	5	6	7	8	9	10	11	12	13	14	15	16	17	18	19	20	21	22
All fields, total	**91,309**	**65,383**	**6,400**	**4,840**	**11,846**	**675**	**2,165**	**45,916**	**34,618**	**2,389**	**2,301**	**5,135**	**343**	**1,130**	**45,393**	**30,765**	**4,011**	**2,539**	**6,711**	**332**	**1,035**
Dentistry (D.D.S. or D.M.D.)	4,795	3,030	221	261	926	24	333	2,661	1,866	86	119	422	14	154	2,134	1,164	135	142	504	10	179
Medicine (M.D.)	15,646	10,232	1,147	747	3,230	132	158	7,935	5,455	396	363	1,565	66	90	7,711	4,777	751	384	1,665	66	68
Optometry (O.D.)	1,304	822	46	40	305	2	89	445	320	8	12	78	0	27	859	502	38	28	227	2	62
Osteopathic medicine (D.O.)	3,232	2,388	118	125	550	28	23	1,581	1,235	38	58	230	10	10	1,651	1,153	80	67	320	18	13
Pharmacy (Pharm.D.)	10,932	7,053	781	443	2,314	69	272	3,716	2,528	248	137	677	32	94	7,216	4,525	533	306	1,637	37	178
Podiatry (Pod.D. or D.P.) or podiatric medicine (D.P.M.)	555	375	71	30	61	1	17	305	233	27	12	23	0	10	250	142	44	18	38	1	7
Veterinary medicine (D.V.M.)	2,504	2,272	42	78	90	10	12	580	537	9	17	11	5	1	1,924	1,735	33	61	79	5	11
Chiropractic medicine (D.C. or D.C.M.)	2,639	2,125	100	120	179	17	98	1,683	1,370	47	73	123	12	58	956	755	53	47	56	5	40
Naturopathic medicine	182	154	5	3	10	3	7	36	30	2	0	2	2	0	146	124	3	3	8	1	7
Law (LL.B. or J.D.)	43,769	32,939	3,002	2,821	3,865	370	772	23,197	18,388	1,109	1,378	1,753	189	380	20,572	14,551	1,893	1,443	2,112	181	392
Theology (M.Div, M.H.L., B.D., or Ord.)	5,751	3,993	867	172	316	19	384	3,777	2,656	419	132	251	13	306	1,974	1,337	448	40	65	6	78

NOTE: Degree-granting institutions grant associate's or higher degrees and participate in Title IV federal financial aid programs. Includes degrees that require at least 6 years of college work for completion (including at least 2 years of preprofessional training). Race categories exclude persons of Hispanic ethnicity. Reported racial/ethnic distributions of students by level of degree, field of degree, and sex were used to estimate race/ethnicity for students whose race/ethnicity was not reported.

SOURCE: U.S. Department of Education, National Center for Education Statistics, 2007–08 Integrated Postsecondary Education Data System (IPEDS), Fall 2008. (This table was prepared June 2009.)

Historical summary of faculty, students, degrees, and finances in degree-granting institutions: Selected years, 1869–70 through 2007–08

Selected characteristic	1869–70	1879–80	1889–90	1899–1900	1909–10	1919–20	1929–30	1939–40	1949–50	1959–60	1969–70	1979–80	1989–90	1999–2000	2005–06	2006–07	2007–08
1	2	3	4	5	6	7	8	9	10	11	12	13	14	15	16	17	18
Total institutions[1]	563	811	998	977	951	1,041	1,409	1,708	1,851	2,004	2,525	3,152	3,535	4,084	4,276	4,314	4,352
Total faculty[2]	5,553[3]	11,522[3]	15,609	23,868	36,480	48,615	82,386	146,929	246,722	380,554	450,000[4]	675,000[4]	824,220[5]	1,027,830[5]	1,290,426[5]	—	1,371,390[5]
Males	4,887[3]	7,328[3]	12,704[3]	19,151	29,132	35,807	60,017	106,328	186,189	296,773	346,000[4]	479,000[4]	534,254[5]	602,469[5]	714,453[5]	—	743,812[5]
Females	666[3]	4,194[3]	3,105[3]	4,717	7,348	12,808	22,369	40,601	60,533	83,781	104,000[4]	196,000[4]	289,966[5]	425,361[5]	575,973[5]	—	627,578[5]
Total fall enrollment[6]	52,286	115,817	156,756	237,592	355,213	597,880	1,100,737	1,494,203	2,444,900	3,639,847	8,004,660	11,569,899	13,538,560	14,791,224	17,487,475	17,758,870	18,248,128
Males	41,160[3]	77,972[3]	100,453[3]	152,254[3]	214,648[3]	314,938	619,935	893,250	1,721,572	2,332,617	4,746,201	5,682,877	6,190,015	6,490,646	7,455,925	7,574,815	7,815,914
Females	11,126[3]	37,845[3]	56,303[3]	85,338	140,565[3]	282,942	480,802	600,953	723,328	1,307,230	3,258,459	5,887,022	7,348,545	8,300,578	10,031,550	10,184,055	10,432,214
Earned degrees conferred																	
Associate's, total	—	—	—	—	—	—	—	—	—	—	206,023	400,910	455,102	564,933	713,066	728,114	750,164
Males	—	—	—	—	—	—	—	—	—	—	117,432	183,737	191,195	224,721	270,095	275,187	282,521
Females	—	—	—	—	—	—	—	—	—	—	88,591	217,173	263,907	340,212	442,971	452,927	467,643
Bachelor's, total[7]	9,371	12,896	15,539	27,410	37,199	48,622	122,484	186,500	432,058	392,440	792,316	929,417	1,051,344	1,237,875	1,485,242	1,524,092	1,563,069
Males	7,993	10,411	12,857	22,173	28,762	31,980	73,615	109,546	328,841	254,063	451,097	473,611	491,696	530,367	630,600	649,570	667,928
Females	1,378	2,485	2,682	5,237	8,437	16,642	48,869	76,954	103,217	138,377	341,219	455,806	559,648	707,508	854,642	874,522	895,141
Master's, total[8]	0	879	1,015	1,583	2,113	4,279	14,969	26,731	58,183	74,435	208,291	298,081	324,301	457,056	594,065	604,607	625,023
Males	0	868	821	1,280	1,555	2,985	8,925	16,508	41,220	50,898	125,624	150,749	153,653	191,792	237,896	238,189	246,491
Females	0	11	194	303	558	1,294	6,044	10,223	16,963	23,537	82,667	147,332	170,648	265,264	356,169	366,418	378,532
First-professional, total[7]	—	—	—	—	—	—	—	—	—	—	34,918	70,131	70,988	80,057	87,655	90,064	91,309
Males	—	—	—	—	—	—	—	—	—	—	33,077	52,716	43,961	44,239	44,038	45,057	45,916
Females	—	—	—	—	—	—	—	—	—	—	1,841	17,415	27,027	35,818	43,617	45,007	45,393
Doctor's, total	1	54	149	382	443	615	2,299	3,290	6,420	9,829	29,866	32,615	38,371	44,808	56,067	60,616	63,712
Males	1	51	147	359	399	522	1,946	2,861	5,804	8,801	25,890	22,943	24,401	25,028	28,634	30,251	31,215
Females	0	3	2	23	44	93	353	429	616	1,028	3,976	9,672	13,970	19,780	27,433	30,365	32,497
Finances																	
In thousands of current dollars																	
Current-fund revenue	—	—	—	—	$76,883	$199,922	$554,511	$715,211	$2,374,645	$5,785,537	$21,515,242	$58,519,982	$139,635,477	—	—	—	—
Educational and general income	—	—	$21,464	$35,084	67,917	172,929	483,065	571,288	1,833,845	4,688,352	16,486,177	—	—	—	—	—	—
Current-fund expenditures	—	—	—	—	—	—	507,142	674,688	2,245,661	5,601,376	21,043,113	56,913,588	134,655,571	—	—	—	—
Educational and general expenditures	—	—	—	—	—	—	377,903	521,990	1,706,444	4,685,258	16,845,212	44,542,843	105,585,076	—	—	—	—
Value of physical property	—	—	95,426	253,599	457,594	747,333	2,065,049	2,753,780[9]	4,799,964	13,548,548	42,093,580	83,733,387	164,635,000	—	—	—	—
Market value of endowment funds	—	—	78,788[10]	194,998[10]	323,661[10]	569,071[10]	1,372,068[10]	1,686,283[10]	2,601,223[10]	5,322,080[10]	11,206,632	20,743,045	67,978,726	—	—	—	—

—Not available.

[1]Prior to 1979–80, excludes branch campuses.

[2]Total number of different individuals (not reduced to full-time equivalent). Beginning in 1959–60, data are for the first term of the academic year.

[3]Estimated.

[4]Estimated number of senior instructional staff based on actual enrollment data for the designated year and enrollment/staff ratios for the prior staff survey. Excludes graduate assistants.

[5]Because of revised survey procedures, data may not be directly comparable with figures prior to 1989–90. Estimated number of senior instructional staff based on actual enrollment data for the designated year and enrollment/staff ratios for the prior survey. Excludes graduate assistants.

[6]Data for 1869–70 to 1939–40 are for resident degree-credit students who enrolled at any time during the academic year.

[7]From 1869–70 to 1959–60, first-professional degrees are included under bachelor's degrees.

[8]Figures for years prior to 1969–70 are not precisely comparable with later data.

[9]Includes unexpended plant funds.

[10]Book value. Includes other nonexpendable funds.

NOTE: Data through 1989–90 are for institutions of higher education, while later data are for degree-granting institutions. Degree-granting institutions grant associate's or higher degrees and participate in Title IV federal financial aid programs. The degree-granting classification is very similar to the earlier higher education classification, but it includes more 2-year colleges and excludes a few higher education institutions that did not grant degrees. (See Appendix A: Guide to Sources for details.) Detail may not sum to totals because of rounding.

SOURCE: U.S. Department of Education, National Center for Education Statistics, *Biennial Survey of Education in the United States; Education Directory, Colleges and Universities; Faculty and Other Professional Staff in Institutions of Higher Education; Fall Enrollment in Colleges and Universities; Earned Degrees Conferred; Financial Statistics of Institutions of Higher Education;* Higher Education General Information Survey (HEGIS), "Fall Enrollment in Institutions of Higher Education," "Degrees and Other Formal Awards Conferred," and "Financial Statistics of Institutions of Higher Education" surveys; and 1989 through 2008 Integrated Postsecondary Education Data System, "Fall Enrollment Survey" (IPEDS-EF:89–99), "Fall Staff Survey" (IPEDS-S:89–99), "Finance Survey" (IPEDS-F:FY90–00), "Completions Survey" (IPEDS-C:90–00), "Institutional Characteristics Survey" (IPEDS-IC:89–99), Winter 2005–06, Winter 2007–08, Spring 2007, Spring 2008, Fall 2007, and Fall 2008. (This table was prepared July 2009.)

Total fall enrollment in degree-granting institutions, by attendance status, sex of student, and control of institution: Selected years, 1947 through 2008

Year	Total enrollment	Attendance status			Sex of student			Control of institution			
		Full-time	Part-time	Percent part-time	Male	Female	Percent female	Public	Private		
									Total	Not-for-profit	For-profit
1	2	3	4	5	6	7	8	9	10	11	12
1947[1]	2,338,226	—	—	—	1,659,249	678,977	29.0	1,152,377	1,185,849	—	—
1948[1]	2,403,396	—	—	—	1,709,367	694,029	28.9	1,185,588	1,217,808	—	—
1949[1]	2,444,900	—	—	—	1,721,572	723,328	29.6	1,207,151	1,237,749	—	—
1950[1]	2,281,298	—	—	—	1,560,392	720,906	31.6	1,139,699	1,141,599	—	—
1951[1]	2,101,962	—	—	—	1,390,740	711,222	33.8	1,037,938	1,064,024	—	—
1952[1]	2,134,242	—	—	—	1,380,357	753,885	35.3	1,101,240	1,033,002	—	—
1953[1]	2,231,054	—	—	—	1,422,598	808,456	36.2	1,185,876	1,045,178	—	—
1954[1]	2,446,693	—	—	—	1,563,382	883,311	36.1	1,353,531	1,093,162	—	—
1955[1]	2,653,034	—	—	—	1,733,184	919,850	34.7	1,476,282	1,176,752	—	—
1956[1]	2,918,212	—	—	—	1,911,458	1,006,754	34.5	1,656,402	1,261,810	—	—
1957	3,323,783	—	—	—	2,170,765	1,153,018	34.7	1,972,673	1,351,110	—	—
1959	3,639,847	2,421,016	1,218,831 [2]	33.5	2,332,617	1,307,230	35.9	2,180,982	1,458,865	—	—
1961	4,145,065	2,785,133	1,359,932 [2]	32.8	2,585,821	1,559,244	37.6	2,561,447	1,583,618	—	—
1963	4,779,609	3,183,833	1,595,776 [2]	33.4	2,961,540	1,818,069	38.0	3,081,279	1,698,330	—	—
1964	5,280,020	3,573,238	1,706,782 [2]	32.3	3,248,713	2,031,307	38.5	3,467,708	1,812,312	—	—
1965	5,920,864	4,095,728	1,825,136 [2]	30.8	3,630,020	2,290,844	38.7	3,969,596	1,951,268	—	—
1966	6,389,872	4,438,606	1,951,266 [2]	30.5	3,856,216	2,533,656	39.7	4,348,917	2,040,955	—	—
1967	6,911,748	4,793,128	2,118,620 [2]	30.7	4,132,800	2,778,948	40.2	4,816,028	2,095,720	2,074,041	21,679
1968	7,513,091	5,210,155	2,302,936	30.7	4,477,649	3,035,442	40.4	5,430,652	2,082,439	2,061,211	21,228
1969	8,004,660	5,498,883	2,505,777	31.3	4,746,201	3,258,459	40.7	5,896,868	2,107,792	2,087,653	20,139
1970	8,580,887	5,816,290	2,764,597	32.2	5,043,642	3,537,245	41.2	6,428,134	2,152,753	2,134,420	18,333
1971	8,948,644	6,077,232	2,871,412	32.1	5,207,004	3,741,640	41.8	6,804,309	2,144,335	2,121,913	22,422
1972	9,214,860	6,072,389	3,142,471	34.1	5,238,757	3,976,103	43.1	7,070,635	2,144,225	2,123,245	20,980
1973	9,602,123	6,189,493	3,412,630	35.5	5,371,052	4,231,071	44.1	7,419,516	2,182,607	2,148,784	33,823
1974	10,223,729	6,370,273	3,853,456	37.7	5,622,429	4,601,300	45.0	7,988,500	2,235,229	2,200,963	34,266
1975	11,184,859	6,841,334	4,343,525	38.8	6,148,997	5,035,862	45.0	8,834,508	2,350,351	2,311,448	38,903
1976	11,012,137	6,717,058	4,295,079	39.0	5,810,828	5,201,309	47.2	8,653,477	2,358,660	2,314,298	44,362
1977	11,285,787	6,792,925	4,492,862	39.8	5,789,016	5,496,771	48.7	8,846,993	2,438,794	2,386,652	52,142
1978	11,260,092	6,667,657	4,592,435	40.8	5,640,998	5,619,094	49.9	8,785,893	2,474,199	2,408,331	65,868
1979	11,569,899	6,794,039	4,775,860	41.3	5,682,877	5,887,022	50.9	9,036,822	2,533,077	2,461,773	71,304
1980	12,096,895	7,097,958	4,998,937	41.3	5,874,374	6,222,521	51.4	9,457,394	2,639,501	2,527,787	111,714 [3]
1981	12,371,672	7,181,250	5,190,422	42.0	5,975,056	6,396,616	51.7	9,647,032	2,724,640	2,572,405	152,235 [3]
1982	12,425,780	7,220,618	5,205,162	41.9	6,031,384	6,394,396	51.5	9,696,087	2,729,693	2,552,739	176,954 [3]
1983	12,464,661	7,261,050	5,203,611	41.7	6,023,725	6,440,936	51.7	9,682,734	2,781,927	2,589,187	192,740
1984	12,241,940	7,098,388	5,143,552	42.0	5,863,574	6,378,366	52.1	9,477,370	2,764,570	2,574,419	190,151
1985	12,247,055	7,075,221	5,171,834	42.2	5,818,450	6,428,605	52.5	9,479,273	2,767,782	2,571,791	195,991
1986	12,503,511	7,119,550	5,383,961	43.1	5,884,515	6,618,996	52.9	9,713,893	2,789,618	2,572,479	217,139 [4]
1987	12,766,642	7,231,085	5,535,557	43.4	5,932,056	6,834,586	53.5	9,973,254	2,793,388	2,602,350	191,038 [4]
1988	13,055,337	7,436,768	5,618,569	43.0	6,001,896	7,053,441	54.0	10,161,388	2,893,949	2,673,567	220,382
1989	13,538,560	7,660,950	5,877,610	43.4	6,190,015	7,348,545	54.3	10,577,963	2,960,597	2,731,174	229,423
1990	13,818,637	7,820,985	5,997,652	43.4	6,283,909	7,534,728	54.5	10,844,717	2,973,920	2,760,227	213,693
1991	14,358,953	8,115,329	6,243,624	43.5	6,501,844	7,857,109	54.7	11,309,563	3,049,390	2,819,041	230,349
1992	14,487,359	8,162,118	6,325,241	43.7	6,523,989	7,963,370	55.0	11,384,567	3,102,792	2,872,523	230,269
1993	14,304,803	8,127,618	6,177,185	43.2	6,427,450	7,877,353	55.1	11,189,080	3,115,715	2,888,897	226,818
1994	14,278,790	8,137,776	6,141,014	43.0	6,371,898	7,906,892	55.4	11,133,680	3,145,110	2,910,107	235,003
1995	14,261,781	8,128,802	6,132,979	43.0	6,342,539	7,919,242	55.5	11,092,374	3,169,407	2,929,044	240,363
1996	14,367,520	8,302,953	6,064,567	42.2	6,352,825	8,014,695	55.8	11,120,499	3,247,021	2,942,556	304,465
1997	14,502,334	8,438,062	6,064,272	41.8	6,396,028	8,106,306	55.9	11,196,119	3,306,215	2,977,614	328,601
1998	14,506,967	8,563,338	5,943,629	41.0	6,369,265	8,137,702	56.1	11,137,769	3,369,198	3,004,925	364,273
1999	14,791,224	8,786,494	6,004,730	40.6	6,490,646	8,300,578	56.1	11,309,399	3,481,825	3,051,626	430,199
2000	15,312,289	9,009,600	6,302,689	41.2	6,721,769	8,590,520	56.1	11,752,786	3,559,503	3,109,419	450,084
2001	15,927,987	9,447,502	6,480,485	40.7	6,960,815	8,967,172	56.3	12,233,156	3,694,831	3,167,330	527,501
2002	16,611,711	9,946,359	6,665,352	40.1	7,202,116	9,409,595	56.6	12,751,993	3,859,718	3,265,476	594,242
2003	16,911,481	10,326,133	6,585,348	38.9	7,260,264	9,651,217	57.1	12,858,698	4,052,783	3,341,048	711,735
2004	17,272,044	10,610,177	6,661,867	38.6	7,387,262	9,884,782	57.2	12,980,112	4,291,932	3,411,685	880,247
2005	17,487,475	10,797,011	6,690,464	38.3	7,455,925	10,031,550	57.4	13,021,834	4,465,641	3,454,692	1,010,949
2006	17,758,870	10,957,305	6,801,565	38.3	7,574,815	10,184,055	57.3	13,180,133	4,578,737	3,512,866	1,065,871
2007	18,248,128	11,269,892	6,978,236	38.2	7,815,914	10,432,214	57.2	13,490,780	4,757,348	3,571,150	1,186,198
2008	19,102,814	11,747,743	7,355,071	38.5	8,188,895	10,913,919	57.1	13,972,153	5,130,661	3,661,519	1,469,142

—Not available.

[1]Degree-credit enrollment only.

[2]Includes part-time resident students and all extension students (students attending courses at sites separate from the primary reporting campus).

[3]Large increases are due to the addition of schools accredited by the Accrediting Commission of Career Schools and Colleges of Technology.

[4]Because of imputation techniques, data are not consistent with figures for other years.

NOTE: Data through 1995 are for institutions of higher education, while later data are for degree-granting institutions. Degree-granting institutions grant associate's or higher degrees and participate in Title IV federal financial aid programs. The degree-granting classification is very similar to the earlier higher education classification, but it includes more 2-year colleges and excludes a few higher education institutions that did not grant degrees. (See Appendix A: Guide to Sources for details.)

SOURCE: U.S. Department of Education, National Center for Education Statistics, *Biennial Survey of Education in the United States*; *Opening Fall Enrollment in Higher Education*, 1963 through 1965; Higher Education General Information Survey (HEGIS), "Fall Enrollment in Colleges and Universities" surveys, 1966 through 1985; and 1986 through 2008 Integrated Postsecondary Education Data System, "Fall Enrollment Survey" (IPEDS-EF:86–99), and Spring 2001 through Spring 2009. (This table was prepared September 2009.)

Total fall enrollment in degree-granting institutions, by control and type of institution: 1963 through 2008

	All institutions					Public institutions					Private institutions				
		4-year					4-year					4-year			
Year	Total	Total	University	Other 4-year	2-year	Total	Total	University	Other 4-year	2-year	Total	Total	University	Other 4-year	2-year
1	2	3	4	5	6	7	8	9	10	11	12	13	14	15	16
1963[1]	4,779,609	3,929,248	—	—	850,361	3,081,279	2,341,468	—	—	739,811	1,698,330	1,587,780	—	—	110,550
1964[1]	5,280,020	4,291,094	—	—	988,926	3,467,708	2,592,929	—	—	874,779	1,812,312	1,698,165	—	—	114,147
1965[1]	5,920,864	4,747,912	—	—	1,172,952	3,969,596	2,928,332	—	—	1,041,264	1,951,268	1,819,580	—	—	131,688
1966[1]	6,389,872	5,063,902	—	—	1,325,970	4,348,917	3,159,748	—	—	1,189,169	2,040,955	1,904,154	—	—	136,801
1967	6,911,748	5,398,986	2,186,235	3,212,751	1,512,762	4,816,028	3,443,975	1,510,333	1,933,642	1,372,053	2,095,720	1,955,011	675,902	1,279,109	140,709
1968	7,513,091	5,720,269	2,266,120	3,454,149	1,792,822	5,430,652	3,783,652	1,592,707	2,190,945	1,647,000	2,082,439	1,936,617	673,413	1,263,204	145,822
1969	8,004,660	5,937,127	2,420,429	3,516,698	2,067,533	5,896,868	3,962,522	1,738,493	2,224,029	1,934,346	2,107,792	1,974,605	681,936	1,292,669	133,187
1970	8,580,887	6,261,502	2,534,336	3,727,166	2,319,385	6,428,134	4,232,722	1,832,694	2,400,028	2,195,412	2,152,753	2,028,780	701,642	1,327,138	123,973
1971	8,948,644	6,369,355	2,594,470	3,774,885	2,579,289	6,804,309	4,346,990	1,913,626	2,433,364	2,457,319	2,144,335	2,022,365	680,844	1,341,521	121,970
1972	9,214,860	6,458,674	2,620,749	3,837,925	2,756,186	7,070,635	4,429,696	1,941,040	2,488,656	2,640,939	2,144,225	2,028,978	679,709	1,349,269	115,247
1973	9,602,123	6,590,023	2,629,796	3,960,227	3,012,100	7,419,516	4,529,895	1,950,653	2,579,242	2,889,621	2,182,607	2,060,128	679,143	1,380,985	122,479
1974	10,223,729	6,819,735	2,702,306	4,117,429	3,403,994	7,988,500	4,703,018	2,006,723	2,696,295	3,285,482	2,235,229	2,116,717	695,583	1,421,134	118,512
1975	11,184,859	7,214,740	2,838,266	4,376,474	3,970,119	8,834,508	4,998,142	2,124,221	2,873,921	3,836,366	2,350,351	2,216,598	714,045	1,502,553	133,753
1976	11,012,137	7,128,816	2,780,289	4,348,527	3,883,321	8,653,477	4,901,691	2,079,929	2,821,762	3,751,786	2,358,660	2,227,125	700,360	1,526,765	131,535
1977	11,285,787	7,242,845	2,793,418	4,449,427	4,042,942	8,846,993	4,945,224	2,070,032	2,875,192	3,901,769	2,438,794	2,297,621	723,386	1,574,235	141,173
1978	11,260,092	7,231,625	2,780,729	4,451,222	4,028,467	8,785,893	4,912,203	2,062,295	2,849,908	3,873,690	2,474,199	2,319,422	718,434	1,601,314	154,777
1979	11,569,899	7,353,233	2,839,582	4,513,651	4,216,666	9,036,822	4,980,012	2,099,525	2,880,487	4,056,810	2,533,077	2,373,221	740,057	1,633,164	159,856
1980	12,096,895	7,570,608	2,902,014	4,668,594	4,526,287	9,457,394	5,128,612	2,154,283	2,974,329	4,328,782	2,639,501	2,441,996	747,731	1,694,265	197,505 [2]
1981	12,371,672	7,655,461	2,901,344	4,754,117	4,716,211	9,647,032	5,166,324	2,152,474	3,013,850	4,480,708	2,724,640	2,489,137	748,870	1,740,267	235,503 [2]
1982	12,425,780	7,654,074	2,883,735	4,770,339	4,771,706	9,696,087	5,176,434	2,152,547	3,023,887	4,519,653	2,729,693	2,477,640	731,188	1,746,452	252,053 [2]
1983	12,464,661	7,741,195	2,888,813	4,852,382	4,723,466	9,682,734	5,223,404	2,154,790	3,068,614	4,459,330	2,781,927	2,517,791	734,023	1,783,768	264,136
1984	12,241,940	7,711,167	2,870,329	4,840,838	4,530,773	9,477,370	5,198,273	2,138,621	3,059,652	4,279,097	2,764,570	2,512,894	731,708	1,781,186	251,676
1985	12,247,055	7,715,978	2,870,692	4,845,286	4,531,077	9,479,273	5,209,540	2,141,112	3,068,428	4,269,733	2,767,782	2,506,438	729,580	1,776,858	261,344
1986	12,503,511	7,823,963	2,897,207	4,926,756	4,679,548	9,713,893	5,300,202	2,160,646	3,139,556	4,413,691	2,789,618	2,523,761	736,561	1,787,200	265,857 [3]
1987	12,766,642	7,990,420	2,929,327	5,061,093	4,776,222	9,973,254	5,432,200	2,188,008	3,244,192	4,541,054	2,793,388	2,558,220	741,319	1,816,901	235,168 [3]
1988	13,055,337	8,180,182	2,978,593	5,201,589	4,875,155	10,161,388	5,545,901	2,229,868	3,316,033	4,615,487	2,893,949	2,634,281	748,725	1,885,556	259,668
1989	13,538,560	8,387,671	3,019,115	5,368,556	5,150,889	10,577,963	5,694,303	2,266,056	3,428,247	4,883,660	2,960,597	2,693,368	753,059	1,940,309	267,229
1990	13,818,637	8,578,554	3,044,670	5,533,884	5,240,083	10,844,717	5,848,242	2,290,464	3,557,778	4,996,475	2,973,920	2,730,312	754,206	1,976,106	243,608
1991	14,358,953	8,707,053	3,065,429	5,641,624	5,651,900	11,309,563	5,904,748	2,301,222	3,603,526	5,404,815	3,049,390	2,802,305	764,207	2,038,098	247,085
1992	14,487,359	8,764,969	3,050,345	5,714,624	5,722,390	11,384,567	5,900,012	2,283,834	3,616,178	5,484,555	3,102,792	2,864,957	766,511	2,098,446	237,835
1993	14,304,803	8,738,936	3,022,728	5,716,208	5,565,867	11,189,088	5,851,760	2,259,692	3,592,068	5,337,328	3,115,715	2,887,176	763,036	2,124,140	228,539
1994	14,278,790	8,749,080	3,009,072	5,740,008	5,529,710	11,133,680	5,825,213	2,244,636	3,580,577	5,308,467	3,145,110	2,923,867	764,436	2,159,431	221,243
1995	14,261,781	8,769,252	2,999,641	5,769,611	5,492,529	11,092,374	5,814,545	2,235,939	3,578,606	5,277,829	3,169,407	2,954,707	763,702	2,191,005	214,700
1996	14,367,520	8,804,193	2,984,965	5,819,228	5,563,327	11,120,499	5,806,036	2,226,529	3,579,507	5,314,463	3,247,021	2,998,157	758,436	2,239,721	248,864
1997	14,502,334	8,896,765	2,995,886	5,900,879	5,605,569	11,196,119	5,835,433	2,231,273	3,604,160	5,360,686	3,306,215	3,061,332	764,613	2,296,719	244,883
1998	14,506,967	9,017,653	3,021,136	5,996,517	5,489,314	11,137,769	5,891,806	2,249,825	3,641,981	5,245,963	3,369,198	3,125,847	771,311	2,354,536	243,351
1999	14,791,224	9,198,525	3,044,369	6,154,156	5,592,699	11,309,399	5,969,950	2,266,494	3,703,456	5,339,449	3,481,825	3,228,575	777,875	2,450,700	253,250
2000	15,312,289	9,363,858	3,061,812	6,302,046	5,948,431	11,752,786	6,055,398	2,280,122	3,775,276	5,697,388	3,559,503	3,308,460	781,690	2,526,770	251,043
2001	15,927,987	9,677,408	3,126,907	6,550,501	6,250,579	12,233,156	6,236,455	2,336,922	3,899,533	5,996,701	3,694,831	3,440,953	789,985	2,650,968	253,878
2002	16,611,711	10,082,332	3,210,271	6,872,061	6,529,379	12,751,993	6,481,613	2,403,149	4,078,464	6,270,380	3,859,718	3,600,719	807,122	2,793,597	258,999
2003	16,911,481	10,417,247	3,242,639	7,174,608	6,494,234	12,858,698	6,649,441	2,419,631	4,229,810	6,209,257	4,052,783	3,767,806	823,008	2,944,798	284,977
2004	17,272,044	10,726,181	3,258,982	7,467,199	6,545,863	12,980,112	6,736,536	2,426,495	4,310,041	6,243,576	4,291,932	3,989,645	832,487	3,157,158	302,287
2005	17,487,475	10,999,420	3,271,620	7,727,800	6,488,055	13,021,834	6,837,605	2,443,682	4,393,923	6,184,229	4,465,641	4,161,815	827,938	3,333,877	303,826
2006	17,758,870	11,240,330	3,306,973	7,933,357	6,518,540	13,180,133	6,955,013	2,459,874	4,495,139	6,225,120	4,578,737	4,285,317	847,099	3,438,218	293,420
2007	18,248,128	11,630,198	3,349,214	8,280,984	6,617,930	13,490,780	7,166,661	2,490,615	4,676,046	6,324,119	4,757,348	4,463,537	858,599	3,604,938	293,811
2008	19,102,814	12,131,436	3,412,435	8,719,001	6,971,378	13,972,153	7,331,809	2,544,529	4,787,280	6,640,344	5,130,661	4,799,627	867,906	3,931,721	331,034

—Not available.

[1] Data for 2-year branch campuses of 4-year institutions are included with the 4-year institutions.

[2] Large increases are due to the addition of schools accredited by the Accrediting Commission of Career Schools and Colleges of Technology.

[3] Because of imputation techniques, data are not consistent with figures for other years.

NOTE: Data through 1995 are for institutions of higher education, while later data are for degree-granting institutions. Degree-granting institutions grant associate's or higher degrees and participate in Title IV federal financial aid programs. The degree-granting classification is very similar to the earlier higher education classification, but it includes more 2-year colleges and excludes a few higher education institutions that did not grant degrees. (See Appendix A: Guide to Sources for details.) Some data have been revised from previously published figures.

SOURCE: U.S. Department of Education, National Center for Education Statistics, *Opening Fall Enrollment in Higher Education*, 1965; Higher Education General Information Survey (HEGIS), "Fall Enrollment in Institutions of Higher Education" surveys, 1966 through 1985; and 1986 through 2008 Integrated Postsecondary Education Data System, "Fall Enrollment Survey" (IPEDS-EF:86–99), and Spring 2001 through Spring 2009. (This table was prepared September 2009.)

Total fall enrollment in degree-granting institutions, by sex, age, and attendance status: Selected years, 1970 through 2018
[In thousands]

Sex, age, and attendance status	1970	1980	1990	1995	2000	2001	2002	2003	2004	2005	2006	2007	Projected 2009	2013	2018
1	2	3	4	5	6	7	8	9	10	11	12	13	14	15	16
All students	8,581	12,097	13,819	14,262	15,312	15,928	16,612	16,911	17,272	17,487	17,759	18,248	19,037	19,710	20,620
14 to 17 years old	259	247	177	148	145	133	202	150	200	199	231	179	146	142	161
18 and 19 years old	2,600	2,901	2,950	2,894	3,531	3,595	3,571	3,479	3,578	3,610	3,769	3,978	4,162	4,032	4,175
20 and 21 years old	1,880	2,424	2,761	2,705	3,045	3,408	3,366	3,472	3,651	3,778	3,648	3,761	4,021	4,157	4,128
22 to 24 years old	1,457	1,989	2,144	2,411	2,617	2,760	2,932	3,482	3,036	3,072	3,193	3,362	3,438	3,750	3,820
25 to 29 years old	1,074	1,871	1,982	2,120	1,960	2,014	2,102	2,107	2,386	2,384	2,401	2,522	2,667	2,800	3,097
30 to 34 years old	487	1,243	1,322	1,236	1,265	1,290	1,300	1,369	1,329	1,354	1,409	1,428	1,525	1,716	1,856
35 years old and over	823	1,421	2,484	2,747	2,749	2,727	3,139	2,853	3,092	3,090	3,107	3,017	3,078	3,113	3,383
Males	5,044	5,874	6,284	6,343	6,722	6,961	7,202	7,260	7,387	7,456	7,575	7,816	8,210	8,359	8,505
14 to 17 years old	130	99	87	61	63	54	82	60	78	78	82	75	77	74	81
18 and 19 years old	1,349	1,375	1,421	1,338	1,583	1,629	1,616	1,557	1,551	1,592	1,705	1,805	1,851	1,768	1,784
20 and 21 years old	1,095	1,259	1,368	1,282	1,382	1,591	1,562	1,491	1,743	1,778	1,673	1,633	1,793	1,829	1,773
22 to 24 years old	964	1,064	1,107	1,153	1,293	1,312	1,342	1,605	1,380	1,355	1,470	1,551	1,588	1,699	1,669
25 to 29 years old	783	993	940	962	862	905	890	930	1,045	978	1,051	1,020	1,110	1,139	1,243
30 to 34 years old	308	576	537	561	527	510	547	592	518	545	557	659	697	766	811
35 years old and over	415	507	824	986	1,012	961	1,164	1,025	1,073	1,130	1,037	1,074	1,094	1,083	1,144
Females	3,537	6,223	7,535	7,919	8,591	8,967	9,410	9,651	9,885	10,032	10,184	10,432	10,827	11,351	12,115
14 to 17 years old	129	148	90	87	82	79	121	91	122	121	149	104	69	68	81
18 and 19 years old	1,250	1,526	1,529	1,557	1,948	1,966	1,955	1,921	2,027	2,018	2,064	2,173	2,311	2,264	2,391
20 and 21 years old	786	1,165	1,392	1,424	1,663	1,817	1,804	1,981	1,908	2,000	1,975	2,129	2,227	2,328	2,356
22 to 24 years old	493	925	1,037	1,258	1,324	1,448	1,590	1,877	1,657	1,717	1,724	1,811	1,850	2,051	2,151
25 to 29 years old	291	878	1,043	1,159	1,099	1,110	1,212	1,177	1,341	1,406	1,350	1,502	1,557	1,661	1,854
30 to 34 years old	179	667	784	675	738	780	753	777	812	809	852	770	829	949	1,044
35 years old and over	409	914	1,659	1,760	1,736	1,767	1,976	1,828	2,018	1,960	2,070	1,943	1,984	2,030	2,239
Full-time	5,816	7,098	7,821	8,129	9,010	9,448	9,946	10,326	10,610	10,797	10,957	11,270	11,833	12,290	12,932
14 to 17 years old	242	223	144	123	125	122	161	120	165	131	166	153	103	101	117
18 and 19 years old	2,406	2,669	2,548	2,387	2,932	2,929	2,942	2,953	3,028	3,037	3,155	3,379	3,548	3,454	3,625
20 and 21 years old	1,647	2,075	2,151	2,109	2,401	2,662	2,759	2,766	2,911	3,030	2,944	3,021	3,246	3,375	3,409
22 to 24 years old	881	1,121	1,350	1,517	1,653	1,757	1,922	2,144	2,074	2,097	2,093	2,133	2,187	2,412	2,524
25 to 29 years old	407	577	770	908	878	883	1,013	1,072	1,131	1,136	1,217	1,263	1,312	1,395	1,547
30 to 34 years old	100	251	387	430	422	494	465	512	490	549	605	549	596	682	747
35 years old and over	134	182	471	653	599	602	684	758	812	818	778	772	842	870	963
Males	3,505	3,689	3,808	3,807	4,111	4,300	4,501	4,638	4,739	4,803	4,879	5,029	5,292	5,383	5,513
14 to 17 years old	124	87	71	54	51	43	65	50	63	36	66	58	56	54	59
18 and 19 years old	1,265	1,270	1,230	1,091	1,250	1,329	1,327	1,307	1,313	1,357	1,409	1,532	1,574	1,509	1,535
20 and 21 years old	990	1,109	1,055	999	1,106	1,249	1,275	1,218	1,385	1,460	1,331	1,344	1,480	1,513	1,481
22 to 24 years old	650	665	742	789	839	854	936	1,041	960	951	1,003	1,007	1,035	1,114	1,114
25 to 29 years old	327	360	401	454	415	397	467	503	509	439	562	585	595	614	688
30 to 34 years old	72	124	156	183	195	216	183	242	201	238	232	228	253	280	307
35 years old and over	75	74	152	238	256	212	247	277	310	321	275	275	300	299	329
Females	2,311	3,409	4,013	4,321	4,899	5,148	5,445	5,688	5,871	5,994	6,078	6,240	6,541	6,907	7,419
14 to 17 years old	117	136	73	69	74	78	96	71	103	94	100	95	47	47	57
18 and 19 years old	1,140	1,399	1,318	1,296	1,682	1,600	1,615	1,645	1,716	1,680	1,746	1,847	1,974	1,946	2,090
20 and 21 years old	657	966	1,096	1,111	1,296	1,413	1,484	1,548	1,526	1,569	1,612	1,677	1,766	1,862	1,928
22 to 24 years old	231	456	608	729	814	903	985	1,103	1,113	1,146	1,090	1,127	1,152	1,298	1,410
25 to 29 years old	80	217	369	455	463	486	546	569	622	697	654	678	716	781	860
30 to 34 years old	28	127	231	247	227	277	282	270	289	311	372	320	343	402	440
35 years old and over	59	108	319	415	343	390	437	482	502	497	503	497	542	571	634
Part-time	2,765	4,999	5,998	6,133	6,303	6,480	6,665	6,585	6,662	6,690	6,802	6,978	7,204	7,421	7,688
14 to 17 years old	17	38	32	25	20	11	41	30	35	68	65	26	43	42	45
18 and 19 years old	194	418	402	507	599	666	628	526	549	573	614	600	614	578	550
20 and 21 years old	233	441	610	596	644	746	607	706	741	748	704	740	775	782	719
22 to 24 years old	576	844	794	894	964	1,003	1,010	1,338	963	976	1,100	1,229	1,251	1,339	1,296
25 to 29 years old	668	1,209	1,213	1,212	1,083	1,132	1,088	1,035	1,255	1,248	1,184	1,259	1,355	1,405	1,550
30 to 34 years old	388	905	935	805	843	796	835	856	839	805	805	880	930	1,033	1,109
35 years old and over	689	1,145	2,012	2,093	2,150	2,126	2,456	2,094	2,280	2,272	2,329	2,245	2,237	2,243	2,420
Males	1,540	2,185	2,476	2,535	2,611	2,661	2,701	2,622	2,648	2,653	2,696	2,786	2,918	2,976	2,992
14 to 17 years old	5	17	16	7	11	11	17	10	15	41	16	17	21	20	21
18 and 19 years old	84	202	191	246	333	300	288	250	239	235	297	273	276	260	249
20 and 21 years old	105	201	313	283	276	342	287	274	358	318	341	288	314	316	292
22 to 24 years old	314	392	365	365	454	458	405	564	419	405	466	544	553	586	555
25 to 29 years old	456	594	539	508	447	508	423	427	536	539	488	435	515	525	555
30 to 34 years old	236	397	381	378	332	294	364	350	317	306	325	430	444	486	504
35 years old and over	340	382	672	748	757	749	917	748	764	809	762	799	795	784	815
Females	1,225	2,814	3,521	3,598	3,692	3,820	3,964	3,963	4,014	4,038	4,106	4,192	4,286	4,444	4,696
14 to 17 years old	12	20	17	18	9	1	24	20	19	27	48	9	22	21	23
18 and 19 years old	110	215	211	261	266	366	340	276	311	338	318	327	338	318	301
20 and 21 years old	128	240	297	313	368	404	320	433	382	430	363	452	461	466	427
22 to 24 years old	262	452	429	529	510	545	605	774	543	571	634	685	698	753	740
25 to 29 years old	212	616	674	704	636	624	666	608	720	709	696	824	840	880	994
30 to 34 years old	151	507	554	427	511	502	471	507	523	499	480	449	486	547	605
35 years old and over	349	762	1,340	1,345	1,393	1,377	1,539	1,346	1,516	1,464	1,567	1,446	1,442	1,459	1,605

NOTE: Distributions by age are estimates based on samples of the civilian noninstitutional population from the U.S. Census Bureau's Current Population Survey. Data through 1995 are for institutions of higher education, while later data are for degree-granting institutions. Degree-granting institutions grant associate's or higher degrees and participate in Title IV federal financial aid programs. The degree-granting classification is very similar to the earlier higher education classification, but it includes more 2-year colleges and excludes a few higher education institutions that did not grant degrees. (See Appendix A: Guide to Sources for details.) Detail may not sum to totals because of rounding.

SOURCE: U.S. Department of Education, National Center for Education Statistics, Higher Education General Information Survey (HEGIS), "Fall Enrollment in Colleges and Universities" surveys, 1970 and 1980; 1990 through 2008 Integrated Postsecondary Education Data System, "Fall Enrollment Survey" (IPEDS-EF:90–99), and Spring 2001 through Spring 2008; and *Projections of Education Statistics to 2018.* U.S. Department of Commerce, Census Bureau, Current Population Survey (CPS), October, selected years, 1970 through 2008. (This table was prepared September 2009.)

Recent high school completers and their enrollment in college, by sex: 1960 through 2008

[Numbers in thousands]

Year	Number of high school completers[1]						Enrolled in college[2]								
	Total		Males		Females		Total				Males				Females			
							Number		Percent		Number		Percent		Number		Percent	
1	2		3		4		5		6		7		8		9		10	
1960	1,679	(43.8)	756	(31.8)	923	(29.6)	758	(40.9)	45.1	(2.13)	408	(29.5)	54.0	(3.18)	350	(28.2)	37.9	(2.80)
1961	1,763	(46.0)	790	(33.2)	973	(31.3)	847	(42.9)	48.0	(2.09)	445	(30.8)	56.3	(3.10)	402	(29.9)	41.3	(2.77)
1962	1,838	(43.6)	872	(31.5)	966	(30.0)	900	(43.2)	49.0	(2.05)	480	(31.1)	55.0	(2.96)	420	(30.0)	43.5	(2.80)
1963	1,741	(44.2)	794	(32.1)	947	(30.0)	784	(41.5)	45.0	(2.09)	415	(29.8)	52.3	(3.11)	369	(28.8)	39.0	(2.78)
1964	2,145	(43.0)	997	(31.9)	1,148	(28.5)	1,037	(45.6)	48.3	(1.89)	570	(32.9)	57.2	(2.75)	467	(31.4)	40.7	(2.54)
1965	2,659	(47.7)	1,254	(35.1)	1,405	(32.0)	1,354	(51.4)	50.9	(1.70)	718	(36.7)	57.3	(2.45)	636	(35.8)	45.3	(2.33)
1966	2,612	(45.0)	1,207	(33.8)	1,405	(29.0)	1,309	(50.2)	50.1	(1.72)	709	(36.0)	58.7	(2.49)	600	(34.8)	42.7	(2.32)
1967	2,525	(37.9)	1,142	(28.4)	1,383	(24.3)	1,311	(40.9)	51.9	(1.42)	658	(28.9)	57.6	(2.09)	653	(28.9)	47.2	(1.92)
1968	2,606	(37.3)	1,184	(28.2)	1,422	(23.8)	1,444	(41.7)	55.4	(1.39)	748	(29.6)	63.2	(2.00)	696	(29.3)	48.9	(1.89)
1969	2,842	(36.0)	1,352	(26.8)	1,490	(23.7)	1,516	(42.5)	53.3	(1.34)	812	(30.3)	60.1	(1.90)	704	(29.7)	47.2	(1.85)
1970	2,758	(37.4)	1,343	(26.1)	1,415	(26.8)	1,427	(42.2)	51.7	(1.36)	741	(29.7)	55.2	(1.94)	686	(29.8)	48.5	(1.90)
1971	2,875	(38.0)	1,371	(26.6)	1,504	(27.1)	1,538	(43.2)	53.5	(1.33)	790	(30.3)	57.6	(1.90)	749	(30.8)	49.8	(1.84)
1972	2,964	(37.8)	1,423	(27.0)	1,542	(26.4)	1,459	(43.1)	49.2	(1.31)	750	(30.4)	52.7	(1.89)	709	(30.5)	46.0	(1.81)
1973	3,058	(37.1)	1,460	(27.6)	1,599	(24.6)	1,424	(43.0)	46.6	(1.29)	730	(30.6)	50.0	(1.87)	694	(30.2)	43.4	(1.77)
1974	3,101	(38.6)	1,491	(27.8)	1,611	(26.8)	1,475	(43.7)	47.6	(1.28)	736	(30.8)	49.4	(1.85)	740	(31.1)	45.9	(1.77)
1975	3,185	(38.6)	1,513	(27.3)	1,672	(27.2)	1,615	(44.8)	50.7	(1.26)	796	(31.2)	52.6	(1.83)	818	(32.1)	49.0	(1.75)
1976	2,986	(39.8)	1,451	(28.9)	1,535	(27.3)	1,458	(43.6)	48.8	(1.31)	685	(30.4)	47.2	(1.87)	773	(31.2)	50.3	(1.82)
1977	3,141	(40.7)	1,483	(29.7)	1,659	(27.7)	1,590	(45.4)	50.6	(1.29)	773	(31.8)	52.1	(1.87)	817	(32.4)	49.3	(1.77)
1978	3,163	(39.7)	1,485	(29.3)	1,677	(26.7)	1,585	(45.2)	50.1	(1.28)	759	(31.6)	51.1	(1.87)	827	(32.4)	49.3	(1.76)
1979	3,160	(40.0)	1,475	(29.2)	1,685	(27.2)	1,559	(45.1)	49.3	(1.28)	744	(31.4)	50.4	(1.88)	815	(32.4)	48.4	(1.76)
1980	3,088	(39.4)	1,498	(28.4)	1,589	(27.3)	1,523	(44.6)	49.3	(1.30)	700	(30.9)	46.7	(1.86)	823	(32.0)	51.8	(1.81)
1981	3,056	(42.2)	1,491	(30.4)	1,565	(29.1)	1,648	(45.8)	53.9	(1.30)	817	(32.4)	54.8	(1.86)	831	(32.4)	53.1	(1.82)
1982	3,100	(40.4)	1,509	(29.0)	1,592	(28.2)	1,569	(46.9)	50.6	(1.36)	741	(32.7)	49.1	(1.95)	828	(33.6)	52.0	(1.90)
1983	2,963	(41.6)	1,389	(30.4)	1,573	(28.2)	1,562	(46.7)	52.7	(1.39)	721	(32.3)	51.9	(2.03)	841	(33.6)	53.4	(1.91)
1984	3,012	(36.5)	1,429	(28.7)	1,584	(21.9)	1,663	(46.0)	55.2	(1.37)	801	(32.7)	56.0	(1.99)	862	(32.3)	54.5	(1.90)
1985	2,668	(40.1)	1,287	(28.7)	1,381	(27.9)	1,540	(45.1)	57.7	(1.45)	755	(31.6)	58.6	(2.08)	785	(32.1)	56.8	(2.02)
1986	2,786	(38.6)	1,332	(28.5)	1,454	(26.0)	1,498	(45.0)	53.8	(1.43)	743	(31.7)	55.8	(2.06)	755	(31.9)	51.9	(1.99)
1987	2,647	(40.9)	1,278	(29.8)	1,369	(28.0)	1,503	(45.1)	56.8	(1.46)	746	(31.9)	58.3	(2.09)	757	(31.9)	55.3	(2.04)
1988	2,673	(47.0)	1,334	(34.1)	1,339	(32.3)	1,575	(50.3)	58.9	(1.57)	761	(35.6)	57.1	(2.24)	814	(35.4)	60.7	(2.20)
1989	2,450	(46.5)	1,204	(32.9)	1,246	(32.8)	1,460	(48.7)	59.6	(1.64)	693	(34.0)	57.6	(2.35)	767	(34.8)	61.6	(2.27)
1990	2,362	(43.0)	1,173	(30.6)	1,189	(30.2)	1,420	(45.9)	60.1	(1.60)	680	(32.2)	58.0	(2.29)	740	(32.6)	62.2	(2.24)
1991	2,276	(41.0)	1,140	(29.0)	1,136	(29.0)	1,423	(44.8)	62.5	(1.62)	660	(31.4)	57.9	(2.33)	763	(31.9)	67.1	(2.22)
1992	2,397	(40.4)	1,216	(29.1)	1,180	(28.1)	1,483	(45.4)	61.9	(1.58)	729	(32.3)	60.0	(2.24)	754	(31.8)	63.8	(2.23)
1993	2,342	(41.4)	1,120	(30.6)	1,223	(27.7)	1,467	(45.4)	62.6	(1.59)	670	(31.9)	59.9	(2.33)	797	(32.1)	65.2	(2.17)
1994	2,517	(38.1)	1,244	(27.9)	1,273	(25.9)	1,559	(43.0)	61.9	(1.43)	754	(30.6)	60.6	(2.05)	805	(30.2)	63.2	(1.99)
1995	2,599	(40.9)	1,238	(29.9)	1,361	(27.7)	1,610	(44.5)	61.9	(1.41)	775	(31.3)	62.6	(2.03)	835	(31.5)	61.3	(1.95)
1996	2,660	(40.5)	1,297	(29.5)	1,363	(27.7)	1,729	(46.1)	65.0	(1.42)	779	(32.4)	60.1	(2.09)	950	(32.5)	69.7	(1.92)
1997	2,769	(41.8)	1,354	(31.0)	1,415	(27.9)	1,856	(47.3)	67.0	(1.38)	860	(33.6)	63.6	(2.01)	995	(32.9)	70.3	(1.87)
1998	2,810	(43.9)	1,452	(31.0)	1,358	(31.0)	1,844	(48.3)	65.6	(1.38)	906	(34.4)	62.4	(1.96)	938	(33.9)	69.1	(1.93)
1999	2,897	(41.5)	1,474	(29.9)	1,423	(28.8)	1,822	(47.8)	62.9	(1.38)	905	(34.1)	61.4	(1.95)	917	(33.4)	64.4	(1.95)
2000	2,756	(45.3)	1,251	(33.6)	1,505	(29.7)	1,745	(48.4)	63.3	(1.41)	749	(33.4)	59.9	(2.13)	996	(34.4)	66.2	(1.88)
2001	2,549	(46.5)	1,277	(33.7)	1,273	(32.0)	1,574	(47.5)	61.8	(1.48)	767	(33.7)	60.1	(2.11)	808	(33.3)	63.5	(2.08)
2002	2,796	(42.7)	1,412	(31.3)	1,384	(29.0)	1,824	(46.1)	65.2	(1.31)	877	(33.0)	62.1	(1.88)	947	(32.1)	68.4	(1.82)
2003	2,677	(42.2)	1,306	(29.9)	1,372	(29.7)	1,711	(45.2)	63.9	(1.35)	799	(31.5)	61.2	(1.97)	913	(32.3)	66.5	(1.86)
2004	2,752	(40.0)	1,327	(29.1)	1,425	(27.3)	1,835	(44.9)	66.7	(1.31)	815	(31.5)	61.4	(1.95)	1,020	(31.6)	71.5	(1.74)
2005	2,675	(40.8)	1,262	(31.5)	1,414	(24.9)	1,834	(44.8)	68.6	(1.31)	839	(32.2)	66.5	(1.94)	995	(30.6)	70.4	(1.77)
2006	2,692	(44.6)	1,328	(32.7)	1,363	(30.1)	1,776	(46.4)	66.0	(1.33)	875	(33.2)	65.8	(1.90)	901	(32.4)	66.1	(1.87)
2007	2,955	(42.6)	1,511	(30.0)	1,444	(30.3)	1,986	(47.0)	67.2	(1.26)	999	(33.4)	66.1	(1.78)	986	(33.1)	68.3	(1.79)
2008	3,151	(42.8)	1,640	(29.6)	1,511	(30.9)	2,161	(48.0)	68.6	(1.21)	1,080	(34.1)	65.9	(1.71)	1,081	(33.8)	71.6	(1.69)

[1]Individuals ages 16 to 24 who graduated from high school or completed a GED during the preceding 12 months.
[2]Enrollment in college as of October of each year for individuals ages 16 to 24 who completed high school during the preceding 12 months.
NOTE: Data are based on sample surveys of the civilian population. High school completion data in this table differ from figures appearing in other tables because of varying survey pro-cedures and coverage. High school completers include GED recipients. Standard errors appear in parentheses. Detail may not sum to totals because of rounding.
SOURCE: American College Testing Program, unpublished tabulations, derived from statistics collected by the Census Bureau, 1960 through 1969. U.S. Department of Commerce, Census Bureau, Current Population Survey (CPS), October, 1970 through 2008. (This table was prepared August 2009.)

Recent high school completers and their enrollment in college, by race/ethnicity: 1960 through 2008
[Numbers in thousands]

Year	Number of high school completers[1]				Enrolled in college[2]								
	Total	White	Black[3]	Hispanic[3]	Total		White		Black[3]		Hispanic[3]		
					Number	Percent	Number	Percent	Number	Percent	Number	Percent Annual	Percent 3-year moving average
1	2	3	4	5	6	7	8	9	10	11	12	13	14
1960	1,679 (43.8)	1,565 (44.7)	— (†)	— (†)	758 (40.9)	45.1 (2.13)	717 (40.2)	45.8 (2.21)	— (†)	— (†)	— (†)	— (†)	— (†)
1961	1,763 (46.0)	1,612 (46.9)	— (†)	— (†)	847 (42.9)	48.0 (2.09)	798 (42.2)	49.5 (2.19)	— (†)	— (†)	— (†)	— (†)	— (†)
1962	1,838 (43.6)	1,660 (45.2)	— (†)	— (†)	900 (43.2)	49.0 (2.05)	840 (42.4)	50.6 (2.15)	— (†)	— (†)	— (†)	— (†)	— (†)
1963	1,741 (44.2)	1,615 (45.2)	— (†)	— (†)	784 (41.5)	45.0 (2.09)	736 (40.7)	45.6 (2.17)	— (†)	— (†)	— (†)	— (†)	— (†)
1964	2,145 (43.0)	1,964 (45.4)	— (†)	— (†)	1,037 (45.6)	48.3 (1.89)	967 (44.8)	49.2 (1.98)	— (†)	— (†)	— (†)	— (†)	— (†)
1965	2,659 (47.7)	2,417 (50.6)	— (†)	— (†)	1,354 (51.4)	50.9 (1.70)	1,249 (50.4)	51.7 (1.78)	— (†)	— (†)	— (†)	— (†)	— (†)
1966	2,612 (45.0)	2,403 (48.0)	— (†)	— (†)	1,309 (50.2)	50.1 (1.72)	1,243 (49.6)	51.7 (1.79)	— (†)	— (†)	— (†)	— (†)	— (†)
1967	2,525 (37.9)	2,267 (40.3)	— (†)	— (†)	1,311 (40.9)	51.9 (1.42)	1,202 (40.1)	53.0 (1.50)	— (†)	— (†)	— (†)	— (†)	— (†)
1968	2,606 (37.3)	2,303 (40.4)	— (†)	— (†)	1,444 (41.7)	55.4 (1.39)	1,304 (40.9)	56.6 (1.47)	— (†)	— (†)	— (†)	— (†)	— (†)
1969	2,842 (36.0)	2,538 (39.8)	— (†)	— (†)	1,516 (42.5)	53.3 (1.34)	1,402 (42.0)	55.2 (1.41)	— (†)	— (†)	— (†)	— (†)	— (†)
1970	2,758 (37.4)	2,461 (40.7)	— (†)	— (†)	1,427 (42.2)	51.7 (1.36)	1,280 (41.2)	52.0 (1.44)	— (†)	— (†)	— (†)	— (†)	— (†)
1971	2,875 (38.0)	2,596 (41.1)	— (†)	— (†)	1,538 (43.2)	53.5 (1.33)	1,402 (42.5)	54.0 (1.40)	— (†)	— (†)	— (†)	— (†)	— (†)
1972	2,964 (37.8)	2,520 (37.2)	316 (18.3)	101 (14.2)	1,459 (43.1)	49.2 (1.31)	1,252 (39.0)	49.7 (1.42)	141 (16.7)	44.6 (4.62)	46 (11.7)	45.0 (9.74)	— (†)
1973	3,058 (37.1)	2,590 (30.8)	324 (18.5)	119 (13.7)	1,424 (43.0)	46.6 (1.29)	1,238 (39.2)	47.8 (1.40)	105 (15.2)	32.5 (4.30)	64 (13.0)	54.1 (9.01)	48.7 (5.33)
1974	3,101 (38.6)	2,620 (31.4)	325 (19.0)	121 (15.2)	1,475 (43.7)	47.6 (1.28)	1,236 (39.4)	47.2 (1.39)	154 (17.4)	47.2 (4.58)	57 (12.9)	46.9 (8.94)	53.0 (5.09)
1975	3,185 (38.6)	2,701 (31.9)	302 (15.4)	132 (15.8)	1,615 (44.8)	50.7 (1.26)	1,381 (40.5)	51.1 (1.37)	126 (13.6)	41.7 (3.97)	77 (14.5)	58.0 (8.44)	52.5 (4.88)
1976	2,986 (39.8)	2,492 (33.1)	290 (15.8)	152 (16.2)	1,458 (43.6)	48.8 (1.31)	1,217 (39.1)	48.8 (1.43)	129 (13.8)	44.4 (4.08)	80 (14.8)	52.7 (7.97)	53.8 (4.68)
1977	3,141 (40.7)	2,618 (34.0)	325 (19.3)	155 (16.0)	1,590 (45.4)	50.6 (1.29)	1,331 (40.8)	50.8 (1.41)	161 (17.9)	49.5 (4.65)	79 (14.8)	50.8 (7.96)	48.5 (4.72)
1978	3,163 (39.7)	2,615 (33.7)	345 (18.4)	135 (15.3)	1,585 (45.2)	50.1 (1.28)	1,321 (40.6)	50.5 (1.41)	160 (17.7)	46.4 (4.51)	56 (13.0)	42.0 (8.44)	45.9 (4.69)
1979	3,160 (40.0)	2,629 (32.7)	319 (19.7)	155 (16.1)	1,559 (45.1)	49.3 (1.28)	1,313 (40.5)	49.9 (1.41)	149 (17.5)	46.7 (4.69)	70 (14.3)	45.0 (7.92)	46.4 (4.83)
1980	3,088 (39.4)	2,554 (30.9)	350 (19.7)	130 (17.1)	1,523 (44.6)	49.3 (1.30)	1,273 (39.6)	49.8 (1.43)	149 (17.7)	42.7 (4.44)	68 (14.4)	52.3 (8.70)	49.8 (4.78)
1981	3,056 (42.2)	2,490 (34.1)	349 (20.5)	146 (17.6)	1,648 (45.8)	53.9 (1.30)	1,367 (40.5)	54.9 (1.44)	149 (17.8)	42.7 (4.44)	76 (15.1)	52.1 (8.19)	49.2 (4.68)
1982	3,100 (40.4)	2,474 (32.9)	382 (19.6)	173 (18.2)	1,569 (46.9)	50.6 (1.36)	1,303 (41.5)	52.7 (1.52)	137 (17.9)	35.8 (4.33)	75 (15.8)	43.2 (7.96)	49.8 (4.94)
1983	2,963 (41.6)	2,363 (33.1)	390 (21.1)	138 (17.8)	1,562 (46.7)	52.7 (1.39)	1,301 (40.9)	55.0 (1.55)	149 (18.7)	38.2 (4.34)	75 (15.7)	54.2 (8.96)	47.3 (4.73)
1984	3,012 (36.5)	2,331 (29.1)	433 (18.5)	187 (17.0)	1,663 (46.0)	55.2 (1.37)	1,375 (39.9)	59.0 (1.54)	172 (19.4)	39.8 (4.15)	83 (16.2)	44.3 (7.67)	49.9 (4.89)
1985	2,668 (40.1)	2,104 (32.3)	332 (19.3)	141 (19.7)	1,540 (45.1)	57.7 (1.45)	1,264 (39.2)	60.1 (1.62)	140 (17.8)	42.2 (4.78)	72 (17.0)	51.0 (9.76)	46.5 (5.19)
1986	2,786 (38.6)	2,146 (30.3)	378 (18.4)	169 (21.7)	1,498 (45.0)	53.8 (1.43)	1,219 (38.8)	56.8 (1.62)	140 (17.9)	36.9 (4.38)	74 (17.7)	44.0 (8.85)	42.9 (5.21)
1987	2,647 (40.9)	2,040 (32.4)	333 (20.6)	176 (20.9)	1,503 (45.1)	56.8 (1.46)	1,195 (38.7)	58.6 (1.65)	174 (19.3)	52.2 (4.82)	59 (16.1)	33.5 (8.25)	44.9 (5.04)
1988	2,673 (47.0)	2,013 (37.9)	378 (22.3)	179 (26.6)	1,575 (50.3)	58.9 (1.57)	1,230 (42.9)	61.1 (1.79)	168 (21.1)	44.4 (4.91)	102 (23.6)	57.1 (10.14)	48.6 (5.99)
1989	2,450 (46.5)	1,889 (37.3)	332 (21.3)	168 (26.5)	1,460 (48.7)	59.6 (1.64)	1,147 (41.7)	60.7 (1.85)	177 (20.9)	53.4 (5.27)	93 (22.9)	55.1 (10.51)	51.6 (6.33)
1990	2,362 (43.0)	1,819 (32.2)	331 (21.9)	121 (21.8)	1,420 (45.9)	60.1 (1.60)	1,147 (38.5)	63.0 (1.80)	155 (19.7)	46.8 (5.08)	52 (16.0)	42.7 (10.82)	51.7 (5.70)
1991	2,276 (41.0)	1,727 (30.3)	310 (20.2)	154 (23.5)	1,423 (44.8)	62.5 (1.62)	1,129 (37.2)	65.4 (1.82)	144 (18.8)	46.4 (5.25)	88 (19.9)	57.2 (9.58)	51.6 (5.52)
1992	2,397 (40.4)	1,724 (30.9)	354 (21.4)	198 (23.0)	1,483 (45.4)	61.9 (1.58)	1,109 (37.4)	64.3 (1.84)	171 (20.2)	48.2 (4.92)	109 (21.0)	55.0 (8.50)	58.1 (5.04)
1993	2,342 (41.4)	1,719 (32.6)	304 (20.4)	201 (23.1)	1,467 (45.4)	62.6 (1.59)	1,082 (37.9)	62.9 (1.85)	169 (19.6)	55.6 (5.28)	125 (21.9)	62.2 (8.22)	55.4 (4.97)
1994	2,517 (38.1)	1,915 (27.0)	316 (17.9)	178 (17.3)	1,559 (43.0)	61.9 (1.43)	1,236 (35.5)	64.5 (1.61)	161 (16.7)	50.8 (4.42)	87 (14.0)	49.1 (6.28)	55.0 (3.23)

See notes at end of table.

Recent high school completers and their enrollment in college, by race/ethnicity: 1960 through 2008—Continued

[Numbers in thousands]

	Number of high school completers[1]				Enrolled in college[2]								
	Total	White	Black[3]	Hispanic[3]	Total		White		Black[3]		Hispanic[3]		
												Percent	
Year					Number	Percent	Number	Percent	Number	Percent	Number	Annual	3-year moving average
1	2	3	4	5	6	7	8	9	10	11	12	13	14
1995	2,599 (40.9)	1,861 (30.1)	349 (19.2)	288 (19.4)	1,610 (44.5)	61.9 (1.41)	1,197 (36.1)	64.3 (1.64)	179 (17.6)	51.2 (4.20)	155 (17.6)	53.7 (4.92)	51.2 (3.18)
1996	2,660 (40.5)	1,875 (30.8)	406 (17.3)	227 (18.9)	1,729 (46.1)	65.0 (1.42)	1,264 (37.5)	67.4 (1.67)	227 (19.0)	56.0 (4.03)	115 (16.3)	50.8 (5.79)	56.7 (2.97)
1997	2,769 (41.8)	1,909 (31.8)	384 (19.2)	336 (19.0)	1,856 (47.3)	67.0 (1.38)	1,301 (38.1)	68.2 (1.64)	225 (19.4)	58.5 (4.12)	220 (19.7)	65.6 (4.53)	54.6 (2.94)
1998	2,810 (43.9)	1,980 (33.0)	386 (20.2)	314 (20.8)	1,844 (48.3)	65.6 (1.38)	1,357 (39.0)	68.5 (1.61)	239 (20.0)	61.9 (4.05)	149 (18.3)	47.4 (4.92)	51.8 (2.79)
1999	2,897 (41.5)	1,978 (31.8)	436 (15.2)	329 (20.9)	1,822 (47.8)	62.9 (1.38)	1,311 (38.6)	66.3 (1.64)	257 (19.1)	58.9 (3.86)	139 (18.0)	42.3 (4.76)	47.5 (2.84)
2000	2,756 (45.3)	1,938 (32.9)	393 (20.0)	300 (22.4)	1,745 (48.4)	63.3 (1.41)	1,272 (38.8)	65.7 (1.66)	216 (19.5)	54.9 (4.11)	159 (19.2)	52.9 (5.03)	49.0 (2.96)
2001	2,549 (46.5)	1,834 (34.8)	381 (20.3)	241 (21.1)	1,574 (47.5)	61.8 (1.48)	1,178 (38.7)	64.3 (1.72)	210 (19.4)	55.0 (4.17)	124 (17.4)	51.7 (5.63)	52.7 (2.93)
2002	2,796 (42.7)	1,903 (31.3)	382 (19.1)	344 (21.6)	1,824 (46.1)	65.2 (1.31)	1,314 (36.5)	69.1 (1.55)	227 (18.7)	59.4 (3.90)	184 (19.2)	53.6 (4.46)	54.6 (2.75)
2003[4]	2,677 (42.2)	1,832 (30.8)	327 (18.4)	314 (20.9)	1,711 (45.2)	63.9 (1.35)	1,213 (35.9)	66.2 (1.61)	188 (17.4)	57.5 (4.25)	184 (18.9)	58.6 (4.61)	58.0 (2.66)
2004[4]	2,752 (40.0)	1,854 (30.9)	398 (15.5)	286 (19.9)	1,835 (44.9)	66.7 (1.31)	1,276 (36.1)	68.8 (1.57)	249 (17.9)	62.5 (3.77)	177 (18.4)	61.8 (4.76)	58.1 (2.60)
2005[4]	2,675 (40.8)	1,799 (30.5)	345 (16.6)	390 (20.6)	1,834 (44.8)	68.6 (1.31)	1,317 (35.4)	73.2 (1.52)	192 (17.1)	55.7 (4.15)	211 (19.7)	54.0 (4.18)	57.9 (2.51)
2006[4]	2,692 (44.6)	1,805 (33.2)	318 (19.0)	382 (22.1)	1,776 (46.4)	66.0 (1.33)	1,237 (36.7)	68.5 (1.60)	177 (17.9)	55.5 (4.33)	222 (20.5)	57.9 (4.18)	58.6 (2.43)
2007[4]	2,955 (42.6)	2,043 (29.9)	416 (17.6)	355 (22.3)	1,986 (47.0)	67.2 (1.26)	1,421 (36.8)	69.5 (1.49)	232 (19.5)	55.7 (3.78)	227 (20.7)	64.0 (4.22)	61.9 (2.33)
2008[4]	3,151 (42.8)	2,091 (31.3)	416 (19.7)	458 (21.9)	2,161 (48.0)	68.6 (1.21)	1,499 (37.5)	71.7 (1.44)	232 (19.6)	55.7 (3.78)	292 (22.0)	63.9 (3.72)	— (†)

—Not available.
†Not applicable.
[1]Individuals ages 16 to 24 who graduated from high school or completed a GED during the preceding 12 months.
[2]Enrollment in college as of October of each year for individuals ages 16 to 24 who completed high school during the preceding 12 months.
[3]Due to the small sample size, data are subject to relatively large sampling errors. A 3-year moving average is an arithmetic average of the year indicated, the year immediately preceding, and the year immediately following. Moving averages are used to produce more stable estimates.

[4]White and Black data exclude persons identifying themselves as two or more races.
NOTE: High school completion data in this table differ from figures appearing in other tables because of varying survey procedures and coverage. High school completers include GED recipients. Race categories exclude persons of Hispanic ethnicity. Total includes persons of other racial/ethnic groups not separately shown. Standard errors appear in parentheses.
SOURCE: American College Testing Program, unpublished tabulations, derived from statistics collected by the Census Bureau, 1960 through 1969. U.S. Department of Commerce, Census Bureau, Current Population Survey (CPS), October, 1970 through 2008. (This table was prepared August 2009.)

553

Graduation rates of previous year's 12th-graders and college attendance rates of those who graduated, by selected high school characteristics: 1999–2000, 2003–04, and 2007–08

Selected high school characteristic	For 1998–99 school year		College attendance rate of 1998–99 graduates in 1999–2000			For 2002–03 school year		College attendance rate of 2002–03 graduates in 2003–04			For 2006–07 school year		College attendance rate of 2006–07 graduates in 2007–08 at 4-year institutions
	Number of high schools with 12th-graders	Graduation rate of 12th-graders[1]	Total	4-year institutions	2-year institutions	Number of high schools with 12th-graders	Graduation rate of 12th-graders[1]	Total	4-year institutions	2-year institutions	Number of high schools with 12th-graders	Graduation rate of 12th-graders[1]	
1	2	3	4	5	6	7	8	9	10	11	12	13	14
Public high schools	20,000 (230)	87.7 (0.67)	57.4 (0.50)	35.4 (0.43)	22.0 (0.34)	22,500 (400)	85.5 (0.77)	61.8 (0.94)	35.0 (0.61)	26.7 (0.58)	24,100 (540)	81.2 (1.34)	39.5 (0.91)
Percent of students who are Black, Hispanic, Asian, Pacific Islander, American Indian/Alaska Native, or two or more races													
Less than 5 percent	6,400 (170)	94.2 (0.79)	63.2 (0.73)	41.3 (0.67)	21.9 (0.59)	6,100 (220)	95.4 (0.41)	68.8 (0.87)	42.6 (0.96)	26.3 (0.64)	5,200 (270)	90.7 (1.23)	46.8 (1.54)
5 to 19 percent	4,800 (180)	89.1 (1.13)	58.7 (1.11)	36.6 (0.88)	22.1 (0.69)	5,200 (270)	87.8 (1.81)	63.9 (2.41)	38.0 (1.77)	26.0 (1.10)	5,400 (320)	89.9 (1.53)	48.4 (2.06)
20 to 49 percent	4,000 (170)	81.7 (2.02)	54.0 (1.16)	32.5 (0.92)	21.5 (0.70)	4,700 (180)	84.8 (1.68)	61.4 (1.44)	34.1 (1.27)	27.3 (0.94)	6,200 (440)	77.2 (2.85)	35.0 (1.89)
50 percent or more	4,800 (150)	82.5 (1.26)	51.1 (0.96)	28.7 (0.89)	22.3 (0.69)	6,500 (280)	74.8 (2.34)	53.2 (2.52)	25.8 (1.43)	27.4 (1.54)	7,300 (430)	71.4 (2.76)	30.8 (2.00)
Percent of students approved for free or reduced-price lunch													
School does not participate	2,400 (130)	80.1 (2.15)	49.7 (2.32)	30.0 (1.75)	19.7 (1.49)	2,400 (230)	71.2 (2.41)	51.4 (2.83)	23.2 (2.26)	28.1 (1.81)	2,800 (320)	66.7 (3.78)	25.4 (4.12)
0 to 25 percent	8,600 (180)	92.2 (0.55)	65.1 (0.74)	42.6 (0.67)	22.5 (0.44)	6,800 (230)	92.9 (0.59)	73.6 (0.59)	46.9 (0.78)	26.7 (0.65)	6,700 (360)	91.1 (1.24)	52.1 (1.63)
26 to 50 percent	4,800 (160)	87.3 (1.49)	57.5 (0.92)	33.4 (0.81)	24.1 (0.63)	6,700 (220)	89.4 (1.19)	64.2 (0.96)	36.7 (1.08)	27.5 (0.74)	7,300 (350)	86.7 (1.54)	41.5 (1.44)
51 to 75 percent	2,300 (140)	85.9 (2.81)	48.0 (2.18)	29.1 (1.57)	18.9 (0.92)	4,000 (270)	83.8 (2.25)	55.3 (2.76)	27.3 (1.58)	28.1 (1.58)	4,100 (290)	79.0 (3.56)	33.2 (1.91)
76 to 100 percent	2,000 (100)	79.4 (2.35)	43.0 (1.91)	22.2 (1.35)	20.7 (1.61)	2,600 (260)	72.0 (4.90)	42.3 (4.49)	20.7 (2.79)	21.6 (2.22)	3,300 (360)	63.7 (5.55)	26.0 (2.93)
School locale													
City	—	—	—	—	—	4,500 (240)	77.1 (1.80)	59.5 (2.00)	32.5 (1.61)	27.0 (1.28)	4,800 (300)	71.6 (2.81)	36.1 (2.73)
Suburb	—	—	—	—	—	4,800 (200)	83.6 (1.40)	67.4 (1.39)	40.3 (1.11)	27.1 (1.01)	5,400 (360)	80.8 (3.25)	41.2 (2.35)
Town	—	—	—	—	—	3,700 (200)	82.6 (3.24)	57.7 (1.94)	31.1 (1.65)	26.6 (0.97)	3,900 (310)	80.2 (2.61)	35.2 (2.28)
Rural	—	—	—	—	—	9,500 (390)	91.6 (0.97)	61.6 (1.92)	35.2 (1.28)	26.5 (0.99)	10,000 (460)	86.4 (1.70)	41.9 (1.47)
Private high schools	7,600 (240)	97.4 (0.55)	71.6 (1.90)	55.6 (1.74)	16.1 (1.00)	8,200 (260)	94.2 (0.86)	76.6 (1.58)	56.2 (1.77)	20.3 (1.30)	8,900 (280)	93.8 (0.91)	66.5 (1.57)
Percent of students who are Black, Hispanic, Asian, Pacific Islander, American Indian/Alaska Native, or two or more races													
Less than 5 percent	2,700 (150)	95.5 (1.53)	67.9 (3.17)	53.3 (2.85)	14.7 (1.61)	2,500 (180)	95.6 (1.59)	73.2 (3.03)	54.4 (3.31)	18.7 (2.14)	2,100 (160)	96.4 (1.19)	68.2 (3.81)
5 to 19 percent	2,500 (130)	99.1 (0.44)	82.3 (1.68)	63.6 (2.37)	18.7 (2.01)	2,900 (170)	95.2 (1.40)	84.7 (1.82)	64.2 (2.71)	20.5 (2.10)	3,500 (200)	95.6 (1.60)	70.3 (2.24)
20 to 49 percent	1,400 (100)	98.5 (0.59)	70.5 (3.90)	55.3 (3.29)	15.2 (2.24)	1,700 (140)	90.8 (2.36)	75.8 (4.16)	56.7 (3.70)	19.1 (2.52)	2,000 (190)	91.5 (2.13)	58.7 (3.39)
50 percent or more	1,000 (110)	97.0 (1.53)	55.9 (6.56)	41.6 (5.34)	14.3 (2.28)	1,100 (140)	93.6 (1.97)	63.7 (6.03)	38.3 (4.52)	25.4 (4.47)	1,400 (130)	88.6 (2.71)	65.3 (3.37)
Percent of students approved for free or reduced-price lunch													
School does not participate	6,700 (230)	97.9 (0.47)	73.8 (1.73)	57.0 (1.74)	16.8 (1.03)	7,100 (250)	95.3 (0.86)	76.7 (1.76)	56.2 (2.00)	20.5 (1.51)	7,300 (280)	95.7 (0.66)	68.3 (1.77)
0 to 25 percent	700 (70)	98.8 (0.74)	64.9 (6.49)	53.8 (5.69)	11.0 (1.40)	600 (80)	95.0 (3.62)	84.7 (4.28)	66.2 (4.35)	18.5 (2.39)	700 (100)	91.4 (7.18)	73.2 (4.64)
26 to 100 percent	‡	‡	‡	‡	‡	400 (80)	75.1 (7.62)	59.1 (8.13)	38.9 (6.70)	20.2 (4.34)	1,000 (130)	80.8 (4.70)	46.7 (6.86)
School locale													
City	—	—	—	—	—	†	†	†	†	†	3,100 (170)	94.4 (1.52)	71.8 (2.62)
Suburb	—	—	—	—	—	†	†	†	†	†	2,800 (180)	93.0 (1.52)	67.0 (2.99)
Town	—	—	—	—	—	†	†	†	†	†	1,000 (150)	95.7 (2.12)	63.8 (5.02)
Rural	—	—	—	—	—	†	†	†	†	†	2,000 (190)	92.9 (2.88)	58.9 (3.54)

—Not available.
†Not applicable.
‡Reporting standards not met.
[1]Includes only students who were enrolled in 12th grade in fall of the school year and graduated with a diploma by the end of the following summer.

NOTE: Data are based on a sample survey and may not be strictly comparable with data reported elsewhere. Includes all schools, including combined schools, with students enrolled in the 12th grade. Some data have been revised from previously published figures. Detail may not sum to totals because of rounding. Standard errors appear in parentheses.
SOURCE: U.S. Department of Education, National Center for Education Statistics, Schools and Staffing Survey (SASS), "Public School Questionnaire," 1999–2000, 2003–04, and 2007–08, "Private School Questionnaire," 1999–2000, 2003–04, and 2007–08, and "Charter School Questionnaire," 1999–2000. (This table was prepared October 2009.)

Total undergraduate fall enrollment in degree-granting institutions, by attendance status, sex of student, and control of institution: 1967 through 2008

Year	Total	Full-time	Part-time	Males	Females	Males Full-time	Males Part-time	Females Full-time	Females Part-time	Males Public	Males Private	Females Public	Females Private
1	2	3	4	5	6	7	8	9	10	11	12	13	14
1967	6,015,683	4,344,890	1,670,793	3,502,099	2,513,584	2,569,411	932,688	1,775,479	738,105	2,491,831	1,010,268	1,801,574	712,010
1968	6,475,714	4,740,408	1,735,306	3,781,000	2,694,714	2,810,135	970,865	1,930,273	764,441	2,787,269	993,731	1,994,726	699,988
1969	6,884,485	4,992,050	1,892,435	4,007,528	2,876,957	2,952,197	1,055,331	2,039,853	837,104	2,996,025	1,011,503	2,162,292	714,665
1970	7,368,644	5,280,064	2,088,580	4,249,702	3,118,942	3,096,371	1,153,331	2,183,693	935,249	3,236,128	1,013,574	2,384,127	734,815
1971	7,744,254	5,512,996	2,231,258	4,417,873	3,326,381	3,201,118	1,216,755	2,311,878	1,014,503	3,427,012	990,861	2,580,781	745,600
1972	7,942,439	5,489,090	2,453,349	4,428,593	3,513,846	3,120,817	1,307,776	2,368,273	1,145,573	3,465,701	962,892	2,756,903	756,943
1973	8,259,671	5,578,558	2,681,113	4,537,599	3,722,072	3,134,418	1,403,181	2,444,140	1,277,932	3,579,696	957,903	2,942,716	779,356
1974	8,798,728	5,726,346	3,072,382	4,765,582	4,033,146	3,191,770	1,573,812	2,534,576	1,498,570	3,800,052	965,530	3,231,678	801,468
1975	9,679,455	6,168,396	3,511,059	5,257,005	4,422,450	3,459,328	1,797,677	2,709,068	1,713,382	4,244,632	1,012,373	3,581,400	841,050
1976	9,434,591	6,033,233	3,401,358	4,906,277	4,528,314	3,244,339	1,661,938	2,788,894	1,739,420	3,950,985	955,292	3,669,377	858,937
1977	9,716,703	6,094,023	3,622,680	4,897,197	4,819,506	3,188,262	1,708,935	2,905,761	1,913,745	3,937,407	959,790	3,905,573	913,933
1978	9,684,399	5,962,826	3,721,573	4,761,067	4,923,332	3,068,641	1,692,426	2,894,185	2,029,147	3,812,299	948,768	3,974,986	948,346
1979	9,997,977	6,079,415	3,918,562	4,820,123	5,177,854	3,086,696	1,733,427	2,992,719	2,185,135	3,865,030	955,093	4,181,801	996,053
1980	10,475,055	6,361,744	4,113,311	5,000,177	5,474,878	3,226,857	1,773,320	3,134,887	2,339,991	4,015,000	985,177	4,426,955	1,047,923
1981	10,754,522	6,449,068	4,305,454	5,108,271	5,646,251	3,260,473	1,847,798	3,188,595	2,457,656	4,089,975	1,018,296	4,558,388	1,087,863
1982	10,825,062	6,483,805	4,341,257	5,170,494	5,654,568	3,299,436	1,871,058	3,184,369	2,470,199	4,139,766	1,030,728	4,573,307	1,081,261
1983	10,845,995	6,514,034	4,331,961	5,158,300	5,687,695	3,304,247	1,854,053	3,209,787	2,477,908	4,116,682	1,041,618	4,580,436	1,107,259
1984	10,618,071	6,347,653	4,270,418	5,006,813	5,611,258	3,194,930	1,811,883	3,152,723	2,458,535	3,989,549	1,017,264	4,503,942	1,107,316
1985	10,596,674	6,319,592	4,277,082	4,962,080	5,634,594	3,156,446	1,805,634	3,163,146	2,471,448	3,952,548	1,009,532	4,524,577	1,110,017
1986	10,797,975	6,352,073	4,445,902	5,017,505	5,780,470	3,146,330	1,871,175	3,205,743	2,574,727	4,002,471	1,015,034	4,658,245	1,122,225
1987	11,046,235	6,462,549	4,583,686	5,068,457	5,977,778	3,163,676	1,904,781	3,298,873	2,678,905	4,076,349	992,108	4,842,240	1,135,538
1988	11,316,548	6,642,428	4,674,120	5,137,644	6,178,904	3,206,442	1,931,202	3,435,986	2,742,918	4,113,497	1,024,147	4,989,649	1,189,255
1989	11,742,531	6,840,696	4,901,835	5,310,990	6,431,541	3,278,647	2,032,343	3,562,049	2,869,492	4,271,822	1,039,168	5,215,920	1,215,621
1990	11,959,106	6,976,030	4,983,076	5,379,759	6,579,347	3,336,535	2,043,224	3,639,495	2,939,852	4,352,875	1,026,884	5,356,721	1,222,626
1991	12,439,287	7,221,412	5,217,875	5,571,003	6,868,284	3,435,526	2,135,477	3,785,886	3,082,398	4,530,934	1,040,069	5,617,023	1,251,261
1992	12,537,700	7,244,442	5,293,258	5,582,936	6,954,764	3,424,739	2,158,197	3,819,703	3,135,061	4,536,925	1,046,011	5,679,372	1,275,392
1993	12,323,959	7,179,482	5,144,477	5,483,682	6,840,277	3,381,997	2,101,685	3,797,485	3,042,792	4,447,266	1,036,416	5,564,521	1,275,756
1994	12,262,608	7,168,706	5,093,902	5,422,113	6,840,495	3,341,591	2,080,522	3,827,115	3,013,380	4,394,309	1,027,804	5,550,819	1,289,676
1995	12,231,719	7,145,268	5,086,451	5,401,130	6,830,589	3,296,610	2,104,520	3,848,658	2,981,931	4,380,030	1,021,100	5,523,596	1,306,993
1996	12,326,948	7,298,839	5,028,109	5,420,672	6,906,276	3,339,108	2,081,564	3,959,731	2,946,545	4,382,751	1,037,921	5,552,532	1,353,744
1997	12,450,587	7,418,598	5,031,989	5,468,532	6,982,055	3,379,597	2,088,935	4,039,001	2,943,054	4,408,364	1,060,168	5,599,115	1,382,940
1998	12,436,937	7,538,711	4,898,226	5,446,133	6,990,804	3,428,161	2,017,972	4,110,550	2,880,254	4,360,935	1,085,198	5,589,277	1,401,527
1999	12,681,231	7,735,075	4,946,156	5,559,457	7,121,774	3,515,869	2,043,588	4,219,206	2,902,568	4,431,056	1,128,401	5,678,953	1,442,821
2000	13,155,393	7,922,926	5,232,467	5,778,268	7,377,125	3,588,246	2,190,022	4,334,680	3,042,445	4,622,098	1,156,170	5,917,224	1,459,901
2001	13,715,610	8,327,640	5,387,970	6,004,431	7,711,179	3,768,630	2,235,801	4,559,010	3,152,169	4,804,014	1,200,417	6,181,857	1,529,322
2002	14,257,077	8,734,252	5,522,825	6,192,390	8,064,687	3,934,168	2,258,222	4,800,084	3,264,603	4,960,291	1,232,099	6,472,564	1,592,123
2003	14,480,364	9,045,253	5,435,111	6,227,372	8,252,992	4,048,682	2,178,690	4,996,571	3,256,421	4,956,392	1,270,980	6,566,711	1,686,281
2004	14,780,630	9,284,336	5,496,294	6,340,048	8,440,582	4,140,628	2,199,420	5,143,708	3,296,874	5,009,240	1,330,808	6,641,340	1,799,242
2005	14,963,964	9,446,430	5,517,534	6,408,871	8,555,093	4,200,863	2,208,008	5,245,567	3,309,526	5,046,002	1,362,869	6,651,728	1,903,365
2006	15,184,302	9,571,079	5,613,223	6,513,756	8,670,546	4,264,606	2,249,150	5,306,473	3,364,073	5,133,850	1,379,906	6,713,576	1,956,970
2007	15,603,771	9,840,978	5,762,793	6,727,600	8,876,171	4,396,868	2,330,732	5,444,110	3,432,061	5,300,572	1,427,028	6,837,011	2,039,160
2008	16,365,738	10,254,930	6,110,808	7,066,623	9,299,115	4,577,431	2,489,192	5,677,499	3,621,616	5,531,965	1,534,658	7,059,252	2,239,863

NOTE: Data include unclassified undergraduate students. Data through 1995 are for institutions of higher education, while later data are for degree-granting institutions. Degree-granting institutions grant associate's or higher degrees and participate in Title IV federal financial aid programs. The degree-granting classification is very similar to the earlier higher education classification, but it includes more 2-year colleges and excludes a few higher education institutions that did not grant degrees. (See Appendix A: Guide to Sources for details.) Detail may not sum to totals because of rounding.

SOURCE: U.S. Department of Education, National Center for Education Statistics, Higher Education General Information Survey (HEGIS), "Fall Enrollment in Colleges and Universities" surveys, 1967 through 1985; and 1986 through 2008 Integrated Postsecondary Education Data System, "Fall Enrollment Survey" (IPEDS-EF:86–99), and Spring 2001 through Spring 2009. (This table was prepared September 2009.)

Total postbaccalaureate fall enrollment in degree-granting institutions, by attendance status, sex of student, and control of institution: 1967 through 2008

Year	Total	Full-time	Part-time	Males	Females	Males Full-time	Males Part-time	Females Full-time	Females Part-time	Males Public	Males Private	Females Public	Females Private
1	2	3	4	5	6	7	8	9	10	11	12	13	14
1967	896,065	448,238	447,827	630,701	265,364	354,628	276,073	93,610	171,754	351,947	278,754	170,676	94,688
1968	1,037,377	469,747	567,630	696,649	340,728	358,686	337,963	111,061	229,667	410,609	286,040	238,048	102,680
1969	1,120,175	506,833	613,342	738,673	381,502	383,630	355,043	123,203	258,299	457,126	281,547	281,425	100,077
1970	1,212,243	536,226	676,017	793,940	418,303	407,724	386,216	128,502	289,801	496,757	297,183	311,122	107,181
1971	1,204,390	564,236	640,154	789,131	415,259	428,167	360,964	136,069	279,190	513,570	275,561	305,604	109,655
1972	1,272,421	583,299	689,122	810,164	462,257	436,533	373,631	146,766	315,491	506,950	303,214	341,081	121,176
1973	1,342,452	610,935	731,517	833,453	508,999	444,219	389,234	166,716	342,283	523,274	310,179	373,830	135,169
1974	1,425,001	643,927	781,074	856,847	568,154	454,706	402,141	189,221	378,933	538,573	318,274	418,197	149,957
1975	1,505,404	672,938	832,466	891,992	613,412	467,425	424,567	205,513	407,899	560,041	331,951	448,435	164,977
1976	1,577,546	683,825	893,721	904,551	672,995	459,286	445,265	224,539	448,456	555,912	348,639	477,203	195,792
1977	1,569,084	698,902	870,182	891,819	677,265	462,038	429,781	236,864	440,401	535,748	356,071	468,265	209,000
1978	1,575,693	704,831	870,862	879,931	695,762	458,865	421,066	245,966	449,796	519,150	360,781	479,458	216,304
1979	1,571,922	714,624	857,298	862,754	709,168	456,197	406,557	258,427	450,741	503,949	358,805	486,042	223,126
1980	1,621,840	736,214	885,626	874,197	747,643	462,387	411,810	273,827	473,816	507,587	366,610	507,852	239,791
1981	1,617,150	732,182	884,968	866,785	750,365	452,364	414,421	279,818	470,547	496,825	369,960	501,844	248,521
1982	1,600,718	736,813	863,905	860,890	739,828	453,519	407,371	283,294	456,534	493,122	367,768	489,892	249,936
1983	1,618,666	747,016	871,650	865,425	753,241	455,540	409,885	291,476	461,765	493,356	372,069	492,260	260,981
1984	1,623,869	750,735	873,134	856,761	767,108	452,579	404,182	298,156	468,952	484,963	371,798	498,916	268,192
1985	1,650,381	755,629	894,752	856,370	794,011	451,274	405,096	304,355	489,656	484,940	371,430	517,208	276,803
1986	1,705,536	767,477	938,059	867,010	838,526	452,717	414,293	314,760	523,766	503,107	363,903	550,070	288,456
1987	1,720,407	768,536	951,871	863,599	856,808	447,212	416,387	321,324	535,484	497,117	366,482	557,548	299,260
1988	1,738,789	794,340	944,449	864,252	874,537	455,337	408,915	339,003	535,534	495,461	368,791	562,781	311,756
1989	1,796,029	820,254	975,775	879,025	917,004	461,596	417,429	358,658	558,346	504,528	374,497	585,693	331,311
1990	1,859,531	844,955	1,014,576	904,150	955,381	471,217	432,933	373,738	581,643	522,136	382,014	612,985	342,396
1991	1,919,666	893,917	1,025,749	930,841	988,825	493,849	436,992	400,068	588,757	535,422	395,419	626,184	362,641
1992	1,949,659	917,676	1,031,983	941,053	1,008,606	502,166	438,887	415,510	593,096	537,471	403,582	630,799	377,807
1993	1,980,844	948,136	1,032,708	943,768	1,037,076	508,574	435,194	439,562	597,514	537,245	406,523	640,056	397,020
1994	2,016,182	969,070	1,047,112	949,785	1,066,397	513,592	436,193	455,478	610,919	535,759	414,026	652,793	413,604
1995	2,030,062	983,534	1,046,528	941,409	1,088,653	510,782	430,627	472,752	615,901	527,605	413,804	661,143	427,510
1996	2,040,572	1,004,114	1,036,458	932,153	1,108,419	512,100	420,053	492,014	616,405	519,702	412,451	665,514	442,905
1997	2,051,747	1,019,464	1,032,283	927,496	1,124,251	510,845	416,651	508,619	615,632	515,823	411,673	672,817	451,434
1998	2,070,030	1,024,627	1,045,403	923,132	1,146,898	505,492	417,640	519,135	627,763	507,763	415,369	679,794	467,104
1999	2,109,993	1,051,419	1,058,574	931,189	1,178,804	509,852	421,337	541,567	637,237	510,125	421,064	689,265	489,539
2000	2,156,896	1,086,674	1,070,222	943,501	1,213,395	522,847	420,654	563,827	649,568	510,309	433,192	703,155	510,240
2001	2,212,377	1,119,862	1,092,515	956,384	1,255,993	531,260	425,124	588,602	667,391	523,597	432,787	723,688	532,305
2002	2,354,634	1,212,107	1,142,527	1,009,726	1,344,908	566,930	442,796	645,177	699,731	551,729	457,997	767,409	577,499
2003	2,431,117	1,280,880	1,150,237	1,032,892	1,398,225	589,190	443,702	691,690	706,535	555,903	476,989	779,692	618,533
2004	2,491,414	1,325,841	1,165,573	1,047,214	1,444,200	598,727	448,487	727,114	717,086	550,236	496,978	779,296	664,904
2005	2,523,511	1,350,581	1,172,930	1,047,054	1,476,457	602,525	444,529	748,056	728,401	543,221	503,833	780,883	695,574
2006	2,574,568	1,386,226	1,188,342	1,061,059	1,513,509	614,709	446,350	771,517	741,992	545,554	515,505	787,153	726,356
2007	2,644,357	1,428,914	1,215,443	1,088,314	1,556,043	632,576	455,738	796,338	759,705	556,727	531,587	796,470	759,573
2008	2,737,076	1,492,813	1,244,263	1,122,272	1,614,804	656,926	465,346	835,887	778,917	568,550	553,722	812,386	802,418

NOTE: Data include first-professional and graduate-level students. Data through 1995 are for institutions of higher education, while later data are for degree-granting institutions. Degree-granting institutions grant associate's or higher degrees and participate in Title IV federal financial aid programs. The degree-granting classification is very similar to the earlier higher education classification, but it includes more 2-year colleges and excludes a few higher education institutions that did not grant degrees. (See Appendix A: Guide to Sources for details.)

SOURCE: U.S. Department of Education, National Center for Education Statistics, Higher Education General Information Survey (HEGIS), "Fall Enrollment in Colleges and Universities" surveys, 1967 through 1985; and 1986 through 2008 Integrated Postsecondary Education Data System, "Fall Enrollment Survey" (IPEDS-EF:86–99), and Spring 2001 through Spring 2009. (This table was prepared September 2009.)

Total fall enrollment in degree-granting institutions, by state or jurisdiction: Selected years, 1970 through 2007

State or jurisdiction	Fall 1970	Fall 1980	Fall 1990	Fall 2000	Fall 2002	Fall 2003	Fall 2004	Fall 2005	Fall 2006	Fall 2007	Percent change, 2000 to 2007
1	2	3	4	5	6	7	8	9	10	11	12
United States	8,580,887	12,096,895	13,818,637	15,312,289	16,611,711	16,911,481	17,272,044	17,487,475	17,758,870	18,248,128	19.2
Alabama	103,936	164,306	218,589	233,962	246,414	253,846	255,826	256,389	258,408	268,183	14.6
Alaska	9,471	21,296	29,833	27,953	29,546	31,035	30,869	30,231	29,853	30,616	9.5
Arizona	109,619	202,716	264,148	342,490	401,605	435,767	490,925	545,597	567,192	624,147	82.2
Arkansas	52,039	77,607	90,425	115,172	127,372	133,950	138,399	143,272	147,391	152,168	32.1
California	1,257,245	1,790,993	1,808,740	2,256,708	2,474,024	2,340,698	2,374,045	2,399,833	2,434,774	2,529,522	12.1
Colorado	123,395	162,916	227,131	263,872	282,343	289,424	300,914	302,672	308,383	310,637	17.7
Connecticut	124,700	159,632	168,604	161,243	170,606	170,976	172,775	174,675	176,716	179,005	11.0
Delaware	25,260	32,939	42,004	43,897	49,228	49,595	49,804	51,612	51,238	52,343	19.2
District of Columbia	77,158	86,675	79,551	72,689	91,014	95,297	99,988	104,897	109,505	115,153	58.4
Florida	235,525	411,891	588,086	707,684	792,079	840,108	866,665	872,662	885,651	913,793	29.1
Georgia	126,511	184,159	251,786	346,204	397,604	411,102	434,283	426,650	435,403	453,711	31.1
Hawaii	36,562	47,181	56,436	60,182	65,368	67,481	67,225	67,083	66,893	66,601	10.7
Idaho	34,567	43,018	51,881	65,594	72,072	75,390	76,311	77,708	77,872	78,846	20.2
Illinois	452,146	644,245	729,246	743,918	776,622	796,815	801,401	832,967	830,676	837,018	12.5
Indiana	192,668	247,253	284,832	314,334	342,064	350,102	356,801	361,253	368,013	380,477	21.0
Iowa	108,902	140,449	170,515	188,974	202,546	213,958	217,646	227,722	238,634	256,259	35.6
Kansas	102,485	136,605	163,733	179,968	188,049	190,306	191,590	191,752	193,146	194,102	7.9
Kentucky	98,591	143,066	177,852	188,341	225,489	235,743	240,097	244,969	248,914	258,213	37.1
Louisiana	120,728	160,058	186,840	223,800	232,140	244,537	246,301	197,713	224,147	224,754	0.4
Maine	34,134	43,264	57,186	58,473	63,308	64,222	65,415	65,551	66,149	67,173	14.9
Maryland	149,607	225,526	259,700	273,745	300,269	307,613	312,493	314,151	319,460	327,597	19.7
Massachusetts	303,809	418,415	417,833	421,142	431,224	436,102	439,245	443,316	451,526	463,366	10.0
Michigan	392,726	520,131	569,803	567,631	605,835	616,012	620,980	626,751	634,489	643,279	13.3
Minnesota	160,788	206,691	253,789	293,445	323,791	339,597	349,021	361,701	375,899	392,393	33.7
Mississippi	73,967	102,364	122,883	137,389	147,077	148,584	152,115	150,457	151,137	155,232	13.0
Missouri	183,930	234,421	289,899	321,348	348,146	359,749	365,204	374,445	377,098	384,366	19.6
Montana	30,062	35,177	35,876	42,240	45,111	47,240	47,173	47,850	47,501	47,371	12.1
Nebraska	66,915	89,488	112,831	112,117	116,730	119,511	121,053	121,236	124,500	127,378	13.6
Nevada	13,669	40,455	61,728	87,893	95,671	100,849	105,961	110,705	112,270	116,276	32.3
New Hampshire	29,400	46,794	59,510	61,718	68,523	69,608	70,163	69,893	70,669	70,724	14.6
New Jersey	216,121	321,610	324,286	335,945	361,733	372,632	380,374	379,758	385,656	398,136	18.5
New Mexico	44,461	58,283	85,500	110,739	120,997	127,040	131,577	131,337	131,828	134,375	21.3
New York	806,479	992,237	1,048,286	1,043,395	1,107,270	1,126,085	1,141,525	1,152,081	1,160,364	1,172,811	12.4
North Carolina	171,925	287,537	352,138	404,652	447,335	464,437	472,709	484,392	495,633	502,330	24.1
North Dakota	31,495	34,069	37,878	40,248	45,800	48,402	49,533	49,389	49,519	49,945	24.1
Ohio	376,267	489,145	557,690	549,553	587,996	603,399	614,234	616,350	619,942	630,497	14.7
Oklahoma	110,155	160,295	173,221	178,016	198,423	207,791	207,625	208,053	206,236	206,382	15.9
Oregon	122,177	157,458	165,741	183,065	204,565	198,786	199,985	200,033	197,594	202,928	10.9
Pennsylvania	411,044	507,716	604,060	609,521	654,826	676,121	688,780	692,340	707,132	725,397	19.0
Rhode Island	45,898	66,869	78,273	75,450	77,417	79,085	80,377	81,382	81,734	82,900	9.9
South Carolina	69,518	132,476	159,302	185,931	202,007	207,601	208,910	210,444	212,422	217,755	17.1
South Dakota	30,639	32,761	34,208	43,221	47,751	55,816	48,708	48,768	48,931	49,747	15.1
Tennessee	135,103	204,581	226,238	263,910	261,899	276,999	278,055	283,070	290,530	297,785	12.8
Texas	442,225	701,391	901,437	1,033,973	1,152,369	1,175,336	1,229,197	1,240,707	1,252,709	1,269,098	22.7
Utah	81,687	93,987	121,303	163,776	178,932	183,462	194,324	200,691	202,151	203,679	24.4
Vermont	22,209	30,628	36,398	35,489	36,537	37,695	38,639	39,915	41,095	42,191	18.9
Virginia	151,915	280,504	353,442	381,893	404,966	414,945	425,181	439,166	456,172	478,268	25.2
Washington	183,544	303,603	263,384	320,840	338,820	345,566	343,524	348,482	348,154	352,075	9.7
West Virginia	63,153	81,973	84,790	87,888	93,723	97,005	97,884	99,547	100,519	116,848	33.0
Wisconsin	202,058	269,086	299,774	307,179	329,443	329,738	331,506	335,258	340,158	343,747	11.9
Wyoming	15,220	21,147	31,326	30,004	32,605	33,695	33,955	35,334	34,693	35,246	17.5
U.S. Service Academies[1]	17,079	49,808	48,692	13,475	14,420	14,628	14,754	15,265	12,191	15,285	13.4
Other jurisdictions	67,237	137,749	164,618	194,633	211,204	218,058	220,920	223,165	226,175	226,849	16.6
American Samoa	0	976	1,219	297	1,367	1,537	1,550	1,579	1,607	1,767	494.9
Federated States of Micronesia	0	224	975	1,576	2,173	2,558	2,608	2,283	2,539	2,379	51.0
Guam	2,719	3,217	4,741	5,215	5,157	4,710	4,642	6,064	5,789	5,244	0.6
Marshall Islands	0	0	0	328	224	601	623	604	647	557	69.8
Northern Marianas	0	0	661	1,078	1,299	1,237	1,101	967	968	901	-16.4
Palau	0	0	491	581	668	727	651	651	679	668	15.0
Puerto Rico	63,073	131,184	154,065	183,290	197,781	203,951	207,180	208,625	211,458	212,949	16.2
U.S. Virgin Islands	1,445	2,148	2,466	2,268	2,535	2,737	2,565	2,392	2,488	2,384	5.1

[1]Data for 2000 and later years reflect a substantial reduction in the number of Department of Defense institutions included in the IPEDS survey.
NOTE: Data through 1990 are for institutions of higher education, while later data are for degree-granting institutions. Degree-granting institutions grant associate's or higher degrees and participate in Title IV federal financial aid programs. The degree-granting classification is very similar to the earlier higher education classification, but it includes more 2-year colleges

and excludes a few higher education institutions that did not grant degrees. (See Appendix A: Guide to Sources for details.)
SOURCE: U.S. Department of Education, National Center for Education Statistics, Higher Education General Information Survey (HEGIS), "Fall Enrollment in Colleges and Universities" surveys, 1970 and 1980; and 1990 through 2007 Integrated Postsecondary Education Data System, "Fall Enrollment Survey" (IPEDS-EF:90), and Spring 2001 through Spring 2008. (This table was prepared July 2009.)

Total fall enrollment in public degree-granting institutions, by state or jurisdiction: Selected years, 1970 through 2007

State or jurisdiction	Fall 1970	Fall 1980	Fall 1990	Fall 2000	Fall 2002	Fall 2003	Fall 2004	Fall 2005	Fall 2006	Fall 2007	Percent change, 2000 to 2007
1	2	3	4	5	6	7	8	9	10	11	12
United States	6,428,134	9,457,394	10,844,717	11,752,786	12,751,993	12,858,698	12,980,112	13,021,834	13,180,133	13,490,780	14.8
Alabama	87,884	143,674	195,939	207,435	217,883	225,347	226,989	228,153	230,668	237,632	14.6
Alaska	8,563	20,561	27,792	26,559	28,314	29,821	29,515	28,866	28,595	29,381	10.6
Arizona	107,315	194,034	248,213	284,522	307,496	310,679	317,974	320,865	331,441	332,154	16.7
Arkansas	43,599	66,068	78,645	101,775	113,509	119,920	123,973	128,117	131,407	135,525	33.2
California	1,123,529	1,599,838	1,594,710	1,927,771	2,121,106	1,978,831	1,987,283	2,008,155	2,047,565	2,136,087	10.8
Colorado	108,562	145,598	200,653	217,897	233,740	236,883	239,308	234,509	231,901	227,984	4.6
Connecticut	73,391	97,788	109,556	101,027	108,522	108,815	110,354	111,705	112,476	114,072	12.9
Delaware	21,151	28,325	34,252	34,194	37,344	37,621	38,243	38,682	38,118	39,092	14.3
District of Columbia	12,194	13,900	11,990	5,499	5,603	5,424	5,388	5,595	5,769	5,608	2.0
Florida	189,450	334,349	489,081	556,912	617,754	643,784	649,857	648,999	651,908	683,328	22.7
Georgia	101,900	140,158	196,413	271,755	317,180	330,052	335,979	342,012	346,138	359,883	32.4
Hawaii	32,963	43,269	45,728	44,579	48,163	50,316	50,569	50,157	49,990	50,454	13.2
Idaho	27,072	34,491	41,315	53,751	57,996	60,481	60,695	60,303	59,211	60,526	12.6
Illinois	315,634	491,274	551,333	534,155	554,093	566,137	563,593	555,149	552,777	550,940	3.1
Indiana	136,739	189,224	223,953	240,023	258,627	262,957	266,916	267,298	271,704	278,951	16.2
Iowa	68,390	97,454	117,834	135,008	145,798	149,195	149,776	148,907	151,052	154,644	14.5
Kansas	88,215	121,987	149,117	159,976	167,741	169,384	170,149	170,319	170,531	170,054	6.3
Kentucky	77,240	114,884	147,095	151,973	188,518	196,474	197,991	201,579	204,198	211,234	39.0
Louisiana	101,127	136,703	158,290	189,213	197,547	207,923	208,218	181,043	192,554	193,316	2.2
Maine	25,405	31,878	41,500	40,662	44,850	46,714	47,284	47,519	47,770	48,357	18.9
Maryland	118,988	195,051	220,783	223,797	246,792	251,984	256,582	256,073	260,921	269,719	20.5
Massachusetts	116,127	183,765	186,035	183,248	187,874	189,334	187,873	188,295	192,164	198,700	8.4
Michigan	339,625	454,147	487,359	467,861	495,676	501,821	500,873	505,586	511,776	519,449	11.0
Minnesota	130,567	162,379	199,211	218,617	235,513	242,531	241,245	240,853	244,106	250,397	14.5
Mississippi	64,968	90,661	109,038	125,355	134,130	134,318	137,543	135,896	136,626	139,931	11.6
Missouri	132,540	165,179	200,093	201,509	214,022	216,777	214,561	217,722	218,475	223,155	10.7
Montana	27,287	31,178	31,865	37,387	40,615	42,444	42,289	42,997	42,995	42,857	14.6
Nebraska	51,454	73,509	94,614	88,531	92,111	93,432	93,195	93,181	94,486	96,680	9.2
Nevada	13,576	40,280	61,242	83,120	89,547	94,205	96,773	100,043	101,856	104,797	26.1
New Hampshire	15,979	24,119	32,163	35,870	40,958	41,324	40,642	41,007	41,530	41,982	17.0
New Jersey	145,373	247,028	261,601	266,921	289,275	298,906	305,034	304,315	308,374	318,296	19.2
New Mexico	40,795	55,077	83,403	101,450	111,667	117,245	121,339	120,976	121,668	124,773	23.0
New York	449,437	563,251	616,884	583,417	610,756	613,895	623,192	626,222	635,785	652,428	11.8
North Carolina	123,761	228,154	285,405	329,422	367,861	383,720	389,143	396,755	406,068	410,746	24.7
North Dakota	30,192	31,709	34,690	36,014	41,134	43,383	43,275	42,808	42,949	43,016	19.4
Ohio	281,099	381,765	427,613	411,161	441,738	450,369	454,377	453,001	452,962	460,240	11.9
Oklahoma	91,438	137,188	151,073	153,699	171,369	178,612	179,281	179,225	178,015	177,643	15.6
Oregon	108,483	140,102	144,427	154,756	173,698	166,129	165,375	163,752	160,059	165,260	6.8
Pennsylvania	232,982	292,499	343,478	339,229	370,386	381,254	384,525	380,271	388,251	396,774	17.0
Rhode Island	25,527	35,052	42,350	38,458	38,867	39,937	39,920	40,008	40,374	41,503	7.9
South Carolina	47,101	107,683	131,134	155,519	167,563	171,893	172,386	174,686	176,415	180,479	16.0
South Dakota	23,936	24,328	26,596	34,857	37,760	38,179	37,598	37,548	38,028	38,917	11.6
Tennessee	98,897	156,835	175,049	202,530	194,202	196,088	199,904	200,394	205,056	208,524	3.0
Texas	365,522	613,552	802,314	896,534	1,006,549	1,035,872	1,071,926	1,081,335	1,094,139	1,109,666	23.8
Utah	49,588	59,598	86,108	123,046	135,778	140,282	145,182	148,960	148,228	147,982	20.3
Vermont	12,536	17,984	20,910	20,021	21,238	22,607	22,980	24,090	24,385	24,829	24.0
Virginia	123,279	246,500	291,286	313,780	337,286	341,948	343,391	349,195	357,823	370,486	18.1
Washington	162,718	276,028	227,632	273,928	293,007	298,079	293,145	296,756	297,048	301,793	10.2
West Virginia	51,363	71,228	74,108	76,136	79,741	82,273	83,274	85,148	86,501	87,838	15.4
Wisconsin	170,374	235,179	253,529	249,737	268,010	266,805	266,884	268,928	272,246	273,708	9.6
Wyoming	15,220	21,121	30,623	28,715	30,666	31,666	31,597	32.611	32,860	33,705	17.4
U.S. Service Academies[1]	17,079	49,808	48,692	13,475	14,420	14,628	14,754	15,265	12,191	15,285	13.4
Other jurisdictions	46,680	60,692	66,244	84,464	86,484	85,665	83,831	82,341	80,685	80,958	-4.2
American Samoa	0	976	1,219	297	1,367	1,537	1,550	1,579	1,607	1,767	494.9
Federated States of Micronesia	0	224	975	1,576	2,173	2,558	2,608	2,283	2,539	2,379	51.0
Guam	2,719	3,217	4,741	5,215	5,038	4,546	4,470	5,875	5,603	5,077	-2.6
Marshall Islands	0	0	0	328	224	601	623	604	647	557	69.8
Northern Marianas	0	0	661	1,078	1,299	1,237	1,101	967	968	901	-16.4
Palau	0	0	491	581	668	727	651	651	679	668	15.0
Puerto Rico	42,516	54,127	55,691	73,121	73,180	71,722	70,263	67,990	66,154	67,225	-8.1
U.S. Virgin Islands	1,445	2,148	2,466	2,268	2,535	2,737	2,565	2,392	2,488	2,384	5.1

[1]Data for 2000 and later years reflect a substantial reduction in the number of Department of Defense institutions included in the IPEDS survey.
NOTE: Data through 1990 are for institutions of higher education, while later data are for degree-granting institutions. Degree-granting institutions grant associate's or higher degrees and participate in Title IV federal financial aid programs. The degree-granting classification is very similar to the earlier higher education classification, but it includes more 2-year colleges and excludes a few higher education institutions that did not grant degrees. (See Appendix A: Guide to Sources for details.)
SOURCE: U.S. Department of Education, National Center for Education Statistics, Higher Education General Information Survey (HEGIS), "Fall Enrollment in Colleges and Universities" surveys, 1970 and 1980; and 1990 through 2007 Integrated Postsecondary Education Data System, "Fall Enrollment Survey" (IPEDS-EF:90), and Spring 2001 through Spring 2008. (This table was prepared July 2009.)

Total fall enrollment in private degree-granting institutions, by state or jurisdiction: Selected years, 1970 through 2007

State or jurisdiction	Fall 1970	Fall 1980	Fall 1990	Fall 2000	Fall 2002	Fall 2003	Fall 2004	Fall 2005	Fall 2006	Fall 2007	Percent change, 2000 to 2007
1	2	3	4	5	6	7	8	9	10	11	12
United States	**2,152,753**	**2,639,501**	**2,973,920**	**3,559,503**	**3,859,718**	**4,052,783**	**4,291,932**	**4,465,641**	**4,578,737**	**4,757,348**	**33.7**
Alabama	16,052	20,632	22,650	26,527	28,531	28,499	28,837	28,236	27,740	30,551	15.2
Alaska	908	735	2,041	1,394	1,232	1,214	1,354	1,365	1,258	1,235	-11.4
Arizona	2,304	8,682	15,935	57,968	94,109	125,088	172,951	224,732	235,751	291,993	403.7
Arkansas	8,440	11,539	11,780	13,397	13,863	14,030	14,426	15,155	15,984	16,643	24.2
California	133,716	191,155	214,030	328,937	352,918	361,867	386,762	391,678	387,209	393,435	19.6
Colorado	14,833	17,318	26,478	45,975	48,603	52,541	61,606	68,163	76,482	82,653	79.8
Connecticut	51,309	61,844	59,048	60,216	62,084	62,161	62,421	62,970	64,240	64,933	7.8
Delaware	4,109	4,614	7,752	9,703	11,884	11,974	11,561	12,930	13,120	13,251	36.6
District of Columbia	64,964	72,775	67,561	67,190	85,411	89,873	94,600	99,302	103,736	109,545	63.0
Florida	46,075	77,542	99,005	150,772	174,325	196,324	216,808	223,663	233,743	230,465	52.9
Georgia	24,611	44,001	55,373	74,449	80,424	81,050	98,304	84,638	89,265	93,828	26.0
Hawaii	3,599	3,912	10,708	15,603	17,205	17,165	16,656	16,926	16,903	16,147	3.5
Idaho	7,495	8,527	10,566	11,843	14,076	14,909	15,616	17,405	18,661	18,320	54.7
Illinois	136,512	152,971	177,913	209,763	222,529	230,678	237,808	277,818	277,899	286,078	36.4
Indiana	55,929	58,029	60,879	74,311	83,437	87,145	89,885	93,955	96,309	101,526	36.6
Iowa	40,512	42,995	52,681	53,966	56,748	64,763	67,870	78,815	87,582	101,615	88.3
Kansas	14,270	14,618	14,616	19,992	20,308	20,922	21,441	21,433	22,615	24,048	20.3
Kentucky	21,351	28,182	30,757	36,368	36,971	39,269	42,106	43,390	44,716	46,979	29.2
Louisiana	19,601	23,355	28,550	34,587	34,593	36,614	38,083	16,670	31,593	31,438	-9.1
Maine	8,729	11,386	15,686	17,811	18,458	17,508	18,131	18,032	18,379	18,816	5.6
Maryland	30,619	30,475	38,917	49,948	53,477	55,629	55,911	58,078	58,539	57,878	15.9
Massachusetts	187,682	234,650	231,798	237,894	243,350	246,768	251,372	255,021	259,362	264,666	11.3
Michigan	53,101	65,984	82,444	99,770	110,159	114,191	120,107	121,165	122,713	123,830	24.1
Minnesota	30,221	44,312	54,578	74,828	88,278	97,066	107,776	120,848	131,793	141,996	89.8
Mississippi	8,999	11,703	13,845	12,034	12,947	14,266	14,572	14,561	14,511	15,301	27.1
Missouri	51,390	69,242	89,806	119,839	134,124	142,972	150,643	156,723	158,623	161,211	34.5
Montana	2,775	3,999	4,011	4,853	4,496	4,796	4,884	4,853	4,506	4,514	-7.0
Nebraska	15,461	15,979	18,217	23,586	24,626	26,079	27,858	28,055	30,014	30,698	30.2
Nevada	93	175	486	4,773	6,124	6,644	9,188	10,662	10,414	11,479	140.5
New Hampshire	13,421	22,675	27,347	25,848	27,565	28,284	29,521	28,886	29,139	28,742	11.2
New Jersey	70,748	74,582	62,685	69,024	72,458	73,726	75,340	75,443	77,282	79,840	15.7
New Mexico	3,666	3,206	2,097	9,289	9,330	9,795	10,238	10,361	10,160	9,602	3.4
New York	357,042	428,986	431,402	459,978	496,514	512,190	518,333	525,859	524,579	520,383	13.1
North Carolina	48,164	59,383	66,733	75,230	79,474	80,717	83,566	87,637	89,565	91,584	21.7
North Dakota	1,303	2,360	3,188	4,234	4,666	5,019	6,258	6,581	6,570	6,929	63.7
Ohio	95,168	107,380	130,077	138,392	146,258	153,030	159,857	163,349	166,980	170,257	23.0
Oklahoma	18,717	23,107	22,148	24,317	27,054	29,179	28,344	28,828	28,221	28,739	18.2
Oregon	13,694	17,356	21,314	28,309	30,867	32,657	34,610	36,281	37,535	37,668	33.1
Pennsylvania	178,062	215,217	260,582	270,292	284,440	294,867	304,255	312,069	318,881	328,623	21.6
Rhode Island	20,371	31,817	35,923	36,992	38,550	39,148	40,457	41,374	41,360	41,397	11.9
South Carolina	22,417	24,793	28,168	30,412	34,444	35,708	36,524	35,758	36,007	37,276	22.6
South Dakota	6,703	8,433	7,612	8,364	9,991	17,637	11,110	11,220	10,903	10,830	29.5
Tennessee	36,206	47,746	51,189	61,380	67,697	80,911	78,151	82,676	85,474	89,261	45.4
Texas	76,703	87,839	99,123	137,439	145,820	139,464	157,271	159,372	158,570	159,432	16.0
Utah	32,099	34,389	35,195	40,730	43,154	43,180	49,142	51,731	53,923	55,697	36.7
Vermont	9,673	12,644	15,488	15,468	15,299	15,088	15,659	15,825	16,710	17,362	12.2
Virginia	28,636	34,004	62,156	68,113	67,680	72,997	81,790	89,971	98,349	107,782	58.2
Washington	20,826	27,575	35,752	46,912	45,813	47,487	50,379	51,726	51,106	50,282	7.2
West Virginia	11,790	10,745	10,682	11,752	13,982	14,732	14,610	14,399	14,018	29,010	146.9
Wisconsin	31,684	33,907	46,245	57,442	61,433	62,933	64,622	66,330	67,912	70,039	21.9
Wyoming	0	26	703	1,289	1,939	2,029	2,358	2,723	1,833	1,541	19.6
Other jurisdictions	**20,557**	**77,057**	**98,374**	**110,169**	**124,720**	**132,393**	**137,089**	**140,824**	**145,490**	**145,891**	**32.4**
American Samoa	0	0	0	0	0	0	0	0	0	0	†
Federated States of Micronesia	0	0	0	0	0	0	0	0	0	0	†
Guam	0	0	0	0	119	164	172	189	186	167	†
Marshall Islands	0	0	0	0	0	0	0	0	0	0	†
Northern Marianas	0	0	0	0	0	0	0	0	0	0	†
Palau	0	0	0	0	0	0	0	0	0	0	†
Puerto Rico	20,557	77,057	98,374	110,169	124,601	132,229	136,917	140,635	145,304	145,724	32.3
U.S. Virgin Islands	0	0	0	0	0	0	0	0	0	0	†

†Not applicable.
NOTE: Data through 1990 are for institutions of higher education, while later data are for degree-granting institutions. Degree-granting institutions grant associate's or higher degrees and participate in Title IV federal financial aid programs. The degree-granting classification is very similar to the earlier higher education classification, but it includes more 2-year colleges and excludes a few higher education institutions that did not grant degrees. (See Appendix A: Guide to Sources for details.)

SOURCE: U.S. Department of Education, National Center for Education Statistics, Higher Education General Information Survey (HEGIS), "Fall Enrollment in Colleges and Universities" surveys, 1970 and 1980; and 1990 through 2007 Integrated Postsecondary Education Data System, "Fall Enrollment Survey" (IPEDS-EF:90), and Spring 2001 through Spring 2008. (This table was prepared July 2009.)

Total fall enrollment in degree-granting institutions, by attendance status, sex, and state or jurisdiction: 2006 and 2007

State or jurisdiction	Total	Fall 2006 Full-time Males	Full-time Females	Part-time Males	Part-time Females	Total	Fall 2007 Full-time Males	Full-time Females	Part-time Males	Part-time Females
1	2	3	4	5	6	7	8	9	10	11
United States	17,758,870	4,879,315	6,077,990	2,695,500	4,106,065	18,248,128	5,029,444	6,240,448	2,786,470	4,191,766
Alabama	258,408	73,405	97,737	33,387	53,879	268,183	76,106	101,202	34,118	56,757
Alaska	29,853	5,744	7,168	6,078	10,863	30,616	5,648	7,132	6,434	11,402
Arizona	567,192	146,018	217,651	81,709	121,814	624,147	160,867	259,148	82,041	122,091
Arkansas	147,391	39,919	54,902	19,248	33,322	152,168	41,143	55,874	20,193	34,958
California	2,434,774	552,589	687,488	523,741	670,956	2,529,522	570,597	706,796	552,957	699,172
Colorado	308,383	86,463	102,272	48,210	71,438	310,637	89,031	105,588	48,034	67,984
Connecticut	176,716	50,945	62,361	22,744	40,666	179,005	52,795	63,917	22,708	39,585
Delaware	51,238	13,973	19,272	6,166	11,827	52,343	14,371	19,576	6,217	12,179
District of Columbia	109,505	26,975	37,433	16,799	28,298	115,153	26,994	37,464	18,435	32,260
Florida	885,651	217,238	288,201	148,347	231,865	913,793	227,878	296,255	155,277	234,383
Georgia	435,403	123,259	166,642	52,654	92,848	453,711	129,056	173,902	53,880	96,873
Hawaii	66,893	16,814	23,136	10,823	16,120	66,601	16,628	22,422	10,929	16,622
Idaho	77,872	24,598	28,508	9,844	14,922	78,846	24,265	28,454	10,388	15,739
Illinois	830,676	220,542	265,781	136,671	207,682	837,018	225,421	272,747	134,068	204,782
Indiana	368,013	117,783	138,279	45,710	66,241	380,477	121,943	142,960	47,340	68,234
Iowa	238,634	69,222	82,594	32,242	54,576	256,259	72,189	88,157	34,477	61,436
Kansas	193,146	54,728	60,238	31,049	47,131	194,102	54,570	59,833	31,209	48,490
Kentucky	248,914	64,118	88,535	42,322	53,939	258,213	65,573	90,911	46,124	55,605
Louisiana	224,147	68,410	94,260	21,948	39,529	224,754	67,873	92,440	23,059	41,382
Maine	66,149	18,543	22,773	8,084	16,749	67,173	19,005	23,429	8,153	16,586
Maryland	319,460	75,699	96,974	54,867	91,920	327,597	78,836	98,259	56,315	94,187
Massachusetts	451,526	140,366	170,534	51,063	89,563	463,366	144,749	174,317	52,884	91,416
Michigan	634,489	167,380	201,133	103,652	162,324	643,279	172,435	203,719	104,256	162,869
Minnesota	375,899	102,651	131,797	54,036	87,415	392,393	104,918	133,250	58,238	95,987
Mississippi	151,137	46,453	69,470	11,440	23,774	155,232	47,863	71,467	11,962	23,940
Missouri	377,098	101,287	127,839	57,834	90,138	384,366	103,670	130,064	58,602	92,030
Montana	47,501	16,978	18,380	4,626	7,517	47,371	17,003	18,071	4,787	7,510
Nebraska	124,500	38,160	44,017	17,654	24,669	127,378	38,781	43,756	18,703	26,138
Nevada	112,270	22,421	29,708	26,870	33,271	116,276	23,565	30,936	28,202	33,573
New Hampshire	70,669	21,679	26,664	7,767	14,559	70,724	22,516	26,997	7,087	14,124
New Jersey	385,656	108,827	125,028	59,165	92,636	398,136	113,950	129,204	61,710	93,272
New Mexico	131,828	29,590	39,247	25,188	37,803	134,375	30,224	39,158	26,370	38,623
New York	1,160,364	364,706	456,940	124,379	214,339	1,172,811	371,375	463,961	124,486	212,989
North Carolina	495,633	133,179	179,337	65,135	117,982	502,330	136,321	181,090	65,780	119,139
North Dakota	49,519	18,578	18,347	5,089	7,505	49,945	18,312	18,353	5,518	7,762
Ohio	619,942	191,086	232,916	75,639	120,301	630,497	195,594	236,564	77,919	120,420
Oklahoma	206,236	60,289	72,543	28,657	44,747	206,382	60,871	72,237	29,048	44,226
Oregon	197,594	54,973	66,399	31,729	44,493	202,928	55,703	66,514	34,129	46,582
Pennsylvania	707,132	236,656	273,731	69,801	126,944	725,397	243,609	279,687	72,104	129,997
Rhode Island	81,734	27,804	32,023	8,005	13,902	82,900	28,163	32,849	8,130	13,758
South Carolina	212,422	60,844	83,344	22,014	46,220	217,755	63,008	85,337	22,917	46,493
South Dakota	48,931	15,333	17,031	5,779	10,788	49,747	15,332	17,095	6,005	11,315
Tennessee	290,530	89,996	119,283	29,351	51,900	297,785	93,256	122,124	30,241	52,164
Texas	1,252,709	314,819	380,919	225,125	331,846	1,269,098	321,442	384,631	228,537	334,488
Utah	202,151	62,227	59,198	39,837	40,889	203,679	64,111	61,862	38,815	38,891
Vermont	41,095	15,003	15,293	3,584	7,215	42,191	15,764	15,673	3,504	7,250
Virginia	456,172	121,835	156,255	71,188	106,894	478,268	128,162	161,832	75,639	112,635
Washington	348,154	97,051	117,838	54,077	79,188	352,075	97,884	117,979	56,246	79,966
West Virginia	100,519	34,233	40,404	9,574	16,308	116,848	35,779	41,535	19,689	19,845
Wisconsin	340,158	98,424	118,577	48,409	74,748	343,747	102,325	121,490	45,916	74,016
Wyoming	34,693	9,608	9,293	6,190	9,602	35,246	9,491	9,435	6,679	9,641
U.S. Service Academies	12,191	9,894	2,297	0	0	15,285	12,479	2,795	11	0
Other jurisdictions	226,175	67,256	105,052	20,634	33,233	226,849	68,994	104,167	20,391	33,297
American Samoa	1,607	340	475	294	498	1,767	328	509	324	606
Federated States of Micronesia	2,539	823	884	409	423	2,379	888	872	299	320
Guam	5,789	1,045	1,686	1,197	1,861	5,244	1,190	1,917	872	1,265
Marshall Islands	647	284	243	62	58	557	181	146	130	100
Northern Marianas	968	253	468	86	161	901	248	411	89	153
Palau	679	212	240	61	166	668	229	246	80	113
Puerto Rico	211,458	63,967	100,095	18,269	29,127	212,949	65,586	99,114	18,359	29,890
U.S. Virgin Islands	2,488	332	961	256	939	2,384	344	952	238	850

NOTE: Degree-granting institutions grant associate's or higher degrees and participate in Title IV federal financial aid programs.

SOURCE: U.S. Department of Education, National Center for Education Statistics, 2006 and 2007 Integrated Postsecondary Education Data System (IPEDS), Spring 2007 and Spring 2008. (This table was prepared July 2009.)

Total fall enrollment in public degree-granting institutions, by attendance status, sex, and state or jurisdiction: 2006 and 2007

State or jurisdiction	Total	Fall 2006 Full-time Males	Fall 2006 Full-time Females	Fall 2006 Part-time Males	Fall 2006 Part-time Females	Total	Fall 2007 Full-time Males	Fall 2007 Full-time Females	Fall 2007 Part-time Males	Fall 2007 Part-time Females
1	2	3	4	5	6	7	8	9	10	11
United States	**13,180,133**	**3,406,146**	**4,089,417**	**2,273,258**	**3,411,312**	**13,490,780**	**3,516,489**	**4,170,492**	**2,340,810**	**3,462,989**
Alabama	230,668	63,873	84,283	31,543	50,969	237,632	66,526	86,367	32,136	52,603
Alaska	28,595	5,528	6,806	5,834	10,427	29,381	5,460	6,765	6,215	10,941
Arizona	331,441	65,287	76,219	77,293	112,642	332,154	66,897	76,872	76,912	111,473
Arkansas	131,407	34,031	47,843	18,238	31,295	135,525	34,901	48,493	19,153	32,978
California	2,047,565	425,282	516,744	485,506	620,033	2,136,087	443,853	535,862	512,746	643,626
Colorado	231,901	61,417	68,628	40,184	61,672	227,984	62,199	68,058	40,027	57,700
Connecticut	112,476	29,121	35,050	17,513	30,792	114,072	30,340	36,163	17,568	30,001
Delaware	38,118	11,168	15,252	4,073	7,625	39,092	11,526	15,549	4,154	7,863
District of Columbia	5,769	1,294	1,492	992	1,991	5,608	1,272	1,524	1,031	1,781
Florida	651,908	147,182	194,674	118,784	191,268	683,328	156,632	201,991	126,358	198,347
Georgia	346,138	94,138	123,448	46,550	82,002	359,883	99,715	129,595	46,887	83,686
Hawaii	49,990	12,448	15,284	8,807	13,451	50,454	12,513	15,218	8,920	13,803
Idaho	59,211	17,470	19,114	8,871	13,756	60,526	17,670	19,184	9,279	14,393
Illinois	552,777	134,055	150,458	107,476	160,788	550,940	136,205	152,372	104,963	157,400
Indiana	271,704	82,951	93,122	40,033	55,598	278,951	85,816	95,455	40,854	56,826
Iowa	151,052	46,792	49,105	23,190	31,965	154,644	48,334	49,877	23,689	32,744
Kansas	170,531	47,664	51,520	28,512	42,835	170,054	47,683	51,436	27,975	42,960
Kentucky	204,198	51,758	68,343	38,120	45,977	211,234	52,727	69,661	41,527	47,319
Louisiana	192,554	58,408	78,426	20,094	35,626	193,316	58,150	76,850	21,198	37,118
Maine	47,770	12,811	14,812	6,774	13,373	48,357	13,115	14,865	6,984	13,393
Maryland	260,921	60,534	75,309	46,542	78,536	269,719	63,124	76,833	48,613	81,149
Massachusetts	192,164	49,987	58,688	29,412	54,077	198,700	52,295	60,095	30,869	55,441
Michigan	511,776	137,103	158,950	85,526	130,197	519,449	141,431	161,878	85,416	130,724
Minnesota	244,106	71,128	78,089	38,658	56,231	250,397	73,283	79,329	40,336	57,449
Mississippi	136,626	42,152	61,732	10,780	21,962	139,931	43,366	63,482	11,128	21,955
Missouri	218,475	60,205	73,495	31,545	53,230	223,155	62,035	75,021	32,066	54,033
Montana	42,995	15,513	16,273	4,304	6,905	42,857	15,507	15,989	4,423	6,938
Nebraska	94,486	28,061	30,081	15,531	20,813	96,680	28,562	29,822	16,262	22,034
Nevada	101,856	18,704	23,825	26,544	32,783	104,797	19,642	24,419	27,795	32,941
New Hampshire	41,530	11,910	14,468	5,349	9,803	41,982	12,545	14,860	4,906	9,671
New Jersey	308,374	82,726	97,734	49,289	78,625	318,296	86,689	100,797	51,817	78,993
New Mexico	121,668	26,441	34,111	24,542	36,574	124,773	27,141	34,127	25,939	37,566
New York	635,785	187,340	227,520	82,402	138,523	652,428	194,215	233,729	85,151	139,333
North Carolina	406,068	100,115	135,303	61,084	109,566	410,746	102,646	136,457	61,261	110,382
North Dakota	42,949	16,536	15,212	4,735	6,466	43,016	16,347	15,124	4,930	6,615
Ohio	452,962	136,472	159,535	61,701	95,254	460,240	140,007	161,652	63,479	95,102
Oklahoma	178,015	48,811	59,732	26,961	42,511	177,643	48,932	59,234	27,367	42,110
Oregon	160,059	42,616	48,639	28,709	40,095	165,260	43,563	48,954	30,948	41,795
Pennsylvania	388,251	129,510	142,160	41,473	75,108	396,774	133,756	144,510	42,466	76,042
Rhode Island	40,374	9,777	13,679	5,653	11,265	41,503	10,165	14,277	5,792	11,269
South Carolina	176,415	48,873	65,577	19,980	41,985	180,479	50,467	67,016	20,859	42,137
South Dakota	38,028	12,980	12,941	4,193	7,914	38,917	12,949	13,080	4,410	8,478
Tennessee	205,056	59,874	77,883	24,292	43,007	208,524	61,659	78,674	24,853	43,338
Texas	1,094,139	261,490	314,088	208,132	310,429	1,109,666	267,117	316,753	212,006	313,790
Utah	148,228	39,287	35,249	36,401	37,291	147,982	40,348	36,500	35,593	35,541
Vermont	24,385	7,473	8,557	2,619	5,736	24,829	7,735	8,694	2,541	5,859
Virginia	357,823	91,224	110,560	62,196	93,843	370,486	95,113	114,109	64,303	96,961
Washington	297,048	80,176	94,838	49,346	72,688	301,793	81,347	95,679	51,541	73,226
West Virginia	86,501	29,749	33,181	8,794	14,777	87,838	30,217	33,598	8,878	15,145
Wisconsin	272,246	78,958	89,869	41,988	61,431	273,708	82,251	91,485	39,596	60,376
Wyoming	32,860	7,849	9,219	6,190	9,602	33,705	8,022	9,363	6,679	9,641
U.S. Service Academies	12,191	9,894	2,297	0	0	15,285	12,479	2,795	11	0
Other jurisdictions	**80,685**	**24,645**	**38,843**	**6,493**	**10,704**	**80,958**	**25,872**	**39,340**	**6,133**	**9,613**
American Samoa	1,607	340	475	294	498	1,767	328	509	324	606
Federated States of Micronesia	2,539	823	884	409	423	2,379	888	872	299	320
Guam	5,603	985	1,600	1,185	1,833	5,077	1,124	1,842	865	1,246
Marshall Islands	647	284	243	62	58	557	181	146	130	100
Northern Marianas	968	253	468	86	161	901	248	411	89	153
Palau	679	212	240	61	166	668	229	246	80	113
Puerto Rico	66,154	21,416	33,972	4,140	6,626	67,225	22,530	34,362	4,108	6,225
U.S. Virgin Islands	2,488	332	961	256	939	2,384	344	952	238	850

NOTE: Degree-granting institutions grant associate's or higher degrees and participate in Title IV federal financial aid programs.

SOURCE: U.S. Department of Education, National Center for Education Statistics, 2006 and 2007 Integrated Postsecondary Education Data System (IPEDS), Spring 2007 and Spring 2008. (This table was prepared July 2009.)

Total fall enrollment in private degree-granting institutions, by attendance status, sex, and state or jurisdiction: 2006 and 2007

State or jurisdiction		Fall 2006				Fall 2007				
			Full-time		Part-time			Full-time		Part-time	
	Total	Males	Females	Males	Females	Total	Males	Females	Males	Females
1	2	3	4	5	6	7	8	9	10	11
United States	**4,578,737**	**1,473,169**	**1,988,573**	**422,242**	**694,753**	**4,757,348**	**1,512,955**	**2,069,956**	**445,660**	**728,777**
Alabama	27,740	9,532	13,454	1,844	2,910	30,551	9,580	14,835	1,982	4,154
Alaska	1,258	216	362	244	436	1,235	188	367	219	461
Arizona	235,751	80,731	141,432	4,416	9,172	291,993	93,970	182,276	5,129	10,618
Arkansas	15,984	5,888	7,059	1,010	2,027	16,643	6,242	7,381	1,040	1,980
California	387,209	127,307	170,744	38,235	50,923	393,435	126,744	170,934	40,211	55,546
Colorado	76,482	25,046	33,644	8,026	9,766	82,653	26,832	37,530	8,007	10,284
Connecticut	64,240	21,824	27,311	5,231	9,874	64,933	22,455	27,754	5,140	9,584
Delaware	13,120	2,805	4,020	2,093	4,202	13,251	2,845	4,027	2,063	4,316
District of Columbia	103,736	25,681	35,941	15,807	26,307	109,545	25,722	35,940	17,404	30,479
Florida	233,743	70,056	93,527	29,563	40,597	230,465	71,246	94,264	28,919	36,036
Georgia	89,265	29,121	43,194	6,104	10,846	93,828	29,341	44,307	6,993	13,187
Hawaii	16,903	4,366	7,852	2,016	2,669	16,147	4,115	7,204	2,009	2,819
Idaho	18,661	7,128	9,394	973	1,166	18,320	6,595	9,270	1,109	1,346
Illinois	277,899	86,487	115,323	29,195	46,894	286,078	89,216	120,375	29,105	47,382
Indiana	96,309	34,832	45,157	5,677	10,643	101,526	36,127	47,505	6,486	11,408
Iowa	87,582	22,430	33,489	9,052	22,611	101,615	23,855	38,280	10,788	28,692
Kansas	22,615	7,064	8,718	2,537	4,296	24,048	6,887	8,397	3,234	5,530
Kentucky	44,716	12,360	20,192	4,202	7,962	46,979	12,846	21,250	4,597	8,286
Louisiana	31,593	10,002	15,834	1,854	3,903	31,438	9,723	15,590	1,861	4,264
Maine	18,379	5,732	7,961	1,310	3,376	18,816	5,890	8,564	1,169	3,193
Maryland	58,539	15,165	21,665	8,325	13,384	57,878	15,712	21,426	7,702	13,038
Massachusetts	259,362	90,379	111,846	21,651	35,486	264,666	92,454	114,222	22,015	35,975
Michigan	122,713	30,277	42,183	18,126	32,127	123,830	31,004	41,841	18,840	32,145
Minnesota	131,793	31,523	53,708	15,378	31,184	141,996	31,635	53,921	17,902	38,538
Mississippi	14,511	4,301	7,738	660	1,812	15,301	4,497	7,985	834	1,985
Missouri	158,623	41,082	54,344	26,289	36,908	161,211	41,635	55,043	26,536	37,997
Montana	4,506	1,465	2,107	322	612	4,514	1,496	2,082	364	572
Nebraska	30,014	10,099	13,936	2,123	3,856	30,698	10,219	13,934	2,441	4,104
Nevada	10,414	3,717	5,883	326	488	11,479	3,923	6,517	407	632
New Hampshire	29,139	9,769	12,196	2,418	4,756	28,742	9,971	12,137	2,181	4,453
New Jersey	77,282	26,101	27,294	9,876	14,011	79,840	27,261	28,407	9,893	14,279
New Mexico	10,160	3,149	5,136	646	1,229	9,602	3,083	5,031	431	1,057
New York	524,579	177,366	229,420	41,977	75,816	520,383	177,160	230,232	39,335	73,656
North Carolina	89,565	33,064	44,034	4,051	8,416	91,584	33,675	44,633	4,519	8,757
North Dakota	6,570	2,042	3,135	354	1,039	6,929	1,965	3,229	588	1,147
Ohio	166,980	54,614	73,381	13,938	25,047	170,257	55,587	74,912	14,440	25,318
Oklahoma	28,221	11,478	12,811	1,696	2,236	28,739	11,939	13,003	1,681	2,116
Oregon	37,535	12,357	17,760	3,020	4,398	37,668	12,140	17,560	3,181	4,787
Pennsylvania	318,881	107,146	131,571	28,328	51,836	328,623	109,853	135,177	29,638	53,955
Rhode Island	41,360	18,027	18,344	2,352	2,637	41,397	17,998	18,572	2,338	2,489
South Carolina	36,007	11,971	17,767	2,034	4,235	37,276	12,541	18,321	2,058	4,356
South Dakota	10,903	2,353	4,090	1,586	2,874	10,830	2,383	4,015	1,595	2,837
Tennessee	85,474	30,122	41,400	5,059	8,893	89,261	31,597	43,450	5,388	8,826
Texas	158,570	53,329	66,831	16,993	21,417	159,432	54,325	67,878	16,531	20,698
Utah	53,923	22,940	23,949	3,436	3,598	55,697	23,763	25,362	3,222	3,350
Vermont	16,710	7,530	6,736	965	1,479	17,362	8,029	6,979	963	1,391
Virginia	98,349	30,611	45,695	8,992	13,051	107,782	33,049	47,723	11,336	15,674
Washington	51,106	16,875	23,000	4,731	6,500	50,282	16,537	22,300	4,705	6,740
West Virginia	14,018	4,484	7,223	780	1,531	29,010	5,562	7,937	10,811	4,700
Wisconsin	67,912	19,466	28,708	6,421	13,317	70,039	20,074	30,005	6,320	13,640
Wyoming	1,833	1,759	74	0	0	1,541	1,469	72	0	0
Other jurisdictions	**145,490**	**42,611**	**66,209**	**14,141**	**22,529**	**145,891**	**43,122**	**64,827**	**14,258**	**23,684**
American Samoa	0	0	0	0	0	0	0	0	0	0
Federated States of Micronesia	0	0	0	0	0	0	0	0	0	0
Guam	186	60	86	12	28	167	66	75	7	19
Marshall Islands	0	0	0	0	0	0	0	0	0	0
Northern Marianas	0	0	0	0	0	0	0	0	0	0
Palau	0	0	0	0	0	0	0	0	0	0
Puerto Rico	145,304	42,551	66,123	14,129	22,501	145,724	43,056	64,752	14,251	23,665
U.S. Virgin Islands	0	0	0	0	0	0	0	0	0	0

NOTE: Degree-granting institutions grant associate's or higher degrees and participate in Title IV federal financial aid programs.

SOURCE: U.S. Department of Education, National Center for Education Statistics, 2006 and 2007 Integrated Postsecondary Education Data System (IPEDS), Spring 2007 and Spring 2008. (This table was prepared July 2009.)

Total fall enrollment in private not-for-profit degree-granting institutions, by attendance status, sex, and state or jurisdiction: 2006 and 2007

State or jurisdiction	Total	Fall 2006				Total	Fall 2007			
		Full-time		Part-time			Full-time		Part-time	
		Males	Females	Males	Females		Males	Females	Males	Females
1	2	3	4	5	6	7	8	9	10	11
United States	**3,512,866**	**1,145,995**	**1,469,564**	**343,886**	**553,421**	**3,571,150**	**1,168,466**	**1,496,036**	**347,328**	**559,320**
Alabama	22,588	8,008	10,945	1,465	2,170	22,527	8,150	10,855	1,337	2,185
Alaska	855	180	303	137	235	719	134	261	99	225
Arizona	8,592	3,099	3,320	990	1,183	7,789	3,144	2,319	1,080	1,246
Arkansas	14,349	5,279	6,098	961	2,011	14,766	5,552	6,289	978	1,947
California	274,931	86,206	114,407	30,990	43,328	277,554	85,998	113,346	32,390	45,820
Colorado	31,667	8,627	11,642	4,782	6,616	31,948	8,792	11,645	4,698	6,813
Connecticut	60,956	21,107	26,185	4,858	8,806	61,646	21,649	26,537	4,763	8,697
Delaware	13,120	2,805	4,020	2,093	4,202	13,251	2,845	4,027	2,063	4,316
District of Columbia	72,783	22,687	31,229	7,800	11,067	73,460	22,764	31,073	8,233	11,390
Florida	149,448	45,345	56,101	22,759	25,243	150,807	45,473	55,732	23,257	26,345
Georgia	63,562	21,923	31,983	3,514	6,142	65,720	22,252	32,683	3,829	6,956
Hawaii	14,278	3,609	6,091	1,991	2,587	13,119	3,274	5,416	1,904	2,525
Idaho	16,871	6,451	8,369	900	1,151	16,672	5,973	8,344	1,026	1,329
Illinois	214,533	66,854	87,006	22,602	38,071	220,491	70,254	92,342	21,235	36,660
Indiana	80,263	30,112	37,208	4,552	8,391	83,110	30,998	38,657	4,837	8,618
Iowa	55,430	19,367	24,962	3,783	7,318	56,170	19,494	25,221	3,939	7,516
Kansas	21,191	6,674	7,828	2,509	4,180	22,452	6,487	7,502	3,173	5,290
Kentucky	30,097	9,638	13,630	2,523	4,306	31,913	10,052	14,400	2,811	4,650
Louisiana	24,630	8,100	11,121	1,685	3,724	24,204	7,824	10,867	1,653	3,860
Maine	16,958	5,590	7,265	1,213	2,890	17,308	5,737	7,809	1,074	2,688
Maryland	52,590	13,338	18,484	7,833	12,935	52,673	13,732	18,924	7,306	12,711
Massachusetts	254,962	88,270	110,398	21,214	35,080	260,400	90,390	112,897	21,525	35,588
Michigan	114,353	26,864	37,872	17,654	31,963	116,000	27,705	38,178	18,258	31,859
Minnesota	70,249	21,998	30,032	6,554	11,665	71,851	22,455	30,596	6,869	11,931
Mississippi	12,781	3,930	6,493	635	1,723	13,461	4,193	6,647	796	1,825
Missouri	140,695	35,402	44,823	25,120	35,350	143,481	35,826	46,124	25,310	36,221
Montana	4,506	1,465	2,107	322	612	4,514	1,496	2,082	364	572
Nebraska	27,039	9,244	12,182	1,999	3,614	28,177	9,430	12,513	2,326	3,908
Nevada	761	241	396	47	77	1,504	534	817	60	93
New Hampshire	24,419	8,829	10,233	1,876	3,481	24,629	9,027	10,345	1,833	3,424
New Jersey	71,714	24,170	24,644	9,383	13,517	73,822	25,112	25,545	9,429	13,736
New Mexico	3,450	886	1,305	371	888	2,932	908	1,084	252	688
New York	477,439	162,253	204,486	39,294	71,406	474,411	162,681	206,315	36,683	68,732
North Carolina	83,596	31,488	40,846	3,767	7,495	85,809	32,013	41,700	4,146	7,950
North Dakota	5,555	1,931	2,800	258	566	5,723	1,842	2,771	446	664
Ohio	138,359	47,182	57,359	12,091	21,727	138,712	47,809	57,703	12,210	20,990
Oklahoma	21,430	8,443	9,120	1,658	2,209	21,490	8,580	9,214	1,608	2,088
Oregon	29,390	9,453	13,578	2,563	3,796	29,602	9,354	13,701	2,605	3,942
Pennsylvania	273,765	90,709	114,147	24,166	44,743	280,713	93,431	117,513	24,519	45,250
Rhode Island	40,747	17,856	17,902	2,352	2,637	40,758	17,865	18,153	2,309	2,431
South Carolina	33,441	11,060	16,611	1,930	3,840	33,875	11,372	16,855	1,875	3,773
South Dakota	7,788	1,896	3,257	862	1,773	7,702	1,936	3,166	888	1,712
Tennessee	67,197	23,766	31,838	4,245	7,348	69,572	24,662	32,944	4,509	7,457
Texas	125,017	41,646	50,141	14,528	18,702	126,003	42,934	51,656	13,865	17,548
Utah	44,443	19,017	20,025	2,950	2,451	47,173	20,187	21,707	2,782	2,497
Vermont	16,177	7,185	6,548	965	1,479	16,725	7,624	6,747	963	1,391
Virginia	69,273	21,924	30,632	7,078	9,639	77,753	23,910	32,563	9,228	12,052
Washington	41,520	12,829	19,403	3,702	5,586	41,726	12,904	19,342	3,733	5,747
West Virginia	11,271	3,798	5,635	569	1,269	11,965	4,094	5,968	617	1,286
Wisconsin	61,837	17,261	26,554	5,793	12,229	62,368	17,614	26,941	5,635	12,178
Wyoming	0	0	0	0	0	0	0	0	0	0
Other jurisdictions	**124,539**	**34,476**	**56,708**	**12,866**	**20,489**	**124,148**	**35,180**	**54,672**	**12,823**	**21,473**
American Samoa	0	0	0	0	0	0	0	0	0	0
Federated States of Micronesia	0	0	0	0	0	0	0	0	0	0
Guam	186	60	86	12	28	167	66	75	7	19
Marshall Islands	0	0	0	0	0	0	0	0	0	0
Northern Marianas	0	0	0	0	0	0	0	0	0	0
Palau	0	0	0	0	0	0	0	0	0	0
Puerto Rico	124,353	34,416	56,622	12,854	20,461	123,981	35,114	54,597	12,816	21,454
U.S. Virgin Islands	0	0	0	0	0	0	0	0	0	0

NOTE: Degree-granting institutions grant associate's or higher degrees and participate in Title IV federal financial aid programs.

SOURCE: U.S. Department of Education, National Center for Education Statistics, 2006 and 2007 Integrated Postsecondary Education Data System (IPEDS), Spring 2007 and Spring 2008. (This table was prepared July 2009.)

Fall enrollment in degree-granting institutions, by race/ethnicity of student and by state or jurisdiction: 2008

State or jurisdiction	Number							Percentage distribution						
	Total	White	Black	Hispanic	Asian/Pacific Islander	American Indian/Alaska Native	Non-resident alien	Total	White	Black	Hispanic	Asian/Pacific Islander	American Indian/Alaska Native	Non-resident alien
1	2	3	4	5	6	7	8	9	10	11	12	13	14	15
United States	**19,102,814**	**12,088,781**	**2,584,478**	**2,272,888**	**1,302,797**	**193,289**	**660,581**	**100.0**	**63.3**	**13.5**	**11.9**	**6.8**	**1.0**	**3.5**
Alabama	310,941	199,837	90,446	7,066	5,198	2,536	5,858	100.0	64.3	29.1	2.3	1.7	0.8	1.9
Alaska	30,717	21,392	1,041	1,276	1,837	4,329	842	100.0	69.6	3.4	4.2	6.0	14.1	2.7
Arizona	704,245	429,869	101,276	106,780	25,489	20,032	20,799	100.0	61.0	14.4	15.2	3.6	2.8	3.0
Arkansas	158,374	114,839	29,981	5,277	2,795	1,805	3,677	100.0	72.5	18.9	3.3	1.8	1.1	2.3
California	2,652,241	1,066,385	216,554	764,410	491,873	24,635	88,384	100.0	40.2	8.2	28.8	18.5	0.9	3.3
Colorado	325,232	239,719	22,548	38,204	12,967	4,776	7,018	100.0	73.7	6.9	11.7	4.0	1.5	2.2
Connecticut	184,178	128,546	20,710	17,649	8,631	611	8,031	100.0	69.8	11.2	9.6	4.7	0.3	4.4
Delaware	53,088	36,057	10,726	2,303	2,140	176	1,686	100.0	67.9	20.2	4.3	4.0	0.3	3.2
District of Columbia	126,110	55,529	49,143	6,746	8,081	629	5,982	100.0	44.0	39.0	5.3	6.4	0.5	4.7
Florida	972,699	527,133	178,502	197,330	35,480	4,277	29,977	100.0	54.2	18.4	20.3	3.6	0.4	3.1
Georgia	476,581	271,277	153,597	15,909	20,144	1,576	14,078	100.0	56.9	32.2	3.3	4.2	0.3	3.0
Hawaii	70,104	17,204	1,577	2,237	43,579	382	5,125	100.0	24.5	2.2	3.2	62.2	0.5	7.3
Idaho	80,456	70,007	851	4,551	1,849	1,072	2,126	100.0	87.0	1.1	5.7	2.3	1.3	2.6
Illinois	859,242	544,284	128,408	105,411	50,374	2,987	27,778	100.0	63.3	14.9	12.3	5.9	0.3	3.2
Indiana	401,956	323,978	38,515	13,483	9,122	1,538	15,320	100.0	80.6	9.6	3.4	2.3	0.4	3.8
Iowa	286,891	218,295	18,612	10,539	29,465	1,589	8,391	100.0	76.1	6.5	3.7	10.3	0.6	2.9
Kansas	198,991	156,395	13,004	10,510	5,258	3,363	10,461	100.0	78.6	6.5	5.3	2.6	1.7	5.3
Kentucky	257,583	221,049	24,463	3,725	3,280	818	4,248	100.0	85.8	9.5	1.4	1.3	0.3	1.6
Louisiana	236,375	144,792	71,320	6,298	5,575	1,706	6,684	100.0	61.3	30.2	2.7	2.4	0.7	2.8
Maine	67,796	61,778	1,451	1,041	1,321	958	1,247	100.0	91.1	2.1	1.5	1.9	1.4	1.8
Maryland	338,914	188,394	95,918	14,871	23,943	1,460	14,328	100.0	55.6	28.3	4.4	7.1	0.4	4.2
Massachusetts	477,056	334,907	39,942	34,159	35,567	1,998	30,483	100.0	70.2	8.4	7.2	7.5	0.4	6.4
Michigan	652,799	489,548	91,614	19,112	22,381	5,477	24,667	100.0	75.0	14.0	2.9	3.4	0.8	3.8
Minnesota	411,055	323,793	41,034	10,128	18,878	5,088	12,134	100.0	78.8	10.0	2.5	4.6	1.2	3.0
Mississippi	160,441	91,364	63,030	1,645	1,580	678	2,144	100.0	56.9	39.3	1.0	1.0	0.4	1.3
Missouri	396,409	307,449	51,397	12,414	10,659	2,550	11,940	100.0	77.6	13.0	3.1	2.7	0.6	3.0
Montana	47,840	40,324	338	946	650	4,454	1,128	100.0	84.3	0.7	2.0	1.4	9.3	2.4
Nebraska	130,458	110,434	6,359	5,592	3,388	1,084	3,601	100.0	84.7	4.9	4.3	2.6	0.8	2.8
Nevada	120,490	70,446	10,217	20,734	14,626	1,700	2,767	100.0	58.5	8.5	17.2	12.1	1.4	2.3
New Hampshire	71,739	63,703	1,557	2,071	1,904	537	1,967	100.0	88.8	2.2	2.9	2.7	0.7	2.7
New Jersey	410,160	236,420	58,324	60,887	35,480	1,302	17,747	100.0	57.6	14.2	14.8	8.7	0.3	4.3
New Mexico	142,413	59,204	4,419	58,749	2,837	12,912	4,292	100.0	41.6	3.1	41.3	2.0	9.1	3.0
New York	1,234,858	725,899	172,500	148,670	104,298	5,066	78,425	100.0	58.8	14.0	12.0	8.4	0.4	6.4
North Carolina	528,977	348,983	128,676	17,455	14,961	6,344	12,558	100.0	66.0	24.3	3.3	2.8	1.2	2.4
North Dakota	51,327	43,435	963	630	562	3,150	2,587	100.0	84.6	1.9	1.2	1.1	6.1	5.0
Ohio	653,585	518,970	83,104	14,968	14,707	2,727	19,109	100.0	79.4	12.7	2.3	2.3	0.4	2.9
Oklahoma	206,757	142,831	19,433	8,793	5,540	21,106	9,054	100.0	69.1	9.4	4.3	2.7	10.2	4.4
Oregon	220,474	174,776	5,937	14,479	14,846	3,866	6,570	100.0	79.3	2.7	6.6	6.7	1.8	3.0
Pennsylvania	740,288	569,310	80,331	28,136	33,475	2,095	26,941	100.0	76.9	10.9	3.8	4.5	0.3	3.6
Rhode Island	83,893	64,408	5,203	6,617	3,913	433	3,319	100.0	76.8	6.2	7.9	4.7	0.5	4.0

See notes at end of table.

Fall enrollment in degree-granting institutions, by race/ethnicity of student and by state or jurisdiction: 2008—Continued

State or jurisdiction	Number							Percentage distribution						
	Total	White	Black	Hispanic	Asian/Pacific Islander	American Indian/Alaska Native	Non-resident alien	Total	White	Black	Hispanic	Asian/Pacific Islander	American Indian/Alaska Native	Non-resident alien
1	2	3	4	5	6	7	8	9	10	11	12	13	14	15
South Carolina	230,695	154,165	63,614	4,621	3,920	915	3,460	100.0	66.8	27.6	2.0	1.7	0.4	1.5
South Dakota	50,444	43,666	851	595	553	3,579	1,200	100.0	86.6	1.7	1.2	1.1	7.1	2.4
Tennessee	307,610	226,329	61,323	6,598	6,320	1,173	5,867	100.0	73.6	19.9	2.1	2.1	0.4	1.9
Texas	1,327,148	647,092	170,169	377,176	73,325	7,078	52,308	100.0	48.8	12.8	28.4	5.5	0.5	3.9
Utah	217,224	184,828	3,642	12,645	7,757	2,323	6,029	100.0	85.1	1.7	5.8	3.6	1.1	2.8
Vermont	42,946	38,802	926	1,050	1,063	248	857	100.0	90.4	2.2	2.4	2.5	0.6	2.0
Virginia	500,796	327,310	103,226	22,944	31,281	2,514	13,521	100.0	65.4	20.6	4.6	6.2	0.5	2.7
Washington	362,535	265,756	16,684	26,469	34,961	6,169	12,496	100.0	73.3	4.6	7.3	9.6	1.7	3.4
West Virginia	125,333	107,184	9,141	3,596	2,182	635	2,595	100.0	85.5	7.3	2.9	1.7	0.5	2.1
Wisconsin	352,875	296,715	20,743	12,151	11,428	4,038	7,800	100.0	84.1	5.9	3.4	3.2	1.1	2.2
Wyoming	35,936	31,778	398	1,869	441	644	806	100.0	88.4	1.1	5.2	1.2	1.8	2.2
U.S. Service Academies	15,539	12,193	740	1,373	913	151	169	100.0	78.5	4.8	8.8	5.9	1.0	1.1
Other jurisdictions	**236,167**	**633**	**2,025**	**221,700**	**10,575**	**29**	**1,205**	**100.0**	**0.3**	**0.9**	**93.9**	**4.5**	**#**	**0.5**
American Samoa	1,806	4	0	2	1,599	0	201	100.0	0.2	0.0	0.1	88.5	0.0	11.1
Federated States of Micronesia	2,457	0	0	0	2,457	0	0	100.0	0.0	0.0	0.0	100.0	0.0	0.0
Guam	5,351	227	40	43	4,708	11	322	100.0	4.2	0.7	0.8	88.0	0.2	6.0
Marshall Islands	689	0	0	0	689	0	0	100.0	0.0	0.0	0.0	100.0	0.0	0.0
Northern Marianas	791	15	1	2	587	0	186	100.0	1.9	0.1	0.3	74.2	0.0	23.5
Palau	502	0	0	25	476	0	1	100.0	0.0	0.0	5.0	94.8	0.0	0.2
Puerto Rico	222,178	249	59	221,474	43	14	339	100.0	0.1	#	99.7	#	#	0.2
U.S. Virgin Islands	2,393	138	1,925	154	16	4	156	100.0	5.8	80.4	6.4	0.7	0.2	6.5

#Rounds to zero.
NOTE: Race categories exclude persons of Hispanic ethnicity. Degree-granting institutions grant associate's or higher degrees and participate in Title IV federal financial aid programs. Detail may not sum to totals because of rounding.

SOURCE: U.S. Department of Education, National Center for Education Statistics, 2008 Integrated Postsecondary Education Data System (IPEDS), Spring 2009. (This table was prepared September 2009.)

Enrollment and degrees conferred in degree-granting women's colleges, by selected characteristics and institution: Fall 2007 and 2007-08

Institution[1]	State	Type and control[2]	Enrollment, fall 2007							Degrees awarded to females, 2007–08			
			Total	Females	Percent female	Males, full-time	Females, full-time	Males, part-time	Females, part-time	Associate's	Bachelor's	Master's	Doctor's
1	2	3	4	5	6	7	8	9	10	11	12	13	14
Total	†	†	98,168	92,104	93.8	2,414	64,505	3,650	27,599	623	14,134	5,967	220
Judson College	AL	3	311	300	96.5	3	238	8	62	†	48	†	†
Mills College	CA	3	1,446	1,349	93.3	85	1,221	12	128	†	194	153	6
Mount Saint Mary's College	CA	3	2,366	2,141	90.5	108	1,546	117	595	130	357	72	10
Scripps College	CA	3	920	908	98.7	8	902	4	6	†	185	†	†
Saint Joseph College	CT	3	1,773	1,662	93.7	17	854	94	808	†	184	191	†
Trinity Washington University	DC	3	1,630	1,486	91.2	45	770	99	716	3	136	208	†
Agnes Scott College	GA	3	892	889	99.7	3	859	0	30	†	191	7	†
Brenau University	GA	3	2,577	2,274	88.2	125	1,407	178	867	5	367	218	†
Spelman College	GA	3	2,343	2,343	100.0	0	2,236	0	107	†	483	†	†
Wesleyan College	GA	3	691	675	97.7	8	404	8	271	†	76	29	†
Lexington College	IL	3	57	57	100.0	0	49	0	8	2	7	†	†
Saint Mary-of-the-Woods College	IN	3	1,677	1,595	95.1	4	480	78	1,115	7	174	32	†
Saint Mary's College	IN	3	1,604	1,602	99.9	0	1,570	2	32		330	†	†
Midway College	KY	3	1,422	1,237	87.0	102	923	83	314	67	227	†	†
College of Notre Dame of Maryland	MD	3	3,402	2,934	86.2	25	638	443	2,296	†	412	347	5
Bay Path College	MA	3	1,603	1,557	97.1	23	1,128	23	429	49	264	57	†
Mount Holyoke College	MA	3	2,204	2,204	100.0	0	2,154	0	50	†	548	3	†
Pine Manor College	MA	3	472	466	98.7	6	451	0	15	1	47	0	†
Simmons College	MA	3	4,733	4,379	92.5	64	2,376	290	2,003	†	482	909	58
Smith College	MA	3	3,065	3,015	98.4	46	2,954	4	61	†	708	149	6
Wellesley College	MA	3	2,380	2,309	97.0	1	2,237	70	72	†	604	†	†
College of Saint Benedict	MN	3	2,086	2,086	100.0	0	2,051	0	35	†	441	†	†
College of St. Catherine	MN	3	5,238	4,960	94.7	121	3,085	157	1,875	166	518	308	21
Cottey College	MO	4	323	323	100.0	0	321	0	2	101	†	†	†
Stephens College	MO	3	1,050	1,001	95.3	33	800	16	201	1	136	19	†
College of Saint Mary	NE	3	973	969	99.6	4	720	0	249	78	109	68	3
College of Saint Elizabeth	NJ	3	2,044	1,854	90.7	53	860	137	994	†	236	180	†
Georgian Court College	NJ	3	3,045	2,686	88.2	103	1,543	256	1,143	†	374	149	†
Barnard College	NY	3	2,346	2,346	100.0	0	2,292	0	54	†	572	†	†
College of New Rochelle	NY	3	6,226	5,667	91.0	366	4,185	193	1,482	†	878	362	†
Marymount College of Fordham U.[3]	NY	3	243	194	79.8	33	142	16	52	†	†	†	†
Bennett College for Women	NC	3	678	678	100.0	0	655	0	23	†	108	†	†
Meredith College	NC	3	2,202	2,173	98.7	0	1,780	29	393	†	349	32	†
Peace College	NC	3	692	691	99.9	0	642	1	49	†	125	†	†
Salem College	NC	3	992	955	96.3	12	628	25	327	†	155	44	†
Bryn Mawr College	PA	3	1,790	1,687	94.2	68	1,510	35	177	†	311	113	14
Carlow College	PA	3	2,178	2,024	92.9	78	1,248	76	776	†	322	187	0
Cedar Crest College	PA	3	1,888	1,790	94.8	16	972	82	818	†	317	23	†
Chatham University	PA	3	1,860	1,635	87.9	95	1,078	130	557	†	134	220	46
Moore College of Art and Design	PA	3	558	558	100.0	0	497	0	61	†	86	†	†
Wilson College	PA	3	724	648	89.5	7	358	69	290	9	87	†	†
Columbia College	SC	3	1,510	1,463	96.9	16	1,159	31	304	†	216	199	†
Converse College	SC	3	1,881	1,633	86.8	32	752	216	881	†	171	178	†
Texas Woman's University	TX	1	12,168	11,095	91.2	593	6,362	480	4,733	†	1,355	1,265	51
Hollins University	VA	3	1,049	1,002	95.5	11	829	36	173	†	181	85	†
Mary Baldwin College	VA	3	1,685	1,563	92.8	48	1,085	74	478	†	234	58	†
Sweet Briar College	VA	3	815	789	96.8	17	741	9	48	†	130	9	†
Alverno College	WI	3	2,654	2,606	98.2	19	1,824	29	782	4	346	49	†
Mount Mary College	WI	3	1,702	1,646	96.7	16	989	40	657	†	219	44	†

†Not applicable.

[1]Data are for colleges and universities identified by the Women's College Coalition as women's colleges in 2009. Excludes women's colleges whose IPEDS data are reported together with a coed institution or coordinate men's college. The following institutions were excluded for this reason: The Women's College of the University of Denver; Newcomb College Institute of Tulane University; Douglass Residential College of Rutgers University; and Russell Sage College of the Sage Colleges.

[2]1 = public, 4-year; 3 = private not-for-profit, 4-year; and 4 = private not-for-profit, 2-year.
[3]Institution closed in 2007.
NOTE: Degree-granting institutions grant associate's or higher degrees and participate in Title IV federal financial aid programs.
SOURCE: U.S. Department of Education, National Center for Education Statistics, 2007 and 2007–08 Integrated Postsecondary Education Data System (IPEDS), Spring 2008 and Fall 2008. (This table was prepared August 2009.)

Fall enrollment and degrees conferred in degree-granting tribally controlled institutions, by institution: Fall 2000 through fall 2007, and 2006–07 and 2007–08

Institution	Type and control[1]	Total fall enrollment							2007				Degrees to American Indians/ Alaska Natives			
													Associate's		Bachelor's	
		2000	2001	2002	2003	2004	2005	2006	Total	Total American Indian/ Alaska Native	Percent American Indian/ Alaska Native	Undergraduate American Indian/ Alaska Native	2006–07	2007–08	2006–07	2007–08
1	2	3	4	5	6	7	8	9	10	11	12	13	14	15	16	17
Tribally controlled institutions[2]	†	13,680	14,075	15,468	17,776	17,605	17,167	17,255	17,418	13,820	79.3	13,699	1,245	1,263	144	173
Alaska																
Ilisagvik College	2	322	279	316	417	214	278	203	439	300	68.3	300	5	4	†	†
Arizona																
Diné College	2	1,712	1,685	1,822	1,878	1,935	1,825	1,669	1,657	1,632	98.5	1,632	215	229	†	†
Tohono O'odham Community College	2	—	—	—	181	169	270	198	154	147	95.5	147	20	21	†	†
Kansas																
Haskell Indian Nations University	1	918	967	887	918	928	918	889	894	894	100.0	894	106	100	50	68
Michigan																
Bay Mills Community College	2	360	368	430	386	401	406	550	427	262	61.4	262	8	16	†	†
Saginaw Chippewa Tribal College	2	—	—	41	66	109	123	125	127	110	86.6	110	10	10	†	†
Minnesota																
Fond du Lac Tribal and Community College	2	999	1,023	1,315	1,735	1,775	1,981	2,181	2,197	333	15.2	333	39	44	†	†
Leech Lake Tribal College	2	240	174	244	162	195	189	198	243	220	90.5	220	15	10	†	†
White Earth Tribal and Community College	4	—	79	99	81	67	61	106	99	85	85.9	85	3	0	†	†
Montana																
Blackfeet Community College	4	299	341	418	546	561	485	467	471	444	94.3	444	55	62	†	†
Chief Dull Knife College	2	461	442	268	442	356	554	359	437	393	89.9	393	18	17	†	†
Fort Belknap College	2	295	170	158	215	257	175	161	244	185	75.8	185	13	15	†	†
Fort Peck Community College	2	400	419	443	419	504	408	441	422	322	76.3	322	14	31	†	†
Little Big Horn College	2	320	203	275	394	291	259	312	272	262	96.3	262	36	37	†	†
Salish Kootenai College	3	1,042	976	1,109	1,100	1,130	1,142	1,092	1,040	749	72.0	749	60	36	17	30
Stone Child College	2	38	242	83	434	347	344	397	305	290	95.1	290	22	34	†	†
Nebraska																
Little Priest Tribal College	4	141	88	146	130	154	109	95	120	104	86.7	104	8	5	†	†
Nebraska Indian Community College	2	170	191	118	190	190	107	115	89	78	87.6	78	3	3	†	†
New Mexico																
Institute of American Indian and Alaska Native Culture	1	139	44	155	154	176	113	192	231	215	93.1	215	13	7	22	14
Navajo Technical College	2	841	299	283	300	306	333	392	367	367	100.0	367	32	40	†	†
Southwestern Indian Polytechnic Institute	2	304	723	777	936	772	614	561	600	600	100.0	600	56	38	†	†
North Dakota																
Candeska Cikana Community College	2	9	169	160	190	197	198	233	223	217	97.3	217	29	19	†	†
Fort Berthold Community College	2	50	50	249	274	285	241	196	201	182	90.5	182	14	24	†	†
Sitting Bull College	1	22	194	214	317	289	287	286	290	262	90.3	262	33	22	3	6
Turtle Mountain Community College	3	686	684	897	959	787	615	788	928	889	95.8	889	44	67	0	4
United Tribes Technical College	4	204	302	463	466	536	885	606	604	571	94.5	571	98	80	†	†
South Dakota																
Oglala Lakota College[2]	1	1,174	1,270	1,279	1,441	1,501	1,302	1,485	1,456	1,337	91.8	1,264	69	83	39	37
Sinte Gleska University[2]	3	900	895	787	1,055	1,400	1,123	969	971	780	80.3	732	54	66	13	14
Sisseton-Wahpeton College	2	250	275	285	287	287	290	279	245	204	83.3	204	22	17	†	†
Washington																
Northwest Indian College	1	524	600	667	643	519	495	623	584	498	85.3	498	37	45	†	†
Wisconsin																
College of the Menominee Nation	4	371	407	530	499	507	532	513	505	424	84.0	424	37	38	†	†
Lac Courte Oreilles Ojibwa Community College	2	489	516	550	561	460	505	574	576	464	80.6	464	57	43	†	†

—Not available.

†Not applicable.

[1]1 = public, 4-year; 2 = public, 2-year; 3 = private not-for-profit, 4-year; and 4 = private not-for-profit, 2-year.

[2]"Total American Indian/Alaska Native" enrollment (column 11) includes graduate students and therefore does not equal "Undergraduate American Indian/Alaska Native" enrollment (column 13).

NOTE: This table only includes institutions that were in operation during the 2007–08 academic year. They are all members of the American Indian Higher Education Consortium and, with few exceptions, are tribally controlled and located on reservations. Degree-granting institutions grant associate's or higher degrees and participate in Title IV federal financial aid programs. Totals include persons of other racial/ethnic groups not separately identified.

SOURCE: U.S. Department of Education, National Center for Education Statistics, 2000 through 2007, 2006–07, and 2007–08 Integrated Postsecondary Education Data System (IPEDS), Spring 2001 through Spring 2008, Fall 2007, and Fall 2008. (This table was prepared July 2009.)

Fall enrollment, degrees conferred, and expenditures in degree-granting historically Black colleges and universities, by institution: 2006, 2006–07, 2007, and 2007–08

Institution	State	Type and control[1]	Total enrollment, fall 2006	Enrollment, fall 2007		Degrees conferred, 2007–08					Total expenditures, 2006–07 (in thousands)
				Total	Black enrollment	Associate's	Bachelor's	Master's	First-professional	Doctor's	
1	2	3	4	5	6	7	8	9	10	11	12
Total[2]	†	†	**308,774**	**306,515**	**253,415**	**3,763**	**31,070**	**7,129**	**1,778**	**495**	**$6,608,479**
Alabama A&M University[3]	AL	1	6,076	5,706	5,129	†	631	256	†	25	126,372
Alabama State University	AL	1	5,565	5,608	5,373	†	457	184	†	21	109,972
Bishop State Community College	AL	2	4,070	2,811	1,586	268	†	†	†	†	32,781
Concordia College	AL	3	827	555	512	18	47	†	†	†	7,059
Gadsden State Community College	AL	2	5,206	5,514	1,121	494	†	†	†	†	46,158
H. Councill Trenholm State Technical College, Trenholm	AL	2	1,318	1,340	869	127	†	†	†	†	18,472
J. F. Drake Technical College	AL	2	690	694	444	49	†	†	†	†	7,808
Lawson State Community College	AL	2	3,141	3,320	2,769	248	†	†	†	†	34,030
Miles College	AL	3	1,738	1,210	1,197	†	220	†	†	†	23,291
Oakwood College	AL	3	1,771	1,824	1,674	5	257	†	†	†	34,852
Shelton State Community College, C. A. Fredd campus	AL	2	5,413	5,323	1,586	229	†	†	†	†	43,913
Stillman College	AL	3	815	915	888	†	106	†	†	†	20,709
Talladega College	AL	3	425	350	350	†	29	†	†	†	10,930
Tuskegee University[3]	AL	3	2,842	2,936	2,775	†	335	44	50	2	104,149
Arkansas Baptist College	AR	3	408	602	589	27	15	†	†	†	3,771
Philander Smith College	AR	3	580	561	547	†	82	†	†	†	11,822
University of Arkansas at Pine Bluff[3]	AR	1	3,128	3,200	3,033	†	365	21	†	†	66,402
Delaware State University[3]	DE	1	3,690	3,756	3,070	†	455	139	†	4	92,997
Howard University	DC	3	10,771	10,125	9,132	†	1,400	384	434	106	793,362
University of the District of Columbia[3]	DC	1	5,534	5,371	4,353	152	318	52	†	†	119,389
Bethune-Cookman College	FL	3	3,111	3,434	3,270	†	383	9	†	†	54,840
Edward Waters College	FL	3	842	811	770	†	126	†	†	†	25,876
Florida A&M University[2]	FL	1	11,907	11,562	10,479	96	1,430	238	265	11	267,848
Florida Memorial College	FL	3	1,867	1,750	1,555	†	184	52	†	†	37,623
Albany State College	GA	1	3,927	4,033	3,677	3	505	110	†	†	57,633
Clark Atlanta University	GA	3	4,514	4,271	4,179	†	573	175	†	36	88,954
Fort Valley State University[3]	GA	1	2,176	2,562	2,463	11	268	22	†	†	54,320
Interdenominational Theological Center	GA	3	466	442	409	†	†	†	91	16	9,311
Morehouse College	GA	3	2,933	2,810	2,723	†	521	†	†	†	81,917
Morehouse School of Medicine	GA	3	286	300	239	†	†	12	51	3	117,790
Paine College	GA	3	913	917	902	†	100	†	†	†	20,092
Savannah State University	GA	1	3,241	3,169	3,001	†	300	45	†	†	47,275
Spelman College	GA	3	2,290	2,343	2,279	†	483	†	†	†	75,297
Kentucky State University[3]	KY	1	2,498	2,696	1,716	37	231	47	†	†	56,144
Dillard University	LA	3	1,124	956	932	†	176	†	†	†	40,808
Grambling State University	LA	1	5,065	5,161	4,550	36	537	93	†	3	85,481
Southern University and A&M College[3]	LA	1	8,624	8,288	7,772	4	940	305	†	9	161,780
Southern University at New Orleans	LA	1	2,197	2,648	2,554	16	229	143	†	†	34,773
Southern University at Shreveport	LA	2	2,387	2,337	1,934	252	†	†	†	†	25,539
Xavier University of Louisiana	LA	3	3,012	3,088	2,440	†	343	31	152	†	87,865
Bowie State University	MD	1	5,291	5,464	4,913	†	616	333	†	9	72,756
Coppin State College	MD	1	4,104	3,932	3,666	†	293	97	†	†	68,168
Morgan State University	MD	1	6,705	7,208	6,454	†	813	130	†	42	166,627
University of Maryland, Eastern Shore[3]	MD	1	4,130	4,086	3,273	†	448	74	†	13	87,755
Alcorn State University[3]	MS	1	3,584	3,668	3,299	40	442	143	†	†	72,316
Coahoma Community College	MS	2	1,838	2,216	2,135	199	†	†	†	†	21,523
Hinds Community College, Utica Campus	MS	2	1,125	1,125	1,046	87	†	†	†	†	—
Jackson State University	MS	1	8,256	8,698	8,127	†	915	370	†	52	180,269
Mississippi Valley State University	MS	1	3,162	3,009	2,865	†	375	129	†	†	69,185
Rust College	MS	3	920	979	912	5	119	†	†	†	14,913
Tougaloo College	MS	3	913	856	851	2	127	†	†	†	27,309

See notes at end of table.

Fall enrollment, degrees conferred, and expenditures in degree-granting historically Black colleges and universities, by institution: 2006, 2006–07, 2007, and 2007–08—Continued

Institution	State	Type and control[1]	Total enrollment, fall 2006	Enrollment, fall 2007		Degrees conferred, 2007–08					Total expenditures, 2006–07 (in thousands)
				Total	Black enrollment	Associate's	Bachelor's	Master's	First-professional	Doctor's	
1	2	3	4	5	6	7	8	9	10	11	12
Harris-Stowe State College	MO	1	1,868	1,882	1,697	†	106	†	†	†	23,741
Lincoln University[3]	MO	1	3,224	3,156	1,175	82	245	63	†	†	42,459
Bennett College for Women	NC	3	607	678	663	†	108	†	†	†	17,179
Elizabeth City State University	NC	1	2,681	3,061	2,442	†	389	22	†	†	64,960
Fayetteville State University	NC	1	6,301	6,692	5,035	†	775	160	†	13	97,796
Johnson C. Smith University	NC	3	1,470	1,463	1,450	†	213	†	†	†	34,732
Livingstone College	NC	3	907	960	935	†	118	†	†	†	16,623
North Carolina A&T State University[3]	NC	1	11,098	10,498	9,363	†	1,172	437	†	32	219,772
North Carolina Central University	NC	1	8,675	8,383	6,996	†	854	390	141	†	160,073
Saint Augustine's College	NC	3	1,247	1,284	1,251	†	168	†	†	†	27,090
Shaw University	NC	3	2,882	2,866	2,747	10	421	6	22	†	46,608
Winston-Salem State University	NC	1	5,650	5,870	4,781	†	867	131	†	†	119,860
Central State University	OH	1	1,766	2,022	1,950	†	170	2	†	†	50,762
Wilberforce University	OH	3	863	834	792	†	172	3	†	†	16,277
Langston University[2]	OK	1	2,788	2,823	2,224	14	320	41	†	7	40,268
Cheyney University of Pennsylvania	PA	1	1,667	1,438	1,395	†	147	49	†	†	42,990
Lincoln University of Pennsylvania	PA	1	2,423	2,449	2,298	†	227	213	†	†	55,194
Allen University	SC	3	530	651	641	†	45	†	†	†	15,232
Benedict College	SC	3	2,531	2,641	2,617	†	343	†	†	†	49,922
Claflin College	SC	3	1,758	1,763	1,653	†	274	31	†	†	36,302
Clinton Junior College	SC	4	108	93	92	16	†	†	†	†	2,370
Denmark Technical College	SC	2	1,377	1,571	1,496	133	†	†	†	†	12,137
Morris College	SC	3	824	871	871	†	106	†	†	†	16,325
South Carolina State University[2]	SC	1	4,384	4,933	4,730	†	554	98	†	13	111,902
Voorhees College	SC	3	710	587	581	†	124	†	†	†	16,549
Fisk University	TN	3	953	814	711	†	107	16	†	†	27,673
Lane College	TN	3	1,370	1,766	1,758	†	175	†	†	†	19,739
Le Moyne-Owen College	TN	3	714	592	583	†	100	†	†	†	13,978
Meharry Medical College	TN	3	730	752	609	†	†	11	141	7	117,224
Tennessee State University[3]	TN	1	9,038	9,065	6,746	149	942	419	†	†	163,194
Huston-Tillotson College	TX	3	742	768	583	†	93	†	†	†	15,051
Jarvis Christian College	TX	3	675	712	666	†	66	†	†	†	12,669
Paul Quinn College	TX	3	784	567	500	†	132	†	†	†	11,695
Prairie View A&M University[3]	TX	1	8,006	8,382	7,467	†	758	699	†	10	153,729
Saint Philip's College	TX	2	9,264	9,256	1,452	691	†	†	†	†	56,287
Southwestern Christian College	TX	3	202	201	186	31	8	†	†	†	4,950
Texas College	TX	3	755	774	682	1	82	†	†	†	12,111
Texas Southern University	TX	1	11,224	9,540	8,045	†	807	212	307	25	159,589
Wiley College	TX	3	862	926	828	1	157	†	†	†	13,531
Hampton University	VA	3	6,152	5,658	5,167	2	988	105	37	13	140,994
Norfolk State University	VA	1	6,238	6,155	5,526	54	737	222	†	4	127,826
Saint Paul's College	VA	3	681	700	682	†	124	†	†	†	15,942
Virginia State University[3]	VA	1	4,872	4,720	4,507	14	599	99	†	9	108,298
Virginia Union University	VA	3	1,599	1,535	1,488	†	203	†	87	2	23,851
Virginia University of Lynchburg	VA	3	178	217	210	6	26	†	0	8	980
Bluefield State College	WV	1	1,923	1,804	214	85	219	†	†	†	20,512
West Virginia State College	WV	1	3,502	3,218	617	†	442	9	†	†	57,161
University of the Virgin Islands[3]	VI	1	2,4,88	2,384	1,931	69	193	53	†	†	74,146

—Not available.
†Not applicable.
[1]1 = public, 4-year; 2 = public, 2-year; 3 = private not-for-profit, 4-year; and 4 = private not-for-profit, 2-year.
[2]Total includes fall 2006 enrollment data for Lewis College of Business. This institution is excluded from other columns since it no longer operates as a degree-granting institution.
[3]Land-grant institution.
NOTE: Degree-granting institutions grant associate's or higher degrees and participate in Title IV federal financial aid programs. Excludes historically Black colleges and universities that are not participating in Title IV programs. Historically Black colleges and universities are degree-granting institutions established prior to 1964 with the principal mission of educating Black Americans. Federal regulations, 20 U.S. Code, Section 1061 (2), allow for certain exceptions to the founding date. Totals include persons of other racial/ethnic groups not separately identified. Detail may not sum to totals because of rounding.
SOURCE: U.S. Department of Education, National Center for Education Statistics, 2006 through 2008 Integrated Postsecondary Education Data System (IPEDS), Fall 2007, Fall 2008, Spring 2007, and Spring 2008. (This table was prepared August 2009.)

Fall enrollment in degree-granting historically Black colleges and universities, by type and control of institution: 1976 through 2007

Year	Total enrollment	Males	Females	4-year	2-year	Public Total	Public 4-year	Public 2-year	Private Total	Private 4-year	Private 2-year
1	2	3	4	5	6	7	8	9	10	11	12
All students											
1976	222,613	104,669	117,944	206,676	15,937	156,836	143,528	13,308	65,777	63,148	2,629
1977	226,062	104,178	121,884	209,898	16,164	158,823	145,450	13,373	67,239	64,448	2,791
1978	227,797	104,216	123,581	211,651	16,146	163,237	150,168	13,069	64,560	61,483	3,077
1979	230,124	105,494	124,630	214,147	15,977	166,315	153,139	13,176	63,809	61,008	2,801
1980	233,557	106,387	127,170	218,009	15,548	168,217	155,085	13,132	65,340	62,924	2,416
1981	232,460	106,033	126,427	217,152	15,308	166,991	154,269	12,722	65,469	62,883	2,586
1982	228,371	104,897	123,474	212,017	16,354	165,871	151,472	14,399	62,500	60,545	1,955
1983	234,446	106,884	127,562	217,909	16,537	170,051	155,665	14,386	64,395	62,244	2,151
1984	227,519	102,823	124,696	212,844	14,675	164,116	151,289	12,827	63,403	61,555	1,848
1985	225,801	100,698	125,103	210,648	15,153	163,677	150,002	13,675	62,124	60,646	1,478
1986	223,275	97,523	125,752	207,231	16,044	162,048	147,631	14,417	61,227	59,600	1,627
1987	227,994	97,085	130,909	211,654	16,340	165,486	150,560	14,926	62,508	61,094	1,414
1988	239,755	100,561	139,194	223,250	16,505	173,672	158,606	15,066	66,083	64,644	1,439
1989	249,096	102,484	146,612	232,890	16,206	181,151	166,481	14,670	67,945	66,409	1,536
1990	257,152	105,157	151,995	240,497	16,655	187,046	171,969	15,077	70,106	68,528	1,578
1991	269,335	110,442	158,893	252,093	17,242	197,847	182,204	15,643	71,488	69,889	1,599
1992	279,541	114,622	164,919	261,089	18,452	204,966	188,143	16,823	74,575	72,946	1,629
1993	282,856	116,397	166,459	262,430	20,426	208,197	189,032	19,165	74,659	73,398	1,261
1994	280,071	114,006	166,065	259,997	20,074	206,520	187,735	18,785	73,551	72,262	1,289
1995	278,725	112,637	166,088	259,409	19,316	204,726	186,278	18,448	73,999	73,131	868
1996	273,018	109,498	163,520	253,654	19,364	200,569	182,063	18,506	72,449	71,591	858
1997	269,167	106,865	162,302	248,860	20,307	194,674	175,297	19,377	74,493	73,563	930
1998	273,472	108,752	164,720	248,931	24,541	198,603	174,776	23,827	74,869	74,155	714
1999	274,212	108,398	165,814	249,169	25,043	199,704	175,364	24,340	74,508	73,805	703
2000	275,680	108,164	167,516	250,710	24,970	199,725	175,404	24,321	75,955	75,306	649
2001	289,985	112,874	177,111	260,547	29,438	210,083	181,346	28,737	79,902	79,201	701
2002	299,041	115,466	183,575	269,020	30,021	218,433	189,183	29,250	80,608	79,837	771
2003	306,727	117,795	188,932	274,326	32,401	228,096	196,077	32,019	78,631	78,249	382
2004	308,939	118,129	190,810	276,136	32,803	231,179	198,810	32,369	77,760	77,326	434
2005	311,768	120,023	191,745	272,666	39,102	235,875	197,200	38,675	75,893	75,466	427
2006	308,774	118,865	189,909	272,770	36,004	234,505	198,676	35,829	74,269	74,094	175
2007	306,515	118,640	187,875	270,915	35,600	233,807	198,300	35,507	72,708	72,615	93
Black students											
1976	190,305	84,492	105,813	179,848	10,457	129,770	121,851	7,919	60,535	57,997	2,538
1978	192,243	82,452	109,791	181,862	10,381	132,987	125,391	7,596	59,256	56,471	2,785
1980	190,989	81,818	109,171	181,237	9,752	131,661	124,236	7,425	59,328	57,001	2,327
1982	182,639	78,874	103,765	171,942	10,697	126,368	117,562	8,806	56,271	54,380	1,891
1984	180,803	76,819	103,984	171,401	9,402	124,445	116,845	7,600	56,358	54,556	1,802
1986	178,628	74,276	104,352	167,971	10,657	123,555	114,502	9,053	55,073	53,469	1,604
1988	194,151	78,268	115,883	183,402	10,749	133,786	124,438	9,348	60,365	58,964	1,401
1990	208,682	82,897	125,785	198,237	10,445	144,204	134,924	9,280	64,478	63,313	1,165
1991	218,366	87,380	130,986	207,449	10,917	152,864	143,411	9,453	65,502	64,038	1,464
1992	228,963	91,949	137,014	217,614	11,349	159,585	149,754	9,831	69,378	67,860	1,518
1993	231,198	93,110	138,088	219,431	11,767	161,444	150,867	10,577	69,754	68,564	1,190
1994	230,162	91,908	138,254	218,565	11,597	161,098	150,682	10,416	69,064	67,883	1,181
1995	229,418	91,132	138,286	218,379	11,039	159,925	149,661	10,264	69,493	68,718	775
1996	224,201	88,306	135,895	213,309	10,892	156,851	146,753	10,098	67,350	66,556	794
1997	222,331	86,641	135,690	210,741	11,590	153,039	142,326	10,713	69,292	68,415	877
1998	223,745	87,163	136,582	211,822	11,923	154,244	142,985	11,259	69,501	68,837	664
1999	226,407	88,057	138,350	213,729	12,678	156,115	144,124	11,991	70,292	69,605	687
2000	227,239	87,319	139,920	215,172	12,067	156,706	145,277	11,429	70,533	69,895	638
2001	238,638	90,718	147,920	224,417	14,221	164,354	150,831	13,523	74,284	73,586	698
2002	247,292	93,538	153,754	231,834	15,458	172,203	157,507	14,696	75,089	74,327	762
2003	253,257	95,703	157,554	236,753	16,504	180,104	163,977	16,127	73,153	72,776	377
2004	257,545	96,750	160,795	241,030	16,515	184,708	168,619	16,089	72,837	72,411	426
2005	256,584	96,891	159,693	238,030	18,554	186,047	167,916	18,131	70,537	70,114	423
2006	255,150	96,508	158,642	238,446	16,704	185,894	169,365	16,529	69,256	69,081	175
2007	253,415	96,313	157,102	236,885	16,530	185,344	168,906	16,438	68,071	67,979	92

NOTE: Historically Black colleges and universities are degree-granting institutions established prior to 1964 with the principal mission of educating Black Americans. Federal regulations, 20 U.S. Code, Section 1061 (2), allow for certain exceptions to the founding date. Data through 1995 are for institutions of higher education, while later data are for degree-granting institutions. Degree-granting institutions grant associate's or higher degrees and participate in Title IV federal financial aid programs. The degree-granting classification is very similar to the earlier higher education classification, but it includes more 2-year colleges and excludes a few higher education institutions that did not grant degrees. (See Appendix A: Guide to Sources for details.)

SOURCE: U.S. Department of Education, National Center for Education Statistics, Higher Education General Information Survey (HEGIS), "Fall Enrollment in Colleges and Universities," 1976 through 1985 surveys; and 1986 through 2007 Integrated Postsecondary Education Data System, "Fall Enrollment Survey" (IPEDS-EF:86–99), and Spring 2001 through Spring 2008. (This table was prepared August 2009.)

Degree-granting institutions, by control and type of institution: Selected years, 1949–50 through 2008–09

Year	All institutions			Public			Private								
								4-year, total	2-year, total	Not-for-profit			For-profit		
	Total	4-year	2-year	Total	4-year	2-year	Total			Total	4-year	2-year	Total	4-year	2-year
1	2	3	4	5	6	7	8	9	10	11	12	13	14	15	16
Excluding branch campuses															
1949–50	1,851	1,327	524	641	344	297	1,210	983	227	—	—	—	—	—	—
1959–60	2,004	1,422	582	695	367	328	1,309	1,055	254	—	—	—	—	—	—
1969–70	2,525	1,639	886	1,060	426	634	1,465	1,213	252	—	—	—	—	—	—
1970–71	2,556	1,665	891	1,089	435	654	1,467	1,230	237	—	—	—	—	—	—
1971–72	2,606	1,675	931	1,137	440	697	1,469	1,235	234	—	—	—	—	—	—
1972–73	2,665	1,701	964	1,182	449	733	1,483	1,252	231	—	—	—	—	—	—
1973–74	2,720	1,717	1,003	1,200	440	760	1,520	1,277	243	—	—	—	—	—	—
1974–75	2,747	1,744	1,003	1,214	447	767	1,533	1,297	236	—	—	—	—	—	—
1975–76	2,765	1,767	998	1,219	447	772	1,546	1,320	226	—	—	—	—	—	—
1976–77	2,785	1,783	1,002	1,231	452	779	1,554	1,331	223	—	—	—	—	—	—
1977–78	2,826	1,808	1,018	1,241	454	787	1,585	1,354	231	—	—	—	—	—	—
1978–79	2,954	1,843	1,111	1,308	463	845	1,646	1,380	266	—	—	—	—	—	—
1979–80	2,975	1,863	1,112	1,310	464	846	1,665	1,399	266	—	—	—	—	—	—
1980–81	3,056	1,861	1,195	1,334	465	869	1,722	1,396	326 [1]	—	—	—	—	—	—
1981–82	3,083	1,883	1,200	1,340	471	869	1,743	1,412	331 [1]	—	—	—	—	—	—
1982–83	3,111	1,887	1,224	1,336	472	864	1,775	1,415	360 [1]	—	—	—	—	—	—
1983–84	3,117	1,914	1,203	1,325	474	851	1,792	1,440	352	—	—	—	—	—	—
1984–85	3,146	1,911	1,235	1,329	461	868	1,817	1,450	367	—	—	—	—	—	—
1985–86	3,155	1,915	1,240	1,326	461	865	1,829	1,454	375	—	—	—	—	—	—
Including branch campuses															
1974–75	3,004	1,866	1,138	1,433	537	896	1,571	1,329	242	—	—	—	—	—	—
1975–76	3,026	1,898	1,128	1,442	545	897	1,584	1,353	231	—	—	—	—	—	—
1976–77	3,046	1,913	1,133	1,455	550	905	1,591	1,363	228	1,536	1,348	188	55	15	40
1977–78	3,095	1,938	1,157	1,473	552	921	1,622	1,386	236	—	—	—	—	—	—
1978–79	3,134	1,941	1,193	1,474	550	924	1,660	1,391	269	1,564	1,376	188	96	15	81
1979–80	3,152	1,957	1,195	1,475	549	926	1,677	1,408	269	—	—	—	—	—	—
1980–81	3,231	1,957	1,274	1,497	552	945	1,734	1,405	329 [1]	1,569	1,387	182	165	18	147
1981–82	3,253	1,979	1,274	1,498	558	940	1,755	1,421	334 [1]	—	—	—	—	—	—
1982–83	3,280	1,984	1,296	1,493	560	933	1,787	1,424	363 [1]	—	—	—	—	—	—
1983–84	3,284	2,013	1,271	1,481	565	916	1,803	1,448	355	—	—	—	—	—	—
1984–85	3,331	2,025	1,306	1,501	566	935	1,830	1,459	371	1,616	1,430	186	214	29	185
1985–86	3,340	2,029	1,311	1,498	566	932	1,842	1,463	379	—	—	—	—	—	—
1986–87	3,406	2,070	1,336	1,533	573	960	1,873	1,497	376	1,635	1,462	173	238	35	203
1987–88	3,587	2,135	1,452	1,591	599	992	1,996	1,536	460	1,673	1,487	186	323	49	274
1988–89	3,565	2,129	1,436	1,582	598	984	1,983	1,531	452	1,658	1,478	180	325	53	272
1989–90	3,535	2,127	1,408	1,563	595	968	1,972	1,532	440	1,656	1,479	177	316	53	263
1990–91	3,559	2,141	1,418	1,567	595	972	1,992	1,546	446	1,649	1,482	167	343	64	279
1991–92	3,601	2,157	1,444	1,598	599	999	2,003	1,558	445	1,662	1,486	176	341	72	269
1992–93	3,638	2,169	1,469	1,624	600	1,024	2,014	1,569	445	1,672	1,493	179	342	76	266
1993–94	3,632	2,190	1,442	1,625	604	1,021	2,007	1,586	421	1,687	1,506	181	320	80	240
1994–95	3,688	2,215	1,473	1,641	605	1,036	2,047	1,610	437	1,702	1,510	192	345	100	245
1995–96	3,706	2,244	1,462	1,655	608	1,047	2,051	1,636	415	1,706	1,519	187	345	117	228
1996–97	4,009	2,267	1,742	1,702	614	1,088	2,307	1,653	654	1,693	1,509	184	614	144	470
1997–98	4,064	2,309	1,755	1,707	615	1,092	2,357	1,694	663	1,707	1,528	179	650	166	484
1998–99	4,048	2,335	1,713	1,681	612	1,069	2,367	1,723	644	1,695	1,531	164	672	192	480
1999–2000	4,084	2,363	1,721	1,682	614	1,068	2,402	1,749	653	1,681	1,531	150	721	218	503
2000–01	4,182	2,450	1,732	1,698	622	1,076	2,484	1,828	656	1,695	1,551	144	789	277	512
2001–02	4,197	2,487	1,710	1,713	628	1,085	2,484	1,859	625	1,676	1,541	135	808	318	490
2002–03	4,168	2,466	1,702	1,712	631	1,081	2,456	1,835	621	1,665	1,538	127	791	297	494
2003–04	4,236	2,530	1,706	1,720	634	1,086	2,516	1,896	620	1,664	1,546	118	852	350	502
2004–05	4,216	2,533	1,683	1,700	639	1,061	2,516	1,894	622	1,637	1,525	112	879	369	510
2005–06	4,276	2,582	1,694	1,693	640	1,053	2,583	1,942	641	1,647	1,534	113	936	408	528
2006–07	4,314	2,629	1,685	1,688	643	1,045	2,626	1,986	640	1,640	1,533	107	986	453	533
2007–08	4,352	2,675	1,677	1,685	653	1,032	2,667	2,022	645	1,624	1,532	92	1,043	490	553
2008–09	4,409	2,719	1,690	1,676	652	1,024	2,733	2,067	666	1,629	1,537	92	1,104	530	574

—Not available.

[1] Large increases are due to the addition of schools accredited by the Accrediting Commission of Career Schools and Colleges of Technology.

NOTE: Data through 1995–96 are for institutions of higher education, while later data are for degree-granting institutions. Degree-granting institutions grant associate's or higher degrees and participate in Title IV federal financial aid programs. The degree-granting classification is very similar to the earlier higher education classification, but it includes more 2-year colleges and excludes a few higher education institutions that did not grant degrees. (See Appendix A: Guide to Sources for details.) Changes in counts of institutions over time are partly affected by increasing or decreasing numbers of institutions submitting separate data for branch campuses.

SOURCE: U.S. Department of Education, National Center for Education Statistics, *Education Directory, Colleges and Universities*, 1949–50 through 1965–66; Higher Education General Information Survey (HEGIS), "Institutional Characteristics of Colleges and Universities" surveys, 1966–67 through 1985–86; and 1986–87 through 2007–08 Integrated Postsecondary Education Data System, "Institutional Characteristics Survey" (IPEDS-IC:86–99), and Fall 2000 through Fall 2008. (This table was prepared July 2009.)

Degree-granting institutions and branches, by type and control of institution and state or jurisdiction: 2008–09

State or jurisdiction	Total	All public institutions	Public 4-year institutions — Total	Research university, very high[1]	Research university, high[2]	Doctoral/research university[3]	Masters[4]	Baccalaureate[5]	Special focus[6]	Public 2-year	All not-for-profit institutions	Not-for-profit 4-year institutions — Total	Research university, very high[1]	Research university, high[2]	Doctoral/research university[3]	Masters[4]	Baccalaureate[5]	Special focus[6]	Not-for-profit 2-year	For-profit institutions — Total	For-profit 4-year	For-profit 2-year
1	2	3	4	5	6	7	8	9	10	11	12	13	14	15	16	17	18	19	20	21	22	23
United States	**4,409**	**1,676**	**652**	**63**	**75**	**27**	**261**	**181**	**45**	**1,024**	**1,629**	**1,537**	**33**	**27**	**45**	**344**	**532**	**556**	**92**	**1,104**	**530**	**574**
Alabama	72	39	14	1	3	0	9	1	0	25	19	19	0	0	1	2	10	6	0	14	10	4
Alaska	7	5	5	1	0	0	2	0	0	2	1	1	0	0	0	1	0	0	0	1	0	0
Arizona	75	24	3	2	1	0	0	0	0	21	10	10	0	0	0	2	2	6	0	41	28	13
Arkansas	50	33	11	0	1	1	5	3	1	22	12	12	0	1	0	1	9	2	0	5	3	2
California	426	147	35	8	1	0	19	5	2	112	146	138	3	1	11	26	22	75	8	133	60	73
Colorado	80	27	12	3	1	1	2	5	0	15	12	11	0	0	0	3	3	4	1	41	23	18
Connecticut	46	22	10	1	0	0	4	4	1	12	18	16	1	0	2	6	5	2	2	6	4	2
Delaware	10	5	2	1	0	0	1	0	0	3	5	4	0	0	1	1	1	1	1	0	0	0
District of Columbia	16	2	2	1	0	0	2	0	1	0	11	11	1	3	2	3	0	3	0	3	3	0
Florida	188	40	20	3	3	2	2	9	1	20	56	55	1	1	2	11	21	19	1	92	51	41
Georgia	135	73	25	2	1	1	13	7	1	48	35	32	1	1	0	4	17	9	3	27	18	9
Hawaii	21	10	4	1	0	0	0	3	0	6	5	5	0	0	0	2	2	1	0	6	4	2
Idaho	14	7	4	0	1	1	1	1	0	3	4	4	0	0	2	1	1	0	0	3	2	1
Illinois	180	60	12	2	2	1	7	0	0	48	84	80	2	0	2	16	22	36	4	36	21	15
Indiana	107	29	15	2	1	2	6	4	0	14	43	42	1	0	0	9	21	11	1	35	19	16
Iowa	66	19	3	2	0	0	1	0	0	16	36	35	0	0	0	5	20	10	1	11	10	1
Kansas	66	32	8	2	0	0	4	0	1	24	24	22	0	0	1	6	13	3	2	10	5	5
Kentucky	73	24	8	1	1	1	5	1	0	16	27	27	0	0	1	3	14	9	0	22	8	14
Louisiana	85	51	17	1	2	1	9	2	3	34	10	10	1	0	0	2	4	3	0	24	4	20
Maine	30	15	8	0	1	0	1	6	0	7	13	12	0	0	0	3	6	3	1	2	0	2
Maryland	57	29	13	1	1	1	8	1	1	16	21	21	1	0	0	4	7	9	0	7	4	3
Massachusetts	124	30	14	1	0	2	7	2	2	16	84	80	5	3	1	14	25	32	4	10	4	6
Michigan	106	45	15	3	2	2	7	1	0	30	52	52	0	0	1	9	23	19	0	9	6	3
Minnesota	114	42	11	1	2	0	8	2	0	31	37	36	0	0	3	6	11	16	1	35	29	6
Mississippi	40	24	9	0	4	0	4	0	1	15	11	11	0	0	0	3	4	4	0	5	0	5
Missouri	131	34	13	2	3	0	6	3	0	21	56	52	1	1	0	12	12	26	4	41	20	21
Montana	23	18	6	0	2	0	1	3	0	12	5	4	0	0	0	1	2	1	1	0	0	0
Nebraska	42	15	7	1	1	0	3	2	1	8	19	17	0	0	0	3	9	5	2	8	5	3
Nevada	21	7	6	0	2	0	0	4	0	1	2	2	0	0	0	0	1	1	0	12	7	5
New Hampshire	28	12	5	0	1	0	2	2	0	7	14	13	1	0	0	2	6	3	1	2	1	1
New Jersey	63	33	14	1	2	0	9	1	1	19	25	25	1	1	0	9	3	10	0	5	3	2
New Mexico	42	28	8	1	3	0	4	0	1	20	5	5	0	0	0	4	1	0	0	9	8	1
New York	307	78	43	3	3	2	20	13	4	35	186	166	6	5	6	39	30	80	20	43	18	25
North Carolina	133	75	16	3	2	0	6	3	1	59	45	44	1	0	0	5	28	9	1	13	10	3
North Dakota	22	14	8	0	2	0	1	4	0	6	6	5	0	0	0	1	1	3	1	2	2	0
Ohio	209	60	30	2	7	1	1	16	3	30	77	71	1	1	1	18	25	25	6	72	10	62
Oklahoma	59	29	17	0	2	0	6	7	2	12	14	14	1	0	1	3	5	4	0	16	7	9
Oregon	60	26	9	1	1	1	3	1	1	17	25	25	0	2	2	3	9	11	0	9	5	4
Pennsylvania	262	65	44	2	6	1	16	22	2	21	114	101	2	3	3	30	36	28	13	83	9	74
Rhode Island	13	3	2	1	1	0	1	0	0	1	9	9	1	0	0	4	1	3	1	1	0	1
South Carolina	69	33	13	1	1	1	4	5	1	20	25	23	0	0	0	5	14	4	2	11	7	4
South Dakota	24	12	7	0	1	0	0	3	2	5	8	7	0	0	0	1	3	3	1	4	4	0
Tennessee	105	22	9	1	2	0	5	1	0	13	48	46	1	1	1	10	17	17	2	35	16	19
Texas	218	109	45	2	6	3	21	5	8	64	57	53	1	1	2	16	17	16	4	52	15	37
Utah	38	14	7	1	1	0	2	3	0	7	4	3	0	1	0	1	1	0	1	20	17	3

See notes at end of table.

Degree-granting institutions and branches, by type and control of institution and state or jurisdiction: 2008–09—Continued

State or jurisdiction	Total	Public institutions									Not-for-profit institutions									For-profit institutions		
		All public insti-tutions	Public 4-year institutions							Public 2-year	All not-for-profit insti-tutions	Not-for-profit 4-year institutions							Not-for-profit 2-year	Total	4-year	2-year
			Total	Research university, very high[1]	Research university, high[2]	Doctoral/research university[3]	Master's[4]	Bacca-laureate[5]	Special focus[6]			Total	Research university, very high[1]	Research university, high[2]	Doctoral/research university[3]	Master's[4]	Bacca-laureate[5]	Special focus[6]				
1	2	3	4	5	6	7	8	9	10	11	12	13	14	15	16	17	18	19	20	21	22	23
Vermont	25	6	5	0	1	0	2	2	0	1	17	16	0	0	0	5	9	2	1	2	2	0
Virginia	114	39	15	2	4	0	6	3	0	24	35	35	0	0	1	7	20	7	0	40	21	19
Washington	78	43	13	2	0	0	6	4	1	30	18	18	0	0	0	10	3	5	0	17	12	5
West Virginia	44	23	12	1	1	0	1	9	0	11	9	9	0	0	0	2	6	1	0	12	2	10
Wisconsin	75	31	14	1	1	0	9	3	0	17	30	28	0	1	0	10	10	7	2	14	10	4
Wyoming	11	8	1	0	1	0	0	0	0	7	0	0	†	†	†	†	†	†	†	3	2	†
U.S. Service Academies	5	5	5	0	0	0	0	5	0	0	†	†	†	†	†	†	†	†	†	†	†	†
Other jurisdictions	**86**	**25**	**18**	**0**	**1**	**0**	**2**	**12**	**3**	**7**	**44**	**38**	**0**	**0**	**2**	**5**	**19**	**12**	**6**	**17**	**8**	**9**
American Samoa	1	1	1	0	0	0	0	1	0	0	0	0	0	0	0	0	0	0	0	0	0	0
Federated States of Micronesia	1	1	0	0	0	0	0	0	0	1	0	0	0	0	0	0	0	0	0	0	0	0
Guam	3	2	1	0	0	0	1	0	0	1	1	1	0	0	0	0	0	1	0	0	0	0
Marshall Islands	1	1	0	0	0	0	0	0	0	1	0	0	0	0	0	0	0	0	0	0	0	0
Northern Marianas	1	1	1	0	0	0	0	1	0	0	0	0	0	0	0	0	0	0	0	0	0	0
Palau	1	1	0	0	0	0	0	0	0	1	0	0	0	0	0	0	0	0	0	0	0	0
Puerto Rico	77	17	14	0	1	0	1	9	3	3	43	37	0	0	2	5	19	11	6	17	8	9
U.S. Virgin Islands	1	1	1	0	0	0	1	0	0	0	0	0	0	0	0	0	0	0	0	0	0	0

†Not applicable.

[1] Research universities with a very high level of research activity.

[2] Research universities with a high level of research activity.

[3] Institutions that award at least 20 doctor's degrees per year, but did not have a high level of research activity.

[4] Institutions that award at least 50 master's degrees per year.

[5] Institutions that primarily emphasize undergraduate education.

[6] Four-year institutions that award degrees primarily in single fields of study, such as medicine, business, fine arts, theology, and engineering. Includes some institutions that have 4-year programs, but have not reported sufficient data to identify program category. Also includes institutions classified as 4-year under the IPEDS system, which had been classified as 2-year in the Carnegie classification system because they primarily award associate's degrees.

NOTE: Relative levels of research activity for research universities were determined by an analysis of research and development expenditures, science and engineering research staffing, and doctoral degrees conferred, by field. Further information on the research index ranking may be obtained from http://www.carnegiefoundation.org/classifications/index.asp?key=798#related. Degree-granting institutions grant associate's or higher degrees and participate in Title IV federal financial aid programs.

SOURCE: U.S. Department of Education, National Center for Education Statistics, 2008–09 Integrated Postsecondary Education Data System (IPEDS), Fall 2008. (This table was prepared July 2009.)

Number and percentage of degree-granting institutions with first-year undergraduates using various selection criteria for admission, by type and control of institution: Selected years, 2000–01 through 2008–09

Selection criteria	All institutions			Public institutions			Private institutions			Not-for-profit			For-profit		
	Total	4-year	2-year	Total	4-year	2-year	Total	4-year	2-year	Total	4-year	2-year	Total	4-year	2-year
1	2	3	4	5	6	7	8	9	10	11	12	13	14	15	16
	Number of institutions with first-year undergraduates														
2000–01	3,717	2,034	1,683	1,647	580	1,067	2,070	1,454	616	1,383	1,247	136	687	207	480
2005–06	3,880	2,198	1,682	1,638	588	1,050	2,242	1,610	632	1,351	1,240	111	891	370	521
2007–08	3,983	2,313	1,670	1,639	608	1,031	2,344	1,705	639	1,334	1,244	90	1,010	461	549
2008–09	4,034	2,351	1,683	1,632	609	1,023	2,402	1,742	660	1,333	1,243	90	1,069	499	570
Open admissions	Percent of institutions														
2000–01	40.2	12.9	73.2	63.8	12.1	91.9	21.4	13.3	40.7	14.0	11.7	34.6	36.5	22.7	42.5
2005–06	44.7	18.3	79.3	66.1	13.6	95.4	29.2	20.1	52.4	15.3	13.1	40.5	50.2	43.5	54.9
2007–08	44.5	19.5	79.2	65.7	14.5	95.9	29.7	21.3	52.1	15.3	13.3	42.2	48.7	42.7	53.7
2008–09	45.7	20.2	81.3	65.7	14.9	96.0	32.1	22.0	58.6	15.7	13.4	46.7	52.5	43.3	60.5
Some admission requirements[1]															
2000–01	58.4	85.8	25.1	35.4	87.4	7.1	76.6	85.2	56.3	84.5	86.8	63.2	60.7	75.4	54.4
2005–06	53.4	80.5	18.0	33.6	86.1	4.3	67.9	78.5	40.8	84.2	86.5	57.7	43.2	51.6	37.2
2007–08	52.6	78.8	16.3	34.1	85.4	3.9	65.5	76.4	36.3	83.9	86.1	53.3	41.2	50.3	33.5
2008–09	51.8	78.3	14.7	34.1	84.9	3.9	63.7	76.0	31.4	83.8	86.1	52.2	38.7	50.9	28.1
Secondary grades															
2000–01	34.6	58.7	5.5	23.9	63.4	2.4	43.0	56.7	10.7	60.1	64.1	23.5	8.7	12.6	7.1
2005–06	34.1	57.1	4.2	25.9	68.4	2.2	40.1	53.0	7.4	62.8	66.2	25.2	5.7	8.6	3.6
2007–08	34.2	56.3	3.6	26.7	68.8	1.9	39.4	51.8	6.3	65.1	67.8	27.8	5.5	8.9	2.7
2008–09	34.2	56.1	3.5	27.0	69.1	2.0	39.0	51.5	5.9	65.2	68.1	25.6	6.4	10.4	2.8
Secondary class rank															
2000–01	13.7	24.3	1.0	10.9	30.3	0.3	16.0	21.9	2.3	23.2	25.1	5.9	1.6	2.4	1.3
2005–06	11.3	19.4	0.7	10.4	28.7	0.2	11.9	16.0	1.6	19.3	20.5	6.3	0.7	0.8	0.6
2007–08	10.3	17.4	0.6	10.2	27.1	0.2	10.5	13.9	1.3	18.1	18.9	6.7	0.4	0.4	0.4
2008–09	9.6	16.0	0.6	9.4	24.6	0.4	9.7	13.0	0.9	17.1	17.9	5.6	0.5	0.8	0.2
Secondary school record															
2000–01	45.8	70.3	16.2	29.4	72.9	5.8	58.7	69.2	34.1	73.2	75.5	52.2	29.5	30.9	29.0
2005–06	48.5	73.3	15.9	30.8	78.2	4.2	61.4	71.6	35.4	77.6	79.7	55.0	36.7	44.3	31.3
2007–08	47.5	71.1	14.7	31.3	78.1	3.7	58.7	68.6	32.4	77.2	79.2	50.0	34.4	40.1	29.5
2008–09	46.7	70.6	13.2	31.2	77.3	3.7	57.2	68.3	27.9	77.0	79.1	47.8	32.5	41.3	24.7
College preparatory program															
2000–01	15.5	27.3	1.2	16.2	44.0	1.1	14.9	20.7	1.3	22.1	24.1	4.4	0.4	0.5	0.4
2005–06	15.2	26.4	0.6	17.4	47.1	0.8	13.6	18.8	0.3	22.4	24.3	1.8	0.2	0.5	0.0
2007–08	15.5	26.3	0.5	18.1	47.7	0.7	13.6	18.7	0.2	23.8	25.4	1.1	0.2	0.4	0.0
2008–09	15.1	25.5	0.5	17.9	46.8	0.7	13.2	18.1	0.2	23.6	25.2	1.1	0.2	0.4	0.0
Recommendations															
2000–01	20.4	34.4	3.5	2.7	7.4	0.2	34.4	45.1	9.3	46.6	49.2	22.8	10.0	20.8	5.4
2005–06	19.2	31.9	2.5	2.9	7.7	0.2	31.1	40.8	6.3	49.1	51.5	23.4	3.7	5.1	2.7
2007–08	18.0	29.5	2.1	2.6	6.7	0.2	28.8	37.6	5.2	49.0	50.6	25.6	2.1	2.4	1.8
2008–09	17.9	29.1	2.3	2.8	7.2	0.2	28.1	36.7	5.6	48.8	50.5	24.4	2.4	2.2	2.6
Demonstration of competencies[2]															
2000–01	8.0	12.1	3.0	2.2	5.0	0.7	12.7	15.0	7.1	12.1	12.7	7.4	13.7	29.0	7.1
2005–06	7.0	9.8	3.3	2.3	6.1	0.2	10.3	11.1	8.4	10.2	10.3	9.0	10.5	13.8	8.3
2007–08	6.1	8.7	2.5	1.8	4.8	0.1	9.0	10.1	6.3	9.4	9.3	11.1	8.5	12.1	5.5
2008–09	6.2	8.7	2.7	2.1	5.3	0.2	9.0	9.9	6.7	9.4	9.3	11.1	8.5	11.4	6.0
Test scores[3]															
2000–01	47.2	72.5	16.7	33.2	83.4	5.8	58.5	68.2	35.6	70.3	73.4	41.9	34.6	36.7	33.8
2005–06	36.5	62.5	2.6	31.1	82.3	2.4	40.5	55.2	3.0	65.7	70.5	12.6	2.2	4.1	1.0
2007–08	34.8	58.4	2.1	31.6	81.7	2.0	37.0	50.0	2.2	64.4	67.9	15.6	0.8	1.7	0.0
2008–09	33.8	56.6	2.1	31.3	80.5	2.1	35.6	48.2	2.1	63.3	66.9	14.4	0.9	1.8	0.2
TOEFL[4]															
2000–01	43.4	71.2	9.9	30.2	77.4	4.6	54.0	68.7	19.2	66.2	70.1	30.9	29.3	60.4	15.8
2005–06	41.5	67.9	7.1	31.0	79.3	3.9	49.3	63.8	12.3	67.0	70.6	27.0	22.4	41.1	9.2
2007–08	41.4	66.3	6.8	30.9	77.5	3.5	48.6	62.3	12.1	67.5	70.0	32.2	23.8	41.6	8.7
2008–09	41.1	65.8	6.7	31.0	77.5	3.3	48.0	61.7	11.8	66.7	69.4	28.9	24.7	42.5	9.1
No admission requirements, only recommendations for admission															
2000–01	1.4	1.2	1.7	0.8	0.5	0.9	1.9	1.5	2.9	1.5	1.4	2.2	2.8	1.9	3.1
2005–06	1.8	1.1	2.7	0.3	0.3	0.3	2.9	1.4	6.8	0.5	0.4	1.8	6.6	4.9	7.9
2007–08	2.9	1.7	4.6	0.2	0.2	0.2	4.8	2.3	11.6	0.8	0.6	4.4	10.1	6.9	12.8
2008–09	2.6	1.5	4.0	0.1	0.2	0.1	4.2	2.0	10.0	0.5	0.5	1.1	8.8	5.8	11.4

[1]Many institutions have more than one admission requirement.
[2]Formal demonstration of competencies (e.g., portfolios, certificates of mastery, assessment instruments).
[3]Includes SAT, ACT, or other admission tests.
[4]Test of English as a Foreign Language.

NOTE: Degree-granting institutions grant associate's or higher degrees and participate in Title IV federal financial aid programs. Detail may not sum to totals because of rounding. SOURCE: U.S. Department of Education, National Center for Education Statistics, 2000–01 through 2008–09 Integrated Postsecondary Education Data System, Fall 2000 through Fall 2008. (This table was prepared August 2009.)

Number of applications, admissions, and enrollees; their distribution across institutions accepting various percentages of applications; and SAT and ACT scores of applicants, by type and control of institution: 2008–09

Application, admission, enrollment, and SAT and ACT score	All institutions Total	4-year	2-year	Public Total	4-year	2-year	Private Total	4-year	2-year	Private Not-for-profit Total	4-year	2-year	Private For-profit Total	4-year	2-year
	2	3	4	5	6	7	8	9	10	11	12	13	14	15	16
Number of undergraduate institutions reporting application data [1]	4,025	2,343	1,682	1,632	609	1,023	2,393	1,734	659	1,330	1,240	90	1,063	494	569
Percentage distribution of institutions by their acceptance of applications	100.0	100.0	100.0	100.0	100.0	100.0	100.0	100.0	100.0	100.0	100.0	100.0	100.0	100.0	100.0
No application criteria	45.8	20.2	81.4	65.7	14.9	96.0	32.2	22.1	58.7	15.7	13.5	46.7	52.8	43.7	60.6
90 percent or more accepted	7.7	9.3	5.3	3.8	8.2	1.2	10.3	9.7	11.7	9.2	9.3	3.3	11.6	10.9	12.1
75.0 to 89.9 percent accepted	12.0	18.2	3.2	9.0	22.7	0.9	14.0	16.7	6.8	18.4	19.5	3.3	8.4	9.5	7.4
50.0 to 74.9 percent accepted	23.2	35.2	6.6	16.1	40.6	1.5	28.1	33.3	14.6	38.8	40.2	20.0	14.8	16.0	13.7
25.0 to 49.9 percent accepted	9.7	14.5	2.9	4.6	11.5	0.5	13.1	15.6	6.7	13.9	14.1	11.1	12.1	19.2	6.0
10.0 to 24.9 percent accepted	1.4	2.0	0.5	0.7	2.0	0.0	1.8	2.1	1.2	3.2	2.8	7.8	0.2	0.2	0.2
Less than 10 percent accepted	0.3	0.5	0.1	0.1	0.2	0.0	0.5	0.6	0.3	0.8	0.6	2.2	0.2	0.4	0.0
Number of applications (in thousands)	7,428	7,271	158	4,128	4,055	73	3,300	3,216	84	3,065	3,047	18	235	169	67
Percentage distribution of applications by institutions' acceptance of applications	100.0	100.0	100.0	100.0	100.0	100.0	100.0	100.0	100.0	100.0	100.0	100.0	100.0	100.0	100.0
No application criteria	†	†	†	†	†	†	†	†	†	†	†	†	†	†	†
90 percent or more accepted	3.6	3.2	23.8	4.2	3.8	25.2	2.9	2.4	22.6	1.9	1.9	6.1	15.7	11.3	26.9
75.0 to 89.9 percent accepted	15.4	15.4	14.6	18.3	18.4	13.5	11.8	11.7	15.6	11.6	11.6	0.8	14.5	12.5	19.5
50.0 to 74.9 percent accepted	47.1	47.1	43.5	51.3	51.3	52.3	41.7	41.9	35.9	42.6	42.6	48.0	29.4	28.1	32.7
25.0 to 49.9 percent accepted	26.0	26.2	16.2	22.3	22.5	9.0	30.7	30.9	22.4	30.0	30.0	30.7	39.6	47.3	20.2
10.0 to 24.9 percent accepted	6.6	6.7	1.9	3.8	3.9	0.0	10.0	10.2	3.5	10.7	10.7	14.1	0.6	0.5	0.7
Less than 10 percent accepted	1.4	1.4	#	0.1	0.1	0.0	3.0	3.1	0.0	3.2	3.2	0.2	0.2	0.2	0.0
Number of admissions (in thousands)	4,252	4,140	111	2,542	2,487	55	1,710	1,654	57	1,563	1,554	9	147	99	48
Percentage distribution of admissions by institutions' acceptance of applications	100.0	100.0	100.0	100.0	100.0	100.0	100.0	100.0	100.0	100.0	100.0	100.0	100.0	100.0	100.0
No application criteria	†	†	†	†	†	†	†	†	†	†	†	†	†	†	†
90 percent or more accepted	6.0	5.3	33.2	6.5	5.9	33.6	5.3	4.3	32.8	3.5	3.4	11.5	24.4	18.5	36.7
75.0 to 89.9 percent accepted	22.0	22.1	17.5	24.5	24.7	15.7	18.2	18.2	19.3	18.1	18.2	1.2	19.2	17.5	22.6
50.0 to 74.9 percent accepted	51.9	52.2	39.2	52.7	52.8	45.7	50.7	51.3	33.0	52.7	52.7	58.2	28.6	28.7	28.3
25.0 to 49.9 percent accepted	17.7	18.0	9.5	15.1	15.3	5.0	21.7	22.0	13.8	21.2	21.1	23.4	27.6	35.0	12.1
10.0 to 24.9 percent accepted	2.2	2.3	0.6	1.3	1.3	0.0	3.6	3.7	1.1	3.9	3.9	5.8	0.2	0.2	0.3
Less than 10 percent accepted	0.2	0.2	#	#	#	0.0	0.5	0.5	#	0.6	0.6	#	#	#	0.0
Number of enrollees (in thousands)	1,578	1,495	83	982	944	38	596	551	46	479	473	5	118	77	40
Percentage distribution of enrollees by institutions' acceptance of applications	100.0	100.0	100.0	100.0	100.0	100.0	100.0	100.0	100.0	100.0	100.0	100.0	100.0	100.0	100.0
No application criteria	†	†	†	†	†	†	†	†	†	†	†	†	†	†	†
90 percent or more accepted	8.4	6.9	35.4	8.2	7.1	35.5	8.8	6.6	35.4	5.7	5.6	17.6	21.5	13.1	37.7
75.0 to 89.9 percent accepted	22.0	22.3	18.1	24.7	25.0	17.9	17.6	17.5	18.3	18.0	18.2	1.7	15.9	13.6	20.4
50.0 to 74.9 percent accepted	48.5	49.2	36.1	51.3	51.6	43.3	43.8	44.9	30.2	47.5	47.6	45.8	28.6	28.8	28.2
25.0 to 49.9 percent accepted	17.8	18.3	9.8	14.1	14.6	3.3	24.0	24.7	15.2	21.6	21.5	26.0	33.8	44.3	13.7
10.0 to 24.9 percent accepted	2.8	2.9	0.6	1.7	1.7	0.0	4.7	5.0	1.0	5.8	5.8	8.8	0.2	0.2	0.0
Less than 10 percent accepted	0.4	0.4	#	0.0	0.0	0.0	1.1	1.1	#	1.3	1.3	#	#	#	0.0
SAT scores of applicants															
Critical reading, 25th percentile [2]	473	474	413	457	459	409	481	482	419	481	482	419	439	439	‡
Critical reading, 75th percentile [2]	584	585	528	566	567	532	593	595	523	594	595	523	550	550	‡
Mathematics, 25th percentile [2]	477	479	413	468	470	408	482	483	420	483	484	420	421	421	‡
Mathematics, 75th percentile [2]	589	590	527	579	580	534	594	595	519	595	596	519	548	548	‡
ACT scores of applicants															
Composite, 25th percentile [2]	20.0	20.1	16.9	19.2	19.4	16.5	20.5	20.5	18.0	20.5	20.5	17.6	19.2	19.0	‡
Composite, 75th percentile [2]	25.1	25.2	21.8	24.1	24.2	21.3	25.6	25.7	23.1	25.7	25.7	22.9	24.1	24.0	‡
English, 25th percentile [2]	19.0	19.1	15.3	18.1	18.2	15.2	19.5	19.6	15.8	19.6	19.6	15.8	17.6	17.6	‡
English, 75th percentile [2]	25.2	25.3	22.0	24.1	24.3	21.9	25.8	25.9	22.5	25.9	25.9	22.5	23.8	23.8	‡
Mathematics, 25th percentile [2]	18.9	19.0	16.3	18.4	18.5	15.9	19.2	19.2	17.4	19.3	19.3	17.4	16.3	16.3	‡
Mathematics, 75th percentile [2]	24.8	24.9	20.8	24.1	24.3	20.4	25.2	25.2	21.6	25.2	25.3	21.6	22.2	22.2	‡

†Not applicable.
#Rounds to zero.
‡Reporting standards not met.
[1] Excludes institutions not enrolling first-time degree/certificate-seeking undergraduates. The total on this table differs slightly from other counts of undergraduate institutions because approximately 0.3 percent of undergraduate institutions did not report application information.

[2] Data are only for institutions that require test scores for admission. Relatively few 2-year institutions require test scores for admission.
NOTE: Detail may not sum to totals because of rounding.
SOURCE: U.S. Department of Education, National Center for Education Statistics, 2008–09 Integrated Postsecondary Education Data System, Fall 2008. (This table was prepared August 2009.)

Average scores on Graduate Record Examination (GRE) general and subject tests: 1965 through 2008

			General test sections				Subject tests									
Academic year ending	Number of GRE takers	GRE takers as a percent of bachelor's degrees[1]	Verbal	Quantitative	Analytical reasoning	Analytical writing	Biochemistry, cell and molecular biology	Biology	Chemistry	Computer science	Education	Engineering	Literature	Mathematics	Physics	Psychology
1	2	3	4	5	6	7	8	9	10	11	12	13	14	15	16	17
1965	93,792	18.7	530 (124)	533 (137)	† (†)	†	† (†)	617 (117)	628 (114)	† (†)	481 (86)	618 (108)	591 (95)	— (†)	— (†)	556 (91)
1966	123,960	23.8	520 (124)	528 (133)	† (†)	†	† (†)	610 (115)	618 (110)	† (†)	474 (87)	609 (106)	588 (94)	— (†)	— (†)	552 (91)
1967	151,134	27.0	519 (125)	528 (134)	† (†)	†	† (†)	613 (114)	615 (104)	† (†)	476 (90)	603 (104)	582 (91)	— (†)	— (†)	553 (93)
1968	182,432	28.8	520 (124)	527 (135)	† (†)	†	† (†)	614 (114)	617 (104)	† (†)	478 (87)	601 (105)	572 (91)	— (†)	— (†)	547 (93)
1969	206,113	28.3	515 (124)	524 (132)	† (†)	†	† (†)	613 (112)	613 (104)	† (†)	477 (88)	591 (103)	569 (89)	— (†)	— (†)	543 (89)
1970	265,359	33.5	503 (123)	516 (132)	† (†)	†	† (†)	603 (111)	613 (113)	† (†)	462 (92)	586 (110)	556 (90)	— (†)	— (†)	532 (91)
1971	293,600	35.0	497 (126)	512 (134)	† (†)	†	† (†)	603 (113)	618 (117)	† (†)	457 (95)	587 (115)	546 (91)	— (†)	— (†)	530 (92)
1972	293,506	33.1	494 (125)	508 (136)	† (†)	†	† (†)	606 (115)	624 (124)	† (†)	446 (93)	594 (114)	544 (96)	— (†)	— (†)	528 (92)
1973	290,104	31.5	497 (125)	512 (135)	† (†)	†	† (†)	619 (110)	630 (114)	† (†)	459 (96)	593 (114)	545 (96)	— (†)	— (†)	529 (92)
1974	301,070	31.8	492 (126)	509 (137)	† (†)	†	† (†)	624 (110)	634 (115)	† (†)	452 (93)	591 (121)	547 (99)	— (†)	— (†)	530 (95)
1975	298,335	32.3	493 (125)	508 (137)	† (†)	†	† (†)	— (†)	— (†)	— (†)	— (†)	— (†)	— (†)	— (†)	— (†)	— (†)
1976	299,292	32.3	492 (127)	510 (138)	† (†)	†	† (†)	627 (112)	627 (107)	— (†)	454 (93)	594 (119)	539 (101)	— (†)	— (†)	531 (93)
1977	287,715	31.3	490 (129)	514 (139)	† (†)	†	† (†)	625 (113)	630 (109)	— (†)	453 (93)	592 (115)	532 (101)	— (†)	— (†)	532 (95)
1978	286,383	31.1	484 (128)	518 (135)	† (†)	†	† (†)	622 (113)	624 (108)	— (†)	452 (91)	594 (114)	530 (102)	— (†)	— (†)	529 (97)
1979	282,482	30.7	476 (130)	517 (135)	† (†)	†	† (†)	621 (117)	623 (104)	— (†)	451 (89)	592 (115)	525 (102)	— (†)	— (†)	530 (97)
1980	272,281	29.3	474 (131)	522 (136)	† (†)	†	† (†)	619 (115)	618 (105)	— (†)	449 (90)	590 (116)	521 (105)	— (†)	— (†)	534 (98)
1981	262,855	28.1	473 (128)	523 (136)	† (†)	†	† (†)	617 (115)	615 (103)	— (†)	453 (90)	590 (116)	520 (99)	— (†)	— (†)	532 (97)
1982	256,381	26.9	477 (126)	533 (137)	498 (126)	†	† (†)	616 (114)	616 (105)	— (†)	456 (89)	593 (115)	521 (100)	— (†)	— (†)	532 (97)
1983	263,674	27.2	473 (131)	541 (138)	504 (128)	†	† (†)	623 (114)	620 (105)	— (†)	459 (90)	599 (114)	527 (98)	— (†)	— (†)	542 (95)
1984	265,221	27.2	475 (130)	541 (139)	512 (129)	†	† (†)	622 (115)	619 (102)	— (†)	461 (90)	604 (114)	530 (97)	— (†)	— (†)	543 (96)
1985	271,972	27.8	474 (126)	545 (140)	516 (129)	†	† (†)	619 (114)	621 (101)	— (†)	459 (89)	615 (120)	531 (95)	— (†)	— (†)	541 (95)
1986	279,428	28.3	475 (126)	552 (140)	520 (129)	†	† (†)	612 (114)	628 (106)	— (†)	464 (87)	616 (119)	527 (96)	— (†)	— (†)	542 (97)
1987	293,560	29.6	477 (126)	550 (140)	521 (128)	†	† (†)	605 (113)	629 (104)	— (†)	465 (86)	619 (119)	526 (95)	— (†)	— (†)	536 (95)
1988	303,703	30.5	483 (123)	557 (140)	528 (128)	†	† (†)	606 (114)	631 (108)	— (†)	467 (85)	622 (120)	525 (94)	— (†)	— (†)	537 (94)
1989	326,096	32.0	484 (125)	560 (142)	530 (129)	†	† (†)	620 (116)	642 (117)	— (†)	465 (87)	626 (116)	528 (91)	— (†)	— (†)	538 (95)
1990	344,572	32.8	486 (123)	562 (143)	534 (131)	†	† (†)	612 (114)	662 (123)	— (†)	461 (84)	617 (111)	523 (92)	— (†)	— (†)	537 (95)
1991	379,882	34.7	485 (122)	562 (141)	536 (131)	†	† (†)	609 (113)	660 (123)	— (†)	457 (85)	611 (111)	523 (93)	— (†)	— (†)	535 (95)
1992	411,528	36.2	483 (120)	561 (140)	537 (129)	†	† (†)	605 (113)	654 (128)	— (†)	462 (82)	610 (117)	525 (92)	— (†)	— (†)	536 (95)
1993	400,246	34.4	481 (117)	557 (140)	541 (129)	†	† (†)	606 (114)	662 (133)	— (†)	462 (80)	602 (115)	516 (94)	— (†)	— (†)	536 (97)
1994	399,395[2]	34.2	479 (116)	553 (139)	545 (129)	†	—	620 (116)	627 (113)	— (†)	493[3] (104)	601 (115)	517 (95)	— (†)	— (†)	538 (96)
1995	389,539[2]	33.6	477 (115)	553 (140)	544 (131)	†	—	622 (116)	675 (138)	— (†)	488[3] (102)	596 (113)	513 (96)	— (†)	— (†)	544 (98)
1996	376,013[2]	32.3	473 (114)	558 (139)	549 (131)	†	—	614 (114)	678 (135)	— (†)	489[3] (104)	604 (119)	512 (97)	— (†)	— (†)	547 (99)
1997	376,062[2]	32.1	472 (113)	562 (139)	548 (129)	†	—	620 (115)	684 (143)	— (†)	487[3] (103)	602 (114)	525 (100)	— (†)	— (†)	554 (99)
1998	364,554[2]	30.8	471 (113)	569 (141)	543 (133)	†	—	628 (113)	686 (137)	— (†)	477[3] (100)	609 (118)	530 (100)	— (†)	— (†)	563 (100)
1999	396,330	33.0	468 (114)	565 (143)	542 (133)	†	—	626 (114)	684 (137)	— (†)	† (†)	604 (115)	527 (100)	— (†)	— (†)	559 (99)

See notes at end of table.

Average scores on Graduate Record Examination (GRE) general and subject tests: 1965 through 2008—Continued

Academic year ending	Number of GRE takers	GRE takers as a percent of bachelor's degrees[1]	General test sections				Subject tests									
			Verbal	Quantitative	Analytical reasoning	Analytical writing	Biochemistry, cell and molecular biology	Biology	Chemistry	Computer science	Education	Engineering	Literature	Mathematics	Physics	Psychology
1	2	3	4	5	6	7	8	9	10	11	12	13	14	15	16	17
2000[4]	397,489	32.1	465 (116)	578 (147)	562 (141)	† (†)	— (†)	629 (114)	686 (133)	— (†)	† (†)	—	530 (99)	— (†)	— (†)	563 (98)
2001	432,667	34.8	— (†)	— (†)	— (†)	† (†)	— (†)	— (†)	— (†)	— (†)	† (†)	†	— (†)	— (†)	— (†)	— (†)
2002	520,547	40.3	473 (123)	597 (151)	571 (139)	† (†)	— (†)	— (†)	— (†)	— (†)	† (†)	†	— (†)	— (†)	— (†)	— (†)
2003[5,6]	571,606	42.4	470 (120)	593 (147)	†	4.2 (0.96)	517 (100)	635 (114)	682 (125)	712 (97)	† (†)	†	538 (98)	620 (131)	669 (151)	580 (101)
2004[5,6,7]	418,463	29.9	469 (120)	597 (148)	†	4.2 (1.00)	517 (101)	643 (115)	675 (120)	715 (93)	† (†)	†	537 (97)	621 (130)	665 (148)	586 (101)
2005[5,6,7]	431,783	30.0	467 (118)	591 (148)	†	4.2 (0.90)	518 (100)	647 (117)	675 (117)	715 (91)	† (†)	†	540 (97)	623 (130)	672 (151)	592 (101)
2006[5,7,8]	508,604	34.2	465 (117)	584 (149)	†	4.1 (0.90)	519 (99)	650 (118)	677 (116)	717 (92)	† (†)	†	541 (97)	627 (129)	678 (153)	598 (101)
2007[5,7,8]	561,060	36.8	462 (119)	584 (151)	†	4.0 (0.90)	521 (97)	650 (120)	689 (115)	715 (91)	† (†)	†	542 (98)	636 (130)	686 (155)	600 (101)
2008[5,7,8]	553,375	35.4	457 (121)	586 (152)	†	3.9 (0.90)	525 (97)	651 (120)	694 (116)	712 (92)	† (†)	†	541 (98)	640 (131)	692 (156)	603 (101)

—Not available.

†Not applicable.

[1]GRE takers include examinees from inside and outside of the United States, while the bachelor's degree recipients include U.S. institutions only.

[2]Total includes examinees who received no score on one or more general test measures.

[3]Data reported for 1994 through 1998 are from the revised education test.

[4]Subject test score data reflect the three-year average for all examinees who tested between October 1 three years prior to the reported test year and September 30 of the reported test year. These data are not directly comparable with data for most other years.

[5]Subject test score data reflect the three-year average for all examinees who tested between July 1 three years prior to the reported test year and June 30 of the reported test year. These data are not directly comparable with previous years, except for 1999 and 2000.

[6]Analytical writing test score data reflect the average for all examinees who tested between October 1, 2002, and June 30 of the reported test year.

[7]Verbal and quantitative test score data reflect the three-year average for all examinees who tested between July 1 three years prior to the reported test year and June 30 of the reported test year. These data are not directly comparable with previous years.

[8]Analytical writing test score data reflect the three-year average for all examinees who tested between July 1 three years prior to the reported test year and June 30 of the reported test year.

NOTE: GRE data include test takers from both within and outside of the United States. GRE scores for the verbal, quantitative, and analytical reasoning sections range from 200 to 800. Scores for the analytical writing section range from 0 to 6, in half-point increments. The range of scores is different for the various subject tests, from as low as 200 to as high as 990. The analytical reasoning section of the GRE, a multiple-choice test, was discontinued in September 2002, and replaced by the analytical writing section, an essay-based test. The education subject test was administered for the final time in April 1998. The engineering subject test was administered for the final time in April 2001. Some data have been revised from previously published figures. Standard deviations appear in parentheses.

SOURCE: Graduate Record Examination Board, *Examinee and Score Trends for the GRE General Test, 1964–65 through 1985–86; A Summary of Data Collected From Graduate Record Examinations Test-Takers During 1986–87; Guide to the Use of Scores,* 1987–88 through 2001–02; *Sex, Race, Ethnicity, and Performance on the GRE General Test,* 2000–01 through 2001–02; *Factors That Can Influence Performance on the GRE General Test,* 2003–04; *GRE Volumes by Country, 2000–2007;* and *Interpreting Your GRE Scores,* 2005–06 through 2008–09. U.S. Department of Education, National Center for Education Statistics, Higher Education General Information Survey (HEGIS), "Degrees and Other Formal Awards Conferred" surveys, 1964–65 through 1985–86; and 1986–87 through 2007–08 Integrated Postsecondary Education Data System (IPEDS), "Completions Survey" (IPEDS-C:87–99), and Fall 2000 through Fall 2008. (This table was prepared October 2009.)

Expenditures of public degree-granting institutions, by type of institution, purpose of expenditure, and state or jurisdiction: 2004–05, 2005–06, and 2006–07

[In thousands of current dollars]

State or jurisdiction	Total expenditures, 2004–05	Total expenditures, 2005–06	All institutions Total[1]	Operating	4-year institutions Total	Operating expenditures Total[1]	Instruction	Nonoperating	2-year institutions Total	Operating expenditures Total[1]	Instruction	Nonoperating
1	2	3	4	5	6	7	8	9	10	11	12	13
United States	$215,794,343	$226,549,889	$238,828,801	$230,398,826	$196,121,062	$188,683,105	$50,755,304	$7,437,956	$42,707,739	$41,715,721	$16,432,945	$992,018
Alabama	4,440,310	4,732,672	5,120,941	5,017,885	4,500,497	4,413,982	993,274	86,515	620,443	603,903	239,650	16,540
Alaska	625,319	649,612	692,853	678,634	676,339	662,168	178,968	14,171	16,515	16,466	5,168	49
Arizona	3,521,306	3,809,011	4,098,686	3,968,843	2,978,201	2,882,412	867,045	95,790	1,120,485	1,086,432	408,170	34,053
Arkansas	2,329,165	2,538,362	2,711,428	2,648,555	2,371,643	2,317,004	505,083	54,639	339,786	331,551	131,055	8,235
California	32,218,384	34,026,467	33,939,568	32,529,138	24,931,656	23,921,821	5,488,783	1,009,836	9,007,912	8,607,317	3,293,808	400,595
Colorado	3,311,032	3,515,871	3,766,780	3,657,989	3,325,789	3,233,518	914,912	92,271	440,992	424,471	174,640	16,521
Connecticut	2,306,275	2,393,182	2,482,496	2,424,928	2,136,157	2,081,578	530,745	54,579	346,339	343,350	133,069	2,989
Delaware	757,382	798,725	853,410	852,120	732,635	731,345	287,241	1,290	120,775	120,775	53,490	0
District of Columbia	100,155	116,830	125,484	125,484	125,484	125,484	47,484	0	0	0	0	0
Florida	7,460,740	7,793,877	8,307,928	8,175,067	6,831,020	6,701,901	2,055,162	129,119	1,476,908	1,473,166	501,022	3,743
Georgia	4,666,410	5,008,710	5,318,459	5,260,223	4,399,784	4,353,242	1,201,475	46,542	918,675	906,981	367,492	11,694
Hawaii	1,055,358	1,148,545	1,266,174	1,141,369	1,084,624	965,001	272,456	119,622	181,550	176,367	75,617	5,183
Idaho	865,207	895,666	917,108	906,112	797,100	786,818	270,467	10,281	120,009	119,294	37,990	715
Illinois	7,707,684	8,147,811	8,317,879	8,158,185	6,165,239	6,057,410	1,489,320	107,829	2,152,640	2,100,776	707,175	51,865
Indiana	4,579,970	4,732,305	4,929,528	4,807,294	4,533,044	4,420,622	1,582,351	112,422	396,483	386,672	137,955	9,811
Iowa	3,261,661	3,524,403	3,632,046	3,571,653	2,944,714	2,897,529	539,819	47,184	687,333	674,123	281,192	13,210
Kansas	2,395,901	2,533,777	2,607,366	2,576,566	2,066,568	2,042,646	610,159	23,922	540,798	533,920	197,523	6,878
Kentucky	3,351,737	3,649,151	3,976,747	3,921,017	3,477,752	3,437,763	802,942	39,989	498,995	483,254	188,991	15,741
Louisiana	3,311,847	3,303,679	3,519,436	3,463,839	3,134,451	3,086,097	843,937	48,353	384,985	377,741	162,273	7,244
Maine	685,520	710,855	746,481	734,490	648,997	637,026	173,421	11,971	97,484	97,464	42,881	20
Maryland	4,129,836	4,413,784	4,643,844	4,566,313	3,632,676	3,566,550	950,677	66,125	1,011,168	999,762	383,019	11,406
Massachusetts	3,076,812	3,345,954	3,515,544	3,466,578	2,878,503	2,831,777	744,642	46,726	637,041	634,801	238,655	2,240
Michigan	9,599,856	10,130,974	10,563,666	10,416,084	9,006,741	8,883,456	2,214,738	123,285	1,556,925	1,532,628	513,597	24,297
Minnesota	3,637,085	3,878,041	4,112,919	4,035,112	3,269,141	3,197,633	893,251	71,508	843,778	837,479	369,266	6,298
Mississippi	2,759,232	2,894,694	3,111,365	3,054,043	2,431,612	2,379,043	482,601	52,569	679,753	675,000	253,074	4,752
Missouri	3,351,500	3,522,278	3,648,634	3,588,079	3,049,125	3,000,416	783,911	48,709	599,509	587,663	235,684	11,845
Montana	748,026	797,297	819,680	803,847	736,491	722,813	180,020	13,678	83,189	81,033	26,185	2,156
Nebraska	1,518,562	1,639,823	1,722,136	1,688,225	1,456,223	1,424,021	410,410	32,202	265,912	264,204	107,934	1,708
Nevada	1,117,126	1,212,202	1,315,804	1,267,253	1,255,533	1,207,534	433,373	48,000	60,271	59,719	25,567	552
New Hampshire	637,403	695,153	725,778	707,478	642,137	623,837	177,699	18,300	83,641	83,641	28,021	0
New Jersey	5,271,538	5,569,181	5,695,452	5,556,009	4,703,335	4,564,980	1,226,719	138,356	992,117	991,029	356,482	1,087
New Mexico	2,286,513	2,427,203	2,565,733	2,524,659	2,087,008	2,053,824	351,978	33,184	478,725	470,835	175,682	7,889
New York	10,305,243	11,031,705	12,607,530	11,987,124	10,001,228	9,426,387	2,679,670	574,841	2,606,302	2,560,737	1,021,127	45,566
North Carolina	6,501,732	7,037,662	7,649,176	7,388,234	6,062,212	5,801,774	1,885,931	260,438	1,586,965	1,586,460	736,594	505
North Dakota	716,180	753,586	787,853	772,493	691,508	677,609	212,252	13,899	96,345	94,884	37,641	1,461
Ohio	8,494,328	9,091,243	9,638,217	9,448,904	8,385,429	8,210,639	2,267,977	174,790	1,252,787	1,238,265	462,646	14,523
Oklahoma	2,521,594	2,746,540	2,982,655	2,926,543	2,582,340	2,542,758	762,183	39,582	400,315	383,785	148,319	16,530
Oregon	3,476,027	3,722,085	3,961,130	3,798,609	3,127,798	3,007,851	594,330	119,946	833,332	790,757	313,392	42,575
Pennsylvania	8,345,982	8,736,935	9,093,770	9,056,929	8,202,039	8,181,556	2,076,334	20,483	891,731	875,372	360,441	16,359
Rhode Island	538,384	567,607	587,678	581,533	490,838	484,929	124,982	5,909	96,840	96,604	42,852	237
South Carolina	2,716,391	2,902,490	3,123,388	3,079,651	2,517,205	2,478,479	793,141	38,726	606,182	601,172	236,507	5,010
South Dakota	485,499	500,890	546,221	539,217	495,842	488,873	163,364	6,969	50,379	50,345	22,280	34
Tennessee	3,011,156	3,123,980	3,289,781	3,257,253	2,809,053	2,777,581	972,666	31,472	480,728	479,672	205,941	1,056
Texas	19,467,672	18,401,632	20,016,371	16,906,941	16,643,997	13,662,236	4,326,243	2,981,761	3,372,375	3,244,705	1,296,558	127,670
Utah	2,882,837	3,074,335	3,291,002	3,247,786	3,032,819	2,990,835	537,344	41,984	258,182	256,951	100,324	1,232
Vermont	556,927	594,285	647,066	632,687	622,659	608,280	169,583	14,379	24,407	24,407	8,544	0
Virginia	5,423,809	5,846,089	6,311,272	6,217,176	5,555,781	5,464,200	1,473,496	91,581	755,491	752,976	360,441	2,515
Washington	5,417,079	5,674,037	5,980,733	5,904,415	4,714,330	4,642,644	1,282,235	71,685	1,266,403	1,261,771	554,336	4,632
West Virginia	1,147,417	1,250,615	1,324,271	1,294,269	1,249,041	1,219,772	360,091	29,269	75,230	74,497	28,499	733
Wisconsin	4,564,833	4,706,156	4,904,966	4,757,563	3,800,231	3,681,248	1,042,991	118,983	1,104,735	1,076,314	577,998	28,420
Wyoming	467,251	486,855	522,738	516,802	334,864	332,574	102,477	2,291	187,874	184,229	66,177	3,645
U.S. Service Academies	1,669,152	1,745,065	1,791,631	1,791,631	1,791,631	1,791,631	422,954	0	0	0	0	0
Other jurisdictions	1,438,206	1,461,202	1,549,127	1,521,349	1,479,810	1,452,135	462,559	27,675	69,317	69,214	24,570	103
American Samoa	9,599	10,036	11,419	11,419	11,419	11,419	4,389	0	0	0	0	0
Federated States of Micronesia	17,822	18,132	19,306	19,306	0	0	0	0	19,306	19,306	5,367	0
Guam	89,316	92,412	96,492	92,969	71,771	68,351	16,680	3,420	24,721	24,618	8,297	103
Marshall Islands	5,878	6,323	7,833	7,833	0	0	0	0	7,833	7,833	4,201	0
Northern Marianas	16,010	16,168	13,132	13,132	13,132	13,132	7,220	0	0	0	0	0
Palau	8,514	8,913	8,359	8,359	0	0	0	0	8,359	8,359	1,979	0
Puerto Rico	1,226,385	1,242,436	1,318,439	1,296,444	1,309,343	1,287,348	420,820	21,995	9,096	9,096	4,726	0
U.S. Virgin Islands	64,682	66,782	74,146	71,886	74,146	71,886	13,451	2,260	0	0	0	0

[1]Includes other categories not separately shown.

NOTE: Degree-granting institutions grant associate's or higher degrees and participate in Title IV federal financial aid programs. Includes data for public institutions reporting data according to either the Governmental Accounting Standards Board (GASB) or the Financial Accounting Standards Board (FASB) questionnaire. Detail may not sum to totals because of rounding.

SOURCE: U.S. Department of Education, National Center for Education Statistics, 2004–05 through 2006–07 Integrated Postsecondary Education Data System (IPEDS), Spring 2006 through Spring 2008. (This table was prepared July 2009.)

Total expenditures of private not-for-profit degree-granting institutions, by purpose and type of institution: 1996–97 through 2006–07

Type of institution and year	Total expenditures, by purpose											
	Total	Instruction	Research	Public service	Academic support	Student services	Institutional support	Auxiliary enterprises[1]	Net grant aid to students[2]	Hospitals	Independent operations	Other
1	2	3	4	5	6	7	8	9	10	11	12	13
	In thousands of current dollars											
All institutions												
1996–97	$67,399,563	$21,126,357	$6,702,520	$1,621,583	$4,942,411	$4,430,241	$8,226,648	$7,079,116	$1,529,456	—	—	$11,741,232
1997–98	69,300,699	23,404,428	7,267,877	1,672,991	5,738,254	4,903,988	9,138,895	7,698,614	1,297,749	$6,395,808	$1,782,095	—
1998–99	75,516,696	25,181,848	7,779,001	1,521,440	6,349,076	5,295,059	9,901,658	8,027,492	1,222,565	7,258,939	2,979,619	—
1999–2000	80,613,037	26,012,599	8,381,926	1,446,958	6,510,951	5,688,499	10,585,850	8,300,021	1,180,882	7,355,110	2,753,679	2,396,563
2000–01	85,625,016	27,607,324	9,025,739	1,473,292	7,368,263	6,117,195	11,434,074	9,010,853	1,176,160	7,255,376	3,134,609	2,022,132
2001–02	92,192,297	29,689,041	10,035,480	1,665,884	7,802,637	6,573,185	12,068,120	9,515,829	1,188,690	7,633,043	3,397,979	2,622,409
2002–03	99,748,076	32,062,218	11,079,532	1,878,380	8,156,688	7,096,223	13,157,744	9,936,478	1,173,845	7,586,208	3,879,736	3,741,024
2003–04	104,317,870	33,909,179	12,039,531	1,972,351	8,759,743	7,544,021	13,951,408	10,508,719	1,101,738	8,374,128	4,222,980	1,934,070
2004–05	110,394,127	36,258,473	12,812,857	2,000,437	9,342,064	8,191,737	14,690,328	10,944,342	1,069,591	9,180,775	4,223,779	1,679,741
2005–06	116,817,913	38,465,058	13,242,343	1,941,519	10,217,274	8,965,704	15,667,101	11,741,258	708,158	9,645,428	4,203,523	2,020,548
2006–07	124,557,725	41,223,483	13,704,450	2,036,588	10,882,028	9,591,334	16,831,353	12,451,087	728,139	10,400,055	4,680,393	2,028,816
4-year												
1996–97	66,668,808	20,922,069	6,701,053	1,616,019	4,902,188	4,294,812	8,095,791	7,011,791	1,502,866	—	—	11,622,219
1997–98	68,677,274	23,164,693	7,267,228	1,669,650	5,704,216	4,817,585	8,988,203	7,621,887	1,276,848	6,395,610	1,771,355	—
1998–99	74,805,484	24,823,398	7,778,900	1,513,641	6,308,251	5,224,455	9,766,020	7,957,265	1,198,516	7,257,021	2,978,017	—
1999–2000	79,699,659	25,744,199	8,376,568	1,438,544	6,476,338	5,590,978	10,398,914	8,228,409	1,162,570	7,355,110	2,752,019	2,176,011
2000–01	85,048,123	27,413,897	9,019,966	1,467,325	7,333,851	6,036,478	11,292,310	8,957,973	1,160,660	7,253,479	3,133,099	1,979,086
2001–02	91,612,337	29,492,583	10,035,394	1,658,781	7,768,870	6,497,127	11,914,149	9,470,557	1,173,725	7,632,942	3,396,831	2,571,376
2002–03	99,137,236	31,866,310	11,079,332	1,871,274	8,122,181	7,014,149	12,996,836	9,876,937	1,161,441	7,586,208	3,854,471	3,708,098
2003–04	103,733,257	33,712,542	12,039,080	1,964,898	8,726,505	7,466,472	13,774,084	10,464,984	1,084,880	8,374,128	4,221,611	1,904,075
2004–05	109,789,731	36,051,084	12,812,326	1,993,767	9,307,600	8,101,214	14,516,197	10,899,456	1,051,216	9,180,775	4,223,779	1,652,317
2005–06	116,247,359	38,249,125	13,241,769	1,931,804	10,177,381	8,894,330	15,524,004	11,696,510	699,462	9,645,428	4,203,523	1,984,024
2006–07	124,061,478	41,056,590	13,703,502	2,028,364	10,850,270	9,522,535	16,693,987	12,414,609	714,398	10,400,055	4,680,393	1,996,775
2-year												
1996–97	730,755	204,288	1,467	5,564	40,223	135,429	130,857	67,324	26,590	—	—	119,013
1997–98	623,424	239,735	649	3,341	34,038	86,403	150,692	76,726	20,901	198	10,740	—
1998–99	711,212	358,450	101	7,799	40,826	70,603	135,638	70,226	24,049	1,917	1,602	—
1999–2000	913,378	268,400	5,358	8,415	34,612	97,521	186,936	71,612	18,311	0	1,660	220,553
2000–01	576,893	193,428	5,772	5,967	34,412	80,717	141,764	52,880	15,500	1,896	1,510	43,046
2001–02	579,960	196,459	86	7,102	33,767	76,058	153,971	45,271	14,965	100	1,147	51,033
2002–03	610,840	195,909	200	7,106	34,506	82,074	160,908	59,541	12,404	0	25,265	32,926
2003–04	584,612	196,637	451	7,453	33,238	77,549	177,324	43,735	16,859	0	1,369	29,995
2004–05	604,395	207,389	532	6,670	34,464	90,523	174,131	44,886	18,375	0	0	27,425
2005–06	570,554	215,934	574	9,715	39,893	71,374	143,096	44,748	8,696	0	0	36,524
2006–07	496,247	166,893	947	8,224	31,758	68,799	137,366	36,478	13,741	0	0	32,041
	Percentage distribution											
All institutions												
1996–97	100.00	31.34	9.94	2.41	7.33	6.57	12.21	10.50	2.27	—	—	17.42
1997–98	100.00	33.77	10.49	2.41	8.28	7.08	13.19	11.11	1.87	9.23	2.57	—
1998–99	100.00	33.35	10.30	2.01	8.41	7.01	13.11	10.63	1.62	9.61	3.95	—
1999–2000	100.00	32.27	10.40	1.79	8.08	7.06	13.13	10.30	1.46	9.12	3.42	2.97
2000–01	100.00	32.24	10.54	1.72	8.61	7.14	13.35	10.52	1.37	8.47	3.66	2.36
2001–02	100.00	32.20	10.89	1.81	8.46	7.13	13.09	10.32	1.29	8.28	3.69	2.84
2002–03	100.00	32.14	11.11	1.88	8.18	7.11	13.19	9.96	1.18	7.61	3.89	3.75
2003–04	100.00	32.51	11.54	1.89	8.40	7.23	13.37	10.07	1.06	8.03	4.05	1.85
2004–05	100.00	32.84	11.61	1.81	8.46	7.42	13.31	9.91	0.97	8.32	3.83	1.52
2005–06	100.00	32.93	11.34	1.66	8.75	7.67	13.41	10.05	0.61	8.26	3.60	1.73
2006–07	100.00	33.10	11.00	1.64	8.74	7.70	13.51	10.00	0.58	8.35	3.76	1.63
4-year												
1996–97	100.00	31.38	10.05	2.42	7.35	6.44	12.14	10.52	2.25	—	—	17.43
1997–98	100.00	33.73	10.58	2.43	8.31	7.01	13.09	11.10	1.86	9.31	2.58	—
1998–99	100.00	33.18	10.40	2.02	8.43	6.98	13.06	10.64	1.60	9.70	3.98	—
1999–2000	100.00	32.30	10.51	1.80	8.13	7.02	13.05	10.32	1.46	9.23	3.45	2.73
2000–01	100.00	32.23	10.61	1.73	8.62	7.10	13.28	10.53	1.36	8.53	3.68	2.33
2001–02	100.00	32.19	10.95	1.81	8.48	7.08	13.00	10.34	1.28	8.33	3.71	2.81
2002–03	100.00	32.14	11.18	1.89	8.19	7.08	13.11	9.96	1.17	7.65	3.89	3.74
2003–04	100.00	32.50	11.61	1.89	8.41	7.20	13.28	10.09	1.05	8.07	4.07	1.84
2004–05	100.00	32.84	11.67	1.82	8.48	7.38	13.22	9.93	0.96	8.36	3.85	1.50
2005–06	100.00	32.90	11.39	1.66	8.75	7.65	13.35	10.06	0.60	8.30	3.62	1.71
2006–07	100.00	33.09	11.05	1.63	8.75	7.68	13.46	10.01	0.58	8.38	3.77	1.61
2-year												
1996–97	100.00	27.96	0.20	0.76	5.50	18.53	17.91	9.21	3.64	—	—	16.29
1997–98	100.00	38.45	0.10	0.54	5.46	13.86	24.17	12.31	3.35	0.03	1.72	—
1998–99	100.00	50.40	0.01	1.10	5.74	9.93	19.07	9.87	3.38	0.27	0.23	—
1999–2000	100.00	29.39	0.59	0.92	3.79	10.68	20.47	7.84	2.00	0.00	0.18	24.15
2000–01	100.00	33.53	1.00	1.03	5.96	13.99	24.57	9.17	2.69	0.33	0.26	7.46
2001–02	100.00	33.87	0.01	1.22	5.82	13.11	26.55	7.81	2.58	0.02	0.20	8.80
2002–03	100.00	32.07	0.03	1.16	5.65	13.44	26.34	9.75	2.03	0.00	4.14	5.39
2003–04	100.00	33.64	0.08	1.27	5.69	13.27	30.33	7.48	2.88	0.00	0.23	5.13
2004–05	100.00	34.31	0.09	1.10	5.70	14.98	28.81	7.43	3.04	0.00	0.00	4.54
2005–06	100.00	37.85	0.10	1.70	6.99	12.51	25.08	7.84	1.52	0.00	0.00	6.40
2006–07	100.00	33.63	0.19	1.66	6.40	13.86	27.68	7.35	2.77	0.00	0.00	6.46

See notes at end of table.

Total expenditures of private not-for-profit degree-granting institutions, by purpose and type of institution: 1996–97 through 2006–07—Continued

Type of institution and year	Total	Instruction	Research	Public service	Academic support	Student services	Institutional support	Auxiliary enterprises[1]	Net grant aid to students[2]	Hospitals	Independent operations	Other
1	2	3	4	5	6	7	8	9	10	11	12	13
Expenditure per full-time-equivalent student in current dollars												
All institutions												
1996–97	$27,880	$8,739	$2,772	$671	$2,044	$1,833	$3,403	$2,928	$633	—	—	$4,857
1997–98	28,270	9,547	2,965	682	2,341	2,000	3,728	3,141	529	$2,609	$727	—
1998–99	30,291	10,101	3,120	610	2,547	2,124	3,972	3,220	490	2,912	1,195	—
1999–2000	31,751	10,246	3,301	570	2,564	2,241	4,169	3,269	465	2,897	1,085	944
2000–01	33,069	10,662	3,486	569	2,846	2,363	4,416	3,480	454	2,802	1,211	781
2001–02	34,841	11,220	3,793	630	2,949	2,484	4,561	3,596	449	2,885	1,284	991
2002–03	36,479	11,725	4,052	687	2,983	2,595	4,812	3,634	429	2,774	1,419	1,368
2003–04	37,240	12,105	4,298	704	3,127	2,693	4,980	3,751	393	2,989	1,508	690
2004–05	38,472	12,636	4,465	697	3,256	2,855	5,120	3,814	373	3,199	1,472	585
2005–06	40,156	13,222	4,552	667	3,512	3,082	5,386	4,036	243	3,316	1,445	695
2006–07	42,060	13,920	4,628	688	3,675	3,239	5,684	4,204	246	3,512	1,580	685
4-year												
1996–97	28,327	8,890	2,847	687	2,083	1,825	3,440	2,979	639	—	—	4,938
1997–98	28,740	9,694	3,041	699	2,387	2,016	3,761	3,190	534	2,676	741	—
1998–99	30,706	10,189	3,193	621	2,589	2,145	4,009	3,266	492	2,979	1,222	—
1999–2000	32,064	10,357	3,370	579	2,605	2,249	4,184	3,310	468	2,959	1,107	875
2000–01	33,359	10,753	3,538	576	2,877	2,368	4,429	3,514	455	2,845	1,229	776
2001–02	35,139	11,312	3,849	636	2,980	2,492	4,570	3,633	450	2,928	1,303	986
2002–03	36,742	11,810	4,106	694	3,010	2,600	4,817	3,661	430	2,812	1,429	1,374
2003–04	37,504	12,188	4,353	710	3,155	2,699	4,980	3,784	392	3,028	1,526	688
2004–05	38,726	12,716	4,519	703	3,283	2,858	5,120	3,845	371	3,238	1,490	583
2005–06	40,394	13,291	4,601	671	3,536	3,091	5,394	4,064	243	3,352	1,461	689
2006–07	42,256	13,984	4,667	691	3,696	3,243	5,686	4,228	243	3,542	1,594	680
2-year												
1996–97	11,426	3,194	23	87	629	2,118	2,046	1,053	416	—	—	1,861
1997–98	10,094	3,882	11	54	551	1,399	2,440	1,242	338	3	174	—
1998–99	12,514	6,307	2	137	718	1,242	2,387	1,236	423	34	28	—
1999–2000	17,148	5,039	101	158	650	1,831	3,510	1,345	344	0	31	4,141
2000–01	14,494	4,860	145	150	865	2,028	3,562	1,329	389	48	38	1,081
2001–02	14,890	5,044	2	182	867	1,953	3,953	1,162	384	3	29	1,310
2002–03	16,846	5,403	6	196	952	2,263	4,438	1,642	342	0	697	908
2003–04	16,561	5,570	13	211	942	2,197	5,023	1,239	478	0	39	850
2004–05	17,552	6,023	15	194	1,001	2,629	5,057	1,304	534	0	0	796
2005–06	18,240	6,903	18	311	1,275	2,282	4,575	1,431	278	0	0	1,168
2006–07	19,498	6,557	37	323	1,248	2,703	5,397	1,433	540	0	0	1,259
Expenditure per full-time-equivalent student in constant 2007–08 dollars[3]												
All institutions												
1996–97	$37,142	$11,642	$3,694	$894	$2,724	$2,441	$4,533	$3,901	$843	—	—	$6,470
1997–98	37,002	12,496	3,881	893	3,064	2,618	4,880	4,111	693	$3,415	$952	—
1998–99	38,973	12,996	4,015	785	3,277	2,733	5,110	4,143	631	3,746	1,538	—
1999–2000	39,705	12,812	4,128	713	3,207	2,802	5,214	4,088	582	3,623	1,356	1,180
2000–01	39,984	12,892	4,215	688	3,441	2,857	5,339	4,208	549	3,388	1,464	944
2001–02	41,393	13,330	4,506	748	3,503	2,951	5,418	4,272	534	3,427	1,526	1,177
2002–03	42,407	13,631	4,710	799	3,468	3,017	5,594	4,224	499	3,225	1,649	1,590
2003–04	42,365	13,771	4,889	801	3,557	3,064	5,666	4,268	447	3,401	1,715	785
2004–05	42,488	13,955	4,931	770	3,596	3,153	5,654	4,212	412	3,533	1,626	646
2005–06	42,721	14,067	4,843	710	3,736	3,279	5,730	4,294	259	3,527	1,537	739
2006–07	43,619	14,436	4,799	713	3,811	3,359	5,894	4,360	255	3,642	1,639	710
4-year												
1996–97	37,738	11,843	3,793	915	2,775	2,431	4,583	3,969	851	—	—	6,579
1997–98	37,617	12,688	3,981	915	3,124	2,639	4,923	4,175	699	3,503	970	—
1998–99	39,507	13,110	4,108	799	3,332	2,759	5,158	4,202	633	3,833	1,573	—
1999–2000	40,096	12,952	4,214	724	3,258	2,813	5,232	4,140	585	3,700	1,385	1,095
2000–01	40,334	13,001	4,278	696	3,478	2,863	5,355	4,248	550	3,440	1,486	939
2001–02	41,747	13,440	4,573	756	3,540	2,961	5,429	4,316	535	3,478	1,548	1,172
2002–03	42,713	13,730	4,774	806	3,499	3,022	5,600	4,255	500	3,269	1,661	1,598
2003–04	42,665	13,866	4,952	808	3,589	3,071	5,665	4,304	446	3,444	1,736	783
2004–05	42,768	14,044	4,991	777	3,626	3,156	5,655	4,246	410	3,576	1,645	644
2005–06	42,974	14,140	4,895	714	3,762	3,288	5,739	4,324	259	3,566	1,554	733
2006–07	43,822	14,502	4,840	716	3,833	3,364	5,897	4,385	252	3,674	1,653	705
2-year												
1996–97	15,222	4,256	31	116	838	2,821	2,726	1,402	554	—	—	2,479
1997–98	13,212	5,081	14	71	721	1,831	3,194	1,626	443	4	228	—
1998–99	16,100	8,115	2	177	924	1,598	3,071	1,590	544	43	36	—
1999–2000	21,444	6,302	126	198	813	2,290	4,389	1,681	430	0	39	5,178
2000–01	17,524	5,876	175	181	1,045	2,452	4,306	1,606	471	0	39	1,308
2001–02	17,690	5,992	3	217	1,030	2,320	4,696	1,381	456	58	46	1,557
2002–03	19,583	6,281	6	228	1,106	2,631	5,159	1,909	398	3	35	1,056
2003–04	18,840	6,337	15	240	1,071	2,499	5,715	1,409	543	0	810	967
2004–05	19,384	6,651	17	214	1,105	2,903	5,585	1,440	589	0	44	880
2005–06	19,405	7,344	20	330	1,357	2,427	4,867	1,522	296	0	0	1,242
2006–07	20,221	6,800	39	335	1,294	2,803	5,597	1,486	560	0	0	1,306

—Not available.

[1]Essentially self-supporting operations of institutions that furnish a service to students, faculty, or staff, such as residence halls and food services.

[2]Excludes tuition and fee allowances and agency transactions, such as student awards made from contributed funds or grant funds.

[3]Constant dollars based on the Consumer Price Index, prepared by the Bureau of Labor Statistics, U.S. Department of Labor, adjusted to a school-year basis.

NOTE: Degree-granting institutions grant associate's or higher degrees and participate in Title IV federal financial aid programs. Detail may not sum to totals because of rounding.
SOURCE: U.S. Department of Education, National Center for Education Statistics, 1996–97 through 2006–07 Integrated Postsecondary Education Data System, "Fall Enrollment Survey" (IPEDS-EF:96–99) and "Finance Survey" (IPEDS-F:FY97–99), and Spring 2001 through Spring 2008. (This table was prepared December 2008.)

Total expenditures of private not-for-profit degree-granting institutions, by purpose and type of institution: 2006–07

Type of institution	Total expenditures, by purpose											
	Total	Instruction	Research	Public service	Academic support	Student services	Institutional support	Auxiliary enterprises[1]	Net grant aid to students[2]	Hospitals	Independent operations	Other
1	2	3	4	5	6	7	8	9	10	11	12	13
	In thousands of current dollars											
Total	$124,557,725	$41,223,483	$13,704,450	$2,036,588	$10,882,028	$9,591,334	$16,831,353	$12,451,087	$728,139	$10,400,055	$4,680,393	$2,028,816
4-year	124,061,478	41,056,590	13,703,502	2,028,364	10,850,270	9,522,535	16,693,987	12,414,609	714,398	10,400,055	4,680,393	1,996,775
Research university, very high[3]	56,159,417	17,194,478	10,785,995	754,701	3,974,363	1,993,599	4,762,547	3,867,893	312,242	7,778,072	4,201,512	534,015
Research university, high[4]	9,977,921	3,466,605	988,568	136,050	1,432,918	683,031	1,320,978	1,368,681	34,816	482,204	53,225	10,847
Doctoral/research[5]	6,590,351	2,783,960	145,213	108,219	758,972	659,060	1,248,729	800,650	16,167	0	31,660	37,721
Master's[6]	20,146,364	7,772,940	253,073	189,285	1,986,195	2,730,713	3,785,369	2,710,386	144,220	101,901	117,105	355,176
Baccalaureate[7]	18,372,232	6,469,167	198,744	181,894	1,629,221	2,768,271	3,547,407	3,029,730	146,190	0	89,384	312,225
Specialized institutions[8]	12,815,193	3,369,439	1,331,910	658,215	1,068,602	687,862	2,028,957	637,268	60,764	2,037,879	187,507	746,791
Art, music, or design	1,646,802	628,743	917	24,904	163,221	145,412	329,984	167,705	3,799	0	8,637	173,480
Business and management	469,655	164,899	4,725	19	44,852	74,904	107,905	64,889	3,070	0	0	4,391
Engineering or technology	327,318	137,246	8,884	52	22,712	46,156	68,859	36,405	6,662	0	0	342
Law	475,311	210,845	4,338	4,394	76,004	52,680	103,854	13,918	695	0	288	8,295
Medical or other health	7,846,861	1,588,086	1,299,963	591,460	571,443	190,212	840,019	157,778	12,927	2,037,879	169,687	387,407
Theological	1,560,676	492,313	4,711	19,988	150,081	139,376	444,418	169,206	30,274	0	8,003	102,305
Tribal[9]	48,836	13,230	383	4,829	2,179	5,549	13,638	1,573	1,355	0	0	6,099
Other specialized	439,734	134,076	7,988	12,568	38,110	33,571	120,280	25,793	1,983	0	891	64,472
2-year	496,247	166,893	947	8,224	31,758	68,799	137,366	36,478	13,741	0	0	32,041
Associate's of arts	446,323	157,670	5	4,039	28,822	60,315	125,380	34,810	10,369	0	0	24,914
Tribal[9]	49,924	9,224	942	4,186	2,936	8,485	11,986	1,668	3,372	0	0	7,127
	Percentage distribution											
Total	100.00	33.10	11.00	1.64	8.74	7.70	13.51	10.00	0.58	8.35	3.76	1.63
4-year	100.00	33.09	11.05	1.63	8.75	7.68	13.46	10.01	0.58	8.38	3.77	1.61
Research university, very high[3]	100.00	30.62	19.21	1.34	7.08	3.55	8.48	6.89	0.56	13.85	7.48	0.95
Research university, high[4]	100.00	34.74	9.91	1.36	14.36	6.85	13.24	13.72	0.35	4.83	0.53	0.11
Doctoral/research[5]	100.00	42.24	2.20	1.64	11.52	10.00	18.95	12.15	0.25	0.00	0.48	0.57
Master's[6]	100.00	38.58	1.26	0.94	9.86	13.55	18.79	13.45	0.72	0.51	0.58	1.76
Baccalaureate[7]	100.00	35.21	1.08	0.99	8.87	15.07	19.31	16.49	0.80	0.00	0.49	1.70
Specialized institutions[8]	100.00	26.29	10.39	5.14	8.34	5.37	15.83	4.97	0.47	15.90	1.46	5.83
Art, music, or design	100.00	38.18	0.06	1.51	9.91	8.83	20.04	10.18	0.23	0.00	0.52	10.53
Business and management	100.00	35.11	1.01	#	9.55	15.95	22.98	13.82	0.65	0.00	0.00	0.94
Engineering or technology	100.00	41.93	2.71	0.02	6.94	14.10	21.04	11.12	2.04	0.00	0.00	0.10
Law	100.00	44.36	0.91	0.92	15.99	11.08	21.85	2.93	0.15	0.00	0.06	1.75
Medical or other health	100.00	20.24	16.57	7.54	7.28	2.42	10.71	2.01	0.16	25.97	2.16	4.94
Theological	100.00	31.54	0.30	1.28	9.62	8.93	28.48	10.84	1.94	0.00	0.51	6.56
Tribal[9]	100.00	27.09	0.79	9.89	4.46	11.36	27.93	3.22	2.77	0.00	0.00	12.49
Other specialized	100.00	30.49	1.82	2.86	8.67	7.63	27.35	5.87	0.45	0.00	0.20	14.66
2-year	100.00	33.63	0.19	1.66	6.40	13.86	27.68	7.35	2.77	0.00	0.00	6.46
Associate's of arts	100.00	35.33	#	0.90	6.46	13.51	28.09	7.80	2.32	0.00	0.00	5.58
Tribal[9]	100.00	18.48	1.89	8.38	5.88	17.00	24.01	3.34	6.75	0.00	0.00	14.28
	Expenditure per full-time-equivalent student in current dollars											
Total	$42,060	$13,920	$4,628	$688	$3,675	$3,239	$5,684	$4,204	$246	$3,512	$1,580	$685
4-year	42,256	13,984	4,667	691	3,696	3,243	5,686	4,228	243	3,542	1,594	680
Research university, very high[3]	129,651	39,696	24,901	1,742	9,175	4,602	10,995	8,930	721	17,957	9,700	1,233
Research university, high[4]	38,616	13,416	3,826	527	5,546	2,643	5,112	5,297	135	1,866	206	42
Doctoral/research[5]	25,888	10,936	570	425	2,981	2,589	4,905	3,145	64	0	124	148
Master's[6]	19,860	7,662	249	187	1,958	2,692	3,732	2,672	142	100	115	350
Baccalaureate[7]	25,858	9,105	280	256	2,293	3,896	4,993	4,264	206	0	126	439
Specialized institutions[8]	48,374	12,719	5,028	2,485	4,034	2,596	7,659	2,406	229	7,692	708	2,819
Art, music, or design	32,307	12,335	18	489	3,202	2,853	6,474	3,290	75	0	169	3,403
Business and management	16,562	5,815	167	1	1,582	2,641	3,805	2,288	108	0	0	155
Engineering or technology	24,851	10,420	675	4	1,724	3,504	5,228	2,764	506	0	0	26
Law	28,294	12,551	258	262	4,524	3,136	6,182	828	41	0	17	494
Medical or other health	105,227	21,296	17,433	7,931	7,663	2,551	11,265	2,116	173	27,328	2,276	5,195
Theological	22,881	7,218	69	293	2,200	2,043	6,516	2,481	444	0	117	1,500
Tribal[9]	23,456	6,354	184	2,320	1,047	2,665	6,550	755	651	0	0	2,930
Other specialized	40,883	12,465	743	1,168	3,543	3,121	11,183	2,398	184	0	83	5,994
2-year	19,498	6,557	37	323	1,248	2,703	5,397	1,433	540	0	0	1,259
Associate's of arts	18,607	6,573	#	168	1,202	2,514	5,227	1,451	432	0	0	1,039
Tribal[9]	34,101	6,300	644	2,859	2,005	5,796	8,187	1,139	2,303	0	0	4,868

#Rounds to zero.
[1]Essentially self-supporting operations of institutions that furnish a service to students, faculty, or staff, such as residence halls and food services.
[2]Excludes tuition and fee allowances and agency transactions, such as student awards made from contributed funds or grant funds.
[3]Research universities with a very high level of research activity.
[4]Research universities with a high level of research activity.
[5]Includes institutions that award at least 20 doctor's degrees per year, but did not have high levels of research activity.
[6]Master's institutions award at least 50 master's degrees per year.
[7]Baccalaureate institutions primarily emphasize undergraduate education. Also includes institutions classified as 4-year under the IPEDS system, which had been classified as 2-year in the Carnegie classification system because they primarily award associate's degrees.

[8]Special-focus 4-year institutions award degrees primarily in single fields of study, such as medicine, business, fine arts, theology, and engineering.
[9]Tribally controlled colleges are located on reservations and are members of the American Indian Higher Education Consortium.
NOTE: Relative levels of research activity for research universities were determined by an analysis of research and development expenditures, science and engineering research staffing, and doctoral degrees conferred, by field. Further information on the research index ranking may be obtained from http://www.carnegiefoundation.org/classifications/index.asp?key=798#related. Degree-granting institutions grant associate's or higher degrees and participate in Title IV federal financial aid programs. Detail may not sum to totals because of rounding.
SOURCE: U.S. Department of Education, National Center for Education Statistics, 2006–07 Integrated Postsecondary Education Data System (IPEDS), Spring 2007 and Spring 2008. (This table was prepared December 2008.)

Total expenditures of private for-profit degree-granting institutions, by purpose and type of institution: 1998–99 through 2006–07

Year and type of institution	Total	Instruction	Research and public service	Student services, academic and institutional support	Auxiliary enterprises[1]	Net grant aid to students[2]	Other
1	2	3	4	5	6	7	8
			In thousands of current dollars				
All institutions							
1998–99	$3,153,591	$1,132,766	$27,060	$1,823,453	$135,398	$34,913	—
1999–2000	3,846,246	1,171,732	24,738	2,041,594	144,305	26,278	$437,599
2000–01	4,235,781	1,310,054	22,896	2,337,151	181,243	43,788	340,649
2001–02	5,087,292	1,517,389	16,632	2,977,225	213,195	23,283	339,567
2002–03	6,110,378	1,747,725	17,987	3,670,218	240,380	36,031	398,037
2003–04	7,364,012	1,883,733	8,606	4,592,730	249,472	56,467	573,004
2004–05	8,830,792	2,313,895	7,583	5,693,200	269,883	54,819	491,411
2005–06	10,208,845	2,586,870	8,445	6,569,329	276,587	66,569	701,044
2006–07	12,152,366	2,884,481	6,087	7,760,044	332,887	68,300	1,100,568
4–year							
1998–99	1,484,139	499,337	6,703	876,636	81,411	20,052	—
1999–2000	2,022,622	595,976	4,393	1,104,001	92,071	11,805	214,377
2000–01	2,414,655	726,328	4,878	1,385,095	113,371	18,519	166,465
2001–02	3,046,929	883,899	3,192	1,842,373	134,740	8,229	174,495
2002–03	3,754,727	1,030,470	5,339	2,337,388	153,528	14,813	213,190
2003–04	4,821,864	1,143,050	3,705	3,108,697	168,069	32,603	365,740
2004–05	5,989,792	1,430,196	3,513	4,110,514	180,036	38,639	226,894
2005–06	7,218,830	1,680,603	4,065	4,985,531	179,064	54,291	315,276
2006–07	8,837,598	1,857,765	4,303	5,909,914	228,624	56,930	780,063
2–year							
1998–99	1,669,451	633,429	20,357	946,817	53,987	14,861	—
1999–2000	1,823,624	575,756	20,345	937,593	52,234	14,473	223,223
2000–01	1,821,126	583,727	18,019	952,056	67,872	25,269	174,184
2001–02	2,040,363	633,490	13,440	1,134,853	78,455	15,054	165,071
2002–03	2,355,650	717,255	12,648	1,332,830	86,853	21,218	184,846
2003–04	2,542,148	740,683	4,901	1,484,033	81,403	23,864	207,264
2004–05	2,840,999	883,699	4,070	1,582,687	89,846	16,181	264,517
2005–06	2,990,015	906,267	4,381	1,583,798	97,523	12,278	385,768
2006–07	3,314,768	1,026,716	1,784	1,850,129	104,264	11,370	320,505
			Percentage distribution				
All institutions							
1998–99	100.00	35.92	0.86	57.82	4.29	1.11	—
1999–2000	100.00	30.46	0.64	53.08	3.75	0.68	11.38
2000–01	100.00	30.93	0.54	55.18	4.28	1.03	8.04
2001–02	100.00	29.83	0.33	58.52	4.19	0.46	6.67
2002–03	100.00	28.60	0.29	60.07	3.93	0.59	6.51
2003–04	100.00	25.58	0.12	62.37	3.39	0.77	7.78
2004–05	100.00	26.20	0.09	64.47	3.06	0.62	5.56
2005–06	100.00	25.34	0.08	64.35	2.71	0.65	6.87
2006–07	100.00	23.74	0.05	63.86	2.74	0.56	9.06
4–year							
1998–99	100.00	33.64	0.45	59.07	5.49	1.35	—
1999–2000	100.00	29.47	0.22	54.58	4.55	0.58	10.60
2000–01	100.00	30.08	0.20	57.36	4.70	0.77	6.89
2001–02	100.00	29.01	0.10	60.47	4.42	0.27	5.73
2002–03	100.00	27.44	0.14	62.25	4.09	0.39	5.68
2003–04	100.00	23.71	0.08	64.47	3.49	0.68	7.59
2004–05	100.00	23.88	0.06	68.63	3.01	0.65	3.79
2005–06	100.00	23.28	0.06	69.06	2.48	0.75	4.37
2006–07	100.00	21.02	0.05	66.87	2.59	0.64	8.83
2–year							
1998–99	100.00	37.94	1.22	56.71	3.23	0.89	—
1999–2000	100.00	31.57	1.12	51.41	2.86	0.79	12.24
2000–01	100.00	32.05	0.99	52.28	3.73	1.39	9.56
2001–02	100.00	31.05	0.66	55.62	3.85	0.74	8.09
2002–03	100.00	30.45	0.54	56.58	3.69	0.90	7.85
2003–04	100.00	29.14	0.19	58.38	3.20	0.94	8.15
2004–05	100.00	31.11	0.14	55.71	3.16	0.57	9.31
2005–06	100.00	30.31	0.15	52.97	3.26	0.41	12.90
2006–07	100.00	30.97	0.05	55.81	3.15	0.34	9.67

See notes at end of table.

**Total expenditures of private for-profit degree-granting institutions, by purpose and type of institution:
1998–99 through 2006–07—Continued**

Year and type of institution	Total	Instruction	Research and public service	Student services, academic and institutional support	Auxiliary enterprises[1]	Net grant aid to students[2]	Other
1	2	3	4	5	6	7	8
	Total expenditures per full-time-equivalent student in current dollars						

Year and type of institution	Total	Instruction	Research and public service	Student services, academic and institutional support	Auxiliary enterprises[1]	Net grant aid to students[2]	Other
Total expenditures per full-time-equivalent student in current dollars							
All institutions							
1998–99	9,685	3,479	83	5,600	416	107	—
1999–2000	10,000	3,046	64	5,308	375	68	1,138
2000–01	10,781	3,334	58	5,949	461	111	867
2001–02	11,144	3,324	36	6,522	467	51	744
2002–03	11,301	3,232	33	6,788	445	67	736
2003–04	11,381	2,911	13	7,098	386	87	886
2004–05	11,205	2,936	10	7,224	342	70	624
2005–06	11,336	2,873	9	7,295	307	74	778
2006–07	12,880	3,057	6	8,225	353	72	1,166
4–year							
1998–99	9,117	3,068	41	5,385	500	123	—
1999–2000	9,688	2,855	21	5,288	441	57	1,027
2000–01	10,588	3,185	21	6,074	497	81	730
2001–02	11,021	3,197	12	6,664	487	30	631
2002–03	10,862	2,981	15	6,762	444	43	617
2003–04	11,291	2,677	9	7,279	394	76	856
2004–05	10,818	2,583	6	7,424	325	70	410
2005–06	10,897	2,537	6	7,526	270	82	476
2006–07	12,551	2,638	6	8,393	325	81	1,108
2–year							
1998–99	10,252	3,890	125	5,815	332	91	—
1999–2000	10,370	3,274	116	5,332	297	82	1,269
2000–01	11,048	3,541	109	5,776	412	153	1,057
2001–02	11,333	3,519	75	6,303	436	84	917
2002–03	12,081	3,678	65	6,835	445	109	948
2003–04	11,557	3,367	22	6,747	370	108	942
2004–05	12,120	3,770	17	6,752	383	69	1,128
2005–06	12,558	3,806	18	6,652	410	52	1,620
2006–07	13,848	4,289	7	7,729	436	47	1,339
Total expenditures per full-time-equivalent student in constant 2007–08 dollars[3]							
All institutions							
1998–99	12,449	4,472	107	7,198	534	138	---
1999–2000	12,493	3,806	80	6,631	469	85	1,421
2000–01	11,208	3,466	61	6,184	480	116	901
2001–02	13,226	3,945	43	7,740	554	61	883
2002–03	13,125	3,754	39	7,884	516	77	855
2003–04	12,935	3,309	15	8,067	438	99	1,006
2004–05	12,363	3,239	11	7,970	378	77	688
2005–06	12,049	3,053	10	7,753	326	79	827
2006–07	13,344	3,167	7	8,521	366	75	1,209
4–year							
1998–99	11,719	3,943	53	6,922	643	158	---
1999–2000	12,104	3,566	26	6,607	551	71	1,283
2000–01	12,790	3,847	26	7,337	600	98	882
2001–02	13,080	3,795	14	7,909	578	35	749
2002–03	12,615	3,462	18	7,853	516	50	716
2003–04	12,832	3,042	10	8,273	447	87	973
2004–05	11,935	2,850	7	8,191	359	77	452
2005–06	11,582	2,696	7	7,999	287	87	506
2006–07	13,004	2,733	6	8,696	336	84	1,148
2–year							
1998–99	13,178	5,000	161	7,474	426	117	---
1999–2000	12,956	4,090	145	6,661	371	103	1,586
2000–01	13,345	4,278	132	6,977	497	185	1,276
2001–02	13,451	4,176	89	7,481	517	99	1,088
2002–03	14,030	4,272	75	7,938	517	126	1,101
2003–04	13,135	3,827	25	7,668	421	123	1,071
2004–05	13,372	4,160	19	7,450	423	76	1,245
2005–06	13,348	4,046	20	7,070	435	55	1,722
2006–07	14,347	4,444	8	8,008	451	49	1,387

—Not available.
[1]Essentially self-supporting operations of institutions that furnish a service to students, faculty, or staff, such as residence halls and food services.
[2]Excludes tuition and fee allowances and agency transactions, such as student awards made from contributed funds or grant funds.
[3]Constant dollars based on the Consumer Price Index, prepared by the Bureau of Labor Statistics, U.S. Department of Labor, adjusted to a school-year basis.

NOTE: Degree-granting institutions grant associate's or higher degrees and participate in Title IV federal financial aid programs. Detail may not sum to totals because of rounding.
SOURCE: U.S. Department of Education, National Center for Education Statistics, 1998–99 through 2006–07 Integrated Postsecondary Education Data System, "Fall Enrollment Survey" (IPEDS-EF:98–99) and "Finance Survey" (IPEDS-F:FY99), and Spring 2001 through Spring 2008. (This table was prepared December 2008.)

Total expenditures of private for-profit degree-granting institutions, by purpose and type of institution: 2006–07

Type of institution	Total expenditures, by purpose						
	Total	Instruction	Research and public service	Student services, academic and institutional support	Auxiliary enterprises[1]	Net grant aid to students[2]	Other
1	2	3	4	5	6	7	8
	In thousands of current dollars						
Total........................	**$12,152,366**	**$2,884,481**	**$6,087**	**$7,760,044**	**$332,887**	**$68,300**	**$1,100,568**
4–year................................	8,837,598	1,857,765	4,303	5,909,914	228,624	56,930	780,063
Doctoral/research[3]......................	1,211,652	221,494	346	987,558	1,853	0	401
Master's[4]...............................	2,212,224	336,177	1,123	1,305,508	57,052	495	511,868
Baccalaureate[5].........................	2,043,793	533,503	1,698	1,333,274	43,926	12,199	119,194
Specialized institutions[6].............	3,369,930	766,591	1,137	2,283,574	125,792	44,235	148,600
Art, music, or design................	1,437,931	364,793	475	902,531	105,421	29,676	35,034
Business and management..........	908,093	123,565	0	728,893	9,069	8,332	38,233
Engineering or technology...........	772,577	209,831	70	504,847	7,440	1,535	48,854
Law....................................	50,881	11,040	0	29,489	0	4,666	5,686
Medical or other health.............	86,994	25,574	592	47,770	853	26	12,179
Other specialized.....................	113,454	31,788	0	70,044	3,009	0	8,613
2–year................................	3,314,768	1,026,716	1,784	1,850,129	104,264	11,370	320,505
	Percentage distribution						
Total........................	**100.00**	**23.74**	**0.05**	**63.86**	**2.74**	**0.56**	**9.06**
4–year................................	100.00	21.02	0.05	66.87	2.59	0.64	8.83
Doctoral/research[3]......................	100.00	18.28	0.03	81.51	0.15	0.00	0.03
Master's[4]...............................	100.00	15.20	0.05	59.01	2.58	0.02	23.14
Baccalaureate[5].........................	100.00	26.10	0.08	65.24	2.15	0.60	5.83
Specialized institutions[6].............	100.00	22.75	0.03	67.76	3.73	1.31	4.41
Art, music, or design................	100.00	25.37	0.03	62.77	7.33	2.06	2.44
Business and management..........	100.00	13.61	0.00	80.27	1.00	0.92	4.21
Engineering or technology...........	100.00	27.16	0.01	65.35	0.96	0.20	6.32
Law....................................	100.00	21.70	0.00	57.96	0.00	9.17	11.18
Medical or other health.............	100.00	29.40	0.68	54.91	0.98	0.03	14.00
Other specialized.....................	100.00	28.02	0.00	61.74	2.65	0.00	7.59
2–year................................	100.00	30.97	0.05	55.81	3.15	0.34	9.67
	Expenditure per full-time-equivalent student in current dollars						
Total........................	**$12,880**	**$3,057**	**$6**	**$8,225**	**$353**	**$72**	**$1,166**
4–year................................	12,551	2,638	6	8,393	325	81	1,108
Doctoral/research[3]......................	6,056	1,107	2	4,936	9	0	2
Master's[4]...............................	13,407	2,037	7	7,912	346	3	3,102
Baccalaureate[5].........................	15,888	4,147	13	10,364	341	95	927
Specialized institutions[6].............	16,016	3,643	5	10,853	598	210	706
Art, music, or design................	19,358	4,911	6	12,150	1,419	400	472
Business and management..........	11,422	1,554	0	9,168	114	105	481
Engineering or technology...........	18,357	4,986	2	11,996	177	36	1,161
Law....................................	27,165	5,894	0	15,744	0	2,491	3,036
Medical or other health.............	13,661	4,016	93	7,502	134	4	1,913
Other specialized.....................	18,014	5,047	0	11,122	478	0	1,368
2–year................................	13,848	4,289	7	7,729	436	47	1,339

[1]Essentially self-supporting operations of institutions that furnish a service to students, faculty, or staff, such as residence halls and food services.

[2]Excludes tuition and fee allowances and agency transactions, such as student awards made from contributed funds or grant funds.

[3]Includes institutions that award at least 20 doctor's degrees per year, but did not have high levels of research activity.

[4]Master's institutions award at least 50 master's degrees per year.

[5]Baccalaureate institutions primarily emphasize undergraduate education. Also includes institutions classified as 4-year under the IPEDS system, which had been classified as 2-year in the Carnegie classification system because they primarily award associate's degrees.

[6]Special focus 4-year institutions award degrees primarily in single fields of study, such as medicine, business, fine arts, theology, and engineering.

NOTE: Degree-granting institutions grant associate's or higher degrees and participate in Title IV federal financial aid programs. Detail may not sum to totals because of rounding.

SOURCE: U.S. Department of Education, National Center for Education Statistics, 2006–07 Integrated Postsecondary Education Data System (IPEDS), Spring 2007 and Spring 2008. (This table was prepared December 2008.)

Total expenditures of private not-for-profit and for-profit degree-granting institutions, by level and state or jurisdiction: 1999–2000 through 2006–07

[In thousands of current dollars]

State or jurisdiction	Not–for–profit institutions											For–profit institutions	
								2006–07					
	1999–2000	2000–01	2001–02	2002–03	2003–04	2004–05	2005–06	Total	4–year	2–year	2005–06	2006–07
1	2	3	4	5	6	7	8	9	10	11	12	13
United States ...	$80,613,037	$85,625,016	$92,192,297	$99,748,076	$104,317,870	$110,394,127	$116,817,913	$124,557,725	$124,061,478	$496,247	$10,208,845	$12,152,366
Alabama	393,465	400,987	419,872	435,190	440,158	459,250	473,626	505,523	505,523	†	66,036	75,727
Alaska.....................	19,042	19,106	19,823	20,561	20,916	21,076	23,276	14,740	14,740	†	667	4,885
Arizona	143,698	160,787	162,471	182,548	141,307	147,825	144,560	136,677	136,677	†	1,301,977	1,942,229
Arkansas.................	230,860	197,313	213,645	216,809	224,969	239,357	239,460	251,234	249,738	1,496	15,111	17,443
California................	7,871,651	8,682,192	9,588,524	10,268,563	10,838,473	10,728,872	11,328,736	12,121,864	12,094,455	27,409	1,343,174	1,514,687
Colorado..................	376,887	399,613	430,242	450,245	486,523	524,349	562,544	585,013	582,369	2,644	431,326	525,249
Connecticut.............	2,094,981	2,193,752	2,343,067	2,517,664	2,684,855	2,882,963	3,074,362	3,279,174	3,261,561	17,613	45,242	50,793
Delaware.................	52,533	56,670	62,625	70,783	80,634	87,617	93,079	105,469	101,926	3,543	†	†
District of Columbia ..	2,267,409	2,230,368	2,387,245	2,530,695	2,673,493	2,824,081	2,922,770	3,134,498	3,134,498	†	149,019	215,804
Florida....................	2,031,623	2,247,374	2,472,362	2,695,985	2,908,264	3,067,443	3,239,855	3,598,947	3,597,346	1,600	889,222	1,007,789
Georgia...................	2,635,438	2,795,105	2,946,777	3,188,042	3,266,674	3,442,374	3,694,276	3,863,137	3,839,024	24,114	305,720	339,673
Hawaii....................	209,135	138,660	146,050	152,348	173,261	195,152	199,857	199,856	199,856	†	26,844	32,583
Idaho......................	118,150	130,256	139,029	147,022	152,512	164,694	176,300	188,165	188,165	†	14,859	15,517
Illinois....................	5,668,566	5,910,538	6,188,489	6,304,076	6,666,469	7,113,842	7,310,521	8,003,782	7,989,215	14,568	753,796	797,643
Indiana...................	1,343,315	1,425,665	1,525,312	1,612,609	1,702,487	1,796,767	1,879,185	1,996,634	1,990,321	6,313	234,536	283,192
Iowa.......................	740,760	767,891	800,428	847,857	875,162	921,320	961,673	1,025,119	1,022,535	2,584	227,505	346,343
Kansas....................	208,729	222,036	232,720	237,781	252,050	265,476	277,289	306,622	296,854	9,768	12,324	20,212
Kentucky.................	400,513	406,358	437,092	458,584	457,484	470,392	495,803	517,782	517,782	†	128,781	143,861
Louisiana	746,629	773,107	828,300	876,419	909,744	940,075	1,088,847	902,642	902,642	†	57,319	67,261
Maine.....................	316,114	341,350	373,835	384,085	399,609	422,938	451,904	479,171	477,367	1,804	6,764	10,375
Maryland..................	2,205,880	2,410,284	2,725,616	3,019,626	3,271,571	3,497,182	3,716,510	3,965,788	3,965,788	†	48,230	58,081
Massachusetts..........	7,591,344	8,187,834	8,831,619	9,506,793	10,037,913	10,799,206	11,622,482	12,192,561	12,176,017	16,544	65,825	68,934
Michigan	995,384	1,065,100	1,134,361	1,206,723	1,259,243	1,327,051	1,407,082	1,433,884	1,433,884	†	61,321	72,457
Minnesota...............	1,004,427	1,093,937	1,164,763	1,157,173	1,222,082	1,297,457	1,358,101	1,446,858	1,444,862	1,996	471,346	547,492
Mississippi	150,123	156,292	158,464	167,822	170,290	178,142	192,778	195,996	195,996	†	9,143	19,908
Missouri..................	2,144,299	2,380,876	2,561,036	3,355,385	2,961,937	3,128,635	3,336,361	3,486,983	3,464,094	22,888	292,903	336,966
Montana..................	69,426	74,446	72,297	78,561	86,364	91,446	91,423	97,769	87,920	9,849	†	†
Nebraska.................	387,569	422,879	445,634	840,326	510,418	557,724	590,420	637,536	635,415	2,121	31,320	36,084
Nevada	7,006	9,130	10,919	9,657	8,677	9,637	11,116	30,311	30,311	†	113,511	119,143
New Hampshire	589,823	654,213	719,549	786,283	837,504	883,914	932,584	992,159	991,030	1,130	47,395	50,844
New Jersey..............	1,362,090	1,479,492	1,588,295	1,641,561	1,765,956	1,873,156	2,038,712	2,143,312	2,143,312	†	81,044	89,642
New Mexico	54,280	63,824	60,571	59,119	52,502	54,076	60,376	59,510	59,510	†	36,476	40,065
New York................	12,519,671	13,099,910	14,177,942	15,800,433	16,557,418	17,680,799	18,471,543	20,111,096	20,035,345	75,751	625,590	685,646
North Carolina	3,530,337	3,845,125	3,978,481	4,219,294	4,439,832	4,808,306	5,158,463	5,540,302	5,524,895	15,407	52,150	62,947
North Dakota	56,000	59,677	63,207	68,513	83,942	88,860	92,921	95,061	67,153	27,908	10,759	6,135
Ohio.......................	2,211,035	2,368,824	2,530,980	2,637,737	2,843,939	3,017,764	3,205,370	3,334,147	3,315,770	18,377	261,728	316,518
Oklahoma	338,276	360,772	363,611	370,604	367,119	392,427	419,638	463,629	463,629	†	78,814	76,520
Oregon....................	456,683	447,516	473,270	487,996	512,749	550,322	578,958	620,302	620,302	†	91,337	98,436
Pennsylvania...........	7,590,629	7,841,530	8,397,080	8,894,900	9,386,083	9,960,675	10,603,066	11,252,008	11,143,422	108,587	585,001	640,768
Rhode Island	828,715	897,056	978,710	1,062,719	1,141,689	1,237,106	1,287,905	1,367,600	1,367,600	†	9,585	10,278
South Carolina........	408,127	432,035	483,551	507,157	532,950	563,952	570,769	605,736	593,639	12,097	20,998	31,925
South Dakota	69,555	75,488	90,290	91,028	93,352	99,575	107,581	111,659	108,195	3,464	26,652	31,541
Tennessee	1,971,564	2,131,732	2,367,380	2,609,840	2,819,415	3,140,336	3,435,062	3,717,946	3,709,725	8,221	166,173	186,957
Texas	2,490,597	2,662,275	2,921,130	3,142,104	3,266,787	3,379,710	3,542,703	3,718,549	3,702,153	16,395	374,290	413,618
Utah.......................	648,035	694,025	741,519	785,441	824,774	867,956	888,654	935,899	925,947	9,952	75,959	78,794
Vermont	347,293	369,832	382,794	400,154	426,338	510,623	553,310	620,608	598,415	22,193	24,009	24,088
Virginia...................	944,905	1,000,236	1,057,465	1,109,551	1,224,687	1,311,743	1,400,161	1,503,421	1,503,421	†	309,961	350,179
Washington..............	600,315	594,393	639,129	674,622	737,957	778,678	803,657	847,942	847,942	†	118,880	117,630
West Virginia............	170,653	185,101	194,652	201,085	197,437	181,181	181,222	184,220	184,220	†	22,726	64,316
Wisconsin	999,502	1,062,053	1,160,074	1,258,006	1,321,899	1,410,625	1,521,060	1,628,880	1,618,969	9,911	48,284	67,990
Wyoming..................	†	†	†	†	†	†	†	†	†	†	37,211	37,195
Other jurisdictions..	431,216	456,532	494,476	680,257	578,021	615,990	648,562	661,324	646,760	14,563	79,139	86,526
Guam......................	†	†	1,160	1,161	999	1,535	2,635	2,797	2,797	†	†	†
Puerto Rico..............	431,216	456,532	493,316	679,096	577,023	614,455	645,927	658,526	643,963	14,563	79,139	86,526

†Not applicable.

NOTE: Degree-granting institutions grant associate's or higher degrees and participate in Title IV federal financial aid programs. Detail may not sum to totals because of rounding.

SOURCE: U.S. Department of Education, National Center for Education Statistics, 1999–2000 through 2006–07 Integrated Postsecondary Education Data System, "Finance Survey" (IPEDS-F:FY98–99), and Spring 2002 through Spring 2008. (This table was prepared July 2009.)

Revenues of public degree-granting institutions, by source of revenue and state or jurisdiction: 2006–07

[In thousands of current dollars]

State or jurisdiction	Total revenues	Operating revenue							Nonoperating revenue[1]			Other revenues and additions
		Total	Tuition and fees[2]	Federal grants and contracts	State and local grants and contracts	Sales and services of auxiliary enterprises[3]	Sales and services of hospitals	Independent operations and other	Total	State appropriations	Local appropriations	
1	2	3	4	5	6	7	8	9	10	11	12	13
United States	**$268,556,045**	**$148,770,382**	**$44,773,470**	**$30,779,946**	**$15,789,626**	**$20,398,261**	**$22,575,459**	**$14,453,621**	**$103,341,970**	**$63,204,939**	**$8,818,685**	**$16,443,693**
Alabama	5,867,964	3,572,873	902,807	867,683	255,739	276,326	1,034,142	236,177	2,122,230	1,532,416	10	172,860
Alaska.....................	733,960	357,121	84,928	145,898	67,687	40,083	0	18,525	336,057	287,414	0	40,782
Arizona	4,403,536	2,144,299	900,192	653,446	158,060	320,321	0	112,280	2,157,911	1,151,631	635,756	101,326
Arkansas.................	2,817,132	1,758,797	320,869	232,638	147,012	197,424	672,528	188,326	982,640	682,379	24,579	75,695
California	37,469,868	20,532,754	3,609,319	4,102,143	2,627,327	2,893,301	3,591,449	3,709,215	14,883,667	9,233,141	2,340,897	2,053,448
Colorado	4,124,319	3,502,215	1,212,564	882,428	497,225	372,657	275,675	261,665	403,162	16,918	61,730	218,942
Connecticut............	2,693,529	1,453,823	448,463	207,454	76,891	193,970	222,828	304,216	1,005,120	891,977	0	234,587
Delaware.................	1,070,908	537,138	269,478	124,806	30,654	91,727	0	20,473	523,064	231,428	0	10,706
District of Columbia ...	130,048	50,199	17,401	15,532	11,938	1,471	0	3,857	77,013	6,516	62,636	2,836
Florida.....................	9,686,162	3,737,876	1,293,194	878,558	807,938	593,523	0	164,663	4,739,613	3,632,755	0	1,208,673
Georgia	5,604,670	3,017,354	965,236	761,679	421,657	521,561	197,255	149,967	2,328,607	2,065,879	0	258,708
Hawaii	1,417,682	607,340	137,996	318,062	55,048	74,711	0	21,522	654,579	514,988	0	155,763
Idaho......................	1,001,986	527,582	194,345	146,988	60,869	90,125	0	35,254	415,372	351,950	8,198	59,033
Illinois....................	8,815,964	4,628,746	1,613,668	782,094	341,057	772,648	424,211	695,068	3,927,439	1,671,782	795,108	259,779
Indiana...................	5,500,271	3,439,212	1,481,610	655,469	318,079	674,736	0	309,319	1,929,415	1,359,913	7,460	131,644
Iowa	3,914,634	2,696,613	594,592	561,410	128,786	365,680	792,585	253,561	1,156,814	831,047	80,541	61,207
Kansas...................	2,755,339	1,556,652	576,316	349,082	112,435	237,063	0	281,755	1,129,531	759,922	219,384	69,156
Kentucky	4,449,342	2,819,260	653,431	570,281	339,072	219,963	901,310	135,203	1,400,841	1,045,794	12,857	229,241
Louisiana	3,730,468	2,191,923	558,896	503,199	395,429	271,082	384,717	78,600	1,412,815	1,270,820	0	125,731
Maine......................	790,603	453,360	176,989	74,073	63,045	89,848	0	49,404	316,380	243,198	0	20,864
Maryland.................	5,248,953	3,022,150	1,185,911	702,492	355,169	507,527	0	271,050	1,862,026	1,225,201	283,634	364,777
Massachusetts..........	3,786,138	2,372,059	818,755	407,568	227,301	286,391	0	632,044	1,299,961	1,143,743	0	114,118
Michigan.................	12,687,298	7,775,288	2,582,844	1,465,166	433,484	870,554	1,983,636	439,603	4,516,295	1,610,778	575,550	395,715
Minnesota...............	4,579,156	2,534,124	1,048,391	568,675	359,979	538,951	0	18,128	1,744,477	1,237,370	0	300,555
Mississippi	3,385,385	1,977,648	371,480	672,985	177,618	204,698	454,072	96,796	1,218,474	877,807	58,166	189,263
Missouri..................	4,020,421	2,503,105	796,646	325,473	139,619	539,939	529,530	171,898	1,441,623	891,523	133,449	75,692
Montana..................	877,781	592,583	218,937	175,345	35,838	94,330	0	68,134	262,765	157,125	6,781	22,433
Nebraska.................	1,853,336	962,068	273,884	187,867	171,043	224,598	21,795	82,881	846,875	568,781	84,249	44,392
Nevada	1,415,816	641,605	236,451	170,285	79,682	92,373	0	62,814	729,669	582,558	0	44,542
New Hampshire.........	826,982	585,948	258,372	102,266	46,244	156,804	0	22,262	173,568	119,078	0	67,466
New Jersey..............	6,024,226	3,782,601	1,405,361	599,531	468,186	422,679	734,350	152,495	2,107,970	1,565,374	203,338	133,656
New Mexico.............	2,868,202	1,582,850	191,472	540,996	165,771	118,549	449,519	116,542	1,141,451	741,110	92,000	143,901
New York.................	12,460,994	6,466,623	1,848,381	1,010,026	1,119,814	722,697	1,621,459	144,245	5,446,494	4,021,727	651,770	547,877
North Carolina	9,071,307	3,508,147	1,104,655	827,823	304,049	1,126,044	0	145,576	4,398,784	3,190,505	170,547	1,164,376
North Dakota	823,319	555,113	220,579	168,698	32,994	80,955	0	51,887	256,312	209,801	1,959	11,895
Ohio........................	10,658,533	7,073,131	2,635,225	917,327	559,182	813,412	1,810,767	337,218	3,302,662	1,881,090	133,803	282,740
Oklahoma................	3,253,858	1,883,533	530,707	360,858	258,330	380,942	0	352,696	1,202,842	886,467	46,846	167,483
Oregon....................	4,166,886	2,870,456	674,752	677,899	230,662	320,553	774,289	192,301	1,197,543	581,557	167,657	98,886
Pennsylvania...........	10,571,313	7,251,468	2,708,439	1,126,470	342,394	770,825	1,816,555	486,785	3,233,063	1,438,787	117,397	86,783
Rhode Island	631,191	404,210	194,607	79,922	22,617	81,701	0	25,363	188,945	175,497	0	38,036
South Carolina........	3,496,269	2,172,178	898,938	466,809	304,684	290,084	0	211,662	1,082,164	804,836	53,058	241,926
South Dakota	577,515	383,431	139,906	108,553	41,670	46,805	0	46,497	180,003	164,247	165	14,082
Tennessee	3,662,832	1,631,177	668,629	287,633	286,670	244,276	0	143,970	1,846,442	1,154,530	4,749	185,213
Texas	25,590,798	10,851,583	3,205,643	2,604,837	1,356,277	955,606	1,131,549	1,597,672	10,973,697	4,717,666	1,093,086	3,765,518
Utah	3,862,546	2,569,390	431,631	411,813	135,666	160,519	883,032	546,730	1,014,271	707,415	0	278,885
Vermont	703,588	511,958	252,326	114,104	44,495	79,039	0	21,994	172,508	70,244	0	19,122
Virginia...................	8,061,349	4,334,777	1,454,534	807,185	191,437	849,030	900,313	132,279	2,778,597	1,618,445	2,261	947,975
Washington..............	7,000,962	4,094,835	994,880	1,019,495	501,333	419,509	857,101	302,518	2,348,805	1,403,518	0	557,321
West Virginia...........	1,499,874	932,821	376,447	200,223	145,619	165,541	0	44,991	417,226	374,863	273	149,826
Wisconsin...............	5,336,795	2,830,374	977,050	677,000	296,467	406,361	0	473,495	2,133,928	1,039,886	650,880	372,493
Wyoming.................	713,905	230,526	53,854	61,348	37,331	45,949	0	32,044	357,613	261,541	37,910	125,766
U.S. Service Academies..........	1,860,131	297,482	1,491	100,346	2,052	82,799	110,794	0	1,562,648	0	0	0
Other jurisdictions	**1,591,068**	**419,586**	**81,380**	**196,521**	**49,832**	**17,568**	**48,604**	**25,681**	**1,142,452**	**943,527**	**47,193**	**29,030**
American Samoa......	10,638	6,834	1,607	4,961	0	265	0	0	3,804	0	0	0
Federated States of Micronesia	18,606	13,025	540	10,759	0	838	0	889	5,581	0	0	0
Guam......................	99,367	46,565	11,934	25,268	1,284	3,059	0	5,021	52,799	32,142	14,221	3
Marshall Islands........	12,666	3,910	185	3,251	85	389	0	0	3,248	1,988	0	5,507
Northern Marianas	13,524	7,064	1,326	5,479	0	0	0	260	6,460	5,948	0	0
Palau......................	8,987	6,044	1,419	3,061	327	943	0	295	2,648	2,385	0	295
Puerto Rico..............	1,355,838	303,816	53,827	129,487	45,709	7,259	48,604	18,930	1,031,989	901,064	3,057	20,033
U.S. Virgin Islands	71,442	32,327	10,544	14,254	2,428	4,814	0	287	35,923	0	29,915	3,192

[1]Includes other categories not separately shown.
[2]Net of allowances and discounts.
[3]After deducting discounts and allowances.
NOTE: Degree-granting institutions grant associate's or higher degrees and participate in Title IV federal financial aid programs. Includes data for public institutions reporting data according to either the Governmental Accounting Standards Board (GASB) or the Financial Accounting Standards Board (FASB) questionnaire. Detail may not sum to totals because of rounding.
SOURCE: U.S. Department of Education, National Center for Education Statistics, 2006–07 Integrated Postsecondary Education Data System, Spring 2008. (This table was prepared July 2009.)

Endowment funds of the 120 colleges and universities with the largest endowments, by rank order: 2006 and 2007

Institution	2007 rank order[1]	Market value of endowment, as of June 30 (in thousands)		Percent change, 2006 to 2007[2]	Institution	2007 rank order[1]	Market value of endowment, as of June 30 (in thousands)		Percent change, 2006 to 2007[2]
		2006	2007				2006	2007	
1	2	3	4	5	1	2	3	4	5
United States (all institutions).................	†	$336,908,009	$409,710,539	21.6					
120 institutions with the largest amounts	†	252,447,149	309,946,346	22.8					
Harvard University (MA).....................	1	29,219,430	34,912,068	19.5	Carnegie Mellon University (PA)	61	936,797	1,110,555	18.5
Yale University (CT).........................	2	17,949,088	22,364,717	24.6	University of California, Los Angeles	62	786,532	1,107,810	40.8
Stanford University (CA)	3	14,084,676	17,164,836	21.9	Berea College (KY)..........................	63	948,738	1,102,272	16.2
Princeton University (NJ)	4	13,458,440	16,379,771	21.7	Georgetown University (DC)....................	64	898,217	1,086,645	21.0
University of Texas System	5	12,118,550	14,186,815	17.1	Lehigh University (PA)........................	65	939,473	1,085,639	15.6
Massachusetts Institute of Technology	6	8,368,066	9,980,409	19.3	Syracuse University (NY)	66	870,906	1,045,952	20.1
Columbia University in the City of New York (NY)	7	5,937,814	7,149,803	20.4	Tulane University of Louisiana	67	887,839	1,041,112	17.3
University of Michigan, Ann Arbor	8	5,566,433	6,986,769	25.5	Weill Cornell Medical College (NY).............	68	832,748	1,037,137	24.5
University of Pennsylvania	9	5,300,000	6,635,000	25.2	Baylor University (TX)........................	69	870,168	1,014,044	16.5
University of California System	10	5,541,931	6,439,437	16.2	U. of Illinois at Urbana-Champaign	70	812,393	1,005,859	23.8
University of Notre Dame (IN)................	11	4,487,838	6,066,310	35.2	Trinity University (TX)	71	814,672	991,112	21.7
University of Chicago (IL)	12	4,662,286	5,832,226	25.1	Saint Louis University, Main Campus............	72	824,851	959,486	16.3
Emory University (GA).......................	13	5,024,779	5,782,439	15.1	University of Kentucky........................	73	767,693	948,306	23.5
Washington U. in Saint Louis (MO)	14	4,746,021	5,658,008	19.2	Middlebury College (VT)......................	74	782,115	936,354	19.7
Duke University (NC)	15	3,915,925	5,255,938	34.2	University of Florida..........................	75	820,809	919,574	12.0
Rice University (TX)	16	3,977,226	4,669,544	17.4	University of Tulsa (OK)	76	817,517	917,967	12.3
Cornell University (NY)	17	3,549,583	4,384,680	23.5	Oberlin College (OH)	77	765,952	893,017	16.6
University of Virginia, Main Campus.............	18	2,466,810	4,370,209	77.2	School of the Art Institute of Chicago	78	810,626	889,063	9.7
Dartmouth College (NH)	19	3,355,775	4,200,212	25.2	University of Arkansas, Main Campus	79	763,069	876,839	14.9
University of Southern California	20	3,065,935	3,715,272	21.2	Vassar College (NY)	80	741,655	869,122	17.2
Vanderbilt University (TN)	21	2,915,620	3,488,258	19.6	U. of Texas Southwestern Med. Center at Dallas	81	759,370	862,860	13.6
Northwestern University (IL)	22	2,388,257	2,871,512	20.2	University of California, Berkeley	82	700,375	856,666	22.3
The University of Texas at Austin...............	23	2,473,963	2,836,489	14.7	Bowdoin College (ME)	83	673,440	827,716	22.9
Johns Hopkins University (MD)	24	2,218,144	2,655,382	19.7	Rensselaer Polytechnic Institute (NY)	84	682,894	812,290	18.9
Brown University (RI)	25	2,166,633	2,633,924	21.6	Indiana University, Bloomington................	85	144,506	810,417	460.8
Ohio State University, Main Campus	26	1,986,570	2,301,869	15.9	University of Louisville (KY)	86	622,013	796,812	28.1
U. of Pittsburgh, Pittsburgh Campus (PA).......	27	1,791,058	2,248,122	25.5	Hamilton College (NY)	87	660,808	783,925	18.6
U. of North Carolina at Chapel Hill	28	1,687,838	2,178,925	29.1	University of Oklahoma, Norman Campus	88	688,223	783,268	13.8
University of Washington, Seattle Campus......	29	1,786,595	2,155,752	20.7	The Juilliard School (NY)	89	654,132	781,386	19.5
New York University	30	1,823,975	2,139,643	17.3	Brigham Young University (UT)	90	666,853	780,444	17.0
California Institute of Technology	31	1,624,377	1,977,210	21.7	Lafayette College (PA)........................	91	689,850	780,196	13.1
University of Wisconsin, Madison	32	1,698,735	1,957,555	15.2	Carleton College (MN)	92	649,832	761,230	17.1
Case Western Reserve University (OH)	33	1,598,566	1,841,234	15.2	University of Miami (FL)	93	620,435	741,382	19.5
Williams College (MA)	34	1,462,131	1,832,269	25.3	University of Tennessee......................	94	578,449	727,581	25.8
Pomona College (CA)	35	1,459,036	1,762,680	20.8	Pepperdine University (CA)	95	521,791	711,617	36.4
Boston College (MA)	36	1,520,296	1,752,760	15.3	Wesleyan University (CT)	96	619,761	710,774	14.7
Purdue University, Main Campus (IN)	37	1,460,065	1,745,156	19.5	Colgate University (NY)	97	558,378	706,657	26.6
University of Rochester (NY)	38	1,494,605	1,732,437	15.9	Northeastern University (MA)	98	612,184	699,559	14.3
Grinnell College (IA)	39	1,471,804	1,718,313	16.7	Santa Clara University (CA)	99	598,657	697,881	16.6
Wellesley College (MA)	40	1,412,604	1,672,473	18.4	Washington and Lee University (VA)	100	586,968	692,797	18.0
Amherst College (MA)	41	1,337,158	1,662,377	24.3	Brandeis University (MA)	101	579,654	691,371	19.3
University of Richmond (VA)	42	1,387,833	1,654,988	19.2	Berry College (GA)	102	542,465	683,253	26.0
Pennsylvania State U., Main Campus.........	43	1,303,476	1,587,197	21.8	Macalester College (MN)	103	578,020	672,356	16.3
Polytechnic University[1] (NY)	44	132,495	1,456,263	999.1	Rochester Institute of Technology (NY)	104	572,779	661,501	15.5
Tufts University (MA)	45	1,148,868	1,452,058	26.4	College of the Holy Cross (MA)	105	544,347	660,609	21.4
Swarthmore College (PA)	46	1,245,282	1,441,232	15.7	Bryn Mawr College (PA)	106	567,458	659,571	16.2
George Washington University (DC)	47	1,156,256	1,398,151	20.9	Washington State University	107	351,162	650,236	85.2
Smith College (MA)	48	1,156,350	1,360,966	17.7	Denison University (OH)	108	535,327	647,876	21.0
Southern Methodist University (TX)	49	1,127,671	1,329,274	17.9	Drexel University (PA)	109	515,108	628,467	22.0
Texas Christian University...................	50	1,197,453	1,316,402	9.9	Indiana University-Purdue University, Indianapolis	110	25,646	623,617	2,331.6
University of Delaware	51	1,118,393	1,279,711	14.4	Mount Holyoke College (MA)	111	516,148	615,376	19.2
Yeshiva University (NY)	52	1,142,730	1,255,445	9.9	Cooper Union for the Advan. of Science and Art (NY)	112	435,247	601,075	38.1
University of Kansas	53	66,598	1,253,802	1,782.6	Bucknell University (PA)......................	113	522,059	599,399	14.8
Baylor College of Medicine (TX)	54	1,059,392	1,253,405	18.3	Colby College (ME)	114	482,019	598,729	24.2
Wake Forest University (NC)	55	1,042,558	1,248,466	19.8	Rutgers University, New Brunswick (NJ)	115	497,914	593,396	19.2
Michigan State University	56	1,060,977	1,247,236	17.6	Soka University of America (CA)	116	487,678	567,295	16.3
U. of Cincinnati, Main Campus (OH)	57	1,099,721	1,185,615	7.8	DePauw University (IN)	117	490,548	558,115	13.8
University of Minnesota, Twin Cities	58	836,316	1,150,625	37.6	Mount Sinai School of Medicine (NY)	118	479,489	556,889	16.1
Boston University (MA)	59	946,377	1,137,977	20.2	University of Missouri, Columbia..............	119	511,429	547,400	7.0
Princeton Theological Seminary (NJ)............	60	948,758	1,114,268	17.4	Furman University (SC)	120	478,834	544,610	13.7

†Not applicable.

[1]Institutions ranked by size of endowment in 2007.

[2]Change in market value of endowment. Includes growth from gifts and returns on investments, as well as reductions from expenditures and withdrawals.

NOTE: Degree-granting institutions grant associate's or higher degrees and participate in Title IV federal financial aid programs. Some data have been revised from previously published figures.

SOURCE: U.S. Department of Education, National Center for Education Statistics, 2005–06 and 2006–07 Integrated Postsecondary Education Data System (IPEDS), Spring 2007 and Spring 2008. (This table was prepared July 2009.)

Employees in degree-granting institutions, by sex, employment status, control and type of institution, and primary occupation: Selected years, fall 1987 through fall 2007

Sex, employment status, control and type of institution, and primary occupation	1987	1989	1991	1993	1995	1997	1999	2001	2003	2005	2007	Percent change 1997 to 2007
1	2	3	4	5	6	7	8	9	10	11	12	13
All institutions	2,337,534	2,473,116	2,545,235	2,602,612	2,662,075	2,752,504	2,883,175	3,083,353	3,187,907	3,379,087	3,561,428	29.4
Professional staff	1,437,975	1,531,071	1,595,460	1,687,287	1,744,867	1,835,916	1,950,861	2,132,150	2,268,268	2,459,885	2,629,401	43.2
Executive/administrative/managerial	133,719	144,670	144,755	143,675	147,445	151,363	159,888	152,038	184,913	196,324	217,518	43.7
Faculty (instruction/research/public service)	793,070	824,220	826,252	915,474	931,706	989,813	1,027,830	1,113,183	1,173,593	1,290,426	1,371,390	38.6
Graduate assistants	161,464	163,298	197,751	202,819	215,909	222,724	239,738	261,136	292,061	317,141	328,979	47.7
Other professional	349,722	398,883	426,702	425,319	449,807	472,016	523,405	605,793	617,701	655,994	711,514	50.7
Nonprofessional staff	899,559	942,045	949,775	915,325	917,208	916,588	932,314	951,203	919,639	919,202	932,027	1.7
Males	1,164,067	1,212,924	1,227,591	1,256,037	1,274,676	1,315,311	1,365,812	1,451,773	1,496,867	1,581,498	1,650,350	25.5
Professional staff	850,451	880,766	895,591	930,933	946,134	982,870	1,026,882	1,105,053	1,160,417	1,240,030	1,302,131	32.5
Executive/administrative/managerial	82,882	87,951	85,423	82,748	82,127	81,931	83,883	79,348	91,604	95,223	102,258	24.8
Faculty (instruction/research/public service)	529,413	534,254	525,599	561,123	562,893	587,420	602,469	644,514	663,723	714,453	743,812	26.6
Graduate assistants	98,608	98,887	119,125	120,384	123,962	125,873	132,607	142,120	156,881	167,529	173,121	37.5
Other professional	139,548	159,674	165,444	166,678	177,152	187,646	207,923	239,071	248,209	262,825	282,940	50.8
Nonprofessional staff	313,616	332,158	332,000	325,104	328,542	332,441	338,930	346,720	336,450	341,468	348,219	4.7
Females	1,173,467	1,260,192	1,317,644	1,346,575	1,387,399	1,437,193	1,517,363	1,631,580	1,691,040	1,797,589	1,911,078	33.0
Professional staff	587,524	650,305	699,869	756,354	798,733	853,046	923,979	1,027,097	1,107,851	1,219,855	1,327,270	55.6
Executive/administrative/managerial	50,837	56,719	59,332	60,927	65,318	69,432	76,005	72,690	93,309	101,101	115,260	66.0
Faculty (instruction/research/public service)	263,657	289,966	300,653	354,351	368,813	402,393	425,361	468,669	509,870	575,973	627,578	56.0
Graduate assistants	62,856	64,411	78,626	82,435	91,947	96,851	107,131	119,016	135,180	149,612	155,858	60.9
Other professional	210,174	239,209	261,258	258,641	272,655	284,370	315,482	366,722	369,492	393,169	428,574	50.7
Nonprofessional staff	585,943	609,887	617,775	590,221	588,666	584,147	593,384	604,483	583,189	577,734	583,808	-0.1
Full-time	1,689,069	1,779,044	1,812,912	1,783,510	1,801,371	1,828,507	1,918,676	2,043,208	2,083,142	2,179,864	2,281,223	24.8
Professional staff	947,733	1,000,396	1,031,797	1,039,094	1,066,510	1,104,834	1,180,173	1,283,684	1,337,568	1,432,107	1,526,823	38.2
Executive/administrative/managerial	128,809	138,454	139,116	137,834	140,990	144,529	153,722	146,523	178,691	190,078	210,257	45.5
Faculty (instruction/research/public service)	523,420	524,426	535,623	545,706	550,822	568,719	590,937	617,868	630,092	675,624	703,463	23.7
Other professional	295,504	337,516	357,058	355,554	374,698	391,586	435,514	519,293	528,785	566,405	613,103	56.6
Nonprofessional staff	741,336	778,648	781,115	744,416	734,861	723,673	738,503	759,524	745,574	747,757	754,400	4.2
Part-time	648,465	694,072	732,323	819,102	860,704	923,997	964,499	1,040,145	1,104,765	1,199,223	1,280,205	38.6
Professional staff	490,242	530,675	563,663	648,193	678,357	731,082	770,688	848,466	930,700	1,027,778	1,102,578	50.8
Executive/administrative/managerial	4,910	6,216	5,639	5,841	6,455	6,834	6,166	5,515	6,222	6,246	7,261	6.2
Faculty (instruction/research/public service)	269,650	299,794	290,629	369,768	380,884	421,094	436,893	495,315	543,501	614,802	667,927	58.6
Graduate assistants	161,464	163,298	197,751	202,819	215,909	222,724	239,738	261,136	292,061	317,141	328,979	47.7
Other professional	54,218	61,367	69,644	69,765	75,109	80,430	87,891	86,500	88,916	89,589	98,411	22.4
Nonprofessional staff	158,223	163,397	168,660	170,909	182,347	192,915	193,811	191,679	174,065	171,445	177,627	-7.9
Public 4-year	1,184,934	1,307,524	1,341,914	1,333,533	1,383,476	1,418,661	1,470,842	1,558,576	1,569,870	1,656,709	1,741,699	22.8
Professional staff	711,714	791,319	826,633	855,913	893,345	932,972	987,622	1,069,161	1,115,312	1,200,168	1,278,894	37.1
Executive/administrative/managerial	55,967	64,343	63,674	59,678	60,590	61,984	64,336	60,245	70,397	74,241	81,364	31.3
Faculty (instruction/research/public service)	322,635	350,720	358,376	374,021	384,399	404,109	417,086	438,459	450,123	486,691	518,221	28.2
Graduate assistants	125,603	131,970	144,344	170,916	178,342	182,481	196,393	218,260	239,600	257,578	266,429	46.0
Other professional	207,509	244,286	260,239	251,298	270,014	284,398	309,807	352,197	355,192	381,658	412,880	45.2
Nonprofessional staff	473,220	516,205	515,281	477,620	490,131	485,689	483,220	489,415	454,558	456,541	462,805	-4.7
Private 4-year	720,474	722,841	734,509	762,034	770,004	786,634	857,820	912,924	988,895	1,073,764	1,157,226	47.1
Professional staff	418,340	431,403	442,524	473,372	495,383	517,485	569,579	627,364	701,244	789,179	867,234	67.6
Executive/administrative/managerial	56,307	57,861	57,148	59,230	62,314	62,580	69,626	65,739	84,306	90,415	103,183	64.9
Faculty (instruction/research/public service)	224,870	232,980	232,893	251,948	262,660	278,541	296,737	325,713	364,166	430,305	472,628	69.7
Graduate assistants	24,896	22,231	23,989	28,880	33,853	36,064	38,597	41,611	52,101	59,147	62,550	73.4
Other professional	112,267	118,331	128,494	133,314	136,556	140,300	164,619	194,301	200,671	209,312	228,873	63.1
Nonprofessional staff	302,134	291,438	291,985	288,662	274,621	269,149	288,241	285,560	287,651	284,585	289,992	7.7
Public 2-year	401,327	413,245	441,414	478,980	482,454	512,086	517,967	578,394	593,466	610,978	620,784	21.2
Professional staff	285,512	287,418	306,631	337,371	336,661	358,367	364,703	408,792	422,756	440,536	449,372	25.4
Executive/administrative/managerial	18,203	19,289	20,772	21,531	21,806	22,822	21,459	22,566	25,872	26,770	27,363	19.9
Faculty (instruction/research/public service)	230,114	226,578	222,532	276,413	272,434	290,451	296,239	332,665	341,643	354,497	358,925	23.6
Graduate assistants	10,767	8,928	29,216	2,762	3,401	3,561	4,170	1,215	323	374	0	-100.0
Other professional	26,428	32,623	34,111	36,665	39,020	41,533	42,835	52,346	54,918	58,895	63,084	51.9
Nonprofessional staff	115,815	125,827	134,783	141,609	145,793	153,719	153,264	169,602	170,710	170,442	171,412	11.5
Private 2-year	30,799	29,506	27,398	28,065	26,141	35,123	36,546	33,459	35,676	37,636	41,719	18.8
Professional staff	22,409	20,931	19,672	20,631	19,478	27,092	28,957	26,833	28,956	30,002	33,901	25.1
Executive/administrative/managerial	3,242	3,177	3,161	3,236	2,735	3,977	4,467	3,488	4,338	4,898	5,608	41.0
Faculty (instruction/research/public service)	15,451	13,942	12,451	13,092	12,213	16,712	17,768	16,346	17,661	18,933	21,616	29.3
Graduate assistants	198	169	202	261	313	618	578	50	37	42	0	-100.0
Other professional	3,518	3,643	3,858	4,042	4,217	5,785	6,144	6,949	6,920	6,129	6,677	15.4
Nonprofessional staff	8,390	8,575	7,726	7,434	6,663	8,031	7,589	6,626	6,720	7,634	7,818	-2.7

NOTE: Degree-granting institutions grant associate's or higher degrees and participate in Title IV federal financial aid programs. Beginning in 2007, includes institutions with fewer than 15 full-time employees; these institutions did not report staff data prior to 2007. By definition, all graduate assistants are part-time.

SOURCE: U.S. Department of Education, National Center for Education Statistics, 1987 through 2007 Integrated Postsecondary Education Data System (IPEDS), "Fall Staff Survey" (IPEDS-S:87–99), and Winter 2001–02 through Winter 2007–08. (This table was prepared October 2008.)

Full-time instructional faculty in degree-granting institutions, by race/ethnicity, sex, and academic rank: Fall 2003, fall 2005, and fall 2007

Sex and academic rank	Total	White	Selected racial/ethnic groups Number[1]	Percent[2]	Black	Hispanic	Asian/Pacific Islander	American Indian/Alaska Native	Race/ethnicity unknown	Nonresident alien[3]
1	2	3	4	5	6	7	8	9	10	11
2003										
Total	630,092	505,186	97,164	15.6	33,106	20,046	41,043	2,969	6,589	21,153
Professors	165,521	144,116	19,402	11.8	5,323	3,415	10,161	503	821	1,182
Associate professors	132,729	109,106	20,763	15.8	7,199	3,860	9,178	526	902	1,958
Assistant professors	152,688	112,657	28,579	19.0	9,449	5,301	13,172	657	2,008	9,444
Instructors	93,087	73,292	16,688	18.2	6,757	4,786	4,314	831	1,349	1,758
Lecturers	23,307	18,338	3,578	15.6	1,202	1,078	1,198	100	315	1,076
Other faculty	62,760	47,677	8,154	13.2	3,176	1,606	3,020	352	1,194	5,735
2005										
Total	675,624	527,900	109,964	16.5	35,458	22,818	48,457	3,231	9,703	28,057
Professors	169,192	145,936	20,856	12.4	5,484	3,793	11,060	519	1,014	1,386
Associate professors	138,444	112,507	22,429	16.4	7,402	4,319	10,144	564	1,296	2,212
Assistant professors	159,689	114,470	31,253	19.9	9,897	5,728	14,922	706	2,809	11,157
Instructors	98,555	76,359	18,368	19.0	7,462	5,261	4,740	905	1,853	1,975
Lecturers	27,215	20,982	4,342	16.2	1,286	1,233	1,714	109	480	1,411
Other faculty	82,529	57,646	12,716	15.8	3,927	2,484	5,877	428	2,251	9,916
Males	401,507	313,685	62,923	15.9	17,029	12,486	31,711	1,697	5,668	19,231
Professors	126,788	109,128	15,706	12.5	3,498	2,680	9,180	348	764	1,190
Associate professors	84,783	68,383	13,893	16.5	3,947	2,551	7,099	296	835	1,672
Assistant professors	86,182	60,244	16,671	19.7	4,459	3,003	8,903	306	1,601	7,666
Instructors	46,481	36,034	8,360	18.4	2,987	2,581	2,320	472	978	1,109
Lecturers	12,976	9,898	1,980	15.6	595	495	839	51	264	834
Other faculty	44,297	29,998	6,313	14.7	1,543	1,176	3,370	224	1,226	6,760
Females	274,117	214,215	47,041	17.4	18,429	10,332	16,746	1,534	4,035	8,826
Professors	42,404	36,808	5,150	12.2	1,986	1,113	1,880	171	250	196
Associate professors	53,661	44,124	8,536	16.0	3,455	1,768	3,045	268	461	540
Assistant professors	73,507	54,226	14,582	20.2	5,438	2,725	6,019	400	1,208	3,491
Instructors	52,074	40,325	10,008	19.5	4,475	2,680	2,420	433	875	866
Lecturers	14,239	11,084	2,362	16.8	691	738	875	58	216	577
Other faculty	38,232	27,648	6,403	17.2	2,384	1,308	2,507	204	1,025	3,156
2007										
Total	703,463	540,460	119,906	17.3	37,930	24,975	53,661	3,340	11,875	31,222
Professors	173,395	147,867	22,734	13.2	5,839	4,128	12,239	528	1,309	1,485
Associate professors	143,692	115,274	24,255	17.1	7,855	4,714	11,082	604	1,628	2,535
Assistant professors	168,508	117,618	34,940	21.2	10,642	6,329	17,290	679	3,593	12,357
Instructors	101,429	77,609	19,470	19.7	7,480	5,800	5,225	965	2,350	2,000
Lecturers	31,264	23,470	5,326	17.4	1,602	1,492	2,081	151	661	1,807
Other faculty	85,175	58,622	13,181	15.9	4,512	2,512	5,744	413	2,334	11,038
Males	409,115	314,375	67,147	16.7	17,782	13,468	34,178	1,719	6,660	20,933
Professors	127,488	108,404	16,882	13.3	3,646	2,874	10,018	344	973	1,229
Associate professors	86,660	68,982	14,760	17.2	4,110	2,768	7,570	312	1,038	1,880
Assistant professors	88,741	60,407	18,207	21.0	4,607	3,265	10,037	298	1,945	8,182
Instructors	46,599	35,795	8,665	19.0	2,928	2,782	2,463	492	1,066	1,073
Lecturers	14,784	11,045	2,367	16.4	721	613	956	77	347	1,025
Other faculty	44,843	29,742	6,266	14.4	1,770	1,166	3,134	196	1,291	7,544
Females	294,348	226,085	52,759	18.2	20,148	11,507	19,483	1,621	5,215	10,289
Professors	45,907	39,463	5,852	12.8	2,193	1,254	2,221	184	336	256
Associate professors	57,032	46,292	9,495	16.8	3,745	1,946	3,512	292	590	655
Assistant professors	79,767	57,211	16,733	21.4	6,035	3,064	7,253	381	1,648	4,175
Instructors	54,830	41,814	10,805	20.2	4,552	3,018	2,762	473	1,284	927
Lecturers	16,480	12,425	2,959	18.3	881	879	1,125	74	314	782
Other faculty	40,332	28,880	6,915	17.6	2,742	1,346	2,610	217	1,043	3,494

[1]Combined number of Black, Hispanic, Asian/Pacific Islander, and American Indian/Alaska Native faculty.
[2]Combined Black, Hispanic, Asian/Pacific Islander, and American Indian/Alaska Native faculty as a percentage of total faculty, excluding race/ethnicity unknown.
[3]Race/ethnicity not collected.
NOTE: Degree-granting institutions grant associate's or higher degrees and participate in Title IV federal financial aid programs. Beginning in 2007, includes institutions with fewer than 15 full-time employees; these institutions did not report staff data prior to 2007. By definition, all graduate assistants are part-time. Race categories exclude persons of Hispanic ethnicity. Totals may differ from figures reported in other tables because of varying survey methodologies.
SOURCE: U.S. Department of Education, National Center for Education Statistics, 2003, 2005 and 2007 Integrated Postsecondary Education Data System (IPEDS), Winter 2003–04, Winter 2005–06, and Winter 2007–08. (This table was prepared October 2008.)

Average salary of full-time instructional faculty on 9-month contracts in degree-granting institutions, by sex, academic rank, and control and type of institution: Selected years, 1999–2000 through 2008–09

[In current dollars]

Academic year, control and type of institution	All faculty			Academic rank									
				Professor			Associate professor			Assistant professor	Instructor	Lecturer	No academic rank
	Total	Males	Females	Total	Males	Females	Total	Males	Females				
1	2	3	4	5	6	7	8	9	10	11	12	13	14
1999–2000													
All institutions	$55,888	$60,084	$48,997	$74,410	$76,478	$67,079	$54,524	$55,939	$52,091	$44,978	$34,918	$38,194	$47,389
Public	55,011	58,984	48,714	72,475	74,501	65,568	54,641	55,992	52,305	45,285	35,007	37,403	47,990
4-year	57,950	62,030	50,168	75,204	76,530	69,619	55,681	56,776	53,599	45,822	33,528	37,261	40,579
Doctoral[1]	62,686	67,294	52,605	81,651	82,900	75,116	57,938	59,190	55,332	48,438	33,334	39,184	39,068
Master's[2]	52,664	55,505	48,068	66,505	67,062	64,715	53,001	53,665	51,888	43,394	33,223	34,208	42,995
Other 4-year	48,280	50,263	44,957	61,327	61,653	60,236	49,888	50,390	48,987	42,304	35,829	36,007	38,345
2-year	48,240	50,033	46,340	57,806	59,441	55,501	48,056	49,425	46,711	41,984	37,634	40,061	48,233
Not-for-profit	58,172	62,788	49,881	78,512	80,557	70,609	54,300	55,836	51,687	44,423	34,670	40,761	41,415
4-year	58,425	63,028	50,117	78,604	80,622	70,774	54,388	55,898	51,809	44,502	34,813	40,783	41,761
Doctoral[1]	74,347	79,678	61,442	97,751	99,341	89,614	63,780	65,347	60,477	53,946	41,820	43,538	46,135
Master's[2]	51,202	54,326	46,413	65,331	66,591	61,378	51,202	52,474	49,167	41,922	33,913	37,266	44,364
Other 4-year	47,743	49,962	44,218	62,007	62,613	59,974	47,285	47,564	46,876	38,937	31,978	33,531	34,809
2-year	37,583	39,933	34,733	39,454	38,431	40,571	36,349	37,342	35,608	31,818	27,696	25,965	40,373
For-profit	29,543	30,023	28,942	45,505	44,248	49,693	48,469	53,548	43,389	33,043	29,894	—	27,958
2005–06													
All institutions	66,172	71,569	58,665	91,208	94,733	81,514	65,714	67,654	62,860	55,106	50,883	45,896	50,425
Public	64,158	69,191	57,462	87,599	91,080	78,412	65,107	67,077	62,231	55,029	52,297	44,628	50,096
4-year	67,951	73,353	59,437	91,600	93,976	83,946	66,745	68,475	64,013	56,181	40,044	44,598	47,107
Doctoral[1]	73,985	80,186	62,865	100,403	102,366	92,511	70,259	72,242	66,876	59,777	39,961	45,422	46,126
Master's[2]	60,338	63,599	55,992	77,776	78,734	75,465	62,045	62,996	60,709	52,352	39,424	43,241	45,777
Other 4-year	56,117	58,617	52,836	72,348	74,162	68,815	59,091	60,179	57,427	49,860	42,287	43,941	51,912
2-year	55,405	56,858	54,082	65,740	67,782	63,544	54,870	55,825	54,004	48,425	57,224	45,427	50,513
Not-for-profit	71,203	77,136	61,985	98,253	101,638	88,144	66,877	68,753	64,074	55,278	41,302	49,777	53,231
4-year	71,419	77,314	62,212	98,378	101,713	88,379	66,981	68,818	64,226	55,367	41,494	49,786	53,907
Doctoral[1]	89,278	96,862	74,490	122,784	125,275	112,800	78,684	81,043	74,518	67,151	46,016	51,647	55,222
Master's[2]	61,186	64,596	56,637	78,400	80,151	74,214	61,777	63,056	60,038	50,948	41,530	45,110	57,098
Other 4-year	58,344	60,800	54,868	76,571	77,504	74,285	57,964	58,039	57,860	47,877	38,394	45,837	45,605
2-year	39,101	38,817	39,307	47,174	48,786	45,945	42,433	43,628	41,753	35,437	36,264	38,908	39,399
For-profit	42,480	42,878	42,027	60,111	59,423	61,417	56,621	55,546	58,393	47,598	35,661	—	41,579
2007–08													
All institutions	71,085	76,935	63,347	98,548	102,555	88,301	70,826	72,940	67,816	59,294	55,325	49,392	54,405
Public	68,981	74,389	62,129	94,723	98,753	84,839	70,289	72,373	67,353	59,433	56,934	47,840	53,552
4-year	72,857	78,673	64,226	99,092	101,952	90,663	72,079	73,894	69,327	60,766	43,927	47,812	51,177
Doctoral[1]	79,165	85,985	67,719	108,727	110,982	100,390	75,823	77,967	72,317	64,545	43,279	47,936	50,108
Master's[2]	64,908	68,220	60,757	84,110	85,157	81,818	67,116	67,977	65,957	56,727	42,201	47,708	50,202
Other 4-year	59,515	61,692	56,768	73,901	76,668	69,301	62,785	63,714	61,455	53,208	50,222	46,591	54,092
2-year	59,646	61,166	58,318	69,905	71,845	67,931	58,354	59,289	57,533	51,607	62,646	48,652	53,965
Not-for-profit	76,289	82,853	66,655	106,056	109,775	95,725	71,867	74,016	68,744	59,042	44,666	54,023	59,772
4-year	76,471	83,008	66,834	106,162	109,843	95,906	71,952	74,082	68,848	59,125	44,785	54,033	60,132
Doctoral[1]	93,742	102,556	78,277	131,417	134,431	120,488	84,164	87,143	79,185	70,023	49,025	56,288	64,028
Master's[2]	64,760	68,274	60,296	82,946	84,728	79,017	65,075	66,371	63,392	53,942	44,814	49,252	60,114
Other 4-year	62,909	65,512	59,359	83,437	84,067	81,980	62,525	62,580	62,447	51,356	40,944	48,342	51,660
2-year	44,318	43,229	45,072	52,077	53,951	50,488	48,563	46,818	49,684	41,308	41,046	34,622	46,027
For-profit	47,246	48,932	45,121	55,400	55,365	55,473	60,719	66,938	55,388	51,813	38,788	—	35,862
2008–09													
All institutions	73,570	79,706	65,638	102,346	106,759	91,522	73,439	75,634	70,375	61,550	56,918	51,188	56,370
Public	71,237	76,897	64,231	98,097	102,488	87,777	72,700	74,939	69,611	61,544	58,505	49,376	55,233
4-year	75,245	81,394	66,393	102,806	105,939	93,960	74,591	76,553	71,684	62,881	45,365	49,315	53,717
Doctoral[1]	81,485	88,691	69,864	112,569	115,095	103,686	78,375	80,617	74,812	66,754	44,238	49,714	53,990
Master's[2]	66,700	70,072	62,579	86,611	87,689	84,368	69,092	70,039	67,838	58,373	43,533	48,658	53,527
Other 4-year	62,475	65,129	59,242	78,568	81,811	73,346	65,679	67,152	63,704	55,553	53,317	48,375	53,134
2-year	61,433	62,870	60,195	71,802	73,766	69,873	59,953	60,938	59,101	53,445	64,577	51,194	55,491
Not-for-profit	79,358	86,228	69,478	110,486	114,653	99,369	74,877	76,966	71,893	61,572	46,771	56,219	63,252
4-year	79,554	86,380	69,690	110,626	114,748	99,597	74,990	77,043	72,048	61,650	46,971	56,226	63,718
Doctoral[1]	97,702	106,983	81,798	138,584	141,639	127,667	87,777	90,646	83,138	73,289	52,785	58,218	68,175
Master's[2]	67,324	70,874	62,845	85,704	87,791	81,334	67,879	69,101	66,285	56,333	45,976	51,676	62,932
Other 4-year	65,522	68,374	61,749	87,036	87,877	85,178	65,088	65,260	64,853	53,328	42,692	52,925	52,523
2-year	44,302	44,254	44,331	55,182	58,434	52,153	46,686	46,989	46,504	43,515	40,360	39,443	39,968
For-profit	52,557	54,816	50,074	79,589	82,037	74,310	68,058	70,509	65,649	59,043	43,000	—	50,212

—Not available.

[1]Institutions that awarded 20 or more doctor's degrees during the previous academic year.
[2]Institutions that awarded 20 or more master's degrees, but less than 20 doctor's degrees, during the previous academic year.
NOTE: Degree-granting institutions grant associate's or higher degrees and participate in Title IV federal financial aid programs.

SOURCE: U.S. Department of Education, National Center for Education Statistics, 1999–2000 through 2008–09 Integrated Postsecondary Education Data System, "Salaries, Tenure, and Fringe Benefits of Full-Time Instructional Faculty Survey" (IPEDS-SA:99), and Winter 2005–06 through Winter 2008–09. (This table was prepared July 2009.)

Average salary of full-time instructional faculty on 9-month contracts in degree-granting institutions, by control and type of institution and state or jurisdiction: 2008–09

[In current dollars]

State or jurisdiction	All institutions	Public institutions						Not-for-profit institutions						For-profit institutions
		Total	4-year institutions				2-year	Total	4-year institutions				2-year	
			Total	Doctoral[1]	Master's[2]	Other			Total	Doctoral[1]	Master's[2]	Other		
1	2	3	4	5	6	7	8	9	10	11	12	13	14	15
United States	$73,570	$71,237	$75,245	$81,485	$66,700	$62,475	$61,433	$79,358	$79,554	$97,702	$67,324	$65,522	$44,302	$52,557
Alabama	63,086	64,645	69,198	72,769	59,032	68,352	53,220	54,675	54,675	68,717	54,022	47,876	†	†
Alaska	68,104	68,659	68,603	70,151	67,492	†	75,472	54,209	54,209	†	54,209	†	†	†
Arizona	75,466	76,007	80,469	80,469	†	†	67,921	55,739	55,739	†	40,237	64,448	†	63,912
Arkansas	54,600	54,828	59,677	66,021	51,993	55,010	43,128	53,319	53,319	†	55,943	51,399	†	†
California	87,736	86,049	89,809	102,078	77,680	71,245	81,765	94,773	94,909	105,468	79,040	88,890	62,991	68,821
Colorado	68,753	67,636	71,528	78,352	57,697	55,539	49,338	76,485	76,485	78,473	75,991	51,824	†	51,390
Connecticut	90,314	83,590	87,922	99,894	76,374	†	70,449	98,126	98,126	118,151	84,013	77,179	†	45,490
Delaware	85,476	85,941	90,935	94,470	65,480	†	63,686	81,080	81,080	61,582	100,835	†	†	†
District of Columbia	88,635	78,932	78,932	†	78,454	85,278	†	91,487	91,487	92,640	78,241	†	†	52,283
Florida	68,068	67,215	71,664	76,734	63,243	60,518	52,738	70,522	70,522	83,157	66,826	53,037	†	88,304
Georgia	67,190	66,001	68,128	81,422	57,028	50,282	46,760	70,456	70,666	93,680	62,981	55,540	55,528	42,000
Hawaii	78,957	81,325	86,586	91,265	71,505	70,071	69,049	68,855	68,855	†	63,240	86,087	†	†
Idaho	57,786	58,458	60,118	61,869	59,757	49,141	49,160	50,935	50,935	†	49,020	52,415	†	†
Illinois	75,346	70,507	73,756	79,571	61,667	†	64,566	82,725	82,901	105,247	64,206	62,201	38,004	33,192
Indiana	69,408	69,076	72,799	78,145	59,200	54,592	45,219	70,111	70,259	95,408	60,436	59,845	43,093	39,985
Iowa	67,526	71,915	82,343	86,921	65,847	†	51,400	59,879	59,879	58,024	59,357	60,444	†	†
Kansas	62,666	65,322	72,275	78,223	58,819	60,351	48,888	46,137	46,390	†	49,453	41,076	39,941	40,000
Kentucky	60,003	61,384	66,203	78,108	59,534	†	49,103	54,474	54,474	61,304	48,837	56,889	†	†
Louisiana	63,098	61,824	63,980	72,432	55,885	57,807	50,573	69,400	69,400	82,084	63,366	52,693	†	45,000
Maine	70,138	67,178	70,224	76,500	73,173	56,479	54,586	75,565	75,565	†	54,660	86,301	58,264	†
Maryland	73,023	72,457	76,057	88,029	65,484	†	65,426	75,103	75,103	91,836	68,430	72,324	†	†
Massachusetts	91,612	74,391	79,992	90,300	69,726	†	60,200	99,351	99,494	114,790	81,855	80,206	52,515	53,878
Michigan	77,147	79,589	80,787	84,356	68,284	54,918	74,237	63,349	63,349	45,630	61,108	65,375	†	†
Minnesota	70,044	71,351	77,573	94,300	68,319	59,220	61,523	67,425	67,433	67,223	63,823	69,581	41,256	40,126
Mississippi	55,302	55,667	60,225	62,602	50,465	†	49,495	52,073	52,073	†	56,707	39,662	†	†
Missouri	66,082	63,537	66,698	73,326	58,098	57,068	53,540	71,233	71,612	88,555	55,798	50,605	48,030	52,745
Montana	56,689	58,350	61,125	64,168	55,677	48,435	41,786	43,354	44,769	†	40,822	45,848	34,077	†
Nebraska	64,340	66,923	72,146	78,026	58,195	†	49,373	57,693	57,732	71,232	52,888	50,095	45,240	†
Nevada	79,794	80,216	81,709	89,145	†	67,202	63,195	62,802	62,802	†	62,802	†	†	53,580
New Hampshire	80,335	76,729	84,608	93,396	71,060	79,127	49,874	86,103	86,103	112,768	66,806	60,516	†	47,364
New Jersey	89,013	86,968	94,427	98,116	90,170	†	68,821	93,781	93,781	111,787	72,640	62,959	†	58,640
New Mexico	61,853	61,500	67,632	73,274	55,896	45,087	47,062	70,995	70,995	†	76,805	64,217	†	†
New York	82,642	76,180	80,096	92,583	77,077	70,554	67,773	89,041	89,288	99,952	72,568	79,701	47,620	41,892
North Carolina	67,498	64,880	77,643	83,046	68,898	67,639	47,331	76,300	76,416	101,230	55,743	55,496	36,389	†
North Dakota	54,551	56,877	58,822	64,538	52,085	45,853	44,119	40,935	46,552	49,011	†	44,381	20,339	†
Ohio	69,235	70,766	74,227	76,439	69,724	57,588	58,185	65,988	66,046	79,927	59,383	66,066	56,651	37,780
Oklahoma	61,106	61,223	64,758	74,679	55,535	47,723	47,932	60,590	60,590	†	63,477	42,909	†	†
Oregon	64,928	63,880	66,497	70,070	54,558	56,705	60,211	68,151	68,151	59,234	71,672	67,562	†	†
Pennsylvania	77,822	75,247	78,274	85,872	74,055	63,882	58,666	80,862	81,101	98,297	69,413	71,990	41,565	36,960
Rhode Island	82,332	71,330	75,110	81,830	62,994	†	59,617	89,110	89,110	93,215	83,485	114,596	†	†
South Carolina	59,920	61,508	68,918	77,755	62,230	53,103	46,492	52,851	53,182	†	53,650	52,491	38,577	125,743
South Dakota	55,667	57,484	59,903	60,589	61,041	41,736	44,556	48,579	48,579	†	47,598	49,155	†	36,775
Tennessee	63,167	60,962	65,308	68,345	59,946	†	46,984	67,685	67,685	92,784	51,874	54,094	†	27,532
Texas	69,131	68,029	74,035	79,941	60,852	51,206	54,510	74,682	74,908	87,080	64,911	59,610	33,137	21,430
Utah	71,309	64,770	67,810	77,045	58,361	57,961	49,790	89,305	89,658	92,672	65,180	†	56,641	†
Vermont	69,851	69,505	69,505	75,162	58,219	55,326	†	70,193	73,487	†	76,985	52,172	43,065	†
Virginia	71,924	74,242	78,740	85,851	64,873	66,540	57,742	64,539	64,539	63,943	66,522	63,239	†	†
Washington	67,287	67,215	74,658	81,718	66,315	54,137	55,328	67,637	67,637	71,754	66,582	66,715	†	58,968
West Virginia	57,440	59,333	61,764	73,454	57,638	51,321	45,352	45,924	45,924	49,092	45,745	44,552	†	†
Wisconsin	68,531	70,148	69,973	79,971	58,249	86,476	70,493	62,286	62,384	72,233	58,235	55,381	49,631	†
Wyoming	68,020	68,020	76,719	76,719	†	†	58,089	†	†	†	†	†	†	†
U.S. Service Academies	113,473	113,473	113,473	†	†	113,473	†	†	†	†	†	†	†	†
Other jurisdictions	58,497	58,822	62,896	†	69,777	56,251	31,329	33,971	33,971	†	33,971	†	†	†
American Samoa	28,336	28,336	28,336	†	†	†	28,336	†	†	†	†	†	†	†
Federated States of Micronesia	20,727	20,727	†	†	†	†	20,727	†	†	†	†	†	†	†
Guam	56,815	56,815	63,389	†	63,389	†	47,327	†	†	†	†	†	†	†
Marshall Islands	26,335	26,335	†	†	†	†	26,335	†	†	†	†	†	†	†
Northern Marianas	41,592	41,592	41,592	†	†	41,592	†	†	†	†	†	†	†	†
Palau	17,321	17,321	†	†	†	†	17,321	†	†	†	†	†	†	†
Puerto Rico	64,208	64,772	64,772	†	72,836	58,603	†	33,971	33,971	†	33,971	†	†	†
U.S. Virgin Islands	59,906	59,906	59,906	†	59,906	†	†	†	†	†	†	†	†	†

†Not applicable.

[1]Institutions that awarded 20 or more doctor's degrees during the previous academic year.

[2]Institutions that awarded 20 or more master's degrees, but less than 20 doctor's degrees, during the previous academic year.

NOTE: Degree-granting institutions grant associate's or higher degrees and participate in Title IV federal financial aid programs. Data include imputations for nonrespondent institutions.
SOURCE: U.S. Department of Education, National Center for Education Statistics, 2008–09 Integrated Postsecondary Education Data System (IPEDS), Winter 2008–09. (This table was prepared July 2009.)

Average salary of full-time instructional faculty on 9-month contracts in 4-year degree-granting institutions, by type and control of institution, rank of faculty, and state or jurisdiction: 2008–09
[In current dollars]

State or jurisdiction	Public doctoral[1]			Public master's[2]			Not-for-profit doctoral[1]			Not-for-profit master's[2]		
	Professor	Associate professor	Assistant professor	Professor	Associate professor	Assistant professor	Professor	Associate professor	Assistant professor	Professor	Associate professor	Assistant professor
1	2	3	4	5	6	7	8	9	10	11	12	13
United States	$112,569	$78,375	$66,754	$86,611	$69,092	$58,373	$138,584	$87,777	$73,289	$85,704	$67,879	$56,333
Alabama............................	103,801	73,722	59,697	76,781	63,969	52,613	89,618	65,125	54,899	66,063	58,835	48,676
Alaska...............................	94,952	70,881	60,221	90,258	72,071	59,002	†	†	†	66,779	55,340	48,804
Arizona.............................	110,591	77,146	66,260	†	†	†	†	†	†	†	†	†
Arkansas...........................	93,019	69,195	60,875	67,083	57,180	49,379	†	†	†	66,507	58,494	48,779
California...........................	129,851	85,526	75,646	94,241	76,107	66,642	140,030	92,441	77,996	102,854	79,092	64,372
Colorado...........................	109,418	81,866	67,634	77,591	62,739	53,940	111,467	79,158	64,916	101,639	65,436	58,539
Connecticut.......................	133,017	91,837	73,913	92,419	72,900	59,448	169,425	90,566	77,557	110,729	79,667	66,367
Delaware...........................	129,217	86,890	73,807	79,651	65,318	60,437	72,189	65,987	57,209	122,169	97,891	63,639
District of Columbia	†	†	†	95,427	74,403	58,871	134,608	89,854	71,797	100,660	70,853	58,683
Florida..............................	106,877	74,042	65,740	87,715	69,380	56,991	120,410	79,455	67,237	88,554	65,450	56,605
Georgia.............................	114,573	79,045	68,590	74,824	60,389	52,409	139,944	89,196	74,839	68,644	61,191	52,909
Hawaii...............................	114,730	87,935	75,535	90,663	74,818	67,107	†	†	†	81,522	71,609	58,753
Idaho................................	83,140	65,913	55,754	78,330	64,013	55,225	†	†	†	59,150	49,712	40,870
Illinois..............................	111,880	75,645	68,945	85,310	67,414	57,367	153,784	93,045	81,918	78,177	65,105	54,282
Indiana.............................	108,606	75,481	65,026	80,688	61,974	55,637	133,470	84,253	71,292	78,849	60,077	53,204
Iowa.................................	118,184	81,445	71,553	85,451	68,185	55,490	72,334	54,969	50,438	77,261	59,767	49,505
Kansas..............................	107,416	75,489	62,734	82,156	62,599	51,456	†	†	†	57,547	50,440	45,543
Kentucky...........................	103,336	74,082	63,641	82,471	64,597	55,117	76,734	61,727	51,771	56,659	49,732	43,379
Louisiana..........................	103,844	75,878	63,964	74,437	62,404	52,819	126,621	82,876	63,848	86,441	62,993	53,922
Maine................................	93,920	74,081	60,627	92,785	71,247	57,734	†	†	†	76,530	61,024	50,712
Maryland...........................	126,152	88,311	76,175	85,313	69,406	61,459	135,506	94,468	80,440	89,359	68,271	58,748
Massachusetts...................	116,037	89,378	70,453	83,787	67,391	58,497	156,132	96,334	83,783	110,773	80,459	65,496
Michigan............................	116,268	79,895	66,918	84,467	68,713	59,326	57,510	47,474	38,768	73,617	61,031	51,499
Minnesota.........................	130,692	85,843	74,596	84,184	67,433	58,295	87,285	68,829	57,776	78,582	63,265	52,595
Mississippi........................	90,822	69,399	58,401	61,472	56,036	49,088	†	†	†	72,893	56,369	49,496
Missouri............................	98,571	71,972	60,753	75,997	60,018	50,550	130,473	78,126	67,552	70,542	58,415	49,131
Montana............................	79,967	64,277	57,158	68,655	58,021	53,518	†	†	†	47,809	42,090	37,409
Nebraska...........................	103,250	75,684	63,886	72,904	61,409	48,552	101,287	69,004	59,146	63,905	53,126	47,418
Nevada.............................	122,641	89,235	70,659	†	†	†	†	†	†	73,986	55,250	51,141
New Hampshire	114,042	85,870	70,370	85,769	69,868	58,294	145,656	96,911	72,127	84,588	61,242	54,020
New Jersey........................	131,438	93,125	73,267	113,882	88,023	70,998	154,864	91,321	75,324	92,681	77,430	60,349
New Mexico........................	95,069	69,537	60,645	68,592	57,742	50,408	†	†	†	74,587	55,343	†
New York...........................	122,234	86,258	70,253	100,474	76,912	64,250	141,349	91,976	74,936	94,716	73,524	59,806
North Carolina....................	119,714	82,667	72,238	91,096	73,680	62,830	146,917	93,703	72,597	65,406	58,336	50,242
North Dakota......................	84,361	67,466	60,349	68,828	56,701	50,795	61,009	52,754	45,091	†	†	†
Ohio..................................	105,617	74,306	62,308	88,909	69,912	58,663	108,913	73,660	63,820	73,945	60,457	50,626
Oklahoma..........................	102,972	72,955	62,839	71,381	59,566	51,654	†	†	†	81,409	63,627	52,346
Oregon..............................	93,846	70,490	62,776	68,864	54,625	44,677	70,050	60,286	51,393	95,129	67,130	58,189
Pennsylvania......................	120,970	84,707	66,972	97,316	77,665	62,269	137,168	90,778	76,087	91,568	71,494	59,907
Rhode Island......................	101,943	74,364	65,885	73,460	63,958	54,266	136,734	77,913	68,797	102,161	85,246	68,427
South Carolina...................	109,135	76,987	68,575	78,144	65,518	56,388	†	†	†	56,967	59,861	49,764
South Dakota.....................	82,966	63,991	55,852	80,395	63,268	53,269	†	†	†	60,003	49,950	44,101
Tennessee.........................	91,893	69,966	57,695	77,078	60,921	50,649	132,254	84,430	66,876	61,769	53,162	46,857
Texas................................	113,333	76,831	68,281	81,075	66,446	57,697	118,586	83,876	75,814	83,589	63,822	53,749
Utah..................................	99,881	72,635	67,210	72,486	60,589	51,715	118,530	87,354	77,212	79,639	64,331	57,672
Vermont.............................	104,378	77,824	65,836	69,127	53,616	43,078	†	†	†	104,387	74,220	61,734
Virginia.............................	118,958	84,101	68,437	82,879	67,284	56,605	77,479	64,769	56,210	85,581	68,864	54,461
Washington........................	106,677	79,846	70,533	82,307	67,471	60,507	91,973	69,553	57,907	82,600	68,628	60,250
West Virginia......................	101,800	72,067	59,019	71,895	58,641	48,971	65,369	49,688	46,019	54,655	49,446	43,035
Wisconsin..........................	102,907	73,222	66,288	71,943	59,682	53,736	101,679	73,898	59,379	69,719	60,298	51,153
Wyoming............................	104,607	75,001	65,567	†	†	†	†	†	†	†	†	†
U.S. Service Academies	†	†	†	†	†	†	†	†	†	†	†	†
Other jurisdictions	†	†	†	79,982	64,492	58,177	†	†	†	†	32,400	44,565
American Samoa	†	†	†	†	†	†	†	†	†	†	†	†
Federated States of Micronesia...............	†	†	†	†	†	†	†	†	†	†	†	†
Guam................................	†	†	†	82,219	66,239	53,640	†	†	†	†	†	†
Marshall Islands	†	†	†	†	†	†	†	†	†	†	†	†
Northern Marianas	†	†	†	†	†	†	†	†	†	†	†	†
Palau................................	†	†	†	†	†	†	†	†	†	†	†	†
Puerto Rico........................	†	†	†	79,721	66,131	61,178	†	†	†	†	32,400	44,565
U.S. Virgin Islands	†	†	†	80,899	55,028	54,672	†	†	†	†	†	†

†Not applicable.
[1]Institutions that awarded 20 or more doctor's degrees during the previous academic year.
[2]Institutions that awarded 20 or more master's degrees, but less than 20 doctor's degrees, during the previous academic year.

NOTE: Degree-granting institutions grant associate's or higher degrees and participate in Title IV federal financial aid programs. Data include imputations for nonrespondent institutions.
SOURCE: U.S. Department of Education, National Center for Education Statistics, 2008–09 Integrated Postsecondary Education Data System (IPEDS), Winter 2008–09. (This table was prepared July 2009.)

Percentage of full-time instructional staff with tenure for degree-granting institutions with a tenure system, by academic rank, sex, and control and type of institution: Selected years, 1993–94 through 2007–08

Academic year, control and type of institution	Percent with tenure														
	Total			Professor			Associate professor			Assistant professor			Instructor	Lecturer	No academic rank
	Total	Male	Female	Total	Male	Female	Total	Male	Female	Total	Male	Female			
1	2	3	4	5	6	7	8	9	10	11	12	13	14	15	16
1993–94															
All institutions..................	56.2	62.6	42.7	91.9	92.8	87.7	76.8	77.5	75.1	14.4	13.6	15.5	38.3	10.8	26.0
Public institutions	58.9	65.4	45.6	92.6	93.6	87.5	80.8	81.6	78.9	17.1	16.1	18.5	45.5	7.2	28.6
4-year......................	56.3	63.5	39.3	94.3	94.7	92.0	80.4	81.2	78.4	13.8	13.0	14.8	4.4	5.4	6.1
Doctoral[1]................	54.5	62.1	35.0	94.2	94.7	90.1	81.3	82.1	79.2	7.3	6.7	8.3	2.8	2.1	5.4
Master's[2]...............	60.5	67.7	46.1	95.4	95.5	95.0	79.3	80.0	77.7	23.0	23.0	22.9	6.4	11.7	11.0
Other	51.1	56.3	40.0	88.4	88.8	86.4	76.5	77.3	74.8	22.7	22.8	22.6	4.6	15.0	6.4
2-year......................	69.9	75.4	63.0	80.7	83.7	75.5	84.2	86.4	81.5	47.7	51.1	44.6	68.9	39.9	65.7
Not-for-profit institutions.	49.5	56.0	35.5	90.3	90.8	88.1	67.6	68.1	66.5	9.0	8.7	9.4	6.1	21.9	18.9
4-year......................	49.5	56.0	35.4	90.3	90.8	88.0	67.6	68.1	66.5	9.0	8.7	9.4	5.5	21.6	15.7
Doctoral[1]................	47.6	53.5	31.9	90.5	90.8	88.5	62.5	63.4	60.0	3.7	3.7	3.7	8.9	29.2	15.4
Master's[2]...............	51.8	59.2	38.2	90.8	91.1	89.8	71.3	72.2	69.6	13.4	13.6	13.1	2.6	0.7	10.5
Other	50.4	57.4	37.2	89.4	90.4	85.1	70.6	70.9	70.2	11.9	11.9	11.9	3.9	3.4	20.0
2-year......................	47.9	54.5	38.5	88.0	84.3	94.3	63.8	65.1	62.7	12.0	12.3	11.9	20.0	86.7	68.6
For-profit institutions	33.8	39.0	27.8	95.2	94.1	100.0	—	—	—	‡	‡	‡	32.9	—	—
1999–2000															
All institutions..................	53.7	59.6	43.2	92.8	93.1	91.2	76.8	76.9	76.7	11.8	11.0	12.9	34.1	3.4	18.3
Public institutions	55.9	62.0	45.6	93.9	94.4	91.9	81.0	81.2	80.7	14.1	13.1	15.4	39.8	4.1	21.2
4-year......................	53.2	60.3	39.3	94.2	94.6	92.5	80.8	81.0	80.3	10.0	9.5	10.6	3.9	3.0	4.0
Doctoral[1]................	50.4	58.0	34.5	92.9	93.6	89.3	79.9	80.2	79.4	4.7	4.4	5.2	2.1	1.5	1.4
Master's[2]...............	59.1	66.0	48.0	96.9	96.9	96.8	82.7	83.0	82.1	18.1	17.8	18.5	6.4	5.9	25.3
Other	54.7	61.2	43.2	94.9	95.1	94.0	80.7	81.3	79.7	21.8	24.1	18.8	5.8	7.2	49.3
2-year......................	67.7	70.6	64.5	91.2	92.2	89.7	83.3	83.6	83.1	53.8	56.0	52.0	60.4	21.2	64.4
Not-for-profit institutions.	48.2	54.2	36.8	90.3	90.5	89.7	68.0	67.8	68.4	7.5	6.8	8.2	1.8	1.2	7.4
4-year......................	48.1	54.1	36.7	90.3	90.5	89.7	68.0	67.8	68.5	7.4	6.8	8.1	1.6	1.2	4.1
Doctoral[1]................	43.4	49.6	29.6	88.6	88.7	87.6	62.6	62.8	62.2	3.0	2.8	3.2	1.0	1.3	0.5
Master's[2]...............	52.3	59.4	41.4	91.2	91.6	90.0	72.0	73.0	70.3	12.1	11.9	12.3	0.9	0.8	22.3
Other	53.5	59.3	44.0	93.5	93.8	92.8	73.1	71.2	76.0	9.9	9.4	10.5	3.6	1.6	23.5
2-year......................	59.7	63.3	53.6	96.0	96.0	96.0	57.1	61.3	54.3	31.6	36.7	28.3	30.2	—	65.8
For-profit institutions	77.4	77.2	77.6	47.4	50.0	33.3	—	—	—	—	—	—	86.1	—	71.9
2005–06															
All institutions..................	49.6	55.2	41.0	91.3	91.6	90.5	73.6	73.0	74.5	8.0	7.4	8.6	28.4	1.8	26.1
Public institutions	51.5	57.1	43.3	92.8	93.1	91.8	77.7	77.3	78.4	9.8	9.1	10.6	33.8	2.3	29.9
4-year......................	48.7	55.4	37.8	93.1	93.3	92.7	77.7	77.3	78.5	6.1	5.8	6.6	2.1	1.6	3.8
Doctoral[1]................	47.2	54.2	34.5	91.6	92.0	90.1	75.9	75.7	76.4	2.7	2.6	2.8	1.2	1.3	2.1
Master's[2]...............	52.3	58.7	43.6	96.5	96.6	96.5	81.0	80.3	82.0	11.4	10.9	11.9	2.9	2.1	5.1
Other	49.1	54.0	42.2	95.4	95.0	96.2	82.6	83.0	81.9	17.6	18.3	16.8	4.9	2.3	34.3
2-year......................	64.1	67.2	61.2	89.5	90.7	88.2	77.9	77.8	77.9	44.1	46.8	41.8	56.2	22.4	70.3
Not-for-profit institutions.	45.1	51.1	35.5	88.3	88.5	87.6	65.4	64.7	66.6	4.6	4.3	4.9	0.7	0.5	9.8
4-year......................	45.1	51.1	35.4	88.3	88.5	87.6	65.4	64.7	66.6	4.6	4.3	4.9	0.4	0.5	9.4
Doctoral[1]................	40.7	47.2	28.3	86.2	86.7	84.1	57.7	57.5	58.1	1.8	1.8	1.8	0.2	0.3	1.8
Master's[2]...............	49.1	55.0	41.1	89.7	90.2	88.3	71.6	71.6	71.6	8.5	8.1	8.8	0.7	1.1	20.9
Other	52.5	57.8	44.8	92.7	92.3	93.9	74.5	73.5	75.9	5.5	5.4	5.6	0.7	1.5	45.7
2-year......................	45.2	50.0	41.2	86.3	91.7	81.5	69.7	92.9	52.6	15.4	8.6	20.9	34.5	‡	50.0
For-profit institutions	69.3	67.1	72.5	70.3	65.6	100.0	—	—	—	—	—	—	78.9	‡	—
2007–08															
All institutions..................	48.8	54.5	40.4	90.6	90.9	89.6	74.0	73.7	74.6	7.8	7.4	8.2	27.8	1.4	25.2
Public institutions	50.5	56.2	42.6	92.1	92.4	91.2	77.7	77.5	78.0	9.4	8.7	10.2	33.2	1.8	29.8
4-year......................	47.8	54.5	37.4	92.3	92.5	91.8	77.7	77.5	78.1	5.8	5.4	6.2	2.0	1.2	4.8
Doctoral[1]................	46.1	53.2	33.9	90.6	91.0	89.2	75.0	74.8	75.3	2.2	2.0	2.5	1.1	0.7	1.1
Master's[2]...............	51.9	58.5	43.7	97.1	97.1	97.0	83.8	83.9	83.6	12.1	11.9	12.3	3.0	1.9	6.1
Other	49.1	53.5	43.2	92.2	93.5	89.8	81.3	81.8	80.5	16.3	17.1	15.4	5.1	3.1	41.6
2-year......................	63.6	66.7	60.7	89.7	91.1	88.3	77.6	77.9	77.4	45.3	48.7	42.6	56.2	21.8	68.1
Not-for-profit institutions.	44.7	50.9	35.2	87.5	87.9	86.4	66.8	66.2	67.9	4.7	4.8	4.6	0.6	0.3	8.5
4-year......................	44.7	50.9	35.2	87.5	87.9	86.4	66.8	66.2	67.9	4.7	4.7	4.6	0.4	0.3	8.2
Doctoral[1]................	40.1	46.9	28.5	84.9	85.6	82.2	59.4	59.4	59.2	2.8	2.8	2.7	0.2	0.2	1.9
Master's[2]...............	49.8	56.1	41.7	89.9	90.5	88.4	73.7	73.9	73.4	8.3	8.9	7.8	0.7	0.6	18.0
Other	52.7	58.2	44.9	93.2	93.0	93.8	77.2	75.2	80.0	5.0	5.2	4.9	1.0	1.4	41.5
2-year......................	41.3	46.4	37.4	92.5	96.2	85.7	60.0	61.5	59.5	17.9	14.3	20.4	17.8	‡	51.6
For-profit institutions	51.3	58.0	42.1	77.4	77.8	76.5	23.7	35.3	8.0	16.0	23.8	10.3	77.9	‡	‡

—Not available.
‡Reporting standards not met.
[1]Institutions that awarded 20 or more doctor's degrees during the previous academic year.
[2]Institutions that awarded 20 or more master's degrees, but less than 20 doctor's degrees, during the previous academic year.
NOTE: The coverage of this table differs from similar tables published in editions of the *Digest* prior to 2003. Previous tenure tabulations included only instructional staff classified as full-time faculty; this table includes all staff with full-time instructional duties, including faculty and other instructional staff. Data for 1993–94 are for institutions of higher education, while later data are for degree-granting institutions. Degree-granting institutions grant associate's or higher degrees

and participate in Title IV federal financial aid programs. The degree-granting classification is very similar to the earlier higher education classification, but it includes more 2-year colleges and excludes a few higher education institutions that did not grant degrees. (See Appendix A: Guide to Sources for details.) Beginning in 2007–08, includes institutions with fewer than 15 full-time employees; institutions with fewer than 15 employees did not report staff data prior to 2007–08. Some data have been revised from previously published figures.
SOURCE: U.S. Department of Education, National Center for Education Statistics, 1993–94 through 2007–08 Integrated Postsecondary Education Data System, "Fall Staff Survey" (IPEDS-S:93–99), Winter 2005–06, and Winter 2007–08. (This table was prepared July 2009.)

Average undergraduate tuition and fees and room and board rates charged for full-time students in degree-granting institutions, by type and control of institution: 1964–65 through 2008–09

Year and control of institution	Constant 2007–08 dollars: Total tuition, room, and board — All institutions	4-year All	2-year	Current dollars: Total tuition, room, and board — All institutions	4-year All	4-year Universities	Other 4-year	2-year	Tuition and required fees (in-state for public institutions) — All institutions	4-year All	4-year Universities	Other 4-year	2-year	Dormitory rooms — All institutions	4-year All	4-year Universities	Other 4-year	2-year	Board (7-day basis)[1] — All institutions	4-year All	4-year Universities	Other 4-year	2-year
1	2	3	4	5	6	7	8	9	10	11	12	13	14	15	16	17	18	19	20	21	22	23	24
All institutions																							
1976–77	$8,207	$9,295	$5,763	$2,275	$2,577	$2,647	$2,527	$1,598	$924	$1,218	$1,210	$1,223	$346	$603	$611	$649	$584	$503	$748	$748	$788	$719	$750
1977–78	8,148	9,211	5,758	2,411	2,725	2,777	2,685	1,703	984	1,291	1,269	1,305	378	645	654	691	628	525	781	780	818	752	801
1978–79	7,994	9,016	5,650	2,587	2,917	2,967	2,879	1,828	1,073	1,397	1,370	1,413	411	688	696	737	667	575	826	825	860	800	842
1979–80	7,660	8,636	5,398	2,809	3,167	3,223	3,124	1,979	1,163	1,513	1,484	1,530	451	751	759	803	729	628	895	895	936	865	900
1980–81	7,579	8,552	5,450	3,101	3,499	3,535	3,469	2,230	1,289	1,679	1,634	1,705	526	836	846	881	821	705	976	975	1,020	943	1,000
1981–82	7,850	8,888	5,569	3,489	3,951	4,005	3,908	2,476	1,457	1,907	1,860	1,935	590	950	961	1,023	919	793	1,083	1,082	1,121	1,055	1,094
1982–83	8,362	9,503	5,853	3,877	4,406	4,466	4,356	2,713	1,626	2,139	2,081	2,173	675	1,064	1,078	1,150	1,028	873	1,187	1,189	1,235	1,155	1,165
1983–84	8,668	9,874	5,937	4,167	4,747	4,793	4,712	2,854	1,783	2,344	2,300	2,368	730	1,145	1,162	1,211	1,130	916	1,239	1,242	1,282	1,214	1,208
1984–85	9,133	10,329	6,364	4,563	5,160	5,236	5,107	3,179	1,985	2,567	2,539	2,583	821	1,267	1,282	1,343	1,242	1,058	1,310	1,311	1,353	1,282	1,301
1985–86[2]	9,503	10,708	6,650	4,885	5,504	5,597	5,441	3,367	2,181	2,784	2,770	2,793	888	1,338	1,355	1,424	1,309	1,107	1,365	1,365	1,403	1,339	1,372
1986–87	9,908	11,351	6,272	5,206	5,964	6,124	5,857	3,295	2,312	3,042	3,042	3,042	897	1,405	1,427	1,501	1,376	1,034	1,489	1,495	1,581	1,439	1,364
1987–88	10,041	11,463	5,963	5,494	6,272	6,339	6,226	3,263	2,458	3,201	3,168	3,220	809	1,488	1,516	1,576	1,478	1,017	1,549	1,555	1,596	1,529	1,437
1988–89	10,251	11,748	6,241	5,869	6,725	6,801	6,673	3,573	2,658	3,472	3,422	3,499	979	1,575	1,609	1,665	1,573	1,085	1,636	1,644	1,715	1,601	1,509
1989–90	10,349	12,024	6,177	6,207	7,212	7,347	7,120	3,705	2,839	3,800	3,765	3,819	978	1,638	1,675	1,732	1,638	1,105	1,730	1,737	1,850	1,663	1,622
1990–91	10,373	12,017	6,213	6,562	7,602	7,709	7,528	3,930	3,016	4,009	3,958	4,036	1,087	1,743	1,782	1,848	1,740	1,182	1,802	1,811	1,903	1,751	1,660
1991–92	10,840	12,618	7,077	7,077	8,238	8,390	8,142	4,092	3,286	4,385	4,368	4,394	1,189	1,874	1,921	1,996	1,875	1,210	1,918	1,931	2,026	1,872	1,692
1992–93	11,070	13,008	7,452	7,452	8,758	8,934	8,648	4,207	3,517	4,752	4,665	4,795	1,276	1,939	1,991	2,104	1,926	1,240	1,996	2,015	2,165	1,927	1,692
1993–94	11,483	13,460	7,931	7,931	9,296	9,495	9,186	4,449	3,827	5,119	5,104	5,127	1,399	2,057	2,111	2,190	2,068	1,332	2,047	2,067	2,201	1,992	1,718
1994–95	11,690	13,692	8,306	8,306	9,728	9,863	9,646	4,633	4,044	5,391	5,287	5,441	1,488	2,145	2,200	2,281	2,155	1,396	2,116	2,138	2,295	2,049	1,750
1995–96	12,059	14,154	8,800	8,800	10,330	10,560	10,195	4,725	4,338	5,786	5,733	5,812	1,522	2,264	2,318	2,423	2,260	1,473	2,199	2,226	2,404	2,123	1,730
1996–97	12,264	14,442	9,206	9,206	10,841	11,033	10,726	4,895	4,564	6,118	6,055	6,150	1,543	2,365	2,422	2,518	2,368	1,522	2,276	2,301	2,460	2,208	1,830
1997–98	12,549	14,760	9,588	9,588	11,277	11,382	11,205	5,192	4,755	6,351	6,232	6,408	1,695	2,444	2,507	2,575	2,469	1,598	2,389	2,419	2,576	2,327	1,900
1998–99	12,964	15,296	10,076	10,076	11,888	12,123	11,752	5,291	5,013	6,723	6,713	6,728	1,725	2,557	2,626	2,710	2,578	1,616	2,506	2,540	2,700	2,446	1,950
1999–2000	13,061	15,446	10,444	10,444	12,352	12,613	12,198	5,408	5,238	7,044	7,026	7,052	1,721	2,682	2,749	2,845	2,695	1,733	2,524	2,559	2,741	2,451	1,954
2000–01	13,081	15,624	10,818	10,818	12,922	13,177	12,775	5,460	5,377	7,372	7,360	7,377	1,698	2,819	2,893	2,999	2,833	1,744	2,622	2,658	2,818	2,565	2,017
2001–02	13,520	16,204	11,380	11,380	13,639	13,942	13,468	5,718	5,646	7,786	7,788	7,785	1,800	2,981	3,060	3,184	2,992	1,848	2,753	2,793	2,970	2,692	2,070
2002–03	13,966	16,786	12,014	12,014	14,439	14,827	14,233	6,252	6,002	8,309	8,406	8,264	1,903	3,179	3,263	3,377	3,201	2,077	2,832	2,867	3,044	2,767	2,272
2003–04	14,736	17,639	12,953	12,953	15,505	16,096	15,205	6,705	6,608	9,029	9,268	8,924	2,174	3,359	3,448	3,599	3,368	2,208	2,986	3,028	3,230	2,914	2,322
2004–05	15,231	18,232	13,792	13,792	16,509	17,219	16,164	7,086	7,122	9,706	10,051	9,559	2,338	3,569	3,661	3,813	3,582	2,336	3,100	3,142	3,355	3,023	2,413
2005–06	15,563	18,561	14,629	14,629	17,447	18,229	17,075	7,231	7,601	10,279	10,666	10,119	2,417	3,804	3,899	4,050	3,821	2,396	3,224	3,269	3,513	3,135	2,418
2006–07	16,057	19,156	15,483	15,483	18,471	19,304	18,085	7,466	8,092	10,931	11,404	10,738	2,496	4,019	4,116	4,261	4,041	2,527	3,372	3,424	3,640	3,306	2,443
2007–08	16,159	19,323	16,159	16,159	19,323	20,302	18,874	7,637	8,412	11,414	11,997	11,175	2,519	4,214	4,317	4,487	4,229	2,635	3,534	3,592	3,818	3,470	2,483
2008–09[3]	16,907	20,154	17,143	17,143	20,435	21,518	19,949	8,230	8,941	12,075	12,716	11,821	2,601	4,446	4,554	4,741	4,458	2,777	3,756	3,807	4,060	3,669	2,852
Public institutions																							
1964–65	6,439	—	4,324	950	—	1,051	867	638	243	—	298	224	99	271	—	291	241	178	436	—	462	402	361
1965–66	6,522	—	4,445	983	—	1,105	904	670	257	—	327	241	109	281	—	304	255	194	445	—	474	408	367
1966–67	6,599	—	4,566	1,026	—	1,171	947	710	275	—	360	259	121	294	—	321	271	213	457	—	490	417	376
1967–68	6,623	—	4,912	1,064	—	1,199	997	789	283	—	366	268	144	313	—	337	292	243	468	—	496	437	402
1968–69	6,630	—	5,241	1,117	—	1,245	1,063	883	295	—	377	281	170	337	—	359	318	278	485	—	509	464	435
1969–70	6,742	—	5,330	1,203	—	1,362	1,135	951	323	—	427	306	178	369	—	395	346	308	511	—	540	483	465
1970–71	6,859	—	5,319	1,287	—	1,477	1,206	998	351	—	478	332	187	401	—	431	375	338	535	—	568	499	473
1971–72	6,981	—	5,520	1,357	—	1,579	1,263	1,073	376	—	526	354	192	430	—	463	400	366	551	—	590	509	515
1972–73	7,210	—	5,920	1,458	—	1,668	1,460	1,197	407	—	566	455	233	476	—	500	455	398	575	—	602	550	566
1973–74	6,888	—	5,785	1,517	—	1,707	1,506	1,274	438	—	581	463	274	480	—	505	464	409	599	—	621	579	591
1974–75	6,389	—	5,473	1,563	—	1,760	1,558	1,339	432	—	599	448	277	506	—	527	497	424	625	—	634	613	638
1975–76	6,360	—	5,291	1,666	—	1,935	1,657	1,386	433	—	642	469	245	544	—	573	533	442	689	—	720	655	699
1976–77	6,453	6,980	5,376	1,789	1,935	2,067	1,827	1,491	479	617	689	564	283	582	592	614	572	465	728	727	763	692	742
1977–78	6,380	6,888	5,373	1,888	2,038	2,170	1,931	1,590	512	655	736	596	306	621	631	649	616	486	755	752	785	720	797
1978–79	6,161	6,629	5,226	1,994	2,145	2,289	2,027	1,691	543	688	777	622	327	655	664	689	641	527	796	793	823	764	837

See notes at end of table.

Average undergraduate tuition and fees and room and board rates charged for full-time students in degree-granting institutions, by type and control of institution: 1964–65 through 2008–09—Continued

	Constant 2007–08 dollars			Current dollars																			
	Total tuition, room, and board			Total tuition, room, and board					Tuition and required fees (in-state for public institutions)					Dormitory rooms					Board (7-day basis)[1]				
					4-year institutions					4-year institutions					4-year institutions					4-year institutions			
Year and control of institution	All institutions	All 4-year	2-year	All institutions	All 4-year	Universities	Other 4-year	2-year	All institutions	All 4-year	Universities	Other 4-year	2-year	All institutions	All 4-year	Universities	Other 4-year	2-year	All institutions	All 4-year	Universities	Other 4-year	2-year
1	2	3	4	5	6	7	8	9	10	11	12	13	14	15	16	17	18	19	20	21	22	23	24
1979–80	5,904	6,347	4,967	2,165	2,327	2,487	2,198	1,822	583	738	840	662	355	715	725	750	703	574	867	865	898	833	893
1980–81	5,800	6,233	4,954	2,373	2,550	2,712	2,421	2,027	635	804	915	722	391	799	811	827	796	642	940	936	969	904	994
1981–82	5,990	6,458	5,003	2,663	2,871	3,079	2,705	2,224	714	909	1,042	813	434	909	925	970	885	703	1,039	1,036	1,067	1,006	1,086
1982–83	6,351	6,894	5,154	2,945	3,196	3,403	3,032	2,390	798	1,031	1,164	936	473	1,010	1,030	1,072	993	755	1,136	1,134	1,167	1,103	1,162
1983–84	6,564	7,140	5,270	3,156	3,433	3,628	3,285	2,534	891	1,148	1,284	1,052	528	1,087	1,110	1,131	1,092	801	1,178	1,175	1,213	1,141	1,205
1984–85	6,821	7,369	5,618	3,408	3,682	3,899	3,518	2,807	971	1,228	1,386	1,117	584	1,196	1,217	1,237	1,200	921	1,241	1,237	1,276	1,201	1,302
1985–86[2]	6,948	7,507	5,799	3,571	3,859	4,146	3,637	2,981	1,045	1,318	1,536	1,157	641	1,242	1,263	1,290	1,240	960	1,285	1,278	1,320	1,240	1,380
1986–87	7,242	7,875	5,688	3,805	4,138	4,469	3,891	2,989	1,106	1,414	1,651	1,248	660	1,301	1,323	1,355	1,295	979	1,398	1,401	1,464	1,348	1,349
1987–88	7,401	8,047	5,602	4,050	4,403	4,619	4,250	3,066	1,218	1,537	1,726	1,407	706	1,378	1,410	1,410	1,409	943	1,454	1,456	1,482	1,434	1,417
1988–89	7,466	8,172	5,560	4,274	4,678	4,905	4,526	3,183	1,285	1,646	1,846	1,515	730	1,457	1,496	1,483	1,506	965	1,533	1,536	1,576	1,504	1,488
1989–90	7,509	8,295	5,501	4,504	4,975	5,324	4,723	3,299	1,356	1,780	2,035	1,608	756	1,513	1,557	1,561	1,554	962	1,635	1,638	1,728	1,561	1,581
1990–91	7,520	8,288	5,482	4,757	5,243	5,585	5,004	3,467	1,454	1,888	2,159	1,707	824	1,612	1,657	1,658	1,655	1,050	1,691	1,698	1,767	1,641	1,594
1991–92	7,871	8,721	5,549	5,138	5,693	6,050	5,458	3,623	1,628	2,117	2,409	1,931	936	1,731	1,785	1,789	1,782	1,074	1,780	1,792	1,852	1,745	1,612
1992–93	7,989	8,942	5,643	5,379	6,020	6,442	5,740	3,779	1,782	2,349	2,604	2,192	1,025	1,756	1,816	1,856	1,787	1,106	1,841	1,854	1,982	1,761	1,668
1993–94	8,245	9,216	5,785	5,694	6,365	6,710	6,146	3,996	1,942	2,537	2,820	2,360	1,125	1,873	1,934	1,897	1,958	1,190	1,880	1,895	1,993	1,828	1,681
1994–95	8,396	9,388	5,823	5,965	6,670	7,077	6,409	4,137	2,057	2,681	2,977	2,499	1,192	1,959	2,023	1,992	2,044	1,232	1,949	1,967	2,108	1,866	1,712
1995–96	8,572	9,611	5,778	6,256	7,014	7,448	6,730	4,217	2,179	2,848	3,151	2,660	1,239	2,057	2,121	2,104	2,133	1,297	2,020	2,045	2,192	1,937	1,681
1996–97	8,699	9,771	5,867	6,530	7,334	7,792	7,035	4,404	2,271	2,987	3,323	2,778	1,276	2,148	2,214	2,187	2,232	1,339	2,111	2,133	2,282	2,025	1,789
1997–98	8,918	10,044	5,902	6,813	7,673	8,210	7,318	4,509	2,360	3,110	3,486	2,877	1,314	2,225	2,301	2,285	2,312	1,401	2,228	2,263	2,438	2,130	1,795
1998–99	9,144	10,328	5,924	7,107	8,027	8,625	7,631	4,604	2,430	3,229	3,640	2,974	1,327	2,330	2,409	2,408	2,410	1,450	2,347	2,389	2,576	2,247	1,828
1999–2000	9,141	10,347	5,902	7,310	8,275	8,912	7,852	4,720	2,506	3,349	3,768	3,091	1,338	2,440	2,519	2,516	2,521	1,549	2,364	2,406	2,628	2,239	1,834
2000–01	9,172	10,463	5,851	7,586	8,653	9,321	8,218	4,889	2,562	3,501	3,979	3,208	1,333	2,569	2,654	2,657	2,652	1,600	2,455	2,499	2,686	2,358	1,906
2001–02	9,530	10,926	6,104	8,022	9,196	9,948	8,715	5,137	2,700	3,735	4,273	3,409	1,380	2,723	2,816	2,838	2,801	1,722	2,598	2,645	2,837	2,504	2,036
2002–03	9,883	11,378	6,512	8,502	9,787	10,604	9,280	5,601	2,903	4,046	4,686	3,668	1,483	2,930	3,029	3,023	3,032	1,954	2,669	2,712	2,895	2,580	2,164
2003–04	10,519	12,143	6,839	9,247	10,674	11,679	10,063	6,012	3,319	4,587	5,363	4,141	1,702	3,106	3,212	3,232	3,199	2,089	2,822	2,875	3,084	2,724	2,221
2004–05	10,894	12,618	7,041	9,864	11,426	12,588	10,734	6,375	3,629	5,027	5,939	4,512	1,849	3,304	3,418	3,427	3,413	2,174	2,931	2,981	3,222	2,809	2,353
2005–06	11,122	12,882	6,906	10,454	12,108	13,424	11,335	6,492	3,874	5,351	6,399	4,765	1,935	3,545	3,664	3,654	3,672	2,251	3,035	3,093	3,372	2,899	2,306
2006–07	11,458	13,272	7,067	11,049	12,797	14,215	11,983	6,815	4,102	5,666	6,842	5,020	2,018	3,757	3,878	3,875	3,881	2,407	3,191	3,253	3,498	3,083	2,390
2007–08	11,573	13,429	6,975	11,573	13,429	14,921	12,590	6,975	4,291	5,943	7,173	5,285	2,061	3,952	4,082	4,079	4,083	2,506	3,331	3,404	3,668	3,221	2,409
2008–09[3]	12,113	14,060	7,463	12,283	14,256	15,875	13,343	7,567	4,544	6,319	7,630	5,618	2,137	4,185	4,322	4,335	4,313	2,654	3,554	3,616	3,911	3,412	2,777
Private institutions																							
1964–65	12,926	—	9,862	1,907	—	2,202	1,810	1,455	1,088	—	1,297	1,023	702	331	—	390	308	289	488	—	515	479	464
1965–66	13,303	—	10,330	2,005	—	2,316	1,899	1,557	1,154	—	1,369	1,086	768	356	—	418	330	316	495	—	529	483	473
1966–67	13,660	—	10,798	2,124	—	2,456	2,007	1,679	1,233	—	1,456	1,162	845	385	—	452	355	347	506	—	548	490	487
1967–68	13,726	—	10,969	2,205	—	2,545	2,104	1,762	1,297	—	1,534	1,237	892	392	—	455	366	366	516	—	556	501	504
1968–69	13,776	—	11,135	2,321	—	2,673	2,237	1,876	1,383	—	1,638	1,335	956	404	—	463	382	391	534	—	572	520	529
1969–70	14,179	—	11,169	2,530	—	2,920	2,420	1,993	1,533	—	1,809	1,468	1,034	436	—	503	409	413	561	—	608	543	546
1970–71	14,591	—	11,207	2,738	—	3,163	2,599	2,103	1,684	—	1,980	1,603	1,109	468	—	542	434	434	586	—	641	562	560
1971–72	15,007	—	11,246	2,917	—	3,375	2,748	2,186	1,820	—	2,133	1,721	1,172	494	—	576	454	449	603	—	666	573	565
1972–73	15,024	—	11,241	3,038	—	3,512	2,934	2,273	1,898	—	2,226	1,846	1,221	524	—	622	490	457	616	—	664	598	595
1973–74	14,366	—	10,943	3,164	—	3,717	3,040	2,410	1,989	—	2,375	1,925	1,303	533	—	622	502	483	642	—	720	613	624
1974–75	13,910	—	10,591	3,403	—	4,076	3,156	2,591	2,117	—	2,614	1,954	1,367	586	—	691	536	564	700	—	771	666	660
1975–76	13,983	—	10,349	3,663	—	4,467	3,385	2,711	2,272	—	2,881	2,084	1,427	636	—	753	583	572	755	—	833	718	712
1976–77	14,089	14,345	10,716	3,906	3,977	4,715	3,714	2,971	2,467	2,534	3,051	2,351	1,592	649	651	783	604	607	790	791	882	759	772
1977–78	14,055	14,332	10,640	4,158	4,240	5,033	3,967	3,148	2,624	2,700	3,240	2,520	1,706	698	702	850	648	631	836	838	943	800	811
1978–79	13,951	14,246	10,475	4,514	4,609	5,403	4,327	3,389	2,867	2,958	3,487	2,771	1,831	758	761	916	704	700	889	890	1,000	851	858
1979–80	13,396	13,669	10,230	4,912	5,013	5,891	4,700	3,751	3,130	3,225	3,811	3,020	2,062	827	831	1,001	768	766	955	957	1,078	912	923

See notes at end of table.

Average undergraduate tuition and fees and room and board rates charged for full-time students in degree-granting institutions, by type and control of institution: 1964–65 through 2008–09—Continued

Year and control of institution	Total tuition, room, and board (Constant 2007–08 dollars)			Total tuition, room, and board (Current dollars)					Tuition and required fees (in-state for public institutions)					Dormitory rooms					Board (7-day basis)[1]				
	All institutions	All 4-year	2-year	All institutions	All 4-year	Universities	Other 4-year	2-year	All institutions	All 4-year	Universities	Other 4-year	2-year	All institutions	All 4-year	Universities	Other 4-year	2-year	All institutions	All 4-year	Universities	Other 4-year	2-year
1	2	3	4	5	6	7	8	9	10	11	12	13	14	15	16	17	18	19	20	21	22	23	24
1980–81	13,368	13,670	10,516	5,470	5,594	6,569	5,249	4,303	3,498	3,617	4,275	3,390	2,413	918	921	1,086	859	871	1,054	1,056	1,209	1,000	1,019
1981–82	13,870	14,239	10,677	6,166	6,330	7,443	5,947	4,746	3,953	4,113	4,887	3,853	2,605	1,038	1,039	1,229	970	1,022	1,175	1,178	1,327	1,124	1,119
1982–83	14,926	15,370	11,570	6,920	7,126	8,536	6,646	5,364	4,439	4,639	5,583	4,329	3,008	1,181	1,181	1,453	1,083	1,177	1,300	1,306	1,501	1,234	1,179
1983–84	15,617	16,139	11,587	7,508	7,759	9,308	7,244	5,571	4,851	5,093	6,217	4,726	3,099	1,278	1,279	1,531	1,191	1,253	1,380	1,387	1,559	1,327	1,219
1984–85	16,417	16,915	12,417	8,202	8,451	10,243	7,849	6,203	5,315	5,556	6,843	5,135	3,485	1,426	1,426	1,753	1,309	1,424	1,462	1,469	1,647	1,405	1,294
1985–86[2]	17,285	17,953	12,669	8,885	9,228	11,034	8,551	6,512	5,789	6,121	7,374	5,641	3,672	1,553	1,557	1,940	1,424	1,500	1,542	1,551	1,720	1,490	1,340
1986–87	18,416	19,107	12,150	9,676	10,039	12,278	9,276	6,384	6,316	6,658	8,118	6,171	3,684	1,658	1,673	2,097	1,518	1,266	1,702	1,708	2,063	1,587	1,434
1987–88	19,210	19,480	12,935	10,512	10,659	13,075	9,854	7,078	6,988	7,116	8,771	6,574	4,161	1,748	1,760	2,244	1,593	1,380	1,775	1,783	2,060	1,687	1,537
1988–89	19,546	20,043	13,917	11,189	11,474	14,073	10,620	7,967	7,461	7,722	9,451	7,172	4,817	1,849	1,863	2,353	1,686	1,540	1,880	1,889	2,269	1,762	1,609
1989–90	20,038	20,481	14,456	12,018	12,284	15,098	11,374	8,670	8,147	8,396	10,348	7,778	5,196	1,923	1,935	2,411	1,774	1,663	1,948	1,953	2,339	1,823	1,811
1990–91	20,408	20,926	14,705	12,910	13,237	16,503	12,220	9,302	8,772	9,083	11,379	8,389	5,570	2,063	2,077	2,654	1,889	1,744	2,074	2,077	2,470	1,943	1,989
1991–92	21,280	21,839	14,755	13,892	14,258	17,572	13,201	9,632	9,419	9,759	12,037	9,060	5,754	2,221	2,241	2,825	2,042	1,788	2,252	2,257	2,709	2,098	2,090
1992–93	21,736	22,294	14,710	14,634	15,009	18,898	13,882	9,903	9,942	10,294	13,055	9,533	6,059	2,348	2,362	3,018	2,151	1,970	2,344	2,354	2,825	2,197	1,875
1993–94	22,435	23,026	15,067	15,496	15,904	20,097	14,640	10,406	10,572	10,952	13,874	10,100	6,370	2,490	2,506	3,277	2,261	2,067	2,434	2,445	2,946	2,278	1,970
1994–95	22,811	23,368	15,723	16,207	16,602	21,041	15,363	11,170	11,111	11,481	14,537	10,653	6,914	2,587	2,601	3,469	2,347	2,233	2,509	2,520	3,035	2,362	2,023
1995–96	23,580	24,132	15,845	17,208	17,612	22,502	16,198	11,563	11,864	12,243	15,605	11,297	7,094	2,738	2,751	3,680	2,473	2,371	2,606	2,617	3,218	2,429	2,098
1996–97	24,032	24,569	15,926	18,039	18,442	23,520	16,994	11,954	12,498	12,881	16,552	11,871	7,236	2,878	2,889	3,826	2,602	2,537	2,663	2,672	3,142	2,520	2,181
1997–98	24,236	24,960	16,913	18,516	19,070	24,116	17,717	12,921	12,801	13,344	17,229	12,338	7,464	2,954	2,964	3,756	2,731	2,672	2,762	2,761	3,132	2,648	2,785
1998–99	24,919	25,641	17,137	19,368	19,929	25,443	18,430	13,319	13,428	13,973	18,340	12,815	7,854	3,075	3,091	3,914	2,850	2,581	2,865	2,865	3,188	2,765	2,884
1999–2000	25,243	25,893	17,463	20,186	20,706	26,534	19,127	13,965	14,081	14,588	19,307	13,361	8,235	3,224	3,237	4,070	2,976	2,808	2,882	2,881	3,157	2,790	2,922
2000–01	25,836	26,426	17,880	21,368	21,856	27,676	20,247	14,788	15,000	15,470	20,106	14,233	9,067	3,374	3,392	4,270	3,121	2,722	2,993	2,993	3,300	2,893	3,000
2001–02	26,628	27,202	18,801	22,413	22,896	29,115	21,220	15,825	15,742	16,211	21,176	14,923	10,076	3,567	3,576	4,478	3,301	3,116	3,104	3,109	3,462	2,996	2,633
2002–03	27,133	27,653	20,638	23,340	23,787	31,043	21,965	17,753	16,383	16,826	22,716	15,416	10,651	3,752	3,764	4,724	3,478	3,116	3,206	3,197	3,602	3,071	3,870
2003–04	28,012	28,520	22,250	24,624	25,099	32,886	23,153	19,558	17,315	17,763	24,128	16,284	11,545	3,945	3,952	4,979	3,647	3,581	3,364	3,354	3,778	3,222	4,432
2004–05	28,505	28,998	22,190	25,810	26,257	34,761	24,274	20,093	18,154	18,604	25,643	17,050	12,122	4,171	4,170	5,263	3,854	4,243	3,485	3,483	3,855	3,370	3,728
2005–06	28,607	29,061	22,522	26,889	27,317	36,510	25,282	21,170	18,862	19,292	26,954	17,702	12,450	4,380	4,386	5,517	4,063	3,994	3,647	3,639	4,039	3,517	4,726
2006–07	29,493	29,990	21,035	28,439	28,919	38,437	26,823	20,284	20,048	20,517	28,580	18,848	12,708	4,606	4,613	5,691	4,302	4,147	3,785	3,788	4,166	3,672	3,429
2007–08	30,258	30,778	21,685	30,258	30,778	40,634	28,531	21,685	21,462	21,979	30,251	20,190	13,126	4,804	4,808	6,006	4,466	4,484	3,992	3,991	4,376	3,875	4,074
Not-for-profit	31,921	32,050	18,857	31,921	32,050	40,634	29,679	18,857	23,201	23,328	30,251	21,451	11,789	4,725	4,730	6,006	4,347	3,796	3,994	3,991	4,376	3,880	3,272
For profit	25,115	25,665	23,522	25,115	25,665	†	25,665	23,522	14,778	15,226	†	15,226	13,363	6,445	6,781	†	6,781	4,901	3,892	3,658	†	3,658	5,258
2008–09[3]	30,803	31,267	22,429	31,233	31,704	42,841	29,344	22,742	21,982	22,449	31,969	20,720	13,632	5,034	5,041	6,254	4,697	4,519	4,216	4,214	4,617	4,091	4,591
Not-for-profit	33,270	33,398	19,991	33,734	33,864	42,841	31,394	20,270	24,557	24,692	31,969	22,720	12,424	4,953	4,958	6,254	4,570	3,983	4,224	4,214	4,617	4,103	3,863
For profit	24,667	24,916	24,016	25,011	25,264	†	25,264	24,352	14,472	14,603	†	14,603	13,853	6,667	7,073	†	7,073	4,810	3,872	3,587	†	3,587	5,689

—Not available.

†Not applicable.

[1]Data for 1986–87 and later years reflect a basis of 20 meals per week rather than meals 7 days per week. Because of this revision in data collection and tabulation procedures, data are not entirely comparable with figures for previous years. In particular, data on board rates are somewhat higher than in earlier years because they reflect the basis of 20 meals per week rather than meals served 7 days per week. Since many institutions serve fewer than 3 meals each day, the 1986–87 and later data reflect a more accurate accounting of total board costs.

[2]Room and board data are estimated.

[3]Preliminary data based on fall 2007 enrollment weights.

NOTE: Data are for the entire academic year and are average total charges for full-time attendance. Tuition and fees were weighted by the number of full-time-equivalent undergraduates, but were not adjusted to reflect student residency. Room and board were based on full-time students. Data through 1995–96 are for institutions of higher education, while later data are for degree-granting institutions. Degree-granting institutions grant associate's or higher degrees and participate in Title IV federal financial aid programs. The degree-granting classification is very similar to the earlier higher education classification, but it includes more 2-year colleges and excludes a few higher education institutions that did not grant degrees. (See Appendix A: Guide to Sources for details.) Because of their low response rate, data for private 2-year colleges must be interpreted with caution. Some data have been revised from previously published figures. Detail may not sum to totals because of rounding.

SOURCE: U.S. Department of Education, National Center for Education Statistics, Higher Education General Information Survey (HEGIS), "Institutional Characteristics of Colleges and Universities" surveys, 1965–66 through 1985–86; "Fall Enrollment in Institutions of Higher Education" surveys, 1965 through 1985; and 1986–87 through 2008–09 Integrated Postsecondary Education Data System, "Fall Enrollment Survey" (IPEDS-EF:86–99), "Institutional Characteristics Survey" (IPEDS-C:86–99), Spring 2001 through Spring 2008, and Fall 2000 through Fall 2008. (This table was prepared August 2009.)

Average undergraduate tuition and fees and room and board rates charged for full-time students in degree-granting institutions, by type and control of institution and state or jurisdiction: 2007–08 and 2008–09

[In current dollars]

State or jurisdiction	Public 4-year						Private 4-year						Public 2-year, tuition and required fees (in-state)	
	2007–08		2008–09[1]				2007–08		2008–09[1]				2007–08	2008–09[1]
	Total	Tuition and required fees (in-state)	Total	Tuition and required fees (in-state)	Room	Board	Total	Tuition and required fees	Total	Tuition and required fees	Room	Board		
1	2	3	4	5	6	7	8	9	10	11	12	13	14	15
United States	$13,429	$5,943	$14,256	$6,319	$4,322	$3,616	$30,778	$21,979	$31,704	$22,449	$5,041	$4,214	$2,061	$2,137
Alabama....................	11,031	4,916	12,166	5,538	3,288	3,340	21,383	14,428	22,444	15,358	3,538	3,548	2,823	2,823
Alaska......................	11,725	4,747	12,970	5,008	4,367	3,595	26,380	18,401	28,837	19,517	4,284	5,036	2,920	3,119
Arizona....................	12,275	4,951	13,995	5,580	4,915	3,500	22,858	14,188	21,813	13,124	4,962	3,727	1,475	1,612
Arkansas..................	10,615	5,425	11,669	5,762	3,234	2,673	19,967	14,025	21,053	14,860	3,105	3,089	1,921	2,128
California..................	14,885	4,870	15,683	5,254	5,425	5,004	35,182	24,616	37,017	26,032	5,958	5,026	588	586
Colorado..................	13,342	5,262	14,240	5,683	4,352	4,205	30,126	19,587	29,331	19,293	5,698	4,340	2,077	2,197
Connecticut..............	16,253	7,459	17,364	7,891	5,075	4,399	40,209	29,321	42,268	30,911	6,295	5,063	2,829	2,982
Delaware..................	16,162	7,819	17,185	8,288	5,261	3,636	20,251	12,523	21,454	13,005	4,345	4,105	2,490	2,684
District of Columbia	†	3,140	†	3,140	†	†	35,592	24,826	37,554	26,152	7,424	3,978	†	†
Florida......................	10,698	2,967	11,506	3,309	4,592	3,605	27,996	19,645	28,185	19,325	4,809	4,051	1,864	2,099
Georgia....................	10,962	3,988	11,540	4,270	4,360	2,911	28,988	20,074	30,594	21,283	5,323	3,988	1,873	1,890
Hawaii......................	12,178	4,630	13,434	5,391	3,936	4,107	21,465	11,344	22,957	12,297	4,588	6,071	1,567	1,757
Idaho.......................	9,861	4,380	10,408	4,612	2,626	3,170	10,886	6,015	11,724	6,335	1,794	3,596	2,110	2,242
Illinois.....................	16,782	8,968	18,213	9,847	4,366	4,001	30,853	21,504	32,359	22,599	5,370	4,390	2,375	2,519
Indiana....................	14,084	6,590	14,973	6,923	3,898	4,152	29,639	22,101	31,310	23,350	4,021	3,938	2,819	2,930
Iowa........................	13,189	6,219	13,831	6,435	3,593	3,804	24,122	17,680	25,280	18,643	3,079	3,558	3,264	3,415
Kansas.....................	11,335	5,402	12,012	5,746	3,075	3,191	22,642	16,589	23,842	17,522	2,880	3,439	2,029	2,091
Kentucky..................	12,611	6,330	13,190	6,828	3,328	3,034	22,407	15,817	23,691	16,779	3,424	3,488	2,772	2,929
Louisiana.................	9,462	3,826	10,384	4,085	3,598	2,700	30,320	22,157	32,013	23,454	4,839	3,720	1,634	1,713
Maine.......................	14,818	7,275	16,112	8,018	4,028	4,066	32,495	23,651	34,784	25,059	4,672	5,053	3,287	3,272
Maryland..................	15,661	7,155	16,111	7,249	4,963	3,899	36,213	26,883	38,453	28,483	5,886	4,083	3,014	3,071
Massachusetts...........	16,167	7,928	17,112	8,201	5,212	3,699	41,396	30,408	43,522	32,086	6,453	4,984	3,070	3,255
Michigan..................	16,014	8,479	17,039	9,078	4,236	3,725	21,890	14,828	22,862	15,552	3,684	3,626	2,186	2,255
Minnesota................	14,173	7,696	15,105	8,292	3,474	3,338	30,076	22,595	31,706	23,860	4,101	3,745	4,532	4,614
Mississippi	10,794	4,764	11,047	4,942	3,419	2,686	18,372	12,659	19,358	13,276	2,942	3,140	1,725	1,770
Missouri...................	13,383	6,641	14,009	6,904	4,258	2,847	25,091	17,529	26,509	18,576	4,022	3,911	2,384	2,456
Montana...................	11,606	5,418	11,970	5,462	2,986	3,522	21,355	14,982	22,884	16,054	3,107	3,723	2,993	3,092
Nebraska..................	11,857	5,446	12,641	5,878	3,320	3,443	22,642	16,189	23,722	17,079	3,416	3,228	2,129	2,220
Nevada....................	12,152	3,034	12,869	3,348	5,469	4,052	25,764	15,025	25,897	15,998	5,583	4,316	1,763	1,920
New Hampshire	18,266	9,601	19,242	10,193	5,405	3,644	34,859	25,483	36,786	26,817	5,714	4,255	5,975	6,001
New Jersey...............	19,479	9,636	20,735	10,375	6,597	3,763	35,073	24,804	37,156	26,305	5,849	5,002	3,057	3,193
New Mexico..............	10,619	4,147	11,266	4,413	3,666	3,186	24,441	16,057	25,458	16,720	4,371	4,367	1,267	1,272
New York..................	14,143	5,060	14,865	5,103	5,818	3,943	36,394	26,044	38,488	27,527	6,486	4,475	3,422	3,525
North Carolina	10,894	4,300	11,333	4,373	3,848	3,112	29,143	21,492	30,963	22,904	4,185	3,874	1,376	1,404
North Dakota	11,137	5,757	11,418	5,780	2,479	3,159	14,804	10,108	15,614	10,666	2,159	2,790	3,599	4,104
Ohio........................	16,353	8,083	16,582	8,067	4,697	3,817	30,119	22,360	31,611	23,542	4,085	3,985	3,200	3,150
Oklahoma.................	10,607	4,470	12,333	5,011	3,441	3,881	22,898	16,221	24,762	17,420	3,612	3,730	2,360	2,531
Oregon.....................	13,852	5,926	15,179	6,286	4,611	4,282	31,765	23,906	33,763	25,254	4,435	4,074	2,893	2,937
Pennsylvania.............	17,218	9,608	18,124	10,132	4,557	3,435	35,939	26,559	37,964	28,057	5,395	4,512	3,185	3,308
Rhode Island	15,809	7,147	17,266	7,648	5,776	3,842	36,586	26,782	39,072	28,409	5,870	4,792	2,846	3,090
South Carolina..............	15,091	8,375	16,136	8,976	4,587	2,574	24,944	18,307	25,336	18,553	3,315	3,468	3,231	3,361
South Dakota..............	10,530	5,393	11,373	5,755	2,543	3,074	20,559	15,242	21,697	15,774	2,757	3,167	3,707	3,931
Tennessee................	11,343	5,361	12,026	5,680	3,431	2,915	25,810	18,510	27,364	19,659	4,122	3,583	2,631	2,778
Texas......................	12,337	5,535	13,222	6,030	3,778	3,414	27,241	19,735	29,228	21,124	4,423	3,681	1,430	1,471
Utah........................	9,685	4,025	10,352	4,262	2,579	3,510	12,817	6,144	13,482	6,598	3,400	3,484	2,439	2,553
Vermont...................	18,295	10,443	19,661	11,316	5,302	3,043	33,883	25,148	36,101	26,788	5,121	4,192	4,420	4,684
Virginia....................	13,926	6,890	14,868	7,448	4,084	3,336	25,684	18,551	27,280	19,673	3,937	3,669	2,486	2,666
Washington...............	13,512	5,378	14,165	5,704	4,188	4,273	31,408	23,442	33,455	24,955	4,489	4,010	2,768	2,850
West Virginia..............	11,425	4,383	12,131	4,703	3,935	3,493	21,950	15,221	19,859	12,625	3,463	3,770	2,704	2,790
Wisconsin.................	11,750	6,182	12,406	6,554	3,531	2,322	28,410	21,329	30,001	22,520	3,839	3,642	3,375	3,536
Wyoming..................	10,068	2,990	10,556	3,057	3,346	4,153	10,890	10,890	†	11,325	†	†	1,920	2,007

†Not applicable.

[1]Preliminary data based on fall 2007 enrollment weights.

NOTE: Data are for the entire academic year and are average charges. Tuition and fees were weighted by the number of full-time-equivalent undergraduates, but were not adjusted to reflect student residency. Room and board are based on full-time students. (See Appendix A: Guide to Sources for details.) Degree-granting institutions grant associate's or higher degrees and participate in Title IV federal financial aid programs. Some data have been revised from previously published figures. Detail may not sum to totals because of rounding. SOURCE: U.S. Department of Education, National Center for Education Statistics, 2007–08 and 2008–09 Integrated Postsecondary Education Data System (IPEDS), Fall 2007, Fall 2008, and Spring 2008. (This table was prepared August 2009.)

Undergraduate tuition and fees and room and board rates for full-time students in degree-granting institutions, by percentile of charges and control and type of institution: 2000–01 through 2008–09

[In current dollars]

Control and type of institution, and year	Tuition, room, and board					Tuition and required fees				
	10th percentile	25th percentile	Median (50th percentile)	75th percentile	90th percentile	10th percentile	25th percentile	Median (50th percentile)	75th percentile	90th percentile
1	2	3	4	5	6	7	8	9	10	11
All public institutions[1]										
2000–01	$5,701	$6,878	$8,279	$9,617	$11,384	$612	$1,480	$2,403	$3,444	$4,583
2001–02	6,153	7,342	8,602	10,136	12,207	468	1,539	2,529	3,648	4,815
2002–03	6,385	7,801	9,138	10,885	13,094	479	1,629	2,656	3,950	5,281
2003–04	6,909	8,522	10,029	12,085	14,440	900	1,800	2,913	4,464	6,149
2004–05	7,265	9,081	10,797	12,842	15,401	900	1,920	3,152	4,977	6,752
2005–06	7,700	9,623	11,348	13,543	16,264	990	2,070	3,329	5,322	6,972
2006–07	8,337	10,125	12,042	14,505	16,965	1,080	2,190	3,490	5,652	7,530
2007–08	8,827	10,890	12,690	15,446	17,979	1,144	2,245	3,666	5,988	7,969
2008–09[2]	9,379	11,534	13,616	16,283	18,866	1,144	2,377	3,988	6,394	8,488
Public 4-year[1]										
2000–01	6,503	7,347	8,468	9,816	11,611	2,118	2,516	3,314	4,094	5,085
2001–02	6,998	7,697	8,881	10,525	12,416	2,272	2,648	3,489	4,373	5,536
2002–03	7,325	8,121	9,446	11,250	13,408	2,356	2,929	3,784	4,780	6,259
2003–04	7,924	9,023	10,447	12,292	14,655	2,609	3,251	4,254	5,702	6,882
2004–05	8,380	9,574	11,022	13,031	15,622	2,880	3,582	4,665	6,081	7,542
2005–06	8,863	10,219	11,596	13,830	16,443	3,094	3,822	5,084	6,458	8,097
2006–07	9,461	10,797	12,272	14,748	17,160	3,206	4,074	5,376	6,825	8,667
2007–08	10,012	11,471	13,035	15,819	18,384	3,355	4,262	5,689	7,272	8,907
2008–09[2]	10,616	12,136	13,911	16,583	19,291	3,702	4,399	6,068	7,844	9,428
Public 2-year[1]										
2000–01	3,321	3,804	4,627	5,750	6,871	310	724	1,387	1,799	2,455
2001–02	3,613	4,078	4,921	6,187	7,060	308	768	1,440	1,888	2,534
2002–03	3,730	4,475	5,347	6,510	7,829	308	780	1,544	2,078	2,680
2003–04	3,874	4,725	5,562	6,983	8,360	478	1,024	1,700	2,325	2,844
2004–05	4,097	4,889	6,021	7,420	9,015	710	1,048	1,803	2,459	3,033
2005–06	4,380	4,822	6,234	7,567	8,993	691	1,109	1,920	2,589	3,100
2006–07	4,487	5,199	6,376	8,035	9,719	670	1,184	2,059	2,713	3,316
2007–08	4,637	5,361	6,777	8,138	10,471	590	1,200	2,091	2,819	3,384
2008–09[2]	4,900	5,633	6,935	8,823	11,183	590	1,200	2,208	2,930	3,480
All private institutions										
2000–01	13,514	17,530	22,398	27,280	32,659	7,520	10,716	14,880	18,795	24,336
2001–02	14,675	18,673	23,585	28,788	33,993	7,950	11,350	15,560	19,700	25,485
2002–03	15,400	19,657	24,885	30,453	35,753	8,210	11,356	16,078	20,702	26,646
2003–04	16,332	20,833	26,455	32,242	37,710	8,650	12,020	16,930	21,790	28,400
2004–05	17,144	21,746	27,872	34,342	39,565	9,184	12,750	17,590	22,712	29,786
2005–06	18,243	23,044	29,279	35,783	41,707	9,285	12,840	18,120	24,030	31,444
2006–07	19,102	24,350	31,009	38,448	43,770	10,200	14,010	19,125	25,414	33,210
2007–08	19,982	25,762	32,710	40,778	46,203	10,684	14,360	21,074	27,856	35,089
2008–09[2]	21,297	27,318	34,658	43,214	48,524	11,288	13,821	21,260	28,700	36,504
Not-for-profit[2]	21,668	27,438	34,849	43,246	48,524	12,030	18,415	24,954	31,576	37,125
For-profit[2]	17,150	17,150	25,834	29,959	32,742	11,176	12,570	12,840	16,356	19,350
Private 4-year										
2000–01	13,972	17,714	22,493	27,430	32,659	8,305	11,548	15,420	19,200	24,336
2001–02	14,740	18,790	23,645	28,907	34,064	8,700	12,150	16,200	20,200	25,533
2002–03	15,592	19,755	24,981	30,459	35,743	8,570	12,300	16,620	21,175	26,910
2003–04	16,364	20,833	26,536	32,242	37,710	9,082	12,660	17,524	22,420	28,440
2004–05	17,156	21,808	27,925	34,468	39,565	9,570	13,200	18,170	23,386	29,910
2005–06	18,350	23,238	29,294	35,912	41,707	9,675	12,956	18,900	24,366	31,452
2006–07	19,187	24,500	31,099	38,448	43,792	10,560	14,880	19,924	26,120	33,318
2007–08	20,005	25,876	32,768	40,778	46,203	11,066	15,600	21,500	28,630	35,187
2008–09[2]	21,454	27,368	34,658	43,232	48,524	11,700	14,248	22,014	29,300	36,504
Not-for-profit[2]	21,668	27,827	34,967	43,348	48,524	12,430	18,700	25,190	31,825	37,125
For-profit[2]	17,150	17,150	25,834	29,959	30,400	11,288	12,840	12,840	16,356	20,435
Private 2-year										
2000–01	6,650	6,850	13,220	16,400	21,845	5,013	6,887	8,329	11,064	13,995
2001–02	10,314	11,527	16,118	17,391	24,214	6,085	7,575	9,102	11,704	14,500
2002–03	11,293	12,189	16,919	21,374	29,777	6,353	7,995	9,600	12,280	15,260
2003–04	11,955	14,119	17,124	26,560	40,780	6,800	8,325	10,462	12,892	17,500
2004–05	13,807	15,486	19,844	27,276	34,385	7,008	8,813	10,629	13,548	18,025
2005–06	11,560	15,680	18,410	22,809	43,425	7,560	9,285	11,180	14,196	17,995
2006–07	8,685	16,568	19,115	26,677	40,130	7,980	9,688	11,600	14,833	18,710
2007–08	15,529	17,460	20,362	26,727	40,232	8,160	10,150	11,840	15,015	18,760
2008–09[2]	16,085	18,714	22,347	26,863	43,382	9,000	10,770	12,725	16,356	18,325
Not-for-profit[2]	16,085	17,568	19,860	24,878	39,463	3,740	8,760	11,791	15,207	18,440
For-profit[2]	21,442	23,327	26,863	43,382	43,382	9,334	11,000	12,790	16,356	18,325

[1]Average undergraduate tuition and fees are based on in-state students only.
[2]Preliminary data based on fall 2007 enrollment weights.
NOTE: Data are for the entire academic year and are average rates for full-time students. Student charges were weighted by the number of full-time-equivalent undergraduates, but were not adjusted to reflect student residency. The data have not been adjusted for changes in the purchasing power of the dollar. Degree-granting institutions grant associate's or higher degrees and participate in Title IV federal financial aid programs. Some data have been revised from previously published figures.
SOURCE: U.S. Department of Education, National Center for Education Statistics, 2000–01 through 2008–09 Integrated Postsecondary Education Data System (IPEDS), Fall 2000 through Fall 2008 and Spring 2001 through Spring 2008. (This table was prepared August 2009.)

Average graduate and first-professional tuition and required fees in degree-granting institutions, by first-professional field of study and control of institution: 1987–88 through 2008–09

| Year and control | Average full-time graduate tuition and required fees | | Average full-time first-professional tuition and required fees in current dollars | | | | | | | | | |
	Current dollars	Constant 2007–08 dollars	Chiropractic	Dentistry	Medicine	Optometry	Osteopathic medicine	Pharmacy	Podiatry	Veterinary medicine	Law	Theology
1	2	3	4	5	6	7	8	9	10	11	12	13
All institutions												
1987–88	$3,599	$6,577	$6,996	$9,399	$9,034	$7,926	$10,674	$5,201	$12,736	$4,503	$6,636	$3,572
1988–89	3,728	6,512	7,972	9,324	9,439	8,503	11,462	4,952	13,232	4,856	7,099	3,911
1989–90	4,135	6,894	8,315	10,515	10,597	9,469	11,888	5,890	14,611	5,470	8,059	4,079
1990–91	4,488	7,095	9,108	10,270	10,571	9,512	12,830	5,889	15,143	5,396	8,708	4,569
1991–92	5,116	7,837	10,226	12,049	11,646	9,610	13,004	6,731	16,257	6,367	9,469	4,876
1992–93	5,475	8,132	11,117	12,710	12,265	10,858	14,297	6,635	17,426	6,771	10,463	5,331
1993–94	5,973	8,648	11,503	14,403	13,074	10,385	15,038	7,960	17,621	7,159	11,552	5,253
1994–95	6,247	8,793	12,324	15,164	13,834	11,053	15,913	8,315	18,138	7,741	12,374	5,648
1995–96	6,741	9,237	12,507	15,647	14,860	11,544	16,785	8,602	18,434	8,208	13,278	5,991
1996–97	7,111	9,474	12,721	16,585	15,481	12,250	17,888	9,207	19,056	8,668	14,081	6,558
1997–98	7,246	9,484	13,144	17,695	16,310	12,679	18,668	9,744	19,355	9,013	14,992	6,832
1998–99	7,685	9,887	13,582	19,051	17,107	14,066	20,000	9,735	19,547	9,392	15,601	7,171
1999–2000	8,071	10,093	14,256	19,576	17,818	14,354	20,903	10,740	20,158	9,867	16,491	7,725
2000–01	8,429	10,192	15,093	22,097	19,151	15,448	21,784	11,273	20,455	10,365	17,795	7,868
2001–02	8,857	10,523	15,632	22,597	19,795	16,148	22,970	12,259	20,886	11,070	18,707	8,737
2002–03	9,226	10,725	16,758	24,517	21,206	16,439	24,379	13,597	21,633	12,142	19,810	9,485
2003–04	10,312	11,731	17,264	26,124	22,892	17,439	26,059	14,987	22,645	13,420	21,305	9,850
2004–05	11,004	12,153	18,535	28,455	24,293	18,048	27,900	15,951	23,631	14,535	22,935	10,412
2005–06	11,621	12,363	19,445	29,729	25,699	18,717	29,320	17,224	24,347	15,526	24,474	10,811
2006–07	12,312	12,768	21,473	32,004	27,086	19,886	30,604	18,634	25,594	16,551	26,042	11,628
2007–08	12,962	12,962	22,815	34,699	28,040	21,046	32,163	19,542	26,112	17,012	27,670	11,346
2008–09[1]	13,542	13,355	23,979	37,543	29,890	22,125	33,607	20,842	27,118	18,223	29,585	11,983
Public[2]												
1987–88	1,827	3,339	†	4,614	5,245	2,789	5,125	2,462	†	3,523	2,810	†
1988–89	1,913	3,342	†	5,286	5,669	3,455	6,269	2,218	†	3,889	2,766	†
1989–90	1,999	3,333	†	5,728	6,259	3,569	6,521	2,816	†	4,505	3,196	†
1990–91	2,206	3,487	†	5,927	6,437	3,821	7,188	2,697	†	4,840	3,430	†
1991–92	2,524	3,866	†	6,595	7,106	4,161	7,699	2,871	†	5,231	3,933	†
1992–93	2,791	4,146	†	7,006	7,867	5,106	8,404	2,987	†	5,553	4,261	†
1993–94	3,050	4,416	†	7,525	8,329	5,325	8,640	3,567	†	6,107	4,835	†
1994–95	3,250	4,575	†	8,125	8,812	5,643	8,954	3,793	†	6,571	5,307	†
1995–96	3,449	4,726	†	8,806	9,585	6,130	9,448	4,100	†	6,907	5,821	†
1996–97	3,607	4,805	†	9,434	10,057	6,561	9,932	4,884		7,343	6,565	†
1997–98	3,744	4,900	†	9,762	10,555	7,366	10,358	5,046	19,541	7,472	7,125	†
1998–99	3,897	5,013	†	10,259	11,141	7,890	10,858	5,476	19,818	7,707	7,510	†
1999–2000	4,043	5,056	†	10,795	11,610	7,922	11,377	5,997	19,578	8,271	7,824	†
2000–01	4,243	5,131	†	11,946	12,188	8,452	11,866	6,476	20,228	8,720	8,414	†
2001–02	4,496	5,341	†	13,092	13,186	9,619	12,708	7,187	21,254	9,375	9,115	†
2002–03	4,842	5,628	†	13,992	14,591	10,187	13,497	8,304	21,992	10,396	10,172	†
2003–04	5,544	6,307	†	15,613	16,500	11,537	14,994	9,424	22,638	11,763	11,838	†
2004–05	6,080	6,715	†	17,690	18,078	12,387	16,467	10,332	24,788	12,878	13,155	†
2005–06	6,493	6,908	†	19,177	19,473	13,229	17,653	11,444	24,808	13,849	14,544	†
2006–07	6,894	7,150	†	20,701	20,627	14,392	18,102	12,523	26,242	14,915	15,658	†
2007–08	7,415	7,415	†	22,037	21,206	15,489	19,310	13,490	27,322	15,838	16,962	†
2008–09[1]	7,914	7,805	†	24,787	22,959	16,285	20,898	14,476	28,942	17,070	18,461	†
Private												
1987–88	6,769	12,370	6,996	16,201	14,945	11,635	13,311	8,834	12,736	12,544	9,048	3,572
1988–89	6,945	12,132	7,972	16,127	15,610	12,050	13,536	9,692	13,232	13,285	9,892	3,911
1989–90	7,881	13,140	8,315	16,800	16,826	13,640	14,117	10,656	14,611	14,184	10,901	4,079
1990–91	8,507	13,448	9,108	18,270	17,899	13,767	15,009	11,546	15,143	14,159	12,247	4,569
1991–92	9,592	14,693	10,226	20,318	19,225	14,366	16,098	12,937	16,257	15,816	12,946	4,876
1992–93	10,008	14,866	11,117	21,309	19,585	14,459	17,098	13,373	17,426	17,103	13,975	5,331
1993–94	10,790	15,622	11,503	23,824	20,769	14,156	17,720	14,838	17,621	17,433	15,193	5,253
1994–95	11,338	15,959	12,324	24,641	21,819	14,497	18,422	14,894	18,138	17,940	16,201	5,648
1995–96	12,083	16,556	12,507	25,678	23,001	15,235	19,619	15,618	18,434	19,380	17,251	5,991
1996–97	12,537	16,702	12,721	26,618	24,242	15,949	20,714	15,934	19,056	19,526	18,276	6,558
1997–98	12,774	16,720	13,144	29,985	25,249	16,550	21,707	16,575	19,316	18,624	19,311	6,832
1998–99	13,299	17,110	13,582	31,917	26,495	17,848	22,867	16,874	19,492	19,617	20,253	7,171
1999–2000	13,782	17,234	14,256	32,268	27,702	18,317	23,791	18,220	20,259	20,128	21,393	7,725
2000–01	14,420	17,435	15,093	35,234	30,077	19,838	24,719	19,022	20,498	20,883	23,063	7,868
2001–02	15,165	18,017	15,632	36,184	30,438	20,374	25,909	20,325	20,825	21,772	24,019	8,737
2002–03	14,983	17,418	16,758	39,085	31,895	20,197	27,552	21,561	21,551	22,813	25,243	9,485
2003–04	16,209	18,440	17,264	40,414	32,913	20,955	29,095	23,022	22,647	23,941	26,746	9,850
2004–05	16,751	18,500	18,535	43,228	34,296	21,532	30,707	24,152	23,365	25,027	28,175	10,412
2005–06	17,244	18,345	19,445	45,633	35,895	22,162	32,349	25,439	24,240	26,191	29,782	10,811
2006–07	18,108	18,779	21,473	49,135	37,569	23,474	33,986	26,681	25,432	27,135	31,561	11,628
2007–08	19,208	19,208	22,815	51,803	39,280	24,503	35,299	27,884	25,928	23,558	33,481	11,346
2008–09[1]	19,430	19,162	23,979	54,774	41,289	25,757	36,708	29,618	26,842	24,646	35,622	11,983

†Not applicable.

[1]Preliminary graduate tuition average based on fall 2007 enrollment weights and first-professional tuition average based on 2007–08 degrees.

[2]Data are based on in-state tuition only.

NOTE: Average graduate student tuition weighted by fall full-time-equivalent graduate enrollment. Average first-professional tuition weighted by number of degrees conferred during the academic year. Some year-to-year fluctuations in tuition data may reflect nonreporting by individual institutions. Excludes institutions not reporting degrees conferred and institutions not reporting tuition. Data through 1995–96 are for institutions of higher education, while later data are for degree-granting institutions. Degree-granting institutions grant associate's or higher degrees and participate in Title IV federal financial aid programs. The degree-granting classification is very similar to the earlier higher education classification, but it includes more 2-year colleges and excludes a few higher education institutions that did not grant degrees. (See Appendix A: Guide to Sources for details.) Some data have been revised from previously published figures.

SOURCE: U.S. Department of Education, National Center for Education Statistics, 1987–88 through 2008–09 Integrated Postsecondary Education Data System, "Fall Enrollment Survey" (IPEDS-EF:87–99); "Completions Survey," (IPEDS-C:88–99); "Institutional Characteristics Survey" (IPEDS-IC:87–99); Fall 2000 through Fall 2008; and Spring 2001 through Spring 2008. (This table was prepared August 2009.)

Percentage of undergraduates receiving aid, by type and source of aid and selected student characteristics: 2007–08

Selected student characteristic	Number of undergraduates[1] (in thousands)	Any aid Total[2]	Any aid Federal	Any aid Nonfederal	Grants Total	Grants Federal	Grants Nonfederal	Loans Total	Loans Federal[3]	Loans Nonfederal	Work study Total[4]
1	2	3	4	5	6	7	8	9	10	11	12
All undergraduates	20,928 (0.4)	65.6 (1.20)	48.2 (0.85)	48.0 (0.77)	51.7 (0.96)	27.6 (0.47)	38.5 (0.72)	38.7 (0.24)	34.9 (0.18)	14.8 (0.21)	7.4 (0.20)
Sex											
Male	9,013 (126.0)	61.4 (1.38)	43.1 (0.98)	45.7 (1.01)	46.7 (1.16)	21.7 (0.59)	37.0 (0.95)	35.0 (0.45)	31.1 (0.38)	13.8 (0.26)	7.2 (0.31)
Female	11,915 (125.7)	68.8 (1.04)	52.0 (0.74)	49.7 (0.62)	55.5 (0.78)	32.0 (0.37)	39.5 (0.61)	41.5 (0.26)	37.8 (0.24)	15.5 (0.28)	7.6 (0.18)
Race/ethnicity											
White	12,924 (109.7)	63.5 (1.32)	44.4 (0.99)	47.8 (0.83)	48.2 (0.95)	20.7 (0.39)	38.5 (0.79)	38.5 (0.54)	34.6 (0.52)	15.0 (0.28)	7.3 (0.25)
Black	2,925 (59.1)	76.2 (1.56)	63.5 (1.57)	50.5 (0.93)	63.5 (1.31)	46.4 (1.19)	38.4 (0.84)	49.6 (1.05)	46.1 (1.02)	17.7 (0.62)	7.2 (0.35)
Hispanic	2,960 (93.0)	69.0 (0.76)	53.4 (0.72)	48.8 (0.85)	58.1 (0.99)	39.5 (0.63)	39.2 (0.93)	39.2 (1.09)	30.3 (1.15)	14.1 (0.44)	7.2 (0.33)
Asian	1,236 (38.0)	53.4 (1.96)	36.7 (1.21)	42.1 (1.71)	43.1 (1.54)	22.7 (0.96)	36.0 (1.37)	25.6 (0.89)	22.4 (0.90)	9.3 (0.57)	8.7 (0.56)
American Indian/Alaska Native	176 (18.7)	70.8 (2.92)	54.3 (3.17)	48.4 (3.06)	60.4 (3.12)	39.3 (3.51)	41.8 (2.74)	35.5 (3.34)	31.9 (3.49)	12.0 (2.09)	5.3 (1.12)
Native Hawaiian/Pacific Islander	151 (11.6)	61.5 (3.28)	42.4 (3.32)	44.5 (2.97)	49.3 (3.10)	26.6 (3.02)	36.3 (2.83)	35.5 (3.01)	27.9 (2.83)	12.3 (1.57)	7.7 (1.46)
Other	61 (5.2)	64.1 (4.03)	49.2 (3.84)	41.1 (4.13)	51.1 (3.96)	33.2 (3.10)	33.1 (3.88)	35.5 (4.02)	32.8 (3.88)	12.7 (2.37)	6.1 (1.60)
Two or more races	495 (25.9)	68.1 (1.51)	53.2 (1.46)	49.7 (1.58)	53.8 (1.43)	31.2 (1.31)	40.7 (1.31)	41.6 (1.55)	38.6 (1.60)	14.0 (0.98)	11.4 (1.02)
Age											
15 to 24 years old	12,490 (60.2)	66.9 (1.02)	49.3 (0.67)	51.4 (0.72)	52.5 (0.94)	25.0 (0.40)	42.7 (0.76)	40.4 (0.25)	36.3 (0.24)	15.6 (0.21)	10.4 (0.26)
24 to 29 years old	3,621 (37.1)	66.3 (1.60)	52.5 (1.10)	43.0 (1.12)	52.0 (1.10)	36.5 (0.72)	30.6 (0.93)	41.6 (0.61)	37.4 (0.49)	16.3 (0.53)	3.8 (0.23)
30 years old or over	4,817 (52.5)	61.8 (1.55)	42.1 (1.35)	42.7 (0.95)	49.4 (1.16)	27.4 (0.77)	33.4 (0.84)	32.3 (0.55)	29.5 (0.50)	11.7 (0.42)	2.3 (0.18)
Marital status											
Not married[5]	16,761 (59.2)	66.4 (1.28)	49.6 (0.89)	49.2 (0.84)	52.7 (1.05)	28.1 (0.51)	39.8 (0.77)	40.2 (0.32)	36.2 (0.26)	15.4 (0.25)	8.6 (0.23)
Married	3,763 (58.7)	60.8 (1.01)	40.4 (0.96)	42.3 (0.71)	45.7 (0.80)	22.0 (0.54)	33.1 (0.78)	31.0 (0.50)	28.2 (0.51)	11.7 (0.39)	2.6 (0.20)
Separated	404 (13.1)	77.1 (2.32)	64.8 (1.94)	47.8 (2.75)	67.9 (2.69)	55.3 (1.97)	32.9 (2.69)	48.9 (1.66)	45.3 (1.62)	18.0 (1.49)	3.2 (0.53)
Attendance status[6]											
Full-time, full-year	8,220 (59.4)	79.5 (0.37)	63.0 (0.32)	62.9 (0.43)	64.4 (0.38)	33.0 (0.38)	52.8 (0.52)	53.3 (0.42)	49.6 (0.42)	20.1 (0.29)	13.5 (0.29)
Part-time or part-year	12,708 (59.2)	56.6 (1.86)	38.6 (1.48)	38.3 (1.13)	43.5 (1.50)	24.0 (0.97)	29.2 (0.99)	29.3 (0.63)	25.5 (0.55)	11.4 (0.34)	3.5 (0.23)
Dependency status and family income											
Dependent	11,081 (65.7)	66.5 (1.06)	48.2 (0.71)	52.5 (0.78)	51.4 (0.94)	22.1 (0.37)	43.9 (0.81)	40.6 (0.33)	36.5 (0.31)	15.9 (0.23)	11.0 (0.29)
Less than $20,000	1,263 (22.5)	80.7 (1.13)	71.4 (0.82)	57.5 (1.13)	76.7 (1.25)	68.2 (0.84)	50.4 (1.23)	40.0 (1.01)	36.7 (0.98)	12.5 (0.55)	12.1 (0.59)
$20,000–$39,999	1,853 (23.2)	78.5 (1.07)	68.5 (0.78)	59.7 (0.88)	71.8 (1.10)	59.3 (0.76)	52.2 (0.98)	44.6 (0.81)	41.7 (0.89)	15.1 (0.46)	14.6 (0.51)
$40,000–$59,999	1,852 (26.1)	66.8 (1.69)	49.3 (1.31)	54.9 (1.29)	53.1 (1.41)	23.7 (0.94)	46.5 (1.21)	43.2 (0.81)	39.0 (0.71)	17.3 (0.58)	12.5 (0.53)
$60,000–$79,999	1,646 (28.8)	63.3 (1.27)	41.6 (0.99)	51.4 (1.15)	41.7 (1.17)	1.7 (0.18)	41.2 (1.19)	43.2 (0.91)	38.5 (0.92)	18.1 (0.61)	11.0 (0.71)
$80,000–$99,999	1,398 (23.8)	63.1 (0.98)	40.0 (0.78)	51.1 (1.01)	41.7 (1.02)	0.5 (0.14)	41.6 (1.02)	43.2 (0.76)	37.7 (0.76)	18.4 (0.62)	10.2 (0.60)
$100,000 or more	3,070 (42.8)	56.4 (1.06)	32.9 (0.80)	45.9 (0.81)	37.4 (0.81)	0.6 (0.08)	37.3 (0.80)	34.4 (0.71)	30.2 (0.77)	14.5 (0.36)	8.0 (0.31)
Independent	9,847 (65.6)	64.6 (1.42)	48.2 (1.08)	42.9 (0.87)	52.0 (1.06)	33.7 (0.63)	32.3 (0.76)	36.6 (0.35)	33.2 (0.28)	13.6 (0.34)	3.3 (0.16)
Less than $10,000	2,268 (31.4)	74.0 (1.25)	63.3 (0.70)	45.9 (1.04)	67.4 (1.08)	58.3 (0.59)	33.4 (0.97)	45.0 (0.80)	40.6 (0.93)	16.0 (0.59)	6.8 (0.33)
$10,000–$19,999	1,714 (30.2)	71.5 (1.74)	62.4 (1.24)	42.9 (1.28)	62.3 (1.50)	52.3 (1.09)	30.7 (1.04)	45.6 (0.78)	42.0 (0.77)	15.8 (0.66)	3.7 (0.30)
$20,000–$29,999	1,502 (27.4)	68.6 (2.17)	54.8 (1.85)	42.9 (1.60)	51.5 (1.89)	34.9 (1.31)	30.8 (1.22)	45.6 (0.89)	36.9 (0.93)	15.4 (0.76)	3.0 (0.37)
$30,000–$49,999	2,001 (34.5)	62.9 (1.74)	44.6 (1.63)	43.9 (1.17)	49.3 (1.27)	28.4 (1.08)	33.6 (1.10)	34.9 (0.89)	31.8 (0.80)	13.1 (0.65)	1.8 (0.22)
$50,000 or more	2,362 (40.8)	49.7 (1.07)	22.4 (1.02)	39.1 (0.76)	32.4 (0.79)	0.3 (0.09)	32.3 (0.79)	20.9 (0.75)	18.4 (0.75)	9.0 (0.44)	1.2 (0.18)
Housing status											
School-owned	2,964 (111.5)	80.1 (1.21)	70.1 (1.00)	60.7 (1.14)	66.6 (1.14)	23.5 (0.57)	62.3 (1.11)	57.9 (0.84)	53.7 (0.75)	22.0 (0.57)	22.5 (0.85)
Off-campus, not with parents	11,296 (219.5)	65.5 (1.53)	45.5 (1.31)	48.4 (0.91)	51.3 (1.19)	29.9 (0.77)	35.0 (0.78)	38.4 (0.51)	34.8 (0.47)	14.5 (0.33)	4.5 (0.21)
With parents	5,002 (143.6)	56.1 (1.66)	40.4 (1.14)	38.7 (1.19)	43.9 (1.67)	24.5 (0.95)	32.5 (1.26)	25.8 (0.45)	22.1 (0.40)	10.6 (0.30)	4.9 (0.26)

[1]Numbers of undergraduates may not equal figures reported in other tables, since these data are based on a sample survey of students who enrolled at any time during the school year. Includes all postsecondary institutions.
[2]Includes students who reported they were awarded aid, but did not specify the source or type of aid.
[3]Includes Parent Loans for Undergraduate Students (PLUS).
[4]Details on federal and nonfederal work-study participants are not available.
[5]Includes students who were single, divorced, or widowed.
[6]Full-time, full-year includes students enrolled full time for 9 or more months. Part-time or part-year includes students enrolled part time for 9 or more months and students enrolled less than 9 months either part time or full time.

NOTE: Excludes students whose attendance status was not reported. Detail may not sum to totals because of rounding and because some students receive multiple types of aid and aid from different sources. Data include undergraduates in degree-granting and non-degree-granting institutions. Data include Puerto Rico. Race categories exclude persons of Hispanic ethnicity. Standard errors appear in parentheses.
SOURCE: U.S. Department of Education, National Center for Education Statistics, 2007–08 National Postsecondary Student Aid Study (NPSAS:08). (This table was prepared August 2009.)

School boards revenue and expenditures

	2004	2005	2006	2007	2008
			$ thousands		
Total revenue	**39,494,601**	**41,742,462**	**45,465,066**	**45,964,481**	**48,226,782**
Own source revenue	10,645,706	11,145,911	11,355,924	11,940,556	12,149,440
Property and related taxes	8,605,737	8,852,678	8,992,363	9,465,488	9,653,893
Other taxes	681	705	721	768	770
Sales of goods and services	1,911,195	2,135,853	2,186,749	2,294,554	2,312,765
Interest income and investment income	91,300	105,785	130,669	133,315	134,986
Other revenue from own sources	36,793	50,890	45,422	46,431	47,026
Transfers	28,848,895	30,596,551	34,109,142	34,023,925	36,077,342
Federal government	109,462	136,480	106,643	110,669	113,545
Provincial government	28,555,159	30,264,440	33,819,289	33,724,229	35,771,485
Municipal government	184,274	195,631	183,210	189,027	192,312
Total expenditures	**39,398,230**	**42,979,682**	**47,199,448**	**47,712,377**	**48,751,414**
Education	38,683,838	42,251,024	46,446,081	46,918,561	47,967,632
Debt charges	714,392	728,658	753,367	793,816	783,782
Surplus or deficit	**96,371**	**-1,237,220**	**-1,734,382**	**-1,747,896**	**-524,632**

Note: Year ending December 31.
Source: Statistics Canada, CANSIM, table (for fee) 385-0009.
Last modified: 2009-08-31.

School boards revenue and expenditures, by province and territory
(Newfoundland and Labrador, Prince Edward Island, Nova Scotia, New Brunswick)

	2008[1]				
	Canada	N.L.	P.E.I.	N.S.	N.B.[2]
	$ thousands				
Total revenue	**48,226,782**	**670,928**	**191,836**	**1,142,155**	**0**
Own source revenue	**12,149,440**	5,763	1,003	72,276	0
Property and related taxes	**9,653,893**	..	0	0	0
Other taxes	**770**	0	0	0	0
Sales of goods and services	**2,312,765**	4,796	896	63,034	0
Investment income	**134,986**	568	..	3,527	0
Other revenue from own sources	**47,026**	399	107	5,715	0
Federal government	**113,545**	4,767	111	..	0
Education	**113,545**	4,767	111	..	0
Provincial and territorial governments	**35,771,485**	660,398	190,722	896,979	0
Education	**35,357,414**	660,398	190,722	896,979	0
Debt charges (interest)	**414,071**	0	..	..	0
Municipal governments	**192,312**	0	0	172,900	0
Education	**192,312**	0	0	172,900	0
Total expenditures	**48,751,414**	**753,066**	**192,084**	**1,135,675**	**0**
Education	**47,967,632**	751,974	192,084	1,135,521	0
Debt charges	**783,782**	1,092	..	154	0
Surplus or deficit	**-524,632**	**-82,138**	**-248**	**6,480**	**0**

.. : not available for a specific period of time.
1. Year ending December 31.
2. Schools boards of New Brunswick are administrated by provincial general government.
Source: Statistics Canada, CANSIM, table (for fee) 385-0009.
Last modified: 2010-03-08.

School boards revenue and expenditures, by province and territory
(Quebec, Ontario, Manitoba, Saskatchewan)

	2008[1]				
	Canada	Que.	Ont.	Man.	Sask.
	$ thousands				
Total revenue	48,226,782	10,562,826	20,303,106	1,755,103	2,004,870
Own source revenue	12,149,440	2,623,469	7,125,848	666,942	875,076
Property and related taxes	9,653,893	1,443,160	6,625,492	576,460	802,967
Other taxes	770	0	..	0	770
Sales of goods and services	2,312,765	1,180,309	421,817	84,728	59,729
Investment income	134,986	0	57,389	4,778	8,961
Other revenue from own sources	47,026	0	21,150	976	2,649
Federal government	113,545	20,113	76,609	2,370	334
Education	113,545	20,113	76,609	2,370	334
Provincial and territorial governments	35,771,485	7,903,826	13,100,649	1,085,791	1,129,460
Education	35,357,414	7,557,859	13,100,649	1,050,063	1,129,460
Debt charges (interest)	414,071	345,967	0	35,728	..
Municipal governments	192,312	15,418	0	..	0
Education	192,312	15,418	0	..	0
Total expenditures	48,751,414	10,711,065	21,115,440	1,854,208	1,725,630
Education	47,967,632	10,383,276	20,735,032	1,813,368	1,719,872
Debt charges	783,782	327,789	380,408	40,840	5,758
Surplus or deficit	-524,632	-148,239	-812,334	-99,105	279,240

.. : not available for a specific period of time.
1. Year ending December 31.
Source: Statistics Canada, CANSIM, table (for fee) 385-0009.
Last modified: 2010-03-08.

School boards revenue and expenditures, by province and territory
(Alberta, British Columbia, Yukon)

	2008[1]			
	Canada	Alta.	B.C.	Y.T.[2]
	$ thousands			
Total revenue	**48,226,782**	**6,421,226**	**5,120,235**	**0**
Own source revenue	12,149,440	509,379	258,804	0
Property and related taxes	9,653,893	197,412	..	0
Other taxes	770	0	0	0
Sales of goods and services	2,312,765	274,067	221,432	0
Investment income	134,986	31,251	28,145	0
Other revenue from own sources	47,026	6,649	9,227	0
Federal government	113,545	92	8,341	0
Education	113,545	92	8,341	0
Provincial and territorial governments	35,771,485	5,907,761	4,853,090	0
Education	35,357,414	5,875,385	4,853,090	0
Debt charges (interest)	414,071	32,376	..	0
Municipal governments	192,312	3,994	0	0
Education	192,312	3,994	0	0
Total expenditures	**48,751,414**	**5,848,342**	**5,367,071**	**0**
Education	47,967,632	5,820,864	5,366,808	0
Debt charges	783,782	27,478	263	0
Surplus or deficit	**-524,632**	**572,884**	**-246,836**	**0**

.. : not available for a specific period of time.
1. Year ending December 31.
2. Schools boards of Yukon are administrated by territorial general government.
Source: Statistics Canada, CANSIM, table (for fee) 385-0009.
Last modified: 2010-03-08.

School boards revenue and expenditures, by province and territory
(Northwest Territories, Nunavut)

	2008[1]		
	Canada	N.W.T.	Nvt.[2]
	$ thousands		
Total revenue	**48,226,782**	**54,497**	**0**
Own source revenue	12,149,440	10,880	0
Property and related taxes	9,653,893	8,402	0
Other taxes	770	0	0
Sales of goods and services	2,312,765	1,957	0
Investment income	134,986	367	0
Other revenue from own sources	47,026	154	0
Federal government	113,545	808	0
Education	113,545	808	0
Provincial and territorial governments	35,771,485	42,809	0
Education	35,357,414	42,809	0
Debt charges (interest)	414,071	0	0
Municipal governments	192,312	..	0
Education	192,312	..	0
Total expenditures	**48,751,414**	**48,833**	**0**
Education	47,967,632	48,833	0
Debt charges	783,782	425	0
Surplus or deficit	**-524,632**	**5,664**	**0**

.. : not available for a specific period of time.
1. Year ending December 31.
2. Schools boards of Nunavut are administrated by territorial general government.
Source: Statistics Canada, CANSIM, table (for fee) 385-0009.
Last modified: 2010-03-08.

Universities and colleges revenue and expenditures

	2005	2006	2007	2008	2009
			$ thousands		
Total revenue	**29,484,455**	**31,296,336**	**33,442,589**	**36,219,454**	**37,441,581**
Own source revenue	13,336,261	14,074,771	14,891,573	16,244,024	16,779,804
Sales of goods and services	10,520,144	10,958,828	11,473,607	12,429,235	12,897,731
Tuition fees	6,152,681	6,416,268	6,784,499	7,405,380	7,681,008
Other sales of goods and services	4,367,463	4,542,559	4,689,108	5,023,855	5,216,723
Investment income	645,905	818,219	971,183	1,078,078	1,100,739
Other own source revenue	2,170,212	2,297,724	2,446,782	2,736,711	2,781,334
Transfers from other levels of government	16,148,194	17,221,565	18,551,016	19,975,431	20,661,777
Transfers from federal government	2,678,489	2,907,421	2,967,236	3,297,089	3,366,952
Transfers from provincial governments	13,444,014	14,278,561	15,546,441	16,636,515	17,253,880
Transfers from local governments	25,691	35,583	37,339	41,827	40,945
Total expenditures	**29,609,613**	**31,055,528**	**33,016,662**	**35,686,476**	**36,966,708**
Education	28,976,903	30,383,330	32,337,751	34,946,384	36,193,420
Postsecondary education	28,699,579	30,093,079	32,027,595	34,600,485	35,836,590
Administration	5,377,969	5,673,367	6,578,901	7,318,420	7,422,256
Education	14,250,885	14,947,966	15,780,869	17,007,798	17,691,098
Support to students	1,031,730	1,100,234	1,191,590	1,335,982	1,359,762
Other postsecondary education expenses	8,038,995	8,371,513	8,476,235	8,938,284	9,363,476
Debt charges	606,483	643,871	650,094	709,514	740,786
Surplus or deficit	**-125,158**	**240,808**	**425,927**	**532,978**	**474,872**

Note: Fiscal year ending March 31.
Source: Statistics Canada, CANSIM, table (for fee) 385-0007.
Last modified: 2009-08-31.

Universities and colleges revenue and expenditures, by province and territory (Newfoundland and Labrador, Prince Edward Island, Nova Scotia, New Brunswick)

| | 2009 | | | | |
	Canada	N.L.	P.E.I.	N.S.	N.B.
			$ thousands		
Total revenue	**37,441,581**	**613,274**	**171,382**	**1,189,594**	**624,295**
Own source revenue	16,779,804	195,663	80,915	679,041	293,451
Sales of goods and services	12,897,731	163,696	70,370	564,103	225,675
Tuition fees	7,681,008	85,259	39,698	356,137	169,586
Other sales of goods and services	5,216,723	78,436	30,672	207,966	56,088
Investments income	1,100,739	4,418	2,446	36,355	22,070
Other own source revenue	2,781,334	27,549	8,099	78,582	45,707
Transfers from other levels of governments	20,661,777	417,611	90,467	510,553	330,843
Federal government	3,366,952	72,528	20,120	109,523	49,088
Provincial governments	17,253,880	344,239	70,347	400,998	281,686
Local governments	40,945	843	..	32	69
Total expenditures	**36,966,708**	**590,411**	**191,412**	**1,173,312**	**577,608**
Education	36,193,420	589,630	188,374	1,156,490	574,831
Postsecondary education	35,836,590	589,630	183,833	1,156,490	574,831
Administration	7,422,256	164,443	52,913	234,939	78,135
Education	17,691,098	286,365	93,287	582,055	305,626
Support to students	1,359,762	20,852	2,989	53,305	12,270
Other postsecondary education expenses	9,363,476	117,970	34,644	286,191	178,798
Debt charges	740,786	781	3,039	16,822	2,778
Surplus or deficit	**474,872**	**22,863**	**-20,030**	**16,282**	**46,686**

.. : not available for a specific period of time.
Note: Fiscal year ending March 31.
1. Excludes Yukon for confidentiality purposes.
Source: Statistics Canada, CANSIM, table (for fee) 385-0007.
Last modified: 2009-08-31.

607

Universities and colleges revenue and expenditures, by province and territory
(Quebec, Ontario, Manitoba, Saskatchewan)

	2009				
	Canada	Que.	Ont.	Man.	Sask.
	$ thousands				
Total revenue	**37,441,581**	**8,237,509**	**14,783,404**	**1,115,742**	**1,308,460**
Own source revenue	16,779,804	2,535,621	7,918,614	463,367	513,807
Sales of goods and services	12,897,731	1,770,622	6,109,985	326,889	394,249
Tuition fees	7,681,008	790,321	3,835,904	214,475	201,217
Other sales of goods and services	5,216,723	980,300	2,274,081	112,413	193,032
Investments income	1,100,739	154,111	517,883	26,079	51,301
Other own source revenue	2,781,334	610,888	1,290,747	110,398	68,257
Transfers from other levels of governments	20,661,777	5,701,889	6,864,789	652,375	794,653
Federal government	3,366,952	841,311	1,337,247	93,274	123,796
Provincial governments	17,253,880	4,857,944	5,514,424	559,088	670,349
Local governments	40,945	2,634	13,119	12	508
Total expenditures	**36,966,708**	**8,488,777**	**14,126,047**	**1,109,825**	**1,311,740**
Education	36,193,420	8,027,193	13,916,912	1,097,501	1,304,482
Postsecondary education	35,836,590	7,918,007	13,718,204	1,097,501	1,278,836
Administration	7,422,256	1,535,920	2,858,874	209,471	264,641
Education	17,691,098	4,211,403	6,422,107	580,352	670,553
Support to students	1,359,762	226,878	704,033	19,690	43,403
Other postsecondary education expenses	9,363,476	1,943,807	3,733,190	287,988	300,238
Debt charges	740,786	429,081	209,136	12,324	7,258
Surplus or deficit	**474,872**	**-251,267**	**657,356**	**5,916**	**-3,280**

Note: Fiscal year ending March 31.
1. Excludes Yukon for confidentiality purposes.
Source: Statistics Canada, CANSIM, table (for fee) 385-0007.
Last modified: 2009-08-31.

Universities and colleges revenue and expenditures, by province and territory
(Alberta, British Columbia, Northwest Territories, Nunavut)

	2009				
	Canada	Alta.	B.C.	N.W.T.	Nvt.
	$ thousands				
Total revenue	**37,441,581**	**4,238,497**	**5,015,373**	**85,913**	**27,235**
Own source revenue	16,779,804	1,777,632	2,251,125	48,443	10,598
Sales of goods and services	12,897,731	1,393,792	1,810,316	47,697	10,156
Tuition fees	7,681,008	806,121	1,170,681	2,262	8,676
Other sales of goods and services	5,216,723	587,672	639,634	45,435	1,479
Investments income	1,100,739	127,871	156,510	716	442
Other own source revenue	2,781,334	255,968	284,298	30	..
Transfers from other levels of governments	20,661,777	2,460,866	2,764,248	37,471	16,638
Federal government	3,366,952	314,110	403,723	2,230	..
Provincial governments	17,253,880	2,130,595	2,352,957	35,240	16,638
Local governments	40,945	16,161	7,567	..	..
Total expenditures	**36,966,708**	**4,063,626**	**5,194,474**	**81,719**	**27,471**
Education	36,193,420	4,048,669	5,149,955	81,627	27,471
Postsecondary education	35,836,590	4,030,803	5,149,955	81,627	27,471
Administration	7,422,256	1,086,297	913,658	11,517	5,440
Education	17,691,098	1,869,591	2,556,002	70,100	22,031
Support to students	1,359,762	132,342	143,179	10	..
Other postsecondary education expenses	9,363,476	942,575	1,537,116	..	..
Debt charges	740,786	14,956	44,518	92	..
Surplus or deficit	**474,872**	**174,872**	**-179,101**	**4,194**	**-236**

.. : not available for a specific period of time.
Note: Fiscal year ending March 31.
1. Excludes Yukon for confidentiality purposes.
Source: Statistics Canada, CANSIM, table (for fee) 385-0007.
Last modified: 2009-08-31.

Undergraduate tuition fees for full time Canadian students, by discipline, by province
(Canada)

	2006/2007 r	2007/2008	2008/2009	2009/2010	2010/2011
	average ($)				
Canada	**4,400**	**4,558**	**4,747**	**4,942**	**5,138**
Agriculture, Natural Resources and Conservation	3,869	4,064	4,366	4,697	4,791
Architecture and Related Services	3,839	3,999	4,503	4,826	5,140
Humanities	4,336	4,342	4,364	4,525	4,660
Business Management and Public Administration	4,195	4,637	4,978	5,191	5,422
Education	3,373	3,545	3,652	3,739	3,859
Engineering	4,943	5,099	5,319	5,577	5,881
Law	7,155	7,382	8,030	8,229	8,697
Medicine	9,659	10,029	9,821	9,815	10,244
Visual and Performing Arts & Comm. Technologies	3,991	4,239	4,377	4,592	4,768
Physical and Life Sciences and Technologies	4,270	4,534	4,679	4,885	5,041
Math., Computer and information Sciences	4,650	4,746	4,987	5,299	5,550
Social and Behavioural Sciences	4,041	4,165	4,251	4,431	4,590
Other Health, Parks, Recreation and Fitness	4,996	4,400	4,539	4,477	4,715
Dentistry	..	12,516	13,290	13,917	14,701
Nursing	..	4,267	4,422	4,558	4,679
Pharmacy	..	4,215	8,366	8,783	9,250
Veterinary medicine	..	4,296	4,422	5,358	5,611

r : revised.

.. : not available for a specific period of time.

Notes:

Using the most current enrolment data available, average tuition fees have been weighted by the number of students enrolled by institution and field of study.

Since the distribution of enrolment across the various programs varies from period to period, caution must be exercised in making long-term historical comparisons.

Revised data for 2006/2007 and for 2007/2008 resulting from the modifications to the questionnaire (implementation of the Classification of Instructional Programs (CIP) for both undergraduate and graduate programs) and the expansion of the survey universe.

For Nova Scotia and Quebec, both in- and out-of-province students are included in the weighted average calculations.

Source: Statistics Canada, Centre for Education Statistics.

Last modified: 2010-09-24.

University degrees, diplomas and certificates granted by sex, by province (Both sexes)

	2004	2005	2006	2007	2008
	Both sexes				
	number				
Canada	**211,902**	**216,240**	**227,085**	**242,787**	**244,380**
Newfoundland and Labrador	3,111	3,126	3,597	3,585	3,399
Prince Edward Island	672	750	792	798	831
Nova Scotia	9,576	9,522	10,110	10,455	9,738
New Brunswick	4,944	5,244	5,463	5,268	5,439
Quebec	61,212	62,973	62,832	63,684	64,407
Ontario	80,436	84,138	89,244	102,153	99,387
Manitoba	6,309	6,339	6,771	6,948	7,308
Saskatchewan	5,778	3,747	3,747	3,741	3,906
Alberta	18,705	18,015	19,185	19,917	18,510
British Columbia	21,159	22,386	25,350	26,238	31,455

Note: The reconciliation of data is not completed yet for University of Saskatchewan, 2008; for University of British Columbia, for years 2006 to 2008; for Nipissing University, 2008. The following institutions, previously colleges, have now the status of universities and are included in the 2008 counts for British Columbia. These are: Capilano University, Vancouver Island University, Emily Carr University of Art and Design, Kwantlen Polytechnic University and University of the Fraser Valley. Counts for qualifications awarded were revised from 2004 to 2007. Also, the graduates for the Institut de pastorale des Dominicains were removed for 2006 and 2007 data. Due to the revision of the institutions in the survey, the following are not included in the 2008/2009 data: in Ontario, Institut de pastorale des Dominicains, Tyndale University College and Seminary, Redeemer University College, Royal Military College of Canada; in Alberta, Newman Theological College; in British Columbia, Vancouver School of Theology, Trinity Western University, and Seminary of Christ the King. For University of Regina, qualifications awarded since 2005 are not available. The 2004 qualifications awarded for University of Alberta have been updated. For Quebec institutions, qualifications awarded do not include micro programs and attestations. The Classification of Instructional Programs (CIP) 2000 codes assigned to programs are under review for 2008 for all Quebec and Alberta institutions, as well as Thompson Rivers University, Capilano University, Vancouver Island University, Emily Carr University of Art and Design, Kwantlen Polytechnic University and University of the Fraser Valley. Field of study was updated for years 1999 to 2007 for some institutions.
Source: Statistics Canada, CANSIM, table (for fee) <u>477-0014</u>.
Last modified: 2010-07-14.

University degrees, diplomas and certificates granted by sex, by province (Males)

	2004	2005	2006	2007	2008
	Males				
	number				
Canada	**85,320**	**86,970**	**90,102**	**95,367**	**97,620**
Newfoundland and Labrador	1,143	1,116	1,329	1,356	1,284
Prince Edward Island	222	231	285	255	276
Nova Scotia	3,792	3,804	3,984	3,993	3,876
New Brunswick	1,947	2,007	2,025	1,953	2,079
Quebec	24,828	25,665	25,296	25,755	26,205
Ontario	32,574	33,864	35,391	39,285	39,447
Manitoba	2,412	2,409	2,505	2,721	2,826
Saskatchewan	2,193	1,500	1,500	1,491	1,563
Alberta	7,533	7,137	7,548	7,839	7,341
British Columbia	8,679	9,246	10,233	10,722	12,720

Note: The reconciliation of data is not completed yet for University of Saskatchewan, 2008; for University of British Columbia, for years 2006 to 2008; for Nipissing University, 2008. The following institutions, previously colleges, have now the status of universities and are included in the 2008 counts for British Columbia. These are: Capilano University, Vancouver Island University, Emily Carr University of Art and Design, Kwantlen Polytechnic University and University of the Fraser Valley. Counts for qualifications awarded were revised from 2004 to 2007. Also, the graduates for the Institut de pastorale des Dominicains were removed for 2006 and 2007 data. Due to the revision of the institutions in the survey, the following are not included in the 2008/2009 data: in Ontario, Institut de pastorale des Dominicains, Tyndale University College and Seminary, Redeemer University College, Royal Military College of Canada; in Alberta, Newman Theological College; in British Columbia, Vancouver School of Theology, Trinity Western University, and Seminary of Christ the King. For University of Regina, qualifications awarded since 2005 are not available. The 2004 qualifications awarded for University of Alberta have been updated. For Quebec institutions, qualifications awarded do not include micro programs and attestations. The Classification of Instructional Programs (CIP) 2000 codes assigned to programs are under review for 2008 for all Quebec and Alberta institutions, as well as Thompson Rivers University, Capilano University, Vancouver Island University, Emily Carr University of Art and Design, Kwantlen Polytechnic University and University of the Fraser Valley. Field of study was updated for years 1999 to 2007 for some institutions.
Source: Statistics Canada, CANSIM, table (for fee) 477-0014.
Last modified: 2010-07-14.

University degrees, diplomas and certificates granted by sex, by province (Females)

	2004	2005	2006	2007	2008
	Females				
	number				
Canada	**126,549**	**129,255**	**136,941**	**147,381**	**146,721**
Newfoundland and Labrador	1,962	2,004	2,259	2,226	2,112
Prince Edward Island	453	519	507	543	552
Nova Scotia	5,772	5,718	6,108	6,456	5,859
New Brunswick	3,000	3,240	3,441	3,312	3,357
Quebec	36,384	37,311	37,533	37,929	38,205
Ontario	47,862	50,274	53,853	62,871	59,940
Manitoba	3,897	3,930	4,266	4,227	4,479
Saskatchewan	3,585	2,244	2,244	2,247	2,343
Alberta	11,169	10,878	11,628	12,066	11,160
British Columbia	12,471	13,134	15,102	15,504	18,711

Note: The reconciliation of data is not completed yet for University of Saskatchewan, 2008; for University of British Columbia, for years 2006 to 2008; for Nipissing University, 2008. The following institutions, previously colleges, have now the status of universities and are included in the 2008 counts for British Columbia. These are: Capilano University, Vancouver Island University, Emily Carr University of Art and Design, Kwantlen Polytechnic University and University of the Fraser Valley. Counts for qualifications awarded were revised from 2004 to 2007. Also, the graduates for the Institut de pastorale des Dominicains were removed for 2006 and 2007 data. Due to the revision of the institutions in the survey, the following are not included in the 2008/2009 data: in Ontario, Institut de pastorale des Dominicains, Tyndale University College and Seminary, Redeemer University College, Royal Military College of Canada; in Alberta, Newman Theological College; in British Columbia, Vancouver School of Theology, Trinity Western University, and Seminary of Christ the King. For University of Regina, qualifications awarded since 2005 are not available. The 2004 qualifications awarded for University of Alberta have been updated. For Quebec institutions, qualifications awarded do not include micro programs and attestations. The Classification of Instructional Programs (CIP) 2000 codes assigned to programs are under review for 2008 for all Quebec and Alberta institutions, as well as Thompson Rivers University, Capilano University, Vancouver Island University, Emily Carr University of Art and Design, Kwantlen Polytechnic University and University of the Fraser Valley. Field of study was updated for years 1999 to 2007 for some institutions.
Source: Statistics Canada, CANSIM, table (for fee) <u>477-0014</u>.
Last modified: 2010-07-14.

University enrolments by program level and instructional program
(All programs)

	All programs				
	2004/2005	2005/2006	2006/2007	2007/2008	2008/2009
	number				
Total, instructional programs	**1,021,521**	**1,050,225**	**1,066,905**	**1,072,488**	**1,112,370**
Education	73,119	74,052	75,222	75,129	75,492
Visual and performing arts and communications technologies	37,041	37,443	37,830	37,800	41,859
Humanities	161,073	170,355	170,916	167,664	176,817
Social and behavioural sciences and law	176,919	182,010	187,770	189,996	191,016
Business, management and public administration	165,306	168,678	175,428	177,537	189,201
Physical and life sciences and technologies	88,188	90,441	92,328	93,372	94,113
Mathematics, computer and information sciences	40,983	36,636	34,242	32,724	33,219
Architecture, engineering and related technologies	86,520	85,533	86,313	88,470	91,890
Agriculture, natural resources and conservation	14,910	15,252	15,708	16,032	17,091
Health, parks, recreation and fitness	98,775	104,748	109,176	113,157	118,941
Personal, protective and transportation services	1,827	1,761	2,244	2,217	2,823
Other instructional programs	76,767	83,007	79,518	78,165	77,016

Note: The reconciliation of data is not completed yet for University of Saskatchewan for 2008/2009; for University of British Columbia, for years 2006/2007 to 2008/2009. The following institutions, previously colleges, have now the status of universities and are included in the 2008/2009 counts for British Columbia. These are: Capilano University, Vancouver Island University, Emily Carr University of Art and Design, Kwantlen Polytechnic University and University of the Fraser Valley. Enrolments counts were revised from 2004/2005 to 2007/2008. Also, the enrolments for the Institut de pastorale des Dominicains were removed from the 2006/2007 and 2007/2008 data. For University of Regina, enrolments since 2005/2006 are not available. Due to a revision of the institutions in the survey, the following are not included in the 2008/2009 data : in New Brunswick, Bethany Bible College; in Ontario, Institut de pastorale des Dominicains, Tyndale University College and Seminary, Redeemer University College, Royal Military College of Canada; in Alberta, Newman Theological College; in British Columbia, Regent College, Vancouver School of Theology, Trinity Western University, and Seminary of Christ the King. For University of Saskatchewan, the definition of full-time and part-time enrolments has changed: the registration status for enrolments in 2008/2009 refers to the September to December period. In the previous years, it referred to the September to April period. As well, their residency enrolments in the health-related programs are not included in the 2008/2009 counts. The Classification of Instructional Programs (CIP) 2000 codes assigned to programs are under review for 2008/2009 for all Quebec and Alberta institutions, as well as Thompson Rivers University, Capilano University, Vancouver Island University, Emily Carr University of Art and Design, Kwantlen Polytechnic University and University of the Fraser Valley. Field of study was updated for years 1999/2000 to 2007/2008 for some institutions.
Source: Statistics Canada, CANSIM, table (for fee) 477-0013.
Last modified: 2010-07-14.

University enrolments by program level and instructional program
(Bachelor's and other undergraduate degree)

	Bachelor's and other undergraduate degree				
	2004/2005	2005/2006	2006/2007	2007/2008	2008/2009
	number				
Total, instructional programs	**724,404**	**743,958**	**756,708**	**756,579**	**766,935**
Education	45,849	46,554	47,877	47,958	47,772
Visual and performing arts and communications technologies	31,044	31,824	32,157	32,154	34,293
Humanities	135,864	145,791	145,248	141,675	144,753
Social and behavioural sciences and law	146,046	148,353	152,622	151,323	149,817
Business, management and public administration	107,130	111,795	116,184	118,740	124,215
Physical and life sciences and technologies	70,230	72,165	73,299	73,509	73,749
Mathematics, computer and information sciences	30,993	26,982	24,366	23,061	23,073
Architecture, engineering and related technologies	64,545	63,660	64,095	65,337	66,540
Agriculture, natural resources and conservation	9,348	9,666	9,864	9,957	10,551
Health, parks, recreation and fitness	71,286	74,895	77,970	79,893	82,080
Personal, protective and transportation services	891	996	1,530	1,407	1,542
Other instructional programs	11,175	11,274	11,499	11,568	8,547

Note: The reconciliation of data is not completed yet for University of Saskatchewan for 2008/2009; for University of British Columbia, for years 2006/2007 to 2008/2009. The following institutions, previously colleges, have now the status of universities and are included in the 2008/2009 counts for British Columbia. These are: Capilano University, Vancouver Island University, Emily Carr University of Art and Design, Kwantlen Polytechnic University and University of the Fraser Valley. Enrolments counts were revised from 2004/2005 to 2007/2008. Also, the enrolments for the Institut de pastorale des Dominicains were removed from the 2006/2007 and 2007/2008 data. For University of Regina, enrolments since 2005/2006 are not available. Due to a revision of the institutions in the survey, the following are not included in the 2008/2009 data : in New Brunswick, Bethany Bible College; in Ontario, Institut de pastorale des Dominicains, Tyndale University College and Seminary, Redeemer University College, Royal Military College of Canada; in Alberta, Newman Theological College; in British Columbia, Regent College, Vancouver School of Theology, Trinity Western University, and Seminary of Christ the King. For University of Saskatchewan, the definition of full-time and part-time enrolments has changed: the registration status for enrolments in 2008/2009 refers to the September to December period. In the previous years, it referred to the September to April period. As well, their residency enrolments in the health-related programs are not included in the 2008/2009 counts. The Classification of Instructional Programs (CIP) 2000 codes assigned to programs are under review for 2008/2009 for all Quebec and Alberta institutions, as well as Thompson Rivers University, Capilano University, Vancouver Island University, Emily Carr University of Art and Design, Kwantlen Polytechnic University and University of the Fraser Valley. Field of study was updated for years 1999/2000 to 2007/2008 for some institutions.
Source: Statistics Canada, CANSIM, table (for fee) 477-0013.
Last modified: 2010-07-14.

University enrolments by program level and instructional program
(Master's degree)

	Master's degree				
	2004/2005	2005/2006	2006/2007	2007/2008	2008/2009
	number				
Total, instructional programs	**94,053**	**94,197**	**96,273**	**101,403**	**102,654**
Education	11,361	11,637	11,502	11,880	12,141
Visual and performing arts and communications technologies	2,169	2,304	2,538	2,709	2,817
Humanities	6,969	7,128	7,278	7,695	6,717
Social and behavioural sciences and law	12,471	12,489	13,458	14,304	14,004
Business, management and public administration	22,101	21,783	21,885	22,740	23,487
Physical and life sciences and technologies	8,565	8,505	8,775	9,309	9,381
Mathematics, computer and information sciences	5,439	5,202	5,103	4,938	4,800
Architecture, engineering and related technologies	13,026	12,492	12,318	12,879	13,407
Agriculture, natural resources and conservation	2,898	2,934	3,063	3,183	3,231
Health, parks, recreation and fitness	8,586	9,195	9,705	10,962	11,997
Personal, protective and transportation services	318	315	306	342	174
Other instructional programs	150	216	342	468	504

Note: The reconciliation of data is not completed yet for University of Saskatchewan for 2008/2009; for University of British Columbia, for years 2006/2007 to 2008/2009. The following institutions, previously colleges, have now the status of universities and are included in the 2008/2009 counts for British Columbia. These are: Capilano University, Vancouver Island University, Emily Carr University of Art and Design, Kwantlen Polytechnic University and University of the Fraser Valley. Enrolments counts were revised from 2004/2005 to 2007/2008. Also, the enrolments for the Institut de pastorale des Dominicains were removed from the 2006/2007 and 2007/2008 data. For University of Regina, enrolments since 2005/2006 are not available. Due to a revision of the institutions in the survey, the following are not included in the 2008/2009 data : in New Brunswick, Bethany Bible College; in Ontario, Institut de pastorale des Dominicains, Tyndale University College and Seminary, Redeemer University College, Royal Military College of Canada; in Alberta, Newman Theological College; in British Columbia, Regent College, Vancouver School of Theology, Trinity Western University, and Seminary of Christ the King. For University of Saskatchewan, the definition of full-time and part-time enrolments has changed: the registration status for enrolments in 2008/2009 refers to the September to December period. In the previous years, it referred to the September to April period. As well, their residency enrolments in the health-related programs are not included in the 2008/2009 counts. The Classification of Instructional Programs (CIP) 2000 codes assigned to programs are under review for 2008/2009 for all Quebec and Alberta institutions, as well as Thompson Rivers University, Capilano University, Vancouver Island University, Emily Carr University of Art and Design, Kwantlen Polytechnic University and University of the Fraser Valley. Field of study was updated for years 1999/2000 to 2007/2008 for some institutions.
Source: Statistics Canada, CANSIM, table (for fee) 477-0013.
Last modified: 2010-07-14.

University enrolments by program level and instructional program
(Earned doctorate)

	Earned doctorate				
	2004/2005	2005/2006	2006/2007	2007/2008	2008/2009
			number		
Total, instructional programs	**34,734**	**36,795**	**38,985**	**41,112**	**42,801**
Education	2,682	2,640	2,742	2,844	2,952
Visual and performing arts and communications technologies	627	729	792	921	969
Humanities	4,128	4,299	4,467	4,656	4,854
Social and behavioural sciences and law	6,996	7,323	7,785	8,409	8,739
Business, management and public administration	1,449	1,521	1,566	1,560	1,599
Physical and life sciences and technologies	7,602	8,100	8,694	8,925	9,204
Mathematics, computer and information sciences	2,154	2,352	2,526	2,646	2,727
Architecture, engineering and related technologies	5,487	5,958	6,396	6,711	7,026
Agriculture, natural resources and conservation	1,065	1,125	1,134	1,179	1,215
Health, parks, recreation and fitness	2,301	2,484	2,553	2,868	3,096
Personal, protective and transportation services	42	48	42	39	42
Other instructional programs	192	216	285	348	378

Note: The reconciliation of data is not completed yet for University of Saskatchewan for 2008/2009; for University of British Columbia, for years 2006/2007 to 2008/2009. The following institutions, previously colleges, have now the status of universities and are included in the 2008/2009 counts for British Columbia. These are: Capilano University, Vancouver Island University, Emily Carr University of Art and Design, Kwantlen Polytechnic University and University of the Fraser Valley. Enrolments counts were revised from 2004/2005 to 2007/2008. Also, the enrolments for the Institut de pastorale des Dominicains were removed from the 2006/2007 and 2007/2008 data. For University of Regina, enrolments since 2005/2006 are not available. Due to a revision of the institutions in the survey, the following are not included in the 2008/2009 data : in New Brunswick, Bethany Bible College; in Ontario, Institut de pastorale des Dominicains, Tyndale University College and Seminary, Redeemer University College, Royal Military College of Canada; in Alberta, Newman Theological College; in British Columbia, Regent College, Vancouver School of Theology, Trinity Western University, and Seminary of Christ the King. For University of Saskatchewan, the definition of full-time and part-time enrolments has changed: the registration status for enrolments in 2008/2009 refers to the September to December period. In the previous years, it referred to the September to April period. As well, their residency enrolments in the health-related programs are not included in the 2008/2009 counts. The Classification of Instructional Programs (CIP) 2000 codes assigned to programs are under review for 2008/2009 for all Quebec and Alberta institutions, as well as Thompson Rivers University, Capilano University, Vancouver Island University, Emily Carr University of Art and Design, Kwantlen Polytechnic University and University of the Fraser Valley. Field of study was updated for years 1999/2000 to 2007/2008 for some institutions.
Source: Statistics Canada, CANSIM, table (for fee) 477-0013.
Last modified: 2010-07-14.

University degrees, diplomas and certificates granted, by program level and instructional program
(All programs)

	All programs				
	2004	2005	2006	2007	2008
	number				
Total, instructional programs	**211,902**	**216,240**	**227,085**	**242,787**	**244,380**
Education	26,079	25,929	27,027	27,606	27,723
Visual and performing arts, and communications technologies	8,214	7,917	8,298	8,826	9,348
Humanities	23,643	24,303	25,479	27,381	26,199
Social and behavioural sciences, and law	40,965	42,087	45,714	50,730	50,169
Business, management and public administration	44,364	45,369	45,897	48,822	49,968
Physical and life sciences, and technologies	14,619	15,675	17,055	18,915	18,627
Mathematics, computer and information sciences	10,938	10,041	9,474	8,616	8,214
Architecture, engineering and related technologies	17,616	17,976	18,579	19,527	20,142
Agriculture, natural resources and conservation	3,690	3,369	3,693	3,954	4,059
Health, parks, recreation and fitness	20,169	21,876	23,916	26,253	26,841
Personal, protective and transportation services	360	327	474	492	882
Other instructional program	1,248	1,341	1,437	1,620	1,659

Note: The reconciliation of data is not completed yet for University of Saskatchewan, 2008; for University of British Columbia, for years 2006 to 2008; for Nipissing University, 2008. The following institutions, previously colleges, have now the status of universities and are included in the 2008 counts for British Columbia. These are: Capilano University, Vancouver Island University, Emily Carr University of Art and Design, Kwantlen Polytechnic University and University of the Fraser Valley. Counts for qualifications awarded were revised from 2004 to 2007. Also, the graduates for the Institut de pastorale des Dominicains were removed for 2006 and 2007 data. Due to the revision of the institutions in the survey, the following are not included in the 2008/2009 data: in Ontario, Institut de pastorale des Dominicains, Tyndale University College and Seminary, Redeemer University College, Royal Military College of Canada; in Alberta, Newman Theological College; in British Columbia, Vancouver School of Theology, Trinity Western University, and Seminary of Christ the King. For University of Regina, qualifications awarded since 2005 are not available. The 2004 qualifications awarded for University of Alberta have been updated. For Quebec institutions, qualifications awarded do not include micro programs and attestations. The Classification of Instructional Programs (CIP) 2000 codes assigned to programs are under review for 2008 for all Quebec and Alberta institutions, as well as Thompson Rivers University, Capilano University, Vancouver Island University, Emily Carr University of Art and Design, Kwantlen Polytechnic University and University of the Fraser Valley. Field of study was updated for years 1999 to 2007 for some institutions.
Source: Statistics Canada, CANSIM, table (for fee) 477-0014.
Last modified: 2010-07-14.

University degrees, diplomas and certificates granted, by program level and instructional program
(Bachelor's and other undergraduate degree)

	Bachelor's and other undergraduate degree				
	2004	**2005**	**2006**	**2007**	**2008**
	number				
Total, instructional programs	148,857	152,028	161,766	176,025	171,882
Education	18,639	18,414	19,206	19,653	19,875
Visual and performing arts, and communications technologies	6,552	6,231	6,645	7,107	7,272
Humanities	17,574	18,486	19,644	21,477	20,217
Social and behavioural sciences, and law	33,192	33,975	37,263	41,529	40,128
Business, management and public administration	23,685	24,633	25,776	28,740	28,554
Physical and life sciences, and technologies	11,046	12,054	13,131	14,922	14,421
Mathematics, computer and information sciences	7,839	7,014	6,531	5,808	5,367
Architecture, engineering and related technologies	11,778	11,670	12,216	13,122	13,011
Agriculture, natural resources and conservation	2,058	1,815	2,043	2,262	2,190
Health, parks, recreation and fitness	15,429	16,596	18,048	20,067	19,638
Personal, protective and transportation services	204	228	297	306	240
Other instructional program	864	912	972	1,038	978

Note: The reconciliation of data is not completed yet for University of Saskatchewan, 2008; for University of British Columbia, for years 2006 to 2008; for Nipissing University, 2008. The following institutions, previously colleges, have now the status of universities and are included in the 2008 counts for British Columbia. These are: Capilano University, Vancouver Island University, Emily Carr University of Art and Design, Kwantlen Polytechnic University and University of the Fraser Valley. Counts for qualifications awarded were revised from 2004 to 2007. Also, the graduates for the Institut de pastorale des Dominicains were removed for 2006 and 2007 data. Due to the revision of the institutions in the survey, the following are not included in the 2008/2009 data: in Ontario, Institut de pastorale des Dominicains, Tyndale University College and Seminary, Redeemer University College, Royal Military College of Canada; in Alberta, Newman Theological College; in British Columbia, Vancouver School of Theology, Trinity Western University, and Seminary of Christ the King. For University of Regina, qualifications awarded since 2005 are not available. The 2004 qualifications awarded for University of Alberta have been updated. For Quebec institutions, qualifications awarded do not include micro programs and attestations. The Classification of Instructional Programs (CIP) 2000 codes assigned to programs are under review for 2008 for all Quebec and Alberta institutions, as well as Thompson Rivers University, Capilano University, Vancouver Island University, Emily Carr University of Art and Design, Kwantlen Polytechnic University and University of the Fraser Valley. Field of study was updated for years 1999 to 2007 for some institutions.
Source: Statistics Canada, CANSIM, table (for fee) 477-0014.
Last modified: 2010-07-14.

University degrees, diplomas and certificates granted, by program level and instructional program
(Master's degree)

	Master's degree				
	2004	2005	2006	2007	2008
	number				
Total, instructional programs	32,751	33,012	34,152	34,971	36,423
Education	3,723	3,498	3,909	4,059	4,089
Visual and performing arts, and communications technologies	645	735	729	819	858
Humanities	2,511	2,247	2,388	2,397	2,652
Social and behavioural sciences, and law	3,972	4,281	4,467	4,623	4,863
Business, management and public administration	10,047	9,690	9,636	10,212	10,419
Physical and life sciences, and technologies	2,241	2,304	2,538	2,409	2,544
Mathematics, computer and information sciences	1,953	2,046	2,085	1,944	1,959
Architecture, engineering and related technologies	4,365	4,557	4,440	4,347	4,311
Agriculture, natural resources and conservation	831	855	855	906	1,050
Health, parks, recreation and fitness	2,388	2,763	3,018	3,168	3,528
Personal, protective and transportation services	45	9	24	15	9
Other instructional program	21	30	60	78	138

Note: The reconciliation of data is not completed yet for University of Saskatchewan, 2008; for University of British Columbia, for years 2006 to 2008; for Nipissing University, 2008. The following institutions, previously colleges, have now the status of universities and are included in the 2008 counts for British Columbia. These are: Capilano University, Vancouver Island University, Emily Carr University of Art and Design, Kwantlen Polytechnic University and University of the Fraser Valley. Counts for qualifications awarded were revised from 2004 to 2007. Also, the graduates for the Institut de pastorale des Dominicains were removed for 2006 and 2007 data. Due to the revision of the institutions in the survey, the following are not included in the 2008/2009 data: in Ontario, Institut de pastorale des Dominicains, Tyndale University College and Seminary, Redeemer University College, Royal Military College of Canada; in Alberta, Newman Theological College; in British Columbia, Vancouver School of Theology, Trinity Western University, and Seminary of Christ the King. For University of Regina, qualifications awarded since 2005 are not available. The 2004 qualifications awarded for University of Alberta have been updated. For Quebec institutions, qualifications awarded do not include micro programs and attestations. The Classification of Instructional Programs (CIP) 2000 codes assigned to programs are under review for 2008 for all Quebec and Alberta institutions, as well as Thompson Rivers University, Capilano University, Vancouver Island University, Emily Carr University of Art and Design, Kwantlen Polytechnic University and University of the Fraser Valley. Field of study was updated for years 1999 to 2007 for some institutions.
Source: Statistics Canada, CANSIM, table (for fee) 477-0014.
Last modified: 2010-07-14.

University degrees, diplomas and certificates granted, by program level and instructional program
(Earned doctorate)

	Earned doctorate				
	2004	2005	2006	2007	2008
	number				
Total, instructional programs	**4,251**	**4,191**	**4,446**	**5,010**	**5,421**
Education	348	372	351	339	357
Visual and performing arts, and communications technologies	54	66	78	90	87
Humanities	528	420	405	381	462
Social and behavioural sciences, and law	717	774	792	852	942
Business, management and public administration	147	129	165	174	183
Physical and life sciences, and technologies	1,137	1,098	1,161	1,386	1,431
Mathematics, computer and information sciences	225	228	252	309	357
Architecture, engineering and related technologies	636	639	732	897	1,017
Agriculture, natural resources and conservation	147	126	144	177	174
Health, parks, recreation and fitness	285	309	327	366	384
Personal, protective and transportation services	0	6	9	3	3
Other instructional program	27	24	27	36	33

Note: The reconciliation of data is not completed yet for University of Saskatchewan, 2008; for University of British Columbia, for years 2006 to 2008; for Nipissing University, 2008. The following institutions, previously colleges, have now the status of universities and are included in the 2008 counts for British Columbia. These are: Capilano University, Vancouver Island University, Emily Carr University of Art and Design, Kwantlen Polytechnic University and University of the Fraser Valley. Counts for qualifications awarded were revised from 2004 to 2007. Also, the graduates for the Institut de pastorale des Dominicains were removed for 2006 and 2007 data. Due to the revision of the institutions in the survey, the following are not included in the 2008/2009 data: in Ontario, Institut de pastorale des Dominicains, Tyndale University College and Seminary, Redeemer University College, Royal Military College of Canada; in Alberta, Newman Theological College; in British Columbia, Vancouver School of Theology, Trinity Western University, and Seminary of Christ the King. For University of Regina, qualifications awarded since 2005 are not available. The 2004 qualifications awarded for University of Alberta have been updated. For Quebec institutions, qualifications awarded do not include micro programs and attestations. The Classification of Instructional Programs (CIP) 2000 codes assigned to programs are under review for 2008 for all Quebec and Alberta institutions, as well as Thompson Rivers University, Capilano University, Vancouver Island University, Emily Carr University of Art and Design, Kwantlen Polytechnic University and University of the Fraser Valley. Field of study was updated for years 1999 to 2007 for some institutions.
Source: Statistics Canada, CANSIM, table (for fee) 477-0014.
Last modified: 2010-07-14.

Average weekly earnings (including overtime), educational and related services, by province and territory

	2005	2006	2007	2008	2009
	current dollars				
Canada	**779.60**	**808.15**	**834.62**	**862.64**	**877.75**
Newfoundland and Labrador	758.08	774.90	813.68	854.64	890.62
Prince Edward Island	763.80	776.41	799.46	x	811.11
Nova Scotia	726.28	712.74	765.85	760.47	768.82
New Brunswick	767.64	778.44	825.01	831.64	881.38
Quebec	762.09	775.51	813.13	814.96	810.70
Ontario	793.67	832.01	849.72	885.58	913.98
Manitoba	711.31	737.97	801.13	818.71	816.82
Saskatchewan	755.66	781.99	820.94	843.00	854.67
Alberta	771.40	797.66	836.55	896.22	917.48
British Columbia	825.80	872.38	862.70	906.81	913.82
Yukon	948.69	1,010.51	1,040.14	x	x

x : suppressed to meet the confidentiality requirements of the *Statistics Act*

Note: Excludes owners or partners of unincorporated businesses and professional practices, the self-employed, unpaid family workers, persons working outside Canada, military personnel, and casual workers for whom a T4 is not required.

Source: Statistics Canada, CANSIM, table (for fee) 281-0027 and Catalogue no. 72-002-XIB.

Last modified: 2010-03-31.

Employment, educational and related services, by province and territory

	2005	2006	2007	2008	2009
			Employees[1]		
Canada	**1,058,974**	**1,082,942**	**1,109,718**	**1,135,454**	**1,151,367**
Newfoundland and Labrador	18,404	18,790	18,907	19,983	21,166
Prince Edward Island	4,462	4,466	4,636	x	5,112
Nova Scotia	35,884	36,964	35,642	36,429	36,023
New Brunswick	22,621	24,327	24,249	24,972	25,438
Quebec	257,734	260,997	265,890	270,977	274,868
Ontario	393,207	403,082	415,559	426,352	431,202
Manitoba	44,710	44,242	44,592	46,159	47,956
Saskatchewan	38,603	38,818	39,897	40,328	43,191
Alberta	110,010	112,382	117,496	121,893	123,796
British Columbia	129,031	134,665	138,489	139,086	137,925
Yukon	1,200	1,234	1,300	x	x

x : suppressed to meet the confidentiality requirements of the *Statistics Act*
1. Excludes owners or partners of unincorporated businesses and professional practices, the self-employed, unpaid family workers, persons working outside Canada, military personnel, and casual workers for whom a T4 is not required
Source: Statistics Canada, CANSIM, table (for fee) 281-0024 and Catalogue no. 72-002-XIB.
Last modified: 2010-03-31.

Full-time teaching staff at Canadian universities, by rank and sex

	2004/2005	2005/2006	2006/2007	2007/2008	2008/2009
			number		
Both sexes					
Total rank	**38,572**	**39,615**	**40,567**	**41,306**	**41,954**
Full professor	14,024	14,027	14,039	14,187	14,382
Associate professor	12,142	12,647	13,195	13,618	14,208
Assistant professor	10,238	10,646	10,910	10,986	10,824
Rank or level below assistant professor[1]	1,951	2,074	2,181	2,203	2,196
Other ranks (not elsewhere classified)[2]	217	221	242	312	344
Males					
Total rank	**26,280**	**26,676**	**27,008**	**27,186**	**27,341**
Full professor	11,376	11,290	11,183	11,172	11,195
Associate professor	7,917	8,168	8,450	8,634	8,958
Assistant professor	6,002	6,164	6,233	6,178	5,995
Rank or level below assistant professor[1]	887	950	1,026	1,064	1,032
Other ranks (not elsewhere classified)[2]	98	104	116	138	161
Females					
Total rank	**12,292**	**12,939**	**13,559**	**14,120**	**14,613**
Full professor	2,648	2,737	2,856	3,015	3,187
Associate professor	4,225	4,479	4,745	4,984	5,250
Assistant professor	4,236	4,482	4,677	4,808	4,829
Rank or level below assistant professor[1]	1,064	1,124	1,155	1,139	1,164
Other ranks (not elsewhere classified)[2]	119	117	126	174	183

Notes:
1. Rank or level below assistant professor includes lecturers, instructors and other teaching staff.
2. Other ranks include staff that do not fit in the above categories.
Source: Statistics Canada, CANSIM, table (for fee) 477-0017.
Last modified: 2010-12-23.

People employed, by educational attainment

	2010		
	Both sexes	Men	Women
	%		
Total	**61.6**	**65.4**	**57.9**
15 to 24 years	55.0	53.4	56.6
25 to 44 years	80.5	84.4	76.7
45 and over	51.3	56.5	46.5
Less than Grade 9	19.8	27.5	12.7
15 to 24 years	24.2	27.3	20.5
25 to 44 years	51.0	62.4	35.1
45 and over	15.8	22.6	10.1
Some secondary school	40.3	45.7	34.5
15 to 24 years	37.4	36.5	38.4
25 to 44 years	63.6	70.2	54.1
45 and over	34.7	43.7	26.3
High school graduate	61.7	67.7	55.9
15 to 24 years	64.5	65.2	63.7
25 to 44 years	75.9	81.3	69.5
45 and over	53.0	59.6	48.0
Some postsecondary	60.7	62.9	58.6
15 to 24 years	57.1	55.3	58.8
25 to 44 years	73.8	77.8	69.2
45 and over	54.6	58.8	50.8
Postsecondary certificate or diploma[1]	70.8	74.0	67.6
15 to 24 years	75.3	73.1	77.3
25 to 44 years	84.6	88.4	80.7
45 and over	59.4	62.8	56.1
Bachelor's degree	75.3	77.8	73.2
15 to 24 years	73.2	68.7	75.9
25 to 44 years	85.0	88.9	82.1
45 and over	64.3	67.5	61.1
Above bachelor's degree	75.4	74.6	76.4
15 to 24 years	66.1	57.8	71.9
25 to 44 years	85.0	87.7	82.5
45 and over	67.9	66.5	69.9

1. Includes trades certificate.
Source: Statistics Canada, CANSIM, table (for fee) 282-0004 and Catalogue no. 89F0133XIE.
Last modified: 2011-01-28.

Intellectual property in the higher education sector

	2004	2005	2006	2007	2008
	$ thousands				
Total operational expenditures for intellectual property management[1]	36,927	41,544	42,492	41,851	51,124
Income from intellectual property[1]	51,210	55,173	59,689	52,477	53,183
	number				
Full-time equivalent employees engaged in intellectual property management	280	292	323	285	321
Invention disclosures[2]	1,432	1,452	1,356	1,357	1,613
Inventions protected[2]	629	761	707	668	820
Patent applications[3]	1,264	1,410	1,442	1,634	1,791
Patents issued[3]	397	376	339	479	346
Patents held[3]	3,827	3,961	4,784	4,185	5,908
New licenses and options[4,5]	494	621	437	538	524
Active licenses and options[4,5]	2,022	2,836	2,038	2,679	3,343

Note: Data were not collected for 2000 and 2002 since this survey was done on an occasional basis between 1998 and 2003.
1. Intellectual property refers to any creation of the human mind that can be protected by law.
2. An invention is any patentable product, process, machine, manufacture or composition of matter, or any new and useful improvement of any of these.
3. A patent is a document that protects the rights of an inventor. Patents are granted by the governments of countries.
4. A license is an agreement with a client to use the institution's intellectual property for a fee or other consideration.
5. An option is the right to negotiate for a license.
Source: Statistics Canada, CANSIM, table (for fee) 358-0025 and Catalogue nos. 88-222-X and 88F0006XIE.
Last modified: 2010-08-23.

Glossary of Education Terms

Accountability
measurable proof, usually in the form of student results on various tests, that teachers, schools, divisions and states are teaching students efficiently and well, usually in the form of student success rates on various tests; Virginia's accountability programs is known as the Standards of Learning which includes curriculum standards approved by the Board of Education and required state tests based on the standards.

Accreditation
a process used by the Virginia Department of Education to evaluate the educational performance of public schools in accordance regulations.

Achievement gap
the difference between the performance of subgroups of students, especially those defined by gender, race/ethnicity, disability and socioeconomic status.

ACT
one of the two commonly used tests designed to assess high school students' general educational development and their ability to complete college-level work in four skill areas: English, mathematics, reading, and science reasoning.

Adequate yearly progress (AYP)
a measurement indicating whether a school, division or the state met federally approved academic goals required by the federal Elementary and Secondary Education Act/No Child Left Behind Act (ESEA/NCLB).

Adult/Continuing education
a program of instruction provided by an adult/continuing education instructional organization for adults and youth beyond the age of compulsory school attendance including basic education and English literacy, English for speakers of other languages, civics education, GED testing services, adult secondary education and Individualized Student Alternative Education Plan (ISAEP) programs.

Advanced Placement (AP)
college-level courses available to high school students which may allow a student to earn college credit provided through the College Board.

Alignment
effort to ensure that what teachers teach is in accord with what the curriculum says will be taught and what is assessed on official tests.

Alternative assessment
a method to measure student educational attainment other than the typical multiple-choice test which may include portfolios, constructed response items and other performance-measurement tools.

Alternative education
a school or center organized for alternative programs of instruction.

Assessment
method of measuring the learning and performance of students; examples include achievement tests, minimum competency tests, developmental screening tests, aptitude tests, observation instruments, performance tasks, etc.

At-risk students
students who have a higher than average probability of dropping out or failing school.

Average daily membership (ADM)
the K-12 enrollment figure used to distribute state per pupil funding that includes students with disabilities ages 5-21, and students for whom English is a second language who entered school for the first time after reaching their 12th birthday, and who have not reached their 22nd birthday; preschool and post-graduate students are not included in ADM.

Benchmark
a standard for judging performance.

Block scheduling
a way of organizing the school day into blocks of time longer than the typical 50-minute class period; with the 4X4 block students take four 90-minute classes each day allowing for completion of an entire course in one semester instead of a full year; with an A/B or rotating block students take six to eight classes for an entire year but classes in each subject meet on alternate days for 90 minutes.

Charter school
a school controlled by a local school board that provides free public elementary and/or secondary education to eligible students under a specific charter granted by the state legislature or other appropriate authority, and designated by such authority to be a charter school.

Class period
a segment of time in the school day that is approximately 1/6 of the instructional day.

Cohort
a particular group of people with something in common.

College Board
the organization that administers SAT, AP and other standardized tests to high school students planning on continuing their educations at a post-secondary level.

Combined school
a public school that contains any combination of or all K-12 grade levels that are not considered an elementary, middle or secondary school .

Composite index of local ability to pay
a formula to determine the state and local government shares of K-12 education program costs, which is expressed as a ratio, indicating the local percentage share of the cost of education programs; for example, a locality with a composite

index of 0.3000 would pay 30 percent and the state would pay 70 percent of the costs.

Confined
due to physical, medical or emotional impairments based on certification of need, a student is restricted or limited from attendance at a regular public school during the regular school hours; this does not apply to situations where a student is restricted for discipline or non-medically based situations.

Core curriculum
the body of knowledge that all students are expected to learn in the subjects of English, mathematics, history/social science and science.

Curriculum
a plan or document that a school or school division uses to define what will be taught and the methods that will be used to educate and assess students.

Curriculum alignment
occurs when what is taught includes or exceeds the content defined by the Standards of Learning (SOL).

Data-based decision making (also referred to as "research-based decision making")
organizing, analyzing and interpreting existing sources of information and other data to make decisions.

Direct aid to public education
funding appropriated for the operation of public schools including funding for school employee benefits, Standards of Quality, incentive-based programs, allotment of sales tax and lottery revenues and specific appropriations for programs such as Governor's Schools and adult literacy initiatives.

Disaggregated data
presentation of data broken into subgroups of students instead of the entire student body which allows parents and teachers to measure how each student group is performing; typical subgroups include students who are economically disadvantaged, from different racial or ethnic groups, those who have disabilities or have limited English fluency.

Distance learning
method of instruction in locations other than the classroom or places where teachers present the lessons, which uses various forms of technology to provide educational materials and experiences to students.

Dropouts
students who leave high school before receiving a diploma.

Early childhood education
the education of young children, especially under the age of 5.

Economically disadvantaged
a student who is a member of a household that meets the income eligibility guidelines for free or reduced-price school meals (less than or equal to 185% of Federal Poverty Guidelines).

Elementary & Secondary Education Act (ESEA)
the primary federal law affecting K-12 education; the most recent reauthorization of the law is also known as the No Child Left Behind Act of 2001 (NCLB).

Elementary school
a public school with grades kindergarten through five.

Eligible students
the total number of students of school age enrolled in the school at a grade or course with a Standards of Learning test; does not include students who are allowed an exclusion such as limited English proficient (LEP) students or some students with disabilities.

English as a second language (ESL)
a program of instruction and services for non-English-speaking or limited-English-proficient students to help them learn and succeed in schools.

English-language learners (ELL)
a student whose first language is other than English and who is in a special program for learning English.

Enrollment
the act of complying with state and local requirements for registration or admission of a child for attendance in a school within a local school division; also refers to registration for courses within the student's home school or within related schools or programs.

Even Start
a federally funded program that provides family-centered education projects to help parents become full partners in the education of their children.

First time
the student has not been enrolled in the school at any time during the current school year.

Four core subject/academic areas
English, mathematics, science and history/social science for purposes of SOL testing.

Free and appropriate public education (FAPE)
requirement through the federal Individuals with Disabilities Education Act (IDEA) that education of students with disabilities (between the ages of 3 and 22) must be provided at public expense, under public supervision, at no charge to the parents and based on the child's unique needs and not on the child's disability.

General education
K-12 instruction that meets the commonwealth's Standards of Learning and prepares children for elementary, secondary and postsecondary success.

Gifted
programs that provide advanced educational opportunities including accelerated promotion through grades and classes and an enriched curriculum for students who are endowed with a high degree of mental ability.

Governor's school

a school serving gifted high school students who meet specific admissions criteria for advanced educational opportunities in areas including the arts, government and international studies, mathematics, science, and technology; both academic-year and summer governor's schools are offered.

Graduate

a student who has earned a Board of Education recognized diploma: advanced studies, advanced technical, standard, standard technical, modified standard, special or general achievement.

Head Start

a federally funded child-development program that provides health, educational, nutritional, social and other services to pre-school children from economically disadvantaged families.

Home-based instruction

non-reimbursable educational services provided in the home setting (or other agreed upon setting) in accordance with the student's individual education program who were removed from school for disciplinary or other reasons, but not the result of a medical referral.

Homebound instruction

academic instruction provided to students who are confined at home or in a health-care facility for periods that would prevent normal school attendance based upon certification of need by a licensed physician or licensed clinical psychologist. For a student with a disability, the Individual Education Program (IEP) team must determine the delivery of services, including the number of hours of services.

Home instruction (also referred to as "home schooling")

instruction of a student or students by a parent or parents, guardian or other person having control or charge of such student or students as an alternative to attendance in a public or private school in accordance with the provisions of the Code of Virginia provisions (§22.1-254.1).

Home tutoring

instruction by a tutor or teacher with qualifications prescribed by the Virginia Board of Education, as an alternative to attendance in a public or private school and approved by the division superintendent in accordance with the provisions of the Code of Virginia §22.1-254; often used as an alternative form of home schooling.

Individuals with Disabilities Education Act (IDEA)

federal law guiding the delivery of special education services for students with disabilities which includes the guarantee of "free and appropriate public education" for every school-age child with a disability and allows parental involvement in the educational planning process, encourages access to the general curriculum and delineates how school disciplinary rules and the obligation to provide a free appropriate public education for disabled children mesh.

Individualized education program (IEP)

a written plan created for a student with disabilities by the student's teachers, parents or guardians, the school administrator, and other interested parties. The plan is tailored to the student's specific needs and abilities, and outlines attainable goals.

Individualized education program team (IEP Team)

team charged with developing, reviewing and revising a student's IEP and consisting of the parent(s), the child (if appropriate), a regular education teacher, a special education teacher, an administrator qualified to supervise the provision of services and an individual who can interpret the instructional implications of evaluation results.

Individualized family service plan (IFSP)

a written plan outlining the procedure necessary to transition a child with disabilities to preschool or other appropriate services.

International Baccalaureate (IB)

a program established to provide an internationally recognized; interdisciplinary; pre-collegiate course of study offered through the International Baccalaureate Organization, headquartered in Switzerland, and examination results are accepted by more than 100 countries for university admission.

Licensed clinical psychologist

a psychologist licensed by the Virginia Board of Psychology who must either be in a treatment relationship or establishing a treatment relationship with the student to meet eligibility requirements for requesting homebound services.

Licensed physician

an individual who has been licensed by the Virginia Board of Medicine to practice medicine who can certify medical conditions for requesting homebound services.

Licensed teacher

an individual who has met all the current requirements for a teacher in the Virginia and holds a license from the Virginia State Board of Education, or, if teaching on-line, a license from Virginia or another state.

Limited-English proficient (LEP) -see English-language learners Linear weighted average

a calculation, approximating what most school divisions spend to operate their schools, used to establish the funded cost of many components of the Standards of Quality (SOQ), such as instructional salaries.

Literary fund

established in the Constitution of Virginia (Article VIII, § 8) as a permanent and perpetual school fund that provides low-interest loans to school divisions for capital expenditures, such as construction of new buildings or remodeling of existing buildings.

Locally awarded verified credit

a verified unit of credit awarded by a local school board in accordance with the SOA.

Magnet school/center (also referred to as "specialty school/center")

a public school that focuses on a particular area of study, such as performing arts or science and technology but also offer regular school subjects.

Middle school
a public school with grades 6 through 8.

Migrant Education
a program of instruction and services for children who move periodically with their families from one school to another in a different geographical area to secure seasonal employment.

National Assessment of Educational Progress (NAEP) (also referred to as "the Nation's Report Card")
the only nationally representative and continuing assessment of what America's students know and can do in various subject areas including mathematics, reading, science, writing, U.S. history, geography, civics and the arts; the federally funded program (currently contracted to Educational Testing Service in Princeton, N.J.) tests a representative sample of students in grades 4, 8 and 12 and provides information about the achievement of students nationally and state-by-state.

National Blue Ribbon Award
honors public and private K-12 schools that are either academically superior in their states or that demonstrate dramatic gains in student achievement; awarded annually by the U.S. Department of Education through the Blue Ribbon Schools Program.

Nation's Report Card
see "National Assessment of Educational Progress (NAEP)".

No Child Left behind Act of 2001 (NCLB)
see "Elementary & Secondary Education Act".

Norm-referenced tests
standardized tests designed to measure how a student's performance compares with that of other students.

Phonological Awareness Literacy Screening (PALS)
state-provided K-3 screening tool to help reduce the number of children with reading problems by detecting those problems early and providing research-based, small-group intervention.

Pedagogy
the art of teaching.

Planning period
one class period per day (or the equivalent) unencumbered of any teaching or supervisory duties.

Portfolio
a collection of student work chosen to exemplify and document a student's learning progress over time.

Pre-school child care
a school-operated program that provides custodial care of pre-school students enrolled in a school or system before school day starts and/or after a school day ends.

Proficient
test results indicating that the student demonstrated the skills and knowledge outlined in the Standards of Learning (SOL).

Professional/staff development
training for teachers, principals, superintendents, administrative staff, local school board members and Board of Education members designed to enhance student achievement and is required by the Standards of Quality (SOQ).

Psychiatrist
an medical doctor who has been licensed by the Virginia Board of Medicine and trained to practice in the science of treating mental diseases.

Reading First
federal program focuses on putting proven methods of early reading instruction into classrooms to ensure all children learn to read well by the end of third grade.

Recess
a segment of free time during the standard school day in which students are given a break from instruction.

Reconstitution
for a school rated accreditation denied, it is a process to initiate a range of accountability actions to improve pupil performance and to address deficiencies in curriculum and instruction; may include, but is not limited to, restructuring a school's governance, instructional program staff or student population.

Regular school year
the period of time between the opening day of school in the fall and the closing day of school for that school term that is at minimum 180 teaching days or 990 teaching hours.

Remedial program
a program designed to remedy, strengthen and improve the academic achievement of students who demonstrate substandard performance.

Research-based decision making
see "data-based decision making".

Response to intervention (RTI)
a method designed to identify and provide early, effective assistance to children who are having difficulty learning: Tier 1 students need extra help understanding the core curriculum, Tier 2 students consistently showing a discrepancy between their current level of performance and the expected level of performance, and Tier 3 students need even more support.

Restructuring
the implementation of a new organizational pattern or style of leadership and management to bring about renewed, more effective schools. It can mean reorganizing the school day or year and changing conventional practices, such as grouping students by age for an entire school year or giving competitive grades. Or it may refer to changing the roles of teachers and administrators, allocating more decision-making power to teachers, and involving parents in decisions.

Sampling
a way of estimating how a whole group would perform on a test by testing representative members of the group or giving different portions of the test to various subgroups.

SAT
one of the two commonly used tests designed to assess high school students' general educational development and required

for college entrance by many institutions of higher education; administered by The College Board.

School
a publicly funded institution where students are enrolled for all or a majority of the instructional day; those students are reported in fall membership at the institution and the institution, at minimum, meets requirements adopted by the Board of Education.

School age
a child who is age 5 on or before September 30 and has not reached age 20; compulsory attendance school age is 5-18.

Secondary school
a public school with any grades 9 through 12.

Special education (SPED)
a service especially designed and at no cost to the parent/guardian that adapts the curriculum, materials or instruction for students identified as having educational or physical disabilities and tailored to each student's needs and learning style and provided in a general education or special education classroom, home, hospital, separate school or other setting.

Specialty school
see "magnet school/center".

Standardized testing
tests administered and scored under uniform (standardized) conditions. Because most machine-scored, multiple-choice tests are standardized, the term is sometimes used to refer to such tests, but other tests may also be standardized.

Standard school day
a calendar day that averages at least five and one-half instructional hours for students in grades 1-12, excluding breaks for meals and recess, and a minimum of three instructional hours for students in kindergarten.

Standard school year
a school year of at least 180 teaching days or a total of at least 990 teaching hours per year.

Standard unit of credit
earned credit based on a minimum of 140-clock hours of instruction and successful completion of the requirements of the course.

Standards of Accreditation (SOA)
the Board of Education's regulations establishing criteria for approving public schools in Virginia as authorized in the Standards of Quality (SOQ).

Standards of Learning (SOL)
the minimum grade level and subject matter educational objectives, described as the knowledge and skills "necessary for success in school and for preparation for life," that students are expected to meet in Virginia public schools and specified by the Standards of Quality (SOQ).

SOL curriculum frameworks
teacher resource guides for mathematics, science, English and history/social sciences delineating essential knowledge, skills and processes required by the Standards of Learning (SOL).

Standards of Quality (SOQ)
the minimum program that every public school division in Virginia must meet; a major portion of state funding for direct air to public education is based on the SOQ; the standards are established in the Constitution of Virginia, defined in the Code of Virginia and prescribed by the Board of Education, subject to revision only by the General Assembly.

Student
a child age 5 on or before September 30 up to age 18; a child with disabilities age 2-21; a child of limited English proficiency who entered a Virginia school after age 12 but not age 22.

Student periods
means the number of students a teacher instructs per class period multiplied by the number of class periods taught.

Substitute tests
tests approved by the Board of Education as substitutes for SOL end-of-course tests for awarding verified credit for high school; examples include Advanced Placement (AP), International Baccalaureate (IB), SAT II, as well as a number of certifications and licensing examinations in career and technical fields.

Title I
federal funding program authorized by Title I of ESEA/NCLB to support instructional needs of students from low-income families to ensure that all children have a fair and equal opportunity to obtain a high-quality education and reach (at a minimum) proficiency on state academic achievement standards and assessments.

Title 1 school
a school with a high rate of disadvantaged students making it eligible for participation in federal Title I programs.

Title 1 school-wide assistance
Title 1 schools with 40 percent or greater high-poverty, student population may use federal funding to meet the needs of all students at the school.

Title 1 targeted assistance
federal funding is used to meet the needs of the educationally disadvantaged students only and the poverty percentages must be at least 35% or above the district wide average.

Transition plan
plan provided by the licensed physician or licensed clinical psychologist to explain the need for extended homebound instruction which includes the name of the student, justification for the extension of homebound instruction, additional time homebound instruction is anticipated and specific steps planned to return the student to classroom instruction.

Verified unit of credit
earned credit based on a standard unit of credit, plus a passing score on the end-of-course SOL test or substitute test approved by the Board of Education.

Vocational
a school or center organized for a program that offers a sequence of courses that are directly related to the preparation of individuals for paid or unpaid employment in current or emerging occupations requiring other than a baccalaureate or advanced diploma

Source: Virginia Department of Education

Boldface listings are parent organizations.

Boldface listings are parent organizations.

Boldface listings are parent organizations.

Boldface listings are parent organizations.

Boldface listings are parent organizations.

Boldface listings are parent organizations.

Boldface listings are parent organizations.

E

Boldface listings are parent organizations.

F

Boldface listings are parent organizations.

I

Boldface listings are parent organizations.

J

Journal of Multicultural Counseling & Development, 4412

Journal of Negro Education, 4151

Journal of Physical Education, Recreation and Dance, 4535

Journal of Positive Behavior Interventions, 4152

Journal of Reading Recovery, 3684

Journal of Recreational Mathematics, 4498

Journal of Research and Development in Education, 4153

Journal of Research in Character Education, 4154

Journal of Research in Childhood Education, 4330, 4349

Journal of Research in Rural Education, 4155

Journal of Research in Science Teaching, 4584

Journal of Research on Computing in Education, 4640

Journal of School Health, 4156

Journal of Sex Education & Therapy, 4413

Journal of Special Education, 4157

Journal of Special Education Technology, 4641

Journal of Student Financial Aid, 3942

Journal of Teaching Writing, 4447

Journal of Teaching in Physical Education, 4536

Journal of Urban & Cultural Studies, 4158

Journal of Vocational Education Research, 4365

Journal on Excellence in College Teaching, 3466

Journalism Education Association, 277, 692, 3467

Journalism Quarterly, 4448

Journey Education, 5755

Joy Carpets, 5441

Joyce Foundation, 2408

Jubail British Academy, 1471

Jules & Doris Stein Foundation, 2270

Julia R & Estelle L Foundation, 2618

Julio R Gallo Foundation, 2271

July in Rensselaer, 3621

Jumeirah English Speaking School, 1472

Jump Start Math for Kindergartners, 5934

JuneBox.com, 5848

Junior Achievement, 4821

Just 4 Teachers, 5841

Justrite Manufacturing Company, 5594

K

K'nex Education Division, 3622

K-12 District Technology Coordinators, 4043

K-6 Science and Math Catalog, 4025

K12jobs.Com, 3497

KI, 5442

KIDSNET, 3864

KIDSNET Media Guide and News, 3864

KLM Bioscientific, 5595

KSBA Annual Conference, 3289

KSJ Publishing Company, 3904

Kabira International School, 1022

Kaeden Corporation, 4822

Kaiserslautern Elementary School, 1735

Kaiserslautern High School, 1736

Kaiserslautern Middle School, 1737

Kaleidoscope, 3623, 4159

Kaludis Consulting Group, 899

Kanawha County Public Library, 2777

Kane/Miller Book Publishers, 4823

Kansai Christian School, 1138

Kansas Association of School Librarians, 439

Kansas Business Education Association, 440

Kansas City Public Library, 2538

Kansas City School District, 612

Kansas Department of Education, 2982

Kansas Education Association, 441

Kansas Library Association, 442

Kansas School Boards Association Conference, 3290

Kansas State Department of Education, 2983, 2984, 2985

Kansas State University, 277, 692, 3467

Kaohsiung American School, 1139

Karachi American Society School, 2105

Karl C Parrish School, 1345

Karnak Corporation, 5518

Karol Media, 5121

Kathleen Price and Joseph M Bryan Family Foundation, 2645

Kean College of New Jersey, 3230

Keep America Beautiful, 4824

Kellems Division, 5749

Kellett School, 1140

Ken Cook Education Systems, 5756

Ken Haycock and Associates, 4474

Ken-a-Vision Manufacturing Company, 5596

Kenan Center, 2649

Kendale Primary International School, 1738

Kendall-Hunt Publishing Company, 4825

Kennedy Center Alliance for Arts Education, 301

Kenneth T & Eileen L Norris Foundation, 2272

Kensington Microwave, 5757

Kensington School, 1739

Kensington Technology Group, 5443

Kent H. Smith Library, 2670

Kent State University, 3624, 4477

Kentland Foundation, 2766

Kentucky Association of School Administrators, 900

Kentucky Department of Education, 2990, 2987, 2988, 2989, 2993, 2994

Kentucky Library Association, 443

Kentucky School Boards Association, 3289

Kentucky School Media Association, 444

Kentucky School Superintendents Association Meeting, 3291

Kentucky State University, 3625

Kepro Circuit Systems, 5597

Kestrel Manor School, 1023

Kettering Fund, 2662

Kewaunee Scientific Corporation, 5598

Key-Bak, 5255

Keyboard Instructor, 5256

Keystone Schoolmaster Newsletter, 4284

Khartoum American School, 1024

Kid Keys 2.0, 5944

Kids Percussion Buyer's Guide, 5257

Kids at Heart & School Art Materials, 5258

KidsAstronomy.com, 6083

KidsCare Childcare Management Software, 3498

Kidstamps, 5259

Kidstuff Playsystems, 5674

Kiev International School, 1401

Kigali International School, 1025

Kilmer Square, 2557

Kilmore International School, 1141

Kimball Office Furniture Company, 5444

Kimbo Educational, 5122

Kinabalu International School, 1142

Kinder Magic, 5945

King Fahad Academy, 1740

King Faisal School, 1473

King George V School, 1143

King's College, 1741, 505

Kingsgate English Medium Primary School, 1026

Kingston Press Services, Ltd., 4449

Kingsway Academy, 1917

Kisongo Campus, 1002

Kisumu International School, 1027

Kitakyushu International School, 1144

Kitzingen Elementary School, 1742

Kleine Brogel Elementary School, 1743

Kleiner & Associates, 901

Kluwer Academic/Human Sciences Press, 4136, 4143, 4217, 4324, 4339, 4384, 4386, 4404, 4569

Knex Education, 5260, 5599

Knex Education Catalog, 5260, 5599

Knowledge Adventure, 4826, 5934, 5944

Knowledge Unlimited, 4827, 5289

Koc School, 1474

Kodaikanal International School, 1145

Kodaly Teaching Certification Program, 3626

Koffler Sales Company, 5600

Komodo Dragon, 5601

Kompan, 5675

Kongeus Grade School, 2106

Kool Seal, 5519

Kooralbyn International School, 1146

Koret Foundation, 2273

Kowloon Junior School, 1147

Kraus International Publications, 4828

Kreonite, 5602

Kresge Foundation, 2503

Kruger & Eckels, 5603

Kulas Foundation, 2663

Kuwait English School, 1475

Kyoto International School, 1148

L

LA Steelcraft Products, 5676

LASPAU (Latin America Scholarship Program), 4376

LCD Products Group, 6110

LD Forum, 4160

LDSystems, 5520

LEGO Data, 5604

LG Balfour Foundation, 2477

LINC, 364

LINX System, 5605

LMS Associates, 4488

LPR Publications, 4305, 4310, 4372

LRP Publications, 4091, 4094, 4102, 4106, 4134, 4234, 4275, 4278, 4280, 4287, 4288, 4304, 4307, 4308, 4311, 4325, 4425

LRP Publishing, 4374

LSBA Convention, 3292

LSBA Quarter Notes, 4285

La Chataigneraie International School, 1744

La Maddalena Elementary School, 1745

Lab Safety Supply, 5606

Lab Volt Systems, 3627, 5607

Lab-Aids, 5608

Lab-Volt, 5395

Labconco Corporation, 5609

Labelon Corporation, 5370

Labor Department Building, 2923

Lahore American School, 1149

Lajes Elementary School, 1746

Lajes High School, 1747

Lake Education, 4829

Lakenheath Elementary School, 1748

Lakenheath High School, 1749

Lakenheath Middle School, 1750

Lakeside Manufacturing, 5610

Lakeview Corporate Center, 2354

Lakewood Publications, 4317

Lancing College, 1751

Landmark Editions, 4830

Landscape Structures, 5677

Landstuhl Elementary and Middle School, 1752

Lane Family Charitable Trust, 2274

Lane Science Equipment Company, 5611

Langenseheidt Publishing, 4831

Language & Speech, 4449

Language Arts, 4450

Language Schools Directory, 3983

Language Travel Magazine, 5982

Language, Speech & Hearing Services in School, 4451

Lanna International School Thailand, 1150

Lapis Technologies, 5758

Boldface listings are parent organizations.

Boldface listings are parent organizations.

Boldface listings are parent organizations.

Boldface listings are parent organizations.

O

Boldface listings are parent organizations.

Overseas Family School, 1179
Overseas School of Colombo, 1180
Overview of Prevention: A Social Change Model, 3556
Owens Community College, 3646
Owens-Corning Foundation, 2671
Oxton House Publishers, LLC, 4891, 4243, 4958
Oxton Publishers, LLC, 5341

P

P. Lambda Theta, Int'l Honor & Professional Assn., 4112
PACER Center, 130, 3413
PASCO Scientific, 5627
PBS TeacherSource, 5775, 3513
PBS Video, 5133
PCTE Bulletin, 4457
PDK International Conference, 3350
PEN American Center, 3934
PF Collier, 4892
PICS Authentic Foreign Video, 5134
PRO-ED, 4893, 3971
PSBA School Board Secretaries and Affiliates Conference, 3351
PTA National Bulletin, 4198
PTA in Pennsylvania, 4199
Pacific Harbour International School, 1181
Pacific Northwest Council on Languages Annual Conference, 3352
Pacific Northwest Library Association, 290, 424, 781
Pacific Regional Educational Laboratory, 5061
Pacific Telesis Group Corporate Giving Program, 2288
Pagestar, 3512
Paideia Group, 3647
Pakistan International School-Peshawar, 1479
Palache Bilingual School, 2130
Palisades Educational Foundation, 2625
Palmer Foundation, 2411
Palmer Snyder, 5460
Pamela Joy, 941
Pamela Sims & Associates, 3648, 3696
Pan American Christian Academy, 1356
Pan American School-Bahia, 1357
Pan American School-Costa Rica, 1358
Pan American School-Monterrey, 1359
Pan American School-Porto Alegre, 1360
Panama Canal College, 1361
Panasonic Communications & System Company, 5382
Panic Plan for the SAT, 6179
Panterra American School, 1795
Paoli Publishing, 3781
Paradigm Lost: Leading America Beyond It's Fear of Educatio, 3795
Paraeducator's Guide to Instructional & Curricular Modific, 3472
Paragon Furniture, 5461
Parek Stuff, 5699
Parent Educational Advocacy Training Center, 5062
The Parent Institute, 3451, 4333, 4351, 4565, 4575, 4576
Parent Involvement Facilitator: Elementary Edition, 3867
Parent Link, 5776
Parent Training Resources, 3413
Parenting Press, 4894
Parents Make the Difference!, 4351
Parents Make the Difference!: School Readiness Edition, 4333
Parents Still Make the Difference!, 4575
Parents Still Make the Difference!: Middle School Edition, 4576

Parents as Teachers National Center, 749, 4200, 5063
Parents, Let's Unite for Kids, 131
Paris American Academy, 1796
Parlant Technologies, 5909
Parlant Technology, 5776
Parsifal Systems, 942
Partners in Learning Programs, 5290
Pasir Ridge International, 1182
Passing Marks, 4201
Patrick Henry Elementary School, 1797
Patterson's American Education, 3796
Patterson's Elementary Education, 3868
Patterson's Schools Classified, 3797
Paul & Mary Haas Foundation, 2750
Paul H Rosendahl, PHD, 943
Pawling Corporation, 5462
Peace & Justice Studies Association, 132
Peace Corp, 2131
Peak School, 1183
Pearson Education, 3931, 3941
Pearson Education Communications, 3828
Pearson Education Technologies, 5291
Peel Productions, 5225
Peerless Sales Company, 5463
Penco Products, 5527
Penguin USA, 4895
Peninsula Community Foundation, 2289
Pennsylvania Assn. of Secondary School Principals, 4284
Pennsylvania Council for the Social Studies, 3353, 4617, 4621
Pennsylvania Council of Teachers of English, 4457
Pennsylvania Department of Education, 3139, 3134, 3135, 3136, 3137, 3138, 3473
Pennsylvania Education, 3473
Pennsylvania Home Schoolers Newsletter, 4202
Pennsylvania Library Association (PaLA), 521
Pennsylvania PTA, 4199
Pennsylvania School Boards Association, 3351
Pennsylvania School Librarians Association, 522
Pennsylvania Science Teachers Association, 3354
Pennsylvania State Education Association, 4203
Pennsylvania State Education Association (PSEA), 523
Pennsylvania State University, 3600, 3676, 4598
Pennsylvania State University-Workforce Education & Develop, 3649
Pentel of America, 5292
Penton Overseas, 5135
People to People International, 261
Peopleware, 5777
Percussion Marketing Council, 5257
Perfect PC Technologies, 944
Perfection Learning, 4896, 4959
Perfection Learning Corporation, 4896
Performa, 945
Performance Improvement Journal, 3474
Performance Learning Systems, 3650
Performance Resource Press, 3558, 5116, 5141, 5309
Pergamon Press, Elsevier Science, 4479
Perma Bound Books, 4897
Permagile Industries, 5528
Permanent School Fund, 3178
Perot Foundation, 2751
Perry High School, 414
Perse School, 1798
A Personal Planner & Training Guide for the Substitute Tea, 3687
Personal Planner and Training Guide for the Paraprofession, 3414
Personalized Software, 5937
Personalizing the Past, 4898
Personnel Services, 3106
Persons as Resources, 3798
Perspective, 4618
Perspectives for Policymakers, 4295

Perspectives on History Series, 4899
Peter D & Eleanore Kleist Foundation, 2359
Peter Li Education Group, 4306
Peter Loring/Janice Palumbo, 2483
Peter Norton Family Foundation, 2290
Peterhouse, 1035
Peterson's Competitive Colleges, 3799
Peterson's Grants for Graduate and Postdoctoral Study, 3950
Peterson's Guide to Four-Year Colleges, 3800
Peterson's Guide to Two-Year Colleges, 3801
Peterson's Guides, 3765
Peterson's Private Secondary Schools, 4020
Peterson's Regional College Guide Set, 3802
Peterson's Sports Scholarships and College Athletic Progra, 3951
Peterson's, A Nelnet Company, 3799, 3800, 3801, 3802, 3807, 3822, 3950, 3951, 3994, 4020, 4039, 5690, 6173, 6174, 6179
Pew Charitable Trusts, 2702
Peyton Anderson Foundation, 2380
Peytral Publications Inc, 4900
Phelps Publishing, 4901
Phi Delta Kappa Educational Foundation, 4204, 3386, 3387, 3402, 3424, 3429, 3570, 3713
Phi Delta Kappa International, 262, 3615, 3774, 3845, 4205
Phi Delta Kappan, 4205
Phil Hardin Foundation, 2531
Philip H Corboy Foundation, 2412
Phillip Roy Multimedia Materials, 5967
Phillips Broadband Networks, 5778
Phoenix Films/BFA Educ Media/Coronet/MII, 5136
Phoenix Learning Group, 5136
Phoenix Learning Resources, 4902
Phoenix Learning Resources Conference, 790
Phoenix Public Library, 2227
Phonics Institute, 4552
Phuket International Preparatory School, 1184
Phyllis A Beneke Scholarship Fund, 2778
Physical Education Digest, 4540
Physical Educator, 4541
Physics Teacher, 4587
Piano Workshop, 3651
Picture Book Learning Volume-1, 3984
Pike Publishing Company, 3430
Pin Man, 5293
Pine Peace School, 2132
Pinewood Schools of Thessaloniki, 1799
Pioneer New Media Technologies, 5779
Pittsburg State University, 3652, 3606
Pittsburgh Office And Research Park, 2695
Place in the Woods, 3753, 4092, 4486, 4554
Planning & Changing, 4296
Planning & Evaluation Service, 2865
Planning for Higher Education, 4206
Planning, Research & Evaluation, 2957
Planning, Results & Information Management, 3015
PlayConcepts, 5294
PlayDesigns, 5684
Playground Environments, 5685
Playnix, 5686
Playworld Systems, 5687
Pleasant Company Publications, 4903
Plough Foundation, 2724
Plymouth State College, 2555
Pocket Books/Paramount Publishing, 4904
Poetry Alive!, 946
Polaroid Corporation, 5780
Polaroid Education Program, 3653
Policy & Planning, 2972, 3156
Policy & Practice, 4207
Policy, Assessment, Research & Information Systems, 3195
Polk Brothers Foundation, 2413
Polyform Products Company, 5295

Q

R

Boldface listings are parent organizations.

S

Boldface listings are parent organizations.

Boldface listings are parent organizations.

U

Boldface listings are parent organizations.

V

Boldface listings are parent organizations.

W

Boldface listings are parent organizations.

X

Y

Z

Alabama

Alabama Business Education Association, 373
Alabama Education Association, 374
Alabama Library Association, 375
Alabama State Department of Education, 2877
American Educational Studies Association, 630, 3225
Assistant Superintendent & Financial Services, 2878
Association for Science Teacher Education Science Annual Meeting, 329, 653
Auburn University at Montgomery Library, 2212
Benjamin & Roberta Russell Educational and Charitable Foundation, 2213
Birmingham Public Library, 2214
Carolina Lawson Ivey Memorial Foundation, 2215
Deputy Superintendent, 2879
Disability Determination Division, 2880
FPMI Communications, 871
General Administrative Services, 2881
Huntsville Public Library, 2216
Instructional Services, 2883
Inter-Regional Center, 242
International Association of Educators for World Peace, 66
JL Bedsole Foundation, 2217
Jefferson State Community College, 3620
Mildred Weedon Blount Educational and Charitable Foundation, 2218
Mitchell Foundation, 2219
Post Secondary Educational Assistance, 947
Rehabilitation Services, 2885
Student Instructional Services, 2887
Superintendent, 2888
University of South Alabama, 2220

Alaska

Alaska Association of School Librarians, 376
Alaska Commission on Postsecondary Education, 2890
Alaska Department of Education Administrative Services, 2891
Alaska Department of Education & Early Development, 2892
Alaska Department of Education Bilingual & Bicultural Education Conference, 3258
Alaska Library Association, 377
Libraries, Archives & Museums, 2893
School Finance & Data Management, 2894
Special Education Service Agency, 973
Teaching And Learning Support Program, 2895
University of Alaska-Anchorage Library, 2221

Arizona

AZLA/MPLA Conference, 611
Annual Academic-Vocational Integrated Curriculum Conference, 640
Annual Challenging Learners with Untapped Potential Conference, 641
Annual Conference on Hispanic American Education, 642
Annual Effective Schools Conference, 643
Annual Microcomputers in Education Conference, 645
Arizona Department of Education, 2222
Arizona Governor's Committee on Employment of People with Disabilities, 2223
Arizona Library Association, 378
Arizona School Boards Association, 379
Center for Image Processing in Education, 3581

Conference on Information Technology, 671
Council of Education Facility Planners-International, 232
Education Services, 2224
Evo-Ora Foundation, 2225
Flinn Foundation, 2226
Grand Canyon University College of Education, 3608
High School Reform Conference, 681
Increasing Student Achievement in Reading, Writing, Mathematics, Science, 685
Infusing Brain Research, Multi-Intelligence, Learning Styles and Mind Styles, 687
Integrated/Thematic Curriculum and Performance Assessment, 689
International Studies Association (ISA), 253
National Association for Developmental Education (NADE), 79
National Council of State Supervisors of Music, 2897
National School Conference Institute, 742
North Central Association Annual Meeting, 3339
Northern Arizona University, 3644
Peace & Justice Studies Association, 132
Phoenix Public Library, 2227
Professional Office Instruction & Training, 380
Restructuring Curriculum Conference, 3356
Special Programs, 2228
Staff Development Workshops & Training Sessions, 3664
Technology in 21st Century Schools, 760
Tesseract Group, 982
Vocational Technological Education, 2230
www.learningpage.com, 3508

Arkansas

Arkansas Business Education Association, 381
Arkansas Department of Education, 2898
Arkansas Department of Education: Special Education, 2899
Arkansas Education Association, 382
Arkansas Library Association, 383
Charles A Frueauff Foundation, 2231
Children's Educational Opportunity Foundation, 820
Dawson Education Cooperative, 838
Dawson Education Service Cooperative, 839
Dimensions of Early Childhood, 164
Federal Programs, 2900
Roy and Christine Sturgis Charitable and Educational Trust, 2232
Southern Early Childhood Annual Convention, 3361
The Jones Center For Families, 2233
University of Arkansas at Little Rock, 3677
Walton Family Foundation, 2234
Westark Community College, 2235
William C & Theodosia Murphy Nolan Foundation, 2236
Winthrop Rockefeller Foundation, 2237

California

Advance Infant Development Program, 798
Aguirre International Incorporated, 799
Ahmanson Foundation, 2238
Alice Tweed Tuohy Foundation, 2239
American Honda Foundation, 2785
Arrillaga Foundation, 2240
Asian American Curriculum Project, 286
Assessing Student Performance: Exploring the Purpose and Limits of Testing, 3384
Association for Environmental and Outdoor Education (AEOE), 18

Association for Play Therapy, 21
Association for Play Therapy Conference, 652
Association for Refining Cross-Cultured International, 803
Association of Educational Therapists, 190
Atkinson Foundation, 2241
BankAmerica Foundation, 2242
Bechtel Group Corporate Giving Program, 2243
Bernard Osher Foundation, 2244
Boys-Viva Supermarkets Foundation, 2245
CCAE/COABE National Conference, 3268
CPM Educational Program, 810
CSBA Education Conference & Trade Show, 3269
Caldwell Flores Winters, 811
California Biomedical Research Association, 331
California Business Education Association, 384
California Classical Association-Northern Section, 385
California Community Foundation, 2246
California Department of Education, 2902
California Department of Education's Educational Resources Catalog, 2903
California Department of Special Education, 2904
California Foundation for Agriculture in the Classroom, 386
California Kindergarten Conference and PreConference Institute, 3270
California Library Association, 387
California Reading Association, 388
California School Library Association, 389
California Teachers Association, 390
Carnegie Foundation for the Advancement of Teaching, 813
Carrie Estelle Doheny Foundation, 2247
Center for Civic Education, 31
Center for Critical Thinking and Moral Critique Annual International, 586
Center for Research on the Context of Teaching, 5008
Center on Disabilities Conference, 666
Cisco Educational Archives, 3524
Coalition of Essential Schools, 823
College Bound, 824
Computer Using Educators, Inc (CUE), 359
Concern-America Volunteers, 229
Consortium on Reading Excellence, 830
Constitutional Rights Foundation, 37
Council on Islamic Education, 237
Council on Library Technical Assistants (COLT), 288
Creative Learning Systems, 837
Curriculum & Instructional Leadership Branch, 2905
Dan Murphy Foundation, 2248
Darryl L Sink & Associates, 3591
David & Lucile Packard Foundation, 2249
Department Management Services Branch, 2906
Disability Rights Education & Defense Fund, 42
Division for Research, 5017
Education, Training and Research Associates, 52
Effective Training Solutions, 865
Energy Education Group, 334
Epistemological Engineering, 868
Evelyn & Walter Haas Jr Fund, 2250
Excell Education Centers, 870
Executive Office & External Affairs, 2907
Field Services Branch, 2908
Foundation Center-San Francisco, 2251
Foundation for Critical Thinking, 3605
Foundation for Critical Thinking Annual Conference, 3279
Foundation for Critical Thinking Regional Workshop & Conference, 679
Foundations Focus, 2252
Francis H Clougherty Charitable Trust, 2253
Freitas Foundation, 2254
Fritz B Burns Foundation, 2255
George Frederick Jewett Foundation, 2256

Colorado

Connecticut

Delaware

District of Columbia

Florida

Georgia

Hawaii

Information & Telecommunications Services Branch, 2946
James & Abigail Campbell Foundation, 2390
Oceanic Cablevision Foundation, 2391
Office of Curriculum, Instruction and Student Support, 2947
Pacific Regional Educational Laboratory, 5061
Paul H Rosendahl, PHD, 943
Samuel N & Mary Castle Foundation, 2392
Special Education Department, 2948
State Public Library System, 2949
University of Hawaii, 2393

Idaho

Boise Public Library, 2394
Claude R & Ethel B Whittenberger Foundation, 2395
Idaho Education Association, 422
Idaho Library Association, 423
Idaho State Department of Education, 2950
Moore Express, 930
Northwest Association of Schools & Colleges Annual Meeting, 128, 3343
Pacific Northwest Library Association, 290, 424, 781, 781
Walter & Leona Dufresne Foundation, 2396

Illinois

ALA Annual Conference, 609
American Academy of Pediatrics, 5
American Association of French Teachers Conference, 619
American Association of School Librarians National Conference, 622
American Association of Teachers of French, 269
American Library Association, 285
American Library Association Annual Conference, 632
Ameritech Foundation, 2397
Annual Ethics & Technology Conference, 644
Association for Library & Information Science Education Annual Conference, 287, 3265
Awards and Recognition Association, 27
Career Evaluation Systems, 812
Carus Corporate Contributions Program, 2398
Center for the Study of Reading, 5011
Chauncey & Marion Deering McCormick Foundation, 2399
Chicago Community Trust, 2400
Chicago Principals Association Education Conference, 3274
Clearinghouse on Early Education and Parenting (CEEP), 171
Coleman Foundation, 2401
Community Foundation for Jewish Education, 827
Creative Learning Consultants, 836
Curriculum Center - Office of Educational Services, 3590
DeVry University, 3592
Dellora A & Lester J Norris Foundation, 2402
Dillon Foundation, 2403
Dr. Scholl Foundation, 2404
Easter Seals Communications, 48
Eastern Illinois University School of Technology, 3595
Educational Specialties, 859
Educator & School Development, 2952
Educator Certification, 2953
Energy Concepts, 3602
Evanston Public Library, 2405
Executive Deputy Superintendent, 2954
Farny R Wurlitzer Foundation, 2406
Finance & Support Services, 2955

Grover Hermann Foundation, 2407
How to Raise Test Scores, 3400
IASB Joint Annual Conference, 3281
Illinois Affiliation of Private Schools for Exceptional Children, 425
Illinois Assistant Principals Conference, 3284
Illinois Association of School Business Officials, 426
Illinois Business Education Association (IBEA), 427
Illinois Citizens' Education Council, 428
Illinois Department of Education, 2956
Illinois Education Association, 429
Illinois Library Association, 430
Illinois Library Association Conference, 767
Illinois Principals Professional Conference, 3285
Illinois Resource Center Conference of Teachers of Linguistically Diverse Students, 3286
Illinois School Library Media Association, 431
Illinois Vocational Association Conference, 768
Independent Schools Association of the Central States, 63, 149
Innovative Learning Group, 881
Institute of Cultural Affairs, 240
International Awards Market, 593
International Council on Education for Teaching, 3236
Janice Borla Vocal Jazz Camp, 3619
Joyce Foundation, 2408
Kodaly Teaching Certification Program, 3626
Lloyd A Fry Foundation, 2409
Lutheran Education Association, 73
Lutheran Education Association Convention, 694
Management Simulations, 912
Midwestern Regional Educational Laboratory, 5032
National Council of English Teachers Conference, 3326
National Council of Teachers of English Annual Convention, 279, 3327
National Lekotek Center, 111
North American Students of Cooperation, 127
North Central Business Education Association (NCBEA), 479
North Central Regional Educational Laboratory, 5057
Northern Trust Company Charitable Trust, 2410
Orff-Schulwerk Teacher Certification Program, 3645
Palmer Foundation, 2411
Philip H Corboy Foundation, 2412
Planning, Research & Evaluation, 2957
Polk Brothers Foundation, 2413
Prince Charitable Trust, 2414
Recognition & Supervision of Schools, 2958
Regenstein Foundation, 2415
Region 5: Education Department, 2959
Requirements for Certification of Teachers & Counselors, 3420
Richard H Driehaus Foundation, 2416
Robert E Nelson Associates, 964
Robert R McCormick Tribune Foundation, 2417
Rockford Systems, 3658
School Improvement & Assessment Services, 2961
Sears-Roebuck Foundation, 2418
Sigma Tau Delta, 283
Spencer Foundation, 2419
Student Development Services, 2963
Sulzer Family Foundation, 2420
Teaching for Intelligence Conference, 757
Top Quality School Process (TQSP), 3437
United Airlines Foundation, 2421
Valenti Charitable Foundation, 2422
Wavelength, 3571, 3680
Workforce Education and Development, 3682

Indiana

Agency for Instructional Technology, 354, 3221
Allen County Public Library, 2423
American Camping Association National Conference, 624
Art to Remember, 2808
Arvin Foundation, 2424
Association for Educational Communications & Technology Annual Convention, 357, 3264
Ball State University, 3577
Before the School Bell Rings, 3386
Beyond Tracking: Finding Success in Inclusive Schools, 3387
C/S Newsletter, 3452
Center for Professional Development & Services, 817
Center for School Assessment & Research, 2965
Clearinghouse on Reading, English & Communication, 315
Clowes Fund, 2425
Community Relations & Special Populations, 2966
Dekko Foundation, 2426
ERIC Clearinghouse for Social Studies Education, 348
East Central Educational Service Center, 846
Educational Services Company, 858
Eli Lilly & Company Corporate Contribution Program, 2427
External Affairs, 2967
Foellinger Foundation, 2428
History of Science Society, 336
Hoosier Science Teachers Association Annual Meeting, 766
ISBA/IAPSS Annual Conference, 3283
Indiana Association of School Business Officials, 432
Indiana Business Education Association, 433
Indiana Department of Education, 2968
Indiana Library Federation, 434
Indiana State Teachers Association, 435
Indiana University-Purdue University of Indianapolis, IUPUI, 3612
Indianapolis Foundation, 2429
International Curriculum Management Audit Center, 3615
International Listening Association Annual Convention, 598
John W Anderson Foundation, 2430
July in Rensselaer, 3621
Law of Teacher Evaluation: A Self-Assestment Handbook, 3402
Lilly Endowment, 2431
Moore Foundation, 2432
National Educational Service, 109
National Student Exchange, 119
Office of Legal Affairs, 2969
Office of School Financial Management, 2970
Office of the Deputy Superintendent, 2971
PDK International Conference, 3350
Phi Delta Kappa International, 262
Piano Workshop, 3651
Priority Computer Services, 950
Professional Computer Systems, 952
Professional Learning Communities at Work, 3417
Revolution Revisited: Effective Schools and Systemic Reform, 3424
School Improvement & Performance Center, 2973
Teachers Association in Instruction Conference, 3364
Teachers as Leaders, 3429
Voices in the Hall: High School Principals at Work, 3570
W Brooks Fortune Foundation, 2433
Wilderness Education Association, 140

BBX Teacher Clearinghouse, 3378
Beverly Celotta, 808
CHADD: Children & Adults with Attention Deficit/Hyperactivity Disorder, 29, 661
Career & Technology Education, 3007
Center for Organization of Schools, 5007
Center for Social Organization of Schools, 5009
Center for Technology in Education, 5010
Certification & Accreditation, 3008
Childhood Education Association International, 587
Childrens Youth Funding Report, 2809
Clarence Manger & Audrey Cordero Plitt Trust, 2455
Clark-Winchcole Foundation, 2456
Commonwealth Foundation, 2457
Compensatory Education & Support Services, 3009
Division of Business Services, 3010
Dr. Anthony A Cacossa, 842
Dresher Foundation, 2458
ERIC Clearinghouse on Assessment & Evaluation, 46
Educational Productions Inc, 3537
Educational Systems for the Future, 860
Edward E Ford Foundation, 2459
Enoch Pratt Free Library, 2460
France-Merrick Foundation, 2461
Grayce B Kerr Fund, 2462
Henry & Ruth Blaustein Rosenberg Foundation, 2463
Hummel Sweets, 2815
Instruction Division, 3011
International Association for the Exchange of Students for Technical Experience, 244
International Baccalaureate American Global Centre, 246
International Clearinghouse for the Advancement of Science Teaching, 3549
International Dyslexia Association (IDA), 276
International Dyslexia Association Annual Conference, 596
International Performance Improvement Conference Expo, 690
James M Johnston Trust for Charitable and Educational Purposes, 2464
John W Kluge Foundation, 2465
Learner-Centered, 603
Learning Independence Through Computers, 364
Library Development & Services, 3012
Longview Foundation for Education in World Affairs/International Understanding, 2767
Marion I & Henry J Knott Foundation, 2466
Maryland Center for Career and Technology Education, 3634
Maryland Department of Education, 3013
Maryland Educational Media Organization, 454
Maryland Educational Opportunity Center, 914
Maryland Elco Incorporated Educational Funding Company, 915
Maryland Library Association, 455
Maryland State Teachers Association, 456
NCSS Summer Workshops, 3640
National Association for Bilingual Education, 278, 710
National Association of School Psychologists Annual Convention, 194, 719
National Clearinghouse for Alcohol & Drug Information, 5046
National Council for History Education Conference, 3324
National Council for Social Studies Annual Conference, 3325
National Council for the Social Studies, 349
National Data Bank for Disabled Student Services, 159
National Institute of Child Health and Human Development, 2850
National School Public Relations Association, 116

National School Supply & Equipment Association, 743
National Women's Studies Association, 123, 3241
Performance Improvement Journal, 3474
Planning, Results & Information Management, 3015
President's Council on Fitness, Sports & Nutrition, 314
Professional Development Institutes, 3654
Robert G & Anne M Merrick Foundation, 2467
School Equipment Show, 752
Special Education/Early Intervention Services Division, 3016
Success for All Foundation, 977
T-Shirt People/Wearhouse, 2823
Teacher Magazine, 3484
University Research, 984

Massachusetts

ART New England Summer Workshops, 3574
Annual New England Kindergarten Conference, 3262
Associated Grantmakers of Massachusetts, 2468
Association for the Education of Gifted Underachieving Students Conference, 656
Beacon Education Management, 807
Boston Foundation, 2469
Boston Globe Foundation II, 2470
Boston Public Library, 2471
Carney Sandoe & Associates, 814
Center on Families, Schools, Communities & Children's Learning, 5013
Civic Practices Network, 36
Corporate Design Foundation, 832
Critical Issues in Urban Special Education: The Implications of Whole-School Change, 3588
Critical and Creative Thinking in the Classroom, 3589
Dean Foundation for Little Children, 2472
E-S Sports Screenprint Specialists, 2811
EF Educational Tours, 44
Education Development Center, 50, 851
Educational Placement Sources-US, 3455
Educational Register, 54
Educational Technology Center, 362
Effective Strategies for School Reform, 3598
Efficacy Institute, 866
Excellence in Teaching Cabinet Grant, 3246
Facing History & Ourselves, 56
George I Alden Trust, 2791
Harvard Institute for School Leadership, 3609
Harvard Seminar for Superintendents, 3610
Hyams Foundation, 2473
International Physicians for the Prevention of Nuclear War, 249
Irene E & George A Davis Foundation, 2474
James G Martin Memorial Trust, 2475
Jessie B Cox Charitable Trust, 2476
KidsCare Childcare Management Software, 3498
LG Balfour Foundation, 2477
Leadership and the New Technologies, 3628
Learning & The Enneagram, 3629
Linkage, 904
List of Regional, Professional & Specialized Accrediting Association, 3407
Little Family Foundation, 2478
MESPA Spring Conference, 3296
Massachusetts Business Educators Association, 457
Massachusetts Department of Education, 3017
Massachusetts Department of Educational Improvement, 3018
Massachusetts Library Association, 458
Massachusetts School Boards Association Meeting, 3300
Massachusetts Teachers Association, 459

Media and American Democracy, 3635
Meeting the Tide of Rising Expectations, 697
Merrimack Education Center, 921, 5029
NASDTEC Knowledge Base, 3411
NELMS Annual Conference, 3313
National Association of State Directors of Teacher Education & Certification, 156, 3237
National Coalition of Advocates for Students, 91
National Commission for Cooperative Education, 94
National Evaluation Systems, 934
New England History Teachers Association, 350
New England Kindergarten Conference, 3332
Pennsylvania School Librarians Association, 522
Polaroid Education Program, 3653
Principals' Center Spring Institute Conference, 3355
Project Zero Classroom, 3656
Recruiting New Teachers, 3242
Region 1: Education Department, 3019
Rogers Family Foundation, 2479
Standards and Accountability: Their Impact on Teaching and Assessment, 3665
State Street Foundation, 2480
Sudbury Foundation, 2481
TERC, 5080
TUV Product Service, 3671
Technical Education Research Centers, 981
Time to Teach, Time to Learn: Changing the Pace of School, 3436
Timothy Anderson Dovetail Consulting, 983
Trustees of the Ayer Home, 2482
Uplinc, 986
Weld Foundation, 2483
Western Massachusetts Funding Resource Center, 2484
William E Schrafft & Bertha E Schrafft Charitable Trust, 2485
Women's Educational & Industrial Union, 141
Women's International League for Peace & Freedom, 186
Woodstock Corporation, 2486
Worcester Public Library, 2487

Michigan

AVKO Educational Research Foundation, 5003
Accuracy Temporary Services Incorporated, 796
Adult Extended Learning Office, 3021
Alex & Marie Manoogian Foundation, 2488
Association for Asian Studies, 203
Association for Behavior Analysis Annual Convention, 649
Association for Gender Equity Leadership in Education, 19
Charles Stewart Mott Foundation, 2489
Childs Consulting Associates, 821
Chrysler Corporate Giving Program, 2490
Clonlara School Annual Conference Home Educators, 764
Community Foundation for Southeastern Michigan, 2491
Community Foundation of Greater Flint, 2492
Cronin Foundation, 2493
Detroit Edison Foundation, 2494
Effective Schools Products, 864
Extensions - Newsletter of the High/Scope Curriculum, 3457
Ford Motor Company Fund, 2495
Frey Foundation, 2496
General Motors Foundation, 2497
Grand Rapids Foundation, 2498
Harry A & Margaret D Towsley Foundation, 2499
Henry Ford Centennial Library, 2500
Herbert H & Grace A Dow Foundation, 2501
Herrick Foundation, 2502
Higher Education Management Office, 3023

677

Innovator, 3460
Instructional Programs, 3024
Kresge Foundation, 2503
Leona Group, 903
MASB Annual Fall Conference, 3295
MEMSPA Annual State Conference, 695
Malpass Foundation, 2504
McGregor Fund, 2505
Michigan Association for Media in Education, 461
Michigan Association of Elementary and Middle School Principals Conference, 3301
Michigan Association of School Administrators, 462
Michigan Department of Education, 3025
Michigan Education Association, 463
Michigan Education Council, 922
Michigan Elementary & Middle School Principals Association, 464
Michigan Library Association, 465
Michigan Science Teachers Association Annual Conference, 3302
Michigan State University Libraries, 2506
NCRTL Special Report, 3468
National Center for Community Education, 3238
National Center for Research on Teacher Learning, 5040
National Heritage Academies, 935
National Student Assistance Conference, 745
Office of School Management, 3026
Office of the Superintendent, 3027
Postsecondary Services, 3028
Professional Development Workshops, 3655
Rebus, 958
Richard & Helen DeVos Foundation, 2507
Rollin M Gerstacker Foundation, 2508
SAP Today, 3558
School Program Quality, 3029
Society for Research in Child Development, 754, 5073
Steelcase Foundation, 2509
Student Financial Assistance, 3031
Teacher & Administrative Preparation, 3032
University of Michigan-Dearborn Center for Corporate & Professional Development, 3679
Wayne State University, 2510
Whirlpool Foundation, 2511

Minnesota

Andersen Foundation, 2512
Bush Foundation, 2513
Cargill Foundation, 2514
Center for Global Education, 3580
Charles & Ellora Alliss Educational Foundation, 2515
Closing the Gap, 668
Communicating for America, 228
Data & Technology, 3033
Data Management, 3034
Designs for Learning, 840
Duluth Public Library, 2516
Education Funding, 3035
Education Minnesota, 466
Emerging Technology Consultants, 867
Examiner Corporation, 869
FR Bigelow Foundation, 2517
Financial Conditions & Aids Payment, 3036
First Bank System Foundation, 2518
Graduate Programs for Professional Educators, 3607
Hiawatha Education Foundation, 2519
Higher Education Consortium, 876
Human Resources Office, 2901, 3038
IA O'Shaughnessy Foundation, 2520
INFOCOMM Tradeshow, 683
Innovative Programming Systems, 882

Insight, 883
Marbrook Foundation, 2521
Medtronic Foundation, 2522
Minneapolis Foundation, 2523
Minneapolis Public Library, 2524
Minnesota Business Educators, 467
Minnesota Congress of Parents, Teachers & Students/Minnesota PTA, 468
Minnesota Department of Children, Families & Learning, 3039
Minnesota Department of Education, 3040
Minnesota Leadership Annual Conference, 3305
Minnesota Library Association, 469
Minnesota School Administrators Association, 3306
Minnesota School Boards Association, 470
Minnesota School Boards Association Annual Meeting, 3307
National Computer Systems, 3642
Otto Bremer Foundation, 2525
PACER Center, 130
Parent Training Resources, 3413
Residential Schools, 3041
Saint Paul Foundation, 2526
Scholarship America, 2837
TCF Foundation, 2527
Training & Presentations, 3368

Mississippi

Community Outreach Services, 3042
Educational Consultants of Oxford, 853
Educational Innovations, 3043
External Relations, 3044
Foundation for the Mid South, 2528
JJ Jones Consultants, 892
Jackson-Hinds Library System, 2529
Management Information Systems, 3045
Mississippi Advocate For Education, 471
Mississippi Business Education Association, 472
Mississippi Department of Education, 3046
Mississippi Employment Security Commission, 3047
Mississippi Library Association, 75
Mississippi Power Foundation, 2530
Office of Accountability, 3048
Phil Hardin Foundation, 2531
Vocational Technical Education, 3049

Missouri

Advocates for Language Learning Annual Meeting, 612
Ameren Corporation Charitable Trust, 2532
Clearinghouse for Midcontinent Foundations, 2533
College of the Ozarks, 3586
Danforth Foundation, 2534
Deputy Commissioner, 3050
Division of Instruction, 3051
Enid & Crosby Kemper Foundation, 2535
Hall Family Foundation, 2536
Instructional Materials Laboratory, 5026
James S McDonnell Foundation, 2537
Kansas City Public Library, 2538
MNEA Fall Conference, 3297
MSBA Annual Conference, 3298
Mary Ranken Jordan & Ettie A Jordan Charitable Foundation, 2539
McDonnell Douglas Foundation, 2540
Missouri Association of Elementary School Principals, 473
Missouri Association of Secondary School Principals, 474

Missouri Congress of Parents & Teachers/Missouri PTA, 475
Missouri Department of Education, 3052
Missouri LINC, 5033
Missouri Library Association, 476
Missouri Library Association Conference, 785
Missouri National Education Association, 477
Missouri State Teachers Association, 478
Missouri State Teachers Association Conference, 3308
Monsanto Fund, 2541
Montana Association of School Librarians (MASL), 481
National Council on Alcoholism & Drug Abuse, 731
Parents as Teachers National Center, 749, 5063
People to People International, 261
Region 7: Education Department, 3053
Senior Researcher Award, 3252
Special Education Division, 2951, 3054
Supplemental Instruction, Supervisor Workshops, 3669
Urban & Teacher Education, 3055
Vocational & Adult Education, 2875, 3056
Vocational Rehabilitation, 2896, 3057
World Trade Centers Association, 142

Montana

Accreditation & Curriculum Services Department, 3058
American Council on Rural Special Education (ACRES), 9
Council for Indian Education, 347
Division for Early Childhood, 165
Division of Information-Technology Support, 3059
Eastern Montana College Library, 2542
Montana Association of County School Superintendents, 480
Montana Association of Elementary School Principals Conference, 3309
Montana Department of Education, 3060
Montana High School Association Conference, 778
Montana Library Association, 482
Montana School Boards Association, 928
Montana State Library, 2543
Operations Department, 3061
Parents, Let's Unite for Kids, 131
Western Business and Information Technology Educators (WBITE), 483

Nebraska

Administrative Services Office, 3020, 3062
Division of Education Services, 3063
Dr. CC & Mabel L Criss Memorial Foundation, 2544
Mountain Plains Business Education Association (M-PBEA), 496
Mountain-Plains Business Education Association (M-PBEA), 445
National Contact Hotline, 318
Nebraska Department of Education, 3064
Nebraska Library Association, 484
Nebraska School Boards Association Annual Conference, 779
Nebraska State Business Education Association, 485
Nebraska State Education Association, 486
Rehabilitation Services Division, 3065
Thomas D Buckley Trust, 2545
W Dale Clark Library, 2546

Guild Notes Bi-Monthly Newswletter, 3458
Hagedorn Fund, 2608
Hasbro Children's Foundation, 2609
Henry Luce Foundation, 2610
Herman Goldman Foundation, 2611
Hess Foundation, 2612
Higher & Professional Education, 3087
Hitting the High Notes of Literacy, 682
Horace W Goldsmith Foundation, 2613
Human-i-Tees, 2814
IBM Corporate Support Program, 2614
Information Center on Education, 5023
Institute of International Education, 241
International Association of Students in
    Economics & Business Management (AIESC),
    245
International Center for Leadership in Education,
    888
Island Drafting & Technical Institute, 3618
J&Kalb Associates, 890
JI Foundation, 2615
JP Associates Incorporated, 893
JP Morgan Charitable Trust, 2616
Jewish Education Service of North America, 69
Jewish Educators Assembly, 70
Jewish Foundation for Education of Women, 2835
Joukowsky Family Foundation, 2617
Julia R & Estelle L Foundation, 2618
Leon Lowenstein Foundation, 2619
Levittown Public Library, 2620
Life Skills Training, 3406
Literacy Volunteers of America National
    Conference, 693
Louis & Anne Abrons Foundation, 2621
MacMillan Guide to Correspondence Study, 3408
Magi Educational Services Incorporated, 910
Margaret L Wendt Foundation, 2622
McGraw-Hill Foundation, 2623
Modern Language Association Annual
    Conference, 698
Mosaica Education, 931
NCSIE Inservice, 3469
NYSSBA Annual Convention & Expo, 3317
National Academy Foundation Annual Institute
    for Staff Development, 707
National Center for Learning Disabilities, 89
National Center for the Study of Privatization in
    Education, 5042
National Child Labor Committee, 5045
National Clearinghouse for Information on
    Business Involvement in Education, 5048
National Guild of Community Schools of the Arts
    Conference, 306, 734
National Reading Styles Institute, 936
National Reading Styles Institute Conference, 738
National Research Center on English Learning
    and Achievement, 282
National Society for the Study of Education (N
    SSE), 118
New York Department of Education, 3088
New York Foundation, 2624
New York Library Association (NYLA), 501
New York School Superintendents Association
    Annual Meeting, 3334
New York Science Teachers Association Annual
    Meeting, 3335
New York State Council of Student
    Superintendents Forum, 771
New York State United Teachers (NYSUT), 502
New York State United Teachers Conference,
    3336
New York Teachers Math Association
    Conference, 3337
Northeast Regional Center for Drug-Free Schools
    & Communities, 5058
Operation Crossroads Africa, 259
Orators & Philosophers: A History of the Idea of
    Liberal Education, 3412
Palisades Educational Foundation, 2625

Phoenix Learning Resources Conference, 790
Princeton Review, 949
ProLiteracy Worldwide, 319
Professional Responsibility Office, 3089
Public Relations Student Society of America, 133
Quality Education Development, 956
Quality School Teacher, 3419
Quantum Performance Group, 957
Region 2: Education Department, 3090
Regional Learning Service of Central New York,
    960
Robert Sterling Clark Foundation, 2626
Rochester Public Library, 2627
Ronald S Lauder Foundation, 2628
Rookey Associates, 965
SH & Helen R Scheuer Family Foundation, 2629
SUNY College at Oswego, 3659
Samuel & May Rudin Foundation, 2630
Scholarships in the Health Professions, 2838
Seth Sprague Educational and Charitable
    Foundation, 2631
Sexuality Information & Education Council of the
    US, 135
Sidney Kreppel, 971
Starr Foundation, 2632
Stewart Howe Alumni Service of New York, 975
Superintendents Work Conference, 3362
Teachers & Writers Collaborative, 284
Teachers College: Columbia University, 3673
Tiger Foundation, 2633
Tisch Foundation, 2634
Travelers Group, 2635
Tribeca Learning Center-PS 150, 173
United Nations Development Program, 266
United States-Japan Foundation, 2801
Vocational & Educational Services for Disabled,
    3091
White Plains Public Library, 2636
William Randolph Hearst Foundation, 2637
William T Grant Foundation, 2638
www.nprinc.com, 3510

North Carolina

AE Finley Foundation, 2639
Association of Boarding Schools, 23
Auxiliary Services, 3092
Cannon Foundation, 2640
Dickson Foundation, 2641
Duke Endowment, 2642
Financial & Personnel Services, 3093
First Union University, 2643
Foundation for the Carolinas, 2644
Kathleen Price and Joseph M Bryan Family
    Foundation, 2645
Mary Reynolds Babcock Foundation, 2646
Master Woodcraft Inc., 696
Measurement, 919
Musikgarten, 3638
NCASA Annual Conference, 3311
National Association of Academic Advisors for
    Athletics, 312
National Early Childhood Technical Assistance
    System, 167, 5050
National Society for Experiential Education
    Conference, 117, 744
Non-Profit Resource Center/Pack Memorial
    Library, 2647
North Carolina Association of Educators (NCAE),
    504
North Carolina Business Education Association
    (NCBEA), 505
North Carolina Department of Education, 3094
North Carolina Department of Instructional
    Services, 3095
North Carolina Department of Public Instruction
    (DPI), 506

North Carolina Library Association (NCLA), 507
Poetry Alive!, 946
SERVE, 5068
SERVE Conference, 751
Staff Development & Technical Assistance, 3096
State Library of North Carolina, 2648
William R Kenan Jr Charitable Trust, 2649
Winston-Salem Foundation, 2650
Z Smith Reynolds Foundation, 2651

North Dakota

ATEA Journal, 3445
American Technical Education Association
    Annual Conference, 639
Myra Foundation, 2652
North Dakota Department of Education, 3097
North Dakota Department of Public Instruction
    Division, 3098
North Dakota Education Association (NDEA),
    508
North Dakota Library Association, 509
North Dakota State Board for Vocational &
    Technical Education, 3099
North Dakota Vocational Educational Planning
    Conference, 780
Study & State Film Library, 3100
Tom & Frances Leach Foundation, 2653

Ohio

AIS Annual Conference, 608
Akron Community Foundation, 2654
American Association for Employment in
    Education Annual Conference, 614
American Foundation Corporation, 2655
Analog & Digital Peripherals, 3495
Association for Integrative Studies, 20
Balance Sheet, 3450
Blind School, 3101
Brief Legal Guide for the Independent Teacher,
    3389
Burton D Morgan Foundation, 2656
Citizens for Educational Freedom, 35
Curriculum, Instruction & Professional
    Development, 3102
Dayton Foundation, 2657
Direct Instructional Support Systems, 841
E-Z Grader Software, 3496
Early Childhood Education, 3103
Edison Welding Institute, 3596
Education Concepts, 849
Educational REALMS-Resources for Engaging
    Active Learners in Mathematics and Science,
    332
Educational Theatre Association Conference, 677
Eisenhower National Clearinghouse for
    Mathematics and Science Education, 292, 333
Emco Maier Corporation, 3601
Eva L & Joseph M Bruening Foundation, 2658
Fastech, 3603
Federal Assistance, 3104
GAR Foundation, 2659
George Gund Foundation, 2660
Gold Medal Products, 2813
Hobart Institute of Welding Technology, 3611
Hoover Foundation, 2661
Industrial Training Institute, 3613
Institute for Development of Educational
    Activities, 885
International Thespian Society, 300
Journal on Excellence in College Teaching, 3466
Kent State University, 3624
Kettering Fund, 2662
Kulas Foundation, 2663

Oklahoma

Oregon

Pennsylvania

National Association of Catholic School Teachers, 82

National Center on Education in the Inner Cities, 5044

Northeast Conference on the Teaching of Foreign Languages, 3341

Northeast Regional Christian Schools International Association, 772

Office of Elementary and Secondary Education, 3137

Office of the Comptroller, 3138

Opportunities Industrialization Centers International (OIC), 260

PSBA School Board Secretaries and Affiliates Conference, 3351

Parsifal Systems, 942

Pennsylvania Council for the Social Studies Conference, 3353

Pennsylvania Department of Education, 3139

Pennsylvania Education, 3473

Pennsylvania Library Association (PaLA), 521

Pennsylvania Science Teachers Association, 3354

Pennsylvania State Education Association (PSEA), 523

Pennsylvania State University-Workforce Education & Development Program, 3649

Pew Charitable Trusts, 2702

Prevention Service, 948

Region 3: Education Department, 3140

Research for Better Schools, 5067

Research for Better Schools Publications, 3421

Richard King Mellon Foundation, 2703

Rockwell International Corporation Trust, 2704

SIGI PLUS, 5069

Samuel S Fels Fund, 2705

Sarah Scaife Foundation, 2706

Satellites and Education Conference, 775

Search Associates, 3243

Shore Fund, 2707

Stackpole-Hall Foundation, 2708

Total Quality Schools Workshop, 3676

United States Steel Foundation, 2709

Westinghouse Foundation, 2802

William Penn Foundation, 2710

Rhode Island

American Mathematical Society, 633

Career & Technical Education, 3022, 3141

Champlin Foundations, 2711

East Bay Educational Collaborative, 845

Equity & Access Office, 3142

Human Resource Development, 3143

Instruction Office, 3144

National Education Association Rhode Island (N EARI), 524

Northeast and Islands Regional Educational Laboratory, 5059

Office of Finance, 3145

Outcomes & Assessment Office, 3146

Providence Public Library, 2712

Resource Development, 3147

Rhode Island Association of School Business Officials, 525

Rhode Island Department of Education, 3148

Rhode Island Educational Media Association, 526

Rhode Island Foundation, 2713

Rhode Island Library Association, 527

School Food Services Administration, 3149

Special Needs Office, 3150

Teacher Education & Certification Office, 3151

South Carolina

Annual Conductor's Institute of South Carolina, 3575

Association for Education in Journalism and Mass Communication Convention, 650

Association of Schools of Journalism and Mass Communication (ASJMC), 273

Budgets & Planning, 3152

Charleston County Library, 2714

Communications Services, 2987, 3153

Computers on Campus National Conference, 669

General Counsel, 2882, 3154

George Dehne & Associates, 874

Internal Administration, 3155

National Dropout Prevention Center, 5049

National Dropout Prevention Center/Network Conference, 732

Policy & Planning, 2972, 3156

Sally Foster Gift Wrap, 2818

Satellite Educational Resources Consortium, 5070

South Carolina Department of Education, 3157

South Carolina Education Association (SCEA), 528

South Carolina Library Association, 529

South Carolina Library Association Conference, 3359

South Carolina State Library, 2715

Support Services, 2229, 3158

Teaching Education, 3487

South Dakota

Finance & Management, 3159

John McLaughlin Company, 896

Services for Education, 3160

South Dakota Community Foundation, 2716

South Dakota Department of Education & Cultural Affairs, 3161

South Dakota Education Association (SDEA), 531

South Dakota Library Association, 532

South Dakota State Historical Society, 3162

South Dakota State Library, 2717

Special Education Office, 3163

Tennessee

Alliance for Technology Access Conference, 355

Benwood Foundation, 2718

Center for Appalachian Studies & Services Annual Conference, 662

Christy-Houston Foundation, 2719

Frist Foundation, 2720

Institute of Higher Education, 3614

JR Hyde Foundation, 2721

Lyndhurst Foundation, 2722

Mental Edge, 3499

Modern Red Schoolhouse Institute, 927

Nashville Public Library, 2723

Oosting & Associates, 940

Plough Foundation, 2724

RJ Maclellan Charitable Trust, 2725

School Memories Collection, 2820

Special Education, 2962, 3030, 3110, 3110, 3131, 3164

Teaching and Learning, 3165

Tennessee Association of Secondary School Principals (TASSP), 533

Tennessee Department of Education, 3166

Tennessee Library Association, 534

Tennessee School Boards Association, 535

Tennessee School Boards Association Conference, 3365

Vocational Education, 2889, 3084, 3167, 3167

Texas

Accountability Reporting and Research, 3168

Albert & Ethel Herzstein Charitable Foundation, 2726

Annual State Convention of Association of Texas Professional Educators, 3263

Apple Education Grants, 3244

Association for Business Communication (ABC), 15

Burlington Northern Foundation, 2727

Burnett Foundation, 2728

Center for Educational Leadership Trinity University, 3579

Center for Occupational Research & Development, 3583

Center for Play Therapy, 170, 3584

Center for Play Therapy Fall Conference, 3272

Center for Play Therapy Summer Institute, 784

Chief Counsel, 3134, 3169

Children's Literature Festival, 788

Choristers Guild's National Festival & Directors' Conference, 667

Clinical Play Therapy Videos: Child-Centered Developmental & Relationship Play Therapy, 3526

Conference for Advancement of Mathematics Teaching, 670

Continuing Education, 3170

Cooper Industries Foundation, 2729

Corpus Christi State University, 2730

Cullen Foundation, 2731

Curriculum Development & Textbooks, 3171

Curriculum, Assessment & Professional Development, 3172

Curriculum, Assessment and Technology, 3173

Dallas Public Library, 2732

Drug Information & Strategy Clearinghouse, 43

Education of Special Populations & Adults, 3174

Educational Technology Design Consultants, 861

El Paso Community Foundation, 2733

Ellwood Foundation, 2734

Eugene McDermott Foundation, 2735

Ewing Halsell Foundation, 2736

Exxon Education Foundation, 2737

Field Services, 3175

Fondren Foundation, 2738

GTE Foundation, 2790

George Foundation, 2739

Gordon & Mary Cain Foundation, 2740

Haggar Foundation, 2741

Health Occupations Students of America, 180

Hobby Foundation, 2742

Houston Endowment, 2743

Houston Public Library, 2744

Internal Operations, 3176

International Exhibit, 597

Intervention in School and Clinic, 3462

James R Dougherty Jr Foundation, 2745

Journal of Classroom Interaction, 3463

Learning for Life, 3403

Leland Fikes Foundation, 2746

MD Anderson Foundation, 2747

Meadows Foundation, 2748

Moody Foundation, 2749

Multicorp, 932

National Athletic Trainers' Association, 313

National Educational Systems (NES), 168

Operations & School Support, 3177

Paul & Mary Haas Foundation, 2750

Permanent School Fund, 3178

Perot Foundation, 2751

Psychological Corporation, 162

RW Fair Foundation, 2752

Records Consultants, 959

Region 6: Education Department, 3179

Sid W Richardson Foundation, 2753

Utah

Vermont

Virginia

Arts

A&F Video's Art Catalog, 6140
ART New England Summer Workshops, 3574
Alarion Press, 4666
All Art Supplies, 6141
American Academy of Arts & Sciences Bulletin, 4507
American Art Clay Company, 6142
American Art Therapy Association, 295
American Dance Therapy Association, 296
American Musicological Society, 297
Annual Conductor's Institute of South Carolina, 3575
Annual Summer Institute for Secondary Teachers, 3576
Arnold Grummer, 6143
Arrowmont School of Arts & Crafts, 6144
Art & Creative Materials Institute, 6145
Art Education, 4508
Art Image Publications, 4682
Art Instruction Schools, 6146
Art Visuals, 4683
Art to Remember, 6147
ArtSketchbook.com, 6148
Arts & Activities, 4509
Arts Education Policy Review, 4510
Arts Institutes International, 6149
Choral Journal, 4512
Choristers Guild's National Festival & Directors' Conference, 667
Clavier, 4513
College Guide for Visual Arts Majors, 3994
Coloring Concepts, 4725
Community Outreach and Education for the Arts Handbook, 3995
Creative Teaching Press, 4734
Crizmac Art & Cultural Education Materials Inc, 5213
Dover Publications, 4748
Dramatics, 4514
ERIC Clearinghouse for Social StudiesEducation, 348
Educational Theatre Association Conference, 677
Flute Talk, 4515
Future Music Oregon, 298
Graphic Arts Education & Research Foundation, 178
Graphix, 5244
Harmonic Vision, 6056
Instrumentalist, 4516
International Conference, 594
International Thespian Society, 300
International Trombone Festival, 602
International Workshops, 3617
Italic Letters, 3996
Janice Borla Vocal Jazz Camp, 3619
Journal of Experiential Education, 4517
July in Rensselaer, 3621
Kennedy Center Alliance for Arts Education, 301
Kodaly Teaching Certification Program, 3626
Mel Bay Publications, 4859
Midnight Play, 6057
Mondo Publishing, 4865
Money for Visual Artists, 3946
Museum Stamps, 6150
Music Ace 2, 6151
Music Educators Journal, 4518
Music Educators Journal and Teaching Music, 4519
Music Educators National Conference, 699
Music Teacher Find, 6058
Music Teachers Association National Conference, 700
Music Teachers Guide to Music Instructional Software, 3999
Music Teachers National Association, 302
Music and Guitar, 6059

Musikgarten, 3638
NAEA News, 4520
National Art Education Association, 303
National Art Education Association Annual Convention, 709
National Association for Music Education, 304
National Association of Schools of Music (NASM), 305
National Council of State Supervisors of Music, 2897
National Guild of Community Schools of the Arts, 306
National Guild of Community Schools of theArts Conference, 734
National Institute of Art and Disabilities, 307
National Standards for Dance Education News, 4539
Oranatics Journal, 4522
Orff-Schulwerk Teacher Certification Program, 3645
Phelps Publishing, 4901
Piano Workshop, 3651
Pure Gold Teaching Tools, 6060
Resource Booklet for Independent Music Teachers, 4000
Rhythms Productions, 4920
School Arts, 4001
SchoolArtsDavis Publications, 4523
SchoolArts Magazine, 4524
Studies in Art Education, 4525
Teaching Journal, 4526
Teaching Music, 4527
Ultimate Early Childhood Music Resource, 4528
http://library.thinkquest.org, 6061
http://members.truepath.com/headoftheclass, 6062
www.sanford-artedventures.com, 6064
www.songs4teachers.com, 6065

Civics & Government

AppleSeeds, 4600
Boletin, 4601
Center for Civic Education, 31
Children's Book Council, 4716
Choices Education Project, 4721
Cobblestone, 4605
Colloquoy on Teaching World Affairs, 4606
Congressional Quarterly, 4730
Directory of Central America Classroom Resources, 4030
ERIC Clearinghouse for Social StudiesEducation, 348
Educators Guide to FREE Social Studies Materials, 4031
Facts on File, 4776
Focus, 4608
Footsteps, 4609
Frog Publications, 4784
Goethe House New York, 4787
Greenhaven Press, 4789
Hands-On Prints, 4794
High Touch Learning, 4800
Horn Book Guide, 4804
Houghton Mifflin Books for Children, 4805
Houghton Mifflin Company: School Division, 4806
Hyperion Books for Children, 4807
Jacaranda Designs, 4816
Keep America Beautiful, 4824
Knowledge Unlimited, 4827
Lynne Rienner Publishing, 4845
Media and American Democracy, 3635
Middle States Council for the Social Studies Annual Regional Conference, 3304
NASDTEC Knowledge Base, 3411
NCSS Summer Workshops, 3640

National Council for Social Studies Annual Conference, 3325
National Council for the Social Studies, 349
National Council for the Social Studies, 4875
National Women's History Project, 4882
National Women's History Project Annual Conference, 746
New Press, 4885
NewsBank, 4886
Organization of American Historians, 4890
Pennsylvania Council for the Social Studies Conference, 3353
Perspectives on History Series, 4899
Phi Delta Kappa Educational Foundation, 4204
Population Connection, 4905
Rand McNally, 4914
Roots & Wings Educational Catalog-Australia for Kids, 4923
Routledge/Europa Library Reference, 4925
Sharpe Reference, 4936
Social Issues Resources Series, 4940
Social Science Education Consortium, 4941
Social Studies School Service, 4942
USA Today, 4970
VIDYA Books, 4973
West Educational Publishing, 4982
Western History Association Annual Meeting, 795
Winston Derek Publishers, 4986
World & I, 4989
World Bank, 4991
World Book Educational Products, 4992
World Eagle, 4993
World Resources Institute, 4994
World of Difference Institute, 4996
Worth Publishers, 4997
www.ushistory.com, 6066

Economics

American Educational Studies Association, 630
Bluestocking Press Catalog, 4697
Capitalism for Kids, 4604
Chicago Board of Trade, 4715
Junior Achievement, 4821
National Council on Economic Education, 4877

English

ABDO Publishing Company, 4656
AGS, 4657
Accelerated Reader, 5709
American Educational Studies Association, 630
Amsco School Publications, 4679
Australian Press-Down Under Books, 4689
Ballantine/Del Rey/Fawcett/Ivy, 4691
Barron's Educational Series, 4692
Beech Tree Books, 4694
Black Butterfly Children's Books, 4695
Bluestocking Press Catalog, 4697
BridgeWater Books, 4699
Brown & Benchmark Publishers, 4701
Capstone Press, 4708
Carolrhoda Books, 4710
Center for Critical Thinking and Moral Critique Annual International, 586
Center for Education Studies, 346
Center for Learning, 5006
Charles Scribner & Sons, 4714
Children's Book Council, 4716
Children's Literature Festival, 788
Children's Press, 4717
Chime Time, 4720
Clearinghouse on Reading, English &Communication, 315
Cottonwood Press, 4732

Foreign Language

Geography

History

Art Visuals, 4683
Asian American Curriculum Project, 4684
Bluestocking Press Catalog, 4697
Boletin, 4601
California Weekly Explorer, 4602
Calliope, 4603
Center for Education Studies, 346
Center for Learning, 5006
Choices Education Project, 4721
Cobblestone, 4605
Colloquoy on Teaching World Affairs, 4606
Council for Indian Education, 347
Dinocardz Company, 4744
Editorial Projects in Education, 4756
Educators Guide to FREE Social Studies
    Materials, 4031
Ethnic Arts & Facts, 4770
Faces, 4607
Facts on File, 4776
Goethe House New York, 4787
History Matters Newsletter, 4610
History of Science Society, 336
Jacaranda Designs, 4816
Lerner Publishing Group, 4839
Middle States Council for the Social Studies
    Annual Regional Conference, 3304
NYSTROM, 4871
National Council for History Education
    Conference, 3324
National Council on Economic Education, 4877
National Women's History Project, 4882
National Women's History Project Annual
    Conference, 746
New England History Teachers Association, 350
New Press, 4885
Organization of American Historians, 4890
Pennsylvania Council for the Social Studies
    Conference, 3353
Personalizing the Past, 4898
Perspectives on History Series, 4899
Pleasant Company Publications, 4903
Routledge/Europa Library Reference, 4925
Runestone Press, 4926
Sharpe Reference, 4936
Social Science Education Consortium, 4941
Society for History Education, 352
VIDYA Books, 4973
Western History Association, 353
Western History Association Annual Meeting, 795
World & I, 4989
World of Difference Institute, 4996
www.ushistory.com, 6066

Mathematics

AIMS Education Foundation, 4658
Accelerated Math, 5708
Advantage Learning Systems, 6155
American Mathematical Society, 633
Association for Advancement of Computing
    inEducation (AACE), 328
Association for Science Teacher Education
    Science Annual Meeting, 653
Association of Science-Technology Centers, 330
Conference for Advancement of Mathematics
    Teaching, 670
Didax Educational Resources, 4742
ETA - Math Catalog, 4751
Education Development Center, 851
Educational REALMS-Resources for
    EngagingActive Learners in Mathematics and
    Science, 332
Eisenhower National Clearinghouse
    forMathematics and Science Education, 292
Eisenhower National Clearinghouse
    forMathematics and Science Education, 333
Everyday Learning Corporation, 4772

Extra Editions K-6 Math Supplements, 4774
F(G) Scholar, 4775
Focus on Learning Problems in Math, 4495
Games2Learn, 5745
Increasing Student Achievement in
    Reading,Writing, Mathematics, Science, 685
Ingenuity Works, 5751
Iowa Council Teachers of Math Conference, 3287
Journal for Research in Mathematics Education,
    4496
Journal of Computers in Math & Science, 4497
Journal of Recreational Mathematics, 4498
K'nex Education Division, 3622
K-6 Science and Math Catalog, 4025
Lawrence Hall of Science, 4832
Math Notebook, 4499
MathSoft, 4856
Mathematical Association of America, 293
Mathematics & Computer Education, 4500
Mathematics Teacher, 4501
Mathematics Teaching in the Middle School, 4502
Mimosa Publications, 4863
NCTM Annual Meeting & Exposition, 3312
NCTM Educational Materials, 4870
NCTM News Bulletin, 4503
National Council of Teachers of Mathematics, 294
National Council of Teachers of Mathematics
    Conference, 3328
Notices of the American Mathematical Society,
    4504
Options Publishing, 4889
SSMart Newsletter, 4505
Summing It Up: College Board Mathematics
    Assessment Programs, 6139
Summit Learning, 4948
Teaching Children Mathematics, 4506
WH Freeman & Company, 4976
Wolfram Research, Inc., 4987
Word Associates, 5817

Reading & Language Arts

ABC Feelings Adage Publications, 4655
ADE Bulletin, 4429
AGS, 4657
Accelerated Reader, 5709
Advantage Learning Systems, 6155
Australian Press-Down Under Books, 4689
Beyond Words, 4430
Brown & Benchmark Publishers, 4701
Carolrhoda Books, 4710
Carson-Dellosa Publishing Company, 4711
Center for Learning, 5006
Christian Literacy Outreach, 4545
Classroom Notes Plus, 4434
Classroom Strategies for the English Language
    Learner, 3975
Clearinghouse on Reading, English
    &Communication, 315
Cognitive Concepts, 4723
Concepts to Go, 4729
Conover Company, 829
Continental Press, 4731
Cottonwood Press, 4732
Council-Grams, 4438
Counterforce, 4439
Creative Teaching Press, 4734
Curriculum Associates, 4736
Diagnostic Reading Inventory for Bilingual
    Students in Grades 1-8, 4004
Diagnostic Reading Inventory for Primary and
    Intermediate Grades K-8, 4005
Diagnostic Reading Inventory for Primaryand
    Intermediate Grades K-8, 6131
Dinah-Might Activities, 4743
Dominic Press, 4746
DynEd International, 4750

English Education, 4440
English for Specific Purposes, 4443
Essential Learning Products, 4769
Exercise Exchange, 4546
Formac Distributing, 4780
Forum for Reading, 4547
Frog Publications, 4784
Games2Learn, 5745
Gareth Stevens, 4785
Getting Funded: The Complete Guide to
    WritingGrant Proposals, 3930
Greenwillow Books, 4790
Henry Holt Books for Young Readers, 4799
Hidden America, 3753
Higher Education & National Affairs, 4129
Hitting the High Notes of Literacy, 682
Increasing Student Achievement in
    Reading,Writing, Mathematics, Science, 685
International Reading Association, 316
International Reading Association Annual
    Convention, 599
Iowa Reading Association Conference, 3288
Italic Handwriting Series-Book A, 3976
Italic Handwriting Series-Book B, 3977
Italic Handwriting Series-Book C, 3978
Italic Handwriting Series-Book D, 3979
Italic Handwriting Series-Book E, 3980
Italic Handwriting Series-Book F, 3981
Italic Handwriting Series-Book G, 3982
Journal of Adolescent & Adult Literacy, 4548
Journal of Basic Writing, 4445
Kaeden Corporation, 4822
Language Arts, 4450
Language Schools Directory, 3983
Laubach LitScape, 4549
Laubach Literacy Action Directory, 4007
Lauri, 5261
Learning Connection, 4834
Literacy Volunteers of America National
    Conference, 693
Mari, 4854
McCracken Educational Services, 4857
National Contact Hotline, 318
National Council of English Teachers Conference,
    3326
National Council of Teachers of English, 279
National Council of Teachers of English Annual
    Convention, 3327
National Reading Styles Institute Conference, 738
National Writing Project, 4883
News for You, 4551
Options Publishing, 4889
PF Collier, 4892
PRO-ED, 4893
Phoenix Learning Resources, 4902
Phoenix Learning Resources Conference, 790
Phonics Institute, 4552
Picture Book LearningVolume-1, 3984
Prentice Hall School Division, 4906
Process of Elimination - a Method of Teaching
    Basic Grammar - Teacher Ed, 3985
Process of Elimination: A Method of Teaching
    Basic Grammar - Student Ed, 3986
Put Reading First: The Research BuildingBlocks
    For Teaching Children To Read, 3987
RIF Newsletter, 4553
Rand McNally, 4914
Reading Improvement, 4555
Reading Psychology, 4556
Reading Recovery Council of North America, 320
Reading Research Quarterly, 4557
Reading Research and Instruction, 4558
Reading Teacher, 4559
Reading Today, 4560
Ready to Read, Ready to Learn, 4008
Recorded Books, 4917
Rhythms Productions, 4920
Scott & McCleary Publishing Company, 4934
Social Studies School Service, 4942

NCLB Reform Oriented Listings

Science

Special Education

Technology

General Reference

American Environmental Leaders: From Colonial Times to the Present
An African Biographical Dictionary
Encyclopedia of African-American Writing
Encyclopedia of American Industries
Encyclopedia of Emerging Industries
Encyclopedia of Global Industries
Encyclopedia of Gun Control & Gun Rights
Encyclopedia of Invasions & Conquests
Encyclopedia of Prisoners of War & Internment
Encyclopedia of Religion & Law in America
Encyclopedia of Rural America
Encyclopedia of the United States Cabinet, 1789-2010
Encyclopedia of Warrior Peoples & Fighting Groups
Environmental Resource Handbook
From Suffrage to the Senate: America's Political Women
Global Terror & Political Risk Assessment
Historical Dictionary of War Journalism
Human Rights in the United States
Nations of the World
Political Corruption in America
Speakers of the House of Representatives, 1789-2009
The Environmental Debate: A Documentary History
The Evolution Wars: A Guide to the Debates
The Religious Right: A Reference Handbook
The Value of a Dollar: 1860-2009
The Value of a Dollar: Colonial Era
University & College Museums, Galleries & Related Facilities
Weather America
World Cultural Leaders of the 20th & 21st Centuries
Working Americans 1880-1999 Vol. I: The Working Class
Working Americans 1880-1999 Vol. II: The Middle Class
Working Americans 1880-1999 Vol. III: The Upper Class
Working Americans 1880-1999 Vol. IV: Their Children
Working Americans 1880-2003 Vol. V: At War
Working Americans 1880-2005 Vol. VI: Women at Work
Working Americans 1880-2006 Vol. VII: Social Movements
Working Americans 1880-2007 Vol. VIII: Immigrants
Working Americans 1770-1869 Vol. IX: Revol. War to the Civil War
Working Americans 1880-2009 Vol. X: Sports & Recreation
Working Americans 1880-2010 Vol. XI: Entrepreneurs & Inventors

Bowker's Books In Print®Titles

Books In Print®
Books In Print® Supplement
American Book Publishing Record® Annual
American Book Publishing Record® Monthly
Books Out Loud™
Bowker's Complete Video Directory™
Children's Books In Print®
Complete Directory of Large Print Books & Serials™
El-Hi Textbooks & Serials In Print®
Forthcoming Books®
Law Books & Serials In Print™
Medical & Health Care Books In Print™
Publishers, Distributors & Wholesalers of the US™
Subject Guide to Books In Print®
Subject Guide to Children's Books In Print®

Business Information

Directory of Business Information Resources
Directory of Mail Order Catalogs
Directory of Venture Capital & Private Equity Firms
Food & Beverage Market Place
Grey House Homeland Security Directory
Grey House Performing Arts Directory
Hudson's Washington News Media Contacts Directory
New York State Directory
Sports Market Place Directory
The Rauch Guides – Industry Market Research Reports

Statistics & Demographics

America's Top-Rated Cities
America's Top-Rated Small Towns & Cities
America's Top-Rated Smaller Cities
Comparative Guide to American Suburbs
Comparative Guide to Health in America
Profiles of... Series – State Handbooks

Health Information

Comparative Guide to American Hospitals
Comparative Guide to Health in America
Complete Directory for Pediatric Disorders
Complete Directory for People with Chronic Illness
Complete Directory for People with Disabilities
Complete Mental Health Directory
Directory of Health Care Group Purchasing Organizations
Directory of Hospital Personnel
HMO/PPO Directory
Medical Device Register
Older Americans Information Directory

Education Information

Charter School Movement
Comparative Guide to American Elementary & Secondary Schools
Complete Learning Disabilities Directory
Educators Resource Directory
Special Education

TheStreet.com Ratings Guides

TheStreet.com Ratings Consumer Box Set
TheStreet.com Ratings Guide to Bank Fees & Service Charges
TheStreet.com Ratings Guide to Banks & Thrifts
TheStreet.com Ratings Guide to Bond & Money Market Mutual Funds
TheStreet.com Ratings Guide to Common Stocks
TheStreet.com Ratings Guide to Credit Unions
TheStreet.com Ratings Guide to Exchange-Traded Funds
TheStreet.com Ratings Guide to Health Insurers
TheStreet.com Ratings Guide to Life & Annuity Insurers
TheStreet.com Ratings Guide to Property & Casualty Insurers
TheStreet.com Ratings Guide to Stock Mutual Funds
TheStreet.com Ratings Ultimate Guided Tour of Stock Investing

Canadian General Reference

Associations Canada
Canadian Almanac & Directory
Canadian Environmental Resource Guide
Canadian Parliamentary Guide
Financial Services Canada
History of Canada
Libraries Canada

Grey House Publishing

4919 Route 22, PO Box 56, Amenia NY 12501-0056 | (800) 562-2139 | www.greyhouse.com | books@greyhouse.com